New International Dictionary of Old Testament Theology & Exegesis

Volume 3

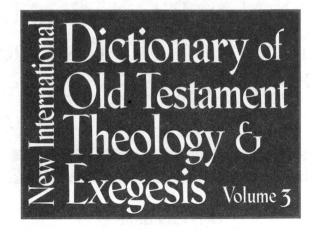

The New International Dictionary of Old Testament Theology and Exegesis

EDITORIAL BOARD

New International Dictionary of Old Testament Theology & Exegesis

Volume 3

Willem A. VanGemeren
General Editor

ZONDERVAN™

GRAND RAPIDS, MICHIGAN 49530

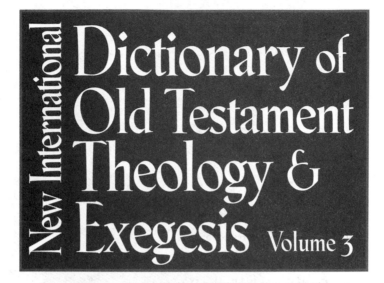

ZONDERVAN™

New International Dictionary of Old Testament Theology and Exegesis, Volume 3

Requests for information should be addressed to:

Zondervan, *Grand Rapids, Michigan 49530*

Library of Congress Cataloging-in-Publication Data

New International dictionary of Old Testament theology and exegesis /
Willem VanGemeren, general editor.
p. cm.
Includes bibliographical references and index.
ISBN 0-310-20218-3
1. Bible. O. T.—Dictionaries. 2. Bible. O. T.—Dictionaries—Hebrew. 3. Bible. O. T.—Theology—Dictionaries. 4. Bible O. T.—Criticism, interpretation, etc.—Dictionaries 5. Bible. O. T.—Theology—Dictionaries—Hebrew. 6. Bible. O. T.—Criticism, interpretation, etc.—Dictionaries—Hebrew. I. VanGemeren, Willem.
BS440.N438 1996
221.3—dc20 96-15006

This edition printed on acid-free paper.

Designed and typeset by Teknia Software

Printed in the United States of America

01 02 03 04 05 06 07 08 /DC/ 10 9 8 7 6 5

TABLE OF CONTENTS

Contributors

† Deceased

ABEGG, MARTIN G., JR
M.Div., M.Phil., Ph.D.; Assistant Professor of Old Testament, Trinity Western University, Langley, British Columbia, Canada

AITKEN, KENNETH T.
B.D., Ph.D.; Lecturer in Hebrew and Semitic Languages, University of Aberdeen, Aberdeen, Scotland

ALDEN, ROBERT L. †
B.A.,M.Div., Ph.D.; Late Professor of Old Testament, Denver Seminary, Denver, Colorado, United States of America

ALEXANDER, T. DESMOND
B.A., Ph.D.; Lecturer in Semitic Studies, The Queen's University of Belfast, Belfast, Northern Ireland

ALLEN, LESLIE C.
M.A., Ph.D., D.D.; Professor of Old Testament, Fuller Theological Seminary, Pasadena, California, United States of America

AMES, FRANK RITCHEL
B.A., M.Div., M.A.L.S., Ph.D. cand.; University Librarian, Colorado Christian University, Lakewood, Colorado, United States of America

ARNOLD, BILL T.
B.A., M.Div., Ph.D.; Professor of Old Testament and Semitic Languages, Asbury Theological Seminary, Wilmore, Kentucky, United States of America

AUSTEL, HERMANN J.
M.Div., Ph.D.; Professor of Old Testament at Northwest Baptist Seminary, Tacoma, Washington, United States of America

AVERBECK, RICHARD E.
B.A., M. Div., Ph. D.; Associate Professor of Old Testament and Semitic Languages, Trinity Evangelical Divinity School, Deerfield, Illinois, United States of America

BAILEY, WILMA A.
B.S., M.Div., Ph.D.; Assistant Professor of Old Testament, Messiah College, Grantham, Pennsylvania, United States of America

BAER, DAVID. A.
B.A., M.Div., Ph.D. cand. at University of Cambridge, United Kingdom; Lecturer in Old Testament and Biblical Languages, Seminario ESEPA, San José, Costa Rica

BAKER, D. W.
A.B., M. of Christian Studies, M. of Phil., Ph.D.; Professor of Old Testament and Semitic Languages, Ashland Theological Seminary, Ashland, Ohio, United States of America

BALDWIN, JOYCE G. †
B.A., B.D.; Freelance Writer, Late Principal, Trinity College, Bristol, United Kingdom

BALOIAN, BRUCE E.
B.A., M.Div., M.A., Ph.D.; Associate Professor, Azusa Pacific University, Azusa, California, United States of America

BECK, JOHN A.
B.A., M.Div., Th.M., Ph.D. cand.; Assistant Professor of Biblical Languages, Concordia University Wisconsin, Mequon, Wisconsin, United States of America

BEYER, BRYAN E.
B.A., M. Div., Ph.D.; Academic Dean, Columbia Bible College, Columbia, South Carolina, United States of America

BLOCK, DANIEL
B.Ed., B.A., M.A., Ph.D.; Professor of Old Testament Interpretation, Southern Baptist Theological Seminary, Louisville, Kentucky, United States of America

BOSMAN, HENDRIK L.
B.A. (Hons.), D.D.; Professor of Old Testament, University of Stellenbosch, Stellenbosch, South Africa

BRACKE, JOHN M.
B.A., M.Div., D.Min., Ph.D.; Professor of Old Testament; Dean for Academic Life, Eden Theological Seminary, St. Louis, Missouri , United States of America

BRENSINGER, TERRY L.
B.A, M.Div., M.A., M.Phil., Ph.D.; Associate Professor of Biblical Studies, Messiah College, Grantham, Pennsylvania, United States of America

BRISCO, THOMAS V.
B.A., M.Div., Ph.D.; Associate Professor of Biblical Backgrounds and Archaeology, Southwestern Baptist Theological Seminary, Fort Worth, Texas, United States of America

BROOKE, GEORGE J.
M.A., Ph.D.; Senior Lecturer in Intertestamental Literature, University of Manchester, Manchester, United Kingdom

BROWN, MICHAEL L.
B.A., M.A., Ph.D.; Adjunct Professor of Old Testament and Jewish Studies, Regent University School of Divinity, Virginia Beach, Virginia, United States of America

BURGE, GARY M.
B.A., M.Div., Ph.D.; Professor of New Testament, Wheaton College, Wheaton, Illinois, United States of America

BUTTERWORTH, GEORGE MICHAEL (MIKE)
B.Sc., B.D., M. Phil., Ph.D.; Academic Dean, Oak Hill College, London, United Kingdom

CARAGOUNIS, CHRYS C.
B.D., Th.D.; Associate Professor, Lund University, Lund, Sweden

CAREW, M. DOUGLAS
B.S., P.G.D.E., M.Div., Ph. D. cand. at Trinity Evangelical Divinity School, Deerfield, Illinois; Instructor at Sierra Leone Bible College, Freetown, Sierra Leone, West Africa

CARPENTER, EUGENE E.
A.B., M.Div., Ph.D.; Director of Graduate Studies; Professor of Old Testament and Hebrew, Bethel College, Mishawaka, Indiana, United States of America

CARROLL R., M. DANIEL
B.A., Th.M., Ph.D.; Professor of Old Testament, Denver Seminary, Denver, Colorado, United States of America

CARTLEDGE, TONY W.
B.S., M.Div., Ph.D.; Pastor, Woodhaven Baptist Church, Apex, North Carolina, United States of America

CATHCART, K. J.
M.A., Ling. Or.D., M.R.I.A.; Professor of Near Eastern Languages, University College, Dublin, Ireland

CHAN, KAM-YAU ALAN
M.Div.; Th.M.; Pastor of Chinese Christian Union Church, North Highland Park, Illinois, United States of America

CHHETRI, CHITRA
B.D., Th.M., Ph.D. cand.; Principal of Nepal Bible Ashram, Nepal

CHISHOLM, ROBERT B.
B.A., M.Div., Th.M., Th.D.; Professor of Old Testament Studies, Dallas Theological Seminary; Dallas, Texas, United States of America

CLARK, DAVID G.
B.A., Ph.D.; Director, Graduate Studies in Religion, Professor of New Testament, Southern California College, Costa Mesa, California, United States of America

COLLINS, JACK
S.B., S.M., M.Div., Ph.D.; Associate Professor of Old Testament, Covenant Theological Seminary, St. Louis, Missouri, United States of America

COOK, JOHANN
B.A., B.Th., M.A., D.Litt.; Associate Professor, Department of Ancient Near Eastern Languages, University of Stellenbosch, Stellenbosch, South Africa

CORNELIUS, I.
D.Litt.; Senior Lecturer, Department of Ancient Near Eastern Studies, University of Stellenbosch, South Africa

COTTERELL, PETER
B.D., B. Sc., Ph.D., D.Univ.; Former principal, London Bible College, London, United Kingdom; Fellow of the Institute of Linguists, Fellow of the Royal Society of Arts, United States of America

CREACH, JEROME F. D.
B.A., M. Div., Th.M., Ph.D.; Assistant Professor, Barton College, Wilson, North Carolina, United States of America

DENNINGER, DAVID
B.A., M.Div., Ph.D., Trinity International University, Deerfield, Illinois, United States of America

DIAMOND, A. R. PETE
B.S., Dip. Christian Studies, Th.M., Ph.D.; Adult Education Coordinator, All Saints By-the-Sea Episcopal Church, Santa Barbara, California, United States of America

DICKENS, OWEN P.
B.A., M.A., M.Div., Ph.D.; Associate Professor of Religion, Asbury College, Wilmore, Kentucky, United States of America

DOCKERY, DAVID S.
B.S., M.Div., M.A., Ph.D.; President, and Professor of Christian Studies, Union University, Jackson, Tennessee, United States of America

DOMERIS, WILLIAM R.
B.A., M.A., Ph.D.; Senior Lecturer in Old Testament, University of the Witwatersrand, Johannesburg, South Africa

DREYTZA, MANFRED
D.Th.; Lecturer in Old Testament, Geistliches Rüstzentrum Krelingen, Walsrode, Germany

DUMBRELL, WILLIAM J.
B.A., M.A., B.D., M.Th., Th.D.; Senior Lecturer, Trinity Theological College, Singapore.

ELLIS, ROBERT R.
B.S., M.Div, Ph.D.; Associate Professor of Old Testament and Hebrew, Logsdon School of Theology, Hardin Simmons University, Abilene, Texas, United States of America

ELS, P. J. J. S.
M.A., Ph.D. cand., D.Th., D.Litt.; Professor of Old Testament Studies, University of the Western Cape, Bellville, South Africa

ENNS, PETER
B.A., M.Div., M.A., Ph.D.; Associate Professor of Old Testament, Westminster Theological Seminary, Philadelphia, Pennsylvania, United States of America

FOULKES, FRANCIS
M.Sc., B.A., M.A., B.D.; Formerly Warden, St. John's College, Auckland, New Zealand

FOUTS, DAVID M.
B.A., Th.M., Th.D; Associate Professor of Bible, Bryan College, Dayton, Tennessee, United States of America

FREDERICKS, DANIEL C.
B.A., M.Div., Ph.D.; Provost and Vice President for Academic Affairs; Professor of Biblical Studies, Belhaven College, Jackson, Mississippi, United States of America

FRETHEIM, TERENCE E.
B.A., M.Div., Th.D.; Professor of Old Testament, Luther Seminary, St. Paul, Minnesota, United States of America

FULLER, RUSSELL T.
B.S., M.A., M.Phil., Ph.D.; Associate Professor of Biblical Studies, Mid-Continent College, Mayfield, Kentucky, United States of America

FUTATO, MARK D.
B.A., M.Div., M.A., Ph.D.; Associate Professor of Old Testament, Westminster Theological Seminary in California, Escondido, California, United States of America

GIESE, RONALD, JR
B.S., M.A., Ph.D.; Associate Professor of Biblical Studies, Liberty University, Lynchburg, Virginia, United States of America

GORDON, ROBERT P.
M.A., Ph.D.; Regius Professor of Hebrew and Fellow of St. Catharine's College, University of Cambridge, Cambridge, United Kingdom

GRISANTI, MICHAEL A.
B.A., M.Div., Th.M., Ph.D.; Associate Professor of Old Testament at Central Baptist Theological Seminary, Minneapolis, Minnesota, United States of America

HADLEY, JUDITH M..
B.A., M.A., Ph.D.; Assistant Professor of Theology and Religious Studies, Villanova University, Villanova, Pennsylvania, United States of America

HAGUE, STEPHEN
B.A., M.A., M.Div.; Ph.D. candidate at Bristol University and Wycliffe Hall, Bristol and Oxford, United Kingdom

HALL, GARY H.
B.A., M.Div., M.Th., Ph.D.; Professor of Old Testament, Lincoln Christian Seminary, Lincoln, Illinois, United States of America

HAMILTON, VICTOR P.
B.A., B.D., Th.M., M.A., Ph.D.; Professor of Religion, Asbury College, Wilmore, Kentucky, United States of America

HARMAN, ALLAN M.
B.A., B.D., M.Litt., Th.M., Th.D.; Professor of Old Testament, Presbyterian Theological College, Melbourne, Australia

HARRISON, ROLAND K. †
B.D., Th.M., Ph.D., D.D.; Late Professor Emeritus, Wycliffe College, Toronto, Ontario, Canada

HARTLEY, JOHN E.
B.A., B.D., M.A., Ph.D.; Professor of Old Testament in the C. P. Haggard Graduate School of Theology, Azusa Pacific University, Azusa, California, United States of America

HARVEY, JOHN E.
B.A., M.C.S., Ph.D. cand. at Wycliffe College, University of Toronto, Toronto, Ontario, Canada

HASEL, GERHARD F. †
B.A., M.A., Ph.D.; Late Professor of Old Testament and Biblical Theology; Theological Seminary, Andrews University, Berrien Springs, Michigan, United States of America

HAYDEN, ROY E.
B.A., B.D., Th.M., M.A., Ph.D.; Professor of Old Testament, Oral Roberts University Graduate School of Theology, Tulsa, Oklahoma, United States of America

HESS, RICHARD S.
B.A., M.Div., Th.M., Ph.D.; Reader in Old Testament, Roehampton Institute London, United Kingdom

HILL, ANDREW E.
B.A., M.A., M.Div., Ph.D.; Professor of Old Testament, Wheaton College, Wheaton, Illinois, United States of America

HOFFMEIER, JAMES K.
B.A., M.A., Ph.D.; Professor of Old Testament and Archaeology, Wheaton College, Wheaton, Illinois, United States of America

HOLMSTEDT, ROBERT
B.A., M.A., Ph.D. cand. at University of Wisconsin, Madison, Wisconsin, United States of America

HOOKS, STEPHEN M.
B.A., M.Div., Ph.D.; Professor of Biblical Studies at Atlanta Christian College, East Point, Georgia, United States of America

HORSNELL, MALCOLM J. A.
B.A., B.D., Th.M., Ph.D.; Professor of Old Testament Interpretation, McMaster Divinity College, Hamilton, Ontario, Canada

HOSTETTER, EDWIN C.
B.A., M.A.R., Ph.D.; Professor of Biblical Studies, Ecumenical Institute of Theology, Baltimore, Maryland, United States of America

HOWARD, DAVID M., JR
B.S., M.A., A.M., Ph.D.; Associate Professor of Old Testament and Semitic Languages, Trinity Evangelical Divinity School, Deerfield, Illinois, United States of America

HUBBARD, ROBERT L., JR
A.B., B.D., M.A., Ph.D.; Professor of Biblical Literature, North Park Theological Seminary, Chicago, Illinois, United States of America

JENSON, PHILIP P.
M.A., S.T.M., Ph.D.; Lecturer in Old Testament and Hebrew, Trinity College, Bristol, United Kingdom

JOB, JOHN B.
M.A., B.D.; Former Vice-Principal and Lecturer in Old Testament at Immanuel College, Ibadan, Nigeria and at Cliff College, Calver, United Kingdom; Minister in the South Bedford and Ampthill Methodist Circuit, United Kingdom

JOHNSTON, GORDON H.
B.A., Th.M., Ph.D.; Associate Professor of Old Testament Studies, Lancaster Bible College, Lancaster, Pennsylvania, United States of America

JONKER, LOUIS
M.A., D.Th.; Part-time Lecturer (and Minister of Religion) at University of Stellenbosch, Stellenbosch, South Africa

KAISER, WALTER C., JR
B.A., B.D., M.A., Ph.D.; Colman M. Mockler Distinguished Professor of Old Testament, President-Elect, Gordon Conwell Theological Seminary, S. Hamilton, Massachusetts, United States of America

KEOWN, GERALD L.
B.S., M.Div., Ph.D.; Associate Professor of Old Testament Interpretation, The Southern Baptist Theological Seminary, Louisville, Kentucky, United States of America

KIUCHI, NOBUYOSHI
Ph.D.; Associate Professor of Old Testament, Tokyo Christian University, Chiba, Japan

KLEIN, GEORGE L.
B.A., Th.M, M.Div., M.A., Ph.D.; Professor of Old Testament and Semitics, Acting Graduate Dean, Criswell College, Dallas, Texas, United States of America

KLINGBEIL, GERALD A.
B.A. Theology, B.A. Honors, M.A., D. Litt.; Professor of Old Testament and Semitic Languages at Universidad Peruana Unìon, Lima, Peru

KLINGBEIL, MARTIN
B.A., B.A. Honors, M.A., D. Litt.; Professor of Old Testament and Semitic Languages at Universidad Adventista Bolivia, Chochabamba, Bolivia

KONKEL, A. H.
B.R.E., M. Div., Ph.D.; Chairman of Biblical Studies, Providence Theological Seminary, Otterburne, MB, Canada

KOOPMANS, WILLIAM T.
B.A., M.Div., Th.M., Th.D.; Pastor of Cephas Christian Reformed Church, Peterborough, Ontario, Canada

KRUGER, PAUL A.
D.Litt., B.Th.; Senior Lecturer, The University of Stellenbosch, Stellenbosch, Republic of South Africa

LATOUNDJI, DAVID P.
B.A., M.Div., Th.M., M.A., Ph.D. cand. at Trinity Evangelical Divinity School, Deerfield, Illinois, United States of America

LONG, GARY ALAN
B.A., M.A., Ph.D.; Assistant Professor of Semitic Languages and Chair, Department of Hebrew Language, Jerusalem University College, Mt. Zion Campus, Jerusalem, Israel

LONG, V. PHILIPS
B.A., B.S., M.Div., Ph.D.; Professor of Old Testament, Covenant Theological Seminary, St. Louis, Missouri, United States of America

LONGMAN, TREMPER, III
B.A., M.Div., M.Phil, Ph.D.; Professor of Old Testament, Westminster Theological Seminary, Philadelphia, Pennsylvania, United States of America

LU, JEFFREY S.
B.A., M.A., M.Div., Ph.D.; Adjunct Professor at Logos Evangelical Seminary (Los Angeles, California) and Assistant Pastor at the Atlanta Chinese Christian Church, Atlanta, Georgia, United States of America

LUC, ALEX T.
B.Th., B.A., M.Div., M.A., Ph.D.; Professor of Old Testament and Semitic Languages, Columbia Biblical Seminary and Graduate School of Missions, Columbia, South Carolina, United States of America

LUND, JEROME A.
B.R.E., M.Div., M.A., Ph.D.; Associate Research Scholar - Comprehensive Aramaic Lexicon at Hebrew Union College - Jewish Institute of Religion, Cincinnati, Ohio, United States of America

MAGARY, DENNIS R.
B.A., M.Div., M.A., Ph.D.,; Associate Professor of Old Testament and Semitic Languages, Trinity Evangelical Divinity School, Deerfield, Illinois, United States of America

MARTENS, ELMER A.
B.A., B.Ed., B.D., Ph.D.; Professor Emeritus of Old Testament, Mennonite Brethren Biblical Seminary, Fresno, California, United States of America

MASON, REX A.
M.A., B.D., Ph.D.; Emeritus University Lecturer in Old Testament and Hebrew, Oxford University, Oxford, United Kingdom

MASSOUH, SAMIR
B.A., M.A., M.Div.; Chairman, Associate Professor Department of Biblical Studies, College of Arts and Sciences, Trinity International University, Deerfield, Illinois, United States of America

MATTIES, GORDON H.
B.A., M.A., Ph.D.; Associate Professor of Biblical Studies, Concord College, Winnipeg, Manitoba, Canada

MCCANN, J. CLINTON, JR.
A.B., D.Min., Th.M., Ph.D.; Evangelical Professor of Biblical Interpretation, Eden Theological Seminary, St. Louis, Missouri, United States of America

MCCONVILLE, J. GORDON
M.A., B.D., Ph.D.; Senior Lecturer in Religious Studies; Cheltenham and Gloucester College of Higher Education, The Park, Cheltenham, United Kingdom

MEIER, SAMUEL A.
B.A., Th.M., Ph.D.; Associate Professor of Hebrew and Comparative Semitics, Ohio State University, Columbus, Ohio, United States of America

MERRILL, EUGENE H.
B.A., M.A., M.Phil., Ph.D.; Professor of Old Testament Studies, Dallas Theological Seminary, Dallas, Texas, United States of America

MILLARD, ALAN
M.A., M.Phil.; Rankin Professor of Hebrew and Ancient Semitic Languages, The University of Liverpool, United Kingdom

MOBERLY, WALTER
M.A., Ph.D., Lecturer in Theology, University of Durham, Durham, United Kingdom

MOORE, MICHAEL S.
B.A., M.A., M.Div., Th.M., M.Ph., Ph.D.; Adjunct Assistant Professor of Old Testament at Fuller Theological Seminary, Phoenix, Arizona and Preaching Minister at Tatum Boulevard Church of Christ, Phoenix, Arizona, United States of America

MOULDER, WILLIAM J.
B.A., M.Div., Ph.D.; Professor of Biblical Studies, Trinity International University, Deerfield, Illinois, United States of America

NAUDÉ, JACOBUS (JACKIE) A.
M.A., M.Th., M.A., D.Litt.; Senior Lecturer, Department of Near Eastern Studies, The University of the Free State, Bloemfontein, Republic of South Africa

NEL, PHILIP J.
B.Th., D. Litt.; Professor in Semitic Languages, University of the Orange Free State, Bloemfontein, Republic of South Africa

NEWMAN, ROBERT
B.S., M.Div., S.T.M., Ph.D.; Professor of New Testament at Biblical Theological Seminary, Hatfield, Pennsylvania, United States of America

NICOLE, EMILE
Doctorat d'Etat en théologie protestante; Professor of Old Testament, Faculté Libre de Thélogie Évangélique, Vaux-sur-Seine, France

NIEHAUS, JEFFREY J.
B.A., M.A., Ph.D., M.Div.; Professor of Old Testament, Gordon-Conwell Theological Seminary, South Hamilton, Massachusetts, United States of America

NIXON, ROSEMARY
B.D., M.A., M.Th.; Principal, Theological Institute of the Scottish Episcopal Church, Edinburgh, Scotland

NOGALSKI, JIM
Th.D.; Assistant Professor of Old Testament Interpretation, Southern Baptist Theological Seminary, Louisville, KY, United States of America

NOLL, STEPHEN F.
B.A., M.A., Ph.D.; Associate Professor of Biblical Studies, Academic Dean, Trinity Episcopal School for Ministry, Ambridge, Pennsylvania, United States of America

NUNNALLY, W. E.
B.A., M.A. (Hebrew Language); M.A. (Old Testament); M. Phil., Ph.D.; Associate Professor of Early Judaism and Christian Origins at Central Bible College, Springfield, Missouri, United States of America

O'CONNELL, ROBERT H.
B.A., Th.M., Th.D., Ph.D.; presently freelance editor and writer; formerly Associate Professor of Old Testament at Colorado Christian University, Denver, Colorado, United States of America

O'KENNEDY, D. F.
B.A., B.Th., M.Th., D.Th.; Minister at Dutch Reformed Church, Helderberg, Somerset West, and part-time lecturer, University of Stellenbosch (Faculty of Theology, Department of Old Testament) Stellenbosch, South Africa

OLIVER, ANTHONY
B.Th., M.A., Ph.D.; Dean Caribbean Graduate School of Theology, Kingston, Jamaica

OLIVIER, J. P. J. (HANNES)
M.Th., D.Litt.; Professor of Old Testament, University of Stellenbosch, Stellenbosch, South Africa

OSBORNE, WILLIAM
M.A., M.Phil.; Head of Department of Old Testament; Director for Postgraduate Studies, Bible College of New Zealand, Auckland, New Zealand

OSWALT, JOHN N.
B.A., B.D., Th.M., M.A., Ph.D.; Ralph W. Beeson Professor of Biblical Studies, Asbury Theological Seminary, Wilmore, Kentucky , United States of America

PAN, CHOU-WEE
B.A., Ph.D.; Old Testament Lecturer, Trinity Theological College, Singapore

PARK, SANG HOON
Th.M., Ph.D., Senior Pastor, Seungdong Presbyterian Church, Seoul, South Korea

PATTERSON, RICHARD D.
A.B., M.Div., Th.M., M.A., Ph.D.; Distinquished Professor Emeritus, Liberty University, Lynchburg, Virginia, United States of America

PAUL, MAARTEN J.
Th.D.; Teacher of Old Testament, Theologische Hogeschool "Calvijn," Ede, and Pastor of Hervormde Kerk, Dirksland, The Netherlands

PEELS, HENDRIK G. L.
Th.D.; Professor of Old Testament, Theologische Universiteit van de Christlijke Gereformeerde Kerken in Nederland, Apeldoorn, The Netherlands

PENNANT, DAVID F.
M.A., B.D., Ph.D.; Former Curate-in-Charge, St. Savior's Church, Brookwood, Woking, Surrey, United Kingdom

PHELPS, MARK ANTHONY
B.A., M.T.S., M.A.; Instructor, Ozarks Technical/Community College, Springfield, Missouri, United States of America

PIENAAR, DANIEL N.
B.A. Honns, B.A., M.A. Phil. Licenciate; Professor, Head of the Department of Biblical Studies, The University of the Orange Free State, Bloemfontein, South Africa

POWELL, TIMOTHY
B.S., M.Div., Ph.D.; Adjunct Professor, Mennonite Brethren Biblical Seminary; Senior Pastor, Christian Life Assembly, Fresno, California, United States of America

PRICE, JAMES D.
B.S., M.Div., Ph.D.; Professor of Hebrew and Old Testament, Temple Baptist Seminary, Chattanooga, Tennessee, United States of America

PROVAN, IAIN W.
M.A., B.A., Ph.D.; Senior Lecturer in Hebrew and Old Testament Studies, University of Edinburgh, Edinburgh, Scotland

PUTNAM, FREDERIC CLARKE
B.S., M.Div., S.T.M., M.A., Ph.D.; Associate Professor of Old Testament, Biblical Theological Seminary, Hatfield, Pennsylvania, United States of America

RASMUSSEN, CARL G.
B.D., Th.M., Ph.D.; Professor of Old Testament, Bethel College, St. Paul, Minnesota, United States of America

REED, STEPHEN A.
M.Div., M.A., Ph.D.; Winthrop, Iowa, United States of America

REID, DEBRA K.
B.D., M.A., Ph.D.; Tutor in Hebrew, Old Testament and Church History at Spurgeon's College, London, United Kingdom

REIMER, DAVID
B.Th., B.A., M.A., D. Phil.; Fellow and Tutor in Hebrew and Old Testament at Regent's Park College, University of Oxford, Oxford, United Kingdom

ROGERS, JR. CLEON L.
B.A., Th.B., Th.M., Th.D.; Founder and Former Director of the German Theological Seminary, Giessen, Germany

ROOKER, MARK
B.A., Th.M., M.A., Ph.D.; Associate Professor of Old Testament Southeastern Baptist Theological Seminary, Wake Forest, North Carollina, United States of America

VAN ROOY, HARRY F.
M.A., Th.B., D. Litt.; Professor of Old Testament and Semitic Languages at Portchefstroom University for Christian Higher Education, Potchefstroom, South Africa

ROSS, ALLEN P.
Th.M., Th.D., Ph.D.; Professor of Biblical Studies at Trinity Episcopal School for Ministry, Ambridge, Pennsylvania., United States of America

SATTERTHWAITE, PHILIP E.
B.A., M.A., Ph.D.; Affiliated Lecturer at the Faculty of Oriental Studies, University of Cambridge; Research Fellow at Tyndale House, Cambridge, United Kingdom

SCHIBLER, DANIEL
B.A., M.A., Docteur en Etudes Orientales; Visiting Lecturer at Trinity Evangelical Divinity School, Deerfield, Illinois; Pastor, Swiss Reformed Church, Vevey, Switzerland

SCHOVILLE, KEITH N.
B.A., M.A., Ph.D.; Professor Emeritus of Hebrew and Semitic Studies, University of Wisconsin, Madison, Wisconsin, United States of America

SCHULTZ, RICHARD
B.A., M.Div., M.A., Ph.D.; Associate Professor of Old Testament, Wheaton College, Wheaton, Illinois, United States of America

SEEVERS, BOYD
B.A., Th.M., Ph.D. cand. at Trinity Evangelical Divinity School, Deerfield, Illinois, United States of America

SELMAN, MARTIN J.
B.A., M.A., Ph.D.; Deputy Principal, Spurgeon's College, London, United Kingdom

SHEPHERD, JERRY
M.A.R., Ph.D. Associate; Assistant Professor of Old Testament at Edmonton Baptist Seminary, Edmonton, Alberta, Canada

SKJOLDAL, NEIL O.
B.A., S.T.M., Ph.D.; Assistant Professor of Biblical Studies, Trinity International University, Miami, Florida, United States of America

SMICK, ELMER B. †
B.A., Th.B., S.T.M., Ph.D.; Late Professor of Old Testament, Gordon-Conwell Theological Seminary, South Hamilton, Massachusetts, United States of America

SMITH, GARY V.
B.A., M.A., Ph.D., Professor of Old Testament, Bethel Theological Seminary, Minneapolis, Minnesota, United States of America

SONG, THOMAS
B. Th., M. Div., Ph.D. cand. at Trinity Evangelical Divinity School, Deerfield, Ill., United States of America

SOUTHWELL, PETER J. M.
M.A.; Senior Tutor, Wycliffe Hall; Chaplain and Lecturer in Theology, The Queen's College, Oxford, United Kingdom

SPENDER, ROBERT D.
B.A., M.A., Ph.D.; Professor of Biblical Studies, The King's College,. Briarcliff Manor, New York, United States of America

SPINA FRANK ANTHONY
B.A., M.Div., M.A., Ph.D.; Professor of Old Testament, Seattle Pacific University, Seattle, Washington, United States of America

STALLMAN, ROBERT C.
B.A., M.Div., Ph.D. cand. Westminster Theological Seminary; Assistant Professor of Bible and Theology at Central Bible College, Springfield, Missouri, United States of America

STRONG, JOHN T.
B.A., M.Div., M.A.R., Ph.D.; Lecturer, Southwest Missouri State University, Springfield, Missouri, United States of America

STRUTHERS, GALE B.
B.A., M.A., Ph.D. cand. at Trinity Evangelical Divinity School, Deerfield, Illinois; Instructor at Oak Hills Bible College, Bemidji, Minnesota, United States of America

SWART, IGNATIUS
B.A., B.A. (Hons.), M.A., B.Th., D. Phil.; Candidate at the Department of Religious Studies, University of Stellenbosch, Stellenbosch, South Africa

TALLEY, DAVID
B.A., M.A., Th.M., Ph.D. cand. at Trinity Evangelical Divinity School, Deerfield, Illinois, United States of America

TAYLOR, J. GLEN
B.A., Th.M., Ph.D.; Associate Professor, Wycliffe College, Toronto, Ontario, Canada

TAYLOR, MARION A.
B.A., M.A., M.Div., S.T.M., Ph.D.; Associate Professor of Old Testament, Wycliffe College, University of Toronto, Toronto, Ontario, Canada

TAYLOR, RICHARD A.
B.A., M.A., Ph.D., M.A., Ph.D.; Professor of Old Testament Studies, Dallas Theological Seminary, Dallas, Texas, United States of America

THOMPSON, DAVID L.
A.B., B.D., Th.M., Ph.D.; F. M. and Ada Thompson Professor of Biblical Studies, Asbury Theological Seminary, Wilmore, Kentucky, United States of America

THOMPSON, JOHN ARTHUR
M.A., M.Sc., B.Ed., B.D., Ph.D.; Former Reader, University of Melbourne, Department of Middle Eastern Studies, Melbourne, Australia

TOMASINO, ANTHONY
B.A., M.Div., Ph.D.; Lecturer, University of Chicago, Chicago, Illinois, United States of America

TREBILCO, PAUL R.
B.Sc., B.D., Ph.D.; Professor of New Testament Studies, Knox College, and Sub-Dean, Faculty of Theology, University of Otago, Dunedin, New Zealand

TSUMURA, DAVID T.
B.Sc., M.Div., M.A., Ph.D.; Professor of Old Testament, Japan Bible Seminary, Hamura, Tokyo, Japan

TUELL, STEVE S.
B.A., M.Div., Ph.D.; Associate Professor of Religious Studies; Randolph-Macon College, Ashland, Virginia, United States of America

VAN DAM, CORNELIS
B.A., B.D., Th.M., Th.D.; Professor of Old Testament, Theological College of the Canadian Reformed Churches, Hamilton, Ontario, Canada

VANGEMEREN, WILLEM A.
B.A., B.D., M.A., Ph.D; Professor of Old Testament and Semitic Languages, Trinity Evangelical Divinity School, Deerfield, Illinois, United States of America

VANHOOZER, KEVIN
B.A., M.Div., Ph.D.; Senior Lecturer in Theology, New College, Edinburgh University, Edinburgh, Scotland

VAN LEEUWEN, CORNELIS
D.Th.; Emeritus Professor of Old Testament, State University, Utrecht, Netherlands

VAN LEEUWEN, RAYMOND C.
B.A., B.D., M.A., Ph.D.; Professor of Bible and Theology, Dept. of Bible and Theology, Eastern College, St. Davids, Pennsylvania, United States of America

VANNOY, J. ROBERT
B.A., M. Div., S.T.M., Th.D.; Professor of Old Testament at Biblical Theological Seminary, Hatfield, Pennsylvania, United States of America

VAN PELT, MILES V.
B.A., M.A; Lecturer in Greek, Gordon College, Wenham, Massachusetts, United States of America

VAN ROOY, HARRY F.
M.A., Th.B., D. Litt.; Professor of Old Testament and Semitic Languages at Portchefstroom University for Christian Higher Education, Potchefstroom, South Africa

VASHOLZ, ROBERT
B.A., M.A., B.D., M.A., Th.M., Th.D.; Chairman, Old Testament Department, Covenant Theological Seminary, St. Louis, Missouri, United States of America

VERHOEF, PIETER A.
M.A., M.Th., D.Th.; Emeritus Professor, University of Stellenbosch, Stellenbosch, Republic of South Africa

VOS, HOWARD F.
B.A., Th.M., Th.D., M.A., Ph.D.; Professor of History and Archaeology, Department Chair, The King's College, Briarcliff Manor, New York, United States of America

WAKELY, ROBIN
B.A., Ph.D.; Senior Lecturer in Hebrew and Old Testament Studies, Rhodes University, Grahamstown, South Africa

WALKER, LARRY L.
B.A., B.D., M.A., Ph.D.; Chairman of Old Testament Department, Professor of Old Testament and Semitic Languages, Mid-America Baptist Theological Seminary, Memphis, Tennessee, United States of America

WALTKE, BRUCE K.
Th.D., Ph.D.; Marshall Sheppard Professor of Biblical Studies, Regent College, Vancouver, British Columbia, Canada; Professor of Old Testament, Reformed Theological Seminary, Orlando, Florida, United States of America

WALTON, JOHN H.
A.B., M.A., Ph.D.; Professor of Bible, Moody Bible Institute, Chicago, Illinois, United States of America

WAY, ROBERT J.
M.A. (Univ. of St. Andrews), M.A. (Univ. of Cambridge); Minister, Headingley St. Columba United Reformed Church, Leeds, United Kingdom

WEGNER, PAUL
B.A., M.Div., Th.M., Ph.D.; Associate Professor at Moody Bible Institute, Chicago, Illinois, United States of America

WENHAM, GORDON J.
M.A., Ph.D.; Professor of Old Testament, The Cheltenham and Gloucester College of Higher Education, Cheltenham, United Kingdom

WILLIAMS, TYLER F.
B.A., M.Div., Ph.D. cand. at University of St. Michaels College, Wycliffe College, University of Toronto, Toronto, Ontario, Canada

WILLIAMS, WILLIAM C.
B.A., M.A., M.A. Rel., Ph.D.; Professor of Old Testament, Southern California College, Costa Mesa, California, United States of America

WILLIAMSON, HUGH G. M.
M.A., Ph.D., D.D., F.B.A.; Regius Professor of Hebrew, The University of Oxford, Oxford, United Kingdom

WILSON, GERALD H.
B.A., M.Div., M.A., M.A., Ph.D.; Assistant to the Dean and Director of Special Programs at Western Evangelical Seminary, Portland, Oregon, United States of America

WILSON, IAN
B.Sc., M.Phil., M.A., Ph.D.; Clare Hall, Cambridge, United Kingdom

WILSON, MARVIN R.
B.A., M.Div., M.A., Ph.D.; Harold J. Ockenga Professor of Biblical and Theological Studies, Gordon College, Wenham, Massachusetts, United States of America

WISEMAN, D.J.
M.A., D.Lit., F.B.A.; Professor Emeritus of Assyriology, The University of London, London, United Kingdom

WOLF, HERBERT M.
B.A., Th.M., Ph.D.; Professor of Theological Studies (Old Testament) at Wheaton College Graduate School, Wheaton, Illinois, United States of America

WOLTERS, AL
B.A., M.A., Doctorandus, Ph.D.; Professor of Biblical Studies, Redeemer College, Ancaster, Ontario, Canada

WRIGHT, CHRISTOPHER J.H.
M.A., Ph.D.; Principal, Lecturer in Old Testament, All Nations Christian College, Ware, United Kingdom

YAMAUCHI, EDWIN M.
B.A., M.A., Ph.D.; Professor of History, Miami University, Oxford, Ohio, United States of America

YARCHIN, WILLIAM S.
B.A., M.A., Ph.D.; Associate Professor of Religion at Azusa Pacific University, Azusa, California, United States of America

YOUNGBLOOD, RONALD F.
B.D., Ph.D.; Professor of Old Testament and Hebrew, Bethel Theological Seminary (West), San Diego, California, United States of America

YOUNGER, K. LAWSON, JR.
B.A., Th.M., Ph.D.; Associate Professor Biblical Studies, LeTourneau University, Longview, Texas, United States of America

Abbreviations

General

abbr.	abbreviated, abbreviation
abs.	absolute
acc.	accusative
act.	active
AD	*anno Domini* (after Christ)
adj.	adjective (adjectival)
adv.	adverb (adverbial)
af.	afel
Akk.	Akkadian
ANE	ancient Near East(ern)
Apoc.	Apocrypha
apoc.	apocalyptic
Aq.	Aquila's Greek version
Arab.	Arabic
Aram.	Aramaic
art.	article
Assyr.	Assyrian
AT	Altes (Ancien) Testament
BAram	Biblical Aramaic
BC	before Christ
BCE	before the Common Era
BH	Biblical Hebrew
bibl.	biblical
BTalm	Babylonian Talmud
ca.	*circa* (about, around)
Can.	Canaanite
cent.	century
cf.	*confer* (compare)
ch(s).	chapter(s)
Christ.	Christian
col(s).	column(s)
conj.	conjecture
const.	construct
Copt.	Coptic
D	Deuteronomist(ic) (source/stratum)
deut.	deuteronomic
dial.	dialect
disleg.	*dis legomenon* (occurring twice)
diss.	dissertation
DSS	Dead Sea Scrolls
du.	dual
E	Elohist(ic) (source/stratum)
EA	(Tell) el-Amarna (Tablet)
ed(s).	edited by, editor(s), edition(s)
e.g.	*exempli gratia* (for example)
Egyp.	Egyptian
EgypAram	Egyptian Aramaic
Einl.	Einleitung
Eng.	English
ep(s).	epistle(s)
ESA	Epigraphic South Arabic
esp.	especially
ET	English translation
et al.	*et alii* (and others)
Eth.	Ethiopic
etp.	etpe'el/etpa'al
EV(V)	English version(s)
f(f).	*folio* (*foliis*) ([and] on the [following] page[s])
fem.	feminine
fig(s).	figure(s)

fn.	footnote
frg(s).	fragment(s)
FS	Festschrift (for)
G	Greek
GN	geographical name
H	Holiness Code (Lev 17-26)
ha.	haphel
hapleg.	*hapax legomenon* (occurring once)
HB	Hebrew Bible
Heb.	Hebrew
hi.	hiphil
hisht.	hishtaphel
hitp.	hitpael
hitpalp.	hitpalpel
hitpol.	hitpolel
Hitt.	Hittite
ho.	hophal
idem	the same
i.e.	*id est* (that is)
ImpAram	Imperial Aramaic
impf.	imperfect
impv.	imperative
inf.	infinitive
intrans.	intransitive
ipht.	iphta'al
J	Yahwist(ic) (source/stratum)
JAram	Jewish Aramaic
Jew.	Jewish
JPAram	Jewish Palestinian Aramaic
Jud.	Judean
juss.	jussive
K	kethib
Lat.	Latin
LH	Late Hebrew
lit.	literal(ly)
loc. cit.	*loc citato* (in the place cited)
LXX	Septuagint
Mand.	Mandean
masc.	masculine
mg.	margin
Midr.	Midrash (midrashic)
Mish.	Mishnah (mishnaic)
MS(S)	manuscript(s)
MT	Masoretic Text
n(n).	note(s)
NA	Neo-Assyrian
Nab.	Nabatean
n.d.	no date
NE	Near East(ern)
ni.	niphal
no(s).	number(s)
nom(s).	noun(s)
NS	New Series
NT	New (Neues, Nouveau) Testament
obj.	object
OG	Old Greek (version)
OL	Old Latin (version)
Onk.	Onkelos (Targum)
op. cit.	*opere citato* (in the work cited)
OS	Old Series
o.s.	oneself (in lexical definition)
OSA	Old South Arabic
OT	Old Testament
P	Priestly (source/stratum)
p(p).	page(s)
pa.	pael

Pal.	Palestinian
par.	parallel(s)/and parallel passages
part(s).	participle(s)
pass.	passive
pe.	peal
Pent.	Pentateuch
Pesh.	Peshiṭta
pf.	perfect
Phoen.	Phoenician
pi.	piel
pilp.	pilpel
pl.	plural
PN	proper name
pol.	polel/polal
pred.	predicate
prp.	proposed reading
PS	Proto-Sinaitic
Pseud.	Pseudepigrapha
PTalm	Palestinian (Jerusalem) Talmud
pu.	pual
Q	qere
q.	qal
QL	Qumran literature
Rabb.	Rabbinic
repr.	reprint(ed)
rev.	revised (by)
RH	Rabbinic Hebrew
RL	Rabbinic literature
RS	Ras Shamra (Ugarit)
Sab.	Sabean (dialect of OSA)
Sam.	Samaritan
Sem.	Semitic
sg.	singular

sim.	similar(ly)
sing.	singular
s.o.	someone (in lexical definition)
s.t.	something (in lexical definition)
subj.	subject
subst.	substantive
suff.	suffix
Sum.	Sumerian
supp.	supplement(ary)
s.v(v).	*sub verbo* (under the word[s])
Symm.	Symmachus's Greek version of the OT
Syr.	Syriac (language)
Talm.	Talmud (talmudic)
Tg(s).	Targum(s) (targumic)
Th.	Theodotion's Greek version of the OT
tiph.	tiphil
Tosef.	Tosefta
TR	Textus Receptus (Received Text)
tr.	translation, translated (by)
trans.	transitive
Ugar.	Ugaritic
v(v).	verse(s)
var(s).	variant(s)
vb(s).	verb(s)
Vg.	Vulgate
viz.	namely
VL	Vetus Latina
Vrs.	versions (ancient)
W.	West
WestSem.	West Semitic

Symbols

‖	parallel with
<	derived from
>	transformed to
*	hypothetical form
→	cross-reference (within *NIDOTTE)*
#	Hebrew number (Goodrick-Kohlenberger system)
x: Theology	see article (x) in the fourth volume

Publications

AANLM	Atti dell'Academia nazionale dei Lincei: Memorie
AARSBLA	American Academy of Religion/Society of Biblical Literature Abstracts
AARSR	American Academy of Religion Studies in Religion
AASOR	Annual of the American Schools of Oriental Research
AB	Anchor Bible
ABD	*Anchor Bible Dictionary*, ed. D. N. Freedman, 6 vols., New York, 1992
ABL	R. F. Harper, *Assyrian and Babylonian Letters*, 14 vols., Chicago, 1892-1914
ABRL	Anchor Bible Reference Library
AbrN	*Abr-Nahrain*
AcOr	*Acta orientalia*
ADOG	*Abhandlungen der Deutschen Orient-Gesellschaft*
AEO	A. H. Gardiner, *Ancient Egyptian Onomastica*, 3 vols., London, 1947
AER	*American Ecclesiastical Review*
ÄF	Ägyptologische Forschungen
AfO	*Archiv für Orientforschung*
ÄgAbh	Ägyptologische Abhandlungen
AGJU	Arbeiten zur Geschichte des antiken Judentums und des Urchristentums
AGM	*Archiv für Geschichte der Medizin*, ed. K. Sudhoff, 20 vols., Leipzig, 1907-1928
AGMN	*Sudhoffs Archiv für Geschichte der Medizin* (*und Naturwissenschaften*), vols. 21- , 1929-
AHw	W. von Soden, *Akkadisches Handwörterbuch*, 3 vols., Wiesbaden, 1959-1981.
AJBA	*Australian Journal of Biblical Archaelogy*

AJBI	Annual of the Japanese Biblical Institute
AJSL	*American Journal of Semitic Languages and Literatures*
ALUOS	Annual of Leeds University Oriental Society
AnBib	Analecta biblica
AncIsr	R. de Vaux, *Ancient Israel: Its Life and Institutions*, 2 vols., tr. J. McHugh, New York, 1961, 1965
ANEP	*The Ancient Near East in Pictures*, ed. J. B. Pritchard, Princeton, 1954, 1969[2]
ANESTP	*Ancient Near East: Supplementary Texts and Pictures*, ed. J. B. Pritchard, Princeton, 1969
ANET	*Ancient Near Eastern Texts Relating to the Old Testament*, ed. J. B. Pritchard, Princeton, 1950, 1955[2], 1969[3]
Ang	*Angelicum*
AnOr	Analecta orientalia
ANQ	*Andover Newton Quarterly*
AnSt	*Anatolian Studies*
AO	Der alte Orient
AOAT	Alter Orient und Altes Testament
AOB	*Altorientalische Bilder zum AT*, ed. H. Gressmann, Berlin, 1927[2]
AOS	American Oriental Series
AOSTS	American Oriental Society Translation Series
AOT	*Altorientalische Texte zum AT*, ed. H. Gressmann, Berlin, 1926[2]
AOTS	*Archaeology and Old Testament Study*, ed. D. W. Thomas, Oxford, 1967
APFC	A. E. Cowley, *Aramaic Papyri of the Fifth Century B.C.*, Oxford, 1923
APNM	H. B. Huffmon, *Amorite Personal Names in the Mari Texts*, Baltimore, 1965
APOT	*Apocrypha and Pseudepigrapha of the Old Testament*, ed. R. H. Charles, 2 vols., Oxford, 1913; repr. 1978
ARAB	*Ancient Records of Assyria and Babylonia*, ed. D. D. Luckenbill, 2 vols., Chicago, 1926-1927; repr. 1968
ArbT	Arbeiten zur Theologie
ARE	*Ancient Records of Egypt*, ed. J. H. Breasted, 5 vols., Chicago, 1905-1907; repr. New York, 1962
ARM	Archives royales de Mari
ArOr	*Archiv orientální*
ARW	*Archiv für Religionswissenschaft*
AS	D. D. Luckenbill, *The Annals of Sennacherib*, OIP 2, Chicago, 1924

ASG	*Archiv für Schweizerische Geschichte*
ASNU	Acta seminarii neotestamentici upsaliensis
ASOR	American Schools of Oriental Research
ASTI	*Annual of the Swedish Theological Institute*
ASV	American Standard Version
ATAbh	Alttestamentliche Abhandlungen
ATANT	Abhandlungen zur Theologie des Alten und Neuen Testaments
ATAT	Arbeiten zu Text und Sprache im Alten Testament
ATD	Das Alte Testament Deutsch
ATDA	*Aramaic Texts from Deir 'Alla*, ed. J. Hoftijzer and G. van der Kooij, DMOA 19, Leiden, 1976
ATDan	Acta theologica danica
ATR	*Anglican Theological Review*
AusBR	*Australian Biblical Review*
AuSP	G. H. Dalman, *Arbeit und Sitte in Palästina*, 7 vols., Gutersloh, 1928-1942; repr. 1964
AUSS	*Andrews University Seminary Studies*
AUSSDS	Andrews University Seminary Studies: Dissertation Series
AV	Authorized (King James) Version
BA	*Biblical Archaeologist*
BAfO	Beihefte zur Archiv für Orientforschung
BAGD	W. Bauer, W. F. Arndt, F. W. Gingrich, F. W. Danker, *Greek-English Lexicon of the NT*, Chicago, 1957, 1979[2]
BARev	*Biblical Archaeology Review*
BASOR	*Bulletin of the American Schools of Oriental Research*
BASS	Beiträge zur Assyriologie und semitischen Sprachwissenschaft
BAT	Die Botschaft des Alten Testaments
BBB	Bonner biblische Beiträge
BBC	Broadman Bible Commentary
BBET	Beiträge zur biblischen Exegese und Theologie
BBLAK	Beiträge zur biblischen Landes- und Altertumskunde
BBR	*Bulletin for Biblical Research*
BDB	F. Brown, S. R. Driver, and C. A. Briggs, *Hebrew and English Lexicon of the OT,* Oxford, 1907; repr. with corrections, 1953
BDT	*Baker's Dictionary of Theology*, ed. E. F. Harrison, Grand Rapids, 1960
BEATAJ	Beiträge zur Erforschung des Alten Testaments und des Antiken Judentums
BeO	*Bibbia e oriente*

BethM	*Beth Miqra*
BETL	Bibliotheca ephemeridum theologicarum lovaniensium
BETS	*Bulletin of the Evangelical Theological Society*
BEUP	*Babylonian Expedition of the University of Pennsylvania,* ed. H. V. Hilprecht; Series A, Cuneiform Texts, Philadelphia 1893-1914
BEvT	Beiträge zur evangelischen Theologie
BFT	Biblical Foundations in Theology
BGBE	Beiträge zur Geschichte der biblischen Exegese
BHEAT	Bulletin d'histoire et d'exégèse de l'Ancien Testament
BHH	*Biblisch-historisches Handwörterbuch*, ed. B. Reicke and L. Rost, 3 vols., Göttingen, 1962-1966
BHK	*Biblia hebraica,* ed. R. Kittel, Stuttgart, 1905-1906, 1973[16]
BHS	*Biblia hebraica stuttgartensia,* ed. K. Elliger and W. Rudolf, Stuttgart, 1969-1975, 1984[3]
BHT	Beiträge zur historischen Theologie
Bib	*Biblica*
BibLeb	*Bibel und Leben*
BibOr	Biblica et orientalia
BibRev	*Bible Review*
BibS	*Biblische Studien* (Freiburg, 1895-1930; Neukirchen, 1951-)
Biella	J. C. Biella, *Dictionary of Old South Arabic: Sabaean Dialect*, HSS 25, Chico, Calif., 1982
BIES	*Bulletin of the Israel Exploration Society* (= *Yediot*)
BIFAO	*Bulletin de l'institut français d'archéologie orientale*
Bijdr	*Bijdragen*
BIN	*Babylonian Inscriptions in the Collection of James B. Nies, Yale University*, New Haven, 1917-1954
BIOSCS	*Bulletin of the International Organization for Septuagint and Cognate Studies*
BJPES	*Bulletin of the Jewish Palestine Exploration Society*
BJRL	*Bulletin of the John Rylands University Library of Manchester*
BJS	Brown Judaic Studies
BKAT	Biblischer Kommentar: Altes Testament
BL	H. Bauer and P. Leander, *Historische Grammatik der hebräischen Sprache,* Halle, 1918-1922; repr. 1962
BL	*Bibel-Lexikon*, ed. H. Haag, Zurich, 1951; Einsiedeln, 1968[2]
BN	*Biblische Notizen*
BO	*Bibliotheca orientalis*

BR	*Biblical Research*
BRL	K. Galling, *Biblisches Reallexikon*, HAT 1/1, Tübingen, 1937, 1977[2]
BRM	*Babylonian Records in the Library of J. Pierpont Morgan*, ed. A. T. Clay, New York, 1912-1923
BSac	*Bibliotheca Sacra*
BSC	Bible Study Commentary
BT	*Bible Translator*
BTB	*Biblical Theology Bulletin*
BTGP	H.-J. Kraus, *Die biblische Theologie: ihre Geschichte und Problematik*, Neukirchen-Vluyn, 1979
BuA	B. Meissner, *Babylonien und Assyrien*, 2 vols., Heidelberg, 1920, 1925
BurH	*Buried History*
BVC	*Bible et vie chrétienne*
BVSAW	Berichte über die Verhandlungen der sächsischen Akademie der Wissenschaften zu Leipzig
BWANT	Beiträge zur Wissenschaft vom Alten und Neuen Testament
BWL	W. G. Lambert, *Babylonian Wisdom Literature*, Oxford, 1960
BZ	*Biblische Zeitschrift*
BZAW	Beihefte zur Zeitschrift für die alttestamentliche Wissenschaft
CAD	*The Assyrian Dictionary of the Oriental Institute of the University of Chicago*, Chicago, 1956-
CAH	*Cambridge Ancient History*, 12 vols., Cambridge, 1923-1939, 1961-1971[2], 1970-[3]
CahRB	Cahiers de la Revue biblique
CahThéol	Cahiers théologiques
CAT	Commentaire de l'Ancien Testament
CB	Century Bible
CBC	Cambridge Bible Commentary
CBET	Contributions to Biblical Exegesis and Theology
CBQ	*Catholic Biblical Quarterly*
CBQMS	Catholic Biblical Quarterly Monograph Series
CBSC	Cambridge Bible for Schools and Colleges
CC	Communicator's Commentary
CGTC	Cambridge Greek Testament Commentary
CHALOT	*A Concise Hebrew and Aramaic Lexicon of the Old Testament*, ed. W. L. Holladay, Grand Rapids, 1971
ChiSt	*Chicago Studies*
CII	*Corpus inscriptionum iudaicarum*, Vatican City, 1936-

CIS	*Corpus inscriptionum semiticarum*, Paris, 1881-
CIWA	*The Cuneiform Inscriptions of Western Asia*, ed. H. C. Rawlinson, 5 vols., London, 1861-1884, 1891^{2}; repr. 1909
CJ	*Concordia Journal*
CJT	*Canadian Journal of Theology*
CML	*Canaanite Myths and Legends*, ed. G. R. Driver, Edinburgh, 1956; ed. J. C. L. Gibson, 1978^{2}
ConBNT	Coniectanea biblica, New Testament Series
ConBOT	Coniectanea biblica, Old Testament Series
ConCom	Continental Commentaries
COT	Commentaar op het Oude Testament, ed. G. C. Aalders, Kampen, 1955-1957
CPTOT	J. Barr, *Comparative Philology and the Text of the Old Testament*, Oxford, 1968; Winona Lake, Ind., 1987^{2}
CRAI	Comptes rendus des séances de l'Académie des inscriptions et belles lettres
CRINT	Compendia rerum iudaicarum ad Novum Testamentum
CTA	A. Herdner, *Corpus des tablettes en cunéiformes alphabétiques découvertes à Ras Shamra-Ugarit*, 2 vols., Paris, 1963
CTBT	*Cuneiform Texts from Babylonian Tablets... in the British Museum*, London, 1896-
CTJ	*Calvin Theological Journal*
CTM	Calwer theologische Monographien
CTM	*Concordia Theological Monthly*
CurTM	*Currents in Theology and Mission*
DB	*Dictionnaire de la Bible*, ed. F. Vigouroux, Paris, 5 vols., 1895-1912
DBHE	*Diccionaria Biblico-Hebreo-Español*, ed. L. Alonso-Schökel, V. Morla, and V. Collado, 12 vols., Valencia, 1990-1993
DBI	*A Dictionary of Biblical Interpretation*, ed. R. J. Coggins and J. L. Houlden, Philadelphia, 1990
DBSup	*Dictionnaire de la Bible: Supplément*, ed. L. Pirot et al., Paris, 1928-
DBT	X. Léon-Dufour, *Dictionary of Biblical Theology*, tr. P. J. Cahill and E. M. Stewart, New York, 1973^{2} (ET of *Vocabulaire de théologie biblique*, Paris, 1968^{2})
DCH	*Dictionary of Classical Hebrew*, ed. D. J. A. Clines, Sheffield, 1993-
DDD	*Dictionary of Deities and Demons in the Bible*, ed. K. van der Toorn, B. Becking, and P. W. van der Horst, Leiden, 1995
DHRP	Dissertationes ad historiam religionum pertinentes

DISO	C.-F. Jean and J. Hoftijzer, *Dictionnaire des inscriptions sémitiques de l'ouest*, Leiden, 1965
DJD	Discoveries in the Judaean Desert, Oxford, 1955-
DLE	*A Dictionary of Late Egyptian*, ed. L. H. Lesko and B. S. Lesko, 4 vols., Berkeley, Calif., 1982-1989
DME	*A Concise Dictionary of Middle Egyptian*, ed. R. O. Faulkner, Oxford, 1962
DMOA	Documenta et monumenta orientis antiqui
DNWSI	J. Hoftijzer and K. Jongeling, *Dictionary of the North-West Semitic Inscriptions*, 2 vols., Leiden, 1995
DÖAW	Denkschriften: Österreichischer Akademie der Wissenschaften
DOTT	*Documents from Old Testament Times*, ed. D. W. Thomas, London, 1958
DSB	Daily Study Bible
DTC	*Dictionnaire de théologie catholique*, 15 vols., Paris, 1903-1950
DTT	*Dansk teologisk tidsskrift*
EAEHL	*Encyclopedia of Archaeological Excavations in the Holy Land*, ed. M. Avi-Yona, 4 vols., Englewood Cliffs, N.J., 1975-1978
EBC	*The Expositor's Bible Commentary*, ed. F. E. Gaebelein, 12 vols., Grand Rapids, 1976-1995
EBib	Etudes bibliques
ECT	*The Egyptian Coffin Texts*, ed. A. de Buck and A. H. Gardiner, Chicago, 1935-1947
EDB	*Encyclopedic Dictionary of the Bible*, ed. and tr. L. F. Hartman, New York, 1963
EDNT	*Exegetical Dictionary of the New Testament*, ed. H. Balz and G. Schneider, 3 vols., Grand Rapids, 1990- (ET of *Exegetisches Wörterbuch zum NT*, 3 vols. Stuttgart, 1980-1982)
EDT	*Evangelical Dictionary of Theology*, ed. W. A. Elwell, Grand Rapids, 1984
EHAT	Exegetisches Handbuch zum Alten Testament
EMiqr	*Entsiqlopedia miqra'it-Encyclopaedia biblica*, 8 vols., Jerusalem, 1950-1982
EncBib	*Encyclopaedia Biblica*, ed. T. K. Cheyne, 4 vols., London, 1899-1903, 1914^2; repr., 1958
EnchBib	*Enchiridion biblicum*
EncJud	*Encyclopedia Judaica*, Jerusalem, 1971-1972
EOTT	C. Westermann, *Elements of Old Testament Theology*, tr. D. W. Stott, Atlanta, 1982

ER	*The Encyclopedia of Religion*, ed. Mircea Eliade, 16 vols., New York, 1987
ERE	*Encyclopaedia of Religion and Ethics*, ed. J. Hastings, 13 vols., New York, 1908-1927; repr., 13 vols. in 7, 1951)
ErfTS	Erfurter theologische Studien
ErIsr	Eretz Israel
ErJb	*Eranos Jahrbuch*
ESE	M. Lidzbarski, *Ephemeris für semitische Epigraphik*, Giessen, 1900-1915
EstBib	*Estudios bíblicos*
ETL	*Ephemerides theologicae lovanienses*
ETR	*Etudes théologiques et religieuses*
Even-Shoshan	*A New Concordance of the Bible*, ed. A. Even-Shoshan, Jerusalem, 1977, 1983[4]
EvK	Evangelische Kommentare
EvQ	*Evangelical Quarterly*
EvT	*Evangelische Theologie*
ExpTim	*Expository Times*
FOTL	Forms of Old Testament Literature
FOTT	*The Flowering of Old Testament Theology*, ed. B. C. Ollenburger, E. A. Martens and G. F. Hasel, Sources for Biblical and Theological Study 1, Winona Lake, Ind., 1992
FRLANT	Forschungen zur Religion und Literatur des Alten und Neuen Testaments
FuF	*Forschungen und Fortschritte*
FzB	Forschung zur Bibel
GAG	W. von Soden, *Grundriss der akkadischen Grammatik*, AnOr 33, Rome, 1952
GKC	*Gesenius' Hebrew Grammar*, ed. E. Kautzsch, tr. and ed. A. E. Cowley, Oxford, 1910[2] (ET of W. Gesenius, *Hebräische Grammatik*, ed. E. Kautzsch, Halle, 1909[28])
GLECS	Comptes rendus du Groupe linguistique d'études chamito-sémitiques
GPL	Z. S. Harris, *A Grammar of the Phoenician Language*, AOS 8, New Haven, 1936; repr. 1990
GSAT	Gesammelte Studien zum Alten Testament
GTJ	*Grace Theological Journal*
Guide	Guide to Old Testament Theology and Exegesis (vol. 1 of *NIDOTTE*)
GVGSS	C. Brockelmann, *Grundriss der vergleichenden Grammatik der semitischen Sprachen*, 2 vols., Berlin, 1908-1913; repr. 1961

HAD	*Hebrew and Aramaic Dictionary of the OT*, ed. G. Fohrer, tr. W. Johnston, London, 1973 (ET of *Hebräisches und aramäisches Worterbuch zum AT*, Berlin, 1971)
HAHAT	W. Gesenius, *Hebräisches und aramäisches Handwörterbuch über das Alte Testament,* ed. F. Buhl, Berlin, 1915[17]; ed. R. Meyer and H. Donner, 1987-[18]
HAIJ	*A History of Ancient Israel and Judah*, ed. J. M. Miller and J. H. Hayes, Philadelphia, 1986
HALAT	*Hebräisches und aramäisches Lexicon zum Alten Testament*, ed. L. Koehler, W. Baumgartner, and J. J. Stamm, 5 vols., Leiden, 1967-1995[3]
HALOT	*The Hebrew and Aramaic Lexicon of the Old Testament*, 1994- (ET of *HALAT*)
HAR	*Hebrew Annual Review*
HAT	Handbuch zum Alten Testament
HAW	E. König, *Hebräisches und aramäisches Wörterbuch zum Alten Testament*, Leipzig, 1910
HBC	*Harper's Bible Commentary*, ed. J. L. Mays et al., San Francisco, 1988
HBD	*Harper's Bible Dictionary*, ed. P. J. Achtemeier, San Francisco, 1985
HBT	*Horizons in Biblical Theology*
HDB	*Hastings' Dictionary of the Bible*, ed. J. Hastings, 5 vols., New York, 1898-1904; repr. Peabody, Mass., 1994
HDR	Harvard Dissertations in Religion
Herm	Hermanthena
HeyJ	*Heythrop Journal*
HG	J. Friedrich, *Die hethitischen Gesetze*, DMOA 7, Leiden, 1959
HKAT	Handkommentar zum Alten Testament
HL	E. Neufeld, *The Hittite Laws*, London, 1951
HNE	M. Lidzbarski, *Handbuch der nordsemitischen Epigraphik*, Weimar, 1898
HO	Handbuch der Orientalistik
HR	E. Hatch and H. A. Redpath, *Concordance to the Septuagint and Other Greek Versions of the Old Testament,* 2 vols. and supp. vol., Oxford, 1897 (vols. 1-2), 1906 (supp.); repr., 3 vols. in 2, Grand Rapids, 1983
HS	*Hebrew Studies*
HSAT	*Die heilige Schrift des Alten Testaments*, ed. E. Kautzsch and A. Bertholet, Tübingen, 1922-1923[4]
HSM	Harvard Semitic Monographs
HSS	Harvard Semitic Studies

HSyn	C. Brockelmann, *Hebräische Syntax*, Neukirchen, 1956
HTR	*Harvard Theological Review*
HTS	Harvard Theological Studies
HUCA	*Hebrew Union College Annual*
HUCM	Monographs of the Hebrew Union College
IB	*The Interpreter's Bible*, ed. G. A. Buttrick et al., 12 vols., New York, 1951-1957
IBD	*The Illustrated Bible Dictionary*, ed. J. D. Douglas and N. Hillyer, 3 vols., Leicester, 1980
IBHS	B. K. Waltke and M. O'Connor, *An Introduction to Biblical Hebrew Syntax*, Winona Lake, Ind., 1990
IBS	*Irish Biblical Studies*
ICC	International Critical Commentary
IDB	*The Interpreter's Dictionary of the Bible*, ed. G. A. Buttrick, 4 vols., New York, 1962
IDBSup	*The Interpreter's Dictionary of the Bible*, Supplementary Volume, ed. K. Crim, Nashville, 1976
IEJ	*Israel Exploration Journal*
IH	J. de Rougé, *Inscriptions hiéroglyphiques copiées en Egypte*, Etudes égyptologiques 9-11, 3 vols., Paris, 1877-1879
IJH	*Israelite and Judaean History*, ed. J. H. Hayes and J. M. Miller, Philadelphia, 1977
ILC	J. Pedersen, *Israel: Its Life and Culture*, tr. A. Møller (vols. 1-2) and A. I. Fausbøll (vols. 3-4), 4 vols. in 2, London, 1926, 1940; repr. 1973 (ET of *Israel*, vols. 1-2: *Sjaeleliv og Samfundsliv*; vols. 3-4: *Hellighed of Guddeomelighed*, Copenhagen, 1920, 1934)
IndES	*Indian Ecclesiastical Studies*
Int	*Interpretation*
Interp	Interpretation
IOS	*Israel Oriental Studies*
IOSOT	The International Organization for the Study of the Old Testament
IOT	R. K. Harrison, *Introduction to the Old Testament*, Grand Rapids, 1969
IOTS	B. S. Childs, *Introduction to the Old Testament as Scripture*, Philadelphia, 1979
IPN	M. Noth, *Die israelitischen Personennamen im Rahmen der gemeinsemitischen Namengebung*, BWANT 3/10, Stuttgart, 1928; repr., Hildesheim, 1980
IRT	Issues in Religion and Theology

ISBE	*International Standard Bible Encyclopedia*, ed. G. W. Bromiley, 4 vols., Grand Rapids, 1979-1988[2]
ITC	International Theological Commentary
ITQ	*Irish Theological Quarterly*
JAAR	*Journal of the American Academy of Religion*
JANESCU	*Journal of the Ancient Near Eastern Society of Columbia University*
JAOS	*Journal of the American Oriental Society*
JAOSSup	Supplement to the Journal of the American Oriental Society
JARG	Jahrbuch für Anthropoologie und Religionsgeschichte
JASA	*Journal of the American Scientific Affiliation*
Jastrow	M. Jastrow, *Dictionary of the Targumim, the Talmud Babli and Yerushalmi, and the Midrashic Literature*, 2 vols., New York, 1886-1903
JB	Jerusalem Bible
JBC	*The Jerome Biblical Commentary*, ed. R. E. Brown et al., 2 vols. in 1, Englewood Cliffs, N.J., 1968
JBL	*Journal of Biblical Literature*
JBQ	*Jewish Bible Quarterly* (1989-) (formerly *Dor leDor* [1972-1989])
JBR	*Journal of Bible and Religion*
JCS	*Journal of Cuneiform Studies*
JEA	*Journal of Egyptian Archaeology*
JEOL	*Jaarbericht van het Vooraziatisch-Egyptisch Genootschap "Ex oriente lux"*
JES	*Journal of Ecumenical Studies*
JETS	*Journal of the Evangelical Theological Society*
JewEnc	*The Jewish Encyclopedia*, ed. I. Singer, 12 vols., New York, 1901-1906
JFSR	*Journal of Feminist Studies in Religion*
JHNES	Johns Hopkins Near Eastern Studies
JJS	*Journal of Jewish Studies*
JMEOS	*Journal of the Manchester Egyptian and Oriental Society*
JNES	*Journal of Near Eastern Studies*
JNSL	*Journal of Northwest Semitic Languages*
JPOS	*Journal of the Palestine Oriental Society*
JPSV	Jewish Publication Society Version
JQR	*Jewish Quarterly Review*
JQRMS	Jewish Quarterly Review Monograph Series
JR	*Journal of Religion*
JSem	*Journal for Semitics*

JSJ	*Journal for the Study of Judaism in the Persian, Hellenistic, and Roman Period*
JSNT	*Journal for the Study of the New Testament*
JSOT	*Journal for the Study of the Old Testament*
JSOTSup	Journal for the Study of the Old Testament Supplement Series
JSP	*Journal for the Study of the Pseudepigrapha*
JSS	*Journal of Semitic Studies*
JSSR	*Journal for the Scientific Study of Religion*
JTC	*Journal for Theology and the Church*
JTS	*Journal of Theological Studies*
JTVI	*Journal of Transactions of the Victoria Institute*
Jud	*Judaica: Beiträge zum Verständnis...*
KAI	H. Donner and W. Röllig, *Kanaanäische und aramäische Inschriften*, 3 vols., Wiesbaden, 1967-1969^2
KAJI	E. Ebeling, *Keilschrifttexte aus Assur juristischen Inhalts*, WVDOG 50, Leipzig, 1927
KARI	E. Ebeling, *Keilschrifttexte aus Assur religiösen Inhalts*, WVDOG 28, Leipzig, 1915-
KAT	Kommentar zum Alten Testament
KAVI	O. Schroeder, *Keilschrifttexte aus Assur verschiedenen Inhalts*, WVDOG 35, Leipzig, 1920
KB	L. Koehler and W. Baumgartner, *Lexicon in Veteris Testamenti libros*, 2 vols., Leiden, 1958^2
KB	*Keilinschriftliche Bibliothek*, ed. E. Schrader, 6 vols., Berlin, 1889-1915
KBANT	Kommentare und Beiträge zum Alten und Neuen Testament
KBL^2	see KB
KBL^3	see *HALAT*
KBo	*Keilschrifttexte aus Boghazköi*, WVDOG 30, 36, 68-70, 72, 73, 77-80, 82-86, 89-90, Leipzig, 1916-
KD	K. F. Keil and F. Delitzsch, *Biblical Commentary on the Old Testament*, tr. J. Martin et al., 25 vols., Edinburgh, 1857-1878; repr. 10 vols., Grand Rapids, 1973 (ET of *Biblischer Kommentar über das AT*, 15 vols., Leipzig, 1861-1870, 1862-1875^2)
KD	*Kerygma und Dogma*
KEHAT	Kurzgefasstes exegetisches Handbuch zum Alten Testament, ed. O. F. Fritzsche, 17 vols., Leipzig, 1838-1862
KHAT	Kurzer Hand-Commentar zum Alten Testament
KJV	King James (Authorized) Version

KlSchr	*Kleine Schriften* (A. Alt, 3 vols., Munich, 1953-1959, 1964^{3}; O. Eissfeldt, 6 vols., Tübingen, 1962-1979; K. Elliger, Munich, 1966)
KP	E. H. Merrill, *Kingdom of Priests: A History of Old Testament Israel*, Grand Rapids, 1987
KPG	Knox Preaching Guides
KQT	K. G. Kuhn, *Konkordanz zu den Qumrantexten*, Göttingen, 1960
KSGVI	A. Alt, *Kleine Schriften zur Geschichte des Volkes Israel*, 3 vols., Munich, 1953-1959, 1964^{3}
KTU	*Die keilalphabetischen Texte aus Ugarit*, I, ed. M. Dietrich, O. Loretz, and J. Sanmartín, AOAT 24, Neukirchen-Vluyn, 1976
KuAT	*Die Keilinschriften und das Alte Testament*, ed. E. Schrader, Berlin, 1903^{3}
Lange	Lange Commentaries
LB	*Linguistica biblica*
LBC	Layman's Bible Commentaries
LBI	Library of Biblical Interpretation
Leš	*Lešonénu*
LexÄg	W. Helck and E. Otto, *Lexikon der Ägyptologie*, Wiesbaden, 1972-
LexSyr	C. Brockelmann, *Lexicon Syriacum*, Berlin, 1895; Halle, 1968^{2}
LHA	F. Zorell, *Lexicon hebraicum et aramaicum Veteris Testamenti*, Rome, 1946-1954, 1962^{2}
LLA	A. Dillmann, *Lexicon linguae aethiopicae*, Leipzig, 1865
LLAVT	E. Vogt, *Lexicon linguae aramaicae Veteris Testamenti documentis antiquis illustratum*, Rome, 1971
LQ	*Lutheran Quarterly*
LR	*Lutherische Rundschau*
LS	*Louvain Studies*
LSS	Leipziger semitistische Studien
LTK	*Lexicon für Theologie und Kirche*, ed. J. G. Herder, second series, 10 vols., Freiburg, i.B., 1957-1965
LTP	*Laval théologique et philosophique*
LUÅ	Lunds universitets årsskrift
MAL	C. Saporetti, *The Middle Assyrian Laws*, Malibu, Calif., 1984
MAOG	Mitteilungen der altorientalischen Gesellschaft
McCQ	*McCormick Quarterly*
MDB	*Le monde de la Bible*
MdD	E. S. Drower and R. Macuch, *A Mandaic Dictionary*, Oxford, 1963
MDP	Mémoires de la délégation en Perse

MedHab	*Medinet Habu*, Epigraphic Expedition, OIP 8, Chicago, 1930; OIP 9, 1932
MEOL	Mededelingen en Verhandelingen van het Vooraziatisch-Egyptisch Genootschap "Ex oriente lux"
MGWJ	*Monatsschrift für Geschichte und Wissenschaft des Judentums*
Moscati	S. Moscati, *An Introduction to the Comparative Grammar of Semitic Languages*, Wiesbaden, 1969
MSL	*Materialen zum sumerischen Lexikon*, Rome, 1937-
MTZ	*Münchener theologische Zeitschrift*
Mus	*Muséon: Revue d'études orientales*
MVÄG	Mitteilungen der vorderasiatisch-ägyptischen Gesellschaft
NAB	New American Bible
NAC	New American Commentary
NASB	New American Standard Bible
NAWG	Nachrichten der Akademie der Wissenschaften in Göttingen
NBC	*The New Bible Commentary*, ed. D. Guthrie and J. A. Motyer, London, 1970[3]
NBD	*The New Bible Dictionary*, ed. J. D. Douglas, London, 1982[2]
NCB(C)	New Century Bible (Commentary)
NEB	New English Bible
NedTT	*Nederlands theologisch tijdschrift*
NERTROT	*Near Eastern Religious Texts Relating to the Old Testament*, ed. W. Beyerlin, Philadelphia, 1978 (ET of *Religiongeschichtliches Textbuch zum AT*, Grundrisse zum AT 1, Göttingen, 1975)
NFT	New Frontiers in Theology
NGTT	*Nederduits gereformeerde teologiese tydskrif*
NICNT	New International Commentary on the New Testament
NICOT	New International Commentary on the Old Testament
NIDBA	*The New International Dictionary of Biblical Archaeology*, ed. E. M. Blaiklock and R. K. Harrison, Grand Rapids, 1983
NIDNTT	*The New International Dictionary of New Testament Theology*, ed. C. Brown, 4 vols., Grand Rapids, 1975-1978 (ET of *Theologisches Begriffslexicon zum NT*, ed. L. Coenen et al., 4 vols., Wuppertal, 1965-1971)
NIDOTTE	*The New International Dictionary of Old Testament Theology and Exegesis* (the present work)
NIV	New International Version
NIVEC	*The NIV Exhaustive Concordance*, ed. E. W. Goodrick and J. R. Kohlenberger III, Grand Rapids, 1990

NJBC	*The New Jerome Biblical Commentary*, ed. R. E. Brown et al., Englewood Cliffs, N.J., 1990
NJPSV	New Jewish Publication Society Version
NKJV	New King James Version
NKZ	*Neue kirchliche Zeitschrift*
NorTT	*Norsk teologisk tidsskrift*
NovT	*Novum Testamentum*
NRSV	New Revised Standard Version
NRT	*Nouvelle revue théologique*
NTD	Das Neue Testament Deutsch
NTOA	Novum Testamentum et orbis antiquus
NTS	*New Testament Studies*
OBL	Orientalia et biblica lovaniensia
OBO	Orbis biblicus et orientalis
OBT	Overtures to Biblical Theology
OECT	Oxford Editions of Cuneiform Texts
OED	*The Oxford English Dictionary*
OIP	Oriental Institute Publications
OLP	Orientalia lovaniensia periodica
OLZ	*Orientalistische Literaturzeitung*
OMRM	*Oudheidkundige Mededeelingen uit het Rijksmuseum van Oudheden te Leiden*
Or	*Orientalia*
OrAnt	*Oriens antiquus*
OTE	*Old Testament Essays*
OTG	Old Testament Guides
OTL	Old Testament Library
OTM	Old Testament Message: A Biblical-Theological Commentary
OTS	*Oudtestamentische Studiën*
OTT	G. von Rad, *Old Testament Theology*, tr. D. M. G. Stalker, 2 vols., New York, 1962, 1965 (ET of *Theologie des ATs*, Einfuhrung in die evangelische Theologie 1, 2 vols., Munich, 1957, 1960)
OTTCT	B. S. Childs, *Old Testament Theology in a Canonical Context*, London, 1985
OTTO	W. Zimmerli, *Old Testament Theology in Outline*, tr. D. E. Green, Atlanta, 1978 (ET of *Grundriss der alttestamentlichen Theologie*, Theologische Wissenschaft 3, Stuttgart, 1972)
OTWSA	Die Ou Testamentiese Werkgemeenskap in Suid Afrika

PAAJR	*Proceedings of the American Academy of Jewish Research*
Palache	J. L. Palache, *Semantic Notes on the Hebrew Lexicon*, tr. and ed. R. J. Z. Werblowsky, Leiden, 1959
Peake	*Peake's Commentary on the Bible*, ed. M. Black and H. H. Rowley, New York, 1962[2]
PEQ	*Palestine Exploration Quarterly*
PJ	*Palästina-Jahrbuch*
PL	*Patrologia Latina*, ed. J.-P. Migne, 221 vols., Paris, 1841-1864
PNPI	J. K. Stark, *Personal Names in Palmyrene Inscriptions*, Oxford, 1971
POT	De Prediking van het Oude Testament
POTT	*Peoples of Old Testament Times*, ed. D. J. Wiseman, Oxford, 1973
POTW	*Peoples of the Old Testament World*, ed. A. E. Hoerth, G. L. Mattingley, and E. M. Yamauchi, Grand Rapids, 1994
PPG	J. Friedrich and W. Röllig, *Phönizisch-punische Grammatik*, AnOr 46, Rome, 1970[2]
PRU	*Le Palais royal d'Ugarit*, ed. C. F.-A. Schaeffer and J. Nougayrol, Paris, 1956-
PSB	*Princeton Seminary Bulletin*
PSTJ	*Perkins (School of Theology) Journal*
PTR	*Princeton Theological Review*
PTS	*Pretoria Theological Studies*
PTU	F. Gröndahl, *Die Personennamen der Texte aus Ugarit*, Rome, 1967
Pyr	K. Sethe, *Die altägyptischen Pyramidentexte*, 4 vols., Leipzig, 1908-1922
QD	*Quaestiones disputatae*, ed. K. Rahner and H. Schlier, Freiburg, i.B., 1958-; Eng. ed., New York, 1961-
QDAP	*Quarterly of the Department of Antiquities in Palestine*
QJRM	*Quarterly Journal for Reflection on Ministry*
RA	*Revue d'assyriologie et d'archéologie orientale*
RAC	*Reallexikon für Antike und Christentum*, ed. T. Klauser, 10 vols., Stuttgart, 1950-1978
RANE	Records of the Ancient Near East
RÄR	H. Bonnet, *Reallexikon der ägyptischen Religionsgeschichte*, Berlin, 1952
RArch	*Revue archéologique*
RB	*Revue biblique*
RE	*Realencyklopädie für protestantische Theologie und Kirche*, ed. A. Hauck, Leipzig, 1896-1913
REB	Revised English Bible

RECA	*Real-Encyclopädie der classischen Altertumswissenschaft*, ed., A. Pauly, 6 vols., Stuttgart, 1839; ed. G. Wissowa et al., first series, 24 vols., 1894-1963; second series, 10 vols., 1914-1972; supplements, 16 vols., 1903-1980
RechBib	Recherches bibliques
REg	*Revue d'égyptologie*
REJ	*Revue des études juives*
RelS	*Religious Studies*
RES	*Répertoire d'épigraphie sémitique*
ResQ	*Restoration Quarterly*
RevExp	*Review and Expositor*
RevistB	*Revista bíblica*
RevQ	*Revue de Qumran*
RevScRel	*Revue de sciences religieuses*
RevSém	*Revue sémitique*
RGG	*Die Religion in Geschichte und Gegenwart*, H. Gunkel and L. Zscharnack, 5 vols., Tübingen, 1927-1931[2]; ed. K. Galling, 7 vols., 1957-1965[3]
RHLR	*Revue d'histoire et de littérature religieuses*
RHPR	*Revue d'histoire et de philosophie religieuses*
RHR	*Revue de l'histoire des religions*
RLA	*Reallexikon der Assyriologie*, ed. G. Ebeling and B. Meissner, Berlin, 1, 1932; 2, 1938; 3, 1957-1971; 4, 1972-1975; 5, 1976-1980; 6, 1980-1983; 7, 1987-1990
RR	*Review of Religion*
RSO	*Rivista degli studi orientali*
RSP	*Ras Shamra Parallels: The Texts from Ugarit and the Hebrew Bible*, ed. L. R. Fisher, vols. 1-2, AnOr 49-50, 1972, 1975; ed. S. Rummel, vol. 3, AnOr 51, 1981
RSR	*Recherches de science religieuse*
RSV	Revised Standard Version
RTL	*Revue théologique de Louvain*
RTR	*Reformed Theological Review*
RV	Revised Version
RVV	Religionsgeschichtliche Versuche und Vorarbeiten
SAHG	A. Falkenstein and W. von Soden, *Sumerische und akkadische Hymnen und Gebete*, Zurich, 1953
SANT	Studien zum Alten und Neuen Testament
SAOC	Studies in Ancient Oriental Civilization

SAT	*Die Schriften des Alten Testaments in Auswahl*, tr. and ed. H. Gunkel et al., Göttingen, 1909-1915, 1920-1925[2]
SBB	Stuttgarter biblische Beiträge
SBLDS	Society of Biblical Literature Dissertation Series
SBLMS	Society of Biblical Literature Monograph Series
SBM	Stuttgarter biblische Monographien
SBS	Stuttgarter Bibelstudien
SBT	Studies in Biblical Theology
ScrHier	Scripta Hierosolymitana
Scrip	*Scriptura*
SDIOAP	Studia et documenta ad iura orientis antiqui pertinentia
SE	*Studia Evangelica 1, 2, 3,* etc. (= TU 73, 1959; 87, 1964; 88, 1964; etc.)
SEÅ	*Svensk exegetisk årsbok*
SEAJT	*South East Asia Journal of Theology*
Sem	*Semitica*
Seux	J. M. Seux, *Epithètes royales akkadiennes et sumériennes*, Paris, 1967
SGL	A. Falkenstein, *Sumerische Götterlieder*, Heidelberg, 1959
SGV	Sammlung gemeinverständlicher Vorträge und Schriften aus dem Gebiet der Theologie und Religionsgeschichte
SJ	Studia judaica
SJLA	Studies in Judaism in Late Antiquity
SJOT	*Scandinavian Journal of the Old Testament*
SJT	*Scottish Journal of Theology*
SNovT	Supplements to Novum Testamentum
SNumen	Supplements to Numen
SOTBT	Studies in Old Testament Biblical Theology
SPIB	Scripta pontificii instituti biblici
SR	*Studies in Religion/Sciences religieuses*
SSN	Studia semitica neerlandica
SSS	Semitic Study Series
ST	*Studia theologica*
STÅ	*Svensk teologisk årsskrift*
STDJ	Studies on the Texts of the Desert of Judah
STK	*Svensk teologisk kvartalskrift*
Str-B	H. L. Strack and P. Billerbeck, *Kommentar zum NT aus Talmud und Midrasch*, 6 vols., Munich, 1922-1961

STT	*The Sultantepe Tablets*, vol. 1, ed. O. R. Gurney and J. J. Finkelstein, London, 1957; vol. 2, ed. O. R. Gurney and P. Hulin, London, 1964
StudBib	Studia biblica
StudBT	*Studia biblica et theologica*
StudOr	*Studia orientalia*
SUNT	Studien zur Umwelt des Neuen Testaments
SVT	Supplements to Vetus Testamentum
SVTP	Studia in Veteris Testamenti pseudepigrapha
SWBA	Social World of Biblical Antiquity
SWJT	*Southwestern Journal of Theology*
Syria	*Syria: Revue d'art oriental et d'archéologie*
TAPA	*Transactions of the American Philological Association*
TArb	Theologische Arbeiten
TBT	*The Bible Today*
TBü	Theologische Bücherei
TCL	Textes cunéiformes du Musée du Louvre
TDNT	*Theological Dictionary of the New Testament*, ed. G. Kittel and G. Friedrich, tr. and ed. G. W. Bromiley, 10 vols., Grand Rapids, 1964-1976 (ET of *Theologisches Wörterbuch zum NT*, 10 vols., Stuttgart, 1933-1979)
TDOT	*Theological Dictionary of the Old Testament*, ed. G. J. Botterweck, H. Ringgren, and H.-J. Fabry, tr. J. T. Willis, Grand Rapids, 1974- (ET of *TWAT*)
TEH	Theologische Existenz Heute
TEV	Today's English Version
TGI	K. Galling, *Textbuch zur Geschichte Israels*, Tübingen, 1950, 1968^3
TGUOS	*Transactions of the Glasgow University Oriental Society*
THAT	*Theologisches Handbuch zum Alten Testament*, ed. E. Jenni and C. Westermann, 2 vols., Munich, 1971, 1976
Them	*Themelios*
ThStud	*Theologische Studiën*
TigrWb	E. Littmann and M. Höfner, *Wörterbuch der Tigre-Sprache*, Wiesbaden, 1962
TLZ	*Theologische Literaturzeitung*
TNT	G. E. Ladd, *A Theology of the New Testament*, Grand Rapids, 1974
Torch	Torch Bible Commentaries
TOT	W. Eichrodt, *Theology of the Old Testament*, tr. J. A. Baker, 2 vols., Philadelphia, 1961, 1967 (ET of *Theologie des AT*, 3 vols., Leipzig, 1933-1939; 3 vols. in 2, Stuttgart, 1957-1961^2)

TOTC	Tyndale Old Testament Commentaries
TPQ	*Theologisch-praktische Quartalschrift*
TPs	H.-J. Kraus, *Theologie der Psalmen*, BKAT 15/3, Neukirchen-Vluyn, 1979
TQ	*Theologische Quartalschrift*
TRE	*Theologische Realenzyklopädie*, ed. G. Krause and G. Müller, Berlin, 1977-
TREg	P. Lacau, *Textes religieux égyptiens*, part 1, Paris, 1910
TrinJ	*Trinity Journal*
TRu	*Theologische Rundschau*
TSSI	*Textbook of Syrian Semitic Inscriptions*, ed. J. C. L. Gibson, 3 vols., London, 1971-1982
TToday	*Theology Today*
TTS	Trierer theologische Studien
TTZ	*Trierer theologische Zeitschrift*
TU	Texte und Untersuchungen
TV	Theologische Versuche
TViat	Theologia viatorum
TWAT	*Theologisches Wörterbuch zum Alten Testament*, ed. G. J. Botterweck, H. Ringgren, and H.-J. Fabry, 8 vols., Stuttgart, 1970-1995
TWBB	*A Theological Wordbook of the Bible*, ed. A. Richardson, London, 1950
TWOT	*Theological Wordbook of the Old Testament*, ed. R. L. Harris et al., 2 vols., Chicago, 1980
TynBul	*Tyndale Bulletin*
TZ	*Theologische Zeitschrift*
UAA	*Urkunden des ägyptischen Altertums*, ed. G. Steindorff, Leipzig, 1903-
UCPNES	University of California Publications in Near Eastern Studies
UE	Ur Excavations, ed. C. L. Woolley, London, 1927-
UF	*Ugarit-Forschungen*
USQR	*Union Seminary Quarterly Review*
UT	C. Gordon, *Ugaritic Textbook*, AnOr 38, Rome, 1965
UUÅ	Uppsala universitetsårsskrift
VAB	*Vorderasiatische Bibliothek*, 7 vols., Leipzig, 1907-1916
VASKMB	*Vorderasiatische Schriftdenkmäler der königlichen Museen zu Berlin*, ed. O. Schroeder, Leipzig, 1907-
VDI	*Vestnik drevnej Istorii*
VE	*Vox evangelica*
VF	*Verkündigung und Forschung*

VT	*Vetus Testamentum*
WbÄS	A. Erman and H. Grapow, *Wörterbuch der ägyptischen Sprache*, 5 vols., Berlin, 1926-1931; repr. 1963
WBC	Word Biblical Commentary
WbMyth	*Wörterbuch der Mythologie*, ed. H. W. Haussig, Stuttgart, 1961-
WC	Westminster Commentaries
WD	*Wort und Dienst*
WEC	Wycliffe Exegetical Commentary
Wehr	H. Wehr, *A Dictionary of Modern Written Arabic*, ed. J. M. Cowan, Ithaca, 1961, 1976^3
WF	Wege der Forschung
Whitaker	R. E. Whitaker, *A Concordance of the Ugaritic Literature*, Cambridge, Mass., 1972
WMANT	Wissenschaftliche Monographien zum Alten und Neuen Testament
WO	*Die Welt des Orients*
WTJ	*Westminster Theological Journal*
WTM	J. Levy, *(Neuhebräisches und chaldäisches) Wörterbuch über die Talmudim und Midraschim*, 4 vols., Leipzig, 1876-1889; Berlin, 1924^2; repr. 1963
WUNT	Wissenschaftliche Untersuchungen zum Neuen Testament
WUS	J. Aistleitner, *Wörterbuch der ugaritischen Sprache*, BVSAW 106/3, 1963, 1974^4
WVDOG	Wissenschaftliche Veröffentlichungen der deutschen Orientgesellschaft
WW	*Word and World*
WZ	Wissenschaftliche Zeitschrift (der Karl-Marx-Universität, Leipzig/der Wilhelm-Pieck-Universität, Rostock)
YJS	Yale Judaica Series
YOSBT	Yale Oriental Series, Babylonian Texts
ZA	*Zeitschrift für Assyriologie*
ZAH	*Zeitschrift für Althebraistik*
ZÄS	*Zeitschrift für ägyptische Sprache und Altertumskunde*
ZAW	*Zeitschrift für die alttestamentliche Wissenschaft*
ZB	Zürcher Bibelkommentare
ZDMG	*Zeitschrift der deutschen morgenländischen Gesellschaft*
ZDPV	*Zeitschrift des deutschen Palästina-Vereins*
ZEE	*Zeitschrift für evangelische Ethik*
ZKT	*Zeitschrift für katholische Theologie*

ZNW	*Zeitschrift für die neutestamentliche Wissenschaft*
Zorell	F. Zorell, *Lexicon hebraicum et aramaicum Veteris Testamenti*, Rome, 1946-1954, 1962[2]
ZPEB	*The Zondervan Pictorial Encyclopedia of the Bible*, ed. M. C. Tenney, 5 vols., Grand Rapids, 1975
ZRGG	*Zeitschrift für Religions und Geistesgeschichte*
ZTK	*Zeitschrift für Theologie und Kirche*

Old Testament and New Testament

Gen	Ezra	Joel	John	Philem
Exod	Neh	Amos	Acts	Heb
Lev	Esth	Obad	Rom	James
Num	Job	Jon	1 Cor	1 Peter
Deut	Ps	Mic	2 Cor	2 Peter
Josh	Prov	Nah	Gal	1 John
Judg	Eccl	Hab	Eph	2 John
Ruth	S of Songs	Zeph	Phil	3 John
1 Sam	Isa	Hag	Col	Jude
2 Sam	Jer	Zech	1 Thess	Rev
1 Kgs	Lam	Mal	2 Thess	
2 Kgs	Ezek	Matt	1 Tim	
1 Chron	Dan	Mark	2 Tim	
2 Chron	Hos	Luke	Titus	

Apocrypha

1 Esdr	1 Esdras
2 Esdr	2 Esdras
Tob	Tobit
Jdt	Judith
Add Esth	Additions to Esther
Wisd	Wisdom of Solomon
Sir	Sirach (Ecclesiasticus)
Bar	Baruch
Ep Jer	Epistle (Letter) of Jeremiah
S of Three	Song of the Three Young Men
Sus	Susanna

Bel	Bel and the Dragon
Pr Man	Prayer of Manasseh
1 Macc	1 Maccabees
2 Macc	2 Maccabees

Pseudepigrapha

Adam and Eve	*Life of Adam and Eve*
As. Mos.	*Assumption of Moses*
Asc. Isa.	*Ascension of Isaiah*
2 Bar.	*2 (Syriac Apocalypse of) Baruch*
3 Bar.	*3 (Greek Apocalypse of) Baruch*
1 En.	*1 (Ethiopic) Enoch*
2 En.	*2 (Slavonic) Enoch*
3 En.	*3 (Hebrew) Enoch*
Ep. Arist.	*Epistle of Aristeas*
4 Ezra	*4 Ezra*
Jub.	*Jubilees*
3 Macc.	*3 Maccabees*
4 Macc.	*4 Maccabees*
Mart. Isa.	*Martyrdom of Isaiah*
Pss. Sol.	*Psalms of Solomon*
Sib. Or.	*Sibylline Oracles*
T. 12 Patr.	*Testaments of the Twelve Patriarchs*
T. Reub.	*Testament of Reuben*
T. Sim.	*Testament of Simeon*
T. Levi	*Testament of Levi*
T. Jud.	*Testament of Judah*
T. Iss.	*Testament of Issachar*
T. Zeb.	*Testament of Zebulun*
T. Dan	*Testament of Dan*
T. Naph.	*Testament of Naphtali*
T. Gad	*Testament of Gad*
T. Ash.	*Testament of Asher*
T. Jos.	*Testament of Joseph*
T. Benj.	*Testament of Benjamin*

Dead Sea Scrolls and Related Texts

Initial Arabic numeral indicates cave number; Q=Qumran; p=pesher (commentary)

CD	Cairo (Genizah text of the) *Damascus* (*Document*)
Ḥev	Naḥal Ḥever texts
8ḤevXII gr	Greek Scroll of the Minor Prophets from Naḥal Ḥever
Mas	Masada texts
MasShirShabb	*Songs of the Sabbath Sacrifice* or *Angelic Liturgy* from Masada
Mird	Khirbet Mird texts
Mur	Wadi Murabba'at texts
1Q34^{bis}	*Prayer for the Feast of Weeks* (Fragment of Liturgical Prayer Scroll = 1Q Prayers)
1QapGen	*Genesis Apocryphon*
1QDM (or 1Q22)	*Sayings of Moses*
1QH	*Thanksgiving Hymns*
1QIsa^{a}	First copy of Isaiah
1QIsa^{b}	Second copy of Isaiah
1QM	*War Scroll*
1QpHab	*Pesher on Habakkuk*
1QpMic	*Pesher on Micah*
1QpPs	*Pesher on Psalms*
1QS	*Manual of Discipline / Rule of the Community*
3QInv (or 3Q15)	*Copper* (Treasure) *Scroll*
4QFlor	*Florilegium* (*Eschatological Midrashim*)
4QPBless	*Patriarchal Blessings*
4QpIsa^{a,b,c,d}	Copies of the *Pesher on Isaiah*
4QpNah	*Pesher on Nahum*
4QpPs37	*Pesher on Ps 37*
4QSam^{a,b,c}	Copies of Samuel
4QTestim	*Testimonia* text
6QD (or 6Q15)	Fragments of the *Damascus Document*
11QPs^{a}DavComp	Apocryphal Psalms (Prose Supplement)
11QtgJob	*Targum to Job*
11QTemple^{a,b}	*Temple Scroll*

For further sigla, see J. A. Fitzmeyer, *The Dead Sea Scrolls: Major Publications and Tools for Study*, SBL Sources for Biblical Study 20, Atlanta, 1990

Ancient Authorities

Ant.	*Antquities of the Jews*, by Flavius Josephus
Eccl. Hist.	*Ecclesiastical History*, by Eusebius
Nat. Hist.	*Natural History*, by Pliny
Wars	*Wars of the Jews*, by Flavius Josephus

Transliterations

Hebrew and Aramaic

א = ʼ	ו = *w*	כ, ך = *k*	ע = ʻ	שׂ = *ś*
ב = *b*	ז = *z*	ל = *l*	פ, ף = *p*	שׁ = *š*
ג = *g*	ח = *ḥ*	מ, ם = *m*	צ = *ṣ*	ת = *t*
ד = *d*	ט = *ṭ*	נ, ן = *n*	ק = *q*	
ה = *h*	י = *y*	ס = *s*	ר = *r*	

No distinction is made between the *bgdkpt* with or without the dagesh lene.
Compare: תּוֹרָה = *tôrâ* הַתּוֹרָה = *hattôrâ* תּוֹרָתוֹ = *tôrātô*

Vowels

◌ָה = *â*	◌ֵ = *ē*	◌ִ = *i*
◌ָ = *ā*	◌ֵי = *ê*	◌ִי = *î*
◌ַ = *a*	◌ֶ = *e*	וֹ = *ô*
◌ֲ = ^{a}	◌ְ = ^{e} (if vocal)	◌ֹ = *ō*
וּ = *û*	◌ֱ = ^{e}	◌ָ = *o*
◌ֻ = *u*		◌ֳ = ^{o}

Other semitic languages: Transliterations follow standard practice.

Greek

α = *a*	μ = *m*	ψ = *ps*	ηυ = *ēu*
β = *b*	ν = *n*	ω = *ō*	οι = *oi*
γ = *g*	ξ = *x*		ου = *ou*
δ = *d*	ο = *o*	γγ = *ng*	υι = *ui*
ε = *e*	π = *p*	γκ = *nk*	
ζ = *z*	ρ = *r*	γξ = *nx*	ῥ = *rh*
η = *ē*	σ, ς = *s*	γχ = *nch*	ʽ = *h*
θ = *th*	τ = *t*	αι = *ai*	
ι = *i*	υ = *u*	αυ = *au*	ᾳ = *ā*
κ = *k*	φ = *ph*	ει = *ei*	ῃ = *ē*
λ = *l*	χ = *ch*	ευ = *eu*	ῳ = *ō*

THE NEW INTERNATIONAL DICTIONARY OF OLD TESTAMENT THEOLOGY AND EXEGESIS

Lexical Articles נ to שׂ

נ

5528 (*nā'*, enclitic particle), → Particles

5532	נֹאד

נֹאד (*nō'd*), nom. skin-bottle, scroll (6x) (# 5532).

ANE Akk. *nādu(m)*, water skin, leather pouch for precious metals; Tg. Aram. *nôdā'*, leather skin.

OT Three times this word refers to a wineskin (Josh 9:4, 13; 1 Sam 16:20) and once to a skin-bottle for milk (Judg 4:19). A wordplay on *nō'd* as leather used as a skin-bottle and as a scroll is likely in Ps 56:8[9]. In writing *śîmâ dim'ātî b^enō'dekā* ("place my tears in your skin-bottle" or "list my tears on your scroll") in co-text with verbal action of recounting/recording, the psalmist is requesting that his tears be placed (*śîmâ*) in a skin-bottle, emphasizing the level of his distress, and that the reasons for his tears should be recorded (*śîmâ*) on leather, i.e., a scroll. In Ps 119:83, *nō'd* occurs in a simile in the phrase "like a wineskin in the smoke." Most scholars believe that the simile refers to distress, the bottle being likely unused and shriveled. Bergler believes that the simile refers to a swaying to and fro to describe human inconsistency (274).

P-B The uses of this word echo the senses in the OT. The word is attested in the DSS and the Talm.

Skin, leather: → *'ādām* II (leather, # 133); → *'ah^abâ* II (leather, # 174); → *'ôb* I (wine-skin, # 199); → *gēled* (skin, # 1654); → *ḥēmet* (waterskin, # 2827); → *nō'd* (bottle, scroll, # 5532); → *'ôr* (skin, hide, # 6425); → *ṣhl* II (shine [of healthy skin], # 7413); → *taḥrā'* (leather collar?, # 9389); → *taḥaš* I (leather?, # 9391)

Bibliography

S. Bergler, "Der längste Psalm—Anthologie oder Liturgie?" *VT* 29, 1979, 257-88; L. DeVries, "Skin," *ISBE* 4:535-36.

Gary Alan Long

5533	נאה

נאה (*n'h*), q. be lovely, appropriate, suitable (# 5533); נָאוֶה (*nā'weh*), lovely, suitable, desirable (# 5534).

OT 1. Some confusion exists over the vb. *n'h* as to whether it exists as a ni. from *'wh*, desire; (→ # 203; GKC 75x), a pi'lel (BDB, 610), or pa'el (Westermann, 250). *HALAT* is undecided, first listing it as a ni. under *'wh* (20), but later suggesting that it may be a q. derived from a mixing of the roots *nwh* II, praise (→ # 5658) and *'wh* (621). The three uncontested citations found in the OT are Ps 93:5; S of Songs 1:10; Isa 52:7, although *HALAT* emends Ps 141:5 from MT *yānî'* to *y*ᵉ*nā'*, making it a pi. (juss.). Sir 15:9 reads *lō' nā'*ᵃ*tâ t*ᵉ*hillâ b*ᵉ*pî rāšā'*, "a prayer is not appropriate (*n'h*) in the mouth of a wicked man" (Segal, 93).

2. Most agree that the word means beautiful in the sense of appropriate, suitable, although any contact with the root *'wh*, whether from the mixing of the roots *nwh* and *'wh* or as a corrupted ni. from the latter, would argue for a meaning nuanced toward "desirable." NIV accordingly translates Ps 93:5 as "holiness adorns your house . . . O LORD." Shenkel, however, argues that the vb. in Ps 93:5 should be interpreted in light of its variant form (*nwh*) in Exod 15:2 and also here rendered "glorify, praise," thus reading "in your temple the holy ones shall glorify you" (401-16). Dahood agrees, offering the meaning "laud," interpreting the vb. as q. (*Psalms II*, 342-43). If the traditional idea of "appropriate" be accepted, the adj. *nā'weh* would mean beautiful, with a nuance of suitability, appropriateness, and thus of desirability. Beautiful in the sense of "desirable" would seem to be the sense of the word in S of Songs 1:5; 2:14; 4:3; 6:4 (where it parallels *yph*), whereas Ps 33:1; 147:1; Prov 17:7; 19:10; 26:1 seem to lean toward "appropriate, fitting." Yet if Shenkel is correct, the latter category needs to be examined further, for he argues persuasively that both Ps 33:1 and 147:1 are vbs. (with *t*ᵉ*hillâ* following) and should be rendered, "to glorify [with praise]."

Beauty, beautiful, desire, desirable, fair: → *'wh* (desire, regard as beautiful, desirable, # 203); → *ḥemed* (grace, comeliness, beauty, # 2774); → *yph* (become fair, beautiful, adorn, # 3636); → *n'h* (be lovely, # 5533); → *p'r* (beautify, glorify, # 6995); → *špr* (be beautiful, # 9182)

BIBLIOGRAPHY

M. Dahood, *Psalms II*, AB, 1968, 342-43; H. Ringgren, *TDOT* 6:218-20; M. T. Segal, *Sēper ben sira'haš-šālēm,* Jerusalem, 1958, 93-94; J. D. Shenkel, "An Interpretation of Psalm 93,5," *Bib* 46, 1965, 401-16; P. W. Skehan and A. A. DiLella, *The Wisdom of Ben Sira*, AB, 1987; C. Westermann, *Isaiah 40-66*, OTL, 1966, 250.

William C. Williams

5534 (*nā'weh*, beautiful, becoming, suitable), → # 5533

5536 (*n*ᵉ*'um*, declaration, decision), → Prophecy

5537	נאף

נאף (*n'p*), q. commit adultery, (metaphorical) idolatry; pi. commit adultery, (metaphorical) idolatry (# 5537); nom. נַאֲפוּפִים (*na'*ᵃ*pûpîm*), marks of adultery (only in Hos 2:4: "the children of adultery") (# 5538); נִאֻפִים (*ni'upîm*), adultery (only in Jer 13:27; Ezek 23:43) (# 5539).

ANE The vb. *nâku* appears with the meaning "to have illicit sexual intercourse" in Akk. The ancient law codes condemn adultery and prescribe the death penalty. However, the husband may waive or mitigate the punishment if he wishes (see Laws of

Eshnunna 28; Code of Hammurabi 129-32, 155, 156; Middle Assyr. Laws 12, 14, 17, 18, 22-24; Hitt. Laws 195, 197-98; *ANET* 162, 171-72, 180-97).

OT 1. *n'p* occurs 34x in its nom. and vb. forms; 3 noms., 16 q. stem, and 15 pi. stem. Over half the vb. forms are part(s). used as substantives. The root occurs only 6x in the Pent. but 24x in the prophets (esp. Jer, Ezek, and Hos). *n'p* occurs in contexts with harlotry/prostitution 9x.

2. Adultery is forbidden in the Decalogue (Exod 20:14; Deut 5:18). What adultery is and is not may be best understood from the casuistic laws. It involves the sexual liaison of a man with a married woman (Lev 18:20; 20:10), a married woman with a man (Ezek 16:32; Hos 4:13) or a man with a betrothed girl (Deut 22:23-27). The texts are silent on the marital status of the man. Seduction of an unpledged virgin by a man was forbidden, but was not called adultery (Exod 22:16; Deut 22:28-29). Unless one assumes that the man was married every time, one could consider that only the woman's status defined adultery. Even in Ezek 16:32 and Hos 4:13 one can only consider it "probable" that married men were involved (Durham, *Exodus*, WBC, 293).

3. Adultery was detrimental on both sociological and theological grounds. First, since the extended family was the cornerstone of Israelite society, threats to its stability could not be tolerated. Second, marriage, grounded in a divine ordinance (Gen 2:24), was a covenant arrangement (cf. Mal 2:14) that required faithfulness and love. It was a mirror of God's covenant with his people. Therefore, adultery was a sin against God (Gen 39:9) and a shattering of the sexual integrity of the God ordained family (Wright, 123-24). Third, adultery was also an issue of personal integrity, as John I. Durham observes, "Adultery ... was, like idol worship, a turning away from commitment to Yahweh" (*Exodus*, WBC, 294).

The prophets, too, include adultery in a list of expressions of covenantal infidelity. Hosea said, "There is only cursing, lying and murder, stealing and adultery; they break all bounds, and bloodshed follows bloodshed" (Hos 4:2). Jeremiah charges the people with duplicity, "Will you steal and murder, commit adultery and perjury, burn incense to Baal and follow other gods you have not known, and then come and stand before me in this house, which bears my Name, and say, 'We are safe'—safe to do all these detestable things?" (Jer 7:9-10). Other passages also lead to the conclusion that the adulterer readily breaks any one of the Ten Commandments (*TWAT* 5:126-27).

4. The penalty for adultery according to the Law was death (Lev 20:10; Deut 22:22), by stoning (Deut 22:24) or by burning (Lev 20:14; 21:9). The actual practices varied (cf. Prov 6:32-35; see also John 8:4-5). The death penalty did not apply to either party if the girl was a betrothed slave (Lev 19:20-21). It was applied only to the man if the liaison occurred in the open country (Deut 22;25-27). This protected the innocent girl. The wife was also protected from a jealous or insensitive husband by two laws (see Num 5:11-31; Deut 22:13-19).

The laws pertaining to adultery allowed the husband to confirm or allay his suspicions and protect his family name and progeny (Num 5:11-31). Instances of adultery are not rare in the OT (2 Sam 11; Prov 2:16; Jer 7:9; 23:10; Hos 4:2, 13-14; Mal 3:5, etc.), but there is no explicit reference to the death penalty being applied. This is not surprising, considering that two witnesses were needed for capital cases (Deut 17:6).

5. The Wisdom literature, while ignoring the criminal penalty, details the personal, social, and economic consequences of adultery (Prov 2:12-22; 5:1-14; 6:26,

33-35). Adultery is folly because the adulterer is not a person of integrity, destroys the network of family relations, and may come to financial and professional ruin. On rare occasions even the desire for another woman is condemned, "I made a covenant with my eyes not to look lustfully at a girl. ... If my steps have turned from the path, if my heart has been led by my eyes, or if my hands have been defiled, then may others eat what I have sown, and may my crops be uprooted" (Job 31:1, 7-8; cf. Exod 20:17; Prov 6:25-26; Matt 5:28).

6. One-third of the occurrences of *n'p* have a nonliteral sense. Several texts are ambiguous, referring to either literal or metaphorical adultery, or both (Jer 9:2[1]; 23:10; Hos 4:13-14; 7:4). Hosea, Jeremiah, and Ezekiel vividly condemn religious idolatry as spiritual adultery, the epitome of unfaithfulness.

When Hosea portrayed the relationship between God and Israel as a marriage and condemned the Canaanite fertility cult, the emotionally loaded concept became appropriate for apostasy. There were no stronger terms, especially when combined with harlotry language (→ *znh*, # 2388), for Israel's unfaithfulness.

Jeremiah charges Israel with a pagan and idolatrous lifestyle, "Your adulteries (*ni'upîm*) and lustful neighings, your shameless (*zimmâ*, → # 2365) prostitution (*z^{e}nût*)! I have seen your detestable acts (*šiqqûṣ*) on the hills and in the fields. Woe to you, O Jerusalem! How long will you be unclean?" (Jer 13:27; see J. A. Thompson, *Jeremiah*, NICOT, 374-75). Israel had been unfaithful from the beginning (see chs. 2-3; 5:7).

Ezekiel developed two long, scathing diatribes against the two whores, Israel and Judah. They were unfaithful from the very beginning (Ezek 16 and 23; esp. 16:32, 38; 23:37, 43, 45).

7. Other phrases in the OT describe the act of adultery: *škb*, lie with (→ # 8886; see Num 5:13, 19, 20; Deut 22:22-27); *šgl*, violate, ravish (→ # 8711; see Deut 28:30; Isa 13:16); *bw' 'el*, go to (see Gen 16:4; 30:4; 2 Sam 16:21, 22); *qrb 'el*, go near to (see Gen 20:4); *kr' 'al*, crouch over (→ # 4156; see Job 31:10).

8. The adulteress woman is referred to as an *'iššâ zārâ*, foreign woman, in Prov 2:16; 5:3, 20; 7:5, or as a *nokriyyâ*, alien woman; NIV wayward wife) in 2:16; 5:20; 6:24; 7:5; 23:27.

P-B In Judaism adultery remained a serious moral, sociological, and criminal offense. The author of Sir condemns unfaithful men and women (Sir 23:16-27; 25:2). Children suffer from it (Wisd 3:16-19; see also 14:24-26). Sexual sins are the worst kind in the Testament of the Twelve Patriarchs (T. Reub 1:6, 9; 3:10-4:2; 5:3-4; 6:1; T. Levi 9:9, T. Sim 5:3; T. Jud 12:1-9; 18:2-6, etc.). Temptation to adultery should be met with fasting and prayer (T. Jos 4:6, 8; 5:1). The Sib. Or 3:36-45 connects adultery and idolatry. The Mishnah upheld the death penalty (Mish. Sanh. 7.3, 9; B. Sanh. 52b, 55b, 66b). The tractate Sota provided the interpretation of the Num 5 passage, stating that the bitter water test ceased when adultery became common (Mish. Sota 9.9)! The spirit of adultery (Sota 4b) and lust were censured (Yoma 29a, Nid. 13b). Philo denounced adultery (Decal. 121-31). The LXX renders *n'p* by vb., nom., and adj. forms of *moichaō* and *moicheuō,* with no distinction between the q. and pi. vb. forms. *Moichaō* forms occur only in Jer and Ezek.

NT The NT continues the OT strictures against adultery and sexual looseness (Matt 5:27; 15:19; 19:18 and par.; Rom 13:9; 1 Cor 6:9-10; Gal 5:19; Eph 5:5; James 2:11; Rev 22:15). The NT also uses the metaphorical sense to denote wickedness (Matt 12:39; 16:4; Mark 8:38) and idolatry (James 4:4; Rev 2:22), though these latter are ambiguous and could be either literal or metaphorical. Jesus restricts and amplifies the OT understanding. He taught that divorce may only take place when adultery has taken place (Matt 5:31-32; 19:19) and that adultery can occur in the heart apart from the act (Matt 5:28), but he did not affirm the penalty of stoning the adulterer. (→ *NIDNTT* 2:582-84)

Prostitution: → *znh* I (commit fornication, act as a harlot, # 2388); → *qādēš* I (sacred person, temple prostitute, # 7728)

BIBLIOGRAPHY

TDNT 4:729-35; *TWAT* 5:123-29; M. Fishbane, "Accusations of Adultery: A Study of Law and Scribal Practice in Num 5:11-31," *HUCA* 45, 1974, 25-45; R. Gordis, "On Adultery in Biblical and Babylonian Law—A Note," *Judaism* 33, 1984, 210-11; S. Greengus, "Textbook Case of Adultery in Ancient Mesopotamia," *HUCA* 40-41, 1969, 33-44; G. Hall, "The Marriage Imagery of Jeremiah 2 and 3," diss. Union Theol. Sem., Virginia, 1980; W. Kornfeld, "L'adultère dans l'orient antique," *RB* 57, 1950, 92-109; Henry McKeating, "Sanctions Against Adultery in Israelite Society, with Some Reflections on Methodology in the Study of Old Testament Ethics," *JSOT* 11, 1979, 57-72; J. Milgrom, "On the Suspected Adulteress (Num 5:11-31)," *VT* 35, 1985, 368-69; W. L. Moran, "The Scandal of the 'Great Sin' at Ugarit," *JNES* 18, 1959, 280-81; Anthony Phillips, *Ancient Israel's Criminal Law: A New Approach to the Decalogue*, 1970; idem, "Another Look at Adultery," *JSOT* 20, 1981, 3-25; J. J. Rabinowitz, "The 'Great Sin' in Ancient Egyptian Marriage Contracts," *JNES* 18, 1959, 73; J. H. Tigay and H. H. Cohn, "Adultery," *EncJud* 2:313-16; Christopher J. H. Wright, "The Israelite Household and the Decalogue: The Social Background and Significance of Some Commandments," *TynBul* 30, 1979, 101-24.

Gary H. Hall

5538 (*na'ᵃpûpîm*, children of adultery), → # 5537

5539 (*nī'upīm*, adultery), → # 5537

5540	נאץ

נאץ (*n'ṣ*), q. reject, disdain; pi. treat disrespectfully; hitpo. be reviled (# 5540); נְאָצָה (*nᵉāṣâ*), nom. shame, disgrace (# 5541); nom. נֶאָצָה (*ne'āṣâ*), shame, disgrace (# 5542).

ANE The root *n'ṣ* is attested in Akk. as *nâṣu* and *na'āṣu*, scorn, treat with contempt (*AHw*, 758a; *CAD*, 11:53) and in Ugar. as *n'ṣ* with the same meaning (*WUS*, # 1731).

OT The vb. *n'ṣ* occurs in its three attested stems in the OT 24x, all but three with a human subject. It is worth noting that God is the subject only in the q., and in these three uses the vb. means not to show contempt but to reject or spurn. Clearly it is only humans who, ironically and despite their own finiteness, look with contempt on God and others.

1. In the q. Yahweh is said to have rejected his wayward people in the desert (Deut 32:19). Jeremiah, viewing Jerusalem's destruction, laments that the Lord has

spurned both king and priest (Lam 2:6), something the prophet had prayed would not happen (Jer 14:21). For God to despise his people would dishonor (*nbl* II, pi., treat with contempt, → # 5571) his own throne and, in effect, break his covenant with them. On the other hand, God's people despise his counsel (Ps 107:11), spurn his advice (Prov 1:30), and reject correction (5:12). This reveals their foolishness, for only a fool spurns his father's discipline (15:5).

2. The pi. use of *n'ṣ* is factitive, declaring someone or something to be contemptible. Most abhorrent of all is Israel's unspeakable disrespect for Yahweh. Plaintively God asks how long his people will thus treat him (Num 14:11; cf. 16:30). Only wicked (Ps 10:3, 13) and foolish (74:18) people do such things, but Isaiah accuses his own contemporaries of doing so (Isa 1:4). This habit breaks covenant (Deut 31:20) and invites such punishment as denial to the Promised Land (Num 14:23). Moreover, when God's people show him contempt, his enemies are all the more encouraged to do so (2 Sam 12:14)—sometimes, it seems, without end (Ps 74:10). All who do so will, however, eventually bow in submission to him (Isa 60:14), including those who treat his word (Isa 5:24) and his sacred offerings (1 Sam 2:17) contemptuously. In an intensive use of the vb. (hitpo.), Yahweh complains that his name is constantly blasphemed (Isa 52:5).

3. As a nom. *n'ṣ* is attested with two spellings, *n^{e}'āṣâ* and *ne'āṣâ*, the former referring to a "day of disgrace" (2 Kgs 19:3 = Isa 37:3) and the latter to blasphemy against Yahweh (Neh 9:18, 26; Ezek 35:12).

P-B Talmudic Heb. attests "insult, blaspheme" (pi.) and "be insulted" (hitp.).

Rejection, refusal, disgrace, shame: → *gdp* (revile, blaspheme, # 1552); → *znḥ* II (reject, # 2396); → *m'n* (refuse, # 4412); → *m's* I (reject, refuse, # 4415); → *n'ṣ* (reject, disdain, treat disrespectfully, # 5540); → *n'r* (abandon, renounce, # 5545); → *slh* I (despise, reject, # 6136)

Bibliography

THAT 2:3-6; *TWAT* 5:129-37; *TWOT* 2:543-44; Jastrow 2:866; M. Mulder, "Un euphémisme dans 2 Sam. XII 14?" *VT* 18, 1968, 108-14.

Eugene H. Merrill

5541 (*n^{e}'āṣâ*, shame, disgrace), → # 5540

5542 (*ne'āṣâ*, shame, disgrace), → # 5540

5543	נאק

נאק (*n'q*), q. groan (# 5543); נְאָקָה (*n^{e}'āqâ*), nom. groan (# 5544).

ANE Akk. *nâqu* denotes bitter crying, groaning, moaning. A byform, *nhq*, to cry, groan, bray, appears in postbiblical Aram. Postbiblical Heb. also has *n^{e}'āqâ*, groaning.

OT 1. The vb. names the groaning of one severely wounded or dying. In a judgment oracle, it is said Pharaoh will groan, his arms broken by Yahweh at the hands of the king of Babylon (Ezek 30:24). In Job's complaint (24:12a) the dying groan under oppression (reading *mētîm* with Syr. ‖ the cry [*šw'*] of the mortally wounded).

2. The nom. *n^{e}'āqâ* reflects closely the semantic range of the vb., in a nom. form commonly denoting sounds (Waltke and O'Connor, *IBHS* 5.3). All of the

occurrences express a groaning in desperate supplication, before the Babylonian king (Ezek 30:24) and in prayer to God (Exod 2:24; 6:5; Judg 2:18). Exod 2:24 associates the nom. with the vbs. *'nḥ*, groan (→ # 634); *z'q*, cry (→ # 2410); and the nom. *šaw'â*, cry (→ # 8784).

P-B Cf. NT *stenagmos* (Rom 8:26).

Groan, sigh, growl: → *'nḥ* (sigh, groan, # 634); → *'nq* (groan, # 650); → *hgh* I (groan, moan, sigh, meditate, muse, chirp, mutter, # 2047); → *hāgîg* (groan in prayer, # 2052); → *z'q* (cry, howl, wail, # 2410); → *n'q* (groan, # 5543); → *nhm* (growl, groan, # 5637); → *nwḥ* II (groan in anticipation, # 5664); → *p'h* (groan in childbirth, # 7184); → *š'g* (roar, # 8613)

David Thompson

5544 (*n^e'āqâ*, groan), → # 5543

5545 נאר

נאר (*n'r*), pi., abandon, renounce (# 5545).

OT In both occurrences of this vb. in the OT, Yahweh is the subject and the issue is his abandonment of his covenant with his chosen ones. The use of *n'r* in Ps 89:39[40] is especially interesting in that with v. 38[39] it is part of a collocation of synonyms (*znḥ* II, *m's* I) employed by the poet to express his fear that Yahweh has renounced the Davidic monarchy. In Lam 2:7, it is the sanctuary that has been abandoned; here *n'r* is synonymously parallel to *znḥ* II (→).

Rejection, refusal, disgrace, shame: → *gdp* (revile, blaspheme, # 1552); → *znḥ* II (reject, # 2396); → *m'n* (refuse, # 4412); → *m's* I (reject, refuse, # 4415); → *n'ṣ* (reject, disdain, treat disrespectfully, # 5540); → *n'r* (abandon, renounce, # 5545); → *slh* I (despise, reject, # 6136)

BIBLIOGRAPHY
TWOT 2:544.

Eugene H. Merrill

5547 (*nb'*, speak or behave as a prophet), → Prophecy

5553 (*n^ebû'â*, prophetic word, prophecy), → Prophecy

5554 (*nābûb*, hollow), → # 5117

5560 נבח

נבח (*nbḥ*), q. bark, howl (# 5560).

ANE Arab. *nabaḥa*; Akk. *nabāḫu*.

OT The word occurs metaphorically in Isa 56:10 to describe the watchmen of Israel as dogs who are mute, not able to bark (*nbḥ*). They do not warn the people (cf. Isa 29:9-10; Job 30:1).

P-B The LXX uses *hylakteō*, bark; metaporically, cry out.

Animal sounds: → *g'h* (bellow, low [cattle], # 1716); → *hgh* I (groan, moan, sigh, meditate, muse, chirp, mutter, # 2047); → *nbḥ* (bark [dogs], # 5560); → *nhq* (bray [ass], shriek, # 5640);

→ *nḥr* (snort, # 5723); → *'yṭ* (yell, shriek, swoop down [w. shrieks], # 6512); → *ṣhl* I (neigh, shout, # 7412)

Eugene Carpenter

5564	נבט

נבט (*nbṭ*), pi. look at; hi. look, look around, behold, to accept as an act of grace (# 5564); מַבָּט (*mabbāṭ*), nom. hope (# 4438).

ANE Akk. *nabāṭu*, light (up), illuminate; Ugar. *nbṭ* appear, it is seen (although these meanings have not met with general acceptance).

OT 1. The vb. is frequently paralleled to the vb. *r'h*, to see; to the vb. *ḥzh*, to see, usually of prophetic seeing; to the vb. *šwr*, to see, regard, and to the vb. *šqp*, to look down. The vb. occurs 69x.

2. The pi. and hi. of the vb. represent that which one does with the eye, i.e., the act of looking (Ps 94:9; Isa 5:30). To experience the multitude of his offspring, Abram must look up at the heavens and count the stars (Gen 15:5). As Lot and his family flee, they must not look back (Gen 19:17, 26). One typical feature of the worship of God was the watching of Moses by the people, who rose and stood at the entrances to their tents. This was practiced when the Tent of Meeting was in use during the interval between the time at Sinai and the completion and dedication of the tabernacle (Exod 33:8). Moses made a bronze snake and put it up on a pole. When anyone was bitten by a snake and looked at the bronze snake, he lived (Num 21:9). Thus Israel was taught that only in God was there deliverance. The simple invitation to look and live was a test of faith. The one who looked at the land would observe darkness and distress caused by the Assyrian army of terrifying precision and ferocity (Isa 5:30).

3. The hi. is also used for the act of seeing, namely, embracing everything in a mere glance (1 Sam 17:42). Balaam stated that no misfortune was seen in Jacob, i.e., he could discern no misfortune for Israel (Num 23:21). The former promise that the house of Eli should be the permanent holders of the priestly office was revoked by the distress that Eli would see in his dwelling, namely, that the male persons of the family were all to die in the prime of life (1 Sam 2:32). In Ps 94:9 the vb. is used in the question whether he who formed the eye could see, in order to stress that the Creator must be greater than his creatures, i.e., he who made doors of access to the human mind must have power and right of entry. In the description of the eagle's powers and habits, it is stated that his eyes see/detect his food from afar (Job 39:29).

4. The hi. relates to considering/acknowledging, i.e., a careful, sustained, and favorable contemplation (Ps 74:20; 119:6, 15; Isa 5:12). In Ps 119:6, 15 the vb. refers to concentrated attention to the commandments or ways of the Lord. Samuel was not to consider the outward appearance or height of Eliab, Jesse's oldest son, as a reason for anointing him as king (1 Sam 16:7). The vb. relates to the distinctly chastened attitude that the Lord considers/acknowledges, e.g., humbleness and contrition in spirit (Isa 66:2). The divine rejection of Israel's current religious practice is expressed as God's having no regard for fellowship offerings (Amos 5:22). Habakkuk complainingly asked why the sins of Israel were regarded by God, i.e., went unpunished, and why the wicked Chaldeans were used as instrument by God, who cannot, by his nature, regard wrong (Hab 1:3, 13). The afflictions of Israel are not only observed but are considered

by God with a view to taking them in hand, i.e., they would become occasions of divine action (Ps 10:14).

5. The vb. is used both of a person's looking to/upon God and God's looking upon a person. In Exod 3:6 Moses looks upon what he thought was the divine essence. Later God says that Moses, unlike all other true prophets, will continue to look upon his form, i.e., he will be able to converse with him in a unique way (Num 12:8). No person, however, has ever seen the divine essence.

6. People are to look to, i.e., fix their eyes on and thus guide their lives according to the will of, the Lord as their only help (Ps 34:5[6]; Isa 51:1, 6), and also on his means, e.g., the covenantal framework (Ps 74:20; Isa 51:2). Zech 12:10 states that the tribes of Judah and the inhabitants of Jerusalem will look on the one they have pierced. Various suggestions have been made in an attempt to identify the pierced one: historical personages (e.g., Onias III, Simon the Maccabee or Zerubbabel), the suffering Messiah, or the Lord himself. Most scholars prefer the last identification, namely, that the one they have pierced refers to the Lord himself (see, e.g., Merrill). The Lord here speaks in a human way, meaning that he is wounded by the sins of his people. The NT relates Zech 12:10 to Jesus. John 19:37 indicates that the piercing of Jesus' side by the Roman soldier is a fulfilment of the Scripture of Zech 12:10. This passage must convince readers that by the similar events associated with the crucifixion the will of God was done (Schnackenburg, 342-45). The reference in Rev 1:7 extends to all those of every age whose careless indifference to Jesus is typified in the act of piercing. At his coming the non-Christian world, represented in terms of ethnic divisions, will mourn for him. The mourning of Zech 12:10 was that of repentance, but the mourning of Rev is the remorse accompanying the disclosure of divine judgment at the coming of Christ. The thrust of the verse is that upon the imminent return of Christ, unbelievers will mourn the judgment that follows from their rejection (Mounce, 72-73). The ungodly do not regard God's working (Isa 5:12), or appointed leader (Ps 22:17[18]) properly.

7. The divine comprehensiveness is stressed by the vb. From heaven the Lord looks to earth and scans all humanity (Ps 33:13). God observes all (Job 28:24; Ps 33:13; 102:19[20]; 104:32). Just as the shimmering heat in the sunshine and the mist high over the land, the Lord looks calmly down from above (Isa 18:4). An appeal is made to God to look on despairing need in Ps 13:3[4]; 84:9[10]; Lam 1:11; 2:20; 5:1. The prophets and priests who failed to proclaim the true message are treated as lepers, and the Lord no longer considers/acknowledges them (Lam 4:16).

8. The nom. refers to hope which is looked forward to. The nom. relates to the support pledged to Ashdod by Egypt and Ethiopia in the fight against Assyria. Judah was approached, and Isaiah's powerful opposition to such a step turned out to be fully justified: Egypt failed to fight, Ashdod was subjugated, and Ethiopia handed the ringleader, who had fled to Ethiopia, over to the Assyrians (Isa 20:5-6). A similar situation pertains to Ekron, whose hopes were confused (Zech 9:5). 1QIsa reads *mbṭḥm*, their confidence, at Isa 20:5. Although this reading was preferred by some long before the discovery of the Qumran texts in all three cases, the original can be maintained (Wildberger, 749).

P-B In Tg. II Esth 1:2 the vb. is used to refer to the illumination/shining of naphtha, an inflammable substance drained from bitumen beds.

Look, observation, perception, sight, vision, watch: → *ḥdh* II (gaze on, appear, # 2526); → *ḥzh* (see, perceive, behold, # 2600); → *ḥmh* I (see, watch out for, become visible, # 2778); → *nbṭ* (look around, accept as an act of grace, # 5564); → *pls* II (observe, # 7143); → *ṣwṣ* II (look at, # 7438); → *r'h* (see, have visions, choose, perceive, # 8011); → *rṣd* (keep one's eye on, # 8353); → *śqd* (take note of, # 8567); → *š'h* III (stand gazing, # 8617); → *šgḥ* (gaze, stare, # 8708); → *šwr* I (gaze on, regard, see, # 8800); → *šzp* (catch sight of, tan, scorch, # 8812); → *š'h* (look, care about, gaze about, # 9120); → *šqp* (look down, # 9207); → *št'* (gaze, look, regard, look anxiously about, # 9283)

Bibliography

TDNT 5:324-40; *TWOT* 2:546; E. H. Merrill, *Haggai, Zechariah, Malachi*, 1994; R. H. Mounce, *The Book of Revelation*, 1977; R. Schnackenburg, *Das Johannes-evangelium 3*, 1975; H. Wildberger, *Jesaja 2*, 1978.

Jackie A. Naudé

5566 (*nābî'*, prophet), → Prophecy

5567 (*n^ebiyyâ*, prophetess), → Prophecy

5570	נבל

נבל (*nbl* I), q. wither, fade, decay, languish, fall; pi. treat with contempt, dishonor (# 5570); נְבֵלָה (*n^ebēlâ*), corpse (→ # 5577); נֹבֶלֶת (*nōbelet*), shriveled fig (act. ptc.), hapleg. in Isa 34:4.

OT 1. The vb. is used 25x. Most frequent is the meaning of fading or withering of flowers and leaves as a metaphor for the transitoriness of human life (Ps 37:2; Isa 1:30; 28:1; 40:7-8) or of the failure of strength (Exod 18:18; 2 Sam 22:46; Ps 18:45[46]). Ezekiel contrasts the expected fading of leaves with the supernatural fruit trees of the new age whose leaves will not wither (Ezek 47:12). So also is the situation of the person who delights in the law of the Lord (Ps 1:3), for that one's leaf does not wither.

2. The condition of persons, their loss of vitality because of the judgment of God, is likened to leaves and grass that are fading (Isa 1:30; 34:4). The description of Ephraim's city, a personification of leadership, is a "fading flower" (28:1, 4).

3. The sovereignty and omnipotence of God are expressed by his drying up of the earth (Isa 24:4), the erosion and crumbling of mountains (Job 14:18), and by his causing the starry hosts to wither (Isa 34:4).

4. The pi. form of *nbl* is found in four passages with the meaning of, dishonor, hold in contempt, and scoff (Deut 32:15; Jer 14:21; Mic 7:6; Nah 3:6).

Feeble, despair, faint, frail, tender: → *'ml* I (be weak, be feeble, languish, # 581); → *ḥlh* I (become weak, tired, ill, # 2703); → *ylh* (languish, # 3532); → *k'h* (be disheartened, frightened, # 3874); → *nbl* I (wither, fade, languish, dishonor, # 5570); → *'ṭp* II (grow weak, faint, be feeble, # 6494); → *'lp* (cover, faint, # 6634); → *'šš* (become weak, # 6949); → *pwg* (be feeble, numb, be prostrated, # 7028); → *rzh* (destroy, waste away, # 8135); → *rkk* (be tender, timid, gentle, # 8216); → *rph* (become slack, lose heart, discourage, # 8332)

Dry, withering, parched: → *'bl* II (dry up, # 62); → *baṣṣārâ* (dearth, destitution, # 1314); → *zrb* (cease, dry up, # 2427); → *ḥrb* I (be dry or desolate, ruined, # 2990); → *ḥrr* II (be parched, # 3081a); → *ybš* (be dry, dried up, withered, dry up, # 3312); → *mll* I (wither, be dry,

4908); → *nšt* (dry, parched, # 5980); → *qml* (wither, become moldy, musty, infected w. insects, # 7857)

Roy E. Hayden

5570a (*nōbelet*, withered fruit), → # 7238

5571	נבל

נבל (*nbl* II), q. act disdainfully; pi. treat disdainfully (# 5571); נָבָל (*nābāl* I), nom. fool (# 5572); נְבָלָה (*n*ᵉ*bālâ*), nom. stupidity (# 5576).

ANE To date scholars are still uncertain whether *nbl* I, wither, and *nbl* II are derived from the same root (*TWAT* 5:171-73; *THAT* 2:26-31). Suggestions are that *nbl* II is derived from Arab. *nabal*, wretched thing (*HALAT* 626), and Akk. *nbl/npl*, tear out (Roth, 394-409). According to *HALAT* 626-27 the vb. *nbl* II, act foolishly, treat disdainfully, the nom. *nabal* I, foolish one (intellectually and morally), *nābāl* II, the name of Abigail's husband, and *n*ᵉ*bālâ*, stupidity, sacrilege, are cognates.

OT 1. In the OT, the vb. *nbl* II occurs 5x (once each in Deut, Prov, Jer, Mic, and Nah), the substantive/adjective *nābāl* I occurs 18x (Ps 5x; Prov 3x; Deut, 2 Sam, Job, and Isa 2x each; Jer and Ezek 1x each), and the nom. *n*ᵉ*bālâ* occurs 13x (Judg 4x; Isa 2x; Gen, Deut, Josh, 1 Sam, 2 Sam, Job, and Jer 1x each).

2. In Proverbs, *nābāl* is a synonym of *k*ᵉ*sîl*, fool (Prov 17:21; cf. v. 25). A son who is *nābāl* will never bring pleasure to his father (17:21). He can never have refined speech (17:7; McKane, *Proverbs*, 1970, 507f; cf. RSV, NEB, NJPSV). It is said, humorously, that it is an impossible thing for a fool to become prosperous; it would make the earth tremble (30:22). It is advised that if a person acts foolishly (*nbl*) by exalting himself, or if he has been devising evil, he should put his hand on his mouth (30:32).

3. Other than the passages mentioned, where *nbl* refers to mental deficiency, more often *nbl* and its cognates in the OT refer to one who acts foolishly in a moral or religious sense, breaking social orders or behaving treacherously towards God. Phillips (*VT* 25, 1975, 241) asserts that "*n*ᵉ*bālâ* is a general expression for serious, disorderly and unruly action resulting in the breaking up of an existing relationship whether between tribes, within the family, in a business arrangement, in marriage or with God" (cf. Roth, 402-7; Gerleman, 153; G. von Rad, *Genesis*, 1961, 332). The action is commonly expressed in an idiomatic phrase *n*ᵉ*bālâ b*ᵉ*yiśrā'ēl*, sacrilege in Israel, which describes a person who "commits an act of crass disorder or unruliness" or acts "in an utterly disorderly or unruly fashion."

Phillips has identified the use of *n*ᵉ*bālâ* according to three categories. (a) *n*ᵉ*bālâ* is applied to sexual acts. Shechem committed "a sacrilege in Israel" (an outrage NRSV) by raping Dinah (Gen 34:7). Promiscuity and loss of virginity are a "sacrilege in Israel" (disgraceful act NRSV, cf. Judg 19:23; 20:6, 10; Deut 22:21). Similarly Ammon's sexual assault on his half sister Tamar is "sacrilege in Israel," and his action makes him a *nābāl* in Israel (2 Sam 13:12, 13). More generally, committing adultery with a neighbor's wife is also "sacrilege in Israel" (Jer 29:23). (b) When *n*ᵉ*bālâ* is applied to nonsexual offences, it refers to disorderly and unruly action in breaking a custom. Achan violated the covenant of the Lord and committed "sacrilege in Israel" by taking from the banned spoil, which, according to customary law of the holy war, was the Lord's property (Josh 7:15). By custom David was entitled to the payment of tribute for protecting Nabal's properties. Nabal's refusal to pay anything reflected his *n*ᵉ*bālâ* (1 Sam 25:25). (c) *n*ᵉ*bālâ* is applied to the spoken word especially about God. Job's friends are guilty of *n*ᵉ*bālâ* because they have not spoken about God correctly as Job has done (Job 42:8). Their disorderly views, *n*ᵉ*bālâ,* have prevented any constructive theological discussion of the suffering of the righteous (Phillips, 240). In the coming righteous kingdom the corrupted leader of Israel (collective use), who is the fool, *nābāl*, and the scoundrel will be put to shame and punished. For the fool speaks folly, *n*ᵉ*bālâ*. His mind plots iniquity: to practice ungodliness, to utter error concerning the Lord, to starve the hungry, and to refuse drink to the thirsty. The scoundrel devises wicked devices to destroy the poor with lies, even when the plea of the needy is just (Isa 32:5-7; cf. 9:17[16]). In Jer 29:23, *n*ᵉ*bālâ* refers not only to the adultery of the false prophets Ahab and Zedekiah, but also to their lying words.

4. *nābāl,* applied to a nation, refers to a people that does not know God or revere him. The Israelites are foolish, *nābāl,* and unwise, *lō' ḥākām,* because they repay God's righteous and just dealings with their perversity (Deut 32:6). Foolish, *nābāl,* people, who have despised and blasphemed God, are God's enemies (Ps 74:18, 22; cf. Deut 32:21). *nābāl*, applied to individuals, refers to an atheist or an ungodly person, one who denies God's existence (Ps 14:1 = 53:2[1]). The *nābāl* mocks at those who trust in the Lord (Ps 39:9[8]). Job's wife is likened to one of the *n*ᵉ*bālôt* (foolish women; Job 2:10). Prophets who prophesy out of their own minds are the foolish prophets (Ezek 13:3). The *nābāl* and the nameless (*b*ᵉ*lî šēm*) are the outcasts of the earth (Job 30:8). Only a foolish man (*nābāl*) would gain riches by unjust means (Jer 17:11).

5. When *nbl* (pi.) is used, it connotes the breach of the relationship with God or within a social order. Israel is accused of apostasy because they have abandoned God and dishonor, *nbl*, him in their prosperity. They have broken the covenant of the Lord (Deut 32:15; cf. Jer 14:21). In the deplorable situation of Micah's time, the son dishonors (*nbl*) the father, the daughter rises up against the mother, and a man's enemies are the members of his own household (Mic 7:6).

P-B The same connotations of *nābāl* continue in the Apocrypha. Sometimes *nābāl* refers to mental deficiency (Sir 4:27; 20:14f; 33[36]:5); at other times it refers to evil actions (Sir 18:18; 50:26). In QL *nābāl* (1QS 7:9; CD 10:18) and *n*ᵉ*bālâ* (1QS 10:21f) refers to indecent and deceitful speech (*TWAT* 5:185; *THAT* 2:31).

Folly, fool, madness, shameless: → *'*ᵉ*wîl* I (foolish, fool, # 211); → *b'r* IV (be stupid, # 1279); → *hll* III (be confused, foolish, behave like mad, # 2147); → *ksl* I (be foolish, # 4071); → *lhh* (behave like a madman, # 4263); → *nbl* II (act disdainfully, # 5571); → *skl* (behave foolishly, make foolish, frustrate, # 6118); → *pth* I (be inexperienced, be naive, deceive, persuade, # 7331); → *šg'* (raving, crazy, # 8713); → *tpl* I (talk nonsense, # 9520)

Wisdom, knowledge, skill: → *byn* (understand, discern, # 1067); → *ḥkm* (be wise, become wise, act wisely, # 2681); → *yd'* (understand, know, # 3359); → *ysr* I (admonish, correct, discipline, # 3579); → *leqaḥ* (teaching, gift of persuasion, # 4375); → *m*ᵉ*zimmâ*, consideration, plan, evil plan, plot, # 4659); → *'oqbâ* (cunning, craftiness, # 6817); → *'rm* II (be cunning, be crafty, make crafty, # 6891); → *śkl* I (have success, understand, make wise, act with insight, # 8505); → *taḥbulôt* (advice, guidance, # 9374)

Bibliography
IDB 2:303-4; *ISBE* 2:331; *THAT* 2:26-31; *TWAT* 5:171-88; *TWOT* 2:547-48; T. Donald, "The Semantic Field of 'Folly' in Proverbs, Job, Psalms, and Ecclesiastes," *VT* 13, 1963, 285-92; G. Gerleman, "Der Nicht-Mensch. Erwägungen zur hebräischen Wurzel NBL," *VT* 24, 1974, 147-58; D. Kidner, *Proverbs*, 1964, 39-41; S. A. Mandry, *There Is No God!: A Study of the Fool in the OT, Particularly in Proverbs and Qoheleth*, 1972; W. O. E. Oesterley, *The Book of Proverbs*, 1929, lxxxiv-vii; A. Phillips, "NEBALAH—A Term for Serious Disorderly and Unruly Conduct," *VT* 25, 1975, 237-42; W. M. W. Roth, "NBL," *VT* 10, 1960, 394-409.

Chou-Wee Pan

5572 (*nābāl* I, foolish), → # 5571

5574 (*nēbel* I, jar, pitcher, bottle), → # 3998

5575	נֵבֶל

נֵבֶל (*nēbel* II), uncertain stringed instrument: (large/standing) lyre(?); harp(?) (27x, 8 in Ps; # 5575; *HALAT* 627b).

OT Heb. *nēbel* I refers to a leather or ceramic storage vessel (1 Sam 1:24; cf. Ugar. *nbl*, flagon, *UT*, # 1598; Pun. *nbl*, amphore, vaisseau, *DISO*, 173). The name of the musical instrument may derive from the similarity of its shape or construction to that of the vessel (Foxvog-Kilmer). In the OT, *nēbel* usually appears with *kinnôr*, (small/portable) lyre. Although on one occasion both instruments are said to have been made from precious almug wood for use in Solomon's temple (1 Kgs 10:12), the more common resonator box may have been made from wood, perhaps overlaid with leather. The designation *nēbel 'āśôr*, ten-stringed (large/standing) lyre/harp (Ps 33:2; 144:9), may refer to a modified version of the *nēbel* (Foxvog-Kilmer), unless the specification *'āśôr*, ten-stringed, describing a typical *nēbel*, was added only for the sake of poetic meter or parallelism (cf. Ps 92:3[4]; 1QM 4:4-5). Since the *nēbel* was one of the processional instruments of the Israelite ensemble used by the cult prophets of 1 Sam 10:5 (including also *kinnôr*, *tōp*, and *ḥālîl*), it need not have been too large to be carried and played by one person. Isa 5:12 denounces the use of the same four instruments, "(small) lyre and *nēbel*, frame-drum and pipe/shawm," during self-indulgent banquets. Thus, it was an instrument used both in cult worship (Amos 5:23) and for nonreligious festive occasions (Amos 6:5). Unless the text should be emended, MT Isa 14:11 *hemyat n[e]bāleykā*, the sound of your lyres/harps (cf. Isa 5:12), may offer a paronomasis for *hammôt niblāt'kā*, your corpse [Th., Vg.] to death [Symm., Pesh., Vg., 1QIsa[a]; cf. MT Isa 5:25], befitting the irony of the funerary taunt song in 14:4b-23.

P-B Postbiblical Heb. *nēbel* means "hollow musical instrument, lyre (with a leather body)" (Jastrow, 869b); Jewish Aram. *niblā'*, lyre (Jastrow, 869b); Syr. *nablā'*, lyre. Josephus alleges that the *kinnôr* was ten-stringed and played with the plectrum, whereas the *nēbel* was twelve-stringed and played with the fingers (*Ant*. vii.12.3, §306). PTalm. Sukka V, 55c concurs that "*nebel* and *kinnor* (cithern) are the same, with the only difference of more strings (for the former)." 1QM 4:4-5, however, personifies *nēbel 'āśôr* as a group of ten men. Mish. Qinnim 3:6 reports that the strings for the *nēbel* were fashioned from large intestines, whereas those for the *kinnôr* were made from small intestines. Mish. 'Arakin 2:3, 5 describes the orchestration of a Levitical ensemble as comprising no fewer than two (large) lyres/harps (*n^{e}bālîn*), one reed flute (*'abbûb šel qāneh*), two trumpets, nine (small) lyres (*kinnôrôt*), and one cymbal (*ṣelṣāl*). Jewish Aram. *niblā'*, lyre, appears in Tg. Onk. Gen 4:21 for Heb. *kinnôr*.

Musical instruments/terms: → *gittît* (musical instrument?, # 1787); → *hemyâ* (sound, din, # 2166); → *ḥll* (make the pipe played, # 2727); → *ḥṣṣr* (make the trumpet sound, # 2955); → *yôbēl* (ram, # 3413); → *kinnôr* (lyre, # 4036); → *mēn* (string, # 4944); → *m^{e}na'an'îm* (rattle, # 4983); → *nēbel* II (unstringed instrument, # 5575); → *ngn* (play the lyre, # 5594); → *'ûgāb* (flute?, # 6385); → *prṭ* (improvise, # 7260); → *ṣll* I (ring, quiver, # 7509); → *šôpār* (ram's horn, # 8795); → *šālîš* II (musical instrument, # 8956); → *šema'* I (sound, # 9049); → *tpp* (drum, beat, # 9528); → *tq'* (drive, thrust, clap one's hands, blow trumpet, pledge, # 9546)

BIBLIOGRAPHY

R. D. Barnett, "New Facts About Musical Instruments from Ur," *Iraq* 31, 1969, Plates XIId, XVIc, XVIIa/b; B. Bayer, "The Finds That Could Not Be," *BARev* 8/1, 1982, 24, 27-29; idem, "Music: History: Biblical Period, Second Temple Period," *EncJud* 12, col. 564, Fig. 2e; S. B. Finesinger, "Musical Instruments in OT," *HUCA* 3, 1926, 36-44; D. A. Foxvog and A. D. Kilmer, "Music," *ISBE* 3:441a-42a, 437b Fig., 441 Fig.; E. Gerson-Kiwi, "Musique (dans la Bible)," *DBSup* 5, 1957, cols. 1422-24; L. Goldberg, *TWOT* 2:546a-47b; H. Gressmann, *Musik und Musikinstrumente im AT*, 1903, 21-24; O. Keel, *The Symbolism of the Biblical World*, tr. T. J. Hallett, 1985, s.v. "Music and Song," 346a-49a, Figs. 472, 474 and 475; E. Kolari, *Musikinstrumente und ihre Verwendung im AT*, 1947, 58-64; J. D. Prince, "Music," *EncBib* 3, cols. 3232-38 Figs. 13, 17 and 25; C. Sachs, *History of Musical Instruments*, 1940, 115-18; O. R. Sellers, "Musical Instruments of Israel," *BA* 4, 1941, 38-40, Figs. 6, 7b and 8a; K. Seybold, *TWAT* 5:185-88; H. Shanks, et al., "Ancient Musical Instruments," *BARev* 8/1, 1982, 18; idem, "World's Oldest Musical Notation Deciphered on Cuneiform Tablet," *BARev* 6/5, 1980, 25; D. G. Stradling and K. A. Kitchen, "Music and Musical Instruments," *IBD* 2:1032, 1035-37; M. Wegner, *Die Musikinstrumente des alten Orients*, 1950, 38, 42-43; E. Werner, "Musical Instruments," *IDB* 3:475b, Figs. 90, 91, and 92.

Robert H. O'Connell

5576 (*n^{e}bālâ*, stupidity), → # 5571

5577	נְבֵלָה

נְבֵלָה (*n^{e}bēlâ*), nom. corpse, carcass (# 5577); נבל (*nbl*), wither (→ # 5570).

ANE Cognates occur in Akk. (*nabultu*), Aram. (*nabīlat*), Sam., and Arab.

OT *n^{e}bēlâ* is the term most frequently used to refer to a human corpse or animal carcass; it occurs 48x, usually with negative connotations on account of its close association with death. Death is not only totally opposite to life (cf. "living God," Jer 10:10), but is regarded in the OT as an enemy. Of these occurrences approximately one-third come in Lev in regulations concerning contact with animal carcasses, which are deemed unclean on account of either the species (Lev 11:2-47) or the manner of death (11:39; 17:15; 22:8). Whoever touches such a carcass is considered ritually unclean till evening and must wash his clothes (11:24-28, 40; 17:15). Various household objects are also polluted if they come into contact with an unclean carcass (11:32-38). These regulations are referred to briefly in Deut 14:8, 21; Ezek 4:14; 44:31. By eating honey from a lion's carcass Samson blatantly disregards these rules

(Judg 14:6-9; cf. 13:4, 7, 14). The corpse of someone hanged for a capital offence must be buried on the same day of the execution, otherwise the continued exposure of the corpse desecrates the land (Deut 21:22-23; cf. Josh 8:29). Among the curses listed in Deut 28:15-68 the Israelites are warned of the possibility that their "carcasses will be food for all the birds of the air and the beasts of the earth" (v. 26). This motif recurs in Ps 79:2 and several times in Jeremiah (7:33; 16:4; 19:7; 34:20). In an unusual but provocative use of *n^ebēlâ*, Jeremiah describes how the people have defiled the land through "the corpses of pagan idols" (16:18). These idols are not only lifeless, unlike Yahweh the "living God," but were significantly like human corpses in that they made ritually unclean those who touched them.

Corpse: → *g^ewiyyâ* (body, corpse, # 1581); → *gûpâ* (corpse, # 1590); → *mappelet* (carcass, # 5147); → *n^ebēlâ* (carcass, corpse, # 5577); → *peger* (carcass, corpse, # 7007)
Death: → *'bd* I (perish, # 6); → *'^adāmâ* (ground, piece of land, soil, earth, realm of the dead, # 141); → *'āsôn* (mortal accident, # 656); → *gw'* (expire, die, # 1588); → *hrg* (kill, murder, # 2222); → *zrm* I (put an end to life, # 2441); → *ḥedel* (realm of the dead, # 2535); → *ḥnṭ* II (embalm, embalming, # 2846); → *mwt* (die, kill, execute, # 4637); → *qṭl* (murder, slay, # 7779); → *r^epā'îm* I (shades, departed spirits, # 8327); → *š^e'ôl* (sheol, netherworld, # 8619); → *šaḥat* (pit, grave, # 8846)

T. Desmond Alexander

5578	נַבְלוּת

נַבְלוּת (*nablût*), nom. genitals (private parts of women) (# 5578).

ANE Akk. *bāltu*, genitals.

OT The nom. refers to the private parts of a woman. In the allegory of the wife's exposure, the Lord let her stand naked and publicly exposed (Hos 2:10[12]). With her genitals exposed, she was given up to complete contempt, disgrace, and shame. Her lovers stood by like helpless spectators. In this way the Lord illustrated to Israel that he was the first and the last stage of appeal.

Sexual relations: → *'ešek* (testicle, # 863); → *zirmâ* (phallus, emission, # 2444); → *m^ebûšîm* (genitals, # 4434); → *nablût* (genitals, # 5578); → *n^eḥōšet* II (menstruation, lust, # 5734); → *'gn* (keep oneself secluded, # 6328); → *'ōnâ* (cohabitation, sexual intercourse, # 6703); → *škb* (lie down, be ravished, be bedded down, # 8886); → *škh* (exhibit strong testicles, to have strong carnal desire, # 8889); → *šopkâ* (fluid duct of male organ, urinary tubule/organ, # 9163); → **Sexual ordinances: Theology**

Jackie A. Naudé

5580	נבע

נבע (*nb'*), q. bubble; hi. pour forth, bubble up, cause to bubble (# 5580); nom. מַבּוּעַ(*mabbûa'*), spring (# 4430).

OT 1. The vb. is used of water only one time (Prov 18:4). Figurative usages refer to bubbling forth with folly (Ps 59:7[8]; 94:4; Prov 15:2, 28; Eccl 10:1), God's praise (Ps 19:2[3]; 78:2; 119:171; 145:7), or God's wisdom (Prov 1:23).

2. The nom. occurs only 3x in the OT, though it does occur in later Heb. and in Aram. Twice it refers to springs that appear as part of God's special blessing when he restores his people to their land (Isa 35:7; 49:10). Eccl 12:6 speaks of a "pitcher broken by the spring," a figurative reference to death.

Fountain, spring: → *mabbāk* (spring, # 4441); → *ma'yān* (spring, # 5078); → *māqôr* (spring, # 5227); → *nb'* (bubble, # 5580)
Cistern, well, pool, reservoir: → *b^e'ēr* I (well, # 931); → *bôr* (cistern, well, grave, # 1014); → *b^erēkâ* (pool, # 1391); → *gēb* I (cistern, # 1463); → *mîkāl* (reservoir, # 4782); → *miqweh* (accumulation of water, # 5224)

BIBLIOGRAPHY
ISBE 2:356; *TWOT* 2:794; N. Glueck, *Rivers in the Desert*, 1959.

Bryan E. Beyer

5582 (*negeb*, south, Negev), → Negev

5583	נגד

נגד (*ngd*), denom.(?); hi. make known, disclose, declare (334x + Deut 13:10[?]; 1 Sam 12:7[?]; Isa 41:27[?]; Mic 1:10[?]); ho. be made known, disclosed, declared (35x + 2 Sam 15:31[?]; Mic 6:8[?]) (# 5583; *HALAT* 629a-b).

ANE Cognates of this vb. appear in Ancient Aram. *ngd*, report (*DISO*, 174; *KAI*, 2:268 no. 224); Aram. *ngd*, drag, draw; lead (cf. nom. *nāgōdā'*, leader); Egyp. Aram. *ngd*, describe, report (*DISO*, 174; *KAI*, 2:314 no. 266); Arab. *nǧd*, rise above, surpass; be conspicuous; II, inform, notify; make known; X, make oneself bold, conspicuous (Wehr, 943b-44a); Eth. *ngd*, travel, (carry on) trade; Tigre (*TigrWb*, 342b); and Amharic, (carry on) trade. The Heb. vb. is also attested in the Lachish ostraca (iii 2 [hi. inform], iii 13 [ho. be communicated]; cf. Torczyner, *Lachish*, 1:45-73; *DISO*, 174; *KAI*, no. 193).

OT 1. Heb. *ngd* (hi. make known, disclose, declare) is the standard diction vb. corresponding to the poetic diction vb. *ḥwh* I (pi. make shown, declared, explained) (cf. Driver, 30). As a rule, it indicates audible, verbal communication (e.g., Ps 51:15[17]; Isa 48:20), whether relaying the words of a message (Gen 44:24; Exod 19:9; 1 Sam 18:26; 25:12) or describing a situation to someone (1 Sam 19:7; 2 Kgs 6:12). Of 334 OT uses of the hi., 48 occur in the Pentateuch (Gen 31x [Joseph saga 14x]), 138 in the Former Prophets (Judg 26x [Samson saga 23x]; 1-2 Sam 80x; 1-2 Kgs 20x), 70 in the Latter Prophets (Isa 50x; Jer 28x), and 78 in the Writings (Ps 20x; Job 17x). The ho. appears 35x in the OT (Gen 5x; 1-2 Sam 9x; 1-2 Kgs 7x).

2. The vb. is usually used in the profane sphere in connection with a broad range of human affairs that involve communicating something previously unknown, whether telling of a condition (Gen 3:11), relating facts or a report (1 Sam 4:13-14; Job 1:15-17, 19), answering a question (Gen 32:29[30]; 43:7), disclosing a secret (Josh 2:14, 20; Judg 16:6, 10, 13, 15, 17-18), or solving a riddle (Judg 14:12). On the other hand, it also appears regularly in the OT in connection with human interpretations of something understood to have been revealed by Yahweh/God, whether that be a dream (Gen 41:25; Dan 2:2) or a ritual symbol or sign (Ezek 24:19; 37:18). In the Joseph

saga, for example, Pharaoh complains of his magicians, saying that "none could explain [the dream(s)] to me (*wᵉ'ên maggîd lî*)" (Gen 41:24), a clause that parallels clauses in Gen 40:8 and 41:15: "(we/I had dreams/a dream), but there was no one to interpret it (*ûpōter 'ên 'ōtô*)." The synonymous vb., *ptr*, interpret (Aram. and Syr. *pšr*, dissolve; solve, interpret), is used in the OT only in Gen 40 and 41 to denote the interpretation of dreams (so 40:16, 22; 41:8, 12, 13; cf. similarly Heb. *ngd* in Dan 2:2 with Aram. *ûpišrā' nᵉḥawwēh*, "and we will interpret it" in Dan 2:4). When Joseph finally comes to interpret Pharaoh's dream, he explains that through the dreams, "God has revealed (*higgîd*) to Pharaoh what he is about to do" (Gen 41:25).

Thus, in general, when Yahweh/God is the subject of *ngd*, it may be understood as indicating some form of divine revelation to humans of something previously unknown (Gen 41:25; Deut 4:13; 2 Sam 7:11; Amos 4:13). The use of *ngd* in connection with divine revelation is especially pertinent to the prophets (Isa 21:2), whose role it was to reveal to others the divine message (Isa 42:9 [cf. v. 5a]; 45:19 [cf. 18a]). Thus, the vb. appears in Isa 19:12, taunting Egypt's prophets as ineffectual in revealing the divine will concerning Egypt, and in Jer 9:12[11], where the prophet despairs of the dearth of true prophets in Israel who reveal what the mouth of Yahweh has spoken. As part of Yahweh's claim to incomparability among the gods (Isa 41:21-24, 26-29), he taunts other gods to do what only a true god could do, namely, reveal future events (41:22). A characteristic example of the prophetic use of *ngd* appears in Mic 3:8, where the prophet describes his role: "But as for me, I am filled with power, with the spirit of the LORD, and with justice and might, to delcare (*lᵉhaggîd*) to Jacob his trangression, to Israel his sin."

3. Among figurative uses, Ps 19:1[2] uses *ngd* to personify the celestial realm: "The heavens declare (*mᵉsappᵉrîm*) the glory of God; the skies proclaim (*maggîd*) the work of his hands" (cf. Ps 50:6; 97:6). Similarly, in Job 12:7, Job contends that even animals can attest to Yahweh's sovereignty over all earthly life-forms: "But ask the animals, and they will teach you (*wᵉtōrekā*), or the birds of the air, and they will tell you (*wᵉyagged-lāk*)."

Although *ngd* usually denotes an act that involves speaking orally, it may convey figuratively the nonverbal act of showing or attesting. Ps 111:6 states that Yahweh "has shown (*higgîd*) his people the power of his works, giving them the lands of other nations." Similarly, Ezra 2:59 uses *ngd* of showing or proving Israelite lineage by means of written documentation.

P-B Late cognates include postbiblical Heb. *ngd* pi. oppose, hi. tell, testify (Jastrow, 871b; cf. the Qumranic uses of the hi. also in 1QM 10:1; 11:5, 8); Jewish Aram. *ngd* stretch; draw, pull (cf. nom. forms *nogdā'*, distance; path, and *nāgôdā'*, leader; Jastrow, 871b-72b; cf. Prijs, 279). In the RL, the important Aram. nom. *'aggādâ* or Heb. nom. *haggādâ*, tale; lesson, homily (Jastrow, 11a, 330b) denotes a literary (i.e., nonhalakic, nonlegal) midrash on some biblical text or principle (cf. Dietrich, *RGG*³ 3:23-24). Other cognates occur in Syr. *ngd* draw, lead; attract, persuade (cf. nom. forms *nᵉgādā'*, attraction, and *nāgūdā'*, guide, leader; J. Payne Smith, *A Compendious Syriac Dictionary*, 1903, 326b-27b); and Mand. (*MdD*, 288b).

Speech: → *'lm* I (be bound, speechless, grow silent, # 519); → *'mr* I (say, speak, mention, # 606); → *bl'* II (make conveyed, reported, # 1181); → *dbr* II (speak, threaten, promise, command, # 1819); → *ḥwh* I (make declared, explained, # 2555); → *lšn* (slander, # 4387); → *mll* III (speak, say, declare, # 4910); → *ngd* (make known, disclose, declare, # 5583); → *rākîl* (peddler, huckster, deceiver, slanderer, # 8215); → *šnn* II (make repeated, recounted, # 9112)

Bibliography

THAT 2:31-37; *TWAT* 5:188-201; *TWOT* 2:549b-50b; G. R. Driver, "Hebrew Poetic Diction," in *Congress Volume, Copenhagen 1953*, SVT 1, 1953, (26-39) 30; B. M. Levinson, "'But You Shall Surely Kill Him!': The Text-Critical and Neo-Assyrian Evidence for MT Deuteronomy 13:10," in *Bundesdokument und Gesetz: Studien zum Deuteronomium*, ed. G. Braulik, 1995, 37-63; L. Prijs, "Ergänzungen zum talmudisch-aramäischen Wörterbuch," *ZDMG* 117, 1967, (266-86) 279; H. Torczyner, *The Lachish Letters*, 1938, 1:45-73.

Robert H. O'Connell

5585	נגה

נגה (*ngh*), q. shine; hi. cause to shine (# 5585); נֹגַהּ (*nōgah*), nom. brightness, radiance (# 5586); נְגֹהָה (*n^e^gōhâ*), nom. brightness (Isa 59:9) (# 5588); נְגַהּ (*n^e^gah*), (Aram.), nom. first light (Dan 6:19[20]) (# 10459).

ANE Ugar. *ngh*, be bright; Akk. *na/egû*, sing for joy; Aram. *n^e^gah*, be bright, shine; *nûg^e^hâ* light, morning, evening; Syr. *n^e^gah*, be bright; Hatra *ngh*, dawn (?).

OT 1. The nom. *nōgah* denotes brilliant or radiant light. Its physical meaning includes the brightness of the sky at dawn (Prov 4:18; Isa 60:3) or after rain (2 Sam 23:4), or the glow of fire (2 Sam 22:13 ‖ Ps 18:12[13]; Isa 4:5; this meaning is also probable in Isa 62:1 against NIV's "dawn," which is unsupported by the parallelism).

2. The root *ngh* is primarily associated, however, with several different aspects of theophany, such as God's glory (Ezek 10:4), lightning (Ezek 1:4; Hab 3:4, 11), and a rainbow (Ezek 1:28). As in the case of *'wr* (# 239), the precise form of the brightness of God's presence is less significant than the fact that wherever God is, he shines with unusual brilliance. This is especially important to Ezekiel, who sees a theophany in Babylon in which God is enthroned in human form (Ezek 1:4, 13, 27-28).

3. Though the vb. *ngh* refers to various forms of light, such as the moon, a lamp, and fire (2 Sam 22:29 ‖ Ps 18:28[29]; Job 18:5; Isa 13:10), its usage is mainly metaphorical. It can refer to God's shining into the lives of individuals (2 Sam 22:29 ‖ Ps 18:28[29]) or to the messianic age (Isa 9:2[1]). It emphasizes light that shines brightly in the darkness and is easily seen.

P-B Though the vb. *ngh* refers once to the brilliance of a jewel, it is used mainly for looking over or revising manuscripts. The Aram. nom. and vb. are used of shining, especially of morning light (cf. Dan 2:19[20]), but the nom. has a special form *nag^e^he*, found in cultic texts meaning evening—i.e., the beginning of the calendar day.

Light, radiance, brightness: → *'wr* (be light, bright, shine, # 239); → *bāhîr* (bright, brilliant, # 986); → *zrḥ* I (rise [of sun], shine, # 2436); → *yp'* I (shine out, # 3649); → *ngh* (shine, cause to shine, # 5585); → *nhr* II (be radiant, # 5642); → *qrn* (send out rays, be radiant, # 7966)

Bibliography

TWOT 2:550-51; S. Aalen, *Die Begriffe "Licht" und "Finsternis" im AT, im Spätjudentum und im Rabbinismus*, 1951; W. D. Reece, *The Concept of Light in the Old Testament: A Semantic Analysis*, 1989.

Martin J. Selman

5586 (*nōgah*, brightness, radiance), → # 5585

5588 (*n^e^gōhâ*, brightness), → # 5585

5590	נגח

נגח (*ngḥ*), q. gore; pi. push, thrust; hitp. engage in thrusting with (*'im*), (# 5590); נַגָּח (*naggāḥ*), liable to gore, vicious (# 5591).

ANE Arab. *ngḥ* I, be lucky; IV, overcome. There are interesting parallels provided by ANE iconography that correspond to the intention of *ngḥ*: caps, helmets, or crowns with horns attached, worn by ANE deities, symbolize the strength of the goring ox with a strong connotation of victory, while various gods (e.g., Ba'al) also appear theriomorph in the form of a bull (cf. Keel, 127-29, figs. 59-61).

OT The vb. and its derivative is attested 13x in the OT and consistently refers to the pushing activity of a horned animal, which metaphorically can also be applied to the king or the people of Israel.

1. The majority of occurrences in the Pent. (Exod 21:28, 29, 31, 32, 36) are of a legal nature and describe laws pertaining to the goring ox. Differentiation is made between a first-time offender and a repeated gorer (indicated by the usage of the adjective *naggāḥ*). Only in the latter case is the owner liable for the animal's action. Malul establishes the relationship between the laws of the goring ox in the OT and in other ANE law codes (Malul, 113-52; see J. J. Finkelstein, *The Ox That Gored*, 1991).

2. The remainder of the occurrences of the vb. refer to the victory over an enemy illustrated by the imagery of an attacking horned animal. In Deut 33:17 the offspring of Joseph is said to be victorious over his enemies like a goring ox. Zedekiah makes two iron horns (probably a horned cap—see above under ANE) in order to symbolize Ahab's prospective victory over the Arameans (2 Kgs 22:11 = 2 Chron 18:10). In Dan 8:4 a ram with two horns is "pushing" towards west, north, and south, and in 11:40 kings are clashing with each other as fighting horned animals would do. In Ps 44:5[6] the theological implication of the imagery becomes apparent: although it is Israel who pushes back their enemies, it is only in the strength of God that they can do so.

P-B In Targ. Yerushalmi Gen 21:10 the vb. is used as a military term "to wage war" (Jastrow, 873).

Pushing, goring, thrusting: → *dḥh* (push, overthrow, be cast down, # 1890); → *dpq* (push, drive hard, knock, # 1985); → *hdp* (push, thrust, # 2074); → *yrṭ* (shove, push, be reckless, # 3740); → *ngḥ* (gore, push, thrust, # 5590); → *'ll* II (thrust in, # 6619); → *tq'* (drive, thrust, clap one's hands, blow trumpet, pledge, # 9546)

Bibliography

HALAT 630; *TWOT* 2:551; M. Jastrow, *A Dictionary of the Targumim, the Talmud Babli and Yerushalmi, and the Midrashic Literature,* 1903; O. Keel, *Wirkmächtige Siegeszeichen im Alten Testament, OBO* 5, 1974, 125-34; M. Malul, *The Comparative Method in Ancient Near Eastern and Biblical Legal Studies,* AOAT 227, 1990, 113-52; M. L. Suring, *Horn Motifs in the Hebrew Bible and Related Ancient Near Eastern Literature and Iconography,* AUSSDS 4, 1982.

Martin G. Klingbeil

5591 (*naggāḥ*, liable to gore, vicious), → # 5590

5592	נָגִיד

נָגִיד (*nāgîd*), prince, ruler, leader (# 5592).

ANE *ngd* occurs in Phoen. as a designation for a military commander. An old Aram. cognate is found in Sefire 3:10, where it evidently refers to palace officials. In standard Aram. *nāgôdā'* denotes leader in a variety of capacities.

OT 1. Both the etymology and the primary significance of Heb. *nāgîd* have been widely but inconclusively debated (see *HALAT* 630; *TWAT* 5:206-8). The word is found both as a general term for a leader and as a royal designation. As a general term, it is chiefly found in Chron, where it may variously denote a tribal chief (1 Chron 12:27[28]; 2 Chron 19:11), military commander (1 Chron 13:1; 27:4), palace official (2 Chron 28:7), or temple officials serving in various administrative capacities (1 Chron 9:20; 26:24; 2 Chron 31:12; cf. Jer 20:1). The expression "official (*nāgîd*) in charge of the temple of God" (2 Chron 31:13) designates Azariah, the chief priest under Hezekiah (cf. v. 10; cf. 1 Chron 9:11). The "prince of the covenant" in Dan 11:22 is probably a reference to the high priest Onias III (cf. 2 Macc 4:33-34). Whether *māšîaḥ nāgîd*, "the Anointed One, the ruler" in Dan 9:25 is a priestly or a royal figure is uncertain. In Job 29:10 the *n^egîdîm* are the leaders and dignitaries of the city (NIV nobles).

2. (a) As a royal designation, *nāgîd* is only occasionally used of foreign monarchs (Ps 76:12[13]; Ezek 28:2). The term denotes Solomon as the crown prince, appointed by David as his successor (1 Kgs 1:35; cf. 2 Chron 11:22). This may have been the original significance of the term (Mettinger, 158-62; differently Halpern, 8-11). However, in Sam-Kgs the term is otherwise used theologically to present the king-designate as the one chosen and appointed by God to rule his people Israel. It has been suggested this usage represents an early prophetic view of kingship, later taken up in the Davidic theology of the royal Psalms (Fritz, 352). In related expressions the term is applied to Saul (1 Sam 9:16; 10:1), David (e.g., 1 Sam 13:14; 2 Sam 7:8), Jeroboam (1 Kgs 14:7), Baasha (16:2) and Hezekiah (2 Kgs 20:5). Saul's disobedience resulted in God's rejection of him and the designation of David as *nāgîd* in his place (1 Sam 13:14). Likewise, the sins of Jeroboam and Baasha are viewed as a failure to fulfill the responsibilities for which they had been appointed *nāgîd* of God's people—unlike God's servant David (1 Kgs 14:8). God's choice of David as *nāgîd* is expressed through *bḥr*, choose, elect (→ # 1047; 2 Sam 6:21; cf. Ps 78:70), a term also associated with God's covenant with David (e.g., Ps 89:3[4]). The expression "leader (*nāgîd*) ... of the peoples" in Isa 55:4 reflects the universal rule of David as the recipient of God's

covenant (cf. v. 3; Ps 89:25[26]), otherwise connected with his rule as *melek*, king (e.g., Ps 2:5-9).

(b) In Chron, the theological use of the term is restricted to David. Outside his sources, the word serves the Chronicler's emphasis on the centrality of the temple and David's provision for it. Thus it occurs as a key word linking David's speech when he gives Solomon the plans for the temple, and Solomon's speech after it has been built. God had not allowed David to build the temple, but had chosen (*bḥr*) Judah as *nāgîd*, David as king, and Solomon to succeed him and to build the temple (1 Chron 28:4-6). Indeed, God had not chosen anyone as *nāgîd* over his people before he chose (*bḥr*) David, nor appointed any city for the site of his temple before he chose (*bḥr*) Jerusalem (2 Chron 6:5-6).

P-B The term is normally trans. in the LXX by *hēgoumenos,* occasionally by *archôn* (1 Sam 10:1; 13:14). Both serve as general words for leaders and are used to translate a variety of terms (e.g., see *nāśî',* # 5954).

Leaders: → *'ādôn* (lord, master, # 123); → *'allûp* II (tribal chief, # 477); → *'āṣîl* II (eminent, noble, # 722); → *zāqēn* (elder, # 2418); → *ḥōr* I, free man, freeborn, # 2985); → *maptēaḥ* (badge of office, # 5158); → *nāgîd* (prince, ruler, leader, # 5592); → *nāśî'* I (chief, king, # 5954); → *sārîs* (eunuch, court official, # 6247); → *seren* II (Philistine prince, # 6249); → *'attûd* (he-goat, leader, # 6966); → *peḥâ* (governor, # 7068); → *pāqîd* (officer, # 7224); → *qāṣîn* (commander, leader, # 7903); → *rab* II (captain, chief, # 8042); → *rzn* (rule, # 8142); → *šôa'* I (noble, # 8777)

Bibliography

THAT 2:34-35; A. Alt, "The Formation of the Israelite State in Palestine," *Essays on Old Testament History and Religion*, 1966, 171-237; J. W. Flanagan, "Chiefs in Israel," *JSOT* 20, 1981, 47-73; V. Fritz, "Die Deutungen des Königtums Sauls in den Überlieferungen von seiner Entstehung 1 Sam 9-11," *ZAW* 88, 1976, 346-62; B. Halpern, *The Constitution of the Monarchy in Israel*, HSM 25, 1981; G. F. Hasel, "נָגִיד" *TWAT* 5:203-19; T. N. D. Mettinger, *King and Messiah: The Civil and Sacral Legitimation of Israelite Kings*, ConBOT 8, 1976; M. Noth, *Das System der zwölf Stämme Israels*, BWANT, 4/1, 1930; J. van der Ploeg, "Les chefs du peuple d'Israēl et leurs titres," *RB* 57, 1950, 40-61; W. Richter, "Die *nāgîd*-Formel," *BZ* 9, 1965, 71-84; H. N. Rösel, "Jephtah und das Problem der Richter," *Bib* 61, 1980, 251-55; S. Shaviv, "*Nābî'* and *Nāgîd* in 1 Samuel 9:1-10:16," *VT* 34, 1984, 108-13.

Kenneth T. Aitken

5593 (*n*^e^*gînâ*, music, song?), → # 5594

5594	נגן

נגן (*ngn*), q. play (the stringed instrument); pi. make (the stringed instrument) played (15x; # 5594; *HALAT* 631a); nom. מַנְגִּינָה (*mangînâ*), (mocking) song (hapleg.; # 4947; *HALAT* 567a); נְגִינָה (*n*^e^*gînâ*), (string) music(?), (taunt) song(?) (14x; # 5593; *HALAT* 631a).

ANE Akk. *nigûtu* (< *nagû* II, to sing [joyfully]) means (joyful) song/music (*AHw* 2:788a) but bears no etymological relation to Heb. *n*^e^*gînâ.*

OT In the q., only the part. *nōg*^e^*nîm*, players (of [stringed] instruments), is used in the OT (Ps 68:25[26] ‖ *šārîm*, singers). The pi. vb. recurs in 1 Sam 16:16-18, 23, describing playing the (small) lyre (*m^{e}naggēn bakkinnôr*, v. 16) with the hand (*w^{e}lāqaḥ dāwid 'et-hakkinnôr w^{e}niggēn b^{e}yādô*, v. 23; cf. Ps 33:2-3). Often the context implies that the playing of a taunt song or lament against the enemy would have been appropriate (2 Kgs 3:15; Isa 23:16), though the vb. may refer to playing in praise of Yahweh for deliverance (Ps 33:3; Isa 38:20).

The term *n^{e}gînâ* is used to designate taunt songs (Job 30:9 ‖ *millâ*, byword; Lam 3:14 ‖ *ś^{e}ḥōq*, laughingstock) and the song of drunkards (Ps 69:12[13]), though it is unclear whether *n^{e}gînâ* means specifically taunt song or is simply broad enough to include that sense. The use of *'al-n^{e}gînôt* in the postscripts of Ps 3, 5, 53, 54, 60 (MT *'al-n^{e}gînat*), 66, 75 (the putative superscriptions of Ps 4, 6, 54, 55, 61, 67, 76) and Hab 3 (*bingînôtāy*) may indicate not so much the genre of these psalms as the method of their performance ("in the manner of taunt songs" or, more traditionally, "upon stringed instruments"; cf. Waltke). Foxvog-Kilmer compare this use of *'al-n^{e}gînôt* to the Sumerian hymnic subscript *zā-mí*, lyre or praise. The related nom. *mangînâ*, used only in Lam 3:63, refers to mocking in song and may mean specifically taunting song.

Musical instruments/terms: → *gittît* (musical instrument?, # 1787); → *hemyâ* (sound, din, # 2166); → *ḥll* (make the pipe played, # 2727); → *ḥṣṣr* (make the trumpet sound, # 2955); → *yôbēl* (ram, # 3413); → *kinnôr* (lyre, # 4036); → *mēn* (string, # 4944); → *m^{e}na'an'îm* (rattle, # 4983); → *nēbel* II (unstringed instrument, # 5575); → *ngn* (play the lyre, # 5594); → *'ûgāb* (flute?, # 6385); → *prṭ* (improvise, # 7260); → *ṣll* I (ring, quiver, # 7509); → *šôpār* (ram's horn, # 8795); → *šālîš* II (musical instrument, # 8956); → *šema'* I (sound, # 9049); → *tpp* (drum, beat, # 9528); → *tq'* (drive, thrust, clap one's hands, blow trumpet, pledge, # 9546)

Taunt: → *ḥrp* II (taunt, mock, insult, defy, # 3070); → *mangînâ* (taunting song, # 4947); → *š^{e}nînâ*, taunt, # 9110)

Bibliography

D. A. Foxvog and A. D. Kilmer, "Music," *ISBE* 3:448a; E. Kolari, *Musikinstrumente und ihre Verwendung im AT*, 1947, 56; C. Sachs, *History of Musical Instruments*, 1940, 124-27; B. K. Waltke, "Superscripts, Postscripts, or Both," *JBL* 110, 1991, 583-96; E. Werner, "Music," "Musical Instruments," *IDB* 3:459b, 476b; H. Wolf, *TWOT* 2:551.

Robert H. O'Connell

5595	נגע

נגע (*ng'*), q. touch, hurt, reach, arrive; ni. afflict; pu. be afflicted; hi. touch, reach, happen (# 5595); נֶגַע (*nega'*), plague, affliction (→ # 5596).

ANE The vb. *ng'* is not a common Sem. root (Egypt. Aram., Jewish Aram., Mand., and Eth.).

OT The vb. *ng'* occurs 150x, 107 of which are q., and it covers a wide semantic range: touch, strike, reach, and arrive. A preposition commonly precedes the item/person touched (most often *b^e*, but also *'el*, *'ad*, *'al*).

1. The primary meaning of *ng'* is to touch (some kind of physical contact), although its specific nuance varies in different contexts. The vb. can depict things touching (angels' wings, 1 Kgs 6:27) or the prohibited touch of something unclean (Lev 5:2) or sacred (Exod 19:12). An angel touched Daniel and brought him to his feet (Dan 8:18), and another angel caused a coal to touch the prophet's lips (Isa 6:7) in his

vision of Yahweh's majesty. An angel's powerful touch gave Jacob a lifelong limp (Gen 32:25, 32[26, 33]). A causative nuance depicts houses that adjoin (Isa 5:8) or applying (dabbing) blood to something (Exod 4:25; 12:22; see Propp, 496, n. 6). To touch a woman is a euphemism for having sexual relations with her (Gen 20:6; Prov 6:29; cf. *yd'*, Gen 4:1).

Yahweh touched the mouth of his prophet to symbolize the impartation of his word to Jeremiah and to depict his provision of enablement for the prophet's verbal ministry (Jer 1:9). In 1 Sam 10:26, God touches the hearts of certain valiant men to provide support to the newly chosen king. Theophanic language emphasizes God's power and his sovereignty over all creation. He melts the land by touching it (Amos 9:5) and causes the mountains to smoke by his touch (Ps 104:32; 144:5).

Drawing on the fundamental concept of holiness, Yahweh prohibited his people from touching certain things consecrated to him (Exod 19:13—Mount Sinai; Num 4:15—temple utensils; cf. Lev 12:4; Hag 2:12-13) as well as things that were unholy (e.g., Num 19:16—a corpse; Num 19:22; Isa 52:11—any unclean thing). Because Yahweh is holy, he sets apart certain things for himself. Those things are dedicated to him alone and can only be touched by those who have themselves been purified (e.g., priests). Since defilement was infectious (but not holiness, contra Durham, 264-65, cf. Hag 2:12-13), God's people were to be careful not to violate or defile their holy/consecrated status as God's chosen people.

2. In several instances *ng'* possesses a clearly negative connotation, to strike, afflict, or inflict harm. It can depict the powerful force of wind that withers crops (Ezek 17:10) or causes a building's collapse (Job 1:19). Abimelech warns his people against harassing Isaac and his wife (Gen 26:11, 29), and Boaz prohibits his servants from treating Ruth roughly (Ruth 2:9). Even though "touching" a woman can signify cohabitation, contextual indicators (e.g., *klm* and *g'r* in Ruth 2:15-16) suggest that Boaz warns against physical or emotional abuse rather than sexual molestation. Because of their covenant with the Gibeonites, the elders of Israel caution the Israelites about harassing or inflicting injury on their covenant partners (Josh 9:19).

In addition to the trauma of military conflict (Josh 8:15), *ng'* can signify affliction sent by God. Job's experience of Yahweh's "touch" occasions his desparate cry for sympathy (Job 19:21; cf. 1:11; 2:5). Yahweh also strikes pagan rulers (Gen 12:17; cf. 1 Sam 6:9) and disobedient covenant mediators (2 Kgs 15:5 = 2 Chron 26:20) with disease and affliction. Asaph complains that the wicked around him have never experienced this touch of God (Ps 73:5). The servant in Isaiah 53 is struck by Yahweh (Isa 53:4).

The cognate nom., *nega'*, occurs 78x, 61 of which serve as a technical term for leprosy of skin, material, or houses (Lev 13-14; Deut 24:8). As part of the Mosaic covenant, it also connotes interpersonal assaults (Deut 17:8; 21:5) that demand adjudication. The other fourteen instances refer to some kind of plague, suffering, physical blow, or covenant curse (Gen 12:17; Exod 11:1; 1 Kgs 8:37; Ps 38:11[12]; 39:10[11]; 91:10; Prov 6:33).

3. With a spatial nuance (reach, extend to), *ng'* describes the topographical extent of a valley (Zech 14:5) or vegetation (Isa 16:8; Jer 48:32). Because of the thoroughgoing nature of Israel's wickedness ("touching the heart," Jer 4:18; cf. Mic 1:9) her sense of security is groundless. While they expect peace, a sword is poised at (*ng'*)

their throat (Jer 4:11). Hyperbolically, *ng'* describes the intensity of an emotion ("a rage that reaches to heaven," 2 Chron 28:9), the immense proportions of Israel's divine judgment ("reaches to the skies," Jer 51:9; cf. Deut 1:28), or the seeming infinite reach of a ladder in Jacob's dream (Gen 28:12).

4. *ng'* can connote the arrival or approach of persons (1 Sam 14:9; Esth 4:14; Isa 30:4), an animal (Dan 8:7), a message (Jon 3:6), a royal decree (Esth 4:3; 8:17; 9:1), calamity (Judg 20:34, 41; Job 5:19; Ps 32:6), or the arrival of a certain time (Ezra 3:1; Neh 7:72; Eccl 12:1; S of Songs 2:12; Ezek 7:12) or period of time (Esth 2:12, 15).

P-B The Qumran texts use *ng'* with reference to partaking of the sacred community meal (1QS 5:13; 6:16; 7:19; 8:17; CD 10:13; 12:17), regarding those smitten (with some uncleanness or blemish, 1QSa 2:3-6:10), or to coming near or reaching (1QM 17:11; CD 15:5). In addition to the customary meanings in BH, the q. part. can signify an "interested" witness (Qiddušin, 43^{b}). Both the hi. and the q. at times denote "to come to pass" (q.—Gen Rabbah 84 [Yalk, ib. 141]; hi. Gen Rabbah 84; Tosef. Ṭoharot 6, 14). The pi. and nitp. serve as denominative vbs. of *nega'* (plague, affliction) and respectively mean to afflict with leprosy (Nega'im 13, 9; 'Erubin 8, 2) and to be afflicted with leprosy (Keritot 2, 3) (Jastrow 2:874-75).

Happening, meeting, attack: → *'nh* III (happen, # 628); → *hwh* II (become, # 2093); → *hyh* (be, become, happen, # 2118); → *y'd* (appoint, appear, come, meet, # 3585); → *ng'* (touch, hurt, # 5595); → *pg'* (encounter, attack, # 7003); → *pgš* (meet, # 7008); → *qdm* (be before, meet, confront, # 7709); → *qr'* II (happen, # 7925); → *qrh* I (happen, build, odain, direct, select, # 7936)

Beating, crushing, grinding: → *b'ṭ* (kick, # 1246); → *dwk* (pound, # 1870); → *dk'* (crush, be crushed, # 1917); → *dkh* (be crushed, # 1920); → *dqq* (crush, # 1990); → *hlm* (beat, # 2150); → *ḥbṭ* (beat from, # 2468); → *ṭḥn* (grind, mill, # 3221); → *ktš* (grind down, # 4197); → *ktt* (beat fine, pound up, disperse, # 4198); → *mḥṣ* (beat to pieces, # 4731); → *m'k* (press, squeeze, crush, # 5080); → *ngp* (strike, # 5597); → *nk'* (be whipped out, flogged out, # 5777); → *nkh* (be hit, be battered, ruined, destroyed, # 5782); → *ṣrr* I (bind, tie up, # 7674); → *r'ṣ* (beat down, # 8320); → *rṣṣ* (crush, mash, break, # 8368); → *šwp* I (crush, # 8789); → *šḥq* (grind down, # 8835)

BIBLIOGRAPHY

THAT 2:37-39; *TWAT* 5:219-26; *TWOT* 2:551; Durham, *Exodus*, 1987; W. Propp, "That Bloody Bridegroom," *VT* 43, 1993, 495-518.

Michael A. Grisanti

5596	נֶגַע

נֶגַע (*nega'*), nom. plague, stroke (# 5596); < נגע (*ng'*), touch, harm, strike, smite (→ # 5595).

OT 1. In some passages the vb. specifically denotes the idea of striking someone with the intention to harm or kill, or to inflict a disastrous blow upon that person. In this sense *ng'* is closely related to *ngp*. Human beings harm one another (Gen 26:11, 29) or strike one another with the intention of killing (Josh 9:19), but God in his judgment also strikes human beings with disastrous blows (Gen 12:17), disease, and death (2 Kgs 15:5; 2 Chron 26:20; Ps 73:5). In Ps 73:14 *ng'* also expresses physical affliction, viz., the mental distress and inward tension that the psalmist suffers because of the prosperity and behavior of the wicked over against his own suffering (A. Weiser, *The Psalms*, OTL, 1975, 510).

2. The nom. *nega'* is a term used of a stroke or plague (Exod 11:1; Ps 39:10[11]), an assault (Deut 17:8; Prov 6:33), or a disfiguring skin disease (Deut 24:8). The condition described in Lev 13:30; 14:54 was probably ringworm, which is produced by several different tinea parasites. Related forms are *tinea kerion* (inflammatory ringworm of the scalp and beard), *tinea sycosis* (ringworm of the beard), and *tinea tonsurans* (ringworm of the scalp).

3. The nom. form is also closely related to *negep* (# 5598) and *maggēpâ* (→ # 4487) and denotes virtually always a divinely meted out plague or disastrous blow by which God executes his punishment (Exod 11:1; Ps 39:11); in Deut 17:8 and 21:5, on the other hand, *nega'* denotes some form of human assault inflicted on another person. God usually strikes without human intervention but also punishes through a human agent, e.g., hostile nations (2 Sam 7:14; Jer 4:10). In 1 Kgs 8:37 and 2 Chron 6:28 *nega'* appears to be a collective nom. for different forms of divine plagues: famine, pest, scorching (of grain), mildew, locusts, other insects(?), human enemies, and disease. In Prov 6:33 *nega'*, referring to a fatal blow, is also said to be the lot of the adulterer (v. 32).

4. God, however, not only strikes sinful people; his faithful servant received a deadly blow (*ng'*) for the transgressions of God's people (Isa 53:4, 8). Furthermore, God is not only the one who punishes and strikes, but he is also the one who protects the faithful from plague and disaster (*nega'*; Ps 91:10).

Disease—plague: → *deber* I (bubonic plague, # 1822); → *ṭ^eḥōrîm* (plague, # 3224); → *maggēpâ* (plague, # 4487); → *nega'* (plague, affliction, # 5596); → *rešep* I (pestilence, # 8404); → *ṣr'* (suffer from skin disease, # 7665). For related entries → *ḥlh* I (become weak, tired, ill, # 2703); → **Plagues: Theology**

Disease—blister, boil, skin disease, scar, wound: → *'^aba'bu'ōt* (blisters, # 81); → *bōhaq* (skin condition, # 993); → *baheret* (white patch on skin, # 994); → *gārāb* (festering eruption, # 1734); → *zrr* I (press out [wounds], # 2452); → *ḥeres* I (itch, # 3063); → *yabbelet* (wart?, # 3301); → *yallepet* (skin disease, # 3539); → *y^eraqraq* (discoloration, # 3768); → *k^ewiyya* (scar, # 3918); → *m'r* (be sore, # 4421); → *māzôr* I (boil, # 4649); → *makkâ* (blow, # 4804); → *mispaḥat* (skin eruption, # 5030); → *mrḥ* (rub, polish, # 5302); → *neteq* (scalp infection, # 5999); → *sappaḥat* (hair disease, # 6204); → *'ōpel* I (abscesses, # 6754); → *'āš* II (pus, # 6932); → *ṣāpâ* (pus?, # 7597); → *ṣarebet* (scar, # 7648); → *ṣr'* (suffer from skin disease, # 7665); → *ś^e'ēt* II (swelling, # 8421); → *śtr* (break out [tumor], # 8609); → *š^eḥîn* (boil, # 8825). For related entries → *ḥlh* I (become weak, tired, ill, # 2703)

BIBLIOGRAPHY

ISBE 1:532, 953-60, 3:103-6; *THAT* 2:37-39; *TWAT* 5:219-26; T. D. Hanks, *God So Loved the Third World: The Biblical Vocabulary of Oppression*, 1983, 3-39; Y. I. Kim, "The Vocabulary of Oppression in the Old Testament," Ph.D. diss. Drew University, 1981; C. F. Marriottini, "The Problem of Social Oppression in the Eighth Century Prophets," Ph.D. diss. Southern Baptist Theological Seminary, 1983; J. Miranda, *Communism in the Bible*, 1982, 37-39; J. Pons, *L'oppression dans l'Ancien Testament*, 1981; E. Tamez, *Bible of the Oppressed*, 1982, 1-30.

R. K. Harrison/I. Swart

5597	נגף

נגף (*ngp*), q. strike, smite, injure, stumble against; ni. be stricken, smitten; hitp. stumble (# 5597); מַגֵּפָה (*maggēpâ*), nom. plague, stroke, blow, defeat, slaughter (→ # 4487); נֶגֶף (*negep*), nom. striking, blow, plague, stumbling (# 5598).

OT 1. In nearly all instances *ngp* and its derivatives denote a divine plague or blow executed by God with disastrous consequences for the victims (→ *ng'*, touch, # 5595). In cases where the stroke is executed by a human force, God remains the actual instigator of the act (Judg 20:35; 1 Sam 4:2-3; 2 Chron 21:14-17). The stroke is most often executed in the context of the battlefield. God is the divine warrior who executes his judgment on rebellious and sinful people (Israel, the nations, individuals) (Exod 12:13, 23, 27; Josh 22:17; 1 Kgs 8:33; 2 Chron 13:20; Ps 106:29), but who also intervenes on behalf of his threatened or defeated people (Deut 28:7; 1 Sam 7:10), especially in the messianic age (Ps 89:24; Zech 14:12). The outcome of the stroke, then, always takes on disastrous proportions, viz., death and deadly disease (2 Sam 12:15; 2 Chron 21:14, 15, 18). The fierceness of the stroke is seen at its most extreme in the extermination of a whole army or people (Num 16:46-49[17:11-14]; 25:9; Judg 20:35). In Exod 21:22 the verbal form denotes a severe hit or knock that merely injures but does not result in death.

2. *ngp* and the nom. form *negep* are also used metaphorically in the figure of "striking one's foot against rocks." Such accidents easily happened on the stony roads of Palestine. This image expresses misfortune and divine judgment (Isa 8:14; Jer 13:16) but is also used in connection with divine protection (Ps 91:12). Following the ways of wisdom also warrants a secure path, as against stumbling over the rocks of life (Prov 3:23).

Beating, crushing, grinding: → *b'ṭ* (kick, # 1246); → *dwk* (pound, # 1870); → *dk'* (crush, be crushed, # 1917); → *dkh* (be crushed, # 1920); → *dqq* (crush, # 1990); → *hlm* (beat, # 2150); → *ḥbṭ* (beat from, # 2468); → *ṭḥn* (grind, mill, # 3221); → *ktš* (grind down, # 4197); → *ktt* (beat fine, pound up, disperse, # 4198); → *mḥṣ* (beat to pieces, # 4731); → *m'k* (press, squeeze, crush, # 5080); → *ngp* (strike, # 5597); → *nk'* (be whipped out, flogged out, # 5777); → *nkh* (be hit, be battered, ruined, destroyed, # 5782); → *ṣrr* I (bind, tie up, # 7674); → *r'ṣ* (beat down, # 8320); → *rṣṣ* (crush, mash, break, # 8368); → *šwp* I (crush, # 8789); → *šḥq* (grind down, # 8835)
Disease—plague: → *deber* I (bubonic plague, # 1822); → *ṭᵉḥōrîm* (plague, # 3224); → *maggēpâ* (plague, # 4487); → *nega'* (plague, affliction, # 5596); → *rešep* I (pestilence, # 8404); → *ṣr'* (suffer from skin disease, # 7665). For related entries → *ḥlh* I (become weak, tired, ill, # 2703); → **Plagues: Theology**

BIBLIOGRAPHY
T. D. Hanks, *God So Loved the Third World: The Biblical Vocabulary of Oppression*, 1983, 3-39; Y. I. Kim, "The Vocabulary of Oppression in the Old Testament," Ph.D. diss. Drew University, 1981; C. F. Marriottini, "The Problem of Social Oppression in the Eighth Century Prophets," Ph.D. diss. Southern Baptist Theological Seminary, 1983; J. Miranda, *Communism in the Bible*, 1982, 37-39; J. Pons, *L'oppression dans l'Ancien Testament*, 1981; E. Tamez, *Bible of the Oppressed*, 1982, 1-30.

I. Swart

5598 (*negep*, striking, blow), → # 5597

5599	נגר

נגר (*ngr*), ni. run, flow; hi., pour out, pour down; ho. be poured out (# 5599).

ANE In Syr. *ngr* means be long (of time). In Aram. it means to flow.

OT 1. Several times the vb. is used in connection with judgment. In 2 Sam 14:14 death is compared to water spilled on the ground, and in Job 20:28 God's wrath is as destructive as the rushing waters of a flood. God compels the wicked to drink the cup of foaming wine he pours out (Ps 75:8[9]), and when he appears as judge, the mountains melt "like water rushing down a slope" (Mic 1:4 [ho.]). Two verses later the destruction of Samaria is described as the pouring of stones into a valley (1:6).

2. The hi. is used 3x of handing people over to the power of the sword, twice with reference to the fall of Jerusalem (Jer 18:21; Ezek 35:5; cf. Ps 63:10[11]).

3. In the difficult Ps 77:2[3] the psalmist's hands are stretched out (lit., poured out) in a context of prayer. Since the pouring out of one's heart is combined with lifting hands in prayer in Lam 2:19, perhaps the two figures are compressed into one in Ps 77:2 (cf. Coppes, *TWOT* 2:553). The rare vb. *pwg* (→ # 7028) occurs both in Ps 77:2 and Lam 2:18 (relief). A nom. derived from *pwg* (*h^apugôt*) appears with *ngr* in Lam 3:49, also in a context of weeping and prayer.

Pouring out, casting, spilling: → *yṣq* (pour out, cast, # 3668); → *ngr* (run, flow, be poured out, # 5599); → *ntk* (pour out, melt, # 5988); → *špk* (pour out, spill, ebb away, flow out, # 9161)

Herbert M. Wolf/Robert Holmstedt

5600	נִגֶּרֶת

נִגֶּרֶת (cj. *niggeret*), nom. torrent (hapleg., Job 20:28, # 5600); < נגר (*ngr*, deliver, flow, pour, → # 5599).

OT In its only occurrence (Job 20:28) this term parallels a term for flood (*y^ebûl*) and is either a pl. nom. (from *niggeret*) or a substantivally used part. from *ngr* (those which flow = torrents) after the pattern of another part. (*$nōz^e$lîm*, the flowing ones = springs, Exod 15:8; Isa 44:3; et al.). Consequently, the second line of Job 20:28 reads: "Torrents (or waters which flow) on the day of God's wrath."

Flood, deluge, torrent: → *bz'* (wash away, # 1021); → *grp* (wash away, # 1759); → *mabbûl* (heavenly ocean, deluge, # 4429); → *niggeret* (torrent, # 5600); → *ṣwp* (flood, rise up, make float, # 7429); → *šibbōlet* II (torrent, undulation, # 8673); → *šôṭ* II ([sudden] flood, # 8766); → *šṭp* (wash away, flood, overflow, # 8851); → *šeṣep* (flooding, # 9192)

Michael A. Grisanti

5601	נגשׂ

נגשׂ (*ngś*), q. oppress, exact, force, press; ni. be oppressed, pressed, oppress one another (# 5601); נֹגֵשׂ (*nōgēś*), act. part. oppressor, ruler.

ANE In the East Semitic languages the vb. *nagāšu* occurs with the meaning to go away, to leave, to wander around. In Ugar. *ngṯ* means seek (cf. C. H. Gordon, *UT*, 441). In RL the vb. *ngś* occurs with both the meanings, to drive and to press for something or to "exact" payment. It does not occur in Bibl. Aram.

OT 1. *ngś* connotes the exertion of cruel and dehumanizing pressure on another person by forced labor, tribute, or repayment of debt. Such action reduced people to an existence of slavery. The vb. *ngś* correlates with the negative meaning of *kbš* and refers to the execution of power with the intention of harming and subduing individuals. The nom. derivative can be translated oppressor (Isa 9:4[3], 14:4; Zech 9:8) or slave drivers (Exod 5:6, 10). The vb. in the q. form is also used with reference to the requirements of payment (Deut 15:2.3; Dan 11:20). The vb. in the ni. form designates the feeling of "hard pressed" or being "in distress" (1 Sam 13:6; 14:24).

2. In Job 39:7 *ngś* expresses the harsh pressing of a wild ass by its driver. The same treatment was inflicted on the people of Israel who were forced to do hard labor by their slave drivers in Egypt (Exod 3:7; 5:6, 10, 13, 14). Centuries later Judah was compelled to pay tribute to Pharaoh Neco of Egypt, and in order to pay the tribute, King Jehoiakim pressed (*ngś*) his people to make them supply the tribute money (2 Kgs 23:35; cf. Dan 11:20, NIV). *ngś* also describes the severe toil and bondage that the people of God suffered under Assyria and Babylon (Isa 9:4[3]; 14:2, 4).

3. *ngś* also expresses the pressing of debtors by their creditors (Deut 15:2-3). The law of the Sabbatical Year was intended to protect persons in Israelite society who would not have been in a position to repay their debts if they exceeded their real income. According to the law no pressure was to be brought (*ngś*) on such persons, for such pressuring would lead to the enslavement of defaulting debtors and their dependents, whereas the enslavement of an Israelite by a fellow Israelite was strictly forbidden by Israelite law (Lev 25:46; 2 Chron 28:8-11). The people of Israel were meant to be a brotherly society, not oppressing one another but caring for one another's needs. However, in the period of the prophets the ruling class in Israelite society pressed (*ngś*) the socially weak into unpaid servitude and forced labor by their economic exploitation (Isa 3:12; 58:3).

4. In Exod 3:7 the use of *ngś* evokes the physical anguish of the afflicted: the oppressed people cried out to God for deliverance because of their slave drivers (→ *lḥṣ*). In 1 Sam 13:6 (also v. 7b) *ngś* reflects the suffering by Saul's army of a great deal of anxiety and panic because of the Philistines.

5. The opposite of living in the oppressive situation of the Egyptian bondage is stated in Exod 3:8 as living in "a good and spacious land, a land flowing with milk and honey." However, a prosperous society ruled (*ngś*) by peace and righteousness (Isa 60:17), wherein the roles of ruler (*nōgēś*) and subordinate are reversed (Isa 14:2) and which will be permanently protected by God against the oppressor (*nōgēś*, Zech 9:8), is yet to be realized in the eschatological age.

Affliction, oppression: → *dḥq* (oppress, # 1895); → *ḥms* I (do violence, # 2803); → *ḥmṣ* II (oppress, # 2807); → *ynh* (oppress, # 3561); → *lḥṣ* (press, # 4315); → *māṣôr* I (affliction, siege, # 5189); → *mrr* I (be bitter, distraught, afflict, # 5352); → *nega'* (plague, affliction, # 5596); → *ngś* (exact, # 5601); → *'nh* II (afflict, humble, afflict one's soul, fast, oppress, submit, # 6700); → *'wq* I (crush?, # 6421); → *'mr* II (deal tyrannically with, # 6683); → *'šq* I (wrong, # 6943); → *ṣwq* I (constrain, press in/upon, harass, vex, # 7439); → *ṣwr* II (deal tyrannically with, # 7444); → *rhb* (assail, press, pester, alarm, confuse, # 8104); → *rṣṣ* (crush, # 8368); → *tôlāl* (oppressor, # 9354); → *tōk* (oppression, # 9412)

Beating, crushing, grinding: → *b'ṭ* (kick, # 1246); → *dwk* (pound, # 1870); → *dk'* (crush, be crushed, # 1917); → *dkh* (be crushed, # 1920); → *dqq* (crush, # 1990); → *hlm* (beat, # 2150); → *ḥbṭ* (beat from, # 2468); → *ṭḥn* (grind, mill, # 3221); → *ktš* (grind down, # 4197); → *ktt* (beat fine, pound up, disperse, # 4198); → *mḥṣ* (beat to pieces, # 4731); → *m'k* (press, squeeze, crush, # 5080); → *ngp* (strike, # 5597); → *nk'* (be whipped out, flogged out, # 5777); → *nkh* (be hit, be battered, ruined, destroyed, # 5782); → *ṣrr* I (bind, tie up, # 7674); → *r'ṣ* (beat down, # 8320); → *rṣṣ* (crush, mash, break, # 8368); → *šwp* I (crush, # 8789); → *šḥq* (grind down, # 8835)

Kingship, rule, supervision, dominion: → *bʿl* I (marry, rule over, own, # 1249); → *g^ebîrâ/g^eberet* (lady, queen, mistress, # 1485/1509); → *ykḥ* (dispute, reason together, prove, judge, rule, reprove, # 3519); → *kbš* (make subservient, subdue, # 3899); → *mlk* I (rule, # 4887); → *mšl* II (rule, govern, # 5440); → *nṣḥ* (supervise, # 5904); → *rdd* (repel, subdue, # 8096); → *rdh* I (rule, govern, # 8097); → *rʿh* I (feed, graze, shepherd, rule, # 8286); → *śrr* I (rule, direct, superintend, # 8606); → *šlṭ* (gain power, # 8948); → *špṭ* (get justice, act as a judge, rule, # 9149)

BIBLIOGRAPHY
T. D. Hanks, *God So Loved the Third World: The Biblical Vocabulary of Oppression*, 1983, 3-39; Y. I. Kim, "The Vocabulary of Oppression in the Old Testament," Ph.D. diss. Drew University, 1981; C. F. Marriottini, "The Problem of Social Oppression in the Eighth Century Prophets," Ph.D. diss. Southern Baptist Theological Seminary, 1983; J. Miranda, *Communism in the Bible*, 1982, 37-39; J. Pons, *L'oppression dans l'Ancien Testament*, 1981; E. Tamez, *Bible of the Oppressed*, 1982, 1-30.

I. Swart/Philip J. Nel

5602	נגשׁ

נגשׁ (*ngš*), q. draw near, approach, step forth; ni. draw near, approach; hi. bring near, offer; ho. be brought near; hitp. draw near (only in Isa 45:20) (# 5602).

ANE Among cognate Sem. languages, this root is attested only in Ugar., with the meaning to meet (*KTU* 1.6:II:21, 1.23:68).

OT 1. Like its synonym *qrb*, this root involves being near or in close proximity to an object. In the restoration predicted by Jeremiah, the coming prince will approach Yahweh with Yahweh's blessing (Jer 30:21). In other contexts, *ngš* involves drawing near to a person of venerable position (Gen 45:4; 2 Kgs 5:13).

The most important theological context in which this root is used is when priests draw near to the altar to minister before God (Exod 28:43; Ezek 44:13). This is often paralleled by entering (*bw'*) the tabernacle or temple (Exod 30:20). Its cultic uses are nearly identical to those of *qrb*. Isaiah condemned Israel's cultic practices because of the ironic way in which they had drawn near with their mouths to honor him with their lips, while their hearts were far from him (Isa 29:13; see the parallel in Jer 12:2, where the synonym *qrb* is used).

Other physical uses of this root include drawing near in preparation for battle, as David drew near to Goliath (1 Sam 17:40, notice the uses of *qrb* in this passage). In Joel 3:9[4:9], the warriors are summoned to "draw near" and beat their plowshares into swords and their pruning hooks into spears in preparation for warfare. Drawing near may also, like *qrb*, have sexual connotations (Exod 19:15).

2. Instead of having a pass. ni., *ngš* is a mixed root that uses a q. impf. but a ni. pf. (GKC 220; Waltke-O'Connor, *IBHS* 392-93). The seventeen occurrences of the ni. have the same basic meanings as the q. The hi. is used much like those of *bw'* and *qrb*. As a "two-place Hiphil," it is used when one brings an offering to God (Lev 2:8 contains the hi. of all three roots).

Coming, approaching, entering: → *'th* (come, bring, # 910); → *bw'* (go, come, arrive, enter, # 995); → *zrq* II (creep in, # 2451); → *ngš* (draw near, approach, offer, # 5602); → *qrb* (draw near, approach, offer, # 7928)

BIBLIOGRAPHY
TDNT 3:860-66; *THAT* 1:264-69, 674-81; *TWAT* 5:232-37; *TWOT* 2:553-54, 811-13; J. A. Fitzmyer, "More About Elijah Coming First," *JBL* 104, 1985, 295-96; H. Fleddermann, "John and the Coming One (Matt 3:11-12—Luke 3:16-17)," *Society of Biblical Literature: Seminar Papers*, 1984, 377-84; E. Jenni, "'Kommen' im theologischen Sprachgebrauch des AT," *Wort-Gebot-Glaube. W. Eichrodt zum 80.Geburtstag. ATANT* 59, 1970, 251-61; C. F. D. Moule, "A Reconsideration of the Context of Maranatha," *NTS* 6, 1959-60, 307-10; F. Schnutenhaus, "Das Kommen und Erscheinen Gottes im AT," *ZAW* 76, 1964, 1-21; G. von Rad, "The Origin of the Day of the Yahweh," *JSS* 4, 1959, 97-108.

Bill T. Arnold

5603	נֵד

נֵד (*nēd*), nom. heap, wall (# 5603).

ANE Most probably this nom. comes from the root *ndd* II, which occurs also in Arab., rather than *ndd* I, flee. The Arab. *naddun* is probably a cognate nom., as it means a "high hill."

OT In contrast to *gal* I, heap (→ # 1643), and *'ᵃrēmâ* (→ # 6894), the word *nēd* is used exclusively of the piling up of waters (Exod 15:8; Ps 78:13 [of the Red Sea]; Josh 3:13, 16 [of the Jordan]; Ps 33:7 [of the gathering of the waters at creation]).

The nom. is used in Exod 15:8 to designate the wall of water raised by the blast of air from the Lord's nostrils. The psalmist, recalling God's saving activities at the crossing of the sea, naturally used *nēd* as he recounted the event in Ps 78:13. As a *maskil*, the psalm draws upon the mighty acts of God to teach later generations to trust in the Lord.

Heap, mound, pile: → *gal* I (heap, pile, # 1643); → *ḥᵃmôr* II (heap, # 2790); → *mᵉdûrâ* (pile, # 4509); → *nēd* (heap, # 5603); → *sll* (heap, pile up, esteem highly, resist, # 6148); → *'rm* I (be dammed up, # 6890); → *ṣbr* (pile up, # 7392)

Wall, heap of stones: → *gdr* (erect a wall, # 1553); → *ḥômâ* (wall, # 2570); → *ḥayiṣ* (flimsy wall, # 2666); → *ṭîrâ* (row of stones, # 3227); → *kōtel* (wall, # 4185); → *nēd* (heap, wall, # 5603); → *qîr* (wall, # 7815); → *šûr* I (wall, # 8803)

Allan M. Harman/Keith N. Schoville

5604	נדא

נדא (*nd'*), hi. seduce, alienate s.o. affections (hapleg.; # 5604).

ANE Eth. *nad'a*, drive or incite (cattle), has been suggested as a cognate (*HALAT* 634). The Heb. *nd'* stems from *ndh* (# 5612), displace.

OT In its sole occurrence the vb. describes the actions of Jeroboam II alienating/luring the people from Yahweh (2 Kgs 17:21).

Seduction, incitement, enticement: *ḥlq* I (be smooth, be deceptive, make slippery, flatter, # 2744); → *ndḥ* I (banish, be scattered, be cast out, seduce, # 5615); → *swt* (entice, draw away, incite, # 6077); → *šgh* (stray, err, go/do wrong, mislead, # 8706; → t'h (wander off, lead astray, # 9494)

Ronald Youngblood

5605	נדב

נדב (*ndb*), q. to incite, offer freely, give a free-will offering, to make willing, to move to do something; hitp. to offer of one's own accord, freely (# 5605); נְדָבָה (*n^e^dābâ*), nom. freewill offering, voluntary gift, free inclination (# 5607); נָדִיב (*nādîb*), nom./adj. noble man, willing man; willing, generous, noble (# 5618); נְדִיבָה (*n^e^dîbâ*), nom. something noble, honorable, dignity (# 5619).

ANE This word or its cognates occurs in other Sem. languages (e.g., Akk. *nindabû*, cereal offering; Aram. *n^e^dab*, voluntary; *nidbûtā'*, willingness). Northwest Sem. provides some examples close to biblical usage: Phoen. *ndb*, offer, incite (Harris, 123); Aram. *ndbh*.

OT 1. The vb. describes the inner motivation of persons, that attitude or impulse or decision that moves them to act or speak. Its nom./adj. forms are used with it as emphatic cognates.

The vb. describes the condition under which people respond favorably to Yahweh's request for freewill offerings for the tabernacle (Exod 35:29). It is used in the q. stem with heart as the subject in this context. Much later in Israel, in the same theological, cultural, and religious contexts, the call for gifts for the temple of Solomon (1 Chron 29:17) and also for the second temple under Zerubbabel (Ezra 1:6; 2:68), resulted in the same response. In the latter uses the hitp. stem is used and the people themselves are the subject. The word is used in other contexts to designate anyone's volunteering freely for various services or projects (Judg 5:2, 9; 2 Chron 17:16).

2. The general concept of freewill offering permeates all of the uses of *n^e^dābâ*. Yahweh's love is a free love for his people (Hos 14:4[5]) as they return to him even after adultery and rebellion. The reciprocal love of his people is to be free and freely expressed to him in various ways and settings. The Lord's anointed (Ps 110:3) will be followed by troops who are willingly his. The construction of the tabernacle was possible because of the gifts freely given by the people at Yahweh's invitation (Exod 35:29)—only those whose hearts moved (*ndb*) them were to give. Similar gifts were received at the building of the first temple (2 Chron 31:14).

The freewill offering was a major part of Israel's sacrificial system (Lev 7:16). At Israel's festive meals (Deut 16:10) freewill offerings (*zebaḥ*, → # 2285) were presented. They are among the offerings of well-being (Lev 7:16; *šelem*, → # 8968) that Ezekiel envisioned as continuing in the new temple (Ezek 46:12). Vows that were made freely had to be carried out; they could not be rescinded (Lev 22:23). Freewill offerings could be given for no other reason than an expression of love for Yahweh, or they could be given to express thanks for deliverance (Ps 54:6[8]). The offering could be presented only at those sacred sites that Yahweh chose for his offerings (Deut 12:6-7).

3. The word *nādîb* describes the noble man who counsels generous/noble things and possesses a magnanimity of character (Isa 32:8). It also describes a heart that is generous, willing, even noble, such as was possessed by those who gave freely to the tabernacle and the temple when they were under construction (Exod 35:5, 22; 2 Chron 29:31). Similarly, a willing spirit (*rûaḥ*) is open to God (Ps 51:12[14]). The nom. overlaps necessarily with *ṣaddîq*, righteous (→ # 7404) (Prov 17:26), but the *nābāl*, fool (→ # 5572), lacks any nobility of character and is boorish besides (Isa 32:5). A person

of nobility can be described as one apart from God, for at times God opposes him and even shames him with contempt (Job 12:21).

4. The nom. *n^e dîbâ* describes deeds, actions, and thoughts that are counseled by a magnanimous person and reflect a dimension of integrity desirable in God's people. The generous/noble man (*nādîb*) counsels/offers (*y'ṣ*; → # 3619) generous things (Isa 32:8) and also establishes (*qwm*; → # 7756) himself by them. Even the noble person (*n^e dîbâ*) can suffer the loss of this dimension of integrity during times of terror and affliction (Job 30:15).

The major OT synonyms of *ndb* are *'bh*, be willing (→ # 14), *ḥpṣ*, desire (→ # 2913), and *rṣh*, want (→ # 8354). The vb. *ndb* never occurs par. to these, being virtually limited to cultic contexts. As noted, its principal nuance is that of voluntariness, acting out of a willing spirit. The vb. *'bh*, occurring almost exclusively with a negative particle, has to do with intention and is never used as a technical cultic term. A general translation might be unwilling, to refuse, and the like. The vb. *ḥpṣ*, on the other hand, contains the idea of desire or taking pleasure in someone or something. It is used commonly in religious contexts to speak of God's taking pleasure (or not taking pleasure) in some cultic activity. In such cases it is synonymous with *rṣh*; in fact, the two verbs are par. or in juxtaposition in several passages in which Yahweh displays his reaction to certain religious practices (cf. Ps 51:6, 16[8, 18]; Mal 1:10-13).

P-B At Qumran the vb. and the nom./adj. are used in accordance with OT usage, but also with peculiar sectarian images, nuances and allusions (e.g., CD 16:13; 1QS 9:5; 1QH 14:26; CD 6:2-10). The word continued to be used in Late Heb. profusely within the semantic range noted above: that done, given by means of a free will, gladly, agreeable (Jastrow 2:877).

Offering, sacrifice: → *'azkārâ* (sign-offering, # 260); → *'iššeh* (offering by fire, # 852); → *'āšām* (guilt offering, # 871); → *zbḥ* (slaughter, sacrifice, # 2284); → *ḥaṭṭā'at* (sin offering, # 2633); → *ṭbḥ* (slaughter, # 3180); → *minḥâ* (gift, present, offering, sacrifice, # 4966); → *ma'^a śēr* (tithe, # 5130); → *ndr* (make a vow, # 5623); → *nwp* I (move back and forth, wave, # 5677); → *nsk* I (pour out, be consecrated, libation, # 5818); → *'ōlâ* I (burnt offering, # 6592); → *'^a rîsâ* (meal/dough offering, # 6881); → *qorbān* (offering, gift, # 7933); → *šḥṭ* I (slaughter, # 8821); → *šelem* (settlement sacrifice, # 8968); → *tāmîd* (regular offering, # 9458); → *t^e rûmâ* (tribute, contribution, # 9556); → **Aaron: Theology**; → **Offering: Theology**; → **Priests and Levites: Theology**

Voluntary, freewill, generosity: → *ndb* (offer freely, give a freewill offering, # 5605)

Bibliography

TDNT 6:694-700; *TWOT* 2:554-55; Z. Harris, *A Grammar of the Phoenician Language*, 1936; J. Licht, "The Concept of *nedabah* in the DSS," in *Essays on the Dead Sea Scrolls*, 1961, 77-84; R. Rendtorff, *Studien zur Geschichte des Opfers im Alten Israel*, WMANT 24, 1967.

Eugene Carpenter/Michael A. Grisanti

5607 (*n^e dābâ*, freewill offering, voluntary gift), → # 5605

5609 (*nidgālôt*, bannered host?), → # 3919

5610	נדד

נדד (*ndd* I), q. retreat, flee, depart, stray, wander, put to flight, flutter, banish; po. flee; hi.

drive out, put to flight; ho. be banished (# 5610); נְדוּדִים (*n^e dûdîm*), nom. restlessness (Job 7:4 only) (# 5611).

ANE Ugar. *ndd*, go wander, hurry; Arab. *nadda*, flee; and Late Bab. *nadādu*, disappear.

OT 1. The q. form, *ndd*, flee, stray, occurs both in crisis situations with threats of danger and in less drastic situations. *ndd*, wander, characterizes the wicked who in their lostness are "food for vultures" (Job 15:23) and are "banished from the world" (Job 18:18; 20:8; 2 Sam 23:6). Those who are not content with staying at home, but restlessly move about (*ndd*), are likened to birds that stray (*ndd*) from their nest (Prov 27:8). The vb. is frequently used in connection with birds, suggesting rapid fluttering (Isa 16:2; Jer 4:25; 9:10b[9b]; "flapped a wing" Isa 10:14). A "woe" is pronounced on those who wander away (*ndd*) from God (Hos 7:13).

2. Most occurrences of *ndd* are within scenes of destruction from which people escape or flee (*ndd*; e.g., Isa 21:15). The vb. occurs almost exclusively in poetry (exceptions are in Gen 31:40; Esth 6:1, sleep fled), where the part. form *nōdēd* lends an onomatopoeic effect as oracles of judgment are pronounced over Moab (Isa 16:2-3; cf. 21:14, ones fleeing = fugitives) and Ammon (Jer 49:5). Isaiah, in whose book eight of the twenty-seven vb. forms are found, describes how the Assyrians with their destructive tactics put people to flight (Isa 10:31).

3. In the judgment on the cosmos, birds will flee (*ndd*; Jer 4:25; cf. 9:10[9]), as will people (*ndd*) (Isa 33:3). The term is apt for describing the effect of God's judgment generally.

Roaming, wandering, homeless: → *hl'* (stray, be removed far off, # 2133); → *ṭ'h* (roam around, lead astray, # 3246); → *ndd* I (flee, stray, wander, # 5610); → *nwd* (sway, be homeless, # 5653); → *nwṣ* (flee, # 5680); → *rwd* (roam, # 8113); → *šgh* (stray, err, go/do wrong, mislead, # 8706); → *šwṭ* I (roam, # 8763); → *t'h* (wander off, # 9494)
Disappearance, flight, escape: → *brḥ* I (run away, flee, disappear, # 1368); → *ḥlp* I (pass by, disappear, violate, change, renew, # 2736); → *ḥrh* II (disappear, be few in number, # 3014); → *nws* (flee, escape, slip away, # 5674); → *pṭr* (vanish, escape, let out, # 7080); → *plṭ* (save, bring to safety, # 7117); → *parš^e dōn* (loophole [for escape]?, # 7307); → *śrd* (run away, escape, # 8572)

Bibliography

THAT 2:48; *TWAT* 5:245-50; *TWOT* 2:555.

Elmer A. Martens

5611 (*n^e dudîm*, restlessness), → # 5610

5612	נדה

נדה (*ndh* I), pi. exclude, suppose far away (# 5612).

ANE The root *ndh* occurs also in other Sem. literature: Akk. *nadu,* throw.

OT The vb. occurs only in one verbal form, i.e., as a pi. part. and that merely in two instances. In Isa 66:5 it expresses exclusion in the sense of social excommunication of the faithful believer on account of his commitment to Yahweh by his wicked/godless compatriots. In Amos 6:3 it has the sense of putting away/thrusting off/excluding (from their minds): "They (the guilty people of Israel) that thrust off the evil day [of divine judgment]," i.e., refuse to think of it.

P. J. J. S. Els

5614 (*niddâ*, menstrual flow, pollution), → # 1864

5615	נדח

נדח (*ndḥ* I), q. banish; ni. be scattered, banished, seduced; pu. be cast out; hi. scatter, divert, banish, seduce (# 5615); מַדּוּחִים (*maddûḥîm*), nom. repudiation (# 4505).

OT 1. The vb. *ndḥ* is used 55x, 19x in Jerermiah. The most prominent stems are the ni. and hi. (the one use of q., 2 Sam 14:14, is overlooked in *HALAT*). Its basic meaning is drive out. It is used of the banishment of Absalom from David (2 Sam 14:14) and of the expulsion of legitimate priests from Israel (2 Chron 13:9).

2. In line with the other terms of this word group, this vb. focuses on "scatter," particularly in the dispersion of Israel known as the Exile. The ni. can refer to those who have been taken from the land after the destruction of Judah in fulfillment of the covenant curse of expulsion because of sin (Deut 30:4). Some part. forms in the ni. denote the "exiles" or "those who have been scattered" (e.g., Neh 1:9; Jer 30:17; Zeph 3:19), but in several cases the more specific participial construction *nidd*ᵉ*ḥê yiśrā'ēl* ("the scattered/the exiles of Israel") is used (Isa 11:12; Ps 147:2); in all these passages, the émigrés have God's promise that they will be restored to their land. The hi. forms forcefully express that the eviction from Palestine is Yahweh's work. Note the use of the first person in his declarations of judgment (Jer 8:3; 24:9; 27:10, 15; Ezek 4:13; cf. Jer 16:15). Nevertheless, a number of texts that announce his chastisement also proclaim that this same Yahweh in his mercy and faithfulness will gather his people after their time of banishment, as they will then repent and call upon him (Deut 30:1, 4; Jer 23:3, 8; 29:14; 32:37; 46:28). The restoration of this communion between Yahweh and his people and their cleansing unto holiness is the purpose of Yahweh's refining judgment. His infinite grace, however, extends even to other nations, whose exiles will also be gathered in the future (Jer 49:5, 36; Isa 16:3-4, *BHS*).

3. There are cases, however, where the idea of being forced out is not apparent in the use of this vb. Deut 22:1, e.g., alludes to animals that have strayed. The notion of straying or being led astray can also be applied to the people of God, who are presented as the flock that wanders off God's prescribed path or is led to a destructive end. In this figurative usage the themes of judgment or the Exile can still be in the background. Ezek 34 condemns the false shepherds, who do not care for the sheep and do not seek out the "strays" (v. 4, NIV); Yahweh, the good shepherd, will bring them back from the other nations to the pastures of Palestine (v. 16). Deuteronomy warns of being enticed to worship other deities (Deut 4:19; 30:17; both ni.) and decrees harsh penalties for those who lead the nation into idolatry (13:6, 11, 14[5, 10, 13]; cf. Prov 7:21; all hi.). The theological explanation that 2 Kgs gives as the fundamental reason for the destruction of Israel at the hands of Assyria and the subsequent deportation is the straying of the people away from Yahweh after other deities, which had begun under Jeroboam and continued throughout the history of the northern kingdom (2 Kgs 17:21; Q see *BHS*).

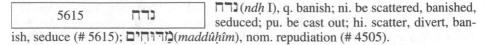

4. Of this vb.'s several synonyms, two are especially worthy of mention. Some scholars consider *dḥh*, push (down), and *dḥḥ*, push, as variations of or perhaps even derived from *ndḥ*. Pace Driver and *HALAT* (363), the articles in *TWAT* and *TWOT* consider that there is only one root *ndḥ* and include the three passages listed under *ndḥ* II (Deut 19:5; 20:19; 2 Sam 15:14) in their discussion of that vb. *TWOT* (2:556) even proposes that the two texts of Deut are the key for grasping the "basic meaning of the root."

5. The sole derivative of *ndḥ* is the hapleg. *maddûḥîm* (Lam 2:14). English versions, though, offer different translations: "worthless, deceptive" (NIV, NRSV, NEB; cf. Tg.) or "banishment" (i.e., oracles leading to banishment; NEB note, cf. *TWAT* 5:259, LXX).

P-B 1. A number of G words translate the various Heb. terms of this word group, and several of the most prominent are mentioned in the study of *pwṣ* (→ # 7046). The G term used most for *ndḥ* but not alluded to in that discussion, however, is *exōtheō*, expel; 18x). Half of these passages occur in Jer (e.g., 8:3; 16:5; 23:2, 3, 8).

2. The vb. *ndḥ* appears only a few times in the Qumran material. For example, in the Thanksgiving Hymns the author (the Teacher of Righteousness?) indicts the false religious leadership of Jerusalem for having driven him and his followers away from the land (1QH 4:8-9), but he trusts in the eventual vindication of his person and cause. The faithful remnant praise God after the eschatological battle in a hymn of thanksgiving of the War Scroll. The God of the covenant will have kept the evil ones of "Belial" from driving the community away from covenant loyalty and obedience (1QM 14:9-10).

Scattering, dispersion: → *bzr* (scatter, # 1029); → *zrh* I (scatter, sprinkle, spread, # 2430); → *zr'* (sow, scatter seed, # 2445); → *zrq* I (sprinkle, scatter, # 2450); → *ndḥ* I (banish, be scattered, be cast out, seduce, # 5615); → *ndp* (blow away, scatter, # 5622); → *npṣ* II (spread out, scatter, be dispersed, # 5880); → *pwṣ* (scatter, disperse, be spread, # 7046); → *pzr* (scatter, spread, # 7061)

BIBLIOGRAPHY

TWAT 5:254-60; *TWOT* 2:556-57; G. R. Driver, "Hebrew Roots and Words," *WO* 1, 1950, 406-15 (esp. 408-9).

M. Daniel Carroll R.

5616	נדח

נדח (*ndḥ* II), q. wield (with an axe); ni. put (a hand) to the axe; hi. bring (ruin) on (# 5616).

ANE The vb. *ndḥ* is attested in Aram. *n^edaḥ* (rare), Sam. *nāda*, Eth. *nadḥa*, and Arab. *nadaḥa,* with meanings that correspond to the Heb. *ndḥ* I, thrust or scatter.

OT Most lexical works (*HAHAT*, BDB, *TWAT*, *TWOT*) do not list two separate roots for *ndḥ*; indeed, the LXX does not appear to recognize two. *HALAT* (636) follows Driver, who distinguished them based on the direction of action, like our use of "expel" and "impel." *ndḥ* II, then, is more restricted, being used of axes, except for 2 Sam 15:14, where David expresses fear that Absalom will "bring" ruin (*rā'â*) on Jerusalem (cf. commentaries for textual discussion).

P-B 1QH 4:8-9 uses *ndḥ* to lament being thrust from the land. A tradition that Isaiah met his death at the hands of Manasseh by being sawed in two appears in *Asc. Isa.* 5:1-16 and also finds expression in the Babylonian and Jerusalem Talmuds (Yebamot 49b; PTalm Sanhedrin 10.2).

Axe, chisel: → *'ēt* III (plowshare?, axe, # 908); → *garzen* (axe, chisel, # 1749); → *kaššîl* (axe, hand axe, # 4172); → *magzērâ* (axe, # 4477); → *m^e gērâ* (stone saw, # 4490); → *maśśôr* (saw, # 5373); → *ndḥ* II (wield [with an axe], # 5616); → *s^e gōr/sāgār* (double axe or javelin, # 6038); → *qardōm* (axe, adze, # 7935)

Robert C. Stallman

5618 (*nâdîb*, willing man, generous, noble), → # 5605

5619 (*n^e dîbâ*, something noble, honorable, dignity), → # 5605

5620 (*nādān* I, sheath), → # 2995

5621	נָדָן

נָדָן (*nādān* II), nom. gift, wages of love (hapleg., Ezek 16:33, # 5621).

ANE Akk. *nudunnû* is the Akk. semi-technical term for gift. According to the Code of Hammurabi (§ 171-72), the *nudunnû* was given after the consummation of the marriage (Neufeld, 114; cf. *HALAT* 597); cf. Middle Heb. *n^e dûnyā'*, bride's outfit, wedding equipment.

OT This Akk. loanword occurs in Ezek 16:33 in par. with *nēdeh* (# 5613; hapleg.). Both refer to the money paid for a harlot's services. These par. terms make the same point as the double use of *'etnan* in 16:34 (→ # 924) and *šḥd* in 16:33 (→ *šḥd*, # 8815). Not only is Israel playing the harlot (and committing covenant infidelity), but she is paying her lovers for this abomination.

Gift: → *'ahab* (gifts of love, charm, # 172); → *zbd* (endow, # 2272); → *mgn* I (deliver, # 4481); → *nādān* II (gift, wages of love, # 5621); → *ntn* (give, present, offer, # 5989); → *skr* II (hand over, # 6127); → *ṣbṭ* (give, # 7381); → *šḥd* (give a gift, # 8815); → *šay* (gift, present, # 8856); → *šalmōnîm* (gift, # 8988)
Bribe, gift: → *beṣa'* (piece of s.t., gain, bribe, # 1299); → *kōper* IV (bribe, # 4111); → *skr* III (bargain, # 6128); → *šḥd* (give a gift, # 8815); → *šalmōnîm* (gift, # 8988)
Tax, gift, offering, tribute: → *'eškār* (tribute, payment, # 868); → *ybl* I (bring [gift, tribute], # 3297); → *middâ* II (tax, # 4501); → *mas* (tribute, tax, forced labor, # 4989); → *maśśā'* I (carrying, burden # 5362); → *maś'ēt* (tax, offering, # 5368); → *sēbel* (forced labor, burden, # 6023); → *t^e rûmâ* (tribute, contribution, # 9556)

BIBLIOGRAPHY

E. Neufeld, *Ancient Hebrew Marriage Laws*, 1944.

Michael A. Grisanti

5622	נדף

נדף (*ndp*), scatter, blow away (# 5622).

OT The use of this root is similar to *npḥ*. The primary meaning is "to scatter," and since the wind is usually the subject, "blowing away" is the connotation. The wind blows chaff (Ps 1:4; Isa 41:2), leaves (Lev 26:36; Job 13:25), crops (Isa 19:7), and smoke (Ps 68:2[3]). All of these symbolic instances contribute to texts depicting divine retribution. In one other text the gains from dishonesty are compared with an ephemeral breath/vapor (Prov 21:6).

Blowing (wind, breath): → *hzh* (pant in sleep, # 2111); → *ndp* (blow away, scatter, # 5622); → *npḥ* (blow, # 5870); → *nšb* (blow, # 5959); → *nšp* (blow, # 5973); → *pwḥ* (blow, blast, malign, # 7032)

D. C. Fredericks

5623	נדר

נדר (*ndr*), q. make a vow (# 5623); נֶדֶר (*neder*), נֵדֶר (*nēder*), nom. vow (# 5624).

ANE The vb. *ndr* is found in Ugar., Phoen-Pun., Egyp.-Aram., Palm., Jewish-Aram., Sam., and Syr.-Mand. Other verbal forms that occur are Arab. *naḏara*; Tigre *naddara*; and Akk. *nazāru*, curse, damn, execrate. The following nom. forms also occur: *ndr* (Ugar., Phoen.-Pun., and Egyp.-Aram.); *nidrā'* (Jewish-Aram.); *nedrā*, *n^{e}dārā* (Syr.); *na/idra'* (Mand.).

OT 1. In the overwhelming majority of cases where the vb. *ndr* occurs, it is used in tandem with the nom. The nom. is also used in combination with the following vbs.: *šlm* in pi., pay, fulfil, complete, consummate (cf. 2 Sam 15:7; Ps 22:25[26]; 50:14; 61:8[9]; 116:14, 18), and in pu. (Ps 65:1[2]); *'śh* in q., fulfil, perform (Judg 11:39; Jer 44:25); *nś'* in q., take (Deut 12:26); *qwm* in q., stand (Num 30:4[5], 7[8], 9[10], 11[12], 12[13]), and in hi., establish, ratify, confirm (Num 30:13[14], 14[15]; Jer 44:25); *'sr* in q., bind [upon oneself] (Num 30:4[5], 5[6], 9[10]); *pl'* in pi., fulfil (Lev 22:21; Num 15:3, 8), and in hi., make [a special vow] (Lev 27:2; Num 6:2); and *prr* in hi., make void, annul (Num 30:8[9], 12[13], 13[14], 15[16]).

Neither the vb. *ndr* nor the nom. that derives from it is used of God, but, as Davies (793) points out, divine promises, oaths, and covenants to individuals as well as to Israel could be considered God's vows (cf. e.g., Gen 12:2-3, 7; 15:5-6; 22:16-18; 26:3-5; 28:13-15; 35:11-12; 2 Sam 7; Ps 89:3-4[4-5]). Vows were normally made by individuals, but sometimes they were offered on behalf of the nation as a whole. In Ps 65:1[2], there is a call to perform vows in thanksgiving for a good harvest and possibly, too, for the end of a drought and the averting of a threatened famine (cf. G. W. Anderson, 1964, 426). Both Ps 76:11[12] and Nah 1:15[2:1] (cf. Smith, 304-5; Achtemeier, 17; Roberts, 54-55; Robertson, 84-85) seem to indicate that, when Israel was under threat from another power, vows were made on behalf of the country as a whole, the fulfilment of which was contingent on Yahweh's deliverance of the nation from oppression.

Num 30:2-15[3-16], which deals with abstinence vows, makes it clear that, while both men and women were entitled to make them, only the vows of men and independent women (the widow and the divorcée [v. 9]) were considered to be unconditionally binding. The majority of women had no independent right to make a vow (cf. *'issār*, # 674). The most plausible explanation for this role differentiation is that, given the economic dependence of most women on men in ancient Israel, it was felt necessary to protect fathers and husbands from excessive commitments made by women who were not ultimately responsible for finding the resources necessary to fulfil those commitments (Rylaarsdam, 527; Olson, 205; Budd, 324). An unmarried woman was under the jurisdiction of her father, and he had the power either to establish or to repudiate any vow she made. When she married, a woman came under the authority of her husband, and he was entitled either to ratify or to nullify his wife's vows. To afford some measure of protection to women and the integrity of their vows, the law required that fathers or husbands should indicate clearly and immediately their approval or disapproval of the vows the women made. Should a father or husband annul a woman's vow after it had been established, he would be considered to have broken the vow and would have to bear the guilt for the default (v. 15[16]). Once the father or the husband had ratified the woman's vow, it became his responsibility to fulfil whatever obligation(s) she had incurred (cf. 1 Sam. 1:21 [however, see LXX which reads, "and his vows and all the tithes of his land"]).

2. With one exception (Jer 44:25), where apostate Jewish women, refugees in Egypt, are excoriated for their worship of "the queen of heaven"—a reference to the Babylonian-Assyrian goddess Ishtar [cf. Canaanite Astarte, Greek Aphrodite, Roman Venus]—vows made by Israelites in the OT were directed at Yahweh. Vows were chiefly aimed at securing Yahweh's aid, protection, or provision, e.g., for success in realizing an ambition (cf. Gen 28:20-22; 2 Sam 15:7-12; Ps 132:2-5), for the birth of a longed-for child (cf. 1 Sam 1:11; Prov 31:2), for a bountiful harvest (Ps 65:1[2]), for victory in battle (76:11[12]), for deliverance from danger (cf. Ps 61:5[6], 8[9]; Jon 1:16), or for recovery from an illness or some other crisis (cf. Job 22:27; Ps 22:25[26]; 66:13-15; 116:14, 18). The evidence suggests that the completion of all vows was made in retrospect, when the votaries' crises had passed (cf. Durham, 300). All the vows in the OT were apparently in the nature of a kind of contract: the petitioner would promise something to God on condition that a favor was granted (de Vaux, 465). However, it must not be assumed that all vows were merely conditional promises of gifts. Not only were some vows expressions of certainty that God had accepted the votaries' prayers (cf. A. A. Anderson, 449), but they were also expressions of a commitment not to discontinue the association with God after the worshipers had been delivered from their predicaments (Westermann, cited by Kraus, 299).

Given the fact that many vows were made by those in dire straits (cf. Jon 2:9[10]!), it is not surprising that several texts contain stern reminders that vows were binding and so were not to be made in a rash, ill-considered, or unrealistic way; and that they had to be discharged without undue deferment (cf. Deut 23:21-23[22-24]; Prov 20:25; Eccl 5:4-5[3-4]). Vowing was optional, but while it was no sin to refrain from making a vow, a person who made a solemn promise to God was required to keep it (cf. Num 30:2[3]; Judg 11:35). The OT demanded not only honesty of intention, but equally honesty of execution (Cunliffe-Jones, 134). Those who had made a vow but later changed their minds and retracted the promise after the emergency had passed were to be penalized by a twenty percent surcharge on the vow (cf. Wenham, 1979, 342). In contrast to the Phoen. practice of devoting money earned by temple prostitutes to the upkeep of the temple, Deut 23:18[19] forbids an Israelite to pay a vow with the hire of a prostitute (cf. Myers, 1041). Money acquired by sinful means could not form part of a gift or offering to God (Craigie, 302).

3. Vows could be either positive, the suppliant promising to devote something to God (e.g., Gen 28:20-22; Num 21:1-3; Judg 11:30-31), or negative, the worshiper undertaking to abstain from some comfort or necessity of life (e.g., Num 6:1-21; 21:1-3; 30:13[14]; Ps 132:2-5; cf. 1 Sam 14:24 [where the hi. of *'lh*, put under an oath, is used]). Among those texts dealing with vows of abstinence, Num 6:1-21, which focuses on the vow of the Nazirite, is of particular interest. The fact that the vb. *pl'* in hi. is used in v. 2 indicates that this kind of vow was something outstanding and unusual (Wenham, 1981, 86). The word "Nazirite," which is derived from the vb. *nzr*, dedicate, consecrate, was applied to those holy members of the laity (men and women, free or slave) who, by means of a vow made either by themselves or by another on their behalf, were separated to Yahweh (Num 6:2, 5, 21; cf. Judg 13:5, 7; 16:17; 1 Sam 1:11; Amos 2:11-12). The special vows taken by those consecrating themselves to God could be either for life (cf. Judg 13:7; 1 Sam 1:11) or, as shown by Num 6:1-21, of temporary duration.

During the period of their vows, according to Num 6, Nazirites were obligated to abstain from: (a) consuming wine and all products of the vine (vv. 3-4); (b) cutting their hair (v. 5); and (c) making contact with a corpse, even that of a close relative (v. 7). Accidental defilement caused by the sudden death of a person beside the Nazirite necessitated the performance of rites of purification followed by reconsecration. In such a case, whatever period of the original vow that may have elapsed was considered null (vv. 9-12). When the specified term of the temporary vow expired, the Nazirite offered certain sacrifices (vv. 13-17), shaved the head, offered the hair on the altar, and returned to ordinary life (vv. 18-21). Sometimes, the desire to undertake the vow of consecration and abstinence may have been motivated by private and personal reasons, but in many cases it seems to have been the expression of a religious and patriotic zeal that aimed to express loyalty to Yahweh and to protect Israel from the corrupting and enervating influences of other cultures and religions (Dummelow, 104-5; cf. Rylaarsdam, 526; Guthrie, 87; Budd, 74; Myers, 752). According to Noth (1968, 54), Nazirites were considered to manifest, in a particular way, the divine presence and to be symbols and mediators of divine grace.

4. Most vows in the OT fall into the category of votive offerings or gifts promised to Yahweh. When divine assistance had been secured, then that which had been promised was offered to God in thanksgiving (cf. Ps 56:12-13[13-14]; 66:13-15). Votive offerings could consist of a human being (Lev 27:2-8; Num 6:1-21); an animal (Lev 27:9-13); a house (27:14-15); a tract of land (27:16-25); worship, shrine, and tithe (Gen 28:20-22); or a commitment to undertake holy war (Num 21:1-3). From early times, a person could be vowed to Yahweh. This meant time spent (either by the person who made the vow [cf. 2 Sam 15:8] or by a member or members of the family) in the performance of auxiliary cultic services at the sanctuary (cf. Lev 27:2-8; 1 Sam 1:9-11). On the basis of Judg 11:29-40, it has been deduced that originally a vow of persons required a human sacrifice and was undertaken only in extreme circumstances in a desperate attempt to secure God's favor and his aid (cf. 2 Kgs 3:26-27). However, human sacrifice was generally viewed with abhorrence in ancient Israel (cf. 2 Kgs 16:3; 17:17; 21:6; Ps 106:37; Jer 7:31; Mic 6:6-7), and either an animal (cf. Gen 22:13) or payment of money (cf. 2 Kgs 12:4[5]) was substituted. Schofield (312) thinks that Judg 11:39-40, which refers to the custom of annual mourning, indicates that

Jephthah's daughter became the cause of an ordinance banning child sacrifice. However legitimate this view, human sacrifice was clearly forbidden in OT law (Lev 18:21; 20:2-5; Deut 12:31; 18:10).

As regards animal votive offerings, in early times these could be made at any sanctuary in ancient Israel, but Deut 12:11, 17, 26 sought to restrict votive and other sacrificial offerings to a single sanctuary. This law of restricting sacrifical worship to a sole sanctuary (*pace,* e.g., Thompson, 162-64) was more of an old ideal expressed in a new way (cf. G. W. Anderson, 1966, 126) than a sweeping innovation in the history of the Israelite cultus (Weinfeld, 190). Votive offerings, which arose from a vow or promise, are to be distinguished from freewill offerings, which were spontaneous and free from any prior commitment. Both burnt offerings (Lev 22:18; Num 15:3, 8) and fellowship offerings (22:21) could be presented as votive offerings.

Some of the criteria by which priests assessed the suitability of sacrifices made in fulfilment of a vow or as a freewill offering are outlined in Lev 22:17-30. Normally, animals to be sacrificed, whether as votive or freewill offerings, had to be perfect and unblemished (22:18-22). However, 22:23, thought by some to be a secondary addition (cf., e.g., Faley, 75), asserts that while certain defects in an animal to be sacrificed as a freewill offering were permitted (presumably because it was being offered spontaneously and purely from motives of devotion), no blemished or mutilated animal could serve as a votive offering (presumably because only a perfect animal would have been promised by the vow). Mal 1:14 (where the q. act. part. of *ndr* occurs without the nom.) complains that the law was not being properly observed and that God was being dishonored with mean and imperfect offerings. Disrespect in cultic matters was symbolic of indifference towards God; it constituted "an outward and visible sign of an inward and spiritual *dis*-grace...." (Dentan, 1119).

5. As already indicated, any vow carried with it a solemn obligation of fulfilment (cf. e.g., Num 30:2-3[3-4]; Deut 23:21-23[22-24]). However, a trend developed towards converting commitments, both people and real property (houses and buildings), into their monetary equivalents. Regulations governing such commutation are found in Lev 27. The q. act. part. of the vb. *ndr* (the one making a vow) is used in v. 8; in v. 2 the nom. occurs in tandem with hi. of *pl'*, make a special vow (RSV; NEB; REB; NIV; TEV). Specific monetary substitutes were to be paid in order to redeem those who had been dedicated to Yahweh (vv. 2-7). Presumably, these amounts, which varied according to the sin, gender, and age of those redeemed, were calculated according to an assessment of working capacity (so Noth, 1965, 205; *pace* Hayes, 180). In the case of the poor man who could not afford to pay according to the fixed scale, there was a relaxation of restrictions, and it was left to the discretion of the priest to arrive at a satisfactory figure (v. 8). Knight (169) considers this kind of vow a form of voluntary income tax for the upkeep of the temple.

Any vowed animal that was fit for sacrifice could not be redeemed, exchanged, or substituted (vv. 9-10). If a votary were caught trying to circumvent this regulation forbidding substitution or exchange, he would have to forfeit both animals (vv. 9-10). While unclean animals could be vowed, it was unlawful to sacrifice them. Consequently, they would be used by the priests, sold for profit, or redeemed by the dedicator, who would pay into the sanctuary the appraised monetary value plus twenty percent (vv. 11-13). The firstlings of the herd and of the flock could not be the object of a vow, since they were considered to belong to Yahweh already (vv. 26-27; cf. Exod 13:2). The case of Hannah's vow (1 Sam 1:11) seems to be an exception to the general rule governing firstlings.

Houses and lands vowed to Yahweh could be redeemed by votaries on payment of the appropriate amounts that were calculated by the priests according to a fixed formula of valuation (vv. 14-25). In the case of land that had been devoted, there were regulations to protect both priests (vv. 20-21) and the original owners (vv. 22-24). No person, animal, or thing that had been devoted (the root *ḥrm* means put to the ban; i.e., set apart as belonging to Yahweh) could be redeemed (vv. 28-29).

6. Isaiah describes how Yahweh will make himself known to the Egyptians, who will then worship him faithfully, offer sacrifices, and make and perform vows (Isa 19:21). Following a period of sanctification and healing (v. 22), Egypt will be found acceptable to Yahweh and will turn and offer supplication to him. Remarkable for his inclusivism, the author envisions a time when Egypt and Assyria, traditionally his nation's most feared and hated enemies, will be united with Israel by the bond of their common allegiance to Yahweh. All three will share equal privilege in this triple alliance of God's holy people and will be Yahweh's agents through whom the divine blessing will permeate the whole world and unite all peoples in the worship of the living God (cf. Gen 12:1-3; 22:18; 26:4; Ps 86:9; 87).

P-B The Heb. vb. *ndr* (and the Aram. vb. *n^edar* I) means (keep off), vow (abstinence); q. pass. part. *nādûr*, being under the obligation of a vow; being the legitimate subject of a vow; ni. be made the subject of a vow; have one's personal value dedicated to the sanctuary; be vowed for a sacrifice; hi. put a person under the influence of a vow; prohibit, forbid; ho. be forbidden by a vow; be subjected to the influence of a vow. The Heb nom. *neder* and the Aram. nom. forms *n^edar* III, *nidrā'*, *nîdrā'* all mean vow. Other nom. forms which occur are *nādērā'*, he who vowed, and *nadrān*, *nôd^erān*, *nadrānît*, *naddārît*, one wont to make vows (Jastrow 2:879-80).

Offering, sacrifice: → *'azkārâ* (sign-offering, # 260); → *'iššeh* (offering by fire, # 852); → *'āšām* (guilt offering, # 871); → *zbḥ* (slaughter, sacrifice, # 2284); → *ḥaṭṭā'at* (sin offering, # 2633); → *ṭbḥ* (slaughter, # 3180); → *minḥâ* (gift, present, offering, sacrifice, # 4966); → *ma^{ca}śēr* (tithe, # 5130); → *ndr* (make a vow, # 5623); → *nwp* I (move back and forth, wave, # 5677); → *nsk* I (pour out, be consecrated, libation, # 5818); → *'ōlâ* I (burnt offering, # 6592); → *'^arîsâ* (meal/dough offering, # 6881); → *qorbān* (offering, gift, # 7933); → *šḥṭ* I (slaughter, # 8821); → *šelem* (settlement sacrifice, # 8968); → *tāmîd* (regular offering, # 9458); → *t^erûmâ* (tribute, contribution, # 9556); → **Aaron: Theology**; → **Offering: Theology**; → **Priests and Levites: Theology**

Pledge, security: → *'issār* (binding obligation, pledge, vow of abstention, # 674); → *ḥbl* II (take in pledge, exact a pledge, # 2471); → *ḥôb* (pledge, collateral, # 2550); → *nš'* I (lend against a pledge, # 5957); → *'bṭ* (borrow, take a pledge from, # 6292); → *'rb* I (stand security for, give security for, # 6842); → *piqqādôn* (deposited goods, store, supply, provision, # 7214); → *tq'* (drive, thrust, clap one's hands, blow trumpet, pledge, # 9546)

Vow, obligation: → *'issār* (binding obligation, pledge, vow of abstention, # 674); → *bṭ'/bṭh* (chatter, babble, vow rashly, # 1051); → *ndr* (make a vow, # 5623)

BIBLIOGRAPHY

E. A. Achtemeier, *Nahum-Malachi*, Interpretation, 1986; A. A. Anderson, *The Book of Psalms. Volume 1: Introduction and Psalms 1-72*, NCBC, 1972; G. W. Anderson, "The Psalms," in

Peake, 1964, 409-43; idem, *The History and Religion of Israel*, 1966; P. J. Budd, *Numbers*, WBC, 1984; P. C. Craigie, *The Book of Deuteronomy*, NICOT, 1983; H. Cunliffe-Jones, *Deuteronomy: Introduction and Commentary*, Torch, 1964; G. H. Davies, "Vows," in *IDB*, 1962, 4:792-93; R. C. Dentan, "The Book of Malachi: Introduction and Exegesis," *IB*, 1956, 6:1115-44; J. R. Dummelow ed., *A Commentary on the Holy Bible*, 1909; J. I. Durham, "Psalms," in *BBC* 1972, 4:153-464; R. J. Faley, "Leviticus," in *NJBC*, 1990, 61-79; H. H. Guthrie, "The Book of Numbers," in *The Interpreter's One-Volume Commentary on the Bible*, 1971, 85-99; J. H. Hayes, "Leviticus," in *HBC*, 1988, 157-81; G. A. F. Knight, *Leviticus*, 1984; H.-J. Kraus, *Psalms 1-59: A Commentary*, 1988; A. C. Myers, ed., *The Eerdmans Bible Dictionary*, 1987; M. Noth, *Leviticus: A Commentary*, OTL, 1965; idem, *Numbers: A Commentary*, OTL, 1968; D. T. Olson, "Numbers," in *HBC*, 1988, 182-208; J. J. M. Roberts, *Nahum, Habakkuk, and Zephaniah: A Commentary*, OTL, 1991; O. P. Robertson, *The Books of Nahum, Habakkuk, and Zephaniah*, NICOT, 1991; J. C. Rylaarsdam, "Nazirite," in *IDB*, 1962, 3:526-27; J. N. Schofield, "Judges," in *Peake*, 1964, 304-15; J. M. P. Smith, "A Commentary on the Book of Nahum," in *A Critical and Exegetical Commentary on Micah, Zephaniah, Nahum, Habakkuk, Obadiah and Joel*, ICC, 1974, 284-360; J. A. Thompson, *Deuteronomy: An Introduction and Commentary*, TOTC, 1974; R. de Vaux, *AncIsr*, 1968; M. Weinfeld, *Deuteronomy and the Deuteronomic School*, 1972; G. J. Wenham, *The Book of Leviticus*, NICOT, 1979; idem, *Numbers: An Introduction and Commentary*, TOTC, 1981.

Robin Wakely

5624 (*nēder*, vow), → # 5623

5627	נהג

נהג (*nhg* I), q. drive, lead, guide, lead forth; pi. drive off, lead forth (# 5627); מִנְהָג (*minhāg*), nom. manner of driving (# 4952).

ANE An Arab. cognate signifies proceeding along a road, with the extended meaning of taking a course of action. Eth. uses this word for cattle herding (*HALAT* 637).

OT 1. A common literal use of the vb. describes driving or leading something from one place to another. The q. stem, and at times also the pi. stem, has this function, and describes animals (Gen 31:18; Exod 3:1) and people (1 Sam 30:22). Humans so described are at times prisoners of war (1 Sam 30:2; Isa 20:4; pi.—Gen 31:26; Deut 4:27; 28:37; for animals wrongfully appropriated, see 1 Sam 23:5; 30:20; Job 24:3). A child will be able to lead or guide wild animals in the messianic kingdom (Isa 11:6; Oswalt, 283). This active, "hands-on" type of personal involvement with God's holy ark by one not authorized to do so could result in death (2 Sam 6:3, 6-7).

Based on this literal usage of the term, a metaphorical extension is encountered in which Yahweh, like a shepherd, leads his own (Ps 78:52; 80:1[2]; Isa 63:14; cf. 49:10). Right choices result from following the guidance of one's wise heart, fleeing experiences in hedonism and clinging to God's ways (Eccl 2:3; Gordis, 216). Just as an army can rely on the leadership of its commanders (1 Chron 20:1; 2 Chron 25:11), so those who are God's will always experience his beneficial guidance (Ps 48:14[15]). Those who oppose him, however, God will drive away into darkness (Lam 3:2).

2. The derived nom. *minhāg* describes the reckless, or at least readily identifiable, driving practices of Jehu (2 Kgs 9:20; G. H. Jones, *1 and 2 Kings*, 1984, 459) and does not significantly contribute to the theological understanding of the concept.

P-B Later rabbinic usage of the word group included the above meanings, but also extended it to describe one's personal conduct (Sifre Deut 323) and the customary activities of different people (Tosefta Beṣa 11.15; Talm. Pesaḥim IV.80-82).

Guidance, leading: → *nhg* I (drive, guide, # 5627); → *nhl* (lead, guide, # 5633); → *nḥh* (lead, # 5697); → *šš'* (lead a child, # 9255)

Bibliography

TWOT 2:558-59; R. Gordis, *Koheleth—The Man and His World*, 3rd ed., 1968; J. N. Oswalt, *The Book of Isaiah 1-39*, 1986.

David W. Baker

5628 (*nhg* II, sob), → # 1963

5629	נהה

נהה (*nhh*), q. lament (# 5629); נְהִי (n^e*hî*), nom. lament (# 5631).

ANE This lexeme is more widely known outside the Scriptures in later writings; the vb. *nhy* is found in later Syr., meaning groan, and the Eth. *nehya* means to unburden.

OT 1. The vb. is found at Ezek 32:18 in the introduction to the lament of Egypt; it is also found in Mic 2:4 in a taunt song against Judah and Jerusalem because of their oppression against the weak. It is proposed for the lament of Ps 102:7[8], changing the psalmist's words of being alone like a bird to moaning like a bird, but if the comparison is to being alone, as indicated by the second half of the verse, any change may be superfluous (Kraus, 1989, 282). (→ Lament: Theology)

2. The nom. n^e*hî*, lament (# 5631), is found 4x in Jer 9 in the lament for Jerusalem; in v. 10[9] it is used with weeping (*bky*) and lament song (*qînâ*) because the countryside has been devastated; it is used in vv. 18-20[17-19] as a description of the professional mourners who wail, shed tears, and teach others the lament songs over the destruction of the land. The nom. describes the lament of Rachel over the loss of her children in 31:15. Amos, in his funeral dirge over Israel, calls to the professional mourners to lament over the land (Amos 5:16). In every instance it is found as a description of the cry of lament uttered by someone in mourning. Each of the biblical contexts has to do with war and the destruction of a land.

P-B In postbiblical writings the vb. is found in connection with tears of lament for the dead in Sir 38:16; the nom. n^e*hî* is also found in the Talm.

Lament, mourning: → *'bl* I (mourn, observe mourning rites, # 61); → *'nh* I (lament, # 627); → *bkh* (weep, bewail, # 1134); → *dm'* (shed tears, # 1963); → *z'q* (call for help, call to arms, assemble, utter a plaintive cry, # 2410); → *nhh* I (lament, # 5629); → *spd* (sound of lament, mourn, # 6199); → *qdr* (be dark, mourn, # 7722); → *qînâ* I (dirge, # 7806); → **Lament: Theology**

A. H. Konkel

5631 (*n^{e}hî*, lament), → # 5629

5633	נהל

נהל (*nhl*), pi. lead, guide, help along; hitp. move along (# 5633); nom. נַהֲלֹל (*nah^{a}lōl* I), watering place (# 5635).

ANE Akk. *na'ālu*, water, moisten (*CAD,* N, 1:6); in Arab. the cognates deal with drinking (Wehr 1966, 1004).

OT 1. This vb. has only one nonhuman object in the OT, when God, like a shepherd tending his flock, gently leads nursing animals with loving care (Isa 40:11). The arms that created the universe and continue to sustain it also shelter those who are helpless. This is metaphorically compared to the loving care of Yahweh for his people Israel, a concept that is stated in nonmetaphorical terms elsewhere using the same vb. (2 Chron 32:22). God, through his gentle care, will provide for nations and individuals the sustenance they need and the tranquility in which to enjoy it (Ps 23:2; 31:3[4]). The physical goal of this direction and guidance is God's holy dwelling (Exod 15:13).

Humans also can and should show compassionate guidance for others, whether those over whom they exercise political control (Gen 47:17), newly released prisoners (2 Chron 28:15), or their nation with its capital (Isa 51:18), because God does so (49:10).

The combined idea of drinking and transference from place to place is found beautifully in Ps 23:2, where God guides the author to the waters of refreshment and tranquility.

2. The related form *nah^{a}lōl* describes a geographical location in the desert, apparently a "water hole" (Isa 7:19), but does not add significantly to the theological understanding of the root word.

P-B Rabbinic interpreters only use the vb. in discussing OT passages in which it occurs and do not add significantly to the discussion (Num Rabbah 12).

Guidance, leading: → *nhg* I (drive, guide, # 5627); → *nhl* (lead, guide, # 5633); → *nḥh* (lead, # 5697); → *šš'* (lead a child, # 9255)

David W. Baker

5635 (*nah^{a}lôl*, watering place), → # 5633

5637	נהם

נהם (*nhm*), q. growl, roar, groan (# 5637); נַהַם (*naham*), nom., growl, snarl, groan (# 5638); נְהָמָה (*n^{e}hāmâ*), nom., roar, groan, anguish (# 5639).

ANE Forms of *nhm* appear in postbiblical Heb., Jewish Aram., Syr., and Mand., meaning growl, roar, coo, sigh. Related to these are the Arab. *nahama*, roar, and the Egyp. *nhm*, shout for joy. Jewish Aram. noms. *nehāmâ* and *nah^{a}mûtā'*, roaring, shrieking, excitement, appear, along with Sam. *nyamtwn*, Syr. *nehāmā'*, *nūhāmā'*, and *nemetā'*, roar, and Mand. *(a)nhimtā*, groan.

OT 1. The vb. denotes the sound the lion makes, seizing its prey or charging with a growl or roar (Prov 28:15; Isa 5:29, 30). Isaiah likens this to the thunderous noise of the sea (Isa 5:30). The lion's roar provides the image for the terror and havoc produced by a wicked ruler (Prov 28:15) and the noise of the army Yahweh summons for judgment (Isa 5:29-30). Figuratively it describes the groaning of the disillusioned profligate (Prov 5:11) and the exiles' response in grief at Jerusalem's fall (Ezek 24:23).

2. The nom. *naham* is used exclusively of the lion's growl or snarl, likening the king's wrath and terror to it (Prov 19:12; 20:2). *n*[e]*hāmâ* denotes the roar of the sea (Isa 5:30). In Ps 38:8[9] it names the heart groan of one crushed by guilt and illness, or may perhaps connote the cause of such groaning, i.e., anguish of heart (so NAB; cf. NASB).

P-B In CD 10:33, *nhmh* describes groaning in response to impending judgment. Cf. NT *metamelomai* (Matt 27:3; 2 Cor 7:8), in sense of regret, and *stenagmos* (Rom 8:26).

Groan, sigh, growl: → *'nḥ* (sigh, groan, # 634); → *'nq* (groan, # 650); → *hgh* I (groan, moan, sigh, meditate, muse, chirp, mutter, # 2047); → *hāgîg* (groan in prayer, # 2052); → *z'q* (cry, howl, wail, # 2410); → *n'q* (groan, # 5543); → *nhm* (growl, groan, # 5637); → *nwḥ* II (groan in anticipation, # 5664); → *p'h* (groan in childbirth, # 7184); → *š'g* (roar, # 8613)
Lion(ess): → *'*[a]*rî* (lion, # 787)

David Thompson

5638 (*naham*, growl, snarl, groan), → # 5637

5639 (*n*[e]*hāmâ*, roar, groan), → # 5637

5640	נהק

נהק (*nhq*), q. cry, shriek; bray (ass) (# 5640).

ANE Ugar. *nhqt* (*UT*, # 1622); Arab. *nahaqa*; Eth. *nehqa*; Tigre. *naḥaqa*; Akk. *nâqu* A, cry, groan.

OT The word occurs twice. In Job 6:5 it indicates the braying of the wild ass (*pere'*) when in need of grass (*deše'*). In 30:7 the word metaphorically describes the actions of young social outcasts, "braying" among the bushes.

Animal sounds: → *g'h* (bellow, low [cattle], # 1716); → *hgh* I (groan, moan, sigh, meditate, muse, chirp, mutter, # 2047); → *nbḥ* (bark [dogs], # 5560); → *nhq* (bray [ass], shriek, # 5640); → *nḥr* (snort, # 5723); → *'yṭ* (yell, shriek, swoop down [w. shrieks], # 6512); → *ṣhl* I (neigh, shout, # 7412)

Eugene Carpenter

5641 (*nhr* I, stream), → # 5643

5642	נהר

נהר (*nhr* II), q. be radiant (# 5642); נְהָרָה (*n*[e]*hārâ*), nom. light (Job 3:4) (# 5644); נְהוֹר/נְהִיר (*n*[e]*hôr*[Q]; *n*[e]*hîr*[K]), Aram. nom. light (Dan 2:22) (# 10466); נַהִירוּ (*nahîrû*), Aram. nom. insight (Dan 5:11, 14) (# 10467).

ANE Cognate with Aram. *nhr,* shine, beam; Akk. *nūru,* nom. light, fire, lamp; *namāru,* vb. shine brightly, become happy, radiant; Arab. *nahār,* day.

OT The vb. is used of people whose faces beam with light. This may be the result of Yahweh's light shining on them (Isa 60:5; cf. vv. 1-3), through their gazing at him (Ps

34:5[6]), or simply because of God's goodness (Jer 31:12; NIV rejoice). It is probably related to the idea of God's face shining in blessing (→ *'wr*).

Light, radiance, brightness: → *'wr* (be light, bright, shine, # 239); → *bāhîr* (bright, brilliant, # 986); → *zrḥ* I (rise [of sun], shine, # 2436); → *yp'* I (shine out, # 3649); → *ngh* (shine, cause to shine, # 5585); → *nhr* II (be radiant, # 5642); → *qrn* (send out rays, be radiant, # 7966)

BIBLIOGRAPHY
S. Aalen, *Die Begriffe "Licht" und "Finsternis" im AT, im Spätjudentum und im Rabbinismus*, 1951; W. D. Reece, *The Concept of Light in the Old Testament: A Semantic Analysis*, 1989.

Martin J. Selman

5643	נָהָר

נָהָר (*nāhār*), river (# 5643); נהר (*nhr* I), stream (# 5641).

ANE The word *nāhār,* which depicts a perpetual flow of water, is attested in Ugar., Akk., Aram., and Arab. The vb. *nhr* has a cognate in Arab. *nahara*, flow, run. In the Bible the vb. is used for people flowing to Jerusalem at the restoration (Isa 2:2; Jer 31:12; Mic 4:1).

Another word for river is *y^{e}'ōr* (# 3284); it also means the Nile. In fact, the term is a loanword from Egyptian *'itrw* (*'irw*, later), meaning watercourse, river. In Akk. *ia'uru* is a stream, and *'Iaru'û* is the Nile.

OT The HB uses a number of terms for "river"; they refer to actual rivers, of course, but can also be used figuratively in a number of ways.

1. The nom. *nāhār* means a river in the strict sense. It is first used of the river that flowed out of Eden to water the garden and then divided into four major rivers (Gen 2:10-14). *nāhār* is also used to identify the rivers that define the boundaries of the Promised Land, i.e., from the river of Egypt to the great river Euphrates (15:18). Sometimes "the river" is used without a proper name and is understood to refer to the Euphrates (31:21; Josh 24:2, 14; Isa 7:20). But the word can also refer to other rivers (Gen 2:14, the Tigris) or to canals (Ezek 1:1, 3, the Kebar).

(a) In Job 28:11 *nāhār* appears to indicate underground streams that are kept from overflowing. In Jon 2:13 the term describes water currents in the deep sea that engulfed Jonah.

(b) In a similar use, Ps 24:2 tells how the Lord founded the earth upon the seas and established it upon the floods (*n^{e}hārôt*). At first glance this psalm appears to be a praise for creation over the primordial waters of the deep, but it turns out to be a celebration of a military victory. Ps 93:3 also uses *n^{e}hārôt* in the sense of the floods that lifted their voices, their waves, but were controlled by the sovereign Lord. These psalms contain an allusion to, if not a polemic against, Canaanite mythology. One of the Canaanite deities of chaos is Prince Sea (*Yam*), also called Judge River (*Nahar*). This strong and daring god enslaved Baal and had to be defeated before Baal could return to his mountain. The Bible portrays the Lord controlling the sea and the rivers (which are not deified), both at creation and in giving his people victory over their Canaanite enemies. In the miracles of Elijah and Elisha the river motif also demonstrated the Lord's victory over Canaanite gods. Both prophets smote the river Jordan with the mantel of Elijah and the waters parted for them (2 Kgs 2:8, 14). Again, Job 9:8

declares that the Lord treads on the waves of the sea, or, from the Canaanite perspective, the back of Yam.

(c) The image of a river naturally suggests the provision of life. Flowing water is living water. The psalmist employs the image to describe God's gracious provisions of life for Jerusalem: "There is a river (*nāhār*) whose streams (*peleg* I; # 7104) make glad the city of God" (Ps 46:4[5]).

2. The word *naḥal* I (# 5707) applies most readily to a temporary river that flows with great force in the winter or rainy season but leaves only dry channels or deep ravines in the summer. Thus, the word can refer to either a fast flowing stream or torrent, or to the dry river bed.

This phenomenon is vividly portrayed in the story of Elijah. He had the provision of God that he could drink from the brook (1 Kgs 17:4); but because he proclaimed that there would be no rain, after a while the brook dried up (v. 7). Without rain there will be no stream of water in these riverbeds.

(a) The literal meaning of *naḥal* applies to a rushing torrent or a flowing stream, rather than to a deeper, steadier river. It would be a wonderful, but temporary, provision of fresh water that could be collected in cisterns. It was also seen as a blessing from God by a people who depended on the rains for all their needs. One primary use of the fresh water is drinking. Ps 110:7 records the natural picture of the Warrior Messiah who will drink from the brook in the way. In Deut 9:21 the rushing stream provided Moses with the means of washing away the crushed remains of the golden calf. These fast flowing torrents were short-lived. In the dry season people would be disappointing to find water in them. Job uses this as an illustration of his deceitful friends (Job 6:15).

(b) The presence of such anticipated torrents of water provided the biblical writers with a number of images. Isaiah forewarned the nation that in the coming judgment their "streams will be turned into pitch" (Isa 34:9). Jeremiah saw the invading armies that would cover the land as an overflowing torrent (Jer 47:2). And with a series of bold descriptions of the Lord in judgment, Isaiah says that his breath will be like a flowing stream (Isa 30:28), indicating that wrath will be poured out swiftly.

On the more hopeful side, Amos called, "Let righteousness [roll on] like a never-ending stream" (Amos 5:24). And Isaiah (Isa 66:12) anticipated a time when God would "extend peace to her like a river (*nāhār*), and the wealth of nations like a flooding stream (*naḥal*)." Ps 36:8, making an allusion to the Garden of Eden, describes one of the spiritual privileges of believers as being able to "drink from your river (*naḥal*) of delights (*'ēden*)."

(c) As indicated above, the word *naḥal* can also refer to the dry riverbed (Gen 26:17) or a deep ravine (Job 30:6). In Gen 26:17 Isaac pitched his tent in the Valley (*naḥal*) of Gerar. Because of the frequent flows of water through such valleys, the water table under the surface was often higher than elsewhere. Thus, trees grew there, and digging wells there could be successful. So in the dry season it would be one of the best places to camp in the wilderness region. From such a river bed David selected the smooth, round stones for his fight with Goliath (1 Sam 17:40). And it was in such a valley that the people later made their corrupt sacrifices (Isa 57:5).

A *wadi*, as these river beds are called, is often named just as a river would be. The "river of Egypt" (*naḥal miṣraim*) is a wadi between Egypt and the Promised Land (Num 34:5; Josh 15:4).

3. Heb. *y^e'ōr* is used most frequently for the Nile (Gen 41:1; Exod 1:22; 2:3). In Egypt the Nile was considered sacred, because it was the source of all the life of Egypt. But the God of Israel could turn it to blood, the evidence of death (Exod 8:1), or even interrupt its flow (Isa 19:5-9). When *y^e'ōr* is in the plural, it refers to the tributaries or canals of the Nile (Exod 8:1). Isaiah uses it in this sense when he announces that the Lord will hiss for the fly from the rivers of Egypt, meaning the Egyptian armies (Isa 7:18).

But *y^e'ōr* has other uses as well. It can refer to rivers in general, such as those the Lord dried up in besieged places (Isaiah's word in 2 Kgs 19:24; see also Zech 10:11). Job 28:10 uses it in the sense of mining shafts. In Dan 12:5 it refers to the Tigris. And Isaiah uses it when he compares the value of great rivers in general to the Lord's abundant provision: "The LORD ... will be like a place of broad rivers" (Isa 33:21).

4. The name *šîḥôr* (# 8865) occurs a few times in the Bible. This word means "Pool of Horus" and refers to the east branch of the Nile. Josh 13:3 refers to Sihor as being "on the east (*'al p^enê*) of Egypt." In 1 Chron 13:5, when David was preparing to move the ark of the covenant, he gathered Israel together from as far south as Sihor and north as Hamath. Jeremiah also uses the word to refer to the entrance to Egypt: "Now why go to Egypt to drink the water from the Shihor? And why go to Assyria to drink water from the River?" (Jer 2:18). Because of their sin the people would end up either in Egypt or Mesopotamia, in spite of the prophet's pleading.

5. The vb. *nzl*, flow, trickle, drop (→ # 5688), is also used for flowing rivers. Ps 147:18 announces that God causes the waters to flow. In the Song of Moses we read how "the surging waters (*nōzēl*; # 5689) stood firm like a wall" (Exod 15:8). Here the word is paralleled with "waters" (*mayim*; → # 4784) and "deep" (*t^ehôm*; → # 9333). Ps 78:44 refers to the Nile River when it says that God turned their floods to blood so that they could not drink the water. Forms of *nzl* also are used for water flowing from the rock (Isa 48:21), dew distilling on the ground (Deut 32:2), or the blessing of rainwater poured upon the dry ground (44:3; see also Job 36:28).

Other uses of this vb. that are analogous with the imagery of rivers include Isa 45:8, which says, "You heavens above, rain down righteousness," and Judg 5:5, which describes the great military victory of the Lord in part with "the mountains quaked (*nzl*) before the LORD."

6. Several other words occur occasionally for these descriptions of rivers. *yûbal* (# 3414) is a stream of water (Jer 17:8). It is related to the vb. meaning conduct, bear along. The Arab. *wabala* means pour down rain. And so *yābāl* I (# 3298) is a "watercourse" (Isa 30:25; 44:4). And *'ûbal* (# 67) is a stream or river (Dan 8:3, 6).

So the several words for river in the OT clearly describe the Lord's provision for life. And since that was so clear, the idea of a river, or all the ideas related to it, naturally lent themselves to descriptions of all the gracious provisions that flowed from God.

7. Not only did the torrents of rainwater dig or find ravines and gullies throughout the hills and rocks of the land, but the people themselves also developed canals,

irrigation ditches, and channels for the water. Several words describe this type of watercourse.

(a) The nom. *peleg,* division (# 7104), comes from the vb. *plg,* which means divide, split (→ # 7103)—cf. the same vb. in Arab. and Aram. The nom. *palgu* in Akk. is a canal. And in Eth. the related nom. is a ravine, stream. In Gen 10:25 the word forms a wordplay on the naming of Peleg, saying, "because in his time the earth was divided." Some have suggested that this is a general reference to the making of irrigation ditches or canals. But it may also refer to the event at the Tower of Babel (11:1-9). Accordingly, Ps 55:10 uses the word to refer to the dividing of speech.

But *peleg* frequently describes channels for water. Ps 1:3 says, "He [the blessed individual] is like a tree planted by streams of water (*palgê māyim*)." In that context the simile compares the channels of water to the life-giving Torah. Similarly, Ps 46:5 refers to irrigating canals from a nearby river. The nom. *p*ᵉ*laggâ* (# 7106) refers to streams in Job 20:17 (but to tribal divisions in Judg 5:15-16).

In a poetic way, Job 38:25 expresses the idea that God prepared the watercourses that the rain follows: "Who cuts a channel for the torrents of rain, and a path for the thunderstorm." This same idea may inform Ps 65:9[10]: "You care for the land and water it; you enrich it abundantly. The streams of God (*peleg ʾ*ᵉ*lōhîm*) are filled with water." Another poetic use of the word expresses the prosperity that Job had had from God; it was a time when "the rock poured out for me streams of olive oil" (Job 29:6).

(b) Another word for channel is *ʾapîq* (# 692), which describes deep rock walls, dry riverbeds, or ravines. Like *naḥal* it can refer to the empty channel or to its contents. The meaning of riverbed or channel is found in Isa 8:7, where the prophet compares the Assyrian army to an enormous river (*nāhār*) that was to come up over its channels (*ʾ*ᵃ*pîqāyw*) and its banks. Note also Joel 1:20: "the streams of water have dried up" (Joel 1:20). Such channels can even be cut by currents in the sea, as 2 Sam 22:16 may allude to in its song of military victory ("the valleys of the sea were exposed").

The word is also used for streams or torrents of water (Ezek 31:12). The psalmist prays, "Restore our fortunes, O LORD, like streams in the Negev" (Ps 126:4). He compares the road from the east to a dry river bed and desires that God will abundantly bless so that people will fill the road back to the land to overflowing its banks.

(c) *ṣinnôr* (# 7562) is a pipe, conduit, or waterspout of some kind. In 2 Sam 5:8 it refers to the conquest of Jerusalem. Someone had to go up through the "watershaft" (natural or man-made is not clear) to take the Jebusite stronghold.

This word is also used in Ps 42:7[8]: "Deep calls to deep at the roar of your waterfalls (*ṣinnôreykā*); all your waves and breakers have swept over me." Some have suggested that this is figurative for the sluices of heaven that have been opened. But more likely it refers to waterfalls in the area. The psalmist has been separated from Jerusalem, the formal place of worship, and finds himself in hiding in the region of Jordan, near Mount Hermon and Mizor. Perhaps one of God's mighty waterfalls has impressed him with his isolation from the holy city.

(d) *t*ᵉ*ʿālâ* (# 9498), trench, conduit, water channel, is a kind of trench used for conveying rain or water of any sort. Note its use in the story of Elijah on Mount Carmel. Before praying for fire to fall from heaven, the prophet had men pour water on his altar and dig a trench around it to retain the water (1 Kgs 18:32, 35, 38). When the fire fell, it also lapped up the water in the trench.

This nom. is also used for the conduit for the water supply to the city of Jerusalem. When Ahaz went to inspect it, he was met by Isaiah and his son (Isa 7:3). With the same sense of a conduit the word poetically describes the Lord's channels for rain (Job 38:25).

(e) The use of the rare word *'ēd* (# 116) in Gen 2:6 poses a special problem. The traditional translation was "but a *mist* went up from the earth and watered the whole face of the ground" (RSV). This harmonized fairly well with the other occurrence of the word in Job 36:27, for which the AV used the gloss "vapor." The NIV chose for the Genesis passage "streams came up from the earth," and for the Job passage, "He draws up the drops of water, which distill as rain to the streams" or, in a note, "distill from the mist as rain." The choice of "streams" over "mist" was influenced by the Akk. word *'idu*, meaning subterranean waterways or underground springs that would well up or flood the surface. But other evidence argues the reverse, the meaning of a "rain cloud," which fits the Job passage rather well too.

8. *Theological reflections*. Rivers and canals served many purposes in the life of the ANE. Essentially, they were the source of life to all the inhabitants, whether it was the Nile in Egypt, the Euphrates in Mesopotamia, or the Jordan in Canaan. These and many other rivers and channels brought people water for drinking (Exod 7:18), washing (2:5), or irrigation. They brought fish for food (Lev 11:9), enabled transport from place to place (Isa 18:2), provided natural boundaries between territories (Josh 1:4), and served as a line of defense (Nah 3:8). They were a common setting for religious experiences, no matter what the religion was. Entering the Land of Promise by crossing a major river was associated with divine intervention (e.g., Josh 3) or a theophany (Gen 32:22-23). Healings (2 Kgs 5:10), baptisms (Matt 3:6), and prayer meetings (Acts 16:13) were appropriately conducted by rivers that symbolized life.

It is no wonder that rivers and channels of water figured prominently in the religious ideas of Israel. Fresh water meant life. The people of the Bible lands could not have survived without the constant supply of fresh, living water. The Israelites did not deify rivers as some nations had, but they treasured them as God's provision of life. Some water came from the Jordan River, which had its source in several springs at the foot of Mount Hermon, being fed from the melting snow and the run-off water from the rainy season. And some water came from the swift running torrents in the ravines and gullies in the rainy seasons, directed and collected in cisterns for future use. And for all this running water they were dependent on the Lord, who sent the rains as a token of his blessing on the land. Indeed, the Lord was the Creator and the Sustainer of life; what better sign of his bounty than the precious flow of fresh, living water.

God's provision of fresh water also became a symbol for prosperity, for the abundant provisions of life that flowed from God (Ps 65:9). If this was true of physical life, how much more was it true of the spiritual life, whether in the present or at the end of the age (Isa 66:12; Ezek 47:1-12). So the prophets began to turn their attention to the age to come, when peace and righteousness would flow like a river, when living water would flow out of Jerusalem (Zech 14:8).

NT The same imagery is used in the NT in connection with the grace of our Lord Jesus Christ. He told the woman at the well that if she drank of the water that he gave her, she would never thirst again, but the water would become in her a spring of water welling up to eternal life (John 4:13-14). Then, in the temple, citing the prophets, Jesus said that whoever believes in him, streams of living water would flow from within him. By this he meant the life that was to be produced by the Spirit (John 7:37-39). Finally, John saw a river of the water of life flowing from the throne of God (Rev 22:1-2). Just as the river flowing out of Eden in Paradise sustained God's creation, so in John's vision of the new paradise a river, clear as crystal, signified God's bountiful provision of life—perfect, spiritual, and eternal.

River: → *nāhār* (river, # 5643); → *šelaḥ* II (canal, water-channel, # 8940); → **River: Theology**

Bibliography

TDOT 5:359-63; Y. Aharoni, *The Land of the Bible: A Historical Geography,* 1967; L. Bronner, *The Stories of Elijah and Elisha,* 1968; M. Dahood, "Eblaite *i-du* and Hebrew *'ed,* Rain Cloud," *CBQ* 43, 1982, 534-38; M. Hareuveni, *Desert and Shepherd in Our Biblical Heritage:* Neot Kedumim, *The Biblical Landscape Reserve in Israel,* 1991; T. O. Lambdin, "Egyptian Loan Words in the Old Testament," *JAOS* 73, 1953, 145-55; Y. T. Radday, "The Four Rivers of Paradise [Gen. 1:10-14]," *Hebrew Studies* 23, 1982, 23-31; E. A. Speiser, "*'ED* in the Story of Creation," *Oriental and Biblical Studies, Collected Writings of E. A. Speiser,* 1955, 19-22; idem, "The Rivers of Paradise," *Oriental and Biblical Studies, Collected Writings of E. A. Speiser,* 1959, 23-34.

Allen P. Ross

5644 (n^e*hārâ*, light), → # 5642

5648	נוא

נוא (*nw'*), hi. hinder, prevent, thwart (# 5648); תְּנוּאָה (t^e*nû'â*), nom. opposition, (cause for) displeasure (only in Num 14:34; Job 3:10; → # 9481).

ANE The word *nw'* is cognate with the Akk. *nê'u,* turn.

OT 1. The verbal root occurs 8x in the OT, always in the hi., and generally denotes a negative response to a planned action. Half of these references are found in the laws on vows in Numbers 30 (vv. 5[6], 8[9], 11[12]). According to P. J. Budd, (*Numbers,* WBC, 1984, 322), the root *nw'*, forbid or frustrate, takes on a technical legal sense here, viz., disallow. That is, a father may annul the vow(s) of his unmarried daughter. Likewise, the husband may legally waive the vow(s) made by his wife. However, the vows of widows and divorced women are binding and stand as uttered. (On the waiving of vows, see G. J. Wenham, *Numbers,* TOTC, 1981, 205-9.)

2. Elsewhere *nw'* means "discourage," as in Moses' speech to the tribes of Reuben and Gad when he implored them to aid their brother tribes in the settlement of the land west of the Jordan River (Num 32:7, 9). Their failure to participate in the Conquest would have been a cause of discouragement to the rest of the tribes of Israel. In fact, Moses likens the situation to the "evil" report delivered by the unbelieving spies who scouted out the land of Canaan after the Exodus (Num 13:25-14:12).

3. Finally, the psalmist lauds the Lord God as one who "thwarts" (*nw'*) the (self-serving) plans of the nations according to his own (righteous) purposes (Ps 33:10). The faithful of Israel may trust their Sovereign Lord, whose invisible hand

"sets up kings and deposes them," thereby shaping the history of both his chosen nation and all humankind (Dan 2:21; cf. Gen 50:20).

Discouragement: → *mss* (waste away, melt, dissolve, lose courage, # 5022); → *sar* (sullen, discouraged, # 6234); → *'gm* (be afflicted, distressed, grieved, # 6327); → *ṣwq* I (constrain, bring into straits, vex, # 7439); → *qṣr* II (be short, be/become discouraged, worn out, # 7918); → *rph* (become slack, lose heart, discourage, # 8332); → *šyḥ* (melt away, be in despair, # 8863)

BIBLIOGRAPHY

ISBE 2:79; R. Gordis, "Studies in Hebrew Roots of Contrasted Meanings," *JQR* 27, 1936, 33-58.

Andrew E. Hill

5649	נוב

נוב (*nwb*), q. grow, prosper, flourish; polel (# 5649); נֹוב (*nôb*), (נִיב Q [*nîb*]), nom. fruit (hapleg.; # 5650); נִיב (*nîb*), nom. fruit (# 5762); תְּנוּבָה (*tᵉnûbâ*), fruit, produce (→ # 9482).

ANE The vb. is related to Aram. *nôb,* fruit.

OT The vb. *nwb* occurs 3x in the q., always in a figure. Ps 62:10[11] denotes the flourishing of riches, Prov 10:31 affirms that the mouth of the righteous produces wisdom, while Ps 92:14 [15] testifies that even in old age the righteous continue to produce fruit. Zech 9:17, the sole use of the polel, refers to the blessings of the kingdom (cf. *dāgān* and *tîrôš*) that will cause God's people to prosper.

P-B The Qumran texts (in the polel) appear to build on the imagery of Zech 9:17 (4Q285 frag. 1, line 6), with the possible addition that the earth of the messianic age will echo that of creation (4Q381 1 8). 1QH 8:13 affirms that the unrighteous will not be allowed to partake of the bounty.

Fruit: → *nîb* (fruit, # 5762); → *prh* I (bear fruit, make fruitful, # 7238); → *qayiṣ* (summer, summer-fruit, # 7811)
Fruitful: → *prh* (bear fruit, make fruitful, # 7238)
Growth, greatness, luxuriance, ripening, sprouting: → *bqq* II (grow luxuriantly, # 1328); → *gdl* I (grow up, become great, make great, boast, # 1540); → *nwb* (grow, prosper, flourish, # 5649); → *sāḥîš* (what grows on its own accord, # 6084); → *sāpîaḥ* I (what grows on its own accord, # 6206); → *ṣmḥ* (sprout, spring up, grow, prosper, make grow, # 7541); → *r'n* (be luxuriant, green, # 8315); → *śg'/śgh* (grow great, increase, exalt, # 8434/8436)

M. G. Abegg, Jr.

5650 (*nôb*, fruit), → # 5649

5653	נוד

נוד (*nwd*), q. sway (e.g., a reed in water), be aimless, be(come) homeless, express sympathy and condolence by shaking the head; hi. make homeless, shake; hitpol. sway back and forth, shake oneself, bemoan one's fate (# 5653); מָנוֹד (*mānôd*), nom. shaking of the head (as gesture of mockery; # 4954); נִיד (*nîd*), nom. shaking of the head, gesture of condolence (# 5764); נִידָה (*nîdâ*), nom. shaking of the head (# 5765).

OT 1. The vb. *nwd*, signifying oscillation, a movement back and forth, can apply to a bird's wings that flutter (Prov 26:2), to a head that is moved back and forth (Jer 18:16), and to a person who goes hither and yon as a fugitive or wanderer (Gen 4:12). Of its twenty-five occurrences, thirteen are found in Isa and Jer, though the word is also represented in the Torah and the Writings.

2. In the Torah the word is limited to the sense of "wandering off," "be a fugitive" (→ *ndd* I [# 5610]). God's judgment of Cain, in which Cain is consigned to homelessness and wandering, anticipates the prophets who, in describing the fate of God's judgment on cities, seize on the "homelessness" dimension of the experience.

3. For the prophets the word *nwd* is linked with the tragedy brought on by God's judgment. The counsel for those in Babylon on whose city God's judgment comes is to flee the city (Jer 50:8; cf. v. 3). To shake the head can be idiomatic for showing concern, a cultural way of showing sympathy. The word *nwd*, sympathize, occurs several times in parallel with pi. *nḥm*, comfort (→ # 5714; cf. Job 2:11; 42:11; Ps 69:20[21]). Both Jeremiah and Isaiah inquire whether, when Jerusalem is destroyed, anyone will be sorry (lit. "shake for you") (Isa 51:19, KJV; "who will comfort you" NIV; cf. Jer 15:5). "Shaking the head" may also mean surprise (Jer 18:16) or scorn (48:27). The swaying of "a hut in the wind" is descriptive of the earth under judgment in the Little Apocalypse (Isa 24:20; cf. 1 Kgs 14:15). As a symbol of the seriousness of the coming judgment, Jeremiah was instructed not to participate at funerals in the rite of mourning or to "show sympathy" (*nwd*) (Jer 16:5). A similar directive to refrain from mourning was issued by the prophet for the death of King Jehoahaz (Jer 22:10).

4. In the Writings *nwd* is found in Job. His friends come to sympathize (*nwd*) and comfort (pi. *nḥm*) (Job 2:11; cf. 42:11; cf. D. J. A. Clines, *Job 1-20*, 57). This personal touch of offering condolences surfaces also in the Psalms (69:20[21]). Prov 26:2 likens a groundless curse to a fluttering sparrow (*nwd*) or a darting (*'wp*, → # 6414) swallow. The curse, when it is unfounded, will not find a landing place.

5. The single occurrence of *nîd*, shaking of the head, as an expression of condolence is translated "comfort from my lips" and is of no theological significance (Job 16:5).

6. *nîdâ*, shaking of the head, occurs only in a description of Jerusalem who had sinned (Lam 1:8) and was rendered "therefore she is removed" (KJV; mg. "become a removing, or wandering"; cf. "people shake their heads at her" in D. Hillers, *Lamentations* [AB], 9-10). So understood, the connection between sin and wandering ("homelessness"), a connection found first in Gen (4:10, 12) and later in the Prophets (Jer 50:8), is sustained. Most recent translations move in a different direction: "And so has become unclean" (NIV; cf. NEB, JB, and N. Gottwald, *Lamentations*, 78).

7. *mānôd*, shaking of the head as in a gesture of mockery, has a single occurrence in Ps 44:14[15] in parallel with being a "byword among the nations." It is nontheological in nature.

Roaming, wandering, homeless: → *hl'* (stray, be removed far off, # 2133); → *ṭ'h* (roam around, lead astray, # 3246); → *ndd* I (flee, stray, wander, # 5610); → *nwd* (sway, be homeless, # 5653); → *nwṣ* (flee, # 5680); → *rwd* (roam, # 8113); → *šgh* (stray, err, go/do wrong, mislead, # 8706); → *šwṭ* I (roam, # 8763); → *t'h* (wander off, # 9494)

Bibliography
THAT 2:61; *TWAT* 5:291-93; *TWOT* 2:560-61.

Elmer A. Martens

5657	נוה

נוה (*nwh* I), q. rest (hapleg.; # 5657); nom. נָוֶה (*nāweh*), pasturage, pl. *nᵉ'ôt* (except for hapleg. *nᵉwôt in* Zeph 2:6) (# 5659); נָוָה (*nāwâ*), pasturage (# 5661); נָוֹות (*nāwôt*), pasturage, abode, residence (# 5662).

ANE The Akk. cognate *naw/mûm* denotes pastureland.

OT 1. As a vb. *nwh* occurs only at Hab 2:5. If the text is accepted as it is, the meaning is something like "reach the goal of travel" or "rest (from travels)." At best this rendering captures the rather impermanent sense of temporary dwelling associated with this root.

2. The noms. *nāwâ, nāweh,* and *nāwôt* refer consistently to a rural setting, removed from villages, towns, and society. In connection with shepherds (Jer 33:12; Amos 1:2; Zeph 2:6), flocks (*ṣō'n,* Isa 65:10; Jer 49:20; 50:45), and camels (Ezek 25:5), the term designates that remote territory on the fringes of the desert areas that was employed for seasonal grazing of domesticated animals (especially sheep, goats, and camels) and should not be confused with fenced, private pastureland, as in the modern period. Perhaps the nearest parallel in the Northwest Hemisphere is the open range land exploited for the production of beef cattle in the Americas during the last century. The pleasantness and peacefulness of such a place can be stressed (Isa 33:20; Jer 25:37; Hos 9:13) and suggests, perhaps, a predilection for rural simplicity over against the complications of city life. On occasion remoteness of the setting is emphasized by the association of the term with the nearby desert, as in *nᵉ'ôt midbār,* "desert pastures" (Jer 9:9; 23:10; Joel 1:19, 20; 2:22).

3. In conjunction with other terms, the nom. becomes a potent image of remote, inhospitable territory occupied chiefly by wild (undomesticated) animals. Chief among the wild beasts mentioned in this connection are the jackals (*tannîm*; Isa 34:13; 35:7). Elsewhere the reference to "pastures of violence" (*nᵉwôt ḥāmās*—Ps 74:20) conjures up a vision of a land beset by brigands, robbers, and wild beasts, in which all human society is at risk. These phrases are often used in speeches of divine judgment (Isa 27:10; 34:13; 35:7), threatening the destruction of cities, reversion to an uninhabited state, and the consequent dissolution of the blessings of human society for which the earth/land (*hā'āreṣ*) was created (cf. Isa 45:18).

4. By extension the nom. takes on more specific, related meanings. With a possessive pronominal suffix, the term can indicate an individual's "homeland" (Ps 79:7; Jer 10:25; 25:30) or "house" (Job 5:3; 18:15), or even personal, moveable "property" (Job 5:24).

In several instances, occurrences of the nom. are not easily related to the basic meaning (remote spot, temporary residence). Additional difficulty stems from the poetic contexts in which most of these are found. For the most part the NIV follows the interpretation "habitation, dwelling, homeland." Other alternatives may be preferable, however.

(a) The nom. occurs 3x in military contexts and may refer to remote military outposts destroyed by the enemy (Ps 79:7; Jer 10:25; 25:30).

(b) Twice in Job (5:24; 18:15) the terms are paralleled by *'ōhel*, tent, in a broader context of threat. In 5:17-23 the poet celebrates how the one whom God reproves is preserved in the midst of troubles. The trouble/threat is described as the stress associated with living in remote, inhospitable regions, populated by "wild beasts." Nevertheless, "you will know that your tent is secure, you will take stock of your property (*nwh*—NRSV "fold") and find nothing missing" (5:24). Job describes the opposing experience of the wicked (cf. 18:5-21, who "is torn from the security of his tent, and marched off to the king of terrors. Fire resides in his tent; burning sulphur is scattered over his dwelling (*nwh*)" (18:14-15). Such language recalls the fate of Job's sheep and shepherds, who fell prey to fire from heaven (1:16). Along with 5:24, the nom. may suggest some temporary shelter for the protection of the flock from predators in remote areas. A third occurrence in Job (5:3) shares the context of threat, but lacks clarity as to the meaning of the nom. "Resentment kills a fool, and envy slays the simple. I myself have seen a fool taking root, but suddenly his house (*nwh*) was cursed. His children are far from safety, crushed in court without a defender" (5:2-4).

5. It is a small step to employ the nom. to refer to the dwelling place of God. In 2 Sam 15:25, the grammar of the sentence makes it difficult to know whether the reference is to the dwelling place of Yahweh or the Ark of the Covenant. Elsewhere the reference is clearly to the dwelling place of Yahweh, but it is not certain whether the temple, the city of Jerusalem, or the land is intended (Exod 15:13). On two other occasions the nom. is related to the presence/dwelling of Yahweh or the Ark of the Covenant. In Exod 15:13 we learn that Yahweh in his steadfast love "will lead the people you have redeemed. In your strength you will guide them to your holy dwelling (*nwh*)." In 2 Sam 15:25, as David flees Jerusalem before his rebellious son Absalom, he forbids the removal of the Ark of the Covenant from the city when he says, "Take the ark of God back into the city. If I find favor in the LORD's eyes, he will bring me back and let me see it and his dwelling place (*nwh*—NRSV the place where it stays) again." As a reference to the resting place of the mobile ark, *nwh* would seem a most appropriate lexical choice. The same is true of the use of this term to describe God's temporary presence among humans.

6. A final set of theologically significant renderings appear in Jer 31:23 and 50:7, both in conjunction with the nom. *ṣedeq* (→ # 7406). In the former passage, the restoration of Judah is in view and onlookers exclaim in wonder, "The LORD bless you, O righteous dwelling (*n^{e}'ôt ṣedeq*), O sacred mountain!" The prophet then emphasizes how Judean farmers and shepherds will experience replenishing. In the second passage, the people of Judah are described as errant sheep, led astray on the mountains by their leaders and devoured by their enemies who justify themselves by claiming, "We are not guilty, because they (Judah) have sinned against the LORD, their true pasture (*n^{e}'ôt ṣedeq*), the LORD, the hope of their fathers." In a wonderful way Yahweh is here proclaimed the ultimate satisfaction of those hopes the people of Israel had pinned on the land. Yahweh is the "true pasture."

7. Original meanings of terms of this root seem to reflect temporary, nomadic circumstances, as with shepherds who travel with their flock, living removed from settled society. Only secondarily have these terms been connected with more settled

residences. The contexts in which these terms are employed may reflect some nostalgia for rural living, although risk and danger are also noted.

House, dwelling, tabernacle: → *bayit* I (house, dwelling, building, family, dynasty, # 1074); → *yšb* (dwell, # 3782); → *mā'ôn* II (den, dwelling, # 5061); → *nwh* I (rest, # 5657); → *škn* (settle, # 8905)
Pasture: → *nwh* I (rest, # 5657); → *r'h* I (feed, graze, shepherd, rule, # 8286)

BIBLIOGRAPHY
D. O. Edzard, "*Altbabylonisch* nawûm," *ZAA* 19, 1959, 168-73; F. I. Anderson, *Job: An Introduction and Commentary*, TOTC, 1976; F. D. Coggan, "The Meaning of חטא in Job v.24" JMEOS 17, 1932, 53-56; S. R. Driver, *Notes on the Hebrew Text and the Topography of the Books of Samuel*, 1943[2], 156-59.

Gerald H. Wilson

5658	נוה

נוה (*nwh* II), hi. praise (# 5658).

ANE Arab. *nawwaha*, call loudly; Mish. Heb. pi., hi. adorn, praise.

OT This vb. belongs to the vocabulary of praise. It occurs only in Exod 15:2, in Moses' victory song after the crossing of the Red Sea. Yahweh is celebrated as "my God": by his saving deed he had proved his divine power to the contemporary generation.

Praising, singing, thanksgiving: → *hll* II (praise, be praiseworthy, boast, exult, # 2146); → *zmr* I (make music, sing praise, # 2376); → *ydh* II (acknowledge, give thanks, praise, # 3344); → *nwh* II (praise, # 5658); → *'nh* IV (sing, # 6702); → *psḥ* I (break forth with or break into singing, # 7200); → *rômēm* (exalt, # 8123a); → *šbḥ* I (commend, praise, honor, # 8655); → *šyr* (sing, # 8876); → *tnh* (recite, commemorate, # 9480)

Leslie C. Allen

5659 (*nāweh*, pasturage), → # 5657

5661 (*nāwâ*, pasturage), → # 5657

5662 (*nāwôt*, pasturage), → # 5657

5663	נוח

נוח (*nwḥ* I), q. settle, take a rest, wait, get relief from; hi. I, procure relief for, let come down, cause to cease; hi. II, station, deposit, leave, keep safe; ho. be left behind (# 5663); הֲנָחָה (*h^anāḥâ*), nom. holiday (remission of taxes?) (# 2182); מָנוֹחַ (*mānôaḥ* I), nom. resting place (# 4955); מְנוּחָה (*m^enûḥâ*), nom./adj. resting place, quieting, calming (# 4957); נוֹחַ (*nôaḥ*), nom. place of rest (# 5665); נַחַת (*naḥat* II), nom., rest, calmness (# 5739); נִיחוֹחַ (*nîḥôaḥ*), adj. soothing, pleasing (# 5767).

ANE This root appears in several of the Sem. languages, including Ugar., Akk., and Aram., with the meaning rest. It also appears in Arab. with a related meaning, making a camel kneel down.

OT 1. The basic idea of this root is found in the idea of roosting or landing upon. This is made clear in the first occasion in Gen (8:4, 9) where, on the one hand, Noah's ark "lands" upon Mt. Ararat, and, on the other, the dove was unable to find a "place (*mānôaḥ*) to set its feet." This idea is especially clear in the noms. *mānôaḥ* and *m^enûḥâ*. So, in addition to the above reference, Isa 34:14 speaks of the night creatures finding "places of rest" in abandoned palaces, and Deut 28:65 makes the metaphor explicit when it says that the Israelites who have sinned against God will find no "resting place for the soles of your feet" (a duplicate of what was said of the dove in Gen 8:9). Interestingly, both Deut 28:65 and Isa 34:14 parallel a hi. form of *rg'* (find a place of repose) with *mānôaḥ*.

Not only do birds find a place to land or roost, so do people, including widows (Ruth 1:9; 3:1) and the people of God (Gen 49:15; Num 10:33; Deut 12:9; 1 Kgs 8:56; Ps 95:11; Isa 32:18; Lam 1:3). In about half of these latter references the point is made that a sinful people will not find a place to land. But not only do people need something to land upon, so does the ark of God. In seven different places reference is made to the ark of God (and, by extension, God himself) finding a place to land upon in Jerusalem (1 Chron 6:31[16]; 28:2; 2 Chron 6:41; Ps 132:8, 14; Isa 11:10; 66:1). However, the last of these references makes it clear that just because the house of God may be located in Jerusalem does not mean that God's resting place is confined to that location.

Connected with the idea of a place to land are the ideas of safety and security. Thus, the waters beside which the shepherd leads his sheep are "quiet" and restful (Ps 23:2). In the same way the king's decision will give "rest" to the troubled mind of the Tekoaite woman (2 Sam 14:17), and the person to whom the Lord has responded can find "rest" (Ps 116:7). Ultimately, the only place where human beings can land in absolute confidence and safety is in the promises of God, but that requires an abandoning of self-reliance, which is perennially distasteful to fallen humans (Isa 28:12).

2. In the vb. forms of the root, the same general range of connotations as those just discussed in the nom. form appear. Among the 144x the vb. appears, by far the most common meaning is that of coming to rest upon some place, or of being caused to rest, or being placed, in a certain spot. At least 53x have this meaning. Some representative examples are: locusts "settled down in every area of the country" (Exod 10:4); the Spirit "rested" upon the seventy elders (Num 10:36); the soles of the priests' feet "rested" in the water (Josh 3:13); the hand of the Lord will "rest on this mountain" (Isa 25:10); "wisdom reposes (rests) in the heart of the discerning" (Prov 14:33); Ezekiel is "set" by God in the valley of dry bones (Ezek 37:1); Moses is commanded to "place" the manna in the ark for purposes of memory (Exod 16:33-34); the ark was "set" on a large stone (1 Sam 6:18); the body of the disobedient Judean prophet was "laid" in the tomb of the Israelite prophet (1 Kgs 13:30); and God promises to "settle" his people in their land after the Exile (Ezek 37:14).

In the hi. II (marked by a doubling of the initial *nun*) and ho. the meaning of set or place is expanded into the idea of "leave behind" or "permit to remain," or even "leave alone." Thus, Joseph commands the brothers to "leave" one of their number behind (Gen 42:33), and Aaron is required to "leave" his sacred garments in the Tent of Meeting (Lev 16:23; see also Ezek 42:14, 19). So also David "left" behind his concubines when he fled Jerusalem before Absalom (2 Sam 16:21; 20:3), God allows certain nations to "remain" (Judg 2:23; 3:1; Jer 27:11), and there are "open areas" in the temple structure (KJV that which was left; Ezek 41:9, 11). Finally, God did not "allow" anyone to oppress his people when they were faithful (Ps 105:14), and "the abundance of a rich man *permits* him no sleep" (Eccl 5:12).

3. A second meaning of this root is to cease activity. This idea is possibly derived from the thought that when one alights upon a roost, all activity, whether flying, feeding, or fighting, stops. Thus God "rested from," or ceased, his creative activity on the seventh day (Exod 20:11), and expected that his people would also cease from their activities on that day (Exod 23:12; Deut 5:14). Such cessation of activity should promote both inner and outer tranquility. When the Judeans rested from defending themselves, they celebrated a joyous feast (Esth 9:17, 18). So also, when Babylon is destroyed, all the lands "are at rest and at peace" (Isa 14:7). God offers such rest and repose, but the people reject it and find nothing but weariness in their own efforts to care for and defend themselves (Isa 28:12; 63:14; Lam 5:5). In Ezek cessation is expressed in a causal way when God promises through the prophet that he will make his anger cease (NIV subside; Ezek 5:13; 16:42; 21:17[22]; 24:13). The ultimate expression of cessation is the rest of death (Job 3:13, 17; Isa 57:2; Dan 12:13).

4. The connotation of causing anger to rest or subside is evident in the nom./adj. *niḥôaḥ*, soothing, pleasing, which occurs 43x in Gen-Num and Ezek, all as an attributive of *reah,* odor, aroma, in connection with burnt offerings. The odor of the burning sacrifice is not pleasing in a sensuous way, but it is restful. Because a sacrifice is offered in faith, God's anger is put to rest. It is ironic that in Ezek (where NIV somewhat unaccountably translates, fragrant incense), instead of causing God's anger to subside through the offering of a pleasing aroma, the ones sacrificing actually provoke him to greater anger because they are offering it to the idols (Ezek 6:13; 16:19; 20:28). Perhaps the most theologically significant of all the occasions of the word is the last one (20:41), where God says that the people themselves will be the "fragrant incense" to the Lord when he brings them home from the nations. As all the prophets had said again and again, it was not the people's sacrifices that God wanted, but it was themselves, as symbolized in their sacrifices.

5. The frequent occurrences of God's promises to give his people "rest" include all of the preceding ideas: a place to land on, a place of serenity, and cessation from effort. But they also include a fourth idea, and that is safety and security. This is made clear by the several references to giving "rest from his/their enemies on every side" (Deut 12:10; 25:19; Josh 23:1; 2 Sam 7:1, 11; 2 Chron 14:7[6]; Neh 9:28; Esth 9:16, 22; Isa 14:3). The sense is to get, or provide, relief from threat or attack. So God not only promises to give his people a place to settle, but he also promises to give them a place of security. It is this latter sense that is operative in the promises to the Transjordanian tribes that they may return to their home territories, once God has given their brothers rest (Deut 3:20; Josh 1:15; 22:4). It is this same idea that occurs in connection with David's and Solomon's decision to build the temple: God has now given them the security and leisure necessary to such an undertaking (e.g., 1 Kgs 5:4[18]). A further extension of this idea is to keep something safe. So Potiphar's wife "kept" Joseph's cloak until her husband came home (Gen 39:16), and the Hebrew people are commanded to "save" the manna gathered on the day before the Sabbath (Exod 16:23-24), as they are also commanded to "store" the tithe in their towns (Deut 14:28).

The range of meanings that this root contains is rather well represented in the 7 uses of the nom. *naḥat*. It speaks of that which is placed on a table (Job 36:16), the cessation of activity in death (Job 17:16; Eccl 6:5), the cessation of self-reliance (Isa 30:15), and the contrast between the tranquility of wisdom and the turmoil of folly (Prov 29:9; Eccl 4:6; 9:17). See also *šqṭ* be undisturbed, at peace (# 9200, # 9201).

Rest, quiet, repose: → *dmh* II (come to an end, rest, be dumb, silent, # 1949); → *nwh* I (rest, # 5657); → *nwḥ* I (settle, take a rest, wait, station, deposit, # 5663); → *rg'* (crust over, come to rest, be quiet, # 8088/89); → *š'n* (be at ease, untroubled, # 8631); → *šbḥ* II (hush, soothe, quiet, # 8656); → *šebet* (sitting quietly, rest, # 8699, 8700); → *štq* (become calm, # 9284)

BIBLIOGRAPHY

TWOT 2:562-63; J. Hausman, *Israel's Rest: Studien zum Selbverstandnis der nachexilischen Gemeinde,* 1987; W. Kaiser, *Toward an Old Testament Theology*, 1978, 127-30; G. von Rad, "There Still Remains a Rest for the People of God," *The Problem of the Hexateuch and Other Essays,* 1966, 94-102; G. Robinson, "The Idea of Rest in the OT and the Search for the Basic Character of the Sabbath," *ZAW* 92, 1980, 32-42; W. Roth, "Deuteronomic Rest Theology: A Redaction Critical Study," *BiblRes* 21, 1976, 5-14.

John N. Oswalt

5664	נוח

נוח (*nwḥ* II), q. groan (# 5664).

ANE *KTU* 1.15:I:7 attests a vb. clearly meaning to groan or moan, most likely *nwḥ* (Driver, *CML*, 156, n. 10, comparing Arab. *nāḥu*, sigh, coo; Aistleitner, *WUS*, 887).

OT Hab 3:16 presents the sole OT occurrence proposed to this point. Even-Shoshan omits a separate *nwḥ* II entry; E. Goodrick and J. Kohlenberger III, *NIV Exhaustive Concordance*, list # 5664 as an unused variant. If the meaning to groan is demanded, taking the MT as from this root might be preferable to emending to a form of *'nḥ*. Most likely 3:16-19 expresses Habakkuk's faith response to 3:2-15, with *nwḥ* I, meaning wait quietly (in anticipation), as in 1 Sam 25:9 (cf. Dan 12:13).

Groan, sigh, growl: → *'nḥ* (sigh, groan, # 634); → *'nq* (groan, # 650); → *hgh* I (groan, moan, sigh, meditate, muse, chirp, mutter, # 2047); → *hāgîg* (groan in prayer, # 2052); → *z'q* (cry, howl, wail, # 2410); → *n'q* (groan, # 5543); → *nhm* (growl, groan, # 5637); → *nwḥ* II (groan in anticipation, # 5664); → *p'h* (groan in childbirth, # 7184); → *š'g* (roar, # 8613)

BIBLIOGRAPHY

TWAT 5:299; G. R. Driver, *Studies in the Vocabulary of the Old Testament,* 1, *JTS* 34, 1933, 377; J. J. M. Roberts, *Nahum, Habakkuk, and Zephaniah,* OTL, 1991, 129, 146, 149.

David Thompson

5665 (*nôaḥ*, place of rest), → # 5663

5667	נוט

נוט (*nwṭ*), q. shake, quake (# 5667).

ANE A cognate byform has been suggested in Ugar. *nṭṭ*, stagger, totter.

OT *nwṭ* occurs only in Psalm 99:1, where it describes the quaking of the earth because of the reigning theophanic presence of Yahweh amidst the cherubim. It is synonymously parallel with the more frequently occurring *rgz* (→ # 8074), which means to tremble or be agitated.

Shaking, terror, trembling: → *g'š* (rise and fall noisily, swell, surge, # 1723); → *zw'* (tremble, quake, be afraid, # 2316); → *zll* II (shake, quake, tremble, # 2362); → *ḥalḥālâ* (shaking, trembling, anguish, # 2714); → *ḥrg* (come out trembling, # 3004); → *ḥrd* (tremble, shudder, startle, # 3006); → *yr'* (tremble, be fainthearted, # 3760); → *mwṭ* (waver, reel, stagger, shake, reel, # 4572); → *m'd* (slip, slide, shake, totter, # 5048); → *nwd* (shake, totter, waiver, wander, mourn, flee, # 5653); → *nwṭ* (shake, quake, # 5667); → *nw'* (shake, tremble, stagger, totter, wave, # 5675); → *n'r* II (shake, shake off, # 5850); → *smr* (shudder, have goose-bumps, bristle, # 6169); → *'iw'îm* (distortion, stagger, dizzy, # 6413); → *pwq* I (stagger, wobble, reel, totter, # 7048); → *pḥd* I (tremble, be in dread, # 7064); → *plṣ* (shudder, shake, tremble, # 7145); → *qwṣ* I (feel disgust, frighten, cause dread, # 7762); → *rgz* (agitate, quiver, shake, excite, rouse up, agitate, # 8074); → *rnh* I (rattle, # 8261); → *r'd* (tremble, shake, tremble, # 8283); → *r'l* I (brandish, make to quiver, # 8302); → *r'š* I (quake, shake, leap, # 8321); → *rpp* (shake, quake, rock, # 8344); → *r^etēt* (terror, panic, trembling, # 8417); → *ś'r* I (be afraid, terrified, bristle with horror, # 8547)

BIBLIOGRAPHY
RSP 1:26-27; *TWOT* 2:563; M. Dahood, *Psalms 1-100*, AB, 1968.

M. V. Van Pelt/W. C. Kaiser, Jr.

5670	נום

נום (*nwm*), q. sleep (# 5670); נוּמָה (*nûmâ*), sleep (# 5671); תְּנוּמָה (*t^enûmâ*), sleep (# 9484).

ANE Sem. cognates occur in Akk. *nâmu*, Arab. *nām*, Aram./Syr. *nûm*, to slumber; Eth. *nōma*, to sleep; cf. Ugar. *nhmmt*, slumber; Syr. *nawmā'*, slumber.

OT Since *nwm* is used only in prophetic and poetic literature (Job 33:15; Ps 76:5[6]; 121:3-4; 132:4; Prov 6:4, 10; 23:21; 24:33; Isa 5:27; 56:10; Nah 3:18), Schüpphaus disagrees with any effort to distinguish *nwm* from *yšn*, seeing the former only as a poetic synonym for the latter (*TDOT* 6:438-41). In light of its cognates, however, it seems better to consider the root *nwm* as indicating a lighter form of sleep than *yšn* or *rdm*, bespeaking a loss of conscious thought as one slips toward *šēnâ* (Ugar. *nhm*; cf. Syr. *nawmā'*; Arab. *nām*; Thomson, 421-22; cf. *HALAT*, doze off, slumber). The words *šnt*, *škb* (lie), and *nhmmt* appear in Krt 33-34: *šnt tl'u'a?n wyškb/nhmmt wyqmṣ*, which H. L. Ginsberg renders, "Sleep prevails over him and he lies; / Slumber and he reclines" (*ANET*, 143). Similar parallels appear in the Bible. Psalm 121:4 appears to differentiate *nwm* from *yšn*: *hinnēh lō'-yānûm w^elō yîšān šōmēr yisrā'ēl*; NIV, "Indeed, he who watches over Israel will neither slumber nor sleep" (cf. Isa 5:27). Job 33:15 seems to distinguish *nwm* from *rdm*: "In a dream, in a vision of the night, when deep sleep (*tardēmâ*) falls on men as they slumber (*t^enûmôt*) in their beds." While dreams normally occur in deep sleep, they can also occur in *t^enûmâ*, as the last reference indicates. Accordingly, the nom. *t^enûmâ*, sleep (→ # 9484), signifies the closing of the eyes and dozing off, an idea seemingly supported by Ps 132:4 and Prov 6:4.

P-B The root is attested in DSS and postbiblical Heb. (See Jastrow 2:887, 1680).

Sleep: → *dlp* II (be sleepless, # 1941); → *yšn* I (sleep, # 3822); → *nwm* (sleep, # 5670); → *rdm* I (go to sleep, # 8101)

BIBLIOGRAPHY

RSP 1:215; 2:14; *TDOT* 6:438-41; B. F. Batto, "The Sleeping God: An Ancient Near Eastern Motif of Divine Sovereignty," *Bib* 68, 1987, 153-77; A. R. Ceresko, "Psalm 121: A Prayer of a Warrior?" *Bib* 70, 1989, 496-510; J. Cheryl Exum, "Of Broken Pots, Fluttering Birds and Visions in the Night: Extended Simile and Poetic Technique in Isaiah," *CBQ* 43, 1982, 331-52; J. G. S. S. Thomson, "Sleep: an Aspect of Jewish Anthropology," *VT* 5, 1955, 421-33.

William C. Williams

5671 (*nûmâ*, sleep), → # 5670

5674	נוס

נוס (*nws*), q. flee, escape, slip away; polel drive onward; hi. drive out (# 5674); מָנוֹס (*mānôs*), place of escape (→ # 4960); מְנוּסָה (*m^e^nûsâ*), flight (→ # 4961).

ANE Old Aram. haphel *hns,* remove (Zakur, 2, 20); Arab. *nās*, move to and fro, be in a state of commotion or agitation. According to Jenni (1993, 56), Heb. *nws* is semantically equivalent to Akk. *naparšudu*.

OT 1. The vb. often implies open flight of a human from mortal danger, whether physical or spiritual: soldiers from the hot pursuit of their enemies (Gen 14:10; Josh 8:20; 2 Sam 18:3; 19:3[4]); a king by means of his chariot from the clutches of those formerly subservient to him (1 Kgs 12:18 = 2 Chron 10:18); the enemies of Israel from before them, because of the Lord's presence (Deut 28:7); a nursemaid with the child she kept for fear that he would be killed by enemies of his dead father (2 Sam 4:4); a murderer (*rōṣēaḥ*) to a city of refuge to escape from the blood-redeemer (*gō'ēl haddām*) (Num 35:6; Deut 4:42; Josh 20:3-4); a godfearer from sexual temptation (Gen 39:12); people from natural disasters associated with divine judgment (Gen 19:20; Num 16:34; Zech 14:5); and a human from a serpent (Exod 4:3) or lion (Amos 5:19).

2. In oracles of judgment against the nations, the enemies of God's people flee in fright, seeking refuge from annihilation (Egypt: Jer 46:5, 21; Moab: 48:6, 44; Edom: 49:8; Damascus: 49:24; Hazor: 49:30; Babylon: 50:16; cf. Isa 13:14). Then, too, the northern kingdom Israel is chided, as if there was somewhere to flee and escape from the judgment of God (Isa 10:3). Even the bravest Israelite warrior will flee naked on the day God's judgment comes (Amos 2:16).

3. In oracles of judgment and hope, the Judean exiles are exhorted to flee from Babylon to Jerusalem for safety, as God's judgment is about to fall on Babylon (Jer 51:6; Zech 2:6[10]).

4. In describing the joy of those returning to Zion from exile, sorrow and sighing "flee away" from the redeemed (Isa 35:10 = 51:11).

5. The sea reacts to the powerful appearance of God when Israel came out of Egypt by fleeing in fright (Ps 114:3, 5; cf. Ps 104:7).

6. At the end of his life Moses was still physically strong; his vigor had not "dissipated" (Deut 34:7).

7. In love poetry the lovers remain together "until the day breaks and the shadows flee" (S of Songs 2:17).

8. The polel appears once, meaning drive onward, in a context of judgment against the adversaries of the Lord (Isa 59:19).

9. The hi. means both put the enemy to flight (Deut 32:30) and put someone/something in a safe place (Exod 9:20; Judg 6:11).

P-B Usage in QL (1QM 3:5-6) and Tannaitic Heb. is conditioned by usage in BH. By far the most frequently attested formal equivalent in the LXX is *phygō*, flee.

Disappearance, flight, escape: → *brḥ* I (run away, flee, disappear, # 1368); → *ḥlp* I (pass by, disappear, violate, change, renew, # 2736); → *ḥrh* II (disappear, be few in number, # 3014); → *nws* (flee, escape, slip away, # 5674); → *pṭr* (vanish, escape, let out, # 7080); → *plṭ* (save, bring to safety, # 7117); → *paršᵉdōn* (loophole [for escape]?, # 7307); → *śrd* (run away, escape, # 8572)
Refuge, escape: → *ḥsh* (seek refuge, # 2879); → *mālôn* (lodging place, # 4869); → *mānôs* (place of escape, # 4960); → *miqlāṭ* (refuge, asylum, # 5236); → *'wz* (take refuge, # 6395); → *plṭ* (save, bring to safety, # 7117); → *śrd* (run away, escape, # 8572)

Bibliography
NIDNTT 1:55-59; *THAT* 2:47-50; *TWOT* 2:563-64; B. Grossfeld, "The Relationship Between Biblical Hebrew ברח and נוס and Their Corresponding Aramaic Equivalents in the Targum—ערק, אפך, אזל: A Preliminary Study in Aramaic-Hebrew Lexicography," *ZAW* 91, 1979, 107-23; E. Jenni, "Response to P. Swiggers," *ZAH* 6, 1993, 55-59; idem, "'Fliehen' im akkadischen und im hebräischen Sprachgebrauch," *Or* 47, 1978, 351-59; J. Kennedy, *Studies in Hebrew Synonyms,* 1898.

Jerome A. Lund

5675	נוע

נוע (*nw'*), q. shake, tremble, stagger, totter, wave; ni. be shaken; hi. make wander, unsteady, shake (# 5675).

ANE Aram. *nw'*, waver, stagger.

OT *nw'* occurs 42x in 36 different verses throughout the OT. In general, it depicts the repetitive back-and-forth movement of a number of different subjects. Such movement is variously termed as shaking, trembling, staggering, tottering, waving, roaming, and wandering.

1. On several occasions, *nw'* is used to describe the movement of various body parts. In 1 Sam 1:13 the grief of Hannah became so overwhelming that while praying, her lips moved back and forth like a person who might be drunk. A certain waving gesture of the hands is an action showing contempt for another (Zeph 2:15). The body part most associated with *nw'*, however, is the head. Apparently, the waving or wagging of the head functioned as a figure of speech or Heb. idiom for the contemptuous mocking of another person (2 Kgs 19:21; Job 16:4; Ps 22:7[8]; 109:25; Isa 37:22; Lam 2:15).

2. *nw'* also describes the shaking of the trees by the wind (Judg 9:9, 11, 13). This same reality also functions metaphorically to depict fear or the shaking of hearts: "His heart and the heart of his people *shook* as the trees of the forest *shake* with the wind" (Isa 7:2, NASB).

3. When a person becomes drunk and his way unsteady, one's manner of locomotion is often described as staggering. Typically, this is a description of sinfulness and judgment, or better, judgment resulting from sinfulness. Both the earth (Isa 24:20) and people (Ps 107:27; Isa 29:9) are described as staggering. Both *nwd*, sway, totter,

and *hgg*, reel, as from festival excess (BDB, 290), appear as parallel vbs. to *nw'* in this context. With regard to the context of judgment, *nw'* as shaking is used to describe the force of judgment, whether concretely (Ps 59:11[12]; Amos 9:9) or metaphorically (Nah 3:12).

4. As with other words in this semantic field, *nw'*, shaking, describes a physical response to the presence of the Lord, especially in theophanic (→) appearance (Exod 20:18; Isa 6:4; 19:1). The term *nw'* also describes Daniel's response to a vision and the appearance of a numinous messenger (Dan 10:10).

5. *nw'* describes the aimless wandering of the vagrant or dispossessed (2 Sam 15:20; Ps 109:10; Lam 4:15). Therefore, the idea of wandering is primarily a negative one. It was the Lord's curse for Cain to be a wanderer about the earth (Gen 4:12, 14). Because of Israel's disobedience, she was made to wander for forty years in the wilderness before crossing over into the Promised Land (Num 32:13). The disobedient are described as those who love to wander or stagger about (Jer 14:10; Amos 4:8; 8:12). Such wanderers are further described as unstable and blind (Prov 5:6; Lam 4:14).

Shaking, terror, trembling: → *g'š* (rise and fall noisily, swell, surge, # 1723); → *zw'* (tremble, quake, be afraid, # 2316); → *zll* II (shake, quake, tremble, # 2362); → *ḥalḥālâ* (shaking, trembling, anguish, # 2714); → *ḥrg* (come out trembling, # 3004); → *ḥrd* (tremble, shudder, startle, # 3006); → *yr'* (tremble, be fainthearted, # 3760); → *mwṭ* (waver, reel, stagger, shake, reel, # 4572); → *m'd* (slip, slide, shake, totter, # 5048); → *nwd* (shake, totter, waiver, wander, mourn, flee, # 5653); → *nwṭ* (shake, quake, # 5667); → *nw'* (shake, tremble, stagger, totter, wave, # 5675); → *n'r* II (shake, shake off, # 5850); → *smr* (shudder, have goose-bumps, bristle, # 6169); → *'iw'îm* (distortion, stagger, dizzy, # 6413); → *pwq* I (stagger, wobble, reel, totter, # 7048); → *pḥd* I (tremble, be in dread, # 7064); → *plṣ* (shudder, shake, tremble, # 7145); → *qwṣ* I (feel disgust, frighten, cause dread, # 7762); → *rgz* (agitate, quiver, shake, excite, rouse up, agitate, # 8074); → *rnh* I (rattle, # 8261); → *r'd* (tremble, shake, tremble, # 8283); → *r'l* I (brandish, make to quiver, # 8302); → *r'š* I (quake, shake, leap, # 8321); → *rpp* (shake, quake, rock, # 8344); → *r^etēt* (terror, panic, trembling, # 8417); → *ś'r* I (be afraid, terrified, bristle with horror, # 8547)

Fear, dread, terror: → *'āyōm* (terrible, awesome, majestic, # 398); → *'êmâ* (terror, dread, # 399); → *bhl* (be dismayed, terrified, dismay, terrify, hasten, hurry, # 987); → *b't* (overtaken by sudden terror, stupefied, be terrified, assail, # 1286); → *gwr* III (be afraid of, dread, stand in awe, # 1593); → *d'g* (be anxious, concerned, fear, dread, # 1793); → *zḥl* II (fear, be afraid, # 2324); → *ḥrd* (tremble, shudder, startle, # 3006); → *ḥtt* (be shattered, dismayed, terrified, scare, terrify, # 3169); → *ygr* (fear, dread, terror, # 3336); → *yr'* I (fear, be afraid, held in honor, # 3707); → *yrh* (be afraid, terrified, paralyzed with fright, # 3724); → *'rṣ* (be alarmed, terrified, dreadful, dreadful, be in terror, # 6907); → *pḥd* I (tremble, be in dread, # 7064); → *qwṣ* I (feel disgust, frighten, cause dread, # 7762)

BIBLIOGRAPHY

E. Jenni, "Verba gesticulatimis im Hebräischen," in *Text, Methode und Grammatik,* Wolfgang Richtes zum 65 Geburtstag, Walter Gross et al., eds. 1991, 191-203.

M. V. Van Pelt/W. C. Kaiser, Jr.

5677	נוף

נוף (*nwp* I), vb. hi. move back and forth; ho. be moved back and forth; po. swing the hand in threatening (# 5677); הֲנָפָה (*h^anāpâ*), vb. or nom. waving (of wave offering, # 2185); תְּנוּפָה(*t^enûpâ*), nom. wave offering (# 9485).

ANE 1. The vb. *nwp* I, wave, has numerous parallels in the Sem. languages: Akk. *nâpu* B, totter (*AHw*, 742, but questionable according to *TWAT* 5:318; *CAD* N1, 327 says the meaning is uncertain), Jewish Aram., move to and fro, Syr. bend, Mish. Heb. swing, and in Soqotri (see the list in *HALOT* 682, and *TWAT* 5:318). Ugar. *np*, height; and Arab. *nwf*, be high, elevated, might also be treated as part of the background etymology (see *HALOT* 682, *nwp* III), but see below.

2. The etymology of the nom. *t^enûpâ*, wave offering, has been debated. Traditionally, it has been derived from the hi. form of the vb. *nwp* I, wave, and translated "wave offering" (Milgrom, 1991, 461; Anderson, 1992, 133). Some have argued for a parallel cultic term in Ugar. *šnpt* (i.e., from the Ugar. Shaphel = Heb. hi. vb.; see Gaster, 578; Hillers), meaning wave offering or more likely presentation (i.e., elevated) offering, as in the OT (see now Tarragon, 64-65, for a list of its four occurrences, following Milgrom, "The Alleged Wave Offering," and most recently idem, 1991, 461-73; cf. Arab. *nwf*, be high, elevated).

Others have suggested a different derivation from Akk. *nâpu* A, make a payment in addition (to rent) (*CAD* N1, 327), combined with *nûptu*, additional payment (*CAD* N2, 343). This would be a close parallel to Heb. *hēnîp t^enûpâ*, make a *t^enûpâ* offering (Anderson, 1992, 134-35). Indeed, it seems unlikely that a motion of waving or even physically elevating is intended, for example, in Num 8:11, where Aaron was ordered to present (*hēnîp*) the whole tribe of Levi as a *t^enûpâ* before the Lord.

No firm conclusion can be reached at this time regarding the derivation of Heb. *t^enûpâ*, but it is difficult to deny the close connection between the nom. and the vb., esp. since they are used together in the expression "wave(?) a wave offering(?) before the Lord." It is possible that at one time there was a kind of gesture or mode of presentation that was intended but, at a later time, the expression could be used more generally for the special presentation of an offering, whether the original gesture was performed or not. It is interesting, however, that even in the dedication of the Levities the Israelites were "to lay their hands on them" and Aaron was to "present the Levites before the LORD as a wave offering from the Israelites" (Num 8:10-11; cf. OT sec. 3).

OT 1. The nom. *t^enûpâ* (30x) is a technical priestly term. *h^anāpâ* occurs only 1x in the expression, "He shakes (*h^anāpâ*) the nations in the sieve of destruction" (Isa 30:28, note the play on words with "sieve"), and apparently originated as an Aram. haphel (= Heb. hi.) inf. (*HALOT* 252-53; BDB, 631 lists it as a hi. inf.). According to *HALOT* 682, the vb. *nwp* I occurs 35x, excluding the q. vb. in Prov 7:17 ("I have perfumed my bed with myrrh, aloes and cinnamon") and the hi. in Ps 68:9a[10a] ("You gave abundant showers, O God"), which it puts under *nwp* II (contra 37x for *nwp* I as in BDB, 629-30, and Even-Shoshan, 749). It is used for shaking or striking the hand (2 Kgs 5:11; Job 31:21; Isa 10:32; 11:15; 13:2; 19:16; Zech 2:9[13]), wielding or shaking tools or weapons of various kinds (Exod 20:25; Deut 23:25[26]; 27:5; Josh 8:31; Isa 10:15 [2x]; → *mizbēaḥ*, altar, # 4640, OT sec. 4, for its use in the altar law passages: "If you make an altar of stones for me, do not build it with dressed stones, for you will defile it if you use a tool on it," Exod 20:25, etc.), and the waving of the grain offering of jealousy before the Lord (Num 5:25).

The largest block of references associate the vb. with the waving, elevating, or presenting of various kinds of *t^enûpâ* offerings: (a) the fat, right thigh (cf. Heb. *t^erûmâ*, tribute, contribution [# 9556] in Exod 29:27) and bread offerings of the "ordination (peace) offering," for the ordination of Aaron and his sons as priests, all of which were burned on the altar (Exod 29:22-25, 27; Lev 8:27); (b) the breast of the "ordination (peace) offering," which Moses ate (Exod 29:26; Lev 8:29); (c) the *t^e rûmâ*, contribution (Exod 35:5, 21) for the construction of the tabernacle (35:22); (d) the breast and right thigh of the inaugural peace (fellowship) offerings (Lev 9:21); (e) the guilt offering and oil brought for the cleansing of the leper (14:12, 24); (f) the first sheaf (23:11-12); (g) the sin and peace offerings along with the firstfruits presented for the celebration of the Feast of Weeks (23:20; cf. vv. 16-19); (h) the shoulder of the peace offering ram and portions of the bread offered for the completion of a Nazirite vow (Num 6:20); (i) the Levites as an offering to the Lord (8:11, 13, 15, 21); (j) the breast of the wave offering and the thigh of the contribution (Heb. *t^e rûmâ*), along with the fat of both (Lev 10:14-15); (k) and esp. the breast of the standard peace offering (7:30).

2. There are two major portions of the peace offering animal that were offered to the priests: the breast (*ḥāzeh*, # 2601, 13x in the OT, all referring to the wave offering breast of slaughtered sacrificial animals; see esp. Lev 7:30, 31, 34) was given as a wave offering to all the priests (*t^e nûpâ*; see 7:29-31, 34); and the right thigh was given as a contribution to the particular priest who officiated at the offering of the particular peace offering (→ *t^e rûmâ*, tribute, contribution, # 9556; note esp. 7:32-33). These were the standard prebends for the priests (7:34). They could be eaten in any clean place (10:14; i.e., they were holy, not most holy, contrast the grain offering prebend in vv. 12-13). Therefore, not only the priests themselves, but also all who lived in their households and were clean could eat of these portions of the peace offerings (22:10-16). Of course, for a common person to eat of these portions would be to violate the holy things of the Lord.

3. As the survey of vb. usage above suggests the term *t^e nûpâ*, wave offering, also refers to the Levites as an offering to the Lord (Num 8:11-20), to the contribution presented as a waving offering for the building of the tabernacle (Exod 35:2; 38:24, 29; cf. the word "contribution" referring to the same articles in 25:2-3; 35:5, 21, 24; 36:3, 6; for the second temple, see Ezra 8:25), and to both the wave offering and the contribution in general: "The thigh that was presented and the breast that was waved must be brought with the fat portions of the offerings made by fire, to be waved before the LORD as a wave offering" (Lev 10:15a). Thus, the same materials on the same occasion could be referred to as both a contribution and a wave offering because the former refers simply to the fact that something was turned over to the Lord as a contribution while the latter refers to the manner in which the contribution was presented to the Lord. The manner of presenting a wave offering was apparently a conspicuous act meant to draw attention to the parts actually offered to the Lord in contexts where this needed to be communicated ritually. Therefore, *t^e nûpâ*, wave offering, was the broader term since it could also include a *t^e rûmâ*, tribute, contribution.

Milgrom has understood the meanings and connection between these two terms differently. He points out that *t^e nûpâ* is done "before the Lord," while *t^e rûmâ* is done "to the Lord," never "before the Lord" (Milgrom, 1991, 461). He concludes from this that "the *t^e nûpâ* must be a cultic ritual because the expression 'before the Lord' always refers to an action within the sanctuary. Conversely, the *t^e rûmâ*, which is always 'to the Lord', has no connection with either ritual or the sanctuary" (ibid., 462). The latter, in fact, "is carried out outside the sanctuary, without a rite" (ibid., 475). More specifically, "*t^{e}nûpâ* is a ritual of dedication that is performed in the sanctuary, with the result that the offering is removed from the domain of the owners and transferred to the domain of God" (ibid., 464), and even more precisely, "*t^{e}nûpâ* is a ritual of raising or lifting intended to dedicate the offering to God" (ibid., 470). It should, therefore, be translated "elevation offering," not "wave offering." Finally, "*t^{e}rûmâ*, then, is a necessary step preceding *t^{e}nûpâ*. An offering requiring *t^{e}nûpâ* must undergo a previous stage of *t^{e}rûmâ*, that is to say, its separation from the profane to the sacred" (ibid., 476).

There is much that is true and important in these observations, but his final conclusion is too rigid. He makes *t^{e}rûmâ* always prior to *t^{e}nûpâ* in the ritual sequence, rather than allowing them in certain cases to stand side by side as terms for the standard twofold distinction between certain priestly portions (i.e., the breast as wave offering and the thigh as contribution; see esp. Lev 7:29-34), with *hēnîp t^{e}nûpâ*, "make a *t^{e}nûpâ* offering," on occasion referring to the manner in which not only the *t^{e}nûpâ* but also the *t^{e}rûmâ* was presented to the Lord. His overly rigid conclusion forces him to argue for diachronic revision in two passages. First, according to Lev 9:21, at the inauguration of the tabernacle, "Aaron waved the breasts and the right thigh (of the communal peace offerings) before the LORD as a wave offering, as Moses commanded." He argues here that "and the right thigh" is due to a later hand. Second, as noted above, according to 10:14-15 both the *t^{e}nûpâ* breast and the *t^{e}rûmâ* thigh were to be presented as a *t^{e}nûpâ*. Milgrom argues that the whole of v. 15 must have been added later and develops an extended explanation of the historical development of prebend regulations from this supposed datum (ibid., 477-81).

4. It is especially significant that these two terms also occur together in the ordination offering ritual for the consecration and ordination of the priests (Exod 29:22-28). Here, as in all peace offerings, the breast is a wave offering (v. 26; cf. Lev 7:30-31), and the right thigh is a contribution that is waved (Exod 29:22, 24, 27), but the latter is then consumed on the altar rather than eaten by the priests (vv. 22, 25; Moses received the normal wave offering breast as his prebend for functioning as the priest here, Exod 29:26; Lev 8:29). This was not the normal procedure (cf. Lev 7:32-33). The summary in 7:37 refers to all five of the major offerings and adds one, the ordination offering (i.e., the installation offering; cf. the use of this term for stones to be set [i.e., installed] in their settings, Exod 25:7; 35:9, 27; 1 Chron 29:2). There are no special directions given for this offering in Lev 1-7 because it was on all counts basically a peace offering. Even the associated grain offering is mentioned (Exod 29:23, 32; Lev 8:26, 31).

This was, however, a special kind of peace offering, one that was only offered in the tabernacle for the installation of the priests in their office (see only Exod 29:19-34 and Lev 7:37 with 8:22-33). Also, the prescribed animal was a ram, even though the peace offering could normally be either a male or a female of the herd, the flock, or the goats (Lev 3:1, 6). The point is that this is a modified peace offering which was modified in a manner similar to the sin offering presented on the behalf of the priest or the congregation (i.e., the meat normally eaten by the priests was burned, not eaten, in these instances, 6:30[23]).

P-B 1. The Qumran Temple Scroll calls for the ordination offering as an annual obligation (11QT 15:12; cf. the remarks in Yadin, 2:61), recounts the standard regulations for the wave and heave offerings (11QT 20:14-21:05; 22:8-14; see Yadin 2:90-93 and 100-101), and develops the *t^enûpâ* and *t^erûmâ* and other regulations underlying Deut 18:1-8 in some detail beyond those delineated in the HB (11QT 50:1-10; Yadin 1:163-68 and 2:271-73).

2. The term *t^enûpâ* occurs nowhere else in the Qumran sectarian documents, but the hi. vb. *nwp* I, to wave, move, shake, occurs, for example, in the War Scroll: "And you, the sons of His Covenant, be strong in the ordeal of God! His mysteries shall uphold you until He moves His hand for His trials to come to an end" (1QM 17:9; translation from Vermes, 123). A few other instances refer to the "lifting" or not lifting of the hand as an indication of strength or the lack thereof (e.g., the Thanksgiving Hymns, 1QH 8:22, 33; 17:26).

3. The LXX uses several different terms to render *t^enûpâ*, some meaning tribute and some additional (offering). The concept of the wave offering does not seem to cross over into the NT. The rabbis thought the wave offering referred to the presentation of an offering to the Lord in a horizontal motion of "extending and bringing back" (Milgrom, 1991, 461).

Offering, sacrifice: → *'azkārâ* (sign-offering, # 260); → *'iššeh* (offering by fire, # 852); → *'āšām* (guilt offering, # 871); → *zbḥ* (slaughter, sacrifice, # 2284); → *ḥaṭṭā'at* (sin offering, # 2633); → *ṭbḥ* (slaughter, # 3180); → *minḥâ* (gift, present, offering, sacrifice, # 4966); → *ma^{a}śēr* (tithe, # 5130); → *ndr* (make a vow, # 5623); → *nwp* I (move back and forth, wave, # 5677); → *nsk* I (pour out, be consecrated, libation, # 5818); → *'ōlâ* I (burnt offering, # 6592); → *'^{a}rîsâ* (meal/dough offering, # 6881); → *qorbān* (offering, gift, # 7933); → *šḥṭ* I (slaughter, # 8821); → *šelem* (settlement sacrifice, # 8968); → *tāmîd* (regular offering, # 9458); → *t^erûmâ* (tribute, contribution, # 9556); → **Aaron: Theology**; → **Offering: Theology**; → **Priests and Levites: Theology**

Bibliography

TWAT 5:318-22; G. A. Anderson, "Sacrifice and Sacrificial Offerings (OT)," *ABD*, 1992, 5:870-86; idem, *Sacrifices and Offerings in Ancient Israel*, HSM, 41, 1987; H. Danby, *The Mishnah*, 1933; T. H. Gaster, "The Service of the Sanctuary: A Study in Hebrew Survivals," *Melanges syriens offerts a Monsieur Rene Dussaud*, 2, 1939, 577-82; J. E. Hartley, *Leviticus*, WBC, 1992; D. R. Hillers, "Ugaritic *šnpt* 'Wave-Offerings'," *BASOR* 198, April 1970, 42; B. A. Levine, *Leviticus*, The JPS Torah Commentary, 1989; J. Milgrom, "The Alleged Wave-Offering in Israel and the Ancient Near East," *IEJ* 22, 1972, 33-38 and reprinted in his *Studies in Cultic Terminology*, SJLA 36, 1983, 133-38; idem, *Leviticus 1-16*, AB, 1991; idem, *Numbers*, The JPS Torah Commentary, 1990; idem, "The Shoulder for the Levites," in Yadin, *The Temple Scroll*, 1, 1983, 169-76; R. Rendtorff, *Leviticus*, BKAT III3, 1992; J.-M. de Tarragon, *Le culte à Ugarit*, 1980; G. Vermes, *The Dead Sea Scrolls in English*, 3d ed., 1987; M. Weinfeld, "Social and Cultic Institutions in the Priestly Source Against Their Ancient Near Eastern Background," *Proceedings of the Eight World Congress of Jewish Studies*, 1983, 95-129; G. J. Wenham, *The Book of Leviticus*, NICOT, 1979; Y. Yadin, *The Temple Scroll*, vols. 1-2, 1983.

Richard E. Averbeck

5678	נוף

נוף (*nwp* II), sprinkle (bed with myrrh) is a dis-leg. (# 5678).

ANE The vb. is cognate with Arab. *naffa*, sprinkle, and Eth. *näfnäfä*, drizzle, sprinkle.

OT The vb. occurs once in the q. (Prov 7:17, "I [the seductress] have perfumed my bed with myrrh"), and once in the hi. (Ps 68:9[10], "You gave abundant showers, O God," or Dahood [*Psalms* II, AB, 131], "Your generous rain pour down, O God," taking the impf. as an impv.). See also Sir 43:17, where the vb. is used with snow ("He makes his snow fly like birds" [*The Wisdom of Ben Sira*, AB, 486]).

BIBLIOGRAPHY

G. R. Driver, "Problems in 'Proverbs'," *ZAW* 50, 1932, 142.

Victor P. Hamilton

5679	נוֹף

נוֹף (*nôp*), nom. height (# 5679).

OT The nom. describes part of Zion (Ps 48:2[3]), but though associated with the Canaanite religious term *ṣāpôn* and cognate with Ugar. *np šmm*, it is probably no more than a simple superlative, viz., "the most beautiful peak" (Dahood).

Mountain, hill, high place: → *bāmâ* (cultic high place, # 1195); → *gib'â* I (hill, # 1496); → *har* (mountain, hill, # 2215); → *y^erēkâ* (thigh, rear portion of mountain, # 3752); → *nôp* (height, # 5679); → *m^eṣād* (stronghold, # 5711); → *'wz* (take refuge, # 6395); → *'lh*, go up, ascend, bring up, # 6590); → *ṣûr* I (rock, boulder, # 7446); → *ṣāpôn* I (north, # 7600); → *rwm* (be high, exalted, proud, # 8123); → *śgb* (be high, fortified, protect, # 8435)

Martin J. Selman

5680	נוץ

נוץ (*nwṣ*), q. distance oneself (# 5680).

OT The single occurrence in Lam 4:15, "When they flee" (*nwṣ*), is nontheological.

Elmer A. Martens

5681	נוֹצָה

נוֹצָה (*nôṣâ*), nom. feathers, plumage (# 5681).

OT The occurrence of this word has occasioned problems in two texts (Lev 1:16; Job 39:13b), but is unambiguous in two other texts (Ezek 17:3, 7). First, the meaning "plumage" does not fit in Lev 1:16. Several proposals have been made, one of which is reflected in the NIV: "crop with its contents" (see mg. note: "crop and the feathers"; see also *HALAT* 645). For the exegetical problems of Job 39:13b, see Hartley, *Job*, 509. Second, the word "feathers" (*nôṣâ*) applies to the plumage of a *nešer* ("eagle, vulture"). "A great eagle with powerful wings (*kānāp*), long feathers (*'ēber*) and full plumage (*nôṣâ*) of varied colors came to Lebanon. ... But there was another great eagle with powerful wings (*kānāp*) and full plumage (*nôṣâ*)" (Ezek 17:3, 7). So Ezekiel contrasts the glory of Babylon with the lesser glory of Egypt (see W. Zimmerli, *Ezekiel*, Hermeneia, 1979, 1:362-63).

Flying, wing: → *'br* (fly, # 87); → *gwz* (fly away, pass, # 1577); → *d'h* (fly swiftly, # 1797); → *ṭwś* (rush, dart, # 3216); → *kānāp* (wing, skirt, outermost edge, # 4053); → *mr'* (spring, fly?, # 5257); → *nôṣâ* (feathers, # 5681); → *'wp* I (fly, fly about, fly away, # 6414)

Birds, flying creatures: → *'br* (fly, # 87); → *bêṣâ* (egg, # 1070); → *barbur* (species of fowl, # 1350); → *gôzāl* (young bird, # 1578); → *dgr* (hatch eggs, # 1842); → *ḥ^asîdâ* (stork, # 2884); → *yônâ* I (dove, # 3433); → *ya'^anâ* (ostrich, eagle-owl?, # 3613); → *kānāp* (wing, skirt, outermost edge, # 4053); → *nešer/n^e^šar* (vulture [eagle], # 5979); → *'ôp* (flying creatures, # 6416); → *'ayiṭ* (birds of prey [collective], # 6514); → *'ōrēb* I (raven, # 6854); → *ṣippôr* I (birds, # 7606); → *qōrē'* I (partridge, # 7926); → *ś^e^lāw* (quails, # 8513)

George L. Klein

5684	נזה

נזה (*nzh*), q. spatter; hi. sprinkle (# 5684).

ANE The vb. may be connected with Syr. *ndy*, sprinkle; Arab. urinate, and Akk. *nezû*, spatter (*AHw*, 784a), void urine (*CAD* 11:200). See 1QS 3:9; 4:21.

OT The vb. occurs infrequently in the q., and here it is intransitive and carries the meaning to spatter (Lev 6:20; 2 Kgs 9:33; Isa 63:3). Much more common is the hi. with the meaning "to sprinkle, cast." All of these instances are in Exod-Num.

Several times there is reference to a sevenfold sprinkling, conveyed by the hi. of *nzh*. These are: (1) with the blood of the sin offering (Lev 4:6, 17; 16:14, 15, 19; Num 19:4); (2) with the oil mixture of water and blood used in the purification/cleansing of the individual with an infectious disease (Lev 14:51); (3) the anointing oil for the altar (8:11). Thus, there is a sprinkling on objects (altars, houses) and on people. It would appear in some of these instances that the purpose of sprinkling blood is purgative, esp. in conjunction with (1). So, the sevenfold sprinkling purges the Holy of Holies on Yom Kippur (16:14, 15, 19), and similarly purges the Holy Place when the High Priest sprinkles the blood before the veil either for his own sin offering or for the sin offering of the community. On the other hand, the multiple sprinkling of the altar in Lev 8:11 gives the altar additional consecration. In the case of Lev 14:16 and Num 19:4 the sprinkling of the blood is a dedicatory rite. Thus, sevenfold sprinkling can be either purificatory or dedicatory. Sevenfold sprinkling played a part as well in Mesopotamian cult, as is witnessed by this sentence, "and sprinkle it seven and seven times over the door and the handle of the door wedge" (*CAD* S:86a). More than likely a hyssop branch was used for such sprinkling (Lev 14:6; Num 19:18).

P-B *nzh* is rendered mostly in the LXX by *rhainō* or a related vb. The only exception is Isa 63:3 (q.), where MT's "their blood spattered my garments" is rendered by LXX "I brought down (*katagō*) their blood to the earth." Sometimes even within one chapter both *rhainō* and a related vb. may be used. For example, LXX renders *nzh* [hi.] in Lev 4:17 with *rhainō*, but earlier in v. 6 renders *nzh* with *prosrainō*. Or again, LXX renders *nzh* in Num 19:4 with *rhainō*, but later uses *perirainō* for the same vb. in vv. 8, 19, 21.

NT *rhainō* and related forms occur most frequently in Hebrews: (1) Heb 9:13, "the blood of goats and bulls and the ashes of a heifer sprinkled [*rhantizousa*] on those who are unceremonially unclean sanctify them so that they are outwardly clean"; (2) Heb 9:19, "Moses...sprinkled [*errantisen*] the scroll and all the people"; (3) Heb 9:21, "In the same way, he sprinkled [*errantisen*] with the blood both the tabernacle and everything used in its ceremonies"; (4) Heb 10:22, "let us draw near to God with a sincere heart...having our hearts sprinkled [rh*erantismenoi*] to cleanse us from a guilty conscience"; (5) Heb 12:24, "to Jesus the mediator of a new covenant, and to the sprinkled [*rhantismou*] blood that speaks a better word than the blood of Abel." Uses not in Hebrews are possibly as many as three: (1) possibly Mark 7:4, "...they do not eat unless they wash," where the reading *baptisōntai* appears in some manuscripts (B) as *rhantisōntai*, "unless they sprinkle themselves"; (2) 1 Peter 1:2, "who have been chosen...for obedience to Jesus Christ and sprinkling [*rhantismon*] by his blood"; (3) possibly Rev 19:13, where one reading for "he is dressed in a robe dipped in blood" is *bebammenon*, but a variant reading is "he is dressed in a robe sprinkled with blood," with different forms of *rhainō* (see J. M. Ford, *Revelation*, AB, 1975, 313-14, 320-21). At least in the five Hebrews references, especially as one moves to Heb 12:24, it appears that the writer is referring to the blood of Christ (by which a new covenant is initialed) sprinkled at Calvary as the antitype of the blood sprinkled around Sinai, which inaugurated the old covenant.

Sprinkling: → *'ᵃguddâ* (sprinkling brush, # 99); → *zrh* I (scatter, sprinkle, be scattered, scatter, spread, be strewed, # 2430); → *zrp* (sprinkle, # 2449); → *zrq* I (sprinkle, scatter, # 2450); → *mlḥ* II (sprinkle salt, # 4873); → *nwp* II (sprinkle, # 5678); → *nzh* (sprinkled, spatter, # 5684)

BIBLIOGRAPHY

TDNT 6:976-84; *TWAT* 5:322-26; *TWOT* 2:566; J. Milgrom, *Leviticus 1-16*, AB, 1991, 233-34; N. Snaith, "The Sprinkling of Blood," *ExpTim* 82, 1970, 23-24; T. C. Vriezen, "The Term *hizza* Lustration and Consecration," *OTS*, 1950, 201-35.

Victor P. Hamilton

5686 נָזִיד

נָזִיד (*nāzîd*), a boiled dish, boilage; pottage; (leguminous) stew (6x; # 5686; *HALAT* 645b).

ANE Cognates of this nom. appear to be limited to Heb. and its dialectal congeners (e.g., Sam. *nazzᵉd*).

OT The Heb. nom. *nāzîd* is related to the vb. *zwd/zyd* (q. boil, seethe; be presumptuous; hi. cause to boil; act presumptuously; → # 2326) and may derive either from a ni. pass. part. form (so GKC §85n) or from a hi. part. form *maqtîl/mēqîm* (GKC §85l; preformative **m* < *n* by dissimilation; cf. R. Meyer, *Hebräische Grammatik*, 1966-1972, §40, 5 [2:35]; cf. the hi. cognate *hēzîd*, cause to boil, in Gen 25:29).

The nom. seems to refer to a composite of legumes or vegetables cooked in water. A cognate acc. construction appears in Gen 25:29: *wayyāzed...nāzîd*, he [Jacob] boiled for his brother a boilage/porridge/stew, which is defined in v. 34 as *nᵉzîd ᶜᵃdāšîm*, a boilage/porridge/stew of lentils. The three uses of the nom. in 2 Kgs 4:38-41 suggest that a *nāzîd* consisted of a porridge/stew of herbs or, on this occasion, poisonous gourds that were cut up, boiled in a pot of water, and here symbolically purified with flour (cf. 2:21, where Elisha's salt symbolically purifies water), then poured out into individual servings. Hag 2:12, which assumes the ritual imputation of sanctity from consecrated meat to the fold of the garment used to carry it (cf. Lev 6:27[20]), presents a case against any secondary imputation of sanctity from the fold of the garment to other food that the garment may touch (including bread, stew [*nāzîd*], wine, oil, etc.).

P-B Postbiblical Heb. *nāzîd*, pottage, dish, appears in Mish. Ṭoharot 2:3, where it designates *nᵉzîd haddemaʿ*, a pottage/dish of (first)fruits [i.e., priest's-due], and in Ṭoharot 2:4, where it refers to *nᵉzîd haqqōdeš*, pottage/dish containing what is consecrated (Jastrow, 891a).

Food: broth, pottage: → *mārāq* (broth, stock, # 5348); → *nāzîd* (dish, boilage, pottage, # 5686)

Bibliography
J. Bottérro, "The Cuisine of Ancient Mesopotamia," *BA* 48, 1985, 36-47; J. F. Ross, "Food," *IDB* 2:(304b-8a) 305a; L. J. Wood, *TWOT* 1:239a-40a; Z. Yeivin, "Food: The Biblical Period," *EncJud* 6, col(s). (1414-18) 1415.

Robert H. O'Connell

5687 (*nāzîr*, consecrated, Nazirite), → # 5692

5688	נזל

נזל (*nzl*), q., hi. flow, trickle (# 5688); נֹזֵל (*nōzēl*), stream (# 5689).

OT 1. The terms used for drips and dripping have broad semantic ranges. The noms. *'ēgel*, drop, *delep*, drop, *mar* II, drop, *neṭep*, drop, and *rāsîs* I, drop, refer to drops of water or of dew. *zôb*, discharge, has reference to something other than water. It describes the bodily discharges in Lev 15.

Among the vbs., there is a variety of usages that can be distinguished according to the subjects that do the dripping or flowing. Many instances seem to be concerned with atmospheric precipitation of one sort or another; i.e., *nzl*, flow, trickle, *nṭp*, drip, in the q., *'rp* I, drip, and *r'p*, drip. *nzl*, flow, trickle, in the q., can also refer to flowing waters on the earth, whether found in rivers, streams, or wells. *pkh*, trickle, in the pi., is used in the image of water trickling from a corner of the temple. Organic substances can drip, including tears from the eyes (*nzl*, *dlp*) and bodily discharges (*zwb*, *ryr*). Other physical substances that can drip or flow include new wine (*nṭp* in the q.), honey, myrrh, and other fragrances (again *nṭp* in the q., and *nzl*), oil (*rss*), the 'juice' of mallows (*ryr*), and milk and honey (*zwb*).

Many of the same vbs. are used to describe nonphysical subjects such as righteousness (*r'p*, *nzl*), words/teaching (*nṭp*) in the q., (*'rp* I), and prophetic preaching (*nṭp* in hi.).

2. In Exod 15:8, *nōzᵉlîm* that "stand like a wall" appear in parallel with waters (*mayim*) and deep waters (*tᵉhōmōt*). The parallel passage of Ps 78:13 (Halpern, 52) uses "waters" (*mayim*). The association of *nzl* with flowing *mayim* (waters) on the land can also be found in Num 24:7; Ps 78:16; 147:18; S of Songs 4:15; Isa 44:3; 48:21 (the single example of a hi. form); Jer 18:14.

3. The vb. easily lends itself to poetic imagery. Jer 9:18[17] describes how "our eyelids" stream with water. Ps 78:44 uses the part. in parallel with "their rivers" to describe streams of blood. Prov 5:15, in an allusion to marital fidelity, commends the drinking of "running water from your own well." The fragrance of the beloved's garden may also "flow forth," *nzl* (S of Songs 4:16).

In Job 36:27-28 Elihu portrays God's great power and care for creation in the imagery of the clouds, whose rain benefits creation, including humankind, "He draws up the drops (*neṭep*) of water, which distill (*zqq*) as rain to the streams; the clouds pour down (*nzl*) their moisture and abundant showers fall (*r'p*) on mankind."

Similar is the use of *nzl* in Deut 32:1-2: "Listen, O heavens, and I will speak; hear, O earth, the words of my mouth. Let my teaching fall (*'rp*) like rain and my words descend (*nzl*) like dew, like showers on new grass, like abundant rain on tender plants." Here *nzl* has the sense of the necessity and blessing produced by the proclamation of God's revelation in God's creation. It, like rain, pours down upon the earth.

Isaiah affirms God's sovereignty in creation and in redemption as he proclaims God's purposes for his people. He confirms to the people that the Lord has his purpose in the Exile and in the restoration from exile (Isa 45:7). He alone is working out his plan (v. 6), and he will bring about the new order in which righteousness dwells, "You heavens above, rain down (*r'p*) righteousness; let the clouds shower it down (*nzl*). Let the earth open wide, let salvation spring up, let righteousness grow with it; I, the LORD, have created it" (v. 8).

Isaiah describes the new state against the backdrop of the Exodus and wilderness wandering, "They did not thirst when he led them through the deserts; he made water flow (*nzl*) for them from the rock; he split the rock and water gushed out (*zwb*)" (Isa 48:21). Isaiah proclaims the new act of God in the language of the psalmist, "He split the rocks in the desert and gave them water as abundant as the seas; he brought streams (*nzl*) out of a rocky crag and made water flow down like rivers" (Ps 78:15-16).

Does *nzl* appear in Judg 5:5, in the expression "the mountains flowed before the LORD?" Or should the vb. be repointed as a passive form of the root *zll* (→ # 2362), convulse, as found in similar contexts in Isa 63:19 and 64:3[2]? The repointing is accepted by Boling (108) and endorsed by Gray (425), who relates it chiastically to the "quaking earth" in v. 4. However, Hauser (31) finds that both the sounds of the words and the ideas in the previous line are continued in the line under discussion. He suggests that the water that dropped from the clouds now flows down the mountains.

P-B In 1QH 8.4 *nzl* is found in the expression "you have placed me by a source of flowing waters in a dry land." This usage was the most frequent one in the Bible.

Dripping, flowing, trickling: → *'ēgel* (drop, # 103); → *dlp* I (drip, # 1940); → *zwb* (flow, # 2307); → *ṭrd* (continuous dripping, # 3265); → *mar* II (drop, # 5254); → *ngr* (flow, gush forth, pour out, # 5599); → *nzl* (flow, trickle, # 5688); → *ntp* (drip, pour, # 5752); → *'rp* I (drip, # 6903); → *pkh* (trickle, # 7096); → *r^{e}wāyâ* (overflow, # 8122); → *ryr* (flow, # 8201); → *rss* I (moisten, # 8272); → *r'p* (drip, flow, rain, # 8319)

BIBLIOGRAPHY

R. G. Boling, *Judges: A New Translation with Introduction and Commentary*, AB, 1975; A. Globe, "The Test and Literary Structure of Judges 5, 4-5," *Bib* 55, 1974, 174-75; J. Gray, "Israel in the Song of Deborah," 421-55 in L. Eslinger and G. Taylor, eds., *Ascribe to the Lord: Biblical and Other Studies in Memory of Peter C. Craigie*, JSOTS 67, 1988; B. Halpern, "Doctrine by Misadventure," 41-74 in R. E. Friedman, ed., *The Poet and the Historian: Essays in Literary and Historical Biblical Criticism*, HSS 26, 1983; A. Hauser, "Judges 5," *JBL* 99, 1980, 23-41.

Richard S. Hess

5689 (*nōzēl*, stream), → # 5643, # 5688

5690	נֶזֶם

נֶזֶם (*nezem*), nom. ring, nose-ring (of woman), earring (of man or woman) (# 5690).

ANE Aram. *z^{e}mamā'*, muzzle, nose-ring, rein; Arab. *zimām*, nose-ring (cf. *HALAT* 646).

OT Always of gold when material mentioned (Exod 35:22; Hos 2:15; etc.). For a discussion on jewelry, see *'dh* (put on ornaments, # 6335).

Malcolm J. A. Horsnell

5691	נֶזֶק

נֶזֶק (*nēzeq*), nom. injury, damage (# 5691); נזק (*nzq*; Aram.), pe., haph. suffer injury/loss/damage (# 10472).

ANE Mari Akkadian often uses the vb. *nazāqum* in much the same way: *ana annī[tim] libbi bēli[ya] ammīnim izzi[q]*, "Why is (the heart of) [my] lord worri[ed] about th[is]?" (ARM 5, 53:17); *šīr bēliya ušazziq*, "He upset (the flesh of) my lord" (ARM 5, 71:26).

OT 1. The vb. is used only of threats to the interests of the Persian king (Ezra 4:13, 15, 22; Dan 6:2[3]).

2. Like the Aram. vb. *nzq* (# 10472), the Heb. nom. *nēzeq* refers to injury or damage suffered by the king (Esth 7:4): "disturbing" the king (NIV), "the loss (the king) would suffer" (NIV marg.).

Hurt: → *klm* (be shamed, humiliated, hurt, # 4007); → *mrṣ* (be hurtful, painful, irritate, # 5344); → *nēzeq* (injury, damage, # 5691); → *'ṣb* II (hurt, grieve, offend, # 6772)

Ronald F. Youngblood

5692	נזר

נזר (*nzr*), ni. dedicate oneself to a deity, forsake, desert someone, treat with awe, fast; hi. restrain o.s. from, accept the obligations of Nazirite (# 5692); מִנְזָר (*minzār*), courtier (# 4694); נָזִיר (*nāzîr*), consecrated, left to unfettered growth, one consecrated, Nazirite (# 5687); נֵזֶר (*nēzer*), consecration, ordination, diadem (# 5694).

ANE Akk. *nazāru*, curse; Aram. *nzr*, to vow, to make a promise (*KAI* 201 4); Arab. *nḏr*, show great reserve.

OT 1. The ni. is used to denote treatment with respect of the sacred offerings of the Israelites to the Lord (Lev 22:2), the act of fasting (Zech 7:3), the act of deserting/dissociation of oneself from the Lord (Ezek 14:7) and the act of self-consecration to an idol (Hos 9:10).

2. The hi. is used to denote the act of restraining oneself from things that defile (Lev 15:31; Num 6:3) or the acceptance of the obligations of the Nazirite (Num 6:2, 5, 6, 12).

3. (a) The nom. *nāzîr* refers to a person who marks his or her status of special sanctity or vow of self-dedication by letting the hair grow and abstaining from wine and strong drink. The Nazirite was a sacred person by virtue of a mysterious/divine endowment and/or the vow of his mother. In later times such a person acquired special status by a self-made vow. In the case of Samson no razor should be used on his head, because he was to be a Nazirite, set apart to God from birth (Judg 13:5, 7; 16:17).

(b) In a Nazirite's status the motif of consecration predominated. They were devotees who separated themselves, or found themselves separated, to God (Num 6:2,

6-8, 12; Judg 13:5, 7; 16:17). The consecration was not an ascetic separation but an expression of loyalty to God, in which forms of abstinence were illustrative rather than constitutive.

(c) The institution was standardized and regulated by law, so that any person who made a vow to observe a specified pattern of conduct could become a Nazirite for a temporary period (Num 6:18, 20). When the Nazirite vow was terminated, the Nazirite was brought to the door of the Tent of Meeting, where a gift was presented, the consecrated head shaved, and the hair burned. Hair symbolized the divine strength that was given to persons. The conclusion of the Nazirite vow was celebrated with a family sacrificial meal and the drinking of wine. Thus, the Nazirite was no longer primarily a sacred person because of a special endowment, but a person vowed to perform a sacred duty.

(d) Amos mentions the prophet and the Nazirite together as persons with a special vocation whose role has been frustrated (Amos 2:11-12).

(e) The nom. is also used to denote someone who is singled out from ordinary life for a specific aim (Lam 4:7). In this way, Joseph is separated to preeminence among his brothers in Jacob's death-bed blessings (Gen 49:26; Deut 33:16). Some suggest that the nom. designated Joseph as a warrior chieftain (*IDB* 3:526). In Lev 25:5, 11 the nom. is used metaphorically to denote untended/unpruned vines.

4. The nom. *nēzer* denotes the Nazirite's vow of separation (Num 6:5, 9) and state of separation (6:4, 5, 8). The nom. has also as referent a diadem. Kings wore a diadem as a badge of royalty or eminence (2 Sam 1:10; 2 Kgs 11:12; 2 Chron 23:11; Ps 89:39[40]; 132:18). The high priest also wore a holy headband as a sign of consecration (Exod 29:6; 39:30; Lev 8:9). See further # 5694

P-B The Mishnah says that the duration of a Nazirite's consecration was to be thirty days if such specification is lacking (*Nazir* 1:3). Gentiles could not become Nazirites (*Nazir* 9:1), but women and slaves could, though under certain circumstances a father or husband could void a woman's vow.

Holy, ban, consecration: → *ḥrm* I (banish, devote to the ban, # 3049); → *nzr* (dedicate oneself to a deity, # 5692); → *qdš* (be holy, consecrate, # 7727)

Bibliography
IDB 3:526-27; *THAT* 2:50-53.

Jackie A. Naudé

5694	נֵזֶר

נֵזֶר (*nēzer*), diadem, a sign of consecration (# 5694); < נזר (*nzr*), dedicate (# 5692).

OT 1. *nēzer* is associated with the root *nzr*, to dedicate, and is thus a symbol of dedication. Both kings and priests were dedicated to the service of God. In the case of Joash, at least, a copy of the covenant statutes was placed in his hands (2 Kgs 11:12; cf. Ps 132:11, 12; 89:39[40]), which associates the *nēzer* (Ps 89), or at least the kingly line (Ps 132), with the covenant and its statutes. Von Rad (cols. 211-18) considers the blessings of the covenant to be chiefly in mind here, but the circumstances surrounding the anointing of Joash (2 Kgs 11:1-21), and the character of Ps 89 and 132 as prayers for deliverance from trouble, make it likely that the covenant's sanctions and duties are as much in mind as its blessings (so also Gray, 518-19).

2. It is uncertain what form the *nēzer* took, except that it was worn on the head by kings (2 Sam 1:10; 2 Kgs 11:12; NIV crown) and by the high priest (Exod 29:6; NIV diadem). Though Saul wore a *nēzer* at his final battle (2 Sam 1:10), he is said to have been appointed by anointing (1 Sam 10:1) and proclamation (1 Sam 10:24), and there is no reference to his being crowned (cf. de Vaux, 103-6, 465). The *nēzer* was, however, an accepted symbol of kingship (Ps 89:39; 132:18). The high priest wore a *nēzer* on his turban (Exod 29:6). According to Exod 28:36 *ṣîṣ* was worn on the turban (→ *miṣnepet*) and inscribed "HOLY TO THE LORD." *ṣîṣ* usually means flower in OT (e.g., Isa 40:6-8), but there is an ancient tradition that in the context of the priestly vestments it meant plate (LXX *petalon*, Vg. *lamina*). According to Josephus (*Ant.* 3:178) this plate bore the name of God in sacred, that is, ancient characters. BTalm. Šabbat (63b) proposes that the *ṣîṣ* on the high priest's turban was a gold plate reaching across the forehead from ear to ear, and of two fingers' breadth. Others maintain that a flower symbol adorned the *miṣnepet;* see Egyptian parallels in it (so A. de Buck *OTS* 9, 1951, 18ff.).

Exod 28:36; 29:6; 39:30 and Lev 8:9 try to solve what could appear to be a contradiction by making *ṣîṣ* another term for *nēzer*. Noth (*Exodus*, 226) reverses the reasoning and understands *nēzer* to be another term for *ṣîṣ*, and supposes the high priest to have carried a golden flower on his forehead as a sign of consecration. He sees a parallel in the serpent worn by the Pharaohs for the same purpose. This equation, whichever way it is taken, may be reflected in Ps 132:18. "The crown (*nēzer*) on [David's] head will be resplendent." Here a verbal form of *ṣîṣ* is used for NIV "resplendent" (lit. "flower, flourish" LXX *exanthēsei*). On the other hand, Josephus (*Ant.* 3:178) considers the *ṣîṣ* to be a plate that forms but a part of the *miṣnepet* (see H. St. J. Thackeray's notes to *Jewish Antiquities* 4:390-91). Lev 8:9 refers to *miṣnepet, ṣîṣ* and *nēzer*, three of the major words for crown, diadem in OT.

The prominent position ascribed to the engraved plate declares the fundamental nature of the high priest as God's agent among the people. Its presence upon him (Exod 28:36-38) enabled him to carry the guilt for any blemishes or shortcomings there may have been in the offerings of the people. According to late rabbinic sources its power extended to making expiation for blemishes found in those who brought the offerings as well. However, its power was annulled if the priest himself were not a godly man (Milgrom, 3:512). If this reflects the ancient view, when a prophet (e.g., Hos 4:7-9) declared the priest to be ungodly, he made a grave charge.

The practice of marking men upon their foreheads whether for good (Ezek 9:4; Rev 7:3; 14:1) or for ill (Rev 13:16; 17:5) sets a context within which the significance of the high priest's *nēzer* can be considered.

Crown: → *ktr* III (wear as ornament, # 4194); → *'ṭr* (surround, crown, # 6496/7)

Clothing—Turban: → *ṭᵉbûlîm* (turban, # 3178); → *miṣnepet* (turban, diadem, # 5200); → *nēzer* (diadem, # 5694); → *ṣānîp* (turban, diadem, # 7565)

BIBLIOGRAPHY

NIDNTT 1:405-6; *TDNT* 7:615-36; A. deBuck, "La fleur au front du grandprêtre," *OTS* 9, 1951, 18-30; J. Gray, *1 & 2 Kings*, 1964, 518-19; J. Milgrom, *Leviticus 1-16*, AB 3, 1991, 511-13;

M. Noth, *Exodus*, 1962, 226; G. von Rad, *Das judische Königsritual*, 72, 1947, cols. 211-18; R. de Vaux, *AncIsr*, 1961, 103-6, 465.

Robert. J. Way

5695 (*nōaḥ*, Noah), → Noah

5697	נחה

נחה (*nḥh*), q. lead; hi. lead (# 5697).

ANE Arab. *nḥw,* go in direction of.

OT The vb. occurs 39x in OT, 11x in q. and 28x in hi. but with no discernible difference of meaning between the stems. Not unexpectedly in light of its predominant use in poetry and wisdom (24x, 18x in Ps), the vb. is to be taken metaphorically of (usually) divine direction in life and destiny. There are, however, many instances of human leadership in mundane circumstances as well as divine leading in physical or at least nonfigurative contexts.

1. *Human subject.* When his efforts to have Balaam curse Israel failed, Balak led (hi.) the false prophet to another place (Num 23:27). Job boasted of having guided (hi.) widows (Job 31:18), and David was extolled for leading (hi.) Israel (Ps 78:72). The commands of a father are to provide guidance (Prov 6:22); indeed, one's own integrity can guide the upright (11:3).

2. *Divine subject.* (a) Figurative uses of vb. The OT describes Yahweh as one who leads in general (hi. Ps 31:4; Isa 57:18 [eschat. context]; q. 58:11). More particularly, he leads the nations (hi. Ps 67:4[5]) and individuals, the latter in or toward righteousness (q. 5:8[9]; hi. 23:3), a straight path (q. 27:11), the everlasting way (q. 139:24), and concerning his will for them (hi. 143:10). This he can do even if one is in heaven above, the sea beneath, or at the very limits of creation (hi. 139:10). More literally, he leads his people to the rock (i.e., to himself; hi. 61:2[3]) or, as elsewhere, to Edom (q. 60:9[11]; q. 108:11). His means of leading is by light, truth, and otherwise (hi. 43:3; hi. 73:24).

(b) Literal uses of vb. In the nature of the case God as spirit leads indirectly through self-manifestations and other phenomena. The vb. *nḥh* occurs frequently to speak of this leading in and after the Exodus event (q. Exod 13:17; hi. 13:21; 15:13 [to his holy dwelling]; q. 32:34 [to Canaan]; Deut 32:12; Neh 9:12, 19; Ps 77:20[21]; 78:14, 53). Abraham's servant declared that God had led him to Rebekah (q. Gen 24:27; hi. 24:48), Job speaks of Yahweh's leading the Bear constellation (Job 38:32), and the psalmist says that God leads mariners to safe harbor (hi. Ps 107:30).

P-B LXX regularly renders *nḥh* by *hodēgō*; cf. Mish. Heb. *nḥy/nḥh,* bring to rest (Ex. R. s. 20).

Guidance, leading: → *nhg* I (drive, guide, # 5627); → *nhl* (lead, guide, # 5633); → *nḥh* (lead, # 5697); → *šš'* (lead a child, # 9255)

Bibliography

TWAT 5:334-42; J. A. Emerton, "Notes on Jer 12:9," *ZAW* 81, 1969, 182-91.

E. H. Merrill

5702 (*nāḥûš*, copper), → # 5733

5703 (*n^{e}ḥûšâ*, copper), → # 5733

5704 (*n^{e}ḥîlôt*, musical term), → # 2727

5705 (*naḥîr*, nostrils [of animal]), → # 5723

5706	נחל

נחל (*nḥl*), vb. denom., q. have or get as a possession or inheritance; pi. divide up for possession; hitp. possess o.s. of; hi. cause to inherit, or give as a possession; ho. be allotted (# 5706); נַחֲלָה (*naḥ^{a}lâ* I), nom. inheritance, property, permanent possession (# 5709).

ANE Arab. *naḥala*; Ugar. *nḥl*, *nḥlt*; Phoen. *nḥl* are all cognates to the Heb.

OT The nom. occurs 221x and the denominative vb. in its various forms 59x. The most common literal meaning of both refers to the division of the land within the kinship structure of Israel and thus signifies the permanent family property allotted to the tribes, clans, and households of Israel. The sense of kinship and of specially significant property inherent in the words leads to a wide metaphorical use, of which the most theologically important is the use of both nom. and vb. to express the relationship between Israel and Yahweh. There is a flexible "triangular" usage of both *nḥl* and *naḥ^{a}lâ* to signify the land as Israel's inheritance, the land as Yahweh's inheritance, Israel as Yahweh's inheritance, and even Yahweh as Israel's (or at least the Levites') inheritance.

1. *The land as Israel's inheritance.* (a) To begin at the most concrete level, the land that belonged to the individual Israelite and his household was his *naḥ^{a}lâ*. It was the land allotted to the family within the tribal division of territory (Num 32:18; Deut 19:14). The only two uses of the pl. *naḥ^{a}lôt* refer to these family plots of allotted land (Josh 19:51; Isa 49:8). The *naḥ^{a}lâ* was the place of the family's security (breached by greedy oppressors, Mic 2:2), the place to which one returned after assembly or battle (Josh 24:28; Judg 21:24), and the place of burial (Josh 24:30). The family patrimony was inalienable (Lev 25:23). It was not "owned" by the current generation, but was held from "the fathers" for the sake of posterity; hence Naboth's staunch rejection of Ahab's proposal (1 Kgs 21:3-4).

Sometimes the importance of kinship obligation (such as levirate marriage) and the importance of preserving one's own *naḥ^{a}lâ* might come into conflict, as the nearer kinsman to Naomi recognized when he refused to take Ruth along with Elimelech's land, because the economic cost of raising an heir to Mahlon while caring for his land might place too much strain on his own *naḥ^{a}lâ* (Ruth 4:5-6, 10). A similar conflict between the preservation of *naḥ^{a}lâ* and the kinship demand of vengeance is seen in 2 Sam 14:4-16 (esp. v. 16). The importance of having a share in the land through the family *naḥ^{a}lâ* is seen both in the strength of the prophetic attack on those whose economic and judicial actions threatened the fabric of such widespread family land holdings (Mic 2:2; cf. Wright, 104-9), and in Ezekiel's vision of the restoration, which seeks to ensure that even aliens will have a share in the blessing through being allotted their own *naḥ^{a}lâ* (Ezek 47:22-23), and also to protect the individual's *naḥ^{a}lâ* from the royal encroachment so prevalent in the preexilic period (46:18).

(b) In Israel's kinship structure, the extended family ("father's house") was the basic unit of the clan (*mišpāḥâ*; → # 5476) and the tribe (*šēbeṭ* [→ # 8657], *maṭṭeh*

[→ # 4751]). The division of land followed this social pattern, and so *naḥ^{a}lâ* can also be used of the territory of clans (Num 33:54; Josh 15:20; 18:28) and of tribes (Gen 48:6; Num 32:32). The Levites alone among the tribes had no tribal *naḥ^{a}lâ* (Deut 10:9; 18:1). Two principles operated at this level. (i) There was an ideal goal of broad equality among the tribal groups in the allocation of land. Groups should receive a large or a small *naḥ^{a}lâ* according to the number of names—i.e., presumably of family heads (Num 26:53-56; 33:54). (ii) Land should remain within such family patrimonies. The exceptional arrangements made in the case of Zelophehad, who had no male heirs and whose daughters therefore requested inheritance (which must have stood as legal precedent), only proves the strength of the basic principle of the inalienability of land within the broader kinship circle (Num 27:1-11; 36).

(c) Finally, at the national level, the land is portrayed as the inheritance of Israel as a whole. The occurrence of *naḥ^{a}lâ* or *nḥl* is less common in this national usage (the actual expression *naḥ^{a}lat [bet-] yiśrā'ēl* is found only twice: Judg 20:6; Ezek 35:15). Although it can obviously refer simply to the national territory as a geographical entity (Deut 19:3, 10), the use of inheritance language of the land as a whole is verging on the metaphorical, in comparison with the concrete meanings in (a) and (b) above, since it draws attention to that unique relationship between Yahweh and Israel of which the possession of this particular land was proof. It is associated with the divine promise to the ancestors of Israel (Exod 32:13; Josh 1:6; Ps 105:11); therefore to enter into and live on the land thus promised was to enjoy the inheritance (Deut 4:21; 26:1, and passim).

But because of the relational dimension inherent in the term, living in the land as *naḥ^{a}lâ* brought moral responsibilities. To do evil would also "bring sin upon the land the LORD your God is giving you as an inheritance" (Deut 24:4). Conversely, obedience and loyalty to the covenant demands would enable Israel "to feast on the inheritance of your father Jacob" (Isa 58:14).

The use of *naḥ^{a}lâ* or *nḥl* in relation to the national territory also speaks of the sovereignty of Yahweh in international history, as does the closely related *yrš* (→ # 3769) and *y^{e}ruššâ* (# 3772). Deuteronomy, so strongly convinced that Israel's possession of the land was by Yahweh's gift for their inheritance, saw the same hand of the same God in the national migrations and histories of conquest among the surrounding nations, affirming, e.g., that Yahweh had "given Ar to the descendants of Lot as a possession (*y^{e}ruššâ*)," in a way expressly comparable to what he was about to do for Israel (Deut 2:9, 11, 19, 22). Moreover Yahweh's sovereignty over other nations was such that he could promise to restore them to their own inheritances in the aftermath of the Babylonian ravages if they would turn to him, in terms that mirror the promise made to Israel in the same context (Jer 12:14-17). So the conquest of Canaan, through which Israel gained possession of what had been the inheritance of other nations (Ps 111:6; *naḥ^{a}lat gôyîm*), was not unique in itself (any more than the Exodus as a national migration was unique at one level, Amos 9:7). What made it unique was the context of election, redemption, covenant, and law that surrounded the events (Ps 111:7-9; cf. 147:19-20; also Deut 4:32-38).

The ultimately universal goal of these realities in the blessing of the nations themselves explains the paradox of the summons to the nations in Ps 47 to rejoice in the conquest by which God gave their land to be Israel's inheritance (47:3-4[4-5]). It was part of a history through which eventually they, the nations, would belong to the very people of Abraham themselves (47:9[10]; cf. 82:8; Isa 19:24-25, and 3. below). Hence, note the baffled grief when that history seemed to have been thrown into reverse by the nations' entering into Israel's inheritance, not in eschatological blessing, but in destructive violence and divine judgment (Lam 5:2). Beyond that judgment, however, the climax of God's purpose is seen by Paul to be the inclusion of the nations into the people of God through the gospel and in the Messiah, Jesus—a reality he describes using strongly OT inheritance language (Eph 3:6; cf. 2:11-22).

2. *The land as Yahweh's inheritance.* The land Israel gained possession of had been, at one level, the inheritance of other nations (Ps 111:6), but in a deeper sense, it could be given by Yahweh because it already belonged to him as his *naḥ^{a}lâ*. This use of this expression connotes not so much family inheritance (from whom could Yahweh have "inherited" the land of Canaan?), as a special, permanent, and precious possession. In the Song of Moses, one of the earliest poetic texts, the land is described as "the mountain of your inheritance," because Yahweh made his dwelling there (Exod 15:17). Hence, at one level of popular thought, to be driven out of the land as Yahweh's inheritance would be to be forced to worship other gods (1 Sam 26:19). The term conveyed the special love and care Yahweh had for the land (Ps 68:9[10]), and thus the special favor it was for Israel to be given it (Jer 3:19) and the special folly it was for them to mistreat it (2 Sam 20:19; Jer 2:7). The precious relationship of the land to Yahweh added poignancy and pain to the destruction of the land, the city, and temple, which represented the whole inheritance, by the Babylonians (Ps 79:1; Jer 50:11).

3. *Israel as Yahweh's inheritance.* The land, however, always stood as a kind of fulcrum in the primary relationship between Yahweh and his people. The precise expression *naḥ^{a}lat yhwh* occurs only 4x, two of which refer to the land (1 Sam 26:19; 2 Sam 20:19) and one describes "sons" (Ps 127:3). The fourth probably refers to Israel as a people (2 Sam 21:3). However, the use of the possessive suffixes "his," "my," and "your" *naḥ^{a}lâ*, all referring to Israel in relation to Yahweh, is found through a wide range of narrative and poetic texts and clearly expresses a strong theological conviction.

Possibly the oldest occurrence is Deut 32:8-9 (*ḥēleq yhwh* ‖ *naḥ^{a}lātô*), in which the origin of the special relationship between Yahweh and Israel is located before even the election of the ancestors, in the cosmic realm of God's sovereignty over all international geography. Such election for inheritance, in the context of God's universal creation and providence, is a cause of joy and blessing (Ps 33:12). The contrast between Yahweh and idols lies not only in the fact that he is "the Maker of all things," but also that Israel is "his inheritance" (Jer 10:16 = 51:19). Significant parts of the salvation history are linked with this, including the Exodus and wilderness (Deut 4:20 = 1 Kgs 8:51) and the gift of kings (1 Sam 10:1; Ps 78:71). It was thus a natural prayer that God as Israel's eternal shepherd would continue to save and bless his inheritance (Ps 28:9).

Such expectations were shaken, however, in the fires of judgment. Yet from Yahweh's standpoint, the necessity of judgment was so painful precisely because of the precious relationship between himself and Israel as his inheritance (2 Kgs 21:14; Isa 47:6). Jeremiah gave the most poignant expression to this feeling (Jer 12:7-9). The concept, however, could also be a vehicle for hope. Some of the most theologically profound prayers in the OT express the plea that Yahweh should restore Israel on the grounds of them being his *naḥ^{a}lâ*—a basis that suggests that the term had connotations of *permanent* possession (Exod 34:9; Deut 9:26, 29; 1 Kgs 8:52-53; Isa 63:17; Joel 2:17). Behind all these prayers lay the fundamental conviction that "the LORD will not reject his people; he will never forsake his inheritance" (Ps 94:14). Such confidence is related to the permanence of the relationship of sonship of Israel to Yahweh as father, which could be the basis of appeal even when the covenant appeared to have been shattered (Isa 63:16; 64:8; → *'āb* [# 3]; cf. Wright, 15-23).

Naturally, the attitude to those nations who attacked Israel was normally a hostile anticipation of Yahweh's judgment on them for their oppression of his *naḥ^{a}lâ* (Ps 94:5; Joel 3:2[4:2]). However, just as the land as inheritance could function eschatologically in relation to the universal hope of blessing to the nations (see conclusion to sec. 1, above), so also the language of inheritance applied to people could be amazingly extended to include other nations. This may be based on the understanding of God as universal ruler and judge of all the earth, on which basis all the nations could be called his *naḥ^{a}lâ* (Ps 82:8), or even offered by Yahweh to the messianic Davidic king as the inheritance attached to his status as divine son (Ps 2:7-8); but it is given remarkable eschatological force with the specific prophecy that even Egypt and Assyria, the archenemies of Israel, will one day be included in the composite description, "my people, ... my handiwork, ... my inheritance" (Isa 19:25). The hope of restoration of Judah as his inheritance is linked to the vision that "many nations will be joined with the LORD on that day and will become my people" (Zech 2:11). The beginning of the fulfillment of that hope in the NT gentile mission is, not surprisingly, described by Paul in the language of sonship and inheritance (cf. Gal 3:7, 14, 18; 3:26-4:7).

4. *Yahweh as Israel's inheritance*. A few texts reverse the direction of the previous section and give *naḥ^{a}lâ* or its equivalent an even more metaphorical sense. Just as Israel is the people specially bonded to Yahweh as *his naḥ^{a}lâ*, so Yahweh is the God bonded to Israel as *their* most precious "possession." Obviously such a concept did not threaten the universality of Yahweh in relation to the earth and all nations, but was another way of expressing the possessive relationship otherwise implicit in phrases like "the LORD our/your God" or "the LORD the God of Israel." By inversion of Deut 32:9, Yahweh is "the Portion (*ḥēleq*) of Jacob" (Jer 10:16 = 51:19), and the sense can be personalized as well (Ps 119:57; Lam 3:24).

The most interesting use of *naḥ^{a}lâ* for Yahweh himself, however, takes us back to the primary meaning of the division of the land and the tribal inheritances. Levi alone among the tribes was to have no territorial *naḥ^{a}lâ*. Rather, their economic survival was to be ensured through the gifts, offerings, and sacrificial portions brought by the rest of the people. All these would constitute their *naḥ^{a}lâ* (Num 18:20-32; Josh 13:14). And because these offerings were ultimately made to Yahweh, though physically enjoyed by the Levites, Yahweh himself could be described as the *naḥ^{a}lâ* of the Levites, "in exchange" for a territorial *naḥ^{a}lâ*: "They shall have no *naḥ^{a}lâ* among their brothers; the LORD is their *naḥ^{a}lâ*" (Deut 18:2).

5. *General meanings*. Both *naḥ^{a}lâ* and *nḥl* can be used in a weak or metaphorical sense simply to express what one may "get" as the "allotted" result of some action or in the context of some relationship (Prov 3:35; 11:29; 14:18). Particularly, it can describe what one "gets" from God in judgment for wickedness (Job 20:29; 27:13; 31:2-3), in blessing for righteousness (Ps 37:18; 119:111; cf. 61:5[6]—*y^{e}ruššâ*), in

protection and vindication (Isa 54:17), or through his natural gifts of creation (Ps 127:3). Negatively, it can be used to express the severing or denial of a relationship between human communities, as when the northern tribes rejected kingship of the house of David, first in the rebellion of Sheba (2 Sam 20:1) and later in the secession under Jeroboam (1 Kgs 12:16; 2 Chron 10:16).

Inheritance: → *yrš* I (take possession of, be dispossessed, drive out, destroy, dispossess, # 3769); → *nḥl* (have as a possession/inheritance, divide up for possession, # 5706)

BIBLIOGRAPHY
ABD 2:761-69; 4:143-54; *NIDNTT* 2:295-302; *TDNT* 3:769-76; *THAT* 2:55-59; *TWAT* 5:342-66; *TWOT* 2:569-70; E. W. Davies, "Inheritance Rights and the Hebrew Levirate Marriage," *VT* 31, 1981, 138-44 and 257-68; idem, "Land: Its Rights and Privileges," *The World of Ancient Israel*, 1989, 349-69; H. O. Forshey, "The Construct Chain *naḥ^{a}lat YHWH/'^{e}lōhîm*," *BASOR* 220, 1975, 51-53; C. H. J. de Geus, *The Tribes of Israel*, 1976; N. K. Gottwald, *The Tribes of Yahweh*, 1979, 237-92; M. Weinfeld, *The Promise of Land: The Inheritance of the Land of Canaan by the Israelites*, 1993; C. J. H. Wright, *God's People in God's Land*, 1990.

Christopher J. H. Wright

5707 (*naḥal* I, stream-bed, wadi, stream, tunnel), → # 5643

5709 (*naḥ^{a}lâ* I, inheritance, property), → # 5706

5710 (*naḥ^{a}lâ* II, infirmity, ill health), → # 2703

5714	נחם

נחם (*nḥm*), ni. be sorry, console oneself; pi. comfort, console; pu. be comforted, consoled, relieved (hapleg.); hitp. be sorry, have compassion, repent, comfort oneself, be relieved, ease oneself (by taking vengeance) (# 5714); נֹחַם (*nōḥam*), nom. pity, compassion (hapleg.) (# 5716); נֶחָמָה (*neḥāmâ*), comfort (# 5717); נִחוּמִים (*niḥûmîm*), consolation, comfort (# 5719); תַּנְחוּמִים/תַּנְחוּמוֹת (*tanḥûmîm/tanḥûmôt*), consolation (# 9487 and 9488).

ANE The root occurs in later Heb., and Christian Pal. and Jud. Aram. (*HALAT* 650; *TWAT* 5:367).

OT The detailed classification of the meanings of this root is difficult, but there are some firm starting points.

1. *The meaning of comfort or console.* (a) The vb. is used of being comforted in bereavement, as in Gen 24:67, "Isaac was comforted after his mother's death," and the cause of his being comforted was his new wife Rebekah. In 2 Sam 13:39 we read that David "was consoled concerning Amnon's death," which implies that he had got over his grief for Amnon and was again able to see Absalom, who had killed Amnon. We may also compare 2 Sam 12:19-23, where David no longer mourns after his child is dead; in v. 24 he comforts (pi.) his wife Bathsheba.

A similar use is found in Gen 38:12 of Judah. *HALAT* (608) separates this occurrence off as meaning simply "keep the time of mourning," but it seems likely that it includes the idea of "getting over the grief." In Gen 37:35, Jacob's sons try to comfort him (pi.), but he refuses to be comforted (ni.). In Jer 31:15 Rachel refuses to be comforted for the loss of her children. The pi. is used of David's well-meaning attempt to console Hanun after the death of his father Nahash (2 Sam 10:2-3 = 1 Chron 19:2-3).

(b) The meaning "comfort" is found in the ni. where it is not a case of bereavement but of some other sorrow (Ps 77:2[3]; Ezek 14:22; 31:16 [used metaphorically of trees]; 32:31).

(c) The pi. consistently means "comfort, console," although the contexts may differ and the type of consolation may vary: those killed in battle (Isa 22:4); those who suffer in exile (Isa 40:1; 49:13; Jer 31:13; Lam 1:2, 16-17; Zech 1:17; etc.).

In the psalms of individual lament, where comfort is sought, it is seldom possible to specify the nature of the distress suffered; see Ps 69:20[21]; 71:21; 86:17; cf. 23:4; 119:76, 82. The word is used in Job, mostly of Job's friends, in their attempts to comfort him (2:11; 7:13; 16:2; 21:34; 29:25; 42:11).

2. *The meaning of be sorry, repent, change one's mind.* (a) The word is used to express two apparently contrasting sentiments in 1 Sam 15, where God says, "I am grieved (*nḥm*) that I have made Saul king" (v. 11; cf. v. 35), but where Samuel also announces that "the Glory of Israel does not lie or change his mind (*nḥm*), for he is not a man, that he should change his mind (*nḥm*)" (v. 29). The explanation seems to be that God does not capriciously change his intentions or ways of acting. It is the change in Saul's behavior that leads to this expression of regret. The reference is notable as being one of the rare occasions when God is said to repent or change his mind concerning something intended as good (cf. Gen 6:6).

(b) In many cases the Lord's "changing" of his mind is a gracious response to human factors. Thus in Jeremiah we often read that repentance on the part of the people (usually *šwb*, but *nḥm* in Jer 8:6 and 31:19) will make it possible for God to repent, change his mind (*nḥm*): 18:8, 10; 20:16; 26:3, 13, 19; cf. 42:10. Note also God's response to Amos's pleas on behalf of Israel (Amos 7:3, 6).

(c) In other places we are told or are left to infer that the change is due to feelings of compassion for a person or people. The ni. sometimes means "have compassion." So the Lord "had compassion" on the people because of their groaning, although they deserved their punishment (Judg 2:18), and the people of Israel had compassion for Benjamin (Judg 21:6, 15) after they had vowed not to give them their daughters in marriage; having made a decision to punish them they tried to find a way of lessening the effects of the punishment (cf. Ps 90:13; Jer 15:6).

(d) In all but five occurrences of *nḥm* the subject is God. The vb. occurs in the set formula describing God as "gracious (*ḥannûn*) and compassionate (*raḥûm*), slow to anger and abounding in love (*ḥesed*), and he relents (*nḥm*) from sending calamity" (Joel 2:13; Jon 4:2, cf. 3:9-10).

3. The nom. *nōḥam* occurs only in Hos 13:14.

4. *niḥumîm* occurs in Isa 57:18 and Zech 1:13, meaning comfort/comforting. Hos 11:8 shows the emotional content that this word can carry: "How can I give you up, O Ephraim.... My heart is changed within me; all my compassion is aroused."

5. The words *tanḥûmîm* and *tanḥûmôt* are pl. in form and have the meaning consolation(s), comfort: Job 15:11; 21:2; Ps 94:19; Isa 66:11 (of Jerusalem's consoling breasts); Jer 16:7.

6. *neḥāmâ* also means comfort or consolation (Job 6:10; Ps 119:50).

Compassion, comfort, consolation: → *ḥws* (pity, look upon with compassion or regret, # 2571); → *ḥml* (spare, have compassion, # 2798); → *maʿadannîm* (dainties, comfort, delight, # 5052); → *nḥm* (be sorry, comfort, have compassion, repent, # 5714); → *ʿgm* (have pity, # 6327); → *rḥm* (love, have compassion, # 8163); → *taʿanûg* (comfort, delight, enjoyment, # 9503)

BIBLIOGRAPHY
THAT 2:59-66; *TWAT* 5:366-83; G. M. Butterworth, "You Pity the Plant: A Misunderstanding," *Indian Journal of Theology* 27, 1978, 32-34; A. H. Friedlander, "Judaism and the Concept of Forgiving," *Christian Jewish Relations* 19, 1986, 6-13.

Mike Butterworth

5716 (*nōḥam*, pity, compassion), → # 5714

5717 (*neḥāmâ*, comfort), → # 5714

5718 (*nᵉḥemyāh*, Nehemiah), → Nehemiah

5719 (*niḥûmîm*, consolation, comfort), → # 5714

5722	נחץ

נחץ (*nḥṣ*), urge; q. part. pass. only used (# 5722). The vb. may come from the root לחץ (*lḥṣ*), squeeze, press, oppress (→ # 4315), which is known in other Sem. languages.

OT This word is used in the OT only in 1 Sam 21:8[9], where David goes to Ahimelech, the priest at the Nob sanctuary, and asks of him a sword, saying that "the king's business was urgent." This was "a clever way of explaining why David was unarmed, and at the same time suggested that he was on a royal mission" (J. Baldwin, *1 and 2 Samuel,* TOTC). It should be said, however, that some suggest that rather than reading *naḥûṣ*, *neḥraṣ* should be read (cf. the vb. in Dan 9:26 with the sense of "decide, decree"). We are largely dependent on the context in 1 Sam 21 in giving meaning to the Heb. word.

Urgency: → *ʾwṣ* (urge, # 237); → *ʾns* (urge, # 646); → *nḥṣ* (compel, # 5722); → *pṣr* (urge, press, push, # 7210)

Francis Foulkes

5723	נחר

נחר (*nḥr*), q. snort; blow; pant at; pi. (?) to be angry at (# 5723); נָחִיר (*nāḥîr*), nostrils (hapleg. in Job 41:12; # 5705); nom. נַחַר (*naḥar*), snorting (# 5724); נַחֲרָה (*naḥᵃrâ*), snorting (# 5725).

ANE Arab. *naḥara*; Eth. *neḥra*; Tigre. *manḥar*; Akk. *naḫāru*, *nāḫiru*; Ugar. *ʾnḫr* (*UT*, # 246).

OT 1. The vb. occurs 2x. In Jer 6:29 (q.) the bellows (*mappûaḥ*) are said to blow fiercely (RSV, NIV) but in vain, for the wicked among the people of God cannot be purged since the ore (the people) is so impure (vv. 27-30). In S of Songs 1:6 (pi.) it most likely means to become angry with. Its object is indicated by the preposition *bᵉ*.

2. The noms. *naḥar*/*naḥ^a^râ* both refer to the snorting of horses (Job 39:20; Jer 8:16). Cf. Ezek 32:2 for a conjectural usage of the term.

P-B The LXX translates as follows: S of Songs (1:6), *machomai*, contend, strive; Jer (6:29) *argyrokopeō*, refine silver.

Animal sounds: → *g'h* (bellow, low [cattle], # 1716); → *hgh* I (groan, moan, sigh, meditate, muse, chirp, mutter, # 2047); → *nbḥ* (bark [dogs], # 5560); → *nhq* (bray [ass], shriek, # 5640); → *nḥr* (snort, # 5723); → *'yṭ* (yell, shriek, swoop down [w. shrieks], # 6512); → *ṣhl* I (neigh, shout, # 7412)

BIBLIOGRAPHY

M. Dahood, "Ugaritic and the Old Testament," *ETL* 44, 1968, 36 [35-45].

Eugene Carpenter

5724 (*naḥar*, snorting), → # 5723

5725 (*naḥ^a^râ*, snorting), → # 5723

5727	נחשׁ

נחשׁ (*nḥš* I), pi. seek or give an omen, practice divination (# 5727); נַחַשׁ (*naḥaš*), nom. magic curse, bewitchment, omen (# 5728).

ANE Arab. *naḥusa*, be disastrous, sinister, ominous; *niḥsat*, (evil) omen; *naḥs*, misfortune; Syr. *neḥšā'*, omen.

OT A complete list of texts is: Gen 30:27; 44:5, 15 (cf. 12, 16, 17, 20); Lev 19:26; Num 23:23; 24:1; Deut 18:10; 1 Kgs 20:33; 2 Kgs 17:17; 21:6 ‖ 2 Chron 33:6.

For a discussion on mantic practices, see *qsm*, practice divination (# 7876).

Malcolm J. A. Horsnell

5728 (*naḥaš*, magic curse, bewitchment, omen), → # 5727

5729	נָחָשׁ

נָחָשׁ (*nāḥāš* I), nom. snake (# 5729). Other noms. for snake, serpent, viper are: אֶפְעֶה (*'ep'eh*), adder (# 704); בָּשָׁן (*bāšān* II, cj.), serpent (# 1422); עַכְשׁוּב (*'akšûb*), viper (hapleg.; # 6582); פֶּתֶן (*peten*), cobra (# 7352); צֶפַע (*ṣepa'*), viper (hapleg.; # 7625); צִפְעֹנִי (*ṣip'ōnî*), viper (# 7626); קִפּוֹז (*qippôz*), snake? (hapleg.; # 7889); שָׂרָף (*śārāp* I), venomous snake (# 8597); שְׁפִיפֹן (*š^e^pîpōn*), viper (hapleg.; # 9159). The vb. for a snake bite is: נשׁך (*nšk* I), q. bite; q. pass. be bitten; pi. bite (# 5966).

ANE *nāḥāš* I is related to the Ugar. *nḥš* and corresponds to the LXX *ophis.* The Heb. vb. *śrp* and Ugar. *šrp* both mean to burn and form the basis for understanding *śārāp* I as fiery (cf. Akk. *sārāpā*). The nom. *peten* and the conjectured *bāšān* I have many cognates, all meaning either literal or mythical snakes (Ugar. *bṯn;* Akk. *bašmu;* Syr. *patnā;* Arab. *baṯan*). The nom. *'ep'eh* corresponds to ESA *'p'w*, Arab. *'af'an,* and Eth. *'af'ōt.* For *'akšûb* there may be an Arab. root meaning to bend backwards. No Sem. cognates have been found for *ṣepa'* or *ṣip'ōnî*. If *qippôz* indeed denotes a snake, it would accord with the Arab. *qafāzat,* arrow snake. The *š^e^pîpōn* in Gen 49:17 is ignored by the LXX but translated as *šāfāfôn* in the Sam. Pent. The Akk. *šibbu* is a mythological snake. For *nšk*, cf. Ugar *nṯk* and Akk. *našāku*.

The snake was universally feared throughout the ANE and symbolized sovereignty, life, fertility, wisdom, chaos, and death. Dating back to Chalcolithic times, snakes in Mesopotamia appeared as cultic symbols on pottery and bronze castings. In the Gilgamesh Epic the wise serpent robs the hero of a plant that could give him immortality. Egyptian pharaohs wore headgear with an erect cobra in front, signifying divine power and protection. The snake, however, is also symbolic of death and chaos, evident in Marduk's victory over the sea serpent Tiamat and Re's subjugation of the evil Apep. The Canaanites borrowed the serpent symbol from the Hyksos and used it to represent the divine power of life.

OT 1. *Identification*. Palestine today is home to over thirty species of snakes; only six are poisonous. These species are presumed in nearly all biblical references to snakes. The "f" sound in many of the Heb. terms is likely onomatopoeic for the snake's puffing noise. The generic term is *nāḥāš,* which appears in parallel with *š^e^pîpōn* (viper, Gen 49:17, NIV), *peten* (cobra, Ps 58:4[5], NIV), *'akšûb* (viper, Ps 140:3[4], NIV), *ṣip'ōnî* (viper[s], Prov 23:32; Jer 8:17, NIV), *ṣepa'* (viper, Isa 14:29, NIV), and also refers to Leviathan, the monster *(tannîn)* of the sea (Isa 27:1). The adj. *śārāp* modifies *nāḥāš* to indicate either its reddish color or inflammatory bite (Num 21:6; Deut 8:15). Moses cast a bronze or copper (*n^e^ḥōšet*) snake, which was later named Nehushtan (Num 21:9; 2 Kgs 18:4). When *śārāp* appears as a nom., it indicates either seraphs (Isa 6:2, 6), the snakes in the wilderness (Num 21:8), or some other kind of snake characterized as *m^e^'ōpēp* (lit. flying; Isa 14:29; 30:6). The understanding of this last type as "flying serpents" rests on a report by Herodotus (3:107, 109), but the biblical description could also indicate a jab or prick, thus NIV "darting." Ps 58:4-5[5-6] associates the act of charming with the *peten,* likely the Egyptian cobra (also called *uraeus, Naja ḥaje*). It appears in parallel with *tannîn* (serpent[s], Deut 32:33; Ps 91:13, NIV), *'ep'eh* (adder, Job 20:16, NIV), *nāḥāš* (snake, Ps 58:4[5], NIV), and *ṣip'ōnî* (viper, Isa 11:8). The *'ep'eh* (NIV adder) may be the deadly sand viper (*Echis colorata*). The hapleg. *'akšûb* appears only in Ps 140:3[4], where it is clearly a snake (maybe the horned viper, *Cerastes cornutus*), though the Tg. and 11QPs^a^ understood it as a corruption of *'akbîš*, spider (cf. Job 8:14; Isa 59:5). The LXX translates it with *aspis,* asp (cf. Rom 3:13). The NIV translates both *ṣip'ōnî* (and the collective, *ṣepa'*, Isa 14:29 only) as viper. The MT's accentuation of Jer 8:17 understands *ṣip'ōnîm* as an attributive adj. modifying *n^e^ḥāšîm,* yielding the translation "deadly snakes" (the NIV takes the words as two noms.). This creature is likely the largest and most dangerous snake in Palestine, the yellow *Vipera xanthina.* The NIV construes the hapleg. *qippôz* (Isa 34:15) as a dialectical equivalent of *qippôd* (owl, as in 34:11; Zeph 2:14), and indeed the passage does concern birds, though some understand the creature as the harmless arrow snake (*Eryx jaculus*) or the common tree snake (*Coluber jugularis*). The *š^e^pîpōn* appears only in Gen 49:17 and may be the horned viper. The vb. *nšk* I usually refers to the biting of snakes but once metaphorically describes false prophets as biters, signifying the deadly effect of their appetite (Mic 3:5). In Hab 2:7 it forms a wordplay with *nešek,* interest in the financial sense.

2. *The Garden of Eden*. Genesis 3 introduces the snake (*nāḥāš*, LXX *ophis*) as one of God's creations, not a dualistic counterpart to Yahweh. Still, the snake is

exceedingly crafty (*'ārûm*, forming a wordplay with the adj. *'êrōm* in 2:25 and 3:7, meaning nude). This being is further distinguished from the other animals in the garden in that it is aware of divine matters, has the power of speech, and is clearly not "good" (1:31). Its shrewd conversation with Eve is full of half-truths: having one's eyes opened and becoming like God only result in shame and separation. The curse on the snake (3:14-15) is not an etiology concerning the age-old antipathy between human beings and snakes, but a rich theological statement full of reversals. Once more crafty (*'ārûm*) than all the animals, now it is more cursed (*'ārûr*); once superior, now it is inferior and must forever crawl on its belly. Although Tg. Ps.-J., Josephus (*Ant* I.1.50), and Gen. Rab. 20:5 claim the snake then lost its legs, the text is silent and may simply be interpreting its natural mode of locomotion. Eating dust is characteristic of an enemy's humiliation (Ps 72:9; Isa 49:23; Mic 7:17), and even when God restores creation's harmony and renders the snake harmless, its degradation will remain (Isa 11:8; 65:25 [*ṣip'ônî; peten*]). Creeping on the earth is the essential characteristic of unclean animals (Lev 11:42; Deut 32:24 of snakes). As for the relationship between the snake and the woman, affability turns to animosity. Genesis does not name the woman's seed, but from a canonical perspective this figure can only be Christ, who turns conflict into conquest (Rev 20:1-10). The enemy is Satan himself, appearing as a gigantic red dragon with seven heads and ten crowns—"that ancient serpent (*ophis*) called the devil" (Rev 12:1-9). The enmity (Gen 3:15) that God placed between him and the woman finally comes to full expression. No longer content to deceive, his intent is to wage war against all heaven (Rev 12:17; 13:4; 16:13-14).

3. *The Exodus.* The transformation of Moses' staff into a snake (*nāḥāš*) served two purposes: first, to weaken his resistance to obey God (Exod 4:1-5), and second, to strengthen Pharaoh's resolve to oppress God's people (7:8-13; the change in terminology from *nāḥāš* to *tannîn* in the second account is insignificant). This staff became the preeminent tool for the display of God's wonders in Egypt and at the Red Sea.

When the Israelites in the wilderness complained against Moses and God, he afflicted them with venomous snakes (*hann^{e}ḥāšîm haśś^{e}rāpîm*, Num 21:4-9; Deut 8:15). Healing from these deadly bites came only from looking at a bronze snake that Moses had made and elevated on a pole according to Yahweh's instructions. Interestingly, excavations in this region at Timna yielded a small bronze snake from a Midianite sanctuary (ca. 1150 BC). The Egyptians used snake models as charms to prevent snake bites, but in this instance the snake is an instrument of healing. While some suggest a Canaanite background for this bronze snake as a symbol of life (Joines), its meaning fits naturally into the inverse logic of the OT sacrificial system (Wenham). Just as innocent animals died to confer life to death-deserving worshipers, so the image of a dead snake becomes an agent that brings life. In Hezekiah's time the bronze snake reappears as an object of idolatrous worship named Nehushtan and is destroyed (2 Kgs 18:4). Even though the Bible is silent regarding the whereabouts of the bronze snake in the interim, the identification of Nehushtan with the Mosaic snake is entirely credible. Rowley, however, understands the snake as a Jebusite fertility symbol associated with the Zadokite priesthood and the narrative in the Pent. as an etiology explaining its later presence in the Jerusalem cult. Joines adopts a mediating position: Israel actually had two bronze snakes. Moses constructed his under Egyptian influence, but the alleged

Elohist interpreted it according to Mesopotamian notions of fertility associated with Nehushtan in eighth-century Palestine.

A prophetic oracle of judgment against Judah suggests a retrograde Exodus by mentioning a voluntary return through snake-infested territory (Isa 30:6; cf. Jer 8:17).

4. *Figurative and didactic use.* Snakes used in simile and metaphor indicate wicked behavior that wounds society (Deut 32:33; Ps 58:4[5]; 140:3[4]; Isa 59:5), the misery of a hangover (Prov 23:32), and the ultimate anguish of the wicked, whose pleasures are only short-lived (Job 20:14, 16). In prophetic rebukes, vanquished pagan nations will lick dust like a snake (Mic 7:17), and Egypt will flee in terror like a hissing snake (Jer 46:22; cf. Egypt as the sea monster Rahab in Isa 30:7). Isaiah warns the Philistines not to gloat prematurely over the Assyrian king's fall from power (Isa 14:29). By metonymy, this enemy ruler (likely Sennacherib) is called a staff (*šēbeṭ*), and although his power is broken, Philistia will yet suffer the might of his kingdom through his successors. Combining imagery of serpents and trees, Isaiah likens this king to a snake; from his root will spring a viper (*ṣepa'*), whose fruit will be a darting, venomous serpent (*ṣārāp* m^e*'ôpēp*).

The sage compares romantic love between a young man and woman to the motion of the eagle, ship, and snake, all of which move in an intriguing, undulating manner without leaving a trace (Prov 30:19). Amos likens those who mistakenly long for the Day of Yahweh to an exhausted man who leans against a wall only to be bitten by a snake lurking in its cracks (Amos 5:19). Qohelet uses snakes to illustrate life's uncertainty and the corresponding need for skill to live it (Eccl 10:8, 11; note the rhyming of *nāḥāš,* snake, and *lāḥāš*, the act of snake charming).

5. *Other creatures.* The word *śārāp* (→ # 8597) refers to literal and figurative snakes (Num 21:6, 8; Isa 14:29) as well as the seraphs in Isaiah's vision (Isa 6:2, 6), which need not be understood as winged serpents and thus symbols of sovereignty that have been imported from Egypt. The word *tannîn* designates a range of creatures, from those in the sea (Gen 1:21; Ps 148:7), to land snakes (Exod 7:9, 10, 12; Deut 32:33; Ps 91:13), to a mythological sea monster (Job 7:12) that signifies the kings of enemy nations (Jer 51:34; Ezek 29:3; 32:2) and appears in parallel with Leviathan (Ps 74:13; Isa 27:1) and Rahab (Isa 51:9). *bāšān* is a geographical name and may stand in Ps 68:22[23] as the extreme opposite of the bottom of the sea (cf. similar language in Amos 9:3), but on the strength of Ugar. evidence might also be another name of *tannîn,* the sea monster (Fensham).

P-B The LXX translators were apparently uncomfortable with the figures Rahab and Leviathan, twice omitting reference to these sea monsters (Job 9:13 and Isa 51:9; Ps 74[73]:14 B, Codex Vaticanus). In Isa 27:1 they construed "Leviathan the gliding serpent" (*liwyātān nāḥāš bārîaḥ*) as "the dragon, the fleeing serpent" (cf. Job 26:13 and Ps 89[88]:10 for similar interpretive moves).

Postbiblical literature frequently mentions the snake. It is a metaphor for temptation and deceit (4 Macc 18:8; Pss Sol 4:9) and strength (Add Esth 1:1e; 10:3d). Daniel killed a venerated snake (*drakōn)* in the Apocryphal Bel and the Dragon. The Pseudepigrapha picture Leviathan as a sea monster; in the messianic future the righteous will eat it in victory (1 En. 60:7; Ladder of Jacob 6:13; 2 Bar. 29:4). Unlike the Apocrypha (Wisd 2:24), the earlier parts of the Pseudepigrapha do not connect the snake in Eden to the devil (*Jub.* 3:17-25; *2 Bar.* 48:42), but eventually they are equated

(*3 Bar.* 9:7; Life AE 16:1-19:3; Liv. Pro 12:13) as in RL (Lev. Rab. 26 on 21:4; 'Abot R. Nat. 1 M). Jewish interpreters attributed credit for healing in the wilderness to God, not the bronze snake (Wisd 16:5-7; Ros Has. 3:8). The Qumran community understood the snakes of Deut 32:33 as metaphors for pagan rulers (CD 8:10, 11; 19:22, 23).

NT Figurative use of snakes continues with John the Baptist and Jesus calling the enemies of the gospel a brood of vipers (Matt 3:7 ǁ Luke 3:7; Matt 23:33). Jesus told his disciples to be shrewd as snakes (Matt 10:16; cf. Gen 3:1). In two similar sayings, he used the unlikely scene of a father's giving his unsuspecting child a snake as a didactic tool to encourage trusting prayer (Matt 7:10 ǁ Luke 11:11).

Images of the Edenic snake appear in a warning against apostasy (2 Cor 11:3) and in the Apocalypse (Rev 9:19; 12:9; 20:2). Images of the Edenic snake appear in a prediction of an imminent crushing victory over Satan (Rom 16:20), a warning against apostasy through deception (2 Cor 11:3), and in the Apocalypse (Rev 9:19; 12:9; 20:2). Ironically, when Satan tempted Jesus, he lifted a text from a psalm that, in fact, promises victory over the evil serpent (Ps 91:11-13; cf. Gen 3:15). The authority of the disciples to walk on snakes signals Satan's defeat and recalls the ancient promise (Gen 3:15; Luke 10:19; cf. the longer ending of Mark and Acts 28:1-6). To teach Nicodemus about eternal life, Jesus likened his future crucifixion and exaltation to the elevation of the bronze snake in the wilderness (John 3:14-15).

Animals: → *bᵉhēmâ* (quadrupeds, # 989); → *zānāb* (tail, # 2387); → *ḥᵃzîr* (pig, # 2614); → *ḥayyâ* I (animal, # 2651); → *keleb* (dog, # 3978); → *'akbār* (mouse, # 6572); → *ṣᵉpardēa'* (frog, # 7630); → *qippod* (hedgehog/owl?, # 7887); → *rmś* (creep, swarm, # 8253); → *šrṣ* (swarm, teem, # 9237); → *tan* (jackal, # 9478); → **Reptiles: Theology**; see the Index for Birds; Camel; Deer; Donkey; Dove; Flock; Gazelle; Insects; Lion; Maggot; Snake, etc.
Leviathan: → *liwyātān* (Leviathan, # 4293); → *tannîn* (sea creatures, # 9490)

BIBLIOGRAPHY
IDB 4:289-91; *ISBE* 4:417-18, 988-89; *NIDNTT* 1:507-11; *TDNT* 5:566-82; *TWAT* 5:384-97; *TWOT* 571-72; I. Aharoni, "On Some Animals Mentioned in the Bible," *Osiris* 5, 1938, 461-78; F. S. Bodenheimer, *Animal and Man in Bible Lands*, 1960, 65-68; G. Cansdale, *All the Animals of the Bible Lands*, 1970, 202-10; F. C. Fensham, "Ps 68:23 in the Light of Recently Discovered Ugaritic Tablets," *JNES* 19, 1960, 292-93; K. R. Joines, *Serpent Symbolism in the Old Testament*, 1974; idem, "Winged Serpents in Isaiah's Inaugural Vision," *JBL* 86, 1967, 410-15; idem, "The Bronze Serpent in the Israelite Cult," *JBL* 87, 1968, 245-56; H. H. Rowley, "Zadok and Nehushtan," *JBL* 58, 1939, 113-41; G. J. Wenham, *Genesis 1-15*, WBC 1, 1987; D. J. Wiseman, "Flying Serpents?," *TynBul* 23, 1972, 108-10.

Robert C. Stallman

5733	נְחֹשֶׁת

נְחֹשֶׁת (*nᵉḥōšet* I), copper, bronze (# 5733); נָחוּשׁ (*nāḥûš*), copper (# 5702); נְחוּשָׁה (*nᵉḥûšâ*), copper, bronze (# 5703).

ANE The meaning of the verbal root of the nom. is unknown, although the occurrence of cognate noms. is widespread in Sem. languages, occurring in Phoen., Palmyrene, Syr., Arab., and Eth.

1. The nom. *nᵉḥōšet* occurs about 140x in the OT. The term is normally translated "copper, bronze." The nom. may refer to copper as ore (Gen 4:22; Deut 8:9;

2 Chron 24:12), to copper as a material hardened with an alloy forming bronze (Exod 38:30; 1 Sam 17:5, 6; 1 Kgs 7:14; 14:27), or to a tool of bronze (Gen 4:22; Lev 6:28[21]; Num 16:39[17:4]; 2 Kgs 25:14; Jer 52:18). Congruent with the latter connotation is the use of the term to refer to fetters of bronze (Judg 16:21; 2 Sam 3:34; 2 Chron 33:11; 36:6; Jer 52:11). Most of the occurrences of the term appear in texts that describe the components of the tabernacle and temple. Copper items in these constructions include sockets (NIV bases; Exod 26:37), utensils (27:3), rings of the altar (27:4), as well as the "bronze" Sea (1 Kgs 7:23-27; 2 Kgs 25:13).

2. The cognate nom. *n^eḥûšâ* (# 5703) occurs 9x and also refers to "copper, bronze," as it is from the same root as *n^eḥōšet*. This metal was used in making materials such as tubes (Job 40:18), bows and arrows (2 Sam 22:35 = Ps 18:34[35]; Job 20:24), and gates (Isa 45:2). As a tough, durable metal the nom. took on a figurative meaning as it was associated with strength (Job 40:18; Mic 4:13). Another cognate form, the adj, *nāḥûš* (# 5702), occurs only in Job 6:12 with the same meaning (NIV bronze), where it qualifies the nom. *bāśār* "flesh."

3. The theological significance of "copper, bronze" is readily apparent from the fact that it was an essential metal used in the construction of the tabernacle and the temple in Jerusalem. In addition, it should be noted that in the listing of the covenant curses in Lev 26 and Deut 28, *n^eḥûšâ* and *n^eḥōšet* are used respectively to describe the discipline God will bring upon the earth and sky for Israel's disobedience. The idea seems to be that if Israel disobeys the Lord, one of the judgments the nation will experience is that of a scarcity of produce. Hence, the terms might rightly be considered to be components of "curse" language. The use of the terms in this parallel manner indicates that there was little if any difference in meaning between the two cognate noms.

NT In the NT one finds cognate terms *chalkolibanon*, *chalkos*, and *chalkion* for "copper, bronze." Of particular theological interest is the use of *chalkolibanon* in Rev 1:15 and 2:18 in describing the Messiah's feet. This appears to be a figurative expression for strength, a usage common in the OT. The imagery in the Apocalypse is similar to the description of the vision of the man in Dan 10:6 and of the creature in Ezek 1:7. Both of these passages contain the expression *n^eḥōšet qālāl*, burnished bronze. The LXX translations of the Heb. text in these passages is similar to the G expression of Rev 1:15 and 2:18. With the exception of gold, copper was the first metal utilized by man. It is rarely used in pure form, being often alloyed with tin to produce "bronze." In Palestine copper adzes from at least 3400 BC have been uncovered. Archaeologists have also uncovered copper spears, vases, statues, cooking utensils, and balances.

Copper, bronze: → *n^eḥōšet* I (copper, bronze, # 5733); → *sēper* II (bronze, plate, # 6220)

BIBLIOGRAPHY

ISBE 1:771; *TWOT* 2:572-73; *ZPEB*, 4:207-12; G. R. Beasley-Murray, *The Book of Revelation*, NCB, 1974, 67; R. H. Mounce, *The Book of Revelation*, NICNT, 1977, 79; H. B. Swete, *Commentary on Revelation*, 17; R. J. Forbes, *Studies in Ancient Technology*, 1972, 9:66-74; B. Rothenberg, *The Ancient Metallurgy of Copper*, 1990; K. H. Singer, *Die Metalle Gold, Silber, Bronze, Kupfer und Eisen im alten Testament und ihre Symbolik*, 1980, 45-48, 104-20.

Mark Rooker

5734	נְחֻשֶׁת

נְחֻשֶׁת (n^e*ḥōšet* II), nom. menstruation, lust (# 5734).

ANE Akk. *naḫšātu*, menstruation.

OT The nom. refers to the lust (of a harlot; NIV wealth). In Ezek 16:36 the imagery of a harlot is used to describe the behavior of Jerusalem. The guilty party is solemnly addressed and once more rebuked for the loathsomeness of her behavior in trifling away her husband's protection and throwing herself into the arms of strangers. She thus brings about her own punishment by the merciless justice of those strangers.

Sexual relations: → *'ešek* (testicle, # 863); → *zirmâ* (phallus, emission, # 2444); → m^e*bûšîm* (genitals, # 4434); → *nablût* (genitals, # 5578); → n^e*ḥōšet* II (menstruation, lust, # 5734); → *'gn* (keep oneself secluded, # 6328); → *'ōnâ* (cohabitation, sexual intercourse, # 6703); → *škb* (lie down, be ravished, be bedded down, # 8886); → *škh* (exhibit strong testicles, to have strong carnal desire, # 8889); → *šopkâ* (fluid duct of male organ, urinary tubule/organ, # 9163); → **Sexual ordinances: Theology**

Jackie A. Naudé

5737	נחת

נחת (*nḥt*), march down, descend, penetrate, settle (# 5737); נַחַת (*naḥat*), descending (# 5738); נְחִתִּים (n^e*ḥittîm*), marching down (# 5741).

OT 1. In the q. the basic meaning is descend (into battle, Jer 21:13 [NIV's "Who can come against us?" is more literally, "Who can come down against us?" a complacent rhetorical question implying invulnerability]; or into Sheol, Job 17:16; 21:13). The ni. has the meaning, penetrate, sink into, as in Ps 38:2[3]: "for your [viz., Yahweh] arrows have pierced me," a reference probably to some kind of illness. The notion of "to penetrate deeply" is also found in q.: "a rebuke impresses (penetrates) a man of discernment" (Prov 17:10). In the pi. the meaning is "stretch, press down, bend," or even "make a bow" (2 Sam 22:35 [=Ps 18:34(35)]), or lower the ridges or furrows by a soaking rain (Ps 65:10[11]). The only use of the vb. with the hi. is Joel 3:11[4:11], "Bring down your warriors, O LORD!"

Words related to the vb. are *naḥat*, descent, only in Isa 30:30, "The LORD...will make them see his arm coming down" (in judgment against Assyria), and *nāḥēt*, descending, marching down. The latter occurs only in the pl., n^e*ḥittîm*, and only in 2 Kgs 6:9, "Beware...because the Arameans are going down there [into battle]."

2. 2 Sam 22:35b (‖ Ps 18:34b[35b]), supported now by *HALAT* (654), is rendered by NIV as "my arms can bend (pi. of *nḥt*) a bow of bronze." Other renderings are "[God] who lowered the miraculous bow into my hands" (*Psalms*, AB, 1:103). To support both the translation "lowered" and the idea of lowering celestial weapons into the arms of terrestrial warriors, Dahood (115) appeals to *UT* 68:11, where the god Kothar lowers clubs for Baal to use against Yamm: *ktr ynḥt ṣmdn*, "Kothar lowers the two clubs." Another possibility is that the phrase in question should be translated, "he shaped the bows of my arms" (*II Samuel*, AB, 454). McCarter (470, 471) appeals to Arab. *naḥata*, hew, shape, dress (stone or wood), and suggests that Ugar. *ktr ynḥt ṣmdn* means "Kothar fashioned a pair of clubs." In favor of McCarter's reading is the fact

that the pi. of both Ugar. and Heb. *nḥt* means "to press down [i.e., engrave, fashion]" rather than simply "lower, descend," which is covered by the q.

3. The defiant question raised by the self-deifying Jerusalemites in Jer 21:13, "Who can come (down) against us?" is strange. Given the fact that Jerusalem is an acropolis, one might expect, "Who can come (up) against us?" Do they think of their would-be aggressors as birds, or do they think themselves impervious even to visitations by their high and holy God?

Marching, stepping: → *ḥšl* (unfit to march, straggle, shatter, # 3129); → *nḥt* (march down, descend, penetrate, settle, # 5737); → *s'n* (tramp along, tread, # 6008); → *pś'* I (step forth, march, # 7314); → *ṣ'd* (step, march, # 7575)

Victor P. Hamilton

5738 (*naḥat* I, descending), → # 5737

5739 (*naḥat* II, rest, calmness), → # 5663

5741 (n^e*ḥittîm*, marching down), → # 5737

5742	נטה

נטה (*nṭh*), extend, stretch out, spread out, bend down, turn, incline, divert, mislead, refused, disavowed (# 5742); מַטֶּה (*maṭṭeh*), tribe (→ # 4751); מִטָּה (*miṭṭâ*), bed (→ # 4753); מֻטֶּה (*muṭṭeh*), injustice (→ 4754); מֻטָּה (*muṭṭâ*), nom. stretching of wings (# 4755).

ANE Cognates in other Sem. languages are few. *HALAT* connects it with Arab. *naṭa*^{w}, spread out, and with Akk. *naṭû*, hit, beat, strike (cf. *AHw*, 768b, *CAD* N, part II, 113-14).

OT 1. The vb. occurs about 130x in the q., with the basic meanings of "stretch out, spread out, turn." The hi. occurs 75x, most frequently with the meaning "turn, incline." The ni. appears 3x (Num 24:6, Israel's tents appear from the heights to Balaam like stretched-out valleys or palm groves; Jer 6:4, the shadows of evening "grow long"; Zech 1:16, the stretching out of a measuring line over Jerusalem). There are many Eng. equivalents for *nṭh*. In the Psalter alone in the NIV renders the vb.: strayed from (44:18[19]); turned from (119:51); evening (102:11[12]); throw (17:11); turned to (40:1[2]); leaning (62:3[4]); slipped (73:2); set (119:112); parted (18:9[10]); plot (21:11[12]); turn aside (125:5); be drawn to (141:4); give (ear) (45:10[11]); turn away (27:9).

2. There is a cluster of uses of *nṭh*, all in the q. and with the object "hand" or "staff," in the narration of the plagues (Exod 6:6; 7:5, 19; 8:5, 6[1, 2]; 8:16, 17[12, 13]; 9:22, 23; 10:12, 13, 21, 22) or the victory at the sea (14:16, 21, 26, 27; 15:12). The subj. of the vb. can be Yahweh (6:6; 7:5; 15:12), Aaron (7:19; 8:5, 6[1, 2], or Moses (9:22, 23). The same motif is present with Joshua, except with the object "javelin" (Josh 8:18 [2x], 26). Note that the stretching of the hand and the use of the staff by Moses and Aaron, though like magical practices, do not serve any magical purpose in Exodus. They are not intrinsically powerful. The only power invoked is God's.

3. In a number of places there is a reference to God's outstretched hand. The phrase in Exod 6:6, *bizrôa' n*^{e}*ṭûyâ ûbišpāṭîm g*^{e}*dōlîm* ("with an outstretched arm and with mighty acts of judgment") should be distinguished from the phrase *b*^{e}*yad ḥ*^{a}*zākâ*

ûbizrôaʿ nᵉṭûyâ ("by a mighty hand and an outstretched arm") in Deut 4:34. This latter phrase also occurs in 5:15; 7:19; 11:2; 26:8, and in the literature influenced by Deuteronomy (1 Kgs 8:42; Ps 136:12; Jer 32:21; Ezek 20:33, 34; cf. also 2 Chron 6:32). "Mighty hand" may appear alone (Deut 3:24; 6:21; 7:8; 9:26; Josh 4:24), as may "outstretched arm" (Exod 6:6; Deut 9:29). Both expressions have their counterpart in Egyptian royal typology. Thus, in the Amarna texts there is reference to the Egyptian king's "strong arm" (*zuruḫ dannu*; in EA 286:12; 287:27; 288:14, 34) by Abdi-hepa, king of Jerusalem. For the phrase "outstretched arm" (cf. Egyptian *pḏ ḏrt*, or *pḏʿ*, or *pḏ ʾimnt*) and the representations of the outstretched arm of kings and gods in Egyptian iconography, see Keel, 158-60.

4. In several instances the vb. is used to describe one's relationship with God and his ways and word. For example, while the phrase "(not) turn to the right (n)or to the left" may be used for a promise given to the residents as they traverse their territory (Num 20:17; Deut 2:27 [with *swr* rather than *nṭh*]), the phrase also has a moral thrust, as in Prov 4:27, "Do not swerve to the right or to the left; keep your feet from evil." This phrase occurs in Deut (5:32[29]; 17:11, 20; 28:14) and in deuteronomistic literature (Josh 1:7; 23:6; 2 Kgs 22:2; cf. also 2 Chron 34:2, said of Josiah). In all of these references, except Prov 4:27, the vb. used is *swr* instead of *nṭh*, but the meaning is the same.

Of interest is the frequent use of *nṭh* with "heart" (*lēb*). Others can turn one's heart after other gods, as did Solomon's wives and concubines (1 Kgs 11:2, 3, 4 [all hi., but 1 Kgs 11:9 q.]). His sin of idolatry was actually more heinous than his sin of polygamy, and if polygamy is the agent or the means, idolatry is the sad end. On the other hand, one can turn one's heart to God (Josh 24:23), or God can turn a person's heart to him (1 Kgs 8:58). Note also the testimony (Ps 119:112) and the prayer (119:36; 141:4) of the psalmist. There are also instances where "heart" is not used, only *nṭh*, but the reference is still faithfulness to God and his ways (44:18[19]; 119:51, 157). In 44:18[19] "heart" occurs in the first line (with *swg*), "our hearts had not turned back," and in the second line, "our feet (*ʾᵃšur*) had not strayed (*nth*) from your path."

5. *nṭh* is used not only with hand and heart, but also with ear, and almost always in the context of prayer. All of these use the hi. (i.e., "cause your ear to bend/turn"). Those that are in the impv. and addressed to God include: Ps 17:6; 31:2[3]; 71:2; 86:1; 88:2[3]; 102:2[3] (cf. 2 Kgs 19:16; Dan 9:18). The idiom in Ps 116:2 is in the indicative rather than the imperative. On a few occasions in the Psalter the writer asks his audience to incline their ear to him (45:10[11]; 78:1), and this is the same line used by the wise father addressing his child (Prov 4:20). On occasion it is God who asks people to incline their ear to him (Isa 55:3).

6. There are several places in the OT where *nṭh* is used of subverting/perverting/thrusting aside justice (Exod 23:6; Deut 16:19; 24:17; 27:19; 1 Sam 8:3; Prov 17:23; Lam 3:35; Amos 2:7, all with *mišpāṭ* as the object of the vb.). Of particular interest is Amos 2:7-8, where the prophet uses the hi. of *nṭh,* but with different meanings. In v. 7 he denounces the people of Israel for "denying justice (*yaṭṭû*, hi. imperfect, 3rd pl.) to the oppressed" (lit., "they thrust/push the humble off the road/way"). In verse 8, the prophet continues, "They lie down (*yaṭṭû*, hi. imperfect, 3rd pl.) [or stretch themselves out] beside every altar on garments taken in pledge." As if to add insult to injury, not only are the people guilty of violating a fundamental law of justice and

fairness (v. 7), but even while by God's altar they are insensitive to the immorality of their acts (v. 8). With reference to Samuel's sons, 1 Sam 8:3 has two patterns of *nṭh*: "They turned aside (*wayyiṭṭû*, q.) after dishonest gain...and perverted (*wayyaṭṭû*, hi.) justice." The first is the means by which the second is accomplished.

7. The nom. *muṭṭâ*, stretching of wings, is a hapleg. in Isa 8:8, in which Assyria's invasion of Judah is likened first to the flooding Euphrates, and then to a bird who with "outstretched wings" covers the breadth of the land. The invading army will invade like a spreading flood, like a bird of prey spreading its wings.

P-B DSS; late Heb. (Jastrow 2:898-99).

Spreading, extending, stretching: → *hdh* (stretch out the hands, # 2063); → *zrh* I (scatter, sprinkle, spread, # 2430); → *ṭpḥ* I (spread out, # 3253); → *yšṭ* (hold out, extend, # 3804); → *mtḥ* (spread out, # 5501); → *nṭh* (extend, # 5742); → *npṣ* II (spread out, scatter, be dispersed, # 5880); → *pwṣ* (scatter, disperse, be spread, dispersed, # 7046); → *pzr* (scatter, scatter, spread, be scattered, # 7061); → *prś* (spread out, spread, # 7298); → *pśh* (spread [of disease], # 7313); → *rpd* (spread out, support, refresh, # 8331); → *šṭḥ* (spread out, pour out, # 8848)

BIBLIOGRAPHY
TWOT 2:573-75; O. Keel, *Wirkmächtige Siegeszeichen im Alten Testament*, 1974; M. Weinfeld, *Deuteronomy and the Deuteronomic School*, 1972/1992; idem, *Deuteronomy 1-11*, AB, 1991.

Victor P. Hamilton

5744	נָטִיל

נָטִיל (*nāṭîl*), nom. weigher of silver (# 5744).

The word occurs only in Zeph 1:11. For a discussion on weights → *šql,* weigh, weigh out, pay, # 9202.

Jerry E. Shepherd

5745 (*nāṭîa'*, plant), → # 5749

5746	נְטִישׁוֹת

נְטִישׁוֹת (*n^eṭîšôt*), tendrils, shoots (# 5746).

OT The word is found only 3x (Isa 18:5; Jer 5:10; 48:32) and lacks illumination from cognates. Isa 18:5, "For, before the harvest ... he will cut off the shoots (*zalzal*, # 2360) with pruning knives, and cut down and take away the spreading branches" (*n^eṭîšôt*, # 5746). In Jer 5:10 the word is used in a judgment scene, "Go through her vineyards and ravage them, but do not destroy them completely. Strip off her branches (*n^eṭîšôt*, # 5746), for these people do not belong to the LORD." Also, the larger context of 48:32 is a judgment scene, "Your branches (*n^eṭîšôt*) spread as far as the sea; they reached as far as the sea of Jazer." The term itself refers to good growth of foliage, but in all three uses in the OT it is found in a larger scene of judgment.

Shoot, bud, growth, sprig, sprout, tendril: → *'ēb* (shoot, # 4); → *gēza'* (shoot, stump, # 1614); → *zalzal* (shoot of vine, # 2360); → *ḥōṭer* (rod, shoot, # 2643); → *yôneqet* (shoot, stripling, # 3438); → *n^eṭîšôt* (tendrils, shoots, # 5746); → *nēṣer* (sprout, shoot, # 5916); → *ṣmḥ* (sprout, spring up, grow, prosper, make grow, # 7541)

Larry Walker

5747	נטל

נטל (*nṭl*), q./pi. lift, bear, carry, weigh (down) (# 5747); נֵטֶל (*nēṭel*), nom. burden, weight (# 5748).

OT 1. In a literal sense the vb. is used of the Lord, who weighs the islands as though they were fine dust (Isa 40:15). Figuratively, he has laid a yoke on a man in one situation (Lam 3:28) and lifted his people up in another (Isa 63:9). In 2 Sam 24:12 the Lord says to David, "I am giving you three options." "Giving" here is lit. "laying upon" (*nṭl ʿl*). The 1 Chron 21:10 parallel reads *nṭh ʿl*, lit., stretching out upon, which would be unique in the sense of give to. Some Heb. MSS read *nṭl* in 1 Chron 21:10, and that is the preferable reading in both passages.

The form *nāṭîl* (# 5774) is often given as a separate entry in lexicons. It is simply a q. passive participle of *nṭl*, however. Found only once (Zeph 1:11), it refers to those who trade with/in (lit., are weighed down by) silver.

2. The hapleg. *nēṭel*, burden, weight, is used of the heaviness of sand as a burden (Prov 27:3).

Burden, load, weight: → *ʾamtaḥat* (sack, bag, burden, pack, # 623); → *ṭʿn* II (load, # 3250); → *ṭrḥ* (burden, load, # 3267); → *y^{e}hāb* (burden, anxious care, # 3365); → *kinʿâ* (bundle, burden, # 4045); → *maśśāʾ* I (carrying, burden # 5362); → *nṭl* (bear, weigh, # 5747); → *nśʾ* (lift, raise high, pardon, contain, bear, exalt o.s., # 5951); → *sbl* (carry, bear a burden, # 6022); → *ʿms*/*ʿmś* (carry a burden, load, # 6673)

Ronald F. Youngblood

5748 (*nēṭel*, burden, weight), → # 5747

5749	נטע

נטע (*nṭʿ*), q. plant; establish; drive (# 5749); מַטָּע (*maṭṭāʿ*), nom. plot for planting, act of planting, plant (# 4760); נָטִיעַ (*nāṭîaʿ*), plant (hapleg.; # 5745); נֶטַע (*neṭaʿ*), nom. planting, plant, slip (# 5750); נְטָעִים (*n^{e}ṭāʿîm*), PN Netaim (# 5751).

ANE Ugar. and Arab. with the same meaning.

OT 1. The vb *ntʿ*, occurs 59x, all but once (Lev 19:23 in the ni./old passive of the q.?) in the q. stem. Although a metaphorical use is frequent, a literal sense also exists and dominates in the book of Genesis. God planted a garden in Eden (Gen 2:28), Noah planted a vineyard (9:20), and Abraham planted a tamarisk tree (21:33). Prov (31:16) and Eccl (2:4, 5; 3:2) continue to use the word with this meaning.

2. Deut 6:11 reveals a theological motif in the use of the literal sense as God's blessing is epitomized by Israel's enjoyment of vineyards and olive trees that they did not plant. In contrast to this stands the curse of disobedience as the landowner is pictured planting vineyards but not enjoying the produce (Deut 28:30, 39); they are instead given to Israel's enemy (28:31, 33) or devoured by the worm (28:39). The prophets capitalize on this figure in order to warn first Israel (Amos 5:11) and then Judah (Zeph 1:13) of the ramifications of their disobedience. Captive Israel is reminded that their repentance brings God's blessing, the return to the land to plant vineyards and gardens and to enjoy their product (Jer 31:5; Ezek 28:26; 36:36; Amos 9:14). Ultimately, a synthesis of the theme of blessings and curses is reached in

Isaiah's discussion of the new heavens and new earth (Isa 65:21-22). It is noteworthy that the vbs. *zr'* (→ # 2445), *ṣmḥ* (→ # 7541), and *štl* (→ # 9278) do not form the basis of a like motif.

3. A legal ruling is established in Lev 19:23, stipulating that in the first three years after planting fruit trees, the crop is forbidden and may not be eaten. The fourth year's crop was counted as the firstfruits and dedicated to God (v. 24). Deut 20:6 specifies that a soldier who has not yet completed this four-year process and begun to use the fruit of his vineyard is exempt from battle (cf. 1 Cor 9:7), lest he die and another man benefit, a sign of God's curse (Deut 28:30, 39).

4. The length of Israel's Babylonian exile was pictured as long enough to plant gardens and eat the produce (Jer 29:5, 28).

5. Metaphorically, Israel itself is the plant that has been transplanted from Egypt (Ps 80:15[16]) and planted in the Land of Promise (Exod 15:17). Although God cared for this choice plant, it produced only worthless fruit (Isa 5:2; Jer 2:21; 11:17; 12:2). God uprooted what he had planted (Ps 44:2[3]; Jer 45:4), sending Israel into exile. The majority of figurative use is, however, reserved for God's message of restoration. Echoing the keynote of the covenant with David (2 Sam 7:10), Israel was to be planted and disturbed no more (1 Chron 17:9; Jer 24:6; 32:41; 42:10; Amos 9:15).

6. Less frequently, Jeremiah records that God also established or planted the nations (Jer 1:10; 18:9).

7. Other figurative instances include the establishment of the heavens (Isa 51:16), the forming of the ear (Ps 94:9), the pitching of a tent (Dan 11:45), and the driving of nails (Eccl 12:11).

8. Built on the *qāṭîl* pattern common to other agricultural activities (e.g., *zāmîr*, vine pruning), *nāṭîa'* may have a pass. sense, that which is planted. The only BH instance of the word in Ps 144:12 is metaphorical, likening youthful sons to mature (*m^{e}guddālîm*) plants.

9. The Tgs. (*niṣbā'*) and the Pesh. (*neṣbā'*) translate the Heb. word *maṭṭā'* with a word meaning planting (place or act) or plant (slip, start). G and Eng. translations, possessing no term with a similar semantic range, have attempted to determine from the context whether the text refers to the act or place of planting, or the actual plant. No consensus has been reached. One possible distribution suggests that Isa 60:21; 61:3 refer to the act of planting, while Ezek 17:7; 31:4, 29; 34:29; Mic 1:6 designate the place. Although used literally at Mic 1:6, the word is used metaphorically elsewhere, referring to the place where Israel is to be eternally established (Ezek 31:4; 34:29) or to the direct act of God as he establishes them (Isa 60:21; 61:3).

10. All four occurrences of *neṭa'* can be understood as plant, slip. The semantic field may, however, include the meanings of the act of planting (Isa 17:11) or the place of planting (5:7). Used literally in Job 14:9, the sprouting of the rootstock is likened to the growth of a young plant. Isa 17:10-11 also designates literal plants, either in a picture of judgment (no harvest, v. 11) upon those who have forsaken God (NIV), or in allusion to the cult of a pagan god (RSV). In Isa 5:7, the conclusion of the Song of the Vineyard, *neṭa'* is a figure for Judah.

P-B 1. Sirach continues the figurative use of *nṭ'*: planting the humble in the land (Sir 10:15), establishing islands in the sea (43:23), and consecrating Jeremiah to build and plant (49:7). In addition to these familiar images, the prideful are pictured as having an evil plant that has taken root within (3:28[26]; cf. Heb 12:15). Although the Qumran community based much of their liturgy on the paradigm of blessing and curse, and used a derivative of *nṭ'* as a designation for their community (*maṭṭa'at 'ôlām*, eternal planting, 1QS 8:5; 11:8) the biblical pattern established on Deut 6:11 and 28:30 is not found. Similarly, the NT discontinues the theme of blessing and curse and Paul adapts the figure of planting to speak of the witness of the Gospel (1 Cor 3:6-8; cf. 4Q504 1-2 ii:13).

2. The Qumran texts use *maṭṭā'* with the same semantic range as the Bible (1QH 7:19; 16:5, 20, 21). The fem. form *maṭṭa'at* (not BH) is used frequently as a designation for the community (*maṭṭa'at 'ôlām,* eternal planting, 1QS 8:5; 11:8; 1QH 6:15; 8:6; 4Q418 81:13; cf. 1QH 8:10). The Qumran theme is not present in the NT.

3. *neṭa'* is used literally at Sir 3:9b (plant) and 40:19c (plantation?). For Sir 3:28[26b], an evil plant that has taken root in the heart of the proud, see Heb 12:15. The only occurrence in the Qumran texts (4Q266 13 2) is with the expression *niṭ'ê hakkerem,* orchard plants, followed by *'ᵃṣê happᵉrî*, fruit trees (cf. Mic 1:6 with *maṭṭā'ê hakkerem,* planting *places* for a vineyard).

Planting: → *yônēq* (young child, infant, suckling, # 3437); → *nṭ'* (plant, establish, drive, # 5749); → *štl* (plant, transplant, # 9278)

Bibliography

TWAT 5:415-24; R. de Vaux, "The Cults of Adonis and Osiris: A Comparative Study," *The Bible and the Ancient Near East,* 1971, 210-37.

Martin G. Abegg, Jr.

5750 (*neṭa'*, planting, plant, slip), → # 5749

5752	נטף

נטף (*nṭp*), q., hi. drip, pour (# 5752); נָטָף (*nāṭāp*), nom. drops of stacte (→ # 5753); נֶטֶף (*neṭep*), nom. drop (# 5754); נְטִפָה (*nᵉṭipâ*), nom. earring (→ # 5755); טוֹטָפֹת (*ṭôṭāpōt*), nom. meaning uncertain; a kind of symbol (→ # 3213).

ANE Aram. *deir 'Allā* 2, 35-36 *ttpn*, drip (see Hackett, 132).

OT 1. In the q. the vb. is used in four ways. (a) It describes the actions of "the sky" and "clouds" (*'ābîm*) in pouring down "water" (Judg 5:4; Ps 68:8[9]). The psalmist makes a connection between the phenomena of nature, God's blessing on his people, and theophany: "The earth shook, the heavens poured down (*nṭp*) rain, before God, the One of Sinai, before God, the God of Israel. You gave abundant showers, O God; you refreshed your weary inheritance" (68:8-9[9-10]).

(b) A second usage appears in prophetic contexts, where it describes the transformation of creation and the great blessing of the redeemed in the imagery of mountains dripping with "new wine" (*'āsîs*). For example, Joel 3:18[4:18]: "In that day the mountains will drip (*nṭp*) new wine, and the hills will flow (*hlk*) with milk; all the ravines of Judah will run (*hlk*) with water. A fountain will flow out (*yṣ'*) of the LORD's house and will water (*šqh*) the valley of acacias." The use of *nṭp* in the hi. in Amos 9:13 is similar.

(c) A third usage is distinctive to poetic literature, where the imagery of lips or hands dripping with "honey" (*nōpet*) or "myrrh" (*môr*) expresses the joys and the deceptiveness of love. S of Songs 5:5, 13 gives such a positive expression, "I arose to open for my lover, and my hands dripped (*nṭp*) with myrrh, my fingers with flowing myrrh, on the handles of the lock. ... His cheeks are like beds of spice yielding perfume. His lips are like lilies dripping with myrrh" (cf. 4:11). The deceptiveness of love comes to expression in Prov 5:3: "For the lips of an adulteress drip (*nṭp*) honey, and her speech is smoother than oil."

(d) Of interest is the usage in Job 29:22, where Job describes his words as poured out upon others: "After I had spoken, they spoke no more; my words fell (*nṭp*) gently on their ears."

2. Other than Amos 9:13, the usages in the hi. describe prophetic preaching, whether in ordering Ezekiel to preach judgment (Ezek 20:46[21:2]), in commanding true prophets to stop preaching (Amos 7:16; Mic 2:6), or in referring to false prophets (Mic 2:6, 11). This usage may be illustrated from Micah. The prophet in dialogue with the false prophets cites them as saying, "Do not prophesy (*nṭp*) ... Do not prophesy (*nṭp*) about these things" (2:6). He responds by showing the folly of their way in that they open themselves up to deception and close themselves to the truth of God's word, "If a liar and deceiver comes and says, 'I will prophesy (*nṭp*) for you plenty of wine and beer,' he would be just the prophet for this people!" (v. 11).

3. The nom. *neṭep* appears only in Job 36:27, drops of water (*niṭ*^{e}*pê māyim*), where it is part of Elihu's description of God's creation of rain.

P-B 1QpHab 10.9, 1QpMic 10.3 (though this latter reading is disputed, see Horgan, 46, 60), and CD 19.25 use the hi. part. to describe "the one who proclaims (*nṭp*) the lie." CD 1.14 combines both senses of a preacher and the pouring or dripping of water in a reference to "the scoffer" who "pours (*nṭp*) over Israel the waters of lies." In a reference to Mic 2:6, CD 4.19 observes that "precept was a preacher (*nṭp*)." Again, CD 8.13 suggests a combination of the images of raining and preaching: "one who poured out lies preached (*nṭp*) to them."

Dripping, flowing, trickling: → *'ēgel* (drop, # 103); → *dlp* I (drip, # 1940); → *zwb* (flow, # 2307); → *ṭrd* (continuous dripping, # 3265); → *mar* II (drop, # 5254); → *ngr* (flow, gush forth, pour out, # 5599); → *nzl* (flow, trickle, # 5688); → *nṭp* (drip, pour, # 5752); → *'rp* I (drip, # 6903); → *pkh* (trickle, # 7096); → *r*^{e}*wāyâ* (overflow, # 8122); → *ryr* (flow, # 8201); → *rss* I (moisten, # 8272); → *r'p* (drip, flow, rain, # 8319)

BIBLIOGRAPHY

J. Hackett, *The Balaam Text from Deir 'Alla*, 1980; M. P. Morgan, *Pesharim: Zumran Interpretations of Biblical Books*, CBQMS 8, 1979.

Richard S. Hess

5753	נָטָף

נָטָף (*nāṭāp*), nom. gum resin (# 5753); < נטף (*nṭp*, drip, → # 5752).

OT Appears only in Exod 30:34 as one of several ingredients in the special formula for the incense that was to be burned only in the tabernacle.

Resin, balm, myrrh: → *mōr* (myrrh, # 5255); → *nāṭāp* (gum resin, # 5753); → *ṣ*^{o}*rî/ṣ*^{e}*rî* (balm, resin, # 7661); → *q*^{e}*ṣîa'* (cassia, # 7904)

Incense: → *l^e bōnâ* I (frankincense, white resin, # 4247); → *qṭr* (let go up in smoke, # 7787)

Gary H. Hall

5754 (*neṭep*, drop), → # 5752

5755	נְטִ(י)פָה

נְטִ(י)פָה (*n^e ṭi/îpâ*), nom. earring (with likeness to drop of water, BDB, 643; # 5755), cf. נָטָף (*nāṭāp*), drop (# 5753); < נטף (*nṭp*), q. drip, flow; hi. let drip, let flow (→ # 5752).

ANE Aram. *ṭiptēp*, *ṭ^e pā'*; Arab. *naṭafa*, to drip (cf. *HALAT*, 656); *naṭafat*, earring (ibid.).

OT Representative usage of the term is found in Judg 8:26; Isa 3:19.

For a discussion on jewelry, see *'dh* (put on ornaments, # 6335).

Malcolm J. A. Horsnell

5757	נטר

נטר (*nṭr*), q. keep (# 5757); מַטָּרָא/מַטָּרָה (*maṭṭārâ/maṭṭārā'*), nom. guard, ward, prison; target, mark (# 4766).

ANE *nṭr* is found in Aram. and Syr.; verbal and nominal forms appear in 1QH, 1QS, and CD; forms of *nṭr* continue in Tgs and in Arab.

OT 1. Of the nine occurrences of *nṭr*, six are verbal. Dan 7:28 contains the Aram. form (*niṭrēt*). The modest phonological variant *ṭ/ṣ* and semantic similarity suggest that *nṭr* and *nṣr* (# 5915) are equivalent. Both are synonyms for *šmr* (→ # 9068); however, usage suggests a nuanced difference between the two. The four occurrences of *nṭr* in the S of Songs (1:6 [2x]; 8:11, 12) relate to protecting a vineyard (used metaphorically) and its fruit. The other five usages all have wrath, anger, or grudge as the object nursed, suggesting that *nṭr* may be used as a technical term by some biblical writers. This usage is also attested in two DSS sectarian documents. In Lev 19:18 a human subject is commanded not to bear a grudge, but to have a genuine concern for one's neighbor (cf. Matt 19:19; Mark 12:31). The Lord is the subject in the other occurrences. He either retains anger against his people (Jer 3:5) and his enemies (Nah 1:2), or he does not nurse anger endlessly against unfaithful Judah (Jer 3:12) or the psalmist (Ps 103:9). Clearly the Lord may be justly angry with the rebellious of his people and his enemies, but he is generously moderate because of his compassionate and merciful nature.

2. *maṭṭārâ* (# 4766) appears 13x signifying a guard, the equivalent of *mišmār* (# 5464). It is an expression predominantly used in exilic and postexilic Heb., particularly employed as a part of the technical term identifying the place in which Jeremiah was held, the court of the guard. Neh 3:25 employs the same expression, although whether the reference is to the identical place is open to question. In the same book "the Gate of the Guard" is mentioned (Neh 12:39). Twice *maṭṭārâ* equates to a target toward which arrows are shot (1 Sam 20:20; Lam 3:12); this is an extension of the idea of a spot under surveillance. In Lam the poet sees himself as the target of God's arrows of wrath. Despite his depression, he finds hope in knowing that the steadfast love of the Lord never ceases, his mercies are endless (Lam 3:22).

Guarding, watching: → *nṭr* (keep, # 5757); → *nṣr* I (watch, guard, keep, # 5915); → *ṣph* I (keep guard, watch attentively, post, # 7595); → *šmr* I (watch, guard, revere, # 9068); → *šqd* (watch, wake, # 9193)

BIBLIOGRAPHY

TWOT 2:576-77; R. D. Patterson, *Nahum, Habakkuk, Zephaniah*, 1991; W. J. Odendaal, *A Compartive Study of the Proto-Semitic Root nṭr*, Stellenbosch (Master's Thesis), 1966; M. Held, "Studies in Biblical Homonyms in the Light of Akkadian," *ANES* 3, 1971, 46-55.

Keith N. Schoville

5759	נטשׁ

נטשׁ (*nṭš*), q. abandon, forsake; ni. abandoned, unattended; pu. unattended (# 5759); נְטִישׁוֹת (*n^eṭîšôt*), tendrils (→ # 5746).

ANE The Akk. *naṭāšu*, give up, has a similar meaning.

OT 1. Though much less common than *'zb*, the root *nṭš*—with 34 occurrences in q., 5 in ni., and 1 in pu.—has essentially the same meaning and a similar distribution. In five vv. *nṭš* is parallel to *'zb*: 1 Kgs 8:57; Ps 27:9; 94:14; Isa 32:14; Jer 12:7.

2. On several occasions it means "spread out" (branches, Isa 16:8) or "deploy" (army, Judg 15:9; 1 Sam 4:2; 30:16; 2 Sam 5:18). In Gen 31:28 *nṭš* means "allow." In Exod 23:11 *nṭš* is best translated "let lie (unplowed)" or "leave to rest"; the referent is the land during the sabbatical year. Num 11:31 uses *nṭš* of the quail that the wind "let fall." Isa 21:15 speaks of a "drawn" sword and Isa 33:23 of "loose" tackle.

Jer 18:14 has the vb. *ntš*, vis-à-vis *nṭš*. Normally the root *ntš* means "pluck up." In this text *ntš* is possibly a misspelling of *nṭš*; the latter meaning would fit better. Another possibility is that *ntš* is a metathesized *nšt*, a thrice-occurring root with the meaning "dry up" (# 5980; Isa 19:5, like Jer 18:14, uses it with "water" as the subj., which argues for the latter explanation of this anomaly).

Abandonment: → *bdd* (be alone, # 969); → *yāḥîd* (only one, abandoned, # 3495); → *nṭš* (abandon, forsake, # 5759); → *'zb* I (abandon, # 6440)

BIBLIOGRAPHY

TWAT 5:436-42; *TWOT* 2:577.

Robert Alden

5762 (*nîb*, fruit), → # 5649

5764 (*nîd*, shaking of the head), → # 5653

5765 (*nîdâ*, shaking of the head), → # 5653

5767 (*nîḥôaḥ*, soothing, pleasing), → # 5663

5769	נִין

נִין (*nîn*), offspring, posterity (# 5769).

OT The term occurs in the same three verses cited under *neked* (Gen 21:23; Job 18:19; Isa 14:22; # 5781). More exactly *nîn* designates immediate offspring, *neked* more distant posterity.

Descendant, offspring, seed: → *dôr* II (generation, # 1887); → *zr'* (sow, scatter seed, form seed, # 2445); → *yld* (bear, bring forth, be born, # 3528); → *nîn* (offspring, # 5769); → *neked* (progeny, # 5781); → *'ēqer* (descendant, # 6830); → *ṣe'eṣā'îm* (offspring, # 7368); → *ribbēa'* (member of fourth generation, # 8067); → *šillēš* (member of sixth generation, # 9000); → *tarbût* (brood, # 9551)

Victor P. Hamilton

5774	ניר

ניר (*nyr* II), q. break up (unplowed ground) (# 5774); נִיר (*nîr* II), nom. unplowed ground (# 5776).

ANE *nîr* is related to Ugar. *nr,* unplowed ground, (see *HALAT* 658).

OT 1. Whether the vb. and nom. from the root *nyr* refer to plowing virgin ground or plowing ground left fallow for sometime is not clear from the limited occurrences (see Carroll, *Jeremiah*, 157, and Holladay, *Jeremiah*, 129).

2. Prov 13:23 teaches that newly plowed fields (*nîr*) of nobles may produce much food, but in the end all will be lost if the venture is based on injustice (McKane, *Proverbs*, 462-63). The NIV has "poor" for "nobles," presuming that *rā'šîm* (MT) should be emended to *rāšîm*. There is no need for this conjectural emendation (Plöger, *Sprüche*, 157), since the MT makes good sense. (See further # 5776)

3. The phrase *nîrû lākem nîr* occurs in Jer 4:3 and Hos 10:12, the former probably being a quotation of the latter (Andersen, 568 and Holladay, 129). In both texts plowing unplowed ground is metaphorical for deep repentance. Just as the ground must be plowed to produce a crop, the hard heart must be broken to bear fruit. In Hos 10:12 breaking up unplowed ground is in anticipation of the coming of the Lord under the figure of the early rains: repentance will result in blessing. In Jer 4:3 breaking up unplowed ground is coordinate to not planting among thorns, since one function of plowing was the removal of noxious weeds that would inhibit a fruitful harvest. "The imagery is indicative of depth of repentance and a cleansing of the heart, and these are conditions of the renewal of a fruitful relationship with Yahweh" (McKane, *Jeremiah*, 87-88).

Plowing: → *'ēt* III (plowshare?, axe, # 908); → *gedûd* I (ridge, # 1521); → *ḥrš* I (plow, engrave, prepare, plan, # 3086); → *ma'anâ* (furrow-length, # 5103); → *nyr* II (break up [unplowed ground], # 5774); → *telem* (furrow, # 9439)

BIBLIOGRAPHY

F. Andersen and D. Freedman, *Hosea*, 1980; R. Carroll, *Jeremiah*, 1986; W. Holladay, *A Commentary on the Book of Jeremiah*, 1986; W. McKane, *Jeremiah*, 1986; idem, *Proverbs: A New Approach*, 1970; O. Plöger, *Sprüche Salomos*, 1984.

Mark D. Futato

5775 (*nîr* I, lamp), → # 5944

5776	נִיר

נִיר (*nîr* II), nom. ground newly broken and cleared (# 5776).

ANE Ugar. *nr* III (in conj. form *nr[t]*), newly broken land (*KTU* 1.16.III:10; *WUS*, 214, §1851; *CML*, 98).

OT This nom. occurs 3x (Prov 13:23; Jer 4:3; Hos 10:12) with the general meaning of unbroken soil. The prophets Jeremiah (Jer 4:3) and Hosea (Hos 10:12) exhort Israel to plow or break up their *nîr*. In both cases the nom. *nîr* II and the vb. *nîr* are cognates. Jeremiah connects his exhortation to break up this ground with the warning not to sow their seed among the thorns. The plowing of the ground removes the thorns and helps transform a wilderness of weeds to a source of abundant harvest. Jeremiah focuses only on the soil. He provides no contrast between good and bad seed, but only properly prepared or unprepared soil. If seed falls among thorns, it will produce nothing (cf. Matt 13:7), but the fault is not with the seed planted, rather the soil. The hard ground cannot be penetrated by scattered seeds; the harshness must be broken up first. For Hosea, the kind of seeds to be planted is of great importance. True, he also challenges Israel to break up their hard ground, exhorting them to plow the *nîr*, but he also urges them to sow the proper seed, righteousness (*ṣ*^{e}*dāqâ*), which will produce the fruit of unfailing love. Because they had sown wickedness (*rāšā'*), they reaped evil.

Prov 13:23 affirms that a poor man's field may yield abundantly, but the produce is often misappropriated (McKane, 462). Hubbard (346) translates the v.: "Much food is in the fallow ground of the poor, and for lack of justice there is waste."

At the very least, *nîr* II signifies land that must be broken up for planting and harvesting. Holladay (129) and Wolff (186) contend that *nîr* II refers to land that either has never been plowed or has lain fallow for a period of time. A number of scholars (Andersen and Freedman, 568; Craigie, Kelley, Drinkard, 67; McComiskey, 177; Thompson, 214) contend that *nîr* II must refer to virgin or unbroken soil, i.e., not ground hard from a lack of plowing, but virgin soil. It appears that there is insufficient contextual evidence, however, to require this more limited meaning of *nîr* II.

P-B Mish. Heb. *nîr* II, newly broken land; Jewish Aram. *nîr* II, newly broken land.

Field, ground, rural area: → *'ădām* IV (ground, # 135); → *bar* IV (wild, open country, # 1340); → *gāzēr* (infertile land, # 1620); → *ḥûṣôt* (open fields, # 2575a); → *yāgēb* (field, # 3321); → *m*^{e}*lēḥâ* (barren land, salt-plain, # 4877); → *mimšāq* (ground overrun with weeds, # 4940); → *m*^{e}*'ārâ* II (bare field, # 5118); → *nîr* II (ground newly broken & cleared, # 5776); → *'āqob* (ground [uneven and bumpy], crafty heart, # 6815); → *p*^{e}*rāzôn* (fertile field, # 7251); → *rekes* (rugged ground, # 8221); → *śādeh* (open country, open field, fields, domain, # 8441); → *š*^{e}*dēmâ* (terrace, # 8727); → *šāmān* (fertile field, # 9044)

BIBLIOGRAPHY

F. Andersen and D. Freedman, *Hosea*, 1980; P. Craigie, P. Kelley, J. Drinkard, Jr., *Jeremiah 1-25*, 1991; W. Holladay, *Jeremiah 1*, 1986; D. Hubbard, *Proverbs*, 1989; T. McComiskey, "Hosea," in *The Minor Prophets*, 1992, 1:1-237; W. McKane, *Proverbs*, 1970; J. Thompson, *The Book of Jeremiah*, 1980; H. Wolff, *Hosea*, 1974.

Michael A. Grisanti

5777	נכא

נכא (*nk'*), a byform of *nkh* (→ # 5782); ni. be whipped out, flogged out (only in Job 30:8; Ps 109:16) (# 5777); נָכָא (*nākā'*), adj. beaten, broken (hapleg. Isa 16:7; # 5778), נָכֵא (*nākē'*), beaten, broken (only in Prov 15:13; 17:22; 18:14; Isa 66:2; # 5779).

OT The adj. *nākē'*, beaten or broken, is a figurative expression for depression in the idiomatic usage with *rûaḥ*, spirit: "A cheerful heart is good medicine, but a crushed spirit dries up the bones" (Prov 17:22; see 15:13; 18:14). But in Isa 66:2 the expression "contrite (lit. broken) in spirit" signifies the humble with whom the Lord is pleased to dwell. True contrition comes to expression in submissiveness to God's word and obedience.

Beating, crushing, grinding: → *b'ṭ* (kick, # 1246); → *dwk* (pound, # 1870); → *dk'* (crush, be crushed, # 1917); → *dkh* (be crushed, # 1920); → *dqq* (crush, # 1990); → *hlm* (beat, # 2150); → *ḥbṭ* (beat from, # 2468); → *ṭḥn* (grind, mill, # 3221); → *ktš* (grind down, # 4197); → *ktt* (beat fine, pound up, disperse, # 4198); → *mḥṣ* (beat to pieces, # 4731); → *m'k* (press, squeeze, crush, # 5080); → *ngp* (strike, # 5597); → *nk'* (be whipped out, flogged out, # 5777); → *nkh* (be hit, be battered, ruined, destroyed, # 5782); → *ṣrr* I (bind, tie up, # 7674); → *r'ṣ* (beat down, # 8320); → *rṣṣ* (crush, mash, break, # 8368); → *šwp* I (crush, # 8789); → *šḥq* (grind down, # 8835)

Cornelis Van Dam

5778 (*nākā'*, beaten, broken), → # 5777

5779 (*nākē'*, beaten, broken), → # 5777

5780 (*n^ekō't*, resin), → # 7661

5781	נֶכֶד

נֶכֶד (*neked*), progeny, posterity, descendants (only in Gen 21:23; Job 18:19; Isa 14:22; # 5781).

OT One use of *neked* would suggest that the term designates grandchildren, the third generation (Gen 21:23). Abimelech the king of Gerar, with his commander at his side, asks favor of Abraham, a powerless shepherd, for the present moment and generations to come!

Descendant, offspring, seed: → *dôr* II (generation, # 1887); → *zr'* (sow, scatter seed, form seed, # 2445); → *yld* (bear, bring forth, be born, # 3528); → *nîn* (offspring, # 5769); → *neked* (progeny, # 5781); → *'ēqer* (descendant, # 6830); → *ṣe'eṣā'îm* (offspring, # 7368); → *ribbēa'* (member of fourth generation, # 8067); → *šillēš* (member of sixth generation, # 9000); → *tarbût* (brood, # 9551)

Victor P. Hamilton

5782	נכה

נכה (*nkh*), ni. be hit, be struck down; pu. be battered, ruined, destroyed; hi. strike, hit, beat, strike dead, wound, batter, destroy; ho. be struck down (dead), be taken, be hit (# 5782); nom. מַכָּה (*makkâ*), blow, stroke, wound, plague, defeat (# 4804); נָכֶה (*nākeh*), crippled, beaten down (→ # 5783); nom. נָכוֹן (*nākôn* I), kick (only in Job 12:5; # 5787).

ANE This vb. occurs in Old Aram. as *nky* (*DISCO*, 178). It probably entered Akk. as a WestSem. loanword, *nakû*, (*AHw*, 724a, *HALAT*, 658b; but, cf. *CAD*, N.1, 197a). Cognates are also found in Arab. and Eth.

OT 1. Of the 504x the vb. *nkh* occurs, it only appears in ni. once (2 Sam 11:15) and in pu. twice (Exod 9:31, 32). The vast majority of occurrences are in hi., with some in ho.

2. The meaning of the vb. ranges from hitting to killing. The vb. is used of one person hitting another (Exod 2:11, 13), striking one on the cheek (Ps 3:7[8]; Lam 3:30), clapping hands (2 Kgs 11:12), and killing (Josh 10:26; 2 Sam 2:23). Any manner of blow or smiting can be described by *nkh*, such as hitting a donkey (Num 22:23, 25, 27), a river (2 Kgs 2:8, 14), striking a house to demolish it (Amos 3:15; 6:11), hitting weapons (Ezek 39:3), a loaf striking a tent (Judg 7:13), smiting and so killing a lion or bear (1 Sam 17:35), or a lion killing a man (1 Kgs 20:36). The heart can strike one, in the sense that the conscience protests (1 Sam 24:5[6]). The sun and the moon can smite (Ps 121:6). A worm can strike a plant and kill it (Jon 4:7). A city can be struck and its inhabitants killed (Josh 19:47; 2 Kgs 15:16). Indeed entire nations can be smitten (Isa 14:6).

3. Israel was expected to strike (*nkh*), and even to wipe out utterly (*ḥrm*) the inhabitants of Canaan, "And when ... you have defeated (*nkh*) them, then you must destroy them totally (*haḥ*^{a}*rēm taḥ*^{a}*rîm*). Make no treaty with them, and show them no mercy" (Deut 7:2). Similarly, in Joshua the vbs. *nkh* and *ḥrm* (destroy) occur side by side, "That day Joshua took Makkedah. He put (*nkh*) the city and its king to the sword and totally destroyed (*ḥrm*) everyone in it. He left no survivors. ... They captured it that same day and put (*nkh*) it to the sword and totally destroyed (*ḥrm*) everyone in it, just as they had done to Lachish" (Josh 10:28, 35).

4. Beating has a role in discipline and teaching wisdom, "Flog a mocker, and the simple will learn prudence" (Prov 19:25a). Disciplining with the rod saves life, "Do not withhold discipline from a child; if you punish (*nkh*) him with the rod, he will not die. Punish (*nkh*) him with the rod and save his soul from death" (Prov 23:13-14).

5. Of special significance is the usage of *nkh* with God or Yahweh as subject. God struck and destroyed all living creatures with the Flood because he was grieved with humanity's wickedness (Gen 8:21; cf. 6:5-7). Egypt as a whole (and in the climactic stage, especially the firstborn) was the object of God's striking because Yahweh wanted to rescue his people from their power and take them to the promised land of Canaan (Exod 3:20; 12:12, 29; cf. 3:7-8, 16-17).

6. In his covenant with his people God promised blessings for obedience and curses for disobedience (Lev 26; Deut 28), warning that he would afflict (*nkh*) his people for their sins seven times over (Lev 26:24; cf. v. 21 where *makkâ* is used in a similar context). God's punishments could include striking with disease (Deut 28:22, 27, 28; cf. Isa 1:5; Jer 14:19), with crop failures (Amos 4:9; Hag 2:17), with death (2 Sam 6:7), and with unspecified judgments (1 Kgs 14:15; Isa 5:25). Such divine action and its results are often designated by *makkâ* (cf., e.g., Deut 28:59; Isa 1:6; Jer 14:17). Yet, the God who strikes is also the healer-God (→ *mḥṣ*), that is, he forgives, reconciles, and redeems, "'But I will restore you to health and heal your wounds (*makkâ*),' declares the LORD, 'because you are called an outcast, Zion for whom no one cares'" (Jer 30:17).

7. It is not surprising that in his law God also instructed Israel to strike the wrongdoer, "If the guilty man deserves to be beaten (*nkh*), the judge shall make him lie down and have him flogged (*nkh*) ... with the number of lashes his crime deserves, but he must not give him more than forty lashes" (Deut 25:2-3a). Nehemiah beat some of

those who had taken foreign wives (Neh 13:25). Sometimes the sword was to be used in the striking of judgment. Indeed, an entire city was to be smitten with the sword if another god was worshiped there (Deut 13:15[16]). Thus sin had to be countered and Israel disciplined in holiness.

The death penalty could result from striking a fellow human. "Anyone who strikes (*nkh*) a man and kills him shall surely be put to death. However, if he does not do it intentionally, but God lets it happen, he is to flee to a place I will designate" (Exod 21:12-13; cf. vv.18-27; Lev 24:17, 21). Respect for parents was so important that striking them could result in the death penalty (Exod 21:15).

8. Ultimately, the suffering servant would stand in the place of God's people and bear the blows they deserved. "Surely he took up our infirmities and carried our sorrows, yet we considered him stricken by God, smitten (*nkh*) by him, and afflicted" (Isa 53:4). He had offered his back to those who beat him (Isa 50:6). The person of the suffering servant pointed to and was fulfilled in Christ (Matt 8:17; cf. 26:67; 27:26-30).

The smitten messianic figure is also evident in Zech 13:7. "'Awake, O sword, against my shepherd, against the man who is close to me!' declares the LORD Almighty. 'Strike (*nkh*) the shepherd, and the sheep will be scattered ...'" (cf. Zech 12:10; Mark 14:27).

9. *makkâ*, blow, wound. The translation of the term *makkâ* ranges from the literal "blow" or "wound" to the more metaphorical "plague." (The same range of meaning is evident in the G *plēgē,* which the LXX uses most often to translate *makkâ,* → # 4804.) The ten blows that Yahweh dealt Egypt are usually called plagues. Indeed, in 1 Sam 4:8 *makkâ* refers to these plagues (C. Isbell in D. J. A. Clines, D. M. Gunn, and A. J. Hauser, eds., *Art and Meaning: Rhetoric in Biblical Literature*, JSOTSup 19, 1982, 48). These devastating blows are alluded to in Rev 8, 9, and 16 where future calamities are prophesied. (See, e.g., H. B. Swete, *The Apocalypse of St. John*, 1968 [1st pub. 1908], 106-16, 200-212 passim.)

10. *nākôn*, which occurs only in Job 12:5, most likely means kick, strike, or beating (as, e.g., NEB) and its formation from the vb. *nkh* is probably analogous, e.g., to the formation of *ḥāzôn*, vision, from the vb. *ḥzh*, see, perceive (→ # 2600). On this understanding, Job complains that those who are at ease and hold calamity in contempt (Job 12:5a) do not support the needy but rather give those who stumble a final blow (v. 5b). On the other hand, others (e.g., RSV) understand *nākôn* as "ready" (ni. part of *kwn*). The sense of the passage then is that calamity and misfortune is ready for those whose feet slip. See E. Dhorme, *A Commentary on the Book of Job*, 1984 (1967), 169-70.

P-B In Qumran the vb. *nkh* is used in hi. to describe Yahweh's striking his people with hunger and nakedness (4QpHos[a] 2:12). Other uses in the context of judgment include 4QpNah frg. 3-4 1:5 and 11QTemple 55:6, 8. Zech 13:7 is quoted as a warning of God's wrath on the sin of his people (CD 19:8).

Beating, crushing, grinding: → *b'ṭ* (kick, # 1246); → *dwk* (pound, # 1870); → *dk'* (crush, be crushed, # 1917); → *dkh* (be crushed, # 1920); → *dqq* (crush, # 1990); → *hlm* (beat, # 2150); → *ḥbṭ* (beat from, # 2468); → *ṭḥn* (grind, mill, # 3221); → *ktš* (grind down, # 4197); → *ktt* (beat fine, pound up, disperse, # 4198); → *mḥṣ* (beat to pieces, # 4731); → *m'k* (press, squeeze, crush, # 5080); → *ngp* (strike, # 5597); → *nk'* (be whipped out, flogged out, # 5777); → *nkh* (be hit, be battered, ruined, destroyed, # 5782); → *ṣrr* I (bind, tie up, # 7674); → *r'ṣ* (beat down, # 8320); → *rṣṣ* (crush, mash, break, # 8368); → *šwp* I (crush, # 8789); → *šḥq* (grind down, # 8835)

Bibliography
TWAT 5:445-54; *TWOT* 2:577-79.

Cornelis Van Dam

5783	נָכֶה

נָכֶה (*nākeh*), smitten (# 5783); < נכה (*nkh*), be smitten, be broken down, whether fatally or not (→ # 5782).

OT The adj. is used of the physical crippling of Mephibosheth in 2 Sam 4:4; 9:3. In Isa 66:2 Yahweh says that the one he esteems is the person who is humble (*'ānî*) and contrite in spirit (*nekēh rûaḥ*). Thus, one must be "crippled" in the inner person in the sense of complete subjection to God if he or she expects his favor.

Handicaps, disfigurement, blind, lame, stammer, speechless: → *'illēm* (speechlessness, # 522); → *gibbēn* (hunchbacked, # 1492); → *ḥārûṣ* IV (mutilation [animal], # 3024); → *ḥērēš* (speechless, # 3094); → *kšḥ* (be lame, crippled, # 4171); → *mûm* (blemish, # 4583); → *mišḥāt* (disfigured, # 5425); → *nākeh* (crippled, smitten, # 5783); → *'wr* I (be blind, # 6422); → *'illēg* (stammering, stuttering, # 6589); → *psḥ* (be lame, crippled, # 7174); → *ṣl'* I (limping condition, # 7519); → *qlṭ* I (defective [animal], # 7832); → *śr'* (deformed, mutilated, # 8594); → *t^eballul* (white spot in eye, # 9319)

R. K. Harrison/E. H. Merrill

5787 (*nākôn* I, kick), → # 5782

5791	נָכֹחַ

נָכֹחַ (*nākōaḥ*), nom. straight way, correct conduct, justice, truth; adj. straight, rightful, appropriate (# 5791).

ANE It is uncertain whether *nākōaḥ* derives from the root *ykḥ* or from *nkḥ*. The root *ykḥ* appears only in Heb. and Jud. Aram. Although uncertain, the following cognates of the root *nkḥ* can be mentioned: *nakkīḥ* in Syr. (mild, soft) and *nağaḥa* in Arab. (to be successful).

OT Derivatives of this word occur 8x in the OT. It is used as nom. in Isa 57:2 (straight path) and 26:10; 30:10; 59:14; Amos 3:10 (the rightful, truth). In 2 Sam 15:3; Prov 8:9; 24:26, however, it is used as an adj. (with the meaning of rightful/appropriate). Liedke (*THAT* 1:731) points out that *nākōaḥ* is "Kennzeichen weisheitlicher Sprache" (cf. also Wolff, 38-40). In the article on *yšr*, be straight, level (# 3837; *THAT* 1:791), Liedke also mentions that the vb. under discussion originally had the literal semantic value of straight (in contrast to crooked), but that it is mainly used figuratively in the OT with the meaning of rightful, true, correct, appropriate (in contrast to bad, false, inappropriate). Liedke suggests the same pattern of usage with regard to *nākōaḥ* and *tqn*, straighten (pi.; → # 9545). In the OT Wisdom literature the goal of correct, appropriate conduct is constantly put forward. However, it should be noted that the didactic function of biblical wisdom is far broader than that which is usually implied by the term ethics. The challenge to pursue wisdom not only involved moral decisions regarding right behavior, "but was an intellectual and pragmatic activity which sought to encompass the totality of experience" (cf. B. S. Childs, *Old Testament Theology in a Canonical Context*, 211).

P-B *nākōaḥ* (derivatives) occur as adj. also in Sir 6:22 (with the meaning of "accessible"), 11:21 (with the meaning of "understandable"), and as nom. in 1QH 2:15 (with the meaning of "the truth").

Level, straight: → *'šr* I (walk straight, # 886); → *yšr* (be straight, level, right, # 3837); → *nākōaḥ* (straight way, correct conduct, justice, truth, # 5791); → *pls* I (clear way, make a path, # 7142); → *šwh* I (be/become like, be alike, make level, # 8750); → *tqn* (straighten, set in order, # 9545)

BIBLIOGRAPHY

THAT 1:730-32; *TWOT* 2:579; H. W. Wolff, *Amos' geistige Heimat*, 1964.

Louis Jonker

5792	נכל

נכל (*nkl*), q. knave, deceiver, cheat (part. only); pi. deceive, to deal cleverly with, beguile; hitp. to plan cleverly, cunningly (# 5792); נֵכֶל (*nēkel*), nom. craft, cunningness (# 5793).

ANE Arab. *nakala*, frighten, mistreat; OSA *nkl*, elaborate production; Eth. and Akk. *nkl*, devise cunningly.

OT 1. The vb. is used 4x (Gen 37:18; Num 25:18; Ps 105:25; Mal 1:14). In Gen 37:18 the brothers of Joseph plot cunningly (hitp.) to kill Joseph. Their evil intent in the process is asserted in Gen 50:20. The Midianites, because of their deceitful treatment of Israel (Num 25:18, pi.) are to be regarded as enemies by Moses and Israel alike. Mal 1:14 describes the one who does not give God his best available sacrifice as a deceiver or knave (q. part.). Ps 105:25 records how Yahweh turned the Egyptians to conspire/deal cunningly (hitp.) with his people to kill them. The word basically means to lead astray, cause to wander, by words or by one's behavior.

2. In every instance the essence of the meaning is to engage in deception, guile, craft through a deliberate plan/act, conscious or otherwise, even if orchestrated by Yahweh, who can with moral integrity "catch the wise/deceitful in their craftiness" (Job 5:13).

P-B Late Heb. continued to use this word in its OT meanings. Hypocrite is used to translate the nom. as well (Gen R 5.49; for refs. see Jastrow 2:910-11).

Deception, falsehood, fraud, guile, iniquity, lie: → *'āwen* (mischief, iniquity, deception, # 224); → *bd'* (invent, devise, lie, # 968); → *kzb* I (lie, be a liar, deceive, # 3941); → *kḥš* (fail, deceive, grow lean, # 3950); → *nkl* (knave, deceiver, cheat, # 5792); → *nš'* II (be deceived, deceive, cause a deception, # 5958); → *sārâ* II (rebellion, crime, revolt, falsehood, # 6240); → *'qb* I (seize the heel, overreach, deceive, # 6810); → *rmh* II (betray, deal treacherously with, # 8228); → *śwṭ* (turn away to falsehood, entangled in lies, # 8454); → *šqr* (deal/act falsely, betray, # 9213); → *tll* (deceive, mock, trifle, # 9438)

Eugene Carpenter/Michael A. Grisanti

5793 (*nēkel*, craft, cunningness), → # 5792

5794	נְכָסִים

נְכָסִים (n^e*kāsîm*), nom. (pl. only), possessions, wealth, riches (# 5794).

ANE The Akk. cognate is *nikkassu* meaning property, wealth, or gain. BDB, 647 suggests that n^e*kāsîm* is probably an Assyr. or Aram. loanword, but the Sum. *nig-ka* is a better possibility (*HALAT* 660). See the Aram. *niksîn* in Ezra 6:8 and 7:26, with the sense of possessions, goods.

OT 1. The semantic field of wealth and riches consists primarily of three terms: *'šr* (wealth, riches in opposition to poverty), *hôn* (material possessions including riches), and n^e*kāsîm* (possessions in general, including livestock), of which the first is the most important. By contrast, the OT has a wide variety of words for poverty and oppression, indicating a greater familiarity with those conditions than with wealth (→ *'ebyôn*, poor [# 36]).

2. n^e*kāsîm* occurs only 5x in the OT. In the Deuteronomistic writings, Joshua blesses the tribes of Reuben, Gad, and Manasseh, who are conspicuous for their great wealth, including large herds of livestock, silver, gold, bronze, iron, and clothing (Josh 22:8). In the incident of Solomon's dream, the king chooses wisdom above riches, wealth (n^e*kāsîm*), and honor (2 Chron 1:11), and so God rewards him by giving him these also (v. 12). The idea of God as the giver of wealth is to be found also in Eccl 6:2 and 5:19[18]. A striking difference is found between these two verses. In the case of the former, the rich person is unable to enjoy his wealth, but in the latter case God supplies also the ability to enjoy his/her wealth. The writer discerns that this is in itself a gift from God. In both the passages from Chron and Eccl our term occurs in parallel with *'ōšer* (# 6948). Usually no difference is intended, but in the phrase rendered in the NIV of Eccl 6:2 as "wealth (*'ōšer*), possessions (n^e*kāsîm*) and honor (*kābôd*)" one may discern a sense of progression from the acquisition of riches, through the power implicit in the ownership of great possessions, to the honor that attends such a person. Just as power, possession, and prestige attends the wealthy, so the poor, by contrast, experience economic, material, and psychological deprivation. The Bible stresses an understanding of wealth or poverty, which presses beyond the narrow economic sense (which we tend to use today) to a fuller sense of the terms. So in a theology of wealth, one needs to understand that wealth in itself is not a corrupting influence, but the power and prestige that attends wealth has the potential to destroy one's spiritual being. The question is not whether one is rich or not, but rather how one became rich and how one handles the power and prestige (honor) that accompany wealth.

P-B Jastrow 2:911 indicates that the talmudic sages used n^e*kāsîm* to include a range of meanings from belongings in general (Yebamot 4:3) through to possessions marking wealth, such as property or a business (Berakot 46a).

NT In his interaction with the wealthy, Jesus witnesses the despair of a young man who had great possessions (Matt 19:21) and the joy of Zachaeus in giving his wealth to the poor (Luke 19:8).

Riches, wealth: → *hwn* (consider easy, risk, # 2103); → n^e*kāsîm* (possessions, wealth, riches, # 5794); → *'šr* (be rich, become rich, make rich, # 6947)

BIBLIOGRAPHY
H. L. Bosman, *Plutocrats and Paupers*, 1991; *CAD* 11:2, 223-30; M. A. Eaton, *Ecclesiastes*, 1983; H. Wolff, *Anthropology of the Old Testament*, 1974, 128-33.

W. R. Domeris

5795	נכר

נכר (*nkr* I), ni. pretend, be recognized; pi. misrepresent, deface, deliver, consider carefully; hi. investigate, recognize, know (how to); hitp. disguise, make known (# 5795); הַכָּרָה (*hakkārâ*), bias (→ # 2129); נֵכָר (*nēkār*), foreign, foreigner (→ # 5797); נֵכֶר (*nēker*), misfortune (disleg. in Job 31:3; Obad 12; # 5798); נָכְרִי (*nokrî*), foreign, strange, alien (→ # 5799).

ANE The root is widely attested in the Sem. languages. On the debate over whether there are two *nkr* roots, see *TWAT* 5:456.

OT 1. The vb. occurs 48x (12x in Job-Proverbs; 9x in Genesis) and carries various senses, most commonly: to recognize a person or object (Gen 27:23; 37:33); to acknowledge a person (Deut 21:17); to have regard for others (Job 34:19); to distinguish (Ezra 3:13); to take notice of (Ruth 2:10, 19). In Gen 42:7, two senses of the word occur together; Joseph recognized his (*nkr,* hi.) brothers, but disguised himself (*nkr,* hitp.), treating them like strangers (cf. 1 Kgs 14:5-6).

2. Theological use of this root is uncommon. In Isa 61:9, when God has redeemed Israel, they will be acknowledged by the nations as a people whom God has blessed; in 63:16, Israel is not acknowledged by its ancestors, only God is their Father. One case where God is subject (Jer 24:5) carries the sense of God's special regard for the exiles. The psalmist complains that no one has regard for him (142:4[5]), implying that God is the one who should assume that role. In Ps 103:16 (cf. Job 7:10), unlike the wind that no longer knows a flower once it has passed over, God is one whose steadfast love for his people endures forever. God knows the deeds of the wicked (Job 34:25), who are friends of darkness rather than light (Job 24:13, 17), and will judge them.

Knowledge, discernment, shrewd, wisdom: → *byn* (understand, discern, # 1067); → *ḥkm* (become wise, act wisely, # 2681); → *ṭ'm* (taste, test, sense, discern, # 3247); → *yd'* I (observe, care about, # 3359); → *nkr* (pretend, be recognized, # 5795); → *'rm* II (be cunning, be crafty, make crafty, # 6891); → *śkl* I (have success, understand, make wise, act with insight, # 8505)

BIBLIOGRAPHY
TWAT 5:454-63.

Terence E. Fretheim

5797	נֵכָר

נֵכָר (*nēkār*), nom. foreign, foreigner (# 5797); נָכְרִי (*nokrî*), nom. and adj. foreign, strange, foreigner, alien (# 5799) < נכר (*nkr*), ni. feign oneself as a stranger; hitp. make oneself unrecognizable (→ # 5795).

ANE These words are well attested in all Sem. languages. The Akk. *nakru*, *nakiru* has more the nuance of enemy or hostility; the nom. *nukru* means something strange or foreign. The Ugar. nom. *nkr* is found in the story of Keret, where the newlywed soldier must give up his wife to a stranger (*KTU* 1.14 ii 50; iv 29). In imperial Aram. *nkry* is found in the story of Aḥiqar (*DISO*, 179).

OT The words *nēkār* (36x) and *nokrî* (45x) are used of that which is alien and to be excluded. The foreigner designated by these terms is usually perceived as dangerous or hostile. The nom. *nēkār* often appears in a construct relationship to indicate that which is morally unacceptable. It may refer to those outside the covenant who may join (Gen 17:12; Exod 12:43) or to those unqualified to participate in the cult (Ezek 44:9). It is frequently used of idolatry in terms of foreign gods (Josh 24:20; Jer 5:19; Mal 2:11) or idols (Jer 8:19). It also refers to hostile foreign people (Neh 9:2; 13:30) or enemies (2 Sam 22:45, 46). The adj. *nokrî* is predominantly used of foreign peoples (Exod 2:22; 18:3; 21:8; Deut 14:21; 17:15; Isa 2:6) or of foreign wives (1 Kgs 11:1; Ezra 10:2; et al.). In Proverbs the strange woman is the adultress who has betrayed her husband and family (Prov 2:16; 5:20; 7:5; 23:27; et al.). Jeremiah speaks of the "strange vine" as a metaphor for the apostasy of Israel (Jer 2:21), and Isaiah of the strange action of God (Isa 28:21). Only in the eschatological vision of Isaiah are foreigners given a positive relationship (56:3, 6) and role (60:10; 61:5), when God has reversed the old orders.

P-B The nom. *nēkār* is found in the Qumran writings in continuity with the OT meaning of a foreign or hostile people (6x). In 4QFlor 1.4 the stranger or outsider is categorized with the Ammonite, Moabite, or bastard (cf. Deut 23:3-4). It is common in later Heb. and Aram., and in the Talmud it occurs in the sense of stranger or Gentile.

Alien, foreigner, stranger: → *gwr* I (dwell as a stranger, # 1591); → *zār* (foreign, surprising, # 2424); → *nēkār* (foreign, foreigner, # 5797); → *tôšāb* (alien, settler, # 9369)

Bibliography

THAT 2:66-68; *TDNT* 1:264-67; 5:1-36; M. Guttmann, "The Term 'Foreigner' (*nkry*) Historically Considered," *HUCA* 3, 1926, 1-20; J. Hoftijzer, "EX xxi 8," *VT* 7, 1957, 388-91.

A. H. Konkel

5798 (*nēker*, misfortune), → # 5795

5799 (*nokrî*, foreign, strange, alien), → # 5797

5800	נְכֹת

נְכֹת (n^e*kōt*), treasure house, (# 5800).

ANE Heb. *bêt* n^e*kōtōh* may be connected with Akk. *bit nakamti* (*CAD* N, Part 1, 156) or *bit nakkamāti* (*CAD* N, Part I, 182-4; *AHw*, 721-22).

OT The nom. appears only in Isa 39:2 and its parallel (2 Kgs 20:13). Hezekiah is visited by envoys from powerful Babylon. What he chooses to do on that memorable occasion is, regrettably, to show them "what was in his *storehouses*—the silver, the gold, the spices, the fine oil, his entire armory and everything found among his treasures (b^e*'ōṣrōtāyw*)." Rather than seize this occasion to speak to his elite but pagan visitors about his God, Hezekiah "succumbed to the temptation to glorify himself and to prove to the Chaldeans that he was a worthy partner for any sort of coalition they might have in mind" (Oswalt, 695).

Close to Isa 39:2 ‖ 2 Kgs 20:13 are the cuneiform lines from Ashurbanipal boasting about his conquest of Susa: *aptēma bīt nakkamātišu(nu) ša kaspu ḫurāṣu bušû makkûru nukkumū qerebšun*, "I opened his treasury wherein silver, gold, valuables and property were stored" (Cohen, 40). Both passages describe the opening of a royal treasury before an alien king.

P-B The expression *byt nktyw* appears in IQIS[a].

Storehouse, treasure: → *'āsām* (stores, # 662); → *'āsōp* (store, # 667); → *'ṣr* (accumulate, amass, store up, # 732); → *gizbār* (treasurer, # 1601); → *genez* I (treasury, # 1709); → *ganzak* (treasury, # 1711); → *ḥsn* (be stored up, # 2889); → *kms* (stored up, # 4022); → *maṭmôn* (treasure [hidden], # 4759); → *misk*[e]*nôt* (stores, # 5016); → *n*[e]*kōt* (treasure house, # 5800); → *niškâ* (storeroom[s], cell, room, # 5969); → *piqqādôn* (deposit, # 7214); → *ṣpn* (hide, hidden, # 7621)

Bibliography

H. R. Cohen, *Biblical Hapax Legomena in the Light of Akkadian and Ugaritic*, SBL DissSer 37, 1978, 40-41, 67 (nn 108, 109, 110, 111, 112), 113; J. Oswalt, *Isaiah 1-39*, NICOT, 1986.

Victor P. Hamilton

5805 (*n*[e]*mālâ*, ant), → # 6856

5807 (*nāmēr*, panther), → # 9478

5812	נֵס

נֵס (*nēs*), nom. banner, standard (# 5812); < נסס (*nss* II), denom. vb. hitpol. (only in Ps 60:4[6]; Zech 9:16) disputed meaning: rally around the banner, or, that it may be displayed (# 5824).

ANE Synonyms and Egyp. terminology are discussed by Couroyer, "Le *nēs* biblique." Its function is "to signal."

OT 1. *nēs* has been described as a "signal with rags." While a ship's sail can be described as *nēs* (Isa 33:23; Ezek 27:7), the primary biblical usage of *nēs* is in a military context. In war a banner was hoisted on high ground, often a hilltop; widely visible, it signaled the rallying point for troops in preparation for battle. Raising a banner on bare hilltop, for example, is used by Isaiah as summoning the warriors (Isa 13:2). Assyria is said to panic at the sight of the battle standard, apparently a signal for them that the enemy was preparing for war or even declaring war (Isa 31:9; Jer 51:12). Raising the banner, together with the blowing of the trumpet (*šôpār*) constituted a war alert (Jer 51:12, 27). A raised banner could mean "Attack!" After Israel's battle with the Amalekites, Moses memorialized God's help in the name, "Yahweh-Nissi" ("Yahweh is my banner," Exod 17:15). The explanation of the name follows the sense of "attack": "The Lord will be at war against the Amalekites from generation to generation" (17:16b).

2. A banner might also announce victory in battle. Part of the meaning of Yahweh-Nissi (Exod 17:15) is undoubtedly the victory granted by Yahweh. In the act of naming, Moses continues with the explanation: "For hands were lifted up to the throne (*kēs*) of the Lord" (17:16 NIV). B. S. Childs, who reviews the options of

meaning in this debated text, plausibly argues that *kēs* (throne) should be *nēs* (banner). In his words, "The point of the naming is to bear witness to Yahweh's role in the battle" (*Exodus*, 315). From start to finish, so the name suggested, the battle belonged to God. The name embodies a theology that holds that God is not outside the fray, but that he is decidedly within the fray. (→ Divine Warrior: Theology)

3. In war, however, if the campaign went badly, the commander might hoist a banner signaling not "fight" but "flight." Ps 60:4[6] is a debated text. If the vb. echoes the earlier "banner," the sense is one of confidence, as in the NIV: "For those who fear you, you have raised a banner to be unfurled against the bow." However, if the vb. derives from the root *nws*, flee, the intent is to list one more piece of deflating news, that of flight "the heaviest blow yet" (Kidner, *Psalms*, 1:217). It is possible, however, to stay with the banner-related vb. and still see the meaning as one of "flight," a sense compatible with the context.

4. The banner represented a focal point. In the plague of poison serpents, God ordered the erection of a bronze serpent on a pole (*nēs*). The victims who cast a look to the focal point, the bronze serpent, would be healed (Num 21:8). So also when God announces he is bringing the exiles to their homeland, he announces that he will raise a banner, to which they will rally and under which they will march (Isa 42:22; 62:10).

Banner: → *dgl* II (lift the banner, being under banners, # 1839); → *nēs* (banner, standard, # 5812)

Bibliography

TWAT 5:468-73; B. Couroyer, "Les *nēs* biblique: signal ou enseigne?" *RB* 91, 1984, 5-29; M. Gorg, "*Nes*—Ein Herrschaftsembleur?" *BN* 14, 1981, 11-17; R. Gradwohl, "Zum Verständnis von Ex. XVII 15f," *VT* 12, 1962, 491-94; M. Weippert, "'Heiliger Krieg' in Israel und Assyrien," *ZAW* 84, 1972, 489n.136.

Elmer A. Martens

5813 (*n^esibbâ*, turn of affairs), → # 6015

5814	נסה

נסה (*nsh*), ni. be trained, accustomed; pi. put to the test, exercise, train (# 5814); nom. מַסָּה (*massâ* I), temptation, trial (# 4999).

OT The vb. *nsh* occurs 36x in the OT. Unlike *bḥn, nsh* appears more frequently in narrative than in poetry, being found 15x in the Torah, 7x in the Former Prophets, only once in the Latter Prophets, and 13x in the Writings. This again suits the root, for *nsh* regularly denotes religious as well as secular forms of testing, and both the means and objectives are typically specified. In this way, *nsh* involves a mode of testing that is more concrete and less intuitive than *bḥn*.

1. In common usage, *nsh* denotes two distinct activities. (a) *nsh* captures the idea of attempting or trying to do something, such as speaking with an exceedingly distraught and seemingly irrational person (Job 4:2) or freeing a nation from captivity (Deut 4:34). In these cases, that which is being done lies outside of normal or recommended behavior; one is in a sense testing common practice.

(b) *nsh* denotes the act of testing people or items in order to determine something about them. Aware of his reputation, the queen of Sheba tested Solomon for the specific purpose of verifying or disproving the claims (1 Kgs 10:1; 2 Chron 9:1). David refused to wear Saul's armor because it was unfamiliar to him; i.e., he had never tested it to determine its usefulness and liabilities (1 Sam 17:39). Qoheleth remarks on the testing of life's meaning through both pleasure and wisdom (Eccl 2:1; 7:23), and the special diet suggested by Daniel had to pass the test of time before final implementation (Dan 1:12, 14). In each instance, specific means are selected as a way of testing the validity, value, or usefulness of the person or item in question.

2. As is the case with *bḥn*, *nsh* appears with some regularity to denote testing in the religious realm. Unlike *bḥn*, however, *nsh* denotes people testing Yahweh nearly as often as it does Yahweh's own acts of testing. People are not to test God, but are instead to obey (Deut 6:16). Nevertheless, people do test God, and they do so with some regularity. Here, the paradigmatic event occurred at Rephidim, renamed Massah ("testing") and Meribah ("quarreling"), where the people complained because of a lack of water (Exod 17:7). Such complaining, particularly given previous divine provisions, is viewed as a clear test of God, a test to determine whether he was actually present with the people or not. Later reflection not only condemned this episode, but used it as a model *not* to be emulated (Deut 6:16; Ps 95:8).

In this and other examples, people test Yahweh either by forgetting his works on their behalf and subsequently calling into question his covenantal faithfulness (Num 14:22; Ps 106:14), or by directly violating his commands (Ps 78:41, 56). Both of these dimensions are insightfully depicted in the progressing ideas of Ps 78. The wilderness community tested God by demanding food (v. 18) and repeatedly rebelling (v. 41), and those who entered the land fared no better, refusing to keep God's commands (v. 56). To question Yahweh's covenantal faithfulness is to entice him to prove himself again and again. To violate his commands is to test the boundaries and doubt his authority.

With respect to Yahweh's testing his people, *nsh* appears in connection with several specific testing devices: the proposed sacrifice of Isaac (Gen 22:1), instructions concerning particular activities (Exod 15:25; 16:4), the Sinai theophany (20:20), the wilderness wandering (Deut 8:2, 16), false prophets (13:3[4]), Canaanites dwelling in the land (Judg 2:22; 3:1, 4), and moments of individual temptation (2 Chron 32:31). These tests are accompanied by particular objectives or goals: to measure obedience (Exod 15:25; 16:4; Deut 8:2; Judg 2:22), instill fear (Exod 20:20), prevent sinning (20:20), discern what is in the heart (Deut 13:3[4]; 2 Chron 32:31), and to ensure future prosperity (Deut 8:16). At issue here is Yahweh's desire both to evaluate specific aspects of his peoples' character as well as to influence and shape them. Given this, it comes as no surprise that individuals occasionally welcomed such testing as a means of affirming their personal piety and commitment (Ps 26:2). For others, testing was proof of infidelity and unfaithfulness.

P-B The LXX normally employs *peirazō* ("try, test, put on trial") and *peiraō* ("try, attempt") when translating *nsh*.

Test, trial, discipline: → *bḥn* (test, # 1043); → *nsh* (test, train, exercise, # 5814); → *ṣrp* (smelt, refine, test, # 7671); → *twh* II (trouble, provoke, # 9345)

Complaint, grumbling: → *'nn* (complain, # 645); → *lwn* I (howl, grumble, # 4296); → *rgn* (murmur, complain, # 8087)

Bibliography
TDOT 2:69-72; *TWOT* 2:581; B. Gerhardsson, *The Testing of God's Son (Matt. 4:1-11 & Par.)*, ConBOT 2:1, 1966.

Terry L. Brensinger

5815	נסח

נסח (*nsḥ*), q. tear down (a house; Prov 15:25) (# 5815); tear away (people in judgment; Ps 52:5[7]; Prov 2:22); ni. be torn away (of people in judgment; Deut 28:63); מַסָּח (*massāḥ*), nom. alternating ? (# 5005) (see, e.g., *HALAT* 572a; BDB, 587a).

ANE Cognate roots are found in Akk. and Arab. (*HALAT* 663b).

OT 1. This vb. is used to describe the wrath of God in punishing sin by tearing the wicked man away from his tent (q., Ps 52:5[7]), destroying the house of the proud (q., Prov 15:25), and in having his people torn from the Promised Land (ni., Deut 28:63). Similarly the treacherous are uprooted from the earth (q., Prov 2:22, par. *krt*).

2. The mng. of nom. *massāḥ* (only in 2 Kgs 11:6) remains uncertain and has been omitted in tr. (e.g., LXX, RSV, NRSV; see D. J. Wiseman, *1 & 2 Kings*, 1993, 231; T. R. Hobbs, *2 Kings*, 1985, 134). NIV renders "take turns" (*HALAT* 572b).

Tearing, prey: → *gzr* II (cut, slaughter, tear, prey, # 1616); → *ḥth* (take, fetch, # 3149); → *ṭrp* (tear in pieces, # 3271); → *mlḥ* I (be torn in pieces, dissipate, # 4872); → *nsḥ* (tear down, tear away, # 5815); → *ns'* (tear out, # 5825); → *ntṣ* (tear down, # 5997); → *ntq* (tear away, # 5998); → *pšḥ* (pluck, pull, leave fallow, # 7318); → *qwṣ* II (tear apart, # 7763); → *qr'* (tear up, # 7973); → *šs'* (tear, divide, # 9117)

Cornelis Van Dam

5816 (*nāsîk* I, wine-contribution), → # 5818

5818	נסך

נסך (*nsk* I), vb. q. pour, pour out; ni. be consecrated, exalted; pi. pour out as a consecration gift; hi. contribute a drink offering, libation (# 5818); נֶסֶךְ (*nesek* I), nom. drink offering (# 5821); נָסִיךְ (*nāsîk* I), nom. wine contribution (# 5816).

ANE 1. The Akk. vb. *nasāku* A, to throw, throw down, tear down (*CAD*, N2, 15-20), appears to be related to the Heb. root *nsk* but is used neither for pouring out as a libation nor pouring out metal into a cast as in Heb. There is, however, a Sumerian loanword in Akk. *nisakku*, offering, which derives from Sumerian *ne-sag* (*AHw*, 794). The Sumerian term occurs, for example, in the temple building hymn of Gudea: "Its (the shrine's) first offering (*ne-sag*) is a mountain dripping with wine" (Gudea Cylinder A col. 28 line 10, quoted from Averbeck, 675; cf. Gudea Cylinder B col. 17 line 5, ibid., 704 referring to offerings presented in bronze vessels). The connection to "a mountain dripping with wine" seems significant here. It might relate to the concept of libations, esp. since the next line refers to the "brewhouse" of the newly constructed temple of the god Ningirsu, which the ruler Gudea was building. Of course, libations were a common offering to the gods throughout the ANE (see Weinfeld, 99, for the Hittites; *CAD*, ŠII, 423-24, for the Babylonians; cf. next two secs.).

2. Ugar. has a vb. *nsk* that means pour out. It is used for pouring out dew and showers upon Anat that she might wash herself clean from the blood of battle (*CML*, 48, lines 40-41 and 52, lines 87-88; cf. Fisher 1:276). In another place Anat is ordered to "pour a peace-offering in the heart of the earth, honey from a pot in the heart of the fields" (*CML*, 49, lines 13-14; cf. 51, lines 68-69). In a different context Aqhat laments, "What does a man get as (his) final lot? Glaze will be poured [on] (my) head, quicklime on to my crown" in burial (*CML*, 109, lines 36-37). Another whole set of occurrences of this root refer to the metal smith (e.g., the one who pours silver into a cast; see *WUS*, 207; Fisher 2:61-62).

3. In the Aram. Sefire Treaties the vb. *nsk* occurs 4x with the meaning to provide (*nsk*) or to not provide (with negative particle) food (*lḥm*) (Fitzmyer, 14-15, line 26; 18-19, line 38; 96-97, lines 5 and 7, and the remarks on 108-9). Similarly, in biblical Aram. we find, "Then King Nebuchadnezzar fell prostrate before Daniel and paid him honor and ordered that an offering and incense be presented (*l^{e}nassākâ*) to him" (Dan 2:46, pael inf. const. vb.); note also, "With this money be sure to buy bulls, rams and male lambs, together with their grain offerings and drink offerings (*nsk*), and sacrifice them on the altar of the temple of your God in Jerusalem" (Ezra 7:17). In other inscriptions we find also the meaning to cast (various metals) (*DISO*, 180; cf. also Syr., to smelt or cast metal). This is the exclusive meaning of the root in Phoen. and Pun. (see *DISO*, 180; R. S. Tomback, *A Comparative Semitic Lexicon of the Phoenician and Punic Languages*, SBLDS 32, 1978, 214-15, *nsk*, caster (of metals), and *nskt*, molten image, statue or metal jar). Arab. has the same vb. meaning to worship (J. M. Cowan (ed.), H. Wehr, *A Dictionary of Modern Written Arabic*, 3d ed., 1976, 962), which derives originally from the meaning pour out (BDB, 650).

OT 1. The vb. *nsk* I occurs 24x overall in the OT (Even-Shoshan, [764] 26x, but Prov 8:23 and Isa 25:7 belong under *nsk* II, entwine, weave, according to *HALAT* 703; cf. also Dan 2:46 for biblical Aram.). The 7x in the q. stem are diverse: 2x with the meaning pour out in the casting of metal idols (Isa 40:19; 44:10), 3x for pouring out drink offerings (Exod 30:9; Hos 9:4; also Isa 30:1, where forming an alliance is lit. to pour out a drink offering; cf. esp. the hi. below), 1x in the expression "The LORD has brought (lit., poured) over you a deep sleep" (Isa 29:10), and 1x in Ps 2:6, "I have installed my King on Zion, my holy hill," where the underlying expression might mean "I have poured out (my libation in the consecration of) my king" (*HALAT* 703 puts it under ni. rather than q. [cf. the LXX passive translation], but the essential meaning is the same; cf. also the other option given there from *skk* II, be shaped). In the latter instance, another possible derivation is another Akk *nasāku* A, which can mean to assign s.o. to a work assignment (*CAD* N 2, 18, meaning 4).

The single pi. and all the hi. and ho. occurrences apply to the pouring out of libations. The first canonical occurrence of both the vb. and its corresponding nom. is in Gen 35:14, "Jacob set up a stone pillar at the place where God had talked with him, and he poured out (*wayyassēk*) a drink offering (*nesek*) on it; he also poured (vb. *yṣq*, # 3668) oil on it." Here and elsewhere a different vb. is used for consecration by means of the pouring out of oil. In another instance David refused to drink but, instead, poured out (*nsk*) the water that his three mighty men risked their lives to obtain for him (2 Sam 23:16 hi. = 1 Chron 11:18 pi.). On these occasions the pouring out of the water was a means of offering it to the Lord as an indication of devotion. The same act was sometimes done to show devotion to other gods in Israel, an act that provoked the Lord to anger against his people (e.g., Ezek 20:28; Jer 7:18; 19:13; 32:29; esp. Jer 44:17-19 [4x], 25 to the Queen of Heaven, apparently the well-known Babylonian goddess Ishtar; cf. 2 Kgs 16:13 for Ahaz pouring out libations on his new altar in the temple). Special libation vessels were made for the tabernacle in association with the table for the bread (Exod 25:29; 37:16, both ho.).

Ps 16:4 is peculiar and difficult (cf. Kraus, 237; Craigie, 157): "The sorrows of those will increase who run after other gods. I will not pour out (vb. *nsk*) their libations (nom. *nesek*) of blood or take up their names on my lips." It seems to refer to the illegitimate offering of blood as if it were something that one would normally drink, which was an abomination in Israel (cf. Lev 7:22-27).

2. Like the vb., the nom. derivatives can refer either to libations (many times) or to statues of cast metal. *nesek* (64x in the OT; cf. also biblical Aram. in Ezra 7:17) occurs with the latter meaning only in Isa 41:29; 48:5; Jer 10:14; 51:17 (listed as *nesek* II in *HALAT* 703), and *nâsîk*, which occurs only 2x in the OT, has this meaning in Dan 11:8a, "He will also seize their gods, their metal images." In Deut 32:38 it refers to "the (foreign) gods who ate the fat of their sacrifices and drank the wine of their drink offerings." The term *massēkâ* (# 5011, 26x in the OT; normally "metal image") derives from the same vb. root and means libation only once, "Woe . . . to those who carry out plans that are not mine, forming an alliance (*massēkâ*), but not by my Spirit" (Isa 30:1).

Like the burnt and peace (fellowship) offerings, the practice of offering drink offerings (i.e., libations) predates the tabernacle system (e.g., Gen 35:14) and continued at other altars even after the tabernacle and temple were available, but in this case all such references are to illegitimate worship of foreign gods (e.g., Jer 19:13; 32:29; Ezek 28:28) or on a foreign altar in the temple (2 Kgs 16:13, 15).

3. Within the sanctuary system libations constituted a significant part of the ritual procedures even on a regular daily basis (Exod 29:40-41; Num 28:5-8), and it was specifically legislated that libations along with grain offerings should normally accompany any burnt or peace offering (Num 15:1-15; cf. Lev 23:13, 18, 37). The idea behind this combination of food offerings seems to be that a good meal would not be complete without meat and bread as well as drink combined (see Offerings and Sacrifices: Theology, sec. 3). Furthermore, libations were poured out at the burnt offering altar outside rather than inside the tabernacle tent (see Exod 30:9), so the fact that the libation vessels that were made for the tabernacle were made in association with and normally placed on the table for the bread of the Presence that was inside the tent also suggests this meal-like conception of things (Exod 25:29; 37:16; Num 4:7).

According to Num 28:7, "The accompanying drink offering is to be a quarter of a hin of fermented drink (*šēkār*, # 8911) with each lamb. Pour out the drink offering to the LORD at the sanctuary." The term for "strong drink" does, indeed, seem to refer to intoxicating beverage elsewhere in the OT. It is probably related to Akk. *šikaru*, beer, which was used in Babylonian libations (Ashley, 564-65; cf. *CAD*, ŠII, 423-24). It seems to be the drink that is made from grain crops in contrast to that of the grape, as Num 6:3 suggests, "He (the Nazirite) must abstain from wine and other fermented drink (*šēkār*)." According to Lev 10:9, priests who were on duty were forbidden this drink, but Deut 14:26 lists it as a normal part of sacrificial meals. Apparently, since it could be consumed by the people in their celebrations of God, it could also be poured out to the Lord as a libation (cf. P-B sec. 1).

The MT in Num 28:15 appears to suggest that a libation of wine might also be offered with a sin offering, "Besides the regular burnt offering with its drink offering, one male goat is to be presented to the LORD as a sin offering." The Heb. text has a masc. suff. on *nesek* (drink offering), which seems to link it to the sin offering goat (masc.), not the burnt offering (fem.). The Sam. Pent. has the fem. suff. like v. 10 in the MT. Milgrom, however, suggests that the masc. suff. here refers to Heb. *tāmîd*, regular offering (masc.), not the term for burnt offering.

A famine or plague could cause the libation and grain offering to be removed from Israel because of lack of grain and wine (Joel 1:9, 13; cf. 2:14). This was a sign of the impending Day of the Lord in Joel (cf. 1:15; 2:1, 11).

P-B 1. The Qumran Temple Scroll makes numerous references to libations. Two points are of particular interest. (a) The vb. is used only once, but it relates to the discussion of *šēkār* in Num 28:7. According to 11QT 21:10, "pour out a strong drink (*škr*) offering, a new wine on the altar of the Lord year by year" (Yadin 2:95; see OT sec. 3). (b) Contrary to the later rabbinic teachings, according to 11QT 18:4-6 and 25:5-6, 12-15 not only burnt and peace offerings, but also sin offerings were accompanied by grain offerings and libations (see the discussion in Yadin 1:143-46; cf. the remarks on Num 28:15). *nsk* occurs nowhere else in the Qumran sectarian literature.

2. Sir 50:14-15 reads as follows: "Finishing the service at the altars, and arranging the offering to the Most High, the Almighty, he reached out his hand to the cup and poured a libation of the blood of the grape; he poured it out at the foot of the altar, a pleasing odor to the Most High, the King of all" (RSV, Metzger, 195).

3. Specific regulations regarding libation wine are given in Mish. 'Abodah Zarah 4:8; 5:1-2, 7-10. The major concerns are with the care that must be taken to avoid contamination of libation wine (or its grapes) by contact with common wine (or grapes), and the regulations concerning using wine earned from a Gentile for wages.

NT The LXX uses primarily G *spondē* for the Heb. nom. *nesek* I and *spendō* for the corresponding Heb. vb. The nom. does not occur in the NT, but the vb. occurs 2x: "But even if I am being poured out like a drink offering on the sacrifice and service coming from your faith, I am glad and rejoice with all of you" (Phil 2:17), and, "For I am already being poured out like a drink offering, and the time has come for my departure" (2 Tim 4:6). Thus, like many of the other OT sacrificial terms, this too is used metaphorically and implicationally for absolute commitment in the Christian life and esp. ministry.

Offering, sacrifice: → *'azkārâ* (sign-offering, # 260); → *'iššeh* (offering by fire, # 852); → *'āšām* (guilt offering, # 871); → *zbḥ* (slaughter, sacrifice, # 2284); → *ḥaṭṭā'at* (sin offering, # 2633); → *ṭbḥ* (slaughter, # 3180); → *minḥâ* (gift, present, offering, sacrifice, # 4966); → *ma'ᵃśēr* (tithe, # 5130); → *ndr* (make a vow, # 5623); → *nwp* I (move back and forth, wave, # 5677); → *nsk* I (pour out, be consecrated, libation, # 5818); → *'ōlâ* I (burnt offering, # 6592); → *'ᵃrîsâ* (meal/dough offering, # 6881); → *qorbān* (offering, gift, # 7933); → *šḥṭ* I (slaughter, # 8821); → *šelem* (settlement sacrifice, # 8968); → *tāmîd* (regular offering, # 9458); → *tᵉrûmâ* (tribute, contribution, # 9556); → **Aaron: Theology**; → **Offering: Theology**; → **Priests and Levites: Theology**

Bibliography

TWAT 5:488-93; T. R. Ashley, *The Book of Numbers*, NICOT, 1993; R. E. Averbeck, "A Preliminary Study of Ritual and Structure in the Cylinders of Gudea," Ph.D. diss., Dropsie College, 1987; C. Brown, "Sacrifice, First Fruits, Altar, Offering," *NIDNTT*, 3:415-38; P. C. Craigie, *Psalms 1-50*, WBC, 1983; L. R. Fisher, *Ras Shamra Parallels*, AnOr 49 and 50, vols. 1 and 2, 1972, 1975; J. E. Hartley, *Leviticus*, WBC, 1992; H.-J. Klauck, "Sacrifice and Sacrificial Offerings (NT)," *ABD*, 1992, 5:886-91; H.-J. Kraus, *Psalms 1-59*, BKAT, 5th ed., ET, 1988; B. A. Levine, *Leviticus*, The JPS Torah Commentary, 1989; B. M. Metzger (ed.), *The Oxford Annotated Apocrypha, Revised Standard Version*, 1965; J. Milgrom, *Leviticus 1-16*, AB, 1991; idem, *Numbers*, The JPS Torah Commentary, 1990; J.-M. de Tarragon, *Le culte à Ugarit*, 1980; G. Vermes, *The Dead Sea Scrolls in English*, 3d ed., 1987; M. Weinfeld, "Social and Cultic Institutions in the Priestly Source Against Their Ancient Near Eastern Background," *Proceedings of the Eighth World Congress of Jewish Studies*, 1983, 95-129; Y. Yadin, *The Temple Scroll*, vols. 1-2, 1983.

Richard E. Averbeck

5819 (*nsk* II, weave, intertwine), → # 6115

5821 (*nesek* I, drink-offering), → # 5818

5822 (*nesek* II, cast statuette, or gold/silver plating), → # 5011

5823	נסס

נסס (*nss* I), falter (# 5823).

OT In Isa 10:18 this vb. occurs as a hapleg. in the phrase *kimsōs nōsēs*. Largely because of the seeming link between *nōsēs* and the Syr. *nāssîs* or *n*^{e}*sîs*, sick, the common translation of this phrase has been, "like a sick man wasting away." Cf. also the G *nosos*. Other suggestions have been that the vb. is related to Akk. *nasāsu*, to sway to and fro, or to the Heb. *nēs*, signal.

NT → *NIDNTT* 1:606-11; 2:705-10.

Falling, tottering, stumbling: → *bṭḥ* II (fall to ground, # 1054); → *hwh* I (fall, # 2092); → *kšl* (stumble, totter, be brought to ruin, # 4173); → *nss* I (falter, # 5823); → *npl* (fall, lie prostrate, # 5877); → *ntr* I (fall, # 6000); → *šmṭ* (release, remit, drop, throw down, fall, stumble, # 9023)

Allan M. Harman

5824 (*nss* II, rally around the banner), → # 5812

5825	נסע

נסע (*ns'*), q. tear out; start out, march on; ni. be torn out; hi. take (a plant) away (from its place); quarry (stones); make (people) start out (# 5825); מַסַּע (*massa'*), nom. journey (→ # 5023); מַסָּע (*massā'*), nom. quarry (→ # 5024).

ANE Cognates are found in Ugar. and Phoen., and perhaps in Arab. and Eth., while the Heb. *nsḥ* appears to be a parallel form (*TWAT* 5:493-94).

OT 1. Whether the original meaning of the vb. is "to pull up tent pegs" or "to break up" (cf. *TWAT* 5:494; Guillaume, 28-29; Delcor, 313), the vb. is most often used in contexts of setting out and traveling and then virtually always in q.

ns' (q.) describes the wandering of Abraham (Gen 12:9; 20:1) and Jacob (Gen 33:17; 35:5, 16, 21; 46:1) through the Promised Land. The fact that they lived in tents and regularly broke camp underlined their status as strangers and aliens in the land of Canaan. They looked forward to the fulfillment of the promises of a country of their own with a lasting city built by God (Heb 11:8-16).

2. The vb. (q.) is also used for the journeying of the Israelites (along with all their possessions) from Rameses to Mount Sinai and their subsequent wandering in the desert for forty years (e.g., Exod 12:37; 13:20; 14:15; 16:1; Num 33:3-48; Deut 1:19). The Lord went with them and directed them (Exod 13:21-22). He instructed them to start out (*ns'*) and cross the Red Sea (14:15), and the angel of God and the pillar of cloud moved (*ns'*) from in front and went behind them shielding them from the Egyptians (14:19). Later the tabernacle accompanied Israel, and the cloud of God's presence that covered it determined when they would set out (*ns'*, 40:36-37; cf. Num 2:34; with the tabernacle and the ark as subjects with *ns'* see resp. Num 1:51; 10:35; cf. 2:17). At the sound of the trumpet blasts, Israel would start the journey (*ns'*) in careful formations as the Lord's army (10:5, 6, 17-25 passim). Whenever the ark set out (*ns'*), Moses would say "Rise up, O LORD! May your enemies be scattered" (10:35; cf. Ps 68:1[2])! The church today is still en route through the desert of this world to the Promised Land (cf. Heb 3:7-4:11; Rev 12:6), in the sure knowledge that Jesus Christ goes with his people (Matt 28:20) and that the enemy has been defeated (Col 2:15).

3. In hi. the vb. can describe God's or Moses' making Israel go forth (Exod 15:22; Ps 78:52; 80:8[9]) or God's causing an east wind to blow to bring quail for food to Israel in the wilderness (Ps 78:26; cf. Num 11:31 q.). Disobedience can lead to God's sending a "destroyer of nations" who sets out (*ns'* q.) for Zion (Jer 4:7), but in mercy he can also cause the scourge of his anger, like Sennacherib, to break camp (*ns'* q.) and withdraw from his people (2 Kgs 19:36, par. Isa 37:37).

4. Why Israel under King Jehoram departed (*ns'* [q.]) and gave up on their siege of Kir Hareseth (2 Kgs 3:27) when complete triumph appeared within their grasp is not clear. The Bible records that "the fury against Israel was great," subsequent to the king of Moab's last desperate attempt to save his city by sacrificing his oldest son (3:27). Perhaps God took victory away from Israel because of his displeasure with Ahab's dynasty (cf. 3:2-3). Another explanation is that when the Israelites witnessed this sacrifice, they were moved with pity for the king and withdrew (Josephus, *Ant*, IX.iii.2; cf. tr. "dismay upon Israel" [cf. J. Gray, *I & II Kings*, OTL, 2nd ed., 1970, 490-91]).

5. In Isa 33:20 redeemed Zion is pictured as "a tent that will not be moved (*ṣ'n* [q.]); its stakes will never be pulled up (*ns'* [q.]), nor any of its ropes broken (*ntq* [ni.])" (NIV). It is noteworthy that the image of a tent is used, probably alluding to the portable precursor of the temple, the tabernacle, as the dwelling place of God (cf. similar language used of the temple in, e.g., 1 Chron 9:19, 21, 23; 2 Chron 31:2; cf. for fulfilment, Rev 21:16, 22).

6. King Hezekiah compared his life, while deathly ill, to a shepherd's tent that had departed or been pulled up (*ns'* ni., Isa 38:12; cf. Job 4:21 ni.). Cf. for a similar image 2 Cor 5:1, 4; 2 Peter 1:13. Job compared his life's anguish with a tree being uprooted (*ns'* hi., Job 19:10).

P-B 1. In CD 1:16, *ns'* hi. designates the removal of the boundary marker (cf. Deut 19:14; *swg* hi.).

2. The rabbinic usage is similar to the biblical. The vb. *ns'* is also used for removing idols (hi.) and of being deposed (hof.) from the high priesthood (see Jastrow, 918).

Journey, going, marching, walking, wandering: → *'rḥ* (be on the road, wander, # 782); → *'šr* I (walk straight, # 886); → *drk* (tread, march, # 2005); → *hlk* (go, walk, behave, # 2143); → *zḥl* I (slide away, # 2323); → *yṣ'* (go out, come forward, # 3655); → *yrd* (go down, go up, descend, # 3718); → *massa'* (setting out, # 5023); → *nḥt* (march down, descend, settle, # 5737); → *s'n* (tramp along, tread, # 6008); → *'dh* I (stride, # 6334); → *'lh* (go up, ascend, bring up, # 6590); → *pś'* I (step forth, march, # 7314); → *ṣ'd* (step, march, # 7575); → *šwr* I (descend, caravan, # 8801)
Separation, breaking down, removal: → *'ṣl* (set apart, withdraw, shorten, # 724); → *bdl* (separate o.s., # 976); → *br'* I (create, separate, # 1343); → *hgh* II (separate, remove, # 2048); → *mwš* II (depart, remove, take away, # 4631); → *ns'* (tear out, march out, # 5825); → *ntq* (tear away, # 5998); → *prq* (pull away, # 7293); → *ṣ'n* (pack up, # 7585); → *rḥq* (be far away, remove, # 8178)

BIBLIOGRAPHY
TWAT 5:493-97; M. Delcor, "Quelques cas de survivances du vocabulaire nomade en hébreu biblique," *VT* 25, 1975, 307-22, esp. 312-13; A. Guillaume, *Hebrew and Arabic Lexicography*, 1965, 28-29 (= *AbrN* 1, 1959, 28-29).

Cornelis Van Dam

5830 נְעוּרִים

נְעוּרִים (*nᵉ'ûrîm*), youth (# 5830); נְעֻרוֹת (*nᵉ'ûrôt*), youth (# 5831).

OT The fem. form occurs only once (Jer 32:30) and is not demonstrably distinct from the masc. form in meaning. Both forms are abstractions from the *n'r* group of noms. This is a general categorization. One's youth can possibly refer back to childhood (e.g., Gen 8:21), though no context unarguably refers to a child. Youths take part in battle (1 Sam 17:33) and can be married (Prov 2:17; 5:18; Mal 2:14-15). Youth can be a time of rebellion (Ps 25:7) and sin (Job 13:26), or of religious instruction (Ps 71:17) and worship (1 Kgs 18:12).

Israel is portrayed in the prophets as a youth (Jer 2:2; 3:4, 24-25; Ezek 23:3, 8, 19, 21; Hos 2:15[17]). The metaphor refers to the wilderness period when Yahweh took her, a vulnerable orphan, under his protection. It also serves as a metaphor for Israel's wayward, rebellious behavior, thus epitomizing the frustrations of a loving parent with offspring who are ungrateful and indiscriminate.

Youth: → *bāḥûr* I (young man, # 1033); → *bᵉtûlâ* (young girl, # 1435); → *nᵉ'ûrîm* (youth, # 5830); → *'ᵃlûmîm* (youth, # 6596); → *ṣā'îr* I (little, small, young, trifling, # 7582); → *qāṭōn* (small, trifling, young, # 7785); → *šaḥᵃrût* (dark hair, prime of youth, # 8841)

John Walton

5831 (*nᵉ'urôt*, youth), → # 5830

5833 (*nā'im*, agreeable, pleasant, lovely), → # 5838

5835	נעל

נעל (*n'l*), q. tie, lock; hi. provide sandals (# 5835); nom. נַעַל (*na'al*), sandal (→ # 5837); מַנְעוּל (*man'ûl*), bolt (# 4980); מִנְעָל (*min'āl*), bolt (# 4981).

OT 1. The vb. *n'l* means tie, lock, in "He shut the doors of the upper room behind him and locked them" (Judg 3:23; cf. v. 24; 2 Sam 13:17, 18; S of Songs 4:12).

2. The vb. appears twice with the meaning "provide sandals," in a list of garments provided for prisoners (2 Chron 28:15) and in a description of the foundling Jerusalem (Ezek 16:10).

3. The nom. *man'ûl* designates a "bolt" in Neh 3:3, 6, 13, 14, 15; S of Songs 5:5.

4. In Deut 33:25 *min'āl* refers to the bolt of a gate.

Closing, shutting: → *'ṭm* (stopped up, # 357); → *'ṭr* (close [mouth], # 358); → *gwp* I (shut, close, # 1589); → *ṭḥḥ* (besmeared, stuck, shut, # 3220); → *ṭmh* (stopped up, # 3241); → *n'l* I (tie, lock, # 5835); → *sgr* I (shut, close, deliver up, # 6037); → *stm* (stop up, # 6258); → *'ṣh* I (shut, # 6781); → *'ṣm* III (shut one's eyes, # 6794); → *ṣrr* I (bind, shut up, be narrow, in straits, distress, # 7674); → *qpṣ* I (draw together, shut, # 7890); → *š''* I (smear, smooth, shut, # 9129)

Bill T. Arnold

5837	נַעַל

נַעַל (*na'al*), sandal (# 5837); < נעל (*n'l*), tie, lock (→ # 5835).

ANE The Heb. word is the same as Syr. *na'alā'*, Mand. *nala*, Arab. *na'l*, and Ugar. *n'l* (*UT*, # 1664). Among the products made by the artisan-god Kothar (*CTA* 4:I:26-44) is *n'l il*, El's sandals (see Schaeffer, *AfO* 20, 1963, 206-7, Fig 21 for a picture of a bronze statue of El with open sandals overlaid with gold).

1. Upon returning from rescuing Lot and defeating the kings, Abram rejects the king of Sodom's gracious offer with "I will accept nothing belonging to you, not even a thread or the thong of a sandal (*miḥûṭ w^{e}'ad ś^{e}rôk na'al*)" (Gen 14:23). Speiser (*Genesis*, AB, 105) connected this phrase with the Aram. formula, *min ḥam w^{e}'ad ḥuṭ*, be it a blade of straw or piece of string, and older Akkad. *lu ḫāmu lu ḫuṣābu*, be it a blade of straw or splinter of wood. The Aram. formula is used in the division of marriage property after a divorce, while the Akk. formula is found in a discussion of dissolving partnership holdings. Gen 14 applies to neither of these circumstances. Much closer to Gen 14 is a Ugar. text (RS 17.340 = *PRU* 4:48-52) in which Niqmaddu, plundered by his enemies and rescued by the Hittite king, Suppiluliuma, attempts to give Suppliliuma a gift as a sign of his appreciation. The restored text reads, "Suppiluliuma, the Great King, saw the loyalty of Niqmaddu and as far as what belongs to Ugarit .... Suppiluliuma, the Great King, will not touch anything, be it straw or splinter ([*ḫāma u*]*ḫuṣāba*)" (Muffs, 86; *CAD* 6:259a).

2. Both Moses (Exod 3:5) and Joshua (Josh 5:15) are told to remove their sandals when in the presence of deity. Apart from a sign of respect and humility, such a command may be dictated by the following factors: (a) in the presence of God there is neither dirt nor possibility of injury, and so sandals are unnecessary; (b) sandals, being made of animal skins, are impure in regard to the sacred and thus not to be worn into a sacred precinct. The fact that the OT, when dealing with priestly vestments, never says

anything about covering for the feet may indicate that the priests ministered barefooted.

3. Sandal removal also plays a part in the law about levirate marriage (Deut 25:5-10) and in the story of Ruth and Boaz (Ruth 4:7-8) with reference to the legal transfer of a right of redemption. Different shoe rites played symbolic roles in property transactions, as the Nuzi texts make clear (Lacheman, 53-54). In the OT sandal removal is also a symbol of disgracing a disagreeable brother (Deut 25).

Leg, loins, foot, thigh: → *b^{e}hôn* (thumb, big toe, # 984); → *ḥ^{a}lāṣayim* (loins, # 2743); → *yārēk* (thigh, leg, # 3751); → *kesel* I (loins, flank/side, # 4072); → *midrāk* (foot-print, # 4534); → *marg^{e}lôt* (place of feet, # 5274); → *motnayim* (loins, hips, # 5516); → *na'al* (sandal, # 5837); → *paḥad* II (thigh, # 7066); → *pa'am* (foot, step, time, # 7193); → *qarsōl* (ankle, # 7972); → *regel* (foot, # 8079); → *šôq* (thigh, leg, # 8797)

BIBLIOGRAPHY

E. R. Lacheman, "Note on Ruth 4:7-8," *JBL* 56, 1937, 53-54; Y. Muffs, "Abraham the Noble Warrior: Patriarchal Politics and Laws of War in Ancient Israel," *JJS* 33, 1982, 81-107.

Victor P. Hamilton

5838	נעם

נעם (*n'm*), q. be pleasing, be agreeable, be dear (# 5838); מַנְעַמִּים (*man'ammîm*), nom. delicacies (# 4982); נָעִים (*nā'îm*), adj. agreeable, pleasant, lovely (# 5833); נֹעַם (*nō'am*), nom. kindness (# 5840).

ANE The root *n'm* is well attested in other Sem. languages (Phoen., Arab., ESA, Aram., Ugar.). Two roots with related meaning will also be covered below.

OT There are two reciprocal, and often overlapping, dimensions to the concept: the intrinsic attractiveness of an object or action, and conversely, an individual's free reception of an object or consent to an action, whether the action or object is pleasing or not. The vb. that primarily indicates the former is *n'm*, be pleasant (appearing only in poetry: Gen 49:15; 2 Sam 1:26; Ps 141:6; Prov 2:10; 9:17; 24:25; S of Songs 7:6[7]; Ezek 32:19), while the vb. expressing the latter is primarily *'bh*, be willing, accede, consent (# 14; less frequently *'wt*, this root being found only in Heb.). The only two contexts in the Bible where *'wt* (# 252) appears, describing the mutual consent between Jacob's sons and the Shechemites (Gen 34:15, 22, 23) and the priests' acceptance of King Jehoash's directives (2 Kgs 12:8[9]), reflect an individual's acquiescence to what are perceived as less than ideal conditions. The same significance applies to *'bh*, but most of its occurrences appear in contexts where the individual refuses to acquiesce or cooperate within the constraints imposed. The root *'bh*, related to the Heb. roots *y'b* (→ # 3277) and *t'b* (→ # 9289) and the nom. *'ebyôn*, poor (→ # 36), is attested in other languages, meaning either not willing, refuse, deny (Arab., Eth., ESA) or willing, wish (Aram., Egyp.).

1. *Intrinsic quality.* (a) The term that focuses on the intrinsic appeal of an object to observers surfaces in personal names for males and females, both Israelite and non-Israelite (Naomi in Ruth 1:2, Naaman in 2 Kgs 5:1, Naam in 1 Chron 4:15, Naamah in 1 Kgs 14:21). It is difficult to determine in such names where a divine element is lacking whether the pleasant quality refers to a deity or to the individual who

bears the name. When this element appears in names of cities, it likely reflects an aesthetic appraisal of the environs (Naamah in Josh 15:41; cf. Gen 49:15).

(b) The intrinsic agreeableness of an object is identified by reference to many of the five physical senses. The tongue finds certain foods pleasing to the taste (Ps 141:4). The eyes discern forms that are pleasing to see (S of Songs 1:16; 7:6[7]). The ears discriminate not only words that are pleasant (Ps 141:6; Prov 15:26; 16:24; 23:8) but also sounds that are pleasing to hear: the lyre (*kinnôr*) in comparison with other instruments, such as percussion and wind instruments, is described as *nā'îm* and so particularly appropriate in praising Yahweh (Ps 81:2[3]). Because the physical sensation is so prominent in this root, references to God should be often understood as marking physical manifestations or theophanies of God (Levenson). Like the vb. *n'm*, the adj. *nā'îm* appears only in poetry (13x: 2 Sam 1:23; 23:1; Job 36:11; Ps 16:6, 11; 81:2[3]; 133:1; 135:3; 147:1; Prov 22:18; 23:8; 24:4; S of Songs 1:16). Unfortunately, the senses of many humans are deadened and unable to appreciate what is *n'm* (Prov 23:8).

(c) The quality is something that is neither everywhere available nor equally available to all, and where it does appear, it may in some cases prove to be ultimately destructive. Not all that is attractive and desirable should be pursued (Prov 9:17), for what is superficially appealing may ultimately lead to one's demise (Gen 49:15). Individuals can intentionally exploit what is attractive as a lure to trap the unsuspecting (Ps 141:4; Prov 9:17). For this reason, one petitions God for help in distancing oneself from the deceptively enticing delicacies of the wicked (Ps 141:4).

2. *Subjective response.* (a) The acceptance (*'wt* [# 252], *'bh* [# 14]) of an object or action by an individual, often coerced by circumstances or another's will, is to be distinguished from Heb. terms such as *rṣh*, be pleased with(→ # 8354), *ndb*, volunteer (→ # 5605), or *ḥpṣ*, desire (→ # 2911), that in contrast focus on the individual's driving desire independent of outside coercion. Only two (Job 39:9; Isa 1:19) of the 54x of *'bh* in the Bible describe positive acceptance and consent to another's status or proposition (contrast the positive reception described in all four of the appearances of *'wt* [Gen 34:15, 22, 23; 2 Kgs 12:8[9]). All other appearances of *'bh* are preceded by a negative particle: "not willing." The remarkably consistent emphasis on an unwillingness to agree or assent to another's status or proposition is perhaps indicative of this term's specific focus or nuance, appearing as it does in primarily negative contexts (cf. meaning of the root in Eth. and Arab.). This vb. cannot stand alone but assumes the action of some other vb. usually present as an infinitive: one is (not) willing *to act* in a specified fashion.

(b) Humans such as Pharaoh (Exod 10:27) are depicted as unwilling to cooperate with God. The most frequent humans in the Bible so described are Israelites who do not wish to listen or obey (Lev 26:21; Isa 28:12; Ezek 3:7; 20:8) or walk in God's ways (Isa 42:24). God, in turn, may be unwilling to cooperate with humans such as Balaam (Deut 23:5[6]; Josh 24:10). The most common dissent, however, is the unwillingness of humans to cooperate with other humans (Deut 2:30; Judg 19:10, 25; 20:13; 1 Sam 22:17; 26:23; 2 Sam 2:21; 13:14, 16, 25; 14:29; 23:16, 17; Ezek 3:7). All four of the appearances of *'wt* relate the cooperation of humans with other humans (Gen 34:15, 22, 23; 2 Kgs 12:8[9]).

Agreeable, lovely, pleasing: → *ṭwb* (please, be in favor, be joyous, be valuable, # 3201); → *kšr* (succeed, prosper, be pleasing, # 4178); → *n'h* (be lovely, # 5533); → *n'm* (be pleasing, be agreeable, be dear, # 5838); → *'rb* III (be pleasant, # 6844); → *rṣh* I (be pleased with, to treat favorably, # 8354)

Bibliography

TDOT 1:24-26; *TWAT* 5:500-506; A. M. Honeyman, "Some Developments of the Semitic Root *'by*," *JAOS* 64, 1944, 81-82; E. Jenni, "Wollen und 'Nichtwollen' im Hebräischen," *Mélanges A. Dupont-Sommer*, 1971, 201-7; E. Kutsch, *Verheisung und Gesetz*, BZAW 131, 1973, 34-38; J. D. Levenson, "A Technical Meaning for N'M in the Hebrew Bible," *VT* 35, 1985, 61-67.

Samuel A. Meier

5840 (*nō'am*, kindness), → # 5838

5848	נַעֲצוּץ

נַעֲצוּץ (*na'ᵃṣûṣ*), thornbush (# 5848).

ANE This term does not appear in cognate languages (*HALAT* 622).

OT In Isa 55:13, it is paired with *sirpad* and contrasted to trees (which represent the blessings of the kingdom to come). On the other hand, it can be used in a description of the land as the result of God's future judgment (Isa 7:19).

P-B In postbiblical Heb. and Aram., *n'ṣ* ocurs as a vb. meaning "to prick, stick" (e.g., PTalm Berakot 4.7b). The nom. form also occurs with the meaning "thorn" (Megilla 10b).

Thornbush, nettle, sting, thistle, thorn: → *'āṭād* (thornbush, # 353); → *barqōn* (thorn, brier, # 1402); → *deber* II (thorny sting, # 1823); → *dardar* (thistle, # 1998); → *ḥēdeq* (brier, # 2537); → *ḥôaḥ* I (thorn, # 2560); → *mᵉsûkâ* (thorn hedge, # 5004); → *na'ᵃṣûṣ* (thornbush, # 5848); → *sîrâ* (thorny bush, # 6106); → *sillôn* (thorn, # 6141); → *sᵉneh* (thorny shrub, # 6174); → *sirpād* (stinging nettle, # 6252); → *ṣe'ᵉlîm* (thorny lotus, # 7365); → *ṣᵉnînîm* (thorns, # 7564); → *qôṣ* I (thornbush, # 7764); → *qimmôś* (weeds, nettles, # 7853); → *śēk* (thorn, splinter, # 8493); → *šāmîr* I (Christ's thorn, # 9031)

Bibliography

TWOT 2:585.

K. Lawson Younger, Jr.

5849 (*n'r* I, growl [of lion]), → # 787

5850	נער

נער (*n'r* II), q. shake; ni. be shaken out, shaken free; pi. shake off, out; hitp. shake oneself free (# 5850); נְעֹרֶת (*nᵉ'ōret*), nom. tow (# 5861).

OT 1. As a vb. *n'r* II is used only 11x in the OT. This vb. can be applied to the shaking of a tree that loses its leaves (Isa 33:9), the shaking of a hand that rejects a bribe (33:15), or the shaking of a garment to dislodge unwanted items (Neh 5:13). Twice it describes what the Lord did to the Egyptians at the Red Sea: "Then the Lord *overthrew* the Egyptians in the midst of the sea" (Exod 14:27 NASB; Ps 136:15). This vb. also describes release from the bonds of captivity, both literally (Judg 16:20) and figuratively (Isa 52:2). Finally, the phrase "to be shaken off" can be used to express rejection (Job 38:13; Ps 109:23).

2. As a nom., this root occurs only 2x (Judg 16:9; Isa 1:31). In both instances it may be translated as "tow," that highly flammable material shaken from flax.

Shaking, terror, trembling: → *g'š* (rise and fall noisily, swell, surge, # 1723); → *zw'* (tremble, quake, be afraid, # 2316); → *zll* II (shake, quake, tremble, # 2362); → *ḥalḥālâ* (shaking, trembling, anguish, # 2714); → *ḥrg* (come out trembling, # 3004); → *ḥrd* (tremble, shudder, startle, # 3006); → *yr'* (tremble, be fainthearted, # 3760); → *mwṭ* (waver, reel, stagger, shake, reel, # 4572); → *m'd* (slip, slide, shake, totter, # 5048); → *nwd* (shake, totter, waiver, wander, mourn, flee, # 5653); → *nwṭ* (shake, quake, # 5667); → *nw'* (shake, tremble, stagger, totter, wave, # 5675); → *n'r* II (shake, shake off, # 5850); → *smr* (shudder, have goose-bumps, bristle, # 6169); → *'iw'îm* (distortion, stagger, dizzy, # 6413); → *pwq* I (stagger, wobble, reel, totter, # 7048); → *pḥd* I (tremble, be in dread, # 7064); → *plṣ* (shudder, shake, tremble, # 7145); → *qwṣ* I (feel disgust, frighten, cause dread, # 7762); → *rgz* (agitate, quiver, shake, excite, rouse up, agitate, # 8074); → *rnh* I (rattle, # 8261); → *r'd* (tremble, shake, tremble, # 8283); → *r'l* I (brandish, make to quiver, # 8302); → *r'š* I (quake, shake, leap, # 8321); → *rpp* (shake, quake, rock, # 8344); → *r^e^tēt* (terror, panic, trembling, # 8417); → *ś'r* I (be afraid, terrified, bristle with horror, # 8547)

Bibliography
TWOT 2:585.

M. V. Van Pelt/W. C. Kaiser, Jr.

5853	נַעַר

נַעַר (*na'ar*), boy, youth, servant (# 5853); נַעֲרָה (*na'^a^râ*), newly married woman; maidservant (# 5855).

ANE 1. The word *n'rn* occurs in Egyptian texts of the Ramseside period, and is most likely a Canaanite loanword. *n'rn* are those engaged in some kind of military role. Thus, in the account of the battle between Ramses II and the Hittite king Muwatallis at Kadesh we read, "The arrival of the *Nearin* troops of Pharaoh—life prosperity, health!—from the land of Amurru..." (*ANET*, p. 256 and n. 12). In what is known as the Papyrus Anastasi (late nineteenth dynasty, near the end of the 13th century BC), Hori, a royal official, says to Amen-em-Opet, "Thou are sent on a mission to *Djahan* at the head of the victorious army, to crush those rebels called *Nearin* ... O Who-Is-It, thou choice scribe, *mahir* who knows (how to use) his hand, foremost of the *nearin*, first of the army host" (*ANET*, p. 476 and n. 21; p. 478).

2. *n'r* also appears frequently in the Ugar. texts (*WUS*, # 1808), where the word describes (a) an overseer or a supervisor; (b) some category of palace personnel; (c) military personnel, and probably high-ranking ones at that (Cutler, MacDonald 1976). The Ugar. texts have the corresponding feminine *n'rt* for masculine *n'r*.

3. The root is present a few times in Phoen. texts (*KAI* 37:A 8, 10. B 11; 24:12). While Akk. does not have the same nom., the semantic equivalent is *ṣuḫāru* (*CAD* Ṣ 231b-235a; MacDonald 1976).

OT 1. *na'ar* appears 239x in the OT. About a third (86) of these are found in Samuel (1 Sam—60x; 2 Sam—26x), followed by Kings with 35 (1 Kgs—11x; 2 Kgs—24x), Genesis (27x), Judges (23x), Isaiah (11x), Nehemiah (8x). Attempts have been made to understand this word by appealing to etymology. Among the more frequent suggestions is that *na'ar* is related either to *n'r* I, growl (i.e., a reference to the voice breaking at puberty), or to *n'r* II, shake (i.e., a reference to the child leaving its mother's womb). Both of these are unconvincing; in fact, it is most unlikely that one may ascertain the meaning of *na'ar* simply by etymological considerations. Rather, one will have to use the contextual approach more than etymology *per se*.

2. *na'ar* appears with *zāqēn* as a merism, "from the young (and) unto the old" (Gen 19:4; Josh 6:21; Esth 3:13) and as permerismos ("old and young") in Jer 51:22, and in reverse order in Exod 10:9; Isa 20:4; and Lam 2:21. Thus, a *na'ar* can never be *zāqēn*, or vice-versa.

3. The word is used to cover a wide range of age-groups, from an unborn child (Judg 13:5, 7, 8, 12), to one just born (1 Sam 4:21), to a three-month-old child (Exod 2:6), to a child not yet weaned (1 Sam 1:22), to a child recently weaned (1 Sam 1:24), to a seventeen-year-old (Gen 37:2 [NIV, "a young man"]), to a thirty-year-old (Gen 41:12; cf. v. 46, [NIV "a young Hebrew"]). There seems to be no case where a *na'ar* was married. Thus, we may conclude that one meaning of *na'ar* is that it refers to any young person from infancy to just before marriage.

4. Jeremiah attempted to evade obedience to God's call on his life by protesting, "I do not know how to speak; I am only a child" (*na'ar*, Jer 1:6). His youth, he felt, disqualified him from public service, especially in a society that gave preference to the sagacity of the elders.

5. There is much evidence (MacDonald 1976) that *na'ar* refers not only to "youngsters" but to a servant or employee who served under the authority of a superior. Samuel and Kings abound with references to *n^e'ārîm* where this interpretation fits. Thus, Gen 18:7 refers to Abraham's *na'ar*, hardly "Abraham's boy," but "Abraham's servant," i.e., the patriarch's most immediate attendant. Cf. also Gen 22:3, 5, 19.

Later in Genesis Pharaoh is told of the presence of a Hebrew *na'ar* (Gen 41:12). Is it likely that later Pharaoh would say of a young boy, "Can we find anyone like this man (*'îš*), one in whom is the spirit of God?" (v. 38), or "You shall be in charge of my palace, and all my people are to submit to your orders" (v.40)? In Josh 2:1 Joshua sent out two scouts who are called "men" (*'^{a}nāšîm*). The king of Jericho also refers to them as "men" (2:3) as does Joshua himself later (6:22). But in the very next verse (6:23) they are called *n^e'ārîm*. Thus a *na'ar* might designate not only a minor (under the authority of his father), but also a (civil) servant or soldier/scout (under the authority of his superior).

6. *na'ar* may reflect a range of meanings as does the Eng. word "boy" ("It's a boy"—gender; "a small boy"—age and size; "he's our boy"—family relationships; "our boys are over there fighting"—soldiers; "I'm playing golf with the boys at the office"—companions).

7. In Gen 22 Abraham uses the absolute form (*hanna'ar*) when referring to Isaac (22:5) as does the angel (v. 12), and here the meaning is clearly "young person." But Abraham uses the construct form (with pronominal suffixes) when referring to his companions (vv. 3, 5, 19), and here the meaning is clearly the less personal "servants."

8. There is an interesting shift between *yeled* and *na'ar* in describing Ishmael. The narrator calls him *yeled* (Gen 21:8, 14), as does Hagar (v. 16). But God/the angel calls him a *na'ar* (vv. 12, 17, 18). The narrator also calls Ishmael a *na'ar* (v. 20) when speakinq of his relationship with God. *yeled* seems to speak here only of a biological relationship, while *na'ar* speaks of care and concern.

9. Abraham is accompanied by two servants (*na'ar*) on a three-day journey (Gen 22:3), as is Balak (Num 22:22, cf. also Saul on his trip to En-dor, 1 Sam 28:8). The theme of two servants may be a literary stereotype. That is, when a man of eminence sets out on a journey, two people attend on him.

10. Twice *na'ar* is used by Isaiah in reference to a special child who is a sign from God (Isa 7:16; 11:6). "A child, not a strutting monarch, is the one whom God chooses to rule this world's great. In innocence, simplicity, and faith lie the salvation of a globe grown old in sophistication, cynicism, and violence" (Oswalt, *Isaiah*, NICOT, 1:283-84).

11. The NIV renders the word *na'ᵃrâ* by "maids" (Gen 24:61); "attendants" (Exod 2:5); "girl(s)" (Deut 22:19); "young woman" (Ruth 4:12); "servant girls" (2:8).

12. When used in the pl. with pronominal suffix, *na'ᵃrâ* invariably means "servants, attendants." Cf. Gen 24:61 (Rebekah's); Exod 2:5 (Pharaoh's daughter's); Ruth 2:8, 22; 3:2 (Boaz's); 1 Sam 25:42 (Abigail's); Esth 2:9; 4:16 (Esther's); Prov 9:3 (Lady Wisdom's); 27:27 (one possessing riches and a crown, v. 24); 31:15 (belonging to "a wife of noble character" [NIV rendering of *'ēšet ḥayil*], but whose husband is prominent enough to sit at the city gate, v. 23).

13. Often *na'ᵃrâ* is qualified with *bᵉtûlâ* ("virgin"), as in Gen 24:16; Deut 22:23, 28; Judg 21:12; 1 Kgs 1:2; Esth 2:2. Gen 24:16 and Judg 21:12 add the further qualification that the young girl(s) had never known a man. The addition of this phrase may either be a reinforcement of the virginity of the woman, or else it alone may suggest virginity and thus indicate that *bᵉtûlâ* is not necessarily "virgin," but rather one of marriageable age (who in most instances obviously would be a *bᵉtûlâ*).

14. Unlike *na'ar*, *na'ᵃrâ* is applied to a married woman (Deut 22:15, 16, 19, 20, 21) in a law that begins "if a man takes a wife, after lying with her." Thus, the marriage has been consummated. In Ruth 2:6 (blurred by NIV) and 4:12 the term refers to a young widow.

15. Among the sins for which Amos condemns Israel is "Father and son use the same *girl* and so profane my holy name" (Amos 2:7). This cannot be a reference to cultic prostitution, for the woman referred to is not a *qᵉdēšâ*, but a *na'ᵃrâ* (a term without any cultic connotations—but cf. Andersen, Freedman, *Amos*, AB 24A, 318-19). Nor can this verse be connected with the Hittite law (*ANET*, p. 196), "If father and son sleep with (the same) slave girl, or harlot, there shall be no punishment," because the *na'ᵃrâ* is neither a slave girl nor a harlot. Rather, for Amos, the *na'ᵃrâ* is another member of the defenseless and exploited persons mentioned in this verse, along with the poor and the oppressed.

16. Num 30:3[4] speaks of a young unmarried woman (literally "a woman ... in her youth"), whose father has the authority to annul any vows or oaths on the day they are made. The expression "a woman in her youth" covers childhood and up until she is married. Rabbinic tradition limits this period to the short time when the first signs of puberty are visible, that is, a girl between eleven years and one day and twelve years and one day (Sipre Num 123). "When a woman has attained puberty, her father no longer has authority over her" (Nedarim 47b).

Male: → *'ādām* (Adam, people, # 132); → *'îš* I (man, husband, # 408); → *'ᵉnôš* I (men, single man, # 632); → *'āšîš* (man, # 861); → *geber* I (young man, # 1505); → *zākār* (male, # 2351); → *mᵉtîm* I (men, people; # 5493); → *na'ar* (boy, # 5853)

Female: → *'iššâ* (woman, # 851); → *g^ebîrâ/g^eberet* (lady, queen, mistress, # 1485/1509); → *na'^arâ* I (girl, # 5855); → *n^eqēbâ* (female, # 5922); → *pîlegeš* (concubine, # 7108); → *šiddâ* (lady, # 8721)
Youth: → *bāḥûr* I (young man, # 1033); → *b^etûlâ* (young girl, # 1435); → *n^e'ûrîm* (youth, # 5830); → *'^alûmîm* (youth, # 6596); → *ṣā'îr* I (little, small, young, trifling, # 7582); → *qāṭōn* (small, trifling, young, # 7785); → *šaḥ^arût* (dark hair, prime of youth, # 8841)
Child: → *gōlem* (embryo, # 1677); → *ṭap* I (children, # 3251); → *yônēq* (young child, # 3437); → *yld* (bear, bring forth, be born, # 3528); → *yātôm* (orphan, # 3846); → *mamzēr* (bastard, # 4927); → *na'ar* (boy, # 5853); → *'ôlēl* (child, # 6402); → *t'm* (bear twins, # 9298); → **Adoption: Theology**

BIBLIOGRAPHY
TWAT 5:507-18; *TWOT* 2:585-86; N. Avigad, "New Light on the *Na'ar* Seals," *Fs. G. E. Wright*, 1976, 294-300; B. J. Bamberger, "Qetanah, Na'arah, Bogereth," *HUCA* 32, 1961, 281-94; H. Barilqu, "The Case of the *ne'ārîm*," *Beth Mikra* 27, 1981/82, 101-8; S. Ben-Reuven, "*Ben* in Contrast to *yeled* and *na'arim* in the Bible," *Beth Mikra* 28, 1982/83, 147-49; B. Cutler and J. Macdonald, "Identification of the *na'ar* in the Ugaritic Texts," *UF* 8, 1976, 27-35; J. Macdonald, "The Status and Role of the *na'ar* in Israelite Society," *JNES* 35, 1976, 147-70; idem, "The Role and Status of *ṣuḫārû* in the Mari Correspondence," *JAOS* 96, 1976, 57-68; C. M. Miller, "Maidenhood and Virginity in Ancient Israel," *ResQ* 22, 1979, 242-46; A. R. Schulman "The *N^ern* at the Battle of Kadesh," *Journal of the American Research Center in Egypt* 1, 1962, 47-53; H. P. Stähli, *Knabe—Jüngling—Knecht. Untersuchungen zum Begriff n'r im Alten Testament*, 1978.

Victor Hamilton

5855 (*na'^arâ* I, newly married woman), → # 5853

5861 (*n^e'oret*, tow), → # 5850

5864 נָפָה

נָפָה (*nāpâ* I), sieve (# 5864).

ANE *nāpâ* is related to Eth. *näpäyä*, sift, see *HALAT* 669.

OT *nāpâ* occurs only in Isa 30:28, where God judges the nations by shaking them in the sieve used for the final cleaning of winnowed grain.

Winnow: → *zrh* I (scatter, winnow, # 2430); → *nāpâ* I (sieve, # 5864); → *raḥat* (winnowing shovel, # 8181)
Sieve: → *ḥašrâ* (sieve, # 3142); → *k^ebārâ* I (sieve, # 3895); → *nāpâ* I (sieve, # 5864)

BIBLIOGRAPHY
ABD 1:95-98; J. Feliks, "Agricultural Implements in Ancient Ereṣ Israel," *EncJud*, 1971; S. Paul and W. Dever, *Biblical Archaeology*, 1974.

Mark D. Futato

5865 (*nāpâ* II, hilly hinterland), → # 2215

5870 נפח

נפח (*npḥ*), blow (# 5870); מַפָּח (*mappāḥ*), blowing (# 5134); מַפֻּחַ (*mappuaḥ*), blowing (# 5135); תַּפּוּחַ (*tappûa* I), apple (→ # 9515).

OT 1. The root means snort or denegrate in Mal 1:13, where the wicked dishonor the sacred sacrifices. Most of the contexts in which this root and derivatives occur depict the just retribution of a sovereign God who in one way or another uses bursts of breath or air to vindicate his righteousness to Israel and her neighbors (e.g., Isa 54:16; Jer 1:13; Ezek 22:20, 21; Hag 1:9).

2. *mappāḥ*, blowing, refers to the final expiration of one's *nepeš* in Job 11:20 (cf. Job 31:39; Jer 15:9), which is an appropriate expression since it was God who inspired the *nepeš* initially (Gen 2:7; also Ezek 37:9; cf. *n^ešāmâ*).

3. The derivative nom., *mappuaḥ*, denotes a blacksmith's bellows that blow in vain, like the prophets' words that do not refine Israel (Jer 6:29).

Blowing (wind, breath): → *hzh* (pant in sleep, # 2111); → *ndp* (blow away, scatter, # 5622); → *npḥ* (blow, # 5870); → *nšb* (blow, # 5959); → *nšp* (blow, # 5973); → *pwḥ* (blow, blast, malign, # 7032)
Breath, life: → *hebel* I (breath, # 2039); → *nepeš* (breath, life, desire, # 5883); → *n^ešāmâ* (breath, # 5972); → *š'p* I (pant, gasp, # 8634)

D. C. Fredericks

5872 (*n^epîlîm*, giants), → Giants

5876	נֹפֶךְ

נֹפֶךְ (*nōpek*), unidentified semiprecious stone (# 5876).

ANE Note the Egypt. *mfk't*, turquoise, malachite.

OT 1. The rare word is cited among the variety of gemstones set in the breastpiece of the high priest (first stone of the second row, Exod 28:18; 39:11), along with *kadkōd* as a medium of exchange for barter (Ezek 27:16), and figuratively as part of Tyre's adornment marking special status (Ezek 28:13). The NIV reads turquoise, the JB reads carbuncle, while the NEB and Allen (*Ezekiel 20-48*, WBC, 1990, 90) agree with Zimmerli (83-84) and more correctly understand garnet—specifically ruby-red garnet or almandine.

2. For a theological introduction to the topic of gems in the OT, see *'ōdem* (# 138).

Precious Stones: → *'eben* (stone, rock, # 74); → *'ōdem* (precious stone, # 138); → *'aḥlāmâ* (jasper, # 334); → *'eqdāḥ* (beryl, # 734); → *bahaṭ* (precious stone, # 985); → *bāreqet* (emerald, # 1403); → *yah^alōm* (precious stone, # 3402); → *yāš^epēh* (jasper, # 3835); → *kadkōd* (ruby?, # 3905); → *lešem* I (precious stone, # 4385); → *nōpek* (semi-precious stone, # 5876); → *sōḥeret* (mineral stone, # 6090); → *sappîr* (lapis lazulli, # 6209); → *piṭdâ* (chrysolite, # 7077); → *š^ebô* (precious stone, # 8648); → *šōham* I (precious stone, # 8732); → *šāmîr* II (emery, diamond?, # 9032); → *šēš* II (alabaster, # 9253); → *taršîš* II (precious stone, # 9577)
Jewelry, ornaments: → *'dh* II (adorn o.s., # 6335)

BIBLIOGRAPHY

IDB 2:898-905; *ISBE* 4:623-30; *NIDNTT* 3:395-98; J. S. Harris, "An Introduction to the Study of Personal Ornaments, of Precious, Semi-Precious and Imitation Stones Used Throughout Biblical History," *ALUOS* 4, 1962, 49-83; L. Koehler, "Hebräische Vokabeln II," *ZAW* 55, 1937, 161-74;

H. Quiring, "Die Edelsteine im Amtsschild des jüdischen Hohenpriesters und die Herkunft ihrer Namen," *AGM* 38, 1954, 193-213; W. Zimmerli, *Ezekiel 25-48*, 1983, 82-84.

Andrew E. Hill

5877	נפל

נפל (*npl*), q. fall; hi. make fall; hitp. fall on, lie prostrate (# 5877); מַפָּל (*mappāl*), folds (of a crocodile's flesh; Job 41:23[15]), sweepings (of grain; Amos 8:6) (# 5139); נְפִילִים (*n*[e]*pîlîm*), giants (→ # 5872); נֵפֶל (*nēpel*), miscarriage (→ # 5878).

ANE While the root *npl* is common in Sem. languages, some meanings such as the Akk. *napālum*, destroy or demolish, have no real equivalent in Heb. In general, Ugar. and Aram. usages are the closest to the range of meanings of *npl* in the OT.

OT 1. The vb. *npl* occurs ca. 433x in the OT, the majority of which (367x) are in the q. Another 61 occurrences are in the hi. and 5 in the hitp., while the one case in the pilal form (Ezek 28:23) is often emended on the basis of some Heb. manuscripts, the LXX, Syr., and Vg. to a q. form. In translating *npl*, the LXX in over 250 cases uses *piptō*, while *empiptō* appears 25x and *epipiptō* 35x.

2. The most common usage is in the literal sense of falling over or falling down, usually with the idea of unintentional falling. Often some indication is given of the direction of the fall (e.g., backward, into, through). It is used indiscriminately of both people and objects (e.g., tent, wall). It can also be employed for getting down from an animal (Gen 24:64) or alighting from a chariot (2 Kgs 5:21).

3. There are two distinct technical uses of *npl* in the OT. The first is in connection with the casting of lots. The q. form is used to describe the literal fact of the lot falling (1 Chron 26:14; Ezek 24:6; Jon 1:7) and the hi. form the casting of lots (Neh 10:34[35]; 1 Chron 24:31; 26:13). As an extension of this usage it is employed to indicate assignment of the Promised Land to the various tribes of Israel (Josh 13:6; 23:4; Ezek 45:1). The full formula occurs in Num 34:2, *tippōl lākem b*[e]*naḥ*[a]*lâ*, "to you it will fall as an inheritance," but more common is the vb. in the hi. plus the preposition *l*[e] (Josh 13:6; 23:4; Isa 34:17). Ps 78:55 even attributes the action of casting lots to the Lord as he dispossessed others in order to settle the tribes of Israel in Canaan.

The second technical usage is a group of passages in which "fall" is used in the sense of "fail." The Lord does not allow Samuel's word to fail (1 Sam 3:19), nor Elijah's (2 Kgs 10:10), and especially does not permit his own word to fail (Josh 21:45; 23:14 [2x]; 1 Kgs 8:56). Similar is the usage in the promissory oath that not a hair of the head will fall (1 Sam 14:45; 2 Sam 14:11; 1 Kgs 1:52).

4. The vb. is often used of an act of self-humiliation, when someone falls on his or her face before a superior (Ruth 2:10; 2 Sam 9:6; 1 Kgs 18:7, 39). Sometimes an additional indication is given, such as falling on the ground (Gen 44:14) or falling at the feet (1 Sam 25:24; 2 Kgs 4:37). The expression is of importance theologically because it is used in the religious sense of prostrating oneself before the Lord (Gen 17:3, 17; 1 Chron 21:16; 2 Chron 20:18) or before his representative (Josh 5:14; 7:6). In some of these cases it appears along with the vb. *ḥwh* II (→ # 2556; e.g., Josh 5:14; 2 Chron 20:18), which emphasizes the aspect of humble submission to the Lord and worship of him. The connection of *npl* with worship would be further strengthened if it could be conclusively demonstrated that *npl* and the root indicating prayer (*pll*) are

really developments of the same biliteral stem meaning "to fall." If the text of Ezek 28:23 is correct, *niplal* in this passage would mean "to be cast down," and an easy transition from this would be a derived meaning "to pray" (cf. Ap-Thomas, "Notes on Some Terms," 231-32). *npl* is used several times in Jeremiah and Daniel to indicate prayer, along with the nouns *t^eḥinnâ* (Jer 36:7; 37:20; 38:26; 42:9; Dan 9:20; → # 9382) and *taḥ^anûn* (Dan 9:18; → # 9384).

5. *npl* also occurs with a variety of military connotations, including attacking one's enemies (without preposition, Job 1:15; with *b^e* Josh 11:7; with *'al*, Jer 48:32). Moreover, it can mean surrendering or deserting to one's enemies, especially so in the concluding period in the history of the kingdom of Judah when it is used to describe those who went over to the Babylonians (2 Kgs 25:11; Jer 21:9; 37:14; 39:9; 52:15). Here, the q. part. *nôp^elîm* takes on the meaning of "deserters." Earlier the expression was used in a good sense to describe the Manassites who defected to David (1 Chron 12:19-20[20-21]), and the northerners who came over to Asa when they saw that divine assistance was given to him (2 Chron 15:9). David's attachment to Achish is also conveyed by this idiom (1 Sam 29:3). The word *n^epilîm* in Gen 6:4 and Num 13:33 (2x) may possibly be related to this military meaning of *npl*, and if so would convey the idea of attackers or violent men. This interpretation would certainly fit the Gen 6 context, both in its wider setting, with the violence of Gen leading on to the violence in ch. 6, and with the further reference in 6:4 to the *n^epilîm* as "heroes," "men of renown." The context in Num 13 also has military overtones, for it forms part of the narrative concerning the investigation of Canaan by the spies.

6. This vb. is also used of experiences of falling where injury is caused or where "falling" is equivalent to "death." It is an easy transition from the one meaning to the other, for while some passages make injury or death explicit, many others are indeterminate and merely leave open the possibility that the injury caused by the fall was fatal. After a fight, a man may fall into his bed but not die (Exod 21:18). Ahaziah, king of Israel, fell through the lattice of an upper room and sent messengers to inquire from Baal-Zebub whether he would recover (2 Kgs 1:2). Other passages, however, show that the falling is equivalent to death. When the Lord intervenes, the helper will stumble, the helped will fall, and both will perish (Isa 31:3). Over a quarter of all occurrences of this vb. are in contexts dealing explicitly with death. Particularly graphic is the reference to Sisera's death in Judges 5:27, where the threefold use of *npl* climaxes the account. Often reference is made to the cause of death, the most common being *baḥereb*, "by the sword" (Num 14:3; Isa 3:25; Amos 7:17), which occurs 25x.

The hi. form is often used with a causative meaning. It is used of death being caused to someone, including references to divine action (Israel in the wilderness, Ps 106:26; inhabitants of Jerusalem, Jer 19:7). Frequently, *npl* occurs in the sense of violent death (96x), especially of death in battle. This is true collectively (Sisera's troops, Judg 4:16; the Philistines, 1 Sam 14:13; the Arameans, 1 Kgs 20:25; Edom, Jer 49:21) and also of individuals (Asahel, 2 Sam 2:23; Ahab, 1 Kgs 22:20). Sometimes the dead are described as lying prostrate (Deut 21:1; Judg 3:25; 1 Sam 31:8). "To fall into the hands of" frequently has the implication of being killed (Judg 15:18; 1 Chron 5:10; 21:13; Lam 1:7).

Falling, tottering, stumbling: → *bṭḥ* II (fall to ground, # 1054); → *hwh* I (fall, # 2092); → *kšl* (stumble, totter, be brought to ruin, # 4173); → *nss* I (falter, # 5823); → *npl* (fall, lie prostrate, # 5877); → *ntr* I (fall, # 6000); → *šmṭ* (release, remit, drop, throw down, fall, stumble, # 9023)
Death: → *'bd* I (perish, # 6); → *'ᵃdāmâ* (ground, piece of land, soil, earth, realm of the dead, # 141); → *'āsôn* (mortal accident, # 656); → *gw'* (expire, die, # 1588); → *hrg* (kill, murder, # 2222); → *zrm* I (put an end to life, # 2441); → *ḥedel* (realm of the dead, # 2535); → *ḥnṭ* II (embalm, embalming, # 2846); → *mwt* (die, kill, execute, # 4637); → *qṭl* (murder, slay, # 7779); → *rᵉpā'îm* I (shades, departed spirits, # 8327); → *šᵉ'ôl* (sheol, netherworld, # 8619); → *šaḥat* (pit, grave, # 8846)

BIBLIOGRAPHY
NIDNTT 1:606-11; 2:705-10; *TDNT* 6:161-73; *TWAT* 5:521-31; D. R. Ap-Thomas, "Notes on Some Terms Relating to Prayer," *VT* 6, 1956, 225-41; M. Delcor, "Quelques cas de survivances du vocabulaire nomade en hébreu biblique," *VT* 25, 1975, 313-15; J. C. Greenfield, "Lexicographical Notes I," *HUCA* 29, 1958, 215-17.

Allan M. Harman

5878	נֵפֶל

נֵפֶל (*nēpel*), nom. stillborn child, miscarriage (# 5878); < נפל (*npl*, fall, → # 5877).

OT The nom. occurs 3x in the genre of protest and prayer. It is used in a first-person question (Job 3:16), in which Job even wonders why he was born; by a writer of one of the lament psalms who is being persecuted (Ps 58:8[9]); and in an aphoristic statement (Eccl 6:3). To be a stillborn child is a terrible fate (Ps 58:8[9]); next to a life of misery it is, however, desirable (Job 3:16); in fact such a situation may even have its advantages (Eccl 6:3).

NT → *NIDNTT* 1:176-88.

Barren, childless, miscarriage: → *galmûd* (barren, # 1678); → *nēpel* (still-born child, miscarriage, # 5878); → *'āqār* (barren, childless, # 6829); → *'ᵃrîrî* (childless, # 6884); → *škl* (be bereaved, bereavement, miscarry, # 8897)

BIBLIOGRAPHY
R. K. Harrison, "Untimely Birth," *IDB* 4:735; G. Lee, "Miscarriage," *ISBE* 3:383.

Victor P. Hamilton

5879	נפץ

נפץ (*npṣ* I), 18x, vb. q. break; pi. smash, break up; pu. be smashed, be pulverized (# 5879); מַפָּץ (*mappāṣ*), 1x, nom. beating (# 5150); נֶפֶץ (*nepeṣ*), 1x, nom. pelting storm (# 5881); מַפֵּץ (**mappēṣ*), 1x, nom. war club (# 5151).

ANE Akk. *napāṣu*, kick, strike, crush; Arab. *nafaḍa*, shake; Official Aram. *npṣwn*, press, crush (but perhaps to be read *'pṣwn* [< root *'pṣ*, squeeze, press]); Tg. Aram. *nᵉpaṣ*, scatter, shake out, shatter, break; Syr. *nᵉpaṣ*, shake, pa. break to pieces.

OT 1. The vb. is used 3x to refer to the breaking (q., Judg 7:19; Jer 22:28) or smashing (pi., Jer 48:12) of pottery. Once it refers to the breaking up of timber for transport (1 Kgs 5:9[23]), once to pulverized chalk (Isa 27:9), and once, more figuratively, to the smashing of power. The balance of its use refers to bringing about the destruction of people, sometimes including an item closely related to the people or profession slated for destruction. In Jer 51:20-23 the vb. is used 9x in a poetic stanza where Yahweh refers to Babylon or Cyrus as a war club (*mappēṣ*; see below at 4) with which Yahweh smashes nations, horse and rider, man and woman, and the like.

2. *nepeṣ* occurs only in Isa 30:30 in a poetic colon containing *zerem*, downpour, and *'eben bārād*, hailstones. The context in Isa 30:30 suggests that the word refers to a pelting storm, i.e., a storm that smashes or causes destruction. Isaiah uses the imagery to refer to Yahweh's destruction of the Assyrians.

3. *mappāṣ*, beating, occurs only in Ezek 9:2, where it appears as a synonym of *mašḥēt*, ruin, destruction. The word is used in a construct chain, as the genitive, *k^e lî mappāṣô*, "his weapon for beating," referring to the instrument used by six executioners who are to go through Jerusalem killing on behalf of Yahweh; the executioners do indeed carry a "deadly weapon" (so NIV).

4. *mappēṣ*, war club, is used only by Jeremiah as a metaphor referring to Babylon or Cyrus (Jer 51:20).

P-B The senses carried by the verbal root are attested in this time period.

Shattering, breaking, destroying: → *mḥq* (strike, # 4735); → *npṣ* I (break, smash, # 5879); → *pṣṣ* (pulverize, crush, # 7207); → *rṭš* (smash, strike down, # 8187); → *r'ṣ* (shatter, # 8320); → *ršš* (destroy, crushed, # 8406); → *šbr* I (break, shatter, # 8689)

BIBLIOGRAPHY

TWOT 2:587.

Gary Alan Long

5880	נפץ

נפץ (*npṣ* II), q. spread out, scatter, be dispersed (# 5880).

ANE This root is attested in Akk. (*napāṣu*) and is understood to be a foreign loanword from Aram. (*AHw*, 736; *HALAT* 671).

OT The three occurrences of this vb., all in q., speak of the dispersion of people: the descendants of Noah, who would fill the earth after the Flood (Gen 9:19); Saul's army out of fear of the Philistines (1 Sam 13:11); and the nations because of the judgment of Yahweh, who is exalted over every natural or human power (Isa 33:3). *TWOT* prefers to consider *npṣ* II as an intransitive sense of a single root *npṣ*.

Scattering, dispersion: → *bzr* (scatter, # 1029); → *zrh* I (scatter, sprinkle, spread, # 2430); → *zr'* (sow, scatter seed, # 2445); → *zrq* I (sprinkle, scatter, # 2450); → *ndḥ* I (banish, be scattered, be cast out, seduce, # 5615); → *ndp* (blow away, scatter, # 5622); → *npṣ* II (spread out, scatter, be dispersed, # 5880); → *pwṣ* (scatter, disperse, be spread, # 7046); → *pzr* (scatter, spread, # 7061)

BIBLIOGRAPHY

TWOT 2:587.

M. Daniel Carroll R.

5881 (*nepeṣ*, pelting storm), → # 5879

5882 (*npš*, be refreshed), → # 5883

5883	נֶפֶשׁ

נֶפֶשׁ (*nepeš*), breath, life, desire (# 5883); < נפשׁ (*npš*), be refreshed (# 5882).

ANE *nepeš* has many cognates in the Sem. languages, most importantly Akk., Arab., Ugar., where there is comparable variety in meaning, yet basic identity as to the root meaning of the nom. as "breath." Other ANE meanings include "life, person, self, desire," of which Hebrew also avails itself. In rare instances, e.g., Ps 69:1[2], Jon 2:5[6], an Akk. rendering, "throat," may be found in the OT, but most of the *HALAT* examples are adequately rendered alternatively.

OT 1. Comparable roots in Ugar. and Akk. confirm the basic biblical meaning for *nepeš* to be "breath" (as do the three verbal instances, Exod 23:12; 31:17; 2 Sam 16:14). Care should be taken not to import a Greek paradigm of psychology to *nepeš*; though at times in its over 700 appearances it refers to the inner person, it seldom denotes a "soul" in any full sense. Initially, it means the literal breath of both animals (Gen 1:20-30; 7:22, *nešāmâ*) and humans (2:7; Ps 107:5; 1 Kgs 17:17, *nešāmâ*). Since breath is tantamount to life itself, *nepeš* essentially means "life" on numerous occasions, e.g., Gen 9:5, "I will require the *nepeš* of man;" (also 2 Sam 23:17). The relationship of breath and life is taken a semantic step farther when *nepeš* is used to denote the living being itself, e.g., Lev 4:2, "If a person (*nepeš*) sins ..." (Josh 11:14, *n^e^šāmâ*). In this sense *nepeš* becomes a synecdoche, representing the total person, both one's physical and nonphysical composition. In fact, *nepeš* is so identified with the whole person that ironically it can denote a nonbreathing corpse! (e.g., Lev 21:11 "nor shall he approach any dead *nepeš*."). This identity of *nepeš* with the entire person gives the word its frequent function as a reference to the self, e.g., Ps 7:2[3], "or they will tear me (my *nepeš*) like a lion"; Lev 26:11, "I (my *nepeš*) will not abhor you."

2. In some cases *nepeš* stands for the inner person rather than the entire individual. *nepeš* represents the desires and inclinations of animals and humans. Perhaps the panting breath that is associated with intense desire is the reason for this nuance in *nepeš* (see other words in this semantic group used for "panting" [*š'p* I, *pwḥ*]). These desires range from the sexual drive of a wild donkey in heat (Jer 2:24), to the physical appetite (Prov 23:2; Eccl 6:7), to the holy preferences of those who love God with all their "heart ... *nepeš* and ... strength" (Deut 6:5). Even Sheol has an appetite for the wicked (Isa 5:14; Hab 2:5), as the wicked do for the righteous, e.g., Ps 27:12, "Do not turn me over to the *nepeš* of my foes." One's *nepeš* can be angry or bitter (Judg 18:25; Prov 14:10; Isa 19:10; Ezek 25:6), yet fortunately it can be encouraged as well (Ps 86:4).

3. The vb. *npš*, be refreshed, occurs 3x and only in the ni. to designate the refreshment that comes from catching one's breath during rest, as instructed in Sabbath theology (Exod 23:12; 31:17; 2 Sam 16:14).

Breath, life: → *hebel* I (breath, # 2039); → *nepeš* (breath, life, desire, # 5883); → *n^e^šāmâ* (breath, # 5972); → *š'p* I (pant, gasp, # 8634)
Blowing (wind, breath): → *hzh* (pant in sleep, # 2111); → *ndp* (blow away, scatter, # 5622); → *npḥ* (blow, # 5870); → *nšb* (blow, # 5959); → *nšp* (blow, # 5973); → *pwḥ* (blow, blast, malign, # 7032)

Bibliography
THAT 2:71-95; *TWOT* 2:587-91; C. A. Briggs, "The Use of *npsh* in the Old Testament," *JBL* 16, 1897, 17-30.

D. C. Fredericks

5884 (*nepet*, hill?), → # 2215

5885	נֹפֶת

נֹפֶת (*nopet*), nom. honey, honey from the comb (# 5885), used as parallel to d^e*baš* (→ # 1831).

ANE In Ugar. *nbt* seems to be the common term for honey (*UT*, # 1602; *WUS*, # 1733). A precious liquid poured like wine in a golden bowl by King Kirtu (KRT 4, 164-65), it served some sacrificial function (note the OT prohibition, Lev 2:11). It is listed as a commodity for trade (*CTA* 142:2, 8, 15; cf. Heltzer, 19). According to Fensham (20), "we have in Ugaritic a development in meaning from bee to honey, as is also the case in Biblical Hebrew." The Akk. cognate *nūbtu* (*AHw*, 800) designates bee, not honey. It is also attested in Punic, but its meaning remains uncertain (*DISO*, 184).

OT The simile "honey" has both positive and negative associations. On the one hand, the psalmist likens the word of God to honey from the honeycomb ("sweeter than honey, than honey from the comb," Ps 19:10[11]), and the sage encourages the seeker of wisdom with fullness of life, likened to the sweetness of honey ("Eat honey, my son, for it is good; honey from the comb is sweet to your taste" [Prov 24:13; cf. v. 14]). The poet celebrates the sweetness of the lover, "Your lips drop sweetness as the honeycomb, my bride; milk and honey are under your tongue" (S of Songs 4:11). On the other hand, the sage warns against a sickening sweetness, such as that of the adulteress, whose lips also drip with honey (Prov 5:3), and against the enjoyment of the pleasures of life too greatly, which like honey may make one sick (27:7; cf. 25:16, 27).

Honey: → d^e*baš* I (honey, # 1831); → *ya'ar* II (honeycombs, # 3624); → *nopet* (honey, honey from the comb, # 5885); → *ṣûp*, I (virgin honey, # 7430)

Bibliography
F. C. Fensham, "Remarks on Keret 59-72," *JNSL*, 4, 11-21; M. Heltzer, *Goods, Prices and the Organization of Trade in Ugarit*, 1978.

J. P. J. Olivier

5887 (*naptûlîm*, struggle), → # 7349

5890 (*nēṣ* I, blossom), → # 7255

5891 (*nēṣ* II, hawk), → # 6416

5893	נצב

נצב (*nṣb* I), ni. stand, station oneself, step up to, approach, stand firm; ni. part. one who is in charge, supervisor; hi. station, set up, establish; ho. be set up (# 5893); מַצָּב (*maṣṣāb*), nom. place (where feet stand), outpost, garrison, station, office (# 5163); מֻצָּב (*muṣṣāb*), nom. pillar, tower (# 5164); מַצָּבָה (*maṣṣābâ*), nom. outpost, sentry (# 5165); מַצֵּבָה (*maṣṣēbâ*), nom. sacred stone, standing stone pillar (# 5167); מַצֶּבֶת

(*maṣṣebet*), nom. standing stone, stump (# 5169 and # 5170); נְצִיב (*nᵉṣîb* I), nom. (military) post, garrison (# 5907); נִצָּב (*niṣṣāb* II), hilt (of sword, → # 5896).

ANE The vbs. in Ugar. *nṣb*, to put up, as well as the Arab. vb. *naṣaba*, set up, correspond with the Heb. *nṣb* (cf. Amarna *naṣābu* B, settle ?, *CAD* 11:33).

OT 1. Texts in the Pentateuch employ *nṣb*, stand, in conjunction with God's miracle-working power, most impressive of which was Israel's march through the Reed Sea, where the "surging waters stood firm (ni. *nṣb*, "statuesque") like a wall" (Exod 15:8, but hi. in Ps 78:13). Moses stood (*nṣb*) on a hilltop with the staff of God in his hands as Israel successfully faced off against the Amalekites (Exod 17:9). In theophanies, which are miracle-like events, God or his angel takes his stand (Gen 28:13; Num 22:23, 31).

2. In prophetic and poetic material the vb. *nṣb*, establish, is linked with divine authoritative action comparable to an overseer or foreman (1 Sam 19:20, ni. part.). God presides (ni. *nṣb*) in the heavenly council, where justice is a critical concern (Ps 82:1; cf. Isa 3:13). By his authority he sets (hi. *nṣb*) the boundaries of the world (Ps 74:17), boundaries within which people groups live in order that his revelation be disseminated through Israel (Deut 32:8), and ensures that the widow's boundaries remain intact (Prov 15:25).

3. *maṣṣāb* as "a place to stand" occurs fewer than a dozen times and largely in military contexts: outpost, garrison (e.g., 1 Sam 14:4, 6). No theological importance attaches to it.

4. *muṣṣāb*, a ho. part., is an uncertain military term without theological significance. It is traditionally rendered "siege wall" (Isa 29:3, tower NIV).

5. *maṣṣābâ* occurs only once, with the meaning of outpost or sentry (1 Sam 14:12).

6. *maṣṣēbâ*, pillar or sacred stone, refers to setting up sacred stones, a practice of the inhabitants of Canaan, such as the Amorites (Exod 23:24). It is illustrated by the Gezer excavations, where ten pillars, some as high as three meters, were aligned in a north/south direction (see M. Avi-Yonah, *Encyclopedia of Archaeological Excavations in the Holy Land*, 429-43, esp. 437). The practice was also known in Egypt (Jer 43:13).

(a) The directives in the Pentateuch in regard to the *maṣṣēbâ*, sacred stone, are along two lines. Israel, upon coming into the land and finding pillars (usually in a cult complex that included altars and Asherah poles), was to smash them (Exod 23:24; 34:13; Deut 7:5; 12:3). A second directive prohibited the setting up of such sacred stones; Yahweh hated them (Deut 16:22; cf. G. Braulik, "Zur Abfolge der Gesetze in Deuteronomium 16, 18-21, 23," *Bib* 69, 1988, 73). The setting up of pillars as memorials to Yahweh (Gen 28:18; 35:14) or as stones of witness (Gen 31:45; cf. Exod 24:4) is of another order and is appropriate.

(b) The Former Prophets report the response to these Torah directives. Certain rulers, notably Hezekiah and Josiah, eliminated sacred stone pillars as part of their religious reform (2 Kgs 18:4; 23:14; cf. Joram, 3:2; Jehu, 10:26-27). Contrary to the instructions in the Torah, Israel erected its own sacred stones (Hos 10:1), a practice for which the punishment was exile (2 Kgs 17:10).

7. *maṣṣebet* is a pillar, usually of stone (2 Sam 18:18). In Isa 6:13, however, the term signifies a tree stump—that which is left standing after the tree is cut or burnt. It is

with this stump that the prophet compares "the holy seed," namely, Israel's righteous remnant. The earlier interpretation of a root stock (hence, new growth) is now questioned (e.g., Wildberger, *Isaiah 1-12*, 274-75; J. D. W. Watts, *Isaiah 1-33*, 69-70, 76). Perhaps the remnant was a monument to Judah's past failure. (→ Isaiah: Theology)

8. *n*^{e}*ṣîb* is primarily a military term with the sense of an outpost or garrison (e.g., 1 Sam 10:5; cf. governor, 1 Kgs 4:19).

Stand, station: → *yṣb* (stand, take stand, # 3656); → *kwn* (stand firm, stand fast, be durable, prepare, establish, # 3922); → *nṣb* I (stand, station oneself, stand firm, # 5893); → *'md* (stand, take one's stand, station, appoint, # 6641); → *qwm* (stand up, stand upright, arise, perform, # 7756)
Pillar, knob: → *kaptôr* II (knob, capital [of pillar], # 4117); → *māṣûq* (pillar, # 5187); → *nṣb* I (stand, # 5893); → *'md* (stand, # 6641)

Bibliography
ISBE 3:869-71; *TDOT* 5:555-65; *TWOT* 2:591-92; N. A. Silberman, "Glossary. Standing Stones: *Masseboth* and Stelae," *BARev* 15, March/April 1989, 58-59; Y. Yadin, *Hazor*, 1975, 43-48.

Elmer A. Martens

5894	נצב

נצב (*nṣb* II), ni. wretched, exhausted (# 5894); not to be confused with *nṣb* I, ni. stand (→ # 5893).

ANE The Heb. *nṣb* II is attested in Arab. *nasiba*, wretched, weak, sick (Barth, 117-19).

OT This vb. is only used once as part of the shepherd's narrative (Zech 11:4-16). Exegetes have not reached agreement about the interpretation of the ni. part. of *nṣb* (v. 16). Some understand it to have a positive connotation, as most of the versions seem to have done, and to link it with *nṣb* I, stand, stand up, be firm (Otzen, 259; Meyers & Meyers, 288). Others consider it to be a negative concept and postulate a vb. *nṣb* II, wretched, due to a similar Arab vb. (*HALAT* 675; Petersen, 86, 88). In v. 15 God calls the prophet a second time to become like a foolish shepherd who would not care for the sheep—not even the healthy (positive) or exhausted one (negative) in v. 16 (Redditt, 684).

P-B 1. LXX. The G tr., *holoklēros*, reads that which is whole or healthy. This corresponds with the Syr. and Lat. versions.

2. RL. In the Midr. Rabbah to Num s. 18 the ni. of *nṣb* is used as stand defiantly (Jastrow 2:927).

Tired, exhausted, feeble, weak, weary: → *'ml* I (be weak, be feeble, languish, # 581); → *ḥlh* I (become weak, tired, ill, # 2703); → *ḥlš* I (be enfeebled, be weakened, # 2764); → *ḥallāš*, weakling, # 2766); → *yg'* (be tired, # 3333); → *mss* (lose courage, melt, become weak, # 5022); → *nṣb* II (wretched, exhausted [animal], # 5894); → *pgr* (be too feeble, tired, # 7006); → *'yp* (be weary, # 6545); → *rph* (become slack, lose heart, discourage, # 8332)

Bibliography
J. Barth, "הַנִּצָּבָה Sach 11, 16," *ZAW* 36, 1916, 117-19; E. H. Merrill, *Haggai, Zechariah, Malachi*, 1994; C. L. & E. M. Meyers, *Zechariah 9-14*, AB, 1993; B. Otzen, *Studien über*

Deutero-Sacharja, 1964; D. L. Petersen, *Zechariah 9-14 and Malachi*, 1995; P. L. Redditt, "The Two Shepherds in Zechariah 11:4-17," *CBQ* 55, 1993, 676-86.

Hendrik L. Bosman

5896 (*niṣṣāb* II, hilt [of a sword]), → # 2995

5897	נצה

נצה (*nṣh* I), ni. struggle with each other; hi. engage in a struggle (# 5897); nom. מַצָּה (*maṣṣâ* II), strife, contention (# 5175); מַצּוּת (*maṣṣût*), those who strive (# 5194).

ANE The Heb. *nṣh* is related to the Aram. *n^{e}ṣā'*, quarrel. There are also Eth. and Arab. cognates.

OT 1. The five uses of the ni. all refer to physical altercations between two persons. Two of the occurrences (Exod 21:22; Deut 25:11) are in legal codes; two others are in narratives, in which there is adjudication of a quarrel by a third party (Lev 24:10; 2 Sam 14:6). In Exod 2:13, which concerns Moses' authority, Moses intervenes in a fight between two Hebrews in Egypt.

2. The hi. occurrences refer to the conflicts between groups: a rebellion among the clan of Reuben against Moses, Aaron, and the Lord (Num 26:9), and in the heading of Ps 60, referring to David's war with Aram.

3. The nom. form *maṣṣâ* occurs 3x in the OT, each time indicating conflict within Israel of which the text is critical: Prov 13:10; 17:19; Isa 58:4.

4. The nom. *maṣṣût* occurs only in Isa 41:12 as part of an assurance of God's salvation for Israel: "those who wage war against you (*'anšê-maṣṣutekā*) will be as nothing at all."

Contention, strife, struggle: → *gl'* (break out in a dispute, # 1679); → *grh* (stir up strife, # 1741); → *nṣh* I (struggle, # 5897); → *ptl* (twist, be wily, shrewd, # 7349); → *ryb* (strive, # 8189); → *r^e'ût* II (longing, striving, # 8296); → *śrh* I (contend, struggle, # 8575)

John M. Bracke

5898	נצה

נצה (*nṣh* II), q. fall in ruins (of cities; Jer 4:7); ni., be destroyed, devastated (of cities, Jer 2:15; of land, 9:12[11] ‖ *'bd*; # 5898).

OT The vb. *nṣh* describes God's judgment on his unrepentant people. Using the "lions" (Assyria and Babylon respectively), he, in his anger, devastates cities so that they become without inhabitants (ni., Jer 2:15[K]; q., 4:7; cf. ni., 2 Kgs 19:25). Thus, Judean cities that were once regarded as places of refuge are defenseless and deserted. See further Holladay, 93-94, 153-54; Thompson, 172-73, 221. If someone asks, "Why has the land been ruined (q., *'bd)* and laid waste (ni., *nṣh)* like a desert?" Yahweh's answer is, "They have forsaken my law ... they have followed the stubbornness of their hearts; they have followed the Baals" (Jer 9:12-14[11-13]). Egypt is also the object of God's wrath, and her land will be similarly devastated (ni., Jer 46:19).

Destruction, annihilation, devastation, disfigurement, ruin: → *'bd* I (perish, # 6); → *'êd* (disaster, # 369); → *blq* (devastate, # 1191); → *dmh* III (ruin, # 1950); → *dmm* III (perish,

1959); → *hrs* (demolish, # 2238); → *ḥbl* III (treat badly, # 2472); → *ḥlq* III (destroy, # 2746); → *ḥt'* (be destroyed, # 3148); → *klh* (be complete, perish, destroy, # 3983); → *krt* (cut, cut off, exterminate, cut a covenant, circumcise, # 4162); → *mḥh* I (wipe off, wipe out destroy, # 4681); → *nṣh* II (fall in ruins, # 5898); → *nts* (break up, # 5995); → *ntṣ* (tear down, # 5997); → *ntš* (root up, pull down, destroy, # 6004); → *p'h* (dash to pieces, # 6990); → *pîd* (ruin, misfortune, # 7085); → *prr* (break, invalidate, nullify, frustrate, foil, thwart, # 7296); → *ṣdh* II (be devastated, # 7400); → *rzh* (destroy, waste away, # 8135); → *šdd* (devastate, # 8720); → *šḥt* (become corrupt, ruin, spoil, # 8845); → *šmd* (be exterminated, destroyed, # 9012); → *tablît* (annihilation, # 9318)

BIBLIOGRAPHY

NIDNTT 1:462-71; W. L. Holladay, *Jeremiah 1*, Hermeneia, 1986; J. A. Thompson, *The Book of Jeremiah,* NICOT, 1980.

Cornelis Van Dam

5900 (*niṣṣâ*, blossom), → # 7255

5901 (*nôṣâ* I, feathers), → # 7606

5902 (*nōṣâ* II, falcon?), → # 6416

5903 (*n^e ṣûrîm*, secret places, caves ?), → # 5117

5904	נצח

נצח (*nṣḥ*), pi. supervise (# 5904); נֵצַח (*nēṣaḥ* I), glory, lastingness (→ # 5905).

ANE Imperial Aram. uses the vb. to designate excelling or doing one's best (*DISO*, 184), while Arab. uses it of counseling and advice (Wehr, 969-70).

OT Uses of the vb. *nṣḥ* occur in two separate contexts. One involves building the temple and serving in its physical maintenance (1 Chron 23:4; Ezra 3:8, 9). The use of the preposition "over" in conjunction with the vb. suggests the idea of supervision or direction of a workforce, as most translations state. In two cases, participial forms are used of "foremen" over the workforce (2 Chron 2:2[1], 18[17]).

Another context is that of the musical worship of the temple (1 Chron 15:21 and in fifty-five psalm headings, with pi. part. e.g., Ps 4, 19, 42, 109). In light of the meaning in the first studied context, a supervisor or director of either the music of the temple or of its liturgical service as a whole is suggested (Sawyer, 35-36).

P-B In the intertestamental period, the vb. is used of God directing or urging on natural phenomena such as the sun (Sir 43:5) and lightning (43:13). This shows his power and control over nature not only as its creator, but also as a continuing overseer. In the Qumran community, the vb. is used to describe priests "conducting" a battle (1QM 9:2; 16:9).

Kingship, rule, supervision, dominion: → *b'l* I (marry, rule over, own, # 1249); → *g^e bîrâ/g^e beret* (lady, queen, mistress, # 1485/1509); → *ykḥ* (dispute, reason together, prove, judge, rule, reprove, # 3519); → *kbš* (make subservient, subdue, # 3899); → *mlk* I (rule, # 4887); → *mšl* II (rule, govern, # 5440); → *nṣḥ* (supervise, # 5904); → *rdd* (repel, subdue, # 8096); → *rdh* I (rule, govern, # 8097); → *r'h* I (feed, graze, shepherd, rule, # 8286); → *śrr* I (rule, direct, superintend, # 8606); → *šlṭ* (gain power, # 8948); → *špṭ* (get justice, act as a judge, rule, # 9149)

Bibliography
J. F. A. Sawyer, "An Analysis of the Context and Meaning of the Psalm Headings," *Glasgow University Oriental Society. Transactions* 22, 1967-1968, 26-38; H. Wehr, *A Dictionary of Modern Written Arabic*, 1966.

David W. Baker

5905	נֶצַח/נֵצַח

נֶצַח/נֵצַח (*nēṣaḥ* I / *neṣaḥ*), nom. luster, glory, lastingness, successful (?) (# 5905).

ANE This nom. is related to the vb. *nṣḥ* I, be perpetual (ni.; → # 5904), and has cognates based on the root *nṣḥ* in Aram., Phoen., and Ugar. in the semantic realm, successful, victorious; and in Arab. and Eth., to be pure.

OT We may follow the *HALAT* arrangement (more insightful than BDB) in seeing that there are two (or perhaps three, see below) basic senses that we may relate to each other. Note that though the nom. is found with two spellings, *nēṣaḥ* (4x) and *neṣaḥ* (37x), this has no semantic effect (cf. Joüon-Muraoka §96Af).

1. *Luster, glory.* In 1 Sam 15:29 the Lord is called *neṣaḥ yiśrā'ēl*, the Glory of Israel (NIV; cf. S. R. Driver); the context, in which Samuel claims that the Lord neither lies nor repents, suggests that some element of God's unchangeableness is specifically in view (cf. Kiel, Keil, *HALAT*). In 1 Chron 29:11 David says that to the Lord belong *hagg^{e}dullâ w^{e}hagg^{e}bûrâ w^{e}hattip'eret w^{e}hannēṣaḥ w^{e}hahôd*, the greatness and the power and the glory/beauty and the *nēṣaḥ* and the majesty. The LXX renders our word here as *nikē*, victory; whereas this is contextually possible (and cf. the Mish. word *niṣṣāḥôn*, victory, strength), it is just as easy to see a connection with 1 Sam 15:29 and sense 2 below, and suppose that God's everlastingness is in view as an aspect of his majesty. Lam 3:18 contains the phrase *'ābad niṣḥî*, my *nēṣaḥ* has perished. The NIV interprets it as splendor; others (cf. Keil) connect it with *nēṣaḥ* II, juice, in the sense vital juice, strength, while still others (e.g., Moskovitz, who cites Rashi; Reyburn) take it as everlastingness, with the idea either that his expectation for a long life is ended, or that his eternal hope is destroyed. This latter line of thought suits the context better; but in any case, emendation (cf. *HALAT*) is unnecessary.

2. *Lastingness, perpetuity.* In the sense lastingness, perpetuity, the nom. can appear with an adverbial sense, forever, always: e.g., Isa 34:10 *nēṣaḥ n^{e}ṣāḥîm*, forever and ever (‖ *l^e'ôlām ... middôr lādôr*, forever ... from generation to generation); cf. Ps 13:1[2]; 16:11; Jer 15:18; Amos 1:11. Once, in Ps 74:3, it is a genitive, *maššū'ôt nēṣaḥ*, eternal ruins.

The most common usage in this sense is in the prepositional phrase *lāneṣaḥ*, forever (twice *'ad-neṣaḥ* with same meaning). In this sense it is synonymous with *'ôlām* and *'ad* and, like them, refers to perpetuity, with the context supplying just how perpetual: e.g., cf. Ps 16:11; 49:9, 19[10, 20]; Isa 25:8, where the contextually supplied nuance is "for all eternity." (→ Time and Eternity: Theology)

Thomas (and cf. Emerton for support) argues, based on his reconstructed semantic history of the Syr. cognate, that sometimes the nom. *nēṣaḥ* (or *lāneṣaḥ*) has the adverbial use, to a preeminence, completely, utterly, and applied this to, e.g., Ps 13:1[2]; 74:10; 79:5; 89:46[47]. The difficulty with this approach is that the ordinary meaning of the expressions yields an intelligible meaning within the legitimate range of literary devices (as Thomas acknowledges in his footnotes), and hence we may suppose that language users would have taken them in the ordinary sense. Perhaps it would be possible, however, to see this intensifying as one of the pragmatic possibilities for the phrases in their ordinary meaning. Hence, in Sir 40:14, *lāneṣaḥ yittōm* may be rendered, it will utterly come to an end (cf. Greek); but there are severe textual difficulties here (cf. Oesterley, Segal, Skehan-DiLella), and the Skehan-DiLella interpretation, once and for all it will come to an end, makes adequate sense.

3. *Success. HALAT* finds this third sense in Prov 21:28 (cf. G. R. Driver): a false witness will perish, *wᵉʾîš šômēaʿ lāneṣaḥ yᵉdabbēr*, and a man who hears will speak forever (cf. NASB). Driver argued that the second half of the verse should be rendered, "the successful witness will speak (on)," assuming *nēṣaḥ* had the meaning success; Emerton proposed, "and he who listens will subdue him completely"; and NIV has, "and whoever listens to him will be destroyed forever." Space does not permit a full analysis of the questions (cf. Collins, 651-53, 656-57), but note that the views of Driver, Emerton, and NIV assume the presence of *dbr* II, to drive out, destroy (elsewhere only found in hi.), either here in the pi. (*yᵉdabbēr*) or by repointing to a hi. or ho. These founder on the simple fact that MT (including accents, which associate *lāneṣaḥ* with *yᵉdabbēr*) is quite intelligible using more ordinary vocabulary: either in the sense, "[even though] a false witness will perish, the man who listens [to him] will speak forever," or else (cf. Kidner; Prov 12:19), "a false witness will perish, and a man who hears [God] will speak forever."

4. *Semantic conclusions.* From the above discussion it appears that senses 1 and 2 actually existed in BH. Can sense 1, used to describe God (traditionally rendered glory, splendor), be related to sense 2, the dominant use? Contextually, some element related to everlastingness suits the passages and may be provisionally accepted as the proper interpretation.

P-B In the Heb. frgs. of Sir, we find the word *neṣaḥ* used twice: once in the phrase *lāneṣaḥ*, forever (Sir 40:14, see sense 2 above), and once as in Isa 34:10, *lᵉnēṣaḥ nᵉṣāḥîm lōʾ ʾeṭṭeh mimmennâ*, "I will never turn away from her [wisdom]" (MS B only; contrast Skehan-DiLella, based on 11QPs^a reading). In the DSS we find quite a few instances of *neṣaḥ* in the syntaxes and meaning discussed under sense 2 above. The RL provides a few instances of *neṣaḥ* in sense 2; the dominant use of this root, however, is in the (Aram. influenced?) sense to be victorious: e.g., *nṣḥ*, vb. to prevail; *niṣṣāḥôn*, nom. victory, strength.

The LXX most commonly translated the expressions listed under sense 2 with *eis ton aiōna*, forever, *eis telos*, to the end, and *eis nikos* (sometimes spelled *neikos*), unto victory (lit.).

NT It is worth noting that in the NT the expression *eis nikos* appears twice, and in both places would make better sense if translated "forever": Matt 12:20 (quoting Isa 42:3, which lacks a corresponding term; Matt's quote is not identical to LXX); 1 Cor 15:54 (quoting Isa 25:8, but not quite from LXX; Theodotion renders Isaiah's *lāneṣaḥ*, forever, with *eis nikos*, and taken this way Paul's quote is close in meaning to MT).

Glory, honor, majesty: → *ʾdr* (be magnificent, majestic, splendid, # 158); → *hdr* (swell, honor, adorn, # 2075); → *hôd* I (splendor, majesty, # 2086); → *yᵉqār* (honor, riches, respect, price, splendor, # 3702); → *kbd* (be heavy, unresponsive, honored, # 3877); → *nēṣaḥ* I (luster, glory, lastingness, successful, # 5905); → *p'r* II (beautify, glorify, # 6995); → *ṣ*^{e}*bî* I (ornament, glory, # 7382)

Time: → *'ōbēd* (ever after, # 7); → *'ōpen* (right time, # 698); → *gîl* I (stage of life, # 1636); → *zmn* (be appointed, # 2374); → *'ôlām* (long time or duration, # 6409); → *'ēt* (time, # 6961); → *pa'am* (foot, step, time, # 7193); → *peta'* (instant, # 7353); → *tāmîd* (continuance, unceasingness, regular offering, # 9458)

Bibliography

C. J. Collins, "Homonymous Verbs in Biblical Hebrew: An Investigation of the Role of Comparative Philology," Ph.D. diss., 1989; G. R. Driver, "Problems in 'Proverbs'," *ZAW* 50, 1932, 141-48; S. R. Driver, *Notes on the Hebrew Text and the Topography of the Books of Samuel*, 1912; J. A. Emerton, "The Interpretation of Proverbs 21, 28," *ZAW* 100, Sup, 1988, 161-70; C. F. Keil, *The Books of Samuel* (KD); idem, *Lamentations* (KD); D. Kidner, *Proverbs*, TOTC, 1964; Y. Kiel, *Sēper Š*^{e}*mû'ēl* (Da'at Miqra), 1981; Y. Moskovitz, "*'êkâ* [Lamentations]," in *Ḥāmēš M*^{e}*gillôt* (Da'at Miqra), 1973; W. Oesterley, *Ecclesiasticus*, CBSC, 1912; W. Reyburn, *A Handbook on Lamentations*, UBS Handbook series, 1992; M. Segal, *Sēper Ben-Sîra' Haššālēm*, 1958; P. Skehan and A. DiLella, *The Wisdom of Ben Sira*, AB, 1987; D. W. Thomas, "The Use of *nēṣaḥ* as a Superlative in Hebrew," *JSS* 1, 1956, 106-9.

C. John Collins

5906	נֵצַח

נֵצַח (*nēṣaḥ* II), juice (only in Isa 63:3, 6) (# 5906).

OT Isaiah uses this rare word for "juice" (="blood") 2x in a poetic description of the battle against the nations from which the Lord returns victoriously. He fuses two images into one: the farmer whose garments are stained with the "juice" of the trampled grapes and the warrior who leaves the battle scene with his garments stained with "blood." The images encourage the godly to hope in the fullness of redemption: "I have trodden the winepress alone; from the nations no one was with me. I trampled them in my anger and trod them down in my wrath; their blood (*nēṣaḥ*) spattered my garments, and I stained all my clothing. For the day of vengeance was in my heart, and the year of my redemption has come. ... I trampled the nations in my anger; in my wrath I made them drunk and poured their blood (*nēṣaḥ*) on the ground" (Isa 63:3-4, 6).

Blood: → *dām* (blood, bloodshed, blood-guilt, murder, # 1947); → *nēṣaḥ* II (juice, blood, # 5906)

Paul Trebilco

5907 (*n*^{e}*ṣîb* I, post, garrison), → # 5893

5910 (*nāṣîr*, preserved), → # 5915

5911	נצל

נצל (*nṣl*), n. be rescued, save o.s.; pi. take away, plunder; hi. to rescue, save, plunder, snatch away, pull out, extricate; ho. be saved, pulled out; hitp. remove, give up (# 5911); הַצָּלָה (*haṣṣālâ*), nom. deliverance (# 2208).

ANE The root *nṣl* occurs only in Northwest (Aram. and Heb.) and Southwest Sem. (Arab.), and the attested forms clearly share close meanings. Akk. attests one example of *naṣālu*, but it seems to derive from *natālu* (CAD N/2, 33, 125). Lachish letter No. 1 has pr. nom. *hṣlyhw*.

OT 1. The vb. ni. primarily has the passive sense, to be delivered. Jacob named the site of his famous wrestling match Peniel because his life was saved although he had seen God face to face (Gen 32:30[31]). The Assyrian emissary, Rabshekah, warned Hezekiah that he would not be saved from Sennacherib's wrath (2 Kgs 19:11; Isa 37:11), but Micah predicts that Judah will be rescued from Babylon (Mic 4:10). With biting irony Amos promises that Samaria will be "saved"—in pieces (Amos 3:12)! One falsely accused Israelite's complaint asks to be delivered from his enemies (Ps 69:14[15]). According to Isaiah, Judah will regret ever assuming she would be saved from Assyria by Egypt and Ethiopia (Isa 20:6). "We are safe" is Judah's misguided cry in temple worship, arrogantly banking on that building for security (Jer 7:10). If judgment falls, says Ezekiel, righteous intermediaries like Noah, Daniel, and Job would be saved, but their presence would not help anyone else (Ezek 14:16, 18).

In several places the vb. ni. has the reflexive sense to save oneself or escape. Deut 23:15[16] prohibits an Israelite from returning to his master a slave who escapes (i.e., saves himself). Ps 33:16 cautions soldiers that they would not save themselves by their strength rather than by Yahweh's. Habakkuk declares woe on the wicked who seek to save themselves from harm (Hab 2:9), but Prov 6:3, 5 urges a child to save himself from an unwise verbal promise to a neighbor.

2. The three occurrences of the vb. pi. have the sense to rob or plunder. In a lengthy vocation report, Yahweh tells Moses that Israel will plunder the Egyptians—and with their cooperation!—a prediction fulfilled in the plague report (Exod 3:22; 12:36). Jehoshaphat and his army helped themselves (vb. pi.) to the booty left when their enemies killed each other off (2 Chron 20:25). In Ezek 14:14 MT [pi.] should be read as hi. to save (cf. v. 20; so *BHS*; *THAT* 2:98; contra LXX; *TWAT* 5:571 [ni.]).

3. The vb. occurs mainly in causative forms (hi.; Aram. ha.; 191x), and overwhelmingly with God as its subject (120x). In general, it designates the snatching away or freeing from the firm grip of some distress. The root appears throughout the OT without association with any specific OT literary genres or traditions.

(a) In the Pentateuch. The vb. hi. appears 19x in the books of Moses with various meanings. Gen 31:9 reflects the root's original sense to snatch. Jacob tells his wives that God has snatched away their father's livestock and given it to him (Gen 31:9), a view they themselves affirm (v. 16). In several examples *miyyad* (from the hands of) goes with the vb., describing deliverance from the control of hostile hands (i.e., oppressors). Reuben did so for Joseph against his vengeful brothers (37:21, 22), Moses did so for the priest of Midian's daughters against shepherds denying them water (Exod 2:19), and citizens of a city of refuge did so for an accused murderer against the blood avenger (Num 35:25). A wife may intervene to rescue her husband by separating him from the grip of someone with whom he is fighting (Deut 25:11).

Yahweh, of course, is the deliverer *par excellence*. Terrified of Esau's wrath, Jacob prays that God will deliver him from his brother's power (Gen 32:11[12]). Israel's deliverance from Egyptian power motivated Yahweh's appearance to Moses

(Exod 3:8; cf. 6:6), although Moses complained that Yahweh was too slow about it (5:23). That great rescue inspired children's names (18:4) and was worth retelling (18:8-10). Indeed, in the Song of Moses Yahweh declares that, as the only God, there is no deliverer (*maṣṣîl*) strong enough to free anything from his mighty grip (Deut 32:39).

According to Deut 23:14, Yahweh traveled with Israel to deliver them by handing their enemies into their power. Here to deliver means to spare disaster, i.e., to prevent Israel's captivity or destruction rather than to extricate them from an imminent or already present disaster (cf. the Passover recollection, Exod 12:27).

(b) In historical narratives. The vb. hi. may describe the action of a human toward other objects or people. In exchange for her cooperation, Rahab asks the Israelite spies to deliver—i.e., snatch away—the lives of her family from the death grip of Israelite annihilation (Josh 2:13). Joshua's covenant with the wily Gibeonites saved them from that same annihilation (9:26; cf. 22:31). Later victorious military actions rescued Israel from enemy oppression (Judg 9:17 [Midian]; 1 Sam 14:48 [Amalek]), and people cited one such deliverance to justify David's return as king from temporary exile (2 Sam 19:9[10]). Early in life David saved a lamb from wild animals (1 Sam 17:35).

Deliverance from the oppressive hands of enemies was something the king did for his people. Because there was no deliverer (*maṣṣîl*) to separate them, one brother killed the other (2 Sam 14:6). So his widowed mother asked King David to deliver her from the hand of someone avenging her son's death (v. 16). On the other hand, David sought Sheba's immediate death for sympathizing with Absalom lest Sheba escape into hiding (lit., snatch away our eyes, 20:6).

Sometimes the vb. hi. means to recover or regain possession of objects previously lost (Judg 11:26 [cities]; 1 Sam 7:14 [land]; 30:8, 18, 22 [wives, children]). In another case it means to defend property against (i.e., to snatch it from) imminent dispossession by invaders (2 Sam 23:12; 1 Chron 11:14). Geographically isolated, the city of Laish had no deliverer (*maṣṣîl*)—i.e., no allied city—to prevent its falling to Israel (Judg 18:28).

When Yahweh's ark entered Israel's camp, the Philistines wondered who would deliver them from the hand of the gods (sic) who had decimated Egypt (1 Sam 4:8). A prophetic oracle ridiculed King Amaziah's worship of Edomite gods who had failed to deliver their worshipers (2 Chron 25:15; cf. Samuel's warning about idols [1 Sam 12:21]).

By contrast, as the OT's model rescuer Yahweh snatched Israel from many dangerous grips. Joshua's farewell speech recalls their rescue from Balaam (Josh 24:10), and Samuel's speech to Israel reminded them of their deliverance from Egypt (1 Sam 10:18; cf. Judg 6:9). Sometimes Israel forgot those rescues (Judg 8:34), but often their recall led Israel to cry for Yahweh to deliver them again from enemies (10:15; 1 Sam 12:10-11; Neh 9:28; cf. 1 Chron 16:35). David especially experienced Yahweh's rescue from wild animals, Goliath (1 Sam 17:37; cf. 26:24), and Saul (2 Sam 12:7). His retrospective thanksgiving song celebrates all his deliverances by Yahweh (2 Sam 22:1, 18, 49; see also Ezra's memoir, Ezra 8:31; the title of Ps 18).

Samuel warned early Israel that repentance was the precondition for Yahweh's deliverance from the Philistines (1 Sam 7:3). Later, D noted that the northern kingdom had ignored Yahweh's promise of deliverance from enemies along with the rest of the covenant (2 Kgs 17:39).

Finally, the vb. hi. plays a prominent role (11x) in the Assyrian diatribes against Hezekiah and Jerusalem (2 Kgs 18-19; para. Isa 36-37; 2 Chron 32). According to the Rabshekah, neither the king (2 Kgs 18:29; Isa 36:14) nor Yahweh himself (2 Kgs 18:30, 32, 35b; Isa 36:15, 18) would successfully snatch Jerusalem from Assyrian hands. The gods of previously conquered nations did not (2 Kgs 18:33, 34, 35a; 19:12; Isa 36:19, 20; 37:12)! But, the Assyrian rhetoric notwithstanding, Yahweh reassured Hezekiah that divine deliverance was certain (2 Kgs 20:6; Isa 38:6).

(c) In the Psalms. With three exceptions Yahweh is the only subject of the vb. hi. in the psalms. The exceptions involve the phrase *'ên maṣṣîl*, without deliverer, which underscores someone's defenselessness against pursuers (Ps 7:2[3]; 71:11) or even against God himself (50:22; cf. Judg 18:28; 2 Sam 14:6; Job 5:4; 10:7).

Petitions to Yahweh for rescue from violent, dangerous hands, lying mouths, or other enemies dominate prayers of complaint (Ps 7:1[2]; 25:20; 31:15[16]; 59:1, 2 [2, 3]; 71:2; 109:21; 120:2; 142:6[7]; 143:9; 144:7, 11 [a royal psalm]; cf. 119:43 [a wisdom psalm]). In the heavenly council, God himself asks the gods to rescue the needy from the wicked by guaranteeing them justice (82:4). Some complaints plead for deliverance from sin and its physical effects (39:8[9]; cf. the prayer of confession, 51:14[16]). One writer's complaint invokes the vb. hi. to say "Come quickly to my rescue" (31:2[3]; cf. 40:13[14]; 70:1[2])—a reflection of the root's original sense to snatch away. The unusual petition that Yahweh not remove (vb. hi.) the word of truth from the psalmist's mouth apparently aims to buttress his personal hope and public testimony for Yahweh (119:43).

Affirmations of confidence (Ps 35:10), vows of thanksgiving (54:7[9]), and offerings of thanksgiving (86:13) bank on Yahweh as the deliverer of those falsely accused or thankfully look back on rescue already received (e.g., from death, 56:13[14]; 86:13). One communal complaint pleads that Yahweh deliver Israel because Jerusalem lies in ruins and many citizens are in captivity (79:9). That Yahweh rescues his people supports the promise of divine protection in a psalm of trust (91:3 [from physical dangers]) and in one praising Yahweh's kingship (97:10 [from the wicked]). The king's personal thanksgiving mentions his own deliverance by Yahweh from deathly danger (18:17[18], 48[49]).

Praise hymns and thanksgiving songs affirm Yahweh's past deliverance of people from fear and trouble (Ps 34:4[5]; 107:6; cf. 106:43) and extol his vigilance to rescue his people from danger (34:17[18], 19[20]) and death (33:19). The prayer for the king (at his coronation?) remembers how Yahweh delivers the needy (72:12). Mockingly, the psalmist's enemies urge him to let Yahweh deliver him (22:8[9])—and he does (v. 20[21]).

(d) In the Prophets. The phrase *'ên maṣṣîl* occurs 7x in the Prophets. In oracles of disaster it underscores the inescapability of present (Isa 42:22) or future judgment (5:29; Hos 5:14). In oracles of salvation it highlights the inevitability of Judah's future victory (Mic 5:8[7]) and the irreversibility of Yahweh's plans (Isa 43:13). In Daniel's vision, the phrase highlights the invincible powers of various nations (Dan 8:4, 7).

Prophetic oracles of hope promise deliverance for Israel from the Assyrians by a new David (Mic 5:6[5]) and for oppressed Egypt, one of God's other peoples, by a divinely sent deliverer (Isa 19:20).

In several places, the vb. hi. with *nepeš* as dir. obj. means to save oneself. According to Isaiah, idolaters are deluded, crying futilely to their man-made god for deliverance (Isa 44:17) but ending up unsaved (v. 20; cf. 57:13). Babylon's foolishness is in trusting in astrologers who cannot save themselves, much less Babylon (47:14). God twice reassures Ezekiel that he will save his own life by faithfully warning exiled Israel to repent (Ezek 3:19, 21; 33:9). On the other hand, he declares that even if the righteous Noah, Daniel, and Job were in a condemned land, the threesome would only save their own lives (14:14 [read as hi.], 20; cf. v. 18).

Twice Jeremiah warns the king to rescue robbery victims from their oppressors' hands by implementing justice (Jer 21:12; 22:3). Other oracles of judgment advise Israel that neither her wealth (Ezek 7:19; Zeph 1:18) nor her righteousness (Ezek 33:12) can save her from the judgment due her sin. The divinely provided plant shades (i.e., protects) pouting Jonah from the scorching sun (Jon 4:6).

Consistent with other usage with Yahweh as its subject, the vb. hi. portrays Yahweh as the deliverer par excellence. He hovers over Jerusalem to deliver (i.e., protect) it from invaders—something the Egyptians cannot do (Isa 31:5). He certainly has the power to deliver his people—witness how he dries up seas and rivers and darkens the skies (50:2). Even Nebuchadnezzar (Dan 3:29) and Darius (6:27[28]) decree empire-wide respect for God after personally seeing him protect Daniel from certain death (Aram.; cf. 6:16[17]). In announcing Jeremiah's prophetic vocation, however, Yahweh stresses more his promised presence to deliver Jeremiah than his power (Jer 1:8, 19), a promise reiterated to answer one of Jeremiah's complaints (15:20, 21) and given also to Ebed-Melech (39:17) and Judah's survivors (42:11). In these cases to deliver means to prevent from falling into the power of others rather than to extricate (cf. the metaphors of fortified city and bronzed wall; cf. 20:13).

But Yahweh also delivers (i.e., snatches away) his people from the preying clutches of false prophets (Ezek 13:21, 23), from abuse by faithless leaders (34:10), and from slavery to other nations (vv. 12, 27). But when Yahweh refuses to rescue, Israel cannot escape the grip of oppression (Zech 11:6), and when he grips Israel in judgment, no one stops him or breaks his grasp (Hos 2:9, 10[11, 12]).

(e) In Wisdom books. The vb. hi. occurs 3x in the book of Job, twice in Eliphaz's rebuttal of Job's claim of innocence. To deny his guilt, he warns, may doom Job's children to a future without a legal defender, either divine or human (*'ên maṣṣîl*, Job 5:4). On the other hand, assures Eliphaz, Almighty God, who corrects the errant, will deliver a repentant Job from any trouble (v. 19). Later, in interrogating his absent God, Job concedes his vulnerability before God's judgment (*'ên maṣṣîl*, 10:7), then pleads that God let him die in peace (vv. 20-22).

In Proverbs the vb. hi. means to rescue from potential, not actual, disaster by steering one away from calamitous paths. Parental instruction teaches that wisdom delivers a child from a wicked lifestyle (Prov 2:12) and adultery (v. 16), thus sparing it the resulting disaster and death (vv. 19, 22). Two parallel antithetical proverbs glorify righteousness as delivering one from death—a deliverance not provided by ill-gotten gain (10:2) or even ordinary wealth (11:4). Other proverbs observe how righteousness

(11:6) and honest speech (12:6) rescue (i.e., spare or prevent) the upright from suffering catastrophes of their own making, and how a truthful witness in court spares the life of a condemned but innocent defendant (14:25). One wise saying urges parents to punish their children to save them from death, i.e., from the fatal consequences of wicked conduct (23:14), while another warns of harsh divine repayment for anyone who fails to spare the life of a condemned felon by withholding exonerating testimony (24:11). On the other hand, another proverb advises against saving hot-tempered people from their self-made disasters; only by suffering the consequences will they learn self-control (19:19).

4. Both occurrences of the vb. ho. involve the phrase "a brand snatched from the fire," a metaphor of being quickly saved from utter disaster (Amos 4:11 [Israel]; Zech 3:2 [the high priest Joshua]).

5. The vb. hitp. occurs only in Exod 33:6 as the reflexive of the pi., reporting that the Israelites took off their offensive ornaments to avoid Yahweh's wrath. Though the context precludes precise translation, the vb. seems to mean tear off or get rid of (NRSV stripped themselves of).

6. The nom. *haṣṣālâ* rescue, relief, occurs only in Esth 4:14, where Mordecai affirms that if Esther fails to obtain deliverance for the Jews from Xerxes, deliverance will arise from somewhere else. Whether he alludes to an expected divine rescue is a matter of dispute, but the book's present canonical status certainly favors such a view.

P-B The root is well attested in postbiblical Heb. and Aram. Indeed, the nom. *haṣṣālâ,* rescue, relief, actually occurs more often in such literature than in MT (6x versus 1x). LXX renders *nṣl* primarily with *rhuomai*, to snatch away, and *exaireō*, to save (for other renderings, see *TWAT* 5:571-72). Twice it presupposes a variant text (Prov 2:16; 19:19), and twice it uses *skiazō*, to shroud in darkness (2 Sam 20:6; Jon 4:6), implying a form of *ṣll* III rather than *nṣl*.

Forms of *nṣl* abound at Qumran ([ni.] 5x, [hi.] 16x, [ho.] 1x), primarily in hymns and prayers, though with much less frequency than its closest synonym *yš'* and with a narrower range of meaning than in MT. With one exception (CD 14:2 [God's covenant guarantees he will save (vb. hi.) from death]), God is the root's exclusive subject, with persons its objects. Universally the root concerns God's deliverance of the faithful or the futility of expecting help from another source. The ungodly have no deliverer (*'ên maṣṣîl*, 1QM 14:11), but Yahweh is deliverer (*maṣṣîl*) of the upright (11QPsa 18 [Syr. II]:17). In CD 4:18 the vb. means to save oneself by flight, i.e., to escape Satan's temptation of riches.

In Qumran hymns, individuals thank God for saving them ([hi.]) from various dangers (e.g., 1QH 2:31; 3:5; 5:13; 19 [Plea], 10; cf. 11QPsa 18 [Syr. II], 17) or deny having done enough righteous deeds to be saved ([ni.]; 1QH 7:17). One prayer affirms that God will even save the faithful from sinning (4Q 504:1-2, II, 16). Qumran commentaries explain that God will save (i.e., spare) his faithful from the coming eschatological judgment (1QHab 8:2 [hi.]; 1Q 14:8-10, 8 [ni.]), something other gods cannot do (1QHab 12:14 [hi.]). In the meantime, says one pesher, the community will be saved (ni.) from the traps of Belial (4QpPs 37:1-2, II, 10). (For other examples, see *TWAT* 5:577.)

NT The NT seldom uses the root's LXX equivalents noted above, but one hears an echo of OT *nṣl* in the familiar petition from the Lord's Prayer, "deliver us from evil" (*rhuomai*, Matt 6:13).

Salvation, deliverance, ransom, rescue: → *g'l* I (redeem, deliver, ransom, # 1457); → *yš'* (be victorious, receive help, save, rescue, # 3828); → *mlṭ* I (get to safety, escape, deliver, give birth to, # 4880); → *nṣl* (rescue, # 5911); → *pdh* (ransom, redeem, deliver, # 7009); → *plṭ* (save, bring to safety, # 7117); → *śrd* (run away, escape, # 8572); → *šālôm* (peace, friendship, happiness, prosperity, health, salvation, # 8934)

Bibliography

TDNT 6:998-1003; 7:965-1024; *THAT* 2:96-99; *TWAT* 5:570-77; U. Bergmann, *Rettung und Befreiung*, 1968; E. Gerstenberger, *Psalms 1*, FOTL 14, 1988; P. Hugger, *Jahwe meine Zuflucht*, 1971, 94-99; E. Jenni, *Das hebräische Pi'el*, 1968, 240, 258; E. Lohse, ed., *Die Texte aus Qumran*, 1964; J. Sawyer, *Semantics in Biblical Research*, SBT 2/24; I. Seeligmann, "Zur Terminologie für das Gerichtsverfahren im Wortschatz des bibl. Hebräische," SVT 16, 1967, 254; G. Vermes, *The Dead Sea Scrolls in English*[3], 1987.

Robert L. Hubbard, Jr.

5913	נצץ

נצץ (*nṣṣ*), q. gleam, sparkle; hi. flower (# 5913); נִיצוֹץ (*nîṣôṣ*), nom. spark (Isa 1:31) (# 5773).

OT 1. The hapleg. q. vb. refers to the intense light or gleaming of the cherubim's feet (Ezek 1:7). For the hi. see Eccl 12:5; S of Songs 6:11; 7:13.

2. The nom. refers to a fiery particle thrown off from a burning substance. No difference with *kîdôd*, spark, can be determined. The nom. is used metaphorically in Isa 1:31 to illustrate that the mighty, who believe that they are not subject to God's ordinances, will recognize how much they have fallen prey to error: just as a spark sets tinder on fire, their own deeds will ultimately rebound against them and destroy them without mercy.

Fire, flame: → *'ûd* (log, burning stick, # 202); → *'ēš* I (fire, # 836); → *b'r* I (burn, blaze up, be consumed, # 1277); → *gaḥelet* (burning charcoal, # 1625); → *goprît* (sulphur, # 1730); → *yṣt* (kindle, burn, set on fire, # 3675); → *yqd* (burn, be burning, kindled, # 3678); → *kîdôd* (spark, # 3958); → *lbb* II (bake cakes, # 4221); → *lahab* (flame, blade, # 4258); → *lhṭ* I (glow, burn, # 4265); → *lappîd* (torch, lightning, # 4365); → *nîṣôṣ* (spark, # 5773); → *peḥām* (charcoal, # 7073); → *reṣep* I (live coal, # 8363); → *rešep* I (flame, glow, arrow, plague, # 8404); → *śrp* (burn, be burnt, # 8596); → *šābîb* (flame, # 8663)
Light, radiance, brightness: → *'wr* (be light, bright, shine, # 239); → *bāhîr* (bright, brilliant, # 986); → *zrḥ* I (rise [of sun], shine, # 2436); → *yp'* I (shine out, # 3649); → *ngh* (shine, cause to shine, # 5585); → *nhr* II (be radiant, # 5642); → *qrn* (send out rays, be radiant, # 7966)

Martin J. Selman/Jackie A. Naudé

5915	נצר

נצר (*nṣr* I), q. watch, guard, keep (# 5915); נָצִיר (*nāṣîr*), adj. (only pl. const., Isa 49:6 K) preserved (# 5910); נִצְּרָה (*niṣṣ*^{e}*râ*), nom. watch, guard (# 5917).

ANE Cognates for *nṣr* occur in Akk., Anc. Aram., Ugar., Arab., Phoen., Syr., and Pun.

OT 1. *nṣr* is equivalent in semantic value to *šmr* (→ # 9068). Forms of *nṣr* occur 61x, but 21 are part., primarily functioning nominally. The similarity between *nṣr* and *šmr* is strikingly illustrated by Ps 119: *nṣr* is used 10x, *šmr* 21x. In Prov, *nṣr* occurs 19x compared to 30x for *šmr*. Poetic parallelism places the two words in balancing stichs in six verses: 2:8, 11; 4:6; 13:3; 16:17; and 27:18.

2. The objects governed by *nṣr* are instructive. Material things are guarded: a fig tree (Prov 27:18), a vineyard (Job 27:18), and a fortress (Nah 2:1[2]). Besiegers (Jer 4:16) and besieged (Isa 1:8) may be kept under scrutiny.

3. The Lord, too, watches his vineyard = his people (Isa 27:3), but his watching of humankind can be critical (Job 7:20). Yet the Lord also is "he who guards your life" (Prov 24:12). Wisdom, too, as a divine manifestation, keeps those who do not forsake her (4:6). The Lord guarded his people, "the apple of his eye" (Deut 32:10). The Lord preserves the faithful (Ps 31:23[24]); his love and truth can protect commoner (40:11[12]) and king (61:7[8]). At the same time, he guards those who keep his covenant (25:10), and the result is that uprightness and integrity provide self-protection (25:21). Part of that protection has to do with appropriate speech. The Lord can set a guard for the mouth, a watch over the lips (141:3), but at the same time, "he who guards (*nṣr*) his lips guards (*šmr*) his life" (Prov 13:3).

Fidelity in adhering to the Lord's will is a major emphasis. Ps 119 employs *nṣr* 10x to affirm the author's intent to keep the statutes of the Lord (119:2, 22, 129), his decrees (119:33, 34, 145), his precepts (119:56, 69, 100), his commands (119:115), and his Torah (119:34). As with this psalm, the preponderance of appearances of *nṣr* are in Ps and Prov, for the focus of these writings is primarily on the intimate relationship between the individual's keeping of the covenant and the Lord's protection.

Guarding, watching: → *nṭr* (keep, # 5757); → *nṣr* I (watch, guard, keep, # 5915); → *ṣph* I (keep guard, watch attentively, post, # 7595); → *šmr* I (watch, guard, revere, # 9068); → *šqd* (watch, wake, # 9193)

BIBLIOGRAPHY

THAT 2:99-101; *TWOT* 2:594-95; M. Held, "Studies in Biblical Homonyms in the Light of Accadian," *ANES* 3, 1970, 46-55; C. Rabin, *"Noṣerim," Textus* 5, 1966, 44-52.

Keith N. Schoville

5916	נֵצֶר

נֵצֶר (*nēṣer*), sprout, shoot (# 5916).

OT This word is found 4x (Isa 11:1; 14:19; 60:21; Dan 11:7) and is probably related to the same root that gives us the place name Nazareth, although the city is not mentioned in the OT. This word may be in the background of Matt 2:23, which notes, "What was said through the prophets: 'He will be called a Nazarene.'" There is no such exact quotation found anywhere in the Prophets. The term *ṣemaḥ* (# 7542) seems to imply more than the idea of a small beginning of growth (sprout or shoot); *nēṣer* implies more mature growth. The fact that the NIV took *ṣemaḥ* as messianic is reflected in the capitalized "Branch" in Isa 4:2; Jer 23:5; 33:15; Zech 3:8; 6:12. It would have been better if the NIV used a different term here for *nēṣer* in Isa 11:1. This difference in messianic titles is found in the NAB's "bud shall blossom," the REB's "shoot," and the NJPSV's "new shoot." The term is used to denote a sprout springing from a root and is from a common Sem. root, to be green, fresh, although the vb. is not used in the OT.

In Isa 11:1, *nēṣer* is used in the famous promise: "A shoot (*ḥōṭer*; # 2643) will come up from the stump (*gēza'*) of Jesse; from his roots (*šōreš*, # 9247) a Branch (*nēṣer*) will bear fruit." The term was understood as Messiah by the ancient Tg. and is capitalized in the NIV to carry this meaning (B. D. Chilton, *The Isaiah Targum*, 1987, 2:28). *nēṣer* is also used figuratively in the prophecy against Babylon, where Isaiah describes the king of Babylon, "But you are cast out of your tomb like a rejected branch" (Isa 14:19). And during the glorious days of Zion, the Lord describes his people as "the shoot (*nēṣer*) I have planted, the work of my hands, for the display of my splendor" (Isa 60:21). All the new EVV properly render shoot or bud.

Finally, *nēṣer* is used in a family tree sense in Dan 11:7, which says that "one from her family line will arise to take her place." This is lit. "branch (*nēṣer*) of her roots" (KJV).

Shoot, bud, growth, sprig, sprout, tendril: → *'ēb* (shoot, # 4); → *gēza'* (shoot, stump, # 1614); → *zalzal* (shoot of vine, # 2360); → *ḥōṭer* (rod, shoot, # 2643); → *yôneqet* (shoot, stripling, # 3438); → *n*ᵉ*ṭîšôt* (tendrils, shoots, # 5746); → *nēṣer* (sprout, shoot, # 5916); → *ṣmḥ* (sprout, spring up, grow, prosper, make grow, # 7541)

Larry Walker

5917 (*niṣṣ*ᵉ*râ*, watch, guard), → # 5915

5918	נקב

נקב (*nqb*), q. pierce, bore; designate, distinguish, note; designate as bad, curse; ni. be designated, registered (by name) (# 5918); מַקֶּבֶת (*maqqebet* I), nom. hammer (→ # 5216); מַקֶּבֶת (*maqqebet* II), nom. quarry (# 5217); נֶקֶב (*neqeb*), nom. (perforated) mounting(?) (# 5920); נְקֵבָה (*n*ᵉ*qēbâ*), nom. female (→ # 5922).

ANE Akk. (Old and Standard Babylonian) *naqābu,* deflower, rape; Arab. *naqaba,* to bore, pierce, perforate, *naqb,* digging, excavation, hole, tunnel; Epigraphic South Arab. *nqb,* to cut, excavate; Tg. Aram. *n*ᵉ*qab,* to perforate, *niqbā',* hole, perforation; Inscriptional Heb. *hnqb,* piercing (ni. inf. const.) and *nqbh,* tunnel (nom.); Nab. *nqybyn,* designated, marked (q. pass. part.); Syr. *n*ᵉ*qab,* to bore, pierce, dig through, *neqbā',* hole, opening; Ugar. *nqbn,* harness, perforated straps (associated with a donkey) (B. Margalit, *UF* 15, 1983, 105).

OT 1. Seven times the vb. in the q. stem refers to piercing or boring through something: 2 Kgs 12:9[10], lid of a chest; 18:21 = Isa 35:6, a hand; Hab 3:14, a head; Hag 1:6, a moneybag; Job 40:24, the nose of Behemoth; 41:2[40:26], the jaw of Leviathan. Twice it refers to designating or naming: Gen 30:28, wages, "*Name* your wages" (NIV); Isa 62:2, designating or bestowing a new name for Jerusalem. Once, as a q. pass. part., the vb. refers to notable people (Amos 6:1).

Five times in the q. the root seems to signify designate something as bad, i.e., to curse or blaspheme, though this sense for the root is not without question. In three of these occurrences morphological ambiguity clouds the analysis. The impf. or prefix conjugation is used: *yiqq*ᵉ*buhû* (2x; Job 3:8; Prov 11:26) and *wayyiqqōb* (Lev 24:11). Morphologically, these spellings could be transitive forms of a q. impf. of the root *nqb* or the root *qbb*, curse. Such a quasi-Aramaic spelling of the q. impf. of the root *qbb*, where the first root consonant is doubled, is not uncommon among geminate roots in BH. That the root *nqb* carries a sense of curse or blaspheme seems clearer in Lev 24:16, where both a q. act. part (*nōqēb*) and q. inf. const. occur after the ambiguous impf. form and the root *qll*, curse, and where the textual environment demands a sense of blaspheme for this root. These occurrences argue for the probability that *nqb* underlies the three morphologically ambiguous forms, though the root *qbb* must remain a possibility. The three occurrences in Leviticus (Lev 24:11, 16 [2x]) refer to a disrespectful or inappropriate treatment of Yahweh's name.

The root occurs 6x in the ni. In all cases it refers to designated or registered names.

2. The meaning of *neqeb* is uncertain. The lexical item occurs once in Lev 19:33 as part of a geographical name, perhaps a pass, and its occurrence in Ezek 28:13 is far from clear, though the textual environment seems to support a sense of a perforated mounting or setting for precious stones.

P-B For the vb. senses of to bore, to perforate, to curse, to designate are attested. The nom. *neqeb* refers to a hole, perforation, or incision.

Penetration: → *nḥt* (march down, descend, penetrate, settle, # 5737)

BIBLIOGRAPHY

TWOT 2:595-96; H. C. Brichto, "The Problem of 'Curse' in the Hebrew Bible," *SBL Monograph* 13, 1963, 200-202.

Gary Alan Long

5920 (*neqeb*, [perforated] mounting?), → # 5918

5922 (*n*ᵉ*qēbâ*, female), → # 2351

5923	נָקֹד

נָקֹד (*nāqōd*), speckled (# 5923).

OT All nine occurrences of *nāqōd* are found in the episode of Jacob's breeding speckled sheep and goats in order to augment his herd and diminish that of his Laban (Gen 30:32-33, 35, 39; 31:8, 10, 12). *nāqōd* always appears with one of these words: *ṭālû'*, spotted, and *'āqōd*, streaked: "And they bore young that were streaked (*'ᵃqudîm*) or speckled (*n*ᵉ*qōdîm*) or spotted (*ṭ*ᵉ*lû'îm*)" (30:39).

In the story, Jacob and Laban made much of determining Jacob's wages in relation to the color of the animals: speckled (*nāqōd*) and spotted (*ṭālû'*) sheep, streaked (*'āqōd*) and spotted (*ṭālû'*) male goats, speckled (*nāqōd*) and spotted (*ṭālû'*) female goats, as well as "dark-colored" (*ḥûm*) lambs (30:32, 35; 31:8-10). While the precise details of the negotiations are not without difficulty (see Westermann, 2:481-82), the details serve the narrator to develop the theme of God's blessing and protection. God richly blesses Jacob, in spite of his conniving and of Laban's countermeasures.

Laban recognized God's blessing on Jacob through his work with Laban's flock (30:27, 30). Jacob interpreted the blessing as a confirmation of his righteous or honest treatment of the unscrupulous Laban (30:33; 31:12, 38-40). The allocation of the spotted and speckled sheep to Jacob later became part of the reason for Jacob's return to the Promised Land (31). God had promised to bless Jacob before he went to Laban

(28:3-4, 13-15) and to bring him back to the land of Canaan. Through the mysterious proliferation of Jacob's sheep and the rift this caused with Laban, God fulfilled these two promises.

Jacob (→) finally recognized God's hand in his prosperity, "The angel of God ... said, 'Look up and see that all the male goats mating with the flock are streaked (*'āqōd*), speckled (*nāqōd*) or spotted (*bārōd*), for I have seen all that Laban has been doing to you'" (31:11-12).

Colors—spotted, dappled: → *'āmōṣ* (pie-bald?, # 600); → *bārōd* (dappled, spotted, # 1353); → *ṭl'* (spotted, gaudy, # 3229); → *nāqōd* (speckled, # 5923); → *'āqōd* (striped, streaked, # 6819)

Robert Alden

5924	נֹקֵד

נֹקֵד (*nōqēd*), shepherd, herdsman, sheep-dealer (Amos 1:1; 7:14; # 5924).

ANE In Ugar. *nqd* is the title of the priest-scribe, *'il-malk* (*KTU* 1.6:VI:55; cf. *RSP* 2:63-64). Akk. *nāqidu* (*AHw*, 744; *CAD*, 11 (1), 333-35) is used for a herdsman.

OT 1. The word is used of King Mesha of Moab in 2 Kgs 3:4. It can be translated "shepherd" because there is nothing religious in the contexts, but some prefer "augurer" (cf. J. Gray, *I & II Kings* [OTL], 1977^3, 484-85).

2. Amos is also described by the same term. He was part of the Tekoan shepherds (1:1); in 7:14 he refutes Amaziah by stating that he is not a professional prophet, but a *nōqēd*. In the light of the Ugar. texts where the word can refer to a priest, some have described Amos as a cultic official or part of the temple personnel (literature and views discussed in S. M. Paul). The best argument against the cultic interpretation seems to be Amos 7, where he is clearly described as a breeder of cattle (*bôqēr* v. 14) and a herdsman in charge of the sheep (*ṣō'n* v. 15a). (→ Amos: Theology)

Arts, crafts, professions: → *'ommān* (craftsman, # 588); → *'ōpeh* (baker, # 685); → *gōdēr* (mason, # 1553); → *gallāb* (barber, # 1647); → *dayyāg* (fisherman, # 1900); → *ḥōṣēb* (stonecutter, # 2935); → *ḥārāš* (craftsman, # 3093); → *ḥōšēb* (weaver, # 3110); → *ṭabbāḥ* (butcher, # 3184); → *yôṣēr* (potter, # 3450); → *yāqûš* (fowler, # 3687); → *kbs* (wash, # 3891); → *kōrēm* (vinedresser, # 4144); → *mašqeh* (butler, # 5482); → *nōqēd* (shepherd?, # 5924); → *ṣayyād* I (hunter, # 7475); → *ṣōrēp* (goldsmith, # 7671); → *rō'eh* (shepherd, # 8286a); → *rōqēaḥ* (ointment-mixer, # 8382)

BIBLIOGRAPHY

S. M. Paul, *Amos*, 1991, 34-35.

I. Cornelius

5925	נְקֻדָּה

נְקֻדָּה (*n^{e}quddâ*), small globules of silver (# 5925).

OT The nom. occurs only in S of Songs 1:11; a possible cognate, *nāqōd*, speckled (→ # 5923), is found in Gen 30:32 and 31:12 of spotted sheep and goats, and *n^{e}qud-dîm*, crumbled bread, small cake (→ # 5926), in Josh 9:5 and 1 Kgs 14:3 of a dry crumbly food, but lexicographers usually separate the two roots. There are several problems in understanding this verse. First, it is not clear whether the silver is added to the gold or the gold to the silver; perhaps judging that the more precious metal would be added, JPSV translated, "We will add wreathes of gold to your spangles of silver." If spangles is used in the usual sense of small glittering dots, this hardly makes sense, but it could mean a clasp or a stud. A second problem is the type of gold object; it clearly is some type of ornamentation worn on the cheeks of the horse, which could be compared to a woman's jewelry (vv. 9-10). This word is found in Ugar. in texts dealing with chariots, but none of them make clear what it is, and it is also uncertain whether we are dealing with the same thing. Finally, the exact nature of the silver can only be conjectured, but it would seem to be some small type of bead.

P-B In postbiblical Heb. *n^equddôt* is the term used for the signs in the Tiberian system of vocalization.

Metals: → *'^anāk* (lead, # 643); → *b^edîl* (dross, # 974); → *barzel* (iron, # 1366); → *zāhāb* (gold, # 2298); → *ḥel'â* I (rust, # 2689); → *ḥašmal* (glow?, electrum, glowing metal, # 3133); → *kesep* (silver, money, # 4084); → *masgēr* II (metal worker, # 4994); → *ma'^abeh* (foundry, # 5043); → *n^eḥōšet* I (copper, bronze, # 5733); → *sîg* (lead oxide, # 6092); → *sēper* II (bronze, plate, # 6220); → *'ōperet* (lead, # 6769); → *paḥ* II (thin sheet, # 7063); → *p^elādōt* (steel?, # 7110); → *ṣwr* III (cast [metal], # 7445); → *ṣa'^aṣu'îm* (things formed by metal coating, # 7589); → *ṣph* II (arrange, overlay, plate, glaze, # 7596); → *ṣrp* (melt, smelt, refine, # 7671); → *qālāl* (polished metal, # 7838); → *šḥṭ* II (alloyed, # 8822)

BIBLIOGRAPHY

T. N. D. Mettinger, "Nominal Pattern *'qetulla'* in Biblical Hebrew," *JSS* 16, 1971, 6; M. H. Pope, *Song of Songs*, AB, 1977, 343-46.

A. H. Konkel

5926 (*n^equddîm*, cakes sprinkled with aromatic seeds), → Bread

5927	נקה

נקה (*nqh*), ni. be free, exempt from guilt, responsibility; pi. remain unpunished, to be acquitted (# 5927); נָקִי (*nāqî*), adj. free from, exempt, pure, innocent (# 5929); נִקָּיוֹן (*niqqāyôn*), nom. cleanness, whiteness, innocence (# 5931).

ANE Heb. *nqh* is related to Akk. *naqû*, pour out (libations), sacrifice (*AHw*, 744f), which occurs mostly in cultic contexts (Dhorme, 224-25). According to Cross (302, 306n 16) it also conveys the meaning to be pure, clean, spotless. It occurs in Aram., denoting some act of purification by means of a libation (*DISO*, 186), and in Arab. as "cleanse pure." The etymology of a Heb. derivative *m^enaqqiyâ*, sacrificial cups (cf. Exod 25:29; 37:16; Num 4:7; Jer 52:19), suggests an original general Sem. root meaning "to empty out, pour"; hence, "be clean, innocent, free." The derived juridical meaning, to be acquitted, or to be free from punishment, is exclusive to the OT.

OT 1. The root *nqh* conveys the notion of freedom in a forensic sense: on the one hand, the exemption from obligations and duties that have been legally imposed; on the other, the acquittal of guilt incurred and punishment deserved on account of God's forgiveness. By declaring a person *nāqî* he is set free.

2. The most frequent occurrence of *nāqî* (21 of the 43x) is as an adj. in the fixed expression *dām nāqî*, innocent blood (Deut 19:10; 2 Kgs 24:4; Jer 22:17, etc.),

referring to guiltless people who are threatened with murder (Deut 27:25; 1 Sam 19:5) or who have actually been killed (Deut 19:13; 2 Kgs 21:16; Jon 1:14). It forms an integral part of the prophetic accusation (Jer 2:34; 7:6; 19:4; 22:3; 26:15; cf. Ps 106:38; Isa 59:7). Parallel concepts like *ṣaddîq* (Exod 23:7; Ps 94:21), *yāšār* (Job 4:7), *tām* (9:22), *'ānî* (Ps 10:8), etc., indicate from a juridical point of view who these innocent persons were: clearly the powerless, guiltless, and blameless (2 Sam 14:9).

3. The adj. *nāqî* (var. *nāqi'*) is also used in a positive sense to describe someone's exemption from charges or obligations, hence his "freedom." It entails, e.g., the freedom (exemption) from military service of the newly wed (Deut 24:5). It also designates freedom from slavery (Gen 44:10) or hard labor (1 Kgs 15:22). Furthermore, it describes freedom from the obligations of an oath or an agreement (Gen 24:8, 41; Num 32:22; Josh 2:17, 20) or the effects of a curse (Num 5:19, 28, 31). The word *nāqî* thus embodies the notion of freedom in a juridical sense, i.e., acquitted, exempt, or freed from, declared innocent of legal or ethical obligations, punishment, or guilt. It is never associated with the cult, which explains why the word is absent from Leviticus. The term *n^eqî kappayim* (clean hands) in Ps 24:4 refers to an ethical conduct that is undergirded by juridical acquittal (similarly *niqqāyôn* in Gen 20:5; Ps 26:6; 73:13). The nom. *niqqāyôn* also refers to innocence (Hos 8:5) and cleanness (Amos 4:6).

4. The vb. *nqh* occurs 44x in the OT (ni. 25x; pi. 18x; q. inf. abs. once, modifying a ni.), most frequently in an ethical, moral, or forensic sense, denoting the release from an obligation, guilt, or punishment. Thus the husband is declared free from guilt (*w^eniqqâ mē'āwōn*) and innocent if, in declaring his wife unfaithful, he adheres to the correct legal procedures (Num 5:31). The word also designates release from punishment or responsibility (Exod 21:19). The expression *nāqî mē'im yhwh* refers to the exemption from punishment by the Lord. It is sometimes negativized, stating a reprimand. "Be sure of this: The wicked will not go unpunished, but those who are righteous will go free" (Prov 11:21; cf. 16:5; Ps 19:13[14]; Jer 2:35; 25:29; 49:12). The pi., "to acquit," is used consistently with God as subject, with the exception of 1 Kgs 2:9 (where Solomon is addressed). He is the one to whom the innocent turns for acquittal (Ps 19:12[13] and forgiveness, knowing that God forgives but does not leave the guilty unpunished (Exod 34:7; Num 14:18; cf. Exod 20:7; Job 9:28; Jer 30:11; 46:28; Nah 1:3).

Freedom, innocence, cleanness, liberation: → *d^erôr* III (release, freedom, # 2002); → *ḥpš* (freed, # 2926); → *ḥōr* I (free man, freeborn, # 2985); → *nqh* (be free, exempt from guilt, remain unpunished, # 5927); → *ntr* III (set free, # 6002); → *qôm^emiyyût* (walk erect, # 7758); → *rwḥ* A (become wide or spacious, be spacious, # 8118)

Guilt, evil, unrighteousness: → *'šm* (become guilty, incur guilt, bear guilt, pronounce guilty, # 870); → *dām* (blood, bloodshed, blood-guilt, murder, # 1947); → *wāzār* (unjust, laden with guilt, # 2261); → *ḥwb* (be the cause of guilt, # 2549); → *ḥēṭ'* (sin, guilt, punishment of sin, # 2628); → *nqh* (be free, exempt from guilt, remain unpunished, # 5927); → *rš'* (act wickedly, unrighteously, be guilty, pronounce guilty, # 8399)

Punishment and sin: → *ḥṭ'* (sin, commit a sin, purify, # 2627); → *ykḥ* (dispute, reason together, prove, judge, rule, reprove, # 3519); → *ysr* I (admonish, correct, discipline, # 3579); → *'wh* (do wrong, pervert, # 6390); → *'wl* I (act wrongly, # 6401); → *p^e'ullâ* (wages punishment, reward, payment, deeds, # 7190); → *pqd* (punish, assemble, record, appoint, # 7212)

Bibliography

ISBE 3:118-22; F. M. Cross, "The Cave Inscriptions from Khirbet Beit Lei," *FS Glueck,* 1970, 299-306; E. Dhorme, *Les religions de Babylonie et d'Assyrie,* 1949.

J. P. J. Olivier

5929 (*nāqî,* free from, exempt, pure, innocent), → # 5927

5931 (*niqqāyôn,* cleanness, whiteness, innocence), → # 5927

5932 (*nāqîq,* cleft, crack), → # 5117

5933	נקם

נקם (*nqm*), q. avenge, take vengeance, revenge, entertain revengeful feelings; ni. be avenged, take vengeance, avenge o.s.; hitp. take (oneself's) vengeance (# 5933); nom. נָקָם (*nāqām*), vengeance, revenge, requital (# 5934); נְקָמָה (*n*[e]*qāmâ*), vengeance, revenge, requital (# 5935).

ANE The root *nqm* is of WestSem. origin and is well attested in Late Aram., Arab., and Eth. languages. Regarding the literature that historically speaking coincides with the OT period, *nqm* appears in the nomenclature of the second millennium BC (expression of the hope of divine protection?), in two Mari letters (in the context of criminal law), and in two Aram. documents: Sefire III (in the context of covenant law) and a legal text from Elephantine (in the context of sacral law). The root does not occur in the Amarna literature (cf. W. T. Pitard, 5-25; versus G. E. Mendenhall, 69-104, and J. N. Musvosvi). The word group *nqm* seems to have been preferred for its legal connotations and should, therefore, be associated with the maintenance of justice.

OT 1. In view of the history of exegesis (Marcion!) it is of great importance to understand the OT preaching of God's "vengeance" correctly. For modern man the word "vengeance" has strongly negative connotations (immorality, arbitrariness, illegitimacy, cruelty); "vengeance" and love are antipodes. In the OT, however, the concept of "vengeance" has a positive connotation, both from a semantic as well as from a theological point of view: "vengeance" has to do with lawfulness, justice, and salvation. As such, the theme of "vengeance" takes up an important position in OT theology, particularly in the writings of the prophets Isa, Jer, and Ezek.

2. The root *nqm* is used 79x; in ca. 85 percent God is subject, either directly or in a derivative sense. In the OT, *nqm* is normally God's prerogative or that of the people used by him as instruments (judge, king, court, people). The idea of legitimacy and competent authority is inherent in the root *nqm*. In the case of (human) individual or illegitimate revenge, the use of *nqm* is either avoided or this vocable is given a negative semantic value (see under 8) because it lacked God's legitimation. Nowhere in the OT does *nqm* refer to blood-vengeance (versus E. Lipiński).

3. Divine "vengeance" is usually set in the context of lawfulness or war. Metaphors like God as King, God as Judge, and God as Warrior play a great part in the *nqm*-texts, God as King being the overall thought. God's "vengeance" in the OT can be described as the punitive retribution of God, who, as the sovereign King—faithful to his covenant—stands up for the vindication of his glorious name in a judging and fighting mode, while watching over the maintenance of his justice and acting to save his

people. The notion of "vengeance" is no foreign element in the OT revelation of God, but is a consequence of his holiness (Jer 50:28-29); zeal (Isa 59:18), coupled with his wrath (Mic 5:14), is subordinate to his justice (Isa 63:1, 4). Yahweh is the *'ēl n^e qāmôt*, God of vengeance (Ps 94:1), threefold *nōqēm* (Nah 1:2). In history, God reveals his bilateral acting up to his covenant: he is both a forgiving and a revengeful God (Ps 99:8). Forgiveness and vengeance, lawfulness and grace, love and wrath are not contradictions within Yahweh.

4. The vengeance of the God of the covenant can turn against Israel. God sends a sword that takes vengeance for the breaking of the covenant (Lev 26:15). Reacting to the infringement of lawfulness and the violation of the covenant God cannot but send vengeance (Jer 5:9, 29; 9:9[8]). God's vengeance is usually disciplinary in nature and aims at the restoration of lawfulness and the covenant in order that Zion (→ Theology) will turn into a "city of righteousness," a "faithful city" (Isa 1:24-26), again. God's vengeance calls to a halt the wickedness and the crying injustice in Zion (59:17-18). Yahweh, the supreme judge, sees to it that the blood that is shed cannot be covered in the blood-city of Jerusalem, but, so to speak, gets on to "a bare rock": God is permanently reminded of the injustice by the clearly visible blood, namely, in order to intervene out of "vengeance" (Ezek 24:8). Likewise, God's vengeance is the result of the lawsuit between Saul and David (1 Sam 24:13; cf. 2 Sam 4:8), between Jeremiah and his opponents (Jer 11:20; 15:15; 20:12).

5. Usually God's "vengeance" is turned against the nations because they attempt to reach out for world power in their unlimited lust of power: Assur (Nah 1:2), Babel (Isa 47:3; Jer 50-51), Egypt (Jer 46:10); because they recklessly rise against himself and injure his honor (Deut 32 from v. 26; Mic 5:14); and because they try to destroy his people Israel (Num 31:2; Deut 32:35; Jer 50-51 *passim*; Ps 79:10). There is often a close relationship between vengeance over the enemy and the salvation of God's people: one is the reverse of the other, as, e.g., in Isa 34:8; 35:4; 59:18; 61:2; 63:4; Jer 51:36; Nah 1:2; cf. 1:15 [2:1]). God's vengeance marks the turn from destruction to restoration, from injustice to peace, and as such can be the object of joy (Ps 58:11) or contents of worldwide jubilation (Deut 32:43). More and more God's vengeance gets eschatological purport in the prophetic teachings: one day God's vengeance will prepare the way for the new Zion (Isa 34:8; 61:2); all obstacles for perfect joy and peace will be eliminated by God's vengeance (Ps 149:7; Mic 5:14).

6. The call for God's vengeance in the Psalms (the so-called imprecatory psalms) and the confessions of Jeremiah is to be seen in the light of the previous. These passages imply (in a situation of uttermost threat!) an abandonment of private revenge and a total surrender to him who judges righteously. In no instance is the satisfaction of feelings of hatred of embittered people at stake. The prayer for vengeance is the prayer for victory of lawfulness and the revelation of the God of the covenant, who, while judging, keeps his word (Ps 58:11; 79:10; 94:1; 149:7). From a hermeneutical point of view allowance must be made for the specific situation of the OT believer and his time (little sight of a final judgment after death; the curse as a legitimate legal remedy; a specific covenantal relationship, etc.). The imprecation, in its deepest intention, is a cry for the breakthrough of God's kingdom in liberation and vengeance. Without God's vengeance there is no justice (Ps 58:12) and no future (Deut 32:43; Ps 149:7-9).

7. The passages in which *nqm* takes a human subject are placed in the context of lawfulness or war. In Gen 4:15 a potential murderer is threatened by sevenfold vengeance: *nqm* means legal protection for Cain. Lamech grabs this privilege in a godless *conservatio sui* (v. 24). The legal community watches over justice, especially when blood-vengeance does not function properly (Exod 21:20-21—the slave is subj. in both vv.). The adulterer is officially judged on the "day of vengeance" (*yôm nāqām*), no hush money can prevent that (Prov 6:34). Making war can also be characterized as *nqm*. In the ANE war is frequently described by means of juridical metaphors and is considered as a "lawsuit" in which the godhead passes sentence (cf. Judg 11:36 after 11:27; 2 Sam 18:19, 31; 22:48). Besides, in the OT the idea of Yahweh-war (Von Rad: "holy war") is of importance. In that way Joshua (Josh 10:13), Saul (1 Sam 14:24; 18:25), and the Israelites (Esth 8:13) have their vengeance on their enemies. Even Samson's "revenge," better "vindication" (Judg 15:7; 16:28), is in accordance with the redemptive struggle against the enemy (Judg 14:4).

8. In a few texts *nqm* denotes (negative) human vengefulness. The word group *nqm* is used as an utterance of an evil, resentful disposition in Lev 19:18: revengefulness is in conflict with a holy life in covenantal communion and as such is forbidden. A "revengeful person" and an "enemy" can be synonymous (Ps 8:3; 44:17; cf. Lam 3:60; Ezek 25:12, 15). Jeremiah's opponents put their (forbidden) revengefulness in the golden frame of lawfulness (Jer 20:10).

P-B Apoc., Pseudep., and QL link up with the OT in broad outline (prohibition of human revengefulness; vengeance as a divine prerogative; the eschatological day of vengeance); as a result of the great frequency and intensity of the theme in these writings, they, however, breathe a different atmosphere than the OT does. (→ Retribution: Theology)

Judgment: → *dyn* (judge, contend, govern, administer, # 1906); → *miśpāḥ* (breach of law, # 5384); → *pll* I (sit in judgment, arbitrate, expect, # 7136); → *ṣdq* (be just, righteous, justified, # 7405); → *špṭ* (judge, execute judgment, govern, # 9149)

Vengeance: → *gmr* (cease, fail, requite, # 1698); → *nqm* (avenge, revenge, avenge o.s., # 5933)

Bibliography

THAT 2:106-9; *TWAT* 5:602-12; W. Dietrich, "Rache. Erwägungen zu einem alttestamentlichen Thema," *EvT* 36, 1976, 450-72; K. Koch (ed.), *Um das Prinzip der Vergeltung in Religion und Recht des Alten Testaments*, WF 125, 1972; H. McKeating, "Vengeance Is Mine. A Study of the Pursuit of Vengeance in the Old Testament," *ExpTim* 74, 1963, 239-45; J. L. McKenzie, "Vengeance Is Mine," *Scripture* 12, 1960, 33-39; G. E. Mendenhall, "The 'Vengeance' of Yahweh," *The Tenth Generation. The Origins of Biblical Tradition*, 1973, 69-104; E. Merz, *Die Blutrache bei den Israeliten*, BZAW 20, 1916; J. N. Musvosvi, *The Concept of Vengeance in the Book of Revelation in Its Old Testament and Near Eastern Context*, 1987; H. G. L. Peels, *The Vengeance of God: The Meaning of the Root NQM and the Function of the NQM-Texts in the Context of Divine Revelation in the Old Testament*, OTS 31, 1995; idem, "Passion or Justice? The Interpretation of b^e*yôm nāqām* in Prov vi 34," *VT*, 44, 1994, 270-74; W. T. Pitard, "Amarna *ekēma* and Hebrew *nāqam*," *Maarav* 3, 1981, 5-25; R. H. Swartzback, "A Biblical Study of the Word 'Vengeance'," *Int* 6, 1952, 451-57.

H. G. L. Peels

5934 (*nāqām*, vengeance, revenge, requital), → # 5933

5935 (*n^eqāmâ*, vengeance, revenge, requital), → # 5933

5936	נקע

נקע (*nq'*), q. disengage oneself, turn away from someone (# 5936).

ANE The Arab. cognate *naqa'a* means cause to yield.

OT Found only in Ezekiel, the vb. describes a break-up in a lover's relationship: God's turning in disgust because of Judah's promiscuity with her paramours (neighbors) (Ezek 23:22, 28). A related form with similar meaning *yq'*, turn aside (→ # 3697), appears in Ezek 23:17, 18 (*HALAT* 2:412; 3:681).

J. A. Thompson

5937	נקף

נקף (*nqp* I), pi. cut/chop down; destroy (# 5937); nom. נֹקֶף (*nōqep*), beating; cutting (# 5939).

ANE Arab. cf. *naqafa*.

OT 1. In Isa 10:34 the word describes figuratively the action of the Lord with an iron tool (ax) as he cuts down the enemies (Assyria) of his people. "Forest thickets/Lebanon" have both a figurative referent, Assyria, and a literal referent, the forest of Lebanon and its mighty cedars. In Job 19:26 *nqp* refers to a laceration destruction (NIV, RSV) of Job's skin (*'ôrî*), resulting in his death. The NJPSV renders this "after my skin will have been peeled off" (26a). The LXX renders v. 26a, "stand/arise afterwards when my skin has suffered (*anantlein*) these things." The Vg. rendering *in rursum circumdabor pelle mea*, "and afterwards I will be wrapped in/supplied with my skin," understands *'ôrî* as "my skin," but *nqp* as = *circumdare*, put something around something else/purify, almost the opposite of some of the other translations. Based on the use of the word elsewhere in the OT this translation seems wrong.

Job goes on to assert that in his flesh he will/does see/catch a vision of God (26b). This verse is full of translation difficulties (e.g., *'ôrî* may mean when I awake, q. inf. const. > *'wr* + 1cs pron. suff.). The root *nqp* is associated with violent acts and destruction. In Isa 10:33-34 it is used as a near synonym to *šsp*, lop off (→ # 9119), *gd'*, fell, cut (→ # 1548), *špl*, bring low (→ # 9164), *npl*, fall (→ # 5877).

2. The nom. is used in the simile/idiom *k^enōqep zayit*, as the beating of an olive tree, to describe the condition of Damascus (Isa 17:6) and the earth itself (Isa 24:13) after God judges/devastates it. It is paralleled by "some gleanings will remain (after the harvest of grapes)."

P-B The LXX translates *nqp* using *piptō*, fall, lose (Isa 10:34) and with a part. of *anetlēn*, bear, suffer, sustain.

Cutting, destruction, extermination, shearing, trimming: → *bṣ'* (cut away, get gain, cut off, break up, # 1298); → *br'* III (clear out trees, cut, destroy, # 1345); → *btr* (cut into pieces, # 1439); → *gd'* (cut short, # 1548); → *gzh* (bring forth, # 1602); → *gzz* (cut, shear, # 1605);

→ *gzr* I (cut, take away, # 1615); → *grz* (be cut off, # 1746); → *gr'* I (cut out, reduce, # 1757); → *ḥlp* II (cut through, pierce, # 2737); → *ksḥ* (cut, cut down, # 4065); → *krsm* (make cropped, trimmed off, # 4155); → *krt* (cut, cut off, exterminate, cut a covenant, circumcise, # 4162); → *melqāḥāyim* (snuffers for trimming/cleaning of lights/lamps, # 4920); → *nqp* I (cut/chop down, destroy, # 5937); → *ntḥ* (cut in pieces, # 5983); → *qṣb* (cut off, shear, # 7892); → *šsp* (hew into pieces, # 9119); → *tzz* (cut away, # 9372)

Eugene Carpenter

5938	נקף

נקף (*nqp* II), q. go round (in time); hi. surround, go round (in time) (# 5938); נִקְפָּה (*niqpâ*), nom. cord (hapleg. in Isa 3:24; # 5940); (?) תְּקוּפָה (*tᵉqûpâ*), nom. turning (→ # 9543).

ANE Ugar. *nqpt* seems to mean cycle (of time). Syr. *nqp* means cling to, while Arab. *waqafa* means stand still.

OT 1. The vb. is used of military hostility in 2 Kgs 6:14 and thence in laments: (a) in pitiful descriptions of personal enmity at Ps 17:9; 22:16[17] in order to solicit God's help, and (b) in protests against God's own hostility (Job 19:6; Ps 88:17[18]; Lam 3:5). In Job 19:6 Bildad's view of a natural moral law of destruction for the wicked (18:7-10) is contested with an insistence that in Job's case God is personally responsible (19:6-12).

2. A sacred procession is in view at Ps 48:12[13]. In Josh 6:3, 11 both a religious procession and a military march are envisaged.

P-B In 1QpHab 4:7 the vb. is used of the military activity of the Kittim or Romans.

Circle, turn: → *'pp* (surround, # 705); → *ḥdr* I (surround, enclose, # 2539); → *ḥwg* (describe a circle, # 2552); → *ktr* II (surround, # 4193); → *nqp* II (go round, surround, # 5938); → *sbb* (turn go round, surround, # 6015); → *'āgōl* (round, # 6318); → *'ṭr* (surround, crown, # 6496/7)

BIBLIOGRAPHY

TWAT 5:612-16.

Leslie C. Allen

5939 (*nōqep*, beating; cutting), → # 5937

5940 (*niqpâ*, cord, rope), → # 5938

5941	נקר

נקר (*nqr*), q. pick out, hew out; pi. bore out, dig out, cut out; pu. be broken out (# 5941); נְקָרָה (*nᵉqārâ*), nom. cleft in rock, cavern (# 5942).

ANE Arab., OSA *naqara*, hollow out, excavate; Akk. *naqāru*, scrape out.

OT 1. The vb., used 6x with the meaning to pull, pluck, dig, hew, or bore out something, is used with different objects both figuratively and literally. In the q. it is used twice to describe the gouging out of a person's eye (1 Sam 11:2; Prov 30:17; cf. Judg 16:20). Nahash, the Ammonite, threatened this gruesome punishment for the people of Jabesh Gilead (1 Sam 11:2). The haughty eye is an evil to be removed (Prov 30:17).

2. Two of the uses in the pi. are metaphorical, referring to blinding men by deception (Num 16:14) and to the debilitating effect of the night (Job 30:17).

3. The single pu. usage refers to Abraham as the source or quarry (*maqqebet*; deleting *bôr*) from which God hewed his people (*nqr*; ‖ to *ḥṣb* in pu. also) (Isa 51:1).

4. The nom. is found in Exod and Isa with the meaning cleft in a rock (*ṣûr*) or clefts. Both times it involves persons seeking shelter from the presence of God (the day of judgment [Isa 2:21], the day of God revealing himself to Moses [Exod 33:22]).

Digging: → *ḥpr* I (dig, seek out, # 2916); → *ḥṣb* (quarry, hew out, dig, # 2933); → *ḥtr* (dig, break through, # 3168); → *krh* I (dig, be dug, # 4125); → *nqr* (pick out, hew out, dig out, # 5941); → *qwr* I (dig, bubble, # 7769)
Bricks, stone: → *gāzît* (ashlar stone, # 1607); → *ḥṣb* I (break, dig, quarry, hew out, # 2933); → *lbn* II (make, produce, mold bricks, # 4236); → *massāʿ* (quarry [stones], # 5024); → *nqr* (pick out, hew out, dig out, # 5941)
Rock, stones: → *'eben* (stone, rock, # 74); → *gābîš* (rock-crystal, # 1486); → *ḥallāmîš* (flint, # 2734); → *ḥāṣāṣ* (gravel, # 2953); → *kēp* (rock, # 4091); → *sōḥeret* (mineral stone, # 6090); → *selaʿ* (rock, # 6152); → *sql* (throw stones, # 6232); → *ṣûr* I (rock, boulder, # 7446); → *ṣûr* II (pebble, flint, # 7447); → *ṣōr* I (flint knife, # 7644); → *rgm* (stone, # 8083); → *talpiyyôt* (courses of stones, # 9444)

Eugene Carpenter/Michael A. Grisanti

5942 (*n*ᵉ*qārâ*, cleft, gap [in rock]), → # 5117, # 5941

5944	נֵר

נֵר (*nēr* I), nom. lamp, light (# 5944); נִיר (*nîr* I), nom. lamp (# 5775).

ANE Cognate with Akk. *nūru*, nom. light, fire, lamp, frequently used as a divine epithet, especially of the sun god Shamash. Compare also the Old Aram. divine name *nr* (Sefire), the Ugar. divine epithet *nyr* (also Ugar. *nr*, lamp), and a Punic personal name (*bʿlnr*, Ba'al is a lamp).

OT 1. As a familiar symbol of domestic and working life (Jer 25:10), the lamp (*nēr*) is a natural metaphor for life. It is used primarily as a symbol for the quality and length of life. The recurring phrase "the lamp (of the wicked) goes out," which occurs several times in the Wisdom literature (e.g., Job 18:5; Prov 13:9; 20:20), appears to mean that life for the wicked is shortened and unfulfilled. This is suggested by Prov 24:20, which affirms that the wicked have no future (Heb. *'aḥ*ᵃ*rît*; → # 344).

2. Although the comparable phrase "the lamp of the righteous" does occur (Prov 13:9; Heb. *'ôr*, → # 240), the OT seems to assume that without God human lives are in darkness and that even the righteous have no lamp of their own. Only Yahweh can give light to a person's lamp, that is, his life (Ps 18:28[29]; the parallel verse says simply "You are my lamp, O LORD" (2 Sam 22:29). Yahweh, in fact, gives light to human beings through his own lamp. This idea is applied both to the guidance given by God's word (Ps 119:105) and to the spiritual and physical growth resulting from the gift of Yahweh's life or breath (Prov 20:27, "The lamp of the LORD searches the spirit [breath] of a man"; cf. Gen 2:7).

3. The separate metaphor of a lamp shining in darkness gives rise to two further distinctive concepts. First, the lamps on the tabernacle or temple lampstand were to be kept burning all night (Exod 30:7-8; Lev 24:3-4; contrast 2 Chron 29:7). As with the lampstand, the lamps probably represent the light of God's continuing presence. Second, specific representatives of the Davidic line are described as a lamp (2 Sam

21:17; 1 Kgs 11:36; Ps 132:17; in this sense always *nîr* (II) in Kgs and Chron). The context usually refers to some potentially fatal threat (2 Sam 21:17), notably through David's own family (2 Kgs 8:18-19 ‖ 2 Chron 21:4-7). The meaning here is neither life nor "yoke, dominion" (Hanson), but a guarantee that David's house will survive even the darkest days because of God's covenant promise.

P-B *nēr* is generally used for the lights on the candlestick in the temple. The expression "God's lamp" may refer either to the candlestick or to the Law, and "lamp of Israel" is often used to describe a great scholar or teacher.

NT Though Jesus is once called a lamp (Rev 21:23), as is John the Baptist (John 5:35), the NT mainly refers to a lamp to encourage believers not to hide God's light but give it maximum exposure (Matt 5:15; Mark 4:21; Luke 8:16). The eye as the lamp of the body enables others to see a person's inner light (Matt 6:22-23; Luke 11:34-36). The lampstand is used mainly in Revelation as a symbol for individual churches (Rev 1:12-20). However, churches are only light-bearers, for the true light of the Messiah, and their lampstand, may be removed if they do not repent (Rev 2:5).

Lamp: → *m^e^nôrâ* (lamp, lampstand, # 4963); → *nēr* I (lamp, light, # 5944)

Bibliography

NIDNTT 2:484-96; *TDNT* 4:16-28, 324-27; *TWOT* 2:565-66; P. D. Hanson, "The Song of Heshbon and David's *Nir*," *HTR* 61, 1968, 297-320.

Martin J. Selman

5948 (*nērd*, aromatic ointment), → # 8379

5951	נשׂא

נשׂא (*nś'*), q. lift, raise high, pardon, contain, bear, support; ni. raise o.s.; pi. carry; hi. burden s.o; hitp. exalt o.s. (# 5951); מַשָּׂא (*maśśā'* I), burden (→ # 5362); מַשָּׂא (*maśśā'* II), pronouncement (→ # 5363); מַשֹּׂא (*maśśō'*), partiality (→ # 5365); מַשְׂאֵת (*maś'ēt*), lifting, gift (→ # 5368); נְשׂוּאָה (*n^e^śû'â*), burden, idol (→ # 5953); נָשִׂיא (*nāśî'* I), chief (→ # 5954).

ANE See discussion under OT, # 2.

OT 1. The vb. occurs 654x in the OT, most of which are in the q. (597x). Derivatives from the vb. are (a) *śî'*, height (NIV pride), a hapleg. in Job 20:6; (b) *ś^e^'ēt*, raising o.s. up; diginity, nobility; exaltation. Seven of the fourteen occurrences of this nom. are in Lev 13-14, where *ś^e^'ēt* refers to the swelling on one's skin, one criterion for diagnosing skin diseases. The word *ś^e^ēt* may refer to the discoloration of the skin rather than to its rising or swelling, for Lev 13:3 states that this *ś^e^'ēt* appears lower than the rest of the skin (see NIV footnote) and so hardly can be a swelling.

2. The root occurs frequently in related Sem. languages. There are even instances where *nś'* in a word pair occurs both in BH and in ANE texts. One of these word pairs is *nś'/sbl* (Held, 90-96). Thus, Isa 46:7 speaks of those who take their own crafted god in time of panic and siege, and "lift it (*nś'*) to their shoulders and carry (*sbl*) it." The suffering servant, says Isaiah, "took up (*nś'*) our infirmities and carried (*sbl*) our sorrows" (Isa 53:4). The same pair occurs in Aram. (Ahiqar: 89-90): "From fear of

the lion, the ass left his burden and will not carry (*sbl*) it. He shall bear (*nś'*) shame before his fellow and shall bear (*nś'*) a burden which is not his." Cf. also the parallelism of the roots in Akk. (Borger: Esarhaddon 20:17), "I put (*aššima*) a basket on my head, and carried (*ušazbil*) it myself."

Another word pair involving *nś'* common to the OT and ANE texts is *nś'/'ms* (Greenfield, 253-68). God refers to the house of Jacob as "you whom I have upheld (*'ms*) since you were conceived, and have carried (*nś'*) you since your birth" (Isa 46:3). This pair is found in Ugar. (*CTA* 6 [62] I: 10-15)—"Loudly she calls unto the gods' torch Shapsh, lift (*'ms*) Puissant Baal, I pray unto me." Hearkening the gods' torch, Shapsh picks up (*tšu*) Puissant Baal and sets him on Anath's shoulder. The word pair is also present in the Phoenician Eshmenezer inscription (*KAI* 14:5-6)—"May he not take (*nś'*) the casket in which I am resting, and may he not carry me away (*'ms*) from this resting place."

One might also note the pair *nś'/šyt* in Exod 23:1, "Do not spread (*nś'*) false reports. Do not help (*šyt*) a wicked man by being a malicious witness," and compare it with Ugar. (*CTA* 19 [1 Aqht]: 58-60), "Weeping she lifts (*tšu*) her father. She rests (*tštnn*) him on the back of the ass, on the beautiful back of the donkey." In both of these texts the second action is a continuation of the first. Spreading false rumors leads to joining hands with the wicked.

Finally, there is the frequent expression (41x) in Ugar. *nšu g/ṣyḥ*, "lifting one's voice and crying," which compares to Isa 42:11.

3. Related to this last phrase, but with the vb. *nś'*, is the expression *nś' qôl*, "lifting, raising one's voice." The phrase is followed by vbs. such as *bkh*, "weep" (Gen 21:16 [Hagar]; 27:38 [Esau]; 29:11 [Jacob]; Judg 2:4 [the Israelites]; 21:2 [the men of Israel over Benjamin]; 1 Sam 11:4 [Saul's people after hearing about the debacle of Jabesh Gilead]; 24:16[17] [Saul], etc.). In almost all of these the context is one of deep, personal anguish, and the lifting of one's voice in weeping is a way of ventilating one's emotional pain.

nś' qôl is also used with *qr'*, "call" (Judg 9:7); with *ṣ'q*, "cry out" (the suffering servant, Isa 42:2); and with *rnn*, "sing" (24:14; 52:8). Frequently, the objects of this vb. are "lamentation" (*qînâ*), as in Jer 7:29; Ezek 19:1; 27:2, 32; 28:12; 32:2; Amos 5:1; "prayer" (*t^epillâ*), as in 2 Kgs 19:4 (= Isa 37:4; Jer 7:16; 11:14); and "oracle" (*māšāl*), as in Num 23:7, 18; 24:3, 15; Isa 14:4; Mic 2:4; Hab 2:6).

4. The expression *nś' nepeš 'el/l^e* ("lift one's soul to") occurs 9x in the OT, 7x in q. and 2x in pi. In six of these nine the object is a thing and the basic meaning of the phrase is "direct one's desire towards, long for" (Deut 24:15; Ps 24:4; Prov 19:18; Jer 22:27; 44:14; Hos 4:8).

In the remaining three, however, the object is Yahweh (Ps 25:1; 86:4; 143:9[8]). Is lifting one's soul to Yahweh an activity of prayer and worship or something other? This expression with Yahweh as object occurs only in the petition section of individual lament psalms, in which the vb. *bṭḥ*, trust, is used in proximity to *nś' nepeš 'el* (Ps 25:2; 86:2; 143:8). Appealing to a similar idiom in Mesopotamian literature, Barré (46-54), suggests that *nś'* here means "lift up and take (away)." The expression does not then mean to long for God, but rather to "flee for protection to Yahweh, seek refuge in Yahweh."

5. The expression *nś' rō'š*, "lift up the head," occurs in a transitive form (one raises the head of another), as can be observed in Gen 40:20. There is an unusual wordplay here in that the pharaoh lifted up the head of the chief cupbearer by pardoning him and lifted up the head of the chief baker by hanging him. This double entendre for *nś' rō'š* is spelled out clearly in Gen 40:13, 19. See also Jer 52:31, where *nś' rō'š* describes Evil-Merodach's pardoning of Jehoiachin and the latter's release from prison.

This expression also occurs as a reflexive form (one lifts up one's own head). In such instances the phrase means a proud show of autonomy and independence (Judg 8:28; Job 10:15; Ps 83:2[3]; Zech 1:21[2:4]). This reflexive form is also present in Ps 24:7, 9, in which the psalmist, using metonymy, speaks to the gatekeepers with an apostrophe to the gates themselves. The expression "lift up your heads, O you gates" is a command to the gatekeepers to stand proudly as the King of glory enters (Cooper, 37-60).

6. The phrase *nś' pānîm*, the reflexive "lift up one's own face," occurs only in Num 6:26 and in Deut 28:50 (NIV's "a fierce looking nation without respect for the old" is literally "a nation strong of face that does not lift the face upon an elder"). In both instances the meaning of "lift up the face " is "smile," i.e., a facial expression of favor.

Much more frequent is the transitive use of the phrase, "lift up the face of PN." This phrase connotes "show favor to" 5x: "receive me" (Gen 32:20[21], NIV); "I will accept him," i.e., "I will lift up his face" (Job 42:8, NIV); "the people do not respect the priests" (Job 42:9; Lam 4:16, NIV). Extensions of this meaning, "show favor to," are "show deference to" (e.g., "Very well, I will grant this request too," Gen 19:21, NIV); "expiate sin," "Would he accept you?" (Mal 1:8, NIV); "show partiality, display favoritism" (Lev 19:15; Job 13:8; 32:21; 34:19; Ps 82:2; Prov 18:5).

7. The third commandment of the Decalogue, "You shall not misuse the name of the LORD your God" (Exod 20:7, NIV) is literally, "You shall not lift up the name of Yahweh your God for what is worthless." One way of abusing God's name was to use it in order to lend credence to a false oath, "Do not swear falsely by my name" (Lev 19:12). If such was the original setting of the third commandment, later reflections on this prohibition expanded its meaning and application for the community of faith.

8. One must distinguish between lifting the hand (sing.) for the purpose of oath-taking (Exod 6:8; Num 14:30; Ezek 20:5) or of rebellion (2 Sam 20:21), and lifting the hands (pl.) for blessing (Lev 9:22; Ps 134:2; 1 Tim 2:8).

9. Particularly important is the phrase *nś' 'āwōn/ḥēṭ'*. Of the 29x the phrase *nś' 'āwōn* occurs in the OT, God is the subject of the vb. 7x (Exod 34:7; Num 14:18; Ps 32:5; 85:2[3]; Isa 33:24; Hos 14:2[3]; Mic 7:18). In such cases the phrase means "remove iniquity." If, however, the subject of the vb. is a person, then the idiom means "bear responsibility, punishment" (Exod 28:43; Lev 5:1, 17; 7:18; 17:16; 19:8; Num 5:31; 18:1, 23) and suggests capital punishment, which, at least in the case of Lev 5:1-13, can be commuted by remorse and confession to a sin/purification offering.

There are a few instances in which the phrase *nś' ḥaṭṭā't* with the meaning of "remove iniquity, forgive sin" has a person as a subject: (1) Joseph is asked to forgive the sins of his brothers (Gen 50:17); (2) Pharoah asked for forgiveness from Moses (Exod 10:17); and (3) Saul asked Samuel to forgive his sin (1 Sam 15:25). In each of these cases a superior, and one favored by God, is besought by one with lower status for forgiveness. In two other instances, the priest, as God's representative on earth and in the sanctuary, is authorized to remove the sin (*nś' 'awôn*, Exod 28:38; Lev 10:17) of the congregation (see Milgrom, 422-23, 622-25, 1041).

A key part of the ritual of the Day of Atonement is the mention in Lev 16:22 that the scapegoat will carry the sins (*nś' 'āwōn*) of the people to a solitary place. This is the only time an animal is the subject of this phrase. It is probably reading too much into this v. to see here an instance of atonement via vicarious suffering. The expression suggests to carry away rather than to suffer, given the prepositional phrase that follows (to a solitary place), which modifies a vb. of motion (Whybray, 48-49).

While the phrase *nś' ḥēṭ'* occurs 9x in the OT (Lev 19:17; 20:20; 22:9; 24:15; Num 9:13; 18:22, 32; Isa 53:12; Ezek 23:49), Isa 53:12 is the only one of these in which a person bears the sin of another ("he bore the sin of many"), and as such the phrase is functionally equivalent to the one in the previous verse (11), "he will bear their iniquities" (*sbl 'āwōn*). This servant of the Lord, says the prophet, is one who has shared, undeservedly and intensely, in the sins and hurts of others.

Height: → *g'h* (rise up, be exalted, # 1448); → *gbh* (be high, exalt, be haughty, # 1467); → *gēwâ* I (pride, # 1575); → *nś'* (lift, raise high, pardon, bear, exalt o.s., # 5951); → *sll* (lift up, exalt, # 6148); → *rwm* (be high, exalted, proud, # 8123)
Arrogance, pride, presumption: → *g'h* (rise up, be exalted, # 1448); → *zyd* (act presumptuously, prepare food, # 2326); → *yāhîr* (haughty, # 3400); → *sll* (lift up, exalt, # 6148); → *'pl* (swell, lift up, # 6752); → *'ātāq* (old, arrogant, # 6981); → *pḥz* (be reckless, arrogant, # 7069); → *rwm* (be high, exalted, proud, # 8123); → *šaḥaṣ* (pride, # 8832)
Forgiveness, pardon: → *nś'* (lift, raise high, pardon, bear, exalt o.s., # 5951); → *slḥ* (practice forbearance, pardon, forgive, # 6142)

Bibliography

THAT 2:109-17; *TWAT* 1:506-9; 5:658-63; 9:57-89; *TWOT* 2:600-602; M. L. Barré, "Mesopotamian Light on the Idiom *nasa' nepeš*," *CBQ* 52, 1990, 46-54; G. Bertram, "'Hochmut' und verwandte Begriffe im griechischen und hebräischen Alten Testament," *WO* 3, 1964, 32-43; A. Cooper, "Ps 24:7-10: Mythology and Exegesis," *JBL* 102, 1983, 37-60; E. P. Dhorme, "L'Emploi metaphorique des noms de parties du corps en hébreu et en akkadien," *RB* 29, 1920, 465-506; 30, 1921, 347-99, 517-40; 31, 1922, 215-33, 489-547; 32, 1923, 185-212; D. E. Gowan, *When Man Becomes God: Humanism and Hybris in the Old Testament,* 1975; J. C. Greenfield, "Scripture and Inscription," *Near Eastern Studies in Honour of W. F. Albright,* 1971, 253-68; M. I. Gruber, "The Many Faces of Hebrew *ns' panim*, 'Lift Up the Face'," *ZAW* 95, 1983, 252-60; M. Held, "The Root ZBL/SBL in Akkadian, Ugaritic, and Biblical Hebrew," *JAOS* 88, 1968, 90-96; P. Humbert, "Demesure et chute dans l'Ancien Testament," *Hommage á Wilhelm Vischer,* 1960, 63-82; R. Knierim, *Die Hauptbegriffe für Sünde im Alten Testament,* 1967; J. Milgrom, *Leviticus 1-16,* AB, 1991; G. Olafson, "The Use of Ns' in the Pentateuch and Its Contribution to the Concept of Forgiveness," Ph. D. Dissertation, Andrews University, 1992; R. N. Whybray, *Thanksgiving for a Liberated Prophet,* JSOTSup 4, 1978.

Victor Hamilton

5952	נשׂג

נשׂג (*nśg*), hi. overtake, catch up, attain, reach; afford; become rich/prosperous (# 5952); מַשֶּׂגֶת (*maśśeget*), nom. overtaking (# 5371).

ANE The vb. *našağa,* hunt for, search or seek after, strive for, occurs in Arab.

OT The vb., which is used only in the hi., occurs 50x (*NIVEC*, 1549) and the nom. 2x.

1. (a) The vb., which is identified as a hunting term (Baldwin, 91; C. L. Meyers and E. M. Meyers, 96), is most frequently used with the meaning overtake or catch up. When Jacob and his family fled from his father-in-law and crossed the Euphrates, Laban pursued them for seven days and overtook them in the hill country of Gilead (Gen 31:25). Joseph ordered his steward to follow and overtake his brothers and to challenge them with the theft of a silver cup (probably a sacred vessel used for divination) (Gen 44:4, 6). Pharaoh's horses and chariots, horsemen and army overtook the Israelites encamped at the sea by Pi Hahiroth, opposite Baal Zephon (Exod 14:9). Moses and the people celebrated in song Yahweh's deliverance of Israel from their powerful enemy, who had boasted how he would pursue, overtake, and destroy them (Exod 15:9). To limit the ancient tribal law of blood revenge (see Num 35), three cities of refuge were established, where the manslayer could find refuge, thereby minimizing the possibility of his death at the hands of the avenger of blood, who, in hot anger, would otherwise pursue and overtake him (Deut 19:6). When the king of Jericho sent to Rahab asking her to bring forth the two Israelite spies who had come to her, she pretended that they had already left the city at dark and urged hot pursuit in order to overtake them (Josh 2:5).

When he enquired of Yahweh whether he should pursue and overtake the Amalekites, David was told to pursue for he would surely overtake them and rescue the women and children of Ziklag, who had been carried away captive (1 Sam 30:8). When news reached him of Absalom's revolt, David instructed all his servants in Jerusalem to flee with him in haste lest Absalom should overtake them quickly (2 Sam 15:14). When Nebuchadnezzar's siege forces made a breach in the wall of Jerusalem, Zedekiah and all his men of war fled by night towards the Arabah, but the Babylonians pursued and overtook them in the plains of Jericho (2 Kgs 25:5; par. Jer 39:5; 52:8). Following the destruction of Jerusalem by the Babylonians in 587/586 BC, the city, personified as a widow, lamented the fact that Judah's pursuers had all overtaken her in the midst of her distress (Lam 1:3). In a strong protestation of innocence, a psalmist who is being harried by relentless foes asks God to let the enemy pursue, overtake, and kill him (Ps 7:5[6]) if he had committed any crime (vv. 3-5[4-6]). Yahweh is thanked for his intervention in a battle that turned defeat into victory by empowering the Israelite king to pursue, overtake, and slay his enemies (Ps 18:37[38]).

The subject of the vb. can also be blessings, curses, iniquities, a promiscuous wife, war, a sword, Yahweh's burning anger, Yahweh's words and statutes, terrors, disgrace, righteousness, and joy and gladness. Israel was assured that obedience to Yahweh would result in the promised blessings overtaking (NIV has "accompany"; NEB has "light upon" [cf. REB]) them (Deut 28:2). Contrariwise, disobedience would lead to curses pursuing and overtaking them (28:45).

Yahweh's help is urgently requested by a helpless individual who is acutely conscious that his numerous iniquities have overtaken him (Ps 40:12[13]).

In a daring use of the marriage metaphor, which seems to have been borrowed from the cult of Baal, Israel is portrayed as a promiscuous wife who, having been fenced in behind a divinely erected hedge of thorns and a wall, first exhausts herself in futile attempts to catch up (*wᵉlōʾ-taśśîg ʾōtām*, but she will not overtake them) with her lovers (a reference to the immoral fertility rites of Canaanite religion), and then comes to her senses and resolves to return to her first husband, Yahweh (Hos 2:7[9]).

Given that Yahweh's rebellious people have sinned from the days of Gibeah (cf. Judg 19 [the incident of the homosexual rapists]; Hos 5:8; 9:9), the rhetorical question is posed: "Shall not war overtake them in Gibeah?" (Hos 10:9, NRSV). The destructive war will involve the whole of the northern kingdom, Gibeah here being a synecdoche for sinful Israel (Stuart, 168). If one were to follow Andersen and Freedman (560, 565) and construe *taśśîgēm* in the past tense (cf. NIV), the implication would be that just as God had punished Israel by war for the crime described in Judg 19, so he would inflict the same kind of judgment on them on this occasion.

Jeremiah advised his compatriots against flight to Egypt and warned that those who were determined to go there would be overtaken by the sword (Jer 42:16) and become the victims of famine (vv. 16-17) and pestilence (v. 17). The awesome strength of the terrifying monster Leviathan is such that, even if one could get close enough to strike him with a sword (*maśśîgēhû ḥereb*, lit., a sword overtaking him), a spear, a lance (or dagger [NEB], dart [RSV; NRSV; NIV; Hartley, 529], or arrow [Dhorme, 640]), or a javelin, it would have no effect (Job 41:26[18]).

One in deep affliction and humiliation invokes a curse upon his malignant persecutors, enjoining Yahweh to pour out his indignation on them and let his burning anger overtake them (Ps 69:24[25]).

The contrast between human mortality and the enduring power of Yahweh's words is highlighted in Zech 1:6 (cf. Isa 40:8; 55:11), where Zechariah, calling the community to repentance, reminds the people that their fathers, who had refused to heed the prophetic summons to repent and suffered the Babylonian conquest and subsequent exile, had been overtaken by (i.e., experienced the fulfillment of) the divine words and statutes. Some (e.g., Thomas, 1956, 1059-60; Ackroyd, 1964, 646-47; Mason, 33) read "you" as the object of the vb. overtake, instead of MT "your fathers," but Baldwin (92) considers this alteration arbitrary.

In what may well be the continuation of the third discourse of either Zophar (A. B. Davidson, 217; Peake, 241-45; Dummelow, 310; Franks, 359; Strahan, 227-30; Irwin, 401; Pope, 187-88, 191-95; Gordis, 291, 296; May and Metzger, 638; cf. Watts, 105; Bergant, 137) or of Bildad (Hartley, 355, 358-61) (Job 27:13-23), the wicked are portrayed as being the victims of terrors that overtake them either with the speed and power of a flood (so RSV; NRSV; NEB; REB; NIV; TEV; A. B. Davidson, 222; Driver and Gray, 1:232; 2:188; Gordis, 292, 295; Hartley, 359-60) or in broad daylight (changing MT *kammayim*, like waters, to *bayyôm* or *yômām* [so JB; Dhorme, 396; Pope, 188, 194]) (v. 20).

In response to his warning that the people would experience a grievous destruction for their social and moral abuses, members of the community (the people as a whole [Laberge, 251]; false prophets [May and Metzger, 1124; cf. NIV; March, 732-33; Allen, 294-96]; nobles [Dummelow, 580]; the authorities [Wolff, 80-81]; the rich [J. M. P. Smith, 60; Thomas, 1964, 631]; the rapacious rich [Hillers, 36]; the affluent aristocracy [Dahlberg, 485]; greedy laymen/greedy oppressors/greedy land-grabbers/swindlers [J. M. P. Smith, 26-27]) reprimand Yahweh's prophet for preaching of such things and arrogantly assert that disgrace (of a humiliating catastrophe) will not overtake them (reading with Hillers, 34 [cf. RSV; NRSV; JB; NIV; *BHS*; Allen, 292; J. M. P. Smith, 25-26; *pace* Archer, 754] *tassîgēnû = taśśîgēnû*, it will overtake us, for MT *yissag*, it will draw back or depart) (Mic 2:6; cf. 3:11).

Rebellion against the divine not only creates alienation from God, but also leads inevitably to moral bankruptcy, misery, helplessness, hopelessness, disillusionment, and bitterness, all of which contribute to the collapse of society. Confession of guilt is the first step in the process of renewal and restoration. In a call to national repentance (Isa 59:1-21), it is pointed out that corruption has so contaminated the community that Judeans grope in the darkness of social and spiritual depravity (May and Metzger, 896; cf. Isa 8:22; 50:10; 58:8, 10; Jer 13:16; Amos 5:18-20), acknowledging that "justice is far from us, and righteousness does not overtake us" (v. 9, RSV [NEB, NRSV, and NIV have "does not reach us"]). According to Jones (531), *ṣ^{e}dāqâ* here means "rightness" in human relationships. However, most commentators take the word as having a soteriological meaning: deliverance (Muilenburg, 690; cf. Motyer, 486), salvation (Skinner, 190; Kelley, 358; Scullion, 167; cf. G. A. Smith, 1927b, 234-40, 455; Smart, 254; Whybray, 1975, 223), redemption (Smart, 254), or vindication (Clifford, 589). Given that the ethical and soteriological senses of the word constitute the obverse and reverse of the same coin, *s^{e}dāqâ* here may have a double meaning (cf. Whybray, 1975, 196-97, 223). As Herbert (151) points out, justice and righteousness are essential not only for honest living before God, but also for the divine subjugation of everything that constricts or destroys human existence.

The ransomed of Yahweh who will return to Zion with singing will be overtaken, or overwhelmed (cf. Oswalt, 626), by joy and gladness and, with the departure of sorrow and sighing, will experience uninterrupted happiness (Isa 35:10; par. 51:11; cf. Ps 23:6). However, as G. A. Smith (1927a, 462) and Motyer (275), amongst others, have noted, the words *śāśôn w^{e}śimḥâ yaśśîgû[m]* could equally well be translated "they overtake gladness and joy," in which case the meaning would be that the joy that had been previously eluding their grasp will now at last be caught and possessed.

(b) It is clear from some of the texts cited in (a) above (see, e.g., the way that NEB, NRSV, and NIV translate *taśśîgēnû* in Isa 59:9) that the vb. can have the meaning reach. The vb. is used with this meaning in the context of time spans. When Pharaoh asked him his age, Jacob replied that the years of his life had been few and hard (lit., evil) and had not attained to (*w^{e}lō' hiśśîgû* [JB has "falling short of"; NIV translates "they do not equal"]; Hamilton, 609, has "They come nowhere near comparing with") the years of his fathers in their sojournings (Gen 47:9). Some (e.g., von Rad, 408; Davies, 288; May and Metzger, 61) think that Jacob's statement may refer to the spread of evil, which, in turn, resulted in a sharp increase in the number of afflictions and adversities besetting human existence and a corresponding diminishing of human vitality manifested in a progressively decreasing life span. However, others (e.g., R. Davidson, 284; Maher, 256) take it to be a purely factual statement, the difficult years having been caused in large part by Jacob's own shortcomings.

One of the blessings Israelites were promised as a reward for obedience was fertility of the soil and abundant yield of the harvest (cf. Amos 9:13): their threshing would last (RSV; NEB; REB; Wenham, 324; cf. NIV, "will continue until" [NRSV has "overtake"]) to the time of vintage (*w^{e}hiśśîg lākem dayiš 'et-bāṣîr*), and the vintage would last to the time for sowing (*ûbāṣîr yaśśîg 'et-zāra'*) (Lev 26:5).

The vb. is once used of reaching the hand to the mouth. During a hard battle with the Philistines in the vicinity of Michmash, Saul laid an oath on his soldiers prohibiting them from eating food until the evening (fasting was considered pleasing to God), by which time he hoped to be avenged on his enemies (1 Sam 14:24). Consequently, when the army came across a rich supply of honey, ideal for renewing vigor, no man put his hand to his mouth (*w*ᵉ*'ên-maśśîg yādô 'el-pîw*; v. 26).

The vb. is used with the meaning reach/regain in Prov 2:19: those who visit the smooth-spoken *'iššâ zārâ* (strange woman, v. 16) do not regain (*w*ᵉ*lō'-yaśśîgû*) the paths of life (on the concept of dying as a journey to the netherworld, from which no return is possible, see Scott, 43; McKane, 288; Whybray, 1994, 57). The reference here may not be, primarily, to sexual immorality, as many (e.g., Fritsch, 796; Dentan, 307; Walls, 552; Whybray, 1994, 54) think, but to participation in a strange cult. It has been argued that the woman concerned (either a foreigner [so Boström, 103-4] or an Israelite who has become an outsider, one who is beyond the pale [so McKane, 285]) may be a devotee of a foreign cult (possibly that of Ishtar, the goddess of love), in which case her promiscuity may be a cultic act aimed at fulfilling her religious obligations (Boström, 103-4; McKane, 287; cf. Scott, 43; Tate, 19 [this approach is, however, rejected by, among others, Whybray, 1994, 54-55]).

(c) When the vb. occurs in combination with the nom. *yād*, it means afford or become rich/prosperous, depending on the context. Special concessions were made to the poor in respect of sacrifices (Lev 5:7-13). The indigent who could not afford a she-goat or a ewe-lamb were permitted to offer much less expensive gifts as a sacrifice. Either two turtledoves or two young pigeons would suffice, one of the birds being offered for the sin offering and the other for the burnt offering (Lev 5:7-10). However, the extremely poor man who could not afford (*lō' taśśîg yādô*, v. 11) even two turtledoves or two young pigeons was instructed to bring, instead, a tenth of an ephah of fine flour, which was accepted as satisfying the sin offering requirements (vv. 11-13).

The same compassionate consideration for the poor is shown in the regulations governing the offerings made by lepers for cleansing (Lev 14:1-32). In the case of a leper who could not afford the offerings for his cleansing (*'*ᵃ*šer lō'-taśśîg yādô b*ᵉ*ṭoh*ᵒ*rātô*, v. 32), two turtledoves or two young pigeons, such as he could afford (*'*ᵃ*šer taśśîg yādô*, vv. 22, 30), would suffice, one of the birds for a sin offering and the other for a burnt offering.

Sensitivity to socioeconomic status is shown in other laws, too. As a result of poverty, a man could be obliged to sell part of his land (Lev 25:25-28). Should he have no next of kin to redeem what has been sold and later becomes prosperous (*w*ᵉ*hiśśîgâ yādô*, v. 26), then he may redeem it himself, computing the years that have elapsed since the sale and refunding the difference to the person who had bought it (i.e., paying to the purchaser the sum due for the time still to run to the Jubilee Year).

In the case of extreme poverty, a man might have no alternative but to sell himself to a resident foreigner who had become rich (*taśśîg yad gēr w*ᵉ*tôšāb*, lit., the hand of a stranger or sojourner [that] acquires, Lev 25:47). It was possible for such a man to be redeemed either by a relative or, should he become rich (*hiśśîgâ yādô*), by himself (v. 49), by paying the man who purchased him a sum that was calculated in accordance with a formula that took account of his period of service with his owner (which was reckoned at the rate of a hired servant) and the time remaining until the Jubilee Year.

Those who vow themselves or another person to Yahweh (i.e., dedicate themselves or another to his service) may be released from the fulfillment of the vow on payment of a monetary substitute (Lev 27:1-8). Special provision is made for the man who is too poor to pay the valuation normally prescribed: He is instructed to bring before the priest the person whom he has dedicated, and the priest will determine the amount to be paid according to what the man who makes the vow can afford (*'al-pî 'ašer taśśîg yad hannōdēr*, v. 8).

The offering of the Nazirite who took a vow was to be according to his vow as a Nazirite, in addition to whatever else he could afford (*milleᵉbad 'ašer-taśśîg yādô*, Num 6:21): He was encouraged to make extra offerings, as much as he could afford, over and above the minimum required, and these additional commitments had to be fulfilled before he could be released from his vow and reintegrated into the ranks of ordinary citizens.

According to the regulations concerning the offerings to be made in the restored temple (Ezek 46:1-8), on the day of the new moon (i.e., the first day of the month), the prince is to offer a young, unblemished bull together with six lambs and a ram without defect (v. 6) and, as a grain offering, he is to provide one ephah with the bull, one ephah with the ram, and, with the lambs, whatever he can afford (REB; cf. NEB; RSV), as much as he wishes (NRSV; cf. JB "and what he pleases"), or whatever he wants to give (NIV; cf. JB) (*ka'ašer taśśîg yādô*, v. 7), together with a hin of oil for each ephah (the laws for the Sabbath and the New Moon sacrifices in Ezek 46:1-8 differ from the legislation in Num 28:9-10 [Sabbath] and in 28:11-15 [New Moon]).

(d) In one text, the vb. appears, at first sight, to have the meaning move away, remove. In a searing indictment of God's irresponsible absence and/or his callous indifference to the ruthless actions of rapacious oppressors and ruffians as well as to the prayers of the suffering innocent, Job refers to those who remove boundary stones (*gᵉbulôt yaśśîgû*, Job 24:2). The removal of boundary markers, which was tantamount to violent appropriation of another person's property, was prohibited in ancient Israel (and throughout the ANE), and those who violated the prohibition were severely condemned (Deut 19:14; 27:17; Prov 22:28; 23:10; Hos 5:10). It is doubtful that the vb. here is *nśg*. It is much more likely that *yaśśîgû* is a variant spelling of *yassîgû* (hi. of *swg*, push back), which is the vb. used in all the passages cited in the previous sentence (cf. Driver and Gray, 2:164; Dhorme, 354; Gordis, 264; Hillers, 34; Hartley, 343).

2. The word *maśśeget*, which many (e.g., BDB, 673) take to be the fem. sing. hi. part. of the vb. but which some (e.g., *HALAT*) consider a nom., occurs twice (Lev 14:21; 1 Chron 21:12). As noted above, there are special procedures to be followed for the cleansing of leprosy (Lev 14:1-32). Those suffering from the disease are instructed to offer appropriate sacrifices (vv. 10-20), but a special concession, involving a considerable modification in the size of the sin offering and the burnt offering together with a reduction of the grain offering (the guilt offering, the main element in the sacrificial procedure, is unchanged), is made in the case of the one who is poor "and cannot afford much" (*wᵉ'ên yādô maśśeget*, v. 21).

As Curtis and Madsen (250) point out, triads of divine judgment are not uncommon in the OT (Lev 26:25-26; 1 Chron 21:11-12; 2 Chron 20:9; Jer 14:12; 21:7-9; 24:10; 27:8, 13; 29:17-18; 32:24, 36; 34:17; 38:2; 42:17, 22; 44:13; Ezek 5:12; 6:11-12; 7:15; 12:16; cf. 1 Kgs 8:37). After David had incurred the divine wrath by taking a census, Yahweh instructed Gad to tell the king to choose one of three forms of punishment: three years of famine, three days of pestilence (the sword of Yahweh), or three months of devastation "and close pursuit by the sword of your enemy" (*w^e ḥereb 'ôy^e bekā l^e maśśeget*, NEB; REB) (1 Chron 21:12). Most translators, however, prefer a verbal formulation (e.g., "while the sword of your enemies overtakes you" [RSV; NRSV]; "with the sword of your enemies overtaking you" [Braun, 1986, 212]; "with their swords overtaking you" [NIV]; "with the sword of your enemies thrusting at you" [JB]).

Perhaps the most significant of 1 Chron 21's variations from its Samuel source is that David is incited to number Israel by Satan (a proper name [*pace* Japhet, 373-75] in 1 Chron 21:1 [cf. Job 1:6; 2:2; Zech 3:1-2, where it is a common noun]), rather than by "the anger of Yahweh" (2 Sam 24:1). This change seems to reflect a developing piety that balked at attributing evil to God and preferred to use the figure of Satan (elsewhere, the adversary), a member of the divine entourage, to account for evil and misfortune (May and Metzger, 518; Myers, 147; Coggins, 107; Braun, 1986, 216-17; 1988, 353). Some (e.g., Coggins, 107) think that, by the Chronicler's time, Satan had come to be a personal enemy, whose purpose was to frustrate God's actions. Others (e.g., Ackroyd, 1973, 74; Williamson, 143-44) maintain that Satan is not, here, a wholly alien, independent force opposed to God; rather, he is under divine control and operates within Yahweh's purpose.

Hunting: → *yqš* (lay a trip wire, set a trap, # 3704); → *paḥ* I (trap, snare, # 7062); → *ṣwd* (hunt, # 7421); → *rešet* (net, # 8407); → *šûḥâ* I (pit, # 8757)
Pursuit: → *dbq* (stick, cling, cleave, pursue, # 1815); → *dlq* (set on fire, burn, hotly pursue, # 1944); → *rdp* (be behind, pursue, persecute, # 8103)
Riches, wealth: → *hwn* (consider easy, risk, # 2103); → *n^e kāsîm* (possessions, wealth, riches, # 5794); → *'šr* (be rich, become rich, make rich, # 6947)

BIBLIOGRAPHY

P. R. Ackroyd, "Zechariah," in *Peake*, 1964, 646-55; idem, *I & II Chronicles, Ezra, Nehemiah*, Torch, 1973; L. C. Allen, *The Books of Joel, Obadiah, Jonah and Micah*, NICOT, 1976; F. I. Andersen and D. N. Freedman, *Hosea: A New Translation With Introduction and Commentary*, AB, 1980; G. L. Archer, "Micah," in *NBC*, 1972, 752-61; J. G. Baldwin, *Haggai, Zechariah, Malachi: An Introduction and Commentary*, TOTC, 1974; D. Bergant, *Job, Ecclesiastes*, OTM, 1982; G. Boström, *Proverbia Studien: Die Weisheit und das fremde Weib in Spr. 1-9*, 1935; R. L. Braun, *1 Chronicles*, WBC, 1986; idem, "1 Chronicles," in *HBC*, 1988, 342-56; R. J. Clifford, "Isaiah 40-66," in *HBC*, 1988, 571-96; R. J. Coggins, *The First and Second Books of the Chronicles*, CBC, 1976; E. L. Curtis and A. A. Madsen, *A Critical and Exegetical Commentary on the Books of Chronicles*, ICC, 1965; B. T. Dahlberg, "The Book of Micah," in *The Interpreter's One-Volume Commentary on the Bible*, 1971, 483-90; A. B. Davidson, *The Book of Job With Notes, Introduction and Appendix*, CBSC, 1962; R. Davidson, *Genesis 12-50*, CBC, 1979; G. H. Davies, "Genesis," in *BBC*, 1970, 1:101-304; R. C. Dentan, "The Proverbs," in *The Interpreter's One-Volume Commentary on the Bible*, 1971, 304-19; E. Dhorme, *A Commentary on the Book of Job*, 1967; S. R. Driver and G. B. Gray, *A Critical and Exegetical Commentary on the Book of Job Together With a New Translation*, ICC, 1964; J. R. Dummelow, ed., *A Commentary on the Holy Bible*, 1909; R. S. Franks, "Job," in *Peake*, 1920, 346-65; C. T. Fritsch, "The Book of Proverbs: Introduction and Exegesis," in *IB*, 1955, 4:765-957; R. Gordis, *The Book of Job: Commentary, New Translation and Special Studies*, 1978; V. P. Hamilton, *The Book of*

Genesis Chapters 18-50, NICOT, 1995; J. E. Hartley, *The Book of Job*, NICOT, 1988; A. S. Herbert, *The Book of the Prophet Isaiah Chapters 40-66*, CBC, 1975; D. R. Hillers, *Micah*, Hermeneia, 1984; W. A. Irwin, "Job," in *Peake*, 1964, 391-98; S. Japhet, *I & II Chronicles: A Commentary*, OTL, 1993; D. R. Jones, "Isaiah—II and III," in *Peake*, 1964, 516-36; P. H. Kelley, "Isaiah," in *BBC*, 1972, 5:149-374; L. Laberge, "Micah," in *NJBC*, 1990, 249-54; W. McKane, *Proverbs: A New Approach*, OTL, 1970; M. Maher, *Genesis*, OTM, 1982; W. E. March, "Micah," in *HBC*, 1988, 731-35; R. Mason, *The Books of Haggai, Zechariah and Malachi*, CBC, 1977; H. G. May and B. M. Metzger, eds., *The New Oxford Annotated Bible*, 1973; C. L. Meyers and E. M. Meyers, *Haggai, Zechariah 1-8: A New Translation With Introduction and Commentary*, AB, 1988; J. A. Motyer, *The Prophecy of Isaiah: An Introduction & Commentary*, 1993; J. Muilenburg, "The Book of Isaiah Chapters 40-66: Introduction and Exegesis," in *IB*, 1956, 5:381-773; J. M. Myers, *1 Chronicles: Introduction, Translation, and Notes*, AB, 1973; J. N. Oswalt, *The Book of Isaiah Chapters 1-39*, NICOT, 1986; A. S. Peake, *Job*, CB, 1905; M. H. Pope, *Job: Introduction, Translation, and Notes*, AB, 3d ed., 1979; G. von Rad, *Genesis: A Commentary*, OTL, 3d ed., 1972; R. B. Y. Scott, *Proverbs, Ecclesiastes: Introduction, Translation, and Notes*, AB, 1965; J. Scullion, *Isaiah 40-66*, OTM, 1982; J. Skinner, *The Book of the Prophet Isaiah Chapters XL-LXVI*, CBSC, 1960; J. D. Smart, *History and Theology in Second Isaiah: A Commentary on Isaiah 35, 40-66*, 1967; G. A. Smith, *The Book of Isaiah. Volume I: Chapters I-XXXIX*, new and revised ed., 1927 (1927a); idem, *The Book of Isaiah. Volume II: Chapters XL-LXVI*, new and revised ed., 1927 (1927b); J. M. P. Smith (with W. H. Ward and J. A. Bewer), *A Critical and Exegetical Commentary on Micah, Zephaniah, Nahum, Habakkuk, Obadiah and Joel*, ICC, 1974; J. Strahan, *The Book of Job Interpreted*, 1913; D. Stuart, *Hosea-Jonah*, WBC, 1987; M. E. Tate, "Proverbs," in *BBC*, 1972, 5:1-99; D. W. Thomas, "The Book of Zechariah Chapters 1-8: Introduction and Exegesis," in *IB*, 1956, 6:1051-88; idem, "Micah," in *Peake*, 1964, 630-34; A. F. Walls, "Proverbs," in *NBC*, 1972, 548-69; J. D. W. Watts (with J. J. Owens and M. E. Tate), "Job," in *BBC*, 1972, 4:22-151; G. J. Wenham, *The Book of Leviticus*, NICOT, 1979; R. N. Whybray, *Isaiah 40-66*, NCBC, 1975; idem, *Proverbs*, NCBC, 1994; H. G. M. Williamson, *1 and 2 Chronicles*, NCBC, 1982; H. W. Wolff, *Micah: A Commentary*, 1990.

Robin Wakely

5953	נְשׂוּאָה

נְשׂוּאָה (*n^e^śû'â*), thing carried; load, burden (# 5953); < **נשׂא** (*nś'*), lift up, carry (→ # 5951).

OT The term occurs only in Isa 46:1, where it is in parallel to *'^a^ṣabbîm*: "their idols (*'^a^ṣṣabbêhem*) ... The images that are carried (*n^e^śu'ōt*)" (NIV). An alternate reading (cf. *BHS*) is, "Their images are a burden for animals, like heavy loads *carried* by weary cattle." The context names the gods (Bel, Nebo); thus these are images of these gods, not idols themselves.

Idolatry: → *'^e^lîl* (Nothing, # 496); → *'^a^šērâ* (wooden cult-object, pole, goddess, # 895); → *gillûlîm* (images, idols, # 1658); → *dāgôn* (Dagon, # 1837); → *k^e^môš* (Chemosh [god of the Moabites], # 4019); → *mōlek* (Molech, # 4891); → *massēkâ* I (cast statuette, # 5011); → *mipleṣet* (terrible thing, dreadful object, # 5145); → *semel* (image, # 6166); → *'āṣāb* (god-image, # 6773); → *'aštōret* (Astarte, # 6956); → *pesel* (cultic image, statue of a god, # 7181); → *tōmer* II (scarecrow, # 9473); → *t^e^rāpîm* (figurines, mask, # 9572); → **Idolatry: Theology**

Judith M. Hadley

5954	נָשִׂיא

נָשִׂיא (*nāśîʾ* I), chief, king (# 5954); < נשׂא (*nsʾ*), lift up (→ # 5951).

ANE Cognates exist in an Aram. dialect, *anši*, and in Phoen.

OT 1. The word, occurring 131x, derives from *nśʾ*, lift, and appears to have originally signified "one lifted up, chief." It occurs most often in Numbers, esp. in enumerations of the chiefs of the Israelite tribes (cf. chs. 1, 2, 7, 34). They are typically described as "the leaders of their ancestral tribes ... the heads (*rāʾšîm*) of the clans of Israel" (1:16; cf. 7:2; Josh 22:14). Together they comprise the "twelve leaders of Israel" (1:44; cf. 17:2[17]), and are the "leaders of the community" (*ʿēdâ*, 4:34; 31:13; cf. Exod 16:22; 34:31) or tribal "assembly" (*ʿēdâ*, Josh 9:15, 18). The term can also be used for the leader of a clan (Num 25:14; cf. 1 Chron 4:38). Eleazer is the "chief leader" (*n^{e}śîʾ n^{e}śîʾîm*) of the levitical clans (Num 3:32). Reference is also made to a wider body of 250 "leaders of the community" who rebelled against Moses (16:2). Abraham is called a "mighty *nāśîʾ*" by the Hittites (Gen 23:6).

2. The *n^{e}śîʾîm*, leaders, chiefly appear as leaders and tribal representatives alongside Moses (Num 36:1), with the priest Aaron (4:46) or his son Eleazar (27:2), and later with Joshua (Josh 9:15) and the priest Phinehas (22:32). Reference is primarily made to them in contexts concerned with tribal matters, such as the census of the tribes (Num 1:5, 44; 4:46), the arrangement of the camp (2:3, 5, etc.), the assignment of land (32:2; 34:18), and the settling of questions of inheritance (27:2; 36:1; cf. Josh 17:4). The leaders ratify Joshua's treaty with the Gibeonites by swearing an oath and later insist on keeping their word despite the complaints of the Israelites (Josh 9:15-21). They also represent the tribes in religious affairs. They present the offerings for the tabernacle (Num 7:11; cf. Exod 35:27), and they and Phinehas are sent by the Israelites to reproach the tribes in Transjordan for apostasy (Josh 22:14). Lev 4:22 makes provision for the forgiveness of unintentional sin by a *nāśîʾ*. Cursing a *nāśîʾ*, alongside blaspheming God, is prohibited (Exod 22:28[27]).

3. In Ezek, *nāśîʾ* is commonly used as a royal title in preference to *melek*, king. The latter is mostly reserved for the monarchs of the imperial powers of Babylon (Ezek 17:12; 19:9) and Egypt (29:3; 30:21). Thus, the word is applied to the last kings of Judah (19:1), esp. to Zedekiah (7:27; 12:10, 12; 21:25[30]) and his royal house (21:12[17]; 22:6). These passages center on the failure and judgment of the Israelite monarchy. In this context, the term may reflect an evaluation of the rulers against an ideal of leadership of God's people drawn from the tribal era. At all events, in the context of Israel's restoration, the term is used constructively to define the proper status and role of the ruler within the religious community in subordination to the priests as against the absolutist claims associated with the word *melek* (cf. 1 Sam 8:11-18). This perspective is developed in Ezek 40-48, where the duties (45:16, 17, 22; 46:4) and privileges (44:3; 45:7-9) of the *nāśîʾ* are carefully set out. In less priestly and more prophetic vein, the word is also used in Ezek to designate the Davidic ruler whom God will appoint to "shepherd the flock," in contrast with the rulers and leaders who cared for themselves instead of the flock (34:23-24; cf. vv. 2, 21). The "king over them" (37:24-25) will be a "*nāśîʾ* among them" (34:24).

P-B The word is regularly trans. in the LXX by *archōn,* except in Ezek 40-48, where it is rendered by *hegoumenos* (e.g., 44:3) or *aphēgoumenos* (e.g., 46:2). In Gen 23:8 Abraham is a "king (*basileus*) from God." At Qumran, the word is used to designate tribal leaders (1QM 3:3, 14-15, etc.). Further, the expression *n^eśî' kol hā'ēdâ,* the Prince of the whole congregation, occurs as a designation of the King-Messiah, who will accompany the Priest-Messiah. In 6QD 7:20 they are respectively the "star" and "scepter" of Num 24:17 (cf. also 1QM 5:1). In the Talm., the term is used of the head of the Sanhedrin (see Zeitlin).

Kingship, rule, supervision, dominion: → *b'l* I (marry, rule over, own, # 1249); → *g^ebîrâ/g^eberet* (lady, queen, mistress, # 1485/1509); → *ykḥ* (dispute, reason together, prove, judge, rule, reprove, # 3519); → *kbš* (make subservient, subdue, # 3899); → *mlk* I (rule, # 4887); → *mšl* II (rule, govern, # 5440); → *nṣḥ* (supervise, # 5904); → *rdd* (repel, subdue, # 8096); → *rdh* I (rule, govern, # 8097); → *r'h* I (feed, graze, shepherd, rule, # 8286); → *śrr* I (rule, direct, superintend, # 8606); → *šlṭ* (gain power, # 8948); → *špṭ* (get justice, act as a judge, rule, # 9149)

Leaders: → *'ādôn* (lord, master, # 123); → *'allûp* II (tribal chief, # 477); → *'āṣîl* II (eminent, noble, # 722); → *zāqēn* (elder, # 2418); → *ḥōr* I, free man, freeborn, # 2985); → *maptēaḥ* (badge of office, # 5158); → *nāgîd* (prince, ruler, leader, # 5592); → *nāśî'* I (chief, king, # 5954); → *sārîs* (eunuch, court official, # 6247); → *seren* II (Philistine prince, # 6249); → *'attûd* (he-goat, leader, # 6966); → *peḥâ* (governor, # 7068); → *pāqîd* (officer, # 7224); → *qāṣîn* (commander, leader, # 7903); → *rab* II (captain, chief, # 8042); → *rzn* (rule, # 8142); → *šôa'* I (noble, # 8777)

BIBLIOGRAPHY

THAT 2:109-17; *TWAT* 5:647-57; A. Alt, "The Formation of the Israelite State in Palestine," *Essays on Old Testament History and Religion*, 1966, 171-237; J. W. Flanagan, "Chiefs in Israel," *JSOT* 20, 1981, 47-73; J. D. Levenson, *Theology of the Program of Restoration of Ezekiel 40-48*, HSM 10, 1976; M. Noth, *Das System der zwölf Stämme Israels*, BWANT, 4/1, 1930; J. van der Ploeg, "Les chefs du peuple d'Israël et leurs titres," *RB* 57, 1950, 40-61; E. A. Speiser, "Background and Function of the Biblical *Nāśî'*," *CBQ* 25, 1963, 111-17; R. de Vaux, *AncIsr*, 1961; idem, *The Early History of Israel*, 2, 1978; S. Zeitlin, "The Titles High Priest and the Nasi of the Sanhedrin," *JQR* 48, 1957-58, 1-5; W. Zimmerli, *Ezekiel*, Hermeneia, 1979, 1983.

Kenneth T. Aitken

5956	נשק

נשק (*nśq*), ni. catch/take fire, be kindled, be/become inflamed, break out; hi. burn, kindle, light, set on fire, ignite, inflame (# 5956).

ANE In Egypt. Aram., the vb. occurs with the meaning burn, scorch, singe.

OT 1. The ni. pf. occurs in Ps 78:21, although some scholars (e.g., BDB, 969) consider *niśś^eqâ* to be from *ślq* while others (e.g., Anderson, 567) remain undecided as to whether the root is *ślq* or *nśq*. In this verse, the ni. pf. is used in tandem with the nom. *'ēš* and in parallelism with *b'r* as a graphic description of God's destructive or punitive anger—"fire broke out against Jacob" (v. 21; cf. Num 11:1-3; Ps 97:3; Isa 30:27; 66:15-16; Jer 4:4; Lam 2:3; Ezek 21:31[36]; 22:31; 38:19)—which blazed up (cf. NEB; REB) in response to perverse and rebellious Israel's incomprehensible lack of faith, short memory, insolence, defiant demanding, and failure to trust in God's willingness, power, and ability to save the people from any peril that might threaten them (v. 22). (Buttenwieser's argument [121-47] that v. 21 originally belonged at the beginning of v. 59 is ingenious, but does not carry conviction.)

2. The hi. occurs, also in parallelism with *bʿr*, in Isa 44:15, though some scholars (e.g., BDB, 969) consider *yaśśîq* to be from *ślq*. This verse is part of a polemical taunt-song (Isa 44:9-20) directed at the Jewish exiles, which ridicules idolatry by representing it in the form of a caricature (see esp. Westermann, 144-52). This caustic satire exposes the preposterous inconsistency of using as fuel for warmth and for baking ("he kindles a fire and bakes bread") the same perishable tree from which a god to be worshiped has been laboriously carved. Whereas in Gen 1:26-27 God made human beings in his image and likeness, this passage in Isaiah 44 unveils the absurdity and ignominy of deluded man, trying to make God in his image (McKenzie, 68; cf. Knight, 80). A similar satirical attitude towards the ridiculous futility and self-deception of idol makers and the folly of a quasi-magical veneration of images is found in chs. 13-14 (particularly, 13:11-13) of the deutero-canonical book of Wisdom, written in Alexandria in the mid-first century BC, and in the Roman poet Horace's *Satires*, I, viii, 1-3 (Skinner, 57; Scullion, 64).

3. The hi. is again used in parallelism with *bʿr* in Ezek 39:9, part of the legendary, almost apocalyptic-style, description of Yahweh's victory over the huge forces of the mysterious Gog from the country of Magog, the chief prince of Meshech and Tubal (38:2, 3; 39:1) and self-willed leader of the hostile northern nations (on the enemy from the north, see Isa 14:31; Jer 1:13-15; 4:5-6; Joel 2:20; Zeph 1:10-13), who recklessly transgressed his divine commission and misused his power (see esp. Eichrodt, 524). The idea of a final assault by hostile powers on the people of God, which ends in the annihilation of the aggressors, is echoed in 1 En 56:5-8 (see Charles, 222); 4 Ezra 13:1-13, 25-53 (see Box, 616, 618); Rev 20:7-9 (see, e.g., Cooke, 406).

The account of Yahweh's defeat of Gog's invasion in Ezek 38-39 emphasizes the irrevocable nature of the divine promise for Israel's future (Klein, 166) and climaxes in the vindication of Yahweh's holiness in the sight of many nations (39:27). When, after the annihilation of Gog and his mighty hordes, the inhabitants of the cities of Israel will gather up the enormous quantities of abandoned military equipment, the aggressors' weapons will be so abundant as to provide a seven-year supply of firewood for domestic uses. The burning of an enemy's weapons is echoed in Sib Or iii, 725-31 (see, e.g., Cooke, 418). The motif of destroying armaments to emphasize Yahweh's superiority over the nations or to underscore the folly of trusting in, or being afraid of, weapons occurs in several OT texts (Ps 46:9[10]; 76:3[4]; Isa 9:5[4]; Hos 2:18[20]; see Klein, 163). However, in Ezek 39 it is the people who destroy the weapons, and this task, together with the burial of the enemy's corpses, is Israel's only contribution to the annihilation of Gog and his heathen allies. Some commentators (e.g., Vawter and Hoppe, 179) take the fact that the Israelites use the combustible weapons as a source of fuel as an indication that the defeat of Gog would be the final battle, rendering armaments obsolete (cf. Isa 66:15-23; Joel 3:19-21[4:19-21]; Zech 14:1-21). According to Fisch (260) and Stalker (266), the burning of the enemy's weapons signifies that military equipment is now obsolete, given the state of security assured by God.

Others, however (e.g., Zimmerli, 316) do not think that the final elimination of war is envisaged here. As regards the combination *ûbiʿᵃrû wᵉhiśśîqû* (and use ... for fuel and burn them up Ezek 39:9), this has been regarded with suspicion in some quarters. The LXX seems to omit *w^{e}hiśśîqû,* while the Pesh. substitutes *w^{e}hiśśîqû* with *'ēš*, giving the reading "and they shall kindle fire...." Although some commentators follow the lead of the LXX and Pesh., others (e.g., Cooke, 423) see no reason to do so. Some scholars (e.g., GKC § 66e; Cooke, 423) consider *w^{e}hiśśîqû* to be from *ślq*, with *śin* doubled to compensate for the assimilation of the *lamedh*. Wevers (292) takes the words "and burn them" to be a late gloss aimed at explaining the rare word "make fires."

Burning, blazing, glowing, scorching, singeing: → *b'r* I (burn, blaze up, be consumed, # 1277); → *gaḥelet* (burning charcoal, # 1625); → *dlq* (set on fire, burn, hotly pursue, # 1944); → *ḥmr* III (be in ferment, be heated, be red, glow, blaze, # 2813); → *ḥrr* I (glow, blaze, # 3081); → *yṣt* (light, kindle, ignite, burn, scorch, # 3675); → *yqd* (burn, kindle, # 3678); → *kwh* (burn, blaze, singe, # 3917); → *lhṭ* I (burn, glow, blaze, # 4265); → *nśq* (catch fire, be kindled, burn, # 5956); → *ṣwt* (light, kindle, ignite, set in flames, # 7455); → *qdḥ* (kindle, light, ignite, set ablaze, catch or take fire, # 7706); → *śrp* (burn, scorch, cauterize, # 8596)

Fire, flame: → *'ûd* (log, burning stick, # 202); → *'ēš* I (fire, # 836); → *b'r* I (burn, blaze up, be consumed, # 1277); → *gaḥelet* (burning charcoal, # 1625); → *goprît* (sulphur, # 1730); → *yṣt* (kindle, burn, set on fire, # 3675); → *yqd* (burn, be burning, kindled, # 3678); → *kîdôd* (spark, # 3958); → *lbb* II (bake cakes, # 4221); → *lahab* (flame, blade, # 4258); → *lhṭ* I (glow, burn, # 4265); → *lappîd* (torch, lightning, # 4365); → *nîṣôṣ* (spark, # 5773); → *peḥām* (charcoal, # 7073); → *reṣep* I (live coal, # 8363); → *rešep* I (flame, glow, arrow, plague, # 8404); → *śrp* (burn, be burnt, # 8596); → *šābîb* (flame, # 8663)

BIBLIOGRAPHY

A. A. Anderson, *The Book of Psalms: Volume 2, Psalms 73-150,* 1972; G. H. Box, "IV Ezra," in R. H. Charles ed., *The Apocrypha and Pseudepigrapha of the Old Testament in English. Volume II: Pseudepigrapha,* 1913, 542-624; M. Buttenwieser, *The Psalms Chronologically Treated with a New Translation,* 1969; A. F. Campbell, "Psalm 78: A Contribution to the Theology of Tenth Century Israel," *CBQ* 41, 1979, 51-79; R. P. Carroll, "Psalm LXXVIII: Vestiges of a Tribal Polemic," *VT* 21, 1971, 133-50; R. H. Charles, "I Enoch," in R. H. Charles, ed., *The Apocrypha and Pseudepigrapha of the Old Testament in English. Volume II: Pseudepigrapha,* 1913, 163-281; R. J. Clifford, "In Zion and David a New Beginning: An Interpretation of Psalm 78," in B. Halpern and J. D. Levenson, eds., *Traditions in Transformation: Turning Points in Biblical Faith,* 1981, 121-41; G. W. Coats, *The Murmuring Motif in the Wilderness Traditions of the Old Testament: Rebellion in the Wilderness,* 1968; G. A. Cooke, *A Critical and Exegetical Commentary on the Book of Ezekiel,* 1936; W. Eichrodt, *Ezekiel: A Commentary,* 1970; S. Fisch, *Ezekiel: Hebrew Text and English Translation with an Introduction and Commentary,* 1950; R. W. Klein, *Ezekiel: The Prophet and His Message,* 1988; G. A. F. Knight, *Servant Theology: A Commentary on the Book of Isaiah 40-55,* 1984; A. Maclaren, *The Psalms: Volume II, Psalms xxxix-lxxxix,* 1903; J. L. McKenzie, *Second Isaiah: Introduction, Translation, and Notes,* 1968; J. Moltmann, *The Crucified God: The Cross of Christ as the Foundation and Criticism of Christian Theology,* 1976; J. Scullion, *Isaiah 40-66,* 1982; J. Skinner, *The Book of the Prophet Isaiah Chapters XL-LXVI,* 1922; D. M. G. Stalker, *Ezekiel: Introduction and Commentary,* 1968; M. E. Tate, *Psalms 51-100,* 1990; B. Vawter and L. J. Hoppe, *A New Heart: A Commentary on the Book of Ezekiel,* 1991; C. Westermann, *Isaiah 40-66: A Commentary,* 1969; J. W. Wevers, *Ezekiel,* 1969;

W. Zimmerli, *Ezekiel 2: A Commentary on the Book of the Prophet Ezekiel Chapters 25-48*, 1983.

Robin Wakely

5957	נשׂא

נשׂא (*nš'* I), (נשׁה [*nšh* II], same), q. lend/be a creditor against a pledge; hi. advance a loan against a pledge (# 5957); מַשָּׁא (*maššā'*), nom. loan against pledge; collateral (# 5391); מַשָּׁאָה (*maššā'â*), secured/guaranteed loan (# 5394); מַשֶּׁה (*maššeh*), nom. that which is pledged as security for a loan (hapleg.; # 5408); נְשִׁי (*n^e šî*), nom. loan against pledge (hapleg.; # 5963).

ANE The following nom. forms occur: Arab. *nasa'a*, delay of payment; OSA *rāšû*, creditor; and OSA *rašûtu*, balance in one's favor.

OT 1. The vb. is often mistakenly understood to refer to the practice of lending money at interest. Doubtless this is due in no small measure to the wording of Exod 22:25[24]. Here, the person who lends money to a poor compatriot is prohibited from behaving towards the borrower as a *nōšeh* (masc. sing. q. act. part. [the words *nōšeh* and *nôšeh* seem to be variant spellings of *nōše'*]). The second line of the v. reads *lō'-t^e śîmûn 'ālāyw nešek*, do not impose interest upon him (cf. Lev 25:35-37; Deut 23:19-20[20-21]). Many understand the reference in the second line to the taking of interest to be an allusion to the practice of a *nōšeh*. Thus, e.g., JB translates *nōšeh* as usurer: "You must not play the usurer with him [the poor borrower]: you must not demand interest from him" (cf. NIV: "Do not be like a moneylender; charge him no interest").

However, there is strong support from Pesh., Tgs., and Vg. for the insertion of a *waw* conjunction before the adv. of negation that begins the second line. This may well indicate that the second line, with its reference to the exaction of interest, is not necessarily an allusion to the way in which a *nōšeh* operates. Furthermore, an examination of the use of the vb. in other passages suggests that it means lending against a pledge, in which case a better translation of the word *nōše'/nōšeh* is creditor (RSV; NRSV). As regards the theological value of Exod 22:25[24], the intense concern for the poor in this v. is characteristic of the OT. Those who claim to be in a covenant relationship with God have a moral obligation to shun exploitative practices and to mirror the divine compassion by showing kindness to their less fortunate fellows and by protecting the right of the poor to the basic necessities of life (cf. Childs, 479).

While the exaction of interest was prohibited in ancient Israel, except in the case of a loan made to a foreigner (Deut 23:20[21]), the taking of a pledge (i.e., an article [or person] pledged as security for debt) was permitted. However, the OT aimed to protect the domestic life and dignity of the debtor and prevent undue privation by imposing strict conditions on the potentially oppressive practice of taking collateral (Nelson, 229-30). To minimize the possibility of economic oppression, the OT legislation sought to prevent the lender from abusing his legitimate rights or from enforcing them in such a way as to harass the debtor (Driver, 1965, 276). In Deut 24:10 (where the hi. [followed by prep. *b^e*] is used in tandem with nom. *maššā'â* [in the const.]), the person who demands collateral in respect of a loan is forbidden to violate the sanctity of the debtor's home. In 24:11 (where the masc. sing. q. act. part. is used), the person making the loan is directed to remain standing outside the house and to wait for the pledge (*ha'ᵃbôṭ*) to be brought out to him. This requirement, which protected the privacy of the borrower's home and left the selection of the article offered to his discretion (cf., e.g., Craigie, 308), is peculiar to Deut. In 24:12-13, as in Exod 22:26-27[25-26] (cf. Job 22:6; Ezek 18:7; Amos 2:8), the lender is instructed that if the borrower has nothing save his cloak (used as a blanket at night) to give in pledge, then the garment must not be retained by the creditor overnight. The restoration of the garment at sundown is commended as an act righteousness before Yahweh. Some (e.g., Gottwald, 115) think that, in practice, either no pledge at all was taken or it was taken ceremonially for one day or on periodic occasions as a reminder that the debt was still owing. This may have been the case with respect to the majority of small loans to the indigent (though see Amos 2:8), but there is evidence of instances where creditors insisted on, and sometimes seized, pledges of property and even of people from those to whom more substantial loans had been advanced.

When a debtor offered a pledge to his creditor, this often took the form of property. Sometimes, however, the borrower offered to put his dependants at the disposal of the creditor. A creditor was legally entitled to recover a debt from an insolvent debtor by taking into service the man's wife and children (cf. Exod 21:7). Attempts were made by legislators to mitigate the practice of debt slavery (Lev 25:39-43; Deut 15:12-18), and the Sabbath year and Jubilee laws demanded remission of both debts and bondages every seventh and fiftieth year, respectively. The sabbatical principle was based on the recognition of the need for God's people to show compassion, care, and concern in their dealings with one another and, in particular, in their treatment of their less fortunate fellows. In Deut 15:2, part of the law on the seventh year of release (vv. 1-6), the hi. of *nš'[h]* is used with the const. of nom. *maššeh*, in the interesting sentence *šāmôṭ kol-ba'al maššēh yādô 'ᵃšer yaššeh bᵉrē'ēhû*. This probably means: "Every creditor who holds a loan-pledge shall release what has been pledged to him by the one indebted to him" (cf. C. J. H. Wright, 1992, 858; NEB; REB; JB; Phillips, 103). Almost certainly, this verse is referring to pledges given for debt and not simply to the debt itself (see especially Horst; North; C. J. H. Wright, 1984; 1992, 858). The hand referred to (*yādô*, his hand) is almost certainly that of the creditor, who had a legal right to call in that which had been pledged to settle an unpaid debt (cf. Driver, 1965, 175, and Smith, 200, both of whom, however, in common with many others, take *maššeh* to mean the loan itself). While it may be conceded that the Heb. is difficult, there is no need to assume the accidental omission of words from the MT (*pace BHS*; Mayes, 248).

The author of Deut 15:2 certainly seems to have in mind the case of a debtor who has pledged either land or dependants in respect of a loan. If this be correct, then Israelites are being asked here to restore all pledges, whether of property or persons, to their rightful owners. This would certainly have provided debtors with welcome relief, but what about the debt itself? Some scholars (e.g., C. J. H. Wright, 1992, 858) think that the pledge would not only have provided security until a debt was settled, but would also have served to repay the loan. In such an "antichretic" arrangement, the produce of the pledged land or the service of the dependant put at the creditor's disposal would belong to the creditor and would constitute the payment of the debt (C. J. H. Wright, 1992, 858; cf. idem, 1990, 171-72). This is a compelling view in the case of Deut 15:1-3. It is uncertain whether this law is prescribing a complete, permanent cancellation of the debt, or a temporary suspension of repayment for one year. However, a temporary respite is suggested both by the wording of v. 2 (lit., "he [the creditor] shall not press [*ngś*] his neighbor") and by the fact that a special Year of Jubilee would have been unnecessary if the intention of the sabbatical law had been the total, permanent cancellation of all debts and the permanent restoration of all mortgaged property (C. J. H. Wright, 1992, 859; cf., e.g., Craigie, 236; *pace*, e.g., Smith, 198-99; G. E. Wright, 428; Mayes, 247; Payne, 93; Nelson, 223). It seems, then, that 15:1-3 is instructing creditors to return pledges to debtors and not to press for any loan repayments for the duration of the year of release.

In Prov 22:26, there is a warning against entering injudiciously into a contract to guarantee another's loan. The first stich refers to those who go guarantor by striking hands (the vb. used is *tq'*, strike, followed by nom. *kap*, hand), which symbolizes the making of a contract. In the second stich, the vb. *'rb*, put up security, is used in conjunction with nom. *maššā'ôt*, and the meaning is to become surety (RSV; NRSV)/go surety (JB; McKane, 1970, 246)/pledge oneself as surety (NEB; REB; Scott, 137) for debts. While recognizing the moral obligation of charity and the importance of being a generous benefactor (cf. 21:26), Prov is also aware of the grave risks involved when one enters into an agreement to provide surety without having adequate financial resources to cope with any contingency that might arise (cf. McKane, 1970, 379). Failure to settle a debt guaranteed by a pledge could mean being reduced to abject poverty or even to slavery (cf. Gen 44:32-33; 2 Kgs 4:1). Concerned to prevent the reckless gambling of one's security in high risk financial dealings, the book warns against rash impulses to guarantee the debts of other people (cf. 6:1-5; 17:18; 20:16; 27:13).

2. The anxiety and distress caused by callous or unscrupulous moneylending practices are alluded to in several texts. In 1 Sam 22:2, at Adullam, where David had taken refuge, he attracted to himself a motley band of marginal people, which included those in straitened circumstances, those who were discontented, and those who were in debt (*[w^{e}]kol-'îš '^{a}šer-lô nōše'*, and every one who had a lender [creditor]). In the past, there was a tendency to interpret the rivalry between Saul and David almost exclusively as a flare up in the tensions between northern and southern groups. However, some older commentators (e.g., Kirkpatrick, 1899, 186) recognized that much more was involved, for the text clearly indicates that some of those resorting to David were smarting under the oppression of tyranny, that some were victims of the neglect of the laws forbidding usury, and that some were in despair at the way the country was being run and hoped for better things under a new leader. More recent studies from a sociological perspective have confirmed the impression that one of the most important factors in the struggle between Saul and David was the tension between the rich, landed populace determined to maintain the status quo and the economically disadvantaged, who were embittered by deprivation and eager for change (cf. Brueggemann, 156-57; McCarter, 357, 359; Klein, 1983, 222-23).

According to 2 Kgs 4:1, the destitute widow of one of the sons of the prophets appealed to Elisha for help when the creditor (*hannōšeh*) came to take her two children to be his slaves. The author of 4:1-7 is concerned to show that while the prophet was unable to prevent a legal foreclosure, the providence of God was able miraculously to provide sufficient oil not only to sustain the woman and her children, but also to pay back either the loan that had been taken against pledge or the creditors (v. 7). Following Q, the word *nišyēk*^{e}*y* in v. 7 is understood by some to be a corrupt form of *nišyēk*, your loan taken against pledge, from an otherwise unattested nom. *n*^{e}*šî* (see, e.g., *HALAT*; Jones, 404; Cogan and Tadmor, 56). Others (e.g., Montgomery and Gehman, 371; *BHS*; Hobbs, 41), influenced by LXX and Tg., prefer to emend the word to *nōšayik* or *nōšeykî*, your creditors.

In Neh 5:7, 10, where the masc. pl. q. act. part. is used in tandem with the nom. *maššā'*, it is recorded that in the postexilic community in Judah, certain Jews were taking advantage of their economically deprived brethren by acting as *nōšîm* in respect of loans. Some (see, e.g., RSV; NRSV; NIV) have understood Nehemiah's charge to be directed against the illegal exaction of interest. Significantly, however, in their complaints (5:2-5), the debtors said nothing about the taking of interest. Those commentators (e.g., Bowman, 709; Williamson, 233, 238; Clines, 168; Klein, 1988, 381; Blenkinsopp, 259) are almost certainly correct who think that the main point at issue was not the exaction of interest, but the practice of seizing from insolvent debtors persons and property pledged against nonpayment of debt. After all, in v. 10 Nehemiah points out, without the slightest trace of guilt, that he himself, together with the members of his family and party, have been acting as *nōšîm*. It seems highly probable, therefore, that Nehemiah and other members of the community have been advancing loans against pledge and that when he advocates abolishing *'et-hammaššā' hazzeh*, Nehemiah is referring to "this practice of demanding pledges/surety in respect of loans." The charge made by Nehemiah against the nobles and officials was almost certainly that in their role as creditors, they were seizing pledges of property and/or people either for nonpayment of loans advanced, or in lieu of loan repayment.

In Neh 5:11, the masc. pl. q. act. part. occurs again, probably in conjunction with nom. *maššā'â*. Many (e.g., Davies, 202; Batten, 243; Oesterley, 1920, 332; Bowman, 710-11; JB; NRSV; NIV; R. North, 394) see the need to emend the word *ûm*^{e}*'at*, and the hundredth of. If *BHS*, *HALAT*, and others are right, then MT *ûm*^{e}*'at* should be emended to *ûmašša't* (const. of nom. *maššā'â*), and the secured/guaranteed loan of. While the fundamental problem was almost certainly the practice of making loans on pledge, one cannot, of course, entirely exclude the possibility that interest was also levied (Williamson, 240). The precise measures implemented by Nehemiah to relieve the socioeconomic crisis are disputed, but the evidence from Neh 5:7, 10-11 indicates that one of them was the restoration to their rightful owners of all pledges (fields, vineyards, olive orchards, and houses) and the cessation of demands for pledges.

3. Neh 10 describes a solemn, public commitment to the *tôrâ,* which was recorded in writing and signed by the community's civic and religious leaders. One of the specific covenant stipulations mentioned is described in 10:31[32], where the nom. *maššā'* occurs in tandem with *kol-yād*, lit. that pledged of every hand (cf. Deut 15:2), the hand referred to presumably being the one that held the document proving debt (see Driver, 1965, 175; Bowman, 763). Here, as has frequently been pointed out (see, e.g., Ryle, 272-73; Clines, 206; Williamson, 334-35; Blenkinsopp, 316; Fensham, 240), the law of the seventh fallow year (Exod 23:10-11; Lev 25:1-7)—which was to the disadvantage of farmers—is combined with the law requiring the septennial remission of debt slaves and the restoration of people and property taken in pledge (Deut 15:1-18; cf. Exod 21:2-6)—which was to the disadvantage of merchants and employers. By

combining these two regulations, neither sector of the communtity would profit from the other's sacrificial observance of the law (Clines, 206; Klein, 1988, 385). It is uncertain whether the signatories to the document obeyed these idealistic stipulations. The earliest testimony to their observance comes from the second century BC (1 Macc 6:49, 53; cf. Josephus, *Ant* 13:8.1).

4. The profoundly negative connotation of the words associated with the practice of lending against pledges is capitalized on in a number of passages. The q. is used in Jer 15:10, part of the prophet's second personal lament (vv. 10-21), where Jeremiah likens the strife and rejection he is experiencing in his role as prophet of disaster to the hostility and ostracism that could be experienced by both debtors and creditors. Protesting at the fact that he has become a social outcast, the prophet asserts that he has been neither a lender (*lō'-nāšîtî*, I have not lent) nor a borrower (*[wᵉ]lō'-nāšû-bî*, they [men] have not lent to me). The reference to lending and borrowing, which may have been a popular saying or proverb (Hyatt, 939), has been variously interpreted. It is unnecessary to think that this is an allusion to those involved in dubious financial transactions. The text probably refers to those who lend and those who borrow against a pledge. Even apparently straightforward monetary and business dealings are, in any age, a potential and ready source of friction and strife (on this, see especially McKane, 1986, 344-47).

The masc. sing. q. act. part. is used in Ps 109:11, part of a section (vv. 6-20, 28-29) where a speaker first expresses the hope that the enemy will die prematurely (v. 8) and that his wife and children will be robbed of their inheritance (v. 8) and become destitute beggars (v. 10); he then makes the wish that the creditor (*nôšeh*) will seize everything the aggressor owns (v. 11). There is debate about the identity of the speaker in vv. 6-19. Whereas in the rest of the psalm the enemies are referred to in the pl., in vv. 6-19 the sing. is used almost exclusively. Some think that the enemies are here collectively designated by singular pronouns or that an outstanding individual among them, perhaps the ringleader, has been singled out. If this be correct, then the speaker is the psalmist who, in a state of righteous indignation created by the fact that his love and prayer for his enemies have been rewarded with words of hate, false accusations (vv. 2-5), and scorn (v. 25), employs violent and repellent language to provide a counter-imprecation that will ensure that the potent curses of his enemies will not avail (see Delitzsch, 176-80; C. A. and E. G. Briggs, 364, 369-71; Kirkpatrick, 1957, 651-58; Oesterley, 1959, 457-61; McCullough, 582; Kissane, 1964, 501-7; May and Metzger, 742-43; M'Caw and Motyer, 521; A. A. Anderson, 758-59; Durham, 394-95; Eaton, 259-60; Kidner, 389-90; Rogerson and McKay, 59-60, 63; Bratcher and Reyburn, 936, 938-43; Mays, 348-50). However, others (e.g., G. W. Anderson, 437; Toombs, 292-93; Weiser, 690-91; Kraus, 338-42; Allen, 76-77; Stuhlmueller, 483; Kselman and Barré, 545) argue that the psalmist is here quoting the words of hate (v. 3) that were leveled at him by his malicious adversaries. A minority view is that of Dahood (99, 102), who thinks that in vv. 6-19 the beleagured psalmist is cursing the judge who considered that the charges brought by the enemies warranted a hearing. This seems unlikely; but whatever be the correct interpretation, it is clear from this psalm that only when God intervenes in human affairs is the web of human deceit and hatred broken, injustice replaced by truth and righteousness, cursing turned into blessing, and fear transformed into joy (Weiser, 692).

The q. act. part. is also used in Isa 50:1, where Yahweh asks Zion's children in exile if they can produce their mother's bill of divorce and if they can determine the identity of the creditor to whom he has sold them. Here, Yahweh seems to be responding to the complaint that he has abandoned Jerusalem (cf. 49:14-16). The majority of commentators think that the rhetorical questions in 50:1 demand negative answers and that the point being made is that Yahweh has not irrevocably repudiated his people, either by an unalterable divorce or by selling them irretrievably into slavery; rather, he has caused a temporary separation in order to punish them for their disloyalty and flagrant disobedience. Just as it is preposterous to imagine that God could have a creditor, so it is inconceivable that he should ever surrender his rights over his children (Skinner, 1960, 111; cf. Whitehouse, 168-69; C. R. North, 1967, 198; 1971, 115; Muilenburg, 580-81; McKenzie, 112-14; Herbert, 94; Scullion, 103-4; Sawyer, 130; Knight, 143; Watts, 1987, 193). According to this interpretation, the way is open for reconciliation (Skinner, 1960, 110). A different perspective is offered by Westermann (224). He argues that the two metaphors in v. 1a, b contain Israel's charge that God has repudiated her, despite having bound himself to her in the covenant. In v. 1c, the rejoinder to the charge does not dispute the fact of repudiation, which signifies Israel's destruction as a nation, but rather justifies the act of repudiation on the ground of Israel's transgression.

5. Catastrophes are no respecters of persons. In Isa 24:1-6, it is announced that, as a result of humankind's breach of "the everlasting covenant" (v. 5), universal judgment is imminent. The earth will be laid waste and made desolate (vv. 1, 3) and its inhabitants scattered (v. 1). Very few will survive (v. 6). Two forms of the masc. sing. q. act. part. occur in Isa 24:2 in the phrase *kannōšeh ka'ᵃšer nōše' bô*, as with the creditor, so with the debtor (RSV; NRSV; Kaiser, 180; cf. JB; REB; TEV; Watts, 1985, 313). G. B. Gray (405) reads: "He of whom interest is taken like him that taketh interest." However, not only is it unlikely that the vb. *nš'[h]* means to exact interest, but there is no warrant for reversing the order of the words in MT (others who reverse the order include Oswalt, 438, "like debtor, like the one who gives credit to him"; NIV "[the same] for debtor as for creditor"; NEB "[the same for] debtor and creditor"; Kissane, 1960, 265, "The debtor like the creditor"; cf. RV; Skinner, 1909, 181). The contrasting pairs in v. 2, which embrace the religious, domestic, and commercial sectors of society, convey a picture of totality (Motyer, 197). There will be no immunity from the catastrophe: all human beings, irrespective of rank, wealth, and power, must face the judgment decreed by Yahweh.

6. There are two cases (1 Kgs 8:31 [par. 2 Chron 6:22] and Jer 23:39) where it is hotly disputed whether the vb. used is, in fact, *nš'* I. 1 Kgs 8:31 (par. 2 Chron 6:22) deals with an oath taken in the sanctuary to determine guilt or innocence in the case of a legal dispute where no evidence is procurable (cf., e.g., Skinner, 1893, 148). Some (e.g., RSV; NRSV; NEB; REB; NIV; Slotki, 62; Dillard, 45-46) take the vb. here to mean to make/require/adjure/exact/impose [an oath]. The plaintiff would impose an oath on the defendant, requiring him to swear his innocence before the altar in the temple. Similar procedures were used in cases involving trusteeship (Exod 22:7-15[6-14]) and in the case of a woman suspected of adultery (Num 5:11-31). In the latter case, the oath was accompanied by a self-maledictory curse. However, there is widespread scepticism about whether the vb. used in 1 Kgs 8:31 is *nš'* I. In their version of both 1 Kgs

8:31 and 2 Chron 6:22, some MSS read *nś'*, take (up), instead of *nš'*, and not a few commentators think that this is more tenable (see, e.g., Montgomery and Gehman, 202; J. Gray, 222).

Most translators and commentators (cf. e.g., NEB; REB; Driver, 1906, 141; Peake, 271; Bright, 151; Davidson, 36) see in Jer 23:39 a continuation of the play on the word *maśśā'*, burden, found in vv. 33-38 and emend the words *[wᵉ]nāšîtî* [from *nāšâ* I, forget] *'etkem nāšō'*, "[and] I will surely forget you" [NIV]), to *[wᵉ]nāśîtî* (i.e., *[wᵉ]nāśā'tî) 'etkem nāśō'*, "[and] I will surely lift you up/carry you like a burden." H. Torczyner (followed by H. M. Weil) has argued that the word *maśśā'*, burden or oracle, in vv. 33-40 should be read as *maššā'*, loan or pledge. Israel, he maintains, is about to be abandoned and is depicted here as Yahweh's possession or property, which he will give as a pledge or loan out. This pledge or loan will not be made as a temporary measure or with a view to redeeming the people at a later stage. However, this interpretation is not compelling and has commanded only limited support (on this, see especially McKane, 1986, 598-99).

Borrowing and lending: → *lwh* II (borrow, lend, # 4278); → *nš'* I (lend against a pledge, # 5957); → *nšk* II (pay/exact interest, # 5967); → *'bṭ* (borrow, take a pledge from, # 6292); → *šmṭ* (release, remit, drop, throw down, # 9023)

BIBLIOGRAPHY

L. C. Allen, *Psalms 101-150*, WBC, 1983; A. A. Anderson, *The Book of Psalms. Vol. 2: Psalms 73-150*, NCBC, 1972; G. W. Anderson, "The Psalms," in *Peake*, 1964, 409-43; L. W. Batten, *A Critical and Exegetical Commentary on the Books of Ezra and Nehemiah*, 1961; J. Blenkinsopp, *Ezra-Nehemiah: A Commentary*, OTL, 1988; R. A. Bowman, "The Book of Ezra and the Book of Nehemiah: Introduction and Exegesis," *IB*, 1954, 3:549-819; R. G. Bratcher and W. D. Reyburn, *A Translator's Handbook on the Book of Psalms*, 1991; C. A. and E. G. Briggs, *A Critical and Exegetical Commentary on the Book of Psalms*. Vol. II, ICC, 1960; J. Bright, *Jeremiah: Introduction, Translation, and Notes*, AB, 1965; W. Brueggemann, *First and Second Samuel*, 1990; B. S. Childs, *Exodus: A Commentary*, OTL, 1974; D. J. A. Clines, *Ezra, Nehemiah, Esther*, NCBC, 1984; M. Cogan and H. Tadmor, *II Kings: A New Translation With Introduction and Commentary*, AB, 1988; P. C. Craigie, *The Book of Deuteronomy*, NICOT, 1983; M. Dahood, *Psalms III: 101-150*, AB, 1970; R. Davidson, *Jeremiah (Volume 2) and Lamentations*, 1985; T. W. Davies, *Ezra, Nehemiah and Esther*, 1909; F. Delitzsch, *Biblical Commentary on the Psalms*. Vol. III, KD, 2d ed., 1885; R. B. Dillard, *2 Chronicles*, WBC, 1987; S. R. Driver, *The Book of the Prophet Jeremiah*, 1906; idem, *A Critical and Exegetical Commentary on Deuteronomy*, ICC, 3rd ed., 1965; J. I. Durham, "Psalms," in *BBC*, 1972, 4:153-464; J. H. Eaton, *Psalms: Introduction and Commentary*, 1972; F. C. Fensham, *The Books of Ezra and Nehemiah*, NICOT, 1983; N. K. Gottwald, "The Book of Deuteronomy," in *The Interpreter's One-Volume Commentary on the Bible*, 1971, 100-121; G. B. Gray, *A Critical and Exegetical Commentary on the Book of Isaiah I-XXVII*, ICC, 1975; J. Gray, *I & II Kings: A Commentary*, OTL, 2d revised, ed., 1970; A. S. Herbert, *The Book of the Prophet Isaiah Chapters 40-66*, 1975; T. R. Hobbs, *2 Kings*, WBC, 1985; F. Horst, *Das Privilegerecht Jahves*, 1930; J. P. Hyatt, "The Book of Jeremiah: Introduction and Exegesis," in *IB*, 1956, 5:775-1142; G. H. Jones, *1 and 2 Kings. Volume II: 1 Kings 17:1-2 Kings 25:30*, NCBC, 1984; O. Kaiser, *Isaiah 13-39: A Commentary*, OTL, 1974; D. Kidner, *Psalms 73-150: A Commentary on Books III-V of the Psalms*, TOTC, 1977; A. F. Kirkpatrick, *The First Book of Samuel, With Map, Notes and Introduction*, 1899; idem, *The Book of Psalms*, 1957; E. J. Kissane, *The Book of Isaiah Translated From a Critically Revised Hebrew Text With*

Commentary. Vol. I (I-XXXIX), 1960; idem, *The Book of Psalms Translated from a Critically Revised Hebrew Text With a Commentary*, 1964; R. W. Klein, *1 Samuel*, WBC, 1983; idem, "Nehemiah," in *HBC*, 1988, 379-86; G. A. F. Knight, *Servant Theology: A Commentary on the Book of Isaiah 40-55*, 1984; H.-J. Kraus, *Psalms 60-150: A Commentary*, 1989; J. S. Kselman and M. L. Barré, "Psalms," in *NJBC*, 1990, 523-52; P. K. McCarter, *I Samuel: A New Translation With Introduction, Notes and Commentary*, AB, 1980; L. S. M'Caw and J. A. Motyer, "The Psalms," in *NBC*, 1972, 446-547; W. S. McCullough, "The Book of Psalms: Exegesis Psalms 72-92, 94, 97-99, 101-119, 139," in W. S. McCullough et al., "The Book of Psalms," *IB*, 1955, 4:1-763; W. McKane, *Proverbs: A New Approach*, OTL, 1970; idem, *A Critical and Exegetical Commentary on Jeremiah. Volume 1: An Introduction and Commentary on Jeremiah I-XXV*, ICC, 1986; J. L. McKenzie, *Second Isaiah: Introduction, Translation, and Notes*, AB, 1968; H. G. May and B. M. Metzger, eds., *The New Oxford Annotated Bible*, 1973; A. D. H. Mayes, *Deuteronomy*, NCBC, 1979; J. L. Mays, *Psalms*, 1994; J. A. Montgomery and H. S. Gehman, *A Critical and Exegetical Commentary on the Books of Kings*, 1967; J. A. Motyer, *The Prophecy of Isaiah: An Introduction & Commentary*, 1993; J. Muilenburg, "The Book of Isaiah Chapters 40-66: Introduction and Exegesis," *IB*, 1956, 5:381-773; R. D. Nelson, "Deuteronomy," in *HBC*, 1988, 209-34; C. R. North, *Isaiah 40-55*, 1971; idem, *The Second Isaiah: Introduction, Translation and Commentary to Chapters XL-LV*, 1967; R. North, "The Chronicler: 1-2 Chronicles, Ezra, Nehemiah," in *NJBC*, 1990, 362-98; W. O. E. Oesterley, "Ezra-Nehemiah," in *Peake*, 1920, 323-35; idem, *The Psalms Translated With Text-Critical and Exegetical Notes*, 1959; J. N. Oswalt, *The Book of Isaiah Chapters 1-39*, NICOT, 1986; D. F. Payne, *Deuteronomy*, 1985; A. S. Peake, *Jeremiah Vol. I: Jeremiah I-XXIV*, 1910; A. Phillips, *Deuteronomy*, 1973; J. W. Rogerson and J. W. McKay, *Psalms 101-150*, 1977; H. E. Ryle, *The Books of Ezra and Nehemiah With Introduction, Notes and Maps*, 1893; J. F. A. Sawyer, *Isaiah.* Volume 2, 1986; R. B. Y. Scott, *Proverbs, Ecclesiastes: Introduction, Translation, and Notes*, 1965; J. Scullion, *Isaiah 40-66*, 1982; J. Skinner, *Kings*, 1893; idem, *The Book of the Prophet Isaiah Chapters I-XXXIX*, 1909; idem, *The Book of the Prophet Isaiah Chapters XL-LXVI*, 1960; I. W. Slotki, *Kings: Hebrew Text & English Translation With an Introduction and Commentary*, 1961; G. A. Smith, *The Book of Deuteronomy*, 1918; C. Stuhlmueller, "Psalms," in *HBC*, 1988, 433-94; L. E. Toombs, "The Psalms," in *The Interpreter's One-Volume Commentary on the Bible*, 1971, 253-303; J. D. W. Watts, *Isaiah 1-33*, WBC, 1985; idem, *Isaiah 34-66*, WBC, 1987; A. Weiser, *The Psalms: A Commentary*, OTL, 1965; C. Westermann, *Isaiah 40-66: A Commentary*, 1969; O. C. Whitehouse, *Isaiah XL-LXVI*. Vol. II, 1908; H. G. M. Williamson, *Ezra, Nehemiah*, NCBC, 1985; C. J. H. Wright, "What Happened Every Seven Years in Israel? Old Testament Sabbatical Institutions for Land, Debt and Slaves," *EvQ* 56, 1984, 129-38, 193-201; idem, *God's People in God's Land: Family, Land, and Property in the Old Testament*, 1990; idem, "Sabbatical Year," in *ABD*, 1992, 5:857-61; G. E. Wright, "The Book of Deuteronomy: Introduction and Exegesis," *IB*, 1953, 2:309-537.

Robin Wakely

5958	נשׁא

נשׁא (*nš'* II), ni. be deceived; hi. to deceive, cause a deception (+ acc., אֶת, - ל) (# 5958); מַשָּׁאוֹן (*maššāʾôn*), nom. guile, deceit, dissimulation (hapleg., Prov 26:26, # 5396); מַשּׁוּאוֹת(*maššûʾôt*), deception, deceit (# 5397).

OT The vb. occurs 16x (hi. all but once). The word is considered to be related to *šāw'* (→ # 8736), deceit, the hi. of the form arising directly from *šāw'* and the ni. being a secondary development. This seems to be acceptable based upon present knowledge. At its center lies the idea of deception, passing for reality that which is, in fact, not the case. The word overlaps greatly with *kzb* (→ # 3941) and *kḥš* (→ # 3950), but *kzb* usually emphasizes lying through the use of words. It is close to *kḥš*, since both emphasize accepting a deception for reality. The vb. *nš'* can suggest a process of self-deception, while *kḥš* usually communicates conscious deception of others.

1. The first record of deception is found in Gen 3:13, where Eve asserts that the serpent deceived her. The deception consisted of the false picture of reality painted for Eve by the words of the serpent, whose words were a direct challenge to the words of the Lord God. True reality lay in the interpretation of reality presented by Yahweh God (2:15-17). Any understanding of reality that differed from a reality presented and defined by God's words (here with respect to the tree of the knowledge of good and evil) could only be deceitful and false. However, the account in Gen 3 also makes clear that Eve's claim was not entirely accurate, for she acted on her own evaluation of the tree (3:6). She herself took part in the deception, deceiving herself (cf. 1 John 2:15-16). Self-deception of this nature is found later in the OT as is well attested by this word and synonyms.

2. In the Prophets the king of Assyria raises the issue of deception, exhorting (in hi. jussive forms + *'al*) Hezekiah not to be deceived by the expectation that his God would deliver him (2 Kgs 18:29 ‖ Isa 36:14) and exhorting the people not to let Hezekiah deceive them into believing that the Assyrians would not destroy Jerusalem (2 Kgs 19:10 ‖ Isa 37:10). Here again the enemy of Israel exhorts the people of Yahweh not to trust his words, much as the serpent/Satan had done to Eve. In the parallel passage in 2 Chron 32:15 (‖ Isa 36:14; 2 Kgs 18:29) the writer uses the vb. *swt* (lead astray; → # 8454), in parallelism with *nš'*, again echoing the serpent's efforts to lead Eve from the truth of Yahweh's character and words.

3. *nš'* II is used to indicate the possibility of self-deception by Israel (lit. do not deceive yourselves). The Israelites repeatedly assured themselves that the king of Babylon would not enter the city to destroy it (Jer 37:9).

False prophets were a constant source of deception. Their false words consistently tempted Israel to believe in that which Yahweh had not approved of or delivered to his people (Jer 4:10 [2x]; 29:8), thereby creating false hopes. There is no deception found in Yahweh's words. Jeremiah (4:10), however, accuses Yahweh of a total deception by allowing false prophets to confuse his people. Yet Yahweh urges his people not to be fooled by deceptions presented by the false prophets and diviners (29:8). It is because of the people's moral and ethical rejection of God's words in the Torah/Prophets that the Lord, with moral integrity, deals with his people in this "deceptive" way.

4. The hubris and pride of Edom is what caused them to be deceived, and they are warned against letting the "pride of your heart" deceive them. The pride of Edom will be rewarded when their own friends deceive them (Obad 3, 7). The pride of humankind's heart is thus able to cause persons to deceive themselves, refusing to recognize their limitations.

Mighty Memphis, the ancient religious capital of Egypt, had become deceived (ni., Isa 19:13, par. with *y'l* I, be foolish) by her trust in her gods and false idols, even though they had been known at one time for their wisdom (1 Kgs 4:29-30).

5. Ps 55:15[16] has many mss. that may read a hi. of *nš'*, giving a possible translation, "let death work a deception (*yaššîmāwet*) upon them, let them go down to Sheol alive." This is far from certain, however. The NIV translates this as "surprise them"; the NJPSV has "Let him incite death against them." The translation of the preposition *'al* may favor the NJPSV (cf. also 89:22[23]).

6. The nom. *maššā'ôn* only occurs in Prov 26:26. The man consumed by hate covers his malice with deception/deceit. The nom. *maššû'ôt* might occur in Ps 73:18 and 74:3. Several scholars derive this term (repointing it *m*^{e}*šô'ôt*) from *šāw'* (emptiness, vanity, see # 8736) with the translation, "ruins." Tate (227) combines both ideas in his translation, "deceptive places of ruin." In light of the par. terms, Anderson (534, 539) prefers *maššû'ôt* in Ps 73:18 and *m*^{e}*šô'ôt* in Ps 74:3.

P-B The word is used in Late Heb. in the hi. stem to mean to carry away; to incite, allure (e.g., Gen R 3:19), but with other meanings as well (see Jastrow 2:938-39).

Deception, falsehood, fraud, guile, iniquity, lie: → *'āwen* (mischief, iniquity, deception, # 224); → *bd'* (invent, devise, lie, # 968); → *kzb* I (lie, be a liar, deceive, # 3941); → *kḥš* (fail, deceive, grow lean, # 3950); → *nkl* (knave, deceiver, cheat, # 5792); → *nš'* II (be deceived, deceive, cause a deception, # 5958); → *sārâ* II (rebellion, crime, revolt, falsehood, # 6240); → *'qb* I (seize the heel, overreach, deceive, # 6810); → *rmh* II (betray, deal treacherously with, # 8228); → *śwṭ* (turn away to falsehood, entangled in lies, # 8454); → *šqr* (deal/act falsely, betray, # 9213); → *tll* (deceive, mock, trifle, # 9438)

Bibliography

THAT 2:882-83; *TWAT* 5:657-58; *TWOT* 2:603-4; A. Anderson, *Psalms*, NCBC, 1972; M. Tate, *Psalms 51-100*, WBC, 1990.

Eugene Carpenter/Michael A. Grisanti

5959	נשב

נשב (*nšb*), blow (# 5959); nom. אֶשְׁנָב (*'ešnāb*), lattice (→ # 876).

OT The sovereignty of God is illustrated by this root's only two occurrences. As Creator and Provider he causes the wind to blow (Ps 147:18), and the expiration of his breath can consume grass and flowers, but just as easily, people (Isa 40:7).

Blowing (wind, breath): → *hzh* (pant in sleep, # 2111); → *ndp* (blow away, scatter, # 5622); → *npḥ* (blow, # 5870); → *nšb* (blow, # 5959); → *nšp* (blow, # 5973); → *pwḥ* (blow, blast, malign, # 7032)

D. C. Fredericks

5960	נשה

נשה (*nšh* I), q. forget; ni. be forgotten; pi. cause to forget (# 5960); נְשִׁיָּה (*n*^{e}*šiyyâ*), nom. oblivion (# 5964). In Deut 32:18 the strange form *tešî* is usually emended to *tiššeh,* you forget (NIV). In Job 11:6 some scholars relate to *nšh* II, demand payment (cf. NRSV). In Jer 23:39 the vb. is probably to be repointed to a form of *nś'*, lift up, with much ancient support. In Ezek 39:26 MT *w*^{e}*nāśû* (= *w*^{e}*nāś*^{e}*'û*, and they will bear [their shame]) need not be emended to *w*^{e}*nāšû,* they will forget (cf. NIV); cf. Zimmerli, 295, 320. In Mic 6:10 MT *ha'iš,* (= *h*^{a}*yēš,* are there?) is generally emended to *ha'eššeh*, Am I to forget? (NIV).

ANE The root accords with Ugar. *nšy*; Arab. *nasiya,* OSA *nsy,* Tigre *nasā,* and Eth. *tänāsäyä* (cf. Akk. *mašû*).

OT 1. This much less common vb., which is synonymous with *škḥ,* forget, and occurs in parallelism with it in Deut 32:18, echoes part of its range of uses. It is employed with human subjects in Deut 32:18, where it signifies neglect of the covenant God "who gave you birth," and in Lam 3:17, where crisis causes past happiness to be forgotten. The nom. *n*ᵉ*šiyyâ,* oblivion, in Ps 88:12[13] is an epithet of Sheol, where the dead are forgotten. Gen 41:51 is comparable in relating to a change of human fortune: the name Manasseh is explained in terms of God's causing trouble to be forgotten.

2. In other passages God is subject or implicit subject. The vb. is used in a positive context at Isa 44:21 in an assurance of salvation: God would not forget Israel. It appears in negative contexts concerning divine punishment in Job 11:6 and Mic 6:10.

Forgetting: → *nšh* I (forget, # 5960); → *škḥ* I (forget, # 8894)
Death: → *'bd* I (perish, # 6); → *'ᵃdāmâ* (ground, piece of land, soil, earth, realm of the dead, # 141); → *'āsôn* (mortal accident, # 656); → *gw'* (expire, die, # 1588); → *hrg* (kill, murder, # 2222); → *zrm* I (put an end to life, # 2441); → *ḥedel* (realm of the dead, # 2535); → *ḥnṭ* II (embalm, embalming, # 2846); → *mwt* (die, kill, execute, # 4637); → *qṭl* (murder, slay, # 7779); → *r*ᵉ*pā'îm* I (shades, departed spirits, # 8327); → *š*ᵉ*'ôl* (sheol, netherworld, # 8619); → *šaḥat* (pit, grave, # 8846)

Bibliography

THAT 2:898-904; S. Balentine, *The Hidden God: The Hiding of the Face of God in the Old Testament,* 1982, 136-43; W. Zimmerli, *Ezekiel* 2, 1983.

Leslie C. Allen

5963 (*n*ᵉ*šî,* loan against pledge), → # 5957

5964 (*n*ᵉ*šiyyâ,* oblivion), → # 5960

5965 (*n*ᵉ*šîqâ,* kiss), → # 5975

5966 (*nšk* I, bite; be bitten; bite), → # 5729

5967	נשך

נשך (*nšk* II), q. pay/give/earn interest; hi. charge/exact/lend at interest (# 5967); נֶשֶׁךְ (*nešek*), interest, usury (# 5968).

ANE Nom. forms occur in Sam. *nēšêk*, and Ugar. *ntk.*

OT 1. The q. and hi. forms of the vb. occur in tandem with the nom. in Deut 23:19[20], which prohibits Israelites from charging interest on loans made to their compatriots. The hi. is used again (2x) in v. 20[21], which permits the levy of interest on loans made to foreigners only. Deut 23:19[20] has parallels in Exod 22:25[24] and Lev 25:35-37, but Deut 23:20[21] has no parallel. Interest rates in ancient Israel are not known, but those in some other countries of the ANE varied considerably, sometimes ranging up to 50 percent (Barrois, 809; Hyatt, 243). Although precluded from taking interest on loans made to their fellow citizens, Israelite lenders were permitted to take pledges; but while these were supposed to be strictly regulated so as to protect the livelihood and dignity of the debtor and to prevent undue hardship (Deut 24:6, 10-13), not every lender conformed to the regulations (e.g., Amos 2:8).

Most scholars maintain that loans made to Israelites were almost exclusively acts of charity for the relief of destitution as opposed to loans of a commercial nature for the purpose of expanding business (see Driver, 1953, 232; 1965, 265-66; G. A. Smith, 274; Dummelow, 71; Cooke, 199; G. E. Wright, 472; Cunliffe-Jones, 132-33; Dahood, 84; Gottwald, 115; Harford, 187; Stalker, 159; Gray, 58; Eaton, 57; Thompson, 242; Taylor, 150; Craigie, 302; Clifford, 1982, 91, 126; 1990, 54; Cox, 225; Payne, 132; Miller, 173; cf. Robinson, 175; Manley and Harrison, 223). However, Hyatt (243; cf. Rylaarsdam, 1008) questions whether lending in Israel would have been restricted mainly to charity or distress loans to the poverty-stricken. He argues that it would be strange if there had not been Israelite farmers who, on occasion, required loans at the beginning of planting, to be repaid at harvest time, or Israelite entrepreneurs who needed to borrow instant capital for business ventures of one kind or another.

According to Deut 15:1-11, all debts were to be released every seventh year. There is debate about whether this passage envisions a cancellation of all debts or only their suspension for the year during which the fields would lie fallow (→ *nš'* I, # 5957). Although Jewish tradition holds that it refers to cancellation, many think the text calls for a postponement of payment (see Clifford, 1982, 91). However, despite such legislation, the evidence available indicates that debt was a perennial social problem in ancient Israel (Chilton, 114).

The masc. pl. q. act. part. with suff. occurs in Hab 2:7, part of a section (vv. 6-20) consisting of woes against a wicked nation. Opinion is divided on whether the word means "your debtors [those who pay you interest]" or "your creditors [those who take interest from you]," but, given the context, the reading "your creditors" is the more probable (see, especially, Patterson, 186-87; 189-90; Roberts, 119; Robertson, 189). In vv. 6-7, an assurance is given that the oppressor who loads himself with pledges (i.e., the booty and tribute he has exacted from other nations) will experience a complete reversal of circumstances. There is debate about the relationship between the nom. *nešek* and the vb, *nšk,* to bite. However, even if Rashi, GB, BDB, Dahood (84), Childs (479), and Brownlee (285) are wrong to subsume the nom. under this vb., there is almost certainly a fine play on the words interest and bite in Hab 2:7 (see, e.g., Dummelow, 590; Roberts, 119; cf. Pusey, 418; Driver, 1906, 79; Garland, 259; Robertson, 186-90). The debtors turned creditors (i.e., the exploited nations forced by the oppressor to pay him for use of what he considered to be his land) will become the biters, and the oppressor will himself be bitten (i.e., the plundered nations will demand payment from the oppressor for what they consider to be the loans they have made to him). Although originally directed at the rapacious, unjust, iniquitous, violent, and idolatrous nation that plundered many peoples (v. 8), acquired gain by violence (v. 9), built towns with blood (v. 12), degraded its neighbors (v. 15), and put its trust in lifeless objects that had no breath (vv. 18-19), the condemnation here has universal reference, indicting all human tyranny (May and Metzger, 1137-38; Stephens-Hodge, 770; R. L. Smith, 1984, 111).

2. The nom. *nešek* occurs in Exod 22:25[24] and Lev 25:36-37, both of which prohibit the exaction of interest from a brother Israelite. Clearly, the covenant

relationship with God was understood to preclude Israelites from exploiting their poverty-stricken fellows. It is significant that in Exod 22:25[24] the borrower is referred to as *he'ānî*, the poor, and that in Lev 25:35 the debtor is described as one who, having become indigent (*mûk* is the vb. used), needs to be strengthened (the vb. is *ḥzq*), i.e., set on his feet again, and treated with the same consideration as that shown to the stranger (*gēr*) and the sojourner (*[wᵉ]tôšāb*). This strongly suggests that in the situation envisaged by these passages, the person in need is a pauper and that the money borrowed would have been for the bare necessities, not for any commercial undertaking (see Noth, 1966, 187).

In Lev 25:36-37 the word *nešek* is used of interest on money while the word *tarbît* refers to interest charged on food stuffs and paid in kind (Kennedy, 168; Chapman and Streane, 143; Noth, 1965, 191). According to Snaith (166; cf. Eichrodt, 239), the *nešek* type of interest was paid regularly, and in the end the original loan was repaid in a single payment, whereas in the case of the *tarbît* there was no interim payment of interest, but an increased sum was repaid in the end. McKane (626) and Tate (88), following Gemser, think that *nešek* may refer to the practice of discounting, where the borrower is given less than the full amount of the loan requested but is required to pay back the full amount. Lev 25, which is based on several central affirmations of Israel's faith and particularly on the concepts of justice and righteousness, is of great theological importance. Focusing on the sabbatical year and the Year of Jubilee, it shows a profound concern for personal rights and human dignity (Faley, 78). There is uncertainty, however, about whether some or all of these laws designed to prevent economic exploitation were carried out in practice or were a purely theoretical scheme for the alleviation of poverty. How is one to explain the fact that no historical observance of the directives to return land, resolve debts, and release slaves is recorded in the OT? There is intense debate (see, e.g., C. J. H. Wright) both about whether the regulations were considered real and practicable or academic and utopian, and about whether they formed an integral part of ancient law that later fell into disuse or were a late, idealistic formulation, a social blueprint never put into effect. Nevertheless, despite these uncertainties, the two major themes of Lev 25:1-55, viz., release/liberty and return/restoration, deserve to be acknowledged as a powerful guide and critique in the formulation of Christian biblical ethics in the modern world (C. J. H. Wright, 1028-29).

Regrettably, it seems that the laws against lending at interest were not strictly obeyed. The nom. is used in Prov 28:8, which condemns the rapaciousness and injustice of the ruthless wealthy who, in their insatiable appetite for money, capitalize on the misfortunes of their fellow Israelites. In itself, the possession of riches was not viewed as a mark of impiety, but wealth divorced from compassion and generosity was considered incompatible with righteousness and an affront to brotherhood (McKane, 626). The nom. is used in Ezek 22:12, part of an indictment against faithless Jerusalem (22:1-31) for violating the *tôrâ* (especially the central laws of the "Holiness Code" [Lev 17-26]). Various sins, all symptomatic of inner alienation from God (Eichrodt, 310), are catalogued, including the exaction of interest and increase (v. 12). The prophet declares that in response to the crimes they have committed against both God and their fellows, the people will be scattered in exile among the nations and all the impurities in Jerusalem will be destroyed (vv. 13-22). Yahweh's plaintive words "and you have forgotten me" (v. 12) indicate that social morality is dependent on remembrance of God (Cooke, 242; cf. Wevers, 174; Taylor, 167).

The nom. also occurs in Ezek 18:8, 13, 17 and Ps 15:5, which demand of the faithful the highest ethical standards. In Ezek 18:8, 17, the righteous man is defined as one who does not lend at interest (*nešek*) or take any increase (*tarbît*). In contrast, the wicked man is callous and more concerned with making a profit out of another's misfortune than with helping someone in time of need (v. 13). Speaking in a period characterized by cynicism, despair, and rebellious questioning of God's righteousness, Ezekiel assures his people of divine faithfulness and exhorts them to accept God's invitation to life by adhering strictly to his covenant demands. Ps 15, which may well have been an entrance liturgy used when a group of pilgrims arrived at the gates of the sanctuary, catalogues the requisite moral qualities of the person who may be admitted to the worshiping congregation. In v. 5, the man who loans money without charging interest is declared worthy of acceptance to the sanctuary and to personal communion with God.

P-B The nom. forms *nešek* ([bite], usury, interest) and *naškānît* (an animal wont to bite, biter) occur, as does the vb. *nāšak*, q. bite; take interest; ni. bite; hi. cause to bite; pay interest (Jastrow 2:940).

Borrowing and lending: → *lwh* II (borrow, lend, # 4278); → *nš'* I (lend against a pledge, # 5957); → *nšk* II (pay/exact interest, # 5967); → *'bṭ* (borrow, take a pledge from, # 6292); → *šmṭ* (release, remit, drop, throw down, # 9023)

Bibliography

G. A. Barrois, "Debt, Debtor," in *IDB*, 1962, 1:809-10; W. H. Brownlee, *Ezekiel 1-19*, WBC, 1986; A. T. Chapman and A. W. Streane, *The Book of Leviticus*, 1914; B. S. Childs, *Exodus: A Commentary*, OTL, 1974; B. Chilton, "Debts," in *ABD*, 1992, 2:114-16; R. Clifford, *Deuteronomy*, 1982; idem, "Exodus," in *NJBC*, 1990, 44-60; G. A. Cooke, *A Critical and Exegetical Commentary on the Book of Ezekiel*, ICC, 1967; D. Cox, *Proverbs With an Introduction to Sapiential Books*, 1982; P. C. Craigie, *The Book of Deuteronomy*, NICOT, 1983; H. Cunliffe-Jones, *Deuteronomy: Introduction and Commentary*, 1964; M. Dahood, *Psalms I:1-50. Introduction, Translation, and Notes*, AB, 1966; S. R. Driver, *The Minor Prophets: Nahum, Habakkuk, Zephaniah, Haggai, Zechariah, Malachi*, 1906; idem, *A Critical and Exegetical Commentary on Deuteronomy*, ICC, 3d ed., 1965; idem, *The Book of Exodus*, 1953; J. R. Dummelow, ed., *A Commentary on the Holy Bible*, 1909; J. H. Eaton, *Psalms: Introduction and Commentary*, 1972; W. Eichrodt, *Ezekiel: A Commentary*, 1970; R. J. Faley, "Leviticus," in *NJBC*, 1990, 61-79; D. D. Garland, "Habakkuk," in *BBC*, 1972, 7:245-69; N. K. Gottwald, "The Book of Deuteronomy," in *The Interpreter's One-Volume Commentary on the Bible*, 1971, 100-121; J. Gray, "The Book of Exodus," in *The Interpreter's One-Volume Commentary on the Bible*, 1971, 33-67; G. Harford, "Exodus," in *Peake*, 1964, 168-95; J. P. Hyatt, *Exodus*, 1971; A. R. S. Kennedy, *Leviticus and Numbers*, 1910; W. McKane, *Proverbs: A New Approach*, OTL, 1970; G. T. Manley and R. K. Harrison, "Deuteronomy," in *NBC*, 1972, 201-29; H. G. May and B. M. Metzger, eds., *The New Oxford Annotated Bible*, 1973; E. H. Merrill, *Deuteronomy*, NAC, 1994; P. D. Miller, *Deuteronomy*, 1990; M. Noth, *Leviticus: A Commentary*, 1965; idem, *Exodus: A Commentary*, 1966; R. D. Patterson, *Nahum, Habakkuk, Zephaniah*, 1991; D. F. Payne, *Deuteronomy*, 1985; E. B. Pusey, *The Minor Prophets With a Commentary*, 1891; J. J. M. Roberts, *Nahum, Habakkuk, and Zephaniah: A Commentary*, OTL, 1991; O. P. Robertson, *The Books of Nahum, Habakkuk, and*

Zephaniah, NICOT, 1991; H. W. Robinson, *Deuteronomy and Joshua*, 1907; J. C. Rylaarsdam, "The Book of Exodus: Introduction and Exegesis," *IB*, 1952, 1:831-1099; G. A. Smith, *The Book of Deuteronomy*, 1918; R. L. Smith, *Micah-Malachi*, WBC, 1984; N. H. Snaith, *Leviticus and Numbers*, 1967; D. M. G. Stalker, *Ezekiel: Introduction and Commentary*, 1968; L. E. H. Stephens-Hodge, "Habakkuk," in *NBC*, 1972, 767-72; M. E. Tate, "Proverbs," in *BBC*, 1972, 5:1-99; J. B. Taylor, *Ezekiel: An Introduction and Commentary*, TOTC, 1971; J. A. Thompson, *Deuteronomy: An Introduction and Commentary*, 1974; G. J. Wenham, *The Book of Leviticus*, NICOT, 1979; J. W. Wevers, *Ezekiel*, NCBC, 1969; C. J. H. Wright, "Jubilee, Year of," in *ABD*, 1992, 3:1025-30; G. E. Wright, "The Book of Deuteronomy: Introduction and Exegesis," *IB*, 1953, 2:309-537.

Robin Wakely

5968 (*nešek*, interest, usury), → # 5967

5969	נִשְׁכָּה

נִשְׁכָּה (*niškâ*), nom. storeroom(s), cell, room; living quarters, chamber (# 5969).

OT Part of the work on the Jerusalem wall was made opposite the living chambers/quarters of Meshullam, son of Berekiah (Neh 3:30; cf. Neh 13:7). The nom. also refers to a kind of collection/storage room for contributions, firstfruits, and tithes (12:44). The word is used in theologically nuanced contexts, for at this time the wall of Jerusalem was being built under the supervision of Nehemiah (Neh 3-4), and proper gifts, firstfruits, and tithes were being collected and stored for the priests and Levites according to instructions from the Torah (12:44).

Cellar: → *ḥānût* (vaulted cell, vault, dungeon, # 2844); → *niškâ* (storeroom(s), cell, room, # 5969); → *ṣ^{e}rîaḥ* (cellar, vault, pit, stronghold, # 7663)
Storehouse, treasure: → *'āsām* (stores, # 662); → *'āsōp* (store, # 667); → *'ṣr* (accumulate, amass, store up, # 732); → *gizbār* (treasurer, # 1601); → *genez* I (treasury, # 1709); → *ganzak* (treasury, # 1711); → *ḥsn* (be stored up, # 2889); → *kms* (stored up, # 4022); → *maṭmôn* (treasure [hidden], # 4759); → *misk^{e}nôt* (stores, # 5016); → *n^{e}kōt* (treasure house, # 5800); → *niškâ* (storeroom[s], cell, room, # 5969); → *piqqādôn* (deposit, # 7214); → *ṣpn* (hide, hidden, # 7621)

Eugene Carpenter/Michael A. Grisanti

5970	נשל

נשל (*nšl*), q. slip or drop off, draw off, clear away; pi. clear out (# 5970).

ANE Aram. *n^{e}šal*; Arab. *nasala*; Punic *nšl*, clear away.

OT The word occurs 7x in the OT, mostly in the q. stem. It can refer to an ax head slipping off its handle and causing the death of a bystander (Deut 19:5), or to olives wasting away and falling unused from their trees (Deut 28:40). The word can refer to removal of one's sandals, as with Moses before the burning bush (Exod 3:5) and Joshua in the presence of the commander of the Lord's army (Josh 5:15). In two occurrences of the q. and in the lone occurrence of the pi. the word refers to the clearing away of adversarial peoples, whether Canaanite nations from before Israel (Deut 7:1, 22) or Judeans from before Edom (2 Kgs 16:6).

P-B The Heb. word occurs in RL (in q., pi., ni., hi.) with the sense of to strike off or chip, slip or fall off. It may refer to the chipping of wood with an ax (e.g., *Tosef. Macc.* 2.6). A number of times it refers to limbs falling off a body due to sudden decay (e.g., *Lev. Rab.* 22:4; 37:4; *Gen. Rab.* 10:7). The Aram. word appears in the aphel in the Targumim (e.g., *Targ. Y.* Deut 24:1) with the sense of to send off. In the DSS the word may occur in 1QLiturgy of the Three Tongues of Fire 2.4, although the text is uncertain at this point. (See *DJD*, 1, 1955, 131, and plate XXX.) If the textual restoration of *lamed* is correct, *nšl* seems here to refer to the priest removing his shoes.

Sliding, slipping: → *m'd* (slip, slide, shake, totter, # 5048); → *nws* (flee, escape, slip away, # 5674); → *nšl* (slip off, drop, clear away, # 5970)

BIBLIOGRAPHY
E. Jenni, *Das hebräische Pi'el*, 1968, 144.

Richard A. Taylor

5971 (*nšm*, gasp), → # 5972

5972	נְשָׁמָה

נְשָׁמָה (n^e*šāmâ*), breath (# 5972); < נשׁם (*nšm*), gasp (# 5971).

OT 1. n^e*šāmâ* is used primarily as "breath" in rich poetic and theological passages. The creative breath of God (Gen 2:7) inspires breath in humans (Job 33:4; Prov 20:27; Isa 42:5; 57:16), inspires wise understanding (Job 32:8), and breathes out the frost (37:10). But the n^e*šāmâ* of God can also destroy the wicked (4:9) as easily as wood (Isa 30:33) and lay bare his own creations (2 Sam 22:16; Ps 18:15[16]).

2. The vb. *nšm* is used but once, to describe God's pursuit of Israel in judgment, namely his "panting" to crush them for their unfaithfulness (Isa 42:14).

Breath, life: → *hebel* I (breath, # 2039); → *nepeš* (breath, life, desire, # 5883); → n^e*šāmâ* (breath, # 5972); → *š'p* I (pant, gasp, # 8634)

D. C. Fredericks

5973	נשׁף

נשׁף (*nšp*), blow (# 5973); נֶשֶׁף (*nešep*), nom. twilight, darkness (# 5974); יַנְשׁוּף (*yanšûp*), nom. great owl (→ # 3568).

ANE The vb. is attested in Aram. *nšp*, and Arab. *nasafa*, as well as Akk. *našāpu*, blow away. The nom. is attested in Aram. n^e*šap* and *nišpā'*.

OT 1. The vb. occurs in the q. stem twice in the OT, only in poetry. It is used of the Lord's blowing on the Red Sea to drown the Egyptians (Exod 15:10), and of his blowing destruction on the crops of idolaters (Isa 40:24).

2. *nešep*, nom. twilight, darkness (# 5974). This nom. is possibly associated with the evening breeze and its accompanying darkness. This word occurs 12x in the OT, sometimes ∥ with, *'ereb*, evening (# 6847), *'^{a}pēlâ*, darkness (# 696), or *laylâ*, night (# 4326); and sometimes opposed to *bōqer*, morning (# 1332), *yôm*, day (# 3427), and *ṣoh^{o}rayim*, noon (# 7416). At times it refers to evening twilight or dusk: "At twilight (*nešep*), as the day was fading, as the dark of night set in" (Prov 7:9; see

also 1 Sam 30:17; 2 Kgs 7:5, 7; Job 24:15; Isa 21:4; 59:10). However, Toy regarded the passage in Proverbs to refer to the "darkness of the dread of night." Isaiah pronounced "woe to those who rise early in the morning to run after their drinks, who stay up late at night [lit. linger after dusk (*nešep*)] till they are inflamed with wine" (Isa 5:11). At times it refers to morning twilight or dawn: Job complained, "When I lie down I think, 'How long before I get up?' The night drags on, and I toss till dawn" (Job 7:4; see also Ps 119:147). At times it is used in const. with another word, much like an adj. in Eng.: "darkening hills" (lit., hills of twilight) (Jer 13:16), and "morning stars" (lit., stars of dawn) (Job 3:9).

Darkness: → *'ōpel* (darkness, gloom, # 694); → *'ešûn* (approach of darkness, # 854); → *ḥšk* (be, grow dark, grow dim, darken, conceal, confuse, # 3124); → *ṭuḥôt* (darkness, obscurity, inward parts, # 3219); → *kamrîr* (blackness, deep gloom, # 4025); → *laylâ* (night, # 4326); → *nešep* (twilight, darkness, # 5974); → *'wp* II (be dark, # 6415); → *'alāṭâ* (darkness, dusk, # 6602); → *'mm* II (darken, dim, # 6670); → *'arāpel* (deep darkness, thick darkness, heavy cloud, # 6906); → *ṣll* III (be/grow dark, cast a shadow, # 7511); → *ṣalmāwet* (darkness, shadow of death, # 7516); → *qdr* (be dark, mourn, # 7722)

BIBLIOGRAPHY

TWOT 2:605; C. H. Toy, *Proverbs*, ICC, 147.

James D. Price

5974	נֶשֶׁף

נֶשֶׁף (*nešep*), nom. dusk, twilight, dawn; darkness (# 5974); < נשׁף (*nšp*), blow (→ # 5973).

ANE The vb. *našāpu*, blow, is found in Akk., and the form *naššibtå* occurs in Sam.

OT The word is used of both the twilight of sunset (2 Kgs 7:5, 7; Job 24:15; Prov 7:9; Isa 5:11; 21:4; 59:10; Jer 13:16) and the twilight before dawn (Job 3:9; 7:4; Ps 119:147). In one text in particular (1 Sam 30:17), opinion is divided as to whether the word refers to the evening twilight or to the morning twilight.

1. There can be no certainty whether *nešep* in 1 Sam 30:17 means the first light of dawn or the evening twilight (see Smith, 248; Klein, 283). If Kirkpatrick (227), JB, NEB, REB, TEV, Wevers (1971a, 169), Ackroyd (1971a, 222-23), Philbeck (85-86), Baldwin (168), Klein (279), McCarter (430, 435), Hobbs (90), and Nelson (190) are correct, then David launched his attack on the Amalekites at early dawn. There are others, however, who argue that the assault began at dusk (Smith, 247-48; Bennett, 286; Dummelow, 195; RSV; NRSV; NIV). Kennedy (185), Smith (247-48), and Bennett (285-86) consider MT *lemoḥorātām* (of the next day) a copyist's error and maintain that David's slaughter of the enemy would have lasted only over the period before and after sunset of the same day. Caird (1035) is also of the opinion that *lemoḥorātām* cannot be original since the attack was a sudden one and cannot have lasted more than twenty-four hours. He suggests omitting *lemoḥorātām* or, following others (e.g., Kennedy, 185; Driver, 1966, 223), emending it so that it reads "to put them to the ban" (*leha ḥarimām*). Although this emendation is rejected by some (e.g., Philbeck, 86; cf. McKane, 1963, 168; Mauchline, 1971, 190), it is accepted by others (e.g., Ackroyd, 1971a, 223).

However, many scholars argue that it is incorrect to interpret the text as if it is saying that David gained a lightning victory. Ackroyd (1971a, 222-23), Herztberg (228), and Baldwin (168) take *mēhannešep* to mean from the dawn, and point out that the attack would have been most effective very early in the morning when the opposing troops would have been sleeping off the soporific effects of their carousing and least able to defend themselves. Baldwin (168) thinks that the fighting continued through until the afternoon of the following day when the sun was declining (cf. Klein, 279). However, others, while accepting that *nešep* here means early dawn, argue that the fighting is unlikely to have lasted two full days. Thus, e.g., Kirkpatrick (227) and Wevers (1971a, 169), who also read "from (the) dawn" for *mēhannešep*, argue that David's forces waited until the dawn of the following day before launching their attack and that the slaughter continued until sunset (or beyond) of the same day that battle was engaged (cf. Goldman, 179). A similar position is adopted by Philbeck (85-86), who also takes *hannešep* to mean the dawn, and who thinks that a single day of battle is more likely than two days of fighting. Hertzberg (228) points out that *'ereb*, which is given as the *terminus ad quem* of the battle, refers to the time when the sun is on the decline, i.e., from the middle of the day until it becomes dark (*laylâ* normally being reserved for the hours of darkness). He concludes that the battle may have lasted from the early morning twilight until the early, middle, or late afternoon of the same day.

2. In three texts, the word almost certainly means the first light of dawn (Job 3:9; 7:4; Ps 119:147). Coming perilously close to cursing God without actually saying the words (Good, 411), Job asks that the day of his birth be cursed, that the stars of its dawn be dark, and that it fail to see the light of the morning (Job 3:9; cf. Davidson, 24-25; Peake, 1905, 72; Driver, 1906, 7; Strahan, 53; Driver and Gray, 34-35; Irwin, 393; Pope, 30; Dhorme, 28; Andersen, 104; Janzen, 63; Clines, 68, 87; Hartley, 94; *pace* Franks, 349, who thinks the reference is to the stars of the twilight that end the night). Strahan (53), followed by others (e.g., Driver and Gray, 34; Pope, 30; Clines, 87-88; Hartley, 94) think the reference to the morning stars is to Venus and Mercury, which appear as the harbingers of the arrival of day and which, if darkened, would result in an endless night waiting for a dawn that would never come. Many (e.g., Dummelow, 295; Terrien, 925-26) maintain that the days of the year were thought to have an existence of their own, so that Job is not cursing a day that has long ceased to exist, but one that returns each year to blight his happiness and that of others. However, Clines (78-80, 83-84) argues that it is more likely that the focus, both here and in the previous v. (3), is on the original day of his birth. In this case, the malediction is a parody of a curse, and although its language is fierce, its power is wholly literary (Clines, 79).

The purpose of Job's malediction may have been either to give frank expression of his pain and grief (cf. Clines, 79-80), or to evoke pity, human and divine (Andersen, 101). Experiencing the creation as the very opposite of the "good, very good" of Gen 1, Job begins his maledictions with a parodic reversal of God's first word of creation recorded in Gen 1:3, "Let there be light" (Clines, 84; on the similarities and differences between Job 3:1-10 and Jer 20:14-18, see, Clines, 80-81). Fishbane (154) goes so far as to say that Job 3:1-13 is a "counter-cosmic incantation" aimed at reversing the world-ordering events of Gen 1. However, as Clines (81) points out, Job is less concerned with the entire created order than he is with those elements of it that were responsible for his own personal existence.

In Job 7:4, Job complains that, owing to his psychic and physical torment (Clines, 196), he spends the whole night not in deep, refreshing sleep, but in anguished tossing until the dawn (see Strahan, 79, 82; Driver and Gray, 68; Pope, 57; Hartley, 143; *pace* Dhorme, 98-99, who argues that *nešep* here means the twilight of evening).

The early morning twilight was a recognized time for communing with God (cf. Wisd 16:28; Anderson, 842). At the dawning of the light, a psalmist, beset by enemies who are far from the *tôrâ*, cries to God for help (Ps 119:147, 150).

3. In the majority of cases, the word refers to the evening twilight.

(a) During Ben-Hadad's siege of Samaria, which was repulsed by Yahweh's intervention, four lepers who were confined in isolation to the entrance to the gate of the city and who had decided to take the risk of defecting to the Syrians rather than face certain death from the famine, set off for the enemy's camp at evening twilight (2 Kgs 7:5; *pace* Wevers, 1971b, 200, and Nelson, 190-91, who think that *nešep* here refers to the first break in the darkness of the night). They found the Syrian camp deserted. Either because Yahweh had created the sound of chariots, horses, and many soldiers (so, e.g., Keil, 330-31; Nelson, 190), or as a result of a rumor of the approach of Hebrew reinforcements (so, e.g., Wevers, 1971b, 199; Honeycutt, 245; J. Gray, 524-25; Hobbs, 86, 91), the Syrians panicked and fled away in the twilight in disarray, abandoning all their tents, weapons, animals, and provisions (2 Kgs 7:7). Comic effect is created both by the coincidence of the four harmless lepers arriving at the front of the camp as the Syrians flee out the back and by the fact that it is the outcasts of society who open the way for the city to be relieved in fulfilment of the prophetic word given in vv. 1-2 (e.g., Hobbs, 91-92; Nelson, 190).

(b) A deeply disturbing vision of the fall of Babylon (Isa 21:2) caused Isaiah such psychological trauma that he suffered from insomnia. The evening twilight he longed for, normally a period of calm and quiet (and, possibly, of visionary communications), had become filled with dark foreboding and fear, depriving him of sleep (21:4). The suggestion of Mauchline (1970, 164-65) that the reference may be to the twilight of the prophet's life when he hoped to enjoy some peace and security does not commend itself.

The distraught prophet's anxiety has been variously explained. Some think it may have been caused by his anticipation of the repercussions Babylon's defeat would have for Judah (see Dummelow, 430) or for those Jews living in Babylonia (see Peake, 1920, 451). Kidner (602) thinks that Isaiah was showing empathy for the future exiles for whom Babylon was both prison and home. Others (see Thomson and Skinner, 76; Oswalt, 393) are of the view that the prophet was moved with compassion and empathy for the personal horrors to be experienced by Israel's enemies. G. B. Gray (353; cf. Scott) attributes the prophet's distress to the ecstatic state in which the vision was received. Kaiser (125) points out that it is not uncommon in the prophetic literature for the horror of a vision or word of disaster to have a profound physical effect on the recipient (cf. Jer 4:19-22; 6:24; 8:18-9:1[8:18-23]; 23:9; 30:5-7; Ezek 30:4, 9; Nah 2:11). Later, Kaiser continues, descriptions of the horror overcoming prophetic recipients of a vision became a stylistic device aimed at reinforcing the genuineness of their pronouncements. Ackroyd (1971b, 344) suggests that the prophet's anguish was caused by the overpowering nature of the divine word (cf. Kelley, 253), together with the uncertainty created when one great power overthrows another. Bright (503-4) thinks that the passage was written against the background of the events of 691-689 (cf. Wright, 61-62) or those of 652-648, in both of which periods Assyria was the dominant power in the region and Babylon was involved in a revolt. While linking the original context of the oracle to 689, Motyer (172) argues that on one level the horror of the vision pertains to the fall of the historical Babylon, but on another, it is describing the ultimate horror of Yahweh's final dealing with sin, its agents, and the world system in which it is embodied (174-75; cf. Seitz, 163-64).

(c) Evening twilight is sometimes associated with the outrageous conduct of those (the murderer, the thief, and the adulterer [Job 24:14-16]) who "rebel against the light" (Job 24:13; cf. John 3:19-20), i.e., who prefer to perpetrate their crimes stealthily under cover of the darkness. The adulterer waits for the dusk to conceal his identity (Job 24:15), and it is at dusk that the gullible youth takes to walking the streets near the house of the loose woman, the adventuress (Prov 7:9). In connection with the latter text, Cox (144) points out that twilight, that brief moment immediately before the darkness of night overwhelms the light of day, is used in the sapiential tradition to represent the half world of temptation that is being considered but that has not yet been entered. Included among the wicked denounced by Isaiah in a series of six reproaches (5:8-23) are the debauched carousers who imbibe liquor from early in the morning until late in the evening (*m*^{e}*'aḥ*^{a}*rê bannešep*, "who tarry late into the evening" [5:11; RSV]), with the result that their critical faculties, judgment, and sensitivity to responsibilities and values are dulled and their ability to discern the meaning of existence and the will and activity of God is severely impaired.

(d) Just as light is often used as a metaphor for God's salvation and of the prosperity and safety enjoyed by those living in true obedience to him, so blindness and darkness frequently symbolize rebellion against, denial of, and separation from God together with the distress and disaster resulting from the failure to abide by Yahweh's moral will (see McKenzie, 170). A last opportunity to repent is offered to wayward Judah in Jer 13:16: The defiantly disobedient people are urged to give glory to Yahweh (i.e., obey him) before he turns their light into impenetrable darkness and they become like those whose feet stumble "on the darkening hills" (*'al-hārê nāšep*). The reference here may be to travelers on mountain paths overtaken by the gathering gloom before reaching their destination (see Cunliffe-Jones, 112; Frost, 383; Cawley and Millard, 637; Green, 87); or to shepherds guarding their flocks on the mountains by night and waiting for the light of a dawn that may never come (see Carroll, 300; Thompson, 369); or to a flock of sheep marooned at night on precipitous crags, deserted by their shepherds, and awaiting the light of dawn when they can move with safety (cf. McKane, 1986, 301). In a later generation, the advent of the new age is delayed by those who are alienated from God, who have repudiated his love and who grope and stumble in the darkness of social and spiritual depravity, their noon becoming for them like the evening twilight, i.e., the light of their hope rapidly diminishing to the point of extinction (Isa 59:10; cf. Deut 28:29; Lam 4:14; Amos 5:18-20; John 3:19; 12:35-40).

P-B The vb. *nšp* (Aram. *n*^{e}*šap*), blow, breathe, occurs, as does the nom. *nešep* (Aram. *nišpā'*), [zephyr,] early morning; sunset (Jastrow 2:941).

Sunrise, dawn, sunset: → *'ôr* (light, daylight, dawn, lightning, # 240); → *zeraḥ* I (dawn, sunrise, # 2437); → *mābô'* (entrance, sunset, west, # 4427); → *ma'ᵃrāb* II (setting of the sun, west, # 5115); → *nešep* (dusk, twilight, dawn, darkness, # 5974); → *šaḥar* (pre-dawn twilight, # 8840)

BIBLIOGRAPHY

P. R. Ackroyd, *The First Book of Samuel*, CBC, 1971 (1971a); idem, "The Book of Isaiah," in *The Interpreter's One-Volume Commentary on the Bible*, 1971, 329-71 (1971b); F. I. Andersen, *Job: An Introduction and Commentary*, TOTC, 1976; A. A. Anderson, *The Book of Psalms. Vol. 2: Psalms 73-150*, NCBC, 1972; J. G. Baldwin, *1 and 2 Samuel: An Introduction and Commentary*, TOTC, 1988; W. H. Bennett, "I. and II. Samuel," in *Peake*, 1920, 273-93; J. Bright, "Isaiah-I," in *Peake*, 1964, 489-515; G. B. Caird, "The First and Second Books of Samuel: Introduction and Exegesis," in *IB*, 1953, 2:853-1176; R. P. Carroll, *Jeremiah: A Commentary*, OTL, 1986; F. Cawley and A. R. Millard, "Jeremiah," in *NBC*, 1972, 626-58; D. J. A. Clines, *Job 1-20*, WBC, 1989; D. Cox, *Proverbs With an Introduction to Sapiential Books*, OTM, 1982; H. Cunliffe-Jones, *Jeremiah: God in History*, Torch, 2nd ed., 1972; A. B. Davidson, *The Book of Job With Notes, Introduction and Appendix*, CBSC, 1962; E. Dhorme, *A Commentary on the Book of Job*, 1967; S. R. Driver, *Notes on the Hebrew Text and the Topography of the Books of Samuel With an Introduction on Hebrew Palaeography and the Ancient Versions and Facsimiles of Inscriptions and Maps*, 2d ed., 1966; idem, *The Book of Job in the Revised Version*, 1906; S. R. Driver and G. B. Gray, *A Critical and Exegetical Commentary on the Book of Job Together With a New Translation*, ICC, 1964; J. R. Dummelow, ed., *A Commentary on the Holy Bible*, 1909; M. Fishbane, "Jeremiah IV 23-26 and Job III 3-13: A Recovered Use of the Creation Pattern," *VT* 21, 1971, 151-67; R. S. Franks, "Job," in *Peake*, 1920, 346-65; S. B. Frost, "The Book of Jeremiah," in *The Interpreter's One-Volume Commentary on the Bible*, 1971, 372-404; S. Goldman, *Samuel: Hebrew Text & English Translation with an Introduction and Commentary*, Soncino, 1962; E. M. Good, "Job," in *HBC*, 1988, 407-32; G. B. Gray, *A Critical and Exegetical Commentary on the Book of Isaiah I-XXVII*, ICC, 1975; J. Gray, *I & II Kings: A Commentary*, OTL, 2d ed., 1970; J. L. Green, "Jeremiah," in *BBC*, 1972, 6:1-202; J. E. Hartley, *The Book of Job*, NICOT, 1988; H. W. Hertzberg, *I & II Samuel: A Commentary*, OTL, 1974; T. R. Hobbs, *2 Kings*, WBC, 1985; R. L. Honeycutt (with M. P. Matheney), "1-2 Kings," in *BBC*, 1971, 3:146-296; W. A. Irwin, "Job," in *Peake*, 1964, 391-408; J. G. Janzen, *Job*, Interp, 1985; O. Kaiser, *Isaiah 13-39: A Commentary*, OTL, 1974; C. F. Keil, *The Books of the Kings*, KD, 2d ed., ca. 1872; P. H. Kelley, "Isaiah," in *BBC*, 1972, 5:149-374; A. R. S. Kennedy, *Samuel*, CB, 1905; D. Kidner, "Isaiah," in *NBC*, 1972, 588-625; A. F. Kirkpatrick, *The First Book of Samuel, With Map, Notes and Introduction*, CBSC, 1899; R. W. Klein, *1 Samuel*, WBC, 1983; P. K. McCarter, *1 Samuel: A New Translation With Introduction, Notes and Commentary*, AB, 1980; W. McKane, *I & II Samuel: Introduction and Commentary*, Torch, 1963; idem, *A Critical and Exegetical Commentary on Jeremiah Volume 1: An Introduction and Commentary on Jeremiah I-XXV*, ICC, 1986; J. L. McKenzie, *Second Isaiah: Introduction, Translation, and Notes*, AB, 1968; J. Mauchline, *Isaiah 1-39*, Torch, 1970; idem, *1 and 2 Samuel*, NCB, 1971; J. A. Motyer, *The Prophecy of Isaiah: An Introduction & Commentary*, 1993; R. D. Nelson, *First and Second Kings*, Interp, 1987; J. N. Oswalt, *The Book of Isaiah Chapters 1-39*, NICOT, 1986; A. S. Peake, *Job*, CB, 1905; idem, "Isaiah I-XXXIX," in *Peake*, 1920, 436-59; B. F. Philbeck, "1-2 Samuel," in *BBC*, 1971, 3:1-145; M. H. Pope, *Job: Introduction, Translation, and Notes*, AB, 3d ed., 1979; R. B. Y. Scott, "Isaiah XXI:1-10: The Inside of a Prophet's Mind," *VT* 2, 1952, 278-82; C. R. Seitz, *Isaiah 1-39*, Interp, 1993; H. P. Smith, *A Critical and Exegetical Commentary on the*

Books of Samuel, ICC, 1961; J. Strahan, *The Book of Job Interpreted*, 1913; S. Terrien, "The Book of Job: Introduction and Exegesis," in *IB*, 1954, 3:875-1198; J. A. Thompson, *The Book of Jeremiah*, NICOT, 1987; C. H. Thomson and J. Skinner, *Isaiah I-XXXIX*, 1921; J. W. Wevers, "The First Book of Samuel," in *The Interpreter's One-Volume Commentary on the Bible*, 1971, 155-69 (1971a); idem, "The Second Book of the Kings," in *The Interpreter's One-Volume Commentary on the Bible*, 1971, 197-207 (1971b); G. E. Wright, *Isaiah*, LBC, 1965.

Robin Wakely

5975	נשׁק

נשׁק (*nšq* I), q. kiss; pi. kiss (# 5975); נְשִׁיקָה (n^{e}*šîqâ*), nom. kiss (# 5965). *HALAT* enters the hi. part. מַשִּׁיקוֹת(*maššîqôt*), touching (only in Ezek 3:13), under *nšq* II (# 5976); while BDB and Even-Shoshan have it as the hi. of *nšq* I with the same meaning.

ANE Cognate vbs. attested in Ugar (*nšq*), Aram. (*nšq*), Akk. *našāqu,* all meaning kiss; this favors an etymon **nšq*. The Arab. cognate is problematic: BDB connect with *nasaqa,* to fasten, arrange in order (favored by other cognates); while *HALAT* connect with *našiqa,* to smell (because Kopf, 265-67, connects *nasaqa* with *nšq* II). The unusual phonology of the *HALAT* arrangement is then unexplained.

OT 1. *Syntax.* Three syntactic patterns are found: (a) reciprocal; only q., Ps 85:10[11]: *<A> <B> nāš*^{e}*qû,* "*A* and *B* kiss each other;" (b) with accusative or suffix, q.; for pi., see below on Ps 2:12: *<A> nšq ('et-) <B>,* and (c) with dative object; q. and pi.: *<A> nšq l*^{e} *<B>,* both "*A* kissed B."

2. *Usage.* The key to the significance of the kiss is who is kissing whom or what, and in what social setting. (a) Most examples are of people kissing relatives or friends to express affection: e.g., Jacob (as Esau) kissing Isaac (Gen 27:26-27); Laban kissing Jacob, then Jacob's wives and children (Gen 29:13; 31:28, 55[32:1]); David and Jonathan (1 Sam 20:41, *wayyišš*^{e}*qû 'îš 'et-rē'ēhû* "and they kissed one another," emphasizing reciprocity); see also Gen 33:4; 45:15; 48:10; 50:1; Exod 4:27; 18:7; Ruth 1:9, 14; 2 Sam 14:33; 15:5; 19:39[40]; 1 Kgs 19:20; Prov 24:26. Pretended affection is seen in Joab's kiss for Amasa (2 Sam 20:9; cf. Prov 27:6). Many of these are in public without embarrassment. Jacob's kiss of Rachel at the well (Gen 29:11), though some see romantic overtones in it, is explained in v. 12 as an act of a kinsman's affection. Probably Samuel's kiss for Saul at his anointing (1 Sam 10:1) should be in this category, rather than be seen as an act of homage; in Samuel-Kings kings are supposed to be subject to prophets (see 1 Sam 15, and Long, 135-36). In Ps 85:10[11] personified righteousness and peace kiss each other.

(b) The romantic kiss appears in S of Songs 1:2, where the woman wishes her lover would kiss her. Such displays of affection were reserved for private contexts: in 8:1 she wishes he were her brother so she could kiss him outdoors without shame. Thus, the "wayward wife" is shockingly brazen when she kisses her paramour in the street (Prov 7:13; bad enough that she is adulterous but in public too!).

(c) Kissing can also express religious homage: e.g., Israelite mouths have not kissed Baal (1 Kgs 19:18; cf. Job 31:27; Hos 13:2).

3. *Problem passages.* In Ps 2:12 heathen kings are told *našš*^{e}*qû bar,* "Kiss the Son" (NIV). *HALAT* favors emending the problematic *bar* to *b*^{e}*raglāyw* to get "kiss his feet" (cf. RSV), while others (e.g., Hakham [8-9], who also considers the otherwise

unattested meaning, purity) parse it as an adverb meaning "purely"; but (a) *nšq* does not govern its object with b^e-; (b) the adverbial construction leaves an unspecified object, which is not an attested pattern for *nšq*; (c) a kiss can express religious homage (usage c above), and the "son" of this psalm deserves it (vv. 2, 7, 8); and (d) the referent for *bar* is "son" in the context (v. 7; see Craigie [64] for discussion of this apparent "Aramaism"). The difficult *w^e'al-pîkā yiššaq kol-'ammî* (Gen 41:40), does not conform to the normal syntax of *nšq* (see Delitzsch, 300); hence the suggestion of Kitchen (noted with approval in Vergote, 97 n.1; cf. Redford, 166 n.4) is most helpful: he compares Egyptian *sn-t3*, kiss the earth, to render homage or submission, yielding for Gen 41:40 "and according to your command shall all my people kiss [the earth in submission]."

P-B In the DSS the vb. appears only in CD 13:3, in a form dependent on Gen 41:40; it does not appear in the Heb. frgs. of Sir, but probably underlies 29:5 (see Segal ad loc.), where one kisses a lender's hand to express servility.

NT The NT has examples of usage: e.g., Judas' kiss, Matt 26:46-49 par. (cf. 2 Sam 20:9!); the "holy kiss" within the "family" of believers; and perhaps Luke 7:38, 45 (the woman kissing Jesus' feet). The RL provides examples of the continued use of the Heb. words, along the lines of BH (Jastrow, 940-42).

BIBLIOGRAPHY

ABD 4:89-92; *HDB* 3:5-6; *ISBE* 3:43-44; *TWAT* 5:676-80; *TWOT* 2:606; J. M. Cohen, "An Unrecognized Connotation of *nšq peh* with Special Reference to Three Biblical Occurrences," *VT* 32, 1982, 416-24; P. C. Craigie, *Psalms 1-50*, WBC, 1983; F. Delitzsch, *Genesis*, (Engl) 1894; A. Hakham, *Sēfer T^{e}hillîm*, Da'at Miqra, 1979; E. Jenni, *Das hebräische Pi'el*, 1968, 148-49; K. A. Kitchen, "The Term *nšq* in Genesis xli.40," *ExpTim* 69:1, Oct. 1957, 30; L. Kopf, "Arabische Etymologien und Parallelen zum Bibelwörterbuch," *VT* 9, 1959, 247-87; V. P. Long, *The Reign and Rejection of King Saul*, SBLDS 118, 1989; A. A. Macintosh, "A Consideration of the Problems Presented by Psalm ii.11 and 12," *JTS* n.s. 27, 1976, 1-14; D. B. Redford, *A Study of the Biblical Story of Joseph*, SVT 20, 1970; M. Z. Segal, *Sēfer Ben Sîrā' Haššālēm*, 1958; J. Vergote, *Joseph en Égypte*, 1959; C. Westermann, *Genesis 37-50*, BKAT, 1982 (Engl 1986).

C. John Collins

5976 נשק

נשׁק (*nšq* II), vb. q. part. const. pl. armed (3x in MT; # 5976; נֶשֶׁק (*nešeq* I), nom. weapon(s), armory, battle, fray (10x in MT; # 5977).

ANE 1. *Philology*. The nom. is semantically connected to the root *nšq*, meaning to arm, to be equipped [for war]. Ironically, the same root can have the meaning to kiss (cf. *nšq* I; # 5975). Many have seen a connection between the two seemingly opposite meanings via the Arab. cognate, which has the meaning fasten together, arrange in order (BDB, 676; *TWOT* 2:606).

2. *History*. The second millennium was apparently the most important period in the history of the development of armaments. The innovations that took place at this time did not change radically until the advent of gunpowder. For example, the beginning of the biblical period witnessed the invention of the composite bow, the sickle sword, the coat of mail, the battering ram, and the horse-drawn war chariot. Other

weapons like the spear and sling underwent improvement during this period (*World History of the Jewish People*, 128). During the early Israelite period the Canaanites and Philistines enjoyed technological superiority over the Hebrews, which resulted in their continued occupation of the lowlands. This situation was especially due to their use of iron chariots (Judg 1:19; 4:3; Hobbs, 111). With the rise of the united monarchy and Israel's entrance into the Iron Age, weapons of all kinds became much more numerous among the Hebrews. The subjugation of the Philistines by David broke their monopoly over the manufacture of metal objects, and the weapons industry came under the control of the king (Hobbs, 112; cf. 1 Sam 8:12). From this time on the use of conventional weapons by the Israelites is well attested.

3. *Description*. ANE armaments may be categorized in terms sim. to those of the modern day: offensive and defensive weaponry. Offensive weaponry can be further subdivided into three categories. Long-range weapons consisted of the sling (*qela'* → # 7845), the bow (*qešet* → # 8008), and later the catapult. Medium-range weapons included the javelin and lighter spear (*ḥ^{a}nît* → # 2851). These long- and medium-range weapons served as artillery and were thus used to initiate the conflict. Short-range weapons were then used in hand-to-hand combat and consisted of the larger spear (*ḥ^{a}nît* → # 2851), the sword and dagger (cf. *ḥereb* # 2995), and the axe and the mace (unattested in OT; cf. Yadin, 1:6; Gonen, 14; Hobbs, 109-27). The chariot (*merkābâ* → # 5324) and battering ram (*kar* → # 4119; *q^{e}bōl* → # 7692) were deployed in cavalry and siege operations, respectively. Defensive armaments consisted of the helmet, coat of mail, girdle (*ḥgr* → # 2520), greaves (*miṣḥâ*, # 5196), and shield (*māgēn* → # 4482).

OT 1. In the MT, the state of being armed for battle is sometimes reflected by several terms: *nšq* (1 Chron 12:2; 2 Chron 17:17; Ps 78:9 [LXX 77:9]); *ḥmš*, be fully armed for battle (→ # 2821); *ḥlṣ*, arm (→ # 2741); *ḥgr*, put on arms (→ # 2520); *šlp*, overthrow (# 8990), etc. In the vast majority of these instances the Heb. terms describe a state of readiness for conflict (cf. Eph 6:11-17). That the verbal form occurs so seldom may suggest that it is derived from the noun *nešeq*. This term is translated variously as weapon(s) (1 Kgs 10:25; 2 Kgs 10:2; 2 Chron 9:24; Job 20:24; Isa 22:8; Ezek 39:9, 10), armory (Neh 3:19), and battle/fray (Job 39:21; Ps 140:7[8]). Most of these passages use the term lit. Ps 140:7[8], however, is highly poetic, indicating the superiority of God's power over human weapons of destruction. Isa 22:8 occurs in a context that sets up the typical contrast between self-reliance and reliance upon God (cf. also Deut 20:1; Judg 7:2; 1 Sam 17:45, 47; Ps 2:12; 20:7[8]; 33:16-7; 44:1-3[2-4], 5-7[6-8]; 60:12[14]; Isa 63:1-9; Zech 4:6, etc.). Ezek 39:9-10 speaks futuristically of a time when the abandonment and destruction of weapons represents victory and peace brought by God (cf. Ps 46:9[10]; 76:3[4]; Isa 2:4; Ezek 39:3; Hos 2:18; Mic 4:3-4; 5:10; Zech 9:10, etc.).

Implements are often referred to collectively in the OT by the terms *kēlîm* (Gen 27:3; 49:5; 1 Sam 16:21; 17:54; 2 Sam 23:37, etc.), *k^{e}lê milḥāmâ* (Deut 1:41; Judg 18:11, 16, 17; 1 Sam 8:12; 2 Sam 1:27; Jer 21:4; 51:20, etc.), or *nešeq*. Other words for armament are: בֵּית כְּלִי (*bêt k^{e}lî*), nom. const. armory (2x in MT; # 2045+3998); כּוֹבַע (*kôba'*), nom. helmet(s) (6x in MT; # 3916); מִצְחָה (*miṣḥâ*), nom. const. [?] (hapleg; # 5196); סִרְיוֹן (*siryôn*), nom. armor (2x in MT; # 6246); קוֹבַע (*qôba'*), nom.

helmet(s) (2x in MT; # 7746); שִׁרְיוֹן (*širyôn*), nom. (coat[s] of) armor (5x in MT; # 9234); שִׁרְיָן (*širyān*), nom. armor, breastplate (3x in MT; cf. # 9234).

With the development of a standing army in the monarchial period, weaponry became more standardized. It was the responsibility of the king to ensure the manufacture and issue of conventional weapons (1 Sam 8:9, 12; 2 Chron 14:8[7]; 25:5; 26:14; 32:5). These weapons were often stored in a special place when not in use, called the "armory" (*bêt k^elî*, 2 Kgs 20:13; Isa 39:2; *nešeq*, Neh 3:19). At times, even the temple and the palace served as repositories for armaments (cf. 1 Kgs 10:16-7; 2 Kgs 11:10; 2 Chron 23:9; Isa 22:8, etc.).

On the basis of biblical and archaeological evidence it appears that the emphasis of the Israelite armies was on offensive rather than defensive weaponry. For example, the Bible has much to say about implements such as the sword and the spear. In comparison, there is little said to suggest that the wearing of armor was emphasized until the time of Uzziah (Hobbs, 110, 127; cf. 2 Chron 26:14; Neh 4:16[10]; Jer 46:4 [LXX 26:4]; 51:3 [LXX 28:3]). When armor is mentioned, it is employed by either foreigners (1 Sam 17:5) or by the elite (1 Sam 17:38; 1 Kgs 22:34; 2 Chron 18:33; Hobbs, 132). Armor was costly and sophisticated (Hobbs, 127, 131; Yadin 1:15). The scaled armor described in the Bible was heavy, often comprising 400-600 large plates of metal, which were attached with great difficulty to a leather undercoat (*EncJud* 16:266, 269; Gonen, 77, 79). Originally armor seems to have been developed to free the hands of charioteers from having to hold a shield, thus enabling them to drive and wield the bow (Hobbs, 131-32; *World History of the Jewish People*, 133; cf. 1 Kgs 22:34). It was eventually employed by the infantry (1 Sam 17:5, 38), but only became popular in Israel in the later monarchial period (2 Chron 26:14). That the Heb. word for armor is attested by three variant spellings (*siryôn* [# 6246]; *širyôn* [# 9234]; *širyān*) suggests a foreign origin. Figurative use of the term is restricted to Isa 59:17 (cf. Eph 6:14).

2. Apparently the helmet has a history par. to that of body armor. It originated outside Israel (Hobbs, 128-30), was originally made of leather and later metal (Warry, 12, 14; Yadin 1:134-35), was primarily the possession of the upper class (1 Sam 17:38), and became a conventional form of personal defense in Israel only in the late monarchial period (2 Chron 26:14). The term seldom appears in the Bible and was usually possessed by foreign armies (1 Sam 17:5; Jer 46:4 [LXX 26:4]; Ezek 23:14; 27:10; 38:5). Its two spellings (*kôbâ* [# 3916]; *qôbâ* [# 7746]) suggest that it also is a loanword (Hobbs, 128; *TWOT* 1:432). In Isa 59:17 God is pictured as donning the "helmet of righteousness" in arming himself for the defense of humanity. When couched in such terms, it would appear that the prophet is describing salvation as the crowning act of God. The ultimate preparation for new life in the spirit and the inevitable conflict that follows in the life of the Christian is described in sim. terms (Eph 6:17).

The term "greaves" is of interest in that it appears only in the description of Goliath's armor (1 Sam 17:6). That it appears in the sing. in the MT renders the term an even greater challenge, leading some to question the traditional translation (Hobbs, 132). It is well within the conventions of Heb. (and G; cf. Polybius 6:23, greave) diction, however, to speak of things pl. in terms of a collective sing. This is the way the ancient versions understood the term, which seems to require a pl. due to the context, "on his *legs* he wore bronze greaves." It is also possible that the Masoretes should have vocalized the term *miṣḥōt*. Although most ANE soldiers are generally pictured bare-legged (Yadin, 2:388, 422-3, etc.), there is evidence that some Assyrian soldiers wore leg coverings (Hobbs, 132). Because of the ethnic connection between the Philistines and the Aegean peoples, however, it is even more important to note that bronze greaves from 1400 BC were found at Dendra, on the Greek mainland. They are also mentioned prominently in the writings of Homer and were still being worn by Greek infantrymen as late as their wars against the Persians (Warry, 12, 14, 35). Because the Bible uses an unknown term to describe an unfamiliar object in a well-known passage such as this, and because its existence is so clearly documented as being a unique possession of Goliath's people group, its occurrence here evidences the historical accuracy of the account.

P-B/NT From Qumran, the most informative passage on the armaments of this time is found in 1QM 5:3-14. Many commentators suggest that the weaponry described here more closely resembles that of the Greco-Roman world than the biblical world, though Davies urges caution (*1QM, The War Scroll from Qumran*, 12, 58). Other important descriptions may be found in Polybius 6:23; 1 Macc 6:35; and esp. Josephus, *Wars* 3:93-95, who uses G terms sim. to those found in Luke 11:22; Rom 13:12; Eph 6:11-17; Rev 9:9; cf. 2 Cor 10:4.

Battle: → *lḥm* I (do battle, fight, # 4309); → *nšq* II (be armed, # 5976); → *'rk* (set, put in rows, enter into battle, # 6885); → *q^e rāb* (battle, # 7930)

BIBLIOGRAPHY

TWOT 2:1435; P. Davies, *1QM, The War Scroll from Qumran*, 1977; *EncJud* 16:266-82; R. Gonen, *Weapons of the Ancient World*, 1975; T. R. Hobbs, *A Time for War*, 1989; B. Mazar, ed., *World History of the Jewish People: Patriarchs*, vol. 2, part 1:127-59, 1970; J. G. Warry, *Warfare in the Classical World*, 1980; Y. Yadin, *The Art of Warfare in Biblical Lands*, 1963.

W. E. Nunnally

5977 (*nešeq* I, weapon, armory, battle, fray), → # 5976

5978 (*nešeq* II, fragrant substance [myrrh?]), → # 8379

5979	נֶשֶׁר

נֶשֶׁר (*nešer*), נְשַׁר (*n^e šar*), vulture (eagle) (# 5979).

ANE The lexeme is well attested throughout the Sem. languages: Ugar. *nšr,* Akk. *naš/sru*, Syr. *nešrā'*, Arab. *na/isr.*

OT This word appears 28x in OT and refers to various kinds of eagles or vultures. It is advisable to translate the term according to the context, i.e., either vultures or eagles; e.g., when *nešer* is said to have baldness of head and neck, it is the vulture (see *Fauna and Flora in the Bible*, 1980, 83-84). In Mic 1:16, *nešer* is more easily identified with the griffon vulture.

Apart from its being unclean (Lev 11:13), probably because of its making contact with carcasses and blood, vultures appear figuratively in the descriptions of God's strength, vigor, and gentleness in the handling of his people (Exod 19:4; Deut 32:11). The vulture plays a significant role in the description of Ezekiel's vision of God's glory (Ezek 1:10; 10:14). In other passages vultures are used as metaphors for swiftness

(2 Sam 1:23; Job 9:26; Jer 4:13; Lam 4:19), high-flying (Prov 23:5; Obad 4), soaring on wings (Job 39:27; Isa 40:31), ever-renewing might (Ps 103:5), pride (Jer 49:16; Obad 4), and atrociousness in attacking preys (Jer 48:40; 49:22; Hos 8:1; Hab 1:8).

P-B In DSS *nešer* appears in 1QpHab 3:6-12 and 4Q504, 6:7. LXX consistently renders *nešer* as *aetos,* which in the NT appears in the description of judgmental scenes (Matt 24:28; Luke 17:37) and as one of the four living creatures (Rev 4:7), a reminder of Ezekiel's vision (Ezek 1).

Birds, flying creatures: → *'br* (fly, # 87); → *bêṣâ* (egg, # 1070); → *barbur* (species of fowl, # 1350); → *gôzāl* (young bird, # 1578); → *dgr* (hatch eggs, # 1842); → *ḥ^{a}sîdâ* (stork, # 2884); → *yônâ* I (dove, # 3433); → *ya'^{a}nâ* (ostrich, eagle-owl?, # 3613); → *kānāp* (wing, skirt, outermost edge, # 4053); → *nešer/n^{e}šar* (vulture [eagle], # 5979); → *'ôp* (flying creatures, # 6416); → *'ayiṭ* (birds of prey [collective], # 6514); → *'ōrēb* I (raven, # 6854); → *ṣippôr* I (birds, # 7606); → *qōrē'* I (partridge, # 7926); → *ś^{e}lāw* (quails, # 8513)

BIBLIOGRAPHY

EMiqr 5:976-78; *TWAT* 5:680-89; M. Greenberg, *Ezekiel 1-20*, 1983.

N. Kiuchi

5980	נשת

נשת (*nšt*), q. be dry, parched, fail; ni. be dried up (# 5980).

OT The vb. occurs 3x, possibly 4x. The throat is dry or parched (Isa 41:17), the strength of the warrior fails (Jer 51:30), and the waters of the river dry up (Isa 19:5). If the word in question in Jer 18:14 is emended (the *š* and *t* are reversed, *yinnāt^{e}šû* becomes *yinnāš^{e}tû*), then the passage reads (NIV), "Do its cool waters from distant sources ever cease to flow?"

Dry, withering, parched: → *'bl* II (dry up, # 62); → *baṣṣārâ* (dearth, destitution, # 1314); → *zrb* (cease, dry up, # 2427); → *ḥrb* I (be dry or desolate, ruined, # 2990); → *ḥrr* II (be parched, # 3081a); → *ybš* (be dry, dried up, withered, dry up, # 3312); → *mll* I (wither, be dry, # 4908); → *nšt* (dry, parched, # 5980); → *qml* (wither, become moldy, musty, infected w. insects, # 7857)

Roy E. Hayden

5981 (*ništ^{e}wān*, letter), → Writing

5983	נתח

נתח (*ntḥ*), pi. to cut up into pieces (# 5983); nom. נֵתַח (*nētaḥ*), piece of meat of animal or persons (# 5984).

ANE Arab. *nataḥa*, remove hair; Tigre. *natḥa*, tear out.

OT 1. The vb. *ntḥ* is used in a cultic context, signifying the process of cutting animals into parts (Exod 29:17; Lev 1:6, 12; 8:20), each time referring to the preparation of a (whole) burnt offering. The story of the Levite's concubine (Judg 19:9; 20:6) and of Saul's cutting up of two oxen have ritualistic overtones. The people were threatened with death, if they did not rally to the cause.

2. The nom. *nētaḥ* is often found as a cognate nom. to the vb. The parable in Ezek 24:4-6 refers to the people of Jerusalem as pieces *(nētaḥ)* that will be both boiled and then cast out indiscriminately.

P-B Mish. Heb., split up, cut up, carve up; Jew. Aram., tear down, pull down; snatch away.

Cutting, destruction, extermination, shearing, trimming: → *bṣʻ* (cut away, get gain, cut off, break up, # 1298); → *brʼ* III (clear out trees, cut, destroy, # 1345); → *btr* (cut into pieces, # 1439); → *gdʻ* (cut short, # 1548); → *gzh* (bring forth, # 1602); → *gzz* (cut, shear, # 1605); → *gzr* I (cut, take away, # 1615); → *grz* (be cut off, # 1746); → *grʻ* I (cut out, reduce, # 1757); → *ḥlp* II (cut through, pierce, # 2737); → *ksḥ* (cut, cut down, # 4065); → *krsm* (make cropped, trimmed off, # 4155); → *krt* (cut, cut off, exterminate, cut a covenant, circumcise, # 4162); → *melqāḥāyim* (snuffers for trimming/cleaning of lights/lamps, # 4920); → *nqp* I (cut/chop down, destroy, # 5937); → *ntḥ* (cut in pieces, # 5983); → *qṣb* (cut off, shear, # 7892); → *šsp* (hew into pieces, # 9119); → *tzz* (cut away, # 9372)

Eugene Carpenter

5984 (*nētaḥ*, piece), → # 5983

5985	נָתִיב

נָתִיב (*nātîb*), path (# 5985); נְתִיבָה (*n^e tîbâ*), path, way (# 5986).

OT Closely akin to *derek* and *'ōraḥ* but with the meaning path, as opposed to journey, is *nātîb* and its related fem. form, *n^e tîbâ*. These apparently derive from a vb. *ntb*, which, if cognate to Arab. *ntb*, may suggest "to be raised up, to be prominent"; that is, the elevation of a pathway above the surrounding terrain. The vb. is never attested in the OT, however. A Ugar. cognate *ntb(t)* occurs a couple times with the same general sense as the Heb. noms. (*WUS*, # 1870).

1. The theological value of this term lies in its use as a metaphor for lifestyle, pattern of behavior, or course of life. God's ways can be described as a *nātîb* as well as a *derek* or *'ōraḥ*. The pathway of human life is similarly and more commonly so designated. Thus the psalmist, in the former case, understands his covenant relationship with Yahweh in terms of walking in the path, *nātîb*, i.e., within covenant stipulations (*miṣwôt*) (Ps 119:35). Job sees this path as one of light (Job 24:13), illuminated by the revelation of God's own word (Ps 119:105). Wisdom, as a personification representing God himself, is said by the wise man to provide paths (*n^e tîbôt*) of peace, that is, a life characterized by wholeness and leading to a destination of ultimate well-being (Prov 3:17).

2. As for human ways, as always the OT speaks of them as being either righteous or evil. But life in general is also seen as a pathway, as both *derek* and *'ōraḥ* make clear. In accordance with this understanding *nātîb/n^e tîbâ* occurs in the Wisdom literature especially as a picture of human experience. In fact, the *nātîb/n^e tîbâ* complex, as opposed to its synonyms, is seldom used apart from a metaphorical way. Bildad says that the evil man encounters traps in the way of life (Job 18:10). Job must concede that God has made his pathway dark (19:8). Moreover, his enemies have broken up his path, making the journey of life exceedingly difficult (30:13). (→ Job: Theology)

David was aware, however, that though the enemy might try to ensnare him along the way, Yahweh knew his path and therefore could guide him unerringly (Ps 142:3[4]). This is also the promise that inspired the prophets as they looked to a day of future deliverance. Yahweh says that he will bring the blind by a way (*derek*) they know not and lead them through an unfamiliar path (*n*e*tîbâ*) (Isa 42:16). For the disobedient, however, life will not be so smooth and easy, for Yahweh will hedge off their way (*'ōraḥ*) with thorns and wall off their path (*n*e*tîbâ*) with a barrier (Hos 2:6[8]).

3. The way of the righteous is the way of wisdom who, personified again, says that she provides righteousness (*ṣ*e*dāqâ*) and justice (*mišpāṭ*) (Prov 8:20). Only in this way (*'ōraḥ*) is life to be found (Prov 12:28), or, as the parallel line puts it, only in this pathway (*derek n*e*tîbâ*) is there "no death" (Dahood, 340). These, Jeremiah says, are the paths of old (*n*e*tîbôt 'ôlām*), the "good way" (*derek haṭṭôb*) (Jer 6:16).

As for the wicked, their path is to be avoided (Prov 1:15). A striking example is that of the harlot (probably folly, the antithesis of lady wisdom), against whom the young man in Proverbs is repeatedly warned. He must not turn aside to her way (*derek*) or go astray in her path (*n*e*tîbâ*, Prov 7:25). Isaiah, speaking of sinners more generally, points out that they do not know the way (*derek*) of peace and there is no justice in their path (*n*e*tîbâ*, Isa 59:8). In fact, Jeremiah adds, Israel's sinful nature, having wandered from the ways of old, has become sidetracked to a path (*n*e*tîbâ*) that was not constructed as a proper roadway (Jer 18:15).

Path, way: → *'rḥ* (be on the road, wander, # 782); → *derek* (way, distance, journey, manner, # 2006); → *madrēgâ* (steep way, # 4533); → *m*e*sillâ* (highway, # 5019); → *ma'gāl* II (track, # 5047); → *miš'ôl* (hollow way, # 5469); → *nātîb* (path, # 5985); → *pls* I (clear way, make a path, # 7142); → *š*e*bîl* (path, # 8666); → *š*e*pî* I (track, # 9155)

Wisdom, knowledge, skill: → *byn* (understand, discern, # 1067); → *ḥkm* (be wise, become wise, act wisely, # 2681); → *yd'* (understand, know, # 3359); → *ysr* I (admonish, correct, discipline, # 3579); → *leqaḥ* (teaching, gift of persuasion, # 4375); → *m*e*zimmâ*, consideration, plan, evil plan, plot, # 4659); → *'oqbâ* (cunning, craftiness, # 6817); → *'rm* II (be cunning, be crafty, make crafty, # 6891); → *śkl* I (have success, understand, make wise, act with insight, # 8505); → *taḥbulôt* (advice, guidance, # 9374)

BIBLIOGRAPHY

M. Dahood, "Hebrew-Ugaritic Lexicography VII," *Bib* 50, 1969, 340.

Eugene H. Merrill

5986 (*n*e*tîbâ*, path), → # 5985

5987	נָתִין

נָתִין (*nātîn*), temple servant (# 5987). Aram. נְתִין (*n*e*tîn*), temple servant (# 10497); < נתן (*ntn*), give, present, offer, allow, permit, surrender, deliver, set, put, place (→ # 5989).

ANE Ugar. *ytmn* (*UT*, 301:I:1 = UM Glossary, 1169) refers to members of a guild. In the Aram. Hatra inscription (*KAI*, 243), *ntyn'* describes King 'TLW as given/dedicated (to the temple).

OT *n*e*tînîm* is a designation for the lowest order of temple personnel, a term appearing exclusively in postexilic texts (1x in 1 Chron, 8x in Ezra [Ezra 7:24 in Aram.], 9x in Neh), always with the definite article and never in the singular. The KJV simply transliterated the Heb. word as Nethinims, but more recent translations render it "temple servants." Derived from the vb. *ntn*, give, in its cultic sense (cf. *TWAT* 5:706-12), the term describes those who have been given or devoted to service in the sanctuary, this interpretation being confirmed by the G translation of 1 Chron 9:2. This designation may be compared with (and possibly derived from) the term *n^e tunîm* (the given ones; cf. the K of Ezra 8:17) used in Num 3:9; 8:16, 19; 18:6 to describe the Levites as belonging to God but given as a gift (18:6) to the Aaronic priests. According to Ezra 8:20, the temple servants, in turn, were appointed (lit., given) by David and his officials to serve the Levites. Their origin is, thus, chronologically close to that of the sons of Solomon's servants, with whom they are mentioned (Ezra 2:58; Neh 7:60; 11:3).

According to Jewish tradition, these temple servants are to be identified with the Gibeonites (Josh 9:23, 27); onomastic studies suggest that some of them were of foreign origin, possibly prisoners of war. However, there is no solid basis for viewing them, on the basis of ANE analogies or rabbinic sources, as foreigners or temple slaves, i.e., as temple property (so KB and Mendelsohn, 105; cf. Levine), but rather as members of a cultic guild who are listed as returning from exile in order to take up their duties in the second temple. Their service may have been menial, but it accorded them a status as one of five divisions of temple personnel (along with the priests, Levites, singers, and gatekeepers), occupying a prominent place in public life (Neh 10:28-29[29-30]); the psalmist considered such service for the LORD to be a truly high calling (Ps 134:1; 135:1-2).

P-B The LXX usually transliterates the Heb. term except for 1 Chron 9:2, where it translates *n^e tînîm* as *dedomenoi*.

NT Paul may be influenced by this cultic use of *ntn* when he describes the church leaders as gifts of the ascended Christ to the church (Eph 4:7-13).

Servant, slave: → *'āmâ* (female slave, # 563); → *n^e tînîm* (temple slaves, # 5987); → *'ebed* (servant, # 6269); → *šiphâ* (female slave, maidservant, # 9148)

BIBLIOGRAPHY

ABD 4:1085-86; *TWAT* 5:706-12; *TWOT* 2:609; M. Haran, "The Gibeonites, the Nethinim, and the Sons of Solomon's Servants," *VT* 11, 1961, 159-69; A. Levine, "The *netînîm*," *JBL* 82, 1963, 207-12; idem, "Later Sources on the *netînîm*," Orient and Occident, *AOAT* 22, 1973, 101-7; I. Mendelsohn, *Slavery in the Ancient Near East*, 1949; E. A. Speiser, "Unrecognized Dedication," *IEJ*, 13, 1963, 69-73; J. P. Weinberg, "*Nethînîm* und 'Söhne der Sklaven Salomos' in 6.-4. Jh.v.u.Z.," *ZAW* 87, 1975, 355-71; H. G. M. Williamson, *Ezra, Nehemiah*, WBC 16, 1985.

Richard Schultz

5988 נתך

נתך (*ntk*), q., pour out; ni., be poured out, be melted; hi., pour out, melt; ho., be melted (# 5988); nom. הִתּוּךְ (*hittûk*), melting (# 2247).

ANE The Akk. vb. *natāku* means drip. In Ugar. *ntk* is pour (Krt 28).

OT 1. Like *spk*, *ntk* can refer to pouring out one's heart in prayer, especially in the midst of great sorrow (Job 3:24). Twice *ntk* is used of rain: the deluge that poured down during the plague of hail (Exod 9:33), or the rain that marked the end of a drought during David's rule (2 Sam 21:10).

2. Most cases (9x) refer to the pouring out of God's anger and wrath, a wrath that burned like fire and enveloped Judah and Jerusalem because of their idolatry (2 Chron 34:21, 25; Jer 7:20; 44:6). Even after Jerusalem was destroyed, God threatened to pour out his anger on the remnant that fled to Egypt (Jer 42:18). Daniel recognized that God's wrath justly carried out the curses of the Law (Dan 9:11), and Gabriel told Daniel that in the end times the anger of God will be unleashed (*ntk*) against the one who "will set up an abomination that causes desolation" (9:27).

3. The hi. is used of paying the workers repairing the temple (2 Kgs 22:9 = 2 Chron 34:17). The term is used to describe the forming of the human fetus as being poured out like milk or curdled like cheese (Job 10:10).

4. Several times in Ezekiel the vb. refers to the melting of metals in a furnace to describe the judgment on Jerusalem. Instead of purifying her, this outpouring of God's wrath will serve to destroy Jerusalem (Ezek 22:20-22; 24:11). Cf. *yṣq*, to cast metal (# 3688).

5. The nom. *hittûk* occurs only in Ezek 22:22 in connection with the melting of the people of Jerusalem.

Pouring out, casting, spilling: → *yṣq* (pour out, cast, # 3668); → *ngr* (run, flow, be poured out, # 5599); → *ntk* (pour out, melt, # 5988); → *špk* (pour out, spill, ebb away, flow out, # 9161)

Bibliography

NIDNTT 2:853-55; *TDNT* 2:467-69; *TWAT* 5:689-93; *TWOT* 1:395-96; 2:553; J. G. Baldwin, *Haggai, Zechariah, Malachi*, 1972, 119-20; J. P. Louw & E. A. Nida, eds., *Greek-English Lexicon of the New Testament Based on Semantic Domains*, 1, 1988-89, 522-23, 535.

Herbert M. Wolf/Robert Holmstedt

5989	נתן

נתן (*ntn*), give, present, offer, allow, permit, surrender, deliver, set, put, place (# 5989); אֶתְנָה (*'etnâ*), nom. gift to prostitute, pay (hapleg., Hos 2:12[14]; # 921); אֶתְנַן (*'etnan*), nom. gift to prostitute, pay (# 924); מַתָּן (*mattān* I), nom. gift, present (# 5508); מַתָּנָה (*mattānâ* I), nom. gift, present (# 5510); מַתַּת (*mattat*), nom. gift (# 5522); נָתִין (*nātîn*), temple servant (→ # 5987).

ANE *ntn* is a common Sem. root, e.g., Heb. and Aram. (*ntn*); Amor., Ugar., Phoen., and Punic (*ytn*); Akk. (*nadānu*), give (see *HALAT* for cognates in less common languages). In Aram. the verbal root *yhb* replaced *ntn* relatively early.

OT The Heb. verbal root *ntn* is the fifth most common root, occurring ca. 2010x in the OT. It is attested only in the q. and ni. (since a more accurate designation for the form *yuttan* is a q. pass. rather than a ho., Joüon, 167, §58, *IBHS*, 373-76, §22.6b). For a book by book statistical analysis, see *THAT* 2:118-19.

Several theological dictionaries suggest that *ntn* possesses three primary meanings: give; set/set up/put; make/do (*HALAT* 692-94, *TWOT* 2:608-9, *HAHAT*, 529-31, *LHA*, 539-41). Labuschagne, however, contends that *ntn* basically marks the act through which an object or matter is set in motion (*THAT* 2:119). This primary meaning manifests itself in two semantic fields. The first field of meaning is descriptive: to set in motion, i.e., to displace an object (put in motion, place, lay, furnish someone with something, give). The second field of meaning is causative/factitive: to set in motion (cause, effect, produce, bring about). As Labuschagne correctly points out, the common foundational meaning precludes an absolute demarcation between these two semantic fields. In both realms of meaning, prepositions play a significant role in the meaning of *ntn*.

1. *In the descriptive semantic realm. ntn* (set in motion [displace/put/give]), occurs with several prepositions (*'el, l^e^, b^e^, b^e^qereb, b^e^tōk, ʿal, baʿad, taḥat, 'ēt, ʿim*). A pronom. suffix on *ntn* designates the recipient of the giving, i.e., a dative suffix (Ezek 16:38; 17:19; 21:27[32]). A pronom. suffix on a nom. following *ntn* can also function as a dative suffix.

(a) With fluid/abstract noms. In certain cases where *ntn* has fluid or abstract noms. as its object (rain, hail, blood, spirit, fear, disgrace, jealousy, signs, miracles, etc.), the vb. can signify "pour out, bring over" (Deut 21:8; 1 Kgs 2:5; Job 5:10; Ps 105:32; et al.; cf. van Dijk, 16-30; Reif, 114-16).

(b) With persons as object. In several passages *ntn* becomes a technical term for "put in prison" (2 Chron 16:10; Jer 37:4, 15, 18; 52:11). *ntn* also occurs as part of a summons to surrender the accused (2 Sam 14:7; 20:21) or connotes "to hand over" in judgment (esp. when Yahweh is the subj. — Num 2:13; 1 Kgs 13:26; 14:16; Isa 34:2; et al.). It designates "to devote/make available/entrust/place at one's disposal," with regard to the firstborn (Exod 22:29-30[28-29]); a child dedicated to Yahweh by vow (1 Sam 1:11); children devoted to Molech (Lev 20:2); horses dedicated to the sun (2 Kgs 23:11); a technical term for Levites (*n^e^tûnîm*, Num 3:9; 8:16; 16:19); and a class of servants dedicated to the Levites (*n^e^tînîm*, 1 Chron 9:2; Ezra 2:43, 58, 70).

(c) The act of retribution. The idiom "bring upon one's head" (*ntn + ʿal +* suffix or *nātan + ʿal + rō'š* [head]) depicts the retribution given for an abomination (Ezek 7:3, 4, 9), wicked ways (1 Kgs 8:32; Ezek 9:10; 11:2), or covenant treachery (Ezek 17:19).

(d) "Attribute/assign." The general idea "to furnish" someone with something leads to the more specialized meaning of "attribute/assign"—whether it be to confer the honor of kingship on someone (Dan 11:21), to attribute impropriety to God (Job 1:22), or to ascribe righteousness (36:3), majestic power (Ps 68:35[36]), or honor (1 Sam 6:5; Jer 13:16; Mal 2:2). To this field of meaning belongs the technical expression of confession of guilt in a legal context (*ntn tôdâ*, Josh 7:19; Ezra 10:11).

(e) Technical legal term. In the legal sphere of trading, wages and prices, marriage, and bestowal of inheritance, *ntn* also has a technical meaning.

(i) Trade, wages, and prices. The expression *ntn l^e^* generally means to furnish someone with something, either through barter (1 Kgs 21:2), a loan (Deut 15:10; Ps 37:21), a purchase (Gen 23:9; 47:16; Deut 14:25-26; 1 Kgs 21:15), restitution (Exod 22:7, 10[6, 9]), repayment of a loan (Exod 21:19, 30; Num 5:7; Prov 6:31), payment of fines (Exod 21:22; Deut 22:19), or wages paid for services rendered (Gen 30:28; Exod 2:9; 1 Kgs 5:6[20]; Ezek 16:33; Jon 1:3) (a derivative of *ntn* [*'etnan*] and two related terms [*nēdeh, nādān*] occur in Ezek 16:33, see below). Finally, in this realm of commerce, *ntn b^e^nešek* signifies loaning money with interest, a practice forbidden among Israelites (Exod 22:25[24]; Lev 25:35-38; Ps 15:5; Ezek 18:8, 13).

(ii) Marriage. The near juxtaposition of *l^e^'iššâ* (for a wife) with *ntn* refers to the involvement of the bride's parents or others in the marriage arrangement (Gen 16:3;

29:28; 30:4, 9; 34:8, 12; et al.), just as the vb. *lqḥ* signifies the activity of the groom or his parents (Gen 12:19; 25:20; 28:9; 34:4, 21; et al.). In the mouth of the groom or his parents, the imperatival form of *ntn* becomes a stereotypical speech form for the acquisition of a bride (Gen 34:8, 12; 2 Kgs 14:9 = 2 Chron 25:18). *ntn* also signifies the act of giving a dowry (1 Kgs 9:16) or a wedding present to a daughter (Josh 15:19).

(iii) Inheritances. *ntn* commonly occurs with the objects *'ᵃḥuzzâ* (Num 27:4, 7) and *naḥᵃlâ* (27:9-11; 36:2) to signify the granting of an inheritance to family members. In a more global fashion, *ntn* frequently connotes the tribal land inheritances of the Israelites (once again with *'ᵃḥuzzâ* [Gen 17:8; Lev 14:34; Num 32:5, 29; et al.] and *naḥᵃlâ* [Num 16:14; 26:54; et al.] as objects). In addition to family and tribal inheritances, *ntn* occurs with regard to the following inheritance issues: slaves (Lev 25:45-46), Levitical tithes (Num 18:21, 24), nations of the world (Ps 2:8), inheritances of aliens (Ezek 47:23), and the sale of an inheritance (1 Kgs 21:3). Context determines whether *ntn* signifies the act of giving or the foundational intent to give.

(iv) Miscellaneous. *ntn* describes the official delivery of a legal instrument, whether it is a divorce letter (Deut 24:13) or a bill of sale (Jer 32:12).

(f) *ntn* and derived noms. Two derivatives of *ntn* (*'etnan* [11x] and *'etnâ*, hapleg.—Hos 2:12[14]) denote the wages of a harlot. The verbal root (*ntn*) and one of these cognates occur together 3x (Ezek 16:34, 41; Hos 2:12[14]) and highlight the exchange of money for services. Ezek 16:34, 41 (cf. 16:31) deliver a pointed indictment against Israel. The nation of Israel had chosen to play the harlot instead of remaining faithful to Yahweh. Israel, however, was unique in her harlotry. Israel "disdained" money, i.e., instead of receiving payment for her prostitution, she paid her customers. Mic 1:7 predicts Yahweh's judgment on Israel's prostitution. Her prostitute's wages (emblematic either for the prosperity gained from Baal [Smith, 18] or the many gold and silver images formed for use in her idolatry [Waltke, 2:620-21]) will serve to fund her attackers' idolatrous temples (see Loretz, 134-35, for the Ugar. par., *tnn*, and its meaning, esp. as it relates to Mic 1:7; cf. Watson, 464-67 for an alternative explanation). Von Soden (309-11) contends that the Heb. *'etnan* does not derive from *ntn*, but finds its source in 2 Hurrian terms (*uatnannu/uatnannuḫli*), which respectively mean "allotment" and an official involved with that allotment.

Three other derivatives of *ntn* (*mattānâ* I, *mattān*, and *mattat*) signify the general idea of "gift," with the specific nuance provided by the respective context. In ceremonial texts *mattānâ* I (17x) refers to gifts offered at the sanctuary of Yahweh (Exod 28:38; Lev 23:38; Num 18:29; Deut 16:17; Ezek 20:26), or an idolatrous sanctuary (Ezek 20:31, 39), as well as to Yahweh's provision of the Levites as a gift for Israel (Num 18:6-7). This nom. can also signify gifts that are part of an inheritance (Ezek 46:16-17), something beyond the inheritance (Gen 25:6; 2 Chron 21:3), tribute (Ps 68:18[19]), gifts for the poor (Esth 9:22), and a bribe (Prov 15:27; Eccl 7:7). The other two derivatives (*mattān* I [5x] and *mattat* [6x]) are generally less specific in nuance. While both refer to gifts or abundance (*mattān* I, Prov 18:16; 19:6; 21:14; *mattat*, 1 Kgs 13:7; Prov 25:14; Eccl 3:13; 5:19[18]), *mattān* I can specify a wave offering (Num 18:11) or a bridal gift (Gen 34:12). Wyatt (437-38, n. 14) suggests that *mattān* I here represents the Ugar. *trḫt* (cf. Akk. *tirḫatu*, bride-price), just as the Heb. *mōhar* corresponds to the Ugar. *mhr* (dowry) (e.g., *KTU* 1.24:17-22). In this case (Gen 34:12) *mattān* I connotes the "bride-price" given by the groom (cf. Exod 22:17[16]) or the groom's family (cf. Akk. *nudunnû*; Neufeld, 113-14). *mattat* occurs twice in an idiomatic expression (lit., "the gift of his hand") that means "according to his ability" (Ezek 46:5, 11; cf. Deut 16:17, where *mattānâ* I functions in the same fashion).

(g) *ntn* with other vbs. *ntn* occurs with *'mr* and *š'l* in contexts where someone (human or divine) either negotiates a price/wage, makes a request, and/or offers to grant a petition (human relationships, Gen 30:31; 34:11-12; 38:16-18; Esth 5:6; 7:2; divine-human relationships, Gen 15:2; 1 Kgs 3:5; Ps 2:8; 21:5). With regard to Ps 21:5, notice the par. Ugar. expression "ask silver and I will give (it) you, ask life and I will give (it) you" (*KTU* 1.17.VI:17, 25; *CML*, 108-9).

ntn and *lqḥ* (→ # 4374) often occur together to form a stereotypical expression "take and give," a kind of hendiadys that has a juridical nuance in several contexts (par. to the Akk. pair, *našū-nadānu* [to take or make available and give; *AHw*, 754, §III/5], an expression found in the Akk. legal documents at Ugarit, which connotes the transfer of property initiated by the king). Although the exact Heb. counterpart to the Akk. pair does not occur until postbiblical Heb. (cf. Speiser, 161; Jastrow, 848, s.v. *maśśā'*), *ntn—lqḥ* provides the BH equivalent. In addition to the nonjuridical uses (Gen 18:8; 21:14; Exod 12:7; Num 6:18-19; 19:17; et al.), the *ntn-lqḥ* pair signifies the power of a ruler to transfer property (Gen 20:14; 21:27; 1 Sam 8:14-16; cf. 1 Kgs 9:16), the disposing power of Moses (Exod 30:16; Num 7:6; 31:47), and most significantly, Yahweh's ability to dispose of his creation (Lev 7:34; Num 8:18-19; 2 Sam 12:11; 1 Kgs 11:35; Job 1:21) (cf. *nṣl/'ṣl-ntn* pair; Gen 31:9; Num 11:25).

2. *In the causative/factitive realm.* In several passages *ntn* signifies causation ("he causes me to learn") or describes an effected state (factitive, e.g., "he made me learned").

(a) With an accusative object (and without a dative object). Within this category, *ntn* normally provides a causative nuance, e.g., Prov 13:10, "pride only breeds quarrels" (cf. 10:10; 13:15; 23:31; 29:15, 25), perfume spreads its fragrance (S of Songs 1:12; 2:13; 7:13[14]), land gives forth its fruit (Ps 67:6[7]; 85:12[13]; Prov 28:19; Ezek 34:27; Zech 8:12), and the rock will pour out its water (Num 20:8).

The juxtaposition of *qôl* (→ # 7754) and *ntn* signifies a loud sound. Of the thirty times this construction occurs, the pl. *qôlôt* appears 3x (Exod 9:23; 1 Sam 12:17-18) with reference to a thunderstorm sent by Yahweh. When human beings (or personifications, e.g., wisdom) serve as the subj. of *ntn*, the expression refers to lamenting (Gen 45:2; Num 14:1; Jer 22:20; 48:34), hostile shouting (Jer 4:16), a public announcement (Prov 1:20; 2:3; 8:1; 2 Chron 24:9), or simply a loud noise (Jer 51:55; Lam 2:7). This collocation (*ntn* + *qôl*) also connotes the sounds of lions (Jer 2:15; 12:8; Amos 3:4) and birds (Ps 104:12) and describes the utterance of the deep (*t^ehôm*, Hab 3:10) and the skies (Ps 77:17[18]) at the sight of Yahweh. The instances with Yahweh as their subj. highlight his awesome power (2 Sam 22:14 = Ps 18:13[14]); Ps 46:6[7]); 68:33[34]); Jer 10:13 = 51:16; 25:30; Joel 2:11; 3:16[4:16]). The construction *l^eqôl tittô* in Jer 10:13 (= 51:16) has vexed many scholars. Althann (7-11) contends that this expression requires no emendation or addition, but was deliberately inverted from the normal word order (*l^etittô qôl*) to draw attention to the storm as the Lord's utterance.

When an abstract nom. serves as the object of *ntn*, the meaning of "procure, grant" is likely. Yahweh procures or grants for the stated recipient favor (Gen 39:21; 43:14; Exod 3:21; 11:23), mercy (Deut 13:17[18]), perpetual reproach (Ps 78:66), rest

(Josh 1:13; 1 Kgs 8:56), and vengeance (2 Sam 4:8). The dative idea (for him/them) is signified either by the preposition *l*^e^ or less directly by the construct relationship (between noms. or between a nom. and suffix, e.g., Gen 39:21; Exod 3:21; cf. Joüon, 467, §29h).

(b) "To make." Three constructions occur to signify "to make": *ntn k*^e^, *ntn* + two acc., or *ntn* + acc. + *l*^e^. The first possibility (*ntn k*^e^) normally signifies "to make as" (Ruth 4:11; Isa 41:2; Jer 19:12; Ezek 3:9; 16:7; 26:19; et al., cf. Gen 42:30; Ps 44:11[12]).

In several instances the combination of *ntn* with two acc. connotes "to appoint" or "ordain," i.e., "to make someone something." Yahweh is the most common subj. and he appoints a person(s) to a position or function (father, Gen 17:5; prophet, Jer 1:5; watchman, Ezek 3:17; sign, 12:6; firstborn, Ps 89:27[28]). Yahweh also assigns people or lands to devastation (Ezek 22:4; 32:15), waste (33:29), and desolation (26:19; 32:15). The prophetic proclamations of judgment are sometimes juxtaposed with the hostile expression *naṭâ yād*, "to stretch out the hand against" (Jer 51:25; Ezek 25:7, 13; 35:3; cf. *ntn yād* below). An adj. (Deut 26:19; Ps 18:32[33]; Ezek 3:8) or a part. (Num 5:21) occasionally replaces the second acc.

Whereas the preceding construction (*ntn* + two acc.) generally signifies a factitive nuance (the object is in an effected state, *IBHS*, 349, §20.2m), the expression *ntn* + acc. + *l*^e^ primarily presents a causative connotation. In several instances this construction manifests the noncausative nuance of *ntn* (Neh 4:4[3:36]; Isa 43:28; Ezek 15:6; 23:46; 25:4; 29:5; 33:27; 39:4). Nevertheless, Yahweh is most often the subj. who affirms his intention to make/appoint a person(s) for a specific function or position. Yahweh will make Abraham into a great nation (Gen 17:6, 20), he will appoint Moses to serve as "God" to Pharaoh (Exod 7:1), and he will appoint the servant as a light of the nations (Isa 49:6). Once again, the construction is common among prophetic utterances of judgment. Yahweh appoints his words to be a fire (Jer 5:14) and will make Israel to serve as a spectacle before the nations (Ezek 28:17) (cf. *śîm* and *šît* in similar constructions).

(c) *mî yittēn*. The collocation *mî yittēn* occurs 25x in the OT and serves to introduce a wish. The construction is most abundant in Job (11x—6:8; 11:5; 13:5; 14:4, 13; 19:23 [2x]; 23:3; 29:2; 31:31, 35) and is followed either by a nom. form (nom., part., inf.), pronom. suffix, or a finite vb. In certain instances it retains the basic meaning of *ntn*, to give (e.g., Judg 9:29, "If only this people were under my command [lit., given/entrusted to me]"; Ps 55:6[7], "Oh, would that I were given wings" = "Oh, that I had the wings"). In other cases the basic meaning of *ntn* is weakened or even lost, in which case *mî yittēn* simply signifies a wish (e.g., 2 Sam 18:33[19:1], "If only I had died instead of you!"; Deut 5:29, "Oh, that their hearts would be inclined to fear me") (Joüon, 616, §164d; cf. Jongeling, 32-40).

3. *ntn with certain body parts*. The juxtaposition of *ntn* with certain body parts leads to various idiomatic expressions (cf. Akk. *nadānu šēpē*, "to set out, depart," *AHw*, 702, § II/3).

(a) Shoulder/back. In relatively few instances *ntn* occurs with the noms. *kātēp* (shoulder) and *'ōrep* (neck/back). The expression "to stiffen the shoulder" (*ntn kātēp sôreret*) depicts the animal that stiffens his muscles in an attempt to reject the yoke (Neh 9:29; Zech 7:11). Of the three occurrences of the phrase "to turn the neck/back" (*ntn ʿōrep*), three refer to the flight of an enemy, exposing their back (Exod 23:27; 2 Sam 22:41 = Ps 18:40[41]), and one instance describes Israel's rejection of Yahweh (2 Chron 29:6).

(b) Hand. *ntn* occurs more frequently with *yād* (→ # 3338) as its object. The expression *ntn yād* can simply depict the extension of a hand (Gen 38:28) or a handshake of friendship (2 Kgs 10:15). More significantly, it represents the gesture that seals a formal alliance (Ezra 10:19; Lam 5:6; Ezek 17:18) or demonstrates one's commitment or loyalty to another person or divine being (1 Chron 29:24; 2 Chron 30:8).

ntn bᵉyad has a number of possible meanings: simply to place something in someone's hand (Gen 27:17; Deut 24:1, 3; Judg 7:16), allow/permit (Exod 10:25), hand over/commit (2 Sam 16:8; 2 Chron 34:16; Isa 22:21), place in the care of/under one's authority (Gen 9:2; 30:35; 32:16[17]; 39:4, 8, 22) (cf. *ntn ʿal yād*, Gen 42:37; Esth 6:9).

Most prominently, *ntn bᵉyad* occurs in military and legal settings (cf. *ntn bᵉkap*; Judg 6:13; Jer 12:7) and signifies the delivery or abandonment of a person(s) or matter into the power of another. In human relationships, a military commander can turn over the leadership of his men to another leader (2 Sam 10:10; 1 Chron 19:11), the elders can hand over a murderer to the blood avenger (Deut 19:12), and a political ruler can refuse to deliver a person to a mob bent on murder (Jer 26:24; 38:16). The Philistines give their god Dagon credit for capturing Samson (Judg 16:23-24). Yahweh promises to deliver Israel's enemies (Deut 7:24; 21:10; Josh 21:44[42]; Judg 3:28; 11:21) and the land itself (Josh 2:24; Judg 1:2; 18:10) into her authority. However, because of Israel's covenant infidelity, Yahweh affirms his intention to make them subject to other peoples (Judg 2:14; 6:1). Albrektson (38-39) points out that in ANE literature a king used the expression, "the gods delivered it into my hand," to express the belief that the course of events was directed by the gods and that his victory was a divine gift.

(c) Heart. In connection with *lēb/lᵉbāb* (→ # 4213), *ntn lēb bᵉ* describes a person's intense devotion (or lack of it) to a given task/person/truth (1 Chron 22:19; 2 Chron 11:16; Eccl 1:17; 7:21; 8:9, 16; Dan 10:12). The expression *ntn bᵉlēb* always has Yahweh as its subj. and describes what Yahweh provides for someone's inner being, whether it be plans to carry out (Neh 2:12; 7:5), wisdom/ability (Exod 35:34; 36:2; 2 Chron 9:23), fear (Jer 32:40), or rejoicing (Ps 4:7[8]).

(d) Face. The collocation *ntn pānîm* offers four potential nuances of meaning. *ntn pānîm el* indicates the direction one faces (Gen 30:40; Dan 9:3; cf. 10:15, *ntn pānîm* + nom. with a locative *he*). When followed by an inf. *ntn pānîm lᵉ* connotes "to intend or determine" (2 Chron 20:3; cf. *śîm pānîm lᵉ*, 2 Kgs 12:17[18]; Isa 42:16; Dan 11:17). Ezekiel uses a variation of this expression, *ntn pānîm lᵉʿummat pᵉnêhem*, to compare the prophet's face to that of his obstinate audience (Ezek 3:8). As Layton (179) suggests, "Yahweh will make the prophet's brow just as hard as that of those who oppose him." Finally, *ntn pānîm bᵉ* signifies hostility. In all these occurrences (Lev 17:10; 20:3, 6; 26:17; Ezek 14:8; 15:7a) only Yahweh is the subj., and in four instances a form of *krt* (to cut off) follows this idiom. The reading of the Syriac Peshiṭta and Targum Onkelos for Lev 17:10, "I will set my anger against," illustrates this nuance (Layton [169-81] also points out several clear ANE parallels).

4. All the earth and its abundance belongs to Yahweh as their Lord and Creator (Ps 24:1; 50:9-12). According to Jer 27:5 Yahweh declares, "With my great power and

outstretched arm I made the earth and its people and the animals that are on it, and I give it to anyone I please." In the realm of all humanity Yahweh gives and causes breath and life (Isa 42:5) and all that goes along with existence. However, Yahweh's disposals concern Israel especially. As the sole owner of the earth, Yahweh grants his chosen people their land and special existence. Yahweh's giving is not only motivated by beneficence, but grounded in relationship. In preparation for their entrance into the Promised Land (Deut 1-4), Moses provides an overview of Yahweh's self-revelation through numerous historical events. As their covenant Lord and Redeemer, these events provide the foundation for Yahweh's claim of sovereignty over them. Since he gives them this land as a covenant grant, Israel must wholeheartedly serve their suzerain. As their benefactor, Yahweh is worthy of (and demands) their loyalty and offerings. The Psalter also presents Yahweh as the One to whom all things are subject. The only acceptable response to God is trust and praise, manifested in inner attitudes as well as by means of proper stewardship of those provisions.

P-B The verbal root *ntn* occurs 58x in the Qumran sectarian documents, where it conforms to OT usage. The LXX primarily uses *didōmi* to translate *ntn*.

NT See *NIDNTT* 2:39-44; *TDNT* 2:166-73.

Gift: → *'ahab* (gifts of love, charm, # 172); → *zbd* (endow, # 2272); → *mgn* I (deliver, # 4481); → *nādān* II (gift, wages of love, # 5621); → *ntn* (give, present, offer, # 5989); → *skr* II (hand over, # 6127); → *ṣbṭ* (give, # 7381); → *šḥd* (give a gift, # 8815); → *šay* (gift, present, # 8856); → *šalmōnîm* (gift, # 8988)

Bribe, gift: → *beṣa'* (piece of s.t., gain, bribe, # 1299); → *kōper* IV (bribe, # 4111); → *skr* III (bargain, # 6128); → *šḥd* (give a gift, # 8815); → *šalmōnîm* (gift, # 8988)

Tax, gift, offering, tribute: → *'eškār* (tribute, payment, # 868); → *ybl* I (bring [gift, tribute], # 3297); → *middâ* II (tax, # 4501); → *mas* (tribute, tax, forced labor, # 4989); → *maśśā'* I (carrying, burden # 5362); → *maś'ēt* (tax, offering, # 5368); → *sēbel* (forced labor, burden, # 6023); → *t^erûmâ* (tribute, contribution, # 9556)

BIBLIOGRAPHY

THAT 2:117-41; *TWAT* 5:693-712; *TWOT* 2:608-9; Jastrow 2:863, 944; B. Albrektson, *History and the Gods*, 1967; R. Althann, "The Inverse Construct Chain and Jer 10:13, 51:16," *JNSL* 15, 1989, 7-11; H. J. van Dijk, "A Neglected Connotation of Three Hebrew Verbs," *VT* 18, 1968, 16-30; R. Ellis, "Divine Gift and Human Response: An Old Testament Model for Stewardship," SWJT 37, 1995, 4-14; B. Jongeling, "L'Expression *my ytn* dans l'Ancien Testament," *VT* 24, 1974, 32-40; P. Joüon, *A Grammar of Biblical Hebrew*, 1991; S. Layton, "Biblical Hebrew 'To Set the Face,' in Light of Akkadian and Ugaritic," *UF* 17, 1986, 169-81; O. Loretz, "Ugaritische und hebräische Lexikographie (II)," *UF* 13, 1981, 127-35; E. Neufeld, *Ancient Hebrew Marriage Laws*, 1944; S. C. Reif, "A Note on a Neglected Connotation of NTN," *VT* 20, 1970, 114-16; D. J. Reimer, "A Problem in the Hebrew Text of Jeremiah 10:13, 51:16, *VT* 38, 1988, 348-53; W. von Soden, "Hurritisch *uatnannu* > Mittelassyrisch *utnannu* und > Ugaritisch *itnn* > Hebräisch *'ätnan* 'ein Geschenk, Dirnenlohn," *UF* 20, 1988, 309-11; E. Speiser, "Akkadian Documents from Ras Shamra," *JAOS* 75, 1955, 154-65; R. L. Smith, *Micah-Malachi*, 1984; B. K. Waltke, "Micah," *The Minor Prophets*, 1993, 2:591-764; W. Watson, *Traditional Techniques in Classical Hebrew Verse*, 1994; N. Wyatt, "The Story of Dinah and Shechem," *UF* 22, 1990, 431-58.

Michael A. Grisanti

5995	נתס

נתס (*nts*), q. break up (only in Job 30:13; # 5995); usually treated as cognate to *nts̱*, tear down (→ # 5997).

ANE This root is probably attested in Ugar. (*UT* 68:4) (Ceresko, 66).

OT In Job 30:13 *nts* is used for the figurative breaking up of a path. Job compares himself to a besieged city whose enemies want his downfall and therefore cut off his means of escape. For the text, see Dhorme, 438-39.

Destruction, annihilation, devastation, disfigurement, ruin: → *'bd* I (perish, # 6); → *'êd* (disaster, # 369); → *blq* (devastate, # 1191); → *dmh* III (ruin, # 1950); → *dmm* III (perish, # 1959); → *hrs* (demolish, # 2238); → *ḥbl* III (treat badly, # 2472); → *ḥlq* III (destroy, # 2746); → *ḥt'* (be destroyed, # 3148); → *klh* (be complete, perish, destroy, # 3983); → *krt* (cut, cut off, exterminate, cut a covenant, circumcise, # 4162); → *mḥh* I (wipe off, wipe out destroy, # 4681); → *nṣh* II (fall in ruins, # 5898); → *nts* (break up, # 5995); → *ntṣ* (tear down, # 5997); → *ntš* (root up, pull down, destroy, # 6004); → *p'h* (dash to pieces, # 6990); → *pîd* (ruin, misfortune, # 7085); → *prr* (break, invalidate, nullify, frustrate, foil, thwart, # 7296); → *ṣdh* II (be devastated, # 7400); → *rzh* (destroy, waste away, # 8135); → *šdd* (devastate, # 8720); → *šḥt* (become corrupt, ruin, spoil, # 8845); → *šmd* (be exterminated, destroyed, # 9012); → *tablît* (annihilation, # 9318)

BIBLIOGRAPHY

NIDNTT 1:462-71; A. R. Ceresko, *Job 29-31 in the Light of Northwest Semitic*, BibOr 36, 1980; E. Dhorme, *A Commentary on the Book of Job*, 1967/1984.

Cornelis Van Dam

5997	נתץ

נתץ (*ntṣ*), q. tear down, break down, demolish; break (teeth; Ps 58:6[7] ‖ *hrs*); q. pass. (pointed as ho., see GKC, § 53u), be torn up; ni. be torn down, destroyed; pi. tear down; pu. be demolished (# 5997).

OT 1. Of the 42x that this root is used, it occurs most often (31x) in q. Its meaning is similar to that of *hrs* (see above) and can denote the destruction of a variety of structures, such as an illicit altar (pu., Judg 6:28; q. 6:30-32; cf. v. 25 [*hrs*]; Exod 34:13), high places (pi., 2 Chron 31:1), and the walls of a city (q. 2 Kgs 25:10).

2. Used figuratively, God can tear down his people (collectively, q., Jer 31:28, or as an individual, q., Ps 52:5[7]; cf. also *nsḥ* [→ # 5815]; q., Job 19:10) and other nations (q., Jer 18:7; also see 1:10). It is noteworthy that in 1:10 and 31:28 *ntṣ* is used with *ntš*, *hrs*, and *'bd* (cf. 18:7, where *hrs* is lacking). But what God tears down, he will also build up (1:10; 31:28; on 1:10, see Thiel, 69-71; on 31:28, see Brueggemann, 67-69). This building up and planting after the time of judgment for sin sets the stage for the new covenant, announced in 31:31, in which God's grace and faithfulness will be revealed as never before (31:32-37).

3. One was obliged to demolish a stove or oven and tear down a house when these had become unclean (q. pass., Lev 11:35; q., 14:45).

P-B The term *ntṣ* is also used in Talmudic literature for breaking down an unclean house or oven (cf. 3 above; Jastrow 2:945).

Destruction, annihilation, devastation, disfigurement, ruin: → *'bd* I (perish, # 6); → *'êd* (disaster, # 369); → *blq* (devastate, # 1191); → *dmh* III (ruin, # 1950); → *dmm* III (perish, # 1959); → *hrs* (demolish, # 2238); → *ḥbl* III (treat badly, # 2472); → *ḥlq* III (destroy, # 2746); → *ḥt'* (be destroyed, # 3148); → *klh* (be complete, perish, destroy, # 3983); → *krt* (cut, cut off, exterminate, cut a covenant, circumcise, # 4162); → *mḥh* I (wipe off, wipe out destroy, # 4681); → *nṣh* II (fall in ruins, # 5898); → *nts* (break up, # 5995); → *ntṣ* (tear down, # 5997); → *ntš* (root up, pull down, destroy, # 6004); → *p'h* (dash to pieces, # 6990); → *pîd* (ruin, misfortune, # 7085); → *prr* (break, invalidate, nullify, frustrate, foil, thwart, # 7296); → *ṣdh* II (be devastated, # 7400); → *rzh* (destroy, waste away, # 8135); → *šdd* (devastate, # 8720); → *šḥt* (become corrupt, ruin, spoil, # 8845); → *šmd* (be exterminated, destroyed, # 9012); → *tablît* (annihilation, # 9318)

BIBLIOGRAPHY

NIDNTT 1:462-71; *TWAT* 5:713-19; W. Brueggemann, *To Build, To Plant*, 1991, 67-69; E. Jenni, *Das hebräische Pi'el*, 1968, 184; W. Thiel, *Die deuteronomistische Redaktion von Jeremia 1-25*, WMANT 41, 1973, 69-71.

Cornelis Van Dam

5998	נתק

נתק (*ntq*), q. tear away; draw away (military); ni. be snapped in two; be pulled loose; let o.s. be drawn away (military); be drawn out; pi. tear up, pull up; hi. separate; draw s.o. away (military) (# 5998); נֶתֶק (*neteq*), itch, infection (→ # 5999).

ANE Cognates are found in Deir Alla Aram., Nabatean Arab., and Eth. (*HALAT* 695). *ntq* is also related to Heb. *ntḥ* and *ntk* (*TWAT* 5:720).

OT 1. The primary meaning of *ntq* is tear away and tear out (*TWAT* 5:720). It can refer to tearing off a ring. God prophesies in judgment against Jehoiachin that even if he were a signet ring on his right hand, the Lord would pull him off and hand him over to his enemies (Jer 22:24, q.), a judgment God later graciously reversed in his descendants (Hag 2:23). The vb. can also refer to the refining process, an image of separating the wicked from God's people, which is all in vain for they are too corrupt (Jer 6:29 ni.).

2. Cords can also be torn and broken, such as those that held Samson (Judg 16:9, pi., ni.; 12, pi.) and tent cords (Jer 10:20, ni.; Isa 33:20, ni., → *ns'*, # 5825).

A proverb also found outside Israel is: "A cord of three strands is not quickly broken" (Eccl 4:12, ni.), indicating there is safety in companionship (M. A. Eaton, *Ecclesiastes*, TOTC, 1983, 94-95).

3. Used with *môsērâ*, fetters (→ # 4593), *ntq* describes the breaking of the bonds of dominion. It is telling that when Israel tore off the Lord's bonds (Jer 2:20, pi.), they became fettered to Baal and enslaved to prostitution (Jer 2:20-25; cf. Rom 1:18-32). Such breaking of the Lord's covenant bonds (Jer 5:5, pi.) leads to judgment, although God will not destroy them completely (5:6-13). Indeed, he will eventually break the bonds of the enemies he has set over them (30:8, pi.; Nah 1:13, pi.; Ps 107:14, pi.). Although the kings of the world may rally against the Lord and his anointed and seek to break his bonds (Ps 2:3, pi.), God in heaven laughs and holds them in derision (2:4; cf. Acts 4:25-28).

4. Used with reference to body parts, *ntq* can refer to torn testicles that makes a sacrificial animal unacceptable for offering to the Lord (Lev 22:24, q. pass.; cf. Mal 1:13-14). Likewise, the priests must be perfect (cf. Lev 21:20). In Ezek 23:34 (pi.), Judah's (Oholibah's) tearing of her own breasts (once fondled by illicit lovers, Ezek 23:21) forms part of God's judgment for her promiscuity in violation of her covenant with him (cf. 23:35-39).

5. In Isa 58:6 God reminds his people that true fasting is "to loose (*ptḥ* [pi.]; → # 7336) the chains of injustice and untie (*ntr* [hi.]; → # 6002) the cords of the yoke, to set the oppressed free (*šlḥ* [pi.]) and break (*ntq* [pi.; for retaining the pl. form of *ntq*, see Dahood, 340-41]) every yoke."

6. Frustrated by the prosperity of the wicked and concerned for God's honor, Jeremiah demands that God drag them off (*ntq*, hi.) like sheep to be butchered (Jer 12:3, cf. vv. 1-2; cf. Hab 1-2). Cf. A. R. Diamond, *The Confessions of Jeremiah in Context*, JSOTSup 45, 1987, 46-47, 214-15.

7. In military contexts, the vb. is used of luring soldiers away through diversionary tactics to effect victory over them (Josh 8:6, hi.; 16, ni.; Judg 20:31, hof., 32 q.).

P-B 1. Although the vb. is not found in extant DSS, the meaning of the vb. is found in a nom. *ntq* (unattested in OT), after *l'yn* (1QH 5:37; cf. S. Holm-Nielsen, *Hodayot. Psalms From Qumran*, ATDan 2, 1960, 100, 111).

2. Besides the major OT uses of *ntq*, RL also contains the meanings: q. to secrete (of fruit juices), pi. be discontented, be transformed (Jastrow, 945).

Separation, breaking down, removal: → *'ṣl* (set apart, withdraw, shorten, # 724); → *bdl* (separate o.s., # 976); → *br'* I (create, separate, # 1343); → *hgh* II (separate, remove, # 2048); → *mwš* II (depart, remove, take away, # 4631); → *ns'* (tear out, march out, # 5825); → *ntq* (tear away, # 5998); → *prq* (pull away, # 7293); → *ṣ'n* (pack up, # 7585); → *rḥq* (be far away, remove, # 8178)

Bibliography

TWAT 5:719-23; M. Dahood, "Hebrew-Ugaritic Lexicography VII," *Bib* 50, 1969, 337-56, esp. 340-41; E. Jenni, *Das hebräische Pi'el*, 1968, 176, 183.

Cornelis Van Dam

5999	נֶתֶק

נֶתֶק (*neteq*), itch, infection (# 5999).

OT A rare word describing a scalp infection resulting in *Alopecia area*ta, in which circumscribed patches of baldness are produced (Lev 13:30-37; 14:54). Eng. versions generally render the term itch (# 5999).

Disease—blister, boil, skin disease, scar, wound: → *'ᵃba'bu'ōt* (blisters, # 81); → *bōhaq* (skin condition, # 993); → *baheret* (white patch on skin, # 994); → *gārāb* (festering eruption, # 1734); → *zrr* I (press out [wounds], # 2452); → *ḥeres* I (itch, # 3063); → *yabbelet* (wart?, # 3301); → *yallepet* (skin disease, # 3539); → *yᵉraqraq* (discoloration, # 3768); → *kᵉwiyya* (scar, # 3918); → *m'r* (be sore, # 4421); → *māzôr* I (boil, # 4649); → *makkâ* (blow, # 4804); → *mispaḥat* (skin eruption, # 5030); → *mrḥ* (rub, polish, # 5302); → *neteq* (scalp infection, # 5999); → *sappaḥat* (hair disease, # 6204); → *'ōpel* I (abscesses, # 6754); → *'āš* II (pus, # 6932); → *ṣāpâ* (pus?, # 7597); → *ṣarebet* (scar, # 7648); → *ṣr'* (suffer from skin disease, # 7665); → *śᵉ'ēt* II (swelling, # 8421); → *śtr* (break out [tumor], # 8609); → *šᵉḥîn* (boil, # 8825). For related entries → *ḥlh* I (become weak, tired, ill, # 2703)

Bibliography
ISBE 1:532, 953-60; 3:103-6; J. Milgrom, *Leviticus*, AB, 793.

R. K. Harrison

6000	נתר

נתר (*ntr* I), q. fall (metaphor of discouragement); hi. drop(?) (# 6000).

OT 1. The vb. *ntr* occurs twice in BH, only in Job, and both instances are problematical. In Job 6:9 (hi.) the reference is to God's letting his hands become free or untied (cf. Ps 105:20; 146:7; Isa 58:6) and so cutting Job off in death. A possible connection with Ugar. has been cited for the combination *ntr yd,* together with a divine subject (*THAT* 2:725-26).

2. In Job 37:1 (q.) "fall" is a metaphor for an emotion of the heart. In the context Elihu is responding to the thought of the might and power of God and declares that his heart trembles. The parallel phrase then uses *ntr* plus the prepositional phrase *mimm^{e}qômô*, from its place.

P-B The Tg. takes the word to mean leap (= *ntr* II; → # 6001), while a derivation from the root *trr*, which in Akk. means tremble, quake, is feasible.

NT → *NIDNTT* 1:606-11; 2:705-10.

Falling, tottering, stumbling: → *bṭḥ* II (fall to ground, # 1054); → *hwh* I (fall, # 2092); → *kšl* (stumble, totter, be brought to ruin, # 4173); → *nss* I (falter, # 5823); → *npl* (fall, lie prostrate, # 5877); → *ntr* I (fall, # 6000); → *šmṭ* (release, remit, drop, throw down, fall, stumble, # 9023)

Allan M. Harman

6001	נתר

נתר (*ntr* II), q. start, spring; pi. leap; hi. start, leap back (# 6001).

ANE Aram. and Syr. *n^{e}tar*, fall, fall off, drop; Arab. *natala,* jump from a resting position.

OT 1. In Job 37:1 *ntr* describes the trembling of one's heart in fearful excitement before a mighty thunderstorm, which portends the appearance of Yahweh. For 2 Sam 22:33 reading *wayyattēr*, there have been many proposals: "and it springs from" (KB), "and he sets free" (BDB, from *ntr* III), "and he gives" (following parallel text in Ps 18:32[33] *wayyittēn*), "and he mapped out" (defective spelling of MT for *wayy^{e}tā'ēr* (cf. Isa 44:13; so P. McCarter, Jr., *II Samuel*, AB, 1984, 470). This lack of consensus indicates how difficult the MT text is.

2. The vb. in the pi. represents the leaping ability of insects with specially formed back legs (Lev 11:21).

3. In Hab 3:6 the vb. in the hi. pictures the nations' leaping back before the overwhelming, theophanic presence of Yahweh.

Jumping, leaping, skipping: → *glš* (skip, jump, # 1683); → *dwṣ* (dance, # 1881); → *dlg* (leap, # 1925); → *znq* I (jump before, # 2397); → *ntr* II (start, spring, # 6001); → *sld* (jump, spring,

6134); → *pwš* (skip, leap, # 7055); → *pzz* II (be quick, agile, hop, # 7060); → *rqd* (skip, leap, # 8376); → *šqq* (run about, jump, # 9212)

John E. Hartley

6002	נתר

נתר (*ntr* III), hi. set free, let prisoners go free, unfasten the thongs of a yoke (# 6002).

OT The root *ntr* III only occurs in the hi. It conveys the meaning of release or set free a captive, e.g., Ps 105:20 (cf. Ps 146:7): "The king sent and released (*ntr*) him, the ruler of peoples set him free (*ptḥ*)" (cf. Ps 102:20[21]). Its usage in the Psalms is closely connected with God's care and deliverance of the oppressed and less privileged. It occurs in a similar context in Isa 58:6, where it is said that "to loose (*ptḥ* [pi.] → # 7336) the chains of injustice and untie (*ntr*) the cords of the yoke," denotes figuratively the freedom of the emancipated captives (*ḥopšîm*).

The word is theologically highly significant because it describes God's concern and liberating acts towards those helplessly bound by the yoke of captivity and need.

Freedom, innocence, cleanness, liberation: → *d^e^rôr* III (release, freedom, # 2002); → *ḥpš* (freed, # 2926); → *ḥōr* I (free man, freeborn, # 2985); → *nqh* (be free, exempt from guilt, remain unpunished, # 5927); → *ntr* III (set free, # 6002); → *qôm^e^miyyût* (walk erect, # 7758); → *rwḥ* A (become wide or spacious, be spacious, # 8118)

J. P. J. Olivier

6003	נֶתֶר

נֶתֶר (*neter*), nom. nitre, an alkaline solution made from wood ashes used as a cleansing agent (# 6003).

OT Both uses of the term (lye, KJV) are in a parabolic context (Prov 25:20; Jer 2:22). For NIV's, soda, see *ISBE* 3:191.

Wash, washing: → *bōr* II (potash, # 1342); → *dwḥ* (rinse, # 1866); → *ṭbl* I (immerse, # 3188); → *kbs* (wash, pound, # 3891); → *neter* (nitre, # 6003); → *rḥṣ* (wash, # 8175); → *šeleg* II (soapwort, # 8921)

BIBLIOGRAPHY

ISBE 1:439-40; 3:191-92; 4:1022; *NIDNTT* 1:143-45, 150-52.

Elmer A. Martens

6004	נתשׁ

נתשׁ (*ntš*), q. pluck up, root out, pull down; ni. be rooted up, destroyed; q. pass. be rooted up (# 6004).

ANE There is a similar root in Syr. and Aram.

OT 1. Psalm 80:8-9[9-10] speaks of Israel as being like a vine brought out of Egypt, planted in their land, taking root and filling the land. Many passages indicate that continued life and fruitfulness in the land was dependent on obedience; others give warning that unfaithfulness must lead to their being rooted out (e.g., Deut 29:28[27]; 1 Kgs 14:15; 2 Chron 7:19-20).

2. Jeremiah often spoke in these terms to Judah, and at his call the Lord told him he would be the means of the fulfilling of this purpose of the Lord: "I appoint you over nations and kingdoms to uproot and tear down, to destroy and overthrow, to build and to plant" (Jer 1:10). The theme of uprooting and planting again "articulates God's decisive judgment and God's resilient hope" (W. Brueggemann, in *Interpreting the Prophets*, eds. J. L. Mays and P. J. Achtemeier, 119). Both are Jeremiah's message to Judah, but the plural "nations" has a significance. In 18:7-8 the word of the Lord is, "If at any time I announce that a nation or kingdom is to be uprooted, torn down and destroyed, and if that nation I warned repents of its evil, then I will relent—" (cf. 12:14-17). There was the judgment of uprooting, but then the message of hope that Jeremiah brought, "I will plant and not uproot them" (24:6). "Just as I watched over (Israel and Judah) to uproot and tear down ... so I will watch over them to build and to plant," and in particular the city of Jerusalem would "never again be uprooted or demolished" (31:28, 40). (→ Jeremiah: Theology)

Uproot: → *ntš* (root up, pull down, destroy, # 6004); → *'qr* (root up, # 6827); → *šrš* (root up, # 9245)

Destruction, annihilation, devastation, disfigurement, ruin: → *'bd* I (perish, # 6); → *'êd* (disaster, # 369); → *blq* (devastate, # 1191); → *dmh* III (ruin, # 1950); → *dmm* III (perish, # 1959); → *hrs* (demolish, # 2238); → *ḥbl* III (treat badly, # 2472); → *ḥlq* III (destroy, # 2746); → *ḥt'* (be destroyed, # 3148); → *klh* (be complete, perish, destroy, # 3983); → *krt* (cut, cut off, exterminate, cut a covenant, circumcise, # 4162); → *mḥh* I (wipe off, wipe out destroy, # 4681); → *nṣh* II (fall in ruins, # 5898); → *nts* (break up, # 5995); → *ntṣ* (tear down, # 5997); → *ntš* (root up, pull down, destroy, # 6004); → *p'h* (dash to pieces, # 6990); → *pîd* (ruin, misfortune, # 7085); → *prr* (break, invalidate, nullify, frustrate, foil, thwart, # 7296); → *ṣdh* II (be devastated, # 7400); → *rzh* (destroy, waste away, # 8135); → *šdd* (devastate, # 8720); → *šḥt* (become corrupt, ruin, spoil, # 8845); → *šmd* (be exterminated, destroyed, # 9012); → *tablît* (annihilation, # 9318)

BIBLIOGRAPHY
TWAT 5:727-28.

Francis Foulkes

ס

6006 (*sē'â*, seah), → # 406

6007 (*s*^{e}*'ôn*, boot), → # 6008

6008	סאן

סאן (*s'n*), tramp along, tread (# 6008); a hapleg. in Isa 9:5[4]; denom. vb. from סְאוֹן (*s*^{e}*'ôn*), boot (# 6007).

ANE Akk. *šênu* is a denom. from *šēnu*, to put on a shoe (*HALAT* 697). The shoe, while not strictly a boot, is a foot covering worn by soldiers.

OT The vb. and nom. appear in the same v., and only in this verse. Through a child God will bring an end to war and other forms of oppression. NIV's rendering of the first part as "every warrior's boot used in battle ... will be destined for burning" is an attempt to make sense of the Heb., which reads literally, "every boot booting with shaking" (*kol s*^{e}*'ôn sō'ēn b*^{e}*ra'aš*).

Marching, stepping: → *ḥšl* (unfit to march, straggle, shatter, # 3129); → *nḥt* (march down, descend, penetrate, settle, # 5737); → *s'n* (tramp along, tread, # 6008); → *pś'* I (step forth, march, # 7314); → *ṣ'd* (step, march, # 7575)

Victor P. Hamilton

6010	סבא

סבא (*sb'*), q. drink excessively (# 6010); סֹבֶא (*sōbe'*), nom. beer, drink (# 6011).

OT 1. *sōbe'* is probably some sort of grain beer, comparable to Akk. *sību* (*CAD* 15, 231). The image in Isa 1:22 of dissipated leaders fits better watered-down beer (J.-J. Hess, *MGWJ* 78, 1934, 6-9, "Was bedeutet *sōbe'* Jesaias 122?"), since wine was generally diluted. The passage may echo Deut 21:20, which also refers to rebelliousness and drunkenness. Hos 4:18 links drunkenness and prostitution, possibly reflecting behavior in the fertility cult (G. I. Emmerson, "A Fertility Goddess in Hosea IV 17-19?" *VT* 24, 1974, 492-97).

2. Ezek 23:42 has a part. *sōb*^{e}*'îm* (K) or a noun *sābā'îm* (Q), which would be the only occurrence of *sābā'*, drunkard. Others read "Sabeans" (*s*^{e}*bā'îm*; REB) or omit by dittography (*HALAT* 697; Zimmerli, *Ezekiel*, 1:478-79).

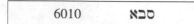

3. The four passages with the denominative vb. *sb'* describe those who drink too much beer (Isa 56:12) or wine (Prov 23:20). The text of Nah 1:10 is uncertain, but it may refer to the helplessness of the Assyrian army. The drunkenness of a rebellious son represents a deadly refusal to abide by the standards of community life (Deut 21:20).

Drinking, intoxication: → *sb'* (drink excessively, # 6010); → *škr* (be or become drunk, # 8910); → *šth* II (drinking, # 9272)

P. P. Jenson

6011 (*sōbe'*, beer, drink), → # 6010

6015	סבב

סבב (*sbb*), q. turn, go round, surround; ni. turn round; pi. change; pol. go round, surround; hi. cause to turn, change, bring round, surround; ho. be turned, surrounded (# 6015); מֵסַב (*mēsab*), nom. circle, table, divan, surrounding; adv. around (# 4990); מְסִבָּה (*m*[e]*sibbâ*), adv. around (# 4991); נְסִבָּה (*n*[e]*sibbâ*), nom. (strictly, ni. part.), turn of affairs (hapleg.; # 5813); סִבָּה (*sibbâ*), nom. turn of affairs (hapleg.; # 6016); סָבִיב (*sābîb*), adv. and prep. around (# 6017).

ANE The vb. is well attested: Ugar. *sbb,* turn; Old Aram. surround; Akk. *šibbu,* girdle; Arab. *sabab*, rope; Tigre *šabīb*, cord. In the Heb. of the Lachish ostraca *tsbt* signifies turning point or course (of time). In Moabite an adv. *sbbt* occurs with the sense of round about.

OT 1. The vb. is often used in a hostile (e.g., Gen 19:4; Judg 19:22) or military (e.g., 2 Sam 18:15; 2 Kgs 6:15) sense. This usage is echoed in lament contexts, where crisis or enemies have beset the speaker, who either prays for deliverance (Ps 17:11; 88:17[18]; cf. 49:5[6]; Job 16:13; 19:10, 12) or gives thanks for it (Ps 18:5[6]; 22:12, 16[13, 17]; 118:10-12; 140:9[10]; Jon 2:3, 5[4, 6]). In Hos 7:2 Israel's wicked deeds surround and trap them; in 11:12[12:1] Israel has surrounded God with lies as their weapons.

2. A liturgical procession is in view in Ps 26:6; 48:12[13]. In Josh 6:3-15 Israel's marching around Jericho has both military and religious connotations. In Ps 32:7 God's surrounding the psalmist "with songs of deliverance" refers to God as the agent of a deliverance, which is celebrated by a singing group around the psalmist (cf. 142:7[8]).

3. The vb. relates to protection in 2 Chron 14:7[6] and hence to God's encircling care of his people in Deut 32:10 (shielded) and to the "unfailing love" around the faithful in Ps 32:10. The adverb *sābîb* (around) is used in contexts of divine protection in Ps 34:7[8]; 125:2; Zech 2:5[9]; cf. the usc of the preposition *sābîb* in 2 Kgs 6:17.

4. The vb. is also used in various judgment contexts. In Ps 7:7[8] God is urged to vindicate the psalmist by convening a court to judge his enemies. In Ezek 7:22 God's turning his face from the Judeans refers to the withdrawal of his favor. In Hab 2:16 Yahweh's cup of wrath is to "come round" to the Babylonians.

5. The vb. is used of a change of king in 1 Kgs 2:15; 1 Chron 12:23[24], and of human manipulation of the course of affairs in 2 Sam 14:20. A new reign is ascribed to God's providential control in 1 Chron 10:14. Similarly in Ezra 6:22 (cf. 1:1) God

"changed the attitude" of Darius so that he helped the Jews. Elijah's prayer in 1 Kgs 18:37 is ambiguous: it refers to God either as the cause of Israel's conversion (NIV; cf. Hauser and Gregory, *From Carmel*, 49-50) or as the ultimate cause of Israel's apostasy (cf. Montgomery and Gehman, *Kings*, 305).

6. Jer 31:22 enigmatically announces a new thing that God would create, "a woman will surround (*t*^{e}*sôbēb*) a man." Jerome's interpretation in terms of Mary's carrying Jesus inside her womb hardly respects the context. Possibly it refers to God's gift of sons to "Virgin Israel" (v. 21) after restoration to the land (cf. v. 27) (cf. Anderson, 476-77).

7. The noms. *sibbâ* and *n*^{e}*sibbâ*, turn of affairs, denote the divinely ordered removal of kingship in 1 Kgs 12:15 and 2 Chron 10:15. These changes are related to God's control over history in fulfillment of his prophetic word. According to 1 Kgs 12:15 Rehoboam's negative response to the people was the occasion (*sibbâ*, the turn of events) of the division of the kingdom. The parallel account (2 Chron 10:15) makes an even stronger statement. The word *n*^{e}*sibbâ* expresses the Chronicler's theological perspective, according to which the kingdom is God's, and the division of the kingdom is to be viewed in the same light as the removal of the kingdom from Saul (1 Chron 10:14; see Williamson, *I and II Chronicles*, 95-96).

8. The nom. *mēsab* denotes the couch or divan of the king (S of Songs 1:12; cf. v. 16; see Murphy, *Song*, 131, n. 12; NIV at his table) or in the pl. the surroundings of the royal city Jerusalem (2 Kgs 23:5).

9. The preposition *sābîb*, around, is used in descriptions of theophany, the awesomeness of the appearing God (Ps 18:11[12] = 2 Sam 22:12; Ps 50:3; 97:2). The adv. *sābîb*, around, is so used in Ezek 1:4, 27-28. (→ Theophany: Theology) Similarly, the adv. *m*^{e}*sibbâ* in a vivid description of God's glory in the thunderstorm (Job 37:12).

10. The phrase *māgôr missābîb*, terror on every side, is a cry or statement of alarm that is used in a lament context in Ps 31:13[14]; in Lam 2:22 such a crisis is ascribed to God's doing. In Jer 6:25; 46:5; 49:29 it describes divine punishment that takes the form of military attack. In Jer 20:3 it is a new name given to Jeremiah's priestly persecutor Pashhur as an omen of the personal fate that would overwhelm him and his fellow persecutors at the fall of Judah (cf. McKane, 462-65). In Jer 20:10 Jeremiah complains that the people mock him by throwing his prophetic coinage back at him. (→ Jeremiah: Theology)

P-B The Qumran Hymns echo the usage of the vb. [OT 1] in lamenting descriptions of hostility (1QH 2:25) and sorrow (1QH 5:35).

Circle, turn: → *'pp* (surround, # 705); → *ḥdr* I (surround, enclose, # 2539); → *ḥwg* (describe a circle, # 2552); → *ktr* II (surround, # 4193); → *nqp* II (go round, surround, # 5938); → *sbb* (turn go round, surround, # 6015); → *'āgōl* (round, # 6318); → *'ṭr* (surround, crown, # 6496/7)

BIBLIOGRAPHY

TWAT 730-43; B. W. Anderson, "'The Lord Has Created Something New': A Stylistic Study of Jer 31:15-22," *CBQ* 40, 1978, 463-78; A. J. Hauser, R. Gregory, *From Carmel to Horeb: Elijah in Crisis*, 1990.

Leslie C. Allen

6016 (*sibbâ*, turn of affairs), → # 6015

6017 (*sābîb*, around), → # 6015

6019	סְבַךְ

סְבַךְ (*s^{e}bak*), thicket (# 6019); סְבֹךְ (*s^{e}bōk*), thicket (# 6020); < סבך (*sbk*), intertwine (in Job 8:17; # 6018).

OT 1. In Gen 22:13 a ram was caught in a thicket so that God could provide a sacrifice for Abraham, a substitute for his only son Isaac.

2. The destruction of the sanctuary is likened to the cutting down of a thicket of trees with axes (Ps 74:5). Jer 4:7 uses the word metaphorically when referring to the destroyer from the north (Babylonia), which is like a lion that left his lair to destroy the land. Wickedness sets ablaze the thicket of the forest in Isa 9:18[17] and will be cut off by an axe (10:34).

Forest, park, thicket: → *gā'ôn* (height, eminence, # 1454); → *ḥōreš* (forest, woodland, # 3091); → *ya'ar* I (forest, wood, # 3623); → *s^{e}bak* (thicket, # 6019); → *pardēs* (park, forest, # 7236)

I. Cornelius

6020 (*s^{e}bōk*, thicket), → # 6019

6022	סבל

סבל (*sbl*), q. bear a burden/load; pu. be firmly established (Ps 144:14), hitp. drag oneself along (Eccl 12:5) (# 6022); סֵבֶל (*sēbel*), nom. (compulsory) labor (# 6023); סֹבֶל (*sōbel*), nom. (oppressive) burden (# 6024); סַבָּל (*sabbāl*), nom. burden-bearer (# 6025); סְבָלוֹת (*s^{e}bālôt*), nom. forced labor (# 6026).

ANE In all periods of Akk. the various nuances of *zabālu* include carry a load, bear punishment, suffer misery, and *zābilu* is used in the sense of carrier, corvée worker. In Old Babylonian, *nazbaltum* means load, burden, and *nazbalum* means load carried in brick-making processes. According to M. Weinfeld *sbl* is to be compared to the Akk. *tupšikku* when used of corvée ("The Counsel of the 'Elders' to Rehoboam and Its Implications," *Maarav* 31, 1982, 27-53).

OT 1. The vb. *sbl* and its cognate noms. are all concerned with the bearing of burdens or loads, both literal and figurative. Jacob uses the vb. to refer to his son Issachar in a forced-labor context (Gen 49:15). An idol finds itself in the unenviable position of having to be carried by its devotees in Isa 46:7 ("They lift it [*yiśśā'ūhû*] to their shoulders and carry it [*yisb^{e}lūhû*]")—in stark contrast to the Lord of the universe, who tenderly carries his people (v. 4: "I ... will sustain you [*'esbōl*] ... I will carry you [*'eśśā'*]; I will sustain you [*'esbōl*]"). Ps 144:14 is a fine example of how difficult it sometimes is to choose between a translation that involves a literal use of a vb. and one that leans toward a more figurative usage: "Our oxen will draw heavy loads (*m^{e}sūbbālîm*)" (NIV), "Our chieftains will be firmly established" (NIV, mg.). The allegory of the aging person parallels the muting of sexual desire with a grasshopper that "drags himself along (*yistabbēl*)" (Eccl 12:5).

Lam 5:7, which speaks of children bearing the punishment for their parents' sinful behavior, beautifully paves the way for the use of *sbl* twice in the Song of the

Suffering Servant in Isa 52:13-53:12. "He took up (*nś'*) our infirmities and carried (*sbl*) our sorrows" (53:4) is quoted in Matt 8:17 in connection with the healing ministry of Christ. "He will bear (*yisbōl*) their iniquities" (53:11) is paralleled by "he bore (*nś'*) the sin of many" in v. 12. In particular, the crushing burden implicit in the root *sbl* reminds us again of the enormous price Jesus paid for our redemption and justifies Polycarp's profound characterization of the fourth Servant Song as "the golden passion of the Old Testament."

2. Solomon appointed Jeroboam to supervise the whole labor force (*sēbel*) of the house of Joseph (1 Kgs 11:28). Among the builders of Jerusalem's wall in the days of Nehemiah were "those who carried materials (*hannōśᵉ'îm bassēbel 'ōmᵉśîm*)" (Neh 4:17[11]). Forced labor is clearly in view in Ps 81:6[7], a reference to the time of Israel's slavery in Egypt prior to the Exodus.

3. Restricted to Isaiah, *sōbel* is always used in parallelism with the (metaphorical) yoke an oppressor forces down on the shoulders of his subjects (Isa 9:4[3]; 10:27; 14:25).

4. A *nomen opificer/professionis*, the nom. *sabbāl* is translated as "laborers" in the NIV in 2 Chron 34:13; Neh 4:10[4] and "carriers" in 1 Kgs 5:15[29]; 2 Chron 2:2[1], 18[17] (in the 1 Kgs reference *nôśē' sabbāl* is the idiom used).

5. Attested only in Exodus, *siblâ* (always pl. *siblôt*) refers to the burdensome toil of the Israelites under their Egyptian oppressors: forced labor (Exod 1:11), hard labor (2:11), work (5:4, 5), yoke (6:6, 7).

Burden, load, weight: → *'amtaḥat* (sack, bag, burden, pack, # 623); → *ṭ'n* II (load, # 3250); → *ṭrḥ* (burden, load, # 3267); → *yᵉhāb* (burden, anxious care, # 3365); → *kin'â* (bundle, burden, # 4045); → *maśśā'* I (carrying, burden # 5362); → *nṭl* (bear, weigh, # 5747); → *nś'* (lift, raise high, pardon, contain, bear, exalt o.s., # 5951); → *sbl* (carry, bear a burden, # 6022); → *'ms/'mś* (carry a burden, load, # 6673)

Bibliography

TWOT 2:616.

Ronald F. Youngblood

6023 (*sēbel*, [compulsory] labor), → # 6022

6024 (*sōbel*, burden), → # 6022

6025 (*sabbāl*, burden-bearer), → # 6022

6026 (*siblâ*, forced labor), → # 6022

6032	סגד

סגד (*sgd*), q. bow down (# 6032).

ANE The root *sgd* appears with this meaning in Aram., Arab. and Eth.

OT The vb. appears only 4x, in the impf., always in conjunction with *ḥwh*, always of false worship; it reinforces the idea of obeisance (Isa 44:15, 17, 19; 46:6). In the Aram. of Dan 2:46; 3:5-28, however, it appears, instead of, and as an equivalent of, *ḥwh*.

Worship, bow down, serve: → *ghr* (down, bend over, # 1566); → *ḥwh* II (worship, bow, make obeisance, # 2556); → *kpp* (bow down, bow oneself down, # 4104); → *kr'* (bend, # 4156); → *sgd* (bow down, # 6032); → *'bd* (work, serve, worship, # 6268); → *qdd* (bow down, kneel down, # 7702); → *šrt* (wait on, be an attendant, serve, minister, # 9250)

Terence E. Fretheim

6033 (*s^e gôr*, enclosure), → # 6037

6034	סָגוּר

סָגוּר (*sāgûr*), nom. gold plate; finest gold (# 6034).

ANE The word is, perhaps, found in Ugar. *sgrt* and in Akk. *ḫurāṣu sag(i)ru*, solid/pure (hidden) gold.

OT 1. The form and derivation of the word are uncertain (see below). It occurs 9x in the combination *zāhāb sāgûr*, pure gold. Both the inner sanctuary and the inside of the temple itself are said to have been overlaid (*ṣph*) with pure gold (1 Kgs 6:20-21). The ten lampstands (1 Kgs 7:49 [‖ 2 Chron 4:20]) as well as the cups, snuffers, basins, incense dishes, and fire pans (1 Kgs 7:50 [‖ 2 Chron 4:22]) were all made of pure gold. All the vessels of the House of the Forest of Lebanon were also of pure gold (1 Kgs 10:21 [‖ 2 Chron 9:20]).

2. Gray (1970, 170) thinks that the word *sāgûr* qualifying *zāhāb* is a pass. part. that may be cognate with Arab. *sajara*, heat an oven. He maintains that *zāhāb sāgûr* denotes gold heated in a crucible. Montgomery and Gehman (152) think that the word is a translation of a technical term of Akk. origin denoting a certain monetary value. Others (e.g., Mauchline, 341; NEB; REB) take the word to mean "red." According to BDB, *sāgûr* is a masc. sing. q. pass. part. of the vb. *sgr*, shut, close (hence, prized, rare), but Driver (80, commenting on *s^e gôr* in Job 28:15) does not think that this is the most probable derivation.

Job 28:15 may indicate that the word is a nom. How is one to account for the pointing of MT (*s^e gôr*) in this v.? The fact that the word is used in parallelism with *kesep* suggests three possibilities. It could be that *s^e gôr* is an abbreviation for *zāhāb sāgûr*. A second suggestion is that *s^e gôr* could be a separate nom. meaning solid gold, which has been poetically used here instead of *zāhāb sāgûr* (so Driver and Gray, 195-96; Dhorme, 407–8; Pope, 204; cf. *BHS*). A third possibility is that the pointing of MT is wrong, in which case the word should be read *sāgûr*. At any rate, the context demands the reading gold (so RSV; NRSV), solid gold (so JB), fine gold (Davidson, 229), finest gold (so NIV), or refined gold (Peake, 251). NEB and REB have "red gold." The point made by Job 28:15-19 is that wisdom is of incomparable value: it cannot be purchased even with the most precious and exotic metals or gemstones.

Gold: → *'ôpîr* (gold of Ophir, # 234); → *beṣer* I (gold ore, # 1309); → *zāhāb* (gold, # 2298); → *ḥārûṣ* I (gold, # 3021); → *ketem* (gold, # 4188); → *sāgûr* (pure gold, # 6034); → *paz* (pure gold, # 7058); → *ṣrp* (melt, smelt, refine, # 7671)

Bibliography

A. B. Davidson, *The Book of Job With Notes, Introduction and Appendix*, 1962; E. Dhorme, *A Commentary on the Book of Job*, 1967; S. R. Driver, *The Book of Job in the Revised Version*, 1906; S. R. Driver and G. B. Gray, *A Critical and Exegetical Commentary on the Book of Job*

Together with a New Translation, ICC, 1964; J. Gray, *I & II Kings: A Commentary*, OTL, 2d, rev, ed., 1970; J. Mauchline, "I and II Kings," in *Peake*, 1964, 338-56; J. A. Montgomery and H. S. Gehman, *A Critical and Exegetical Commentary on the Books of Kings*, ICC, 1967; A. S. Peake, *Job*, 1905; M. H. Pope, *Job: Introduction, Translation, and Notes*, AB, 3d ed., 1979.

Robin Wakely

6035	סְגֻלָּה

סְגֻלָּה (s^e*gullâ*), nom. personal possession, treasure; crown jewel (# 6035).

ANE Ugar. *sglt*, treasure (?) (*UT*, # 1735); Akk. *sug/kullu*, herd; *sikiltu*, possession.

OT 1. In a profane, secular sense the word refers to one's personal possessions (1 Chron 29:3), in this case, David's presentation of his own gold and silver to the temple of his God (cf. 27:25-31; cf. also Eccl 2:8).

2. In the theological usage of the term its most important referent is Israel, whom God makes into his s^e*gullâ* (Exod 19:5), his own unique possession. Although all nations are his, Israel will become the "crown jewel" among all the nations. Her unique quality lies in her position/function/character as his kingdom of priests and a holy nation (set aside unto him; see also Deut 7:6; 14:2; 26:18; Ps 135:4).

In Malachi the nom. refers to the community that has a heart to fear the Lord (Mal 3:17). They are the Lord's and have a glorious future, unlike the complacent and rebellious (3:18-4:1).

P-B The LXX translates it as *laos periousios* in Exod 19:5.

NT In Titus 2:14 in the NT the same word is used to refer to God's new people through Christ. 1 Pet 2:9 quotes Exod 19:5, using *peripoiēsis*, which means the same thing—a special possession, "a people belonging to God."

Treasure: → *'āsām* (stores, # 662); → *'āsōp* (store, # 667); → *'ṣr* (accumulate, amass, store up, # 732); → *gizbār* (treasurer, # 1601); → *genez* I (treasury, # 1709); → *ganzak* (treasury, # 1711); → *ḥmd* (desire, treasure, # 2773); → *ḥsn* (be stored up, # 2889); → *kms* (stored up, # 4022); → *maṭmôn* (treasure [hidden], # 4759); → *misk*^{e}*nôt* (stores, # 5016); → n^e*kōt* (treasure house, # 5800); → *niškâ* (storeroom(s), cell, room, # 5969); → s^e*gullâ* (property, treasured possession, # 6035); → *piqqādôn* (deposit, # 7214); → *ṣpn* (hide, hidden, # 7621)

Bibliography

THAT 2:142-44; M. Greenberg, "Hebrew s^e*gulla:* Akkadian *sikiltu*," *JAOS* 71, 1951, 172-74; J. Durham, *Exodus*, 3, 1987, 256; U. Cassuto, *Exodus*, 1967, 227; B. Childs, *Exodus*, OTL, 1975, 341, 367; E. A. Speiser, "סְגֻלָּה" *Or* 25, 1956, 1-3; M. Weinfeld, *Deuteronomy* 1-11, AB, 1991, 368.

Eugene Carpenter

6036 (*segen*, community head), → # 2985

6037	סגר

סגר (*sgr* I), q. shut, close; ni. be shut up, closed; pi. deliver up; pu. be shut up; hi. deliver up, shut up, hand over (# 6037); nom. מַסְגֵּר (*masgēr* I), dungeon (→ # 4993); מִסְגֶּרֶת

(*misgeret*), border, rim, fastness, bulwark (→ # 4995); סְגוֹר (s^e*gôr*), enclosure (hapleg.; # 6033); סְגֹר (s^e*gōr*), nom. javelin (hapleg. in Ps 38:3; → # 6038); סוּגַר (*sûgar*), wooden collar (hapleg; # 6050).

ANE The Phoen. Eshmunazar inscription has two examples of this root in the causative stem, meaning to deliver s.o. up/over for submission or death (lines 9 and 21, cf. Gibson, *TSSI* 3:106-9). Eighth century Aram. had a nom. from this root for prison (Panammuwa Inscription, lines 4 and 8; Gibson 2:78-79). The root was also used in Ugar. (*UT*, 449, # 1738), Arab. *šağara*; Akk. *sekēru/sakāru, šigaru*.

OT 1. This vb. is the ordinary designation for the closing of doors and gates (26 of its 91 occurrences specifically have "door" or "gate" as direct object). Isaiah describes the renewed splendor of Zion when Yahweh becomes her shining light: her gates will always stand serenely open and never shut (ni. impf.), so that nations may bring her their wealth (Isa 60:11). Often the vb. is used for being closed up behind doors or gates for protection (Gen 7:1; Judg 9:51). Jericho was "bolted and barred" (Josh 6:1; NEB, a double use of this root, q. act. part. and pu. part.) or "tightly shut up" as in NIV. Thus, the miracle about to be described in Josh 6 was all the more striking.

2. The pi. and hi. may use the idiom "to shut up into s.o.'s hand," which means to deliver over for severe punishment or even death (see ANE above). David believed that Yahweh would deliver Goliath into his hand in order to show that there is a living God in Israel (1 Sam 17:46). The psalmist can rejoice that God has not closed him up in the hand of his enemies, but instead has set his feet "in a spacious place" (Ps 31:8[9]).

3. The noms. derived from this root usually designate a place or manner of confinement.

(a) The word s^e*gôr*, enclosure, in the phrase "confinement of the heart" (Hos 13:8) is an idiom for the chest protecting the heart, the symbol of life (Wolff, *Hosea*, 226).

(b) *sûgar*, wooden collar, is a hapleg. in Ezekiel's allegory of the lioness and the young lion (19:9; Jehoiachin). The lion is placed in such a collar and brought to the king of Babylon (Zimmerli, *Ezekiel*, 1:395-96; *HALAT* 703).

(c) The word *masgēr*, dungeon, is a metaphor for duress or affliction. In Isa 24:22, the kings of the earth, held accountable for their acts, are placed in "prison" (‖ *bôr*) awaiting the final trial. Isaiah also portrays the Servant of the Lord as someone who will release captives from prison (Isa 42:7). The psalmist asked Yahweh to set him free from prison (Ps 142:7[8]; → *masgēr*, # 4993 sub # 4995).

(d) *misgeret* (border, rim, stronghold, den) occurs 17x, mainly in the description of the table of the presence in the Holy Place (Exod 25:25, 27) and the movable stands in the temple (1 Kgs 7:28-29, 31-32, 35-36). The other 3x it has the meaning stronghold or den (Ps 18:46 ‖ 2 Sam 22:45[46]; Mic 7:17), from where the enemies of God capitulate. (→ *misgeret* # 4995)

(e) s^e*gōr* in Ps 38:3 is the band enclosing the shaft. It probably refers by metonymy to the entire weapon, probably a javelin of some kind (cf. 1QM V, 7, 9).

Closing, shutting: → *'ṭm* (stopped up, # 357); → *'ṭr* (close [mouth], # 358); → *gwp* I (shut, close, # 1589); → *ṭḥḥ* (besmeared, stuck, shut, # 3220); → *ṭmh* (stopped up, # 3241); → *n'l* I (tie, lock, # 5835); → *sgr* I (shut, close, deliver up, # 6037); → *stm* (stop up, # 6258); → *'ṣh* I (shut,

6781); → *'ṣm* III (shut one's eyes, # 6794); → *ṣrr* I (bind, shut up, be narrow, in straits, distress, # 7674); → *qpṣ* I (draw together, shut, # 7890); → *š''* I (smear, smooth, shut, # 9129)
Prison, restraint, closure: → *'ᵃsēpâ* (imprisonment, # 669); → *'sr* (bind, imprison, fetter, hitch, # 673); → *kl'* I (detain, imprison, close, shut up, # 3973); → *misgeret* (stronghold, dungeon, rim, table, # 4995); → *sgr* (close, # 6037); → *sōhar* (prison, # 6045); → *'ṣr* (restrain, imprison, stop, close, # 6806)

BIBLIOGRAPHY
NIDNTT 2:729-34; *TWAT* 5:753-56; M. Held, "Pits and Pitfalls in Akkadian and Biblical Hebrew," *JANESCU* 5, 1973, 184-85; J. Ovellette, "The Basic Structure of the Solomonic Temple and Archaeological Research," in *The Temple of Solomon*, ed. J. Gutmann, 1976, 1-20.

Bill T. Arnold

6038 (*sᵉgōr*, double axe or javelin), → # 7935

6039	סַגְרִיר

סַגְרִיר(*sagrîr*), downpour (# 6039).

ANE *sagrîr* is related to Arab. *sağara*, fill with water (see *HALAT* 702).

OT *sagrîr* occurs only in Prov 27:15. A downpour's power to cause dripping within a house (see Dalman) provides material for a simile of a quarrelsome wife's power to create misery in a home.

Rain, dew, drizzle, hail, showers: → *'ēgel* (drop [of dew], # 103); → *brd* I (hail, # 1351); → *gšm* (make rain, # 1772); → *zrm* II ([clouds] pour out [water], # 2442); → *ḥᵃnāmal* (sleet, hail?, # 2857); → *ṭal* (dew, light rain, drizzle, # 3228); → *yrh* II (give drink, cause rain, # 3722); → *mṭr* (make rain, # 4763); → *malqôš* (late rain, # 4919); → *sagrîr* (downpour, # 6039); → *sāpîaḥ* II (violent storm, # 6207); → *rᵉbîbîm* (showers, # 8053); → *rāsîs* (dew drop, # 8268); → *r'p* (drip, flow, rain, # 8319); → *śā'îr* IV (heavy rain, # 8540); → *šikbâ* (layer of dew, emission/ discharge of seed, # 8887)

BIBLIOGRAPHY
G. Dalman, *AuS*, 1:189.

Mark D. Futato

6040	סַד

סַד (*sad*), nom. stocks, shackles (hapleg. in Job 13:27; # 6040).

OT The prisoner's feet were placed in such stocks. In Job, the word has a figurative usage, "You fasten my feet in shackles; you keep close watch on all my paths by putting marks on the soles of my feet" (Job 13:27; cf. 33:11).

Chain, fetter: → *'sr* (bind, imprison, fetter, hitch, # 673); → *zēq* I (chain, fetter, # 2414); → *ḥarṣōb* (chain, fetter, # 3078); → *kebel* (shackle, # 3890); → *migbālôt* (chains, # 4456); → *mahpeket* (stocks, # 4551); → *mōsēr* (fetters, chains, # 4591); → *sad* (stocks, shackles, # 6040); → *pḥḥ* (be captured, chained, # 7072); → *rtq* (be bound, # 8415); → *šaršᵉrâ* (chain, # 9249)

T. Desmond Alexander

6041	סָדִין

סָדִין (*sādîn*), nom. linen garment (# 6041).

ANE Akk. *saddinnu*; cognates in Syr., Arab., and G. Note the use of *sindōn*, linen, in Matt 27:59; Mark 14:51-52; 15:46.

OT The word occurs twice in connection with Samson's challenge to the Philistines to solve his riddle (Judg 14:12-13). His reward, if they failed, was "thirty linen garments" (RV, NIV et al.; KJV sheets). Prov 31:24 lists these as products that the noble wife sells, along with sashes, to the merchants. The fourth and last occurrence is in Isaiah's list of women's clothing (Isa 3:23).

Clothing, garment: → *beged* II (clothes, garment, # 955); → *g^elôm* (garment, # 1659); → *ḥob* (fold of garment, # 2460); → *ḥōṣen* (fold of garment, # 2950); → *k^etonet* (garment, # 4189); → *lbš* (put on, clothe, wear, # 4252); → *mad* (garment, clothes, # 4496); → *madeweh* I (garment, # 4504); → *maḥ^alaṣot* (festive garments, # 4711); → *meltāḥâ* (wardrobe, # 4921); → *mešî* (costly garments, # 5429); → *sādîn* (costly garments, # 6041); → *sut* (garment, # 6078); → *p^etîgîl* (fine clothing, # 7345); → *ṣeba'* (colorful garments, # 7389); → *śimlâ* (garment, cloth, # 8529); → *šōbel* (flowing skirt, # 8670); → *šît* (garment, attire, # 8884)
Linen: → *sādîn* (linen garment, # 6041); → *pēšet* (flax linen, # 7324)

Robert L. Alden

6042 (*s^edōm*, Sodom), → Sodom

6043	סֵדֶר

סֵדֶר (*sēder*), arrangement, order, regulation (# 6043) a hapleg. in Job 10:22, where in his preoccupation with death Job uses five different expressions for the darkness of Sheol. The last of these five expressions is that Sheol is a land of "disorder" (*w^elō' s^edārîm*). The darkness of the underworld causes disorder and confusion for its occupants.

Order, battle: → *sēder* (order, # 6043); → *'rk* (set, put in rows, enter into battle, # 6885); → *tqn* (straighten, set in order, # 9545)

BIBLIOGRAPHY
E. Dhorme, *A Commentary on the Book of Job*, 1984, 155-56; J. Hartley, *The Book of Job*, NICOT, 1988, 191, 191n.5; W. Michel, *Job in the Light of Northwest Semitic*, Biblica et Orientalia 42, 1987, 1:250; N. H. Tur-Sinai, *The Book of Job*, 1957, 185-86.

Victor P. Hamilton

6044	סַהַר

סַהַר (*sahar*), nom. round enclosure (# 6044); סֹהַר (*sōhar*), prison (house) (→ # 6045).

ANE The etymology is uncertain, despite possible Egypt. and Akk. cognates. The context of Ugar. *shr* (*CML*, 146) is insufficient for firm conclusions. The root idea may be "round," so that the *bêt hassōhar* is the round outside wall of the prison where Joseph (Gen 39:20-23) and his brothers (40:3, 5) are incarcerated.

OT *sahar* is only found in S of Songs 7:2[3], where the navel or vulva may be compared to a "rounded goblet" (O. Keel, *The Song of Songs*, 1994, 232).

Enclosure: → *gnn* (enclose, protect, # 1713); → *ḥdr* I (surround, enclose, # 2539); → *sahar* (round enclosure, # 6044); → *ṣwr* I (besiege, enclose, # 7443); → *śwk* (hedge, shut in, # 8455)

P. P. Jenson

6045	סֹהַר

סֹהַר (*sōhar*), nom. prison (house) (# 6045).

ANE The word *sōhar* is known only in the story of Joseph and is always in the form *bêt hassōhar* (Gen 39:20-23; 40:3, 5).

OT 1. The expression *bêt hassōhar*, house of the prison, is a technical term to designate the prison in which Joseph was kept; the narrator explains it as the place "where the king's prisoners were confined" (Gen 39:20). The explanatory nature of this phrase is seen by the unusual use of the word king instead of pharaoh. The fact that this term occurs only in a story set in Egypt has led to the search for an Egyptian background to the expression, but none of the proposed comparisons are linguistically acceptable (Redford, 47-48).

The word *sōhar* probably derives from a stem *shr*, with the meaning to be round, found in S of Songs 7:2[3] (→ # 6044). In this text it describes a vessel identified archaeologically as a large, deep, ring-based bowl (Pope, 618).

The prison in which Joseph was kept was on the property of Potiphar, the chief vizier of Pharaoh (Gen 39:1), as is seen in the sequel when the chief cupbearer and baker are thrown into the same prison, described as being "in the vizier's house" (40:3-4). The situation described here may be like that of a certain vizier Rekhmire, who served under Thutmose III (1501-1447 BCE) in the eighteenth dynasty. The duties of the vizier listed in the inscriptions on the walls of his tomb indicate that he was the grand steward of all Egypt and that all activities of the state were under his control. This included the judiciary, in which reference is made to the hearing of cases in his hall. The text refers to "the great prison" in which those who are not able to disprove the charges made against them are detained for a hearing of the case (Breasted 2:276). The chief cupbearer and baker in similar fashion were "put ... in custody" (*b^e^mišmār*) under the supervision of Joseph (40:3-4).

The situation of Joseph's imprisonment is not altogether clear. The expected fate of a servant who sexually assaulted his master's wife would be execution. It is probable Potiphar did not entirely believe his wife's story, indicated in part by the fact that the charge she reported to her husband (Gen 39:17) was less explicit than the one she gave to the servants (39:14). In any case, Joseph was assigned duties as the administrator of the prison (39:22-23; 41:12). His capacity is only given in a general sense in each case, and there is no reason to assume two versions of the story, as asserted by Redford (146-48) and others.

2. The story of Joseph including his imprisonment is interpreted in Ps 105:16-22, in which imprisonment becomes another means of showing that God takes what is evil and makes it good (Gen 50:20). The word of God tested (*ṣrp*) Joseph (Ps 105:19). The vb. *ṣrp* literally means to refine, forming a play on the iron fetters of imprisonment mentioned in the v. previous (105:18). The physical imprisonment also fettered Joseph's aspirations, testing and transforming his character until the time that the divine word should come true (105:19). God in his time brings good out of evil,

showing his redemptive power over the evils in the world brought about because humankind determined to choose what was good and evil (Gen 3:5).

P-B In Mish. Heb. the word *shr* means enclosed place, stable, or moon. It is also used to designate the place where the Sanhedrin met.

Prison, restraint, closure: → *'ᵃsēpâ* (imprisonment, # 669); → *'sr* (bind, imprison, fetter, hitch, # 673); → *kl'* I (detain, imprison, close, shut up, # 3973); → *misgeret* (stronghold, dungeon, rim, table, # 4995); → *sgr* (close, # 6037); → *sōhar* (prison, # 6045); → *'ṣr* (restrain, imprison, stop, close, # 6806)

Bibliography

J. H. Breasted, *Ancient Record of Egypt*, 1962, 2:266-95; W. Lee Humphreys, *Joseph and his Family: A Literary Study*, 1988; J. Gerald Janzen, *Genesis 12-50*, 1993, 157-63; M. H. Pope, *Song of Songs*, 1977, 617-19; D. B. Redford, *A Study of the Biblical Story of Joseph*, 1970, 47-48, 146-48; L. Ryken, *Words of Delight*, 1987, 100-105.

A. H. Konkel

6047	סוג

סוג (*swg* I), q. deviate, diverge; digress; depart from; decline, deflect; be faithless, disloyal, rebellious; ni., give way, fall back, shrink back; give ground; recede; recoil; retreat, withdraw; turn away; be turned back; give in; make off, run away, take to one's heels; become disloyal, rebellious; revolt; desert; be turned back; turn apostate; hi., displace, shift, remove; put away (?); ho., be forced or driven back; repelled, repressed (# 6047).

ANE The vb. *swǧ* occurs in Arab. with the meaning go carefully, cautiously, prudently, warily, circumspectly.

OT 1. The q. occurs 3x. The wilfully perverse man who reaps the reward of his conduct (Prov 14:14) is described as *sûg* (masc. sing. q. act. part. in the const.) *lēb*, lit. turned away/faithless of heart (McKane, 232, 474, followed by REB, translates renegade). Writing in a cynical, degenerate, and unrighteous age, a psalmist (Ps 53:3[4]) bemoans the universal collapse of morals and condemns all human beings for having fallen away, or turned aside, from God (Dahood, 1973, 18, 20 has "Each is miscreant"). The par. Ps 14:3 has *sār*, turned aside (or, less likely, stubborn, rebellious, taking the vb. to be *sārar* [Dahood, 1966, 80-81; cf. Anderson, 1972a, 133]). C. A. and E. G. Briggs (110) think that Ps 14 and Ps 53 were derived from a common origin that may have had both vbs. Be that as it may, the point made by 53:3[4] (and by 14:3) is that the result of ignoring the demands that the reality of God makes on human life is social and religious disintegration (cf. Weiser, 165).

In a communal lament, Israel the vine, which had been carefully cultivated but is now forsaken, prays for restoration and promises more faithful conduct in the future (Ps 80:18[19]). It is better to take the words *wᵉlō'-nāsôg mimmekā* as a vow of fidelity ("we will not turn back from you") rather than as a statement ("we have not turned away from you") (see Delitzsch, 389; Tate, 308, 316; Bratcher and Reyburn, 718; *pace* Dahood, 1973, 255, 261; NEB). This is probably a solemn assertion not to relapse into idolatry or rebellion (Anderson, 1972b, 586). The striking relationship between this declaration of obligation and the vow made by the people at the assembly at Shechem (Josh 24:16-18) has often been noted (see Westermann, 60; Kraus, 143). Interestingly, the middle letter *'ayin* in the word "forest" in Ps 80:13[14] is elevated above the line in Heb. MSS: the letter's name means eye, and its spiritual significance is that the eye of the compassionate God is always upon his people (Stuhlmueller, 472). If, in his compassion, Yahweh will restore his people, they will consecrate their lives anew to his service (Weiser, 551).

2. In the ni., the vb. is used of Jonathan's insatiable bow, which did not turn back empty from battle (2 Sam 1:22, where, unusually, *nāśôg* has been written for *nāsôg* [see, e.g., Driver, 1966, 237]). In this v. eulogizing the heroic courage and superior military skills and ability of two of Israel's greatest warriors, Jonathan's bow and Saul's sword are depicted as drinking the blood and eating the fat of their victims (cf. Deut 32:42; Isa 34:6; Jer 46:10). The ni. is also used of the panic-stricken Egyptian warriors at the battle of Carchemish in 605 BC, breaking ranks and fleeing in disarray, confusion, and terror from the Babylonians, who are executing Yahweh's vengeance (Jer 46:5). The imagery of repelling an attacking force is used in prayers where oppressed supplicants make an urgent plea that hostile adversaries (mainly, but perhaps not exclusively, personal enemies in Ps 35:4; 40:14[15]; 70:2[3]; Zion's in Ps 129:5) be thrown into ignominious and uncontrolled retreat.

3. The ni. is often used of faithless conduct, of a treacherous desertion of one to whom a firm commitment had been made (cf. Roberts, 173). Only once is the vb. used of one whose faithfulness was exemplary. Despite suffering profound humiliation and even maltreatment in a hostile environment, Yahweh's dedicated servant did not shrink from his assigned task: he did not turn backwards (*'āḥôr lō' n^{e}sûgōtî*, lit., backward Isa did not turn back, Isa 50:5).

Jeremiah warned the insecure and vacillating Zedekiah that if he were to refuse to surrender to the Babylonians, Jerusalem would be burned and the members of the royal household captured (Jer 38:17-23). Jeremiah paints a striking picture of the women of the harem being led out to the officers of the king of Babylon while chanting what was probably a sneering taunt song (see Carroll, 687; Boadt, 97; Streane, 255; Driver, 1906, 235) rather than a haunting dirge or lament (see Peake, 173-74; Cunliffe-Jones, 226; Davidson, 127-28). This song about the plight of their former king includes the line "those trusted friends of yours ... have deserted you" (v. 22; cf. 20:10, where the motif of treachery among familiar friends also occurs). The trusted friends (lit., the men of your welfare) were the king's advisors who deceived Zedekiah by urging him to resist the Babylonians, a course of action that would lead to him sinking in the mud, as Jeremiah had done when he had been incarcerated in Malchiah's cistern (38:6).

The reference in Zeph 1:6 to those who have turned back from following Yahweh is probably not to syncretists (already mentioned in v. 5), but to the indifferent and self-sufficient who neglect the divine commands and who make their own plans without bothering to seek guidance from Yahweh (cf. Achtemeier, 65; Patterson, 304, 306-7; Roberts, 173-74; Robertson, 265-66). They are warned that the day of Yahweh's exterminating judgment is imminent. Elsewhere, those guilty of a sinful devotion to other deities are warned that they themselves will be turned back, repulsed, in bitter shame as a result of God's judgment (Isa 42:17). The way in which inexplicably perverse and disloyal Israel repeatedly turned away from God, despite his many mercies and blessings, is likened to the twisting of a defective, unreliable bow (Ps 78:57;

cf. Hos 7:16). Here, *wayyissōgû*, and/but they turned away, is translated by NEB and REB as "they were renegades." This psalm testifies to the fact that God's love defies all human expectations and calculations (Weiser, 542): the just and forgiving mercy of God can outlast the folly, obstinacy, and inconstancy of humankind (Rogerson and McKay, 1977b, 140, 151). But it also serves as a salutary warning that only those who submit to God in faith and obedience may participate in the history of salvation (Weiser, 543).

Having suffered a humiliating defeat at the hand of an unnamed foreign nation, an anguished and perplexed Israel considers itself betrayed and insists that the calamity is unmerited since the heart (considered the center of the will and intellect, which determined behavior) of the people has not turned back, i.e., been unfaithful (Ps 44:18[19]). This confident assertion of the nation's basic fidelity to God's covenant (vv. 17-22) makes Ps 44 unique (Rogerson and McKay, 1977a, 206).

In an impressive call to national repentance (Isa 59:1-21), the community in Jerusalem confesses the magnitude of its offenses. The people's rebellion (transgressing, v. 12), faithlessness (denying Yahweh, v. 13), and desertion (turning away from following God [*w^{e}nāsôg mē'aḥar '^{e}lōhênû*], v. 13) have eliminated justice (in v. 14, the ho. pf. is used with *'āḥôr* [justice is turned back]), righteousness, truth, and integrity (vv. 9a, 14-15). As a consequence, a barrier has been created between the community and God; salvation is being delayed.

4. With one exception (Mic 6:14), the hi. is used of removing a neighbor's landmark (Deut 19:14; 27:17; Job 24:2; Prov 22:28; 23:10; Hos 5:10). In Mic 6:14, the context suggests that the meaning of the vb. is hold back (of storing provisions). Some have felt it necessary to emend the MT (see, e.g., *BHS*; Allen, 376; Hillers, 80-81). However, Wolff (196) thinks that if the occurrence of the vb. here is original, then it may suggest a deceitful practice, perhaps a secret storage of food that would endanger the neighbor just as much as the malicious removal of the boundary stone. There were laws enshrining the right of Israel's ancestral families to property, which they believed was theirs under an ancient divine land grant (Habel, 51). The removal of a landmark (i.e., a property boundary stone), which defined the limits of one's divinely allotted portion/inheritance (see Mays, 89; Thompson, 266), was forbidden (Deut 19:14; cf. *ANET*, 422 [The Instruction of Amen-em-opet, ch. 6]). To displace a boundary marker was condemned as a severe violation of the integrity of Yawheh's holy land (Clifford, 105).

A gift from Yahweh, the land had to be honored by exemplary conduct. Misuse of the land constituted a violation of the sacral order (Mayes, 289). The person who transgressed the prohibition came under the curse of God (Deut 27:17). In the absence of hedges or other natural borders, ownership of plots that were conterminous was frequently the subject of dispute (see Job 24:2; Prov 22:28; 23:10; Hos 5:10; Mic 2:2) (Davies, 239). The evidence (e.g., Prov 23:10) suggests that some wealthy, avaricious landowners perpetrated acts of aggression upon poorer neighbors in order to acquire their land fraudulently (see Brueggemann, 90-98; Thompson, 217; Craigie, 268; Payne, 116; Wright, 128-31). Some (e.g., Craigie, 332-33) think that in Deut 27:17 the reference may be to a stone that was not simply a marker, but an inscribed stone monument similar to the Mesopotamian *kudurru* stone (Oppenheim, 123, 159; Craigie, 332; Hartley, 345-46), which detailed property rights. If this is correct, then the crime envisaged here may be the total appropriation of a neighbor's plot. Any form of encroachment on a neighbor's boundary was potentially destructive, not only of the individual and his immediate household, but also of his entire ancestral line (Wright, 129).

P-B In Heb. and Aram., the vb. *swg* I occurs with the meaning [cut off, separate], fence in, mark off; guard against trespassing a law, make a prohibition more restrictive; exaggerate; pi. fence in; hi. remove the landmark. The nom. forms *swg* ([partition], large chest or basket, class, species) and *sûgâ* (fence, enclosure) are also found (Jastrow 2:960-61).

Unfaithful, fraudulent, perfidious, rebellious, treacherous: → *bgd* (act faithlessly, treacherously, perfidiously, # 953); → *m'l* (behave or act contrary to one's duty, faithless, # 5085); → *mrh* (be refractory, obstinate, # 5286); → *m*^{e}*šûbâ* (unfaithfulness, apostasy, defection, # 5412); → *swg* I (deviate, diverge, decline, be faithless, rebellious, # 6047); → *sē'ēp* (disunited, divided in heart and mind, conflicting, schismatic, # 6189); → *srr* I (be stubborn, rebellious, # 6253); → *rmh* II (betray, deal treacherously with, # 8228); → *šqr* (deal/act falsely, betray, # 9213)

BIBLIOGRAPHY

E. Achtemeier, *Nahum-Malachi*, Interp, 1986; L. C. Allen, *The Books of Joel, Obadiah, Jonah and Micah*, NICOT, 1976; A. A. Anderson, *The Book of Psalms. Volume I: Introduction and Psalms 1-72*, NCBC, 1972 (1972a); idem, *The Book of Psalms. Volume 2: Psalms 73-150*, 1972 (1972b); L. Boadt, *Jeremiah 26-52, Habakkuk, Zephaniah, Nahum*, OTM, 1982; R. G. Bratcher and W. D. Reyburn, *A Translator's Handbook on the Book of Psalms*, 1991; C. A. and E. G. Briggs, *A Critical and Exegetical Commentary on the Book of Psalms*, 1, ICC, 1960; W. Brueggemann, *The Land*, 1978; R. P. Carroll, *Jeremiah: A Commentary*, OTL, 1986; R. Clifford, *Deuteronomy With an Excursus on Covenant and Law*, OTM, 1982; P. C. Craigie, *The Book of Deuteronomy*, NICOT, 1983; H. Cunliffe-Jones, *Jeremiah: God in History*, Torch, 2d ed., 1972; M. Dahood, *Psalms I: 1-50. Introduction, Translation, and Notes*, AB, 1966; idem, *Psalms II: 51-100. Introduction, Translation, and Notes*, AB, 1973; R. Davidson, *Jeremiah Volume 2 and Lamentations*, DSB, 1985; T. W. Davies, "Deuteronomy," in *Peake*, 1920, 231-43; F. Delitzsch, *Biblical Commentary on the Psalms*. Vol. II, KD, 2d ed., 1889; S. R. Driver, *The Book of the Prophet Jeremiah: A Revised Translation With Introductions and Short Explanations*, 1906; idem, *Notes on the Hebrew Text and the Topography of the Books of Samuel With an Introduction on Hebrew Palaeography and the Ancient Versions and Facsimiles of Inscriptions and Maps*, 2d ed., 1966; N. C. Habel, *The Land Is Mine: Six Biblical Land Ideologies*, 1995; J. E. Hartley, *The Book of Job*, NICOT, 1988; D. R. Hillers, *Micah*, Hermeneia, 1984; H.-J. Kraus, *Psalms 60-150: A Commentary*, 1989; W. McKane, *Proverbs: A New Approach*, OTL, 1970; A. D. H. Mayes, *Deuteronomy*, NCBC, 1979; J. L. Mays, *Hosea: A Commentary*, OTL, 1969; A. L. Oppenheim, *Ancient Mesopotamia: Portrait of a Dead Civilization*, 1965; R. D. Patterson, *Nahum, Habakkuk, Zephaniah*, 1991; D. F. Payne, *Deuteronomy*, DSB, 1985; A. S. Peake, *Jeremiah and Lamentations Vol. II: Jeremiah XXV to LII, Lamentations*, CB, 1912; J. J. M. Roberts, *Nahum, Habakkuk, and Zephaniah: A Commentary*, OTL, 1991; O. P. Robertson, *The Books of Nahum, Habakkuk, and Zephaniah*, NICOT, 1991; J. W. Rogerson and J. W. McKay, *Psalms 1-50*, CBC, 1977 (1977a); idem, *Psalms 51-100*, CBC, 1977 (1977b); A. W. Streane, *The Book of the Prophet Jeremiah, Together With the Lamentations, With Map Notes and Introduction*, CBSC, 1891; C. Stuhlmueller, "Psalms," in *HBC*, 1988, 433-94; M. E. Tate, *Psalms 51-100*,

WBC, 1990; J. A. Thompson, *Deuteronomy: An Introduction and Commentary*, TOTC, 1974; A. Weiser, *The Psalms: A Commentary*, OTL, 1965; C. Westermann, *The Praise of God in the Psalms*, 1966; H. W. Wolff, *Micah: A Commentary*, OTL, 1990; C. J. H. Wright, *God's People in God's Land: Family, Land, and Property in the Old Testament*, 1990.

Robin Wakely

6048	סוג

סוג (*swg* II), q. fenced about, bordered by (hapleg. S of Songs 7:2[3]; # 6048).

Border, boundary, corner, edge, rim: → *gbl* I (bound, border, # 1487); → *zāwît* (corner, # 2312); → *kānāp* (wing, skirt, outermost edge, # 4053); → *karkōb* (rim, edge, # 4136); → *mḥh* II (border on, # 4682); → *swg* II (border by, # 6048); → *pē'â* I (corner, # 6991); → *pinnâ* (corner, # 7157); → *ṣad* (side, # 7396); → *ṣēlā'* I (side, rib, side-chamber, # 7521); → *qēṣ* (limit, boundary, # 7891); → *qāṣeh* (end, border, # 7895); → *qṣ'* II (made with corners, # 7910)

Gordon H. Matties

6050 (*sûgar*, cage, prison), → # 6037

6054	סוּחָה

סוּחָה (*sûḥâ*), nom. offal (# 6054).

OT The only clear use of this word is in Isa 5:25. Isaiah expresses the anger of God against his people and says that their dead bodies will be like refuse (offal) in the streets. It has been conjectured that a word spelled with a *ś* instead of *s* in Job 9:31 (NIV slime pit) may be from the same root (D. J. A. Clines, *Job 1-20*, WBC, 1989, 220, n. 31a). For the textual issues in Ps 80:16[17], see W. VanGemeren, "Psalms," *EBC*, 1991, 5:526.

Dung, excrement, refuse, urine: → *'ašpōt* (ash-heap, refuse-heap, dung-hill, # 883); → *gll* II (befoul, dirty o.s., # 1671); → *dōmen* (dung, manure, # 1961); → *ḥ^a^rā'îm* (dung, # 2989); → *yešaḥ* (filth, diarrhea, # 3803); → *madmēnâ* I (dung pit, # 4523); → *sûḥâ* (offal, # 6054); → *pereš* I (offal, contents of stomach, # 7302); → *ṣē'â* (filth, human excrement, # 7362); → *ṣāpîa'* (dung [of cattle], # 7616); → *śîg* (excrement, # 8485); → *šyn* (urinate, # 8874)

Roy E. Hayden

6056	סוך

סוך (*swk* I), stir up, provoke (# 6056); מְסוּכָה (m^e*sûkâ*), hedge (→ # 5004).

ANE Possibly the vb. may be connected with Arab. *šwk/šauk*, sting (vb. and nom.), but especially with Eth. *säksäkä*, incite.

OT A disleg. in the pilpel in Isa 9:11[10], "the LORD has strengthened Rezin's foes against them and *has spurred* their enemies on," and in Isa 19:2: "I will *stir up* Egyptian against Egyptian."

Stirring, tossing: → *grš* II (toss up, # 1764); → *ḥmr* II (foam, surge, # 2812); → *swk* I (stir up, # 6056); → *'wr* II (stir oneself, # 6424); → *rḥš* (be stirred up, # 8180)

BIBLIOGRAPHY
W. Leslau, *Ethiopic and South Arabic Contributions to the Hebrew Lexicon*, 1958, 36; J. A. Motyer, *The Prophecy of Isaiah*, 1993, 107; H. Wildberger, *Isaiah 1-12*, 1991, 220-21.

Victor P. Hamilton

6057	סוך

סוך (*swk* II), q. anoint, pour out; hi. anoint o.s.; ho. be anointed with (# 6057).

ANE *swk* II is not attested outside of BH.

OT 1. The most frequent usage (8x) refers to putting oil on the body for cosmetic purposes, usually after washing (Exod 30:32; Judg 3:24; Ruth 3:3; 2 Sam 12:20; 14:2; 2 Chron 28:15; Dan 10:3 [2x]). Failure to use oil in this way was associated with distress of some sort, whether grief (2 Sam 12:20; 14:2), mental anguish (Dan 10:3), or deprivation (2 Chron 28:15). On the other hand, to be able to put on oil was apparently considered an integral part of looking and being at one's best (Ruth 3:3; 2 Sam 12:20; 2 Chron 28:15; Ezek 16:9). The latter two occurrences suggest a possible medicinal use as well. Chronicles refers to prisoners who are given food, water, clothing and shoes, and who have oil put on them, while Ezekiel recounts the figurative story of God's finding Israel as an abandoned child, whom he washed and put oil upon (cf. Luke 10:34 for an explicit example of oil being used medicinally).

2. Two other references occur in the context of the failure of the olive crop (an expression of divine judgment). Because the crop has failed, there is no olive oil to pour out (Deut 28:40; Mic 6:15).

3. A third usage is somewhat strange, occurring as it does in a euphemistic expression for elimination of body waste: "to cause the feet to pour" (Judg 3:24; 1 Sam 24:3[4]).

Anoint: → *mšḥ* I (anoint, spread a liquid, # 5417); → *swk* II (anoint, pour out, # 6057)

John N. Oswalt

6061	סוּס

סוּס (*sûs* I), horse (# 6061); סוּסָה (*sûsâ*), mare (# 6063).

ANE Ugar. *ssw*, Akk. *sīsû*, Phoen. *ss*, Deir Alla *ssh* (?), Old Aram. *ssyh*, Egypt. Aram. *sws*, Jewish Aram. *susyā'*, Syr. *susyā'*, Man. *susyā'*, Nab. *swsy'*, Palm. *swsy*, Arab. *sīsī*.

OT 1. The term most often appears in military contexts, frequently in conjunction with references to chariots. During the second millennium BC horse-drawn chariots became an essential part of NE armies and were greatly valued by kings. For example, in the Ugaritic Legend of Kirtu, King Pabil offers Kirtu silver, gold, slaves, horses, and chariots if he will terminate his siege of Pabil's city (*CTA* 14 iii 128; see Gibson, *CML*, 85). The OT frequently describes powerful armies, including those of Egypt, Assyria, and Babylon, as containing horses and chariots (Exod 14:9, 23; Josh 11:4; 1 Kgs 20:1; 2 Kgs 6:14-15; Isa 5:28; Jer 4:13; 46:9; Ezek 26:10-11; Nah 3:2; Zech 9:10; see *CAD* 15:331-32 for examples from Akk. literature). Some of the northern hordes, such as the

Scythians, rode on horses in battle (cf. Jer 6:23; 50:42; Ezek 38:4, 15). The horse was a symbol of military might, and its very appearance and mannerisms struck fear into the heart of those being attacked (Jer 8:16; Hab 1:8).

2. Because of its military importance the horse was understandably viewed as a guarantee of security (cf. Isa 30:16, where it is viewed as a safety valve that would allow even a defeated army to flee quickly and escape capture) and an object of trust (Ps 20:7a). In the Phoenician Karatepe inscription (*KAI* 26 A i 6-7; Gibson, *SSI*, 3:46-47; *ANET*, 499-500) Azitawadda boasts that he "added horse to horse" with the aid of Baal and the gods. However, Yahweh, the covenant God of Israel, wanted his people to trust in his ability to protect and deliver, not in horses and chariots. Moses urged Israel not to fear horses and chariots and assured them that Yahweh would give them victory in battle (Deut 20:1). The Law of Moses prohibited Israel's king from accumulating horses and developing a chariot force (Deut 17:16), but Solomon and several other kings blatantly disregarded this command (1 Kgs 4:26[5:6]; 10:25-29; 22:4; 2 Kgs 3:7; Isa 2:7; 31:1; Ezek 17:15). According to Micah, Yahweh would someday purify Judah by ridding it of horses and chariots (Mic 5:10[9]).

3. Faithful Yahwists recognized that the war horse, though stronger and faster than men (cf. Jer 12:5), was composed of flesh, susceptible to physical weakness (cf. 1 Kgs 18:5) and unable to resist Yahweh's supernatural power (Isa 31:3). One might prepare the horse for battle, but success comes from Yahweh (Prov 21:31). Men of faith trust in Yahweh, not horses, for their security (Ps 20:7; Hos 14:3[4]) because they realize that he bestows his favor on the obedient and faithful, not the strong (Ps 33:17-19; 147:10-11). In Israel the powerful word of Yahweh's prophets takes the place of horses and chariots (cf. 2 Kgs 2:11-12 and Beek, 1-10).

4. This faith in Yahweh was wisely placed, for time and again Yahweh demonstrated his superiority to horses and chariots on the battlefield. When Pharaoh's horses and chariots marched against Israel, Yahweh miraculously destroyed them in the Red Sea (Exod 15:1, 19, 21; cf. Deut 11:4; Isa 43:22). After Israel routed Jabin's army, Joshua, in obedience to Yahweh's instructions, burned the chariots and hamstrung the horses as a public testimony to Yahweh's superiority over the armies of men (Josh 11:4-11; cf. 2 Sam 8:4). The prophets frequently depict Yahweh destroying horses and chariots in conjunction with his judgment on disobedient and proud nations (Jer 50:37; 51:21; Amos 2:15; 4:10). Though he sometimes uses human armies as his instruments (Jer 50:37; 51:21), he does not need to use such methods (Hos 1:7). With a mere battle cry he disposes of horses and chariots (Ps 76:6[7]) and then invites the scavengers to devour the flesh of the dead horses (Ezek 39:20). The postexilic prophets Haggai and Zechariah picture the culminating eschatological battle as being highlighted by Yahweh's defeat of horses and chariots (Hag 2:22; Zech 10:5; 12:4; 14:15). He will rid Jerusalem of chariots and war horses as he establishes universal peace (Zech 9:10).

5. In his role as warrior Yahweh is sometimes portrayed as possessing horses and chariots (Hab 3:8, 15). He has "horses and chariots of fire" at his disposal (2 Kgs 6:17; cf. 2 Kgs 2:11). He can even strike panic into his enemies' hearts by making them hear imaginary horses and chariots (2 Kgs 7:6).

6. Various characteristics of the horse are utilized in the metaphorical language of OT writers. David likens sinners to a stubborn horse (Ps 32:9), while Solomon compares a fool to a horse that needs to be whipped before it will cooperate (Prov 26:3).

Jeremiah accuses God's people of pursuing their own sinful ways with the aggressiveness of horses charging into battle (Jer 8:6), and he compares Judah's idolaters/spiritual adulterers to lusty sex-starved stallions (5:8). In a similar vein Ezekiel compares Judah's preoccupation with political alliances to a lusty mare that longs for a large dose of a stallion's semen (Ezek 23:20). On a more positive note, Isaiah likens Moses' generation, the recipients of God's watchful care and protection, to a horse running in open country without stumbling (Isa 63:13), and Zechariah looks forward to a day when God's protection will cause his people to be as confident as a "proud horse in battle" (Zech 10:3).

7. A synonym for *sûsâ*, mare, is *rammākâ*, swift mare (# 8247), a hapleg. in Esth 8:10.

Horse: → *dhr* (gallop, # 1851); → *sûs* I (horse, # 6061); → *pārāš* (horseman, rider, horse, # 7304); → *rekeš* (team of horses, # 8224); → *ra'mâ* II (mane, # 8310); → *š^e'ātâ* (stamping [of hoofs], # 9121)
Chariot, cart, wagon, riding: → *rkb* (ride/mount, # 8206); → *šālîš* III (third man in war-chariot, adjutant, # 8957); → **Warfare: Theology**

BIBLIOGRAPHY

ADB 1:888-92; 6:1136-37; *ANET* 499-500; *CAD* 15:328-34; *IDB* 2:646-48; *TDNT* 3:336-39; *TWAT* 5:782-91; M. A. Beek, "The Meaning of the Expression 'The Chariots and the Horsemen of Israel' (II Kings ii 12)," *OTS* 17, 1972, 1-10; S. Dalley, "Foreign Chariotry and Cavalry in the Armies of Tiglath-pileser III and Sargon II," *Iraq* 47, 1985, 31-48; Y. Ikeda, "Solomon's Trade in Horses and Chariots in Its International Setting," in *Studies in the Period of David and Solomon and Other Essays*, ed. by T. Ishida, 1982, 215-38; M. A. Littauer and J. H. Crouwel, *Wheeled Vehicles and Ridden Animals in the Ancient Near East*, 1979; W. D. McHardy, "The Horses in Zechariah," BZAW 103, 1968, 174-79; S. Mowinckel, "Drive and/or Ride in O.T.," *VT* 12, 1962, 278-99; Y. Yadin, *The Art of Warfare in Biblical Lands*, 1963.

Robert B. Chisholm

6063 (*sûsâ*, mare), → # 6061

6066	סוּף

סוּף (*swp*), q. and hi. come to an end (# 6066); סוֹף (*sôp*), nom. end (# 6067); סוּפָה (*sûpâ* I), storm wind (→ # 6070).

ANE An Aram. cognate means to end, to perish; Arab. *swf*, to die of an epidemic.

OT 1. The Heb. verbal root *swp* occurs only 7x in the OT. The meaning come to an end in the sense of destroy is appropriate in the contexts where divine judgment is the theme (Ps 73:19; Isa 66:17; Amos 3:15). The only other occurrence of the root in the q. stem is in Esth 9:28, in the injunction that the Feast of Purim shall not "cease" among Israelite descendants (NRSV). The hi. form appears twice in Zeph 1:2-3 (sweep away, NRSV) and once in Jer 8:13 (a disputed text in which the Heb. consonants are usually revocalized).

2. The nom. *sôp*, end, appears 5x in the OT (2 Chron 20:16; Eccl 3:11; 7:2; 12:13; Joel 2:20). In Ecclesiastes the sage bemoans the limitations of humanity, which prevent a full understanding of God's ways (Eccl 3:11). He also soberly reminds the reader that "the end" for everyone is the grave (7:2). In Joel 2:20 the word has the

meaning "rear guard," as in a military convoy that Yahweh will overthrow on behalf of Israel.

3. The Aram. verbal root *swp* occurs twice in Dan (be fulfilled, 4:30; bring to an end = annihilate, 2:44).

End, cessation, outcome: → *'aḥ^{a}rît* (end, outcome, # 344); → *'ps* (cease, come to an end, # 699); → *bṭl* (cease working, # 1060); → *gmr* (be at an end, cease, fail, # 1698); → *ḥdl* I (end, stop, # 2532); → *swp* (come to an end, # 6066); → *sārâ* I (stopping, # 6239); → *qēṣ* (end, limit, boundary, # 7891); → *qṣh* I (bring about the end, shorten, # 7894)

BIBLIOGRAPHY

ISBE 2:79; R. Gordis, "Studies in Hebrew Roots of Contrasted Meanings," *JQR* 27, 1936, 33-58; W. A. Ward, "The Semitic Biconsontal Root SP," *VT* 24, 1974, 339-49.

Andrew E. Hill

6067 (*sôp*, end), → # 6066

6068 (*sûp* I, [sea of] reeds), → # 7866

6070	סוּפָה

סוּפָה (*sûpâ* I), nom. destructive windstorm, whirlwind (# 6070; > סוּף + ה loc (*HALAT* 706) or < *swp*, come to an end (→ # 6066; *HAHAT*, 539; BDB, 693). Synonyms: *s/śa'ar*, gale, windstorm (→ # 6193), *s/ś^{e}ārâ*, gale, windstorm (→ # 8554), *rûaḥ*, air in motion, wind (→ # 8120).

OT 1. The nom. occurs 14x in the OT, only in poetic texts. The word includes the semantic components "swiftness" and (in contrast to *rûaḥ*) "destructiveness."

2. In Isa 5:28b; 66:15; Jer 4:13 the wheeling of chariots is compared with *sûpâ*, "like a whirlwind." Job 37:9 describes God's wisdom that is seen in the realm of weather phenomena, e.g., the tempest that comes out "from its chamber."

3. According to the destructive effect of the whirlwind, *sûpâ* is aptly used for describing God's punitive acts either against Israel's enemies or against Israel itself and for salvation of his people.

(a) Isa 29:5-8 describes God's destroying Israel's enemies who fight against Ariel (Jerusalem). God's coming for judgment is accompanied by signs of theophany: thunder, earthquake, tempest, fire, his most available agents. The everyday experience of a storm that drives chaff and thistles away becomes a metaphor for God's sovereign "blowing" away his enemies. They are compared to *qaš*, chaff (→ # 7990; Ps 83:15[14]), *mōṣ*, chaff (→ # 5161; Isa 17:13), or *teben*, straw (→ # 9320; Job 21:18).

(b) *sûpâ* may also metaphorically denote the woe that overwhelms s.o., especially the *rāšā'*, godless (→ # 8401; Prov 1:27), but the believer can find shelter with God. The "stormy day" (*yôm sûpâ*, Amos 1:14) stands in parallel with "day of battle"; it is the day of Rabbat-Ammon's destruction in war that is effected by God. The metaphorical language leaves the question open whether it is a "real" storm accompanying the battle, or a poetic, interpretative element. "The categories of natural and supernatural are not distinguished in this kind of thinking" (Anderson/Freedman, *Amos,* 284; AB, 24A). Compare Nah 1:3b: "His way is in the whirlwind and the storm." *sûpâ* and *ś^e'ārâ* are God's agents, revealing and concealing his approaching for judgment.

Job 27:20 and Prov 10:25 imply God's sweeping the godless away by a tempest. Hos 8:7a speaks of man's own responsibility for his actions: Samaria's inhabitants worship other gods, and by this they are sowing *rûaḥ* and will reap *sûpâ*. This clause has by translation become a proverb in many European languages. Humans not only reaps what they sow, but the reaping will be the full consequence of their evil deeds.

P-B *sûpâ* occurs in Sir 43:17 in a wisdom context that describes God's creating all kinds of weather phenomena. The Qumran text CD 19:25 uses *rûaḥ* and *sûpâ* in the same climactic way as Hos 8:7. The LXX mainly translates *sûpâ* by *kataigis* (8x), the apt word for "storm wind, tornado."

Wind, storm: → *zal'āpâ* (scorching [wind], # 2363); → *ḥāzîz* (cloud, strong wind, thunderclap, # 2613); → *yôm* II (wind, storm, breath, # 3428); → *m*e*zārîm* (north-winds, # 4668); → *sûpâ* I (destructive wind-storm, whirlwind, # 6070); → *s'h* (calumniate, rush [storm], # 6185); → *rûaḥ* (wind, Spirit, # 8120); → *r'm* I (storm, thunder, # 8306); → *ś'r* II (carry off in a storm-wind, # 8548)

Bibliography

TWAT 5:800-3; A. D. Crown, "Toward a Reconstruction of the Climate of Palestine 8000 B.C. to 0 B.C.," *JNES* 31, 1972, 312-30; H. Lugt, "Wirbelstürme im Alten Testament," *BZ* 19, 1975, 195-204; R. B. Y. Scott, "Meteorological Phenomena and Terminology in the Old Testament," *ZAW* 64, 1952, 11-25.

Manfred Dreytza

6073	סוּר

סוּר (*swr*), q. turn aside from one's course; avert, turn away, turn toward, go away, desert, become disaffected, cease, desist; hi., push back, put s.o. at a distance, get rid of; ho., be estranged (# 6073); סוּר (*sûr* I), nom. faithless, disloyal, turn apostate (# 6074); סָרָה (*sārâ* I), cease (hapleg. in Isa 14:6) (# 6239).

ANE Cognates occur in the following: Phoen. *sur,* alienate; OSA *śwr*, separate; and Akk. *sâru*, dance.

OT 1. A common meaning for this vb., which occurs about 300x, is to "turn aside" physically from what one is doing (e.g., Exod 3:4) or from the road one is traveling (Judg 18:3, 15). The word is employed for s.o. or s.t. departing, e.g., glory cloud (Num 12:10), jealousy (Ezek 16:42), or a perverse heart (Ps 101:4). The hi. is found many times in conjunction with the rituals of sacrifice (Lev 3:4, 10, 15; 4:9; 7:4). For a comparison of *swr* with *šwb* and *pnh,* see *šwb*, # 8740.

2. For the most part *swr* has to do with the moral/spiritual direction someone is taking. Persons turn from the right road. Not unlike the story of Adam and Eve in the garden, Israel after a new beginning at the Exodus was "quick to turn aside (*swr*) from the way I [God] commanded them" (Exod 32:8) by making a calf to be god. Israel turned aside from the way the ancestors had walked (Judg 2:17) and from God's ordinances (Mal 3:7). Or, put another way, given an already sinful direction, as in Jeroboam's example, succeeding kings continued in (departed not from) the evil way: Jehoram (2 Kgs 3:3); Jehu (10:29; 13:11).

A frequent exhortation by pious leaders, prophets, and wisdom teachers is not to turn aside (*swr*) from the good and right way (Deut 17:20; Josh 23:6; 1 Sam 12:20, 21). To turn from the way God commanded is to invite a curse (Deut 11:28) and worse (Jer 17:13). *swr* is prominent in Deut and the Deuteronomic history in expressions such as turning aside from the commandment (Deut 17:20) or statutes (2 Sam 22:23).

To those traveling the road of wickedness, the admonitions are to leave that way and take the path of righteousness (Prov 3:7). Warnings are issued to keep one's distance from evil and wickedness (Num 16:26; Prov 3:7; Isa 52:11) and to remove (hi. *swr*) strange gods (Gen 35:2; Josh 24:14; 1 Sam 7:3), false worship (Amos 5:21, 23), lying (Ps 119:29), perversity (Prov 4:24), or evil generally (Isa 1:16). To depart from the way of evil is understanding (Job 28:28; cf. 1:8; Prov 14:16), but fools detest doing that (Prov 13:19). By the fear of the Lord one avoids (*swr*) evil (16:6).

3. There are instances of persons keeping a straight and steady course by following after God: Hezekiah (2 Kgs 18:6), Josiah (2 Kgs 22:2), and the psalmist (Ps 119:102). To stay on course is to turn neither to the right or to the left (Deut 2:27; 5:32[29]; Josh 1:7; 2 Kgs 22:2). Certain kings (e.g., Asa) removed (hi. *swr*) ancestral idols (2 Chron 14:3[2]). Israel on occasion removed (hi. *swr*) the offensive Baals and served the Lord (Judg 10:16; 1 Sam 7:4).

4. The alienation factor may be observed as twofold. The wicked call on God to depart from them (Job 21:14; 22:17). God in turn demands that the wicked depart from him (Ps 119:115; 139:19).

5. God is the subject of *swr*. He removed Isaiah's iniquity (Isa 6:7; cf. Joshua's sin in Zech 3:4). For an obedient people he will remove illness (Deut 7:15). It is God who removes the stony heart and in a work of transplant provides a heart of flesh (Ezek 36:26).

God's presence in the symbol of the pillar of cloud and fire stayed (did not depart from, *swr*) with the tabernacle (Num 12:10). God's Spirit departed from Saul (1 Sam 16:14; 18:12; 28:15; cf. Judg 16:20). Because of Israel's sin God threatened to remove her supports (Isa 3:1); he threatened to remove Judah (2 Kgs 23:27).

Turning, apostasy, returning, faithlessness, repentance: → *zwr* II (turn away, # 2319); → *ḥmq* (turn aside, # 2811); → *yq'* (turn aside, # 3697); → *nq'* (disengage, # 5936); → *sbb* (turn, go round, surround, # 6015); → *swr* (turn aside, # 6073); → *pnh* (turn to the side, # 7155); → *śṭh* (turn aside, # 8474); → *šwb* I (repent, turn, return, revert, withdraw, # 8740); → *tᵉqûpâ* (turning point, # 9543)

Bibliography

THAT 2:148-50; *TWOT* 2:620-21.

J. A. Thompson/Elmer A. Martens

6074 (*sûr* I, faithless), → # 6073

6077	סות

סות (*swt*), hi. entice, draw away, urge (on), mislead, woo, incite (# 6077).

ANE The vb. has no readily recognized cognates.

OT 1. The vb. *swt* in the sense of urging someone to action may occur in a morally neutral context. Othniel, the judge, is urged by Acsah to ask her father Caleb for a field

(Josh 15:18 = Judg 1:14). Ahab urges (*swt*) Jehoshaphat to attack the Arameans at Ramoth-Gilead (2 Chron 18:2).

2. In human interaction *swt* refers to suspicions or charges that someone has enticed or incited another. Baruch is unjustly accused of inciting Jeremiah against certain arrogant men (Jer 43:3). An Assyrian commander falsely accuses Hezekiah of misleading the people of Jerusalem (2 Kgs 18:32; 2 Chron 32:11, 15; Isa 36:18).

A related usage of *swt* has to do with a warning about enticement by riches (Job 36:18). The text about close relatives and friends who entice to idol worship (Deut 13:6-11[7-12]) gave rise to extensive Rabbinic pronouncements concerning the *mēsît*, one who leads individuals and towns away from God and who is subject, therefore, to the most severe punishments. Some of the NT texts that hint at a negative public response to the ministry of Jesus may suggest that the hatred reserved for the *mēsît* could, on occasion, have been directed toward him.

3. God may be the object of Satan's *swt* (Job 2:3), but more often God is the subject of *swt*, as when God draws Job away (*swt*) from the jaws of distress (36:16; cf. 2 Chron 18:31). David is unsure concerning whether God or human beings have incited Saul against him (1 Sam 26:19). A similar uncertainty, though deriving from entirely different causes, swirls around the question of whether it was God (2 Sam 24:1) or Satan (1 Chron 21:1) who incited David to take a census of Israel's (and Judah's) fighting men. Although alternative solutions to the problem have been suggested (cf., e.g., Sailhamer, 37-44), the traditional harmonistic approach remains the best of the available options: God's permissive action is highlighted in 2 Sam 24:1, while Satan's instrumentality (cf. Rev 12:9) is emphasized in the later text. Thus, the Lord through Satan incited David (cf. further Youngblood, 1095-96).

Seduction, incitement, enticement: → *nd'* (seduce, # 5604); → *ndḥ* I (banish, be scattered, be cast out, seduce, # 5615); → *swt* (entice, draw away, incite, # 6077); → *šgh* (stray, err, go/do wrong, mislead, # 8706); → *t'h* (wander off, lead astray, # 9494)

Bibliography

D. Neale, "Was Jesus a *Mesith*? Public Response to Jesus and His Ministry," *TynBul* 44/1, 1993, 89-101; J. H. Sailhamer, "1 Chronicles 21:1—A Study in Inter-Biblical Interpretation," *TrinJ* 10, 1989, 33-48; R. F. Youngblood, "1, 2 Samuel," *EBC* 3:1095-96.

Ronald Youngblood

6078	סוּת

סוּת (*sût*), nom. garment (hapleg. in Gen 49:11) (# 6078).

OT In Jacob's blessing of Judah, he speaks of a ruler that will come out of Judah. This ruler will bring an era of prosperity, likened to a vine, which will produce such benefits as an abundance of wine. This "winy" age is imaged as a time when the ruler will wash his "garment" in "the blood (*dam*, → # 1947) of grapes" (Gen 49:11).

Clothing, garment: → *beged* II (clothes, garment, # 955); → *g*ᵉ*lôm* (garment, # 1659); → *ḥob* (fold of garment, # 2460); → *ḥōṣen* (fold of garment, # 2950); → *k*ᵉ*tonet* (garment, # 4189); → *lbš* (put on, clothe, wear, # 4252); → *mad* (garment, clothes, # 4496); → *madeweh* I (garment, # 4504); → *maḥ*ᵃ*laṣot* (festive garments, # 4711); → *meltāḥâ* (wardrobe, # 4921); → *mešî* (costly garments, # 5429); → *sādîn* (costly garments, # 6041); → *sut* (garment, # 6078);

→ *p^e tîgîl* (fine clothing, # 7345); → *ṣeba'* (colorful garments, # 7389); → *śimlâ* (garment, cloth, # 8529); → *šōbel* (flowing skirt, # 8670); → *šît* (garment, attire, # 8884)

Robert L. Alden

6079	סחב

סחב (*sḥb*), q. drag, drag away (# 6079).

ANE A cognate is found in the Mesha Inscription, where *w'sḥb* refers to the "altar hearth of [Israel's] DWD" and to the vessels of Yahweh, each dragged before Kemosh (ll. 12-13, 18). There are also Phoen., Arab., and Eth. cognates.

OT This vb. occurs once in 2 Sam and 4x in Jer. In 2 Sam 17:13, Hushai suggests to the usurper Absalom that if David—exiled with his men from Jerusalem—seeks refuge in a city, Absalom's forces should simply drag (*sḥb*) that city into the valley with ropes. In Jer 15:3, the Lord threatens Judah with four kinds of destroyers, one of which consists of "dogs to drag away" the corpses of those killed by the sword. In Jer 22:19, the prophet threatens Jehoiakim with an unlamented death: "He will have the burial of a donkey—dragged away and thrown outside the gates of Jerusalem." Finally, Edom and Babylon suffer an identical verdict at Jer 49:20 and 50:45, respectively: "The young of the flock will be dragged away." In all five occurrences, something dead or destroyed is dragged away from its original location. In each, the actor exerts a clear supremacy or control over the thing dragged, a denigration of the victim that seems crucial for the verb's meaning in all five instances. This notion also occurs in the two appearances of the vb. in the Mesha Inscription.

Dragging, pulling out: → *gll* I (roll, roll away, flow down, drag, wallow, # 1670); → *grr* (drag out, ruminate, sawn up, # 1760); → *mšh* (pull out [of water], # 5406); → *mšk* (seize, drag off, delay, # 5432); → *sḥb* (drag off, pull away, # 6079); → *šll* I (pull out, # 8963)

D. A. Baer

6080	סְחָבוֹת

סְחָבוֹת (*s^e ḥābôt*), nom. rags (pl.) (# 6080).

OT The word occurs in Jer 38:11-12. Ebed-Melech took some "old rags" (*s^e ḥābôt*) and "worn-out clothes" (*m^e lâḥîm*) for Jeremiah to put under his arm pits so that he could be lifted from the pit.

Clothes—rags: → *b^e lôy* (rags, # 1170); → *melaḥ* I (worn out clothes, # 4874); → *s^e ḥabôt* (rags, # 6080)

Robert L. Alden

6081	סחה

סחה (*sḥh*), pi. scrape away (hapleg.; # 6081); סְחִי (*s^e ḥî*), nom. scraping(s), offscouring, scum (hapleg.; # 6082); סוּחָה (*sûḥâ*), nom. scraping(s), dung (hapleg.; → # 6054), from the putative root סוח (*swḥ*), a byform of *sḥh*: "The dead bodies are like refuse (*sûḥâ*) in the streets" (Isa 5:25).

ANE Eth. *sh'* (*saha*), nom. refuse. Arab. *sḥy*, sweep away (*HALAT* 707).

OT The vb. *sḥh* functions in a context where God threatens people with divine judgment and punishment. Three other vbs. are also used in conjunction with *sḥh*, viz., *šḥt,* destroy, *ns'*, remove, and *ntn*, give (her over to be a bare rock). This clearly expresses the ultimate aim of Yahweh (i.e., to remove even the ruins so that the city will be a desolate and empty place).

In this way not even a vague memory or sign will be left of Tyre under divine judgment. The Lord says of her, "I will scrape away (*w^esiḥêtî*) her rubble and make her a bare rock" (Ezek 26:4). Of Jerusalem and her people after the Babylonian destruction of 586 BC Jeremiah says to the Lord, "You have made us scum (*s^eḥî*) and refuse among the nations" (Lam 3:45). A similar idea is expressed by Paul: "Up to this moment we have become the scum of the earth, the refuse of the world" (1 Cor 4:13).

Dung, excrement, refuse, urine: → *'ašpōt* (ash-heap, refuse-heap, dung-hill, # 883); → *gll* II (befoul, dirty o.s., # 1671); → *dōmen* (dung, manure, # 1961); → *ḥ^arā'îm* (dung, # 2989); → *yešaḥ* (filth, diarrhea, # 3803); → *madmēnâ* I (dung pit, # 4523); → *sûḥâ* (offal, # 6054); → *pereš* I (offal, contents of stomach, # 7302); → *ṣē'â* (filth, human excrement, # 7362); → *ṣāpîa'* (dung [of cattle], # 7616); → *śîg* (excrement, # 8485); → *šyn* (urinate, # 8874)

Scraping: → *grd* (scrape oneself, # 1740); → *mll* IV (scrape, # 4911); → *sḥh* (scrape away, # 6081); → *qṣh* I (trim off, maim, shorten, scrape off, # 7894); → *qṣ'* I (scrape off, # 7909); → *rdh* II (scrape out, # 8098)

Ronald Youngblood

6082 (*s^eḥî*, scraping), → # 6081

6084	סָחִישׁ

סָחִישׁ (*sāḥîš*), what grows on its own accord (second year after harvest) (hapleg.; # 6084).

ANE Akk. *sippîḫu.* wild growth.

OT The sole instance occurs at 2 Kgs 19:29, where *sāḥîš* is likely a byform of *šāḥîs* (Isa 37:30). Contextually, the word refers to that which grows from the *sāpîaḥ*, which is random growth following a year of sowing.

Growth, greatness, luxuriance, ripening, sprouting: → *bqq* II (grow luxuriantly, # 1328); → *gdl* I (grow up, become great, make great, boast, # 1540); → *nwb* (grow, prosper, flourish, # 5649); → *sāḥîš* (what grows on its own accord, # 6084); → *sāpîaḥ* I (what grows on its own accord, # 6206); → *ṣmḥ* (sprout, spring up, grow, prosper, make grow, # 7541); → *r'n* (be luxuriant, green, # 8315); → *śg'/śgh* (grow great, increase, exalt, # 8434/8436)

BIBLIOGRAPHY
T. R. Hobbs, *2 Kings*, WBC, 1985; G. H. Jones, *1 and 2 Kings*, 1984; R. D. Patterson and H. J. Austel, "1, 2 Kings," *EBC*, 1988, 4:267-68, 270.

M. G. Abegg, Jr.

6086	סחר

סחר (*sḥr*), travel, trade (# 6086); סֹחֵר (*sōḥēr*), part. trader; סַחַר (*saḥar*), nom. profit (# 6087); סְחֹרָה (*s^eḥōrâ*), merchandise (# 6088).

ANE Akk. *saḫāru*, turn, surround (*HALAT* 708a); Arab. *saḥira*, rise early.

OT 1. Although the Israelite patriarchs were not so much traders (Gen 34:10 and 42:34 refer to traveling and not trade [Elat, 527-8 with literature; but cf. M. Silver, *Prophets and Markets*, 1983, 8]), Abraham buys Hittite land for the burial of Sarah according to the standard price (*šeqel kesep*) of the traders (23:16). Solomon buys horses and linen through royal traders (*sōḥ*ᵃ*rē hammelek*, 1 Kgs 10:28-29 = 2 Chron 1:16). He also received revenue from traders (1 Kgs 10:15 = 2 Chron 9:14).

2. The root is used for the Midianites (Gen 37:28) and great trading cities, like Tyre (Isa 23:2, 8; Ezek 27 [cf. *TWAT* 4:815-16]) and her trading partners (e.g., Aram, Tarshish, Damascus, Arabia, etc., in Ezek 27) and Babylonia (Isa 47:15; Ezek 17:4). Tyre's immoral profits will be given to God (Isa 23:3, 18). The wise woman does profitable business (*ṭôb saḥrāh*) (Prov 31:18).

P-B A merchant is not the right person to get information from on prices (Sir 37:11).

Trade, merchandise, buying, selling: → *k*ᵉ*na'an* (trader, # 4047); → *krh* (get by trade, # 4126); → *m*ᵉ*ḥîr* I (price, payment, # 4697); → *mkr* I (trade, sell, # 4835); → *sḥr* (travel, trade, # 6086); → *qnh* (acquire, buy, # 7864); → *rkl* (trade, # 8217); → *šbr* II (buy, # 8690)

BIBLIOGRAPHY

TWAT 4:815-17; M. Elat, "The Monarchy and the Development of Trade in Ancient Israel," *State and Temple Economy in the Ancient Near East*, 2, 1979, 527-31; B. Landsberger, *Hebräische Wortforschung*, 1967, 187-90; E. A. Speiser, *Oriental and Biblical Studies*, 1967, 96-105.

I. Cornelius

6087 (*saḥar*, profit), → # 6086

6088 (*s*ᵉ*ḥōrâ*, merchandise), → # 6086

6089	סֹחֵרָה

סֹחֵרָה (*sōḥērâ*), rampart (# 6089).

OT *sōḥērâ* occurs only in Ps 91:4 and likely derives from *sḥr*, go around (→ # 6086). It may be related to Syr. *sakk*ᵉ*rā'*, shield; thus the frequent translation buckler, or to Akk. *siḫirtu*, wall enclosing a town, city wall, thus rampart. The context of the lone occurrence in BH suggests a protective devise; God's faithfulness is the protective shield or enclosure for those who dwell in the shelter of the Most High, in the shadow of the Almighty.

BIBLIOGRAPHY

E. Klein, *A Comprehensive Etymological Dictionary of the Hebrew Language for Readers of English*, 1987; A. A. Macintosh, "Psalm XCI 4 and the Root *sḥr*," *VT* 23, 1973, 52-62; M. E. Tate, *Psalms 51-100*, WBC, 1990, 448; W. A. VanGemeren, "Psalms," *EBC*, 5:599-600.

Keith N. Schoville

6090	סֹחֶרֶת

סֹחֶרֶת (*sōḥeret*), mineral stone in pavement mosaic (# 6090).

ANE See the Akk. *siḫru*, a variety of *šubû*, stone (*CAD* 15:239-40).

OT The nom. occurs only Esth 1:6. NIV understands the mosaic pavement to have included "costly stones" (cf. JB "precious stones"; NEB "turquoise"). The NRSV opts for "colored stones," following Moore (*Esther*, AB 7B, 1971, 1).

Rock, stones: → *'eben* (stone, rock, # 74); → *gābîš* (rock-crystal, # 1486); → *ḥallāmîš* (flint, # 2734); → *ḥāṣāṣ* (gravel, # 2953); → *kēp* (rock, # 4091); → *sōḥeret* (mineral stone, # 6090); → *sela'* (rock, # 6152); → *sql* (throw stones, # 6232); → *ṣûr* I (rock, boulder, # 7446); → *ṣûr* II (pebble, flint, # 7447); → *ṣōr* I (flint knife, # 7644); → *rgm* (stone, # 8083); → *talpiyyôt* (courses of stones, # 9444)

Bibliography

ISBE 3:205-6; 4:622-30; *NIDNTT* 2:731-34; 3:381-99.

Andrew E. Hill

6092 סִיג

סִיג (*sîg*), lead oxide (# 6092).

OT The nom. is unique to the OT and appears always in the context of refining silver. Enough of the ancient art of smelting and refining silver was known generally so the prophets and wisdom writers could use it as a symbol for purification and judgment. The primary prophetic text is Isa 1:22, 25, where the prophet compares the nation to dross that will pass through the refiner's kiln and become pure silver.

Silver was found bound with lead ores and had to be separated in a two stage process. The first stage consisted of reducing the lead ore to lead containing the silver. This process contained two steps: the lead ore (commonly galena) was heated leaving lead sulfate and lead oxide (litharge); the mixture was then heated, in charcoal at a high temperature in a relative absence of air to reduce it to crude lead. The result of the smelting process was a small amount of silver (in practice usually less than one-half percent) with lead and other metals. In ancient practice there was little differentiation of the chemical changes involved; primitive metallurgy was a really complicated mess of reactions, so the description of the city corrupted by its leaders as dross (Isa 1:22) was an apt picture. The second stage for the metallurgist to extract the silver from the crude lead was refinement through a process known as cupellation. The metal was placed in a cupel, a shallow vessel made of a porous substance as bone ash, and the furnace was heated until the molten lead was bright red; a blast of air turned it into lead oxide, which was absorbed by the cupel, leaving behind the silver. This is the process described in Isa 1:25 as the prophet concludes the metaphor to assure the purification of the leaders of Jerusalem.

In Jer 6:27-29 this image is taken up in a variant manner; the prophet functions as a refiner, but the result is a failure with no yield of silver. The MT apparently has an improper word division in Jer 6:29a, which should read, "The bellows are scorched by the fire, the lead (*'ōperet*) is consumed." Lead was also added by the refiner as a flux to carry away unwanted alloys, but in this case the lead was used up and only a mess remained (it is possible this mess is indicated by the metals mentioned in v. 28).

In Ezek 22:17-22 the image is given a new turn with reference only to the preliminary stage of smelting, ruling out the possibility of refining for silver as in Isa 1:25. The raw material is described in 22:18 as devoid of silver (the MT text is corrupt in this verse, the word silver is a gloss, as is evident in comparison with the LXX). The description is elaborated in terms of the process in 22:19-22; the image for worthlessness is also made to be one of judgment. The people will be gathered to Jerusalem, just as the crude metal would be placed into a furnace, heated with bellows, and smelted.

The other OT references to lead oxide are also metaphorical: Prov 25:4-5 compares the removal of alloy to produce silver to the removal of the wicked to form a just kingdom; Ps 119:119 refers to the wicked of the earth as alloy. There appears to be an error of word division in the MT in Prov 26:23a; the text should say, "As a white glaze (*kspsg*) covers a clay pot," based on the Ugar. *spsg* (*UT*, 451). White glaze on a clay pot is a striking emblem of heated (or perhaps flattering) lips concealing an evil mind.

P-B The nom. is found in Mish. Heb. with the sense of dross, base metal, unrefined silver, or refuse.

NT The image of refining metal is used in a positive sense in the NT, where the trial of faith is more precious than gold that has passed through the refiner's fire (1 Peter 1:6-7).

Metals: → *'anāk* (lead, # 643); → *bedîl* (dross, # 974); → *barzel* (iron, # 1366); → *zāhāb* (gold, # 2298); → *ḥel'â* I (rust, # 2689); → *ḥašmal* (glow?, electrum, glowing metal, # 3133); → *kesep* (silver, money, # 4084); → *masgēr* II (metal worker, # 4994); → *ma'abeh* (foundry, # 5043); → *neḥōšet* I (copper, bronze, # 5733); → *sîg* (lead oxide, # 6092); → *sēper* II (bronze, plate, # 6220); → *'ōperet* (lead, # 6769); → *paḥ* II (thin sheet, # 7063); → *pelādōt* (steel?, # 7110); → *ṣwr* III (cast [metal], # 7445); → *ṣa'aṣu'îm* (things formed by metal coating, # 7589); → *ṣph* II (arrange, overlay, plate, glaze, # 7596); → *ṣrp* (melt, smelt, refine, # 7671); → *qālāl* (polished metal, # 7838); → *šḥṭ* II (alloyed, # 8822)

BIBLIOGRAPHY
L. C. Allen, *Ezekiel 20-48*, WBC, 1990; R. J. Forbes, *Studies in Ancient Technology*, 8, 1964, 228-39; W. L. Holladay, *Jeremiah 1*, 1986, 230-32; J. A. Motyer, *The Prophecy of Isaiah*, 1993.

A. H. Konkel

6105	סִיר

סִיר (*sîr*), nom. (cooking) pot; tub, basin (# 6105).

ANE Cognates are found in Can., Akk., and possibly Egyp. Aram. (*HALAT* 710).

OT 1. The nom. *sîr* can denote a domestic cooking pot of various sizes, which was set on the fire for cooking (Exod 16:3; 2 Kgs 4:38-41; Eccl 7:6 [note the play on words with *sîrîm*, meaning thorns; → # 6106]). It can also refer to the bronze pots used to remove ashes from the altar of the whole burnt offering in the tabernacle and temple service (Exod 27:3; 38:3; 1 Kgs 7:45). Interestingly, in Jer 52:18-19, *sîr* is listed not only with the bronze articles that were taken from the temple by the Babylonians, but also among the gold and silver ones. *sîr* is also noted in the vessels (→ *kelî*, # 3998) used for Josiah's Passover (2 Chron 35:13; first in the list with *dûd* and *ṣallaḥat*). Finally, the term can also denote a washing basin (Ps 60:8[10]; 108:9[10]). From the above, it appears that *sîr* is a general term for pots.

2. The image of the pot functioned effectively in prophetic literature. In Mic 3:3, Israel's cruel and evil leaders are described as chopping up God's own people like

meat for the pot (*sîr* ‖ *qallaḥat*). Their injustice will be answered by God's judgment (3:4).

The ominous vision Jeremiah received of a boiling pot (*sîr nāpûaḥ*) tilted away from the north and ready to pour disaster on Judah was a vivid portrayal of coming divine judgment (Jer 1:13-14; cf. Sauer, 59-61, who links the image with ritual hostile to Yahweh). In Ezek 24:1-14, Jerusalem is likened to the cooking pot and her inhabitants to the pieces of meat that would be boiled in God's wrath (cf. 11:1-12).

On a more positive note, the cooking pots at the temple (used by worshipers) were singled out as an example of how even these lowly objects will (like the more sacred bowls in front of the altar) be holy to the Lord on the great day of the Lord (Zech 14:20). There will then be no more distinction between the common and the holy. Every pot (*sîr* used generically for all cooking pots) in Jerusalem and Judah will be sacred (14:21). It is interesting to note that pots inscribed *qdš* (and thus apparently consecrated for holy use) have been found in Iron II sites (see further Gordon, 120-22).

Pan, pot: → *'ᵃgarṭāl* (bowl, basin, # 113); → *dûd* (cooking pot, # 1857); → *maḥtâ* (censer, fire pan/tray, # 4746); → *marḥešet* (baking pan, # 5306); → *maśrēt* (baking pan, # 5389); → *sîr* (cooking pot, # 6105); → *pārûr* (cooking pot, # 7248); → *qallaḥat* (pot, # 7831)

BIBLIOGRAPHY

R. Amiran, *Ancient Pottery of the Holy Land*, 1970; R. P. Gordon, "Inscribed Pots and Zechariah XIV 20-1," *VT* 42, 1992, 120-23; A. M. Honeyman, "The Pottery Vessels of the Old Testament," *PEQ* 71, 1939, 85; J. L. Kelso, *The Ceramic Vocabulary of the Old Testament*, BASOR, Suppl. Studies, nos. 5-6, 1948, esp. §§ 26 and 63; J. L. Kelso, "Pottery," *IDB* 3, 846-53, esp. 850; C. L. and E. M. Meyers, *Zechariah 9-14*, 1993, 481-82; G. Sauer, "Mandelzweig und Kessel in Jer 1:11ff.," *ZAW*, 78, 1966, 56-61.

Cornelis Van Dam

6106	סִירָה

סִירָה (*sîrâ*), thorny bush; barb; hook (# 6106).

OT 1. The term is clearly used to describe the thorny burnet (a shrub; *Poterium spinosum*, Löw) in contexts of judgment on the nations: Edom (Isa 34:13), Israel (Hos 2:6), and Nineveh (Nah 1:10). In Eccl 7:6, the laughter of fools is likened to the crackling sound of thorns (*sîrâ*) under a pot.

2. The word is also used of the thorny hook (taken from *Poterium spinosum*) used as a fishhook for the removal of prisoners by the Assyrians (Amos 4:2).

Thornbush, nettle, sting, thistle, thorn: → *'āṭād* (thornbush, # 353); → *barqōn* (thorn, brier, # 1402); → *deber* II (thorny sting, # 1823); → *dardar* (thistle, # 1998); → *ḥēdeq* (brier, # 2537); → *ḥôaḥ* I (thorn, # 2560); → *mᵉsûkâ* (thorn hedge, # 5004); → *na'ᵃṣûṣ* (thornbush, # 5848); → *sîrâ* (thorny bush, # 6106); → *sillôn* (thorn, # 6141); → *sᵉneh* (thorny shrub, # 6174); → *sirpād* (stinging nettle, # 6252); → *ṣe'ᵉlîm* (thorny lotus, # 7365); → *ṣᵉnînîm* (thorns, # 7564); → *qôṣ* I (thornbush, # 7764); → *qimmôś* (weeds, nettles, # 7853); → *śēk* (thorn, splinter, # 8493); → *šāmîr* I (Christ's thorn, # 9031)

BIBLIOGRAPHY

TWOT 2:623; Löw, *Die Flora der Juden*, 1928; M. Zohary, *Plants of the Bible*, 1982, 156.

K. Lawson Younger, Jr.

6107	סָךְ

סָךְ (*sāk*), nom. number, multitude, crowd, throng (hapleg.; # 6107); perhaps < סכך (*skk* I), cover, protect (→ # 6115).

ANE This nom. is poorly attested and of uncertain origin: Phoen. *msk,* number, multitude (*DISO*, 160; *CIS*, 1:3; Cooke, 33); Egyp. *saki* > *sk,* warrior, soldier; troops (multitude of soldiers?) (Lesko 3:106; Budge 2:639).

OT 1. The Heb. nom. *sāk* in Ps 42:4[5] is a hapleg. The matter is complicated by the presence of several Heb. homonyms, leading to a variety of views. The nom. probably denotes crowd, festive throng in BH, just as it is used in Modern Heb.

2. The context seems to demand that *sāk* be nuanced "large crowd, throng, multitude." The psalmist describes his past customary action of leading a festive throng in a liturgical procession to the temple. Because it is the antecedent of the pl. suffix on *'eddaddēm,* I led them, the nom. *sāk* probably refers to a group of worshipers. It appears to be a synonym for *hāmôn ḥôgēg,* festive throng. NIV has handled it admirably:

> I used to go with the multitude (*sāk*),
> leading the procession to the house of God,
> with shouts of joy and thanksgiving
> among the festive throng (*hāmôn*).

3. However, others argue that *sāk* is a synonym for *bêt 'elōhîm*, house of God, and so render it as "tent, tabernacle" (Gesenius, 542; Kraus, 435, 437). The nom. is then connected to the common Sem. root *skk*: Sum. *sukku,* sanctuary, temple; Akk. *sukku,* shrine, sanctuary, temple; Arab. *šākaka,* cover a roof; *šukuku,* roof, roofed building. Linguists then derive *sāk* from the variably spelled Heb. root *skk/śkk* I, which has many derivatives: *skk,* cover; *māsāk,* covering; *mesukâ,* covering; *mûsāk,* covered structure; *sōkēk,* covering shield; *śkk,* cover; *śōk,* booth, pavillion. As attractive as this might be, it fails to explain the antecedent of the pl. suff. on *'edaddēm,* I led them.

4. Textual variants in Ps 42:4[5] confuse the hapleg. *sāk,* multitude, with the common homonym *sōk* (thicket, lair): LXX *skēnēs,* tent; and Syr. *setārā',* protection, covering; and Heb. mss. *sōk,* covert, lair. So some relate *sāk* to the variably spelled Heb. root *skk/śkk* II, which has many derivates: *skk,* weave together; *sōk,* thicket; *sukkâ,* woven booth, tabernacle; Succoth; *śkk,* weave. This derivation leads to the proposals of "interwoven mass, throng" (BDB, 697) or "booth" (Gesenius, 542). The former sees *sāk* as a synonym for *hāmôn,* throng, while the latter is a synonym for *bêt 'ĕlōhîm,* house of God.

5. Still others relate *sāk* to *śwk,* hedge up, fence about; *meśûkâ* nom. hedge. Dahood proposes the nuance "barrier," referring to the temple enclosure that separated the court of the Gentiles (Dahood, 257). This does not fit the context; it creates a questionable title for the dividing wall; and it does not explain the a-class vowel.

P-B 1. The nom. *sāk,* crowd, does not appear in DSS or RL. Rabbinic exegesis of Ps 42:4[5] mistakenly derived *sāk* from the homonymic word *sak,* shade: "When I traversed the land in shade, I struck them dumb for as long as the house of God [was standing]" (Braude, 2:442).

2. The nom. *sāk* reappears in Modern Heb. as “crowd, festive throng.” Modern Heb. has four distinct homonyms: *sāk*, lubricate, oil; *sāk*, crowd; *sak*, cover, screen, shade; *sak*, sum (of money), total, amount (Klein, 445; Segal and Dagut, 377; Sivan and Levenston, 502).

3. The nom. *sāk* in Ps 42 should not be confused with the homonym *sak* (amount), which did not arise until Mish. Heb.: *sak*, amount, sum, number; *s^{e}kā’*, add up, total, gather, assemble (Jastrow, 988; Levy, 521). For example, “The number (*sak*) of pupils for a teacher in the primary class is twenty-five” (Baba Bathra 21a). This is connected to Syr. *sākā’,* nom. end.

NT The NT term *ochlos*, crowd (# 4063), parallels Heb. *sāk*, festive throng, when it describes the festive crowd accompanying Jesus into Jerusalem during the Triumphal Entry in a manner similar to a liturgical procession going into the temple (Matt 21:8, 46).

Crowd of people, congregation, rabble: → *’^{a}sapsup* (rabble, # 671); → *hāmôn* (noise, crowd, agitation, bustle, turmoil, # 2162); → *h^{a}mullâ* (noise, noisy crowd, crowd, # 2167); → *sāk* (number, multitude, throng, # 6107); → *‘^{a}ṣārâ* (festive assembly, # 6809); → *qhl* (assemble, summon, # 7735); → *rigmâ* (noise, noisy crowd, # 8086)

BIBLIOGRAPHY

TWAT 5:838-56; *TWOT* 2:623-24; W. G. Braude, *Midrash on the Psalms*, 1959, 2:442; E. A. W. Budge, *An Egyptian Hieroglyphic Dictionary*, 1978, 2:639; G. A. Cooke, *A Textbook of North-Semitic Inscriptions*, 33; P. Craigie, *Psalms 1-50*, 1983, 323; M. Dahood, *Psalms I*, 1966, 257; M. Jastrow, *A Dictionary of the Targumim, the Talmud Babli and Yerushalmi, and the Midrashic Literature*, 988; E. Klein, *A Comprehensive Etymological Dictionary of the Hebrew Language*, 1987, 445; H.-J. Kraus, *Psalms 1-59: A Commentary*, 1978, 435-37; L. H. Lesko, *A Dictionary of Late Egyptian*, 3:106; J. Leveen, “Textual Problems in the Psalms,” *VT* 21, 1971, 48-58; J. Levy, *Wörterbuch über die Talumudim und Midraschim*, 1:521; J. Schreiner, “Verlangen nach Gottes Nähe und Hilfe: Auslegung von Psalm 42/43,” *BibLeb* 10, 1969, 254-64; M. Segal and M. B. Dagut, *Hebrew-English Dictionary of Contemporary Israeli Hebrew*, 1985, 377; R. Sivan and E. A. Levenston, *The Megiddo Modern Dictionary*, 1987, 502.

Gordon H. Johnston

6108	סֹךְ

סֹךְ (*sōk*), thicket, shelter, hut (# 6108).

ANE The word *sōk* is probably derived from the Heb. root *skk* III, overshadow, screen, cover (see also *sukkâ*, hut, booth, thicket). The Heb. root *skk* is cognate with the Arab. *sakka,* to close, choke up.

OT 1. The term *sōk* occurs 5x in the OT with a range of meanings. Even as the Lord established his *sōk* in Jerusalem (tent, NIV; booth, NRSV), so too he permitted it to be destroyed like a garden in the Babylonian invasion of Judah (Lam 2:6). Here Yahweh’s *sōk* is to be identified with the Jerusalem temple, the symbol of God’s abiding presence with his people.

2. In Ps 10:9 the wicked are said to devour the poor like a lion springing from cover. However, the psalmist sings a song of trust because the Lord shelters the righteous in his *sōk* (Ps 27:5; cf. 76:2[3]).

3. Yahweh's anger will come against Judah like the lion springing from cover (Jer 25:38). The imagery of a lion stalking prey in stealth and then pouncing to devour is a motif for divine wrath in Jer 4:7; 5:6; Hos 5:14; 13:7-8. Theologically, the passage is a vivid reminder that Yahweh's sovereignty extends to all the nations.

Hiding: → *ḥb'* (hide, conceal, # 2461); → *ḥbh* (hide, # 2464); → *ḥāgû* (refuge, cleft, # 2511); → *ḥpp* I (screen, shelter, # 2910); → *ṭmn* (hide, # 3243); → *kḥd* (be hidden, hide, # 3948); → *knp* (hide oneself, # 4052); → *sōk* (hiding-place, shelter, thicket, hut, # 6108); → *str* (hide, kept secret, # 6259); → *'lm* (hidden things, secrets, # 6623); → *ṣpn* (hide, # 7621); → *śpn* (conceal, # 8561)
Shelter: → *ḥpp* I (screen, shelter, # 2910); → *maḥseh* (refuge, shelter, # 4726); → *mālôn* (lodging place, # 4869); → *mistôr* (shelter, # 5039); → *skk* I (cover, shelter, # 6114)

BIBLIOGRAPHY

ISBE 2:705-7; *TWOT* 2:623-24; R. Gordis, "Studies in Hebrew Roots of Contrasted Meanings," *JQR* 27, 1936-37, 33-58.

Andrew E. Hill

6109 (*sukkâ*, tabernacle, hut), → # 6109a, 6114

6109a	סֻכּוֹת

סֻכּוֹת (*sukkôt*), Feast of Tabernacles, traditional tr. booths or tabernacles (used by Vg.; # 6109a); sg. סֻכָּה (*sukkâ*), thicket, hut, (# 6109).

ANE The nom. *sukkôt* is usually linked with *skk* III, cover (→ # 6114; *HALAT* 712). There is considerable difference of opinion amongst scholars about the usage of *skk*, and caution must be exercised when using OT dictionaries (*TWAT* 5:839-40). Cognates with a meaning similar to *skk*, shrine III, are Akk. *sukku,* chapel; and Arab. *sakka* VIII, dense (vegetation).

OT 1. *Usage*. In the OT a *sukkâ* can refer to a thicket used as a lion's den (Job 38:40) or to a temporary dwelling such as a hut (Lev 23:43; 2 Sam 11:11; Isa 1:8; 4:6). More common is the use of the pl. in *ḥag hassûkkôt*, festival of the huts, to refer to the Feast of the Booths/Tabernacles/Succoth (Lev 23:34, 42-43; Deut 16:13, 16; 31:10; 2 Chron 8:13; Ezra 3:4; Neh 8:15-17; Zech 14:16, 18-19).

2. *Succoth in recent interpretation.* The interpretation of the Succoth Feast is one of the most controversial areas of OT scholarship, and divergent opinions exist. Mowinckel (1953, 1963) saw the feast as the cultic vehicle by means of which the blessing of God was transferred to the individual and the community. This was especially true of the fall festival that as cultic drama Mowinckel related to the ascendence of God as King to the throne, symbolized by the procession of the ark during the covenant celebration (2 Sam 6). Weiser rejected the ascension to the throne as the center of the Succoth Feast and replaced it with the renewal of the covenant as proclamation of the salvific acts of God. Kraus (879) is convinced that a royal Zion festival that commemorated the election of the Davidic dynasty, not covenant renewal, was at the heart of the Succoth Feast. The reconstruction put forward by von Rad identifies Shechem as the venue for the celebration of the covenant by proclaiming the Torah during the Feast of Succoth.

3. *Possible development of the Feast of Succoth.* (a) The Feast of Succoth is closely associated with the Feast of Ingathering (*ḥag h'āsîp*; Exod 23:16). This indicates an intention to observe the end of the agricultural year during the fall, and it is likely that it started on the full moon in the middle of the seventh month and lasted one day (Ps 81:3). The Feast of Succoth is often referred to as "the feast/festival" (*ḥag*; 1 Kgs 8:2, 65; 12:32; 2 Chron 5:3; 7:8; Neh 8:14, 18; Ezek 45:25).

(b) More details are found in Deut 16:13-15, where the festival is called Feast of Succoth and is to last seven days. The dedication of Solomon's temple took place during the time of this festival and so it points to the importance of this feast (1 Kgs 8:2, 65-66). The location of the feast is now "at the place the LORD will choose," and this probably indicates the centralizing of Israelite worship in the Jerusalem temple (Deut 16:15).

(c) Lev 23:33-42 describes the Feast of Succoth as a joyous occasion; the sojourn in the wilderness is provided as motivation for the dwelling in tents/booths (de Vaux, 496). This feast was the last important feast of the year and was celebrated on 15-22 Tishri (7th month) after the autumn harvest (Grabbe, 93-94). Persons taking part in the festival made booths or temporary shelters from leaves and branches (Neh 8:15). The length of the feast is now eight days, and an elaborate series of sacrifices is mentioned in Num 29:12-39. Each day had its own cultic events—i.e., a specific order of sacrifices (Num 29:12-38), and perhaps also a water libation ceremony (Isa 12:13) and the singing of Hallel (Ps 113-118) and the Psalms of Ascent (Ps 120-134).

4. *Theological interpretation of the Feast of Succoth.* This feast can also be understood within the theological framework of blessing, rejoicing, and kindness to the poor (McConville, 1984, 110-11). (a) It is much more than a mere reminder that God provides for the needs of Israel with each agricultural season. Joy and gratitude are appropriate because the feast is a commemoration and a reenactment of God's salvific acts during the Exodus and the years in the wilderness (*TWOT* 2:624).

(b) There seems to be an increasing emphasis on sin and the reconciliation between God and humankind by means of the detailed information about sacrifices in Lev 23 and Num 29 (*TWAT* 5:852-53). The Feast of Succoth is significant for the absolving of sin within the context of cultic expiation by means of substitution. Thus, the effect of the sin perpetrated by humankind falls on the sacrificial animal, and reconciliation is established (Otto & Schramm, 82-84).

P-B 1. *LXX.* The nom. *sukkâ* is translated 26x with *skēnē*, tent. The Feast of Succoth is referred to by the setting up of tents (Deut 16:16, etc).

2. *RL.* The tractate Sukkah in the Mishnah discusses the Feast of Succoth and concludes that it was also to be considered days of "holy convocation."

3. *Qumran.* Lev 23 and Num 29 are still adhered to (*TWAT* 5:855-56). There seems to be a preference in the Temple Scroll for the sin offering as opposed to the initial burnt sacrifice during the Succoth Feast (Maier, 89).

NT John 7:2 also uses *skēnopēgia* to refer to "a Jewish feast." Peter wants to build booths/tents in Mark 9:5 (Matt 17:4; Luke 9:33), similar to the Succoth Feast, to establish a locus for the appearance of the glory of God (*EDNT* 3:251).

Feasts & festivals: → *bikkûrîm* (early or firstfruits, # 1137); → *ḥag* (procession, round dance, festival, feast, # 2504); → *ḥ^{a}nukkâ* (dedication, Feast of Dedication, # 2853); → *mô'ēd* (appointed time, # 4595); → *maṣṣôt* (Feast of the Unleavened Bread, # 5174a); → *marzēaḥ* (cultic feast, funeral meal, # 5301); → *sukkôt* (Feast of Tabernacles, # 6109a); → *ʿaṣārâ* (festive assembly, # 6809); → *pûrîm* (festival of Purim, # 7052a); → *pesaḥ* (Feast or sacrifice of Passover, # 7175 [→ **Passover: Theology**]); → *rō'š ḥōdeš* (festival of the new Moon, # 8031a); → *rō'š haššānâ* (beginning of the year, # 8031b); → *šābu'ôt* (feast of Weeks, # 8651a); → *šabbāt* (sabbath, # 8701 [→ **Sabbath: Theology**])

BIBLIOGRAPHY

EDNT 3:251-52; *TWAT* 5:838-56; *TWOT* 2:623-24; L. Grabbe, *Leviticus*, 1993; H.-J. Kraus, *Psalmen*, 1966; J. Maier, *Die Tempelrolle vom Toten Meer*, 1978; J. G. McConville, *Law and Theology in Deuteronomy*, 1984; S. Mowinckel, *Religion und Kultus*, 1953; idem, *The Psalms in Israel's Worship*, 1963; E. Otto & T. Schramm, *Festival and Joy*, 1981; G. von Rad, *The Problem of the Hexateuch and Other Essays*, 1966; A. Weiser, *The Psalms*, 1962.

Hendrik L. Bosman

6114	סכך

סכך (*skk* I), q. cover, guard, overshadow; hi. cover, protect, shut up (# 6114); סָךְ (*sāk*), nom. multitude (hapleg.; → # 6107); סֹכֵךְ (*sōkēk*), nom. cover (hapleg.; → # 6116). סכך (*skk* II), q. weave (→ # 6115). סכך (*skk* III), hi. cover, shelter (# 6114); מְסֻכָּה/מְסֻכָה ((*m^esukâ/m^esukkâ*), cover (# 5010); סֹךְ (*sōk*), cover, hide (→ # 6108); סֻכָּה (*sukkâ*), nom. tabernacle, tent, hut, shelter (→ # 6109). Possible derivative: מָסָךְ (*māsāk*), nom. cover, curtain, shield (# 5009).

ANE Cognates include the Akk. *sakāku*, choked up (*AHw*, 1010b); Arab. *sakka*, blocked.

OT 1. *skk* I (used 18x) is one of a list of Heb. words rendering the idea of cover (→ *ksh*, cover, # 4059). *skk* II means knit together or weave (Ps 139:13), while according to *HALAT*, *skk* III means cover, shelter (e.g., Judg 3:24 and cf. the festival of Sukkoth). This threefold division is not without its problems, as *TWAT* 5:840, makes clear. *skk* I, like *ksh* (→ # 4059), is used in a literal sense of the action of concealment. So a curtain (*pārōket*, → # 7267) is to conceal (*skk* I—NIV, shield) the ark of the covenant from view (Exod 40:3, 21). Or the term is used in the sense of overshadow, as the wings of the cherubim overshadow the atonement cover of the ark (Exod 37:9; cf. 1 Kings 8:7 and 1 Chron 28:18).

2. In the prophets, *skk* I is used in Ezek 28:14, 16, where the king of Tyre, is called "the anointed cherub that covers" (NIV, guardian cherub, in line with the ANE idea of the cherubim as guardians of the king's throne, cf. Zimmerli, 85, 92-93). The idea of protection occurs also in Nah 2:5[6] of a protective shield (lit., the covering) in parallel to the city wall.

3. In the Writings, the q. *skk* I occurs with a literal sense (Behemoth is covered by the shadow of lotus plants, Job 40:22). The hi. (or perhaps of *skk* III, so *HALAT* 712, and see *TWAT* 5:840) is used in Job 3:23 (hedge in). The same sense of closing in or limiting, as in God's shutting in the sea, occurs in 38:8.

4. Theologically, the key idea of God's protection occurs in Ps 91:4, where the psalmist uses the powerful imagery of a mother bird to speak of God who covers (*skk* I) with his feathers and spreads the protection of his wings over the righteous (cf. 5:11[12]). In 140:7[8], God covers (NIV, shields) one's head in the day of battle.

5. *skk* I has at least two derivatives (so *HALAT*), both occurring only once. *sōkēk* is found in Nah 2:5[6] with the sense of a protective shield, but not in Neh 2:6 as *HALAT* 712. *sāk* (→ # 6107) occurs in Ps 42:4[5], with the sense of throng or multitude, referring to the worshipers who proceed into the house of God. The nom. *māsāk* (following *HALAT* and BDB) belongs to the root (*skk*), but whether *skk* I, II, or III is intended is unclear. The probability is that *skk* I (→ # 6114) is intended, but in the absence of a definite conclusion, the nom. will be treated separately. *māsāk* (used 25x in all) is found mostly in Exod (16x) and Num (6x), where the reference is to the tabernacle, and in particular to the curtains that served as doors or symbolic boundaries between one area and another. So there was a screen at the gate of the court (Exod 27:16; 38:18; Num 3:26), a screen at the opening of the tent itself (Exod 26:36-7; 35:15; Num 3:26), and most important of all, at the entrance to the Most Holy Place (Exod 35:12; 39:34; 40:21; Num 3:31). The latter is literally the veil (*pārōket*, → # 7267) of the covering (*māsāk*). Here was the boundary between the realm of the human and the divine, which only the high priest might cross and then only on the Day of Atonement. Within the idea of the veil is to be found the most important theological contribution of the term *māsāk*. The veil denies access, but also points to the awesome mystery that God inhabits and so signifies the gulf between the holiness of God and humankind's profanity.

6. In 2 Sam 17:19 *māsāk* refers to some form of lid used to cover a well in order to hide Jonathan and another person. Grain was then sprinkled across the lid to conceal it completely from view. The cloud that God spreads as a cover (Ps 105:39) is both the sign of his presence and protection against the sun, while conversely the pillar of fire is the sign and giver of light. Thus the protection of God assumes a practical dimension for the desert wanderers (cf. Isa 4:5; *ḥuppâ*, # 2903). God speaks of removing Jerusalem's cover in order to spy out the defense secrets of the City of David (Isa 22:8).

7. *skk* II (so *HALAT*) occurs in q. in Ps 139:13 and the po. in Job 10:11, both describing the creative act of God in the womb of a mother, in knitting together (so NIV) bone and sinew, leading the psalmist to exclaim, "I praise you because I am fearfully and wonderfully made" (Ps 139:14a), and Job to acknowledge "You gave me life" (Job 10:12). The ni. should probably be read in Prov 8:23, where Wisdom proclaims her preexistence as the entity, fashioned (NIV margin) from eternity, before the world began. The alternative is to read *nsk* III (# 5820; so *NIVEC*) or *nsk* II (# 5819; so *HALAT* 664b) with the sense of appointed. *HALAT* offers conjecturally also the ni. of *skk* II in Ps 2:6. The psalmist speaks there of either God's induction of the king in Zion (NIV installed makes good sense, given that v. 7a speaks of a decree) or of his creation (reading the ni. of *skk* II) of the king as a son (cf. v. 7b, today I have begotten you, NIV margin). The advantage of the creation reading is that it undercuts the view of the king as the *adopted* son of God (as in Dahood, 1:11-12) and implies the closer (relational) sense of Creator and created. Generally, for *skk* II, the theology of cover goes beyond the idea of God as Protector to include that of God as Creator, thus overlapping with the semantic domain of creation (→ *br'* I, create, separate [# 1343]), and so giving this root its distinctive theological contribution.

8. *skk* III (following *HALAT*) occurs twice in the hi. The phrase "cover one's feet" is used in both Judg 3:24 (Eglon, king of Moab) and 1 Sam 24:3[4] (Saul) as a euphemism for "relieving oneself." *HALAT* offers also the conjectured reading of the

q. of *skk* III in Lam 3:43-44. Here graphically illustrated is a deep sense of abandonment and frustration as experienced by the writer. Lamentations sees God as covered with anger (v. 43) and as judge who is covered with a cloud so that no prayer can penetrate (v. 44). The people have become the scum and refuse of the nations (v. 45). Even in Lam, few descriptions can match this sense of despair when faced with a God whom even prayer cannot reach! The linguistic contribution of *skk* III lies in the sense of cover as concealment. Three derivatives are adduced by *HALAT*.

(a) *sōk* (# 6108) continues the sense of concealment, referring to the lair of a lion (Ps 10:9; Jer 25:38) and to a hiding place, provided by God in the day of trouble (Ps 27:5b; NIV has tabernacle in view of the parallel with God's dwelling, v. 5a). Ps 76:2[3] again parallels *sōk* with God's dwelling but lacks the element of concealment.

(b) *m^{e}sukâ* occurs only once in Ezek 28:13, where the ruler of Tyre is described in his primal glory as adorned with jewels, representing either royal or priestly wear (so Zimmerli, 92). The connections with Eden (v. 13a), cherubim (vv. 14, 16), and the holy mountain of God (v. 14) suggest that the writer may be drawing on an elaborate sacral or royal mythology.

(c) The third derivative is *sukkâ*, usually rendered as hut or shelter (→ *sukkoth*, # 6109a).

P-B The LXX uses a variety of G words (see *TWAT* 5:855), including *skiazō*, meaning to overshadow, and *skepazō*, meaning shelter or cover. The LXX uses *to katapetasma*, meaning covering veil or curtain, to translate both *māsāk* and *pārōket* (see further *NIDNTT* 3:794-95).

NT The account of the torn curtain (*to katapetasma*) in Mark 15:38 (and parallels) carries both the sense of revelation (as the opposite of cover) and access (which the veil denied). The G *episkiazo* is used in the sense of overshadow (Matt 17:5; Luke 1:35) while the form *skepasma* occurs once in 1 Tim 6:8, meaning either clothing (so NIV) or shelter. Reminiscent of Ps 91:4 is Jesus' comparison of himself to a mother hen who would gather the people of Jerusalem as her chicks (Matt 23:37; Luke 13:34).

Covering, guard, shield: → *ḥph* (cover, sheath, overlay, panel, # 2902); → *ksh* (cover, conceal, cover, put on, clothe, # 4059); → *lwṭ* (cover, enfold, wrap, # 4286); → *skk* I (cover, guard, overshadow, protect, # 6114); → *spn* (cover, roof, panel, # 6211); → *'lp* (cover, faint, # 6634)

BIBLIOGRAPHY

TWAT 5:838-56; *TWOT* 2:623-24; *AncIsr*, 312-30; B. Childs, *Exodus*, 1974; M. Dahood, *Psalms*, 2, 1968; M. Haran, *Temples and Temple Service in Ancient Israel*, 1978; M. Pope, *Job*, 1965; W. Zimmerli, *Ezekiel 2*, 1983.

W. R. Domeris

6115	סכך

סכך (*skk* II), q. weave, form hapleg. in Ps 139:13; pol. interweave, interlace (only in Job 10:11; # 6115); נסך (*nsk* II), q. intertwine (hapleg. in Isa 25:7); ni. be woven (hapleg. in Prov 8:23; # 5819).

OT *skk* II and *nsk* II, weave (# 5819) are probably byforms of an original two biradical root (*sk*). One vb. took the form of a geminate and the other of a ni. The nom. and q. pass. part. appear in Isa 25:7: "the sheet that covers (*nsk*)."

1. Psalm 139:13 (q.) and Job 10:11 (pol.) have nearly identical forms of the vb. *skk* in the two masc. sg. q. impv. with one common sg. pronom. suff. "you knit me together." It is apparent that these two roots have the same fundamental meaning, whether used literally of weaving or figuratively of prenatal formation, or of the creation of an alliance, the meshing of wills. M. Dahood relates the vb. to the meaning "cover" in Ps 139:13 (*Psalms III*, AB, 292).

2. The ni. of *nsk* occurs once in Prov 8:23, speaking of Lady Wisdom who claims to have been "formed (NIV appointed; marginal note, fashioned) from eternity, from the beginning, before the world began."

Spinning, sewing, weaving, embroidering: → *'rg* (spin, weave, # 755); → *dallâ* I (hair, thrum, loom, # 1929); → *ḥōšēb* (weaver, # 3110); → *ṭwh* (spin, # 3211); → *kîšôr* (distaff, # 3969); → *mānôr* (rod, # 4962); → *skk* II (weave, intertwine, # 6115); → *'ēreb* I (knitted material, # 6849); → *pelek* I (spindle-whorl, # 7134); → *rqm* (embroider, weave together, # 8387); → *śᵉrād* (woven, # 8573); → *šbṣ* I (weave, # 8687); → *šᵉtî* I (woven material, # 9274); → *tpr* (sew, # 9529)

Robert L. Alden

6116	סֹכֵךְ

סֹכֵךְ (*sōkēk*), mantelet (# 6116).

OT The nom. *sōkēk* occurs only in Nahum 2:5[6] to signify a protective cover set up against a city wall to allow sappers to undermine the wall while protected from the defenders above.

Fortification, citadel, siege-mound, stronghold: → *'armōn* (citadel, # 810); → *bîrâ* (citadel, acropolis, # 1072); → *bṣr* III (be inaccessible, # 1307); → *dāyēq* (siege-mound, # 1911); → *ḥêl* (rampart, # 2658); → *millô'* (terrace, # 4864); → *misgeret* (stronghold, dungeon, rim, table, # 4995); → *mᵉṣād* (stronghold, # 5171); → *māṣôr* II (fortification, fortified city, # 5190); → *sōḥērâ* (rampart, # 6089); → *sōkēk* (mantelet, # 6116); → *ṣᵉrîaḥ* (cellar, vault, pit, stronghold, # 7663); → *śgb* (be high, fortified, protect, # 8435); → **Fortification: Theology**

BIBLIOGRAPHY

TWOT 2:623-24; J. J. M. Roberts, *Nahum, Habakkuk, and Zephaniah*, 1991.

Keith N. Schoville

6118	סכל

סכל (*skl*), ni. behave foolishly; pi. make foolish, frustrate; hi. act foolishly (# 6118); סָכָל (*sākāl*), nom. foolish, fool (# 6119); סֶכֶל (*sekel*), nom. fool (# 6120); סִכְלוּת/ שִׂכְלוּת (*siklût/śiklût*), nom. foolishness (# 6121/8508).

ANE The root *skl* is related to Arab. *šakela*, "dubious, be ambiguous"; and is attested by Akk. *saklu*, "simple, ponderous, foolish," and by Syr. *seklā'*, "foolish," *saklūtā'*, "folly" (*HALAT* 712-13). According to Roth (70), the Akk. adj. refers to a man with little or no intellectual capacity.

OT 1. In the OT, the vb. *skl* occurs 8x: 4x in ni. (1 Sam 13:13; 2 Sam 24:10; 1 Chron 21:8; 2 Chron 16:9), 2x in pi. (2 Sam 15:31; Isa 44:25), and 2x in hi. (Gen 31:28; 1 Sam 26:21). The adj. *sākāl* occurs twice (Jer 4:22; 5:21); the substantive, *sākāl* occurs 5x, all in Eccl (2:19; 7:17; 10:3[2x], 14); *sekel* occurs once (10:6); and the denominative abstract nom. *siklût* occurs 7x, all in Eccl (1:17; 2:3, 12, 13; 7:25; 10:1, 13). The words *śkl* in Isa 44:25 and *śiklût* in Eccl 1:17 are believed to be the misspelled forms or other forms of the root *skl*.

2. Certain nuances are discernible in pi., hi., and ni. vb. usage. In 2 Sam 15:31, David asks the Lord to "turn Ahithophel's counsel into foolishness (*skl* pi.)." Here *skl* is used in parallel to the vb. *prr*, "frustrate" (v. 34; 17:14), which means to cause Ahithophel's counsel to become inherently bad and inappropriate (Roth, 72). Again, in Isa 44:25, *škl* pi. is used in parallel to *prr* to describe the Lord, the creator God, the one who "fails the signs of false prophets and makes fools (*hll* III) of diviners, who overthrows the learning of wise men and turns it into nonsense (*škl*)." When *skl* hi. is used, it connotes foolish error in judgment (Roth, 73-74). Jacob acts foolishly (*skl*) in misjudging both Laban's sentiments toward him and breaking the custom of bidding farewell (Gen 31:28; cf. Saul, 1 Sam 26:21). When *skl* ni. is used, it refers to acting foolishly in not putting one's trust in the Lord (1 Sam 13:13; Roth, 74-77). David, in his confession, acknowledges he has done a foolish thing (*skl*) in putting confidence in his troops by counting them (2 Sam 24:10 = 1 Chron 21:8, cf. Asa, 2 Chron 16:9). Roth (77) suggests that "*skl* ni. was a (rare) technical term alive in late preexilic prophetic circles of the South to identify the failure of the anointed of the LORD to rely solely on Yahweh in military and political matters."

3. The only two occurrences of the adj. *sākāl* are found in Jeremiah. *sākāl* and *'ewîl* are used in parallel: "My people are fools (*'ewîl*).... They are senseless (*sekālîm*) children; they have no understanding. They are skilled in doing evil; they know not how to do good" (Jer 4:22). Similarly, in 5:21, *sākāl* is used in parallel to *'ên lēb*, senseless (lit., "without heart"), to describe spiritual blindness and deafness associated with idolatry and rebellion (5:19, 23).

4. In Ecclesiastes, the *sākāl*, who is synonymous with the *kesîl* (Eccl 10:2-3, 12-14; cf. 2:12-16), is senseless (10:3). He is talkative (10:14). A fool cannot hide his inadequacy, for it inevitably reveals itself in public places (10:3; cf. Murphy, *Ecclesiastes*, 1992, 101). When the *sekel*, fool, is set in high position and the rich sit in low place, it is a sign of the collapse of society (10:6; cf. Whybray, *Ecclesiastes*, 1989, 152). While the nom. *sākāl* is the opposite of *ḥākām*, wise (2:19; 10:2-3; cf. 7:16-17), *siklût* is the opposite of *ḥokmâ*, wisdom (1:17; 2:3, 12, 13; 7:25; 10:1; cf. 10:13). Wisdom excels *siklût* as light excels darkness (2:13). *siklût* is close to *hôlēlôt*, madness; they frequently appear as a word pair (1:17; 2:12; 7:25; 10:13). In 7:17, 25 the meanings of *sākāl* and *siklût* come close to *reša'*, wickedness.

Folly, fool, madness, shameless: → *'ewîl* I (foolish, fool, # 211); → *b'r* IV (be stupid, # 1279); → *hll* III (be confused, foolish, behave like mad, # 2147); → *ksl* I (be foolish, # 4071); → *lhh* (behave like a madman, # 4263); → *nbl* II (act disdainfully, # 5571); → *skl* (behave foolishly, make foolish, frustrate, # 6118); → *pth* I (be inexperienced, be naive, deceive, persuade, # 7331); → *šg'* (raving, crazy, # 8713); → *tpl* I (talk nonsense, # 9520)

Frustration: → *mig'eret* (fierce anger, frustration, # 4486); → *skl* (behave foolishly, make foolish, frustrate, # 6118); → *slp* (frustrate, overthrow, twist, mislead, # 6156); → *prr* (break, invalidate, nullify, frustrate, foil, thwart, # 7296)

Wisdom, knowledge, skill: → *byn* (understand, discern, # 1067); → *ḥkm* (be wise, become wise, act wisely, # 2681); → *yd'* (understand, know, # 3359); → *ysr* I (admonish, correct, discipline, # 3579); → *leqaḥ* (teaching, gift of persuasion, # 4375); → *mezimmâ*, consideration, plan, evil plan, plot, # 4659); → *'oqbâ* (cunning, craftiness, # 6817); → *'rm* II (be cunning, be crafty, make crafty, # 6891); → *śkl* I (have success, understand, make wise, act with insight, # 8505); → *taḥbulôt* (advice, guidance, # 9374)

Bibliography

IDB 2:303-4; *ISBE* 2:331; *THAT* 2:824; *TWOT* 2:624-25; T. Donald, "The Semantic Field of 'Folly' in Proverbs, Job, Psalms, and Ecclesiastes," *VT* 13, 1963, 285-92; S. A. Mandry, *There Is No God! (A Study of the Fool in the OT, Particularly in Proverbs and Qoheleth)*, 1972; W. M. W. Roth, "A Study of the Classical Hebrew Verb SKL," *VT* 18, 1968, 69-78.

Chou-Wee Pan

6119 (*sākāl*, foolish, fool), → # 6118

6120 (*sekel*, fool), → # 6118

6121 (*siklût*, foolishness), → # 6118

6122 (*skn* I, be of use), → # 6125

6125	סֹכֵן

סֹכֵן (*sōkēn*), steward, take care (# 6125); < סכן (*skn* I), q. be of use, service; ni. incur danger; hi. be accustomed (# 6122).

OT 1. The term *sōkēn* (# 6125) comes from the root *skn* I (# 6122), meaning be of use, service (cf. *skn* II, # 6124) and in the ni. in Eccl 10:9 (to incur danger). *skn* occurs 9x mainly in Job, where it means benefit or profit (Job 15:3; 22:2; 34:9; 35:3). The hi. is used in Job 22:21, where the NIV renders submit. For a double use of the vb. in reference to Balaam's ass, see Num 22:30 (NIV been in the habit) and Ps 139:3 (NIV familiar).

2. The part. *sōkēn* (used 3x) primarily carries the sense of steward or overseer (so also in Ugar. *skn bt melek*, the overseer of the king's palace), as in Isa 22:15. Also, within the semantic field of nurse *sōkēn* describes Abishag's care of the elderly David (1 Kgs 1:2, 4). The KJV rendering as "cherish" is far richer than the NIV attend (v. 2) and take care (v. 4).

Leaders: → *'ādôn* (lord, master, # 123); → *'allûp* II (tribal chief, # 477); → *'āṣîl* II (eminent, noble, # 722); → *zāqēn* (elder, # 2418); → *ḥōr* I, free man, freeborn, # 2985); → *maptēaḥ* (badge of office, # 5158); → *nāgîd* (prince, ruler, leader, # 5592); → *nāśî'* I (chief, king, # 5954); → *sārîs* (eunuch, court official, # 6247); → *seren* II (Philistine prince, # 6249); → *'attûd* (he-goat, leader, # 6966); → *peḥâ* (governor, # 7068); → *pāqîd* (officer, # 7224); → *qāṣîn* (commander, leader, # 7903); → *rab* II (captain, chief, # 8042); → *rzn* (rule, # 8142); → *šôa'* I (noble, # 8777)

W. R. Domeris

6126	סכר

סכר (*skr* I), ni. be stopped up; pi. be shut up (# 6126).

OT 1. This root is probably related to *sgr*, close (→ # 6037), through consonantal interchange (Waltke-O'Connor, *IBHS*, 94). It is closely related to Akk. *sekēru*, frequently used of stopping up water sources (*AHw*, 1035). There are cognates in epigraphic South Arabian, Aram., and Ugar. (*UT*, 449, # 1738).

2. It is variously used for stopping up mouths (Ps 63:11[12]) or fountains of the deep (Gen 8:2 ‖ *kl'*).

Closing, shutting: → *'ṭm* (stopped up, # 357); → *'ṭr* (close [mouth], # 358); → *gwp* I (shut, close, # 1589); → *ṭḥḥ* (besmeared, stuck, shut, # 3220); → *ṭmh* (stopped up, # 3241); → *n'l* I (tie, lock, # 5835); → *sgr* I (shut, close, deliver up, # 6037); → *stm* (stop up, # 6258); → *'ṣh* I (shut, # 6781); → *'ṣm* III (shut one's eyes, # 6794); → *ṣrr* I (bind, shut up, be narrow, in straits, distress, # 7674); → *qpṣ* I (draw together, shut, # 7890); → *š''* I (smear, smooth, shut, # 9129)

Bill T. Arnold

6127	סכר

סכר (*skr* II), pi. hand over (give) (hapleg. in Isa 19:4, # 6127).

ANE Old Aram. *skr*, hand over, deliver.

OT Since the LXX, Targum, and Peshitta render this phrase "I will deliver," scholars contend that this verbal root stands distinct from *skr* I. Rowlands (196) suggests that *skr* II is a dialectal variant of *sgr*, shut up, close (cf. Wildberger, *Jesaja*, 700).

As with the common idiom *ntn* b^e*yad*, this hapleg. belongs to a similar construction, *skr* b^e*yad*, describing the judgment Yahweh intends to bring on the Egyptians.

Gift: → *'ahab* (gifts of love, charm, # 172); → *zbd* (endow, # 2272); → *mgn* I (deliver, # 4481); → *nādān* II (gift, wages of love, # 5621); → *ntn* (give, present, offer, # 5989); → *skr* II (hand over, # 6127); → *ṣbṭ* (give, # 7381); → *šḥd* (give a gift, # 8815); → *šay* (gift, present, # 8856); → *šalmōnîm* (gift, # 8988)

Bibliography

E. Rowlands, "The Targum and the Peshiṭta Version of the Book of Isaiah," *VT* 9, 1959, 178-91; H. Wildberger, *Isaiah 1-12*, 1991.

Michael A. Grisanti

6128	סכר

סכר (*skr* III), bargain, bribe (hapleg. in Ezra 4:5, # 6128); the vb. is an alternative form of *śkr*, barter, buy (→ # 8509).

OT The payment made by the enemies of the returned exiles to discourage them from rebuilding the temple was intended to frustrate them and, hence, could be seen as a form of bribery: "They hired (*skr*) counselors to work against them and frustrate their plans during the entire reign of Cyrus king of Persia and down to the reign of Darius king of Persia" (Ezra 4:5).

Similarly, the word *mattānâ* I (< *ntn*) has a neutral meaning of gift. However, often a gift is used to purchase influence. Its refusal is a mark of godliness, "A greedy man (*bôṣē'a bāṣa'*) brings trouble to his family, but he who hates bribes (*mattānōt*) will live" (Prov 15:27).

Bribe, gift: → *beṣa'* (piece of s.t., gain, bribe, # 1299); → *kōper* IV (bribe, # 4111); → *skr* III (bargain, # 6128); → *šḥd* (give a gift, # 8815); → *šalmōnîm* (gift, # 8988)

Gift: → *'ahab* (gifts of love, charm, # 172); → *zbd* (endow, # 2272); → *mgn* I (deliver, # 4481); → *nādān* II (gift, wages of love, # 5621); → *ntn* (give, present, offer, # 5989); → *skr* II (hand over, # 6127); → *ṣbṭ* (give, # 7381); → *šḥd* (give a gift, # 8815); → *šay* (gift, present, # 8856); → *šalmōnîm* (gift, # 8988)

J. Clinton McCann

6131	סלא

סלא (*sl'*), pu. paid (with gold); weighed (against gold) (# 6131); *sl'* = *slh* II, pu. paid (with gold); weighed (against gold) (# 6137).

ANE Cognates are found in Arab. and OSA (see *HALAT* 714; Müller, 312.) Perhaps it is denom. of *sal*, basket, which is used as measurement in barter trade (Geller, 181, n. 23).

OT 1. *sl'* is used as a pu. part. in Lam 4:2, in a description of the esteem the precious sons of Zion once had ("weighed against fine gold," i.e., "worth their weight in gold," NIV). With the destruction of Jerusalem, they are regarded as earthen jars (Lam 4:2). All this may allude to the fact that Zion was to be for Yahweh a crown of beauty (Isa 62:3) and her people like the jewels of a crown (Zech 9:16).

2. The pricelessness of wisdom is indicated by the fact that it cannot be weighed (*slh*) against or bought with fine gold (Job 28:16, 19).

Payment, rent, reward, wages: → *'ᵃgôrâ* (payment, # 102); → *'eškār* (tribute, payment, # 868); → *mᵉḥîr* I (price, payment, # 4697); → *sl'* (be paid, # 6131); → *slh* II (be paid, # 6137); → *pᵉ'ullâ* (wages, punishment, reward, payment, # 7190); → *rṣh* II (pay for, make good, make amends, # 8355); → *śkr* (hire, # 8509); → *šlm* (repay, reward, retribute, make peace, # 8966); → **Retribution: Theology**

BIBLIOGRAPHY

S. A. Geller, "'Where Is Wisdom?': A Literary Study of Job 28 in Its Settings," in J. Neusner, B. A. Levine, E. S. Frerichs, eds., *Judaic Perspectives on Ancient Israel*, 1987, 181, n. 23; W. W. Müller, "Altsüdarabische Beiträge zum Hebräischen Lexikon," *ZAW* 75, 1963, 304-16, esp. 312.

Cornelis Van Dam

6134	סלד

סלד (*sld*), pi. spring, jump for joy (hapleg.; # 6134).

OT Job 6:10 is a difficult line. Possibly Job asserts that if God would answer his petition, he would leap in joy despite excruciating pain. This is the most frequent reading of this line. On the other hand, it is possible that this vb. means "leap back." Clines (*Job 1-20*, WBC, 1989, 156, 159) thus translates the line, "even while I recoiled in unrelenting pain." The latter reading coincides best with the context.

Jumping, leaping, skipping: → *glš* (skip, jump, # 1683); → *dwṣ* (dance, # 1881); → *dlg* (leap, # 1925); → *znq* I (jump before, # 2397); → *ntr* II (start, spring, # 6001); → *sld* (jump, spring, # 6134); → *pwš* (skip, leap, # 7055); → *pzz* II (be quick, agile, hop, # 7060); → *rqd* (skip, leap, # 8376); → *šqq* (run about, jump, # 9212)

John E. Hartley

6136	סלה

סלה (*slh* I), q. despise, pi. reject, treat as worthless (# 6136).

ANE Akk. attests the meaning of cognate *šalû* (*salû', šalā'u*), reject, throw away (*CAD*, 17:272-73; *AHw* 1015a, 1152). Cf. Aram/Syr. *s^{e}lā'*, despise, reject.

OT Yahweh is the subject of both occurrences of the vb. In the q. it is said that he rejects all who stray from his decrees (Ps 119:118), i.e., who break covenant with him. Jeremiah, speaking for Jerusalem, laments that Yahweh has disregarded (pi. *slh*) all the warriors of Judah and brought in foreigners to wreak destruction (Lam 1:15). Hillers (*Lamentations,* 12-13) suggests a root *sll,* heap up (→ # 6148).

Rejection, refusal, disgrace, shame: → *gdp* (revile, blaspheme, # 1552); → *znḥ* II (reject, # 2396); → *m'n* (refuse, # 4412); → *m's* I (reject, refuse, # 4415); → *n'ṣ* (reject, disdain, treat disrespectfully, # 5540); → *n'r* (abandon, renounce, # 5545); → *slh* I (despise, reject, # 6136)

BIBLIOGRAPHY
TWOT 2:625; D. Hillers, *Lamentations*, AB, 1972, 12-13.

Eugene H. Merrill

6137 (*sl'* II, be paid), → # 6131

6141	סִלּוֹן

סִלּוֹן (*sillôn*), thorn; pl. *sallônîm* (# 6141).

ANE Judaeo-Aram. *silwā'*; Arab. *sullā'*.

OT This is a spiny desert perennial that grows to a height of one meter. It produces a large pink flower. The mature plants tumble through the desert (Ezek 2:6; 28:24). Zohary suggests that the proper name Zillah, the wife of Lamech (Gen 4:23), may be derived from this plant.

Thornbush, nettle, sting, thistle, thorn: → *'āṭād* (thornbush, # 353); → *barqōn* (thorn, brier, # 1402); → *deber* II (thorny sting, # 1823); → *dardar* (thistle, # 1998); → *ḥēdeq* (brier, # 2537); → *ḥôaḥ* I (thorn, # 2560); → *m^{e}sûkâ* (thorn hedge, # 5004); → *na'^{a}ṣûṣ* (thornbush, # 5848); → *sîrâ* (thorny bush, # 6106); → *sillôn* (thorn, # 6141); → *s^{e}neh* (thorny shrub, # 6174); → *sirpād* (stinging nettle, # 6252); → *ṣe'^{e}lîm* (thorny lotus, # 7365); → *ṣ^{e}nînîm* (thorns, # 7564); → *qôṣ* I (thornbush, # 7764); → *qimmôś* (weeds, nettles, # 7853); → *śēk* (thorn, splinter, # 8493); → *šāmîr* I (Christ's thorn, # 9031)

BIBLIOGRAPHY
Irene and Walter Jacob, "Flora," *ABD*, 1992, 2:816; M. Zohary, *Plants of the Bible*, 1982, 166.

K. Lawson Younger, Jr.

6142	סלח

סלח (*slḥ*), q. practice forbearance, pardon, forgive (33x); ni. to be pardoned, forgiven (13x) (# 6142); nom. סַלָּח (*sallāḥ*), ready to pardon (hapleg. in Ps 86:5; # 6143); סְלִיחָה (*s^{e}lîḥâ*), forgiveness, pardon (# 6145)

ANE In Akk. the vb. *salāḫu* (*AHw*, 1013), usually occurring in nonreligious texts (*TWAT* 5:860), conveys the meaning sprinkle (water, oil, tears, urine). In an Akk. ritual text relating to the New Year's Festival the sprinkling of Tigris and Euphrates water coincides with the rites of purification (*kuppuru*) of the temple (*ANET*, 333), which were destined to avert and to destroy threatening evil (Janowski, 55). In *Ludlul bēl Nēmeqi* the expression "I was sprinkled with water of purification" is paralleled by "I was released from my bond (debt or obligation)," and also by "I was given prosperity" (lines 79-88), thereby alluding to some form of atonement achieved at Esagila (Lambert, 61). Stamm (*THAT* 2:150) favors the use of this etymology to determine the original meaning of the root *slḥ*.

The word also occurs in an Ugar. ritual text (*KTU* 1.46). Because of its fragmentary state the exact meaning of the expression *slḥ npš* cannot be ascertained, despite attempts by Gordon to translate it as "forgiveness (of soul)" (*Ugaritic Literature*, 133) or, alternatively, by the vb. sprinkle (*UT*, # 1757).

OT Considering the fundamental theological importance and frequent occurrence of the subject matter it addresses, *slḥ* is used sparingly in the OT literature, and then primarily in cultic contexts. In all instances, however, God is the subj. of the vb. and its derivative forms (*TWAT* 5:861). Hence, the denotation of *slḥ* is an act of pardon by God alone.

God's forgiveness of sins is fundamental to biblical faith as epitomized in the "Apostles' Creed." Although the OT does not contain a systematized exposition of divine pardon, nothing said about God is as important as that he forgives sins (Koch, 224) and that humans are in constant need of his forgiveness (von Rad, 348). In the OT forgiveness comprises the removal of sin and the restoration of communion between God and humanity (*TOT* 2:455). It depends solely on God's love, mercy, and compassion towards the sinner (C. Westermann,125) and on his readiness to initiate the processes of reconciliation and atonement. It requires, and usually goes hand in hand with, the confession of sin, repentance, restitution, and renewal. Though it remains closely connected with the cult and sacrificial practices, it actually encompasses all spheres of life for the individual and the community. It entails the nullification of guilt, the release of obligations, and the reduction or total relinquishment of punishment (*TOT* 2:453). According to Sakenfeld (*CBQ*, 327) forgiveness is understood basically as the preservation of the covenant community and is thus implied in the total concept of God's salvation (McKeating, 69). Forgiveness is not restricted exclusively to spiritual blessings but is also used in connection with the restoration of earthly blessings such as health, honor, children, etc. The OT contains several words and expressions denoting forgiveness, among them first and foremost *slḥ,* usually rendered *hileōs* in the Septuagint (*TDNT* 3:300).

1. *slḥ in the context of the cult.* Koch (226) contends correctly that the particular situations in life of the various cultic contexts in which the word functions remain almost impossible to determine. The word *slḥ* occurs most regularly in connection with the offering prescripts in Leviticus and Numbers (*THAT* 2:153), which are firmly rooted in, and emanate from, belief in God's forgiveness.

The so-called *kipper…w*^{e}*nislaḥ* formula designates God's forgiveness subsequent to, and as an essential element of, the atonement ritual performed by the intercessory priest on behalf of an individual or the community for sins committed unintentionally (Lev 4:20, 26, 31, 35; 5:10, 13, 16, 18; 6:7[5:26]; 19:22; Num 15:25-28) or even without a priest's mediation (Num 14:20; cf. 30:5[6], 8[9], 12[13];

2 Chron 7:14). While God is not mentioned *expressis verbis* in the formula (as the implied subject of *slḥ,* ni.), it is clear that no one other than God grants forgiveness. Moreover, the mere bringing of sin and guilt offerings does not release guilt and secure forgiveness. The priestly ritual first leads to the acknowledgment of God as the merciful forgiver of (unintentional) sins, and only then to the actual declaration by the priest that the sinner is forgiven and thus released from his guilt (Janowski, 254). The ritual in its entirety depends on God's willingness to forgive and does not operate mechanistically (*TOT* 2:443). Sacrificial atonement has definite limitations (1 Sam 3:14), especially if the offense is one of contempt (*n'ṣ*) for God (Sakenfeld, 321), as is the case in Num 14 (cf. vv. 11, 23). It is equally clear that the ritual inherently requires a confession of guilt (Ps 32:3-5), which underlines its personal character (Vriezen, *RGG* 6:508).

The cultic ordinances regarding the binding obligations of the vows of women (Num 30:3-16[4-17]) contain Yahweh's promise of releasing a woman from her obligation in the event that her father or husband forbade her to do so, without requiring an obligatory offering or intercession by a priest. *slḥ* thus embodies the meaning of "release from an obligation." Köhler (208) argues that *slḥ* in this particular instance means "to practice forbearance."

Closely connected with the cult are the hymns and prayers that contain thanksgiving and pleas for God's forgiveness respectively. In Ps 103 the reasons for this individual song of thanksgiving are stated: the Lord "forgives (*slḥ*) all [my] sins and heals (*rp'*, [# 8324]) all [my] diseases; he redeems (*g'l*) [my] life from the pit and crowns (*'ṭr*) [me] with love and compassion" (vv. 3-4). The strong relationship between forgiveness and healing (implicitly, redemption from threatening death) reveals God's real motive for forgiveness, namely, to restore to alienated human beings fellowship and communion with himself (Hasel, 202). Only God's forgiveness safeguards against death and destruction (Gunneweg, 12). God's forgiveness implies hope for the God-fearing who constantly wait on the Lord (Kraus, 872): "If you, O LORD kept a record of sins, O Lord, who could stand? But with you there is forgiveness (*s^e lîḥâ*); therefore you are feared" (Ps 130:3-4). The true ground of God's forgiveness is to be found in the goodness of his being: "You are forgiving (*sallāḥ*) and good (*ṭôb*), O LORD, abounding in love (*ḥesed*) to all who call to you" (Ps 86:5). This echoes the ancient cultic praise formula: "The LORD, the LORD, the compassionate (*raḥûm*) and gracious (*ḥannûn*) God, slow to anger, abounding in love and faithfulness (*ḥesed we'^e met*), maintaining love (*ḥesed*) to thousands, and forgiving (*nś'*) wickedness, rebellion and sin"; on account of this Moses asked for forgiveness and the privilege of living as reconciled people (Exod 34:6-9). In all these hymns and prayers God's forgiveness is experienced in an act of mercy and compassion (cf. Dan 9:9: "The LORD our God is merciful and forgiving"), which revitalizes hope and trust.

A *carpe diem* philosophy of life that is not founded on the principle of divine pardon is a life under ordeal (Isa 22:14) and death (27:9-11) (Janowski, 117, 250). It is theologically important to realize that the concept of God's forgiveness prevents any deterministic trends in Israelite religion, in particular, the view that affliction derives automatically from wrongdoing.

The temple dedication prayer (1 Kgs 8:14-66 = 2 Chron 6:3-42) contains five requests for God's forgiveness of his people as they find themselves in various predicaments resulting from their sins. An indispensable condition of God's forgiveness is repentance (Jacob, 289), comprising confession of guilt, expiation, and a return to the covenant God who dwells in the temple. Forgiveness entails, accordingly, the removal of sins (cf. Ps 25:11-18), the aversion of punishment, and the restoration of people by means of a redemptive act (Dan 9:19). Prayers in or toward the temple where the Name of the Lord dwells are suggestive of the importance of the cult as the major setting for God's forgiveness (Vriezen, *RGG* 6:510). It is because of God's Name that sinners can humbly pray and hope for his forgiveness (Num 14:19; Ps 25:11) and his restoration (lit. "healing") of the land by keeping it free from all sorts of calamities and natural disasters (2 Chron 7:14). This close connection between God's compassion and his willingness to forgive is also apparent in the Qumran literature (*THAT* 2:155).

2. *slḥ in other contexts.* The word *slḥ* occurs 8x in the prophetic literature, mostly in the book of Jeremiah. In Amos 7:2 the prophet's prayer of intercession on behalf of Jacob leads the Lord to relent and postpone his impending judgment; *slḥ* here actually concerns the prevention of punishment, not the pardoning of sins. Jer 5:1 also alludes to a similar situation. God is eager to forgive Jerusalem her sins and to avert his judgment, provided the prophet "can find one person who deals honestly and seeks the truth," i.e., one who will really turn from his wicked ways (36:3, 7). Jeremiah makes it clear that forgiveness is not granted unconditionally and cheaply in accordance with Jerusalem's belief that the Lord will never abandon Zion regardless of what his people have done. The consequences of sin cannot be ignored; forgiveness does not necessarily exclude punishment (cf. Num 14:19) or exempt one from the obligation to obey the Lord. Von Rad (*OTT* 2:211) argues that it was towards the end of his career that Jeremiah envisaged a completely new covenant in which forgiveness is granted from the outset: "For I will forgive their wickedness and will remember their sins no more" (Jer 31:34). It is on account of his unconditional forgiveness of all their guilt that God will rebuild Judah and Israel (33:8), thereby constituting the eschatological community of the faithful (50:20; see Levin, 135; Gunneweg, 12).

According to Stamm (*THAT* 2:158) an expression with a cultic-forensic background, *mḥh pešaʿ*, blot out transgression, is used rather than *slḥ* to designate forgiveness in Isa 43:25; 44:22. Isa 55:7, nevertheless, contains all accompanying aspects of forgiveness: seek (*drš*) the Lord, forsake (*ʿzb*) evil ways, and turn (*šwb*) to the Lord in the expectation and firm belief that he will show his mercy (*rḥm*) and will be ready to forgive (*slḥ*). In such cases God's forgiveness is acknowledged as "the central act of succour without which all other goods lost their value" (Eichrodt, *TOT* 2:458).

slḥ is used sparingly in the narrative literature of the OT. Apart from the above-mentioned prayers and specific cultic matters, *slḥ* occurs only in 2 Kgs 5:18, where Naaman requested God's absolution in regard to a foreign cultic rite that he had to perform. Though Elisha did not explicitly pronounce God's forgiveness, Naaman left in the hope that God would show his forbearance.

In a few instances (Deut 29:20[19]; 2 Kgs 24:4) it is said that God refuses to grant his forgiveness, for example, because of his anger against the sins of Manasseh who had filled Jerusalem with innocent blood. A similar situation is pictured in Jer 5:7 and Lam 3:42: "We have sinned and rebelled and you have not forgiven." Persistence in going one's own way (Deut 29:20[19]; cf. Num 15:30) incurs God's wrath. Without repentance forgiveness is in danger of becoming inoperative (Jacob, 289). God's forgiveness cannot be taken for granted; it can never be procured by sacrifices alone, but requires an awareness and confession of sin, repentance, and an appeal to God (Vriezen, *RGG* 6:508). If God forgives the sin of anyone, the awareness of that forgiveness must show itself by the desire to please God and to live faithfully within the covenant community (McKeating, 74).

3. *Forgiveness* (*slḥ*) *in diachronic perspective.* Because there is no uniform notion of forgiveness in the OT, Koch (266) warns against too easy an identification between the OT concept of forgiveness and its Christian counterpart. The concept may have emanated originally from some cultic ritual (cf. *slḥ* as general Sem. word meaning "sprinkle") and was attached to certain cultic practices that included intercessory prayers, sacrificial and expiatory rites, and purification ceremonies, at particular places and times. But there was no development of a systematic doctrine of forgiveness in preexilic times. During exilic and postexilic times the perception of God's preparedness to forgive gained new dimensions in regard to cultic practices and popular faith. This may account for the fact that the word *slḥ* occurs almost exclusively in exilic and postexilic literature (Levin, 134). Moreover, the theme of unconditional forgiveness was first articulated by the promise of the new covenant (Jer 31:34), whereby the Lord would nullify and remove all the sin of Israel and Judah, never to recall it again (*TWAT* 5:863). The promise of God's pardoning of sin and remittance of guilt is therefore to be seen as the basis of all God's blessings, *fundamentum huius beneficii* (Calvin). To designate God as the merciful redeemer from, and forgiver of, sins is perhaps the greatest achievement of OT times (Koch, 237). God's gracious and unconditional forgiveness forms the essential cord between the OT and the NT, for it is God's Servant who vicariously suffers (Isa 53:5) the burden of sin, thereby redeeming the "us" of the so-called Fourth Servant Song.

4. *Related words for "forgiveness."* While *slḥ* is the only word that is used comprehensively and exclusively of God's forgiveness, some other expressions also express the same concept or particular aspects of it, e.g., *nś' ḥaṭṭā't/peša'/'āwōn,* remove sin (cf. Exod 32:32; 34:7; Num 14:18; Josh 24:19); *kpr* (pi.), cover or atone (Isa 22:14; Jer 18:23; Ezek 16:63); *mḥh peša',* blot out rebellion or guilt (Isa 43:25; 44:22; Jer 18:23); *rp',* heal, i.e., restore (Ps 103:3; Isa 57:18; Jer 3:22; Hos 14:4[5]); *'br* (hi.), take away or let (guilt) pass by (Mic 7:18); *kbs* (pi.), cleanse (Jer 2:22); *ṭhr* (pi.), purify (Ps 51:2[4]); *šlk* (hi.) *'aḥ^{a}rê,* cast behind (one's back) (Isa 38:17; Mic 7:19); *str* (hi.) *pānîm min,* conceal from (Ps 51:9[11]); *lō' ḥšb,* never to consider guilt (2 Sam 19:19[20]; Ps 32:2); *lō' zkr,* never to remember (Isa 43:25).

P-B In the Qumran texts the word *slḥ* is used in conjunction with *kpr*, and both embody the meaning "forgive." In both the Late Aram. literature of Militz and the Sam. Pentateuch, Heb. *kpr* is constantly equated with Aram. *slḥ*. Contrary to the OT usage where God is exclusively subject of *slḥ,* a holy priest can forgive (*slḥ*) and perform atonement (*kpr*) (Janowski, 76, 261). *slḥ* also occurs in the personal name *yslḥ,* may (God) forgive, in the Elephantine papyri. The root *slḥ* has retained its meaning of "forgiveness, pardon" in modern Heb. (Stamm, 57).

Atonement: → *kpr* I (cover, paint, smear, atone, appease, # 4105); → *rṣh* II (pay for, make good, make amends, # 8355)

Offering, sacrifice: → *'azkārâ* (sign-offering, # 260); → *'iššeh* (offering by fire, # 852); → *'āšām* (guilt offering, # 871); → *zbḥ* (slaughter, sacrifice, # 2284); → *ḥaṭṭā'at* (sin offering,

2633); → *ṭbḥ* (slaughter, # 3180); → *minḥâ* (gift, present, offering, sacrifice, # 4966); → *ma‘^{a}śēr* (tithe, # 5130); → *ndr* (make a vow, # 5623); → *nwp* I (move back and forth, wave, # 5677); → *nsk* I (pour out, be consecrated, libation, # 5818); → *‘ōlâ* I (burnt offering, # 6592); → *‘^{a}rîsâ* (meal/dough offering, # 6881); → *qorbān* (offering, gift, # 7933); → *šḥṭ* I (slaughter, # 8821); → *šelem* (settlement sacrifice, # 8968); → *tāmîd* (regular offering, # 9458); → *t^{e}rûmâ* (tribute, contribution, # 9556); → **Aaron: Theology**; → **Offering: Theology**; → **Priests and Levites: Theology**

Forgiveness, pardon: → *nś’* (lift, raise high, pardon, bear, exalt o.s., # 5951); → *slḥ* (practice forbearance, pardon, forgive, # 6142)

Sin, guilt, rebellion, transgression, wrong: → *’āwen* (mischief, iniquity, deception, # 224); → *ḥṭ’* (sin, commit a sin, purify, # 2627); → *‘wh* (do wrong, pervert, # 6390); → *‘wl* I (act wrongly, # 6401); → *pš‘* (rebel, violate, transgress, # 7321); → **Fall: Theology**

BIBLIOGRAPHY

TDNT 3:300-339; *THAT* 2:150-60; *TWAT* 5:859-68; R. P. Gordon, “Micah vii 19 and Akkadian *kabāsu*,” *VT* 28, 1978, 355; A. H. J. Gunneweg, “Schuld ohne Vergebung?” *EvT* 36, 1976, 2-14; G. Hasel, “Health and Healing in the Old Testament,” *AUSS* 21, 1983, 191-202; E. Jacob, *Theology of the Old Testament*, ET, 1958; B. Janowski, *Sühne als Heilsgeschehen. Studien zur Sühnetheologie der Priesterschrift und zur Wurzel KPR im Alten Orient und im Alten Testament*, 1982; K. Koch, “Sühne und Sündenvergebung um die Wende von der exilischen zur nachexilischen Zeit,” *EvT* 26, 1966, 217-39; L. Köhler, *Theologie des Alten Testaments*, 1957; H.-J. Kraus, *Psalmen 60-150*, BKAT XV/2, 1978; W. G. Lambert, *BWL*, 1960; C. Levin, *Die Verheissung des neuen Bundes in ihrem theologiegeschichtlichen Zusammenhang ausgelegt*, 1985; H. McKeating, “Divine Forgiveness in the Psalms,” *SJT* 18, 1965, 69-83; K. D. Sakenfeld, “The Problem of Divine Forgiveness in Num 14,” *CBQ* 37, 1975, 317-30; J. J. Stamm, *Erlösen und Vergeben im Alten Testament*, 1940; G. von Rad, *OTT* 2, 1965; Th. C. Vriezen, *Hoofdlijnen der Theologie van het Oude Testament*, 1966; idem, “Sündenvergebung,” *RGG* 6:507-11; C. Westermann, *Die Theologie des Alten Testaments in Grundzügen*, 1978.

J. P. J. Olivier

6143 (*sallāḥ*, ready to pardon), → # 6142

6145 (*s^{e}lîḥâ*, forgiveness, pardon), → # 6142

6148 סלל

סלל (*sll*), q. heap, pile up; pilp. extol, esteem highly; hitp. resist like a barrier (# 6148); מְסִלָּה (*m^{e}sillâ*), nom. raised highway (# 5019); מַסְלוּל (*maslûl*), nom. highway (# 5020); סֹלְלָה (*sōl^{e}lâ*), nom. siege ramp (# 6149); סֻלָּם (*sullām*), nom. staircase (hapleg. in Gen 28:12; # 6150).

ANE None of the other Sem. languages have a vb. with a similar meaning. It is most probably derived from the Akk. *sulû*, highway, and became in Heb. a denom. vb.

OT 1. The vb. *sll* only occurs 12x in the OT, and four of these are in the Isaianic passages where the q. impv. *sōllû* is repeated (Isa 57:14; 62:10), occurring with *m^{e}sillâ* as the object in the second of these passages and with *derek*, way, road (→ # 2006). *derek* serves as the object of other q. vb. forms (Job 19:12; Jer 18:15), while *’orḥâ*, path (→ # 784), is used in Job 30:12 and Prov 15:19. The vb. most commonly refers to the action of building up a roadbed above or higher than the surrounding terrain (cf. our English word "highway" for a similar development), and in some contexts the implication is the erection of siege works against an invading army. The destruction of Babylon is referred to in Jer 50:26, with the call going out to open her granaries and pile her up like the heaps of grain that had been stored there.

In several passages it is used metaphorically of lifting up. The first of these is Prov 4:8 (pilp.), where the sage commands the disciple to "lift up" wisdom, i.e., esteeming her highly. Another occurrence is Exod 9:17 (hitp.), where the pharaoh is accused of exalting himself against God's people. In Ps 68:4[5] the impv. *sōllû* is used in parallel with *sîrû*, sing (→ # 2376), and *zammerû*, sing praises (→ # 2376).

2. Of the related noms., by far the most common and important is *mesillâ*, occurring 27x. While at times the semantic range of *mesillâ* is similar to that of *derek*, yet for the majority of its usages it has a more restricted range of meaning. *derek* (from the root *drk*, tread down) often refers to a path created by constant use, and it has a wide metaphorical usage that commonly refers to the settled character of people (cf. "the way of the righteous" and "the way of the wicked" in Ps 1:6).

mesillâ is used once with a similar metaphorical meaning of the road of life in Prov 16:17 (NIV the highway of the upright), but its most common usage is to denote a prepared road. In some instances *derek* and *mesillâ* are used in parallel. For example, in Num 20:17-19 the Israelites request permission to travel through Edom using the king's highway (*derek hammelek*). When the request is denied, they claim that they will only go along the main road (*mesillâ*). In Judg 20:31-32, 45 it refers to the roads leading to Bethel and Gibeah, and these appear to be roads or highways specifically constructed by heaping up stones or earth. Nowhere is it ever used of streets within a city. It is used by the Chronicler to denote the steps made out of algum wood for the temple and the royal palace (2 Chron 9:11). It has often been suggested that this is an error for the word *miṣ'ād* used in the parallel passage in 1 Kgs 10:12. However, *miṣ'ād* is a hapleg. and *mesillôt* is best retained.

The most important theological usage of *mesillâ* is in regard to the highway prepared for the returning exiles. Just as there was a highway for Israel when leaving Egypt, so there will be a highway for the remnant as they return from Assyria (Isa 11:16). It is clearly a word used in eschatological passages, as is marked out by its appearance in Isa 19:23 which describes a highway that connects Assyria with Egypt, so that the two former enemies will be united in worship of the Lord. In Isa 40:3 *mesillâ* occurs in parallel with *derek*, in a passage in which the call is for God's people ("my people," v. 1) to prepare a highway for the Lord as he comes to deliver his people. Here the highway is not for the people but for the Lord. It has been suggested that the language may reflect the practice of compelling inhabitants of a region to prepare a road for an advancing army (cf. the language of Esarhaddon in D. J. Wiseman, *The Vassal Treaties of Esarhaddon,* line 54). The word is also known in Moabite (cf. J. C. L. Gibson, *Syrian Semitic Inscriptions,* 1, 75). Comparison has also been made with Babylonian festal processions, in which a statue of Marduk was carried to Babylon. However, the picture in Isa 40 is of an eschatological coming of the Lord himself, when his glory will be universally revealed. It seems to be a combination of "the ancient picture of the Lord coming to his people's aid (Deut 33:2; Judg 5:4; Ps 68:4[5], 7[8]) with the practice of constructing processional ways for visiting dignitaries"

(J. A. Motyer, *The Prophecy of Isaiah*, 1993, 300). The one occurrence of *maslûl* (Isa 35:8) shows that its meaning is basically the same as *m^esillâ* (→ # 5019).

3. Another derivative from *sll* is *sōl^elâ*, siege ramp, which occurs 11x. The case of Joab and his troops besieging Sheba in Abel Beth Maacah by building a siege ramp is an excellent illustration of the use of *sōl^elâ* (2 Sam 20:15). Stones and earth were used to build a ramp against the wall of a city to allow the attackers close access in order to break through the walls. As in this passage, it commonly occurs with the vb. *špk*, build up (2 Sam 20:15; 2 Kgs 19:32 = Isa 37:33; Jer 6:6; Ezek 4:2; 17:17; 21:22[27]; 26:8). In addition to its occurrence in historical passages, *sōl^elâ* is used in prophetical passages in which the Lord is threatening Jerusalem, especially by the attack of Nebuchadnezzar (Jer 6:6; Ezek 4:2; 26:8), or in which reference is made to the siege ramps as already existing (Jer 32:24; 33:4). The passages in Ezekiel in which *sōl^elâ* are found are important in that they contain a cluster of military terminology related to attack on a city (*māṣôr*, siege; *dayeq*, siege works; *maḥ^anôt*, camps; *kārîm*, battering rams). Good examples of siege ramps can be seen at Lachish (built by Sennacherib) and the even larger one at Masada (built by the Romans).

4. *sullām* in Gen 28:12 is a hapleg. and appears to be derived from *sll*. In Phoenician inscriptions the pl. *slmt* occurs twice, while in Akkadian there is a building term *simmiltu*. The Ugar. usages of *sll, slmn,* and *mslmt* are probably personal or place names (for details see C. Houtmann, *VT* 27, 339). The two most common interpretations of *sullām* are that it is either a ladder or a staircase (probably in the form of a ziggurat). The LXX and the Vg. do not help greatly, because their renderings (*klimax* and *scala* respectively) are ambiguous in that both words can be used for staircase and ladder. While in G *klimax* is normally a ladder, yet it is used occasionally to denote a staircase (*Odyssey* i.330; x.558).

However, it is most probable these versions intended a ladder to be understood, and hence they originated the long line of interpretation of the word *sullām*. The origin of the word and the idea are debatable. J. G. Griffiths has argued for Egyptian influence, citing texts in which the deceased king ascends to heaven (*ET* 76, 1964/65, 229-30; *ET* 78, 1966/67, 54-55). The Babylonian parallels may well be nearer the mark, as they depict the *simmiltu* as intended for the passage of divine messengers (see A. R. Millard, *ET* 78, 1966/67, 86). But it is not necessary to seek precise sources as the word occurs in a dream, and ultimately the context in Gen 28 must be decisive. The *sullām* rests on the earth, with angelic messengers ascending and descending on it (v. 12). Beside it stands the Lord (taking *'ālāw* to refer to the Lord rather than to the *sullām*), who identifies himself as the God of Abraham and Isaac (v. 13). When he awakens from sleep, Jacob recognizes that the Lord is in that place, and he declares it to be "the house of God" and "the gate of heaven" (vv. 16-17). The place itself he calls "Bethel" (v. 19). In the dream, therefore, there is a meeting of heaven and earth, and while that very place was "the gate of heaven," yet there was a way (whether "ladder," or "staircase," or "road") reaching to heaven, with angelic messengers using it. John 1:51 seems to be an allusion to this incident, and the Christological interpretation given there to an open heaven with angels ascending and descending upon the Son of Man can be seen as a ready adaptation of the incident at Bethel (for Christian interpretations of Jacob's ladder, see C. A. Patrides).

P-B Only once does the vb. occur in the DSS (4Q 177), though the root occurs on four other occasions (1QS 8, 14; 4Q 185, 1-2 II 2, 4Q 511, 2 I 6; 2Q 23, 6, 2). The first three of these are basically quoting from Isa 40:3. The LXX translators clearly had difficulty with this vb., using vbs such as *hodopoieō* (Isa 62:10; Ps 68:4[5]; Job 30:12) and *tribein* (Prov 15:19), but also *pericharakoō*(Prov 4:8) and *empoieō* (Exod 9:17).

Heap, mound, pile: → *gal* I (heap, pile, # 1643); → *ḥ^{a}môr* II (heap, # 2790); → *m^{e}dûrâ* (pile, # 4509); → *nēd* (heap, # 5603); → *sll* (heap, pile up, esteem highly, resist, # 6148); → *'rm* I (be dammed up, # 6890); → *ṣbr* (pile up, # 7392)

Bibliography

TWAT 5:867-72; *TWOT* 2:626-27; H. Cohen, *Biblical Hapax Legomena in the Light of Akkadian and Ugaritic*, 1978, 34; J. G. Griffiths, "The Celestial Ladder and the Gate of Heaven (Genesis xxviii. 12 and 17)," *ExpTim* 76, 1964/65, 229-30; idem, "The Celestial Ladder and the Gate of Heaven in Egyptian Ritual," *ExpTim* 78, 1966/67, 54-55; C. Houtmann, "What Did Jacob See at Bethel?" *VT* 27, 1977, 337-51; A. R. Millard, "The Celestial Ladder and the Gate of Heaven (Genesis xxviii. 12, 17)," *ExpTim* 78, 1996/67, 86-87; C. A. Patrides, "Renaissance Interpretations of Jacob's Ladder" *TZ* 18, 1962, 411-18; C. Westermann, *Genesis* III, 454; E. J. Young, *Isaiah III*, 27-28.

Allan M. Harman

6149 (*sōl^{e}lâ*, siege ramp), → # 6148

6150 (*sullām*, staircase), → # 6148

6152	סֶלַע

סֶלַע (*sela'*), rock, stone (# 6152).

ANE Syr. has a cognate meaning, cliff; Arab. *sala'a*, split.

OT 1. The word *sela'* is a common nom. in the OT, occurring some 56x. The term is used interchangeably with *ṣûr* I, although *sela'* more often suggests rocks of smaller size than does *ṣûr*. These rocks are places where the wild animals live (Job 39:1; Ps 104:18), places where fugitives hide (1 Sam 13:6), especially those facing the wrath of God's judgment in the form of invasion by foreign armies (Isa 7:19; Jer 16:16; 48:28), and places that lend themselves to the building of fortifications and strongholds (Jer 49:16; Obad 3). This word *sela'* is the expression used to describe the rock of provision from which Moses was to command to bring forth water to nourish the Israelites in the desert (Num 20:8, 10-11). Moses' sin of disobedience in striking the rock and his sin of insubordination in usurping Yahweh's place (Num 20:11-12) prevented him from entering the Promised Land.

2. Like the word *ṣûr* I, *sela'* also is a name for God (2 Sam 22:2; Ps 42:10[9]), symbolizing his unshakable faithfulness, permanence, protection, care, and provision for his people (Ps 71:3; 78:16; Isa 32:2).

3. *sela'* is also a metaphor for Israel's sin and rebellion against God (Jer 5:3), and the brazenness of the people as they flaunted their evil deeds publicly (Ezek 24:7-8).

4. The word *sela'* is also used as a proper name in the OT, identified with the Nabatean Petra in 2 Kgs 14:7, an unidentified Amorite border fortress in Judg 1:36, and an unknown site in Moab (Isa 16:1). Elsewhere, the location where King Saul had

to abandon his pursuit of David due to a Philistine incursion was called Sela Hammahlekoth (1 Sam 23:28), and a site known as *sela'-rimmon* or the "rock of Rimmon" (a rock outcropping or cave near Gibeah) is mentioned 3x in the OT (Judg 20:45, 47; 21:13).

Rock, stones: → *'eben* (stone, rock, # 74); → *gābîš* (rock-crystal, # 1486); → *ḥallāmîš* (flint, # 2734); → *ḥāṣāṣ* (gravel, # 2953); → *kēp* (rock, # 4091); → *sōḥeret* (mineral stone, # 6090); → *sela'* (rock, # 6152); → *sql* (throw stones, # 6232); → *ṣûr* I (rock, boulder, # 7446); → *ṣûr* II (pebble, flint, # 7447); → *ṣōr* I (flint knife, # 7644); → *rgm* (stone, # 8083); → *talpiyyôt* (courses of stones, # 9444)

Bibliography

NIDNTT 2:731-34; 3:381-99; *ISBE* 3:205-6; 4:622-30.

Andrew E. Hill

6155 (*sol'ām*, katydid), → # 746

6156	סלף

סלף (*slp*), pi. frustrate, overthrow, distort, twist, mislead (# 6156); סֶלֶף (*selep*), nom. deceit, perversity, subversion, duplicity (only in Prov 11:3; 15:4) (# 6157).

OT 1. Legal texts warn against perverting or twisting (*sillēp*) justice through either offering or receiving bribes (Exod 23:8; Deut 16:19). Bribery subverts the very foundations of society (Mayes, *Deuteronomy*, 265; → *šḥd,* give a gift, # 8815; *šōḥad*, gift, bribe, # 8816). Several words overlap in meaning and use. The literal and the nonliteral meanings of the Heb. words blend as they denote subversion of order and its consequences: human injustice and divine justice (*slp*); conspiracy (*'bt*); a winding path, perversion of justice (*'ql*); twist, struggle, shrewd, crooked (*ptl*). The Law, Prophets, and the Writings witness to God's justice in contrast to the human tendency to subvert it, and call on the wise to distance themselves from the lawless. After all, those who distort and subvert exemplify folly.

2. The Wisdom tradition amplifies the law by encouraging the wise to lead a life of integrity in contradistinction from the fools. Goodness and uprightness should be the norm. A departure from them is a skewing or purposeful distortion from this expected and desired good.

Fools ruin their own lives as well as those of others because they are not content, have little regard for people, and even rage against God (Prov 13:6; 19:3). But God justly overthrows those who have subverted his order. He frustrates their plans and words (Job 12:19; Prov 22:12). Thus, he maintains and restores justice in his world.

3. The nom. *selep* signifies a destructive way of life. A sharp contrast is drawn in Wisdom literature between the upright who act with integrity and the treacherous who act in just the opposite manner, with duplicity (*selep*). First, they have a different effect on people. The righteous bring healing, whereas the fools by their perverted, twisted, and distorted way take life away from others, "The tongue that brings healing is a tree of life, but a deceitful tongue crushes the spirit" (Prov 15:4). Second, both the righteous and the wicked reap the yield of the seed that they have sown, "The integrity of the upright guides them, but the unfaithful are destroyed by their duplicity (*selep*)" (Prov 11:3).

P-B In the intertestamental period, Ben Sirach encouraged the godly to examine anything carefully before finding fault or criticizing (Sir 11:7). The Temple Scroll warns against "perverting" the words of the righteous, an action compared to blinding the wise and perverting justice through bribes (51:13). Similar uses occur in RL (Jastrow, 996).

Distortion, perversion, shrewdness, twisting: → *hēpek* (opposite, perversity, # 2201); → *kpn* (twist, # 4102); → *lwz* (let out of sight, go wrong way, # 4279); → *slp* (frustrate, overthrow, twist, mislead, # 6156); → *'bt* (conspire together, # 6309); → *'wh* (do wrong, pervert, # 6390); → *'wl* I (act wrongly, # 6401); → *'wt* (make crooked, pervert, bent, # 6430); → *'ql* (perverted, # 6823); → *'qš* (be perverse, make crooked, # 6835); → *ptl* (twist, be wily, shrewd, # 7349); → *r"* I (be bad, injure, # 8317)

BIBLIOGRAPHY
TWOT 2:627.

David W. Baker

6157 (*selep*, deceit, perversity), → # 6156

6159	סֹלֶת

סֹלֶת (*sōlet*), wheat flour (# 6159).

OT This common word for flour, used 52x in the OT, probably refers to a more roughly ground wheat (J. Milgrom, *Leviticus 1-16*, AB, 1991, 179). It may be related to the Akk. word *salātu,* meaning crush, and there are significant cognates throughout the ANE (e.g., Akk. *siltu*, a kind of grain; Arab. *sult*, a kind of barley without husks). The LXX uses the word *semidalis* and the Vg. *simila,* both referring to a fine flour, which suggests that this grain is made from the heart of the grain. Later Heb. and Aram. derivatives (*sôl^{e}tā'*, *sûltā'*) continued to connote a finely ground flour, but it appears to be grain-like portions left after grinding. R. D. Patterson believes that this word is distinguished from *qemaḥ*, meal (cf. 1 Kgs 5:2; → # 7854), which denotes the whole kernel or bran ground together with the heart of the grain (*TWOT* 2:628). This word is used predominantly for the flour of various grain offerings (Lev 2:1, 2, 4, 5, 7; 6:8; 7:12; etc.), and in most cases *sōlet* could be substituted for more expensive offerings when the person was poor (5:11; 14:21). However, this kind of flour was significantly more expensive than barley (2 Kgs 7:1, 16, 18) and was used in fine cuisine (Ezek 16:13), proper for entertaining guests (Gen 18:6).

P-B Two passages from RL explain what the word *sōlet* means: "a sieve lets through the flour but retains the *sōlet*" (Mish. 'Abot 5:15), and, "When you sift the flour beneath (the sieve), the *sōlet* is above" (PTalm Šabbat 7, 10b, 17c).

Grain, barley, millet, rice, etc.: → *'ābîb* (ears of grain, # 26); → *bisqālôn* (fresh stalks [cj.], # 1303); → *bar* III (grain, corn, # 1339); → *gādîš* I (stack of grain, # 1538); → *gereś* (grits, # 1762); → *dāgān* (grain, # 1841); → *dōḥan* (sorghum, millet, # 1893); → *ḥiṭṭâ* (wheat, # 2636); → *kussemet* (emmer-wheat, # 4081); → *karmel* IV (grain, fresh, newly ripened grain, # 4152); → *m^{e}lîlâ* (grain, grains, # 4884); → *minnît* (rice, # 4976); → *mōṣ* (chaff, # 5161); → *sōlet* (wheat flour, # 6159); → *pannāg* (parched? grain, meal or flour, # 7154); → *ṣebet* (grain, bundle of grain, # 7395); → *ṣānum* (hard, barren [ears of grain], # 7568); → *qālî* (parched grain,

7833); → *qāmâ* (crops, grain, standing grain, # 7850); → *śôrâ* (millet, # 8463); → *śᵉʿōrâ* (barley, # 8555); → *šibbōlet* I (ear of grain, # 8672); → *šeber* II (grain, # 8692)

Paul D. Wegner

6160 (*sam*, fragrant perfumes), → # 8379

6163 (*sᵉmādar*, blossom cluster [of vine]), → # 7255

6164	סמך

סמך (*smk*), q. support, lean; ni. lean against; pi. refresh (# 6164); שְׂמִיכָה (*śᵉmîkâ*), curtain (→ # 8526).

ANE The root is widely used in the Sem. languages with a similar range of meaning to the OT usage.

OT 1. This vb. occurs 48x in the OT, of which fourteen are in Leviticus and eleven in the Psalms. The root also appears in the personal names Ahisamach (Exod 31:6), Semakiah (1 Chron 26:7), and Ishmakiah (2 Chron 31:13), with the verbal element describing help or support.

2. In general this word refers to support or strengthening provided, often in parallel with other vbs. connoting help, such as *ʿzr*, *yšʿ* (→ # 3828), *zqp*, and *pgʿ* (→ # 7003), or in contrast with vbs. such as *npl*, fall (→ # 5877; cf. Ps 37:24; 145:14). In Gen 27:37 Isaac speaks of sustaining Jacob with corn and wine, a usage extended in the pi. to refreshing with food (S of Songs 2:5). Amos 5:19 is an excellent example of its use with both a direct and indirect object: The Day of the Lord "will be as though a man fled from a lion only to meet a bear, as though he entered his house and rested his hand on the wall only to have a snake bite him." Frequently the Lord is the subject of the vb., for he upholds the righteous and bowed down (Ps 37:17, 24; 119:116; 145:14). The pass. part. has the meaning "constant, enduring" (111:8; 112:8; Isa 26:3).

3. In the ni. *smk* is used of leaning on a staff (2 Kgs 18:21 ‖ Isa 36:6) or leaning against pillars (Judg 16:29). It is also used of Israel's trust in God (Isa 48:2) or of an individual's confidence in his God as his refuge (Ps 71:6).

4. On two occasions *smk ʿal* has the sense of "exercise pressure, attack, come against" (Ps 88:7[8]; Ezek 24:2).

5. A major use of *smk* occurs in passages describing two types of ritual in the OT, in both of which the vb. is used with "hands" or "his hand" as the object.

(a) There is a clear distinction between *smk* and the two synonymous vbs. *śym* I (# 8492) and *šyt* (# 8883). The former involves the exercise of some force, while the latter pair involve touching without the application of physical pressure. The actions described by the use of these vbs. differ markedly, for *smk* is a technical term used of certain specified situations (see below), while *śym* I and *šyt* are less technical and have a far wider range of application (cf. Daube, *The NT and Rabbinic Judaism*, 224-29).

(b) *smk* is used over 20x to describe the leaning of hands on an animal about to be sacrificed. This applies to the burnt, fellowship, and sin offerings (Lev 1:4; 3:2; 4:4) and especially to the ritual of the Day of Atonement (Lev 16). In the specifications for this latter ceremony it is stated that both hands were to be laid on the goat (Lev 16:21), whereas in the other sacrifices only one hand is mentioned. Various theories to explain this laying on of hands have been advanced (for a summary cf. *THAT* 2:884). The Day of Atonement provides the clearest case involving the imposition of hands as transference of sin is made explicit (Lev 16:22). It has been proposed that in the other cases there is identification of the offerer with the animal, not transference of his sin to it (Milgrom, 765; Sansom, 323-26), but all the cases can be explained satisfactorily on the basis of transference.

(c) Three times *smk* describes Moses' act in setting apart his successor Joshua (Num 27:18, 23; Deut 34:9), and once when the formal consecration of the Levites is described (Num 8:10). In both situations transference of authority is in view.

6. Imposition of hands also took place when a blasphemer was being executed (Lev 24:14). The gesture may in this case have been a way whereby the community both identified the offender and also identified themselves as witnesses.

P-B 1. In QL the pass. ptc. appears, describing the enduring resoluteness of the Essenes. The finite vb. occurs most commonly with God as the subject. The occurrences in 1QapGen 20:22, 29 are important as they form the first mention in Jewish sources of laying on of hands in healing (J. A. Fitzmyer, *The Genesis Apocryphon of Qumran Cave 1: A Commentary*, 140).

2. In RL *smk* is restricted to the sacrifices and to the ordination of a rabbi.

NT The NT has various references to laying on of hands, some of which seem to be nontechnical (e.g., Jesus' blessing the children, laying on hands for healing), while others, e.g., the appointment of the seven in Acts 6, the appointing of Paul and Barnabas as missionaries in Acts 13, and the statements in 1 Tim 4:14; 5:22; 2 Tim 1:6 regarding the imposition of hands, seem to have the OT use of *smk* as their background (→ *NIDNTT* 2:150-53).

Help, support, sustenance: → *zqp* (rise, lift up, # 2422); → *smk* (support, lean, refresh, # 6164); → *s'd* (sustain, support, # 6184); → *'zr* (help, support, find help, # 6468); → *rpq* (lean, # 8345); → *š'n* (lean, depend on, # 9128)

Bibliography

TDNT 9:424-34; *THAT* 2:160-62; *TWAT* 5:880-93; D. Daube, *The NT and Rabbinic Judaism*, 224-46; J. E. Hartley, "Excursus: Laying on of Hand(s)," *Leviticus*, WBC, 1992, 19-21; J. Milgrom, *IDBSup*, 763-71; J. K. Parratt, "The Laying on of Hands in the New Testament: A Re-Examination in the Light of the Hebrew Terminology," *ExpTim* 80, 1968-69, 210-14; M. C. Sansom, "Laying on of Hands in the Old Testament," *ExpTim* 94, 1982-83, 323-26.

Allan M. Harman

6166	סֶמֶל

סֶמֶל (*semel*), image of a god (# 6166), (synonym of *pesel*, # 7181); possibly specifically Asherah (→ # 895).

ANE Sam., Mish. Heb., Phoen. (*KAI*, 26, 41). Etymology unknown.

OT The nom. occurs 5x. In Deut 4:16 it is part of the piling up of nouns that attempts to drive home the point that no likeness of any kind may be made. The parallel passages (4:23, 25; cf. 4:15; 5:8; Exod 20:4) do not have *semel,* which therefore may be a gloss on *psl* in v. 16. 2 Chron 33:7 exactly reproduces 2 Kgs 21:7 (with NRSV: "carved image of Asherah") except that *semel* replaces "the Asherah."

2 Chron 33:15 also uses *semel* where "Asherah" would be expected. This may suggest that *semel* is specifically the goddess Asherah (in Phoenician *sml b'l* is a consort of Baal), but it is more likely that the Chronicler wished to remove any suggestion that an existent deity was involved, and asserted it was merely an image (an image of another image or idol).

Ezek 8:3, 5 describes a *semel* that stirs up powerful emotions (jealousy? anger? fury? sexual passion is unlikely). This item stands at the entrance of the northern gate of the inner court. Stadelmann (also Schroer) thinks that this is specifically a statue of Asherah, but it might also be some kind of guardian of the portal (e.g., a lion) that the new orthodoxy (formed in opposition to Babylonian usage) found extremely offensive (cf. *gillûlîm* in Ezekiel). While cherubim may be verbally described, apparently they must not be carved (Ezek 10).

Idolatry: → *'ᵉlîl* (Nothing, # 496); → *'ᵃšērâ* (wooden cult-object, pole, goddess, # 895); → *gillûlîm* (images, idols, # 1658); → *dāgôn* (Dagon, # 1837); → *kᵉmôš* (Chemosh [god of the Moabites], # 4019); → *mōlek* (Molech, # 4891); → *massēkâ* I (cast statuette, # 5011); → *mipleṣet* (terrible thing, dreadful object, # 5145); → *semel* (image, # 6166); → *'āṣāb* (god-image, # 6773); → *'aštōret* (Astarte, # 6956); → *pesel* (cultic image, statue of a god, # 7181); → *tōmer* II (scarecrow, # 9473); → *tᵉrāpîm* (figurines, mask, # 9572); → **Idolatry: Theology**

BIBLIOGRAPHY
C. Dohmen, "Heisst סֶמֶל 'Bild, Statue'?" *ZAW* 96, 1984, 263-66; C. Frevel, *Aschera und der Ausschlieslichkeitsanspruch YHWHs*, 1995; J. M. Hadley, "Yahweh and 'His Asherah,'" *Ein Gott allein?* 1994, 235-68; J. W. McKay, *Religion in Judah Under the Assyrians: 732-609 B.C.*, 1973; S. Schroer, *In Israel gab es Bilder*, 1987; R. Stadelmann, *Syrisch-Palästinenische Gottheiten in Ägypten*, 1967; W. Zimmerli, *Ezekiel*, 1979.

Judith M. Hadley

6169	סמר

סמר (*smr*), q. shudder, have goose bumps; pi. bristle (# 6169); מַסְמֵר (*masmēr*), nom. pin, nail (# 5021); סָמָר (*sāmār*), adj. bristling (# 6170).

ANE Arab. *sammara*, to nail; Akk. *samrūtum*, a nail.

OT The Heb. root *smr* occurs 7x: 2x as a vb. (Ps 119:120; Job 4:15, q. and pi. respectively), 4x as the nom. *masmēr* (1 Chron 22:3; 2 Chron 3:9; Isa 41:7; Jer 10:4), and 1x as the adj. *sāmār* (Jer 51:27).

The two verbal occurrences of *smr* appear in connection with the flesh (*bāśār*, → # 1414) and probably describe the physical reaction of goose bumps (the involuntary flexing of the skin's arector pilli muscles) caused by fear or terror. Adjectivally, this root describes either a particular type of locust or its bristly, hairy appearance. As a nom. this root has come to represent the technical Heb. term for nail.

Shaking, terror, trembling: → *g'š* (rise and fall noisily, swell, surge, # 1723); → *zw'* (tremble, quake, be afraid, # 2316); → *zll* II (shake, quake, tremble, # 2362); → *ḥalḥālâ* (shaking, trembling, anguish, # 2714); → *ḥrg* (come out trembling, # 3004); → *ḥrd* (tremble, shudder, startle, # 3006); → *yr'* (tremble, be fainthearted, # 3760); → *mwṭ* (waver, reel, stagger, shake, reel, # 4572); → *m'd* (slip, slide, shake, totter, # 5048); → *nwd* (shake, totter, waiver, wander, mourn, flee, # 5653); → *nwṭ* (shake, quake, # 5667); → *nw'* (shake, tremble, stagger, totter, wave, # 5675); → *n'r* II (shake, shake off, # 5850); → *smr* (shudder, have goose-bumps, bristle, # 6169); → *'iw'îm* (distortion, stagger, dizzy, # 6413); → *pwq* I (stagger, wobble, reel, totter, # 7048); → *pḥd* I (tremble, be in dread, # 7064); → *plṣ* (shudder, shake, tremble, # 7145); → *qwṣ* I (feel disgust, frighten, cause dread, # 7762); → *rgz* (agitate, quiver, shake, excite, rouse up, agitate, # 8074); → *rnh* I (rattle, # 8261); → *r'd* (tremble, shake, tremble, # 8283); → *r'l* I (brandish, make to quiver, # 8302); → *r'š* I (quake, shake, leap, # 8321); → *rpp* (shake, quake, rock, # 8344); → *reṭēṭ* (terror, panic, trembling, # 8417); → *ś'r* I (be afraid, terrified, bristle with horror, # 8547)

Fear, dread, terror: → *'āyōm* (terrible, awesome, majestic, # 398); → *'êmâ* (terror, dread, # 399); → *bhl* (be dismayed, terrified, dismay, terrify, hasten, hurry, # 987); → *b't* (overtaken by sudden terror, stupefied, be terrified, assail, # 1286); → *gwr* III (be afraid of, dread, stand in awe, # 1593); → *d'g* (be anxious, concerned, fear, dread, # 1793); → *zḥl* II (fear, be afraid, # 2324); → *ḥrd* (tremble, shudder, startle, # 3006); → *ḥtt* (be shattered, dismayed, terrified, scare, terrify, # 3169); → *ygr* (fear, dread, terror, # 3336); → *yr'* I (fear, be afraid, held in honor, # 3707); → *yrh* (be afraid, terrified, paralyzed with fright, # 3724); → *'rṣ* (be alarmed, terrified, dreadful, dreadful, be in terror, # 6907); → *pḥd* I (tremble, be in dread, # 7064); → *qwṣ* I (feel disgust, frighten, cause dread, # 7762)

BIBLIOGRAPHY

TWOT 2:629.

M. V. Van Pelt/W. C. Kaiser, Jr.

6170 (*sāmār*, bristling), → # 6169

6172 (*sanballaṭ*, Sanballat), → Geshem

6174	סְנֶה

סְנֶה (*seneh*), thorny shrub (# 6174).

ANE It is possible that *seneh* is cognate to Akk. *sinû* or *zinû* (*AHw* 3:1529; *CAD* 21:123-24). The term also appears in Syr. and Arab.

OT The word is used 4x in Exod 3 in connection with the theophany of the burning bush. In Deut 33:16 the reference is to the same event in the life of Moses. Some scholars think that this was a "varicolorous blackberry bush" (*HALAT* 661), but the botanical identification is uncertain.

P-B The word *sanyā'*, thorn, is found in a number of postbiblical Heb. contexts (e.g., Midr. S of Songs 1.1).

Thornbush, nettle, sting, thistle, thorn: → *'āṭād* (thornbush, # 353); → *barqōn* (thorn, brier, # 1402); → *deber* II (thorny sting, # 1823); → *dardar* (thistle, # 1998); → *ḥēdeq* (brier, # 2537); → *ḥôaḥ* I (thorn, # 2560); → *mesûkâ* (thorn hedge, # 5004); → *na'aṣûṣ* (thornbush, # 5848); → *sîrâ* (thorny bush, # 6106); → *sillôn* (thorn, # 6141); → *seneh* (thorny shrub, # 6174); → *sirpād* (stinging nettle, # 6252); → *ṣe'elîm* (thorny lotus, # 7365); → *ṣenînîm* (thorns, # 7564); → *qôṣ* I (thornbush, # 7764); → *qimmôś* (weeds, nettles, # 7853); → *śēk* (thorn, splinter, # 8493); → *šāmîr* I (Christ's thorn, # 9031)

BIBLIOGRAPHY

TWOT 2:629; Zohary, *Plants of the Bible*, 1982, 140-41.

K. Lawson Younger, Jr.

6178 (*sanḥērîb*, Sennacherib), → Sennacherib

6180 (*sansinnâ*, blossom cluster of dates), → # 7255

6184	סעד

סעד (*s'd*), q. sustain, support (# 6184); nom. מִסְעָד (*mis'ād*), architectural term (# 5026).

ANE The root occurs with wide distribution in the Sem. languages, and always with similar meaning. In bibl. Aram. it is found once in Ezra 5:2, with the meaning of "support."

OT 1. As compared to the other vbs. for support, *s'd* tends to emphasize the general idea as distinct from specific connotations such as holding (up), with the idea of nourishment or physical support being prominent. The instances of its use in the OT fall into two categories:

(a) Seven times *s'd* occurs with the general meaning of "support," "strengthen." The majority of these references are in the Psalter. David experienced God's shield of victory and knew that he was sustained by God's right hand (Ps 18:35[36]). One instance specifies help from the Lord during a time of sickness (41:3[4]). The other passages in Psalms either refer to help given (94:18, with *ḥasdᵉkā* as the subject) or appeal for support to be afforded (20:2[3]; 119:117). The other passages concern the support of the king's throne. In Isa 9:7[6] the Davidic throne is to be established and sustained, while Prov 20:28 declares that covenant love (*ḥesed*) supports the king's throne.

(b) On five occasions *s'd* is used in contexts concerning food (Gen 18:5; Judg 19:5, 8; 1 Kgs 13:7; Ps 104:15), and, of these, only in 1 Kgs 13:7 is the vb. unaccompanied by the object *lēbab*, heart (→ # 4213). To strengthen the heart clearly means "to eat" or "take refreshment," with "heart" being equivalent to the life of man. On three occasions the food indicated is expressly said to be *leḥem*, bread (→ # 4312).

2. The nom. *mis'ād* occurs only in 1 Kgs 10:12, in a description concerning the almug-(elsewhere algum-)wood that Hiram's ships brought from Ophir. Solomon is said to have used it to make a *mis'ād* for the temple and for the royal palace, and also used it for the harps and lyres. The parallel passage in 2 Chron 9:11 has *mᵉsillōt*, pathways, but there is no evidence to support the equation of *mis'ād* with *mᵉsillôt*. Clearly the wood was used for musical instruments as well as for some furniture or fitting for the temple and palace, and therefore "balustrade" or "fretwork" seems most likely.

Help, support, sustenance: → *zqp* (rise, lift up, # 2422); → *smk* (support, lean, refresh, # 6164); → *s'd* (sustain, support, # 6184); → *'zr* (help, support, find help, # 6468); → *rpq* (lean, # 8345); → *š'n* (lean, depend on, # 9128)

BIBLIOGRAPHY

THAT 2:160-62, 256-59, *TWAT* 5:880-93; D. Daube, *The NT and Rabbinic Judaism*, 224-46; J. Milgrom, *IDBSup*, 763-71.

Allan M. Harman

6185	סעה

סעה (*s'h*), q. calumniate, rush (hapleg.; # 6185).

OT The word occurs only in Ps 55:8[9]. Its meaning is uncertain. BDB, relating it to Syr. and Arab. roots, translates "*rush*, storm-wind" (BDB, 703; cf. *TWOT* 2:629). LXX reads *apo oligopsuchias kai kataigidos*, "from faint-heartedness and storminess," which may reflect a different Heb. original. Kraus deletes *s'h* (H.-J. Kraus, *Psalmen*, 1978, 1:401) as apparently does NEB's "from wind and storm." Dahood (*Psalms 51-100*, AB 17, 1968, 33), on the basis of Ugar. *s't*, translates "sweeping." Tate (*Psalms 51—100*, WBC, 1991, 20:52) concludes "the meaning is probably something like 'raging' or 'sweeping'—metaphorical in nature, of course." At best, "calumniate" (KB 662) can only be an extrapolation of the metaphorical sense of the term within the context of Ps 55. The psalmist laments the slanderous treatment he receives from his adversaries. His agony is so intense he confesses his desire to flee far away: "I would hurry to my place of shelter, far from the [slanderous] tempest and storm" (Ps 55:8, NIV).

P-B No significant occurrences of this root appear.

Wind, storm: → *zal'āpâ* (scorching [wind], # 2363); → *ḥāzîz* (cloud, strong wind, thunderclap, # 2613); → *yôm* II (wind, storm, breath, # 3428); → *m^e^zārîm* (north-winds, # 4668); → *sûpâ* I (destructive wind-storm, whirlwind, # 6070); → *s'h* (calumniate, rush [storm], # 6185); → *rûaḥ* (wind, Spirit, # 8120); → *r'm* I (storm, thunder, # 8306); → *ś'r* II (carry off in a storm-wind, # 8548)

Tim Powell

6186 (*sā'îp* I, cleft, crack), → # 5117

6187 (*sā'îp* II, branch), → # 580

6188	סעף

סעף (*s'p* II), cut down (branch) (# 6188); סְעִיף/סְעַפָּה (*sā'îp* II, *s^e 'appâ*), nom. branch (→ # 6187/6190); סֵעֵף (*sē'ēp*), adj., disunited, divided in heart and mind, conflicting, schismatic, fickle, changeable, inconstant, inconsistent (hapleg.; → # 6189); סְעִפִּים (*s^e 'ippîm*), crutches (# 6191); סַרְעַפָּה (*sar'appâ*), branch (→ # 6250).

OT The nom. *s^e 'ippîm* in 1 Kgs 18:21 has at least two potential meanings. It could denote "crutches" made out of tree limbs, or it could indicate "alternatives" set forth as choices, that is, "sides, parties." (A pair of related terms are *sā'îp,* branch, in Isa 17:6; 27:10, and *s'p,* cut down or lop off, in Isa 10:33; cf. *s^e 'appâ* and *sar'appâ* in Ezek 31:5-6, 8.)

Branch (of tree): → *'āmîr* (branch, bough, # 580); → *s'p* II (cut down, # 6188); → *'ānāp* (branches, # 6733)

Edwin C. Hostetter

6189	סֵעֵף

סֵעֵף (*sē'ēp*), adj., disunited, divided in heart and mind, conflicting, schismatic; fickle, changeable, inconstant, inconsistent (hapleg.; # 6189); < סעף (*s'p*), pi. cut off; cut down; cut short; lop off (hapleg.; → # 6188).

ANE In Arab. the adj. *sa'f* occurs with the meaning common, general, ordinary; low, vulgar, mean, base; contemptuous, scornful, disdainful; despicable, contemptible.

OT 1. The masc. pl. adj. occurs in Ps 119:113, where the psalmist, denouncing his enemies, expresses his hatred for *sē'ᵃpîm*. The word has been interpreted in different ways. LXX reads *paranomoi*, transgressors (of the law). Vg. has "wicked." Tg. translates "people who think vain thoughts." C. A. and E. G. Briggs (413, 432) read "those that swerve with their mouth" (from truth and the law). Delitzsch (239, 257), Kirkpatrick (722-23), Oesterley (495-96), RSV, NRSV, NIV, Dahood (168), Eaton (277), and Kidner (427) take the reference to be to the doubleminded (cf. NEB; REB). JB translates "those whose allegiance is divided"; TEV reads "those who are not completely loyal to you"; and Allen (131) has "people with divided loyalties." Kraus (407; cf. Rogerson and McKay, 107) translates "fickle people." The word may describe those who are hypocritical or duplicitous. However, the primary reference seems to be to those who lack single-minded devotion and commitment to Yahweh and who are not prepared to accept the yoke of the *tôrâ* without equivocation or vacillation (cf. Bratcher and Reyburn, 1030). Kirkpatrick (723; cf. Kissane, 1964, 553, 561) refers to these people as "unstable waverers, half Israelites, half heathen." Anything less than wholehearted commitment and loyalty to Yahweh is faithlessness.

2. The pi. part. is used in Isa 10:33 of Yahweh, the axe-wielding forester, who, with terrifying power, will lop off the boughs. The identity of "the boughs" has occasioned considerable debate. Many (e.g., Smith, 149-52, 173-74; Whitehouse, 173; Skinner, 94; Thomson and Skinner, 43; Peake, 444; Bright, 498; Mauchline, 125-26; Kelley, 230; Sheppard, 558; Oswalt, 273-76; Motyer, 120; Seitz, 95) take the reference to be to Assyria. Kissane (1960, 125) and Kaiser (157) maintain that it is the Davidic kingdom, both the royal house and the commoners, that is condemned to ruin. Jensen (237) thinks that the object of Yahweh's judgment is neither presumptuous Assyria nor the Davidic kingdom as a whole, but the leaders who are responsible for Judah's dangerous policies. Wright (49) maintains that vv. 33-34 constitute an independent prophecy of judgment directed against Israel or Judah or both. Gray (211) is noncommittal on the subject of the identity of the boughs, merely pointing out that vv. 33-34 describe the approaching destruction of some people whose pride has provoked Yahweh to wrath.

Unfaithful, fraudulent, perfidious, rebellious, treacherous: → *bgd* (act faithlessly, treacherously, perfidiously, # 953); → *m'l* (behave or act contrary to one's duty, faithless, # 5085); → *mrh* (be refractory, obstinate, # 5286); → *mᵉšûbâ* (unfaithfulness, apostasy, defection, # 5412); → *swg* I (deviate, diverge, decline, be faithless, rebellious, # 6047); → *sē'ēp* (disunited, divided in heart and mind, conflicting, schismatic, # 6189); → *srr* I (be stubborn, rebellious, # 6253); → *rmh* II (betray, deal treacherously with, # 8228); → *šqr* (deal/act falsely, betray, # 9213)

BIBLIOGRAPHY

L. C. Allen, *Psalms 101-150,* WBC, 1983; R. G. Bratcher and W. D. Reyburn, *A Translator's Handbook on the Book of Psalms,* 1991; C. A. and E. G. Briggs, *A Critical and Exegetical Commentary on the Book of Psalms. vol. 2,* ICC, 1960; J. Bright, "Isaiah-1," in *Peake,* 1964, 489-515; M. Dahood, *Psalms III: 101-150,* AB, 1970; F. Delitzsch, *Biblical Commentary on the Psalms,* Vol. III, KD, 2d ed., 1885; J. H. Eaton, *Psalms: Introduction and Commentary,* Torch, 1972;

G. B. Gray, *A Critical and Exegetical Commentary on the Book of Isaiah. Vol. I: Introduction, and Commentary on I-XXVII*, ICC, 1975; J. Jensen (with W. H. Irwin), "Isaiah 1-39," in *NJBC*, 1990, 229-48; O. Kaiser, *Isaiah 1-12: A Commentary*, OTL, 1977; P. H. Kelley, "Isaiah," in BBC, 1972, 5:149-374; D. Kidner, *Psalms 73-150: A Commentary on Books III-V of the Psalms*, TOTC, 1977; A. F. Kirkpatrick, *The Book of Psalms*, CBSC, 1957; E. J. Kissane, *The Book of Isaiah Translated from a Critically Revised Hebrew Text With Commentary. Vol. I (I-XXXIX)*, 1960; idem, *The Book of Psalms Translated from a Critically Revised Hebrew Text With a Commentary*, 1964; H.-J. Kraus, *Psalms 60-150: A Commentary*, 1989; J. Mauchline, *Isaiah 1-39*, Torch, 1970; J. A. Motyer, *The Prophecy of Isaiah: An Introduction & Commentary*, 1993; W. O. E. Oesterley, *The Psalms Translated With Text-Critical and Exegetical Notes*, 1959; J. N. Oswalt, *The Book of Isaiah Chapters 1-39*, NICOT, 1986; A. S. Peake, "Isaiah I-XXXIX," in *Peake*, 1920, 436-59; J. W. Rogerson and J. W. McKay, *Psalms 101-150*, CBC, 1977; C. R. Seitz, *Isaiah 1-39*, Interp, 1993; G. T. Sheppard, "Isaiah 1-39," in *HBC*, 1988, 542-70; J. Skinner, *The Book of the Prophet Isaiah Chapters I-XXXIX*, CBSC, 1909; G. A. Smith, *The Book of Isaiah. Volume I: Chapters I-XXXIX*, rev. ed., 1927; C. H. Thomson and J. Skinner, *Isaiah I-XXXIX*, 1921; O. C. Whitehouse, *Isaiah I-XXXIX*, CB, 1905; G. E. Wright, *Isaiah*, LBC, 1965.

Robin Wakely

6192 (*s'r* I, be stormy; be raged), → # 8548

6193 (*sa'ar*, gale, tempest), → # 8548

6194 (*sᵉ'ārâ*, gale, tempest), → # 8548

6195 (*sap* I, bowl, basin, cup, goblet), → # 3998

6197 (*sap* II, threshold), → # 6214

6199 (*spd*, sound of lament, mourn), → Lament

6200	ספה

ספה (*sph*), q. sweep away; ni. be swept away; hi. to hurl (s.t.) (# 6200).

OT 1. In Gen 18:23-24 it is used in association with the designations righteous and wicked. "Will you sweep away (*sph*), the righteous with the wicked?" In Deut 29:18 *sph* is used in a phrase that describes the result of a stubborn attitude that would sweep the watered land away. The good land is replaced by a parched or dry land because of disobedience. The same idea of dramatic change or removal is also present in Isa 7:20. Here divine judgment and calamity is portrayed once again. The removal of an old age beard is an extreme form of humiliation and dishonor. In this way the victim's honor was being swept away. Hence, the word has a negative connotation in this passage.

2. In Ps 40:14[15] *sph* also functions in a context of threat and disaster. Here the word is used in a synonymous parallel construction. "May those who seek to take my life be put to shame and confusion; may all who desire my ruin be turned back to disgrace." The psalmist appeals to God to bring shame and humiliation on his antagonist. These people are dangerous because they are out to kill and sweep him away. Therefore, God must sweep them away as one does refuse. This rendering is more dramatic than merely "taking" something away or destroying it. The word *sph* is used then in a very hostile manner in this poem.

3. In Num 32:14 the vb. can be translated "to sweep away." This can be considered as a problematic verse in BH. Many Bible translations, lexicons, and theological dictionaries depart from the MT (i.e., *lispôt*, sweeping up) and follow the reading (i.e., *lāsepet*, to add). This text-critical choice is based on the evidence of various versions. Such a position, however, is not necessary since *sph* can also be translated as "sweeping up" (i.e., the anger of the Lord). This translation makes more sense, especially if one thinks of the idea of fanning or heaping it up like a fire. Israel is, therefore, charged with sweeping up (i.e., sin upon sin), thus making God more angry in the process (cf. also Isa 30:1).

4. The vb. also appears in the ni. form in a number of passages. Here it can be rendered with a passive meaning: "to be swept away" or "to be snatched away." The context is one in which divine judgment and disaster is about to befall a city. In fact, the angels warn Lot to make haste to leave Sodom, lest they "be swept away" (*sph*) when the city is punished (Gen 19:15). In Num 16:25-35 we have a similar situation. Moses warns the assembly of Israel to distance themselves from the tents and belongings of rebellious Korah, Dathan, and Abiram (→ Korah's Rebellion: Theology), lest they be swept away because of all their sins and transgressions. Once again *sph* is employed in the sense of being swept away in divine judgment (cf. also 1 Sam 12:25, where Israel and the king are threatened with being swept away if they persist in their evil ways).

5. In 1 Sam 26:10, the idea is being conveyed that Yahweh himself will cause Saul to be swept away (hi. *sph,* i.e., cause or orchestrate his demise). The context is one in which David is fleeing from Saul. David does not undertake to remove Saul himself. "'As surely as the LORD lives,' he said, 'the LORD himself will *strike* him (*sph*).'" Thus, the translation should be rendered "he will be swept away" (i.e., by God). In fact, the narrator takes great pains to convey the idea that it is Yahweh himself who is causing Saul to go down.

Sweeping (away): → *y'h* (sweep, # 3589); → *sḥh* (scrap away, scrap, # 6081); → *sph* (sweep away, # 6200)

BIBLIOGRAPHY

F. I. Andersen, & A. D. Forbes, "יעה", "סחה" and "ספה," in *The Vocabulary of the Old Testament*, 1992.

P. J. J. S. Els

6202	ספח

ספח (*sph* I), q. attach, associate; ni. attach oneself; pi. join; hith. join oneself, adhere to (# 6202).

ANE There are no known cognates (*HALAT* 721).

OT This vb. occurs 5x in the OT and has the nuance of being associated with someone or something in order to participate in their inheritance or share. Two of the occurrences are in 1 Sam. In the condemnation of the house of Eli, which is at the same time a speech in favor of the faithful Zadok, Eli is told that those left in his family will come to implore Zadok to be associated with one of the priests for sustenance (1 Sam 2:36). In the other passage, David tells Saul how he has been effectively disinherited: "they have driven me out today from my share (*histappēaḥ*) in the heritage of the LORD" (1 Sam 26:19; *NRSV*). Job describes how the outcasts of society join together under the nettles (Job 30:7). The term is also used in parallel with *lwh* of the joining of aliens to the house of Jacob to benefit from Israel's inheritance (Isa 14:1). Whereas scholars had frequently emended Hab 2:15 to read "from the goblet of" (*missap*; BDB, 705; *HALAT* 721), the same reading as MT is preserved in 1QpHab 11:2, and the sense of association is entirely negative, both in the biblical text and in the pesher (see W. H. Brownlee, *The Midrash Pesher of Habakkuk*, 1979, 180-82). In this sense of association for sharing, the nuance of this vb. in its OT contexts may be echoed in Jesus' reply to Peter in John 13:8.

P-B The vb. is used with *ś* for *s* in CD 4:11 (see most recently D. R. Schwartz, "'To Join Oneself to the House of Judah' (Damascus Document IV, 11)," *RevQ* 10, 1981, 435-46) to imply that it is to one's great advantage to join the House of Judah before the age when Belial is overtly against Israel. In Mish. Heb. the general meaning continues and is best exemplified through its forceful use in Ruth Rabbah to Ruth 1:1: "they became citizens in the fields of Moab" (Jastrow, 1012).

Association, cleaving, companionship: → *dbq* (stick, cling, cleave, pursue, # 1815); → *ḥōbᵉlîm* (union, # 2482); → *ḥbr* II (unite, be joined, charm, make an ally, # 2489); → *yḥd* (be united, # 3479); → *lwh* I (accompany, join, attach oneself, # 4277); → *spḥ* I (attach, associate, join oneself, # 6202); → *ʿrb* II (associate with, mingle with, be intermixed with, # 6843); → *rʿh* II (associate with, be best man, make friends with, # 8287); → *šlb* (joined, dovetailed, # 8917)

George J. Brooke

6204	סַפַּחַת

סַפַּחַת (*sappaḥat*), a rare term possibly denoting *Alopecia pityrodes*, in which bodily hair falls off and is accompanied by a shedding of the cuticle in bran-like scales or shreds (Lev 13:2; 14:56; # 6204).

Disease—blister, boil, skin disease, scar, wound: → *ʾᵃbaʿbuʿōt* (blisters, # 81); → *bōhaq* (skin condition, # 993); → *baheret* (white patch on skin, # 994); → *gārāb* (festering eruption, # 1734); → *zrr* I (press out [wounds], # 2452); → *ḥeres* I (itch, # 3063); → *yabbelet* (wart?, # 3301); → *yallepet* (skin disease, # 3539); → *yᵉraqraq* (discoloration, # 3768); → *kᵉwiyya* (scar, # 3918); → *mʾr* (be sore, # 4421); → *māzôr* I (boil, # 4649); → *makkâ* (blow, # 4804); → *mispaḥat* (skin eruption, # 5030); → *mrḥ* (rub, polish, # 5302); → *neteq* (scalp infection, # 5999); → *sappaḥat* (hair disease, # 6204); → *ʿōpel* I (abscesses, # 6754); → *ʿāš* II (pus, # 6932); → *ṣāpâ* (pus?, # 7597); → *ṣarebet* (scar, # 7648); → *ṣrʿ* (suffer from skin disease, # 7665); → *śᵉʾēt* II (swelling, # 8421); → *śtr* (break out [tumor], # 8609); → *šᵉḥîn* (boil, # 8825). For related entries → *ḥlh* I (become weak, tired, ill, # 2703)

BIBLIOGRAPHY

ISBE 1:532, 953-60; 3:103-6; G. J. Wenham, *Leviticus*, NICOT, 1979, 189-214.

R. K. Harrison

6206	סָפִיחַ

סָפִיחַ (*sāpîaḥ* I), what grows on its own accord (# 6206).

OT Contextually, *sāpîaḥ* denotes produce that grows unintentionally during the sabbatical (Lev 25:5) or Jubilee (Lev 25:11) years from that which is spilled during the previous harvest. The use of the word at 2 Kgs 19:29 (Isa 37:30) suggests the possibility that Sennacherib's siege of Jerusalem took place in a sabbatical year, followed by a Jubilee.

P-B *sapîaḥ* continues to be used in RL for spontaneous growth of the sabbatical year (BTalm Pesaḥim 51b).

Growth, greatness, luxuriance, ripening, sprouting: → *bqq* II (grow luxuriantly, # 1328); → *gdl* I (grow up, become great, make great, boast, # 1540); → *nwb* (grow, prosper, flourish, # 5649); → *sāḥîš* (what grows on its own accord, # 6084); → *sāpîaḥ* I (what grows on its own accord, # 6206); → *ṣmḥ* (sprout, spring up, grow, prosper, make grow, # 7541); → *r'n* (be luxuriant, green, # 8315); → *śg'/śgh* (grow great, increase, exalt, # 8434/8436)

BIBLIOGRAPHY
R. D. Patterson and H. J. Austel, *1, 2 Kings*, EBC, 1988, 4:267-68, 270; G. H. Jones, *1 and 2 Kings*, 1984.

M. G. Abegg, Jr.

6207	סָפִיחַ

סָפִיחַ (*sāpîaḥ* II), violent storm (# 6207).

ANE *sāpîaḥ* is related to Arab. *sapaḥa*, pour (see BDB, 705, and Zorell, *Lexicon*, 559).

OT *sāpîaḥ* occurs only in Job 14:19. A violent storm's power to erode soil provides material for a simile of God's power to dash the hopes of people. The NIV translates *sāpîaḥ* as "torrents," perhaps based on the widely accepted emendation to *s^{e}ḥîpâ*, rainstorm (see *HALAT* 721 and Hartley, *Job*, 239). The conjectured form would occur only here and is based on *māṭār sōḥēp*, a driving rain (Prov 28:3), and a presumed Arab. *saḥīfeh*, rainstorm, torrential rain (see Clines, *Job*, 284, who, however, questions the existence of the Arab. word). Perhaps *sāpîaḥ* itself is a nom. with the sense "downpour" (see Holladay, *Lexicon*, 259) or "violent storm" (see Zorell, *Lexicon*, 559), based on the context, which includes erosion (v. 18) and power (v. 20), and on the Arab. cognate *sapaḥa*, pour out.

Rain, dew, drizzle, hail, showers: → *'ēgel* (drop [of dew], # 103); → *brd* I (hail, # 1351); → *gšm* (make rain, # 1772); → *zrm* II ([clouds] pour out [water], # 2442); → *ḥ^{a}nāmal* (sleet, hail?, # 2857); → *ṭal* (dew, light rain, drizzle, # 3228); → *yrh* II (give drink, cause rain, # 3722); → *mṭr* (make rain, # 4763); → *malqôš* (late rain, # 4919); → *sagrîr* (downpour, # 6039); → *sāpîaḥ* II (violent storm, # 6207); → *r^{e}bîbîm* (showers, # 8053); → *rāsîs* (dew drop, # 8268); → *r'p* (drip, flow, rain, # 8319); → *śā'îr* IV (heavy rain, # 8540); → *šikbâ* (layer of dew, emission/ discharge of seed, # 8887)

BIBLIOGRAPHY
D. Clines, *Job 1-20*, 1989; J. Hartley, *The Book of Job*, 1988.

Mark D. Futato

6208 (*s^{e}pînâ*, deck, ship), → # 6211

6209	סַפִּיר

סַפִּיר (*sappîr*), sapphire, lapis lazuli or lazurite (# 6209).

ANE Cognates in Aram., Syr., and Eth.; perhaps ultimately derived from Sanskrit. That the OT understands the softer stone, azure lapis lazuli, is assumed from the Ugar. *ṭhr/iqnim* (lapis lazuli) and the association of the Heb. *ṭāhôr*, pure, with *sappîr* in Exod 24:10.

OT Most of the modern Eng. versions, including the NIV, translate "sapphire" and read "lapis lazuli" in the margin or footnote. Blue lapis lazuli was a beautiful and valuable gemstone, one in demand in the ancient world. For this reason it is part of the royal vestment (Ezek 28:13) and is included among the twelve gemstones adorning the breastpiece of Israel's high priest (Exod 28:18; 39:11). And yet, according to Job's hymn, wisdom is of far greater value than gold and precious stones like lapis lazuli (Job 28:16). The beauty and costliness of the stone is also evidenced by its inclusion in the decor of God's heavenly throne room (Exod 24:10; Ezek 1:26; 10:1). According to Isaiah, the restored Zion will rest on foundations of lapis lazuli (Isa 54:11; cf. Rev 21:19). The word is also used metaphorically of personal beauty, as in the case of the maiden's description of her beloved (S of Songs 5:14) and the princes of Judah prior to the Babylonian invasion (Lam 4:7)!

For a theological introduction to the topic of gems in the OT, see *'ōdem* (# 138).

Precious Stones: → *'eben* (stone, rock, # 74); → *'ōdem* (precious stone, # 138); → *'aḥlāmâ* (jasper, # 334); → *'eqdāḥ* (beryl, # 734); → *bahaṭ* (precious stone, # 985); → *bāreqet* (emerald, # 1403); → *yah^a^lōm* (precious stone, # 3402); → *yāš^e^pēh* (jasper, # 3835); → *kadkōd* (ruby?, # 3905); → *lešem* I (precious stone, # 4385); → *nōpek* (semi-precious stone, # 5876); → *sōḥeret* (mineral stone, # 6090); → *sappîr* (lapis lazulli, # 6209); → *piṭdâ* (chrysolite, # 7077); → *š^e^bô* (precious stone, # 8648); → *šōham* I (precious stone, # 8732); → *šāmîr* II (emery, diamond?, # 9032); → *šēš* II (alabaster, # 9253); → *taršîš* II (precious stone, # 9577)
Jewelry, ornaments: → *'dh* II (adorn o.s., # 6335)

BIBLIOGRAPHY
IDB 2:898-905; *ISBE* 4:623-30; *NIDNTT* 3:395-98; *TWOT* 2:631; J. S. Harris, "An Introduction to the Study of Personal Ornaments, of Precious, Semi-Precious and Imitation Stones Used Throughout Biblical History," *ALUOS* 4, 1962, 49-83; L. Koehler, "Hebräische Vokabeln II," *ZAW* 55, 1937, 161-74; H. Quiring, "Die Edelsteine im Amtsschild des jüdischen Hohenpriesters und die Herkunft ihrer Namen," *AGM* 38, 1954, 193-213; W. Zimmerli, *Ezekiel 25-48*, 1983, 82-84.

Andrew E. Hill

6210 (*sēpel*, bowl, basin), → # 3998

6211	ספן

ספן (*spn*), q. cover with, panel (# 6211); ; conj. סְפִינָה (*s^e^pînâ*), nom. ship, deck (# 6208); סִפֻּן (*sippun*), nom. ceiling, roof (# 6212).

ANE The Arab. *sfn*, peel, and Akk. *sapānu* (*AHw*, 1025), flush down, level, are suggested cognates.

OT 1. The q. occurs in descriptions of wooden roofing beams and decorative paneling, made of cedar, and is probably a specialized architectural term (see Wolff, 30). Cedar was used in monumental buildings because it offered a greater span than other building timbers like sycamore. Such usage is also attested in Assyrian and Babylonian inscriptions (see AR, n653). The temple of Solomon (1 Kgs 6:9) and the Hall of Justice (1 Kgs 7:3) are said to be roofed (covered) with beams of cedar. In 1 Kgs 7:7, Gray (169) and Wiseman (783) suggest reading the *sāpun* (MT) as *sāpan* and rendering it, following the versions, as paneled (so too NIV, which reads *sippun*). Moreover, the Heb. speaks somewhat confusingly of the covering of cedar being from floor to floor. The Syr. and the Vg. has simply from floor to ceiling (so also NIV and cf. 1 Kgs 6:15).

2. Jer 22:14 calls down judgment on those kings who panel (so NIV) their palaces with cedar. Roof with cedar would also be acceptable. Hag 1:4 is capable of being rendered as either "roof" or "panel." NIV (see also Petersen, 48 and Ackroyd, 155) opts for the latter, so that the contrast is between houses that are paneled (implying luxury) and the poverty of the temple ruins. Wolff (30) and Verhoef (57-59) prefer the former, suggesting that the people have simply roofed (finished) houses while the temple lies in ruin. The likelihood of paneled houses they deem to be remote, given the probable financial situation of the time, unless the question was an ironical one. The prophet would then be castigating the people for the excesses in their own building, whatever the nature of these were.

3. The nom. *sippun* is used in the description of the construction of the temple of Solomon, concerning the extent of the interior wooden paneling, which apparently stretched all the way from floor to ceiling (1 Kgs 6:15). This is the only occurrence of the term unless one reads it (with NIV) in 1 Kgs 7:7. Similarly, *s^e^pînâ* is used only once (Jon 1:5), indicating that Jonah had gone "below deck" (NIV; lit. into the recesses of the *s^e^pîna*). *s^e^pînâ* may signify here deck ("a remote place below deck," D. Stuart, *Hosea-Jonah*, WBC, 1987, 454) or ship ("the lowest part of the ship," H. W. Wolff, *Obadiah and Jonah*, 1986, 105).

BIBLIOGRAPHY

P. Ackroyd, *Exile and Restoration*, 1972; J. Gray, *I and II Kings*, 1964; C. L. Meyers and E. M. Meyers, *Haggai, Zechariah 1-8*, 1987; D. L. Petersen, *Haggai and Zechariah*, 1984; P. A. Verhoef, *The Books of Haggai and Malachi*, 1987; H. W. Wolff, *Haggai*, 1988.

W. R. Domeris

6212 (*sippun*, ceiling, roof), → # 6211

6214	ספף

ספף (*spp*), denom. vb. hitpol. lie at the threshold (# 6214); סַף (*sap* III), nom. threshold, lintel (# 6197).

ANE Akk. *sippu*, doorframe, door jambs (Zimmern, 31), Aram. *sippā'*, doorsill (Kaufman, 92), Phoen. *sp*, doorsill.

OT 1. The use of the vb. *spp* in Ps 84:10[11] (NIV be a doorkeeper) occurs only here. It describes the psalmist's preference for this task in the house of God over and above any association with the wicked. However, this position seems to be a humble one in contrast to other descriptions of doorkeepers in the temple of Jerusalem (cf.

2 below). Therefore, it may not describe an official role. More likely it depicts one who stand at the entrance to the temple, awaiting permission to enter (Anderson, 606; Kidner, 306).

2. *sap* most often occurs in the expression "doorkeepers" (*šōm^{e}rê hassap*), which is virtually synonymous with *šō'ēr*, gatekeeper. Most often this refers to guards of a sanctuary (2 Kgs 12:9[10]; 22:4; 23:4; 25:18; 2 Chron 34:9; Jer 35:4; 52:24; similar expressions in 1 Chron 9:22; 2 Chron 23:4). However, palace guards are described by the use of the same term in Esth 2:21 and 6:2.

3. The *sap* appears with other architectural features in the temple of Ezekiel (40:6, 7; 41:16), in Solomon's temple (2 Chron 3:7), and in Isaiah's vision of God's house (Isa 6:4).

4. In Judg 19:27 the corpse of the violated concubine is portrayed as having her hands on the threshold, as though seeking safety.

P-B In the Qumran Copper Scroll treasure is twice buried *tḥt hsp* (beneath the threshold, 3Q15 II.12; XII.2). An occurrence on the Temple Scroll mentions the distance from the threshold to *hsp* as the height of a gate (11QT 36.9).

NT → *NIDNTT* 2:29-31.

Door, gate, threshold: → *'ayil* (doorpost, # 382); → *'ōmnâ* (pillar?, doorpost?, # 595); → *b^{e}rîaḥ* (bar, # 1378); → *delet* (door, # 1946); → *lûl* (trapdoor, # 4294); → *m^{e}zûzâ* (doorpost, # 4647); → *miptān* (threshold, # 5159); → *mašqôp* (lintel, # 5485); → *spp* (lie at threshold, # 6214); → *ṣîr* I (door pivot, # 7494); → *ša'ar* I (gate, # 9133)

BIBLIOGRAPHY

A. A. Anderson, *The Book of Psalms*, NCB 2, 1972; S. A. Kaufman, *The Akkadian Influences on Aramaic*, 1974; D. Kidner, *Psalms 73-150: A Commentary on Books III-V of the Psalms*, TOTC, 1975; H. Zimmern, *Akkadische Fremdwörter als Beweis für babylonischen Kultureinfluss*, 1915.

Richard S. Hess

6216 (*spq* II, be in abundance), → # 8563

6217 (*sepeq*, abundance), → # 8563

6218	ספר

ספר (*spr* I), q. count, number, reckon, ni. be counted, numbered; pi. recount, rehearse, declare, count; pu. be recounted, related, rehearsed (# 6218); nom. מִסְפָּר (*mispār* I), number, tale (→ # 5031); nom. סֵפֶר (*sēper* I), missive, document, writing, book (→ # 6219); nom. סֹפֵר (*sōpēr*), enumerator, master officer, secretary, scribe (→ # 6221); nom. סְפָר (*s^{e}pār* I), enumeration, census (hapleg.; → # 6222); nom. סִפְרָה (*siprâ*), book (hapleg.; → # 6225).

ANE For a careful discussion of the disputed etymology (cf. *HALAT* 723; BDB, 707) with a review of relevant literature and related synonyms, see *THAT* 2:162-65; *TWAT* 5:911-12.

OT 1. The straightforward sense of enumeration is concretely illustrated in the q. (26x): festal seasons are calculated (Lev 15:13); populations are counted (2 Sam 24:10); stars and grains of sand are numbered (Gen 15:5; Ps 139:18), etc. This sense is continued in the ni. (8x) and also occasionally in the pi. (Ps 22:17[18]; 50:16 and 40:5[6] are ambiguous between count/recount). Some uses of the q. and ni. occur in theologically interesting contexts. Innumerable progeny constitute one of the blessings of the promise to the fathers (Gen 15:5; 16:10; 32:13; cf. 1 Kgs 3:8). God counts an individual's steps in a figure of divine attention both as saving care (Ps 56:8[9]) and ironically as sadistic pestering (Job 14:16; so ICC, 130; Dhorme, 203; AB, 109; contrast Gordis, 150-51; Habel, 235) or moral inquisition (Job 31:4). When David is incited by God to conduct a census, this sinful act elicits divine wrath (2 Sam 24; cf. 1 Chron 21:1; 27:23, 24; see further, *THAT* 1:635-39; *TWAT* 4:978-79; *AncIsr,* 228, 258-65; Gerhard von Rad, *Holy War in Ancient Israel*, 1991).

2. The vb., however, finds explicit and preeminent theological relevance in the Psalter (cf. 1 Chron 16:24; Isa 43:21; Jer 51:10) in pi. and pu. stems. There it constitutes a verbal act of worship or praise. It is a laudatory recital or declaration of God's saving deeds and character, termed variously: his wonders (Ps 9:1[2]; 26:7; 40:5[6]; 75:1[2]), work or acts (44:1[2]; 73:28; 107:22; 118:17), glory (96:3), righteousness (71:15), loyal love (88:11[12]), greatness (145:6). This recounting offers as the focus of Israel's worship, Yahweh, the praiseworthy Savior who rescues the life of the community gathered in praise of his name (22:22[23]; 102:21[22]). Taken at its most literal and elaborate level of performance, this act entails the sacred narration of the nation's history as a saving story that embraces Israel's history of distress, rebellion, and forgetfulness with divine punishment, forgiveness, forbearance, and rescue (78:1-72). At this level of elaboration, saving deeds include more than rescue from periodic moral and physical crisis; there is also the gift of social institutions, namely, covenant and Torah, the Davidic kingship, as perennial saving presences (78:5-6, 65-72). It is no surprise, then, that a growing Torah-centered piety could view the meditative rehearsal of covenantal statues both a sign of faith and a self-transforming, identity-preserving, sanctifying, worshipful act (119:13; cf. 50:16).

Israel's life as projected in the imagery and idiom of the Psalter is cult-centered. Israel as a social, national, religious, ideational entity is legitimated by worship of Yahweh. Israel exists to praise (cf. Exod 9:16; 10:2; 18:8). The totality of the community history and experience is poured through this legitimating grid. The laudatory recital finds its significance within this structure. The narrative representation in the cultic community of its past saving experiences is not only the appropriate grateful response (Ps 107:22), but also the model for future historical experience, generating hope (118:17). Thus, for those in present distress, the narrative representation guides their present expectation, complaint, and petition on the one hand, motivating divine action, and on the other, offering assurance to the distressed (44:1[2]; 102:21[22]). Past participation in this cultic act signals one's integrity and fidelity (26:7); so too the vow to participate in cultic actions, on the other side of distress (22:22[23]; 71:15). Both lay a claim on the Savior, anchoring his honor in the well-being of the suppliant and the continued existence of a worshiping Israel. This laudatory recital of God's saving deeds is generative; Israel creates and re-creates itself through it from one generation to the next (145:4-7; cf. 78:5-6). The alternative is to forget, shattering the memory and the identity of the worshiping community (78:7, 11, 42). There is, however, the threat of deception; recital in the cult may serve a mask for the wicked (50:16). (→ Psalms: Theology)

3. Several noms. are discussed under Writing: Theology.

P-B This sense of laudatory recital continues in the Qumran hymns (1QH 1:30, 33; 6:11; 11:6, 28; 17:17; see further *TWAT* 5:920-21). The vb. is translated in LXX primarily by *arithmeō* (for q.) and *diēgeomai* (for pi.). The latter occurs once in the NT of a noncultic laudatory declaration of God's saving action on behalf of a demoniac (Luke 8:39; see further *NIDNTT* 1:575-76).

Counting, recounting, record: → *ḥšb* (consider, reckon, # 3108); → *kss* (determine, # 4082); → *mnh* (count, reckon, assign, appoint, ordain, # 4948); → *spr* I (count, number, reckon, rehearse, # 6218); → *pqd* (number, appoint, # 7212)
Praising, singing, thanksgiving: → *hll* II (praise, be praiseworthy, boast, exult, # 2146); → *zmr* I (make music, sing praise, # 2376); → *ydh* II (acknowledge, give thanks, praise, # 3344); → *nwh* II (praise, # 5658); → *'nh* IV (sing, # 6702); → *pṣḥ* I (break forth with or break into singing, # 7200); → *rômēm* (exalt, # 8123a); → *šbḥ* I (commend, praise, honor, # 8655); → *šyr* (sing, # 8876); → *tnh* (recite, commemorate, # 9480)

BIBLIOGRAPHY
TWAT 5:910-21; W. Brueggemann, *Abiding Astonishment: Psalms, Modernity, and the Making of History*, 1991; idem, *Israel's Praise: Doxology, Idolatry and Ideology*, 1988; E. Dhorme, *A Commentary on the Book of Job*, 1984; R. Gordis, *The Book of Job*; N. C. Habel, *The Book of Job*, OTL, 1985; G. H. Jones, "The Concept of Holy War," in *The World of Ancient Israel*, ed. R. E. Clements, 1989, 299-321; H.-J. Kraus, *Theology of the Psalms*, 1986, 84-100, 137-43; C. Westermann, *Praise and Lament in the Psalms*, 1981, 52-81.

A. R. Pete Diamond

6219 (*sēper* I, written document), → Writing

6219a (*sēper ḥayyîm*, book of life), → Book of Life

6219b (*sēper zikkārôn*, book of remembrance), → Book of Life

6220	סֵפֶר

סֵפֶר (*sēper* II), bronze (?) (# 6220).

OT Some understand the nom. *sēper* in Exod 17:14; Job 19:23; Isa 30:8; to be the Akk. loanword *siparru*, bronze, borrowed into Heb. (*HALAT* 724). This rendering certainly makes sense in each of the contexts, yet the NIV as most other translations has resisted this option, understanding the nom. to be the common term *sēper* meaning book, scroll.

For a discussion on copper, see *n^eḥōšet* I (copper, bronze, # 5733).

Mark Rooker

6221 (*sōpēr*, scribe), → Writing

6222 (*s^epār* I, census), → # 5031

6225 (*siprâ*, book), → Writing

6228 (*s^epōrôt*, numbers, measure), → # 5031, Writing

6230 (*sōperet*, writer?), → Writing

6232	סקל

סקל (*sql*), q. to stone, throw stones; ni. be stoned; pi. throw stones, cast away stones, pu. be stoned (# 6232).

ANE Aram. *sql*, stone.

OT 1. The vb. *sql* is customarily employed to indicate execution by stoning in OT legal texts. For example, violation of civil law as in cursing the king was a capital offense and punishable by stoning (cf. Ahab's trumped up charge against Naboth, 1 Kgs 21:10-15; note the civil law also calls for the "goring ox" to be stoned, Exod 21:28-32). Israelite ceremonial law called for execution by stoning for idolatry (Deut 13:10; 17:5) and for violation of the ban on booty during holy war (Josh 7:25), while moral law decreed death by stoning for certain types of sexual misconduct (Deut 22:21, 24).

2. Shimei shows his contempt and hostility for King David by throwing stones at him (and cursing him) when David flees Jerusalem in the face of Absalom's coup (2 Sam 16:6, 13). As a descendant of Saul, Shimei was no doubt seeking vengeance for David's part in the deaths of Abner, Ish-Bosheth, and the seven members of Saul's family surrendered to the Gibeonites (2 Sam 3:26-28; 4:7-8; 21:1-13). Stoning was apparently a common mob reaction against leadership in the face of intolerable distress, as Moses fretted during the hardships of the desert trek (Exod 17:4).

3. Twice the pi. of *sql* is used as a poetic metaphor of Yahweh's work on behalf of Israel, initially in establishing them as his vineyard by "clearing the stones" from a fertile hillside (Isa 5:2); and later in "removing the stones" and restoring Israel in the land of covenant promise (62:10). In both cases, the vb. *sql* is part of a sequence of activities demonstrating God's compassion and painstaking care in nurturing Israel as his elect.

Rock, stones: → *'eben* (stone, rock, # 74); → *gābîš* (rock-crystal, # 1486); → *ḥallāmîš* (flint, # 2734); → *ḥāṣāṣ* (gravel, # 2953); → *kēp* (rock, # 4091); → *sōḥeret* (mineral stone, # 6090); → *sela'* (rock, # 6152); → *sql* (throw stones, # 6232); → *ṣûr* I (rock, boulder, # 7446); → *ṣûr* II (pebble, flint, # 7447); → *ṣōr* I (flint knife, # 7644); → *rgm* (stone, # 8083); → *talpiyyôt* (courses of stones, # 9444)

Shooting, throwing: → *dḥh* (push, overthrow, be cast down, # 1890); → *ṭwl* (throw, # 3214); → *ydh* I (shoot, # 3343); → *yrh* I (shoot, throw, # 3721); → *mgr* (throw, # 4489); → *rbb* II (shoot, # 8046); → *rmh* I (throw, shoot, # 8227); → *šlk* I (throw, hurl, # 8959); → *šmṭ* (release, remit, drop, throw down, # 9023)

BIBLIOGRAPHY

ABD 5:546-56, 1073-74; *ISBE* 3:205-6; 4:630; *NIDNTT* 2:731-34; 3:381-99; *THAT* 2:538-42; *TWOT* 2:634.

Andrew E. Hill

6234 (*sar*, sullen, discouraged), → # 6253

6239	סרה

סרה (*srh* I), stopping (hapleg.; # 6239).

OT The root *srh* occurs only in Isa 14:6, in the prophet's taunt song against the king of Babylon (14:4-21), an idealized personage according to Wolf (*Isaiah*, 1985, 112).

The word, usually translated "unceasing" (so NIV, NRSV), is constructed in parallelism with *b^{e}lî ḥāśāk,* "relentless." J. H. Oswalt (*Isaiah 1-39*, NICOT, 1986, 316) notes, "the picture here of increasing and relentless oppression accords very well with the claims of the Assyrian kings.... They mastered the technique of ruling through terror." Yet Isaiah assured the Israelites that the Lord's might is greater than that of the king of Babylon. The God of Israel will break the scepters of human kings like matchsticks and bring down the wicked even to Sheol (14:5, 15).

End, cessation, outcome: → *'aḥ^{a}rît* (end, outcome, # 344); → *'ps* (cease, come to an end, # 699); → *bṭl* (cease working, # 1060); → *gmr* (be at an end, cease, fail, # 1698); → *ḥdl* I (end, stop, # 2532); → *swp* (come to an end, # 6066); → *sārâ* I (stopping, # 6239); → *qēṣ* (end, limit, boundary, # 7891); → *qṣh* I (bring about the end, shorten, # 7894)

Andrew E. Hill

6240 (*sārâ* II, rebellion, crime, revolt, falsehood), → # 6253

6242 (*sārûaḥ*, hanging over), → # 6243

6243	סרח

סרח (*srḥ* I), hang over, grow luxuriantly, sprawl (# 6243); סָרוּחַ (*sārûaḥ*), projecting, hanging over, flowing, sprawled (# 6242); סֶרַח (*seraḥ*), nom. what hangs over # 6245).

ANE Arab. *saraḥa*, move away, roam freely.

OT 1. This vb. appears in the q. stem in two places. (a) In Exod 26:12 it describes how the back (western end) of the tabernacle is to be provided with a curtain of goat hair (v. 7), whose "additional length ... that is left over" (also described as "the half curtain") will "hang down" (*srḥ*) at the back of the tabernacle (Haran, *Temples*, 152). (b) In the parable of Ezek 17:6 *srḥ* describes a stage in the growth of a vine (*gepen*). After the vine "sprouted" (*ṣmḥ*), it "became a low, spreading (*srḥ*) vine."

2. The nom. form of *seraḥ* occurs only once in the Bible. It is found with its cognate vb. in the description of the tabernacle construction in Exod 26:12.

3. *sārûaḥ*, pass. part., appears in the same context in Exod 26:13 (see above), where it describes how the outer curtains will be made an additional cubit in length: "will hang over the sides (i.e., the north and the south) of the tabernacle so as to cover it."

(a) In Ezek 23:15 the Babylonian officers are handsome, with their belts around the waist and with "flowing turbans on their heads." Such seems more likely as appropriate military dress than "long hair with a band" (Zimmerli, *Ezekiel 1*, 487, with reference to Herodotus). Thus the Babylonian ruler Merodach-Baladan is portrayed (*ANEP*, 156 no. 454) with a helmet/turban hardly dignified with a flowing "streamer" emerging from the top of the headdress and reaching to his waist.

(b) *sārûaḥ* appears in Amos 6:4 and 7. In both verses it is used to describe the feasting of the wealthy without regard for those who are oppressed. Whether or not *sārûaḥ* here implies drunkenness to the point of loss of control of one's limbs (Wolff, *Joel and Amos*, 276) is not clear, but the root suggests a posture in which limbs hang over couches. Semitic rulers were unaccustomed to being so portrayed at the time of Amos. A portrait of an Assyrian king reclining at a feast does not appear until more than a century later, with Ashurbanipal (King, *Amos*, 149). The feast portrayed in v. 7 is described in as a *mizraḥ*, a likely reference to the Canaanite funerary feast known as the *marzeaḥ* (→ # 5301), which included the variety of elements found in this text (King, *Amos*, 137-61; Andersen and Freedman, *Amos*, 568). Amos' use of *sārûaḥ* and the preceding two words in v. 7 suggest an alliterative wordplay, *w^esār mizraḥ s^erûḥîm*, "and the feast of sprawling will cease."

Hanging, dangling, sprawling, strangling: → *dlh* II (dangle, # 1927); → *dll* II (dangle, # 1938); → *ḥnq* (strangle, # 2871); → *ḥpṣ* II (let hang?, # 2912); → *srḥ* I (hang over, # 6243); → *tlh/tl'* (hang, # 9434)

Bibliography

F. I. Andersen and D. N. Freedman, *Amos: A New Translation with Introduction and Commentary*, AB 24A, 1989; M. Haran, *Temples and Temple-Service in Ancient Israel*, 1985; P. J. King, *Amos, Hosea, Micah—An Archaeological Commentary*, 1988; H. W. Wolff, *Joel and Amos*, Hermeneia, 1977; W. Zimmerli, *Ezekiel 1*, Hermeneia, 1979; idem, *Ezekiel 2*, Hermeneia, 1983.

Richard S. Hess

6244	סרח

סרח (*srḥ* II), ni. stink, spoil (# 6244).

ANE There is a possible occurrence of the root in *KAI* 10, 15 (destroy?).

OT In Jer 49:7 *srḥ* describes how the wisdom of the Edomites has decayed. It is in the third phrase of a verse with parallels in *'ayin*, nonexistence, and *'bd*, perish. BDB (710) relates this to *srḥ* I, go free, be unrestrained (cf. REB "dispersed abroad"). However, this would be the only occurrence in the ni., and *HALAT* (726) distinguishes for this one verse *srḥ* II, stink, decay.

P-B The vb. is also found in Sir 42:11 (with *APOT* I, 470, reading *šēm srḥ*, a bad name) and in later Heb. (Jastrow, 1024).

Smell, stench: → *b'š* (stink, become odious, # 944); → *zwr* III (stink, be offensive, # 2320); → *znḥ* I (become foul-smelling, # 2395); → *ḥnn* II (be stinking, loathsome, # 2859); → *srḥ* II (stink, spoil, # 6244); → *ṣaḥ^anâ* (stench, # 7462); → *rwḥ* B (smell, # 8193); → **Smell: Theology**

P. Jenson

6245 (*seraḥ*, what hangs over), → # 6243

6246 (*siryôn*, armor), → # 5976

6247	סָרִיס

סָרִיס (*sārîs*), nom. court official (early), eunuch (late) (# 6247).

ANE 1. All the related Sem. roots are derived from original Akk. title: *ša rēši/rîši* (*šarri*), the one at the head (of king), he who is the head > *ša-riš*, nom. high-ranking court official, royal attendant, palace steward, chief manager, chamberlain (early: Middle-Neo Assyrian/Babylonian); eunuch, harem guard, court official, royal attendant, chamberlain (late: Neo-Assyrian and Neo-Babylonian) (*AHw*, 974; *GAG*, §46d; *MSL*, 8:1:74; 12:230:5-6; Jensen, 91-93; Zimmern, 116).

2. The Akk. title is reflected throughout the Sem. world: Nuzi *ša rēši,* the one who is head, chief official (*HSS* 14:99. 17; *AHw*, 974); Ugar. *ša rēšu* (*šarri*), the one at the head (of the king) (*PRU* 4:237. 22; 203. 13); Phoen. *srs,* eunuch (*RES* 1206. 1-3); Old Aram. *srs/srs',* nom. royal official, eunuch (Degen, 46, 52; Lidzbarski, 331; Cook, 86); Aram. *srs,* nom. eunuch (*DISO*, 197); Emp. Aram. *srs,* nom. eunuch (*DISO*, 197, 271); Egyp. Aram. *srs/srs',* nom. eunuch (*DISO*, 197; *HALAT* 2:769); JAram/CPA nom. *s^{e}rîsā'*, eunuch, castrate; vb. *sārîsā',* to castrate, emasculate (*DISO*, 197; *HALAT* 2:769); Syr. nom. *s^{e}rîsā',* eunuch, castrate; vb. *sārîsā',* to casterate, emasculate (Brockelmann, 239b); Eth. *šariš,* chief, court official (Dalmann, 694); Arab. *sarīs,* nom. castrate; *sarsisa,* vb. to be impotent; Mand. *srs,* vb. to castrate (Drower, 338a); Mid. Egyp. vb. *srs,* to take command of (military corps); Late Egyp. *srs,* nom. royal official (*DME*, 237).

3. The Akk. title is an idiom similar to the title *ša šarri,* representative of the king, royal commissioner (*CAD* 17:2:114). The title *ša rēši* exhibits a twofold range of meaning that developed historically. Throughout the early and late periods it designated a court official, while in the later period the technical meaning of eunuch arose with the development of the practice of utilizing castrated men within the royal court. This twofold development is mirrored in Northwest Semitic (Phoen., Aram., Heb.). Only the early meaning (royal official) appears in Ugar., Nuzi, and Egyp.; however, only the later meaning (eunuch) appears in Arab. (derived from Emp. Aram.).

4. Beginning in the Neo-Assyrian and Neo-Babylonian periods, kings of the eastern empires began to employ eunuchs for certain tasks, such as the supervision of the royal harem or the royal children. Because these tasks had previously been assigned to "normal" palace attendants, the title *ša rēši* acquired the technical meaning eunuch, as several cunieform inscriptions show. Thus, the meaning eunuch arose with the practice of utilizing castrated men in key positions in Assyria, Babylon, and Persia (*TWOT* 2:635). Eunuchs formed a most important part of the Assyrian bureaucracy and were numerous (Grayson, 605). In the Middle and Neo-Assyrian periods, the eunuch was a highly trained and important person in the royal palace (Weidner, 264-65).

5. A major institution in the Assyrian court was the harem, which consisted of a number of wives, concubines, serving maids, and eunuch harem guards. There was a strict order of precedence within the harem, with the queen mother at the top. Immediately under her in authority was the chief wife of the reigning king, her status being determined by the fact that she was the first wife to give the king a male offspring. Princes normally spent their early years in the harem. There was much rivalry and jealousy within the Assyrian harem, and since the heir to the throne spent his early years there, harem plots to overthrow the king were not uncommon (Grayson, 749-50).

6. WestSem. noms. in the Iron Age generally refer to eunuchs employed by kings as royal officials, palace stewards, and personal attendants: Emp. Aram. *srs,* nom. eunuch (Aḥiqar 61, 63, 69; *CIS* 2:75. 3), e.g., *rb srs,* chief eunuch (*CIS* 2. 38. 6); Old Aram. *mr srsy srgn,* the head of the eunuches of Sargon (Sefiré 3. 5); Phoen. *rb srsrm,* chief of eunuchs (*RES*, 1206. 1-3), and Emp. Aram. *rb srs,* chief eunuch (*CIS* 2:38. 6) (*AHw*, 974; *DISO*, 271).

7. Akk. loanword reflected in Mid. Egyp. *srs,* vb. to take command of (military corps) (*DME*, 237) and Late Egyp. *srs,* nom. official (*DLE* 3:145). The nuance eunuch

does not occur in Egyptian, and there is no conclusive evidence that Egypt employed eunuchs in this capacity.

OT 1. As in other WestSem. languages, *sārîs* is an Akk. loanword. Akk. *ša rēši/rīši* had a basic twofold range of meaning in its historical development: court official, steward (early), and eunuch = harem guard (late). Likewise, *sārîs* exhibits the same twofold range of meanings corresponding to a common historical development: court official, royal steward (preexilic); and eunuch = royal steward, harem guard (exilic and postexilic) (see *HALAT* 2:769; *TWOT* 2:634-35). Morphologically, *sārîs* (official) exhibits the *qātîl* nom. pattern that is used often for professional vocations, e.g., *pāqîd,* appointed officer, *nāgîd,* leader, *nābî',* prophet (see Waltke-O'Connor, §5. 3c; Bauer-Leander, §470n).

2. Before more recent scholars related *sārîs* to Akk. *ša rēši,* royal official (*AHw*, 974), the relatively late nuance eunuch was naively assigned to all BH usages. BDB represents outdated scholarship in assigning eunuch for all BH usages and relating it to admittedly denom. vbs. for to castrate in Syr., Aram., and Arab. (BDB, 710). In reality, *sārîs* is not to be translated eunuch unless context or other evidence demands it (*TWOT* 2:634-35). Because castrates were prohibited from the assembly (Lev 21:20; Deut 23:2), the only referents to eunuchs are foreigners (Assyrians, Babylonians, Persians) or Judeans castrated in exile (2 Kgs 9:32; 18:17 (?); Esth 1:10, 12, 15; 2:3, 14-15, 21; 6:2, 14; 7:9; Isa 56:3; Dan 1:3, 7-11, 18).

3. In the preexilic period *sārîs* is a title designating a high-ranking official in the political or military spheres (*HALAT* 2:769; de Vaux 1:121; Koehler, 26-27; Selmsdorf, 557). It refers to a military official in Middle Kingdom Egypt (Gen 37:36; 39:1; 40:2, 7) and in the Neo-Assyrian army (2 Kgs 18:17; Jer 39:3, 13). It is used in reference to court officials in the royal court of the early united monarchy (1 Sam 8:15; 1 Chron 28:1; 2 Chron 18:8), and in the royal courts of Israel (1 Kgs 22:9; 2 Kgs 8:6; 9:32) and Jerusalem (2 Kgs 23:11; 24:12, 15; 25:19; Jer 29:2; 34:19; 38:17; 41:16; 52:25) during the divided kingdom period. During the exilic and postexilic periods, it refers to royal officials or personal attendants of the royal family in Babylon (Dan 1:3, 7-11, 18) and Susa (Esth 1:10, 12, 15; 2:21; 6:2, 14; 7:9).

4. In the Joseph narrative *sārîs* designates three Egyptian officials: Potiphar, captain of the guard (Gen 37:36; 39:1), and the chief cupbearer and chief baker (Gen 40:2, 7). BDB suggested eunuch (BDB, 710); however, that nuance developed only later in BH, and research has failed to turn up any evidence for the use of eunuchs as officials in Egypt (*TWOT* 2:635). BH *sārîs* probably reflects Mid. Egyp. *srs,* royal official, commander (of military corps), which is an Akk. loanword from *ša rēši* (*šarri*), royal official (lit., he who is of the king's head) (*DME*, 237). The use of *sārîs* to designate a military commander (Potiphar) and royal attendants (chief cupbearer, chief baker) reflects the original Akk. loanword, which was often used to designate a military official or royal household attendant (e.g., chief cupbearer) (*AHw*, 974). Although later uses of *sārîs* designate eunuchs, neither the original Akk. etymology nor the Egyptian usage of the term had any connotation of sexual impotence. Besides, a eunuch would hardly have a wife (Gen 39:7-19). LXX inconsistently renders *sārîs* with *spadontos*, guard (Gen 37:36), and *eunochos*, eunuch (Gen 39:1; 40:2, 7). The military connotation of Mid. Egyp. *srs* harmonizes with the BH description of Potiphar: as *sārîs* of Pharoah, he was *śar haṭṭabbāḥîm,* captain of the bodyguards

(Gen 37:36; 39:1). While Mid. Egyp. *srs* denotes a commander, Late Egyp. *srs* denotes a Persian official; therefore a Middle Kingdom date for Joseph (E. H. Merrill, *Kingdom of Priests*, 49-55) is consistent with the Mid. Egyp. nuance.

5. Pointing to contemporary models of ANE kingship, Samuel (ca. 1120-1020 BC) designates members of such a royal court whose support would burden Israel as *sārîsāyw,* his officials, and *ʿᵃbādāyw,* his attendants (NIV 1 Sam 8:15). This nuance of *sārîs* parallels contemporary Mid. Assyr. (1380-911 BC) usage of *ša rēšu*(*m*) designating members of the Assyrian royal court: royal official, superintendent, palace attendant (*AHw*, 974). Burdensome taxation would be required to support such a royal court in Israel, as in other empires such as Assyria and Babylon (Saggs, 238-60).

6. The earliest use of *śārîs* to designate historical members of Israel's royal court are the palace officials (*haśśārîsîm*) of David (1 Chron 28:1). Nothing is specified about their duties; however, they evidently played a significant administrative role because David summmoned them with the officials (*śārîm*) of Israel and palace guards (*haggibôrîm*) at the time of Solomon's succession to instruct them about building the temple (1 Chron 28:1-19). It is not clear whether they were royal officials with some kind of authority or simply palace attendants who carried out the whims of the king.

7. During the divided monarchy, *sārîs* designates a member of the royal court charged with tasks and errands by the king: Ahab sent a *sārîs* (NIV official) to summon Micah (1 Kgs 22:9 = 2 Chron 18:8), and Joram charged a *sārîs* (NIV official) to restore a woman's land that had been lost when she left the country (2 Kgs 8:6). Again, it is unclear whether *sārîs* denotes an official with authority or merely a royal attendant with delegated tasks. In any case, the tasks assigned to the Israelite *sārîs* are similar to the errands and duties assigned to the Assyrian *ša rēši,* court official (North, 87). Some suggest that these were eunuch-attendants who were introduced into Israel by Jezebel (see sec. 8 below); however, there is no reason to assume that here *sārîs* denotes anything more than the basic nuance royal official, attendant.

8. Eunuchs were employed as royal attendants of queens in many ANE kingdoms during the Iron Age (Saggs, 749-50). However, the first mention of eunuchs in the royal household of Israel are the eunuch-attendants (*sārîsîm*) of Jezebel; Jehu persuaded them into throwing Jezebel down from the window of the royal palace (2 Kgs 9:32). It is likely that Jezebel had imported these eunuch-attendants from her Phoenician homeland when she married Ahab. The fact that intentionally castrated men were excluded from the congregation by Mosaic law (Lev 22:24; Deut 23:2) only underscores Jezebel's lack of concern for the laws of Yahweh.

9. 2 Kgs 18:17 lists three Neo-Assyr. officials who played a role in Sennacherib's siege of Jerusalem in 701 BC: *tartān,* supreme commander, *rab sārîs,* chief officier, and *rab šāqēh*, field commander (NIV). These are not personal names (as KJV), but derived from Neo-Assyr. titles for high-ranking military officials (Grayson, 605; Tadmor, 279-85; Patterson-Austel, 259). The title *rab sārîs* is derived from Akk. *rabû ša rēši,* lit., chief who is the head (*AHw*, 974), which is also reflected in Phoen. *rb srsrm,* chief of eunuchs (*RES* 1206. 1-3) and Emp. Aram. *rb srs,* chief eunuch (*CIS* 2:38. 6; *AHw*, 974; *DISO*, 271). The Akk. title designated a military commander or, later, chief eunuch (*AHw*, 974; *GAG* §46d; *MSL* 8:1:74; Zimmern, 116). While both nuances are present in Neo-Assyr., the other two titles in 2 Kgs 18:17 suggest the military connotation. However, this might designate a eunuch serving as a royal official,

because eunuchs did play important roles in the Neo-Assyr. bureaucracy (Grayson, 605). The second title, *tartān,* supreme field commander, is derived from Akk. *turtannu/tartanu,* which refers to a high military and administrative official, second in rank only to the king (*KAJI* 245:17; Unger, 204-10). The third title, *rab šāqēh,* field commander (# 8042), is derived from Akk. *rab šaqû*, commandant, commander of the march, chief officer, chief cupbearer (*AHw*, 933-38, 1182; Klauber, 73-75; Ellenbogen, 152), which is reflected in Emp. Aram. *rb šwq,* inspector of the march (*CIS* 2:3932. 5; *DISO*, 271). Assyrian records indicate that the *rab šaqû* occupied an important position in royal affairs (Grayson, 605; Weidner, 264-65).

10. Isaiah prophesied that members of the Davidic royal family would be taken hostage and would become *sārîsîm* (KJV/NIV: eunuchs) in the Babylonian palace (2 Kgs 20:18 = Isa 39:7). This might depict the castration of Hezekiah's male descendants and reflect the Neo-Babylonian practice of employing eunuchs as palace attendants and stewards (Grayson, 605). However, Isaiah might merely be predicting the well-known Neo-Babylonian practice of taking foreign princes and nobles as hostages to the Babylonian royal court, where they were placed into subordinate roles as state officials (Grayson, 750). In fulfillment of this prophecy, Hezekiah's son Manasseh was captured by the Assyrians and held prisoner in Babylon (2 Chron 33:11), and many more descendants of Hezekiah were taken by Nebuchadnezzar II to Babylon, where they maintained a noble status (2 Kgs 24:15; 25:7; Dan 1:3).

11. Sometimes *sārîs* designates an official appointed with authority over a particular area. For example, the title *sārîs* designates an official named Nathan-Melek, who had a room in the temple and was in charge of the chariots and horses King Amon quartered in the temple court that he had converted into stables (2 Kgs 23:11). This is most clearly seen in an unnamed Jerusalem official (*sārîs*) who was the appointed officer (*pāqîd*) over the fighting men (2 Kgs 25:19; Jer 52:25). De Vaux notes: "Perhaps he was a commander-in-chief, or a civilian in charge of the administration of the army, i.e., a minister of national defense, for the supreme command was exercised by the king himself" (de Vaux, 225).

12. The title *hassārîsîm*, the court officials (NIV), is juxtaposed with the leaders (*śārîm*) of Jerusalem and Judah during the reign of Zedekiah (Jer 34:19). Likewise, *sārîsîm* designates members of the royal court of King Jehoiachin (2 Kgs 24:12, 15; Jer 29:2; 41:16), who were taken captive by Nebuchadnezzar II, along with Jehoiachin and his royal family, *'ªbādāyw*, his attendants, *śārāyw,* his nobles, and *sārîsāyw,* his officials (2 Kgs 24:12).

13. In the case of Ebed-Melech, an Ethiopian who served in the royal palace as the personal attendant of King Zedekiah, the technical nuance eunuch is indicated by the grammatical construction *'îš sārîs*, a eunuch (NIV margin) (Jer 38:7).

14. Nebu-Sheziban (NIV: Nebo-Sareskim) bears the title *rab-sārîs,* chief officer (Jer 39:3, 13), as one of the three Neo-Babylonian officials (*śārê melek-bābel*) who established control of Jerusalem after its conquest by Nebuchadnezzar II in 588-86 BC. *nᵉbû-šazbān* (conj., cf. Jer 39:13) reflects the personal name *Nabū-šēzibanni,* "Nabu, save me!" (Tallqvist, 160; Stamm, 170; Zimmern, 399-401), and *rab-sārîm* reflects the title *rab ša rēši* (lit., chief who is at the head), which designates a Babylonian political/military official, often a provincial governor of newly conquered

provinces (*AHw*, 974; *GAG*, 46d; *MLS* 8/1:74; *HALAT* 2:769-70; Zimmern, 116; Selmsdorf, 557).

15. The Neo-Babylonian official Ashpenaz, whom Nebuchadnezzar II charged with the care of the Judean royal family and nobility, is entitled *rab sārîsāyw,* chief of his court officials (Dan 1:3) and *śar hassārîsîm,* the chief official (1:7-11, 18). These parallel titles reflect Akk. *rabû ša rēši* (lit., chief who is the head), which designated a royal official throughout all periods, but had developed a technical meaning designating the chief eunuch by this period (*AHw*, 974; *MSL* 8:1:74; Zimmern, 116). The latter is reflected in Phoen. *rb srsrm* chief of eunuchs (*RES* 1206. 1-3), and Emp. Aram. *rb srs,* chief eunuch (*CIS* 2:38. 6; *DISO*, 271). (On this, see ANE, sec. 4-5.) During this period, *rab sārîsîm* could denote chief eunuch (Kitchen, 165-66). While the general nuance (non-castrated) royal attendant is acceptable, it would make sense that eunuchs were used to attend the personal needs of the royal family in their daily contact in their personal apartments.

16. In Esther the term *sārîs* has a polysemantic range of meaning and referents, designating four kinds of Persian royal officials who were eunuchs: eunuchs in charge of the harem (Esth 2:3, 14-15), eunuch attendants of the queen (4:4-5), eunuch guards of the king's private apartment (2:21; 6:2), and eunuch attendants of the king (1:10, 12, 15; 6:14; 7:9) (Bardtke, 284). The polysemantic nature of *sārîs* encompasses their physical condition (eunuchs) and their official position (royal attendants). The eunuch Hegei was in charge of the harem of the young virgins (2:3), and the eunuch Shaashga was in charge of the harem of the concubines (2:14-15). (Note: Herodotus 9:33 mentions a eunuch of Xerxes with a name similar to Hegei.) While eunuchs are usually associated with the king's harems and the queen's attendants, they also played important roles in administrative affairs. Xerxes employed seven eunuchs as attendants to carry out menial tasks and errands (1:10, 12, 15; 6:14; 7:9).

17. The nuance eunuch is clear in Isa 56:3-4 ("I am a dry tree"), a passage describing the new covenant blessings that would be extended to the group excluded in Lev 21:20 and Deut 23:1, conditioned upon genuine covenant repentance. God's offer of salvific blessings are all-embracing and inclusive of those who were often viewed as excluded (foreigners and eunuchs). Those who were formerly excluded may be included if they repent and keep the covenant. No one would be excluded from membership of God's people, either by nationality and ancestry (foreigners) or by accident of birth or former affiliation to another god (eunuchs). The middle walls of partition have come tumbling down between Jews and Gentiles, including repentant eunuchs, who would be welcome within the house of God—not just within the temple precincts, but into the very divine presence. The salvific and eschatological blessings will be far beyond those that an earthly family would have brought. Note: Aramaic Targum renders Isa 56:3-4 with *sārîsā'* nom. castrate.

18. Consistent with the fact that the nuance eunuch developed later, *sārîs* is not used in the lawcodes that excluded those who were castrated from the assembly (Lev 21:20; Deut 23:2). Although neither text clearly indicates the cause of the castrations, the most common view is that their physical defects were not due to simple accidents but rather to pagan rites. Such physical mutilation was contrary to the design of God's creation and destroyed the procreative power of the Israelites. Apart from the apostate

policies of Jezebel, it is unlikely that eunuchs were employed in the royal court of Israel or Judah.

P-B 1. The early nuance steward remains in use, but the predominate usage refers to a eunuch through castration or a male who is sexually impotent due to malformation: *sārîs*, nom. eunuch, one who is impotent or castrated; steward, manager; *sarsā'*, nom. steward, manager, agent; *sārîsā'*, nom. castrate; *sāras*, vb. to mutilate, emasculate, make impotent; *sērûs*, vb. to castrate; *sarsāyā'*, adj. mutilated or reduced coin (Jastrow, 1027-29; *HALAT* 2:769; BDB, 710).

2. RL discusses the three ways a male could become a eunuch: deformity at birth, involuntary castration (of a slave by his owner), and voluntary castration (forbidden) (*Y'bamoth* 8:4, 80).

3. The impotency of an idol is compared to a eunuch: "What good does it do to offer to an idol? For it can neither eat nor smell; so is he who is persecuted by the Lord. He sees with his eyes and groans, like a eunuch who embraces a virgin and sighs" (Sir 30:20).

NT 1. LXX renders *sārîs* once as *spadontos*, guard (Potiphar: Gen 37:36), and everywhere else as *eunochos*, eunuch. This is reflected in the NT nom. *eunochos*, eunuch (Matt 19:12; Acts 8:27, 34, 38-39) and the vb. *eunochidzō*, to make (someone) a eunuch (Matt 19:12).

2. The ANE practice of castrating and employing eunuchs as palace officials, particularly as personal attendants of a queen, was still in vogue in the case of the Ethiopian eunuch (*eunochos*), who served under Candace (Acts 8:27-39). Ironcially, it was Isaiah who promised new covenant blessings for believing eunuchs and foreigners (Isa 56:3-4), and this believing foreign eunuch was saved through reading and believing Isaiah's prophecy of the Servant who provided new covenant blessings (Isa 53:7-8).

3. Christ states that some are born eunuchs, others are made eunuchs by men, and others make themselves eunuchs for the sake of the kingdom of heaven (Matt 19:12) (see P-B sec. 2, above). Just as some males submitted to castration to become eunuchs so that they could serve without distraction as the personal attendants of ANE kings, some believers make themselves eunuchs (by renouncing marriage?) to more effectively serve the kingdom of heaven without sexual distraction (Matt 19:12). This might be behind Paul's advice to singles to remain unmarried, if possible, to secure undistracted devotion to the service of Christ (1 Cor 7:25-35).

Leaders: → *'ādôn* (lord, master, # 123); → *'allûp* II (tribal chief, # 477); → *'āṣîl* II (eminent, noble, # 722); → *zāqēn* (elder, # 2418); → *ḥōr* I, free man, freeborn, # 2985); → *maptēaḥ* (badge of office, # 5158); → *nāgîd* (prince, ruler, leader, # 5592); → *nāśî'* I (chief, king, # 5954); → *sārîs* (eunuch, court official, # 6247); → *seren* II (Philistine prince, # 6249); → *'attûd* (he-goat, leader, # 6966); → *peḥâ* (governor, # 7068); → *pāqîd* (officer, # 7224); → *qāṣîn* (commander, leader, # 7903); → *rab* II (captain, chief, # 8042); → *rzn* (rule, # 8142); → *šôa'* I (noble, # 8777)

Bibliography

AHw 2:974; *CIS* 2:38. 6; 2:75. 3; *DISO*, 197; *HALAT* 2:769; *TDNT* 2:766-67; *TWOT* 2:634-35; A. Y. Aikhenwald, "Some Names of Officials in the Later Books of the Old Testament," *Vestnik drevnej Istorii* 3, 1985, 58-65 [Russian]; C. Brockelmann, *Lexicon Syriacum*, 1966, 239; G. Dalmann, *Aramäisches-neuhebräisches Wörterbuch*, 1938, 694; R. Degen, *Altaramäische*

Grammatik, 46-52; E. S. Drower-R. Macuch, *A Mandaic Dictionary*, 338; R. O. Faulkner, *A Concise Dictionary of Middle Egyptian*, 1964, 237; A. K. Grayson, "Mesopotamia, History of," in *ABD*, 1992, 4:749-50; G. Haddad, "An Ethiopian Officer Forces the Hand of King Zedekiah: Jeremiah 38:1-13," *TRu* 5, 1982, 58-62; C. F. Jean-J. Hoftijzer, *Dictionnaire des inscriptions sémitiques de l'ouest*, 1965, 197; G. E. Kadish, "Eunuchs in Ancient Egypt?" *Studies in Ancient Oriental Civilizations*, 35, 1969, 55-67; K. A. Kitchen, *Ancient Orient and Old Testament*, 1966, 165-66; R. W. Klein, "Ezra and Nehemiah in Recent Studies," in *Magnalia Dei: The Mighty Acts of God*, 1976, 361-76; L. Koehler, *Der hebräische Mensch*, 1953, 26-27; B. Landsberger, *Materialien zum sumerischen Lexikon*, 8:1-74; 12:230:5-6; L. F. Lesko, *A Dictionary of Late Egyptian*, 1987, 3:145; M. Lidzbarski, *Ephemeris für semitische Epigrahik*, 1966, 331; B. Reicke and L. Rost, *Biblisch-historisches Handwörterbuch*, 1962-66, 1:448; H. Tadmor, "Rab-Saris and Rab-Shakeh in 2 Kings 18," in *The Word of the Lord Shall Go Forth*, 1983, 279-85; R. de Vaux, *AncIsr*, 1965, 1:115-22, 225; E. Weidner, "Hof- und Harems-Erlasse assyricher Könige," *AfO* 17, 1956, 264-65; E. M. Yamauchi, "Was Nehemiah the Cupbearer a Eunuch?" *ZAW* 92, 1980, 132-42; H. Zimmern, *Akkadische Fremdwörter*, 1917, 116.

Gordon H. Johnston

6248 (*seren* I, axle), → # 8206

6249	סֶרֶן

סֶרֶן (*seren* II), nom. Philistine prince (# 6249).

ANE 1. *seren* II is a Philistine loanword whose etymology is debated, with scholars proposing three options for its etymological origin: Hitt. nom. *tarwanas/sarawanas,* judge, king, (Rabin, 113-39; Andrews, 22; Kitchen, 67; Sanders, 166; Brug, 197; Howard, 243); G nom. *tyrannos*, tyrant, ruler, lord (Klostermann, 2:739-40; *HALAT* 2:770); and Indo-Aryan nom. *ser,* ruler, commander (*TWOT* 2:635). The debate about whether the origin of the Philistines was Aegean or Anatolian factors into discussions about the etymological origin of this term (Dothan, 21-23). The etymological debate probably will not be resolved until the Philistine language is recovered and the term is documented.

2. Many early scholars suggested that *seren* II derived from G *tyrannos*, tyrant, king, absolute ruler (Klostermann 2:739-40, MacLaurin, 472, Dothan, 18), which is reflected in RSV and ASV translations: lord, tyrant. This G term referred to the despotic ruler of the Greek city-state. According to Hippias, *tyrannos* was first used of monarchs in the time of Archilleus (Alc. 37a), where it was interchangeable with *basileus*, king. Only later did it denote a chief or prince (first cent. BC). G *tyrannos* itself was borrowed from another language: Neo-Hittite, Lydian, or Phrygian (Liddell-Scott, 1836; Rabin, 113-39).

3. Recent scholars suggest that *seren* II is derived from Neo-Hittite *tarwanas/sarawanas*, judge, king (Albright, 516; Andrews, 22; Barnett, 373; Brug, 197; Dothan, 22; Howard, 243; Kitchen, 67; Rabin, 113-39; Sanders, 166). This was a title commonly borne by Neo-Hittite kings in the late Luvian (Hittite hieroglyphic) inscriptions in eleventh-seventh centuries BC (Laroche, 197-98, §371; Meriggi, 125). Similarly, the word for Goliath's helmet, *kōba'* (1 Sam 17:5), may have entered Heb. from the Philistines and be of Anatolian origin, related to Hittite *kupaḫḫi* (Kitchen, 67; Barnett, 373). Neo-Hittite/Lydian *tarwanas/sarawanas* passed into proto-Greek Illyrian and later entered the G language, forming the basis for *tyrannos* (Albright, 516;

Andrews, 22; Barnett, 373; Brug, 197; Dothan, 22; Howard, 243; Kitchen, 67; Liddell-Scott, 1836; Sanders, 166).

4. In the Sem. languages, *seren* II occurs only in a few Northwest dialects beside BH: Ugar. nom. *srn/śrn,* prince; vb. *srn,* to act like a prince (*UT* §1797; *WGU* §1952); Egyp. Aram. *srn,* nom. prince (*KAI* 2:325 §271a; Ellenbogen, 126-27).

5. Ugar. nom. *srn/śrn,* prince, is synonymous with *mlk,* king (*CTA* 85:3; 1059:3; 1146:7; 60:10; 323:III:2; 2085:12). The royal title *bn srn/śrn,* son of prince (*CTA* 2078:22; 3321:I:42), appears to be synonymous with *bn mlk,* son of king = prince. The phrase *yn srnm* (*CTA* 124:18) probably means wine fit for kings. The personal names *'bdmlk bn śrn* (*CTA* 323:III:2) and *'l bn srn* (*CTA* 306:7) are used of individuals in the royal position of prince, that is, son of the king.

OT 1. *seren* II, prince, ruler (*HALAT* 2:770), should not be confused with *seren* I axle (*HALAT* 2:770; *TWOT* 2:635). It appears only in pl.: *s*ᵉ*rānîm* (absolute) and *sarnê* (construct). The segholate pattern reflects a morphology that can be reconstructed from the original Hittite: *sarawanas* > *sarānas* > *saranu* > *sarnu* > *sarn* > *saren* > *seren* (see ANE 3 above).

2. *seren* II is used only in reference to the rulers of the five city-states of the Philistine pentapolis: Ashdod, Ashkelon, Ekron, Gath, and Gaza (Josh 13:3; Judg 3:3; 16:5, 8, 18, 23, 27, 30; 1 Sam 5:8, 11; 6:4, 12, 16; 7:7; 29:2, 6-7; 1 Chron 12:20).

3. Relatively little is stated in Scripture about the position which the Philistine *seren* held over his individual city-state. However, many historians believe that the nature of the pentapolis and the position of the *seren* was modeled on the league of Greek city-states, each under a semiautonomous ruler (*tyrannos*), The independent nature of the Iron Age Philistine city-states is similar to the structure of Mycenean society of this period. There are several other close connections between the Philistines and the Myceneans, e.g., Philistine pottery seems to derive from Mycenean IIIc pottery types from the end of the thirteenth century BC.

4. Historians and archaeologists generally describe the social organization of the Philistines as a military aristocracy (Dothan, 18-19). Until the Philistines were conquered by David and assimilated into the population, they were the ruling class in the territory they conquered, dominating Canaanites and Israelites alike. This is borne out in Philistine royal title *seren,* which has both royal and military connotations. In terms of its royal nuance, *seren* II and *melek* are used interchangeably, just as Ugar. *srn* (prince) and *mlk* (king) are used interchangeably (see ANE 2 above). For example, Achish, one of the Philistine *s*ᵉ*rānîm* (1 Sam 29:2), is called the king (*melek*) of Gath (1 Sam 21:10, 12; 27:2). Thus, the *seren* may have borne the title king (*melek*) as well. Later Neo-Assyrian records refer to Philistine kings, but whether they bore the title *seren* is not known (Kitchen, 77; Katzenstein, 327-28). The titles *s*ᵉ*rānîm* and *śarîm* (military commanders) are used interchangeably at times (1 Sam 29:2-6). Each *seren* ruled his own city-state and commanded his own army (1 Sam 13:5; 31:3). The dual role of ruler/commander was necessary to control the civilian populations of Canaanite and Israelites, whom the Philistines dominated during the early Iron Age.

5. The Philistine structure of leadership/government is only described vaguely in BH; however, some aspects seem fairly clear. At the head of each Philistine city-state stood the *seren*—one over each city (1 Sam 5:8; 6:4, 16). The *seren* was the governor/ruler of his Philistine city-state. The *s*ᵉ*rānîm* were distinct from the ordinary

citizens (Judg 16:27, 30; 1 Sam 5:8, 11), local Canaanites (Judg 3:3), and nearby villagers (1 Sam 6:18). They were invested with authority and wielded executive civil power (Judg 16:5, 8; 1 Sam 5:11; 6:16). They were qualified to offer sacrifice to their gods on behalf of their cities (Judg 16:23). And in time of war they possessed military authority (1 Sam 7:7; 29:1-7; 1 Chron 12:19). They function as the military and civil governors of their city-state.

6. While the Philistine *seren* wielded supreme executive authority, there were limitations to his power. This can be assessed from the meeting of the Philistine rulers in Ashdod during the plague brought about by the capture of the ark (1 Sam 4-6) and from the disagreement between the Philistine princes (*śārîm*) and Achish about whether David could take part in the battle against Saul at Gilboah (1 Sam 29:4-10). Both show that the Philistine rulers did not have absolute power over major political or military decisions (Dothan, 18-19).

7. Although each Philistine *seren* generally acted autonomously, they cooperated when common cause necessitated. They conspired together to solicit Delilah to subdue Samson (Judg 16:5); they acted in concert in the crisis involving the ark at Ashdod and Ekron (1 Sam 5-6); and they repeatedly fought together against the Israelites (1 Sam 7:7; 29:2; 1 Chron 12:19).

8. There is no direct evidence whether the position of *seren* II was an elected or inherited office. Neo-Assyr. annals suggest that the royal office was hereditary in Philistia; however, this does not necessarily indicate similar practices early in the Iron Age when the Philistine *s^erānîm* are mentioned in the HB. However, the Philistine populace occasionally was able to depose their ruler, as was the case of Padi, king of Ekron, ca. 701 BC (*ANET*, 286).

P-B 1. *seren* II does not appear in DSS or ancient Heb. inscriptions, nor does it appear in the RL. It only occurs 1x in Mish. Heb., and even there it follows the pattern of BH usage: it is a plural form and is used in reference to Philistine rulers (Sir 46:18). The passage recounts the events of 1 Sam 7 in a glowing resume of the heroic deeds of Samuel: "He called upon Yahweh of Hosts when his enemies pressed upon him on every side, when he offered the sacrifice. Yahweh thundered from heaven, and with a great noise made his voice heard. He destroyed the rulers of Tyre and all the princes (*sarnê*) of the Philistines" (Sir 46:16-18).

2. *seren* II essentially dropped out of usage in Mish. and Late Heb. However, it has been revived in modern Hebrew, taking on a general denotation "captain" (Zilkha, 217).

Leaders: → *'ādôn* (lord, master, # 123); → *'allûp* II (tribal chief, # 477); → *'āṣîl* II (eminent, noble, # 722); → *zāqēn* (elder, # 2418); → *ḥōr* I, free man, freeborn, # 2985); → *maptēaḥ* (badge of office, # 5158); → *nāgîd* (prince, ruler, leader, # 5592); → *nāśî'* I (chief, king, # 5954); → *sārîs* (eunuch, court official, # 6247); → *seren* II (Philistine prince, # 6249); → *'attûd* (he-goat, leader, # 6966); → *peḥâ* (governor, # 7068); → *pāqîd* (officer, # 7224); → *qāṣîn* (commander, leader, # 7903); → *rab* II (captain, chief, # 8042); → *rzn* (rule, # 8142); → *šôa'* I (noble, # 8777)

Bibliography

TWOT 2:635; W. F. Albright, "*ts-ran*," *Studies Presented to D. M. Robinson*, 1951, 228; idem, "Syria: The Philistines and Phoenicia," *CAH*, 3/33, 1975, 516; A. Andrews, *The Greek Tyrants*,

22; R. D. Barnett, "The Sea Peoples," *CAH*, 2/28: 17; idem, *The Sea Peoples*, 1969, 70-78; J. F. Brug, *A Literary and Archaeological Study of the Philistines*, 1985, 197; H. Donner and W. Röllig, *Canaanite and Aramaic Inscriptions*, 1966-69, 2:325; T. Dothan, *The Philistines and Their Material Culture*, 1982, 18-23; idem, "What We Know About the Philistines," *BARev* 8:4, 1982, 30; M. Ellenbogen, *Foreign Words in the Old Testament*, 1962, 126-27; D. N. Freedman, "Early Israelite History in the Light of Early Israelite Poetry," *Unity and Diversity: Essays in the History, Literature, and Religion of the Ancient Near East*, 1975, 9-10; G. Garbini, "On the Origin of the Hebrew-Philistine Word *seren*," *Semitic Studies in Honor of Wolf Leslau*, 1991, 516-19; W. Helck, "Ein sprachliches Indiz fur due Herkunft der Philister," *BN* 21, 1983, 31; D. M. Howard, "Philistines," *POTW*, 1994, 243; H. J. Katzenstein, "Philistines," *ABD*, 1992, 5:326-30; K. A. Kitchen, "Philistines," *POTT*, 1973, 67; E. Klostermann, "τύραννος," *Das Onomastikon der biblischen Ortsnamen*, 1966, 2:739-40; E. Laroche, *Les hiéroglyphes hittites*, 1960-, 1:197-98, §371; E. C. B. Maclaurin, "ANAK/ ANAQ," *VT* 15, 1965, 472-74; P. Meriggi, *Hieroglyphisch-hethitishes Glossar*, 1962, 125; C. Rabin, "Hittite Words in Hebrew," *Or* 32, 1963, 113-39; N. K. Sandars, *The Sea Peoples*, 1985, 166; F. Stäehlin, *Die Philister*, 1918, 20-25, 40; H. Tikten, *Kritische Untersuch zu Texte des Samuel-büchern*, 1920, 10; A. Zilkha, *Modern Hebrew-English Dictionary*, 1989, 217; H. Zimmern, *Akkadische Fremdwörter*, 1917, 7.

Gordon H. Johnston

6251 (*srp*, burn), → # 8596

6252	סַרְפַּד

סַרְפַּד (*sirpad*), stinging nettle (# 6252).

OT Occurring only once in the OT, *sirpad* may be one of three words used synonymously for the nettle (*Urtica urens* or *Urtica pilulifera*; see Zohary, 162). In Isa 55:13 it is contrasted to a valuable tree (*HALAT* 668).

Thornbush, nettle, sting, thistle, thorn: → *'āṭād* (thornbush, # 353); → *barqōn* (thorn, brier, # 1402); → *deber* II (thorny sting, # 1823); → *dardar* (thistle, # 1998); → *ḥēdeq* (brier, # 2537); → *ḥôaḥ* I (thorn, # 2560); → *m*ᵉ*sûkâ* (thorn hedge, # 5004); → *na'*ᵃ*ṣûṣ* (thornbush, # 5848); → *sîrâ* (thorny bush, # 6106); → *sillôn* (thorn, # 6141); → *s*ᵉ*neh* (thorny shrub, # 6174); → *sirpād* (stinging nettle, # 6252); → *ṣe'*ᵉ*lîm* (thorny lotus, # 7365); → *ṣ*ᵉ*nînîm* (thorns, # 7564); → *qôṣ* I (thornbush, # 7764); → *qimmôś* (weeds, nettles, # 7853); → *śēk* (thorn, splinter, # 8493); → *šāmîr* I (Christ's thorn, # 9031)

BIBLIOGRAPHY

Irene and Walter Jacob, "Flora," *ABD*, 1992, 2:805; M. Zohary, *Plants of the Bible*, 1982, 162.

K. Lawson Younger, Jr.

6253	סרר

סרר (*srr* I), q. be stubborn, headstrong, be rebellious, (# 6253); adj. סַר (*sar*), sullen, downcast (# 6234); nom. סָרָה (*sārâ* II), rebellion, crime, revolt; falsehood (# 6240).

ANE Akk. *sarāru*, be unstable, deceitful; Arab. *šarra*, be evil; Ugar. *srr*, be rebellious (*KTU* 1.4.VII:48). For the noms.: Akk. *sarru,* false, unreliable; Akk. *sartu,* falsehood, lie, crime.

OT The vb. occurs 18x to describe rebellion, possibly stressing the attitude more than the rebellious deed (*TWOT* 2:635).

1. *A rebellious son*. The vb. *srr* occurs 4x as a par. term of *mrh* (see # 5286) in the expression, "stubborn and rebellious" (Deut 21:18, 20; Ps 78:8; Jer 5:23). In Deut it describes the rebellious son brought before the tribal elders by his grieving parents. Because his life is characterized by *srr*, this one receives the death penalty (by stoning, Deut 21:21).

2. *Israel's rebellious attitude*. In response to the reading of God's law, the Israelites in Jerusalem joined Nehemiah to confess the sins of the nation (Neh 9:1-37). The psalm-like prayer/confession of 9:29 presents many idioms that bring out the character of Israel that sent her into exile: they would not turn (*lô' šwb*) to the Torah, acted presumptuously (*zyd*), did not listen (*šm'* + *l*ᵉ) to the commandments, and sinned (*ḥṭ'*) against the judgments (*b*ᵉ + *mišpāṭ*). They (lit.) "presented a shoulder (*kātēp*) of rebellion (*sôreret*) and hardened their necks."

Their forefathers were a stubborn and rebellious generation (Ps 78:8) with stubborn and rebellious hearts (Jer 5:23), who departed from Yahweh in disloyalty. They turned a "stubborn back" to Yahweh (and plugged their ears, Zech 7:11) and acted like a stubborn heifer resisting its master, refusing to submit to Yahweh's authority (Hos 4:16). Israel's leaders led the way in rebellion (Isa 1:23; Hos 9:15), devoting themselves to injustice and oppression rather than caring for the needy and oppressed. Israel's penchant for establishing foreign alliances served as a key manifestation of their betrayal of Yahweh (Isa 30:1). Although Yahweh longed for his people to return (65:2), the opportunity for restoration was eventually withdrawn. Yahweh pronounced a woe (*hôy*) upon his covenant nation (30:1) and promised to drive this rebellious nation from the land of promise (Hos 9:15).

These hardened rebels (Jer 6:28) eventually experience the trauma of covenant curses. The repetition of *srr* in the construction *sārê sôr*ᵉ*rîm* (6:25) has occasioned significant discussion. Holladay (228, 230; cf. McKane, 154-55; *TWAT* 5:959) prefers to emend *sārê* to *śārê* (following a similar construction in Isa 1:23, *śārayik sôr*ᵉ*rîm* [your rulers are rebels]), which could be rendered "princely rebels" or "arch-rebels" (NEB). Driver (85) suggested that the two words were homonyms from distinct roots that were juxtaposed to express a superlative idea, "persons turning aside (*sûr*) in disobedience (*srr*)" or "rebels in revolt." It appears best to accept the MT and regard these two words as a superlative construction and translate it "rebels of rebels" or "the most stubborn of rebels" (Bright, 47).

3. *Yahweh's sovereignty over rebels*. In his call for the entire world to praise God for his kingship, the psalmist (Ps 66:7) depicts Yahweh as one who sovereignly decimates the feeble attempts by rebels to thwart his rule. In another psalm of praise and thanksgiving, the psalmist (68:6[7]) revels in God's commitment to vindicate the oppressed righteous and to banish all rebels to hardship. Even the rebellious enemies must submit to his sovereignty and bring him gifts (68:18[19]).

4. *The rebellious harlot*. In Prov 7, the *locus classicus* for the description of the adulteress, the wise sage depicts the harlot as a loud (*hmh*) and defiant (*srr*) woman, who shamelessly lurks in several places, like an animal ready to ambush her prey. This woman cares little about God's demand for personal purity or covenant conformity.

5. *The adj. sullen*. The adj. *sar* is found 4x, meaning downcast, sullen, disheartened (1 Kgs 20:43; 21:4-5; Jer 6:28). In addition to its occurrence in Jer 6:28 (see

sec. 2), this adj. describes Ahab's frame of mind in the wake of the prophet's forceful rebuke (1 Kgs 20:43) or because he was not able to carry out his intentions (21:4-5).

6. *The nom. rebellion.* The nom. *sārâ* II occurs 7x (Deut 13:5[6]; 19:16; Isa 1:5; 31:6; 59:13; Jer 28:16; 29:32). Jenni (205-7) suggest that the defendant in Deut 19:16 was accused of lying (*sārâ* II) rather than rebellion. From this he argues (211) that four other instances of *sārâ* II also signify lying or falsehood (Deut 13:5[6]; Isa 59:13; Jer 28:16; 29:32). Although the falsehood nuance is clear in Deut 19:16, the other six occurrences of *sārâ* II could also connote rebellion. The difficulty lies in the fact that 3x the indictment is directed at those who are preaching *sārâ* II (Deut 13:5[6]; Jer 28:16; 29:32). Their false teaching constitutes rebellion because through their messages they lead God's children in rebellion against his demands. The stress on rebellion is also appropriate in light of Isaiah's and Jeremiah's repeated emphasis on this unfortunate reality.

P-B In the DSS the CD scroll contains most of the uses of this root. Its meaning takes on a new cultural/contextual meaning with reference to the Qumran community and its own view of itself. Those who separate from the Qumran community are the rebellious par excellence (cf. CD 1:12, 13; 2:6; esp. 1QS 10:20-21). Falsity and falsehood are found described by this root more often than in the OT (CD 5:21; 12:3). The root seems to take on the meaning of *sûr*, turn away (cf. *HALAT* 727; Ruppert, *TWAT* 5:962).

The root continued to mean rebel, to lord it in Late Heb. It refers to the rebellious son (see Jastrow 2:1030). The nom. *sār*, one who is low-spirited, is found (cf. BH *sar*; see Jastrow 2:1021; Exod R.s. 2).

NT In the NT the stubborn, rebellious nature of the Jews/Israelites continued to be a major problem (cf. Mark 3:5; 16:14; Tit 1:9, 10; Heb 3:8, 15; Jude 11).

Rebellion, conspiracy, stubbornness, obstinacy: → *ysd* II (conspire together, # 3570); → *kšh* (become stubborn, headstrong, # 4170); → *lāṣôn* (bragging, foolish talk, # 4371); → *lṣṣ* (rebel, scoff, # 4372); → *mrd* (revolt, rebel, # 5277); → *mrh* (be refractory, obstinate, # 5286); → *srr* I (be stubborn, rebellious, # 6253); → *'bt* (conspire together, # 6309); → *'ēṣâ* II (disobedience?, revolt?, # 6784); → *'ātāq* (old, hard, stubborn, arrogant, # 6981); → *pš'* (revolt, rebel, # 7321); → *qᵉšî* (stubbornness, # 8001); → *qšr* (ally together, conspire, bind, # 8003); → *šᵉrîrût* (stubbornness, # 9244)

BIBLIOGRAPHY

TWAT 5:957-63; *TWOT* 2:635; J. Bright, *Jeremiah*, 1965; G. Driver, "Two Misunderstood Passages of the Old Testament," *JTS* 6, 1955, 82-87; W. Holladay, *Jeremiah 1*, 1986; E. Jenni; "Dtn 19,16: *sarā*, Falschheit," in *Mélanges bibliques et orientaux en l'honneur de M. Henri Cazelles*, 1981, 201-11; W. McKane, *A Critical and Exegetical Commentary on Jeremiah*, 1986.

Eugene Carpenter/Michael A. Grisanti

6258	סתם

סתם (*stm*), q. stop up, make unrecognizable, keep close, secret; ni. be closed; pi. stop up (# 6258).

ANE The root occurs throughout the range of Sem. languages with the meaning "hide."

OT 1. This term is the standard expression for stopping up or blocking off sources of water supply (7x out of 13).

2. By extension, it came to designate the closing off of words, visions, or wisdom, thereby making them hidden and secret. At the conclusion of Daniel's book, he is commanded to close up the words and seal the scroll until the end of time (Dan 12:4, 9; cf. 8:26; Ezek 28:3). At the pivotal point in David's agonizing confession of his sinful condition, he avers that God desires to impart truth and wisdom to him in the hidden, private place (NIV inmost place, Ps 51:6[8]). Knowing that God wants him to internalize divine wisdom, David continues his prayer with the bold requests "cleanse me...wash me...," etc.

Closing, shutting: → *'ṭm* (stopped up, # 357); → *'ṭr* (close [mouth], # 358); → *gwp* I (shut, close, # 1589); → *ṭḥḥ* (besmeared, stuck, shut, # 3220); → *ṭmh* (stopped up, # 3241); → *n'l* I (tie, lock, # 5835); → *sgr* I (shut, close, deliver up, # 6037); → *stm* (stop up, # 6258); → *'ṣh* I (shut, # 6781); → *'ṣm* III (shut one's eyes, # 6794); → *ṣrr* I (bind, shut up, be narrow, in straits, distress, # 7674); → *qpṣ* I (draw together, shut, # 7890); → *š''* I (smear, smooth, shut, # 9129)

Bill T. Arnold

6259	סתר

סתר (*str*), ni., pi., hi. hide; pu. kept secret; hitp. keep o.s. hidden (# 6259); nom. מִסְתּוֹר (*mistôr*), shelter (hapleg. in Isa 4:6; # 5039); מַסְתֵּר (*mastēr*), read hi. part. מַסְתִּיר (*mastîr*, so NIV, hapleg. in Isa 53:3; # 5040); מִסְתָּר (*mistār*), hiding place (# 5041); סֵתֶר (*sēter*), hiding place, shelter (# 6260); סִתְרָה (*sitrâ*), refuge (hapleg. in Deut 32:38; # 6261).

ANE The root *str* occurs in Arab., Aram., Egypt. (*mśtr.t*).

OT 1. The vb. *str* means to hide oneself or others for the sake of protection from life-threatening situations. For example, Moses hid his face in the presence of God (Exod 3:6); David hid himself from the wrath of King Saul (1 Sam 20:5, 19, 24); the prophet Elijah hid himself from King Ahab (1 Kgs 17:3); Joash was hidden from Athaliah by Jehosheba (2 Kgs 11:2 ‖ 2 Chron 22:11[12]); and Baruch and Jeremiah are commanded by God to hide from King Jehoiakim (Jer 36:19, 26).

The term may also describe the attempt to hide the sin of adultery from a spouse (Num 5:13), or unintentional hidden faults (Ps 19:12[13], or even the concealment of information (1 Sam 20:2). Job laments he was not hidden from trouble (Job 3:10; 14:13), while by contrast the Lord's servant refused to hide his face from those abusing him (Isa 50:6).

2. *str* may also refer to the residual mystery of the transcendent God, who is free to remain hidden (Job 34:29; Prov 25:2; Isa 45:15) or free to involve himself in his creation (Ps 22:24[25]). Despite assumptions of the wicked, God has not ignored injustice (NIV covered his face; Ps 10:11). Likewise, the secret things like wisdom belong to God (Deut 29:28; Job 28:21). This contributes to the hiddenness of human destiny and purpose in life (Job 3:23), making divine revelation all the more essential (Ps 119:19).

3. Theologically, the verbal *str* reveals Yahweh as a God from whom human sin cannot be hidden (Job 34:22; Jer 16:17; 23:24), nor the secret plans of those plotting evil (Isa 29:14-15; cf. Amos 9:3). The idiom "I will hide my face" symbolizes covenant violation and a breach of fellowship between God and Israel (some 20x, e.g., Deut 31:17, 18; Isa 59:2; 64:7[6]; Mic 3:4). The expression signifies the wrath of God, the

rejection of his people (temporarily), and the initiation of covenant curses against Israel for their sin and rebellion (even exile, Ezek 39:23, 24, 29). Yet, in his compassion God hides his face but briefly, and in his grace he has hidden Israel's past troubles (i.e., forgotten them, Isa 65:16). He shelters or hides the upright from the schemes of the wicked (Ps 17:8; 31:20[21]; 64:2[3]), and his face is not hidden from the prayers of the righteous in distress (27:9; 69:17[18]; 102:2[3]; 143:7).

4. The righteous Branch of the Lord will be a *mistôr* (NIV refuge) from the elements for the survivors of the day of God's wrath (parallel with *maḥseh,* place of refuge; Isa 4:6).

5. For *mastēr* in Isa 53:3 read *mastîr* (hi. part.), "Like one from whom men hide their faces" (NIV), or "like one hiding his face from us" (so Watts, *Isaiah 34-66*, WBC 25, 1987, 224; cf. NRSV).

6. The nom. *mistār* conveys the sense of "hiding in ambush" in five of the ten cases where the form appears (usually the wicked lying in wait for the righteous, as in Ps 10:8, 9; 17:12; 64:4[5]; but note God lying in ambush for Judah like a lion, Lam 3:10). Elsewhere, Israel wept in hiding over her sins during the Exile (Jer 13:17), knowing God's pervasive presence makes it impossible to hide sin and rebellion from him (23:24; 49:10). On *mistār* in Isa 45:3, see *maṭmôn* (→ # 4759); on Ps 10:8-9, see *skk* (→ # 6114).

7. The nom. *sēter* occurs 35x in the OT with a variety of connotations. The term may refer to animal (Job 40:21; metaphorically in S of Songs 2:14), human (1 Sam 19:2), or even divine hiding places—where the darkness and thick clouds of the thunderstorm are the Lord's covering or veil (Job 22:14; Ps 18:11[12]). Yahweh himself is a hiding place or shelter for the righteous, preserving those who trust in him in his tent or tabernacle (Ps 27:5; 31:20[21]; 32:7; 61:4[5]; 91:1). By contrast, the wicked have made "lies" their shelter—but to no avail (Isa 28:17).

Elsewhere *sēter* conveys a meaning of secret activity, like Abigail covertly aiding David (1 Sam 25:20). More commonly, this activity is evil or malicious, as in the case of David's adultery with Bathsheba (2 Sam 12:12), idolatry and murder committed in secret (Deut 27:15, 24), or slanderous accusations made in secret (Ps 101:5). However, Job recognized human sin can never be kept secret from God, who knows all things (Job 24:15). On one occasion, the psalmist uses *sēter* to describe the mystery of divine activity in human procreation (Ps 139:15).

Lastly, Jeremiah uses *sēter* in a technical way to indicate private conversation (Jer 37:17; 38:16; 40:15; cf. Judg 3:19). Conversely, Isaiah the prophet proclaims that Yahweh's revelation of himself to Israel has not been spoken in secret—God's redemptive truth has been published openly from the beginning (Isa 45:19; 48:16).

8. The unique word *sitrâ* occurs only in the Song of Moses (Deut 32:38), a satire on the inability of the false gods (to which the Hebrews would inevitably turn) to provide shelter and protection for Israel.

NT → *NIDNTT* 2:211-20; 3:553-56.

Hiding: → *ḥb'* (hide, conceal, # 2461); → *ḥbh* (hide, # 2464); → *ḥāgû* (refuge, cleft, # 2511); → *ḥpp* I (screen, shelter, # 2910); → *ṭmn* (hide, # 3243); → *kḥd* (be hidden, hide, # 3948); → *knp* (hide oneself, # 4052); → *sōk* (hiding-place, shelter, thicket, hut, # 6108); → *str* (hide, kept secret, # 6259); → *'lm* (hidden things, secrets, # 6623); → *ṣpn* (hide, # 7621); → *śpn* (conceal, # 8561)

Refuge, escape: → *ḥsh* (seek refuge, # 2879); → *mālôn* (lodging place, # 4869); → *mānôs* (place of escape, # 4960); → *miqlāṭ* (refuge, asylum, # 5236); → *'wz* (take refuge, # 6395); → *plṭ* (save, bring to safety, # 7117); → *śrd* (run away, escape, # 8572)

BIBLIOGRAPHY
ISBE 2:705-7; *THAT* 2:174-82; *TWOT* 2:636; S. E. Balentine, "A Description of the Semantic Field of Hebrew Words for Hide," *VT* 30, 1980, 137-53; R. Gordis, "Studies in Hebrew Roots of Contrasted Meanings," *JQR* 27, 1936-37, 33-58.

Andrew E. Hill

6260 (*sēter*, hiding place, shelter), → # 6259

6261 (*sitrâ*, refuge), → # 6259

ע

6264 (*'āb* I, canopy [NIV overhang]), → # 1215

6265 (*'āb* II, cloud), → # 6380

6268	עבד

עבד (*'bd*), q. work, perform, serve, worship, carry out, honor; ni. to be tilled, worked; pu. to be worked; hi. enslave, make work, make serve; ho. be caused/influenced to serve, be led to worship (# 6268); מַעֲבָד (*ma'ᵃbad*), nom. deed(s), act(s) (# 5042); עֶבֶד (*'ebed* I), nom. slave, servant, subordinate (# 6269); עֲבָד (*'ᵃbad*), work, labor (# 6271); עֲבֹדָה (*'ᵃbōdâ*), nom. service, work, labor; worship (# 6275); עֲבֻדָּה (*'ᵃbuddâ*), nom. servants, workforce (# 6276); עַבְדוּת (*'abᵉdût*), nom. servitude, bondage (# 6285).

ANE The root is witnessed in many Sem. languages, but is different in meaning sometimes, although the same radicals are employed. Cf. Ugar. *'bd*, Arab. *'abada*, OSA *'bd,* which mean, serve, work (cf. also Eth. *'abäṭä*, lay oppressive labor upon); Aram/Syr. *'ᵃbad*, Phon. *'bd*, which mean make, do (cf. Heb. *'śh*, make, do).

For substantives note: *'ebed*, Ugar. *'bd*, Phoen. *'bd*, Aram. *'abdā'*, Arab. *'abd*, OSA *'bd*. It occurs in Akk. as a loanword [*abdu*; cf. *(w)ardu*]. It is clear that the content of the activity indicated by the root will be cultural-religious specific to each national group.

OT 1. According to Westermann's count (*THAT* 2:183) the vb. *'bd* is used 317x (Heb. 289x; Aram. 28x) in BH. It is employed 271x in the q. stem, and its use encompasses both secular and religious/theological importance. What may appear to be a merely nontheological usage is sometimes seen to be a religious usage upon closer examination.

2. Gen 2:5 indicates clearly that one of the purposes for the creation of *'ādām*, humankind, was to till (*'bd*) the ground *before* the Fall. So it was always God's design that humans would work the ground the Lord/God had created in Eden, an inherent religious act when done to fulfill the Creator's purposes. In 2:15, two infinitives construct indicating purpose, work/till, in parallel with watch over/keep (*šmr*), establish this point farther. But there is no indication that this was "forced labor," such as the Israelites were made to perform for Pharaoh. Working the ground became a

burdensome task after the rebellion of humankind (3:17-19). The alienation of Cain from the land (*'ᵃdāmâ*) furthered this alienation (4:12), because the earth would no longer yield the reward for cultivating (*'bd*) it. So the "profane" use of the word takes on a profound theological significance when set within a larger canonical context in Gen 1-4. The response of the ground itself is ultimately dependent on humankind's spiritual relation to God and, hence, to the ground.

Work in the sense of the kinds of duties carried out to earn one's living becomes subsumed in the word. Esau's servitude to Jacob was both a result of and foretold in a divine word of Yahweh attending their birth (Gen 25:23). Hence, the relationships among various persons/nations are dependent in various ways on God's sovereignty.

Yahweh limited the work week of his people, as an act of grace (cf. Egyptian 10-day work week), to six days with a seventh day of refreshment and rest for not only humans but animals as well (Exod 20:9; Deut 5:13). Ecclesiastes can even assert that the sleep of the laborer (*'bd*) is sweet (Eccl 5:12[11]).

On the other hand, forced labor in building Pharaoh's supply cities was imposed upon the Israelites by Pharaoh and termed "oppressive/harsh labor," carried out under intolerable conditions (Exod 1:13; 5:18), the purpose of which was to destroy God's people (5:18). This cruel oppression was both foretold and subsequently punished/judged according to God's pronouncements in Gen 15:14. Servitude to the Philistines was likewise a burden suffered in Canaan (1 Sam 4:9).

Hezekiah, on the other hand, could refuse to serve the Assyrian king, and God blessed him (2 Kgs 18:7), for God had given him the freedom to do so. But Zedekiah was directed by Jeremiah's word to serve the king of Babylon in his day. Who serves whom is ultimately Yahweh's decision, but is tied to the moral, ethical, and religious condition of the persons/peoples involved (cf. Exod 14:5). Israel rightly refused to serve (*'bd*) Solomon's son Rehoboam (1 Kgs 12:7).

Furthermore, an Israelite slave could *choose* to be a perpetual "slave" under a Master whom he had come to love, not hate (Exod 21:6; Deut 15:12, 18). Faithful service to the Lord was rewarded by God's mercy in sparing those who truly served him, true service accentuating the difference between the righteous and the wicked (Mal 3:17). These examples illustrate some of the various ways in which the concepts of service, servitude, labor, and work are put into use in various settings: toward God, other persons, animals, and activities in general.

3. The vb. form in the q. is often used theologically with respect to the cult of Israel in its service and care for the tabernacle, temple, its appurtenances, and its personnel.

After the age of fifty, a Levite could no longer serve in the services of the cult (Num 8:25). The word refers to "observing" the Feast of Unleavened Bread (Exod 13:5-6) and similar festivals in the process of worship. Num 3:7-10 and 16:9 refer to the "work of the tabernacle" regarding both the mundane duties of carrying it and putting it together, and the supervision of the actual worship activities (cf. Num 8:11; Josh 22:27). The vb. is used specifically regarding sacrifices to worship (*'bd*) Yahweh (Isa 19:21).

Thus, the vb. refers to the performance of the cult in the sense of worship, honor, serve in a purely religious sense, in addition to caring (*'bd*) for its physical upkeep and maintenance. The goal of the Exodus was the worship (*'bd)* of the Lord at

Sinai (Exod 3:12; cf. 1 Chron 28:9; Mal 3:18). "To serve Yahweh" ([*'bd*] *yhwh*) is found 56x (e.g., Exod 4:23; Deut 6:13; 1 Sam 7:3; Ps 100:2; Jer 2:20), all referring to worship, cultic service or faithfully keeping his covenant as his people.

In a negative application the word refers to the observance/worship of other gods 41x, esp. the gods in Canaan (Exod 23:33; Deut 4:28; Josh 23:7; Judg 2:19; Jer 5:19). They are *not* to be worshiped. Other objects besides the so-called "gods" were venerated (*'bd*): stars (Deut 4:19), Baals, (Judg 2:11; 10:6, 10; 1 Sam 22:10), the *gillûlîm*, gods (2 Kgs 17:12). Ahab became infamous for his service to Baal (1 Kgs 16:31).

4. The ni. and pu. add little to the discussion, although the pu. describes Jacob as the object of bondage at the hands of Babylon. The vb. is used in the hi. to describe the forced slavery placed upon Israel by Pharaoh (Exod 1:13; 6:5; cf. 2 Chron 2:18[17]; Ezek 29:18). Isa 43:23-24 indicates in an ironic use of the vb. *'bd* that, in effect, the Lord says "I have not burdened/belabored (*'bd*) you with grain offerings (*b^eminḥâ*) (236x) ... but you have burdened/belabored (*'bd*) me with your sins ... (*b^eḥaṭṭô'te[y]kā*)." In a great reversal of God's deliverance in the Exodus, he will enslave (*'bd*) Israel to her enemies (Jer 17:4). The ho. is used to give the sense "be caused/enticed to serve/go into servitude to." Often it means to the gods of Canaan (Exod 20:5; 23:24; Deut 5:9; 13:2[3]).

5. The nom. *'ebed* is used 800x in the OT (plus 7x in Aram.). Since Yahweh was the Lord/God of all the earth, the word was, of course, used to express the relationship of all beings to this Creator and Ruler of all. The word is used in ways that are expected from the use of the vb. *'bd*. Here the major theological uses of the word will be summarized (see esp. *HALAT* 732; *THAT* 2:191-95; *TWAT* 5:994-1010). (→ Servant, slave: Theology)

The first five categories are based on *HALAT*'s analysis, informed by *THAT*.

(a) The word often expresses the position of a human being before God. The chief servant of Abraham became, in reality, the servant of the Lord God in order to find Isaac a wife (Gen 24:2, 9, 14; cf. 24:34), binding himself by an oath. Israel as a nation was/were the servant/servants of Yahweh (Lev 25:55; Isa 41:9; 65:9). The prophets were not servants of men but of Yahweh, doing his bidding (2 Kgs 17:13; Jer 7:25; 26:5; Ezek 38:17). The refusal of Israel to heed and obey the prophets, Yahweh's servants, resulted in their devastation, as Daniel recognized in exile (Dan 9:6; cf. Ezra 9:11). The prophets were special servants, privy to the plans of the Sovereign Lord (Amos 3:7; cf. Deut 32:43). The Lord avenges the blood of his prophetic servants (2 Kgs 9:7).

(b) My servant (*'abdî*), his servant (*'abdô*) is used of many persons in the OT, meaning the Lord God's servant. For persons of distinctive character or role; such as: Abraham, Isaac, Jacob (Exod 32:13; Deut 9:27); Caleb (Num 14:24); Moses, *par excellence* in the old covenant (Exod 14:31; Num 12:7; Deut 34:5; 1 Kgs 8:53; Mal 4:4[3:22]); Joshua (Josh 24:29); Isaiah (Isa 20:3); David (1 Sam 23:10; 25:39); Eliakim, Job, etc.; Israel as a nation (Isa 41:8); and Jacob as a nation (Isa 44:1-2; 45:4). My servant, the Branch (*ṣemaḥ*), refers to the Messiah and/or a revived/restored line of David (Zech 3:8). Both Cyrus and Nebuchadnezzar are servants of Yahweh to do his bidding as he exercises his sovereignty over the nations (Isa 44:28; 45:1; cf. Jer 25:9; 27:6; 43:10).

(c) An especially significant use of *'ebed* describes the "servant of Yahweh" (*'ebed yhwh*). It is used of Moses (Deut 34:5), Joshua (24:29), and David (Ps 18, title [18:1]). But it is especially significant in Isaiah 40-55, where it describes a person/servant whose specific identity may be somewhat fluid. This servant has the stupendous duty of not only bringing back the tribes of Jacob, but of bringing salvation to all nations (cf. Gen 12:3; Isa 42:1-7; 49:5-6). The servant is vindicated by the Lord (Isa 50:8-9). His work involves suffering and death on behalf of others (52:13-53:12; cf. also 41:8; 42:1, 19; 44:2). He is separate from the servant(s) of the psalms who cry out for help. He does not cry out, and a solidarity of the servant with Yahweh and the "we," the observers (esp. 53:1-6), is evident as he suffers on behalf of those who are watching him (vv. 4-6); yet he is vindicated, although stricken for the transgressions of the Lord's people (vv. 7-9). All of this process of tragedy was assigned to the servant by the Lord with a specific purpose in mind (v. 10). This servant not only makes intercession for others, but justifies many (v. 11) and has borne the sins of many (v. 12). He becomes so united with the will of Yahweh for his people that it is difficult to separate the two. While many see Israel, a righteous remnant of Israel, or a righteous person within Israel (e.g., Moses, Jeremiah, Isaiah, Josiah, Manasseh!) as the servant, the NT clearly identifies the ultimate fulfillment of the servant as Jesus (Acts 8:26-40). This is the servant *par excellence* of the new covenant, who literally surrenders his life (vv. 10-12) in order to fulfill his Master's wishes (vv. 7-10). (→ Isaiah: Theology)

(d) The "servant of God" is further singled out as one who had a specific task to perform. Moses the servant of God wrote the law of God (Dan 9:11). The one who was chosen as the servant of God always had a good Master, always had a task to perform that involved doing the will of the covenant God, did not speak or act on his own behalf, but solely at the behest of his divine Sovereign Master. To be a servant of Yahweh was an honor, raising the status of the person involved. It did not mean degradation but exaltation in Yahweh's service. To be a servant of God had no negative connotations for the servant, after all things were considered, even though his task might have been one of delivering a word or parable of judgment.

(e) In Psalms the word is used in a religious sense. In Ps 119 (14x) the *'ebed* is the one who obeys God's word/law in various contexts: he obeys God's word (v. 17 *dābār*), meditates upon his ordinances (v. 23, *ḥûqqîm*), and fears his God (v. 38, *yir'eh*). He calls on God to supply his word to him (v. 49), etc. The other thirteen uses in the psalms picture God's servant calling for help (e.g., 27; 35; 69; 109). The servant of Ps 143:12 implores the Lord to act in his behalf, "for (*kî*) I am your servant (*'ᵃnî 'abdekā*)."

6. The nom. *'abōdâ* is found 145x. Its dominant theological sphere of use can be presented as follows:

(a) Service for God in the cult, which involved many areas. Some were appointed to take care of the vessels and instruments (1 Chron 9:28), while some were appointed particular tasks (28:14; 2 Chron 34:13). The movement of the tabernacle was described as the work of the service (*'ᵃbōdat 'ᵃbōdâ*) of the Tent of Meeting (Num 4:47). The word describes all the work done in the construction of the tabernacle (Exod 39:42), just as God had said. It is used to refer to both the religious service performed at the tabernacle and the actual work on the tent (Exod 30:16; cf. Num 3:7; 1 Chron 23:24). The nom. can refer to the ceremony (*hā'ᵃbōdâ*) of the Passover (Exod 12:25;

13:5) itself. In fact, the word *ʿᵃbōdâ* refers in most places to service at the sanctuary/holy place. The priests and Levites are especially involved (Num 4:4, 19; 2 Chron 8:14; cf. Ezek 44:14).

(b) In a more general sense the word describes God's work (Isa 28:21) as a strange/alien work he will perform against his people. It also describes the work/fruit of righteousness in the restoration/messianic era of Isaiah (Isa 32:17).

(c) In a general sense *ʿᵃbōdâ* describes service of many kinds—in particular, the service performed for Yahweh (Josh 22:27) involving burnt offerings, sacrifices, and offerings of well-being (fellowship).

7. The other noms. are used only 8x all together. Eccl 9:1 is surprisingly theological as it ties the works of both the wise and the righteous to the sovereignty of God. Their works (*ʿᵃbād*) are in the hand of God (*bᵉyad hāʾᵉlōhîm*). *ʿᵃbuddâ* refers to servants in Job 1:3 and also to God's increase of Isaac's good fortune (servants) in Gen 26:14. In both cases this blessing of wealth is through a covenantal blessing of God. *ʿabᵉdût*, servitude, refers to the bondage Israel was still suffering at the hands of the nations and as a result of God's judgments on them (Ezra 9:8; cf. Neh 9:17). *maʿᵃbād* refers to the deeds/acts of the wicked in Job 34:25 whom God overthrows them. The Aram. term (# 10434) ascribes justice to all of the works of God (Dan 4:37[34]).

P-B The root *ʿbd* is found often in the DSS, and its usage is basically the same as in the OT. The verbal usage is the same, except the "righteous" and the "wicked" have their particular sectarian meanings. The nom. *ʿebed* is the self-designation of the worshiper in the psalms of praise (1QH 5:15, 18; 9:11; 11:30; cf. 1QS 11:16). It refers, as the OT, to the prophets of God (1QpHab 2:9; 7:5; 1QS 1:3) and to David (1QM 11:2). The sale or oppression of a slave was forbidden (CD 11:12). Egypt is called *bêt ʿᵃbādîm*, house of slaves.

ʿᵃbōdâ is used often as in the OT, but also has developed a wider usage in these texts: the service of (for) the truth, falsehood, justice, uncleanness, power of oppression, (resp. 1QpHab 7:11; 10:11; 1QS 4:9; 1QH 6:19; 1QS 4:10; 1Qsa 1:22). In contrast to Eccl 9:1, these sections ascribe the works of men to the "two spirits" (1QS 3:26). The word is used to refer to service in the military (1QM 2:9; 15). The manifestation of nature is also controlled by and does its service toward God (1QH 1:12).

In Judaism the servant, *ʿebed*, was understood to refer to Israel most often (see bibliog.). In mishnaic Heb. the word continued to be used profusely, especially to indicate priestly service (Ḥullin, 246) or worship (Temura 6:1), whether good or bad. It was found in the ni. nitpael, hi. (enslave, oppress; Yalkut Exod 162); pi. (for further references see Jastrow 2:1034-35). The noms. (*ʿebed*, *ʿᵃbād*, *ʿabᵉdût*, *ʿᵃbōdâ*) were also used. *ʿᵃbōdâ* was especially lively in its usage. Theological usage indicated divine service, priest's service; worship; *ʿᵃbōdâ zārâ* was used to indicate idolatry.

The LXX employed *douleuō*, serve (114x), *latreuō*, worship (75x), *ergazomai*, effect, do, work (37x), *leitourgeō* (13x). Other vbs. were used once or twice each. For *ʿebed* the noms. found are: *doulos* (314x), *pais* (336x), *therapōn* (42x). *ʿᵃbōdâ* is translated with *leitourgeia*, worship, most often, also by *ergon*, work, deed, act. Other words used were *douleia*, servitude; *ergasia*, work, employment; *latreia*, worship, sacrifice.

NT In the NT the concept of the servant of the Lord in Isa is found often. Of major significance is the fact Jesus explains his ministry/life/death in terms drawn from the Suffering Servant of Isaiah. Jesus fulfills the promises (Lk 4:16-21; cf. Isa 61:1-3). Isa 52:13-53:12 is the Suffering Servant that Jesus modeled himself after (Lk 24:44-47). On the basis of the inspired author of Acts 8:26-40, the Servant of Isaiah 53 is none other than Jesus (v. 35). Among the followers of Christ, those who are greatest must be servants first of all (Matt 20:6; 23:11). A true servant is always about his Master's assignment (24:46). Romans reminds us that the authorities of this world are also no more than servants of God (Rom 13:6). The apostles are to be considered servants of Christ (1 Cor 4:1), and we also are to live as servants of God (1 Peter 2:16). The servants of God are also flames of fire (Heb 1:7). Revelation recalls the prophets as God's servants (Rev 10:7; 11:18). Finally, the ultimate goal of history will be realized as God's servants serve him (Rev 22:3).

Deed, act, misdeed, work: → *gml* (accomplish, commit, achieve, ripen, # 1694); → *mᵉlā'kâ* (work, duties, task, # 4856); → *'ll* I (act, wipe out, deal with, harm, glean, # 6618); → *'śh* I (make, do, prepare, create, work, service, # 6913); → *p'l* (do, make, produce, practice, accomplish, perform, # 7188)
Worship, bow down, serve: → *ghr* (down, bend over, # 1566); → *ḥwh* II (worship, bow, make obeisance, # 2556); → *kpp* (bow down, bow oneself down, # 4104); → *kr'* (bend, # 4156); → *sgd* (bow down, # 6032); → *'bd* (work, serve, worship, # 6268); → *qdd* (bow down, kneel down, # 7702); → *šrt* (wait on, be an attendant, serve, minister, # 9250)

Bibliography

ISBE 4:419-23; *NBD* 2:763-72; *TDNT* 2:264-83; 5:655-72; *THAT* 2:182-200; *TWAT* 5:981-1012; F. F. Bruce, *Sure Mercies of David*, 1954; J. Coppens, "La mission du serviteur de Yahwe et son statut eschatologique," *ETL* 48, 1972, 343-71; I. Engnell, "The 'Ebed Yahweh Songs and the Suffering Messiah in Deutero-Isaiah," *BJRL* 31, 1948, 54-93; J. P. Floss, "Jahwe dienen—Göttern dienen," *BBB* 45, 1975; P. Grelot, "Les poemes du serviteur: de la lecture critique à l'herméneutique," *Lectio Divina* 103, 1981; D. R. Hillers, "*Berît 'ām*: Emancipation of the People," *JBL* 97, 1978, 175-82; A. S. Kapelrud, "The Identity of the Suffering Servant," *Fest. W. F. Albright*, 1971, 307-14; G. Knight, *Servant Theology*, International Theological Commentary, 1984; H.-J. Kraus, *Gottesdienst im Israel*, 1962; W. S. LaSor, *Israel: A Biblical View*, 1976; N. Lohfink, "'Israel' in Jes 49, 3," *FzB* 2, 1972, 217-29; K. Nakazawa, "The Servant Songs—A Review After Three Decades," *Orient*, 1982, 65-82; C. R. North, *The Suffering Servant in Deutero-Isaiah*, 1956; H. M. Orlinsky, "The So-called 'Servant of the Lord' and 'Suffering Servant' in Second Isaiah," *VTSup* 14, 1967, 1-133; I. Riesener, "Der Stamm עבד im Alten Testament," *BZAW* 149, 1979; H. Ringgren, *Messiah in the OT*, SBT 1/18, 1956; H. H. Rowley, *The Servant of the Lord and Other Essays*, 1965; J. Sailhammer, "Genesis," *EBC*, 1990, 44-45; N. W. Tidwell, "My Servant Jacob, Isa xliii 1," *VTSup* 26, 1974, 84-91; J. P. M. van der Ploeg, "Slavery in the Old Testament," *VTSup* 22, 1972, 72-87; G. von Rad, "Das Werk Yahwes," *TBü* 48, 1973, 236-44; L. E. Wilshire, "The Servant City: A New Interpretation of the 'Servant of the Lord' in the Servant Songs of Dt-Is," *JBL* 94, 1975, 356-67; E. J. Young, *Studies in Isaiah*, 1955; Z. Zevit, "The Use of עֶבֶד as a Diplomatic Term in Jeremiah," *JBL* 88, 1969, 74-77; W. Zimmerli, "Zur Vorgeschichte von Jes. 53," *VTSup* 17, 1969, 236-44.

Eugene Carpenter

6269 (*'ebed* I, slave), → Servant

6271 (*ʿᵃbād*, work), → # 6268

6275 (*ʿᵃbōdâ*, work), → # 6268

6276 (*ʿᵃbuddâ*, servants), → # 6268

6285 (*ʿabdut*, servitude), → # 6268

6286	עבה

עבה (*ʿbh*), q. be thick, fat, gross (# 6286); מַעֲבֶה (*maʿᵃbeh*), foundry, mold (# 5043); עֲבִי (*ʿᵃbî*), thickness (# 6295).

OT 1. The nom. is used of physical thickness of the reservoir or sea of cast metal in the temple (1 Kgs 7:26; 2 Chron 4:5), of the pillars of the temple (Jer 52:21), and of a shield (Job 15:26). (See further # 5043)

2. The vb. is used in the reply given by Rehoboam to those who asked that he might lighten the yoke that his father Solomon laid on the people: "My little finger is thicker than my father's waist. My father laid on you a heavy yoke; I will make it even heavier" (1 Kgs 12:10-11 = 2 Chron 10:10-11).

3. In Deut 32:15 the adj. is used of Israel becoming proud and complacent: "Jeshurun grew fat and kicked; filled with food, he became heavy and sleek. He abandoned the God who made him and rejected the Rock his Savior" (cf. the use of *qpʾ* in Zeph 1:12).

4. In contrast to the root *ʿbh*, the root *kbd*, be heavy, is extended to denote honor and dignity, especially the nom. *kābôd*, glory (→ # 3883).

Thick: → *ʿbh* (be thick, # 6286); → *qpʾ* (thicken, congeal, # 7884)

Francis Foulkes

6287 (*ʿᵃbôṭ*, pledge, security, deposit), → # 6292

6290/6291	עָבוֹת

עבות (*ʿābôt* I), (thickly) branching (# 6290); עָבוֹת (*ʿābôt* II), branch (# 6291).

OT In Ezek 19:11; 31:3, 10, 14 one should probably read "clouds," from *ʿāb*, rather than "branches," from *ʿābôt*. Furthermore, the nom. *ʿᵃbōt* in Ps 118:27 likely means "cord" instead of "branch"; there is, however, an adj. *ʿābôt*, leafy, that surfaces in Lev 23:40; Neh 8:15; Ezek 6:13; 20:28. At the encouragement of Ezra, the Israelites gathered branches from shade (*ʿābôt*) trees, among others, as had been instructed by Moses in Lev 23:33-43 for observing the Feast of Tabernacles (Neh 8:13-18).

Branch (of tree): → *ʾāmîr* (branch, bough, # 580); → *sʿp* II (cut down, # 6188); → *ʿānāp* (branches, # 6733)

Edwin C. Hostetter

6292	עבט

עבט (*ʿbṭ* I), q. borrow; take as pledge/security/deposit/guarantee; hi. lend [out] on pledge (# 6292); denom. vb. < עֲבוֹט (*ʿᵃbôṭ*), nom. pledge, security, deposit, guarantee

(# 6287); עַבְטִיט (*'abṭîṭ*), nom. weight of pledges, heavy debts, or extortion (hapleg.; # 6294).

ANE The vb. occurs in Akk. *ḫabātu*, borrow. Nom. forms are found in Sam. *'āboṭ*; Akk. *ebuṭṭum*, *ebuttum*, interest-free loan.

OT 1. The q. (borrow) and the hi. (lend) both occur in Deut 15:6, part of the law dealing with the septennial year of release (15:1-11). The reward for obedience to the law will be Yahweh's blessing, as a result of which Israel will become a major, self-sufficient, mercantile power, exporting (lending) to and having financial control over many nations without having to import (borrow) goods or capital from any other country. The hi. is used again in v. 8, which calls on Israelites to give generously and cheerfully to the poor brother and to lend to him sufficiently for his need (15:7-8). Israelites who enjoyed financial security had a moral obligation to ensure that their less fortunate compatriots were not deprived by force of circumstance of the necessities of life. In v. 8, NEB and REB correctly read "lend him on pledge" It is not charity in the sense of almsgiving that is being called for here; rather, it is charitable disposition and conduct towards the needy person who pledges to repay the loan in due course (cf. e.g., Craigie, 237; Mayes, 249). Israelites were expected to mirror the compassionate nature of the God they worshiped (cf. e.g., Phillips, 163).

Deut 24:10-13 minimizes the oppressive power of taking pledges (cf. e.g., Nelson, 230). In 24:10, where the q. inf. const. is used in tandem with nom. *'ᵃbôṭ*, the creditor is forbidden to enter the house of the debtor to fetch a pledge. Instead, he must wait outside until the debtor brings the pledge out to him (v. 11). This instruction, which is unique to Deut., served a twofold purpose: it preserved the privacy of the debtor's home (cf. e.g., Cunliffe-Jones, 137; Wright, 475; Phillips, 163; Thompson, 247; Craigie, 308), and by leaving the selection of the pledge to the debtor, it prevented the creditor from pressuring the borrower into payment by carrying off something the poor man could not spare (cf. e.g., Dummelow, 133; G. A. Smith, 281; Wright, 475; Gottwald, 115; Craigie, 308). The command that follows in vv. 12-13 (the nom. *'ᵃbôṭ* occurs in each v.) not to sleep in the pledge (the outer garment) of a poor man, but to return it to its rightful owner before nightfall is also found in Exod 22:26-27[25-26]. Significantly, Deut 24:13 assures the creditor that obedience to this law will be considered righteousness before Yahweh, i.e., it will put the creditor in right relationship with God. Such legislation was designed to alleviate the hardship of the economically marginal while preventing the rich from profiting from the need of the weaker members of society to take a loan (cf. e.g., Nelson, 229-30). Unfortunately, it is clear from a number of texts that some creditors acted contrary to the law and retained garments taken in pledge (cf., Job 22:6; Prov 20:16 [par. 27:13]; Amos 2:8).

The scandal of religious punctilio combined with social ruthlessness (Kidner, 620) is roundly condemned in Isa 58. The people are first quoted, and then Yahweh, through the medium of the prophet, replies (Isa 58:3). In response to the people's demand to know why God has taken no notice of their assiduous fasting, Yahweh points out that self-interested, self-righteous religiosity that divorces faith from kindness and justice is a sham that results in estrangement from God, no matter how meticulously public worship is observed (cf. Knight, 22-23). People are infinitely more important than cultic rites, and, however ostentatious, fasting can never substitute for compassion, particularly for the oppressed and the destitute (Scullion, 163). Many translators take the words *w^e^kol-'aṣṣ^e^bêkem tingōśû* to refer either to the oppression of workers ("and [you] oppress all your workers" [RSV; NRSV; cf. JB; TEV]) or to their exploitation (NIV), by forcing them to work even harder (NEB; REB). Muilenburg (679) prefers to translate "you press your occupations" (i.e., business affairs), but this is rather weak, for the vb. *ngś* is used of Egyptian oppression (cf. Exod 3:7; 5:10, 13) and carries overtones of slave-driving (Herbert, 146). However, a number of scholars suggest emending the somewhat uncertain word *'aṣṣ^e^bêkem*, your workers, to *'ōb^e^ṭêkem* (masc. pl. q. act. part. of *'bṭ* with suff. 2nd p. masc. pl.), those who borrow from you against a pledge (e.g., *BHS*; *HALAT*; cf. Peake, 469; Westermann, 336). While this emendation has the support of Vg., which reads *debitores vestros*, your debtors, it has not been widely accepted.

In Isa 58, Yahweh stresses that he does not require self-mortification, self-abasing gestures, symbols of humiliation, or shallow external ritual devoid of integrity. Worshipers who oppress or neglect the poor pervert religion (Stuhlmueller, 345). The fast acceptable to God is the loosing of unjust bonds (v. 6), the liberation of the oppressed (v. 6), the feeding of the hungry (vv. 7, 10), the housing of the homeless (v. 7), the clothing of the naked (v. 7), compassion for the afflicted (v. 10), and a return to proper motivation for religious observances (v. 13), plus the removal of oppression (v. 3), quarrels and contentions (v. 4), callousness (v. 7), contemptuous action (v. 9), wicked speech (v. 9), hypocrisy, self-indulgence, and flagrant indifference to God's will (v. 13). To the author of this passage, the quality of one's relationship with God is indicated by the quality of one's relationship with one's fellows (May and Metzger, 895).

2. The nom. *'abṭîṭ* occurs in Hab 2:6, part of a section (vv. 6-20) consisting of woes against a rapacious, iniquitous, violent, and idolatrous nation, which plundered many peoples. An assurance is given that the wicked tyrant who loads himself with *'abṭîṭ* will experience a complete reversal of circumstances (2:6-7). There is dispute about the meaning of the word *'abṭîṭ*, which occurs only here. AV divides it into two words (*'āb*, mass, and *ṭîṭ*, mud) and reads thick clay. This is supported by some Heb. MSS, as well as Syr. and Vg. Some (e.g., Pusey, 417-18; Dummelow, 590; Robertson, 187) think it possible that Habakkuk deliberately created a double entendre, the word conveying both wealth derived from oppressive pledges and the heap of clay with which the greedy, grasping nation has burdened itself. However, the majority of commentators take *'abṭîṭ* to be an intensive form from *'bṭ*, give or receive a pledge as security for a debt (see, e.g., GKC, § 84^b, m). RSV, JB, and Robertson (186) translate "pledges." NEB, REB and NRSV have "goods taken in pledge." NIV reads "[and makes himself wealthy by] extortion!" It is uncertain whether *'abṭîṭ* means "a heavy debt of loans borrowed from others" or "a weight of pledges taken to secure loans made to others" (cf. Roberts, 118). The word seems to refer to the booty and tribute exacted by the oppressor from other nations (cf. e.g., Achtemeier, 49-50; Ceresko, 263).

A plausible interpretation of v. 7 is that the plundered nations that were forced to pay the oppressor for use of what he considered to be his land will be changed from debtors to creditors and will demand payment from the oppressor for what they consider to be the loans they have made to him. Although there is lack of clarity about the relationship between the vb. *nšk*, pay or give interest, and the vb. *nšk*, bite, there is almost certainly a fine play on these words in v. 7: those bitten (i.e., those who have been forced to pay interest) will now bite the former creditor and demand payment for the loans they have advanced him (see, e.g., Dummelow, 590; Roberts, 119; cf. Pusey, 418; Driver 79; Garland, 259; Patterson, 189-90; Robertson, 186-90). Whatever the original referent of Hab 2:6-7 may have been, the condemnation here has universal reference, indicting all human economic tyranny (May and Metzger, 1137-38; Stephens-Hodge, 770; R. L. Smith, 111).

P-B The following. nom. forms occur in Heb.: *ʿᵃbôṭ*, (fastening) pledge, security; saddle, saddlebag, saddle cushions, rugs, baggage; *ʿābîṭ*, (fastening, pressing) sumpter saddle; saddle cushion; large carrying basket for the transport of grapes; large vessel for the collection of wine. In Aram. the nom. *ʿᵃbîtāʾ* (sumpter saddle; burden, obligation) occurs as does the denom. vb. *ʿᵃbaṭ*, seize a pledge; itp. have one's goods seized (Jastrow 2:1036-37).

Borrowing and lending: → *lwh* II (borrow, lend, # 4278); → *nšʾ* I (lend against a pledge, # 5957); → *nšk* II (pay/exact interest, # 5967); → *ʿbṭ* (borrow, take a pledge from, # 6292); → *šmṭ* (release, remit, drop, throw down, # 9023)

Pledge, security: → *ʾissār* (binding obligation, pledge, vow of abstention, # 674); → *ḥbl* II (take in pledge, exact a pledge, # 2471); → *ḥôb* (pledge, collateral, # 2550); → *nšʾ* I (lend against a pledge, # 5957); → *ʿbṭ* (borrow, take a pledge from, # 6292); → *ʿrb* I (stand security for, give security for, # 6842); → *piqqādôn* (deposited goods, store, supply, provision, # 7214); → *tqʿ* (drive, thrust, clap one's hands, blow trumpet, pledge, # 9546)

Bibliography

E. Achtemeier, *Nahum-Malachi*, Interpretation, 1986; A. R. Ceresko, "Habakkuk," in *NJBC*, 1990, 261-64; P. C. Craigie, *The Book of Deuteronomy*, NICOT, 1983; H. Cunliffe-Jones, *Deuteronomy: Introduction and Commentary*, 1964; S. R. Driver, *The Minor Prophets: Nahum, Habakkuk, Zephaniah, Haggai, Zechariah, Malachi*, 1906; J. R. Dummelow, ed., *A Commentary on the Holy Bible*, 1909; D. D. Garland, "Habakkuk," in *BBC*, 1972, 7:245-69; N. K. Gottwald, "The Book of Deuteronomy," in *The Interpreter's One-Volume Commentary on the Bible*, 1971, 100-121; A. S. Herbert, *The Book of the Prophet Isaiah Chapters 40-66*, CBC, 1975; D. Kidner, "Isaiah," in *NBC*, 1972, 588-625; G. A. F. Knight, *The New Israel: A Commentary on the Book of Isaiah 56-66*, ITC, 1985; H. G. May and B. M. Metzger, eds., *The New Oxford Annotated Bible*, 1973; A. D. H. Mayes, *Deuteronomy*, NCBC, 1979; J. Muilenburg, "The Book of Isaiah Chapters 40-66: Introduction and Exegesis," *IB*, 1956, 5:381-773; R. D. Nelson, "Deuteronomy," in *HBC*, 1988, 209-34; R. D. Patterson, *Nahum, Habakkuk, Zephaniah*, 1991; A. S. Peake, "Isaiah I-XXXIX," in *Peake*, 1920, 436-73; A. Phillips, *Deuteronomy*, CBC, 1973; E. B. Pusey, *The Minor Prophets With a Commentary*, 1891; J. J. M. Roberts, *Nahum, Habakkuk, and Zephaniah: A Commentary*, OTL, 1991; O. P. Robertson, *The Books of Nahum, Habakkuk, and Zephaniah*, NICOT, 1991; J. Scullion, *Isaiah 40-66*, 1982; G. A. Smith, *The Book of Deuteronomy*, 1918; R. L. Smith, *Micah-Malachi*, WBC, 1984; L. E. H. Stephens-Hodge, "Habakkuk," in *NBC*, 1972, 767-72; C. Stuhlmueller, "Deutero-Isaiah and Trito-Isaiah," in *NJBC*, 1990, 329-48; J. A. Thompson, *Deuteronomy: An Introduction and Commentary*, TOTC, 1974; C. Westermann, *Isaiah 40-66: A Commentary*, OTL, 1969; G. E. Wright, "The Book of Deuteronomy: Introduction and Exegesis," *IB*, 1953, 2:309-537.

Robin Wakely

6294 (*'abṭîṭ*, pledges, debts), → # 6292

6295 (*'ᵃbî*, thickness), → # 6286

6296	עבר

עבר (*'br* I), q. pass through; ni. be forded; pi. cause to pass through or over; hi. make pass through (# 6296); מַעֲבָר (*ma'ᵃbār*), ford, pass (# 5044); מַעְבָּרָה (*ma'bārâ*), ford (# 5045); nom. עֵבֶר (*'ēber* I), side (# 6298); עֲבָרָה (*'ᵃbārâ*), ford (# 6302).

ANE The root is common to most of the Sem. languages with the exception of Eth., occurring with meanings similar to Heb. in Aram., Syr., Arab., and Ugar.

OT 1. This vb. is used to describe the movement of people (Gen 18:5) or of inanimate objects, such as a razor (Num 6:5) or time (1 Chron 29:30). In those cases in which there is no mention of specific points or boundaries, the meaning is similar to other vbs. of movement, and it is used in parallelism with *bw'* (→ # 995; Amos 5:5), *hlk* (→ # 2143; Amos 6:2), and *ng'* (→ # 5595; Jer 48:32). While human beings are usually the subject, the vb. occurs with a divine subject when the description is given of the glory of God passing in front of Moses at Sinai (Exod 33:22; 34:6) and similarly in front of Elijah (1 Kgs 19:11).

2. Frequently *'br* is used to designate movement from one place to another. Gen 31:21 illustrates this usage well, in that *'br* describes the movement of Jacob as he crosses the Euphrates when fleeing from Laban. Similarly it is employed to describe Israel's crossing the Jordan into the Promised Land, especially so in Deut (3:18, 21, 25, 27, 28, etc.) and Josh (1:2, 11, 14; 2:23; 3:1, 2, etc.). It is also used of progression through a specified territory, such as Israel's request to march through Edomite and Amorite territory (Num 20:17-21; 21:22-23). Traversing a more restricted area such as a camp (Josh 3:2) or a specific district (1 Sam 9:4) is also a common use of *'br* in the OT.

From the literal meaning of *'br* various metaphorical nuances developed. To exceed others in wealth or wickedness (Jer 5:28) were appropriate extensions of the basic idea, as was the idea of men dying and passing from this life (Job 30:15; Prov 22:3). The vb. was also utilized in a series of technical expressions, such as *'ōbēr yām*, seafaring (Isa 23:2); *kesef 'ōbēr*, silver of the current weight (Gen 23:16); *môr 'ōbēr*, liquid myrrh (S of Songs 5:5); and *kol hā'ōbēr 'al happᵉqudîm*, everyone who moves over into the counted group (Exod 30:13-14; 38:26).

3. The hi. form of *'br* has wide usage, designating the causation of movement of people or things. It is used to describe God's causing wind to blow over the earth after the Flood (Gen 8:1) and of a person's causing a sound or voice to be heard (Exod 36:6; Lev 25:9; 2 Chron 30:5; 36:22). It designates a razor passing over the body (Num 8:7) or an arrow passing beyond someone (1 Sam 20:36). On several occasions it is used in expressions that describe God's gracious action in forgiving sin, and at times in parallel with other well-known terms for the removal of sin (e.g., see Job 7:21 [*nś' peša'*]; Mic 7:18 [q. part. with *nś' 'āwôn*; → # 5951]). The most specialized usage of the hi. is in connection with the sacrifice of children. There are only two specific instances, once when Ahaz made his son pass through the fire (2 Kgs 16:3) during the Syro-Ephraimitic war and the other time when Manasseh did likewise while facing a threat from the Assyrians (2 Kgs 21:6). However, there are other references to this practice in

both the law (Lev 18:21; Deut 12:31) and the prophets (Jer 3:24; 7:31; 19:5; 32:35; Ezek 20:31), two of which specify that it was an offering to *mōlek* (Lev 18:21; Jer 32:35) and several that specify it was with fire (Deut 18:10; 2 Kgs 16:3; 17:17; 21:6; 2 Chron 33:6; Ezek 20:31). The practice was never a permitted Israelite ritual and only occurs as an alien influence late in the history of Judah (cf. R. de Vaux, *AncIsr*, 444-46).

4. *'br* can also have covenantal overtones. It is used to describe the action of passing between the dismembered animal pieces in a covenant inauguration ceremony (*'br bên*, Gen 15:17; Jer 34:18, 19); possibly from this developed the expression *'br* b^e to denote entry into covenant with Yahweh (Deut 29:12[11]). When used with the prep. *'el*, *'br* denotes rejecting an existing regime and aligning with an opposing party, as when David and his six hundred men "went over to Achish son of Maoch king of Gath" (1 Sam 27:2), or when Ishmael made captives of the people remaining in Mizpah and went over to the Ammonites (Jer 41:10; see also the same terminology in the pact between Jacob and Laban, Gen 31:52). Most frequently, though, *'br* is used with an object such as "covenant" (Deut 17:2; Josh 7:11, 15; Judg 2:20; 2 Kgs 18:12; Jer 34:18; Hos 6:7; 8:1) or "commands (of the covenant)" to indicate violation of a covenant relationship (Deut 26:13; 1 Sam 15:24; 2 Chron 24:20; Ps 148:6; Isa 24:5; Dan 9:11), with some contexts like Josh 23:16 indicating that such transgression was equivalent to walking after and serving other gods.

5. There are several noms. derived from *'br* that have the meaning of passage through the water. *'ᵃbārâ* occurs once in the sense of "ford" (2 Sam 19:18[19]) and twice in the expression "fords in the desert" (2 Sam 15:28; 17:16). The nom. *ma'ᵃbār* only occurs in the const. with the meaning of ford or passage (Gen 32:22[23], "the ford of the Jabbok") or pass (1 Sam 13:23, "the pass at Michmash"), with one occurrence referring to the sweep of a rod (Isa 30:32). *ma'ᵃbārâ* is used more frequently with similar meanings of ford or pass, including the reference in Jer 51:32 to the enemy's seizing the defensive crossing surrounding Babylon. The connection in idea between *'ābār* (only occurring in the pl. *'ᵃbārîm*) and the vb. is not so clear. It appears by itself as a place name in Jer 22:20 and in the expression "mountain(s) of the Abarim" (Num 27:12; 33:47-48; Deut 32:49) to describe the northwestern part of the Moabite mountains, including Mt. Nebo. It also occurs in the place name *'iyyê hā'ᵃbārîm* (Num 21:11; 33:44), an unidentified place in southern Moab.

6. There are several important usages in the OT involving *'ēber*. It is used both as a nom. and as a preposition indicating location or direction. As a nom. it means "side" or possibly "edge, shore." The latter meaning may well apply in the case of the expression *'ēber hayyardēn*, "beyond/along the Jordan," which occurs 38x in the OT (29x in Deut and Josh). In many contexts this expression is further defined to make clear whether west or east of the Jordan is intended. Thus Josh 9:1 clearly uses it of the west bank of the Jordan, while later in the same chapter it describes the Transjordanian territories of Sihon and Og (9:10). By itself it does not designate with precision the relationship to the Jordan but requires either context or added specification to do so. The expression is equivalent to "Jordanside," with further detail being required for accurate description.

When *'ēber* is used without further precise definition, it often marks out a region across a boundary or a body of water. Thus Moses reminds the covenant people that God's word is not beyond (*'ēber*) the sea (Deut 30:13). The word can also be used in a more general relationship, such as of the position of the pillars in the temple to the fretwork (1 Kgs 7:20). In the expression *'ēber hānnāhār*, *nāhār* always refers to the Euphrates, and the term assumed a political and administrative meaning. The cognate Akk. expression *'eber nāri*, first documented during the reign of Esarhaddon, refers to the area west of the Euphrates. It is also expressed that way in the OT, as when Solomon's empire is described as embracing "all the kingdoms west of the River, from Tiphsah to Gaza" (1 Kgs 4:24[5:4]). The standpoint is that of a person in Palestine, yet the phrase is used of a precise geographical area. The same geographical reference occurs in the use of the Aram. phrase *'ᵃbar-nahᵃrâ* in Ezra 4:10. (→ Jordan Valley, Theology)

P-B Only the verbal form occurs in the DSS, with a similar range of meaning as noted for the OT. It is used of crossing the Jordan (1Q 22.1,9; 2,2) as well as of entry into God's covenant (1QS 1.18,20). The LXX uses vbs. compounded with *para* and *dia* to express the idea of going through or beyond, while *parabainō* and *parerchomai* are used to translate passages in which *'br* denotes breach of the covenant.

Passing, fording: → *gwz* (pass by, # 1577); → *ḥlp* I (pass by, disappear, # 2736); → *'br* I (pass through, ford, # 6296)

Bibliography

THAT 2:200-204; *TWAT* 5:1015-33; B. Gemser, "*Be'eber hajjarden*: In Jordan's Borderland," *VT* 2, 1952, 349-55; E. W. Hengstenberg, "The Other Side Jordan," *Dissertations on the Genuineness of the Pentateuch*, II, 1847, 256-64; J. P. U. Lilley, "By the River-Side," *VT* 28, 1978, 165-71; A. F. Rainey, "The Satrapy Beyond the River," *Australian Journal of Biblical Archaeology* 1,2, 1969, 51-78; M. Weinfeld, "Burning Babies in Ancient Israel: A Rejoinder to Morton Smith's Article, *JAOS*, 1975, 477-79," *UF* 10, 1978, 411-13.

Allan M. Harman

6297	עבר

עבר (*'br* II), hitp. show o.s. infuriated (# 6297); עֶבְרָה (*'ebrâ*), nom. excess, arrogance, anger, fury (# 6301).

ANE The etymology of the vb. is uncertain.

OT The nom. *'ebrâ* occurs 34x in the OT—1x in the Pent., 12x in the poetical books, and 21x in the prophetic books. In the majority of the occurrences the Lord is the subject. The vb. occurs 8x; all uses are in the hitp. stem—1x in the Pent. and 7x in the poetical books.

1. The nom. *'ebrâ* is par. to *'ap*, anger; *ḥarôn 'ap*, fierce anger; *'êd*, calamity; *za'am*, indignation; *'ṣārâ*, distress; *'akzārî*, cruel; *gē'*, pride; *ga'ᵃwâ*, pride; *gā'ôn*, exaltation; *ḥrh*, burning anger. It is modified by *yôm*, day; *'ap*, anger; *ṣrr*, enemies; *zēdôn*, arrogance; *šēbeṭ*, rod; *'ēš*, fire; *qin'â*, jealousy. *'ebrâ* is described as being *qšh*, hard (Gen 49:7); *ybl*, borne along (Job 21:30); *'sp*, gathered (Ps 85:3[4]); *pwḥ*, blown out (Ezek 21:31[36]); *npḥ*, blown with the result of being *ntk*, poured forth (22:21); something that will *klh*, consume (22:31); *špk*, be poured out (Hos 5:10); and *nṣḥ*, enduring (Amos 1:11). *'ebrâ* is contrasted with *ṭôb*, good (Prov 11:23), and *rāṣôn*, delight (14:35).

The day of the Lord's fury (*b^{e}yôm 'ebrat yhwh*; Zeph 1:18) is described in 1:15 by using the following words: *ṣārâ*, distress, and *m^{e}ṣûqâ*, stress; *šô'â*, devastation, and *m^{e}šô'â*, desolation; *ḥōšek*, darkness, and *'^{a}pēlâ*, gloominess; *'ānān*, clouds, and *'^{a}rāpel*, heavy clouds. This day arises as a consequence of human sin (1:17). Consequently, the word "wrath" (*'ebrâ*) in 1:18 is "suggestive of the overwhelming nature of the divine anger against sin" (Patterson, 322). The Lord's fury (*'ebrâ*) is something from which people will not be delivered (*nṣl*) (Ezek 7:19). In the Lord's fury (*'ebrâ*) strongholds will be torn down (*hrs*) (Lam 2:2). The above passages refer to events that find partial fulfillment in the destruction of Jerusalem in 586 BC, with their final consummation in the eschatological Day of the Lord (cf. VanGemeren, 174-76).

2. *Pentateuch.* The nom. *'ebrâ* can denote "fury," which conveys the idea of an intense, possibly destructive rage. Gen 49:5-7 contains Jacob's blessing for Simeon and Levi, in which he refers to their anger (*'ap*) and fury (*'ebrâ*). The destruction these brothers brought upon the inhabitants of Shechem on account of the rape of their sister Dinah (Gen 34:25-29) is the likely incident underlying Jacob's assessment of their volatile emotions. In this instance *'ebrâ* clearly depicts a destructive rage on the part of the two sons of Jacob.

3. *Poetical books. 'ebrâ* is used 5x in Prov. In two instances it is contrasted with positive virtues. Prov 11:23 compares the desire of the righteous, which ends in good (*ṭôb*), with the hope of the wicked, which ends in wrath. In 14:35 the delight (*rāṣôn*) of the king is contrasted with his wrath (*'ebrâ*).

The vb. *'br* is found 4x in Ps and 3x in Prov. It occurs 3x in Ps 78, a psalm that recounts the unfaithfulness of the Israelites up to the time David was made king. The result of the Lord's fury was fire breaking out against Jacob and anger (*'ap*) against Israel (v. 21). The reason behind this fury was the people's disbelief and lack of trust (v. 22). The Lord's fury led to a rejection (*m's*) of the people (v. 59, cf. v. 62).

4. *Prophetic books. 'ebrâ* is used the majority of times (19x) with a direct reference to the fury of the Lord. "By the wrath of the LORD Almighty the land will be scorched and the people will be fuel for the fire.... Each will feed on the flesh of his own offspring" (Isa 9:19[18]-20[19]). According to 13:31, the heavens will tremble and "the earth will shake from its place." People will be "thrust through" as they are captured; "their infants will be dashed to pieces before their eyes; their houses will be looted and their wives ravished" (13:15-16). The images portrayed are ones of intense, destructive rage.

In Isa 14:6 *'ebrâ* also has the sense of a destructive rage. On the day the Israelites receive relief they will take up a taunt against the king of Babylon and will proclaim that the Lord has broken the rod of the wicked. It was this rod that struck the people in fury with "unceasing blows." The image is of a cruel overlord mercilessly beating the people.

P-B The vb. *'br* in Aram. carries the meanings in the hitp. and nitpael of swell, become wroth; become pregnant; be extended; be added to (Jastrow, 1039). The Aram. nom. *'ebrâ* denotes anger and indignation (Jastrow, 1040a). In the LXX *'br* is translated with a variety of words; *'ebrâ* is translated with either *thymos* or *orgē*.

Anger, rage, wrath: → *'np* (be angry, # 647); → *z'm* (curse, be angry, # 2406); → *z'p* I (rage, # 2406); → *ḥēmâ* (rage, # 2779); → *ḥrh* I (be hot, become angry, # 3013); → *k's* (be irritated, angry, # 4087); → *'br* II (show anger, # 6297); → *qṣp* I (become angry, # 7911); → *rgz* (shake, agitate, # 8074); → **Anger: Theology**

BIBLIOGRAPHY

THAT 2:200-207; *TWOT* 2:643-44; B. E. Baloian, *Anger in the Old Testament,* 1992; S. Erlandsson, "The Wrath of YHWH," *TynBul* 23, 1973, 111-16; A. J. Heschel, *The Prophets,* 2, 1962; R. L. Mayhue, "The Prophet's Watchword: Day of the Lord," *GTJ* 6, 1985, 231-46; L. Morris, "The Wrath of God," *ExpTim* 63, 1952, 142-45; R. D. Patterson, *Nahum, Habakkuk, Zephaniah,* 1991; W. A. VanGemeren, *Interpreting the Prophetic Word,* 1990.

Gale B. Struthers

6298 (*'ēber* I, side), → # 6296

6301 (*'ebrâ*, arrogance, anger), → # 6297

6302 (*'ᵃbārâ*, ford), → # 6296

6309	עבת

עבת (*'bt* II), pi. conspire together (hapleg.) (# 6309); nom. עֲבֹת (*'ᵃbōt*), rope, cord (→ # 6310).

ANE Akk. *ebēṭu* (*ebētu*), (be) tie(d), girt or restrict, occurs mainly in medical texts, but also in other contexts (*CAD* E, 13-14; *AHw*, 182-83; cf. *nībittu*, girdle [*CAD* N 2:201]).

OT The vb. *'bt* occurs only in Mic 7:3, where the prophet shows the depressing picture of the misery that besets Israel, with those entrusted with the authority to guide the people aright turning against them. The judge seeks bribes, the powerful make exorbitant demands; all "conspire together."

Distortion, perversion, shrewdness, twisting: → *hēpek* (opposite, perversity, # 2201); → *kpn* (twist, # 4102); → *lwz* (let out of sight, go wrong way, # 4279); → *slp* (frustrate, overthrow, twist, mislead, # 6156); → *'bt* (conspire together, # 6309); → *'wh* (do wrong, pervert, # 6390); → *'wl* I (act wrongly, # 6401); → *'wt* (make crooked, pervert, bent, # 6430); → *'ql* (perverted, # 6823); → *'qš* (be perverse, make crooked, # 6835); → *ptl* (twist, be wily, shrewd, # 7349); → *r''* I (be bad, injure, # 8317)

David W. Baker

6310	עֲבֹת

עֲבֹת (*'ᵃbōt*), nom. twisted cord/rope, twine, braid (# 6310).

OT The word *'ᵃbōt* (24x; for cognates and etymology see *AHw*, 774a; *HALAT* 740), more limited in scope than its synonym *ḥebel* II, refers primarily to fetters or bindings (e.g., Judg 15:13), and also to decorative plaited work (e.g., Exod 28:14). One metaphorical usage in connection to human moral life—i.e., willful attachment to sin—provides theological interest (Isa 5:18). In this woe oracle, the prophet castigates those in the community who arrogantly oppose and disbelieve his proclamations. Their actions "draw sin with cords of deceit (*bᵉḥablê haššāw'*), and wickedness as with cart ropes (*wᵉka'ᵃbôt hā'ᵃgālâ*)." The obscurity of the first expression, "cords of deceit," inclines many to emend the text to "cords of an ewe" (reading *šû'* or *śeh* instead of *šāw'*; see NCB, 65; OTL, 64; NICOT, 163 n. 1; G. R. Driver, "Isaiah I-XXXIX: Textual and Linguistic Problems," *JSS* 13, 1968, 38; contrast BKAT, 178; WBC, 59). Then "cart rope" is repointed to "calf rope" (reading *hā'ēgel* instead of *hā'ᵃgālâ*). The alternatives affect the particulars of the figure but not its overall import: the prophet's opponents are firmly hitched or tethered to their sins, which renders their destruction inevitable (cf. *TDOT* 4:176-77). On Hos 11:4 and Ps 129:4, see *ḥebel* II, cord (→ # 2475).

Cord, rope: → *gādil* (tassel, # 1544); → *ḥebel* II (cord, rope, land, region, # 2475); → *nᵉ'ōret* (tow, # 5861); → *niqpâ* (cord, rope, # 5940); → *'ᵃbōt* (twisted cord, # 6310); → *qaw* I (measuring cord, # 7742)

Bibliography

NIDNTT 3:591-92, 858; *TDNT* 2:43, 896-901; *TDOT* 4:172-79; *TWAT* 6:1223-25; R. J. Forbes, *Studies in Ancient Technology*, 4, 1956, 2-80.

A. R. Pete Diamond

6314 (*'ugâ*, cake of bread), → Baking, Bread

6316	עָגִיל

עָגִיל (*'āgîl*), nom. round ornament (for men and women), possibly earring (# 6316), cf. עָגֹל (*'āgōl*), round (# 6318).

ANE Aram. *'argēl*, roll.

OT 1. Two examples of *'āgîl*, round ornament, are Num 31:50; Ezek 16:12. For a discussion on jewelry, see *'dh* (put on ornaments, # 6335).

2. The word *'āgōl* defines several temple furnishings: the Sea of cast metal (1 Kgs 7:23 ‖ 2 Chron 4:2), the bronze basin on the movable stand (1 Kgs 7:31, 35), and Solomon's throne (10:19).

Circle, turn: → *'pp* (surround, # 705); → *ḥdr* I (surround, enclose, # 2539); → *ḥwg* (describe a circle, # 2552); → *ktr* II (surround, # 4193); → *nqp* II (go round, surround, # 5938); → *sbb* (turn go round, surround, # 6015); → *'āgōl* (round, # 6318); → *'ṭr* (surround, crown, # 6496/7)

Leslie C. Allen/Malcolm J. A. Horsnell

6317	עֲגִילָה

עֲגִילָה (*'agîlâ*), round shield (# 6317). The meaning of the root is derived from the hypothetical root *'gl*, go in circles, and determined by its translation equivalent in the Septuagint (*thuros*).

OT The word occurs 1x in the OT, in a passage that describes the actions of the divine warrior (→): "He makes wars cease to the ends of the earth; he breaks the bow and shatters the spear, he burns the shields with fire" (Ps 46:9[10]). It is worth noting that Craigie (342) and some translations (NKJV) dispute this translation, based on the Septuagint, to support the rendering "war-wagons" or "chariots." Besides the Septuagint, the word's lone postbiblical occurrence supports the translation "shields."

P-B 1QM6:15 has the expression *mgny 'glh*, which Yadin (1962, 121) renders "round shield."

Shield: → *māgēn* I (shield, protection, # 4482); → *ʿᵃgîlâ* (round shield, # 6317); → *ṣinnâ* II (long shield, # 7558); → *šeleṭ* (shield, # 8949)

BIBLIOGRAPHY

TWAT 4:646-59; P. C. Craigie, *Psalms 1-50*, 1983; O. Keel, *The Symbolism of the Biblical World*, 1978, 222-25; Y. Yadin, *The Scroll of the War of the Sons of Light Against the Sons of Darkness*, 1962; idem, *The Art of Warfare in Biblical Lands*, 1963.

Tremper Longman

6318 (*ʿāgōl*, round), → # 6316

6319	עֵגֶל

עֵגֶל (*ʿēgel*), nom. calf, calves (# 6319); עֶגְלָה (*ʿeglâ*), nom. heifer (# 6320).

ANE 1. This common term for calf appears in many Sem. dialects: *agalum* in Akk., *ʿgl* in Ugar., *ʿîgla'* in Aram., and *ʿajla* in Arab. (cf. BDB 722). This term derives from *ʿgl*, round, probably expressing the leaping around of the calves (cf. Ps 29:6; Mal 4:2).

OT 1. Like *par* (→ # 7228), *ʿēgel* is a gender distinctive term, with a fem. form *ʿeglâ* (# 6320).

2. The calf of one year or older was used as a sacrificial animal (Lev 9:3); however, *ʿēgel* is not a principal animal for sacrifice. Since this term refers to the calf of a younger age, *par* (bull, → # 7228) is far more frequently found in sacrificial laws.

Like *pārâ*, heifer, *ʿeglâ*, heifer, is never used for the burnt offering or sin offering. When, at the anointing of David, Samuel offered a heifer (*ʿeglat bāqār*) it must have been a peace (fellowship) offering (1 Sam 16:2). An unusual use of *ʿeglâ* is found in the expiation for the bloodshed of an unknown murder (Deut 21:3-4, 6). A heifer that had never been worked was put to death in the place of the murderer so that the bloodshed was atoned.

3. The most significant use of this term is an image of a calf. No less than 17x (out of 36x) *ʿēgel* depicts the making of a calf-idol. There were two instances of apostasy: Aaron's golden calf (Exod 32), and Jeroboam's golden calf (1 Kgs 12:25-33). Both are severely condemned in the Bible. The authors of the Kgs and the Chron repeatedly condemned this sin (2 Kgs 10:29; 17:16; 2 Chron 11:15; 13:8).

4. The heifer (*ʿeglâ*) was useful for agricultural purposes, such as plowing (e.g., Deut 21:3) and treading the grain on the threshing ground (Hos 10:11). The calves that were not reserved for breeding purposes were used for food (*ABD* 6:1129). They were often castrated to increase fat content. The fattened calf was choice food (1 Sam 28:24), which only the rich could afford (Amos 6:4).

P-B See *bāqār*: P-B.

NT The NT does not use a specific term for calf. It uses a general term *moschos*. The fattened calf (*moschos*) is the appropriate food for celebrating the reunion of the lost son (Luke 15:23, 27, 30). The making of a calf image is expressed with a vb. derived from *moschos* (Acts 7:14).

Herd: → *bāqār* (cows, cattle, # 1330); → *ʿēgel* ([bull-]calf, # 6319); → *par* (bull, # 7228); → *šôr* I (bull, ox, steer, # 8802)

Bibliography
ABD 5:870-86; 6:1129-30; *IBD* 1:254-55; *IDB* 1:543-44, 724; 3:614; *ISBE* 1:623-25, 798; 3:624; *NIDNTT* 1:113-19; 2:410-14; *TDNT* 2:760-62; *TDOT* 2:6-20 (esp. 13-17), 209-16; *TWOT* 1:121, 124-25, 524; F. S. Bodenheimer, *Animal and Man in Bible Lands*, 1960; J. Feliks, *Animal World of the Bible*, 1962; J. Milgrom, "The Paradox of the Red Cow (Num 19)," *VT* 31(1), 1981, 62-72; J. N. Oswalt, "The Golden Calves and the Egyptian Concept of Deity," *EQ* 45:13-20; R. Pinney, *Animals of the Bible*, 1964; S. Wefing, "Beobachtungen zum Ritual mit der roten Kuh (Num 19:1-10a)," *ZAW* 93, 1981, 341-64.

Jeffrey S. Lu

6320 (*'eglâ*, heifer), → # 6319

6322 (*'ªgālâ*, cart), → # 8206

6327	עגם

עגם (*'gm*), q. have pity on, be afflicted, distressed, grieved (hapleg.) (# 6327).

OT The word occurs only in Job 30:25, where Job testifies to his concern for the poor: "Have I not wept (*bkh*) for those in trouble? Has not my soul grieved for the poor?" Job argues that he has been deeply concerned for those who are languishing. He identified (emotionally) with their plight and implies that he has done something about it (cf. 29:12-17; 31:16-23). See J. E. Hartley, *The Book of Job*, NICOT, 1988, 404-5.

P-B *'gm* is attested in postbiblical Heb. and Aram. with the meaning "grieved."

Compassion, comfort, consolation: → *ḥws* (pity, look upon with compassion or regret, # 2571); → *ḥml* (spare, have compassion, # 2798); → *maʿªdannîm* (dainties, comfort, delight, # 5052); → *nḥm* (be sorry, comfort, have compassion, repent, # 5714); → *'gm* (have pity, # 6327); → *rḥm* (love, have compassion, # 8163); → *ta'ªnûg* (comfort, delight, enjoyment, # 9503)
Affliction, oppression: → *dḥq* (oppress, # 1895); → *ḥms* I (do violence, # 2803); → *ḥmṣ* II (oppress, # 2807); → *ynh* (oppress, # 3561); → *lḥṣ* (press, # 4315); → *māṣôr* I (affliction, siege, # 5189); → *mrr* I (be bitter, distraught, afflict, # 5352); → *nega'* (plague, affliction, # 5596); → *ngś* (exact, # 5601); → *'nh* II (afflict, humble, afflict one's soul, fast, oppress, submit, # 6700); → *'wq* I (crush?, # 6421); → *'mr* II (deal tyrannically with, # 6683); → *'šq* I (wrong, # 6943); → *ṣwq* I (constrain, press in/upon, harass, vex, # 7439); → *ṣwr* II (deal tyrannically with, # 7444); → *rhb* (assail, press, pester, alarm, confuse, # 8104); → *rṣṣ* (crush, # 8368); → *tôlāl* (oppressor, # 9354); → *tōk* (oppression, # 9412)

G. M. Butterworth

6328	ענן

ענן (*'gn*), ni. keep o.s. secluded (from marital intercourse) (# 6328).

OT The vb. occurs 1x. The meaning is uncertain but possibly refers to the act of keeping oneself secluded from marital intercourse. In reply to the protestations of Orpah and Ruth, Naomi argued that in their case the law of levirate marriage could not possibly apply. She had no more sons and was unlikely to have any. Therefore it would not make sense to wait and seclude themselves from marital intercourse for this reason (Ruth 1:13).

P-B In Mish. Heb. the vb. is used in the legal situation of bereft women the whereabouts of whose husbands were in doubt. In the Talmud the nom. *ʿᵃgûnâ* refers to a woman who lived retired in her own house without a husband.

Sexual relations: → *'ešek* (testicle, # 863); → *zirmâ* (phallus, emission, # 2444); → *mᵉbûšîm* (genitals, # 4434); → *nablût* (genitals, # 5578); → *nᵉḥōšet* II (menstruation, lust, # 5734); → *ʿgn* (keep oneself secluded, # 6328); → *ʿōnâ* (cohabitation, sexual intercourse, # 6703); → *škb* (lie down, be ravished, be bedded down, # 8886); → *škh* (exhibit strong testicles, to have strong carnal desire, # 8889); → *šopkâ* (fluid duct of male organ, urinary tubule/organ, # 9163); → **Sexual ordinances: Theology**

Jackie A. Naudé

6330 (*ʿad*, to, until), → Particles

6332 (*ʿēd*, witness), → # 6386

6334	עדה

עדה (*ʿdh* I), q. stride; hi. remove (garment) (# 6334).

OT The q. vb., occurring only in Job 28:8, is parallel to the hi. of *drk*, thus requiring the meaning of walking on (the path). Prov 25:20a (if not a dittograph of 19b) attests *ʿdh* as a hi. part. and, in context, suggests the idea of removing clothing. It is difficult to see how the two meanings derive from *ʿdh* I, unless Job 28:8 is to be taken as "pass by, aside," or the like (Toy, *Proverbs*, 467).

Journey, going, marching, walking, wandering: → *'rḥ* (be on the road, wander, # 782); → *'šr* I (walk straight, # 886); → *drk* (tread, march, # 2005); → *hlk* (go, walk, behave, # 2143); → *zḥl* I (slide away, # 2323); → *yṣ'* (go out, come forward, # 3655); → *yrd* (go down, go up, descend, # 3718); → *massaʿ* (setting out, # 5023); → *nḥt* (march down, descend, settle, # 5737); → *s'n* (tramp along, tread, # 6008); → *ʿdh* I (stride, # 6334); → *ʿlh* (go up, ascend, bring up, # 6590); → *pśʿ* I (step forth, march, # 7314); → *ṣʿd* (step, march, # 7575); → *šwr* I (descend, caravan, # 8801)

Eugene H. Merrill

6335	עדה

עדה (*ʿdh* II), q. put on ornaments, adorn o.s./s.o. (# 6335); עֲדִי (*ʿᵃdî*), nom. ornament(s) (# 6344).

ANE Aram. *ʿîdût*, ornament (BDB, 725); Ugar. *ʿdy* (*UT* 1820).

OT 1. *General introduction.* Wearing of jewelry and ornaments was an accepted part of human dress (both male and female). Ornaments were used to decorate sacred appurtenances, such as the ark. When, in the monarchy, class distinctions between rich and poor widened considerably, the prophets proclaimed oracles against wearing of jewelry and ornaments by the ruling rich upper classes, since the wearing of such became a sign of haughtiness, associated among others things with the oppression of the poor and weak.

2. *General interpretation.* Jewelry was a valued possession and included the following: necklace, shell necklace, ring, head decoration/turban, earring, nose/earring, anklet, bracelet, crescent, headband/sun-like ornament, and pearls. A general term used

for jewelry/ornaments is *ʿᵃdî*; the term *kᵉlî*, vessel, is also used of jewelry. The rich could afford the more opulent jewelry, especially those made with gold, silver, and precious stones, which signaled their wealth. Ornaments such as signets could be used to identify personal property. Signets and other precious jewelry signified the authority and position of the one wearing it. Jewelry could also be used to adorn animals, such as camels or horses. It was a prized spoil of warfare taken by victors as a sign of their triumph. Prostitutes adorned themselves with jewelry as part of their allure in attracting customers.

The wearing of jewelry expressed a positive, joyful attitude to life experienced as good. In times of mourning jewelry was inappropriate. Jewelry enhanced human attractiveness, added to the sensual appeal of lovers, and was a part of wedding attire. It could be used as a special gift for someone on a special occasion; it could also be a sign of regal status and office.

Jewelry was used in Israelite worship an atonement offering or as a wave offering to Yahweh. Presumably, such a gift expressed the giver's adoration of Yahweh and symbolized Yahweh's holiness and great value in the eyes of the giver. In the tabernacle, gold rings and filigree settings were used in the carrying staves for the ark (→ # 7778), the altar of burnt offering, and the altar of incense. The ephod and breastpiece of the priest Aaron had gold rings and filigree settings.

During the monarchy, class distinctions between the rich and the poor widened considerably and incensed the prophets, who denounced jewelry as a negative thing, not because it was intrinsically evil but because it had been given a wrong place in life. It had become an ostentatious sign of the rich and powerful, who oppressed the poor and weak. At times it was wrongly used for pagan practices of worship or as a magical amulet to ward off evil.

3. *The OT usually speaks of ornamentation positively*. It signaled a positive and joyful attitude to life rather than one of mourning (cf. Exod 33:4, 5, 6; 2 Sam 1:24; Isa 49:18; Jer 2:32). A faithful people will remember Yahweh just as a "maiden" or "bride" will not forget to wear her "jewelry" (*ʿᵃdî*) and "ornaments" (Jer 2:32). At the eschatological restoration, the nation Israel will be adorned with her children as "ornaments" (*ʿᵃdî*) (Isa 49:18).

(a) Ornamentation is used as a metaphor of positive ethical and spiritual values. A wise man's rebuke is like a gold "earring" (*nezem*) and a gold "ornament" (*ḥᵃlî*) (Prov 25:12). A father's instruction and a mother's teaching are a "chain"/necklace (*ʿᵃnāqîm*) adorning the neck (Prov 1:9). Wisdom and knowledge are valued more than "rubies"/corals (*pᵉnînîm*) (Job 28:18; Prov 3:15; 8:11; 20:15); in Prov 31:10 the object valued is a good wife.

Jerusalem, before becoming unfaithful, is described as a woman who rose to become a queen, a most beautiful "jewel"/ornament (*ʿᵃdî; ʿᵃdāyim*), famous among the nations, because Yahweh had beautified her with fine clothing and jewelry, including "bracelets" (*ṣᵉmîdîm*), "necklace" (*rābîd*), "ring"/nosering (*nezem*), and "earrings" ("round ornaments," *ʿᵃgîlîm*); see Ezek 16:7, 11-12 (cf. Jer 2:32).

(b) Ornamentation enhances, or is a symbol of, the romantic and sensual appeal of lovers. The lover is attracted to his beloved by a "jewel" (*ʿᵃnāq*) of her "necklace" (*ṣawwārôn*) (S of Songs 4:9). The beloved's "graceful legs" are like "jewels"/ornaments (*ḥᵃlāʾîm*) (S of Songs 7:1[2]. The lover sees the beloved's beauty enhanced by "earrings"/pendants (*tōrîm*), "strings of pearls"/necklace of shells (*ḥᵃrûzîm*), and silver studded gold "earrings"/pendants (*tôrê zāhāb*) (S of Songs 1:10-11). It is said of the royal bride at her wedding: "her gown is interwoven with gold" (NIV) or, more literally, "her gown is (made) from gold filigree (*mišbᵉṣôt*)" (Ps 45:13[14]).

(c) Jewelry could be a gift for someone on a special occasion. Abraham's servant, in search of a wife for Isaac, gives a gold "nose ring" (*nezem*) and two gold "bracelets" (*ṣᵉmîdîm*), presumably bridal gifts, to Rebekah (Gen 24:22, 30, 47).

(d) Jewelry could be worn by men. The Midianites/Ishmaelites customarily wore gold "earrings" (*nezem*) (Judg 8:24-26); Midianite kings wore "ornaments"/crescents (*śahᵃrôn*) and "pendants"/earrings (*nᵉṭîpâ*) (8:26). The Amalekite who killed Saul took from him his crown and a "band"/armlet (*'eṣ'ādâ*) from his head (2 Sam 1:10).

Kings wore signet rings, e.g., Pharaoh (Gen 41:42) and Persian kings (Esth 3:10, 12; 8:2, 8, 10), as sign of their official authority and for sealing documents. When Joseph is put in charge of Egypt, Pharaoh placed his "signet ring" (*ṭabba'at*) on Joseph's finger and had him dressed in fine clothes with a gold "chain"/necklace (*rābîd*) for his neck (Gen 41:42).

(e) Ornaments could be used to decorate animals. Gideon removed the "ornaments"/crescents (*śahᵃrōnîm*) and "chains"/necklaces (*'ᵃnāqôt*) from the necks of the camels of the dead Midianite kings, Zebah and Zalmunna, whom he had defeated (Judg 8:21). Horses of Persian royalty were decorated on the head with a royal "crest" (*keter*) (Esth 6:8).

(f) Jewelry was taken as plunder by victorious armies. The plunder taken by the Israelites from the defeated Midianites included "gold earrings" (*nezem/nizmê zāhāb*), "ornaments"/crescents (*śahᵃrōnîm*), "pendants"/earrings (*nᵉṭipôt*), as well as "ornaments"/crescents (*śahᵃrōnîm*) and "chains"/necklaces (*'ᵃnāqôt*) from the necks of camels (Judg 8:21, 24-26).

(g) Jewelry could be presented to Yahweh as an offering, presumably as a sign of his holiness and of the people's adoration of him; he is valued highly and worthy of expensive gifts. When Moses sent the Israelites to defeat the Midianites, they brought to Yahweh as an atonement offering booty of gold, including "armlets"/bracelets (*'eṣ'ādâ*), "bracelets" (*ṣāmîd*), "signet rings" (*ṭabba'at*), "earrings"/round ornaments (*'āgîl*) and "necklaces"/ornaments (of neck or breast) (*kûmāz*) (Num 31:50). Among the objects offered by the Israelites to Yahweh as a wave offering for the tabernacle were "earrings"/rings (*nezem*), "rings"/signet rings (*ṭabba'at*), and "ornaments" (for neck or breast) (*kûmāz*) (Exod 35:22).

Gold "rings" (*ṭabbā'ōt*) were used for carrying the ark (Exod 25:12-15; 37:3, 5), the sacred table (25:26-27; 37:13-14), the altar of burnt offering (27:4, 7; 38:5, 7) the altar of incense (30:4; 37:27), as well as to attach Aaron's breastplate to the ephod (28:23-28; 39:16-17, 19-20).

The two gold "filigree settings" (*mišbᵉṣôt*) (in which onyx stones engraved with "the names of the sons of Israel" were mounted) were worn on the shoulder pieces of Aaron's ephod (Exod 28:11; 39:6). Twelve precious stones, symbolizing the twelve sons of Israel, were mounted on the breastpiece in four rows of three gold "filigree settings" (39:13). Other gold "filigree settings" were used in attaching the breastpiece to the ephod (28:13-14, 25; 39:16-17).

4. *Jewelry is occasionally spoken of negatively (by the prophets).* Ornamentation with "rings"/earrings (*nezem*) and "jewelry"/ornament (*ḥelyâ*) could be a sign of pagan worship (Baalism) and forsaking Yahweh (Hos 2:13[15]).

Ornamentation, with "ornaments jingling" (vb. *'ks*) on the ankles of women, together with ostentatious "finery," including "bangles"/anklets (*'ᵃkāsîm*), "head-bands" (*šᵉbîsîm*), "crescent necklaces"/crescents (*śahᵃrōnîm*), "earrings" (*nᵉṭîpôt*), "bracelets" (*šērôt*), "ankle chains"/anklets (*ṣᵉ'ādôt*), "signet rings" (*ṭabbā'ôt*), and "nose rings" (*nizmê hā'āp*), were worn by men (mostly) and women, who were in positions of social and political power and used their positions to aggrandize themselves (see L. G. Running, *ISBE* 2, 407a). The words are associted with oppression of the poor and with Yahweh's judgment on the nation (Isa 3:16-22, in the context of vv. 11-26).

Oholah (Samaria) and Oholibah (Jerusalem) are metaphorically presented as two sisters, unfaithful wives of Yahweh, who, because of their lusting after foreign alliances and religion, are pictured as prostitutes decked out in fine "jewelry" (*'ᵃdî*) and given "bracelets" (*ṣᵉmîdîm*) by their customers (Ezek 23:40, 42; Jer 4:30 ['*ᵃdî*]). The people of Israel, says Ezekiel, are proud of their beautiful "jewelry" of gold and silver (7:19a); consequently, it was an "unclean thing," causing Israel to "stumble into sin" (v. 19), for they had used it to make pagan idols (7:20).

5. *Jewelry could be used for magical purposes.* R. K. Harrison suggests that the "crescents" (*śahᵃrōnîm*, "ornaments" NIV) of Judg 8:21, 26 and possibly the "ear-rings" (*nezem*) of Exod 32:2 functioned as magical charms/amulets to protect against evil spirits (*ISBE* 1, 119 under "Amulet"). Similarly, I. Ben-Dor suggests the possibility that, since "the 'crescents' [*śahᵃrōnîm*] worn by animals (Judg 8:21) and by human beings (Isa 3:20 [sic, 3:18]) symbolize the moon-deity," these crescents may have amuletic character (*IDB* 1:122; NIV tr. "ornaments" in Judg 8:21 and "crescent necklaces" in Isa 3:18). Ben-Dor also suggests that the ornaments in Isa 3:18-23 and elsewhere in the OT may also be amulets. E. E. Platt has shown that many of the items of jewelry and clothing mentioned in Isa 3:18-23 were worn by men (*AUSS* 17, 1979, 71-84).

NT The NT has essentially the same approach to jewelry/ornamentation as the OT, namely, it is an acceptable part of human dress and is therefore used as a positive symbol. It may, however, be used in wrong ways and be a symptom of a wrong lifestyle.

Precious jewels symbolically express the marvelous nature of the reign of God in the eschaton of the new Jerusalem (Rev 21:11, 18-21). Similarly, the kingdom of God present now is likened to a pearl of great value (Matt 13:45).

Women are advised to dress "modestly," not with excessive and expensive clothes and ornaments; the quality of their lives ("good deeds") and not their outward adornment is what should clothe them (1 Tim 2:9-10).

The "woman sitting on a scarlet beast" (Rev 17:3), is, in prophetic fashion, depicted and implicitly denounced as a "great prostitute" (v. 1), dressed in finery and "glittering with gold, precious stones and pearls" (v. 4).

Jewelry, ornaments: → *ḥᵃlî* I (ornament, jewel, # 2717); → *ḥᵃrûzîm* (necklace of shells, # 3016); → *ṭabba'at* (ring, # 3192); → *kûmāz* (ornament, # 3921); → *mišbᵉṣôt* (settings, # 5401); → *nezem* (ring, # 5690); → *nᵉṭi(î)pâ* (ear-ring, # 5755); → *'āgîl* (ear-ring?, # 6316); → *'dh* II (adorn o.s., # 6335); → *'ks* (jingle, # 6576); → *'nq* (put on as a necklace, # 6735);

→ *p^e nînîm* (corals, pearls, # 7165); → *ṣawwārôn* (necklace, # 7454); → *ṣāmîd* I (bracelet, # 7543); → *ṣ^e ʿādâ* (anklets, # 7577); → *rābîd* (necklace, # 8054); → *śah^a rônîm* (crescents, # 8448); → *šābîs* (ornament, # 8667); → *šēr* I (bracelet, # 9217); → *tôr* (pendant, # 9366)

Bibliography

I. Ben-Dor, "Amulets," *IDB* 1:122; E. A. W. Budge, *Amulets and Superstitions*, 1930; R. G. Bullard, "Stones, Precious," *ISBE* 4:623-30; D. R. Edwards, "Dress and Ornamentation," *ABD* 2:232-38; P. L. Garber and R. W. Funk, "Jewels and Precious Stones," *IDB* 2:898-905; K. R. M. Hyslop, *Western Asiatic Jewelry c. 3000-612 B.C.*, 1971; J. M. Meyers, "Dress and Ornaments," *IDB* 1:869-71; M. S. and J. L. Miller, "Jewelry," *Harper's Encyclopedia of Bible Life*, 1978[3], 55-65; W. M. F. Petrie, *Amulets*, 1914; E. E. Platt, "Jewelry, Ancient Israelite," *ABD* 3:823-34; idem, *AUSS* 17, 71-74, 189-202; L. G. Running, "Garments, IX. Ornaments," *ISBE* 2:406-7; E. D. van Buren, "Amulets in Ancient Babylonia," *Or* 14, 1945, 18-23.

Malcolm J. A. Horsnell

6337	עֵדָה

עֵדָה (*ʿēdâ* I), nom. community, gathering, band, troop(s), swarm, flock, assembly, congregation, herd, family/household (# 6337); < יעד (*yʿd*), appoint (→ # 3585).

ANE Ugar. *ʿdt*, *mʿd*, indicating a gathering of the gods (*WUS*, 1195; *UT* 1816; cf. *UT* # 2037, *WUS* 2215); Sam. *īda*; Mish. Heb., Jew. Aram. *ʿdt*'; Egyp. Aram. *ʿd(t')*; Syr. *ʿedtā*'; cf. Akk. *puḫur-ilī*, an assembly of gods; *puḫru* = assembly; cf. Aram. *k^e ništā*, assembly; Egyp. *sḥwy*, assemblage.

OT 1. The nom. *ʿēdâ* is employed 149x in the OT, 129x in the books of Gen-Num, Josh (source critics find it mostly in P). It is not found in Deut. It evidently comes from the verbal root *yʿd*, determine, decide, ascertain, in the ni., gather together. Levy/Milgrom see its usage mainly in two areas (*TWAT* 5:1081): (a) reference to a general assembly/gathering of the people, the legal/juristic community(ies), and the worshiping community. Its major referent is the religious community; (b) a swarm/hoard of animals, which is transferred to various groups of persons of differing descriptions: mobs, troops, bands, rabble, hordes (cf. *HALAT* 746). The latter classification can involve, however, groups with good characteristics as well. Also, the word refers to gatherings/groups of divine/spiritual/heavenly beings, a usage well attested in other ANE literature.

2. Briefly, the following materials will serve to be illustrative of these general categories in reverse order.

(a) A swarm of bees (*ʿ^a dat d^e bôrîm*) (Judg 14:8) were found in the corpse of a dead lion by Samson (cf. Hos 7:12).

(b) Ps 22:16[17] identifies the *ʿ^a dat m^e rēʿîm* as a mob/band of evil persons seeking the godly man as he suffers. The herd of bulls in Ps 68:30[31] refers to humans, who are probably princes who support the rulers/pharaohs of foreign nations (cf. 86:14, "a group/band of ruthless men," *ʿ^a dat ʿ^a rîṣîm*). In Job 16:7 the nom. refers to Job's close relatives and friends. On the other hand, 1:5 speaks of the congregation of the righteous (*ʿ^a dat ṣaddîqîm*).

(c) The term *ʿēdâ* refers to gatherings of the people in general. Judg 20:1 records the gathering of the whole congregation, all the sons of Israel, *kol b^e nê yiśrāʾēl*, to fight the Benjaminites (cf. Judg 21:10, 13). 1 Kgs 8:5 refers to the gathered community (*'ēdâ*) who were congregated (*y'd*) about Solomon. The community was often summoned by trumpets for travel in the desert (*miqrā' hā'ēdâ*, Num 10:2).

(d) Several terms employing the root *'ᵃdat* are used to describe Israel in various settings. The *'ᵃdat yiśrā'el* can be a worshiping community, as at Passover (Exod 12:3), or a congregation under a curse (Josh 22:20). The *'ᵃdat bᵉnê yiśrā'ēl* can be a travel procession (Exod 16:1) or part of all of Israel gathered for civil war (Josh 22:12). The congregation/assembly (*hā'ēdâ*, Lev 8:4) or the whole assembly (*kōl-hā'ēdâ*, 8:3) refers to the worshiping community or the group as a court of law (Josh 20:9) or simply the group in a secular setting (9:21). So, no inherently theological meaning is intrinsic to its meaning, except as based on its usage.

Exod 12:6; Num 14:5 feature what may be termed pleonastic uses of *qāhāl/'edâ: qᵉhal 'ᵃdat (bᵉnê) yiśrā'ēl*, the people of the community of Israel.

Several words used with *'ēdâ* indicate that there were persons standing at the head of the *'ēdâ/qāhāl*, assembly: the king (1 Kgs 8:5), princes/nobles/leaders (*nᵉśî'îm*, Exod 16:22; 34:31; elders (*ziqnê hā'ēdâ*, Lev 4:15; Judg 21:16); officials of the community (*qᵉrî'îm*, Num 1:16; 26:9). Those enrolled in the community were designated as *pᵉqûdê hā'ēdâ* (Exod 38:25).

3. The difference between *qāhāl* and *'ēdâ* is hard to note. *'ēdâ* means largely those Israelites gathered together for a specific goal (cf. vb. *y'd*, appoint, determine); *qāhāl* came to mean all Israel gathered by God as his special people. But it also appears that this generalization proposed by Farrer (*NBD*², 226), is far too sweeping. His statement that the LXX translates *'ēdâ* by *ekklēsia* also appears to be incorrect. The vb. *qhl* is used to designate the calling of both the *'ēdâ* and the *qāhāl*. The terms are *nearly* synonymous. *'ēdâ* stands parallel with *sôd* in Ps 111:1 (cf. Gen 49:6, where *qhl* parallels *sôd*). *sôd* indicates a group among whom decisions/plans are created and confirmed.

Assemblies of divine beings were referred to in Israel and outside of Israel in the ANE. Ps 82:1 speaks of God having taken his place in the assembly of God/the divine assembly (*ba'ᵃdat-'ēl*; cf. NIV, "the great assembly," taking *'ēl* as a superlative adj.). And the peoples of the earth are referred to as the "assembled peoples" (Ps 7:7[8], *'ᵃdat lᵉ'ummîm*) whom Yahweh will judge (7:8[9]).

P-B The LXX translated the word mostly with *synagōgē* (132x), gathering, assembly; *episystasis* (11x), gathering, tumult, riotous meeting; and *plēthos* (4x), crowd, throng, the mass. Significantly, it is never rendered with *ekklēsia* (cf. NT). *qāhāl* is so translated 68x and with *synagōgē* (36x) (see entry on *qhl*). It has been cogently argued that *'ēdâ/qāhāl* are the forerunners of the NT *synagōgē/ekklēsia* respectively, although this conclusion is currently challenged (cf. *TDNT* 3:528-32, 802-6). Backgrounds for the NT terms have been found in Hellenistic Jewish Christianity and the intertestamental period (cf. *TWAT* 6:1222).

In LH the word meant assembly, congregation, court, or even a gathering for prayer. An assembly capable of rendering judgments had to consist of ten persons (Sanhedrin 1:6; see Jastrow 2:1043). In Sir 4:7; 7:7; 42:11; 44:15, the "assembly" (*'ēdâ*) of the wicked (*rᵉšā'îm*), of the public (*š'r*), and of the people (*'am*) are found, closely reflecting OT usage.

In the DSS *'ēdâ* occurs ca. 100x. It has its OT meanings, but in the earlier scrolls also depicts the Qumran group as the "holy community" (CD 20:2; 1QS 5:20). It is later replaced by *yaḥad*, community. It is used to designate the community as both an earthly or a heavenly assembly (1QM 1:10; 4:9). In the scrolls it can even reflect various hostile groups (11QM 15:9; 1QH 2:22). Through the addition of suffixes the *'ēdâ* can be related to various persons (1QSb 3:3, e.g., the high priest). It describes the congregation of the chosen (4QpIsa[d]).

NT The NT uses of *synagōgē/ekklēsia* are noted above (see comments to LXX above). *Synagōgē,* meaning synagogue, Jewish house of worship, legal assembly (cf. Matt 10:17), assembly, or worship meeting, may have OT *'ēdâ* as its OT forerunner (LXX = *synagōgē*). *Ekklēsia* refers to the church or a congregation; an assembly for religious, political, and other groups (even unofficial) may have *qāhāl* (LXX = *ekklēsia, synagōgē*) as its forerunner. The NT use of *ekklēsia* probably indicates the church's desire to distance itself from the synagogue of the Jews (*THAT* 1:746).

Congregation, community, society: → *gēw* II (community, society, # 1569); → *yḥd* (join, # 3479); → *y'd* (determine, designate, appoint, assemble, # 3585); → *s^egullâ* (property, treasured possession, # 6035); → *'ēdâ* I (community, gathering, band, # 6337); → *qhl* (assemble, summon, # 7735)

BIBLIOGRAPHY
*IDB 1:*669-70; *NIDNTT* 1:270-73, 291-93, 295-304, 306; *TDNT* 3:487-536; *THAT* 1:742-48; *TWOT* 1:388; G. W. Anderson, "Israel: Amphictyony: *'am; ḳāhāl; 'ēdah,*" *FS H. G. May,* 1970, 135-51; H. Cazelles, "Élans, état monarchique et tribus," *Understanding Poets and Prophets: Essays in Honour of George Wishart,* JSOTSup 152, 1993, 77-92; N. A. Dahl, *Das Volk Gottes,* 1941, 61-76; G. Evans, "Ancient Mesopotamian Assemblies," *TAOS,* 78, 1958, 1-11, 114-15; H. J. Fabry, "Studien zur Ekklesiologie des AT und der Qumrangemeinde," Diss., Bonn. 1979, 200-212; L. E. Frizzell, "The People of God: A Study of the Relevant Concepts in the Qumran Scrolls," Diss., Oxford, 1974, esp. 223-26; R. Gordis, "Democratic Origins in Ancient Israel—The Biblical *'edâ,*" *A. Marx Jubilee Vol.*, 1949, 369-88; H. W. Hertzberg, *Werdende Kirche im AT,* 1950; S. N. Kramer, "'Vox Populi' and the Sumerian Literary Documents," *RA* 58, 1964, 149-56; J. Milgrom, "Priestly Terminology and the Political and Social Structure of Pre-Monarchic Israel," *JQR* 69, 1979, 65-81; L. Rost, *Die Vorstufen von Kirche and Synagogue im Alten Testament,* BWANT 4/24, 1938, 2:1967; J. M. Shaw, "The Concept of the 'People of God' in Recent Biblical Research," Diss. Princeton Theol. Sem., 1958; M. Weinfeld, "Congregation," *EJ* 3:893-96; W. P. Wood, "The Congregation of Yahweh: A Study of the Theology and Purpose of the Priestly Document," Diss. of Union Theol. Sem., Virginia, 1974.

Eugene Carpenter

6338 (*'ēdâ* II, witness), → # 6386

6340 (*'iddâ*, menstrual period), → # 1864

6343	עֵדוּת

עֵדוּת (*'ēdût*), nom. statutes, stipulations, warning sign, reminder (# 6343); < עוד (*'wd* II), encircle, call to witness (→ # 6386).

ANE Sam. *īdot*.

OT 1. The nom. occurs 46x in OT, most frequently in the Ps (15x, 9x in Ps 119), Exod (20x), and Num (11x). It often refers to nonspecified laws or commands from God to his people, particularly in Psalms (e.g., 19:7[8]; 119:14, 88, 129, 157; cf. 1 Kgs 2:3; 2 Kgs 23:3; 1 Chron 29:19; 2 Chron 34:31; Neh 9:34; Jer 44:23). It also refers to the law given during the exodus generation in Ps 78:5 and to the Passover in 81:5[6]. Although the meaning is not entirely clear, the use of *'ēdût* in the superscripts to Ps 60 [60:1] and 80 [80:1] seems to refer to the covenant. Throughout Exod, Lev, and Num, it is used in combination with ark (*'ᵃrôn*), tent (*'ōhel*), and tabernacle (*miškān*), and is variously translated "ark of the Testimony" (NIV), "ark of the covenant" (NRSV), etc. D. Hillers has made a good case for translating the nom. as "covenant" or "part" rather than "testimony" (*Covenant: A History of a Biblical Idea*, 1969, 160-68). In the context of the Sinai narratives, Hillers argues, *bᵉrît* (→ # 1382) pertains to "oaths that bind God alone," whereas *'ēdût* lays "the yoke of obligation on Israel," i.e., the Israelites have an obligation to maintain the covenant stipulations.

2. In several places, *'ēdût* alone is used to refer to the ark (e.g., Exod 16:34; 27:21; 30:36). Elsewhere it refers to the two tablets that are to be placed in the ark (25:21; 40:20).

P-B The LXX consistently translates *'ēdût* as *martyrion*, witness (S. H. Blank, "The LXX Renderings of Old Testament Terms for Law," *HUCA* 7, 1930, 280).

Law of God: → *ḥōq* (portion, obligation, boundary, law, order, # 2976); → *miṣwâ* (command, commandment, # 5184); → *mišpāṭ* (judgment, decision, legal case, legal claim, # 5477); → *'ēdût* (statutes, stipulations, warning sign, reminder, # 6343); → *piqqûdîm* (directions, order, # 7218); for *tôrâ* (direction, instruction, law, the law, # 9368); → **Decalogue: Theology**; → **Ethics: Theology**; → **Law of God: Theology**

Bibliography

TDNT 4:474-508; *THAT* 2:209-21; *TWOT* 2:649-50.

Peter Enns

6344 (*'ᵃdî*, ornament), → # 6335

6349 (*'ādîn*, given to pleasure), → # 6357

6357	עדן

עדן (*'dn*), pi. delight; hitp. luxuriate, revel (# 6357); מַעֲדַנִּים (*maᵃdannîm*), nom. dainties, comfort, delight (# 5052); עָדִין (*'ādîn*), adj. given to pleasure (# 6349); עֵדֶן (*'ēden* I), nom. luxury, dainty, delight (# 6358); עֵדֶן (*'ēden* II), Eden (→ # 6359); עֶדְנָה (*'ednâ*), nom. delight (# 6366).

ANE The vb. is used only in the hitp. stem in the OT, but it is attested in postbiblical Heb. in the pi. stem. Thus, it is regarded by some as a denominative derived from the nom. *'ēden* I (# 6358 below). The vb. is also attested in Syr. *'aden*. Words derived from this vb. are attested in Arab. *ǵadan*, languor, Palm. *'dn'*, good fortune, in postbiblical Heb. *'îdûn*, luxuriousness, and Ugar. *'dn*, delicacies.

OT 1. The vb. is used once in the hitp. in the OT. In the days of Nehemiah, when the Israelites stood to praise God and to confess their sins, they rehearsed how God gave them possession of their land: "They ate to the full and were well-nourished; they reveled (*ht'dn*) in your great goodness" (Neh 9:25).

2. *'ēden* I, nom. luxury, dainty, delight (# 6358). This nom. is used 3x in the OT. It may refer to fine clothes: In David's lament over the death of King Saul and Jonathan, he said, "O daughters of Israel, weep for Saul, who clothed you in scarlet and finery (*'ēden*), who adorned your garments with ornaments of gold" (2 Sam 1:24). It may refer to fine food: in Jeremiah's lament over the downfall of Jerusalem, he said, "Nebuchadnezzar king of Babylon has devoured us, he has thrown us into confusion, he has made us an empty jar. Like a serpent he has swallowed us and filled his stomach with our delicacies (*'ēden*), and then has spewed us out" (Jer 51:34). It may refer to pleasurable delights: the psalmist praised God for his goodness to humankind, "You gave them drink from your rivers of delights (*'ēden*)" (Ps 36:8[9]).

3. *'ednâ*, nom. delight, pleasure (# 6366). This nom. occurs only once in the OT. When Sarah heard the Lord promise Abraham that she would bear a son, she laughed to herself as she thought, "After I am worn out and my master is old, will I now have this [conjugal] pleasure?" (Gen 18:12).

4. *'ādîn*, adj. given to pleasure (# 6349). This adj. occurs only once in the OT and is used as a subst. In Isaiah's oracle against Babylon, he addressed the personified city, "Now then, listen, you wanton creature (*'ādîn*), lounging in your security and saying to yourself, 'I am, and there is none besides me. I will never be a widow or suffer loss of children'" (Isa 47:8).

5. *ma'ᵃdannîm*, nom. dainties, comfort, delight (# 5052). This nom. occurs 3x in the OT, only in poetry. It refers to fine food, delicacies. In blessing Asher, Jacob said, "Asher's food will be rich; he will provide delicacies (*ma'ᵃdannîm*) fit for a king" (Gen 49:20); in lamenting the suffering of the nobles of Jerusalem, Jeremiah spoke of them as "those who once ate delicacies" (*ma'ᵃdannîm*) (Lam 4:5); and Solomon praised a good son, saying, "Discipline your son, and he will give you peace; he will bring delight (*ma'ᵃdannîm*) to your soul" (Prov 29:17).

P-B In Mish. Heb. the vb. occurs in the pi. stem, meaning to smooth, make tender, make delicate, to refresh, invigorate. In the hitp. stem it means to luxuriate, indulge in luxury. The nom. occurs in the QL.

Delight, enjoyment, pampering: → *'dn* (delight, luxuriate, revel, # 6357); → *'ng* (delight oneself, # 6695); → *pnq* (pamper o.s, pamper, # 7167); → *ṣhq* (laugh, play, insult, # 7464); → *š''* II (play, take delight in, # 9130)

Desire, coveting, craving, delight, happiness, longing, pleasure: → *'ᵃrešet* (desire, request, # 830); → *ḥmd* (desire, crave, long for, covet, treasure, # 2773); → *ḥpṣ* I (want, desire, wish, care, # 2911); → *ḥšq* (desire, longing, lust, # 3137); → *y'b* (long for, yearn, desire, # 3277); → *kāleh* (longing, # 3985); → *kmh* (long after, lust for, # 4014); → *ksp* II (desire, long after, # 4083); → *môrāš* II (wish, desire, # 4626); → *'rg* (long after, pant after, # 6864); → *š'l* (ask, request, wish, # 8626); → *t'b* I (desire, long after, # 9289); → *tᵉšûqâ* (desire, longing, appetite, # 9592)

Bibliography

TWOT 1:646-47; M. Dahood, *Psalms I*, AB, 222; S. R. Driver, *Notes on the Hebrew Text and the Topography of the Books of Samuel*, 1912, 238; P. K. McCarter, Jr., *II Samuel*, AB, 72-73.

James D. Price

6358 (*'ēden* I, luxury, dainty, delight), → # 6357

6359	עֵדֶן

עֵדֶן (*'ēden* II), גַּן עֵדֶן (*gan 'ēden*), nom. Eden, garden of Eden (# 6359); < עדן (*'dn* I, delight, luxuriate, → # 6357).

ANE A derivation from the Sumerian/Akk. EDIN/*edinu*, steppe, is less likely (*HALAT*). The nearest (and oldest) etymology is the Aram. *'dn,* which occurs in the ninth century BC Tell Fekheriye inscription (*m'dn*), meaning abundance (F. C. Fensham, *JNSL* 15, 1989, 89). This is related to the Heb. vb. *'dn* I and nom. *'ēden* I (luxuriate, delight). In Ugar. the geographical name *'dn* occurs (*RSP* 2:307).

OT 1. *gan 'ēden*, Garden of Eden, specifies the garden in Gen 2-3. In 2:8 the garden is located *in* Eden (*b*^{e}*'ēden*); also in Ezek 28:13, where it is further specified as the garden of God (→ *gan,* # 1703), but in v. 10 the river of the garden flows *from* Eden (*mē'ēden*). The difference in the use of the prepositions (*b*^{e} = "in" and *min* = "from") may indicate that Eden refers to the general location or region in which the garden was situated. There has been much speculation on the location of the Garden of Eden (*ISBE* 2:16-17), but the meaning (quality) is of greater importance. "Eden" may be related to the Heb. vb. *'dn* I and nom. *'ēden* I (luxuriate, delight) as in the LXX. Humanity was placed by God in the Garden of Eden to take care of it (2:15). After the episode described in Gen 3, they are banished and have to work the soil (3:23). Paradise is lost (Milton), guarded by the cherubim on the east side of Eden (v. 24). The term is also used metaphorically in Ezek 36:35 and Joel 2:3. Ezekiel promises that the wasted land will be like the Garden of Eden. Joel has it in the reverse meaning when describing the Day of the Lord.

2. In Ezek 31:9 ("in the garden of God," [→ *gan,* # 1703]), 16, 18 are "the trees of Eden" (*'*^{a}*ṣē-'ēden*), a ch. comparing Egypt to a garden.

3. Eden is mostly used in relation to the garden, but Eden alone is used in Gen 2:8, 10. Cain sojourned in a land east of Eden (Gen 4:16).

4. Eden is identified with the garden of God (Ezek 28:13) or stands in parallelism to the garden of Yahweh (Isa 51:3), the latter describing the restoration of Zion, when the deserts will be like Eden.

P-B LXX transliterates the Heb. *'ēden* as *edem* and translates *gan 'ēden* with *paradeisos tryphēs*, "garden of pleasure." In Sir 40:27 the fear of the Lord is like a blessed *'ēden* (G *paradeisos eulogias* = fruitful garden, cf. v. 17). The Qumran text 1QH 6:16 compares the righteous with a tree watered by the rivers of Eden (reminiscent of Ps 1:3).

Garden, orchard: → *gan/gannâ* (garden, orchard, # 1703/1708); → *karmel* I (orchard, # 4149); → *[gan] 'ēden* II ([garden of] Eden, # 6359); → *'*^{a}*rûgâ* (garden bed, terrace, # 6870); → *pardēs* (park, forest, # 7236)

BIBLIOGRAPHY

ISBE 2:399-400; *TWAT* 6:1093-1103; *TWOT* 2:646-47; *ZPEB* 2:199-201; I. Cornelius, "Paradise motifs in the 'Eschatology' of the Minor Prophets and the Iconography of the ANE," *JNSL* 14,

1988, 41-83; H. N. Wallace, *The Eden Narrative*, 1985, 70-89; C. Westermann, *BKAT* I/1, 284-87.

I. Cornelius

6366 (*'ednâ,* delight), → # 6357

6371	עדר

עדר (*'dr* I), ni. be weeded (# 6371); nom. מַעְדֵּר (*ma'dēr*), hoe (# 5053).

OT The activity of weeding kept a land from being overgrown. An uncultivated field was only suitable for shepherding, "As for all the hills once cultivated (*'dr*) by the hoe (*ma'dēr*), you will no longer go there for fear of the briers and thorns; they will become places where cattle are turned loose and where sheep run" (Isa 7:25, cf. 5:6; see Dalman, *AuSP*, 2:328). In these texts Isaiah uses the vb. negatively to describe the Promised Land under the curse because of Israel's failure to keep the covenant stipulations.

Agriculture—implements: → *ḥārîṣ* II (hoe?, # 3044); → *migrāp* (shovel?, # 4493); → *ma'dēr* (hoe, # 5053)

Mark D. Futato

6372	עדר

עדר (*'dr* III), ni. be missing, lacking; pi. cause to lack (# 6372).

ANE The root is attested elsewhere only in Arab.

OT The vb. is confined in the Bible to the poetry of two prophets (Isa 34:16; 40:26; 59:15; Zeph 3:5) and the narratives of Sam-Kgs (1 Sam 30:19; 2 Sam 17:22; 1 Kgs 4:27[5:7]). The lack in view is typically a few objects from among a large quantity of similar objects that together comprise a totality (1 Sam 30:19; 2 Sam 17:22; 1 Kgs 4:27[5:7]; Isa 34:16; 40:26). In this regard it differs from *ḥsr*, the most common Heb. root for "lack," which more frequently identifies the complete deprivation of the object(s) in view. In nearly every biblical passage except Isa 59:15, the vb. is preceded by the negative particle *lō'*, not.

Lack, need, want: → *ḥsr* (diminish, decrease, lack, deprive, # 2893); → *ḥpṣ* I (want, desire, wish, care, # 2911); → *'dr* III (be missing, lacking, # 6372); → *ṣōrek* (need, # 7664)

Sam Meier

6373 (*'ēder* I, herd), → # 7366

6380	עוב

עוב (*'wb*), hi. cover with a cloud (# 6380); nom. עָב (*'āb* II), cloud (# 6265).

ANE The root *'wb*/*'yb* is represented in several cognates with the meaning "darken" or "cloud" (*HALAT* 730; *THAT* 5:978-79).

OT 1. The verbal form occurs only in Lam 2:1, "How the Lord has covered the Daughter of Zion with the cloud of his anger!" The alternative rendering of *'wb* by "deal with contempt" is possible (S. Bergler, "Threni V," *VT* 27, 1977, 316), and is reflected in the NIV marginal note: "How the Lord in his anger has treated the Daughter of Zion with contempt!"

2. The nom. *'āb* occurs 30x, thirteen of which are straightforward references to rain clouds (e.g., Judg 5:4; 1 Kgs 18:45; Ps 77:17[18]). Often such texts stress God's sovereignty over the clouds in demonstration of the wonder and wisdom of his creative power. "Do you know how the clouds hang poised, those wonders of him who is perfect in knowledge?" (Job 37:16). This sovereignty over the clouds demonstrates particularly God's power in blessing and in cursing. On the one hand, God is the giver of rain that makes life on earth possible: "He covers the sky with clouds (*'āb*); he supplies the earth with rain and makes grass grow on the hills" (Ps 147:8). On the other hand, when he withholds rain, the earth becomes desolate: "I will make it a wasteland, neither pruned nor cultivated, and briers and thorns will grow there. I will command the clouds (*'āb*) not to rain on it" (Isa 5:6).

3. In Job *'āb* occurs 8x. Job's friends refer to the clouds as an object lesson in their common condemnation of Job. Zophar argues that though the pride of the wicked may reach the clouds, they will be brought down (Job 20:6). Eliphaz cites the wicked as believing that God does not see what happens on earth: "Thick clouds (*'āb*) veil him, so he does not see us as he goes about in the vaulted heavens" (22:14). Elihu argues that God's power in nature (37:11) is beyond human comprehension (36:29) and, particularly, beyond Job's ability to understand (37:16).

Job agrees with his friends that God's power in creation is awesome: "He wraps up the waters in his clouds, yet the clouds do not burst under their weight" (26:8). Further, he laments his alienation from the God whose ways he cannot fathom: "Terrors overwhelm me; my dignity is driven away as by the wind, my safety vanishes like a cloud" (30:15). By a series of questions, God challenges Job, as well as his friends, to look to him alone for wisdom: "Do you know the laws of the heavens? Can you set up God's dominion over the earth? Can you raise your voice to the clouds (*'āb*) and cover yourself with a flood of water?" (38:33-34). (→ Job: Theology)

4. *'āb* occurs in figures of speech to denote transitoriness (Job 30:15), pride (20:6), favor (Prov 16:15), and speed (Isa 60:8, see the comment on 16:8 by Oswalt, *Isaiah*, 362, also n. 16).

5. *'āb* pertains to concealment or theophany 8x. In Job 22:14 the *'ābîm* hide God from human vision. The occurrences of *'āb* in the context of theophany are of interest, such as the theophany at Mount Sinai (Exod 19:9). (→ Theophany: Theology)

As a vehicle of revelation the *'ābîm* provide transportation in Ps 104:3 and Isa 19:1 (cf. Futato, 16-17). For texts using related vocabulary for the motif of God riding on clouds, etc., cf. Deut 33:26, where God rides on the "heavens" (*šāmayim*) and on the "clouds" (*š^{e}ḥāqîm*); 2 Sam 22:11 ‖ Ps 18:10[9], where God rides on the "cherub" (*k^{e}rûb*) and the "wings of the wind" (*kan^{e}pê rûaḥ*); and Ps 68:4[5], 33[34], where God rides on the "clouds" (*'^{a}rābôt*) and the "ancient skies above" (*š^{e}mê š^{e}mê qedem*), respectively; see Fitzgerald, 267-69. For Baal as the "rider of the clouds" (*rkb 'rpt*) in Ugar. literature, see *UT* 51 III 11; 51 V 122; 67 II 7.

God's theophanic presence in or on the *'ābîm* may bring judgment (Isa 19:1) or salvation (2 Sam 22:12 ‖ Ps 18:12[13]). The psalmist imagines how all of creation is at God's command as he comes to deliver his people and to judge the adversaries: "The clouds poured down water, the skies resounded with thunder; your arrows flashed back and forth. Your thunder was heard in the whirlwind, your lightning lit up the world; the earth trembled and quaked" (Ps 77:17-18[18-19]).

Cloud: → *ḥāzîz* (cloud, strong wind, thunderclap, # 2613); → *miplāś* (spreading [of a cloud], # 5146); → *'wb* (cover w. cloud, # 6380); → *'ānān* (clouds, # 6727); → *'ᵃrāpel* (deep darkness, thick darkness, heavy cloud, # 6906); → *šaḥaq* (dust, clouds of dust, # 8836)
Heaven: → *'ᵃguddâ* (firmament, sprinkling brush, # 99); → *rāqîa'* (firmament, plate, # 8385); → *šaḥaq* (clouds of dust, # 8836); → *šāmayim* (heaven, sky, air, # 9028)
Thunder: → *hēd* (thunderclap?, # 2059); → *ḥāzîz* (cloud, strong wind, thunderclap, # 2613); → *qôl* (voice, sound, thunder, cry, # 7754); → *r'm* I (storm, thunder, # 8306)

BIBLIOGRAPHY
TWAT 5:978-82; G. Dalman, *Arbeit und Sitte*, 1928-42, repr. 1987, 1:103-14; A. Fitzgerald, "The Lord of the East Wind," diss. Pontifical Biblical Institute, 1983; M. Futato, "Meteorological Analysis," diss. The Catholic University of America, 1984; J. Luzarraga, *Las Tradiciones de la Nube en la Biblia y en el Judaismo Primitivo*, AnBibl 54, 1973, 15-41; G. E. Mendenhall, *The Tenth Generation: The Origins of the Biblical Tradition*, 1973, 32-66; P. Reymond, *L'eau, sa vie, et sa signification dans l'AT*, 1958, 11-18, 29-31, 35-41; P. Sabourin, "The Biblical Cloud: Terminology and Tradition," *BTB* 4, 1974, 290-312; R. Scott, "Meteorological Phenomena," *ZAW* 64, 1952, 11-25; E. F. Sutcliffe, "The Clouds as Water-Carriers in Hebrew Thought," *VT* 3, 1953, 99-103.

Mark D. Futato

6383 (*'wg*, bake), → Baking

6384 (*'ôg*, Og), → Og

6385	עוּגָב

עוּגָב (*'ûgāb*), uncertain: (vertical) flute(?); harp(?) (4x; *HALAT* 751a; # 6385).

ANE The word is attested in the Sam. Pent. *wāgåb* (with *waw* copulative); Arab. *ğa'bat*, quiver, tube, pipe.

OT Tg. always translates Heb. *'ûgāb* as *'abbûbâ*, reed-pipe, flute; Vg. always as *organon*, panpipe. The LXX and Pesh. translations view the instrument as either stringed (*kithara/kinārā'* in Gen 4:21; *psalmos/mēnē'* in Job 21:12; *psalmos/zᵉmārā'* in Job 30:31), or of the winds (*organon*, [pan]pipe/*ḥalyatā'*, flute in Ps 150:4). Most scholars have inferred that *'ûgāb* designates the (vertical) flute. Bayer finds here the term for "harp" (*EJ* 12, col. 565; *BARev* 8/1, 33). The pairing in Ps 150:4 of *minnîm*, strings, and *'ûgāb* (cf. *nēbel*, [large] lyre/harp, and *kinnôr*, [small] lyre, in 150:3) may support the view that *'ûgāb* signifies a stringed instrument, but such pairing may indicate no more than simultaneous performance (cf. *tôp*, frame-drum, and *māḥôl*, dancing in 150:4). Since the *kinnôr* and *'ûgāb* are mentioned in the primordial saga (Gen 4:21), one could infer that they were considered archetypal instruments. However, their mention together may alternatively serve as a syntheton for all (stringed?) musical instruments.

P-B Parallelism between *'ûgāb* and *kinnôr* in Ps 151:2[4] (11QPsᵃDavComp, *DJD* 4:49) offers no certainty that the author of this work considered these instruments as two forms of the harp/lyre (so NRSV) or as different types of instrument (so LXX, where they are translated as *organon*, [pan]pipe, and *psaltērion*, psaltery, respectively).

Musical instruments/terms: → *gittît* (musical instrument?, # 1787); → *hemyâ* (sound, din, # 2166); → *ḥll* (make the pipe played, # 2727); → *ḥṣṣr* (make the trumpet sound, # 2955); → *yôbēl* (ram, # 3413); → *kinnôr* (lyre, # 4036); → *mēn* (string, # 4944); → *m^ena'an'îm* (rattle, # 4983); → *nēbel* II (unstringed instrument, # 5575); → *ngn* (play the lyre, # 5594); → *'ûgāb* (flute?, # 6385); → *prṭ* (improvise, # 7260); → *ṣll* I (ring, quiver, # 7509); → *šôpār* (ram's horn, # 8795); → *šālîš* II (musical instrument, # 8956); → *šema'* I (sound, # 9049); → *tpp* (drum, beat, # 9528); → *tq'* (drive, thrust, clap one's hands, blow trumpet, pledge, # 9546)

BIBLIOGRAPHY

B. Bayer, "The Finds That Could Not Be," *BARev* 8/1, 1982, 33; idem, "Music: History: Biblical Period, Second Temple Period," *EJ* 12, col. 565; S. B. Finesinger, "Musical Instruments in OT," *HUCA* 3, 1926, 52-53; D. A. Foxvog and A. D. Kilmer, "Music," *ISBE* 3:443b; E. Gerson-Kiwi, "Musique (dans la Bible)," *DBSup* 5, 1957, cols. 1428-29; P. Grelot, "L'orchestre de Daniel iii 5, 7, 10, 15," *VT* 29, 1979, 26; H. Gressmann, *Musik und Musikinstrumente im AT*, 1903, 28-29; O. Keel, *The Symbolism of the Biblical World*, tr. T. J. Hallett, 1985, s.v. "Music and Song," 340b, 344b-45a, Fig. 462; E. Kolari, *Musikinstrumente und ihre Verwendung im AT*, 1947, 36-39; J. D. Prince, "Music," *EncBib* 3, cols. 3229-30; C. Sachs, *The History of Musical Instruments*, 1940, 106; O. R. Sellers, "Musical Instruments of Israel," *BA* 4, 1941, 40-41, Fig. 8b; D. G. Stradling and K. A. Kitchen, "Music and Musical Instruments," *IBD* 2:1032, 1038; E. Werner, "Musical Instruments," *IDB* 3:471b.

Robert H. O'Connell

6386	עוד

עוד (*'wd*), pi. surround, encircle; po./hitpol. help; hi./ho. warn, admonish, call to witness (# 6386), a denom. vb. from עֵד (*'ēd*), nom. witness (# 6332); עֵדָה (*'ēdâ* II), nom. witness (# 6338); תְּעוּדָה (*t^e'ûdâ*), nom. attestation, testimony (# 9496).

ANE Ugar. *'d* (possibly in personal names, Gordon, *UT*, # 1817) and *t'dt* (Gordon, *UT*, # 1832); Inscriptional Heb. *'d*, *'wd* (*DNWSI*, 825, 831).

OT 1. The vb. sometimes means warn, give assurance (Gen 43:3; Exod 21:29; 1 Kgs 2:42; Neh 13:15, 21). Used in this sense it occasionally refers to prophetic warnings. At Sinai Yahweh told Moses to warn the people about the consequences of getting too close to the holy mountain (Exod 19:21). In his capacity as prophetic covenant mediator Moses warned Israel that rejection of Yahweh would result in destruction (Deut 8:19). Yahweh instructed Samuel to warn Israel solemnly (note the emphatic infinitive absolute preceding the finite verbal form) about the consequences of having a king like all the nations (1 Sam 8:9). Jeremiah lamented that no one would listen to his warnings of judgment because Yahweh's word was "offensive" to the people of Judah (Jer 6:10). The Levitical prayer recorded in Neh 9 recalls that Israel rejected the prophets' warnings and exhortations to repent (vv. 26, 29-30). Zech 3:6 uses the vb. of the angel's assuring promise to Joshua that he would be allowed to serve in the rebuilt temple if he was obedient to Yahweh's word (see v. 7).

2. In several passages the vb. means to command, prohibit, usually in a covenantal context. At Sinai Yahweh commanded Moses to "put limits around the

mountain and set it apart as holy" (Exod 19:23). In his final speech to Israel Moses urged the people to observe carefully the covenant regulations he had commanded (Deut 32:46). Later prophets commanded Israel to "turn from [their] evil ways [and] observe" the covenant stipulations (2 Kgs 17:13), but the people consistently rejected Yahweh's commandments (17:15; cf. Neh 9:34). Ps 81:8-9[9-10] recalls that Yahweh prohibited his people from serving other gods, while Jer 11:7 encapsulates Yahweh's covenantal demands under the basic command, "Obey me." (The vb. *'wd* appears 3x in this verse, which we might translate as follows: "I solemnly commanded [infinitive absolute + perfect] your fathers when I brought them out of Egypt, and to this day I have continually commanded [infinitive absolute] them, saying: 'Obey me'".)

3. At times the vb. carries the sense testify against, accuse (see 1 Kgs 21:10, 13) in a legal or covenantal setting. In theological contexts Yahweh's prophets sometimes function as his witnesses who testify and/or accuse. During the reign of King Joash of Judah, prophets testified on Yahweh's behalf against his sinful people (2 Chron 24:19). Yahweh commissioned Amos to testify against Israel (Amos 3:13). The prophet's "testimony" took the form of a judgment announcement laced with accusatory elements (see vv. 14-15). Jeremiah testified against the remnant of Judah, pointing out that they had "made a fatal mistake" when they flippantly claimed they would obey Yahweh (Jer 42:19-20). A few days before, following the murder of the governor Gedaliah, this remnant urged Jeremiah to find out if Yahweh wanted them to stay in Judah or flee to Egypt, and assured him that they would do whatever Yahweh said (vv. 2-3). When Jeremiah agreed (v. 4), the people solemnly called on Yahweh to be a legal accuser or witness against (the related nom. *'ēd* is used) them if they did not obey Yahweh's instructions in the matter (vv. 5-6). However, when Jeremiah told them Yahweh wanted them to stay in Judah, they rejected his word and insisted on going to Egypt.

In the role of a legal or covenantal witness, Yahweh himself sometimes appears as the subject of the vb. In the covenantal lawsuit recorded in Ps 50 he accuses (v. 7) his people of hypocrisy and covenantal violations (vv. 8-21). In Mal 2:14 he testifies against husbands who have divorced their wives and denounces them for their breach of promise (vv. 15-16).

4. The vb. can also have the nuance of adjure, formally designate as a legal witness. Moses adjured the heavens and earth as witnesses (Deut 4:26; 30:19; 31:28) that the people had agreed to keep Yahweh's covenant and to subject themselves to its curses (or judgments) in the case of disobedience. The appeal to covenantal witnesses has parallels in ANE treaties, which call upon various gods to perform this function (*TDOT* 1:397; Baltzer, *The Covenant Formulary*, 14; Weinfeld, *Deuteronomy and the Deuteronomic School*, 62). In some cases the heavens and earth are included among the witnesses, probably designating by metonymy the deities who inhabit these realms. In the monotheistic context of Deut, the covenantal idiom, while retained, has been reduced to a metaphorical level, where the heavens and earth are personified or stand by metonymy for the watching world (see Kline, *The Structure of Biblical Authority,* 116, n. 6). In either case the phrase suggests totality and permanence and lends a solemn tone to Moses' appeal (see Craigie, *Deuteronomy*, 139). Isaiah calls upon two men to witness the naming of his son Maher-shalal-hash-baz (Isa 8:2). Associating witnesses with the naming ceremony formally designated the boy as a sign-child whose name and growth pattern would verify the prophet's message as authentic when the

events prophesied were fulfilled. Jeremiah chose men to witness a land transaction in Anathoth (Jer 32:10) that served as a reminder that the exiles would eventually return to the land in fulfillment of Yahweh's promise (vv. 15, 37-44).

5. The related nom. *'ēd* often refers to a legal witness to the truth of a matter. Such a witness can testify as an eyewitness to actions, statements, and legal transactions (see Ruth 4:9-11; Isa 8:2; Jer 32:10, 12, 25). The Mosaic Law carefully regulated legal testimony. A man could not be condemned by the testimony of only one witness (Num 35:30; Deut 17:6; 19:15). In a case involving a capital offense, the witnesses who bring the incriminating evidence must be the primary executioners (Deut 17:7). Individuals were not to withhold testimony (Lev 5:1) or bear false witness against an innocent man (Exod 20:16 = Deut 5:20; Exod 23:1). False witnesses received the same penalty as the falsely accused individual would have suffered if condemned as guilty (Deut 19:16-21). The Proverbs also denounce false legal testimony (Prov 12:17; 14:5, 25; 19:5, 9, 28; 21:28; 24:28; 25:18) and list "a false witness" as one of the seven special objects of Yahweh's hatred (6:19).

6. When referring to a personal witness, *'ēd* appears in several theologically significant contexts. When the covenant was renewed at Shechem following the conquest of the land, the people who had just sworn allegiance to Yahweh agreed to stand as witnesses against themselves (Josh 24:22). (Form-critical considerations suggest that their affirmation was a legal oath. See Koopmans, *Joshua 24 as Poetic Narrative*, 406.) If they proved unfaithful in the future, the vow of allegiance made on that day ("We will serve Yahweh," v. 21) would serve as self-incriminating evidence against them.

In Isa 43:10 and 44:8 Yahweh commissioned Israel to serve as his witnesses. Before the nations, their gods, and their witnesses, Israel was to affirm that Yahweh is the incomparable God who decrees and acts, demonstrating his infinite superiority to the man-made deities of the pagan world. In establishing a new covenant with Israel, Yahweh promised to make the nation his witness to the Gentiles, a role he had earlier assigned to the Davidic kings (Isa 55:3-5). As military conquerors of and rulers over the surrounding nations, David and his descendents were to testify of God's greatness. (See Eaton, "The King as God's Witness," 25-38, and *Kingship and the Psalms*, 182-85.)

God himself appears as a "witness" in several passages. In this role he did not merely testify to the truth, but also served as the vindicator of wronged parties and the judge of wrongdoers. Laban reminded Jacob that the stone heap they had erected was a tangible reminder that God was the real witness to their contract in that he would judge Jacob if he mistreated Laban's daughters (Gen 31:50). Laban apparently refers to Yahweh here (see v. 49), though shortly after this he seems to make a distinction between the God of Abraham (= Yahweh) and the god of Nahor, making it possible that he has the latter deity in mind (see v. 53, where the vb. "judge" in MT [cf. SP and LXX, however] is pl.).

Samuel, in his farewell speech to Israel, appealed to Yahweh as a "witness" to the fact that he had treated the people justly and was innocent of any charges of wrongdoing (1 Sam 12:5). The people's affirmation ("He is witness") was a legal formula (see Koopmans, 384) by which they formally agreed with Samuel's assertion and renounced any future claims to the contrary. If they should violate their oath, Yahweh would serve as Samuel's vindicator. In this way Samuel protected himself from the whims of the fickle nation.

Twice in Jeremiah's prophecies Yahweh stood as the witness-judge against Israel. In the prophet's letter to the exiles Yahweh announced that he would severely judge the prophets Ahab and Zedekiah for their adulterous deeds and false prophecies, to which Yahweh himself was a "witness" (29:20-23, see esp. v. 23). Later the people appealed to Yahweh as a "true and faithful witness" and promised they would obey his instructions (42:5). When the people disobeyed, Jeremiah warned them that Yahweh, the witness to their broken promise, would come as their judge (v. 22, see vv. 13-18).

Micah's prophecy opens with the announcement that Yahweh intended to testify against the nations of the earth (1:2). This introduction is a rhetorical trap designed to get Israel's attention. The following judgment speech makes it clear that Yahweh was coming in universal judgment, but Israel and Judah, not the nations, were the focal point of his angry gaze.

Yahweh's dual role of witness-judge is especially apparent in Mal 3, where he comes as a witness to testify of Israel's sins (v. 5) and as the enforcer (lit. "messenger") of the covenant (v. 1), who purifies the nation through fiery judgment (vv. 2-4) (see Verhoef, *Haggai and Malachi,* 288-89, 293).

7. By extension *'ēd* can refer to supporting evidence that functions like a witness (see Exod 22:13[12], where a sheep's bodily remains are offered as proof that the animal was killed by a wild beast and not stolen). Job uses the term in this sense when he laments that his emaciated physical condition is like a hostile "witness" that serves as a constant reminder of God's disapproval and anger (Job 16:8). (Despite the presence of this seeming incontrovertible "witness" against him, he is confident that he has a heavenly witness [16:19] who will appeal his case before God. On the identity of this witness, see *śāhēd,* witness [→ # 8446].) Job's physical ailments and pain may also be in view in 10:17, where he accuses God of bringing new witnesses against him.

In Deut 31 both the law scroll (v. 26) and Moses' song (vv. 19, 21; see Deut 32:1-43) serve as witnesses against Israel. If Israel breaks Yahweh's covenant, the law scroll can be brought forward as evidence supporting Yahweh's accusation, establishing Israel's guilt, and justifying divine judgment. Likewise Moses' song, which anticipates Israel's apostasy and God's judgment, would serve as an incriminating witness to Israel's ingratitude and as a verbal testimony vindicating Yahweh's implementation of the covenant curses (see E. H. Merrill, *Deuteronomy,* 402-3).

8. The nom. *'ēd* can also refer to a tangible reminder that an agreement has been made. Objects that function as witnesses/reminders of an agreement include the stone heap built by Jacob and Laban (Gen 31:48, 52), the altar built by the Transjordanian tribes to remind them of their commitment to remain loyal to Yahweh (Josh 22:27-28, 34), and the eschatological altar and pillar to be built on Egypt's border, called a "sign" (*'ôt*) or reminder to the Egyptians of Yahweh's ability (or promise?) to help them (Isa 19:20). (The altar and pillar [v. 19], viewed as a unified witness or sign, are the probable subjects of the 3 masc. sg. vb. in v. 20. See G. B. Gray, *Isaiah*, 337-40, 342.)

9. The identity of the "witness" mentioned in Ps 89:37[38] is uncertain. The preceding context affirms the unalterability of God's promises to David. God promised David a royal line that would be as enduring as the sun and moon in the skies. The precise translation of v. 37b has been debated. Though some (for example, NIV) take

ne'^{e}mān as an attribute adjective ("a faithful/enduring witness in the sky"), the word order suggests that it is predicative ("a/the witness in the sky is faithful," cf. NASB). Ahlström (*Psalm 89*, 130) and others identify the "witness" with the rainbow of Gen 9, but this seems unlikely, since the rainbow is never associated with the Davidic covenant elsewhere (Mosca, 28, n. 3; Tate, 426). Mosca argues that the throne itself (v. 36b) is the witness (32). He appeals to parallels from the ANE where royal thrones are "divinized" or localized in the heavens (34), but the biblical parallels he offers (34-35) are weak and nowhere else does a throne function as a witness (see Tate, 425). Mullen proposes that a covenantal witness to the Davidic royal grant is in view. He suggests one of the "olden gods," a member of the heavenly assembly (perhaps the sun or moon), is the witness that "stands as legal guarantor to the promise" (218). Tate supports Mullen's general line of argument, but prefers to see an "unidentified" witness, rather than a "definite figure" (427). Veijola contends that Yahweh himself, though a partner to the covenant, also serves as the heavenly witness to the agreement (416-17).

Of course, some argue that "witness" is not the correct reading here. (For a summary of such approaches, see Mullen, 211-13.) One option is to connect *w'd* to the preceding and read "forever and ever" (for other examples of this phrase, see BDB, 723). However, in this case the relationship of the second line to the first is unclear. Others take *'ēd* as a synonym of *kissē'*, throne, understanding it as cognate with Ugar. *'d*, throne, dais (*CTA* 16 vi 22 ‖ *ks'*; Gibson, *CTA* 101). Emending *baššaḥaq*, in the heavens, to *kaššaḥaq*, like the heavens (*bet/kaph* confusion is widely attested), one could then read, "(his) throne like the heavens (is) firm/stable." The enduring nature of the heavens has already been alluded to in the psalm (v. 29), while Job 37:18 speaks of God spreading out the heavens (*š^{e}ḥāqîm*) and compares their strength to a bronze mirror. (Ps 89:29 uses *šāmayim*, which frequently appears in parallelism to *š^{e}ḥāqîm*; see BDB, 1007.)

10. The fem. nom. *'ēdâ* is used of tangible reminders that an agreement has been made. It refers specifically to the seven lambs Abraham offers Abimelech (Gen 21:30) as a reminder of their treaty and oath (see E. A. Speiser, *Genesis,* 160) and the pillar erected by Laban (Gen 31:52). In Josh 24:27 the word refers to the stone Joshua set up to testify against the people. Much like the heavens and earth (Deut 4:26; 30:19; 31:28), the personified stone functions in the role of a covenantal witness.

11. The nom. *t^e'ûdâ* refers to prophetic testimony or instruction in Isa 8:16, 20 (note the parallelism with *tôrâ*) and to a legally binding symbolic act in Ruth 4:7.

12. A homonymic vb. *'wd* occurs in the Psalms. (Though some have tried to relate this root to *'wd* II [which occurs in the hi./ho. stems], it is probably better to treat it as etymologically distinct [see BDB, 728, 730; and *HALAT* 751-52]. *HALAT* [751] lists cognates in Arab., ESA, Eth., Syr., and Palmyrene.) This vb. carries the semantic nuance surround, bind in Ps 119:61, where it is used in the pi. stem to describe how the wicked seek to entrap the psalmist with their "ropes." The vb. also means help, sustain, relieve. In Ps 146:9 and 147:6 it is used in the polel stem to describe how the Lord, in his role of just king, helps the vulnerable and weak by opposing their oppressors. In Ps 20:8[9] the psalmist boasts that he and his people are sustained by the Lord's enabling presence.

Witness: → *yāpēaḥ* (witness?, # 3641); → *'wd* (surround, encircle, admonish, call to witness, # 6386); → *śāhēd* (witness, # 8446)

Bibliography
HALAT 744-46, 751-52, 1627; *NIDNTT* 3:1038-51; *TDNT* 4:483-85; *THAT* 2:209-21; *TWAT* 5:1107-30; G. W. Ahlström, *Psalm 89: Eine Liturgie aus dem Ritual des leidenden Königs*, 1959, 130; K. Baltzer, *The Covenant Formulary*, 1971, 14; P. C. Craigie, *Deuteronomy*, NICOT, 1976; M. Delcor, "Les attachés litteraires, l'origine et la signification de l'expression biblique 'prendre à temoin le ciel et la terre,'" *VT* 16, 1966, 8-25; J. H. Eaton, "The King as God's Witness," *ASTI* 7, 1970, 25-40; F. C. Fensham, "*'d* in Exodus xxii 12," *VT* 12, 1962, 337-39; idem, *Kingship and the Psalms*, SBT, 1976; G. B. Gray, *Isaiah*, 1912, 337-40, 342; M. G. Kline, *The Structure of Biblical Authority*, 1972, 116, n. 6; W. T. Koopmans, *Joshua 24 as Poetic Narrative*, JSOTSup, 1990; P. G. Mosca, "Once Again the Heavenly Witness of Ps 89:38," *JBL* 105, 1986, 27-37; E. T. Mullen, Jr., "The Divine Witness and the Davidic Royal Grant: Ps 89:37-38," *JBL*, 102, 1983, 207-18; M. Tate, *Psalms*, 1990, 424-27; J. A. Thompson, "Expansions of the עד Root," *JSS* 10, 1965, 222-40; G. M. Tucker, "Witnesses and 'Dates' in Israelite Contracts," *CBQ* 28, 1966, 42-45; T. Veijola, "The Witness in the Clouds," *JBL* 107, 1988, 413-17; idem, "Zu Ableitung und Bedeutung von *Hēʿîd* I im Hebräischen," *UF* 8, 1976, 343-51; P. A. Verhoef, *Haggai and Malachi*, NICOT, 1987, 288-89, 293; M. Weinfeld, *Deuteronomy and the Deuteronomic School*, 1992.

Robert B. Chisholm

6390	עוה

עוה (*ʿwh*), q. do wrong; ni. be disturbed, distressed; pi. agitate; hi. pervert, do wrong (# 6390); עָוֺן (*ʿāwōn*), nom. iniquity, punishment of sin, transgression (→ # 6411).

OT The vb. appears 17x in the OT, in different conjugations. In the q. it appears in Esth 1:16 and Dan 9:5 with the meaning to do wrong. With basically the same meaning it appears in the hi. in 2 Sam 7:14; 19:19[20]; 24:17; 1 Kgs 8:47; 2 Chron 6:37; Ps 106:6; Jer 9:5[4] (cf. *BHS* n[a]). It is frequently used with the vb. to sin and indicates wrongdoing against God. With the meaning to pervert, it appears in the hi. in Job 33:27 and Jer 3:21.

The vb. appears 4x in the ni. In 1 Sam 20:30 the part. is used in a derogatory sense to describe Jonathan's mother as a perverse and rebellious woman. The same use occurs in Prov 12:8 to describe a man with a warped mind. In Isa 21:3 it points to the distress experienced upon receiving bad news. In Ps 38:6[7] the NIV translates it as, "I am bowed down." It can also point to the poet's agitation because of the burden of his guilt.

The vb. occurs 2x in the pi. In Isa 24:1 the face of the earth is the object (to ruin its face) and in Lam 3:9 the paths of the poet, with the meaning ruin or make crooked.

P-B The vb. occurs 7x in Qumran. In 1QS 1:24 it is related to a confession of sin as in Ps 38:7. In the other instances it denotes someone who is perverted, with no insight (1QH 1:22), a perverted spirit (3:21; 11:12; 13:15) or a perverted heart (7:27).

The vb. appears in Mish. Heb. and Jewish Aram. with the meaning to do wrong.

In the LXX the word is usually translated with *talaipgreg*, to experience distress.

Confusion, agitation: → *bwk* (be agitated, wander in agitation, # 1003); → *bll* (confuse, mix, # 1176); → *blʿ* III (be confused, confused, # 1182); → *hwm* (throw into confusion, be in uproar,

2101); → *kmr* (agitated, # 4023); → *'wh* (disturb, distress, agitate, pervert, do wrong, # 6390); → *p'm* (be disturbed, feel disturbed, # 7192); → *rhb* (assail, press, pester, alarm, confuse, # 8104); → *r'm* II (be agitated, be confused, # 8307); → *tmh* (be benumbed, be stunned, shocked, gaze, # 9449)

Bibliography

THAT 6:43-244, 248; *NIDNTT* 3:859.

Harry F. van Rooy

6395	עוז

עוז (*'wz*), q. take refuge; hi. bring to safety (# 6395); מָעוֹז (*mā'ôz*), nom. refuge, place of safety (# 5057).

ANE Arab. *'wḏ*, seek refuge, and Ugar. *'wd*.

OT 1. The root *'wz* occurs twice in the q. stem in the OT (Ps 52:7[9]; Isa 30:2). The NIV translates "grew strong" in Ps 52:7[9] (agreeing with the JB and reading *'zz*) and "help" in Isa 30:2 (in synonymous parallelism with *ḥāsût*). The NEB and NRSV read "take refuge," rendering more accurately the emphatic construction with the preceding *mā'ôz*. Those who take refuge in wealth (NRSV following Syr.), or those who take refuge in wild lies (NEB), come to nothing because they refuse to take refuge in God (Ps 52:7[9]).

2. The nom. *mā'ôz* occurs 35x in the OT. The NIV translates "refuge" in eight instances (Ps 31:2, 4; Prov 10:29; Isa 25:4; Nah 1:7; 3:11), with "fortress" and "stronghold" the other prominent renderings of the word. The term may designate natural (e.g., Judg 6:26; Isa 23:4) or artificial havens (e.g., Isa 17:9; Ezek 24:25). It may also be used in a figurative sense of rulers who provide protection by virtue of their political savvy or military prowess (Isa 30:2-3). Predominantly, the word is a metaphor for Yahweh, who is a refuge to his people (2 Sam 22:33; Ps 27:1; 28:8). God is a place of safety for those in distress and trouble (Ps 37:39; Nah 1:7) and for the poor and needy (Isa 25:4). However, the righteous make Yahweh their refuge only through faith and obedience in the way of the Lord (Prov 10:29), so that joy of worship and service before God becomes a refuge to the faithful (Neh 8:10). (→ # 5057)

Hiding: → *ḥb'* (hide, conceal, # 2461); → *ḥbh* (hide, # 2464); → *ḥāgû* (refuge, cleft, # 2511); → *ḥpp* I (screen, shelter, # 2910); → *ṭmn* (hide, # 3243); → *kḥd* (be hidden, hide, # 3948); → *knp* (hide oneself, # 4052); → *sōk* (hiding-place, shelter, thicket, hut, # 6108); → *str* (hide, kept secret, # 6259); → *'lm* (hidden things, secrets, # 6623); → *ṣpn* (hide, # 7621); → *śpn* (conceal, # 8561)
Refuge, escape: → *ḥsh* (seek refuge, # 2879); → *mālôn* (lodging place, # 4869); → *mānôs* (place of escape, # 4960); → *miqlāṭ* (refuge, asylum, # 5236); → *'wz* (take refuge, # 6395); → *plṭ* (save, bring to safety, # 7117); → *śrd* (run away, escape, # 8572)

Bibliography

ISBE 4:65-66; *TDOT* 5:64-75; *TWOT* 1:307-8; S. E. Balentine, "A Description of the Semantic Field of Hebrew Words for 'Hide,' *VT* 30, 1980, 137-53; L. Delekat, "Zum hebräischen Wörterbuch," *VT* 14, 1964, 28-33.

Andrew E. Hill

6396 (*ʿ^{a}wîl*, young boy), → # 6407

6401	עול

עול (*ʿwl* I), pi. act wrongly (# 6401); nom. עָוֶל (*ʿāwel*), wrong, injustice (# 6404); עַוָּל (*ʿawwāl*), transgressor, criminal (# 6405); עַוְלָה (*ʿawlâ*), perversity, wickedness (# 6406); עֹלָה (*ʿōlâ*; # 6593) is a byform of *ʿawlâ*; the textual variant עַלְוָה (*ʿalwâ* I), evildoer (# 6594), in Hos 10:9 may be explained as metathesis (see below).

ANE Cognates are the Arab. *ʿwl*, deviate; Syr. act unjustly; Geez rot.

OT 1. The largest group of words within this root are the segholate noun *ʿāwel* and its feminine counterpart *ʿawlâ*. The latter has a byform *ʿōlâ,* a result of the phonetic contraction from *ʿaw* to *ʿō* (Gesenius-Kautsch 24f). They total almost sixty cases.

The realm of legal and social practice is home for the majority of the occurrences. They are specific acts that are done (over a dozen times as the direct object of vbs. of doing, *ʿśh* and *pʿl*) and are specifically contrasted to righteousness and good behavior (Deut 32:4, opposing *ṣaddîq* and *yāšār*; cf. also Job 6:29; Ps 58:2[3]; 92:15[16]; 107:42; 125:3; Zeph 3:5; IQS 3:20-21), therefore indicating a meaning "perversity" and "inequity." Skewing judicial rectitude (Lev 19:15; Isa 61:8; Zeph 3:5 with *mišpāṭ*) by such practices as bribery (Ezek 18:8) is called *ʿāwel*, injustice, and is strongly proscribed. So are unfair business and trade practices, which are also called *ʿāwel* (Lev 19:35; Deut 25:16; Ezek 28:18).

The meaning of the word group to describe physical acts as "wickedness" and "injustice" is illustrated by its frequent use in conjunction with other words for wickedness: *rʿʿ* I [be bad, → # 8317]—Ps 37:1; *ršʿ* [act wickedly, → # 8399]—Hos 10:13; *gzl* [robbery, → # 1608]—Isa 61:8; *dām* [bloodshed, → # 1947]—Isa 59:3; Mic 3:10; Hab 2:12; *ḥms* I [violence, → # 2803]—Ps 58:2[3]; *ʾlḥ* [corruption and abomination, → # 480] and *tʿb* [be detestable, → # 9493]—Job 15:16; *ʾāwen* [sin, mischief, → # 224]—Job 11:14; *ʿawōn* [iniquity, → # 6411]—Isa 59:3; see also probably Hos 10:9 in the context of sin [*ḥṭʾ*, → # 2627], where apparently there was a transposition of letters during the transmission of the text to the *ʿalwâ* of the MT; *ʿnh* II [oppression, → # 6700]—2 Sam 7:10; Ps 89:22[23]; and *r^{e}miyyâ* [deceit]—Job 13:7; 27:4; cf. Ps 43:1; Zeph 3:13; and *šeqer* [lies]—Isa 59:3. While including physical acts of evil, the injustice can also be an oral pronouncement, as indicated by its association at times with the lips or speaking (Job 6:30; 13:7; 27:4; Isa 59:3; Mal 2:6). This wickedness leads to the death and destruction of its practitioners (Job 24:20; Prov 22:8; Ezek 3:20; 18:24, 26; 33:13, 18). Life is still available if this evil is abandoned (Ezek 33:15). The collocation of the terms with some of these more specific designations of wrongdoing seems to indicate that it is a more abstract, generic, word for "wickedness" and "evil," encompassing any number of undesirable activities.

The meaning of the word group designating "wickedness/injustice" can also be perceived through the other words to which it is contrasted, for example, mercy or covenant love (*ḥesed* II [→ # 2876]—Ps 43:1; Hos 10:13), blamelessness (*tāmîm* [→ # 9459]—Ezek 28:15), and one who keeps the law of God (Ps 119:3) or returns to him (Job 22:23).

Theologically, these wicked actions have absolutely no part in the character of God (Deut 32:4; Job 34:10). God even goes as far as expressing shock at Israel's rejection of him, as if he were an evil person (Jer 2:5), a situation antithetical to God's very nature. Such actions are to be expunged by his followers from their own life (Job 34:32; Ps 7:3[4]). Those who practice them are to be abhorred (Prov 29:27) and avoided, since they are fools (Ps 53:1[2]) who do not deserve the support or protection of anyone (82:2).

Another aspect of the word group appears in Deut 32:4, in its context of God's truthfulness (*'ᵉmûnâ* [→ # 575] ; cf. 1QS 3:19; 4:17-20, 23; 1QH 11:26). Here iniquity is expressed as "falsity" or "lying" in such a way as to pervert justice.

The complete contrast to anything godly is shown by "wickedness" being an action of an atheist in Ps 53:1[2], one who denies God's very existence. In the parallel Ps 14:1 *'awel* is replaced by *'ᵃlîlâ* [→ # 6613], describing ruthless and wanton behavior.

2. The marked opposition to God is explicit in two of the five occurrences of *'awwāl*. Such evil ones do not even know God (Job 18:21). The righteous God, who is just and without wrong (*ṣdq*, *mišpāṭ*), is exactly their opposite (Zeph 3:5). These wicked are compared in simile to carnivorous beasts with rending fangs (Job 29:17), and those who receive their evil ministrations hope for their ultimate ruin (Job 27:7; 31:3). The person so described is not just a one-time delinquent but a repeat offender, as is shown by the pattern of the Heb. nom (*IBHS* 5.4).

3. The verbal form *'wl*, which only occurs twice, draws a contrast between God's majesty and human unrighteousness (Isa 26:10) and those wrong actions that are characterized by cruelty (*ḥmṣ* II, → # 2807) on the part of the wicked (*rāšā'*; Ps 71:4). The pi. form is a denominative (*IBHS* 24.4), deriving from the much more common and earlier nominal forms. Grammarians (Gevirtz, 57-66; *IBHS* 5.6) note the forcefulness of the word because of the initial '. This coupled with the one occurrence in the form of a participle (Ps 71:4) indicates a person who was characteristically and decidedly evil, and this in direct opposition to God.

4. The fem. nom. *'awlâ* indicates an abstract concept (*IBHS* 6.4.2b). As in previously discussed forms of the same root, the entire concept of wickedness and evil is antithetical to the person of God (2 Chron 19:7; Job 36:23; Ps 92:15[16]; Zeph 3:5) and to those who are truly his people (Job 11:14; Mal 2:6).

5. *'ōlâ*, wrong, is easily misread as being *'ōlâ*, burnt offering. The contexts of four occurrences of the noun preclude them from having the latter meaning. God abhors the wickedness that is associated with robbery (*gzl* [→ 1608]—Isa 61:8), violence (*ḥms* [→ # 2803]—Ps 58:2[3]), and cunning plots (*'āmōq* [→ # 6678]—Ps 64:6[7]). These are contrasted with things of which he approves, such as justice (*mišpāṭ*—Isa 61:8), righteousness, and uprightness (*ṣedeq* and *mêšārîm*—Ps 58:1[2]).

P-B RL often uses the pi. of the vb. in the context of dishonest business practice, cheating in measurement and false (*šqr*) weights (Tosefta Baba Qamma 7:7; Yalkut Num 765; Tanḥuma Balak 12).

Corruption: → *'lḥ* (be corrupted, # 480); → *muṭṭeh* (corruption of justice, # 4754); → *sûr* (corrupt, # 6074); → *šḥt* (become corrupt, ruin, spoil, # 8845)
Bad, vicious, wicked: → *zmm* (plan, purpose, plan evil, # 2372); → *kîlay* (scoundrel, # 3964); → *'wl* I (act wrongly, # 6401); → *ṣdh* I (act intentionally, # 7399); → *r''* I (be bad, injure, # 8317); → *rš'* (act wickedly, unrighteously, be guilty, pronounce guilty, # 8399)
Guilt, evil, unrighteousness: → *'šm* (become guilty, incur guilt, bear guilt, pronounce guilty, # 870); → *dām* (blood, bloodshed, blood-guilt, murder, # 1947); → *wāzār* (unjust, laden with

guilt, # 2261); → *ḥwb* (be the cause of guilt, # 2549); → *ḥēṭ'* (sin, guilt, punishment of sin, # 2628); → *nqh* (be free, exempt from guilt, remain unpunished, # 5927); → *rš'* (act wickedly, unrighteously, be guilty, pronounce guilty, # 8399)

Sin, guilt, rebellion, transgression, wrong: → *'āwen* (mischief, iniquity, deception, # 224); → *ḥṭ'* (sin, commit a sin, purify, # 2627); → *'wh* (do wrong, pervert, # 6390); → *'wl* I (act wrongly, # 6401); → *pš'* (rebel, violate, transgress, # 7321); → **Fall: Theology**

BIBLIOGRAPHY

S. Gevirtz, "Formative ע in Biblical Hebrew," *Eretz-Israel* 16, 1982, 57*-66*.

David W. Baker

6402	עול

עול (*'wl* II), q. suckle, nurse (# 6402); עֲוִיל (*'ᵃwîl*), nom. young boy (only in Job 19:18 and 21:11; → # 6396); עוּל (*'ûl*), nom. sucking child, infant (disleg.: Isa 49:15; 65:20; # 6403); עוֹלֵל (*'ôlēl*), nom. boy, child (→ # 6407).

ANE The Ugar. *'l* means suckling animal; likewise the Syr. *'îlâ*. The Arab. *ǵwl* has the sense of suckling; *'wl* refers to nurturing.

OT 1. The semantic field of "nurse" deals with nursing, nurse, suckling (breast-feeding), and infants; the subject is developed under *ynq* (→ # 3567).

2. The care of mothers for their young is well illustrated by *'wl* II, e.g., cows nursing their calves (Gen 33:13). By extension, the term may come to mean calves (1 Sam 6:7, 10). David is taken from tending his sheep and suckling (part. of *'wl* II) ewes to be the shepherd of Israel (Ps 78:71). In such a passage the basic sense of caring and protecting comes to the fore.

3. Isaiah is the key for understanding the theology of these terms. In one of the most powerful pictures of the love of God, Isa 40:11 speaks of God gently leading the exiled Israel back to her land, like a shepherd, carrying his lambs and gently leading those of his flock who have young (part. of *'wl* II). The picture is one of infinite care and a slow pace. The nom. *'ûl* occurs in 49:15, when the prophet asks whether a woman might forget her sucking child. Surely not. God's love supersedes even the strongest of all loves, for while a mother may forget her nursing child, according to Isaiah, God never does! The power of the two words "But God" underlines the compassion of God in a dramatic way. Isa 65:20 speaks of the eschatological Jerusalem, where never again will a child (*'ûl*) die within a few days, nor will an old person fail to enjoy the fullness of old age.

P-B In RL *'ûlā'* I has the sense of that which is carried, and by implication an infant or nursing child (Baba Batra 9a). Again a protective sense may be found here.

NT Jesus as the good shepherd (John 10:14) is the NT counterpart of the protective God of the OT (cf. Isa 40:11).

Nurse: → *ynq* (suck, suckle, infant, nurse, # 3567); → *'wl* II (suckle, nurse, # 6402)

BIBLIOGRAPHY

TWAT 5:1131-35; J. E. Gardner, *Women in Roman Law and Society*, 1986, 241-44; A. Cameron and A. Kuhrt (eds.), *Images of Women in Antiquity*, 1993, 273-87.

W. R. Domeris

6403 (*'ûl*, nursing child), → # 6402; # 6407

6404 (*'āwel*, unrighteousness), → # 6401

6405 (*'awwāl*, unrighteous one), → # 6401

6406 (*'awlâ*, perversity, wickedness), → # 6401

6407	עוֹלֵל

עוֹלֵל (*'ôlēl*), boy, child (# 6407); עֲוִיל (*'ᵃwîl*), young boy, found only in Job 19:18 and 21:11 (# 6396); עוּל (*'ûl*), nursing, suckling child (disleg. in Isa 49:15; 65:20; # 6403); < עול (*'wl II*), nurse (→ # 6402)

OT 1. Yahweh's compassion for his own is compared to a mother's love for her *'ûl* (Isa 49:15). She may forget her *'ûl,* but Yahweh will never forget his children. Throughout the OT long life is a sign of Yahweh's favor and a reward for virtue. But in the new Jerusalem normal life span will rival that of the antediluvians (65:20). (See further # 6402)

2. In Job 19:18 the force of *'ᵃwîl* is "urchins." Job protested juvenile disrespect for elders (see 2 Kgs 2:23).

3. *'ôlēl* is paired with *yônēq* (→ *ynq*, suck, # 3567). Other pairings for *'ôlēl* are *bᵃḥûrîm* (young men, Jer 6:11; 9:21[20]) and *bānîm* (sons, Ps 17:14). In some references, all violent, there is mention of children being "dashed" to pieces: *rṭš* (2 Kgs 8:12; 13:16[14:1]; Isa 13:16; Nah 3:10); *npṣ* (Ps 137:9). The pronouncement of a blessing by Jews exiled to Babylon on anyone who seizes a Babylonian *'ôlēl* and dashes him against a rock (Ps 137:9) is unexpected and may be revolting. The individual who thus speaks is "typical of that man in every age who is godly and devoted to the things of God, yet who—theologically speaking—lives in BC ... Christ judges this man's hate. But he does not expurgate the passionate involvement that created it" (J. Bright, *The Authority of the Old Testament*, 1967/1975, 238, 240-41).

Child: → *gōlem* (embryo, # 1677); → *ṭap* I (children, # 3251); → *yônēq* (young child, # 3437); → *yld* (bear, bring forth, be born, # 3528); → *yātôm* (orphan, # 3846); → *mamzēr* (bastard, # 4927); → *na'ar* (boy, # 5853); → *'ôlēl* (child, # 6402); → *t'm* (bear twins, # 9298); → **Adoption: Theology**
Nurse: → *ynq* (suck, suckle, infant, nurse, # 3567); → *'wl* II (suckle, nurse, # 6402)

Victor P. Hamilton

6409	עוֹלָם

עוֹלָם (*'ôlām*), nom. long time, constancy, for all time (# 6409). Derivation is uncertain. The nom. is often derived from the root < *'lm* I, hidden, so that the basic meaning of the nom. would be an "obscure time." But if the root were *'lm*, the base form of the nom., as suggested by the Aram. cognate *'ālam*, would be *qātal*. This form is unattested as a nom. base in a Sem. language. Consequently, it has been suggested that the *-am* ending of the nom. is an adverbial ending and not part of the root. On this basis, suggested roots include *w'l* (cf. Eth. *wa'alu*, tarry) or *'ll*, cognate with the Akk. *ullû*, ascend (see further Jenni, 199-202).

ANE The nom. is widely attested. Ugar. *'lm*, long time, perpetuity, is used in many of the same constructions as in the Heb. (e.g., *'d 'lm*, *l'lm*, forever; cf., e.g., *KTU* 1.2, IV, 10; 1.4, IV, 42; 4.360, 2). In Moab. and Phoen., *'lm*, perpetuity, is used in various constructions. It appears in several Aram. dialects; Old Aram., BA, Syr., Nab., Pal., *'ālmā'* eternity, age, world, Eth. *'ālam*, world, age, eternity.

OT 1. The basic meaning of the nom. is farthest time, distant time (Jenni, 25). It does not seem to mean eternity in the philosophical sense of the word (i.e., neither unbounded time nor eternal timelessness), although there are a few vv. where the meaning of the nom. is very much like the idea of eternity. In most cases, however, like other Heb. terms for time, the meaning of *'ôlām* is closely linked to the occurrence of events. Thus, *'ôlām* is usually used to describe events extended into the distant past or future. Such distant time is clearly relative: it can be a time in one's own life (Ps 77:5 [6]), a life span (Exod 21:6), or the furthest conceivable time (15:18).

2. When referring to the past, the nom. is frequently used in construct phrases to modify other noms. In such cases, it essentially means "ancient." The gates of Jerusalem are described as the *pîṯḥê 'ôlām*, the "ancient gates" (Ps 24:7, 9), and Proverbs warns against moving an ancient boundary-marker (Prov 22:28; 23:10). The "ancient hills" (*gib'ôt 'ôlām*) are considered a source of blessings and bounty (Gen 49:26; Deut 33:15; cf. Hab 3:6), while the "ancient path" or "way" is regarded as the road of the wicked and idolaters (Job 22:15; Jer 18:15; but cf. Thompson, 43, and Hartley, 328, who take the nom. in these vv. to mean dark, obscure). The book of Isaiah predicts the eschatological restoration of the "ancient ruins," the destroyed cities of Israel (Isa 58:12; 61:4). Elsewhere, Jeremiah warns Judah that God is bringing against them an "ancient nation," i.e., the Babylonians (Jer 5:15), and the psalmist laments that his enemy has made him like one of the "ancient dead" (NIV like those long dead, Ps 143:3). The nom. may also be combined with different words for time. Deut 32:7 urges the rebellious Israelites to remember the "ancient days" (*y^emôt 'ôlām*), i.e., the salvation history of the nation. Cf. also Mic 7:14, where the events of the "ancient days" refers specifically to the Exodus. In Ps 77:5[6], the troubled author states that he remembered the "years of old" (*'ôlāmîm*, using the plural variant, perhaps with extensive force, that occurs 12x in the OT) and his songs in the night—not the distant past, but happier times in the psalmist's life.

The divine title *'ēl 'ôlām* (Gen 21:33; cf. also Isa 40:28; # 446) might also be best understood as a reference to God's antiquity. "The Ancient One" is a common epithet for the god El in Ugar. texts (Cross, 16-19), and the same image is applied to Israel's God in Dan 7:9, where the Lord is described as the "Ancient of Days" (*'attîq yômîn*). The text of Genesis probably preserves an old epithet for God that was common to the Syro-Canaanite milieu and adopted by the Israelites as an appropriate description of the Lord.

3. The nom. is also used with the preposition *min*, meaning "from ancient times, from antiquity." The *nephilim* are described as "heroes of old" (*gibbôrîm 'ašer mē'ôlām*) in Gen 6:4. Similarly, the Geshurites, Girzites, and Amalekites are described as people who had lived in the land from Shur to Egypt "from ancient times" (1 Sam 27:8). Often, the nom. is used in designations of times within Israel's history: Josh 24:2 states that Israel's fathers dwelt beyond the river "long ago"; Jer 2:20 speaks of the deliverance from Egypt as from "long ago"; Mal 3:4 uses the same language of the

period of the monarchy; while Jer 28:8 refers to the prophets who prophesied "from early times." Mic 5:2[1] predicts the coming of a messianic king from Bethlehem, whose origin was "from of old, from ancient times" (*mîmê 'ôlām*). Here, the nom. phrase could well refer to the pristine days of the Davidic monarchy (as the reference to Bethlehem, David's home town, suggests; cf. Smith, 43-44). It probably expresses the hope for a "new David" who would take control of the decrepit monarchy and restore Israel's glory (cf. Ezek 34:23-24; 37:24-25). While it is tempting to see here a reference to the eternal preexistence of the Messiah, no such an idea is found in biblical or postbiblical Jewish literature before the Similitudes of Enoch (1 cent. BC-1 cent. AD; see 1 En 48:2-6).

Various aspects of God are also described as being "from antiquity." According to Ps 25:6, God's mercy and lovingkindness have been from old (*mē'ôlām*), probably alluding to his acts of compassion on behalf of the Israelites. A more distant time is meant in Prov 8:23, where wisdom is described as the first of God's works, which was "appointed from eternity . . . before the world began." The author uses a series of terms for age or antiquity, driving home the point that wisdom is the most ancient of all creations (Whybray, 131-32). In Joel 2:2, which says that the Day of the Lord was "such as never was of old," the phrase essentially means forever: there has never been a day like it before. In Ps 93:2, the nom. *'ôlām* might approach the idea of eternity in a more abstract sense. Here, God is described as "from all eternity," which probably means more than merely the distant past.

4. Much more frequently, *'ôlām* refers to the future. It can refer to a future of limited duration; i.e., to conditions that will exist continuously throughout a limited period of time, often a single life span. The nom. is sometimes used in a construct phrase to modify another nom. (perpetual, continual). According to Prov 10:25, while a wicked person is blown away by the whirlwind, the righteous "stand firm forever" (*y^{e}sôd 'ôlām*), which lasts one's entire life. In Exod 21:6, a slave who chooses to remain with his master for life is called a "servant for life" (see also Deut 15:17; cf. 1 Sam 27:12). Similar constructions are found in Jer 20:11, where the prophet predicts that his oppressors will be "thoroughly disgraced" (lit., disgrace of perpetuity), and Jer 20:17, where he wishes that his mother's womb had been "enlarged forever" (i.e., that he had never been born). In each of these cases, the nom. essentially means "his/her whole life."

The same is true in many cases where the nom. is used to modify a vb., sometimes standing alone, but usually with prepositions *l-* or *'ad*. In Exod 19:9, the Lord tells Moses that he will come to him in a thick cloud, so that the people will trust Moses *l^e'ôlām*, ever after, for the rest of his life. In 1 Sam 1:22, Hannah vows that her child will remain in the house of God at Shiloh *'ad 'ôlām*, the rest of his life. Likewise, when Jonathan asks David to swear not "ever" (*'ad 'ôlām*, 1 Sam 20:15) to harm Jonathan's descendants, they agree that the Lord is witness "between me and you forever" (*'ad 'ôlām*, 20:23), i.e., that God oversee the vow all their lives. In Ps 45:2[3], the king is "blessed ... forever" by God, while in 61:7[8], he is enthroned in God's presence perpetually. According to Ps 21:4[5], God grants the king "length of days, for ever and ever"—a phrase that calls to mind the cry of royal veneration, "May my lord King David, live forever" (1 Kgs 1:31; Neh 2:3). In each case, the expected blessing is not eternal life, but long life.

Also in the Psalms, the Lord tells a king that he is "a priest forever, in the order of Melchizedek" (Ps 110:4)—probably referring to royal prerogative to exercise a certain amount of priestly power, just as Melchizedek had been both priest and king of Salem (cf. Kraus, 351). Elsewhere, authors of different psalms declare that they will do various acts *'ad 'ôlām* or *l^e'ôlām* (perpetually): praise the Lord (Ps 52:9[11]), give thanks (30:12[13]; 79:13), glorify the Lord's name (86:12; 145:2), bless the Lord's name (145:1), sing praises (61:7[8]; 89:1[2]), declare the Lord's justice (75:9[10]), trust in the Lord's mercy (52:8[10]), and abide in God's dwelling/presence (41:12[13]; 61:4[6], 7[8]). The nom. is also used in negative constructions: the righteous person will "never be shaken" (15:5; Prov 10:30; cf. Ps 30:6[7]; 55:22[23]); the psalmist prays that he should not ever be put to shame (Ps 31:1[2]). In each of these vv., the phrase obviously means the rest of the speaker's life.

5. In many more cases, the nom. is used with longer time periods in view—indeed, it often implies unceasingness or perpetuity. The nom. is used in this fashion to describe aspects of creation: in Ps 78:69; 104:5; Eccl 1:4, the earth is said to have been established "forever," i.e., it will continue to exist into the most distant future. Similarly, the heavens and their denizens are established forever (Ps 148:6). Zion, the mountain of God, is also established perpetually (48:8[9]). Less permanent creations can also be described in this manner. Joshua sets up stones at the site of the Jordan crossing to serve as a "memorial ... forever" for the Israelites (Josh 4:7). Similarly, Isaiah is told to inscribe a judgment oracle on a tablet and a scroll, in order that it might serve as a witness against the wicked perpetually (*l^e'ad 'ad-'ôlām*; Isa 30:8). Nations, such as Babylon, can aspire to exist forever (Isa 47:7; Obad 10; Ps 81:15[16]). Such aspirations are manifestations of their pride and invariably provoke God's wrath. People, too, can aspire to live forever, as did Adam and Eve (Gen 3:22). Moreover, the Lord swears that his spirit will not strive with humanity perpetually (6:3). Rather, there is a strict limit to humanity's violent time upon the earth. Dan 12:2 predicts that after the final conflict between the saints and the forces of the evil king, many of those who sleep in the dusty earth shall be resurrected, "some to everlasting life, others to shame and everlasting contempt."

States of affairs, too, can be perpetual. In 1 Kgs 8:13, the temple is established as a place where the Lord would dwell perpetually. (The fact that the temple was eventually destroyed does not invalidate its original purpose.) In 2 Sam 3:28, David claims that he and his kingdom will be perpetually innocent of Abner's death, so that no guilt should fall on him or his descendants. Elijah's servant Gehazi and his descendants are perpetually cursed with Naaman's leprosy as a result of Gehazi's greed (2 Kgs 5:27). The enmity between Israel and some of its neighboring nations was to continue perpetually (Deut 23:3[4], 6[7]; Ezra 9:12; Ezek 25:15, 35; cf. Ps 78:66, "everlasting shame"). God's anger/enmity can also be described as perpetual. Several times the question is posed, "Will (the Lord) always be angry (with Judah)?" (Jer 3:5; 17:4; cf. Ps 85:5[6]), in light of the judgment of exile. In Jer 14:4, the Lord states that his anger will burn perpetually against Judah; in Mal 1:4, his anger burns perpetually against Edom.

6. The nom. is used frequently in connection with the idea of covenants between God and humanity. God's unconditional promises to his people are often described as perpetual or eternal (→ *b^erît*, covenant, # 1382). In Gen 9:12, 16, God

makes an "everlasting covenant" (*b^e^rît 'ôlām*) that he will not destroy the earth again by water forever. The covenant with Abraham is also described as an "everlasting covenant" (Gen 17:7, 13, 19; cf. Judg 2:1; 2 Sam 7:24; 1 Chron 16:15; Ps 105:10), especially the promise of land to Abraham and his descendants (Gen 13:15; 17:18; 48:4; Exod 32:13; 1 Chron 16:17). Phinehas, because of his zeal for the Lord, receives a covenant of perpetual priesthood for himself and his descendants (Num 25:13). Frequently, God's covenant with David is presented as a perpetual covenant (2 Sam 7:13, 16, 25, 29; 22:51; 23:5; 1 Kgs 2:33, 45; 9:5; 2 Chron 13:5; Ps 18:50[51]; 89:4[5], 28[29], 36[37], 37[38]; cf. Hillers, 106-19). The throne of his line will be established to perpetuity because of David's early piety and desire to build the temple (2 Sam 7), regardless of his later failures. While the Babylonian exile and the destruction of the monarchy seemed to have invalidated this promise for some of the prophets, this covenant became the basis for the belief in a messianic king, a new Davidic monarch (or Davidic line), who would rule the people forever (Isa 55:3; Ezek 37:24-25). The cases of Phinehas and David may be contrasted with those of the high priest Eli (1 Sam 2:30) and King Saul (13:13), who would have received perpetual offices and dynasties, but lost favor due to their disobedience. The use of *'ôlām* in these cases does not mean that the covenants could never be abrogated. Rather, it means that they were made with no anticipated end point. Walton (132) argues that aspects of the covenant fulfilled in Christ remained intact, while others became obsolete. So while the covenant with Phinehas became obsolete after the destruction of the temple, the covenant with David continued in altered form through the Messiah. For a continuity perspective, see W. A. VanGemeren, *The Progress of Redemption* (1995).

The requirements of conditional covenants, too, are described as "perpetual." Circumcision, the sign of God's covenant with Abraham, is called a "perpetual covenant" that the Israelites were required to keep (Gen 17:13). Keeping the Sabbath is called an "everlasting covenant" (*b^e^rît 'ôlām*) between God and Israel (Exod 31:16, 17), as is the arrangement of the Bread of the Presence (Lev 24:8). Many of the prescriptions in the Pentateuch are called "a lasting ordinance" (*ḥuqqat 'ôlām*), which were to be carried out regularly: the observance of the Passover and other feasts (Exod 12:14, 17, 24; Lev 23:14, 21, 41), the lighting of lamps in the temple (Exod 27:21; 28:43), the blowing of the trumpets for assembly (Num 10:8), and the various regulations regarding the preparations and presentations of sacrifices (Exod 29:9, 28; 30:21; Lev 3:17; 6:18[11]; 7:34, 36; 10:9, 15; 16: 29, 31, 34; Num 15:15; 18:8, 11, 19, 23; Ezek 46:14). On the other hand, the outcomes of conditional covenants can also be everlasting or perpetual. By keeping the laws of the covenant, the Israelites will enjoy perpetual blessing (Deut 5:29[26]); but failure to follow the laws result in curses that will serve as a sign for Israel and its descendants forever (Deut 28:46).

7. As different aspects of God stretch back to antiquity, so do various aspects stretch forward into perpetuity. According to Isa 60:19, 20, the Lord is an eternal light for his people, contrasting the darkness that covers the Gentiles. God's word is also eternal. In Isa 40:8, God's word is probably his prophetic pronouncements, which are not annulled by the passage of time; in Ps 119:89, God's word refers to the law, which is not subject to change (see also 111:8; 119:152). God's covenant faithfulness (*ḥesed*), his commitment to his people, is also eternal (1 Chron 16:34; 2 Chron 20:21; Ezra 3:11; Ps 89:2[3]; 100:5; 106:1; 107:1; 118:1, 2, 3, 4, 29; 136:1, 2, 3, etc.; Jer 33:11; cf.

Ps 117:2). Deut 33:27 speaks of God's eternal arms, whereby he protects Israel. In a number of vv., it is stated that God reigns as king forever (Exod 15:18; Ps 9:7[8]; 10:16; 29:10; 66:7; 145:13; 146:10; Jer 10:10; Lam 5:19). Only a few vv., however, state that God himself will continue to exist perpetually: Ps 135:13 says that the name of the Lord endures forever, a metonymy for God himself. In Deut 32:40, God swears to take vengeance on his adversaries, as he lives forever, whereas Ps 102:12[13] says that God abides forever, in contrast to the psalmist himself.

8. There are a few references in which the nom. *'ôlām* is used to denote all time, stretching both forward and backward. The phrase *mē'ôlām 'ad 'ôlām*, from everlasting to everlasting, is used in Ps 41:13[14] ("Praise be to the LORD ... from everlasting to everlasting") and as a description of God's covenant faithfulness (*ḥesed*) in Ps 103:17. In these cases, it does not mean boundless eternity, but from ancient times until the distant future. In Ps 90:2, however, where the same phrase is used to describe God himself, it most likely means boundless time, stretching forward and backwards into perpetuity.

The most controversial reference, however, is found in Eccl 3:11. Here, it is written that God "has placed eternity (*hā'ōlām*) in the hearts of men; yet they cannot fathom what God has done from beginning to end." This v. is the only place in the OT where the nom. *'ôlām* is used as either the subject or object of a vb. Such use is common, however, in postbiblical Heb. and should not be considered a serious difficulty. More problematic is the meaning of the nom. in this phrase. Numerous suggestions have been made, including emending the text (cf. Murphy, 34, for several possibilities). "Eternity" here can well be understood as a circumlocution for "the idea of eternity" (cf. Isa 63:4, "the day of vengeance was in my heart," i.e., the idea of the time for vengeance), and so the phrase can be understood to mean that God has given humanity an innate sense of eternity. In the context of Eccl 3, this statement probably refers to the knowledge that all events occur in their proper time (seasons, life, death, etc.; cf. 3:1-9). The relationship between this statement and the phrase "what God has done from beginning to end" (v. 11) is obscure; the prepositional phrase *mibbᵉlî 'ᵃšer* (translated "yet" in the NIV) is used only here. While it is usually translated as a disjunction, in view of Ecclesiastes' sometimes unique turns of phrase, a word-for-word translation, "without which they cannot comprehend what God has done," should not be eliminated from consideration.

P-B The nom. is frequently attested in postbiblical Heb. It is used extensively in the DSS, in many of the same constructions found in the OT. Here, too, it can refer to either the distant past or the perpetual future. It is used far more frequently in the pl. than in the OT, apparently with an intensive force. In the LXX, it is usually translated *aiōn*, which means "age." In Mish. Heb., the nom. takes on the additional meanings of "age" and "world," especially in the phrases *'ôlām hazzeh*, the present age (or world), and *'ôlām habbā'*, the age (or world) to come, the messianic age.

Time: → *'ōbēd* (ever after, # 7); → *'ōpen* (right time, # 698); → *gîl* I (stage of life, # 1636); → *zmn* (be appointed, # 2374); → *'ôlām* (long time or duration, # 6409); → *'ēt* (time, # 6961); → *pa'am* (foot, step, time, # 7193); → *peta'* (instant, # 7353); → *tāmîd* (continuance, unceasingness, regular offering, # 9458)

→ Time and Eternity: Theology

BIBLIOGRAPHY
THAT 2:228-43; *TWAT* 5:1144-59; J. Barr, *Biblical Words for Time*, 1962; F. M. Cross, *Canaanite Myth and Hebrew Epic*, 1973; S. DeVries, *Yesterday, Today and Tomorrow: Time and History in the Old Testament*, 1975; J. Hartley, *Job*, NICOT, 1988; D. Hillers, *Covenant: The History of a Biblical Idea*, 1969; E. Jenni, "Das Wort *'ôlām* im Alten Testament," *ZAW* 64, 1952, 197-248, and 65, 1953, 1-35; H.-J. Kraus, *Psalms 60-150: A Commentary*, 1989; J. Muilenburg, "The Biblical View of Time," *HTR* 54, 1961, 225-71; R. Murphy, *Ecclesiastes*, WBC, 1992; H. W. Robinson, *Inspiration and Revelation in the Old Testament*, 1946, ch. 8; R. B. Y. Scott, *Proverbs-Ecclesiastes*, AB, 1965, 221; M. Sekine, "Erwägungen zur hebräischen Zeitauffassung," in *Congress Volume: Bonn, 1962, SVT* 9, 1963, 66-80; R. Smith, *Micah-Malachi*, WBC, 1984; N. Snaith, "Time in the Old Testament," in F. F. Bruce (ed.), *Promise and Fulfilment*, 1963, 175-86; J. A. Thompson, *Jeremiah*, NICOT, 1980; J. Walton, *Covenant: God's Purpose, God's Plan*, 1994; R. N. Whybray, *Proverbs*, NCBC, 1994; idem, *Ecclesiastes*, NCBC, 1989; J. Wilch, *Time and Event: An Exegetical Study of 'ēth in the Old Testament in Comparison to Other Temporal Expressions in Clarification of the Concept of Time*, 1969, 1-19; H. W. Wolff, *Anthropology of the Old Testament*, 1973.

Anthony Tomasino

6409a ([*'el*] *'ôlam*, Everlasting God), → # 446a

6411 עָוֹן

עָוֹן (*'āwōn*), nom. iniquity, punishment of sin, transgression (# 6411); < עוה (*'wh*), do wrong, pervert (→ # 6390).

OT Unlike the broad usage of *ḥṭ'*, the term *'āwōn*, iniquity, has predominantly religious and ethical function, a function already seen frequently in the early part of the Pentateuch (Gen 4:6; 15:16; 19:15; Exod 20:5; 34:9; Num 14:34). This word occurs 231x in OT (R. Knierim, *THAT* 2:243-46), and its pl. form sometimes serves as a summary word for all sins against God. In Lev 16:21-22, the word functions as the "key term," as Milgrom calls it, in the confession of sins. Here it is the only term repeated in the summation (v. 22) to include the other two common terms (sin [*ḥṭ'*] and transgression [*pš'*]) in the immediate context (J. Milgrom, *Leviticus 1-16,* 1991, 25, 1043). These three Heb. words, being the most common terms for sin, often occur together in the same context as a phrase (13x in OT), with *'āwōn* frequently standing before the other two (7x). It is not surprising to see that in Exod 34:7, the phrase "wickedness, rebellion, and sin" is used in God's proclamation of his mercy to forgive. While this phrase is intended to signify the totality of sins against God, it also directs our attention to the completeness of God's forgiveness for those who repent.

For a discussion of sin, → *ḥṭ'* (sin, commit a sin; make a sin offering, purify, # 2627).

Sin, guilt, rebellion, transgression, wrong: → *'āwen* (mischief, iniquity, deception, # 224); → *ḥṭ'* (sin, commit a sin, purify, # 2627); → *'wh* (do wrong, pervert, # 6390); → *'wl* I (act wrongly, # 6401); → *pš'* (rebel, violate, transgress, # 7321); → **Fall: Theology**

Alex Luc

6413	עִוְעִים

עִוְעִים (*'iw'îm*), nom. distortion, stagger, dizziness (# 6413).

OT This Heb. nom. occurs only in Isa 19:14: "The LORD has poured into them a spirit of *dizziness*; they make Egypt stagger in all that she does, as a drunkard staggers around in his vomit." It is generally assumed that this nom. is derived from the Heb. root *'wh* (→ # 6340), bend, twist, distort, stagger (cf. Isa 21:3). In this context Isaiah uses *'iw'îm* to depict the unsteady stagger associated with intoxication. The language of intoxication is symbolic of divine judgment.

Shaking, terror, trembling: → *g'š* (rise and fall noisily, swell, surge, # 1723); → *zw'* (tremble, quake, be afraid, # 2316); → *zll* II (shake, quake, tremble, # 2362); → *ḥalḥālâ* (shaking, trembling, anguish, # 2714); → *ḥrg* (come out trembling, # 3004); → *ḥrd* (tremble, shudder, startle, # 3006); → *yr'* (tremble, be fainthearted, # 3760); → *mwṭ* (waver, reel, stagger, shake, reel, # 4572); → *m'd* (slip, slide, shake, totter, # 5048); → *nwd* (shake, totter, waiver, wander, mourn, flee, # 5653); → *nwṭ* (shake, quake, # 5667); → *nw'* (shake, tremble, stagger, totter, wave, # 5675); → *n'r* II (shake, shake off, # 5850); → *smr* (shudder, have goose-bumps, bristle, # 6169); → *'iw'îm* (distortion, stagger, dizzy, # 6413); → *pwq* I (stagger, wobble, reel, totter, # 7048); → *pḥd* I (tremble, be in dread, # 7064); → *plṣ* (shudder, shake, tremble, # 7145); → *qwṣ* I (feel disgust, frighten, cause dread, # 7762); → *rgz* (agitate, quiver, shake, excite, rouse up, agitate, # 8074); → *rnh* I (rattle, # 8261); → *r'd* (tremble, shake, tremble, # 8283); → *r'l* I (brandish, make to quiver, # 8302); → *r'š* I (quake, shake, leap, # 8321); → *rpp* (shake, quake, rock, # 8344); → *r^{e}ṭēt* (terror, panic, trembling, # 8417); → *ś'r* I (be afraid, terrified, bristle with horror, # 8547)
Drinking, intoxication: → *sb'* (drink excessively, # 6010); → *škr* (be or become drunk, # 8910); → *šth* II (drinking, # 9272)

M. V. Van Pelt/W. C. Kaiser, Jr.

6414	עוף

עוף (*'wp* I), q. fly; pol. fly about; hitpol. fly away (# 6414); עוֹף (*'ôp*), nom. bird (→ # 6416); עַפְעַפַּיִם (*'ap'appayim*), eyelids (→ # 6757).

ANE The cognate term *'p'p* occurs in Ugar. with the same meaning.

OT 1. The vb. denotes a movement, frequently a very rapid movement, and refers variously to forces who "swoop down" on their enemies (Isa 11:14), arrows (Ps 91:5), birds (Gen 1:20; Deut 4:17; Hab 1:8), the days of ones life (Ps 90:10), dreams (Job 20:8), clouds (Isa 60:8), locusts (Nah 3:16), a flying scroll carrying away the curse and the accursed (Zech 5:1, 2; → Curse), riches (Prov 23:5), seraphim (Isa 6:2), serpents (Isa 14:29; see Wiseman), sparks of fire (Job 5:7), sword (Ezek 32:10, NIV brandish), and Zion's treasure-laden ships (Isa 60:8).

2. The sight of birds in the sky was a marvel for the ancient Hebrews. Far from looking at the flight of birds for omens or signs, they saw these creatures as part of God's creation. Nevertheless, large birds, such as the *nešer*, inspired them with awe, "There are three things that are too amazing for me, four that I do not understand: the way of an eagle (*nešer*) in the sky, the way of a snake on a rock, the way of a ship on the high seas, and the way of a man with a maiden" (Prov 30:18-19). It is little wonder that the way of birds became a metaphor for God's relation with the world. On the one

hand, God is awe-inspiring as he makes his entry into the world of creation. On the other hand, God is loving as he cares for his people.

3. In a derived way, the metaphor of flight also expresses something about human kings. But, unlike God, they are all too often characterized as filled with power and pride. Like birds, they swoop on the nations and loot and destroy, as if they were birds of prey. Yet, human kingdoms are also are in God's hands. He uses them for his purposes, and he sets them aside in his judgment.

Many of these occurrences are figurative or metaphorical. The images convey encouragement or rebuke and judgment. For example, Isaiah comforts the people with these words, "Like birds hovering overhead, the LORD Almighty will shield Jerusalem; he will shield it and deliver it, he will 'pass over' it and will rescue it" (Isa 31:5). Hosea likens God's judgment on Israel to a sudden disaster: "Ephraim's glory will fly away like a bird—no birth, no pregnancy, no conception" (Hos 9:11).

The vb. also appears in theophanic imagery: "He (Yahweh) mounted the cherubim and flew; he soared on the wings of the wind" (Ps 18:10[11] = 2 Sam 22:11; see *d'h*).

Flying, wing: → *'br* (fly, # 87); → *gwz* (fly away, pass, # 1577); → *d'h* (fly swiftly, # 1797); → *ṭwś* (rush, dart, # 3216); → *kānāp* (wing, skirt, outermost edge, # 4053); → *mr'* (spring, fly?, # 5257); → *nôṣâ* (feathers, # 5681); → *'wp* I (fly, fly about, fly away, # 6414)

Birds, flying creatures: → *'br* (fly, # 87); → *bêṣâ* (egg, # 1070); → *barbur* (species of fowl, # 1350); → *gôzāl* (young bird, # 1578); → *dgr* (hatch eggs, # 1842); → *ḥᵃsîdâ* (stork, # 2884); → *yônâ* I (dove, # 3433); → *yaᶜᵃnâ* (ostrich, eagle-owl?, # 3613); → *kānāp* (wing, skirt, outermost edge, # 4053); → *nešer/nᵉšar* (vulture [eagle], # 5979); → *'ôp* (flying creatures, # 6416); → *'ayiṭ* (birds of prey [collective], # 6514); → *'ōrēb* I (raven, # 6854); → *ṣippôr* I (birds, # 7606); → *qōrē'* I (partridge, # 7926); → *śᵉlāw* (quails, # 8513)

BIBLIOGRAPHY

G. R. Driver, "Birds in the OT," *PEQ* 86, 1955, 5-20; 87, 1955, 129-40; idem, "Once Again: Birds in the Bible," *PEQ* 90, 1958, 56-58; D. J. Wiseman, "Flying Serpents?" *TynBul* 23, 1972, 108-10.

George L. Klein

6415	עוף

עוף (*'wp* II), q. be dark (# 6415); מוּעָף (*mû'āp*), nom. gloom (→ # 4599); מָעוּף (*mā'ûp*), nom. gloom (# 5066); עֵיפָה (*'êpâ* I), nom. darkness (# 6547); תְּעֻפָה (*tᵉ'upâ*), nom. darkness conj. (# 9507).

ANE The vb. is not attested in the other Sem. languages except possibly in a derived nom. in Akk. *upû*, cloud. Akk. *apû* = become dim/cloudy—is used only of the eyes and may not be relevant—although the nom. is similarly employed.

OT 1. The vb. occurs only once in the OT and that only in the q. stem with the meaning to be dark, figurative of misery and gloom. Zophar counseled Job that if he would repent of his sins, "Your life would be brighter than noonday, though it is dark (*'wp*), it would be like morning" (Job 11:17, lit. tr.); but see the discussion below under *tᵉ'upâ,* darkness (# 9507).

2. The nom. *mû'āp*, gloom, occurs only once in the OT: "Nevertheless, there will be no more gloom for those who were in distress" (Isa 9:1[8:23]). Cf. *mā'ûp*, gloom, in 8:22.

3. The nom. *mā'ûp*, gloom, occurs only once in the OT in const. with another word—"fearful gloom" (lit. gloom of anguish): "Then they will look toward the earth and see only distress and darkness (*ḥ^a šēkâ*) and fearful gloom (*mā'ûp*), and they will be thrust into utter darkness" (*'apēlâ*, Isa 8:22). Cf. *mû'āp*, gloom in Isa 9:1[8:23].

4. The word *'êpâ* I or *'êpātâ*, darkness, occurs 2x in the OT, only in poetry. Speaking of God's creative power, Amos referred to him as "he who turns dawn to darkness (*'êpâ*)" (Amos 4:13). Figuratively, it is used of the darkness of the grave or the netherworld. In Job's complaint to God, he said, "Are not my few days almost over? Turn away from me so I can have a moment's joy before I go to the place of no return, to the land of gloom (*ḥōšek*, # 3125) and deep shadow (*ṣalmawet*, # 7516), to the land of deepest (*'ōpel*, # 694) night (*'êpātâ*), of deep shadow (*ṣalmawet*, # 7516) and disorder, where even the light is like darkness (*'ōpel*, # 694)" (Job 10:20-22).

5. The word *t^e 'upâ*, nom. darkness (conj.), occurs only once in the OT, "and darkness will become like morning" (Job 11:17). The MT reads *tā'upâ*, which is morphologically a vb. meaning "though it be dark"; but NIV follows *HALAT* in conjecturally emending the form to *t^e 'upâ* as a nom. Such an emendation of the MT is questionable, since the text makes sense as it stands (cf. ASV and NKJV). Franz Delitzsch prefers the vb. form because the word is accented on the penult, as required for this form of the vb.; the nom. form requires the accent on the ultima.

P-B In Modern Heb. the nom. *t^e 'ûpâ*, means "flight, aviation," and the nom. *mā'ûp* means "flight." In the Tg. *'êpā'* means cover or veil.

Darkness: → *'ōpel* (darkness, gloom, # 694); → *'^e šûn* (approach of darkness, # 854); → *ḥšk* (be, grow dark, grow dim, darken, conceal, confuse, # 3124); → *ṭuḥôt* (darkness, obscurity, inward parts, # 3219); → *kamrîr* (blackness, deep gloom, # 4025); → *laylâ* (night, # 4326); → *nešep* (twilight, darkness, # 5974); → *'wp* II (be dark, # 6415); → *'^a lāṭâ* (darkness, dusk, # 6602); → *'mm* II (darken, dim, # 6670); → *'^a rāpel* (deep darkness, thick darkness, heavy cloud, # 6906); → *ṣll* III (be/grow dark, cast a shadow, # 7511); → *ṣalmāwet* (darkness, shadow of death, # 7516); → *qdr* (be dark, mourn, # 7722)

BIBLIOGRAPHY

TWOT 2:655; F. Delitzsch, *Job*, I, KD 187-88; E. J. Young, *The Book of Isaiah*, 1:321-24.

James D. Price

6416	עוֹף

עוֹף (*'ôp*), flying creatures (# 6416).

ANE Sem. cognates: Ugar. *'p*, Aram. *'ôpā'*, Sam., Syr. *'aupā'*, Arab. *'auf*.

OT 1. In the OT *'ôp* is a generic term for flying creatures, including insects (Gen 7:14, 21; Lev 11:20-23; Deut 14:19). In God's creation the flying creatures were designed, along with animals, to be controlled and governed by man (Gen 1:26, 28). After the Flood, flying creatures were also allowed as food for humankind (Gen 9:2-3).

2. In worship, therefore, clean birds, as part of the daily food of the Israelites, could be an offering to God. Such a distinction between clean and unclean birds was already known by Noah (Gen 8:20, → *'ōrēb*). Since birds were entrusted to the hand of

humankind at the creation, they were inevitably affected by human sins, which became evident in the judgment of God. Birds frequently appear in the pronouncement of judgment in prophetic literature with two aspects: sharing the destiny of humans (Gen 6:7; Jer 4:25; Hos 4:3; Zeph 1:3) and implementing the divine punishment (Deut 28:26; Jer 15:3; Ezek 29:5, etc.). In the latter case, "the birds of the air" are obviously birds of prey and, therefore, unclean. Hence, it could be maintained, as in the case of unclean animals devouring corpses (→ *ḥayyâ,* # 2651), that God uses the force of death in his punishment on human sins (→ *ya'ᵃnâ*).

3. In the restoration of Israel (Hos 2:18[20]) the birds, along with other creatures, are partners in the covenant God makes for humans (as in Gen 9:10).

4. In Wisdom literature, birds evidence skill (Job 12:7; Eccl 10:20) beyond that of humans. In Job 38-39 God reminds Job of a series of birds (among them, the ostrich [*rᵉnānîm,* 39:13, # 8266], the falcon [*nēṣ* II, 39:26, # 5891, NIV hawk], the cock [? *śēkwî,* 38:36, # 8498, NIV the mind, see *HALAT*], *nōṣâ* II, # 5902 [falcon ?] in 39:13 is not used in NIV), the wisdom or folly of which is given by God's unfathomable wisdom. In Prov 30:19, 31 the eagle and rooster (*zarzîr,* # 2435) are part of the creation that gives to human beings not only the wonder and mystery of God's world, but also enjoyment.

P-B In the DSS *'ôp* appears mostly in 1QH (e.g., 8:9) and 11QTemple (e.g., 48:4). It is also found extensively in Late Heb. in the forms of *'ôp, 'ôpôt.* The biblical phrase *'ôp kānāp* is also found, though relatively small in number (e.g., Pirqe Rabbi Eliezer 8a). LXX almost always renders *'ôp* by *peteinon*, mostly its pl. form. The latter term occurs 6x in the Apoc. In the NT the latter term occurs 14x, in 9x of which it is paired with *ouranos* (heaven, e.g., Matt 6:26; 8:20; 13:32).

Birds, flying creatures: → *'br* (fly, # 87); → *bêṣâ* (egg, # 1070); → *barbur* (species of fowl, # 1350); → *gôzāl* (young bird, # 1578); → *dgr* (hatch eggs, # 1842); → *ḥᵃsîdâ* (stork, # 2884); → *yônâ* I (dove, # 3433); → *ya'ᵃnâ* (ostrich, eagle-owl?, # 3613); → *kānāp* (wing, skirt, outermost edge, # 4053); → *nešer/nᵉšar* (vulture [eagle], # 5979); → *'ôp* (flying creatures, # 6416); → *'ayiṭ* (birds of prey [collective], # 6514); → *'ōrēb* I (raven, # 6854); → *ṣippôr* I (birds, # 7606); → *qōrē'* I (partridge, # 7926); → *śᵉlāw* (quails, # 8513)

Bibliography

ABD 6:1109-67; V. P. Hamilton, *Genesis* 1-17, 1990; W. Houston, *Purity and Monotheism: Clean and Unclean Animals in Biblical Law,* 1993; G. J. Wenham, *Genesis 1-15*, 1990.

N. Kiuchi

6418 ('wṣ, make plans), → # 3619

6421	עוק

עוק (*'wq* I), q. crush(?), break(?), totter(?); hi. crush(?), break(?), cause to totter(?) (# 6421); nom. מוּעָקָה (*mû'āqâ*), distress, hardship (# 4601); עָקָה (*'āqâ* I), misery, hardship (# 6821).

ANE Arab. *'aqqa,* to split open; Ugar. *'qq,* rend, devour (*KTU* 1.12:I:27; Gibson, *CML*² 154, "ravenous beast").

OT The verbal (i.e., q. and hi.) and nom. forms are all hapleg. The precise meaning of these three words is difficult to determine. However, from the contexts wherein the nom. forms are used (Ps 55:3[4]; 66:11), it becomes clear that they denote some form of affliction. These two words are clearly used in contexts where the psalmists suffer persecution, insult, distress, and captivity at the hand of enemies (55:3[4]) and God (66:11). In the latter psalm *mû'āqâ* is used in the context of divine visitation: God refines his people and tests their trust in, and loyalty to, him (v. 10) by bringing distress (note the NIV's translation of *mû'āqâ* with "burden") upon them. In Amos 2:13 the vb. describes the nature of God's judgment of Israel.

Affliction, oppression: → *dḥq* (oppress, # 1895); → *ḥms* I (do violence, # 2803); → *ḥmṣ* II (oppress, # 2807); → *ynh* (oppress, # 3561); → *lḥṣ* (press, # 4315); → *māṣôr* I (affliction, siege, # 5189); → *mrr* I (be bitter, distraught, afflict, # 5352); → *nega'* (plague, affliction, # 5596); → *ngś* (exact, # 5601); → *'nh* II (afflict, humble, afflict one's soul, fast, oppress, submit, # 6700); → *'wq* I (crush?, # 6421); → *'mr* II (deal tyrannically with, # 6683); → *'šq* I (wrong, # 6943); → *ṣwq* I (constrain, press in/upon, harass, vex, # 7439); → *ṣwr* II (deal tyrannically with, # 7444); → *rhb* (assail, press, pester, alarm, confuse, # 8104); → *rṣṣ* (crush, # 8368); → *tôlāl* (oppressor, # 9354); → *tōk* (oppression, # 9412)

BIBLIOGRAPHY

T. D. Hanks, *God So Loved the Third World: The Biblical Vocabulary of Oppression*, 1983, 3-39; Y. I. Kim, "The Vocabulary of Oppression in the Old Testament," Ph.D. diss. Drew University, 1981; C. F. Marriottini, "The Problem of Social Oppression in the Eighth Century Prophets," Ph.D. diss. Southern Baptist Theological Seminary, 1983; J. Miranda, *Communism in the Bible*, 1982, 37-39; J. Pons, *L'oppression dans l'Ancien Testament*, 1981; E. Tamez, *Bible of the Oppressed*, 1982, 1-30.

I. Swart

6422	עור

עור (*'wr* I), pi. blind s.o.; be blind (# 6422); עִוֵּר (*'iwwēr*), blind (# 6426); עִוָּרוֹן (*'iwwārôn*), loss of sight (# 6427); עַוֶּרֶת (*'awweret*), blindness (# 6428).

OT 1. The vb. *'wr,* make blind, is used to speak of the physical blindness of King Zedekiah (2 Kgs 25:7; Jer 39:7; 52:11), and it occurs also metaphorically to describe the judicial blindness of judges who succumb to bribes (Exod 23:8; Deut 16:19).

2. The nom. *'iwwēr*, blind, is used with both literal and figurative meanings. God makes people with sight or blindness (Exod 4:11), but he is able to heal blindness (Ps 146:8) and will do so in the eschatological day (Isa 29:18; 35:5; 42:7, 16; Jer 31:8). Meanwhile, it is a serious violation of covenant to cause the blind to stumble (Lev 19:14) or lead them astray (Deut 27:18). On the other hand, blind priests cannot serve God (Lev 21:18), nor may blind animals be offered to him for his own perfections call for perfection in his ministers and in the gifts presented to him (Deut 15:21; Mal 1:8).

Blindness is also a metaphor for confusion or spiritual insensitivity. Covenant disobedience will cause one to stagger like a blind man (Deut 28:29; cf. Lam 4:14; Zeph 1:17). Israel, whose history was marked by such defection, is therefore described as blind (Isa 59:10), a servant people whose spiritual sight has been lost (42:18, 19; 43:8). Her very watchmen (i.e., her prophets) have, ironically, lost their capacity to watch by virtue of having become blind to truth (56:10).

3. The nom. *'awweret*, blindness, is used in Lev 22:22 alone, speaking there of the disqualification of blind animals for sacrifice.

4. The rare derivative *'iwwārôn*, loss of sight, occurs in Deut 28:28 as divine punishment for disobeying covenant provisions, and also in Zech 12:4 as an affliction imposed by God upon the horses of those forces attacking Jerusalem.

NT → *NIDNTT* 1:218-20.

Handicaps, disfigurement, blind, lame, stammer, speechless: → *'illēm* (speechlessness, # 522); → *gibbēn* (hunchbacked, # 1492); → *ḥārûṣ* IV (mutilation [animal], # 3024); → *ḥērēš* (speechless, # 3094); → *kšḥ* (be lame, crippled, # 4171); → *mûm* (blemish, # 4583); → *mišḥāt* (disfigured, # 5425); → *nākeh* (crippled, smitten, # 5783); → *'wr* I (be blind, # 6422); → *'illēg* (stammering, stuttering, # 6589); → *psḥ* (be lame, crippled, # 7174); → *ṣl'* I (limping condition, # 7519); → *qlṭ* I (defective [animal], # 7832); → *śr'* (deformed, mutilated, # 8594); → *t^eballul* (white spot in eye, # 9319)

R. K. Harrison/E. H. Merrill

6424	עור

עור (*'wr* II), q. stir oneself, be awake; ni. set in motion; polel stir up, brandish; hi. rouse, order, disturb; summon; hitpol. rouse o.s. (# 6424).

ANE For cognate Sem. roots cf. Ugar *'r* (*WUS*, # 2092; *UT*, # 1849), *'rr* (*UT*, # 1926), awaken, and *ǵr*, be awake; Akk. *êru(m)*, awake (*AHw*, 247a; *CAD* 4:326); Arab. *'arra* VI, be restless and *ǵyr*, agitate for/against s.t. (Leslau: *Ethiopic and South Arabic Contributions to the Hebrew Lexicon*, 1958, 38). The root is present also in Syr., Mand., and Aram. (cf. Sefire II B 4, *ym zy y'wrn*, "YM who are watchful" [J. A. Fitzmyer, *The Aramaic Inscriptions of Sefire*, 1967, 80-81, 86-87]). For an alternate reading of the Aram. vb., see A. Lemaire and J.-M. Durand, *Les inscriptions araméennes de Sfiré et l'Assyrie de Shamshi-ilu*, 1984, 117, 127, 141, "who are under treaty obligations" (*y'dwn*).

OT 1. In the simple and passive stems the vb. is used for being aroused or excited to some activity. In the factitive and causative stems the vb. is used for arousing or stirring somebody to action. The activities to which one is aroused are those that require extra effort, such as war, work, or love.

2. *'wr* II occurs several times in conjunction with *qyṣ* (→ # 7810): (1) Ps 73:20, "As a dream when one awakes (*mēhāqîṣ*), O Lord, on awakening (emending MT *bā'îr* to *b^ehā'îr* [see *BHS* and Avishur, 681]) you will despise them as fantasies"; (2) in syndetic parataxis, "Awake (*hā'îrâ*), and rise (*w^ehāqîṣâ*) to my defense!" (35:23); (3) in reverse order, "Woe to him who says to wood, 'Come to life' (*hāqîṣâ*)! Or to lifeless stone 'Wake up' (*'ûrî*)!" (Hab 2:19); (4) in parallelism, "Awake (*'ûrâ*), O Lord ... Rouse yourself (*hāqîṣâ*)...." (Ps 44:23[24]); (5) in parallelism between two verses, "Arise (*'ûrâ*) to help me; look on my plight" (Ps 59:4[5]), and "rouse yourself (*hāqîṣâ*) to punish all the nations" (59:5[6]).

While different vbs. are used in the OT for "stir, wake up," the subj. and obj. of the vb. varies. For example, the stirring of water is conveyed by *grš* II (Isa 57:20; Amos 8:8) and *ḥmr* II (Hab 3:15). When God is the subj., the vb. may be *swk* I (Isa 19:2) or *yqṣ* (Ps 78:65), and when God is the obj. (normally in an impv.), the vb. is either *qyṣ* (Ps 44:23) or *'wr* II (Ps 35:23). When God is the subj. of the vb., the emphasis is on the affirmation of faith in the power and authority of God. No nation, whatever its superpower status, operates autonomously. And no nation, however dominant militarily, is immune to his hand of judgment. He incites the Medes against Babylon and Egyptian against Egyptian. God even rouses enemies against Israel; e.g., against Rezin (*swk* I, Isa 9:11[10]), against Jehoram (*ʿwr* II, 2 Chron 21:16), against Israelite tribes (*ʿwr* II, 1 Chron 5:26). But God also arouses and stirs nations that would become the means of Israel's deliverance (Cyrus, *ʿwr* II, 2 Chron 36:22). Thus, the aroused nations of the earth are Yahweh's servants for weal or woe.

The emphasis is changed when God is the object of these vbs. If, when God is subj. the emphasis is on the affirmation of faith, then when God is the object, the emphasis is on the challenge to faith. The first is doxological. The second is skeptical. The first uses the indicative. The second uses the impv. The first is testimony. The second is protest. The concern here is not so much that God is hostile, but that he is indifferent or neglectful, or entirely too passive. And this concern may be expressed in either a community complaint (Ps 44:23[24]; 80:2[3]) or an individual complaint (35:23). For the faithful the protracted silences of God, especially in times of tension or crisis, have always been a conundrum. Noting how such psalms combine reverence with disappointment, hope with despair, confidence in the character of God with exasperation at his inaction, R. Foster (*Prayer: Finding the Heart's True Home*, 1992, 23) suggests that such psalms "give us permission to shake our fist at God one moment and break into doxology the next."

3. Apart from Job 41:10[2], S of Songs 5:2, and Mal 2:12, all other uses of *ʿwr* II in the q. are in the impv. (fem.: Judg 5:12[3x]; S of Songs 4:16; Isa 51:9[3x]; 52:1[2x]; Hab 2:19; Zech 13:7; masc.: Ps 7:6[7]; 44:23[24]; 57:8[9](2x); 59:4[5]; 108:2[3]). Those summoned to awake include the wind for refreshment (S of Songs 4:16), Zion to joy (Isa 52:1), a songstress to celebration (Judg 5:12), lifeless stone (Hab 2:19), the sword to judgment (Zech 13:7), musical instruments to playing (Ps 57:8[9] 108:2[3]), God himself for intervention (Ps 7:6[7]; 44:23[24]; 59:4[5]), and God's arm (Isa 51:9).

The last group is the most interesting, those in which God is told to rouse himself. This prayer can also be conveyed by the polel impv. (Ps 80:2[3]: "...Awaken [*ʿôr^{e}râ*] your might; come and save us") and by the hi. impv. (35:23, "Awake [*hāʿîrâ*], and rise to my defense!"). In only one of these Psalm references (44:23[24]) is there a reference to God's sleeping (cf. 78:65, which refers to Yahweh's waking [*yqṣ*] like one who had slept), and the presence of a v. like Ps 121:4 ("he who watches over Israel will neither slumber nor sleep") suggests that the writer of Ps 44 is using sleep metaphorically, to refer to a perceived sense of inexplicable divine inactivity.

One might also suggest that references in the Psalms calling upon God to rouse or bestir himself (and similar phrases such as "Arise, O LORD!" [Ps 3:7(8); 9:19(20); 10:12, etc.]) reflect an OT tradition that God saves his chosen when the light of the sun appears in the morning. Thus, it was "at daybreak" that God delivered his people from the pursuing Egyptians (Exod 14:27); and it was when God's people "got up the next morning" (2 Kgs 19:35) that they saw God's judgment on the Assyrians. For the theme of deliverance in the morning in Isaiah, when darkness gives way to light, see Isa 8:22-9:2; 17:14; 33:2; 42:16; 49:9; 58:10; 60:1. Little wonder then that the psalmist proclaims (Ps 30:5[6]), "...weeping may remain for a night, but rejoicing comes in the morning." The morning is the time when God does his work.

4. If frequently God is the object of the vb. when it is in the q., then as frequently he is the subject of the vb. when it is in the hi. That is to say, God not only is aroused to action, but arouses others to actions. This idea is especially prominent when *rûaḥ* is the object of the vb.

For example, Hag 1:14 states that "the LORD stirred up the spirit of Zerubbabel ... and the spirit of the whole remnant ... [and they] began to work on the house of the LORD." So when used with *rûaḥ*, the hi. of *'wr* II means to arouse to action. Normally there is a political context for the activity in question. Yahweh stirred up the kings of the Medes against Babylon (Jer 51:11); the spirit of a destroyer against Babylon (Jer 51:1); the spirit of the king of Assyria against several Israelite tribes (1 Chron 5:26); the spirit (NIV hostilities) of the Philistines and Arabs against Jehoram and Judah (2 Chron 21:16); the spirit of Cyrus (NIV moved the heart) to make a proclamation regarding the building of the Jerusalem temple (2 Chron 36:22; Ezra 1:1). The same idea is present in Isa 13:17 ("I will stir up against them [Babylon] the Medes") but without the object *rûaḥ*.

Only in Hag 1:14 (cited above) and Ezra 1:5 does "stir/arouse the spirit" refer to action by Israelites. And since all the other usages are patently political, the appearance of the phrase in Hag 1:14 suggests that the action of rebuilding the temple is not totally devoid of political import (i.e., a reflection of limited autonomy and internal self-rule).

5. If God stirs up agents of destruction (see above), he also stirs up messiahs and saviors for his people, i.e., Cyrus (Isa 41:2, 25; 45:13 [NIV raise up]); he stirs up his own exiled people and prepares them for restoration and as agents of judgment against the nations (Jon 3:7[4:7]); and God compares himself to an eagle that stirs up its nest, hovers over its young, and catches them on his wings as a powerful figure of speech of his love for his people (Deut 32:11).

6. On a few occasions the hi. is used to refer to humans rather than God, stirring up other persons against a third party (Dan 11:2; Jon 3:9[4:9]).

7. In addition to the activity of war to which one is aroused, one may also be aroused to an activity like love. Three times in the S of Songs (2:7; 3:5; 8:4) the daughters of Jerusalem are admonished: "Do not arouse (*'wr* II, hi.) or awaken (*'wr* II, polel) love until it so desires." "Arouse ... awaken" might also be rendered "incite ... excite." The prohibition is clear enough. Love personified as a force, a power, should not be artificially or prematurely stimulated. Let it emerge in its proper time.

P-B For the vb. in the Qumran texts see CD 12:18; 13:7; 19:7; 1QH 6:29; 9:3.

Stirring, tossing: → *grš* II (toss up, # 1764); → *ḥmr* II (foam, surge, # 2812); → *swk* I (stir up, # 6056); → *'wr* II (stir oneself, # 6424); → *rḥš* (be stirred up, # 8180)

Stirring, waking up: → *yqṣ* (awake, # 3699); → *'wr* II (stir oneself, # 6424); → *qyṣ* II (awake, # 7810)

BIBLIOGRAPHY

TDNT 2:333-39 (= *TWNT* 2:332-37); *TWAT* 5:1184-90; *TWOT* 2:655-56; Y. Avishur, *Stylistic Studies of Word-Pairs in Biblical and Semitic Literatures*, 1984; C. C. Broyles, *The Conflict of Faith and Experience in the Psalms*, JSOTSup 52, 1989, 76-80; J. J. Stamm, "Ein ugaritisch-hebräisches Verbum und seine Ableitungen," *TZ* 35, 1979, 5-9; J. Thompson, "Sleep:

An Aspect of Jewish Anthropology," *VT* 5, 1955, 420-33; R. J. Tournay, *Seeing and Hearing God with the Psalms*, JSOTSup 118, 1991, 155-56.

Victor P. Hamilton

6425	עוֹר

עוֹר (*'ôr*), nom. (human) skin, hide, leather (99x, # 6425). The root underlying this nom. is unclear: *'wr* II, be naked, *'rr* I, strip oneself, lay bare, and *'rh* I, lay bare (pi.), make naked (hi.) all have merit.

ANE Punic *'rt* leather, skin (*KAI* 69, 74), and *'wr* [?]; Ugar. **'r*, though unattested in alphabetic texts, a polyglot vocabulary list cites (Sum.) SU= (Akk.) *ma-aš-ku* = (Hurrian) *aš-ḫé* = (Ugar.) [*ú*]*-ru*, leather, skin (J. Nougayrol, et al., *Ugaritica* 5, 1968, text 130 ii 6'). *uru/ūru* is the closest that Akk. writing could vocalize the likely Ugar. vocalization **'ōru*. Additionally, in an economic text listing garments, one entry written with Akk. signs but representing a Ugar. word is "2 *túgú-ra-tu*." Most likely, this entry denotes "2 leather garments," the Ugar. word here being pl. and vocalized /*'ōrātu*/, cf. BH *'ôrôt* (Huehnergard, 159). It is unlikely that Ugar. *ġr* (or *ġr*), cited in *HALAT* as a possible cognate, refers to "skin, hide," since the spelling *túgú-ra-tu* rules out /*ġ*/ as the initial consonant: Akk. *ḫ*-signs are used for Ugar. /*ġ*/, while *ú* can represent initial /'/, /h/, or /'/.

OT 1. The word refers to human and animal skin. It is used nonfiguratively to refer to the human organ that covers the body (Job 7:5) and as synecdoche to refer to the whole person (Exod 22:27[26] NIV body).

2. The use of this word in "I am left with the skin of my teeth" (Job 19:20; NIV I have escaped with only the skin of my teeth) is difficult to understand. The surrounding context suggests that Job has been delivered from death but in a condition where death might have been a better alternative. Job is saying that he escaped nothing, in contrast to the common English usage of this idiom to refer to a narrow, but genuine escape (Clines, 452; Clines also offers a good review of scholarly opinions, 430-32).

3. Many consider the phrase "skin for skin" (Job 2:4) to come from the world of bartering, a phrase referring to fair exchange, pelt for pelt. "Skin" may be synecdoche here for "person": Job has given up his family and household members, and the adversary claims that anybody will forfeit other people's lives to save oneself. Borrowing the idea of an outer and inner skin from Arab. literature, some have suggested that the phrase refers to vengeance, similar to "an eye for an eye": Job will pay back any harm done to him.

4. Animal skin or hide is often the sense of the word. Animal skin was used for garments in Gen 3:21, where God, in a meaningful gesture of kindness, clothes the human couple with skin graments. Animal skins also cover the tabernacle (Exod 26:14). The word also refers to leather articles (Lev 11:32; 13:48-59).

P-B The senses of "skin" and "hide/leather" continue to be connected with this word.

Skin, leather: → *'ādām* II (leather, # 133); → *'ahᵃbâ* II (leather, # 174); → *'ôb* I (wine-skin, # 199); → *gēled* (skin, # 1654); → *ḥēmet* (waterskin, # 2827); → *nō'd* (bottle, scroll, # 5532);

→ *'ôr* (skin, hide, # 6425); → *ṣhl* II (shine [of healthy skin], # 7413); → *taḥrā'* (leather collar?, # 9389); → *taḥaš* I (leather?, # 9391)

Bibliography

TWOT 2:657; D. J. A. Clines, *Job 1-20*, WBC, 1989; L. DeVries, "Skin," *ISBE* 4:535-36; J. Huehnergard, *Ugaritic Vocabulary in Syllabic Transcription*, 1987; R. Reed, *Ancient Skins, Parchment and Leathers*, 1972; J. C. Trever, "Leather," *ISBE* 3:97.

Gary Alan Long

6426 (*'iwwēr*, blind), → # 6422

6427 (*'iwwārôn*, loss of sight), → # 6422

6428 (*'awweret*, blindness), → # 6422

6430	עות

עות (*'wt*), pi. make crooked, pervert; pu. bent; hitp. bend (6430); עַוָּתָה (*'awwātâ*), oppression (hapleg.; # 6432).

ANE A possible cognate *'tt*, cheat, twist, in Syr. might be related to a secondary Heb. root *'wh*, Akk. (Old Babylonian) *ewû*, overcharge, or Arab. *ǵwy*, go astray (see *HALAT* 752-53, 760).

OT 1. An allegorical description of the increasing decrepitude of old age uses a physical sense of the word in the hitp. Among other things, the "strong men," i.e., the legs (cf. Ps 147:10) "bend" (RSV; *stoop,* NIV, REB; Eccl 12:3). The vb. here indicates an abnormal, degenerative state, as is also the case with the pi., which is parallel with "what is lacking" (*ḥsr*) in 1:15. It is contrasted with something straightened or made right (*tqn*; 1:15; 7:13), though in the last reference any negative connotation is lacking. What is twisted, especially if by God himself (7:13), may not be rectified by mortals, even in their pursuit for wisdom (1:12-18).

2. More commonly, *'wt* has a metaphorical use in the area of ethical practice, signifying a moral deviation from the correct path. Someone can commit a specific wrongdoing, such as using dishonest scales to "cheat" (NIV) or "swindle" (JB; Amos 8:5). This is a similar use to the concept of being "crooked" or "bent" as we have in Eng. A legal dispute (*rîb*) can also be "subverted" (NRSV; Lam 3:36) when decided on grounds other than its own merits.

The term also signifies a more general, undefined perversion of justice (Ps 119:78). The fact that this kind of activity is unthinkable on the part of God (Job 8:3; 34:12) leads to a theological quandary for Job. He believes in the justice of God, who "frustrates" (NIV, JB) or makes crooked the way of the wicked (Ps 146:9) as a fitting punishment for their perversity. If Job's friends are correct in claiming that Job is a sinner suffering for his own misdeeds (Job 19:5), it must be because God has in fact made him such (v. 6), God has perverted him, since Job views himself as innocent. He does not deny that God is having him suffer, since that is evident to all around him (vv. 7-20). He does not have complete understanding of why this is happening, but he knows that he is innocent and that God cannot pervert justice. He can only rely on the assurance that God, his Redeemer, is alive and that Job will ultimately see God, a privilege reserved for one exonerated from any guilt (vv. 25-27). All theological rationalizing cannot take the place of assurance of his own innocence and God's justice.

Corruption: → *'lḥ* (be corrupted, # 480); → *muṭṭeh* (corruption of justice, # 4754); → *sûr* (corrupt, # 6074); → *šḥt* (become corrupt, ruin, spoil, # 8845)

BIBLIOGRAPHY
TWOT 2:657.

David W. Baker

6432 (*'awwātâ*, oppression), → # 6430

6434 (*'az*, strong, defiant, shameless), → # 6451

6435 (*'āz*, strength), → # 6451

6436	עֵז

עֵז (*'ēz*), goat, fabric made out of goat's hair (# 6436).

OT During the wilderness wanderings, the women spun a fabric from this abundant material (Exod 35:26). These fabrics were used for making the curtains of the tabernacle (36:14).

For a discussion on goat, see *ṣō'n,* (flock, # 7366).

Fabrics, material: → *b^erōmîm* (fabric of two colors, # 1394); → *ḥ^aṭubôt* (colored fabric, # 2635); → *'ēz* (fabric made out of goat's hair, # 6436); → *ṣeba'* (colored, dyed fabric, # 7389); → *ša'aṭnēz* (material, linen?, # 9122); → *tl'* II (clad in scarlet material, # 9433)
Spinning, sewing, weaving, embroidering: → *'rg* (spin, weave, # 755); → *dallâ* I (hair, thrum, loom, # 1929); → *ḥōšēb* (weaver, # 3110); → *ṭwh* (spin, # 3211); → *kîšôr* (distaff, # 3969); → *mānôr* (rod, # 4962); → *skk* II (weave, intertwine, # 6115); → *'ēreb* I (knitted material, # 6849); → *pelek* I (spindle-whorl, # 7134); → *rqm* (embroider, weave together, # 8387); → *ś^erād* (woven, # 8573); → *šbṣ* I (weave, # 8687); → *š^etî* I (woven material, # 9274); → *tpr* (sew, # 9529)

Robert L. Alden

6437 (*'ōz*, strength, power, strong), → # 6451

6439	עֲזָאזֵל

עֲזָאזֵל (*'^azā'zēl*), nom. Azazel, demon, scapegoat (# 6439).

OT This word appears 4x in the prescriptions governing the Day of Atonement: Lev 16:8, 10 [*bis*], 26. Its undetermined origin and limited use in the OT has resulted in much speculation and uncertainty with regard to its precise and original meaning. Translations such as the RSV and ASV have simply transliterated the Heb. word, "Azazel." The NIV and NASB translations, however, have rendered this term "scapegoat." In each instance the *lamed* inseparable preposition, "to, for," is affixed to the disputed term. Four major explanations have been suggested for this word (see Hartley, 237-38; Kaiser, 1112).

1. The first position proposes that this is a descriptive term for the goat itself. Thus the word is a combination of the Heb. nom. *'z*, goat, and the vb. *'zl*, to go, go

away. Such a rendering is supported by the LXX, Vg., Theodotion, Aquila, and Ibn Ezra. The result of such an etymological configuration is the rendering of the NIV and NASB, scapegoat, or the better, "escape-goat." If this is the case, it becomes difficult to understand why the goat (*śāʿîr* III) is sent (*šlḥ*) to itself or for itself: 16:10, to send him to *ʿᵃzāʾzēl,* and 16:26, the one who sends the goat to *ʿᵃzāʾzēl.* These statements make it difficult to support this interpretative option.

2. A second position proposes that this term be understood abstractly in the sense of entire removal (Feinberg, 331-33). The existence of the Arab. cognate *ʿazala,* banish, remove, certainly makes this a valid option. This position is found wanting, however, because there are few abstract terms in Lev (Hartley, 237) and it does not adequately account for the parallel "for the LORD" in 16:8.

3. A third position stems from rabbinic tradition, which suggests that this is a term designating the place to which the goat departs (Hartley, 237-38). Like the second position, this would not sufficiently account for the parallel expression "for the LORD" in 16:8. Also, "solitary place" (*ʾereṣ gᵉzērâ*; 16:22) and "desert" (*midbār*; 16:10) already designate the place to which the goat is to be sent.

4. The fourth position suggests that the Azazel is a reference to a desert demon or the devil himself (Hartley, 238; Keil & Delitzsch, 398). In support of this position is the book of Enoch, which uses this name for a chief demon (En 8:1; 9:6; 10:4-8; 13:1-2; 54:5; 55:4; 69:2). The OT also associates the appearance of goats with demons (see *śāʿîr* III; this might account for the name Azazel. Furthermore, the desert or wilderness is frequently described by both the OT and NT as the abode of evil spirits (Isa 13:1; 34:13; Matt 12:43; Luke 11:24; Rev 18:2). This interpretation also balances the parallel expression "for the LORD" in 16:8 and makes sense of the remaining grammatical expressions. The difficulty of this position, however, is the theological problem stemming from the relationship between evil spirits and the worship rites of the Day of Atonement.

In truth, no one position can be maintained with absolute certainty. The limited use of the terminology along with the unusual grammatical-logical relationships leaves this issue unclear. Each position carries with it a set of solutions supported by some evidence, answering some questions and leaving others unanswered. Either the first or the fourth position, however, is supported by the most reasonable sets of evidence. The first position makes the best theological sense while the fourth makes the most grammatical sense. (→ Azazel: Theology)

Spirit, ghost, demon: → *ʾôb* II (medium, spiritist, necromancer, ghost, # 200); → *ʾiṭṭîm* I (ghosts, ghosts of the dead, spirits, # 356); → *lîlît* (night monster, night creature, # 4327); → *ʿᵃzāʾzēl* (Azazel, demon, scapegoat, # 6439); → *ṣî* II (desert dweller, crier, yelper, wild beast, # 7470); → *rûaḥ* (wind, breath, transitoriness, volition, disposition, temper, spirit, Spirit, # 8120); → *rᵉpāʾîm* I (shades, departed spirits, # 8327); → *śāʿîr* III (satyr, goat demon, goat idol, # 8539); → *šēd* (demon, # 8717)

BIBLIOGRAPHY

TWOT 2:657-58; G. L. Archer, *Encyclopedia of Bible Difficulties,* 1982, 127-28; G. Deiana, "Azazel in Lv 16," *Lateranum* 54, 1988, 16-33; E. L. Feinberg, "The Scapegoat of Leviticus Sixteen," *BSac* 115, 1958, 320-31; J. E. Hartley, *Leviticus,* WBC 4, 1992; W. C. Kaiser, Jr., "Leviticus," *The New Interpreter's Bible,* 1, 1994; idem, *More Hard Sayings of the Old Testament,*

1992, 94-97; J. Milgrom, *Leviticus 1-16*, AB, 1991; G. J. Wenham, *The Book of Leviticus*, NICOT, 1979.

M. V. Van Pelt/W. C. Kaiser, Jr.

6440	עזב

עזב (*'zb* I), q. abandon; ni., q. pass. be abandoned (# 6440).

ANE The Heb. *'zb* is cognate with the Akk. *ezēbu*, leave, with the Arab. *'azab*, be distant, single, and with the Eth. The Aram. shaph'el *šêzēb*, deliver, represents a polar meaning. Problems occur where *'zb* cannot have any of the usual meanings. In Exod 23:5 it seems to mean "help" (but see Cooper, "The Plain Sense of Exod 23:5," *HUCA* 1988, 16), where he proposes the standard meaning, viz. "You must leave the animal alone. By no means meddle with someone else's fallen donkey." Neh 3:8 and 4:2[3:34] require the meaning fortify (KJV), restore (NIV), or the like. Nehemiah's word may be *'zb* II, cognate with OSA *'d̲b*, restore, repair, and with Ugar. *'db*, prepare, make (*UT*, # 1818, or Segert, *A Basic Grammar of the Ugaritic Language*, 1985; Dahood, "The Root," 303-9; Williamson, "Reconsideration," 74-85).

OT 1. The root occurs in thirty of the OT books. It is least represented in the Pent. and the Minor Prophets. Of the 214 occurrences of the vb., 203 are in the q., nine in ni., and two in pu. Within these patterns most vbs. are pf. and impf. with eleven infinitives, thirty participles, and five imperatives.

2. God, the nation Israel, and individual men and women are the most common subjects of the vb. When God is the subj., the most common objects are the nation (Jer 12:7), an individual king (2 Chron 32:31), or a psalmist (Ps 71:11). In many sentences the vb. is negated—God will *not* forsake his people (Gen 28:15; Deut 31:6, 8). Or the psalmists often pray, "Do not forsake me" (Ps 38:21[22]; 71:9, 18; 119:8). When human beings are the subj., they forsake or abandon the Lord (Judg 2:12-13; 2 Kgs 21:22), his covenant (Jer 22:9), law (2 Chron 12:1), or statutes (1 Kgs 18:18).

Less frequently people leave other people (Ruth 2:11; 2 Chron 28:14). Sometimes people leave objects such a coat (Gen 39:13), herds (Gen 50:8), or cities (1 Chron 10:7). In even rarer cases people abandon conceptual things such as wisdom or folly (Prov 4:6; 9:6).

3. The phrase *'āṣûr w^{e} 'āzûb*, a polar word pair ("restricted and free"), is an antithetical merismus whose meaning is unclear (Deut 32:36; 1 Kgs 14:10; 21:21; 2 Kgs 9:8; 14:26). Noth had concluded that the original meaning was lost (*Überlieferungsgeschichtliche Studien*, 1957^{2}, 75). Kutsch explained the phrase contextually by reference to the royal family. If so, the *'āṣûr* signifies the children who are under parental authority and the *'āzûb* as those males who are independent ("Die Wurzel," 57-69). He did not fully take into account the usage in Deut 32:36, as Saydon has argued (371-74). Saydon concludes that the bipolar terms are synonymous ("helpless and destitute") and signify members of the lowest class of society. Gray (*I & II Kings*, OTL, 1970, 337) follows Noth in holding that the original meaning has been lost, rendering it "to the very last" (335). DeVries explains it as "an alliterative phrase of utter loathing," rendering it, like Saydon, "helpless and abandoned" (*1 Kings*, WBC, 1985, 179).

4. The phrase *'^{a}zûbâ*, abandoned, occurs 3x with reference to Israel. Israel's abandonment by God in exile is likened to a woman who has been abandoned by her

husband (Isa 54:6; 60:15; 62:4). In 60:15 it is parallel with *śᵉnû'â*, hated. Here *'zb* signifies a temporary abandonment occasioned by offensive acts. Yet, it is also a process by which the Lord brought Israel to her senses and to the recognition of her need of God. See, in contrast, Isa 60:15b: "I will make you the everlasting pride and the joy of all generations."

5. The root *'zb* is a covenantal term that is frequently (more than 100x) used to denote the act of breaking the covenant (Deut 29:25[24]; Jer 2:13, 17, 19; 22:9; Dan 11:30; → *bᵉrît*, # 1382). In this regard, it is synonymous with *prr* I, end, (Deut 31:16; → # 7296), *znh* I, play the prostitute (Hos 4:10; → # 2388), *n'ṣ*, reject (Isa 1:4; → # 5540). God charged Israel with having broken the covenant. When the curses of the covenant were unleashed, the covenant people were treated as a noncovenant people. Yahweh abandoned his people to someone he had promised to be present (54:7-8). The divine abandonment was temporary, however. The prophets who proclaimed the divine abandonment, judgment, and alienation also spoke of the renewal of the covenant, of the greater involvement of God in the person of the messianic King and in the ministry of the Holy Spirit, of the spiritual transformation of Israel and of the nations, and of the opening up of a new era of fulfillment in anticipation of the final transformation of all things.

6. On several occasions the vb. appears twice in the same verse or in paired verses. Deut 31:16b-17a, e.g., reads: "They will forsake me and break the covenant I made with them. On that day I will become angry with them and forsake them"; 2 Chron 12:5b reads similarly: "This is what the LORD says, 'You have abandoned me; therefore, I now abandon you to Shishak.'" Other double and opposite uses of *'zb* are in 2 Chron 13:10-11; 15:2; 24:20; Ezra 9:9-10.

Abandonment: → *bdd* (be alone, # 969); → *yāḥîd* (only one, abandoned, # 3495); → *nṭš* (abandon, forsake, # 5759); → *'zb* I (abandon, # 6440)

BIBLIOGRAPHY

THAT 2:249-52; *TWAT* 5:1200-1208; *TWOT* 2:658-59; M. Dahood, "The Root עזב II in Job," *JBL* 78, 1959, 303-9; E. Kutsch, "Die Wurzel עצר im Hebräischen," *VT* 2, 1952, 57-69; P. P. Saydon, "The Meaning of the Expression עָצוּר וְעָזוּב," *VT* 2, 1952, 371-74; H. G. M. Williamson, "A Reconsideration of עזב II in Biblical Hebrew," *ZAW* 97, 1985, 74-85.

Robert L. Alden

6445 (*'azzâ*, Gaza), → Gaza

6449 (*'ᵉzûz*, strength, power), → # 6451

6450 (*'izzûz*, powerful), → # 6451

6451	עזז

עזז (*'zz*), q. be or prove oneself strong; prevail over, overpower; give or impart strength; pi., establish; ni., be insolent, impudent, bold; hi., (make strong [the face] =) be insolent, impudent, bold, brazen, shameless (# 6451); עַז (*'az*), adj. strong; fierce/cruel; defiant, shameless; hard, stern, severe, grim, brazen; turbulent (# 6434); עָז (*'āz*), nom. strength (hapleg.; # 6435); עֹז (*'ōz* I), nom. strength, power (# 6437 [*HALAT* distinguishes between *'ōz* I, strength, power; and *'ōz* II, refuge, shelter; defence, protection (derived from *'wz*, take or seek refuge]); עֱזוּז (*"ezûz*), nom., strength, power (# 6449); עִזּוּז (*'izzûz*), adj. powerful (# 6450).

ANE Cognate forms are found in Ugar., *'z*; OSA, Eth., *azaza*; Akk. *ezēzu*, be annoyed or angry, fall into a rage; Sam. *'az* (with suff. *bazzåk*); Aram. *'zz*, be strong; Syr. *'az*, be powerful; Phoen. *'z*, power, force.

OT 1. The vb. occurs at least 10x (*NIVEC*, 1565) and possibly 12x.

(a) In three texts, the vb. has the meaning be strong or show oneself strong. God is urged to show his strength (*'ûzzâ*, q. emph. impv., lit., show yourself strong) (Ps 68:28[29]). Different translations have been suggested for *'ûzzâ*, some of which are based on emendations. However, there is no necessity to change MT (cf. Knight, 315), and the most likely translation is "Be strong/show yourself strong" (cf. Kirkpatrick, 393). Toombs (282; cf. Kirkpatrick, 393; Weiser, 489-90) takes vv. 28-31[29-32] to be an appeal to God to reenact the ancient victories over the Canaanites against those enemies currently threatening Israel. This v. has also been interpreted as a request to God to continue to be the source of Israel's strength and coherence (M'Caw and Motyer, 493).

The power of Yahweh, the creator and sovereign over everything that has been created (Kraus, 1989, 211), is incomparable; he who created the heavens, the world, and everything in it (Ps 89:11[12]), who stills the raging sea (v. 9[10]), who crushed the primeval sea dragon, Rahab (v. 10a[11a]), and who scattered his enemies (v. 10b[11b]) has a mighty arm, his hand is strong, or shows strength (*tā'ōz yādᵉkā*, your hand is strong or shows strength), and his right hand is high (v. 13[14]). Some (e.g., Dahood, 1966, 160, 163; 1973, 198, 203, 315) think that *yādᵉkā* denotes the left hand when paired, as here, with "right hand." Dahood (1973, 308) translates the phrase "your left hand is triumphant." What is certain is that, like his arm, "the hand" and "right hand" of Yahweh are symbols of his power (cf. Exod 15:6-12; Ps 17:7; 18:35[36]; 139:10; Isa 48:13). If, as seems plausible, the phrase *tā'ōz yādᵉkā* is to be translated "your hand shows strength," then this emphasizes the thought that God not only possess incomparable power, but also exercises it (Kirkpatrick, 535; cf. Rogerson and McKay, 192, commenting on the arm and right hand of God; Tate, 1990, 421-22, commenting on Yahweh's raised right hand). The references in Ps 89:9-13[10-14] to Yahweh's triumph over the forces of chaos (see, especially, Kraus, 1989, 206-7), which so clearly illustrate Yahweh's power, are echoed elsewhere in the OT (cf. Job 9:13b; 26:12-13; Ps 104:5-9; Isa 51:9-10).

Using the majestic unfolding of the seasons and the mighty phenomena of nature to illustrate the ineffably great and benevolent works of the Creator, Elihu points out that it is God who commands the snow to fall and who tells the shower and the rain to show their strength, be fierce (NEB) or violent (REB, i.e., be a mighty downpour, NIV), or pour down in torrents (JB, reading *'ōzzû*, "show strength" or "be strong" [see, e.g., Dhorme, 562], for MT *'uzzô*, his strength [Job 37:6]). The power of God manifest in the awe-inspiring wonders of nature is beyond human comprehension (36:26, 29; 37:5; Watts, 1972, 134).

(b) In four texts, the vb. means prevail over. The heroic and sometimes extraordinary feats performed by the judges were accomplished not by mere human strength, vigor, bravery, and resolve, but by the empowerment of the Spirit of Yahweh (cf. Exod 31:3; 35:31; Judg 6:34; 11:29; 13:25; 14:6, 19; 15:14; 1 Sam 10:10; 11:6; 16:13; 2 Sam 23:2; 1 Kgs 18:12, 46; 2 Kgs 2:16; Isa 11:2; 28:6; Ezek 3:24) (cf. Strahan, 260). After the people cried unto Yahweh when he punished them for their sin by selling them into the power of King Cushan-Rishathaim of Aram Naharaim for a period of eight years, the Spirit of Yahweh empowered Othniel, the son of Kenaz, Caleb's younger brother, and his hand prevailed over, *wattā'oz yādô 'al* ([Judg 3:10] so RV; RSV; NRSV; Slotki, 178), Cushan-Rishathaim. NIV translates *wattā'oz yādô 'al* as "overpowered him"; JB has "he overcame"; NEB and REB have "[he] was too strong for"; Moore, 88, translates "He got the upper hand of"; and Lindars, 127, reads "and his hand was powerful against."

When, as a result of their sin, Yahweh gave his people into the power of Midian for seven years (Judg 6:1), the hand of Midian prevailed over (RSV; NRSV; Slotki, 204) Israel (*wattā'oz yad-midyān 'al yiśrā'ēl*, v. 2). NEB and REB translate the phrase as "The Midianites were too strong for Israel [NEB]/the Israelites" [REB]; TEV has "The Midianites were stronger than Israel"; JB reads, "and Midian bore down heavily on Israel"; and NIV translates, "Because the power of Midian was so oppressive."

The angel who interprets the vision of history unfolding informs Daniel (Dan 11:11-13) that though the king of the south (Ptolemy IV Philopator [221-203 BC]) will achieve some success in battle (the battle at Raphia, 217 BC) against the king of the north (Antiochus III the Great [223-187 BC]), he will not ultimately prevail (RSV and NRSV, translating *w^{e}lō' yā'ôz* [Dan 11:12]), maintain his advantage (NEB; REB), remain triumphant (NIV), continue to be victorious (TEV), or be bold (Jeffery, 519). The Egyptian army under Ptolemy V Epiphanes, 203-181 BC, was crushed by Antiochus at Paneion, near modern Banias, 199/98 BC). Bevan (179-80) rightly understands the phrase to mean that Ptolemy IV failed to press his advantage by following up his victory with a vigorous pursuit of Antiochus, but, instead, made peace with the Seleucids as soon as possible and contented himself with the occupation of Coele-Syria (cf. Jeffery, 519; R. A. Anderson, 132). Charles (123) attributes Ptolemy IV's tactical blunder to his effeminate and dissolute character (cf. Polybius 14.12.3-4), and Driver (1922, 171; cf. Porteous, 162) thinks it also had a lot to do with his natural indolence.

In a prayer for deliverance from the wicked, a supplicant entreats Yahweh to arise and let not mortals prevail, *'al-yā'ōz '^{e}nôs* (Ps 9:19[20]; RSV; NRSV; C. A. and E. G. Briggs, 69; Oesterley, 143; Kissane, 39; Craigie, 114; Mays, 1994, 75), or have the upper hand (JB). The phrase has also been translated "give man no chance to boast his strength" (NEB); "restrain the power of mortals" (REB); "let not mortal man wax strong" (Kirkpatrick, 50); "let not man triumph" (NIV); "let not mortal man be defiant" (Delitzsch, 1889, 159); "do not let men defy you!" (TEV); "so that human beings may not be defiant" (Kraus, 1988, 189); "let men not be overweening any longer" (Buttenwieser, 422); and "lest men should boast" (Dahood, 1966, 54).

(c) In one text, the q. is used in the sense of imparting strength to someone. Wisdom is praised for making the wise man more powerful (*tā'ōz leḥākām*, lit., she gives strength to the wise man) than ten rulers in a city (Eccl 7:19). The number ten has often been explained as being purely figurative, suggesting perfection (see, e.g., Martin, 256-57). However, many of the Hellenistic cities were ruled by a committee consisting of ten prominent citizens (cf. Rankin, 67; Peterson, 120; Scott, 1965, 237; Gordis, 269; Crenshaw, 142; Davidson, 52; [though see Grieve, 415; Jones, 321;

Whybray, 1989, 122]). The v., then, may well mean more than that the power of wisdom is greatly superior to brute force (Plumptre, 169; Dummelow, 397). It may be making the point that an individual whose source of strength is wisdom is stronger and more effective than an entire city council (Martin, 257; Grieve, 415; cf. Ryder, 464).

(d) Once, the vb. (in the pi.) is used with the meaning establish. Personified wisdom declares that she was present when Yahweh "fixed securely the fountains of the deep" (NIV), "fixed fast the springs of the deep" (JB), "set the springs of ocean firm in their place" (NEB), "contained" (McKane, 223), or "confined the springs of the deep" (REB) (reading *b*[e]*'azz*[e]*zô*, the pi. inf. const. with prefixed prep. and suff. of 3rd pers. masc. sg. [so the versions; see McKane, 355] for MT *ba'*[a]*zôz*, the q. inf. const. with prep. [Prov 8:28]). Both the upper and the lower oceans had to be contained. The clouds dammed the upper ocean, (8:28a) and the springs of the nether deep were fixed fast to prevent them from breaking through the disc of the earth (v. 28b; McKane, 355). Wisdom's role as the witness of God is unparalleled: she was the first of his acts of creation (8:22) and witnessed the primeval events; she enjoys a unique relationship with the Creator (8:30); and among the things created by God, her authority and power are unequalled (cf. Tate, 1972, 32-34).

(e) In three texts, the vb. has the meaning be insolent, impudent, bold. In the new age, when Israel's enemies are incapacitated and Zion is inviolable, immovable, and occupied by righteous citizens (Kelley, 286), the city will see no more the insolent (RSV; NRSV), arrogant (NIV; TEV), or overweening (JB) people (*'am nô'āz* [masc. sing. ni. part.], Isa 33:19). Some (e.g., BDB, 418) take *nô'āz* to be a ni. part. of the vb. *y'z* and translate the word as "barbarous" (NEB; REB; Watts, 1985, 425); some translate *'am nô'āz* as "people of barbarous speech" (see Skinner, 252). However, *nô'āz* is almost certainly to be derived from *'zz* (Wildberger, cited by Watts, 1985, 426). The reference is to foreign conquerors.

The skilful and unscrupulous seductress, who is bold in both action and invitation (Tate, 1972, 29), seizes the senseless young man, kisses him, and speaks to him with an impudent (RSV; NRSV), brazen (NIV; Scott, 1965, 64), or hard (McKane, 221) face (*hē'ēzâ pāneyhā*, lit., she made strong [hi.] her face [Prov 7:13]). JB translates *hē'ēzâ pāneyhā* as "the bold-faced creature," and NEB and REB have "brazenly she accosted him."

Whereas the man of integrity, anxious to do what is right, gives careful consideration to his conduct, the wicked man puts on a bold (RSV; NRSV), brazen (Fritsch, 906), or brass (McKane, 562) face (*hē'ēz ... b*[e]*pānāyw*, lit., he makes strong [hi.] with his face, Prov 21:29). NEB and REB translate *hē'ēz ... b*[e]*pānāyw* as "puts a bold face on it"; NIV reads "puts up a bold front"; and JB has "assumes an air of confidence." The meaning may be that the wicked person, who is both unprincipled and inconsiderate of anyone else, brazenly does whatever suits him without showing any regard for others (Dummelow, 387; Fritsch, 906). Another possibility is that the wicked man has to rely on bluff, bogus posturing and effrontery so as to maintain the appearance of being confident and business-like when extricating himself from difficult situations, deviously concealing his true character (McKane, 562; Tate, 1972, 68; cf. Martin, 135).

2. The adj. *'az* occurs at least 23x (*NIVEC*, 1564) and possibly 24x.

(a) In two texts it is used of an individual. Yahweh, who controls all heavenly and earthly powers (Kaiser, 101), declares that he will hand over the Egyptians into the hand of a hard master: a fierce (RSV; NRSV; REB; NIV; Kissane, 1960, 204; Wright, 59)/cruel (JB; NEB; TEV) king (*ûmelek ʿaz*), probably (Skinner, 146; Kissane, 1960, 207; Kaiser, 101), though not necessarily (Scott, 1956, 279) a foreigner, who will rule over them (Isa 19:4). Oswalt (364) reads "a strong king," and Watts (1985, 248) has "powerful," but the fact that *ʿaz* is used in parallelism with *qāšeh* (hard, harsh, severe, fierce, cruel) suggests that *ʿaz* here means fierce or cruel.

A wise man is mightier than a strong man (reading [with LXX, Syr., Vg., Tg., *BHS*, RSV; Scott, 1965, 144, McKane, 248, 397] *gābar* [he is mighty] for MT *geber* [man], and *mēʿāz* [than a strong one] for MT *baʿôz* [in strength]) (Prov 24:5). Intellectual ability is more powerful than physical strength or brute force (cf. e.g., Whybray, 1994, 345).

(b) In five texts, the adj. is applied to people(s). After their reconnaissance of Canaan, the majority of the spies reported that although the land was fertile, the fact that the indigenous people were strong (*ʿaz hāʿām*) and had powerful fortifications (Num 13:28) would prove an insurmountable obstacle to Israel's entry.

Ants are of limited physical strength (*ʿam lōʾ-ʿāz*, lit., a people not strong), but they compensate for their severe physical limitations by foresight, discipline, and industry, as illustrated by the fact that they make provision for the winter by gathering and storing food in the summer (Prov 30:25; McKane, 661). Their exceptional achievement, which is out of proportion to their seemingly inadequate size or power (Cox, 246), provides a useful model for human wisdom (cf. 6:6-11; Tate, 1972, 96). By acquiring wisdom, human beings too can overcome their natural limitations (Whybray, 1994, 419).

In response to his mighty acts against the ruthless tyrants, strong or cruel people(s) (*ʿam-ʿāz*) will glorify Yahweh (Isa 25:3). NEB and REB understand the adj. to mean cruel here (REB reads "many a cruel nation holds you in honour"), and this translation receives some support from the fact that the word is used in parallelism with the adj. *ʿārîṣîm*, ruthless. On this reading, the meaning is that formerly imperious people(s) will be forced to acknowledge Yahweh's supremacy (cf. Scott, 1956, 303). An alternative possibility is that the overthrow of the oppressive power(s) will lead many other powerful nations to glorify God (cf. Gray, 426).

Because bloody crimes are committed throughout Judah and Jerusalem is full of violence, Yahweh will bring the worst of the nations (possibly a cypher for the Babylonians [cf. Jer 6:22-23; Hab 1:13; May, 104; Boadt, 313]) to take possession of his people's houses, and he will put an end to the arrogance/pride of the strong (*g*^{e}*ʾôn ʿazzîm*, Ezek 7:24). JB translates *ʿazzîm* as "their grandees." Not a few (e.g., *BHS*; Cooke, 83, 88; Zimmerli, 200) emend MT *ʿazzîm* to *ʿuzzām* (their bastion/stronghold), a change supported by the fact that variations of the phrase *g*^{e}*ʾôn ʿuzzām* occur elsewhere in the book (24:21; 30:6, 18; 33:28). On the other hand, others acknowledge that the more difficult reading may be retained (cf. Brownlee, 113).

Yahweh, who created all and governs all (Vawter, 55), makes destruction flash forth against the strong (Amos 5:9a; on the meaning flash forth for *hammablîg* [lit., he smiles/causes to smile], see Driver, 1901, 180; Hammershaimb, 81; R. L. Smith, 111-12 [this translation of the vb., though, is considered dubious by Snaith, 1958, 90, and Paul, 169]). Some (e.g., *BHS;* JB; NIV; Hubbard, 170) suggest emending the MT *'āz* (strong) to *'ōz* (stronghold), but this is unnecessary. The argument that v. 9 contains words that are partly corrupted names of starry constellations (so, e.g., NEB; Duhm, 68; Snaith, 1958, 90-92; 1960, 32; McKeating, 40) is unconvincing (cf. Hayes, 161). This v. makes the point that human strength is no match for Yahweh's destructive powers (Driver, 1901, 180; R. L. Smith, 112; Stuart, 348); v. 9b stresses that no human fortifications are impregnable to divine judgment (cf. Mays, 1976, 96; Hubbard, 171).

(c) In three texts, the adj. is used of enemies. One who, without the divine assistance, would have been engulfed by destructive foes, praises Yahweh for graciously intervening to deliver his loyal and obedient servant from a strong (Kirkpatrick, 92, suggests fierce as an alternative) enemy (*mē'ōy^ebî 'āz*, from my strong enemy) (2 Sam 22:18; par. Ps 18:17[18]). A slandered and persecuted individual entreats Yahweh to deliver him from sinister and murderous enemies (Ps 59:2[3]), who are fierce (RSV; NIV; Kissane, 1964, 255)/ruthless (Kissane, 1964, 254)/savage (NEB)/cruel (TEV)/violent (REB) (reading *'azzîm* for MT *'zîm*, v. 3[4]).

(d) Once the adj. is used of corrupt community leaders, who are described as greedy dogs, predators who have a voracious, insatiable appetite (*'azzê-nepeš*, lit., strong of appetite), and who are more concerned with their own profit and pleasure than with the needs of those in their care (Isa 56:11).

(e) In two verses, the adj. is applied to a lion. The riddle Samson put to the thirty Philistine guests at his wedding feast was, "Out of the eater, something to eat; out of the strong (*ûmē'az*), something sweet" (Judg 14:14). Having obtained, at the last minute, the answer to the riddle from his wife, whom they had threatened to kill, the Philistines said to Samson "What is sweeter than honey? What is stronger than a lion (*ûmeh 'az mē'^arî*)?" (Judg 14:18).

(f) In two passages, the adj. is used of turbulent waters. An archetypal image of the liberative power of Yahweh is the Exodus image (Miscall, 108) of the one who makes a way in the sea, a path in the mighty (RSV; NRSV; NEB; REB; NIV; Watts, 1987, 124), fierce (McKenzie, 55), or swirling (TEV) waters (*ûb^emayim 'azzîm*, Isa 43:16). According to another text (Neh 9:11), Israel's Egyptian pursuers were cast by Yahweh into the depths as a stone into mighty (RSV; NRSV; NIV; Williamson, 301), rushing (JB), raging (TEV), or turbulent (NEB; REB) waters (*b^emayim 'azzîm*). Neh 9:9-11 consists of a pastiche of quotations from the Exodus account (Ryle, 1893, 255-56; 1917, 100; Williamson, 313), but the adj. *'azzîm* seems to have been borrowed from Isa 43:16 (Ryle, 1893, 256; Clines, 194).

(g) In one text, the adj. is used of a powerful wind. A singular testimony to the sovereign power and absolute lordship of Yahweh was his victory over the sea, which symbolized chaos (Honeycutt, 385). When Moses stretched out his hand over the seemingly impassable Reed Sea, Yahweh drove back the waters with a strong east wind (*b^erûaḥ qādîm 'azzâ*) and made the sea dry land (Exod 14:21). Durham (194) translates *b^erûaḥ qādîm 'azzâ* "with a gale." The obstacle that had trapped Israel is transformed by Yahweh into the means of the entrapment and death of their oppressors (Durham, 198).

(h) Once the adj. is used as the epithet of a boundary/border or territory/country. If the MT of Num 21:24 (*'az g^ebûl b^enê 'ammôn*) be retained (with NRSV; NEB; NIV; TEV; Snaith, 1964, 264; Owens, 140; Wenham, 161; Ashley, 415, 420), then the

Israelites were unable to further their conquests because the boundary/border of the Ammonites was strong (NRSV; Owens, 140; Ashley, 415, 420)/strongly defended (TEV)/fortified (NIV), or because the country (NEB)/territory (REB) of the Ammonites became difficult. Snaith (1964, 264) translates, "Because that [the frontier of Ammon] was rough ground," which he takes to mean that the boundary was ill-defined. However, many (e.g., LXX; *BHS*; RSV; JB; Kennedy, 313; Wade, 224; Marsh, 245; Guthrie, 95; Thompson, 190; Noth, 160, 163; Budd, 241-42, 246; cf. Davies, 229) emend *'az* to *ya'zēr* (Jazer), which gives the translation, "For Jazer was the boundary/frontier of the Ammonites."

(i) Twice the adj. conveys the intensity of anger. Simeon and Levi were cursed because of their fierce (RSV; NRSV; NEB; REB; NIV; TEV; Speiser, 361; Westermann, 218; Hamilton, 650) or ruthless (JB) anger (Gen 49:7). Elsewhere, a covert gift is said to placate anger and a concealed bribe to appease raging fury (JB's translation of *ḥēmâ 'azzâ* [Prov 21:14], lit., strong wrath).

(j) In one text, the adj. describes the intensity of love. Love (the genuine kind that is undivided, unfeigned, complete, and enduring [Delitzsch, 1877, 145; cf. Murphy, 197]) is as strong/irresistible (cf. Davidson, 152) as death, which is an unrelenting, overpowering, and destructive power from which no one escapes (S of Songs 8:6; on the usage of the word "love" in the OT, see Gledhill, 228-31). With a power as awesome and compelling as that of death, love, like death, overpowers and masters its victims (Gledhill, 231).

(k) In two passages, the adj. occurs in combination with *pānîm* (face) with the sense strong/bold/hard/severe/stern/grim countenance. Disobedience will result in Yahweh's sending against Israel a nation of stern countenance (*gôy 'az pānîm*), which will show no regard for the elderly or for the young (Deut 28:50). Driver (1965, 315) translates "[a nation of] fierce countenance"; NIV has "a fierce-looking nation"; and Craigie (1983a, 347) reads "a nation of fierce appearance." However, as G. A. Smith (315) and Driver (1965, 315) rightly point out, the meaning of the adj. here is not so much fierce as hard, inflexible, or unyielding, for this defiant nation will be unmoved by considerations of pity.

The unyielding, defiant Antiochus IV Epiphanes, who is portrayed as the personal embodiment of all iniquity and as the epitome of imperial pretension (R. A. Anderson, 101), is described as a king of bold, stern, hard, or insolent countenance (*'az-pānîm*, Dan 8:23). JB has "proud-faced," and R. A. Anderson (101) suggests "brazen-faced." Charles (92) and Driver (1922, 123) think that the expression *'az-pānîm* here was borrowed from Deut 28:50.

(l) Once, the fem. pl. adj. is used with the sense strong (i.e., defiant) things. Whereas the poor man, who is dependent on others for help, speaks in an ingratiating way (in wheedling tones [McKane, 239]), the rich man, who has the power and wealth to give or acquire without much regard for others (Tate, 1972, 60), answers defiantly/roughly (RSV; NRSV; Scott, 1965, 113)/harshly (NIV; cf. NEB; REB)/brusquely (McKane, 239) (*ya'aneh 'azzôt* [Prov 18:23], lit., he answers strong things). The meaning is probably that, just as civility, deference, and flattery are necessary for the poor man's survival, so brusqueness is part of the rich man's defence against the unrelenting demands that are made on his generosity (McKane, 518).

3. The nom. *'āz* occurs once. In Jacob's blessing on his twelve sons (Gen 49:1-28), the firstborn, Reuben, is described as being preeminent/foremost/excelling in power (*[wᵉ]yeter 'āz*, v. 3; the translation preeminent/foremost/excelling in defiance is possible, but less likely [see Westermann, 224]). Before being reduced to insignificance as early as the eleventh century BC, the tribe of Reuben once enjoyed political prominence (Maher, 265).

4. The nom. *'ōz* occurs 94x (*NIVEC*, 1565).

(a) The word is used in a wide range of contexts and applied to a wide range of subjects. Strength resides in Leviathan's neck (Job 41:22[14]). The firmament, here a synonym for heavens (A. A. Anderson, 1972b, 956; cf. JB; NEB; REB; NIV; TEV), is mighty (Ps 150:1). Yahweh empowers the Judaean king, making his scepter mighty so that he can exercise dominion over all his foes (110:2). When the destroyer sent by Yahweh has demolished the renowned strongholds of Moab, all those round about will be in awe at how the mighty scepter has been broken (Jer 48:17). Likening Judah to a vine (Ezek 19:10-14), Ezekiel describes Zedekiah as its strongest stem that towered aloft (19:11), but then, when the vine was plucked up in fury and cast down to the ground, was withered by the east wind (Nebuchadnezzar) (19:12). When the vine was transplanted in the wilderness (i.e., taken to Babylon, 19:13), the fire that consumed its branches and fruit left no strong stem (19:14). Though strong, Tyre's pillars will collapse when Nebuchadnezzar attacks the city (26:11). Even if Babylon were to fortify her strong height (RSV; NRSV)/high towers (NEB)/her towers in the heights (REB)/towering citadel (JB)/her lofty stronghold (NIV), destroyers sent by Yahweh to execute his judgment will come upon her (Jer 51:53).

When Abimelech encamped against Thebez, the city's inhabitants took refuge in a strong tower (Judg 9:51). The good wife girds her loins with strength (Prov 31:17); strength and dignity are her clothing (31:25). David danced before Yahweh with all his might when the ark was transferred to Jerusalem (2 Sam 6:14); he and all Israel celebrated before God with all their might with music and singing (1 Chron 13:8). At Hezekiah's great Passover festival, those Israelites who were in Jerusalem kept the Feast of Unleavened Bread seven days, during which period the Levites and the priests praised Yahweh daily, singing with all their might (2 Chron 30:21, emending MT *bikᵉlê-oz*, with instruments of strength, to *bᵉkol-'ōz*, with all strength [*BHS*; *pace* Dillard, 239]). Inspired by the dramatic victory over Sisera, the composer of the Song of Deborah bids his or her soul to march on with might (Judg 5:21). After having drunk deeply of the cup of Yahweh's wrath, Zion is bidden to awake and put on her strength (Isa 52:1). A grateful psalmist praises Yahweh for having increased his strength of soul (Ps 138:3, reading [with, e.g., *BHS;* A. A. Anderson, 1972b, 902] *tarbēnî*, lit., you increase[d] me, instead of MT *tarhibēnî*, you make [made] me [arrogant]). Another psalmist thanks Yahweh for having made him more stable than a strong mountain (Ps 30:7[8], following the translation of Dahood, 1966, 181, 183; cf. A. A. Anderson, 1972a, 243). One has strong confidence (RSV; NRSV; cf. JB), or a secure fortress (NIV) or stronghold (McKane, 232), in the fear of Yahweh (Prov 14:26). The possession of wisdom changes the hardness (lit., strength) of a man's countenance (Eccl 8:1).

(b) In four passages, the nom. occurs in combination with *zᵉrôa'*, arm. With heavy sarcasm, Job thanks Bildad for having saved the arm that had no strength (*zᵉrôa' lō'-'ōz*, with *lō'-'ōz* having the force of an adj. [Dhorme, 377]) (Job 26:2). It is with his mighty arm that Yahweh scatters his enemies (Ps 89:10[11]). God is reminded of his victory over the forces of chaos (Rahab, the dragon [Isa 51:9b]) at creation and over the waters of the sea at the time of the Exodus (51:10), and the arm of Yahweh is urged to awake and put on strength (51:9a). A prophet underscores the certainty of his proclamation of Zion's imminent vindication, with the assurance that Yahweh has sworn by his right hand and by his mighty arm that he will never again permit foreigners to overrun the land of Israel (Isa 62:8).

(c) In four texts the word is used of a powerful city, whether literal or figurative. In celebration of God's victory over their enemies, the people of Judah will sing a song in gratitude for the fact that, thanks to divine protection, they have a strong city (Isa 26:1). A rich man's wealth is his strong city (Prov 10:15; par 18:11). Prov 18:19 has been variously interpreted: "A brother saved by his brother is like a town fortified and elevated" (LXX); "A brother helped is like a strong city" (RSV; cf. JB); "Help your brother and he will protect you like a strong city wall" (TEV); "An ally offended is stronger than a city" (NRSV); "An aggrieved brother *is more inaccessible* than a fortified city" (McKane, 239, 520); "An offended brother is more unyielding than a fortified city" (NIV); "A reluctant brother is more unyielding than a fortress" (NEB; REB).

(d) In several texts, the word seems to have the meaning strong refuge, secure fortress, fortification. A wise man scales (RSV), can scale (JB), or attacks (NIV) the city of the mighty and throws down the stronghold or rampart (JB) in which they trust (Prov 21:22, reading *'ōz mibṭeḥāh*, lit. the strength of her trust, instead of MT *'ōz mibṭeḥâ;* REB translates "its boasted strength"). This v. probably means that a seemingly impregnable fortress is vulnerable to a tactician who is both talented and enterprising (McKane, 551). Israel is warned that, because of her transgressions, an enemy will tear down her stronghold (NEB; REB; cf. NIV) or defenses (RSV; TEV; cf. NRSV) (Amos 3:11). Yahweh established a bulwark (RSV; NRSV; REB) or stronghold (JB) to still his enemies (Ps 8:2[3]). Here, *'ōz* may be a poetic name for heaven (A. A. Anderson, 1972a, 102; JB footnote). If the translations of Prov 14:26 by NIV and McKane (232) are followed, a person has a secure fortress or stronghold in the fear of Yahweh. A psalmist who is experiencing affliction expresses his trust in Yahweh, his strong refuge (Ps 71:7).

(e) In five texts, the word occurs in combination with *gā'ôn*, pride. As a result of Israel's disobedience, Yahweh will break the pride of her power, i.e., her stubborn pride (NEB; REB; NIV; TEV) (Lev 26:19; Ezek 24:21). Those seeking to take possession of Palestinian property belonging to those deported to Babylonia are warned that Yahweh will make the land a desolation and a waste, and her proud might will come to an end (Ezek 33:28). When the day of Yahweh comes, Egypt's proud might will come down (30:6) and come to an end (30:18).

(f) The nom. is most frequently used in connection with God. Power belongs to God (Ps 62:11[12]). Might characterizes his reign (99:4 [on attempts to translate this difficult colon, see Tate, 1990, 526-27]): the divine king who reigns is robed in majesty and girded with strength (93:1). With him are strength and wisdom (Job 12:16). Might and joy are in his dwelling place (1 Chron 16:27). Strength and beauty are in his sanctuary (Ps 96:6). In time to come, even those who were once his enemies will confess that only in him are righteousness (RSV; NRSV; NIV), salvation (Westermann, 176), or victory (NEB; REB; JB; TEV) and strength (Isa 45:24). Yahweh is the strength of his people (Exod 15:2; Ps 28:8; 46:1[2]; 59:17[18]; 81:1[2]; 118:14 [par. Isa 12:2b]). Yahweh is the glory of his worshipers' strength (Ps 89:17[18]); it is he who gives power to his people (68:35[36]; cf. 29:11). All those whose strength or refuge (NEB; REB) is in Yahweh are blessed (84:5[6]). Yahweh is the strong deliverer who shields the head of the faithful in the day of battle (140:7[8]). He is the strength of the faithful in the day of trouble (Jer 16:19); he is their strength and shield when they are attacked by enemies (Ps 28:7).

From the region of Sinai (Hab 3:3), God came with power (3:4) to rescue his people. It was by his power that Yahweh guided the people to his holy dwelling, i.e., Sinai or, more probably, Zion (Durham, 208) (Exod 15:13). It is Yahweh who empowers his servant for the task with which he has entrusted him (Isa 49:5). Yahweh is the source of the Israelite king's strength (1 Sam 2:10). Yahweh is exalted in his strength (Ps 21:13[14]), and the king rejoices in the divine power (21:1[2]). It is by Yahweh's strength that the ruler of Israel is empowered to feed his flock (Mic 5:4[3]). The congregation is urged to seek Yahweh and his strength continually (Ps 105:4; par. 1 Chron 16:11). God is a strong tower affording the righteous protection against the enemy (Ps 61:3[4]; Prov 18:10). He is a mighty rock on whom his followers can depend for protection (Ps 62:7[8]). The faithful can confidently call upon him to summon his might (68:28[29], reading *ṣawwēh*, command, for MT *ṣiwwâ*, he commanded). The faithful who are beset by ruthless enemies can ask him for strength (86:16), confident of deliverance. His followers who are in affliction encourage themselves by recalling his mighty deeds in the past, when he manifested his might among the peoples (77:14[15]). Yahweh has power over nature; by his might he is able to control the south wind (78:26b) and to divide the sea (74:13). He overcomes those forces opposed to him with his mighty arm (89:10[11]). So great is Yahweh's power that his enemies cringe before him (66:3). The power of Yahweh's wrath is against all who forsake him (Ezra 8:22).

Although it is seldom that people consider the power, or triumph (A. A. Anderson, 1972b, 653), of God's anger (Ps 90:11), no one can withstand his powerful wrath (76:7[8], reading [with, e.g., *BHS*] *mē'ōz*, before the strength of, for MT *mē'āz*, from then). Yahweh's power is manifest in the sanctuary (63:2[3]), whether experienced in the form of a theophany (Weiser, 454-55), in the form of a rite using fire, smoke, and the blowing of a horn (cf. Tate, 1990, 127), as an internalized apprehension (cf. Tate, 1990, 127), as a conviction generated by the presence of the ark of the covenant (A. A. Anderson, 1972a, 456), by the protection afforded by the sanctuary (A. A. Anderson, 1972a, 457), or by a divine act that delivered the psalmist from his enemies (Kissane, 1964, 269). It is only fitting that worshipers should sing aloud to God their strength or refuge (NEB; REB) (81:1[2]) and proclaim to others his might in song (59:16[17]). Both humans (96:7; par. 1 Chron 16:28; cf. Ps 68:34[35]) and the heavenly beings (Ps 29:1) are enjoined to ascribe to Yahweh glory and might.

(g) In three texts the word is used of the ark of the covenant, the ancient symbol of Yahweh's presence and power. Echoing the ancient song of the ark (Num 10:35-36), which reflected the belief that this object was Yahweh's throne, on which he was invisibly seated when holy war was waged against enemies, Yahweh is bidden to arise and go to his resting place, "you and the ark of your might" (Ps 132:8 [par. 2 Chron 6:41a]). When Israel acted treacherously, provoking him to great wrath, Yahweh punished his faithless people by forsaking his dwelling at Shiloh (Ps 78:60) and surrendering his power (i.e., the ark) to captivity (78:61).

5. The nom. *ʿᵉzûz* occurs 3x. For the benefit of the coming generation, the congregation tells of his power, reciting the glorious deeds of Yahweh and the wonders he has wrought (Ps 78:4). In a hymn extolling the character of the God of Israel, a psalmist asserts that he will declare Yahweh's greatness and people will proclaim the power of his awe-inspiring acts (*[we]ʿᵉzûz nôr'ōteykā*, 145:6). As a result of his people's disobedience, Yahweh poured on them the heat of his anger and the might, fury (NEB; REB; NRSV; cf. JB), or violence (NIV; TEV) of battle (*[we]ʿᵉzûz milḥāmâ*, Isa 42:25).

6. The word *ʿizzûz* is found 2x. Yahweh, the king of glory, is strong and mighty (*ʿizzûz wᵉgibbôr*, Ps 24:8). Yahweh is the one who brought forth the Egyptian chariots and horses, army (*ḥayil*) and warrior (*wᵉʿizzûz*; RSV; NRSV), men of valor (NEB), or reinforcements (NIV), and then snuffed them out like a wick (Isa 43:17).

P-B The vb. *ʿzz* (Aram. *ʿᵃzaz*, same) occurs with the meaning (sting, be pointed, flinty) be hard, strong; hi. (of color) be bright, intense; set one's face against; dare, be insolent, defy; strengthen, encourage; hitp. become strong; be daring, defiant. The following nom. forms are found: *ʿᵃzā'zēl* (Azazel, [Fort], a rough and rocky mountain); *ʿôz* I, *ʿōz* (fortitude, strength, majesty); *ʿazzût* (insolence, effrontery; harshness); *ʿazzîzā'* (sting, insult); and *ʿᵃzîzûtā'* (hardihood; obduracy). The following adjectives also occur: *ʿaz* (strong, firm; vehement, rough; [of colors] bright, intense; [of smell and taste] pungent, acrid; insolent, impudent); *ʿizzûz* (majestic); *ʿazzîz*, *ʿazzîzā'* (strong, intense) (Jastrow, 2:1048-49, 1060-61).

Power, strength: → *'ābîr* (strong, powerful, # 51); → *'ôn* I (generative power, strength, # 226); → *'ayil* I (man of power, # 380); → *'ēl* IV (strength, power, # 445); → *'mṣ* (be strong, strengthen, be superior over, # 599); → *'āpîq* II (strong, # 693); → *'šš* (take courage, # 899); → *gbr* (accomplish, excel, swell, rise, be strong, # 1504); → *dōbe'* (strength, # 1801); → *zimrâ* II (strength, # 2380); → *ḥzq* (be strong, overpower, support, seize, # 2616); → *ḥayil* (capacity, power, property, # 2657); → *ḥāsōn* (strong, # 2891); → *ykl* (able, endure, be victorious, conquer, # 3523); → *ysr* II (strengthen, # 3580); → *kabbîr* (strong, # 3888); → *kōaḥ* I (strength, power, possession, means, # 3946); → *kellaḥ* I (maturity, full vigor, # 3995); → *mᵉ'ōd* (power, might, # 4394); → *ma'ᵃmāṣ* (exertion, # 4410); → *nśg* (overtake, be able to, afford, appear, # 5952); → *ʿzz* (be strong, defy, show a shameless, # 6451); → *ʿṣm* I (be mighty, vast, numerous, make strong, # 6793); → *tqp* (overpower, # 9548)

BIBLIOGRAPHY

THAT 2:252-56; A. A. Anderson, *The Book of Psalms. Volume I: Introduction and Psalms 1-72*, NCBC, 1972 (1972a); idem, *The Book of Psalms. Volume 2: Psalms 73-150*, NCBC, 1972 (1972b); R. A. Anderson, *Signs and Wonders: A Commentary on the Book of Daniel*, ITC, 1984; T. R. Ashley, *The Book of Numbers*, NICOT, 1993; A. A. Bevan, *A Short Commentary on the Book of Daniel for the Use of Students*, 1892; L. Boadt, "Ezekiel," in *NJBC*, 1990, 305-28; R. G. Bratcher and W. D. Reyburn, *A Translator's Handbook on the Book of Psalms*, 1991; C. A. and E. G. Briggs, *A Critical and Exegetical Commentary on the Book of Psalms. Vol. I*, ICC, 1960; W. H. Brownlee, *Ezekiel 1-19*, WBC, 1986; P. J. Budd, *Numbers*, WBC, 1984; M. Buttenwieser, *The Psalms Chronologically Treated With a New Translation*, 1969; R. H. Charles, *The Book of Daniel*, CB, 1913; D. J. A. Clines, *Ezra, Nehemiah, Esther*, NCBC, 1984; G. A. Cooke, *A Critical and Exegetical Commentary on the Book of Ezekiel*, ICC, 1967; D. Cox, *Proverbs With an Introduction to Sapiential Books*, OTM, 1982; P. C. Craigie, *The Book of Deuteronomy*, NICOT, 1983 (1983a); idem, *Psalms 1-50*, WBC, 1983 (1983b); J. L. Crenshaw, *Ecclesiastes: A Commentary*, OTL, 1987; M. Dahood, *Psalms I: 1-50. Introduction, Translation, and Notes*, AB, 1966; idem, *Psalms II: 51-100. Introduction, Translation, and Notes*, AB, 1973; R. Davidson, *Ecclesiastes and the Song of Solomon*, DSB, 1986; E. W. Davies, *Numbers*, NCBC, 1995; F. Delitzsch, *Commentary on the Song of Songs and Ecclesiastes*, K-D, 1877; idem, *Biblical Commentary on the Psalms. Volume I*, K-D, 1889; E. Dhorme, *A Commentary on the Book of Job*, 1967; R. B. Dillard, *2 Chronicles*, WBC, 1987; S. R. Driver, *The Books of Joel and Amos With Introduction and Notes*, CBSC, 1901; idem, *The Book of Daniel With Introduction and Notes*, CBSC, 1922; idem, *A Critical and Exegetical Commentary on Deuteronomy*, ICC, 3d ed., 1965; B. Duhm, *The Twelve Prophets: A Version in the Various Poetical Measures of the Original Writings*, 1912; J. R. Dummelow, ed., *A Commentary on the Holy Bible*, 1909; J. I. Durham, *Exodus*, WBC, 1987; C. T. Fritsch, "The Book of Proverbs: Introduction and Exegesis," in *IB*, 1955, 4:765-957; T. Gledhill, *The Message of the Song of Songs: The Lyrics of Love*, 1994; R. Gordis, *Koheleth—The Man and His World*, 1955; G. B. Gray, *A Critical and Exegetical Commentary on the Book of Isaiah I-XXVII*, ICC, 1975; A. J. Grieve, "Ecclesiastes," in *Peake*, 1920, 411-17; H. H. Guthrie, "The Book of Numbers," in *The Interpreter's One-Volume Commentary on the Bible*, 1971, 85-99; V. P. Hamilton, *The Book of Genesis Chapters 18-50*, NICOT, 1995; E. Hammershaimb, *The Book of Amos: A Commentary*, 1970; J. H. Hayes, *Amos the Eighth-Century Prophet: His Times and His Preaching*, 1988; R. L. Honeycutt, "Exodus," in *BBC*, 1970, 1:305-472; D. A. Hubbard, *Joel and Amos: An Introduction and Commentary*, TOTC, 1989; A. Jeffery, "The Book of Daniel: Introduction and Exegesis," *IB*, 1956, 6:339-549; E. Jones, *Proverbs and Ecclesiastes: Introduction and Commentary*, Torch, 1961; O. Kaiser, *Isaiah 13-39: A Commentary*, OTL, 1974; P. H. Kelley, "Isaiah," in *BBC*, 1972, 5:149-374; A. R. S. Kennedy, *Leviticus and Numbers*, CB, 1910; D. Kidner, *Psalms 1-72: An Introduction and Commentary on Books I and II of the Psalms*, TOTC, 1979; A. F. Kirkpatrick, *The Book of Psalms*, CBSC, 1957; E. J. Kissane, *The Book of Isaiah Translated From a Critically Revised Hebrew Text With Commentary. Vol. I (I-XXXIX)*, 1960; idem, *The Book of Psalms Translated From a Critically Revised Hebrew Text With a Commentary*, 1964; G. A. F. Knight, *The Psalms. Volume I*, DSB, 1982; H.-J. Kraus, *Psalms 1-59: A Commentary*, 1988; idem, *Psalms 60-150: A Commentary*, 1989; B. Lindars, *Judges 1-5: A New Translation and Commentary*, 1995; L. S. M'Caw and J. A. Motyer, "The Psalms," in *NBC*, 1972, 446-547; W. McKane, *Proverbs: A New Approach*, OTL, 1970; H. McKeating, *The Books of Amos, Hosea and Micah*, CBC, 1971; J. L. McKenzie, *Second Isaiah: Introduction, Translation, and Notes*, AB, 1968; M. Maher, *Genesis*, OTM, 1982; J. Marsh, "The Book of Numbers: Introduction and Exegesis," in *IB*, 1953, 2:135-308; G. C. Martin, *Proverbs, Ecclesiastes and Song of Songs*, CB, 1908; H. G. May, "The Book of Ezekiel: Introduction and Exegesis," in *IB*, 1956, 39-338; J. L. Mays, *Amos: A Commentary*, OTL, 1976; idem, *Psalms*, Interp, 1994; P. D. Miscall, *Isaiah*, Readings, 1993; G. F. Moore, *A Critical and Exegetical Commentary on Judges*, ICC, 2d ed., 1918; R. E. Murphy, *The Song of Songs: A Commentary on the Book of Canticles or the Song of Songs*, Hermeneia, 1990; M. Noth, *Numbers: A Commentary*, OTL, 1968; W. O. E. Oesterley, *The Psalms Translated With Text-Critical and Exegetical Notes*, 1959; J. N. Oswalt, *The Book of Isaiah Chapters 1-39*, NICOT, 1986; J. J. Owens, "Numbers," in *BBC*, 1971, 2:75-174; S. M. Paul, *Amos*, Hermeneia, 1991; W. H. Peterson, "Ecclesiastes," in *BBC*, 1972, 5:100-127; E. H. Plumptre, *Ecclesiastes; Or, the Preacher, With Notes and Introduction*, CBC, 1898; N. W. Porteous, *Daniel: A Commentary*, OTL, 1965; O. S. Rankin, "The Book of Ecclesiastes: Introduction and Exegesis," in *IB*, 1956, 5:1-88; J. W. Rogerson and J. W. McKay,

Psalms 51-100, CBC, 1977; E. T. Ryder, "Ecclesiastes," in *Peake*, 1964, 458-67; H. E. Ryle, *The Books of Ezra and Nehemiah With Introduction, Notes and Maps*, CBSC, 1893; idem, *The Books of Ezra and Nehemiah*, CBSC, 1917; R. B. Y. Scott et al., "The Book of Isaiah," in *IB*, 1956, 5:149-773; idem, *Proverbs, Ecclesiastes: Introduction, Translation, and Notes*, AB, 1965; J. Skinner, *The Book of the Prophet Isaiah Chapters I-XXXIX*, CBSC, 1909; J. J. Slotki (with H. Freedman), *Joshua and Judges: Hebrew Text & English Translation With an Introduction and Commentary*, Soncino, 1961; G. A. Smith, *The Book of Deuteronomy*, CBSC, 1918; R. L. Smith, "Amos," in *BBC*, 1972, 7:81-141; N. H. Snaith, *The Book of Amos. Part Two: Translation and Notes*, 1958; idem, *Amos, Hosea and Micah*, 1960; idem, "Numbers," in *Peake*, 1964, 254-68; E. A. Speiser, *Genesis: Introduction, Translation, and Notes*, AB, 1964; J. Strahan, "Judges," in *Peake*, 1920, 256-70; D. Stuart, *Hosea-Jonah*, WBC, 1987; M. E. Tate, "Proverbs," in *BBC*, 1972, 5:1-99; idem, *Psalms 51-100*, WBC, 1990; J. A. Thompson, "Numbers," in *NBC*, 1972, 168-200; L. E. Toombs, "The Psalms," in *The Interpreter's One-Volume Commentary on the Bible*, 1971, 253-303; B. Vawter, *Amos, Hosea, Micah, With an Introduction to Classical Prophecy*, OTM, 1981; G. W. Wade, "Numbers," in *Peake*, 1920, 213-30; J. D. W. Watts (in collaboration with J. J. Owens and M. E. Tate), "Job," in *BBC*, 1972, 4:22-151; idem, *Isaiah 1-33*, WBC, 1985; idem, *Isaiah 34-66*, WBC, 1987; A. Weiser, *The Psalms: A Commentary*, OTL, 1965; G. J. Wenham, *Numbers: An Introduction and Commentary*, TOTC, 1981; C. Westermann, *Genesis 37-50: A Commentary*, 1986; R. N. Whybray, *Ecclesiastes*, NCBC, 1989; idem, *Proverbs*, NCBC, 1994; H. G. M. Williamson, *Ezra, Nehemiah*, WBC, 1985; G. E. Wright, *Isaiah*, LBC, 1965; W. Zimmerli, *Ezekiel 1*, Hermeneia, 1979.

Robin Wakely

6459 (*'uzziyyāh*, Uzziah), → Uzziah

6460 (*'uzziyyāhû*, Uzziah), → Uzziah

6465 (*'ozniyyâ*, black vulture), → # 7606

6466	עזק

עזק (*'zq*), pi. break up, loosen (# 6466).

OT 1. The vb. *'zq* is used only in Isa 5:2. Here the vinedresser (God) executes his plan for developing a quality vineyard. He breaks up (*'zq*) the ground, removes the stones, and then plants the vines. The reference is to the deep breaking up of the soil before the planting of the vines (cf. H. Wildberger, *Isaiah 1-12*, 1991, 181). The use of *'zq* in the "Song of the Vineyard"—an extended agricultural metaphor—powerfully describes how the Lord had lovingly provided Israel with the perfect environment for producing the righteousness requisite for maintaining the covenant relationship. God's gracious provisions stand in sharp contrast with Israel's rebellion.

P-B In Mish. Heb. the vb. *'zq* refers to breaking up soil, and the nom. *'ᵃzēqâ* refers to soil that has been broken up.

Agriculture—farming: → *'ikkār* (farmer, # 438); → *ygb* (be a farmer, # 3320); → *'dr* I (be weeded, # 6371); → *'zq* (break up, loosen, # 6466); → *śdd* (harrow, # 8440)

Mark D. Futato

6468	עזר

עזר (*'zr*), q. help, support; ni. find help (# 6468); עֵזֶר (*'ēzer* I), nom. help, support (# 6469); עֶזְרָה (*'ezrâ* I), nom. help, support (# 6476).

ANE The root appears in almost all the Sem. languages (the only exceptions are Akk. and Eth.). It also appears in a variety of Sem. personal names.

OT 1. The vb. occurs 80x, with almost all of these (76x) in the q., and it is most common in the Psalms (16x), Isaiah (16x), 2 Chronicles (12x), and 1 Chronicles (10x). Along with either El or Yah it appears in personal names such as Eliezer (Exod 18:4, "God is my helper"), Azarel (Ezra 10:41, "God has helped"), Azriel (1 Chron 5:24, "My help is God"), and Azariah (2 Kgs 14:21, "The LORD has helped").

2. The general meaning is, help, support, succor, but it also takes on some more specific meanings.

(a) The vb. is used with a subject that indicates divine intervention to assist the object of the vb., such as heathen gods (Deut 32:28; 2 Chron 28:23), an angel (Dan 10:13), or the God of Israel (Ps 79:9). Often the divine help to Israel took the form of military assistance (1 Chron 12:18; 2 Chron 14:11[10]; 25:8; 26:7). Though other writers also express the same concept (e.g., Ps 46:5[6]), the Chronicler in particular gives emphasis to it, perhaps due partly to the decreased use of the vbs. *yš'*, save, and *nṣl*, deliver, in later Hebrew. No indication is given of the precise way in which God's help was given. The three passages detailing God's help to the Judean kings Asa (14:12[11]), Amaziah (25:8), and Uzziah (26:7) all use the vb. *'zr* prior to mention of God's intervention, but in each case the reader is left to assume that God did so by aiding the armies in their task. The Cushites were "struck down" by the Lord and were crushed before him. Amaziah marshaled his army and led them out to a victorious battle over Seir, while Uzziah was so helped that the Ammonites had to bring tribute to him.

In Isa 41:10-50:9 *'zr* occurs 7x, four of which are addressed to the nation of Israel. It occurs in oracles using the formula "Do not fear," and in the three occurrences in ch. 41 it may well imply some form of military action (41:10, 13, 14). In 44:2 it is not military action that is in view but blessing upon Jacob's descendants. E. W. Conrad has argued that the former are related to the war oracles in Deut 3:2 (‖ Num 21:34); Josh 8:1-2; 10:8; and 11:6, which offer comfort and reassurance before a battle, while the latter are similar to the four patriarchal "Fear not" oracles in Gen (15:1; 21:17; 26:24; 46:3). What is important in Isa 44:2 is that the promise element is formulated in the first person sing. ("The 'Fear Not' Oracles"). The other three occurrences all have the servant of the Lord as the object (49:8; 50:7, 9).

In the Psalms there are numerous references to divine help provided to a variety of people (the righteous, the poor, the fatherless) and in various circumstances (illness, personal distress, oppression).

The nom. *'ēzer* occurs ca. 20x and is predominantly used in reference to Israel's God, as thirteen of the occurrences relate to declarations concerning the Lord's ability to save and deliver. It comes in parallelism with *nṣl* hi. (Exod 18:4) and with *plṭ* pi. (Ps 70:5[6]). The idea of defense is emphasized by the fact that *'ēzer* is on six occasions linked with the epithet "shield" (Deut 33:29; Ps 33:20; 89:18-19[19-20]; 115:9-11; the MT text of Ps 89:19[20] is often emended to *nēzer* as in v. 39[40], but there is no MS evidence to support this change). When used along with "shield," the combined expression has the connotation of divine protection afforded to Israel, just as the warrior in battle was protected by his shield. The fem. nom. *'ezrâ* occurs slightly more frequently (ca. 26x), and together with the preposition *l*^{e} it is almost equivalent to *l*^{e} plus the inf. const. of the vb. What is distinctive about *'ezrâ* is that it is used in the Psalms exclusively of divine help and appears 4x in the standard expression, "Come quickly to help me" (Ps 22:19[20]; 38:22[23]; 40:13[14]; 70:1[2]; and cf. also 40:17[18], "You are my help and my deliverer; O my God, do not delay."

(b) The vb. *'zr* is also used of help among humans, either of a general kind (Isa 41:6; Ezra 10:15) or specifically of military help afforded (Josh 1:14; 10:4; 2 Sam 8:5; 18:3 [Q]; 1 Kgs 20:16; 1 Chron 12:1). Similarly the noms. can refer to human assistance, including military help (Isa 30:5; Dan 11:34). Of the two noms. *'ezrâ* is used more frequently than *'ēzer* of help for the Lord, as in the case of Meroz (Judg 5:23 [2x]). The most distinctive use of *'ēzer* with this meaning is the way in which it is used in Gen 2:18, 20. The Lord God declares that it is not fitting for man to be alone, but that he should be provided with an *'ēzer*. It need not necessarily imply divine assistance, and the context rather suggests it is used in a general way to denote mutual assistance in the marriage relationship by one who corresponds (*k*^{e}*negdô*) to man.

P-B The OT usage of *'zr* continues in the QL. The LXX usually employs *boētheō* to translate it, though the NT use of this vb. is far less prominent than in Josephus.

Help, support, sustenance: → *zqp* (rise, lift up, # 2422); → *smk* (support, lean, refresh, # 6164); → *s'd* (sustain, support, # 6184); → *'zr* (help, support, find help, # 6468); → *rpq* (lean, # 8345); → *š'n* (lean, depend on, # 9128)

BIBLIOGRAPHY

THAT 2:256-59; *TWAT* 6:14-21; E. W. Conrad, "The 'Fear Not' Oracles in Second Isaiah," *VT* 34, 1984, 129-52; M. Dahood, *Psalms III*, 95-96.

Allan M. Harman

6469 (*'ēzer* I, help support), → # 6468

6474 (*'ezrā'*, Ezra), → Ezra

6476 (*'ezrâ* I, help, support), → # 6468

6478	עֲזָרָה

עֲזָרָה (*'^{a}zārâ*), border (of altar) or court (# 6478).

ANE The nom. may be cognate to the Arab. root *'ḏara*, protecting, screening, and a Sabean nom. *m'ḏr,* which refers to a border or setting.

OT The word occurs in the OT with two distinct meanings, both related to the temple. In Ezekiel's vision of the temple this term is often used in reference to the border or edge of the altar and is thus translated by NIV as "ledge" (Ezek 43:14 [3x], 17, 20; 45:19). The word is also used this way in the Temple Scroll.

The remaining occurrences, which are confined to Chronicles, refer to the "court" of the temple (2 Chron 4:9 (2x); 6:13). This meaning corresponds to *ḥāṣēr* and is believed to be the postexilic equivalent for the earlier *ḥāṣēr*. The nom. is believed to have arisen from Aram. influence, especially illustrated from the Aram. Targum translation of Isa 1:12, where the Targum translates *ḥāṣēr* of the MT with *'zrty*.

P-B The nom. occurs very frequently in postbiblical Heb., notably the Mishnah and the Tosefta.

Court, enclosure: → *gizrâ* (cutting, separate room, forecourt, # 1619); → *ḥāṣēr* (enclosure, court, settlement, village, # 2958); → *'ᵃzārâ* (border, court, # 6478); → *parbār* (court, # 7232)

BIBLIOGRAPHY

TDOT 5:131-39; E. Ben Yehuda, *Thesaurus Totius Hebraitatis,* 1947-59, 5:4416 (in Heb.); A. Hurvitz, "The Evidence of Language in Dating the Priestly Code. A Linguistic Study in Technical Idioms and Terminology," *RB,* 81, 1974; idem, A *Linguistic Study of the Relationship Between the Priestly Source and the Book of Ezekiel,* 1982; J. Levy, *Neuhebräische und Chaldäisches Wörterbuch über die Talmudim und Midraschim,* 1876-89, 3:633; M. F. Rooker, *Biblical Hebrew in Transition: The Language of the Book of Ezekiel,* 170-71.

Mark F. Rooker

6485 (*'ēṭ*, pen, stylus), → Writing

6486	עטה

עטה (*'ṭh* I), q., wrap o.s., hi., cover, wrap up (# 6486); מַעֲטֶה (*maᵃṭeh*), nom. garment (# 5073).

ANE Akk., Arab., and Aram. cognates lean in the direction of conceal, be dark, extinguish.

OT 1. The vb. *'ṭh* occurs less than 15x, mainly in the Psalms. Isa 61:10 is problematic; most modern scholars read "wrap" (*'ṭh*) instead of MT "covered" (*y'ṭ*); (see *BHS*; *HALAT* 401, 769; Watts, *Isaiah 34-66*, 301). For the parallelism with *lbš*, see *lbš*.

2. Most often the vb. has a figurative meaning—so the prayer of Ps 71:13, "may [they] ... be covered with scorn" and Ps 109:29, "My accusers will be clothed (*lbš*) with disgrace and wrapped (*'ṭh*) in shame as in a cloak (*mᵉ'îl*)." Ps 104:2 speaks of God's covering himself with light, and Isa 59:17 of God's wrapping himself in zeal.

3. The nom. *maᵃṭeh* appears only in Isa 61:3, where God will give his people "a garment of praise instead of a spirit of despair."

Clothing—Wear clothes: → *lbš* (put on, clothe, wear, # 4252); → *'ṭh* I (cover, wrap, # 6486); → *'ṭp* I (wrap, # 6493); → *ṣnp* I (wrap, turn, # 7571)

Robert L. Alden

6487	עטה

עטה (*'ṭh* II), q. delouse (# 6487).

ANE The Arab. *'ṭw* means to grasp, seize, or reach for something.

OT A homonym for *'ṭh* (wrap) with the meaning "delouse" was first established by von Gall (105-21) on the basis of an Arab. cognate. The simile in Jer 43:12 evidently involves a witty double meaning (Holladay, 302). At first sight the simile would seem to be that Nebuchadnezzar will wrap himself with Egypt as a shepherd wraps himself with his garment. A shepherd could suggest a ruler (cf. 2:8), but the presence of the garment suggests the second far less elegant meaning. Nebuchadnezzar will delouse Egypt as a shepherd his garment, that is, he will absolutely pillage it. The same vb. may also be found in the threat against Shebna in Isa 22:17 (*HALAT* 768).

Insects: → *d^ebôrâ* I (bee, wasp, # 1805); → *kēn* V (mosquito, gnat, louse, # 4031); → *'ṭh* II (delouse, # 6487); → *'aqrāb* (scorpion, # 6832); → *'ārōb* (fly, swarm of flies, flying insects, # 6856); → *'āš* I (moth, # 6931); → *ṣir'â* (hornet, destruction, fear, terror, depression, discouragement, # 7667); → *qml* (wither, become moldy, musty, infected w. insects, # 7857)

BIBLIOGRAPHY

A. G. E. K. von Gall, "Jeremias 43, 12 und das Zeitwort עטה," *ZAW* 24, 1904, 105-21; W. L. Holladay, *Jeremiah 2*, Hermeneia, 1989, 302.

A. H. Konkel

6488 (*'āṭûp*, weakened, feeble, sickly), → # 6494

6490	עֲטִישָׁה

עֲטִישָׁה (*'^aṭîšâ*), nom. sneeze (# 6490).

ANE Arab. *'uṭas*, Eth. *'eṭas*, *'eṭās*, Syr. *'ṭāšā'*, *'uṭāšā'*, *'uṭš^etā'*. The nom. is translated sneeze in each case.

OT The nom. is onomatopoeic in Heb. and appears solely in Job 41:18[10] in a poetic and hyperbolic description of Leviathan, a great mythic monster, whose "snorting throws out flashes of light" (NIV). Dhorme proposes that "when the animal sneezes, the tiny drops which he causes to spurt out from the water glint in the sun, and it is in this way that 'his sneezing makes the light to sparkle'" (Dhorme, *Job*, 636).

Sneeze: → *zrr* II (sneeze, # 2453); → *'^aṭîšâ* (sneeze, # 6490)

BIBLIOGRAPHY

E. Dhorme, *A Commentary on the Book of Job*, 1984; M. Pope, *Job*, 1965, 340.

Wilma Ann Bailey

6491 (*'^aṭallēp*, bat), → # 7606

6493	עטף

עטף (*'ṭp* I), q. bend, wrap o.s. (# 6493); מַעֲטֶפֶת (*ma'^aṭepet*), nom. outer garment (hapleg. in Isa 3:22) (# 5074).

ANE The root occurs in several Semitic languages (*HALAT* 770).

OT 1. The root occurs in poetry and is used metaphorically of a valley covered with grain (Ps 65:13[14]), of violence covering evil persons like a garment (Ps 73:6), and of God hiding (*'ṭp*) himself (Job 23:9).

2. The vb. *'ṭp* is parallel with *lbš* in Ps 65:13[14] and expresses the rich glory of nature: "The meadows are covered (*lbš*) with flocks and the valleys are mantled (*'ṭp*) with grain," but also the abundant evil of the wicked (Ps 73:6). The vb. in Job 23:9—"when he turns (*'ṭp*) to the south, I catch no glimpse of him"—could possibly be rendered by "cover," in the sense that God is enveloped in the clouds (see n. 2 in J. Hartley, *Job*, NICOT, 339).

Clothing—Wear clothes: → *lbš* (put on, clothe, wear, # 4252); → *'ṭh* I (cover, wrap, # 6486); → *'ṭp* I (wrap, # 6493); → *ṣnp* I (wrap, turn, # 7571)

Robert L. Alden

6494	עטף

עטף (*'ṭp* II), q. grow weak; ni. faint; hi. be feeble; hitp. feel faint (# 6494); עָטוּף (*'āṭûp*), weakened, feeble, sickly (# 6488); not to be confused with *'ṭp* I, wrap (→ # 6493).

ANE The vb. is linked to Arab. *'aṭafa*, perish, and possibly to *'aṭiba*, to be ruined (*Wehr*, 557a).

OT The vb. occurs 11x; the nom. 2x. In Gen 30:42 a hi. const. and a pass. part. of *'ṭp* are used to refer to the weak animals in the narrative about how Jacob ensured that the strong offspring came his way (Brenner, 77-80; Wenham, 252).

Isa 57:16 contains God's promise that he will not accuse forever or remain angry "for then the spirit/life-breath of man would grow faint." God gives and upholds life also for those who become "faint/weak" (Watts, 262-63).

In Lam 2 no less than three references to *'ṭp* are found as part of the description about the disaster that struck Jerusalem; the first two by the narrator and the third by Zion. Lam 2:11 reports about the children and infants that faint (possibly as a result of hunger and thirst during the siege of Jerusalem) in the city streets; the fainting children are compared to wounded men (v. 12), and in v. 19 the same example of distress (fainting children) is refered to (*TWOT* 2:662; Provain, 70-77).

Jon 2:7[8] forms part of the prophet's prayer, in which the hitp. of *'ṭp* plus *napšî* can be tr. "my life was ebbing away/was growing weak," or it can be interpreted as an idiom "to lose consciousness" (Stuart, 467).

The highest concentration of references to *'ṭp* is found in the Psalms. The subjects of the vb. vary from the *rûaḥ*, spirit (77:3[4]; 142:3[4]; 143:4), to the heart (61:2[3]) and the *nepeš*, soul, self (107:5; *TWOT* 2:662). In Ps 61:2[3] the "fainting heart" probably indicates an ebbing vitality as one of the reasons for the lament (Tate, 110). Ps 77:4 uses the faintness/weakness of the spirit to indicate that God has become a source of spiritual distress. Whenever God's help in bygone days is recalled, the circumstances of the psalmist make his spirit grow faint/weak (Tate, 274; Anderson, 557). Ps 102:1 [HB] contains the only use of the vb. in a psalm title, where the afflicted man is described as being "faint." Ps 107:5 again refers to the ebbing away of life as the growing weak of the *nepeš*. Ps 142:3[4] and 143:4 both refer to the spirit of the psalmist that "grows faint/weak" within him and lead to an individual complaint addressed to God (Allen, 279, 282).

P-B 1. *Qumran*. 1QH 8:29 reads, "For (my life) has come near the pit (Sheol/netherworld) and my soul faints day and night" (cf. Ps 61:2[3]; 77:3[4]; 107:5; 142:3[4]; 143:4; Isa 57:16; Jon 2:7[8]).

2. *Rabbinical literature*. In the Midrash Till. on Ps 61:3 it is asked how long one must remain in prayer? The answer is: till your heart is "faint/weak" (Jastrow 2:1064).

NT In Luke 16:9 *ekleipō*, cease, come to an end refers to a time when mammon "runs out" (cf. LXX in Lam. 2:1; Jon 2:8). In Heb 1:12 this word indicates that the years of God will never end (*EDNT* 1:417). *eklyomai*, tire, become weak, lose courage (cf. LXX in Lam 2:12, 19) is used for physical exhaustion in Matt 15:32 and Mark 8:3, and in the reprimand not to lose heart in Heb 12:3 (*EDNT* 1:419).

Feeble, despair, faint, frail, tender: → *'ml* I (be weak, be feeble, languish, # 581); → *ḥlh* I (become weak, tired, ill, # 2703); → *ylh* (languish, # 3532); → *k'h* (be disheartened, frightened, # 3874); → *nbl* I (wither, fade, languish, dishonor, # 5570); → *'ṭp* II (grow weak, faint, be feeble, # 6494); → *'lp* (cover, faint, # 6634); → *'šš* (become weak, # 6949); → *pwg* (be feeble, numb, be prostrated, # 7028); → *rzh* (destroy, waste away, # 8135); → *rkk* (be tender, timid, gentle, # 8216); → *rph* (become slack, lose heart, discourage, # 8332)

BIBLIOGRAPHY

EDNT 1:417, 419; *TWOT* 2:661-62; L. C. Allen, *Psalms 101-150*, WBC, 1983; A. A. Anderson, *The Book of Psalms*, 2, 1992; A. Brenner, "*atupim* and *qissurin* (Gen 30:31-42)," *BethM* 24, 1978, 77-80; I. W. Provain, *Lamentations*, 1991; K. Seybold, *Das Gebet des Kranken im AT*, 1973; D. Stuart, *Hosea-Jonah*, WBC, 1987; M. E. Tate, *Psalms 51-100*, WBC, 1990; J. D. W. Watts, *Isaiah 34-66*, WBC, 1987; G. J. Wenham, *Genesis 16-50*, WBC, 1994; R. N. Whybray, *Isaiah 40-66*, Hermeneia, 1990.

Hendrik L. Bosman

6496/6497	עטר

עטר (*'ṭr*), q. surround (# 6496); pi. crown; hi. bestow crowns (# 6497); עֲטָרָה (*'aṭārâ* I), nom. crown, wreath; "that which surrounds" (# 6498).

ANE The Arab. *'ṭr* means surround.

OT 1. In 1 Sam 23:26 the vb. *'ṭr*, surround, encircle, is used intransitively with a bad sense of one army closing in upon another. In Ps 5:12[13] the vb. is doubly transitive in that both the psalmist and God's favor are the objects: "You surround them with your favor as with a shield" (NIV). Jerome and LXX render *'ṭr* by crown, but fail to notice that a crown can scarcely be described as a shield.

2. The only unambiguous occurrence of the pi. of *'ṭr*, crown, is S of Songs 3:11, where the context determines that *'ṭr* must be rendered crowned. Elsewhere the choice between crown and surround must be carefully weighed, such as in the phrase, "You crowned him with glory and honor" (Ps 8:5[6]). This phrase may be understood as consequent upon the previous phrase, "You made him a little lower than the heavenly beings." The sense is then that although humankind significantly lacks (*ḥsr*) something of the heavenly beings' attributes, he still has a significant position in God's creation. In this case the translation "surrounded" is to be preferred, and the emphasis of the verse is on a human being's subordinate but protected status. On the other hand, the phrase in question may be regarded as introductory to the following, "You made him ruler over the works of your hands." In this case the translation "crowned" is to be preferred, and the emphasis of the verse is on a human being's power and his role as steward of God's creation. The problem is only one of translation. The verse serves both these functions, and pi. *'ṭr* bridges them in a way no Eng. translation can accomplish.

Ps 65:11[12], "You surround the year *of* your goodness" (MT) presents difficulties. NIV is representative of EVV in providing an indirect object, "You crown the year *with* your bounty." Jerome *volvetur annus in bonitate tua* reflects the sense encircle for pi. *'ṭr*. Considered in the light of the context of the annual round of nature referred to in

vv. 9-13[10-14], this suggests the rendering, "You bring the year of your bounty full circle." If crown is kept, the syntax of the MT may be retained, "You crown your bounteous year," and the second stichos, "your carts overflow with abundance," is to be taken as epexegetical of crown.

Ps 103:4 EVV and ancient versions translate "crown," but the verse stands in the context of rescue and speaks of the protection rather than of the dignity that people receive from God. The translation "and surrounds you with love and compassion" should be considered.

3. The nom. *'ᵃṭārâ*, crown, signifies that which surrounds. The crown of the king of Rabbah (or maybe of the god Milcom, NIV margin) was a symbol of authority. With an estimated weight of 34 kilograms it was too heavy for wear (2 Sam 12:30; 1 Chron 20:2). Mordecai was able to walk about with an *'aṭārâ,* which he wore (Esth 8:15); his crown may have been lighter. In Israel the status of the king derived from God (Ps 21:3); rule that disregarded his authority lost legitimacy, and its symbol's significance was traduced.

The crown of Joshua (Zech 6:9-14) was kept in the temple as a memorial, either as a reminder that sovereignty derives from God or as a reminder to God of the blessing he had promised (so Ackroyd, 200). It is not certain that this crown is intended in 1 Macc 1:22, for Antiochus IV removed such crowns when he stripped the temple. They were replaced at the rededication (1 Macc 4:57). These crowns may have been the metal borders that surrounded some of the temple furniture (cf. Exod 30:3, 4; 37:2, 11, 12, 26, 27; NIV moulding). The payment of a crown tax to the Seleucids was a galling reminder to the Jews that their sovereignty derived de facto from the Gentiles (1 Macc 10:29; 11:35; 13:39).

4. The nom. *'ᵃṭārâ*, crown, is used by metonymy for "rule," whether legitimate (Isa 28:5) or illegitimate (Isa 28:1, 3; Ezek 21:26[31]). A crown was part of the bridegroom's regalia (S of Songs 3:11; cf. Isa 61:10; *AncIsr*, 33), and by natural extension the word symbolized "honor" (Job 19:9; Lam 5:16) and personal dignity (Ezek 16:12; 23:42).

Crown: → *ktr* III (wear as ornament, # 4194); → *'ṭr* (surround, crown, # 6496/7)
Circle, turn: → *'pp* (surround, # 705); → *ḥdr* I (surround, enclose, # 2539); → *ḥwg* (describe a circle, # 2552); → *ktr* II (surround, # 4193); → *nqp* II (go round, surround, # 5938); → *sbb* (turn go round, surround, # 6015); → *'āgōl* (round, # 6318); → *'ṭr* (surround, crown, # 6496/7)

BIBLIOGRAPHY

P. R. Ackroyd, *Exile and Restoration*, 1972, 200; R. de Vaux, *AncIsr*, 1961, 33.

Robert J. Way

6498 (*'ᵃṭārâ*, crown), → # 6496/7

6504 (*'ay*, Ai), → Ai

6507 (*'êbāl*, Ebal), → Ebal

6512	עיט

עיט (*'yṭ*), yell; shriek; swoop down in shrieks (# 6512); עַיִט (*'ayit*), birds of prey (→ # 6514).

ANE Cf. Arab. *'yṭ*; Syr. *'ayṭā'*.

OT This word occurs 2x (in q., 1 Sam 15:19; 25:14). In 15:19 it describes Saul's act of disobedience when he swooped upon (*'yṭ*) Agag, king of the Amalekites, and his people and kept him and some spoil for himself. He had acted as a bird of prey that would attack and keep the prey for itself to devour and gloat over. In 25:14 it refers to the foolish, boorish, disrespectful language used by Nabal ("fool") when he "shrieked, railed" (*y'ṭ*, impf.) at them. Both of these verses emphasize an unreasoning verbal/military attack/maneuver on other persons/things. The two sure occurrences are used with *'el, b^e*, respectively.

P-B The LXX translates the vb. with *hormaō*, lay hold of (1 Sam 15:19), and *ekklinō*, turn away from (1 Sam 25:14).

Animal sounds: → *g'h* (bellow, low [cattle], # 1716); → *hgh* I (groan, moan, sigh, meditate, muse, chirp, mutter, # 2047); → *nbḥ* (bark [dogs], # 5560); → *nhq* (bray [ass], shriek, # 5640); → *nḥr* (snort, # 5723); → *'yṭ* (yell, shriek, swoop down [w. shrieks], # 6512); → *ṣhl* I (neigh, shout, # 7412)

Eugene Carpenter

6514	עַיִט

עַיִט (*'ayiṭ*), birds of prey (collective; # 6514).

ANE The nom. is attested in Ugar. *'t* and Sam. *īṭ* (cf. *CPTOT*, 128).

OT The nom. appears 8x and mostly represents an enemy or an adversary. In Gen 15:11 Abram wards off the birds of prey while making a covenant with the Lord. It is generally understood that the sacrifices here represent Israel, while the birds of prey represent unclean nations, Gentiles, possibly Egypt (M. Douglas, G. Wenham, N. Sarna). In other passages *'ayiṭ* sometimes represents foreign invaders (Isa 46:11; Jer 12:9).

P-B In some of the midrashic literature *'ayiṭ* in Gen 15:11 is taken to refer to "the son of David" or "Jerusalem" in reference to Jer 12:9 (e.g., Pirqe R. El. 27a).

Birds, flying creatures: → *'br* (fly, # 87); → *bêṣâ* (egg, # 1070); → *barbur* (species of fowl, # 1350); → *gôzāl* (young bird, # 1578); → *dgr* (hatch eggs, # 1842); → *ḥ^asîdâ* (stork, # 2884); → *yônâ* I (dove, # 3433); → *ya^{'a}nâ* (ostrich, eagle-owl?, # 3613); → *kānāp* (wing, skirt, outermost edge, # 4053); → *nešer/n^ešar* (vulture [eagle], # 5979); → *'ôp* (flying creatures, # 6416); → *'ayiṭ* (birds of prey [collective], # 6514); → *'ōrēb* I (raven, # 6854); → *ṣippôr* I (birds, # 7606); → *qōrē'* I (partridge, # 7926); → *ś^elāw* (quails, # 8513)

Bibliography

ABD 6:1109-67; M. Douglas, *Purity in Danger*, 1966; V. P. Hamilton, *Genesis 1-17*, 1990; W. Houston, *Purity and Monotheism: Clean and Unclean Animals in Biblical Law,* 1993; W. McKane, *Jeremiah,* 1986; N. Sarna, *Genesis,* 1989; G. J. Wenham, *Genesis 1-15*, 1990.

N. Kiuchi

6523	עין

עין (*'yn*), denom. vb. view with suspicion (hapleg. in 1 Sam 18:9; # 6523); עַיִן (*'ayin*), eye, look, appearance, spring (# 6524; for the meaning "spring" → # 5078).

ANE The root *'yn*, eye, is a common Sem. nom., but a denom. vb. *'yn* also occurs in Aram., Arab., and Ugar.

OT 1. The vb. only occurs in a participial form in 1 Sam 18:9(Q). The nom., however, occurs ca. 866x in the OT and 5x in bibl. Aram. (Dan 4:34[31]; 7:8 [2x], 20; Ezra 5:5). For a full tabulation including the separate meanings of "eye" and "source," see *THAT* 2:260. The dual *'ênayim* is much more common than the singular *'ayin*. The "eye" is used in its literal meaning and in connection with expressions relating to seeing. It is also employed in prepositional phrases to denote presence before someone or judgments of favor or disfavor on persons or activities. A variety of emotional and spiritual conditions can be indicated by it, and God's omniscience is frequently represented by anthropomorphic use of eye/eyes. (→ Anthropomorphism: Theology)

2. The word *'ayin* is repeatedly used to designate the literal eye of both people and animals. It appears when other parts of the body are being mentioned (2 Kgs 4:34) but especially in combination with "ears" (Deut 29:4[3]; Neh 1:6; Ps 115:5-6; Isa 6:10). At times the two eyes are mentioned, while the expression "between the eyes" (Exod 13:9, 16; Deut 6:8; 14:1; Dan 8:5, 21) is equivalent to "forehead." Although the wearing of the law "between the eyes" (Deut 6:8) could be taken literally, similar instructions concerning the Feast of Unleavened Bread and the rules concerning the firstborn (Exod 13:9, 16) must have a figurative meaning, or else these are to be like frontlets between their eyes, i.e., visible signs to everyone that they are the people of God.

References also occur to the eyes of various animals, including small animals (Gen 30:41) and birds (Job 28:7; Prov 1:17). The beauty of eyes is a thing to be noted (of David, 1 Sam 16:12), while "weak" or "delicate" eyes appears to be a comment drawing attention to absence of beauty (of Leah, Gen 29:17).

3. Under the provisions of the *lex talionis*, if harm was done to a person, then restitution was to be made: "fracture for fracture, eye for eye, tooth for tooth" (Lev 24:19-20; cf. Exod 21:24, 26; Deut 19:21). This law applied to the offended person and was intended to establish a standard of justice and to limit retaliation to the exact extent of the injury inflicted (cf. Kaiser, 72-73, 299-301). Goring out of eyes of prisoners, including kings, was a regular happening during warfare (Judg 16:21; 2 Kgs 25:7). The importance of the eye for person's welfare is emphasized by the fact that if a slave's eye was destroyed, he was allowed his freedom (Exod 21:26).

4. Several varieties of prepositional phrases are employed with *'ayin*, many of them standard expressions with the prepositions b^e or l^e. "To find favor in the eyes of" (Gen 6:8; 19:19; 32:5[6]; 34:11) is used to describe the approval and blessing that righteous people receive from God as well as insecure attempts to bribe favor out of another person (33:8, 10, 15). "Before the eyes of" = "in the presence of" (23:11, 18; Exod 7:20; 17:6; 40:38) describes actions that are done right in front of people; thus they are fully responsible for the information that is revealed to them. The opposite condition of the absence from the presence of someone is expressed by the use of the preposition *min* (cf. Num 15:24). The expression "in the eyes of" occurs frequently with an adjective, especially "good" (*ṭôb*) or "upright" (*yāšār*) and "evil" (*ra'*), to express favorable and unfavorable judgments respectively being passed on persons and events. It forms one of the recurring phrases that gives an assessment of the period of the judges: "Every man did what was right in his own eyes" (lit., Judg 17:6; 21:25). In

the monarchical narratives it is often part of the formulaic introduction of divine approval or disapproval that commences the account of a king's reign (e.g., Asa, 1 Kgs 15:11; Nadab, 15:26; Baasha, 15:34; Hezekiah, 2 Kgs 18:3; Josiah, 22:2).

5. *'ayin* is also used in various expressions to denote mental or emotional states. It is regularly used in conjunction with a negative particle (*lō'* and *'al*) and the vb. *ḥws*, show mercy (→ # 2571), to denote the deprivation of compassion (Gen 45:20; Deut 7:16; 13:8[9]; Ezek 5:11; 7:4; 20:17; without "eyes"—Jer 13:14; 21:7; Ezek 24:14). In conjunction with the vb. *r''*, do evil, it indicates the absence of compassion or an eye that looks with disfavor on someone (Deut 15:9; 28:54, 56). With the vb. *rwm*, exalt o.s., "eye" is used to denote a haughty spirit (Ps 18:27[28]; 131:1; Prov 6:17; 21:4; Isa 10:12), but in other constructions it indicates attitudes such as mockery (Prov 30:17), humility (Job 22:29), stinginess (Deut 15:9), and arrogance (Ps 101:5; Isa 2:11; 5:15). Several times it appears in construct relationships to indicate what is good to the eyes (Gen 3:6), desirable to the eyes (Ezek 24:16), or an abomination of the eyes (Ezek 20:7). In other passages "eye" describes a human desire (Num 15:39; 1 Kgs 20:6; Job 31:1, 7; Eccl 2:10; Jer 5:3; 22:17; Lam 2:4).

6. The nom. *'ayin* can refer to spiritual rather than physical sight. The opening of the eyes of Adam and Eve after they had eaten from the forbidden fruit (Gen 3:5, 7) indicates a perception on a spiritual level that is accompanied by an awareness of their alienation from God (→ Fall of Humankind). Eyes can be blinded by God (Isa 6:10), and this Isaianic usage may be echoed in Jer 5:21. Idol worshipers are said to have their eyes plastered over so that they cannot see that their idols are merely worthless pieces of wood that deceive idol worshipers (Isa 44:18). In crisis situations God can open eyes so that reality can be seen, as Balaam experienced when he saw the angel of the Lord standing before him with a drawn sword (Num 22:31), or as Elisha's servant encountered when he saw the chariots of God's army (2 Kgs 6:17). Eyes that look to the Lord express confidence and expectancy as he hears prayer (Ps 123:2), while God gives spiritual enlightenment to the eyes by his word (Ps 19:8[9]; 119:18).

7. The eye is mentioned in connection with other bodily functions related to the eye. The eyes are the source of tears, being used both with the vb. *dm'*, shed tears (→ # 1963), and the nom. *dim'â*, tear (→ # 1965); both together in Jer 13:17; with *dim'â*, Ps 116:8; Jer 9:1[8:23]; 31:16; with the vb. *yrd*, flow down (→ # 3718; Ps 119:136; Jer 9:18[17]; 13:17). This may be the origin of the metaphorical use of "eye" meaning "source" (see 9 below). Eye is not the subject of the common Heb. vb. for weeping, *bkh* (→ # 1134), and only in Jer 9:1[8:23]; 13:17; 31:16 and Lam 1:16 do "weeping eyes" and the vb. *bkh* come in parallelism. Tears in the eyes may be due to a prophet's deep sorrow over the destruction that God is planning to bring on his people (Jer 9:1[8:23]; 13:17) or the sorrow of people who have been destroyed and have no one to comfort them (Lam 1:16), but the removal of tears (Jer 31:16) is connected to God's new work of hope in the lives of his people.

8. The singular and plural are used in anthropomorphic expressions, such as declarations that the Lord's eyes are on the land of Canaan continually (Deut 11:12) or that the Lord's eyes are on the righteous. They watch over the sinful (Amos 9:8) and can be hidden from humankind (Isa 1:15). God is declared to be of purer eyes than to look on evil (Hab 1:13), and when he appeared to Israel, he did so in a very personal, visible way, "eye to eye" (Num 14:14; cf. the similar idiom with *pānîm*,

Gen 32:30[31]; Exod 33:11; Deut 5:4; 34:10; Judg 6:22; Ezek 20:35). In an interesting idiom God's eyes are said to be open to the pleas of his people (1 Kings 8:29, 52), whereas in European languages "ears" would be the expected means of reception. These anthropomorphic expressions account for almost a quarter of all instances of *'ayin* in the OT. Several facts concerning them should be noted.

(a) The most common form is *'ên/'ênê yhwh,* which occurs over 100x, describing God's sovereign knowledge of, care for, and control of events and people, as well as his moral approval or disapproval of people.

(b) It is rare to find this anthropomorphic use of "eyes" with *'ᵉlōhîm*, God. The only cases are Num 23:27; 1 Chron 21:7; Prov 3:4. This same phenomenon is also apparent with all the other anthropomorphisms (→), which are applied almost exclusively to *yhwh*, not to *'ᵉlōhîm* (cf. the presence of *yad yhwh*, hand of the LORD, in an otherwise elohistic psalm, Ps 75:8[9]).

(c) Some anthropomorphic expressions throw back upon God an attribute of human beings when speaking of his omniscience. Thus it is not surprising that expressions used of people are also applied to God, including "to find favor in the eyes of" (Exod 33:17) and "to be great in the eyes of" (1 Sam 26:24). A series of approbatory or condemnatory phrases are applied to God as they are to various individuals ("good/upright/evil in the sight of the LORD").

(d) Job wondered if the explanation for his suffering was perhaps that God sees things differently than people on earth (Job 10:4). Although Job recognized God's transcendence, he was less certain about the nature of God's rule of humankind, based on his unique perspective of seeing what was happening on earth. The use of an anthropomorphism such as "the eyes of the LORD" is used to teach concerning God's nature in terms that are intelligible to us. These expressions are ostensive in design, not descriptive. They are intended to bring God close to human beings in the fullness of his personal revelation.

(e) The anthropomorphisms of the OT have to be considered against the background of the prohibition against making images of God. Consistent anthropomorphism leads toward idolatry. The God revealed in the OT could not be confined within limits set by men, and adoration of him was not through the medium of physical representations. Even when images were made of gods, they were impotent and their eyes could not see (Ps 115:5; 135:16). For a general discussion of anthropomorphisms in the OT see Jacob, 39-42, and A. Heschel, *The Prophets*, II, 39-58. (→ Anthropomorphism: Theology)

(f) The translator of the LXX had difficulty with the anthropomorphisms and attempted to remove certain of them (cf. the discussion by Fritsch, *Anti-Anthropomorphisms*).

9. Closely connected with the anthropomorphic expressions are those in which eyes are employed as a symbol for the divine presence. Thus, in Ezek 1:18 in Ezekiel's opening vision the wheels were full of eyes, as were the cherubim's back, hands, wings, and wheels in a later vision (10:12; cf. also Rev 4:8, where the four living creatures have eyes all around). This usage is employing the expression symbolically to convey the idea of God's all-seeing presence, and Zech 3:9 would seem to fall into the same category. The seven lamps in the prophet's vision (Zech 4:10) were "the eyes of the LORD, which range throughout the earth." Along with these there can be grouped

passages in which people are spoken of metaphorically as "eyes." Such is the case of Hobab, who as leader was to be Israel's "eyes" in the wilderness (Num 10:31).

10. In a group of passages *'ayin* appears with what BDB called "transferred meanings" (744). Thus, "the eye of the land" (Exod 10:5, 15; Num 22:5, 11) is used to indicate the surface of the land covered by locusts or by people. It can also denote the appearance of something (mildew, Lev 13:55; resin, Num 11:7). The reflection of metal or jewels can be described using *'ayin* (Ezek 1:4, 7, 16, 27; 8:2; 10:9; Dan 10:6), as well as the sparkle of wine (Prov 23:31 ‖ *hit'addām*, be red) or ice (Ezek 1:22).

11. In addition to the meaning "eye," *'ayin* is found 23x in the OT with the meaning of "source," the majority of these instances being in the Pentateuch. Lexicons in the tradition of Gesenius, such as BDB, separate this root from the root for "eye," but KB and *HALAT* relate "eye" and "source" to an identical root. Since the eye is the source of tears (see 7 above), it is called a fountain (*māqôr*, Jer 9:1[8:23]). With the meaning spring, *'ayin* is present in numerous compound names in the OT, such as En-gedi, Endor, Enrogel, and Enshemesh (*HALAT* 774-75; → # 5078).

12. Activities of the eye.

(a) Frequently *'ayin* appears in close connection with expressions for "seeing," especially the vb. *r'h* (→ # 8011). "Eyes" often form the subject of *r'h* (Gen 45:12 [2x]; Deut 3:21; 4:3, 9), and also *ḥzh* (Ps 11:4; → # 2600). The common expression "to lift up one's eyes and see" (*nś' 'ênāyim*, Gen 13:10; 18:2; Josh 5:13; 1 Sam 6:13; 2 Sam 13:34) can use vbs. other than *r'h* (e.g., with *nbṭ*, hi. Isa 51:6; with *nkr*, hi. Job 2:12). When used with *r'h*, the conjunction and demonstrative particle *hinnēh* often follows in order to draw emphatic attention to the object of the vb. The same idea can be conveyed by the synonymous expression *śam 'ênê 'al* (Gen 44:21). A similar expression occurs in Bibl. Aram. with the vb. *nṭl* (Dan 4:34[31]).

(b) A variety of vbs., including *glh*, reveal (→ # 1655, e.g., Num 22:31; 24:4, 16; Ps 119:18), *ptḥ*, open (→ # 7337, e.g., 1 Kgs 8:29, 52; Neh 1:6), and *pqḥ*, open (→ # 7219, e.g., Gen 21:19; 2 Kgs 4:35; Isa 42:7) are used to designate the opening of the eyes of God to the situation of his people, or the opening of the eyes/understanding of his people to the ways of God.

(c) Several other vbs. have a more negative connotation: *qrṣ*, wink (→ # 7975), and *rzm*, wink (→ # 8141).

P-B The LXX uniformly uses *ophthalmos* to translate *'ayin* and carries over many of the Heb. idioms, including to find *charis*, grace, or *eleos*, mercy, in someone's eyes. Many of the OT usages are continued in the NT, though figurative reference to the eyes of God is rare (Heb 4:13; 1 Peter 3:12).

Eye, wink: → *'îšôn* (pupil of eye, # 413); → *bābâ* (pupil of eye, # 949); → *'yn* (view with suspicion, # 6523); → *'ap'appayim* (flashing of eye, # 6757); → *qrṣ* (wink, pinch, # 7975); → *rzm* (flash, # 8141); → *teballul* (spot in eye, # 9319)

Fountain, spring: → *mabbāk* (spring, # 4441); → *ma'yān* (spring, # 5078); → *māqôr* (spring, # 5227); → *nb'* (bubble, # 5580)

BIBLIOGRAPHY

NIDNTT 3:511-21; *TDNT* 5:375-78; *THAT* 2:259-68; *TWAT* 6:31-55; T. J. Finley, "'The Apple of his Eye' (*bābat 'ênô*) in Zechariah ii 12," *VT* 38, 1988, 337-38; C. T. Fritsch, *The Anti-Anthropomorphisms of the Greek Pentateuch*, 1943; E. Jacob, *Theology of the Old Testament*, 1958;

W. C. Kaiser, Jr., *Toward Old Testament Ethics*, 1983; C. McCarthy, "The Apple of the Eye," in *Melanges Dominique Barthelemy*, ed. P. Casetti, O. Keel, and A. Schenker, 1981, 289-95; L. A. Oppenheim, "The Eyes of the Lord," in *Essays in Memory of E. A. Speiser*, ed. W. W. Hallo, 1968, 173-80; S. C. Reif, "A Root to Look Up? A Study of the Hebrew *nś' 'yn*," in *VTSup* 36, ed. J. Emerton, 1985, 230-44; E. Robertson, "The Apple of the Eye in the Masoretic Text," *JTS* 138, 1937, 56-59; G. J. Wenham, *The Book of Leviticus*, NICOT, 1979; C. Wright, *An Eye for an Eye: The Place of Old Testament Ethics Today*, 1983; E. M. Yamauchi, "Magic in the Biblical World," *TynBul* 34, 1983, 169-200.

Allan M. Harman

6524 (*'ayin*, spring; eye), → # 5078, # 6523

6545	עיף

עיף (*'yp* I), q. be weary (# 6545); which developed by the transposition of the first two consonants (metathesis) from יעף (*y'p* I), q. be weary, faint (→ # 3615) (GKC, 70; *HALAT* 402, 775); עָיֵף (*'āyēp*), adj. exhausted, faint (# 6546); יָעֵף (*yā'ēp*), nom./adj. fatigued or tired (# 3617); יְעָף (*y*^{e}*'āp*), flight (# 3618), are both derived from *y'p* I.

ANE The root *'yp* might be related to the Syr. vb. *'āp*, be tired, since the adj. *'āyēp* has a cognate in the Syr. adj. *'ayîp*, weary, and in the Sam. *īf*, tired. The root *y'p* is possibly linked with the Arab. *waġafa*, to walk fast, and the Christian Aram. *Y'P* (*HAHAT*, 476). *y*^{e}*'āp* is an aramaism and used only in Dan 9:21 (BDB, 419).

OT 1. *Distribution*. *'yp* and its derivatives are found in ten books of the OT. The vb. is used 4x in narrative texts—three of them in the Samuel books (Judg 4:21; 1 Sam 14:28, 31; 2 Sam 21:15) and only once in prophetic literature (Jer 4:31). The adj. appears 7x in narrative texts (Gen 25:29-30; Deut 25:18; Judg 8:4-5; 2 Sam 16:14; 17:29) and, with one exception, seems to be paired in twos. In prophetic literature the adj. occurs 6x, with a high concentration in Isaiah (Isa 5:27; 28:12; 29:8; 32:2; 46:1; Jer 31:25), while it occurs twice each in Wisdom (Prov 25:25; Job 22:7) and lyrical literature (Ps 63:1[2]; 143:6).

y'p appears in only five books of the OT. There are similar concentrations of usage as with *'yp*, with a significant number of occurrences in Isaiah. The vb. occurs primarily (8x) in prophetic literature (Isa 40:28, 30, 31; 44:12; Jer 2:24; 51:58, 64; Hab 2:13), while the adj. is found twice each in narrative (Judg 8:15; 2 Sam 16:2) and prophetic literature (Isa 40:29; 50:4).

The semantic field of tiredness and weariness embraces the total range of physical, emotional, and spiritual incapacity. It is clear from the distribution of usage that references to being weary or tired are most prevalent in narrative (1 and 2 Sam) and prophetic literature (Isa).

The nom. *y*^{e}*'āp* flight, will be discussed as part of apocalyptic literature because it is only attested in Dan 9:21.

2. *Narrative texts*. In the short narrative about the sale of the birthright (Gen 25:29-34), Esau came home exhausted from the hunt (v. 29; Westermann, 1985, 416-17). The famished Esau asks for the stew, inarticulately referred to as the "red, red stuff" (Alter, 44). Therefore, Ibn Ezra was correct when he interpreted *'āyēp* as referring to the state of being in dire need of food and drink (Sarna, 182, 363). Jacob

exploits his famished brother. Esau is depicted as lacking in wisdom and restraint by selling his birthright for some lentil stew (Clifford, 400-401).

Deut 25:17-19 calls for the extermination of the Amalekites because of the hostility they displayed when they cut off the wearied and worn-out Israelites camping at Rephidim without water (cf. Exod 17:1-16; Carmichael, 244). *'āyēp* refers to a weariness caused by thirst and is used parallel to *yāgēa'*, worn out, thus emphasizing the exhaustion of the Israelites. Amalek's lack of compassion for the weary and the thirsty caused the divine judgment to blot out their memory (Thompson, 253; Miller, 177; Merrill, 331). Amalek becomes the symbol of inhuman behavior and of the oppression of the weak—even Haman has an Amalekite ancestry in Esth 3:1 (Braulik, 121; Rose, 255).

The narrative describing the flight and death of Sisera in Judg 4:17-22, refers in v. 21 to Sisera's lying fast asleep because he was exhausted (*y'p*). Lindars (203-4) suggests "collapsed" instead of "weary." According to ANE laws of hospitality (Gen 19:5, 8) a guest must be protected, an obligation that Sisera assumes. There is an ironic twist in the narrative when the mighty warrior becomes weary and vulnerable in his sleep, to be killed by a woman who had other loyalties than being hospitable (Soggin, 78). The narrative in Judges that concerns Gideon in the Transjordan has numerous references to being weary or exhausted (Judg 8:4-21). Verse 4 has a good example of hendiadys (a single expression consisting of two parts) with "exhausted (*'yp*) yet keeping up the pursuit," a combination of words that is more or less repeated in v. 5. The further reference to "exhausted" in v. 15 forms a strong inclusio with vv. 4-5 (Boling, 154-57). All three references to being weak or exhausted in Judg 8 have some bearing on the law of hospitality that was not adhered to by the inhabitants of Succoth.

In 1 Sam 14:24-35 the narrative about the battle between Israel and the Philistines is interrupted by an account of Saul's vow to kill any Israelite who eats that day (v. 24). The entire army keeps the vow (vv. 25-26), but Jonathan violates the vow in ignorance (v. 27). The weariness of the army is linked to the keeping of the vow, a weariness in stark contrast to the bright-eyed Jonathan, who had just eaten honey (Brueggemann, 1990, 104-5). 1 Sam 14:31 describes the Israelite attack on Michmash and how they were exhausted (*wayyā'ap*). This creates not only an inclusio with v. 28, but also provides a reason for eating the plunder (cf. the wordplay *wayya'aś* with *wayya'aṭ*, they pounced on, v. 32; Van Zyl, 178).

Ziba tries to win David's favor with gifts of food and wine (2 Sam 16:1-4; Robinson, 235-36). He refers to the soldiers becoming exhausted in the desert as the reason for his gifts (v. 2). The following narrative gives an account of how Shimei curses David and closes with a description of how David arrives at the destination exhausted (16:5-14). Although the destination is not specified in the MT, it is clear from 17:22, one MS of the LXX, and Josephus (*Ant* 7, 210), that it was the Jordan River (McCarter, 369). The motif of the Jordan being a place of refreshment for the weary is a common motif in Jewish and Christian piety (Robinson, 238). Conroy (142) is impressed by the frequent use of key words, refrains, and the interweaving of vocabulary in 2 Sam 13-20, and uses the references to weariness in 16:2, 14 as an example of material inclusion. 2 Sam 17:27-29 is a compound sentence that explains how David and his soldiers are fed in the wilderness (Fokkelman, 235). As in 16:2, the reason for the provision of food and drink is the weariness caused by the wilderness. This might be an allusion to the law of hospitality that prevails in communities living in desert or wilderness areas (Robinson, 245). Brueggemann (1971, 329-31) is of the opinion that weariness constitutes a common motif that forms an inclusio in 2 Sam 16:14-17:29 and that weariness and rest (an approximate synonym for *šālôm*, peace) are juxtaposed in such a way in these narratives that weariness becomes equivalent to the absence of harmony or peace. 2 Sam 21:15-22 contains four episodes, each of which reports the killing of a Philistine giant by a soldier of David. The exhausted older David is in stark contrast to the younger heroic figure of the past (Brueggemann, 1990, 338-39). The weary David causes the army to refuse him any access to the battlefront "so that the lamp of Israel will not be extinguished" (v. 17).

3. *Prophetic literature*. Isa 5:8-30 combines a series of woe oracles and sentences of judgment (Seitz, 49-50). In vv. 26-30 distant nations (probably Assyria) are summoned to execute the judgment of God on Israel, and the inevitable judgment is reflected by the terse but remorseless reference in v. 27 that "not one of them grows tired or stumbles" (Clements, 69-70). There is a chiasm linking the negatively formulated statements in v. 27 with the positively formulated v. 28 (Oswalt, 169). Thus, the lack of tiredness or sleep among the soldiers in v. 27 is closely related to the readiness of the horses and the chariots in v. 28. The second subsection in Isa 28 is found in vv. 7-13 and consists of a judgment oracle over the priest and prophet who presume to teach Israel but in fact only speak gibberish (Seitz, 209; Tanghe, 235-60). A chiasmus in v. 12 portrays the cohesion between God's offer to Israel of rest in Canaan and Israel's responsibility of giving rest to the weary (Watts, 1985, 364). Israel accused other nations, such as the Amalekites and the inhabitants of Succoth, that they did not take care of the weary. Now they are themselves accused of the same lack of care for the tired and the weary!

Isa 29:1-8 starts in the first four verses with a woe oracle against Ariel, which is besieged, first by God and later by the nations. A shift takes place in the last four verses, when God fights the enemies of Mount Zion, thereby indicating that the judgment against Jerusalem also includes the other nations and that God acts independently of them (Routledge, 181-90; Seitz, 212-14). The reference in v. 8 to the hungry and thirsty person who only dreams that he is eating and drinking and who awakens faint and thirsty is applied to the nations and constitutes an explanation of the dream mentioned in v. 7 (Werlitz, 316). God is portrayed as the only reality, and the threats of the nations are unreal—being faint or weary expresses the ephemeral quality of the threat of the nations (Watts, 1985, 382-83). Some exegetes also interpret this pericope as a deliverance upon Zion that is equivalent to a divine eschatological event (*TDOT* 6:154).

Isa 32:1-8 breaks the preceding pattern of woe oracles with the introduction of righteous royal figures (Seitz, 228-29). In v. 2 *ʿᵃyēpâ* refers to a thirsty land that forms part of four vivid similes depicting the royal figures and the good leaders as sources for protection and support, the last simile being "the shadow of a great rock in a thirsty land" (Oswalt, 580).

The disputation in Isa 40:12-31 comes to a climax in vv. 27-31, when complaints and doubts are confronted by the proclamation of God's sovereignty and grace (Hanson, 26-27). Any interpretation of this pericope must keep in mind that it functions as a theological introduction for the rest of the book of Isaiah (Van Oorschot, 28).

Four references to being tired or weary are found in vv. 28-31; they are preceded by Jacob's (Israel's) complaint about the inscrutable way in which God had acted (Westermann, 1969, 58-59). This complaint is answered in v. 28 by appealing to different aspects of Israel's faith: God is everlasting, the Creator who "will not grow tired or weary" (Whybray, 1990, 58-59). The Tg. tr. is "not by work and not by tiring" and the LXX "not by labor nor by exhaustion." All in all the expression points to the effortless way in which creation was performed by God (Beuken, 54). In v. 29 the description of the Creator continues with the reminder that "he gives strength to the weary," which is interpreted by the Tg. as "he gives to the righteous who are weary of his word, wisdom" (Watts, 1987, 88). The frailty of human strength at its best (youths and young men) is juxtaposed with the strength God provides to those who hope in the Lord (vv. 30-31; Whybray, 1990, 59). In the early church this introduction to the second half of the book of Isaiah was chosen as an Advent lesson. Part of the essence of biblical faith is expressed in this answer to the doubting Israel by describing God as the everlasting Creator, who does not faint or grow weary and who gives power and strength like that of the eagles to the faint and the weary (Hanson, 31-32).

Isa 44:9-20 is a masterpiece of taunting satire against idols, idolmakers and their worshipers (Watts, 1987, 143). Two types of idols are discussed: the metal idol in 44:12 and a wooden one in vv. 13-20. The means of manufacturing the metal idol emphasizes that an object made by human hands is subject to human weakness—lack of food results in loss of strength, and thirst causes the blacksmith to become faint (Whybray, 1990, 100). The description of the weakness in v. 12 is contrasted with God as Creator in 40:27-31: the blacksmith may grow faint but God never tires (Beuken, 212).

Isa 46:1-4 uses a number of key words to draw a devastating contrast between the Babylonian gods and the Lord of Israel (Whybray, 1990, 113). The idols have to be carried and supported, while God carries and supports his people (Watts, 1987, 167). Weariness is part of the effect that the idols have on those (the beasts of burden) who have to carry them (46:1; Franke, 34). Isa 50:4-9 is the third Servant Song and begins by referring to the prophetic call and mission. As a true prophet, God provides him the ability to speak. The word given by God sustains the weary (Whybray, 1990, 151). The Servant is awakened to hear the word that has to be passed on to the weary Israel, who, because of weariness is not in a position to hear the word of the Lord (Westermann, 1969, 228-29).

Jer 2:20-28 makes use of a series of metaphors to express Judah's continued idolatry and stubborn refusal to return to God (Huey, 66). Judah is compared to a wild donkey in heat (2:24; Bailey & Holladay, 1968, 256-60). Israel's availability for other gods is likened to the accessibility of the wild donkey to other animals of the species that "need not tire themselves" to find her (Carroll, 133). The warning of judgment in 4:27-31 contains a rhetorical address to Jerusalem in the image of a woman in labor in v. 31 (Jones, 118). The perfect fem. of *'yp* is not otherwise attested and expresses the ebbing away of Jerusalem's life before her murderers or enemies. Stark irony is portrayed in the dying woman in labor: She who brings forth life is dying (Holladay, 146, 171-72). Jer 31:23-26 expands the theme of restoration beyond the Exile by using reversal motifs, such as the rebuilding of the temple or the unexpected solidarity of farmers and shepherds (Carroll, 605-6). The reference to the weary and the faint in the poetic v. 25, forms part of a parallelism, structured as a chiasmus (Jones, 397). Therefore, the weary and the faint in exile can look forward to being refreshed and satisfied by the Lord Almighty, the God of Israel, who will bring them back from captivity (31:23).

Another warning of Babylon's coming destruction is found in Jer 51:49-58. In v. 58 a climax is reached when the destruction of Babylon's famous walls is announced and it is indicated that the defenders will exhaust themselves for nothing (Huey, 429-30; Reimer, 98-99). The last part of the sentence can be tr. "and the nations weary themselves only for fire." This also indicates the futility of the mighty Babylon to resist the punishment of God (Carroll, 853). Note must be taken that similar references to "and they weary themselves" can be found in 51:64 and Hab 2:13; this might point to the quoting of an existing popular saying (Holladay, 431). Seraiah's symbolic act against Babylon to throw a scroll with an oracle of doom in the Euphrates is described in Jer 51:59-64 (Huey, 430). As the scroll will sink into the river, so will Babylon sink and her people fall (lit., "they will weary themselves").

Hab 2:11-13 contains the third in a series of woe oracles found in 2:5-20, which describe the fate of the enemy (Haak, 16, 66-67). In v. 13 the parallel use of *yg'* and *y'p* denote the effort and the wearisome effects of hard work, and this might reflect some wisdom influence as indicated by Prov 23:4 (Patterson, 197). Roberts (122-23) considers it to be an indictment of Babylon, whose oppression of the other nations prevents them from enjoying the fruits of their own labors.

4. *Lyrical literature*. Ps 63 is one of the prayer songs that starts with a lamentation that expresses the longing for the presence and the help of God (vv. 1-2[2-3]; Kraus, 18)). The "dry and weary land" in 63:1[2] forms part of a metaphor where thirst expresses the poet's longing for God just as an exhausted wanderer has for water in a waterless desert (63:1[2]; Anderson, 1992, 455). In the early church Ps 63 introduced the singing during the Sunday service because of the focus on the thirst of the soul for God and the eventual quenching of that thirst through God's presence in the sanctuary (Mays, 217). Ps 143 is another prayer song or complaint of an individual who is persecuted by enemies (Kraus, 535). The extended hands in v. 6 express the psalmist's dependence on God (cf. 28:2; 44:20). There is no vb. in v. 6b, "my soul thirsts for you like a parched land," while 11QPsa 25 has "in a dry land my soul (looks) for you" (Anderson, 1992b, 928). The use of *'yp* in the expression "a parched land" must be understood within the context of hopeful penitence: The thirst of the soul is like a parched land that turns to God for salvation (Mays, 434).

5. *Wisdom literature*. The third speech of Eliphaz lists a number of Job's offenses (Job 22:6-11; Course, 130). These offenses are related to Job's former wealth and imply greed and miserliness. The offenses of denying water to the weary (or the thirsty) and food to the hungry are mentioned in v. 7 (Alden, 231). The seriousness of the accusation is suggested by the syntactically strained position of the *lō'*, not, at the beginning of the sentence (Witte, 36). Amalek's crime of not caring for the thirsty in Deut 25:18 can also be kept in mind and possibly presupposes an ANE wisdom definition of what a righteous person must do. Job later denies any guilt in this regard (Job 29:12-16; 31:13, 16-17, 21).

Prov 25:23-28 consists of metaphorical proverbs of which vv. 25-26 both have water in common (Whybray, 1994, 368). The tr. of *nepeš* as "soul" might be reconsidered because "throat" makes more sense in conjunction with the preceding "cold water." "Thirsty or tired throat" is attested by the LXX, Pesh. and Vg. Thirst makes the throat tired and becomes the focal point where fatigue is most acutely experienced (McKane, 590).

6. *Apocalyptic literature.* The expression *mu'āp bî'āp* in Dan 9:21 can be tr. wearied with weariness; it would then depict a difficult-to-understand, tired angel Gabriel. Some of the ancient versions connected it with the vb. *'wp*, fly, and assumed the part. construction to be an imitation of the underlying Aram. (Hartman & Di Lella, 243). Collins (351-52) cautions that we should not be too hasty in deciding what is appropriate to an angel, but the notion of an angel in flight would perhaps make more sense.

P-B 1. *Qumran.* 1QH 8:36 uses *'yp* in the form of an orthographic variant *''p*, tired (*TDOT* 6:152).

2. *Rabbinical literature.* The *Pesik. Zakhor* 28a uses "faint from thirst" and the *Exodus Rabbah* 19, "They were fainting from the smell" (of the Passover sacrifice) (Jastrow 2:1073). The *Talmud Sanhedrin* 94b uses *'āyēp* as a synonym for industrious, hardworking. On numerous occasions *'yp* II or *'wp* can be tr. to bend, to double (*Targ. Ex.* 26:9; 28:16; 39:9). In *Tanh. Vayera* 22 the pi. is used, "Satan came to annoy/tire (*y'p*) us" (Jastrow 1:585).

NT *astheneō/astheneia/asthenēs* signify weakness and lack of power in connection with the physical existence of humankind (Mark 14:38), weakness (Heb 7:28), sickness (Matt 8:17, etc.), the inability to understand (Rom 6:19), and ethical weakness (5:6) (*EDNT* 1:170-71). *dipsaō* is used for thirst as a bodily need (1 Cor 4:11-13) and for thirsting for eternal life (John 6:35; 7:37) (*EDNT* 1:337-38). *peinaō* is also used for hunger in a literal sense (Matt 4:2, etc.) and in a citation of Prov 25:21 in Rom 12:20 (*TDNT* 6:12-22). *kopos* is used for work or the trouble accompanying labor (Matt 26:10, etc.). It can also be used for making trouble or causing hardship (Mark 14:6; Gal 6:17) (*TDNT* 3:827-30).

Feeble, despair, faint, frail, tender: → *'ml* I (be weak, be feeble, languish, # 581); → *ḥlh* I (become weak, tired, ill, # 2703); → *ylh* (languish, # 3532); → *k'h* (be disheartened, frightened, # 3874); → *nbl* I (wither, fade, languish, dishonor, # 5570); → *'ṭp* II (grow weak, faint, be feeble, # 6494); → *'lp* (cover, faint, # 6634); → *'šš* (become weak, # 6949); → *pwg* (be feeble, numb, be prostrated, # 7028); → *rzh* (destroy, waste away, # 8135); → *rkk* (be tender, timid, gentle, # 8216); → *rph* (become slack, lose heart, discourage, # 8332)

Tired, exhausted, feeble, weak, weary: → *'ml* I (be weak, be feeble, languish, # 581); → *ḥlh* I (become weak, tired, ill, # 2703); → *ḥlš* I (be enfeebled, be weakened, # 2764); → *ḥallāš*, weakling, # 2766); → *yg'* (be tired, # 3333); → *mss* (lose courage, melt, become weak, # 5022); → *nṣb* II (wretched, exhausted [animal], # 5894); → *pgr* (be too feeble, tired, # 7006); → *'yp* (be weary, # 6545); → *rph* (become slack, lose heart, discourage, # 8332)

Bibliography

EDNT 1:170-71, 337-38; *TDNT* 3:827-30; 6:12-22; *TDOT* 6:148-56; R. L. Alden, *Job*, NBC, 1993; R. Alter, *The Art of Biblical Narrative*, 1981; A. A. Anderson, *The Book of Psalms I*, 1992a; idem, *The Book of Psalms II*, 1992b; K. E. Bailey, "The 'Young Camel' and 'Wild Ass' in Jer 2:23-25," *VT* 18, 1968, 256-60; W. A. M. Beuken, *Jesaja IIA*, 1979; R. G. Boling, *Judges*, AB, 1975; G. Braulik, *Deuteronomium II*, 1992; W. Brueggemann, "Kingship and Chaos," *CBQ*

33, 1971, 317-32; idem, *First and Second Samuel*, 1990; C. M. Carmichael, *The Laws of Deuteronomy*, 1974; R. P. Carroll, *Jeremiah*, OTL, 1986; R. E. Clements, *Isaiah 1-39*, NCBC, 1987; R. J. Clifford, "Genesis 25:19-34," *Int* 45, 1991, 397-401; J. J. Collins, *Daniel*, Hermeneia, 1993; C. Conroy, *Absalom Absalom!* 1978; J. E. Course, *Speech and Response: A Rhetorical Analysis of the Introductions to the Speeches of the Book of Job (chaps 4-24)*, 1994; J. P. Fokkelman, *Narrative Art and Poetry in the Books of Samuel*, 1, 1981; C. Franke, *Isaiah 46, 47, and 48: A New Literary-Critical Reading*, 1994; R. D. Haak, *Habakkuk*, 1992; P. D. Hanson, *Isaiah 40-66*, 1995; L. F. Hartman & A. A. Di Lella, *The Book of Daniel*, 1978; W. L. Holladay, *Jeremiah 1*, Hermeneia, 1986; F. B. Huey, *Jeremiah. Lamentations*, NBC, 1993; D. R. Jones, *Jeremiah*, 1992; H.-J. Kraus, *Psalms 60-150*, 1993; B. Lindars, *Judges 1-5*, 1995; J. L. Mays, *Psalms*, 1994; P. K. McCarter, *II Samuel*, AB, 1984; W. McKane, *Proverbs*, OTL, 1970; E. H. Merrill, *Deuteronomy*, NBC, 1994; P. D. Miller, *Deuteronomy*, 1990; J. N. Oswalt, *The Book of Isaiah*, NICOT, 1986; R. D. Patterson, *Nahum, Habakkuk, Zephaniah*, 1991; D. J. Reimer, *The Oracles Against Babylon in Jeremiah 50-51*, 1993; J. J. M. Roberts, *Nahum, Habakkuk and Zephaniah*, OTL, 1991; G. Robinson, *1 and 2 Samuel*, 1993; M. Rose, *5. Mose. Teilband 1*, 1994; R. L. Routledge, "The Siege and Deliverance of the City of David in Isaiah 29:1-8," *TynBul* 43, 1992, 181-90; N. M. Sarna, *Genesis*, 1989; C. R. Seitz, *Isaiah 1-39*, 1993; J. A. Soggin, *Judges*, OTL, 1981; V. Tanghe, "Dichtung und Ekel in Jesaja xxviii 7-13," *VT* 43, 1993, 235-60; J. A. Thompson, *Deuteronomy*, TOTC, 1974; J. Van Oorschot, *Von Babel zum Zion*, 1993; A. H. Van Zyl, *1 Samuel*, 1988; J. D. W. Watts, *Isaiah 1-33*, WBC, 1985; idem, *Isaiah 34-66*, WBC, 1987; J. Werlitz, *Studien zur literarkritischen Methode: Gericht und Heil in Jesaja 7, 1-17 und 29, 1-8*, 1992; C. Westermann, *Isaiah 40-66*, 1969; idem, *Genesis 12-36*, 1985; R. N. Whybray, *Isaiah 40-66*, Hermeneia, 1990; idem, *Proverbs*, 1994; M. Witte, *Philologische Notizen zu Hiob 21-27*, 1995.

Hendrik L. Bosman

6546 (*'āyēp*, exhausted, faint), → # 6545

6547 (*'êpâ*, darkness), → # 6415

6551	עִיר

עִיר (*'îr* I), nom. city, town (# 6551).

ANE This nom. is not derived from any known root vb., but the nom. is attested in Phoen. *'r*, Ugar. *'r*, and Sabean *'r*, city, and in OSA *'r*, hill, castle. At times the parallel *'r/byt* city/house occurs in Babylonian and Sumerian literature as well as in the OT. Fleming suggested that such pairs should be understood as city/temple pairs.

In the ANE the *'îr* was usually fortified and had its own ruler, who may have been called a king; for example, Melchizedek was called king of Salem [Jerusalem] (Gen 14:18), and Sodom had a king (Gen 14:21). These cities often had surrounding villages that were dependent on them for protection and commerce, and for their temples and shrines. In comparison to modern cities, most of the cities of the ANE were relatively small; thus, Euan Fry suggested that word "town" be used to tr. *'îr* rather than "city," except for the most prominent cities, such as Babylon and Nineveh (434-38).

OT 1. The nom. is used about 1092x in the OT and is the principal word for a city or town, but it can also refer to a village or hamlet as well as a capital city. Thus, the word is used of a wide range of settlements without regard to relative size. Fry suggested that the importance of the *'îr* was not its size but its being protected by a wall and a strong gate. Thus, it is interesting that Cain built a city (*'îr*) early in the history of humankind (Gen 4:17).

2. The word may refer to a fortified city (*'îr māṣôr*) (Ps 31:21[22]; Jer 5:17) as contrasted with unwalled villages: "And the number of the gold rats was according to the number of the Philistine towns (*'îr*) belonging to the five rulers—the fortified towns (*'îr mibṣār*) with their country villages (*kōper*)" (1 Sam 6:18). It may refer to a walled city: "If a man sells a house in a walled city (*'îr ḥômâ*), he retains the right of redemption a full year after its sale" (Lev 25:29). It may refer to a town dependent on another city: "The territory from Aroer on the rim of the Arnon Gorge, and from the town (*'îr*) in the middle of the gorge, and the whole plateau past Medeba to Heshbon and all its towns (*'îr*) on the plateau, including Dibon, Bamoth Baal, Beth Baal Meon" (Josh 13:16-17). Sometimes these dependent villages were referred to as "daughters" (*bat*) of the mother city: "Ekron with its surrounding settlements (*bat*) and villages (*ḥāṣēr*)" (15:45). It may refer to a royal city as opposed to rural towns: "Then David said to Achish, 'If I have found favor in your eyes, let a place be assigned to me in one of the country towns (*'îr haśśādeh*), that I may live there. Why should your servant live in the royal city (*'îr hammamlākâ*) with you?'" (1 Sam 27:5, where the same word is used with different modifiers). It may refer to storage cities: "[Solomon] built up Lower Beth Horon, Baalath, and Tadmor in the desert, within his land, as well as all his store cities (*'îr hammiskᵉnôt*) and the towns (*'îr*) for his chariots and for his horses" (1 Kgs 9:17-19). It may refer to cities of refuge (*'îr miqlāṭ*, → # 5236), cities officially designated for the protection of a person who had committed manslaughter not worthy of the death penalty (Num 35:11). It may refer to a city where a wayfarer may settle (Ps 107:4, 7, 36).

The rulers of a city were responsible for civil law in its surrounding territory. When a crime was committed, the city nearest the crime scene had jurisdiction over the matter (Deut 21:1-9). The people in the outlying villages and settlements would enter the city for protection in time of war (Jer 35:1-11).

3. Theologically, Jerusalem became the principal city, known as the city of David, the covenant king, and as the site of the temple, the central sanctuary. It was known as the habitation of the Lord. In the eschatological kingdom, Jerusalem will be the center of world government and worship (Isa 2:1-5) and the habitation of the Lord, with all its associated benefits (4:2-6). The nom. *'îr* is used with various modifiers to refer to Jerusalem. Thus, Jerusalem is the city of God: "There is a river whose streams make glad the city of God, the holy place where the Most High dwells" (Ps 46:4[5]; see also 48:8[9]; 87:3). It is the city of the Lord: "Every morning I will put to silence all the wicked in the land, I will cut off every evildoer from the city of the LORD" (101:8); "The sons of your oppressors will come bowing before you; all who despise you will bow down at your feet and will call you The City of the LORD, Zion of the Holy One of Israel" (Isa 60:14). It is the city of righteousness: "I will restore your judges as in days of old, your counselors as at the beginning. Afterward you will be called The City of Righteousness (*'îr haṣṣedeq*), the Faithful City (*qiryâ neʾᵉmānâ*)" (1:26). It is called the city of truth: "This is what the LORD says: 'I will return to Zion and dwell in Jerusalem. Then Jerusalem will be called the City of Truth (*'îr hāʾemet*), and the mountain of the LORD Almighty will be called the Holy Mountain'" (Zech 8:3). It is called the

holy city [lit., the city of holiness]: "Awake, awake, O Zion, clothe yourself with strength. Put on your garments of splendor, O Jerusalem, the holy city (*'îr haqqōdeš*)" (Isa 52:1; see also 48:2). Sometimes a derogatory modifier is used when the city is to be condemned. Thus, Jerusalem is called the city of oppressors: "Woe to the city of oppressors (*'îr hayyônâ*), rebellious and defiled!" (Zeph 3:1). And it is called the city of bloodshed: "For this is what the Sovereign LORD says: 'Woe to the city of bloodshed (*'îr haddāmîm*), to the pot now encrusted, whose deposit will not go away!'" (Ezek 24:6; see also 22:2; 24:9).

4. Likewise, *'îr* is used with various modifiers to refer to other important cities: (a) Damascus, the city of renown: "Why has the city of renown (*'îr tᵉhillâ*) not been abandoned, the town (*qiryâ*) in which I delight?" (Jer 49:25); (b) Tyre, the city of renown (*'îr hahullālâ*) (Ezek 26:17); (c) Nineveh, the city of blood (Nah 3:1); (d) [Babylon], the city of merchant traders (Ezek 17:4); and (e) sacred cities of Israel: "Your sacred cities have become a desert: even Zion is a desert, Jerusalem a desolation" (Isa 64:10[9]).

5. At times *'îr* is used of a fortress or other construction within the walls of another city: (a) of the City of David: "David then took up residence in the fortress and called it the City of David" (2 Sam 5:9; see also 5:7; 6:10); (b) of a pagan temple complex: "As soon as Jehu had finished making the burnt offering, he ordered the guards and officers: 'Go in and kill them; let no one escape.' So they cut them down with the sword. The guards and officers threw the bodies out and then entered the inner shrine (*'îr*) of the temple of Baal" (2 Kgs 10:25); Fisher proposed that the expression here be tr. "temple quarter," based on parallels he found in the Nuzi texts (so also in 1 Kgs 20:30; 2 Kgs 20:4 K; cf. Ps 73:20); (c) of a water supply [lit., a city of water]: "Joab then sent messengers to David, saying, 'I have fought against Rabbah and taken its water supply (*'îr*)'" (2 Sam 12:27); and (d) of a fortified place of any size: "The Israelites secretly did things against the LORD their God that were not right. From watchtower to fortified city (*'îr*) they built themselves high places in all their towns (*'îr*)" (2 Kgs 17:9; see also 18:8).

6. Occasionally the word is used figuratively of the inhabitants of a city: "When the man entered the town and told what had happened, the whole town (*'îr*) sent up a cry" (1 Sam 4:13; see also 5:12; Isa 22:2).

P-B This nom. was used often in the QL and in postbiblical literature with essentially the same meaning. In Modern Heb. the fem. form, *'ayārâ*, means a small town, and the term, *'îr habbîrâ*, means capital city.

City, village, country: → *ḥûṣ* (outside, street, # 2575); → *ḥāṣēr* (enclosure, court, settlement, village, # 2958); → *kāpār* (village, # 4107); → *māqôm* (place, town, site, dwelling place, holy place, # 5226); → *miqlāṭ* (city of refuge, asylum, # 5236); → *'îr* I (city, town, # 6551); → *pᵉrāzôn* (fertile field, # 7251); → *qiryâ* (town, city, # 7953); → *rᵉḥōb* I (broad open place, plaza, # 8148); → *šûq* (street [in a town], # 8798)

BIBLIOGRAPHY

NIDNTT 2:801-5; *TDNT* 6:522-29; *THAT* 2:268-71; *TWOT* 2:664-65; C. L. Feinberg, "The Cities of Refuge," *BSac* 103, 1946, 411-17, 104, 1947, 35-48; E. Fry, "Cities, Towns and Villages in the Old Testament," *BT*, 30, 1979, 434-38; Daniel E. Fleming, "House/'City': An Unrecognized

Parallel Word Pair," *JBL* 105, 1986, 689-93; L. R. Fisher, "The Temple Quarter," *JSS* 8, 1963, 34-41;

James D. Price

6555 עַיִר	עַיִר (*'ayir*), stallion of an ass (# 6555).

OT The *'ayir* (Lat. *pulus*), with cognates in Akk., Ugar., Amor., and Arab., is defined by BDB as "male ass (young and vigorous)," and it occurs 8x in the OT, often with related terms such as *'ātôn* (Gen 49:11, in Jacob's patriarchal blessing); *ḥ*[a]*môr* (Zech 9:9, the royal entry of the Messianic king, where *ḥ*[a]*môr* is parallel to *'ayir ben-'*[a]*tōnôt*); *pere'* (Job 11:12, where the *'ayir* is the offspring of the *pere'* [or, *pere' 'ādām*; see # 7230]). One of its more interesting usages occurs in Judg 10:4, where there is a play on words between thirty donkeys (*'*[a]*yārîm*) and thirty cities (*'ārîm*, reading *poleis* with OG).

Donkey: → *'ātôn* (she-ass, # 912); → *ḥ*[a]*môr* I (male ass, donkey, # 2789); → *'ayir* (stallion of an ass, # 6555); → *'ārôd* (wild ass, # 6871); → *pere'* (zebra [wild ass], # 7230); → *pered* (mule, # 7234)

Michael S. Moore/Michael L. Brown

6567 (*'êrôm*, naked), → # 6873

6568 (*'ayiš*, lioness, bear?), → # 787

6571 (*'akkābîš*, spider), → # 6856

6572 עַכְבָּר	עַכְבָּר (*'akbār*), mouse (# 6572).

ANE This word is well attested in various Sem. languages: Akk. *akbaru*; Phoen. *'kbr* (personal nom.); Sam. *'gbrh;* Arab. *'akābir* (pl.).

OT 1. The term appears 6x (4x in 1 Sam 6). It is an unclean animal (Lev 11:29). Some suggest that *'akbār* is a collective nom., subordinating various kinds of mice. When the Philistines returned the ark of God to the Israelites, they sent with it five gold tumors and five gold mice (1 Sam 6:4, 5, NIV rats). The relationship between the plague and the mice is not clear, but the golden mice are specified together with five golden tumors, partly because of the pestiferous mice, and partly with the purpose of giving honor to the God of Israel. In this sense, this prescription may be a sympathetic magic for purgation in Philistia. However, this whole incident should be seen in the light of the theological message that the God of Israel is a universal God, having the command of the foreign priests and diviners (cf. vv. 2-4).

2. Isaiah condemns the cultic practices, espccially those that included the ritualistic eating of pig and rat meat (66:17; *'akbār*).

P-B LXX renders the term *mys*. It is attested in DSS (11QTemple 50:20). Mouse occurs frequently in RL as a polluting animal (e.g., BTalm Pesaḥim 10b) and as the symbol of stealing and loss of memory (BTalm Horayot 13a; Pesaḥim 9b). A certain midrash stresses the evil of Noah's generation by comparing it with mice that do not intermingle with other species (Tanḥuma Buber, Noah 11).

Animals: → *b^ehēmâ* (quadrupeds, # 989); → *zānāb* (tail, # 2387); → *ḥ^azîr* (pig, # 2614); → *ḥayyâ* I (animal, # 2651); → *keleb* (dog, # 3978); → *'akbār* (mouse, # 6572); → *ṣ^epardēa'* (frog, # 7630); → *qippod* (hedgehog/owl?, # 7887); → *rmś* (creep, swarm, # 8253); → *šrṣ* (swarm, teem, # 9237); → *tan* (jackal, # 9478); → **Reptiles: Theology**; see the Index for Birds; Camel; Deer; Donkey; Dove; Flock; Gazelle; Insects; Lion; Maggot; Snake, etc.

Bibliography
EMiqr 6:223-24; R. Gordon, *I & II Samuel*, 1986.

N. Kiuchi

6575 (*'ākān*, Achan), → Achan

6576	עכס

עכס (*'ks*), pi. jingle (with anklets) (# 6576); nom. עֶכֶס (*'ekes*), anklet (of woman) (# 6577).

ANE Arab. *'ikās*, foot-chain/fetter of camel (cf. *HALAT* 779).

OT The terms are found in Prov 7:22 and Isa 3:18.

P-B In QL we find the use of *'ks*, skip (11QPs[a], cf. *HALAT* 779).
For a discussion on jewelry, see *'dh* (put on ornaments, # 6335).

Malcolm J. A. Horsnell

6577 (*'ekes*, anklet), → # 6576

6579	עכר

עכר (*'kr*), q. to bring ruin, agitation, calamity, trouble, destruction; ni. to become distressed (# 6579).

OT This root is used to describe an emotional, psychological, and spiritual state of persons, communities (Israel), and nations, as well as the accompanying external conditions (Judg 11:35; Job 6:4).

Ruin, destruction: → *dmh* III (ruin, # 1950); → *hāwwâ* II (ruin, # 2095); → *h^arîsâ* (ruins, # 2232); → *ḥrb* I (be dry or desolate, ruined, # 2990); → *kšl* (stumble, totter, be brought to ruin, # 4173); → *m^eḥittâ* (terror, ruins, destruction, # 4745); → *nkh* (be hit, be battered, ruined, destroyed, # 5782); → *nṣh* II (fall in ruins, # 5898); → *swr* (corrupt, # 6074); → *pîd* (ruin, misfortune, # 7085); → *šeber* (breach, ruin, # 8691); → *šḥt* (become corrupt, ruin, spoil, # 8845)

Eugene Carpenter

6582 (*'akšûb*, viper), → # 5729

6584 (*'al* II, on), → Particles

6585	עֹל

עֹל (*'ōl*), yoke (# 6585).

ANE Amarna Canaanite *ḫullu*, yoke; Arab. *ġullu*, collar, manacle. It is often stated that the word occurs in Ugar., but this does not appear to be the case.

OT 1. In only three instances does *'ōl* refer to a device that bound a domesticated beast to an implement or a cart (Num 19:2; Deut 21:3; 1 Sam 6:7); in its remaining 37 occurrences it is used figuratively.

2. *'ōl* refers to the servitude of one individual to another or to a people under a monarch: Esau was to serve Jacob until he tore off Jacob's yoke (Gen 27:40); the Israelites demanded that Rehoboam lighten the heavy yoke Solomon had placed on them (1 Kgs 12:4 [2x], 9, 10, 11, 14; see par. 2 Chron 10).

3. In five instances *'ōl* refers to the political bondage from which the Lord delivered his people: in Lev 26:13 the shattering of Israel's yoke is used with reference to the divine deliverance from the oppression of the Egyptians; in Isaiah and Jeremiah the destruction or removal of the yoke refers to the Lord's imminent deliverance of his people from the oppression of the Assyrians (Isa 9:4[3]; 10:27; 14:25) and the Babylonians (Jer 30:8). Following most commentators, *'ōl* of Hos 11:4 should be repointed to *'ûl*, infant (while rendering *l^eḥî* as "cheek" rather than "jaw"), as yokes were not attached to the jaw but to the shoulder (Isa 9:4[3]; 10:27). Moreover, this emendation is consonant with the infant imagery of 11:1-3.

4. *'ōl* is particularly significant in Jeremiah, where salvation for the nations (including Judah) consisted in total surrender and servitude to Nebuchadnezzar. They were to bring their necks under Nebuchadnezzar's yoke (Jer 27:11-12), for it was the Lord who had put this yoke on them (28:14). Any nation that did not put its neck under the yoke of Nebuchadnezzar would be punished by the Lord with sword, famine, and plague (27:8), but the Lord was going to deliver his people from the Babylonians by breaking the yoke from their necks (30:8; cf. Ezek 34:27). (→ Jeremiah: Theology)

5. *'ōl* is also used in Jeremiah with reference to the binding nature of the Torah, which Judah failed to keep and so became idolatrous: "You broke off your yoke and tore off your bonds" (Jer 2:20 [the subject of the verbs in MT is 1st person sing., but the context and the LXX's 2nd person sing. subjects make a reading with the pl. preferable]). So also the rich, who did not did not know the Torah of their God, are described as having "broken off the yoke and torn off the bonds" (Jer 5:5; cf. Nah 1:13, which uses a par. construction with *mōṭ*).

6. In Lamentations *'ōl* refers to the burden that a young man was to bear while he anticipated the salvation of the Lord (Lam 3:27). It may also refer to the domination of sin (1:14), but it is more likely that *'ōl* should be repointed to *'al*, over, reading, "watch has been kept over my sins," following LXX; in further support of this reading is the fact that *šqd*, watch, wake (→ # 9166), is often followed by *'al*.

P-B 1. In RL *'ōl* often pertains to the idea of submission to the will of God: one reads of *'ōl malkût šāmayîm*, the yoke of the kingdom of heaven; *'ōl miṣwôt*, the yoke of the commandments; and *'ōl šel haqqādôš*, the yoke of the holy one. In contrast, there are the demands of government and society: one reads of *'ōl malkût*, the yoke of government; *'ōl derek 'ereṣ*, the yoke of earthly conduct; and *'ōl bāśār w^edām*, the human yoke (*TDNT* 2:900).

2. In the Didache *zygos*, yoke, was used with reference to sexual asceticism (Didache 6:2); and in Barnabas 2:6 it designates the new law of Jesus, where it is more of a gift than an obligation (*TDNT* 2:901).

NT The term *zygos*, yoke, which is the primary translation of *'ol* in the LXX, refers to a balance in Rev 6:5; elsewhere it is used figuratively: for the easy yoke of Jesus (Matt 11:29-30; cf. the use of *'ōl* in RL above), for the burden of the law (Acts 15:10), for the yoke of slavery under the law (Gal 5:1), and for the institution of slavery (1 Tim 6:1).

Yoke: → *môṭâ* (yoke, carrying pole, # 4574); → *'ōl* (yoke, # 6585); → *ṣmd* (be attached, attach oneself, # 7537)

BIBLIOGRAPHY

TDNT 2:896-901; *TWAT* 6:79-83; C. L. Tyer, "The Yoke in Ancient Near Eastern, Hebrew and New Testament Materials," Unpublished Dissertation: Vanderbilt, 1963.

John E. Harvey

6589	עִלֵּג

עִלֵּג (*'illēg*), adj. stammering, stuttering (hapleg.; # 6589).

ANE The root is attested in Ugar. *'lg*, stammering (cf. *UT* Glossary, # 1854a), which renders unlikely the *HALAT* contention that the word results from metathesis in the root *l'g*.

OT The only occurrence of this root is in Isa 32:4. The focus in the literary context is on the reign of the righteous king and its concomitant blessings. When the reign of the righteous king comes, eyes will truly see, ears will genuinely listen, and speech that is stammering or inarticulate will be transformed. "The mind of the rash will know and understand, and the stammering (*'illegîm*) tongue will be fluent and clear" (Isa 32:4). The form of the word fits the pattern of a number of adj. that "denote a bodily or mental fault or defect" (*GKC*, 233). The healing of this defect will be one of the signs of the new kingdom of righteousness.

P-B The root shows no significant use.

Handicaps, disfigurement, blind, lame, stammer, speechless: → *'illēm* (speechlessness, # 522); → *gibbēn* (hunchbacked, # 1492); → *ḥārûṣ* IV (mutilation [animal], # 3024); → *ḥērēš* (speechless, # 3094); → *kšḥ* (be lame, crippled, # 4171); → *mûm* (blemish, # 4583); → *mišḥāt* (disfigured, # 5425); → *nākeh* (crippled, smitten, # 5783); → *'wr* I (be blind, # 6422); → *'illēg* (stammering, stuttering, # 6589); → *psḥ* (be lame, crippled, # 7174); → *ṣl'* I (limping condition, # 7519); → *qlṭ* I (defective [animal], # 7832); → *śr'* (deformed, mutilated, # 8594); → *t^eballul* (white spot in eye, # 9319)

Tim Powell

6590	עלה

עלה (*'lh*), q. go up, ascend; ni. be taken up, be exalted, be taken away, be led up; hi. bring, lead up, bring upon, make high, bring up; ho. be offered; hitp. lift oneself up (# 6590); מַעֲלֶה (*ma'^aleh*), stairs, ascent, rise, stand, platform, story, pass (# 5090); מַעֲלָה (*ma'^alâ*), ascent, return home, step, stairs, processions (# 5092); עָלֶה (*'āleh*), nom. leafage (→ # 6591); עֹלָה (*'ōlâ*), nom. whole burnt offering (→ # 6592); עֱלִי (*'^elî*), nom. pestle (# 6605); עִלִּי (*'illî*), upper (# 6606); עֲלִיָּה (*'^aliyyâ*), nom. upper room (→ # 6608); עֶלְיוֹן (*'elyôn* II), Most High (→ # 6610); תְּעָלָה (*t^e'ālâ* II), nom. trench (→ # 9498).

ANE This word group is well attested in the cognate languages, such as Aram. *'lh*, Akk. *elû*, and Ugar. *'ly*.

OT 1. The nom. *ma'aleh* is a *maqṭal* formation from the vb. *'lh*, rise, go up. Closely related semantically are the q. part. *'ōleh*, going up, ascending, and byform the nom. *ma'ᵃlâ*, step, stair (BDB, 752). The vb. *'lh* occurs nearly 900x, usually to be construed in a nontheological or noncultic manner.

2. The nom. *ma'aleh* appears only 19x in the OT, only twice in possible reference to a religious activity (1 Sam 9:11; 2 Chron 32:33). Even here the only meaning is a literal one, referring to a slope up to a city and to royal sepulchers respectively. In its fem. form *ma'ᵃlâ,* usually rendered "step, stair," occurs in the titles of Psalms 120-34 to describe their nature as "songs of ascent," i.e., psalms that constituted part of the ritual of the pilgrimage procession of those who came to Jerusalem to celebrate the thrice annual convocations (see Lev 23). Even here the meaning is essentially literal, for travelers did indeed ascend when they made their way to the Holy City. It is likely that they sang the appropriate hymns at the various fifteen stages or "steps" of the way.

3. "Ascent" as a theological term must find its meaning, then, in connection with its cognate vb. *'lh*, to ascend. Here the usage is further subdivided between the occurrences where *'lh* is strictly spiritual or metaphorical, namely, when used to speak of ascending to God, and where it is still primarily physical but with intensely religious overtones, when referring to the journey to a holy place. One always ascends to such places whether or not in fact they are topographically elevated.

The notion of ascending to God is attested about 9x, especially in the Pentateuch. It is central to the discourse concerning Yahweh's covenant with Israel, where the great distance between the exalted God and his unworthy slave people is emphasized. Thus, Moses ascended to Yahweh at Sinai (Exod 19:3), but the people were forbidden to do so lest they die (19:24). Following the disclosure of the essence of the covenant text—the Book of the Covenant (20:1-23:33)—Moses once more was invited to meet Yahweh (24:1), this time accompanied by a handful of others (24:12). Later when the people sinned in the incident of the golden calf, Moses said he would again ascend unto Yahweh, this time to intercede on their behalf (32:30). In recounting this episode to a later generation Moses uses the vb. *'lh* to speak of his appearance before Yahweh to receive a new copy of the stone tablets (Deut 10:1).

4. In a most significant passage the annual pilgrimages of the people to the central sanctuary are described as "going up ... to appear before the LORD your God" (Exod 34:24). The vb. *'lh* here should be viewed in connection with the nom. *ma'ᵃlâ* which, as already noted, designates the "songs of ascent" sung by the worshipers winding their way to Jerusalem to encounter Yahweh in worship and praise. They speak of ascent not only because Jerusalem was topographically elevated but because Yahweh was there high and lifted up.

5. The only other occurrence of *'lh* with reference to approaching God is in the Judges pericope concerning the near annihilation of the tribe of Benjamin. There the narrator describes the gathering of the assembly of leaders at Mizpah as an ascent to Yahweh himself (Judg 21:5, 8; cf. 20:1). This suggests unmistakably that assemblies in holy places in the name of Yahweh were tantamount to encounters with the transcendent God. The connection between holy place and holy God is transparently clear.

Perhaps in a greater attempt to minimize the immanental aspect of God's reality and presence, his people far more often are said to ascend to holy places (ca. 15x) than they are to appear before him directly. The juxtaposition of the two does occur, however, in Exod 24, the passage cited above with reference to covenant ceremony. Yahweh had commanded Moses to ascend to him (v. 12), so Moses "went up on the mountain of God" (v. 13).

6. The tendency in the development of OT thought is toward the increasing enhancement of Yahweh's absolute otherness, his transcendence. Hannah goes up to the house of Yahweh (1 Sam 1:7), Samuel goes up to the high place (9:13, 14, 19), and Hezekiah (2 Kgs 19:14; 20:5, 8; 2 Chron 29:20; Isa 37:14; 38:22), Josiah (2 Kgs 23:2; 2 Chron 34:30), and the princes of Judah (Jer 26:10) ascend to the temple. This was not limited to only certain leaders, however, for the psalmist declares that anyone who has "clean hands and a pure heart" can ascend to the hill of Yahweh, his holy place (Ps 24:3-4).

Journey, going, marching, walking, wandering: → *'rḥ* (be on the road, wander, # 782); → *'šr* I (walk straight, # 886); → *drk* (tread, march, # 2005); → *hlk* (go, walk, behave, # 2143); → *zḥl* I (slide away, # 2323); → *yṣ'* (go out, come forward, # 3655); → *yrd* (go down, go up, descend, # 3718); → *massa'* (setting out, # 5023); → *nḥt* (march down, descend, settle, # 5737); → *s'n* (tramp along, tread, # 6008); → *'dh* I (stride, # 6334); → *'lh* (go up, ascend, bring up, # 6590); → *pś'* I (step forth, march, # 7314); → *ṣ'd* (step, march, # 7575); → *šwr* I (descend, caravan, # 8801)

BIBLIOGRAPHY

THAT 2:272-90; *TWOT* 2:666-70, 771-72; G. Brin, "The Formulae 'From ... and Onward/Upward,'" *JBL* 99, 1980, 161-71; S. Paul, "Two Cognate Semitic Terms for Mating and Copulation," *VT* 32, 1982, 492-94; B. Renaud, "Osée II 2: *'lh mn h'rṣ*: Essai d'interprétation," *VT* 33, 1983, 495-500; S. Shibayama, "Notes on *Yārad* and *'Ālāh*: Hints on Translating," *JBR* 34, 1966, 358-62; J. Wijngaards, "הוציא and העלה: A Twofold Approach to the Exodus," *VT* 15, 1964, 91-102.

Eugene H. Merrill

6591	עָלֶה

עָלֶה (*'āleh*), nom. leaf, leafage (# 6591); < עלה (*'lh*), go up, ascend, climb (→ # 6590).

ANE Aram. *'lh*, *'alyā'*; Akk. *elû*, sprout.

OT The word occurs 19x in the OT. It is a general word for a wide variety of types of leaves, such as olive, myrtle, palm, and others (Gen 8:11; Neh 8:15). It can refer to the leaves of both small bushes (Job 30:4) and large oaks (Isa 1:30). Adam and Eve sewed together leaves of a fig tree in an effort to conceal their nakedness (Gen 3:7). The word appears twice in Ezekiel's vision to describe leaves that are not susceptible to change and that possess unusual therapeutic value (Ezek 47:12). Often the word is used to describe the fragility of human life, particularly in an eschatological setting (Isa 34:4; 64:6[5]). In Lev 26:36 fearsome captivity is announced for Israel during which "the sound of a windblown leaf will put them to flight." Similar hyperbole occurs in Job 13:25: "Will you torment a windblown leaf?" Several times the vibrant growth of a healthy leaf becomes a simile for vividly picturing the prosperity of those who are godly (Ps 1:3; Prov 11:28; Jer 17:8).

The total number of OT occurrences increases by two if emendations recorded in the apparatus of *BHS* are accepted. In Jer 11:16 for (*'ālêhā,* upon it), some scholars suggest (*b^{e}'ālēhû,* in its leaves), and in Ps 74:5 for *l^{e}mā'lâ,* upper, some suggest *lô 'āleh,* its [entrance] to a leaf.

P-B The word occurs in RL both in the normal botanical sense and in a symbolic sense. Examples of the latter include *Gen. Rab.* 19:6 ("the leaves that brought grief into the world"; cf. 15:7), which is a reference to Gen 3:7, and Ḥullin 92a ("the leaves thereon [i.e., on the vine Israel] are the untutored"). The normal rendering (14x) of *'āleh* in the LXX is *phyllon,* leaf, foliage, plant. Other, less common, renderings are *anabasis,* going up, leaves, in Ezek 47:12, and *stelechos,* crown of the root, trunk, in Jer 17:8. The word occurs in the DSS in 1QH 8:8, 26; 10:25.

Vegetation: → *'ēzôb* (hyssop, # 257); → *dš'* (become green, sprout, # 2012); → *zr'* (sow, scatter seed, form seed, # 2445); → *ḥāṣîr* I (grass, # 2945); → *ḥ^{a}šaš* (dry grass, # 3143); → *yereq* (green, greenness, # 3764); → *nṭ'* (plant, establish, drive, # 5749); → *'āleh* (leaf, leafage, # 6591); → *'ēśeb* (herb, herbage, weed, # 6912); → *qîqāyôn* (plant of uncertain identity, # 7813); → *rō'š* II (bitter and poisonous herb, # 8032); → *śîaḥ* I (bush, shrub, # 8489); → *šiṭṭâ* (acacia, # 8847)

Bibliography

ISBE 3:96; H. A. Brongers, "Das Zeitwort *'ālā* und seine Derivate," in *Travels in the World of the Old Testament* [Fs M. A. Beek], 1974, 30-40.

Richard A. Taylor

6592	עֹלָה

עֹלָה (*'ōlâ* I), nom. burnt offering (# 6592).

ANE 1. There are several apparent attestations of this sacrificial term outside of the biblical stream of tradition. The Proto-Sinaitic Inscriptions attest the expression *ma'hb (b)'lt,* swear to present a burnt offering (*'lt* = Heb. *'ōlâ*; Albright, 41-43), although it has also been translated "beloved of Baalat" (*TWAT* 6:107). Ugar. uses a different word to refer specifically to the burnt offering (see ANE sec. 3), but the corresponding Ugar. vb. *'ly,* to go up, in the shaphel (i.e., causative = Heb. hi.) stem, is used for offering up incense in the Aqhat epic: *wyq[ry] dbḥ. 'lm. yš'ly. dgṯh bšmym,* "And he presented a sacrifice to the gods, he sent up his incense among the heavenly ones" (*CML* 120 lines 184b-86a and 191-92; cf. also the votive inscriptions cited in W. F. Albright, *BASOR* 110, 1948, 16 n. 52; Tarragon, 63-64).

Similarly, in the Ugar. Keret epic, Keret "did go up on to the tower, did mount the shoulder of the wall," *w'ly lzr . mgdl rkb ṯkmm . ḥmt* (CML, 87 lines 165b-67a), in order to offer sacrifices. We have a sort of biblical parallel to this in 2 Kgs 3:27a, "Then he (Mesha, the Moabite king) took his firstborn son, who was to succeed him as king, and offered him as a sacrifice (*wayya^{a}lēhu 'ōlâ*; translate instead, "offered him up as a burnt offering") on the city wall (*'al haḥōmâ*)." On the basis of this evidence and *yš'ly* in the Aqhat epic (see above), some have argued that the Heb. *'ōlâ* offering was originally a tower offering (see the references cited in *TWAT* 6:106; Levine, "Prolegomenon," XLIII). However, as Levine has noted, "The sense of 'ascending' can have three possible referents: a) The ascent of the offering to heaven in smoke, fire, and aroma. b) The ascent of sacrifice onto the altar. c) The ascent of the officiants to a high place, tower, wall, or the like for the purpose of offering it up" (ibid.; cf. also *TWAT* 6:106). The parallel with Ugar. *šrp* (see ANE sec. 3) suggests Levine's first category and, therefore, the meaning burnt offering.

At Marseilles and Carthage the Punic inscriptions refer to the burnt offering with the term *kll* (= Heb. *kālîl*, entire, whole, complete, # 4003): *b'lp kll 'm św't*, "for an ox, whole offering or *ṣw't* offering" (R. S. Tomback, *A Comparative Semitic Lexicon of the Phoenician and Punic Languages*, SBLDS 32, 1978, 143, and additional references there; cf. also the remarks under OT sec. 1). In one case it occurs with *šlm*: *'m šlm kll*, "or the *šlm* of the burnt offering" (ibid.). The apparent genitive relationship here between burnt offering and peace offering suggests that the relationship between the two terms in Pun. was different from the HB. In later times, however, we find *'lt* in a Neo-Punic dedicatory inscription: *'š h'l' [k]' 'lt 'w m[n(?)ḥt bmqds*, "a man who offered here a burnt offering or a grain offering in the sanctuary" (ibid., 244, 247; cf. *KAI* 1:29 text 159, line 8). Here, once again, the vb. root matches the nom. as in the HB (e.g., Gen 8:20; cf. the Ugar. vb. above).

2. The same term continues to be used for the burnt offering in postbiblical literature as a continuation of the stream of biblical tradition. It occurs 3x in an Achemenid letter from the Elephantine (Egyptian) Jewish community, in which the authors request that Bagoas, governor of Judah, authorize the rebuilding of the Yaho (i.e., Yahweh) temple in Elephantine. If the request were granted, the "meal-offering, incense, and burnt offering" (*mnḥh wlbwnh w'lwh*; also written *w'lwt'*, with the article) that had been suspended since the destruction of the temple (Rosenthal, 11, line 21; *ANET,* 492a) would be offered on behalf of Bagoas (Rosenthal, 11, line 25; *ANET,* 492b). In the same text we also find the combination "burnt offering and sacrifices" in a general statement of sacrificial piety, "And you (Bagoas) shall have a merit before Yaho the god of Heaven more than a man who offers to him burnt offering and sacrifices (*'lwh wdbḥn*) worth a thousand talents of silver ..." (Rosenthal, 11, line 28; *ANET,* 492b).

Of course, both the Heb. and the Aram. term are used in later Jewish literature as well (see P-B).

3. The corresponding sacrificial term in Ugar. is *šrp* (= Heb. *śrp*, burn; cf. Anderson, 1987, 34). It can occur alone as an isolated offering (see Tarragon [63] for some examples), but it appears most frequently in the combination *šrp wšlmm*, burnt offering and peace offering (see the compilation in R. E. Whitaker, *A Concordance of the Ugaritic Literature*, 1972, 610). As an example see: *ṣpn.dqt.šrp.wšlmm[ṯn šm.w'a]lp.lb'l.w'aṯrt*, "(for) Saphon a small animal as a burnt-offering; and as a peace-offering, [two sheep(?) and a] head of cattle for Ba'al and Athirat" (Dijkstra, 71, lines 7-8 and comments on line 2; cf. the discussion in Weinfeld, 107-8; Tarragon, 61-64).

In a few Neo-Assyrian texts, Akk. *šarāpu*, to burn (cf. Ugar. *šrp* above) is used to refer to the burning of humans as burnt offerings to the gods: "(he who initiates a claim against the sold land) burns his eldest son before Sin, burns his eldest daughter before Belet-seri" (*CAD* vol. 17, pt. 2, 52; cf. M. Weinfeld, *UF* 4, 1972, 144-49 for a complete discussion). Some have argued that these texts refer not to actual child sacrifice (e.g., ibid.) but, instead, to the dedication of children to the relevant god(s). This is also said to be the case for Molech worship in the OT (see Lev 18:21; Deut 12:31; 18:10; 2 Kgs 23:10). However, this conclusion has not been accepted by all and seems to be open to question in light of 2 Kgs 3:27a, "Then he (Mesha, the Moabite king) took his firstborn son, who was to succeed him as king, and offered him as a sacrifice on the city wall," and other evidence for child sacrifice in Molech worship (see Heider).

The corresponding Hittite term is also used commonly as a pair with Hittite *keldiya*, peace offerings. For example, according to one treaty text, "rites to the god of burnt offering (*ambašši*) and peace offerings (*keldiya*) are performed on account of the old tablets" (Weinfeld, 98-99 and n. 14; cf. ibid., 106-7).

OT 1. The burnt offering animal from the herd or the flock was completely burned on the altar (including its entrails, Lev 1:9, 13), except for the hide, which went to the officiating priest as his prebend (7:8; see the same in the Punic tariffs, Levine, *In the Presence of the Lord*, 120). The same was true for the burnt offering bird (1:14-17), except that in such a case there was no priestly prebend, and the priest was "to remove the crop with its contents and throw it to the east side of the altar, where the ashes are" (1:16). Milgrom translates here, "He shall remove its crissum by its feathers," and argues that it refers to the cutting off of the tail feather section of the bird and removing its intestines (Milgrom, 1991, 134, 169-71). In any case, one could almost render *'ōlâ* as whole offering or whole burnt offering.

In fact, it has been suggested that the original term for the burnt offering was Heb. *kālîl* (entire, whole complete, # 4003; cf. ANE sec. 2 for the Pun. evidence; also *HALOT* 479, for other primary and secondary literature), which would more naturally be translated "whole offering." The term *'ōlâ* may have been introduced when it became the practice to exclude the skin from the offering. Thus, *'ōlâ* would have become the accepted term and should be translated "burnt offering" because it refers to the "ascending of the offering" up to the Lord in smoke by means of its incineration on the altar (Milgrom, *Leviticus 1-16*, 173-74; cf. the vb. *'ālâ*, to go up, ascend, # 6590; Ugar. *šrp*, ANE sec. 3). Alternatively, *HALOT* argues that *kālîl* was "early suppressed by" *'ōlâ*, without suggesting that *'ōlâ* was not one of the original terms for the "(whole) burnt offering" (*HALOT* 479). It is also proposed that *'ōlâ* alone is an abbreviation for *minḥâ* (# 4966) plus *'ōlâ*, "tribute rising (in the fire)" (*HALOT* 830).

It is probably best to treat *'ōlâ* and *kālîl* as complementary terms, the former referring to the manner of offering and the latter to the extent of it. Whether or not *kālîl* was prior to *'ōlâ* is open to question (cf. Milgrom above). In two instances *kālîl* occurs alone, seemingly as a term meaning whole burnt offering (NIV, Deut 13:16[17]; 33:10). In one such case it may continue to carry its normal adverbial meaning, entirely: 13:16[17] could easily be rendered, "and you shall burn the city and all its plunder with fire entirely to the Lord your God." However, in another context the adverbial translation does not seem appropriate: 33:10b seems to use *kālîl* as a term for some kind of specific offering that would be placed on the altar, "He (Levi) offers incense (*q^eṭôrâ*) before you and whole burnt offerings (*kālîl*) on your altar."

There are two occurrences of *kālîl* and *'ōlâ* together. According to 1 Sam 7:9, "Samuel took a suckling lamb and offered it up as a whole burnt offering (*'ōlâ kālîl*) to the LORD." Ps 51:19[21] is particularly interesting: "Then (after one's heart has become contrite [v. 17] and, therefore, the walls of Jerusalem are rebuilt [v. 18]) there will be righteous sacrifices, whole burnt offerings (lit., burnt offering and whole offering, *'ōlâ w^ekālîl*), to delight you; then bulls will be offered on your altar." The latter passage might suggest that *kālîl* and *'ōlâ* refer to two different kinds of offerings, except that we have here poetic parallelism (see Tate, 8 and 29-30). The conjunction w^e could be epexegetical, meaning that the burnt offering is the kind of offering that is offered completely on the altar, in contrast to the sacrifices referred to previously in this verse (cf. *zbḥ*, # 2283).

2. As far as the usage of the burnt offering is concerned, historically it is important to recognize the distinction between burnt offerings presented at solitary altars (i.e., not in the tabernacle or temple) as opposed to sanctuary altars (i.e., in the tabernacle or the temple; see the full discussion of this distinction and its historical critical implications in Offerings and Sacrifices: Theology, secs. 8-11). The term first occurs in Gen 8:20, referring to its use long before the tabernacle system had been established: "Then Noah built an altar to the LORD and, taking some of all the clean animals and clean birds, he sacrificed burnt offerings on it" (cf. *'ōlâ* also in ch. 22 for the intended offering of Isaac, vv. 2, 3, 6, 7, 8, 13). Moreover, such offerings continued at solitary altars and on high places long after the tabernacle (and even the temple) had been built, whether approved (e.g., Judg 6:26; 1 Sam 7:9-10, 17; 2 Sam 24:22-25; 1 Kgs 18:38-39; with peace offerings, Josh 8:31 [cf. Exod 20:24; Deut 27:5-7]; Judg 21:3-4, etc.) or unapproved (e.g., Judg 11:31; 1 Sam 13:8-14; 1 Kgs 18:25-29).

Of course, the sanctuary system of offerings and sacrifices also included the ancient burnt offering (with grain, drink, and peace offerings) that had been part of solitary altar worship of the faithful from Noah down through most of the preexilic monarchical period (see above). The same external worship system to which the Israelite people were already accustomed before Sinai was tailored to fit into the tabernacle system, where, however, the key features of the rituals could be performed only by the Aaronic priests, not the offerers themselves.

3. From a literary point of view, the rules for burnt, grain, and peace (fellowship) offerings in Lev 1-3 form a unified whole. The repetition of the introductory formula and address to "the Israelites" in 4:1-2 (cf. 1:1-2) separates the rules for sin and guilt offerings in 4:1-6:7 from those in chs. 1-3. This is a literary reflection of the historical reality that before and even after the construction of the tabernacle, the burnt offerings and peace offerings, and the grain and drink offerings that normally came with them, constituted a system of offerings used by the faithful at solitary Yahwistic altars outside the tabernacle.

Of course, the sanctuary system of sacrificial worship required additional offerings and sacrifices, especially the sin and guilt offerings (Lev 4:1-6:7). The primary reason for these additions to the system was that the sanctuary was more than an altar through which one could approach and commune with the God of heaven. It was to be a place of God's perpetual residence (i.e., God's house, or tent in the case of the tabernacle; see esp. Exod 25:8, "have them make a sanctuary for me, and I will dwell among them"; 2 Sam 7:2, 5-7, 13 house versus tent). One could have an altar and altar worship without a sanctuary (→ *mizbēaḥ*, altar, # 4640), but this stands quite apart from the essentials of proper maintenance of the presence of the Lord, which was the primary focus of the tabernacle ritual procedures (Knohl, 152; Milgrom, 1991, 176).

The fact that the Lord actually resided in the tabernacle or temple sanctuary required that special attention be paid to maintaining the sanctity and purity of his presence there. This was accomplished by means of sacrificial atonement. For example,

Lev 15:31 concludes the clean and unclean section of Leviticus (Lev 11-15) with this warning: "You must keep the Israelites separate from things that make them unclean, so they will not die in their uncleanness for defiling my dwelling place, which is among them." This leads naturally and immediately to the regulations for the annual Day of Atonement (Lev 16). The summary at the end of Lev 16 clarifies the fact that the goal of this day was to make atonement for the sanctuary (lit., "atone the sanctuary") on behalf of the people (16:29-34; → *kpr* I, # 4105).

4. The burnt offering was not particularly suited to the tasks of sanctifying or purifying the tabernacle (or later the temple). Nevertheless, there are several instances in which it is said that the burnt offering was used as part of an overall ritual process of purging the tabernacle. In the very introduction to the tabernacle burnt offering procedure in Lev 1:4, "He (the offerer) is to lay his hand on the head of the burnt offering, and it will be accepted on his behalf to make atonement for him." According to 14:18-20, the burnt offering and its associated grain offering were included with the sin and guilt offerings in the making of atonement for the leper (cf. also vv. 29-31 for a more unifying statement of the combined atoning efficacy of all the offerings).

The close relationship between the tabernacle inauguration day (Lev 9) and the Day of Atonement (Lev 16) has been discussed elsewhere (→ *kpr* I, # 4105, OT secs. 32-33). Lev 9:7 binds the burnt and sin offerings together as the means of atoning for the priests and the people on the inauguration day. Similarly, on the Day of Atonement burnt offerings for the priests and the people (Lev 16:24) were included in the making of atonement for the year, that is, after the extended series of sin offering rituals for the priests and the people had been performed (vv. 11-22, including the scapegoat as a sin offering according to vv. 5, 8-11). Moreover, this and other evidence suggests that one would not normally offer a sin offering for atonement without including a burnt offering as part of the overall atonement procedure (e.g., when two birds were brought to make atonement, the first was a sin offering and the second a burnt offering, 5:7; cf. 12:6, 8). Ezekiel assigns atonement to the burnt offering in combination with other offerings (Ezek 45:15, 17; note that even the peace offering is included here).

5. The question that arises at this point is the manner and degree to which the burnt offering atones. There are several views. One scholar has argued that it was the laying of the hand on the burnt offering that would turn it into an offering that made atonement (Levine, 1974, 73, n. 51; see Lev 1:4a). Others suggest that the burnt offering was a required element in a series of atonement offerings because it "completed the self-committal required for full atonement" (Rainey, 498). The animal was completely consumed upon the altar to symbolize the offering of complete "self-committal." Another more general view is that, since it is unrelated to any specific sinful act, the attachment of atoning efficacy to the burnt offering expressed "the idea that the very approach to the holy requires atonement and appeasement" (Knohl, 152).

Some would offer a diachronic explanation of the distinction between the atonement of the burnt offering and that of the sin and guilt offerings. In one form the diachronic approach explains the development of the sin and guilt offerings as a postexilic second temple phenomenon. In essence, "... the consciousness of sin, called forth by the rejection of the people from the face of Jehovah, was to a certain extent permanent," so that "there was always a divine command to be fulfilled, and by thinking of it a man kept himself from following after the desires and lusts of his own heart." Thus, the rituals "no longer draw down the Deity into human life on all important occasions, to take part in its joys and its necessities." Instead, "the chief effect of it, which is always produced with certainty, is atonement" (Wellhausen, 424; cf. the skepticism regarding this approach and the literature cited in Knohl, 151).

Another form of the diachronic explanation argues that the burnt offering was the primary atonement offering in the early history of Israel. The sin and guilt offerings arose only in connection with the "advent of the temple/tabernacle," when "it became imperative to devise specific sacrifices to purge the sacred house and its sancta of their contamination and desecration" (Milgrom, 1991, 176). This pushes the development back before the exile, against the general Wellhausen theory. However, it continues to maintain the diachronic explanation from a theoretical and methodological point of view.

6. On one level the diachronic approach is justified. As we have already observed, there are no occurrences of the sin and guilt offerings before the institution of the tabernacle in Exodus, and there are few references to them outside of the priestly literature of the OT (i.e., major sections of Exod-Num, and Ezek 40-48) even subsequent to the inauguration of the tabernacle (see only 1 Sam 6:3, 4, 8, 17; 2 Kgs 12:16[17]; 2 Chron 29:21-24; Ezra 8:35; Neh 10:33[34]; Isa 53:10). In other words, outside of the sanctuary complex itself, the burnt and peace offering worship system provided the substantial ritual context of worship at the solitary altars and on the high places (see above). This suggests two things. (a) There was no need for such offerings before the tabernacle was initiated. (b) Even after the priestly sanctuary system was established in Israel, the focus of the nonpriestly elements of the population remained on matters of worship and celebration before God rather than sanctuary purity. The latter was the main concern of the priesthood, who bore the responsibility of the sanctuary and its proper maintenance (Lev 10; Num 18).

In one sense, therefore, the burnt and peace offering system of worship at solitary altars was sufficient before there was a sanctuary in Israel (cf. Exod 20:24-26; 24:4). However, this does not mean that the burnt offering had no atoning effect either before or after the sanctuary system arose. Nor does it suggest that the sin and burnt offerings completely replaced burnt offerings in the making of atonement. Instead, the atoning effect of burnt offerings is well established both inside and outside of the sanctuary system, but it arises from a different rationale than the sin and guilt offerings and therefore functions in a different way and accomplishes different purposes (→ Offerings and Sacrifices: Theology, for detailed remarks on the diachronic fallacy as it is applied to the OT sacrificial system).

The foundational meaning of *kpr* (pi.), to make atonement, is to wipe clean (→ # 4105 for arguments). This seems to be the primary significance of the blood manipulation, for example, in the sin offering ritual (see Lev 4 and 16). The burnt offering with its associated grain and drink offerings was a food gift to God (→ Offerings and Sacrifices: Theology; cf. Milgrom, 1991, 176). As such, the burnt offering made atonement not by means of blood manipulation but as a gift that would have the same effect on God as, for example, Jacob's gifts to Esau in Gen 32:20[21], "For he (Jacob) thought, 'I will pacify (*kipper*) him (lit., his faces) with these gifts I am sending on ahead; later, when I see him, perhaps he will receive me" (cf. 33:20; the underlying idea seems to be that Jacob intended to "wipe the anger off Esau's face" with these gifts). The burnt offering carried an atoning effect as a gift that appeased or entreated God rather than as a literal cleansing procedure. One can compare with this, for example, the effect Noah's burnt offering had on God in Gen 8:20-22 (v. 21a, "The LORD smelled the pleasing aroma and said in his heart: 'Never again will I curse the ground because of man'"), or Saul's intent in 1 Sam 13:12, "I thought, 'Now the Philistines will come down against me at Gilgal, and I have not sought the LORD's favor.' So I felt compelled to offer the burnt offering" (cf. 2 Sam 24:22-25; Job 1:5; 42:8; the understanding suggested here is similar to that in Wenham, 57-63).

7. When the burnt offering was incorporated into the sanctuary system of offerings, the very same kind of atoning efficacy came along with it (see Lev 1:4 and OT sec. 4). On the one hand, the burnt offering was the last atoning offering in all attested cases where it was combined in sequence with the sin offering (and other offerings) in the making of atonement. On the other hand, when the burnt offering was combined with the peace offering in a series of rituals, it always came before the peace offering (see Lev 9:8-21). As a gift, the burnt offering carried the effect of the sin offering cleansing atonement forward one further step by appeasing or entreating atonement before God on behalf of the person(s) who had caused the impurity in the first place. It was "an aroma pleasing to the LORD" (Lev 1:9b; cf. Gen 8:20-22). Thus, it followed the sin (and/or guilt) offering(s) in any sequence of offerings.

This was true even on the most important annual occasion of sin offering atonement that cleansed the tabernacle, the Day of Atonement (Lev 16; → *kpr,* # 4105). After offering the sin offerings for the priests and the people, the high priest would then change out of his special garments, bathe himself, and put on his regular priestly garments (vv. 23-24), and would then "come out and sacrifice the burnt offering for himself and the burnt offering for the people, to make atonement for himself and for the people" (v. 24b). Significantly, even though the atoning effect of the sin offerings had been mentioned numerous times previously, nevertheless, the atoning effect of the burnt offerings themselves is still emphasized here. The following verse suggests that the burning of the fat of the sin offering animals was done in association with the incineration of the burnt offerings.

It seems that, in general, the fat of the sin offerings contributed to the gift to God that was the essence of the burnt offerings (cf. Lev 4:10, 19, 26, 31, 35), just as the burnt offerings contributed to the atonement that was the essence of the sin offerings. It is significant that Lev 4:31 uses the same common expression to describe the effect of the burning of the sin offering fat on the altar as was commonly used to describe the effect of the burnt offering as a whole: "the priest shall burn it (the fat) on the altar as an aroma pleasing to the LORD" (Lev 4:31b; cf. 1:9b).

The same was true of the burning of the fat of the peace (fellowship) offerings on the altar (see Lev 3:5, the priest shall burn the fat of the peace offering "as an offering made by fire [*'iššeh*, # 852], an aroma pleasing to the LORD"). In this case, however, the burnt offering gift to God normally preceded the peace offering in a sequence because the latter took the matter still another step forward by enacting the communion between the Lord (the blood and fat went to the altar) and his worshiper(s) (the meat was consumed by the person[s] who brought the offering, with certain portions going to the priest[s] as their prebend; → *šelem*, peace offering, # 8968). In other words, the burning of the fat of all the other animal offerings was their contribution to the gift to

God, which was the primary rationale of burnt offerings, but each of the other kinds of animal offerings emphasized something other than the gift principle. The peace offering emphasized communion, the sin offering emphasized cleansing by atonement (→ *ḥaṭṭā't*, # 2633), and the guilt offering emphasized reparation by atonement (→ *'āšām*, # 871).

The normal way of handling the blood in the burnt, peace, and guilt offerings was the same. The priest would "sprinkle it against the altar on all sides at the entrance to the Tent of Meeting" (Lev 1:5, the main burnt offering section; *zrq*, # 2450 better trans. scatter or splash; cf. Lev 3:2 for the peace offering and 7:2 for the guilt offering). The blood manipulation for the burnt offering came immediately after the killing of the animal (1:5), and it was relatively simple compared to that of the sin offering (cf. 4:5-7, 30). However, the blood was not just disposed of by pouring it out on the ground at the base of the altar (contrast the remainder of the blood in 4:7b; cf. 17:13; Deut 12:16). The splashing of the blood around on the altar was a way of offering it up completely upon the altar, which corresponded to arranging the pieces of the animal's carcass on the altar (Lev 1:8-9). This suggests that the blood participated in the making of the atonement along with the burning of the carcass and even functioned on the same level, as part of the gift to the Lord.

8. The major sections of burnt offering regulations for the tabernacle are Lev 1:3-17; 6:8-13[1-6]; 7:8; Num 15:1-10. It could be from the cattle (Lev 1:3-9), the sheep and goats (vv. 10-13), or the birds (vv. 14-17; usually limited to the poor; e.g., 12:8; 14:22). Lev 1:4 is a particularly important verse: "He is to lay his hand on the head of the burnt offering, and it will be accepted on his behalf to make atonement for him." We have already dealt with the issue of atonement in relation to the burnt offering (secs. 4-7).

Amid the diversity of different kinds of offerings and the many distinctive ways they were offered to the Lord, it appears that there was one constant in the presentation of sacrificial animals (except the birds): the laying on of the hand, or hands (pl.) if more than one person was involved (for the burnt offering see Exod 29:15; Lev 1:4; 8:18; Num 8:12; for the peace offering, Exod 29:19; Lev 3:2, 8, 13; 8:22; for the sin offering, Exod 29:10; Lev 4:4, 15, 24, 29, 33; 8:14; Num 8:12; 2 Chron 29:23; the guilt offering pericope is incomplete with regard to blood manipulation and hand laying but both should be assumed, see Lev 7:2 for the blood manipulation). The purpose of this act was to identify the offerer with his offering (see Wright) and possibly also to designate or consecrate the offering for the purposes of the offering (see, again, 1:4).

Contrary to popular belief, the laying on of the hand did not transfer sin or anything else from the offerer to the offering. One could not offer something laden with sin upon the altar. This would go against the very heart of the logic of the system. In the scapegoat ritual the high priest was to lay both of his hands on the animal and confess the sins of the whole congregation in order to expressly transfer the sins to the goat. But in that case the animal was not offered upon the altar but instead was sent as far away from the altar as possible (e.g., Lev 16:21-22; cf. Num 27:20, 23; Deut 34:9 for another case of transfer by laying on the hands).

9. The acceptance of the burnt offering probably depended on the proper fulfillment of all the regulations (see Milgrom, 1991, 149-50; Hartley, 19). For the burnt offering the animal had to be a male and without defect (Lev 1:3; cf. 22:21 for the

peace offering without defect). No mention is made of a special indication of the acceptability of the offering and, in fact, the offering or offerer could sometimes become unacceptable days after the original presentation of the offering (7:18).

It is easy to confuse the passages that refer to the acceptance of offerings (Lev 1:1-3; 7:18?; 19:7; 22:21, 23, 25, 27; Ps 51:16; Isa 56:7; 60:7; Jer 6:20; Hos 8:13?; Amos 5:22; Mic 6:7; Mal 1:10, 13; 2:13; cf. metaphorically Ps 119:108) with those that refer to the acceptance of offerers (Exod 28:38; Lev 7:18?; 19:5, 7; 22:19, 29; 23:11; 2 Sam 24:23; Jer 14:10, 12; Hos 8:13?; Ezek 20:40; 43:27; cf. metaphorically Ezek 20:41). But in either case the acceptance of the offering was sometimes connected to whether or not the offerer was the kind of person whom the Lord was willing to accept. As David put it: "You do not delight in sacrifice, or I would bring it; you do not take pleasure in burnt offerings. The sacrifices of God are a broken spirit; a broken and contrite heart, O God, you will not despise" (Ps 51:16-17[18-19]). At times the wickedness of the whole nation made the entire sacrificial system unacceptable (see Jer 6:20; Amos 5:22). At other times the Lord anticipated accepting Israel as a pleasing aroma when he brought them back into the land (Ezek 20:41).

10. The offerer normally slaughtered the animal (see "he" in Lev 1:5a, 6; contrast for the bird, 1:15-17), but the priests splashed its blood (v. 5b) and placed its various parts on the altar fire (vv. 7-9a), "to burn all of it on the altar" as a "burnt offering, an offering made by fire, an aroma pleasing to the LORD" (v. 9b). The basic principle behind the burnt offering was that the whole animal was offered on the altar (see "whole burnt offering," Deut 33:10; 1 Sam 7:9; Ps 51:19; cf. Lev 6:22-23[15-16] for the burning of the whole grain offering), including the cut up pieces (*nētaḥ*, # 5984) of the slaughtered animal, the head, as well as the suet (*peder*, # 7022; only 3x in the OT, all in relation to the offering of burnt offerings, Lev 1:8, 12; 8:20), which refers to the internal fatty tissue around the loins and kidneys of the animal (*HALOT* 864; see nom. Levine, *Leviticus*, 7, for Akk., *pitru* as a cognate). The only exceptions were the hide of the larger animals that had been skinned as part of the slaughtering process (Lev 1:6; 7:8) and the crop of the birds with its contents (Lev 1:16, "feathers" in some of the English versions is probably incorrect) or, as Milgrom has suggested, "its crissum by its feathers."

It was the burning of the offering that made it a pleasing aroma to the Lord, which, in turn, caused it to have a certain effect on the Lord and his way of relating to the offerer(s). In the worship at solitary altars it was a way of calling on the Lord to pay attention to the needs, requests, and entreaties of his worshipers either independently (see Num 23:3; 1 Sam 7:9-10; Job 42:7-9; cf. Job 1:5) or in association with the peace offering (see, Judg 20:26-27; 21:3-5; 2 Sam 24:25). Within the levitical system, in addition to its association with atonement procedures (see OT secs. 4-7), the burnt offering, like the peace offering, could be used to express various kinds of worship (Lev 22:18-20; Num 15:3). Moreover, along with its accompanying grain offerings and drink offerings, the burnt offering was the staple of the daily, weekly, monthly, and annual festival cycle cult in the tabernacle (Exod 29:38-45; Num 28:3-8, 10; 1 Chron 16:40; Ezra 3:5; Ezek 46:13-15; Dan 8:11-13; 11:31; 12:11; cf. also Ezra 6:9, *ʿalāwān*, pl. of *ʿalāt*, burnt offering, the only occurrence in Bibl. Aram.).

P-B 1. The term *ʿōlâ* occurs about 50x in the Qumran Temple Scroll (see Yadin). Two special issues arise here. (a) Milgrom has pointed out that the Temple Scroll assigns atonement to all the festival burnt offerings, but then he argues that this was a misunderstanding on the part of the sectarians (Milgrom, 1991, 175). (b) The Temple Scroll required that not only the blood manipulation but also the burning of the sacrificial portions of the sin offering were to be fully accomplished before commencing with the burnt offering. The later rabbis, however, argued that the blood manipulation of the sin offering was to be done before the burnt offering could be slaughtered, but the burning of the parts of the burnt offering was done before the sacrificial portions of the sin offering (Yadin 1:146-48).

The reorganization of the temple worship described in the Qumran War Scroll required that the leaders of the people "attend at holocausts (*'wlwt*) and sacrifices to prepare sweet-smelling incense for the good pleasure of God, to atone (*kpr*) for all His congregation, and to satisfy themselves perpetually before Him at the table of glory" (1QM 2:5; Vermes, 106). This passage suggests that they, like the OT itself, considered the burnt offerings to have an atoning effect as a pleasing aroma to the Lord (cf. OT secs. 4-7). However, in the Manual of Discipline a totally different point is made: "They (the men of perfect holiness) shall atone for guilty rebellion and for sins of unfaithfulness that they may obtain lovingkindness for the Land without the flesh of holocausts and the fat of sacrifice. And the prayer rightly offered shall be as an acceptable fragrance of righteousness, and perfection of way as a delectable free-will offering" (1QS 9:4-5; Vermes, 74). This movement toward a metaphorical understanding of offerings is interesting in light of the same movement in the NT (see below).

The Damascus Document is concerned with other things: "No man on the Sabbath shall offer anything on the altar except the Sabbath burnt-offering; for it is written thus: *Except your Sabbath offerings* (Lev xxiii, 38). No man shall send to the altar any burnt-offering, or cereal offering, or ... by the hand of one smitten with any uncleanness, permitting him thus to defile the altar. For it is written, *The sacrifice of the wicked is an abomination, but the prayer of the just is as an agreeable offering* (Prov xv, 8)" (CD 11:18-19; Vermes, 96).

Of course, various remarks and even full descriptions regarding the burnt offering requirements and procedures can be found in many places in the Mishnah and other later RL (see the citations in Danby, 843).

2. The LXX generally uses G *holokautōma*, holocaust offering, to render Heb. *'ōlâ*. In addition to corresponding OT passages it occurs in the Apocryphal book of 1 Maccabees. 1 Macc 1:45 describes Antiochus Epiphanies's forbidding of proper burnt offerings and sacrifices in the second temple; 4:42-58 records the restoration of proper burnt offerings in the temple by Judas Maccabeus.

NT The G term *holokautōma*, whole burnt offering, is used only in the pair "burnt offerings and sacrifices," and only 3x in the entire NT. According to Mark 12:33, to love the Lord with all the heart ... (cf. Deut 6:5) "is more important than all burnt offerings and sacrifices" (cf. Mic 6:8). Heb 10:6, 8 quote Ps 40:6 twice, "Sacrifice and offering you did not desire, but a body you prepared for me; with burnt offerings and sin offerings you were not pleased." Heb 10:10 goes on to connect these quotations to the logic of the burnt offering as it is applied to Jesus as our sacrifice, "And by that will, we have been made holy through the sacrifice of the body of Jesus Christ once for all."

The same concept is applied to the Christian in Rom 12:1, “Therefore, I urge you, brothers, in view of God’s mercy, to offer your bodies as living sacrifices, holy and pleasing to God—this is your spiritual act of worship.” We have the privilege of offering our bodies back to the one who gave his body for us.

Offering, sacrifice: → *'azkārâ* (sign-offering, # 260); → *'iššeh* (offering by fire, # 852); → *'āšām* (guilt offering, # 871); → *zbḥ* (slaughter, sacrifice, # 2284); → *ḥaṭṭā'at* (sin offering, # 2633); → *ṭbḥ* (slaughter, # 3180); → *minḥâ* (gift, present, offering, sacrifice, # 4966); → *ma'ᵃśēr* (tithe, # 5130); → *ndr* (make a vow, # 5623); → *nwp* I (move back and forth, wave, # 5677); → *nsk* I (pour out, be consecrated, libation, # 5818); → *'ōlâ* I (burnt offering, # 6592); → *'ᵃrîsâ* (meal/dough offering, # 6881); → *qorbān* (offering, gift, # 7933); → *šḥṭ* I (slaughter, # 8821); → *šelem* (settlement sacrifice, # 8968); → *tāmîd* (regular offering, # 9458); → *tᵉrûmâ* (tribute, contribution, # 9556); → **Aaron: Theology**; → **Offering: Theology**; → **Priests and Levites: Theology**

BIBLIOGRAPHY

TWAT 6:105-24; W. F. Albright, *The Proto-Sinaitic Inscriptions and Their Decipherment*, 1969; G. A. Anderson, “Sacrifice and Sacrificial Offerings (OT),” *ABD*, 1992, 5:870-86; idem, *Sacrifices and Offerings in Ancient Israel*, HSM, 41, 1987; C. Brown, “Sacrifice, First Fruits, Altar, Offering,” *NIDNTT*, 3:415-38; H. Danby, *The Mishnah*, 1933; M. Dijkstra, “The Ritual KTU 1.46 (= RS 1.9) and Its Duplicates,” *UF* 16, 1984, 69-76; G. B. Gray, *Sacrifice in the OT*, 1971 (1925); J. E. Hartley, *Leviticus*, WBC, 1992; G. C. Heider, “Molech,” *ABD* 4:895-98; H.-J. Klauck, “Sacrifice and Sacrificial Offerings (NT),” *ABD* 5:886-91; I. Knohl, *The Sanctuary of Silence: The Priestly Torah and the Holiness School*, 1995; B. A. Levine, *In the Presence of the Lord*, SJLA 5, 1974; idem, *Leviticus*, The JPS Torah Commentary, 1989; idem, “Prolegomenon” to G. B. Gray, see above; J. Milgrom, *Leviticus 1-16*, AB, 1991; idem, *Numbers*, The JPS Torah Commentary, 1990; A. F. Rainey, “The Order of Sacrifices in OT Ritual Texts,” *Bib* 51, 1970, 485-98; R. Rendtorff, *Leviticus*, BKAT 3, 1985; F. Rosenthal (ed.), *An Aramaic Handbook*, Part I/1, 1967; J.-M. de Tarragon, *Le culte á Ugarit*, 1980; M. E. Tate, *Psalms 51-100*, WBC, 1990; G. Vermes, *The Dead Sea Scrolls in English*, 3d ed., 1987; M. Weinfeld, “Social and Cultic Institutions in the Priestly Source Against Their Ancient Near Eastern Background,” *Proceedings of the Eight World Congress of Jewish Studies*, 1983, 95-129; J. Wellhausen, *Prolegomena to the History of Israel*, 1878, ET 1885; G. J. Wenham, *The Book of Leviticus*, NICOT, 1979; D. P. Wright, “The Gesture of Hand Placement in the Hebrew Bible and in Hittite Literature,” *JAOS* 106, 1986, 433-46; Y. Yadin, *The Temple Scroll*, vols. 1-2, 1983.

Richard E. Averbeck

6596	עֲלוּמִים

עֲלוּמִים (*'ᵃlûmîm*), youth (# 6596); עֶלֶם (*'elem*), young man (# 6624); עַלְמָה (*'almâ*), young woman (# 6625).

ANE Cognate with Ugar. *ǵlm*, boy, servant; Phoen. *'alam*; Aram. *'alîm*, servant. So, for instance, in the Ugar. texts, Keret is often referred to as *ǵlm il*, which means the same as *'bd il* (Krt: 153, 299). Based on the cognate usage, A. Schoors has suggested that the abstract nom. *'ᵃlûmîm* ought to be translated “bondage” (Isa 54:4). E. Hammershaimb uses the Ugar. material to conclude that *ǵlmt/'almâ* is “a designation for the mother-goddess, that is . . . the queen who gives birth to the royal heir” (“Immanuel Sign,” 1951, 128). Unfortunately, he gives no indication how this meaning would fit with Rebekah or Miriam. Nevertheless, the Ugar. usage, especially in text *CTA* 24:7 (*hl ǵlmt tld bn*, "behold the *ǵlmt* has borne a son") suggests that in that literature "virgin" would be an inaccurate rendering.

OT The fem. sing. *'almâ*, cannot be considered in isolation from its related masc. and abstract forms. The fem. nom. occurs 7x (Gen 24:43; Exod 2:8; Ps 68:25[26]; Prov 30:19; S of Songs 1:3; 6:8; Isa 7:14); the masc. nom. occurs twice (1 Sam 17:56; 20:22); the nom. abstraction *'ᵃlûmîm* occurs 5x (Job 20:11; 33:25; Ps 89:45[46]; 90:8; Isa 54:4). Many have built a case for understanding the meaning of the word through a proposed etymological connection. Jerome argued for a connection between *'almâ* and the root *'lm* (→ # 6623), meaning to hide or conceal. He thus considered such a girl to be more than a virgin, i.e., to be "cloistered" (Kamesar, 1990, 62). G. Gerleman has explored the relationship between the root *'lm* and the adverb *'ôlâm* (# 6409). He builds a case that *'ôlâm* belongs to the range of meaning of "sperren" (limitation, barrier). Thus *'ad 'ôlâm* would take on the meaning of "beyond limitations" (of time or space). An *'elem* or *'almâ* would be someone "shut out" of knowledge or experience, someone "uninformed" or "uninitiated." So in Gen 24 Rebekah is unaware of the test in which she is involved. In 1 Sam 20, Jonathan's servant is unaware of the role he is playing. In Exod 2:8 Miriam pretends to be unaware of the identity of the child (Gerleman, 344-49). All of this is intriguing, but it is not convincing in Isa 7:14 and hardly fits in passages such as Ps 68:25[26] or S of Songs 1:3. H. Wolf suggests that the Ugar. texts use *ǵlmt* in situations where the woman is about to be married (450); but what does this suggest for the Ugar. usage of the masculine singular (ms) forms? Further, though Wolf points out the fact that Rebekah is also about to be married in Gen 24, it does not seem to be appropriate to describe Miriam by the use of such a term. None of these hypotheses takes sufficient account of the masculine and abstract forms, and all are based on methods that are lexically inadequate.

Hypothetical relationship to a verbal root, as with any etymological data, is at best diachronic and thus unreliable as a guide to meaning. Semitic cognates are equally suspect since the relationship between the cognates is based on the assumption of a common proto-Semitic lexical core. Therefore, this is also diachronic information. Nevertheless, the sychronic information that is available, sparse as it is, matches the lexical profile offered by the cognates. We must now summarize the basic elements of the synchronic lexical profile.

In Gen 24:43 the activity in which the *'almâ* (Rebekah) is engaged is drawing water. Her status is young, unmarried, of marriageable age, and a virgin. All of these are clarified by other descriptions in the context (note the use of *na'ᵃrâ*, v. 14, and *bᵉtûlâ*, v. 16). There is no basis in the context, however, for identifying any of these as a nuance of *'almâ*. In Exod 2:8 there is nothing in the context to clarify the nuance of the term aside from what we know of the girl to whom it is applied, Miriam, which is very little. Contributing to the problem in this occurrence is that the term is applied to Miriam by the narrator rather than by any of the other characters. The remainder of the passages do not identify the *'almâ* by name, so we have only the activities described in the passage to assist us. In Ps 68:25[26] the only activity ascribed to the individuals is the playing of tambourines, so no contribution is made. In Prov 30:19 the text speaks of the "way of a man with an *'almâ*" as being one of four incomprehensible things. Even if sexual activity is implied by the term *derek* (way), the text does not indicate whether it might represent an initial sexual encounter; therefore, the status of the *'almâ* is not clarified any further by this context. S of Songs 1:3 speaks vaguely of *'ālāmôt* loving the king.

The two passages providing the most significant information are S of Songs 6:8 and Isa 7:14. The former identifies three classes of women that we infer are distinct and mutually exclusive: queens, concubines, and *'ālāmôt*. Many commentators have suggested that these represent three classifications within the royal harem. If this is true, it is not likely that one of the categories could be identified as virgins. On the other hand, it would be logical to differentiate between those who had borne royal offspring and those who had not. In this case the queens would be the favorites of higher status or important political wives; the concubines would be principally sexual partners and slave girls; the *'ᵃlâmôt* may be either those who have not yet borne children, or those whose primary function in the harem was childbearing. That childbearing is the issue is also suggested by Isa 7:14, for there it is treated as a "sign" that the *'almâ* is pregnant and will bear a son to be named Immanuel.

The masc. sing. is used once referring to David following his succesful bout with Goliath, and once referring to the young man helping Jonathan. Neither of these contexts offers an description of activity characteristic of an *'elem*. Likewise there is nothing concerning the status of either individual that would suggest a nuance for the term.

Finally, of the five occurrences of the abstract nom., the most significant is Isa 54:4. In a context featuring a metaphorical attribution of this term to Israel, she is also described as having a husband (v. 5) and of being barren (v. 1). In parallel phrases the "shame" of her *'ᵃlûmîm* is paired with the shame of her widowhood. As concluded above with regard to the fem. nom. occurrences, the circumstances of this context suggest a close connection with childbearing, the only logical shame of *'ālûmîm* being the barrenness previously referred to. Of the remaining four occurrences, the two in Job refer to males relative to age, though 20:11 may include virility. Ps 89:45[46], likewise, suggests some connection to virility, for there is shame in its being discontinued. Ps 90:8 appears to be more directly related to the verbal root *'lm* and therefore does not contribute to the present discussion.

The lexical profile may now be constructed in light of the following conclusions:

1. At least two of the contexts feature childbearing as a pivotal issue (Isa 7:14; 54:4). We must resolve whether this involves the woman's *status* as a childbearer (i.e., mother), her *ability* to bear children (e.g., age, physical condition, marriageability), or her *opportunity* to be a childbearer (i.e., virginity). The very fact that an *'almâ* can be barren (Isa 54:4) suggests that such a description cannot be exclusively applied to someone who has not had the opportunity to bear children (i.e., a virgin). The fact that a married woman may be labeled an *'almâ* (Isa 54:4; possibly S of Songs 6:8) precludes the term as exclusively appropriate to someone of marriageable age. This leaves the woman's *status* as a childbearer as the logical choice. The fact that a young woman has not borne a child may in fact suggest that she is a virgin, and perhaps even of marriageable age, but the lexical profile of the term does not require either of those to be true. To say this another way, a woman ceases to be an *'almâ* when she becomes a mother—not when she becomes a wife or a sexual partner.

2. How then is this term applied to males? On the basis of Job 20:11 and Ps 89:45[46], where the abstract nom. is applied to males, it appears that the term refers to the ability to be a father. A woman's bearing of a child is comparable to a man's begetting of a child. But the woman's ability to bear a child is demonstrated by the birth process, while a man's ability to beget a child is demonstrated in his virility. The common ground is the potential for procreative activity.

We conclude, then, that applied to a female, the term refers to one who has not yet borne a child and as an abstraction refers to the adolescent expectation of motherhood. This would be captured in Eng. by a combination of the terms "nubility" and "fertility"—a woman so described is full of childbearing potential. When applied to a male it describes a virile young man, (or, more neutrally, "a strapping young man") and as an abstraction refers to youthful virility. None of the overlapping near synonyms refer as explicitly to childbearing interests and status. The passage that is least compliant with this profile is Exod 2:8, for neither this nor any other specific nuance serves any purpose to the narrator.

The most significant theological issues surrounding this term center on its use in Isa 7:14. The citation of this verse in Matt 1:23 and the nature of the doctrinal affirmation at stake have greatly hindered objective lexical analysis through the centuries. It must be immediately recognized that though Matthew cites Isa 7:14 in support of the virgin birth of Christ, he does not depend on the meaning of *'almâ* to establish that doctrine. Likewise *parthenos*, as with *'almâ*, does not refer specifically to a virgin.

> It is evident that the primary meaning of the word has to do with sexual maturity and, by extension, the age of the young woman, not with sexual experience or the lack of it. That the word may be used of a virgin is evident: it is not used, however, to define her virginity, but to define her capacity for marriage. So . . . it may also refer to a married young woman (until the birth of her first child) (Bratcher, 98).

That the G *parthenos* used by Matthew and by the LXX in Isa 7:14 can mean virgin and that an *'almâ* can be a virgin are sufficient for the fulfillment to be identified. The OT need not anticipate in its prophecy every specific element that finds fulfillment in the NT. One only needs to analyze Matthew's quotations of the OT in 2:15, 18, 23 to confirm the loose association that is often sufficient for the identificaiton of fulfillment to be made. For further discussion of the methods involved see Walton. The fulfillment of Isaiah's prophecy in the time of Ahaz concerned the birth of an individual who may not have had a recognizable role to play in the events of his time, but whose name represented the hope of deliverance. That hope was realized in a fuller way in the coming of Jesus, born of a virgin, God with us in incarnate form. This is in every sense a fulfillment of Isaiah's prophecy, but that does not require that Isaiah anticipated the nature of the fulfillment.

Consequently, our lexical study need not be hampered by theological mandates. We are not obliged to find the meaning "virgin" in the lexical profile of *'almâ* in order to justify the NT or our theological creeds.

Youth: → *bāḥûr* I (young man, # 1033); → *b^{e}tûlâ* (young girl, # 1435); → *n^{e}'ûrîm* (youth, # 5830); → *'^{a}lûmîm* (youth, # 6596); → *ṣā'îr* I (little, small, young, trifling, # 7582); → *qāṭōn* (small, trifling, young, # 7785); → *šaḥ^{a}rût* (dark hair, prime of youth, # 8841)

Bibliography

R. G. Bratcher, "A Study of Isaiah 7:14," *BT* 9, 1958, 97-126; G. Gerleman, "Die sperrende Grenze: Die Wurzel *'lm* im Hebräischen" *ZAW* 91, 1979, 338-49; C. H. Gordon, "*'Almah* in Isaiah 7:14," *JBR* 21, 1953, 106, 240-41; E. Hammershaimb, "The Immanuel Sign," *ST* 3, 1951, 124-42; A. Kamesar, "The Virgin of Isaiah 7:14: The Philological Argument From the Second to the Fifth Century" *JTS* 41, 1990, 51-75; M. Rehm, "Das Wort *'almah* in Is 7,14," *BZ* 8, 1964, 89-101; A. Schoors, "Is *liv* 4," *VT* 21, 1971, 503-5; J. Scullion, "An Approach to the Understanding of Isaiah 7:10-17," *JBL* 87, 1968, 289-93; J. E. Steinmueller, "Etymology and the Biblical Usage of *'Almah*," *CBQ* 2, 1940, 28-43; B. Vawter, "The Ugaritic Use of *GLMT*," *CBQ* 14, 1952, 319-22; T. Wadsworth, "Is There a Hebrew Word for Virgin?" *RevQ* 23, 1980, 161-71; J. H. Walton, "Isaiah 7:14—What Is In a Name?" *JETS* 30, 1987, 289-306; P. Wegner, *An Examination of Kingship and Messianic Expectation in Isaiah 1-35*, 1992, 106-22; G. J. Wenham, "*B^{e}tulah,* 'A Girl of Marriageable Age,'" *VT* 22, 1972, 326-48; H. Wildberger, *Isaiah 1-12*, 1991, 306-14; J. T. Willis, "The Meaning of Isaiah 7:14 and Its Application in Matthew 1:23," *RevQ* 21, 1978, 1-17; R. D. Wilson, "The Meaning of *'Alma* (A. V. 'Virgin') in Isaiah VII.14," *PTR* 24, 1926, 308-16; H. M. Wolf, "A Solution to the Immanuel Prophecy in Isaiah 7:14-8:22," *JBL* 91, 1972, 449-56.

John Walton

6598 (*'^{a}lûqâ*, leech), → # 6856

6600	עלז

עלז (*'lz*), q. exult (# 6600); עָלֵז (*'ālēz*), nom./adj. exultant (hapleg., Isa 5:14; # 6601); עַלִּיז (*'allîz*), exultant, wild, haughty, wanton (# 6611).

ANE Mish. Heb. *'^{a}lîzâ*, rejoicing; *'allîz*, wanton, noisy. The similarity of *'lz*, *'ls*, *'lṣ* has caused scholars to debate whether these terms are allophones that connote the same basic meaning (*IBHS*, 94, §5.8b; *GKC*, 68, §19a) or homonyms (words with the same consonants but different meanings, Emerton, 214-20; Rabin, 396-97). Those who identify these forms as homonyms point to the translation diversity in the Vrs. (in several instances connoting the nuance of strength), cite a potential Arab. cognate, *ghalîz*, think, coarse, rude; and finally, they identify several passages where they find the meaning "rejoice" objectionable. However, Vanoni (32; *TWAT* 6:128) correctly points out that neither etymological possibilities nor an examination of the Vrs. demonstrates that *'lz* and *'lṣ* are homonyms. The translation variety in the Vrs. represents attempts to express the meaning of the vb. rather than evidence for homonyms (Millard, 89). The interchangeability of *'lz* and *'lṣ* suggest they are byforms (Ps 68:4-5[5-6]—*'lz* ‖ *'lṣ*; 96:12 = 1 Chron 16:32; *'lz* = *'lṣ*). (For *'lṣ* → # 6636.)

OT 1. The vb. *'lz* occurs 7x in Ps, 4x in Jer, and once each in 2 Sam, Prov, Isa, Hab, and Zeph. It occurs with various cognates that emphasize the enthusiastic, expressive nature of this rejoicing (e.g., *gyl*, Hab 3:18; *śmḥ*, 2 Sam 1:20; Prov 23:15-16; Jer 50:11; Zeph 3:14; *rnn*, Ps 96:11[12]; 149:5; Zeph 3:14).

(a) Malicious joy. In his lament of Saul (2 Sam 1:20), David states the impossible in order to express his fervent wish (Anderson, 17), namely, that no one would provide the Philistines an occasion to gloat over their defeat of Israel. The psalmist (Ps 94:3) wonders in agony how long God will allow the wicked to gloat over the affliction of the righteous.

(b) Short-lived or banished rejoicing. Yahweh will answer Babylon's celebration of her decimation of Judah with severe judgment (Jer 50:11; 51:39). Jeremiah (11:15) indicts the children of Israel for seeking to cover up their covenant treachery by offering sacrifices at the temple. Yahweh will turn their inappropriate rejoicing into sorrow. As with other cognates (*gyl*, *śmḥ*), the banishment of celebration serves as an indication of divine judgment. In Isa 23:12, the loss of Sidon's joy (cf. 23:7, a city of revelry [*'allîzâ*]) accompanies the loss of peace, tenure, and rest.

(c) Rejoicing in/by Yahweh. In the Psalter (Ps 28:7; 68:4[5]; 96:12 = 1 Chron 16:32; 149:5) Yahweh's character provides the ground for jubilation 4x. Habakkuk (Hab 3:18) affirms that he will rejoice in God regardless of his circumstances while Zephaniah (3:14) calls God's people to rejoice in their great and mighty God.

The MT (identical wording) of Ps 60:6[8] and 108:7[8] depict God as the one rejoicing. Noth restructures the MT *''lzh*, I will exult, with *'lh zh*, I will go up now (cf. Num 13:17), since *'lz* does not occur with God as its subject outside of Ps 60:6[8] and 108:7[8]. However, Yahweh repeatedly serves as the subject of cognate vbs. (*gyl*, *śmḥ*, *śwś*). Also, the apparent function of *'lz* as the inclusio counterpart to *rw'* in Ps 108:9[10] supports the MT reading. Consequently, these par. passages in Psalms offer hope to the afflicted people of God because Yahweh rejoices that he alone ultimately controls the status of peoples and lands.

(d) Miscellaneous. Jeremiah (15:17) laments his lonely life, in which he never celebrated with revelers. A son whose speech is without deception brings rejoicing to the depth of his father's being (Prov 23:16).

2. The nom. *'allîz* occurs 7x (Isa [5x], Zeph [2x]); in 5x (Isa 22:2; 23:7; 24:8; 32:13; Zeph 2:15) it depicts a city or multitude devoted to self-satisfaction. Their arrogant commitment to pleasure provides a stark contrast to the numbing silence of a devastated city. The juxtaposition of *'allîz* and *ga'ᵃwâ* in Isa 13:3 and Zeph 3:11 refers to a group of people who exult with pride concerning a certain issue. Isaiah describes the warriors that Yahweh gathers to fight against Babylon, who celebrate their sure victory (cf. GKC 440, §135n), while Zephaniah refers to the civil and religious leaders who exult in their sinful ways (polar opposite of meek and humble in Zeph 3:12; cf. Patterson, 379; Zvi, 232). Since Yahweh calls the warriors to battle in Isa 13, various scholars prefer the rendering, "rejoicing in his majesty/sovereignty" (Ball, 178; Fohrer, 1:162; Oswalt, 302; Watts, 196, Wildberger, 499, 502). Although *ga'ᵃwâ* can signify God's majesty (Deut 33:26; Ps 68:34[35]), neither the soldiers called by Yahweh nor the leaders of Jerusalem appear to rejoice in God's character, but rather, they exult in their own accomplishments.

3. The nom. *'ālēz*. The only instance of this form occurs in Isa 5:14, where it signifies the arrogant revelry of God's people who devoted themselves to satisfying their pleasures rather than submitting to Yahweh. Those for whom satisfying the appetite is preeminent become nourishment for the insatiable appetite of Sheol. Emerton's emendation (135-42, he replaces *w'lz bh*, whoever rejoices in it, with *w'z lbh*, the courage of her heart) has no Vrs. or MSS support.

Happiness, joy, rejoicing: → *'šr* II (be fortunate, # 887); → *blg* (be cheerful, happy, # 1158); → *gad* II (luck, fortune, # 1513); → *gyl* (exult, # 1635); → *ḥdh* (gladden, rejoice, make happy, # 2525); → *'lz* (exult, # 6600); → *'ls* (enjoy, appear glad, # 6632); → *'lṣ* (rejoice, # 6636); → *śwś* (rejoice, # 8464); → *śmḥ* (rejoice, make glad, # 8523)

Bibliography

TWAT 6:126-31; *TWOT* 2:610; L. Allen, *Psalms 101-150*, WBC, 1983; A. Anderson, *2 Samuel*, 1989; I. Ball, Jr., *A Rhetorical Study of Zephaniah*, 1988; J. Bright, "Jeremiah's Complaints—Liturgy or Expressions of Personal Distress?" in *Proclamation and Presence*, 1970, 189-214; D. Clines, *Job 1-20*, 1989; J. Emerton, "The Textual Problems of Isaiah V. 14," *VT* 17, 1967, 135-42; idem, "Notes on Some Passages in the Book of Proverbs," *JTS* 20, 1969, 202-20; G. Fohrer, *Das Buch Jesaja*, 1960; R. Gordis, *The Book of Job*, 1978; A. Guillaume, "Hebrew and Arabic Lexicography: A Comparative Study," *Abr-Nahrain* 1, 1959-60, 3-35; J. Hartley, *The Book of Job*, NICOT, 1988; A. Millard, "עלץ 'To Exult,'" *JTS* 26, 1975, 87-89; C. North, "שְׁכֶם אֶעְלֹזָה אֲחַלְּקָה (Psa. 1x 8 ‖ Psa. cviii 8)," *VT* 17, 1967, 242-43; J. Oswalt, *The Book of Isaiah, Chapters 1-39*, NICOT, 1986; R. Patterson, *Nahum, Habakkuk, Zephaniah*, 1991; C. Rabin, "Etymological Miscellanea," in *SH* 8, 1961, 384-400; M. Tate, *Psalms 51-100*, WBC, 1990; G. Vanoni, "Das Problem der Homonymie beim althebräischen 'LZ/'LṢ," *BN* 33, 1986, 29-33; J. Watts, *Isaiah 1-33*, WBC, 1985; H. Wildberger, *Isaiah 1-12*, 1991; E. Zvi, *A Historical-Critical Study of the Book of Zephaniah*, 1991.

Michael A. Grisanti

6601 (*'ālēz*, exultant), → # 6600

6602	עֲלָטָה

עֲלָטָה (*'ᵃlāṭâ*), nom. darkness, dusk (# 6602).

ANE This nom. is not attested in other Sem. languages, unless possibly by the transposition of the letters *l* and *ṭ* in Arab. *ġaṭala*, be cloudy, and *ġayṭalatu*, darkness.

OT The nom. occurs 4x in the OT and refers to the darkness that follows the setting of the sun: so, "when the sun had set and darkness had fallen" (Gen 15:17), and "at dusk" (Ezek 12:6-7, 12).

P-B In Mish. Heb. the vb. *'lṭ* occurs in the hi. stem, meaning to darken, and the nom. *'eleṭ* occurs, meaning darkness, gloom. In the Talm. literature the word means darkness or mist.

Darkness: → *'ōpel* (darkness, gloom, # 694); → *'ᵉšûn* (approach of darkness, # 854); → *ḥšk* (be, grow dark, grow dim, darken, conceal, confuse, # 3124); → *ṭuḥôt* (darkness, obscurity, inward parts, # 3219); → *kamrîr* (blackness, deep gloom, # 4025); → *laylâ* (night, # 4326); → *nešep* (twilight, darkness, # 5974); → *'wp* II (be dark, # 6415); → *'ᵃlāṭâ* (darkness, dusk, # 6602); → *'mm* II (darken, dim, # 6670); → *'ᵃrāpel* (deep darkness, thick darkness, heavy cloud, # 6906); → *ṣll* III (be/grow dark, cast a shadow, # 7511); → *ṣalmāwet* (darkness, shadow of death, # 7516); → *qdr* (be dark, mourn, # 7722)

Bibliography

TWOT 2:670; G. A. Cooke, *Ezekiel*, ICC, 130.

James D. Price

6603 (*'ēlî*, Eli), → Eli

6605 (*'ᵉlî*, pestle), → # 6590

6606 (*'illî*, upper), → # 6590

6608	עֲלִיָּה

עֲלִיָּה (*ʿaliyyâ*), nom. upper room (# 6608); < עלה (*ʿlh*), go up (→ # 6590).

ANE The nom. *ʿilîtâʾ* occurs in Aram., *ʿellîtāʾ* in Syr., and *ʿlyt* in Palm. In Arab. the nom. developed into *ʿi/ʿulliyyat*.

OT This nom. occurs in different contexts. It is used to refer to the upper room of an ordinary house (1 Kgs 17:19, 23), of a palace (Judg 3:20, 23-25; 2 Kgs 1:2; Isa 38:8), at the temple (1 Chron 28:11; 2 Chron 3:9), over the city gate (2 Sam 19:1), and even as God's seat over the heavenly floods (Ps 104:3, 13).

Room: → *ḥeder* (dark room, chamber of sheol, # 2540); → *liškâ* (hall, # 4384); → *m*[e]*huqṣāʿôt* (corner room, # 4553); → *ʿ*[a]*liyyâ* (upperroom, # 6608)

Louis Jonker

6610 (*ʿelyôn [ʿel]*, [God] Most High), → # 446a

6611 (*ʿallîz*, exultant, wild, haughty, wanton), → # 6600

6612	עֲלִיל

עֲלִיל (*ʿ*[a]*lîl*), clay furnace (hapleg.; # 6612); < עלל (*ʿll* II), thrust (→ # 6619).

OT The words of God are flawless (*ṭhr*), like silver refined (*ṣrp*) in a clay furnace (Ps 12:6[7]).

NT → *NIDNTT* 1:654-56.

Furnace, fireplace, forge, oven, stove: → *ʾaḥ* (brazier, firepot, # 279); → *kibšān* (furnace, forge, # 3901); → *kûr* (forge, # 3929); → *kîr* (small stove, # 3968); → *m*[e]*bašš*[e]*lôt* (fireplaces, # 4453); → *môqēd* (fireplace, # 4611); → *ʿ*[a]*lîl* (clay furnace, # 6612); → *tannûr* (oven, furnace, # 9486)

Bibliography
IBD 531; *ZPEB* 2:614; O. Keel, *The Symbolism of the Biblical World*, 1979, 184.

I. Cornelius

6613 (*ʿ*[a]*lîlâ*, transgression, deed, charge), → # 6618

6617	עֲלִיצוּת

עֲלִיצוּת (*ʿalîṣût*), nom. exultation, gloating (# 6617); עלץ (*ʿlṣ*), q. to rejoice, gloat (# 6636).

ANE Akk. has this root with the meaning exult.

OT 1. The vb. (found 8x) denotes the joyous celebration in the cult, the jubilant gladness that accompanies triumph over one's enemies. Hannah rejoices in the gift of a child as she "boasts over [her] enemies" (1 Sam 2:1). David likewise rejoices in God in connection with turning back his enemies (9:3[4]) and with the protection of saints (5:11[12]). The righteous trust God to protect them from the gloating of their enemies (25:2).

2. In 1 Chron 16:32, the field rejoices in God's goodness toward his creation and his people (‖ Ps 96:12 *'lz*).

3. In Proverbs (11:10; 28:12) the vb. also denotes cultic celebration when the righteous triumph over the wicked, as the parallels show (see Leo G. Perdue, *Wisdom and the Cult*, 1978, 312).

4. The hapleg. *'ᵃlîṣût* describes the joyful gloating of the enemies of God who oppress his people (Hab 3:14). This perverse fiendish gloating delights in victimizing the helpless person, but God will judge this and bring salvation to his people.

Happiness, joy, rejoicing: → *'šr* II (be fortunate, # 887); → *blg* (be cheerful, happy, # 1158); → *gad* II (luck, fortune, # 1513); → *gyl* (exult, # 1635); → *ḥdh* (gladden, rejoice, make happy, # 2525); → *'lz* (exult, # 6600); → *'ls* (enjoy, appear glad, # 6632); → *'lṣ* (rejoice, # 6636); → *śwś* (rejoice, # 8464); → *śmḥ* (rejoice, make glad, # 8523)

Gary V. Smith

6618	עלל

עלל (*'ll* I), q. (?) to drink again and again; poel, to act, to wipe out, deal with, to harm, to glean; poal, to inflict pain upon s.o., s.t.; hitp. to sport with, to deal mischievously with s.o.; hitpoel to deal petulantly, mischievously (# 6618); מַעֲלָל (*ma'ᵃlāl*), nom. deed, practice, act (# 5095); עֲלִילָה (*'ᵃlîlâ*), transgression, wantonness, offence; deed, act, charge (# 6613); עֲלִילִיָּה (*'ᵃlîliyyâ*), (mighty in) deeds; few grapes (# 6614); עוֹלֵלוֹת (*'ôlēlôt*), gleaning(s) of; a few grapes (# 6622); תַּעֲלוּלִים (*ta'ᵃlûlîm*), cruelty, caprice, wantonness, misdeed (# 9500).

ANE Arab. *'alla*, do anything a second time; Eth. *'alälä*, gain practice, get used to.

OT 1. The vb. always has a negative connotation or denotation, appearing 20x in the OT. Obad 16 is probably not a q. of *'ll*, but a q. of *l''* II, 1x in OT (cf. MT *lā'û*; prp. *nā'û*; *HALAT* 506, 789, *'allû*). *'ll* is used to indicate labor activities. The vineyards will not be gleaned (poel, 11x), removing all grapes left after its usual harvesting, but any remaining grapes shall be left for the poor (*'ᵃnî*), alien (*gēr*), orphan (*yātôm*), or widow (*'almānâ*). When used with persons the word indicates a destructive, abusive, or deceitful action/attitude toward others, such as to wipe out, kill; make sport of, mock, dally with; abuse; take advantage of; inflict pain/grief upon; exercise oneself in mischievousness, wantonness. For example, the Egyptians/Pharaoh are made sport of/dallied with by the Lord (hitp. Exod 10:2; 1 Sam 6:6). A Levite's concubine is abused sexually, and Saul and Zedekiah feared abuse from various groups (Judg 19:25; 1 Sam 31:4, hitp.; Jer 38:19, hitp.). The consummate fool was Balaam, whose donkey sported with him (hitp., Num 22:29). In the hitpoel it evidently means to pick off, wipe out, cut down in battle/ambush, as in Judg 20:45, where the Israelites killed the Benjaminites. In Isa the poel is used to describe how the evil rulers of the Lord's people oppress them, "strip them clean" (Isa 3:12), like a vineyard (3:14). Lamentations has several uses of the poel of the word meaning "inflict, afflict, oppress" (Lam 1:12, 22; 2:20). In 1:12 the eyes of the weeping prophet bring him "pain" (poal, 1x) in his soul at the sight of a destroyed Jerusalem. Ps 141:4 (hitpoel, 1x) records the plea of the psalmist to keep back his heart from acting without restraint to do destructive deeds/actions (*'ᵃlîlôt*). While the poel, poal, and hitpoel indicate a straightforward act upon/dealing with someone or something, the reflexive use of the hitp. carries the connotation of dealing with someone to their detriment and one's own mischievous desires/pleasure.

The syntax of the vb. calls for the use of several possible constructions. With the poel, l^e + acc. is found; poal employs l^e; the hitp. has b^e as a preposition; hitpoel employs b^e and *'et*. b^e is regularly used with vbs. indicating touching, striking, striking at, possibly in these cases indicating the action to one's own advantage (*BHS*, 199). The use of the l^e may be a *dativus ethicus* or "reflexive" use, indicating the subjects involvement in the action (*BHS*, 208).

2. The noms., of course, indicate the results of the verbal action, but can refer to good results in certain contexts apart from the vb. *ma'ᵃlāl* is found most often and indicates the actions, good/bad, of people (Deut 28:20; Isa 1:16; Jer 7:3-5). The Lord does not partake in the evil doings of his people (Mic 2:7). His works are good and should not be forgotten (Ps 78:7). *'ᵃlîlâ* is used less often and describes the actions/deeds of those who in Israel produced evil works (Ezek 20:43; Zeph 3:7). The word also denotes actions that God does that should be made known (*yd'*) among the nations, actions that lead to salvation/rescue (Isa 12:4). The nom. *'ôlēlā* denotes gleaning(s) of grapes/olives. God's utter "picking bare" of Edom is more extreme than that which the gatherers of grapes would leave in a vineyard (Jer 49:9; cf. Obad 5). This simile refers to the Israelites who were left with nothing to feed them; they are worse than a vineyard after it has been picked of its grapes (Mic 7:1). The olive garden/tree that has been beaten became a symbol for Jacob when it is judged (Isa 17:6). Even the earth, in apocalyptic fashion, will be as when an olive tree is beaten—desolate (Isa 24:13).

3. The remaining noms. are found 3x total. God's deeds (*'ᵃlîliyyôt*) are great in creation and history and are to be recognized and followed (Jer 32:19). *ta'ᵃlûlîm*, cruelty, caprice, wantonness, misdeed, is used twice, but its meaning is best determined in context. In Isa 3:4 the nom. is parallel with *nᵉ'ārîm*, children/young men. The *ta'ᵃlûlîm* are said to rule over the people. The abstract "cruelty" may best be understood as defining the subject by their wicked, capricious manner of rule (H. Wildberger, *Isaiah 1-12*, Continental, 1991, 131-32). The leaders acted like children by their petty, greedy leadership, resulting in anarchy (Oswalt, *Isaiah 1-39*, NICOT, 1986, 133).

The second text (Isa 66:4) has divine retribution as the subject. Because the evildoers have refused to be obedient to God by defying him, they will receive their just deserts. As they have mistreated people, God will bring them down by "harsh treatment."

P-B The LXX uses many words to render this Heb. root, as might be expected, since its context determines its meaning to a great degree. The G words used more than once are: *empaizō*, mock, *kalamaomai*, do well/good, *epiphyllizō*, glean grapes, *epanatrygaō*, gather, glean. Likewise the noms. are rendered in various ways. Among other words, the ones found most often are: *'ōlēlā*, *epiphyllis*, small grapes for gleaners; *'ᵃlîlā*, *epitēdeuma*, custom, practice; *hamartia*, sin, wrong; *anomia*, lawlessness; *asebeia*, godless; *'ᵃlîliyyā*, *ergon*, work, deed; *ma'ᵃlāl*, *epitēdeuma*, practice, customs; *ergon*, work, deed; *diaboulion*, deliberation.

In the DSS the root is found only in nom. forms. No new theological uses appear, but, as in the OT, God punishes the evil deeds of the evildoer and by his Holy Spirit cleanses them (cf. 1QS 4:17; 1QS 4:21; 1QH 14:9; 15:24; CD 5:16).

In Late Heb. (cf. Jastrow 2:1083) the word continued to be used in the polel (Eccl Rabbah 6:10). In the hitpalel and nitpalel, it bears the meaning sport, abuse (Giṭṭin 58[a]).

Deed, act, misdeed, work: → *gml* (accomplish, commit, achieve, ripen, # 1694); → *m[e]lā'kâ* (work, duties, task, # 4856); → *'ll* I (act, wipe out, deal with, harm, glean, # 6618); → *'śh* I (make, do, prepare, create, work, service, # 6913); → *p'l* (do, make, produce, practice, accomplish, perform, # 7188)

BIBLIOGRAPHY

TWAT 6:151-60; *TWOT* 2:670-71.

Eugene Carpenter

6619	עלל

עלל (*'ll* II), poel, thrust in (hapleg.; # 6619); עֲלִיל (*'[a]lîl*), oven, furnace (hapleg., Ps 12:6[7]; # 6612).

OT 1. Job says he has thrust his brow in the dust, symbolic of the extremity of moral depression (Job 16:15, see Dhorme, *A Commentary on the Book of Job*, 1984, 238). On the ritual of mourning, see D. J. A. Clines, *Job 1-20*, WBC, 1989, 385-86).

2. Since *'[a]lîl* occurs only in Ps 12:6[7], its meaning is determined by the LXX rendering, *dokimion* (oven, crucible). However, Kraus suggested this word was part of an unintelligible marginal phrase incorporated into the text later and had to do with the procedure in the process of smelting (Hans-Joachim Kraus, *Psalms 1-59: A Commentary*, 1988, 207).

Furnace, fireplace, forge, oven, stove: → *'aḥ* (brazier, firepot, # 279); → *kibšān* (furnace, forge, # 3901); → *kûr* (forge, # 3929); → *kîr* (small stove, # 3968); → *m[e]bašš[e]lôt* (fireplaces, # 4453); → *môqēd* (fireplace, # 4611); → *'[a]lîl* (clay furnace, # 6612); → *tannûr* (oven, furnace, # 9486)
Thrust: → *dḥh* (push, overthrow, be cast down, # 1890); → *ngḥ* (gore, push, thrust, # 5590); → *tq'* (drive, thrust, clap one's hands, blow trumpet, pledge, # 9546)

Bill T. Arnold

6622 (*'ôlēlôt*, gleanings), → # 6618

6623	עלם

עלם (*'lm*), q. hidden things, secrets; ni. be hidden; hi. hide; hitp. hide o.s. (# 6623); nom. תַּעֲלֻמָה(*ta'[a]lumâ*), something hidden, secret (# 9502). The root occurs 28x in the OT, most often in the hi. and ni. stems (pass. part. only in q., Ps 90:8).

ANE The Heb. *'lm* has no clear cognates. It is uncertain whether the initial consonant of the root was originally *ayin* or *ghayin*. The primary meaning of the root *'lm* is to hide, conceal, or be hidden. Some now connect the Heb. *'lm* with the Ugar. *ġlm* and Arab *ẓlm*, to be dark (see the discussion and bibliography in Pope, *Job*, AB 15, 53-54). *HALAT* makes a distinction between *'lm* I, hide, and *'lm* II, be dark. The exegete must determine whether the use of *'lm* in a given text should be equated with the meaning "to cover, hide" or "be darkened" (see 5 below).

OT 1. The basic meaning "hidden" is applied to wisdom, either concealed from the living (Job 28:11) or made known to King Solomon (1 Kgs 10:3; 2 Chron 9:2). There was an episode in the life of Elisha when the Lord withheld knowledge from the prophet to encourage faith on the part of the Shunammite woman (2 Kgs 4:27). Clearly, there is nothing hidden from God (Ps 90:8), and he is free to reveal or conceal wisdom and knowledge according to his divine purposes.

2. The root *'lm* may refer to accidental or unintentional sin that has escaped the notice of the individual and/or community, such as unwitting sin committed by the whole congregation (Lev 4:13), ritual uncleanness (Lev 5:2-3), or even a rashly made vow (5:4; in each case the NIV and NRSV read "unaware"). By contrast, *'lm* also describes deliberate sin which the perpetrator attempts to hide or conceal (e.g., Num 5:13; Ps 90:8). In either case, God will judge every secret deed (*kol-ne'lām*) according to standards of good and evil (Eccl 12:14).

3. On occasion the righteous, when assailed by the wicked, perceive that God has hidden himself from them and their plight (Ps 10:1; 55:1[2]; Lam 3:56). Of course, this divine concealment is only apparent and temporary, as the righteous always affirm God's responsive presence in situations of need (cf. Ps 55:16-23). However, Isaiah acknowledged God indeed hides his face from those who worship with only the pretense of religiosity (Isa 1:15) (→ *str,* hide, keep secret [# 6259]).

4. *'lm* is rendered "ignore" (NIV, NRSV) in contexts of covenant obligation, whether the mundane (like retrieving stray animals of a neighbor, Deut 22:1, 3, 4), or the sacrosanct (like aiding the socially disadvantaged, 1 Sam 12:3; Isa 58:7; or even opposing abominations like human sacrifice, Lev 20:4).

5. In two instances the root *'lm* presents translation difficulties. The hitp. *yit'allēm*, hides itself, is awkward in Job 6:16. D. J. A. Clines (*Job* 1-20, WBC 17, 1989, 160) and J. Hartley (*Job*, NICOT, 1988, 136) read *'rm* for *'lm,* claiming intentional alliteration (with the liquids *l* and *m*) and translate "swollen by snow" (so NIV; cf. P. W. Skehan, "Second Thoughts on Job 6:16 and 6:25," *CBQ* 31, 1969, 210-12). Pope reads *'lm* but connects it with the meaning "to be dark" (hence, "darkened with snow"; *Job*, AB 15, 1980, 53; so NRSV). The synonymous parallelism of the poetry would suggest "turbid" or "darkened" is the more likely understanding.

6. Both the NIV and NRSV read the ni. part. *na'ᵃlāmîm* as "hypocrites" in Ps 26:4 (cf. Dahood, *Psalms 1-50*, AB 16, 1965, 162; he renders "benighted" or darkened morally and intellectually). Literally the term suggests those who hide themselves, their thoughts, motives, and activities, just as deceitful men (26:4a), evildoers (26:5a), and the wicked (26:5b) are inclined to do.

7. The nom. *ta'ᵃlumâ* occurs only 3x in the OT. As with *kḥd* (e.g., Ps 69:5[6]), the psalmist acknowledged the omniscience of God who knows the secrets of the heart (44:21[22]). Dahood translated "dark corners of the heart" on the basis of Job 28:11. Either way the term has pejorative connotations, suggesting sins of commission and omission. Zophar equates the *ta'ᵃlumô*t of wisdom with knowledge exclusively the property of God. Theologically, he showcases the tension between the mercy and justice of God as it is played out in the human experience (Job 11:6). In 28:11 the word refers to subterranean mysteries made known as a result of mining technologies (including precious stones and geological features).

NT → *NIDNTT* 2:211-20; 3:553-56.

Hiding: → *ḥb'* (hide, conceal, # 2461); → *ḥbh* (hide, # 2464); → *ḥāgû* (refuge, cleft, # 2511); → *ḥpp* I (screen, shelter, # 2910); → *ṭmn* (hide, # 3243); → *kḥd* (be hidden, hide, # 3948); → *knp* (hide oneself, # 4052); → *sōk* (hiding-place, shelter, thicket, hut, # 6108); → *str* (hide, kept secret, # 6259); → *'lm* (hidden things, secrets, # 6623); → *ṣpn* (hide, # 7621); → *śpn* (conceal, # 8561)

Bibliography

ISBE 2:705-7; *THAT* 2:575-81; *TWOT* 2:671-72; S. E. Balentine, "A Description of the Semantic Field of Hebrew Words for Hide," *VT* 30, 1980, 137-53; R. Gordis, "Studies in Hebrew Roots of Contrasted Meanings," *JQR* 27, 1936-37, 33-58; J. A. Thompson, "The Root '-l-m in Semitic Languages and Some Proposed New Translations in Ugaritic and Hebrew," in *A Tribute to Arthur Voobus: Studies in Early Christian Literature and Its Environment, Primarily in the Syrian East*, R. H. Fischer, ed., 1977; R. F. Youngblood, "Qoheleth's 'Dark House' (Eccl 12:5)," *JETS* 29, 1986, 397-410.

Andrew E. Hill

6624 (*'elem*, young man), → # 6596

6625 (*'almâ*, young woman), → # 6596

6632	עלס

עלס (*'ls*), q. enjoy, appear glad, enjoy o.s. (# 6632).

ANE Arab. *'ls* , to eat and drink, to give to eat. Although certain lexical works (BDB, 763; Zorell, 603) treat all three OT uses under a single root, others posit the existence of *'ls* II (*HALAT*, 791; *TWAT* 6:128). Guillaume ("Lexicography," 29-30) suggested that *'ls* I derives from Arab. *'alasa* and means to enjoy, delight in (Job 20:18; Prov 7:18), while *'ls* II stems from Arab. *'aliza* and means to be restless (Job 39:13) (cf. Guillaume, "Arabic Background," 125; Clines, 475). Although *'ls* II may exist, Job 39:13 does not require a meaning different from rejoice to make sense in the present context. Without a compelling contextual reason for suggesting homonymy, one must remain cautious with regard to homonyms suggested by philological studies (note Barr's [135-55, esp. 154-55] cautions about the growing number of suggested homonyms; cf. Payne, 50-51, 64-65).

OT This vb. occurs only 3x (Job 20:18; 39:13; Prov 7:18) and connotes enthusiastic celebration. In his rebuke of Job, Zophar affirms that the wicked will not endure and, consequently, they will not be able to enjoy the fruit of their labor (Job 20:18; cf. Eccl 2:18-23). Yahweh uses the ostrich to confront Job with the surpassing nature of his wisdom. Just as Job did not understand the divine rationale for his affliction, the ostrich is an unlikely part of God's handiwork. This bird can flap its wings with joyful enthusiasm (*'ls*, Job 39:18) but not fly, leave her eggs exposed to various dangers, and treat her young harshly; and yet the ostrich is still part of God's creation. Finally, in Prov 7:18 the prostitute invites her potential victim to "enjoy ourselves (*'ls*) with love."

Happiness, joy, rejoicing: → *'šr* II (be fortunate, # 887); → *blg* (be cheerful, happy, # 1158); → *gad* II (luck, fortune, # 1513); → *gyl* (exult, # 1635); → *ḥdh* (gladden, rejoice, make happy, # 2525); → *'lz* (exult, # 6600); → *'ls* (enjoy, appear glad, # 6632); → *'lṣ* (rejoice, # 6636); → *śwś* (rejoice, # 8464); → *śmḥ* (rejoice, make glad, # 8523)

BIBLIOGRAPHY

TWAT 6:126-31; J. Barr, *Comparative Philology and the Text of the Old Testament*, 1987; D. Clines, *Job 1-20*, 1989; A. Guillaume, "The Arabic Background of the Book of Job," *Promise and Fulfillment*, 1963, 106-27; idem, "Hebrew and Arabic Lexicography: A Comparative Study," *Abr-Nahrain* 1, 1959-60, 3-35; D. Payne, "Old Testament Exegesis and the Problem of Ambiguity," *ASTI* 5, 1966-67, 46-68.

Michael A. Grisanti

6634	עלף

עלף (*'lp*), pu., hitp. cover, faint (# 6634).

ANE Arab. *ġlf* II, cover, veil.

OT The vb. *'lp* occurs only in the pu. and hitp. forms with the sense of either cover or faint. The wide range in meaning raises the question of two roots: *'lp* I, cover; *'lp* II, faint; *HALAT* only lists one root.

1. Those vv. best rendered as "cover" include S of Songs 5:14, a description of the lover with arms of gold and a body of polished ivory decorated (the pu.) with sapphires. The hitp. of *'lp* in Gen 38:14, describes Tamar's action of veiling herself, either in the fashion of a prostitute or simply as a disguise.

2. Those passages best suited to the translation "faint" are the pu. form found in Isa 51:20, which speaks of young people who, like trapped antelope, lie exhausted at the head (dead ends or cul de sacs) of every street. In similar vein, Amos 8:13 speaks of the Day of the Lord, when the young people will faint (hitp.) because of thirst. Both prophets use the image of exhausted youth to underline the devastation and horror of the punishment unleashed by God. The theological contribution of *'lp* is best located within these passages, serving to underline, in the graphic tragedy of youth destroyed, the dark side of the Day of the Lord.

In the prophetic parable of the great tree, aimed against the pharaoh of Egypt (Ezek 31), v. 15 is best vocalized as the pu. (so *HALAT*), describing the king's fall and the accompanying mourning, which included even the trees of Lebanon (NIV the trees of the field fainted for him). The poetic sense is that of trees that adopt an attitude of mourning, perhaps bowed down and stripped of their leaves. Zimmerli (152) points out the connection elsewhere between withering and mourning in Isa 24:7 and Jer 14:2. Finally, in Jon 4:8 the heat of the sun causes Jonah to feel faint and in the midst of his despair to wish for death.

Covering, guard, shield: → *ḥph* (cover, sheath, overlay, panel, # 2902); → *ksh* (cover, conceal, cover, put on, clothe, # 4059); → *lwṭ* (cover, enfold, wrap, # 4286); → *skk* I (cover, guard, overshadow, protect, # 6114); → *spn* (cover, roof, panel, # 6211); → *'lp* (cover, faint, # 6634)

Feeble, despair, faint, frail, tender: → *'ml* I (be weak, be feeble, languish, # 581); → *ḥlh* I (become weak, tired, ill, # 2703); → *ylh* (languish, # 3532); → *k'h* (be disheartened, frightened, # 3874); → *nbl* I (wither, fade, languish, dishonor, # 5570); → *'tp* II (grow weak, faint, be feeble, # 6494); → *'lp* (cover, faint, # 6634); → *'šš* (become weak, # 6949); → *pwg* (be feeble, numb, be prostrated, # 7028); → *rzh* (destroy, waste away, # 8135); → *rkk* (be tender, timid, gentle, # 8216); → *rph* (become slack, lose heart, discourage, # 8332)

W. R. Domeris

6636	עלץ

עלץ (*'lṣ*), q. to rejoice, gloat (# 6636); עֲלִיצוּת (*'ᵃlîṣût*), nom. exultation, gloating (# 6617).

ANE Middle Heb. *'ls* (hapleg., Erub 53ᵇ), to rejoice; Ugar. *'ls*, to rejoice; OSA *m'ls*, rejoicing; Akk. *elēṣu*, to swell, to rejoice. For the relationship of *'ls* and *'lz*, see *'lz* (# 6600).

OT 1. The vb. *'ls* occurs 4x in Ps (5:11[12]; 9:2[3]; 25:2; 68:3[4]), twice in Prov (11:10; 28:12), and once in Sam (1 Sam 2:1) and Chron (1 Chron 16:32). The juxtaposition of *'ls* with several cognates (*śmḥ*—1 Sam 2:1; Ps 5:11[12]; 9:2[3]; 68:3[4]; *rnn/rnh*—Ps 5:11[12]; 1 Chron 16:32-33; Prov 11:10; *zmr*—Ps 9:2[3]; *śwś*—Ps 68:3[4]) evidences the expressive nature of this root.

As Millard (88) points out, every occurrence of the vb. "has a context of victory, a victory won or to be won by God, giving His people cause and liberty to 'rejoice'." Along with Hannah who celebrates her God-given triumph over childlessness (1 Sam 2:1), nature celebrates Yahweh's rulership (1 Chron 16:32 = Ps 96:12, *'lz*). Those who have Yahweh's name rejoice in his protection (Ps 5:11[12]) while the psalmist (9:2[3]) and the righteous (68:3[4]) revel in God's character.

As with several cognate vbs., *'ls* signifies malicious joy of gloating from which the psalmist pleads for deliverance (Ps 25:2). In the two instances of *'ls* in Prov (11:10; 28:12), the entire community triumphantly celebrates when persons loyal and faithful to God enjoy victory over the forces of evil (Hubbard, 441).

2. The hapleg., *'ᵃlîṣût*, occurs in Hab 3:14, a text which Hiebert (43) describes as "the lengthiest textual puzzle of the chapter." Some scholars do not even offer a translation for the last half of this verse (e.g., Hiebert, 8-9; Albright, 13, 17, n. ww). If the MT is accepted (or some form of *'ls* is retained, cf. Haak, 28, 100-102, O'Connor, 238), *'ᵃlîṣût* depicts the malicious joy of the enemies of God's people who revel in the pursuit and destruction of the humble and poor (Patterson, 246), possibly alluding to the Egyp. pursuit of the children of Israel as a pattern for Gentile attacks.

Happiness, joy, rejoicing: → *'šr* II (be fortunate, # 887); → *blg* (be cheerful, happy, # 1158); → *gad* II (luck, fortune, # 1513); → *gyl* (exult, # 1635); → *ḥdh* (gladden, rejoice, make happy, # 2525); → *'lz* (exult, # 6600); → *'ls* (enjoy, appear glad, # 6632); → *'lṣ* (rejoice, # 6636); → *śwś* (rejoice, # 8464); → *śmḥ* (rejoice, make glad, # 8523)

Bibliography

TWAT 6:126-31; *TWOT* 2:673; W. Albright, "The Psalm of Habakkuk," *Studies in Old Testament Prophecy*, 1950, 1-18; R. Haak, *Habakkuk*, SVT, 44, 1992; T Heibert, *God of My Victory: The Ancient Hymn in Habakkuk 3*, 1986; D Hubbard, *Proverbs*, 1989; A Millard, "עלץ 'To Exult'," *JTS* 26, 1975, 87-89; M. O'Connor, *Hebrew Verse Structure*, 1980; R. Patterson, *Nahum, Habakkuk, Zephaniah*, 1991.

Michael A. Grisanti

6638	עַם

עַם (*'am* I), sing.: populace-member, citizen; kinsman, relative; collective: populace, people; kin (32x; # 6638; *HALAT* 792aB.).

ANE Cognates include Akk. *ummānu(m)* (*AHw* 3:1413-14), Ugar. *'m*, clan, kin (?) (*WUS* # 2042; *UT* # 1864; *KTU* 1, 17 i 27[?]); Syr. *'ammā'*, sing.: plebeian; pagan; collective: populace; and Arab. *'amm*, paternal uncle, relative.

At least two separate lexical derivations have been proposed for Semitic *'am*(*m*), corresponding to the singular (citizen; kinsman) and collective (people; kin) in BH. However, early and widespread attestation of the use of *'am*(*m*) in both senses—e.g., in Amorite, Phoenician, South and North Arabic—makes it "possible to conclude that we are dealing with a single noun and not two separate words" (Good, 141).

OT 1. Both the singular and collective uses of Heb. *'am* may be found either with or without kinship connotations, and there is reason to doubt that the idea of kinship forms the basis of the noun's semantic history (Good, 63). Collective uses of *'am*, such as those in Gen 14:16; Ps 95:7; 100:3; Prov 30:24-26; Isa 65:10; Mic 7:14; Nah 3:18; Zech 9:16, indicate that the basic sense of the collective may be closer to colony, flock, or populace, identifying a common group, than to people or kin, as comprising either humans or consanguineous relations, respectively. Concomitantly, the singular use of the term may designate a member of a common group or populace, be it a kinship group or not. Indeed, kinship connotations are entirely lacking from some singular uses. Yahweh is portrayed as using *'ammî* to refer to a single individual, "one of my people," in apposition to *'et-he'onî 'immāk*, "the poor one with you" (Exod 22:25[24]). In this instance, the term indicates group membership apart from supposed kinship ties. The parallelism of the pl. *'ammîm* with *'amît*, (individual) citizen, *rēa'*, companion, *'aḥ*, brother, fellow, and *b^enê 'ammeykā*, descendants of your people, indicates that *'ammîm* is virtually synonymous with *b^enê 'ammeykā* in designating (fellow) populace-members or (fellow) citizens (Lev 19:16-18). (→ Nation, People: Theology)

2. Whereas the basic sense of Heb. *'am* may be devoid of kinship connotations, there are contexts in which it refers to kinship groups or members of kinship groups and may therefore coincidentally connote kinship identity. Gen 19:38 offers an exquisite example of the use of *'am* in paronomastic mockery of Ammonite ancestry. Although Lot's younger daughter euphemistically names her son, whom she had conceived by her father, *ben-'ammî*, son of my kin, yet the name may be satirically construed as "son of my kinsman," obliquely designating her father the progenitor. Through paronomasia, this "son of incest" turns out to be "the father of the sons of Ammon" (*'^abî b^enê-'ammôn*). Note, in Gen 19:37, a parallel paronomastic satire on *mô'āb*, eponymous ancestor of the Moabites; consonantal *m'b* connotes *mē'āb*, by/from father (LXX *ek tou patros mou* [Gen 19:37]; cf. 19:36 *mē'^abîhem*, by/from their father). Elsewhere, when Jeremiah ventured to return from Jerusalem to Benjamin (i.e., to Anathoth; cf. 1:1) to claim from there his portion among *hā'ām*, it appears that he was in fact seeking his patrimony among his kinsfolk (Jer 37:12; cf. 32:6-12; Ruth 3:11).

3. Although, when Heb. *'am* is used to designate kinship groups, it may bear kinship connotations, it nowhere clearly signifies paternal kinship *per se* (contra "[väterliche] Verwandtschaft," *HALAT* 792a). In Ruth's declaration of kinship loyalty to Naomi (*'ammēk 'ammî*, your kin [shall be] my kin, Ruth 1:16), Ruth reckons herself to be a kin-member with Naomi despite the fact that her marital kinship ties with Naomi are severed and there is no hope that such ties will ever be restored. That the

group designation *'am* may be applied to paternally-determined kinship groups is probably only accidental.

4. The suffixed pl. const. form of *'am* appears in the idiom *nikr^{e}tâ* (*hannepeš hahî'*) *mē'ammêhā* (Gen 17:14; Exod 31:14 [*miqqereb 'ammêyhā*]; Lev 7:20, 21, 25, 27; 19:8; 23:29; Num 9:13) and *nikrat* (*hā'îš hahû'*) *mē'ammāyw* (Exod 30:33, 38; Lev 17:9) "be cut off ... from its/his relatives," which serves as a euphemism for "be killed." In this idiom, *'ammîm* refers exclusively to one's living relatives. Perhaps Ezek 18:18 alludes to this idiom when it affirms that a "father will die for his own sin, because he ... did what was wrong among his people (*b^{e}tôk 'ammâw*)." In all probability, the preceding idiom complements the idiom *yē'āsēp 'el-'ammâw*, be gathered to his relatives (Gen 25:8, 17; 35:29; Num 20:24; 27:13; 31:2), in which the suffixed pl. const. of *'am* refers exclusively to one's deceased relatives (viewed as incorporeal beings). That the latter idiomatic euphemism for "to die" should not be construed as referring to burial in the family tomb may be discerned from its use in Gen 49:29 [read *'ammay*], 33 and Deut 32:50. In only one passage does the suffixed pl. const. of *'am* refer to the corpses of deceased relatives, by contact with which a priest would become defiled (Lev 21:1, 4, 14-15). The priestly prohibition pertains only to more distant *'ammîm*, relatives. Touching deceased members of his close family subgroup, comprising mother, father, son, daughter, brother and unmarried sister, would not defile the priest.

Family, relative, citizen: → *'āb* (father, # 3); → *'aḥ* II (brother, kinsman, relative, countryman, # 278); → *'ēm* (mother, # 562); → *bēn* I (son, grandson, member of a group, # 1201); → *bat* I (daughter, granddaughter, # 1426); → *dôd* (uncle, # 1856); → *ḥām* I (father-in-law, # 2767); → *ḥtn* (become intermarried, become a son-in-law, # 3161); → *mōdā'* (kinsman, relative, # 4530); → *mišpāḥâ* (clan, kind, # 5476); → *'am* I (citizen, kinsman, relative, # 6638); → *ribbēa'* (member of fourth generation, # 8067); → *šillēš* (member of sixth generation, # 9000)

Bibliography

B. Alfrink, "L'expression *ne'^{e}sap 'el-'ammāyw*," *OTS* 5, 1948, 118-31; F. I. Anderson, "Israelite Kinship Terminology," *BT* 20, 1969, 29-39; D. I. Block, "The Foundations of National Identity: A Study in Ancient Northwest Semitic Perceptions," diss., Liverpool, 1982; H. Brichto, "Kin, Cult, Land and Afterlife—A Biblical Complex," *HUCA* 44, 1973, 1-54; M. D. Goldman, "Concerning the Meaning of *'am*," *AusBR* 3, 1953, 51; R. M. Good, *The Sheep of His Pasture: A Study of the Hebrew Noun 'Am(m) and Its Semitic Cognates*, HSM 29, 1983; N. K. Gottwald, *Tribes of Yahweh*, 1979, 235-341; G. B. Gray, "*'ammi*," in *Encyclopaedia Biblica*, 1, 1899, 138-40; A. R. Hulst, *THAT* 2, cols. 290-325; Th. W. Juynboll, "Über die Bedeutung des Wortes *'amm*," in *Orientalische Studien Theodor Nöldeke*, ed., C. Bezold, 1906, 1:353-56; M. A. Klopfenstein, "Alttestamentliche Themen in der neueren Forschung," *TRu* 53, 1988, 331-53, on Heb. *'am(m)* (345-47); L. Köhler, "Der Name Ammoniter," *TZ* 1, 1945, 154-56; M. Krenkel, "Das Verwandtschaftswort *'am*," *ZAW* 8, 1888, 280-84; E. Lipiński, *TWAT* 6, cols. 177-94; L. B. Paton, "*'Amm, 'Ammi*," in *Hastings Encyclopaedia of Religion and Ethics*, 1925, 1:386-89; J. Pedersen, *ILC*, 1-2, 54-57, 59; L. Rost, "Die Bezeichnungen für Land und Volk im AT," in *Festschrift Otto Procksch*, 1934, 125-48 (repr. in *Das kleine Credo und andere Studien zum AT*, 1965, 76-101); E. A. Speiser, "'People' and 'Nation' of Israel," *JBL* 79, 1960, 157-63 (repr. in *Oriental and Biblical Studies*, eds., J. J. Finkelstein and M. Greenberg, 1967, 160-70); J. J. Stamm, "Zum Ursprung des Namens der Ammoniter," *Archiv orientální* 17, 1948, 379-82; H. Tadmor, "'The People' and the Kingship in Ancient Israel: The Role of Political Institutions in the Biblical Period," in *Jewish Society Through the Ages*, ed. H. H. Ben-Sasson and S. Ettinger, 1971, 46-68; C. C. Torrey, "'*amm*," in *JE*, 1901, 1:521; H. M. Weil, "'*Ammî* 'compatriote, consanguin,'" *Revue des études sémitiques et babyloniaca*, 1941-45, 87-88; C. U. Wolf, "Terminology of Israel's Tribal Organization," *JBL* 65, 1946, 45-49.

Robert H. O'Connell

6639 (*'am* II, people, peoples, citizens), → Nations

6641	עמד

עמד (*'md*), q. stand, take one's stand, stand still, stay; hi. set up, station, appoint, restore; ho. be presented, be set upright (# 6641); מַעֲמָד (*ma'ᵃmād*), nom. post, station, position (# 5096); מָעֳמָד (*mo'ᵒmād)*, nom. firm ground, foothold (# 5097); עֹמֶד (*'ōmed*), nom. positions, place to stand (# 6642); עִמָּד (*'immād*), with (# 6643); עֶמְדָה (*'emdâ*), nom. protection (# 6644); עַמּוּד (*'ammûd*), nom. tent pole, post, pillar, column (# 6647).

ANE The Akk. *emēdu*, lean against, lay upon; and the Arab. *'amada*, support/intend, share a general range of meaning with the Heb. *'md*.

OT 1. Among the non-theological nuances of *'md* one may list to stand to one's feet (Neh 8:5; Esth 7:7), to stand at the ready, prepared to serve one's master (1 Sam 16:22), and to remain or stay (Ruth 2:7). The vb. is evenly distributed throughout the OT (525x). Theologically, when viewed in terms of genre, certain nuances attach more often to *'md* in prose material; other nuances predominate in poetic material.

2. A common theological motif associated with *'md* in prose material is that of being in the presence of God. Just as one enters the presence of a human dignitary (e.g., Moses before Pharaoh, Exod 9:10; cf. Num 27:2), so individuals "stand" self-consciously in the presence of God (e.g., Abraham, Gen 18:22; 19:27; cf. Moses, Deut 10:8, 10). Aaron, along with priests and elders, present themselves (q. *'md*) before the Lord (Lev 9:5). The corporate group too, Israel or all Judah, stands (i.e., presents itself) before Yahweh to worship and/or to receive instruction (Deut 4:10; 2 Chron 20:13).

3. A more technical, somewhat idiomatic use of the vb. *'md* relates to government, especially royalty, before whom persons "stand" as messengers or ministers, prepared to take directives (Dan 1:4). As for God, King over all, he can deploy prophets, priests, and others who stand before Yahweh as his messengers. True prophets, for example, are privy to the decisions made in the divine council where they stand (*'md*) (Jer 23:18, 22; cf. 18:20). Elijah introduces himself as the prophet of Yahweh, "before whom I stand" (1 Kgs 17:1; 18:15). God raises up prophets to serve him ("stand before him," Deut 18:5, 7; cf. Jer 15:1). Priests, Levites especially, are acknowledged ministers before the Lord (Deut 10:8; 18:7; Zech 3:1; cf. 2 Chron 29:11) who "perform their service" (*'md*) (1 Kgs 8:11 NIV; cf. Ps 134:1; 135:2). In the heavenly court, hosts are at God's right and left hand (2 Chron 18:18). To be in God's service is a high honor.

4. Court language employs *'md*. The parties stand (*'md*) before the judge (Deut 19:17; 1 Kgs 3:16). God takes his position at the right hand of the needy to safeguard justice (Ps 109:31).

5. In poetic material *'md* in the sense of "endure" is noticeable. God's plans "stand firm" (*'md*) (Ps 33:11). His righteousness and his praise "endure" (*'md*) forever (Ps 111:3, 10 KJV). Indeed, God himself endures (*'md*) (Ps 102:26[27]), as does the

fear of the Lord (Ps 19:9[10]). Wickedness will not endure. The Babylonian warriors, for example, will not stand (*'md*), for the Lord will push them down (Jer 46:15; cf. Mal 3:2).

6. Poetic descriptions of theophany tell of God's coming (cf. *qwm* [→ # 7756]), but also of his standing (Ezek 3:23; 10:18; 11:23). Habakkuk portrays God as standing (*'md*) and surveying the earth (Hab 3:6). In the eschatological battle God will appear and plant his feet (*'md*) on the Mount of Olives (Zech 14:4).

7. In narrative material the hi. form of *'md* in the sense of appoint is used of administrative actions by officials (e.g., singers, 2 Chron 20:21). In poetic material the subject of the hi. *'md* is invariably God. God appoints or establishes his devotee upon the high places (Ps 18:33[34]; cf. 30:7[8]; 31:8[9]). He has made to stand (hi. *'md*) his covenant with Jacob (105:10) and more fundamentally the sun, moon, and stars (148:6). God is an agent who puts things and people in place and does so with firmness.

8. *ma'ᵃmād* as "post" or "station" in its five occurrences is nontheological (e.g., places, 2 Chron 35:15), except for its use by Isaiah in a judgment oracle on Shebna, the steward, whom God will depose from office (*ma'ᵃmād*) (Isa 22:19).

9. *mo'ᵒmād* in its single occurrence is rendered as "foothold" (Ps 69:2[3]) in the context of a lament.

10. *'ōmed* as a place where one stands designates the location of king (2 Chron 34:31), priests, and people (2 Chron 35:10; Neh 8:7). In two instances in Daniel an angel is involved in "making Daniel stand on his standing" (lit., Dan 8:18; 10:11).

11. *'emdâ* occurs only once (Mic 1:11), in the sense of standing place (*HALAT* 797).

12. *'ammûd* designates pillar or column, often in conjunction with tabernacle or temple (e.g., Exod 27:10; 1 Kgs 7:2). (a) Two of the temple pillars that were elaborately decorated stood twenty-seven feet in height and were named Boaz and Jakin (1 Kgs 7:21). Their names probably mean, respectively, "in him is strength" and "he establishes." Their significance may be "as proprietary emblems, claiming the temple for Yahweh" (S. DeVries, *1 Kings*, 1985, 112). (b) A permanent cloud column (*'ammûd*, # 6647) served Israel in the wilderness to guide, illumine, and, when necessary, shade them (Exod 13:21-22).

P-B The QL has discourses about standing (e.g., standing fast (*'md*) with God). Among other claims, it asserts that "those who measure up to thy demands will stand (*'md*) before thee forever" (1QH4:21) (→ preliminary discussion in *TDNT* 7:645; cf. *NIDNTT* 3:224; W. Grundmann, "Stehen und Fallen im qumranischen und ntl. Schrifttum," in *Qumran Probleme*, 1963, 147-66).

Pillar, knob: → *kaptôr* II (knob, capital [of pillar], # 4117); → *māṣûq* (pillar, # 5187); → *nṣb* I (stand, # 5893); → *'md* (stand, # 6641)

Stand, station: → *yṣb* (stand, take stand, # 3656); → *kwn* (stand firm, stand fast, be durable, prepare, establish, # 3922); → *nṣb* I (stand, station oneself, stand firm, # 5893); → *'md* (stand, take one's stand, station, appoint, # 6641); → *qwm* (stand up, stand upright, arise, perform, # 7756)

BIBLIOGRAPHY
TDNT 7:638-46; *THAT* 2:328-31; *TWOT* 2:673-75; G. Yishaq, "'*md*, endure," *BethM* 32, 1986/87, 383-86 (Heb.).

Elmer A. Martens

6642 (*'ōmed*, positions, place to stand), → # 6641

6643 (*'immād*, with), → # 6641

6644 (*'emdâ*, protection), → # 6641

6647 (*'ammûd*, tent pole, post, pillar, column), → # 6641

6648 (*'ammôn*, Ammon), → Ammon

6660	עָמִית

עָמִית (*'āmît*), nom. citizen, community member (# 6660).

ANE Arab. *'āmmat*, nation; ESA *'mt*, community; Aram. *'ămîtā'*, people; Akk. *emūtu*, family of the husband, house of the bride's family; Mish. Heb. *'āmît*. Punic has the expression *'mt 'š'štrt* ("the community/associates of Ashtarte") (*DISO*, 217; Tomback, 251).

OT 1. The nom. *'āmît* occurs 12x in BH, 11x in Leviticus. There the referent is someone who is a member of the Israelite community (Levine, 172), and the term is synonymous with *rēa'* (*THAT* 2:299). Deception of (Lev 6:2[5:21]; 19:11), adultery with the wife of (18:20), partiality toward (19:15), acquiescence in evil with (19:17), harm of (24:19), and taking advantage of (25:14, 15, 17) one's *'āmît* are all forbidden. Of special interest is the condition of 6:2[5:21], which is presented in the context of the laws concerning the reparation offering. This offering provided for blatant sins of lying against and cheating one's fellow community member. That it goes on to deal with perjury in court, with false swearing before God, is even more surprising. This is distinct from the other instances where a reparation offering could be used. The others involve inadvertent sins (Wenham, 108-9).

2. The twelfth occurrence is found in Zech 13:7. There it appears in parallel with *geber*, man, and *rō'î*, my shepherd. The historical identification of the shepherd who is to be struck down is disputed. In part the issue depends on whether vv. 7-9 are connected with 11:17 or with 13:1-6. For a summary of views see Smith, 282-83. Jesus identified himself with this image in Matt 26:31 and Mark 14:27.

P-B The word *'āmît* appears in 1QS VI.26 to describe the figure who is insulted through the rash words of one of the community. It is used in parallel with *rēa'*.

Friend, companion, colleague, community member: → *'allûp* I (familiar, friend, # 476); → *ḥbr* II (unite, be joined, charm, make an alliance with, # 2489); → *k^enāt* (collaegue, # 4056); → *'āmît* (citizen, community member, # 6660); → *r'h* II (associate with, be best man, make friends with, # 8287)

Bibliography
B. Levine, *Leviticus: The Traditional Hebrew Text with the New JPS Translation, Commentary,* 1989; R. L. Smith, *Micah-Malachi,* WBC, 1984; R. Tomback, *A Comparative Semitic Lexicon of the Phoenician and Punic Languages,* 1978; G. Wenham, *The Book of Leviticus,* NICOT, 1979.

Richard S. Hess

6661	עמל

עמל (*'ml*), q. labor, toil (# 6661); עָמָל (*'āmāl*), nom. distress, trouble, toil, effort, misfortune (# 6662); עָמֵל (*'āmēl*), nom. laborer, sufferer (# 6665).

ANE The vb. is common in postbiblical Heb. and Jewish Aram., to labor, toil, appearing as well in Old Aram., Egyp. Aram., Palmyrene, Christian Palestinian Syr., Mand.; cf. Arab. *'amila*, exert oneself, struggle; Eth. *mā'bal*, tool, and Akk. *nēmelu*, gain possession.

OT 1. The vb. *'ml*, all q., denotes labor, often with an eye to its difficulty, its burdensome nature, hence toil. Thirteen of sixteen OT occurrences appear in Ecclesiastes, with the first entry setting the characteristic meaning and expression for its use. Eccl 1:3 describes the entire human enterprise as a laborious task, questioning its value. The characteristic expression is "all his labor at which he toils under the sun," with minor contextual variation in 1:3; 2:18, 19, 20, 22 (cf. 2:11); 5:18[17]; and 9:9. The expression joins *'ml* with its cognate nom. *'āmāl,* both denoting laborious toil (nom. meaning shifts slightly in 2:11, 18, 19; see below). LXX registers the burdensome nature of the effort with *mochtheō* and *mochthos* here. Beyond these set expressions, with only one exception, the vb. in Eccl carries the same meaning of burdensome toil: of the solitary worker's ceaseless toil (4:8), and of toil for nothing (5:16[15]). In 8:17 it seems not to have laborious life in view but humanity's indefatigable effort to comprehend the ways of God. In Eccl 2:11 *'āmal* describes the toil of producing something with one's own hands and of accomplishing tasks (cf. 2:18, 19, 21). The part. highlights the ongoing nature of the toil in Eccl 2:18, 22; 3:9; 4:8; 9:9.

2. Outside Eccl *'ml* also denotes labor, though with no particular attention to its difficulty. It alludes to the work Jonah did *not* invest to grow the plant he grieved (Jon 4:10), and it describes the efforts of house/palace builders (Ps 127:1[2]).

3. Functioning as a nom. the part. *'āmēl* (# 6664) reflects the range of meaning surveyed above. In Judg 5:26 *'āmēl* (pl.) is simply a workman, a worker, as in Prov 16:26. NASB renders this proverb's wordplay with the nom. part. and vb.: "A worker's appetite [*'āmēl*] works [*'ām^{e}lâ*] for him." Uses in Job seem to elevate the sense of burden and difficulty connoted by *'ml* sufficiently so as to warrant translating the nom. part. as one who suffers, one who is in misery. Thus Job, questioning the value of surviving birth at all, asks why God gives light to the sufferer, to the one who labors in misery (LXX *tois en pikriā* [Job 3:20]). Detailing the sad destiny of the wicked, Zophar claims either that "the full force of the *sufferer* [= MT *kol-yad-'āmēl*] will come to him," or, more likely, "the full force of *misery* will come upon him" [NIV, reading *'āmāl* with LXX, Vg.] (20:22).

4. The most common OT derivative of *'ml* (53x) is the nom. *'āmāl*, occurring predominantly in Eccl (22x), Job (8x), and Ps (13x). In Qohelet's lead question it

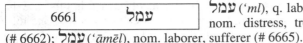

describes the whole life enterprise as a laborious task (Eccl 1:3). Elsewhere in Eccl it is difficult to discern whether *'āmāl* denotes life itself or the more restricted sense of the labor of earning and maintaining a livelihood. The more general meaning of laborious existence itself *may* surface again at 5:15 (from birth to death); 6:7 (driven by appetite); and 9:9. Ps 90:10 shares this estimate of life as essentially toil. *'āmāl* seems to denote man's work, his labor to support himself in Eccl 2:10, 20, 21, 22, 24; 3:13; 4:4, 6, 8, 9; 5:18[17]; 10:15.

5. *'āmāl* denotes not only the act but also the results of the act, in this case the product or fruit of labor. Thus *'āmāl* names the goods or wealth *for which* one toils (Eccl 2:11, 18), eventually passed to and controlled by another (2:19, 21). In 2:10 the word occurs twice, first naming the fruit of the Treacher's toil (accomplishment, NIV) and then the work that produced it. So also the psalmist claims that Israel inherited as God's gift what others had toiled to produce (Ps 105:44).

6. Like the vb. the nom. *'āmāl* can accent the difficulty and burden associated with toil. It then denotes trouble, misery, adversity. Used in this way, *'āmāl* describes the adversity that Manasseh's birth helped Joseph forget (Gen 41:51), Israel's slave labor in Egypt (Deut 26:7), and trouble at the hands of Israel's enemies (Judg 10:16; cf. Num 23:21). *'āmāl* names Jeremiah's difficult life of suffering and adversity (Jer 20:18); it is also used for Job's plight (Job 3:10; 7:3; 11:16). Prov 31:7 suggests drowning this sort of misery in strong drink. *'āmāl* names oppressive labor as the judgment of God (Ps 107:12) and trouble as the implied result of sin (‖ *'ºnî*, affliction, Ps 25:18). In Eliphaz' thought *'āmāl* springs from mischief/evil (Job 4:8; 5:6), though it can also describe more generally humanity's troubled life (5:7). In a moment of skewed perception the psalmist thought the wicked escaped this misery common to humans (Ps 73:5), and then used the same nom. to describe this prospect itself as a burden (73:16). Job insults his associates as a misery-producing lot (Job 16:2).

7. *'āmāl* can narrow to denote trouble associated with or caused by wickedness, or to name that wickedness itself. In several passages it is linked with *'āwen*, which also names both trouble and wickedness (Job 15:35; Ps 7:14[15]; 10:7; 55:10[11]; 90:10; Isa 10:1; 59:4; Hab 1:3; cf. with *'āwen* in Num 23:21 and Ps 90:10 above). Thus, according to Job 15:35, the godless conceive trouble and give birth to evil (similarly *māšāl* in Ps 7:14[15]; Isa 59:4). Ps 55:10[11] associates *'āmāl* with malice and abuse (Ps 7:16[17]). This trouble lies with wickedness under an evil person's tongue (10:7; cf. 140:9[10]), prompting a proverbial warning (Prov 24:2). *'āmāl* describes the behavior of the wicked (Ps 10:14) and the unjust treatment of innocents because of a corrupt throne (94:20; cf. v. 21). Similarly in the prophets, God denounces decrees that produce oppression (*'āmāl*, Isa 10:1). *'āmāl* figures in the kind of society of which Habakkuk complains (Hab 1:3) and which God cannot countenance (Hab 1:13, ‖ *rā'*, evil). This suffering, caused by evil, God's servant endures in Isa 53 (v. 11).

P-B Sir 11:11 coordinates parts. *'āmēl* and *yôgēa'*, describing a person who labors only to fall further behind. In 1QpHab 8:2 *'āmāl* names the adversity of the righteous (also 1QH 11:19 [10:32; 11:1 broken contexts]), and in 10:12 vain labor of the Wicked Priest. 1QS 9:22 coordinates *'āmāl*, fruit of the hands, with *hôn*, wealth. LXX's most common translation of *'āmal* (*mochtheō*) does not occur in the NT. Instead, *kopiaō*, to be weary (e.g., John 4:6), work hard, toil, struggle (e.g., Matt 6:28) and *kakopatheō*, suffer/bear hardship (e.g., 2 Tim 2:9) carry its themes forward. Noms. *'āmāl* and *'āmēl* find clearest NT expression in noms. *kopos, mochthos*, *ponos*, and *odynē*.

Labor, trouble, toil: → *ḥyl* I (be in labor, tremble, # 2655); → *yg'* (be tired, # 3333); → *l'h* I (become tired, # 4206); → *mas* (tribute, tax, forced labor, # 4988); → *sbl* (carry, bear a burden, # 6022); → *'bd* (work, serve, worship, # 6268); → *'ml* (labor, toil, # 6661); → *ṣārâ* I (misery, anguish, affliction, trouble, # 7650)

Bibliography

TWAT 6:214-19; R. Gordis, *Koheleth*, 1951, 418-20.

David Thompson

6662 (*'āmāl* I, distress, trouble, effort, misfortune), → # 6661

6665 (*'āmēl*, laborer, sufferer), → # 6661

6667 (*'ᵃmālēq*, Amalek), → Amalek

6670	עמם

עמם (*'mm*), darken, dim; match, be equal to; ho. be darkened (# 6670). KB still distinguishes two roots (*'mm* I, be like, match and *'mm* II, darken), but *HALAT* treats them together.

ANE This vb. is attested in Aram., *'ᵃmam,* grow dark, and Arab. *ġamma,* cover.

OT This vb. occurs 3x in the OT. In the q. stem it refers to a darkening of its object: thus, figuratively "the cedars . . . could not rival it" [NIV], lit. "could not darken it [with their shadow]" (Ezek 31:8); "Is no secret hidden from you?" [NIV], lit. "held dark" (Ezek 28:3). In the pu. stem it refers to "being darkened": thus, "How the gold has lost its luster" [NIV] (Lam 4:1). In Lam 4:1, D. R. Hillers (*Lamentations,* AB 78) proposed to emend *yû'ām* to *yû'ab*, be despised, so as to be in parallel with a second emendation, *yišne'* to *yiśśānê',* be hated. He justified the emendations by reasoning that gold does not lose its luster or become dull, and that all other references to gold are to its value rather that to its color or brightness. However, such an emendation is based purely on conjecture, not on textual evidence; so it must be rejected. It is true that literal gold retains its luster, but in a metaphor the figure may represent the unexpected. Proud, self-confident Jerusalem (the gold) had indeed lost its glory—it was in ruins.

P-B In RL the vb. is used often. The q. stem refers to a flame becoming dim or coals being quenched. The pu. stem has a similar nuance, and the pilpel stem means to cover up, as to suppress a case in court or to disregard the law.

Darkness: → *'ōpel* (darkness, gloom, # 694); → *'ᵉšûn* (approach of darkness, # 854); → *ḥšk* (be, grow dark, grow dim, darken, conceal, confuse, # 3124); → *ṭuḥôt* (darkness, obscurity, inward parts, # 3219); → *kamrîr* (blackness, deep gloom, # 4025); → *laylâ* (night, # 4326); → *nešep* (twilight, darkness, # 5974); → *'wp* II (be dark, # 6415); → *'ᵃlāṭâ* (darkness, dusk, # 6602); → *'mm* II (darken, dim, # 6670); → *'ᵃrāpel* (deep darkness, thick darkness, heavy cloud, # 6906); → *ṣll* III (be/grow dark, cast a shadow, # 7511); → *ṣalmāwet* (darkness, shadow of death, # 7516); → *qdr* (be dark, mourn, # 7722)

Bibliography

G. A. Cooke, *Ezekiel*, ICC, 315.

James D. Price

6673	עמש/עמס

עמש/עמס (*'mś/'ms*), q. carry a burden, load; hi. place a load (on) (# 6673); מַעֲמָסָה (*ma'amāśâ*), nom. load (# 5098).

OT 1. Pack animals (Gen 44:13; Neh 13:15) were not the only beasts of burden in ancient times. Human beings were often forced to carry their share (Neh 4:17[11]: "those who carried materials [*hannōśe'îm bassēbel 'ōmesîm*]") at the very least (→ *sbl*, # 6022). Especially striking is the contrast between images of false gods that have to be carried about and are therefore "burdensome" (*'amûsôt*, Isa 46:1) on the one hand and the one true God who carries his people—people who have been "upheld" (*'amūsîm*, 46:3) by him since they were conceived—on the other. In addition, he is the God who "bears our burdens" (Ps 68:19[20]). How unlike Rehoboam, who was determined to lay on his people a heavier yoke than his father Solomon had imposed on them (1 Kgs 12:11 = 2 Chron 10:11)!

2. The nom. *ma'amāśâ*, load, is a hapleg., used to describe Jerusalem metaphorically as "an immovable rock (*'eben ma'amāśâ*)" that would defy the efforts of "all who try to move it (*kol-'ōmesêhā*)" (Zech 12:3).

Burden, load, weight: → *'amtaḥat* (sack, bag, burden, pack, # 623); → *ṭ'n* II (load, # 3250); → *ṭrḥ* (burden, load, # 3267); → *yehāb* (burden, anxious care, # 3365); → *kin'â* (bundle, burden, # 4045); → *maśśā'* I (carrying, burden # 5362); → *nṭl* (bear, weigh, # 5747); → *nś'* (lift, raise high, pardon, contain, bear, exalt o.s., # 5951); → *sbl* (carry, bear a burden, # 6022); → *'ms/'mś* (carry a burden, load, # 6673)

Ronald F. Youngblood

6676	עמק

עמק (*'mq* I), q. be deep, mysterious; hi. make deep (# 6676); מַעֲמַקִּים (*ma'amaqqîm*), nom. depths (# 5099); עֵמֶק (*'ēmeq* I), valley (→ # 6677), עָמֹק (*'āmōq*), adj. deep, deeper, impenetrable, mysterious (# 6678); עֹמֶק (*'ōmeq*), nom. depth (# 6679); עָמֵק (*'āmēq*), nom. obscure, unintelligible (# 6680).

ANE There are cognates in Akk. and Aram. Note Aram. *'ammîq* (adj.), deep, inscrutable things (# 10555).

OT 1. The only occurrence of *'mq* in the q. describes the profound nature of Yahweh's thoughts, "How great are your works, O LORD, how profound your thoughts!" (Ps 92:5[6]).

2. The hi. form of the vb. comes only in the Latter Prophets. Hosea denounces Israel's lack of respect for human life by the expression "deep in slaughter" (Hos 5:2; cf. 4:2). This verse has raised textual problems (*BHS*). Wolff emends the text to "a pit in Shittim that was dug deep" (*Hosea*, 94; cf. D. Stuart, 88). Less problematic is Hosea's usage in 9:9, where he likens the depth of Israel's "corruption" to the atrocious acts associated with Gibeah during the period of the judges (Judg 19-21; see Wolff, *Hosea*, 158).

Isaiah rebukes the people for their stubborn insistence at *Realpolitik*, that is, they made many plans without consulting the Lord, "Woe to those who go to great depths (*'mq*) to hide their plans from the LORD" (Isa 29:15). Isaiah confirms that God judges the wicked, including Assyria: "Its fire pit has been made deep (*'mq*) and wide, with an abundance of fire and wood; the breath of the LORD, like a stream of burning sulfur, sets it ablaze" (30:33). If only God's people would realize that they have "so greatly (*'mq*) revolted" against God and that they must return to him (31:6)!

3. The adj. *'āmōq* has the basic meaning of "deep." In Lev 13:3, 4, 25, 30, 31, 32, 34 a man is designated unclean if a sore is judged to be "deeper than the skin" ("more than skin deep," NIV). Sometimes *'āmōq* denotes that which is either profound or complex. In Job 11:8, Zophar questions Job whether he is so knowledgeable as to understand the *profound* mysteries in creation: "They are higher than the heavens ... They are deeper than the depths (*'āmōq*) of the grave—what can you know?" (cf. Eccl 7:24). Job responds that God is wise and that his wisdom is evident in the complexities of history: "He reveals the deep things (*'āmōq*) of darkness and brings deep shadows into the light" (Job 12:22).

Unlike God, the depth of humans is deceptive and cunning: "Surely the mind and heart of man are cunning (*'āmōq*)" (Ps 64:6[7]; cf. Prov 18:4; 20:5). The word *'āmōq* is used figuratively in the expression "deep pit" to describe the danger of associating with either an adulteress (Prov 22:14) or prostitute (Prov 23:27).

4. *'āmēq* comes in the expression *'imqê śāpâ,* denoting speech that is obscure or unintelligible: "You will see those arrogant people no more, those people of an obscure speech, with their strange, incomprehensible tongue" (Isa 33:19). Here Isaiah signifies how the Lord can and will bring deliverance from the destructive Assyrians, whom the people greatly feared (vv. 17-19).

When the exile of Judah to Babylon had begun, the Lord called Ezekiel to be his messenger to the exiles: "You are not being sent to a people of obscure speech and difficult language, but to the house of Israel—not to many peoples of obscure (*'āmōq*) speech and difficult language, whose words you cannot understand. Surely if I had sent you to them, they would have listened to you" (Ezek 3:5-6).

5. The word *'ōmeq* may refer to the depth of the grave, "But little do they know that the dead are there, that her guests are in the depths of the grave" (Prov 9:18). With heaven as a counterpart, it signifies the totality of creation, "As the heavens are high and the earth is deep, so the hearts of kings are unsearchable" (25:3).

6. The pl. nom. *ma'ᵃmaqqîm* usually occurs in a construct chain with either *mayim* (water, Ps 69:2[3], 14[15]; Ezek 27:34) or *yām* (sea, Isa 51:10). Whereas it may have a literal sense as "depths" of the sea (Isa 51:10; Ezek 27:34), it also carries the nonliteral sense of being overwhelmed by disaster or trouble, "I sink in the miry depths.... I have come into the deep waters; the floods engulf me" (Ps 69:2[3], cf. v. 14[15]; 130:1). In the case of the latter, it is similar to the Engl. idiom "to be in deep water."

7. The pl. nom. *'ammîqātā'*, deep things, occurs in Dan 2:22, in parallel with *mᵉsattᵉ rātā'*, hidden things. The content is God's revelation to human beings of things that would otherwise be impenetrable.

Deep: → *mᵉṣôlâ/mᵉṣûlâ* (deep, depths, # 5185); → *'mq* I (be deep, mysterious, make deep, # 6676); → *tᵉhôm* (Primeval ocean, deeps of the sea, subterranean water, deep, # 9333); → *taḥtôn* (lower, lowest, # 9396)

Language, tongue, speech: → *l'z* (speak unintelligibly, # 4357); → *lāšôn* (tongue, language, # 4383); → *lšn* (slander, # 4387); → *śāpâ* (language, lip, shore, # 8557)

Sea and large bodies of water: → *gal* II (wave, # 1644); → *ḥôl* I (mud, sand, # 2567); → *ḥ^a^rîpôt* (cj. grains of sand, # 3041); → *yām* (sea, seas, # 3542); → *m^e^ṣôlâ/m^e^ṣûlâ* (deep, depths, # 5185); → *qarqaʿ* I (floor, bottom of sea, # 7977); → *t^e^hôm* (Primeval ocean, deeps of the sea, subterranean water, deep, # 9333)

BIBLIOGRAPHY
TWAT 6:220-26; H. W. Wolff, *The Anthropology of the OT*, 1973.

T. Desmond Alexander

6677	עֵמֶק

עֵמֶק (*'ēmeq*), valley, plain (# 6677).

OT *ʿēmeq* is evidently related to the Heb. root *ʿmq*, be deep, make deep (→ # 6676). In about forty-three percent of instances, it is found in construct with a nom. and the construct pair form the name of a specific valley. Among those so named are the Valley of Rephaim (Josh 15:8; 18:16; 2 Sam 5:18, 22; 23:13; Isa 17:5; 1 Chron 11:15; 14:9), of Achor (Josh 7:24, 26; 15:7; Isa 65:10; Hos 2:15[17]), of Siddim (Gen 14:3, 8, 10), of Jezreel (Josh 17:16; Judg 6:33; Hos 1:5), of Elah (1 Sam 17:2, 19; 21:9[10]), of Jehoshaphat (Joel 3:2[4:2], 12[4:12]), of Succoth (Ps 60:6[8]; 108:7[8]), of Beracah (2 Chron 20:26), of Shaveh (Gen 14:17), of Hebron (37:14), and of Aijalon (Josh 10:12). In addition, one reads of the King's Valley in Gen 14:17 and 2 Sam 18:18.

It seems that many of the valleys were located in the lower elevations—some among the low rolling hills. These included the Jezreel, Siddim, Elah, Succoth, and Aijalon. Chariots were able to operate in an *ʿēmeq* (Judg 1:19; Isa 22:7), and a cart was able to traverse an *ʿēmeq* (1 Sam 6:13). In one instance an *ʿēmeq* is mentioned in contrast to the mountains (1 Kgs 20:28). On the other hand, some valleys were broader valleys located in the hill country: namely, the Rephaim (near Jerusalem), Achor, Beracah(?), Hebron, and those near Ai (Josh 8:13), Gibeon (Isa 28:21), and Beth Rehob (Judg 18:28). As Israel entered and lived in the land of Canaan, some of its enemies were located in the valleys: the Amalekites and/or the Canaanites (Num 14:25; Josh 17:16; Judg 1:19; 6:33), the Amorites (Judg 1:34); and the Midianites (6:33 and ch. 7).

Besides being places where Israel's enemies lived and where battles took place, grain crops were grown in an *ʿēmeq* (1 Sam 6:13; Job 39:10; Ps 65:13[14]; 84:6[7]; Isa 22:7), and cattle and flocks were tended there (1 Chron 27:29; Isa 65:10). From the above, it is evident that an *ʿēmeq* is wider than a *gay'* (# 1628), but narrower than a *biqʿâ* (# 1326). In valleys typical activities included growing crops, grazing, waging battles, and engaging in illicit worship practices. In addition, they served as boundary markers and were thought of as places of both judgment and blessing. See also → *naḥal* I, stream bed, wadi, stream, tunnel, # 5707.

Valley: → *biqʿâ* (valley, # 1326); → *gay'* (valley, # 1628); → *naḥal* I (stream-bed, wadi, stream, tunnel, # 5707); → *ʿēmeq* (valley, # 6677)

BIBLIOGRAPHY
A. Schwarzenbach, *Die geographische Terminologie im Hebräischen des Altern Testaments*, 1954, 30-39; G. A. Smith, *The Historical Geography of the Holy Land*, 1931, 249-50, 435-38.

Carl Rasmussen

6678 (*'āmōq*, deep, deeper, mysterious), → # 6676

6679 (*'ōmeq*, depth), → # 6676

6682/6683	עמר

עמר (*'mr*), pi. gather grain (# 6682); hitp. deal tyrannically with, treat someone brutally (# 6683); עֹמֶר (*'ōmer* I), ear of grain (# 6684).

ANE In Aram. the vb. *'mr* refers to loading or to gather in the crops, viz. to harvest. It is also used as subst. to indicate a dry measure of capacity (J. Hoftijzer & K. Jongeling, *DNWSI* 2:873).

OT 1. *'mr* as vb. in pi. only occurs once in the pi. part., in Ps 129:7b, when referring to the curse against the haters of Zion who will be like grass (*ḥ^{a}ṣîr*, v. 6a) that does not fill the reaper's (*qōṣēr*) hand, nor the bosom/lap of the binder (*m^e'ammēr*). NIV translates *ḥoṣen*, lap/bosom, with "arms," but misses the point of the legal symbolism involved (cf. M. Malul, *Studies in Mesopotamian Legal Symbolism*, 1988, 336). The JB has "lap." Cf. visual representation in H. Gressmann, *AOB*, No. 166, of gathering of the grain.

2. The hitp. vb. *'mr* occurs only in Deut 21:14; 24:7. In 21:14 another vb. in the "oppression" and "affliction" field is used along with *'mr,* viz., *'nh.* It is clear from both contexts that *'mr,* like *'nh,* intends to express an oppressive deed that has devastating physical and psychological impact on the afflicted person. The latter is mistreated, forced to submit to the will of a stronger party, reduced to servile existence, and his or her whole person degraded.

3. *'ōmer* I, omer, ear of grain, sheaf, is used as a measurement of capacity (R. de Vaux, *AncIsr*, 1974, 200; *ABD* 6:903-4) and is one-tenth of an ephah (Exod 16:36), viz., a daily food ration of about 1 litre. The LXX translates it by *gomor.* It is only used in Exod 16:16, 18, 22, 32, 33, 36 for the measurement of the "bread from heaven," the manna (*TWAT* 4:968-75; "Manna," *ABD* 4:511; also in Num 11:7). One omer has to be collected each day, but two portions in order to make provision for the Sabbath (v. 22). One omer has to be kept in a jar for future generations (v. 33).

The word omer as "sheaf" occurs in the Pentateuchal laws. In Lev 23:10, 11, 12, 15 the Israelites have to bring a sheaf of the first grain of the harvest (*'ōmer rē'šît qāṣîr*) as an offering of the firstfruits to the priest, who must wave (*nwp*, [→ # 5677] subst. *t^{e}nûpâ, TWAT* 5:321) it before it may be used (v. 14).

Deut 24:19 rules that an overlooked sheaf (*škḥ 'ōmer*) should be left for the alien, the fatherless, and the poor (cf. Lev 19:9-10). For the application of this law, see the story of Ruth and Boaz (Ruth 2:7, 15) (→ Ruth: Theology).

In Job 24:10b it is used figuratively when Job complains about the seeming injustice of the world. The righteous carry sheaves, but stay hungry (*r'b*).

Harvest, gleaning: → *'sp* (gather, harvest, # 665); → *bṣr* (harvest grapes, # 1305); → *y^{e}bûl* (produce, yield, # 3292); → *lqṭ* (reap, harvest, # 4377); → *'ll* I (glean, # 6618); → *'mr* (gather grain, # 6682); → *qbṣ* (gather, # 7695); → *qṣr* (harvest, # 7917); → *t^{e}bû'â* (crop, yield, # 9311); → *t^{e}nûbâ*, produce, # 9482)

Oppression: → *dḥq* (oppress, # 1895); → *ḥms* I (do violence, # 2803); → *ḥmṣ* II (oppress, # 2807); → *ynh* (oppress, # 3561); → *lḥṣ* (press, # 4315); → *'nh* II (afflict, humble, afflict one's

soul, fast, oppress, submit, # 6700); → *'šq* I (wrong, # 6943) → *ṣwq* I (constrain, press in/upon, harass, vex, # 7439); → *rṣṣ* (crush, # 8368); → *tôlāl* (oppressor, # 9354); → *tōk* (oppression, # 9412)
Measurement, standard, rule: → *zrh* II (measure, # 2431); → *mdd* (measure, measure off, # 4499); → *š'r* (calculate, # 9132); → *tkn* (regulate by weighing or measuring, # 9419). **For measurements of weight/volume:** → *'êpâ* (an ephah, # 406), **for measurements of length:** → *'ammâ* I (cubit, ell, forearm, # 564)

BIBLIOGRAPHY
ABD 6:903-4; T. D. Hanks, *God So Loved the Third World: The Biblical Vocabulary of Oppression*, 1983, 3-39; Y. I. Kim, "The Vocabulary of Oppression in the Old Testament," Ph.D. diss. Drew University, 1981; C. F. Marriottini, "The Problem of Social Oppression in the Eighth Century Prophets," Ph.D. diss. Southern Baptist Theological Seminary, 1983; J. Miranda, *Communism in the Bible*, 1982, 37-39; J. Pons, *L'oppression dans l'Ancien Testament*, 1981; E. Tamez, *Bible of the Oppressed*, 1982, 1-30.

I. Swart/I. Cornelius

6684 (*'ōmer* I, ear of grain), → # 6682

6685 (*'ōmer* II, omer), → # 406

6686 (*'ᵃmōrâ*, Gomorrah), → Sodom

6687 (*'omrî*, Omri), → Omri

6694	עֵנָב

עֵנָב (*'ēnāb*), nom. grapes, cluster of grapes (# 6694).

ANE The word is found in Ugar. *ġnb* (*UT*, 1976); Old Akk. *inbu(m)*; Aram. *'nb*; Syr. *'enbā'*, but it is used with a variety of meanings. Each usage must be carefully determined. Akk. *inbu* = fruit tree and O. Akk. = fruit (Gelb, *Glossary*, 51); Arab. *'inab*, grape, grape cluster.

OT The nineteen uses of this nom. in the OT closely parallel the use of the words that cluster around it: winepress, vat, wine, vineyard, vines. Together these words were used to indicate the blessing or cursing of Israel/Judah by Yahweh through their abundance or lack of abundance.

1. The Nazirite in Israel was to eat no grapes or any fruit of the vineyard until his vow was completed (Num 6:3-4).

2. The abundance of grapes in Israel served to illustrate Yahweh's covenant blessings; their lack, his covenant curses (Deut 32:14). They could be eaten freely up to a point when in a neighbor's field (23:24), but at harvest some were to be left for the sojourner, widow, and fatherless (24:21). Their backsliding and breaking of the covenant showed Israel to be unfaithful, for when the Lord planned to gather grapes, there were none on the vine (Jer 8:13).

3. The promised land of Canaan yielded grape clusters that required two men to carry them on a pole between them, an illustration and fulfillment of the covenant promises (Num 13:23-24).

4. The biblical writers used the image of grapes in several metaphors/similes. They represented the people of Israel in Isaiah's parable of the vineyard (Isa 5:1-6). Although the Lord planted a choice vine (*šrq*), the vineyard produced wild grapes (*b*^{e}*'uš*, → # 946), not good grapes (*'ēnāb*); although he gave it a tower and a wine vat, it produced stinking grapes. All of the expenditures of the Lord went for naught. When God in elective grace chooses a people for salvation and service, he has a right to expect faithful and obedient compliance.

5. Yahweh's early felicitous relationship with his people was likened to finding grapes in the desert (Hos 9:10), a time when Yahweh found fruitfulness and hope in his people. While two kinds of fruit (figs, grapes) are present, later the people abandoned the Lord who had found and cherished them. At Baal Peor they had become as vile (*šiqqûṣ*, → 9199) as the false gods they worshiped there; i.e., they had become a spoiled fruit (cf. Num 25).

6. Poison grapes from the vine of Sodom (Deut 32:32) metaphorically speak of the noxious origins of pagan religion. The fruit of the worship of false gods leaves a bad taste in the mouth and, even worse, leads to death.

7. The day of judgment and woe for Israel will be a time when Yahweh judges because he finds no grapes or vines in Israel (Jer 8:13).

8. During the sabbatical year fallen grapes were to be left on the ground for the poor of the land (Lev 25:5).

9. The presence of an abundance of grapes marks the marvelous time of fertility during which the one who is to rule from the tribe of Judah reigns (Gen 49:11).

10. A few more words are used once or twice, but do not add anything to the theological discussion above: cf. *b*^{e}*'ûšîm*, stinking, unripe, wild (grapes, → # 946), *mezeg*, mixed wine (→ # 4641).

P-B 1. The LXX translates this Heb. word quite uniformly with *staphulê*, grapes, bunch of grapes.

2. At Qumran the word is found a couple of times. One activity of the priest in charge of a feast is to cut the unripe grapes from the vines.

3. In Mish. Heb. the term meant berry (PTalm Nedarim XI, 42) and is found quite widely but with little OT exegetical value.

Grapes: → *'eškôl* I (cluster[s] of grapes, # 864); → *b*^{e}*'uš* (sour, unripe, wild grapes/berries, # 946); → *zāg* (peel/skins of grapes, seed, kernel, # 2293); → *ḥarṣān* (unripe grapes, # 3079); → *'ēnāb* (grapes, cluster of grapes, # 6694); → *pereṭ* (fallen grapes/berries, # 7261)

Bibliography

HBD 1112-13; *IDB* 4:785-86; *TWAT* 6:227-29; *TWOT* 2:679; J. Döller, "Der Wein in Bibel und Talmud," *Bib* 4, 1923, 143-67, 267-99.

Eugene Carpenter

6695	ענג

ענג (*'ng*), pu. be delicately brought up; hitp. delight o.s. in (# 6695); עֹנֶג (*'ōneg*), enjoyment, pleasure, delight (# 6696); עָנֹג (*'ānōg*), spoiled, pampered (# 6697); תַּעֲנוּג (*ta*^{a}*nûg*), comfort, delight, enjoyment, pleasure, luxury, pampering (# 9503).

ANE The Arab. form *ġanūǧa* carries the sense be coy, pamper. The Eth. form *'a'nūg*, ear, nose ring, has also been noted (*LLA*, 993).

OT 1. *Morphology and syntax.* Two main verbal forms are found in the OT. The pu. part. is used in Jer 6:2; all other forms found (9x) are hitp. Except for one occurrence, the hitp. forms always occur in combination with a preposition. The vb. is found most often (6x) in combination with the prefix *'al*: Job 22:26; 27:10; Ps 37:4, 11; Isa 57:4; 58:14. In Isa 55:2, the preposition is b^e and in 66:11, it is *min*.

2. *Distribution.* The verbal and nominal forms occur a total of 15x in the OT. The verbal lexemes are used 10x (Deut 28:56; Job 22:26; 27:10; Isa 55:2; 57:4; 58:1; 66:11; Jer 6:2). Nom./adj. lexemes occur 5x: *'ānōg* is used 3x (Deut 28:54, 56; Isa 47:1); *'ōneg* occurs 2x (Isa 13:22; 58:13).

The lexemes are most frequent (8x) in the Prophets. One of these is in Jer 6:2, the rest (7x) are in Isaiah (Isa 13:22; 47:1; 55:2; 57:4; 58:13, 14; 66:11). In the Pentateuch the lexeme appears only in Deut 28:54, 56. In poetic books the lexemes occur 4x: Job (2x: Job 22:26; 27:10) and Psalms (2x: Ps 37:4, 11). They appear either in clusters (Isa 55-66), pairs (Ps 37:4, 11; Deut 28:54, 56; Isa 58:13, 14), or adjacent chs. (Isa 57:4; 58:13, 14).

3. *Theological usage.* The various senses of the word can be classified into two distinct realms of usage, the religious and the secular.

(a) The religious usage. Two patterns of usage are evident. The poetic texts (Job 22:26; 27:10; Ps 37:4) share in common the reciprocity idea of the Wisdom tradition, especially in Ps 37:4. A close interplay exists between "delight ... in the LORD," and "desires of your heart." The path to true self-fulfillment does not lie in a preoccupation with self but in selfless preoccupation with God. When the psalmist sets his heart on God, God reciprocates by making him truly fulfilled. The sense of *'ng* here is "take great pleasure in."

The second pattern of usage, with the sense desirable, enjoyable, is found in Isa 58:13-14. The Sabbath element in these two verses calls for comment. Westermann takes it as an addition to vv. 1-12. This is in view of the earlier Sabbath reference in 56:1-8. In seeking the connection between these two verses and vv. 1-12, Motyer (483) contrasts "the feast over against the fast. The Lord is more interested in enjoyment of its blessings through obedience than in self-imposed deprivatons." It perhaps is more likely that the contrast is rather between the "proper observance" and "reckless observance" of both these covenant requirements.

Both religious observances were to be accompanied by just social conduct. The problem is that Israel had reduced these observances to mere external rituals. They had lost sense of the essential link between spiritual demands of worship and the moral responsibilities towards fellow humans and society.

The parallel usage of *'ng* with *ḥpṣ* in v. 13 is instructive. The people had turned to their own desires, *ḥepaṣekā*, because they did not perceive Sabbath observance a delight, *'ōneg*. Thus, they had not honored the Sabbath but had treated it as an empty ritual in pursuit of their own selfish interest. Isaiah calls for a change of disposition. If God's blessing is going to be experienced, they must perceive that true Sabbath observance is not only a profitable religious and social provision, but a true delight.

The usage of *'ng* in Isa 54:4 appears to stand alone. It carries the sense mock, flirt with, act in a familiar way.

(b) The secular usage. (i) Deut 28:56. This text is set in the context of the covenant curses and blessings. The effect of the curse on the family is highlighted. Breakdown of the family ensues with the disintegration of family bonds, loyalty, and commitment. The associations of the lexeme suggest loyalty, faithfulness, and devotion as characteristics of the gentle and sensitive. The effect of the curse is that even the one who is most sensitive and delicate of spirit and heart will grow cold and heartless. The sense of this participial usage is delicate, sensitive, tender.

(ii) Psalm 37:11. The wisdom motif of reward for good and retribution for evil is evident in this context. The picture is one of overabundance. The wise man receives and enjoys to the full an abundance of concrete material blessings. The sense of the lexeme therefore is pleasure, enjoyment, comfort, luxury.

(iii) Prophets. The secular usages in Isaiah are all figurative. They may be classified into two pairs. The first pair (Isa 13:22; 47:1) have in common the theme of the judgment of Babylon. The sense of the adjectival usage in 13:22 may be luxurious, pampered. The connotations suggest loss of privileges and utter desolation. The usage in 47:1 connotes shame and loss of status. The city will lose its exalted position and be brought to shame. The sense of the lexeme in this context is tender, delicate. In each case the second pair (55:2; 66:11) uses symbolic language rooted in vivid concrete images. In 55:2, the tangible "what is not bread" is parallel to the intangible "what does not satisfy." Similarly, these two phrases are parallel to and contrast "what is good" and "the richest of fare." All of these form the object sphere of delight, *'ng*. Thus, to pursue intangible satisfaction through the tangible pleasures of godless living is to pursue the elusive and is demonstrative of a grave lack of discernment/wisdom. *'ng* is to be taken in parallel with the vbs. speaking and eating. The literal sense of the wording in 55:2; 66:11 is therefore take great delight, immerse yourself in. The figurative meaning, however, is be committed, entrust oneself, be faithful to God.

The imagery in 66:11 is maternal. The mother-suckling relationship is graphic portrayal of the fullness and richness of Yahweh's salvation. The connotations are of fruitfulness, abundance of supply, and satisfaction. In this context, *'ng* carries the sense be content, be comforted, be totally satisfied.

4. *Synonyms and antonyms.* *'ng* is different from *š''*, take delight (→ # 9130), in that *'ng* has distinct religious and secular meanings. Furthermore, the secular usages form the majority of its senses. *'ng* is never used as a direct object in a possessive sense. Though there is some overlap in the range of meanings, there are also different emphases. *'ng* in some of its usages is associated with images of pleasure and the sensual. *š''* is never used in this way.

5. *Summary.* The lexeme occurs 15x in the OT: the verbal form is used 10x and the nom. 5x. The root is used with both secular and religious meanings, the secular meanings being more frequent. The semantic range of the root includes: take great pleasure in, enjoyable, desirable, pleasure, enjoyment, comfort, luxurious, pampered, gently, sensitive tender, delicate.

P-B Three distinct senses are employed in LXX. The sense tender, delicate is retained by LXX in Deut 28:56 and Isa 47:10. In the former, *apalē* and *tryphera* translate the verbal form of *'ng*. In the latter, the verbal form *tryphēsēte* is used. The same sense is retained in Isa 66:11. The second sense is that of confidence, trust. This sense, confidence, is used in Job 22:26, *parrhēsiasthēsē*, and 27:10, *parrēsian*. The sense trust is used for Isa 58:14, where *pepoithōs* translates *'ng*. The third sense, riot, appears in Isa 57:4.

The pi. is attested in Mish. Heb. while pa. is found in Pal. Aram. (BCh 2m, 556a). The sense is reflexive, enjoy o.s. (hitp.) is found in DSS (KQT 167).

Delight, enjoyment, pampering: → *'dn* (delight, luxuriate, revel, # 6357); → *'ng* (delight oneself, # 6695); → *pnq* (pamper o.s, pamper, # 7167); → *ṣḥq* (laugh, play, insult, # 7464); → *š''* II (play, take delight in, # 9130)

Bibliography

O. Kaiser, *Isaiah 13-39,* OTL, 1974; D. Kidner, *Proverbs,* 1964; idem, *Psalms 73-150*, 1975; H.-J. Kraus, *Psalms 2,* 1989; J. L. McKenzie, *Second Isaiah*, 1968; J. N. Oswalt, *Isaiah 1-39*, NICOT, 1986; W. A. VanGemeren, "Psalms," *EBC*, 1991; J. D. W. Watts, *Isaiah 1-33,* 1985; C. Westermann, *Isaiah 40-66,* OTL, 1969; E. J. Young, *Isaiah 1, 2,* NICOT, 1965, 1969.

Douglas Carew

6696 (*'ōneg*, enjoyment, pleasure, delight), → # 6695

6697 (*'ānōg*, spoiled, pampered), → # 6695

6698	ענד

ענד (*'nd),* q. wind something around, tie something on (only in Job 31:36; Prov 6:21; # 6698); מַעֲדַנּוֹת(*ma'adannôt),* nom. bands, fetters (# 5051).

OT 1. Job uses the vb. *'nd* in a metaphor for wrapping divine vindication around his head like a crown, "Surely ... I would put it on like a crown" (Job 31:36; cf. Hartley, *Job*, 425). Similarly, in the Wisdom tradition the sages exhort their disciples to heed their teachings by binding it, as it were, around their neck, "Bind (*qšr*) them upon your heart for ever; fasten (*'nd*) them around your neck" (Prov 6:21).

2. Some scholars suggest that *ma'adannôt* is derived from *'nd* by metathesis of the final two consonants (*HALAT* 576). Consequently, we may read in 1 Sam 15:32, "Agag came to him in fetters." R. P. Gordon observes that the manner of Agag's coming is "elusive" (*I & II Samuel*, 1986, 146). Klein follows Bratcher in his rendering: "Agag came to him trembling" (*1 Samuel*, 145). NIV has "confidently" ("trembling" in marginal note).

Less ambiguous is Job 38:31, "Can you bind the chains of the Pleiades?" (NIV mg.). W. Brueggemann sees in this text an allusion to the myth of Orion, who upon his death was "bound" to the sky ("Orion," *IDB* 3:609). Alternative readings, however, are possible.

Band, tie: → *'pd* (put on tightly, # 679); → *'ᵃpēr* (bandage, # 710); → *'eṣ'ādâ* (band, # 731); → *ḥbš* (tie up, saddle, imprison, bind, # 2502); → *ḥgr* (bind, gird, # 2520); → *ḥāšûq* (clasp ring, # 3122); → *ḥtl* (be swaddled, # 3156); → *keset* (band [for magic purposes], # 4086); → *migbā'â* (head-band, # 4457); → *'nd* (wind, tie s.t., # 6698); → *'qd* (tie up, # 6818); → *ṣrr* I (bind, tie up, # 7674); → *qšr* (ally together, conspire, bind, # 8003); → *rks* (bind, tie, # 8220); → *rtm* (tie up, # 8412)

T. Desmond Alexander

6699	עָנָה

עָנָה (*ʿnh* I), q. answer, reply, accede to a request, witness against, with b^e; ni. (5x) reply for o.s. (Ezek 14:4), be answered (Job 11:2); hi. give an answer (Prov 29:19) (# 6699); מַעֲנֶה (*ma*ʿ*a**neh* I), nom. response, answer (# 5101).

ANE This lexeme is attested in the three main Sem. branches. Cognates of the vb. are attested in Akk. *enû*, overturn (*AHw*, 220b); in Ugar. *ʿny*, answer, reply, say (*UT*, 1419; Segert, 196); in Aram. *ʿnh*, respond, speak, answer (Jastrow, 1093a); in Mand. *ʿnh*, answer, reply (*MdD*, 24a); in Arab. *ʿnw*, respond orally and publicly to a request (Biella, *Dictionary*, 373); and in Egyp. *ʿnn*, wind around or encircle (*WbÄS*, I, Part I, 192). Cognate of the nom. is attested in Ugar. *mʿn*, response, answer (*UT*, 1883; *WUS*, 2060a).

OT 1. *Answer, reply.* This lexeme is used 316x in the OT, over 300x in q. The dominant meaning in q. is to answer or reply.

(a) God serves as the grammatical subject of this vb. 67x. In the majority of those occurrences, the divine response comes as a result of a person's call or request. In the Psalms, God is the subject of *ʿnh* in 31 of 33 cases. This response often follows the distressed cry of the writer. "In my anguish I cried to the LORD, and he answered by setting me free" (Ps 118:5). The divine response is not something that the Lord is obligated to give but is a product of the Lord's compassion. "Answer me, O LORD, out of the goodness of your love; in your great mercy turn to me" (69:16[17]). Thus, the object of the vb. can be protection (20:1[2]), deliverance (65:5[6]), or freedom (118:5).

The Lord takes the initiative and answers (*ʿnh*) without someone's request in only 5 instances (Ps 65:5[6]; Hos 2:21[23]; 14:8[9]; Joel 2:19; Zech 10:6. While God may initiate the response without a person's request, it is theologically significant that a mortal never serves as the subject of this vb. in responding to God unless God himself has initiated the process. The response by God may be undefined, as in Isa 65:24, "Before they call I will answer"; or it may be defined: thunder (1 Sam 7:9-10), fire (1 Kgs 18:37, 38; 1 Chron 21:26), awesome deeds of righteousness (Ps 65:5[6]), even *šālôm*, wholeness (Gen 41:16).

The very fact that God is willing to reply often implies divine favor (Isa 58:9; Joel 2:19). Hos 2 is particularly noteworthy. Following words of divine judgment, which include the threat of agricultural ruin, words of restoration reach a climatic conclusion in vv. 21-22[23-24]. Here God's initial response sets off a chain reaction that employs *ʿnh* 5x. This chain of response results in a shower of divine blessing and favor, which includes agricultural restoration (L. J. Wood, "Hosea," *EBC* 7:180).

By contrast, the Lord's refusal to answer (*ʿnh*) is clearly a sign of divine disfavor, even judgment. Samuel makes this point in 1 Sam 8:18, and it is further illustrated in the life of Saul (1 Sam 14:37; 28:6). This connotation is subsequently employed in the Writings. "They cried for help, but there was no one to save them—to the LORD, but he did not answer" (Ps 18:41[42]). The speaker elsewhere laments the fact that God has abandoned him even to the point of not answering (Ps 22:2[3]). This implies that the speaker is regarded as an apostate! For it is only such a person whom God does not answer. Note how the final precative perfect (*IBHS* 30.5.4c,d.) of the lament section repeats the root (22:21[22]). The speaker cries out for resolution to this untenable situation before the thanksgiving can begin. The use of this psalm in the gospels opens up its relevance in Christ's passion. In experiencing the full weight of God's anger at the sins of the world, Jesus underwent the punishment as an apostate. This is not to suggest that Jesus deserved this punishment because of his lack of faithfulness. Rather, he experienced this abandonment as the substitute for a world of sinners who had abandoned God.

(b) A human being may also be the grammatical subject of *'nh*. Here the vb. frequently introduces a reply in direct discourse. However, this discourse is not ordinarily part of a sustained dialogue. The object of the vb. may be a person (Gen 23:14) or a thing (Deut 20:11; 1 Kgs 18:21). Failure to respond to God has serious consequences. "Listen! I am going to bring on Judah and on everyone living in Jerusalem every disaster I pronounced against them. I spoke to them, but they did not listen; I called to them, but they did not answer" (Jer 35:17).

(c) The derived nom. *ma'aneh* is predominantly a verbal answer or reply. The nom. occurs 8x, five of which are in Prov (e.g., Prov 15:1). The nom. *dābār*, word (→ # 1821), is also employed in this sense, as is the nom. *gab*, answer (# 1462), which appears only in Job 13:12, where the NIV translates with the potentially misleading "defenses."

(d) Within the semantic domain of answering one also encounters *'mr*, say (→ # 606), and *šwb*, respond (→ # 8740). *'mr* is used 96x, of which 61x are in Samuel and Kings. It is virtually always part of a dialogue formula. *šwb* in the sense of reply occurs only 20x, of which six are in Job. These generally are not used in dialogue formulas; they are often responses in more emotionally charged situations (1 Kgs 12:6, 9, 16).

2. *Accede to a request. 'nh* is used 65x with the meaning of submit or comply. This sense is the primary one found in Psalms (35x), where the imperative form of this lexeme is employed 14x. The imperative is part of the prayer language of the psalms, heightening the sense of urgency that attends the request being made. "Answer (*'nh*) me when I call to you, O my righteous God. Give me relief from my distress; be merciful to me and hear my prayer" (Ps 4:1[2]). This sense is also found in connection with a mortal response (1 Kgs 12:7) and in connection with a divine response (1 Sam 7:9).

3. *Witness against.* This sense of *'nh* is a product of its collocation with the preposition b^e. This combination of words is used 15x in the OT, of which six are in the Torah. It appears in statutory formulation (Num 35:30), the Decalogue (Exod 20:16; Deut 5:20), and in practical application (2 Sam 1:16). The subject of the vb. may be a person (Deut 19:16), a sin (Isa 59:12; Jer 14:7), or one's appearance (Isa 3:9). Note that the NIV's handling of Mic 6:3 is weak in this respect, since it translates with the generic, "Answer me." An irony may be imported to the text in Gen 30:33, where Jacob uses this word combination (*'nh* b^e) to indicate that his honesty was testifying for him by saying it will testify against him. A more generic type of witnessing or witnessing on behalf of someone is constructed with the Heb. nom. *'ēd*, witness (→ # 6332), as in Gen 21:30.

4. *The vb. 'nh in Job. 'nh* is used over 60x in Job, of which 37 are uses independent of the dialogue formula noted above. As Job struggles to define the mortal versus divine relationship, these 37 instances help drive the reflective debate forward and help to profile the character of Job. In Job 9 *'nh* is used 4x. Here Job states with great frustration that it is impossible for a mortal to respond to God, even if one wished to (9:3)

or were innocent (9:15). This vb. is employed as Job asserts he has both a right to answer God and a right to demand an answer from God (13:22). But God refuses to provide a response to Job's demands (19:7; 30:20). Finally, the Lord himself takes on the role of inquisitor. "Let him who accuses God answer him" (40:2). And Job himself is forced to humbly admit that mortals cannot respond. "I spoke once, but I have no answer—twice, but I will say no more" (40:5). Thus the reflective debate that seeks to define the relationship between God and mortals involves *'nh*. The conclusion is that God operates on such a grand scale that mortals are unable either to receive answer from God nor give answer to him. The Lord refuses to answer those who are treating him as an apostate would. Job's presumptions and arguments took on the flavor of one who had abandoned God; thus, God treats him with the appropriate response—and that is no response.

5. *A dialogue marker. 'nh* is collocated with the vb. (*'mr*) 123x. In the majority of these instances (100 acc. to Joüon), the word pair is used to mark a change in speaker within a dialogue. It is the marker of choice when the change in speaker also involves someone answering a question. *'nh* is also collocated 6x with the vb. *dbr* (5x in Kings). Each, as above (# 3), is in the dialogue formula.

P-B The LXX translates primarily with *apokrinomai* but is sensitive to the various nuances of the vb. described above. The nom. is translated by *apokrisis* or *eisakoē*. In the Tgs. one finds the senses of speaking, singing, and responding. QL employs the vb. 12x, of which eight are in the dialogue formula. Talm. and Mish. use the vb. in the sense of speak, respond, or sing in a chorus in q. In ni. it means to have one's prayer answered, be called to speak, or be sworn to allegiance. Modern Hebrew employs the root for answer or respond.

Asking and Answering: → *'nh* I (answer, reply, witness against, # 6699); → *š'l* (ask, inquire, request, wish, beg, greet, # 8626)

BIBLIOGRAPHY

TDNT 3:944-45; *THAT* 2:842-43; *TWOT* 2:679-80; C. Cox, "*Eisakouō* and *Epakouō* in the Greek Psalter," *Bib* 62, 1981, 251-58; L. Delekat, "Zum Hebräisches Wörterbuch," *VT* 14, 1964, 37-42; A. Guillaume, "Notes and Studies, Hosea 2:23, 24," *JTS* 15, April 1964, 57-58; P. Joüon, "Respondit et Dixit," *Bib* 13, 1932, 309-14.

John A. Beck

6700	ענה

ענה (*'nh* II), q. bowed down; ni. bow; pi. afflict, humble, afflict one's soul, fast, oppress; pu. be humbled; hitp. submit (# 6700); עַנְוָה (*'anwâ*), humility (# 6709); עֱנוּת (*'^{e}nût*), affliction (# 6713); עֳנִי (*'^{o}nî*), misery, affliction (# 6715); תַּעֲנִית (*ta'^{a}nît*), fasting (# 9504).

ANE This vb. has similar meanings in several related Sem. languages (Assyr. *enû*, to thwart, frustrate, do violence to; Ar. *'anā['nw]*, humble, Syr. *'n'* [Eth. pe'el], humble oneself; OSA to be lowly, submissive; Ugar. to be cowed, humbled or punished). It is also found in the Mesha Inscription with the meaning to humble (lines 5, 6).

OT 1. There are a number of Heb. words for oppression or subjugation, probably resulting from the prevalence of such action in the ANE. One of the more common words, *'nh* II, occurs approximately 80x in the OT. Uncertainty as to the actual number of occurrences arises from several passages where it is unclear whether the derivation is *'nh* II, afflict, or its homonym *'nh* I, answer (e.g., Ps 55:19[20] [NASB "answer;" NIV "afflict"]; → # 6699). The lexeme *'nh* II has a range of meaning that covers both the positive and negative aspects of several Eng. words, namely, humble, oppress, and afflict.

2. (a) The vb. *'nh* occurs about six times in the q. and is descriptive of a variety of situations. It refers to near-death affliction (Ps 116:10), hardship used by God to drive the psalmist back to God's word (119:67), and the oppression of wicked leaders (Zech 10:2). A somewhat unusual usage of this word appears in Isa 31:4, where it refers to a lion that cannot be frightened away or disturbed (possibly derived from the meaning humbled) after capturing its prey.

(b) This word occurs only four times in the ni. form, consistently meaning suffer, be oppressed, or be humble (Exod 10:3; Ps 119:107; Isa 53:7; 58:10). L. J. Coppes mistakenly asserts that "the Niphal usages of this word are reflective, emphasizing self-affliction (Ps 119:75; Isa 58:10)" (*TWOT* 2:682). For instance, Ps 119:75 (which is a pi. form anyway) clearly states that God afflicted the psalmist. Even Isa 53:7, which describes "the servant" as being "oppressed (*niggaš*) and afflicted, yet he did not open his mouth," does not necessarily suggest self-inflicted pain.

(c) *'nh* II most commonly appears with pi. and pu. (6x) stems and has a fairly wide range of meanings. It may be used for sexual abuse (Deut 22:24; 2 Sam 13:14); physical or mental oppression (Gen 31:50; Exod 22:22[21]; 1 Kgs 11:39); subjugation (Exod 1:11; Judg 16:5, 19); or even humbling oneself by fasting (Ps 35:13; Isa 58:5). In 2 Sam 13:22 and 32 this word describes Tamar, who is humbled or humiliated in the eyes of her people after being violated by Amnon. Delilah afflicted Samson when she cut his hair so that the Philistines could subjugate and mock their archenemy (Judg 16:19). This word is also used of the pain inflicted on Joseph by ankle fetters (Ps 105:18).

In Lev 16:31 and 23:27 the people were to humble or inflict themselves with inner pain expressing contrition, most likely accompanied by prayer and fasting, in preparation for the Day of Atonement. God sometimes uses affliction for correction or to bring about a desired goal (1 Kgs 11:39; Ps 119:71), resulting in occasional thanks to God for affliction (Ps 88:7[8]; 90:15; 119:75; Lam 3:33). God humbled Israel in the wilderness (Deut 8:2, 16) and the Babylonian exile (Ps 102:23[24]; Isa 64:12[11]) in order to bring them back to him. More often, however, it is used of people afflicting or attempting to humble others, which is invariably humiliating and demeaning (Exod 1:12; Judg 19:24). For example, Sarah treated Hagar so harshly that she fled (Gen 16:6), and Shechem overpowered Dinah to violate her (Gen 34:2). Because the weaker of society (e.g., foreigners [Exod 22:21(20)], widows [Exod 22:22(21)], women captured in war [Deut 21:14]) were often at the mercy of the stronger, God gave specific laws to guard against their abuse and oppression.

(d) Numerous synonyms for *'nh* II appear in the OT: *dḥq*, thrust, crowd, oppress (# 1895); *dk'*, crush, oppress (# 1917); *ynh*, suppress, oppress, maltreat (# 3561); *ng'*, be stricken (# 5595); *ngś*, press, drive, oppress, exact (# 5601); *'wq*, weigh one down (# 6421); and *'šq* I, oppress, wrong, extort (# 6943). These words generally describe the action of subjugation or oppression. Beyond the action itself, the word *ygh*, grief, distress, sorrow (# 3324), expresses the emotional side of oppression; *špl* (# 9166) describes the state of being humble or low; and *kn'* (# 4044) connotes submission to another's will.

3. The nom. *'anwâ* occurs only in Ps 45:[5] and may be an incorrect pointing of *'ᵃnāwâ*, humility. If the latter is the correct pointing of the nom., then the psalmist expects the king to champion truth and display the humility of righteousness.

4. The nom. *'ᵉnût* is a hapleg., which appears in Ps 22:24[25], where the psalmist praises God for not despising or turning away from him in his dire affliction. Instead God heard the psalmist when he called to him and delivered him. The grammatical construction of this phrase is probably a superlative genitive (Waltke and O'Connor, *IBHS*, 154), meaning "the affliction of the afflicted," i.e., the greatest of all afflictions.

5. The nom. *'ᵒnî* occurs 36x in the OT and expresses the condition of pain, suffering, and anguish resulting from affliction. It is expressive of profound national affliction, such as the Egyptian sojourn (Exod 3:7, 17; Deut 16:3; 26:7; Neh 9:9) and Babylonian captivity (Lam 1:3, 9; 3:1; Isa 48:10), as well as individual suffering (Gen 31:42; Ps 88:9[10]). It appears most frequently in the books of Job and Psalms (16x), which often record responses to suffering. *'ᵒnî* can refer to both physical affliction, as in Job (30:16, 27; 36:8), or mental anguish, such as Hannah's despair over her inability to bear children (1 Sam 1:11). God can shield the needy from affliction (Ps 107:41), or he can use it for his purposes (Isa 48:10, God has refined Israel "in the furnace of affliction"). Numerous passages relate how affliction causes those who are afflicted to turn to God (Job 36:15; Ps 9:13[14]; 25:18; 31:7[8]; 119:50, 92, 153).

6. The word *ta'ᵃnît* occurs only in Ezra 9:5 and describes Ezra's reaction to the Israelites' sin of marrying foreign wives. He tore his garment, pulled hair from his head and beard, sat appalled as a sign of his sadness and grief, and then fasted until the evening offering. The nom. probably refers specifically to the fasting that would have been a natural accompaniment to grief (Clines, 1984, 121).

P-B The LXX translates this word group by a variety of words. Talmudic Aramaic has several related words, *'ānî*, *'anyā'*, *'anyāy'*, each meaning afflicted, humble, poor. There are also several denom. noms. similar to those found in BH: *'ᵃniyyût*, *'ᵃniyyûtā'*, *'anyûtā'*, meaning misery or poverty. Modern Hebrew, likewise, has many related words with similar meanings.

Affliction, oppression: → *dḥq* (oppress, # 1895); → *ḥms* I (do violence, # 2803); → *ḥmṣ* II (oppress, # 2807); → *ynh* (oppress, # 3561); → *lḥṣ* (press, # 4315); → *māṣôr* I (affliction, siege, # 5189); → *mrr* I (be bitter, distraught, afflict, # 5352); → *nega'* (plague, affliction, # 5596); → *ngś* (exact, # 5601); → *'nh* II (afflict, humble, afflict one's soul, fast, oppress, submit, # 6700); → *'wq* I (crush?, # 6421); → *'mr* II (deal tyrannically with, # 6683); → *'šq* I (wrong, # 6943); → *ṣwq* I (constrain, press in/upon, harass, vex, # 7439); → *ṣwr* II (deal tyrannically with, # 7444); → *rhb* (assail, press, pester, alarm, confuse, # 8104); → *rṣṣ* (crush, # 8368); → *tôlāl* (oppressor, # 9354); → *tōk* (oppression, # 9412)

Humility, affliction, misery: → *kn'* (be subdued, be humbled, humble o.s., # 4044); → *'nh* II (afflict, humble, afflict one's soul, fast, oppress, submit, # 6700); → *ṣn'* (be modest, humble, # 7570); → *šḥḥ* (stoop, crouch, humble, # 8820); → *špl* (be low, be levelled, humiliate, bring low, # 9164)

BIBLIOGRAPHY
IDB 2:659-60; *ISBE* 2:775-78; 3:609-11; *THAT* 2:341-50; *TWAT* 6:247-70; *TWOT* 2:682-84; D. J. A. Clines, *Ezra, Nehemiah, Esther*, NCBC, 1984; T. D. Hanks, *God So Loved the Third World: The Biblical Vocabulary of Oppression*, 1983, 247-70.

Paul Wegner

6701	ענה

ענה (*'nh* III), q. be troubled about, be occupied with; hi. keep someone busy with (# 6701); nom. עִנְיָן (*'inyān*), affair, concern, business, occupation (# 6721); מַעֲנֶה (*ma'ᵃneh* II), purpose (hapleg.; → # 5102).

OT 1. The usual separation of four homonymic roots, *'nh* I-IV, is problematic (*HALAT* 807-8; BDB, 775-76; L. Delekat, "Zum hebräischen Wörterbuch," *VT* 17, 1964, 38; *THAT* 2:335-36; *TWAT* 6:243-45). But the etymological debate has little significance for theological reflection. Apart from *ma'ᵃneh* II (Prov 16:4), this root is exclusive vocabulary to Ecclesiastes (11x). Qohelet uses the nom. *'inyān* as a general term for the concerns, affairs, or tasks of human existence. It encapsulates all those activities evaluated in his grim vision of reality within the framework of futility (Eccl 1:3, *hebel*; cf. Michael Fox, "The Meaning of HEBEL for Qohelet," *JBL* 105, 1986, 409-27). Nothing is exempted. *'inyān* takes in human vocational pursuits as well as the perennial round of historical patterns in the human-cultural life cycle: aspirations for meaning, fulfillment, and a secure existence; moral, ethical and religious behavior; and even the search for understanding and wisdom (contrast NCB, 49; M. Fox, *Qohelet and His Contradictions,* 152, who limit *'inyān* to the search for understanding). For parallel expressions in Qohelet's vocabulary, cf. *ma'ᵃśeh*, work (→ # 5126) < *'śh*, do (1:13, 14; 2:17), and *'āmāl*, toil (→ # 6662) < *'ml*, labor (1:3).

2. Qohelet's evaluation of human concerns or tasks is negative; they are an evil or misfortune (*rā'*; Eccl 1:13) perpetrated against the human race, causing frustration and pain (2:23) and of no advantage whatever (2:11). This state of affairs exists not because of human moral failure or want of skillful exercise of human industry, but because the Creator has irrevocably determined and arranged it so (1:13; 3:10-11; cf. 1:15). Qohelet's theology of creation is in striking contrast and tension with the profoundly affirmative theology of creation reflected in the Pentateuchal creation accounts or the creation hymns in the Psalms (→ *br'* I, create, separate, # 1343). Qoheleth's theology of creation is also in tension with the early Christian theology of the apostle Paul, who situates the creation-human order within the soteriological framework of primordial human sin and subsequent curse/futility destined for eschatological reversal (Rom 8:20-21). Qohelet, in contrast to Israel's traditional wisdom assumptions, postulates an enigmatic, frustrating created order. For him, the latter reflects the character of a labyrinthine deity, inimical to the triumphalist human quest for a secure and meaningful mastery of existence. On the problem of correlating this aspect of Qohelet's thought with the positive affirmations present in the final form of the book, see M. Fox, *Qohelet and His Contradictions*, 1990. (→ Ecclesiastes: Theology)

3. Three unrelated Heb. roots are masked by the English idea of "concern": *d'g*, of little theological significance (→ # 1793), signifies a feeling of concern—i.e., anxiety, fear, or dread. *śyḥ* ranges from mental/emotional to verbal acts and signifies

concern with—i.e., think about, talk about, express concern about something. Theological significance derives from its use in the vocabulary of worship in the Psalms (→ # 8488). *'nh* III, not properly a theological term in its own right, referring predominantly to any external activity that one is busy with, concerned with, takes on theological interest (see above) within the reflections of Ecclesiastes on the character of human existence and its concerns—i.e., affairs, tasks.

P-B The LXX translates all three roots variously and inconsistently.

NT It is difficult to detect the extent to which, if any, these terms directly influenced the NT. For comparison with parallel terminology, see *NIDNTT* 1:276-78; 2:860-61; 3:798-800; *TDNT* 2:40-41; 4:589-93; 6:23-26.

Concern, business, occupation, trouble: → *d'g* (be anxious, concerned, fear, dread, # 1793); → *'nh* III (be troubled, busy with, # 6701); → *ṣrr* I (bind, shut up, be narrow, in straits, distress, # 7674); → *śyḥ*, complain, muse, study, talk, meditate, # 8488)

Bibliography
J. L. Crenshaw, "Qoheleth in Current Research," *HAR* 7, 1983, 41-56; idem, *Ecclesiastes,* 1987, 23-28, 72-73; D. C. Fredericks, *Qoheleth's Language: Reevaluating Its Nature and Date,* 1988, 235; R. Gordis, *Koheleth: The Man and His World,* 1968, 112-22; Diethelm Michel, *Qohelet,* 1988, 82-107; *TWAT* 6:243, 245-46; M. Wagner, *Die lexikalischen und grammatikalischen Aramäismen im alttestamentlichen Hebräisch,* 1966, 92; C. F. Whitley, *Koheleth: His Language and Thought,* 1978, 12, 56; J. G. Williams, "Proverbs and Ecclesiastes," in *The Literary Guide to the Bible*, eds., R. Alter and F. Kermode, 1987, 277-82.

A. R. Pete Diamond

6702	ענה

ענה (*'nh* IV), q. and pi. sing (# 6702).

ANE Arab. *ġny* II, sing; Syr. *'ny*, sing responsively. It is unlikely that there is an Ugar. *'ny*, sing (Andersen, 109).

OT This vb. is sometimes hard to distinguish from *'nh* I, answer. In Hos 2:15[17] it is to be attributed to the latter (NIV mg.). In other contexts antiphonal singing may be in view (Sasson, 157).

1. The most common usage relates to women's singing of victory songs (Exod 15:21; 1 Sam 18:7; 21:12; 29:5; cf. Jer 51:14).

2. The vb. relates to other communal celebrations of diverse kinds, with reference to the digging of a well in Num 21:17 and to the grape harvest in Jer 25:30. The latter setting is also reflected in Isa 27:2, where the vb. introduces the song of God's vineyard that is a positive counterpart to the song of judgment in 5:1-7.

3. In Exod 32:18 the vb. occurs 3x in Moses' description of the Israelites' revelry over the golden calf (v. 6). The noise is twice described in negative terms, using the q.: it is neither the sound of a song of victory nor that of a song of defeat. In the third case an intensive pi. is used, perhaps with reference to loud singing; the LXX interprets it as drunken cries.

4. It expresses hymnic praise in Ezra 3:11; Ps 147:7. In the heading to Ps 88 *lᵉ'annôt* is of uncertain meaning and generally left untranslated; it may refer to singing (Kraus, *Psalms 60-150,* 190; NAB). In 119:172 the wish to sing of God's word is an

indirect petition for a positive answer to the psalmist's prayer of lament, so that in turn he may praise God in thanksgiving.

NT → *NIDNTT* 3:668-76

Praising, singing, thanksgiving: → *hll* II (praise, be praiseworthy, boast, exult, # 2146); → *zmr* I (make music, sing praise, # 2376); → *ydh* II (acknowledge, give thanks, praise, # 3344); → *nwh* II (praise, # 5658); → *'nh* IV (sing, # 6702); → *psḥ* I (break forth with or break into singing, # 7200); → *rômēm* (exalt, # 8123a); → *šbḥ* I (commend, praise, honor, # 8655); → *šyr* (sing, # 8876); → *tnh* (recite, commemorate, # 9480)

BIBLIOGRAPHY

F. I. Andersen, "A Lexicographical Note on Exodus xxxii 18," *VT* 16, 1966, 108-12; J. M. Sasson, "The Worship of the Golden Calf," *Orient and Occident*, 1973, 151-59.

Leslie C. Allen

6703	עֹנָה

עֹנָה (*'ōnâ*), nom. cohabitation, sexual intercourse (marital intercourse) (# 6703).

OT The nom. refers to conjugal rights, i.e., sexual intercourse. According to Exod 21:10, if another concubine was taken by the master, the first one was not to be deprived of her food, clothing, and marital rights.

Sexual relations: → *'ešek* (testicle, # 863); → *zirmâ* (phallus, emission, # 2444); → *m^ebûšîm* (genitals, # 4434); → *nablût* (genitals, # 5578); → *n^eḥōšet* II (menstruation, lust, # 5734); → *'gn* (keep oneself secluded, # 6328); → *'ōnâ* (cohabitation, sexual intercourse, # 6703); → *škb* (lie down, be ravished, be bedded down, # 8886); → *škh* (exhibit strong testicles, to have strong carnal desire, # 8889); → *šopkâ* (fluid duct of male organ, urinary tubule/organ, # 9163); → **Sexual ordinances: Theology**

Jackie A. Naudé

6705	עָנָו

עָנָו, עָנִי (*'ānāw* [# 6705]; *'ānî* [# 6714]), adj. humble, needy, afflicted, poor; עֲנָוָה (*'^anāwâ*), nom. humility (# 6708); עַנְוָה (*'anwâ*), humility (hapleg. in Ps 18:36; # 6709); עֱנוּת (*'^enût*), affliction (# 6713); עֳנִי (*'^onî*), miser,y affliction (# 6715); תַּעֲנִית (*ta'^anît*), fasting (# 9504); < ענה (*'nh* II), q. be downcast, afflicted; ni. humble o.s. be humbled; pi. afflict humble, do violence to, rape, afflict one's soul, fast; pu. be afflicted, hi. oppress, afflict, hitp. humble s.o., submit (→ # 6700).

ANE The Hebrew root *'nh* emphasizes the use of force leading to humiliation, the basic sense being stoop low (Isa 31:4; Zech 10:2). Arab. *'anā'*, be lowly, submissive. Cognates occur in Syr. and Eth. with the same meaning. The root is attested in Aram. inscriptions: *'nwh*, poverty, humiliation (*Aḥiqar*, 1. 105; *APFC*, 223; *KAI* 11, 206). In Moabite *'nw* is found in the Meša' Inscription, where it describes the oppression of Moab by Omri of Israel (*KAI* 181 5 [cf. 6]).

OT 1. In the semantic relationship of the Heb. adj. *'ānî* and *'ānāw* (humble, poor, needy), the difference or the lack of it between the forms *'ānî* and *'ānāw* is important. *'ānî* means to have been humbled, afflicted by necessity or circumstances, stressing the difficulty of the condition and implying (in distinction from *'ebyôn*, needy [→ # 36], *dal*, impoverished [→ # 1924]—with which words it is often linked) some kind of disability present. In the earlier law codes the meaning for *'ānî* is presented as a technical one of dispossessed, thus without landed property (Lev 19:10; 23:22; Deut 15:11; 24:12) and poor, virtually without citizenship. The *'ānî* was on the same level as the resident alien, the widow, and the orphan, all of whom were disadvantaged because of their social standing and who lived from day to day, dependent on others for their welfare and livelihood. They constituted a third economic class positioned somewhere between the free man and the slave, threatened socially and probably excluded from normal communal life. Yahweh, however, was their defender (cf. Deut 10:17-18). Israel later was exhorted by the prophets to deal justly with the *'ānî* (Isa 10:2; 58:7; cf. Prov 14:21). The godly would do this (Ezek 18:17), while the ungodly would withhold their favors (Job 24:9). In the OT generally, *'ānî* was widely used of physical affliction or suffering endured (Job 24:14; 29:12; 36:15; Ps passim; Isa 51:21; 54:11; Jer 22:16; Ezek 16:49, etc.).

2. *'ānāw* means, basically, bent over (under the pressure of circumstances) and consequently, as affliction does its proper work, humble. The Greek OT renderings of *'ānî* and *'ānāw* confirm this since *'ānî* is normally translated by LXX *penēs*, *ptōchos*, *asthenēs*, *tapeinos*, but *'ānāw* is only rarely translated by *penēs* (Ps 10:17; 22:26) or *ptōchos* (Ps 69:33; Isa 29:19; 61:1) but mostly by *praus* or *tapeinos*. The task of deciding the question of the semantic distinction between the forms has not been made any easier by the confusion in the received Heb. text between the pl. forms, since in the late Heb. script (first century BC to AD 100), Heb. *waw* and *yodh* were difficult to distinguish (as is apparent from the frequent Ketib/Qere variations). The sing. form *'ānāw* occurs only at Num 12:3. The K (*'ᵃnawîm*) is textually written in Ps 9:19; Isa 32:7; Amos 8:4, but a scribal Q is proposed at these places; on the other hand, the K *'ᵃniyyîm* is written in Ps 9:13; 10:12; Prov 3:34; 14:21; 16:19, where the Q *'ᵃnāwîm* is scribally preferred.

3. Two questions now surface: (a) Is the *'ānāw*/*'ānî* distinction an original pairing, and if not, when did it appear in the language? (b) What is the relationship between the *'ᵃnāwîm* and the *'ᵃniyyîm* when the latter is used other than exclusively economically? If *'ānāw*/*'ānî* are original synonyms, then the religious/moral development for *'ᵃnāwîm*, humble, is later, but a distinction between the forms seems there as early as Num 12:3, which is regarded as non-Mosaic by even the most conservative scholars and certainly by Zephaniah's period. It has been suggested that the distinction in the two terms *'ānāw*/*'ānî* was a prophetic one designed to distinguish the poor—*'ānî*, *'ebyôn*, *dal*—from the pious—*'ᵃnāwîm*. Be that as it may, what can be said is that the application of the terms to the emerging remnant entity in Israel emptied them of any necessary economic thrust (particularly in the case of *'ānî*).

4. The designation *'ānî*, afflicted, needy, as opposed to *'ānāw*, humble, is never linked to deserved poverty but always is used to denote those who were exploited and wrongfully impoverished (Job 24:4; Ps 37:14; Isa 32:7). The *'ᵃniyyîm* are Yahweh's special people in a special relationship. Yahweh can refer to them as "my people" (Exod 22:24[25]) and he is their special protector (Prov 22:22-23). Opposed to the *'ānî* are not the rich as we might suppose, but the wicked, *rᵉšā'îm* (Ps 9:18[19]), the violent, *pārîṣ* (Ezek 18:10-12), and the oppressor, *'ōšēq* (cf. Amos 4:1), all words referring to

fellow Israelites. In caring for the *ʿaniyyîm*, pious Israelites manifested their covenant loyalty. While that care was the responsibility of every level of society, it was incumbent on Israel's king to ensure that the *ʿānî* received justice in the courts (Ps 72:2-4; Prov 31:9). After the exile the various groups of the oppressed, the poor, the needy, the humble, obedient to Yahweh, consolidated themselves and move closer together (Ps 119:41). It is consistent with all this that the coming Messiah would be of this disposition (Zech 9:9). But in view of the benefits flowing from affliction, God can be thanked as its author (Ps 88:7[8]; 90:15; 119:75; Lam 3:33).

5. The Heb. noms. *ʿonî* and *ʿanāwâ*. The ambiguous relationship of the adjectives also obtains in regard to the two noms., *ʿonî* coordinate with *ʿānî* as affliction (Gen 16:11; 29:32; 1 Sam 1:11) and *ʿanāwâ* (Prov 15:33; 18:12; 22:4; Zeph 2:3), humility. In the LXX *ʿonî* is rendered by *tapeinōsis*, *penia*, and *thlipsis*, while *ʿanāwâ* by *prautēs*. *ʿanāwâ* is considered the religious term, describing the believing relationship to Yahweh. As hapax legomena, three further noms. occur: *ʿanwâ*, humility (Ps 18:36), *ʿenût*, affliction (Ps 22:25), and *taʿanît*, fasting (Ezra 9:5).

6. Theological Reflections.

(a) *Pentateuch*. The reference at Num 12:3 (*ʿānāw*) is of Moses as more humble than anyone else on the face of the earth. He thus exhibits the true nature of humility in human experience and is therefore paradigmatic for Israel. The reference must be taken closely together with the remark that precedes, "And the LORD heard this" (i.e., the complaint against Moses' leadership leveled by Miriam and Aaron, 12:2). Moses was prepared to submit to this unprovoked and hurtful attack by leaving his vindication to God. This selfless, trustful, nonassertive attitude to life is thus characteristic of the virtue.

The vb. is used in Deut 8:1-3 of Israel humbled by Yahweh in the wilderness. The chapter then presents a contrast to a proud Israel (v.17). An attitude of pride was ill-suited to a people whose life and prosperity had come from the hands of a redeeming God. This passage then becomes the paradigm of how Israel in her history is to relate to Yahweh. Thus, at the beginning of her entry into the Promised Land Israel is aware of the necessity for national humility if the blessings of the land are to be enjoyed.

(b) *The Prophets*.

(i) Amos, who prophesied in the prosperous reign of Jeroboam II (782-753 BC), reflects extensively on the luxurious and indolent life of the rich (Amos 5:11; 6:4). The prime sin of Israel was its treatment of its poor and needy. Concomitant with the socially elevated state of the rich was the position of the small landowners, who had been reduced to peasantry and penury. In these circumstances the rich merchants exploited the new poor and the needy of Israel by their corrupt commercial practices (8:4-6, *ʿaniyyîm*). The judgment context of 2:2-7 indicts Israel for the economic and judicial aggressions perpetrated by the upper classes. In this context the *ʿanāwîm* (2:7, NIV deny justice to the oppressed, but NASB, turn aside the way of the humble; cf. also 8:4 K) are linked in parallelism with the preceding social terms, *'ebyôn*, needy, and *dallîm*, poor, as a defined innocent group within Israel involved with the economically oppressed and judicially disadvantaged, yet conceptually differentiated from them. At this stage they are a viable part of the whole of an Israel who must accept total responsibility for covenant maintenance. Amos may be indicating how the one who has been socially degraded becomes humble ethically. In Amos it is God himself who uncovers the malaise, since conditions in Israel cry out for heavenly intervention. Amos underscores the fact that Israel's deity is Yahweh, the covenant God who had brought Israel out of the land of Egypt (2:10; 3:1; 9:7). The judgment on the rich and powerful has as its aim the creation of the egalitarian society, which Israel's election demanded, in a land that was free from exploitation. The election of Israel brings with it heavy responsibilities; Yahweh will visit upon it a requital for its covenant violation.

(ii) *Isaiah*. The poor (*ʿaniyyîm*) and God's people are paired, while the rich are condemned for striking at the fabric of covenant society (Isa 3:14-15; cf. 10:2). The messianic age, in which all inequities will be removed, is an era where the Spirit of God resting on the Messiah will take Israel back to its Davidic beginnings and build a new dynastic line (11:1-16). The king will show concern for the weakest members of the state. As the product of his divine endowment (vv. 2-3a) there will come the absolute justice of his rule (vv. 3b-5), bringing qualities of security to the people of God that are characterized in vv. 6-9. This ruler is one for whom the welfare of the people is his uppermost thought; this is an unattainable human ideal but can only be satisfied by divine government. His judgment, the exercise of his royal office, will be according to prescribed covenant norms. Thus, he will judge in righteousness the poor, identified by the parallelism with *ʿanāwîm*, meek (v. 4). The typical messianic reversal of circumstances is required because deception and manipulation have distorted reality. Correspondingly the rich and powerful will be judged in accordance with the Messiah's justice (v. 4), their deeds being wicked. The weak will be seen as covenant brothers whose denial of their rights will be avenged. Because a society that impoverishes, enslaves, humiliates, and marginalizes the disadvantaged is not the kingdom of God, the prophets encourage all the godly to look to God for change. It is not difficult to see how the virtue of humility arises from affliction.

In Isa 14:32 Zion has been founded as a refuge for the afflicted (*ʿaniyyîm*). In Isa 26:6 the distressed (*ʿānî*) and the impoverished (*dallîm*) will place their feet on the ruins of the previous inequitable social structure. Isa 29:17-21 constitutes an indictment of Judah's leaders, who had ignored God. The common people had borne the brunt of the ensuing social disasters. Verses 18-19 speak of the coming blessings of the helpless. Above all, the coming age will be concerned with justice for the oppressed, where the humble (*ʿanāwîm*) are mentioned along with the disadvantaged of the community—the deaf, the blind, and the needy (*'ebyônîm*). Comfort will be brought for them in the shape of the heart-changing salvation offered by Isaiah as their relief from the present oppression.

In Isa 40-55, God's intervention, which would bring the Exile to an end, was eagerly awaited. The structure of oppression was not that imposed by one Israelite on another, for the nation as a whole was now the despoiled and was suffering captivity and exploitation at the hands of oppressing nations (41:17-20). It is in these circumstances that the prophet announces the return of the captivity and the advent of the New Jerusalem. The afflicted are now all of God's people, before whom the prophet places the prospect of return. The humiliated and oppressed (*ʿaniyyîm*) are the recipients of divine compassion (49:13). They receive the promise of the new covenant of peace (54:11). But the Servant will be the One who, in being afflicted, will take on himself the afflictions of Israel (Isa 53:7).

The Servant personage in Isa 61:1 announces his messianic charter as one anointed by the Spirit of God to bring good news to the meek (*ʿᵃnāwîm*), the faithful Israelites (though the LXX with its reading of *ptōchois* seems to presuppose *ʿᵃniyyîm*, afflicted). Nothing less than the end-time Jubilee, the restitution of God's original righteousness for his people, will be ushered in, essentially a reconstitution of creation. The *ʿᵃnāwîm* (61:1) prepare themselves for the coming of that day by mourning for Zion and by awaiting the salvation that has not yet arrived. God is with such poor (*ʿānî*) who, by definition, are contrite in spirit (66:2, *ʿānî*).

(iii) Zephaniah moves in the same direction as Amos and Isaiah, but there is a fresh nuance with the identification of the *ʿᵃnāwîm* with the remnant, though perhaps anticipated in Isaiah 40-55. In Zeph 2:1-3 the context is one of the Day of the Lord against Judah. The prophet pauses to exhort the nation to repentance—the prophet's first offer of redemption. The only kind word is directed to the humble of (or from) the land (*ʿᵃnāwîm*, 2:3). These humble righteous are significantly different from the rest of the nation (1:4-13). By seeking righteousness and continued humility, *ʿᵃnāwâ*, they set themselves off from an arrogant generation (2:8, 10, 15; 3:11). Thus, humility is urged upon them in apposition to righteousness, a response in behavior and practice that God demands and which the godly are to strive more fully to do (Dawes, 41). Even so, there is no guarantee of their preservation in this world, because God's anger will affect even the *ʿᵃnāwîm*.

In Zeph 3:11-13 the afflicted (*ʿānî*) and the poor, who, by the juxtaposition of vv. 12 and 13, are the remnant, are truly righteous, while the proud and the haughty are considered enemies of Yahweh. Yahweh will remove all the proud and thus leave only the afflicted (*ʿānî*, 3:11-12), i.e., those who seek refuge in the Lord. In view of the parallelism between the afflicted and the remnant in 3:12-13, the humble in 2:3 are the remnant later designated in 2:7. Thus Zephaniah shows clearly the connection between highly approved ethical conduct and lowly social status. Zeph 3:11-13 makes it clear that the humiliated shun engaging in unjust social action in contrast to those who use violence in society; instead, they seek refuge with God. The people of God involved and characterized as oppressed are the antithesis of the godless upper strata.

The redeemed remnant (see 2:1-3, 7) constitutes a new and powerful people in Zeph 3. These afflicted have an active trust (3:12) and are people of integrity. They are like God in their hatred of lies (3:5), and deceit (3:13). They praise God for his mercy and thus show their dependence on him (3:14-17). They seek God and live righteously (2:1-3). The term *ʿānî*, oppressed, by Zephaniah's time refers to the absence of influence, wealth and notable rank in society. They are the people who are righteousness (2:3) and the only ones who will have no cause for anxiety at the coming horrors of the Day of the wrath of Yahweh. In Zeph 3:6-8 Yahweh's intervention paves the way for the appearance of the remnant/humble and their future blessing. The faithful remnant will return from far lands (3:10), find forgiveness (3:11), remain faithful to God (3:12), be righteous (3:13), and dwell in peace (3:13).

(c) *Psalms*. The movement from outward distress (material poverty) to the humble poor who trust God (Ps 14:6) and recognize themselves as the bearers of the divine promises is clearly seen in the book of Psalms. The designations *ʿānî*, and particularly *ʿānāw*, become the self-chosen titles of those who are in deep need and difficulty, and who humbly seek help from Yahweh alone or who have found it

(Ps 40:17[18]; 102:1). The nom. *ʿᵒnî* deals usually with the situation of great need in which Yahweh is entreated to intervene (Ps 25:18; 31:8; 119:53; cf. Job 30:16; Lam 1:9; Neh 9:9).

A shift in basic meanings in the two adjectives *ʿānî*, afflicted, and *ʿānāw*, meek/humble, appears to have taken place before the Exile and to have been bound up with the emergence of a remnant within the nation with whom the humble/afflicted/needy have been identified (Zeph 2:3; 3:12). God is now clearly the great reverser of circumstances, bringing down the proud and the powerful, delivering the afflicted (Ps 35:10), and choosing and exalting Israel as the lowly of God (afflicted, Ps 68:10[11]; 72:2; 74:19, 21; meek, 76:9). It is the nature of Yahweh to dwell with the lowly and the contrite of heart. God esteems, bestows favor on, looks upon, and does not despise the prayer of the humble afflicted, who are conscious of their enjoyment of the divine goodwill (Ps 74:19), irrespective of their outward circumstances. During the Exile the faithful, often in the Psalms identified as the godly poor, had learned to wait quietly. When the nobles, the rich, and the powerful showed themselves open to foreign religious influences after the Exile, the poor, needy, and humble obedient to Yahweh in all points were further differentiated, perhaps even consolidated.

(i) Psalm 9-10. These two psalms abound with references to the afflicted, poor, and needy. The composite Ps 9-10 is an individual lament in which the psalmist finds his own personal identity with the needy (*ʿaniyyîm*) (9:12[13]), who have not been forgotten by Yahweh. Yahweh will punish the oppressors who have afflicted the disadvantaged people (9:13). He remembers them, i.e., both the *dakkîm*, oppressed/exploited, of v. 9, and the *ʿᵃniyyîm*, the afflicted, of v. 12. Their affliction consists of attacks by the foreign nations before whom Israel has been exposed (v. 12). While in Ps 10:2 the pursuit of the afflicted by the wicked is keen, there is the expectation that Yahweh will intervene. Ps 10:17 concludes with the expression of confidence that God will not forget the desires of the *ʿᵃnāwîm*, the humble (cf. similarly, 9:18[19] K).

(ii) Psalm 18:27[28]. David praises God for the victory going to the afflicted (*ʿānî*), while the proud are afflicted in this typical divine reversal of circumstances. In 18:35[36], in the third part of the verse, we have "and your humility (*ʿᵃnāwâ*) has made me great" (NIV you stoop down to make me great; note 2 Sam 22:36, "and your help [*waʿᵃnōtᵉkā*] has made me great"). Many conjectures have been proposed for the unusual form, but the sense of divine humility in 18:35[36] is not impossible (Ps 113:6). God's condescension has saved David. God had stooped to conquer David's enemies. The divine character had been exhibited in seeking and promoting the welfare of David. There seems to be no incompatibility between humility of this character and the exercise of God's controlled power (Dawes, 46).

(iii) Psalm 22. The prayer portion of the lament moves in two phases (vv. 1-11[2-12] and vv. 12-21[13-22]), each concluding with the theme of the psalm, "be not far off" (vv. 11[12], 19[20]).

In vv. 22-26[23-27] the movement is from prayer for help to praise for aid received (v. 24[25]). The delivered one is surrounded now by a company of people in praise and faith. All the different designations from v. 22[23] onwards refer to this company. They are fearers of the Lord (v. 23[24]), descendants of Jacob/Israel (vv. 23[24], 25[26]), seekers of the Lord (v. 26[27]), and the meek (*ʿᵃnāwîm*, v. 26[27]). These meek, seekers, and fearers see themselves as the true Israel, the real congregation, who live by the praise of the Lord. Without separating themselves from their society, they are thinking and speaking about themselves and their relation to God in a way that is beginning to redefine what it means to be Israel. They have learned that Yahweh does not despise the affliction of the humble but hears their cry for help.

Verses 23-24[24-25] call upon the assembly to join the delivered one in his praise of Yahweh, who is the defender of the poor (*'ānî*) and who satisfies them. The company of believers celebrate not only the salvation of the member but the good news of deliverance (v. 25[26]). The salvation of the one is the ground of hope for all the lowly. In vv. 26-31[27-32], the fate of this afflicted/meek one is further connected with the future of the kingdom of Yahweh. Its message extends to the entire world with its families of many peoples (v. 27[28]) and for future generations yet unborn (vv. 30-31[31-32]). Such a universal recognition will take place through the proclamation of the afflicted ones as the righteousness of God (v. 31[32]). So the vision of the hymn is prophetic in character and eschatological in its hope. And yet Ps 22 is more than the prayer and praise of an afflicted person. It properly pertains to the Davidic king, who like the Servant of Yahweh of Isaiah 40-55 provides a profound example of suffering and inward humility (cf. Isa 53:7). So the psalmist offers a messianic portrait, later to be realized in the ministry of Jesus the Messiah. Jesus identifies himself with the figure of the psalm in his own death. Hence, the psalm is used in the NT to interpret the death and resurrection of Jesus. It is a theodicy for all who commit their ways to Yahweh. Jesus suffered and died as one of the meek for the humble.

(iv) Psalm 25. The Ps begins with an expression of trust and a plea that the psalmist's enemies not be allowed to triumph (vv. 1-3). In vv. 4-7 outward oppression and inward distress are found side by side. In vv. 8-9 Yahweh guides the *'ᵃnāwîm* (v. 9), with whom the psalmist is to be plausibly identified. The *'ᵃnāwîm* of v. 9 are sinners who are taught the way of the Lord (vv. 8b, 9), the righteous covenant keepers (v. 10), who wait on him (v. 21). Verses 12-14 focus on the one who fears Yahweh, a further presentation of the manner of life of the *'ᵃnāwîm*.

(v) Psalm 34. The psalmist refers to his intention to praise Yahweh (vv. 1-3[2-4]). The *'ᵃnāwîm* (v. 2[3]) who join him (v. 3[4]) are the congregation of Israel, who look towards the Lord for his deliverance (v. 5[6]). They are the poor (cf. v. 6[7], *'ānî*, those who fear Yahweh [v. 7(8)], who trust him [v. 8(9)], who seek him [v. 10(11)], and who are righteous [v. 15(16)]). Their plea comes to Yahweh from an absolute submission to his will, being of a broken heart and of a contrite spirit (v. 18[19]).

(vi) Psalm 37. We may note the synonyms whereby the *'ᵃnāwîm* are identified with the righteous (*ṣaddîq*). The righteous in the psalm are the *'ᵃnāwîm* (vv. 11, 29), those "who hope in the LORD" (v. 9); the "meek" (v. 11); "the righteous," (vv. 12, 16a, 17b, 21b, 25b, 29a, 30a, 32a, 39a); the "poor and needy" (v. 14b); "those whose ways are upright" (v. 14c); "the blameless" (vv. 18a, 37a); "those the LORD blesses" (v. 22a); "the just" (v. 28); "the upright" (v. 37a); "man of peace" (v. 37b). The quiet patient acceptance of their lot, without resistance, anger, or complaint, cherishing the hopes of Israel within them, marks them as the true Israel. Yahweh will reverse adversity into blessing (37:11; 147:6; Isa 26:6). God, the ultimate judge (Ps 49:4; 76:9), encourages the lowly to wait in hope for they will receive their reward (37:9).

It can thus be argued that *'ānāw*, and probably *'ānî*, have changed their meaning from a depiction of material disadvantage and the humiliation that follows, to a self-chosen title of people who in their deep need and difficulty turn to Yahweh and find help from him. Doubtless poverty and disadvantage had functioned as fruitful soil for piety and humility. The humble are not reconciled to the situation of oppression and exploitation but seek to break out of the circle of violence. They rely on God, who promises change and blessing, dependent on their relationship with one another. The point of the psalm is to offer hope to all who have been put in adverse circumstances. That hope is not miraculous; it is a change in themselves. By praising God they will experience an inner control over external circumstances. They are heirs to the promises given to Israel. Theirs is the earth. They are the true Israel. The violence of the workers of wickedness will rebound on their own heads (Ps 37:22b).

(vii) Psalm 45. In the presentation of messianic kingship in the OT, the "Messiah" is the supporter of the underprivileged, the impoverished, and the needy. So fittingly in Ps 45:4[5] the Messiah's glory is not to increase for its own sake but for the sake of promoting righteous humility (*'anwâ-ṣedeq* [the only occurrence of *'ānwâ*]) and truth. These attributes fit in well with the expectations of the Messiah (cf. Isa 11:4).

(viii) Psalm 69. The psalm is an individual lament, the occasion for which may be the sickness of the poet (vv. 26[27], 29[30]). He calls on Yahweh, his defence, to act. It is clear that the petition is not an isolated case (v. 6[7]), because he pleads for himself and for others so disposed. The hope of all those who trust in Yahweh is at stake in the answer sought in his prayers. The praise for him from all those who will be rescued (31-34[32-35]; cf. 22:23-27) is ground for assurance to the *'anāwîm* (v. 32[33]). The reversal of circumstances comes about by Yahweh's involvement with the psalmist and is evidence for all the *'anāwîm* (v. 32[33]; cf. v. 6[7]). In saving them Yahweh saves Zion (v. 35[36]), for they are heirs of its legacy.

(ix) Psalm 76. Yahweh, who has made his name known (v. 1[2]) and given his revelation to Israel on Mount Zion (v. 2[3]), will destroy all the instruments of war and create *šālôm* for his people (v. 3[4]). The army of courageous heroes who marched on Jerusalem (v. 5-6[6-7]) were repelled by the fearsome appearance of the God of Zion (v. 4[5]). So from heaven comes the judgment that spreads fear and fright worldwide, but signifies salvation for the *'anwê-'ereṣ*, humble of the earth (v. 9[10], NIV afflicted of the land), who have endured the malice of the kings of the earth (*malkê-'ereṣ*, v. 12[13]), the agents of chaos.

(x) Psalm 147. This is one of the five closing *hallel* psalms. Verses 1-2, framed by praise, proclaim the creative power of the God of Israel. Yahweh takes care of his people, returning health and healing to the community (v. 3). By his authoritative voice the Creator calls the stars by name (v. 4) and demonstrates his inexhaustible power and wisdom (v. 5). This God will bring order by vindicating the poor (*'anāwîm*, v. 6) and by condemning the wicked.

(xi) Psalm 149. The psalm is a further *hallel* psalm in celebration of God's kingship. The hymnic introduction (v. 1) invites the congregation to praise Yahweh (v. 2) as the Creator and the King on Zion. What follows in hymnic substantiation of this request speaks of Yahweh's grace to Israel and thus of the salvation (victory) of the meek (*'anāwîm*). The parallelism of "his people" with "the humble" in v. 4 shows that the *ʿanāwîm* are the totality of Israel and, thus, the remnant. This community on Zion is a group of helpless people who put their trust in Yahweh (cf. Isa 14:32). Note that the gracious activity of Yahweh precedes the activity of Israel described in vv. 5-9: The helpless have received grace and salvation from Yahweh. Having received such grace, they may rule with Yahweh. The community of the saints, *ḥasîdîm* (v. 5), i.e., the *ʿanāwîm*, are to praise God and participate in his just rule as king and judge of the world. The traditional interpretation of v. 4 is the promise that the humble (*ʿanāwîm*) will be victorious in war, but the text may point to a cultic rejoicing in salvation granted to the people of God, described here in the traditional terms of humble/meek.

(d) Wisdom literature. In the Wisdom literature the humble/needy display that reverence for Yahweh by recognizing their place in the basic cosmic order, so that humility means the acquiring of a proper self-estimate. This humility is the human recognition of one's own inadequacy when faced with the evidence for creation and providence. Humility is finally defined not in terms of lowliness but in terms of selflessness and is an essential root of all wisdom (cf. Prov 11:2). The fear of God and humility are necessary concomitants, for true selfhood is to be found in the fear of Yahweh, a point emphasized in 16:18-19. The possession of true humility brings greater joy than sharing in the ill-gotten gain of the proud.

In the book of Proverbs *ʿānî* is almost exclusively used, as we might expect of proverbial and old material, in an economic sense (Prov 22:22; 30:14; 31:9, 20, though cf. 15:15, oppressed). *ʿānāw*/*ʿanāwâ* appear in the general rules of life to be observed by the world at large and not as tied to a particular society. In short, humility, like righteousness in Proverbs, is part of the cosmic ordering of the created universe, one of the essential factors by which life in God's creation proceeds. Yahweh is scornful towards the scorners, but shows favor to the *ʿanāwîm* (3:34). The effect of arrogance is disgrace (11:2). But with the humble (*ṣenûʿîm*) is wisdom. The Heb. nom. occurs only here in the OT but is derived from the vb. *ṣnʿ*, be modest (traditionally "humble"; cf. Micah 6:8), and given the antithesis of this wisdom context in Proverbs, it is probably to be understood as not thinking more highly of oneself that one ought to think. The possession of such a characteristic is not likely to bring its possessor into disgrace, which arrogance will.

"The fear of the LORD teaches a man wisdom, and humility (*ʿanāwâ*) comes before honor" (Prov 15:33). Here the parallel to "humility" is the major wisdom feature of "the fear of the LORD." The whole parallel statement "the fear of the LORD teaches a man wisdom" is a variant of the normal "the fear of the LORD is the beginning of wisdom" (cf. Job 28:28; Ps 111:10; Prov 1:7; 9:10; Eccl 12:13); i.e., the fear of Yahweh is the first principle, that upon which wisdom is based. In short, wisdom has a religious foundation, a positive devotion to God, which means the renunciation of pride and the expression of humility. It means the renunciation of autonomy and trusting Yahweh at every step of life's progress, again an accurate description of what is involved in humility (Prov 3:5-7). The parallel clause to 9:10 ("the fear of the LORD is the beginning of wisdom") is "knowledge of the Holy One is understanding," a phrase requiring the acknowledgment of the distance that separates humanity from God, viz., humility. The usage of *ʿanāwâ* in 15:33 and 22:4 brings out this fact.

ʿanāwâ is thus the personal quality that makes integration into the world order possible and enables the possessor to know his place in the total system. *ʿanāwâ* confesses the limits beyond which human wisdom cannot pass and acknowledges human lowliness before God. The would-be wise man in his world is humbled by his recognition that humankind is not the measure of all things. The opposite to humility is the scornful attitude of the religious despisers, to which Prov 1:7 points. Note that all three occurrences of *ʿᵃnāwâ* in Prov associate humility with social recognition and status. The second clause of 15:33 appears word for word in 18:12: "Before his downfall a man's heart is proud, but humility (*ʿᵃnāwâ*) comes before honor." As pride, the opposite of humility, brings destruction, humility brings honor. Humility is here defined again as the fear of God and, in sharp contrast to arrogance, is revealed in modesty before God and human beings. According to O. Ploeger (*Sprüche Salomos*, 1981[3], 213), humility in 18:12 is to be understood as a sign of self-critical judgment, a sober evaluation of one's own importance, which nevertheless brings one success.

In Prov 22:4 "humility" (*ʿᵃnāwâ*) and "the fear of the LORD" are coupled as appositional parallels. Their compatible reward is "wealth and honor and life." Unlike the prophetic and psalmic literature, humility and poverty are generally not compatible in Wisdom literature. Yet the sages observe that the disassociation of the humble from the evildoers does not guarantee success; "Better to be lowly in spirit (*šᵉpal-rûaḥ*) and among the oppressed (*ʿᵃnāwîm*) than to share plunder with the proud" (16:19). The concept of humility, understood here in very positive terms, is detached from its social base. Now generalized humility is no longer indirectly pitted against the prevailing disorder as in the Psalms.

(e) Postexilic prophecy. Zech 9:1-17 is a divine warrior song, where the humble king of Israel enters Jerusalem, riding on an ass. He has conquered Israel's traditional foes in his progress from Hamath on the northern border of the Promised Land down to the temple city (v. 9). The portrait of the humble (*ʿānî,* NIV gentle) Messiah draws support from line 2 of the Aramaic Zakir Stele, "I am a humble man" (*ANET*, 655). The donkey, in contrast with the horse, was not used in warfare. Thus, the image of the king mounted on a donkey is the coming of the "Prince of Peace." This Messiah does not approach riding a horse or a chariot, i.e., belligerently, but in a peaceful and unaggressive processional, as one who is accepted by Yahweh and granted victory. In 11:7, 11 the flock, i.e., Israel as destined for slaughter, is "poor" (*ʿᵃniyyîm*).

Humility, affliction, misery: → *knʿ* (be subdued, be humbled, humble o.s., # 4044); → *ʿnh* II (afflict, humble, afflict one's soul, fast, oppress, submit, # 6700); → *ṣnʿ* (be modest, humble, # 7570); → *šḥḥ* (stoop, crouch, humble, # 8820); → *špl* (be low, be levelled, humiliate, bring low, # 9164)

Affliction, oppression: → *dḥq* (oppress, # 1895); → *ḥms* I (do violence, # 2803); → *ḥmṣ* II (oppress, # 2807); → *ynh* (oppress, # 3561); → *lḥṣ* (press, # 4315); → *māṣôr* I (affliction, siege, # 5189); → *mrr* I (be bitter, distraught, afflict, # 5352); → *negaʿ* (plague, affliction, # 5596); → *ngś* (exact, # 5601); → *ʿnh* II (afflict, humble, afflict one's soul, fast, oppress, submit, # 6700); → *ʿwq* I (crush?, # 6421); → *ʿmr* II (deal tyrannically with, # 6683); → *ʿšq* I (wrong, # 6943); → *ṣwq* I (constrain, press in/upon, harass, vex, # 7439); → *ṣwr* II (deal tyrannically with, # 7444); → *rhb* (assail, press, pester, alarm, confuse, # 8104); → *rṣṣ* (crush, # 8368); → *tôlāl* (oppressor, # 9354); → *tōk* (oppression, # 9412)

Poor, crushed, needy: → *'ebyôn* (poor, needy, # 36); → *dk'* (crush, be crushed, # 1917); → *dal* II (scanty, helpless, powerless, insignificant, dejected, # 1924); → *dqq* (crush, # 1990); → *mwk* (depressed, grow poor, # 4575); → *miskēn* (poor man, # 5014); → *ʿānāw* (poor, humble,

6705); → *'ānî* (humble, # 6714); → *ṣn'* (be modest, humble, # 7570); → *rwš* (become poor, oppressed, # 8133)

Bibliography

NIDNTT 2:256-64; *TDNT* 2:645-51; 8:6-15; *THAT* 2:341-50; *TWAT* 6:247-56; S. B. Dawes, "ANAWA In Translation and Tradition," *VT* 41, 1991, 38-48; Y. I. Kim, "The Vocabulary of Oppression in the Old Testament," (Ph.D. diss. Drew University), 1981; C. F. Marriottini, "The Problem of Social Oppression in the Eighth Century Prophets," (Ph.D. diss. Southern Baptist Theological Seminary), 1983; P. D. Miscall, "The Concept of the Poor in the Old Testament," *HTR* 65, 1972, 600-612.

W. J. Dumbrell

6708 (*'anāwâ*, humility), → # 6705

6708 (*'anāwâ*, humility), → # 6700

6709 (*'anwâ*, humility), → # 6700, # 6705

6711 (*'anûšîm*, fines), → # 6740

6713 (*'enût*, affliction), → # 6700, # 6705

6714 (*'ānî*, humble), → # 6700, # 6705

6715 (*'onî*, misery affliction), → # 6700, # 6705

6721 (*'inyān*, affair, concern, occupation), → # 6701

6725 (*'nn*, bring clouds), → # 6727

6726 ענן

ענן (*'nn*), denom. of *'ānān*; pi. cause s.t. to appear; po. interpret signs, tell fortunes, conjure up, practice magic/sorcery (# 6726); nom. עָנָן (*'ānān* I), clouds, cloud mass (→ # 6727); *'ānān* II, does not occur in OT, but by comparison with Arab. *'anna* (see below) it may have to do with appearing/manifestation, or with Arab. *ǵanna* (see below) it may mean one who speaks through the nose, who nasalizes.

ANE Akk. cf. *ganānu*, confine (*CAD* 5, 40); Arab. *'anna*, appear (suddenly); *ǵanna*, buzz, hum, mumble; Ugar. *'nn*, recite to music (*UT*, 1885); for עָנָן (*'ānān* II) cf. Phoen. *'nn* and Palmyrene *'nyny*.

OT For samples of the terms, see Gen 9:14; Lev 19:26; Deut 18:10, 14; Judg 9:37; 2 Kgs 21:6 ‖ 2 Chron 33:6; Isa 2:6; 57:3; Jer 27:9; Mic 5:11. For an extended discussion on magic, see *kšp*, practice magic (# 4075).

P-B Tg. *'anan* I, pa. to augur from clouds (Jastrow, 1095); *'ānenā'*, interpreter of clouds (Jastrow, 1096).

Cloud: → *ḥāzîz* (cloud, strong wind, thunderclap, # 2613); → *miplāś* (spreading [of a cloud], # 5146); → *'wb* (cover w. cloud, # 6380); → *'ānān* (clouds, # 6727); → *'arāpel* (deep darkness, thick darkness, heavy cloud, # 6906); → *šaḥaq* (dust, clouds of dust, # 8836)

Malcolm J. A. Horsnell

6727	עָנָן

עָנָן (*'ānān* I), nom. (mass of) clouds (# 6727); עֲנָנָה (*'^{a}nānâ*), a (distinct) cloud (only in Job 3:5; # 6729); ענן (*'nn*), pi. bring clouds (only in Gen 9:14) (# 6725).

OT 1. The meteorological phenomenon referred to by *'ānān* is not a distinct cloud, but a cloud mass, seldom if ever bringing rain (Scott, 24-25). It is often used in reference to the dust cloud of a sirocco/east wind (e.g., Jer 4:13; Nah 1:3; see Fitzgerald, 201). The hapleg. *'^{a}nānâ* in Job 3:5—"May darkness and deep shadow claim it once more; may a cloud (*'^{a}nānâ*) settle over it; may blackness overwhelm its light"—is a *nomen unitatis* or singulative for the collective *'ānān*, and there is no evidence for translating *'^{a}nānâ* by "rain cloud," as in *HALAT* 812a (see J. E. Hartley, *The Book of Job*, NICOT, 1988, 90; D. J. A. Clines *Job 1-20*, WBC, 1989, 85).

2. The nom. *'ānān* is most frequent in figures of speech or metaphors for transitoriness, immensity, and impenetrability. As a metaphor, it signifies transitoriness. For example, in Hos 6:4 the "morning cloud" (NIV morning mist) denotes lack of commitment (see Scott, 21, 24; Wolff, *Hosea*, 119). As a figure for immensity, Ezekiel speaks of the power of Gog as "a cloud covering the land" (Ezek 38:9). The image is in keeping with the primary meaning, "mass of clouds." As a metaphor for impenetrability, the mass of clouds signifies the distance the exilic people felt to exist between themselves and God: "You have covered yourself with a cloud so that no prayer can get through" (Lam 3:44).

3. The majority of the occurrences of *'ānān* (58 out of 87) are used in relation to God's theophanic presence. The visible manifestation of God's glory is frequently in the *'ānān*: on Sinai (Exod 24:16); in the Tent of Meeting (40:34-35); in the temple (1 Kgs 8:11; Ezek 10:4); on the eschatological Mount Zion (Isa 4:5; cf. Luke 21:27). (→ Theophany: Theology)

(a) In some texts God's presence in the *'ānān* serves to guide his people, as in the phrase *'ammûd 'ānān* (pillar of cloud, Exod 13:21; Num 14:14; Deut 31:15). (→ *'ammûd*, pillar # 6647)

(b) God's presence in the *'ānān* also brings judgment, in particular when the meteorological referent of *'ānān* is the sirocco/east wind (Ps 97:2; Jer 4:13; Ezek 30:3; Joel 2:2; Nah 1:3; Zeph 1:15); the majority of these texts explicitly link the theophanic *'ānān* of judgment to the Day of the Lord: "a day of darkness and gloom, a day of clouds (*'ānān*) and blackness (*'^{a}rāpel*, → # 6906). Like dawn spreading across the mountains, a large and mighty army comes, such as never was of old nor ever will be in ages to come" (Joel 2:2; see Fitzgerald, 291-302).

Cloud: → *ḥāzîz* (cloud, strong wind, thunderclap, # 2613); → *miplāś* (spreading [of a cloud], # 5146); → *'wb* (cover w. cloud, # 6380); → *'ānān* (clouds, # 6727); → *'^{a}rāpel* (deep darkness, thick darkness, heavy cloud, # 6906); → *šaḥaq* (dust, clouds of dust, # 8836)

Bibliography

THAT 2:351-53; *TWAT* 6:270-75; G. Dalman, *Arbeit Und Sitte*, 1928-42, repr. 1987, 1:103-14; A. Fitzgerald, "The Lord of the East Wind," diss. Pontifical Biblical Institute, 1983; M. Futato, "Meteorological Analysis," diss. The Catholic University of America, 1984; J. Luzarraga, *Las Tradiciones de la Nube en la Biblia y en el Judaismo Primitivo*, AnBibl 54, 1973, 15-41; G. E. Mendenhall, *The Tenth Generation: The Origins of the Biblical Tradition*, 1973, 32-66; P. Reymond, *L'eau, sa vie, et sa signification dans l'AT*, 1958, 11-18, 29-31, 35-41; P. Sabourin, "The

Biblical Cloud: Terminology and Tradition," *BTB* 4, 1974, 290-312; R. Scott, "Meteorological Phenomena," *ZAW* 64, 1952, 11-25; E. F. Sutcliffe, "The Clouds as Water-Carriers in Hebrew Thought," *VT* 3, 1953, 99-103.

Mark D. Futato

6729 (*ʿanānâ*, distinct cloud), → # 6727

6733 (*ʿānāp*, branches), → # 580

6734 (*ʿānēp*, full of branches), → # 580

6735	ענק

ענק (*ʿnq*), q. put on as a necklace; hi. adorn the neck of s.o. as with a necklace (# 6735); עֲנָק (*ʿanāq* I), nom. necklace (# 6736).

ANE Akk. *unqu*, ring (cf. *AHw*, 1422); Aram. *ʿi/ʿunqāʾ*, neck, throat, necklace (Jastrow, 1096); Syr. *ʿeqqāʾ*, [*ʿeqqāʾ*], necklace; Arab. *ʿnq* II, grasp the neck; *ʿnq* III and VIII, embrace, hug; Eth. *ʿanäqä*, put around the neck; *ʿenqwe*, precious stone (cf. *HALAT* 812).

OT For occurrences, see Judg 8:22; Prov 1:9; S of Songs 4:9.
For a discussion on jewelry, see *ʿdh* (put on ornaments, # 6335).

Malcolm J. A. Horsnell

6736 (*ʿanāq* I, necklace), → # 6735

6740	ענשׁ

ענשׁ (*ʿnš*), q. impose a fine, penalty, levy; ni. be fined, be compelled to make amends for (# 6740); עֲנוּשִׁים (*ʿanûšîm*), fines (q. pass. part., # 6711); עֹנֶשׁ (*ʿōneš*), nom. fine, penalty, levy (# 6741).

ANE The following forms are found: Ugar. *ġnṯ*; Akk. *ḫanāšu/kanāšu*; Sam. hitp. *ijjannaš*; Pun. nom. *ʿnšm*.

OT 1. The ni. is used in Exod 21:22 (part of the Covenant Code [20:22-23:33]), which prescribes that when brawling men hurt (probably inadvertently) a pregnant woman and she suffers a miscarriage (RSV; NRSV; JB; NEB; REB; TEV) or gives birth prematurely (so NIV; Durham, 323), but no further harm follows, then the one who has hurt her shall be fined (*yēʿānēš*) and shall pay the amount levied by the injured woman's husband. As the text stands, the fairness of the demand made by the husband is determined by the judges. However, the last word of MT, *bipᵉlilîm*, is rare and has been variously translated: "as the judges determine" (RSV; NRSV); "subject to the approval of the judges" (TEV); "after arbitration" (JB; cf. Cazelles, cited by Childs, 448; Driver, 219); "after assessment" (NEB; REB); "in accordance with an assessment" (Childs, 443; following Speiser); "in accord with an objective evaluation" (Durham, 308, 312); "[whatever ...] the court allows" (NIV). Budde (cited by, among others, Rylaarsdam, 1000, and Childs, 448) emends the word to *binᵉpilîm*, for the miscarriage (cf. Driver, 219). Some commentators (e.g., Childs, 448) think that the translation "judges" does not fit the context of Exod very well, but others (e.g., Rylaarsdam, 1000; Davies, 178) maintain that this translation is reasonable.

The ni. occurs in Prov 22:3 (and in par. 27:12), which contrasts the alertness and perception of the prudent man (which apprise him of trouble and enable him to take evasive action), with the dullness and myopia of the unwary individual, who continues in ignorance along the way in which danger lurks and suffers the consequences (*w^e^ne'^e^ nāšû*, and they [the simple] suffer [for it].

2. The q. occurs in Deut 22:19, part of a series of laws (22:13-30) regulating sexual behavior, which indicates that in ancient Israel honor and shame were of greater importance than in modern Western society (Clifford, 121) and sex was a concern of the community and not merely a matter of private moral decision (Nelson, 228). According to v. 19, a man who was proved guilty of having wrongfully accused his bride of prenuptial unchastity was compelled to pay a fine of 100 shekels of silver (twice the bridal price?; see v. 29) to the father of the young woman. Phillips (149) argues that the translation "[they shall] fine" in v. 19 is technically incorrect because a fine was a penalty of the criminal law that was imposed by the state and payable to the state, whereas here the money is given to the bride's father as compensation for slander. As additional punishment, the man was to be whipped by the elders (v. 18) and was precluded from ever divorcing his wife. Preventing the man from divorcing his wife meant that even if sexual relations were discontinued, the husband would have to continue to support her, and the legal rights of inheritance belonging to the woman [and her firstborn child, if there were one] would be protected (see Clifford, 119; Craigie, 293). Should the charge brought against the woman be considered proven, then she was stoned to death (vv. 20-21).

The woman's fate hinged on whether or not her father could produce one of two types of evidence in support of his daughter's defense: either a bloodstained garment or item of bedding to prove that his daughter's hymen had been ruptured on the wedding night, or similar indications that the woman had been menstruating shortly before the marriage was consummated (Blenkinsopp, 104-5). Needless to say, this method of determining the guilt or innocence of the woman in question was both crude and uncertain (see Cunliffe-Jones, 129; Payne, 127-28). There can be no denying that women had a subordinate role in ancient Israel. Significantly, the OT insists on the virginity of only the bride, and it was the husband's legal right to expect his spouse to be a virgin on their wedding day.

The bias of a male-dominated society is evident in Deut 22:19 from the double standard of the penalties to be imposed. Whereas a falsely accusing husband was to be whipped, fined, and deprived of the right to divorce, the wife found guilty of prenuptial unchastity forfeited her life. Moreover, if the woman were adjudged to be innocent, the compensation awarded for malicious defamation of character would be given not to her, but to her father (Gottwald, 114). The reputation of the bride's father seems to have been considered more important than that of the woman herself (cf. Mayes, 311). Nevertheless, despite their discriminatory nature, these laws did afford women a degree of protection from the worst excesses of male domination (Nelson, 228). Ancient Israelite law makers can be criticized for their partiality, their one-dimensional perspective of sexual problems, and their totally uncompromising attitude towards punishment. However, while not underestimating these obvious flaws, the regulations in Deut 22:13-30 serve as a salutary reminder to moderns grown accustomed to an excess of liberty and latitude in sexual matters that purity and fidelity are of great importance and need to be jealously guarded (Cunliffe-Jones, 129; Miller, 160-63).

The q. inf. is used in Prov 17:26, which criticizes bad penal practice (see McKane, 506-7), citing the legal abuse of imposing a fine on an innocent person. The q. inf. occurs again in 21:11, which comments on the discipline administered to the unteachable scoffer (the intellectually supercilious). The imposition of a penalty on such a person is considered not only justifiable (cf. Prov 19:25), but also of pedagogical value, in that the untutored youth may learn the lesson that the scoffer himself is incapable of assimilating.

The masc. pl. q. pass. part. is used in Amos 2:8b, part of a pericope (2:6-8) where the prophet excoriates abuse of power and violations of human rights. In 2:8b Amos indicts those Israelites who drink in their place of worship the wine of those who have been fined. The reference seems to be to creditors who, undeterred by their apparent proximity to the deity (Yahweh?) whom they profess to be worshiping at their sacrificial banquets, drink the wine which has been obtained (either legally or illegally; see Paul, 86-87) as a tax, a fine, or as payment or interest on debts (cf. Dummelow, 565; Hayes, 114). The rot of exploitation is to be found in every sphere of society, even at the core of religious life (Kraft, 468), where, to satisfy their own greedy desires and sensual indulgence, the rapacious rich callously manipulate legal process (cf. Fosbroke, 787-88; Mays, 47). In every age, those who profess to worship God need to be reminded that to combine a travesty of justice and purity with religion is to sever the nerve of integrity (cf. Smith, 97; Snaith, 46-47).

The q. is used in 2 Chron 36:3 of imposing a levy (JB; NIV) or indemnity (REB). The ill-fated Jehoahaz, who had reigned for only three months in Jerusalem (v. 2), was deposed by Neco, king of Egypt, who exacted from Judah a levy of 100 talents of silver and a talent of gold. In par. 2 Kgs 23:33, the nom. *'ōneš* is used in combination with the vb. *ntn* and prep. *'al* (lay a levy upon).

3. The nom. *'ōneš* is found in Prov 19:19, an obscure v. considered by some (e.g., Martin, 120; cf. Fritsch, 894) almost an insoluble riddle. The v. seems to advocate letting justice take its course in the case of the incorrigible man of ungovernable passion, who tends to act impulsively and irrationally; such a man must be made to pay the legal consequences of his display of temper (McKane, 529; Tate, 62). By his excesses, a man of intemperate rage creates trouble not only for himself, but for others as well. Should he be relieved of the legal penalty, the likelihood is that he would learn no valuable lesson. On the contrary, such misplaced kindness would almost certainly aggravate his condition and encourage him to commit further acts of mischief, which would in turn involve him in more scrapes with the law (McKane, 529-30).

In 1 Kgs 10:15, a description of some of the sources of Solomon's gold, the words *mē'anšê hattārîm*, lit., from the men of the merchants, are translated "from the traders" by RSV and NRSV (cf. Keil, 161). However, JB reads "from merchants' dues"; NIV translates "the revenues from merchants" (cf. Jones, 226); TEV (cf. Montgomery and Gehman, 219-20; Gray, 263; La Sor, 334) has "the taxes paid by merchants"; de Vries (135) reads "the taxes laid on travelers"; and NEB and REB have "the tolls levied by the customs officers." The latter translations are based on the emendation of MT *mē'anšê* to *mē'onšê*, i.e., prep. with const. masc. pl. of nom. *'ōneš*. There is good support for this reading from the versions: LXX has *phorōn*, fines, taxes; and Tg. has *'ᵃgar*, rental.

The nom. (sing. const.), with the meaning confiscation (lit., punishment) of, is found in Ezra 7:26, part of Artaxerxes' letter (7:12-26), which is written in Aram. In v. 26, the Persian king, who, by recognizing Mosaic law makes it part of his own law, prescribes forms of punishment of decreasing severity for acts of disobedience, viz., the death sentence, corporal punishment, confiscation of goods, and imprisonment (see Fensham, 108; Clines, 106). Such sanctions were Persian state penalties. The pericope in which v. 26 is embedded sheds significant light on the relationship between the law of God and the law of the Persian king and has an important bearing on the difficult question of the distinction between church and state (Williamson, 105-6).

P-B Verbal forms are well attested: Heb. *'nš*, press (cf. Aram. *'ᵃnaš*), punish, fine; pass. part. punishable; ni. be punished; suffer. The nom. forms *'ônes*, *'ōneš*, punishment, penalty, confiscation; responsibility, also occur (Jastrow 2:1055, 1096-97).

Fine, punishment: → *'nš* (impose a fine, penalty, levy, # 6740)
Judgment: → *dyn* (judge, contend, govern, administer, # 1906); → *miśpāḥ* (breach of law, # 5384); → *pll* I (sit in judgment, arbitrate, expect, # 7136); → *ṣdq* (be just, righteous, justified, # 7405); → *špṭ* (judge, execute judgment, govern, # 9149)
Justice, judgment: → *dyn* (judge, contend, govern, administer, # 1906); → *miśpāḥ* (breach of law, # 5384); → *pll* I (sit in judgment, arbitrate, expect, # 7136); → *ṣdq* (be just, righteous, justified, # 7405); → *špṭ* (judge, execute judgment, govern, # 9149)\

BIBLIOGRAPHY

J. Blenkinsopp, "Deuteronomy," in *NJBC*, 1990, 94-109; B. S. Childs, *Exodus: A Commentary*, 1974; R. Clifford, *Deuteronomy*, 1982; D. J. A. Clines, *Ezra, Nehemiah, Esther*, 1984; P. C. Craigie, *The Book of Deuteronomy*, NICOT, 1983; H. Cunliffe-Jones, *Deuteronomy: Introduction and Commentary*, 1964; G. H. Davies, *Exodus: Introduction and Commentary*, 1967; S. R. Driver, *The Book of Exodus*, 1953; J. R. Dummelow, ed., *A Commentary on the Holy Bible*, 1909; J. I. Durham, *Exodus*, WBC, 1987; F. C. Fensham, *The Books of Ezra and Nehemiah*, NICOT, 1983; H. E. W. Fosbroke, "The Book of Amos: Introduction and Exegesis," *IB*, 1956, 6:761-853; C. T. Fritsch, "The Book of Proverbs: Introduction and Exegesis," *IB*, 1955, 4:765-957; N. K. Gottwald, "The Book of Deuteronomy," in *The Interpreter's One-Volume Commentary on the Bible*, 1971, 100-121; J. Gray, *I & II Kings: A Commentary*, OTL, 2d, rev., ed., 1970; J. H. Hayes, *Amos the Eighth-Century Prophet: His Times and His Preaching*, 1988; G. H. Jones, *1 and 2 Kings. Volume 1: 1 Kings 1-16:34*, NCBC, 1984; C. F. Keil, *The Books of the Kings*, KD, 2nd ed., ca. 1872; C. F. Kraft, "The Book of Amos," in *The Interpreter's One-Volume Commentary on the Bible*, 1971, 465-76; W. S. La Sor, "1 and 2 Kings," *NBC*, 1972, 320-68; W. McKane, *Proverbs: A New Approach*, OTL, 1970; G. C. Martin, *Proverbs, Ecclesiastes and Song of Songs*, 1908; A. D. H. Mayes, *Deuteronomy*, NCBC, 1979; J. L. Mays, *Amos: A Commentary*, OTL, 1976; E. H. Merrill, *Deuteronomy*, NAC, 1994; P. D. Miller, *Deuteronomy*, 1990; J. A. Montgomery and H. S. Gehman, *A Critical and Exegetical Commentary on the Books of Kings*, ICC, 1967; R. D. Nelson, "Deuteronomy," in *HBC*, 1988, 209-34; S. M. Paul, *Amos*, 1991; D. F. Payne, *Deuteronomy*, 1985; A. Phillips, *Deuteronomy*, 1973; J. C. Rylaarsdam, "The Book of Exodus: Introduction and Exegesis," *IB*, 1952, 1:831-1099; R. L. Smith, "Amos," in *BBC*, 1972, 7:81-141; N. H. Snaith, *The Book of Amos. Part Two: Translation and Notes*, 1958; E. A. Speiser, "The Stem *PLL* in Hebrew," *JBL* 82, 1963, 301-6; M. E. Tate,

"Proverbs," in *BBC*, 1972, 5:1-99; S. J. de Vries, *1 Kings*, WBC, 1985; H. G. M. Williamson, *Ezra, Nehemiah*, WBC, 1985.

Robin Wakely

6741 (*'ōneš*, fine, penalty, levy), → # 6740

6747	עָסִיס

עָסִיס (*'āsîs*), nom. grape juice (unfermented) (# 6747); < עסס (*'ss*, tread down, # 6748).

ANE Cf. Syr. *'as*, explore; BH *'ss* (vb.), tread.

OT 1. The word may be rendered as grape juice or new wine, depending on the context. In the setting of Joel 1:5, the people are lamenting the absence of the juice because the vines are not bearing grapes. In the conclusion of the book, the prophet encourages them with a vision of restoration, when "the mountains will drip new wine" (Joel 3[4]:18; cf. Amos 9:13). The nom. is also used as a simile to describe the actions of Israel's enemies when God restores Israel's fortunes (Isa 49:26), for they will become drunk on blood as with new wine (NIV wine). It is used by the groom to help intoxicate his new bride with his love (S of Songs 8:2).

2. The vb. occurs only in Mal 4:3[3:21] but its cognate nom. puts its meaning beyond doubt. The normal vb. for treading down in conquest (*drk* → # 2005) is not used here, possibly because the figure of a calf dancing about (4:2[3:20]) lends itself more readily to crushing grapes than standing on the neck or back of a defeated foe.

Grapes—juice, wine: → *gat* I (wine press, # 1780); → *dema'* (juice from wine vat, # 1964); → *ḥōmeṣ* (vinegar, wine, beer, # 2810); → *ḥemer* (wine, foaming wine, # 2815); → *yayin* (wine, # 3516); → *yeqeb* (wine vat/trough, winepress, # 3676); → *yrš* II (tread the wine press/grapes, # 3770); → *mhl* (adulterated wine, # 4543); → *mezeg* (spiced/blended/mixed wine, # 4641); → *mišrâ* (juice, # 5489); → *'āsîs* (grape juice, # 6747); → *śḥṭ* (squeeze, to press out grapes, # 8469); → *šemer* I (dregs, aged wine, # 9069); → *tîrôš* (fresh wine, # 9408)

Bibliography

HBD 1112-13; *IDB* 4:784-86; *ISBE* 4:1068-72; *TDNT* 5:162-66; E. Merrill, *Haggai, Zechariah, Malachi*, 1994, 447-48.

Eugene Carpenter

6748 (*'ss*, tread down), → # 6747

6752	עפל

עפל (*'pl*), pu. to swell, lift up; hi. to be presumptuous (# 6752).

ANE Arab. has the vb. meaning to be neglectful, presumptuous.

OT The vb. metaphorically pictures the person with a high or swollen head. The Israelites who initially refused to go into Canaan because of the spies' report realized their mistake and, being puffed up about their own abilities, presumptuously tried to possess it (Num 14:44 [hi.]; ‖ Deut 1:43 [*zyd*, be presumptuous, → # 2326]). The greedy and violent Babylonians are called *yāhîr*, excessively haughty (Hab 2:5) and *'pl*, puffed up (2:4 [q.]), about their military power.

Arrogance, pride, presumption: → *g'h* (rise up, be exalted, # 1448); → *zyd* (act presumptuously, prepare food, # 2326); → *yāhîr* (haughty, # 3400); → *sll* (lift up, exalt, # 6148); → *'pl* (swell, lift up, # 6752); → *'ātāq* (old, arrogant, # 6981); → *pḥz* (be reckless, arrogant, # 7069); → *rwm* (be high, exalted, proud, # 8123); → *šaḥaṣ* (pride, # 8832)

Gary V. Smith

6754	עֹפֶל

עֹפֶל (*'ōpel* I), abscesses, boils (# 6754).

ANE Akk. *uplu*, boil.

OT The general sense points to a boil (furuncle), a carbuncle, or an abscess. In Deut 28:27 the NIV, NKJV rendered it "tumors," perhaps influenced by 1 Sam 5:6-12; 6:4-5, which would imply plague buboes. Whether the Babylonians extended this meaning to *uplu* is uncertain.

Disease—blister, boil, skin disease, scar, wound: → *'ᵃba'bu'ōt* (blisters, # 81); → *bōhaq* (skin condition, # 993); → *baheret* (white patch on skin, # 994); → *gārāb* (festering eruption, # 1734); → *zrr* I (press out [wounds], # 2452); → *ḥeres* I (itch, # 3063); → *yabbelet* (wart?, # 3301); → *yallepet* (skin disease, # 3539); → *yᵉraqraq* (discoloration, # 3768); → *kᵉwiyya* (scar, # 3918); → *m'r* (be sore, # 4421); → *māzôr* I (boil, # 4649); → *makkâ* (blow, # 4804); → *mispaḥat* (skin eruption, # 5030); → *mrḥ* (rub, polish, # 5302); → *neteq* (scalp infection, # 5999); → *sappaḥat* (hair disease, # 6204); → *'ōpel* I (abscesses, # 6754); → *'āš* II (pus, # 6932); → *ṣāpâ* (pus?, # 7597); → *ṣarebet* (scar, # 7648); → *ṣr'* (suffer from skin disease, # 7665); → *śᵉ'ēt* II (swelling, # 8421); → *śtr* (break out [tumor], # 8609); → *šᵉḥîn* (boil, # 8825). For related entries → *ḥlh* I (become weak, tired, ill, # 2703)

BIBLIOGRAPHY
ISBE 1:532, 953-60; 3:103-6.

R. K. Harrison

6757	עַפְעַפַּיִם

עַפְעַפַּיִם (*'ap'appayim*), flashing, glance of the eye (# 6757).

OT The traditional rendering of *'ap'ap*, which only occurs in the dual construct and sing. fem. forms, is "eyelid." This is probably because it is a derivative of *'wp* I, fly, flap (→ # 6414), but out of 10x in the OT, 5x it is parallel to *'ênayim* (Ps 11:4; 132:4; Prov 4:25; 6:4; Jer 9:18[17]). It may be better to assume it means "(flashing) eyes." The word *šᵉmurôt* in Ps 77:4[5] may mean "eyelids," as they are the eye's guard, while in Lev 14:9 *gabbōt 'ênayim* means "eyebrows." God can hold eyelids open by sending trouble and sleeplessness (Ps 77:4[5]) or open his eyelids to evaluate the lives of his people (11:4). When people keep their eyelids open, they are attentive to their spiritual, social, or other responsibilities.

Eye, wink: → *'îšôn* (pupil of eye, # 413); → *bābâ* (pupil of eye, # 949); → *'yn* (view with suspicion, # 6523); → *'ap'appayim* (flashing of eye, # 6757); → *qrṣ* (wink, pinch, # 7975); → *rzm* (flash, # 8141); → *tᵉballul* (spot in eye, # 9319)

Allan M. Harman

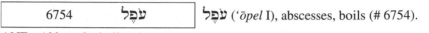

6759	עפר

עפר (*'pr*), denom. vb., pi., kept dusting (him) with dust (# 6759); עָפָר (*'āpār*), nom., dry earth, dust, loose soil, rubble, plaster (# 6760).

ANE The Heb. *'pr* has etymological associations with Ugar. *'pr*, dust.

OT 1. The vb. is used only in 2 Sam 16:13, where Shimei kept throwing dirt at David.

2. The nom. *'āpār* is used 110x in OT in a great variety of ways. It has several literal uses. It is used of dry, loose earth more than 20x. Shimei showers David with dirt (2 Sam 16:13). Blood is to be covered with earth (Lev 17:13; Ezek 24:7), the Philistines use earth to fill wells that Isaac dug (Gen 26:15), torrents wash the soil away (Job 14:19), and the fire burned up the soil with the sacrifice (1 Kgs 18:38). The ostrich warms her eggs in the sand (Job 39:14). In judgment, God says the rain will be turned to powder (Deut 28:24), the dust will be soaked with fat and will turn into burning sulphur (Isa 34:7, 9), and in Beth Ophrah they roll in the dust (Mic 1:10). Dust will be the serpent's food (Gen 3:14; Isa 65:25; Mic 7:17), vipers glide in dust (Deut 32:24), and the dust becomes hard (Job 38:38). Dust is sprinkled on the head as a sign of grief (Josh 7:6; Job 2:12; Lam 2:10; Ezek 27:30), and dust from the tabernacle floor is put into water for an ordeal (Num 5:17).

3. *'āpār* is used 12x of the material from which the human body is composed and to which it will return (Gen 2:7; 3:19; Job 4:19; 8:19; 10:9; 34:15; Ps 103:14; 104:29; Eccl 3:20; 12:7).

4. *'āpār* refers 11x to the surface of the ground. Moses strikes the dust and it becomes gnats (Exod 8:12, 13 [8:16, 17]). God brings city and walls down to the dust (Isa 25:12; 26:5). Twice "holes in the ground" are mentioned (Job 30:6; Isa 2:19). Though the stump may die in the soil (Job 14:8), hardship does not spring from the soil (5:6). There is no equal to leviathan on earth (41:33[25]. Job is confident that his Redeemer will stand upon the earth (19:25).

5. *'āpār* means powder 9x. Moses ground the golden calf to powder as fine as dust and threw this dust into the water (Deut 9:21). David boasts that he beat his enemies as fine as the dust of the earth (2 Sam 22:43; Ps 18:42[43]). Josiah destroyed cultic objects by grinding them to power or reducing them to rubble (2 Kgs 23:6, 12, 15). Eliphaz the Temanite tells Job to assign his nuggets to the dust and allow the Almighty to be his gold (Job 22:24). Num 19:17 mentions the ashes used for cleansing purposes.

6. The debris of ruined cities, either as dust or rubble, is mentioned 6x (1 Kgs 20:10; Neh 4:2[3:24]; 4:10[4:4]; Ps 102:14 [15]; Ezek 26:4, 12.

7. The dust of the earth is equivalent to the grave 9x (Job 7:21; 17:16; 20:11; 21:26; Ps 22:15[16], 29[30]; 30:9[10]; Isa 26:19; Dan 12:2).

8. *'āpār* is also the material used for mortar, clay, or plaster (Lev 14:41, 42, 45). It is the material of which the earth is composed (Prov 8:26; Isa 40:12). Iron ore is taken from the earth (Job 28:2).

9. Several figurative usages of *'āpār* also occur. It is used to express abundance. The descendants of Abraham are likened to the dust of the earth (Gen 13:16; 28:14), as are the people over whom Solomon rules (2 Chron 1:9) and the people of Israel in the prophecy of Balaam (Num 23:10). The wicked heap up silver like dust (Job 27:16), as

did Tyre (Zech 9:3). God rained meat down on the Israelites like dust (Ps 78:27). Figuratively, the people of Israel trample on the poor as upon the dust of the ground (Amos 2:7). Dust is a figure to describe how the king of Aram destroyed most of the army of Israel and made them like the dust at threshing time (2 Kgs 13:7). God turns nations to dust with his sword (Isa 41:2). And as an expression of judgment, the blood of the people will be poured out like dust (Zeph 1:17).

10. Three passages speak of enemies licking the dust (Ps 72:9; Isa 49:23; Mic 7:17). Three others talk of raising someone from the dust: the poor (1 Sam 2:8; Ps 113:7) and Jehu (1 Kgs 16:2). Another one addresses Jerusalem to shake off her dust (Isa 52:2).

11. Humiliation is the subject 8x. Babylon is admonished to sit in the dust (Isa 47:1). Job buries his brow in the dust (Job 16:15), is reduced to dust and ashes (30:19) and is told by God to bury all the wicked in the dust if he has the ability (40:13). David asks to sleep in the dust if he is guilty (Ps 7:5[6]). The psalmist decries his plight of being brought down to the dust (44:25[26]; 119:25). Self-abasement is the theme of three passages: Abraham says he is nothing but dust and ashes (Gen 18:27), Job repents in dust and ashes (Job 42:6), and one who wishes to seek God should bury his face in the dust (Lam 3:29).

Dust, clay, dirt, loose soil: → *'ābāq* (dust, # 85); → *'ēper* (ashes, loose soil, # 709); → *ḥōmer* II (mud, clay, mortar, # 2817); → *ṭîṭ* (mud, mire, clay, # 3226); → *ṭnp* (dirty, # 3245); → *'pr* (dust, # 6759); → *rōba'* II (dust, rubbish, # 8066); → *regeb* (clods of earth, # 8073); → *š^{e}ḥôr* (soot, blackness, # 8818); → *šaḥaq* (dust, clouds of dust, # 8836)

BIBLIOGRAPHY
ISBE 1:998.

Roy E. Hayden

6760 (*'āpār*, dry earth, dust), → # 6759

6762	עֹפֶר

עֹפֶר (*'ōper*), fawn of a gazelle, deer (# 6762).

OT This term (cf. Arab. *ġufur*, young of mountain goat) is found 5x in the OT, all in the S of Songs, 3x parallel with *ṣ^{e}bî* in the beloved's description of her lover ("like a gazelle or a young stag"; 2:9, 17; 8:14) and 2x in the lover's description of his beloved's breasts ("like two fawns, twins of a gazelle"; 4:5; 7:3[4]). For discussion of the imagery, → *ṣ^{e}bî* II/*ṣ^{e}biyyâ*, # 7383, # 7386.

Deer, gazelle: → *'ayyāl* / *'ayyālâ* (deer, # 385/0387); → *zemer* (gazelle, # 2378); → *yaḥmûr* (roebuck, # 3502); → *yā'ēl* I/*yā'^{a}lâ* I (ibex, # 3604, 3607); → *'ōper* (fawn of a gazelle, deer, # 6762); → *ṣ^{e}bî* II/*ṣ^{e}bîyâ* (gazelle, # 7383, 7386)

Michael S. Moore/Michael L. Brown

6769	עֹפֶרֶת

עֹפֶרֶת (*'ōperet*), lead (# 6769).

ANE The Akk. *abāru* appears to be a Sum. loanword that found its way into Aram. and later Heb. as *'^{a}(b)bār* (*AHw*, 4a). It is found in old Babylonian between gold and tin; in the Alalakh tablets it is poured into the mouth of a criminal as punishment for a crime. The term *'ôperet* occurs in a Punic inscription written to the gods of the underworld seeking approval for the money (silver) that has been poured out like lead (*KAI*, 89).

OT The nom. occurs in the OT as part of a list of metals of decreasing value (Num 31:22; Ezek 27:12) or in a list of alloys from which silver is extracted (Jer 6:29; Ezek 22:18, 20). The visions of Zechariah picture the removal of evil from the city of Jerusalem as a woman carried away in a pot with a heavy lead lid (Zech 5:7-8). The weight of lead makes it an ideal image for the way the Egyptians sunk in the sea (Exod 15:10). Job wishes that his words could be inscribed with an iron pen and lead (19:24); Rashi and some modern commentators explain this as lead poured into chiseled out letters to make them sparkle, but it may simply refer to an alloy used in making the stylus. Depictions of scribes and ancient writing tools are provided by Pritchard (*ANEP*², 232-36).

P-B The nom. is found in Mish. Heb. and Aram. *'ᵃbārā'*, Syr., and the Samaritan Aram. dialect. It appears as a simile in the Thanksgiving Hymn (1QH 8.19) to describe wicked trees sinking like lead in torrents of water, in contrast to the trees growing by the springs of sound teaching.

Metals: → *'ᵃnāk* (lead, # 643); → *bᵉdîl* (dross, # 974); → *barzel* (iron, # 1366); → *zāhāb* (gold, # 2298); → *ḥel'â* I (rust, # 2689); → *ḥašmal* (glow?, electrum, glowing metal, # 3133); → *kesep* (silver, money, # 4084); → *masgēr* II (metal worker, # 4994); → *maʻᵃbeh* (foundry, # 5043); → *nᵉḥōšet* I (copper, bronze, # 5733); → *sîg* (lead oxide, # 6092); → *sēper* II (bronze, plate, # 6220); → *'ōperet* (lead, # 6769); → *paḥ* II (thin sheet, # 7063); → *pᵉlādōt* (steel?, # 7110); → *ṣwr* III (cast [metal], # 7445); → *ṣaʻᵃṣu'îm* (things formed by metal coating, # 7589); → *ṣph* II (arrange, overlay, plate, glaze, # 7596); → *ṣrp* (melt, smelt, refine, # 7671); → *qālāl* (polished metal, # 7838); → *šḥṭ* II (alloyed, # 8822)

BIBLIOGRAPHY

KAI, 89; G. Fohrer, *Das Buch Hiob*, KAT XVI, 1989, 317; R. J. Forbes, *Studies in Ancient Technology*, 8, 1964, 228-39; W. L. Holladay, *Jeremiah 1*, 1986, 230-32.

A. H. Konkel

6770	עֵץ

עֵץ (*'ēṣ*), nom. wood, tree (# 6770); עֵצָה (*'ēṣâ* III), wood (# 6785).

ANE *'ēṣ* is a common Sem. root for trees, wood, lumber, timber, sticks, etc. It is used in Akk. *iṣu*; Ugar. *'ṣ*; and in Phoen. Eth. *'eḍ* (cf. OSA *'ḍ*). It appears as *'ā'* in Aram. (cf. Egypt. Aram. *'q*), because of dissimulation. The original root is uncertain; BDB lists *'ṣh*. Obviously, different trees were found in different areas of the ANE, but a similar use of their products and their imagery is attested. The lands of Assyria, Babylon and Egypt were limited in the variety of trees found. In contrast Canaan was noted for an abundance of a variety of trees.

OT The precise identification of various trees mentioned in the HB and in the ANE involves a number of difficulties and uncertainties, especially in regard to conifers. Some of these terms seem so elastic as to appear to be used generically as English "evergreen." Several other words are found only once or a couple of times, leaving few contexts and sometimes few cognates for help in understanding their identification. Realizing that the HB preserves only a fraction of the Canaanite/ancient Heb. vocabulary that was used, the variety of terms that have been preserved in BH is nevertheless surprising. As our knowledge of the ancient languages of the Bible world increases, we will be able to identify clearly more of the trees mentioned in the OT.

In general, trees were valued for food (Ezek 47:12), building material, and shade (Isa 10:18; 33-34; 35:1-2; 41:19). Lev 19:23-25 forbids the eating of fruit during the first four years after planting; wanton deforestation is also forbidden (Deut 20:19-20). Nevertheless, the ancient natural forests in Palestine have been greatly reduced or become extinct. In modern times these lands of the Bible have become largely barren and do not reflect the rich flora of antiquity. The reforestation programs of the modern state of Israel reflect the potential of the land to produce and sustain large forests. Lebanon still has a few significant forests that reflect this ancient situation.

Solomon appears to have had some botanical gardens, and Josephus and Pliny mention a few planted groves. David appointed an overseer in charge of the "olive and sycamore-fig trees in the western foothills" (1 Chron 27:28). But systematic planting of trees in antiquity seems unknown, except in cemeteries and around the tombs of saints. Certain forests in the OT were given specific names, e.g., the Forest of Hereth (1 Sam 22:5), the Forest of Ephraim (2 Sam 18:6). Occasionally salt-encrusted stumps of old palm trees wash up on the shores of the Dead Sea.

Certain highly valued wood was imported from abroad—especially almug wood (# 5233) and the famous cedars from Lebanon.

1. One of the earliest references to the use of wood is the shipbuilding of Noah. He used *gōper* (# 1729) in the construction of the ark. Noah was to build the ark with this wood and to coat (*kpr*; → 4105) it with pitch (*kōper*, → # 4109; Gen 6:14). The Heb. word *gōper* is used only here in the HB. The NIV, RSV, NRSV and REB used cypress to translate this uncertain term; the NAB uses gopherwood and the NJPSV reads resinous wood.

2. Trees are mentioned several times in connection with the travels of the patriarchs. Certain trees or groves of trees became known as landmarkers or became famous through association with some event that took place at the site. They served a practical service or were remembered for personal reasons. It is not necessary to read primitive tree worship into such narratives. A tree was sometimes used as a regional marker. Such seems to be the case with the tree site at Moreh, "Abraham traveled through the land as far as the site of the great tree (*'ēlôn* I; # 471) of Moreh at Shechem" (Gen 12:6). These "great trees of Moreh" are again noted in Deut 11:30 as a territorial marker.

Another tree site note in the patriarchal narrative is Mamre. Abraham "went to live near the great trees of Mamre at Hebron, where he built an altar to the LORD," Gen 13:18). Elsewhere the text reports that Abraham "was living near the great trees of Mamre" (14:13). The famous tree site is mentioned again, "The LORD appeared to Abraham near the great trees of Mamre" (18:1). Sometimes the patriarch himself planted a tree at a site to be remembered. Abraham planted a tamarisk (*'ēšel*; → # 869) at Beersheba in the desert, and "there he called upon the name of the LORD, the Eternal God" (21:33). Jacob's household gave him "all the foreign gods they had and the rings in their ears, and Jacob buried them under the oak (*'ēlâ* I, # 461) at Shechem" (35:4). Rebekah's nurse Deborah was buried "under the oak (*'allôn* I, # 473) below Bethel," and the site was named "Allon Bacuth" (35:8). Other burials in the OT were also under trees.

3. During the time of Joshua and the judges certain significant trees are still being noted in the narrative. Josh 19:33 refers to a "large tree" (*'ēlôn* I; # 471) that was at the boundary of the tribal allotment of Naphtali. Josh 24:26 records that Joshua set up a large stone under the oak (*'ēlâ*, # 464) near the holy place of the Lord. Judg 4:5 describes how Deborah "held court under the Palm (*tōmer* I, # 9472) of Deborah." Judg 4:11 tells us that Heber the Kenite "pitched his tent by the great tree (*'ēlôn*; # 471) in Zaanannim near Kedesh." Judg 6:11, 19 relates that the angel of the Lord sat down "under the oak (*'ēlâ*; # 461) in Ophrah that belonged to Joash the Abiezrite." Judg 9:6 narrates how "all the citizens of Shechem and Beth Millo gathered beside the great tree (*'ēlâ*; # 461) at the pillar in Shechem to crown Abimelech king." Judg 9:37 refers to the "soothsayer's tree" (*'ēlôn*; # 471), although the Heb. here could be rendered in several different ways: Elon-meonenim (NRSV, NAB), Soothsayers' Terebinth (REB), Diviners' Oak (NJB). The AV has "plain of Meonenim."

4. Later Hebrew history continues to use certain tree sites as geographical markers. Even when the city is identified, a tree site may be added for specificity. For example, "Saul was staying on the outskirts of Gibeah under a pomegranate tree (*rimmôn* I, # 8232) in Migron" (1 Sam 14:2). Similarly, 22:6 records that Saul "was seated under the tamarisk (*'ēšel*; → # 869) tree on the hill at Gibeah, with his officials standing around him." 1 Kgs 13:14 notes the "man of God" sitting under an oak tree (*'ēlâ*; # 461), and 1 Chron 10:12 records how the valiant men of Jabesh Gilead buried the bones of Saul and his sons "under the great tree (*'ēlâ*; # 461) in Jabesh." It was the "thick branches of a large oak" (*'ēlâ*; # 461) that caught Absalom's head and left him dangling in mid air (2 Sam 18:9-10, 14).

Sometimes the Heb. reference is understood as a place-name: Saul and the Israelites camped in the Valley of Elah (*'ēlâ*; # 461) (1 Sam 17:2). But this same language could be translated, rather than transliterated, as in NAB's "Vale of the Terebinth" or NJB's "Valley of the Terebinth" and be understood as a place name. In 10:3 "the great tree (*'ēlôn*; # 471) of Tabor" is used as a geographical marker.

5. The availability of wood in ancient Canaan provided ample timber for various secular constructions. Isa 9:10[9] gives a clue to the better wood used for construction in a context where the evil people brag that although "the bricks have fallen down" they will build "with dressed stone," and although the "fig (*šiqmâ*; → # 9204) trees have been felled," they will "replace them with cedars (*'erez*; → # 780)." The preference here was possibly due to appearance as much as durability. The coarse grain of the sycamore-fig is durable, and mummy cases made of it have lasted to present times. The sycamore-fig was common in Egypt and is singled out for mention in Ps 78:47. Cedar logs, lit., woods of cedar (*'erez*; # 780), were used in the construction of David's personal residence (2 Sam 5:11).

One large construction project was shipbuilding. Ezekiel provides valuable information on the kinds of wood used in shipbuilding in his lament over Tyre passage. "They made all your timbers of pine (*b^erôš*; → # 1360) trees from Senir; they took a cedar (*'erez*; # 780) from Lebanon to make a mast for you. Of oaks (*'allôn* I, → # 473) from Bashan they made your oars; of cypress wood (*t*[e]*'aššûr*; → # 9309) from the coasts of Cyprus they made your deck, inlaid with ivory" (Ezek 27:5-6).

In S of Songs 1:17 the lover's house is described as having beams of cedar (*'erez*; # 780) and rafters of fir (*b*[e]*rôš*; # 1360). These woods were likely preferred for their beauty.

6. Besides the lumber used in large construction projects, select woods were also used in woodworking by the specialist carpenters. Such specialists were found throughout the ANE. In ancient Israel the craftsmen who worked with wood were called appropriately workers of wood (*ḥārāš 'ēṣ*; cf. Exod 31:5; 2 Sam 5:11; 1 Chron 22:15; → # 3093). Certain kinds of wood were particularly prized for this trade. Some of these artisans would be called cabinet makers today. They were specialists in carving, decorating, and ornamentation. Undoubtedly they would be the ones paneling and doing the wainscoting in the temple. Such artisans would be the ones responsible for carving idols for use by the general population (see below).

Most of these smaller and finer products have been lost to the ravages of time. Only sporadically fragments of such items are found by archaeologists. (The MB II tombs in Jericho have preserved some tables, bowls, jugs, and toilet boxes).

7. Idols were sometimes made of wood. The OT gives more information—if only in sarcasm—on these products than on other products of the carpenter. Isaiah gives a vivid description of this process: "The carpenter measures with a line and makes an outline with a marker; he roughs it out with chisels and marks it with compasses. He shapes it in the form of man" (Isa 44:13). In biting sarcasm the prophet goes on to describe how the very same wood used for making idols is also used for common household needs as cooking and giving warmth. The wood not used for domestic needs is designed into an idol: "From the rest he makes a god, his idol; he bows down to it and worships. He prays to it and says, 'Save me; you are my god'" (44:17). He also provides information on the kinds of wood used in idol-making: cedar (*'erez*; # 780), cypress (→ *tirzâ*; # 9560), oak (*'allôn* I, # 473), and pine (*'ōren* I; # 815) are specifically listed (44:14).

The prophet Jeremiah also supplies similar information on the manufacture of wooden idols made from the trees of the forest. The craftsman cuts it down, and then "shapes it with his chisel" (Jer 10:3). The people who worship such wooden idols are then described as "senseless and foolish" and "taught by worthless wooden idols" (v. 8).

The several different kinds of wood used in making idols may be based not only on availability but also on economic factors. The more durable and attractive kinds of wood were undoubtedly preferred by the wealthier idolaters, who were able to purchase idols made from the more valuable woods. The poor had to accept inferior wood. Isaiah even refers in irony to idolaters bowing down before a mere "block of wood" (*bûl* II; # 1005; Isa 44:19). This could be mere irony, but it could also represent the cheapest of wooden idols. The Asherah was an idol carved out of wood or some kind of living tree form. It is mentioned often and its presence seems to have been pervasive (see below, # 10).

8. Of special interest is the use of various trees and woods in the Hebrew religion. During the Feast of tabernacles, the people were instructed to take "choice fruit from the trees, and palm fronds (*tāmār* I, → # 9469; *kippâ*, branch, # 4093), leafy branches, and poplars (*'*[a]*rābâ* I; # 6857; 4x [Lev 23:40; Job 40:22; Ps 137:2; Isa 15:7;

44:4]), and rejoice before the LORD" (Lev 23:40). This verse contains some unusual terms. The term "poplars" translates two words: *'ᵃrābâ* I (# 6857) and *naḥal* I (→ # 5707). This combination is unique here and is variously rendered in the new versions: "willows of the brook" (NRSV), "willows from the riverside" (REB), "valley poplars" (NAB), and "flowering shrubs from the river bank" (NJB).

For the construction of the booths during the time of Nehemiah, different tree branches were utilized—"olive (*zayit*; → # 2339) and wild olive, myrtles (*hᵃdas*; # 2072), palms (*tāmār* I; # 9469), and shade trees" (Neh 8:15). And as late as the period of the Maccabbees such use of tree branches is still attested (2 Macc 10:7). And when Simon Maccabeus entered Jerusalem, it was with thanksgiving and "branches of palm trees" (1 Macc 13:51).

The construction of the Tent of Meeting involved specified woods. Acacia (*šiṭṭâ*; # 8847) wood was used in the construction of the altar of burnt offering, which was then overlaid with bronze (Exod 38:1). This same durable wood was also used in the construction of the ark of the covenant (37:1) and for the poles for carrying the tabernacle furniture (37:4). Acacia wood is available in the desert.

The description of the parts of the sacred lampstand stipulates that "three cups shaped like almond flowers (*mᵉšuqqād*; # 5481) with buds and blossoms are to be on one branch, three on the next branch, and the same for all six branches extending from the lampstand" (Exod 25:33; cf. 37:19). Trees or their parts provided ideas for decoration.

In a cleansing ritual, cedar (*'erez*; # 780) wood was stipulated one of the ingredients, along with scarlet yarn, hyssop, and the two live birds (Lev 14:4; cf. Num 19:6). (In this desert context, the use of cedar is uncertain.)

The later construction of the great temple of Solomon involved the use of cedar (*'erez*; # 780) logs imported from Lebanon through the port of Joppa. Huge amounts of cedar were required because the temple was lined with cedar paneling from floor to roof (1 Kgs 6:15). The enormous numbers of workers required to cut and ship the cedar is recorded in 5:13-18[27-32]. The doors on Solomon's temple were made of pine (*bᵉrôš*; # 1360) that rested in "four-sided jambs of olive wood for the entrance to the main hall" (6:33). Doors of olive wood were made for the entrance to the inner sanctuary (6:31).

Especially noted for use in Solomon's temple is the valued almugwood (*'almuggîm*; # 523), which was used "to make supports for the temple of the LORD and for the royal palace, and to make harps and lyres for the musicians" (1 Kgs 10:11-12). The text especially notes that "so much almugwood has never been imported or seen since that day" (10:12). The passage in 2 Chron 2:8[7] refers to algum logs (*'algûmîm*; # 454), a variant spelling and a good sign of a loanword (cf. 2 Chron 9:10). It appears in Ugar. as *'almg* (Aistleitner, *WUS*, # 226). (Another rare imported wood was ebony [*hobnîm*, # 2041], which is mentioned only in Ezek 27:15.)

Solomon's temple was roofed "with beams and cedar (*'erez*; # 780) planks" (1 Kgs 6:9). It also had "cedar columns supporting trimmed cedar beams" (7:2). In Ezekiel's temple, "palm tree decorations" (*timōrâ*; → # 9474) are mentioned (Ezek 40:16, 22, 26; cf. 41:18). The same term is used in 1 Kgs 6:29 of Solomon's temple.

9. Trees are employed as metaphor throughout the OT, especially in the poetry. The Psalms provide many vivid pictures of how trees symbolize people. "The

righteous will flourish like the palm (*tāmār* I; # 9469) tree, they will grow like a cedar of Lebanon.... they will bear fruit in old age, they will stay fresh and green" (Ps 92:12-13[13-14]). But the Psalms also use this imagery of the wicked, as in 37:35, which describes the "wicked and ruthless man flourishing like a green (*ra'ᵃnān*; # 8316) tree in its native soil." Note the different kinds of trees used in these two passages. Tree imagery is used of kings or people of wealth and power (cf. Dan 4:10[7]).

The book of Ecclesiastes utilizes tree imagery in the beautiful white blossoms of the almond tree (*šāqēd*; → # 9196), picturing the gray hair of the aging in the well-known sustained imagery of aging in Eccl 12:5. Trees are mentioned by the psalmist in the famous passage that describes the condition of the exiles in Babylon, "There on the poplars (*'ᵃrābâ*; # 6857) we hung our harps" (Ps 137:2).

10. It is the Hebrew prophets who make the most extensive use of tree symbolism. They were quick to seize on the graphic images possible from this item of nature known to the people at large. Isaiah leads in this use of tree language. In Isa 9:14-15 the prophet uses the palm tree in a merism: "So the LORD will cut off from Israel both head and tail, both palm branch and reed in a single day; the elders and prominent men are the head, the prophets who teach lies are the tail" (cf. Isa 19:15). The lofty palm is contrasted with the lowly reed. Isa 55:13 vividly contrasts the superior pine tree (*bᵉrôš*; # 1360) with the thornbush, and the myrtle (*hᵃdas*; # 2072) with the briers in the time of restoration.

Such imagery is used to represent restoration and abundance. The Lord promised to put in the desert "the cedar (*'erez*; # 780) and the acacia (*šiṭṭâ*; # 8850), the myrtle (*hᵃdas*; # 2072) and the olive" and that he would "set pines (*bᵉrôš*; # 1360) in the wasteland, the fir (*tidhār*; # 9329) and the cypress (*tᵉ'aššûr*; → # 9309) together" (Isa 41:19). When speaking of the glory of Zion to come, Isaiah predicts, "The glory of Lebanon will come to you, the pine (*bᵉrôš*; # 1360), the fir (*tidhār*; # 9329) and the cypress (*tᵉ'aššûr*; # 9309) together, to adorn the place of my sanctuary" (60:13). Isa 14:8 records the sentiments of the trees at the downfall of Babylon: "The pine trees (*bᵉrôš*; # 1360) and the cedars (*'erez*; # 780) of Lebanon exult over you." Use of rich tree imagery is typical of Isaiah's writing.

Other Hebrew prophets also made good use of tree imagery. Zech 11:1-2 graphically describes the trees in a painful condition, "Wail, O pine (*bᵉrôš*; # 1360) tree, for the cedar (*'erez*; # 780) has fallen; the stately trees are ruined! Wail, oaks (*'allôn* I; # 473) of Bashan; the dense forest has been cut down!"

Ezekiel used the term "forest" symbolically to indicate a region or domain; "forest of the southland" denoted the kingdom of Judah (Ezek 20:46). Isaiah represented the kingdoms that God threatened to destroy as a forest destined to be burned (Isa 10:17-19, 34). Here the briars and thorns denoted the common people and the "glory of the forest" nobles and others of high rank (cf. Isa 32:19; 37:24; Jer 21:14; 22:7). "Forest" may be used symbolically to represent the epitome of well-being (Isa 32:15).

The lofty tree is used by the prophets to speak of greatness and that which is impressive. Cedars were uncommonly tall and wide-spreading and therefore provided a graphic image that the Hebrew prophets were quick to utilize; the oaks also stood out as imposing and impressive. Amos describes the Lord's destruction of the Amorites though they were "tall as the cedars (*'erez*; # 780) and strong as the oaks" (*'ōren* I;

473; Amos 2:9). Isaiah uses the same word pair to describe the Lord's judgment on the proud, lofty, and exalted, the "cedars of Lebanon, tall and lofty, and all the oaks of Bashan" (Isa 2:12-13). Similarly, Ezekiel describes the Assyrian as "once a cedar in Lebanon" (Ezek 31:3) and especially notes its "beautiful branches overshadowing the forest; it towered on high, its top above the thick foliage." In fact, the prophet goes on to say, "The cedars (*'erez*; # 780) in the garden of God could not rival it, nor could the pine trees (*b^e rôš*; # 1360) equal its boughs, nor could the plane trees (*'ermôn*, # 6895) compare with its branches—no tree in the garden of God could match its beauty" (Ezek 31:8).

In the story of the two eagles and a vine, Ezekiel is instructed to "tell the house of Israel a parable" about an eagle that went to Lebanon and took "hold of a cedar (*'erez*; # 780) and broke off its topmost shoot (*ṣammeret*, → # 7550) and carried it away to a land of merchants, where he planted it in a city of traders" (Ezek 17:3-4). Other designations for trees in this parable are *qaḥ*, willow (# 7774) and *ṣapṣāpâ*, willow tree (# 7628). *qaḥ*, willow, is found only in 17:5 and not illuminated by cognates. Those who do not understand this term as a reference to a tree in this verse understand it as a vb. indicating placed or planted (usually from the vb. *lqḥ*). The two hapleg. have led to numerous interpretations. Hareuveni believes there is a tree growing on the bank of the Euphrates River that has characteristics of both the willow and the poplar, a tree called the *Populus euphratica*, a member of the *Salid* (willow) family.

Certain trees can represent what is highest and most challenging. So Sennacherib boasted that he had ascended the heights of the mountains, the utmost heights of Lebanon, and cut down its tallest cedars (*'erez*; # 780) and the choicest of its pines (*b^e rôš*, # 1360; Isa 37:24).

Prophets readily used tree imagery, but they were aware of the possible pagan overtones because of Canaanite cults linked to trees. The Canaanite fertility goddess Asherah was symbolized by trees or tree-like pillars. Worship among the trees was condemned by Israel's prophets because of associations with Canaanite religious practices (Deut 12:2; Isa 1:29; 57:5; Jer 2:20; Ezek 6:13; Hosea 4:12-13).

11. The sheer beauty of some trees caused the ancients to use tree imagery to represent the attractive and desirable. The S of Songs uses trees to present beautiful settings, as in a "grove of nut trees" (*'^e gôz*; → # 100) and the blooming pomegranates (*rimmôn*; # 8232; S of Songs 6:11). This book of beauty and love also mentions "under the apple tree (*tappûaḥ*; # 9515) I roused you" (8:5), and the refreshment that apples may bring (2:5). The lover is compared to "an apple tree (*tappûaḥ*) among the trees of the forest" (2:3). Tree language is probably used euphemistically in 7:8, "I will climb the palm tree and take hold of its fruit." Some think the general shape of the tree, as seen from a distance, could resemble a standing woman.

12. The names of trees were adopted and used as both place and personal names. In a few passages there is uncertainty whether the Heb. was intended as a common or proper nom. For example, in the case of *'^a rābâ* I, poplar (# 6857), the reference in Isa 15:7 is undoubtedly a place-name, as the NIV (Ravine of the Poplars), NRSV (Wadi of the Willows), NAB (Gorge of the Poplars), and NJPSV (Ravine of the Willows) reflect. The REB (Wadi Arabim) and the NASB (brook of the Arabim) preferred to transliterate rather than translate the word.

It is easy to see how places could be named after trees that grew there. The palm tree (*tāmār*) yields two or three place-names called Tamar (1 Kgs 9:18; Ezek 47:19; 48:28). Jericho was also called the "City of Palms" (Deut 34:3; cf. Judg 1:16; 3:13; 2 Chron 28:15). The place Jacob named Bethel was formerly called Luz, a name surely based on a rare word for almond preserved in Heb. (*lûz*, # 4280), but occurring commonly in Aram./Syr. (Gen 28:19). The "apple tree" (*tappûaḥ*, # 9515) gave its name to a site in the western foothills (Josh 15:34) and a site in the territory of Ephraim (Josh 16:8); also cf. the site En Tappuah (Josh 17:8; cf. 12:17).

Several variants on the same Heb. root appear in place-names. The Valley of Elah (*'ēlâ*; # 461) is mentioned in 1 Sam 17:2, where David slew Goliath. Elon (*'ēlôn*; # 471) is a place-name in Josh 19:43, a town in the territory of Dan. Elath (# 397) the town and harbor on the Gulf of Elath (Deut 2:8) is a variant on the above terms for trees.

But tree names were also adopted as personal names. Tappuah (*tappûaḥ*; → # 9515), apple, is used as a personal name in 1 Chron 2:43. Tamar (*tāmār* I; # 9469) is a personal name of the daughter-in-law of Judah (Gen 38:6), of the daughter of David (2 Sam 13:1), and of the daughter of Absalom (14:27). Elah (*'ēlâ*; # 461) is the name of a chief of Edom (Gen 36:41), the name of the son of Baasha (1 Kgs 16:6-14), the name of the father of Hoseha, last king of Israel (2 Kgs 15:30), the name of a son of Caleb (1 Chron 4:15), and the name of the son of Uzzi (1 Chron 9:8). Elon (*'ēlôn*; # 471) is the name of a son of Zebulun (Gen 46:14; Num 26:26) and is used also of the father-in-law of Esau. Elon the judge, from the tribe of Zebulon, is mentioned in Judg 12:11-12.

13. Trees provided a good resource in the art of the ANE, and this included Israel. Palm trees were depicted extensively on Jewish coinage and especially on the *Judaea Capta* coins of Vespasian. The palm was depicted on some synagogues as still preserved at Capernaum today.

14. Several other miscellaneous references to trees need to be noted. Jeremiah refers to the almond tree in a pun: "I see the branch of an almond tree" (*šāqēd*; # 9196) and the Lord responds, "You have seen correctly, for I am watching (*šqd*; → # 9193) to see that my word is fulfilled" (1:11-12). The almond tree in Israel blossoms early, in January/February, while the other trees are still bare. Jeremiah seized on vivid imagery to represent the speedy fulfillment of the prophecies of doom.

The almond tree is also mentioned (with a different word) in the strange passage in Gen 30:37, where Jacob tricked Laban in the increase of selected animals. The text states that "Jacob ... took fresh-cut branches from poplar (*libneh*, # 4242), almond (*lûz* I; # 4280) and plane trees (*'ermôn*, # 6895) and made white strips on them by peeling the bark and exposing the white inner wood of the branches." The whole episode is enigmatic, but we can note here the particular trees selected are not specified with common terms.

Yet another episode involving the almond in mentioned in Gen 43:11, where Isaac directed his sons to carry almonds as part of their present to Joseph in Egypt. This would be a special gift since almond trees were not common in Egypt; it would also remind Joseph of his homeland.

A third reference involving the almond tree is the story in Num 17:1-13 about Aaron's staff that "sprouted, budded, blossomed and produced almonds" (*šāqēd*;

9196; v. 8[23]). This passage does use the regular word for almomd. Perhaps almond blossoms are mentioned because of their early blossoming and sheer beauty.

NT Tree imagery continues on into the NT. John the Baptist and Jesus refer to people's faith in terms of trees and their fruit (Matt 3:10; 7:17-20; 12:33). Jesus compares the kingdom of God in its full manifestation to a mighty tree (13:32). (Tree of Life: Theology; →Tree of the Knowledge of Good and Evil: Theology)

Branch (of tree): → *'āmîr* (branch, bough, # 580); → *s'p* II (cut down, # 6188); → *'ānāp* (branches, # 6733)
Olive: → *gargēr* (ripe olive, # 1737); → *zayit* (olive tree, olive, # 2339); → *yiṣhār* I (oil, # 3658); → *šemen* (olive oil, # 9043)
Trees: → *'ēlâ* I (mighty tree, # 461); → *'erez* (cedar, # 780); → *'ōren* I (pine, # 815); → *'ēšel* (tamarisk, # 869); → *b^erôš* (juniper, # 1360); → *lûz* I (almond-tree, # 4280); → *'ēṣ* (trees, tree, wood, timber, sticks, # 6770); → *'ar'ār* (juniper, # 6899); → *ṣammeret* (acacia, [tree-]top, # 7550); → *šāqēd* (almond, # 9196); → *šiqmâ* (sycamore-[fig-] tree, # 9204); → *t^e'aššûr* (cypress, # 9309); → *tāmār* I (date-palm, # 9469); → *tirzâ* (unknown tree, # 9560); (→ **Tree of Knowledge/Life: Theology**)
Vegetation: → *'ēzôb* (hyssop, # 257); → *dš'* (become green, sprout, # 2012); → *zr'* (sow, scatter seed, form seed, # 2445); → *ḥāṣîr* I (grass, # 2945); → *ḥ^ašaš* (dry grass, # 3143); → *yereq* (green, greenness, # 3764); → *nṭ'* (plant, establish, drive, # 5749); → *'āleh* (leaf, leafage, # 6591); → *'ēśeb* (herb, herbage, weed, # 6912); → *qîqāyôn* (plant of uncertain identity, # 7813); → *rō'š* II (bitter and poisonous herb, # 8032); → *śîaḥ* I (bush, shrub, # 8489); → *šiṭṭâ* (acacia, # 8847)

BIBLIOGRAPHY

ABD 2:803-17; 6:656-60; *Corpus Publication*, vol. O-N, 1979, 3562-63; *EJ* 16:630-31; *IDB* 4:695-97; *TWOT* 2:688-89; D. A. Anderson, *All the Trees and Woody Plants of the Bible*, 1979; *Fauna and Flora of the Bible*, 1980; F. N. Hepper, *Baker Encyclopedia of Bible Plants*, 1992; N. Hereunveni, *Tree and Shrub in Our Biblical Heritage*, 1984; D. L. Jeffrey, ed., *A Dictionary of Biblical Tradition in English Literature*, 1992; P. K. Meagher, *Encyclopedic Dictionary of Religion*; *Eerdmans Bible Dictionary* (rev. ed.), 1987, 1018; H. N. and A. L. Moldenke, *Plants of the Bible*, 1952; W. E. Shewell-Cooper, *Plants, Flowers and Herbs of the Bible*, 1977; Y. Waisal, *Trees of the Land of Israel*, 1980; W. Walker, *All the Plants of the Bible*, 1957; M. Zohary, *Plants of the Bible*, 1982.

Larry L. Walker

6772	עצב

עצב (*'ṣb* II), q. hurt, grieve; ni. be distressed, displeased, grieve; pi. grieve, offend; hi. grieve; hitp. feel grieved, outraged (# 6772); nom./adj. **מַעֲצֵבָה** (*ma^{'a}ṣēbâ*), place of torment (# 5107); **עָצֵב/עַצָּב** (*'āṣēb/'aṣṣāb*), (heavy) worker (# 6774); **עֶצֶב** (*'eṣeb* II), hardship, pain, offending (# 6776); **עֹצֶב** (*'ōṣeb* II), hardship, pain, distress (# 6778); **עִצָּבוֹן** (*'iṣṣābôn*), hardship, pain, distress (# 6779); **עַצֶּבֶת** (*'aṣṣebet*), pain, painful spot (# 6780).

ANE The root *'ṣb* occurs in Arab., Aram. (see Dan 6:21), postbiblical Heb., and Eth. (see *TWAT* 6:298-301).

OT 1. The vb. *'ṣb* II occurs 15x. The common reflexive usage and texts such as Isa 54:6 (distressed in spirit) show that it has to do basically with inner feelings (*bkh* and *'bl*, weep, mourn, more externally evident grief, presuppose *'ṣb*; see 2 Sam 19:1-2; Neh 8:9-11).

2. The nom. *'eṣeb* II (6x) refers to laborious activity or, once, offending speech (Prov 15:1), all pain-inducing. All occur in poetry, and five of the six in Wisdom sayings (also Gen 3:16?). The nom. *'iṣṣābôn* (3x), all in Gen 3-5, refers to pain-filled labor. The nom. *'aṣṣebet* (5x), all in poetry, refers to internal sorrow, pain (Ps 147:3) or social strife (Prov 10:10). The nom. *'ōṣeb* II, 3x in Ps 139:24, is of uncertain meaning, commonly "wicked" (NRSV mg., hurtful). The nom. *'āṣēb* 1x (Isa 58:3) refers to laborers. The nom. *ma'ᵃṣēbâ* 1x (Isa 50:11) designates a place of pain, an effect of divine judgment.

3. The majority of nominal forms occur in Wisdom or Wisdom-like material (including Gen 3:16-17). Their orientation is more toward that inner pain and toilsome work that is generally true of the human situation, toward associations with childbirth (Gen 3:16; cf. 1 Chron 4:9), daily work (Ps 127:2) and its rewards (Prov 5:10; 14:23), personal health (15:13), and the complexities of interhuman relationships (10:10; 15:1). Human sin can lead to pain and judgment (Ps 16:4; Isa 50:11; cf. Eccl 10:9), but God can act to relieve pain and toil (Gen 5:29; Ps 147:3; Isa 14:3), for which no human effort can substitute (Prov 10:22, NAB).

The pain includes both physical and psychic dimensions, as does the relief; the psychic is stressed in some texts (Prov 15:1, 13), the physical in others, especially with *'eṣeb* and *'iṣṣābôn* (for discussion of Gen 3:16, see Meyers, 300-301). These words do not name all work as toilsome (→ *'śh* [do, → # 6913]; *'ml* [labor, → # 6661]; *p'l* [do, → # 7188]), but recognize that it is a not uncommon characteristic of a generally positive gift of God in a world filled with sin and its negative effects, even upon ecological realities (Gen 3:17; cf. Hos 4:1-3).

4. The verbal usage specifies an inner grieving in the face of loss (1 Sam 20:34; 2 Sam 19:2) or failure in relationships with God (Neh 8:10-11; Isa 54:6) or other human beings (Gen 34:7; 45:5), or it names the injury resulting therefrom (1 Chron 4:10; Ps 56:5[6]). Three instances have to do with God's grieving, provoked by the sinful response of the human race (Gen 6:6) and by Israel, from its beginnings (Ps 78:40) and throughout its history (Isa 63:10). God is revealed, not as one who remains unmoved by the human response, but as one who is deeply affected by what has happened to the relationship (see T. Fretheim, *The Suffering of God*, 109-13).

Pain, pangs: → *ḥbl* IV (be pregnant, travail, # 2473); → *ḥyl* I (be in labor, tremble, # 2655); → *k'b* (be in pain, cause pain, ruin, # 3872); → *mrṣ* (be hurtful, painful, irritate, # 5344); → *'ṣb* II (hurt, grieve, offend, # 6772)

BIBLIOGRAPHY

TWAT 6:298-301; *TWOT* 2:687-88; C. Meyers, "Gender Roles and Genesis 3:16 Revisited," *The Word of the Lord Shall Go Forth: Essays in Honor of David Noel Freedman in Celebration of his Sixtieth Birthday*, ASOR 1, 1983, 300-301, 337-54; J. Scharbert, *Der Schmerz im AT*, 1955.

Terence E. Fretheim

6773	עָצָב

עָצָב (**'āṣāb*), (only in pl.) nom. god-image (# 6773): the single example of the sing. in MT is pointed *'oṣbî* (# 6777; Isa 48:5), presumably from ***עֹצֶב** (**'ōṣeb*), *'ṣb* pointed with the vowels of בֹּשֶׁת (*bōšet*), shame. This meaning is also conjectured in Ps 139:24. As similarly sounding words from *'ṣb* II mean pain, hard labor, grief, it is probable that the use of this word for the images was meant to carry overtones of that sense.

ANE The vb. form has parallels in the Mish. Heb. stretch, set; Syr. bind up (wounds), repair (boat); Arab. twist, as well as Geez *'aṣäbä*, be hard; Tigrinya *'aṣäbä*, be in misery, distress.

OT 1. The word is used frequently for images used in worship by foreigners, especially of Bel, Nebo, and Marduk (Isa 46:1; Jer 50:2). In Isa 46:1 the term *n[e]śû'â*, load, burden (# 5953), occurs in parallelism to *'[a]ṣabbîm*: "their idols (*'[a]ṣṣabbêhem*) ... the images that are carried (*n[e]śu'ōt*)" (NIV). An alternate reading (cf. *BHS*) is, "Their images are a burden for animals, like heavy loads *carried* by weary cattle." The context names the gods (Bel, Nebo); thus these are images of these gods, not idols themselves. In the Psalms *'āṣāb* is used instead of *pesel* in the idol parodies (Ps 115:4 ‖ 135:15).

2. The word is fairly common in Hosea (4x). While some see here a reference to imported foreign religions, it is more likely that the poet attacks the use of images in the worship of Yahweh. The most common association is with the calf/calves (cf. Hos 8:4-5), which need not be symbols of other gods. For the general prophetic attitude to images see *'[e]lîlîm* (# 496). The more priestly oriented the text, the more the opposition to images. In Ps 106:36, 38, although they are what the deut. history refers to as the "other gods" or "Baals and Astartes," it is the *'[a]ṣabbîm* themselves that are worshiped, and this may be true in some of the other references.

3. In Jer 50:2, where the Babylonian gods are named, the addition of *'[a]ṣabbîm* and *gillûlîm* with the same vbs. suggests an attempt to deny the existence of the gods and to reduce them to images (idols, fetishes).

P-B This word is most commonly translated in LXX by *eidōlon*. It continues to be used in Jewish literature.

Idolatry: → *'[e]lîl* (Nothing, # 496); → *'[a]šērâ* (wooden cult-object, pole, goddess, # 895); → *gillûlîm* (images, idols, # 1658); → *dāgôn* (Dagon, # 1837); → *k[e]môš* (Chemosh [god of the Moabites], # 4019); → *mōlek* (Molech, # 4891); → *massēkâ* I (cast statuette, # 5011); → *mipleṣet* (terrible thing, dreadful object, # 5145); → *semel* (image, # 6166); → *'āṣāb* (god-image, # 6773); → *'aštōret* (Astarte, # 6956); → *pesel* (cultic image, statue of a god, # 7181); → *tōmer* II (scarecrow, # 9473); → *t[e]rāpîm* (figurines, mask, # 9572); → **Idolatry: Theology**

Bibliography

TDNT 2:375-80; *TWAT* 6:301-5; M. I. Gruber, "Azabbim," *DDD*, cols. 238-40; W. M. W. Roth, "For Life, He Appeals to Death (Wis 13:18)," *CBQ* 37, 1975, 20-47; S. Schroer, *In Israel gab es Bilder*, 1987.

Judith M. Hadley

6774 (*'āṣṣāb*, [heavy] worker), → # 6772

6776 (*'eṣeb* II, hardship, pain, offending), → # 6772

6778 (*'ōṣeb* II, hardship, pain, distress), → # 6772

6779 (*'iṣṣābôn*, hardship, pain, distress), → # 6772

6780 (*'aṣṣebet*, pain, painful spot), → # 6772

6781	עצה

עצה (*'ṣh* I), q. shut (hapleg.) (# 6781).

OT In Prov 16:30 it appears to have a meaning related to an Arab. cognate *ġdw*, wrinkle the eyelids (*HALAT*): "He who winks with his eye (shuts his eye) is plotting perversity."

Closing, shutting: → *'ṭm* (stopped up, # 357); → *'ṭr* (close [mouth], # 358); → *gwp* I (shut, close, # 1589); → *ṭḥḥ* (besmeared, stuck, shut, # 3220); → *ṭmh* (stopped up, # 3241); → *n'l* I (tie, lock, # 5835); → *sgr* I (shut, close, deliver up, # 6037); → *stm* (stop up, # 6258); → *'ṣh* I (shut, # 6781); → *'ṣm* III (shut one's eyes, # 6794); → *ṣrr* I (bind, shut up, be narrow, in straits, distress, # 7674); → *qpṣ* I (draw together, shut, # 7890); → *š''* I (smear, smooth, shut, # 9129)

Bill T. Arnold

6782	עָצֶה

עָצֶה (*'āṣeh*), spine, backbone (hapleg. in Lev 3:9; # 6782). For a discussion on bones in the OT, see *'eṣem* I (bone, skin, body, self, # 6795).

Robert B. Chisholm

6783 (*'ēṣâ* I, plan, counsel, advice), → # 3619

6784	עֵצָה

עֵצָה (*'ēṣâ* II), nom. disobedience, resistance, rebellion, contention (# 6784).

OT G. Driver (192-93) was one of the first to contend that a unique root, *'ēṣâ* II (derived from Arab. *'aṣā*, disobeyed, rebelled), existed in several passages. *HALAT* (821) also posits the existence of a nom. *'ēṣâ* II, citing eight examples (Job 10:3; 12:13; 18:7; Ps 13:2[3]; 14:6; 106:43; Isa 16:3; Hos 10:6). However, that entry concludes with the observation that a second root distinct from *'ēṣâ* I (→ # 6783) remains questionable. Most lexical works (*THAT* 1:748-53; *TDOT* 6:156-85; Even-Shoshan, 908-9) disregard Driver's suggestion. Lisowsky (1106) lists two occurrences of this conjectured nom. (Ps 13:2[3]; 106:43). None of the eight posited instances of *'ēṣâ* II contextually requires a meaning other than the customary semantic range of *'ēṣâ* I. The LXX readings unanimously support *'ēṣâ* I as well. Nothing is gained in this instance by multiplying roots.

P-B The LXX translates all of the references listed above with *boulē*, counsel, plan. The word is found in Sir 11:9. It is in the DSS (1QS 8:1). In LH (Jastrow 2:1101) *'ēṣā* (II) means counsel, advice, plan; thus, that this is a distinctive root from *'eṣa* I is suspect (see above).

Rebellion, conspiracy, stubbornness, obstinacy: → *ysd* II (conspire together, # 3570); → *kśh* (become stubborn, headstrong, # 4170); → *lāṣôn* (bragging, foolish talk, # 4371); → *lṣṣ* (rebel, scoff, # 4372); → *mrd* (revolt, rebel, # 5277); → *mrh* (be refractory, obstinate, # 5286); → *srr* I (be stubborn, rebellious, # 6253); → *'bt* (conspire together, # 6309); → *'ēṣâ* II (disobedience?, revolt?, # 6784); → *'ātāq* (old, hard, stubborn, arrogant, # 6981); → *pš'* (revolt, rebel, # 7321);

→ q^e*šî* (stubbornness, # 8001); → *qšr* (ally together, conspire, bind, # 8003); → *š^{e}rîrût* (stubbornness, # 9244)

Bibliography

TDOT 6:156-85; *THAT* 1:748-53; G. R. Driver, "Mistranslations," *ExpTim* 57, 1945-46, 192-93; A. Even-Shoshan, *A New Concordance of the Old Testament*, 1990; G. Lisowsky, *Konkordanz zum Hebräischen Alten Testament*, 1958.

Eugene Carpenter/Michael A. Grisanti

6785 (*'ēṣâ* III, wood), → # 6770

6786 (*'āṣûm*, mighty, vast), → # 6793

6788	עצל

עצל (*'ṣl*), ni. be slow, hesitate (# 6788); nom./adj. עָצֵל (*'āṣēl*), slow, lazy (# 6789); עַצְלוּתעַצְלָה (*'aṣlâ, 'aṣlût*), laziness (# 6790/6791); עֲצַלְתַּיִם (*'^{a}ṣaltayim*), extreme laziness, indolence (# 6792).

ANE An Arab. cognate is *'aṣala*; *'aṣila*, be slow; Akk. *eṣēlu*, D. paralyze; *eṣlu*, heavy of movement, languishing.

OT 1. The single occurrence of the vb. is in the story of Danites attacking the land of Laish. There seemed to be hesitancy to follow the counsel of the young Levite acting as priest for Micah (Judg 18:9). The spies, encouraged by the priest's oracle, "Your journey has the LORD's approval" (Judg 18:6), called on their fellow Danites not to hesitate (*'ṣl*); when they proceeded, they were victorious (18:27-28).

2. The word in its adj. and nom. forms is most frequent in Wisdom literature in discourses about sloth and laziness (16x). The description of the lazy entails ridicule and censorship, perhaps as a motivation to avoid a lifestyle characterized by laziness. The lazy person makes ridiculous excuses, imagining the worst should he venture out (Prov 26:13; cf. 22:13). The sluggard is compared in his turning over in his sleep to a door on its hinges (26:14). The irritation the sluggard brings to the employer is like vinegar to the teeth and like smoke to the eyes (10:26). The indolent earns only the disapproval of his fellows. Sarcastically, the sluggard is characterized as one too lazy even when eating to bring the hand up from the dish to the mouth (19:24; 26:15).

Other motivations to avoid the life of sloth are pragmatic; the laws of God are not invoked, except indirectly, by pointing to the consequences of laziness. A vignette of neglecting one's responsibilities is painted in Prov 24:30-34 as an admonition to avoid a lazy way of life. The lazy man fails to make building repairs and must bear the consequences of deterioration and inconvenience (Eccl 10:18). Laziness results in poverty (Prov 19:15). By contrast, the wife of noble character watches over the affairs of her household and does not eat the bread of idleness (*'aṣlût*). The women of the family of God keep bread on their table because of their diligent work (Prov 31:27).

Since there is no plowing, there will be no reaping (Prov 20:4). The indolent person may have desire and craving, but failure to act means that he or she will have nothing (13:4). Refusal to work could even mean death (21:25). The imperative is to learn from the ant, for the way of wisdom lies in the direction of diligence (6:9).

Lazy, slow, slack: → *'rk* I (become long, # 799); → *'ṣl* (be sluggish, # 6788); → *r^e^miyyâ* (slackness, # 8244); → *rph* (become slack, lose heart, discourage, # 8332)

J. A. Thompson/Elmer A. Martens

6789 (*'āṣēl*, slow, lazy), → # 6788

6790/91 (*'aṣlût*, laziness), → # 6788

6792 (*'^a^ṣaltayim*, extreme laziness), → # 6788

6793	עצם

עצם (*'ṣm* I), be mighty, powerful; be vast, numerous; make strong (# 6793); עָצוּם (*'āṣûm*), adj. mighty, powerful; vast (# 6786); עֹצֶם (*'ōṣem* I), nom. power, vigor (# 6797); עָצְמָה (*'oṣmâ*), nom. power, vigor (# 6800); עֲצֻמוֹת (*'^a^ṣumôt*), nom. proofs (hapleg.; # 6802); תַּעֲצֻמוֹת (*ta'^a^ṣumôt*), nom. power, vigor (hapleg.; # 9508).

ANE Verbal forms are found in Arab., *'aẓuma* (be, become vast, mighty); Arab. *'aẓama* (hinder, impede, obstruct); Tigre., *'aṣma*; Syr. *'^e^ṣam* (quarrel, dispute, fight, struggle, contend). Adjectival forms are found in Sam. *'āṣom*, Ugar. *'ẓm*, and Arab. *'aẓīm* (vast, strong, mighty). The Arab. nom. *'iṣmat* (defence, vindication, advocacy) also occurs.

OT 1. The vb., which in all texts except Ps 105:24 (hi.) is used in the q., occurs 18x in the MT, if the form *'aṣ^e^mâ*, she was strong (*HALAT*; others, e.g., BDB, 782, take the word to be a fem. nom.) in Nah 3:9 is emended to *'oṣmāh*, her strength, and MT *ûk^e^'omdô*, and when he has arisen, in Dan 11:4 is changed to *ûk^e^'oṣmô*, and when he becomes strong.

(a) In eight passages (excluding Nah 3:9), the vb. has the meaning be strong. In three texts, it is used of a potentially threatening force that, as a result of multiplication, has become increasingly powerful ("a strength to be reckoned with" [Durham, 1987, 2, translating the vb. in Exod 1:7]). When, as a result of God's blessing (Gen 26:2-5), Isaac prospered, acquiring much wealth, a great household, and large flocks and herds, Abimelech, the king of the Philistines, in whose territory Isaac was sojourning, told him to leave Gerar because he had become much more powerful than the envious Philistines (*'āṣamtā mimmennû m^e^'ōd*, you are/have become much mightier than we are [Gen 26:16]).

In spite of oppression, the descendants of Abraham multiplied and prospered (cf. 1:28; 9:1, 7 [God's intentions in creation; see Fretheim, 25]) in Egypt, as God had promised (12:2; 15:5; 17:2-8; 22:15-18; 26:2-5, 24; 28:1-4, 13-15; 35:10-12; 48:3-4; Exod 32:13; Deut 10:22; Isa 51:2), and grew immensely powerful (*wayya'aṣmû bim^e^'ōd m^e^'ōd* [Exod 1:7]; *wayya'aṣmû m^e^'ōd* [1:20]). Most translators understand the verb in 1:7, 20 to mean become strong, but some (e.g., NIV; Childs, 1, 5; Houtman, 230, 258) take it to mean become numerous. It is significant that a form of *'ṣm* often occurs alongside a form of *rbb/rbh* (be, become much, many, great [# 8045; # 8049]; e.g., Ps 139:17-18; Jer 5:6) and that the adj. *rab*, many, much, great (# 8041), frequently occurs together with *'āṣûm*, mighty, vast (e.g., Exod 1:9; Num 32:1; Deut 9:14; 26:5) (Houtman, 231). Moreover, the hi. of *prh*, be fruitful (# 7238), is used in parallelism with the hi. of *'ṣm* in Ps 105:24, which describes how Yahweh made his people fruitful in Egypt and stronger than their enemies. Here, some (e.g., RSV; NRSV; NEB; JB; TEV; Delitzsch, 1885, 139; Oesterley, 446; Kraus, 1989, 306; Bratcher and Reyburn, 898) take the vb. to convey the idea of strength or vigor, but others (e.g., NIV; REB; Buttenwieser, 804; Kissane, 1964, 481; Dahood, 1970, 50, 59; Allen, 1983, 36, 38) understand it as expressing size. This suggests that the vb., in some contexts at least, means be, become mighty/strong on account of numbers (Houtman, 231). By translating the vb. in Exod 1:7, 20 as "waxed mighty," S. R. Driver (1953, 2, 7; cf. Montgomery, 349 on Dan 8:24) neatly combines the two senses of becoming larger and becoming powerful.

Those Judeans are denounced who, instead of relying on Yahweh for their security, look for help to Egypt and place their trust in chariots because they are many (*kî rāb*) and in horsemen because they are very strong (*kî-ʿāṣ*^{e}*mû m*^{e}*ʾōd*) (Isa 31:1). Here, too, some translators (e.g., RV; RSV; NRSV; JB; NIV; Watts, 1985, 407) take the vb. to be signifying strength while others (e.g., NEB; REB; Whitehouse, 325; Kaiser, 1974, 311; Oswalt, 569) think it conveys the idea of large numbers. Although Kissane (1960, 339) translates "because they are very powerful," he acknowledges (341) that "numerous" is an equally valid translation. But irrespective of which sense of the verb one prefers here, the point of the verse remains the same: those who choose to make material power (the brute force of soldiers and armaments), whether one's own or that of allies, their primary commitment (see Oswalt, 571) instead of spiritual power that belongs to God and that no human power can thwart or withstand, choose failure (v. 3; cf. Ps 118:8-9; Prov 3:5; Jer 17:5-8; Hos 10:13b) (Thomson and Skinner, 119-20; Kissane, 1960, 341; Kelley, 281; Mauchline, 213). Using Isa 2:7 as an illustration, Skinner (1909, 236) maintains that the prophets considered horses and chariots objectionable in themselves because they were embodiments of irreligious materialism. However, Oswalt (571) seems to suggest that the issue is that of Judah's primary commitment rather than whether the possession of military equipment is incompatible with faith in God.

(b) In four passages, the verb means be, become strong, without any obvious connection between the strength acquired by the person(s) and an increase in number. In Daniel's vision of the ram (the Medo-Persian empire) and the goat (the Greek empire) (Dan 8:1-27), when the he-goat became strong (*k*^{e}*ʿoṣmô*), its great horn was broken, a reference to Alexander the Great's unexpected death at the height of his powers in 323 BC (8:8). In his interpretation of the vision of unfolding history (Dan 11:1-12:13), a celestial visitant explains to Daniel that a mighty king (Alexander the Great) will arise and, once he has become powerful (reading *ûk*^{e}*ʿoṣmô* [see *BHS*; *HALAT*; Bevan, 172; Charles, 119; S. R. Driver, 1922, 164; cf. JB; TEV] in 11:4 instead of MT *ûk*^{e}*ʿomdô*, and when he arises), his kingdom will be broken and divided into four.

In the latter end of Greek rule, the interpreting angel explains to Daniel, a violent and treacherous king (Antiochus IV Epiphanes) will arise whose power will be great (*w*^{e}*ʿāṣam kōḥô*, lit., and his power will become strong [Dan 8:24]). He will make deceit prosper, magnify himself, destroy many (including those belonging to the people of the saints), and even rise up against the prince of princes (i.e., God), before being broken by no human hand (vv. 24-25). In the angel's interpretation of unfolding history (Dan 11:1-12:13), Antiochus IV Epiphanes is described as a contemptible person and a usurper (11:21), who will become strong (*wᵉʿāṣam* [v. 23]). Daniel 8 and 11 make the important point that although mighty human powers may seem unassailable, each one is broken, sometimes when its strength is at its apex (Goldingay, 219).

(c) The vb. is used with the meaning be, become numerous with different subjects (enemies, widows, iniquities, apostasies, sins, God's wondrous deeds, and God's thoughts). A suffering penitent afflicted by severe physical deterioration (Ps 38:3[4], 5-10[6-11], 17[18]), deserted by his friends (v. 11[12]), and relentlessly harassed by treacherous enemies, confesses his iniquity, apologizes for his sin (v. 18[19]), and entreats God to make haste to deliver him from his foes, who attack him without cause (reading *ḥinnām* [so 4QpPs[a], cited by Craigie, 1983b, 302], which is a more suitable parallel to *šāqer*, wrongfully, than MT *ḥayyîm*, life) and are numerous (*ʿāṣēmû*, v. 19[20]). Here, RSV, NRSV, and Kissane (1964, 169) have "mighty" (cf. RV; TEV; G. W. Anderson, 427; Dahood, 1966, 234; A. A. Anderson, 1972a, 307; Kraus, 1988, 410). However, the fact that *ʿāṣēmû* is used in parallelism with *[wᵉ]rabbû* (and they are many) suggests that *ʿṣm* here refers, at least primarily, to the size rather than to the power of the opposition (cf. JB; NEB; REB; NIV; Delitzsch, 1889b, 19; C. A. and E. G. Briggs, 341, 343; Buttenwieser, 579; Craigie, 1983b, 301).

An individual in deep affliction and pain (Ps 69:1-3[2-4]), wrongfully persecuted by enemies (v. 4[5]), ostracized by his own family (v. 8[9]), conscious of his sin (v. 5[6]), but suffering because of his loyalty to God (vv. 6-12[7-13]), prays for divine intervention to deliver him from those who hate him without cause, who seek to destroy him, who attack him with lies, and who are numerous (v. 4[5]). RSV translates *ʿāṣᵉmû* as "[they are] mighty" (cf. REB; TEV; Davison, 339; Taylor, 363; Kissane, 1964, 301, 304; Durham, 1972, 310; Eaton, 175; Weiser, 494; Kraus, 1989, 57). Once again, however, the fact that the vb. is used in parallelism with *rbh* suggests that the primary reference is to the large number of foes rather than their great strength (cf. NEB; NRSV; JB; NIV; Delitzsch, 1889b, 272; C. A. and E. G. Briggs, 113, 116, 121; Buttenwieser, 726; Oesterley, 328; A. A. Anderson, 1972a, 500; Dahood, 1973, 153, 157; Tate, 1990, 187).

As a result of her obdurate rejection of him, Yahweh has no alternative but to destroy Jerusalem (Jer 15:6), winnowing its citizens as with a fork, bereaving them (v. 7), and making their widows more in number than the sand of the sea (*ʿāṣᵉmû-lî ʾalmᵉnōtāw*, lit., their widows have become numerous to me [v. 8]). Peake (1910, 207) argues that the tenses in vv. 6b-9 describing the calamity should be changed from perfects to futures. Others (e.g., NIV; Dummelow, 466; Cunliffe-Jones, 121; Green, 93; Clements, 1988, 96) treat those verbs in Jer 15:5-9 that refer to Yahweh's destructive actions in the perfect tense as "prophetic perfects," describing future events as though they had already happened. However, many think it more probable that this passage is a reflection on the disaster that befell Jerusalem in 587/586 BC (so RSV; NRSV; NEB; REB; TEV; S. R. Driver, 1906, 88; Hyatt, 1956, 937; Bright, 1965, 105, 111; Thompson, 1987, 388-91; Boadt, 119; Carroll, 322-23; Davidson, 1986, 124-25; McKane, 1986, 337-43). On the other hand, McKane (1986, 343) rightly points out that although the events are described as if they lie in the past, the passage may be the result of a prophetic premonition so intense that the downfall of Jerusalem could only be expressed as if it had already been accomplished.

Following his thanksgiving for deliverance from trouble (Ps 40:1-11[2-12]), a psalmist appeals to Yahweh to rescue him from evils (presumably external troubles) that have encompassed him without number and from his iniquities (presumably his own evil acts in the past [Craigie, 1983b, 316]), which have overtaken him and outnumber (*'āṣ^e^mû*) the hairs of his head (v. 12[13]; a similar hyperbolic comparison is used in Ps 69:4[5]).

Had there been but one person of true piety and genuine integrity in the whole of Jerusalem, Yahweh might have pardoned the city (Jer 5:1), but the prophet's thorough search failed to locate anyone committed to justice and truth. Consequently, Yahweh had no alternative but to unleash destructive forces (invaders graphically portrayed as wild animals [cf. Jer 2:15; 4:7; Hos 13:7-8; Hab 1:8; Zeph 3:3]) against his people for their countless transgressions and their numerous apostasies (*kî rabbû piš'êhem 'āṣ^e^mû m^e^šubôtêhem*, lit., for their transgressions are many, numerous are their apostasies [5:6]).

Yahweh will despoil Israel's oppressors (Jer 30:11, 16) and release (v. 8), heal (v. 17), and restore his people (vv. 9-10, 18-22), who have been deserted by former political allies (v. 14; cf. 4:30) and whose wound, inflicted by an enemy sent by Yahweh because of his people's great iniquity and flagrant sins (*'al rōb ^a^wōnēk 'āṣ^e^mû ḥaṭṭō'tāyik*, lit., because your guilt is great, your sins numerous [vv. 14 and 15]), seems, from a human perspective, incurable (vv. 12-13, 15; cf. 8:21-22; 14:17). The God who wounds to punish sin is the same God who, out of infinite grace and compassion, will cure the seemingly incurable wound of his people and restore them to full health (Davidson, 1985, 73-74).

In a thanksgiving for deliverance from trouble (Ps 40:1-10[2-11]), an individual asserts that if he were to undertake to recite Yahweh's wondrous deeds and his thoughts toward his people, the task would prove impossible because these acts of salvation are more than can be numbered/recounted (*'āṣ^e^mû missappēr*, v. 5[6]; cf. 92:5[6]; 104:24; 106:2; 139:17-18). Another psalmist exclaims in reverential wonder at the vastness of God's thoughts (*meh 'āṣ^e^mû rā'šêhem*, lit., how vast is the sum of them, Ps 139:17 [either viewing *rē'eykā* as an Aramaism or reading *dē'eykā*, your thoughts, instead of MT, your friends; *pace* LXX and Vg.]); they cannot be counted because they are more than the sand (v. 18). Human beings are incapable of expressing, let alone of comprehending, the infinite fullness of Yahweh's love (Weiser, 337) or the immeasurable totality of his thoughts (A. A. Anderson 1972b, 911). God's love and penetrating knowledge are unfathomable, transcending the capacity of human imagination and intellectual comprehension (Kraus, 1989, 516-17).

2. The adj *'āṣûm* occurs 31x. (a) Frequently occurring in combination with other adjectives, especially *rab* (many much, great), *'āṣûm* can refer to strength of power or to strength of numbers (cf. Delitzsch, 1889b, 427), depending on the context, although it is not always easy to determine which is the more probable meaning. This difficulty can be illustrated with reference to two texts (Joel 2:11; Amos 5:12). There are different translations of the phrase *kî 'āṣûm 'ōśēh d^e^bārô* in Joel 2:11, where the prophet, calling the nation to national repentance and fasting, warns his people of the great and terrible day of Yahweh, which none can withstand (cf. Rev 6:17). The words *kî rab m^e'^ōd maḥ^a^nēhû kî 'āṣûm 'ōśēh d^e^bārô* are translated "for his host is exceedingly great; he that executes his word is powerful" (RSV); "and indeed his regiments

are innumerable, all-powerful is the one that carries out his orders" (JB); "his forces are beyond number, and mighty are those who obey his command" (NIV). However, NEB and REB, which understand *'āṣûm* here to signify, primarily, size rather than power, read, "His is a mighty army, countless are those who do his bidding." NRSV goes further, taking both *rab m^e'ōd* and *'āṣûm* as connoting large numbers: "How vast is his host! Numberless are those who obey his command." Among commentators, most understand *'āṣûm* here to be signifying physical strength (Pusey, 118; S. R. Driver, 1901, 54; Bewer, 104; Kennedy, 72; Hubbard, 57; Wolff, 1977, 38, 48; Stuart, 247), but some understand it to mean vastness (Duhm, 212; Allen, 1976, 66).

Amos knows firsthand how many are his people's transgressions (*rabbîm piš'êkem*, many are your transgressions) and how *'^{a}ṣumîm* are their sins (Amos 5:12). The phrase *wa'^{a}ṣumîm ḥaṭṭō'têkem* is variously translated: "and how forceful your sins" (G. A. Smith, 167-68); "and (how) formidable are your wrongdoings" (Wolff, 1977, 230, 248); "and the severity of your sins" (Stuart, 342); "and the magnitude of your sins" (Ward, 75); "and how mighty are your sins" (RV; S. R. Driver, 1901, 181); "and mighty your sins" (Pusey, 195); "and how great are your sins" (RSV; NRSV; cf. NIV; Harper, 122); "and your misdeeds are huge" (Snaith, 85, 87); "and your sins enormous" (JB); "how monstrous your sins" (REB); "and manifold your sins" (Duhm, 68); "and how countless your sins" (NEB; Paul, 157; cf. Hubbard, 172); "how numerous are your sins" (Mays, 1976, 96; cf. Hayes, 152); "and how many crimes you have committed" (TEV). Some (e.g., Paul, 174) maintain that *rabbîm* and *'^{a}ṣumîm* are synonymous terms here, signifying "manifold" and "multiple." However, others (e.g., Pusey, 195) argue that the adj. *'^{a}ṣumîm* signifies strength here; the people's sins were not many only, but also strong in the oppression of the poor.

(b) The word is applied to Yahweh's chosen people. Yahweh's decision not to conceal from Abraham what he was proposing to do to Sodom (cf. Amos 3:7 [Yahweh always reveals his plans to his prophetic servants]) was based on two considerations: (i) nothing must obstruct the fulfillment of Yahweh's promise that Abraham would become a great and powerful nation (*l^{e}gôy gādôl w^e'āṣûm*) by whom, or in whom, all the nations of the earth would bless themselves or be blessed (Gen 18:18, 19b); and (ii) the judgment on Sodom would prove a useful didactic tool when Abraham was instructing his children and the members of his household about the maintenance of righteousness and justice (18:19a).

The new pharaoh who did not know Joseph (Exod 1:8) is thought by many (e.g., Harford, 169; Stalker, 209; Honeycutt, 323; Clements, 1972, 11; Clifford, 46; cf. S. R. Driver, 1953, 2; G. H. Davies, 60; Hyatt, 1971, 58) to be Rameses II, 1290-1224/1223 BC, and by some (e.g., Wright and Filson, 37b; H. R. Jones, 121; cf. Rylaarsdam, 836; Hyatt, 1971, 58; Clements, 1972, 11) to be Seti/Sethos I, 1303/1302-1290 BC (see, however, Houtman, 235, who points out that *melek-ḥādāš* in v. 8 is more a figure of speech than a careful historical reference). When he came to power, he considered the large and prolific colony of Israelites in the delta region a serious security risk, saying, "The people of Israel are more numerous and more powerful than us" (*rab w^e'āṣûm mimmennû*, Exod 1:9; on the hyperbole here, see Houtman, 236-37).

Fearful of the Israelites, whom he considered too powerful (RSV; NRSV; JB; NIV; Budd, 249; Ashley, 441; E. W. Davies, 247 [NEB and REB translate "too many" and TEV has "they outnumber us"]) for him, the Moabite king Balak sought to enlist the services of the renowned Mesopotamian diviner Balaam with the intention of securing a divine curse on the interlopers (Num 22:6). The story of Balak and Balaam (Num 22:1-24:25) illustrates that the stratagems of adversaries are incapable of hindering or halting Israel's triumphant progress to the Promised Land (Budd, 273).

At the Feast of Weeks, the autumn harvest pilgrimage festival (Deut 16:9-12), at which Yahweh was thanked for his gift of the land and for his many blessings, Israelites recalled liturgically how their ancestor Jacob went down to Egypt, where he became a great (*gādôl*; # 1524), powerful (*'āṣûm*), and populous (*wārāb*) nation (Deut 26:5). JPSV (cf. Thompson, 1974, 256) translates "a great and very populous nation," but the overwhelming majority of translators take *'āṣûm* here to be a reference to power rather than to size.

Faced with the people's incomprehensible insubordination and lack of trust, Yahweh wished to strike them with pestilence, disinherit them, and make of Moses *l^e gôy-gādôl w^e 'āṣûm*, a nation greater and mightier (RSV; NRSV; JB; Budd, 148; E. W. Davies, 142-43)/stronger (NIV; Ashley, 251)/more powerful (TEV) than they (Num 14:12; NEB and REB have "more numerous"). Yahweh's threat to destroy the wilfully faithless people and to create a new nation from the descendants of Moses, an intention averted only by the intercession of Moses, is found in only two other passages (Exod 32:9-14; Deut 9:13-21). In Deut 9:14, the word *'āṣûm* again occurs. Because of their unceasing rebellion even at Horeb (cf. Exod 32:1-35), Yahweh wanted to destroy his stubborn and disloyal people and to make of Moses a nation more powerful (*'āṣûm*) and more numerous (*wārāb*) than they (Deut 9:14). Here, too, it is only the intercession of Moses that persuades God to preserve Israel from destruction (9:18-21; cf. Amos 7:1-6, where the heart of God was turned by the importuning prayers of the prophet [on the similarities between the two passages, see Miller, 122-24]).

In the new age of peace, when regathering, healing, restoration, and empowerment will replace the suffering, separation, crippling injury, and debilitation experienced during the divine judgment (cf. Scoggin, 210), Yahweh will graciously transform the lame and the rejected into a dynamic remnant (cf. Mic 5:5-9[4-8]), which will become a powerful nation (*l^e gôy 'āṣûm*, Mic 4:7 [Hillers, 54, translates the adj. here as "populous"]). He will also institute his royal dominion anew and forever upon Mount Zion. In what reads like a commentary on this v. (Wolff, 1990, 124), Isa 60:1-22 declares that when Jerusalem will be gloriously restored, its citizens will prosper and flourish, the least of them becoming a clan and the smallest one a mighty nation (*l^e gôy 'āṣûm* [v. 22; cf. Gen 15:5; 17:16; 18:18; 22:17]).

Once the adj. is used of the faithful congregation. A psalmist who entreats Yahweh to rescue him from his enemies promises to offer thanks for divine deliverance in the great congregation (*b^e qāhāl rāb*), in the mighty throng (*b^e 'am 'āṣûm* [Ps 35:18]).

(c) In six texts the adj. is used to describe the indigenous peoples who are overcome by Yahweh to enable his people to take possession of Palestine. The majority of translations take the word to be referring primarily to the power, rather than the size, of these nations. Compared with Israel, these (seven) nations were *rabbîm wa'^a ṣûmîm* (Deut 7:1), more numerous and powerful (NEB; REB)/larger and stronger (NIV)/larger and more powerful (TEV)/greater and mightier (RSV)/greater and stronger (JB). NRSV, however, understands the adj. to be referring here to size: mightier and more numerous. These nations were *gᵉdōlîm waʿᵃṣumîm* (Deut 4:38; 9:1; 11:23; Josh 23:9 [*gᵉdōlîm waʿᵃṣûmîm*]).

Since it was as a result of Yahweh's love for the patriarchs that he brought the Israelites out of Egypt (Deut 4:37) and drove out nations greater and more powerful than they (4:38), Israel's obedience, allegiance, and commitment should be motivated by a responding love (4:37-40; cf. 6:4-5). In a hymn celebrating Yahweh's mighty deeds (Ps 135:1-21), the divine victory over many nations (*gôyim rabbîm*) and slaughter of many/mighty kings (*mᵉlākîm ʿᵃṣûmîm*), which enabled Israel to take possession of the Promised Land, are gratefully recalled (v. 10). The recollection of Yahweh's mighty saving acts on behalf of his people serves to reinforce both the deut. exhortation to complete obedience and uncompromising faith in him (cf. Watts, 1971, 206), and the psalmist's summons to praise the great Creator for his incomparable grace, compassion, and power.

(d) In the divinely inaugurated new age of peace, Jerusalem will serve a divine purpose that will encompass all peoples (Achtemeier, 142). When the city is restored and exalted as the center of worship and salvation for the whole world, Yahweh will judge between many peoples (*ʿammîm rabbîm*) and arbitrate in the disputes of strong nations (*lᵉgôyim ʿᵃṣumîm*) far and wide (Mic 4:3 [Wolff, 1990, 112, translates the latter phrase as "the multitude of nations"]). When Yahweh returns to Zion and graciously restores Jerusalem and Judah (Zech 8:1-23), many peoples and powerful nations (*ʿammîm rabbîm wᵉgôyim ʿᵃṣûmîm*) will come to seek him in Jerusalem and to entreat his favor (v. 22). The salvation wrought in the city by the power and compassion of Yahweh will attract all peoples to worship and serve Israel's God; through Zion, Yahweh will pour out his love and blessing on all peoples (cf. Zech 8:13; Achtemeier, 142-43).

(e) The adj. is sometimes used of a powerful army. In what was to prove a futile attempt to ward off the approach of Antiochus IV Epiphanes, the king of Egypt (Ptolemy VI Philometor) waged war with an exceedingly great and powerful army (*bᵉḥayil-gādôl wᵉʿāṣûm ʿad-mᵉʾōd* [Dan 11:25]).

In one text (Isa 8:7), the powerful military forces of the king of Assyria are described as the mighty and many (*hāʿᵃṣûmîm wᵉhārabbîm*) waters of the river (the surging waters of the turbulent Euphrates at flood tide), which the Judeans would have to face as a result of their lack of trust in Yahweh. Confronted by the Syro-Ephraimite coalition, they rejected their God's proffered assistance (symbolized by the waters of Shiloah, Isa 8:6 [see, further, Kelley, 219-20; Wildberger, 342-45]) and appealed to Assyria for protection (cf. 2 Kgs 16:7).

The adj. is applied 3x to a huge swarm of locusts, described as a mighty invading army (Joel 1:6; 2:2, 5). It may be that in 2:2, 5, the locusts stand in the background as a model of the threatening army proclaimed by prophecy (see, e.g., Wolff, 1977, 44-47, 52-53). Viewing the devastation wrought by the locusts as God's judgment on his people (1:2-2:11), the prophet describes these agents of destruction under the image of a ruthless nation powerful and innumerable (*ʿāṣûm wᵉʾên mispār* [1:6]); a great and powerful army (*ʿam rab wᵉʿāṣûm*, 2:2 [REB has "a vast and countless host"]), spread like the dawn (MT *kᵉšaḥar*) or as blackness (reading *kišḥôr* or *kišḥōr*; cf. Deut 4:11; 5:22-23; Amos 5:18-20; Zeph 1:15) upon the mountains (Amos 2:2); a powerful army (*[k^e]'am 'āṣûm* [REB has "a vast host" and NEB has "a countless host"]) drawn up for battle (2:5). Wolff (1977, 29) argues that, in all three passages, *'āṣûm* connotes more the idea of multitude than power as such. Allen (1976, 46, 64, 65) translates the adj. in all three passages as "massive." According to S. R. Driver (1901, 38) and Hubbard (44), *'āṣûm* here describes both the numerical and the physical strength of the locusts. However, given the combinations of words in 1:6 and 2:2, it seems more likely that the word conveys, primarily, the power of the invaders.

(f) The adj. is also used of the power of strong people in general, of disputants, and of badgers. Yahweh will give his faithful suffering servant a portion among the great (*bārabbîm*), and the servant will divide the spoils with the strong (*w^e'et-'^aṣûmîm*) (Isa 53:12; North [1967, 245; 1971, 140] translates *rabbîm* as "the many" and *'^aṣûmîm* as "numerous"). On this reading of the verse, the meaning is that the servant will split the booty with powerful warriors (see, e.g., Miscall, 125). However, some (e.g., North, 1967, 65, 245; 1971, 140; Ackroyd, 364; Motyer, 442-43; cf. Kelley, 345; Herbert, 115) suggest that "the great" and "the strong" should be taken as direct objects of the vb. divide (this suggestion is rejected by Skinner, 1960, 149). Ackroyd (364) thinks it possible that the meaning is that the nations will be booty for the servant (identified as Israel) to recompense him for his humiliation and for bearing their sin.

Antiochus IV Epiphanes, whose strength will be great, will wreak devastation and destroy powerful men (*'^aṣûmîm* [Dan 8:24]). Some (e.g., Rashi [cited by R. A. Anderson, 102; Collins, 341]; NEB; REB) think that the powerful here are the nations. Others (e.g., Pseudo-Saadia, Ibn Ezra [cited by Collins, 341]; Goldingay, 218) identify them as the Israelites. Collins (341) considers the reference to be to the other claimants to the Syrian throne. Bevan (140), who translates *'^aṣûmîm* as "many," takes the word to refer to the political enemies of Antiochus, members of the upper classes who were strongly opposed to this usurper (cf. Charles, 93; S. R. Driver, 1922, 124; Montgomery, 350; Heaton, 199).

In legal cases where litigation was interminable and indecisive, a dispute between powerful contestants (*'^aṣûmîm*, lit., powerful men [so JB and TEV]) could sometimes be settled by casting the lot, which was a means of determining the will of Yahweh (Prov 18:18; cf. 1 Sam 10:20-21; 14:40-42; Jon 1:7; Matt 27:35; Acts 1:26) (cf. Tate, 1972, 59; McKane, 1970, 521-22). Arguing that MT *'^aṣûmîm* is unsuitable to the context, G. R. Driver (183) suggests that the word be changed to *'ôṣ^emîm*, litigants; although this emendation is accepted by NEB and REB, it is not convincing (McKane, 1970, 522).

Although badgers are creatures of little physical strength (*'am lō'-'āṣûm*, lit., a people not powerful), they have the resourcefulness and the technical ingenuity and application to make their homes in the rocks (Prov 30:26).

(g) In one text, the pl. seems to be used as an abstract nom., power. In a prayer for deliverance from wicked enemies (Ps 10:1-18), an individual complains that the helpless/the oppressed falls by (RSV; NRSV), into (JB), or under (NIV) the powerful tyrant's might (*w^enāpal ba'^aṣûmāyw*, lit., and he [the hapless] falls by his [the tyrant's] might [v. 10]; *pace* C. A. and E. G. Briggs, 80, 87, who translate *ba'^aṣûmāyw* as "because of his great numbers," arguing that the word refers to size/quantity rather than to strength). Some (e.g., Dummelow, 333; Kirkpatrick, 54) understand "his strong ones" to mean the strong-armed ruffians in the wicked man's retinue. Delitzsch

(1889a, 174, 182) and BDB (783) take "his mighty ones" to refer to the powerful claws of a lion. Craigie (1983b, 121-23) supports the translation "into his claws," pointing out the close association between Ugar. *'ẓm* and Heb. *yād* (hand) and arguing that if the "bones" (of the hands) are here poetically described as "claws," this would provide an appropriate heightening of the simile of the lion in v. 9. On the basis of Ugar. *'ẓm*, which he claims means dig or burrow, Dahood (1966, 60, 63-64) postulates a Heb. root *'ṣm* with the same meaning and then translates *ba'ᵃṣûmāyw* as "into his pit." Some resort to emending MT. For example, Buttenwieser (440) follows LXX *bᵉ'oṣmô* (by his might), and Kraus (1988, 189, 191) accepts Gunkel's suggestion, *bᵉmô'ᵃṣōtāyw*, by means of/through his schemes.

(h) In two texts, the word almost certainly means "many" (Num 32:1; Prov 7:26). The sons of Reuben and the sons of Gad owned a very great multitude of cattle (*[û]miqneh rab ... 'āṣûm mᵉ'ōd* [Num 32:1]). The pleonasm is obviated by JB, which translates *'āṣûm* as "fine" (signifying, presumably, the vigorous health of the cattle), and by NEB which reads "large and very numerous flocks."

The smooth-talking adventuress (Prov 7:5) has laid low many victims (*rabbîm ḥᵃlālîm*) and slain *'ᵃṣumîm* (v. 26). The latter word is translated "a mighty host" (RSV; Fritsch, 826); "a mighty throng" (NIV); "a great company" (McKane, 1970, 222); "numerous" (NRSV); "numberless" (Scott, 1965, 64); "without number" (NEB; REB); "too many to count" (TEV); and "many" (Dummelow, 382). The translations given by AV ("many strong men") and JB ("the strongest") do not commend themselves. The meaning "numerous" is preferable (Whybray, 1994, 118).

3. The nom. *'ōṣem* I occurs at least 3x and possibly 4x. Israelites are warned not to succumb to the self-destructive temptation to pride and self-sufficiency (Deut 8:1-20). Such arrogant presumption is tantamount to the deification of self (Wright, 389; cf. Watts, 1971, 225; Thompson, 1974, 137; Mayes, 194; Isa 10:8-11; 14:13-14; Ezek 28:2). They are instructed (Deut 8:18) to remember that it is Yahweh who gives them the power to acquire wealth (JB reads "power" for *ḥāyil*, which is less likely in this context). They must never say: "My power [*kōḥî*] and my vigor [*wᵉ'ōṣem yādî*, lit., and the power of my hand; NEB and REB read energy] have gotten me this wealth [*'et-haḥayil hazzeh*]" (v. 17). Not only is the land God's gift to Israel, but the time, energy, and ability to extract wealth from it are also divine endowments (Manley and Harrison, 217; cf. Craigie, 1983a, 189).

In his final defense (Job 29:1-31:40), Job complains that God has turned cruel in his dealings with him, attacking him with the vigor of his hand (*bᵉ'ōṣem yādᵉkā*, with the vigor of your hand, 30:21; cf. 13:24b; 16:9-14; 19:11; Isa 63:10b).

In a caustic indictment of the Assyrian capital, Nahum seeks to convince Nineveh of her doom by asking her if she seriously considers herself better than Thebes (Nah 3:8), the Egyptian capital, which, despite its formidable natural strength and apparent invincibility, was captured by Ashurbanipal's army in 663 BC. At the time of the collapse of Thebes, Egypt was ruled by Ethiopians and united under one dynasty (the twenty-fifth dynasty [712-663]) with Ethiopia, which (together with Egypt) is described as "her [i.e., Thebes's] boundless strength" (v. 9; NIV, changing MT *'āṣᵉmâ*, she was powerful [*HALAT*], to *'oṣmāh*, her strength [following LXX; Pesh.; Vg.; Tg.; so, too, *BHS*; RSV; NRSV; JB; NEB; J. M. P. Smith, 356; R. L. Smith, 86-87]). Just as the legendary power of the Egyptian capital did not avail in face of the Assyrian threat in 663, so Nineveh's power will fail to withstand the onslaught of the Babylonian-Median-Scythian coalition (vv. 10-15). No fortifications or defense systems, however impressive, and no amount of support from powerful allies can afford protection from the anger of God (Achtemeier, 26; cf. Robertson, 115).

In the day that he will restore and reunite Israel (Isa 11:10-16), Yahweh will utterly destroy (RSV; NRSV), divide (NEB; REB), or dry up (JB; NIV; TEV; Skinner, 1909, 101; Kissane, 1960, 130, 139; Kaiser, 1977, 163; Watts, 1985, 177-78; Wildberger, 486-88) the tongue of the Egyptian sea (the Gulf of Aqaba [Dummelow, 424]; the Gulf of Suez [Skinner, 1909, 101; Peake, 1920, 445; Kelley, 233; Wildberger, 496]; an arm of Lake Menzaleh [Bright, 1964, 499]; the Red Sea [Gray, 227; Kissane, 1960, 139; Herbert, 92; Motyer, 127]; the Nile [Duhm, cited by Scott, 1956, 252]) (v. 15). He will also wave his hand over the river (probably the Euphrates [*pace* Scott, 1956, 252, who argues that here and in 19:5 the reference is to the Nile]) to bring a powerful wind (so REB, changing MT *ba'yām rûḥô* [v. 15], with his scorching wind, to *b*^{e}*'ōṣem rûḥô* [so, too, Pesh. and Vg.; cf. LXX; Tg.]) (v. 15). Whitehouse (180-81), Wildberger (486-88, 497), and Watts (1985, 177-79) all think that the translation "by means of the power/violence of his storm" is justified. No human power will be allowed to frustrate Yahweh's purpose; hostile forces will be neutralized (Seitz, 109).

4. The nom. *'oṣmâ* occurs 2x. The despairing and debilitated exiles are assured that, in marked contrast to the impotent idols, Yahweh, whose power is infinitely great (cf. Isa 40:26) and inexhaustible, is the source of renewal and vitality for those who hope, trust, and believe in him (Miscall, 101): He gives strength (*kōaḥ*) to the faint and invigorates (*'oṣmâ yarbeh*, lit., vigor he increases) the exhausted (Isa 40:29). Despite her many sorceries and the great power or potency of her enchantments (*b*^{e}*'oṣmat ḥ*^{a}*bārayik m*^{e}*'ōd*, Isa 47:9), Babylon will suffer the loss of children and widowhood, suddenly and simultaneously. Whereas RSV, NRSV, NIV, JB, G. A. Smith (212), Skinner (1960, 84), Watts (1987, 168) take the nom. *'oṣmâ* here as signifying power, RV ("the great abundance of"), NEB and REB ("countless"), McKenzie (90 ["many"]), Westermann (187 ["many"]) take it to refer to a large number. The word almost certainly signifies strength, although the overall meaning of the v. would not be altered if the reference were to a large number. The sources of Babylon's false security will be of no avail against the power of Yahweh; they will neither ward off the coming catastrophes nor afford any protection when disaster strikes.

5. The nom. *'*^{a}*ṣumôt* (lit., powerful things [Whybray, 1975, 68] or strengths [Skinner, 1960, 25]), which is used of strong words or arguments (Westermann, 81, 83), i.e., convincing proofs (Herbert, 37), occurs once (Isa 41:21). The pagan deities are challenged to set forth their case (*rîb*^{e}*kem*, your case) and bring their proofs (*'*^{a}*ṣumôtêkem*). AV (cf. Motyer, 315) translates *'*^{a}*ṣumôtêkem* as "your strong reasons"; NIV, McKenzie (33), and North (1971, 56) have "your arguments;" and TEV has "the best arguments you have." The inability of the gods of the nations to show insight into past events or to indicate the course of future history or to intervene actively in history (vv. 22-24) exposes their nothingness. Unlike Yahweh, who, as the Creator, Redeemer and sovereign Lord of history, knows both the past and the future, proclaims what is to happen, and shapes the historical process, these gods are null and void (cf. 42:8-9; 43:9, 16-19; 44:6-8; 45:20-21; 46:8-11; 48:3-8; Ackroyd, 355-56; D. R. Jones, 519; Muilenburg, 460).

6. The nom. *ta'^{a}ṣumôt*, vigor, occurs once (Ps 68:35[36]). The God of Israel, who inspires reverential awe among the faithful and terror among his enemies (cf. Ps 66:3; Rogerson and McKay, 92), gives power (*'ōz*) and strength/vigor/abundant power (*w^{e}ta'^{a}ṣumôt*) to his people. The salvation of Israel depends daily on the victory of the divine warrior, and it is the duty of the congregation to remember and represent Yahweh as the power and strength of his people (Mays, 1994, 228-29).

P-B The vb. *'ṣm* occurs with the meaning press; close (the eyes); [be compressed, hard] be strong; acquire, possess; hitp. and nitp. be closed; be headstrong towards one another; fortify each other, i.e., enter an agreement with the condition of forfeiture. The nom. *'eṣem* ([strength] bone; substance, essence, self; substance, wealth, [especially] livestock) is also found. The adj. *'āṣûm* (strong, mighty) and the nom. *'^{a}ṣûmâ* (possession) also occur (Jastrow 2:1102-3).

Bibliography

E. Achtemeier, *Nahum-Malachi*, Interp, 1986; P. R. Ackroyd, "The Book of Isaiah," in *The Interpreter's One-Volume Commentary on the Bible*, 1971, 329-71; L. C. Allen, *The Books of Joel, Obadiah, Jonah and Micah*, NICOT, 1976; idem, *Psalms 101-150*, WBC, 1983; A. A. Anderson, *The Book of Psalms. Volume I: Introduction and Psalms 1-72*, NCBC, 1972 (1972a); idem, *The Book of Psalms. Vol. 2: Psalms 73-150*, NCBC, 1972 (1972b); G. W. Anderson, "The Psalms," in *Peake*, 1964, 409-43; R. A. Anderson, *Signs and Wonders: A Commentary on the Book of Daniel*, ITC, 1984; T. R. Ashley, *The Book of Numbers*, NICOT, 1993; A. A. Bevan, *A Short Commentary on the Book of Daniel for the Use of Students*, 1892; J. A. Bewer, "A Critical and Exegetical Commentary on Obadiah and Joel," in J. A. Bewer et al., *A Critical and Exegetical Commentary on Micah, Zephaniah, Nahum, Habakkuk, Obadiah and Joel*, ICC, 1974; L. Boadt, *Jeremiah 1-25*, OTM, 1982; R. G. Bratcher and W. D. Reyburn, *A Translator's Handbook on the Book of Psalms*, 1991; C. A. and E. G. Briggs, *A Critical and Exegetical Commentary on the Book of Psalms. Vol. I*, ICC, 1960; J. Bright, "Isaiah—I," in *Peake*, 1964, 489-515; idem, *Jeremiah: Introduction, Translation, and Notes*, AB, 1965; P. J. Budd, *Numbers*, WBC, 1984; M. Buttenwieser, *The Psalms Chronologically Treated With a New Translation*, 1969; R. P. Carroll, *Jeremiah: A Commentary*, OTL, 1986; R. H. Charles, *The Book of Daniel*, CB, 1913; B. S. Childs, *Exodus: A Commentary*, OTL, 1974; R. E. Clements, *Exodus*, CBC, 1972; idem, *Jeremiah*, Interp, 1988; R. J. Clifford, "Exodus," in *NJBC*, 1990, 44-60; J. J. Collins, *Daniel*, Hermeneia, 1993; P. C. Craigie, *The Book of Deuteronomy*, NICOT, 1983 (1983a); idem, *Psalms 1-50*, WBC, 1983 (1983b); H. Cunliffe-Jones, *Jeremiah: God in History*, Torch, 2d ed., 1972; M. Dahood, *Psalms I: 1-50. Introduction, Translation, and Notes*, AB, 1966; idem, *Psalms II: 51-100. Introduction, Translation, and Notes*, AB, 1973; idem, *Psalms III: 101-150*, AB, 1970; R. Davidson, *Jeremiah. Volume I*, DSB, 1986; idem, *Jeremiah Volume 2 and Lamentations*, DSB, 1985; E. W. Davies, *Numbers*, NCBC, 1995; G. H. Davies, *Exodus: Introduction and Commentary*, Torch, 1967; W. T. Davison, *The Psalms I-LXXII*, CB, n.d. (1904?); F. Delitzsch, *Biblical Commentary on the Psalms. Volume 1*, KD, 1889 (1889a); idem, *Biblical Commentary on the Psalms. Vol. II*, 2d ed., 1889 (1889b); idem, *Biblical Commentary on the Psalms. Vol. III*, KD, 2d ed. 1885; G. R. Driver, "Problems in the Hebrew Text of Proverbs," *Bib* 32, 1951, 173-97; S. R. Driver, *The Books of Joel and Amos With Introduction and Notes*, CBC, 1901; idem, *The Book of the Prophet Jeremiah: A Revised Translation With Introductions and Short Explanations*, 1906; idem, *The Book of Daniel With Introduction and Notes*, CBSC, 1922; idem, *The Book of Exodus*, CBSC, 1953; B. Duhm, *The Twelve Prophets: A*

Version in the Various Poetical Measures of the Original Writings, 1912; J. R. Dummelow ed., *A Commentary on the Holy Bible*, 1909; J. I. Durham, "Psalms," in *BBC*, 1972, 4:153-464; idem, *Exodus*, WBC, 1987; J. H. Eaton, *Psalms: Introduction and Commentary*, Torch, 1972; T. E. Fretheim, *Exodus*, Interp, 1991; C. T. Fritsch, "The Book of Proverbs: Introduction and Exegesis," in *IB*, 1955, 6:765-957; J. E. Goldingay, *Daniel*, WBC, 1989; G. B. Gray, *A Critical and Exegetical Commentary on the Book of Isaiah. Vol. I: Introduction, and Commentary on I-XXVII*, ICC, 1975; J. L. Green, "Jeremiah," in *BBC*, 1972, 6:1-202; G. Harford, "Exodus," in *Peake*, 1920, 168-95; W. R. Harper, *A Critical and Exegetical Commentary on Amos and Hosea*, ICC, 1966; J. H. Hayes, *Amos the Eighth-Century Prophet: His Times and His Preaching*, 1988; E. W. Heaton, *The Book of Daniel: Introduction and Commentary*, Torch, 1964; A. S. Herbert, *The Book of the Prophet Isaiah Chapters 40-66*, CBC, 1975; D. R. Hillers, *Micah*, Hermeneia, 1984; R. L. Honeycutt, "Exodus," in *BBC*, 1970, 1:305-472; C. Houtman, *Exodus. Volume 1*, Historical, 1993; D. A. Hubbard, *Joel and Amos: An Introduction and Commentary*, TOTC, 1989; J. P. Hyatt, "The Book of Jeremiah: Introduction and Exegesis," in *IB*, 1956, 5:775-1142; idem, *Exodus*, NCBC, 1971; D. R. Jones, "Isaiah—II and III," in *Peake*, 1964, 516-36; H. R. Jones, "Exodus," in *NBC*, 1972, 115-39; O. Kaiser, *Isaiah 1-12: A Commentary*, OTL, 1977; idem, *Isaiah 13-39: A Commentary*, OTL, 1974; P. H. Kelley, "Isaiah," in *BBC*, 1972, 5:149-374; J. H. Kennedy, "Joel," in *BBC*, 1972, 7:61-80; A. F. Kirkpatrick, *The Book of Psalms*, CBSC, 1957; E. J. Kissane, *The Book of Isaiah Translated From a Critically Revised Hebrew Text With Commentary. Vol. I (I-XXXIX)*, 1960; idem, *The Book of Psalms Translated From a Critically Revised Hebrew Text With a Commentary*, 1964; H.-J. Kraus, *Psalms 1-59: A Commentary*, 1988; idem, *Psalms 60-150: A Commentary*, 1989; W. McKane, *Proverbs: A New Approach*, OTL, 1970; idem, *A Critical and Exegetical Commentary on Jeremiah. Volume I: An Introduction and Commentary on Jeremiah I-XXV*, ICC, 1986; J. L. McKenzie, *Second Isaiah: Introduction, Translation, and Notes*, AB, 1968; G. T. Manley and R. K. Harrison, "Deuteronomy," in *NBC*, 1972, 201-29; J. Mauchline, *Isaiah 1-39*, Torch, 1970; A. D. H. Mayes, *Deuteronomy*, NCBC, 1979; J. L. Mays, *Amos: A Commentary*, OTL, 1976; idem, *Psalms*, Interp, 1994; P. D. Miller, *Deuteronomy*, Interp, 1990; P. D. Miscall, *Isaiah*, Readings, 1993; J. A. Montgomery, *A Critical and Exegetical Commentary on the Book of Daniel*, ICC, 1964; J. A. Motyer, *The Prophecy of Isaiah: An Introduction & Commentary*, 1993; J. Muilenburg, "The Book of Isaiah Chapters 40-66: Introduction and Exegesis," in R. B. Y. Scott et al., "The Book of Isaiah," in *IB*, 1956, 5:149-773; C. R. North, *The Second Isaiah: Introduction, Translation and Commentary to Chapters XL-LV*, 1967; idem, *Isaiah 40-55*, Torch, 1971; W. O. E. Oesterley, *The Psalms Translated With Text-Critical and Exegetical Notes*, 1959; J. N. Oswalt, *The Book of Isaiah Chapters 1-39*, NICOT, 1986; S. M. Paul, *Amos*, Hermeneia, 1991; A. S. Peake, *Jeremiah. Vol. I: Jeremiah I-XXIV*, CB, 1910; idem, "Isaiah I-XXXIX," in *Peake*, 1920, 436-59; E. B. Pusey, *The Minor Prophets With a Commentary Explanatory and Practical and Introductions to the Several Books*, 1891; O. P. Robertson, *The Books of Nahum, Habakkuk, and Zephaniah*, NICOT, 1991; J. W. Rogerson and J. W. McKay, *Psalms 51-100*, CBC, 1977; J. C. Rylaarsdam, "The Book of Exodus: Introduction and Exegesis," in *IB*, 1952, 1:831-1099; B. E. Scoggin, "Micah," in *BBC*, 1972, 7:183-229; R. B. Y. Scott, "The Book of Isaiah Chapters 1-39: Introduction and Exegesis," in R. B. Y. Scott et al., "The Book of Isaiah," in *IB*, 1956, 5:149-773; idem, *Proverbs, Ecclesiastes: Introduction, Translation, and Notes*, AB, 1965; C. R. Seitz, *Isaiah 1-39*, Interp, 1993; J. Skinner, *The Book of the Prophet Isaiah Chapters I-XXXIX*, CBSC, 1909; idem, *The Book of the Prophet Isaiah Chapters XL-LXVI*, CBSC, 1960; G. A. Smith, *The Book of the Twelve Prophets. Vol. I: Amos, Hosea, and Micah*, EB, 10th ed., 1903; J. M. P. Smith, "A Critical and

Exegetical Commentary on the Books of Micah, Zephaniah and Nahum," in J. M. P. Smith et al., *A Critical and Exegetical Commentary on Micah, Zephaniah, Nahum, Habakkuk, Obadiah and Joel*, ICC, 1974; R. L. Smith, *Micah-Malachi*, WBC, 1984; N. H. Snaith, *The Book of Amos. Part Two: Translation and Notes*, 1958; D. M. G. Stalker, "Exodus," in *Peake*, 1964, 208-40; D. Stuart, *Hosea-Jonah*, WBC, 1987; M. E. Tate, "Proverbs," in *BBC*, 1972, 5:1-99; idem, *Psalms 51-100*, WBC, 1990; W. R. Taylor et al., "The Book of Psalms," in *IB*, 1955, 4:1-763; J. A. Thompson, *Deuteronomy: An Introduction and Commentary*, TOTC, 1974; idem, *The Book of Jeremiah*, NICOT, 1987; C. H. Thomson and J. Skinner, *Isaiah I-XXXIX*, 1921; J. M. Ward, *Amos and Isaiah: Prophets of the Word of God*, 1969; J. D. W. Watts, "Deuteronomy," in *BBC*, 1971, 2:175-296; idem, *Isaiah 1-33*, WBC, 1985; idem, *Isaiah 34-66*, WBC, 1987; A. Weiser, *The Psalms: A Commentary*, OTL, 1965; C. Westermann, *Isaiah 40-66: A Commentary*, OTL, 1969; O. C. Whitehouse, *Isaiah I-XXXIX. Vol. I*, CB, 1905; R. N. Whybray, *Isaiah 40-66*, NCBC, 1975; idem, *Proverbs*, NCBC, 1994; H. Wildberger, *Isaiah 1-12: A Commentary*, Continental, 1991; H. W. Wolff, *Joel and Amos*, Hermeneia, 1977; idem, *Micah: A Commentary*, 1990; G. E. Wright, "The Book of Deuteronomy: Introduction and Exegesis," in *IB*, 1953, 2:309-537; G. E. Wright and F. V. Filson eds., *The Westminster Historical Atlas to the Bible*, 1946.

Robin Wakely

6793a (‘*ṣm* II, gnaw the bones), → # 6795

6794	עצם

עצם (‘*ṣm* III), q., pi. shut one's eyes (# 6794).

OT This root is used twice in Isaiah. In Isa 33:14, the godless of Zion cry out in a fashion reminiscent of Ps 15:1: "Who of us can dwell with the consuming fire?" The answer (Isa 33:15-16) lists various characteristics that describe the person who enjoys life in God's presence. After two positive traits of this individual ("walks righteously" and "speaks what is right," v. 15), the prophet enumerates four defensive qualities: he rejects extortion, keeps his hands from bribes, stops (*'ṭm*) his ears from hearing plots of murder, and shuts (‘*ōṣēm*, q. act. part.) his eyes against contemplating evil (lit., "from seeing evil"). In Isa 29:10, the Lord has shut (pi.) the eyes of the prophets because of their persistent rejection of truth (→ *š*‘‘).

Closing, shutting: → *'ṭm* (stopped up, # 357); → *'ṭr* (close [mouth], # 358); → *gwp* I (shut, close, # 1589); → *ṭḥḥ* (besmeared, stuck, shut, # 3220); → *ṭmh* (stopped up, # 3241); → *n‘l* I (tie, lock, # 5835); → *sgr* I (shut, close, deliver up, # 6037); → *stm* (stop up, # 6258); → ‘*ṣh* I (shut, # 6781); → ‘*ṣm* III (shut one's eyes, # 6794); → *ṣrr* I (bind, shut up, be narrow, in straits, distress, # 7674); → *qpṣ* I (draw together, shut, # 7890); → *š*‘‘ I (smear, smooth, shut, # 9129)

Bill T. Arnold

6795	עֶצֶם

עֶצֶם (‘*eṣem* I), bone, skin, body, self (# 6795); עֹצֶם (‘*ōṣem* II), bone (NIV frame) (hapleg., Ps 139:15; # 6798); denom. עצם (‘*ṣm* II), gnaw the bones (hapleg., Jer 50:17; # 6793a).

ANE Ugar. ‘*ẓm* I, bone; Ph./Pu. ‘*ṣm*, bone; Arab. ‘*aẓm*, Akk. *eṣemtu*, bone, frame of the body; Eth. ‘*aḍem*, Aram. ‘*iṭmā'*; Syr. ‘*aṭmā*.

OT 1. The bones were often viewed as the seat of one's physical strength and health (Job 20:11; 21:24; Prov 3:8; 15:30; Isa 58:11; 66:14; Lam 4:7; Akk. texts speak of bones burning with fever [*CAD* 4:342]). Zion's children (the returning exiles) will rejoice over her restoration. Isa 66:14 states that the "bones" of the children (symbolizing their national strength and prosperity here) will flourish "like grass." Those overcome by fear spoke of their bones shaking (Job 4:14; Jer 23:9; Hab 3:16), while those enduring intense physical pain or emotional distress frequently complained that their bones were weakened (Job 33:19, 21; Ps 6:2[3]; 31:10[11]; 32:3; 38:3[4]; 42:10[11]; Lam 1:13; cf. Job 19:20; 30:17, 30; Ps 102:5[6]).

2. The breaking of the bones was an idiom for divine punishment (Ps 51:8[10]; Isa 38:13; Lam 3:4). Similarly, God's protection finds expression in the idiom that bones are not broken (Ps 34:20[21]). The apostle John applied this promise in a literal sense to the circumstances of Jesus' death. The fact that Jesus' legs were not broken on the cross foreshadowed his ultimate vindication (John 19:36).

3. As one might expect, bones were sometimes associated with death (Ps 141:7). Public exposure of one's bones following death was an extreme form of humiliation (cf. 2 Sam 21:12-14). Especially severe divine judgment results in the bones of God's enemies being scattered or exposed (Ps 53:5[6]; Jer 8:1-2; Ezek 6:5; cf. also Akk. texts referring to bones being exposed or scattered, *CAD* 4:342). Contact with a corpse's bones caused ritual contamination (Num 19:18; 1 Kgs 13:2; 2 Kgs 23:14, 16, 20; Ezek 39:14-16). In Ezekiel's vision of the "Valley of Dry Bones," the scattered bones symbolize Israel's national "death" through exile, which would be overcome by the prophetic word and the divine life-giving breath (Ezek 37:1-14). Prophetic authority over death is also vividly illustrated in 2 Kgs 13:21, which tells how mere contact with Elisha's bones caused a corpse to come to life.

4. The idiom "flesh and bone" (NIV flesh and blood) refers to kinship relationships within clan and tribal contexts (Gen 29:14; Judg 9:2; 2 Sam 5:1; 19:12-13[13-14]). The relationship of the first man and woman was defined in kinship terms as well. As the first such relationship in human history, it established a pattern for the marriage institution, which supercedes the closest of blood relationships, even that of parent-child, and constitutes an inseparable bond (Gen 2:23-24; cf. G. Wenham, *Genesis 1-15*, WBC, 1987, 70-71; → *bāśār*, flesh [# 1414]).

5. The movement and placement of the patriarch Joseph's bones have theological significance in the narratives of Israel's early history. Certain that God's oath to the fathers would be realized, Joseph made the sons of Israel vow that they would carry his bones to the Promised Land when they departed from Egypt (Gen 50:24-25), an obligation that Moses was careful to fulfill (Exod 13:19). When Joshua later buried Joseph's bones in Shechem, the act was a testimony to God's sovereignty and faithfulness (Josh 24:32).

Bone: → *gerem* (bone, # 1752); → *'eṣem* I (bone, skin, body, self, # 6795)

Flesh, food, meat: → *bāśār* (meat, food, flesh, # 1414); → *šᵉ'ēr* (meat, food, # 8638)

BIBLIOGRAPHY

CAD 4:341-43; *NIDNTT* 1:240; *TWAT* 6:326-32; *TWOT* 2:690; L. Delekat, "Zum hebräischen Wörterbuch," *VT* 14, 1964, 49-52; W. Eichrodt, *TOT*, 2:146; A. Johnson, *The Vitality of the*

Individual in the Thought of Ancient Israel, 1964, 67-69; H. Wolff, *Anthropology of the OT*, 1981, 27, 29, 67.

Robert B. Chisholm

6797 (*'ōṣem* I, full power), → # 6793

6798 (*'ōṣem* II, bone), → # 6795

6800 (*'oṣmâ*, full power), → # 6793

6802 (*'ᵃṣumôt*, proofs), → # 6793

6806	עצר

עצר (*'ṣr*), q. restrain, detain, arrest, imprison, close; ni. bring to a stop, be closed (# 6806); מַעְצוֹר (*ma'ᵃṣôr*), nom. hindrance (# 5109); מַעְצָר (*ma'ᵃṣār*), self-control (hapleg. in Prov 25:28; # 5110); עֶצֶר (*'eṣer*), nom. ruler? (# 6807); עֹצֶר (*'ōṣer*), nom. barrenness, oppression (# 6808); עֲצָרָה/עֲצֶרֶת (*'ᵃṣārâ/'aṣṣeret*), assembly (→ # 6809).

ANE The vb. *'ṣr* is found in Can. in the Amarna tablets, meaning retained (*ḫaziri*); it is also found in middle Aram. and Arab., meaning to press or squeeze. The nom. *'ōṣer* is found in Ugar., meaning edge or boundary (*ǵṣr*), though earlier this reference was translated as a vb. (*KTU* 1.4 viii 4).

OT 1. The vb. *'ṣr*, retain, shut off, is frequently used to describe phenomena as the stopping a plague (Num 16:48, 50[17:13, 15]), the heavens withholding rain (Deut 11:17; 2 Chron 7:13), or the womb being withheld from conception (Gen 16:2; 20:18). One of the most frequent and puzzling metaphorical uses is in references to leadership, possibly derived from the sense of "bridle" or control (Kutsch, 57). It occurs repeatedly in the collocation *'āṣûr wᵉ'āzûb* (Deut 32:36; 1 Kgs 14:10; 21:21; etc.), variously translated as "slave or free," "young and old," "clean and unclean," etc. (→ *'zb* I, abandon, # 6440). Talmon and Fields, on the basis of an extensive intertextual study, have made a case for taking the expression as a hendiadys rather than a merism and translate it as "ruler-deliverer" (85-112). This helps to explain other difficult references, such as 1 Sam 9:17 and 21:7[8]. In terms of restraint, the vb. may simply refer to detaining someone for hospitality (Judg 13:15, 16), or it may be used to refer to the restriction of a person's movement (1 Chron 12:1; Neh 6:10; Jer 36:5). In Jer 33:1 and 39:15 the vb. describes the prophet's being held in the custody of the king. In 2 Kgs 17:4 it refers to being confined to the prison house (*bêt kele'*) by a conquering king.

2. The singular occurrence of the nom. *'eṣer* in Judg 18:7 should be related to the use of the verb as a ruler (Talmon and Fields, 91-92; cf. Meek, 328, who translates "conqueror of oppression," derived from the verbal sense of restraint or repression). The nom. *'ōṣer* is used once of a barren womb (Prov 30:16) and once as oppression (Ps 107:39). It is possibly a reference to the imprisonment of arrest or custody in its only other occurrence in Isa 53:8. North translates "After arrest and sentence" (240-41), but acknowledges that the picture is not clear and the expression could be a hendiadys ("By reason of oppressive sentence"). The nom. *ma'ᵃṣôr* occurs once (1 Sam 14:6) to say there is nothing that has power to prevent the deliverance of the Lord.

3. Imprisonment as a legal punishment is foreign to ANE conceptions. It is not found in the OT until the time of Ezra, and then only as the authorization of a foreign king. The Aram. word *'esûr* (cf. Heb. *'sr*) is found in a list of possible sentences (Ezra 7:26). Though imprisonment was not a formal punishment, which would involve some form of retribution or compensation for an offense, it was an important part of the penal system. Prisoners of war and political adversaries were held in a type of compound (prison house) so they could be employed for forced labor, as in the case of Samson with the Philistines (Judg 16:21) or Zedekiah under Nebuchadnezzar (Jer 52:11). The house of the mill (Akk. term *bīt ararri*) is a place of detention for forced labor, either as a punishment or for persons under arrest pending the outcome of their case. Ps 107:10-14 is a testimony of imprisonment and hard labor for deported Israelites. Houses of servitude (Akk. *bīt kiššāti*; cf. Heb. *bêt ᵃbādîm*) often included defaulting debtors and their families, who were temporarily reduced to slavery (2 Kgs 4:1; Neh 5:5). Political enemies might be held in prison rather than killed, as indicated in the Aramaic Sefire inscriptions (*KAI* 224.18), possibly in order to avoid a popular uprising, as in the case of John the Baptist (Matt 14:3-5). The imprisonment of Jeremiah (Jer 37:15-16) may have been for similar considerations. Treatment of such prisoners was so harsh they could be considered as being among those doomed to die (Ps 79:11; 102:20[21]). This may have been a convenient way of disposing of enemies without incurring bloodguilt (Gen 37:22-24).

The prison as a means by which society deals with criminal behavior as a form of punishment or deterrence has come into widespread use only within the last 300 years. It is an extremely costly approach, and for many crimes is ineffective for prevention.

4. The broad semantic range of *'ṣr* has led to a great variety of usages, but it is notable how many of them are an expression of divine purpose in relation to humans rather than human restraint of others. The divine action may be judgmental, as in shutting off the heavens, but often the restraint is positive, as in a gathering for worship. If *'āṣûr* describes a leader chosen by God, as some contexts demand (1 Sam 9:17), it is another example of how the divine restraint is to a beneficial end.

P-B In Mish. Heb. the vb. *'ṣr* has the meanings detain, gather together, and store away. The nom *'aṣeret* is often used to refer to a festive gathering. Late Aram. *'ṣr* means to press or squeeze, the nom. *'aṣrā'* is a winepress, *'iṣrā'* is juice. At Qumran the vb. *'ṣr* is used in the biblical sense of retaining strength or ability (cf. Dan 10:8, 16), as in the vision of Samuel (4Q160) or the Hymns (e.g., 1QH 1.3, 10.11, 12). In the words of Moses (1Q22, 2.10) it refers to God holding back the rain of the heavens (cf. Deut 11:17).

Prison, restraint, closure: → *'ᵃsēpâ* (imprisonment, # 669); → *'sr* (bind, imprison, fetter, hitch, # 673); → *kl'* I (detain, imprison, close, shut up, # 3973); → *misgeret* (stronghold, dungeon, rim, table, # 4995); → *sgr* (close, # 6037); → *sōhar* (prison, # 6045); → *'ṣr* (restrain, imprison, stop, close, # 6806)

Bibliography

ABD 5:468-69; *CAD* 8:459-60; E. Kutsch, "Die Wurzel עצר im Hebräischen," *VT* 2, 1952, 57-69; P. K. McCarter, *I Samuel*, 1980, 179, 349-50; T. J. Meek, "Translating the Hebrew Bible," *JBL* 79, 1960, 328-35; C. R. North, *The Second Isaiah*, 1967, 240-41; S. Talmon and

W. W. Fields, "The Collocation *mštyn bqyr w'ṣwr w'zšb* and Its Meaning," *ZAW* 101, 1989, 85-112.

A. H. Konkel

6807 (*'eṣer*, ruler?), → # 6806

6808 (*'ōṣer*, barrenness, oppression), → # 6806

6809	עֲצָרָה

עֲצָרָה (*'ᵃṣārâ*), festive assembly (# 6809); עֲצֶרֶת (*'ᵃṣeret*), assembly (# 6809); < עצר (*'ṣr*), restrain, imprison, stop, close (→ # 6806).

ANE Examples of the root *'ṣr* can be found in Eth. *'äṣärä*; Arab. *'aṣara*; and Aram. and Syr. *'ᵃsār,* to press. The vb. can be trans. in different ways in the OT: detain (1 Kgs 18:44), imprison (2 Kgs 17:4), close (Gen 20:18). Another nom. derived from the root *'ṣr* is *'ᵃṣeret* and is often translated with "solemn assembly" (Lev 23:36).

OT 1. *Usage*. The fem. nom.*'ᵃṣārâ* can refer to different types of assembly (*TWOT* 2:691): a pious gathering accompanied by fasting and pleading (Joel 1:14; 2:15), a general festivity among many others (Isa 1:13), and an idolatrous feast in honor of Baal (2 Kgs 10:20). The term *'ᵃṣeret* is used for the ritual assembly on the eighth day of the Feast of Booths/Succoth (Lev 23:36; Num 29:35; Neh 8:18), the assembly on the eighth day of Solomon's consecration of the temple that corresponds with the eighth day of the feast of Succoth (2 Chron 7:9), the ritual assembly on the seventh day of the Feast of Unleavened Bread/Massot (Deut 16:8), and a crowd of unfaithful people/assembly of deceivers (Jer 9:2[1]).

2. *Theological interpretation*. It is possible that these terms originally referred to the last phase of a feast or assembly, which was not necessarily a religious one (*TWAT* 6:337). The purpose of an *'ᵃṣārâ* and an *'ᵃṣeret*, therefore, depended on the type of feast or assembly that took place beforehand. Similar solemn gatherings are mentioned in conjunction with the New Year's feast in Lev 23:24 and the Day of Atonement in 23:27. It is likely that the festive or solemn assembly denoted a day of restraint or abstinence that marked the end of a feast, or more in particular commemorated the closing of the harvest cycle of festivals (Gaster, 98). The frequency of the term points to the communal nature of Israelite religion.

P-B In the Pesiqta Rabbati: the pi. of *'ṣr* is used to refer to the holding of a festive gathering, whilst *'ᵃṣeret* is used for the concluding Feast of the Succoth festival, which may have been more solemn (Num 29:35). *'ᵃṣeret* became the standard name for the Feast of Weeks in the Midrash and Talmud (Frank, 218). During the second temple period, the day on which the festive assembly was commemorated coincided with an extra day added to the Feast of Succoth, and in the Mishnah the festive assembly is also applied to the Feast of Weeks (Gaster, 98-99). The LXX translates the term with *exodion*. From the eleventh century AD another day was added to the festive assembly, known as the *Simhath Torah* (Rejoicing in the Law), during which Torah scrolls were paraded in a procession around the synagogue. The service in the synagogue on this day included special chants and hymns celebrating the giving of the law on Sinai (Gaster, 101).

Feasts & festivals: → *bikkûrîm* (early or firstfruits, # 1137); → *ḥag* (procession, round dance, festival, feast, # 2504); → *ḥ^{a}nukkâ* (dedication, Feast of Dedication, # 2853); → *mô'ēd* (appointed time, # 4595); → *maṣṣôt* (Feast of the Unleavened Bread, # 5174a); → *marzēaḥ* (cultic feast, funeral meal, # 5301); → *sukkôt* (Feast of Tabernacles, # 6109a); → *'^{a}ṣārâ* (festive assembly, # 6809); → *pûrîm* (festival of Purim, # 7052a); → *pesaḥ* (Feast or sacrifice of Passover, # 7175 [→ **Passover: Theology**]); → *rō'š ḥōdeš* (festival of the new Moon, # 8031a); → *rō'š haššānâ* (beginning of the year, # 8031b); → *šābu'ôt* (feast of Weeks, # 8651a); → *šabbāt* (sabbath, # 8701 [→ **Sabbath: Theology**])

BIBLIOGRAPHY

TWAT 6:333-38; *TWOT* 2:691; Y. Frank, *The Practical Talmud Dictionary*, 1992; T. Gaster, *Festivals of the Jewish Year*, 1978; E. Kutsch, "Die Wurzel עצר im Hebräisch," *VT* 2, 1952, 57-69.

Hendrik L. Bosman

6810	עקב

עקב (*'qb* I), q. seize the heel, overreach, deceive; pi. arrest, rearguard, hinder, hold back (# 6810); nom. עָקֵב (*'āqēb*), heel, hoof, footprint, step (# 6811); עָקֹב (*'āqōb*), adj. insidious, uneven [ground] (→ # 6815); עָקְבָה (*'oqbâ*), cunning, craftiness, deceptive(ly?) (# 6817).

ANE Ugar. *'qb*, held back, hindered (*KTU* 1.18.V:9; *WUS*, 240, §2086; *CML*, 111, 154); rough, be hilly (*KTU* 4.645:1); Arab. *'qb*; Eth. Tigre *'qb*; nom. *'āqēb*; Ugar. *KTU* 1:17; Arab. *'aqib*; Tigre *'eqeb*; nom. *'āqōb*; Eth., Tigre *'aqab*; Arab. *'aqabat*; Ugar. *'qb*. Jewish Aram., Geez *'aqab*, high ground, slope; Amharic *'aqabat*, high ground, slope; Arab. *'aqabat*, steep way; Ugar. *'qb*, rough, hilly.

OT 1. The nom. *'āqēb* occurs 13x. The usage in Gen 3:15 describes the archetypal seizing of the serpent at the heel of humankind. Here the heel serves as the point of impact for the manifestation of hostility between the seed of humankind and the serpent. The serpent strikes at the person's heel while the person strikes at the serpent with his heel. The second son born to Isaac was Jacob (*ya'^{a}qōb*), given this name at birth because he had grasped Esau's heel (*'āqēb*) during the delivery (25:26). Later events delineate the destiny of Jacob, anticipated by his activity and naming at birth. Gen 49:17 depicts the tribe of Dan as a serpent who strikes at a horse's hooves, causing its rider to fall backward. In the same manner that a snake can strike at the legs of a horse and overthrow the stronger animal, Dan, one of the smaller tribes, has the potential of exerting authority beyond its size (Ross, 705). The word can be translated as an ambush (NIV) in Josh 8:13, a deceitful ploy from behind (as the heel imagery would indicate) to trick Ai. Bildad describes the evil person as one who is caught by the heel in a trap (Job 18:9), i.e., he has been attacked from behind, deceitfully. To lift the heel against someone (Ps 41:9[10]) was a symbol and an act of rejection, like turning one's back. Israel's sins have resulted in her body being violently accosted, again from the back (lit., your heels have been treated violently [Jer 13:22]). The prophets point out that Israel will be treated like the harlot/prostitute she has been (Jer 13:22, 26-27; cf. Isa 47:3).

2. The vb., a denom. vb. derived from the nom. *'āqēb*, is found 5x. Three of the four passages allude directly or indirectly to Jacob's grasping Esau's heel at birth. In

the wake of Jacob's surreptitious theft of Esau's blessing, Esau complains that Jacob supplanted him (*'qb*, Gen 27:36) twice (by taking Esau's birthright and blessing). The imagery of supplanting or superseding delineated by Jacob's grabbing of Esau's heel at birth here widens to include the deceptive means Jacob used to accomplish his scheme. The supplanting of Jacob becomes synonymous with the deception of Jacob. The Ugar. usage of *'qb* focuses on the supplanting facet of the vb. (hindering, foiling; cf. Margalit, 95-96; Hamilton, 227, n. 28). Hos (12:3[4]) indicts God's covenant nation (Israel and Judah) for living up to the name of their forefather Jacob. His grasping of Esau's heel at birth appears to serve as a paradigm for his penchant for overcoming, whether it was with regard to God or his brother. Jeremiah (Jer 9:4[3]) describes the social decay of Israel by alluding to Jacob's supplanting ways. Rather than seeking each other's good, brothers sought to hinder each other for their own advancement. Although some identify a different verbal root in Job 37:4 (metaplastic form of *'iqqēb*, hold back, restrain, Gordis, 425), this verse probably signifies Yahweh's open display of his awesome power in nature. He does not supplant the lightning and thunder (i.e., restrain it).

3. The two remaining words have similar usage. The nom. *'oqbâ* (2 Kgs 10:19) refers to Jehu's treacherous actions necessary to destroy the prophets/ministers of Baal. The adj. *'āqōb* is used in three significant passages. The prophet Jeremiah juxtaposes *'āqōb* with *lēb* to describe the spiritual condition of God's people. In light of the parallelism of *mîšôr*, level, straight, and *'āqōb* in Isa 40:4 and the juxtaposition of *yōšer* (a cognate of *mîšôr,* uprightness, steadiness, dependability) with *lēb* in Deut 9:5; 1 Kgs 9:4; Ps 119:7, *'āqōb* in Jer 17:9 might connote the heart that is devious or difficult, i.e., tortuous (Holladay, 1986, 495). Holladay (1974, 100) suggests a translation, "The heart is rougher than anything, and incurable: who understands it?"

4. According to *HALAT* this nom. occurs 3x (Isa 40:4; Jer 17:9; Hos 6:8) and is derived from *'qb* I, to supplant, overreach, take by the heel. Schwarzenbach (5) posits that *'āqōb* means "a demarcated region which is arduous and troublesome." The meaning of *'āqōb* is made clear in Isa 40:4 by its contrast with *mîšôr* (level place, → # 4793). The transformation of rugged places into level places constitutes part of what Isaiah depicts as preparatory to the coming of Yahweh to bring his people home.

In Jer 17:9 *'āqōb* seems to manifest a quite different meaning, crafty, deceitful (LXX, deep; LXX [Lucianic], Vg., heavy, weighty; Syr., hard, difficult). In light of the contrast between *'āqōb* and *mîšôr* in Isa 40:4, Jeremiah may be contrasting *'āqōb* heart with a *yōšer* (cognate of *mîšôr*) heart (Deut 9:5; 1 Kgs 9:4; Job 33:3; Ps 119:7). Holladay (1974, 100) offers a vivid translation of this part of Jer 17:9: "the heart is rougher than anything and incurable."

It is unlikely that *'āqōb* occurs in Hos 6:8. Stuart (98-99) redivides and repoints the last two words of the verse (*"ᵃqubbâ middām* to *'iqbêhem dām*) to produce the translation "whose footprints are bloody" (lit. "their footprints [are] blood"). McComiskey (95-96; cf. Andersen and Freedman, 441) does not alter the MT, but suggests that this form is a denom. of the nom. *'āqēb*, heel, footprint, after the pattern of a pass. adj., trodden/tracked.

5. The exact meaning of the words from the *'qb* root must be determined in context. Lexicons normally list two roots that are identical in orthography. The name Jacob (*ya'ᵃqōb*) comes from the root *'qb* and means supplanter, deceiver. As the character of Jacob was changed by encounter with God, finally his name was changed as

well. The new name given by God was Israel (*yiśrāʾēl* [# 3776]; Gen 32:28[29]; for another explanation, → Jacob: Theology).

P-B Late Heb. employed the root with its OT meanings and added some nuanced usages (pa. to trace, spy). For refs. see Jastrow 2:1104.

Deception, falsehood, fraud, guile, iniquity, lie: → *'āwen* (mischief, iniquity, deception, # 224); → *bd'* (invent, devise, lie, # 968); → *kzb* I (lie, be a liar, deceive, # 3941); → *kḥš* (fail, deceive, grow lean, # 3950); → *nkl* (knave, deceiver, cheat, # 5792); → *nš'* II (be deceived, deceive, cause a deception, # 5958); → *sārâ* II (rebellion, crime, revolt, falsehood, # 6240); → *'qb* I (seize the heel, overreach, deceive, # 6810); → *rmh* II (betray, deal treacherously with, # 8228); → *śwṭ* (turn away to falsehood, entangled in lies, # 8454); → *šqr* (deal/act falsely, betray, # 9213); → *tll* (deceive, mock, trifle, # 9438)

Bibliography

TWAT 6:338-43; *TWOT* 2:691-92; F. Andersen and D. Freedman, *Hosea*, AB, 1980; R. Gordis, *The Book of Job*, 1978; V. Hamilton, *The Book of Genesis, Chapters 18-50*, WBC, 1995; W. Holladay, *Jeremiah 1*, Hermeneia, 1986; idem, *Jeremiah: Spokesman Out of Time*, 1974; B. Margalit, "Lexicographical Notes on the Aqht Epic (Part I: *KTU* 1.17-18)," *UF* 15, 1983, 95-96; T. McComiskey, "Hosea," in *The Minor Prophets*, 1992, 1:1-237; Allen Ross, *Creation and Blessing*, 1988; A. Schwarzenbach, *Die geographische Terminologie im Hebräischen des Alten Testaments*, 1954; D. Stuart, *Hosea—Jonah*, WBC, 1987.

Eugene Carpenter/Michael A. Grisanti

6811 (*'āqēb*, heel, hoof, footprint, step), → # 6810

6815	עָקֹב

עָקֹב (*'āqōb*), adj. showing footprints, deceitful, treacherous (# 6815); עָקְבָּה (*'oqbâ*), nom. trickery, deception (# 6817); < עקב (*'qb* I), q. hold by the heel, attack at the heel, supplant, deceive; pi. hold back, only Job 37:4 (→ # 6810).

ANE The cognates of the root *'qb* may be seen in Ugar., Akk., and Syr., with various meanings based on "heel."

OT 1. Occurring only 1x in OT, the nom. *'oqbâ* describes Jehu's deception in carrying out his plan to eliminate Ahab's influence by destroying the Baal worshipers (2 Kgs 10:19). The adj. *'āqōb* occurs 3x in OT, signifying a deceitful/treacherous act or condition. In Jer 17:9, the human heart is depicted as "deceitful above all things" and as incurable. Though BDB groups *'āqōb* of Isa 40:4 under a different root, the separate groupings are unnecessary. The single grouping in *HALAT* is more reasonable. The Isaianic use of the term for the ground condition need not be totally unrelated to the other usage of the term. Here the prophet calls his audience to prepare the way for the Lord, noting that the "rough ground" (*'āqōb*) shall become level. The description of treacherous acts and of treacherous ground do not necessarily require two different roots. In this verse, the term "level" (*mîšôr*) also carries a dual function: Elsewhere, in Isa 11:4, *mîšôr* means "righteousness," describing one of the characteristics of the messianic rule.

2. The term *'āqōb* is more picturesque than *'ārûm,* "cunning" (# 6874), in depicting a deceitful act because of its close tie to the nom. *'āqēb* (# 6811), which

means "heel." The root *'qb* is best known for its relation to the story of Jacob's grasping the heel of Esau (Gen 25:26; cf. 27:36). The name "Jacob" (*y'qb*) is based on this root. This graphic meaning may be seen in the use of *'āqōb* in Hos 6:8, where Gilead is condemned as a wicked city that is, as NIV vividly translates the term, "stained with footprints of" blood (NRSV tracked with). While *'ārûm* not only means "cunning" but also positively "prudent/wise" (mainly in Proverbs), *'āqōb* does not possess such strong positive meaning. In this respect, the narrow descriptive function of the root *'qb* is similar to that of the negative term *nkl*, "be crafty/deceitful" (Gen 37:18; Num 25:18; Ps 105:25; Mal 1:14).

P-B Sir 36:25 uses *'āqōb* to describe the heart, warning that a "deceitful" mind that causes grief will reap grief. In Sir 6:20, the term depicts the "tough" (NRSV harsh) approach Lady Wisdom takes in dealing with a fool. As Segal (41) has observed, the latter meaning resembles its usage in Isa 40:4, above. Its meaning as "deceitful/crooked" or as "rough" (ground or pathways) continues in Mish. Heb. (see Jastrow 2:1105; Yehuda 5:4668).

Deception, falsehood, fraud, guile, iniquity, lie: → *'āwen* (mischief, iniquity, deception, # 224); → *bd'* (invent, devise, lie, # 968); → *kzb* I (lie, be a liar, deceive, # 3941); → *kḥš* (fail, deceive, grow lean, # 3950); → *nkl* (knave, deceiver, cheat, # 5792); → *nš'* II (be deceived, deceive, cause a deception, # 5958); → *sārâ* II (rebellion, crime, revolt, falsehood, # 6240); → *'qb* I (seize the heel, overreach, deceive, # 6810); → *rmh* II (betray, deal treacherously with, # 8228); → *śwṭ* (turn away to falsehood, entangled in lies, # 8454); → *šqr* (deal/act falsely, betray, # 9213); → *tll* (deceive, mock, trifle, # 9438)

Bibliography

TWAT 6:338-43; N. Ararat, "Scripture's Battle Against Cunning," *BethM* 26, 1980, 67-78; M. H. Segal, *Sefer Ben Sira Haššalem*, 1958; B. Yehuda, *Dictionary and Thesaurus of the Hebrew Language*, 1959, 5:4665-69.

A. Luc

6817 (*'oqbâ*, trickery), → # 6810

6818	עקד

עקד (*'qd*), q. tie up (hapleg. in Gen 22:9; # 6818); עָקֹד (*'āqōd*), adj. striped, streaked (# 6819).

OT 1. The *Akedah*, the story of the "binding" (*'qd*) of Isaac (→), is the Heb. name of the story of Abraham's sacrifice of Isaac.

2. All seven occurrences of *'āqōd* are in Gen 30 and 31, describing the color of the small cattle that Jacob (→) bred. The difference between *'āqōd* and *nāqōd* is brought out clearly in 31:8, "If he (Laban) said, 'The speckled (*nāqōd*) ones will be your wages,' then all the flocks gave birth to speckled (*nāqōd*) young; and if he said, 'The streaked ones (*'āqōd*) will be your wages,' then all the flocks bore streaked (*'āqōd*) young."

Band, tie: → *'pd* (put on tightly, # 679); → *'ᵃpēr* (bandagc, # 710); → *'eṣ'ādâ* (band, # 731); → *ḥbš* (tie up, saddle, imprison, bind, # 2502); → *ḥgr* (bind, gird, # 2520); → *ḥāšûq* (clasp ring, # 3122); → *ḥtl* (be swaddled, # 3156); → *keset* (band [for magic purposes], # 4086); → *migbā'â* (head-band, # 4457); → *'nd* (wind, tie s.t., # 6698); → *'qd* (tie up, # 6818); → *ṣrr* I (bind, tie up,

7674); → *qšr* (ally together, conspire, bind, # 8003); → *rks* (bind, tie, # 8220); → *rtm* (tie up, # 8412)
Colors—spotted, dappled: → *'āmōṣ* (pie-bald?, # 600); → *bārōd* (dappled, spotted, # 1353); → *ṭl'* (spotted, gaudy, # 3229); → *nāqōd* (speckled, # 5923); → *'āqōd* (striped, streaked, # 6819)

T. Desmond Alexander

6819 (*'āqōd*, striped, streaked), → # 6818

6821 (*'āqâ* I, misery), → # 6421

6823	עקל

עקל (*'ql*), pu. perverted (# 6823); עֲקַלְקַל (*'ᵃqalqāl*), adj. crooked, winding (# 6824); עֲקַלָּתוֹן (*'ᵃqallātôn*), nom. coiling (# 6825).

ANE The root *'ql*, twist, pervert, is attested in Arab. and Syr. (*HALAT* 827).

OT 1. The vb. *'ql* is a hapleg., found in the context of Habakkuk's portrayal of his crooked generation. When the law had suffered paralysis and justice was "perverted" (Hab 1:4), the righteous suffered, "The wicked hem in the righteous, so that justice is perverted." Peer pressure made it difficult for the godly to live by the straight and righteous revelation of the Lord. (→ Habakkuk: Theology)

2. *'ᵃqalqāl* has both a literal and a nonliteral significance. On the one hand, it denotes byways. In a description of the destruction during the period of Shamgar (Judg 5:6-7), ordinary life and communication was jeopardized. People, not able to go on regular paths, had to take indirect "winding" (*'ᵃqalqāl*) ways (5:6). On the other hand, the psalmist affirms his faith that God hates and brings to an end the perverted, "crooked ways" (*'ᵃqalqāl*) of the evildoers, "But those who turn to crooked ways the LORD will banish with the evildoers" (Ps 125:5).

3. A possible combination of literal and figurative occurs in the poetic description of Leviathan as a serpent who not only flees, but also "coils" or "twists" (*'ᵃqallātôn*, Isa 27:1). This description of a serpent is entirely fitting, but the perverse, anti-creation nature of Leviathan could well lead to an extended metaphorical description of the serpent as morally "twisted." This "monster must be destroyed ... it is the monster of evil. That, too, God will destroy, and his people may await that day with joy" (Oswalt, *Isaiah*, 491).

P-B In Aramaic RL, the pi. pass. part. of the root describes a "crooked" staff (Sipre Deut., 308; Yalquṭ Deut., 942).

Distortion, perversion, shrewdness, twisting: → *hēpek* (opposite, perversity, # 2201); → *kpn* (twist, # 4102); → *lwz* (let out of sight, go wrong way, # 4279); → *slp* (frustrate, overthrow, twist, mislead, # 6156); → *'bt* (conspire together, # 6309); → *'wh* (do wrong, pervert, # 6390); → *'wl* I (act wrongly, # 6401); → *'wt* (make crooked, pervert, bent, # 6430); → *'ql* (perverted, # 6823); → *'qš* (be perverse, make crooked, # 6835); → *ptl* (twist, be wily, shrewd, # 7349); → *r''* I (be bad, injure, # 8317)
Leviathan: → *liwyātān* (Leviathan, # 4293); → *tannîn* (sea creatures, # 9490)

BIBLIOGRAPHY

C. H. Gordon, "Leviathan: Symbol of Evil," in *Biblical Motifs. Origins and Transformations*, 1966, 1-9; J. A. Emerton, "Leviathan and *LTN*: The Vocalization of the Ugaritic Word for the

Dragon," *VT* 32, 1982, 327-31; P. Wernberg-Møller, *The Manual of Discipline*, STDJ 1, 1957; J. N. Oswalt, "The Myth of the Dragon and the Old Testament Faith," *EQ* 49, 1977, 163-72.

David W. Baker

6824 (*ʿaqalqāl*, crooked, winding), → # 6823

6825 (*ʿaqallātôn*, coiling), → # 6823

6827	עקר

עקר (*ʿqr*), q. root up; ni. be rooted up; pi. hamstring (animal) (# 6827).

ANE Common Semitic; cf. Arab. *aqara* III, hamstring.

OT 1. It is used in the proverbial expression in Eccl 3:2, "a time to be born and a time to die, a time to plant and a time to uproot." M. Dahood ("Phoenician Background of Qohelet," *Bib* 47, 1966, 270) makes the suggestions that the vb. may mean "harvest" rather than "root up" and that at least would make the pi. use of the vb. more understandable.

2. It is used of God's judgment pronounced by Zephaniah on Philistia, including the uprooting of Ekron (Zeph 2:4).

3. It is used of the hamstringing of animals (e.g., Gen 49:6), especially the horses of defeated enemies to prevent their further use in warfare (Jos 11:6-9; 2 Sam 8:4 = 1 Chron 18:4).

Root, uproot: → *ntš* (root up, pull down, destroy, # 6004); → *ʿqr* (root up, # 6827); → *šrš* (root up, # 9245)

Francis Foulkes

6829	עָקָר

עָקָר (*ʿāqār*), childless, barren, sterile (# 6829); < עקר (*ʿqr*, uproot, → # 6827).

OT 1. In the OT barrenness was considered a curse or affliction sent by God (Gen 20:18), primarily because procreation was considered to be both a commandment and a blessing (Gen 1:28; 9:7; Ps 127:3-5). If fertility was one of God's blessings on Israel, how else could barrenness be interpreted? This belief about fertility may explain why Gen 38:9-10 is the sole explicit reference in the Bible to what may be considered as some form of birth control. There are several instances in the OT, however, where barrenness is not attributed to any form of disobedience. Just as all forms of sickness are not to be explained as punishment for sin (e.g., Job), so not all instances of barrenness are to be explained as punishment for sin (Sarah [Gen 11:30]; Rebekah [25:21]; Rachel [29:31]; Manoah's wife [Judg 13:2]; Hannah [1 Sam 1:5]). In fact, it is difficult to find one instance in the OT where a named woman is cursed with childlessness. The nearest example is 2 Sam 6:23, but it is not certain that Michal's childlessness is meant as a punishment.

2. In three of the above cases (Sarah, Rebekah, and Rachel), the barren woman was destined to be one of the ancestresses of Israel. The thrice-repeated emphasis on the barrenness of the ancestress-to-be raises the question of how exactly God's frequent promises of descendants as numerous as the stars of the heaven or the sands of

the seashore are to be realized. Is their sterility an insuperable barrier to the accomplishment of the divine plan and program? Is their barrenness a threat to all that God has said? Or is the overcoming of this obstacle a testimony to God's power and integrity?

3. In none of the above instances was the condition permanent. In two cases the barren woman first attempted to solve her own situation by providing her husband with a surrogate (Gen 16:1-2; 30:3-4). However culturally acceptable such a practice may have been in the patriarchal age, Genesis understands such a move as a human attempt to solve an apparently irremediable problem. Isaac demonstrated that intercessory prayer rather than concubinage could effectively reverse his wife's biological situation (25:21).

4. Twice God promised that when his people were settled in their land, neither husbands nor wives would know childlessness (Exod 23:26; Deut 7:14). Such would be the blessing of God on his people. Presumably this meant the end of childlessness because of a congenital condition, an injury that inhibits the birthing process, or the lack of a spouse because of celibacy, bereavement, or divorce.

5. The barren woman is the special object of God's grace (Ps 113:9).

Barren, childless, miscarriage: → *galmûd* (barren, # 1678); → *nēpel* (still-born child, miscarriage, # 5878); → *'āqār* (barren, childless, # 6829); → *'ariri* (childless, # 6884); → *škl* (be bereaved, bereavement, miscarry, # 8897)

BIBLIOGRAPHY

TWAT 6:343-46; O. Babb, "Barrenness," *IDB* 1:359.

Victor P. Hamilton

6830	עֵקֶר

עֵקֶר (*'ēqer* I), member, descendant (# 6830).

ANE Cognate with Aram. *'qr,* a term appearing in the Aramaic inscriptions of Sefire in Syria (J. Gibson, *TSSI,* 2:28, to no. 7, line 3).

OT The *'ēqer* is a member/offshoot of an alien's family to whom an Israelite may be sold (hapleg. in Lev 25:47).

Descendant, offspring, seed: → *dôr* II (generation, # 1887); → *zr'* (sow, scatter seed, form seed, # 2445); → *yld* (bear, bring forth, be born, # 3528); → *nîn* (offspring, # 5769); → *neked* (progeny, # 5781); → *'ēqer* (descendant, # 6830); → *ṣe'ᵉṣā'îm* (offspring, # 7368); → *ribbēa'* (member of fourth generation, # 8067); → *šillēš* (member of sixth generation, # 9000); → *tarbût* (brood, # 9551)

BIBLIOGRAPHY

H. R. Cohen, *Biblical Hapax Legomena in the Light of Akkadian and Ugaritic,* 1978, 19-20.

Victor P. Hamilton

6832	עַקְרָב

עַקְרָב (*'aqrāb*), nom. scorpion (# 6832).

ANE Syr. *'eqqarbā'*; Old Aram., Egyp. Aram. *'rqb'*; Akk. *aqrabu*; Arab., Eth. *'aqrab*; Tigre *'arqab/'arqab*, scorpion.

OT The term is found 9x in the OT. More than a dozen species of this arachnid of the *Scorpionida* order occur in Palestine. They represent great danger to God's people/prophets (Deut 8:15; Ezek 2:6), literally so in the desert, figuratively so as Ezekiel lived among people who would attack him. In both instances, the Lord kept his prophet/people safe. Scourging with scorpions is used to emphasize the oppression with which Rehoboam threatened northern Israel—a more severe treatment than beating with whips (1 Kgs 12:11, 14; cf. 2 Chron 10:11, 14). The divinely appointed boundaries of the Promised Land included a southern marker called Scorpion Pass (Num 34:4, *ma'ᵃlēh 'aqrabbîm*; cf. Josh 15:3; Judg 1:36).

P-B The LXX transliterates the term (e.g., Num 34:4, *anabasin Akrabin*). In the other six references it employs *skorpios*, scorpion. Use of *'aqrāb* is found in Late Heb. The end result of drinking wine was compared to being stung by the tip of the scorpion's tail (Jastrow 2:1109).

NT The nom. scorpion is used 5x in the NT. It is an undesirable gift (Luke 11:12). Jesus gave his 72 followers power over scorpions (Luke 10:9). Locusts from the Abyss are given power to torture with a scorpion-like sting those who do not have God's seal (Rev 9:3, 5, 10).

Insects: → *dᵉbôrâ* I (bee, wasp, # 1805); → *kēn* V (mosquito, gnat, louse, # 4031); → *'ṭh* II (delouse, # 6487); → *'aqrāb* (scorpion, # 6832); → *'ārōb* (fly, swarm of flies, flying insects, # 6856); → *'āš* I (moth, # 6931); → *ṣir'â* (hornet, destruction, fear, terror, depression, discouragement, # 7667); → *qml* (wither, become moldy, musty, infected w. insects, # 7857)

BIBLIOGRAPHY
IDB 2:246-56; *Fauna and Flora of the Bible*, 1980².

Eugene Carpenter/Michael A. Grisanti

6833 (*'eqrôn*, Ekron), → Ekron

6835	עקשׁ

עקשׁ (*'qš*), ni. be perverse; pi. make crooked; hi. show perverse (# 6835); nom. מַעֲקַשִּׁים (*ma'ᵃqaššîm*), uneven ground (# 5112); adj. עִקֵּשׁ (*'iqqēš* I), perverted, false (# 6836); nom. עִקְּשׁוּת (*'iqqᵉšût*), perversion, falsehood (# 6838).

ANE The Syr. *'qisā'* means twisted, distorted. The Arab. *'aqaṣa* is used for braiding, e.g., hair.

OT 1. The only literal use of the Heb. root is of the nom. *ma'ᵃqaššîm* in a description of God's blessing for those who follow him. For them, darkness becomes light and rough places a plain or a straight path (*yšr*, Isa 42:16). Here the literal nature of the terrain is intended.

2. Other words from this root are metaphorically extended to the moral level. *'iqqᵉšût*, perversion, twice describes the fruit of the mouth in the context of corrupt and vile people (Prov 4:24; 6:12). *'iqqēš* is also used to describe speech (8:8; 19:1), as well as the very heart of a person (Ps 101:4; Prov 11:20; 17:20) and the way or manner of life one leads (Deut 32:5; Prov 2:15; 22:5; 28:6). These distorted or perverse people are compared to the crooked and corrupt (Deut 32:5; Prov 8:8), the evil, slanderers, and

wicked (Ps 101:4-7), and the devious, wrong, and perverse (Prov 28:6). They are contrasted with the blameless, pure, and faithful (2 Sam 22:27; Ps 18:26[27]), the right and faultless (Prov 8:8), and those who are blameless in their character (Prov 19:1; 28:6). God is displeased with those who are perverse and does not allow them success (2 Sam 22:27; Prov 11:20; 17:20; 22:5). The form of the adjective itself shows that it describes a departure from the norm, since the form is generally used to refer to defects (*IBHS*, 89).

3. Verbal forms of the root occur in three stems and are all used metaphorically. The ni. is used in an adjectival and possibly reflexive sense (*IBHS*, 386, possibly a denominative vb. derived from the adj. *'iqqēš*; cf. Prov 28:6). A contrast is drawn between the salvation of one whose walk is blameless (*tāmîm*) and the sudden fall of one whose ways are described as perverse (28:18). The pi., on the other hand, stresses the state being brought about, the factitive use (*IBHS*, 401). Prov 10:9 is largely identical to 28:18, except that in 10:9 the "ways" are the direct object of the vb. rather than as in 28:18, where "ways" are described as perverse (ni. of *'qš*). The wicked, who are without integrity or justice (Isa 59:8), pervert or make crooked the paths they travel (Prov 10:9). Israel's leaders direct her into sin since they take justice and integrity (*yšr*) and distort it (Mic 3:9).

The sole use of the hi. stem is one in which a person, in this case Job, would be declared perverse (guilty, NIV; Job 9:20) by God even if he should declare himself innocent (*IBHS*, 438-39). In each of these verbal examples the vb. denotes a departure from the desired norm of following the will and guidance of God.

Falsehood, perversity, wrong: → *bd'* (invent, devise, lie, # 968); → *hēpek* (opposite, perversity, # 2201); → *kzb* I (lie, be a liar, deceive, # 3941); → *lwz* (let out of sight, go wrong way, # 4279); → *slp* (frustrate, overthrow, twist, mislead, # 6156); → *sārâ* II (rebellion, crime, revolt, falsehood, # 6240); → *'wl* I (act wrongly, # 6401); → *'wt* (make crooked, pervert, bent, # 6430); → *'qš* (be perverse, make crooked, # 6835)

BIBLIOGRAPHY

ISBE 3:802; *TWOT* 2:693; W. Brueggemann, "A Neglected Sapiential Word Pair," *ZAW* 89, 1977, 234-58; M. Dahood, "Hebrew-Ugaritic Lexicography VII," *Bib* 50, 1969, 353-54.

David W. Baker

6836 (*'iqqēš* I, perverted, false), → # 6835

6838 (*'iqq^{e}šût*, perversion, falsehood), → # 6835

6842	ערב

ערב (*'rb* I), q. stand security for; mortgage; barter; give security for; make a wager (# 6842); עֲרֻבָּה (*'^{a}rubbâ*), nom. pledge, security, surety, token (# 6859); עֵרָבוֹן (*'ērābôn*), nom. pledge, security (# 6860); תַּעֲרוּבוֹת (*ta'^{a}rûbôt*), nom., pledges, used in the phrase *b^{e}nê hatta'^{a}rūbôt*, hostages (# 9510).

ANE The vb. is found in Ugar. *'rb*, go security/bail for; Arab. *'rb*, pledge, pawn, mortgage; Akk. *erēbu* (in the phrase *ana qatāti erēbu*, go surety for). The following nom. forms also occur: Syr. *'rābā'*, *'arrābūtā'*, security, bail, surety; Jewish-Aram. *'ār^{e}bā'*, Syr. *'arrābā'*, surety, bail; Akk. *erubbātum*, pledge, security, mortgage, deposit, guarantee; Ugar.-Akk. *e-ru-ub*, pledge, security, mortgage, deposit, guarantee; Ugar. *'rbn*, surety, bail, guarantee; Arab. *'arbān*; Eth. *'rabōn*, *'erbūn*; G *arrabōn*; Lat. *arr(h)abo*, *arrha*, pledge, security, mortgage, deposit, guarantee.

OT 1. The vb. occurs several times in the book of Proverbs (Prov 6:1; 11:15; 17:18; 20:16; 22:26; 27:13), which, while mindful of the need for compassion, generosity, and neighborliness, warns of the grave dangers involved in gambling one's financial security by pledging to cover another's possible business losses. High risk monetary transactions could result in abject poverty and even slavery (cf. e.g., Gen 44:32-33; Prov 20:16; 22:26-27; cf. 2 Kgs 4:1). Prov 6 is usually taken to be admonishing the injudicious person who has ensnared himself by rashly volunteering to go surety for another's debt (v. 1) to importune ([v. 3] *rhb*, act stormily, boisterously (# 8104); G. C. Martin, 52, suggests besiege) his neighbor in order to obtain release from the guaranty (vv. 3-5). Most scholars think that the words *rēa'* and *zār* in 6:1 are synonymous terms. However, Boström (cited by McKane, 321-22) maintains that *'rb* followed by the preposition *l*[e] means giving surety to and not going surety for, in which case the *rēa'* is the creditor and the *zār* the debtor.

The person who underwrites the financial liabilities of a stranger is courting disaster, but one who refrains from becoming implicated in binding financial agreements will avoid the ruin that can result from a debtor defaulting on his financial obligations (Prov 11:15; cf. e.g., McKane, 429). Prov 17:18 (where the vb. occurs with nom. *'*[a]*rubbâ*) asserts that only a senseless individual endangers himself by going surety for someone else's debts. The aim of this v. seems to be to inculcate caution and a realistic evaluation of financial risk before incurring financial liability on behalf of another (cf. McKane, 502-3). Good intentions are a virtue only when the person having them has made a hard-headed analysis of the situation and a careful assessment of whether what has been promised can be accomplished (Collins, 24). Prov 20:16 (par. 27:13) may be taking the view that anyone reckless enough to go surety for another's debt does not deserve to escape the consequences of his stupidity when the debtor has defaulted (cf. e.g., Dummelow, 386; Jones, 173). Alternatively, it may be advising the person dealing with someone who is a bad credit risk, particularly one who is liable for the debts of foreigners (however, see G. C. Martin, 125), to insist on security so as to avoid serious financial loss if the debtor should default (McKane, 543; cf. Tate, 65). In 22:27, the advice against going surety for another person is motivated by concern that the unfortunate guarantor may have his belongings, even his bed, seized by the creditor(s). Far from being a noble sacrifice, to lose one's possessions in this way is nothing less than a lamentable lack of acumen and a failure to take adequate stock of one's financial resources (Collins, 52).

2. The vb. is used of those subsistence farmers mortgaging (i.e., giving as security) their fields, vineyards, and houses in order to obtain grain during a famine (Neh 5:3). In 1753, Guthe (cited, with qualified approval, by Batten, 238, 247) proposed the slight emendation of MT *rabbîm* (many) in v. 2 to *'ōr*[e]*bîm* (mortgaging). This conjecture is convincing and has been accepted by many modern scholars (e.g., Davies, 199-200; *BHS*; *HALAT*; Bowman, 706; NEB; REB; JB; Browne, 379; Clines, 1984, 166; Blenkinsopp, 1988, 253-54). On this reading of v. 2, the economic crisis in Judah at one point in Nehemiah's governorship was so severe and the loan conditions imposed by callous creditors so harsh that some poverty-stricken citizens who owned

no land were driven to the extermity of putting up their children as surety to obtain food. In extreme need, it was permitted to mortgage one's children (Exod 21:7; cf. 2 Kgs 4:1; Isa 50:1) or oneself (Lev 25:39) in order to clear a debt by labor. However, it is thought by some (e.g., Blenkinsopp, 1988, 257) that in lending transactions it was not unusual for the family member's service to begin as soon as the loan was advanced and to continue until the debt was amortized. It is not clear to what extent the remission (Deut 15:1-18; cf. Exod 21:2) and Jubilee (Lev 25) laws, which were designed to mitigate the evils of the mortgage of persons, were implemented in ancient Israel, but in the one case for which evidence exists (Jer 34:8-16), the law was circumvented (cf. e.g., Clines, 1984, 166).

3. The vb. occurs with the sense barter/exchange merchandise (Ezek 27:9, 27). It is used in tandem with nom. *ma*^{a}*rāb*, which occurs only in Ezek 27:9, 13, 17, 19, 25, 27, 33-34 and which many (e.g., *HALAT*; BDB) connect with *'rb* I. Ezek 27:1-36 is a lament over the prestigious Phoenician seaport of Tyre, in which the island city is described as a beautifully constructed, splendidly equipped, and expertly sailed cargo ship that is wrecked by a violent storm. In v. 9b, the image changes to Tyre's harbor thronging with ships, carrying merchants from every seafaring nation of the known world who have come to barter for the high quality and much sought-after Tyrian goods. There has been little support for the view advanced by G. R. Driver (64-65) that, in v. 9b, we are dealing with a root *'rb*, offer (attested in OSA and Syr.), and that we should read here a causative pi. *l*^{e} *'ārēb*, meaning cause to give, obtain. The suggestion made by Dahood (1964, 83, n. 2) that the word be linked to a stem meaning enter and translated import is also unconvincing. In v. 27, where the figure of the ship is resumed, there is a description of how, succumbing to the onslaught of a powerful east wind, the richly-laden vessel capsized and sank into the depths of the sea with the loss of its entire company, including those trading in merchandise (*'ōr*^{e}*bê ma*^{a}*rābēk*). The proud self-sufficiency, arrogant overconfidence, and self-adulation of affluent Tyre, which resulted from its commercial skill, advanced technology, and worldwide trade relationships, not only failed to avert the day of Yahweh's judgment (Zimmerli, 71), but actually precipitated the city's eventual ruin (Blenkinsopp, 1990, 120-21).

4. The vb. occurs in the phrase *'ārab 'et-libbô*, lit., (who is he who) would give his heart in security, i.e., would gamble his life (Jer 30:21; Bright, 1965, 280; cf. S. R. Driver, 1906, 182). This v. refers to the new ruler (the title king may have been deliberately avoided for political and/or religious reasons) who will lead the restored Israel and who will be the perfect intermediary between God and his people. By special dispensation, he will be granted direct access to God, for, given the risk of death when approaching the holy God unbidden (cf. Exod 19:21; 33:20; Num 8:19), no sinful mortal "would dare of himself" (RSV; cf. NRSV)/"would be so bold" (Bright, 1965, 272)/"ventures of himself" (NEB)/"would risk his life" (JB)/"dare risk his life" (REB)/"will devote himself" (NIV) to venture near the divine presence.

5. Twice (Gen 43:9; 44:32), the vb. is used of a man going surety for another in the sense of furnishing a guarantee of that person's safety by standing in his place. According to Speiser (327-28), this technical sense of the vb. is particularly common in Akk. legal usage. In Gen 43:9 and 44:32, the vb. is used of Judah, who eventually persuaded his father Jacob to let Benjamin accompany his brothers to Egypt by undertaking full responsibility for (lit., going surety; i.e., guaranteeing [NIV]) the youngster's

safety. Whereas in the past Judah's conduct had been characterized by jealousy, hatred, violence, and deception, in Gen 43-44 he is portrayed as displaying both self-sacrificing concern for a brother and filial solicitude toward his father. The callous man who had masterminded the sale into slavery of the first favorite now offers to bear the burden of slavery in order to secure the freedom of the second favorite and so protect his father from further grief (Kselman, 123; Maher, 247; Westermann, 136-38; cf. R. Davidson, 260; Gibson, 1982, 287).

In two passages (Ps 119:122; Isa 38:14), the vb. is used of God's affording a man protection or indemnifying him against harm from oppressors in much the same way as a man would go surety for a debtor to defer distraint and offer bail. In Isa 38:14, part of a song (vv. 9-20) traditionally ascribed to Hezekiah, Yahweh is requested to be the security, surety, guarantor, or safeguard of the oppressed supplicant and to bail him out (cf. Watts, 1987, 54). According to Watts (1987, 60), the root *'šq*, oppress (# 6943), is a technical legal term for the pressure that a creditor brings to bear on his debtor. Many (e.g., Peake, 1920, 459; Bright, 1964, 515; Watts, 1987, 60; cf. Skinner, 1909, 280; Herbert, 1973, 212) think that the petitioner, likening himself to a debtor who is being led to jail, appeals to Yahweh, as his creditor, to become his security so that he can escape imprisonment (cf. Job 17:3). Others (e.g., Thomson and Skinner, 142) maintain that it is death that is here depicted as an oppressive creditor, about to seize the person of the unfortunate debtor. However, it seems more probable that Yahweh is the creditor, who is being urged to intervene by posting bail for the debtor who has defaulted. Afflicted by God, the speaker, like Job (cf. Job 9:15; 17:3), can only appeal to God against God (Kaiser, 406; cf. Oswalt, 685; Seitz, 259).

In Ps 119:122, a speaker who complains that he is being oppressed (as in Isa 38:14, the vb. used in Ps 119:121-22 is *'šq*), despite being innocent (v. 121), implores God to be his protector and helper (lit., go surety for—i.e., guarantee [ensure, NIV]—his well-being) or to indemnify him against harm from those oppressing him (cf. Dahood, 1970, 186, who, however, takes the vb. to be from a root meaning enter). Some (cf. e.g., Eaton, 277; *BHS*; Kraus, 410) suggest emending *'ᵃrōb 'abdᵉkā* to *'ᵃrōb dᵉbārᵉkā*, "Give your word as surety....," but this conjecture is not really necessary.

In Job 17:3, part of Job's reply (16:1-17:16) to the second discourse of Eliphaz, the first stich reads *śîmâ-nā' 'orbēnî 'immāk*. Many emend *'orbēnî* (take me on pledge) to *'ērᵉbōnî* (cf. e.g., Clines 1989, 373; Hartley, 266) or *'erbōnî* (cf. e.g., Strahan, 157; Dhorme, 244), my pledge (nom. *'ērābôn* with suff.), which would give the meaning, "Lay down a pledge for me with yourself" (NRSV; cf. RSV), or "Keep my pledge close by you" (Clines, 1989, 368; cf. Dhorme, 244; Pope, 127-28). There is widespread agreement that Job's problem is that no one is prepared either to let himself be used as surety or to offer a pledge on Job's behalf, but opinions differ about what precisely Job is asking for in v. 3. Some think that he is asking God to be his guarantor. Thus, e.g., REB renders, "Be my surety with yourself" (cf. NEB). A. B. Davidson (147-48), one of many scholars who sees in 17:3 the same division of God into two parties as appears in 16:21, argues that Job is entreating the God who alone can uphold his cause to become surety for Job, and to convince the God who persecutes Job of his innocence. A similar line is taken by Peake (1905, 172), who also draws attention to the dichotomy in God in 17:3. In asking God to give bail to God, Job is asking his creditor to become the debtor's guarantor. The pledge that Job asks God to deposit for him is that

God will vindicate him in the future. While the metaphor suggests a pledge to pay a debt, Job is asking God to undertake the task of proving that no debt is due. Driver and Gray (151) understand Job to be asking the friendly God to give the pledge or bail required to secure Job's release from the hostile God who, until he receives the bail, will keep Job a prisoner. Franks (357; cf. Dummelow, 304) understands Job to be urging God, in his capacity as Job's advocate, to give a pledge to God, as Job's creditor, that he will vindicate his client in the future. Gibson (1985, 137-39) reckons that Job, envisaging a future assize in heaven, is appealing to the friendly God to win for him from the other, malevolent, persecuting, and implacable deity the verdict that is his due.

According to Strahan (149-50, 157-58) and Habel (93), Job, who throughout his crises had experienced God as his accuser, oppressor, watchman, and judge, was appealing to the hidden justice and compassion of God. Bergant (101) is of the opinion that Job, the plaintiff, is imploring God, the defendant who is accused of injustice, to supply the legal bond that is demanded in this judicial case. Watts (1972, 75; cf. Hartley, 268) maintains that Job is asking God, not to be the bondsman, but to arrange for such a deposit as will enable Job to get respite from the constant affliction until the case has been decided. Clines (1989, 394) rejects the view that Job is asking for bail money to obtain temporary relief from the wrath of God. While Job certainly yearns to be free from divine suffocation and assault, his primary objective is to have his name cleared.

Clines (1989, 393-94) is one of several scholars who reject the argument that Job is appealing to God to be his guarantor. These scholars argue that, in v. 3, Job requests God to accept him as his own guarantor. Thus, for example, JB translates, "You yourself must take my own guarantee." Terrien (1028) maintains that Job, accepting the inexplicable fact that God is treating him as if he were a criminal, is asking the hostile deity to accept a guarantee until Job's innocence has been established. According to Dhorme (244-45), the only pledge that Job has to offer God is his sufferings. However, Clines (1989, 394) takes a different tack. He asserts that the purpose behind the motif of the pledge here is the eventual declaration of Job's innocence. Job has been assaulted by God (16:7-14), which constitutes prima facie evidence of guilt. Here, Job is affirming his innocence by offering a pledge that will be forfeited should he be proved guilty. A minority view is that of MacKenzie and Murphy (477), who think that Job is beseeching God to find a third-party guarantor who will go bail for Job in his presence.

6. The hitp., to pledge stakes in a wager (J. Gray, 682), conveys the sense of reciprocal action and competition (Cogan and Tadmor, 231). The vb. is used of making a wager (2 Kgs 18:23 [par. Isa 36:8], *pace* Watts, 1987, 19-20, who translates "Please negotiate," and Keil, 438, who incorrectly takes the vb. here to be *'rb*, enter [into contest]). Using psychological warfare to undermine resistance, the Assyrian official, the Rabshakeh, possibly Sennacherib's commander-in-chief in the field (cf. e.g., Kaiser, 380; Watts, 1987, 26, 29-30), taunts the three Judahite officials representing King Hezekiah by offering to donate 2,000 horses if Jerusalem's leaders can provide riders for them. Clearly, the Assyrians considered Hezekiah's troops to be not only inadequate numerically but also inexperienced horsemen (J. Gray, 682). Moreover, unlike the Assyrians, Judah and Israel rarely used cavalry in their battles (Hobbs, 257) and

horses were in short supply (cf. Deut 17:16; 1 Kgs 10:28; Isa 31:1, 3). According to Sennacherib's own account in the Taylor Prism (*ANET*, 287-88), there was large-scale desertion from Hezekiah's ranks.

7. In addition to meaning surety (see above on Prov 17:18), the nom. *'^{a}rubbâ* seems to be used of a token. In 1 Sam 17:18, Jesse asks David to bring provisions to his brothers who were serving in the army and to return with *'^{a}rubbātām*, lit., their pledge. Most translations have "some token [from them]," but NIV reads "some assurance" and suggests as an alternative "some pledge of spoils." Kimchi (cited by Goldman, 101) gives the interesting, but unlikely, explanation that David was to redeem the pledge given by his brothers for the supplies that they had borrowed. Another improbable interpretation is that of Schulz (cited by Hertzberg, 150), who maintains that David was being asked to bring the brothers' pay back to their father. Dummelow (191) understands the word to be a reference to some proof that David had fulfilled his mission. In similar vein, TEV has "something to show that you saw them." Many (e.g., Rashi [cited by Goldman, 101]; Kirkpatrick, 156; Kennedy, 124; S. R. Driver, 1966, 142; Wevers, 164; Ackroyd, 141) think the term refers to some agreed sign of the brothers' continued safety and welfare. McKane (110) and Hertzberg (150) understand the token to be confirmation of both the safe delivery of the gifts and the continued safety of the brothers.

8. As indicated above, the nom. *'ērābôn*, pledge, probably occurs in Job 17:3. It is also found in Gen 38:17-18, 20, part of the story about Judah and Tamar (38:1-30). When Judah promised to send her a kid from the flock as payment for intercourse, Tamar asked him for a pledge until he sent it. The pledge agreed upon consisted of Judah's signet, cord, and staff (the insignia of a man of rank; see Skinner, 1969, 454; Simpson, 760; Herbert, 1962, 128; von Rad, 360; Westermann, 53). By retaining these items, Tamar was later able to prove unequivocally and publicly that Judah was the father of her unborn child (v. 25).

9. The phrase *b^{e}nê hatta'^{a}rubôt* (lit., sons of pledges) occurs with the meaning hostages (2 Kgs 14:14 [par. 2 Chron 25:24]). This is the only reference to the taking of hostages in the OT. Cogan and Tadmor (157) draw attention to a similar nominal construction (*kî līṭūtu*, in the state/condition of being a hostage) that occurs in Assyrian royal inscriptions of the twelfth-eighth centuries BC. After he had defeated Amaziah, king of Judah, Jehoash, king of Israel, came to Jerusalem where he damaged a section of the wall, plundered the gold, silver, and other treasures from the temple and palace, and returned with hostages (probably members of the nobility) to Samaria. J. Gray (611) thinks that the hostages were pledges for war indemnity. Keil (383) and La Sor (358) think that the taking of hostages may have been a measure aimed at enforcing peace (cf. Slotki, 247).

P-B In Heb. the vb. *'ārab* means insert, press into, interweave, mix, confuse; substitute, put in place of, vouch for; pi. mix; create a symbolical community of residence or continuity of action; pledge; and hitp. be mixed. In Aram., the vb. *'^{a}rab*, *'^{a}rêb* means vouch for, be surety for; mix; combine; pa. mix; mix up, confound; create a symbolical community of residence or continuity of action; vouch, be surety; itp. be mixed. The nom. bondsman, surety, occurs in both Heb. (*'ārēb*) and in Aram. (*'arbā'*). The Heb. nom. forms *'ērābôn*, *'êrābôn*, and the Aram. *'arbônā'* mean pledge, earnest money;

going security. The Heb. nom. *ʿărēbût* and the Aram. nom. forms *ʿarbûtāʾ* and *ʿărûbtāʾ* mean security, pledge (Jastrow 2:1109-14).

NT The word *arrabōn* occurs twice in 2 Cor (1:22; 5:5) and once in Eph (1:14). Translations of the word vary greatly. Most translators favor either guarantee (RSV; Phillips; TEV; Barclay, 1969, 67) or pledge (Moffatt; NEB; REB; JB; Hodge, 25, 120; Barclay 1956, 196-98; R. P. Martin, 23, 96, 101, 108-9, 116); either alone or in combination with other expressions (e.g., "foretaste and guarantee" [Barclay, 1969, 67; Mitton, 62-64]). Kerr argues persuasively that neither guarantee nor pledge is a good translation of *arrabōn* in the NT texts. After investigating the use of the term in Heb., G, and Roman law, Kerr concludes that the contract for services is more likely to have been the source of the metaphor than contracts of sale. In a contract for services, the person submitting the *arrabōn* is the one for whom the work is to be carried out and the recipient is the person who will do the work. In a contract of sale, the one who gives the *arrabōn* is the purchaser and the recipient is the seller. Whereas it makes sense to think of God giving an *arrabōn* to those who believe in and serve him, it is difficult to envisage a hypothetical transaction in which Christians sell something to God who, as the buyer, gives them an *arrabōn*.

Guarantee is not a suitable translation of *arrabōn* in 2 Cor 1:22; 5:5; Eph 1:14 because in contracts for services, the prospective loss of the *arrabōn* is borne primarily by the person who is to carry out the work, so that if a guarantee were necessitated by economic pressure, it would be primarily one given by the workman. As Kerr points out, this is a position different from that envisaged in the NT texts. Moreover, even if contracts of sale were the source of the metaphor, the fact that God is the purchaser nullifies the need for a guarantee of payment of the full price. As for pledge, the fact that the strict meaning of this word is something that is deposited as security that a promise will be kept and then reclaimed when the promise has been honored, makes it, too, an unsuitable translation of *arrabōn* in 2 Cor 1:22; 5:5; Eph 1:14. It seems likely that some translators render pledge because they have in mind the generalized modern meaning of the word as promise, as when one pledges a sum of money to an institution or a(nother) good cause. However, this meaning of pledge is problematic because it focuses on a promise of a gift yet to come. While there is certainly a gift of God yet to come, as other texts assure us, it is not part of the meaning of *arrabōn*. Whereas in transactions such as gifts the one party has no obligations, *arrabōn* was given in pursuance of contracts in which both parties had obligations. While conceding that there is no English word or phrase that corresponds in all respects to *arrabōn*, Kerr (97) maintains that "a first installment" probably best conveys the correct sense (as Barclay, 1956, 227, 229; 1969, 71; Barrett, 80-81, 149, 157; NRSV [2 Cor 1:22]; Robinson, 36 [installment]; Plummer, 41, 150 [installment]; Furnish, 137, 145, 149, 271, 301 [down payment]; NIV [deposit]).

Pledge, security: → *ʾissār* (binding obligation, pledge, vow of abstention, # 674); → *ḥbl* II (take in pledge, exact a pledge, # 2471); → *ḥôb* (pledge, collateral, # 2550); → *nšʾ* I (lend against a pledge, # 5957); → *ʿbṭ* (borrow, take a pledge from, # 6292); → *ʿrb* I (stand security for, give security for, # 6842); → *piqqādôn* (deposited goods, store, supply, provision, # 7214); → *tqʿ* (drive, thrust, clap one's hands, blow trumpet, pledge, # 9546)

BIBLIOGRAPHY

NIDNTT 2:39-40; *TDNT* 1:475; P. R. Ackroyd, *The First Book of Samuel*, CBC, 1971; W. Barclay, *The Letters to the Corinthians*, DSB, 2nd ed., 1956; idem, *The New Testament: A New Translation. Volume Two: The Letters and the Revelation*, 1969; C. K. Barrett, *A Commentary on the Second Epistle to the Corinthians*, HNTC, 1973; L. W. Batten, *A Critical and Exegetical Commentary on the Books of Ezra and Nehemiah*, ICC, 1961; D. Bergant, *Job, Ecclesiastes*, OTM, 1982; J. Blenkinsopp, *Ezra-Nehemiah: A Commentary*, OTL, 1988; idem, *Ezekiel*, Interpretation, 1990; R. A. Bowman, "The Book of Ezra and the Book of Nehemiah: Introduction and Exegesis," *IB*, 1954, 3:549-819; J. Bright, "Isaiah-I," in *Peake*, 1964, 489-515; idem, *Jeremiah: Introduction, Translation, and Notes*, AB, 1965; L. E. Browne, "Ezra and Nehemiah," in *Peake*, 1964, 370-80; D. J. A. Clines, *Ezra, Nehemiah, Esther*, NCBC, 1984; idem, *Job 1-20*, WBC, 1989; M. Cogan and H. Tadmor, *II Kings: A New Translation With Introduction and Commentary*, AB, 1988; J. J. Collins, *Proverbs, Ecclesiastes*, 1980; M. Dahood, "Accadian-Ugaritic *dmt* in Ezekiel 27:32," *Bib* 45, 1964, 83-84; idem, *Psalms III: 101-150*, AB, 1970; A. B. Davidson, *The Book of Job With Notes, Introduction and Appendix*, CBC, 1962; R. Davidson, *Genesis 12-50*, CBC, 1979; T. W. Davies, *Ezra, Nehemiah and Esther*, CBC, 1909; E. Dhorme, *A Commentary on the Book of Job*, 1967; G. R. Driver, "Difficult Words in the Hebrew Prophets," in H. H. Rowley ed., *Studies in Old Testament Prophecy Presented to Professor Theodore H. Robinson by the Society for Old Testament Study on His Sixty-Fifth Birthday*, 1950, 52-72; S. R. Driver, *The Book of the Prophet Jeremiah: A Revised Translation With Introductions and Short Explanations*, 1906; idem, *Notes on the Hebrew Text and the Topography of the Books of Samuel With an Introduction on Hebrew Palaeography and the Ancient Versions*, 2d ed., 1966; S. R. Driver and G. B. Gray, *A Critical and Exegetical Commentary on the Book of Job Together With a New Translation*, ICC, 1964; J. R. Dummelow, ed., *A Commentary on the Holy Bible*, 1909; J. H. Eaton, *Psalms: Introduction and Commentary*, Torch, 1972; R. S. Franks, "Job," in *Peake*, 1920, 346-65; V. P. Furnish, *II Corinthians Translated With Introduction, Notes, and Commentary*, AB, 1985; J. C. L. Gibson, *Genesis. Volume 2*, DSB, 1982; idem, *Job*, DSB, 1985; S. Goldman, *Samuel: Hebrew Text & English Translation With an Introduction and Commentary*, Soncino, 1962; J. Gray, *I & II Kings: A Commentary*, OTL, 2d ed., 1970; N. C. Habel, *The Book of Job*, OTL, 1975; J. E. Hartley, *The Book of Job*, NICOT, 1988; A. S. Herbert, *Genesis 12-50: Introduction and Commentary*, Torch, 1962; idem, *The Book of the Prophet Isaiah Chapters 1-39*, CBC, 1973; H. W. Hertzberg, *I & II Samuel: A Commentary*, OTL, 1974; T. R. Hobbs, *2 Kings*, WBC, 1985; C. Hodge, *An Exposition of the Second Epistle to the Corinthians*, 1980; E. Jones, *Proverbs and Ecclesiastes: Introduction and Commentary*, Torch, 1961; O. Kaiser, *Isaiah 13-39: A Commentary*, OTL, 1974; C. F. Keil, *The Books of the Kings*, KD, 2d ed., ca. 1872; A. R. S. Kennedy, *Samuel*, 1905; A. Kerr, "APPABΩV," *JTS* (n.s.) 39, 1988, 92-97; A. F. Kirkpatrick, *The First Book of Samuel With Map, Notes and Introduction*, CBSC, 1899; H.-J. Kraus, *Psalms 60-150: A Commentary*, 1989; J. S. Kselman, "Genesis," in *HBC*, 1988, 85-128; W. McKane, *Proverbs: A New Approach*, OTL, 1970; W. S. La Sor, "1 and 2 Kings," in *NBC*, 1972, 320-68; R. A. F. MacKenzie and R. E. Murphy, "Job," in *NJBC*, 1990, 466-88; M. Maher, *Genesis*, OTM, 1982; G. C. Martin, *Proverbs, Ecclesiastes and Song of Songs*, CB, 1908; R. P. Martin, *2 Corinthians*, WBC, 1986; C. L. Mitton, *Ephesians*, NCBC, 1981; J. N. Oswalt, *The Book of Isaiah Chapters 1-39*, NICOT, 1986; A. S. Peake, *Job*, CB, 1905; idem, "Isaiah I-XXXIX," in *Peake*, 1920, 436-59; A. Plummer, *A Critical and Exegetical Commentary on the Second Epistle of St. Paul to the Corinthians*, ICC, 1951; M. H. Pope, *Job: Introduction, Translation, and Notes*, AB, 3d ed., 1979; G. von Rad, *Genesis: A Commentary*, OTL, 3d ed., 1972; J. A. Robinson,

St. Paul's Epistle to the Ephesians: A Revised Text and Translation With Exposition and Notes, 2d ed., 1904; C. R. Seitz, *Isaiah 1-39*, Interpretation, 1993; C. A. Simpson, "The Book of Genesis: Introduction and Exegesis," *IB*, 1952, 1:437-829; J. Skinner, *The Book of the Prophet Isaiah Chapters I-XXXIX*, CBSC, 1909; idem, *A Critical and Exegetical Commentary on Genesis*, ICC, 2d ed., 1969; I. W. Slotki, *Kings: Hebrew Text & English Translation With an Introduction and Commentary*, Soncino, 1961; E. A. Speiser, *Genesis: Introduction, Translation, and Notes*, AB, 1964; J. Strahan, *The Book of Job Interpreted*, 1913; M. E. Tate, "Proverbs," in *BBC*, 1972, 5:1-99; S. Terrien, "The Book of Job: Introduction and Exegesis," *IB*, 1954, 3:875-1198; C. H. Thomson and J. Skinner, *Isaiah I-XXXIX*, 1921; J. D. W. Watts, et al., "Job," in *BBC*, 1972, 4:22-151; idem, *Isaiah 34-66*, WBC, 1987; C. Westermann, *Genesis 37-50: A Commentary*, 1986; J. W. Wevers, "The First Book of Samuel," in *The Interpreter's One-Volume Commentary on the Bible*, 1971, 155-69; W. Zimmerli, *Ezekiel 2: A Commentary on the Book of the Prophet Ezekiel Chapters 25-48*, Hermeneia, 1983.

Robin Wakely

6843	ערב

ערב (*'rb* II), associate with; mingle with; be intermixed with (# 6843); עֵרֶב (*'ēreb* I), knitted material (→ # 6849); עֵרֶב (*'ēreb* II), mixture, mixed company (# 6850); עָרֹב (*'ārōb*), swarm of insects (→ # 6856).

OT 1. The vb. appears in the hitp. in Ezra 9:2 in the context of concern about those who "have mingled the holy race with the peoples around them," referring to the offspring of Israelites who married non-Israelites. Such a mixing is evidence of faithlessness. See also Ps 106:35, where the Israelites are described as having mixed themselves with the (Canaanite) nations. This mixing led to idolatry and other non-Yahwistic practices within the Israelite community. Where mixing takes on a specifically negative connotation, it is in the context of a threat to Yahwistic faith.

2. The nom. *'ēreb* (# 6850) appears in Exod 12:38 in reference to a miscellaneous collection of people distinct from Israel that joined them in the Exodus from Egypt. In Neh 13:1-3 it refers to descendants of the Moabites and Ammonites (and other foreigners) who settled among Israel but now must be separated out because the Israelites, having read the law, learned that transgressions on the part of some of their ancestors prohibited their participation in Israel. In Jer 25:20, 24 (the latter may be the result of dittography) the nom. appears on a list of condemned kingdoms, which includes all of the nations on earth including Judah. An oracle there against Babylon finds the mixed people (foreigners, NIV) within Babylon caught up in the condemnation. Ezek 30:5 has a similar list (Syr. reads "Arab"). 1 Kgs 10:15 records that Solomon received tribute (or gifts) from the kings of the mixed people. The parallel text in 2 Chron 9:14 reads "Arabs" and *BHS* suggests "Arabs." The nom. appears to refer to people of assorted ethnic groups and is a neutral term in these texts, except for the late text in Nehemiah, where the mixed people (non-Israelites) are excluded from Israel.

The reason for the exclusion in the postexilic period was the fact that the Ammonites and Moabites had refused to provide food and drink to Israel in the desert and, in addition, had hired Balaam to curse Israel (Neh 13:2; cf. Num 22:3-11; Deut 23:3-5). Implicit, however, is the impurity of these peoples by virtue of their descent from the incestuous relationship of Lot and his daughters (Gen 19:30-38). They were, thus, a mixed people with whom intermarriage would contaminate the covenant nation as it, indeed, had done throughout Israel's history (Neh 13:23-27). The Lord had commanded his elect people to be holy as he was holy (Lev 19:1-4), a state that would be impossible were they to enter into marriage and other relationships with the unbelieving nations (Exod 34:16; Deut 7:3).

Association, cleaving, companionship: → *dbq* (stick, cling, cleave, pursue, # 1815); → *ḥōbᵉlîm* (union, # 2482); → *ḥbr* II (unite, be joined, charm, make an ally, # 2489); → *yḥd* (be united, # 3479); → *lwh* I (accompany, join, attach oneself, # 4277); → *spḥ* I (attach, associate, join oneself, # 6202); → *'rb* II (associate with, mingle with, be intermixed with, # 6843); → *r'h* II (associate with, be best man, make friends with, # 8287); → *šlb* (joined, dovetailed, # 8917)
Mixing, mingling, mixture: → *bll* (confuse, mix, # 1176); → *kil'ayim* (two kinds, # 3977); → *msk* (mix, # 5007); → *'rb* II (associate with, mingle with, be intermixed with, # 6843); → *rbk* (stirred, mixed, # 8057); → *rqḥ* (blend, mix, # 8379)

Wilma A. Bailey/ Eugene Merrill

6844	ערב

ערב (*'rb* III), q. be pleasant or agreeable; please; be well-pleasing or liked (# 6844); עָרֵב (*'ārēb*), adj. pleasant, agreeable (# 6853).

ANE This root is attested in Mish. Heb. as a vb. *'rb*, be sweet, agreeable, or pleasant; sweeten, gladden, or humor; and cause to be sweet or pleasing, and as an adj. *'ārēb*, agreeable, or *'ārîb*, spiced, sweet, or pleasing (Jastrow 2:1110-11; *HALAT* 830, 832); cf. Arab. *'aru/ib*, it fits or suits (*HALAT* 830). Klein notes that this word is of uncertain etymology and that it might be a special development of *'rb* II, mix, with the meaning, be well mixed, be duly arranged (484).

OT 1. *Distribution.* The vb. *'rb* occurs 8x in the OT in prophetic literature (2x in Jer, 1x each in Ezek, Mal, and Hos) and in the Wisdom literature (2x in Prov and 1x in Ps). The adj. *'ārêb* occurs 2x in the OT, exclusively in Wisdom literature (1x in Prov and 1x in S of Songs).

2. *Verb.* The vb. appears only in the q. stem. It captures the positive emotional response to some happening in life. This happening can be pleasing to self, as in sleep (Jer 31:26; Prov 3:24) or a realized desire (Prov 13:19), or it can be pleasing to another (exclusively God), as in one's meditation (Ps 104:34), grain offering (Mal 3:4), or sacrifices (Jer 6:20; Hos 9:4).

The term implies that one moves in a direction very strongly. As used in Prov 13:19, Kidner notes that "the lesson of the proverb is that to set your heart on a thing is to weaken the power to assess it" (104). It speaks of the type of emotional response that may blind one to the realities and responsibilities of life. When one uses this term to describe the heart set on something, it implies that the grip is difficult to loosen. However, this proverb generates much controversy. Toy suggests that each line has lost its parallel line, so that we have two incomplete proverbs (274). Perowne does not see a weakening of power to assess as does Kidner; rather, he concludes that fools are simply that, fools, and they do not move toward the sweetness of good desires (103). However, Scott supports Kidner and even suggests changing the text (95). McKane notes that "'pleasurable to a *nepeš*' is a metaphor which has its basis in the sensation of appetizing food" (459). There is somewhat of a parallel in Prov 13:12, which contrasts the emotions of fulfillment and unfulfillment. Both verses clearly demonstrate that to realize a desire is good. Therefore, this word connotes emotion and indicates a strong appraisal, whether it be a positive one (Ps 104:34; Mal 3:4) or a negative one (Jer 6:20; Hos 9:4).

The word also has a satisfying component to it. It is used 2x in the context of sleep (Prov 3:24; Jer 31:26). In Prov 3:24, it is paralleled with "you will not be afraid." It implies that one is at peace. In Jer 31:26, the text is obscure. Bright (282-83), Feinberg (572-73), and Thompson (577) give a good summary of the proposals of the meaning. Feinberg concludes that sleep/dream was sweet because "the truths received in them were comforting foreviews of future glory for God's people (contrast the disappointing dreams in Isa 29:8; cf. Prov 3:24)" (573). The idea of future glory was satisfying to consider. Also in the passages that involve God, the satisfaction theme is prominent (Ps 104:34; Mal 3:4; Jer 6:20; Hos 9:4). God is either satisfied (which brings blessing) or he is not satisfied (which brings judgment).

Furthermore, the word has a moral component to it. The happening is not simply pleasing in and of itself. It is often tied to the uprightness of the heart. In Ps 104:34, the meditation will be pleasing not simply because it is a good meditation, but because of the life of the one who offers the meditation. He is one who sings praise (v. 33), is contrasted to the sinners and the wicked (v. 35), and is glad in the Lord (v. 34). In Mal 3:4; Jer 6:20; Hos 9:4, the acceptability or unacceptability of the sacrifices is not based on the sacrifices themselves, but rather on the obedient lifestyle of the ones who offer them. It does not matter how much the sacrifice might cost (i.e., imported incense and sweet cane or the amount of the sacrifice that is for the Lord), when sin is not forsaken, the sacrifices are worthless. Feinberg notes, "In themselves, sacrifices were never efficacious; all the prophets who speak of them as used in heartless worship deny their validity (cf. Isa 1:11-13; Jer 7:21-23; Hos 6:6; Amos 5:21-27; Mic 6:6-8)" (424). This is also evidenced in Prov 3:24, where the sleep is pleasant not simply because of sleep itself, but also because of one's finding (v. 13) and keeping (v. 21) wisdom. Therefore, the favorability of the happening is not simply a result of the moment, but also of the character of the individual who participates.

Holladay refers to this term as a technical term from the cult "used by priests in announcing the sacrifice worthy" (223). Von Rad also holds to this (261, n. 170).

There is some debate as to whether or not Hos 9:4 uses this root. *HALAT* does not include it, whereas Even-Shoshan does (the LXX supports Even-Shoshan). *HALAT* proposes that the term in Hos 9:4 belongs to a separate root, *'rb* IV, offer or present (830). Others follow this proposal (cf. Holladay, 223; Mays, 124; Driver, 64; Stuart, 140). This proposal is strengthened by the fact that in Hos 9:4, the term is paralleled with *nsk*, pour out (# 5818).

3. *Nom.* The adj. *'ārēb* conveys the positive emotional response one has to an object in life. The objects are bread (Prov 20:17) and another's voice (S of Songs 2:14). In both instances the object appeals to the senses, providing favorable emotions. In Prov 20:17, the response is a physical one coupled with moral implications, for the favorableness of the bread is only temporary in that it is stolen and the person will be found out (cf. Prov 9:17). The satisfaction expressed here is not complete apart from a pure heart.

P-B In the LXX, the G translates the term basically by three words that reflect different nuances: *areskō* (please, be pleasing/acceptable, Mal 3:4), *hēdys* (sweet, gladly; Prov 3:24; S of Songs 2:14; Jer 31:26[25]), and *hēduō* (sweeten, season, Prov 20:17; Ps 104:34; Jer 6:20; Hos 9:4).

Desire, coveting, craving, delight, happiness, longing, pleasure: → *'ᵃrešet* (desire, request, # 830); → *ḥmd* (desire, crave, long for, covet, treasure, # 2773); → *ḥpṣ* I (want, desire, wish, care, # 2911); → *ḥšq* (desire, longing, lust, # 3137); → *y'b* (long for, yearn, desire, # 3277); → *kāleh* (longing, # 3985); → *kmh* (long after, lust for, # 4014); → *ksp* II (desire, long after, # 4083); → *môrāš* II (wish, desire, # 4626); → *'rg* (long after, pant after, # 6864); → *š'l* (ask, request, wish, # 8626); → *t'b* I (desire, long after, # 9289); → *tᵉšûqâ* (desire, longing, appetite, # 9592)

BIBLIOGRAPHY

NIDNTT 1:456; *TDNT* 1:455-57; 2:909-26; J. Bright, *Jeremiah*, AB, 1965; G. R. Driver, *Studies in Old Testament Prophecy*, ed. by H. H. Rowley, 1950; A. Even-Shoshan, *A New Concordance of the Bible,* 1993; C. Feinberg, "Jeremiah," *EBC*, 1986; W. Holladay, *A Commentary on the Book of the Prophet Jeremiah*, Hermeneia, 1986; D. Kidner, *The Proverbs,* TOTC, 1964; E. Klein, *A Comprehensive Etymological Dictionary of the Hebrew Language for Readers of English*, 1987; J. L. Mays, *Hosea*, OTL, 1967; W. McKane, *Proverbs*, OTL, 1970; T. T. Perowne, *The Proverbs*, 1899; R. B. Y. Scott, *Proverbs, Ecclesiastes,* 1965; D. Stuart, *Hosea Jonah*, WBC, 1987; J. A. Thompson, *The Book of Jeremiah,* NICOT, 1980; C. H. Toy, *A Critical and Exegetical Commentary on the Book of Proverbs,* ICC, 1899; G. von Rad, *OTT*, vol. I, 1962.

David Talley

6845 (*'rb* V, become evening), → # 1332

6847 (*'ereb* I, evening), → # 1332

6849	עֵרֶב

עֵרֶב (*'ēreb* I), nom. knitted material (# 6849).

ANE. Common Sem. *'rb*, enter, i.e., a shuttle entering between the vertical thread on a loom.

OT Along with *šᵉtî* (→ # 9274), this technical term alluding to the woven or knitted fabric occurs 9x in Lev 13:48-59. In the KJV, RSV, NASB, and others the pair is translated warp and woof. In the NIV and NAB they are "woven and knitted material." The pericope has to do with clothing contaminated with mildew. Milgrom, however, addresses the question of whether the mold could develop in threads in just one direction and argues that it can (*Leviticus 1-16*, AB, 809; cf. N. Snaith, *Leviticus and Numbers*, NCB, 1967, 98). Mildew, like sin, must be arrested before it spreads and contaminates the whole. Compare Paul's references to yeast in 1 Cor 5:6-8; Gal 5:9.

Spinning, sewing, weaving, embroidering: → *'rg* (spin, weave, # 755); → *dallâ* I (hair, thrum, loom, # 1929); → *ḥōšēb* (weaver, # 3110); → *ṭwh* (spin, # 3211); → *kîšôr* (distaff, # 3969); → *mānôr* (rod, # 4962); → *skk* II (weave, intertwine, # 6115); → *'ēreb* I (knitted material, # 6849); → *pelek* I (spindle-whorl, # 7134); → *rqm* (embroider, weave together, # 8387); → *śᵉrād* (woven, # 8573); → *šbṣ* I (weave, # 8687); → *šᵉtî* I (woven material, # 9274); → *tpr* (sew, # 9529)

Robert L. Alden

6850 (*'ēreb* II, mixture, mixed company), → # 6843

6851 (*'ᵃrab*, Arabia), → Arabia

6853 (*'ārēb*, pleasant), → # 6844

6854	עֹרֵב

עֹרֵב (*'ōrēb* I), raven (# 6854).

ANE Sem. cognates occur in Akk. *āribu/ēribu*, Syr., Mand. *'urba*, Aram. *ôrbā'*, *ôrabtā'*, and Eth. *qura(b)*.

OT In the OT this word appears 10x and is regarded as an unclean bird (Lev 11:15). Ravens first appear in OT when Noah sought to know if the flood had abated (Gen 8:7).

1. In 1 Kgs 17:4, 6 the ravens are ordered by God to feed Elijah when he was in the river of Kerith. Though some medieval lexicographers took this Heb. word as referring to people (merchants) and not birds, perhaps because of the notion that Elijah is fed by the unclean birds, there is no need to take it that way. Moreover, the fact the ch. 17 presents three scenes in which Elijah makes contact with the increasing degrees of death also supports the view that the term refers to ravens.

2. In the judgment oracle in which Isa 34:11 occurs, the raven is an instrument of judgment along with unclean animals, such as the *qippōd*, hedgehog/owl (?) (→ # 7887).

3. In the so-called Wisdom literature the ravens are an object of God's providential care (Job 38:41; cf. Ps 147:9), though apparently it is an instrument of punishment in Prov 30:17.

P-B LXX renders this word as *korax,* which occurs in the NT only in Luke 12:24. In RL rabbis, in the *haggadah*, interpreted God's providential care for the ravens as originating in their cruelty toward their young (e.g., LevR 19,1).

Birds, flying creatures: → *'br* (fly, # 87); → *bêṣâ* (egg, # 1070); → *barbur* (species of fowl, # 1350); → *gôzāl* (young bird, # 1578); → *dgr* (hatch eggs, # 1842); → *ḥᵃsîdâ* (stork, # 2884); → *yônâ* I (dove, # 3433); → *yaᶜᵃnâ* (ostrich, eagle-owl?, # 3613); → *kānāp* (wing, skirt, outermost edge, # 4053); → *nešer/nᵉšar* (vulture [eagle], # 5979); → *'ôp* (flying creatures, # 6416); → *'ayiṭ* (birds of prey [collective], # 6514); → *'ōrēb* I (raven, # 6854); → *ṣippôr* I (birds, # 7606); → *qōrē'* I (partridge, # 7926); → *śᵉlāw* (quails, # 8513)

BIBLIOGRAPHY

EMiqr 6:362-64; Str-B 2:191; N. Kiuchi, "Elijah's Self-Offering: 1 Kgs 17:21," *Bib* 75, 1994, 74-79.

N. Kiuchi

6856	עָרֹב

עָרֹב (*'ārōb*), nom. fly/flies; destructive swarm of flies, various flying insects (?) (# 6856); < ערב (*'rb* II, mingle, → # 6843).

ANE Sam. *'ārᵉb*; Jewish Aram. *'rwb'*; Akk. *urbattu* (synonym of *tultu*, worm); Syr. *'arrûbā*, swarm of vermin and insects.

OT 1. This word is found 9x in the OT. Every use is tied to the fourth plague of flies (Exod 8:20-32[16-28]; Ps 78:45; 105:31). The species of fly is uncertain (cf. *z^e^bûb*, possibly a common housefly). Its scientific classification is usually given as *Stomoxys calitrans,* the bearer possibly of the sixth plague of boils. Their appearance in Egypt was miraculous (Ps 105:31) and so was their absence from Goshen.

Some argue in favor of translating this word as mosquito or gnat (*IDB* 2:255). Exactness is not possible, but the term from *'rb*, mingle with, be intermixed with, may indicate a swarm of mixed insects. Ps 78:45 explains that a swarm of flies bit/devoured the Egyptians. It is possible that the *'ārōb*, swarm, included gnats (*kēn*), featured in plague three.

2. Nine words are used only once or twice to indicate various insects. While their use is limited, sometimes the moral, ethical, and religious teachings accompanying their use is highly significant:

(a) *z^e^bûb*, nom. fly (# 2279). The fly (*z^e^bûb*) refers to Egypt (parallel *d^e^bôrâ* [# 1808], bee = Assyria) in Isa 7:18 as God's avenging instrument against an unbelieving Ahaz/Judah. The corrupting influence of folly's effect on wisdom and honor is likened to dead flies in perfume; though it may be small, folly can detract greatly from wisdom/honor (Eccl 10:1). The people in Ekron had a god named Baal-Zebub, lord of the fly (2 Kgs 1:2-3).

(b) *zîz*, nom. small (ravaging) creatures of the field (# 2328). "Creatures of the field" (Ps 50:11; 80:13[14]) is used in parallelism with "bird" (*'ôp*) of the mountains to indicate the Lord's ownership of all animal and insect life (cf. 50:14-15). The word refers to nations/peoples who ravage the Lord's nation from Egypt (80:13[14]).

(c) *n^e^mālâ*, nom. ant (# 5805). The ways (Prov 6:6) of the ant are an object lesson to make the sluggard wise. Ants wisely store up their food when possible (30:25).

(d) *'akkābîš*, nom. spider (# 6571); *qûr*, nom. spider web (# 7770). Bildad, implicating Job, asserts that the one who does not remember God has as fragile a ground of trust as "spider web" (Job 8:14; cf. 27:18). Isaiah depicts the sorry state of his sinful people and compares their deeds to spider webs (Isa 59:5-6).

(e) *'^a^lûqâ*, nom. leech (# 6598). The leech (Prov 30:15a) becomes a symbol of things that are never satisfied and introduces the 3 + 4 statement about the grave, barren womb, dry land, fire—all never say "Enough" (30:15b-16).

(f) *par'ōš*, nom. flea (# 7282). David disparagingly, and in overstatement, ridicules Saul for coming after him and for regarding him as a mere flea to be dealt with (1 Sam 24:14[15]; 26:20).

(g) *qereṣ*, nom. gadfly (# 7976). The gadfly represents Nebuchadnezzar as he is coming against Egypt to judge her (Jer 46:20).

P-B These words were employed with little or no changes in meaning. For refs., in order discussed above, see Jastrow 1:393; 2:913, 1028, 1425, 1236, 1081, 1009.

NT Jesus referred to the moth to illustrate the instability and ephemeral nature of earthly treasures (Matt 6:19, 20; Luke 12:33; cf. worms, Mark 9:48; Act 12:33; 2 Tim 3:6). In thc NT thc most infamous usc of thc fly is in the name Beelzebub = OT *ba'al z^e^bûb*. It is a name for the devil or the prince of demons (e.g., Matt 10:25; Mark 3:22; Luke 11:19), lit. "lord of flies."

Insects: → *d^ebôrâ* I (bee, wasp, # 1805); → *kēn* V (mosquito, gnat, louse, # 4031); → *'ṭh* II (delouse, # 6487); → *'aqrāb* (scorpion, # 6832); → *'ārōb* (fly, swarm of flies, flying insects, # 6856); → *'āš* I (moth, # 6931); → *ṣir'â* (hornet, destruction, fear, terror, depression, discouragement, # 7667); → *qml* (wither, become moldy, musty, infected w. insects, # 7857)

BIBLIOGRAPHY
IDB 2:246-56, 303, 403-4; 3:144-48; G. Hort, "The Plagues of Egypt," *ZAW* 69, 1957, 84-103; 70, 1958, 48-59; *Fauna and Flora of the Bible*, 1980[2].

Eugene Carpenter/Michael A. Grisanti

6857 (*'ᵃrābâ* I, poplar), → # 6770

6858	עֲרָבָה

עֲרָבָה (*'ᵃrābâ* III), steppe (60x) (# 6858).

OT As a synonym of *midbār*, *'ᵃrābâ* III remains unclear in its precise semantic distinction. For disputed etymology and representation in cognate languages, see *HALAT* 832-33 and BDB, 787; *TWAT* 4:666-67; for antonyms see *THAT* 1:58. Theological importance lies not so much in its lexical and geographical reference as in its thematic associations. For this see the developed thematic discussion on Desert; Arabah: Theology

Desert, wilderness, wasteland: → *bōhû* (waste, # 983); → *bqq* I (lay waste, be agitated, # 1327); → *ḥorbâ* (ruin, waste, # 2999); → *y^ešîmôn* (wilderness, waste, # 3810); → *midbār* I (wilderness, # 4497); → *'ᵃrābâ* III (steppe, # 6858); → *ṣ^eḥîḥâ* (scorched land, # 7461); → *ṣiyyâ* (desert, # 7480); → *š'h* I (lie waste, make s. th. into desolate, # 8615); → *šmm* (be desolate, deserted, lay waste, shudder, be horrified, # 9037); → **Desert: Theology**

A. R. Pete Diamond

6859 (*'ᵃrubbâ*, pledge, security), → # 6842

6860 (*'ērābôn*, security), → # 6842

6861 (*'ᵃrāb*, *'arbî*, Arab[s], Arabian, nomad), → Arabia

6864	ערג

ערג (*'rg*), q. long after, pant after (# 6864).

ANE A cognate may be the Arab. *'rǧ*, mount, ascend; cf. Eth. *'arga*, ascend, come/go up.

OT The vb. is used 3x in the q. impf. forms. It is used metaphorically to describe the soul's longing after God in par. with the deer's longing after flowing streams [Ps 42:1[2] (2x)]. Made in God's image, human beings find their ultimate life in the presence of God and his word (cf. Deut 8:3; Eccl 12:13). It has been suggested that the word could be translated cry out, but on weak contextual evidence. Wild animals in utter despair, when streams of water are dried up, pant after (*'rg*) God, the final source of life (Joel 1:20).

Desire, coveting, craving, delight, happiness, longing, pleasure: → *'ᵃrešet* (desire, request, # 830); → *ḥmd* (desire, crave, long for, covet, treasure, # 2773); → *ḥpṣ* I (want, desire, wish, care, # 2911); → *ḥšq* (desire, longing, lust, # 3137); → *y'b* (long for, yearn, desire, # 3277);

→ *kāleh* (longing, # 3985); → *kmh* (long after, lust for, # 4014); → *ksp* II (desire, long after, # 4083); → *môrāš* II (wish, desire, # 4626); → *'rg* (long after, pant after, # 6864); → *š'l* (ask, request, wish, # 8626); → *t'b* I (desire, long after, # 9289); → *t^e^šûqâ* (desire, longing, appetite, # 9592)

Eugene Carpenter/Michael A. Grisanti

6867	ערה

ערה (*'rh*), q. make (o.s.) bare; ni. be poured out; pi. pour out, make bare; hi. expose; hitp. stripped naked (# 6867); עֶרְוָה (*'erwâ*), nakedness, genitals, shame; euphemism for sexual intercourse (uncover the nakedness), curse formula (to the shame of your mother's nakedness), indecency (shameful thing) (# 6872); עֶרְיָה (*'eryâ*), nakedness, bareness (# 6880).

Related forms: ערר (*'rr*), polel, strip bare; hitpalp., be leveled (# 6910); מַעַר, מַעֲרֶה (*ma'ar, ma'^a^reh*), nom. bare place (# 5113, # 5116); עַרְעָר (*'ar'ār* I), adj., destitute (# 6899), עֲרִירִי (*'^a^rîrî*), adj., childless (→ # 6884). Texts with *'rr* are so designated below.

ANE 1. The root *'rh* is well attested in the cognates. Ugar. *'rw*, take off one's clothes, expose oneself (*HALAT* 834b); Aram. *'rh*, (ni.) be poured out, (pi.) lay bare, (hi.) expose, (hitp.) expose oneself (*HAD*, 213); Phoen. *'ry*, uncover, expose (*DISO*, 221); Akk. *erû/arû*, take off one's clothes (*AHw*, 247); Arab. *'ariya*, be naked (Wehr, 608-9).

2. The nom. *'erwâ* is well attested in the other cognate languages. Ugar. *'ry*, naked (*WUS*, # 2097); Phoen. *'ry*, strip (*DISO*, 221); Aram. nakedness, exposedness, genital (area), sexual organ; with *dābār* (*'erwat d^e^bar*) indecency (*HAD*, 213); Sam. nakedness (*HALAT* 835a); Akk. *ūru(m)* II or *urû*, nakedness, shame (*AHw*, 1435a); Arab. six forms of root *'ry* with meanings of naked, bare (fig. & nonfig.) (Wehr, 608-9). The related *'eryâ* is found in Aram. *'ery^e^tā'*, nakedness, nudity (*HALAT* 836b), and *'erwâ*, nakedness, bareness (*HAD*, 213).

3. The vb. *'rr* II (BDB, 792b, strip oneself; *HALAT* 841b, take one's clothes off) is a secondary form from *'rh*, with Aram. cognate *'rr*, strip oneself, lay bare, demolish (*HAD* 214).

OT 1. The vb. *'rh* occurs 16x in the OT, in five of the vb. stems and in every division (Pent. [3x], Hist. [1x], Poetry [4x], Prophets [8x]). It means to make bare or pour out, both nonfiguratively (expose a shield, strip the clothes off someone) and figuratively (stripped in judgment, the Spirit poured out).

2. *Make bare.* Objects can be made bare. A shield is uncovered in Isa 22:6 (pi.). Babylonian fortresses are stripped bare by the Assyrians (23:13, *'rr* polel), and their thick wall will be leveled (Jer 51:58, *'rr*, hitpalp.). Ps 137:7 has pi. *'rh* in a clever nonfigurative/figurative double usage, with Edom imploring Babylon (2x) to "bare" Jerusalem at her destruction, meaning both to "raze" (lay bare foundations = tear down walls) (Anderson, 900; Briggs 2:486) and to shame her (as prisoners were shamed through baring their buttocks, cf. Isa 20:4). Dahood's "strip her, strip her ... to her buttocks" (3:273) stresses the latter meaning.

Persons can also be bared. In Lev a man exposes the source of blood in a menstruating woman by having sexual relations with her during her period (20:18 [hi.] ‖ *glh*, → # 1655). Having relations with a close relative is forbidden (20:19 [hi.] ‖ *glh*,

→ # 1655) because that would "lay bare one's own flesh" (NRSV; dishonor a close relative, NIV). In Ps 141:8 (pi.) the writer asks God not to leave his soul destitute (abandoned). In Lam 4:21 the nation Edom will be drunk and stripped naked (decimated) (hitp.) by Yahweh in judgment.

3. *Pour out.* A pitcher of water (Gen 24:20) and a chest (2 Chron 24:11) (both pi.) are poured out or emptied. In a related figurative use, the Messiah poured out his life unto death (Isa 53:12, hi.) or "exposed his soul unto death; he voluntarily laid it bare, even to death" (Young 3:359). The Spirit is also "poured out" after God's judgment, turning the desert into a fertile field (abundance) (Isa 32:15, ni.) (Oswalt, 588). But the Messiah and Spirit are poured out (*'rh*) in Isaiah only after Israel is bared (*'rh*) in judgment. In 20:3 God had commanded Isaiah to go about barefoot and naked (see *'ārôm*, # 6873) as a sign of judgment. In 32:11 the prophet warns the rich to strip (*pšṭ*, # 7320) and make themselves bare (q. *'rh*) in light of God's wrath, which will leave the land a waste until the Spirit is "poured out" and abundance returns. This outpouring brings about "a reversal of the present condition, a renewal that is, indeed, revolutionary, the very opposite of the condition described (earlier)" (Young 2:399).

4. *Other.* In Ps 37:35 (hitp.) *'rh* describes a wicked man temporarily flourishing (spreading/exposing himself?) like a green tree. The apparent nom. pl. of *'ārâ* (*'ārôt*) in Isa 19:7 is problematic. BDB "bare place" (788b) and Kelly "meadows" (187) keep the idea of "bare." NIV plants, Clements (lotus, 168), and Bultema (paper reeds, 196) all translate *'ārôt* to make contextual sense, where Yahweh's judgment on Egypt will cause the reeds, rushes, and *'ārôt* to dry up, even at the mouth of the Nile. Young comments, "*'ārôt* is a strong word and apparently refers to naked or bare places. These have often been assumed to be open meadows. . . . Probably the Heb. word may reflect the Egyp. word *'r*, which means papyrus, and thus the reference would be to those places where the papyrus grows" (2:22). If this is correct, the word probably means "reed" (*HALAT* 835a).

5. The nom. *ma'ar* or *ma'areh*, bare place, is used for space on a vessel available to be decorated (1 Kgs 7:36) and the open space of Geba (Judg 20:33). Nahum (3:5) uses *ma'ar* for the nakedness (*qālôn* II, shame, # 7830) of Nineveh that the nations will see when God "lifts (her) skirt over (her) face," referring to the capture and subsequent humiliation of its surviving inhabitants (Roberts, 73).

6. The word *'erwâ* occurs 55x in the OT (Lev [32x], rest of Pent. [9x], 1 Sam [1x], Ezra (Aram. *'arwâ*, 1x, Prophets [12x]). Apart from Lev, where it stands for sexual intercourse (with pi. *glh*, uncover → # 1655), it is used of nakedness/genitals or the closely related shame, or related figurative meanings. The later *'eryâ* is found only 6x, but always in the Prophets with the idea of nakedness or bare as judgment for covenantal disobedience.

(a) Nakedness/genitals. The Pent. uses *'erwâ* for Noah's nakedness in drunken stupor (Gen 9:22-23; see also discussion below); priests' nakedness, which must be concealed (Exod 20:26; 28:42); unprotected land (Gen 42:9, 12); indecent thing (with *dābār*), meaning excrement (Deut 23:14[15]); again indecent thing (*'erwat dābār*) as grounds for divorce (Deut 24:1: not just *'erwâ*, scandalous conduct, but *'erwat dābār*, something indecent, [Jastrow, 1114-15]).

(b) Sexual intercourse. All references in Lev (usually with pi. *glh*, uncover [# 1655]) are euphemisms for sexual intercourse. "The phrase covers intercourse within marriage and outside it. Effectively then these rules define the limits within which a man may seek a wife for himself" (Wenham, 253; cf. Harrison, 186). In contrast to the practices in Egypt and Canaan, God did not permit the Israelites to have intercourse with close blood relatives or women connected through marriage. Thus, the prohibitions against "uncovering the nakedness" of one's mother (18:7), stepmother (18:8), sister (or perhaps half sister) (18:9), granddaughter (18:10), step sister (18:11), paternal and maternal aunts (18:12-14; 20:19-20), daughter-in-law (18:15), or sister-in-law (18:16; 20:21; see Deut 25:5-10 for exception in order to continue the family name). Conspicuous by its absence in this list is the daughter, perhaps because it is understood (cf. account of Lot and daughters in Gen 19:30-38).

In addition to forbidding these close familial relationships, a man must also avoid intercourse with both a woman and her close relatives: daughter (Lev 18:17a, not listed in vv. 7-16), granddaughter (18:17b), sister (18:18; cf. Jacob's earlier troubles with Leah and Rachel in Gen 29-30). He must also abstain from a woman during her menstrual period (Lev 18:19) because of her ritual impurity (cf. 12:2, 5).

These relationships are prohibited because the woman's nakedness literally "belongs to" her husband (Noth, 135) (Lev 18:7, 8, 14, 16; 20:11, 20-21). The phrase has also been understood to mean "she is one with" (Wenham, 254-55). Marriage creates a vertical blood relationship from parent to child and a horizontal relationship between spouses that must not be violated by intercourse (Wenham, 255). Violation of one of these relationships is wickedness (18:17), and the statute should be obeyed because of the special position that the people of God have (18:6). In 20:7-27 the prescribed penalty is death for various sins, including these illicit relationships.

Normally *'erwâ* is used with *glh* in Lev. Only in 20:17 does the author use *r'h* (→ # 8011) of a husband marrying his half sister and each seeing the other's nakedness, again a euphemism for intercourse. Although "see" here means the same as "uncover," this usage along with Ezek 16:37, supports the argument that when Ham saw (*r'h*) Noah's nakedness (Gen 9:22-23), he performed a homosexual act (von Rad, 133). Basset suggests incest between Ham and his mother, but most understand the act as that of looking on his father's nakedness (Cassuto, 151-53; Speiser, 61). Westermann (488) points out that in the Ugar. myth "The Tale of Aqht," a dutiful son is one "who takes (his father) by the hand when he is drunk, carries him when he is sated with wine" (*ANET*, 150a). This ref. supports the understanding that Ham did indeed commit a grave breach of custom in not covering his drunken father, but rather left him in his nakedness to go outside and tell his brothers (cf. also Isa 51:18).

(c) The lexeme *'erwâ* is used in historical and prophetic books most often for dishonor, shame, usually referring to covenantal disobedience. Hab 3:9 (*'rr*) speaks of the Lord uncovering the "nakedness" of his bow (preparing for war to enact judgment). Note also the curse formula in 1 Sam 20:30, "to the shame of your mother's nakedness" (lit.), a comment intended to insult the character of the recipient (Jonathan) rather than his mother (the speaker's wife)!

The word most often refers to Israel's dishonor and shame for their disobedience to their covenant with the Lord. Yahweh had promised that Israel would suffer nakedness (*'êrôm*, # 6567) along with hunger, thirst, and poverty if they did not keep the covenant (Deut 28:48). The prophets frequently use *'erwâ* and *'eryâ* to describe how this curse would or did come true. "Nakedness" refers to vulnerable or conquered

Israel (Ezek 16:39; 23:29 [both *'rr* with *'êrôm*], Mic 1:11 [*'rr* with *bōšet*, shame, # 1425]; Hos 2:9[11] [only here used with pi. *ksh*, cover → # 4059]). Shame is used for prisoners led away with bare buttocks (Isa 20:4) or decimated Jerusalem (Lam 1:8), or the shame of Israel's prostitution (unfaithfulness to the Lord) (Ezek 23:29). Like Leviticus Ezekiel uses *'erwâ* with *glh*, uncover, as a euphemism for sexual intercourse (22:10) and a figure of Israel's unfaithfulness to the Deuteuronomic covenant.

Dishonor without the covenantal meaning appears in Ezra 4:14, where the Persian king faces "dishonor" if Jerusalem rebels. A less negative connotation is found in Ezekiel's allegory in ch. 16, where God contrasts a mature and prosperous Israel with its earlier state of being naked and bare (innocent, unprotected) (Ezek 16:7, 22; both *'eryâ* with *'êrôm*).

The close connection of shame to nakedness after the early chapters of Gen demonstrates that the OT understanding that being naked outside of marriage was always shameful. Nakedness was not tolerated outside of proper sexual relationships (*TWOT* 2:1692). The frequent usage in the Prophets attests to the fulfillment of the deut. curse for covenantal disobedience.

7. The idea of "bare" as "destitute" of honor or fortune occurs in Ps 102:17[18]. Yahweh hears the prayer of the destitute (*'ar'ār*), referring either to the afflicted man of vv. 1-11 or more likely the nation in exile (v. 17b) (Anderson, 709).

8. Bare in the sense of childless (*'arîrî*) is first found in Gen 15:2, where Abraham describes his condition before Sarah gave birth, and it is repeated in Lev 20:20-21 as punishment for certain types of improper sexual relationships. Yahweh later commanded that King Jehoiachin, one of the last kings of Judah, was to be considered childless (*'arîrî*), although he had at least seven children (1 Chron 3:17-18), because none of his sons would succeed him as king.

P-B *'rh* is most often translated in the LXX by *apokalyptō*, reveal, disclose, or *ekkenoō*, empty out, pour out. In DSS it means take off one's clothes, (1QIsa[a] 32:11, *HALAT* 834b); in Mish. Heb. uncover (Jastrow 1:1116a).

The LXX translates *'erwâ*, *'eryâ* with *gymnōsis*, nakedness; *aschēmosynē*, shame of nakedness; *aschēmōn*, unpresentable; *aischynē*, shame, disgrace; *aschēmoneō*, behave improperly. In Mish. Heb. *'erwâ*, *'eryâ* mean nakedness, genitals, unchastity, forbidden relations, lewdness, also understood as something improper, grounds for divorce (cf. Deut. 24:1; Jastrow 1114-15, 1117).

Bare, naked, destitute, stripped: → *ḥśp* I (strip, bare, # 3106); → *'rh* (make bare, be poured out, # 6867); → *'ārôm* (naked, # 6873); → *'rr* (strip bare, be leveled, # 6910); → *pṣl* (strip, # 7202); → *pšṭ* (take off [clothes], attack, strip, # 7320); → *šᵉpî* (barren height, # 9155)

Bibliography

TWOT 2:695; A. A. Anderson, *The Book of Psalms (2:73-150)*, NCB, 1972; F. W. Basset, "Noah's Nakedness & the Curse of Canaan: A Case of Incest?" *VT* 21, 1971, 232-37; H. Bultema, *Commentary on Isaiah*, 1981; C. A. Briggs, *A Critical and Exegetical Commentary on the Book of Psalms*, ICC, 1906; U. Cassuto, *A Commentary on the Book of Genesis: Part Two, From Noah to Abraham*, 1984; R. E. Clements, *Isaiah 1-39*, NCB, 1980; M. Dahood, *Psalms 3:101-150*, AB, 1970; R. K. Harrison, *Leviticus: An Introduction and Commentary*, 1980; W. Kelly, *An Exposition of the Book of Isaiah*, 1947; M. Noth, *Leviticus: A Commentary*, 1977; J. N. Oswalt, *The Book of Isaiah: Chapters 1-39*, NICOT, 1986; G. von Rad, *Genesis: A Commentary*,

1961; J. J. M. Roberts, *Nahum, Habakkuk, and Zephaniah: A Commentary,* 1991; E. A. Speiser, *AB: Genesis,* 1962; G. J. Wenham, *The Book of Leviticus,* NICOT, 1979; C. Westermann, *Genesis 1-11: A Commentary,* 1984; E. J. Young, *The Book of Isaiah* (3 vols.), NICOT 2, chs. 19-39, 1969; 3, chs 40-66, 1972.

Boyd V. Seevers

6870	עֲרוּגָה

עֲרוּגָה (*ʼᵃrûgâ*), nom. bed of plants, plot, terrace? (# 6870).

ANE Arab. *ʻaraǧa,* ascend, zigzag; a connection with *ǧarafa,* a sandy ground suitable for plant production, is questionable.

OT Contextually, the meaning bed for planting, following the KJV (S of Songs 5:13; 6:2; note, however, Ezek 17:7, 10 with furrow), is suitable but not certain (cf. RSV, NASB). The NIV prefers plot at Ezek 17:7, 10. Pope suggests, on the basis of the Arab. root, the meaning steps or terraces.

P-B The LXX (A and B MSS) has *bōlos,* a lump or clod of dirt (Ezek 17:7, 10) but *phialē,* vial, at S of Songs 5:13 and 6:2. T. B. Hull 50a uses the nom. as groove between lobes of the lung, while Mish. Sabb. 9:2 as a garden bed in a fallow field. 4Qpapyrus Hodayot-Like frag 2, lines 4, 9, apparently a description of an eschatological garden, records that the plant (roots?) "shall not be pulled up from its bed of balsam (pleasant plot?)."

Garden, orchard: → *gan/gannâ* (garden, orchard, # 1703/1708); → *karmel* I (orchard, # 4149); → *[gan] ʻēden* II ([garden of] Eden, # 6359); → *ʻᵃrûgâ* (garden bed, terrace, # 6870); → *pardēs* (park, forest, # 7236)

BIBLIOGRAPHY

M. H. Pope, *Song of Songs,* 1977, 540.

Martin G. Abegg, Jr.

6871	עָרוֹד

עָרוֹד (*ʻārôd*), wild ass (# 6871).

OT The only undisputed attestation of Heb. *ʻārôd* (the Arabian Onager, or *Equus hemionus onager,* with attested cognates only in Jew. Aram.) occurs in Job 39:5b, which the NIV omits, due to the parallelism with *pere'* (the slightly smaller Syrian Onager, rendered here as "wild donkey") in 39:5a. Job is asked by the Lord, "Who let thc wild donkey go free? Who untied his ropes?" with vv. 6-8 continuing the graphic imagery of the unencumbered wild donkey roaming the wastelands and hills. In spite of its wildness, however, the Talmud records that the *ʻārôd* was occasionally used for turning millstones (BTalm ʻAboda Zara 16b). Jer 48:6 MT reads *kaʻᵃrôʻēr,* but OG translates *onos agrios,* wild ass, probably reading *kʻrwd.* The Aram. cognate **ʻᵃrād* (det., *ʻᵃrādayyā'*) occurs in Dan 5:21, where it is stated of Nebuchadnezzar in his time of insanity that "he lived with the wild donkeys and ate grass like cattle."

Donkey: → *'ātôn* (she-ass, # 912); → *ḥ^a^môr* I (male ass, donkey, # 2789); → *'ayir* (stallion of an ass, # 6555); → *'ārôd* (wild ass, # 6871); → *pere'* (zebra [wild ass], # 7230); → *pered* (mule, # 7234)

Michael S. Moore/Michael L. Brown

6872 (*'erwâ*, nakedness, genitals, shame), → # 6867

6873	עָרוֹם

עָרוֹם (*'ārôm*; *'ārōm*), naked (# 6873); מַעֲרוֹם (*ma'^a^rōm*), nakedness (hapleg. in 2 Chron 28:15; # 5122); עֵירוֹם (*'êrôm*, *'ērôm*), naked (# 6567).

ANE *'ārôm* and *'êrôm* are attested only in Sam. *'ārôm*, naked (*HALAT* 835b).

OT 1. The adj. *'ārôm* and *'êrôm*/*'ērôm* occur 26x in the OT (Gen [4x], rest of the Historical Books [2x], Job [6x], rest of Poetry [1x], Prophets [13x]). *'ārôm* occurs 16x, and *'êrôm*/*'ērôm* 10x. The adj. forms signify nakedness—most often as a figure for Israel under judgment, less as a figure for a needy person.

2. The nom. *'ārôm* is used for the nakedness of Adam and Eve in Gen 2-3. First they "were both naked, and they felt no shame" (2:25), showing that nudity without sin was not evil. "Since they did not yet know good or evil, nor had they yet learned that sexual desire could also be directed towards *evil ends*, they had no cause to feel ashamed" (Cassuto, 137). After the "crafty" (wordplay with the nearly identical *'ārûm* (→ # 6874) serpent deceived them, they realized their nudity (3:7, *'êrôm*), tried to cover it, feared God because of it (3:10, *'êrôm*), and were challenged by God because of their knowledge (3:11, *'êrôm*). Kidner writes, "The *fig leaves* were pathetic enough, as human expedients tend to be, but the instinct (to hide in shame) was sound and God confirmed it (v. 21), for sin's proper fruit is shame" (69). In the rest of the Bible, nakedness, is often associated with shame, with nakedness and shame even used interchangeably (see *'erwâ*, nakedness, # 6872).

The word *'ārôm* also describes Saul's state as he lay prophesying after stripping off (*pšṭ*, # 7320) his robes (1 Sam 19:24). The lack of negative comment and the context—the leading by "the Spirit of God," the presence of Samuel, and the appearance of normal prophetic behavior (vv. 23-4)—imply that Saul's nakedness was not inappropriate. Perhaps Saul was not completely naked. "*'ārôm* does not always signify complete nudity, but is also applied to a person with his upper garment off" (KD 2:197; cf. 2 Sam 6:20; Isa 20:2; Mic 1:8; esp. John 21:7). Job (1:21[2x]) and Eccl (5:15[14]) also use *'ārôm* as a neutral term, portraying a child at birth and a person at death. Job 26:6 also states that death, a state shrouded in mystery, lies "naked" (exposed) before God.

3. "Naked" also describes the poor person, unprotected in the cold (Job 24:7, 10). Only an unrighteous person would take that person's clothes (as security for debts) (22:6). The prophets also use naked for needy, stating that a righteous person (Ezek 18:7, 16) and Yahweh (Isa 58:7) clothe the "naked" (provide for his needs).

4. In the deut. covenant, God warned Israel that one of the curses she would suffer for disloyalty would be shameful judgment that leads to "nakedness," along with "hunger and thirst . . . and dire poverty" (Deut 28:48, *'êrôm*). This passage provides the basis for most of the prophetic uses of the word. The prophets usually use naked as a figure for Israel's undergoing the shame of Yahweh's judgment. Ezekiel begins his

allegory of unfaithful Jerusalem in ch. 16 by describing her as naked and bare (with *'erwâ*, # 6872) in her youth, (Ezek 16:7, 22 both *'ērôm*) as a picture of innocence, but follows by describing the devastating judgment that she will receive for her unfaithfulness, including the plundering that will leave her "naked and bare" (16:39; 23:29, again both *'ērôm* with *'erwâ*). Hos (2:3[5]) depicts the judgment as God stripping (*pšṭ* # 7320) Israel naked, as at birth (make her barren like a desert).

5. Yahweh tells Isaiah (Isa 20:2-4) to announce the coming judgment against Egypt and Ethiopia by going about naked and barefoot (with *yāḥēp* → # 3504) as a sign of mourning. Yahweh also commanded Micah to go about "barefoot and naked" (*'ārôm* with *šôlāl* [→ # 8768]) as a sign of shame and lament before the coming judgment, this time against Israel (Mic 1:8). "In going about naked, (the prophet) probably was simply wearing an undergarment, and so ... was not acting against what was honorable. He was merely going against custom in such a way that attention would be drawn to himself" (Young 2:55).

The terms *yāḥēp* and *šôlāl* are used without *'ārôm* as well. The former appears in 2 Sam 15:30, where David flees from Absalom barefoot and covers his head as a sign of mourning, and in Jer 2:25, where Yahweh commands Israel not to chase false gods until they are barefoot and their throat is dry (sandals worn out and thirsty from running away from them). When Job speaks of God humbling counselors and priests (powerful men) by leading them about barefoot (Job 12:17, 19), the translation is unclear. BDB (1021), Clines (275-76, 300) and the LXX understand *šôlāl* as barefoot, while NIV and Rowley (95) use stripped. Either way, the author uses *šôlāl* to convey humility.

Although nakedness was not originally shameful, that became its normal connotation after the Fall. Occasionally used to describe the state of the needy person or human at birth or death, *'ārôm* was most often used by the prophets verbally and pictorially to portray the shame and destitution Israel would suffer for her covenantal disloyalty.

P-B LXX uses *gymnos*, naked, bare, for *'ārôm, 'ārōm, 'êrôm, 'ērôm*; DSS (4Q166 11 12), lightly dressed, as in naked and barefoot above; Mish. Heb. stripped, naked, bare (Jastrow, 1115).

Bare, naked, destitute, stripped: → *ḥśp* I (strip, bare, # 3106); → *'rh* (make bare, be poured out, # 6867); → *'ārôm* (naked, # 6873); → *'rr* (strip bare, be leveled, # 6910); → *pṣl* (strip, # 7202); → *pšṭ* (take off [clothes], attack, strip, # 7320); → *š^{e}pî* (barren height, # 9155)

BIBLIOGRAPHY

U. Cassuto, *A Commentary on the Book of Genesis: Part One, From Adam to Noah,* 1961; D. J. A. Clines, *Job 1-20,* WBC, 1989; D. Kidner, *Genesis: An Introduction and Commentary,* 1967; C. F. Keil & F. Delitzsch, *Commentary on the Old Testament,* 1985; H. H. Rowley, *The Book of Job,* NCBC, 1976; E. J. Young, *The Book of Isaiah,* NICOT, 1969.

Boyd V. Seevers

6874 (*'ārûm*, cunning, crafty, shrewd, prudent), → # 6891

6880 (*'eryâ*, nakedness, bare), → # 6867

6881	עֲרִיסָה

עֲרִיסָה (*ʿarîsâ*), nom. a sacrificial offering made out of coarse meal or dough (# 6881).

ANE Syr. *ʾarsānāʾ*, nom. hulled barley, groats.

OT The Israelites were instructed to present as a gift to the Lord the first yield (*rēʾšît*) of their baking as a loaf of bread (*ḥallâ*; Num 15:20-21; Ezek 44:30). Snaith (*Leviticus and Numbers*, NCB, 155) proposes "a batch of loaves from one kneading trough" as the meaning of *ʿarîsâ*. This offering is attested in Nehemiah's time, when the people pledged to make such a contribution to the sanctuary required by the law, including this specific offering (Neh 10:37[38]).

P-B In Mish. Heb. it means kneading trough, dough of a trough, batch (Jastrow, 1117). Its precise, liturgical meaning is not known. LXX renders it *phurama*, paste, dough (NIV "ground meal"), while Tg. uses "kneading trough" (J. Milgrom, *Numbers*, JPS Torah Commentary, 122).

Leaven, unleavened, dough: → *bṣq* (swell, # 1301); → *ḥmṣ* I (be sour, leavened, # 2806); → *maṣṣâ* I (unleavened bread, # 5174); → *ʿarîsâ* (dough, course meal, # 6881)
Offering, sacrifice: → *ʾazkārâ* (sign-offering, # 260); → *ʾiššeh* (offering by fire, # 852); → *ʾāšām* (guilt offering, # 871); → *zbḥ* (slaughter, sacrifice, # 2284); → *ḥaṭṭāʾat* (sin offering, # 2633); → *ṭbḥ* (slaughter, # 3180); → *minḥâ* (gift, present, offering, sacrifice, # 4966); → *maʿašēr* (tithe, # 5130); → *ndr* (make a vow, # 5623); → *nwp* I (move back and forth, wave, # 5677); → *nsk* I (pour out, be consecrated, libation, # 5818); → *ʿōlâ* I (burnt offering, # 6592); → *ʿarîsâ* (meal/dough offering, # 6881); → *qorbān* (offering, gift, # 7933); → *šḥṭ* I (slaughter, # 8821); → *šelem* (settlement sacrifice, # 8968); → *tāmîd* (regular offering, # 9458); → *tᵉrûmâ* (tribute, contribution, # 9556); → **Aaron: Theology**; → **Offering: Theology**; → **Priests and Levites: Theology**

John E. Hartley

6883 (*ʿārîṣ*, master, violent, tyrant), → # 6907

6884	עֲרִירִי

עֲרִירִי (*ʿarîrî*), childless (only in Gen 15:2; Lev 20:20-21; Jer 22:30) (# 6884).

OT 1. The word describes the divine penalty for violation of incest taboos (Lev 20:20-21). It is not clear, however, whether the individuals in the incestuous relationship already have children with other partners or not. For some reason only sexual intercourse with one's aunt (v. 20) or marriage to one's sister-in-law (v. 21) among all the incest violations of Lev 18 and 20 brings childlessness to the participants. Of course, an instance where the prohibition of 20:21 would not apply is the levirate marriage, in which a brother is legally bound to marry the wife of his deceased and childless brother (Deut 25:5-10).

2. "Childless" may be understood nonliterally. Jehoiachin was to be called "childless" (Jer 22:30), not because he never fathered any children (in fact, he was the father of seven children, 1 Chron 3:17-18; see *ANET,* 308, for references to five of his sons in a cuneiform document from Babylon), but because none of his offspring would ever succeed him as king of Judah. Possibly Jeremiah's prophecy was motivated by his conviction that it was not Yahweh's plan to permit a descendant of Jehoiachin to

assume the throne of David. When Jehoiachin's grandson Zerubbabel (1 Chron 3:19) returned from the Exile, he returned not as king but as governor in postexilic Jerusalem under the Persian emperor.

3. Abraham, who was childless, was perplexed as to how God's purposes and promises for a large progeny would be realized (Gen 15:2). The text is one of the few in the OT where "childless" is used of the husband (see above, Jer 22:30). Gen 15:2 represents a lament of a childless father and as such may be compared to the Ugaritic Epic of King Keret, the hero of which at one time lost his wife and children, and to the Epic of Aqhat, in which Dan'el also was a childless husband. Keret's wife had been taken from him before she could give him an heir. He besought El for a wife so that he would have children to carry on his line. Dan'el offered sacrifices and libations to the gods so that he might be blessed with a model son. Present in both of these epics, but absent in Gen 15:2, are elaborate ritual procedures by the suppliant to persuade the gods to alleviate childlessness. In Gen 15:2 the unconditional promises of God take the place of elaborate ritual.

Barren, childless, miscarriage: → *galmûd* (barren, # 1678); → *nēpel* (still-born child, miscarriage, # 5878); → *'āqār* (barren, childless, # 6829); → *'^{a}rîrî* (childless, # 6884); → *škl* (be bereaved, bereavement, miscarry, # 8897)

BIBLIOGRAPHY

O. Babb, "Barrenness," *IDB* 1:359; U. Cassuto, "The Seven Wives of King Keret," *BASOR* 119, 1950, 18-20; R. T. O'Callaghan, "Echoes of Canaanite Literature in the Psalms," *VT* 4, 1954, 164-76; S. Talmon, "'Wisdom' in the Book of Esther," *VT* 13, 1963, 419-55, esp. 438-40.

Victor P. Hamilton

6885	ערך

ערך (*'rk*), set, put in rows; prepare, put in order; keep ready; enter into battle; confront (# 6885); מַעֲרָךְ (*ma'^{a}rāk*), plan, consideration (# 5119); מַעֲרָכָה (*ma'^{a}rākâ*), row, battle line (→ # 5120); מַעֲרֶכֶת (*ma'^{a}reket*), layer (bread) (→ # 5121); עֵרֶךְ, *'ērek*, suitable number of pieces, lay, row (# 6886). All instances of the vb. are in the q.

ANE Phoen., Nab., and Ugar. have a root *'rk*. Thus, in *Ugaritica* v, 12:3-4 *b'l 'rkm* is paired with *b'lt bhtm*, "Mistress of the Palace," leading one to believe that because *'rkm* is parallel with *bhtm*, the former must mean "house, temple." Similarly, Nab. *'rkwt' wbty'* (CIS, II, 350:2) means something like "buildings and houses." And Phoen. *'dr 'rkt* (see *Or* 38, 1969, 159) probably is "superintendent of buildings." This connection of *'rk* with house recalls Job 28:13, "Man does not know [Wisdom's] *'erkâ*." It is unlikely that *'erkāh* means "price, value, worth [NIV]," because the theme of Wisdom's value is raised only later in the ch. (vv. 15-19), and in vv. 12-14 place names dominate. Read, thus, "man does not know her home." (Older sources like BDB, 790 and more recent sources like *BHS,* needlessly emend *'erkāh* to *darkâ.*) The roots *'rk* and *bayit*, house, are also associated in Prov 9:1-2, "Wisdom has built her house (*bêtāh*) ... she has also set (*'ār^{e}kâ*) her table."

The Nuzi texts, at least as far back as the second millennium BC, illustrates that penalties in the form of fixed animal ratios were commutable to currency. The feminine plural *'rkt*, equivalents, is attested in a Punic votive inscription with the vb. *ndr*, vow, pledge, and in another Punic text a tax official is called *r[b] ʿrkt*, supervisor of the taxes. (For both the Nuzi and Punic evidence, see Speiser, 29-33.)

OT 1. The basic meaning of the vb. is "to arrange in order" for the sake of accomplishing a useful purpose. It is never used to describe arranging something arbitrarily or haphazardly. Thus, wood is set in order on an altar for a fire (Gen 22:9; Lev 1:7; 1 Kgs 18:33), a table is arranged for a meal (Ps 23:5; 78:19; Prov 9:2; Isa 21:5; 65:11; Ezek 23:41 [on which incense and oil are placed]), troops draw up in battle order for engaging the enemy (Gen 14:8; Judg 20:20, 22, 33; 1 Sam 4:2; 17:2, 8, 21; 2 Sam 10:9-10), lamps are prepared for proper burning (Ps 132:17), and words and arguments are drawn up in preparation for the presentation of a persuasive legal case (Job 13:18).

2. In conjunction with this last illustration, one notes the use of *ʿrk* as a forensic term (see the above reference to Job 13:18, "Now that I have prepared my case"). See also 23:4: Job about God, "I would state my case before him"; 32:14: Elihu to the three counselors about Job, "But Job has not marshaled his words against me"; 33:5: Elihu's challenge to Job, "Answer me if you can; prepare yourself [i.e., prepare your case] and confront me"; 37:19: Elihu to Job about God, "We cannot draw up our case because of our darkness"; Ps 5:3[4]: "In the morning I lay my request [or, "draw up my case"] before you"; 50:21: God speaking to the wicked, "But I will rebuke you and accuse you to your face" [or, "I will accuse you and draw up a case before your eyes"]; Isa 44:7: "Who is like me?... Let him declare and lay out before me ... what is yet to come."

3. This use of *ʿrk* may clarify the meaning of David's words in 2 Sam 23:5, "Has he not made with me an everlasting covenant, arranged (*ʿ^{a}rûkâ*) and secured in every part?" The use of the participle of *ʿrk* with "covenant" may indicate that the expression is borrowed from legal terminology and is intended to describe the covenant with David, the terms of which have been fully and clearly set forth by God.

4. It is not difficult to discern why *ʿrk* is used both forensically and as a military term for the deployment of troops. A legal dispute is a contest of words, while the other is a dispute involving soldiery and weaponry. The use of *ʿrk* in both legal and military contexts is parallel with *yṣb* (in the hitp.), "take one's stand," also used in a legal context (Job 33:5) and in a military one (1 Sam 17:16).

5. *ʿrk* also appears in the OT as part of the technical vocabulary of the cult. The priests lay out the wood on the fire (Lev 1:7) and arrange or lay out the sections of the sacrifice on the wood after the sacrifice has been flayed and quartered (1:8, 12; in v. 8 the vb. is in the pl. because it requires several priests to do this with the much larger and heavier bull, while in v. 12 the vb. is in the sing. because one person can handle the parts of the smaller animal from the flock). In Exod 40:23 *ʿrk* refers to the placing of the bread on the table in the sanctuary (see also Lev 6:12[5]; Num 23:4).

One wonders if there is a possible connection between *ʿrk* in this cultic context and the use of *ʿrk* for approaching God in prayer (see Ps 5:3[4] and cf. par. 2 above). While the forensic background of *ʿrk* is in view there, it is possible, in light of the many uses of *ʿrk* for the laying of the pieces of the offering in order (Exod-Num), that the psalmist in Ps 5:3[4] conveys by his use of *ʿrk* the idea of bringing an offering. So understood, "we should have to imagine that early in the morning the petitioner brought an offering that accompanied his prayers and pleas for a divine verdict" (Kraus, 154).

6. *ma'ărāk* occurs only in Prov 16:1, "To a man belong the *plans/arrangements* of the heart."

7. *ma'ărākâ* may designate a "row" of lamps (Exod 39:37), or a "battle line" (1 Sam 4:2, 12, 16; 17:20-21, 22) or "ranks, armies" (17:8, 10, 26, 36, 45).

8. The most frequently used nom. related to *'rk* is *'ērek*, referring, for example, to a suit of clothes laid out in order (Judg 17:10), or to the graceful form of Leviathan, praised by Yahweh to Job (Job 41:12[4]). Most often this nom. occurs in Leviticus, either in chs. 5 and 6 in connection with the guilt offering (5:15, 18; 6:6[5:25], or in ch. 27 (21x) in connection with vows or pledges or donations to the sanctuary that may be redeemed. In every instance where the expression *bᵉ'erkᵉkā* (lit., "in/according to your valuation") is used, a monetary payment is stipulated. In the three passages from Lev 5 and 6 NIV renders "the proper value," while in ch. 27 NIV uses simply "the value." Here *'ērek* means "assessed value, equivalent." Thus, in the guilt offering the individual's ram that is brought as a sacrifice must correspond to, or be covertible into, the equivalent in silver (5:15). This indicates that the guilt offering is the only OT sacrifice that is commutable to currency.

Order, battle: → *sēder* (order, # 6043); → *'rk* (set, put in rows, enter into battle, # 6885); → *tqn* (straighten, set in order, # 9545)

BIBLIOGRAPHY

TWOT 2:695-96; M. J. Dahood, "Hebrew-Ugaritic Lexicography VII," *Bib* 50, 1969, 337-56, esp. 355; H.-J. Kraus, *Psalms 1-59*, 1988; E. A. Speiser, "Leviticus and the Critics," in *Y. Kaufmann Jubilee Volume*, 1960, 29-45; G. J. Wenham, *The Book of Leviticus*, NICOT, 1979, 103-12.

Victor P. Hamilton

6886 (*'ērek*, lay, row), → # 6885

6887	ערל

ערל (*'rl*), q. treat as uncircumcised; ni. be uncircumcised (# 6887; but see below [OT 1]); denom. from עָרֵל (*'ārēl*), adj. uncircumcised (# 6888); עָרְלָה (*'orlâ*), nom. foreskin (# 6889).

ANE The root occurs in Akk., Arab., and Aram.

OT 1. The adj. *'ārēl*, uncircumcised, and nom. *'orlâ*, foreskin, are used literally in the passages that relate to circumcision (→ *mwl*, # 4576): Gen 17:11ff.; 34:14; Exod 4:25; 12:48; Lev 12:3; Josh 5:3, 7. In Judg 14:3; 15:18; 1 Sam 14:6; 17:26, 36; 31:4 (= 1 Chron 10:4); 2 Sam 1:20, the adj. is used as a term of ethnic contempt concerning the Philistines, who were probably of Indo-European origin and so did not conform to the West Sem. practice of circumcision. It implies their alien status and, especially in 1 Sam 17:26, 36, their opposition to Israel's God. In Hab 2:16 the vb. *hē'ārēl*, be uncircumcised, may connote "show one's foreskin" and so "be exposed" (NIV), but there is strong textual evidence (cf. NRSV, REB) for a reading *hērā'ēl*, stagger (cf. Isa 51:17, 22). In Isa 52:1 Jerusalem, ruined during the Exile, is promised that the *'ārēl*, uncircumcised, and the unclean, the foreigners who destroyed it, would not invade the holy city again. There is a link with the cultic role of circumcision (→ *mwl*).

2. The vb. and nom. are used in a metaphor at Lev 19:23. The fruit of newly planted trees was for the first three years to be regarded as their uncircumcised foreskins and so could not be offered to God as firstfruits. Again, the cultic role of circumcision is in view.

3. Regarding the metaphorical uses of the nom., for a discussion of Deut 10:16; Jer 9:25[24], see *mwl*, circumcise (Circumcision: Theology [sec. 5]). A similar case occurs in Lev 26:41, which refers to the humbling of Israel's "uncircumcised heart" (*lᵉbābām hā'ārēl*); it is explained in terms of rejecting God's laws (v. 43). In Ezek 44:7 (cf. v. 9) foreigners, who are *'arlê-lēb*, uncircumcised in heart, and *'arlê-bāśār*, uncircumcised in flesh, and thus emphatically not members of the covenant people, are forbidden to serve in the grounds of the new temple, unlike the Carian guards who patrolled the courts of the preexilic temple (cf. 2 Kgs 11:4-16). In Jer 6:10 Israel's ear is called *'ᵃrēlâ*, uncircumcised, in its unresponsiveness to God; the same lack of commitment has been considered above (see *mwl*). In the priestly text of Exod 6:12, 30 Moses objects to God's commission of him on the ground that he (Moses) is *'ᵃral śᵉpātayim*, uncircumcised in lips. It clearly connotes "faltering lips" (NIV), probably via the notion of being unfit for cultic use (cf. Lev 19:23; Isa 6:5 [unclean lips]; 52:1; cf. Hermisson, 71-72).

4. In the satirical lament over Egypt in Ezek 32:18-32, mention of the *'ᵃrēlîm*, uncircumcised, lying in the underworld occurs 9x (in v. 27 a reading *mē'ôlām*, long ago, is preferable; cf. NRSV, NJPSV). Similar language is used in 28:10; 31:18. Since at least in 28:10; 32:29, 30 reference is made to ethnic groups who normally practiced circumcision, it has been suggested that a term for infants who died before being circumcised and were barred from burial in the family tomb is here used of a category of outcasts in Sheol (cf. Lods, 271-83).

Circumcision: → *mwl* I (circumcise, # 4576); → *mll* II (circumcise, # 4909); → *'rl* (treat as uncircumcised, # 6887)

Bibliography

TDNT 6:72-81; *TWAT* 4:734-38; 6:385-87; B. S. Childs, *Exodus*, OTL, 1974; M. V. Fox, "The Sign of the Covenant: Circumcision in the Light of the Priestly *'ôt* Etiologies," *RB* 81, 1974, 557-96; H.-J. Hermisson, *Sprache und Ritus im altisraelitischen Kult*, 1965, 64-76; M. Kessler, "Genesis 34—An Interpretation," *Reformed Review* 19, 1965, 3-8; H. Kosmala, "The 'Bloody Husband'," *VT* 12, 1962, 14-28; A. Lods, "La mort des incirconcis," *Comptes rendus de l'Académie des Inscriptions et Belles-Lettres*, 1943, 271-83; J. Sasson, "Circumcision in the Ancient Near East," *JBL* 85, 1966, 473-76; R. de Vaux, *AncIsr* (Engl), 1961, 46-48; M. Weinfeld, "Jeremiah and the Spiritual Metamorphosis of Israel," *ZAW* 88, 1976, 17-56; C. Westermann, *Genesis 12-36*, ConCom, 1985.

Leslie C. Allen

6888 (*'ārēl*, uncircumcised), → # 6887

6889 (*'orlâ*, foreskin), → # 6887

6890	ערם

ערם (*'rm* I), ni. dam up (# 6890); עֲרֵמָה (*'ᵃrēmâ*), nom. heap (# 6894).

ANE The root *'rm* is known in Ugar., Arab., Syr., and Aram., while in Arab. the nom. *'aramat* refers to unthreshed grain.

OT 1. The vb. occurs only in Exod 15:8, describing the waters of the Red Sea being "piled up" by the Lord's breath.

2. Usually in the OT *'ᵃrēmâ* is used of heaps of grain (Ruth 3:7; Neh 13:15; S of Songs 7:2[3]; Hag 2:16), or of grain and fruit (2 Chron 31:6 [2x], 7, 8, 9). In Jer 50:26 it is used along with the vb. *sll* of the destruction of Babylon, piling her up "like heaps of grain."

Heap, mound, pile: → *gal* I (heap, pile, # 1643); → *ḥᵃmôr* II (heap, # 2790); → *mᵉdûrâ* (pile, # 4509); → *nēd* (heap, # 5603); → *sll* (heap, pile up, esteem highly, resist, # 6148); → *'rm* I (be dammed up, # 6890); → *ṣbr* (pile up, # 7392)

Allan M. Harman

6891	ערם

ערם (*'rm* II), q. be cunning, be crafty, be deceptive, be shrewd; hi. make shrewd, make crafty (# 6891); עָרוּם (*'ārûm*), adj. cunning, crafty, shrewd, prudent (# 6874); עָרְמָה (*'ormâ*), nom. craftiness, shrewdness, prudence (# 6893).

ANE The root *'rm* is attested in Aram. and Syr., shrewd, and Arab., ill-natured. While LXX translates *'rm* in Gen 3:1 with *phronimos*, thoughtful, wise, both the negative and positive meanings ("cunning" and "prudent") of the term are generally rendered with *panourgeuō* (esp. adj. *panourgos* and nom. *panourgia*).

OT 1. The root *'rm* II in its various forms occurs 22x in the OT, but never in the Prophets. While it may carry either a negative or a positive meaning, its positive usage appears mainly in Proverbs, where the vb. *'rm* occurs 2x, the adj. *'ārûm* 8x, and the nom. *'ormâ* 3x. It basically describes an attribute or act that is characterized by prudence and wisdom. The uses of the term suggest that human reason, though tainted by sin, is not automatically condemned. Occurrences outside of Proverbs (among which is the reference to the serpent's subtlety in Gen 3:1) generally convey a negative idea.

Two grammatical matters need to be dealt with briefly. First, according to BDB and *HALAT*, except for the true hi. (*ya'rîm*) in Ps 83:3[4], the other three occurrences of the vb. in the form of *ya'rim*, he is (will be) shrewd, are to be regarded as q. (1 Sam 23:22; Prov 15:5; 19:25). The q. inf. abs. in 1 Sam 23:22 would ordinarily suggest that the vb. *ya'rim* in the verse should also be considered a q. It is possible, however, to follow the analysis of the computerized *BHS* text of *Westminster Hebrew Morphology* (CATBE, 1991) that treats all four occurrences as hi. vbs. The construction that a q. inf. abs. followed by a hi. imperf., though rare, occurs in at least three other instances in the OT (2 Sam 15:8; Jer 8:13; Zeph 1:2). A second matter concerns *'rm* in Job 5:13 (NIV in their craftiness). *NIVEC* and *HALAT* treat it as a vb., which would suggest lit. "in their dealing craftily," while BDB sees it as from the nom. *'ormâ* (or a theorized *'ōrem*). The alternatives, however, rarely cause any significant difference in translation.

2. Outside of Prov, the theological uses of *'rm* also point to shrewdness that is against the will of God. In its first occurrence in Gen 3:1, the author, in describing the serpent as *'ārûm*, crafty, lays an important background for the understanding of

cleverness. Its phonological resemblance to *ʿarûmîm*, naked (Gen 2:25) probably serves to form a link between the Fall narrative and the Creation narrative (V. P. Hamilton, *The Book of Genesis*, 1990, 187). The innocence of Adam and Eve is broken by the "craftiness" of the tempter, but the latter's success is under God's curse. The *ʿārûm* serpent is now *'ārûr*, cursed (Gen 3:14). God's judgment on cleverness that directs people away from his word can be seen throughout the OT (e.g., the false prophets).

Many scholars propose that the use of *ʿārûm* in Gen 3:1 is based on the Wisdom tradition and therefore it is a neutral word without moral connotations. The context of Gen 1-3, however, suggests that it portrays a cleverness that is opposed to the works of God. The same term is used in the book of Job, which is also part of the Wisdom tradition, to depict pejoratively people whom God rejects (Job 5:12; 15:5). In Exod 21:14, *ʿormâ* serves to characterize the scheme of a murderer.

The various forms of *ʿrm* all have a positive meaning in Prov and frequently describe a "prudent" or "shrewd" person. It is used synonymously in parallel with "knowledge" (Prov 1:4; 8:6; 19:25), an important term that represents a central teaching of the book. Its positive usage in the book, however, does not necessarily suggest an unreserved optimism toward the human intellect. In Prov, true wisdom cannot be sought apart from the fear of the Lord (1:7; 9:10), and he who "trusts in his own mind" is a fool (28:26, RSV). In Prov "prudence" (*ʿormâ*) is placed alongside wisdom (*ḥokmâ*) to depict a divine attribute (8:12). In 1QpHab 7:14, God is said to have decreed history according to his *ʿormâ* (M. P. Horgan, *Pesharim: Qumran Interpretations of Biblical Books*, 1979, 17). One who possesses prudence lives in the will of God.

Contrary to a "fool," the prudent person in Prov is crowned with knowledge (Prov 14:18). This person is shrewd and humble (12:23; 13:16), understands the direction of life (14:8, 15), and foresees and deals wisely with dangers (22:3; 27:12). There are many examples in the OT that demonstrate such prudent or shrewd living, e.g., the lives of Moses and David. While the OT says that the first woman failed under the "craftiness" of the tempter, it also recounts to us women who overcame enormous life challenges because of their shrewdness. The lives of Naomi and Esther are colorful examples of prudent persons who played a vital role in God's history of salvation. Though successes in life ultimately come from God, the OT also emphasizes a responsible attitude to the life of faith. Cleverness for the sake of achieving one's own malicious goal is condemned, but exercising it diligently and responsibly in dependence on God brings divine blessings. It is in light of this that Jesus' words, "shrewd as snakes and innocent as doves" (Matt 10:16), take on meaning.

Shrewd, cunning, crafty: → *ʿoqbâ* (cunning, craftiness, # 6817); → *ʿrm* II (be cunning, be crafty, make crafty, # 6891)

BIBLIOGRAPHY

TWAT 6:387-92; N. Ararat, "Scripture's Battle Against Cunning," *Beth Mikra* 26, 1980, 67-78; A. J. Bledstein, "The Genesis of Humans: The Garden of Eden Revisited," *Judaism*, 26/2, 1977, 187-200; D. Carr, "The Politics of Textual Subversion: A Diachronic Perspective on the Garden of Eden Story," *JBL* 112/4, 1993, 589-90; M. B. Fox, "Words for Wisdom," *ZAH* 6, 1993, 149-69; R. L. Hubbard, "Theological Reflections on Naomi's Shrewdness," *TynBul* 40, 1989,

283-92; K. R. Joines, *Serpent Symbolism in the Old Testament,* 1974; R. N. Whybray, *The Intellectual Tradition in the Old Testament,* 1974.

A. Luc

6893 (*'ormâ*, craftiness, shrewdness, prudence), → # 6891

6894 (*'^{a}rēmâ*, heap), → # 6890

6895 (*'ermôn*, plane trees), → # 6770

6899	עַרְעָר

עַרְעָר (*'ar'ār*), juniper (# 6899).

ANE Etymology uncertain. Some (*HALAT*) take it as a reduplication of a root *'wr*, watch.

OT The word is used only 3x: Ps 102:17[18]; Jer 17:6; 48:6. The only instances of it rendered as "juniper" are by the REB in Jer 17:6 and the NASB in 48:6.

Its use in Ps 102:17[18] does not seem to involve any tree and is not taken that way by any translation. Most versions agree with the idea of the NIV here, "He will respond to the plea of the destitute" (*'ar'ār*).

The modern translations of the word in Jer 17:6 are: NIV/NASB bush; KJV heath; NRSV shrub; REB juniper; NAB barren bush; NJPSV scrub.

Jer 48:6 is not listed in some lexicons and is taken by some translations to represent an animal (wild ass in NRSV; wild ass in NAB; and wild donkey in NJPSV). But other versions treat the word as in Jer 17:6: NIV bush; NASB juniper; and KJV heath. The REB renders destitute here.

Trees: → *'ēlâ* I (mighty tree, # 461); → *'erez* (cedar, # 780); → *'ōren* I (pine, # 815); → *'ēšel* (tamarisk, # 869); → *b^{e}rôš* (juniper, # 1360); → *lûz* I (almond-tree, # 4280); → *'ēṣ* (trees, tree, wood, timber, sticks, # 6770); → *'ar'ār* (juniper, # 6899); → *ṣammeret* (acacia, [tree-]top, # 7550); → *šāqēd* (almond, # 9196); → *šiqmâ* (sycamore-[fig-] tree, # 9204); → *t^e'aššûr* (cypress, # 9309); → *tāmār* I (date-palm, # 9469); → *tirzâ* (unknown tree, # 9560); (→ **Tree of Knowledge/Life: Theology**)

Larry L. Walker

6902 (*'ōrep*, neck, back), → # 7418

6903	ערף

ערף (*'rp* I), q. drip (# 6903); עֲרָפֶל (*'^{a}rāpel*), thick darkness (→ # 6906).

ANE *'rp* is related to Ugar. *'rp* (RS 23.28 [*KTU* 4.721] 2, 12, where *'rpm* appears twice after *lbšm* and is understood by Dietrich, Loretz, and Sanmartin, 165, as a dark, black color). Cf. also Akk. *erēpu*, become dusky, dark, and *erpetu*, cloud.

OT In Deut 32:2 the vb. *'rp* in "Let my teaching fall (*'rp*) like rain" is parallel with *nzl*, "and my word descend (*nzl*) like dew." In Deut 33:28, the Promised Land is the place of God's blessing on his people, where "the heavens drop (*'rp*) dew."

P-B Sir 43:22 has a similar description of natural rainfall, "the dripping clouds restore them all; and the scattered dew enriches the parched land" (Skehan and Di Lella, 486).

Dripping, flowing, trickling: → *'ēgel* (drop, # 103); → *dlp* I (drip, # 1940); → *zwb* (flow, # 2307); → *ṭrd* (continuous dripping, # 3265); → *mar* II (drop, # 5254); → *ngr* (flow, gush forth, pour out, # 5599); → *nzl* (flow, trickle, # 5688); → *nṭp* (drip, pour, # 5752); → *'rp* I (drip, # 6903); → *pkh* (trickle, # 7096); → *r^ewāyâ* (overflow, # 8122); → *ryr* (flow, # 8201); → *rss* I (moisten, # 8272); → *r'p* (drip, flow, rain, # 8319)

BIBLIOGRAPHY

M. Dietrich, O. Loretz, and J. Sanmartin, "Zur ugaritischen Lexikographie XIII," *UF* 7, 1975, 157-69; P. W. Skehan and A. A. Di Lella, *The Wisdom of Ben Sira*, AB, 1987.

Richard S. Hess

6904 (*'rp* II, break [neck of an animal]), → # 7418

6906	עֲרָפֶל

עֲרָפֶל (*'ᵃrāpel*), deep darkness, thick darkness, heavy cloud (# 6906).

ANE This nom. may be derived from the root vb. *'rp* I, drip, drop [as of rain] (# 6903) with the prep. *l*, and so designates the deep darkness of a rain cloud (cf. *'ārîp*, cloud; Akk. *erēpu*, become dark, *erpetu*, cloud). Less likely is Arab. *ġpr*, cover, because of the transposition of the letters. The nom. is attested in Aram. *'arpelā'*, Syr. *'arpel*, and Ugar. *ġrpl*, heavy cloud.

OT This nom. occurs 15x in the OT, often in parallel with other words for darkness, such as *ḥōšek* (# 3125), *nešep* (# 5974), *'ᵃpēlâ* (# 696), also *ṣalmāwet*, shadow of death (# 7516), and *'ānān* I, cloud (# 6727); and it appears in opposition to *'ôr*, light (# 240).

The word refers most often to the darkness and clouds associated with a theophany. At Mount Sinai, "the people remained at a distance, while Moses approached the thick darkness (*'ᵃrāpel*) where God was" (Exod 20:21). Later Moses described the event again, "You came near and stood at the foot of the mountain while it blazed with fire to the very heavens, with black (*ḥōšek*) clouds and deep darkness (*'ᵃrāpel*)" (Deut 4:11); and again later, "These are the commandments the LORD proclaimed in a loud voice to your whole assembly there on the mountain from out of the fire, the cloud (*'ānān*) and the deep darkness (*'ᵃrāpel*)" (Deut 5:22). Describing another theophanic appearance of God, David wrote, "Dark clouds were under his feet" (2 Sam 22:10 = Ps 18:9[10]). Discussing the dwelling place of God, Solomon said, "The LORD has said that he would dwell in a dark cloud (*'ᵃrāpel*)" (1 Kgs 8:12 = 2 Chron 6:1). Eliphaz asked Job concerning the abode of God, "Does he judge through such darkness (*'ᵃrāpel*)?" (Job 22:13). And the psalmist said of God, "Clouds (*'ānān*) and thick darkness (*'arāpel*) surround him; righteousness and justice are the foundation of his throne" (Ps 97:2). It refers to the thick darkness that shrouded the primeval ocean, as God described it to Job: "Who shut up the sea behind doors when it burst forth from the womb, when I made the clouds (*'ānān*) its garment and wrapped it in thick darkness (*'ᵃrāpel*)?" (Job 38:8-9).

It refers to the thick darkness that stands in contrast with God's glory that Isaiah described: "See, darkness (*ḥōšek*) covers the earth and thick darkness (*'ᵃrāpel*) is over the peoples, but the LORD rises upon you and his glory appears over you" (Isa 60:2). It refers figuratively to deep gloom brought on by God's judgment, as Jeremiah declared, "Give glory to the LORD your God before he brings the darkness (*ḥšk*), before your feet stumble on the darkening (*nešep*) hills. You hope for light, but he will turn it to thick darkness (*ṣalmawet*) and change it to deep gloom (*'ᵃrāpel*)" (Jer 13:16). It refers to the gloom associated with Israel's captivity, as the Lord promised, "As a shepherd looks after his scattered flock when he is with them, so will I look after my sheep. I will rescue them from all the places where they were scattered on a day of clouds (*'ānān*) and darkness (*'ᵃrāpel*)" (Ezek 34:12). That same expression, "a day of clouds (*'ānān*) and darkness (*'ᵃrāpel*)," is used by both the prophet Joel and Zephaniah to describe the Day of the LORD (Joel 2:2; Zeph 1:15).

P-B In Mish. Heb. this word became the name of the lower sky, and in Modern Heb. it means a mist or fog.

Darkness: → *'ōpel* (darkness, gloom, # 694); → *'ᵉšûn* (approach of darkness, # 854); → *ḥšk* (be, grow dark, grow dim, darken, conceal, confuse, # 3124); → *ṭuḥôt* (darkness, obscurity, inward parts, # 3219); → *kamrîr* (blackness, deep gloom, # 4025); → *laylâ* (night, # 4326); → *nešep* (twilight, darkness, # 5974); → *'wp* II (be dark, # 6415); → *'ᵃlāṭâ* (darkness, dusk, # 6602); → *'mm* II (darken, dim, # 6670); → *'ᵃrāpel* (deep darkness, thick darkness, heavy cloud, # 6906); → *ṣll* III (be/grow dark, cast a shadow, # 7511); → *ṣalmāwet* (darkness, shadow of death, # 7516); → *qdr* (be dark, mourn, # 7722)
Cloud: → *ḥāzîz* (cloud, strong wind, thunderclap, # 2613); → *miplāś* (spreading [of a cloud], # 5146); → *'wb* (cover w. cloud, # 6380); → *'ānān* (clouds, # 6727); → *'ᵃrāpel* (deep darkness, thick darkness, heavy cloud, # 6906); → *šaḥaq* (dust, clouds of dust, # 8836)

BIBLIOGRAPHY
TWOT 2:698; M. Dahood, *Ugaritic-Hebrew Philology. Marginal Notes on Recent Publications*, *BibOr* 17, 68; idem, *Psalms I*, AB 107, 1965.

James D. Price

6907	ערץ

ערץ (*'rṣ*), q. be alarmed, terrified, dreadful; ni. inspiring terror, dreadful; hi. terrify, be in terror (# 6907); מַעֲרָצָה (*maʿᵃrāṣâ*), nom. terrifying power (# 5124); עָרִיץ (*'ārîṣ*), nom. master, violent one, tyrant (# 6883).

ANE Syr., come upon suddenly, violently; Arab. (*'ariṣa*), quiver, flicker (*TWOT* 2:299).

OT The verbal form of *'rṣ* occurs 15x in the OT and has been freely translated as be terrified, terrify, cause terror, torment, shake, dread, and stand in awe. As many as five different synonyms have been suggested: *yr'*, fear (→ # 3707); *pḥd*, tremble (→ # 7064); *gwr*, be afraid (→ # 1593); *ygr*, be afraid (→ # 3336); and *ḥtt*, shattered, filled with terror (→ # 3169; *TWOT* 2:699).

1. In Deut and Josh, this word is used in the prohibition "Do not be terrified" (Deut 1:29; 7:21; 20:3; 31:6; Josh 1:9). In each instance the prohibition is directed to either Israel or one of Israel's leaders (Moses or Joshua). Each prohibition is followed by one of two different motive or purpose clauses explicating the ground for such a prohibition, "For the LORD your God goes with you; he will never leave you nor

forsake you" (Deut 31:6); "For the LORD your God is the one who goes with you to fight for you against your enemies to give you victory" (20:4). In each case the idea of Yahweh's actual presence in the face of a great task or enemy threat functions as the motivation.

2. In Isa and Ps, *'rṣ* describes either the effect of Yahweh's presence or his activity (cf. Isa 29:23 for activity). The earth will tremble at the "*dread* of the LORD and the splendor of his majesty" (Isa 2:19, 21). Furthermore, the heavenly council also stands astonished by Yahweh: "In the council of the holy ones God is *greatly feared*; he is more awesome than all who surround him" (Ps 89:7[8]; cf. Isa 47:12 [ironic use]). In such instances, the characterization of an awesome sight or amazement at tremendous power stands at the forefront of the authors' original use of the word. The idea of fear is most likely a secondary connotation as one possible response to such astonishing realities. The earlier uses in Deut and Josh are related to these later instances in that the early prohibitions against being terrified are further grounded in the later testimony that Yahweh is the ultimate object of astonishment for his people and the supreme terror against the wicked.

'rṣ can be used simply to describe wicked things or people. Isa 8:12 records that the plight of the fatherless and oppressed is due to those who cause terror on earth. Similarly, Job uses this word to describe fear in the midst of adversity (Job 13:25; 31:34).

3. As an adj., *'ārîṣ* occurs 20x; 13x in the prophets Isa, Jer, and Ezek, and 7x in the sacred writings of Job, Ps, and Prov. In the majority of instances this word is used to describe wicked, evil people. Several helpful epexegetical expressions accompany this word, yielding a fuller understanding of what type of wicked or evil person this adj. describes. Such people are characterized as those who "have an eye for evil" (Isa 29:20), or "men without regard for God" (Ps 54:3[5]; 86:14). The terrifying existence of such people is ameliorated by the fact that they will be duly judged by Yahweh in the end (cf. Isa 13:11; 29:5, 20). Similarly, nations are also depicted as "ruthless" (Isa 25:3). Ezekiel repeats the same expression, "the most ruthless of nations" (*'ārîṣê gôyim*), 4x to depict nations who have become the vehicle of God's wrath or judgment (Ezek 28:7; 30:11; 31:12; 32:12). Only once, in Jer 20:11, is this adj. used to describe Yahweh as a "mighty warrior" [dread warrior, NASB].

Fear, dread, terror: → *'āyōm* (terrible, awesome, majestic, # 398); → *'êmâ* (terror, dread, # 399); → *bhl* (be dismayed, terrified, dismay, terrify, hasten, hurry, # 987); → *b't* (overtaken by sudden terror, stupefied, be terrified, assail, # 1286); → *gwr* III (be afraid of, dread, stand in awe, # 1593); → *d'g* (be anxious, concerned, fear, dread, # 1793); → *zḥl* II (fear, be afraid, # 2324); → *ḥrd* (tremble, shudder, startle, # 3006); → *ḥtt* (be shattered, dismayed, terrified, scare, terrify, # 3169); → *ygr* (fear, dread, terror, # 3336); → *yr'* I (fear, be afraid, held in honor, # 3707); → *yrh* (be afraid, terrified, paralyzed with fright, # 3724); → *'rṣ* (be alarmed, terrified, dreadful, dreadful, be in terror, # 6907); → *pḥd* I (tremble, be in dread, # 7064); → *qwṣ* I (feel disgust, frighten, cause dread, # 7762)

BIBLIOGRAPHY

TWOT 2:699; J. Eaton, "Some Misunderstood Hebrew Words for God's Self-Revelation," *BT* 25, 1974, 331-38.

M. V. Van Pelt/W. C. Kaiser, Jr.

6908	ערק

ערק (*'rq*), q. gnaw, rankle (# 6908).

ANE The root with this meaning appears in Syr. and Arab., and possibly Eth. and Ugar. (see *HALAT*).

OT This rare root occurs only twice, both in Job (30:3, 17). Of uncertain nuance, it may have figurative reference to the friends' chewing on Job with their words (30:3) or to Job's pain (30:17).

Pain, pangs: → *ḥbl* IV (be pregnant, travail, # 2473); → *ḥyl* I (be in labor, tremble, # 2655); → *k'b* (be in pain, cause pain, ruin, # 3872); → *mrṣ* (be hurtful, painful, irritate, # 5344); → *'ṣb* II (hurt, grieve, offend, # 6772)

Terence E. Fretheim

6910 (*'rr*, strip bare; be leveled), → # 6867

6911	עֶרֶשׂ

עֶרֶשׂ (*'ereś*), nom. bedstead, couch (# 6911).

ANE Cognates are attested in both Eastern and West. Sem. (BDB, 793; *HALAT* 841; *UT*, 194, 237-38, 461-62).

OT 1. *'ereś* occurs less commonly in Scripture than *miṭṭâ*, bed. Like *miṭṭâ*, *'ereś* was also used for lounging and eating (Amos 6:4) and as a place for a sick person (Ps 41:3[4]). It was the natural place for sexual relations (Prov 7:16) and as such became the symbol for such activity (S of Songs 1:16). When used for sleeping (Job 7:13; Ps 132:3-4) it could be decked with special coverings (*mar^{e}baddîm* [→ *rbd*, prepare a bed, # 8048], McKane, 337) or possibly a canopy (Dahood, "Lexicography," 360-61; Prov 7:16), which may have screened its occupants from view (Carr, 86; Dahood, *Psalms,* 243). The *'ereś* (and probably any formal bed) was a furnishing characteristic of the wealthy, for the poor generally slept on mats covered only by their clothing (Exod 22:26-27; Pfeifer, 273; Anderson, 90). Deut 3:11 may allude to a kingly iron bed for Og of Bashan, although some have suggested it intends a sarcophagus (Craigie, 120) of basalt (Mayes, 144).

2. The perplexing *bidmešeq 'āreś* of Amos 3:12 has yielded much discussion. Some defend the traditional reading which is supported by the ancient versions, interpreting the expression as "Damascus bed" or "damask of a couch" (KD X, 264; Pfeifer, 273). The sense would be a heightened portrait of wealth: not only are they in Samaria sitting on couches, but on divans of Damascus or damask (Barstad, 182). Others, noting the difference between *d^{e}mešeq* in the text and *dammeśeq,* Damascus, urge textual corruption and posit a reconstructed word in its place. Rabinowitz argues for an amalgum of *bad* and *šōq,* yielding the reading *ûbad miššōq 'āreś*, which would allow "a piece [chip] out of the leg of a bed" (Rabinowitz, 228-29; Moeller, 33-34; Waard and Smalley, 72-73, 230). Gese has urged that *d^{e}mešeq* represents an Assyrian word, otherwise unknown in the Bible, spelled *'āmešet* or *'amšat* (Assyr.: *amartu/amaštu*) and meaning "head [of the bed]," corresponding to *pē'â,* meaning "foot [of the bed]" ("Fussende," "Kopfaufbau"; Gese, 431; Wolff, 198; cf. *HALAT* 218).

Bed: → *yṣ'* (spread out a bed, # 3667); → *miṭṭâ* (bed, # 4753); → *miškāb* (bed, # 5435); → *'ereś* (bedstead, # 6911); → *pē'â* II (luxury [of a couch], # 6991); → *rbd* (prepare a bed, # 8048)

BIBLIOGRAPHY

A. A. Anderson, *The Book of Psalms I*, NCB, 1972, 90; H. M. Barstad, *The Religious Polemics of Amos*, 1984, 33-36, 127-41, 182; G. F. Carr, *The Song of Solomon*, TOTC, 1984, 86-87; P. C. Craigie, *The Book of Deuteronomy*, NICOT, 1976, 120; M. Dahood, "Hebrew-Ugaritic Lexicography VI," *Bib*, 49, 1968, 355-69; idem, *Psalms III*, AB, 1966, 243; J. de Waard and W. A. Smalley, *A Translator's Handbook on the Book of Amos*, 1979, 71-73, 128-29, 250; H. Gese, "Kleine Beiträge zum Verständnis des Amosbuches," *VT*, 12, 1962, 417-38; R. Gordis, *The Song of Songs and Lamentations*, 1974, 80; F. Landy, *Paradoxes of Paradise*, 1983, 177-79; A. D. H. Mayes, *Deuteronomy*, NCB, 1979, 144; W. McCane, *Proverbs*, OTL, 1970, 337; H. Moeller, "Ambiguity at Amos 3:12," *BT* 15, 1964, 31-34; G. Pfeifer, "'Rettung' als Beweis der Vernichtung (Amos 3,12)," *ZAW*, 100, 1988, 269-77; M. H. Pope, *Song of Songs*, AB, 1977, 359-60; I. Rabinowitz, "The Crux at Amos III 12," *VT*, 11, 1961, 228-31; J. B. White, *A Study of the Language of Love in the Song of Songs and Ancient Egyptian Poetry*, 1978, 35-47, 194-99; H. W. Wolff, *Joel and Amos*, Hermeneia, 1977, 96-98, 272, 276.

William C. Williams

6912	עֵשֶׂב

עֵשֶׂב (*'ēśeb*), green plants, grass (# 6912).

ANE *'ēśeb* is related to Akk. *ešēbu* (grow abundantly, *AHw*, 253b) and *išbabtu* (grass, *AHw*, 392a), and to Arab. *'ušb* (plants, grass); see *HALAT* 842.

OT 1. *'ēśeb* is used in some texts in the broad sense of plants (e.g., Gen 1:11-12; Dalman, 1:335). Such plants may grow in the wild (e.g., Isa 42:15; Dalman, 1:335) or be a product of agriculture (e.g., Exod 9:22). Agricultural produce is specifically in view in the phrase *'ēśeb haśśādeh* (e.g., Gen 3:18). *'ēśeb haśśādeh* in 2:5 is thus not vegetation in general but agricultural produce, which had not yet sprung up because there was no farmer to work the ground (see Westermann, *Genesis*, 199).

2. Since *'ēśeb* was highly valued as food for people (Gen 1:29) and animals (Deut 11:15), it is used in figures of blessing (Deut 32:2; Ps 72:16; Mic 5:6). *'ēśeb* is also used in figures of divine judgment (Deut 29:22; Isa 37:27; Jer 14:6), because of how quickly it withers.

Grass, plants: → *dš'* (become green, sprout, # 2012); → *ḥāṣîr* I (grass, # 2945); → *ḥ[a]šaš* (dry grass, # 3143); → *yrq* II (be green, # 3762b); → *leqeš* (late grass, # 4381); → *'ēśeb* (green plants, # 6912)

BIBLIOGRAPHY

U. Cassuto, *Commentary on Genesis*, 1944; G. Dalman, *AuSP*, 1928-42; J. Durham, *Exodus*, WBC, 1987; C. Westermann, *Genesis 1-11*, 1974; H. Wolff, *Joel and Amos*, Hermeneia, 1977.

Mark D. Futato

6913	עשׂה

עשׂה (*'śh* I), q. to make, do, prepare, set up, create, deal, effect, bring about, obtain, complete, execute, to commit (s.t.), perform work, service; deal with, act, inflect, serve; ni. to be done, performed, completed, prepared, finished, ready; pu. to be made produced (# 6913); מַעֲשֶׂה (*ma'[a]śeh*), nom. work, deed, product, power, act (# 5126).

OT 1. Of the 2,627x this vb. is used in the OT, 2,527x it is employed in the q., 99x in the ni. stem, and once in the pu. (q. pass?). Its semantic range is enormous, but not all areas are theologically crucial or relevant. The nom. *ma'ᵃśeh* is found ca. 220-236x(?). Several orthographic homonyms occur, II = "to press," III = "to cover," IV = "to turn to/toward." Several personal names are compounded with the root (I); *'ᵃśāh'ēl* (2 Sam 2:18; 3:27, 30; 23:24; 2 Chron 17:8; Ezra 10:15; cf. also *'ᵃśî'ēl*, 1 Chron 4:35); *'ᵃśāyâ* (2 Kgs 22:12, etc.); *'el'āśâ* (Jer 29:3, etc.); *ya'ᵃśî'ēl* (1 Chron 11:47); *ma'ᵃśēyāh(û)* (Ezra 10:21; Jer 21:1); *ma'śay* (1 Chron 9:12); *ya'ᵃśāy* (Ezra 10:37). All of these seem to point to concepts connected with creation, e.g., "El(Yah) has made." In the q. the vb. conforms pretty much to the meanings to make or to do, with many nuances of each of these meanings employed.

2. *With God as subject.* (a) God is the Creator (*'ôśeh*), and this word is the most general word used to describe his creative acts. It is used with *br'*, create; *yṣr*, form, mold, make, create; cf. *qnh*, create; *kwn*, set, found, establish; *ṣlh*, prosper, increase. *'śh* is found 18x in Gen 1-5 to mark the creation of the world and of humankind. In the primeval story of Gen 1-11 this word occurs 32x. In ch. 1 the word is found 7x, indicating that God created: the expanse between the water (v. 7), fruit trees that produced fruit (vv. 11, 12), (appointed ? = *'śh*?) the two lights, sun/moon to regulate seasons, feasts, festivals, time, harvesting, and plowing, and to give light at appointed times (v. 16), and the wild animals, thus including all of the animal world under his Lordship/Creatorship (v. 25). It is the word used when God deliberated about the creation of human beings, "Let us make (*'śh*) man (*'ādām*) in our image, in our likeness" (v. 26). The word summarizes the entire creative activity/account (vv. 1-30) in v. 31 (cf. 2:2-4). God is a God who acts and brings his plans to realization.

A helper, woman, is made (*'śh*) for man in Gen 2:18. The serpent was among the wild creatures God made (*'śh*). Adam and Eve try to make garments to cover their nakedness, but the Lord replaces them with clothes he made for them (3:21). The word describes the act of fratricide committed by Cain (4:10). In 5:1 *'śh* refers to the fact that God made humankind (*'ādām*) in his image—a fact repeated explicitly for the last time in the OT at 9:6.

God grieves/mourns (*nḥm*) that he had made (*'śh*) humankind (*'ādām*) just before the Flood (Gen 6:6-7). Noah fulfilled God's command to make an ark (6:14-16); just as God commanded, he did (6:22; 7:5). In 7:4 the coming destruction of everything God had made (*'śh*) is announced. In 8:21 he vows never to do this destructive process again to all life. The episode of Ham's son centers on "what he had done" (9:24, *'śh*) to Noah. The builders of the Tower of Babel attempt/desire to make a name for themselves (11:4), a thing only God can do for his people through Abraham (12:2). The word is used twice in 11:4 to refer to the people's act of building a city, a rebellious act against God and an act of gross hubris.

This short survey of all of the uses of *'śh* in Gen 1-11 illustrates its character. It is a word whose meaning is determined by the function its context assigns to it. In itself it simply indicates activity of whatever kind its context demands, making/doing. The word occurs another 98x in Genesis. It is a marker with almost no intrinsic restrictions placed upon what it might mean in all possible contexts. The following discussions seek to indicate some of the things the word is used to designate. It will be noted that the word can speak of God's making something as in an act of creation, or simply doing something with what is already at hand. Both *br'* (→ # 1343) and *'śh* can mean to create as a new thing not present before.

(b) God makes the heavens and earth (see section a), but also will make/create a new heaven and new earth for his people. In addition to Gen, Isa 40-66 and Psalms are important here. Gen 14:19, through the lips of Melchizedek, speaks of God Most High, Creator (*qōneh*) of heaven and earth, indicating the Lord, Yahweh, as the High God of the pagan pantheon. His use of *qnh* (→ # 7864) introduces an important synonym (in context) to *'śh*. Recalling Gen 1-2, Isa 45:7, 18 employs *'śh, yṣr, kwn, br'* in parallelism to designate the Lord God as the Creator, fashioner, maker, founder of the earth (cf. 2 Kgs 19:15; Isa 37:16). Ps 146:6 adds the sea to his creative acts. God's creation/making (*'ōśeh*) of a new heaven and earth (*'et* + acc.; cf. Gen 1:1) is designated by this word, and the term encompasses everything in it as well: the descendants of his people, his seed will endure forever, all humanity will bow before the Lord, those who reject him will be a reproach to all who see them. The part. of the vb. encompasses the entire picture (Isa 66:22-24). The word is equal to *bōrē'* in a parallel v. in 65:17-18, where the Lord creates both a new heaven/earth and the new Jerusalem.

The vb. *br'* is more limited in its semantic/grammatical range than is *'śh. br'* always has God as its subject, never indicates the material from which God creates, and is used to indicate the creation of various objects (*THAT* 1:338). *'śh* can be used exactly like *br'*, but is not restricted to the first two items noted with *br'*. Both Isa 65:17-18; 66:22-24 imply/state the creation of God's people in these new circumstances (see c. below). So God is the Creator *par excellence* of both the first heavens and earth and the final eschatological/teleological heavens and earth.

(c) God will, after creating the world and cosmos, make (*'śh*) and have a people, beginning with Gen 1:26-28, but continuing after the fall in 12:1-3; Num 14:12. In Exod his goal is to have a people (Exod 6:7). He has the power of the potter to make and mold them (Jer 18:3). He does/has done all he can possibly do for them (Isa 5:4). He will bring them to completion as Isa 66:22 makes clear, "Your name and descendants will endure" in the new heavens and new earth.

This new people must have a new heart; Ezekiel declares after they have cast off their sins (*peša'*), they must acquire for themselves a new heart (*lēb ḥādāš*). Salvation is from the Lord; indeed, a new heart comes only from him (cf. Ezek 11:19), it is given (*ntn*) by him (36:26-29).

(d) God creates not only physical light and darkness (Gen 1:3) (juss. of *hyh*), but also good/evil in the historical, suprahistorical, and natural realms (cf. Isa 44:24; 45:7). In fact, the last four words of 45:7 assert "I ... do (*'śh*) all these things." He makes the poor (Prov 14:31; 17:5) and the rich (22:2), all classes of people. Since he has done so, anyone who oppresses a poor person shames his Creator (14:31; 17:5).

(e) God brings forth/does/works many things. All of the bountifulness of nature and creation come from him (Gen 1:11; Ps 107:37; Jer 12:2) who brings it about. He works wonders (Exod 11:10) and signs (4:17, 30). Here *'śh* functions as *ntn/śym* often do in relation to these things; that is, setting them in place for his purposes.

(f) *'śh* is used with *ḥayil*, power, strength, army, etc., at times, and its meaning is determined by the contextual function and meaning of *ḥayil.* Num 24:18 indicates that Israel will do strongly (*ḥāyil*; cf. Ps 60:12[14]). *ḥayil* clearly means prosperity in

Deut 8:17. Even the justice of Yahweh works (*'śh*) *ḥayil*, stability(?) (Deut 8:18), a concept that recalls the Egyptian world order, *m³ᶜt*.

(g) *'śh* can take on the meaning to celebrate, keep a festival or feast in a cultic context (Exod 12:48; Josh 5:10; 2 Kgs 23:21), or to discharge a vow or duty (Jer 44:25). It can also mean to appoint priests (1 Kgs 12:31; 13:33).

(h) God brings to pass (*'śh*) whatsoever he will in his function as judge and Lord of the government of the world. In general he does great things (Ps 71:19; 106:21) in creation (Ps 104) and history (Ps 136). He creates righteous things (103:6) and acts of justice (Ezek 5:10, 15; 11:9). He alone works vengeance (*nāqām*; Judg 11:36; Ezek 25:17).

In sum the Lord is the doer (*'ôśeh*) of all things and the proper subject of this ubiquitous vb. in the OT.

3. *With human beings as subject.* (a) Persons also do (*'śh*) certain things. Abraham performed righteousness/justice (*ṣᵉdāqâ/mišpāṭ*; Gen 18:19) as the way of the Lord. To do mercy, to show love, and to show compassionate faith (*ḥesed*) with someone is an act that God has done and wants his people to imitate. This is what Yahweh practiced himself (Exod 20:6; Ps 136), especially toward his anointed (Ps 18:50[51]). To do these things is also expressed by more restrictive vbs. *nṣr*, guard, keep; *šmr*, guard, keep; *zkr*, remember; *rdp*, pursue, that define the act/attitude more clearly. They signify more specifically how one does (*'śh*) the deeds/words of love, mercy, etc. Other things that humankind can do/show/keep are found: *ḥōnep,* profaneness (Isa 32:6, cf. *'wn, tô'â, nᵉbālâ*); *ḥāmās*, violence, etc. Persons can do good (*'śh ṭôb*; Ps 34:14[15]; 37:27) or evil (*ra'*; Mal 2:17). In the cultic sphere *'śh* is used to designate making/doing an offering: an *'ôlâ + zebaḥ* (2 Kgs 5:17); *ḥaṭṭā't* (Lev 14:19); *'iššeh* (Num 15:3). These activities demonstrate and illustrate the moral/religious/spiritual likeness of persons made in the image of their Creator.

(b) *'śh* is used often to indicate the fulfillment or performance of a command. This is especially used of persons carrying out instructions or commands from God: e.g., making the sanctuary (*miqdāš*) exactly as demanded. *'śh* is found 267x in Exod, twice the number of occurrences in any other Pentateuchal book. Yahweh/men are both often subjects. Israel builds Yahweh's sanctuary, Moses and Aaron do his will/instructions just as he says, and Yahweh effects/does to Egypt what he says he will do (Exod 39:1, 6; cf. 25:10-22 with 37:1-9). Noah also carried out the construction of the ark precisely, doing (*'śh*) as the Lord commanded him (Gen 6:22). In these cases to make/to do will fit the context, depending on its demands.

Israel was to do the moral/ethical/religious "blueprint" of the Torah in its demands, not merely its physical accomplishments, such as building the tabernacle (cf. Exod 19:8; 24:7). To be God's people Israel had to do his commandments (Jer 11:4, 6, 7; 32:23; Ezek 9:11). Yahweh's people must do/reflect on Yahweh's *dābār*, word; *rāṣôn*, will; *ḥoq*, ordinance; *miṣwâ*, commandment; *mišpāṭ*, justice; *tôrâ*, teaching; *piqqûdîm*, instructions; *'ᵉmet*, truth; *'ᵉmûnâ*, faithfulness. Men also do/commit sin, evil, wickedness, abomination, harlotry, deceit—things that God never does, thus showing their corrupt nature.

4. The idioms that deal with poetic justice/irony—"As he has acted/done (*'śh*), so shall it be done to him" (Lev 24:19; cf. Deut 19:19)—are found often. Edom is to be repaid in kind for her treatment of Israel (Obad 15). (→ Retribution: Theology) The

oath formula "May God deal with me, be it ever so severely, if ..." (2 Sam 3:35) is common in forensic/cultic settings. "To do good to" employs the idiom *'śh ṭôb 'im* (Judg 9:16; 2 Sam 2:6). The opposite is, of course, found (to do evil, *ra'*; Judg 15:3; cf. Gen 26:29). The expression "What have you done?" is probably a piece of forensic legal language used between persons in informal settings (Gen 12:18; Exod 14:11; Judg 8:1; cf. also "What have I done?" Num 22:28; 1 Sam 13:11). Moses' expression "What am I to do with these people?" (Exod 17:4) is a question calling for a specific forensic answer (cf. Hos 6:4). The expression "works of the hands of (people/God, Lord)" is found 54x. What the "works" are must be determined from the context; they can be good or bad. In Deut the works (*ma'ᵃśeh*) often refer to the evil works of paganism in the land of Canaan or other alien nations (Deut 4:28; 27:15; cf. 2 Kgs 19:18; Isa 2:8; 37:19; Mic 5:13[12], etc.). The works of paganism amounts to nothing (Isa 41:29), vanity, in God's sight. The stereotyped historical idiom/framework that is used to indicate the deeds/acts of the kings in the deut. history forms a key role in its structure (1 Kgs 14:29; 15:7; 24:5). (→ Kings: Theology)

'śh is used to designate Yahweh's activity, for good or evil, in history at a national, universal, or personal level. Amos says God's actions are revealed to his prophets before he does them (Amos 3:7). But, at times his actions seem to be dramatically unexpected (Isa 33:13), especially in Wisdom literature (cf. Job 1-2). 2 Kgs 17 is a classic example, explaining why Yahweh did what he did to Israel (cf. also Jer 5:19; 30:15). As in creation, so in the prophets, Yahweh's word is effective to bring about his deed (Ezek 12:25; 17:24; 22:14). In fact, in history the Lord does everything that he wants (Isa 46:10; 48:14; 55:11). Shalmaneser (2 Kgs 17:3, 4; 18:9), Nebuchadnezzar (Jer 25:9), Cyrus (Isa 45:1)—all do Yahweh's bidding (cf. Ps 115:3; 135:6). In the life of the individual, Yahweh works both good/evil as he does elsewhere (Gen 50:19; Ps 22, esp. v. 31[32]).

5. One of the most critical, disobedient activities of the Israelites, when in a state of rebellion, was the making (*'śh*) of a golden calf at the foot of Sinai (Exod 32:4, 8). It was the archetypal sin of idolatry. It is followed by Micah's idols (Judg 17:4) and Jeroboam's golden calves (1 Kgs 14:9; cf. 2 Kgs 17:29). Hab 2:18 and Isa 2:8 condemn this evil production of idols emphatically. Yahweh is the living God, not a work (*ma'ᵃśeh*) of human hands, like the religious idols of the pagan kings (Isa 37:19).

6. In the ni. no new meanings of the vb. *'śh* are discernible. The forms mean the same, but are merely passive. Ecclesiastes has a large number of passive statements, but none involve a new theological concept, unless it be in the summary way the book refers to "all the things done under the sun" by humankind (1:13, 14; 4:1).

7. The single use of a pu. in Ps 139:15 is possibly a true q. pass. At any rate, it translates as "I was made (*'uśśêtî*) in the secret part/place (*sēter*)." The latter phrase most likely refers to the womb.

8. The use of the nom. *ma'ᵃśeh* follows closely on the employment of the vb., describing what is accomplished by the action, literal or figurative, of the vb. It signifies what is done or what is being done. A summary of its major uses will suffice. Not all uses of it are theologically signficant. Vollmer finds 56 uses of the nom. that are important theologically (*THAT* 2:368). All kinds of God's works/actions and all types of human works/actions are designated by the nom. A few examples follow. The Lord's works/deeds/actions of salvation are theologically paramount (Exod 34:10;

Josh 24:31; Judg 2:7, 1). The Lord's acts of salvation/deliverance that he has done and will do are depicted in the Prophets (Isa 5:12, 19), sometimes because the people refuse to respect them and stand condemned (Isa 5:12). The word refers to the creation (Ps 8:6[7]; 103:22), the entire creation (104:24, 31). The one who needs God's acts of salvation now, remembers them from the past (143:5), for they are the foundation of hope. Yahweh's incomparable works are praised (86:8; 139:14). Elihu describes God's power in nature (Job 37:7) and among humanity (14:15; 34:19).

9. The book of Ecclesiastes declares the inability of a person to comprehend fully God's works (Eccl 3:11, *ma'ᵃśîm*), but other authors, nevertheless, declare the dependability of his works (Ps 92:4[5]; Dan 9:14).

LXX The LXX usually used *poieō*, do, to render *'śh*; *ergon*, deed, works normally translates *ma'ᵃśeh.* Other words used for the vb.: *gignomai*, be, become; *ergazomai*, effect, do, work out; *prassō*, practice, do; *chraō/chraomai*, use, make use of, employ; *synteleō*, complete; *plassō*, do; *hetoimazō*, prepare, make ready; *kataskeuazō*, prepare; *hamartanō*, do/commit sin, fall short. For the noms. the following are also found, all meaning basically "something done, accomplished, deed, act," *poiēma*, *poiēsis*, *ergasia*. A few other words are used one time each. Interestingly *ktizō* is not used for *'śh* (vb), but for *br'*, to create; *ysd*, establish, found; *yṣr*, to form; *kwn*, make, establish, create; *qnh*, create, acquire. The same is true in the NT.

P-B The use of the root *'śh* in the DSS can be noted and the following summary categories given. Nothing new is found in these scrolls of unusual theological significance that goes beyond the OT usage of this ubiquitous word. The usage of the word is to be expected since it is such a general term.

In the Temple Scroll it is found over 100x as a vb. and 3x in its nom. form. Its meanings, determined by its context, correspond to its use in the OT. The Qumran covenanters were expected to follow truth, justice, and righteousness and to fulfill the *ḥuqqîm* of God (1QS 1:5; 5:2), doing always what God commanded (1QS 1:16). In summary, they are doers of the Torah (1QpHab 7:11). Certain combinations found in the OT are used, such as "to do evil/justice" (1QS 1:7; 5:12). At Qumran, "without God nothing has been done or occurs" (1QS 11:11).

The nom. *ma'ᵃśeh* retains the same meanings it had in the OT, with some adaptation to objects of interest to the Qumran community. His people are "his work" (1QH 11:30). Justice/righteousness preceded all of God's works (1QH 14:16; 15:20). All his works/deeds were known beforehand by God alone. They are all great and marvelous (1QM 10:8; 1QH 1:7, 21). Human deeds are deceitful (*rᵉmiyyâ*; 1QH 1:26), God's are righteous altogether (1QH 4:20; 1QM 11:4). The members of the community are to be tested according to their insight and deeds (1QS 5:21, 23, 24), with an indication that works/deeds are tied to the salvation of the person.

Mish. Heb. finds, of course, a lively use of the word, but it often corresponds to *'bd*, do, work, etc. Hence, *'śh* means do, work, prepare (e.g.,Šebi'it VIII, 6; Tosef. VI, 29). It is used in additional stems. In addition to the ni. stem it is used in the hi., meaning "to cause to do; to order" (Baba Batra 9a; Exod Rabbah s. 35). In the pi. it means to force, enforce (Pesiqta Rabbati 33). For further refs. see Jastrow 2:1124-25.

Deed, act, misdeed, work: → *gml* (accomplish, commit, achieve, ripen, # 1694); → *mᵉlā'kâ* (work, duties, task, # 4856); → *'ll* I (act, wipe out, deal with, harm, glean, # 6618); → *'śh* I (make, do, prepare, create, work, service, # 6913); → *p'l* (do, make, produce, practice, accomplish, perform, # 7188)

Bibliography

NIDNTT 3:1152-58; *THAT* 2:359-70; *TWAT* 6:413-32; R. Braun, "Kohelet und die frühhellenistische Popularphilosophie," *BZAW* 130, 1973, 53; D. Edelman, "Saul's Rescue of Jabesh-Gilead (1 Sam 11:1-11)," *ZAW* 96, 1984, 204; D. Hillers, "An Alphabetic Cuneiform Tables from Taanach," *BASOR* 176, 1964, 46; M. R. Lehmann, "Biblical Oaths," *ZAW* 81, 1969, 74-92; T. M. Ludwig, "The Traditions of the Establishing of the Earth in Deutero-Isaiah," *JBL* 92, 1973, 345-57; H. D. Preuss, "Verspottung fremder Religionen in AT," *BWANT* 12, 1971; M. Reisel, "The Relation Between the Creative Function of the Verbs עשה - יצר - ברא in Isa 43:7 and 45:7," *Verkenningen in een stroom-gebred*, 1975, 65-67; H. Ringgren, *The Faith of Qumran*, 1963; H. H. Schmid, *Gerechtigkeit als Weltordnung: Hintergrund und Geschichte des alttestamentlichen Gerechtigkeitsbegriffes*, BHT 40, 1968; E. Sjöberg, "Wiedergeburt und Neuschöpfung in palästinischen Tirdentum," *ST* 4, 1950, 44-85; idem, "Neuschöpfung in den Toten-Meer-Rollen," *ST* 9, 1955, 131-36.

Eugene Carpenter

6917 (*'āśôr*, ten, a decade), → # 6924

6920 (*'ᵃśîrî*, tenth), → # 6924

6923 (*'śr*, take a tenth, tithe), → # 6924

6924	עֶשֶׂר

עֶשֶׂר (*'eśer*), nom. ten (cardinal number) (# 6924); מַעֲשֵׂר (*ma'ᵃśēr*), tithe (→ # 5130); עָשׂוֹר (*'āśôr*), nom. a ten, a decade (# 6917); עֲשִׂירִי (*'ᵃśîrî*), adj. a tenth (ordinal number) (# 6920); עשׂר (*'śr*), q. take a tenth; pi. tithe (# 6923); עָשָׂר (*'āśār*), nom. ten in compound numbers (# 6925); עֶשְׂרֵה (*'eśrēh*), nom. ten in compound numbers (# 6926); עֲשָׂרָה (*'ᵃśārâ*), nom. group of ten, ten (# 6927); עִשָּׂרוֹן (*'iśśārôn*), nom. tenth part (# 6928); עֶשְׂרִים (*'eśrîm*), twenty (# 6929).

OT 1. As the number of fingers on both hands, ten lies close at hand as the archetypal round number and base for counting (though not in every culture). It is uncertain whether there is significance in ten being the sum of the important numbers seven and three (but see the proportions in 1 Kgs 11:3; Job 1:2-3). It is used as a standard unit of reckoning for buildings (Exod 26:16; 1 Kgs 6:3; Ezek 40:11), presents (2 Kgs 5:5), wages (Judg 17:10), and periods of time (Gen 16:3). It is the lowest member of the series 10 - 100 - 1000 - 10,000 (→ hundred, # 4395). It was the smallest military unit (Deut 1:15; Sinuhe's escort consisted of ten men, *ANET*, 21).

2. Ten is used as a round number (cf. the English "dozen"). Jacob complains that Laban has changed his wage ten times (Gen 31:7, 41), and Israel tries God's patience ten times in the wilderness (Num 14:22). Ten times the normal is hyperbole, as when Elkanah considers himself worth more than ten sons (1 Sam 1:8), and Daniel and his friends are found ten times better than all the other young men (Dan 1:20).

3. Ten sometimes implies a note of completeness. In lists such as the Ten Commandments the number may have a mnemonic value, although there are three different ways to divide up the verses into ten. Called the "ten words" (Exod 34:28; Deut 4:13;

10:4), the Decalogue is a summary revelation of God's will for Israel. While the two tablets may be complete duplicates (→ *šᵉnayim*, two, # 9109), the division into two sets of five commandments sums up their content aptly (M. Weinfeld, *Deuteronomy 1-11*, 1991, 245; → Decalogue: Theology). The first pentad expresses love for God (cf. Deut 6:5) and is distinctively Yahwistic and Israelite. The second five encompass the social sphere and encourage love for humankind (cf. Lev 19:18). Though written on stone for permanence, the ten words also required interpretation, elaboration, and application, as may be seen in the different traditions represented by Exod 20 and Deut 5, and the expansion and application of the commandments found in the detailed case laws of Exod 21-23 and Deut 12-26.

4. Ten is frequently found as a literary structuring principle. Although an explicit recognition of a ten is often found only in later texts, it is evident that there are ten plagues revealing the power of God (Exod 7-11). There are ten generations before the Flood (the antediluvians of Gen 5) and after the Flood (leading to Abraham, Gen 10).

5. The chief significance of twelve is that it is the number of the tribes of Israel (Gen 49:28), traced back to the twelve sons of Jacob (Gen 35:22; 42:13). The participation of the tribes is an important feature of Israel's early worship, and significant stages in the Exodus (Exod 24:4) and the crossing of the Jordan (Josh 4:3) are marked by twelvefold ritual acts. The tabernacle is surrounded by twelve tribes (Num 2:17-31), although the special role of Levi requires Ephraim and Manasseh, Joseph's sons, to act as full tribes. Twelve representatives of the tribes fulfil various functions (Num 1:44), and the leaders themselves offer dedications to the tabernacle on twelve days (Num 7). The names of the tribes are inscribed on the stones of the high priestly breastplate (Exod 28:21). The restoration of the twelve tribes of the divided kingdom (1 Kgs 11:30) is a feature of postexilic hope (Ezek 47:13), a hope sustained by the ritual of the rededicated temple (Ezra 6:17; 8:35). Twelve is also a round number, similar to ten (Num 33:9; 2 Sam 2:15). A year has twelve months, and its completion can trigger significant events (Esth 2:12; Dan 4:29[25]). Twelve officials in turn were responsible for supplying food for Solomon one month in the year (1 Kgs 4:7). The threatened exaltation of Joseph over his eleven brothers is a key plot element of the Joseph narrative (Gen 37:9).

P-B Increasing interest in number symbolism led to the multiplication of significant tens, for example in the ten eras of various apocalyptic texts (2 En 91:15-16). Philo called ten the number of perfection (*Vita Mos* 1:96). M. Ab. 5 has various lists that illustrate the systematic and pedagogic use of numbering. Thus, the world was created by ten sayings (Gen 1; M. Ab. 5:1), and Abraham was tested ten times (Mish. 'Abot 5:3; Jub 19:8). The War Scroll refers to the twelve tribes and their commanders (1QM 5:1-2). The group of ten with its commander (1QM 4:5) is the smallest building block of larger groups (1QS 2:22; CD 13:1).

Numbers: → *'eḥād* (one, # 285); → *'elep* II (thousand, military contingent, # 547); → *'arba'* (four, # 752); → *ḥāmēš* (five, # 2822); → *mē'â* I (hundred, # 4395); → *'eśer* (ten, # 6924); → *rᵉbābâ* (ten thousand, myriad, # 8047/8052); → *šeba'* I (seven, # 8679); → *šālōš, šᵉlōšâ* (three, a three, # 8993); → *šᵉmōneh* (eight, # 9046); → *šᵉnayim* (two, # 9109); → *šēš* I (six, # 9252); → *tēša'* (nine, # 9596)

Numbering, counting: → *kss* (reckon, apportion, # 4082); → *mnh* (count, # 4948); → *spr* I (count, number, reckon, rehearse, # 6218); → *pqd* (number, appoint, # 7212)

Bibliography

NIDNTT 2:692-94; *TDNT* 2:36-37; *TWAT* 6:432-38; A. Bea, "Der Zahlenspruch in Hebräischen und Ugaritischen," *Bib* 21, 1940, 196-98; H. A. Brongers, "Die Zehnzahl in der Bibel und ihrer Umwelt," in *Studia Biblica et Semitica: Theodoro Christiano Vriezen qui munere Professoris Theologiae per XXV annos functus est, ab amicis, collegis, discipulis dedicata,* eds. W. C. von Unnik and A. S. van der Woude, 1966, 30-45; A. M. Cartun, "'Who Knows Ten?' The Structural and Symbolic Use of Numbers in the Ten Plagues: Exodus 7:14-13:16," *USQR* 49, 1991, 65-119; W. Herrmann, "Mercatores mandatu missi. Ein Beitrag zum Verständnis der Einheiten "Fünf" und "Zehn" in der kanonischen und deuterokanonischen Literatur des Alten Testaments," *ZAW* 91, 1979, 329-38; Jastrow 2:1127.

P. P. Jenson

6925 (*'āśār*, ten), → # 6924

6926 (*'eśrēh*, ten), → # 6924

6927 (*'ᵃśārâ*, ten), → # 6924

6928 (*'iśśārôn*, tenth part), → # 6924

6929 (*'eśrîm*, twenty), → # 6924

6931	עָשׁ

עָשׁ (*'āš* I), nom. clothes' moth, moth (# 6931).

ANE Jew. Aram., Syr. *'aššā'*; Ugar. *'ṯ*; Arab. *'aṯṯat*; Eth. *'ᵉḍē*; Akk. *ašāšu*.

OT The word is found 7x in the OT. The moth is the avenger/destroyer of the ones who are corrupt and accuse (falsely) the righteous/servant of the Lord (Isa 50:9; 51:8); it will devour those who do not have God's law in their hearts (‖ to *sās* in 51:8). Job compares the fragility of human life to moths (Job 4:19) and to garments weakened by them (13:28). The works of the wicked are unstable and pass away like a moth's cocoon (27:18; lit., "he builds his house like a moth"). Job may be asserting that humans are crushed more quickly than a moth (4:19; cf. 8:14). The moth serves as a symbol of the Lord as he consumes the strength/wealth of men (Ps 39:11[12]) and even his own people (Hos 5:12).

P-B The LXX generally employs *sēs*, moth, to translate these passages. In Job 13:28 it describes a cloth as moth-eaten (*sētobrōton*). Ps 38:12 [= Matt 39:12] interestingly has *arachnēn*, spider, for MT moth; Sir 42:13 holds that as a moth comes from garments (corruption), so evil comes from a woman. In LH it continued to be used with the meaning moth (Deut R. s. 2; Jastrow 2:1124).

NT In the NT the destructive aspects of the moth are stressed with respect to earthly, not heavenly treasure (Matt 6:19-20; Luke 12:33-34). James 5:2 recalls Job 13:28, using the LXX's term *sētobrōton*, moth-eaten, to describe the riches of the wealthy.

Insects: → *debôrâ* I (bee, wasp, # 1805); → *kēn* V (mosquito, gnat, louse, # 4031); → *'ṭh* II (delouse, # 6487); → *'aqrāb* (scorpion, # 6832); → *'ārōb* (fly, swarm of flies, flying insects, # 6856); → *'āš* I (moth, # 6931); → *ṣir'â* (hornet, destruction, fear, terror, depression, discouragement, # 7667); → *qml* (wither, become moldy, musty, infected w. insects, # 7857)

BIBLIOGRAPHY

IDB 2:246-56; 3:451; E. Dhorme, *A Commentary on the Book of Job*, 1984; J. Hartley, *The Book of Job*, 1988; A. R. Hulst, *Old Testament Translation Problems*, 1960; *Fauna and Flora of the Bible*, 1980².

Eugene Carpenter/Michael A. Grisanti

6932	עָשׁ

עָשׁ (*'āš* II), pus (hapleg.; # 6932); a rare derivative of עשׁשׁ (*'šš*), become weak, dissolve (→ # 6949).

OT *'āš* most probably indicates pus, a product of inflammation containing among others elements dead cells and liquefied tissue. The "moth" in Hos 5:12—"I am like a moth to Ephraim" (NIV)—unfortunately conveys the sense of external corruption rather than the internal disintegration that was sapping the moral and spiritual fiber of the apostate nation. The next verse makes this even more explicit, "When Ephraim saw his sickness (*ḥolî*), and Judah his sores (*māzôr*), then Ephraim turned to Assyria, and sent to the great king for help. But he is not able to cure you, not able to heal your sores (*māzôr*)" (5:13). See H. W. Wolff, *Hosea*, Hermeneia, 1974, 115).

Andersen and Freedman (*Hosea*, AB, 1980, 412) prefer to take *'āš* and *rāqāb* together in Hos 5:12 as a reference to maggots. While they view this as a metaphor for the devouring of rotten flesh, recent medical research has suggested that maggots can promote healing of a wound because they feed on only the diseased parts.

Disease—blister, boil, skin disease, scar, wound: → *'aba'bu'ōt* (blisters, # 81); → *bōhaq* (skin condition, # 993); → *baheret* (white patch on skin, # 994); → *gārāb* (festering eruption, # 1734); → *zrr* I (press out [wounds], # 2452); → *ḥeres* I (itch, # 3063); → *yabbelet* (wart?, # 3301); → *yallepet* (skin disease, # 3539); → *yeraqraq* (discoloration, # 3768); → *kewiyya* (scar, # 3918); → *m'r* (be sore, # 4421); → *māzôr* I (boil, # 4649); → *makkâ* (blow, # 4804); → *mispaḥat* (skin eruption, # 5030); → *mrḥ* (rub, polish, # 5302); → *neteq* (scalp infection, # 5999); → *sappaḥat* (hair disease, # 6204); → *'ōpel* I (abscesses, # 6754); → *'āš* II (pus, # 6932); → *ṣāpâ* (pus?, # 7597); → *ṣarebet* (scar, # 7648); → *ṣr'* (suffer from skin disease, # 7665); → *śe'ēt* II (swelling, # 8421); → *śtr* (break out [tumor], # 8609); → *šeḥîn* (boil, # 8825). For related entries → *ḥlh* I (become weak, tired, ill, # 2703)

BIBLIOGRAPHY

ISBE 1:532, 953-60; 3:103-6.

R. K. Harrison

6933 (*'āš* III, Aldebaran?, Arcturus, Bear?, Leo), → # 3919

6934 (*'āšôq*, oppressor), → # 6943

6935 (*'ašûqîm*, oppression), → # 6943

6938 (*'āšîr*, rich, wealthy), → # 6947

6939	עשן

עשן (*'šn*), q. be wrapped in smoke, be angry (# 6939); עָשָׁן (*'āšān* I), nom. smoke (# 6940); עָשֵׁן (*'āšēn*), adj. smoking (# 6942).

OT 1. In the OT the terms for smoke appear chiefly in three contexts: theophanic portrayals, descriptions of mundane events whether actual or prophesied, and comparisons or figurative descriptions. (→ Theophany: Theology)

2. There are three occurrences of the vb. *'šn* in theophanic contexts. When Yahweh descends upon Mount Sinai, it smokes (Exod 19:18). The hills and mountains also smoke when he touches them in theophanic descent (Ps 104:32; 144:5).

3. The vb. also occurs 3x in figurative expressions of anger. Yahweh's wrath will smoke against the persistent idolater (Deut 29:19[20]). The psalmist in lament asks why (Ps 74:1) or how long (80:4[5]) Yahweh's anger will smoke against his people.

4. There are eight occurrences of the nom. *'āšān* in theophanic contexts. Twice it is used figuratively of Yahweh's anger, the smoke out of his nostrils (2 Sam 22:9 = Ps 18:9[8]; cf. Isa 65:5). In other cases, the term is used to describe the smoke that attends actual theophanies: God appears to Abram as a smoking furnace (Gen 15:17), and a similar comparison is used of Mount Sinai when God descends upon it (Exod 19:18 [2x]); the temple is filled with smoke at Isaiah's inaugural vision of Yahweh (Isa 6:4), and Isaiah envisions Yahweh eschatologically dwelling in Zion in a cloud of smoke by day and a glow of flaming fire by night, reminiscent of the wilderness wanderings (4:5; cf. Exod 40:38); Joel prophesies that in the last days there will be blood, fire, and columns of smoke (Joel 3:3[2:30]), a prophecy that Peter applies to the events surrounding Christ's crucifixion (Acts 2:14-23).

5. The nom. also occurs 10x in nontheophanic descriptions. Smoke arises from burning cities (Josh 8:20-21; Judg 20:38, 40) or chariots (Nah 2:14). It heralds a foe (Isa 14:31) or characterizes the future destruction of Israel (9:17[18]) and Edom (34:10). Smoke pours forth from Leviathan's nostrils (Job 41:12[20]). And smoke irritates the eyes (Prov 10:26).

6. The nom. is also used a few times in comparisons or figures of speech to describe the quality of transitoriness (Ps 37:20; 68:3; 102:4[3]; Isa 51:6; Hos 13:3) or the dust cloud of Solomon's chariot (S of Songs 3:6).

7. The adj. *'āšēn* occurs twice in the OT. Once it describes Mount Sinai smoking at Yahweh's descent (Exod 20:18). It also describes sarcastically Rezin, king of Aram, and Pekah, son of Remaliah, king of Israel ("these two smoldering stubs of firewood," Isa 7:4).

P-B The nom. occurs in naturalistic descriptions twice (faces blackened by smoke, Epis. Jer. 1:21; smoke seen in battle, 1 Macc 4:20). It also occurs in comparisons twice (breath of human nostrils like smoke—i.e., transitory, Wisd. Sol. 2:2; cf. 5:14).

Smoke: → *'šn* (be wrapped in smoke, be angry, # 6939); → *qṭr* (let go up in smoke, # 7787); → *tîmārâ* (palm-shaped column of smoke, # 9406)

Bibliography
TWOT 2:705; W. Eichrodt, *Theology of the Old Testament*, 1961, 2:270.

Jeffrey J. Niehaus

6940 (*'āšān* I, smoke), → # 6939

6942 (*'āšēn*, smoking), → # 6939

6943	עשׁק

עשׁק (*'šq* I), q. oppress, wrong, extort; pu. be abused, crushed (# 6943); מַעֲשַׁקּוֹת(*ma'ašaqqôt*), extortion, exploitation (# 5131); עָשׁוֹק (*'āšôq*), oppressor (# 6934); עֲשׁוּקִים (*'ašûqîm*), oppression (# 6935); עֹשֶׁק (*'ōšeq*), nom. oppression, extortion (# 6945); עָשְׁקָה (*'ošqâ*), oppression (# 6946).

ANE Akk. *ešqu,* strong; Arab. *'asiqa,* pursue, *'asaq,* injustice; Aram. *'šq*, wrong.

OT 1. This group of words describes in a minority of instances the oppression of Israel by foreign oppressors (1 Chron 16:21; Ps 105:14; Isa 52:4; Jer 50:33; Hos 5:11; cf. also Isa 23:12; 30:12). On the other hand, they frequently describe various forms of social injustice by which the rich in Israelite society oppressed the poor (→ *ynh*, oppress [# 3561]).

2. It is significant that in a number of usages of *'šq* and its derivatives is explicitly indicated in the context (Deut 24:14; Jer 7:6; Amos 4:1). People most likely to be mistreated and socially oppressed were those without adequate defence of their rights, viz., the widow, orphan, sojourner, and the poor. *'šq* and its derivatives thus have strong overtones of "extortion" and "despoliation": they are often accompanied by the vbs. *gzl* (despoil, rob, → 1608) and *lqḥ* (take, → # 4374); see Lev 6:2, 4 [5:21, 23]; Deut 28:29, 33; 1 Sam 12:3-4. The oppressor robs the oppressed in different ways: by using false scales and doing fraudulent trade (Hos 12:7[8]); by holding back the laborer's wages (Jer 22:13); by bribery, usury, and profit at the expense of the poor and the foreigner (Ezek 22:12, 29). The primary purpose of the oppressor is to accumulate wealth that is only attainable by exploiting and robbing one's neighbor.

3. In one instance God is accused of oppressing the righteous (Job 10:3). On the other hand, God is often described as the one who commits himself to the cause of oppressed people. These people also show their steadfast faith in Yahweh as their deliverer and defender of their cause (Ps 72:4; 103:6; 146:7; Isa 38:14). Oppression of the poor is even equated with an act of oppression against God (Lev 6:2[5:21]; Prov 14:31). In Isa 54:14 *'ōšeq* is contrasted with the promise of a future Zion that "will be established in righteousness."

P-B In 1QpHab 1:6; 10:1 the nom. *'ōšeq* describes social oppression. In 10:1 *'ōšeq* is used in parallel with *gāzēl,* robbery, a term that is often used in the OT (also in vb. form) along with words for oppression to describe the despoliation of the goods of other people.

Affliction, oppression: → *dḥq* (oppress, # 1895); → *ḥms* I (do violence, # 2803); → *ḥmṣ* II (oppress, # 2807); → *ynh* (oppress, # 3561); → *lḥṣ* (press, # 4315); → *māṣôr* I (affliction, siege, # 5189); → *mrr* I (be bitter, distraught, afflict, # 5352); → *nega'* (plague, affliction, # 5596); → *ngś* (exact, # 5601); → *'nh* II (afflict, humble, afflict one's soul, fast, oppress, submit,

6700); → *'wq* I (crush?, # 6421); → *'mr* II (deal tyrannically with, # 6683); → *'šq* I (wrong, # 6943); → *ṣwq* I (constrain, press in/upon, harass, vex, # 7439); → *ṣwr* II (deal tyrannically with, # 7444); → *rhb* (assail, press, pester, alarm, confuse, # 8104); → *rṣṣ* (crush, # 8368); → *tôlāl* (oppressor, # 9354); → *tōk* (oppression, # 9412)
Plunder, spoil, robbing, stealing: → *bzz* (plunder, spoil, # 1024); → *gzl* (steal, rob, # 1608); → *gnb* (steal, rob, # 1704); → *pārîṣ* II (burglar, robber, # 7265); → *pereq* (crossroad?, plunder, # 7294); → *šll* II (take plunder, seize, # 8964); → *šsh* (plunder, loot, # 9115)

BIBLIOGRAPHY
T. D. Hanks, *God So Loved the Third World: The Biblical Vocabulary of Oppression*, 1983, 3-39; Y. I. Kim, "The Vocabulary of Oppression in the Old Testament," Ph.D. diss. Drew University, 1981; C. F. Marriottini, "The Problem of Social Oppression in the Eighth Century Prophets," Ph.D. diss. Southern Baptist Theological Seminary, 1983; J. Miranda, *Communism in the Bible*, 1982, 37-39; J. Pons, *L'oppression dans l'Ancien Testament*, 1981; E. Tamez, *Bible of the Oppressed*, 1982, 1-30.

I. Swart

6945 (*'ōšeq*, oppression, extortion), → # 6943

6946 (*'ošqâ*, oppression), → # 6943

6947	עשׁר

עשׁר (*'šr* I), q. be rich, to become rich; hi. make rich, gain riches; hitp. enrich oneself (# 6947); עָשִׁיר (*'āšîr*), adj. rich, wealthy (# 6938); עֹשֶׁר (*'ōšer*), nom. wealth, riches (# 6948).

ANE *TWAT* 6:447 identifies the Aram. *'tr/'tyr* (*DISO*, 224), the Syr. *'tr*, and Arab. *'ašara* as cognates, meaning abundance and plenty. See also the Sam. *'āššer* with the meaning of riches. *HALAT* 850 suggests that if Ps 65:10 is *'šr* II, following the Ugar., then *'šr* I is the form discussed here.

OT 1. The semantic field of wealth and riches consists primarily of three terms: *'šr* (wealth, riches in opposition to poverty), *hôn* (material possessions, including riches), and *n*^e^*kāsîm* (possessions in general, including livestock), of which the first is the most important. By contrast, the OT has a wide variety of words for poverty and oppression, indicating a greater familiarity with those conditions than with wealth (→ *'ebyôn*, poor [# 36]).

2. The world of the OT was not one of great opulence and wealth. Even the riches of kings, such as Solomon's (see A. R. Millard, *Solomon's Wealth*, 20-34), were insignificant when measured against the wealth of Egypt or Assyria. Archaeology testifies to the building projects of Solomon, Ahab, and Hezekiah, but the most exciting constructions and the most beautiful mosaics date from Roman times and later (e.g., Masada, Sepphoris). For the OT, wealth and riches refer in the tribal period to the material blessings of farmers—cattle, sheep (e.g., Gen 13:2). Idyllic rural life is epitomized in 1 Kgs 4:25, "During Solomon's lifetime Judah and Israel, from Dan to Beersheba, lived in safety, each man under his own vine and fig tree." Long life, good crops, affluence, and power are seen to be signs of God's material blessings (cf. Gen 49:3, 8; Deut 33:13-17). However, with the growth of the monarchy, particularly from the time of Solomon onwards, a clear distinction became obvious between the stratum

of the wealthy and powerful and the bulk of the peasant population (*ABD* 6:84-85). The prophets warned often against the dangers of accumulating possessions at the cost of someone else's welfare (e.g., Isa 5:8; 10:1-3), while the tenth commandment urged people to be content with their share of material possessions (Exod 20:17).

3. The Mosaic laws emphasize the sense of equality of all people, not least with regard to the sabbatical and Jubilee codes. While *'āšîr* and *'ōšer* occur in the Pentateuchal narratives with the general sense of rich or riches (Gen 14:23; 31:16), in the law codes a technical sense comes into play. *'āšîr* means a definable group of people who are known by their position in society as the rich. So in Exod 30:15, the regulation for the half-shekel census tax is laid out with the strict instruction that the rich should not give more nor the poor less than the required half shekel. Thus, the principle of the equality of all people in the sight of God regardless of wealth is underlined.

4. The prophets of the eighth century BC spoke into a context where changing forms of land tenure, from patrimonial to prebendal (see Coote, 24-32) and an economic system, biased against the small land owner, had created a small (about 3 to 5 percent of the population) but powerful ruling elite (owning 50 to 70 percent of the arable land). Amos speaks of their stone mansions and their fertile vineyards (Amos 5:11), but warns that they will not enjoy these, for their sins will be held against them by God (v. 12a). They oppress the poor and deny them justice in the courts (v. 12b). They cheat with false balances and sell the refuse of the wheat to the poor (8:4-8). In similar vein, Isaiah cries out, "Woe to you who add house to house and join field to field till no space is left and you live alone in the land" (Isa 5:8), and follows with the same warning: "Surely the great houses will become desolate, the fine mansions left without occupants" (5:9). The dark face of wealth is graphically depicted here—the lies, cheating, structural violence, oppression, and injustice. Religion has become a screen for injustice (Amos 8:5), and so God will reject their worship until "justice rolls on like a river, righteousness like a never-failing stream!" (5:24).

5. *'āšîr* often refers to the wealthy as a group (see Mic 6:12, which speaks of the violence of the rich, and Jer 9:23[22], which warns against the rich man boasting about his wealth). In some instances *'āšîr* may also refer to an individual, as in the parable of Nathan of the poor man's lamb (2 Sam 12:1-4). In contrast to the wealthy of Amos's time, remorse swept over David as his abuse of power was exposed (12:5-14).

6. In the famous Servant Song of Isa 53, the oppressed Servant of God is assigned a grave with the wicked and the rich (v. 9, following the reading of the MT and 1QIsa, *TWAT* 6:448). The sense is that in his death the servant receives no honor, for he shares a grave with the very people who have oppressed him, being disowned by even family and friends. Here rich (*'āšîr*) and wicked (*rᵉšā'îm*) are in parallel.

7. The Wisdom tradition is a great source for teaching on wealth and poverty and presents both the positive and the negative sides of wealth. On the positive side we have statements like "The blessing of the LORD brings wealth, and he adds no trouble to it" (Prov 10:22), which underlines God's provision for his own. Unfortunately, in modern times this message has sometimes been distorted by the so-called prosperity cults, where wealth and prosperity are overemphasized as the just rewards for righteousness (see Bosman, 25-32). The positive side of wealth is also found in passages like 10:15, "The wealth of the rich is their fortified city"; 3:16, Lady Wisdom has riches and honor in her left hand, long life in her right (cf. Ps 112:3; Prov 8:18)

Prov 14:24, "The wealth of the wise is their crown." Laziness, rather than oppression, is seen as a primary cause of poverty, while hard work is a sure way of bringing wealth (10:4). Such statements presuppose that one is not fighting against the kind of oppressive structures envisaged by Amos or Isaiah. On the negative side, Job threatens the wicked that while they sleep, God will suddenly remove their wealth (Job 27:19). The writer of Proverbs warns that those who trust in riches will fall, but the righteous will thrive (Prov 11:28). In these passages the rich are either aligned with the wicked or contrasted with the righteous.

8. The theology of wealth may be expressed as follows: Wealth is a blessing from God (Prov 10:22), but to pursue wealth for its own sake is a recipe for discontent, loneliness, and emptiness (Eccl 4:8; cf. Prov 28:20). As we enter the world, so shall we depart, naked and empty-handed (Eccl 5:15[14]). Better than riches is a good name (Prov 22:1), and, ultimately, real riches are to be found in the humility and fear of the Lord (22:4). A wise person prays, "Give me neither poverty nor riches, but give me only my daily bread" (30:8). When riches become one's god (Mammon), then one opens the doors to oppressive ideologies, an unquenchable thirst for power, corruption, and violence (Isa 10:1-2). Along such a path other people are dehumanized (Amos 2:6-7), and the door is open to abuse and the creation of structures where violence breeds like a cancer (Mic 6:12). The OT ethic urges a sharing of wealth and a caring for those who are poor and oppressed (Job 31:16-25). Here in v. 25 Job uses two related terms, namely, *ḥayil* (# 2657), used 25x in the OT as "wealth" or "riches," and *kabbîr* (# 3888), used only here as "fortune." Wisdom, righteousness, and wealth in combination are seen to be God's ideal for humankind (Prov 3:13-16).

P-B 1. The LXX uses the word group *plouteō* about 180x, of which 76 instances render the Heb. root *'šr*. Ben Sirach reflects the same dual understanding of wealth as does Proverbs. An industrious person will grow wealthy (Sir 31:3), provided he refrains from wickedness (19:1-3). Wealth brings honor (10:30), peace (44:6), and a full, happy life (44:1-88). However, wealth is also a danger and those who trust in their riches will fall (11:9). Riches cannot be taken into the next life (11:17-19; cf. Eccl 5:12-19[11-18]).

2. RL makes wide use of *'šr* and its derivatives. The dominant sense is one of strength (or power, see Baba Batra 25b) and wealth ('Abot 4:9 and Baba Batra 9b). Control on the abuse of riches is expressed. For example, parents are not permitted to give away their wealth to their children and then throw themselves on charity (Ketubot 48a). Šabbat 25b speaks of true wealth coming to the person who is satisfied with what they possess. In line with the prophets, Yoma 35b condemns those who are rich and yet neglect the poor.

3. The idea of spiritual riches found in the NT (Matt 6:20) is present also in several intertestamental texts (e.g., T. Levi 13:5; *1 En.* 17:3; *Pss. Sol.* 9:9), whereby a place in God's kingdom might be assured.

NT 1. A number of G terms are used, of which *plousios* and *ploutos* are the most common. Jesus gives several warnings about the dangers of riches (e.g., Matt 13:22), addresses three woes to the rich (Luke 6:24-26), and in a number of parables juxtaposes the rich and poor (e.g., Luke 16:19-31). The message of the gospels is not that poor people are closer to God or more loved by God. Rather, the NT stresses God's concern and care for the poor and needy in the absence of societal and legal protection (2 Cor 8:9).

Riches, wealth: → *hwn* (consider easy, risk, # 2103); → *n^{e}kāsîm* (possessions, wealth, riches, # 5794); → *'šr* (be rich, become rich, make rich, # 6947)

BIBLIOGRAPHY
NIDNTT 2:829-53; *TDNT* 6:318-32; *TWOT* 2:706; H. L. Bosman, (ed) *Plutocrats and Paupers*, 1991; R. B. Coote, *Amos Among the Prophets*, 1981; T. Donald, "The Semantic Field of Rich and Poor in the Wisdom Literature of Hebrew and Accadian," *OrAnt* 3, 1964, 27-41; S. Gillingham, "The Poor in the Psalms," *ExpTim* 100, 1989/90, 15-19; M. Hengel, *Earliest Christianity*, 1986; A. R. Millard, "Solomon's Wealth," *BARev* 15, 1989, 20-34; J. Pixley, C. Boff, *The Bible, the Church and the Poor*, 1989; G. von Rad, *Wisdom in Israel*, 1972; R. N. Whybray, "Poverty, Wealth and Point of View in Proverbs," *ExpTim* 100, 1988/89, 332-36.

W. R. Domeris

6948 (*'ōšer*, riches), → # 6947

6949	עשׁשׁ

עשׁשׁ (*'šš*), q. become weak (# 6949).

ANE The vb. refers to darkness: Sam. *'ššh*, darkness; Arab. *'as'asa*, dark. There may be some link to *'š* II and Arab. *ġtt*, be weak, waste away (*HALAT* 850). Delekat (52-55) suggests swelling up, which might point to muscles and being strong.

OT This vb. is only used 3x, all in the Psalms. In Ps 6:7[8] the wasting and the weakness of the eye indicate the deterioration of the psalmist; conversely, a clear eye symbolized strength and good health (Craigie, 94). Ps 31:9-10[10-11] shows a high degree of grammatical and semantic parallelism with *'šš* occurring at the beginning and the end of these two verses (Dion, 187). Exegetes have not yet reached final consensus as to the exact meaning of *'šš* in Ps 31. Collins (187) has suggested that vv. 9-10[10-11] are a description of weeping and tears, while Bons (56-59) opted for a reference to the darkness of the eye. The metaphoric language can be interpreted in different ways, but in general one can accept that, one way or the other, a weakening of the eye refers to sickness or the nearness of death (Craigie, 261).

P-B 1. *LXX*. All three occurrences of *'šš* in the Psalms are translated with *tarassō*, stir up, confuse, trouble, disturb.

2. *Qumran and RL*. The root *'šš* is tr. in 1QH 5:34 to be dark, to be/become dark; this corresponds with the Targum interpretation of Ps 6:8 and 31:11. 1QH 9:5 can be tr. "my eye is like darkness" because of the attestation of *'šš'* as darkness in Christian Pal. Aram. (Nebe, 116-17). In the Midrash Till. on Ps 19:1, *'šš* refers to strength (Jastrow 2:1127).

NT *tarassō* occurs 18x in the NT, 11x in the Gospels (6x in John) (*EDNT* 3:335-36). It refers to the stirring up of people (Acts 17:8), inner agitation (John 11:33), or the troubling of the soul (12:27).

Feeble, despair, faint, frail, tender: → *'ml* I (be weak, be feeble, languish, # 581); → *ḥlh* I (become weak, tired, ill, # 2703); → *ylh* (languish, # 3532); → *k'h* (be disheartened, frightened, # 3874); → *nbl* I (wither, fade, languish, dishonor, # 5570); → *'ṭp* II (grow weak, faint, be feeble,

6494); → *'lp* (cover, faint, # 6634); → *'šš* (become weak, # 6949); → *pwg* (be feeble, numb, be prostrated, # 7028); → *rzh* (destroy, waste away, # 8135); → *rkk* (be tender, timid, gentle, # 8216); → *rph* (become slack, lose heart, discourage, # 8332)

BIBLIOGRAPHY

EDNT 3:335-36; E. Bons, *Psalm 31-Rettung als paradigma*, 1994; T. Collins, "Physiology of Tears in the Old Testament," *CBQ* 33:18-38, 185-197; P. C. Craigie, *Psalms 1-50*, WBC, 1983; L. Delekat, "Zum hebräischen Wörterbuch," *VT* 14, 1964, 7-66; P. E. Dion, "Strophic Boundaries and Rhetorical Structure in Psalm 31," *Église et théologie* 18, 1987, 183-92; G. W. Nebe, "Zu עשׁ in 1QH 9:5," *RevQ* 12, 1985, 115-18.

Hendrik L. Bosman

6950 (*'št* I, sleek), → # 4170

6951	עשת

עשת (*'št* I), hitp. think, consider (# 6951); עַשְׁתּוּת (*'aštût*), nom. opinion, thought (hapleg.; # 6953); עֶשְׁתּוֹן (*'eštôn*), nom. plan (hapleg.; # 6955).

ANE Aram. *'ᵃšat*, ithpe. think; *'eštônā'*, nom. plan.

OT The vb. is used in reference to God's considering favorably the desperate condition of people on board a ship that was about to be torn apart by a mighty storm (Jon 1:6). The nom. *'aštût* is used in Job 12:5 for the "thought" or "opinion" of those who are at ease, i.e., in expressing their opinion Job's comforters make him a laughing-stock. *'eštôn* is used in Ps 146:4 for the plans or ideologies of mortals. Though the source of these great ideas may be an inspiring leader, they should not become the basis of one's trust, no matter how brilliant they seem, for they come apart at the death of their originator. In Sir 3:24(23) this nom. stands for the speculative thinking of the Greeks, which Ben Sira judges to be "evil and misleading fancies (*dimyônôt*)"; for Ben Sira the true wisdom of the law is far better.

Plan, thought, meditation, scheming: → *'zn* II (weigh, consider carefully, # 264); → *bd'* (devise, imagine, # 968); → *higgāyôn* (melody, thought, # 2053); → *zmm* (plan, purpose, plan evil, # 2372); → *ḥms* II (think, invent, # 2804); → *ḥšb* (count, compute, calculate, think, plan, # 3108); → *yēṣer* I (frame of mind, disposition, # 3671); → *'št* I (think, consider, # 6951); → *śîḥâ* (meditation, study, # 8491); → *śᵉ'ippîm* (disquieting thoughts, worries, # 8546); → *tar'ît* (thought, # 9569)

John E. Hartley

6953 (*'aštût*, opinion, thought), → # 6951

6955 (*'eštôn*, plan, thought), → # 6951

6956	עַשְׁתֹּרֶת

עַשְׁתֹּרֶת (*'aštōret*), Astarte (NIV Ashtoreth/s, # 6956; *'aštārōt*, place-name, # 6958). *עַשְׁתֶּרֶת (*'ašteret*), offspring (function of Astarte, # 6957). The vocalization of the name of the goddess in the MT may be that of (*bōšet*), shame. WestSem., עשתרת may be derived from *'šr*, be rich, with infixed /t/ and metathesis. But it may be derived from East Sem. Ishtar with quadriliteral root.

ANE Astarte is not prominent in Ugar. myths, where she is inferior not only to Asherah but also to Baal's "sister" Anat (found in place-names in OT). In the ritual texts and god lists she is more prominent, found, e.g., as "Hurrian Astarte" and "Astarte-name-of-Baal" *'ṯtrt. šm.b'l KTU* 1.16. 6: 56. But no personal names formed with hers have been discovered to date. There is also a god *'ṯtr* (masc. form), son of Asherah and rival of Baal. Astarte was known in Egypt at least from the time of Amenophis II (fifteenth century) and was very prominent in Phoenicia and Carthage in the later first millennium, whence she became known to the Greeks, who identified her with Aphrodite. She was a goddess of sexuality, of fruitfulness, and a warrior goddess.

OT 1. As an (individual) foreign god (singular), Astarte is the/a city god of Sidon in particular. In the deut. condemnation of Solomon (1 Kgs 11:5, 33), Solomon is accused of following "Ashtoreh, the goddess of the Sidonians" (v. 5, along with Chemosh and Milcom). In 2 Kgs 23:13 he is accused of making high places for the three gods (in 1 Kgs 11:7 Astarte is [accidentally?] omitted). Only in 2 Kgs 23:13 is Astarte called the abomination (*šiqquṣ*) of the Sidonians instead of the god; Chemosh and Molech/Milcom are also called abominations (1 Kgs 11:5, 7). This is a further example of the replacement of the word "god" for some term of abuse.

2. Astarte is also a general term for goddess. Prior to the time of the kings, the deut. history sees a recurring apostasy of the Israelites, when they abandon Yahweh and turn to "the Baals and the Ashtoreths" (Judg 10:6; 1 Sam 7:4; 12:10; cf. Judg 2:13). This phrase is equivalent to "other gods" or "foreign gods" (1 Sam 7:3), who within the deut. theology are seen as imports into the worship of the nation.

3. In Deut 7:13; 28:4, 18, 51 the connection with the goddess seems completely lost (as may also be the case with the Asherim/Asherah).

Idolatry: → *'ᵉlîl* (Nothing, # 496); → *'ᵃšērâ* (wooden cult-object, pole, goddess, # 895); → *gillûlîm* (images, idols, # 1658); → *dāgôn* (Dagon, # 1837); → *kᵉmôš* (Chemosh [god of the Moabites], # 4019); → *mōlek* (Molech, # 4891); → *massēkâ* I (cast statuette, # 5011); → *mipleṣet* (terrible thing, dreadful object, # 5145); → *semel* (image, # 6166); → *'āṣāb* (god-image, # 6773); → *'aštōret* (Astarte, # 6956); → *pesel* (cultic image, statue of a god, # 7181); → *tōmer* II (scarecrow, # 9473); → *tᵉrāpîm* (figurines, mask, # 9572); → **Idolatry: Theology**

BIBLIOGRAPHY

TWAT 6:453-63; W. F. Albright, *Yahweh and the Gods of Canaan*, 1968; J. Day, "Ashtoreth (deity)," *ABD* 1:491-94; T. S. Frymer, "Ashtoreth," *EJ* 1:738-39; R. Stadelmann, *Syrisch-Palästinenische Gottheiten in Ägypten*, 1967; N. Wyatt, "Ashtoreth," *DDD*, cols 203-13.

Judith M. Hadley

6957 (*'ašteret*, lambs), → # 7366

6961	עֵת

עֵת (*'ēt*), nom. time, point of time, period of time, the right time (# 6961). < uncertain. The root *'nh*, "answer," in BH has frequently been suggested, but a relationship to the BH vb. is now widely rejected. Other suggested roots included *'dt*, related to the Akk. *'idtu*, agreement; *y'd*, BH appoint, assemble.

ANE 1. The nom. is not widely attested. It could be related to the Akkad. *ittu*, when, time. It appears in several of the Lachish Letters and is also attested in Phoen./Pun *'t*, time.

2. In the ancient NE and ancient Greece, there existed two conceptions of the notion of time. One, a cyclical view (represented in the Egyp. word *tr*; in G by *aiōn),* conceived of time as an endless cycle of regularly recurring events. This conception originated from the observation of the repetitive natural cycles, such as day and night, the procession of the seasons, or in Egypt, the yearly flooding of the Nile. The other conception of time, a more linear view (represented in Egyptian by the word *'.t*; in G often by *kairos*), originated from the observance that events of unique significance can occur within the continuous cycle. The ancient peoples recognized that individuals have very different lifespans, in which noteworthy occurrences (e.g., birth, marriage, death) take place at different times. Consequently, not all life experiences could be viewed in terms of the simple repetition of a cycle, but instead as points on a continuum. This concept of time came to be associated with the idea of individual fate or destiny. Both of these conceptions of time are found in the OT, often in connection with the word *'ēt* (see further Herrman, 103-20).

OT 1. The nom. *'ēt* is the most common Heb. word for the concept of time. While the Heb. ideas about time were not monolithic, it is accurate to say that time in the OT is rarely considered as an abstract concept. Rather, time is usually associated with specific events and their occurrence (Robinson, 109). Thus, the word *'ēt* is most frequently used (with a preposition, usually *b*-, but sometimes *l*-, and where appropriate, *k*-) to designate the time when an event occurs.

2. The relationship between time and event can be expressed in a number of ways. One common means is to use *'ēt* in the construct state with a nom. designating the event. The phrase can designate a point or short period of time, as in (lit.) "the time of her death" (1 Sam 4:20), "the time of the burnt sacrifice" (2 Chron 29:27), or "the time of the discontinuance of the daily sacrifice" (Dan 12:11). It can also designate a longer period of time, as in "the time of old age" (Ps 71:9; 1 Kgs 11:4). Different periods of the day are defined using this same formula, including (lit.) the "time of noon" (Jer 20:16), the "time of the going down of the sun" (2 Chron 18:34), and the "time of the evening" (Gen 8:11; 24:11; Josh 8:29; Isa 17:14; Zech 14:7). The phrase "times of trouble" (*'ēttôt baṣṣarâ*) is used in the book of Psalms for the periods of oppression experienced by God's people. Ps 9:9[10] states that the Lord is a stronghold for the oppressed in the times of trouble (i.e., he gives them protection against their oppressors); but 10:1 asks why the Lord stands aloof in the time of trouble. Jer 14:8 reflects the sentiments of both vv., acknowledging that the Lord is Israel's Savior in times of distress (*'ēt ṣārâ*; cf. Isa 33:2), but expressing dismay that he has not taken action to help his people. A similar phrase is used in Judg 10:14, where the Lord, exasperated with the sinful Israelites, tells them to seek salvation from their idols (lit.) "in the time of your distress" (*'ēt ṣārat^{e}kem*), again meaning the periods of foreign oppression. In each case, God has permitted the oppression of his people because of their sin (see also 2 Chron 28:22).

Israel's eschatological hardships are described in similar terms and phrases. Jer 15:11 seems to say that the time of distress will serve a good purpose for Israel, although the purpose is not defined until later in the book (on the difficulty in translating this v., see Thompson, 392-93). In 30:7, the "time of the distress of Jacob" will be more awful than any day preceding it, but it will result in a time of eschatological bliss, when Israel will be saved and a new David will reign over them (30:9). This same prophet refers to the eschatological judgment as the (lit.) "time of visitation (by the LORD)" (8:12; 10:15; 46:21; 49:8; 50:27; 51:18). Dan 12:1 expresses a similar idea about the eschatological oppression, stating that it will be a "time of distress" greater than any preceding or following, but it will result in the salvation and glorification of the righteous in Israel. Daniel frequently uses the phrase "time of the end" (*'ēt qēṣ*) to designate the period and course of events that initiate the eschaton (8:17; 11:35, 40; 12:1, 4, 9), which is viewed here not as a point of time, but a process (see Collins).

3. A more common formula for expressing the relationship between time and event is with the phrase "at that time" (*bā'ēt hahî'*). This phrase is frequently used in historical narratives to place an event in its temporal context (e.g., Josh 5:2; 6:26; 11:10; Judg 3:29; 4:4; 1 Kgs 8:65; 14:1; 2 Kgs 16:6; 1 Chron 21:28; 2 Chron 28:16; Ezra 8:34; Neh 4:22[16]). In Deuteronomy, Moses often prefaces references to past events and statements with the phrase, "At that time" (Deut 1:9, 16, 18; 2:34; 3:4, 8, 12, 18; 4:14; 5:5; etc.), relating them to other occasions in the Exodus narrative. This same phrase, however, is used in prophetic narratives, like the more common "in that day," to relate events in the future or in the eschaton. Jeremiah uses the phrase for the time of the imminent judgment on Judah (i.e., the Babylonian Exile; Jer 4:11; 8:1), as do Micah (Mic 3:4) and Zephaniah (Zeph 1:12; it should be noted that these last two references are sometimes identified by commentators as glosses; cf. De Vries, 41, although his conclusion that such additions tell us little about the Hebraic understanding of time is untenable). This phrase is also used for the time of eschatological blessing, when God will destroy Judah's enemies, restore its fortunes (Isa 18:7; Zeph 3:19, 20), and establish a Davidic heir as its legitimate king (Jer 33:15). In Dan 12:1, the phrase marks a radical discontinuity in world events: when the king of the North has invaded Egypt and proceeded against Judah (11:42-45), "at that time Michael . . . will arise" to deliver the righteous from their oppression.

4. The nom. is also used to designate the proper time for an event, the time when an event should take place. This proper time can be determined by circumstances. David falls into sin when he remains home in the spring, "the time when kings go off for war" (2 Sam 11:1), when conditions are right for doing battle. In Hag 1:2, the people of Judah have claimed that it is not yet the "time" (i.e., the proper time) for rebuilding the temple; but the Lord replies by asking if it is time for the Jews to live in houses, while his own house lies in ruins (1:4). Prov 15:23 praises a word spoken "timely" (i.e., "in its [proper] time"), an answer aptly given, while Ecclesiastes observes that a wise heart will know the proper time and procedure before a king (Eccl 8:5). The Lord often determines the proper time for events: Hos 10:12 advises that the period before the coming judgment is the "time to seek the LORD" and do works of righteousness. Several biblical books speak of the proper time for judgment: Job laments that the Lord does not establish specific times for the judgment of the wicked (Job 24:1), but Deut 32:35 states that the foot of the wicked will, indeed, slip in due time, the time that the Lord has determined for vengeance. Ezek 7:7, 12 proclaim that "the time" has come, the appropriate time to judge Israel for all of its sins; while 22:3

pronounces woe on those who shed blood in the city in order to bring on its time for judgment.

There is also a sense in which many of life's events have a proper time on the basis of the natural order, a conception sometimes related to a cyclical understanding of time. This idea is most eloquently expressed in Eccl 3:1-9: "There is a time for everything, and a proper time (*'ēt*; NIV season) for every activity under heaven: a time to be born and a time to die (cf. 7:17), a time to plant and a time to uproot" (3:1-2). Indeed, anything may be pleasant when it occurs in its proper time (3:11). There is an order to the world, and life's events occur in the appropriate place in this order (cf. Whybray, 65-73; Wolff, 89-92). This same idea underlies the use of the word *'ēt* to designate a "season": thus, the "time of rain," the proper time for rain to come, is the rainy season (Lev 26:4; Deut 11:14; 28:12; Ezra 10:13; Jer 5:24; Zech 10:1); the time of the singing of birds (S of Songs 2:12) is spring. Jeremiah observes that the birds know the proper time for migration, but God's people are ignorant of his ordinances that are equally well established (Jer 8:7).

5. There are some uses of *'ēt* where its meaning is not intimately linked to the occurrence of events, but rather to the idea of the more abstract idea of chronological time. The statement "at/about this time tomorrow" (1 Sam 9:16; 20:12; 1 Kgs 19:2; 20:6) is certainly using the nom. *'ēt* with a chronological sense, meaning "time of day, hour." Similarly, in Ezek 12:27, the Jews' claim that Ezekiel's prophecies of doom refer to "distant times" also uses the nom. in a fully chronological sense (cf. Wilch, 86). The phrase *bekōl 'ēt* (Exod 18:22, 26; Lev 16:2; Ps 10:5; 34:1[2]; 62:8[9]; etc.), "all the time," also utilizes the chronological aspects of the nom.

6. In other cases, however, the "event" aspect of the nom. is emphasized, so that the chronological aspect is overshadowed or nonexistent. In Neh 9:28, it is related that the Israelites apostatized and cried out to the Lord "many times" (NIV time after time). 1 Chron 29:30 states that the "times" of David's reign—i.e., the events—are recorded in the records of Samuel, Nathan, and Gad. The "event" aspect of *'ēt* might also underlie the phrase "men . . . who understood the times" in 1 Chron 12:32 and Esth 1:13. The phrase describes those skilled in the interpretation of the law and so does not refer to chronology or astrological matters. Rather, the phrase probably describes those familiar with historical precedence, and *'ēt* here means prior events of legal significance (cf. Wilch, 87). Even more generally, the nom. sometimes has the connotation of "circumstance." When Ps 31:15[16] says that "my times are in your hands," it probably means the circumstances or fortunes of human life (cf. also Isa 33:6; perhaps Esth 4:14; Barr, 117). (Indeed, numerous passages affirm God's sovereignty over time; see Robinson, 111-12.) The nom. might also mean "circumstances" in Dan 9:25, which states that the temple will be rebuilt, but *b^{e}ṣôq hā'ittîm*, "in times of trouble" (cf. Wilch, 85).

P-B The nom. is usually translated *kairos*, usually a point of time, in the LXX. Ben Sirach uses the nom. frequently with the sense of appointed time (e.g., Sir 43:6-7) or of proper time for an event (4:23). The nom. also appears often in the major DSS. In the Community Rule (1QS) 1.14, 8.15, 9.12-13 and other scrolls (e.g., CD 16.3; 1QM 14.13), the nom. refers to the proper time for the feasts, sacrifices, etc., required by the Law. In the War Scroll, the period of the eschatological battle is called the "time of salvation" (1QM 1.5), as well as the "time of distress" (1.11; 15.1). In RL, the nom. *'ēt* continues to be used, but it is largely supplanted by *zemān* as the principal word for the general notion of time.

Time: → *'ōbēd* (ever after, # 7); → *'ōpen* (right time, # 698); → *gîl* I (stage of life, # 1636); → *zmn* (be appointed, # 2374); → *'ôlām* (long time or duration, # 6409); → *'ēt* (time, # 6961); → *pa'am* (foot, step, time, # 7193); → *peta'* (instant, # 7353); → *tāmîd* (continuance, unceasingness, regular offering, # 9458)

Bibliography

THAT 2:370-85; *TWAT* 6:463-82; J. Barr, *Biblical Words for Time*, 1969; J. Collins, "The Meaning of 'the End' in the Book of Daniel," in *Of Scribes and Scrolls*, ed. Harold Attridge, John Collins, and Thomas Tobin, 1990, 91-98; S. DeVries, *Yesterday, Today and Tomorrow: Time and History in the Old Testament*, 1975; R. Gordis, *Koheleth—The Man and His World*, 1955, 218; S. Herrmann, *Time and History*, 1981; J. Muilenburg, "The Biblical View of Time," *HTR* 54, 1961, 225-71; H. W. Robinson, *Inspiration and Revelation in the Old Testament*, 1946, ch. 8; R. B. Y. Scott, *Proverbs-Ecclesiastes*, AB, 1965, 221; M. Sekine, "Erwägungen zur hebräischen Zeitauffassung," *Congress Volume: Bonn, 1962, SVT* 9, 1963, 66-80; N. Snaith, "Time in the Old Testament," in F. F. Bruce (ed.), *Promise and Fulfilment*, 1963, 175-86; J. A. Thompson, *The Book of Jeremiah*, NICOT, 1980; J. Wilch, *Time and Event: An Exegetical Study of 'ēth in the Old Testament in Comparison to Other Temporal Expressions in Clarification of the Concept of Time*, 1969; H. W. Wolff, *Anthropology of the Old Testament*, 1973; R. N. Whybray, *Ecclesiastes*, NCBC, 1989.

Anthony Tomasino

6963	עתד

עתד (*'td*), pi. prepare, make ready; hitp. be prepared, destined (# 6963); adj./nom. עָתוּד (*'ātûd*), ready, (pl.) stores/supplies (# 6965); עַתּוּד (*'attûd*), leader (→ # 6966); עָתִיד (*'ātîd*), ready, prepared (# 6969); עֲתִיד (*'ᵃtîd*), Aram. adj., prepared, willing # 10577).

ANE In late Aram. and in many Arab. dialects the root *'td*, prepare, make/be ready, is well attested.

OT 1. Various things in the O.T. are described as being ready, prepared, ready for use. According to Prov 24:27 a man can only build (up) his house(hold) if he is able to provide for its upkeep: He must first make his work in the field ready (*'td*, pi.), i.e., have it in order. The king of Assyria's haughtiness knows no bounds (Isa 10:13); in his appetite for wealth he even plunders food supplies (*'ᵃtîdôt*, K [the prepared things]; *'ᵃtûdôt*, Q [their he-goats, i.e., leaders]: NASB and NIV incorrectly translate, treasures) of the various nations, so that they will eventually starve to death.

2. In the context of judgment *'td* has the connotation of destine for, reserve for. The cities and houses that will be punished by God are destined (*'td*, hitp.) to become a heap of rubble. Only the ungodly want to live in such places (Job 15:28). In Deut 32:35 *'ᵃtidōt* refers to the punishment that God has prepared, i.e., destined or reserved (in the day of their calamity, v. 35b) for the godless nation, cf. Prov 19:29.

3. In a few texts *'td* denotes the preparedness for action. Esth 3:14 and 8:13 (*'ᵃtûdîm* [K.]; *'ᵃtîdîm* [Q.]) are of special theological value. Like in the story of the Exodus (cf. Exod 12:11, 31), the people are urged to prepare for and to be ready for battle (the day of vengeance; → *nqm*, avenge [# 5933]). Within the structure of the

book of Esther, these two texts, which are nearly identical in formulation, function as the two focal points of an ellipse (see J. A. Loader, *Esther*, 1980, 146-47), illustrating the "reversal theme" (see Greenstein, "A Jewish Reading of Esther"). In Job 15:24 the king is ready or prepared for battle. The "professional" cursers (→ *qbb* [# 7686]; *'rr* [# 4423]) of 3:8 are "prepared" to rouse (→ *'wr* II [# 6424]) the powers of chaos (Leviathan), just as one incites a dog to attack another person.

4. Nebuchadnezzar asks Daniel's friends if they are "ready" (*'ᵃtîdîm*, Aram.), i.e., "willing," to worship the golden statue (Dan 3:15).

5. Also the root *kwn* (*hyh nākôn*) contains the notion of preparation (→ *kwn*, # 3922). The theme of preparing oneself for meeting God is also of theological importance, see Exod 19:11, 15; 34:2; Amos 4:12.

P-B The preparedness for the final struggle is of importance in the literature of Qumran, see e.g., 1 QM 7.5; 10.5; 1QS[a] 1.27.

Acceptance: → *qbl* (receive, take, # 7691); → *rṣh* I (be pleased with, to treat favorably, # 8354)

BIBLIOGRAPHY

TWAT 4:95-107; G. Gerleman, *Esther*, BKAT XXI, 1982; E. L. Greenstein, "A Jewish Reading of Esther," in *Judaic Perspectives on Ancient Israel*, ed. J. Neusner, et al., 1987, 235-43.

H. G. L. Peels

6964 (*'attâ*, now), → Particles

6965 (*'ātûd*, ready, stores, supplies), → # 6963

6966	עַתּוּד

עַתּוּד (*'attûd*), ram, leader (# 6966); < עתד (*'td*), pi. prepare, make ready; hitp. be prepared, destined (→ # 6963).

ANE Cognates occur in Arab. *'atū*, a (younger) ram; also in Akk. *atūdu*, *etūdu*, *dūdu*, where an age differentiation seems to be signified.

OT The word lit. means he-goat, but like other words for animals it is also used to designate human beings on the strength of a trait perceived in common.

1. Most of the references to male goats are in the context of prescriptions for sacrifice (e.g., 13x in Num 7) or in discourse about sacrifice (Ps 50:9, 13; 66:15; Isa 1:11). Goats, including male goats, were items of commerce in the cattle industry (Ezek 27:21; cf. Prov 27:26). Jacob, in reporting a dream mentions male goats mating with the speckled of the flock (Gen 31:10, 12).

2. Since a male goat is the leader of the flock (Jer 50:8), the term readily comes to mean leader, ruler. In Isa 14:9 it is used simply as a synonym of *melek*, king. In the condemnation of Israelite rulers in Zech 10:3, however, the underlying pastoral imagery is more apparent through parallelism with "shepherd." This double nuance of the word is exploited most fully in Ezek 34:17, where "the rams and goats" between whom God as the Good Shepherd will judge are evidently the weak and the strong of the flock, the oppressed and the oppressor (cf. vv. 20-21), with "goats" presumably referring to the leaders of Israel. Whether this contrast is equivalent to the earlier one between the "bad shepherds" and the "flock" (vv. 1-10) is not clear. Possibly v. 17 has

in view leaders who were traditionally more closely identified with the people than the king and his royal officials.

3. Apart from Isa 14:9, the application of the term to rulers of foreign nations draws on a different trait of the male goat, viz., its use as a sacrificial victim. Hence, in several passages the word refers to foreign rulers in the context of God's great sacrificial slaughter of the nations, often cast in apocalyptic tones (cf. Isa 34:6; Jer 51:40; Ezek 39:18).

Leaders: → *'ādôn* (lord, master, # 123); → *'allûp* II (tribal chief, # 477); → *'āṣîl* II (eminent, noble, # 722); → *zāqēn* (elder, # 2418); → *ḥōr* I, free man, freeborn, # 2985); → *maptēaḥ* (badge of office, # 5158); → *nāgîd* (prince, ruler, leader, # 5592); → *nāśî'* I (chief, king, # 5954); → *sārîs* (eunuch, court official, # 6247); → *seren* II (Philistine prince, # 6249); → *'attûd* (he-goat, leader, # 6966); → *peḥâ* (governor, # 7068); → *pāqîd* (officer, # 7224); → *qāṣîn* (commander, leader, # 7903); → *rab* II (captain, chief, # 8042); → *rzn* (rule, # 8142); → *šôa'* I (noble, # 8777)
Flock: → *ṣō'n* (flock, small cattle, # 7366)

BIBLIOGRAPHY
TWAT 6:483-86.

Kenneth T. Aitken

6969 (*'ātîd*, ready, prepared), → # 6963

6971 (*'ātîq*, enduring), → # 6980

6972 (*'āttîq*, old, moved), → # 6980

6975 (*'ᵃtalyâ*, Athaliah), → Athaliah

6980	עתק

עתק (*'tq*), q. to move, become old; hi. to move (# 6980); עָתִיק (*'ātîq*), adj. enduring, venerable (hapleg. in Isa 23:18; # 6971); עַתִּיק (*'āttîq*), adj. old, moved (# 6972); עָתָק (*'ātāq*), adj. old, hard, stubborn, arrogant (# 6981); עָתֵק (*'ātēq*), adj. enduring, old (hapleg. in Prov 8:18; # 6982); Aram. עַתִּיק (*'āttîq*), adj. old (# 10578).

ANE Parallel roots are found in Akk. *etēqu*, pass along; Arab. *'ataqa*, grow old, Ugar. *'tq*, pass over, and Aram. *'āttîq*, old.

OT 1. The vb. *'tq* and the adj. *'āttîq* (see below) include the idea of moving or removing of settled or stable things (Job 9:5; 14:18) as well as the idea of becoming old (Job 21:7; Ps 6:7[8]). The central idea of the root points to the enduring quality of things: wealth (*'ātēq*, Prov 8:18), clothing (*'ātîq*, Isa 23:18), or God himself, who is the Ancient of Days (Aram. *'āttîq*, Dan 7:9, 13, 22). The latter phrase is unique in the OT and is generally agreed to refer to Yahweh's eternal existence (cf. Ps 9:7[8]; 29:10; 90:2). Several recent scholars (J. A. Emerton, L. Rost) have suggested that the phrase has Canaanite parallels similar to the name for the Canaanite god, El, who is called *abū šānīma*, father of years (*CTA* 1.3.24; 4.4.24; 6.1.36; 17.6.49). They further argue that the context of Dan 7 is similar to Ugaritic myths in the following ways: (a) Ba'al is subordinant to El as the "one like a son of man" is subordinate to "the Ancient of Days"; (b) one of Ba'al's common epithets is "rider of the clouds" (*CTA*, *passim);* and (c) El is portrayed as an aged god in the Ugaritic texts (*CTA* 4.5.65-66). While these are unquestionably similar ideas, it is difficult to see how and why Canaanite materials would be transmitted over such a long period of time and over so broad a geographical range (i.e., Babylon). J. J. Collins has argued that this is the very reason why there are several differences in the tradition, in that it has undergone significant developments in its transmission (*Daniel*, 1993, 291). Nevertheless, significant doubt remains that these ideas are borrowed from Canaanite traditions. The LXX translates this phrase literally as *palaios tōn hēmerōn*, Ancient of Days, and some have suggested that the phrase "antecedent or head of days" in 1 Enoch (46:1, 2; 47:3) is a parallel phrase (N. Porteous, *Daniel*, 1965, 107).

2. The adj. *ʿātāq* carries connotations of hardened, crusty, stubborn, or arrogant sayings (Ps 31:18[19]; 94:4). Such people speak with an arrogant or stiff (hardened) neck (75:5[6]).

3. The adj. *ʿāttîq*, old or moved, occurs only twice in the OT, and it is uncertain as to how the word can have such different meanings. In Isa 28:9 it refers to a child weaned or removed from the breast, but in 1 Chron 4:22 the adj. refers to an old list or a list handed down from antiquity. The context appears to be more certain in Isa 28:9, suggesting parallel units (i.e., "children [just] weaned from milk" and "those just taken from the breast"), since the words "milk" and "breast" are clearly parallel. Since the word *ʿattîq* is related to the root *ʿtq* with the dual meaning move or transcribe and grow old, it is best to understand the child in Isa 28:9 as being moved on from milk/the breast to more solid food, and the list in 1 Chron 4:22 as being moved on, passed down, or copied from previous generations. This word appears to be similar in meaning to the *ʿātēq* (see below) since money that has been passed down from generation to generation is "enduring wealth and prosperity" (Prov 8:18).

4. *ʿātēq*, hereditary, occurs only in Prov 8:18 in the phrase *hôn ʿātēq*, abundant or lasting wealth, which is used in a parallel construction with *ʿōšer*, riches (→ *ʿšr* [# 6948]). *hôn* by itself means wealth or sufficiency, and the word *ʿātêq* may add the idea of durable wealth.

Old, aged: → *zqn* (be old, grow old, # 2416); → *yašîš* (elderly, very aged, # 3813); → *yšn* II (become old, # 3823); → *ʿtq* (move, become old, to move, # 6980); → *śyb* (be grey, old, # 8482)
Arrogance, pride, presumption: → *gʾh* (rise up, be exalted, # 1448); → *zyd* (act presumptuously, prepare food, # 2326); → *yāhîr* (haughty, # 3400); → *sll* (lift up, exalt, # 6148); → *ʿpl* (swell, lift up, # 6752); → *ʿātāq* (old, arrogant, # 6981); → *pḥz* (be reckless, arrogant, # 7069); → *rwm* (be high, exalted, proud, # 8123); → *šaḥaṣ* (pride, # 8832)
Riches, wealth: → *hwn* (consider easy, risk, # 2103); → *nᵉkāsîm* (possessions, wealth, riches, # 5794); → *ʿšr* (be rich, become rich, make rich, # 6947)

Bibliography

TWOT 2:708; J. A. Emerton, "The Origin of the Son of Man Imagery," *JTS* 9, 1958, 225-42; L. Rost, "Zur Deutung des Menschensohnes in Daniel 7," *Gott und die Götter: Festgabe für Erich Fascher zum 60. Geburtstag*, ed. G. Delling, 1958, 41-43.

Gary V. Smith/Paul D. Wegner

6981 (*ʿātāq*, old, hard, stubborn, arrogant), → # 6980

6982 (*ʿātēq*, enduring, old), → # 6980

6986 (*ʿātār*, fragrance), → # 8379

פ

6990	פאה

פאה (*p'h*), hi. dash to pieces (hapleg.; # 6990).

OT Had Yahweh not feared that the adversaries would gloat and claim victory over Israel, he would have dashed his people to pieces (*p'h*) in jealous wrath for they were not deserving of his salvation (Deut 32:26; cf. Exod 32:12; Num 14:11-20; Isa 10:5-13; Joel 2:17; Mic 7:8-10).

Destruction, annihilation, devastation, disfigurement, ruin: → *'bd* I (perish, # 6); → *'êd* (disaster, # 369); → *blq* (devastate, # 1191); → *dmh* III (ruin, # 1950); → *dmm* III (perish, # 1959); → *hrs* (demolish, # 2238); → *ḥbl* III (treat badly, # 2472); → *ḥlq* III (destroy, # 2746); → *ḥt'* (be destroyed, # 3148); → *klh* (be complete, perish, destroy, # 3983); → *krt* (cut, cut off, exterminate, cut a covenant, circumcise, # 4162); → *mḥh* I (wipe off, wipe out destroy, # 4681); → *nṣh* II (fall in ruins, # 5898); → *nts* (break up, # 5995); → *ntṣ* (tear down, # 5997); → *ntš* (root up, pull down, destroy, # 6004); → *p'h* (dash to pieces, # 6990); → *pîd* (ruin, misfortune, # 7085); → *prr* (break, invalidate, nullify, frustrate, foil, thwart, # 7296); → *ṣdh* II (be devastated, # 7400); → *rzh* (destroy, waste away, # 8135); → *šdd* (devastate, # 8720); → *šḥt* (become corrupt, ruin, spoil, # 8845); → *šmd* (be exterminated, destroyed, # 9012); → *tablît* (annihilation, # 9318)

Bibliography

NIDNTT 1:462-71; *TWAT* 6:491-94.

Cornelis Van Dam

6991	פֵּאָה

פֵּאָה (*pē'â* I), nom. side, corner, rim (# 6991).

ANE Akk. *pû* / *pātu*; Ugar. *pat,* edge, border.

OT Of the over 80x the nom. occurs, more than half are found in Ezek 40-48 to give locations (e.g., north side). The remainder of the occurrences fall into several categories: the corners of pieces of furniture, whether cultic (Exod 25:26) or common (Amos 3:12); the edges of a field that are to be left unharvested to provide for the poor (Lev 19:9); the boundaries or borders of a territory (Josh 18:12, 14); the fringes of hair or beard that are to be left untrimmed (Lev 19:27).

The latter use also extends by metonymy to the temples of the head, most frequently as the target of punishing treatment. The three most significant passages in this regard are Num 24:17; Isa 3:17; Jer 48:45. Num 24:17 juxtaposes *pa'ᵃtê mô'āb* (foreheads of Moab) with *qarqar kol bᵉnê šēt* (NIV: skulls of all the sons of Sheth), in which the NIV has accepted the reading *qodqōd.* This goes contrary to the DSS citations of this passage but aligns with Jer 48:45. Isa 3:17 likewise uses *qodqod,* but the parallel term is *pothēn*, missing the aleph that would be expected if *pē'â* were the root. Most recently *pothēn* has been understood as related to Akk. *pūtu* (forehead). In these judgment oracles the damage to the head represents the victory of one party over the other. The Num 24 passage represents the earliest reference in the text to Israel's victory over her enemies by the hand of God through his royal representative and thus constitutes one of the foundational stepping stones for the development of messianic theology.

Border, boundary, corner, edge, rim: → *gbl* I (bound, border, # 1487); → *zāwît* (corner, # 2312); → *kānāp* (wing, skirt, outermost edge, # 4053); → *karkōb* (rim, edge, # 4136); → *mḥh* II (border on, # 4682); → *swg* II (border by, # 6048); → *pē'â* I (corner, # 6991); → *pinnâ* (corner, # 7157); → *ṣad* (side, # 7396); → *ṣēlā'* I (side, rib, side-chamber, # 7521); → *qēṣ* (limit, boundary, # 7891); → *qāṣeh* (end, border, # 7895); → *qṣ'* II (made with corners, # 7910)

Gordon H. Matties/John Walton

6994 (*p'r* I, knock down [w. stick]), → # 580

6995	פאר

פאר (*p'r* II), vb. pi. beautify, glorify; hitp. glorify o.s. (# 6995); פְּאֵר (*pᵉ'ēr*), nom. headdress (# 6996); תִּפְאָרָה(*tip'ārâ*), nom. beauty, glory; תִּפְאֶרֶת(*tip'eret*), nom. beauty, glory, boasting (# 9514).

ANE No known cognates.

OT 1. *Verb.* (a) Pi. The syntax of the pi. is transitive: A *pē'ēr* (*'et-*) B, A beautified B. The A-elements are God (Ps 149:4; Isa 55:5; 60:7, 9, perhaps 13) and the Persian king (Ezra 7:27). The B-elements are: the temple in restored Jerusalem (*bêt tip'artî*, the house of my beauty/renown, Isa 60:7; *mᵉqôm miqdāšî*, the place of my sanctuary, v. 13; *bêt yhwh*, the house of the Lord, Ezra 7:27); restored Jerusalem itself (Isa 60:9); the meek (*'ᵃnāwîm*, i.e., the humbly pious who endure suffering and await God's act of redemption, Ps 149:4; God will beautify them with *yᵉšû'â*, salvation); and the heir of David (Isa 55:5, identification indicated by second pers. masc. sing. inflections). Fensham (at Ezra 7:27) sees Ezra as presenting the fulfillment of Isa 60:7, 13; this is plausible in light of the vocabulary connections and lends support to the view that the Isaiah passage was antecedent Scripture to Ezra.

(b) Hitp. The later chapters of Isa use the hitp. as the reflexive of the pi., with God as subject: He glorifies himself through his actions of salvation for Israel (Isa 44:23; 60:21; 61:3), or through the Servant, who embodies ideal Israel (49:3). In this usage it refers to God's gaining for himself ascriptions of glory and dignity.

An apparent idiom is C *hitpā'ēr 'al* D: C honored himself over D, i.e., C credited himself with more honor than D. In Exod 8:9[5] Moses invites Pharaoh to honor himself over Moses by setting a time for relief from the plague of frogs; in Judg 7:2 God is concerned lest Israel honor itself above him in claiming credit for the victory over Midian; and in Isa 10:15 Assyria is likened to an axe that would honor itself over its wielder (in the metaphor, this would be the Lord). These are not presented as praiseworthy actions.

2. The noms. *tip'ārâ* and *tip'eret* are identical in meaning and treated here together (as in BDB). There are four basic senses: (a) beauty, adornment; (b) glory, dignity (as inherent and as ascribed); (c) glorying, boasting; (d) in connection with *kābôd*, glory, and the divine presence.

(a) Beauty, adornment. In 2 Chron 3:6 Solomon overlaid the Lord's house with precious stones for adornment (*l^e tip'eret*); in Ezek 16:17, 39; 23:26 we find the expression *k^e lê tip'artēk*, objects of your adornment, referring to jewelry; cf. Isa 3:18. In Isa 52:1 Zion is invited to clothe herself with *bigdê tip'artēk*, your garments of adornment, to celebrate God's coming deliverance. Isa 28:1-5 has a wordplay that emphasizes God's gracious activity: vv. 1, 4 refer to Ephraim in its pride as a fading flower, glorious beauty (*ṣîṣ nōbēl ṣ^e bî tip'eret*), which will be laid low, while in v. 5 the Lord will be a crown of glory, a wreath of beauty (*'^a ṭeret ṣ^e bî, ṣ^e pîrat tip'ārâ*) for the remnant of his people after the foretold act of judgment: i.e., he will be for them in reality what they only have in ephemeral form in their sin.

(b) Glory, dignity, renown (inherent or ascribed). The semantic bridge between senses (a) and (b) can be seen in Exod 28:2, 40: Aaron and his sons will have special clothing *l^e kābôd ûl^e tip'eret*, for glory and for beauty/dignity (of rank). Similarly in Isa 62:3 Zion will be *'^a ṭeret tip'eret*, a crown of beauty/glory, in the Lord's hand; for other examples of this expression see Jer 13:18; Ezek 16:12; 23:42 (cf. 16:17, 39; 23:26 listed under sense [a]); Prov 4:9; 16:31. The semantic link seems to be that the beauty is expressive of the dignity of the bearer and elicits ascriptions of glory. In 20:29 the (ascribed) dignity of young men is their strength (‖ *h^a dar z^e qēnîm*, [ascribed] splendor of old men). Cf. Isa 44:13, where a craftsman makes an idol *k^e tabnît 'îš k^e tip'eret 'ādām*, like the shape of a man, like the beauty/dignity of a human (a desecration of that beauty or dignity); cf. also Esth 1:4; Lam 2:1; Zech 12:7.

In this sense we find *tip'eret* in connection with *šēm*, name, fame, renown: In Deut 26:19 Israel's recognized position of dignity is called *t^e hillâ, šēm, tip'eret* (praise, fame, glory), while Jer 13:11 calls that intention to mind to Judah's shame, and in 33:9 Jerusalem will finally be these things for all the Gentiles, as a result of God's chastising and cleansing; in 1 Chron 22:5 the temple is to be for fame and glory for all lands. In these passages from Deut and Jer, the position of dignity of the covenant people also brings ascriptions of glory to the Lord; in 1 Chron 22:5 the ascription of glory to the Lord is the main point.

This sense is in view when we read of God's *tip'eret* (inherent or ascribed glory): e.g., Isa 63:12, where God's *z^e rôa' tip'eret,* arm of glory, went at Moses' right hand to make for himself an everlasting name (cf. v. 14, where God led his people to make for himself *šēm tip'eret*, a name of glory; see also 1 Chron 29:13); Isa 63:15, where heaven is *z^e bul qodš^e kā w^e tip'arteka*, the habitation of your holiness and your glory (cf. 64:11[10], which refers to the temple as *bêt qodšēnû w^e tip'artēnû*, the house of our holiness and glory; 60:7); 46:13, where God by his deliverance will give to Israel his glory (‖ to Zion *t^e šû'ātô*, his salvation; cf. 4:2; 60:19; Ps 89:17[18]); Ps 71:8, where the psalmist's mouth is filled with God's praise (*t^e hillâ*) and *tip'eret,* (ascribed) glory; 1 Chron 29:11, where to God belong (ascriptions of) greatness, strength, glory, splendor, and majesty (*g^e dullâ, g^e bûrâ, tip'eret, nēṣaḥ, hôd*).

(c) Glorying, boasting. This sense occurs when someone ascribes beauty or glory to himself (cf. hitp. of the vb.). For example, in Judg 4:9 Barak will not have the boasting rights for the victory over Sisera; in Isa 10:12 the Lord will punish the king of Assyria for *tip'eret rûm 'ênāyw*, the (self-) glorying of the height of his eyes (NIV the haughty look in his eyes); cf. 13:19; 20:5; Jer 48:17; Ezek 24:25 (the temple used as an illegitimate object of boasting, cf. v. 21).

But not every instance of the use of *tip'eret* for boasting is negative: in Prov we find it used for commendable things; e.g., Prov 17:6, the boast of sons is their fathers; 19:11, to overlook an offense is something to boast about; 28:12, great is the boasting when the righteous triumph (see Millard on the interpretation of this verse).

(d) Glory as the divine presence. Apparently under the influence of the synonym *kābôd*, glory, *tip'eret* can sometimes designate the manifest presence of God with his people. In Ps 78:61 God's glory (*tip'eret*) went into captivity; this is a reflection on 1 Sam 4, which in vv. 21-22 uses the more normal term for this idea, *kābôd.* In Ps 96:6 it is said that *hôd w^ehādār*, majesty and splendor, are before the Lord, and *'ōz w^etip'eret*, strength and glory, are in his sanctuary. As with *kābôd*, this specialized usage is possible because God's presence with his people in the cult reveals his own inherent glory and importance. The semantic relationship can be seen from Isa 60:7; 63:12, 15, listed under sense (b) above.

3. The nom. *p^e'ēr*, headdress, seems generally to denote ornamental headdress: of priests, Exod 39:28 (made of *šeš*, fine linen, and distinct from *miṣnepet,* turban); Ezek 44:18 (in idealized temple; made of *pištîm,* flax); as an emblem of festivity (opposed to emblems of mourning), Isa 61:3 (wordplay: God will replace *'eper,* ashes, with *p^e'ēr*, festal headgear), 10; Ezek 24:17, 23; and as part of finery worn by extravagant women, Isa 3:20 (figure for the daughters of Zion).

P-B/NT These words all appear in Sirach, DSS, and the RL, basically along the lines of BH usage (but *p^e'ēr* is only found in RL). In the LXX the most common G words to translate words from the *p'r* group are cognates of *doxa,* glory (which it shares with parts of the *kbd*-group), and *kauchaomai,* to boast. It is interesting that, like *p'r*, the boasting denoted by *kauchaomai* can be bad, self-exaltation, *kauchēsis* (e.g., Rom 3:27), or it can be good, delighting in good things (e.g., Rom 5:3, 11).

Glory, honor, majesty: → *'dr* (be magnificent, majestic, splendid, # 158); → *hdr* (swell, honor, adorn, # 2075); → *hôd* I (splendor, majesty, # 2086); → *y^eqār* (honor, riches, respect, price, splendor, # 3702); → *kbd* (be heavy, unresponsive, honored, # 3877); → *nēṣaḥ* I (luster, glory, lastingness, successful, # 5905); → *p'r* II (beautify, glorify, # 6995); → *ṣ^ebî* I (ornament, glory, # 7382)

Bibliography

NIDNTT 1:227-29; *TDNT* 3:645-54; *THAT* 1:387-89; F. C. Fensham, *Ezra and Nehemiah,* NICOT, 1982; A. R. Millard, "'*lṣ* 'to Exult,'" *JTS*, n.s. 26, 1975, 87-89.

C. John Collins

6996 (*p^e'ēr*, headdress), → # 6995

6997 (*pō'râ*, branches, shoots), → # 580

6998 (*pu'râ*, branches), → # 580

7001	פַּג

פַּג (*pag*), nom. unripe fruit (# 7001).

OT *pag* specifically refers to the unripe fruit of the fig tree (S of Songs 2:13).

Fig: → *bikkûrâ* (early fig, # 1136); → *bls* (scratch open, # 1179); → *šiqmâ* (sycamore-[fig-] tree, # 9204); → *t*ᵉ*'ēnâ* (fig, # 9300)

Edwin C. Hostetter

7002 (*piggûl*, impure [unclean meat]), → # 2866

7003	פגע

פגע (*pg'*), q. encounter, fall in with; fall upon, attack; assail; urge strongly; hi. let s.t. strike, intercede, urge strongly (# 7003); פֶּגַע (*pega'*), nom. occurrence, chance, target (# 7004).

ANE *pg'* is attested primarily in NW Sem. languages (Aram., Syr.) as well as Arab. (*fağa'a*) with a wide range of meaning (like BH, see below).

OT *pg'* occurs 46x and can mean arrive, meet, reach, kill, make intercession, or place/lay, and in most cases is followed by the preposition *b*ᵉ. As with other verbal roots in this general semantic field (see synonyms below), the "meeting" signified by *pg'* can be intentional or unintentional.

1. Accidental/unintended encounters. From a human perspective, *pg'* can signify a chance encounter: e.g., between Jacob and angels (Gen 32:1[2]), between Saul and the prophets (1 Sam 10:5), or between a person and an enemy's animal (Exod 23:4). The man who flees from a lion and chances upon a bear evidences the inescapable nature of the coming Day of the Lord (Amos 5:19). Rahab urged the spies to hide in the hills lest the search party from Jericho discover them (Josh 2:16). Moses established cities of refuge to protect the man guilty of unintentional murder from death in case the blood avenger finds him (Num 35:19, 21).

2. Intentional encounters. In fourteen cases *pg'* + *b*ᵉ serves as a synonym for "to kill" (lit., to fall upon). It can signify an attack made with the intent to kill (Judg 15:12; 18:25) or simply describes the act of killing (Judg 8:21; 1 Sam 22:17-18[3x]; 2 Sam 1:15; 1 Kgs 2:25, 29, 31, 32, 34, 46). God is the subject of *pg'* only once, where he stands ready to destroy either by means of plagues or sword (Exod 5:3).

More positively, *pg'* can signify pleading or making intercession with another person (Gen 23:8; Ruth 1:16; Isa 53:12; 59:16; Jer 15:11; 36:25) or with God (Job 21:15; Jer 7:16; 27:18).

In the fourth Servant Song (Isa 53:6) the prophet depicts the Servant upon whom Yahweh lays/places the weight of human iniquity.

3. In a spatial sense, *pg'* describes a person who "arrives" at his or her destination (Gen 28:11) and, more technically, serves as part of a formula for tracing the border of a tribal allotment (Josh 16:7; 17:10; 19:11, 22, 26, 27, 34).

4. The nom. *pega'* occurs in Solomon's affirmation (1 Kgs 15:4[18]) that Yahweh had given him rest from military threat (no adversary or misfortune [*pega'*]). In Eccl 9:11 the nom. signifies chance.

P-B Mish. Heb. utilizes two vb. homonyms and two nom. homonyms (which differ only in vocalization) to cover the same semantic range as Bib. Heb. *pg‘* (to meet/encounter, to strike/attack, to urge/intercede) and *pega‘* (contact/accident) (Jastrow 2:1135). In addition to this, the Mish. Heb. vb. *pg‘* connotes "to plague," and both nom. *pega‘* and *p^{e}ga‘* signify "affliction/plague."

Happening, meeting, attack: → *'nh* III (happen, # 628); → *hwh* II (become, # 2093); → *hyh* (be, become, happen, # 2118); → *y‘d* (appoint, appear, come, meet, # 3585); → *ng‘* (touch, hurt, # 5595); → *pg‘* (encounter, attack, # 7003); → *pgš* (meet, # 7008); → *qdm* (be before, meet, confront, # 7709); → *qr'* II (happen, # 7925); → *qrh* I (happen, build, odain, direct, select, # 7936)

Bibliography

TWAT 6:501-8; *TWOT* 2:715; R. L. Hubbard, "The Hebrew Root PG‘ as a Legal Term," *JETS* 27, 1984, 129-34; F. Rundgren, "פגע_פגשׁ. Eine Wurzeluntersuchung," *AcOr* 21, 1953, 336-45.

Michael A. Grisanti

7004 (*pega‘*, chance), → # 7003

7006	פגר

פגר (*pgr*), pi. be too feeble, tired, exhausted (# 7006).

ANE The vb. is found in Mish. Heb. in pi., Jewish Aram in pa., Christian Pal. Aram., Sam., Syr. *b^{e}gar*, be powerless, and Arab. *faġara*. It is now contested that *peger*, corpse or monument, can be considered as a derivative of *pgr* (*TWAT* 6:508-14).

OT This vb. is used only in 1 Sam 30:10, 21 to describe a group of exhausted soldiers, who were not able to cross the brook of Besor (v. 10) and were too tired to follow David (v. 21)—a hint of more than mere physical feebleness that is also implied by the troublemakers that did not want to share their plunder (Fokkelman, 583, 588; Miscall, 177-81). Although exhaustion is given as reason for a group staying behind, the fact of having a rearguard reserve amounted to good military strategy (Klein, 283).

P-B 1. *LXX*. In 1 Sam 30:10 the tr. *hoitines ekathisan* reflects *'šr yšbw*, who sat down, and not *'šr pgrw*, who were exhausted (McCarter, 431).

2. *Rabbinical literature*. In the BTalm Šabbat 129b the pa. of *pgr* is used to refer to the day on which teachers took a holiday (Jastrow 2:1135).

Tired, exhausted, feeble, weak, weary: → *'ml* I (be weak, be feeble, languish, # 581); → *ḥlh* I (become weak, tired, ill, # 2703); → *ḥlš* I (be enfeebled, be weakened, # 2764); → *ḥallāš*, weakling, # 2766); → *yg‘* (be tired, # 3333); → *mss* (lose courage, melt, become weak, # 5022); → *nṣb* II (wretched, exhausted [animal], # 5894); → *pgr* (be too feeble, tired, # 7006); → *‘yp* (be weary, # 6545); → *rph* (become slack, lose heart, discourage, # 8332)

Bibliography

EDNT 2:224-25; *TWAT* 6:508-14; *TWOT* 2:715; J. P. Fokkelman, *Narrative Art and Poetry in the Books of Samuel*, 2, 1986; R. W. Klein, *1 Samuel*, WBC, 1983; P. K. McCarter, *1 Samuel*, AB, 1980; P. D. Miscall, *1 Samuel*, 1986.

Hendrik L. Bosman

7007	פֶּגֶר

פֶּגֶר (*peger*), nom. corpse, carcass (# 7007); < פגר (*pgr*), be tired (→ # 7006).

ANE In addition to Akk. *pagru*, body or corpse, there are cognates with the same semantic range in Syr. and Mandean.

OT *peger* always denotes human bodies or corpses, except in Gen 15:11 and Lev 26:30, where it refers to animals and idols respectively. Related to the verbal root *pgr*, meaning "grow faint," *peger* frequently denotes the body at the time of death or soon after (e.g., Num 14:29, 32, 33; 2 Kgs 19:35; 2 Chron 20:24-25; Isa 37:36). The proposal of D. Neiman ("*PGR*: A Canaanite Cult-Object in the Old Testament," *JBL* 67, 1948, 55-60) that *peger* should be translated "stele" in Lev 26:30 and Ezek 43:7, 9 has found some support.

Corpse: → *g^e^wiyyâ* (body, corpse, # 1581); → *gûpâ* (corpse, # 1590); → *mappelet* (carcass, # 5147); → *n^e^bēlâ* (carcass, corpse, # 5577); → *peger* (carcass, corpse, # 7007)

T. Desmond Alexander

7008	פגשׁ

פגשׁ (*pgš*), q., ni. fall in with, meet; pi. meet (# 7008).

ANE This verbal root is only attested in Mish. Heb., to strike against, meet.

OT 1. *pgš* primarily signifies some kind of meeting or encounter, whether friendly, neutral (Gen 33:8; Exod 4:27; 1 Sam 25:20; Isa 34:14; Jer 41:6), or hostile (Gen 32:17[18]; Exod 4:24; 2 Sam 2:13; Prov 17:12). Two passages utilize the rage of a she-bear robbed of her cubs to emphasize the intensity of certain meetings. The writer of Prov compares the convergence of the fool and his folly to the violent encounter of a man and an enraged bear (Prov 17:12). Hosea depicts the severity of the covenant sanctions unleashed against Israel by means of the same violent image (Hos 13:8).

2. Two passages in Prov (22:2; 29:13) compare two poles of society (rich and poor, oppressed and oppressor) and affirm that these two groups meet, i.e., they have a common bond. Since Yahweh grants the existence of both, each should treat the other with respect/equity (as covenant partners).

3. The writer of Job emphasizes the vast superiority of God's wisdom over the ingenuity of the crafty. When he brings their plans to naught, the wise and the cunning are overwhelmed (*pgš*) by darkness and can only grope to find their way (Job 5:14).

4. In Ps 85:10[11] steadfast love and truth meet together (*pgš*) and righteousness and peace embrace (*nšq*). These four traits serve as personifications of divine attributes and work in harmony to accomplish Yahweh's intentions for the land of his people.

Happening, meeting, attack: → *'nh* III (happen, # 628); → *hwh* II (become, # 2093); → *hyh* (be, become, happen, # 2118); → *y'd* (appoint, appear, come, meet, # 3585); → *ng'* (touch, hurt, # 5595); → *pg'* (encounter, attack, # 7003); → *pgš* (meet, # 7008); → *qdm* (be before, meet, confront, # 7709); → *qr'* II (happen, # 7925); → *qrh* I (happen, build, odain, direct, select, # 7936)

BIBLIOGRAPHY

TWOT 2:715; F. Rundgren, "פנע_פנשׁ. Eine Wurzeluntersuchung," *AcOr* 21, 1936, 336-45.

Michael A. Grisanti

7009	פדה

פדה (*pdh*), q. ransom, redeem; deliver; hi. to let be redeemed (# 7009); פְּדוּיִם (p^e*dûyim*), nom. ransom (# 7012); פְּדוּת (p^e*dût*), nom. ransom, redemption (# 7014); פִּדְיוֹם (*pidyôm*), nom. ransom, redemption (# 7017); פִּדְיוֹן (*pidyôn*), nom. ransom money (# 7018).

ANE Unlike *g'l*, *pdh* is a common root shared by all Sem. languages except Aram. The Arab. vb. *fadā* has the specific legal sense to redeem a person or thing by providing an equivalent replacement, while its corresponding nom. means ransom (cf. Eth.; OSA). By contrast, Akk. *padû/pedû* reflects the more general helping sense to spare or release. In the Babylonian creation account (VII, 29; cf. VI, 34), the creation of humans freed (*padû*) the rebellious gods from serving the other gods. Ugar. closely resembles Heb. in having both the specific legal and the more general senses.

OT *pdh* has a broader meaning than its frequent parallel *g'l* and also lacks the latter root's specifically legal roots. Occurring primarily as q. vb., however, *pdh* does have a firm place in OT legal literature, partly in marriage laws and partly in cultic regulations.

1. The vb. q. appears in cultic instructions about the redemption of firstborn people and animals. Both the legislation concerning the Feast of Unleavened Bread (Exod 13) and the so-called Ritual Decalogue (Exod 34) share this common theological assumption: All firstborn belong exclusively to Yahweh (13:1-2; 34:19). Graciously, however, Yahweh permits Israel to redeem firstborn donkeys and sons (13:13; 34:20), presumably by offering an animal substitute. By combining ritual slaughter with redemption, Israel recalls the contrasting fates of the firstborn in Egypt and testifies to Yahweh's power in redeeming his own firstborn, Israel (13:15-16).

In later legislation Yahweh grants to priests his exclusive claim to Israel's firstborn but also mandates the redemption of firstborn unclean animals and of humans for five shekels of silver each (Num 18:15-16). All other clean animal firstborn may not be redeemed because they are holy, i.e., set aside for Yahweh's exclusive use (v. 17). The law concerning devoted things permits the redemption of an unclean firstborn animal (Lev 27:27) but forbids it for humans subject to destruction under the ban (*ḥērem*, v. 29; but cf. Ezra 10:8). In short, Yahweh's ownership of humans or animals means their ritual death or their service for him, but their ransom (i.e., replacement by an equivalent being) means continued life on their own.

2. Similar cultic and ritual assumptions underlie the ransom of Jonathan (1 Sam 14). Destined to die for violating Saul's rash oath in ignorance, Jonathan escapes death because his fellow soldiers redeem him. They appeal to his heroics that day on God's behalf (v. 45). Though silent about the price paid (e.g., an animal, prisoner of war, money, etc.?), the soldiers' appeal implies that Jonathan's heroism had earned his ransom.

3. On two occasions David backs up an oath by invoking Yahweh as the one who has redeemed his life (vb. q. + *nepeš*) from every trouble (2 Sam 4:9; 1 Kgs 1:29).

Whether David borrows an existing liturgical formula or frames his own, here *pdh* shares the general sense to save or rescue typical of other roots for salvation. Later, responding to Nathan's dynastic oracle, David's prayer marvels at Israel's unique election—the only people Yahweh redeemed (2 Sam 7:23 = 1 Chron 17:21). Nehemiah's prayer for Persian favor echoes the same sentiment (Neh 1:10).

4. In Deut Yahweh is the exclusive subject of *pdh* as the one who ransomed Israel from Egypt. Since the context refers to Israel as slaves (Deut 7:8; 13:5[6]) and as Yahweh's inheritance (9:26), here *pdh* designates a legal act of redemption from slavery by Yahweh. Israel appeals to that redemption to ask that Yahweh remove bloodguilt from the land (21:8). Similarly, because Israel is a redeemed slave, Moses enjoins them to treat their own slaves generously (15:15) and forbids them to mistreat aliens, orphans, and widows (24:18). Thus, Yahweh's ransom from Egypt both assures Israel of future help and models proper conduct for future Israel.

5. The psalmists employ the vb. q. more times than any other biblical writers (14 of 53x). Most common is the petition "Redeem me!" voiced in complaint psalms seeking legal vindication against a charge of defection from Yahweh (Ps 26:11) or rescue from false accusations by enemies (69:18[19]). In the acrostic Ps 119, *pdh* (vb. q.) opens the "p" line as the psalmist seeks deliverance from oppression (v. 134). Another acrostic concludes with a cry that Yahweh redeem Israel from all its troubles (25:22). In a communal complaint, Israel cries for deliverance from oppressive national enemies, i.e., to save the nation's life (44:26[27]).

Psalmists also use *pdh* in affirmations of confidence or trust. They affirm that Yahweh stands ready and able to rescue, whether from serious illness, from opponents (Ps 31:5[6]; 55:18[19]; 71:23; cf. v. 20), or from the terrible consequences of Israel's own iniquities (130:8). The latter text is the only place where *pdh* occurs with reference to sins, but the reference certainly fits well within the theology of the OT. To conclude, one thanksgiving psalm beautifully asserts that Yahweh redeems the life of his servants, i.e., spares them condemnation (34:22[23]).

A wisdom psalm gives reassurance that God will spare the wise the deathly doom of fools, taking them to himself (Ps 49:15[16]). Though cryptic, the latter text may reflect the psalmist's expectation of a final, perhaps even eschatological, deliverance from death. The unshakable confidence of the above poets sharply contrasts the rebellions of their ancestors, who forgot the God who had powerfully redeemed Israel from their Egyptian enemy (78:42).

6. Yahweh is also the subject of the vb. q. in the Prophets, both in oracles of judgment and hope. Hosea's woe oracle pronounces disaster on rebellious Israel, even though Yahweh would rather redeem them (Hos 7:13). In an ironic question expecting a negative answer, Yahweh declines to ransom Israel from death, a sure sign of his present lack of compassion (13:14). In both Hosean contexts, to redeem means more generally to snatch away or free from danger, and in 13:14 *pdh* parallels *g'l*. In his covenant lawsuit, Yahweh rebuts Israel's weariness with him by recalling his ransom of them from Egypt (Mic 6:4).

As for hope, an unusual messenger formula in Isaiah's Little Apocalypse recalls Yahweh's redemption of Abraham, perhaps from Pharaoh or Abimelech (Gen 12:17-20; 20:3-18), to support an oracle of hope (Isa 29:22). Isaiah twice invokes virtually identical language, including q. pass. part., to picture the redeemed of Yahweh, i.e., those whom God's revenge on nations liberates to return home (35:10 = 51:11; cf. Num 18:16). Responding to Jeremiah's complaint, Yahweh reaffirms his promise to redeem (i.e., to release) the beleaguered prophet from his foes' grip (Jer 15:21; par. *nṣl*). In the Book of Consolation, Yahweh's declaration that he has ransomed Jacob confirms the certainty of his promise to bring scattered Israel back home (31:11; cf. Zech 10:9).

7. In Job, Eliphaz counsels Job to accept God's discipline, secure in the knowledge that God will save (vb. q.) Job's life from death in famine or war (Job 5:20). Elihu's later, lengthy rebuke of Job portrays as righteous someone who publicly sings a thanksgiving psalm, confessing his sin and testifying that God had delivered (*pdh*) his life from deathly sickness (33:28; cf. Sir 51:2). Job's rhetorical question (Job 6:23) denies having ever asked them to risk their lives to ransom him from oppressors. The root here probably has the general sense to save since there is no contextual reference to any monetary payment (but cf. *THAT* 2:392 [legal release of a poor person from debt-slavery]). Here one sees that *pdh* has a broader sense than *g'l* because the ransom involves the voluntary service of a friend rather than the duty of a family member.

8. The vb. hi. only occurs in Exod 21:8, probably the earliest OT occurrence of *pdh* since scholars believe its context (the Covenant Book) to be ancient. The slave law permits the redemption of an Israelite slave who no longer pleases her master, thereby wasting his money. Presumably, a relative of the woman pays a negotiated or standard ransom amount to gain her release (the context is silent). By treating redemption from debt-slavery, here *pdh* closely resembles *g'l*. Further, the case also shows that *pdh* has a secular usage besides its more common religious one (cf. Job 6:23).

9. The vbs. ni. and ho. occur in the marriage law governing sexual relations between an engaged woman and a man not her fiancé (Lev 19:20). They define the woman as a slave permitted to be redeemed (ho. inf. abs.) but not yet actually redeemed (ni. pf.). The law forbids the death penalty since the case involves no adultery in a legal sense since the woman is still a slave. Instead, through a guilt offering the man is to obtain atonement (vv. 21-22). Here *pdh* shows the same secular sense seen in Exod 21:8. The preference for *pdh* over *g'l* here may imply that the case falls outside the realm of family law. The remaining vb. ni. occurs in (Isa 1:27): When divine judgment falls, Zion will be redeemed (i.e., rescued from foes) by justice.

10. The nom. *pidyôm* (Num 3:49) occurs only once (unless one repoints MT *happ^{e}duyyim* [v. 51] to *pidyōm*) and seems textually suspect (Q reads *happ^{e}dûyim* in v. 51; Sam. reads the latter in vv. 49 and 51). On the other hand, if MT preserves the correct consonants, one might read the same phrase (*kesep happidyô/ōm*, money of ransom) in both vv., and *happidyô/ōm* could represent a byform of *pidyôn* (so *HALAT* 863). If so, nom. *pidyôm/n* occurs in two phrases in three contexts.

In Num 3:49 Moses accepts the redemption money (*kesep happidyôm*) for 273 Israelite firstborn males, otherwise they would have belonged to Yahweh. Twice nom. *pidyôn* appears in the phrase *pidyôn napšô*, ransom of (one's) life (see also 2 Sam 4:9; 1 Kgs 1:29; Job 33:28; Ps 34:22[23]; 49:15[16]; 55:18[19]; 71:23). Part of customary law, Exod 21:30 permits the owner of an ox that habitually gores to escape the death penalty by paying a ransom of life, i.e., the release of his own life (contra NRSV). (For similar laws, see the Laws of Eshnuna [§4] and the Code of Hammurabi [§51].) Ps 49, a wisdom psalm, invokes the same phrase in a maxim teaching that the rich cannot buy their way out of death (v. 8[9]; emended after LXX)—the price is simply out of even their reach!

11. The abstract pl. nom. *p^{e}dûyim*, ransom, appears 5x in Num 3 (vv. 46, 48, 49, 51 [txt. emend.]) and in 18:16. Both contexts concern the redemption of Israelite firstborn, both human and animal, which otherwise belonged to Yahweh. Num 18 specifically treats the case of unclean animals. Though the texts' underlying ideology is obscure, nom. *p^{e}dûyim* clearly means the release through a monetary payment of living beings on whom Yahweh has a claim.

12. Two psalmists use nom. *p^{e}dût,* redemption, deliverance, to affirm truths about Yahweh. *p^{e}dût* forms the "p"-line in an acrostic praise psalm, citing Yahweh's redemption of Israel and his covenant as evidence of his awesome, holy name (Ps 111:9). Possibly the allusion is to Israel's early history (e.g., Exodus, Sinai), though the context is unclear. In a Song of Ascent, another psalmist grounds his call for Israel to hope in Yahweh's great power of redemption with respect to her sins (130:7-8). In Isa 50:2 Yahweh berates his exiled people for doubting his power to redeem them from their sins (but cf. LXX, which reads q. inf. constr.). *p^{e}dût* seems out of place in Exod 8:23[19], however, so one should probably follow Davies's suggested reading *prdt,* separation, for MT *p^{e}dût* (i.e., a copyist's omission of original *r*).

P-B Both vb. and noms. *pidyôn* and *p^{e}dût* appear in postbiblical Heb. sources. RL retains the root's juristic sense, using biblical texts concerning the release of devoted things or of the firstborn. In the Midrash and Talmud the vb. also describes the freeing of Israel from captivity, but redemption from sin and error is described with the root *kpr.*

The LXX renders *pdh* with forms of *lytroō,* an appropriate equivalent since it implies a payment or ransom price. The root occurs in Sir 51:2 and is also well attested at Qumran, the vb. in the hymns and nom. *p^{e}dût* almost exclusively in war texts. Qumran hymns thank God for redeeming community members from violent death inflicted by (1QH 2:32, 35) or suffered by (3:19) their enemies. Like MT psalmists, 1QH 17:20 petitions God to redeem the petitioner's life, i.e., to save it from the annihilation that awaits the wicked.

The War Scroll (1QM 14:5) knew Israel as the people of his [God's] redemption (*'am p^{e}dûtô*; cf. 1QM 1:12). In this and similar phrases with *p^{e}dût*, redemption denotes the Qumran community's past (1QM 11:9; 14:5; 17:6) or future rescue (so 1QM 1:12; 14:10; 15:1; 18:11; 4QM^a 8). This redemption is eternal (1QM 1:12; 18:11) and parallels the destruction of all peoples of iniquity (1QM 15:2). As a community rule, CD 16:8 forbids anyone from redeeming (i.e., canceling) the obligations of an oath even at the price of his own life. This usage of the root has no counterpart in the OT itself.

NT NT terms for redemption no longer reflect the OT distinction between *pdh* and *g'l.* The NT bypasses *lytroomai*, their primary equivalent in LXX, in favor of *rhyomai*, a word rarely used in LXX for *g'l* and *pdh*, and *sōzō*, which LXX never uses for *g'l* and rarely (2x) for *pdh*.

Salvation, deliverance, ransom, rescue: → *g'l* I (redeem, deliver, ransom, # 1457); → *yš'* (be victorious, receive help, save, rescue, # 3828); → *mlṭ* I (get to safety, escape, deliver, give birth to, # 4880); → *nṣl* (rescue, # 5911); → *pdh* (ransom, redeem, deliver, # 7009); → *plṭ* (save, bring to safety, # 7117); → *śrd* (run away, escape, # 8572); → *šālôm* (peace, friendship, happiness, prosperity, health, salvation, # 8934)

Bibliography

TDNT 6:998-1003; 7:965-1024; *THAT* 2:389-406; *TWAT* 6:514-22; D. Clines, *Job 1-20*, WBC 17, 1989, 180; G. Davies, "The Hebrew Text of Exodus VIII 19 (Evv. 23): An Emendation," *VT* 24, 1974, 489-92; J. Hartley, *The Book of Job*, NICOT, 1988, 136-39; F. Heinemann, *Erlösung im Alten Testament*, 1982, 438-63; idem, "Auslösung des verwirkten Lebens. Zur Geschichte und Struktur der biblischen Lösegeldvorstellung," *ZThK* 79, 1982, 25-59; C.-H. Hunzinger, "Fragmente einer älteren Fassung des Buches Milhamā," *ZAW* 69, 1957, 142; A. Jepsen, "Die Begriffe des 'Erlösens' im AT," *FS Hermann*, 1957, 153-63; H.-J. Kraus, "Erlösung. II. Im AT," *RGG*³, 2:586-88; A. Macintosh, "Exodus VIII 19, Distinct Redemption, and the Hebrew Roots פדה and פדד" *VT* 21, 1971, 548-55; F. Nötscher, *Zur Theologischen Terminologie der Qumran Texte*, BBB 10, 1955, 188-89; J. Stamm, *Erlösen und Vergeben im Alten Testament*, 1940, 7-30, 87-105; R. Thompson, *Penitence and Sacrifice in Early Israel Outside the Levitical Law*, 1963.

Robert L. Hubbard, Jr.

7012 (*pᵉdûyim*, ransom), → # 7009

7014 (*pᵉdût*, ransom, redemption), → # 7009

7017 (*pidyôm*, ransom, redemption), → # 7009

7018 (*piddāyôn*, ransom money), → # 7009

7022	פֶּדֶר

פֶּדֶר (*peder*), nom. the fat or suet of an animal (Lev 1:8, 12; 8:20) (# 7022).

ANE Sam. *fādār*, Egyp. *pdr*, nom. the fat or suet of an animal; Akk. *pitru*, the suet upon the liver.

OT In each occurrence (Lev 1:8, 12; 8:20) care is taken to note the proximity of the *peder* to the head of the sacrificial animal on the altar. The significance of this practice is unknown. The meaning of *peder* and its relation to *ḥēleb* is also unknown. LXX commonly uses *stear* to translate *ḥēleb*, but uses it also for *peder* in Lev 1:8, 12; 8:20. Vg. uses *adeps*, soft fat of animals, for *ḥēleb* in Lev 8:20, but in 1:8, 12 it renders *peder* by the phrase "all that adheres to the liver," thereby apparently equating the *peder* with the lesser omentum (→ *ḥēleb*).

P-B Mishnah Tamid 4:2 in its comment on this rite repeats *pdr* without further explanation. Milgrom (159) considers the word to be incapable of closer definition and cogently queries the legitimacy of the comparative material offered.

Fat, fatty food, oil: → *'bs* (fatten, # 80); → *br'* II (fatten o.s., # 1344); → *dšn* I (become fat, # 2014); → *ḥēleb* I (fat, # 2693); → *mhḥ* III (fattened, # 4683); → *mᵉrî'* (fattened, # 5309); → *peder* (fat, # 7022); → *pîmâ* (fat, # 7089); → *šmn* I (be fat, # 9042)

Bibliography

H. Danby, *The Mishnah*, 1933; J. Milgrom, *Leviticus 1-16*, AB 3, 1991.

Robert. J. Way

7023	פֶּה

פֶּה (*peh*), nom. mouth (# 7023).

ANE The Heb. *peh*, the common word for mouth, is cognate with Ugar. *p*, Akk. *pû*(*m*), and Arab. *fû*.

OT 1. *peh* occurs 490x in BH. It is used in a general sense for the mouth of humans and animals, as well as for openings (e.g., the neck of a garment [Exod 28:32; Job 30:18], well [Gen 29:2], cave [Josh 10:18]), and is the word for delta (Isa 19:7). The Lord opened the donkey's mouth and it spoke to Balaam (Num 22:28). In the Flood story it is used of a dove's beak (Gen 8:11). A crocodile's mouth emits flashes of fire (Job 41:19[11]). The ground opens its mouth to receive Abel's blood (Gen 4:11). Bones are scattered at the mouth of the grave (Heb. *Sheol*) (Ps 141:7).

2. A number of common phrases make use of the word "mouth": unanimous (with one mouth) (Josh 9:2); face to face (mouth to mouth) (Num 12:8; 2 Kgs 10:21; 21:16; Jer 32:4; 34:3); from one end to another (Ezra 9:11); devour with open mouth (mouth to mouth) (Isa 9:12[11]); Elisha healed the dead boy by lying on him "mouth to mouth" (2 Kgs 4:34); put the hand over the mouth (a gesture of respect) (Job 29:9; 40:4; Prov 30:32); kiss the hand to the mouth, a gesture of worship (Job 31:27); and to ask someone personally (ask his mouth) (Gen 24:57). Sheaths and scabbards in which swords were kept had a "mouth" shaped sometimes as two mouths of a beast. This part of the sheath formed the clasp at the hilt of the sword. The idiom "to the mouth of the sword" (Gen 34:26) signifies the edge of the sword; (cf. "double-edged sword" [sword with two mouths], Judg 3:16).

In a number of passages reference is made to the testimony (mouth) of witnesses (Num 35:30; Deut 17:6). *peh* occurs also in reference to "dictation" (Jer 36:4, 18) and to commands: Pharaoh declared that all his people should submit to Joseph's orders (mouth) (Gen 41:40).

3. Of all the occurrences of this word in the OT, those involving Yahweh are the most significant theologically. The word (mouth) of the Lord refers to some communication from God himself (Deut 8:3; 1 Kgs 8:15, 24; Isa 1:20; 40:5; Jer 9:12[11]). By contrast, idols have a mouth but do not speak (Ps 115:5; 135:16). By the word of the Lord the heavens were made, the starry host by the breath of his mouth (Ps 33:6). God was active in creation by his word. To "inquire from the mouth of Yahweh" (lit.) was to ask Yahweh (Josh 9:14). The expression "the mouth of the LORD has spoken" (Isa 40:5) gives an authoritative tone to what precedes.

Aaron was designated as Moses' mouth (Exod 4:16). God's word to Pharoah was to be mediated through Aaron's mouth on behalf of Moses. Samuel exhorted Israel not to rebel against Yahweh's commands (mouth) (1 Sam 12:14).

A set of idiomatic expressions combine "mouth" with a preposition to mean "according to" (Lev 25:52; Num 6:21; 7:5). Men gathered to David at Hebron as Yahweh had said (according to the mouth of Yahweh, 1 Chron 12:23). Compliance to the Lord's command (mouth, *peh*) (Exod 17:1; Num 3:16, 39, 51; 33:2) and sometimes noncompliance (Deut 1:26, 43; Lam 1:18) are reported.

4. The believer's speech is characterized by his praise of God. Yahweh's praise shall continually be in my mouth (Ps 34:1[2]; cf. 49:3[4]; 51:15[17]; 63:5[6]; 71:15). Others are known for the curses from their mouth (Ps 10:7; cf. Prov 10:6, 11). The Suffering Servant was silent; he did not verbally accuse or retaliate (Isa 53:7).

Mouth: → *ḥēk* (palate, # 2674); → *midbār* II (mouth, # 4498); → *malqôḥayim* (gums of the mouth, # 4918); → *peh* (mouth, # 7023); → *śāpâ* (lip, # 8557)

Bibliography
IDB 3:454-55; *TDNT* 7:692-701; *THAT* 2:406-10; *TWOT* 2:718.

J. A. Thompson/Elmer A. Martens

7028	פוג

פוג (*pwg*), q. be feeble. numb, cold; ni. be prostrated, powerless (# 7028); הֲפוּגָה (*h^apûgâ*), stopping (hapleg.; # 2198); פּוּגָה (*pûgā*), nom. slackening, relaxation (hapleg.; # 7029).

ANE The vb. is attested in Sam. *pygg*, comforting, to be glad; Mish. Heb. q. to loose, pi. comfort; Arab. *fāğa*, be cold. The nom *pûgâ* occurs as a hapleg. in Lam 2:18 (GKC, 80f; Hillers, 101). *hapûgâ* is a nom. from the hi. of *pwg* and is found only in Lam 3:49 (*HAHAT* 283; *HAL* 1:253).

OT 1. The vb. occurs 4x (Gen 45:26; Hab 1:4; Ps 38:8[9]; 77:2[3]). Gen 45:26 describes how Jacob was stunned/his heart became feeble when he heard Joseph was still alive (Wenham, 430).

The description of the psalmist's sickness in Ps 38:3-11[4-12] lists a number of specific complaints, such as festering wounds, backache, and in v. 8[9] a reference to being powerless/being feeble (Craigie, 303-4). This psalm understands sickness as a correcting chastisement for sin, with its impact at physical and psychological levels. It expresses a serious condition of being very ill (Mays, 162-63). Ps 77:2[3] is part of a prayer for help by an individual who tries to seek the Lord by keeping untiring (*pwg*) hands prayerfully outstretched (Jefferson, 87-91; Kselman, 51-58; Kraus, 114-15).

In Hab 1:4 the remarkable reference to the law as being paralyzed/made ineffective (*pwg*) is the result of God's apparent failure to act and punish wrongdoing (M. D. Johnson, 1985, 257-66; Floyd, 397-418; Roberts, 90).

2. The nom. *pûgâ*, slackening, forms part of an anguished appeal to Jerusalem to call on God to take pity with the suffering of his people (Lam 2:18). This cry to the Lord must be an unceasing exhortation to unrelenting prayer (Provan, 74; Huey, 466).

3. The nom *hapûgâ*, stopping, occurs in the phrase *mē'ên hapugôt* (Lam 3:49) and forms a close parallel to 2:18, communicating a similar lack of rest or relief for the poet, who will weep until God answers (Huey, 477). Some translations (Syr.) consider the lack of relief as a reason for the distress; others (LXX) interpret it as its consequence (Provan, 103). The distress is regarded as a punishment aimed at rehabilitation and not at rejection (B. Johnson, 1985, 58-73).

P-B In RL the BTalm Megilla 25b uses *pwg* to refer to the faintness or loss of courage the congregation might experience on hearing curses. In the Midrash Rabbah to Leviticus s.27 the vb. indicates relaxation when a man is described who did not want to argue seriously with his children (Jastrow 2:1139).

Feeble, despair, faint, frail, tender: → *'ml* I (be weak, be feeble, languish, # 581); → *ḥlh* I (become weak, tired, ill, # 2703); → *ylh* (languish, # 3532); → *k'h* (be disheartened, frightened, # 3874); → *nbl* I (wither, fade, languish, dishonor, # 5570); → *'ṭp* II (grow weak, faint, be feeble, # 6494); → *'lp* (cover, faint, # 6634); → *'šš* (become weak, # 6949); → *pwg* (be feeble, numb, be prostrated, # 7028); → *rzh* (destroy, waste away, # 8135); → *rkk* (be tender, timid, gentle, # 8216); → *rph* (become slack, lose heart, discourage, # 8332)

Bibliography

EDNT 1:117; 2:7-8, 239; P. C. Craigie, *Psalms 1-50*, WBC, 1983; M. H. Floyd, "Prophetic Complaints About the Fulfillment of Oracles in Habakkuk 1:2-7 and Jeremiah 15:10-18," *JBL* 110, 1991, 397-418; D. R. Hillers, *Lamentations*, AB, 1992; F. B. Huey, *Jeremiah Lamentations*, NAC, 1993; H. G. Jefferson, "Psalm 77," *VT* 13, 1963, 87-91; B. Johnson, "Form and Message in Lamentations," *ZAW* 97, 1985, 58-73; M. D. Johnson, "The Paralysis of Torah in Habakkuk 1:4," *VT* 35, 1985, 257-66; H.-J. Kraus, *Psalms 60-150*, 1993; J. S. Kselman, "Psalm 77 and the Book of Exodus," *JANESCU* 15, 1983, 51-58; J. L. Mays, *Psalms*, 1994; I. W. Provan, *Lamentations*, 1991; J. J. M. Roberts, *Nahum, Habakkuk and Zephaniah*, 1991; G. J. Wenham, *Genesis 16-50*, WBC, 1994.

Hendrik L. Bosman

7029 (*pûgâ*, slackening, relaxation), → # 7028

7032	פוח

פוח (*pwḥ*), blow, blast (# 7032); יפח (*ypḥ*), blow, blast (# 3640).

OT 1. These byforms are the most versatile of the words in this semantic group in their use. Literally, the breeze and the day blow in on the romantic world of the lovers (S of Songs 4:16; 2:17; 4:6). Figuratively speaking, the painful blowing and gasping of a woman in labor portrays Israel under her Lord's judgment (Jer 4:31, *ypḥ*). This familiar use of a retributive metaphor recurs in Ezek 21:31[36], where God vows to blow his flame of judgment upon Ammon. The wicked can blast the righteous, but only with unjust violence (Ps 27:12).

2. *pwḥ* can mean "to aspirate" in the sense of an utterance, or "to speak"—always in a moral sense and found only in Proverbs (6:19; 12:17; 14:5, 25; 19:5, 9).

3. There are two cases where *pwḥ* is used in the sense of denegration: the wicked "blow" ridicule upon their enemies (Ps 10:5), and scoffers "blast" their own city with mockery (Prov 29:8). A division between roots *pwḥ* I and *pwḥ* II is unnecessary since a single category ably conveys the breadth of meaning that this word has (contra KB).

Blowing (wind, breath): → *hzh* (pant in sleep, # 2111); → *ndp* (blow away, scatter, # 5622); → *npḥ* (blow, # 5870); → *nšb* (blow, # 5959); → *nšp* (blow, # 5973); → *pwḥ* (blow, blast, malign, # 7032)

D. C. Fredericks

7037 (*pûk*, black eye-paint, hard cement), → # 8379

7046	פוץ

פוץ (*pwṣ*), q. scatter, disperse, be pushed out, pour out; ni. be spread, scattered, dispersed; hi. disperse, scatter (# 7046); תְּפוּצָה (*tᵉpûṣâ*), nom./adj. dispersion (# 9518).

ANE The gathering of dispersed peoples is a common motif of Mesopotamian royal ideology. Widengren (234-39) cites examples from a variety of texts that span centuries, from Hammurabi to the Cyrus Chronicle. The returning and restoration of scattered peoples and their deities to their land is presented as a royal virtue and obligation, which on occasion is also ascribed to the gods. The vocabulary and phraseology associated with the theme appear fixed. As in the OT, the vbs. in Akk. for "scatter" and "gather" are frequently utilized in combination. The principal vb. in Akk. for "scatter," however, is a different root (*sapāḫu; AHw*, 1024-25) from any of the Heb. vbs. of this word cluster (*bzr* → # 1029; *zrh* I → # 2430; *pwṣ; ndḥ* I → # 5615; note, however, *npṣ* II → # 5880; *pzr* → # 7061).

OT 1. The vb. *pwṣ* appears over 60x and is used in q., ni., and especially the hi. More than half of these passages are found in the prophets and are particularly concentrated in Jer and Ezek. One of the basic meanings of *pwṣ* is to overflow or spread out. This idea can be applied, e.g., to water overrunning into the street (Prov 5:16) or to the extension of a battle (2 Sam 18:8).

The notion of scattering is more common. The farmer scatters seed (Isa 28:25), and Yahweh proves his power by scattering the lightning (Job 37:11). Military pressure and defeat can cause the dispersal of soldiers and armies, whether those of the nation (1 Sam 13:8; 2 Kgs 25:5 = Jer 52:8; Jer 40:15) or of an adversary (1 Sam 11:11). Yahweh is called upon to help his people by scattering their enemies (Num 10:35; Ps 68:1[2]; possibly 18:14[15]; 144:6, which can refer to either enemies or lightning), and he announces a future scattering of Egypt, one of Israel's enemies (Ezek 29:12; 30:23, 26).

2. Yahweh's involvement in the scattering of people and armies is an act of judgment, and this perspective is evident early on in the biblical account. Gen 10 and 11 juxtapose the voluntary dispersion of the Canaanites with the forced scattering of rebellious humanity at the Tower of Babel (Gen 10:18; 11:8-9). In Gen 1 Yahweh creates humankind and gives them the mandate to fill the earth (1:27-31); Babel (→), among other things, represents a concerted effort not to obey that commission and at once reveals the human tendency toward hubris and disobedience (NIV "so that we may ... not be scattered," 11:4). Even so, because of his mercy and grace, Yahweh chooses Abram in order to create a nation to reach all the families of the earth (12:1-3).

3. The theme of scattering as chastisement is also directed at Yahweh's own people. Jer and Ezek employ pastoral imagery as a stylistic weapon to denounce the wicked leaders of Jerusalem as unprincipled shepherds. They have exploited the flock (i.e., the nation) and led the people into sin and away from their God; now those who govern are held most responsible for bringing Judah to the disastrous point of being scattered among the nations in judgment (Jer 10:21; 23:1-2; Ezek 34:5, 21). Because the leadership has so utterly failed as shepherds, Yahweh will remove them and he himself will take up the shepherding tasks (Jer 23:3-4; Ezek 34:7-16). Yahweh is the good shepherd, who tends and protects his flock (see *TOT* 1:235-37; V. H. Matthews, D. C. Benjamin, *Social World of Ancient Israel 1250-587 BCE,* 1993, 52-66).

At the most fundamental level, this message of impending doom and dispersion is grounded in the covenant warnings of Deut (4:27; 28:64). Jer and Ezek interpret the end of the sovereign state of Judah and the scattering of the people as the manifestation of the holy wrath of God, who fulfills these covenant curses because of the nation's disobedience (Jer 9:16[15]; 13:24; 18:17; 30:11; Ezek 11:16; 12:15). The forced deportation of a portion of the population to Babylon after the destruction of Jerusalem and the subsequent fleeing of another group with the prophet Jeremiah to Egypt (Jer 43-44) is understood as the consequence of the judgment of Yahweh. In Ezek the announcement of the judgment with the vb. *pwṣ* is sometimes accompanied by the parallel vb. *zrh* I (→ # 2430; Ezek 20:23; 22:15; 29:12; 30:23, 26; 36:19).

4. The covenant relationship, however, also is the basis for the hope of the gathering of the dispersed after the time of judgment (Deut 30:3). This promise of restoration is expressed in formulaic fashion by the combination of *pwṣ* with the vb. *qbṣ*, gather (→ # 7695), which interestingly is utilized in a number of passages in these same prophetic books of Jer and Ezek (Jer 23:1-2; Ezek 11:17; 20:34, 41; 28:25; 29:13; 34:12-13; cf. Neh 1:8-9; Isa 11:12). In other words, Yahweh's scattering of his people is not his final word.

Zech takes up the shepherd imagery of earlier prophets. On the one hand, this prophetic book reproves the worthless shepherds who represent the sinful national leadership (Zech 11:8, 15-17; for the identification of these shepherds, see J. Baldwin, *Haggai, Zechariah, Malachi,* TOTC, 1972, 181-83; contrast P. D. Hanson, *The Dawn of Apocalyptic,* 1979, 337-54). On the other hand, Zech also presents the figure of another shepherd, who is intimately related to Yahweh (13:7; cf. 9:16; 10:3). This shepherd, though, will be smitten (cf. Isa 53:4, 10), and the nation, who are the sheep, will be scattered (cf. 1 Kgs 22:17 = 2 Chron 18:16) and will suffer greatly. The references to the shepherd and the sheep in Zech 13:7 were interpreted messianically both at Qumran and in the NT.

5. The nom. *tᵉpûṣâ* occurs only at Jer 25:34. This unique form, which is not translated in the LXX, is sometimes considered a mixed form of a q. and ni. of *pwṣ* (*GKC* 911) or as ultimately derived from *npṣ* (→ # 5880; NIV shattered; see W. McKane, *Jeremiah,* ICC, 1986, 1:652-53; W. Holladay, *Jeremiah 1,* 1988, 677).

P-B 1. The OT perspective that the dispersion of the Jews—that is, their living outside of Palestine—began with the forced deportations into exile after the fall of Israel and later of Judah because of the judgment of God continues in other Jewish literature (e.g., Sir 48:15; Ps Sol 17:18; 2 Bar 1:4), as do the hope and prayer for the future regathering of his people to the Promised Land (e.g., Ps Sol 17:26; Tob 13:5; 2 Bar 78:7). According to this theological perspective, the Exile represents the *terminus a quo* and the explanation for the establishment of Jewish communities outside the land. The historical realities are more complex, as the forces causing Jews to leave Palestine cannot be limited only to the Exile; e.g., the monarchies had representatives and contacts and had set up trading outposts beyond the national borders before the demise of Israel and Judah (e.g., 1 Kgs 9:26-28; 20:34). Many exiles chose to stay in Babylon and did not return with Zerubbabel, Ezra, or Nehemiah. Others later left Palestine voluntarily for economic reasons or to escape the tensions between the Seleucid and Ptolomaic dynasties. The destruction of the temple in AD 70 also had an important impact on national and cultural identity and on the very meaning of worship, with the resulting struggle to define how properly to live out faith in Yahweh. Still later, the suppression of the Bar Kohba revolt in AD 135 resulted in both expulsion from and emigration out of the land. Scholars debate when it was that living outside the land was countenanced and considered as acceptable in God's sight.

The dispersion of the Jews outside of Palestine, whatever its sociohistorical and economic causes, is now labeled the "Diaspora" (from the G). Although there were Jewish communities throughout the Mediterranean world (*Sib. Or.* 3.271), the primary centers were in Babylon and Egypt. Our sources for life in the Diaspora are diverse. Within the biblical materials, information can be gleaned from Esth, Ps 137, Jer, Ezek, and Dan (depending on one's critical stance, other portions are added, such as Isa 40-55). Other insights are available in extrabiblical material, such as the Elephantine papyri and the works of Josephus. Estimates of this Jewish population for the first century BC range from two to four million.

Apparently the quality of life, social status, and political privileges varied from region to region and were subject to the good graces of the rulers and to the particular political context. The impression based on several biblical texts is that those in Babylon prospered (Ezra 1:6; 2:65-69; Jer 29:5-7) and enjoyed a certain autonomy in self-government (the "elders," Ezek 8:1; 14:1; 20:1, 3); the exiled royal family was also treated well (*ANET*, 308; 2 Kgs 25:27-30). In contrast, Josephus's later efforts to disassociate the larger Jewish population from the "seditious" elements that led to the razing of Jerusalem by Titus (Josephus, *Wars*, 5-7), to defend his people beyond the borders of Palestine against slander (*Against Apion*), and to reproduce official documents granting rights to the Jews in order to corroborate their worth to Roman society (*Ant*, 12.2, 3; 14.8, 10; 16.2, 6) suggest that Jews also suffered opposition and discrimination. The Elephantine papyri provide another glimpse of everyday life in the Diaspora in Egypt. Some of these documents describe the business activity of this Jewish military colony (*ANET*, 222-23, 548-49).

Religious practices were also varied. On the one hand, some Jewish communities were syncretistic. Correspondence from Elephantine substantiates this fact: the Jews there had built a temple, and there is evidence that at least some of the colony worshiped the goddess Anat (*ANET*, 491-92; see M. S. Smith, *The Early History of God*, 1990, 61; O. Keel, *Göttinnen, Götter und Gottessymbole,* 1992, 219-20, 445). The prophet Ezekiel accuses those in Babylon of idolatry (14:1-11). At the same time, the Diaspora was the seedbed for a remarkable and variegated production of biblical translations, commentaries, and theological literature: e.g., the LXX, much of the Apocrypha and Pseudepigrapha, the works of Philo, and the Babylonian Talmud. For more details, see the sources in the bibliography.

2. In the LXX the most important G terms used to translate the various Heb. words of this word group are *diaspeirō*, scatter; *diaspora*, dispersion, *diaskorpizō*, scatter, disperse, and *skorpizō,* scatter, disperse. The term *diaspora* itself can refer to the act of dispersing (Deut 28:25; 30:4), the community of the dispersed (Neh 1:9; Isa 49:6; 2 Macc 1:27), or the place where these communities lived (Jth 5:19).

3. Zech 13:7 is quoted in the Qumran text CD 19:6-14. The shepherd figure is applied to the Teacher of Righteousness, and it is the faithful sect community, the sheep, who are scattered at the time of his visitation (also note R. T. France, *Jesus and the Old Testament,* 1971, 176-77). Another interesting passage that utilizes *pwṣ* is the inscription on one of the many trumpets for the final eschatological battle between the sons of light and the sons of darkness. The words on the "trumpets of departure of the camps" are to speak of God's power to disperse the enemies of righteousness (1QM 3:5).

NT The terms of the LXX reappear in the NT: *skorpizō,* (5x); *diaskorpizō,* (9x); *diaspeirō* and *diaspora,* 3x each. The three vbs. are used in the context of persecution that forces the scattering of the followers of Jesus and the early church: out of fear at the time of Jesus' capture and execution (John 16:32), and because of the opposition of the Jews in Jerusalem (Acts 8:1, 4). In Acts, this forced dispersion prompts the fulfillment of the mandate to reach beyond Judea to the rest of the world with the message of new life in the Christ. Jesus himself quotes Zech 13:7 as a reference to his person: he is the good shepherd (Mk 14:27 and par.; cf. John 10:1-16, 26-28; 16:32), who will be smitten by God for the sins of humankind. His disciples are the sheep that will be scattered, who will flee at the time of his capture (see France, *Jesus and the Old Testament,* 107-10, 154, 200-201, 208-9; D. J. Moo, *The Old Testament in the Passion Narratives,* 1983, 173-78, 182-87).

In one passage *diaspora* is a technical word for the Jewish dispersion (John 7:35; NIV where our people live scattered). In 1 Peter 1:1 and James 1:1, however, the term is applied to the church. Commentators differ as to the exact identity of the group within the church to which *diaspora* refers in these two passages and as to its relationship to ethnic and national Israel (see, respectively, P. H. Davids, *The First Epistle of Peter,* NICNT, 1990, 46-47; R. P. Martin, *James,* WBC 48, 1988, 7-11).

Scattering, dispersion: → *bzr* (scatter, # 1029); → *zrh* I (scatter, sprinkle, spread, # 2430); → *zr'* (sow, scatter seed, # 2445); → *zrq* I (sprinkle, scatter, # 2450); → *ndḥ* I (banish, be scattered, be cast out, seduce, # 5615); → *ndp* (blow away, scatter, # 5622); → *npṣ* II (spread out, scatter, be dispersed, # 5880); → *pwṣ* (scatter, disperse, be spread, # 7046); → *pzr* (scatter, spread, # 7061)

Bibliography

IDB 1:854-56; *ISBE* 1:962-68; *NIDNTT* 1:685-86; 2:33-35; *TDNT* 2:98-104; *TWAT* 6:544-47; *TWOT* 2:719-20; P. R. Ackroyd, *Exile and Restoration,* 1968; R. W. Klein, *Israel in Exile: A Theological Interpretation,* 1979; J. M. Miller and J. H. Hayes, *HAIJ,* 429-36; D. L. Smith, *The Religion of the Landless,* 1989; S. Talmon, "The Emergence of Jewish Sectarianism in the Early Second Temple Period," *Ancient Israelite Religion,* ed. P. D. Miller, P. D. Hanson, S. D. McBride, 1987, 587-616; G. Widengren, "Yahweh's Gathering of the Dispersed," *In the Shelter of Elyon: Essays on Ancient Palestinian Life and Literature in Honor of G. W. Ahlstrom,* ed. W. B. Barrick, J. B. Spencer, JSOT Sup 31, 1984, 227-45; H. G. M. Williamson, "The Concept of Israel in Transition," and R. J. Coggins, "The Origins of the Jewish Diaspora," in *The World of Ancient Israel,* ed. R. E. Clements, 1989, 141-61, 163-81, respectively.

M. Daniel Carroll R.

7048	פּוּק

פּוּק (*pwq* I), q. stagger; hi. wobble, reel, totter (# 7048); פּוּקָה (*pûqâ*), nom. stumbling, shaking, tottering (# 7050); פִּק (*piq*), shaking (# 7211).

ANE In Ugar. *pqq* occurs with the nom. head with the sense, the head wobbles.

OT 1. As a vb., *pwq* I occurs only twice in the OT (Isa 28:7; Jer 10:4). The contexts of these occurrences are related to the other words in the semantic field of shaking, trembling. In Isaiah *pwq* is used to describe the physical staggering of drunkenness.

Jeremiah uses the vb. sarcastically to describe wobbly idols that need to be nailed down so that they do not fall over.

2. In Nah 2:10[11] the nom. form *piq* is used to describe the shaking or knocking of knees characteristic of great fear or anguish. The fem. nom. *pûqâ* also occurs once (1 Sam 25:31) to depict grief or anguish.

P-B Late Heb./Aram. *piqpēq*, loosen, shake.

Shaking, terror, trembling: → *g'š* (rise and fall noisily, swell, surge, # 1723); → *zw'* (tremble, quake, be afraid, # 2316); → *zll* II (shake, quake, tremble, # 2362); → *ḥalḥālâ* (shaking, trembling, anguish, # 2714); → *ḥrg* (come out trembling, # 3004); → *ḥrd* (tremble, shudder, startle, # 3006); → *yr'* (tremble, be fainthearted, # 3760); → *mwṭ* (waver, reel, stagger, shake, reel, # 4572); → *m'd* (slip, slide, shake, totter, # 5048); → *nwd* (shake, totter, waiver, wander, mourn, flee, # 5653); → *nwṭ* (shake, quake, # 5667); → *nw'* (shake, tremble, stagger, totter, wave, # 5675); → *n'r* II (shake, shake off, # 5850); → *smr* (shudder, have goose-bumps, bristle, # 6169); → *'iw'îm* (distortion, stagger, dizzy, # 6413); → *pwq* I (stagger, wobble, reel, totter, # 7048); → *pḥd* I (tremble, be in dread, # 7064); → *plṣ* (shudder, shake, tremble, # 7145); → *qwṣ* I (feel disgust, frighten, cause dread, # 7762); → *rgz* (agitate, quiver, shake, excite, rouse up, agitate, # 8074); → *rnh* I (rattle, # 8261); → *r'd* (tremble, shake, tremble, # 8283); → *r'l* I (brandish, make to quiver, # 8302); → *r'š* I (quake, shake, leap, # 8321); → *rpp* (shake, quake, rock, # 8344); → *r^etēt* (terror, panic, trembling, # 8417); → *ś'r* I (be afraid, terrified, bristle with horror, # 8547)

BIBLIOGRAPHY

TWOT 2:720.

M. V. Van Pelt/W. C. Kaiser, Jr.

7050 (*pûqâ*, stumbling, shaking), → # 7048

7051 (*pwr*, break, frustrate), → # 7296

7052	פּוּרִים

פּוּרִים (*pûrîm*), festival of Purim (7052a); < פּוּר (*pûr*), lot (# 7052).

ANE The Heb. nom. *pwr* is commonly understood to be a loanword from Akk. *pûru*, meaning "lot" (Hallo, 21-22), the native Heb. nom. being *gôrāl. purim* is a Hebraized form of the Akk. and suggests a non-Jewish origin for the festival, which is difficult to specify further as a result of the lack of information provided by the sources (*ABD* 2:637). Some scholars have suggested a Babylonian origin because of the equation of Esther and Mordecai with the deities Ishtar and Marduk (Zimmern, 157); others have suggested that the underlying conflict was between the worshipers of Marduk and Mithra during the Persian Farvardigan festival (compare G trans. of Purim in LXX) celebrated at the end of the year (Lewy, 127).

OT The term occurs only in Esther and when used in the singular is equated with *gôrāl* (Esth 3:7; 9:24). The *pûr* was cast (*npl*, hi.) in the presence of Haman in the first month (Nisan) to select a date for destroying the Jews. Providentially, the twelfth month (Adar) was chosen (3:7; cf. Prov 16:33), the tables were turned against Haman, and the Jews were able to defend themselves (Esth 4-9). The day in which the slaughter of the Jews was to have taken place according to lot (*pûr*) cast for their destruction turned into a day of great triumph. "Therefore these days were called Purim, from the word *pûr*" (9:26), days to be celebrated in gladness (9:28-32). So another chapter in the ongoing conflict with Amalek (cf. 3:1) came to an end (cf. Exod 17:8-16; 1 Sam 15).

P-B Josephus (*Ant* 11:6, 13) indicated, using the LXX translation *phrourai* and *phrouraia*, that the Festival of Purim was held on the 14th and 15th Adar as a commemoration of the Jewish revenge upon their Persian enemies. 2 Macc 15:36 refers to the festival as "Mordecai's day" (*IDB* 3:969). Although the feast was preceded by fasting, the two days of festivities were characterized by rejoicing, the reading of the book of Esther in the synagogue, and the giving of presents and alms (de Vaux, 514). Purim "leavens the religious year with the necessary element of fun and cheer" (Gaster, 230).

NT No reference is made of Purim, although some scholars have suggested that the unnamed feast in John 5:1 might be Purim (*ISBE* 3:1056).

Feasts & festivals: → *bikkûrîm* (early or firstfruits, # 1137); → *ḥag* (procession, round dance, festival, feast, # 2504); → *ḥanukkâ* (dedication, Feast of Dedication, # 2853); → *mô'ēd* (appointed time, # 4595); → *maṣṣôt* (Feast of the Unleavened Bread, # 5174a); → *marzēaḥ* (cultic feast, funeral meal, # 5301); → *sukkôt* (Feast of Tabernacles, # 6109a); → *'aṣārâ* (festive assembly, # 6809); → *pûrîm* (festival of Purim, # 7052a); → *pesaḥ* (Feast or sacrifice of Passover, # 7175 [→ **Passover: Theology**]); → *rō'š ḥōdeš* (festival of the new Moon, # 8031a); → *rō'š haššānâ* (beginning of the year, # 8031b); → *šābu'ôt* (feast of Weeks, # 8651a); → *šabbāt* (sabbath, # 8701 [→ **Sabbath: Theology**])
Lots, division, Urim/Thummim: → *'ûrîm* (Urim, # 242); → *gôrāl* (lot, # 1598); → *ḥlq* II (divide, obtain one's share, # 2745); → *ydd* I (cast, # 3341); → *pûr* (lot, # 7052); → *tummîm* (Thummim, # 9460)

BIBLIOGRAPHY

ABD 2:633-43; *IDB* 3:968-69; *ISBE* 3:1056-57; *TWOT* 2:720; R. de Vaux, *AncIsr*, 1961, 514-17; M. V. Fox, *Character and Ideology in the Book of Esther*, 1991; T. H. Gaster, *Festivals of the Jewish Year*, 1978; W. W. Halo, "The First Purim," *BA* 46, 1983, 19-26; J. Lewy, "The Feast of the 14th Day of Adar," *HUCA* 14, 1939, 127-51; C. A. Moore, "Eight Questions Most Frequently Asked About the Book of Esther," *BibRev* 3, 1987, 16-31; idem, *Esther*, AB, 1971; J. Rosenheim "Fate and Freedom in the Scroll of Esther," *Proof* 12, 1992, 125-49; H. Zimmern, "Zur Frage nach dem Ursprunge des Purimfestes," *ZAW* 11, 1891, 157-69.

Hendrik L. Bosman/C. Van Dam

7053	פּוּרָה

פּוּרָה (*pûrâ*), nom. trough of a winepress (# 7053).

ANE There is no known use of a vb. *pwr* in BH, but cognate vbs. are known in other languages, with thc sense of boil or ferment; cf. Arab. *fāra*, spout forth, boil up.

OT The word is found twice in the OT. In Hag 2:16 its use relates to the poverty the people faced when they neglected building the temple: "When anyone went to a wine vat to draw fifty measures, there were only twenty." Then in Isa 63:3 the Lord's coming on the nations in judgment is described as his having "trodden the winepress alone." (The word that properly meant the trough of the press is used here for the press itself.)

Trough: → *'ēbûs* (feeding trough, # 17); → *yeqeb* (wine vat/trough, winepress, # 3676); → *miš'eret* (kneading trough, # 5400); → *pûrâ* (trough [winepress], # 7053); → *rahaṭ* (watering trough, # 8110); → *šōqet* (watering trough, # 9216)

Grapes—juice, wine: → *gat* I (wine press, # 1780); → *dema'* (juice from wine vat, # 1964); → *ḥōmeṣ* (vinegar, wine, beer, # 2810); → *ḥemer* (wine, foaming wine, # 2815); → *yayin* (wine, # 3516); → *yeqeb* (wine vat/trough, winepress, # 3676); → *yrš* II (tread the wine press/grapes, # 3770); → *mhl* (adulterated wine, # 4543); → *mezeg* (spiced/blended/mixed wine, # 4641); → *mišrâ* (juice, # 5489); → *'āsîs* (grape juice, # 6747); → *śḥṭ* (squeeze, to press out grapes, # 8469); → *šemer* I (dregs, aged wine, # 9069); → *tîrôš* (fresh wine, # 9408)

Francis Foulkes

7055	פּוּשׁ

פּוּשׁ (*pwš* I), q. skip, leap, frisk, gambol (# 7055).

OT 1. This vb. is used for the frisking of calves turned out to pasture; this picture serves as a metaphor for exuberant joy (Mal 3:20[4:2]; cf. Jer 50:11).

2. In Hab 1:8 the vb. appears to describe the galloping of horses, though the text is difficult. This vb. occurs in Nah 3:18, ni., but most emend the text to read *nāpōṣû*, be scattered (BDB [807] lists this text under *pwš* II).

Jumping, leaping, skipping: → *glš* (skip, jump, # 1683); → *dwṣ* (dance, # 1881); → *dlg* (leap, # 1925); → *znq* I (jump before, # 2397); → *ntr* II (start, spring, # 6001); → *sld* (jump, spring, # 6134); → *pwš* (skip, leap, # 7055); → *pzz* II (be quick, agile, hop, # 7060); → *rqd* (skip, leap, # 8376); → *šqq* (run about, jump, # 9212)

John E. Hartley

7058	פַּז

פַּז (*paz*), nom. pure gold, fine gold (# 7058); פזז (*pzz* I), denom. vb., ho. part. מוּפָז (*mûpāz*), pure, refined, fine (# 7059).

ANE The occurrence of the word *paz* or its derivatives in other languages is uncertain. It is disputed whether Ugar. *pd* and Arab. *fiḍḍah*, silver, are related (Kedar-Kopfstein, 34). Other possibilities are Dravidian *pačču*, yellow, and Skt. *pita*, golden stone, but Kedar-Kopfstein (34) maintains that these are more likely to be related to Heb. *piṭdâ*, G *topazos*, topaz.

OT 1. The nom. occurs 9x (Kedar-Kopfstein, 34; *NIVEC* 1585), usually in parallel with *zāhāb*, *ḥārûṣ*, or *ketem*. The crown of fine gold (*'^{a}ṭeret pāz*) that Yahweh sets upon the head of the king is more of a token of the powerful blessings and prosperity God intends for his vicegerent than a symbol of earthly authority (Ps 21:3[4]; Kraus, 1988, 286; Rogerson and McKay, 1977a, 94).

The author of Lam 4:2 bewails the fate of Jerusalem's citizens after the siege and sack of the city: Zion's precious children, once worth their weight in fine gold (*paz*), are now treated as though their value were equivalent to that of cheap crockery. In S of Songs 5:11, a lovesick maiden, probably a bride-to-be, describes her beloved's noble head as the finest gold (*ketem pāz*).

The description of a celestial visitant, either an angel (see Collins, 1984, 96-104; 1993, 399, 402) or something more awesome (see R. A. Anderson, 122-24), makes mention of the loins of the supernatural figure that were girded *b^{e}ketem 'ûpāz*

(Dan 10:5-6). Some (RSV; NRSV) retain MT and translate "(with) gold from/of Uphaz," but others (NEB; REB) emend MT *'ûpāz*, Uphaz, to *'ôpîr*, Ophir (the name of a location famed for the high quality of gold it supplied). There is only one other reference to Uphaz (Jer 10:9); here, while some (RSV; NRSV; NIV; TEV) retain MT, *w^{e}zāhāb mē'ûpāz*, and/with gold from Uphaz, others (Tg.; Pesh.; NEB; REB; JB) emend *mē'ûpāz* to *mē'ôpîr*, from Ophir. Another suggestion made in connection with Dan 10:5 is to emend MT *'ûpāz*, Uphaz, to *ûpāz* (i.e., conjunction with nom.), "and fine gold" (see *BHS*). JB reads "pure gold," TEV "fine gold," and NIV "finest gold."

In an oracle against Babylon (Isa 13:1-22), the warning is issued that when Yahweh comes in judgment, the destruction of the wicked throughout the world will be on such a massive scale that human beings will be almost exterminated, becoming rarer than fine gold (*paz*) (v. 12).

2. Yahweh's *tôrâ* is said to be infinitely more valuable than fine gold (Ps 119:127), however great the quantity (19:10[11]). In both these texts, the *tôrâ* is regarded neither as a wearisome duty nor as a reference work to be consulted in time of need; rather, it is held to be of incomparable value because it is a medium of communion with God, a constant source of refreshment, joy, and fulness of life, the ground of hope, the promise of salvation, and the fountain from which everything of supreme value flows (G. W. Anderson, 439; Oesterley, 486-87, 499-500; Toombs, 267-68, 295; Weiser, 202, 740; A. A. Anderson, 807; Rogerson and McKay, 1977b, 93; Kraus, 1988, 273-76; 1989, 412-14, 420-21; Bratcher and Reyburn, 997; Mays, 98-99, 381-85).

paz is used in two passages eulogizing the inestimable value and power of wisdom (Job 28:17; Prov 8:19). Wisdom is the exclusive property of God and beyond price (Job 28:15-19); it cannot be purchased even with the most precious and exquisite jewels of fine gold (*pāz*; 28:17). But while absolute wisdom, by means of which Yahweh created the world and continues to operate the universe is beyond the grasp and understanding of mortals, v. 28 (considered by many, see Strahan [239], Dhorme [414], Pope [206], and Habel [151], to be a gloss) gives the assurance that if persons lead lives of genuine piety and morality, they can attain a measure of (practical) wisdom. The fruit of such wisdom is considered beyond the value of gold, even fine gold (*ûmippāz*) (Prov 8:19 [cf. 8:10-11]). The contrast drawn in 8:19 between wisdom's fruit and precious metals indicates that the riches referred to include more than simply material blessings (Walls, 558; Collins, 1980, 29-30; Cox, 149, 152; cf. Tate, 32). While material riches are considered important, even necessary, they must be subordinated to wisdom (McKane, 350). Moreover, the quality of a life governed by wisdom's discipline and knowledge is a treasure infinitely more to be desired than material wealth. Through wisdom, one is directed towards Yahweh and one enjoys communion with him (Cox, 152).

3. The ho. part. occurs in 1 Kgs 10:18, which relates how Solomon made a great ivory throne overlaid (*ṣph*) with *zāhāb mûpāz*, refined gold (JB). NEB, REB, and NIV read "fine gold" while RSV, NRSV, and TEV have "the finest gold." Another possibility is "solid gold" (cf. Gray, 265; de Vries, 140). The par. 2 Chron 9:17 has *zāhāb ṭāhôr*, pure gold (RSV; NRSV; NEB; REB; NIV; TEV) or purest gold (JB). Montgomery and Gehman (230) emend the MT *mûpāz* of 1 Kgs 10:18 to *ûpāz* (i.e., the conjunction with nom.). The throne was probably made of wood inlaid with ivory and only

those clear (ivory-free) surfaces would have been given a plating of gold (see Skinner, 170; Jones, 227).

P-B Both nom. and vb. forms occur in Heb.: *paz*, fine gold; (name of) a jewel; *pāzaz*, (move to and fro) be bright, glisten; jingle, rustle; be rash; ho. part, made of fine gold; glistening; pi. dance, sport; jingle, rustle. In Aram., the forms *pᵉzôzā'*, *pîzzûzā'*, made of fine gold, occur. The words *pᵉzîzā'*, (masc.) rash, overhasty, impetuous; gilded or glazed, and *pᵉzîzûtā'*, (fem.) rashness, impetuousness, are also found (Jastrow 2:1149-50).

Gold: → *'ôpîr* (gold of Ophir, # 234); → *beṣer* I (gold ore, # 1309); → *zāhāb* (gold, # 2298); → *ḥārûṣ* I (gold, # 3021); → *ketem* (gold, # 4188); → *sāgûr* (pure gold, # 6034); → *paz* (pure gold, # 7058); → *ṣrp* (melt, smelt, refine, # 7671)

BIBLIOGRAPHY

TDOT 4:32-40; A. A. Anderson, *The Book of Psalms. Vol. 2: Psalms 73-150*, NCBC, 1972; G. W. Anderson, "The Psalms," in *Peake*, 1964, 409-43; R. A. Anderson, *Signs and Wonders: A Commentary on the Book of Daniel*, 1984; R. G. Bratcher and W. D. Reyburn, *A Translator's Handbook on the Book of Psalms*, 1991; J. J. Collins, *Proverbs, Ecclesiastes*, 1980; idem, *Daniel With an Introduction to Apocalyptic Literature*, 1984; idem, *Daniel*, Hermeneia, 1993; D. Cox, *Proverbs With an Introduction to Sapiential Books*, 1982; E. Dhorme, *A Commentary on The Book of Job*, 1967; J. Gray, *I & II Kings: A Commentary*, OTL, 2d rev. ed., 1970; N. C. Habel, *the Book of Job*, 1975; G. H. Jones, *1 and 2 Kings. Volume 1: 1 Kings 1-16:34*, NCBC, 1984; H.-J. Kraus, *Psalms 1-59: A Commentary*, 1988; idem, *Psalms 60-150: A Commentary*, 1989; W. McKane, *Proverbs: A New Approach*, OTL, 1970; J. L. Mays, *Psalms*, 1994; J. A. Montgomery and H. S. Gehman, *A Critical and Exegetical Commentary on the Books of Kings*, ICC, 1967; W. O. E. Oesterley, *The Psalms Translated with Text-Critical and Exegetical Notes*, 1959; M. H. Pope, *Job: Introduction, Translation, and Notes*, AB, 3d ed., 1979; J. W. Rogerson and J. W. McKay, *Psalms 1-50*, 1977 (1977a); idem, *Psalms 101-150*, 1977 (1977b); J. Skinner, *I & II Kings*, 1893; J. Strahan, *The Book of Job Interpreted*, 1913; M. E. Tate, "Proverbs," in *BBC*, 1972, 5:1-99; L. E. Toombs, "The Psalms," in *The Interpreter's One-Volume Commentary on the Bible*, 1971, 253-303; S. J. de Vries, *1 Kings*, WBC, 1985; A. F. Walls, "Proverbs," in *NBC*, 1972, 548-69; A. Weiser, *The Psalms: A Commentary*, OTL, 1965.

Robin Wakely

7059 (*pzz* I, refined), → # 7058

7060	פזז

פזז (*pzz* II), q. be quick, agile; pi. show agility, hop quickly, leap (# 7060).

ANE Syr. *paz*, leap, frisk, be agile; *pazzîzā'*, agile, nimble (*HALAT* 870); Arab. *fazza*, jump up, start, bolt.

OT 1. In Jacob's blessing this vb. in q. describes the agility and dexterity of Joseph in handling a strong bow with his arms against archers who harried him (Gen 49:24).

2. In the pi. this vb. describes David's energetic dancing as he led the procession of the Ark of the Covenant from Obed-Edom's house to Jerusalem (2 Sam 6:16). Acting in this fashion, David, though king, humbled himself before God and revealed his wholehearted commitment to serve God.

Jumping, leaping, skipping: → *glš* (skip, jump, # 1683); → *dwṣ* (dance, # 1881); → *dlg* (leap, # 1925); → *znq* I (jump before, # 2397); → *ntr* II (start, spring, # 6001); → *sld* (jump, spring, # 6134); → *pwš* (skip, leap, # 7055); → *pzz* II (be quick, agile, hop, # 7060); → *rqd* (skip, leap, # 8376); → *šqq* (run about, jump, # 9212)

John E. Hartley

7061	פזר

פזר (*pzr*), q. scatter; pi. scatter, spread; ni. be scattered; pu. be scattered (# 7061).

OT Among its ten occurrences, this vb. can refer to the people of God who were forcibly dispersed into exile (Esth 3:8; Jer 50:17, in par. with *ndḥ*; Joel 3:2[4:2]). This meaning agrees with *pwṣ, ndḥ*, and *zrh*. In other passages, Yahweh can scatter the enemies of his people in judgment (Ps 53:5[6]; 89:10[11]; 141:7), yet he also distributes blessings in his grace (112:9). With a human subject, the vb. in a positive vein can refer to the generosity of the wise who distribute goods (NIV gives freely) to others (Prov 11:24); on the other hand, Jeremiah accuses faithless Israel of having (lit.) "scattered your ways" before other gods, possibly an allusion with sexual undertones to non-Yahwistic worship (Jer 3:13; see J. A. Thompson, *The Book of Jeremiah,* NICOT, 1980, 197, 201 (cf. v. 6); yet note W. Holladay, *Jeremiah 1,* Hermeneia, 1988, 59, 119-20; NIV scattered your favors; NEB promiscuous traffic).

Scattering, dispersion: → *bzr* (scatter, # 1029); → *zrh* I (scatter, sprinkle, spread, # 2430); → *zr'* (sow, scatter seed, # 2445); → *zrq* I (sprinkle, scatter, # 2450); → *ndḥ* I (banish, be scattered, be cast out, seduce, # 5615); → *ndp* (blow away, scatter, # 5622); → *npṣ* II (spread out, scatter, be dispersed, # 5880); → *pwṣ* (scatter, disperse, be spread, # 7046); → *pzr* (scatter, spread, # 7061)

BIBLIOGRAPHY

TWAT 6:547.

M. Daniel Carroll R.

7062	פַּח

פַּח (*paḥ* I), nom. trap, snare, bird trap (# 7062); > פחח (*pḥḥ*), denom. vb. ensnare (→ # 7072).

ANE *HALAT* gives a possible Egyp. root *ph3* and the Arab. *faḫḫ,* meaning trap (see also Driver, *Reflections,* 132).

OT 1. *paḥ* may be rendered in several different ways. In the Prophets it is used 11x, usually with the sense of a snare or a net. For a snare to be effective, it needs to be attached to a sapling or light branch and set across a game track, in such a way that when the animal puts its foot or neck into the snare, the sapling springs back and the noose is pulled tight (see Amos 3:5). Jer 18:22 speaks of Jeremiah's enemies digging a pit to capture him and having hidden snares (*paḥîm*) for his feet. *paḥ* also has the more general sense of a trap. Hos 5:1 likens the priests of Israel to a trap (*paḥ*) and a net (*rešet*) spread out on Mount Tabor, to catch the unwary Israelites and to drag them into idolatry.

2. In the Wisdom writings *paḥ* often has the specific sense of a net. So God rains "nets" upon the wicked (Ps 11:6). In Ps 124:7; Prov 7:23; Eccl 9:12 (all in the

context of trapping birds), "bird-net" is a more precise rendering. Elsewhere a more general sense may be appropriate (e.g., the traps of one's enemies as in Ps 141:9).

P-B The LXX regularly uses *pagis* for *paḥ*, with the general sense of trap or snare. The DSS follow the OT usage (e.g., CD 4:14 and 1QH 18:25), and 4QpPs37 speaks of the "traps of Belial."

Hunting: → *yqš* (lay a trip wire, set a trap, # 3704); → *paḥ* I (trap, snare, # 7062); → *ṣwd* (hunt, # 7421); → *rešet* (net, # 8407); → *šûḥâ* I (pit, # 8757)

BIBLIOGRAPHY

F. I. Andersen and D. L. Freedman, *Hosea*, AB, 1980, 385, 533-34; idem, *Amos*, AB, 1989, 395-97; G. R. Driver, "Reflections on Recent Articles," *JBL* 73, 1954, 131-36; A. Negev, ed., *Archaeological Encyclopaedia of the Holy Land*, 1972, 149-50.

W. R. Domeris

7063 פַּח

פַּח (*paḥ* II), nom., sheets, thin sheets (# 7063).

ANE The word is found in Sam. pl. *fim,* const. *fijji*, and in Egyp. *pḫ3*.

OT There are two occurrences of *paḥ*. According to Exod 39:3, part of a description of the manufacture of the priestly vestments (39:1-31), the ephod was made of various materials, including *paḥê hazzāhāb*, gold leaf, which was hammered out (pi. of *rq'*). This is the only technical description of the method of producing the gold thread used in the sewing of sacral garments. The thin plates of gold would have been cut into narrow strips (either wires or threads) and then worked into the fabric along with yarns of various colors (Driver, 395).

In Num 16:38[17:3], Yahweh instructs Moses to command Eleazar, the son of Aaron, to remove from the fire the bronze censers of those (Korah, a subordinate levitical priest, and his followers) who had been slain after revolting against the ecclesiastical leadership of Moses and Aaron. The censers are to be removed so that they can be made into hammered plates (*riqqu'ê paḥîm*) and used as a covering for the altar of burnt offering. Having been offered to Yahweh, they are considered holy, despite the fact that Korah and his company had no authority to offer them and had died as a consequence of their presumption (Kennedy, 284; Wade, 221; Marsh, 225; Snaith, 1964, 262; 1967, 260-61; Noth, 129-30; Thompson, 186; Sturdy, 121; Burns, 251; Wenham, 138). The covering will serve as a perpetual memorial of the incident and a reminder that none save Aaronic priests are entitled to approach the altar. Some have concluded that this account seems to contradict Exod 27:2 and 38:2, according to which the altar of burnt offering had a bronze covering from the beginning (but see Ashley, 325-26).

Metals: → *'ᵃnāk* (lead, # 643); → *bᵉdîl* (dross, # 974); → *barzel* (iron, # 1366); → *zāhāb* (gold, # 2298); → *ḥel'â* I (rust, # 2689); → *ḥašmal* (glow?, electrum, glowing metal, # 3133); → *kesep* (silver, money, # 4084); → *masgēr* II (metal worker, # 4994); → *maʿᵃbeh* (foundry, # 5043); → *nᵉḥōšet* I (copper, bronze, # 5733); → *sîg* (lead oxide, # 6092); → *sēper* II (bronze, plate, # 6220); → *'ōperet* (lead, # 6769); → *paḥ* II (thin sheet, # 7063); → *pᵉlādōt* (steel?, # 7110); → *ṣwr* III (cast [metal], # 7445); → *ṣaʿᵃṣuʿîm* (things formed by metal coating, # 7589); → *ṣph* II (arrange, overlay, plate, glaze, # 7596); → *ṣrp* (melt, smelt, refine, # 7671); → *qālāl* (polished metal, # 7838); → *šḥṭ* II (alloyed, # 8822)

BIBLIOGRAPHY
T. R. Ashley, *The Book of Numbers*, NICOT, 1993; R. J. Burns, *Exodus, Leviticus, Numbers with Excurses on Feasts/Ritual and Typology*, OTM, 1983; S. R. Driver, *The Book of Exodus*, CBSC, 1953; A. R. S. Kennedy, *Leviticus and Numbers*, CB, 1910; J. Marsh, "The Book of Numbers: Introduction and Exegesis," *IB*, 1953, 2:135-308; M. Noth, *Numbers: A Commentary*, OTL, 1968; N. H. Snaith, "Numbers," in *Peake*, 1964, 254-68; idem, *Leviticus and Numbers*, NCB, 1967; J. Sturdy, *Numbers*, CBC, 1976; J. A. Thompson, "Numbers," *NBC*, 1972, 168-200; G. W. Wade, "Numbers," in *Peake*, 1920, 213-30; G. J. Wenham, *Numbers: An Introduction and Commentary*, TOTC, 1981.

Robin Wakely

7064	פחד

פחד (*pḥd* I), q. tremble; pi. be trembling, be in dread; hiph. cause to shake, tremble (# 7064); פַּחַד (*paḥad*), nom. trembling, terror, dread (# 7065); פַּחְדָּה (*paḥdâ*), nom. dread, terror, awe (# 7067).

ANE Aram. vb. p^e*ḥad*; nom. *paḥdā'*; Akk. *paḫādu*, frighten, quake.

OT The verbal form of *pḥd* I occurs only 25x in the OT. In 22 instances it appears in the q. form describing the shaking that can result from either extreme terror or joy. The pi. form appears only twice (Prov 28:14; Isa 51:13). In both instances it occurs in conjunction with *tāmîd,* denoting the iterative aspect, to quake continually. It appears once as the hi. expressing the causative aspect, to cause to quake (Job 4:14). With regard to distribution throughout the OT, it appears most frequently in the Latter Prophets (13x) and Writings (10x). Only twice does it occur in the Pent (Deut 28:66-67). More than half of all occurrences can be found in the books of Isa (8x) and Ps (5x).

1. The vb. *pḥd* I can describe both the quaking of terror as well as the quaking of delight or joy. In the sense of terror Isaiah uses it to describe the dreadfulness of oppression or dire circumstances (Isa 51:13). The unexpected plight of Job serves as a fine example of this use (Job 3:25; 4:14). A more particular use, however, is found in connection with the judgment of Yahweh on the ungodly. Such judgment is found in connection with Israel (Deut 28:66-67; Isa 33:14), Egypt (Isa 19:16-17), foreign nations in general (Mic 7:17), idolaters (Isa 44:8), and the foolish (Ps 14:5; 53:5[6]).

Another related act of God is the revelation of his word. The response to God's word, however, can be either terror (Jer 36:16) or joy (Ps 119:161). The terror of Yahweh's judgment is antithetically related to joy of his salvation. The material prosperity associated with deliverance or returning from exile motivates this type of reaction (Isa 60:5; Jer 33:9; Hos 3:5). There are also important reasons why God's people have no reason to be terrified: God is the source of salvation (Ps 27:1; 78:53; Isa 12:2), he is the only God (Isa 44:8), and he is the one who cares for and protects his people (Prov 3:24).

2. The nominal form *paḥad* I, fear, occurs 50x in the OT. It is formed after the manner of the one-syllable segolate, *paḥad*, meaning trembling or terror (*TDNT* 9:204). In a few instances, *beṭaḥ*, safety (→ # 1055) (Prov 1:33; 3:23-24) and *šālôm*, peace, security (→ # 8934) (Job 21:9) appear in a contrasting relationship. Such terror

can be caused by the threat of an enemy (Ps 64:1[2]; 91:5; Prov 1:26, 27) or the unexpected dread of misfortune (Job 3:25; 4:14). God's presence and activity among the Israelites causes them to be the object of dread before other nations (Deut 2:25; 11:25; Esth 8:17; Ps 105:38). In a similar context, Yahweh's acts of judgment, either potential or actual, are considered dreadful (Exod 15:16; Ps 53:5[6]; 119:120; Isa 24:17; Jer 48:43, 44; 49:5). Likewise, his very presence evokes terror (Job 13:11; 25:2). In this context both *paḥad yhwh*, the dread of Yahweh, and *paḥad 'ᵉlohîm*, the dread of God (Yahweh, 1 Sam 11:7; 2 Chron 14:13; 17:10; 19:7; 20:29; God, Ps 36:1[2]; Isa 2:10, 19, 21), appear to function as descriptive-technical terminology.

3. The unusual designation *paḥad yiṣḥaq*, the fear of Isaac, appears twice in what appears to be some form of a divine name for God (Gen 31:42, 53). There are two interpretative options: "(1) that it is the obj. of Isaac's reverence in the weaker sense of 'respect,' or (2) along the lines of Palmyrene-Aram., Arab. and Ugar. par. it means 'kinsman,' which corresponds to theophorus elements in Isr. proper names such as *'āb*, father, *'aḥ*, brother, *'aḥ*, people, etc." (*TDNT* 9:204).

4. Other Heb. words appearing with *pḥd* I and denoting the aspect of quaking are *ḥrd* (→ # 3006; Isa 19:16), *rgz* (→ # 8074; Jer 33:9; Mic 7:17), and *r'd* (→ # 8283; Job 14:14; Isa 33:14). Words appearing with *pḥd* I denoting the aspect of terror are *yr'* (→ # 3707; Ps 27:1; Isa 44:8; Mic 7:17), *bhl* (→ # 987; Job 23:15), *bwš* (→ # 1017; Ps 53:5[6]; Isa 44:1) and *ygr* (Job 3:25).

Fear, dread, terror: → *'āyōm* (terrible, awesome, majestic, # 398); → *'êmâ* (terror, dread, # 399); → *bhl* (be dismayed, terrified, dismay, terrify, hasten, hurry, # 987); → *b't* (overtaken by sudden terror, stupefied, be terrified, assail, # 1286); → *gwr* III (be afraid of, dread, stand in awe, # 1593); → *d'g* (be anxious, concerned, fear, dread, # 1793); → *zḥl* II (fear, be afraid, # 2324); → *ḥrd* (tremble, shudder, startle, # 3006); → *ḥtt* (be shattered, dismayed, terrified, scare, terrify, # 3169); → *ygr* (fear, dread, terror, # 3336); → *yr'* I (fear, be afraid, held in honor, # 3707); → *yrh* (be afraid, terrified, paralyzed with fright, # 3724); → *'rṣ* (be alarmed, terrified, dreadful, dreadful, be in terror, # 6907); → *pḥd* I (tremble, be in dread, # 7064); → *qwṣ* I (feel disgust, frighten, cause dread, # 7762)

BIBLIOGRAPHY
TDNT 9:197-205; K. Koch, "*Paḥad Jiṣaq*—eine Gottesbezeichnung?" in *Werden und Wirken des AT*, ed. C. Westermann, 1980, 107-15; A. Lemaire, "A propos de *paḥad* dans l'onomastique ouest-semitique," *VT* 35, 1985, 500-501; M. Malul, "More on *Pachad Yitschaq* (Genesis 31:42, 53) and the Oath by the Thigh," *VT* 35, 1985, 192-200; E. Puech, "La crainte d'Isaac en Genèse 31:42 et 53," *VT* 34, 1984, 356-61.

M. V. Van Pelt/W. C. Kaiser, Jr.

7065 (*paḥad* I, terror, dread), → # 7064

7066	פַּחַד

פַּחַד (*paḥad* II), thigh (# 7066).

OT 1. A hapleg. occurs in Job 40:17: "His [Behemoth's] tail sways like cedar, the sinews of his thighs are close-knit."

2. The twofold use of *paḥad yiṣḥāq*, a name for God, by Jacob may be rendered either as "the fear of Isaac" (NIV) or "the thigh of Isaac" (Gen 31:42, 53), i.e., the family of Isaac (Malul). Malul, along with Hillers, takes *paḥad*, thigh, as a euphemism for

the genitals and suggests that the expression refers symbolically to the posterity/family of Isaac (the spirits of the family, invoked by the symbolic gesture accompanying the oath, were supposed to rally to the protection of their descendants and to the defense of the integrity of their line, 200). There are other possibilities for *paḥad* in the Gen 31 passages apart from "thigh." One possibility is to connect it with an Arab. word meaning refuge, hence "the refuge of Isaac" or "the protection of Isaac" (Kopf, 257; Westermann 3:497). And one should not prematurely dismiss the possibility that *paḥad* carries here its normal meaning "fear," not so much in the sense of "the fear of Isaac," but rather "The One of Isaac Who Causes Fear." In other compound phrases with *paḥad*, as in the expression "the fear/terror of the Lord" (1 Sam 11:7), the second term expresses the source or cause of the dread, not the object of the dread (Sarna, 366 n.17). Thus, the name could be an indirect reference to Laban's encounter with his son-in-law's God in a dream that warned him against harming Jacob (Gen 31:29).

Leg, loins, foot, thigh: → *b^ehôn* (thumb, big toe, # 984); → *ḥ^alāṣayim* (loins, # 2743); → *yārēk* (thigh, leg, # 3751); → *kesel* I (loins, flank/side, # 4072); → *midrāk* (foot-print, # 4534); → *marg^elôt* (place of feet, # 5274); → *motnayim* (loins, hips, # 5516); → *na'al* (sandal, # 5837); → *paḥad* II (thigh, # 7066); → *pa'am* (foot, step, time, # 7193); → *qarsōl* (ankle, # 7972); → *regel* (foot, # 8079); → *šôq* (thigh, leg, # 8797)

Fear, dread, terror: → *'āyōm* (terrible, awesome, majestic, # 398); → *'êmâ* (terror, dread, # 399); → *bhl* (be dismayed, terrified, dismay, terrify, hasten, hurry, # 987); → *b't* (overtaken by sudden terror, stupefied, be terrified, assail, # 1286); → *gwr* III (be afraid of, dread, stand in awe, # 1593); → *d'g* (be anxious, concerned, fear, dread, # 1793); → *zḥl* II (fear, be afraid, # 2324); → *ḥrd* (tremble, shudder, startle, # 3006); → *ḥtt* (be shattered, dismayed, terrified, scare, terrify, # 3169); → *ygr* (fear, dread, terror, # 3336); → *yr'* I (fear, be afraid, held in honor, # 3707); → *yrh* (be afraid, terrified, paralyzed with fright, # 3724); → *'rṣ* (be alarmed, terrified, dreadful, dreadful, be in terror, # 6907); → *pḥd* I (tremble, be in dread, # 7064); → *qwṣ* I (feel disgust, frighten, cause dread, # 7762)

Bibliography

D. R. Hillers, "*Paḥad Yiṣḥāq*," *JBL* 91, 1972, 90-92; K. Koch, "*p^aḥad jiṣḥaq*-eine Gottesbezeichnung?" in *Werden und Wirken des Altes Testament*, Fs. Claus Westermann, 1980, 107-8; L. Kopf, "Arabische Etymologien und Parallelen zum Bibelwörterbuch," *VT* 9, 1959, 247-87; M. Malul, "More on *paḥad yiṣḥāq* (Genesis xxxi 42, 53) and the Oath by the Thigh," *VT* 35, 1985, 192-200; N. Sarna, *Genesis*, JPS Torah Commentary, 1989; C, Westermann, *Genesis 12-36*, 1985.

Victor P. Hamilton

7067 (*paḥdâ*, dread, terror, awe), → # 7064

7068 פֶּחָה

פֶּחָה (*peḥâ*), nom. provincial governor (# 7068).

ANE 1. Babylonian/Assyrian loanword: Akk. *pīḫātu/pāḫātu*, provincial governor; *bēl pīḫāti/pāḫāti,* lord of province; Old Aram. *pḥy,* governor; Emp. Aram. *pḥh,* governor; Egyp. Aram. *peḥâ,* governor; Jewish Aram. *peḥâ,* governor; Bib. Aram. *peḥâ,* provincial governor. Note: Morphological changes of Akk. *pīḫātu* > *pīḫtu* > *pīḫḫu* > *pīḫu* (*AHw*, 876-77) help explain Heb./Aram. *peḥâ.*

2. Akk. *pīl/pāḫātu* provincial governor (*AHw*, 862), is an abbreviation of *bēl pāḫete* (Mid. Assyr.) and *bēl pīl/pāḫāti* (New Assyr./Old Babylonian), lord of a

province, provincial ruler (*AHw*, 120, 18), the title of the official who ruled a province on behalf of the king (Klauber, 99-101; Zimmern, 6). Originally, *pīḫātu,* province, commission over district, and *pāḫātu* governorship; but they eventually merged in meaning (*AHw*, 862). The title is related to *pāḫutu,* responsibility over province (*AHw*, 862).

3. The Akk. titles *bēl pīḫāti* (*pīḫātu/pāḫātu*) and *šaknu* designate similar but different administrative positions in Neo-Assyrian administration over vassal states and annexed provinces (Henshaw, 465-69; Lipinski, 1973; Fensham, 124). Cooperative parts of the empire were controlled by treaty arrangements between the Assyrian king and the local ruler, administered through a *šaknu,* vassal-state governor (*AHw*, 1141; Zimmern, 6; *DISO*, 190). If a conquered people would submit to Assyrian suzerainty, it became a vassal, and the local state and ruler would be kept intact (although if the ruler had been resistant, he could be replaced by someone else). However, turbulent parts of the empire were directly controlled by the Neo-Assyrian king through a *bēl pīḫāti* (Grayson, 750; Saggs, 241-47). If the vassal rebelled or if the newly conquered state was resistent, it lost its independence and was annexed as an Assyrian province (Akk. *pīḫâtu*), becoming an Assyrian territory. This involved military action: Certain cities in the region were destroyed, significant elements of the population (including the elite and craftsmen) were deported, and the native king was deposed. The new province was placed under the direct rule of a governor (*bēl pīḫāti*), as noted in several Neo-Assyrian royal inscriptions (*ANET*, 284-85).

4. The provincial governor was the personal representative of the Neo-Assyrian king, appointed to administer a directly ruled province from a provincial center, where he established his official residence (Saggs, 260; Grayson, 750). His duties encompassed civil, fiscal, military, and religious matters. He was responsible to deport parts of the native populace and resettle the imported populations; maintain stability by treating the conquered cities with conciliation; maintain constant communication with the Assyrian central government; promote and provide for the Assyrian cults; and collect tribute (*biltu* and *mandattu/maddattu*), part of which was sent to the king and the remainder of which was used to maintain the provincial administration (Saggs, 247-60).

5. The Neo-Assyrian/Neo-Babylonian provincial governor had a sizeable staff, including scribes, messengers, surveyors, accountants, diviners, astrologers, recruiting officers, and irrigation controllers, plus military officers commanding the armed forces at the disposal of the governor (Saggs, 260). Each province was subdivided into a number of smaller areas, each centered in one of the large towns of the province and under the control of a *rab alani* (chief of the townships), an official subordinate to the governor, who also had military forces at his disposal. The governor had a regiment of standing Assyrian troops at his disposal, raised by the *rab kiṣri* (captain of army), who was responsible to him (Grayson, 747-48). Command of Assyrian troops in the field could be taken by any provincial governor, since they were military officials (Saggs, 260). However, for major operations, the army was usually under the supreme field commander (Akk. *turtanu/tartanu*), chief military officer (Akk. *rab šaqû,* → *sārîs,* # 6247), or the king himself (*ANET*, 281-88). Thus, provincial governors were not mere administrators but military commanders, since the Neo-Assyrian Empire was primarily militaristic in nature.

6. Imp. Aram. *pḥh*, provincial governor (*DISO*, 226), is a loanword from Akk. *pāḫâtu* and an abbreviation of the title *bēl pīḫâti* (see sec. 3 above). It appears in one diplomatic letter (ʻAdon) and several inscriptions (Behistun, Panamuwa, Sam'al, Zenirli). Several times it refers to Assyrian and Babylonian provincial governors. For example, in the ʻAdon Letter (ca. 600 BC), *pḥh* (line 9) refers to a provincial governor whom Nebuchadnezzar II recently installed over newly conquered territory: "For lord of kings, Pharaoh, knows that [your] servant [cannot withstand him. May my lord be pleased] to send an army to deliver me. May [the lord of kings, Pharaoh] not forsake me. For your servant has kept his [oath] and preserved good relations. But this region [is my lord's possession, and the king of Babylon has taken it and set up] a governor (*pḥh*) in the land, and they have replaced the border [ ]" (lines 6-9).

OT 1. Like Aram. *pḥh*/*pḥy* (see ANE secs. 1, 5), Heb. *peḥâ* is a loanword from Akk. *pī*/*pāḫātu,* provincial governor (*AHw*, 862), and is an abbreviation of the title *bēl pī*/*pāḫāti,* lord of a province (*AHw*, 120. 18; *HALAT* 3:872; BDB, 808; *TWOT* 2:721; Delitzsch, 519).

2. *peḥâ* is used as a title in reference to two positions: (a) administrative official: provincial governor ruling over a subjugated province on behalf of a king, and (b) military official: captain/commander of a provincial army (1 Kgs 20:24; 2 Kgs 18:24 = Isa 36:9). The two distinct offices of BH *peḥâ* essentially parallel the dual roles of the Assyrian provincial governor, who administered his province and also commanded the provincial army (see ANE 4-5).

3. BH *peḥâ* occurs 28x and Bib. Aram. *peḥâ* occurs 10x. It refers to provincial officials ruling over provincial territories on behalf of the king of Israel 2x (1 Kgs 10:15 = 2 Chron 9:14); Damascus 1x (1 Kgs 20:24); Assyria 4x (2 Kgs 18:24 = Isa 36:9; Ezek 2:6, 12); Babylon 5x (Jer 51:23, 28, 57; Ezek 23:12, 23); and Persia: throughout the empire 4x (Esth 3:12; 8:9; 9:3; Dan 6:7[8]), in Trans-Euphrates 9x (Ezra 5:3, 6; 6:6, 13; 8:36; Neh 2:7, 9; 3:7; 5:15), and in postexilic Judah 11x (Ezra 5:14; 6:7; Neh 5:14, 15, 18; 12:26; Hag 1:1, 14; 2:2, 21; Mal 1:8).

4. *Israelite provincial governors* (1 Kgs 10:15 = 2 Chron 9:14). Little is known about the "governors of the land" (*paḥôt hā'āreṣ*) except that their main duty was organizing and collecting taxes/tribute for the central government (McEvenue, 359). The well-organized Solomonic administration received revenue internally from national taxation (1 Kgs 10:15a = 2 Chron 9:14a) and externally from three foreign sources: (a) tolls on foreign merchants/tariffs on imports, (b) tribute from Arabic sheiks in the Negev, and (c) tribute collected from these provincial governors (1 Kgs 10:15b = 2 Chron 9:14b). Their provinces were probably the vassal states under Solomon (1 Kgs 4:21[5:1]), which had been subjugated by David previously (2 Sam 8:1-14) (de Vaux, 133-35). The correlation of BH *peḥâ* with Akk. *bēl pīḫâti* and the similarity of their main duties suggest that the Israelite provincial governors functioned in a manner similar to the Assyrian and Babylonian provincial governors, who administered newly conquered territories on behalf of the king (see ANE 4-5 above). On the other hand, these *paḥôt hā'āreṣ* might be the *niṣṣābîm* district prefects (1 Kgs 4:5) appointed over the twelve administrative districts of Israel (4:7-19). Each prefect was responsible to govern his district and raise revenue to supply provisions for the royal court on a rotating monthly basis (4:7-19, 27-28[5:7-9]) (de Vaux, 133-35). The Assyrians, Babylonians, and Persians used a similar system (Saggs, 238-60). Under Cyrus, provinces

were assigned a particular month of the year, four months imposed on Babylonia because of its wealth (Herodotus 1:192).

5. *Aramean provincial military officers* (1 Kgs 20:24). When the coalition of thirty-two Syro-Palestinian states in alliance with Ben-Haded attacked Israel in 856 BC, each military unit was under its own king (1 Kgs 20:16). The thirty-two heterogeneous parts created an incohesive army, which was easy prey to Israel's army under the singular leadership of Ahab and his subordinate district commanders (20:14-21). Seeing his mistake, Ben-Hadad removed the thirty-two coalition kings (*hamm*^{e}*lākîm*) from their commands and replaced them with subordinate military officers (*paḥôt*) to form an integrated army under his command (20:24). This use of *paḥôt* might reflect the military role of the provincial governor, seen in Neo-Assyrian (see ANE sec. 5). However, it may simply denote captains (BDB, 808) over divisions of coalition armies. While he placed their armies under a captain, Ben-Hadad probably did not subjugate the coalition members to provincial status because when Shalmaneser III encountered the Syro-Palestinian coalition in 853 at Qarqar, it was lead by twelve kings (*ANET* 1:190-91).

6. *Neo-Assyrian provincial governors over Israel* (Ezek 23:6). The use of *paḥôt* and *s*^{e}*gānîm* (# 6036) reflects two kinds of Assyrian administrators in the shift of Israel from the status of Assyrian vassal to province. The title *s*^{e}*gānîm* > *sagan* (= Akk. *šaknu* *HALAT* 2:742) designates Assyrian prefects who administered Israel when it became an Assyrian vassal in 841. On the other hand, *paḥôt* (= Akk. *piḫâtu*) refers to Assyrian provincial governors who ruled directly over Israel when it forfeited its independence and was annexed as an Assyrian province in 722. Ezekiel condemned the disastrous political alliances of Israel with Assyria that eventually led to its doom. As documented in the Black Obelisk (*ANET*, 281), Israel became an Assyrian vassal in 841, when Jehu submitted to Shalmaneser III and paid tribute to stave off a siege of Samaria. During the western campaign of Tiglath-Pileser III, Menahem maintained Israel's vassal status by paying the Assyrian tribute in 738 (2 Kgs 15:18-20; *ANET*, 283).

However, when Pekah allied with Damascus in 734 in an anti-Assyrian pact, Tiglath-Pileser III returned and defeated the coalition in 732. Damascus was converted into several Assyrian provinces, the western and eastern territories of Israel were converted to provinces, while the core of Israel around Samaria was allowed to remain a vassal state under a new, seemingly pro-Assyrian ruler Hoshea (*ANET*, 284; Borger-Tadmor, 244-49). However, when Hoshea revolted in 725, Shalmaneser V besieged Samaria from 725-722 until it fell at the beginning of the reign of Sargon II. He converted Samaria and its environs into an Assyrian province and established a provincial governor (*bēl piḫâti*) over the region, who began to collect the annual tribute: "At the beginning of my royal rule, I besieged and conquered Samaria ... I led away as prisoners 27,290 inhabitants ... I rebuilt the town better than it was before and [settled] in it people from countries which I myself had conquered. I placed an officer of mine as governor (*bēl piḫâti*) over them and imposed upon them tribute (*biltu*) as (is customary) for Assyrian citizens" (*ANET*, 284). Archaeological evidence indicates that Assyrian provincial centers were established in Samaria and Megiddo, and perhaps Dor and Gilead (Forrer, 60-63; Eph'al, 284-86). Neo-Assyrian documents name three provincial governors (*bēl piḫâti*) who were important enough to achieve the status of an eponymn year: Itti-Adad-aninu of Megiddo (679), Nabu-kitta-uṣur of Samaria (690), and Nabu-šar-aḫḫešu of Samaria (646/645) (Grayson, 96, 120).

7. *Neo-Assyrian provincial governors over Judah* (Ezek 23:12, 23). Parallel to Ezek 23:6 (see OT sec. 6), *s^e gānîm* in Ezek 23:12, 23 refers to the Assyrian administrators placed over Judah when it became an Assyrian vassal, while *paḥôt* refers to the Assyrian provincial governors who ruled over those portions of Judah that were annexed as an Assyrian province. Ezekiel refers to the disastrous political move of Ahaz, who willingly made Judah an Assyrian vassal to gain protection from Israel and Syria in 734-732 (2 Kgs 16:5-9; Isa 7:1-8:22). When Hezekiah rebelled against this ill-conceived Assyrian suzerainty, Sennacherib retaliated by conquering forty-six fortress cities in 701 (2 Kgs 18:7-16; *ANET*, 287-88) converting most of Judah—except for Jerusalem and its environs—from a vassal state into several Assyrian provinces (2 Kgs 18:7-16).

In 2 Kgs 18:24 (= Isa 36:9), the title *peḥâ* refers to an Neo-Assyrian provincial governor appointed over the newly conquered territory of Judah in the region of Lachish. Following his celebrated conquest of Lachish, Sennacherib sent his three highest ranking military commanders from Lachish to Jerusalem to intimidate the city to surrender (2 Kgs 18:17-37). The famous Hebrew-speaking *rab šāqēh* (= Akk. *rab šaqû*), field commander (# 8042), boasted that Hezekiah's army could not withstand the forces of even one *peḥâ* (= Akk. *bēl pīḫâti*) provincial governor (2 Kgs 18:24 = Isa 36:9). This depiction of an Assyrian *peḥâ* as commanding a provincial military unit accurately reflects the Assyrian policy of placing a regional army under the command of the provincial *bēl pīḫâti* (see ANE sec. 5). And based upon archaeological evidence from Lachish, it appears that an Assyrian provincial governor did, in fact, set up his provincial headquarters in Lachish, shortly after its fall to Sennacherib in 701 (Aharoni-Elat, 63-64). Thus, it is likely that the Assyrian *peḥâ* mentioned here was a recently or soon-to-be appointed provincial governor over recently conquered Lachish. The Assyrian commander also offered terms of surrender (2 Kgs 18:26-36), which harmonize with the treatment accorded by Assyrian provincial governors to conquered peoples (Saggs, 244-47).

8. *Neo-Babylonian provincial governors: exilic period* (Jer 51:23, 28, 57; Ezek 23:23). Similar to Ezek 23:6, 12 (see OT sec. 6), the titles *s^e gānîm* and *paḥôt* designate two kinds of Babylonian administrative officials who ruled (*māšal*, Jer 51:28) Judah when it became a Babylonian vassal (605-586) and later was converted into a Babylonian province (605-539). After Judah became a Babylonian vassal in 605 (2 Kgs 24:1a), it rebelled several times: Jehoiakim in 601 (24:1b); Jehoiachin in 600-597 (24:9-17); Zedekiah in 595-594 (Jer 37:5; Ezek 17:15-16), and again in 589-586 (2 Kgs 24:20). Nebuchadnezzar II finally ended Judah's status as vassal in 586 with the destruction of Jerusalem and conversion of Judah into a province (25:1-21). Taking care to preserve native Israelite rule, Nebuchadnezzar appointed Gedaliah as provincial governor of the surviving Judean community (2 Kgs 25:22; Jer 40:5-11) and established the provincial center at Mizpah (2 Kgs 25:23). As provincial governor, Gedaliah administered Babylonian economic policies to raise tribute and taxes for Babylon (2 Kgs 25:24; Jer 40:9-10). When Gedaliah was assassinated by an anti-Babylonian faction (2 Kgs 25:25; Jer 41:1-10), Nebuchadnezzar retaliated in 581 (Jer 52:30), and Judah came under direct Babylonian administration under a native Babylonian

governor. Ezekiel announced that Yahweh would judge rebellious Judah through these Babylonian officials, while Jeremiah announced that Yahweh would eventually deliver the repentant remnant when Cyrus would destroy the Babylonians and their provincial governors. Note: Jeremiah and Ezekiel employ the same terms to describe these Assyrian and Babylonian administrative officials. This accurately reflects the fact that the Neo-Babylonians adopted the existing Neo-Assyrian administrative structures already in place (Saggs, 261-68).

In Dan 3:2, 3, 37, Bib. Aram. *paḫ^a wātā'* (pl: provincial governors, # 10580) is listed among eight classifications of Babylonian bureaucratic officials under Nebuchadnezzar II. Because five of these titles are of Iranian origin, Dan 3 was probably composed after the rise of the Persian Empire in 539, and the terms used must have replaced those that were actually used in Aram. under Nebuchadnezzar. This harmonizes with the view that Daniel finished this book around 532 when the new Persian titles would have been current (*EBC* 7:51): (a) satraps (*'^a ḥašdarp^e nayyā'* = APers. *kshathrapān* satrap, realm protector), chief representatives of the king in charge of large satrapies; (b) prefects (*signayyā'* > *s^e gan* = Akk. *šaknu*, governor), administrative officials governing vassal states; (c) provincial governors (*paḫ^a wātā'* = Akk. *pāḫâtu,* provincial governor; abbreviation of *bel pāḫâtu,* lord of a provincial district), administrators governing annexed provinces; (d) royal advisors (*'^a dargāzrayyā'* = MPers. *andarzaghar* counselor); (e) treasurers (*g^e dābrayyā'* = Pers. *ganzabara,* royal treasurer); (f) judges (*d^e tābrayyā'* = MPers., *dātabar* judge); (g) magistrates (*tiptāyē'* = APers., *adipati* over-chief); and (h) provincial administrators (*šilṭōnê m^e dînātā'* = Akk. *šulṭānu,* ruler), a general title for government executives ruling over provincial districts or towns. Note: There is some question whether Dan 3:2, 3 lists seven or eight classifications of officials, depending upon whether *w^e kōl šilṭōnê m^e dînātā'* is a separate group (NIV: "and all the other provincial officials") or a concluding appositional statement ("that is, all the provincial officials").

9. *Persian provincial governors over Judah: Cyrus* (Ezra 5:14; Hag 1:1, 14; 2:2, 21). When Cyrus (559-530) conquered Babylon and inherited its provinces in 539, he kept the existing provincial bureaucracy in place. This explains why *peḥâ* continues to designate provincial governors of annexed territories, as in Neo-Assyrian and Neo-Babylonian periods. However, Cyrus did appoint Gubaru as administrator over the Fertile Crescent ("Babylon and the Land Beyond the River") (Williamson, 82). He also allowed the Jews in Babylon to return to Jerusalem under Sheshbazzar, a descendant of Jehoiachin and "the prince (*hannāśî'*) of Judah" (Ezra 1:8), whom Cyrus appointed as the first governor of the postexilic Jewish community in the Judean province. Sheshbazzar bore the administrative title *peḥâ,* provincial governor (Ezra 5:14) and the honorific title *tiršātā',* (his) excellency = governor (OldPers. *tarsa,* one to be feared, respected) (Neh 7:65, 70[69]). Note: There is debate whether Sheshbazzar, governor (*peḥâ*) of Judah in 539, is Zerubbabel, governor (*peḥâ*) of Judah in 520 (Hag 1:1, 14; 2:2, 21).

Several scholars argue that the postexilic meaning of *peḥâ* is vague and may simply denote a special commissioner, concluding that the first governor of Judah was not Sheshbazzar but Nehemiah (Alt, McEvenue, Donnor). However, a good case can be made that Sheshbazzar was the first provincial governor of Judah (Smith, 149-201; Williamson, 1987, 40-50). Archaeological evidence confirms the existence of governors of Judah before Nehemiah: a bulla and seal with the inscription *'lntn hpḥh* (Elnathan the Governor) date to the late sixth century BC—one century before Nehemiah (see P-B sec. 1). Moreover, Nehemiah states that before him were "earlier" *paḥôt*, governors, who received the food allotment of the governor (Neh 5:14-15).

10. *Persian provincial governors over Judah and Trans-Euphrates: Darius I* (Ezra 5:3, 6; 6:6, 7, 13). The meaning of *peḥâ* is somewhat ambiguous during the period of Darius I (522-486), who reorganized the empire in 522 into twenty satrapies, composed of sixty-seven tribes and nations, to create a more effecient method of taxation and control (Herodotus 3:89). Darius appointed Ushtani as administrator over the entire Fertile Crescent, while the Trans-Euphrates ("Beyond the River") was put under a subordinate satrap Tattannu (522-502), identified with Tattenai, "governor (*paḥat*) of Trans-Euphrates" (Ezra 5:3, 6; 6:6, 13) (Williamson, 1988, 82; Rainey, 53; Oppenheim, 563). Not only is *peḥâ* used of Tattenai, it is also used of the governor of Judah (Ezra 6:7), a provincial district within the Trans-Euphrates satrapy. This ambiguity may reflect confusion created when the new satrapy system was superimposed over the existing provincial system. This came to a head in 520, when the authority Darius bestowed on Tattenai as satrap/governor of Trans-Euphrates clashed with the authority Cyrus previously had bestowed on Sheshbazzar, governor (*peḥâ*) of Judah (Ezra 5:1-17). Darius eventually ruled that Judah could function as a semiautonomous province under their own governor, free from interference from the satrap of Trans-Euphrates (Ezra 6:1-12).

11. *Persian provincial governors: Artaxerxes I* (Ezra 8:36; Neh 2:7, 9; 3:7; 5:14-15, 18; 12:26). While Darius organized the empire into twenty satrapies and placed a satrap over each, Xerxes (486-465) created smaller provinces and placed a governor over each. The satrapy of Trans-Euphrates was organized into several provinces under individual governors (Rainey, 57; Williamson, 1988, 82). As Herodotus notes, Judah was administered as an individual provincial district, distinct from Samaria, in the fifth satrapy of Syria (Trans-Euphrates). Archaeological evidence suggests that Sidon was the capital of this satrapy (Cook, 174; Elayi, 25-26) and that subordinate provincial governors dwelt in Lachish, Hazor, Tel Poleg, Shiqmonah, Ramat Rahel, Ein Gedi, Tell Mazar, Tell es-Sadiyeh, Tell es-Hesi, Samaria, Tell el-Farah, and Gezer (Kenyon, 145-47). This elaborate bureaucracy was still in place under Artaxerxes I (464-424), when Ezra returned to Jerusalem in 458 and Nehemiah in 445 and encountered multiple satraps (*'ᵃḥašdarpᵉnê hammelek*) and Trans-Euphrates provincial governors (*paḥᵃwôt 'ēber hannāhār*) (Ezra 8:36; Neh 2:7, 9; 3:7). Artaxerxes appointed Nehemiah governor (*peḥâ*) over the province of Judah from 445-433. Like Sheshbazzar, Nehemiah bore the administrative title *peḥâ'*, governor (Neh 5:14, 15, 18; 12:26), and the honorific title *tiršātā'*, "(His) Excellency" = Governor (Neh 8:9; 10:1) (Klein). An unnamed governor (*peḥâ*) followed Nehemiah, to whom tribute was paid (Mal 1:8) during the late Persian period [see P-B 2].

12. *Persian provincial governors under Xerxes* (Esth 3:12; 8:9; 9:3). In Esther, set during the reign of Xerxes (486-465), *peḥâ* designates the governor of a province within a satrapy. Herodotus (3:89) states that Darius, the father of Xerxes, had organized the empire into twenty satrapies composed of smaller provinces. By the time of Xerxes, there were 127 provinces, each under the control of a provincial governor. Historical records from the reigns of Darius and Xerxes list sixty-seven different tribes and

nations in the Persian satrapy/provincial system (Armayor, 1-9; Cameron, 47-56). Because Judah and Samaria were separate Jewish provinces (see P-B sec. 2 below), 127 provinces is reasonable for sixty-seven different people groups. The book of Esther reflects a four-level hierarchy: the chief administrators over the satraps, satraps over the twenty satrapies, 127 governors over the smaller provincial units, and subordinate provincial officials over the various peoples in each province.

P-B 1. The existence of the office of provincial governor of Judah before the time of Nehemiah is documented in a bulla and seal, dating to the late sixth century BC, which bears the inscription *'lntn hpḥh* Elnathan the Governor (Avigad, 35). Based upon these and other coins and seal impressions (see secs. 2-4 below), a partial list of governors who preceded and followed Nehemiah has been reconstructed (Avigad, 28-35; Cross, 4-18).

2. Two fifth-century BC Aram. inscriptions refer to unnamed provincial governors over Judah and Samaria during the late Persian period, demonstrating that Judah and Samaria were separate provinces around the time of Ezra, Nehemiah, and Esther (see OT secs. 8-9): *pḥt yhwd,* governor of Judah (Cowley 30:1), and *pḥt šmryn,* governor of Samaria (Cowley 30:29).

3. Several fourth-century Hebrew artifacts refer to separate provincial governors over Judah and Samaria in the late Persian period; one fourth-century BC Hebrew bullae: *pḥt šmrn,* governor of Samaria (Davies, 100. 408. 2); and several fourth-century BC Hebrew silver coins from Judah bearing the name of the Judean governor: *yḥzqyh pḥt* Yeḥizqiyyah, the governor (Davies, 106. 043. 1).

4. Details of Judean provincial government during this period are largely unknown. However, fourth-century BC coins bearing the inscription "Yehud" (= Judah), minted in or near Jerusalem, provide insight into the Persian provincial administration of Judah in the fourth century BC (Mildenberg, 183-96; Betlyon, 633-42). One group of Yehud coins (Group III: ca. 340-331 BC) bears the inscription *yḥzqyh pḥt*, "Yeḥizqiyyah the governor," identifying the Persian provincial governor of the Judean satrapy (Mildenberg, 188; Betylon, 634). The group of Yehud coins from the following period continues to bear the inscription *yḥzqyh* but without the title *pḥt* (Group IV: ca. 331-300 BC), reflecting the new administrative situation in Judah after Alexander's conquest of the Persians (Mildenberg, 188-89; Betylon, 634-35).

5. During the Roman period, *peḥâ* (Mish. Heb.) and *pêḥâ* (Pales. Aram.) developed its widest range of referents: provincial governor, high Jewish official, and rabbi (Jastrow, 1151). For example, the nuance governor appears in the Beck edition of the Targum where all other editions use the more common term *šilṭôn* governer, rulership (Targ II Chr IX. 14). It was used of the Sanhedrin and leading Jewish officials in Jerusalem before the destruction of the temple: "the grandees (*paḥôt*), the chiefs, and the treasurers (of the temple) went out to meet them" (Numbers Rabbah §14). After the destruction of Jerusalem, it was used almost exclusively of the rabbis, who were the sole remnant of Jewish authority: "O son of nobility (*bar pêḥâ*)" (Betsah 5. 62c). Correlated with the historical developments and changes in the Jewish state during this period, the term gradually shifted in its primary referent from the Roman governors (prefects and procurators) to the Sanhedrin as the internal ruling body in Judea.

6. After Jerusalem was destroyed in AD 70 and especially after the Bar-Kochba revolt was crushed in AD 132-135, Jewish nationalism was discouraged and the

Sanhedrin was broken up as the central ruling authority over Judaism. After this, the title *peḥâ* began to be used almost exclusively of the rabbis, whose teaching of the Talmud became the sole unifying authority over diaspora Judaism.

NT 1. Before Rome took control of Judea in 64 BC, it had enjoyed nearly eighty years of independence under the Hasmonean dynasty of priest-kings. Octavian confirmed Herod as king of the Jews in 31 BC. When Herod died in 4 BC, Judea and Samaria were bestowed on Archelaus (Matt 2:22), Galilee and Perea went to Herod Antipas, and Decapolis and Gaulanitis went to Philip. When Archelaus was deposed in AD 6 by Augustus, his principality was transformed into a Roman province and placed under the general supervision of the imperial legate of Syria with its own governor of equestrian rank, Quirinius, who ordered a census to determine the amount of tribute that Judea would henceforth pay Rome (e.g., Mark 12:13-17; Luke 23:2).

2. The first Roman provincial governors who ruled over Judea between AD 6-41 were called prefects (cf. Pontius Pilate's designation in a Caesarea inscription), who commanded cohorts of troops stationed at Caesarea and Jerusalem (Antonio Fortress). The prefect had the right of capital punishment, and also appointed and deposed Jewish high priests. However, the internal affairs of the Jewish nation were administered by the Sanhedrin. The governors of Judea from AD 44-66 were called procurators (*epitropos*), Unlike the prefects, they were not allowed to appoint high priests, because this priviledge was given to the descendants of Herod Agrippa.

Leaders: → *'ādôn* (lord, master, # 123); → *'allûp* II (tribal chief, # 477); → *'āṣîl* II (eminent, noble, # 722); → *zāqēn* (elder, # 2418); → *ḥōr* I, free man, freeborn, # 2985); → *maptēaḥ* (badge of office, # 5158); → *nāgîd* (prince, ruler, leader, # 5592); → *nāśî'* I (chief, king, # 5954); → *sārîs* (eunuch, court official, # 6247); → *seren* II (Philistine prince, # 6249); → *'attûd* (he-goat, leader, # 6966); → *peḥâ* (governor, # 7068); → *pāqîd* (officer, # 7224); → *qāṣîn* (commander, leader, # 7903); → *rab* II (captain, chief, # 8042); → *rzn* (rule, # 8142); → *šôa'* I (noble, # 8777)

BIBLIOGRAPHY

TWOT 2:721; Y. Aharoni, *Excavations at Ramat Rahel: 1961-62*, 1964, 19, 28, 43; A. Y. Aikhenwald, "Some Names of Officials in the Later Books of OT," *VDI* 3, 1985, 58-65 [Russian]; A. Alt, *Kleine Schriften*, 1959, 2:316-37; idem, "Das System der assyrischen Provinzen auf dem Boden des Reiches Israel," *ZDPV* 52, 1992, 220-42; idem, "Neue assyrische Nachrichten über Palästina," *ZDPV* 67, 1945, 128-46; O. K. Armayor, "Herodotus' Catalogues of the Persian Empire in the Light of the Monuments and the Greek Literary Tradition," *TAPA* 108, 1978, 1-9; N. Avigad, *Bullae and Seals*, 1976, 28-35; H. Bengston, "Syrien in der Perserzeit," *Fischers Weltgeschichte*, 1965, 371-76; J. W. Betylon, "Provincial Government of Persian Period Judea and the Yehud Coins," *JBL* 105, 1986, 663-42; R. Borger and H. Tadmor, "Zwei Beitrage zur alttestamentlischen wissenschafter Aufgrund der Inschriften Tiglatpilesers III," *ZAW* 94, 1982, 244-51; F. F. Bruce, "Palestine, Administration of (Roman)," *ABD*, 1992, 5:96-99; G. Cameron, "Persian Satrapies and Related Matters," *JNES* 32, 1973, 47-56; C. Cohen, "Neo-Assyrian Elements in the First Speech of the Biblical Rab-šāqê," *IOS* 9, 1979, 32-48; J. M. Cook, *Persian Empire*, 1983, 174; G. A. Cooke, *Textbook of North-Semitic Inscriptions*, 1903, 62, 178; A. Cowley, *Aramaic Papyri of the Fifth Century BC*, 1923, 248-60; F. M. Cross, "A Reconstruction of Judean Restoration," *JBL* 94, 1975, 4-18; G. I. Davies, *Ancient Hebrew Inscriptions*, 1991, 470; F. Delitzsch, *Assyrische Handwörterbuch*, 1896, 519; M. A. Dupont-Sommer, "Le lettre araméenne du roi Adon au Pharaon," *Sem* 1, 1948, 43-68; M. Elat, "Political Status of the Kingdom of Judah Within the Assyrian Empire in the 7th Century BCE," *Investigations at Lachish*, 1975, 61-70; J. Elayi, "Phoenician Provincial Cities in the Persian Period," *JANESCU* 12, 1980, 13-28; F. C. Fensham, "*peḥâ* in the OT and ANE," *Studies in the Chronicler*, 1981, 44-52; J. A. Fitzmyer, "Aramaic Letter of the King Adon to the Egyptian Pharaoh," *Bib* 46, 1965, 41-55; E. Forrer, *Die Provinzeinteilung des assyrischen Reiches*, 1920, 60-63; J. C. Gibson, *Aramaic Inscriptions*, 1975, 21; H. L. Ginsberg, "An Aramaic Contemporary of the Lachish Letters," *BASOR* 111, 1948, 24-27; A. K. Grayson, "The Walters Art Gallery Sennacherib Inscription," *AfO* 20, 1963, 96, 120; idem, "History and Culture of Assyria," *ABD*, 1992, 4:732-55; R. A. Henshaw, "Office of *Šaknu* in Neo-Assyrian Times," *JAOS* 87, 1967, 517-25; 88, 1968, 461-83; K. M. Kenyon, *Bible and Recent Archaeology*, 1987, 145-47; E. G. Klauber, *Assyrische Beamtentum*, 1910, 99-101; R. W. Klein, "Ezra and Nehemiah in Recent Studies," *Magnalia Dei*, 1976, 361-76; B. Landsberger, *Materilien zum sumerischen Lexikon*, 1937, 1:125-27; idem, *Sam'al*, 1948, 69; E. Lipiński, "*skn* et *sgn* dans le semitique occidental du nord," *UF* 5, 1973, 191-207; P. Machinist, "Palestine, Administration of (Assyro-Babylonian)," *ABD*, 1992, 5:69-81; O. Margalith, "The Political Role of Ezra as Persian Governor," *ZAW* 98, 1986, 110-12; S. E. McEvenue, "The Political Structure in Judah from Cyrus to Nehemiah," *CBQ*, 1981, 5-64; L. Mildenberg, *Greek Numismatics and Archaeology*, 1979, 183-96; N. Na'aman, "Sennacherib's 'Letter to God' on His Campaign to Judah," *BASOR* 214, 1974, 25-39; R. North, "Civil Authority in Ezra," *Studi*, 6:377-404; idem, "Palestine, Administration of (Judean Officials)," *ABD*, 1992, 5:86-90; B. Otzen, "Israel Under the Assyrians: Reflections on Imperial Policy in Palestine," *ASTI* 11, 1977-78, 96-110; J. Pecirkova, "The Administrative Organization of the Neo-Assyrian Empire," *ArOr* 45, 1977, 211-28; idem, "The Administrative Methods of the Neo-Assyrian Empire," *ArOr* 55, 1987, 162-75; T. Petit, "L'élovution sémantique des termes hébreux et aramaens *pḥh* et *sgn* et accadiens *pāḫâtu* et *šaknu*," *JBL* 107, 1988, 53-67; J. van der Ploeg, "Les chefs du peuple d'Israel et leurs noms," *RB* 57, 1950, 40-61; J. N. Postgate, "Assyrian Deeds and Documents," *Iraq* 32, 1970, 148; idem, "The Place of the *Šaknu* in Assyrian Government," *AnSt* 30, 1980, 67-76; A. F. Rainey, "The Satrapy 'Beyond the River'," *AJBA* 1, 1969, 51-78; U. Rüterswörden, *Die Beamten der israelitischen Königszeit*, 1985, 117-21; H. W. F. Saggs, *The Greatness That Was Babylon*, 1969, 233-68; H. C. Schmitt, *Elisa*, 1972, 70-71; M. Smith, "Das Judentum in Palästina während der Perserzeit," *Fischers Weltgeschichte*, 1965, 356-70; idem, *Palestinian Parties and Politics*, 1987, 149-50, 193-201; W. T. Smitten, "Der *Tiršātā'* in Esra-Nehemia," *VT* 21, 1971, 618-20; R. de Vaux, "Titres et fonctionnaires égyptiens à la cour de David et de Salomon," *RB* 48, 1939, 394-405; G. Widengren, "The Persian Period," *IJH*, 1977, 510; H. G. M. Williamson, "Palestine, Administration of (Persian)," *ABD*, 1992, 5:81-86; idem, "The Governors of Judah under the Persians," *TynBul* 29, 1988, 59-82; idem, *Ezra and Nehemiah*, 1987, 40-50; H. Zimmern, *Akkadische Fremdwörter*, 1917, 6-7.

Gordon H. Johnston

7069	פחז

פחז (*pḥz*), q. be reckless, arrogant (# 7069); פַּחַז (*paḥaz*), nom. unstable (hapleg. in Gen 49:4; # 7070); פַּחֲזוּת (*paḥ*^{a}*zût*), nom. reckless, arrogant (hapleg. in Jer 23:32; # 7071).

ANE Akk. *paḫāzu* has the idea of acting with arrogance or presumption, while the Arab. root means haughty, reckless.

OT 1. The vb. (used twice) characterizes reckless or arrogant people not restrained by the usual conventions of proper social behavior or the normal expectations for a person in a sacred position (Judg 9:4; Zeph 3:4). They arrogantly follow their own desires and do not care about others.

2. The nom. *paḥaz* is found in Jacob's blessing, when he compares Reuben's reckless behavior to unstable or turbulent water (Gen 49:4).

3. The deceptive words of the false prophets were reckless boastings (*paḥ*^{a}*zût*), because they were not of God and did not help the people in the slightest (Jer 23:32 ‖ *šeqer*).

Arrogance, pride, presumption: → *g'h* (rise up, be exalted, # 1448); → *zyd* (act presumptuously, prepare food, # 2326); → *yāhîr* (haughty, # 3400); → *sll* (lift up, exalt, # 6148); → *'pl* (swell, lift up, # 6752); → *'ātāq* (old, arrogant, # 6981); → *pḥz* (be reckless, arrogant, # 7069); → *rwm* (be high, exalted, proud, # 8123); → *šaḥaṣ* (pride, # 8832)
Deception, falsehood, fraud, guile, iniquity, lie: → *'āwen* (mischief, iniquity, deception, # 224); → *bd'* (invent, devise, lie, # 968); → *kzb* I (lie, be a liar, deceive, # 3941); → *kḥš* (fail, deceive, grow lean, # 3950); → *nkl* (knave, deceiver, cheat, # 5792); → *nš'* II (be deceived, deceive, cause a deception, # 5958); → *sārâ* II (rebellion, crime, revolt, falsehood, # 6240); → *'qb* I (seize the heel, overreach, deceive, # 6810); → *rmh* II (betray, deal treacherously with, # 8228); → *śwṭ* (turn away to falsehood, entangled in lies, # 8454); → *šqr* (deal/act falsely, betray, # 9213); → *tll* (deceive, mock, trifle, # 9438)

Gary V. Smith

7070 (*paḥaz*, unstable), → # 7069

7071 (*paḥ*^{a}*zût*, reckless, arrogant), → # 7069

7072	פחח

פחח (*pḥḥ*), hi, be captured, be chained (# 7072); denom. from פַּח (*paḥ* I), trap (→ # 7062).

OT The vb. occurs only in Isa 42:22, in a poetic description of the suffering of God's people in exile. The phraseology may be adopted from the lament psalms, "to describe her (Israel's) plight as she made lamentation in the presence of God" (Westermann, 112).

Chain, fetter: → *'sr* (bind, imprison, fetter, hitch, # 673); → *zēq* I (chain, fetter, # 2414); → *ḥarṣōb* (chain, fetter, # 3078); → *kebel* (shackle, # 3890); → *migbālôt* (chains, # 4456); → *mahpeket* (stocks, # 4551); → *mōsēr* (fetters, chains, # 4591); → *sad* (stocks, shackles, # 6040); → *pḥḥ* (be captured, chained, # 7072); → *rtq* (be bound, # 8415); → *šarš*^{e}*râ* (chain, # 9249)

T. Desmond Alexander

7073	פֶּחָם

פֶּחָם (*peḥām*), nom. charcoal (# 7073).

OT 1. The nom. refers to the residue of partially burnt wood that is used by blacksmiths as fuel for fire (Isa 44:12; 54:16).

2. In Prov 26:21 the relation of a quarrelsome person and kindling strife is compared to the relation between charcoal and fire. As charcoal is fuel to the flames, so a quarrelsome person stokes the flames of dissension by adding fuel to the flames of

controversy. The quarrelsome person wrecks the basis of corporate life and produces disruption, instability, and chaos.

Fire, flame: → *'ûd* (log, burning stick, # 202); → *'ēš* I (fire, # 836); → *b'r* I (burn, blaze up, be consumed, # 1277); → *gaḥelet* (burning charcoal, # 1625); → *goprît* (sulphur, # 1730); → *yṣt* (kindle, burn, set on fire, # 3675); → *yqd* (burn, be burning, kindled, # 3678); → *kîdôd* (spark, # 3958); → *lbb* II (bake cakes, # 4221); → *lahab* (flame, blade, # 4258); → *lhṭ* I (glow, burn, # 4265); → *lappîd* (torch, lightning, # 4365); → *nîṣôṣ* (spark, # 5773); → *peḥām* (charcoal, # 7073); → *reṣep* I (live coal, # 8363); → *rešep* I (flame, glow, arrow, plague, # 8404); → *śrp* (burn, be burnt, # 8596); → *šābîb* (flame, # 8663)

Jackie A. Naudé

7074	פַּחַת

פַּחַת (*paḥat*), pit (# 7074).

OT The Eng. term "pit" is used to translate several different Heb. words, among them being *mah^{a}mōr*, watery pits (# 4549; Ps 140:10[11]), *paḥat*, pit (# 7074; 2 Sam 17:9; 18:17; Isa 24:18; Jer 48:28, 43, 44; Lam 3:47), *šô'â*, pit (# 8739; Job 30:3, 14; 38:27; Ps 35:8, 17; 63:9[10]; Prov 1:27; Isa 10:3; 47:11; Ezek 38:9; Zeph 1:15), and *š^{e}ḥît*, pit (# 8827; Ps 107:19[20]; Prov 28:10; Lam 4:20). The basic meaning is of a depression or hole in the ground, often a hunting trap (*paḥ* → # 7062). However, the terms are more typically used in a metaphorical sense, denoting sudden, unforeseen destruction that awaits a nation or an individual.

1. Pit may refer to nothing more than a depression or hole in the ground (2 Sam 17:9; Jer 48:28, cave). The root of *paḥat* means to hollow out or bore through in Akk. and Heb. (*HALAT* 873). More often, however, the literature uses the image of a pit to imply a trap. For example, Lam 4:20 states: "The LORD's anointed, our very life breath, was caught in their traps" (*š^{e}ḥît*, see Held, 186, nets; cf. Jer 48:43-44 [= Isa 24:18]). The enemies' setting a trap for the petitioner, as a hunter sets a trap for a lion, is also the dominant motif in Ps 35 (cf. vv. 8 and 17).

2. Because of the sudden death that a hunting pit brings to the prey, vocabulary for pit becomes synonymous with destruction. Thus, the concepts revolving around the ancient trap take on a metaphorical function. For example, Isa 10:3 reads: "What will you do on the day of reckoning, when disaster (*šô'â*) comes from afar?" Heb. *šô'â* (→ # 8739) can even take on the meaning of a sudden storm (cf. *HALAT* 1325; Scott, 24). In Wisdom literature, the destruction of a pit (*šô'â*) takes on a descriptive function, merely registering the character of wicked or undesirable places (Job 30:3, 14; 38:27; Prov 1:27). In prophetic literature, a much more judgmental tone is set. Thus, the sudden death that comes with a trap is commonly threatened in prophetic speech (e.g., Isa 10:3; 47:11; Jer 48:28, 43; Zeph 1:15). Often, both in the Psalms and the prophetic literature, the death involved in the concept of a pit appears in oracles against foreign nations or the enemies of God's people (e.g., Isa 10:3, Assyria; 47:11, Babylon; Jer 48:28, 43, Moab; Zeph 1:15, nations as a whole; cf. Ps 35:8, 17; 63:9[10] [if the MT is followed, cf. Kraus, 18]; 140:11 [*mah^{a}mōr*], enemies of the petitioner).

It is interesting to note that in this metaphorical usage a single pit or trap expands perceptually so that it becomes an entire realm. The metaphorical use of the idea of pit draws upon certain connections with Sheol, the realm of the dead. Sheol was perceived by the ancients as being located under the earth. A pit, likewise, was dug into the earth, and it also brought about death. Note that in the Ugar. material, the city of Mot (the monster representing death) was named *hmry* (*CTA* 4.VIII.12; S.II.15), a form closely related to *mah*^{a}*mōr*, a term translated as "miry pits" in Ps 140:10[11] (# 4549). 2 Sam 18:10 states that Absalom was buried in a pit (*paḥat*), which suggests that upon his death he was removed from the land of the living and placed in the realm of the dead. Moreover, the Heb. nom. *šaḥat* (→ # 8846), which is related to the nom. *š*^{e}*ḥît,* is used both to designate Sheol and a hunting pit (Held, 181-85). Thus, although the concept of a pit as a trap was distinguished from Sheol, when pit was used as a metaphor, it gained force from certain general similarities with the netherworld.

Pit: → *māgôr* III (storage pit, # 4473); → *madmēnâ* I (dung pit, # 4523); → *mikreh* (pit, # 4838); → *paḥat* (pit, # 7074); → *šûḥâ* I (pit, # 8757); → *šaḥat* (pit, grave, # 8846)
Death: → *'bd* I (perish, # 6); → *'*^{a}*dāmâ* (ground, piece of land, soil, earth, realm of the dead, # 141); → *'āsôn* (mortal accident, # 656); → *gw'* (expire, die, # 1588); → *hrg* (kill, murder, # 2222); → *zrm* I (put an end to life, # 2441); → *ḥedel* (realm of the dead, # 2535); → *ḥnṭ* II (embalm, embalming, # 2846); → *mwt* (die, kill, execute, # 4637); → *qṭl* (murder, slay, # 7779); → *r*^{e}*pā'îm* I (shades, departed spirits, # 8327); → *š*^{e}*'ôl* (sheol, netherworld, # 8619); → *šaḥat* (pit, grave, # 8846)
Hunting: → *yqš* (lay a trip wire, set a trap, # 3704); → *paḥ* I (trap, snare, # 7062); → *ṣwd* (hunt, # 7421); → *rešet* (net, # 8407); → *šûḥâ* I (pit, # 8757)

BIBLIOGRAPHY

M. Held, "Pits and Pitfalls in Akkadian and Biblical Hebrew," *JANESCU* 5, 1973, 173-90; H.-J. Kraus, *Psalms 60-150,* 1989; R. B. Y. Scott, "Meteorological Phenomena and Terminology in the Old Testament," *ZAW* 64, 1952, 11-25.

John T. Strong

7076 (*p*^{e}*ḥetet*, hollow), → # 5117

7077	פִּטְדָה

פִּטְדָה (*piṭdâ*), possibly "chrysolith" (# 7077), only Exod 28:17; 39:10; Job 28:19; Ezek 28:13.

ANE Zimmerli (83) cites the Sans. *pta*, yellow, as a cognate.

OT 1. The JB and NIV read topaz, while the NEB and NRSV read chrysolite (so *HALAT*). According to Zimmerli, topaz is the correct translation here, since the stone in mind is the olive chrysolite, a less hard variety of topaz (83).

2. For a theological introduction to the topic of gems in the OT, see *'ōdem* (# 138).

Precious Stones: → *'eben* (stone, rock, # 74); → *'ōdem* (precious stone, # 138); → *'aḥlāmâ* (jasper, # 334); → *'eqdāḥ* (beryl, # 734); → *bahaṭ* (precious stone, # 985); → *bāreqet* (emerald, # 1403); → *yah*^{a}*lōm* (precious stone, # 3402); → *yāš*^{e}*pēh* (jasper, # 3835); → *kadkōd* (ruby?, # 3905); → *lešem* I (precious stone, # 4385); → *nōpek* (semi-precious stone, # 5876); → *sōḥeret* (mineral stone, # 6090); → *sappîr* (lapis lazulli, # 6209); → *piṭdâ* (chrysolite, # 7077); → *š*^{e}*bô* (precious stone, # 8648); → *šōham* I (precious stone, # 8732); → *šāmîr* II (emery, diamond?, # 9032); → *šēš* II (alabaster, # 9253); → *taršîš* II (precious stone, # 9577)
Jewelry, ornaments: → *ḥ*^{a}*lî* I (ornament, jewel, # 2717); → *ḥ*^{a}*rûzîm* (necklace of shells, # 3016); → *ṭabba'at* (ring, # 3192); → *kûmāz* (ornament, # 3921); → *mišb*^{e}*ṣôt* (settings, # 5401); → *nezem* (ring, # 5690); → *n*^{e}*ṭi(î)pâ* (ear-ring, # 5755); → *'āgîl* (ear-ring?, # 6316);

→ *'dh* II (adorn o.s., # 6335); → *'ks* (jingle, # 6576); → *'nq* (put on as a necklace, # 6735); → *pᵉnînîm* (corals, pearls, # 7165); → *ṣawwārôn* (necklace, # 7454); → *ṣāmîd* I (bracelet, # 7543); → *ṣᵉ'ādâ* (anklets, # 7577); → *rābîd* (necklace, # 8054); → *śahᵃrōnîm* (crescents, # 8448); → *šābîs* (ornament, # 8667); → *šēr* I (bracelet, # 9217); → *tôr* (pendant, # 9366)

BIBLIOGRAPHY

IDB 2:898-905; *ISBE* 4:623-30; *NIDNTT* 3:395-98; J. S. Harris, "An Introduction to the Study of Personal Ornaments, of Precious, Semi-Precious and Imitation Stones Used Throughout Biblical History," *ALUOS* 4, 1962, 49-83; L. Koehler, "Hebräische Vokabeln II," *ZAW* 55, 1937, 161-74; H. Quiring, "Die Edelsteine im Amtsschild des jüdischen Hohenpriesters und die Herkunft ihrer Namen," *AGM* 38, 1954, 193-213; W. Zimmerli, *Ezekiel 25-48*, 1983, 82-84.

Andrew E. Hill

7079	פַּטִּישׁ

פַּטִּישׁ (*paṭṭîš*), hammer (# 7079).

ANE Syr. *pᵉṭēš*, snub-nosed, flat-nosed; Arab. *fiṭṭīsat*, pig's nose; *HALAT* 873, refer to W. A. Ward's proposal of the Egyp. *pdš* crush. Note also the personal name *pṭš* in a second-century BC Numidian-Punic bilingual (*KAI*, 101, line 5), hammer (Benz, 390).

OT *paṭṭîš* occurs 3x. In Jer 23:29 it describes an instrument that can smash rock. Here it forms part of a simile describing the power of God's word, whether in judgment against false prophets or within the experience of the prophet Jeremiah (McKane, 591-92). Jer 50:23 describes Babylon by a metaphor in which the city is called the *paṭṭîš* of the whole earth. Surprisingly, *paṭṭîš* is not used in 51:20-23, where Babylon is the instrument God uses to smash others. If *paṭṭîš* is a sledgehammer (23:29) for use in breaking rocks, it may not be a weapon of war, such as is depicted in 51:20. In Isa 41:7 the creation of an idol involves metalworking and the "smoothing" with a hammer (*paṭṭîš*). Fitzgerald ("Isaiah 40:19-20 + 41:6-7," 443-44) considers several possibilities of understanding the process, including one in which the *paṭṭîš* is a stubby-nosed burnisher used to polish the figurine by burnishing. However, he prefers a smooth-faced hammer, which is used to smooth out the surface and to render it shiny.

P-B In RL and modern Heb., *paṭṭîš* refers to a hammer, including the small hammer and the sledgehammer.

Hammer, hammered work: → *halmût* (hammer, # 2153); → *maqqebet* (hollow, hammer, # 5216/17); → *miqšâ* I (hammered work, # 5251); → *paṭṭîš* (hammer, # 7079); → *rq'* (hammer out, # 8392)

BIBLIOGRAPHY

F. L. Benz, *Personal Names in the Phoenician and Punic Inscriptions*, Studia Pohl 8, 1972; A. Fitzgerald, "The Technology of Isaiah 40:19-20 + 41:6-7," *CBQ* 51, 1989, 426-46; W. McKane, *A Critical and Exegetical Commentary on Jeremiah: Volume 1*, ICC, 1986.

Richard S. Hess

7080	פטר

פטר (*pṭr*), q. vanish, escape, let out, left off duty; hi. make a wry mouth (# 7080); פֶּטֶר (*peṭer*), nom. firstborn (→ # 7081); פִּטְרָה (*piṭrâ*), nom. firstborn (hapleg.; → # 7082).

ANE Akk. *paṭāru,* loosen, release; Ugar. *pṭr,* split; Arab. *paṭara,* split; Eth. *fäṭärä,* create; Syr. *pṭr,* leave, depart; Mand. *pṭr* open up, separate; Aram. *pṭr,* release.

OT The vb. is attested 9x in BH, including four occurrences in the nominal phrase *p*[e]*ṭûrê ṣîṣîm.*

1. As Saul tried to cast his spear through David, David "eluded" (*pṭr mipp*[e]*nê*) him (1 Sam 19:10).

2. Since the Levitical singers were on duty day and night, they were "exempt, set free" from other service (1 Chron 9:33; cf. 2 Chron 23:8).

3. In a proverb the beginning of strife is likened to "letting out water" (Prov 17:14). Cf. Akk. *nagbē puṭṭuru,* to open fountains.

4. The nominal phrase *p*[e]*ṭûrê ṣîṣîm,* open flowers, serves as a technical term to describe a type of ornamentation on the cedar paneling in Solomon's temple (1 Kgs 6:18, 29, 32, 35).

5. The hi. appears in a prayer song of an individual in collocation with the adverbial phrase of manner *b*[e]*śāpâ,* with lip, meaning to draw the mouth despisingly; it describes the second of three actions of the mockers (Ps 22:7[8]). The rendering of the NIV, hurl insults, apparently based on analogy with the first action of audible mocking, is questionable. The action may be nonaudible in nature, like the third action of "shaking the head." In other words, the rendering "make mouths at" (NRSV) may be better.

P-B In a section of Sirach where a youth is admonished about proper conduct at a banquet, he is told not to linger (*'t'ḥr),* but to depart (*pṭr*) to his house (Sir 32:11). The ni. in QL means to leave, during a formal session of the community (*mwšb hrbym*) (1QS 7:10, 12). In Mish. Heb., the q. pass. part. means exempt (from), and the ni., be released. Cf. Jastrow 2:1157-58.

Disappearance, flight, escape: → *brḥ* I (run away, flee, disappear, # 1368); → *ḥlp* I (pass by, disappear, violate, change, renew, # 2736); → *ḥrh* II (disappear, be few in number, # 3014); → *nws* (flee, escape, slip away, # 5674); → *pṭr* (vanish, escape, let out, # 7080); → *plṭ* (save, bring to safety, # 7117); → *parš*[e]*dōn* (loophole [for escape]?, # 7307); → *śrd* (run away, escape, # 8572)

BIBLIOGRAPHY

TWAT 6:564-69; *TWOT* 2:722.

Jerome A. Lund

7081	פֶּטֶר

פֶּטֶר (*peṭer*), nom. firstborn (# 7081); פִּטְרָה (*piṭrâ*), nom. firstborn (hapleg.; # 7082); < פטר (*pṭr*), open, escape (→ # 7080).

ANE While the fundamental meaning of the Heb. vb. is "escape," the corresponding roots in other Sem. languages have the meaning, split (*AHw*, 849).

OT 1. The verbal notion "separate, split" (*pṭr*) becomes a nom. used in the expression "to first open (lit. split) the womb," which defines specifically *b*[e]*kôr,* firstborn, whether human or animal (Exod 13:2; Num 3:12). By extension, *peṭer* alone can mean "firstborn" (13:13; 34:19). These firstborn belong to God, but could be redeemed by offering a lamb in their place (13:12-13).

2. The fem. nom. occurs once in description of the firstborn of Israel, who have been redeemed by the Levites (Num 8:16).

NT In Luke 2:27 Jesus the firstborn child was brought to the temple to be redeemed according to biblical law (Num 3:13, 45). Elsewhere Jesus is called the firstborn among many (Rom 8:29), the firstborn of creatures (Col 1:16), and the firstborn of the dead (Rev 1:5). The "assembly of the firstborn" refers to the believers who have died and who live in the heavenly Jerusalem (Heb 12:23). Firstfruits is also applied to new believers (Rom 16:5) as well as spiritual blessings they receive (Rom 8:23).

NT → *NIDNTT* 1:664-70; 3:415-36.

Firstborn: → *bkr* (bear early fruit, treat as first-born, # 1144); → *peṭer* (first-born, # 7081)

Bill T. Arnold

7082 (*piṭrâ*, first-born), → # 7081

7085	פִּיד

פִּיד (*pîd*), nom., ruin, misfortune (# 7085).

ANE For possible Ugar. and Arab. cognates, see *HALAT* 874a.

OT Job indirectly refers to his misfortune as *pîd* (Job 30:24; 31:29 [∥ *rā'*]). God can, therefore, send such calamity even though it was not in order to punish Job for any specific sin, but rather to prove his integrity to Satan (Job 1-2; cf. e.g., Ps 73). On the other hand, *pîd* is also given to those who deserve it (Prov 24:22, ∥ *'êd*). One at ease (*ša'^{a}nān*) has contempt for it (Job 12:5).

Misfortune, trouble: → *'āwen* (mischief, iniquity, deception, # 224); → *'āmāl* I (distress, trouble, misfortune, # 6662); → *pîd* (ruin, misfortune, # 7085); → *ṣārâ* I (misery, anguish, affliction, trouble, # 7650)

BIBLIOGRAPHY

NIDNTT 1:462-71.

Cornelis Van Dam

7088	פִּים

פִּים (*pîm*), nom. pim, 2/3 shekel (# 7088).

OT The word occurs only in 1 Sam 13:21. For a discussion on weights → *šql,* weigh, weigh out, pay, # 9202.

Jerry E. Shepherd

7089	פִּימָה

פִּימָה (*pîmâ*), hapleg. nom. fat (Job 15:27b) (# 7089).

OT In Job 15:27-33 Eliphaz, one of Job's disputants, tells of the ineluctable fate of the wicked man. He says that even the ungodly man's well-nourished body will be no defense against the rigors to come. In 15:27 the otherwise unknown *pîmâ* is parallel to *ḥēleb*, fat (→ # 2693). D. J. A. Clines (360) observes that the vbs. in the v. suggest a deliberate self-nurture and offers the translation "blubber" for *pîmâ*. NIV "and his waist bulges with flesh" then represents Heb. "and has made blubber upon (his) trunk." Eliphaz is suggesting that Job's present plight is a result of hidden wickedness. In vv. 20-35 he alludes to the change that fell on Job between the situations described in 1:1-3 and 2:11-13. The motif is in harmony with the prophetic critique that declares outward prosperity to be of no value when unaccompanied by inner wealth of spirit (e.g., Ps 49:12-20[13-21]; Amos 5:11-13).

Fat, fatty food, oil: → *'bs* (fatten, # 80); → *br'* II (fatten o.s., # 1344); → *dšn* I (become fat, # 2014); → *ḥēleb* I (fat, # 2693); → *mhḥ* III (fattened, # 4683); → *m^e^rî'* (fattened, # 5309); → *peder* (fat, # 7022); → *pîmâ* (fat, # 7089); → *šmn* I (be fat, # 9042)

BIBLIOGRAPHY
D. J. A. Clines, *Job 1-20*, WBC 17, 1989.

Robert J. Way

7095 (*pak*, juglet, flask, vial), → # 3998

7096	פכה

פכה (*pkh*), pi. trickle (# 7096).

OT Its single occurrence is in Ezekiel's vision of the temple, "He then brought me out through the north gate and led me around the outside to the outer gate facing east, and the water was flowing (*pkh*) from the south side" (Ezek 47:2). On the onomatopoeic nature of this form, cf. Jenni, 273; *HALAT* 875. Zimmerli (505) compares the term to *pak*, bottle, jug (# 7095).

P-B The term appears in RL in comments on the Ezekiel passage. Cf. also the reduplicated form *pakpēk*, ooze, drip.

Dripping, flowing, trickling: → *'ēgel* (drop, # 103); → *dlp* I (drip, # 1940); → *zwb* (flow, # 2307); → *ṭrd* (continuous dripping, # 3265); → *mar* II (drop, # 5254); → *ngr* (flow, gush forth, pour out, # 5599); → *nzl* (flow, trickle, # 5688); → *nṭp* (drip, pour, # 5752); → *'rp* I (drip, # 6903); → *pkh* (trickle, # 7096); → *r^e^wāyâ* (overflow, # 8122); → *ryr* (flow, # 8201); → *rss* I (moisten, # 8272); → *r'p* (drip, flow, rain, # 8319)

BIBLIOGRAPHY
E. Jenni, *Der hebräische Pi'el*, 1968; W. Zimmerli, *Ezekiel 2*, Hermeneia, 1983.

Richard S. Hess

7098	פלא

פלא (*pl'*), ni. be difficult, extraordinary, wonderful; pi. fulfill; hi. do something in an extraordinary way; hitp. to show o.s. marvelous (hapleg.) (# 7098); מִפְלָאוֹת (*miplā'ôt*), wonderful works (hapleg.; # 5140); nom. פֶּלֶא (*pele'*), something extraordinary, wonder (# 7099); adj. פִּלְאִי (*pel'î*), marvelous (# 7100). Some distinguish between *pl'* I, marvelous, and *pl'* II, pi. fulfil (a vow); hi. to fulfil (a vow), see *THAT* 2:415. The existence of this separate root is a debated question.

OT 1. The root *pl'* primarily signifies something that, measured by the standards of what people are accustomed to or what they normally expect, appears to be extraordinary and wonderful (Albertz, *THAT* 2:414). Such exceptional events or objects usually evoke a reaction of astonishment and praise from their beholders, which explains the exceptionally high incidence of this root in the hymnic literature.

2. In the secular setting, in which the root appears only a few times, it emphasizes the limitedness of human comprehension and ability (usually the ni. of *pl'* with the preposition *min* is used). It can signify a juridical matter "too difficult" to judge (Deut 17:8), or, in a wisdom context, phenomena in life that are "too amazing" to understand (Prov 30:18). In 2 Sam 1:26 the love of Jonathan for David is praised as a love that was "more wonderful" than that of women. The root *pl'* may also be used of an object: the Solomonic temple was to be large and "magnificent" (2 Chron 2:9[8]). The root sometimes occurs in a negative sense: Jerusalem's downfall was "astounding" (Lam 1:9; see also Dan 11:36).

3. But most often *pl'* is used in a religious context. The substantives *pele'* and *niplā'ôt* (ni. part.) are frequently connected with God's acts of salvation: the Exodus events (Exod 3:20; Mic 7:15), the wonders he worked during the crossing of the sea and the wilderness journey (Ps 78:12ff.), the crossing of the Jordan (Josh 3:5), and his saving acts on behalf of the pious individual (Ps 9:1[2]; 40:5[6]; 71:17; 107:15, 21, 24, 31). God is, furthermore, hailed as "the one who alone does wonders" (Ps 136:4; cf. Neh 9:17; Job 5:9; 9:10; Ps 72:18; 86:10; 98:1; 105:5; 106:22). All his works can have the character of the wonderful: his statutes (Ps 119:129), his apocalyptic deeds (Dan 12:6), and his general rule and judgments in the world (Isa 25:1). In the later Wisdom literature the divine works in nature and creation also occasion wonder (Job 9:10; 37:5).

4. Much space is devoted in the OT to people's reception of God's wonderful works and their reactions to them. It is noteworthy, at the same time, that *pele'* and *miplā'ôt,* being in essence descriptive of the divine saving deeds in history, are almost completely absent in the narrative sections of the Pentateuch (except for Exod 3:20; 34:10). These terms are especially prominent in the hymnic parts of the OT (mostly the Psalms). This situation can be explained as follows: "wonder" has not so much to do with the factuality of a specific event as with people's subjective experience of it, which, due to its extraordinariness and mystery, evokes an emotion of awe (Exod 15:11; Ps 106:22) and praise in the perceiver (*THAT* 2:418). Wonders are, therefore, to be extolled (*ydh,* Ps 89:5[6]; 107:8; 139:14), remembered (*zkr,* 1 Chron 16:12; Ps 105:5), meditated on (*śyḥ,* Ps 105:2; 119:27; 145:5), and proclaimed (*spr,* 1 Chron 16:24; Ps 9:1[2]; 26:7; 75:1[2]; 78:4; 96:3). God's purpose with them is to arouse to faith (*'mn* hi., Ps 78:32) and thoughtfulness (*byn,* hitpo., Job 37:14).

5. The vb. *pl'* is attested 5x (pi. 3x, hi. 2x), with the meaning "fulfil (a vow)." Whether a separate root *pl'* is reflected in these instances is unclear (*HALAT* 876).

P-B. In the LXX, *pl'* is rendered by a variety of words, of which *thaumasios, thaumastos,* and *thaumastoō* predominate (*THAT* 2:420). In the QL more or less half of the occurrences of the root are in the Hymns (1QH) (see K. G. Kuhn, ed., *Konkordanz zu den Qumrantexten,* 144, 176f.), which concurs with the situation in the OT.

Marvel, wonder: → *'ôt* (sign, mark, # 253); → *ṭôṭāpōt* (symbol?, # 3213); → *môpēt* (marvel, sign, # 4603); → *pl'* (be wonderful, difficult, # 7098)

Bibliography
TDNT 3:27-42; 8:113-26, 200-261; *THAT* 2:413-20; *TWAT* 6:569-83; A. R. C. Leaney, *The Rule of Qumran and Its Meaning*, 1966; W. D. Stacey, *Prophetic Drama in the Old Testament*, 1990; F.-E. Wilms, *Wunder im Alten Testament*, 1979.

Paul A. Kruger

7099 (*pele'*, wonder), → # 7098

7100 (*pel'î*, marvelous), → # 7098

7103	פלג

פלג (*plg*), ni. be divided (# 7103); מִפְלַגָּה (*miplaggâ*), nom. subdivision (→ # 5141); פֶּלֶג (*peleg* I), nom. water channel, canal (→ # 7104); פְּלַגָּה (*p^{e}laggâ*), nom. district, stream (→ # 7106); פְּלֻגָּה (*p^{e}luggâ*), nom. division (# 7107); פְּלַג (*p^{e}lag* I), Aram. part (# 10853).

ANE Akk. *palāku*, divide (an area) (*AHw*, 813); Aram. (and Syr.) *plg*, divide (*DISO*, 227). Nom. forms with the meaning ditch, canal, and river appear in several Sem. languages (Kaufman, 79), and they occur in place names in Mesopotamia (Thompson, 306).

OT 1. The vb. is used in Gen 10:25(∥ 1 Chron 1:19). A wordplay on Peleg, the son of Eber, describes how in his generation "the earth was divided (*plg*)." This could refer to the division between Peleg's descendants and those of his brother Joktan, or it could suggest the division of peoples at the Tower of Babel (Gen 11:1-9; Hess).

2. *p^{e}luggâ*, division, appears in the pl. const. twice in the Song of Deborah (Judg 5:15-16) and once in 2 Chron 35:5. In the Song of Deborah it describes the military divisions of the tribe of Reuben, while in 2 Chron 35:5 it designates groupings of the laity at Josiah's Passover. A similar usage occurs in v. 12 of the same chapter, with a different nominal form, *miplaggôt*. In the Aram. of Ezra, the term appears in parallel with *maḥ^{a}lōqet*, division, being used to describe the organization of the priesthood at the dedication of the second temple: "the priests in their divisions (*p^{e}luggâ*) and the Levites in their groups" (Ezra 6:18).

3. *peleg*, part, occurs in the Aram. portion of Daniel (7:25) in the enigmatic description of the assignment of the saints to the ruler who is opposed to them for the duration of "a time, times, and part of a time."

P-B In 1QH 1:16, 18; 13:16 the vb. appears with God as the subject; he "divides" or apportions human history and hardships. God is also the subject in other prayers where this vb. is used (4Q 509 fragments 5-6 II:5; 4Q 511 fragment 42:3).

Division, measurement, portion: → *ḥlq* II (divide, obtain one's share, # 2745); → *ḥṣh* (divide, be divided, # 2936); → *ḥṣṣ*(divide, order, # 2951); → *mnh* (count, # 4948); → *plg* (be divided, # 7103); → *prd* (spread out, be divided, keep apart, # 7233); → *prs* (measure, divide, # 7271); → *šsʿ* (tear, divide, # 9117)

Bibliography
R. S. Hess, "Peleg," *ABD*, 1992, 217-18; S. A. Kaufman, *The Akkadian Influences on Aramaic*, 1974; T. L. Thompson, *The Historicity of the Patriarchal Narratives*, 1974.

Richard Hess

7104 (*peleg* I, water-channel, canal), → # 5643

7106 (*p^e laggâ*, district, stream), → # 5643

7107 (*p^e lûggâ*, division), → # 7103

7108	פִּלֶגֶשׁ

פִּלֶגֶשׁ (*pilegeš*), concubine (# 7108).

ANE The word is attested in no Sem. language except Heb. For example, concubine may be expressed by *šugītu* or *esirtu* in Akk. Thus, either the word is *sui generis*, or else it came into Heb. through some other avenue, such as an Indo-European language.

OT 1. The Heb. word seems to be essentially the same as G *pallakē* (which came into Latin as *paelex* [alongside *concubina*]), but this does not necessarily lead to the conclusion that the Heb. term was coined under G influence (*pallakē* is used everywhere in the LXX to translate *pilegeš*, except in 2 Sam 5:13 and Esth 2:14 [which use *gynē*] and Ezek 23:20 [which use *chaldaioi*]).

2. Rabin (1974) has proposed that the word comes from the Philistines, a Mediterranean people who both had contacts with the Hebrews and who were of Indo-European stock. Note that from the days of the Conquest on, almost everybody in the OT of whom it is said he had a concubine is from either the tribe of Judah or Benjamin, those in closest contact with the Philistines (see next paragraph).

3. There were seven men who had a concubine, starting with the period of the Conquest: (1) Caleb, a Judaean (1 Chron 2:46, 48); (2) Gideon (Judg 8:31), from the tribe of Manasseh, and from Ophra (Judg 6:11) near Beth Shean (where archaeological excavation has unearthed evidence of Philistine occupation); (3) an Ephraimite Levite taking a concubine from Bethlehem in Judah (Judg 19:1-30); (4) Saul, a Benjamite from Gibeah (2 Sam 3:7; 21:11); (5) David, a Judaean (2 Sam 5:13; 15:16; 16:21, 22; 19:5[6]; 20:3; 1 Chron 3:9); (6) Solomon, a Judaean (1 Kgs 11:3); (7) Rehoboam, a Judaean (2 Chron 11:21), the last specific person identified in the OT as having a concubine.

4. In the patriarchal period Nahor (Gen 22:24) and Esau's son Eliphaz (36:12) each had a concubine, while Abraham and Jacob had two. Keturah is so styled (1 Chron 1:32), but Hagar is not, except indirectly in Gen 25:6 ("He gave gifts to the sons of his concubines"). Jacob's Bilhah is so styled (35:22), but Zilpah is not.

5. All four women are also called *'iššâ*, wife, or *nāšîm*, wives; i.e., Hagar (Gen 16:3); Keturah (25:1); Bilhah (30:4); Zilpah (30:9); Bilhah and Zilpah together (37:2). In no other place in the OT is a woman both *'iššâ* and *pilegeš*. For example, in Judg 19-20 *pilegeš* is used 11x, but *'iššâ* is never used.

6. In addition to being available to the man for sexual congress, concubines, at least in the monarchichal period, were given responsibility for caring for the palace (2 Sam 15:16; 16:21; 20:3, all in light of David's quick exit from Jerusalem under duress).

7. To attempt to gain sexual access to the concubines of another in royal office was tantamount to usurpation of the throne (2 Sam 3:7; 16:21; possibly 2 Kgs 2:17, 21-25).

8. From the story in Judg 19-20 (see 5 above), it would seem that a concubine might be a first and sole wife. But this is an exception. Normally the concubine is an

auxiliary wife (Engelkern: *Nebenfrau*). She is subordinated to the *'iššâ* and is a substitute birth-mother at the disposition of her mistress (Hagar, Zilpah, Bilhah). On the other hand, neither is the concubine a slave, and that ranks her above an *'āmâ* or *šipḥâ*.

Male: → *'ādām* (Adam, people, # 132); → *'îš* I (man, husband, # 408); → *'enôš* I (men, single man, # 632); → *'āšîš* (man, # 861); → *geber* I (young man, # 1505); → *zākār* (male, # 2351); → *metîm* I (men, people, # 5493); → *na'ar* (boy, # 5853)
Female: → *'iššâ* (woman, # 851); → *gebîrâ/geberet* (lady, queen, mistress, # 1485/1509); → *na' arâ* I (girl, # 5855); → *neqēbâ* (female, # 5922); → *pîlegeš* (concubine, # 7108); → *šiddâ* (lady, # 8721)

BIBLIOGRAPHY

EJ 5:862-63; *TWOT* 2:724; K. Engelkern, *Frauen im Alten Israel: Eine begriffsgeschichtliche und sozialrechtliche Studie zur Stellung der Frau im Alten Testament*, 1990; S. Levin, "Hebrew *pilegeš*, Greek *pallakē*, Latin *paelex*: The Origin of Intermarriage Among the Early Indo-Europeans and Semites," *General Linguistics* 23, 1983, 191-97; J. Morgenstern, "Additional Notes on '*Beena* Marriage (Matriarchat) in Ancient Israel" *ZAW* 49, 1931, 46-58; W. Plautz, "Monogamie und Polygynie im Alten Testament," *ZAW* 75, 1963, 3-27; C. Rabin, "The Origin of the Hebrew Word *PILEGESH*," *JJS* 25, 1974, 353-64.

Victor P. Hamilton

7110	פְּלָדוֹת

פְּלָדוֹת (*pelādôt*), nom. steel ? (# 7110).

ANE The Syr. *b/pūlād* and the Arab. *fūlāḏ* are found with the meaning sword or dagger. The Ugar. *pld* is found in a list of cloth and various garments referring to a covering or a carpet.

OT The nom. is a hapleg. at Nah 2:3[4], a verse that has a number of textual problems. *BHS* proposes an emendation of *pelādôt* to *lappidôt*, a sensible solution involving simple metathesis, yielding the very nice metaphor of the chariots flashing like fire. However, if a metal is involved, this may refer to the metal fittings of the chariots that appear as fire, an equally suitable image. Based on the Ugar. Dahood follows Dietrich and Loretz in proposing that *pelādôt* in Nahum also means blankets (396-97); he takes chariot to be metonymy for horse (which is attested), and takes the phrase to mean that the horse blankets were flaming red. However, this is a less suitable image and seems to be too reliant on a questionable connection to a Ugar. word.

Metals: → *'anāk* (lead, # 643); → *bedîl* (dross, # 974); → *barzel* (iron, # 1366); → *zāhāb* (gold, # 2298); → *ḥel'â* I (rust, # 2689); → *ḥašmal* (glow?, electrum, glowing metal, # 3133); → *kesep* (silver, money, # 4084); → *masgēr* II (metal worker, # 4994); → *ma'abeh* (foundry, # 5043); → *neḥōšet* I (copper, bronze, # 5733); → *sîg* (lead oxide, # 6092); → *sēper* II (bronze, plate, # 6220); → *'ōperet* (lead, # 6769); → *paḥ* II (thin sheet, # 7063); → *pelādōt* (steel?, # 7110); → *ṣwr* III (cast [metal], # 7445); → *ṣa'aṣu'îm* (things formed by metal coating, # 7589); → *ṣph* II (arrange, overlay, plate, glaze, # 7596); → *ṣrp* (melt, smelt, refine, # 7671); → *qālāl* (polished metal, # 7838); → *šḥṭ* II (alloyed, # 8822)

BIBLIOGRAPHY

K. J. Cathcart, *Nahum in the Light of Northwest Semitic*, 1973; M. Dahood, "Hebrew-Ugaritic Lexicography VIII," *Bib* 51, 1970, 396-97; W. A. Maier, *The Book of Nahum*, 1959;

R. D. Patterson, *Nahum, Habakkuk, Zephaniah,* 1991; J. J. M. Roberts, *Nahum, Habakkuk, and Zephaniah,* OTL, 1991.

A. H. Konkel

7111	פלה

פלה (*plh*), ni. be treated differently, be distinguished; hi. treat with distinction (# 7111).

ANE A related Heb. root, *pl'*, has possible cognates in Ugar. *ply*, and Arab. *falāy*, investigate, test.

OT 1. Most of the seven occurrences of *plh* in the OT point not only to some distinctive dealing with a person or group but to a distinctive dealing revelatory of God's presence and power. Moses, following the incident of the golden calf, argues with God that God's failure to accompany his people will mean loss of the people's distinctive position. "What else (apart from your accompanying us) will distinguish (*plh*) me and your people from all the other people on the face of the earth?" (Exod 33:16). Israel is marked out as a people by the reality of God's presence with them. This remark is reminiscent of the covenant formula, "I will be your God and you will be my people" (Jer 7:23; cf. Exod 6:7; Lev 26:12).

2. Israel is especially set off from "the other people" in the story of the plagues. Specific mention is made in advance of three plagues—swarm of flies, diseased livestock, and the death of the firstborn—that God will exempt Israel in each instance (Exod 8:22; 9:4; 11:7). This exemption is to lead to the recognition that it is Yahweh who makes the distinction (hi. *plh*).

3. Three MT uses of *plh* in the Psalms are questioned by scholars since in each instance (Ps 4:3[4]; 17:7; 139:14) the versions work off a related word *pl'*, wondrous. For example, the NIV reads, "Show the wonder (*pl'*) of your great love" (17:7). On the basis of the MT, however, one would translate, "Demonstrate the distinctiveness (hi. *plh*) of your great love." Then the sense, as in the Exodus texts, would be that by a given action the presence and power of God would be recognized. In 4:3[4] the psalmist calls on those who had disgraced him to know that God had given him the high distinction of being a covenant partner (→ *b^e rît*, treaty, # 1382).

Discrimination, bias: → *hakkārâ* (bias, # 2129); → *maśśō'* (partiality, # 5365); → *nś' pānîm* (discriminate, # 5951); → *plh* (be treated differently, distinguished, # 7111)

Elmer A. Martens

7114	פלח

פלח (*plḥ*), cut into slices, split open, bring forth (# 7114); פֶּלַח (*pelaḥ*), slice, millstone (# 7115).

ANE Arab. *palaḥa,* cleave, plow; Aram./Syr. *p^e laḥ*, till, work, plow.

OT 1. The vb. is used once in the q. in Ps 141:7 for plowing the land, and in parallel with *bq'*. The remaining four uses are all in the pi. (2 Kgs 4:39 ["he cut them up into the pot of stew"]; Job 16:13 ["he (God) pierces my kidneys"]; Job 39:3 ["they (certain animals) bring forth their young"]; Prov 7:23 ["till an arrow pierces his liver"]). Thus, the root covers maiming, the birth process, cutting and mixing foods, and plowing, all of which are an act of cleaving.

2. In Prov 7:23 the vb. is used in a context comparing the temptable, young and naive man who walks into the house of a seductive adulteress like an unsuspecting animal who walks into a trap that will certainly kill him by piercing his vitals. Death awaits those who cannot see through the façade of temptation.

3. But God may also be the subject of the vb. In Job 16:12c-13, Job sees himself as under attack by God who, as commander of his army of archers, targets Job, whose vital organs are pierced in the process. One can only imagine how distressing it must have been for Job to perceive of God as a brutal foe.

4. The nom. *pelaḥ* means either slice (1 Sam 30:12) or millstone (Judg 9:53; 2 Sam 11:21; Job 41:24[16]), with the lower millstone being harder than the upper millstone from which it is separated, because the former must bear the weight of the latter and the brunt of the grinding.

P-B See Jastrow 2:1178.

Split, breach, slice: → *bq‘* (split, break open, # 1324); → *ḥrm* II (split, # 3050); → *ḥtr* (break through, # 3168); → *miśpāḥ* (breach of law, # 5384); → *plḥ* (cut into slices, split open, # 7114); → *pṣm* (split open, # 7204); → *prṣ* I (break through, burst out, be broken down, # 7287); → *r‘‘* II (break in pieces, # 8318); → *rṣṣ* (crush, mash, break, # 8368); → *šbr* I (break, break down, smash, shatter, # 8689)

Victor P. Hamilton

7115 (*pelaḥ*, slice, millstone), → # 7114

7117	פלט

פלט (*plṭ*), q. save; pi. bring to safety, save; hi. save (# 7117); מִפְלָט (*miplāṭ*), nom. place of refuge (→ # 5144); פַּלֵּט (*palleṭ*), nom. deliverance (# 7119); פָּלִיט (*pālîṭ*), nom. escape, escapee (# 7127); פָּלֵט/פָּלֵיט (*pālêṭ/pālēṭ*), nom. fugitive, escapee (# 7128); פְּלֵיטָה (*p^e^lêṭâ*), nom. escape, deliverance, band of survivors (# 7129).

ANE The root *plṭ*, to escape and to save, is widely attested in Sem. languages, esp. its WestSem. branches. Nom. savior occurs in Ugar. (cf. Palmyr. cognate *blṭy*, savior) and salvation in Ammon. and Aram. The root commonly forms proper names and sentence names with divine subject (so also Heb.). Since it shares common meanings and uses with WestSem. *plṭ*, Akk. vb. *balāṭu*, to live, probably represents an E. Sem. innovation of the common Sem. root *plṭ*. It is doubtful, however, that OSA nom. *blṭ* (a coin) shares any etymological connection with *plṭ*. *HALAT* 879 erroneously identifies proper names *plṭ* and *plṭy* as inscriptional Heb. rather than Ammon.

OT While *mlṭ* lacks nom. forms, *plṭ* shows twice as many noms. as vbs. (53x to 27x). The basic meaning of *plṭ* is to escape or get off from mortal danger and arrive at a place or condition of security. The root appears primarily in exilic or postexilic literature.

1. Only the vb. q. in Ezek 7:16 attests the root's basic meaning to escape, get off. A prophecy of judgment announces that even if survivors escape Jerusalem's doom (*pāl^e^ṭû p^e^lîṭêhem*), they will simply roost on the mountains, moaning likes doves over their iniquity (for *pālîṭ* see below).

2. Whatever its context (i.e., narrative books, prophets, etc.), the vb. pi. appears only in poetry (24x).

(a) In Psalms. Several times the pi. part. forms a title for Yahweh (*m^{e}palṭî*, my deliverer). Kings invoke it in affirmations of confidence within a royal victory hymn (Ps 18:2[3] = 2 Sam 22:2; cf. 4Q381 24:7) and a prayer for national deliverance (Ps 144:2). Individual Israelites affirm similar confidence in Yahweh as deliverer in two parallel complaint psalms (40:17[18] = 70:5[6]). Past experiences of divine deliverance of the king from enemies undergird that confidence (18:43[44] = 2 Sam 22:44; Ps 18:48[49]). A didactic psalm about Yahweh's protection, Ps 91 concludes with an oracle of salvation in which Yahweh promises to rescue (i.e., to preserve, set securely out of reach; cf. par. *śgb* [pi.]) those who love him (v. 14).

Psalmists often cry for Yahweh's deliverance with a vb. pi. One calls out, "Rescue me (my life) from the wicked" (*plṭ* pi. + *nepeš* + *min*), appealing to Yahweh for legal vindication against false accusations (17:13; cf. *mlṭ* [pi.] + *nepeš* + *min* in 43:1). In other individual complaints, psalmists (vb. pi.) cry for divine deliverance from sickness (31:1[2]) or from the distress of the elderly (71:2 [par. *nṣl*], 4 [+ *miyyad/mikkap* from the hand of]). To illustrate his dire straits, one psalmist recalls how Yahweh delivered (vb. pi.) Israel's trusting ancestors (22:4[5]), then quotes his opponents' mocking cry, "Let the LORD rescue him" (v. 8[9]; pi. juss.). That Yahweh has not already done so emboldens the enemies to intensify their attacks, thereby intensifying the speaker's suffering. In a session of the heavenly council, God himself pleads with the "gods" to rescue the weak and needy from the wicked, i.e., to guarantee them impartial justice (82:4; par. *nṣl miyyad*).

Ps 37:40 concludes an instructional psalm about the contrasting fates of the wicked and the righteous, strongly affirming that Yahweh rescues (vb. pi.) the latter when they seek refuge in him. The par. vbs. seem to display the divine rescue in a brief semantic chiasm: Yahweh helps (*'zr*, q.) the righteous (i.e., comes to their aid), rescues them (*plṭ* [pi.] [2x], i.e., effects their escape from danger), and saves them (*yš'* [hi.], i.e., comes to their aid; cf. Ps 71:2-4; Jenni, 122-23).

pallēṭ (pi. inf. abs.) in 56:7[8] is problematic (i.e., no psalmist would plead for the wicked to escape their wickedness). Assuming a copyist's error, one might emend the root *plṭ* to *pls* (# 7142), the latter meaning either to weigh out (cf. NRSV repay) or to take notice of (so Kraus, 407-8). A better option is to retain MT, reading the line as a bitter, even ironic, question: "For their evil is their deliverance for them?" (so Tate, 65, 67). Part of an individual complaint, the line petitions Yahweh's help.

Without compelling textual variants the obscure phrase *rānnê pallēṭ* (pi. inf. const.), glad cries of deliverance, seems textually secure (32:7; *TWAT* 6:599-600 discusses proposed emendations). Whatever its precise sense, in the context of the present thanksgiving psalm it affirms that Yahweh surrounds repentant sinners with protection against their troubles.

(b) In Job. Job disputes Zophar's contention that the wicked are always punished by describing their happy prosperity (Job 21). As an example, he observes that their cow bears calves (vb. pi.) without ever miscarrying (v. 10). Though only attested here, the sense to bear calves fits the context (contrast *TWAT* 6:595-96 [escape]). In rebutting Eliphaz (ch. 23), Job longs to argue his innocence with God himself, because then he could "be delivered forever from my judge" (v. 7; vb. pi. + *min*), i.e., to get away from the terrible legal sentence he's currently serving (cf. NRSV be acquitted ... by).

3. Mic 6:14 employs both vbs. pi. and hi. to portray the terrible futility with which Yahweh will punish idolatrous Israel (but cf. *BHS* [emendation of pi. to hi.]). Not only will they eat but still be hungry, they will also seek to make their possessions safe but not save them (vb. hi., lit. cause [them] to escape). Indeed, whatever Israel saves (vb. pi.) Yahweh will hand over to a violent end. Isa 5:29 has the only other instance of vb. hi., an oracle of judgment that compares the invading Assyrians to roaring lions carrying off (vb. hi.) their prey unimpeded.

4. Of the root's derivatives, the nom. *p^e^lêṭâ*, band of escapees or survivors, is the most numerous (28x), concentrated exclusively in narratives and prophets, notably exilic or postexilic ones (e.g., Chron, Dan). It always occurs in the singular as a collective nom. describing primarily a human group that escapes some life-threatening catastrophe. The surviving group may be a family fearing fraternal revenge (Gen 32:8 [Esau]; cf. ni. part. of *š'r*, to remain) or facing death by starvation (45:7 [Joseph]; cf. *š^e^'ērît*, remnant [# 8642]). It may also be the remnant of an entire tribe, i.e., the Benjaminite males who survived tribal judgment (Judg 21:17). But in Exod 10:5 *p^e^lēṭâ* describes not humans but grain stalks and trees that survived the plague of hail only to face the locust plague (cf. Joel 2:3).

Commonly, the group composes a city or nation that escaped death or conquest at the hands of invaders (i.e., all Israel [Isa 4:2]; Jerusalem [2 Kgs 19:30, 31 = Isa 37:31, 32; 2 Chron 12:7; cf. Ezek 14:22]; the northern kingdom [Isa 10:20; 2 Chron 30:6]). In two cases, the group survived only to die in a later attack (1 Chron 4:43 [Amalek]; Isa 15:9 [Moab]). That no one escaped a slaughter attests its ferocity and magnifies the greatness of Yahweh's victory (2 Chron 20:24). In the memoirs of Ezra and Nehemiah, *p^e^lêṭâ* stands for the remnant of Israel that survived the Babylonian exile (Ezra 9:8, 13, 14, 15; Neh 1:2).

p^e^lēṭâ may designate the event of escape by flight (2 Sam 15:14 [from Absalom's coup]) or divine deliverance of Jerusalem from attacking armies (2 Chron 12:7 [Shishak]; Joel 2:32[3:5]; Obad 17). Other texts underscore that the severity of divine judgment makes escape attempts by nations impossible (Jer 25:35; 50:29 [Babylon]; Joel 2:3). In the eschaton Egypt will not escape conquest (lit., will not have *p^e^lêṭâ* [an escape]) by the king of the North (Dan 11:42).

5. Nom. *pālîṭ*, fugitive, escapee, comes from the adj. *palêṭ* (see below) and appears primarily in prophets but also in narratives (5x). In general, it describes individuals who have fled for their lives from violence, especially the siege of a city. When Canaanite kings conquered Sodom and Gomorrah, one such escapee eluded capture to inform Abram (Gen 14:13); and when Jerusalem fell to the Babylonians, an escapee also informed Ezekiel, signaling an end to the prophet's divinely imposed silence (Ezek 33:21-22; cf. 24:26-27). In 2 Kgs 9:15 the nom. still retains its original sense to slip away when Jehu orders his army not to let anyone slip out of besieged Ramoth Gilead to tip off King Joram to Jehu's coup.

The phrase *p^e^lîṭê 'eprayim,* fugitives of Ephraim (Judg 12:4-5), proves troublesome because of an obscure context and textual problems (see *BHS*). Apparently, the Ephraimites hurled it as a snide slur against Jephthah and his fellow Gileadites (cf. NIV renegades of Ephraim), since it sparked a war between the two groups (v. 4). Perhaps fugitives of Ephraim connoted something like "trashy people we Ephraimites kick out." But in v. 5 the phrase clearly refers to Ephraimite fugitives fleeing the war. If so, the episode has a clever ironic touch: controlling the Jordan crossing, the "trashy fugitives" unwelcome in Ephraim kill any real Ephraimite fugitives who try to cross the river enroute there.

The nom. forms part of the fixed phrase *pālîṭ wᵉśārîd*, escapee and fugitive, invoked to stress the total annihilation resulting from military defeats. One narrator applies it to Ai's army (Josh 8:22, but in reverse order), while Jeremiah twice invokes it to warn Judeans that Egypt offered no shelter from divine judgment (Jer 42:17; 44:14 [see also below]). The phrase describes the slaughter when Jerusalem fell (Lam 2:22) and Edom's inexcusable lack of compassion toward Judeans fleeing that disaster (Obad 14).

In Amos' vision of the altar, Yahweh's decree of judgment puns on cognate words: no escapee (*pālîṭ*) will escape (*mlṭ* [ni.]) when he destroys Samaria (9:1). The nom. is most common in exilic prophets, who invoke *pālîṭ* to portray the human cost of divine judgment. Jeremiah warned Judean refugees in Egypt that very few of those who escaped violent death there (lit., fugitives of the sword) would return to Judah (Jer 44:28). According to Ezekiel, when Judah fell, some would escape death there, but in exile those escapees would hate themselves for their idolatry (Ezek 6:8-9). Other Judeans, he said also, would flee to the mountains of Judah in remorse, moaning like doves (7:16).

Isa 45:20 calls for fugitives of the nations (*pᵉlîṭê haggôyim*) to turn to Yahweh from their idols and be saved (cf. v. 22). Though the context is unclear, probably these fugitives are nations who have fled the fall of Babylon to Persia.

6. The nom. *pālêṭ/pālēṭ*, escapee, occurs almost exclusively in prophets and always m. pl. abs. The lone exception appears in the poetic Song of Heshbon, which praises an Amorite victory over Moab. Moabites have fled Moab because of Moab's defeat (Num 21:29). The *qāṭîl* form commonly comprises noms. of specific subgroups of society (e.g., *nābî'*, prophet, *'āsîr*, prisoner, etc.; see Waltke-O'Connor, 5.3e).

In a prose judgment speech Jeremiah employs this nom. to describe the very few Judean fugitives (i.e., those who fled to Egypt from Judah) who will escape divine wrath and actually return home (Jer 44:14). Also, twice the prophet uses it in judgment oracles against Babylon. A brief prose oracle of hope portrays the return of refugees from exile in Babylon on a mission of divine vengeance for Zion and the temple (50:28). Jer 51:50 addresses the exiles as survivors of the sword (i.e., those who survived the fall of Jerusalem), urging them not to forget Yahweh and Jerusalem. Among the comments that conclude the great book of Isaiah is a climactic promise that Yahweh will dispatch survivors—presumably, of the exile—among the nations as a sign (Isa 66:19). They will proclaim Yahweh's glory and gather his scattered people back to Jerusalem (v. 20).

7. The nom. *miplāṭ*, place of refuge (*HALAT* 584), only occurs in Ps 55:8[9], the complaint of someone betrayed by a close friend. The psalmist wishes to fly from the turmoil swirling around him to a restful desert hideaway (*miplāṭ*).

P-B Vbs. and noms. of root *plṭ* appear in postbiblical Heb. and Aram. The LXX renders its derivatives principally with forms of *anasōzō*, to save again (20x), *sōzō*, to save (12x), and *diasōzō,* to bring through safely (11x). The nom. *sōtēria* also translates *pᵉlêṭâ* (6x). The dominance of forms of *sōzô* in effect means the displacement of the word field of vbs. to escape and to run away by that of vbs. to save. Those who in MT escaped, in LXX become those who are saved.

At Qumran, the root occurs in a wide range of texts and genres, though not in the Temple Scroll. For MT *mlṭ* [hi.] (Isa 31:5) 1QIsa[a] even has *plṭ* hi., and the nom. *p[e]lêṭâ* should be restored at 4QpIsa[c] 6-7, 2:10 (quotation of Isa 10:20). In citing Ps 37:40, 4QpPs[a] 1-10, 4:20 substitutes *mlṭ* for MT's first vb. *plṭ* but retains its second one. The root's usage in Qumran hymns echoes its usage in OT psalms. Using the phrase *plṭ* (pi.) *nepeš*, to save (one's) life, one thanksgiving song lauds God's having saved the life of the poor (1QH 5:18), another that he provides his peaceful shelter to save the psalmist's own life (9:33). Another line affirms the psalmist's trust in God to save him forever (9:29; cf. 6:32; 4QpPs[a] 1.4:20 quoting Ps 37:40). The phrase in 1QH 3:10, to escape (death) throes (*plṭ* ni.), refers to a human birth (para. *mlṭ* [hi.], to give birth [3:9]). One noncanonical psalm borrows a phrase from Ps 18:2[3] (= 2 Sam 22:2), including the pi. part. *m[e]palṭî*, my deliverer (4Q381 24:7). 11QPs[a] 23:13 (= Ps 144:2) has the phrase *mplṭ ly*, my hiding place (but see *TWAT* 6:593-94 for alternate pointings).

According to the Damascus Rule, those outside the Qumran covenant will have neither remnant nor survivor (*š[e]'ērît w[e]p[e]lēṭâ*; CD 2:6f.; cf. 1QM 1:6; 1QS 4:14), but God has left a remnant (*p[e]lēṭâ*), the Qumran community, to produce many descendants (CD 2:11-12). The blessing of 1QSb 1:7 petitions God to deliver (*plṭ* pi. per Milik's reconstruction [see DJD 1:120-21]) the blessed. But Qumran eschews coining from root *plṭ* a self-description of the community as a remnant community (but see *š[e]'ērît* in 1QM 14:8).

In Qumran Aram. texts, the root's usage also corresponds to that of the OT. In the Genesis Apocryphon, the flood's survivors thank the Most High for saving them (*plṭ* pa.) from destruction (1QapGen 12:17; cf. Jub 7:34). The post-dream dialogue says that Abraham's life will be saved (q.) on account of Sarah (19:20; cf. Gen 12:13), and the Lot narrative reports how a shepherd had escaped (q.) from captivity (22:2). In the Targum of Job *plṭ* (pa.), to set free, speaks of birth ushering life into the world (11QtgJ 39:3; see also 32:2). For texts of Enoch, see *TWAT* 6:606.

NT As with *mlṭ*, OT *plṭ* comes into the NT through LXX *sōzō*. Hence, it is difficult to determine where the Heb. root stands behind the G rendering. See *TDNT* 7:965-1024 for discussion.

Remnant, profit: → *ytr* I (remain over, be extra, surplus, # 3855); → *śārîd* I (escapee, survivor of battle, # 8586); → *š'r* (remain, # 8636)

Salvation, deliverance, ransom, rescue: → *g'l* I (redeem, deliver, ransom, # 1457); → *yš'* (be victorious, receive help, save, rescue, # 3828); → *mlṭ* I (get to safety, escape, deliver, give birth to, # 4880); → *nṣl* (rescue, # 5911); → *pdh* (ransom, redeem, deliver, # 7009); → *plṭ* (save, bring to safety, # 7117); → *śrd* (run away, escape, # 8572); → *šālôm* (peace, friendship, happiness, prosperity, health, salvation, # 8934)

Bibliography

NIDNTT 3:177-223; *TDNT* 7:965-1024; *THAT* 2:420-27; *TWAT* 6:589-606; E. Gerstenberger, *Psalms 1*, FOTL 14, 1988, 96, 136-40, 169; G. Hasel, "The Remnant: The Origin and Early History of the Remnant Motif in Ancient Israel" (diss. Vanderbilt, 1970); idem, "Remnant," *IDBSup*, 735; M. Horgan, *Pesharim: Qumran Interpretations of Biblical Books*, CBQMS 8, 1979;

E. Jenni, *Das hebräische Pi'el*, 1968; H.-J. Kraus, *Psalmen*, BKAT 15/14, 1972; E. Schuller, *Non-Canonical Psalms from Qumran*, HSS 28, 1986, 11, 113, 119; M. Tate, *Psalms 51-100*, WBC 20, 1990.

Robert L. Hubbard, Jr.

7119 (*pallēṭ*, deliverance), → # 7117

7127 (*pālîṭ*, escapee), → # 7117

7128 (*pālêṭ*, fugitive), → # 7117

7129 (*p^e lēṭâ*, escape), → # 7117

7130 (*pālîl*, judges), → # 7136

7131 (*p^e lîlâ*, decision), → # 7136

7132 (*p^e lîlî*, calling for judgment), → # 7136

7133 (*p^e lîliyyâ*, decision, judgment), → # 7136

7134	פֶּלֶךְ

פֶּלֶךְ (*pélek* I), nom. spindle-whorl (# 7134).

ANE Akk. *pilakku*, spindle-whorl.

OT In Prov 31:19, the noble wife "grasps the spindle with her fingers." This word is also found in 2 Sam 3:29, translated crutch in NIV and spindle in other versions. David's curse of Joab for the coldblooded murder of Abner may be rendered as "May Joab's house never be without someone . . . who leans on a crutch," or as "May Joab's house never be without someone . . . who grasps a spindle." Taken as "spindle" it seems that David wished for the male descendants of Joab to be either effeminate or disabled because it was women and the crippled who did the tasks of weaving. "Crutch" has little support other than that the logic of the verse demands it.

Spinning, sewing, weaving, embroidering: → *'rg* (spin, weave, # 755); → *dallâ* I (hair, thrum, loom, # 1929); → *ḥōšēb* (weaver, # 3110); → *ṭwh* (spin, # 3211); → *kîšôr* (distaff, # 3969); → *mānôr* (rod, # 4962); → *skk* II (weave, intertwine, # 6115); → *'ēreb* I (knitted material, # 6849); → *pelek* I (spindle-whorl, # 7134); → *rqm* (embroider, weave together, # 8387); → *ś^e rād* (woven, # 8573); → *šbṣ* I (weave, # 8687); → *š^e tî* I (woven material, # 9274); → *tpr* (sew, # 9529)

Robert Alden

7135	פֶּלֶךְ

פֶּלֶךְ (*pelek* II), region, district (# 7135).

ANE This word is associated with Akk. *pilku* I, district (*AHw*, 863; Lipiński, 71), though this has been challenged by Demsky (see also Bowman, 688), who associates *pelek* with Akk. *pilku* II, "work duty, tax on conscripted labor." Thus, the leaders were overseers of groups whose labor served as payment of the Persian tax on their region. Though this word appears at Ugarit (Sivan, 258), its occurrence elsewhere in second-millennium Akk. texts suggests that it is Akk. rather than West. Sem. (Huehnergard, 168). The appearance of *pilku* I in first-millenium Akk. suggests that it is the origin of the Heb. *pelek* in Nehemiah. Along with other words for administration, Heb. borrowed this term from Mesopotamian vocabulary (Williamson, 206).

OT This nom. occurs 7x in Neh 3 (vv. 9, 12, 14, 15, 16, 17, 18). In every case it forms part of the designation of an individual responsible for the repair of part of Jerusalem's wall. The formula is PN followed by GN: "leaders of the (half) district of GN." The GNs attached to the half districts include Jerusalem (twice), Keilah (twice), and Beth Zur. The GNs associated with whole districts are Beth Hakkerem and Mizpah. Thus the postexilic province under Nehemiah was divided into five provinces, named according to their major city center (Williamson, 206; Blenkinsopp, 235, adds an unnamed Jericho and Jordan Valley province). See also Aharoni, 418.

District, region: → *'elep* III (clan, tribe, region, # 548); → *g^e lîlâ* (circle, region, Galilee, # 1666); → *ḥebel* II (cord, rope, land, region, # 2475); → *kikkār* (region, environs, # 3971); → *m^e dînâ* (province, district, # 4519); → *p^e laggâ* (district, stream, # 7106); → *pelek* II (region, district, # 7135)

Bibliography

Y. Aharoni, *The Land of the Bible: A Historical Geography,* 1979[2]; J. Blenkinsopp, *Ezra-Nehemiah,* OTL, 1988; R. A. Bowman, "Introduction and Exegesis to the Book of Ezra and the Book of Nehemiah," *IB* 3:551-819, 1954; A. Demsky, "Pelekh in Nehemiah 3," *IEJ* 33, 1983, 242-44; J. Huehnergard, *Ugaritic Vocabulary in Syllabic Transcription,* 1987; É. Lipiński, "Emprunts suméro-akkadiens en Hébreu biblique," *Zeitschrift für Althebraistik* 1, 1988, 61-73; D. Sivan, *Grammatical Analysis and Glossary of the Northwest Semitic Vocables in Akkadian Texts of the 15th-13th C.B.C. from Canaan and Syria,* 1984; H. G. M. Williamson, *Ezra, Nehemiah,* Word 16, 1985.

Richard Hess

7136	פלל

פלל (*pll* A), pi. judge, execute judgment, expect (# 7136); פלל (*pll* B), hitp. pray (→ Prayer: Theology); פָּלִיל (*pālîl*), nom. judge, # 7130); פְּלִילָה (*p^e lîlâ*), nom. decision (# 7131); פְּלִילִי (*p^e lîlî*), nom. calling for judgment (# 7132); פְּלִילִיָּה (*p^e lîliyyâ*), nom. decision, judgment (# 7133); תְּפִלָּה (*t^e pillâ*), nom. prayer (related to *pll* B; # 9525; → Prayer: Theology).

ANE Among the standard lexica, *HALAT* identifies two homophonous roots *pll*: one meaning arbitrate, which occurs exclusively in the piel, and one meaning pray, intercede, which occurs exclusively in the hithpael. The fact that the former meaning may be related to Akk. *palālum*, watch over, supervise (*AHw*, 813), while only a rather dubious Arab. cognate *falla*, cut oneself in worship, or a connection with Heb. *npl*, fall, can be suggested to support the latter probably supports *HALAT*'s distinction. BDB, however, derives both usages from a common root with the suggested basic meaning intervene, interpose. Efforts to relate the rarer judicial usage of *pll* to the more common usage to refer to intercessory prayer are somewhat forced but not demonstrably incorrect (cf. A. Berlin and E. A. Speiser); even the judicial rendering of *pll* in the standard lexica remains uncertain (cf. Gerstenberger, *TWAT* 6:613).

OT 1. The verbal form *pll* occurs 4x; four different derived nom. forms occur only a total of 6x. The vb. *pll* occurs with the derived meaning expect in Gen 48:11 and is used ironically in Ezek 16:52: Jerusalem, by its exceedingly wicked deeds, has "judged" and acquitted her evil sisters Samaria and Sodom, who, by comparison, appear righteous. The narrower judicial sense is attested in the historical Ps 106:30 where it describes Phinehas's execution of two who blatantly joined themselves (*ṣmd* [# 7537]; Num 25:5-8, Allen's translation "in mediation," *Psalm 101-150*, WBC, 1983, 46, is rather weak) to Baal of Peor, thereby stopping the plague. Only in 1 Sam 2:25 does *pll* refer explicitly to divine judgment, though the meaning is disputed. The verse apparently employs a wordplay using the two roots or meanings of *pll*: If one sins against a fellow human being, God will adjudicate (*pll*, piel) his case; if one sins against God, he does not have a prayer (*pll*, hithpael)!

2. The four nom. forms based on the root *pll* all manifest related meanings: *pālîl* refers in Exod 21:22 to those officials who determine damages to be paid in injury cases and in Deut 32:31, in a derived sense, to those enemies who can themselves judge, come to a verdict regarding the uniqueness of Israel's Rock. *pᵉlîlî* in Job 31:11, 28 refers to punishable iniquities (so J. E. Hartley, *Job*, NIC, 1988, 412, 418), i.e., demanding judgment (*'āwôn pᵉlîlî[m]*, the *m* in v. 11 probably enclitic, M. H. Pope, *Job*, AB, 1973, 232). *pᵉlîlâ* in Isa 16:3 refers to the Moabite delegation's plea that the Jerusalem leaders render a favorable decision on their behalf, while *pᵉlîliyyâ* in 28:7 (noting the chiastic word order) describes the inebriated priests as dysfunctional when rendering decisions.

P-B In Mish. Heb. and Aram., *pll* is used widely to refer to investigation, reasoned argument, and debate (vb. *pilpēl*, *palpēl*; nom. *pilpûl*, *pilpûlā'*, Jastrow, 1184).

Justice, judgment: → *dyn* (judge, contend, govern, administer, # 1906); → *miśpāḥ* (breach of law, # 5384); → *pll* I (sit in judgment, arbitrate, expect, # 7136); → *ṣdq* (be just, righteous, justified, # 7405); → *špṭ* (judge, execute judgment, govern, # 9149)

BIBLIOGRAPHY

THAT 2:427-32; *TWAT* 6:606-17; *TWOT* 2:725-26; D. R. Ap-Thomas, "Notes on Some Terms Relating to Prayer," *VT* 6, 1956, 225-41; A. Berlin, "On the Meaning of *pll* in the Bible," *RB* 96, 1989, 345-51; C. Houtman, "Zu 1 Samuel 2:25," *ZAW* 89, 1977, 412-17; E. A. Speiser, "The Stem *PLL* in Hebrew," *JBL* 82, 1963, 301-6; E. F. de Ward, "Superstition and Judgment: Archaic Methods of Finding a Verdict," *ZAW* 89, 1977, 1-19.

Richard Schultz

7142	פלס

פלס (*pls* I), pi. clear way, make a path (# 7142).

ANE The vb. has cognates in Syr. (*pᵉlaš*, break through), Akk. (*palāšu*, penetrate, break into), Aram. (*fls* II, tear open), and Arab. (*flśtm*, exits). See also Tigre *fälsa*, split (cf. Tigrinya *fäläsä*). The use of the root in a Carthaginian inscription is noted in CRAI 1968, 125.

OT The vb. occurs only in the pi. Although *HALAT* distinguishes between *pls* I and *pls* II, it is mostly difficult to decide whether the meaning of the vb. should be understood as "to level" or "to perceive" (e.g., Prov 4:26; 5:6, 21). It seems that all the occurrences in Proverbs derive from *pls* II. However, it should be noted that all the occurrences of *pls* (cf. also Ps 58:2[3]; 78:50; Isa 26:7) have a wisdom background.

(Cf. Seybold, 53-66.) E.g., note the parallelism of *yšr*, be straight, and *pls* in Isa 26:7. Cf. also the discussion of *nākōaḥ*. In two of the instances where *pls* I is used, Yahweh functions as subj. Isa 26:7 states that Yahweh provides a straight and level path to the righteous (*ṣaddîq*). Note that *t^epallēs* stands par. to *mêšārîm*, equity (# 4797; < *yšr*, be straight, → # 3837). The notion of Yahweh leveling the path of the righteous should be understood within the wisdom context of Yahweh rewarding those who act correctly/appropriately by keeping his commandments. In Ps 78:50, where Yahweh also functions as subj. of the vb. *y^epallēs,* a different context applies. The phrase *y^epallēs nātîb l^e'appô* means literally "he cleared the way for his wrath" and should be understood as Yahweh not restraining his anger.

P-B Jastrow (2:1183-85) mentions that the Talmudic vb. *pls* means split, pick to pieces. However, his reference to *plš* I is significant. This vb. has the meaning divide, go through, and it could probably be associated with the BH vb. *pls* I.

Level, straight: → *'šr* I (walk straight, # 886); → *yšr* (be straight, level, right, # 3837); → *nākōaḥ* (straight way, correct conduct, justice, truth, # 5791); → *pls* I (clear way, make a path, # 7142); → *šwh* I (be/become like, be alike, make level, # 8750); → *tqn* (straighten, set in order, # 9545)

BIBLIOGRAPHY

G. R. Driver, "Notes on the Psalms," *JTS* 36, 1935, 147-56; A. R. Hulst, *Old Testament Translation Problems*, 1960, 115-16; K. Seybold, "Psalm LVIII. Ein Lösungsversuch," *VT* 30, 1980, 53-66.

Louis Jonker

7143	פלס

פלס (*pls* II), pi. observe (# 7143).

ANE A cognate is attested in Akk. *palāsu*, look at/away.

OT The vb. relates to paying attention, observing/scrutinizing (McKane, 315). It is used in Prov 5:21 to stress the idea of the all-seeing God. The man who dies through his indiscipline is he who does not reckon with the Lord's constant observation/scrutinizing of all his tracks. In the wisdom metaphor of the adulteress, the writer states that she did not observe/recognize the path of life, i.e., the route followed by this woman led to death (Prov 5:6).

Look, observation, perception, sight, vision, watch: → *ḥdh* II (gaze on, appear, # 2526); → *ḥzh* (see, perceive, behold, # 2600); → *ḥmh* I (see, watch out for, become visible, # 2778); → *nbṭ* (look around, accept as an act of grace, # 5564); → *pls* II (observe, # 7143); → *ṣwṣ* II (look at, # 7438); → *r'h* (see, have visions, choose, perceive, # 8011); → *rṣd* (keep one's eye on, # 8353); → *śqd* (take note of, # 8567); → *š'h* III (stand gazing, # 8617); → *šgḥ* (gaze, stare, # 8708); → *šwr* I (gaze on, regard, see, # 8800); → *šzp* (catch sight of, tan, scorch, # 8812); → *š'h* (look, care about, gaze about, # 9120); → *šqp* (look down, # 9207); → *št'* (gaze, look, regard, look anxiously about, # 9283)

BIBLIOGRAPHY

W. McKane, *Proverbs: A New Approach*, 1970.

Jackie A. Naudé

7144	פֶּלֶס

פֶּלֶס (*peles*), nom. pointer of balance (# 7144).

OT The word occurs only in Prov 16:11 and Isa 40:12. For a discussion on scales → *mō'znayim,* scales, # 4404.

Jerry E. Shepherd

7145	פלץ

פלץ (*plṣ*), hitp. shudder, shake, tremble (# 7145); מִפְלֶצֶת (*mipleṣet*), nom. disgraceful image, horrid thing (# 5145); פַּלָּצוּת (*pallāṣût*), nom. shuddering, shaking, trembling (# 7146); תִּפְלֶצֶת (*tipleṣet*), nom. horror, terror (# 9526).

OT 1. The verbal form of *plṣ* occurs only once in the hitp. form and denotes a continuous or repetitive back-and-forth movement (Job 9:6). Similar to many of the other Heb. words within the semantic field shake, tremble, this word is set in the familiar context of Yahweh's creative-theophanic presence, "He shakes the earth from its place and makes its pillars *tremble*." It occurs with the synonym *rgz* (→ # 8074), shake, tremble, agitate.

2. The nom. *pallāṣût*, shuddering, shaking, trembling, occurs 4x. In each instance it depicts the internal response to a terrible external reality. This strong emotional reaction, resulting in physical shaking, is described as something that falls upon (Isa 21:4, *b't*, → # 1286), overwhelms (Ps 55:5[6]; Ezek 7:18, *ksh*, → # 4059), and even seizes (Job 21:6, *'ḥz*, → # 296) a person.

3. The nom. *mipleṣet* occurs 4x in the OT: 2x in 1 Kgs 15:3 and 2x in the parallel account, 2 Chron 15:6. Apparently, it is used negatively either as a description of an idol or as a technical term for a particular type of idol. The use of such a term emphasizes the extremely negative assessment that idols and idolatry should have been accorded by a faithful Israelite. See further # 5145.

4. The form *tipleṣet* occurs only once in Jer 49:16. It is used to describe Edom's former strength before the nations. Previously Edom had inspired *terror* (49:16), and now she is doomed to become an object of *terror* herself (49:17).

BIBLIOGRAPHY

TWOT 2:726.

M. V. Van Pelt/W. C. Kaiser, Jr.

7146 (*pallāṣût*, shuddering, shaking, trembling), → # 7145

7147	פלשׁ

פלשׁ (*plš*), q. roll (# 7147).

ANE The Ugar. word *plṯ* (*UT*, # 2056) occurs in the story of Baal and Mot, when at the death of Baal the "dust of wallowing" is scattered on the head of El (*KTU* 1.5 vi 15, 16).

OT The vb. *plš* is found 4x in the OT, always in the hitp.; 3x this is a lamentation of wallowing in the dust (Jer 6:26; Ezek 27:30; Mic 1:10), and it is likely that Jeremiah's command to the leaders of the flock to howl and roll (Jer 25:34) is an ellipsis of the same idea. The expression is a description of mourning customs (e.g., Job 2:8, 12).

P-B The vb. is found in RL in reference to the biblical texts.

Rolling: → *gll* I (roll, roll away, flow down, drag, wallow, # 1670); → *glm* (roll up [mantle], # 1676); → *plš* (roll, # 7147); → *qpd* (roll up, # 7886)

BIBLIOGRAPHY
J. C. L. Gibson, *CML*², 73, 155; J. C. de Moor, *An Anthology of Religious Texts from Ugarit*, 1987, 80.

A. H. Konkel

7148 (*p^e lešet*, Philistine, Philistia), → # 7149

7149	פְּלִשְׁתִּי

פְּלִשְׁתִּי (*p^e lištî*), Philistine (# 7149); פְּלֶשֶׁת (*p^e lešet*), Philistine, Philistia (# 7148).

ANE Egyp. *P-r-s-t-w*; Akk. *Pa-la-as-tu*, Philistia; LXX *allophyloi*, foreigners; other G sources refer to *pelasgoi*, sea people. The word Philistines occurs 288x in the OT and its geographical derivative, Philistia, 8x. (→ Philistines: Theology)

The mortuary temple of Ramses III (1190-1150) at Medinet Habu contains a remarkable scene of a naval battle in his eighth year between the Egyptians and the "Sea People." After the battle Ramses is presented with three rows of prisoners, dressed identically in "feathered crown" headgear and kilts, similar to those worn by envoys from the Aegean, Crete, or Syria. The land battle scenes show them fighting from chariots while their families are following on ox-drawn carts (Barnett, 372). Even more significant is the accompanying description of the invaders: "Their confederation was the Philistines, Tjeker, Shekelesh, Denye(n) and Weshesh, lands united" (*ANET*, 262). These associates are depicted with different headgear, notably the horned helmet, similar to that of the Sherdan mercenaries in the army of Ramses II (Brug, 27). Following this battle, so it is generally assumed, they were "allowed" to settle along the southern coastal plain of the eastern Mediterranean seaboard, the region called Philistia, an obvious derivative of Philistine. According to 1 Sam 6:17 the Philistines then occupied five major cities: Gaza, Ashkelon, Ashdod, Ekron, and Gath (commonly referred to as the Philistine Pentapolis). Discoveries at several other Iron Age I sites, e.g., Tel Qasile, Dor, Acco, Beth-Shean, Tel Batash, etc., testify to their presence elsewhere (Dothan, 25-91).

1. *Material culture*. The Philistines' mastery of the superior iron technology (Muhly, 52) gave them a military edge to control the surrounding areas militarily and economically (cf. 1 Sam 13:19-22). Apart from their strong naval interests (Artzy, 82), they expanded their trading activities inland, which brought them into conflict with the early Israelites settling on the highlands (Kitchen, 60). Wood (51) argues that, in fact, they ousted the Egyptians from Canaan and as a consequence consolidated their political hegemony as far as the Jordan valley. The successive phases of the Philistine settlement from their initial mercenary colonies (Beck, 93-95) to their political consolidation constitute a vivid and dynamic process, "during which large planned cities as well as smaller rural settlements were founded and intensively developed in Philistia" (Mazar, 313).

Excavations at different sites have disclosed the introduction of a distinct new type of pottery in terms of shape (e.g., stirrup jars, kraters, pyxis, strainer spout jugs, kernos rings, bottles, etc.) and decoration (bichrome in black and red over a coating of white slip, with spirals, geometric bands, or figures with stylized "swan" or fish motifs) (Dothan, 1982, 94-218).

Though closely related to Mycenean IIIC ware these were locally manufactured (Gunneweg, 15). The extensive spread of Philistine pottery from the Negev to Dan indicates the extent of Philistine connections. This distinctive pottery became obsolete by the end of Iron Age II (Fritz, 192). Moreover, the discovery in Philistine territory of anthropoid clay coffins with lids bearing resemblance to the Philistine headgear is usually taken as an indication of Philistine presence, but it should be kept in mind that it was in reality an Egyptian custom (Weippert, 372).

The clay figurines, noticeably the *Ashdoda* (Keel, 138), several seals (Garbini, 446), approximately sixteen inscriptions (Naveh, 21), and personal names to be identified as "Philistine," albeit from a later period (Kempinski, 20), disclose elements of a distinct culture on the Palestine coast that resembles the Mycenean IIIB and C in more than one way (Karageorghis, 161). The urban planning and buildings, especially the temple at Tel Qasile (Mazar, 320-22), confirm the view that at the end of the LB Age a new and vigorous people had entered Canaan and usurped the political and economic power held earlier by the Egyptians (Wood, 52; but see Singer, 44).

2. *Philistine history*. Philistine origins remain a subject of much debate (Helck, 132). Brug's view (201-5) that they were indigenous Canaanites that had undergone only limited influence from the Aegean mercenaries in the Egyptian army has not met with wide approval. Dothan (21) and Karageorghis (16), on the other hand, overemphasize their Aegean, esp. Cypriot, origins. In recent scholarship the divergent and complex nature of their origins and their material culture has been pointed out (Howard, 321). The distinctive features represented in the Iron Age material culture of the coastal cities of Palestine signal the emergence, development, and disappearance of an immigrant people who did not replace the indigenous population, but became the military and civil aristocracy that initially dominated it but eventually were assimilated into it (Mazar, 327). As seaborne professional warriors they had to seek consorts from the local population over which they had established political and economic control (Mendenhall, 542). Once they had completely assimilated the Canaanite culture, they established excellent trade relations with the Phoenicians.

According to the "Table of Nations" (Gen 10:14), the "Casluhim (from whom the Philistines came) and Caphtorim" originated in Egypt (Rendsburg, 96). In Zeph 2:5 the Philistines are equated with the Cherethites (Cretans), while Jer 47:4 and Amos 9:7 mention the Isle of Caphtor (Crete) as their place of origin. In the prophetic literature from Amos through Zechariah (Amos 1:6-8; Zech 9:5-8) they remained the epitome of Israel's foe. The ark narratives and Samson cycle reflect the conflict between the Philistines and early Israelites, the outcome of which served as catalyst for the institution of the monarchy (Hindson, 148). After Saul's defeat by the Philistines at Mount Gilboa David once and for all brought an end to the powerful Philistine confederation of states (2 Sam 5:25). Their presence in the Shephelah is largely ignored in the OT historical literature, possibly because the Philistine cities functioned independently from the kingdoms of Israel and Judah (Beck, 140). As economically less important vassals to Egypt (and later to Assyria) than the Phoenicians, they became more and more involved in agriculture (esp. the production of olive oil) than trade, as is testified by the results of the archaeological discoveries at, e.g., Tel Miqne (Gitin & Dothan, 208) and Dor (Raban, 121).

The Assyrian records of the eighth and seventh centuries frequently refer to the Philistine cities and the policies of their respective kings. The purpose of Tiglath-Pileser III's invasion of the Levant was to gain control of the Mediterranean maritime trade (Tadmor, 87-88). The Assyrian overlords preferred to keep the Philistine city states as autonomous tribute-paying vassals rather than annexing them to the empire. Mitinti of Ashkelon, Hanno of Gaza, and others became his vassals (*ANET*, 282). Needless to say, several Philistine cities rebelled time and again (727, 713, 705, cf. *IJH,* 444). Sargon campaigned against the anti-Assyrian coalition of Syro-Palestinian states, among which the Philistine cities of Gaza, Ashdod, Ekron, etc., were forced to pay costly tribute (Beck, 151). The Assyrian attacks on Ekron are depicted vividly in bas-relief on the walls of Sargon's palace in Khorsabad (Brug, 38-39). As a result of Hezekiah's leading role in the revolts following the death of Sargon, Sennacherib expropriated territory from Judah (cf. Isa 1:7) and gave it to the loyal Philistine kings "Mitinti, king of Ashdod, Padi, king of Ekron, and Sillibel, king of Gaza" (*ANET*, 288; cf. Mittmann, 92). His successors concentrated a great deal of effort on conquering Egypt, a prerequisite of which was the absolute control of the Philistine cities as their strategic base. Their cautious neutrality did not safeguard them from constant raids by foreign troops passing through their territory, least of all the Egyptians (Zeph 2:4) and Babylonians. Nebuchadnezzar's campaigns against Judah in 597 and 586 also brought their end (Beck, 158). As was the case with the Judeans, many of the Philistines were deported to Babylonia. After the conquest by Alexander in 332, Ashdod, Ashkelon, and Gaza became independent city states again. It is highly unlikely that anything of the original culture at that stage would have remained distinctively Philistine except for their name (Herodotus 1.105; 2.104). Two loanwords in BH seem all that have remained of their once mighty presence in the Holy Land, i.e., *seren* (chieftain, 1 Sam 5:8; 6:4, 16) and *koba'* (helmet, cf. 1 Sam 17:5).

3. *Philistine religion.* Very little is known about the Philistine religion because the gods associated with them in OT, viz., Dagon (1 Sam 5:4), Ashtoreth (1 Sam 31:8-13), and Baal-Zebub (2 Kgs 1:2), are Canaanite (Brug, 182-88). The OT also alludes to their priests, diviners (1 Sam 6:2), and magicians (Isa 2:6), who were highly esteemed (Hindson, 32). It is to be assumed that they adopted Canaanite religious beliefs and customs. Archaeological artifacts indicate the existence of certain religious practices, e.g., the *kernos* (a hollow ring on top of which stand miniature vessels, small birds, or clay animals), which most probably served a special liturgical purpose; similarly the *Ashdoda* (a female figure whose lower half resembles a bed, probably representing a fertility goddess sitting on a throne). The female figurines show a Mycenean religious heritage where female deities were primarily worshiped. The OT allusions to a male-dominated Philistine pantheon most likely reflect the religious beliefs and cultic practices of a later time and of Canaanite character.

The excavations also show that each Philistine city had a sanctuary. The temple at Tel Oasile is unique in Palestine. It comprises three successive layers (Strata XII-X) of three distinct superimposed temples (dating from the 12-10th century) with raised mud brick platforms and benches and a square sacrificial altar, etc. They do not conform to the plans of Canaanite temples but rather to those in the Aegean and in Cyprus

(Mazar, 322). The original square room (7 x 7m) was enlarged to incorporate a vestibule, a main hall, and a room in the back (Mazar, 320). The roof, incidentally, was supported by two free-standing central pillars (cf. Judg 16:29). This independent building tradition apparently ceased at the end of the eleventh century (Fritz, 193). A round pebble-surfaced hearth, a white plastered *bamah,* and a wheeled cult stand were among the religious objects discovered in building 350 at Ekron, which resembles the Philistine temple at Tel Qasile (Dothan & Gitin, 29-30). A four-horned altar was also discovered at Ekron (Bierling, 46).

4. *Philistine legacy*. Because of their bad reputation in the Bible for causing widespread enmity and disorder vis-à-vis the Israelites during the early period (Iron Age I) of the settlement but also as their subsequent adversaries in military, political, and economic affairs, the Philistine are usually viewed in an unfavorable light (Raban & Stieglitz, 35). Their technological and military skills are mentioned only in passing (cf. 1 Sam 13:19-22). Archaeological excavations show, however, that they were industrious artisans, brave fighters, excellent builders, shrewd politicians, highly productive agriculturalists, and deeply religious people. Their contributions to the prosperity, culture, art, and architecture of Iron Age Palestine were indeed considerable.

Philistines: → *'ašdôd* (Ashdod, # 846); → *'ašqᵉlôn* (Ashkelon, # 884); → *gat* (Gath, # 1781); → *'azzâ* (Gaza, # 6445); → *'eqrôn* (Ekron, # 6833); → *pᵉlištî* (Philistine, # 7149); → Philistines: Theology.

BIBLIOGRAPHY

M. Artzy, "On Boats and Sea Peoples," *BASOR* 266, 1987, 75-84; R. D. Barnett, "The Sea Peoples," *CAH* II/2, 1975, 359-78; B. L. Beck, *The International Roles of the Philistines During the Biblical Period,* 1980; N. Bierling, *Giving Goliath His Due. New Archaeological Light on the Philistines*, 1992; J. F. Brug, *A Literary and Archaeological Study of the Philistines*, 1982; T. Dothan, *The Philistines and Their Material Culture,* 1982; idem, "Philistines, Archaeology," *ABD* 5:328-33; idem and M. Dothan, *People of the Sea: The Search for the Philistines,* 1992; idem, "Ekron of the Philistines," Part I, *BARev* 16/1, 1990, 20-36; V. Fritz, *An Introduction to Biblical Archaeology,* 1994; G. Garbini, "Philistine Seals," in *Horn Festschrift,* 1986, 443-48; S. Gitin, "Ekron of the Philistines," Part II, *BARev* 16/2, 1990, 32-42; J. Gunneweg, T. Dothan, I. Perlman, S. Gitin, "On the Origin of Pottery from Tel Miqne-Ekron," *BASOR*, 264, 1986, 3-16; W. Helck, *Die Beziehungen Aegyptens und Vorderasiens zur Aegaeis bis ins 7. Jahrhundert v. Chr.,* 1979; E. Hindson, *The Philistines and the Old Testament,* 1971; D. M. Howard, "Philistines," *POTW,* 231-50; V. Karageorghis, "Exploring Philistine Origins on the Island of Cyprus," *BARev* 10/2, 1984, 16-28; H. J. Katzenstein, "Philistines, History," *ABD* 5:326-28; A. Kempinski, "Some Philistine Names from the Kingdom of Gaza," *IEJ*, 37/1, 1987, 20-24; K. A. Kitchen, "The Philistines," *POTT*, 53-78; A. Mazar, *Archaeology of the Land of the Bible 10,000-586 B.C.E.*, 1990; G. E. Mendenhall, "Cultural History and the Philistine Problem," *Horn Festschrift*, 1986, 525-46; S. Mittmann, "Hiskia und die Philister," *JNSL* 16, 1990, 91-106; J. D. Muhly, "How Iron Technology Changed the Ancient World and Gave the Philistines a Military Edge," *BARev* 8/6, 1982, 40-54; J. Naveh, "Writing and Scripts in Seventh-Century B.C.E. Philistia: The New Evidence from Tell Jemmeh," *IEJ* 35, 1985, 8-21; A. Raban, R. R. Stieglitz, "The Sea Peoples and Their Contributions to Civilization," *BARev* 17/6, 1991, 34-52; G. A. Rendsburg, "Gen 10:13-14: An Authentic Hebrew Tradition Concerning the Origin of the Philistines," *JNSL* 13, 1987, 89-96; I. Singer, "How Did the Philistines Enter Canaan? A Rejoinder," *BARev* 18/6, 1992, 44-46; L. E. Stager, *Ashkelon Discovered. From Canaanites and Philistines to Romans and*

Moslems, 1991; E. Stern, "How Bad Was Ahab?" *BARev* 19/2, 1993, 20-29; H. Tadmor, "Philistia Under Assyrian Rule," *BA* 29/3, 1966, 86-102; H. Weippert, *Palästina in vorhellenistischer Zeit,* 1988; B. Wood, "The Philistines Enter Canaan—Were They Egyptian Lackeys or Invading Conquerors?" *BARev* 17/6, 1991, 44-52; G. E. Wright, "Fresh Evidence for the Philistine Story," *BA* 29/3, 1966, 70-86.

J. P. J. Olivier

7153 (*pen*, lest, otherwise), → Particles

7154	פַּנַּג

פַּנַּג (*pannag*), uncertain term for an (agricultural?) item of trade: (parched?) grain, meal, or flour derived from millet(?); *panakes* (a plant) or opopanax (its gum-resin)(?) (hapleg.; # 7154; *HALAT* 884b).

ANE Possible cognates may be found in Akk. *pannigu*, pastry, confectionary; a kind of meal/flour (*AHw* 2:818b); and Hitt. *punniki-*, a pastry, confectionary (Friedrich, 173a); cf. Lat. *panicium*, anything baked, pastry, and *panicum*, panic-grass/grain (i.e., edible grains from grasses of the genus *Panicum;* cf. Lewis-Short, 1297c). As viewed against this lexical and semantic convergence, it is alternatively possible that we have a related nom. in G *panakes*, all-heal; self-heal (any of a variety of plants credited with remedial virtues; cf. Liddell-Scott, 1295b re *opopanax*, lit., sap of the *panax* [a gum-resin substitute for balsam]; also Stol, 68-71).

OT The only OT occurrence of *pannag* appears in Ezek 27:17 as part of a list of (agricultural?) commodities that Judah and Israel used to trade with Tyre (whose destruction is prophetically lamented in the *qînâ* of Ezek 27:3b-36; cf. Zimmerli, *Ezechiel* 2, 631; ET: *Ezekiel* 2, 48). The list of items includes: (1) either "wheat of Minnith" (MT) or "wheat and storax/labdanum" (< **b^{e}ḥiṭṭîm ûn^{e}kō(')t*; storax, being either the solid resin from the *Styrax officinalis* tree or the liquid balsam from the bark of the *Liquidambar orientalis* [i.e., Levant storax]; labdanum, being the resinous juice from rockroses of the genus *Cistus*; so Cornill; Eichrodt; *BHS*; cf. Gen 37:25; 43:11); (2) our term *pannag*; (3) honey; (4) oil; and (5) *ṣorî*, balsam or balm.

As to the meaning of the hapleg. *pannag*, the ancient versions variously conjecture: the LXX translates doubly with G *myrōn kai kasias,* of unguents/ointments and of cassia; the Tg. with various forms resembling *qûlyā'*, parched grain; flour from parched grain (cf. Jastrow, 1328a; Zimmerli; though Dalman considered Aram. *qlwwy'* [ed. of P. A. de Lagarde, *Prophetae chaldaice,* 1872] a loanword < G *kolbia/kollyba* [see G. Dalman, *Aramäisch-neuhebräisches Wörterbuch,* 1901, 361; 2d ed., 1922, 378a; cf. *qwlwy'*, 3d ed., 1938, 378a); the Pesh. translates with *dûḥnā'*, millet (cf. Heb. hapleg. *dḥn*, millet, in Ezek 4:9; Loew, 1:738-40 on the millet species *Panicum;* Forbes, 3:87-88, 91; so NRSV; meal, REB); and the Vg. with *balsamum*, balsam. Modern commentators and versions have conjectured: wax (< **w^{e}dônag*, so Cornill; Hoffmann, 15; Bertholet[?]); Kraetzschmar; Fohrer-Galling, 157; Eichrodt; JB; cf. BDB 815a); (early) figs (< **ûpaggîm*; cf. S of Songs 2:13; so RSV, NAB); and confections (cf. Akk. *pannigu*, a pastry, confectionary; so NIV).

Most indications are that we should expect Heb. *pannag* to refer to an agricultural commodity whose identity lies where the Akk., Hitt., and Lat. lexical evidence converges with a translational sense shared by the Tg. and Pesh.: some kind of (parched?) grain, meal, or flour derived from millet. However, we should not exclude the possibility that Heb. *pannag* may refer either to the plant *panakes* or its gum-resin, opopanax (so Stol, 71).

P-B As another possible Jewish Aram. cognate, the Palestinian Tg. to Gen 22:20 reads *wpngt* in some eds., though it should probably be emended to read *ûpagnat*, and she entreated/interceded (Jastrow, 1186a; cf. 1134b).

Grain, barley, millet, rice, etc.: → *'ābîb* (ears of grain, # 26); → *biṣqālôn* (fresh stalks [cj.], # 1303); → *bar* III (grain, corn, # 1339); → *gādîš* I (stack of grain, # 1538); → *gereś* (grits, # 1762); → *dāgān* (grain, # 1841); → *dōḥan* (sorghum, millet, # 1893); → *ḥiṭṭâ* (wheat, # 2636); → *kussemet* (emmer-wheat, # 4081); → *karmel* IV (grain, fresh, newly ripened grain, # 4152); → *m^elîlâ* (grain, grains, # 4884); → *minnît* (rice, # 4976); → *mōṣ* (chaff, # 5161); → *sōlet* (wheat flour, # 6159); → *pannāg* (parched? grain, meal or flour, # 7154); → *ṣebet* (grain, bundle of grain, # 7395); → *ṣānum* (hard, barren [ears of grain], # 7568); → *qālî* (parched grain, # 7833); → *qāmâ* (crops, grain, standing grain, # 7850); → *śôrâ* (millet, # 8463); → *ś^e'ōrâ* (barley, # 8555); → *šibbōlet* I (ear of grain, # 8672); → *šeber* II (grain, # 8692)

BIBLIOGRAPHY
A. Bertholet, *Das Buch Hesekiel erklärt,* KHAT 12, 1897; C. H. Cornill, *Das Buch des Propheten Ezechiel,* 1886; W. Eichrodt, *Der Prophet Hesekiel,* ATD 22/1-2, 1965-1966; ET: *Ezekiel,* OTL, 1970, 379; G. Fohrer and K. Galling, *Ezechiel,* HAT 1/13, 2d ed., 1955, 157; R. J. Forbes, *Studies in Ancient Technology,* 3, 2d ed., 1965, 87-88, 91 (on the millet species *Panicum miliaceum,* L.); J. Friedrich, *Hethitisches Wörterbuch,* 1952, 173a; G. Hoffmann, *Über einige phoenikische Inschriften,* 1889, 15; R. Kraetzschmar, *Das Buch Ezechiel,* HKAT, 1900; C. T. Lewis and C. Short, *A Latin Dictionary,* 1879, 1297c; H. G. Liddell and R. Scott, *A Greek-English Lexicon,* 1968, 1295b; I. Loew, *Die Flora der Juden,* 1 and 2, Publications of the Alexander Kohut Memorial Foundation 4, 1928, 1:738-40 (on the millet species *Panicum miliaceum,* L.); M. Stol, *On Trees, Mountains and Millstones in the Ancient Near East,* 1979, 68-71; W. von Soden, "Zum hebräischen Wörterbuch," *UF* 13, 1981, (157-64) 163; W. Zimmerli, *Ezechiel 2,* BKAT 13/2, 1969, 631; ET: *Ezekiel 2,* trans. J. D. Martin, 1983, 48.

Robert H. O'Connell

7155	פנה

פנה (*pnh*), q. turn to the side; turn around; pay attention to; pass on; pi. turn away, make clear, prepare a way; hi. give way (in fight); turn one's back/shoulder; turn tail to tail; ho. be caused to give way; be turned (134x; # 7155); פְּנִימָה (*p^enîmâ*), nom. inside, inwards, (# 7163); פְּנִימִי (*p^enîmî*), adj. inner (# 7164).

ANE The vb. is well attested in other languages: Akk. *panû*, turn towards; Egypt. *pn'*, turn; Ugar. *pn*, turn; in the impv, be careful!; cf. Eth. *fännäwä*, make s.o. turn toward a direction, send.

OT 1. In everyday usage *pnh* refers to striking out in a certain direction (Deut 2:3; Josh 15:2, 7; 1 Sam 13:17; 1 Kgs 17:3), changing direction (Deut 10:5), turning around (2 Sam 1:7), facing in a given direction (1 Kgs 7:25; Ezek 8:3; 43:1).

2. Theologically, *pnh* is associated with a spiritual orientation, such as turning to idols (Lev 19:4) or to the way of one's choosing (Isa 53:6; cf. 56:1; Job 36:21;

cf. *šwb*). Moses warned that people not turn their heart away from the Lord God (Deut 29:18[17]). Israelites were accused of turning their backs to God and not their faces (Jer 2:27; cf. Deut 31:18). For a comparison of *pnh, šwb,* and *swr*, see *šwb* (# 8740).

3. Only seldom is *pnh* employed in the sense of turning to God (Isa 45:22) (cf. *šwb*). A particular nuance of hi. *pnh* is that of "making preparations" for a revival, a spiritual return to God (Isa 40:3; cf. 57:14; 62:10), with the imagery of clearing a road of obstacles (Mal 3:1).

4. In the sense of paying attention, *pnh* is used in prayer (Ps 25:16; 69:16[17]), often with the appeal for God to have mercy (86:16; 119:132). The psalmist was assured that God would respond (*pnh*) to the prayer of the destitute (102:17[18]). In certain situations God does not pay attention (*pnh*) to offerings (Num 16:15; Mal 2:13). At other times God announces readiness to turn (*pnh*) in the sense of showing favor to his people (Ezek 36:9).

5. The adj. *p^{e}nîmî*, inner, occurs in the OT exclusively with regard to structures or parts of buildings, such as palaces (inner court, Esth 4:11; 5:1) or temple courtyards (Ezek 8:16). The term is a favorite of Ezekiel (24x). Aside from the glory cloud filling the inner court (10:3), the term is essentially an architectural one.

Turning, apostasy, returning, faithlessness, repentance: → *zwr* II (turn away, # 2319); → *ḥmq* (turn aside, # 2811); → *yq'* (turn aside, # 3697); → *nq'* (disengage, # 5936); → *sbb* (turn, go round, surround, # 6015); → *swr* (turn aside, # 6073); → *pnh* (turn to the side, # 7155); → *śṭh* (turn aside, # 8474); → *šwb* I (repent, turn, return, revert, withdraw, # 8740); → *t^{e}qûpâ* (turning point, # 9543)

BIBLIOGRAPHY

TWOT 2:727-28.

J. A. Thompson/Elmer A. Martens

7156	פָּנִים

פָּנִים (*pānîm*), face, (features of face); visible, front, attack, assault (# 7156).

ANE The word is common in the Sem. languages. In Phoen. and Ugar. it is used as in Heb., also with regard to its use in conjunction with prepositions. The Akk. word *pānu* is used for the front side and the pl., like the Heb., for face. The Syr. *p^{e}nita'* is used for side and the Arab. *finā'* for an empty space or a forecourt.

OT 1. *Head of a living being*. The nom. is used frequently in the sense of the front side of a living being, denoting specifically the head of a living being. It can be the head of an animal (Ezek 1:10), a heavenly being or its image (Exod 25:20; Isa 6:2), or a human being. With regard to humans, it can denote a human face in general (Gen 9:23), as that part of thc facc that can scc or be seen. A human face can also reflect the inner feelings (31:2; cf. 3 below). The face can become pale because of fear (Jer 30:6).

2. *Front side, surface*. The nom. can refer to the front of an object. In Ezek 2:10 it refers to the front side of a scroll, with *'āḥôr* referring to its back. It can also refer to the front side of a building or structure, such as the temple (Ezek 41:14) or a tent (Exod 26:9). In 28:37 it refers to the front of the priest's turban and in Num 8:2 to the front of the Menorah. In Joel 2:20 it refers to the front of an army and in 2 Sam 10:9 to the front of a battle.

The nom. is also used to refer to the surface of something. In Job 41:13[5] it is used for the exterior of clothes (cf. also Isa 25:7). It is also used for the surface of the earth (Gen 2:6; Isa 14:21) and of the sea (Gen 1:2; Job 38:30). The nom. is also used temporally to denote the earlier, esp. in conjunction with prepositions like *l*^e and *mill*^e (Deut 2:10, 12).

3. *In certain expressions.* The nom. is used in different idiomatic expressions (see *HALAT* 886-87). The expression *bōšet pānîm* means public shame (Jer 7:19), something clearly visible to other people. A sad face was a sign of sorrow (Gen 40:7; cf. also 1 Sam 1:18; Neh 2:2; Prov 25:23; Dan 1:10). Face is, however, also used in a positive sense, such as the light of his face for the pleasure of a king (Prov 16:15; cf. also 15:13; Eccl 8:1). The nom. is also used to denote a person (Deut 7:10; 2 Sam 17:11) and can be used instead of a pronoun (Gen 32:21[22]).

4. *In conjunction with certain vbs..* The nom. is used in conjunction with certain vbs. As object of *sbb* (hi.) it denotes turning in a certain direction (Judg 18:23). The expression "to fall on the face" is often used for falling down on the ground as a sign of respect for an important person or for God (Gen 17:3). It is a greeting coupled with a special mark of honor. It can be a sign of fear at the appearance of divine glory (Lev 9:24). The expression is also used when someone falls in deep mourning on the body of a dead person (Gen 50:1). To cover the face (with a cloak [1 Kgs 19:13] or a veil [Gen 38:15]) was also an action expressing sorrow (2 Sam 19:4[5]). It could also happen during a theophany, with the aim to cover one's face before the presence of the Lord (1 Kgs 19:13).

To set the face towards a certain place denotes movement in a certain direction (Gen 32:20[21]). To set the face towards is also an expression meaning to decide to do something (2 Kgs 12:18; Jer 42:15). With the prepositions *'el* and *'al* the word gets a menacing meaning (Ezek 6:2). To turn the neck and not the face was a sign of rejection (Jer 2:27). *nāśā' pānîm* has the meaning to grant someone's request (Gen 19:21), while the vb. *hēšîb* with the nom. has the meaning to deny someone's request (1 Kgs 2:16). *rā'â pānîm* is used in formal style to see the face of a high official (Gen 43:3) or a king (2 Sam 3:13), i.e., to appear before him. To spit in someone's face is a sign of derision and contempt (Num 12:14). *nkr* (hi.) with the nom. means to recognize someone (Prov 28:21). The expression sometimes has a judicial meaning, viz., to be partial towards a guilty party in court (Deut 1:17). The same meaning also occurs for the expression *nāśâ' pānîm* (Lev 19:15).

5. *In conjunction with prepositions.* The nom. is combined with various prepositions. It is impossible to give a complete survey of all the possibilities (cf. *HALAT* 888-90 and *THAT* 2:443-46, 451, 457-59). The theologically important cases are discussed under the relevant headings. The most common is the combined preposition *lipnē* (before), accounting for about half of the occurrences of the nom. In many of these combinations the nom. has lost its nominal value and it is part of a combined preposition.

6. *With regard to God.* The nom. appears frequently in combination with God or the Lord. "The face of the LORD" did not develop into an independent theological construct in the OT. In some instances this expression is used as the subject of an action (Exod 33:14; Deut 4:37; Isa 63:9; Lam 4:16). In Exod 33:16 the Lord said that his face (NIV my Presence) would go with Moses. This means that God himself would

accompany Moses. The expression is used in the same way in Isa 63:9 and Lam 4:16. In Deut 4:37 Moses said that God led the people from Egypt through his face (NIV his Presence) and his great power. His face is equated with his power as the means through which God did his mighty deeds.

In a larger number of cases the face of the Lord is the object of divine action. As object of *ns'* it points to a show of favor (Num 6:26). The same semantic field is at work with the vb. *h'yr* (hi.) (Num 6:25), in the priestly blessing. Cf. also expressions such as the light of his face in Ps 4:6[7] and 90:8. As object of *ntn* followed by the preposition *b^{e}* it gets a menacing meaning (to set my face against, Lev 17:10; cf. also 20:5 for a similar expression). The absence of the favor of the Lord is expressed by idoms such as to hide the face (Deut 31:17) and to turn the face away (Ezek 7:22). The expression face to face (Gen 32:30[31]) points to a personal encounter with God (cf. also Deut 5:4).

The face of the Lord also appears as the object of human hope or expectations. Vbs. used in this regard include *r'h* (Exod 23:15, to appear before God in the cult), *ḥzh* (Ps 11:7), *bqš* (pi.) (2 Sam 21:1), *qdm* (pi.) (Ps 89:14[15]), and *ḥlh* (pi. [1 Kgs 13:6]). In the cult reference was made to the *leḥem happānîm* (the bread of the Presence), which pointed to the presence of the Lord in the cult (cf. also Num 4:7). The latter is often used in intercession (Exod 32:11) and in prayers for deliverance (2 Kgs 13:4). The expression *nir'â 'et-p^{e}nē yhwh* is used to state that someone is appearing before the Lord. This usually meant in a cultic sense, to appear in the sanctuary during a festival (Exod 34:20, 24; Deut 16:16; 31:11) or when bringing a sacrifice (Isa 1:12). Hannah also used this expression for her son's appearance in the temple (1 Sam 1:22). In Ps 11:7 and 17:15 the vb. *ḥzh* is used with *pānîm* as object. That the just will see God's face points to the lasting relationship between God and his children, a relationship that will not be broken by death. This seeing of God will take place after the awakening of the psalmist—a phrase that may refer to an awakening after death.

P-B Most of the uses of the nom. also appear at Qumran. Especially important is the expression *hē'îr pānîm,* used for the divine enlightenment of the righteous (1QH 3, 3; 4, 5). In the LXX *prosōpon* is the usual translation of the nom., encompassing the normal usages of the Heb. nom.: face, side, front, surface. When the LXX speaks of the face of the Lord it usually points to a relationship between God and man, e.g., his gracious turning to man. It appears also frequently in cultic language related to the temple.

NT The G word *prosōpon* follows the OT usages in the NT. It is used for the face of a person (Matt 6:16) and also metaphorically (Matt 17:6). In 2 Cor 1:11 it denotes a person. In Luke 21:35 it is used for the surface of the earth. It is also used for the face of God or Christ. For the believer the glory of God appeared in the face of Christ (2 Cor 4:6).

Head: → *'ap* (face, anger, # 678); → *gulgōlet* (scull, # 1653); → *l^{e}ḥî* I (eye, nose, jawbone, chin, cheek, # 4305); → *mēṣaḥ* (forehead, # 5195); → *m^{e}tall^{e}'ôt* (jawbone, # 5506); → *pānîm* (face, visible, assault, # 7156); → *pōt* (front, forehead, # 7327); → *qodqōd* (crown of head, # 7721); → *rō'š* I (head, chief, beginning, # 8031); → *raqqâ* (temple [of head], # 8377)

Bibliography
NIDNTT 1:585-87; *THAT* 2:701-15; *TWAT* 6:629-59; *TWOT* 2:727-28.

Harry F. van Rooy

7157	פִּנָּה

פִּנָּה (*pinnâ*), nom. corner, cornerstone (# 7157).

OT 1. *pinnâ* is found most prominently in architectural usage, describing the corner of the altar (Exod 27:2) and ledge of the altar (Ezek 43:20), houses (Job 1:19), gates (Jer 31:40), city walls (Neh 3:24), corner towers (Zeph 1:16; 3:6), and the city itself (2 Chron 28:24). One of Jerusalem's gates was named the "Corner Gate" (2 Kgs 14:13; 2 Chron 26:9; Jer 31:38; Zech 14:10). *pinnâ* refers also to the corner of the street (Prov 7:8, 12).

2. The cornerstone metaphor grows out of architectural usage, but refers also to human leaders, and in particular, to the royal one of David's house, whom God raises up in marvelous ways to create stability and justice. The specific meaning of cornerstone is used primarily in prophetic oracles (Isa 28:16; Zech 10:4). The architectural metaphor in Isa 28:16, alluding either to the Davidic house or to the temple, evokes trust in what God is doing to establish justice and righteousness in Zion. The imagery may also convey a sense of stability and salvation for Judah through a (royal?) cornerstone (Zech 10:4; note the combination of "cornerstone" and "ruler").

3. Related is the evocative royal connotation of *rôš pinnâ,* head of the corner, in Ps 118:22. Once the word is used in relation to creation as the cornerstone of the earth's foundation (Job 38:6). Three times *pinnâ* has an extended meaning referring to leaders of the people (Judg 20:2; 1 Sam 14:38; Isa 19:13).

NT In the teaching of Christ (Matt 21:42; Mark 12:10; Luke 20:17), the preaching of the apostles (Acts 4:11), and the letters of Paul (Eph 2:20) and Peter (1 Peter 2:6-7), the NT picks up the imagery of the cornerstone as one of the principal prophetic metaphors describing the role of Christ. All that the cornerstone represented concerning the foundations of Israel (whether royal house, temple, or justice), Christ personified; he is appropriately seen as the fulfillment of the *pinnâ* concept.

Border, boundary, corner, edge, rim: → *gbl* I (bound, border, # 1487); → *zāwît* (corner, # 2312); → *kānāp* (wing, skirt, outermost edge, # 4053); → *karkōb* (rim, edge, # 4136); → *mḥh* II (border on, # 4682); → *swg* II (border by, # 6048); → *pē'â* I (corner, # 6991); → *pinnâ* (corner, # 7157); → *ṣad* (side, # 7396); → *ṣēlā'* I (side, rib, side-chamber, # 7521); → *qēṣ* (limit, boundary, # 7891); → *qāṣeh* (end, border, # 7895); → *qṣ'* II (made with corners, # 7910)

Bibliography
NIDNTT 3:388-90; K. Jeppesen, "The Cornerstone (Isa 28:16) in Deutero-Isaianic Rereading of the Message of Isaiah," *ST* 38, 1984, 93-99.

Gordon H. Matties/John Walton

7163 (*pᵉnîmâ*, inside), → # 7155

7164 (*pᵉnîmî*, inside), → # 7155

7165	פְּנִינִים

פְּנִינִים (*pᵉnînîm*), nom. corals, pearls (# 7165).

ANE Akk. *panû*, turn (*AHw*, 822).

OT For examples, see Job 28:18; Prov 3:15 (Q, K *p^eniyyîm*); 8:11; 20:15; 31:10; Eccl 4:7; Lam 4:7; conj. Ps 45:14.

For a discussion on jewelry, see *'dh* (put on ornaments, # 6335).

Malcolm J. A. Horsnell

7167	פנק

פנק (*pnq*), pi. pamper (# 7167).

OT The hapleg. occurrence of this lexeme is *m^epannēq* (Prov 29:21). The context of usage is the domain of household labor and the master-slave relationship. Used in disapprobation of the master's conduct, the import of the usage is negative. The domain of usage also suggests that the concern is functional; pampering is an inappropriate way of preparing a person for the arduous tasks of the slave. The meaning of the second half of the verse is uncertain. It is not clear whether the result of the pampering is that the servant becomes proud and rebellious or becomes simply unproductive and unequal to the task.

P-B The word is found in Mish. Heb., with its sense unchanged (Whybray, 414). Pa'el forms are attested in both Pal. Aram. and Syr. with the sense pamper (*MdD*, 37 5a).

Delight, enjoyment, pampering: → *'dn* (delight, luxuriate, revel, # 6357); → *'ng* (delight oneself, # 6695); → *pnq* (pamper o.s, pamper, # 7167); → *ṣhq* (laugh, play, insult, # 7464); → *š"* II (play, take delight in, # 9130)

Bibliography

A. Cohen, *Proverbs*, 1946; D. Kidner, *Proverbs*, 1964; R. B. Y. Scott, *Proverbs, Ecclesiastes*, 1973; R. N. Whybray, *Proverbs*, NCBC, 1994.

Douglas Carew

7174	פסח

פסח (*psḥ*), be lame, limp (# 7174); פִּסֵּחַ (*pissēaḥ*), lame (# 7177).

ANE Akk. attests *pessû*, be lame, limp.

OT 1. The vb. is used in the q. to speak figuratively of limping about between two opinions or courses of action with regard to the worship of Yahweh or Baal (1 Kgs 18:21). It also describes the physical incapacity of Mephibosheth (2 Sam 4:4), and as an ironic twist on Israel's ambivalence, it refers to the priests of Baal as limping about (NIV dancing; 1 Kgs 18:26). It seems best (with BDB but contra *HALAT*) to distinguish *psḥ* I, pass or spring over (# 7173), from *psḥ* II, limp.

2. The nom. *pissēaḥ* describes Mephibosheth's lameness in both feet due to a childhood accident (2 Sam 9:13; 19:26[27]). The term also describes a condition that disqualified a man for the office of priest (Lev 21:18). Lameness made animals unsuitable as sacrificial offerings (Deut 15:21; Mal 1:8, 13). Figuratively, Job speaks of himself as being "feet to the lame" (Job 29:15). The sage says that a proverb in a fool's mouth is like limp legs (Prov 26:7).

NT → *NIDNTT* 2:415.

Handicaps, disfigurement, blind, lame, speechless: → *'illēm* (speechlessness, # 522); → *gibbēn* (hunchbacked, # 1492); → *ḥārûṣ* IV (injured [animal], # 3024); → *ḥērēš* (speechless, # 3094); → *kšḥ* (be lame, crippled, # 4171); → *mûm* (blemish, # 4583); → *mišḥāt* (disfigured, # 5425); → *nākeh* (crippled, smitten, # 5783); → *'wr* I (be blind, # 6422); → *psḥ* (be lame, crippled, # 7174); → *ṣl'* I (limping condition, # 7519); → *qlṭ* I (defective [animal], # 7832); → *śr'* (deformed, mutilated, # 8594); → *t^eballul* (white spot in eye, # 9319)

R. K. Harrison/E. H. Merrill

7175	פֶּסַח

פֶּסַח (*pesaḥ*), Feast or sacrifice of Passover (# 7175).

ANE The etymology of the root *psḥ* is much disputed, and some very tenuous links have been established with the Akk. *pašāḫu,* to appease, and the Arab. *fasaḥa*, be/become wide (*ABD* 6:755; *ISBE* 3:676).

OT 1. *Usage*. The nom. *pesaḥ* is used for the festival celebration (Exod 12:48; 2 Kgs 23:21) and for the Passover sacrifice (Exod 12:11, 21, 27; Deut 16:2; 2 Chron 30:15, 18). The OT combines the Passover (a sacrifice slaughtered on the 14th day of the first month) with the Feast of the Unleavened Bread (a festival starting on the 15th day of the first month and lasting seven days) in its cultic commemoration of the exodus from Egypt (Deut 16:1-8), without either losing its respective distinguishable characteristics (*TWAT* 6:668).

2. *The Passover in recent interpretation.*

(a) Wellhausen (83-120) considered that the Feasts of Passover and Unleavened Bread were only combined during the reign of Josiah and that the agricultural Feast of the Unleavened Bread, not the Passover, was kept as a national Israelite feast before Josiah (Exod 23:14-17; 2 Kgs 23:21-23). Kraus (61-72) argued that the Passover was celebrated at a central shrine during the time of the judges (as part of an amphictionic cult) and that the eating of unleavened bread was already part of the feast at this stage (Judg 4:19-23; 5:10-12). Josiah, therefore, only reestablished an already existing feast during his reformation of the cult. Haran also believes that the Passover was always connected with a temple site and Josiah only revived centralized celebration.

(b) Segal (101-11, 157-65, 187) has pointed out parallels between the Passover and the Bedouin custom of smearing sacrificial blood on the entrance of a dwelling and the eating of the sacrificial meat during a common meal. An apotropaic purpose to ward off evil is thereby postulated as initial reason for the origin of the Passover, as a nomadic New Year's feast. Otto (42-45) postulates a nomadic origin of the Passover as apotropaic blood ritual that developed into a cultic portrayal of God's salvific rescue of Israel in Egypt, while the Feast of the Unleavened Bread is rooted in a feast at Gilgal celebrating the taking of the land by premonarchical Israel. In sharp contrast van Seters (123-26) connects the Passover with Deuteronomy and the Feast of the Unleavened Bread as substitute for the Passover during the Exile.

(c) Despite a lack of scholarly consensus about the origin and development of the Passover, most scholars agree that the Feasts of Passover and Unleavened Bread were originally two separate cultic entities that exhibited some resemblance with non-Israelite feasts (*IDB* 3:664).

3. *Proposals about the combination of the Feasts of Passover and Unleavened Bread.* The references to the feasts in the Pentateuch (Exod 12-13; 23:14-19; 34:18-26; Lev 23:4-8; Num 28:16-25; Deut 16:1-8) show how these two feasts could be combined, linked or juxtaposed, while maintaining their specific characteristics. This fact has led to attempts at reconstructing the development of the two feasts.

(a) There has been speculation about the exact origins of the two feasts, but this is as futile as their etymological interpretation. In the biblical record the Passover sacrifice and the eating of unleavened bread commemorated God's intervention during the Exodus (for theories on origins see *ABD* 6:760).

(b) Some scholars propose a process of historization or, as Johnstone (40) prefers to call it, "secondary association." In this view Deuteronomy provides a rationale for both feasts, the remembering of the affliction and the hasty departure during the Exodus (16:3). It also stipulates one single cultic place selected by God, which is usually connected with Josiah's centralization and which changed the celebration from a family feast to a national festival (2 Kgs 23:21-23). Moreover, in this view the priestly references to the two feasts are historicized by being embedded in the Exodus narrative (Exod 12) and show how the ancient Passover custom of family festivities was reestablished, after Josiah's centralization, during the Exile (Zimmerli, 124). The possible tradition-historical connection between the Exodus narrative and the northern kingdom is being explored (Cooper & Goldstein, 36-37).

4. *Theological interpretation of the Feasts of Passover and Unleavened Bread.*

(a) The two spring feasts commemorate God's springtime intervention when he brought Israel out of Egypt and eventually into the Promised Land. It thereby marked the beginning of Israel's history as God's people (de Vaux, 492-93). In this regard the commemoration of God's intervention with the Exodus should not obliterate the roots of the Feast of the Unleavened Bread in the spring harvest festival. The joy and the gratitude prevalent in the celebration of the gathering of grain produce provides a significant backdrop to God's liberation of Israel. In addition to the safeguarding of the fertility of the land, Israel took on the commemoration of their foundation as God's people (Albertz, 89-91). The commemorative elements of the feasts were the sacrificial blood, which pointed to God's protection against the tenth plague of the firstborn, the unleavened bread, which signified the haste of Israel preparing for the Exodus, and the bitter herbs, which referred to the Egyptian bondage.

(b) Certain important theological focal points can be distinguished in the Deut and priestly descriptions of the two feasts. According to Deut it is the national celebration of the whole of Israel taking place at the temple in Jerusalem. The priestly instructions create religious intimacy with the redevelopment of the Passover as a family feast and maintain the awe with regards to the cultic presence of God by keeping the Feast of the Unleavened Bread linked to the temple (Johnstone, 178). After the destruction of the Jerusalem temple, the families were the vehicles of the Exodus theology, and they did not lose this function with the rebuilding of the temple (Albertz, 410-11).

(c) The selection of the Passover sacrifice falls on the tenth day of the first month, and it is remarkable that the "scapegoat" is driven out on the tenth day of the seventh month with the Day of Atonement (Rost, 101-3). Thus, two important seasonal changes of the agricultural year (spring and fall) are matched by corresponding cultic activity (Passover and Atonement) and open up the possibility of a certain theological coherence. (→ Passover: Theology)

P-B 1. *Elephantine texts*. A letter written in 419 BC apparently refers to the two festivals, and this indicates that biblical prescriptions in this regard were also adhered to in practice outside of Palestine (*ABD* 6:759).

2. *LXX*. The nom. *pesaḥ* is frequently translated with *pascha* and a few times with *phaska*, which probably presuppose Aram. *pasḥā'*. The nom. *maṣṣôt* is translated by *azyma*.

3. *Qumran*. Only the Temple Scroll directly mentions the Passover (17:6-9) and the Feast of the Unleavened Bread (17:10-16).

NT The NT considers Passover and the Feast of the Unleavened Bread as one festival (Mark 14:2, 12) and makes numerous references to both feasts in narrating the Last Supper and Jesus as the paschal sacrifice (Matt 26:1-46; Mark 14:1-51; Luke 22:1-53; John 13:1-38). Only during the second century did the celebration of Easter with the commemoration of Jesus as the Passover lamb become general (*NIDNTT* 1:634).

Feasts & festivals: → *bikkûrîm* (early or firstfruits, # 1137); → *ḥag* (procession, round dance, festival, feast, # 2504); → *ḥ^anukkâ* (dedication, Feast of Dedication, # 2853); → *mô'ēd* (appointed time, # 4595); → *maṣṣôt* (Feast of the Unleavened Bread, # 5174a); → *marzēaḥ* (cultic feast, funeral meal, # 5301); → *sukkôt* (Feast of Tabernacles, # 6109a); → *'^aṣārâ* (festive assembly, # 6809); → *pûrîm* (festival of Purim, # 7052a); → *pesaḥ* (Feast or sacrifice of Passover, # 7175 [→ **Passover: Theology**]); → *rō'š ḥōdeš* (festival of the new Moon, # 8031a); → *rō'š haššānâ* (beginning of the year, # 8031b); → *šābu'ôt* (feast of Weeks, # 8651a); → *šabbāt* (sabbath, # 8701 [→ **Sabbath: Theology**])

BIBLIOGRAPHY

ABD 6:755-65; *IDB* 3:663-68; *ISBE* 3:675-79; *NIDNTT* 1:632-35; *TDNT* 5:898-904; *TWAT* 6:659-82; *TWOT* 2:728-29; R. Albertz, *A History of Israelite Religion in the Old Testament Period*, 1 & 2, 1994; A. Cooper & B. R. Goldstein, "Exodus and *Maṣṣôt* in History and Tradition," *Maarav* 8, 15-37; R. De Vaux, *AncIsr*, 1961, 484-93; M. Haran, *Temples and Temple-Service in Ancient Israel*, 1978; W. Johnstone, *Exodus*, OTG, 1990; idem, "The Two Theological Versions of the Passover Pericope in Exodus," *FS R. Davidson*, ed. R. P. Carroll, JSOTSup 138, 1992, 160-78; H.-J. Kraus, *Gottesdienst in Israel*, 1962; E. Otto, *Das Mazzotfest in Gilgal*, 1975; idem and T. Schramm, *Festival and Joy*, 1980; L. Rost, *Das kleine Credo*, 1965; J. B. Segal, *The Hebrew Passover*, 1963; J. van Seters, *The Life of Moses*, 1994; J. Wellhausen, *Prolegomena to the History of Israel*, 1885; W. Zimmerli, *OTTO*, 1984.

Hendrik L. Bosman

7177 (*pissēaḥ*, lame), → # 7174

7178 (*pāsîl*, cultic image, statue of a god), → # 7181

7180 (*psl*, carve, hew out of stone, dress), → # 7181

7181	פֶּסֶל

פֶּסֶל (*pesel*), pl. *p^esîlîm*, *פָּסִיל (**pāsîl*), cultic image, statue of a god (# 7181, # 7178); פסל (*psl*), q. carve, hew out of stone, dress (# 7180).

ANE In the Northwest Sem. languages (Mish. Heb., Punic, Nab., Jewish Aram., Syr.) *psl* has a general meaning of carve, chisel, dress (stone); cf. Punic *mnṣbt pslt* (*KAI* carved stele). In Ugar. *pslm* is the product of work in stone and wood (cf. *psl qšt, psl ḥẓm*, maker of bows, maker of arrows, *UT*, 1024: rev. 18-19). The meaning of the Heb. nom. form has no parallel in the cognate languages.

OT 1. The vb. occurs only 6x in the OT. Only in 1 Kgs 5:18[32] does it have a neutral meaning (shape the wood and dress the stone for the temple). Elsewhere it is used for the shaping of the stone tablets (Exod 34:1, 4; Deut 10:1, 3), in conscious contrast to the making of proscribed images (cf. Hab 2:18).

2. The nom. forms have a meaning not paralleled in the cognate languages or derivable from the root. The term *pesel* is the most general word for an image of a god and may refer to any form of manufacture, whether sculpted from wood or stone, sculpted from wood and overlaid with gold or silver (Deut 7:25), or cast in a mold. It is not always to be distinguished as a "carved" (archaic "graven") image from the *massēkâ* or cast image, as comes out in the hendiadys *pesel ûmassēkâ*, a gold (or silver) covered image (less likely; consecrated image).

Images are rarely attacked in the deut. history: the sections concerned with images are 1 Kgs 15; 21:25-26 (in parentheses in NIV, probably a gloss); 2 Kgs 17; 21; 23. In all these places Ezekiel's word *gillûlîm* is used, which is rarely used anywhere else. More usually the objects of disapproval are either foreign gods (e.g., "the Baals" [cf. Baal]) or much more commonly the high places (*bāmôt* [→ # 1195]), poles (*'ašērîm*, → # 895), pillars (*maṣṣēbôt*, → # 5167), and cultic prostitutes (*qᵉdēšîm*, # 7728). Outside of Judg 17-18 *psl* is used only in the anti-Israel polemic of 2 Kgs 17:41 and for the image of Asherah that Manasseh had made (2 Kgs 21:7 ‖ "the Asherah pole" in 2 Kgs 23:6). In Judg 17-18 *pesel* appears to represent an image associated with Yahweh. While this is presented in the context of the anarchy of premonarchic Israel, there is none of the horror of images found in some writings. Images are part of the paraphernalia of shrines, along with ephod and teraphim (17:5; cf. altars, pillars, and [Asherah-] poles [Deut 7:5, 25]). Judg 18:31 is particularly significant, for where the shrine in Dan had an image to represent the presence of Yahweh (and ephod and teraphim, Judg 17:5), the temple at Shiloh (Judg 18:31) had the ark (1 Sam 3:3).

3. Some passages see the images as images of gods (e.g., Deut 12:3). They are banned because no image of Yahweh must be made (or can be made because they do not know what he looks like; cf. Deut 4:15-16, again a polemic, for it is most unlikely that people saw their god images as portraits) and other gods must not be worshiped in any way.

4. Some discussions treat the *pesel* itself as the object of worship (2 Kgs 17:41; 2 Chron 33:22; Mic 5:13[12] ‖ pillars). The object, however, is not recognized as the image of a god (i.e., a visual representation of some aspect of the nature of the god, not necessarily a portrait). Rather, it is declared to be merely an image of some natural object (cf. Deut 4:16-17; *tabnît* of man or woman or animal or bird).

5. In the satires the poet makes fun of the idol-maker, who uses the same wood for an image and to make a fire, and then worships the image. This is most clearly seen in the "idol parody" poems (cf. Roth). This kind of polemic is not aimed at proselytizing, since no worshiper of another religion would accept the caricature, but at minimizing the attraction of such worship to the Judaeans of the Diaspora living amongst

Babylonians, Egyptians, and Greeks. Many of these poems have been collected in Isa 40-45; cf. also 48:5. But others may be found in Jer (e.g., 10:1-16), Hab (2:18-19), and (using *'ṣb*) Psalms.

6. In the sections related to the "second commandment" (esp. Deut 5:8; Exod 20:4), it is specifically said that the image is not to be of anything anywhere and that it is not to be worshiped. This corresponds with the theology of the "idol parodies," but it is likely that in the original shorter form of the commandments, it was the making of an image of Yahweh that was interdicted. And Deut 5:11 ǁ Exod 20:7 may have prohibited calling an image Yahweh.

P-B The LXX normally translates *pesel* by *glyptos*. The genre of idol parodies continues in Ep. Jer. (*Bar.* 6), Bel; *Jub.* 12:2-5; 20:8-9; Wisd 13:10-19; 15:7-13. In the canonical Dan 3 it is the statue that is said to be worshiped (vv. 5, 10, 12, 14, 15, 18), and in Bel (additional ch., Dan 14) the "idol" Bel has to be proved to be alive. So the priests, to avoid embarrassment, enter by a secret door and eat the food set aside for Bel to eat (cf. the food of the offering as in the temple of Jerusalem, 1 Kgs 7:48; cf. 1 Sam 21:6).

Idolatry: → *'ᵉlîl* (Nothing, # 496); → *'ᵃšērâ* (wooden cult-object, pole, goddess, # 895); → *gillûlîm* (images, idols, # 1658); → *dāgôn* (Dagon, # 1837); → *kᵉmôš* (Chemosh [god of the Moabites], # 4019); → *mōlek* (Molech, # 4891); → *massēkâ* I (cast statuette, # 5011); → *mipleṣet* (terrible thing, dreadful object, # 5145); → *semel* (image, # 6166); → *'āṣāb* (god-image, # 6773); → *'aštōret* (Astarte, # 6956); → *pesel* (cultic image, statue of a god, # 7181); → *tōmer* II (scarecrow, # 9473); → *tᵉrāpîm* (figurines, mask, # 9572); → **Idolatry: Theology**

Bibliography

TWAT 6:688-97; W. M. W. Roth, "For Life, He Appeals to Death (Wis 13:18)," *CBQ* 37, 1975, 20-47; S. Schroer, *In Israel gab es Bilder*, 1987.

Judith M. Hadley

7184	פעה

פעה (*p'h*), q. groan in childbirth (# 7184).

ANE Arab., Aram., Syr., and postbiblical Heb. attest the vb. meaning to bleat.

OT Attested once in the OT, this vb. describes the battle cry Yahweh will utter as he rouses himself to deliver Israel (Isa 42:14, cf. v. 13), crying out like a woman in childbirth (NIV). No derivatives appear in the OT.

Groan, sigh, growl: → *'nḥ* (sigh, groan, # 634); → *'nq* (groan, # 650); → *hgh* I (groan, moan, sigh, meditate, muse, chirp, mutter, # 2047); → *hāgîg* (groan in prayer, # 2052); → *z'q* (cry, howl, wail, # 2410); → *n'q* (groan, # 5543); → *nhm* (growl, groan, # 5637); → *nwḥ* II (groan in anticipation, # 5664); → *p'h* (groan in childbirth, # 7184); → *š'g* (roar, # 8613)

David Thompson

7188	פעל

פעל (*p'l*), q. do, make, produce, practice, accomplish, perform (# 7188); מִפְעָל (*mip'āl*), nom. work (# 5148); פֹּעַל (*pō'al*), nom. work, deed(s), doing, conduct, wages (# 7189); פְּעֻלָּה (*pᵉ'ullâ*), nom. wages, punishment, reward, payment, deeds (# 7190).

ANE Phon. Pun. *p'l* (*yp'l*); Arab. *p'l*; OA *p'l*; Egyp. Aram *p'l*; Syr. *p^{e}'al*; Arab. *fa'ala*; OSA *f'l*; Ugar. *b'l* (?); cf. Aram. *'bd*.

OT 1. The vb. *p'l* occurs 57x in the OT, seventeen of which have God as subject. It is used exclusively in poetic passages, giving a heightened perspective to the assertions. It is found only in the q. With God as subject a number of things are asserted about him and his activities.

(a) He himself prepared (*p'l*) the mountain of his inheritance (i.e., Sinai and/or Zion in Canaan). It is his work, not the work of his people, and he will dwell there (*yšb*).

(b) Closely tied to this is the fact that Yahweh effects deliverance/salvation for his people and brings prosperity (Num 23:23; Isa 26:12). His works of salvation are his alone, not created by his people. He brings his work of deliverance among his people to the very midst of the earth, thus effecting salvation (*pō'el y^{e}šû'ôt*, Ps 74:12). Moses feared that the nations would, because of Israel's disobedience and failure, claim that Yahweh had not done these things, thus making a mockery of both Israel and Yahweh (Deut 32:27).

(c) Yahweh bestows (*p'l*) his goodness (*ṭûb*) on all those who seek refuge/shelter in him, especially fulfilling his covenant promises and blessings.

(d) Elihu, correctly, calls the Lord his Maker (*p'l*), ascribing righteousness (*ṣedeq*) to him. He continues further to observe that the Lord brings, effects (*p'l*) events and circumstances on persons to bring them back to him, to turn someone back from the pit to enjoy light and life again (Job 33:29). He further claims that Job's "sins" (*hṭ'* ‖ *pš'*) do not really touch or effect God's character or wisdom and asks Job (*l^{e}* or *b^{e}*) what his sins do (*p'l*) to God. According to Elihu, one's deeds do not affect (*p'l*) God (35:6-8). Whether they are sinful or righteous, they do not change God's nature. (→ Elihu; → Job: Theology)

(e) The prophet Habakkuk reveals that God himself is "doing" (*p'l*) something, an evil in his day—the Babylonian Empire to destroy Israel (Hab 1:5). This extends, however, beyond the Babylonians—Yahweh has been doing (*p'l*) this marvel from the beginning with all nations (here = Cyrus, Isa 41:2). However, God's actions (*pō'^{a}lîm*) produce only good; judgment on evil is a righteous act for God.

2. The subject of the vb., of course, makes all the difference. The root (*p'l*) of the vb. does not describe an intrinsically good or bad act or deed. When persons are the subjects, a variety of things are possible that are not possible when God is the subject. While God's works are all righteous, Israel's/a person's deeds are often evil.

(a) Hosea's message to Ephraim is that they practice (*p'l*) deceit (*šqr*) and treachery. God cannot, therefore, heal them (Hos 7:1). These persons can only expect woe; they, unlike God, are producers of evil (*p'l rā'*) even when they should be silent, resting upon their bed (Mic 2:1). The adulteress is especially deceitful in her production/action of evil—she denies it, exclaiming: "I've done nothing wrong (*'āwen*)" (Prov 30:20).

(b) However, humans can work good/righteousness like their Creator. He who follows the Lord's instructions walks blamelessly (*tâmîm*) and practices/does (*p'l*) righteousness (*ṣedeq*); that person will be able to dwell in the Lord's house. It is possible for persons to imitate God, but God never imitates fallen humanity. Humans do their best when they do (*p'l*) no iniquity (*'awlâ*)—i.e., they walk in his ways (Ps 15:2;

cf. Zeph 2:3). Even the clouds, the world of God's creation, do what he commands (*ṣwh*), accomplishing their appointed functions.

3. The nom. *pō'al* can be noted under the same headings above for the vb. It designates the (a) work/s of God, and (b) the work/deeds of human beings. The kinds of things done can be categorized further:

(a) The Lord's works in creation and providence (*p'l*) are complete/perfect (*tāmîm*) and are morally, ethically approved (Deut 32:4). His work is to be extolled and praised (Job 36:24). The word regularly describes God's works/deeds in history and nature (Ps 44:1[2]). These are to be pondered (77:12[13]). As a result, his works (*p'l*) should be declared. His works in history should foster faith and trust in Yahweh (95:9). His future work of rousing nations even exceeds his past deeds (Hab 1:5; cf. vb. above 1.e).

(b) The work (*p'l*) of Levi's hands, the priestly line of Israel, was diligently prayed for by Moses, as he implores that God may be pleased with Levi's leading Israel in worship and teaching the people Yahweh's laws (Deut 33:11).

(c) The son of Jehoiada performed great exploits (2 Sam 23:20-22 [*p'l* ‖ *'śh*]; 1 Chron 11:22) on behalf of Yahweh and King David. This nom. was used to describe good deeds performed by Ruth (Ruth 2:12) on behalf of Naomi. It describes the deeds of persons both good and bad (Ps 28:4), and God points out the evil deeds of persons (Job 36:9). Both the evil works and those responsible are judged (Job 34:11; Prov 24:12; Isa 1:31). Evil persons produce evil, violent actions (Isa 59:6), and whatever is done under the auspices of deceit and evil will not prove to be permanent (Prov 21:6).

(d) Following are other areas where the word is used:

(i) It is used to describe the lot of all humankind—the daily work they must accomplish. Human beings must attend to their work (*p'l*) as one of the regularities of existence, along with the rhythm of the creation (Ps 104:23).

(ii) The Lord not only judges the individual for his or her deeds, but deals with the actions of nations. He repays the nations for evil deeds, Babylon being the prime example (Jer 50:29). She is to be repaid according to what she has done (*p'l* ‖ *'śh*).

(iii) The work God appoints to persons is to be rewarded regularly. In fact, the work (*p'l*) a person performs is to be paid for in wages (Jer 22:13).

(iv) Pagan gods also claimed to have performed great works, but their deeds are considered less than nothing (Isa 41:24) while God's works are effective, real, and true (Isa 43:9-18).

(v) Deeds and behavior are valuable. They indicate the nature of the inner heart of a person, pointing clearly to the character of even a child (Prov 20:11). One is known by his or her deeds.

(vi) The temptation to get vengeance for evil deeds is deadly. Evil deeds should not be repaid (*p'l* ‖ *'śh*), for then one becomes evil also (Prov 24:29).

4. The case is similar with *pe'ullâ*, used 14x in the OT. For instance, much like *pō'al,* it designates the wages due a hired man. They are not to be held back even overnight (Lev 19:13). It describes reforms carried out by King Asa (2 Chron 15:7) to restore Israel to approval before God. It designates the reward to be given to the Servant of Yahweh (Isa 49:4). It refers to the actions of men in a sweeping way in Ps 17:4, condemning them all as deeds of violence. The righteous man keeps himself from these actions. Some uses are just like *pō'al* (e.g., Ps 28:5; cf. Isa 5:12). Evil works are

done by the wicked man (*rāšā'*) (Prov 11:18). Good faithful deeds will be regarded (lit., get a wage; Isa 40:10; 62:11; 65:7; Jer 31:16).

God gives a just reward to the wicked (Ps 109:20). Yahweh has even foreign kings labor for him (e.g., Nebuchadnezzar, Ezek 29:20) and rewards them—this time with victory over Egypt.

5. *mip'ālâ* is used 3x. In Ps 46:8[9] it refers to the judgments of the Lord upon the earth among nations hostile to him and his people. On the other hand, it refers to the great works of deliverance for his people in 66:5. In Prov 8:22 it denotes the creative acts of God in the beginning, which were all preceded and performed by wisdom.

P-B The LXX translates the vb. most often with *ergazomai*, effect, work, bring about; *po'al/pe'ullâ* are usually translated by *ergon/ergasia/misthos*, wage(s). A few other words are employed once each to render these noms.

In the DSS scrolls the vb. is found meaning to practice evil (1QH 14:14; 1QpHab 12:8; 8:13). God is also found functioning as the subject (1QH 11:33). The nom. *p^e'ullâ* is found 6x and indicates the deeds done by human beings according to the scheme of God, who works evidently through the two spirits (cf. 1QH 11:35; 1QS 4:15); 1QS 4:25).

In Mish. Heb. the vb. continued to mean "work" and esp. "deal" (e.g., Lev R. S. 27; Lam R 3:33). Both man and God are used as the subject in different places (see further Jastrow 2:1202). The nom. *pô'ēl* meaning either work or laborer was employed (e.g., MidR Till to Ps 44; B. Mets II 9[3ob]). For further refs. see Jastrow 2:1144-45.

Deed, act, misdeed, work: → *gml* (accomplish, commit, achieve, ripen, # 1694); → *m^{e}lā'kâ* (work, duties, task, # 4856); → *'ll* I (act, wipe out, deal with, harm, glean, # 6618); → *'śh* I (make, do, prepare, create, work, service, # 6913); → *p'l* (do, make, produce, practice, accomplish, perform, # 7188)

BIBLIOGRAPHY

THAT 2:461-66; *TWAT* 6:697-703; R. Humbert, "L'emploi du verbe *pā'al* et de ses dérivés substantifs en hébreu biblique," *ZAW* 65, 1953, 35-44; J. T. Willis, "On the Text of Micah 21aα-β," *Bib* 48, 1967, 534-41, esp. 536.

Eugene Carpenter

7189 (*pō'al*, work, deed, conduct, wages), → # 7188

7190 (*p^e'ullâ*, wages, punishment, reward, deeds), → # 7188

7192	פעם

פעם (*p'm*), q. stir; ni., hitp. be disturbed, feel disturbed (# 7192).

OT The vb. *p'm* appears 5x in the OT, 1x in the q., 3x in the ni., and 1x in the hitp. In the q. (Judg 13:25), Samson was stirred by the Spirit of the Lord. This indicates the power with which he was endowed. The unusual deeds he did was the result of the work of the Spirit of God in him. In Ps 77:4[5] the poet is so much disturbed (ni.) by his worries that he is unable to speak. In Gen 41:8 the ni. describes the emotion of Pharaoh, who was disturbed by his dreams. Also in Dan 2:3 the ni. describes how Daniel's spirit (*rûaḥ*, as in Gen 41:8) was disturbed. The vb. occurs in the same way and with the same meaning in the hitp. in Dan 2:1.

Confusion, agitation: → *bwk* (be agitated, wander in agitation, # 1003); → *bll* (confuse, mix, # 1176); → *bl'* III (be confused, confused, # 1182); → *hwm* (throw into confusion, be in uproar, # 2101); → *kmr* (agitated, # 4023); → *'wh* (disturb, distress, agitate, pervert, do wrong, # 6390); → *p'm* (be disturbed, feel disturbed, # 7192); → *rhb* (assail, press, pester, alarm, confuse, # 8104); → *r'm* II (be agitated, be confused, # 8307); → *tmh* (be benumbed, be stunned, shocked, gaze, # 9449)

Harry F. van Rooy

7193	פַּעַם

פַּעַם (*pa'am*), foot, step, occurrence, time (# 7193).

ANE The nom. appears in Akk. *pēmu/pēnu* (*AHw*, 854), in Ugar. (*p'n*, foot [*UT*, # 2076], and *pam*, time [*UT* # 1998]), and in Phoen. *p'm*, foot, time. Both Heb. and Phoen. use the phrase "hear a voice many times." Thus Ps 106:43-44 states that "many times (*pe'amîm rabbôt*) he delivered them ... when he heard their cry," and may be compared to Phoen. (*KAI* 68.5), "for he heard the voices many times" (*p'mt brbm*). Cf Avishur:13.

OT 1. *pa'am* means not only "time" but "foot" or "sole of the foot." Possibly one way of keeping time was by the beating or pounding of the sole of the foot on the ground, and this would explain the connection between the two different nuances of the word. Heb. shares with other languages the fact that a word for "time" may have another sense. For example, French *temps* is both "time" and "weather."

2. The more frequent word for time (e.g., in a phrase like "at that time," which provides the temporal setting of an incident) is *'ēt*, but where the nuance overlaps with "occasion," as in the expression "three times a year," *pa'am* is more likely to be used (Barr, 108). Thus *pa'am* is to *'ēt* what *fois* in French is to *temps*, and what *Mal* in German is to *Zeit*, i.e., occasion vs. time. But even here this difference between *pa'am* and *'ēt* should not be considered an absolute distinction, for one finds in the postexilic book of Neh (9:28) the phrase *rabbôt 'ittîm*, many times.

3. *pa'am* occurs 106x in the OT. Once it means "hoofbeats" (Judg 5:28), once "anvil" (Isa 41:7); 3x it refers to the feet of the ark (Exod 25:12; 37:3; 1 Kgs 8:30); 12x it means "foot, step" (2 Kgs 19:24; Ps 17:5; 57:6 [7], etc.). The remaining 89x are in expressions or idioms of time.

The dual *pa'āmayim*, twice, occurs 8x (Gen 27:36; 41:2, etc.). Expressions involving various numbers of times (e.g., "three times" or "seven times") occur 44x. Twice (Ps 106:43; Eccl 7:22) the expression "many times" occurs.

4. The idiom *kᵉpa'am bᵉpa'am* is used of successive occurrences (Judg 16:20; 20:30-31; 1 Sam 3:10; 20:25). Cf. also Balaam's decision not to resort to sorcery against Israel "as at other times" (Num 24:1), i.e., a reference to his first two oracles (25:7-10, 18-24).

5. When *pa'am* means feet, the reference may be to one's walk and lifestyle before God. Cf. Ps 17:5; 119:133.

6. Also, feet represent the means by which one may be tripped, and hence they are the exposed and vulnerable part of the body for which the enemy lies in wait (Ps 57:6[7]; 140:4[5]; Prov 29:5).

7. The first use of the nom. in the OT is Gen 2:23, "This is now (*zō't happa'am*) bone of my bones and flesh of my flesh." The thrust of the idiom (cf. NJPSV this one at last) is Adam's way of contrasting this new creature God has brought to him with the animals God had recently (v. 19) brought before him.

8. The idiom "just once more" (*'ak happa'am*) occurs before Abraham's last phrase in his intervention before God on behalf of Sodom and Gomorrah (Gen 18:32). He prefaces his request that God save these two cities (if only because of a nucleus of ten righteous people) with this idiom because "he is aware how audacious is his unremitting questioning" (Westermann, *Genesis* 1:292).

It also is used by Pharaoh to Moses during the eighth plague (Exod 10:17), "Now forgive my sin once more." This request relates to Pharaoh's earlier admission, "This time [*happa'am*] I have sinned" (9:27). The tragedy here is that Pharaoh admitted his sin, but he kept on sinning.

Leg, loins, foot, thigh: → *b^ehôn* (thumb, big toe, # 984); → *ḥ^alāṣayim* (loins, # 2743); → *yārēk* (thigh, leg, # 3751); → *kesel* I (loins, flank/side, # 4072); → *midrāk* (foot-print, # 4534); → *marg^elôt* (place of feet, # 5274); → *motnayim* (loins, hips, # 5516); → *na'al* (sandal, # 5837); → *paḥad* II (thigh, # 7066); → *pa'am* (foot, step, time, # 7193); → *qarsōl* (ankle, # 7972); → *regel* (foot, # 8079); → *šôq* (thigh, leg, # 8797)
Time: → *'ōbēd* (ever after, # 7); → *'ōpen* (right time, # 698); → *gîl* I (stage of life, # 1636); → *zmn* (be appointed, # 2374); → *'ôlām* (long time or duration, # 6409); → *'ēt* (time, # 6961); → *pa'am* (foot, step, time, # 7193); → *peta'* (instant, # 7353); → *tāmîd* (continuance, unceasingness, regular offering, # 9458)

BIBLIOGRAPHY
Avishur, "Studies of Stylistic Features Common to the Phoenician Inscriptions and the Bible," *UF* 8, 1976, 1-22; J. Barr, *Biblical Words For Time*, 1969.

Victor Hamilton

7194	פַּעֲמוֹן

פַּעֲמוֹן (*pa^amôn*), nom. bell (on priest's robe) (# 7194).

OT 1. *pa^amôn* comes 7x in the prescriptive account of Exod 28:33-34 and the corresponding description of the making of the clothing in 39:25-26. The derivation of the word is uncertain, although there may be some connection with the root *p'm*, and BDB, 821-22 suggests that a concept such as the English strike or stroke underlies various meanings of the vb. and nom. *pa'am* as well as the meaning bell for *pa^amôn*.

2. The bells alternate with pomegranates, run round the lower hem of the high priestly robe (*m^e'îl*), and are made of pure gold (39:25), like other elements of the high-priestly dress (28:14) or the furniture in the Holy Place (25:31). It is not known how many bells there were (later sources suggest 12, 24, 36, 50, 70, 71, 72, 360), or whether the bells had clappers or sounded when they touched other bells. The note that they were to sound when the high priest entered or left the Holy Place (28:35) is taken by Houtman as merismus for their continual sounding during his time of ministry. This suggests that their function was not oriented to the people (as stated in Sir 45:9, "as a reminder to his people"), the priests, or the Levites, or even the high priest himself.

Some (e.g., Dölger) think that the bells have an apotropaic function, protecting the high priest from demons inhabiting the threshold (cf. Exod 28:35, "so that he will not die"). However, the priestly texts never associate demons with the sanctuary, and it is implied that any irregularity in the high-priestly dress invites punishment by death (28:43; 11QT 35:6). Their function is more likely to be directed to God, whose attention is drawn to the high priest and his dress, and particularly to the names of the tribes of Israel on the high priest's shoulders and breastpiece (28:12, 29) (Houtman). The purpose of the bells and pomegranates is to minister or to serve (*šrt* [# 9250]; 39:26). The bells provide a dimension of sound that reinforces the senses of smell and sight, all of which reinforce the communication between God and his people that is at the heart of the priestly ritual and is the source of divine presence and blessing.

P-B The alternating bells and pomegranates suggest beauty to Josephus (*Ant* 3, 160) and harmony between the senses of sight and hearing to Philo in *Migr. Abr.* 103-4. In *Vit. Mos.* 2, 119 and *Spec. Leg.* 1, 93 Philo states that the bells represent harmony between earth (symbolized by the flowers) and water (symbolized by the pomegranates).

Priests and levites: → *'abnēṭ* (sash, esp. of priests, # 77); → *'ēpôd* I (ephod, priestly garment, cult object, # 680); → *ḥōšen* (breast-piece of highpriest, # 3136); → *khn* (perform the duties of a priest, # 3912); → *kōmer* (pagan priest, # 4024); → *lēwî* (levite, # 4290); → *migbā'â* (head-band, # 4457); → *miknāsayim* (trousers, # 4829); → *pa'ᵃmôn* (bell [on priest's robe], # 7194); → *tašbēṣ* (checkered work, # 9587); → **Aaron: Theology**; → **Priests and Levites: Theology**

Bibliography

ABD 1:657; *ERE* 6:313-16; B. Bayer, *The Material Relics of Music in Ancient Palestine and Its Environs*, 1963; F. J. Dölger, "Die Glöckchen am Gewande des jüdischen Hohenpriesters nach der Ausdeutung jüdischer, heidnischer und frühchristlicher Schriftsteller," *Antike und Christentum* 4, 1934, 233-44; J. G. Frazer, *Folk-Lore in the Old Testament: Studies in Comparative Religion Legend and Law*, 3, 1919; C. Houtman, "On the Pomegranates and the Golden Bells of the High Priest's Mantle," *VT* 40, 1990, 223-29; E. Nestle, "Die Zahl der Granatäpfel und Glöckchen am Kleid des Hohenpriesters," *ZAW* 25, 1905, 205-6; idem, "Zu den Glocken am Gewand des Hohenpriesters," *ZAW* 32, 1912, 74.

P. Jenson

7196	פער

פער (*p'r*), open wide (# 7196).

ANE Cognates are Arab. *faġara* and Syr./Aram. *pᵉ'ar*.

OT 1. The vb. is used only in the q., and only 4x in BH. In order they are: (1) Job 16:10, used by Job as a figure of the disdain people feel toward him, "Men open their mouths to jeer at me," or "they gape at me with their mouth"; (2) Job 29:23, again by Job, but this time in a positive setting in which Job recalls how people of his community used to hang on his every word: "They ... drank in my words as the spring rain" (NIV), or more literally, "they opened their mouths as for the spring rain"; (3) Ps 119:131: "I open my mouth and pant, longing for your commands"; (4) Isa 5:14, a verse addressed by the prophet to those consumed with pleasure and possessions: "Therefore the grave [Sheol] enlarges its appetite and opens its mouth without limits." That is, death will swallow them up.

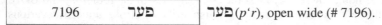

Opening, coming, entrance: → *bw'* (go, come, arrive, enter, # 995); → *p'r* (open wide, # 7196); → *pṣh* (open up, # 7198); → *pqḥ* (open, # 7219); → *ptḥ* I (open, conquer, surrender, set free, loosen, break up, # 7337)

Victor P. Hamilton

7198	פצה

פצה (*pṣh*), q. open up (# 7198).

ANE Arab. *faṣāy*, split (*HALAT* 898).

OT 1. The most frequent object of *pṣh* is mouth. Cf. Gen 4:11; Num 16:30; Deut 11:6; Judg 11:35 ("I have made a vow to the LORD"), 11:36 ("you have given your word to the LORD"); cf. Job 35:16; Ps 22:13[14]; Isa 10:14; Lam 2:16; 3:46; Ezek 2:8. Mouth is not used as the subject of *pṣh* except in Ps 66:14 (where the vb.'s subj. is lips) and 144:7, 11.

2. In a few instances *pṣḥ* is used interchangeably with *ptḥ*. Thus, in the case of the punishment against Korah and others, Moses starts with, "If ... the earth opens (*pṣḥ*) its mouth and swallows them ..." (Num 16:30). Yet in the fulfillment verse (Num 16:32, "and the earth opened its mouth)," *ptḥ* is used. In two subsequent recallings of this event, Deut 11:6 uses the *pṣh* of Num 16:30, while Ps 106:17 uses the *ptḥ* of Num 16:32. Similarly, when God says to Ezekiel, "Open your mouth and eat what I give you" (Ezek 2:8), the word for "open" is *pṣh*. Just four verses later (Ezek 3:2), Ezekiel responds with, "So I opened my mouth, and he gave me the scroll to eat," and here the vb. for "open" is *ptḥ*.

3. The ground is a wide, open-mouthed receptacle that receives anything that comes its way, be it shed blood (Gen 4:11) or the human body (Num 16:30; Deut 11:6). While the vb. open may or may not be present, being swallowed by the earth is a theme present in both epic poetry (Exod 15:12, "and the earth swallowed them") and in the famous incident in Num 16. Cf. also the idea of being swallowed by the watery depths (Ps 69:15[16]).

4. In the case of Dathan and Abiram their consignment to the grave/Sheol via earth's mouth is ironic. Summoned by Moses, they refused to come (up) (*'lh*, Num 16:12, 14). As a result they would go down (*yrd*, 16:30, 33). For complaining that God/Moses had brought them up (*'lh*) only to kill them (*mût*, 16:13), they would go down alive (*yrd ḥayyîm*) to the grave/Sheol (16:30, 33).

5. One may open his mouth in foolishness (Job 35:16), in meanness (Lam 2:6; 3:46), or in savageness (Ps 22:13[14]). In the last three of these four references the expression "open one's mouth" occurs in the genre of lament literature.

6. The meaning "deliver me" (Ps 144:7, 11) is unusual, but, as in the three references listed in the previous paragraph, the vb. appears in a lament psalm in which the psalmist prays to God for deliverance from those who are making life miserable for him.

Opening, coming, entrance: → *bw'* (go, come, arrive, enter, # 995); → *p'r* (open wide, # 7196); → *pṣh* (open up, # 7198); → *pqḥ* (open, # 7219); → *ptḥ* I (open, conquer, surrender, set free, loosen, break up, # 7337)

Victor P. Hamilton

7200	פצח

פצח (*pṣḥ* I), break forth with or break into singing (# 7200); פצח (*pṣḥ* II), pi. break in pieces (hapleg. in Mic 3:3; # 7200).

ANE The vb. *pṣḥ*, defined from its semantic context in the OT, has little in common with possible ANE cognates. The closest vb. to be found is the Akk. *peṣû*, become bright or white (*AHw* 2, 857).

OT 1. The vb. *pṣḥ* occurs several times in Isa (once in Ps 98:4) and mostly in the imperative form. In all contexts it is applied to the happy and joyous reaction of the redeemed—free from suffering and oppression (Isa 14:7; 44:23; 49:13; 52:9; 54:1). In 14:7 it is explicitly used in relation to the eschatological peace (*šālôm*; → # 8934) as result of God's salvation. In all these contexts the vb. designates the joyous "outbreak into singing."

2. The homonym *pṣḥ* II occurs only in an oracle of judgment against the leaders of Judah, who "break their [the people's] bones in pieces" (Mic 3:3).

P-B The Rabb. usage of the vb. *pṣḥ* signifies meanings similar to the Akk. cognate (i.e., be bright) and to its more common usage in the OT (i.e., breaking forth with joy; cf. Jastrow, 1204).

Praising, singing, thanksgiving: → *hll* II (praise, be praiseworthy, boast, exult, # 2146); → *zmr* I (make music, sing praise, # 2376); → *ydh* II (acknowledge, give thanks, praise, # 3344); → *nwh* II (praise, # 5658); → *'nh* IV (sing, # 6702); → *pṣḥ* I (break forth with or break into singing, # 7200); → *rômēm* (exalt, # 8123a); → *šbḥ* I (commend, praise, honor, # 8655); → *šyr* (sing, # 8876); → *tnh* (recite, commemorate, # 9480)

Philip J. Nel

7201 (*peṣîrâ*, blunt?), → # 7210

7202	פצל

פצל (*pṣl*), pi. strip (# 7202); פְּצָלוֹת (*p^eṣālôt*), nom. strips (# 7203).

ANE Aram. *pṣl*, strip, peel, nom. strips (*HAD*, 224); Mish. Heb. *pṣl* (pi.), split, peel, lay bare; hi. split; ni. be peeled/streaked (Jastrow, 1205); Syr. split (Payne Smith, 454); Mand. cut out (*MdD*, 376); Sam. *faṣala*, peel off bark (*HALAT* 898); Arab. divide, cut off (Wehr, 715).

OT *pṣl* is synonymous with *ḥśp*, bare, peel in Gen 30:37-38, where Jacob "peels" (pi. 2x) white "strips" (pl. nom.) on dark branches.

Bare, naked, destitute, stripped: → *ḥśp* I (strip, bare, # 3106); → *'rh* (make bare, be poured out, # 6867); → *'ārôm* (naked, # 6873); → *'rr* (strip bare, be leveled, # 6910); → *pṣl* (strip, # 7202); → *pšṭ* (take off [clothes], attack, strip, # 7320); → *š^epî* (barren height, # 9155)

Boyd V. Seevers

7203 (*p^eṣālôt*, strips), → # 7202

7204	פצם

פצם (*psm*), split open (# 7204).

ANE Cf. Arab. *faṣama*, crush, shatter; Aram. *p^{e}ṣam*, cut out.

OT The vb. is a hapleg. in Ps 60:2[4], "you [God] have shaken the land [Palestine] and torn it open." When God tears open a land, the result is "fractures" (*š^{e}bāreyhā* < *šbr*), which he is implored to heal. God's rejection of his people is comparable to a cosmic catastrophe, possibly an earthquake. All that God's people can do is pray (Ps 60:5[7], 11[13]) and confess (12[14]).

P-B See Jastrow 2:1205.

Split, breach, slice: → *bq'* (split, break open, # 1324); → *ḥrm* II (split, # 3050); → *ḥtr* (break through, # 3168); → *miśpāḥ* (breach of law, # 5384); → *plḥ* (cut into slices, split open, # 7114); → *pṣm* (split open, # 7204); → *prṣ* I (break through, burst out, be broken down, # 7287); → *r''* II (break in pieces, # 8318); → *rṣṣ* (crush, mash, break, # 8368); → *šbr* I (break, break down, smash, shatter, # 8689)

BIBLIOGRAPHY

A. A. Anderson, *Psalms*, NCB, 1:443; M. Dahood, *Psalms*, AB 2:77-78; F. E. Greenspahn, *Hapax Legomena in Biblical Hebrew*, 1984, 151-52.

Victor P. Hamilton

7205	פצע

פצע (*pṣ'*), q. bruise (# 7205); nom. פֶּצַע (*peṣa'*), wound, bruise (# 7206).

ANE Cognates for the Heb. vb. have been suggested in Arab. *faṣa'a*, squeeze (out), and Ugar. *pẓġ*, gash, wound (e.g., *pẓġm ġr*, those who gash [their] skin, *CTA* 19 1:184; *UT*, 246).

OT 1. The root refers to both open wounds and to bruises (the injuring of bodily tissues without actually rupturing the skin, even though subcutaneous hemorrhage may be present). The vb. appears 3x, twice of the results of a physical blow (1 Kgs 20:37; S of Songs 5:7) and once of castration, whether by crushing or cutting the spermatic cord (Deut 23:1[2]).

2. The nom. *peṣa'* occurs 8x, usually of physical wounding. Thus, those who become intoxicated are warned that their condition exposes them to physical harm (Prov 23:29-30). An unhappy Job laments that should he register a complaint with God, doubtless God would respond only by multiplying his wounds (Job 9:17).

(a) Several times the nom. is found in combination with *ḥabbûrâ*, wound, bruise. In Lamech's infamous "sword song" (Vos, 57; KD, *The Pentateuch*, 1956, 1:118-19), he boasts of killing "a man for wounding (*peṣa'*) me, a young man for injuring (*ḥabbûrâ*) me" (Gen 4:23). Similarly, the law of *lex talionis* prescribes "wound for wound" (*peṣa'*) and "bruise for bruise" (*ḥabbûrâ*) (Exod 21:25).

(b) A wound or bruise can have ethical or spiritual implications. Corporal punishment can be a salutary means of discipline and education: "Blows (*ḥabbûrâ*) and wounds (*peṣa'*) cleanse away evil, and beatings (*makkâ*) purge the inmost being" (Prov 20:30). Likewise, "Wounds from a friend can be trusted" (Prov 27:6). Here the emphasis is on nonphysical wounds, i.e., telling a friend the truth can at times be best for his welfare, even though the experience may be psychologically painful (cf. Ps 141:5). Such wounds are more beneficial than an enemy's false tokens of friendship.

(c) A particularly poignant instance of the use of the nom. is found in Isa 1:6, where several synonymous words for wounding occur. Drawing upon a motif of ill health due to wounds suffered in battle, Isaiah laments that the nation's spiritual rebellion has earned for it only "slash wounds (*peṣa'*), lacerations (*ḥabbûrâ*), and bleeding wounds (*makkâ ṭ^{e}rîyyâ*). . . . The political and social catastrophes they were experiencing were the natural results of living in ways contrary to those God designed for them" (Oswalt, 89). Failure to live out God's standards, which have been given to human beings for their good, will lead to spiritual and moral decay for societies and peoples just as surely as physical disease debilitates the body.

P-B The vb. is attested in Mish. Heb. and Aram. with the same senses as BH. The Arab. sense "squeeze out" is also found. Both physical and nonphysical wounding can be attached to the nom. (see Jastrow 2:1205-6). The LXX translates the nom. 5x by *trauma*, wound (Gen 4:23; Exod 21:25 [2x]; Prov 27:6; Isa 1:6) and 3x by *suntrimma*, ruin, destruction (Job 9:17; Prov 20:30; 23:29).

Wound, bruise, sore: → *ḥabbûrâ* (wound, # 2467); → *ḥll* II (pierce, wound, # 2726); → *ṭārî* (fresh [wound], # 3269); → *lḥm* I (battle, come to blows, # 4309); → *m'r* (be sore, # 4421); → *māzôr* I (sore, ulcer, boil, # 4649); → *maḥaṣ* (wound, blow, # 4731); → *makkâ* (wound, # 4804); → *pṣ'* (bruise, # 7205)

BIBLIOGRAPHY

W. McKane, *Proverbs*, OTL, 1970; J. N. Oswalt, *The Book of Isaiah*, NICOT, 1986; G. Vos, *Biblical Theology*, 1948.

R. K. Harrison/R. D. Patterson

7206 (*peṣa'*, wound, bruise), → # 7205

7207	פצץ

פצץ (*pṣṣ*), vb. po. pulverize; hitpol. crumble; pilp. maul, crush (# 7207).

ANE Arab. *faḍḍa*, break open, scatter, breakup; Tg. Aram. *p^{e}'a'*, crush; Nab. **pṣṣ ytpṣṣ* [itpa.], to be divided [?]; Syr. *pa'*, beat down, batter; pa. bruise, crush.

OT Yahweh's word is said to pulverize rocks (Jer 23:29), and Habakkuk speaks of ancient mountains crumbling because of Yahweh, an affirmation of his omnipotence (Hab 3:6). Job describes his experience at the hand of God as having been grabbed by the neck and mauled (Job 16:12; NIV crushed).

Shattering, breaking, destroying: → *mḥq* (strike, # 4735); → *npṣ* I (break, smash, # 5879); → *pṣṣ* (pulverize, crush, # 7207); → *rṭš* (smash, strike down, # 8187); → *r'ṣ* (shatter, # 8320); → *ršš* (destroy, crushed, # 8406); → *šbr* I (break, shatter, # 8689)

Gary Alan Long

7210	פצר

פצר (*pṣr*), q. urge, press; entreat, push, press; hi. "display pushing (i.e. arrogance., presumption)" (BDB) (# 7210); פְּצִירָה (*p^{e}ṣîrâ*), nom. blunt? (# 7201).

ANE The word is used in other Sem. languages (cf. Arab. *faraḍa*, appoint), in Akk. especially of religious duties.

OT 1. The word occurs in relation to an action that one person or group urges on another, as Lot urging the two angels to stay with him (Gen 19:3), the men of Sodom urging Lot to bring the angels out (19:9), Jacob urging Esau to accept his gift (33:11), the company of the prophets urging Elisha to instigate a search for Elijah who had been taken from him (2 Kgs 2:17), and Naaman urging Elisha to accept a gift in thankfulness for the curing of his leprosy (2 Kgs 5:16).

2. The hi. is used in 1 Sam 15:22-23 where, as quoted above, BDB sees the display of pushing leading to the sense of arrogance, presumption. The context is that where Saul has refused to obey the instructions given to him by the Lord, Samuel says, "To obey is better than sacrifice, and to heed is better than the fat of rams. For rebellion is like the sin of divination, and arrogance like the evil of idolatry. Because you have rejected the word of the LORD, he has rejected you as king." Some commentators (see ICC and AB), however, question this one use of the hi. in the OT, and the LXX seems to have read a different vb.

3. The meaning "blunt" of the nom. *p^eṣîrâ* is highly uncertain. The only occurrence is 1 Sam 13:21, where the whole verse is fraught with difficulties and the meaning "bluntness" is only a guess (see S. R. Driver, *Notes on the Hebrew Text and Topography of the Books of Samuel*, Oxford, 1913, in loc.). *HALAT* suggests "price."

Urgency: → *'wṣ* (urge, # 237); → *'ns* (urge, # 646); → *nḥṣ* (compel, # 5722); → *pṣr* (urge, press, push, # 7210)
Pushing, goring, thrusting: → *dḥh* (push, overthrow, be cast down, # 1890); → *dpq* (push, drive hard, knock, # 1985); → *hdp* (push, thrust, # 2074); → *yrṭ* (shove, push, be reckless, # 3740); → *ngḥ* (gore, push, thrust, # 5590); → *'ll* II (thrust in, # 6619); → *tq'* (drive, thrust, clap one's hands, blow trumpet, pledge, # 9546)
Pressure, squeezing: → *'kp* (press hard, # 436); → *'lṣ* (press hard upon, # 552); → *zwr* I (press, wring out, # 2318); → *zrr* I (press out [wounds], # 2452); → *lḥṣ* (press, # 4315); → *mîṣ* (pressing, # 4790); → *m'k* (press, squeeze, crush, # 5080); → *mṣh* (squeeze out, drain, # 5172); → *pṣr* (urge, press, push, # 7210); → *śḥṭ* (squeeze, to press out grapes, # 8469)

Francis Foulkes/P. J. M. Southwell

7211 (*piq*, shaking), → # 7048

7212	פקד

פקד (*pqd*), q. attend to, take note of, care for, punish, muster, assemble, record, enroll, commit, appoint, call to account, avenge; ni. be missed, be lacking, be installed, be called to account; pi. muster; pu. be enrolled, mustered; hi. appoint, entrust, commit; ho. be appointed, entrusted, be deposited; hitp. and hotp. be mustered, enrolled (# 7212); מִפְקָד (*mipqād*), nom. number, appointment (→ # 5152); פְּקֻדָּה (*p^equddâ*), nom. appointment, service, office, guard, punishment, mustering (# 7213); פִּקָּדוֹן (*piqqādôn*), nom. deposit, reserve (→ # 7214); פְּקִדֻת (*p^eqîdut*), nom. commander of the guard (w/ *ba'al*) (hapleg.; # 7215); פְּקוּדִים (*p^equdîm*), nom. amounts (hapleg.; # 7217); *פִּקּוּדִים (*piqqûdîm*), nom. precepts (→ # 7218); פָּקִיד (*pāqîd*), nom. officer (→ # 7224).

ANE The root *pqd* is attested throughout the Sem. languages: Akk. *paqādu*, watch over, entrust, appoint, muster; Ugar. *pqd*, order (hapleg.; *KTU* 1.16. 4.14); Phoen. *pqd*, appoint, authorize; Aram. *pqd*, order; Arab. *faqada*, miss, be missing; etc. The Akk. usage is particularly extensive with *paqādu* attested in all periods and all types of literature. The vb. is found in Tell Arad ostracon 24 ("and he gave them into his care"; reading *bqd* as *pqd*; Y. Aharoni, *Arad Inscriptions*, 1981, 46-49; see OT section 11), and possibly in the Khirbet Beit Lei Burial Cave inscription B. The nom. *mpqd* occurs in the Tell 'Ira ostracon with the meaning "roll call" or "census" (see OT section 3; but J. Garfunkel suggests that it is better rendered "guard"; see his "The Meaning of the Word *MPQD* in the Tel 'Ira Ostracon" [Heb.], *Leš* 52, 1987, 68-74).

OT 1. The vb. *pqd* occurs some 303x in the OT; in Num and Jer it is found 103x and 49x, respectively (this count includes some contested forms; cf. Num 1:22, 4:49 [second occurrence]; *BHS* proposes *pqd* instead of *dbr*, speak, in Num 26:3). Just over three-quarters of these occurrences are q. (235x), though most other stems are also represented (ni. 21x; pi. 1x; pu. 2x; hi. 29x; hitp. 4x; ho. 8x; and hotpael 4x).

2. The wide semantic range of *pqd* has long perplexed scholars. Speiser notes that "there is probably no other Hebrew verb that has caused translators as much trouble as *pqd*" (Speiser, 21). The original meanings that have been proposed are: (a) attend to with care, take note (Speiser, Scharbert, Gehman, McComiskey); (b) look at, carefully observe (*TWAT*, Van Hooser); (c) miss, worry about (H. Gese, *Vom Sinai zum Zion*, 1974, 89 n. 34; KB); and (d) determine the destiny (André). Lübbe rightly questions the relevance of determining an original meaning for *pqd*. Curiously, however, his assessment is based only on an evaluation of the third option (as found in KB), which more than likely represents a later development. The fourth option can similarly be eliminated as it reads too much into the meaning of the vb. Deciding between the first two options is more difficult as they both can account for many of the attested uses of *pqd* in the OT, and they also overlap somewhat. The first option presupposes the second, while the second often implies the first. It is probable, then, that the basic meaning of *pqd* is something like attend to, observe, though the focus here is on the meaning of the word in context.

3. Over one-third of all occurrences of *pqd* in the OT are found with a technical meaning in association with military or taxation censuses (ca. 121x, mostly q.; all hitp. and hotpael [used as passives; see *IBHS*, § 26.3]); most of these occur in the census lists in Num 1-4, and 26 (91x). This use of *pqd* has traditionally been glossed as "number" (cf. RSV, KJV). That *pqd* involves counting or numbering is obvious from the fact that totals are often reported (Exod 38:26; Num 1:46; 2:32; Judg 20:15, 17; 1 Sam 11:8; for the problem of large numbers see Milgrom, *Numbers*, 1990, 336-39), and it is found in conjunction with the phrase *nāśā' rō'š*, take a census (lit. "to lift the head"; cf. Exod 30:12; Num 1:2; 4:2), and with the vbs. *mnh* (→ # 4948) and *spr*, count (→ # 6218), and the nom. *mispār*, number (→ # 5031; Num 1:22; 3:22, 34; 2 Sam 24:1-2; 1 Chron 23:24). Nevertheless, this translation is inadequate, as *pqd* conveys more than the notion of just assigning numbers. On the basis of parallel texts from Mari, Speiser has demonstrated that in census contexts *pqd* invariably has the technical meaning of record, enroll (Speiser, 23). Thus, the material used to construct the tabernacle was "recorded at Moses' command" (Exod 38:21), and each person "entered in the records" contributed a beka of silver towards the construction of the tabernacle

(Exod 38:26, JPS; not "those counted" as the NIV). This sense of enroll is also found in Exod 30:12-14 (cf. 1 Chron 21:6; 23:24).

4. In military contexts *pqd* takes on an even more specialized meaning, i.e., the process of assembling, counting, and ordering of men for battle, and may be more appropriately glossed as "muster, assemble, array." This action is most often executed by military leaders prior to a battle. Joshua, Saul, David, Ahab, Jehoram, and Amaziah all muster their fighting men before engaging in combat (Josh 8:10; 1 Sam 11:8; 13:15; 15:4; 2 Sam 18:1; 1 Kgs 20:15; 2 Kgs 3:6; 1 Chron 25:5). Even the Lord of hosts musters his army for battle against Babylon (Isa 13:4). The census lists in Num 1-4, and 26 are probably best understood in this light (see B. A. Levine, *Numbers 1—20*, 134-5). The first two chapters of Numbers record a census that was undertaken at God's command by Moses and the family heads, and detail the mobilization of the people into a military camp. This census was clearly for military purposes: only those twenty years or older (the age of conscription in Israel; cf. 2 Chron 25:5), who are "able to serve in the army" (*yōṣē' ṣābā',* lit. "go out as an army"; cf. Num 31:27; Deut 20:1; 24:5) are mustered "by their divisions" (Num 1:3; cf. vv. 22, 49). The exemption of the Levites from regular military service accounts for their separate listing (Num 1:47, 49; 2:33). The militaristic connotations associated with censuses in the ANE and the Bible may help explain why David's census in 2 Sam 24 elicited a plague (par. 1 Chron 21). If the taking of a military census almost always preceded a battle, then it is possible that David was either planning an inappropriate military operation or taking steps towards forming a standing army. Either of these actions may have provoked Joab's strong reaction, David's subsequent guilt, and the Lord's wrath (2 Sam 24:3, par. 1 Chron 21:3, 6; 1 Sam 24:10). While McCarter's suggestion that the plague was due to the violation of ritual laws in carrying out the census has some merit (cf. Exod 30:12; P. K. McCarter, Jr., *II Samuel*, 1984, 512-14), it does not do justice to the fact that the plague was only one of three possible punishments (2 Sam 24:13).

5. The vb. *pqd* frequently has the meaning carefully examine, attend to, take note of, with the implied intention of responding appropriately (ca. 80x, almost always q.). This sense occurs occasionally with humans as subj., where it has the notion of "attend to," i.e., "to visit" (cf. Judg 15:1; 1 Sam 17:18 [with *l^{e}šālôm*]). This meaning, however, is most often found with God as subj. God "attends" or "takes note of" someone or something and acts accordingly, whether to bestow divine blessing or judgment. Thus, in positive contexts *pqd* is often glossed as "be concerned about, care for, attend to, help" (Gen 50:24, 25; Exod 4:31; Ruth 1:6; Jer 15:15; Zeph 2:7); while in negative contexts it is typically glossed as "punish" (Exod 20:5; Lev 18:25; 1 Sam 15:2; Isa 13:11; Hos 4:14). Both senses are found in Zech 10:3: "My anger burns against the shepherds, and I will punish (*pqd 'l*) the leaders; for the LORD Almighty will care for (*pqd*) his flock, the house of Judah, and make them like a proud horse in battle." The use of *pqd* in conjunction with vbs. like *zkr* (→ # 2349), remember (Ps 8:4[5]; 106:4; Jer 14:10; 15:15; Hos 8:13; 9:9), and *r'h* (→ # 8011), see (Exod 4:31; Ps 80:14[15]), emphasizes the perception and response implicit in the vb. (see McComiskey, 96).

6. The negative meaning punish is most often construed with the collocation *pqd 'l*, where the prep. indicates the object of divine displeasure (Exod 34:7; Num 14:18; etc.). This construction is responsible for the traditional translation: "to visit sins upon one" (cf. KJV, RSV). The vb. can also bear the meaning punish with an

unmarked obj. (Ps 59:5[6]; 89:32[33]; Jer 14:10; 49:8; Lam 4:22; Hos 9:9), or with the obj. indicated by an independent pronoun (Hos 8:13) or a pronominal suff. (Isa 27:1; Jer 6:15; 49:8; 50:31). The obj. is also indicated once with the prep. *b* (Jer 9:9[8]) and twice with *'l* (46:25 [both *'l* and *'l* occur in this v. with no difference]; 50:18). The reasons for the punishment are commonly indicated by *'t* (Jer 23:2; 25:12; 36:31; Hos 1:4; 2:13[15]; Amos 3:2) or left unmarked (Lev 18:25; Num 14:18, Isa 13:11; Hos 4:9); while the means of punishment are introduced with the prep. *b* (Ps 89:32[33]; Jer 11:22; 27:8; 44:13).

7. God is the only legitimate author of punishment in the OT (see Morris, 63). While his punishment at times extends to non-Israelites (e.g., the kings of Assyria and Babylon [Isa 10:12; Jer 25:12; 50:31], Edom [Lam 4:22], and all nations [Ps 59:5[6]; cf. Isa 13:11; 26:21]), the people of Israel and/or their leaders are most often the object of this punishment (Jer 5:9; Hos 2:13[15]; Amos 3:2; for leaders, cf. Zeph 1:8; Zech 10:3). According to the prophets, Israel was punished for their sins and wickedness (Jer 5:29; 36:31; Hos 9:9; Amos 3:2), for swearing falsely (Jer 14:10), and for burning incense to other gods and sacrificing to the Baals (Jer 44:7-10; Hos 2:13[15]). As a result of this disobedience, plagues and wild animals (Jer 5), drought, famine, and sword (44:13) were going to come upon them, and their wealth was going to be plundered and their houses demolished (Zeph 1). This punishment culminated with the fall of the northern kingdom in 722 BC and with the destruction of Jerusalem and the southern kingdom in 587 BC.

8. God's punishment is not indiscriminate, however, but is based upon the stipulations of the covenant (cf. Lev 26; Deut 27-28; → *b^e^rît*, # 1382) and grounded in his character: "I, the LORD your God, am a jealous God, punishing [*pqd 'l*] the children for the sin of the fathers to the third and fourth generation of those who hate me, but showing love to a thousand generations of those who love me and keep my commandments" (Deut 5:9-10; cf. Exod 20:5; 34:7; Num 14:18). The punishment of the children for the sins of the fathers is an expression of God's righteousness, just as its limited duration and the unlimited blessings for those who love God are expressions of divine mercy (*TDOT* 2:239). Moreover, this punishment presupposes—in accord with this sense of *pqd*—that the children are punished according to their solidarity with and participation in the misconduct of their parents (cf. Josh 7) (Scharbert, 219). This corporate view of responsibility was later modified by Jeremiah and Ezekiel (Jer 31:29-30; Ezek 18:2; but cf. Jer 29:32, where Shemaiah's descendants are also included in his punishment). How the punishment (*pqd 'l*) of the house of Jehu for the "bloodshed of Jezreel" should be understood in this regard is problematic (Hos 1:4). The text appears to condemn Jehu for ending Ahab's line, even though it was commanded by God (2 Kgs 9-10). While some suggest that only the severity of Jehu's massacre is condemned or that Hosea was not aware of the deuteronomic evaluation of Jehu's actions (Wolff, *Hosea*, 18), it is more likely that Hosea contends that in the same way that God used Jehu to put an end to the line of Ahab because of its wickedness, God was going to put an end to Jehu's dynasty for the same reasons (Andersen and Freedman, *Hosea*, 181). That the demise of Jehu's line took place in the Jezreel valley in a move of ultimate irony is possible, though the emendation of 2 Kgs 15:10 to read "at Ibleam" is not certain (*contra* McComiskey, 100).

9. In contrast to the use of *pqd ʿl* in judgment contexts, the object of God's favor or concern is indicated by *ʾt* (Gen 21:1; Exod 4:31; Ruth 1:61; Sam 2:21), a pronominal acc. (Gen 50:24, 25; Exod 3:16; 13:19; Jer 29:10), or a pronominal suff. (Jer 15:15; Zeph 2:7), or it is left unmarked (Ps 65:9[10]; 80:14[15]; Zech 11:16). The positive sense, however, is never construed with the prep. *ʿl*. Thus, while *pqd* occurs with negative connotations without *ʿl*, the collocation *pqd ʿl* never appears with a positive meaning. This leaves room for ambiguity when *pqd* occurs without *ʿl*. For instance, the nature of the Lord's "dealing with" Zedekiah in Jer 32:5 is not clear. While some take it as an indication of divine punishment, it is more likely a promise of divine favor (see C. T. Begg, "Yahweh's 'Visitation' of Zedekiah [Jer 32,5]," *ETL* 63, 1987, 113-17). The same ambiguity is present in Isa 24:22.

10. As with the negative use of *pqd* (see section 6 above), the positive meaning of favor, concern often includes with it an appropriate response. God was not only concerned (*pqd*) for the Israelites in Egypt, but also delivered them from their bondage (Exod 3:16; 4:31; cf. Gen 50:24-25). Similarly, God was not only gracious (*pqd*) to Sarah and Hannah, but he also acted appropriately by blessing them both with a child (Gen 21:1; 1 Sam 2:21). God's great concern for humanity is brought out in Ps 8:4[5], "What are human beings that you are mindful of them, mortals that you care (*pqd*) for them?" (NRSV; cf. Jer 15:15). As v. 5[6] makes explicit, this great concern is grounded in God's status as Creator (but cf. Job 7:17-18; Ps 17:3).

11. In administrative contexts *pqd* often (ca. 59x) involves the transfer of authority from a superior to a subordinate, i.e., appoint someone over someone or something; or the subjecting of someone or something to the subordinate's control, i.e., entrust, commit, deposit someone or something to someone. This meaning is commonly found in the hi. and ho. (29x and 7x, respectively); while these could possibly be understood as causatives of the meaning attend (see section 5 above) (i.e., to cause someone to attend to = appoint over), this does not explain the frequent use of the q. with this sense (ca. 20x). The first sense occurs in a standardized pattern that is found with other vbs. (→ *ṣwh*, command [# 7422; section 9]): the person or sphere over which the person is appointed indicated by the prep. *ʿl* (though other preps. are used: *b* in Esth 2:3; Jer 40:5; 41:2, 18; *ʾl* in Jer 49:19; 50:44; *l* in 1 Kgs 11:28), and the specific task(s) entrusted to the appointee (if expressed) is indicated by *l* + inf. const. Thus, God appoints Jeremiah "(*ʿal*) over nations and over (*w*^{e}*ʿal*) kingdoms to uproot (*ntš*, → # 6004) and tear down (*ntṣ*, → # 5997)" (Jer 1:10; cf. Josh 10:18; 2 Chron 34:12; Ezra 1:2; Neh 12:44; Isa 62:6). The use of *pqd* with the meaning commit, assign is less frequent (ca. 13x). Rehoboam assigns the newly made bronze shields to the commanders of the guard (1 Kgs 14:27, par. 2 Chron 12:10), while the psalmist "commits" his spirit to the Lord (Ps 31:5; cf. Lev 6:4[5:23]; Isa 10:28; Jer 37:21; 41:10).

12. Finally, on a number of occasions *pqd* has the sense of miss, be missed (ca. 15x; predominantly ni.). This meaning is an extension of section 5 above, in that to take note (of someone's absence) means to miss them. Hence, when David plans to be absent from Saul's table Jonathan responds, lit. "you (i.e., your absence) will be noted for your place will be noted," i.e., "you will be missed, because your seat will be empty" (1 Sam 20:18; cf. 20:6, 25, 27). Similarly, when Jehu deceptively brings together the ministers of Baal in order to kill them, he ensures that no priests of Baal

are missing (2 Kgs 10:19). In some contexts *pqd* may also indicate "miss" in the sense of "longing for" (cf. Ezek 23:21).

13. The nom. *p^{e}quddâ* (32x) occurs with roughly the same range of meaning as *pqd*. It is frequently used for various positions of authority (Num 3:32, 36; 2 Kgs 11:18; Isa 60:17; Ezek 44:11) or the notion of punishment (Isa 10:3; Jer 8:12; 10:15; Hos 9:7). It is found once in reference to God's gracious concern (Job 10:12). The nom. *piqqûdîm*, precepts, is found almost exclusively in Ps 119 (21 out of 24x; e.g., vv. 4, 15, 27, 63). The nom. *pāqîd*, officer, denotes one who is placed in a position of authority over others, whether permanently or for a specific duration (13x; Gen 41:34; Judg 9:28; 2 Kgs 25:19; Esth 2:3). The nom. *mipqād* (5x) may refer to an appointment (1 Chron 31:13) or a designated place (Ezek 43:21); it is also found in a construct chain with *mispār*, number, lit. "the number of the record of the people" (2 Sam 24:9, par. 1 Chron 21:5). The nom. *piqqādôn* typically denotes a deposit or reserve (3x.; Gen 41:36; Lev 6:2, 4[5:21, 23]).

P-B A variety of words are used to translate the root *pqd* in the LXX. Over half the occurrences of *pqd* are rendered by the remarkably versatile vb. *episkeptomai*, muster, look at, examine, care for, appoint; and its derivatives. It is also frequently rendered by *ekdikeō*, punish, and *kathistēmi*, appoint, establish. While the significance of the LXX for our understanding of *pqd* should not be overstated (see Gehman and Grossfeld), that the LXX translators rendered *pqd* with *arithmeō* or *arithmos* only a total of 4x illustrates that they also understood *pqd* to signify more than just numbering (Grossfeld, 86; but cf. the Tgs. and the Vg.).

The vb. *pqd* is found ca. 40x among the nonbiblical MSS from Qumran, including 4x in 1QS; 7x in 1QM; 4x in 1QH^a; 2x in 1Q28b; 11x in CD-A; 3x in CD-B; and 2x in 11QTemple^a. Most of these are in line with biblical usage: God musters his celestial army (1QM 12.4), appoints the "Prince of light" (1QM 13.10), and "punishes the depravity of the wicked" (1QH^a 6.24 [14.24]). Some different nuances in the sense of *pqd* are also found: those who freely volunteer to enter the community are "to follow (*pqd*) all the decrees" of the covenant (1QS 5.22; cf. 1QSb 3.24), and after the first year in the community an initiate is "examined (*pqd 'l*) by the command of the Many" (1QS 6.21; cf. CD-A 13.11). Also noteworthy is the absence of the collocation *pqd 'l* in judgment contexts (cf. 1QH^a 14.24; 4Q275 3.6; CD-A 8.2; etc.). The nom. *p^{e}quddâ* is found in reference to the "visitation" (1QS 4.6, 11) or the "moment of visitation" (1QS 3.18; 4.19; cf. CD-B 19.10-11), when the present age is ended and a new age of blessing for the righteous and punishment for the wicked is ushered in.

NT The vb. *episkeptomai* is found a number of times in Luke to denote God's care for and intervention on behalf of his people (Luke 1:68, 78; 7:16; but cf. 19:44). 1 Peter 2:12 refers to Gentiles glorifying God on the day of visitation (*en hēmera episkopēs*; cf. Isa 10:3, LXX). In the OT similar expressions almost always refer to a time of judgment (Isa 10:3; Jer 6:15; 10:15), but in light of Christ, God's visitation becomes a day of both blessing and judgment (cf. QL above; → Punishment, *NIDNTT* 3:92-100). The nom. *episkopos*, used to trans. *p^{e}quddâ* and *pāqîd* in the LXX, refers to church leaders (1 Tim 3:1, 2; → Bishop, *NIDNTT* 1:188-201).

Appointment, commandment, summons: → *zmn* (be appointed, # 2374); → *y'd* (determine, designate, appoint, assemble, # 3585); → *mnh* (count, reckon, assign, appoint, ordain, # 4948);

→ *'md* (stand, take one's stand, station, appoint, # 6641); → *pqd* (punish, assemble, record, appoint, # 7212); → *ṣwh* (order, command, charge, direct, appoint, # 7422); → *šyt* (put, set, lay, appoint, # 8883)

Law of God: → *ḥōq* (portion, obligation, boundary, law, order, # 2976); → *miṣwâ* (command, commandment, # 5184); → *mišpāṭ* (judgment, decision, legal case, legal claim, # 5477); → *'ēdût* (statutes, stipulations, warning sign, reminder, # 6343); → *piqqûdîm* (directions, order, # 7218); for *tôrâ* (direction, instruction, law, the law, # 9368); → **Decalogue: Theology**; → **Ethics: Theology**; → **Law of God: Theology**

Numbers: → *'eḥād* (one, # 285); → *'elep* II (thousand, military contingent, # 547); → *'arba'* (four, # 752); → *ḥāmēš* (five, # 2822); → *mē'â* I (hundred, # 4395); → *'eśer* (ten, # 6924); → *r^ebābâ* (ten thousand, myriad, # 8047/8052); → *šeba'* I (seven, # 8679); → *šālōš, š^elōšâ* (three, a three, # 8993); → *š^emōneh* (eight, # 9046); → *š^enayim* (two, # 9109); → *šēš* I (six, # 9252); → *tēša'* (nine, # 9596)

Speech: → *'lm* I (be bound, speechless, grow silent, # 519); → *'mr* I (say, speak, mention, # 606); → *bl'* II (make conveyed, reported, # 1181); → *dbr* II (speak, threaten, promise, command, # 1819); → *ḥwh* I (make declared, explained, # 2555); → *lšn* (slander, # 4387); → *mll* III (speak, say, declare, # 4910); → *ngd* (make known, disclose, declare, # 5583); → *rākîl* (peddler, huckster, deceiver, slanderer, # 8215); → *šnn* II (make repeated, recounted, # 9112)

BIBLIOGRAPHY

THAT 1:466-86; *TWAT* 6:708-23; G. André, *Determining the Destiny: PQD in the Old Testament*, 1980; H. S. Gehman, "Ἐπισκέπομαι, [*sic*] ἐπισκέπσις, ἐπίσκοπος", and ἐπισκοπή in the Septuagint in Relation to פקד and Other Hebrew Roots — A Case of Semantic Development Similar to that of Hebrew," *VT* 22, 1972, 197-207; B. Grossfeld, "The Translation of the Biblical Hebrew פקד in the Targum, Peshitta, Vulgate and Septuagint," *ZAW* 96, 1984, 83-101; J. B. Van Hooser, "The Meaning of the Hebrew Root פקד in the Old Testament," Harvard Ph. D. thesis, 1962; J. C. Lübbe, "Hebrew Lexicography: A New Approach," *Journal for Semitics* 2, 1990, 1-15; T. E. McComiskey, "Prophetic Irony in Hosea 1.4: A Study of the פקד על Collocation and Its Implications for the Fall of Jehu's Dynasty," *JSOT* 58, 1993, 93-101; P. Middelkoop, "A Word Study: The Sense of PAQAD in the Second Commandment and Its General Background in the OT Regarding to the Translation into the Indonesian and Timorese Languages," *South East Asia Journal of Theology* 4, 1963, 33-47, 56-65; L. Morris, "The Punishment of Sin in the OT," *AusBR* 6, 1958, 62-86; J. Scharbert, "Das Verbum PQD in der Theologie des Alten Testaments," *BZ* 4, 1960, 209-26 (= *Um das Prinzip der Vergeltung in Religion und Recht des Alten Testaments* [WF 125, ed. K. Koch, 1972, 278-99]); E. A. Speiser, "Census and Ritual Expiation in Mari and Israel," *BASOR* 149, 1958, 17-25.

Tyler F. Williams

7213 (*p^equddâ*, appointment, office, punishment), → # 7212

7214	פִּקָּדוֹן

פִּקָּדוֹן (*piqqādôn*), nom. deposited goods; store, stock, supply, provision, reserve; entrusted property (# 7214); < פקד (*pqd*), number, appoint (→ # 7212).

ANE The nom. occurs in Sam. *fiqdon* and in Jewish Aram., *piqq^edônā'*, deposited goods, deposit; Egyp. Aram. *pq[dwn]*, deposit; Nab. *pqdwn*, responsibility or command/order (?); Sam. *pqdwnh*; Akk. *puquddû*, formal surrender/capitulation; entrusted goods.

OT 1. The nom. occurs in Gen 41:36. Found elsewhere in the OT only in Lev 6:2[5:21], 4[5:23], Skinner (468) maintains that the word *piqqādôn*, reserve, was suggested in Gen 41:36 by the word *p^{e}qidîm*, overseers, in v. 34. Be that as it may, 41:36 reports that as part of his plan for minimizing the effects of the seven years of famine that were to follow the seven years of plenty, the sagacious Joseph advocated storing as a reserve 20 percent of the grain produced by Egypt. Perhaps the most important point that emerges from vv. 25-36 is that although God had determined the course of events and hastened to bring them to pass, responsible leaders were expected to devise and implement appropriate, statesmanlike measures for dealing with them (von Rad, 376). The divine purposes required a human counterpart and, as Brueggemann (332) expresses it, in the juxtaposition of divine plan (vv. 9-32) and human action (vv. 33-45) lies the seed of incarnational faith.

2. The nom. is also used in Lev 6:2[5:21], 4[5:23], part of a section (5:14-6:7[5:14-26]) dealing with the guilt offering, prescribed for those offenses against God and neighbor that necessitated not only a reparation sacrifice but restitution to the victim as well. Lev 6:1-7[5:20-26] is concerned with those cases where people not only acquired something through deceit or violence, but also made Yahweh an accessory to the crime by taking an oath of innocnce in his name (Knight, 37; Hayes, 162). According to 6:2[5:21], one of the cases where it was considered appropriate to present a guilt offering by way of atonement was the betrayal of trust in a matter of property given to a friend for safe custody. Here, *piqqādôn*, meaning deposit or entrusted property (Noth, 49), may refer to an item left as security for a loan (Kennedy, 59) or to any valuable article of private property that one person gives to another for safekeeping (Chapman and Streane, 25). The person who fraudulently retained someone else's property was instructed to return the illegal acquisition (6:4[5:23]). In addition, he was required to pay the person he cheated 20 percent of the value of the item as compensation (6:5[5:24]).

The prescriptions relating to the guilt offering are based on some important principles, of which two are of singular significance. (a) Genuine remorse, repentance, voluntary confession of sin, and decisive action to make amends are considered to have a kind of retroactive mitigating effect on deliberate and premeditated wrongs, which renders them eligible for expiation (cf. Hayes, 162; Wenham, 108-9). (b) Restitution (not retribution or revenge) must take place before the guilt offering is acceptable. It is only after rectification has been made with the wronged neighbor (by reparation for damage) that the offender can seek to repair his relationship with God and experience forgiveness, absolution, and renewal (cf. e.g., Milgrom, 72; Wenham, 112; Knight, 37-38; Hayes, 162; Bailey, 34).

P-B In Heb. the vb. *pqd* occurs with the meaning in q. and pi. of (search, examine), visit; (euphem.) have marital connection with; visit, remember, decree upon; count, muster; give in charge, entrust, deposit; command, order; ni. be visited, remembered, decreed upon; be commanded, commissioned; hi. give in charge, deposit; take charge of. The Aram. *p^{e}qad* is also found, with the meaning command; (give in charge), store up; pa. command, commission; af. command, commission; give in charge, deposit; itp. be commanded; be given in charge, be deposited. The Heb. nom. forms, *piqqādôn*, *pîqqādôn*, and the Aram., *piqdônā'*, *pîqdônā'*, also occur with the meaning thing given in charge, deposit. Other forms that occur are Aram. *p^e qadtā'*, order, last will, and Heb. *pāqûd*, mustered, included in the census (Jastrow 2:1206-7).

Pledge, security: → *'issār* (binding obligation, pledge, vow of abstention, # 674); → *ḥbl* II (take in pledge, exact a pledge, # 2471); → *ḥôb* (pledge, collateral, # 2550); → *nš'* I (lend against a pledge, # 5957); → *'bṭ* (borrow, take a pledge from, # 6292); → *'rb* I (stand security for, give security for, # 6842); → *piqqādôn* (deposited goods, store, supply, provision, # 7214); → *tq'* (drive, thrust, clap one's hands, blow trumpet, pledge, # 9546)

BIBLIOGRAPHY
L. R. Bailey, *Leviticus*, KPG, 1987; W. Brueggemann, *Genesis*, Interpretation, 1982; A. T. Chapman and A. W. Streane, *The Book of Leviticus*, CBC, 1914; J. H. Hayes, "Leviticus," in *HBC*, 1988, 157-81; A. R. S. Kennedy, *Leviticus and Numbers*, CB, 1910; G. A. F. Knight, *Leviticus*, DSB, 1984; J. Milgrom, "The Book of Leviticus," in *The Interpreter's One-Volume Commentary on the Bible*, 1971, 68-84; M. Noth, *Leviticus: A Commentary*, OTL, 1965; G. von Rad, *Genesis: A Commentary*, OTL, 3d ed., 1972; J. Skinner, *A Critical and Exegetical Commentary on Genesis*, ICC, 2d ed., 1969; W. A. Ward, "The Egyptian Office of Joseph," *JSS* 5, 1960, 146-47; idem, "Egyptian Titles in Genesis 39-50," *BSac* 114, 1957, 40-59; G. J. Wenham, *The Book of Leviticus*, NICOT, 1979.

Robin Wakely

7215 (*p^e qidut*, commander), → # 7212

7217 (*p^e qûdîm*, amounts), → # 7212

7218	פִּקּוּדִים

פִּקּוּדִים (*piqqûdîm*), nom. directions, order (# 7218); < פקד (*pqd*), number, appoint (→ # 7212).

OT The nom. occurs 24x in OT, exclusively in the Psalms: 21x in Ps 119, once in 19:8[9]; 103:18; 111:7. It refers throughout to God's commands in general. As with the other terms for law found in the Psalms, it is difficult to be more definitive.

P-B The LXX most often translates the term with *entolē*, commandment, although *dikaiōma*, regulation, also occurs several times.

Law of God: → *ḥōq* (portion, obligation, boundary, law, order, # 2976); → *miṣwâ* (command, commandment, # 5184); → *mišpāṭ* (judgment, decision, legal case, legal claim, # 5477); → *'ēdût* (statutes, stipulations, warning sign, reminder, # 6343); → *piqqûdîm* (directions, order, # 7218); for *tôrâ* (direction, instruction, law, the law, # 9368); → **Decalogue: Theology**; → **Ethics: Theology**; → **Law of God: Theology**

BIBLIOGRAPHY
TDNT 2:544-56; *THAT* 2:466-86; *TWOT* 2:731-32.

Peter Enns

7219	פקח

פקח (*pqḥ*), open, always in the q., except for Gen 3:5, 7; Isa 35:5, which are in the ni., be opened (# 7219); פִּקֵּחַ (*piqqēaḥ*), clear-sighted (# 7221), a disleg. in Exod 4:11 (where it is the antonym of blind) and in 23:8 ("a bribe blinds those who see"); פְּקַח־קוֹחַ (p^e*qaḥ-qôaḥ*), opening [of eyesight] (# 7223).

ANE In *HALAT* 903. Cf. Aram. *pqḥ*, to open, make see; Syr. *pqḥ*, bloom; Arab. *faqaḥa*, open the eyes; OSA *pqḥ,* open.

OT 1. Unlike *pṣḥ* (# 7198), which mostly has for its object the mouth, *pqḥ* has mostly for its object or subject the eyes. The only instance where this vb. is used in conjunction with an organ other than the eyes is Isa 42:20 (with ears).

2. God is an opener of eyes (Gen 21:19; 2 Kgs 6:17 [2x], 20 [2x]; Ps 146:8). God calls others to open eyes (Isa 42:7). God's own eyes are open (Job 14:3; Jer 32:19; Zech 12:4). It is not unheard of in OT petitionary prayers for the seeker to ask God to open his eyes (Isa 37:17 [= 2 Kgs 19:16]; Dan 9:18).

3. When God opens eyes it is an indication of his provision for those who stand in desperate need. This applies, for example, to Gen 21:19, when God opened Hagar's eyes and she saw a well. Does this mean that she saw something that did not exist before, that God conjured up a wilderness well? Or was the well there all along, and Hagar did not really see it until God opened her eyes? If it is the latter, then in Gen 21 we have a life-saving resource Hagar could not see without the quickening, eye-opening touch of God.

The same applies to the narrative in 2 Kgs 6. The prophet's servant is able to see the army and horses and chariots of the enemy encircling the city and thus he is prepared to press "the panic button." But he cannot see what the prophet can see, i.e., horses and chariots of fire, until God opens his eyes.

4. One of the promissory statements made by the serpent to Eve was: "Your eyes will be opened," to which he appended, "and you will be like God, knowing good and evil" (Gen 3:5). Whether or not the second part is sequential or explicative to the first is difficult to decide. That is, does the second half of the verse offer a second, distinct promise, or does it expand on and explain the first half of the verse?

In one sense what the serpent promised came true, for verse 7 reads, "Then the eyes of both of them were opened." However, the remainder of the verse does *not* go on to say, "and they became like God." Rather, it states, "and they realized they were naked." That is hardly what they were bargaining for in having their eyes opened and becoming like God. How different is this couple who had their eyes opened from another couple who also had their eyes opened as they walked from Jerusalem to Emmaus ("then their eyes were opened and they recognized him," Luke 24:31)!

5. The phrase p^e*qaḥ-qôaḥ*, opening [of eyesight], appears in Isa 61:1, in which God's Servant says of his ministry, "the LORD has anointed me to ... release from darkness the prisoners" (NIV, cf. Luke 4:18).

Opening, coming, entrance: → *bw'* (go, come, arrive, enter, # 995); → *p'r* (open wide, # 7196); → *pṣḥ* (open up, # 7198); → *pqḥ* (open, # 7219); → *ptḥ* I (open, conquer, surrender, set free, loosen, break up, # 7337)

Victor P. Hamilton

7221 (*piqqēaḥ*, clear-sighted), → # 7219

7223 (p^e*qaḥ-qôaḥ*, opening [eyesight]), → # 7219

7224	פָּקִיד

פָּקִיד (*pāqîd*), nom. officer, commissioner (# 7224); < פקד (*pqd*), miss, visit, take care of, attend to, muster, pass in review, appoint (to task), appoint over, call to account for, seek vengeance, avenge, punish (→ # 7212).

ANE 1. Common Sem. root: vb. is widely attested, but nom. is less so (not in Ugar., Arab., or Eth.): Akk. *paqdu,* officer, administrator, deputy, delegate, representative, agent, magistrate, manager, superintendent, steward of estate, trustee, custodian, curator (*AHw*, 826-27; Eilers, 333); Akk. *pāqidu,* caretaker, overseer (*AHw* 2:827); Pers. (Neo-Babylonian) *pqyd,* officer, magistrate, functionary of administrative branch (Cardascia, 235; *THAT* 2:470); OSA *fqdn,* deputy, official, inspector, overseer (Vincent, 104; *THAT* 2:466); Old Aram. *pqd,* officer, magistrate (*DISO*, 234); Emp. Aram. *pqyd,* officer, magistrate (*DISO* 234); Egyp. Aram. *pqyd,* official, officer (*DISO*, 234); Phoen. *pqyd,* magistrate; *mpqd,* magistrate, administration, appointed work (*GPL*, 138; *DISO*, 234); Pun. *pqd,* officer (*PPG*, 131; *DISO*, 234).

2. In Northeast Sem., the vb. is metonymically related to the nominal title: Akk. *paqādu,* vb. when used in reference to an official: to order, commission, authorize, empower, entrust with (*AHw* 2:824-26); thus, Akk. *paqdu,* nom. person who is commissioned, appointed, empowered, entrusted with responsibility or task, and ordered to perform (*AHw* 2:826-27); and *pāqidu,* nom. someone charged/entrusted with taking care of an area of responsibility (*AHw* 2:827).

3. In Northwest Sem., *pqd* as nom. most often designates a civil official appointed to oversee and administer a city or district: Old Aram. *pqd,* civil official, magistrate (*KAI* 224:4. 10. 13; Sefiré 3:4, 10); Emp. Aram. *mpqd lpqy,* the magistrate/administration of Lepcis (*DISO*, 234; *GPL* 139). As in Northeast Sem., the related vb. describes the appointment of the official and his resultant duties, e.g., Emp. Aram./Phoen./Punic *pqd,* vb. to order, commission, appoint; to watch, inspect, take care of (*DISO*, 233; *GPL*, 138; *PPG*, 131).

OT 1. *pāqîd,* nom. appointed official, officer, commissioner, overseer (*HALAT* 3:904; BDB, 823-24), designates an official appointed to oversee a responsibility/task committed to him (*THAT* 2:466-86). The morphology of *pāqîd* exhibits the *qātîl* pattern often used to designate professional vocations: *nāgîd,* leader, *nābî',* prophet, *sārîs,* official (*IBHS* §5. 3c; *BL* §470n).

2. As in other Sem. languages the nominal connotations of *pāqîd* are related to some denotations of *pqd,* to order, appoint, commission; to oversee, take care of (*KBL* 2:902-3). The hi. of *pqd* often denotes a king appointing an official over an area (Gen 39:4; 2 Kgs 25:23). The *pāqîd* is a subordinate appointed/commissioned by a superior and entrusted with responsibility over a people/region/task (*TWOT* 2:732). This is seen in the cognate accusative *pāqad pāqîd,* to appoint/commission an official/commissioner (to be in charge of something) (Gen 41:34; 2 Chron 31:13).

3. Although *pqd* vb. has a broad range of meanings (Grossfeld, 83-101; Speiser, 21), *pāqîd* has a narrower semantic range: deputy, delegate, agent, representative; official, civil servant, officer; overseer, inspector, supervisor; steward (*THAT* 2:470).

4. *pāqîd* occurs 13x and is used in reference to three kinds of appointed officials: civil, military, and cultic (*HALAT* 3:904; *THAT* 2:470). The *pāqîd* may be a civil official (Gen 41:34; Judg 9:28; Neh 11:9; Esth 2:3), military officer or commander

(2 Kgs 25:19 = Jer 52:25), or cultic official (2 Chron 24:11; 31:13; Neh 11:14, 22; 12:42; Jer 20:1; 29:26) (see secs. 7-9 below).

5. *pāqîd* is often followed by *'al* and a nom. designating the area/people over which the individual has authority: land of Egypt (Gen 41:34), soldiers (2 Kgs 25:19 = Jer 52:25), Benjaminites (Neh 11:9), Levites (11:22), and the singers (12:42). This construction parallels Imp. Aram. *mpqd lpqy,* the magistrate of Lepcis (*DISO*, 234; *GPL*, 139). *pāqîd* is also followed by b^e and a nom. designating the sphere of his authority (Esth 2:3; Jer 20:1; 29:26). *pāqîd* is used in construct to identify the superior over the appointed officer (2 Chron 24:11; 31:13).

6. The high rank of the position is seen in its apposition to *nāgîd,* prince (Jer 20:1), and collocation with *sārîs*, official (2 Kgs 25:19 = Jer 52:25), and *rā'šê hamm^{e}dînâ,* provincial leaders (Neh 11:3). The position may be temporary (Gen 41:34; Esth 2:3) or permanent (Judg 9:28; 2 Kgs 25:19; 2 Chron 24:11; 31:13; Neh 11:9, 14, 22; 12:42; Jer 29:26; 52:25) (BDB, 823-24).

7. *Civil official.* As in the other Sem. languages, the most common referent of *pāqîd* designates a civil official appointed by a king over a city or region (*HALAT* 3:904). The *pāqîd* may function as a governor over a large area: it designates the viziers appointed over the three administrative regions of Egypt (Gen 41:34) and the local commissioners appointed over the 127 provincial districts in the Persian empire (Esth 2:3). The *pāqîd* may function as the deputy of a king over a city-state: it designates the deputy administrator under Abimelech, the king of the city-state Shechem (Judg 9:28). This closely reflects the Amarna administrative usage of Akk. *paqdu,* nom. designating the appointed ruler of the Canaanite city-state (Campbell, 39-54). The *pāqîd* may also function as an official over a provincial capital city: in the community of postexilic Jerusalem, it designates the official over the provincial leaders (Neh 11:9) and the provincial leaders themselves (11:14, 22), who are designated as *rā'šê hamm^{e}dînâ,* leaders of the provincial districts (11:3). LXX appropriately nuances all these usages as civil officials: *toparchas*, regional governors (Gen 41:34), *kōmarchas*, city officials in provincial districts (Esth 2:3), and *episkopos*, city overseer (Judg 9:28; Neh 11:9, 14, 22). Rüterswörden suggests that in the preexilic monarchial period, the terms used to designate the highest-level administrative officials under the king were *pāqîd,* official, *śar,* magistrate, *nāgîd,* prince, *yô'aṣ,* counselor, and *peḥâ,* provincial governor (Rüterswördon, 116-20).

8. *Military official.* It designates the chief official (*sārîs*) who was the commanding officer (*pāqîd*) appointed over the fighting men of Jerusalem (2 Kgs 25:19 = Jer 52:25). This *pāqîd* was probably the commander-in-chief over the army—the minister of national defense (de Vaux, 225). The military nuance is appropriately reflected in LXX *epistatēs*, commander. Related to this is *p^{e}qidut,* commander of the guard (Jer 37:13).

9. *Cultic official. pāqîd* designates the chief officer in charge of the temple (2 Chron 31:13; Jer 20:1; 29:26), the deputy assistant of the high priest (24:11), the overseer in charge of the priests and Levites (Neh 11:14, 22), and the director of the choir (12:42). These nuances are appropriately reflected in LXX: *ho hēgoumenos*, the chief (over the temple) (2 Chron 31:13; Jer 20:1); *prostatos*, deputy officer (of the high priest) (2 Chron 24:11); and *episkopos*, overseer (of the priests and Levites) (Neh 11:14, 22).

P-B 1. The nom. *pqd* occurs 2x in ancient Heb. inscriptions (Davies, 473): it appears in the seal of a Judean provincial official (provenance unknown; second half of sixth century BC), *lpqd yhd,* belonging to the provincial official of Judah (Davies, 106. 012; Bordreuil, 305-7); and in the personal name on a Gezer jar stamp (sixth-fourth centuries BC), *l'bnr pqdyw,* belonging to the officials of PN (?) (Davies, 100. 163; Avigad, 43-46). It might appear in Tel Arad Ostracon 24 (late seventh/early sixth century BC) in collocation with *mlkyhm,* their kings: *whpqydm* and their provincial officials (Davies, 2. 024. 14; Aharoni, 46-47; Müller, 304). The root appears in the Tel 'Ira ostracon (late eighth/seventh century BC): *mpqd* magistrate, administration, or census (?) (Davies, 13. 001; Beit-Arieh, 105-8; Garfunkel, 68-74).

2. The root *pqd* occurs 26x in *DSS* (CD 1. 7; 5. 15; 7. 21; 10. 2; 15. 6; 19. 10,11; 20. 2; 1QS 3. 18; 4. 19, 26; 6:14; 1QSa 1. 9; 1QSb 3. 24; 1QM 2. 4; 13. 10; 1QH 13 1. 7; 16. 5; 1Q26 1 1. 7; 4Q405 20 + 2. 14; 4Q504 23 1. 2; 4QM1 20 1. 2; 4QM1 1 + 1. 8; 4QM5 2 1. 2; 4p Is 2. 2; 4pHs 1. 10). At Qumran the vb. *pqd* often denotes the election or commissioning of a person by God (1QSa 1. 9). The titles *hpqwd* and *hpqyd* ("the Overseer") occur several times in the Zadokite Documents (CD) and the Rule of the Community (1QS), designating the appointed official who presided over the assembly (Charlesworth 1:5). His full title, *hpqyd brw'š hrbym,* the Overseer at the head of the Many (1QS 6:14), indicates his authority. He examined candidates wishing to join the community, then instructed neophytes during their two-year probationary period before they were eligible for full membership (1QS 6. 8-14; CD 14. 6-7).

3. In RL *pāqîd,* officer, commissioner, one appointed to examine (Jastrow, 1209), refers to various kinds of commissioners and officers appointed by Yahweh (Pesik Rab 42). The root has a widespread usage: *pqd,* to visit; to decree; to count, muster; to give in charge, entrust, deposit; to command, order; *p^eqîdâ,* examination, divine visitation (for good or evil), decree, remembrance; *piqqādôn,* thing given in charge, deposit; *p^eqadtâ,* order, last will; *pāqûd,* mustered, included in census; *p^equddâ,* watch, guard; *piqqûd,* charge, trust; count, muster; *piqqûddâ,* command, muster, count; *p^eqîdâ,* examination, divine visitation (for good or evil), remembrance, decree (Jastrow, 1169, 1206-9).

NT The G term that most closely parallels *pāqîd* is *episkopos* (Gehman). The religious leaders appointed over the church are designated by *episkopos*, overseer (Acts 20:28; Phil 1:1; 1 Tim 3:2; Titus 1:7; 1 Peter 2:25) and *episkopē*, overseer (Acts 1:20; 1 Tim 3:1). Roman civil officials in Judea are designated by *hēgeomōn*, governor (Matt 2:6; 10:18; 27:2, 11, 14-15, 21, 23, 27; 28:14; Mark 13:9; Luke 20:20; 21:12; Acts 23:24, 26, 33-34; 24:1, 10; 26:30; 1 Peter 2:14), *hēgeomai*, to govern (Matt 2:6; Luke 22:26; Acts 7:10), and *epitropos*, steward (Matt 20:8; Luke 8:3). Military commanders are *chiliarchos*, chief captain (John 18:12; Acts 21:31-33, 37; 22:24, 26-29; 23:10, 15, 17-19, 22; 24:7, 22; 25:23; Rev 6:15; 19:18).

Leaders: → *'ādôn* (lord, master, # 123); → *'allûp* II (tribal chief, # 477); → *'āṣîl* II (eminent, noble, # 722); → *zāqēn* (elder, # 2418); → *ḥōr* I, free man, freeborn, # 2985); → *maptēaḥ* (badge of office, # 5158); → *nāgîd* (prince, ruler, leader, # 5592); → *nāśî'* I (chief, king, # 5954); → *sārîs* (eunuch, court official, # 6247); → *seren* II (Philistine prince, # 6249); → *'attûd* (he-goat, leader, # 6966); → *peḥâ* (governor, # 7068); → *pāqîd* (officer, # 7224); → *qāṣîn* (commander, leader, # 7903); → *rab* II (captain, chief, # 8042); → *rzn* (rule, # 8142); → *šôa'* I (noble, # 8777)

BIBLIOGRAPHY
AHw, 827; *CAI* 224:4, 10, 13; *DISO*, 233-34; *THAT* 2:466-85; *TWOT* 2:732; Y. Aharoni, *Arad Inscriptions*, 46-47; G. André, *Determining the Destiny: PQD in the Old Testament*, 34-37; N. Avigad, "Epigraphical Gleanings from Gezer," *PEQ* 82, 1950, 43-46; I. Beit-Arieh, "A First Temple Period Census Document," *PEQ* 115, 1983, 105-8; P. Bordreuil, "Charges et fonctions en Syrie-Palestine d'aprés quelques sceaux ouest-sémitiques du second at du premier millénaire," *Comptes rendus des séances de l'académie des inscriptions et belles-lettres*, 305-7; E. F. Campbell, Jr., "Two Amarna Notes: The Shechem City-State and Amarna Administrative Terminology," in *Magnalia Dei: The Mighty Acts of God*, 39-54; G. Cardascia, *Les archives des Murašu*, 235b; B. Chayyim, *The Book of Ben Sirach*, 2:659; A. E. Cowley, *Aramaic Papyri of the Fifth Century BC*, §37. 6; G. I. Davies, *Ancient Hebrew Inscriptions*, §§2. 024. 14; 100. 163; 106. 012; H. Donner and W. Röllig, *Canaanite and Aramaic Inscriptions*, §224:4, 10, 13; G. R. Driver, *Canaanite Myths and Legends*, 1:2; 2:2, 3, 4; 4:1; 6:1, 5; 7:1, 3, 7; 8:1; 9:1; 10:1, 2, 3, 4; 11:2, 3, 4; 12:1; idem, *Aramaic Documents of the Fifth Century BC*, 15-17, 88-90, 103; E. Ebeling, *Das aramäischmittelpersische Glossar Frahang-i-Pahlavik Lichte der assyriologischen Forschung*, 12:4; J. Friedrich, *Phönizisch-punische Grammatik*, §131; J. Garfunkel, "The Meaning of the Word *mpqd* in the Tel 'Ira Ostracon," *Leš* 52, 1988, 68-74 [Hebrew]; H. S. Gehman, "Ἐπισκέμπομαι, ἐπίσκεψις, ἐπισκοπος and ἐπισκοπή in the Septuagint in Relation to פקד and Other Hebrew Roots," *VT* 22, 1972, 197-207; idem, "פקד," *VT* 22, 1972, 199-207; B. Grossfeld, "The Translation of Biblical Hebrew *pqd* in the Targum, Peshitta, Vulgate, and Septuagint," *ZAW* 86, 1984, 83-101; Z. Harris, *A Grammar of the Phoenician Language*, 139; C. F. Jean-J. Hoftijzer, *Dictionnaire des inscriptions sémitiques de l'ouest*, 233-34; K. Koch, *Um das Prinzip der Vergeltung in Religion und Recht*, 175; R. Menahem, "*enīrponog/pāqîd*, in the Parable of the Laborers in the Vineyard," *Immanuel* 24-25, 1990, 118-31; P. Middelkoop, "A Word Study: The Sense of PAQAD in the Second Commandment and Its General Background in the OT in Regard to the Translation into the Indonesian and Timorese Languages," *SEAJT* 4:33-47; L. Müller, *Numismatique de l'ancienne Afrique*, 2:10; 3:192; J. F. Priest, "MEBAQQER, PAQID, and the Messiah," *JBL* 81, 1962, 55-61; E. Qimron and J. H. Charlesworth, "The Rule of the Community (1QS)," in *The Dead Sea Scrolls: Rule of the Community and Related Documents*, 1-51; U. Rüterswörden, *Die Beamten der israelitischen Königszeit*, 116-20; J. Scharbert, "Das Verbum PQD in der Theologie des Alten Testaments," *BZ* 4, 1960, 209-29; E. A. Speiser, "Census and Ritual Expiation in Mari and Israel," *BASOR* 149, 1958, 17-25; J. B. Vanhooser, "The Meaning of the Hebrew Root פקד in the Old Testament," unpublished Ph.D. diss., Harvard University, 1963; R. de Vaux, *Ancient Israel: Social Institutes*, 1:225; B. K. Waltke and M. O'Connor, *Introduction to Biblical Hebrew Syntax*, §5. 3c.

Gordon H. Johnston

7228	פַּר

פַּר (*par*), nom. oxen, bull, cows (# 7228); פָּרָה (*pārâ* I), cow (# 7239).

ANE This term was shared with many Sem. dialects, but in Heb. it had a different referent.

The Heb. term *par* refers to the bovine, i.e., a young steer; however, as a cognate in other Sem. dialects, *par* refers to the caprovine, e.g., *parru*, lamb, in Assyr., *pr* in Ugar., *partâ*, ewe, in Aram. and Syr. (cf. *ABD* 6:1180; BDB 830).

OT 1. *par* occurs 133x in the OT. Its fem. form is *pārâ*. *par* is a subcategory of cattle (*bāqār*, → # 1330). Unlike *bāqār* or *šôr* (bull, → # 8802), *par* has a fem. form, *pārâ* (heifer, # 7239), thus constructing a gender-distinctive pair of noms. Both *šôr* and *bāqār* are generic terms for both sexes of all ages. Like the Eng. word cow *šôr* is used in a general manner, though *šôr* predominantly refers to the male. In the OT Heb., only young cattle have both masc. and fem. forms, such as *par* and *pārâ*, *'ēgel* (calf, → # 6319) and *'eglâ* (heifer, # 6320). The *par/pārâ* and *'ēgel/'eglâ* pairs are the only two distinctive sets that distinguish the sex for the bovine. This phenomenon is probably due to the significant use of young cattle in sacrifice. The bull was accepted as a sacrificial animal, while the heifer was not.

2. The significance of a *par* lies in its prominence in sacrifice. More than any other type of cattle, *par* is a major sacrificial animal. Only 2x (out of 133x) is *par* explicitly unrelated to sacrifice (Gen 32:15; Ps 22:12). Though *bāqār* also refers to sacrificial animals, *par* is virtually a term exclusively used for the sacrificial system. Like *bāqār*, *par* can be used in three types of offerings: (1) burnt offering (*'ôlâ*) to propitiate for sin in general, (2) sin offering (*ḥaṭṭā't*) to atone for specific transgressions, and (3) peace offering (*šᵉlāmîm*) to fellowship with God (→ *bāqār*, # 1330).

As a sin offering, *par* is used on many important occasions: (1) at the consecration of Aaron and his sons (Exod 29:1-14); (2) at the ordination of priests, for their sin (Lev 6:2); (3) for the sins of the high priest (e.g., Lev 4:3-5) or for the unintentional sins of the congregation (Lev 4:13-21); the bull served as a substitute for the guilty party who was to be expelled from the assembly (the blood was sprinkled in the Tent of Meeting and fat was burned on the altar; the expulsion of the guilty was symbolized by burning the animal remains outside the camp); (4) on the Day of Atonement for the sins of the high priest himself (Lev 16:11).

As a burnt offering, *par* is used (1) on the first of each month (Num 28:11); (2) at the Feast of Weeks (28:28); (3) at the Feast of Tabernacles (29:20, 36); (4) for the tabernacle altar dedication, lasting twelve days (Num 7); twenty-four bulls (*par*) were also sacrificed as a peace offering on the same occasion.

3. The cow (*pārâ*) was not to be used as a burnt offering in the OT sacrificial system. The burnt offering of two red heifers was sacrificed by the people of Beth Shemesh when the Philistines returned the ark to Israel (1 Sam 6:14). It should be viewed as a singular event. The incident was problematic, and the Israelites suffered the consequences.

A more interesting case is the red heifer (*pārâ 'ᵃdummâ*) in Num 19:1-10. It is the only case in which a heifer is related to the sin offering. The heifer was slaughtered and burned outside the camp, and its ashes were stored in a clean place outside the camp (19:1). The ashes were mixed with water of cleansing for use in removing impurity from contact with the dead (19:9). Though quite different from the sin offering in the sacrificial system (cf. *bāqār* above), the OT text designates the heifer ashes as a sin offering (*ḥaṭṭā't*).

P-B See *bāqār*: P-B.

NT In the NT the sacrificial language is far less prominent. The reference to bulls (*tauros*) for sacrifice and the ashes of heifers (*damalis*) for purification is only to contrast the complete redemption of Jesus Christ (Heb 9:13; 10:4).

Herd: → *bāqār* (cows, cattle, # 1330); → *ʿēgel* ([bull-]calf, # 6319); → *par* (bull, # 7228); → *šôr* I (bull, ox, steer, # 8802)

BIBLIOGRAPHY

ABD 5:870-86; 6:1129-30; *IBD* 1:254-55; *IDB* 1:543-44, 724; 3:614; *ISBE* 1:623-25, 798; 3:624; *NIDNTT* 1:113-19; 2:410-14; *TDNT* 2:760-62; *TDOT* 2:6-20 (esp. 13-17), 209-16; *TWOT* 1:121, 124-125, 524; F. S. Bodenheimer, *Animal and Man in Bible Lands*, 1960; J. Feliks, *Animal World of the Bible*, 1962; W. Kornfeld, "Reine und unreine Tiere im Alten Testament," *Kairos* 7, 1965, 134-47; J. N. Oswalt, "The Golden Calves and the Egyptian Concept of Deity," *EQ* 45:13-20; R. Péter, "Par et sor note de lexicographie hébraïque," *VT* 25, 1975, 486-96; R. Pinney, *Animals of the Bible*, 1964.

Jeffrey S. Lu

7229 (*pr'*, thrive in fruitfulness), → # 7238

7230	פֶּרֶא

פֶּרֶא (*pere'*), nom. zebra (or wild ass) (# 7230); פִּרְה (*pereh*), fem. nom. zebra (or wild ass) (# 7241).

ANE The Akk. cognate of this term, *parû,* is found in historical and omen texts (*AHw*, 837); note also the cognates in Ugar., Arab., and OSA.

OT The *pere'* is the Syrian Onager (or *Equus hemionus hemihippus*), translated by the NIV as wild donkey 8x and as donkey 1x (Isa 32:14). For a suggested etymology that relates *pere'* to the complex of *pr** vocables with meanings relating to breaking out, see *pered*, # 7234. Known for its independence and its wasteland habitations (cf. Job 39:5-8; → # 6871), it serves as a vivid metaphor, G. Wenham noting that it "is used in the OT as a figure for an individualistic lifestfyle untrammeled by social convention" (WBC, *Genesis 16-50*, 11). According to Job 24:5, "Like wild donkeys in the desert, the poor go about their labor of foraging food," while in Gen 16:12a, Ishmael is prophetically called *pere' 'ādām*, a wild donkey of a man ("countryman" in the LXX, "wild, rough" in the Vg.), expressing in just two words volumes of truth concerning his personality and future (cf. v. 12b!; the rendering of *'ādām* as steppe, as if related to *'ᵃdāmâ*, earth, ground, forwarded by M. J. Dahood, M. H. Pope, and V. Hamilton [cf. *Genesis 1-17*, NICOT, 449, n. 3] does not change the overall meaning; see also immediately below, to Job 11:12).

Hosea rebukes his fickle people by stating, "For they have gone up to Assyria like a wild donkey wandering alone" (Hos 8:9a), speaking not only of their undisciplined behavior but also of their utter lack of divine protection. It is interesting, however, that this verse continues with, "Ephraim has sold herself to lovers," possibly related to the imagery found later in Jer 2:23b-24, where the people of Judah are equated first with a "swift she-camel running here and there," and then with a female wild donkey in heat, sniffing at the air and readily available for mating, a scathing prophetic indictment of the people's unbridled (and unashamed) lust. The fact that the wild donkey is anything but human underscores the outrageousness of Job 11:12 ("But a witless man can no more become wise than a wild donkey's colt can be born a man"; the Heb., however, is difficult, and *pere'* occurs again with *'ādām*, hence NIV's marginal rendering, "a wild donkey can be born tame"; similarly Pope, AB;

D. J. A. Clines, WBC; cf. however, N. C. Habel, OTL, 203, who notes that the proposed varied renderings "tend to soften the paradox of the proverb").

According to Feliks (29), the wild donkey's "numbers steadily dwindled in Israel due to the many yearly droughts," with reference to Jer 14:6: "Wild donkeys stand on the barren heights and pant like jackals; their eyesight fails for lack of pasture" (cf. Ps 104:11). He also notes, "An extremely harsh winter about half a century ago was responsible for their complete extinction even in the Syrian desert."

Donkey: → *'ātôn* (she-ass, # 912); → *ḥ^{a}môr* I (male ass, donkey, # 2789); → *'ayir* (stallion of an ass, # 6555); → *'ārôd* (wild ass, # 6871); → *pere'* (zebra [wild ass], # 7230); → *pered* (mule, # 7234)

BIBLIOGRAPHY

J. Feliks, *The Animal World of the Bible*, 1962.

Michael S. Moore/Michael L. Brown

7232	פַּרְבָּר

פַּרְבָּר (*parbār*), court (# 7232).

OT The nom. *parbār*, court, occurs only one time in 1 Chron 26:18 and possibly in 2 Kgs 23:11 with the variant spelling *parwār*. The nom. *parbār* apparently has no cognate root in Sem. languages; it has been suggested that the word was a foreign loanword from Persian (C. Rabin 4:1079).

Because of the scarcity of usage the meaning of the term is unclear, although the word refers to a structure of the Jerusalem temple. The NIV translates the word as "court" while the word is also translated as "precinct" or "colonnade" in the NRSV. The latter rendering appears to be the meaning of *parwār* in the Temple Scroll.

Court, enclosure: → *gizrâ* (cutting, separate room, forecourt, # 1619); → *ḥāṣēr* (enclosure, court, settlement, village, # 2958); → *'^{a}zārâ* (border, court, # 6478); → *parbār* (court, # 7232)

BIBLIOGRAPHY:

J. Gray, *I & II Kings*, 1970, 737; J. Maier, *The Temple Scroll*, 1985, 90-91; J. Milgrom, "Studies in the Temple Scroll," *JBL*, 97, 1978, 506; E. Qimron, "The Vocabulary of the Temple Scroll," *Annual for the Study of the Bible and the Ancient Near East* 4, 1980, 249-50 (in Heb.); C. Rabin, "Foreign Words," *EMiqr* 4:1079 (in Heb.); Y. Yadin, *The Temple Scroll*, 1983.

Mark F. Rooker

7233	פרד

פרד (*prd*), q. spread out; ni. be divided, be separated; pi. separate, go away; hi. separate, set apart, keep apart; hitp. be parted from one another, be scattered (# 7233); פְּרֻדוֹת (*p^{e}rudôt*), nom. seeds (→ # 7237).

ANE Various of the Sem. languages have cognates, e.g., Ugar. *brd*, divide; Akk. *parādu*, separate (*AHw*, 827 identifies this as a WestSem. loanword in Neo-Babylonian). Syr. *p^{e}rad*, flee, break up; Mand. *prd*, break through, tear apart, flee; Arab. *afrada*, make separate, set aside; Eth. *färädä*, separate.

OT The "separation" described by the root *prd* divides into two general categories: separation observed in the natural and physical world, or the division of individuals or groups from one another. In either case it is usually a literal separation. Where people are involved, the implication is often negative in terms of friends or allies who become hostile or alien.

1. A q. passive part. describes the extension of the wings of the creatures in Ezek 1:11.

2. In the ni. the vb. can be used to describe the separation of rivers into streams (Gen 2:10), of peoples into various nations (10:5, 32; 25:23), of two individuals or groups from each other (13:9, 11, 14; 2 Sam 1:23; Neh 4:19[13]), or of one person from his tribe (Judg 4:11). The ni. of *prd* may also describe an unfriendly person, i.e., one who is "separated" from others (Prov 18:1; 19:4).

3. *prd* is found in Hosea's charge (Hos 4:14) against Israel: "The men *prd* with harlots and sacrifice with shrine prostitutes." This occurrence of a pi. form of the root *prd* is unique in the Bible. The poetic parallelism suggests a synonym for "sacrifice." This is followed by some commentaries and supported by a Ugar. text, "he offers a breast before him [Baal]" (*KTU* 1.3.16; Aistleitner, 58; Wieder, 163; Rudolph, 107). However, the context of the Anat text could support the meaning separate, cut, or carve (de Moor, 3; Caquot, Sznycer, and Herdner, 154). Nor is parallelism the only criterion for determining meaning. Indeed, the preceding context of vv. 13c and 14a suggests a meaning such as separate oneself to or take to one side, with the intent of engaging in some form of sexual cult act (Wolff, 72; Andersen and Freedman, 343, 370). This interpretation agrees more closely with the root's semantic range, including the pu.

4. The pu. appears in Esth 3:8, in a context in which Haman describes the Jews as "a certain people dispersed and scattered among the peoples in all the provinces of your kingdom."

5. The hi. form of *prd* emphasizes the act of separation of two groups of creatures or of persons. Jacob separates part of his flock (Gen 30:40); God separates the nations (Deut 32:8); "a chariot of fire and horses of fire" separate Elijah and Elishah (2 Kgs 2:11); "a gossip (*nirgān*)" or "whoever repeats a matter" separates friends (*'allûp*) (Prov 16:28; 17:9).

6. The hit. form of *prd* is confined to the Wisdom literature. It describes bones that are disjointed (Ps 22:14[15] ‖ 1QH VII.14), evil persons who are dispersed (Ps 92:9[10]), lion cubs that have scattered to seek food (Job 4:11), and the back of leviathan, whose scales cannot be separated (Job 41:17[9]; on the text see Rowley, 336-37).

P-B The hi. form reappears in 1QM X.14 in reference to the separation of the nations in the Tower of Babel account. It occurs in CD VII.12 in a description of the separation of Israel and Judah. The Commentary on Nahum (4Q169 III.7) refers to the "seekers of smooth things," whose gathering (*knstm*) will be dispersed (*nprdh*).

Division, measurement, portion: → *ḥlq* II (divide, obtain one's share, # 2745); → *ḥṣh* (divide, be divided, # 2936); → *ḥṣṣ*(divide, order, # 2951); → *mnh* (count, # 4948); → *plg* (be divided, # 7103); → *prd* (spread out, be divided, keep apart, # 7233); → *prs* (measure, divide, # 7271); → *šs'* (tear, divide, # 9117)

BIBLIOGRAPHY

J. Aistleitner, *Wörterbuch der Ugaritischen Sprache*, 1963; F. I. Andersen and D. N. Freedman, *Hosea: A New Translation with Introduction and Commentary*, AB 24, 1980; A. Caquot, M. Sznycer, and A. Herdner, *Textes ougaritiques. Tome I: Mythes et légendes*, 1974; J. C. de Moor,

An Anthology of Religious Texts, 1987; H. H. Rowley, *Job*, NCB, 1970; W. Rudolph, *Hosea*, KAT 13/1, 1966; A. A. Wieder, "Ugaritic-Hebrew Lexicographical Notes," *JBL* 84, 1965, 160-64; H. W. Wolff, *Hosea: A Commentary on the Book of Hosea*, Hermeneia, 1974.

Richard Hess

7234	פֶּרֶד

פֶּרֶד (*pered*), mule (# 7234); פִּרְדָּה (*pirdâ*), she-mule (# 7235).

OT The *pered* (*mulus*, or more specifically, *Equus asinus mulus*; cf. Akk. *perdum*, "ein Equide" acc. to *AHw*, 855) is the "hybrid offspring of the stallion and she-ass. Both the male and female are sterile" (Feliks, 28). The term is found 17x in the OT, 14x masc. and 3x fem. (with reference to the mule of King David; 1 Kgs 1:33, 38, 44; cf. the comments to Zech 9:9, at *ḥ^a^môr*, # 2789). Etymologically, the nom. would seem to be related to the root **prd* II (flee, flee away), suggesting various aspects of the mule's personality. It is also worth noting that some scholars trace all triliteral roots with *pr** to biliteral *pr*, with the underlying nuance of breaking out, breaking away or the like (cf. *pr'* in Talm. Heb., run, grow [related to *pry*], from which *pere'*, wild donkey (→ # 7230), may be derived; so, e.g., BDB; and note esp. *prd* I, divide; *prh*, be fruitful; **prz*, remove, separate > *p^e^rāzâ*, open region; *prḥ* I, bud, sprout; *prḥ* II, break out [of leprosy]; *prḥ* III, fly; *prṭ*, divide[?]; *prm*, tear, rend garment; *prs*, break in two, divide; **pr'* II, sprout > *pera'*, long hair; *pr'* III, let go, let alone; *prṣ*, break through; *prq*, tear apart, away; *prr* I, break, annul; *prr* II, split divide; *prś*, spread out; *prš* I, make distinct; **prš* III, rip open > *pereš*, offal; note also *pārāš*, horse, steed).

There are several references to the royal family riding mules; cf. 1 Kgs 1:33, 38, 44, where Solomon rides his father David's mule to his coronation at Gihon (note esp. David's words in v. 33, "Set Solomon my son on my own mule," followed by the report of Jonathan to Adonijah, "The king has sent with him Zadok the priest, Nathan the prophet, Benaiah son of Jehoiada, the Kerethites and the Pelethites, and they have put him on the king's mule," v. 44); 2 Sam 13:29 (the sons of David); and 18:9 (Absalom), while in 1 Kgs 10:25 ‖ 2 Chron 9:24 mules are included among the gifts brought by those who sought audience with Solomon (along with "articles of silver and gold, robes, weapons and spices, and horses"; cf. also Ezek 27:14). Both their strength and common use as beasts of burden is reflected in 2 Kgs 5:17, where Naaman requests "as much [Israelite] earth as a pair of mules can carry," and in Ps 32:9, where the mule and horse serve as symbols of self-willed brute beasts (they "have no understanding but must be controlled by bit and bridle or they will not come to you," something that should not be emulated!). According to Zech 14:15, the same plague that strikes those who attack eschatological Jerusalem (cf. v. 12) will strike their horses, mules, camels, donkeys, and other animals in their camps, and, in another end-time context, Isa 66:20 promises that the nations will bring the Jewish people back to their land "on horses, in chariots and wagons, and on mules and camels."

Donkey: → *'ātôn* (she-ass, # 912); → *ḥ^a^môr* I (male ass, donkey, # 2789); → *'ayir* (stallion of an ass, # 6555); → *'ārôd* (wild ass, # 6871); → *pere'* (zebra [wild ass], # 7230); → *pered* (mule, # 7234)

Bibliography
J. Feliks, *The Animal World of the Bible*, 1962.

Michael S. Moore/Michael L. Brown

7235 (*pirdâ*, she-mule), → # 7234

7236	פַּרְדֵּס

פַּרְדֵּס (*pardēs*), park, forest, orchard, later paradise (# 7236).

ANE Akk. *pardēsu* (*AHw*, 833); Persian *paridaida, pairidaêza* (enclosed garden; cf. E. B. Moynihan, *Paradise as a Garden in Persia and Mughal India*, 1979, 1); taken over by Greek (Xenophon).

OT Used for royal gardens, but never employed theologically or symbolically as in later traditions (*NIDNTT* 3:760-64; *TDNT* 5:765-73). Eccl 2:5 mentions a royal project of building gardens and parks (cf. *KAI* 181:21). Neh 2:8 refers to the keeper of the king's park (NIV forest), and in S of Songs 4:13 the beloved is described as plants, which are a park (NIV orchard) of pomegranates. The pomegranate was in the ANE a symbol of life (O. Keel, *Das Hohelied*, ZB, 1986, 134-36).

P-B LXX *paradeisos*, paradise.

NT → *NIDNTT* 2:760-64.

Forest, park, thicket: → *gā'ôn* (height, eminence, # 1454); → *ḥōreš* (forest, woodland, # 3091); → *ya'ar* I (forest, wood, # 3623); → *sᵉbak* (thicket, # 6019); → *pardēs* (park, forest, # 7236)
Garden, orchard: → *gan/gannâ* (garden, orchard, # 1703/1708); → *karmel* I (orchard, # 4149); → *[gan] 'ēden* II ([garden of] Eden, # 6359); → *'ᵃrûgâ* (garden bed, terrace, # 6870); → *pardēs* (park, forest, # 7236)

Bibliography
I. Cornelius, "Paradise Motifs in the 'Eschatology' of the Minor Prophets and the Iconography of the ANE," *JNSL* 14, 1988, 41-42.

I. Cornelius

7237	פְּרֻדוֹת

פְּרֻדוֹת (*pᵉrudôt*), seeds (# 7237); < פרד (*prd*), spread out (→ # 7233).

OT "Dried figs" is the least probable meaning for *pᵉrudôt* (Joel 1:17). A likelier choice is between either "grains of seed" (NIV the seeds are shriveled), or else "stored up supplies."

Sowing: → *zr'* (sow, scatter seed, form seed, # 2445)

Edwin C. Hostetter

7238	פרה

פרה (*prh*), q. bear fruit; hi. make fruitful (# 7238); פְּרִי (*pᵉrî*), fruit, offspring (# 7262).

ANE Ugar. and Phoen. *pr*, fruit; Egyp. *pri*, come out; *prt*, fruit.

OT The following analysis centers on five kinds of settings:

1. *Family size*. Large families are a blessing from Yahweh (Ps 127-28). Parents who have been granted children by Yahweh are fortunate because the fruit (*p*^{e}*rî*) of the belly is a reward (127:3). Descendants are a divine allotment as indicated by the many names composed of the root *ntn*, give, and a theophoric element: e.g., Elnathan and Nethaniah in English. Nevertheless, v. 5 acknowledges a warrior's part in filling one's quiver with arrows—a simile for the fruit of sexual activity. The psalm esteems such activity as participation in the order established at creation. Like Mic 6:7, Ps 127:3-5 evidently refers to the "belly" of the husband rather than the wife.

Having children born in a person's youth offers ample opportunity for rearing offspring and influencing them for life (Ps 127:4; Estes, 305). It was customary in Israel to marry young as reflected in the age of marriage by Judahite kings (between fourteen and sixteen years old) and the expression "wife of youth" (Prov 5:18; Isa 54:6; Mal 2:14-15).

Progeny should be ready to replace their aging parents in society. Such children would be prepared to stand their ground in diverse social situations in interchange with enemies at the "gate" (Ps 127:5). This terminology may refer to lawsuits proceeding at that location (see Keel, 162).

Through careful and godly molding of their children, a couple is able to assuage the pain of ephemerality and achieve lasting significance and a form of immortality. The parents' societal contribution need not be circumscribed by their own temporal and geographical limitations. Offspring keep alive the name of their parents (cf. Gen 48:16; 2 Sam 18:18) and can perpetuate their values (Sir 30:4-6). "As arrows shot from the bow are propelled toward a remote target according to the desire of the archer, so children when properly nurtured extend the effect of their father into human society of the next generation" (Estes, 310).

The wife who has borne children to a righteous husband is analogous to a fruit-bearing (*prh*) grapevine (Ps 128:3; cf. Isa 32:12; Ezek 19:10). Children are a blessing for the person who reveres Yahweh (v. 4). This favor might be linked with the prosperity of Jerusalem (Ps 128:5). The psalmist may be viewing individual and community as mutually interacting (not isolated) entities, so that success by either redounds to the other. Sentiments similar to Ps 127-28 surface in a Sumerian hymn to the goddess Nisaba: "You are the Lady who gives joy to the heart; / you put good seed in the womb, / allow the fruit in the womb to mature, / give a mother's love to the infant" (Keel, 157-58).

Sirach exhibits a different perspective on multiplying (*prh*) offspring (Sir 16:2). Sons and daughters were normally considered a sign of prosperity and well-being (e.g., Gen 24:60; Deut 28:4); to lack a son or daughter was a reproach (e.g., Gen 30:23; 1 Sam 1:6). However, Ben Sira views pride in a large family as inappropriate when that progeny has no fear of God (Sir 16:1-4). A great number of descendants is no grounds for joy unless they revere Yahweh. Sirach holds that a single child who performs the Lord's will is better than a thousand who do not (v. 3). An analogy follows: "For through one intelligent person a city can be filled with people, but through a clan of outlaws it becomes desolate" (v. 4, NRSV). Character comes before quantity; better to die childless than have wicked children—regardless of how many. One should not count on long life for ungodly children and grandchildren, since the wicked come to untimely ends (see Ps 55:23[24]).

2. *Propagation of the species*. The creation account sums up the marvel of reproduction with respect to vegetation. Every tree yields a characteristic fruit (*p*^{e}*rî*) along with its seed, from which in turn another tree of the same species can grow up (Gen 1:11-12). At the creation and after the Flood, God utters a benediction over animals and humans: "Be fruitful and increase in number" (1:22, 28; 8:17; 9:1, 7). The vb. *prh* is contiguous with the root *rbh*, become numerous, in all these verses and also stands near the root *ml'*, fill, in 1:22, 28; 9:1. The vbs. *prh* and *rbh* are juxtaposed regarding the animal creatures—of water or land or air (1:22; 8:17). Human beings are addressed with the same combination (1:28; 9:1, 7). (An ancient blessing formula that would effect the fecundity of a young couple may be reflected [cf. 28:2-3].)

God mandates both sexual and governmental functions to humans; they procreate like animals but rule like deities. "To reproduce and fill the earth on the one hand, and yet to master it on the other, suggest[s] that humans are situated on a cosmic frontier, between terrestrial and supernal realms of existence" (Cohen, 75). People's dominion over earth involves developing earth's potential, utilizing tools of human creativity. "Responsible interaction with the environment offers men and women the deepest personal and spiritual fulfillment, while environmental irresponsibility will lead to their physical and spiritual demise" (Cohen, 77).

3. *Lovemaking*. Love dialogues are found in S of Songs 2:1-3; 4:12-5:1; they entail praise to or about a beloved, and in the latter passage present invitations to lovemaking. Stirred by the delights of the man's affection, the woman proclaims his fruit (*p*^{e}*rî*), or ways of love, as sweet to her taste (2:3). The focus is increasingly on the woman's physical and erotic attractions (ch. 4). Her female charm is likened to an exotic garden of sweet-scented plants (4:12-14). The phrase "choice fruits" in v. 13, where *p*^{e}*rî* is joined and intensified by *meged*, choice fruit, is expressive of a sexual element, a point made more obvious in v. 16. Here the woman invites the man to possess and enjoy her in all her intimate delights. They consummate their love by extending the fullness of themselves to each other.

4. *Punishment for sins*. Two highly respected traditions arose in ancient Israel. One asserted that Yahweh's punishment for sin extended several generations beyond the point of infraction (Exod 20:5-6 = Deut 5:9-10; Exod 34:7; Num 14:18). The second tradition laid stress on individual responsibility and denied that personal ruin depended on ancestral sins (Deut 24:16; 2 Kgs 14:6). On the basis of the former belief, the slogan concerning sour grapes was coined: "The fathers (have) eat(en) sour grapes [*bōser*, unripe grape], and the children's teeth are set on edge" (Jer 31:29 [LXX 38:29]; Ezek 18:2). This proverb, an understandable evaluation of a tragic time, expressed a common mood of bitterness and futility felt by Judahites in the disastrous wake of the first Babylonian deportation—whether they languished among Jerusalem's smoking ruins or in the empire's resettlement ghettos. Apparently the populace concluded that the wrongdoing of a former generation was unfairly loaded on them because of Yahweh's unreasonable anger. Fear of arbitrary divine wrath, where parental iniquities enter the picture, is natural (Waldman, 4-5). However, Jeremiah and Ezekiel rejected the outlook of the proverb, which they predicted would cease being quoted. Instead, only the sinner himself or herself will die (Jer 31:29-30 [LXX 38:29-30]; Ezek 18:3-4).

Ambivalent attitudes persisted, however. On the one hand, Jeremiah admitted that rebellion of an earlier generation weighed heavily upon his contemporaries. Destruction of the southern kingdom was happening because of Manasseh's sins (Jer 15:4). On the other hand, the prophet did not think the people were innocent victims of their parents' guilt; he rebukes both groups for violating God's covenant (11:9-10; 14:20). Jer 32:18-19 [LXX 39:18-19] demonstrates the tension, where Yahweh is said to "bring the punishment for the fathers' sins into the laps of their children after them" as well as to "reward everyone according to his conduct and as his deeds [p^e*rî*] deserve." (An identical dichotomy occurs in Lam 5. Sufferers bear the punishment of their parents who sinned and are no more—which conveys the sense not that parents were punished for iniquity but that they fled the crime scene, leaving the innocent holding the bag [5:7; Hutton, 232]. But this assessment is soon followed by: "Woe to us, for we have sinned!" 5:16.) Did Jeremiah discount the concept of collective historical accountability, or did he accept it under certain conditions? Possibly he anticipated the later rabbinic view that parental guilt befalls children when they continue in the same ways (Waldman, 1-2).

5. *Metaphorical and natural uses.* A common biblical usage of "fruit" refers to the speech (Hos 10:13), thought (Isa 10:12; Jer 6:19), and action (Isa 3:10; Jer 17:10; Mic 7:13) of a human being. These may turn out to be beneficial or injurious. The figure is especially prevalent in the Wisdom literature. For example, Ps 1:3 likens one who trusts in God to a robust tree that always brings forth fruit (cf. Jer 17:8). The industrious homemaker set up a vineyard with what she had earned—lit., "the fruit of her hands" (Prov 31:16). Personified Wisdom commended her fruit as more precious than the finest gold; success is assured to whoever accepts her instruction (8:12-21). People are said to taste the results, good or bad, of their words (12:14; 13:2; 18:20). The relation between seed and plant is analogous to that between deed and consequence.

Besides this sampling of metaphorical uses of *prh* and p^e*rî*, there are naturally many occurrences of the terms with their everyday meanings. Eve and then Adam ate some of the forbidden fruit from the tree that was in the middle of the garden planted in Eden (Gen 3:2-3, 6). Locusts invaded Egypt and devoured every piece of fruit on all the trees in the whole country during one of the ten plagues (Exod 10:15). Whenever the Israelites would plant a new tree, they were supposed to refrain from eating its produce until the fifth year of fruitbearing—after donating the fourth year's yield to Yahweh (Lev 19:23-25). In the middle of the seventh month of each year, the people of Yahweh were supposed to start their celebration of the Feast of Tabernacles by taking choice fruit from the trees (Lev 23:40). The prophet conveys God's promise to bless Jerusalem with vines yielding their fruit amidst general prosperity (Zech 8:12). The Jews under Nehemiah and Ezra agreed to live up to what was expected of them (Lev 27:30), namely, to bring to the temple personnel the tithes from the fruit of their trees (Neh 10:35, 37[36, 38]).

A few additional fruit-related terms appear in scattered passages. The vb. *pr'*, flourish (# 7229), unless it signifies "divide, separate," denotes "thrive in fruitfulness, flourish" in Hos 13:15. The prophet seems to envision Israel as a plant that will die for lack of water. The vb. *nwb*, bear fruit (# 5649), in Ps 92:12-15[13-16] likens the righteous to palm and cedar trees: "they will still bear fruit in old age." Metaphorical and uncertain is the employment of *nîb,* fruit (# 5762), at Isa 57:19 (cf. Sir 32[35]:5). Isaiah's expression "fruit of lips" may indicate the announcement of peace to those far and near. The nom. *nōbelet*, withered fruit (Isa 34:4), is a substantive use of the participle of *nbl*, wither, fade (→ # 5570). Observe the infinitive, *n^ebōl*, previously in that verse: "all the starry host will fall like withered (*n^ebol*) leaves from the vine, like shriveled figs (*nōbelet*) from the fig tree."

P-B At Qumran *p^erî* occurs where a severely fragmentary text (4Q173) quotes and explains Ps 127:3b.

Fruit: → *nîb* (fruit, # 5762); → *prh* I (bear fruit, make fruitful, # 7238); → *qayiṣ* (summer, summer-fruit, # 7811)

BIBLIOGRAPHY

TWOT 2:733-34; J. Cohen, "On Classical Judaism and Environmental Crisis," *Tikkun* 5.2, 1990, 74-77; D. J. Estes, "Like Arrows in the Hand of a Warrior (Psalm cxxvii)," *VT* 41, 1991, 304-11; R. R. Hutton, "Slogans in the Midst of Crisis: Jeremiah and His Adversaries," *Word & World* 10, 1990, 229-36; O. Keel, "Psalm 127: Ein Lobpreis auf Den, der Schlaf und Kinder gibt," in *Ein Gott, eine Offenbarung: Beiträge zur biblischen Exegese, Theologie und Spiritualität*, ed. F. V. Reiterer, 1991, 155-63; N. M. Waldman, "Parents Have Eaten Sour Grapes," *Dor LeDor* 18, 1989, 1-5.

Edwin C. Hostetter

7239 (*pārâ* I, cow), → # 7228

7241 (*pereh*, zebra [wild ass]), → # 7230

7248	פָּרוּר

פָּרוּר (*pārûr*), nom. cooking pot (# 7248).

ANE Etymology is uncertain. Perhaps related to Arab. *fāra*, cook, boil, or to Arab. *'fr*, glow, be hot (see Heb. *pā'rûr*, heat, # 6999); Syr. *n^efar*, roar, rage (*HALAT* 859-60, 908).

OT This type of pot was used to cook the manna (Num 11:8), and Gideon used such a vessel in presenting broth (*māraq*; → # 5348) to the angel of Yahweh (Judg 6:19). It is also mentioned as the last container in which the meat was boiled outside the sanctuary at Shiloh (1 Sam 2:14; along with *dûd*, *kiyyôr* and *qallaḥat*). It thus appeared to have come in different sizes.

P-B From Sir 13:2 it appears that the *pārûr* was normally made of clay. It breaks when striking against the *sîr*, which here must be assumed to be of bronze.

Pan, pot: → *'^agarṭāl* (bowl, basin, # 113); → *dûd* (cooking pot, # 1857); → *maḥtâ* (censer, fire pan/tray, # 4746); → *marḥešet* (baking pan, # 5306); → *maśrēt* (baking pan, # 5389); → *sîr* (cooking pot, # 6105); → *pārûr* (cooking pot, # 7248); → *qallaḥat* (pot, # 7831)

BIBLIOGRAPHY

R. Amiran, *Ancient Pottery of the Holy Land*, 1970; A. M. Honeyman, "The Pottery Vessels of the Old Testament," *PEQ* 71, 1939, 87; J. L. Kelso, *The Ceramic Vocabulary of the Old Testa-*

ment, *BASOR*, Suppl. Studies, nos. 5-6, 1948, esp. §§ 26 and 68; idem, "Pottery," *IDB* 3, 846-53, esp. 850.

Cornelis Van Dam

7251	פְּרָזוֹן

פְּרָזוֹן (*p^e rāzôn*), people who live in open country (# 7251); פְּרָזוֹת (*p^e rāzôt*), nom. open, rural country (# 7252); פְּרָזִי (*p^e rāzî*), nom. open, rural country (# 7253).

ANE This is a contested issue (see below). EA *pu-ru-zi*, rural, unwalled settlement (see # 7253).

OT 1. The nom. *p^e rāzôn* occurs twice in the Song of Deborah (Judg 5:7, 11). Many scholars wrestle not only with the meaning of the term, but the difficulty of finding a meaning that coheres with the argument of both verses in Judg 5. Moore (143) laments, "No rendering which suits the one of the phrases seems to be possible in the other."

(a) Options. Three primary approaches to *p^e rāzôn* exist (see Stager, 225, for other possible etymologies, and Niemann, 235, nn. 7-8, for a concise summary of views with more extensive bibliography). (i) The customary translation of the nom. has been peasantry or village dwellers, i.e., people who dwell outside of walled cities. Proponents (*HALAT* 908; Stager, 224-25; Gottwald, 779-80, n. 516; Niemann, 234-37; Hertzberg, 171) argue for this meaning in light of the meanings of two similar forms, *p^e rāzôt* (# 7252), *p^e rāzî* (# 7253); the Mish. Heb. *pārûz*, one residing in an open place; and the immediate context (see below).

(ii) A second alternative derives *p^e rāzôn* from Arab. *faraza* (according to *HALAT* 908) or *baraza* (going forth in battle, Craigie, 350; Rabin, 127-28) and suggests either the abstract meaning of leadership (Driver, 8; Richter, 72; Soggin, 86; Weiser, 76-77), championship (Rabin, 127-28), or the more precise idea of warriors (Albright, 49, n. 101; Boling, 109; Craigie, 350; Patterson, 132; Wolf, 410). Albright also relates *p^e rāzôn* to a Can. term for warrior (found in an Egyp. transcription). Proponents of this latter view seek to manifest correctly the military overtones of Judg 5:11 and direct attention to a similar term, *perez*, in Hab 3:14 (hapleg.), which may also mean warrior. If correct, 5:7-11 affirms that even though warriors seemed to be nonexistent, the day will come in which Israelites can rejoice in the victorious deeds of Israelite warriors or Yahweh their warrior God.

(iii) Proponents (Garbini, 23-34; Ackroyd, 19-20) of this alternative posit that *p^e rāzôn* derives from OSA *frn*, iron, and they contend that *p^e rāzôn* is a byform of the more common Heb. term *barzel*, the only formal Sem. par. term for *p^e rāzôn*. Garbini links the Judg 5 statements with Israel's lack of iron for weapons during Saul's reign (1 Sam 13:19-21). Ackroyd (20) limits the problem to craftsmanship, not quantity, of iron. He argues that although Israel had no (lit.) iron weapons with which to fight their battle (Judg 5:7), Yahweh's superior might (fig. iron weapon) would accomplish the victory for them.

(b) Suggested meaning. Even though Judg 5:11 has clear military overtones, it is unnecessary to resort to Albright's or Craigie's strained etymology (see Stager's critique ([224-25] and Craigie's own concerns [350, n. 3]). Judg 5:11 refers to the righteous acts of Israel's "irregular army," i.e., conscript soldiers from the many unprotected villages that interspersed Israel's terrain. Ahlström (136) points out that villagers probably would have normally reinforced the regular army. Consequently, the "village life" (NIV) that ceases in Judg 5:7 notes the fact that most village inhabitants had fled to walled towns for protection.

2. The nom. *p^e rāzôt* occurs only 3x (Esth 9:19; Ezek 38:11; Zech 2:4[8]) and signifies villages without walls (see # 7253). That *p^e rāzôt* refers to unwalled villages and not simply open fields is esp. clear in Esth 9:19 and Ezek 38:11. Esth 9:19 describes the celebration by the nonurban Jews of their deliverance from the attack of the Persians. The Jews celebrated in two distinct groups: city dwellers and unwalled village people (those who lived in cities of open country, *b^e ʿārê happ^e rāzôt*). They celebrated on different days because the former fought off Persian attacks for two days while the nonurban Jews fought only for one day. Ezekiel (Ezek 38:10-11) warns of the future day when Gog will devise an attack against restored Israel. Gog describes Israel as "a land of open country" (*'ereṣ p^e rāzôt*), where the people live without walls, gates, or bars (38:11). Zech (2:4[8]) anticipates a time when no walls will be able to contain Jerusalem's vast population. In this instance, *p^e rāzôt* occurs without a preceding word for city or land.

In all three cases, the Jews who lived in unwalled villages or cities were exposed to much more peril than inhabitants of walled cities. However, in each instance Yahweh provides the necessary protection.

3. In two of its three occurrences, the gen. phrase "cities of" (Deut 3:5, *ʿîr*; 1 Sam 6:18, *kōper*) precedes *p^e rāzî*, and the entire phrase stands in contrast to "fortified cities" (*ʿārîm* + *bṣr* III/*mibṣār* [# 4448/# 1307]). The mention of walls, gates, and bars on the fortified city in Deut 3:5 heightens the contrast between the walled cities and the cities of *p^e rāzî*. Both *p^e rāzî* and *p^e rāzôṭ* (see # 7252) occur in Esth 9:19, "rural Jews (Q, *p^e rāzî*), those living in villages (*p^e rāzôt*)." The first term, *p^e rāzî*, is distinct from the similar form, *p^e rāzôt*, in that it directs primary attention to the inhabitants rather than the village.

Na'aman (72-75) contends that the Amarna expression (EA 137) *ālāni pu-ru-zi* parallels *p^e rāzî* and *p^e rāzôt* since they both share the meaning rural, unwalled settlements.

4. Summary. Drawing on the meaning of similar forms, *p^e rāzôt* (# 7252) and *p^e rāzî* (# 7253), it appears that *p^e rāzôt* always signifies unwalled villages in contrast to fortified cities, while *p^e rāzî* refers to the inhabitants of those unwalled cities. The nom. *p^e rāzôn* serves as a collective nom. (see BL, 498, §61c) and connotes either the unwalled villages themselves or, more likely, their inhabitants (Stager, 225).

City, village, country: → *ḥûṣ* (outside, street, # 2575); → *ḥāṣēr* (enclosure, court, settlement, village, # 2958); → *kāpār* (village, # 4107); → *māqôm* (place, town, site, dwelling place, holy place, # 5226); → *miqlāṭ* (city of refuge, asylum, # 5236); → *ʿîr* I (city, town, # 6551); → *p^e rāzôn* (fertile field, # 7251); → *qiryâ* (town, city, # 7953); → *r^e ḥōb* I (broad open place, plaza, # 8148); → *šûq* (street [in a town], # 8798)

BIBLIOGRAPHY

W. Albright, *Yahweh and the Gods of Canaan*, 1968; P. Ackroyd, "Note to **Parzon* 'Iron' in the Song of Deborah," *JSS* 24, 1979, 19-20; G. Ahlström, "Where Did the Israelites Live?" *JNES* 41, 1982, 133-38; R. Boling, *Judges*, AB, 1975; P. Craigie, "Some Further Notes on the Song of Deborah," *VT* 22, 1972, 349-53; G. Driver, "Problems in Judges Newly Discussed," *ALUOS* 4, 1962-1963, 6-25; G. Garbini, "**Parzon* 'Iron' in the Song of Deborah," *JSS* 23, 1978, 23-24;

N. Gottwald, *The Tribes of Yahweh*, 1979; H. Hertzberg, *Die Bücher Josua, Richter, Ruth*, 1959; G. Moore, *A Critical and Exegetical Commentary on Judges*, ICC, 1895; N. Na'aman, "Amarna *ālāni pu-ru-zi* (EA 137) and Biblical *'ry hprzy/hprzwt* ('Rural Settlements')," *ZAH* 4, 1991, 72-75; H. Niemann, "Das Ende des Volkes der Perizziter," *ZAW* 105, 1993, 233-57; R. Patterson, "The Song of Deborah," in *Tradition and Testament*, 1981, 123-60; C. Rabin, "Judges V,2 and the 'Ideology' of Deborah's War," *JJS* 6, 1955, 125-34; W. Richter, *Traditionsgeschichtliche Untersuchungen zum Richterbuch*, 1966; J. Soggin, *Judges*, 1981; L. Stager, "Archaeology, Ecology, and Social History: Background Themes to the Song of Deborah," in *SVT* 40, 1988, 221-34; A. Weiser, "Das Deboralied," *ZAW*, 71, 1959, 67-97; H. Wolf, "Judges," in *EBC* 3, 1992, 375-506.

Michael A. Grisanti

7252 (*pᵉrāzôt*, open, rural country), → # 7251

7253 (*pᵉrāzî*, open, rural country), → # 7251

7255	פרח

פרח (*prḥ* I), q. sprout, bud, break out; hi. bring to bloom (# 7255); פֶּרַח (*peraḥ*), bud, flower, bud- or flower-shaped ornament (# 7258).

ANE Akk. *parāḫu*, ferment/*per'u(m)*, *perḫu*, sprout, descendant; Ugar. *prḫ*, flower; Egyp. *prḫ*, blossom.

OT 1. The vb. *prḥ* occurs in metaphors out of the plant world in the prophets and psalmists. Such is the case for *prḥ*, sprout, as a representation of blooming and growing. The causative sense ("to bring to bud") is clear in the hi. stem of *prḥ* found at Isa 17:10-11. Here, the imagery of planting and fruitfulness is surrounded by an opening mention of the Israelites' neglect of Yahweh and a closing prediction of grief and pain.

The custom apparently was for grain or cuttings to be planted in (possibly shallow) pots or potsherds, watered, and placed in the sun. The plants grew rapidly but wilted equally quickly. The episode represented the rise and death of a deity, who was then mourned with great passion. This tradition of forcing plants to bloom and then allowing them to die symbolized the earth's fertility cycle. (The fertility god with whom these rites were associated may have been Adonis, Baal, Osiris, or Tammuz.) Worshipers believed that by reenacting the ritual of the dying and rising god they would secure a good crop, plus become fecund themselves. But the harvest described by Isaiah would cause disappointment; the finest plants would come to nothing.

2. The book of Leviticus uses the vb. to denote the breaking out of disease on the skin (Lev 13:20), mold on clothing (13:57), or a fungus on the wall of a house (14:43). When the disease did not spread in a person, he or she was declared clean upon the completion of a purification ritual. In the case of a mold or fungus, the affected part had to be removed. However, when the disease kept on spreading, the person was declared unclean; similarly, when a mold or fungus spread persistently, the object became unclean, but unlike a person, it had to be destroyed.

In Exod 9:9-10, *prḥ* refers to the outbreaking of boils as a plague against the Egyptians.

3. The nom. *peraḥ* in Sir 14:17-19 focuses on the motif of human mortality—a motif that underlies the entire pericope, starting at v. 3. In v. 17, as the basis for his

teaching that death will become everybody's lot eventually (cf. v. 12), Ben Sira quotes Scriptural authority (Gen 2:17). Blooming flowers are utilized to depict graphically the precariousness of human existence: "Like abundant (*peraḥ,* bud) leaves on a spreading tree that sheds some and puts forth others, so are the generations of flesh and blood: one dies and another is born" (Sir 14:18 NRSV). Homer employs a similar image: "The generations of people are very much like those of leaves. The autumn wind causes a shedding of the old year's leaves onto the ground, but the forest burgeons with fresh ones when spring returns. So it is with humankind: one generation is born even as another passes away" (*Iliad* 6.146-49).

In Num 17 Yahweh devised a test to prove which leader he chose to minister as priest (v. 20[5]). Yahweh caused dissent to subside by affirming Aaron in a dramatic way. It is not clear whether all three stages—bud, bloom, fruit—were present on the rod simultaneously, or whether the rod had simply passed through those stages (v. 23[8]). In either case, the sprouting rod was placed in the ark, where it continued as a witness to Yahweh's will (v. 25[10]).

The construction and decoration of the bronze reservoir for the temple court is told in considerable detail (1 Kgs 7:23-26). This handiwork of Hiram was cast in one piece, including the lily-like rim (v. 26) and the two rows of gourds. The priests and worshipers used the water to cleanse their hands and feet, to rinse the animal offerings, and to wash blood from the surrounding ground. By contrast, the candelabra were wrought in gold and were among Solomon's own artifacts—special items for the temple's interior (vv. 48-50). Like the reservoir, however, each candelabrum had floral decoration (v. 49).

4. Other words related to flowers.

(a) "Flower" associated with cult: *m^{e}šuqqād* (# 5481). On the central shaft of the tabernacle's lampstand and on all six branches of the lampstand were cups shaped like almond flowers, each consisting of bud and blossom (or perhaps better, calyx and petals). The word for "shaped like almond blossoms" is *m^{e}šuqqād* (Exod 25:33-34; 37:19-20), a part. of a pu. vb. derived in turn from the nom. *šāqēd*, almond (# 9196). The lampstand's design was evidently patterned after an almond tree. The almond is the first tree of spring in southwest Asia, awakening sometimes as early as the middle of December. Before leafing, the tree bedecks itself with radiant white blossoms.

The lampstand likely symbolized the fertility that came from Yahweh. The botanically branched form of the lampstand may even have represented the concept of a sacred tree, a common motif throughout ANE art (→ *'ēṣ*, # 6770). We can locate the same topos in the description of two trees in the middle of Eden's garden (→ # 6359): namely, the tree of life and the tree of the knowledge of good and evil (Gen 2-3).

(b) "Flower" and love poetry: *s^{e}mādar* (# 6163). S of Songs 7:11-14[10-13] constitutes a love monologue. That label refers to a poem in which a single speaker, either male or female, talks to or about a beloved with words of praise, inducements to lovemaking, or descriptions of fantasies. The woman calls the man to the fields for a tryst (v. 11). The awakening of nature—"if the vines have budded, if their blossoms have opened, and if the pomegranates are in bloom" (v. 12[13])—is a recurring theme in this book (see not only 2:11-13 below but also 6:11).

The just-mentioned word "(vine) blossom" translates the Heb. *s^{e}mādar.* The rabbis identified it as the stage of tiny grapes after the blossoms disappear. Yet the statement in 2:13, "the blossoming (s^e*mādar*) vines spread their fragrance," would be meaningless at that phase of development. Recent studies of material from Ebla suggests that the term could really have been the name of a place, *Sumudar/Semadar*, probably in northern Syria. From there, slips of a specially good variety of grapevines might have been carried all over Syria-Palestine and imported into Israel. This understanding of s^e*mādar* would render the phrase "Semadar vines."

The depiction of spring in S of Songs 2 (*nēṣ* [# 5890], blossom, is the lexeme behind "flowers" in 2:12) is one of the most beautiful songs to nature in the HB. The chapter's picture of springtime love may be among the most exquisite anywhere in literature. The meaning of *niṣṣâ* (# 5900) is "blossom" (Job 15:33; Isa 18:5).

(c) "Flower" and season. In Exod 9:31, *gib'ōl* signifies "bud" unless it indicates a month name "Gibeol," equaling Adar, the month of flax blossoms.

(d) Either "branch" (figurative for hair or arm) or else "date blossom cluster" (i.e., breast) translates *sansinnâ* (# 6180) at S of Songs 7:9[8].

(e) The rendering for *qiddâ* (# 7703) is "cassia" (Exod 30:24; Ezek 27:19). For additional cultic associations, → *ṣwṣ*, bloom (→ # 7437).

(f) In S of Songs 5:11, *taltallîm* (# 9446) could have any one of three meanings: date flower clusters, date palm sheaths, or palm branches.

Flower, bud: → *prḥ* I (sprout, bud, bring to bloom, # 7255); → *ṣwṣ* I (sprout, bloom, # 7437)

Bibliography
TWOT 2:734.

Edwin C. Hostetter

7258 (*peraḥ*, bud, flower, flower-shaped ornament), → # 7255

7260	פרט

פרט (*prṭ*), q. uncertain: improvise(?), clap(?), devise(?) (when playing a stringed instrument) (hapleg.; # 7260; *HALAT* 910a); der. פֶּרֶט (*pereṭ*), fallen grapes (→ # 7261).

ANE The vb. is attested in Akk. *parāṭu*, tear/break off, clear away (*AHw* 832b); Amharic *farraṭa*, burst; and Arab. I, precede, escape; II, leave, abandon; separate (Wehr, 631b). The Arab. part. *fāriṭ* means improviser, and the Punic part. *prṭ* may mean one who takes care of (*DISO* 235; *KAI*, # 172, 2) or provider(?) (R. S. Tomback, *A Comparative Semitic Lexicon of the Phoenician and Punic Languages*, 1978, SBLDS 32, 272).

OT The Heb. vb. appears only in Amos 6:5, as a q. part., in the A colon *happōr*^{e}*ṭîm 'al-pî hannābel*, "those who improvise/applaud (LXX *hoi epikrotountes*, Pesh. *d*^{e}*nāqšîn*)/devise upon/at/to the mouth (i.e., synecdoche for 'string'/metonymy for 'sound') of the (large) lyre/harp" (‖ the B colon *ḥāš*^{e}*bû lāhem k*^{e}*lê-šîr*, they invent/scheme for themselves [upon/to] musical instruments).

P-B We find the term in postbiblical Heb., split, separate, specify (Jastrow, 1224a); Jewish Aram. *p*^{e}*raṭ*, break, divide; specify (Jastrow, 1224b); Syr. tear away (J. Payne Smith, *A Compendious Syriac Dictionary*, 1903, 460a); and Mand. *prṭ*.

Musical instruments/terms: → *gittît* (musical instrument?, # 1787); → *hemyâ* (sound, din, # 2166); → *ḥll* (make the pipe played, # 2727); → *ḥṣṣr* (make the trumpet sound, # 2955);

→ *yôbēl* (ram, # 3413); → *kinnôr* (lyre, # 4036); → *mēn* (string, # 4944); → *m^e na'an'îm* (rattle, # 4983); → *nēbel* II (unstringed instrument, # 5575); → *ngn* (play the lyre, # 5594); → *'ûgāb* (flute?, # 6385); → *prṭ* (improvise, # 7260); → *ṣll* I (ring, quiver, # 7509); → *šôpār* (ram's horn, # 8795); → *šālîš* II (musical instrument, # 8956); → *šema'* I (sound, # 9049); → *tpp* (drum, beat, # 9528); → *tq'* (drive, thrust, clap one's hands, blow trumpet, pledge, # 9546)

BIBLIOGRAPHY

H. W. Wolff, *Joel and Amos*, Hermeneia, 1977, 272-73, 276.

Robert H. O'Connell

7261	פֶּרֶט

פֶּרֶט (*pereṭ*), nom. fallen grapes/berries (# 7261).

ANE Jew. Aram. *pirṭā'*; Syr. *p^e rāṭā'*.

OT The word, a hapleg. (Lev 19:10), describes what was left in the vineyards (*kerem*) after the regular harvesting of grapes had taken place. The *pereṭ*, fallen grapes, were to be left for the poor and the stranger. This was a solemn command emphasized by the statement at the end of the verse "I am the LORD your God."

P-B The LXX translates the word with *rhōgas*, what was left/the residue (?). The Vg. translates the Heb. *prṭ* as a general term standing for grapes and grain left over, much as the LXX does.

Grapes: → *'eškôl* I (cluster[s] of grapes, # 864); → *b^e'uš* (sour, unripe, wild grapes/berries, # 946); → *zāg* (peel/skins of grapes, seed, kernel, # 2293); → *ḥarṣān* (unripe grapes, # 3079); → *'ēnāb* (grapes, cluster of grapes, # 6694); → *pereṭ* (fallen grapes/berries, # 7261)

Eugene Carpenter

7262 (*p^e rî*, fruit, offspring), → # 7238

7265	פָּרִיץ

פָּרִיץ (*pārîṣ* II), nom. burglar, robber (# 7265); < פרץ (*prṣ*), break out (→ # 7287).

OT The vb. may carry the sense of committing an act of violence (e.g., Exod 19:22, 24; Ps 106:29). *pārîṣ* I (# 7264), used only once in Isa 35:9, is rendered by the NIV as "ferocious," referring to dangerous animals like the lion. *pārîṣ* II (# 7265), used 5x in the OT, is translated as either "robbers" (Jer 7:11; Ezek 7:22) or "violent" (Ps 17:4; Ezek 18:10; Dan 11:4). In the period just prior to the Babylonian exile, Jeremiah shows how the temple worship became a façade behind which corruption and abuse took place. He stood in the temple gate and accused the people of oppression (Jer 7:6), stealing, murdering, adultery, and the worship of Baal and other gods (v. 9), and then of coming for safety into the house of God (v. 10). They were treating God's house like a refuge (den) of robbers (*p^e rîṣîm*), cries the prophet (v. 11). For this reason God will destroy the house as he destroyed Shiloh (vv. 12-15). Ezek 7:22 also speaks of the destruction of the temple. The treasured place will be desecrated by the robbers (*p^e rîṣîm*) who will enter in.

P-B In the DSS the vb. *prṣ* is used of breaking through a fence (CD 20:25). The nom. *pārîṣ* appears once in a rough quotation of Ezek 18:10 (1QH 6:20-21) and once in a difficult passage (CD 1:18-19), which J. J. Glück renders as "they saw violence (*pārîṣ*) coming and they chose falsehood" ("The Verb *PRṣ* in the Bible and in Qumran Literature," *RevQ* 5, 1964, 123-27).

Plunder, spoil, robbing, stealing: → *bzz* (plunder, spoil, # 1024); → *gzl* (steal, rob, # 1608); → *gnb* (steal, rob, # 1704); → *pārîṣ* II (burglar, robber, # 7265); → *pereq* (crossroad?, plunder, # 7294); → *šll* II (take plunder, seize, # 8964); → *šsh* (plunder, loot, # 9115)

W. R. Domeris

7266	פֶּרֶךְ

פֶּרֶךְ (*perek*), brutal, ruthless (# 7266).

OT This word is found 6x with the meaning of harsh or brutal (Exod 1:13, 14; Lev 25:43, 46, 53; Ezek 34:4). It is used exclusively of treatment of fellow humans, describing the harsh labor conditions of the Israelites in bondage in Egypt (Exod 1:13, 14). It is also used of the mistreatment of fellow countrymen in the Israelite community: "Do not rule over them ruthlessly (*perek*), but fear your God" (Lev 25:43, 46, 53). The only other occurrence is Ezek 34:4, which addresses the shepherds of Israel and the care of their flock: "You have ruled them harshly (*ḥozqâ*, # 2622) and brutally (*perek*)."

Hard, harsh, difficult, severe: → *'akzār* (cruel, # 425); → *ḥzq* (be strong, seize, # 2616); → *ḥms* I (do violence, # 2803); → *kbd* (be heavy, unresponsive, honored, # 3877); → *perek* (brutal, ruthless, # 7266); → *qšh* I (be hard, severe, be stiff-necked, # 7996); → *qšḥ* (treat harshly, harden, # 7998)

Larry Walker

7267	פָּרֹכֶת

פָּרֹכֶת (*pārōket*), nom. curtain in front of the Most Holy Place (# 7267).

ANE 1. There is some question regarding the ANE background of the Heb. word *pārōket*. Akk. has the nom. *parakku*, cult pedestal, sanctuary, shrine (*AHw*, 827b-28b), a loanword in Akk. from Sum. *bara(g)*$_2$, throne room (A. W. Sjoberg (ed.), *The Sumerian Dictionary of the University Museum of the University of Pennsylvania*, vol. 2, B, 1984, 137). *HALAT* 911-12 rejects the connection between this Akk. word and Heb. *pārōket* and suggests, instead, a possible connection to Akk. *parku,* vb. adj., laying across, and the fem. nom. *pariktu*, cross divider (*AHw*, 833-34; cf. the vb. *parāku, AHw*, 828-29). It seems, however, that Heb. *pārōket* is probably related to both Akk. terms mentioned. "The curtain served as a barrier, hindering both entry and sight, and marked at the same time the place in or upon which God was enthroned" (*TWAT* 6:756; my translation).

2. Other cognates for Heb. *pārōket* are: (a) the Phoen. pl. nom. *prkm*, which refers to some kind of cultic functionary, possibly "one who has charge of the temple-curtains" (assuming a connection to Akk. *parāku*; see *DNWSI*, 938, where a possible connection to Heb. *pārōket* is suggested), (b) a nom. in the late Aram. Hatra inscriptions meaning either (incense) altar or chapel, sanctuary (ibid.), and (c) the Syr. words *park^{e}ṯā* and *purk^{e}ṯā* (note the final *t*), meaning veil, curtain (*HALAT* 911).

OT 1. The meaning of *pārōket* (25x) has been much debated. In some places it appears to be the curtain that separates the Holy Place from the Most Holy Place (i.e., the Holy of Holies). For example, in Exod 26:33 the Lord's instructions were to "hang the curtain from the clasps and place the ark of the Testimony behind the curtain. The curtain will separate the Holy Place from the Most Holy Place." Nevertheless, it was also more than that. According to 40:3, Moses was to "place the ark of the Testimony in it and shield the ark with the curtain" (NIV; lit., "cover over the ark with the curtain"), suggesting that the fabric of the *pārōket* stretched not only in front of the ark but also over the top, draped on the frame of acacia wood like a canopy (26:31-32; Friedman, 1992, 295-98).

2. It seems, therefore, that the *pārōket* was not just a curtain or hanging, for which the Heb. word is *qela'* II (# 7846). The latter occurs 15x in the OT, referring consistently to the curtains, hangings that were used to make the surrounding court of the tabernacle (Exod 27:9, 11; 38:9, 12). (As the *BHS* textual note suggests, *qela'* in 1 Kgs 6:34b is most likely a corruption of *ṣela'*, which refers to the two leaves of the doors to the cella of the temple in 1 Kgs 6:34a.) The term *qeres* (# 7971; 9 or 10x, depending on how one reads Exod 26:33) refers to the gold and bronze hooks, rings that were used to link together the curtains of the fabric that was laid over the wooden frame of the tabernacle and the tent that was stretched over the whole structure, respectively (26:6, 11; 35:11; 36:13, 18; 39:33). According to the MT of Exod 26:33a, they were to "hang the curtain from the clasps (lit., hang the *pārōket*/canopy under the *qᵉrāsîm*/rings) and place the ark of the Testimony behind the curtain (*pārōket*)." It is probably better to follow the LXX and read instead *qᵉrāsîm*, (wooden) frames (of the tabernacle framework), which would mean simply that the *pārōket* canopy was to be lower than the frame of the tabernacle so that it could fit underneath it (Friedman, 1992, 296-98).

According to 2 Chron 3:14, "He (Solomon; actually the skilled worker he had hired, Huram-Abi, 2:7, 13) made the curtain (*pārōket*) of blue, purple and crimson yarn and fine linen, with cherubim worked into it" (cf. Exod 26:31). Some question the accuracy of the description here and suggest that there was no *pārōket* in Solomon's temple, arguing that it is not referred to in the parallel 1 Kgs 6:31-32, where doors are indicated rather than a veil (see Williamson [209], who thinks that it is included here by influence of the tabernacle account, Exod 26:31). If it is correct to say that the *pārōket* was not just a veil (i.e., a tent door) but a canopy that was draped over the top of the ark of the covenant suspended from pillars (see 26:32-33), and that this canopy covered the ark underneath the roof of the tent of the tabernacle (see above), then this may have been the case in the temple as well. There would be no necessary contradiction between having doors sealing off the entrance to the *dᵉbîr* (# 1808) of the temple (inner sanctuary; → *miškān*, # 5438; 1 Kgs 6:31-32) as well as a canopy over the ark (2 Chron 3:14) inside the *dᵉbîr* of the temple.

The only thing missing is the mention of that which would have corresponded to the "four posts of acacia wood overlaid with gold and standing on four silver bases" in the tabernacle over which the *pārōket* would have been draped. The "pillars" referred to in 2 Chron 3:17 are Jachin and Boaz, which were placed at the doorway of the outside temple, not in the *dᵉbîr*. Is it possible that the "interwoven chains" and "the pillars" in 2 Chron 3:16 refer to different pillars than Jachin and Boaz, those that were used to suspend the *pārōket* over the ark? This, of course, is all speculative. In any case, whatever one does with the *pārōket* in 3:14, it is interesting that it was this canopy that provided the space known as the Most Holy Place in the tabernacle (Exod 26:33), while it was the *d^ebîr* that did so for the temple (2 Chron 3:8). Apparently, the one was the more appropriate structure for a tent and the latter for a solid house.

P-B *pārōket* occurs 2x in the Qumran Temple Scroll (11QTS 7:13-14; Yadin 2:27-28). The text is broken, but it is clear that they thought that it was a veil of gold (i.e., a gold thread was included with the other threads in a series), for which there is no justification in the OT itself (see the discussion in Yadin 2:27-28).

Later RL seems to confirm that this tradition existed in some circles and, moreover, there is some indication that there were two veils referred to in this broken passage, one made with gold thread and one not (Yadin 2:28). There is a Mishnaic tradition in this regard. It is written that on the Day of Atonement, "he (the high priest) went through the Sanctuary until he came to the space between the two curtains separating the Sanctuary from the Holy of Holies. And there was a cubit's space between them.... The outer curtain was looped up on the south side and the inner one on the north side. He went along between them until he reached the north side; when he reached the north he turned round to the south and went on with the curtain on his left hand until he reached the Ark" (Yoma 5:1; Danby, 167). It has been argued above that in the OT *pārōket* refers to a canopy over the ark, not just a veil separating the Holy Place from the Most Holy Place. The RL does not seem to reflect this interpretation (see the texts cited and discussion in Friedman, 1992, 295).

NT Like *pārōket* in the OT, the G word *katapetasma*, which the LXX uses to render Heb. *pārōket*, is always used in the NT for the inner second curtain of the temple (Heb 9:3). According to Matt 27:51, at the moment of Jesus' death on the cross, "the curtain of the temple was torn in two from top to bottom" (cf. Mark 15:38; Luke 23:45). Heb 10:19b-20 refers to the fact that "we have confidence to enter the Most Holy Place by the blood of Jesus, by a new and living way opened for us through the curtain, that is, his body." Thus, figuratively speaking, Jesus' body was torn for us so that we might have a firm and secure hope that "enters the inner sanctuary behind the curtain" (6:19).

Tabernacle, tent, temple: → *'ōhel* (tent, tent-dweller, # 185); → *d^ebîr* I (Most Holy Place, # 1808); → *mô'ēd* (meeting-place, assembly, tent of meeting, # 4595b); → *miqdāš* (sanctuary, # 5219); → *miškān* (sanctuary, # 5438); → *pārōket* (curtain in front of Most Holy, # 7267); → *sukkâ* (tabernacle, tent, hut, shelter, # 6109); → **Aaron: Theology**; → **Priests and Levites: Theology**

BIBLIOGRAPHY

TWAT 4:744-50; 6:755-57; H. Danby, *The Mishnah*, 1933; R. E. Friedman, "Tabernacle," *ABD*, 1992, 6:292-300; idem, "The Tabernacle in the Temple," *BA* 43, 1980, 241-48; H. G. M. Williamson, *1 and 2 Chronicles*, NCBC, 1982; Y. Yadin, *The Temple Scroll*, vols. 1-2, 1983.

Richard E. Averbeck

7271	פרס

פרס (*prs*), q. measure; hi. divide (# 7271); nom. פַּרְסָה (*parsâ*), hoof (# 7274).

ANE The root is widely attested in other Sem. languages, e.g., Akk. *parāsu*, separate, divide; Aram. *p^e ras*, divide.

OT 1. In the q. stem the vb. describes measuring out or distributing food (*leḥem)* to the needy (Isa 58:7; Jer 16:7).

2. In the code of clean animals (→ # 3197) for eating, the expression "split hoof" (*mapreset parsâ)* describes a class of animal that may be eaten. It appears 7x in a construct relationship (Lev 11:3, 4, 7, 26; Deut 14:6, 7, 8; cf. Ps 69:31[32]). See also Lev 11:6 and Deut 14:7 for usages with the hi. perf.

The nom. *parsâ*, hoof, appears by itself in Deut 14:6, where it describes an animal with two hoofs. Another creature, the unclean carrion eater, *peres* (bearded or black vulture, see Driver, 9-10; → *ṭm'*, unclean, # 3237), may be named for its practice of dropping its victims from great heights to break their bones.

3. In the Aram. of Dan (5:25) the final word written on the wall at Belshazzar's feast is *ûparsîn*, which is interpreted (v. 28): "*p^e rēs*: your kingdom is divided and given to the Medes and the Persians." There is wordplay between the dividing of the kingdom and its being given over to the Persians (*pārās*).

Division, measurement, portion: → *ḥlq* II (divide, obtain one's share, # 2745); → *ḥṣh* (divide, be divided, # 2936); → *ḥṣṣ*(divide, order, # 2951); → *mnh* (count, # 4948); → *plg* (be divided, # 7103); → *prd* (spread out, be divided, keep apart, # 7233); → *prs* (measure, divide, # 7271); → *šs'* (tear, divide, # 9117)

BIBLIOGRAPHY

G. R. Driver, "Birds in the Old Testament: I. Birds in Law," *PEQ* 87, 1955, 5-20.

Richard Hess

7272 (*peres*, vulture), → # 7606

7273 (*pārās*, Persia), → Persia

7274 (*parsâ*, hoof), → # 7271

7277	פרע

פרע (*pr'*), q., ni., let go, let loose, let alone; hi. cause to refrain, show lack of restraint (# 7277); פֶּרַע (*pera'* I), nom. hair (# 7279).

ANE Aram. *p^e ra'*; Syr. *p^e ra'*; Arab. *faraġa*.

OT 1. *pr'* occurs 15x in the OT, 11x in the q. stem, 1x in the ni., 3x in the hi. The basic sense of the word (to loose) may be seen in a variety of related nuances. Sometimes the word suggests the lifting of prior social restraint from people, as when Aaron allowed the Israelites to run wild in the absence of Moses (Exod 32:25bis; cf. 2 Chron 28:19). This is probably the sense of *pr'* in Prov 29:18: "Where there is no revelation, the people cast off restraint." Sometimes the word refers to a willful ignoring of available instructions and thereby suffering the appropriate consequences (1:25; 8:33; 13:18; 15:32). The word can also refer to a wise avoidance of a dangerous alternative, such as the path of evildoers (4:15), or to influencing people to desist from some activity or action, as Moses and Aaron attempted to do with Israelite slave labor in Egypt (Exod 5:4). In Ezek 24:14 the word occurs in Yahweh's warning that he will not refrain from decisive action against rebellious behavior. The word is used 4x in reference to disheveled hair, perhaps caused by removal of the turban or headdress. So the priest dishevels (NIV, loosens) the hair of the woman undergoing moral examination (Num 5:18).

Disheveled hair is part of the assigned lot of the leper (Lev 13:45); it is prohibited for Aaron and his sons (10:6) and for priests (21:10).

2. The nom. *pera'* occurs in the context of the Nazirite (→ # 5692), "He must be holy until the period of his separation to the LORD is over; he must let the (loose, unkempt) hair (*pera' śe'ar*) of his head grow long" (Num 6:5). For the use in Ezek 44:20, see *ksm*, shave (# 4080).

P-B In the RL Heb. *pr'* is used frequently. In the q. it means to tear, destroy, loosen, disarrange, neglect (e.g., the hair); to uncover (e.g., the head); to pay a debt, to settle with, punish. In the ni. it means to uncover one's self (a euphemism for relieving oneself); to collect payment from. In the pi. it means to disarrange, mutilate; to uncover. In the hi. it means to uncover. (For many examples of these meanings see Jastrow, 2:1235.) Aram. *pera'* is common in the Targumim, where it is used in the peal to mean to disarrange, tear open, uncover; to pay, retribute. In the ithpaal it means to be paid (back); to collect, call to account; be revenged, take revenge. The word has similar meanings in Syr. literature, although Syr. *pera'* also assumes the meanings of Heb. *prḥ*, to bud, sprout. (Syr. *peraḥ* means to fly, flee, spread.) In the DSS the word occurs in CD 8:8; 19:21; 1QS 6:26.

Hair: → *zāqān* (beard, # 2417); → *maḥalāpâ* (braid, # 4710); → *miqšeh* (well-dressed hair, # 5250); → *pr'* (untie hair, # 7277); → *ṣîṣit* (hair, tassel, # 7492); → *qewuṣṣôt* (hair, # 7767); → *ś'r* I (be appalled, # 8547); → *śāpām* (moustache, # 8559)
Loose: → *'zq* (break up, loosen, # 6466); → *pr'* (let go, let loose, # 7277); → *ptḥ* I (open, conquer, surrender, set free, loosen, break up, # 7337)

BIBLIOGRAPHY

TWAT 6:757-60; *TWOT* 2:736-37.

Richard A. Taylor

7279 (*pera'* I, hair), → # 7277

7282 (*par'ōš*, flea), → # 6856

7287	פרץ

פרץ (*prṣ* I), q. break through, burst out; ni. spread abroad; pu. be broken down; hitp. break loose (# 7287); nom. מִפְרָץ (*miprāṣ*), inlet, landing (→ # 5153); פָּרִיץ (*pārîṣ* II), robber (→ # 7265); פֶּרֶץ (*pereṣ* I), breach, rupture (# 7288).

ANE Cognates with similar meanings are found in Akk. *parāṣu*, break through, Ugar., *prṣ*, to open, and Arab., *farada*, cut, slit (see *HALAT* 914).

OT 1. The vb. *prṣ* is found about 49x: about 45x in q.; once each in ni. (1 Sam 3:1), pu. (Neh 1:3), and hitp. (1 Sam 25:10). *pereṣ* occurs as a nom. about 19x, as a proper name 15x, and within a geographical name 5x. A good case can be made for understanding the basic meaning to be "break through (a wall)." (For this and other views, see *TWAT* 6:764-68; *HALAT* 914b, and below; also cf. *prṣ* II in *HALAT* 915a.)

2. A city wall provides defence. Thus, to breach a wall is to render a city defenseless (cf., e.g., 2 Kgs 14:13 [par. 2 Chron 25:23]; cf. *bnh*, build, which is in antithetical parallelism to *prṣ* in Neh 4:3[3:35]; Eccl 3:3). Such a broken wall is thus an apt symbol of Yahweh's judgment, whether the wall is of the city (Ps 89:40[41]) or an image of Israel such as a vineyard (Ps 80:12[13]; Isa 5:5). Even a person can be seen as so attacked in judgment by God. "Again and again (lit., with breach upon breach) (*pereṣ ʿal pᵉnê pāreṣ*) he bursts upon me (*yiprᵉṣēnî*)" (Job 16:14; cf. Judg 21:15).

Because of its root meaning, also without the express mention of a wall or breach, the vb. *prṣ* can denote destructive action; e.g., of a plague breaking out against Israel (Ps 106:29), or of a (premature) breaking through of the womb of pregnant cattle (nom. *pereṣ*, Ps 144:14; cf. J. Ziegler, *AOAT* 18, 1973, 192-93). It is also so used of God against the Philistines: "As waters break out (*pereṣ*), the LORD has broken out (*prṣ*) against my enemies" (2 Sam 5:20 [par. 1 Chron 14:11]).

In Mic 2:13 Yahweh is the breaker (*pōrēṣ*) who will break through the enemy lines and go before his people, who will then break through (*pārᵉṣû*) the gate into freedom. (For different interpretations of this passage, see G. Brin, *ZAW* 101, 1989, 118-24.)

The image of a breached wall, and thus a defenseless city, describes a man without self-control (Prov 25:28; cf. 16:32).

The danger that a breached wall posed meant that someone should stand in the breach (*pereṣ*) and ward off the threat (cf. figuratively in Ps 106:23; Ezek 13:5; 22:30), and such a wall needed to be repaired (e.g., Amos 9:11; Neh 6:1).

3. The vb. *prṣ* is also used for the breaching of any restraint (or of invisible walls of restriction). This use occurs in various contexts, including that of blessing and judgment.

It is used of population explosion. In Gen 28:14 Yahweh promises Jacob: "Your descendants will be like the dust of the earth, and you will spread out (i.e., burst forth, *prṣ*) to the west and to the east, to the north and to the south." This blessing is operative in Egypt, where "the more they were oppressed, the more they multiplied and spread (*prṣ*, burst forth)" (Exod 1:12).

In Isa 54:3 the barren one, the people of God, is encouraged with the words: "you will spread out (*prṣ*) to the right and to the left; your descendants will dispossess nations." The promise of innumerable descendants given to Israel, who of herself is as a barren woman without a future, finds fulfillment in the fullness of time when new life is given by the Spirit through the proclamation of the gospel (cf. Isa 44:3-5; Gal 4:24-31). Thus, the NT church becomes the recipient of the old promises of the innumerable seed. (See further E. J. Young, *The Book of Isaiah*, 1972, 3:360-65; *NIDNTT* 1:411-12.)

The vb. *prṣ* can also describe the blessing of a vast increase in livestock and possessions (Gen 30:30, 43; Job 1:10).

Offspring were greatly valued, and thus it was a terrible judgment not to receive children. In Hos 4:10 the warning from Yahweh is sounded that "they will engage in prostitution, but not increase (*prṣ*)." (For the view that the vb. here denotes the ability to penetrate sexually, see Toll, 111-12.) In this light it is striking that when Judah made use of a prostitute (Gen 38:15-18), it resulted in a bursting forth from the womb. Twins were born. Although the hand of the one appeared initially, his brother came out first:

"And she said, 'So this is how you have broken out!' (*pāraṣtā* ... *pāreṣ*). And he was named Perez" (Gen 38:29). God's sovereign grace is highlighted by the fact that irrespective of the circumstance of his conception, Perez, born of Judah and Tamar, was included in the genealogy of Jesus Christ (Matt 1:3; cf. Ruth 4:12, 18).

The breaking out by God in judgment on an unholy people is described in Exod 19 in terms of *prṣ*. Mount Sinai had been fenced off as holy: "The priests and the people must not force their way through (*hrs*) to come up to the LORD, or he will break out (*prṣ*) against them" (Exod 19:24; cf. 22). Uzzah had not respected God's holiness when he touched the ark without being authorized to do so. The result was that Yahweh struck him down in anger and he died. This action is related as "the LORD's wrath had broken out (*prṣ* ... *pereṣ*) against Uzzah" (2 Sam 6:8 [par. 1 Chron 13:11]; cf. 1 Chron 15:13); thus the place was called Perez Uzzah.

When there is no restraint or containment on sin, wickedness multiplies, and "they break all bounds (*prṣ*)" (Hos 4:2). When a slave does not respect the bound with his master, he breaks out (hitp., 1 Sam 25:10). When a plan of action is not hindered by a restraint of time, it bursts forth and is done immediately (1 Chron 13:2; cf. KD); an order not curbed breaks out abroad (2 Chron 31:5). The use of *prṣ* (ni.) in 1 Sam 3:1 is best understood in this light. Visions were not unrestrained and breaking out. They were thus rare. Postbiblical usage of *prṣ*, ni., to be spread, increased, confirms this (see Jastrow, 1237).

In a psychological sense, the barrier that needs to be broken can be unwillingness. Thus, Saul's servants urged (*prṣ*) him to eat (1 Sam 28:23), Absalom pressed (*prṣ*) David (2 Sam 13:25, 27), and Naaman Gehazi (2 Kgs 5:23).

4. More than one root for *prṣ* has been proposed because of passages considered problematic. Using the Akk. cognate *parāṣu*, Driver has suggested that *prṣ* in 1 Chron 13:2; 2 Chron 31:5; 1 Sam 3:1 should be understood as "issue an edict, command, decree, ordain" (*JTS* 23, 1921-22, 72; *JTS*, 25, 1923-24, 177-78; *JTS* 32, 1930-31, 365). Following another root meaning of the same Akk. cognate, Watson has proposed rendering *prṣ* in 1 Sam 3:1 by "false vision" (*BZ*, 29, 90 n. 2). On the basis of Arab., Guillaume has suggested that Gen 38:29 should be rendered "how have you arrived first. Priority is yours" (284-85).

P-B The use of *prṣwt* ("openings") in CD 1:19 has been understood as loopholes in the law (Knibb, *Qumran Community*, 24; cf. Glück, 123-27).

Split, breach, slice: → *bqʿ* (split, break open, # 1324); → *ḥrm* II (split, # 3050); → *ḥtr* (break through, # 3168); → *miśpāḥ* (breach of law, # 5384); → *plḥ* (cut into slices, split open, # 7114); → *pṣm* (split open, # 7204); → *prṣ* I (break through, burst out, be broken down, # 7287); → *rʿʿ* II (break in pieces, # 8318); → *rṣṣ* (crush, mash, break, # 8368); → *šbr* I (break, break down, smash, shatter, # 8689)

BIBLIOGRAPHY

G. Brin, "Micah 2,2-13: A Textual and Ideological Study," *ZAW* 101, 1989, 118-24; G. R. Driver, "Some Hebrew Roots and Their Meanings," *JTS* 23, 1921-22, 69-73, esp. 72; idem, "The Root פרץ in Hebrew," *JTS* 25, 1923-24, 177-78; "Studies in the Vocabulary of the Old Testament," *JTS* 32, 1930-31, 361-66, esp. 365; J. J. Glück, "The Verb *prṣ* in the Bible and in the Qumran Literature," *RevQ* 5, 1964, 123-27; A. Guillaume, "Some Hebrew Roots and Their Meanings: פָּרַץ," *JTS* 24, 1922-23, 318; idem, "Paronomasia in the Old Testament," *JSS* 9, 1964,

282-90, esp. 284-85; M. A. Knibb, *The Qumran Community*, 1987; C. Toll, "Ausdrücke für 'Kraft' im Alten Testament mit besonderer Rücksicht auf die Wurzel BRK," *ZAW* 94, 1982, 111-23; W. G. E. Watson, "The Structure of 1 Samuel 3," *BZ* 29, 1985, 90-93.

Cornelis Van Dam

7288 (*pereṣ* I, breach, rupture), → # 7287

7293	פרק

פרק (*prq*), q. pull away, tear off; pi. pull off, tear off; hitp. pull off from o.s., be pulled off (# 7293; Aram. # 10596); מַפְרֶקֶת (*mapreqet*), nom. neck (hapleg.) (# 5154); פֶּרֶק (*pereq*), nom. crossroad ?; (secured) plunder (# 7294); פָּרָק (*pārāq*), nom. crumbled bread (hapleg.) (# 7295).

ANE This root is widely attested and occurs in Ugar., Old Aram., Akk., Arab., OSA, and Eth. (*HALAT* 916).

OT 1. The basic meaning of tearing off and causing a separation is well illustrated by the vb.'s use in Exod 32 for Israel's tearing off their earrings to make an image of gold (v. 3 [pi.]; cf. v. 2 [pi.], 24 [hitp.]), thus incurring God's wrath (vv. 19-35). In a most vivid image, *prq* refers to the tearing of one's soul by an enemy compared to a lion (Ps 7:2[3] par. *ṭrp*; → # 3271). In Aram. the root can also signify separating oneself from sin (Dan 4:27[24], peal).

2. In the context of judgment, the vb. effectively denotes the tearing of the strong branch (of the royal house) from the vine of Israel (Ezek 19:12, hitp., NASB; cf. 19:10-14). Alternatively one can interpret this passage as Israel's fruit (offspring) being torn off (e.g., NIV). The vb. also graphically portrays the divine judgment of the foolish shepherd eating his own sheep and tearing off the hoofs to get the last morsel of raw meat (Zech 11:16 pi.; cf. C. L. Meyers and E. M. Meyers, *Zechariah 9-14*, AB, 1993, 284-89).

3. In a more positive usage, the term denotes deliverance from enemies and oppressors (Ps 136:24 q.; Lam 5:8, q.) and describes Esau's throwing off the yoke of servitude to Jacob (Gen 27:40, q.; cf. Lev 26:13; for the fulfillment of this prophecy see KD).

4. When the Lord passed by Elijah, preparing to come to him, a great and powerful wind tore the mountains apart (1 Kgs 19:11, pi.), an event reminiscent of God's coming at Mount Sinai (cf. Exod 19:18) and a reminder of his holiness and anger against sin (cf. Ps 18:7[8]; Isa 29:6; Hab 3:6).

5. The nom. *pereq* denotes secured plunder in Nah 3:1, but its meaning in Obad 14 is contested and the testimony of the ancient versions is mixed. In Obad 14 Edom is urged to cease standing at the *pereq* and cutting down those who are escaping. This context can suggest a place where the road pulls away (*prq*) in two directions, the fork of the road or crossroad (so Tg. *prq'* is normally understood), a mountain pass or passage way (so LXX, *diekbolai*), or places of refuge (so Symmachus, *phygadeiai*). See *HALAT* 916. Most modern versions render "crossroads" or "fork of the road" or the like (e.g., NASB, RSV, NAB, NEB, NRSV, REB, NIV). NJPSV renders "passes."

6. The nom *mapreqet*, found only in 1 Sam 4:18, means neck, that which *divides* the head from the body (BDB, 830).

7. The nom. *p^e raq* (constr. of *pārāq*), denotes a fragment (of bread) in Isa 65:4 (K). Q, *m^e raq* (constr. of *mārāq*, broth) is however supported by 1QIs[a], Tg, and LXX.

P-B 1. The root is rare in DSS. Nom. forms of *prq* (*prq wlprqw*, joint to its joint) occur in 4Q386 1:5 in a context similar to Ezek 37:7. See R. Eisenman and M. Wise, *The Dead Sea Scrolls Uncovered*, 1992, 61, 63. Cf. U. Dahmen, "Nachträge zur Qumran-Konkordanz," *Zeitschrift für Althebräistik*, 4, 1991, 230.

2. In Tgs. and RL, the OT meanings of the root *prq* are found in Heb. and Aram. The Heb. vb. also has the ni. (be out of joint, dislocated). The nom. has also a related meaning, such as "period of maturity" (cf. crossroad). Jastrow, 1238-40; also cf. Van Zijl.

Separation, breaking down, removal: → *'ṣl* (set apart, withdraw, shorten, # 724); → *bdl* (separate o.s., # 976); → *br'* I (create, separate, # 1343); → *hgh* II (separate, remove, # 2048); → *mwš* II (depart, remove, take away, # 4631); → *ns'* (tear out, march out, # 5825); → *ntq* (tear away, # 5998); → *prq* (pull away, # 7293); → *ṣ'n* (pack up, # 7585); → *rḥq* (be far away, remove, # 8178)

BIBLIOGRAPHY

TWAT 6:770-73; E. Jenni, *Das hebräische Pi'el*, 1968, 176, 184; J. van Zijl, "The Root פרק in Targum Isaiah," *JNSL* 2, 1972, 60-73.

Cornelis Van Dam

7294 (*pereq*, crossroad?; plunder), → # 7293

7295 (*pārāq*, crumbled), → # 7293

7296/7297	פרר

פרר (*prr*), hi. break, invalidate, nullify, frustrate, foil, thwart; ho. be broken, invalidated, frustrated; hitpol. (with q. inf. abs.) break apart, crumble; pol. and pilp. break apart, shatter (# 7296/7297); פור (*pwr*), hi. break, frustrate (byform, # 7051).

ANE The vb. *prr* is attested in most Sem. languages, though it is not clear whether there is one or more independent roots (see sec. 2 below). The ANE evidence is as follows: Akk. *pararu*, come off, become powerless, break up, disperse (*AHw*, 829-30); Ugar. *prr* I, break, annul; *prr* II, flee (*UT*, 2121 and 2120, respectively; perhaps < *pwr*, cf. *CML*, 156; Ward, 208-9); Pun. *prr* I, break (likely a scribal error; see *DISO*, 237); J.Aram. *prr* I, invalidate, crumble; *prr* II, jerk; Syr. *parpar*, flutter, quiver; Arab. *farra*, escape, flee; *farfara*, shake, tremble (for south Arab. dialects see W. Müller, "Beiträge aus dem Mehri zum etymologischen Teil des hebräischen Lexikons," *Mélanges linguistiques offerts à Maxime Rodinson*, 1985, 273-74). The vb. *prr* I, break, is also found in the Deir 'Alla texts (1.8; *DNWSI*, 944), as is the nom. *pr*, foolishness, mentally deficient (< *prr* II; cf. Akk. *pararu*, become powerless, when said of intelligence = to become confused; see *ATDA*, 181, 246; *DNWSI*, 934). In the Ugar. legend of Kirta *prr* I is found parallel with *ṯbr*, break (*KTU*, 1.2.1.12-13; perhaps < *prr* II, flee, escape; see S. and Sh. Rin, *'Alîlôth Hā'ēlîm*, 1968, 53), and *ṯny*, set aside; the latter in connection with the breaking of a vow (*KTU*, 1.15.3.29-30; see Dahood, 339). Similar associations are found in biblical literature (see sec. 4).

OT 1. The vb. *prr* is found 53x in the OT (the emendation to *swr*, turn aside, in Ps 89:33[34] is unnecessary [*contra TWAT* 6:775; see Dahood, 339]). It is found 46x in the hi. (including 3x as the byform *pwr* [Ps 33:10; 89:33[34]; Ezek 17:19]; for the shift from *pwr* to *prr* see GKC 67a, v; Joüon-Muraoka 82n, o); 3x in the ho.; and 1x each in the q., hitp., pol., and pilp. Its use is concentrated in the Pentateuch (13x; with 3x in Num; 2x each in Lev; Deut; 1x in Gen), and the prophetic books (21x; with 7x in Isa; 6x in Ezek; 5x in Jer; 3x in Zech).

2. Most Heb. lexicons (KBL; BDB; *THAT*) distinguish between *prr* I: hi. break; ho. be broken; and *prr* II: pol. rouse up; hitpol. (with q. inf. abs.) shake to and fro; and pilp. shake (**prr* III, the presumed root of *par*, young bull, steer, and *pārâ*, cow, is not debated). This, however, is not necessary (cf. W. Gesenius, *Hebrew-Chaldee Lexicon*, 1847, 692; J. Levy, *Neuhebräisches und chaldäisches Wörterbuch über die Talmudim und Midraschim*, 1876-89, 4:131-32, 140). Based on the Akk., Ruppert (*TWAT* 6:774-75) ascribes the semantic range to the inflection of the vb. He proposes an original meaning of separate and suggests the following glosses: q. leave, run away, flee (from animals and persons), fall off, come off (with things); hi. drive away, break, dissolve, invalidate (with *bᵉrît*); and in the factitive (pol., pilp., and hitp.) make separate, i.e., scatter, break apart, shatter (the proposed occurrences of *prr* II fit into the factitive sense of the vb.; see sec. 8). Ruppert's suggestions, along with the expected shift in meaning over time, adequately account for the semantic range of *prr*.

3. The vb. *prr* most often denotes a removal or withdrawal (whether purposeful or the result of one's actions) of support for, or validation of, an agreement; thus it may be glossed as annul, break, or invalidate. With this sense it is used transitively, governing a variety of objects: Any Israelite who intentionally breaks Yahweh's commandment (*miṣwâ*) must be cut off (Num 15:31; cf. Ezra 9:14); a husband may nullify or invalidate any vow (*nēder*), oath (*šᵉbû'â*), or rash promise (*mibṭā'*) that his wife makes without his prior knowledge (Num 30:8-15[9-16]); Yahweh asks Job whether he would annul his judgment (*mišpāṭ*) in order to justify himself (Job 40:8); Eliphaz accuses Job of doing away with piety (lit., *yir'â*, fear, i.e., fear of God; 15:4); Ps 89 recalls Yahweh's promise never to break off his steadfast love (*ḥesed*) from David's line (89:33[34]); while in Ps 119 Yahweh is implored to act because his law (*tôrâ*) is being broken (Ps 119:126).

4. *prr* is found 23x with *bᵉrît*, covenant (→ # 1382), as object (21x in the hi. and 2x in the ho. [in Zech 11:11 the obj. is understood from v. 10]). This makes *prr* the most common term used for the violation of a covenant, and as such it may forge a link with the use of *šarra-* in Hittite vassal treaties (see Fensham, 3-5). Other common phrases used for the breaking of a covenant are: *'br bᵉrît*, to transgress, trespass a covenant (Deut 17:2; Josh 7:11, 15; 2 Kgs 18:12; Jer 34:18; Hos 6:7; 8:1; → # 6296); and *'zb bᵉrît*, forsake a covenant (Deut 29:25[24]; 1 Kgs 19:10, 14; Prov 2:17; Jer 22:9; Dan 11:30; → # 6440). *prr* is used to refer to people abrogating covenants/treaties with other people; e.g., Asa king of Judah asks Ben-Hadad king of Aram to break his treaty (*bᵉrît*) with King Baasha of Israel (1 Kgs 15:19 = 2 Chron 16:3; cf. Isa 33:8; Ezek 17:15-16, 18). It is also found, however, in reference to Israel breaking their covenant with Yahweh. In an emotional indictment of covenant violation, God accuses both Judah and Israel of returning to the sins of their ancestors, serving other gods, thereby breaking the covenant he made with their ancestors (Jer 11:10; cf. Ezek 44:7).

Therefore, God will bring disaster on them in accordance with the covenant curses (Jer 11:11; cf. Lev 26:15; Deut 31:16, 20).

5. In stark contrast to Israel's faithlessness is God's faithfulness to the covenant. Among the litany of covenant curses in Lev 26 is the promise that in spite of Israel's continual infidelity, when they are in exile he will not reject them nor abhor them so as to destroy them utterly and break his covenant with them (Lev 26:44; cf. Judg 2:1). So also with regards to the Davidic covenant the Lord says, "If you can break my covenant with the night, so that the day and night no longer come at their appointed time, then my covenant with David my servant ... can be broken" (Jer 33:20-21). The ultimate expression of God's faithfulness, however, is found in his promise of a new covenant: God declares that he is going to make (*krt*) a new covenant (*b^{e}rît ḥ^{a}dāšâ*) with Israel because they broke the covenant he made with their ancestors at Sinai (31:31-32). Similar to this is Ezek 16:60, where Yahweh "will establish an everlasting covenant" (*wah^{a}qimôtî lāk b^{e}rît 'ôlām*) with Israel (cf. *b^{e}rît šālôm*, "covenant of peace" in Ezek 34:25; 37:26). This new covenant is solely God's initiative, and is only possible because God will write his Torah on their hearts (Jer 31:32) or give them a new heart and a new spirit (Ezek 11:19-20; 36:25-28).

6. There are, however, some instances where the possibility of Yahweh's breaking his covenant with Israel is entertained. As much is implied in Jeremiah's impassioned plea for God not to break his covenant with Israel (Jer 14:21), as well as in Ezek 16:59, where Yahweh says that he will do in judgment what Israel has done in unfaithfulness: "Yes, thus says the LORD God: I will deal with you as you have done, you who have despised the oath, breaking the covenant" (NRSV; but cf. NIV). The only direct reference to God's breaking the covenant is found in Zech 11, where in a symbolic act the prophet breaks the staff that represents Yahweh's covenant with all the peoples, i.e., Israel, thus annulling it (11:10-11, 14), though the understanding of this passage is disputed (see C. and E. Meyers, *Zechariah 9-14*, 1993). Noteworthy, however, is that in both Jeremiah and Ezekiel the possibility of Yahweh's breaking the covenant is inextricably linked to the idea of a new covenant (see sec. 5). Nevertheless, this tension should not be smoothed over, as the concept of covenant in the OT is probably not fully homogenized (see B. Childs, *Biblical Theology of the Old and New Testaments*, 1992, 420; cf. e.g., Isa 24:5, where an everlasting covenant [*b^{e}rît 'ôlām*] is said to be broken).

7. On a number of occasions (ca. 10x) *prr* is found with the sense of bringing to naught the purposes, plans, or plots of others; as such it may be glossed as frustrate, thwart, or foil. According to Proverbs, "plans [*maḥ^{a}šābôt*] fail for lack of counsel, but with many advisers they succeed" (Prov 15:22; cf. Ezra 4:5). While fleeing, David sends Hushai to infiltrate Absalom's circle of advisors in order to frustrate Ahithophel's counsel (*'ēṣâ* [# 6783]; 2 Sam 15:34). The plan works, though only because "the LORD had determined to frustrate the good advice of Ahithophel in order to bring disaster on Absalom" (17:14). This typifies its frequent use with God as subject: according to the psalmist, "The LORD foils the plans of the nations [*hēpîr ^{a}ṣat-gôyim*]; he thwarts the purposes of the peoples [*hēnî' maḥš^{e}bôt 'ammîm*]" (Ps 33:10). God also frustrated the plan (*'ēṣâ*) of those who wanted to stop the rebuilding of Jerusalem's walls (Neh 4:15[9]; cf. Job 5:12 [with *maḥ^{a}šābâ*, plan, intention]; Isa 44:25 [with *'otôt*, signs]; implied in Isa 8:10 [with *'ēṣâ*, plan]). In stark contrast to the ease by which

Yahweh frustrates the plans and intentions of others, his plans cannot be foiled; e.g., his judgment of Assyria will not be frustrated, "for the LORD Almighty has purposed, and who can thwart him?" (Isa 14:27).

8. Beyond the reasons provided above (sec. 2), the proposed occurrences of *prr* II (Job 16:12; Ps 74:13; Isa 24:19) do not require specialized meanings. For example, the parallelism of *prr* and *šbr*, break, in Ps 74:13 commends a translation like break apart, or put down (see M. Tate, *Psalms 51-100*, 1990, 243, 251; this is the one place where *prr* is used with the physical act of breaking in mind; in contrast to the vb. *šbr* I, break, break apart [→ # 8689], which is used predominantly with that sense). Similarly, the translation shatter (NIV; NASB) or break (NASB; NJPS) in Job 16:12 is well within the semantic range of *prr* (see BDB; *TWAT* 6:775), as is a rendering like break itself apart, or crumble (NJPS) in Isa 24:19 (taking the hitpol. as a reflexive factitive, i.e., make itself break apart; see *IBHS* §26.2; *TWAT* 6:775).

9. The sole intransitive use of *prr* is found in Eccl 12:5 (*w*[e]*tāpēr hā'*[a]*biyyônâ*; lit., the caper bursts; cf. *HALAT* 917), though many emend it to a ho., i.e., the caper is broken (cf. LXX, Vg., Sym.; see M. Dahood, "Canaanite-Phoenician Influence in Qoheleth," *Bib* 33, 1952, 216). The caper was understood to be an appetite stimulant and possibly an aphrodisiac, hence the tr. "desire is no longer stirred" (NIV; see J. Crenshaw, *Ecclesiastes*, 1988, 187-88).

P-B The vb. *prr* occurs ca. 13x in the nonbiblical mss. from Qumran: 6x in reference to the breaking of a covenant (4QDibHam[a] 5.8; 6.7; 4Q381 frg. 69.8; 4QShir[b] frg. 63.3.5; 4Q418 frg. 131.4; 11QT[a] 59.8); 2x to the breaking of vows (11QT[a] 54.2-3; taken from Num 30); and 1x to the breaking of a precept (*ḥwq*; CD-A 1.20; ‖ *'br bryt*, transgress the covenant). It is found a further 4x with the sense destroy, demolish (1QH 13.12 [5.18]; 2.26 [10.26]; 3.27 [11.27]; frg. 3.5; *contra KQT* 181, which takes the last three references from a different root; see *THAT* 2:488).

Split, breach, slice: → *bq'* (split, break open, # 1324); → *ḥrm* II (split, # 3050); → *ḥtr* (break through, # 3168); → *mišpāḥ* (breach of law, # 5384); → *plḥ* (cut into slices, split open, # 7114); → *pṣm* (split open, # 7204); → *prṣ* I (break through, burst out, be broken down, # 7287); → *r''* II (break in pieces, # 8318); → *rṣṣ* (crush, mash, break, # 8368); → *šbr* I (break, break down, smash, shatter, # 8689)

BIBLIOGRAPHY

THAT 2:486-88; *TWAT* 6:773-80; M. Dahood, "Hebrew-Ugaritic Lexicography IX," *Bib* 52, 1971, 337-56; F. C. Fensham, "Malediction and Benediction in Ancient Near Eastern Vassal-Treaties and the Old Testament," *ZAW* 74, 1962, 1-9; W. A. Ward, "Observations on the Egyptian Biconsonantal Root p3*," *Orient and Occident*, *AOAT* 22, 1973, 207-12.

Tyler F. Williams

7297	פרר

פרר (*prr* II), vb. split, divide, rend, tear (# 7297).

ANE Akk. *parāru*, destroy, shatter.

OT The rarely occurring vb. *prr* II appears 3x: in Isa 24:19 (*bis*; q., hitpol.) and Ps 74:13 (pol.). In each instance the vb. depicts the catastrophic response of nature to

Yahweh's royal power and judgment. In Isaiah *prr* is found in a parallel construction with both *r*'', break, and *mwṭ*, shake, totter. In Ps 74, the vb. *šbr*, break, is used to express the same parallel idea. Given the parallel expressions, *prr* most likely expresses the idea of a splitting or rending of an object caused by violent shaking.

For a discussion on whether this vb. constitutes a separate homonym, see *prr* I (# 9296).

Shaking, terror, trembling: → *g'š* (rise and fall noisily, swell, surge, # 1723); → *zw'* (tremble, quake, be afraid, # 2316); → *zll* II (shake, quake, tremble, # 2362); → *ḥalḥālâ* (shaking, trembling, anguish, # 2714); → *ḥrg* (come out trembling, # 3004); → *ḥrd* (tremble, shudder, startle, # 3006); → *yr'* (tremble, be fainthearted, # 3760); → *mwṭ* (waver, reel, stagger, shake, reel, # 4572); → *m'd* (slip, slide, shake, totter, # 5048); → *nwd* (shake, totter, waiver, wander, mourn, flee, # 5653); → *nwṭ* (shake, quake, # 5667); → *nw'* (shake, tremble, stagger, totter, wave, # 5675); → *n'r* II (shake, shake off, # 5850); → *smr* (shudder, have goose-bumps, bristle, # 6169); → *'iw'îm* (distortion, stagger, dizzy, # 6413); → *pwq* I (stagger, wobble, reel, totter, # 7048); → *pḥd* I (tremble, be in dread, # 7064); → *plṣ* (shudder, shake, tremble, # 7145); → *qwṣ* I (feel disgust, frighten, cause dread, # 7762); → *rgz* (agitate, quiver, shake, excite, rouse up, agitate, # 8074); → *rnh* I (rattle, # 8261); → *r'd* (tremble, shake, tremble, # 8283); → *r'l* I (brandish, make to quiver, # 8302); → *r'š* I (quake, shake, leap, # 8321); → *rpp* (shake, quake, rock, # 8344); → *r^{e}ṭēt* (terror, panic, trembling, # 8417); → *ś'r* I (be afraid, terrified, bristle with horror, # 8547)

Bibliography

TWOT 2:738.

M. V. Van Pelt/W. C. Kaiser, Jr.

7298	פרשׂ

פרשׂ (*prś*), spread out, spread (# 7298); מִפְרָשׂ (*miprāś*), nom. spreading of sails (# 5155).

ANE Cf. OSA *frs*, display, spread out; Ugar. *prš*, expand [land] (*UF*, 7, 1975, 135, 139), or cover with (*UF*, 10, 1978, 61); Akk. *naprušu*, fly (*CAD* N Part I, 314-15).

OT 1. Of the 69 uses of this vb. in the OT, the q. occurs 57x, the ni. 1x (Ezek 17:21, "the survivors will be scattered to the winds"), the pi. 11x (most often with the meaning spread out, but also with the meaning scatter [Ps 68:14(15); Zech 2:6(2)]). The nom. *miprāś* is a disleg. appearing in Job 36:29 (spreading of clouds) and Ezek 27:7 (spreading of sail).

The vb. is distinguished by the few direct objects that follow it with some frequency. Four are especially prominent. There is, first of all, some article of clothing that is spread over an object. Thus, Num 4 has numerous references to the priests spreading a cloth over the holy objects of the tabernacle (vv. 6, 7, 8, 11, 13, 14) before they are ready to be transported by the Kohathite Levites to the next encampment. Over all these objects were at least two coverings. Over the ark, however, there were three coverings (Num 4:5-6). Not only did the spread garment provide protection for the sacred articles, but it also prevented either observation or contact with the holy objects, both of which were fatal.

Another frequent object of *prś* is "net" (9x), spread by God over his apostate people (Ezek 12:13; 17:20; 32:3; Hos 7:12), by foreign nations over Israel (Ezek 19:8), or by an individual bent on entrapment (Ps 140:5[6]; cf. also Prov 29:5; Lam 1:13; Hos 5:1).

A third object of *prś* is *kānāp* (→ # 4053), in the sing. "skirt" (Ruth 3:9; Ezek 16:8), in the pl. "wings" (of birds [Deut 32:11; Job 39:26; Jer 48:40; 49:22], of cherubs [Exod 25:20; 37:9; 1 Kgs 6:27; 8:7; 1 Chron 28:18; 2 Chron 3:13]). More than likely the phrase "spread your skirt over X" means "to marry" (Hubbard, *Ruth*, NICOT, 212).

A fourth object of *prś* is hand (*kap*, palm, 13x; *yad*, hand, 5x). Here the reference is to spreading one's palms/hands in prayer before God. With the q. the object of *prś* is always *kap*. With the pi. the object of *prś* is *yad* (Ps 143:6; Lam 1:17), except for Isa 1:15, where the reference is to prayer. For *prś kap* cf. Exod 9:29, 33; 1 Kgs 8:22, 54; Ezra 9:5; Job 11:13; Ps 44:20[21]. The Heb. phrase is comparable to cognate expressions in other Sem. languages such as Ugar., *ša ydk šmm*, lift your hands to heaven (Krt, 75-76), and Akk. *našû qātu*, pray with uplifted hands, (*CAD* N 2:106-7).

2. The first part of Isa 65:2, "all day long I [Yahweh] have held out (*pēraśtî*) my hands to an obstinate people" is a beautiful picture of God's longsuffering patience with his stubborn people. This part of the verse is quoted by Paul in Rom 10:21. While 10:14-15 ("How, then, can they call on the one they have not believed in? And how can they believe in the one of whom they have not heard...?") is often used as a great missionary text, that is not its contextual use in Rom 10. In effect, Paul is saying to his fellow Israelites that they cannot use the excuse of ignorance to justify their spiritual condition. Not only do they not have any excuse for ignorance but, to the contrary, all day long God has been holding out his hands to his people. They are, therefore, without excuse, as much as are the pagans to whom he refers in 1:20.

Spreading, extending, stretching: → *hdh* (stretch out the hands, # 2063); → *zrh* I (scatter, sprinkle, spread, # 2430); → *ṭpḥ* I (spread out, # 3253); → *yšṭ* (hold out, extend, # 3804); → *mtḥ* (spread out, # 5501); → *nṭh* (extend, # 5742); → *npṣ* II (spread out, scatter, be dispersed, # 5880); → *pwṣ* (scatter, disperse, be spread, dispersed, # 7046); → *pzr* (scatter, scatter, spread, be scattered, # 7061); → *prś* (spread out, spread, # 7298); → *pśh* (spread [of disease], # 7313); → *rpd* (spread out, support, refresh, # 8331); → *šṭḥ* (spread out, pour out, # 8848)

Victor P. Hamilton

7300	פרשׁ

פרשׁ (*prš*), q. explain, adjudicate; ni. be divided; pu. be decided; hi. sting (# 7300); פָּרָשָׁה (*pārāšâ*), nom. exact amount (→ # 7308). The ni. and pu. forms, if they exist, probably represent a form of *prs*.

ANE WestSem. root *prš* should be separated from words for "measure" (Kaufman, 80). For the latter, see the cognates of *prs* (→ # 7271).

OT 1. The vb. is used of divine decisions concerning the fate of someone found guilty of blaspheming (Lev 24:12) or breaking the Sabbath (Num 15:34). It refers to the interpretation of the Book of the Law in Neh 8:8 and describes the reading and explanation of a letter in the Aram. of Ezra 4:18. Cf. the related nom. *pārāšâ*, used to express "the exact amount" of silver (Esth 4:7) or to describe the "account" of Mordecai's fame (10:2).

2. A ni. part. appears in Ezek 34:12, describing something experienced by sheep. *BHS* and Zimmerli (207) suggest *niprāśôt*, scattered, in place of *niprāšôt*. This

seems preferable to the interpretation of *niprāšôt* as wounded, based on a hypothetical Arab. cognate (Ehrlich, 127-28; Willmes, 49-50).

3. A single hi. occurrence in Prov 23:32 likens wine to the actions of a snake in a parallelism: "it bites like a snake and poisons like a viper." Perhaps a separate root *prš* is involved. The LXX (see also Plöger, 261, 264, 278) understands the nom., *rō'š*, poison (LXX *ios*), in place of the MT's hi. form.

P-B The first of the above uses is probably intended in 4Q177.I.11, where the "fathers" explain (*prš*) names. See also 4Q512.42 II.4, where by the command of God the purification of everything is ordered (*npršh*). The nom. *pršh* is found in the copper scroll (3Q15.XII.12) to describe what accompanies a copy of this scroll, i.e., an "explanation."

Division, measurement, portion: → *ḥlq* II (divide, obtain one's share, # 2745); → *ḥṣh* (divide, be divided, # 2936); → *ḥṣṣ*(divide, order, # 2951); → *mnh* (count, # 4948); → *plg* (be divided, # 7103); → *prd* (spread out, be divided, keep apart, # 7233); → *prs* (measure, divide, # 7271); → *šs'* (tear, divide, # 9117)

BIBLIOGRAPHY

A. B. Ehrlich, *Randglossen zur Hebräischen Bibel: Textkritisches, Sorachliches und Sachliches: Fünfter Band*, 1912; S. A. Kaufman, *The Akkadian Influences on Aramaic*, 1974; O. Plöger, *Sprüche Salomos (Proverbia)*, BKAT 17, 1983; B. Willmes, *Die Sogenannte Hirtenallegorie Ez 34: Studien zum Bild des Hirten im Alten Testament*, 1984.

Richard Hess

7302	פֶּרֶשׁ

פֶּרֶשׁ (*pereš* I), offal, contents of stomach (# 7302).

OT The term *pereš*, offal, is found 5x in the Pent. in contexts where the animals (bull and goat) offered for sin offerings, and the red heifer, are to be burned outside the camp (Exod 29:14; Lev 4:11; 8:17; 16:27; Num 19:5). God's disgust with the priests is expressed in an announced action of spreading offal on their faces (Mal 2:3).

Dung, excrement, refuse, urine: → *'ašpōt* (ash-heap, refuse-heap, dung-hill, # 883); → *gll* II (befoul, dirty o.s., # 1671); → *dōmen* (dung, manure, # 1961); → *ḥ^{a}rā'îm* (dung, # 2989); → *yešaḥ* (filth, diarrhea, # 3803); → *madmēnâ* I (dung pit, # 4523); → *sûḥâ* (offal, # 6054); → *pereš* I (offal, contents of stomach, # 7302); → *ṣē'â* (filth, human excrement, # 7362); → *ṣāpîa'* (dung [of cattle], # 7616); → *śîg* (excrement, # 8485); → *šyn* (urinate, # 8874)

Roy E. Hayden

7304	פָּרָשׁ

פָּרָשׁ (*pārāš*), horseman, rider, horse (# 7304).

ANE Old Aram. *prš*, Egypt. Aram. *prš*, Syr. *parrāšā'*, Palm. *prš*, Nab. *prš*, Man. *parrāšā'*, ESA, *prs*, Arab. *faras*, Eth. *faras*.

OT Like *sûs*, horse, this term often appears in military contexts and in descriptions of armies (see, e.g., 1 Sam 13:5; 2 Sam 1:6; 8:4; 10:18; Ezek 26:7, 10; 38:4; Nah 3:3). (See *sûs* [→ # 6061] for a discussion of the significance of horses, chariots, and horsemen in Yahwistic theology.) The word is especially prominent in Exod 14-15, where

Yahweh hardens the Egyptians, causing them to pursue the Israelites (14:9, 17-18). Yahweh then miraculously destroys Pharaoh's horsemen in the Red Sea (14:26, 28; 15:19) in order to reveal his glory (14:17-18) and the reality of his protective presence (the significance of the name, Yahweh, cf. 14:18).

P-B DSS, Late Heb. (Jastrow 2:1243).

Horse: → *dhr* (gallop, # 1851); → *sûs* I (horse, # 6061); → *pārāš* (horseman, rider, horse, # 7304); → *rekeš* (team of horses, # 8224); → *ra'mâ* II (mane, # 8310); → *š^e'ātâ* (stamping [of hoofs], # 9121)
Chariot, cart, wagon, riding: → *rkb* (ride/mount, # 8206); → *šālîš* III (third man in war-chariot, adjutant, # 8957); → **Warfare: Theology**

BIBLIOGRAPHY

TWAT 6:782-87; D. R. Ap-Thomas, "All the King's Horses: A Study of the Term פרש (1 Kings 5.6 [EVV., 4.26] etc.)," in *Proclamation and Presence*, 1970, 135-51; W. R. Arnold, "The Word פָּרָשׁ in the Old Testament," *JBL* 24, 1905, 45-53.

Robert B. Chisholm

7307	פַּרְשְׁדוֹן

פַּרְשְׁדוֹן (*parš^edōn*), loophole (for escape)?, hapleg (# 7307).

ANE This nom. is perhaps related to Akk. *parašdinnu* (*AHw*, 832b: *paraštinnu*), hole; Hitt. *parašdu,* bud, shoot (?).

OT In the story of Ehud's killing of Eglon king of Moab, the phrase *wayyēṣē' happarš^edōnâ* appears at the juncture of the completion of the gruesome deed and the escape (Judg 3:22). The Heb. phrase that follows, *wayyēṣē' 'ēhûd hammisd^erônâ,* "and Ehud went out to the *misd^erôn,*" appears to be an ancient gloss that makes the subject explicit and interprets *parš^edōn* as an architectural term (see LXX). The alternative rendering "filth, dirt," followed in some translations, is based on the etymological connection with Heb. *pereš*, ingested food (→ # 7302; so Tg., Vg.).

P-B The Vg and Tg. offer an etymological exegesis based on Heb. *pereš*, ingested food, and a second element from the second half of the word. The Pesh. guesses that the form is an adverb meaning quickly, describing the manner in which Ehud "went out." LXX-A has a minus, but LXX-B renders *prostada*, portico. Symm. rendered *prothura*, doorway.

Disappearance, flight, escape: → *brḥ* I (run away, flee, disappear, # 1368); → *ḥlp* I (pass by, disappear, violate, change, renew, # 2736); → *ḥrh* II (disappear, be few in number, # 3014); → *nws* (flee, escape, slip away, # 5674); → *pṭr* (vanish, escape, let out, # 7080); → *plṭ* (save, bring to safety, # 7117); → *parš^edōn* (loophole [for escape]?, # 7307); → *śrd* (run away, escape, # 8572)

BIBLIOGRAPHY

R. G. Boling, *Judges*, AB, 1975, 86-87; A. R. Hulst, *Old Testament Translation Problems*, 1960, 20; H. N. Rösel, "Zur Ehud-Erzahlung," *ZAW* 89, 1977, 270-72, esp. 272; W. von Soden, "Zum akkadischen Wörterbuch. 61-66," *Or* 24, 1955, 144-45.

Jerome A. Lund

7308 (*pārāšâ*, exact statement), → Writing

7313	פשׂה

פשׂה (*pśh*), spread (of disease) (# 7313).

OT The vb. appears only in Lev 13 and 14, and there 22x [e.g., Lev 13:5], always in reference to the spread of a skin disease. *pśh* may be connected with Arab. *fašā*, spread, and south Arab. *fš'm,* which are used with skin diseases. More than likely the vb. in Heb. means to spread by increasing in size or number. Thus, the symptom described is the enlargement of localized lesions. On the other hand, the diseases spreading out over the body is conveyed by the vb. *prḥ* in v. 12 (NIV break out).

P-B Mish. Heb. (See Jastrow 2:1144).

Spreading, extending, stretching: → *hdh* (stretch out the hands, # 2063); → *zrh* I (scatter, sprinkle, spread, # 2430); → *ṭpḥ* I (spread out, # 3253); → *yšṭ* (hold out, extend, # 3804); → *mtḥ* (spread out, # 5501); → *nṭh* (extend, # 5742); → *npṣ* II (spread out, scatter, be dispersed, # 5880); → *pwṣ* (scatter, disperse, be spread, dispersed, # 7046); → *pzr* (scatter, scatter, spread, be scattered, # 7061); → *prś* (spread out, spread, # 7298); → *pśh* (spread [of disease], # 7313); → *rpd* (spread out, support, refresh, # 8331); → *šṭḥ* (spread out, pour out, # 8848)

Disease—plague: → *deber* I (bubonic plague, # 1822); → *ṭ^e^ḥōrîm* (plague, # 3224); → *maggēpâ* (plague, # 4487); → *nega'* (plague, affliction, # 5596); → *rešep* I (pestilence, # 8404); → *ṣr'* (suffer from skin disease, # 7665). For related entries → *ḥlh* I (become weak, tired, ill, # 2703); → **Plagues: Theology**

Disease—blister, boil, skin disease, scar, wound: → *'^a^ba'bu'ōt* (blisters, # 81); → *bōhaq* (skin condition, # 993); → *baheret* (white patch on skin, # 994); → *gārāb* (festering eruption, # 1734); → *zrr* I (press out [wounds], # 2452); → *ḥeres* I (itch, # 3063); → *yabbelet* (wart?, # 3301); → *yallepet* (skin disease, # 3539); → *y^e^raqraq* (discoloration, # 3768); → *k^e^wiyya* (scar, # 3918); → *m'r* (be sore, # 4421); → *māzôr* I (boil, # 4649); → *makkâ* (blow, # 4804); → *mispaḥat* (skin eruption, # 5030); → *mrḥ* (rub, polish, # 5302); → *neteq* (scalp infection, # 5999); → *sappaḥat* (hair disease, # 6204); → *'ōpel* I (abscesses, # 6754); → *'āš* II (pus, # 6932); → *ṣāpâ* (pus?, # 7597); → *ṣarebet* (scar, # 7648); → *ṣr'* (suffer from skin disease, # 7665); → *ś^e^'ēt* II (swelling, # 8421); → *śtr* (break out [tumor], # 8609); → *š^e^ḥîn* (boil, # 8825). For related entries → *ḥlh* I (become weak, tired, ill, # 2703)

Disease—fever, illness, infirmity: → *'nš* I (be in poor health, # 653); → *dwb* (wear away, # 1853); → *dalleqet* (fever, # 1945); → *zôb* (discharge, # 2308); → *ḥl'* (fall ill, # 2688); → *ḥlh* I (become weak, tired, ill, # 2703); → *ḥarḥur* (heat of fever, # 3031); → *madeweh* II (disease, # 4504); → *pśh* (spread [of disease], # 7313); → *qaddaḥat* (fever, # 7707); → *šaḥepet* (illness, # 8831). For related entries → *ṣr'* (suffer from skin disease, # 7665)

BIBLIOGRAPHY

M. Höfner, "Eine altsüdarabische sühne-Inschrift," *SVT* 16, 1967, 106-13; B. Levine, *Leviticus,* JPS Torah Commentary, 1989, 77; J. Milgrom, *Leviticus 1-16*, AB, 1991, 781.

Victor P. Hamilton

7314	פשׂע

פשׂע (*pś'* I), step forth, march (# 7314); denom. from פֶּשַׂע (*peśa'*), step (# 7315).

ANE Cf. Aram. and Syr. *ps'*, march; Mand. *psa*, march, cross; Akk. *pasāḫu*, drive out, assemble, draw up; Arab. *fašaḥa*, spread one's legs, take large steps.

OT 1. The vb. is a hapleg. occurring in Isa 27:4, "I would *march* against them in battle," a verse directed by Yahweh, Israel's keeper, against any enemy that would dare attack his vineyard Israel.

2. The nom. derived from this vb., *peśa'*, step, also a hapleg., is found in David's words to Jonathan, "there is only a *step* between me and death" (1 Sam 20:3), as David is hunted by Saul.

Marching, stepping: → *ḥšl* (unfit to march, straggle, shatter, # 3129); → *nḥt* (march down, descend, penetrate, settle, # 5737); → *s'n* (tramp along, tread, # 6008); → *pś'* I (step forth, march, # 7314); → *ṣ'd* (step, march, # 7575)

Victor P. Hamilton

7315 (*pesa'*, step), → # 7314

7318	פשח

פשח (*pšḥ*), leave fallow (hapleg., Lam 3:11, # 7318).

ANE Arab. *fasaḫa*, dislocate, twist, contort, tear up, tear in two.

OT Jenni offers the translation lay idle, in light of the Akk. *pašāḫu*, be still, and Kraus and Plöger posit "he paralyzed me," drawing on Aq.'s *chōlainō* (indicating a form of the Heb. *psḥ*, to be limp, lame).

However, in light of most cognates (see above), *pšḥ* signifies plucking or pulling to pieces. KD (407) points out that the Tg. reading of 1 Sam 15:33 affirms that Samuel *pšḥ* Agag. Whether or not the imagery of a predatory animal continues into v. 11, Lam 3:11 depicts God as both the one who forced the traveler off the path as well as the one who tears him to pieces, a vivid description of the trauma experienced in the horrific fall of Jerusalem.

P-B Mish. Heb. *pšḥ*, to split, tear off, strip; Jewish Aram. *pšḥ*, pe. tear off, pa. tear up, tear in two; Syr. *pšḥ*, pe. cut off, cut into pieces, pa. tear to pieces, mangle, lacerate.

Tearing, prey: → *gzr* II (cut, slaughter, tear, prey, # 1616); → *ḥth* (take, fetch, # 3149); → *ṭrp* (tear in pieces, # 3271); → *mlḥ* I (be torn in pieces, dissipate, # 4872); → *nsḥ* (tear down, tear away, # 5815); → *ns'* (tear out, # 5825); → *ntṣ* (tear down, # 5997); → *ntq* (tear away, # 5998); → *pšḥ* (pluck, pull, leave fallow, # 7318); → *qwṣ* II (tear apart, # 7763); → *qr'* (tear up, # 7973); → *šs'* (tear, divide, # 9117)

Bibliography

E. Jenni, *Das hebräische Pi'el*, 1968; H.-J. Kraus, *Klagelieder (Threni)*, 1956; O. Plöger, "Die Klagelieder," in *Die fünf Megilloth*, 1969, 127-64.

Michael A. Grisanti

7320	פשט

פשט (*pšṭ*), q. take off (clothes), attack; pi. strip; hi. strip, take off; hitp. take off (clothes) (# 7320).

ANE *pšṭ* is attested in the following cognates: Aram. *p^ešaṭ*, q. take off, strip off, undress, shed skin, make straight (*HAD*, 229); Mand. *pšṭ*, stretch out, tear away (*MdD*,

382); Akk. *pāšāṭu(m)*, delete, extinguish (*AHw*, 844a); Arab. *basaṭa* spread, flatten (Wehr, 57-58).

OT 1. The vb. *pšṭ* occurs 43x in the OT in 4 of the vb. stems and in every division (Pent. [6x], Hist. [23x], Writing [4x], Prophets [10x]). It means to take off (clothes) in many different contexts, strip dead soldiers after battle, attack and strip another's clothes (or something figurative), and skin an animal for sacrifice.

2. In q. *pšṭ* often means take off one's clothes at night before bed (Neh 4:23[17]; S of Songs 5:3) or to change sets of clothes (often priests) (Lev 6:11[4]; 16:23; Ezek 44:19). It may also signify mourning (Isa 32:11; Ezek 26:16), a ceremony (1 Sam 18:4, hitp.), or a prophetic experience (1 Sam 19:24). In hi. *pšṭ* is used for taking off *another's* clothes. It may suggest violence (Joseph's brother stripping him of his robe, Gen 37:23) or judgment, as in the case of Moses' removing Aaron's garments after his rebellion to transfer them to his son (Num 20:26, 28; see *TWOT* 2:1845). Unrighteous men "strip" men of clothing as security for debts (Job 22:6) or possibly even as outright thievery (Mic 2:8; see Allen, 296-97).

3. *pšṭ* is also used of a victorious army (Israelite or Philistine) stripping the armor off the dead soldiers after the battle (1 Sam 31:8; 2 Sam 23:10; 1 Chron 10:8; all pi.). The hi. is also used 2x (1 Sam 31:9; 1 Chron 10:9) of the victorious Philistine army stripping Saul's body, perhaps to suggest the more intense attitude of beheading him or of gloating over having killed the king.

Strip in the sense of "to skin" (usually an animal) occurs 4x (all hi.). Normally it describes priests "skinning" an animal for sacrifice (Lev 1:6; 2 Chron 29:34; 35:11). Micah uses it in a graphic depiction of unrighteous Israelites who cruelly mistreat their fellow man (along with tearing flesh from bones, breaking bones, chopping up like meat for the pan, Mic 3:2-3).

4. Another common usage in q. means to attack or advance (against), perhaps "put off" shelter to advance (BDB, 833). Usually an army attacks its target (12x, all in the historical books), the Chaldeans attack Job's camels (Job 1:17), and robbers attack (Hos 7:1).

5. The vb. *pšṭ* also occurs in figurative contexts, usually denoting judgment (hi.). Job accuses God of stripping him of honor (Job 19:9). Ezekiel warns of Yahweh's judgment in sending invaders to strip Israel of her clothing (plunder the nation) (Ezek 16:39; 23:26). Hosea warns that Yahweh will strip Israel and make her naked (*'ārôm*, → # 6873) by making her like a desert (Hos 2:3[5]). Nahum compared Yahweh's judgment on Nineveh to locusts denuding land, a figure of merchants taking the treasures of Nineveh (Nah 3:16).

6. *Synonyms.* The lesser used *ḥśp*, strip, bare (# 3106); and *pṣl*, strip (# 7202) have similar but narrower fields of meaning and appear less frequently than *pšṭ*. The numerous occurrences of *pšṭ* in the Pent. and historical books reflect its nonfigurative meanings, while most of the poetic and prophetic occurrences suggest judgment. In Deut 28:48 Yahweh had threatened nakedness (*'ērôm*, # 6567) for disobeying the covenant, and the prophets use *pšṭ* as one way of showing Yahweh's stripping Israel to bring about that nakedness.

P-B The LXX translates: take off (q.) by *ekdyō*, strip oneself; attack (q.) by *ekteinō*, stretch out, extend, and *epitithēmi*, attack; strip (pi.) by *ekdidyskō*, strip, plunder; strip (hi.) by *ekdyō*, strip; skin (hi.) by *derō*, skin, flay. In Mish. Heb. *pšṭ* means straighten, undress, strip, explain (Jastrow, 1245b).

Bare, naked, destitute, stripped: → *ḥśp* I (strip, bare, # 3106); → *'rh* (make bare, be poured out, # 6867); → *'ārôm* (naked, # 6873); → *'rr* (strip bare, be leveled, # 6910); → *pṣl* (strip, # 7202); → *pšṭ* (take off [clothes], attack, strip, # 7320); → *šᵉpî* (barren height, # 9155)

BIBLIOGRAPHY

TWOT 2:741; L. C. Allen, *The Books of Joel, Obadiah, Jonah and Micah*, NICOT, 1976.

Boyd V. Seevers

7321	פשע

פשע (*pš'*), q. rebel, violate, transgress; ni. be offended (# 7321); **פֶּשַׁע** (*peša'*), nom. rebellion, transgression (→ # 7322).

OT 1. As part of the terminology for sin, *pš'*, transgression, has a narrower meaning than *ḥṭ'* and *'wn*. Originated from the political sphere to mean "rebellion" (e.g., 2 Kgs 1:1) and used 136x in OT, it normally implies willful violations by an inferior against a superior (e.g., Prov 28:24). In biblical theology, the term refers to an open and brazen defiance of God by humans. In Ezek 2:3, its use in parallel with *mrd*, rebel, reinforces its primary connotation: "Son of man, I am sending you to . . . a rebellious nation that has rebelled against me; they and their fathers have been in revolt (*pš'*) against me." The use of this term in Gen 50:17 by the brothers to acknowledge their "sins" against Joseph does not indicate an exception of its normal usage; rather, it highlights the difference of their social positions. However, the meaning of *ḥṭ'* and *'wn* are less restrictive and can often refer to the wrong of a superior against an inferior (e.g., *ḥṭ'* in 1 Sam 19:4; 26:21). Though *'br* (→ # 6296) is often translated in some versions as "transgress," as a term for sin it is not used as frequently as *pš'*. It depicts overstepping the boundaries set by the commandments (e.g., Num 14:41; 1 Sam 15:24).

2. For a discussion of sin, → *ḥṭ'* (sin, commit a sin; make a sin offering, purify, # 2627).

Alex Luc

7322	פֶּשַׁע

פֶּשַׁע (*peša'*), nom. offense(s), rebellion, crime(s), legal offense, personal offense, guilt, wrong(s), property offense, penalty (# 7322); < **פשע** (*pš'*), q. rebel, revolt; sin, offend; wrong; break with, commit (a) crime(s); ni. be offended, alienated (→ # 7321).

ANE Ugar. *pš'*, sin, (*KTU* 1.17.VI:43); Syr. *pᵉsa'*, stiff, be frightened; *pᵉšī'ūtā'*, foolishness.

OT The vb. occurs 41x (q. 40x; ni. 1x), the nom. 93x. It is probably not possible to say whether the vb. or the nom. has precedence (*TWAT* 6:794; cf. *THAT* 489-90). The nom. is juxtaposed with three other key words for sin, *'āwôn* (19x), *ḥaṭā'* (24x), and *rā'â* (6x). Three of these terms, *'āwôn, ḥaṭṭāt'*, and *peša'*, occur together 7x (Exod 34:7; Lev 16:21; Job 13:23; Ps 32:5; Isa 59:12; Ezek 21:24[29]; Dan 9:24), while the *rā'â/ḥaṭā'/peša'* combination only occurs once (Gen 50:17). In these various combinations of different words for sins the biblical writers seek to provide an understanding of the multifaceted nature of sin.

Seebass (*TWAT* 6:799) concludes that the basic meaning of the nom. *peša'*, legal offense (*Rechtsbruch*), serves as an overarching concept for various offenses (*Delikte*) that were especially irritating and offensive. Accordingly, the vb. means to commit a legal offense (*Rechtsbruch begehen*). Seebass's suggestion provides a starting point for a discussion of the meaning of *peša'*. The intentional nature and covenantal background of the term also demands attention. Unlike *ḥṭ'* (which can connote an inadvertent mistake; → # 2627), *peša'* signifies a willful, knowledgeable violation of a norm or standard (*ABD* 6:32). Beyond that, it represents a willful breach of trust. It occurs most frequently to designate the disruption of an alliance through violation of a covenant (see below).

The Mosaic covenant provides the theological backdrop for the primary significance of *peša'*. This fact gathers together the strong and weak points of Seebass's proposal. The Mosaic covenant is a legal document in content and form. Its stipulations/laws comprise the bulk of its content. In this way, *peša'* represents a legal offense. However, *peša'* moves beyond that reality. The idea of a covenant deepens the concept of legal offense. *peša'* does not simply involve external disobedience or breaking a law, but entails the violation of a sacred covenant, i.e., revolt (a deliberate act of disloyalty and disobedience). The commitment of *peša'* may involve social, political, or cultic acts and can occur on an interpersonal (domestic, Exod 22:9[8]), political (1 Kgs 12:19; 2 Kgs 1:1; 3:5, 7), or religious level (1 Kgs 8:50; Isa 1:2; Jer 3:13). In all of this, in a fundamental sense *peša'* represents covenant treachery. The act of *peša'* surely entails a breach of the law, but that legal offense often violates an existing covenantal relationship. Although "transgression" or "legal offense" may adequately serve as a translation for *peša'* in Ps and Prov, it falls short in most historical and prophetic contexts (see below).

1. *Rebellion in the domestic realm.* Offenses with respect to property and persons are covered by *peša'*. Angry because Laban had accused him of theft, Jacob hurls a question at Laban (Gen 31:36): "What is my crime (*peša'*)?" i.e., what have I done to violate the peaceful relationship between us? Out of fear for their lives, Joseph's brothers present to him one of their father's final requests (Gen 50:17), that Joseph might forgive his brothers for their sins (*ḥaṭṭā't*) and wrongs (*peša'*). David spares Saul's life (1 Sam 24:11[12]) in an attempt to demonstrate his innocence of wrongdoing (*rā'â*) or rebellion (*peša'*). In light of David's intimate relationship with Saul's son, Jonathan, it appears that interpersonal offense is in view. However, since Saul was the king and David was anointed to be the next king, David might also be protesting any suggestions of political treachery. To commit *peša'* is to disrupt a relationship of some kind.

Exod 22:7-15[6-14] provides instruction concerning various cases of damage to or loss of deposited goods. Since banks and warehouses of any kind were rare in the ancient world, entrusting goods to the care of another for safekeeping was a common practice. Exod 22:7-8[6-7] concerns the theft of silver or gold and 22:10-13[9-12] deals with loss (death by sickness) or theft of livestock while in the care of another. The beginning of 22:9[8] (*'al kol dᵉbar peša'*, concerning all matters of breach of trust) departs from the form of the other scenarios (case laws) that are introduced by *kî* or *'im*. Consequently, certain scholars (Hyatt, 238; Noth, 184) view v. 9[8] with regard to any kind of property dispute, while others contend that *peša'* signifies contested ownership since entrusted property is in view in the immediate context (Cassuto, 286; Childs, 476; Köhler, 213-18). Although the more general application is possible, the surrounding context and the nom. *peša'* itself suggest that a spec. application is more likely. After specifying silver and gold in the preceding verses, Moses addresses the loss/theft of any property entrusted to another. The grounds for punishment is not simply a property offense or even an infraction of personal rights. This problem is reprehensible because it constitutes a breach of trust or violation of an agreement.

The use of *peša'* in Amos 1-2 provides another illustration of this key distinction. In light of the occurrence of *peša'* in Prov for broader social transgressions (see below), Wolff (152-53; cf. Knierem, 149) contends that in Amos (1:3, 6, 9, 11, 13; 2:1, 4, 6; 3:14; 5:12) *peša'* refers exclusively to transgressions against society, i.e., infractions of property and personal rights. The pl. form of *peša'* serves as a technical term to characterize and summarize cases of this nature (Knierem, 127). Wolff's suggestion, however, misses the main thrust of *peša'* and does not do justice to the theological context of Amos. The repetition of *peša'* in Amos's eight woe oracles implies more than violations of treaties among pagan nations. Their treacherous conduct constituted rebellion against Yahweh himself. Although in most treaty violations a vassal rebels against his suzerain, in Amos *peša'* concerns a "violation of general standards of international morality—universal laws of God—expressed in inhumane treatment of one nation by another" (Andersen and Freedman, 231; cf. Hayes, 71). Each nation indicted for *peša'* in Amos 1 and 2 is guilty of denying Yahweh's authority by asserting their own power.

2. *Rebellion against political rulers or powers*. Several occurrences of the vb. *pš'* in historical literature signify a breaking of a political alliance in concrete terms, whether it be concerning Moab's (2 Kgs 1:1; 3:5, 7) or Edom's (8:20, 22; 2 Chron 21:8, 10) rebellion against Judah/Israel or the hostilities between Israel and Judah (1 Kgs 12:19 = 2 Chron 10:19). These political rebellions provide a conceptual framework for the theological uses of *pš'* (see below).

3. *Rebellion against Yahweh*. The vast majority of the instances of *peša'/pš'* in the OT signify rebellion directed against Yahweh, Israel's suzerain (1 Kgs 8:50). The Mosaic covenant depicts Yahweh as the only one who can grant or refuse to grant forgiveness for *peša'* (Exod 34:7; Num 14:18; cf. Josh 24:19). The Day of Atonement is the only cultic assembly where *peša'*, sin, is removed (Lev 16:16, 21):

The nom. and vb. are esp. abundant in the Prophets, occurring most frequently in Isa (20x), Ezek (13x), and Amos (11x [see above]). These prophets (and others) make repeated use of *peša'/pš'* because their ministries devote significant attention to Israel's past or present covenant treachery. They indict Israel for disrupting their covenant relationship with Yahweh. Isaiah begins his prophecy by depicting Yahweh's relationship with Israel in terms of a father-son relationship. Israel, although a recipient of Yahweh's abundant, tender care, has rebelled against her father (suzerain) (Isa 1:2) and faces severe judgment (1:28). Outside of a single use of *peša'* in 24:20 (in an apocalyptic section delineating God's final judgment and restoration of the earth), the remaining 17x of the vb. and nom. occur in chs. 40-66. In these chapters Isaiah addresses many of the same issues confronted by other writing prophets.

The prophets graphically remind God's covenant nation of their rebellion (called a "rebellious nation," Ezek 2:3; and "a brood of rebels," Isa 57:4), either because they are rushing headlong toward exile or need to realize their responsibility for the Exile (43:27; 50:1; 53:5, 8, 12). There is a cause and effect relationship between their rebellion against Yahweh and their experience of divine punishment (Ezek 20:38; 21:24[29]; 39:24). This painful scenario, however, need not be permanent because Yahweh calls Israel to repent of their rebellion (Ezek 18:30). He is the one who can forgive/blot out their rebellious deeds (Isa 43:25; 44:2; Ezek 37:23). The Lord also affirms that the day is coming when his chosen people will no longer be characterized by covenant treachery (Ezek 14:11). The prophet Isaiah (Isa 53:5, 8, 12) also anticipates the coming of a servant figure along the lines of the ideal Davidic ruler seen in the royal psalms and Isa 9 and 11, who will experience an agonizing death because of the rebellion of his own people.

Daniel anticipates a day future to his own when a king will arise who will desecrate the temple precincts. Because of their rebellion, God will turn over some Israelites to this king's authority (Dan 8:12-13). This king foreshadows another coming king who will arise in a time when rebellion climaxes (8:23; 9:24).

In the Wisdom/poetic literature the word is found 36x (Job-10x, Ps-14x, Prov-12x). In most of these instances the rebellion motif is not as prominent as in historical or prophetic passages because the covenantal background is emphasized less. Consequently, in Wisdom literature *peša'* appears often as a term for legal offense. The primary idea of rebellion appears in a few instances (Job 34:37; Ps 25:7; 36:1[2]) and is understood in the other occurrences. All but one of the instances of *peša'* in Job refer to Job himself, either in one of his laments (Job 7:21; 13:23; 14:17; 31:33) or in Elihu's rebuke of Job (33:9; 34:6, 37; 35:6; 36:9). The psalmist refers to *peša'* as a characteristic of the wicked (Ps 36:1[2]; 107:17) and the cause for divine punishment (5:10[11]; 89:32[33]). The psalmist prays for or refers to the reality of forgiveness (25:7; 32:1, 5; 51:1[3]; 103:12) and asks that God keep him from *peša'* (19:13[14]; 39:8[9]).

In Prov *peša'* is the fruit of the lips of an evil man (Prov 12:13). His words of *peša'* ensnare him (29:6). A righteous man, however, does not have "rebellious lips" (12:13). This *peša'* involves words that create strife and agitation (10:12; 29:22). Confusion/rebellion (*peša'*) causes an entire land to be in turmoil (28:2). Mistreatment and stealing from one's parents constitutes a blatant disregard of natural relational responsibilities toward others (28:24). Acts of *peša'* are the acts of wicked/evil men (29:6, 16). The experience of *pš'* causes alienation between fellow human beings (18:19). These examples illustrate the fact that *peša'/pš'* is a failure to act with wisdom toward others, and especially in ways that create destructive results within society.

Each occurrence of *peša'* in Wisdom literature, whether it is directed toward a fellow human being or God, represents a form of rebellion against God as well. As the suzerain lord who demands obedience from his vassals and expects his subjects to demonstrate mercy and justice to their fellow subjects, any violation constitutes rejection of his authority.

P-B The LXX demonstrates clearly the broad semantic range of meaning *peša'* had within boundaries circumscribing terms/concepts for sin(s). For the vb. the translators employed *asebeō*, act profanely, commit impiety, rebel/sin against the gods/God; *aphistēmi*, cause, make revolt, rebellion; remove from; to stand off from; *anomeō*, act against the law, lawlessly. For the nom. *adikia*, *adikēma*, unrighteousness, unrighteous act/deed; *hamartia*, *hamartēma*, sin, sinfulness, sinful act, deed; *anomia*, *anomēma*, without law, lawless act/deed; *asebeia*, impiety, profaneness; *paraptōma*, transgression, fall away, are all attested. These words do not do full justice to the flexible use of *peša'* in the OT. In general Knierim (*THAT* 1:548) has noted that only six G words are used to render as many as twenty-six Heb. expressions for sin. In the case of *peša'/ḥaṭṭā't* (etc.) the LXX renders these using the first two words above in common, but uses a wider variety of words for *peša'*. The context is all important in catching the nuance of the Heb. word.

In the DSS the vb. (4x+) and the nom. (49x+) are found. It appears in the hi. for the first time (4Q 184:1, 4, 15). The word continues in its OT sense with Isa 59:20; 66:24 highly influencing its meaning (1QS 10:20; 1QH 2:9; 4Q 491:8-10). OT usages are expanded (cf. Ps 25:7; 11QPs(a) 24:11). New parallel pairs are found with *gillûl* ǁ *peša'*. God's purity (*ṭaher*) is contrasted with *peša'* (1QH 3:21; 11:10). The pair *'ašᵉmâ* ǁ *peša'* is also found (1QS 1:23; 9:4). Other interesting pairings and uses occur.

In LH the vb. continues its lively use, meaning to be willful, rebellious (cf. *Yoma* 4:2; 6:2). A *pōšēa'* is a willful transgressor. The vb. also meant, as in the OT, to be faithless (Gen R. s. 52; Prov 18:19). The hi., as in Qumran, is found here also, meaning to cause to transgress (Num R s. 9; Exod 22:8). The nom. *peša'*, meaning rebellion, sin is also found (Gen R. S. 22; see Jastrow 2:1247 for further refs.).

NT In the NT *hamartanō* basically renders *ḥṭ'*, but probably also was intended as a broad term that rendered *pš', nś'*, and *'āwôn* as well (cf. Knierim, *THAT* 2:549, who leaves out *pš'*). All of the words used in the LXX to render *pš'* are used in the NT, but it is difficult to know when the writer might have had *pš'* in mind, since other Heb. words for sin are rendered likewise. *asebia* probably has *pš'* in mind from the OT.

Rebellion, conspiracy, stubbornness, obstinacy: → *ysd* II (conspire together, # 3570); → *kśh* (become stubborn, headstrong, # 4170); → *lāṣôn* (bragging, foolish talk, # 4371); → *lṣṣ* (rebel, scoff, # 4372); → *mrd* (revolt, rebel, # 5277); → *mrh* (be refractory, obstinate, # 5286); → *srr* I (be stubborn, rebellious, # 6253); → *'bt* (conspire together, # 6309); → *'ēṣâ* II (disobedience?, revolt?, # 6784); → *'ātāq* (old, hard, stubborn, arrogant, # 6981); → *pš'* (revolt, rebel, # 7321); → *qᵉšî* (stubbornness, # 8001); → *qšr* (ally together, conspire, bind, # 8003); → *šᵉrîrût* (stubbornness, # 9244)

Sin, guilt, rebellion, transgression, wrong: → *'āwen* (mischief, iniquity, deception, # 224); → *ḥṭ'* (sin, commit a sin, purify, # 2627); → *'wh* (do wrong, pervert, # 6390); → *'wl* I (act wrongly, # 6401); → *pš'* (rebel, violate, transgress, # 7321); → **Fall: Theology**

BIBLIOGRAPHY

ABD 6:31-40; *THAT* 2:488-95; *TWAT* 6:791-810; F. Andersen and D. Freedman, *Amos*, 1989; U. Cassuto, *A Commentary on the Book of Exodus*, 1983; B. Childs, *The Book of Exodus*, 1974; A. Gelin, "Sin in the Old Testament," in *Sin in the Bible*, 1964, 9-39; J. Hayes, *Amos the Eighth Century Prophet: His Times and His Preaching*, 1988; J. Hyatt, *Exodus*, 1971; R. Knierem, *Die Hauptbegriffe für Sünde im Alten Testament*, 1965; L. Köhler, "Zu Ex 22, 8," *ZAW* 46, 1928, 213-18; B. Napier, "Isaiah and the Isaian," in *SVT* 15, 1965, 240-51; M. Noth, *Exodus*, 1962; S. Porubčan, *Sin in the Old Testament*, 1963; H. Wolff, *Joel and Amos*, 1977.

Eugene Carpenter/Michael A. Grisanti

7323 (*pēšer*, solution), → # 7354

7324	פֵּשֶׁת

פֵּשֶׁת (*pēšet*), flax linen (# 7324); פִּשְׁתָּה (*pištâ*), flax linen (# 7325).

OT 1. Linen and wool were the two most common materials used for making textiles in the Levant during OT times (Prov 31:13; Hos 2:5[7], 9[11]). Linen is made from flax (*Linum usitatissmum*), which grew throughout the ANE. The earliest surviving fragments of textile believed to be linen come from Catal Hüyük in Turkey from the Neolithic period (ca. 6000 BC; see James Mellart, *Çatal Hüyük: A Neolithic Town in Anatolia*, 1967, 119-20, plates 116-18). In Egypt, linen is attested from the Fayum A culture, which has been carbon 14 dated to ca. 4000 BC (Fred Wendrof, "Egyptian Prehistory: Some New Concepts," *Science* 169, 1970, 1168.) Between 4000-3000 BC at Teleiât el-Ghassul, a Transjordanian site, linen has survived, while it is found at the Early Bronze IV levels (ca. 2300-2000 BC) at Tell el-Areini in Canaan (Borowski, 98).

Even though linen may have been imported throughout the OT period, the mention of harvesting flax in the Gezer calendar (ca. 900 BC) as a part of the agricultural cycle suggests that linen was widely in use in Israel throughout the OT period. In order to make linen, the flax (*pištâ*) had to undergo a long process from harvesting (pulling) to drying, soaking for some weeks, and drying again for around two years before the fibers were extracted from the stalk and spun into thread (cf. Forbes, 32). The long period of drying is reflected in the story of Rahab hiding the Hebrew spies under the flax on the roof of her house (Josh 2:6). The various phases of linen production is pictorially documented in Upper Egyptian tombs at Deir el-Gebrawi (ca. 2400), Meir, el Bersheh, and Beni Hasan (ca. 2100-2000 BC).

Egyptian linen was especially known for its high quality and sharp, white color. Actual surviving linen garments do not show the original whiteness, but paintings on Book of the Dead papyri show the deceased standing before the divine tribunal for the last judgment decked in piercing white clothes. While Canaan and later Israel grew its own flax and had a good linen industry, Egyptian linen was valued in western Asia (Prov 7:16). The eleventh-century BC papyrus the "Report of Wenamun" records that linen was among the objects brought to Byblos in exchange for timber (M. Lichtheim, *Ancient Egyptian Literature 11*, 1976, 227).

2. Linen is widely mentioned in the OT, and there is a variety of terms for types and qualities of linen. *bad* (# 965) occurs from earliest to latest sources in the OT. This type of linen was used for priestly garments (Exod 28:42; 39:28; Lev 6:10[3]), including the "linen ephod" worn by priests (1 Sam 2:18; 22:18) and is even called "holy linen" in Lev 16:4. The term *šēš* (# 9254), normally translated "fine linen," derives from the Egyptian word *sšr* or *šs* (*HALAT* 1013; *WbÄS* 4:539). Of more than three dozen occurrences of *šēš*, most are used in connection with priestly attire and furnishings for the tabernacle in the book of Exodus. The "fine linen" garment Joseph received from Pharaoh in Egypt was, not surprisingly, made of *šēš*. Only two occurrences (Prov 31:22; Ezek 16:13) are in contexts not closely related to Egypt, while the Exodus references occur within months after the departure from Egypt, and the Joseph story is set in Egypt.

Another term rendered "linen" in English translations is *bûṣ* (# 1009). In the OT it is found only in late period texts, i.e., from the exilic period and beyond (1 Chron 15:27; 2 Chron 2:14[13]; 3:14; 5:12; Esth 1:16; 8:15; Ezek 27:16). *bûṣ* is cognate with

Akk. *bûṣu*. Only in Neo-Assyrian and Neo-Babylonian texts is *bûṣu* found, indicating its late appearance in the Near East (*CAD* 2:350). The term *ḥûr* (# 2580) is used to describe the fine linen string used in the palace of Xerxes in Susa (Esth 1:6; 8:15) and is related to the word meaning "to be white" (*HALAT* 283). *'ēṭûn* (# 355) occurs once in Prov 7:16, in the phrase "colored linens from Egypt." This word appears to derive from the Egyptian term *idmi,* meaning "red cloth" (*HALAT* 36; *WbÄS* 1:153). *karpas* (# 4158) should not be translated as linen. It is a Sanskrit word for cotton and occurs only in Esth 1:6 (*HALAT* 456). Cotton is not introduced to the ANE until around 700 BC, where it is mentioned in Sennacherib's annals; it is not widely known until some centuries later (Forbes 45-46).

3. Garments of linen were cooler than wool and, hence, would have been especially comfortable in the warm climate of the ANE. Consequently, the wide use of linen in priestly attire may not have had any particular symbolic significance in the OT. Linen's use in the tabernacle may also have been used because it was available to the Israelites who had recently left Egypt. There is nothing to suggest from the OT that there was any particular theological significance to God's directive to use linen materials for the priests and in constructing the sanctuary.

The reason for God's prohibition against mixing wool and linen in clothing (Deut 22:11) is unknown. This law, along with those in the preceding verses (vv. 9-10), deal with inappropriate combinations. These could be purely didactic to remind the Israelites that they were a people holy to God, who likewise should not mingle with pagans and their religious and cultural institutions.

BIBLIOGRAPHY

Oded Borowski, *Agriculture in Iron Age Israel*, 1987; R. J. *Forbes Studies in Ancient Technology*, 1956, 4:27-49.

James K. Hoffmeier

7325 (*pištâ*, flax linen), → # 7324

7326 (*pat*, piece, morsel), → Bread

7327	פֹּת

פֹּת (*pōt*), front, forehead (# 7327).

ANE The Akk. nom. *pūtu* means forehead.

OT The nom. appears twice in the OT. In Isa 3:17 it is par. to *qadqōd*. The NIV translates it with scalp, but forehead is more probable. It also appears in 1 Kgs 7:50, where the nom. refers to something connected to the doors of the temple. The NIV translates with sockets, but it could also refer to the front of the doors.

Dahood suggested that this word should be read in Ps 19:7[8]. The MT has *petî*, meaning simple (→ # 7343; NIV "the statues of the Lord are trustworthy, making wise the simple"). Dahood wants to read *pōtî*, translating "my mind." This is a possibility, but the emendation has no textual support.

Head: → *'ap* (face, anger, # 678); → *gulgōlet* (scull, # 1653); → *l^{e}ḥî* I (eye, nose, jawbone, chin, cheek, # 4305); → *mēṣaḥ* (forehead, # 5195); → *m^{e}tall^e'ōt* (jawbone, # 5506); → *pānîm* (face, visible, assault, # 7156); → *pōt* (front, forehead, # 7327); → *qodqōd* (crown of head, # 7721); → *rō'š* I (head, chief, beginning, # 8031); → *raqqâ* (temple [of head], # 8377)

BIBLIOGRAPHY
M. Dahood, *Psalms I*, AB, 1965, 123.

Harry F. van Rooy

7329	פַּת־בַּג

פַּת־בַּג (*pat-bag*), historically: פַּתְבַּג (*patbag*), (royal) food quota, table ration; however, by popular etymology, פַּת (*pat*), bit/morsel + בַּג (*bag*), (Q: בַּז [*baz*] prey, meat, food) > bit/morsel of food (6x; # 7329; *HALAT* 925a).

ANE This term probably derives from Old Persian *pitfa-baga* (cuneiform *pitipabaga*) portion, ration (< *pitav* food + *baga*, distribution quota, though the derivation of the first element is still uncertain [cf. Koschaker, 174-75]) (so, originally, Lagarde, 186; cf. Klein, 536a). The term appears as a loanword in Sanskrit, *bratibāgha*, and in G, *potibazis* (cf. Lagarde, 186; Scheftelowitz, 311; Ellenbogen, 141; Eilers, *Iranische Beamtennamen,* 77); in Egyp. Aram. *ptp'* means food(-ration), food supply, ration (Eilers, 331, 333b; G. R. Driver, 61).

OT Perhaps because several other OT texts use Heb. *pat*, morsel, in the idiom *pat-leḥem*, bit/morsel of bread/food (Gen 18:5; Judg 19:5; 1 Sam 2:36; 28:22; 1 Kgs 17:11; Prov 28:21; or pl. *p^e^tôtê leḥem*; Ezek 13:19), the scribes of the MT posited that the obscure term *patbag* should be presented as two words, *pat* bit/morsel + *bag* (Q: *baz*, prey, meat, food) and, hence, separated the supposed parts of the expression with a metheg, *pat-bag*, bit of food, tidbit, delicacy. Among the ancient versions, the Pesh. calques with *patbāgā'*, a byform of Syr. *paṭbāgā'*, delicacy, choice food. Other ancient versions may preserve a sense that is more akin to the Persian derivation: the LXX translates with *trapeza*, table, dining table, throughout Dan 1 (except for *deipnon,* meal, food, in 1:16), and with *deon*, what is needful, in 11:26; the Vg. translates with *cibus*, food, throughout Dan 1 (except for *mensa*, table, in 1:8), and with *panis,* bread, loaf (of bread), food, in 11:26.

All six OT uses of this expression occur in the book of Daniel (Dan 1:5, 8, 13, 15, 16; 11:26), a book that preserves several technical terms of Old Persian origin (cf. S. R. Driver, 501 n. *, 506-7). The term *patbag*, food quota, table ration, relates to a custom of Persian kings described by Xenophon as the sending of food or drink portions from the royal table to favored friends not present (*Anabasis* I.ix.25-26; *Cyropaedia* VIII.ii.3-4).

P-B In postbiblical Heb., *pat*, bit, piece (of bread), is commonly used alone (without a genitive nom. for the substance) to designate a piece of bread (cf. Jastrow, 1249b-50a); however, the expression *patbag* is entirely lacking from postbiblical Heb. except in 1QIsa[a] (cf. L. Koehler and W. Baumgartner, *Supplementum ad lexicon in Veteris Testamenti libros,* 1958, 181). In Syr., the loanword has become transformed from original *patbāgā'* to the more common *paṭbāgā'*, tidbit, choice morsel (Payne Smith, 442a; cf. Ellenbogen, 141; Wagner, 96), which is joined by nom. *paṭb^e^gā'*, cook, confectioner, and the ethpalal denom. vb. *'etpaṭbag* (< **paṭbāgā'*, to feast on dainties) (Payne Smith, 442a).

Food: portion, provision: → *'kl* (eat, consume, devour, # 430); → *'ᵃruḥâ* (allowance, # 786); → *leḥem* (food, bread, # 4312); → *pat-bag* (food-quota, table-ration, # 7329); → *ṣyd* (provision oneself, outfit o.s, # 7472)

BIBLIOGRAPHY
F. Altheim and R. Stiehl, *Die aramäisch Sprache unter den Achaimeniden,* 1958-, 21; G. R. Driver, *Aramaic Documents of the Fifth Century B.C.*, 2d ed., 1957, 61; S. R. Driver, *Introduction to the Literature of the OT*, 9th ed., 1913, 501 n. *, 506-7; E. D. Klein, *A Comprehensive Etymological Dictionary of the Hebrew Language for Readers of English*, 1987, 536a; P. A. de Lagarde, *Gesammelte Abhandlungen,* 1866, 73, 186; M. Ellenbogen, *Foreign Words in the OT,* 1962, 141; W. Eilers, *Iranische Beamtennamen in der keilinschriftlichen Überlieferung,* Abhandlungen für die Kunde des Morgenlandes, 25/5, 1940, no. 3, **pitfabaga*, 59-81; idem, "Neue aramäkische Urkunden aus Ägypten," *AfO* 17, 1954-1956, (322-35) 331, 333b; P. Koschaker, "Zur Frage der Koranübersetzung: Keilschriftforschung," *OLZ* 47, 1944, 174-75; J. Payne Smith, *A Compendious Syriac Dictionary,* 1903; J. Scheftelowitz, "Zur Kritik des griechischen und massoretischen Buches Esther," *MGWJ*, NS 47, 1903, (24-37, 110-19, 201-13, 289-316) 311; M. Wagner, *Die lexicalischen und grammatikalischen Aramäismen im alttestamentlichen Hebräisch*, BZAW 96, 1966, 96, no. 240.

Robert H. O'Connell

7330	פִּתְגָם

פִּתְגָם (*pitgām*), nom. decree, word (# 7330).

OT Probably of Persian origin (Cameron, 169), this word occurs 6x in the Aram. sections and only twice in the Heb. parts of the OT. Besides a more general meaning (word, response; Ezra 4:17; 5:7, 11; Dan 3:13; also Sir 5:11; 8:9), the word refers to a royal "edict" (Ezra 6:11; Esth 1:20).

In Eccl 8:11, it is not clear whether the "sentence" *(pitgām)* at issue is a divine (so M. E. Eaton, *Ecclesiastes*, TOTC, 1983, 123) or human one. On the decree in Nebuchadnezzar's dream (Dan 4:17[14]), see *gzr*, decree (→ # 1615; Goldingay, *Daniel*, 92). (→ Writing: Theology)

Decree, decision: → *ḥōq* (portion, obligation, boundary, law, order, # 2976); → *ḥrṣ* I (cut, decree, determine, be determined, # 3076); → *ḥtk* (be decreed, # 3155); → *ṭa'am* (taste, disposition, discernment, decree, # 3248); → *pitgām* (decree, # 7330)

BIBLIOGRAPHY
G. Cameron, "Persepolis Treasury Tablets Old and New," *JNES* 17, 1958, 161-76; A. Lacocque, *Daniel et son temps,* 1983, 108-12; F. Nötscher, "Schicksalglaube im Qumran und Umwelt," *BZ* 3, 1959, 205-34; 4, 1960, 98-121; idem, "Himmliche Bücher und Schicksalglaube in Qumran," *RevQ* 1, 1959, 405-11.

Emile Nicole

7331	פתה

פתה (*pth* I), q. be inexperienced, be naive; ni. be made a fool of; hi. deceive, persuade; pu. be seducible, corruptible (# 7331); פֶּתִי (*petî* I), nom. simpleton, naive person (# 7343); פֶּתִי (*petî* II), simplemindedness (# 7344).

ANE The Arab. *fatan* is cognate with the nom. *petî.* As for the vb., cf. Arab. *fatā*, young; Ugar. *pty/w*, weaken, mislead; and Eth. *fätäwä/fätwä*, covet, desire.

OT 1. Most likely *petî* is related to the vb. *pth*, the basic meaning of which is be open. The most common forms of *pth* are in pi., pu., and ni. They connote the meanings of to entice, lure, deceive (Exod 22:16[15]; Judg 14:15; 16:5; 2 Sam 3:25; Prov 1:10; 16:29; 24:28; Hos 2:16), or be enticed, lured, deceived (Job 31:9; Jer 20:7, 10). However the pu. form of *pth* in Prov 25:15 connotes a positive sense: be persuaded. All these occurrences reflect the openness of mind to external influences. When *pth* is used figuratively, it means to be open and ingenuous in mind. The q. part. of *pth* is parallel to *'ên lēb* (he who is senseless; Hos 7:11), *ḥ^{a}sar lēb* (he who is lacking in understanding; Prov 7:7; 9:4, 16), or *'ewîl*, fool (Job 5:2; cf. Prov 14:18). The meaning of the q. part. of *pth* in these two passages is close to *petî.*

2. *petî* (pl. *p^{e}tāyîm, p^{e}tā'yim*) appears 19x in the OT: Proverbs (15x), Psalms (3x), and Ezekiel (1x). In the Torah psalms, *petî*, simpleton, refers to one who lacks wisdom but who can become wise through receiving and learning the law (Ps 19:7[8]; 119:130). *petî* in Ezek 45:20 refers to one who is ignorant (Zimmerli, Eichrodt, NJPSV, RSV, NIV) about the law of the Lord and has committed sin unwittingly (cf. Lev 4).

In Proverbs, *petî*, simpleton, is one who lacks *'ormâ*, prudence (Prov 1:4; 8:5; 19:25), *ḥokmâ*, wisdom (21:11; cf. Ps 19:7[8], or *bînâ*, discernment (Prov 9:6; cf. 19:25; Ps 119:130). *petî* is opposite to *'ārûm*, prudent (Prov 14:15, 18; 22:3; 27:12), but close to *ḥ^{a}sar-lēb*, he who is lacking in understanding (lit., heart; 7:7; 9:4, 16). His mind is not trained and lacks knowledge. He is unable to discern truth from falsehood; he believes in everything (14:15). He does not know how to detect danger and avoid it; he goes straight to it and suffers for it (22:3; 27:12). Though the *petî* is ignorant, yet unlike the *lēṣ*, mocker, he is teachable, and he will learn when he sees that the latter is being punished (19:25; 21:11). In 19:25 and 21:11 the stress is on the teachability and receptivity of the *petî* and those who are *ḥākām*, wise, and *nābôn*, understanding.

In the Wisdom personification passages in Proverbs, though *petî*, simpleton, is used together with *k^{e}sîl*, fool (Prov 1:22, 32; 8:5) and *lēṣ* (mocker; 1:22), the three words are not synonymous. The greatest difference between these words is that *petî* is always used with a neutral sense, without the negative connotation of the other two (Pan, 125-55). Different groups of people have different responses to the invitation of wisdom. The *petî*, like the *na'ar*, young man (1:4; 7:7), whose mind is simple, is easily enticed (1:32; 9:16-18; cf. 7:7, 8). In summary, the *petî* is an ignorant and simple-minded person who does not hate knowledge but is receptive and always prepared to learn or to be taught. (→ Proverbs: Theology)

In Ps 116:6 *petî*, a simple person, is used in an unusual way to connote the psalmist's humility. The positive sense here is reminiscent of "blessed are the pure in heart" in the NT (Matt 5:8).

P-B In QL it is used at least once in a comparable way, when it means the pious and humble of Qumran (1QpHab 12:4; cf. 1QpMicah). Therefore *petî*, a simple person, can mean a childlike person who is humble, teachable, and always prepared to learn. However, most likely this usage of *petî* is limited to occasions where the speaker refers to himself or to the community itself.

P-B *petî* in RL (e.g., BTalm Shab. 32b, 69a, 152a) and in Modern Heb. refers to being easily enticed.

Folly, fool, madness, shameless: → *'ᵉwîl* I (foolish, fool, # 211); → *b'r* IV (be stupid, # 1279); → *hll* III (be confused, foolish, behave like mad, # 2147); → *ksl* I (be foolish, # 4071); → *lhh* (behave like a madman, # 4263); → *nbl* II (act disdainfully, # 5571); → *skl* (behave foolishly, make foolish, frustrate, # 6118); → *pth* I (be inexperienced, be naive, deceive, persuade, # 7331); → *šg'* (raving, crazy, # 8713); → *tpl* I (talk nonsense, # 9520)
Knowledge, discernment, shrewd, wisdom: → *byn* (understand, discern, # 1067); → *ḥkm* (become wise, act wisely, # 2681); → *ṭ'm* (taste, test, sense, discern, # 3247); → *yd'* I (observe, care about, # 3359); → *nkr* (pretend, be recognized, # 5795); → *'rm* II (be cunning, be crafty, make crafty, # 6891); → *śkl* I (have success, understand, make wise, act with insight, # 8505)
Wisdom, knowledge, skill: → *byn* (understand, discern, # 1067); → *ḥkm* (be wise, become wise, act wisely, # 2681); → *yd'* (understand, know, # 3359); → *ysr* I (admonish, correct, discipline, # 3579); → *leqaḥ* (teaching, gift of persuasion, # 4375); → *mᵉzimmâ*, consideration, plan, evil plan, plot, # 4659); → *'oqbâ* (cunning, craftiness, # 6817); → *'rm* II (be cunning, be crafty, make crafty, # 6891); → *śkl* I (have success, understand, make wise, act with insight, # 8505); → *taḥbulôt* (advice, guidance, # 9374)

BIBLIOGRAPHY
THAT 2:495-98; *TWOT* 2:742-43; S. H. Blank, "Folly," *IDB*, 2:303-4; T. Donald, "The Semitic Field of 'Folly' in Proverbs, Job, Psalms, and Ecclesiastes," *VT* 13, 1963, 285-92; S. A. Mandry, *There Is No God! (A Study of the Fool in the OT, Particularly in Proverbs and Qoheleth)*, 1972; W. O. E. Oesterley, *The Book of Proverbs*, 1929, lxxxiv-vii; D. Kidner, *Proverbs*, 1964, 39-41; C-W. Pan, "A Study of the Vocabulary of Education in Proverbs 1-9," dissertation, University of Newcastle upon Tyne, 1987, 124-62.

Chou-Wee Pan

7334 (*pittûaḥ*, engraving), → # 7338

7336 (*pᵉtôt*, morsel), → Bread

7337	פתח

פתח (*pth* I), open, conquer, surrender, set free, loosen, break up (# 7337); nom. מִפְתָּח (*miptāḥ*), opening of lips (# 5157); פֶּתַח (*petaḥ*), opening, entrance (# 7339); פֵּתַח (*pētaḥ*), disclosure, communication (# 7340); פִּתָּחוֹן (*pittāḥôn*), opening (# 7341).

ANE The vb. is widely attested in Sem. languages: Akk. *petû* (*AHw*, 858b-861b); Ugar. *pth* I (*UT*, # 2130); Arab. *fataḥa*; Eth. *fätḥä*; OSA *fth*; Old Aram. (*KAI* 224:8-9); Phoen. (*KAI* 10:4, 5), and even in Egyp. as a Sem. loanword (*WbAS* 1:565).

OT 1. The root *pth* appears 327x in the OT, 136 of which are the vb. *pth* I (and two of these, Dan 6:11 and 7:10, are from the Aram. parts of the OT). These instances break down by stem as follows: q. 97x; ni. 18x; pi. 18x; peil (Aram.) 2x; hitp. 1x.

The most frequent translation, almost the exclusive one, in the q. is open. The same meaning is found for the ni. (be opened, Gen 7:11; Ezek 1:1), but one finds other nuances such as: be loosened (Isa 5:27), be poured out, let loose (Jer 1:14), be wide open to (Nah 3:13). In the pi. one finds, in addition to open (Job 41:14[6]; Isa 48:8; 60:11), free, unload (Gen 24:31), disarm, strip (Isa 45:1), set free (Ps 105:20), remove, take off (Isa 20:2); break up (hardened ground) (28:24).

2. Related to the vb. are the following noms.: (1) *pēṭaḥ*, disclosure, communication, only in Ps 119:130a ("The unfolding of your words gives light"); (2) *pittāḥôn,* opening, only in Ezek 16:63 ("you will ... never again open your mouth" is lit., "you will never again have an opening of the mouth"), and in Ezek 29:21; (3) *miptāḥ*, opening of the lips, a hapleg. in Prov 8:6b; (4) *petaḥ*, opening, entrance.

This last word, *petaḥ*, occurs 165x in the OT, most of which (93x) are found in Exodus-Numbers and Ezekiel. In these four books it normally refers to the entrance to the place of worship, i.e., either the entrance to the tabernacle, i.e., the shrine with its interior chambers (Num 3:25), or else the entrance to the courtyard (3:26). Neither the layperson nor the Levite (3:7) could enter through the opening into the shrine area.

But what is meant by the phrase that a layperson is to bring his offering and present it "at the entrance to the Tent of Meeting" (Lev 1:3)? It is unlikely, as Haran has argued (184), that what is meant by "the entrance to the Tent of Meeting" is merely the thin corridor of the courtyard that extends from the entrance gate to the altar of burnt offering, because the *petaḥ* of a house (Gen 19:11; Deut 22:21; 2 Sam 11:9) or of a gate (1 Kgs 22:10; 2 Kgs 7:3) refers not only to the opening itself, but to the area immediately in front of the opening. Thus, the *petaḥ* of the Tent of Meeting must refer to the entire courtyard, from the entrance to the courtyard to the entrance to the Tent. The very fact that a few verses later (v. 5) the bronze altar is said to be "at the entrance to the Tent of Meeting" means in the area in front of the *petaḥ 'ōhēl mô'ēd*. Unlike the later Herodian temple, which forbade women access to the courtyard by including first an outer court called "The Court of Women," OT law permits women too to approach the *petaḥ 'ōhēl mō'ēd* (Lev 12:6; 15:29; Num 5:16, 18 [where *lipnê yhwh* is functionally equivalent with *lipnê 'ōhēl mō'ēd*]; 6:10, 13 [since the Nazirite office was available to both men and women]).

3. With the vb. *ptḥ* the most frequent object is "mouth" (22x) and "door/gate" (21x). While "mouth" is far and away the most frequent bodily organ used with *ptḥ*, other organs as object of the vb. are lips (Job 11:5; 32:20; Ps 51:15[17]), eyes (1 Kgs 8:29/2 Chron 6:20; 1 Kgs 8:52/2 Chron 6:40; 2 Chron 7:15; Neh 1:6; ears (Isa 35:5; 48:8; 50:5); hands (Deut 15:8, 11; Ps 145:16).

4. The notation in Isa 53:7 that Yahweh's Servant who, despite physical abuse, "did not open his mouth," is a way of saying that the suffering Servant, rather than railing against his tormentors, trusted in God for his vindication. Other sufferers who did not open their mouth against abusers include the writers of Ps 38:13[14] and 39:9[10].

5. The interesting instance of Ezekiel's imposed dumbness (Ezek 3:26) is followed by God's promise that at the appropriate time "I will open your mouth" (Ezek 3:27). Later the prophet is told of a fugitive who will bring Ezekiel news of Jerusalem's fall. At that time "your mouth will be opened" (Ezek 24:27). That fulfillment is described in Ezek 33:22, "and he opened my mouth.... So my mouth was opened." Thus, whatever the nature of Ezekiel's dumbness may have been (and the interpretations differ), it was not only total but temporary, and hence the references to mouth-opening appear as prospect and fact. The mention of the prophet's mouth being opened by God in conjunction with the destruction of Jerusalem may indicate that once judgment had fallen, there was an opportunity for a new word from God to be spoken. He was no longer silent under the constraints of the scroll, filled with lamentation and warning, that he had earlier swallowed.

6. Besides humans, the phrase opening of the mouth is used with caves (Josh 10:22), the earth (Num 16:32; 26:10), and a donkey (22:28).

7. There are a number of references in the OT to the opening of the windows of heaven/the heights. When such windows open, the result is either judgment (Gen 7:11; 8:2; Isa 24:18) or blessing (2 Kgs 7:2, 19; Mal 3:10). Or there may be no use of windows, but simply "the heavens were opened" (Ezek 1:1), thus allowing God to reveal himself to the prophet. Especially in conjunction with the opening of the windows of heaven at the onset of the Flood (Gen 7:11), one may compare the Ugar. text that deals with the building of Baal's palace or mansion (IIAB, VII:17-19), especially the debate between Baal and Kothar-wa-Hasis about putting a window in the palace (i.e., the opening in the heavens through which Baal will rain upon the earth). The three lines read:

(17) *ypt̤.h̤ln.bbhtm*	Let a window be opened in the mansion
(18) *'urbt.bqrb.[h]kl*	a lattice/sluice in the midst of the palace
(19) *m.wy[p]tḥ.bdqt.'rpt.*	and let a rift be opened (in) the clouds.

NT 1. Matthew introduces Jesus' Sermon on the Mount with (lit.) "then he opened his mouth and taught them" (Matt 5:2). It seems that Matthew, in using the phrase "open one's mouth," is employing a Sem. idiom with which one introduces a discourse, and a solemn discourse at that. For OT instances of that same idiom, cf. Job 3:1; 33:2, and for a post-gospel NT reference see Acts 10:34 (Peter at the house of Cornelius). In spite of the frequency of references to opening the mouth in the Bible, Matt 5:2 is the only one that specifically connects opening of the mouth with teaching.

2. Three NT occasions refer to the heavens being opened. (a) The Spirit descends when the heavens are opened (Matt 3:16/Luke 3:21). (b) Stephen sees Jesus when he most needs to when the heavens open (Acts 7:56). (c) New truth about God's concern for Jew and Gentile breaks into Peter's mind when he sees the heavens opened (Acts 10:11).

Opening, coming, entrance: → *bw'* (go, come, arrive, enter, # 995); → *p'r* (open wide, # 7196); → *pṣh* (open up, # 7198); → *pqḥ* (open, # 7219); → *ptḥ* I (open, conquer, surrender, set free, loosen, break up, # 7337)

BIBLIOGRAPHY

TWAT 6:820-52; *TWOT* 2:743-44; E. F. Davis, *Swallowing the Scroll. Textuality and the Dynamics of Discourse in Ezekiel's Prophecy*, Sheffield, 1989; M. Haran, *Temples and Temple Service in Ancient Israel*, Clarendon, 1978; J. Milgrom, *Leviticus 1-16*, AB, 1991; I. Robinson, "*b^{e}petaḥ 'ênayim* in Genesis 38, 14," *JBL* 96, 1977, 569; T. Worden, "The Literary Influence of the Ugaritic Fertility Myth on the Old Testament," *VT* 3, 1953, 273-97, esp. 281.

Victor P. Hamilton

7338	פתח

פתח (*ptḥ* II), pi., pu. carve (# 7338); פִּתּוּחַ (*pittûaḥ*), nom. engraving (# 7334).

ANE Supposed instances in Aram. and Phoen. are open to other interpretations, see *DNWSI*, 950, 951.

OT In 2 Chron 3:7 (cf. Ps 74:6) the pi. of *ptḥ* designates the same decoration in the temple as *ql'* II, carve (→ # 7844), in 1 Kgs 6:29, 32, 35. This vb. is often complemented by *piṭṭûaḥ* to define the methods of inscribing names of the twelve tribes on the stones of the high priest's breastplate and shoulder clasps (Exod 28:9; 39:6 [in 39:14, 30 only *piṭṭûaḥ* occurs]), as on the gold plate for the priestly turban (28:36) and the stone set before Joshua in Zech 3:9. The bronze stands in Solomon's temple were decorated with figures in the same way (1 Kgs 7:36).

Carving, incision, inscription: → *ḥqh* (be incised, # 2977); → *ḥrt* (incise, # 3100); → *ptḥ* II (carve, # 7338); → *ql'* II (carve, # 7844)

Alan Millard

7339 (*petaḥ*, opening, entrance), → # 7337

7340 (*pētaḥ*, disclosure, communication), → # 7337

7341 (*pittāḥôn*, opening), → # 7337

7343 (*petî* I, simpleton, naive person), → # 7331

7344 (*petî* II, simplemindedness), → # 7331

7345	פְּתִיגִיל

פְּתִיגִיל (*p^etîgîl*), nom. fine clothing (Isa 3:24) (# 7345).

OT This hapleg. is probably a loanword. It appears in the catalog of feminine finery: "rich robe" (RSV), "fine clothing" (NIV). See Watts, *Isaiah 1-33*, 44.

Clothing, garment: → *beged* II (clothes, garment, # 955); → *g^elôm* (garment, # 1659); → *ḥob* (fold of garment, # 2460); → *ḥōṣen* (fold of garment, # 2950); → *k^etonet* (garment, # 4189); → *lbš* (put on, clothe, wear, # 4252); → *mad* (garment, clothes, # 4496); → *madeweh* I (garment, # 4504); → *maḥ^alaṣot* (festive garments, # 4711); → *meltāḥâ* (wardrobe, # 4921); → *mešî* (costly garments, # 5429); → *sādîn* (costly garments, # 6041); → *sut* (garment, # 6078); → *p^etîgîl* (fine clothing, # 7345); → *ṣeba'* (colorful garments, # 7389); → *śimlâ* (garment, cloth, # 8529); → *šōbel* (flowing skirt, # 8670); → *šît* (garment, attire, # 8884)

Robert E. Alden

7347 (*p^etîḥâ*, drawn [sword or dagger]), → # 2995

7349	פתל

פתל (*ptl*), ni. twist, struggle, be wily (# 7349); hitp. show o.s. shrewd; נַפְתּוּלִים (*naptûlîm*), nom. struggle (# 5887); פְּתַלְתֹּל (*p^etaltōl*), adj. crooked (hapleg. in Deut 32:5; # 7350).

ANE The root is attested in several Sem. languages (Aram., Syr., Eth., Arab.). Akk. uses *patālu* in its literal sense as "twist, wrap" in describing rope, as well as entrails in divination texts. It is also used to describe a snake (*AHw*, 847).

OT 1. Figurative usage is the rule for the verbal forms of *ptl*. Most commonly the vb. occurs in the context of a contrast between righteousness, blamelessness, and purity on the one hand, and crookedness or wiliness on the other (2 Sam 22:27; Job 5:13; Ps 18:26[27]; Prov 8:8). The vb. *ptl* appears to be close in meaning to *'qš*, distort, pervert, walk in crooked paths, in Prov 8:8, "All the words of my mouth are just; none of them is crooked (*ptl*) or perverse (*'qš*)." The synonyms in Job 5:12-13 are instructive: "He thwarts the plans of the crafty (*'rm* II, → # 6891), so that their hands achieve no success. He catches the wise (*ḥkm*, → # 2681) in their craftiness (*'rm*), and the schemes of the wily (*ptl*) are swept away."

The wise carefully choose words that are expressive of sincerity and integrity, reflect the righteous revelation of God, and shun any possible misunderstanding or deception (Prov 8:8). Even when the people are crooked, the godly need not repay the wicked in kind, because God discriminates between human beings: "to the pure you show yourself pure, but to the crooked you show yourself shrewd" (2 Sam 22:27 = Ps 18:26[27]).

2. The vb. *ptl* has the sense of struggle in Gen 30:8. Rachel, Jacob's beloved wife, when unable to give birth, turns to her maidservant Bilhah, who bears a child in her place. Thereupon, Rachel claims that she has "struggled" greatly with her sister. The root, occurring as a nom. (*naptûlîm*), a vb. (*niptaltî*), and a proper name (*naptālî*; on the grammatical aspects, see Moran, 62), could refer to literal twisting and contortions of a wrestling bout, but this does not fit well into the Genesis context. It can also be a metaphorical extension into the psychological sphere. NAB proposes "play a trick upon," equivalent to our Eng., turn the table on. For a discussion of this difficult verse, see Westermann, *Genesis* 2:474-75; *TWAT* 6:855.

3. The adj. *pᵉtaltōl* (hapleg.) defines the negative response to God's goodness. On the one hand, God is perfect in all his relations: "He is the Rock, his works are perfect, and all his ways are just. A faithful God who does no wrong, upright and just is he" (Deut 32:4). On the other hand, God's people have a history of rebelliousness, "They have acted corruptly (*šḥt*) toward him; to their shame they are no longer his children, but a warped (*'qš*) and crooked (*pᵉtaltōl*) generation" (v. 5). For the translation problems of v. 5, see Craigie, *Deuteronomy*, 377.

P-B In Qumran, the faithful pledged to keep themselves free from the "tortuous" thoughts of his heart (1QS 10:24).

Distortion, perversion, shrewdness, twisting: → *hēpek* (opposite, perversity, # 2201); → *kpn* (twist, # 4102); → *lwz* (let out of sight, go wrong way, # 4279); → *slp* (frustrate, overthrow, twist, mislead, # 6156); → *'bt* (conspire together, # 6309); → *'wh* (do wrong, pervert, # 6390); → *'wl* I (act wrongly, # 6401); → *'wt* (make crooked, pervert, bent, # 6430); → *'ql* (perverted, # 6823); → *'qš* (be perverse, make crooked, # 6835); → *ptl* (twist, be wily, shrewd, # 7349); → *r''* I (be bad, injure, # 8317)

BIBLIOGRAPHY

TWAT 6:852-55; W. L. Moran, "The Hebrew Language in Its Northwest Semitic Background," in *FS Albright*, 1961, 54-72.

David W. Baker

7350 (*pᵉtaltōl*, crooked), → # 7349

7352 (*peten*, cobra), → # 5729

7353	פֶּתַע

פֶּתַע (*peta'*), nom. instant (# 7353).

ANE The nom. is attested in Sam. *fēta* and in the Akk. phrase *ina pitte/i, ina pittima*, suddenly.

OT The nom. is used in every case adverbially, either with or without a preposition, meaning "suddenly." Often, it is used in connection with *pit'ōm* (Num 6:9; Prov 6:15; Isa 29:5; 30:13; # 7328), suddenly, an adverbial form derived from *peta'* by the addition of a *mem*-suffix and the softening of the *'ayin* to *'aleph*. In two cases, the nom. is used in a legal setting. In Num 6:6-9, someone who has taken a Nazirite vow is forbidden to approach a corpse, but if someone dies suddenly (*b^epeta'*) in his presence, he is required to shave his head (6:9). In 35:22, if someone has pushed another suddenly (*b^epeta'*) and without anger, causing his death, he is allowed to flee to a city of refuge to be protected from the vengeance of relatives. The case envisioned is obviously the equivalent of involuntary manslaughter, and so mercy is in order (cf. Milgrom, 510).

More often, however, the nom. is used in the context of judgment, which comes upon sinners without warning. Isa 29:5 predicts that the destruction of the enemy nations that the Lord will bring against Israel will occur suddenly (*l^epeta'*). Hab 2:7 warns Chaldaea that because it had extorted from the nations, its "creditors" (NIV debtors) would suddenly arise and plunder Chaldaea, a clear example of poetic justice. Prov 6:12-15 predicts the end for a wicked man, and 29:1 for one who refuses correction, using identical terms: "He will suddenly be destroyed—without remedy." In one case, Israel itself is threatened with judgment: Isa 30:13 predicts that the iniquity of the Israelites who ally themselves with Egypt and attempt to silence the prophets will be like a breach in a wall that will suddenly break. There is irony in the comparison, since Israel has relied on Egypt for protection, just as one relies on a city wall. Yet just as the damage in a wall can grow undetected for years, so Israel's sin has had insidious effects that will become apparent in an instant (Clements, 247).

P-B The nom. is used, in combination with *pit'ōm*, in Sir 11:21 (the rich may become poor suddenly), and in the Dead Sea Scroll Hodayot text (17:5, a fragmentary section). It is rarely used in Mish. Heb.

Time: → *'ōbēd* (ever after, # 7); → *'ōpen* (right time, # 698); → *gîl* I (stage of life, # 1636); → *zmn* (be appointed, # 2374); → *'ôlām* (long time or duration, # 6409); → *'ēt* (time, # 6961); → *pa'am* (foot, step, time, # 7193); → *peta'* (instant, # 7353); → *tāmîd* (continuance, unceasingness, regular offering, # 9458)

BIBLIOGRAPHY

R. E. Clements, *Isaiah 1-39*, NCBC, 1982; S. DeVries, *Yesterday, Today and Tomorrow: Time and History in the Old Testament*, 1975; J. Milgrom, *Numbers*, JPS Torah Commentary, 1990.

Anthony Tomasino

7354	פתר

פתר (*ptr*), q. interpret (dream) (# 7354); פִּתָּרוֹן (*pittārôn*), nom. interpretation (of dream) (# 7355); פֵּשֶׁר (*pēšer*), nom., solution, interpretation (hapleg. in Eccl 8:1; # 7323); פשׁר (*pšr*), pe. interpret; pa. part. interpreter (# 10599); פִּשְׁרָא (*pišrā'*), nom. interpretation (# 10600).

ANE Akk. *pišrû*, solution, interpretation; Syr. *p^ešārā'*, solution, explanation; Sam. *fitran*, interpretation.

OT This group of words is used mainly in connection with the interpretation of dreams, and in two passages in particular: Gen 40-41 and Dan 2-7. Most of those who have dreams are non-Israelites (Pharaoh's chief cupbearer and chief baker; Pharaoh; Nebuchadnezzar), but the one who gives the interpretation is in each case an Israelite (Joseph; Daniel). The same group of words is used in Dan 5, where Daniel interprets Belshazzar's vision of the writing on the wall; and in Dan 7 Daniel himself has a vision in a dream, which is followed by an interpretation (7:16). Rabinowitz (219-26) notes that *pšr/ptr* and related words do not denote merely an intellectual understanding of a problem: they denote, rather, insight into a future reality that is portended by dreams or visions.

Eccl 8:1 is the only passage in the Bible where the root is apparently not used to denote the interpretation of dreams or visions, though Rabinowitz takes even this passage to refer to the interpretation of a prophetic word.

In both Gen 40-41 and Dan 2-7 there is a great focus on the interpreter. Both Joseph and Daniel give authoritative interpretations, which are immediately accepted as accurate by their hearers (Gen 41:37-40; Dan 2:46-49), and each is increasingly honored as a result (Gen 40:14; 41:9-15, 39-40; Dan 2:48-49; 5:29; 6:28). Though they give their interpretations to non-Israelites, they do so in dependence on the God of Israel (Gen 40:8; 41:16; Dan 2:18-23, 26) as part of a life of faithful service to him.

The non-Israelite setting of Gen 40-41 and Dan 2-7 is, indeed, significant for an understanding of this root. Oneiromancy was widely practiced in Babylon and Egypt and in other ANE civilizations (Oppenheim, 184-245). Like divination and astrology, it was based on the premise that the gods sometimes gave indications of future events. These indications could be duly interpreted: hence dreams were recorded and collections produced, giving guidelines for interpretation (Oppenheim, 246-55 gives a selection of Sum., Akk., Egypt., and Hitt. dream texts; 256-307 is a detailed study of the so-called "Assyrian Dream Book"). The OT shares this belief to the extent that it does contain incidents where individuals receive dreams, which often come from God, and predict events that later come to pass. However, in the OT God more frequently reveals himself to Israelites by other means (law-giving, prophecy; note the negative attitudes to dreams expressed in passages such as Deut 13:1-6; Jer 23:25-32; and Zech 10:2). Perhaps, then, Gen 40-41 and Dan 2-7 imply that God is communicating to non-Israelite rulers using media with which they were familiar; if so, however, he does so in a way that subverts these standard methods of understanding the divine will and demonstrates his own sovereignty.

One aspect of God's sovereignty emerges in both Joseph's and Daniel's insistence that interpretations belong to God alone (Gen 40:8; 41:16; Dan 2:19, 27-8, 30), and humans are dependent on him for them. Hence, Daniel asks his friends to pray for Nebuchadnezzar's vision to be explained, and he gives thanks to God after the explanation has been given (Dan 2:17, 20-23). Both in Genesis and Daniel non-Israelite rulers admit God's role as sole revealer (Gen 41:37-40; Dan 2:47; 4:18; 5:10-16). Strikingly, neither Joseph nor Daniel has any "method" for interpreting dreams and visions (contrast the "Assyrian Dream Book," which has long lists of standard interpretations of events and objects that occur in dreams): they are simply given their interpretations by God.

In both Genesis and Daniel Israelites emerge as having superior wisdom and understanding of the divine will. Thus, in Gen 41 Pharaoh shows his misunderstanding of the two dreams by retelling them to Joseph in a form that destroys the verbal and structural parallels that they have in the narrator's version (cf. vv. 1-7 with vv. 17-24); Joseph shows his understanding by immediately seeing that the two dreams are about the same thing (vv. 25-27; see Sternberg, 394-400). Similarly, in Daniel God's servants are those with the deepest understanding and wisdom: Daniel and his friends are instructed in Babylonian wisdom (Dan 1:5), but God endows them beyond this (1:17-20).

More pointedly, non-Israelite methods of discerning the divine will are presented as ineffectual. In both Genesis and Daniel non-Israelite magicians and astrologers are incapable of giving an interpretation of the dream (Gen 41:8, 15; Dan 2:10-11; 4:6-7; 5:7-9; cf. Exod 7-8, where the Egyptian magicians similarly fail to match the miracles worked by Moses and Aaron). This point is not unduly stressed in Genesis, but is developed in an extended satire in Dan 2 (see Goldingay, 55). In response to Nebuchadnezzar's repeated demands, the Babylonian magicians break down in despair (vv. 10-11), even stating that their skills are no more than human wisdom (v. 11). In contrast, Daniel calmly requests time to interpret the dream (vv. 14-16), and the next day he tells Nebuchadnezzar both the dream and its interpretation (vv. 29-45). In consequence, the Babylonian magicians owe their lives to Daniel (vv. 16, 24), who is later placed in charge of them (v. 48). This is a clear polemic against non-Israelite religious practices and wisdom. By implication, the God of the Israelites is the one true God (so, explicitly, Dan 2:46-47; 6:26-27). One of the most striking features of the root *pšr*, indeed, is the polemical use to which the theological theme of interpretation is put.

God is able to reveal the secrets of history because he is sovereign over history. Daniel has the more explicit picture of God as the one who directs the fates of nations: chs. 2 and 7-12 contain extensive visions ranging over large stretches of history and emphasizing God's sovereignty over a succession of mighty powers, each of which pass away; God is the revealer of mysteries (Dan 2:22, 47), with the implication that the hidden forces that determine human history are in his control. The theme is less explicit, but also unmistakably present in Genesis 37-50: it is God who brings about the survival of Jacob's sons in a most unexpected way (45:4-8; 50:20); indeed, the means he uses to do this, the famine affecting the whole of Egypt and Canaan, have a scope not much smaller than that of the visions in Daniel.

The interpretation of a dream or vision can be favorable or unfavorable. In either case, the question arises as to the certainty of what is foretold. Joseph, for instance, argues from the fact that two dreams have said the same thing, that "the matter has been firmly decided by God, and God will do it soon" (Gen 41:32). At least one dream in the Joseph cycle is not fulfilled: Joseph's dream in 37:9 is not capable of fulfillment even at the time he dreams it, for Rachel (the moon) is already dead by this point. Turner uses this fact, in particular, to argue against a predestinarian interpretation of Gen 37-50 (165-69): the dream comes from God, but is not fulfilled. Gibson takes a different line: the dream of 37:9 is meant to be seen as obviously false and originating in Joseph's own selfish ambition (230-31); hence, the question of the nonfulfillment of God's prediction does not arise. Certainly, the rest of the dreams in Gen 37-50 *do* turn out almost exactly.

In Daniel the dreams are portrayed as accurate depictions of what will happen (Dan 2:45; 4:28; 5:30), and the giving of the interpretation has the effect of the reading of a divine decree. In Dan 2, no response is expected of Nebuchadnezzar except to acknowledge God. Though the vision has spoken of human actions playing a real part in what is to unfold (human kingdoms destroy each other), these actions are under God's control. In Dan 4, Daniel urges Nebuchadnezzar to repent so that, perhaps, the vision may not come about; when Nebuchadnezzar forgets this and boasts of his power, his vision is fulfilled, and he is humbled. In Dan 5, Belshazzar is given no chance for repentance; judgment is simply executed forthwith, in response to the challenge to God that he has in effect thrown down.

Clearly these two passages concerning the interpretation of dreams and vision have strong links with ideas found in the prophets. One thinks of those passages in the prophets where visions are given and then interpreted by words from God (Jer 1:11-15; Amos 7-9). The emphasis on God as the giver of interpretations can be compared with the insistence of prophetic texts that true prophets are those to whom God reveals his counsel (Jer 23:18; Amos 3:7).

P-B The nom. *pšrh* in Sir 38:14 means diagnosis. The term *pēšer* is extensively used in DSS commentaries on biblical texts to introduce explanations of biblical passages, often to explain how things referred to by the biblical texts have been fulfilled in contemporary events: 1QpHab; 4QpIs; 4QPs37, etc. For a discussion of the types of explanations offered, see Roberts, 368-80; Rabinowitz, 226-32. The vocables *ptr* and *pitrôn*/*pitrônā* in Mish. Heb. and Jewish Aram. all mean interpret, interpretation.

NT In the NT *diasapheō* is used in Matt 13:36, where the disciples ask Jesus to interpret the parable of the tares, and *synkrinō* is used at 1 Cor 2:13, where Paul speaks of expressing spiritual truths in spiritual words. There seems to be no direct dependence in these texts on any of the OT passages discussed above.

On the other hand, dreams/visions and interpretations do occur extensively in the intertestamental literature (e.g., *2 Esd.*) and the OT Pseudepigrapha (e.g., *4 Ezra*) and occupy the whole of the book of Revelation. The theological themes discussed above recur in Revelation: the sovereignty of God over history, God's revealing the secrets of history to the faithful, and the futility of pagan religion. (→ Genesis; Daniel)

Dream, revelation, vision: → *ḥzh* (see, perceive, behold, # 2600); → *ḥlm* (dream, revelatory dream, # 2731); → *ptr* (interpret [dream], # 7354); → *r'h* (see, have visions, choose, perceive, # 8011)

Interpretation, explanation: → *b'r* I (make clear, explain, # 930); → *midrāš* (exposition, interpretation, # 4535); → *mēlîṣ* (interpreter, official, heavenly intermediary, # 4885); → *prš* (explain, adjudicate, be divided, # 7300); → *ptr* (interpret [dream], # 7354)

Mantic, divination: → *'aššāp* (conjurer, # 879); → *bad* V (diviner, # 967); → *ḥbr* (engage in astrology, # 2042); → *harṭōm* (soothsayer priest, # 3033); → *yidd^{e}'ōnî* (soothsayer, # 3362); → *kaśdîm* (Chaldeans, astrologers, # 4169); → *lḥš* (conjure, whisper, # 4317); → *nḥš* I (practice divination, # 5727); → *ṣpp* I (whisper, chirp, # 7627); → *qsm* (practice divination, # 7876)

Bibliography

J. C. L. Gibson, *Genesis*, 1981, 1982; J. Goldingay, *Daniel*, WBC 30, 1989; A. L. Oppenheim, *The Interpretation of Dreams in the Ancient Near East (Transactions of the American Philosophical Society)* n.s., 46.3; I. Rabinowitz, "'*Pesher/Pittaron*': Its Biblical Meaning and Its Significance in the Qumran Literature," *RevQ* 8, 1973, 219-32; B. J. Roberts, "Some Observations on the Damascus Document and the Dead Sea Scrolls," *BJRL* 34, 1951-52, 366-87; M. Sternberg,

The Poetics of Biblical Narrative, 1985; L. A. Turner, *Announcements of Plot in Genesis*, JSOTSup 96, 1990.

Philip E. Satterthwaite

7355 (*pittārôn*, interpretation [of dream]), → # 7354

7358 (*patšegen*, copy), → Writing

7359 (*ptt*, crumble), → Bread

צ

7362	צֵאָה

צֵאָה (*ṣē'â*), filth, human excrement (# 7362); צֹאָה (*ṣō'â*), nom. filth, excrement (# 7363); צֹאִי (*ṣō'î*), adj., filthy (# 7364).

ANE A possible root is *yṣ'*, go out (# 3655), in which case Ugar. *ẓu*, exit, could be a cognate (*HALAT* 931).

OT 1. *ṣē'â*, excrement, is found only twice. Deut 23:13[14] commands that upon relieving oneself, a hole is to be dug and the excrement covered. For Ezek 4:12, see *gll* II, be foul (o.s., # 1671).

2. *ṣō'â*, filth, is used figuratively of iniquity; the "filth" of the women of Jerusalem will be washed away (Isa 4:4). After an orgy of drinking, the tables are covered with "filth" from vomit (28:8). Prov 30:12 speaks of those persons, pure in their own eyes, yet are not cleansed of their "filth."

3. *ṣō'î*, filthy, occurs twice in Zechariah's description of the cleansing of Joshua the high priest (Zech 3:3, 4). An angel ordered that the filthy clothes of Joshua be removed. Here, as in Isa 4:4, the word for "filth" signifies "guilt" and not merely stained clothes. The removal of the defiled garments signifies the cleansing from guilt and the new standing of Joshua as a representative of the Lord before the people (D. L. Petersen, *Haggai and Zechariah 1-8*, OTL, 1984, 193-94). (→ Zechariah: Theology)

Dung, excrement, refuse, urine: → *'ašpōt* (ash-heap, refuse-heap, dung-hill, # 883); → *gll* II (befoul, dirty o.s., # 1671); → *dōmen* (dung, manure, # 1961); → *ḥ^a^rā'îm* (dung, # 2989); → *yešaḥ* (filth, diarrhea, # 3803); → *madmēnâ* I (dung pit, # 4523); → *sûḥâ* (offal, # 6054); → *pereš* I (offal, contents of stomach, # 7302); → *ṣē'â* (filth, human excrement, # 7362); → *ṣāpîa'* (dung [of cattle], # 7616); → *śîg* (excrement, # 8485); → *šyn* (urinate, # 8874)

Roy E. Hayden

7363 (*ṣō'â*, filth, human excrement), → # 7362

7364 (*ṣō'î*, filthy), → # 7362

7365	צֶאֱלִים

צֶאֱלִים (*ṣe'ᵉlîm*), a kind of lotus (# 7365).

ANE Cognates for *ṣe'ᵉlîm* are found in Syr. and Eth. (*HALAT* 790).

OT The term occurs twice and seems to indicate the thorny lotus (Job 40:21-22).

Thornbush, nettle, sting, thistle, thorn: → *'āṭād* (thornbush, # 353); → *barqōn* (thorn, brier, # 1402); → *deber* II (thorny sting, # 1823); → *dardar* (thistle, # 1998); → *ḥēdeq* (brier, # 2537); → *ḥôaḥ* I (thorn, # 2560); → *mᵉsûkâ* (thorn hedge, # 5004); → *na'ᵃṣûṣ* (thornbush, # 5848); → *sîrâ* (thorny bush, # 6106); → *sillôn* (thorn, # 6141); → *sᵉneh* (thorny shrub, # 6174); → *sirpād* (stinging nettle, # 6252); → *ṣe'ᵉlîm* (thorny lotus, # 7365); → *ṣᵉnînîm* (thorns, # 7564); → *qôṣ* I (thornbush, # 7764); → *qimmôś* (weeds, nettles, # 7853); → *śēk* (thorn, splinter, # 8493); → *šāmîr* I (Christ's thorn, # 9031)

Bibliography

TWOT 2:749.

K. Lawson Younger, Jr.

7366	צֹאן

צֹאן (*ṣō'n*), flock, small cattle, sheep and goats (# 7366).

ANE An Akk. cognate to Heb. *ṣō'n* occurs in a second-millennium Amarna letter from an unidentified Palestinian official. After the usual bowing and scraping before his "lord" (probably Pharaoh), this official laments his recent loss of money, troops, and flocks (*ṣênu*) to unidentified invaders, probably Habiru-type rebels (EA 263.12). The term he uses for flocks, *ṣênu*, seems to be of Amorite/Can. origin because another term (*zûnu*) appears in the margin as an Akk. equivalent. As is well known, the use of Akk. glosses to explain Can. terms is a frequent occurrence in the Amarna correspondence (note also the Ugar. term *ṣin(u)* discussed by Gordon in *UT*, 2137; note further the Can. gloss *ṣč-č-nu* in EA Akk., and cf. the cognates in Phoen., Moab., Aram., Syr., Arab., and OSA).

Two other Canaanite inscriptions from the first millennium also mention *ṣ'n*. On the Phoenician side of the bilingual Karatepe inscription from the eighth century, for example, a certain Azitiwada publicly predicts that his city will become, by Baal's grace, a place for the raising of bulls (*'lpm*) and flocks (*ṣ'n*, *KAI* 26 A III.9). Further, Mesha the Moabite king and contemporary of Ahab describes the district of Beth Baal-meon as a good place for raising flocks (*ṣ'n*, *KAI* 181.31; see also 2 Kgs 3:4).

OT 1. The Heb. word for flock (*ṣō'n*, Lat *ovis*) can refer in the Bible to groups of sheep (1 Sam 25:2), or goats (Gen 27:9), or to groups of sheep mixed with goats (30:31). Etymologically, the term may be derived from the vb. *yṣ'*, go out (note the G parallel *probaton,* flock, < *probainō,* walk forward; so Lagarde, 136; BDB, 838), but this etymology is not universally accepted (cf. *HALAT* 932). A related Heb. term, *'ēder* (herd, # 6373), can be etymologically derived from the vb. *'dr* III, be lacking, fail (→ # 6372; cf. Arab. *ǧadira*, remain, lag behind, and LXX Gen 35:16, *Gader* [MT 35:21]; see Lagarde, 76-77). Thus, a herd might be defined as something that lags behind or loiters, yet this too is debated. In ancient Israel, flocks were important for food (Amos 6:4), clothing (Gen 31:19), milk (Deut 32:14), and cultic sacrifice

(Num 15:3). Since goat's milk is richer in protein and easier to digest than cow's milk, it was by far the animal nutrient of choice in the ANE. This fact is epitomized by the Talm. saying, "The goat is for milking, the sheep for shearing, the hen for laying eggs and the ox for plowing" (*b. Shab.* 19b).

2. Metaphorically speaking, the notion of flock worked its way deeply into the consciousness of biblical writers, particularly as a metaphor for Israel itself. Israel is often described as a flock in distress (*'ēder*, # 6373; Jer 13:17), a flock destined for sacrifice (Ezek 36:38), or a flock under Yahweh's watchful care (Ps 74:1; Zech 10:3 [*'ēder*]). And this metaphor is not limited to the physical world. In the underworld, even the dead can be styled a flock of sorts, and death itself can be its shepherd (Ps 49:14[15], *māwet;* cf. Mot, Canaanite god of death, in *KTU* 1.4 viii 17).

3. *Sheep.* Biblical writers used several terms for sheep, but the most common are *ṭāleh* (suckling lamb; # 3231), *kebeś/keśeb* (lamb, sheep, # 3897, 4167), *rāḥēl* I (ewe lamb, S of Songs 6:6; # 8161), *'aštārôt* (lambs, # 6957), and *'ayil* I (ram, male sheep, leader; → # 380). The fat-tailed Awassi is the predominant sheep in Israel, typically a white-fleeced animal with a brown or black face. Its height at the shoulders is approx. 68 cm in adult females and 75 cm in males (S. Hirsch, 16). The native goat, known in Arab. as the Ma'az Jebali, can be black, gray, or mottled, and northern breeds appear to be slightly larger than those living in the south (R. Wapnish et al., 37).

Confronted by the Philistines, Samuel instinctively sacrifices the most helpless creature at his disposal; viz., a *ṭāleh* (# 3236; Lat. *agnus,* 1 Sam 7:9). The NIV translates this term as suckling lamb. That it refers to something very young and tender is reinforced by the Syr. cognate *ṭly'* (young boy; see also Aram. *ṭalîthā'*, young girl, in Mark 5:41). Isaiah reimagines this tenderness in his vision of the messianic age as an unnatural time, a time when even wolves and *ṭāleh,* lambs, live together without conflict (Isa 65:25). In the natural world, wolves are the natural predators of *ṭāleh.* In the world to come, however, Yahweh will see to it that even the most helpless of Yahweh's creatures find absolute security, like lambs in the arms of their Shepherd (40:11).

A common word for lamb, sheep, is *kebeś* (Jer 11:19; Hos 4:16; cf. Akk. *kabsu, CAD* "K," 23). Interestingly, this term appears with a metathetical spelling in the Pent. (*keśeb*, Gen 30:32; Lev 1:10; 3:7; 5:6 [*kiśbâ*; # 4167]; Deut 14:4; see GKC 19n).

The term *'aštārôt*, found only 4x in the OT (Deut 7:13; 28:4, 18, 51), always appears in the stock phrase *šᵉgar 'ᵃlāpêkā wᵉ'aštᵉrôt ṣōnekā*, which the NIV translates, "the calves of your herds and the lambs of your flocks." Most scholars are agreed that the clue to deciphering this phrase lies buried in the mists of ancient Canaanite myth. In all likelihood, *šgr* was probably a minor Can. deity charged with catalyzing and protecting the fertility of domesticated animals (*KTU* 1.5 iii 16-17). Ishtar is the well-known goddess of fertility in Mesopotamian, particularly Assyr. myth. A combined deity named *šgr w'štr* clearly appears on the plaster texts discovered at Tell Deir 'Alla in 1967 (I.14, J. Hoftijzer, 273-74; M. Moore, 74). Consequently the writer of Deut appears to be hypostatizing the characteristics of a minor Transjordanian deity into a blessing formula for his particular audience.

The term for ram, *'ayil*, is used literally in passages like Deut 32:14 and 2 Kings 3:4, but its most interesting use, at least from a theological standpoint, is metaphorical. The ancient Song of the Sea, for example, lists the rams (i.e., leaders) of Moab alongside the chiefs of Edom as defeated enemies of Yahweh (Exod 15:15). The designation is apt since the ram, a strong animal, commonly heads the herd of traveling sheep. Late preexilic sources continue to use *'ayil* in this metaphorical sense for leader (Ezek 17:13; 31:11). Such usage continues extrabiblically in the Ma'ub inscription (third-century Phoen.), where a portico of a sanctuary is described as having been built by the "leading men" of the city (lit., the *bn h'lm*, sons of rams, *KAI* 19.2).

4. *Goat.* Similar diversity is found with regard to the biblical terms for goat in the OT: *gᵉdî/gᵉdiyyâ* (kid, # 1531, 1537), *'ēz* (she-goat; # 6436), *'attûd* (ram, he-goat; → # 6966), *śā'îr* II/*śᵉ'îrâ* I (hairy goat, satyr, Isa 13:21; 2 Chron 11:15; # 8538/8544), *'aqqô* (wild goat, Deut 14:5; # 735), and *ṣāpîr* (he-goat, found only in relatively late sources: 2 Chron 29:21; Ezra 8:35; Dan 8:5, 8, 21; # 7618).

The term for kid (*gᵉdî*) is probably best known from the famous command, "You shall not boil a kid in its mother's milk" (repeated verbatim in Exod 23:19; 34:26; Deut 14:21). At least three explanations have been advanced to explain this law. One school of thought argues that this was a pagan practice expressly condemned, even though no extant example of it has yet been found (Keel, 1980; cf. already Maimonides). Another is that pastoralist societies (like ancient Israel), concerned to protect the milk supply, sometimes legislate against contact between meat and milk for magico-religious reasons (Frazer, 150-54). Still another is the argument that prohibitions like this issue from the heart of a benevolent Creator and are ultimately designed to limit cruelty to any helpless creature, human or beast (Philo, *De Virtutibus,* 125-44).

The she-goat or nanny-goat (*'ēz*, Lev 3:12; Deut 14:4) is complemented by the he-goat (*'attûd*, Gen 31:10). Like *'ayil* (ram, leader), this term can also do double duty as a metaphor for leadership. Isaiah, for example, revels in the irony that the *rᵉpā'îm* (NIV: spirits of the departed; → # 8327), parallel with the *'attûdê 'āreṣ* (lit., he-goats of the earth; NIV: leaders in the world), have now "become weak, as we are" (Isa 14:9-10; see Miller).

Eschatologically speaking, Micah alludes to the remnant of Israel as "sheep in a fold, like a flock (*'ēder*) in its pasture" (Mic 2:12), or as a "young lion among the flocks of sheep" (5:8[7]). Yahweh cares for the house of Judah as "his flock" (Zech 10:3).

5. *Theological reflections.* "Know that the LORD is God. It is he who made us, and we are his [the NIV correctly follows the Qere here]; we are his people, the sheep of his pasture" (Ps 100:3). This image was seized upon as a basis for petition in the Psalms. Thus, the psalmist who cries out, "Why have you rejected us forever, O God?" adds poignancy to this with, "Why does your anger smolder against the sheep of your pasture?" These are *your* sheep, Lord! This was also a foundation for praise: "Come, let us bow down in worship, let us kneel before the LORD our Maker; for he is our God and we are the people of his pasture, the flock under his care" (95:6-7a; cf. also 79:13; note that in both Ps 100 and Ps 95, the fact that the Lord made his people is coupled with the fact that they are the flock under his care. Thus, Yahweh's ownership is underscored: He is not only the Shepherd of the flock but also its Creator.)

It was as Shepherd of his flock that the Lord led his people out of Egypt and through the sea (Ps 78:52-53; Isa 63:11), and in like manner he will lead them out of captivity (both Babylonian and eschatological; cf. Isa 40:11, cited above, with its "new exodus" imagery; see also Jer 31:10, "Hear the word of the LORD, O nations; proclaim it in distant coastlands: 'He who scattered Israel will gather them and will watch over his flock like a shepherd'"; cf. Mic 2:12; Zech 9:16). Notice also that Mic 7:14, "Shepherd your people with your staff, the flock of your inheritance, which lives by itself in a forest, in fertile pasturelands. Let them feed in Bashan and Gilead as in days long ago," is followed by the divine response in v. 15, "As in the days when you came out of Egypt, I will show them my wonders," while the (ultimately eschatological) promises in Ezek 36 culminate with, "I will make their people as numerous as sheep, as numerous as the flocks for offerings at Jerusalem during her appointed feasts. So will the ruined cities be filled with flocks of people. Then they will know that I am the LORD" (Ezek 36:37-38; cf. Ps 144:13-14, with literal, not metaphorical intent).

It is only natural, then, that the prophets depicted Yahweh as intensely jealous and protective of his flock, especially when one remembers that it was common in the ANE to designate rulers and leaders as shepherds (for basic references, cf. Sohn, 85, n. 148; see further Seibert). In Jer 13:18-20, the king and queen mother are asked, "Where is the flock that was entrusted to you [*hā'ēder nittān lāk*], the sheep of which you boasted [*ṣō'n tipartēk*]?"; note also 1 Kgs 22:17 (‖ 2 Chron 18:16), Michaiah's vision of the death of Ahab: "I saw all Israel scattered on the hills like sheep without a shepherd, and the LORD said, 'These people have no master. Let each one go home in peace'"; cf. further Moses' prayer for a successor, asking that the Lord would "appoint a man over this community to go out and come in before them, one who will lead them out and bring them in, so the Lord's people will not be like sheep without a shepherd" (Num 27:16b-17). Thus the Lord declares, "My anger burns against the *shepherds*, and I will punish the *leaders*" (Zech 10:3a; my emphasis).

The fundamental sin of these faithless shepherds is expressed in Ezek 34:2, "Woe to the shepherds of Israel who only take care of themselves! Should not shepherds take care of the flock?" (cf. the woe oracle in Zech 11:17). Rather, these senseless sheperds do not seek the Lord, and so the flock is scattered (Jer 10:21), leading to the prophet's agonized weeping "because the LORD's flock will be taken captive" (Jer 13:17; cf. also Ezek 24:5, "take the pick of the flock," viz., for slaughter and boiling, in a judgment parable). The specific indictment against these leaders is that they have "scattered my flock [note again: this is Yahweh's flock!] and driven them away and have not bestowed care on them" (Jer 23:2), expanded on in Ezek 34:3-4, "You eat the curds, clothe yourselves with the wool and slaughter the choice animals, but you do not take care of the flock. You have not strengthened the weak or healed the sick or bound up the injured. You have not brought back the strays or searched for the lost. You have ruled them harshly and brutally" (cf. the ruthless shepherd prophecy in Zech 11:16, and contrast this with Jacob's diligence as a shepherd in Gen 31:38-41). Thus, the helpless, defenseless, sickly, weak, and undernourished sheep were left without a shepherd, consigned to wander on the hills, becoming food for all the wild animals, with no one to seek them out (Ezek 34:5-7).

The Lord himself would have to regather his flock, serving again as a figure for the regathering of the exiles from the nations, expressed most fully in 34:10-16. Interestingly enough, this glorious word of comfort is followed by a judgment oracle: "I will shepherd the flock with justice" (34:16b; cf. v. 22b); "I will judge between one sheep and another, and between rams and goats" (34:17b); "See, I myself will judge between the fat sheep and the lean sheep" (34:20b). There would neither be inequity among the shepherds nor the sheep, as some of the flock began to take on the aggressive and selfish characteristics of the godless shepherds. This promise of justice, however, flows into a messianic prophecy, since ultimately, the only one who could be entrusted with the care of Yahweh's flock was the Davidic Messiah himself: "I will save my flock, and they will no longer be plundered. . . . I will place over them one shepherd, my servant David, and he will tend them; he will tend them and be their shepherd" (34:22-23). Cf. also Jer 23:5-6 ("I will raise up to David a righteous Branch"), which flows out of an identical context.

Of course, David himself was the model shepherd, and the Lord "took him from the sheep pens; from tending the sheep he brought him to be the shepherd of his people Jacob, of Israel his inheritance" (Ps 78:70b-71). Cf. further Mic 5:4a, "He will stand and shepherd his flock in the strength of the LORD." See further Zech 10:4 in light of 10:3, and note that the complex pericope in Zech dealing with shepherds and the flock (11:4-17; cf. also 13:7-9) must be seen against this background. Finally, the metaphor of the people of Israel as Yahweh's flock may underlie the more general expression of Israel's dwelling in safety, expressly stated in Ezek 34:24-31; cf. also Jer 23:6, and, with a slightly different figure, Ps 37:3, "Trust in the LORD and do good; dwell in the land and enjoy safe pasture" (lit., tend, or feed [on?] faithfulness).

There are several other figures taken up in the OT based on the characteristics and behavior of sheep, e.g., straying like sheep serves as an analogy for human sinfulness and frailty of humans (Isa 53:6; cf. also Ps 119:176), while being like a sheep led to slaughter typifies innocent suffering (Isa 53:7; Jer 11:19; note that the similarity of these verses led Sa'adiah Gaon to the singular conclusion that the servant of the Lord in Isa 53 was none other than Jeremiah; cf. also Ps 44:11[12], 22[23], and note further that Isa 53:7 adds the image of the servant being silent like a sheep before her shearers), and calves leaping when released from the stall speaks of the unbounded joy of the righteous in the day of God's judgment (Mal 4:2[3:20]).

In more general terms, with no metaphor intended, Prov 27:23 exhorts, "Be sure you know the condition of your flocks, give careful attention to your herds," since neither riches nor the crown are certain to endure (v. 24), whereas well cared-for flocks (v. 25) will pay rich dividends: "The lambs will provide you with clothing, and the goats with the price of a field. You will have plenty of goats' milk to feed you and your family and to nourish your servant girls" (vv. 26-27). This underscores the fundamental importance of the flock in Israelite life and culture, and it is no surprise that it is found in what is arguably the best-known messianic prophetic passage in the Scriptures. "The wolf will live with the lamb, the leopard will lie down with the goat, the calf and the lion and the yearling together [see also NIV margin]; and a little child with lead them. . . . They will neither harm nor destroy on all my holy mountain, for the earth will be full of the knowledge of the LORD as the waters cover the sea" (Isa 11:6).

P-B The metaphorical usage characteristic of the HB continues well into the LXX. Sirach, for example, contrasts human and divine love via flock imagery. Human love extends only to one's neighbor in a rather vague way. Divine love, however, is concerned for "all flesh," and involves "rebuking, training, and teaching"—which the sage describes as a shepherd "turning his flock around" (*epistrephēn ... to poimnion autou,* Sir 18:13; see also Bar 4:26; 2 Esd 5:18; 15:10; 4 Macc 5:4).

The rabbis continue to use the above terms in the halakhic literature, while in the more haggadic material one discovers a variety of metaphorical images based loosely on the above cited terms.

Some examples: "Great is the ram (*kbś*) who lives among seventy wolves" (Jastrow, 611, a metaphor for Israel's perilous existence in a hostile world). "Where does banished truth go? She goes and sits down in herds (*'drwt*) in the desert" (Jastrow, 1046, a metaphor for the eventual triumph of truth in the face of adversity and falsehood). Then there is the talmudic saying, "When pupils have grown and become like leaders (*'twdym*), then reveal to them the secrets of the law" (Jastrow, 1129).

NT The early Christians often spoke of the church as God's "flock." In John 10:16, Jesus announces his desire to gather all of his "sheep" into one fold, so that there might no longer be sectarian division, but "one flock, one shepherd" (*mia poimnē, heis poimēn*). In Gethsemane, Jesus predicts his disciples will abandon him and quotes Zech 13:7, "(I will) strike the shepherd, and the sheep (of the flock) will be scattered" (Matt 26:31). The LXX of Zech 13:7 translates MT *ṣ'n* as *ta probata* (sheep). Jesus, however (or Matthew?), reads *ta probata tēs poimnēs.* Assuming the LXX has a role in this tradition, either Jesus or the evangelist adds *tēs poimnēs,* perhaps to suggest that not all of the flock is unfaithful to Jesus at his death (e.g., the faithful women mentioned in 27:55-56). At any rate, this flock imagery continues to describe the vulnerability of the church to heresy (Acts 20:28-29), the constant need of the church for spiritual nourishment (1 Peter 5:2-3), and the need to encourage those who faithfully serve Christ's flock as humble, peaceable, and disinterested overseers (1 Clem 44:3).

(→ Azazel: Theology)

Shepherd: → *nwh* I (rest, # 5657); → *ṣō'n* (flock, small cattle, # 7366); → *r'h* I (feed, graze, shepherd, rule, # 8286)

BIBLIOGRAPHY

TDNT 6:689-90; J. Botterweck, "Hirt und Herde im AT und im Alten Orient," in *Die Kirche und ihre Ämter und Stände* (Festgabe J. Kard), 1960; J. Frazer, *Folklore in the Old Testament,* 1975 (originally published in 1918); S. Hirsch, *Sheep and Goats in Palestine,* 1933; J. Hoftijzer and G. van der Kooij, *Aramaic Texts From Deir 'Allā,* 1976; O. Keel, *Das Böcklein in der Milch seiner Mutter und Verwandtes,* OBO 33, 1980; idem, "Tiere als Gefährten und Feinde des biblischen Menschen," *Heiliges Land* 7, 1970, 51-59; P. de Lagarde, *Übersicht über die im aramäischen, arabischen und hebräischen übliche Bildung und Nomina,* 1889; P. D. Miller, "Animal Names As Designations in Ugaritic and Hebrew," *UF* 2, 1970, 177-86; M. S. Moore, *The Balaam Traditions: Their Character and Development,* 1990; I. Siebert, *Hirt-Herde-König: Zur Herausbildung des Königtums im Mesopotamien* (SSA 53, 1969); S. T. Sohn, *The Divine Election of Israel,* 1991, 84-88, 254-56; G. Stein, "Das Tier in der Bibel: Der jüdische Mensch und sein Verhältnis zum Tier," *Judaica* 36, 1980, 14-26, 57-72; P. Wapnish, B. Hesse and A. Ogilvy, "The 1974 Collection of Faunal Remains from Tell Dan," *BASOR* 227, 1977, 35-62.

Michael S. Moore/Michael L. Brown

7368	צֶאֱצָאִים

צֶאֱצָאִים (*ṣe'eṣā'îm*), line of descendants, issue, offspring (# 7368); < יצא (*yṣ'*), go out (→ # 3655).

OT The word *ṣeʾeṣāʾîm* is confined to Isaiah and Job (Job 21:8; 27:14; 31:8; Isa 22:24; 34:1; 42:5; 44:3; 48:19; 61:9; 65:23). Most often it designates the offspring of human beings, but twice the earth's produce (Isa 34:1; 42:5).

Descendant, offspring, seed: → *dôr* II (generation, # 1887); → *zrʿ* (sow, scatter seed, form seed, # 2445); → *yld* (bear, bring forth, be born, # 3528); → *nîn* (offspring, # 5769); → *neked* (progeny, # 5781); → *ʿēqer* (descendant, # 6830); → *ṣeʾeṣāʾîm* (offspring, # 7368); → *ribbēaʿ* (member of fourth generation, # 8067); → *šillēš* (member of sixth generation, # 9000); → *tarbût* (brood, # 9551)

BIBLIOGRAPHY
TDOT 4:143-62; *THAT* 1:443-45.

Victor P. Hamilton

7369 (*ṣāb* I, covered wagon), → # 8206

7370 (*ṣāb* II, great lizard), → Reptiles

7371	צבא

צבא (*ṣbʾ*), q. to go to war, to minister in the cult; hi. to muster troops (# 7371); צָבָא (*ṣābāʾ*), nom. army service; warrior, service in the cult, hard service (# 7372).

ANE The root is fairly common in ancient Sem. Akk. attests the vb. *ṣabāʾu*, to go to war, in the Old Bronze period and the nom. *ṣabu*, group of people, workers, army, from the Old Akk. period on. The root is also attested in Ugar., Arab., and Eth.

OT 1. The vb. occurs only 14x, compared to 479x for the nom. The vb., though, carries the same basic meaning and semantic range, denoting both war and cult activities. While the overlapping of war and cult may be surprising to modern interpreters, the theology of warfare in the OT and the ANE shows that these two spheres are interconnected. According to the OT, Yahweh made his presence known in a special and personal way in the tabernacle-temple, on the one hand, and on the battlefield, on the other. Yahweh's presence is symbolized by the ark of the covenant, which was present in the Holy of Holies except at times of warfare, when it was carried into battle (Longman and Reid, 39-41, 49-52, 86, 92, 182). The connection between Yahweh and war is also noted by the frequent title (lit.) "LORD of Hosts" (*yhwh ṣebāʾôt*, from the nom. *ṣbʾ*).

(a) The q. of the vb. denotes the act of warfare. It can be used to describe the Israelites going to war against (with the preposition *ʿal*) the Midianites at the command of the Lord. In Isa 29:7-8 it is used to describe the aggressive action of the nations against Zion, the symbol of God's own people. In 31:4 it describes the violent action of God. There is some debate as to whether the preposition *ʿal* here means against as usual with *ṣbʾ* in battle contexts. With Oswalt (574) on the basis of context, we take the preposition in another frequent sense (on), as indicating Zion as the place where the battle took place. Instead of fighting against Jerusalem, v. 5 indicates that he rescued it.

(b) Interestingly, the q. can also be used in what at first seems a totally unrelated way. In Exod 38:8 and 1 Sam 2:22 it is used to describe the work of women at the door of the Tent of Meeting. Much discussion concerns the nature of the work these women perform in the cult. Cross (201-3) connects the 1 Sam 2:22 passage, which informs the reader that Eli's sons were copulating with these women, with Num 25:1-15, the sin at Beth Peor, and argues that these women were cult prostitutes. However, such a view is unwarranted or at least not clear. Durham (487-89) rightly points out that in spite of the 1 Sam 2:22 text, the women in Exod 38:8 cannot be conceived as cult prostitutes. After all, they used the copper in their mirrors to construct the laver in the tabernacle. Nonetheless, their role is unclear to the modern reader except to say it had some general association with the cult.

The vb. is not restricted to female workers in the cult. The sons of Gershon are said to serve (*ṣb'*, *ṣābā'*) by carrying various components of the tabernacle as the Israelites wander through the wilderness (Num 4:23). Num 8:24-25 describes the retirement age for Levites and uses the vb. *ṣb'* (v. 24) to describe their work up until that time.

(c) The hi. of the vb. is usually used in a causative sense, to cause someone to go to war, more idiomatically, to muster, draft, or conscript. 2 Kgs 25:19 and its near parallel in Jer 52:25 use the vb. to refer to an officer who was in charge of the conscription.

2. The nom. *ṣābā'* occurs 279x in a divine title. These latter occurrences will not be treated here (→ Yahweh: Theology). The remaining 200 occurrences appear in a variety of contexts, but demonstrate the same semantic range as the vb.

(a) A large proportion of occurrences refer to warfare, either to those who participate in warfare or to army service.

(i) In the first place, and by far the most common usage, the nom. refers to those who participate in warfare, the army or soldiers who compose the army (1 Sam 17:55; 2 Sam 2:8; 10:7; 1 Kgs 16:16). Though the word has no special connection with God's nation, these references are often to the armies of Israel, regular human armies. Troops are often specified as "men of the army" (*'anšê haṣṣābā'*) or the equivalent (see Num 31:53).

An interesting use of the term is in the description of the people of Israel as they wander in the desert from Egypt to Canaan. Both Exod (6:26; 7:4; 12:41) and Num (10:14, 18, 22, 25) use the nom. to refer to the tribes as a whole. This supports the portrayal of Israel in the desert as an army on the march. Their camp is like a war camp and they march like an army into battle, so it is appropriate that they may be likened to an army by the use of the term *ṣābā'*.

God was the one who accompanies the armies of his people when they were obedient to his commands. However, when they disobeyed him, he abandoned them to their fate. The psalmist reflects such a time as well as a longing that God may come back to his people in their struggle against their enemies (Ps 44:9[10]; 60:10[12]; 108:11[12]).

But it is not just human troops who are called *ṣābā'*. A further metaphorical use is common: God's celestial creatures are called a *ṣābā'*. In terms of canonical order, the word first appears in Gen 2:1 in reference to "the vast array" of heaven and earth. Ps 33:6 reflects on God's creation of the "starry host" by the breath of his mouth. Isa 40:26 specifies that the hosts of heaven include the stars (cf. Neh 9:6). The military overtones of the word may be at play here, since the creation itself often fights on behalf of God. Notice in particular Judg 5:20, which mentions the stars fighting from heaven on God's behalf in the war against Midian.

Israel and others sometimes forget the created status of the heavens and earth and their components. When the "starry hosts" (*ṣᵉbā' haššāmayim*) are elevated to the place of the Creator rather than the created, then Israel engages in idolatry (2 Kgs 17:16; 21:3).

(ii) In a few references the word *ṣābā'* means army service. In the census accounts that begin the book of Numbers the word is used because the purpose of the census is to describe the available fighting forces and envisions the tribes of Israel as a vast military force moving toward the battlefield (Num 1:3, 20, 22, 45; 26:2). This use of the word is not just restricted to Numbers (see 1 Chron 5:18, where a force of 44,760 men are counted from the two and one half tribes of Reuben, Gad, and Manasseh and described as "ready for military service").

(b) Like the vb., the nom. occasionally is found in cultic, not war, contexts, once again illustrating the close connection between the two spheres of life in ancient Israel. In Num 4:23, for instance, the nom. is used as a cognate accusative with the vb. of the same root to indicate the work of the Gershonites at the Tent of Meeting. The same chapter so describes the work of the Merarites (4:30) and the Kohathites (4:35; see also Num 8:24, 25).

(c) Lastly, the nom. can be used to describe any kind of hard labor, even that not associated with the cult or the army. Two occurrences are found in Job (7:1; 14:14) and another in Isa (40:2). In such contexts the word can be translated "hard service" (cf. Clines, 183-84).

P-B The root finds extensive use in the literature from Qumran (see *TWAT* 6:875). The Septuagint translates the word in a variety of different ways, perhaps most often with *dynamis* or *stratia*.

War, army, battle, fight: → *gdd* II (band together, # 1518); → *ḥmš* (organized for war, # 2821); → *lḥm* I (do battle, fight, # 4309); → *maḥᵃneh* (camp, encampment, war, # 4722); → *maʿᵃrākâ* (battle-line, # 5120); → *ṣb'* (go to war, serve, muster, conscript, # 7371); → *ṣî* (warship, # 7469); → *ṣrḥ* (yell, call shrilly, raise the war-cry, # 7658); → *qᵉrāb* (battle, # 7930); → *rkb* (ride/mount, # 8206); → *rwʿ* (shout, give war-cry, # 8131); → *šālîš* III (third man in war-chariot, adjutant, # 8957)

BIBLIOGRAPHY

TWAT 6:871-76; D. J. A. Clines, *Job 1-20*, 1989; F. M. Cross, *Canaanite Myth and Hebrew Epic*, 1972; J. I. Durham, *Exodus*, 1987; T. Longman III and D. G. Reid, *God Is a Warrior*, 1995; J. Oswalt, *Isaiah 1-39*, NICOT, 1986.

Tremper Longman III

7372 (*ṣābā'* I, army, warfare, compulsory service), → # 7371

7372a (*ṣᵉbā'ôt [yhwh]*, → Yahweh

7375 (*ṣᵉbō'îm*, Zeboiim), → Sodom

7377	צבה

צבה (*ṣbh* I), q. swell up; hi. make swell up (# 7377); צָבֶה (*ṣābeh*), swollen (# 7379).

OT The concept of swelling and of the causation of a blotch/blemish due to a (skin-)disease is expressed by terms that derive from the verbal roots *ṣbh* I and *nś'*.

1. The forms of *ṣbh* occur 3x and all in a single chapter (Num 5:21, 22, 27)—once in a derived adjectival form and twice as a vb.—in the context of divine judgment on an adulterous woman on account of her presumed extramarital unfaithfulness. In Num 5:11-31 the whole ritual procedure is designed to prove the guilt or otherwise of such a woman under suspicion of her husband. The water potion, which she (having been placed under oath by the priest) is forced to drink before the face of Yahweh and in the presence of the priest and her husband, is intended as a divine oracular indicator. This holy water potion contains some dust of the tabernacle floor. It is potent because of the potency of the sacred area and affects only the guilty person. Such a sin is clearly seen here as effecting personal moral and cultic defilement (cf. v. 19) as well as societal disruption and rejection and ultimately divine judgment (cf. vv. 21-22 and v. 27). The dust or earth taken from the floor of the sanctuary serves to bind the suspected woman to the sanctuary and thereby to its resident God, who is judging her (cf. Levine, 210). In biblical thought a curse (*'ālâ*; # 460) and an oath (*šᵉbû'â*; # 8652) are often related; see Gen 26:28; 1 Sam 14:24; Neh 10:30; Ezek 17:19; Dan 9:11. The oath carries with it an implicit curse that will fall on the oath-breaker (Ashley, 131). Levine (197) rightly points out that the combination of the terms *lᵉ'ālâ wᵉlišbu'â* in v. 21 is best understood as hendiadys and translates it as "an accused oath-violator." The sense seems to be that if the woman is guilty, she will be physically affected by the holy water-dust-and-ink potion, and these physical results, including the loss of her embryo, will signify to her kinsmen that she has sworn falsely as well as committed adultery. She would be held up as an example of the way in which God punishes oath violators (Ashley, 132).

The term *ṣābeh*, therefore, evidently functions in terms of this connotation of curse, humiliation, and divine judgment, since the very belly (= womb) that brings honor to a woman in blessed fertility and consequential childbearing, on the contrary swells up (q. in Num 5:21 and hi. in v. 22) as a proof of guilt and as a means of eradicating evil from the midst of the community. (A. Dillmann, as well as J. Olshausen [*Heb. Gram.* 78c] and B. Stade [*Heb. Gram.* 114a.2] suggest that this hi. inf., *laṣbôt,* be read as a q. inf., *liṣbôt,* which renders a more regular form grammatically, but does not really change the meaning much at this point.) There is quite a range of scholarly opinions as to what the phrase "(Yahweh) causes your thigh to waste away and your abdomen to swell" (cf. vv. 21, 22 NIV) really entails in medical terms. Brichto (60-62) regards "a fallen thigh" to indicate the falling or atrophying of the sexual organ of the woman to make childbearing impossible. He accepts the meaning "to swell" for *ṣbh* and concludes that the fallen thigh and the swollen belly(-womb) in combination are marks of what is called pseudocyesis or hysterical pregnancy (Brichto, 66; cf. Ashley, 133 for some other interpretations suggested by scholars).

Levine (198), in line with the majority of scholars, says it is logical to interpret these terms as indicating a miscarriage, as may be concluded from the contrast between the stated outcome when the woman is guilty and the outcome when she is innocent (v. 28). If innocent, the woman would "retain her seed and her pregnancy would continue." In an excellent discussion of the phenomenology of the ordeal portrayed in Num 5 and the combined interrelatedness of prayer, magic, and judicial aspects integrally present here (to which one may refer for further significant details of this matter), Levine compares the procedure described in this case with similar practices reflected in a text from Mari (ARM X-9, Dossin, 1978) and then pinpoints the central element present here when he says: “the woman suspected of adultery renders herself vulnerable by ingesting dust from the Tabernacle, because her duty to be pure is a duty to the God of Israel, resident in the sanctuary. If the gods in the Mari oath failed in their sworn duty, Mari would be impaired. If the woman of Numbers 5 had failed in her duty, the Tabernacle would be endangered” (Levine, 211).

2. In contrast to *ṣbh*, the other term, *ś*^{e}*’ēt*, swelling (→ # 8421), which refers to a physical swelling, a swollen spot, or a resultant skin blotch never occurs in a negative context of divine judgment/punishment, but rather in a tragic situation of illness and a hope for healing. It is, however, similarly limited in its occurrence (Lev 13 and 14). The context of these two chapters has to do with the matter of ancient Israelite priests having to diagnose the various skin diseases so as to protect the community from the spreading of dangerous contagious diseases. Taking this context into account and particularly noting the various words that occur together with the term *ś*^{e}*’ēt* in each verse leads one to the conclusion that *ś*^{e}*’ēt* sometimes has to be translated by swelling and in other cases by blotch (which may or may not involve a swelling). In Lev 13:2 and 14:56 *ś*^{e}*’ēt* should be rendered by swelling; in 13:10, 19 by a white blotch; in 13:43 by the phrase “an inflamed swelling”; and, finally, in 13:28 by the words a scar/blotch of a burn.

Milgrom presents a good overview of rabbinic sources, the overwhelming number of which render *ś*^{e}*’ēt* as swelling, deriving it from the vb. *nś’*, raise, lift (# 5951). The Tgs., as translations, render this somewhat obscure term with rather more imprecise renderings such as deep spot (Tg. Onq.), prominent mark (Tg. Pesh.—Jonathan), or mark (Tg. Neofiti). Milgrom himself prefers a rendering in line with these Tgs. and translates *ś*^{e}*’ēt* not only in Num 13:2 but also in nearly all its occurrences with the rather vague term discoloration, sometimes in combination with some other adjective. Milgrom tries to support such a rendering by means of the etymological argument that the equivalent Arab. term *si’atu* can mean mark (Driver, 1963, 575b). Milgrom, however, bases his choice against the rabbinic rendering of the term swelling (which incidentally is followed by most modern Bible translations) on a misinterpretation by him of the next verse (3), which he says “states explicitly that the sore appears *lower* than the surrounding skin” (773).

At issue is the basic diagnostic question as to how deep the sore penetrates the flesh. The NIV seems to render it correctly, Lev 13:3: “(if) the sore appears to be more than skin deep.” In light of all the evidence, it therefore still seems best to follow the reading swelling in 13:2 and 14:56 and the other renderings as indicated in this article, which is probably as close as one can get to a correct translation in the light of present knowledge.

Swelling, lifting up: → *bṣq* (swell, # 1301); → *g‘š* (rise and fall noisily, swell, surge, # 1723); → *hdr* (swell, honor, adorn, # 2075); → *‘pl* (swell, lift up, # 6752); → *ṣbh* (swell up, make swell up, # 7377)

BIBLIOGRAPHY

T. R. Ashley, *Numbers*, 1993; H. C. Brichto, “Case of the SOTA and a Reconsideration of Biblical ‘Law,’” *HUCA* 46, 1975, 55-70; P. J. Budd, *Numbers*, WBC 5, 1984; G. Dossin, *Correspondence féminine*, Archives royales de Mari 10:8, 1978; J. L. Hartley, *Leviticus*, WBC 4, 1992; H. Jagersma, *Numeri* (I), De Prediking van het Oude Testament, 1983; B. A. Levine, *Numbers*, AB,

1993; B. Maarsingh, *Leviticus*, De Prediking van het Oude Testament, 1974; J. Milgrom, *Leviticus 1-16*, AB, 1990; M. Noth, *Leviticus*, OTL, 1965; idem, *Numbers*, OTL, 1968; G. J. Wenham, *The Book of Leviticus*, NICOT 1979.

P. J. J. S. Els

7379 (*ṣābeh*, swollen), → # 7377

7380 (*ṣābûa'*, hyena), → # 9478

7381	צבט

צבט (*ṣbṭ*), q. give, pass (hapleg.; Ruth 2:14; # 7381).

ANE Ugar. **ṣbṭ* (only attested in a nom. *mṣbṭm*, tongs); Akk. *ṣabātu(m)*, sieze; Arab. *ḍabaṭa*; Eth. *ḍäbäṭä*, sieze.

OT As with any hapleg., scholars debate the meaning of *ṣbṭ*. In light of the LXX tr. (*bounizō*, heap, pile up; also used in the LXX in Ruth 2:16 for a nom. form of *ṣbt* [note the final radical]; → # 7395), some affirm that *ṣbr*, heap, pile (Gen 41:35, 49; Exod 8:10) provides a better reading (Hubbard, 74; Campbell, 102-3). Others contend that Akk. *ṣabātu(m)*, sieze, provides the etymological foundation for both terms (*ṣbṭ/ṣbt*) in Ruth 2:14, 16 (Sasson, 55-56; Greenspahn, 153). Whether or not *ṣbṭ* in Ruth 2:14 derives from the Akk. *ṣabātu(m)* (cf. Sasson [55] for support of this derivation), the Ugar. cognate (*mṣbṭm*, tongs) and a late Heb. expression (*bēt haṣṣ^{e}bîtâ*, handle) confirm the meaning sieze, grasp, for *ṣbṭ* in the present context. As Ruth sat among the reapers, Boaz took some roasted grain and presented it to her.

Gift: → *'ahab* (gifts of love, charm, # 172); → *zbd* (endow, # 2272); → *mgn* I (deliver, # 4481); → *nādān* II (gift, wages of love, # 5621); → *ntn* (give, present, offer, # 5989); → *skr* II (hand over, # 6127); → *ṣbṭ* (give, # 7381); → *šḥd* (give a gift, # 8815); → *šay* (gift, present, # 8856); → *šalmōnîm* (gift, # 8988)

BIBLIOGRAPHY

E. Campbell, *Ruth*, 1975; F. Greenspahn, *Hapax Legomena in Biblical Hebrew*, 1984; R. Hubbard, Jr., *The Book of Ruth*, 1988; J. Sasson, *Ruth*, 1979.

Michael A. Grisanti

7382	צְבִי

צְבִי (*ṣ^{e}bî*), nom., ornament, glory (# 7382).

ANE *HALAT* connect this word with Aram. *ṣb'*, to desire, and Akk. *ṣibūtu*, desire, plan. If this is correct, then Ugar. *ṣb* (√*ṣby*), to covet, desire, should be included. The Heb. term has gone its own way semantically (from a sense, object of desire?); but perhaps Even-Shoshan is justified in defining the Heb. term as desirable thing, beauty, splendor.

OT 1. *Usages.* The word, which is found 18x, is concentrated in Isa (7x), Ezek (5x), and Dan (4x); the other appearances are 2 Sam 1:19; Jer 3:19.

We find *ṣ^{e}bî* applied to people in 2 Sam 1:19 (Jonathan and Saul are Israel's glory); Isa 4:2 (*ṣemaḥ yhwh*, the Branch of the Lord will be *liṣbî ûl^{e}kābôd*, for beauty and for glory). The word describes the beauty of ornamentation in Isa 23:9; Ezek 7:20.

The nom. refers to the abstract property of beauty or glory in Isa 24:16 (people sing *ṣ^{e}bî laṣṣaddîq*, glory to the Righteous One); 28:1, 4 (*ṣ^{e}bî tip'artô*, the beauty of Ephraim's glory), v. 5 (the Lord himself will be *la'^{a}ṭeret ṣ^{e}bî w^{e}liṣpîrat tip'ārâ*, for a crown of beauty and a wreath of glory, for his remnant).

A major usage applies this term to locations. Palestine as Israel's inheritance is *'ereṣ haṣṣ^{e}bî*, the land of beauty (Dan 11:16, 41; cf. 8:9; Jer 3:19; Ezek 20:6, 15); Zion is called *har-ṣ^{e}bî-qōdeš*, the beautiful holy mountain (Dan 11:45, NIV). Elsewhere Babylon is *ṣ^{e}bî mamlākôt*, the jewel of kingdoms (Isa 13:19, NIV), and sites in Moab are *ṣ^{e}bî 'ereṣ*, the glory of the land (of Moab) (Ezek 25:9).

2. *Literary and semantic observations.* Since *ṣ^{e}bî* can have the shades of meaning beauty, glory, its closest synonym is *tip'eret*, also beauty, glory (→ # 9514). The words appear together in Isa 4:2; 13:19; 28:1, 4, 5. The case of 4:2 is especially interesting with a chiasmus of synonyms: the Branch of the Lord will be *liṣbî ûl^{e}kābôd*, for beauty and for glory, and the fruit of the land will be *l^{e}gā'ôn ûl^{e}tip'eret*, for majesty and for beauty/glory. Similarly *gā'ôn*, majesty, exaltation, pride (→ # 1454), appears often with *ṣ^{e}bî*: 4:2; 13:19; 23:9; 24:16 (cf. v. 14); and in Ezek 7:20 Judah has transformed *ṣ^{e}bî 'edyô*, the beauty of his ornamentation, into *gā'ôn*, pride.

An interesting wordplay comes from the fact that the pl. of *ṣ^{e}bî* would be *ṣ^{e}bā'ôt* (Joüon-Muraoka §96Aq, distinct from *ṣ^{e}bā'îm*, pl. of *ṣ^{e}bî* II, gazelle), and this is the same as the name *ṣebā'ôt*, hosts, in the expression *yhwh ṣebā'ôt,* the Lord of hosts (NIV the Lord Almighty). Hence in Isa 23:9 *yhwh ṣebā'ôt* planned to defile *g^{e}'ôn kol-ṣ^{e}bî*, the majesty/pride of all glory/ornamentation; in 28:5 *yhwh ṣebā'ôt* will become *'^{a}ṭeret ṣ^{e}bî*, a crown of beauty.

P-B *ṣ^{e}bî* is absent from the Heb. frgs. of Sirach Kuhn's concordance of the DSS lists only 1QH 7:29 (in the phrase *kôl ṣ^{e}bî rûaḥ*, which Kuhn calls unclear, while Lohse translates, all glory is wind). In the RL as listed in Jastrow, we find the word used only to refer to Palestine (cf. Jer 3:19; Ezek 20:6; etc.).

Glory, honor, majesty: → *'dr* (be magnificent, majestic, splendid, # 158); → *hdr* (swell, honor, adorn, # 2075); → *hôd* I (splendor, majesty, # 2086); → *y^{e}qār* (honor, riches, respect, price, splendor, # 3702); → *kbd* (be heavy, unresponsive, honored, # 3877); → *nēṣaḥ* I (luster, glory, lastingness, successful, # 5905); → *p'r* II (beautify, glorify, # 6995); → *ṣ^{e}bî* I (ornament, glory, # 7382)

BIBLIOGRAPHY

M. Dahood, "*UT*, 128 IV 6-7, 17-18 and Isaiah 28:8-9," *Or* 44, 1975, 439-41; M. Görg, "Die Bildsprache in Jes 28,1," *BN* 3, 1977, 17-23; E. Lohse, *Die Texte aus Qumran*, 1971.

C. John Collins

7383/7386	צְבִיָּה/צְבִי

צְבִיָּה/צְבִי (*ṣ^{e}bî* II/*ṣ^{e}biyyâ*), gazelle (# 7383, 7386).

OT The *ṣ^{e}bî* (with cognates in Akk., Aram., and Syr.), variously classified as *Gazella dorcas*, *Gazella subgutturosa*, or *Gazella gazella*, is found 14x in the masc., 2x in the fem., most often in the S of Songs (2:7, 9, 17, 18; 3:5; 4:5; 7:3[4]; 8:14), but also in the Torah (Deut 12:15, 22; 14:5; 15:22). The slender, sleek, and swift gazelle conjures up images of speed, beauty, and sexuality. Of Asahel it is stated that he "was as fleet-footed as a wild gazelle" (2 Sam 2:18: *qal b^e raglāyw k^e 'aḥad haṣṣ^e bāyim*; cf. 1 Chron 12:8 for the description of the brave Gadite warriors who defected to David at his stronghold in the desert: "Their faces were the faces of lions, and they were as swift as gazelles in the mountains").

In S of Songs, the references to the gazelle are varied, occurring 2x in the beloved's charge to the "Daughters of Jerusalem ... by the gazelles and by the does of the field" (in the LXX, "by the powers [reading *ṣ^e bā'ôt*?] and forces of the field"; cf. Targ.'s "by the Lord of Hosts and by the strength of the land of Israel") to "not arouse or awaken love until it so desires" (2:7; 3:5); 1x, in a description of her lover ("like a gazelle or a young stag"; 2:9); 2x in hopeful invitations to him (2:17, "turn, my lover, and be like a gazelle or like a young stag on the rugged hills"; and 8:14, the closing verse of the book: "Come away, my lover, and be like a gazelle or like a young stag on the spice-laden mountains"); and 2x in the lover's descriptions of his beloved's breasts ("like twin fawns of a gazelle"; 4:5; 7:3[4], apparently meaning small and youthful, along with well-shaped). This diverse and yet recurrent usage indicates that the gazelle was associated with erotic imagery in general (cf. M. H. Pope, *Job,* AB, 470, who notes that "the gazelle is celebrated in Arabic poetry for its perfection in form and beauty," also pointing out (386) with regard to the deer that "in Mesopotamian incantations to restore sexual potency, the stag is one of the amorous examples used to encourage the impotent").

In Isa 13:14, the beleaguered inhabitants of Babylon (possibly standing for Assyria), withering under enemy attack, are pictured as "a hunted gazelle, like sheep without a shepherd" (cf. Lam 1:6, where Jerusalem's downtrodden and defeated princes are likened to "deer that find no pasture," fleeing before their pursuers). They were unable to free themselves, "like a gazelle from the hand of the hunter, like a bird from the snare of the fowler" (Prov 6:5).

Deer, gazelle: → *'ayyāl/'ayyālâ* (deer, # 385/0387); → *zemer* (gazelle, # 2378); → *yaḥmûr* (roebuck, # 3502); → *yā'ēl* I/*yā^a lâ* I (ibex, # 3604, 3607); → *'ōper* (fawn of a gazelle, deer, # 6762); → *ṣ^e bî* II/*ṣ^e bîyâ* (gazelle, # 7383, 7386)

Michael S. Moore/Michael L. Brown

7389	צֶבַע

צֶבַע (*ṣeba'*), nom. colorful garments (# 7389).

ANE Akk. has *ṣub/pītu*, colored wool. The root with the meaning dyed cloth occurs in Arab., Aram., and Syr.

OT *ṣeba'* occurs just 3x in the OT and all are in Judg 5:30.

Are they not finding and dividing the spoils:
a girl or two for each man,
colorful garments as plunder for Sisera,
colorful garments embroidered,
highly embroidered *garments* for my neck—
all this as plunder?

Clothing, garment: → *beged* II (clothes, garment, # 955); → *g^e lôm* (garment, # 1659); → *ḥob* (fold of garment, # 2460); → *ḥōṣen* (fold of garment, # 2950); → *k^e tonet* (garment, # 4189); → *lbš* (put on, clothe, wear, # 4252); → *mad* (garment, clothes, # 4496); → *madeweh* I (garment,

4504); → *mah͎ªlaṣot* (festive garments, # 4711); → *meltāḥâ* (wardrobe, # 4921); → *mešî* (costly garments, # 5429); → *sādîn* (costly garments, # 6041); → *sut* (garment, # 6078); → *pᵉtîgîl* (fine clothing, # 7345); → *ṣeba'* (colorful garments, # 7389); → *śimlâ* (garment, cloth, # 8529); → *šōbel* (flowing skirt, # 8670); → *šît* (garment, attire, # 8884)

Robert L. Alden

7392	צבר

צבר (*ṣbr*), q. pile up (# 7392); צִבֻּר (*ṣibbur*), nom. heap (# 7393).

OT 1. The vb. is used of collecting grain (Gen 41:35, 49), dead frogs (Exod 8:10), dust (Hab 1:10), and silver (Job 27:16; Zech 9:3). Once it is used without an object (Ps 39:6[7]).

2. The only OT occurrence of the nom. *ṣibbur*, heap, is in the pl. in 2 Kgs 10:8, where it refers to a pile of heads.

Heap, mound, pile: → *gal* I (heap, pile, # 1643); → *ḥªmôr* II (heap, # 2790); → *mᵉdûrâ* (pile, # 4509); → *nēd* (heap, # 5603); → *sll* (heap, pile up, esteem highly, resist, # 6148); → *'rm* I (be dammed up, # 6890); → *ṣbr* (pile up, # 7392)

Allan M. Harman

7393 (*ṣibbur*, heap), → # 7392

7395	צֶבֶת

צֶבֶת (*ṣebet*), grain, bundle of grain (# 7395).

OT This word occurs only in Ruth 2:16 and may come from the vb. *ṣbt,* meaning bind or tie. It has several ANE cognates: Akk. *ṣibtu*, bundle, pack; Aram. *ṣibtā'*, collection, gathering; Arab. *ḍabṭat*, handful, bundle. The LXX translates it as *bebounismenōn*, meaning bundles. Related words continued to be used in later Heb. (*ṣᵉbîtâ*), Mand. (*ṣauta*), and Syr. (*ṣebtā'*), with similar meanings. It is unclear from Ruth 2:16 whether this word refers to a bundle of grain or to the handfuls of grain before they are bundled. See the discussion of *ṣbṭ*, give (→ # 7381).

Grain, barley, millet, rice, etc.: → *'ābîb* (ears of grain, # 26); → *biṣqālôn* (fresh stalks [cj.], # 1303); → *bar* III (grain, corn, # 1339); → *gādîš* I (stack of grain, # 1538); → *gereś* (grits, # 1762); → *dāgān* (grain, # 1841); → *dōḥan* (sorghum, millet, # 1893); → *ḥiṭṭâ* (wheat, # 2636); → *kussemet* (emmer-wheat, # 4081); → *karmel* IV (grain, fresh, newly ripened grain, # 4152); → *mᵉlîlâ* (grain, grains, # 4884); → *minnît* (rice, # 4976); → *mōṣ* (chaff, # 5161); → *sōlet* (wheat flour, # 6159); → *pannāg* (parched? grain, meal or flour, # 7154); → *ṣebet* (grain, bundle of grain, # 7395); → *ṣānum* (hard, barren [ears of grain], # 7568); → *qālî* (parched grain, # 7833); → *qāmâ* (crops, grain, standing grain, # 7850); → *śôrâ* (millet, # 8463); → *śᵉ'ōrâ* (barley, # 8555); → *šibbōlet* I (ear of grain, # 8672); → *šeber* II (grain, # 8692)

BIBLIOGRAPHY

J. Gray, *Joshua, Judges, and Ruth*, 1967, 415; F. E. Greenspahn, *Hapax Legomena in Biblical Hebrew*, 153; R. L. Hubbard, Jr., *The Book of Ruth*, 177.

Paul D. Wegner

7396	צַד

צַד (*ṣad*), nom. side (# 7396).

OT The nom. *ṣad* is used to describe the side of objects (Gen 6:16, a door was put in one side of the ark), the proximity of cities one to another (Josh 3:16), and the left or right side of human beings (Num 33:55; Ezek 4:4) or animals (Ezek 34:21). Isa 60:4 and 66:12 suggests the practice of carrying infants on the hip. Those who trust God need not fear, for through God's protection, thousands will fall at their side and they will not be harmed (Ps 91:7).

Border, boundary, corner, edge, rim: → *gbl* I (bound, border, # 1487); → *zāwît* (corner, # 2312); → *kānāp* (wing, skirt, outermost edge, # 4053); → *karkōb* (rim, edge, # 4136); → *mḥh* II (border on, # 4682); → *swg* II (border by, # 6048); → *pē'â* I (corner, # 6991); → *pinnâ* (corner, # 7157); → *ṣad* (side, # 7396); → *ṣēlā'* I (side, rib, side-chamber, # 7521); → *qēṣ* (limit, boundary, # 7891); → *qāṣeh* (end, border, # 7895); → *qṣ'* II (made with corners, # 7910)

Gordon H. Matties

7399	צדה

צדה (*ṣdh* I), malicious intent (→ 7399); צְדִיָּה (*ṣᵉdiyyâ*), nom. ambush, malice (aforethought) (# 7402).

ANE The nom. is not attested, but Delekat (18) has proposed the Ugar. vb. *ṣdw/y* in *KTU* 1.23, 16, 68. Gibson suggests the meaning "scour" (*CML²*, 156) for the hunt of the gods, a translation adopted by de Moor (121, 127).

OT 1. The vb. *ṣdh* is found in Exod 21:13 and 1 Sam 24:11[12], where the same ambiguities exist; the vb. may refer to the intent or to the manner of the action in each case. The vb. is related to the sense of hunt, as seen in Ugar., as in the example of Saul seeking to ambush David (1 Sam 24:11[12]).

2. The nom. *ṣᵉdiyyâ* is found in Num 35:20, 22, in a section dealing with deliberate and involuntary homicide. Both verses refer to the intent of the action that caused death, but there is a question of how the nom. *ṣᵉdiyyâ* is to be understood (Milgrom, 293). It may be taken as parallel to the words hate or enmity, in which case the ambush is in the mind of the manslayer. Alternately, Rashi took the nom. as defining the manner of the homicide, in which case the action itself is an ambush. Modern commentators are divided in translation, some choosing premeditation (Gray, 473), others lying in wait (Budd, 1780; Ashley, 653).

3. All of these verses have reference to destructive intent, like that of a hunter for his prey; this intent may be indicated by lying in ambush, or it may simply be that the action was obviously premeditated. Ambush is by definition premeditated attack; it is the logical term to use for malicious intent, irrespective of how the actual act is carried out. The action catches the victim unawares, and in that sense is a lying in wait; it is negative and destructive, the kind of thing David would avoid in order not to be like Saul, who was pursuing him (1 Sam 24:13[14]).

P-B The nom. *ṣᵉdiyyâ* in Talm. has the meaning "aiming" (Jastrow, 1262). In Mish. Heb. and later Aram. the vb. *ṣdy/ṣdh* has the meaning of lying in wait, hunt, or capture. In Arab. the vb. *ṣadiya* III means deceive.

Ambush: → *'rb* (lie in ambush, lay an ambush, # 741); → *ṣᵉdiyyâ* (ambush, malice, # 7402); → *śkh* (lie in wait, # 8495)

BIBLIOGRAPHY
T. R. Ashley, *The Book of Numbers*, 1993, 652-53; P. J. Budd, *Numbers*, 1984, 378; L. Delekat, "Zum ugaritischen Verbum," *UF* 4, 1972, 11-26; J. C. de Moor, *An Anthology of Religious Texts from Ugarit*, 1987, 121, 127; J. C. L. Gibson, *CML*^{2}, 124, 127, 156; J. B. Gray, *Numbers*, 1903, 473; J. Milgrom, *Numbers*, 1990, 293.

A. H. Konkel

7400	צדה

צדה (*ṣdh* II), ni. be devastated (of cities; Zeph 3:6; # 7400).

ANE The meaning of this hapleg. can be determined from the Aram., as well as the triple parallelism of *krt*, *šmm*, *ḥrb* (see Sabottka, *Zephanja*, 1972, 110-11, cf. Kopf, 196-97).

OT Yahweh's cutting off (*krt*, hi. [→ # 4162]) nations, demolishing (*šmm*, ni. [→ # 9037]) their strongholds, ruining (*ḥrb*, hi. [→ # 2990]) their streets, and devastating (*ṣdh*, ni. [→ # 7400]) their cities (Zeph 3:6) were to be an object lesson to Jerusalem so that she would fear God, accept correction, and so escape destruction (Zeph 3:7; cf. 2 Chron 36:15-16).

Destruction, annihilation, devastation, disfigurement, ruin: → *'bd* I (perish, # 6); → *'êd* (disaster, # 369); → *blq* (devastate, # 1191); → *dmh* III (ruin, # 1950); → *dmm* III (perish, # 1959); → *hrs* (demolish, # 2238); → *ḥbl* III (treat badly, # 2472); → *ḥlq* III (destroy, # 2746); → *ḥt'* (be destroyed, # 3148); → *klh* (be complete, perish, destroy, # 3983); → *krt* (cut, cut off, exterminate, cut a covenant, circumcise, # 4162); → *mḥh* I (wipe off, wipe out destroy, # 4681); → *nṣh* II (fall in ruins, # 5898); → *nts* (break up, # 5995); → *ntṣ* (tear down, # 5997); → *ntš* (root up, pull down, destroy, # 6004); → *p'h* (dash to pieces, # 6990); → *pîd* (ruin, misfortune, # 7085); → *prr* (break, invalidate, nullify, frustrate, foil, thwart, # 7296); → *ṣdh* II (be devastated, # 7400); → *rzh* (destroy, waste away, # 8135); → *šdd* (devastate, # 8720); → *šḥt* (become corrupt, ruin, spoil, # 8845); → *šmd* (be exterminated, destroyed, # 9012); → *tablît* (annihilation, # 9318)

BIBLIOGRAPHY
NIDNTT 1:462-71; L. Kopf, "Arabische Etymologien und Parallelen," *VT* 8, 1958, 161-215, esp. 196-97; L. Sabbottka, *Zephanja*, BibOr 25, 1972, 110-11.

Cornelis Van Dam

7401 (*ṣādôq*, Zadok), → Zadok

7402	צְדִיָּה

צְדִיָּה (*ṣ*^{e}*diyyâ*), nom. ambush, malice (aforethought) (# 7402); < צדה (*ṣdh* I), do with malicious intent (→ 7399).

ANE The nom. is not attested, but Delekat (18) has proposed the Ugar. vb. *ṣdw/y* in *KTU* 1.23, 16, 68. Gibson suggests the meaning "scour" (*CML*^{2}, 156) for the hunt of the gods, a translation adopted by de Moor (121, 127).

OT The nom. *ṣ*^{e}*diyyâ* is found in Num 35:20, 22, in a section dealing with deliberate and involuntary homicide. Both verses refer to the intent of the action that caused death, but there is a question of how the nom. *ṣᵉdiyyâ* is to be understood (Milgrom, 293). It may be taken as parallel to the words hate or enmity, in which case the ambush is in the mind of the manslayer. Alternately, Rashi took the nom. as defining the manner of the homicide, in which case the action itself is an ambush. Modern commentators are divided in translation, some choosing premeditation (Gray, 473), others lying in wait (Budd, 1780; Ashley, 653).

The vb. *ṣdh* is found in Exod 21:13 and 1 Sam 24:11[12], where the same ambiguities exist; the vb. may refer to the intent or to the manner of the action in each case. The vb. is related to the sense of hunt, as seen in Ugar., as in the example of Saul seeking to ambush David (1 Sam 24:11[12]).

All of these verses have reference to destructive intent, like that of a hunter for his prey; this intent may be indicated by lying in ambush, or it may simply be that the action was obviously premeditated. Ambush is by definition premeditated attack; it is the logical term to use for malicious intent, irrespective of how the actual act is carried out. The action catches the victim unawares, and in that sense is a lying in wait; it is negative and destructive, the kind of thing David would avoid in order not to be like Saul, who was pursuing him (1 Sam 24:13[14]).

P-B The nom. *ṣᵉdiyyâ* in Talm. has the meaning "aiming" (Jastrow, 1262). In Mish. Heb. and later Aram. the vb. *ṣdy/ṣdh* has the meaning of lying in wait, hunt, or capture. In Arab. the vb. *ṣadiya* III means deceive.

Ambush: → *'rb* (lie in ambush, lay an ambush, # 741); → *ṣᵉdiyyâ* (ambush, malice, # 7402); → *śkh* (lie in wait, # 8495)

BIBLIOGRAPHY

T. R. Ashley, *The Book of Numbers*, 1993, 652-53; P. J. Budd, *Numbers*, 1984, 378; L. Delekat, "Zum ugaritischen Verbum," *UF* 4, 1972, 11-26; J. C. de Moor, *An Anthology of Religious Texts from Ugarit*, 1987, 121, 127; J. C. L. Gibson, *CML²*, 124, 127, 156; J. B. Gray, *Numbers*, 1903, 473; J. Milgrom, *Numbers*, 1990, 293.

A. H. Konkel

7404 (*ṣaddîq*, just, righteous), → # 7405

7405	צדק

צדק (*ṣdq*), q. be just, righteous; ni. be justified, put right; pi. justify, make appear righteous; hi. do justice, declare righteous, make right; hitp. justify o.s. (# 7405); צַדִּיק (*ṣaddîq*), adj. just, righteous, correct, lawful (# 7404); צֶדֶק (*ṣedeq*), nom. masc. rightness, righteousness (# 7406); צְדָקָה (*ṣᵉdāqâ*), nom. fem. righteousness, righteous acts (# 7407).

ANE Use of the Sem. root *ṣdq* is widely attested in WestSem. sources.

1. Only one example is known in Akk. in the *CAD*, this from the Amarna Letters: *amur šarru bēlija ṣaduq ana yâši aššur LÚ. MEŠ. GN* "See, my lord, I am right about the people of GN" (*CAD* ṣ:59b; EA 287. 32). Moran (*Amarna Letters*, 342) makes better sense, however, with a different understanding of the syntax: "Consider O king, my lord! *I am in the right*!" (cf. *ANET*, 488). Abdi-Hepa, beleaguered prince of Jerusalem, strikes a pathetic note throughout his correspondence with his Egyptian

overlord; his self-righteous tone is apparent here. The Pal. provenance of this document should be noted; *ṣdq* is otherwise unknown in Akk.

2. In the Ugar. literature, attention has long been drawn to the occurrence of the term in the Keret legend (*KTU* 14 i. 12 = *CML*, 82), where it refers to the king's "lawful" or "legitimate" spouse (in parallel with *yšr*). A letter found in 1978 at Ras Ibn Hani from the king of Ugarit (probably Ammištamru) preserves the use of the term 4x in epithets of the unnamed pharaoh to whom the letter was sent (*IH* 78/3 + 30). It begins: "(To the Sun,) the great king, the king of Egypt, (the goo)d (*n'm*) king, the just (*ṣdq*) king, (the king of ki)ngs, the lord of all the land (of Egyp)t. . . " (*ABD* 6:711; full text in Bordreuil and Caquot; commentary in Milano). This is reminiscent of the titularies used in the EA correspondence and anticipates the use of the term at Byblos in later centuries. It is attractive, then, to think of this as a Sem. rather than Egyp. epithet.

3. The Amman Citadel inscription (*CAI*, No. 59) might preserve an occurrence of the term in the Ammonite language although the reading is disputed. The text (ca. 850) records the words of Milkom at the founding of a sanctuary. Should enemies lay siege to it "(they) shall surely die," while "amid (its) columns (the) just (*ṣdq*[*m*]) will reside" (*CAI*, 154; cf. Smelik, *Writings*, 89-90). These notions resonate with those found in the Psalms, where the temple is the setting for the plea of the righteous to God against the enemy. Ps 125 in particular has several points of contact with the Amman inscription (cf. also Isa 1:21).

4. Phoen. inscriptions provide examples of *ṣdq* over a period of about 700 years, maintaining the sense "legitimate," as seen in the Keret legend from Ugarit. A royal inscription of Yaḥîmilk (*fl.* 950) proclaims that he is "the legitimate (*ṣdq*) and rightful (*yšr*) king in the sight of the holy gods of Byblos" (*TSSI* 3:18; = *KAI* No. 4. 6-7). Similarly, Yaḥawmilk (*fl.* 440) petitions Ba'alat, goddess of Byblos, for long life, "for he is a lawful (*ṣdq*) king" (*TSSI* 3:95 = *KAI* No. 10. 9; but cf. Moscati, *Phoenicians*, 57: "just king"). In the Hellenistic period, a Phoen. votive inscription from Cyprus contains the term in an unfortunately broken context. The speaker lists pious and loyal acts towards Melqart, family and royal court, including cultic offerings "for the legitimate shoot (*ṣmḥ ṣdq*) and for his wife" (*TSSI* 3:137 = *KAI* No. 43. 11). This probably refers to Ptolemy II Philadelphos; the parallels to Jer 23:5 and 33:15 have been widely noted. In light of the letter from Ras Ibn Hani, one wonders whether "legitimate" invariably provides the best translation. It is difficult to arbitrate between "just X" and "legitimate X" in these cases: the former would refer to the individual's behavior (acting rightly), while the latter refers to claims to a given status (having right).

5. Aram. attestations of *ṣdq* are found across several centuries and in a variety of contexts.

(a) Royal inscriptions. The several occurrences of the term in Aram. royal inscriptions have been understood to have the special nuance of loyalty, a case made especially by Donner and Röllig (*KAI* 2:227). Thus, they translate the inscription of Panammu (ca. mid-eighth century): "On the basis of his wisdom and on the basis of his loyalty (*bṣdqh*) he seized the skirt of his lord, the king of Assyria" (*KAI* 2:224 No. 215. 11; also 215. 1, 19; 216. 4-5; 217. 5). Gibson is inclined to accept the nuance of loyalty in these cases, but translates "righteousness" and notes that the sense of "loyalty towards an overlord" is not found in the HB (*TSSI* 2:81-2). On the other hand, the term could carry the same nuance as that in the Phoen. inscriptions examined above. Swetnam argues vigorously for the meaning "righteousness" with the nuance of legitimate succession/legitimacy in these cases (Swetnam, 35-6; cf. the Keret text discussed above). The contexts—which consistently mention either lineage or succession—lend weight to his argument, and this interpretation seems preferable.

(b) Elephantine. It appears that *ṣdq* is used in a technical sense in certain legal papyri found at Elephantine. Muffs argues that the phrase *yhk bdyn wl' yṣdq*, "let him go to court [lit. to trial] and not *win*," is derived from Neo-Assyr. usage. He appeals to functional, etymological, and metrical parallels to the Akk. *ina dēnišu idabbubma lā ilaqqi/dayānu lā išammû* (Muffs, 6, 185).

(c) The proverbs of Ahiqar contain several references to the *ṣdyq* (lines 126, 128, 167, 173) as well as uses of the vb. (ll. 139-40; *ANET*, 429). The *ṣdyq* is one whose lot is consistently maintained by the gods, who protect and take the part of the righteous one. Lindenberger notes several biblical parallels, the most striking being 1 Kgs 2:32 (Lindenberger, 117-19, 170). He renders the vb. as "find innocent," which may be too precise (Lindenberger, 136-37). The situation here is not that of innocence or guilt, but rather of being cleared from false slander, as is also the case in the parallels in Job 9:15; 25:4. The sense is better conveyed by "justified" or "declared right."

6. In Egyp. writings the goddess Ma'at (*m3't*) and the principles she embodies correspond to the notions of WestSem. *ṣdq* (cf. Schmid, "Gerechtigkeit," 402-4). She/it is the foundation of right rule: "Do justice for the Lord of Justice / The justice of whose justice is real.... Speak justice, do justice, for it is mighty; it is great, it endures" ("Eloquent Peasant" B1:304, 320-21; *AEL* 1:181; cf. Prov 8:15).

In sum, the term appears to be used to refer to right comportment: status or behavior in accord with some implied standard. Forensic settings are rare in the extant texts, but the Elephantine papyri show the term to be at home there as well. The high preponderance of royal contexts should not be accorded significance, as this only reflects the nature of surviving documents. The dominant setting is one of ethical assertion, whether the context is secular or religious.

OT 1. Scholars have usually maintained semantic differences between the various forms of *ṣdq* terms (e.g., Ho [in a flawed monograph], Weinfeld cautiously). However, there is a high degree of overlap for these terms, so that nominal constructions can be the semantic equivalent of the verbal form (e.g., cf. Gen 38:26 with 1 Sam 24:17[18]), and the nominal forms are used interchangeably (cf. 2 Sam 22:21, 25 with Ps 18:20[21], 24[25]). While some generalizations may be made about the individual terms, semantic nuance is better derived from context than morphology.

The notions sketched in the survey of ANE material suggest a natural gradation in the word group that comprises both active and stative meanings: one "acts rightly," one can "be righteous." Forensic notions have to do with the adjudication or declaration of right behavior or status. Theological considerations automatically dominate any modern understanding of righteousness; it becomes a sort of verbal shorthand for something true about God, and as such is difficult to define or describe. It will be seen that *ṣdq* terms regularly deal with behavior that, usually by implication, accord with some standard. The standard might be the law, but often this is not the case or, at least, revealed law is not to be understood but rather some natural law or assumed standard. Nuances such as those already seen in the survey of ANE materials can be seen clearly in purely interpersonal settings, and emerge by attending to the function of *ṣdq* in narrative contexts. This, in turn, is suggestive for theological settings, where the deity acts and has his being in a manner analogous to humankind. G. von Rad resisted this division into secular and sacred contexts, while granting them their independence. The danger is that "the impression could be given that there was both a secular concept of *ṣ*[e]*dāqâ* and a purely religious one, and that the latter was possibly a product of later theological reflexion.... But that would be an utterly false description of the case" (*OTT*, 1:374). Still, to separate out these elements—where possible and feasible—assists in the task of understanding what is involved in being righteous in biblical texts.

(a) In fact, such a procedure was unavoidably followed by von Rad in his commentary on Gen 30:33. There we find the story of the separation of Jacob from Laban, after the former's years of service in return for Laban's daughters. As negotiations between the two tricksters proceed, Jacob settles for what appears to be a poor deal. He will not take wages, but will take only the speckled or spotted sheep and goats (30:32) from the flocks to be his own. Thus his flocks would be visibly differentiated from Laban's, so "my *ṣdqh* will testify for me in the future" (30:33). The term is widely translated "honesty"; while this is suitable for the context, it might appear too restricted. Jacob is making the claim that this arrangement will be a guarantee of his right behavior. Laban, while ready to accept the deal, is nonetheless suspicious of his son-in-law, for he, rather than Jacob, separates the flocks and puts three-days' journey between his flock and the spotted sheep. Von Rad comments: "This is one of the few profane examples of that important biblical term which is so difficult to translate. Here, too, it presupposes an existing community relationship and refers to 'loyalty' to an agreement equally binding on both partners. The term is then applied by Israel to Yahweh's relationship to Israel in exactly the same sense" (*Genesis*, 301).

Another story of two schemers in Genesis also uses *ṣdq* (here the vb.) in a "profane" sense. Gen 38 relates the dealings of Judah and his daughter-in-law, Tamar. After the deaths of two of his sons, he sends Tamar away for fear that a third son would die because of her. With the passage of time, Tamar fears she has been forgotten and uses the occasion of the sheep-shearing frolic to lure Judah into having intercourse with her by masquerading as a cultic prostitute. She then takes his ring, cord, and staff as pledge of payment. This encounter results in Tamar's pregnancy, and when Judah hears of it he calls for her execution. Tamar produces the ring, cord, and staff as proof of Judah's paternity. Judah confesses: "She is more righteous than I (*ṣād*[e]*qâ mimmennî*), since I wouldn't give her to my son" (38:26). GKC offers the judgment that "the phrase *ṣdq mn-* expresses not a comparison, but only a relation existing between one person and another; thus in Gn38[26] ... *she is in the right as against me*" (430, n. 2). WOC concur, calling this a "comparison of exclusion": "the subject alone possesses the quality connoted by the adjective or stative vb., to the exclusion of the thing compared," and translate this clause "She is in the right, not I" (265). But this fails to take into account that Tamar as well as Judah was scheming (cf. Sternberg, *Poetics*, 165) and that they dealt falsely with each other. Thus the nuance of exclusion seems to be inadmissible. Wenham (*Genesis 16-50*, 369) further implies this is a judicial context with the nuance of innocence. This seems unlikely in light of 30:33 (and 1 Sam 24:17[18] discussed below). Judah is not admitting his guilt and Tamar's innocence;

rather, he recognizes that her behavior in this affair was more virtuous than his. This does not turn on legal questions, but moral.

Further, the parallel in 1 Sam 24:17[18] suggests that both parties—now Saul and David—had "right" on their side, and again that one's behavior was more virtuous than the other's. The context is the first in the series of three stories about lives David might take (Saul's life in chs. 24 and 26, Nabal's in ch. 25). Saul here expects that David will kill him and "rightly" so (the clear implication of the question posed in 24:19[20]), just as Saul would kill his enemy (i.e., David). David refrains, however, and Saul declares. "You are more righteous than I (*ṣaddîq 'attâ mimmennî*)" (v. 17). This is not, then, a matter of David acting rightly and Saul not at all; rather, David's behavior is more virtuous than Saul's. This is not the usual interpretation, which understands Saul to declare David's innocence and his own culpability. But in this narrative setting we have to reckon with the enmity between them: Saul is seeking David's life, but David is seeking Saul's throne. This brings the interaction into a similar situation as that of Jacob and Laban, or Judah and Tamar. One also notes that the comparative clauses—one of which uses the vb., the other the adjective—are equivalent in meaning. (Cf. also 1 Kgs 2:32 for comparative *min* with *ṣaddîq*.)

Each of these examples shows two individuals in some degree of conflict, with the resolution couched in terms of *ṣdq* where this has the sense of right or virtuous behavior. The standard for evaluating this behavior is not stated but is assumed to be common to both parties. In the cases where the comparative *min* is used, there is also a degree of relativity injected: one party is better behaved than the other.

(b) Nontheological stative uses of the *ṣdq* group are found most clearly with inanimate objects. Just (*ṣedeq*) weights and measures are demanded in the legislation of Lev 19:36 and Deut 25:15. These are to be legitimate measures, rightly conforming to the proper standard and not compromised in any way. Similarly, Deut 4:8 refers to "righteous statutes and ordinances" (RSV)—the single occurrence of *ṣaddîq* without a personal referent in the HB (so Weinfeld, *Deuteronomy 1-11*, 195). In each of these cases there is no possibility of right action or behavior; rather, *ṣdq* refers to some right state of being for each object. This may also be the implication of the blessing of Zebulun and Issachar in Deut 33:19 where it speaks of the people offering "right sacrifices (*zibḥê-ṣedeq*)" (NIV sacrifices of righteousness), although there is more ambiguity here (cf. O'Connor, *HVS*, 214, who translates "legitimate sacrifices").

(c) Returning to narrative, personal contexts also use *ṣdq* with a stative sense. The first occurrence of *ṣaddîq* in the HB seems to carry this meaning. Noah is described as a "righteous man (*'îš ṣaddîq*), blameless (*tāmîm*) among the people of his time" (Gen 6:9). As one who as lived rightly, he has "righteous" status. Similarly, Jehu confronts the people of Jezreel after the slaughter of Ahab's seventy sons and declares, "You are innocent (*ṣaddiqîm 'attem*)" (2 Kgs 10:9). A wide variety of interpretations is given this clause in modern versions. In the context of the narrative, Jehu claims responsibility for the death of Ahab and poses the question of responsibility for the deaths of the seventy. The following verse implies that the wider slaughter is the result of Yahweh's judgment. Of these deaths, then, the people are clear. They have done no wrong, and remain "in the right." In this instance *ṣdq* does not refer to something they have *done*, but to something that they *are*.

The contrast with *rš'*, wicked (→ # 8399), in 2 Sam 4:11 provides a further example of *ṣdq* in its stative sense. Assassins of Ish-Bosheth, Saul's son, bring his head to David, expecting praise for destroying David's enemy. But just as David greeted the news of Saul's death by executing the messenger (2 Sam 4:10; cf. 1:8-16), so here these wicked men (*'ᵃnāšîm rᵉšā'îm*) are executed for having killed a righteous man (*'îš ṣaddîq*). Commentators are united in seeing these antonyms as technical terms, especially in understanding *ṣaddîq* here as "innocent." But it is not simply a matter of David's proceeding as both prosecutor and judge. The explicit comparison with the Amalekite (2 Sam 1) suggests that this is not so much legal as moral judgment. What the Amalekite did was bad; these assassins are worse. In what sense is Ish-Bosheth, the sleeping victim, "innocent"? Anderson (*2 Samuel*, 71) makes the attractive suggestion that it was this situation that rendered the victim "right." The term is used here not so much a comment on the nature of his life (cf. Noah), but rather indicates his victimization. The implication that the assassins were looking for reward for what they thought was a loyal act will have repercussions in consideration of theological notions below.

A more abstract sense of "right" is also possible. 2 Sam 19:28[29] recounts a speech of Mephibosheth, son of Jonathan, which comes near the culmination of a complex story. Ziba, former steward of Saul and Mephibosheth's servant, has dealt deceptively with David during Absalom's rebellion. David fell prey to Ziba's lies (2 Sam 16:1-5) and turned Mephibosheth's property over to him. Mephibosheth's character seems to be of a piece with his father's, and David's rash judgment against him is an act of injustice, not fully redressed in this scenario. In 19:24-30[25-31] Mephibosheth greets the returning David, Absalom's rebellion quelled. He announces Ziba's deceit and praises David's generosity in giving Mephibosheth life and a place at the royal table. He concludes, "Would I still be right (*ûmah-yeš-lî 'ôd ṣᵉdāqâ*) in crying out to the king?" (v. 28[29], lit.; cf. Neh 2:20). Here, *ṣᵉdāqâ* looks like a loaded term, for Mephibosheth has some justification in looking for redress from David's hand, although it is not clear that this is what he is seeking. David's response is to divide the property in half between Ziba and Mephibosheth; the latter's concern seems wholly to be with David's welfare, as he responds, "Let (Ziba) take everything, now that my lord the king has arrived home safely" (19:30[31]). Ironies abound, as Absalom, who intended to give *ṣdq* to all (15:4) has been defeated, while David rewards deceit, unable, it seems, to recognize loyalty.

(d) The sense of innocent implied in several contexts already shades towards the forensic sense of *ṣdq*. Mention has already been made of Absalom's declaration: "If only I were appointed judge in the land! Then everyone who has a complaint or case (*rîb ûmišpāṭ*) could come to me and I would see that he gets justice (*wᵉhiṣdaqtîw*)" (2 Sam 15:4). This is a clearly forensic setting, with Absalom promising fair dealing in law where (it is implied) his father did not. But is this to be taken as a delocutive (thus, "I would declare him innocent") or otherwise (e.g., McCarter: "I would adjudicate it in his favour," *II Samuel*, 353)? Probably, given the setting of Absalom sitting in the gate, the former is more likely: the judge proclaims the innocence of the suitor.

The obligation to dispense justice (*ṣdq*) remains part of royal ideology throughout the history of Israelite and Judaean monarchy. In contrast to Absalom's criticism, the report of the consolidation of David's rule in 2 Sam 8:15 finds him "doing what was just and right (*mišpāṭ ûṣ^{e}dāqâ*) for all his people." This is the first time that this set pair appears in the OT (see also: 1 Kgs 10:9; 1 Chron 18:14; 2 Chron 9:8; Ps 99:4; Isa 9:7[6]; 32:16; 33:5; 59:14; Jer 4:2; 9:24[23]; 22:3, 15; 23:5; 33:15; Ezek 18:5, 19, 21, 27; 33:14, 16, 19; 45:9; Amos 5:7, 24; cf. M. Weinfeld, 228-46). Since the pair forms a hendiadys, precise and distinct meanings for each of the partners should not be sought. Rather, together they represent the ideal of social justice, an ideal lauded by the Queen of Sheba concerning Solomon's kingship in 1 Kgs 10:9, forming part of the excellence of his impressive administration.

Such ideals are also at the heart of instructions concerning the exercise of law in the various legal codes in the Pentateuch (Exod 23:7-8; Lev 19:15; Deut 16:18-20; 25:1 [as preface to law on flogging]; cf. 1:16). The importance of *ṣdq* for the legal adjudication of communal life is emphasized in 16:20 with its insistent "follow justice and justice alone (*ṣedeq ṣedeq tirdōp*)." The just/righteous (*ṣaddîq*) and innocent (*nāqî*) are joined in Exod 23:7; these terms are closely related, but not synonymous, the latter term being more restricted (they occur together only here and Job 22:19; 27:17; Ps 94:21). Together they contrast with the wicked (*rāšā'*). Legal process is to give each of these their due; each of the three main passages include some warning against partiality or bribery. Commenting on Deut 16, D. Patrick (*OT Law*, 117) understands these injunctions to be "simple moral principles that everyone would know," and their enunciation here "to give them greater authority." The Lev legislation makes clear the communal aspect, present to some degree in each context. Lev 19:11-18, a sequence of negative injunctions, is especially concerned with life in community and the proper behavior of members of the community with each other (cf. Noth, *Leviticus*, 141-42). Thus, while the specific use of the term *ṣdq* here is in a legal context, it is actually controlling the *behavior* of those in a position to adjudicate legal claims, as the close connection to the love command in 19:17-18 further suggests. The contrast is thus with "doing injustice" (*'āwel*) rather than simply with guilt or innocence.

(e) Summary. These examples demonstrate the range of meaning for the *ṣdq* group in Heb. narrative and, to a lesser extent, legal contexts. *ṣdq* terminology indicates right behavior or status in relation to some standard of behavior accepted in the community. It also entails the adjudication of such behavior or status as well as the more abstract sense of some claim to it. Nowhere, however, is this standard made explicit, nor is covenant invoked as a ground or basis for *ṣdq*. If a special notion like covenant is assumed, it remains firmly in the background. The picture is rather one akin to natural law, where tacit assumptions about behavior are held in common, but nonetheless real for that. Even in the legal context of standards for judicial behavior, Patrick's comments cited above indicate the self-evident nature of the assumed standard.

2. With a term such as *righteousness* the theological content is often assumed or left only vaguely defined through overuse. Attention paid to the *non*theological uses contributes a fresh perspective when turning to uses of *ṣdq* that involve the deity. The patterns already seen in human interaction can be seen also in relations between God and humanity as well as in the (rare) statements in narrative settings that describe God directly. Predictably, this latter group comes almost exclusively—there appears to be only one exception—from embedded hymns and prayers.

(a) "Right action" in narrative contexts involving Yahweh most often depicts human behavior in divine estimate. The dialogue between Abraham and Yahweh in

Gen 18:22-33 provides a dramatic example. The discussion turns on the question posed by Abraham, "Will you sweep away the righteous (*ṣaddîq*) with the wicked (*rāšā'*)?" (v. 23). The content of this wickedness is spelled out earlier in the tale: "Now the men of Sodom were wicked (*rā'îm*) and were sinning greatly against the LORD" (Gen 13:13). In narrative terms, Abraham's leading question and his continued pushing Yahweh to specify numbers seem to be based in the tour of inspection that Yahweh intends to carry out (as announced in v. 21). The point is to see if the standard of behavior is really as bad as it seems to be (cf. 11:5). Even though Yahweh is appealed to as the judge who must do justice (*mišpāṭ*, v. 25), the adjudication is not over guilt and innocence in forensic terms, for there is no doubt that some bad behavior is taking place (v. 20). Rather, the question is one of standards of behavior and whether those who have acted rightly must be punished as the wicked will be.

A similar pattern may be observed in Deut 9:4-6, in Moses' words at the brink of crossing the Jordan. The Israelites will quickly possess the land, but they are not to suppose that this success is on account of (prep. *b*) their *ṣᵉdāqâ*; rather the reverse is true: Yahweh is driving out the nations because of (prep. *b*) the wickedness (*riš'â*) of the nations. The parallel with "integrity" (NIV; "uprightness of your heart") in v. 5 suggests that the people are claiming reward for good behavior. On the other hand, the Aram. royal inscriptions use *bṣdqh* to provide a basis for some consequence (see above). There it is used in conjunction with wisdom terminology, and controversy persists about the precise meaning of the term (righteousness? loyalty? legitimate successor?). Here there can be little doubt that virtue is in mind. Moses' sermon goes on to recall the episode of the golden calf (Deut 9:7-21) and other examples of rebellion to reinforce the point made in vv. 4-6: Not only did Israel's good behavior not win them the land, they did not, according to Moses, even behave rightly in the first place. Yahweh acts for quite different reasons.

There is reward for *ṣᵉdāqâ* in David's psalm of 2 Sam 22:21 and 25 (= Ps 18:20[21], 24[25]—note that while the Samuel passage uses *ṣedāqâ*, the parallels in Ps 18 use *ṣedeq,* suggesting the basic interchangeability of these terms). David's swan song, as it is used in 2 Sam 22, claims this successful career for a life of *ṣdq*, although the more immediate context (and that of the psalm's superscription) associates Yahweh's beneficent action on David's behalf with deliverance from enemies. The content given to David's *ṣdq* has to do with keeping Yahweh's laws and decrees. (The concentric pattern of this section of the psalm focuses on v. 23: vv. A/A' = vv. 21/25—recompense/*ṣdq*; B/B' = vv. 22/24—general statement/outcome [repeated *šmr*]; C = v. 23—specific "judgments and decree" of Yahweh.) This is the first of the passages considered that explicitly relate the standard of behavior to divine law. The possibility of deut. influence on these verses (so some commentators of both 2 Sam 22 and Ps 18) is of interest in light of Deut 9:4-6. Both carry with them the notion that right behavior, *ṣdq*, can lead to reward from Yahweh.

The hymnic context leads towards a consideration of two hymns—the first, the song of Moses, describes Yahweh's behavior in terms of *ṣdq*. Deut 32:4 is straightforward in its declaration of Yahweh's "name" and greatness. The "ways of the LORD," which David kept (2 Sam 22:22), are here positively described in terms of faithfulness (*'ᵉmûnâ*) and uprightness (*yāšār*), and Yahweh is a *ṣaddîq*. The context, which describes Yahweh's actions towards his people and their reciprocal treatment of him, suggests that *ṣaddîq* here is one who acts rightly.

The other passage is more difficult, containing a number of obscure terms. The song of Deborah (Judg 5) celebrates victory over enemies. Judg 5:11 describes a group extolling (*tnh*, pi.) the *ṣidqôt yhwh* and the *ṣidqôt pirzōnô*, whatever may be intended in this latter group; they are in all likelihood human agents. But how should *ṣidqôt* be understood here? The pl. of *ṣᵉdāqâ* is used 14x, 3 of these cases in construct with *Yhwh* (Judg 5:11; 1 Sam 12:7; Mic 6:5; cf. Ps 103:6; Dan 9:16). One could simply render this "righteous acts" with the NIV, but the consistent context allows for a further nuance for *ṣidqôt* in these cases: On view in these passages are Yahweh's actions (or also, as here, human actions) that have saved or delivered Israel, so that one sometimes sees the translation "victories" (e.g., Boling, *Judges*, 111; but cf. Barr, 380, who fleetingly questions such a meaning). The RSV offers "triumphs" in Judg 5:11—presumably to allow for identical meaning in both parts of the parallelistic line—and "saving deeds/acts" in 1 Sam 12:7 and Mic 6:5, a nuance seen frequently in the Ps and Isa (see below). Certainly here "acting rightly" and on behalf of people in distress makes such translations appealing and more attractive than the colorless NIV.

One confession, ambiguous as regards action or being as well as on other levels, is that of Pharaoh in Exod 9:27, "The LORD is in the right (*yhwh haṣṣaddîq*), and I and my people are in the wrong." Such a rendering suggests a forensic interest, but this is not the case. Syntactically, "the LORD" and "I and my people" are the pred. (cf. Joüon-Muraoka § 137l; Gibson, *Syntax*, § 49[3]), thus, "The *ṣaddîq* (righteous one) is Yahweh; the wicked ones (*hārᵉšā'îm*) are me and my people" might better suggest the flavor of the Hebrew. Pharaoh's failure to let the Israelites leave stands in contrast to Yahweh's justified action in sending the plagues. Moses is not convinced (Exod 9:30), but the confession demonstrates that the main protagonists are Yahweh and Pharaoh rather than Moses and Pharaoh. In any event, Pharaoh seems to concur with the evaluation of Deut 32:4 regarding Yahweh's righteous behavior.

(b) The declarations concerning Yahweh's actions using *ṣdq* shade naturally towards reflections on his being or character. Some ambiguity attaches to Exod 9:27, as well as the confessions of Neh 9:33 and Dan 9:14 which, while predicating *ṣaddîq* to Yahweh, seem to have his actions rather than his being or character in view. The case of the confessions in 2 Chron 12:6; Ezra 9:15; and Neh 9:8 (cf. Ps 119:137; 129:4; also 2 Kgs 10:9 above) is more clear. Here the construction is *ṣaddîq yhwh* or *ṣaddîq 'attâ*, and there is an inevitable contrast between the nature of God and that of his wayward people. This is especially pronounced in Ezra 9:6-15, where, in the space of this short prayer, *'ašmâ* is used 4x and *'āwôn* 3x. While in some sense Yahweh's actions must remain in view, the focus seems rather to be on the divine character.

> They have broken the commandments, which are perhaps regarded as an integral part of the covenant between God and people, while he has remained consistent in his adherence to that relationship. This little phrase thus constitutes the highest form of worship: an acknowledgment of God, even though at the same time it accepts that the worshiper has forfeited his or her right to live before God. *God is thus praised solely for who he is*, and not merely for what the worshiper

hopes to gain from him. (Williamson, *Ezra-Nehemiah*, 138; emphasis added)

It is worth noting that this usage is from the later, postexilic stages of biblical literature.

(c) The aspect of God as judge has already been implied above in discussion of reward for right behavior and brings forensic interests into focus (God as righteous judge, combining the two notions, is clearest in the Ps; see below). Such interests arise in the deut. language of Solomon's dedicatory prayer in the temple (1 Kgs 8). Verses 31-32 deal with sin against a neighbor. Yahweh is called upon to judge (*špṭ*), rendering to the guilty or innocent their due. The condemnation of the wicked (*l^e^haršîa' rāšā'*) is exactly paralleled by the "righteousing" (cf. *Compact OED*, s.v. "righteous") of the righteous (*ûl^e^haṣdîq ṣaddîq*). This entreaty presupposes (v. 31) a case of accusation of some crime for which there is no proof. An oath is taken, leading to the petition of v. 32. The NIV is insistent on this interpretation, rendering the triple use of *ṣdq* as "declare innocent" (vb.), "not guilty" (*ṣaddîq*), and "innocence" (*ṣ^e^dāqâ*). What is left unclear in the prayer is the nature of the consequences for guilt or innocence.

Reward for righteous behavior in a theological setting is most potently expressed in Gen 15:6, a passage that has attracted a great deal of attention. In recent decades discussion has been influenced by von Rad's interpretation of the verse in terms of cultic formulae. Von Rad argued that "credit" or "reckon" (*ḥšb*) derives its particular nuance in this passage from priestly usage, and that the revolutionary aspect of dealings between Yahweh and Abraham resides in the cutting out of the priestly mediation: "There is no cultic intermediary, no priest to speak as the mouthpiece of Yahweh" (1966, 129; critique in Oeming, whose positive proposal is to be rejected). As is often the case in form-critical investigation, von Rad's conclusions rest on a reconstructed *Sitz im Leben* that draws its inspiration from loosely related texts, in this case especially Lev 7:18b and Ezek 18:5-9; but the former does not refer to *ṣdq*, and the latter does not use *ḥšb*! Others (Kline, Hahn, Schmid) see in the verse an anticipation of the Pauline notion of justification by faith. Schmid, who thinks the verse is relatively late (postdeuteronomistic), argues "that righteousness, and the life it makes possible, is to be received as the gift of God, and that the foundation for life is not human behavior, but rather the divine gift of righteousness" (408). According to Schmid, this explains the passivity of Abraham in the passage and excludes interpretations that locate righteousness in *Abraham's* faith.

Although the construction *ṣ^e^dāqâ* plus prep. *l* has been noticed in this connection, insufficient weight has been placed upon it. Westermann (223) mentions Deut 24:13—in which return of a poor man's cloak taken in pledge before nightfall "will be righteousness for you"—as a means of "broadening" von Rad's interpretation. (Notice that the NIV here is unnecessarily neutral in translating the clause generically—"it will be regarded as a righteous act"—and fails to grant any force to *l^e^kâ*, "to/for you.") But this verse (cf. also Deut 6:25; Ps 106:31) does more than this. It obviates the necessity for a cultic *Sitz im Leben* such as that insisted upon by von Rad, and it undermines the notion that, whatever counts as "righteousness" here, it is not any "act" of faith on Abraham's part, as some who hold to a Pauline trajectory would suppose. Whether the keeping of the law (Deut 6:25), the return of the cloak (24:13), the brave intervention of Phineas (Ps 106:30-31), or Abram's [*sic*] belief (Gen 15:6)—all share the notion that an appropriate action has been recognized and approved by the Deity.

Commentators often note that in Gen 15 Abram is struggling to understand how Yahweh's promises concerning an heir can be fulfilled. The promise has, in fact, been queried and countered in 15:2-3. Verse 6 forms the positive counterpart to the previous negative reaction, and this acceptance of the divine promise is affirmed in the accounting by Yahweh of a "righteous" act (cf. Moberly's extensive discussion). In spite of the reluctance on the part of some to see Abram's *act* of faith being rewarded here, no doubt at least in part due to dogmatic constraints, this remains the most cogent reading of the text (*pace* Schmid).

(d) *Summary*. Theological righteousness, then, is closely related to righteousness in an interpersonal context. The spectrum of meanings seen in 1(e) correspond well with those examined where Yahweh is involved. This study of prose/narrative passages prepares the way for the more poetic and theological reflections in Psalms and the Prophets and finds extensive corroboration in the Wisdom literature.

3. *Wisdom literature*. The concentration of uses of *ṣdq* terms is high in the biblical Wisdom literature—not surprising in light of the sages' interest in being right and acting rightly. To compare: of the books examined to this point, Deut uses *ṣdq* most often: 18x of 523x, or roughly 3.4 percent of the total (in Gen it appears 15x; 1-2 Chron only 6x). By contrast, Job, Prov, and Eccl have a combined total of 140x, or 26.7 percent of the occurrences in HB as a whole. This is nearly identical as the usage in the Ps (139x). But given Psalms' greater length (150 chs. *vs.* only 85 in Job/Prov/Eccl), the frequency of *ṣdq* terms in the Wisdom literature is significantly greater than that of the Psalms.

(a) Job. Among other things, the book of Job is about justice, both the possibility of righteous mortals and the nature of divine justice. In attending to the uses of *ṣdq* an interesting pattern emerges: there are no occurrences outside the poetic dialogues of chs. 3-41. This is not for lack of opportunity, for the descriptions of the pious Job as "blameless and upright" (*tām w^{e}yāšār*, 1:1, 8; 2:3) could readily be augmented by a claim for Job's righteousness. This curious feature may be explained several ways. It could be that the term's distinctive usage in the dialogues precludes its more generic use in the prose frame, but this is unlikely. It could be that the prose and the poetry have different origins and concerns—the problematic nature of the interrelationship of prose and poetry has long been noted.

The prologue and epilogue seem to be driven by a different question than the dramatic dialogue. The leading question of the prose frame is put by the Satan in 1:9: "Does Job fear God for nothing?" A good question, and one that ultimately receives a positive answer in Job's capitulation—motivated only by his deepened understanding of the God he worships (42:2-6)—which seems to win divine approval (42:7). Only then is he restored to his former prosperous lifestyle. The leading question of the dialogue is put by Eliphaz in ch. 4. Eliphaz echoes the Satan's question ("Should not your piety be your confidence / and your blameless ways your hope?" 4:6), but this seems to be taken for granted and a new question takes over: "Can mortal man be righteous before God? Can a man be pure before his Maker?" (4:17 RSV; the NIV wrongly understands the prep. *min* to be comparative). This question provides the focus for a consideration of *ṣdq* in the dialogues of Job.

It is widely noted in commentaries that this question comes as the climax of the visionary buildup in 4:12-16; v. 17 provides the content of what the voice in the vision utters. Verses 7-8 seem to prepare the way for a positive answer to the question: One *can* be "innocent" and "upright" (4:7) and live. But the response to the supernatural visitor's question is negative: all are subject to occasional error, even heavenly beings. But, as Clines (132-33) points out, the suffering of Job hardly corresponds to the degree of "error" into which he might have fallen. It is not that Eliphaz—or his visionary interlocutor—here so much *questions* the doctrine of retribution (so Clines, 133) as accounts for it. The implication is thoroughly relational: Error brings separation from the deity; right status ensures life (cf. 4:7-8).

The possibility of human *ṣdq* before God is considered at length by Job in ch. 9. There are strong forensic overtones in this chapter (cf. *rîb* [→ # 8190], v. 3), coloring Job's echo of Eliphaz's question: "But how can a mortal be righteous (*ṣdq*) before God?" (9:2b). Appropriately, some uses of *ṣdq* terms in Job are well translated "innocent" (9:15, 20; 34:5; cf. 22:19; 27:17, with parallel *nāqî*). But these reflections raise another concern: the relationship of divine *ṣdq* to divine power. Job goes on in ch. 9 to recount the awesome power of God, concluding that such a being would not deign to answer him (v. 3), nor could he be coerced to do so (vv. 14, 19). No court or advocate exists to bring them together for adjudication (vv. 32-35). Clines wonders whether Job charges God with "cosmic injustice" (225, citing Gordis, *Book of God and Man*, 80) in ch. 9[10] and decides not: "the speech is best read as a protest that it is hopeless for a person to seek *vindication* (viz. *ṣdq*) from God. For—if God is withholding vindication, as he is in Job's case—no one can be in a position to compel God to give one anything, not even the vindication one deserves" (225-26). But surely, Job would argue, this in itself is unjust and the leading factor in the friends' assuming and developing the notion of Job's guilt. (Clines later notes: "The issue is Job's vindication rather than God's righteousness, though the two are not entirely distinct," 226.) It is not, of course, a matter of power, for this Job concedes at various places in several ways. However, it seems to be assumed in the book that demonstrations of God's power are an indication of his being "right" ("might makes right"; cf. Zophar in 11:7-12; Job in 17:9; Elihu in 34:17; 37:23; possibly all of the Yahweh speeches, chs. 38-41). Thus, Job's lack of vindication is itself evidence that God does indeed pervert justice (*contra* Bildad in 8:3).

So to what does 9:2a refer ("Indeed, I know that this is true")? It seems, at first blush, to suggest that Job is assenting to Bildad's argument of ch. 8, that it is impossible for God to pervert justice (8:3). But Job goes on to posit and explore a basic contradiction, one that arises out of his experience: God is not *supposed* to pervert justice; but this is, in fact, happening. It is an example, then, of cognitive dissonance, and it is no wonder that Job is pushed, *in extremis*, into asserting his own innocence against God's apparent injustice. If, for others, the working equation is that "might equals right," for Job it cannot be the case that both God and Job, in this situation, are *ṣdq* at the same time.

Job, therefore, maintains that he has acted rightly and insists on his own right status against God's seeming indictment: "I will never admit that you are in the right (*ḥālîlâ lî 'im-'aṣdîq 'etkem*); till I die, I will not deny my integrity. I will maintain my righteousness (*b^{e}ṣidqātî*) and never let go of it; my conscience will not reproach me as long as I live" (27:5-6). Such is Job's close relationship to *ṣdq* that he enjoys a reciprocal relationship with it: not only does it describe his character, but his character embodies *ṣdq*. In his summation (29:11-17), Job contradicts Eliphaz's assessment of his life and character (22:6-9). The NIV misinterprets the crucial lines of 29:14 in offering: "I put on righteousness as my clothing; justice was my robe and turban." In line v. 14a, the NIV does not give enough weight to *wayyilbāšēnî*, lit. "and it was clothed (stative) with me" (cf. Driver/Gray, Pope). This is a much stronger statement of Job's *ṣdq* than the NIV allows in representing the vb. in v. 14a with "as my clothing." This is a reciprocal relationship, in which Job is clothed with *ṣdq*, and *ṣdq* is clothed with Job. Likewise, in v. 14b, the NIV undervalues the weight Job attaches to his *mišpāṭ* (justice) by applying the 1 sing. suff. on *mišpāṭî* to the "robe and turban." Rather, it should read "like a robe and turban was my justice." That is, v. 14b carries forward the notion of v. 14a that Job's integrity is the garment. Righteousness and justice are not the metaphorical garments throughout, as in the NIV. This, then, is a strong claim to both right behavior and right status, the assertion of which is the whole point of Job's closing speech.

The Elihu speeches (chs. 32-37) seem especially concerned with *ṣdq*, used 11x in his speech in addition to two occurrences in the introduction (32:1-2). Here the sense is generally that of vindicate, justify, or prove to be right. Elihu's angry outburst is motivated by the sense that Job was "justifying himself rather than God" (32:2), and in this analysis he was exactly right. A key use of the term appears in 33:12; once Elihu has offered his *apologia* for speaking and presented a precis of the debate to that point—in particular that Job is innocent, yet is condemned by God (33:8-11)—he announces: "But I tell you, in this you are not right (*hen-zō't lō'-ṣādaqtā*), for God is greater than man" (33:12). "In this" must mean Job's claims to innocence and God's perversion of justice (33:8-11); that is, the combination of both factors as packaged in Elihu's summary is in view.

"You are not right" (NIV) sounds as if it could mean, "You are not correct." There seem to be at least three possibilities here. Is Job: (a) not correct? (b) not justified? or (c) not vindicated? The first (a) is the simple factual level (and is probably implied automatically in the other two alternatives) and is echoed in 33:32 (if v. 32b is translated as "Speak, for I desire to set you right"); (b) means Job is out of place (colloquially, "out of line") in offering such a view; (c) means that in making his case in this way, Job has not cleared his own name (cf., e.g., 27:1-6). Elihu goes on to challenge Job's assumptions that God does not speak to mortals and that sin is the only reason for divine affliction. The latter point, while strongly suggesting itself (e.g., in 33:17, where suffering is clearly preventative), is still somewhat tenuous, for Elihu can still speak (e.g., in v. 27) of admitting *ḥṭ'*. The most likely option for 33:12, then, is (b): Job has no right to speak this way, not unlike the rude child who speaks insultingly to his or her elders and betters. These notions are also picked up in 34:5-6, 16-20; 35:2-8; 36:6-7; 37:23.

In this consideration of *ṣdq* in Job it is clear that a standard of behavior is implied, but—as in the prose material already examined—the standard remains implicit rather than explicit. There is no appeal to divine law or some external rule of behavior, in spite of such overtly ethical passages as 15:14 and 25:4; nor might such be expected in this non-Israelite context. Only Elihu approaches this notion in his claim to divine inspiration for his insights (ch. 32; cf. 36:3). That there is some agreed standard of behavior is obvious from the disagreements between Job and his friends about Job's conduct (cf. 22:6-9; 29:11-17). One must act in accordance with this (tacit?) standard (i.e., act rightly) in order to be accorded right status before God. However, unlike the clear answer given to the Satan's question (1:9; 42:7), the book remains equivocal about the question posed by Eliphaz's supernatural interlocutor (4:17).

(b) *Proverbs*. More than any other book, Prov prefers one *ṣdq* term dramatically more than the others; this is the adj., *ṣaddîq*. Of the 92x the root occurs in the book, 66x (71.7 percent) the adj. is used. This immediately suggests Prov's interest in the nature of the "one who is *ṣdq*" rather than in abstract conceptions of *ṣdq*. This impression is further strengthened by the observation that 53x in Prov *ṣdq* terms are used in parallelism with *rš'*, act wickedly (→ # 8399), terms; noteworthy in the distribution of these is the single occurrence in chs. 1-9 (in 3:33) as against twenty-five occurrences in chs. 10-12.

McKane (*Proverbs*, 420; cf. 15-16) contends that "the antithesis of *ṣaddîq* and *rāšā'* is a dogmatic classification and that it is expressive of a premise of Yahwistic piety, namely, the doctrine of theodicy. By a doctrine of theodicy I mean the assertion that God enforces a moral order in relation to individuals by rewarding the righteous man and punishing the wicked one." This assessment by McKane is surely correct, although one need not follow him in thinking that this is necessarily a late development. Such correlations in life with the approval (or not) of God (or the gods) are found as early as the third millennium (e.g., *The Instruction of Ptahhotep*), and one need not wait until the Maccabean period for such an articulation to arrive in Heb. literature—in spite of McKane's sweeping aside of such observations (*Proverbs*, 16). The *ṣaddîq* is one who is honest (10:11, 31-32; 13:5; cf. 12:17; 16:13 with *ṣedeq*), generous (21:26), steadfast and bold (11:8-10; 12:7, 12; 14:32; 18:10; 24:15-16; 28:1), loyal (12:5), merciful and just (12:10; 29:7; cf. 31:9), pleasing to God (3:33; 15:28; cf. 15:9; 21:3 with *ṣ^{e}dāqâ*); in short, all his ways lead to life (10:16; 11:19, 30; 12:28; 16:31; 21:21). Significantly, for the sages of Proverbs, the *ṣaddîq* is one who is also wise (*ḥākām*; cf. on Ps 37 below, and Hurvitz, "*ṣaddîq* = 'wise'"), as suggested by the parallelism in 9:9 and 23:24 (cf. Eccl 7:16; 9:1; also 1 En 48:1). The wicked one (*rāšā'*) is equally described by the antonyms of these qualities. This language is often cast in terms of the "way" (*derek*; → # 2006) or "path" (*'ōraḥ*; → # 784) taken by the righteous or wicked, providing a source for the later development of the theme of the "two ways" (2:9, 20; 4:18-19; 8:20; cf. Brock, "The Two Ways," who does not mention these passages in his discussion of HB sources).

The *ṣaddîq*'s relationship to wealth and prosperity in Prov remains problematic. The case as it is usually understood is set out in Prov 13:21: "Misfortune pursues the sinner, but prosperity is the reward of the righteous," or, better, with the NJPSV, "but the righteous are well rewarded" for *y^{e}šallem-tôb*. Such straightforward correlation between prosperity/reward and the good is typically associated with some strands of wisdom thinking (e.g., 15:6). However, a hint of ambivalence towards wealth is introduced by warning against reliance on it (11:4, 28), and against greed for wealth (21:26). In turn, the reward given to the righteous is not great prosperity, but sufficiency (10:3; cf. 16:8). This begins to nuance the "doctrine of theodicy" articulated by McKane (above): These sayings recognize that the wicked (*rāšā'*) do, in fact, have earthly possessions beyond those of the *ṣaddîq*, while at the same time expressing confidence that those who act rightly will, at least, live. (For a nuanced and comprehensive examination of this theme see Whybray, 1990.)

McKane's "doctrine" is, perhaps, most clearly expressed at 11:30-31. Here a concept of payment, for good or ill, is located "on earth" (*bā'āreṣ*). Context—or rather the lack of it—dogs interpretation of these sayings. The "absence" of Yahweh is remarkable in ch. 11; he appears explicitly only in 11:1 and 20. Are we to assume that it is Yahweh who is rewarding and punishing? or, that these results are the inevitable outworking of the order of things in the world? The constraint placed on interpretation by Prov 1-9 tends toward the former. But if these sayings are taken piecemeal, then the latter could equally hold true. No doubt the impression left by the collection as a whole is that Yahweh controls the retributive process that judges all of one's activity (15:9). Still, little comment about the righteous one is specifically "religious," which remains an exceptional implication of the prophetic-sounding 21:3 (cf. 1 Sam 15:22; Ps 51:19[21]; also Hos 6:6).

The association of the *ṣaddîq* with justice arises in two particular ways in Prov. First, the proper administration of justice is the domain of the *ṣaddîq* (Prov 17:15, 26; 18:5, 17; 24:24; 25:26; cf. also 8:15-16; 29:27). Of these, 18:17 sounds remarkably "secular," and McKane classifies it in his A group. (The NIV translation is typical: "The first to present his case seems right (*ṣaddîq*), till another comes forward and questions him." Although "right" is an acceptable translation equivalent in this context, it is unusual in representing *ṣaddîq*; we might usually expect, "The first one is righteous in his case until....") Prov 18:17-19 is concerned with the arbitration of disputes, and McKane's comment that "these sentences are set in the framework of old wisdom and are concerned with the education of the individual for a successful and harmonious life" (***Proverbs***, 11) seems fair. This is not a case of contrast of right against wrong, or *ṣdq* against *rš'*. Rather, it is an appearance of "right" that lasts only up to the cross-examination in due legal process. Perversion of justice is given an explicitly theological assessment in 17:15 and is reminiscent of passages like Deut 25:1 (see above). The second association of the *ṣaddîq* with administration of justice has to do with government. A cluster of passages towards the end of the book relates to proper governance by the *ṣaddîq* (Prov 28:12; 29:2, 16; 31:9), a notion that is introduced in the prologue in the speech by Lady Wisdom (8:15-16). The *rāšā'* still provides the contrast: While the *ṣaddîq*'s rule leads to safety, prosperity, content, and joy, that of the *rāšā'* results in fear, oppression, misery, and discontent.

While the notion of *ṣedeq* and the activities of the *ṣaddîq* are directly related to divine approval, there is little explicit relationship of right action to specially revealed law. Rather, the transition from "secular" to "theological" aspects of the consideration of *ṣdq* in Proverbs is facilitated by the way in which Yahweh is seen to preside over, preserve, and approve the "natural" order of things in the world, an order in which inevitably those who are marked by *ṣdq* shall live, while death awaits those marked by *rš'*.

(c) *Ecclesiastes*. Qoheleth's attitude to *ṣdq* is not easy to discern. He grants a place to the *ṣaddîq* (one who does *ṣedeq*, or *ṭôb* (→ # 3202), cf. Eccl 7:20; 9:1-2), but equivocates on the value he attaches to this behavior and God's regard for it. In 7:15-16, 20, Qoheleth's words imply that, to some extent, the life of the *ṣaddîq* is unattainable, futile, and thus not worth the effort. Further, the "proper" outcomes following on righteous or wicked actions often fail, and the lot that should come to one goes instead to the other (8:14). Yet, Qoheleth seems able also to affirm that God still has all this under control (3:16-17; 9:1-2). This affirmation is qualified by the admission that, even if God is in control, human creatures remain ignorant of his dealings. All this leads to the typical interpretation of Qoheleth: moderation in all things is called for, and this includes the pursuit of a life of *ṣdq*. Whybray has mounted the argument that Qoheleth warns not against excessive righteousness in 7:16, but against *self*-righteousness, "the state of mind which claims actually to have achieved righteousness or perfection" (Whybray, 1978, 191). While such a reading is consonant with other statements in the book, it remains something of a *tour de force,* resting on a fairly atomistic reading of the text.

Despite the problems in wringing consistent sense from Qoheleth, we can be sure that he and his audience shared the notion that a life of *ṣdq* was approved and, in some way, upheld by God, and that good things should happen to good people. Qoheleth puzzles forthrightly with the obvious miscarriages of this assumed standard but maintains, perhaps anticipating the spirit of Pascal's famous wager, that erring on the side of right is to be preferred. The catalogue of balanced pairs in 9:1–2 (cf. the ancient Vrs.) line up the righteous, good, clean, pious (lit. "sacrificers"), against the wicked, evil (so LXX), unclean, and those who fail to sacrifice. Qoheleth does not tell us how one knows the standards by which to live, or where such standards might come from. If anything, Qoheleth works with a sense of "natural" law, taking this concept in a basic sense: A wise person understands through experience and observation what is "right."

4. *Psalms.* The *ṣdq* word group is employed more often in the Psalms than in any other book of the OT, appearing 139x and thus comprising about 26.6 percent of the total occurrences. The psalms are hymns and prayers addressed to God, and the psalmists reflect not only on their own *ṣdq*, but more often on God's *ṣdq* and what it means for their situation. Still, in a few places it means simply what is "right" (Ps 4:5[6]; 23:3; 51:19[21]; 58:1[2]) or "true" (52:3[5]).

Consideration of the *ṣaddîq* draws some psalms into the wisdom sphere. Ps 37 dominates this horizon (37:12, 16, 17, 21, 25, 29, 30, 32, 39), reflecting at length on the circumstances of the *ṣaddîq* and the *rāšā'*, especially emphasizing the ascendence of the former over the latter. God supports the *ṣaddîq* (55:22[23]; 58:10-11[11-12]), but equally the *ṣaddîq* is the one who depends on God. Ps 11 links the notion of God as refuge with the life of the righteous in contrast to the wicked (11:3, 5, 7). Ps 7:8-9[9-10] sets out the reciprocal movement between the God who is *ṣedeq* maintaining the cause of the *ṣaddîq* over against the *rāšā'*. Here, the psalmist's own *ṣdq* is the basis for the plea to God (cf. 4:1; 9:4[5]). To modern ears this can sound perilously like preening self-righteousness, but as Mays (*Psalms*, 64) points out, "It is the righteousness of the Lord that has called forth the righteousness and integrity of the psalmist." Those who live thus are also those who are called to praise God (33:1; cf. 32:11; 64:10[11]; 68:3; 97:11-12).

The Psalms show another side to the lot of the *ṣaddîq*. "Many are the afflictions of the righteous" (RSV) confidently asserts Ps 34:19[20] (better than the NIV's "A righteous man may have many troubles"). The notion that the one who does right is also the one who is oppressed and visited by troubles is found elsewhere in the Psalms. Not only is this equation implied (146:8), but the lamenter in 119:75 states that the affliction (the result of judgment) of one who fears the Lord has a divine origin (cf. 69:26[27]). So 143:1-2 in its plea for God to side with the psalmist confesses that "no one living is righteous before you" (*lō'-yiṣdaq lᵉpāneykā kol-ḥāy*). This in turn translates into a concern for justice for the oppressed (103:6) and even the demand for it (82:3). The latter text has its own problems (in identifying both speaker and referent), but its call for justice in the divine realm to work itself out in care of the needy remains clear.

On the other hand, *ṣdq* also indicates the lot rightly due to the one whose behavior conforms to the desired standard. Ps 24 asks, "Who may ascend the hill of the Lord?" (24:3), and answers: the one who is pure and faithful to the living God (24:4). "He will receive blessing (*bᵉrākâ*) from the LORD and *ṣᵉdāqâ* from God his Savior" (24:5). Modern translations commonly offer "vindication" here, in spite of the fact that this one is in no need of "vindication"! Nor can this slot be filled with "right action/status" as something bestowed on this pious individual. Kraus (*Psalms 1-59*, 314) thinks that of the two parallel, "synonymous" terms, *ṣᵉdāqâ* is the more "concrete" and here has a "clearly shaped meaning, viz., an emanation and declaration from Yahweh, understood in cultic terms: ... he who is declared 'righteous' thereby receives the blessing." The normally wooden LXX translator of the Psalms recognized the problem here, not offering his standard equivalent, *dikaiosynē*, but using rather *eleēmosynē*, mercy, a nuance of the *ṣdq* group that came to the fore towards the Hellenistic period. Something like "just reward" (so JPSV) must be understood here (cf. 18:20, 24[21, 25]; 58:10-11[11-12]). The *reception* of *ṣᵉdāqâ* from Yahweh is noteworthy. Here, the location in the temple (cf. the Amman Citadel Inscription) provides a natural association between *ṣdq* and cultic activity. Their relationship is reciprocal: pious acts result in *ṣdqh*; but only the *ṣdyq* may "ascend the hill of the LORD" (24:3).

Royal psalms make a firm link between the king and the exercise of *ṣdq,* which is itself related to divine *ṣdq* (72:1-3). Just as elsewhere in the Psalms God acts on behalf of his people, so too shall the king. In some way, this royal imitation of divine *ṣdq* accounts for the status the king enjoys (45:7[8]). Thus, maintaining the order of the community contributes to the stability of royal rule: the king's self-interest blends with the custody of his subjects. The exaltation of the king intertwines in a special way with community care in Ps 45:4[5] (following the lead of the LXX in understanding the awkward MT; cf. NIV "in behalf of truth, humility, and righteousness"). In the context of this psalm, the king's glorification in the royal wedding song comes to the fore. Kraus (*Psalms 1-59*, 455) comments: "Here the king appears as the helper of all the disfranchised and as the protector of the mode of existence that is faithful to the community." This theme, while implied (cf. again v. 7[8]), is submerged beneath the general aggrandizement of king as hero in which his mighty deeds are more about vanquishing his own enemies than supporting the cause of the oppressed.

The "twin" psalms, 111-12, provide a fulcrum between divine and human *ṣdq*, the former reflecting on God's works, the latter on the ways of the pious: 111:3, "Glorious and majestic are his deeds, and his righteousness endures forever" (*wᵉṣidqātô 'ōmedet lā'ad*); and 112:3, "Wealth and riches are in his house, and his righteousness endures forever" (= Heb. of 111:3b). If, as commentators Kraus and Tate maintain, this *ṣᵉdāqâ* refers to behavior that is consistent with the covenant, in what sense does it "endure forever"? Baethgen (*Die Psalmen*, 342) rejects the LXX rendering of *eleēmosynē* as "too narrow." He asserts, "The parallelism requires that we think of an acquired rather than an inherent quality. As in Ezek 18:20, *ṣ^e dāqâ* in vv. 3 and 9 is almost identical with "merit" [Verdienst] (cf. Tg.). We approach here a nuance of "generosity," such as that seen already in Prov; the results of *ṣdq* construed this way could, conceivably, be thought to be perpetual. Mays (*Psalms*, 360) finds the connections of Ps 111 and 112 to be "astonishing," since they posit of the *ṣaddîq* what has already been claimed in praise of Yahweh: "This correlation between the praise of the LORD and the commendation of the upright is the psalm's way of teaching that the works of the LORD can and should shape the life of the righteous.... Their goodness is godliness."

The apparent mixing of divine and human *ṣdq* continues into 112:4: "Even in darkness light dawns for the upright, *ḥannûn w^e raḥûm w^e ṣaddîq*." Kraus (*Psalms 1-59*, 364) believes it likely that v. 4b was originally a statement about Yahweh (for which there is both ms. and versional evidence). The RSV ("the LORD is gracious, merciful, and righteous") reflects this conviction as well; the NIV maintains MT ("for the gracious and compassionate and righteous man") and relegates the Vrs. to a note. Delitzsch (*Psalms* 3:200) solves the conundrum by noting that the attributes of v. 4b refer to God (cf. Exod 34:6) and suggests that the "light" that rises is God himself (cf. Baethgen, *Die Psalmen*, 342). Tate (*Psalms 51-100*, 94), on the other hand, relates these adjectives to the human plane, omitting the *waw* on *ṣaddîq* (with some Heb. mss.) and translating: "The righteous person is dutiful and affectionate." The conjunction of the adjectives is itself of interest, for it offers another matrix into which "right" behavior fits, while aligning human *ṣdq* in some way with divine *ṣdq*.

Divine *ṣdq* can inhabit a realm far beyond the earthly pale, as Ps 36:6[7] shows in its likening God's *ṣ^e dāqâ* to the "mountains of God" (RSV, *har^e rê-'ēl*). The combination of terms in 36:5-6a[6-7a] is remarkable:

Your love (*ḥesed*), O LORD, reaches to the heavens,
your faithfulness (*'^e mûnâ*) to the skies.
Your righteousness (*ṣ^e dāqâ*) is like the mighty mountains,
your justice (*mišpāṭ*) like the great deep.

The resonances with Canaanite mythical texts cannot be missed (*pace* Craigie, *Psalms 1-50*, 290, 292). At the same time, these qualities issue in the care of God's creation from greatest to least (36:6b-10[7b-11]). A similar collocation of terms is found in 85:10-13[11-14], where the result is the fertility of the land, bringing life to God's faithful people.

God's *ṣ^e dāqâ*, more often than the psalmist's own, becomes the basis on which favor is sought. The most common context for this language is that of the psalmists' prayer for refuge or deliverance from the enemies (e.g., 31:1[2]). Ps 143:1-2 (already noted above) uses the inevitable lack of human *ṣdq* as a foil to invoke God's action on the psalmist's behalf in "faithfulness" (*'^e mûnâ*) and *ṣ^e dāqâ*, the repeated request in v. 11 providing a frame around the psalm. Ps 5 sees the *ṣaddîq* in a cultic context looking for help from God (cf. comment on Ps 24, above): To be led into Yahweh's *ṣ^e dāqâ* (v. 8[9]) results in life for the psalmist and consequent punishment for the enemy.

The examples already adduced suggest that the figure of God as judge looms large in the use of *ṣdq* in the Psalms, both on the personal (e.g., Ps 9:4[5]) and national or universal (e.g., 9:8[9]) levels. Ps 9 is especially noteworthy for its piling up of related terms: in parallel with *ṣedeq*, 9:4[5] uses *mišpāṭ* (# 5477) and *dîn* (# 1907), while 9:8[9] includes *špṭ* (# 9149) as well as *dîn* (# 1906) and *mēšārîm* (# 4797). Ps 50:6 aligns God's *ṣdq* directly with his activity as *šōpēṭ* in the general context of the cult and the theophanic visitation of the deity. The setting looks like a tribunal, with the heavens bearing witness to the right status of this judge (cf. 97:6). Kraus (*Psalms 1-59*, 492) finds in *ṣedeq* here "(the) actual sense of justice" in forensic terms. God's role as universal judge comes to the fore in the praise psalms of Yahweh the King in 96:13, 98:9, and 99:4, where again *mēšārîm* joins *ṣedeq* and *ṣᵉdāqâ* in the latter two cases. Forensic overtones are present in 69:27[28], where the *ṣaddîq* prays that his enemies may bear their own guilt and not "come into your *ṣᵉdāqâ*." NIV offers for v. 27b "do not let them share in your salvation," while RSV gives the forensic nuance with "may they have no acquittal from thee" (cf. Baethgen, *Die Psalmen*, 217).

The difference between NIV and RSV at 69:27[28] over the equivalent given to *ṣᵉdāqâ* is not an uncommon discrepancy in translations of the Psalter. Many times, *ṣdq* language is used to refer to the action of the deity on behalf of the psalmist. As noted above in discussion of Judg 5:11, *ṣdq* performed on behalf of those in distress can mean something like vindication or salvation (as a rule, the NIV prefers generic "righteousness" in these contexts). Sometimes the language found in the immediate context makes this nuance obvious, as with the use of *plṭ* (71:2), *nṣl* (51:14[16]; 71:2), or *tᵉšû'â* (40:10[11]; 51:14[16]; 71:15). However, this distinction is not always clear, and commentators and modern Vrs. differ frequently over where this meaning is to be discerned. Ps 103:17 provides a good case in point. This psalm is wholly concerned to reflect on God's beneficent actions (cf. 103:6) and offers God praise for them (note connection of 103:8-10 with Exod 34:6-7). Both NIV and RSV offer "and his righteousness [*ṣᵉdāqâ*] to his children's children" for 103:17b. The commentaries, however, rightly tend to find an "extended" meaning for *ṣᵉdāqâ* here, due in part to the frequent mention of *ḥesed* (vv. 4, 8, 11, 17) and *rḥm* (vv. 4, 8, 13): e.g., Baethgen (*Die Psalmen*, 310), noting association with eternal mercy, offers "(helping) righteousness"; Allen (*Psalms 101-150*, 18), "vindication"; Kraus (*Psalms 60-150*, 289), "salvation."

Ps 40:9-10[10-11] is remarkable for its varying of *ṣedeq* and *ṣᵉdāqâ*: v. 9[10], "I proclaim *ṣedeq*..."; v. 10[11], "I do not hide your *ṣᵉdāqâ*..." NIV translates both of these by "righteousness," while RSV offers "deliverance" and "saving help" respectively. "Right action" here involves moving someone from a situation of vulnerability to security. The fluidity with which the psalmist moves from thanksgiving for deliverance to petition in crisis is channeled through this declaration of God's right action on behalf of the psalmist, and the hope (v. 11[12]) that God will also openly support the psalmist in return. Although Kraus translates with "righteousness," his commentary glosses: "Yahweh's 'righteousness' was in Israel no norm, no principle of justice, but deed, bestowal of salvation, proof of his faithfulness of promise and partnership" (*Psalms 1-59*, 427). A rough estimate would see the following verses carrying this sense: 22:31[32]; 24:5; 35:24, 27; 36:10[11]; 37:6; 40:9-10[10-11]; 48:10[11]; 51:14[16]; 65:5[6]; 71:2, 15-16; 88:12[13]; 98:2; 103:6, 17. It is worth noting that as the concentration of lament psalms thin out as the Psalter unfolds, so too does this meaning for *ṣedeq*/*ṣᵉdāqâ*.

In the Psalms, the *ṣaddîq* is one who lives in a way pleasing to God, but God's response is not neatly reciprocal. The *ṣaddîq* is also one who is oppressed, sometimes, it seems, by God himself. Still, there is no other source for life, and so the plea goes forth for *ṣdq* to obtain, and for God's own *ṣdq* to result in, the security and beneficence of the *ṣaddîq* who prays these psalms. Royal psalms offer some consonance between divine and human realms as both earthly and heavenly kings are called upon to exercise *ṣdq*. *ṣdq* works when people conform to God's standards (cf. 19:9[10]; 119:7, 62, 106, 164), and when God maintains the cause of those who live this way.

5. *Prophets*. Given the concerns of the writing prophets, it is no surprise that their use of *ṣdq* revolves around the maintenance of relationship between God and people. Statistically, *ṣdq* terms appear less frequently in these books than one might suppose. In Jer, the largest prophetic book, *ṣdq* terms appear 18x, the same total as Deut, a much smaller book. Ezek has it 43x (found in twenty-seven verses, which are in only nine passages!); Isaiah has the lion's share with 81x.

(a) Eighth-century prophets. Although references are few in the eighth-century minor prophets, each of them uses *ṣdq* language in a distinctive fashion. Amos consistently relates *ṣᵉdāqâ* or the *ṣaddîq* to issues of social justice. The *ṣaddîq* is aligned with the poor oppressed: in Israel "they sell the *ṣaddîq* for silver, and the needy (*'ebyôn*) for a pair of sandals" (Amos 2:6b; 5:12). The dreaded "day of the LORD" (→ # 3427) brings a rejection of Israel's worship, but a plea for a restoration of *mišpāṭ* and *ṣᵉdāqâ* (5:24). The norm has become a calamity; what ought to bring life instead brings death (6:12). Mays (*Amos*, 92-93) comments:

> *ṣᵉdāqā* [*sic*] is the quality of life displayed by those who live up to the norms inherent in a given relationship and thereby do right by the other person or persons involved. The two most important spheres for righteousness were the relationship between Yahweh and Israel defined in the covenant and expressed in the cult, and the relationship of men in the social order of the folk.... In Amos *ṣᵉdāqā* applies to the relational life of the social partners in the people of Israel.

In Amos, then, *ṣdq* operates firmly within a human sphere, although involving norms acceptable to the deity. Hosea, on the other hand, locates *ṣdq* in a more theological context, having to do more with Israel's relationship with Yahweh than within the community (Hos 2:19[21]; 10:12; cf. 14:9[10]). *ḥesed*, loyalty (→ # 2874), is closely related in contexts that concern the renewal of God's people and God's relationship with them. Since Hosea also pictures the people in distress and in need of deliverance, *ṣdq* also bears overtones of salvation (cf. Davies, *Hosea*, 86-87), although this remains secondary to the dominant interest.

Micah brings this element to the fore (although, as in the Psalms in these contexts, the NIV regularly prefers the wooden equivalent of "righteousness"). Especially the use of *ṣidqôt* in 6:5, where a mighty act of deliverance is recalled, makes this nuance clear (thus RSV: "that you may know the saving acts of the LORD"). *ṣdq* in this sense (victory, deliverance) is often associated with the so-called "Second Isaiah" (chs. 40-55); this factor, plus the frequent association of Mic and Isa 1-39, might lead one to expect this usage to be similarly frequent in Isa 1-39, but such is not the case.

The frequency of *ṣdq* language in Isaiah has been noted above; a fairly wide range of nuance attaches to it in this book. Like Amos, Isaiah insists on relating *ṣdq* to the sphere of social justice and the needs of the oppressed. This is the sense we find in the first occurrence of the term in Isa 1:21; the same chapter in looking forward to a brighter future sees the restored judiciary in terms of *ṣedeq* (1:26-27; cf. 11:4-5; 28:17). A distinctive association, shared with some psalms, is the connection between *ṣdq* and peace (*šālôm*; → # 8934), which recurs throughout the book. The presence of *ṣdq* results in *šālôm* (9:2-7[1-6]; 32:16-17; 48:18; 60:17). Scholarly debate over the dating of these passages continues (cf. Williamson, *The Book Called Isaiah*), but these scattered references contribute to the literary unity of the book (see further below). More important for the present purpose is the way in which they link *ṣdq* to God and the beneficent outworking of this divine *ṣdq* in the world and among God's people, following through theologically on the trajectory set for human affairs in Amos.

(b) Prophets of the Babylonian period. Aspects of Jeremiah's usage connect with each of the nuances sketched in the eighth-century prophets, save that of deliverance or victory (but cf. Jer 51:10). In addition, Jeremiah's well-known laments appeal to the God as the *ṣdq* judge, pleading for the prophet's cause to be upheld (11:20; 12:1; 20:12). Like Amos, Jer applies *ṣdq* to the proper ordering of relationships within the community, although the appearance of these sayings among the indictments against the royal house (22:3, 13, 15) might seem a limiting factor. Still, the resonances with, e.g., Ps 24 are apparent; even if addressed to the king, the assumption is that a properly ordered society, one in which *ṣdq* is found, does not allow the powerful to live at the expense of the weak. This issues naturally into the hope for a king who will act according to *ṣdq* (Jer 22:15; 23:5 ‖ 33:15, but note interchange of *ṣaddîq* and *ṣᵉdāqâ*); these notices complement those of Isaiah associating *ṣdq* with *šālôm*. Swetnam argues persuasively that the "righteous Branch" in these verses is best understood as "legitimate Branch" (cf. discussion of Aram. royal inscriptions, above): the rightful (legitimate) successor will do what is right. Only in this way will Judah's future be secured (23:6 ‖ 33:16; cf. Zeph 3:1-5). Jer also uses *ṣdq* terms in contexts concerned with the relationship between God and his people somewhat in the manner of Hosea. Fidelity to Yahweh—or rather, its lack—comes to the fore. Elsewhere, the Jer tradition is surprisingly candid about the fact that worship of the Queen of heaven was common practice in Judah (Jer 44:15-30: both sides grant this premise in their argument). In 4:2 fidelity to Yahweh is expressed *be'ᵉmet bᵉmišpāṭ ûbiṣdāqâ*, while in 9:24[23] the one who knows Yahweh does *ḥesed mišpāṭ ûṣᵉdāqâ*. Behavior that is *ṣdq* maintains the bond of God and people.

Habakkuk's famous dictum ("but the righteous [*ṣaddîq*, unarticulated] will live by his faith [*be'ᵉmûnātô*]" Hab 2:4b; cf. LXX *ho de dikaios ek pisteōs mou zēsetai*) has received much attention, largely because of difficulties in the Heb. text and its varied quotations in the NT. However, we have already seen the relationship between *ṣdq* and life, especially in the expectations of lamenters in the Psalms, but elsewhere as well. Hab is at least in part a theodicy; as such, an interest is expressed in the lot of the *ṣaddîq* against that of the *rāšā'* (1:4, 13), much as the lament psalms. In any case, the close relationship of *ṣdq* with *'ᵉmûnâ* is seen elsewhere, whether in the sphere of human affairs (Prov 12:17a; Isa 59:4), royal/messianic ideals (Isa 11:5), or in the character of God (Deut 32:4). As Mason (90) points out, Hab 2:4 inhabits the same world of thought as Ezek 33:10-16, and the two passages should be read together. While the language of these passages is amenable to notions of a future judgment, in their present contexts they assert that maintenance of *ṣdq* affirms life in *this* world. The discussion of Gen 15:6 (above) also contributes to this interpretation of Hab 2:4b. The justice of God is not impugned, in spite of appearances to the contrary. The *ṣaddiq*, who maintains a faithful or trustworthy lifestyle, is assured of divine approval and support. The woe oracles of Hab 2:6-19 make the opposite case.

As mentioned above, the initial impression that Ezekiel makes heavy use of *ṣdq* terminology is soon modified by the realization that these occurrences are clustered in a small number of passages. Four of these group together (Ezek 3:20-21; 14:12-20; 18:5-32; 33:12-20), each considering in similar terms the fate of the individual who does—or does not do—what is *ṣdq*. Ezek 18:5-9 gives the most comprehensive account of what this behavior looks like, joining matters of purity and equity and summarizing it with reference to divine statutes and ordinances. Observance of this law suggests a cultic interest, one that coheres naturally with Ezekiel's priestly orientation. Beyond this, the prophet's interest is not only in human *ṣdq*, but also the way in which God's regard for it confirms divine justice (cf. 18:29-32; 33:20). Although the precise relationship of these passages is the subject of debate (cf. Joyce), they share the insistence that *ṣdq* is nontransferable: its presence brings life; its absence, death.

(c) Isaiah 40-66. The distinctive use of *ṣdq* language in Isa 40-66, the so-called "Second" or "Deutero-Isaiah," has long been noted (see Olley, "Notes," for brief statement and bibliography). The articles by J. J. Scullion and C. F. Whitely appeared in the early 1970s in quick succession and clearly independent of each other. Scullion argued that the "salvific sense" common in chs. 40-55 continued also through chs. 56-66. Scullion's detailed exegeses of the relevant "Trito-Isaiah" texts (esp. 56:1; 58:2, 8; 59:4, 9-17; 60:17; 61:3, 10-11; 62:1-2; 63:1; 64:5[4]) generally carry conviction, at least sufficiently to make his major case. Secondarily, Scullion also mounts a negative argument: "There is no sign that *ṣedeq-ṣedāqah* [*sic*] have a nomistic or legalistic meaning, nor that the words stand for some 'objective norm' which God or his people follow" (348). Whitely takes a very different course; he seeks to demonstrate that *ṣdq* terms in Deutero-Isaiah have a wide range of nuances. Whitely advances his case largely by appeal to ANE parallels and certain OT passages outside Isa. In particular, he argues that Deutero-Isaiah's monotheism dictated that *ṣdq*—also construed as a divine name—be understood "functionally," and so "merging" with Yahweh's personality. Thus, *ṣedeq* equates to the divine "plan" (41:2; 45:13). While Whitley is right to claim that "*ṣedeq* receives a significantly theological interpretation" in Deutero-Isaiah, his specific proposals have not in most cases been accepted.

More recently, patterns of *ṣdq* usage in Isa have been employed by R. Rendtorff as evidence for the editorial combination of the three sections of the book. Rendtorff urges a view that sees the various links between the sections forming a complex web of relationships. Nonetheless, he finds chs. 40-55 to be the centerpiece towards which chs. 1-39 and 56-66 are oriented: the first and second sections he believes were independent blocks; the third probably did not exist independently of the rest of the Isa traditions. One might say that, for Rendtorff, while chs. 1-39 and 40-55 are stitched together, chs. 40-55 and 56-66 are woven together. He points to distinctive use of *ṣdq* terms to argue his case. Isa 1-39, he claims, links *ṣedeq*/*ṣᵉdāqâ* (162 n. 50: he rightly sees no discernible difference between them) predominantly with *mišpāṭ*, emphasizing human behavior; Isa 40-55, on the other hand, use *ṣdq* in conjunction with forms of *yšʿ* or with *šālôm*, thus speaking of God's actions on behalf of his people. For Rendtorff,

56:1, in which both characteristic usages appear, signals the mixing of these nuances in the third part of the book. For the most part, these generalizations are quite fair.

Isa 51:5-8 provides a good example of Deutero-Isaiah's typical usage. In v. 5 *ṣidqî*, my righteousness, is paralleled by *yišʿî*, my salvation, while in v. 6 *yᵉšûʿātî*, my salvation, and *ṣidqātî*, my righteousness, are paired (cf. 51:8). The referent in each case is to God; here *ṣedeq/ṣᵉdāqâ* carries the nuance of "deliverance" (RSV) or "triumph" (JPSV). Meanwhile, 51:7 speaks of those who know *ṣedeq* and aligns this with *tôrâ*, instruction. In this case, the translation of "right" or "righteousness" is clearly to be preferred. This example also begins to raise a question mark over the way in which Rendtorff concludes his case (164): He asserts that while usages typical for chs. 1-39 and 40-55 find their way to chs. 56-66, what is typical for chs. 40-55 is not found in 1-39. Already in our example from 51:5-8 we see the mixing of the two types; and, contrary to Rendtorff's claims, the theological usage is found in "Proto-Isaiah" as noted above (esp. 9:7[6] and 32:16-17). Even if these are Josianic pieces, they still challenge Rendtorff's claim that chs. 1-39 do not admit the theologically oriented *ṣdq* language (further on this type of phenomena see Williamson, *The Book Called Isaiah*).

(d) Postexilic prophets. Discussion has already provided a trajectory toward the postexilic prophets. While the notion that people must be *ṣdq*—behaving in a manner consonant with right order in the community and before God—persists, *ṣdq* language increasingly is used for future hopes of a secure and beneficent future (cf. Mal 3:17-18). Such is the vision of Zech 8:7-8 in looking forward to the utopian future of God's people, when God will be savior (*môšîaʿ*) for his people, living with them in faithfulness (*ʾᵉmet*) and *ṣᵉdāqâ*.

P-B 1. The LXX translators generally used *dikaio-* words as equivalent for the Heb. *ṣdq* terminology (vb. *ṣdq*, *dikaioō*; nom. *ṣedeq/ṣᵉdāqâ*, *dikaiosynē*; adj. *ṣaddîq*, *dikaios*), although this relationship was not exclusive on either side. Olley's approach (cf. 1980) seems to do justice best to both the G terms in their own right, as well as the contribution of the translation context. Although there is a great deal of semantic overlap in the *ṣdq/dikaio-* partnership, the equivalence is neither complete nor exact. The conceptual shift effected by the move to G seems mostly to involve greater emphasis on legal aspects.

The Apoc. make extensive use of *dikai-* terms (over 200x), and *dikaiosynē* alone appears 73x. It enjoys a high status among these authors. "Love righteousness, you rulers of the earth," begins Wisd 1:1; its initial reflection on death concludes, "For righteousness is immortal" (1:15). Living righteously ensures immortal life (Wisd 5:15; Tob 13:13). So when the angel Raphael is on the point of revealing his true identity to Tobit and Tobias, he counsels them that "a little with righteousness is better than much with wrongdoing" (Tob 12:8-10; cf. Wisd 8:7 with "wisdom"), identifying a righteous life with a charitable, generous life. In spite of this, the righteous are prone to oppression and suffering (Wisd 2:10-11; 5:1; 4 Macc 18:15, quoting Ps 34:19a). Still, Tobit addresses God in prayer: "Righteous are you" (Tob 3:2), just like the canonical postexilic prayers in the OT (Ezra 9:15; Neh 9:8; Dan 9:14); the justice of God results in the salvation of his people (2 Macc 1:25).

2. Postbiblical Jewish literature has an increasing interest in the life and fate of the *ṣaddîq*, an interest seen already in Prov. So, for instance, *4 Ezra*'s "theodicy" asks questions about this that add a future orientation to considerations of righteousness

(cf. 4 Ezra 7:17-18) while carrying on in the trajectory set by Ezek and Hab (cf. 4 Ezra 7:[102]-45[115]). The *Similitudes of Enoch* show similar tendencies (*1 Enoch* 37-71) as each of the three similitudes is concerned in some way with the place of the righteous and wicked in the world and the world-to-come.

3. The DSS have a well-known connection to righteousness in the figure of the Teacher of Righteousness (*môreh [haṣ]ṣedeq*), although the identification and nature of this figure remains enigmatic (cf. Knibb). Przybylski's survey of *ṣdq* terms in the DSS emphasizes the variety of usage among various documents, even those otherwise closely related; only in the CD does Przybylski find *ṣedeq* "used as a major conceptual term" (35). One can generalize only to the extent of suggesting that *ṣdq* denotes right behavior, i.e., conforming to the demands of living in the community, and that these demands are ultimately of divine origin and so implicate God's righteousness as well. "God's righteousness understood in this way is to be the norm for man's righteousness" (ibid.). Unlike the OT, where *ṣedeq* and *ṣ^e^dāqâ* are completely synonymous terms, the DSS show preferences yielding semantic distinction in the pair, with *ṣedeq* referring to human activity and *ṣ^e^dāqâ* to "God's saving, gracious activity" (37-38).

4. The terminology continued to develop in RL. The trend seen in the apocryphal books towards identifying a righteous life with one of good deeds in conformity with the Law—a trajectory deeply rooted in the OT itself—continues. This is not to be understood in a mechanical way; rather, life in accordance with the law reflects knowledge of the ways of God himself: "As God is called merciful and gracious, so be thou merciful and gracious; as God is called righteous, so be thou righteous; as God is called holy, so be thou holy" (*Sifre Deut* 85a; cited by Schechter, 202). Sanders (204-5) further refines this notion out of his study of *ṣdq* terminology in the Tannaitic literature:

> Those who accept the covenant, which carries with it God's promise of salvation, accept also the obligation to obey the commandments given by God in connection with the covenant. One who accepts the covenant and remains within it is "righteous".... Being righteous is not the goal of the religious quest; it is the behavior proper to the one who has accepted the covenant offered at Sinai and the commandments which followed the acceptance of God's kingship. *Tsaddiq* . . . is primarily a word indicating not an achieved, but a maintained status (cf. Przybylski, 39-76).

NT It becomes difficult to continue this survey into the NT, since this article is about Heb. words related to the root *ṣdq*, and none of these terms appears in the Greek NT. Perhaps this does not need to be pointed out in a work of this kind, but sometimes discussions of NT righteousness fail to seize sufficiently onto this concept. The G terminology must be studied in its own right; Heb. meanings cannot simply be imported. The literature on this G terminology is vast and the debates highly nuanced and specialized.

1. *Gospels. dikaio-* terms appear less often than one might suppose; on the most generous conditions, the Synoptics include *dikaio-* terms only 39x, with only 2 of these in Mark. *dikaiosynē* itself occurs 8x (Matt 7x; Luke 1x). John likewise uses this language infrequently (5x for all *dikaio-* related terms; *dikaiosynē* only twice). As in the DSS, this language is less decisive than one might have thought, although the

importance of the concept should not be measured by statistics alone. Jesus' teaching in Matt (5:20; 6:33) is consonant with his Jewish context and does not set him at odds with it. The righteous person behaves in *imitatio Dei*, and in so doing finds life.

2. *Paul*. Although Seebass is right to say that Paul "makes the most frequent use of this whole word-group, and gives it its widest range of meanings," it is surprising to read that "he it is who establishes the closest connection with the OT when speaking of God's righteousness and God's justification of sinners" (*NIDNTT* 3:363). Paul's frequent uses of these terms cluster densely into his letter to the Romans. This book can, perhaps, be understood as Paul's attempt to answer the question of Job: "Can a mortal be righteous before God?" (9:2; cf. Eliphaz in Job 4:17). In this extended response, Paul breaks with his Jewish context as Jesus does not. For Paul, righteousness outside the Law provides hope for life before God (cf. Rom 3:21-22; 9:30-31). For Jews, the law is an expression of God's character; to obey it is to live as God would have us live. Paul, then, in his joining of righteousness primarily to faith rather than behavior, moves outside the orbit of OT/Jewish usage (cf. Ziesler).

Integrity, equity, honesty, loyalty, uprightness: → *ḥsd* II (show o.s. kind, # 2874); → *yšr* (be straight, level, right, # 3837); → *kēn* I (right, sound, honest, aptly, # 4026); → *tmm* (be sound, whole, # 9462)

Justice, judgment: → *dyn* (judge, contend, govern, administer, # 1906); → *miśpāḥ* (breach of law, # 5384); → *pll* I (sit in judgment, arbitrate, expect, # 7136); → *ṣdq* (be just, righteous, justified, # 7405); → *špṭ* (judge, execute judgment, govern, # 9149)

Bibliography

ABD 5:724-73; *NIDNTT* 3:352-77; *TDNT* 2:174-225; *THAT* 2:507-30; L. C. Allen, *Psalms 101-150*, WBC, 1983; F. Baethgen, *Die Psalmen*, 1904; J. Barr, "Common Sense and Biblical Language," *Bib* 49, 1968, 377-87; R. Boling, *Judges*, AB, 1975; P. Bordreuil and A. Caquot, "Les textes en cunéiformes alphabétiques découverts en 1978 à Ibn Hani," *Syr.* 57, 1980, 356-58; S. Brock, "The Two Ways and the Palestinian Targum," in *A Tribute to Geza Vermes*, 1990, 139-52; D. J. A. Clines, *Job 1-20*, 1989; P. C. Craigie, *Psalms 1-50*, WBC, 1983; G. I. Davies, *Hosea*, 1992; F. Delitzsch, *Psalms*, vol. 3, KD, 1880 (1980 rpt.); J. C. L. Gibson, *Davidson's Introductory Hebrew Grammar—Syntax*, 1994; R. Gordis, *The Book of God and Man*, 1965; F. Hahn, "Genesis 15, 6 im Neuen Testament," in *Probleme biblischer Theologie*, 1971, 90-107; A. Ho, *ṣedeq and ṣedāqah in the Hebrew Bible*, 1991; A. Hurvitz, "צדיק = 'Wise' in Biblical Hebrew and the Wisdom Connection of Psalm 37," in *Goldene Äpfel in silbernen Schalen*, 1992, 109-12; P. Joüon and T. Muraoka, *A Grammar of Biblical Hebrew*, 1993; P. Joyce, *Divine Initiative and Human Response in Ezekiel*, 1989; M. Kline, "Abram's Amen," *WTJ* 31, 1968/69, 1-11; M. A. Knibb, "The Teacher of Righteousness—A Messianic Title?" in *A Tribute to Geza Vermes*, 1990, 51-65; J. Krašovec, *La justice (ṣDQ) de Dieu dans la Bible hébraïque et l'interprétation juive et chrétienne*, 1988; H.-J. Kraus, *Psalms 1-59*, 1988; J. Lindenberger, *The Aramaic Proverbs of Ahiqar*, 1983; R. Mason, *Zephaniah, Habakkuk, Joel*, 1994; J. L. Mays, *Amos: A Commentary*, 1969; idem, *Psalms*, 1994; W. McKane, *Proverbs: A Commentary*, OTL, 1970; L. Milano, "Gli epiteti del faraone in una lettera Ugaritica da Ras Ibn Hani," in *Studi Orientalistici in ricordo de Franco Pintore*, 1983, 141-58; R. Moberly, "Abraham's Righteousness (Genesis xv 6)," *Studies in the Pentateuch*, VTSup 41, 1990, 103-30; W. Moran, *The Amarna Letters*, 1992; S. Moscati, *The World of the Phoenicians*, 1968; Y. Muffs, *Studies in the Aramaic Legal Papyri From Elephantine*, 1969; M. Noth, *Leviticus: A Commentary*, 1965; M. Oeming, "Ist Gen 15^6 ein Beleg für die Anrechnung des Glaubens zur Gerechtigkeit?" *ZAW* 95, 1983, 182-97;

J. W. Olley, "Notes on Isaiah XXXII 1, XLV 19, 23 and LXIII 1," *VT* 33, 1983, 446-53; idem, "The Translator of the Septuagint of Isaiah and 'Righteousness,'" *BIOSCS* 13, 1980, 58-74; D. Patrick, *Old Testament Law*, 1985; B. Przybylski, *Righteousness in Matthew and His World of Thought*, 1980; G. von Rad, "Faith Reckoned as Righteousness," in *The Problem of the Hexateuch*, 1966, 125-30 = "Die Anrechnung des Glaubens zur Gerechtigkeit," *TLZ* 76, 1951, 129-32; idem, "'Righteousness' and 'Life' in the Cultic Language of the Psalms," in *The Problem of the Hexateuch*, 1966, 243-66 = "'Gerechtigkeit' und 'Leben' in der Kultsprache der Psalmen," in *Festschrift für Alfred Berthelot*, 1950, 418-37; R. Rendtorff, "The Composition of the Book of Isaiah," in *Canon and Theology*, 1993, 146-69 = "Zur Komposition des buches Jesaja," *VT* 34, 1984, 295-320; idem, "Isaiah 56:1 as a Key to the Formation of the Book of Isaiah," in *Canon and Theology*, 1993, 181-89; E. P. Sanders, *Paul and Palestinian Judaism*, 1977; S. Schechter, *Aspects of Rabbinic Theology*, 1909 (1961); H. Schmid, "Gerechtigkeit und Glaube: Genesis 15,1-6 und sein biblisch-theologischer Kontext," *EvT* 40, 1980, 396-420; J. J. Scullion, "*ṣedeq-ṣedāqah* in Isaiah cc. 40-66 With Special Reference to the Continuity in Meaning Between Second and Third Isaiah," *UF* 3, 1971, 335-48; K. A. D. Smelik, *Writings From Ancient Israel*, 1991; M. Sternberg, *The Poetics of Biblical Narrative*, 1985; J. Swetnam, "Some Observations on the Background of צדיק in Jeremias 23,5a," *Bib* 46, 1965, 29-40; M. E. Tate, *Psalms 51-100*, WBC, 1990; M. Weinfeld, "'Justice and Righteousness'—משפט וצדקה—The Expression and Its Meaning," in *Justice and Righteousness: Biblical Themes and Their Influence*, 1992, 228-46; C. F. Whitely, "Deutero-Isaiah's Interpretation of *ṣedeq*," *VT* 22, 1972, 469-75; N. Whybray, "Qoheleth the Immoralist? (Qoh 7:16-17)," in *Israelite Wisdom: Theological and Literary Essays in Honor of Samuel Terrien*, ed. J. G. Gammie et al., 1978, 191-204; idem, *Wealth and Poverty in the Book of Proverbs*, 1990; H. G. M. Williamson, *The Book Called Isaiah*, 1994; idem, *Ezra, Nehemiah*, WBC, 1985; J. A. Ziesler, *The Meaning of Righteousness in Paul*, 1972.

David J. Reimer

7406 (*ṣedeq*, rightness, righteousness), → # 7405

7407 (*ṣ^e dāqâ*, righteousness, righteous acts), → # 7405

7408 (*ṣidqiyyâ*, Zedekiah), → Zedekiah

7410	צהב

צהב (*ṣhb*), ho. be yellow/copper (# 7410); מֻצְהָב (*muṣhāb*), color of bronze (# 5176); צָהֹב (*ṣāhōb*), white/yellow (# 7411). ṣāhōb ("white/yellow") is a primary color by Brenner's definition (49-105), with a range of color specification from pale to golden or reddish yellow. The root denotes brightness or shiny.

OT 1. The word *ṣāhōb* appears only in Lev 13:30, 32, and 36, in a description of the color of a hair growing from a diseased spot on the skin. The priests determined whether a person was fit to come into the presence of God and worship at the holy temple. The regulations include a set of color tests by which the priests determined whether a disease or fungus brought uncleanness and defiled a person or property. G. J. Wenham's discussion on these complex regulations is most helpful (*Leviticus*, 189-214).

2. The ho. (*muṣhāb*) occurs only in Ezra 8:27 to describe the color of bowls Ezra brought back to Jerusalem. It is a secondary or tertiary color term with a range of yellowish bright to a resemblance of gold (Brenner, 125).

Colors—Green/yellow: → *yrq* II (become green, # 3762b)
Colors—Yellow: → *ṣhb* (yellow/copper, # 7410)

BIBLIOGRAPHY
A. Brenner, *Colour Terms in the Old Testament*, JSOT Sup, 1982; P. L. Garber, "Color," *ISBE* 1:729-32; R. Gradwohl, *Die Farben im Alten Testament*, BZAW 83, 1963.

Robert L. Alden

7411 (*ṣāhōb*, white/yellow), → # 7410

7412	צהל

צהל (*ṣhl* I), q. neigh; shout (# 7412); מִצְהָלוֹת (*miṣhālôt*), neighing (# 5177).

ANE Arab. *ṣahala*; Syr. *ṣ^ehal*.

OT 1. The vb. is used only in the q. 7x. Its usage is largely determined contextually. It describes metaphorically the immoral and unrighteous behavior/character of the people of Judah (Jer 5:8) as they neigh (*ṣhl*) for another's wife (see below). But it also describes the enjoyment Babylon had as she destroyed the Lord's inheritance, neighing as she pillaged the people (50:11). It is also used in a good sense to describe the joyous singing of the people of Zion (Isa 12:6, imper.; Jer 31:7) and the Lord's joyous remnant (Isa 24:14). On the other hand, the term depicts a setting in which persons may need to cry out because of destruction coming upon them (Isa 10:30). In Esth 8:15 it is used with *śmḥ*, rejoice.

2. The nom. *miṣhālôt*, neighings, occurs in Jer 8:16 to describe the horrifying sound of an approaching invasion force. The horses in this powerful enemy army are so numerous that the sound of their neighing precedes them.

3. In his condemnation of Israel's covenant treachery (idolatrous worship), Jeremiah likens Israel to stallions passionately searching for a mate (Jer 5:8). He depicts the Israelites as a stallion neighing (*ṣhl*) before and during the act of mating. The lust illustrated in the neighing of stallions (*miṣhālôt*, 13:27) drove the children of Israel first to participate in pagan cult prostitution and then adultery, both acts of treachery against a covenant (with God or with a spouse).

Animal sounds: → *g'h* (bellow, low [cattle], # 1716); → *hgh* I (groan, moan, sigh, meditate, muse, chirp, mutter, # 2047); → *nbḥ* (bark [dogs], # 5560); → *nhq* (bray [ass], shriek, # 5640); → *nḥr* (snort, # 5723); → *'yṭ* (yell, shriek, swoop down [w. shrieks], # 6512); → *ṣhl* I (neigh, shout, # 7412)

Eugene Carpenter/Michael A. Grisanti

7413	צהל

צהל (*ṣhl* II), hi. make shine (Ps 104:15) (# 7413).

OT The vb. describes the shining effect of skin made healthy through the generous divine provision of olive oil, either in one's diet or as a cosmetic (Ps 104:15).

Healing, health, healthful: → *ghh* (heal, # 1564); → *rp'* (heal, make healthy, drinkable, # 8324); → *šālôm* (peace, friendship, happiness, prosperity, health, salvation, # 8934)

Martin J. Selman

7414	צהר

צהר (*ṣhr*), vb. hi. press out oil (# 7414); יִצְהָר (*yiṣhār* I), nom. (fresh) olive oil (# 3658).

ANE The vb. *ṣhr* has two possible derivations (*HALAT* 945). It could be a denom. vb. from the nom. *yiṣhār* (BDB, 844; cf. below). There is also the possibility, however, that it might be related to the nom. *ṣoh^{o}rayim*, midday, noon (# 7416; see the discussion in *HALAT* 945). It has usually been supposed that *yiṣhār* is derived from the underlying root of the latter term and means etymologically "*shining* oil," in which case the denom. analysis of the vb. *ṣhr* would be a secondary meaning of the root (the primary meaning would be shine).

OT 1. The vb. *ṣhr* occurs only 1x, "They crush olives among the terraces; they tread the winepresses, yet suffer thirst" (Job 24:11). The parallel with "tread the winepresses" suggests the meaning "to crush olives" for the vb. (but see remarks in ANE).

2. The term *yiṣhār*, fresh oil, occurs 21x, most frequently in parallel with new wine (and grain), referring to the fresh olive oil produce of the land (e.g., Deut 7:13; 11:14). Olive trees took a long time to grow and mature, but they also lasted for hundreds of years. Therefore, a good supply of fresh oil was a sign of stability, prosperity, and the Lord's blessing (2 Chron 32:28; Jer 31:12; Hos 2:8, 22; Joel 2:19, 24; cf. 2 Kgs 18:32), while the loss or lack of it was a sign of his judgment (Deut 28:51; Joel 1:10; Hag 1:11; see esp. *TDOT* 6:253-54). The firstfruits or tithe of fresh oil went to the priests and Levites (e.g., Num 18:12; Deut 12:17; 14:23; 18:4; 2 Chron 31:5). Zech 4:14 uses this word to refer to Joshua the high priest and Zerubbabel the governor as "the two who are anointed (lit., the sons of oil) to serve the Lord of all the earth" (cf. Rev 11:4). The image of two olive trees supplying one lampstand with oil suggests that these two men together were the means through which the Lord would bless Israel.

3. The most common word for oil in the OT is *šemen* (oil; → # 9043), which occurs 192x. In the large majority of those cases it refers to olive oil, so much so that the expression "tree(s)/wood of oil" (1 Kgs 6:23, 31-33; Isa 41:19) is a natural way to refer to olive wood.

P-B The nom. *yiṣhār* occurs 7x in the Qumran Temple Scroll (11QTS) and 1x in the Thanksgiving Hymns (1QH). The latter turns the common OT trio of "grain, new wine, and oil" into an expression of worldliness. Warriors rest "on abundant delights, [and on plenty of corn] and wine and oil; they pride themselves in possessions of wealth" (1QH 10:24). The truly godly person does not place his confidence in worldly gain but is, instead, himself like a green tree "beside streams of water, bringing forth leaves and multiplying its branches" (see the context, Vermes, 193; cf. Ps 1). In the Temple Scroll this term is used primarily in references to the "Feast of First Fruits of Oil" (see Yadin 1:111-14 for extensive remarks).

NT The NT word that corresponds to both Heb. *šemen*, oil, and *yiṣhār*, olive oil, is *elaion* (the LXX rendering of both). It occurs 11x and refers exclusively to olive oil (→ *šemen*, # 9043, for the details).

Oil: → *ṣhr* (press out oil, # 7414); → *šemen* (oil, # 9043)

Bibliography
NIDNTT 2:710-13; *TDNT* 2:470-73; *TDOT* 6:253-54; D. E. Fleming, *The Installation of Baal's High Priestess at Emar*, HSS 42, 1992; R. J. Forbes, *Studies in Ancient Technology*, 2d ed., 3:22-26, 104-7, 138-44; H. N. Moldenke and A. L. Moldenke, *Plants of the Bible*, 1952, 157-60; J. F. Ross, "Oil," *The Interpreter's Dictionary of the Bible*, 1962, 3:592-93; J. A. Thompson, "Ointment," *IDB*, 1962, 3:593-95; J. C. Trever, "Oil Tree," *IDB*, 1962, 3:593; G. Vermes, *The Dead Sea Scrolls in English*, 3d ed., 1987; Y. Yadin (ed.), *The Temple Scroll*, 2 vols., 1983; M. Zohary, *Plants of the Bible*, 1982, 56-57.

Richard E. Averbeck

7415 (*ṣōhar*, roof), → # 1511

7416 (*ṣohᵒrayim*, noon, midday), → # 1332

7418	צַוָּאר

צַוָּאר (*ṣawwā'r*), neck (# 7418). Related vocabulary: גַּרְגְּרוֹת (*gargārôt*), neck (# 1738); גָּרוֹן (*gārôn*), throat, neck (# 1744); מַפְרֶקֶת (*mapreqet*), neck (# 5154; < פרק [*prq*], pull away [→ # 7293]); עֹרֶף (*'ōrep*), neck, back (# 6902; < ערף [*'rp* II], break [neck of an animal], # 6904).

ANE The etymology of the primary OT term *ṣawwā'r*, neck, is questionable, although it corresponds to the basic Sem. form *ṣawar/ṣṣaur*, porter or bank/shore; cf. the Akk. *ṣawārum*, neck (*AHw*, 1087a; *TWAT* 6:927). The other primary OT word for neck, *'ōrep*, corresponds to the Arab. *'urfah*, mane, and the Syr. *'urpā*, cock's comb (*TWAT* 6:393; *TWOT* 2:698). Some of these nuances are carried over into the OT.

OT 1. The term most frequently used for neck in the OT is *ṣawwā'r*. It occurs 41x with several related meanings. Its most basic meaning is literal; that is, it refers to the neck as that part of the body joining the head to the trunk.

The OT also links *ṣawwā'r* with strength (cf. Job 39:19; 41:22[14]). Thus, the nobles in Nehemiah are condemned for not putting their "shoulders (*ṣawwā'r*) to the work" (Neh 3:5). The neck as a picture of strength is expressed in military terms in Josh 10:24, where Israel's military victory over the five kings of Jerusalem culminates in stepping "on their necks." Military conquest is also evident in Hab 3:13, although EVV strongly differ on translating the phrase *yᵉsôd 'ad-ṣawwā'r* (NIV you stripped him from head [*ṣawwā'r*] to foot). Isaiah also uses *ṣawwā'r* in a military context, comparing a military predicament with a flood reaching to the neck (8:8 [referring to Israel]; 30:28 [referring to Assyria]). In both instances imminent danger is presupposed. In a different context, one who overestimates his strength by speaking with an "outstretched neck" is guilty of arrogance (Ps 75:5[6], but cf. LXX's "speaking against God"; see also *gārôn* in Isa 3:16).

Neck also is associated with the burdens that individuals or nations bear. In Gen, Isaac prophesies that Esau will wear the yoke of Jacob, that is, he and his family would be Jacob's servants (27:40). In the Prophets, Jeremiah employs the term the most frequently, using it 8x with *'ōl*, yoke (→ # 6585), to picture Yahweh's judgment on the people and their eventual redemption from that judgment (Jer 27:2, 8, 11, 12;

28:10, 11, 12, 14; 30:8; Lam 1:14; cf. Isa 10:27). The yoke that Jeremiah wears on his neck is symbolic of the yoke of captivity that Yahweh was about to place upon the people. In ch. 28, the false prophet Hananiah expressed the prevailing political view that Israel was safe from Babylon by removing the yoke from Jeremiah's neck and breaking it.

Micah underscores the inevitability of the divine judgment: The people would not be able to remove their necks (NIV you cannot save yourselves) from the impending doom (2:3). The neck is where one places necklaces (Gen 41:42) or fine garments (Judg 5:30). See also the description of the woman in S of Songs, whose neck is like a tower (S of Songs 4:4; 7:4), and it is adorned with necklaces (1:10; 4:9). Although the meaning of the tower metaphor is not precise (suggestions include strength, security, dignity—see Crim, 74; *TWAT* 6:928), it is clear that it is indicative of the woman's beauty.

The use of neck in the OT has special connotations with greetings. For example, *ṣawwā'r* is used in the Genesis narratives in conjunction with the greetings of Jacob and Esau (33:4), Joseph and Benjamin (45:14), and Joseph and Jacob (46:29). In each of these instances the biblical writer associates "falling on one's neck" (NIV throwing his arms around him) with weeping, showing the great emotion of these reunions.

2. The nuance of throat is expressed by the term *gārôn*, used 8x in the OT. While it sometimes signifies neck, as do *ṣawwā'r* and *'ōrep* (Isa 3:16; Ezek 16:11), the texts in Ps 69:3[4] and Jer 2:25 identify *gārôn* with thirst. In its other occurrences *gārôn* is primarily associated with the act of speaking. Negatively, the throat of the wicked is described as an open grave—a place of deceitful and destructive words (Ps 5:9[10], where *gārôn* is parallel to *lāšôn*, tongue; cf. the description of idols in 115:7). Positively, *gārôn* is also associated with praising God (Ps 149:6; translations opt for mouth). Sometimes NIV (and most EVV) translate *gārôn* as voice (cf. Isa 58:1).

3. Another term in the semantic field of neck is *gargārôt*. It occurs 4x, exclusively in Prov. There the prominence of the neck is emphasized. That is, by binding love and faithfulness (3:3) or the commandments of their parents (6:20-21) around the neck, one ensures that they will be always with them. In addition, the practice of obedience in the believer's life is likened to the adorning of a neck with an chain or ornament, that is, a highly desired treasure (1:9; 3:22).

4. *mapreqet*, a hapleg. related to the vb. *prq*, tear apart (→ # 7293), is found only in 1 Sam 4:18 to describe the demise of Eli, who fell from his seat and broke his neck upon hearing that the ark of the covenant had been taken.

5. (a) The nom. *'ōrep*, occurring 33x in the OT, is closely related to *ṣawwā'r*. It describes the neck and, more broadly, the back. Military victory is described as being given the neck of one's enemies (Gen 49:8; 2 Sam 22:41 = Ps 18:40[41]; cf. Job 16:12). *'ōrep*, as back, is sometimes paired with the vb. *pnh* (→ # 7155) (or *hpk* [→ # 2200] or *ntn* [→ # 5989]) to describe the act of turning away. In military contexts this turning away is equivalent to retreat (Exod 23:27; Josh 7:8, 12 [NIV translates the phrase as "has been routed" in v. 7, but as "turn their backs" in v. 12]; cf. Jer 48:39). In theological contexts this turning away usually represents Israel's apostasy; e.g., in 2 Chron 29:6 the phrase "turning their backs," together with "unfaithfulness" and "doing evil," describes Israel's sin. Jeremiah also uses *'ōrep* to describe Israel's apostasy, i.e., their unwillingness to listen to Yahweh and to follow his ways (Jer 2:27; 32:33).

Ironically, Yahweh himself will only show the people his back (instead of his face) in the day of their judgment (18:17).

(b) *'ōrep* often connotes obstinacy in the OT (Isa 48:4). It is used with the lexeme *qšh*, harden (→ # 7996), to describe Israel's unwillingness to obey Yahweh's commands. In Jer 7:26; 17:23; 19:15 (see also Neh 9:16, 29), "hardening the neck" is parallel to "not listening" (cf. Couroyer, 215-26; *TWAT* 6:394-95). It was this disobedience that led to God disciplining Israel.

(c) The vb. *'rp*, break the neck, occurs 6x in varied cultic contexts. After commanding the people to redeem their firstborn donkeys with a lamb, both Exod 13:13 and 34:20 mention, "If you do not redeem it, break its neck" (cf. *TWAT* 6:395). Deut 21:4, 6 uses *'rp* to refer to the breaking a heifer's neck as an atonement for an unsolved murder (for a comparison of this pericope with similar ANE literature, see *TWAT* 6:396; Craigie, 278). The other occurrences of the vb. appear in the Prophets. Condemning the cult, Isaiah likens the one who offers a lamb to the one who breaks a dog's neck (Isa 66:3). Hosea uses the same vb. to make a powerful and ironic point about Yahweh's judgment of Israel's temple cult—the neck of their altars will be broken (Hos 10:2; NIV The LORD will demolish their altars; cf. Davies, NCB, 235).

P-B The semantic field of neck is represented in the LXX primarily by *trachēlos*, and also occasionally by *nōton*, *larynx*, *pharanx*, and *ōmos*. The range of *trachēlos* in the postbiblical literature covers the same meanings as found in the OT. "Falling on the neck" indicates a tearful greeting in Tob 11:9, 13. Baruch capitalizes on the military imagery of neck by promising the oppressed people that they will step on the necks of their enemies (Bar 4:25). Sirach offers a slighty different perspective from the OT on wearing wisdom on the neck. Instead of presenting it as an adorning chain, he likens it to a disciplinary yoke. He encourages his readers to put their necks under the yoke of instruction and wisdom (Sir 6:24; 7:23; 30:12; 51:26). On the other hand, a foolish person rejects wise counsel by placing it behind his back, *nōton* (21:15; cf. also the description of traitors in 3 Macc 3:24). Both *nōton* and *trachēlos* are used to form the common phrase "stiff-necked" (Bar 2:33; 1 Esd 1:48), but *sklōrotraxōlos* also is used (Sir 16:11).

NT The word "neck" occurs only a few times in the NT. It is primarily expressed by *trachēlos*, although *nōton* and *larynx* also appear. Some of the meanings attested in the OT are present here.

The imagery of an emotional greeting, "falling on someone's neck," occurs twice in the Lukan writings: in the warm welcome that the father gives to his lost son (Luke 15:20) and the tearful departure of Paul from the Ephesian church (Acts 20:37). Stephen uses *sklōrontraxōlos* (stiff-necked) to describe the disobedient religious leaders of his day (Acts 7:51). The letter of the Jerusalem council depicts the Pharisaic requirements on Gentile Christians as a burden too heavy for the necks of the early church (Acts 15:10; cf. *NIDNTT* 2:1164). This continues the negative connotation given the combination of "yoke" and "neck" in the OT.

Paul's citation of Ps 5:9[10] in Rom 3:13 further associates the throat with all impure speech. Later in Romans, Paul recognizes Priscilla and Aquila as people who had risked their necks (NIV lives) for him (16:4). The neck is also associated with peril in Matt 18:6 and par. (see *NIDNTT* 1:241).

Neck: → *ṣawwā'r* (neck, # 7418); → *qšh* I (be hard, severe, be stiff-necked, # 7996)
Yoke: → *môṭâ* (yoke, carrying pole, # 4574); → *'ōl* (yoke, # 6585); → *ṣmd* (be attached, attach oneself, # 7537)

Bibliography

NIDNTT 1:241; 2:1164; *TDNT* 4:57-58; *TWAT* 6:392-97, 927-29; *TWOT* 2:698, 760-61; P. C. Craigie, *Deuteronomy*, NICOT, 277-80; O. Grotius, "Alttestamentliche Motive im gleichnis vom verlorenen Sohn," *NTS* 24, 1977-78, 240-48; B. Couroyer, "'Avoir la nuque raide': ne pas incliner l'oreille," *RevistB* 88, 1981, 216-25; K. Crim, "'Your Neck Is Like the Tower of David' (The Meaning of a Simile in Song of Solomon 4:4)," *BT* 22, 1971, 70-74.

Neil O. Skjoldal

7421	צוד

צוד (*ṣwd*), q. hunt; pilp. catch (# 7421); מָצוֹד (*māṣôd* I), nom. hunting implement, e.g., net (# 5178); מְצוּדָה (*m*e*ṣûdâ* I), nom. net, prey (# 5180); מְצוֹדָה (*m*e*ṣôdâ*), nom. net (# 5182); צַיִד (*ṣayid* I), nom. hunter, hunting (# 7473); צַיָּד (*ṣayyād*), nom. hunter (hapleg. in Jer 16:16; # 7475).

ANE Cognates are found in several languages. So we have the Akk. *ṣâdu,* the Ugar. *ṣd,* the Phoen. *ṣyd,* and the Arab. *ṣāda,* all bearing the sense of hunting (see *TWAT* 6:930-35).

Assyrian and Egyptian reliefs attest to the practice of hunting, particularly as the sport of kings. Antelope, ostriches, and lions, among other animals, were the prey. The practice of hunting for food (Gen 27:3, 5; Lev 17:13-14) or trapping for skins (Ezek 16:10) was known in the OT. Trappers made use primarily of nets (fine-meshed for birds and thicker for larger animals), pits dug in the ground, snares, and trip wires, which released some means of killing or trapping the animal. These same methods are still in use in parts of Africa today. Fishing made use of hooks and line, or nets. But while the technical details are important, especially because of the confusion that besets even the most modern translations of the OT, the biblical focus is elsewhere. Here in the imagery drawn from these activities we discover the colors for a rich metaphorical tapestry —which has deep theological significance especially for the prophetic and Wisdom sections.

OT 1. The vb. *ṣwd* occurs 18x in its different forms. The Pent. has several instances (Gen 27:3, 5) where *ṣwd* is used of the literal hunting of venison. Lev 17:13-14a commands that the blood of hunted animals and birds must be allowed to drain before the flesh is consumed, for the blood is the life force (v. 14). The nom. *ṣayid* I carries the applied meaning of hunter (Esau, Gen 25:27; Nimrod, Gen 10:9, are said to be skilled or mighty hunters). An Egyptian story from the 20th century BC details the travels of a man called Sinuhe into the general area of Palestine (*ANET*, 18-22). The account describes the region as a good land with an abundance of honey, fruit, and grapes, and a place where one might enjoy roast fowl and desert game, which Sinuhe hunted with his hounds. Today the Negev desert is still home to a wide variety of fauna.

2. In the prophetic section, an important passage is Ezek 13:17-23. Although the passage is difficult to translate (see Zimmerli, 188-89), the oracle appears to be directed against a group of female prophets who make bracelets and veils and use these

as magical charms, perhaps linked to visions and divination (cf. v. 23). Ezekiel then compares these charms to the traps by which fowlers catch birds (v. 20) and warns that God will intervene to set his people free (v. 21).

3. One aspect of the use of *ṣwd* which comes to the fore in the Wisdom section of the OT is the sense of persistence, which accompanies the hunt. Job 10:16 likens God to a fierce lion who hunts him. Lam 4:18 speaks of enemies who "stalked us at every step."

P-B In the DSS, the mention of traps set for the sect by the powers of evil is found in passages like 1QH 3:26; 4:12; CD 16:15.

Hunting: → *yqš* (lay a trip wire, set a trap, # 3704); → *paḥ* I (trap, snare, # 7062); → *ṣwd* (hunt, # 7421); → *rešet* (net, # 8407); → *šûḥâ* I (pit, # 8757)

Bibliography
A. Negev, ed., *Archaeological Encyclopaedia of the Holy Land*, 1972, 149-50; W. Zimmerli, *Ezekiel* I, 1979.

W. R. Domeris

7422	צוה

צוה (*ṣwh*), pi. order, command, charge, direct, appoint, commission, forbid (when negated); pu. be ordered, receive a command (# 7422); מִצְוָה (*miṣwâ*), nom. order, command, commandment (→ # 5184).

ANE The vb. *ṣwh* has no direct parallels in other Sem. languages. Connections have been suggested, however, with the Arab. vb. *wṣy*, II enjoin, make a last testament, give parting charges, IV charge (see Kopf, 197-98); the Egyp. vb. *wḏ*, command, order (R. O. Faulkner, *A Concise Dictionary of Middle Egyptian*, 1986, 73-74) (both assume metathesis); and the Imperial Aram. vb. *ṣwt*, give an order (cf. *APFC* 37.14). The vb. occurs 2x in the Tell Arad ostraca (3 and 18; Y. Aharoni, *Arad Inscriptions*, 1981, 17, 35). In ostracon 18 it is found in a relative clause headed by the nom. *dbr* ("the matter which you commanded me"; see section 6 below).

OT 1. The vb. *ṣwh* is found ca. 496x in the OT (487x in the pi. and 9x in the pu.). Over half of these occurrences are found in the Pentateuch (ca. 252x), with Deut having the highest concentration (88x). Some of these are contested (e.g., Gen 50:16, first occurrence; Ps 44:4[5]; 71:3), and additional occurrences have been proposed (e.g., Ezra 8:17 [Q]; Neh 13:1).

2. While *ṣwh* can be used intransitively (Gen 42:25; 50:16; Exod 36:6), more often than not it is used transitively, governing one or two objects. The direct obj. may be unmarked (Gen 12:20; 2 Sam 7:11) or indicated by *'t* (Gen 7:9; Deut 1:18), a pronoun (Exod 6:13; Josh 1:7), or a prep. (*'l*, Num 15:23; 1 Kgs 11:10; *'l*, Gen 2:16; Esth 2:10; Job 36:32; *l*, Exod 1:22; 1 Sam 20:29), with no appreciable difference in meaning. The indirect object is typically indicated by a prep. (*'l*, Exod 6:13; *'l*, 1 Kgs 11:10; *l*, Num 32:28), though it is also found with *'t* (Exod 34:32). The details of the command are often introduced (in direct address) by *lē'mōr*, saying (ca. 80x; Gen 2:16; Lev 6:9[2]), though a *waw*-relative construction may also be used (Gen 28:1; 42:25).

3. The vb. *ṣwh* denotes the action of a superior stating something with authority and/or force to a subordinate with the purpose of eliciting a response, and may be glossed as "command, order." Alternatively, when negated it may be translated as "forbid" (with *lō'*: Lev 10:1; Deut 17:3; Jer 7:31; with *l^ebiltî*: Gen 3:11; Ruth 2:9). The precise nature of the communication has to be discerned from context. It can range from orders given in a particular situation to elicit a one-time response, to a standing command that has lasting value beyond a single situation (*THAT* 2:532). The latter may be glossed as "command" and the former as "order, charge"—though there is considerable semantic blurring between these terms in English. For instance, Joseph's order for the physicians to embalm his father was (obviously) limited to that particular situation (Gen 50:2; cf. Josh 10:27; 2 Sam 4:12; 13:28; 2 Kgs 16:15; etc.), while Jonadab's command to his children to abstain from wine, among other things, had enduring significance (Jer 35:6, 8, 10, etc.; cf. 2 Kgs 17:35; Amos 2:12). While *ṣwh* is the usual word for command in the OT, both → *'mr* (say, # 606) and → *dbr* (speak, # 1819) are frequently used in connection with *ṣwh* (e.g., 1 Sam 21:2[3]; see *TWAT* 6:943, 950), and occasionally have the meaning of command (cf. Exod 17:10; Deut 1:14; Judg 9:48; 1 Kgs 2:31).

4. Over half of all occurrences of *ṣwh* in the OT have God as subj. (ca. 280x; primarily Yahweh). Antediluvians (Gen 2:16; 6:22), patriarchs (Gen 21:4), prophets (Jer 1:7; 14:14), priests (2 Kgs 11:9; Ezra 9:11), kings (2 Sam 5:25, par. 1 Chron 14:6; 1 Kgs 9:4), and even foreign nations (Isa 10:6; Jer 50:21) are all recipients of God's commands. Most often, however, they are directed to Moses and Israel (esp. in Exod - Num). They also extend to animals (1 Kgs 17:4), the weather (Job 36:32; 37:12; Isa 5:6), the mythical sea-serpent (Amos 9:3), and angels (Ps 91:11). Nothing is beyond God's sovereign command, not even the course of history (Lam 3:37).

The use of *ṣwh* with God as subj. often signifies more than just communication. There is a close connection between God's command and his creative power: the cosmos was created by his command (Ps 148:5; cf. 33:9; Isa 45:12). Implicit in what God commands is the ability to carry it out, e.g., God commanded the building of the tabernacle and its furnishings, and he also empowered Bezalel and Oholiab to be able to accomplish the task (Exod 31:1-11; 35:30-36:1). Similarly, the phrase "I (God) will command my blessing on you" means that God *will* bless them if they follow his decrees and laws concerning the Year of Jubilee (Lev 25:21; cf. Deut 28:8; Ps 133:3; see Rubinstein, 208).

5. Next to God, Moses occurs as the subj. of *ṣwh* the most (ca. 85x), and Joshua follows (14x); both are found typically with Israel as obj. Otherwise *ṣwh* is used for the orders of fathers to sons (Gen 28:1; 1 Sam 17:20), military leaders to subordinates (Josh 1:10), kings to subjects—both Israelite kings (1 Sam 18:22; 2 Sam 21:14) and foreign (Gen 12:20; 26:11; 2 Kgs 17:27)—and employers to employees (Ruth 2:15). Women are the subj. only 5x (Gen 27:8; Ruth 3:6; Esth 4:5, 10, 17). Besides the cases where someone is acting as a spokesperson for God, when *ṣwh* has a human subj. it generally refers to orders bound to a specific situation to evoke a particular response rather than commands with abiding import (see section 3 above). This is esp. the case with orders pertaining to military or state affairs (2 Sam 4:12; 1 Kgs 2:46; 22:31).

6. More than half the occurrences of *ṣwh* are in relative clauses. The most common of these stereotyped phrases is the formula: "just as X commanded (Y)"

(*ka'ᵃšer ṣiwwâ* X *'et-Y*). This form (with variations) is regularly used to indicate that a commanded action (whether commanded by God or a human) has been carried out, and as such is usually called a "completion formula." For example, the Israelites completed the work on the tabernacle "just as the LORD commanded Moses" (Exod 39:32; cf. Gen 7:9; 1 Sam 17:20; Ezra 4:3; the quoted example with God as subj. and Moses as obj. is found ca. 55x in Exod-Num). Rather than looking back to a prior action, the other major use of the latter phrase attempts to justify and/or encourage a future action. This has been dubbed the "authentication formula" (de Vries, 311), and it is found primarily in Deut (but cf. Exod 23:15; Jer 17:22). It regularly occurs as a motive clause attached to a law: "Honor your father and your mother, as the LORD your God has commanded you" (Deut 5:12, 16; cf. v. 12; 20:17). A third stereotyped formula in which *ṣwh* is found is the phrase (with variations): "(the word/commandments) which I (Moses) am commanding you (Israel) today" (*'ᵃšer 'ānōkî mᵉṣawwᵉkā hayyôm* (Deut 6:2; cf. v. 6; 7:11; etc.). This formula occurs almost exclusively in Deut, where it contributes to that book's overall emphasis on the promulgation of the commandments to a new generation. As such it has been called the "promulgation formula" (N. Lohfink, *Das Hauptgebot*, 1963, 59).

7. The frequency of Moses as either sub. or obj. of these stereotyped formulas emphasizes his unique role as mediator and spokesperson for God (→ Moses). This function was passed on to Joshua (→; see section 9 below) and to the prophets that followed after him. The latter fact is not surprising, considering that Moses is portrayed as the archetype and norm of all prophets (cf. Deut 18:14-22). The prophet like Moses will speak "everything I (the LORD) command him" (*kol-'ᵃšer 'ᵃṣawwennû*; Deut 18:18). This notion is picked up in Jer, where Jeremiah is to speak "whatever I (the LORD) command you" (Jer 1:17). It is this faithful transmission of God's word that establishes the genuineness and legitimacy of true prophets of the Lord. In contrast, false prophets are not sent by the LORD and speak lying words, "which I did not tell them to do" (Jer 29:23; cf. 14:14; 23:32; Ezek 13:1-16).

8. Obedience to God's commands brings blessings, while disobedience brings curses (Deut 11:26-28; 27:1-28:68; cf. Gen 3:16-19; 6:22). The dire consequences of disobeying God's commands is illustrated poignantly by the death of Nadab and Abihu. They died because they offered strange fire before the Lord, "contrary to his command" (Lev 10:1-2). Similarly, the author of Sam-Kgs evaluates kings on the basis of whether they have obeyed what the Lord has commanded. The fate of both Saul and Solomon is explicitly linked to their inability to keep the Lord's commands (1 Sam 13:13-14; 1 Kgs 11:10-11, respectively). It always needs to be kept in mind, however, that obedience to God's commands is never a means to salvation, but a response to God's grace.

9. The vb. *ṣwh* is used ca. 15x to denote the appointing or setting aside of someone or something to a specific task, function, or role; in such contexts it may be glossed as appoint, give charge over, commission, ordain. This usage follows a standard pattern (→ *pqd* [section 11; attend to, # 7212]), where the appointee is indicated by *'t* (1 Kgs 1:35; Neh 5:14; 7:2) or a pron. (1 Chron 22:12), and the person or sphere over which the individual is appointed is governed by *'l* (1 Sam 7:11, par. 1 Kgs 1:35; 1 Chron 17:10; other preps. are used; cf. *b* in Neh 5:15). When expressed, the function of the appointment is indicated with *l* + infin. const. (1 Kgs 1:35; Neh 5:14) or *l* alone

(1 Sam 13:14 [first occurrence]; 25:30; 2 Sam 6:21). This formula is employed to describe the appointment of judges and governors (1 Sam 7:11, par. 1 Chron 17:10; Neh 5:14), the Lord's appointment of David "as leader over Israel" (*l^enāgîd 'al-yiśrā'ēl*; 1 Sam 13:14 [first occurrence]; 25:30; 2 Sam 6:21), and even the Lord's appointment of Assyria over Israel (Isa 10:6). The vb. *ṣwh* is also found in a number of contexts, predominantly in the Psalms with the sense ordain, establish. God has "ordained his covenant forever" (Ps 111:9) and "laid down his righteous statutes" (Ps 119:138). A related use of *ṣwh* is found in the accounts of the succession of Joshua as part of a more developed "installation formula" (Num 27:23; Deut 31:14, 23; perhaps Deut 3:23; Josh 1:9; see J. R. Porter, "The Succession of Joshua," in *Proclamation and Presence. FS G. H. Davies*, 1983, 102-32; N. Lohfink, "The Deuteronomistic Picture of the Transfer of Authority from Moses to Joshua," in *Theology of the Pentateuch*, 1994, 234-47). In these passages the vb. governs a single object (i.e., Joshua) and is usually rendered as "commission."

10. In deathbed contexts the vb. *ṣwh* may have a specialized meaning of make a last testament, give parting charges, in line with the Arab. vb. *wṣy* II noted above (cf. *HALAT*; Kopf, 197). This sense has been proposed for 1 Kgs 2:1 (cf. "and he [David] gave a charge to Solomon his son"; J. Gray, *I & II Kings*, 1970, 97), Gen 49:29 (Jacob), as well as for the idiomatic expression *ṣaw l^ebêtekā*, lit. "order your house" (2 Kgs 20:1, par. Isa 38:1; 2 Sam 17:23). While the latter phrase is typically rendered as "put your house in order" (NIV; cf. NRSV, NASB, JPS), it perhaps would be better translated as "give your last directions to your family" (see S. R. Driver, *Notes on the Hebrew Text and Topography of the Books of Samuel*, 1966, 326).

11. The nom. *miṣwâ*, commandment, is found ca. 181x in the OT. While it can refer to the commands of humans (Isa 29:13; Jer 35:14-18) and esp. the commands of a king (1 Kgs 2:43; 2 Kgs 18:36; Esth 3:3; Neh 11:23), it is more often used of God's commands (Num 15:39; Deut 4:2; 1 Kgs 18:18). As such, it is frequently found in conjunction with other legal terms, such as *tôrâ*, law, instruction (→ # 9368), *ḥōq*, statute (→ # 2976), and *mišpāṭ*, ordinance (→ # 5477; → Law of God). It is also the favorite nom. in the antecedent of the relative clause in promulgation formulas (Deut 4:2, 40; 6:2; 7:11; 8:1; etc.; see section 6 above). In some cases *miṣwâ* may be used as a technical term for the prohibitive and command law forms (see G. Liedke, *Gestalt und Bezeichnung alttestamentlicher Rechtssätze*, 1971, 187-95). (See also # 5184.)

P-B Over two-thirds of the occurrences of *ṣwh* in the LXX are translated by *entellomai*, command, order (ca. 345x), while a large majority of the others are rendered by *syntassō*, command, order, or related forms (ca. 115x).

The vb. *ṣwh* is found ca. 50x in the nonbiblical MSS from Qumran (11x in 1QS; 9x in 1QDM; 5x in 11QTemple[a] [all from Deut]; 3x in 1QH[a]; 1x in 1QSb, 1QLitPr[a] and CD-A, and ca. 18x in various cave 4 MSS). It occurs primarily in relative clauses (see section 6 above) with God or Moses as subj., underscoring the need for obedience to the decrees of God and the beliefs of the community (1QS 1.3, 17; 1QDM 2.11; etc.; cf. the "authentication formula"). The Community Rule states forthrightly: "All those who enter in the Rule of the Community shall establish a covenant before God in order to carry out all that he commands ..." (*kkwl 'šr ṣwh*; 1QS 1.16-17). In the para-biblical text 1QDM *ṣwh* occurs in participial form in promulgation formulas that clearly mimic biblical usage (cf. 1QDM 1.9; 2.2, 4).

NT The vb. *entellomai*, command, is used 15x in the NT (→ Command, *NIDNTT* 1:330-43), while vbs. from the root *tassō*, command, are found ca. 100x (→ Determine, *NIDNTT* 1:476-77). Among the occurrences of *entellomai* there are four quotations of the LXX (Matt 4:6 [par. Luke 4:10] quotes Ps 91:11-12; Acts 13:47 quotes Isa 49:6; Heb 9:20 quotes Exod 24:8 [somewhat modified]), and one allusion (Heb 11:22 and Gen 48:15-16).

Appointment, commandment, summons: → *zmn* (be appointed, # 2374); → *y'd* (determine, designate, appoint, assemble, # 3585); → *mnh* (count, reckon, assign, appoint, ordain, # 4948); → *'md* (stand, take one's stand, station, appoint, # 6641); → *pqd* (punish, assemble, record, appoint, # 7212); → *ṣwh* (order, command, charge, direct, appoint, # 7422); → *šyt* (put, set, lay, appoint, # 8883)

Bibliography

THAT 2:530-36; *TWAT* 6:936-59; L. Kopf, "Arabische Etymologien und Parallelen zum Bibelwörterbuch," *VT* 8, 1958, 197-98; E. Rubinstein, "The Verb צוה—A Study in the Syntax of Biblical Hebrew," (Heb.) in *Proceedings of the Sixth World Congress of Jewish Studies,* ed. A. Shinan, 1977, 2:207-12; S. J. de Vries, "The Development of the Deuteronomic Promulgation Formula," *Bib* 55, 1974, 301-16.

Tyler F. Williams

7423	צוח

צוח (*ṣwḥ*), q. shout (# 7423).

OT The vb. is a hapleg., appearing in Isa 42:11. It is parallel to *rnn*, to shout with joy, and occurs in a holy war context. The vb. signifies the response to the appearance of the divine warrior (→).

Shout, (war-)cry, yell: → *hêdād* (shout, # 2116); → *ṣwḥ* (shout, # 7423); → *ṣrḥ* (yell, call shrilly, raise the war-cry, # 7658); → *rw'* (shout, give war-cry, # 8131); → *rnn* (yell, shout [w. joy], moan, # 8264)

Tremper Longman III

7425 (*ṣûlâ*, abyss), → # 5185

7426	צום

צום (*ṣwm*), q. fast (# 7426); nom. צוֹם (*ṣôm*), fasting (# 7427).

OT 1. A fast is a period of complete abstinence from food and sometimes from drink undertaken as a religious observance or as a plea to God.

2. The vb. occurs only in q., to fast, abstain from food. The nom. *ṣôm* designates an act of fasting as a personal observance (e.g., 1 Kgs 21:9, 12), a public ritual (Joel 1:14; 2:15), or state of being in a fast (Neh 9:1).

3. Nom. *ṣôm* is predicated to *qr'*, call (# 7924) 5x (e.g., 1 Kgs 21:9, 12), to *qdš*, consecrate (# 7727) 2x (Joel 1:14; 2:15), and less pertinently to *bḥr*, choose (# 1047) 2x (Isa 58:5, 6). The act of fasting belongs to the semantic field that also contains weep, mourn, wear sackcloth and ashes, deny oneself, and to do no work. The phrase *'nh nepeš*, afflict one's soul (→ # 6700; # 5883), found particularly in Leviticus, is used in apposition to *ṣōm* (Ps 35:13; Isa 58:3, 5). It explicitly includes resting from

work: "you must deny yourselves (*'nh nepeš*) and not do any work" (Lev 16:29, 31; 23:27, 32), and is said in Ps 35:13 (*'nh nepeš*) and in Ezra 8:21 (hitp. *'nh*) to be an end to which fasting may lead. However, the phrase *'nh nepeš* is not a synonym of *ṣôm* (contrary to NIV note on Lev 16:29, which equates self-denial and fasting). Dan 10:3 confirms that the use of *'nh* (hitp.; Dan 10:12) includes fasting. The derived nom. *ta'ᵃnît*, mortification, penitential exercise, occurs in Ezra 9:5 and becomes the standard rabbinic word for a fast.

4. Fasting expresses self-abnegation in order to assert the reality of God and the imperative of his law. Fasting signifies the worshiper's awareness of the sublimity and the holiness of God (W. Eichrodt, *TOT*, 1:406-10). This understanding aggravates the evil of Jezebel's deceit in 1 Kgs 21:9-10. There is no suggestion in the OT that the purpose of fasting is to liberate the spirit from the prison of the flesh or from contact with unspiritual physical matter. The OT is positive in its evaluation of the created world (→ *br'*, create, # 1343). The linking of fasting with the absence of work (Lev 16:29) and self-denial (Lev 16:31; cf. 1 Sam 7:6; 2 Sam 1:11, 12; 1 Macc 3:47) should be understood as a stepping aside from the good gifts of God in order to lay oneself open to their giver. Fasting is open to abuse when it becomes a means to acquire merit, to call oneself to God's attention, or even to put pressure on God.

5. Fasts could be ordered by leaders (Ezra 8:21-23; 2 Macc 13:12) or be undertaken by individuals on their own initiative (Ezra 10:6; Neh 1:4). An oath of self-denial (which included a decision to fast, so N. H. Snaith, "Numbers," *Peake*, §§ 228e, 267) taken by a widow or a divorcee was binding, but in the case of a married woman it needed her husband's expressed or tacit consent (Num 30:9-15[10-16]).

6. The fast of the Day of Atonement was the only regular fast enjoined on Israel from early days, but four other liturgical fasts were introduced after the Exile (Lev 16:1-34; 23:27-32; cf. Esth 9:1-32; Zech 7:3; 8:19). The fasts of Zech 7-8 are traditionally, but not certainly, connected with the events surrounding the fall of Jerusalem. In the LXX Isa 1:13 reads "a fast and laziness" (NIV evil assemblies)—thus placing a temple-based fast before the Exile. The MT exhibits difficulties, but has Vg. support. Fasting did not occur only on the Day of Atonement but occasional fasts were also held (Jer 36:6-9). The distribution of OT references to fasts suggests that they increased with the passage of time. Fasting normally lasted from sunrise to sunset (Judg 20:26; 1 Sam 14:24). The extended fast of Exod 34:28 is abnormal.

7. Some occasional fasts were responsive or reactive for the following purposes: (a) to display conviction of sin publicly (Deut 9:7-19; 1 Sam 7:6; Ezra 10:6; Neh 9:1; Joel 2:12; Jon 3:5; perhaps Jer 36:6-9). Along with some of the penitential Psalms, the book of Lam may conceivably have been composed for use on such occasions, and Isa 59 may embody public confessional forms (P. Ackroyd, *Exile and Restoration*, 1968, 47);

(b) to offer supplication for the deliverance of oneself (Jer 14:11, 12) or of another, even an enemy, from distress (Ps 35:13; cf. Matt 5:44);

(c) to react to the threat of persecution (Esth 4:1-3). The book of Esth is secular in outlook and illustrates how religious practice may take on largely social significance. Ahab's action in 1 Kgs 21:4-7 was not a fast but a sulk;

(d) to mourn the death of a loved one. This fast was observed for varying periods of time (2 Sam 1:12; 3:35): one day (1 Sam 31:13; Jth 16:24), seven days

(Gen 50:10; 2 Sam 12:15-23), or an indefinite period. Judith's lifelong fast was exceptional (Jth 8:5-6). David's refusal to fast after the death of his son by Bathsheba created a stir (2 Sam 12:19-23; see *AncIsr*, 59, 60).

8. Some occasional fasts were proactive:

(a) to call God's attention to the worshiper (Isa 58:3), sometimes with considerable emaciation (Ps 109:24) and personal self-affliction (2 Sam 12:16);

(b) to make a plea to God for deliverance from a natural disaster such as famine (Joel 1:14) or from a military defeat (Joel 2:15-20), or vicariously to gain the deliverance of another from physical (Esth 4:16) or from moral danger (Ezra 10:6);

(c) as a means of gaining spiritual insight either legitimately (Exod 34:28; 2 Chron 20:3; Dan 10:3, 12) or illegitimately (1 Sam 28:20). It is not certain whether Daniel's fast was to gain insight or was a part of his mourning (Dan 10:2-3). To eat is not inimical to fellowship with God, for on Sinai the elders "saw God, and they ate and drank" (Exod 24:11);

(d) as a part of the Holy War (1 Sam 14:24-30; 1 Macc 3:46-60); cf. *AncIsr*, 262, 265.

9. The practice of fasting was also used by some to divert attention from their true need of spirit. Two texts especially not only show the social implications of the righteousness of life for which fasting is a plea, but also make a vivid indictment of the way in which the outward grace of the self-discipline can overlay an attempt to disguise an inward disgrace of heart (Isa 58:1-6; Zech 7:9-10). Fasting of which God approves must be undergirded by the practical embrace of positive virtues (Isa 58:5-12; Jer 14:10-12; cf. Mic 6:6-8; Luke 18:9-14). A similar conviction may underlie Zech 7:4-10, but von Rad understands this passage to reflect the uncertainty of the people over whether their appointed days were intended for fasting or for feasting (*OTT* 2:103).

P-B Official days of fasting were increased as time went by (Mish. Roš Haššana 3:4 and Mish. Ta'anit 1:1-4:8). The usual expression for fasting, *'nh nepeš*, afflict the soul, came to embrace wider self-abnegation than just abstinence from food and could include drinking, washing, anointing, putting on sandals, and marital intercourse (Mish. Ta'anit 1:5). Fasting was intended to create an ethical space in which the worshiper could be met by God. In postexilic times this view was overtaken by its perversion, the belief that the rigors of the fast gave the worshiper a claim on God. Alert to this folly, the midrash on Ps 25:3, "they will be put to shame who are treacherous without excuse," reads: "These are they who fast without repentance" (C. G. Montefiore, *A Rabbinic Anthology*, 1938, 321).

NT By the first century regular fasting was a part of normal religious living (Mark 2:18; Luke 18:12). Jesus caused some indignation by refusing to follow the practice (Luke 7:33-34).

Fast, humility: → *'nh* II (afflict, humble, afflict one's soul, fast, oppress, submit, # 6700); → *ṣwm* (fast, # 7426)

Feasts & festivals: → *bikkûrîm* (early or firstfruits, # 1137); → *ḥag* (procession, round dance, festival, feast, # 2504); → *ḥ^{a}nukkâ* (dedication, Feast of Dedication, # 2853); → *mô'ēd* (appointed time, # 4595); → *maṣṣôt* (Feast of the Unleavened Bread, # 5174a); → *marzēaḥ* (cultic feast, funeral meal, # 5301); → *sukkôt* (Feast of Tabernacles, # 6109a); → *'^{a}ṣārâ* (festive assembly, # 6809); → *pûrîm* (festival of Purim, # 7052a); → *pesaḥ* (Feast or sacrifice of Passover, # 7175 [→ **Passover: Theology**]); → *rō'š ḥōdeš* (festival of the new Moon, # 8031a); → *rō'š haššānâ* (beginning of the year, # 8031b); → *šābu'ôt* (feast of Weeks, # 8651a); → *šabbāt* (sabbath, # 8701 [→ **Sabbath: Theology**])

Bibliography

NIDNTT 1:611-13; *TDNT* 4:926-31; *THAT* 2:536-38; P. Ackroyd, *Exile and Restoration*, 1967; *AncIsr* 59-61, 262-65, 387, 507.

Robert. J. Way

7427 (*ṣôm*, fasting), → # 7426

7429	צוף

צוף (*ṣwp* I), q. flood, overflow; hi. make float (# 7429); צוּף (*ṣûp* I), honeycomb (→ # 7430).

ANE Mish. Heb. *ṣwp*, float on the surface, float; Jewish-Aram. *ṭûp*, inundate, flood; Pal.-Aram. *ṭûp*, to make float; Syr. *ṭāp*, inundate, flood; Mand. *ṭUP*, overflow, inundate.

OT 1. This verbal root occurs 3x (Deut 11:4; 2 Kgs 6:6; Lam 3:54). From the later cognates, *ṣwp* appears to connote flooding and floating. The two hi. instances (Deut 11:4; 2 Kgs 6:6) offer a possible explanation of the rationale for these two diverse meanings for *ṣwp*. The primary meaning may be to pass above or pass over. Consequently, the hi. forms connote to cause to pass above/over. When used with water as the object, *ṣwp* denotes flooding (Deut 11:4—where Yahweh overwhelms the Egyptian army with the collapsing walls of water at the Red Sea), and when juxtaposed with *barzel*, ax, it describes the act of causing the ax to rise to the top of the water, i.e., float (describing Elisha's making the lost axhead to float).

2. A q. form depicts water that passes over a person or thing. In Lam 3 the writer describes Israel's traumatic experience of the siege and destruction of Jerusalem from the perspective of one person. That person becomes totally submerged (*ṣwp*, q.) by the overwhelming flood of devastation, depicting the desperate and almost hopeless nature of Israel's experience of affliction.

P-B In later Heb. this root is well attested. In the q. *ṣwp* connotes to come to the surface, flood or to lie in a conspicuous place. In addition to the causative versions of the preceding meanings, the hi. also signifies, to flood, inundate (Jastrow 2:1268-69).

Flood, deluge, torrent: → *bz'* (wash away, # 1021); → *grp* (wash away, # 1759); → *mabbûl* (heavenly ocean, deluge, # 4429); → *niggeret* (torrent, # 5600); → *ṣwp* (flood, rise up, make float, # 7429); → *šibbōlet* II (torrent, undulation, # 8673); → *šôṭ* II ([sudden] flood, # 8766); → *šṭp* (wash away, flood, overflow, # 8851); → *šeṣep* (flooding, # 9192)

Bibliography

M. Weinfeld, *Deuteronomy 1-11*, AB, 1991.

Michael A. Grisanti

7430	צוף

צוּף (*ṣûp* I), nom. virgin honey (*HALAT* 950) (# 7430).

OT Metaphorically *ṣûp* is used in connection with *d^e baš*, honey (Prov 16:24), and *nōpet*, honey (Ps 19:10[11], NIV honey from the comb), denoting most probably natural honey in its liquid form (Dalman 6:294). McKane (493) argues that both the palatable taste and the medicinal virtue of the honeycomb are here alluded to in order to indicate the therapeutic value of pleasant words.

Honey: → *d^e baš* I (honey, # 1831); → *ya'ar* II (honeycombs, # 3624); → *nopet* (honey, honey from the comb, # 5885); → *ṣûp*, I (virgin honey, # 7430)

BIBLIOGRAPHY
G. Dalman, *AuSP*, VI, repr. 1964.

J. P. J. Olivier

7436 (*ṣôpar*, Zophar), → Zophar

7437	צוץ

צוץ (*ṣwṣ* I), q. sprout; bloom; hi. produce blossoms (# 7437); ציץ (*ṣîṣ* I), צִיצָה (*ṣîṣâ*), blossoms, flower (# 7488, # 7491).

ANE Egyp. *ḏḏ*, flowers.

OT 1. The vb. *ṣwṣ*. The flower that flourishes but soon vanishes was a favorite wisdom image for the ephemeral nature of human life. The poet bewails the transience of humanity with this figure; both the evil and the righteous bloom but also shrivel (Ps 90:3-6). The writer meditates on the destiny of humankind (referred to in the third person) within an address to God. God decreed at the dawn of the universe that people must die: "You turn men back to dust, saying 'Return to dust, O sons of men'" (v. 3). This translation reflects a correct understanding of the verse (Krüger, 198-99). An alternate view considers v. 3b as an advancement, in the sense of a return to life on the part of the dead mentioned in v. 3a. However, the context makes that improbable.

Verse 4 reiterates the theme of v. 2 and illustrates the infinite difference between God's eternity and people's transiency through comparisons involving finite intervals. That difference is further developed with the Heb. vb. *ṣwṣ*, flower, "springs up" (v. 6). Together, vv. 3-6, whose theme v. 10 resumes, comprehend both nascence and disappearance under the work of God. By reciting to the Creator the prevailing transitoriness of human beings (a situation true for all creatures), the lamentation affirms the conviction that humanity can appeal to God. Because God gives life just as he imposes death, humans faced with dying can call on him (Schmidt, 122).

It is possible that Ps 90 bemoans less mortality in general than premature death in particular. Certainly, the bulk of the poem deplores the special suffering of the Israelites, who perished through the agency of God's anger because of their own evil. Either way, human beings have reason to concede their finiteness and renounce their pretensions.

Ps 103:15-18 contrasts the impermanence of people's lives with the permanence of Yahweh's love. On the one hand, human life is ephemeral—like a flower that "flourishes" (*ṣwṣ*), then "is gone." On the other hand, divine love is eternal—persisting down through future generations. The uncertainty of temporal life is stressed in order to set in greater relief the certainty of steadfast love.

The strophe insists that Yahweh can always be depended on to continue demonstrating his merciful character toward the citizens of his kingdom. Thanks to his acts of providence and pardon, the short-lived existence of mortals is somewhat mitigated (see vv. 3-5). Naturally, there are conditions. It is to those who respond to Yahweh's love by walking in harmony with the precepts of his covenants and commandments that his righteous deliverance will come. Yahweh is compassionate toward finite human beings but does expect them to bind themselves closely to himself (Mays, 31).

Yahweh's recognition that individuals will die before long might be exactly what evokes his loving indulgence and righteous concern (Dion, 13, 15, 30). It is the part of wisdom for human beings to discern and embrace their true place before God.

Striking contacts with Ps 103:15-17 are exhibited in Isa 40:6-8. The Isaianic picture of field flowers (here actually the nom. *ṣîṣ*) withering and falling under the hot summer wind stands once more for the finitude of all corporeal strength, which is set against the incontestable infinitude of spiritual power. However, whereas it was divine love that the psalmist contrasted with human life, it is Yahweh's enduring word that the prophet contrasts with people's fading glory. The prophet seems to have done so in order to counter doubt about whether the tidings of God's solace would be fulfilled.

2. The nom. *ṣîṣ* is associated with cultic objects. God instructs Moses to "make a plate of pure gold" (Exod 28:36). The nom. "plate" renders the vocable *ṣîṣ*, which denotes "flower." Hence, the ornament, however stylized, was a flower or blossom of some kind. The object could have been a piece bearing floral decorations or could have had the actual form of a flower. The plate/flower, a golden ornament, belonged to the ancient Israelite high priest. Held onto the forehead by a violet-colored cord, perhaps a band stretching across the forehead from ear to ear or encircling the whole head, it communicated the special position of that priest. Aaron alone—but not his sons during his lifetime—was supposed to wear this reserved sign of consecration on the front of his turban. He and subsequent high priests donned the headdress whenever they officiated inside the tabernacle complex (or, at least, the Tent of Meeting).

Verse 38, which brings the plate/flower into association with the offerings of the people, is turgidly formulated and not altogether intelligible in its details. Should a gift or sacrifice in some instance be unsatisfactory for some reason, perilous guilt would accrue, for which the high priest would be answerable. In such a case, it seems the forehead ornament could shield him from the consequences of that guilt.

The florally shaped or florally engraved accessory may have been regarded as an element of life and of life-giving power. If so, the golden plate/flower itself would have been viewed as efficacious in averting harm. Additionally, it was inscribed with the epigraph "HOLY TO THE LORD," which possibly performed an apotropaic function and reinforced the operation of the ornament (Exod 39:30). (Archaeologists have discovered artifacts used in temple ritual marked with the word "holy".)

An appositive in Exod 39:30; Lev 8:9 qualifies the plate/flower more precisely to have been a "sacred diadem" (compare Exod 29:6). The specification as holy is traceable both to the object's cultic role and to its inscription. A crown was one of the emblems of royal authority that was given the high priest in postmonarchical times.

Apparently one was installed into an office when the vestments were donned (note Num 20:25-26). This may partially account for the Pentateuchal attention paid to the sacerdotal garments and their functions. The symbolic importance of clothing throughout Scripture is attested by the many metaphors that relate moral virtues to apparel: for example, "may your priests be clothed with righteousness" (Ps 132:9), and "he has clothed me with garments of salvation" (Isa 61:10).

3. In Isa 28:4, *ṣîṣâ* denotes "flower."

P-B Large DSS fragments of a poem (4Q185), in which a teacher encourages the people to search for wisdom, preserve two instances of the nom. *ṣîṣ* in a citation from Isa 40:6-8.

Flower, bud: → *prḥ* I (sprout, bud, bring to bloom, # 7255); → *ṣwṣ* I (sprout, bloom, # 7437)

BIBLIOGRAPHY

TWOT 759-60; P. E. Dion, "Psalm 103—A Meditation on the 'Ways' of the Lord," *Église et Théologie* 21, 1990, 13-31; M. Görg, "Die Kopfbedeckung des Hohenpriesters," *BN* 3, 1974, 24-26; T. Krüger, "Psalm 90 und die 'Vergänglichkeit des Menschen,'" *Bib* 75, 1994, 191-219; J. L. Mays, "Psalm 103—Mercy Joined to Loving Kindness," *Austin Seminary Bulletin* 105, 1990, 27-32; W. H. Schmidt, "'Der Du die Menschen lässest sterben': Exegetische Anmerkungen zu Ps 90," in *Was ist der Mensch ...? Beiträge zur Anthropologie des Alten Testaments*, ed. F. Crüsemann et al., 1992, 115-30; T. M. Willis, "'So Great Is His Steadfast Love': A Rhetorical Analysis of Psalm 103," *Bib* 72, 1991, 525-37.

Edwin C. Hostetter

7438	צוץ

צוץ (*ṣwṣ* II), hi. look at (# 7438).

OT The vb. indicates the action of peeping through a narrow opening. In S of Songs 2:9 the lover, who tried to invite his girl to enjoy the beauty of nature with him, peeped through the pierced places of the window, because it would be arrogant to enter the house of her father.

P-B Jastrow mentions the use of this vb. in the sense look out, peep (2:1269).

Look, observation, perception, sight, vision, watch: → *ḥdh* II (gaze on, appear, # 2526); → *ḥzh* (see, perceive, behold, # 2600); → *ḥmh* I (see, watch out for, become visible, # 2778); → *nbṭ* (look around, accept as an act of grace, # 5564); → *pls* II (observe, # 7143); → *ṣwṣ* II (look at, # 7438); → *r'h* (see, have visions, choose, perceive, # 8011); → *rṣd* (keep one's eye on, # 8353); → *śqd* (take note of, # 8567); → *š'h* III (stand gazing, # 8617); → *šgḥ* (gaze, stare, # 8708); → *šwr* I (gaze on, regard, see, # 8800); → *šzp* (catch sight of, tan, scorch, # 8812); → *š'h* (look, care about, gaze about, # 9120); → *šqp* (look down, # 9207); → *št'* (gaze, look, regard, look anxiously about, # 9283)

BIBLIOGRAPHY

G. Gerleman, *Ruth. Das Hohelied*, 1981.

Jackie A. Naudé

7439	צוק

צוק (*ṣwq* I), hi. constrain, bring into straits, close or press in/upon, harass, vex (# 7439); מוּצָק (*mûṣāq*), nom. restriction, distress, affliction, grief, tribulation, trial (# 4608); מָצוֹק (*māṣôq* II), nom. affliction, distress, grief, suffering, stress, tribulation, trial (# 5186); מְצוּקָה (*m*e*ṣûqâ*), nom. straitness, straits, stress, suffering, plight, distress, anguish, affliction, oppression (# 5188); צוֹק (*ṣôq*), nom. constraint, distress, plight, affliction, oppression (hapleg.; # 7441); צוּקָה (*ṣûqâ*), nom. pressure, distress, plight, affliction, oppression (# 7442).

ANE The vb. is well attested: e.g., Ugar. *ṣwq*, exert pressure; Akk. *siāqum, sâqu,* be, become narrow; Arab. *ḍāqa* (*ḍjk*), be, become anxious, uneasy, depressed; annoy, anger, vex, worry, harass, irk; Syr. *'āq* (*'wq*), feel disgust, aversion, loathing, be depressed. Nom. forms are also frequent: Arab. *ḍīq,* narrowness, confinement, restriction, difficulty, dilemma, straits; *ḍaiqat/ḍīqat,* straitened/narrow circumstances, anxiety, uneasiness, oppression; Geez *ṣä'aqä,* compress; Eth. *ṭĕwqat* and *tĕwāqē,* narrowness, straits, distress, affliction, oppression; Syr. *'āqtā',* pain, grief, sorrow, anguish; *'iqūtā,* sorrowfulness, dejectedness.

OT 1. This group of words expresses the severe physical and psychological hardship or distress that individuals or a whole nation (Israel) suffers on account of an external force or party (personal foes or a hostile nation).

2. *ṣwq* and its derivatives describe the terrible suffering and oppressive siege conditions inflicted on the population of northern Israel (Samaria) and Jerusalem by Assyria and Babylonia respectively (Isa 8:22; 9:1[8:23]; 29:2, 7; 30:6; 51:13; Jer 19:9; cf. Deut 28:53, 55, 57). These words appear in contexts where catastrophic conditions caused by siege are described: distress, famine, darkness, destruction, imprisonment, war, desolation, death (Isa 8:21-22; 51:13-14; Jer 19:7-8; Dan 9:25-26). Severe famine was caused by hostile armies who claimed for themselves all the crops and cattle of the land (Deut 28:51). The distress (*māṣôq*) could become so harsh that the suffering people might even eat their children (Deut 28:53, 55, 57; Jer 19:9).

3. The hi. usually conveys the idea of pressure being exerted on an individual or group to grind down resistance, patience, courage, resolve, or moral standards. Samson's Philistine wife "pressed him hard" (RSV) for the explanation of his riddle (Judg 14:17) and "prodded" him to extract the secret of his awesome strength (Judg 16:16). By rejecting God's love, spurning his service, and forfeiting the joyful privileges of the covenant relationship, the Israelites would be reduced to dire straits (Deut 28:53, 55, 57; Jer 19:9, NEB; REB; lit. "in straitness ... they will straiten you"). According to Isa 29:2, Yahweh will "reduce Ariel [Jerusalem] to sore straits" (REB; cf. NEB. NIV has "besiege"; cf., JB), but in Isa 29:7, the threat of annihilation is leveled instead at all who attack and "hem her in" (REB; cf. NIV besiege; RSV distress; NEB her oppressors).

4. The personal calamity of an individual is also expressed by the nom. forms (Ps 25:17; 107:6; 119:143). On the one hand, the distressful situation is caused by personal foes (Ps 25:2; 107:2; 119:139). On the other, personal disaster is the natural consequence of rejecting divine wisdom, knowledge, and the fear of Yahweh (Prov 1:27-29).

(a) The meaning of the nom. *mûṣāq* is well illustrated in Job 36:16, part of a passage bristling with linguistic problems. It is uncertain whether Job is being accused, warned, or encouraged. It is also unclear by what means the sufferer is being (NIV), or was (RSV), or will be (Dhorme, 544-45) enticed "from the jaws of distress to a spacious place free from restriction" (NIV). Moreover, it is difficult to work out whether Job is being persuaded here to see his affliction in terms of corrective discipline or is being assured that his present distress will save him from a worse calamity in the future. However, what is perfectly clear is that *mûṣāq* ("restriction," NIV; "cramping anguish," Dhorme) signifies being hemmed in on every side with no possibility of movement, in contrast with the unrestricted freedom afforded by "a spacious place" (see Smick, "Job," *EBC* 4:1022).

(b) The nom. *māṣôq* describes the condition of those hard-pressed by the pressures of society (1 Sam 22:2) or beset by life's trials and tribulations (Ps 119:143; cf. 32:6 [emending *lᵉ'ēt mᵉṣō' raq*, "while you may be found," accepted by NIV, to *lᵉ'ēt māṣôq*, "at a time of stress/distress/anxiety, trouble," followed by NRSV; RSV; NAB; NEB; REB; JB; C. A. and E. G. Briggs, 280; Anderson, 258; Craigie, 264, 267). An interesting alternative is offered by Buttenwieser (653, 656), who translates "When he comes to search in his heart," on the ground that *mᵉṣō'* is a case of ellipsis, the omitted object being *'et libbô*, "his heart." In support of his translation, he points out that in place of the full phrase, *māṣā' 'abdᵉkā 'et libbô*, which occurs in 2 Sam 7:27, the parallel text, 1 Chron 17:25, uses the ellipsis *māṣā' 'abdᵉkā*]).

Despair is overcome either by meditating on the *tôrâ,* which leads to reassurance of God's protection (Ps 119), or by confessing the guilt of one's sins and experiencing divine forgiveness and healing (Ps 32).

(c) The nom. *mᵉṣûqâ* is used both of the overpowering "anguish" of conscience, which deprives the wicked of enjoyment, security, and peace of mind (Job 15:24), and of the anguish Israelites will experience in the day of Yahweh because of their enmity and rebellion (Zeph 1:15). The phrase "from their distress" occurs 4x in Ps 107, a group thanksgiving in which pilgrims praise Yahweh for the retrieval of disorientated travelers (v. 6), the release of prisoners (v. 13), the restoration of the sick and afflicted (v. 19), and the rescue of storm-tossed mariners (v. 28).

(d) The nom. *ṣûqâ* describes the harsh and dangerous Negev (Isa 30:6), the "fearful gloom" (*mᵉ'ûp ṣûqâ*) to be experienced by those seeking guidance from the occult instead of from Yahweh (8:22), and the calamitous "troubles" that will overwhelm those who despise moral instruction (Prov 1:27).

(e) The nom. forms are frequently used along with the noms. *ṣar* and *ṣārâ,* distress, two words that eminently express the intense inner turmoil and anguish of the afflicted (Job 36:16; Ps 25:17; 107:6; 119:143; Prov 1:27; Isa 8:22; Zeph 1:15; → *ṣrr* [# 7675]). In a few instances the vb. and noms. are used in contexts of severe psychological and emotional distress that the afflicted suffer: they mourn and lament (Isa 29:2) and in their distress cry out to God for help (Ps 107:6; → *lḥs* [# 4315]). In two instances of personal distress (Judg 14:17; 16:16), the vb. appears to express psychological pressure or constraint inflicted on an individual by another person, leading to severe physical exhaustion (note NIV's translation of 16:16: "she prodded him day after day until he was tired to death"). In Job 32:18 *ṣwq* expresses the psychological pressure exerted by a person's own spirit.

5. The terrible siege conditions described by *ṣwq* and its derivatives are at the same time an expression of God's curse and judgment of his disobedient people (Deut 28:53, 55, 57; Jer 19:9). In Zeph 1:15 *mᵉṣûqâ* describes the Day of the Lord, a day of distress, anguish, trouble, ruin, and darkness (cf. Amos 5:18). Yet this situation will not last indefinitely, for God will send his Messiah to his afflicted people, and there will be no more gloom for those who were in distress (*mûṣāq*) (Isa 9:1a[8:23a]).

P-B The nom. *ṣûqâ* is used 3x in 1QH (3:7; 6:33; 9:13), where it represents distress caused by personal foes (or the foes of the community?) similar to that in the OT psalms. In 3:7 the distress is compared to that of a woman in travail, an image used a number of times in the OT to express the nature of oppression and affliction (see also *TWAT* 6:968). The vb. also occurs in other postbiblical texts with the meaning be distressed, worry, and in hi., distress, afflict (Jastrow 2:1270).

Despair, discouragement, grief, trouble: → *'āgēm* (sad, grieved, distressed, # 108); → *y'š* (despair, be hopeless, # 3286); → *mwg* (melt, reel, waver, lose courage, # 4570); → *mss* (waste away, melt, dissolve, lose courage, # 5022); → *'gm* (be afflicted, distressed, grieved, # 6327); → *ṣwq* I (constrain, press in/upon, harass, vex, # 7439); → *ṣrr* I (bind, shut up, be narrow, in straits, distress, # 7674); → *mwg* (melt, reel, waver, lose courage, # 4570); → *qṣr* II (be short, be/become discouraged, worn out, # 7918); → *rph* (become slack, lose heart, discourage, # 8332); → *šyḥ* (melt away, be in despair, # 8863)

Affliction, oppression: → *dḥq* (oppress, # 1895); → *ḥms* I (do violence, # 2803); → *ḥmṣ* II (oppress, # 2807); → *ynh* (oppress, # 3561); → *lḥṣ* (press, # 4315); → *māṣôr* I (affliction, siege, # 5189); → *mrr* I (be bitter, distraught, afflict, # 5352); → *nega'* (plague, affliction, # 5596); → *ngś* (exact, # 5601); → *'nh* II (afflict, humble, afflict one's soul, fast, oppress, submit, # 6700); → *'wq* I (crush?, # 6421); → *'mr* II (deal tyrannically with, # 6683); → *'šq* I (wrong, # 6943); → *ṣwq* I (constrain, press in/upon, harass, vex, # 7439); → *ṣwr* II (deal tyrannically with, # 7444); → *rhb* (assail, press, pester, alarm, confuse, # 8104); → *rṣṣ* (crush, # 8368); → *tôlāl* (oppressor, # 9354); → *tōk* (oppression, # 9412)

BIBLIOGRAPHY

THAT 2:582-83; *TWOT* 2:1844; W. F. Albright, "Palestinian Inscriptions," in *ANET*, 1969, 320-22; A. A. Anderson, *The Book of Psalms. Volume 1: Introduction and Psalms 1-72,* 1972; C. A. and E. G. Briggs, *A Critical and Exegetical Commentary on the Book of Psalms,* vol. 1, 1960; M. Buttenwiser, *The Psalms Chronologically Treated with a New Translation,* 1969; B. S. Childs, *Exodus: A Commentary,* 1974; R. A. Cole, *Exodus: An Introduction and Commentary,* 1973; P. C. Craigie, *Psalms 1-50,* 1983; M. Dahood, *Psalms I: 1-50. Introduction, Translation, and Notes,* 1966; W. T. Davison, *The Psalms: I-LXXII,* n.d.; E. Dhorme, *A Commentary on the Book of Job,* 1967; T. E. Fretheim, *The Suffering of God: An Old Testament Perspective,* 1984; T. D. Hanks, *God So Loved the Third World: The Biblical Vocabulary of Oppression,* 1983, 3-39; Y. I. Kim, "The Vocabulary of Oppression in the Old Testament," Ph.D. diss. Drew University, 1981; A. F. Kirkpatrick, *The Book of Psalms,* 1957; H.-J. Kraus, *Psalms 1-59: A Commentary,* 1988; C. F. Marriottini, "The Problem of Social Oppression in the Eighth Century Prophets," Ph.D. diss., Southern Baptist Theological Seminary, 1983; W. McKane, *Proverbs: A New Approach,* 1970; J. Miranda, *Communism in the Bible,* 1982, 37-39; J. Pons, *L'oppression dans l'Ancien Testament,* 1981; J. F. A. Sawyer, "Spaciousness: An Important Feature of Language About Salvation in the Old Testament," *ASTI* 6, 1967-68, 20-34; E. Tamez, *Bible of the Oppressed,* 1982, 1-30; A. Weiser, *The Psalms: A Commentary,* 1965; H. W. Wolff, *Anthropology of the Old Testament,* 1974.

I. Swart/Robin Wakely

7441 (*ṣôq*, distress, plight, affliction, oppression), → # 7439

7442 (*ṣûqâ*, pressure, distress, oppression), → # 7439

7443	צור

צור (*ṣwr* I), q. besiege, enclose, confine (# 7443); מָצוֹר (*māṣôr* I), nom. oppression, siege, siege-enclosure (→ # 5189); nom. מְצוּרָה(*m*ᵉ*ṣûrâ* II), fortification (# 5193).

OT 1. *ṣwr* I and *ṣrr* I (# 7674) are regarded as byforms, but there are several Semitic roots with closely related meanings of confinement, distress, hostility (cf. *ṣwr* II, *ṣrr* II [→ # 7444; # 7675]). Assignment of a word to the correct root is sometimes uncertain and even inappropriate because of this overlap of meaning.

2. *ṣwr* I probably has a basic meaning of bind, enclose, tie up (as does the related root *ṣrr* I, → # 7674). Thus, Ezekiel binds up his hair in the folds of his robe (Ezek 5:3), and Naaman ties up silver in a bag (2 Kgs 5:23; cf. Deut 14:25). However, binding up gold in a bag is only one interpretation of the vb. in Exod 32:4 (so M. Noth, "Zur Anfertigung," 419-22). Most uses of the vb. occur in a military context, when enclosure means the general idea of distress and the specific one of siege.

3. One purpose of a siege was to capture a wanted person (David, 1 Sam 23:8; the traitor Sheba, 2 Sam 20:15). Material gain is another possibility (silver and slaves in 1 Kgs 20:1), but usually siege is the necessary means for establishing and maintaining the rule of a king (David, 2 Sam 11:1) or emperor (Assyrian, 2 Kgs 18:9; Babylonian, 2 Kgs 24:10-11). It could involve a variety of strategems and equipment, both on the part of attacker (2 Sam 20:15; Isa 29:2-3; Ezek 4:1-3) and defender (e.g., good water supplies, Nah 3:14). For Israel there are rules of siege, which include ecological limits (Deut 20:10-20). In Ps 139:5, God hems the psalmist in on every side. This could be read negatively as a lament, complaining at God's oppressive constraint. However, it might also be a positive assurance of his comprehensive care, or simply an affirmation of absolute sovereignty.

4. For Israel the success or failure of a siege depended on God's will and the people's attitude. Deut 28:52-57 affirms that disobedience will lead to the breakdown of physical, social, and religious life as a result of siege famine. This is worked out in the deuteronomistic history, as Samaria falls before the Assyrian siege because of sin (2 Kgs 17:5), and Jerusalem falls before the Babylonians. Despite the earlier preservation under Hezekiah, divine judgment on Israel's faithlessness made a successful siege inevitable (Isa 29:3; Jer 21:4; Ezek 4; cf. 6:11-12). Yet in turn Babylon will fall to siege (Isa 21:2), and no amount of preparation can save a city under divine sentence (Nineveh, Nah 3:14).

5. *māṣôr* I, oppression, siege (from *ṣwr* I), should be distinguished from *māṣôr* II, *meṣûrâ* II, fortress (→ # 5190; # 5193; *HALAT* 589). *māṣôr* may mean the siege generally, the siege works, or the associated distress (→ # 5189). When a city comes into siege, *māṣôr* refers to the whole process; but it refers to siege works in Deut 20:20. In the phrase *b*ᵉ*māṣôr ub*ᵉ*māṣôq* (lit., "in siege and in distress"; Deut 28:53, 55, 57; Jer 19:9), *māṣôr* probably combines overtones of distress and siege ("dire straits," REB; W. Thiel, *TWAT* 6:970).

Affliction, oppression: → *dḥq* (oppress, # 1895); → *ḥms* I (do violence, # 2803); → *ḥmṣ* II (oppress, # 2807); → *ynh* (oppress, # 3561); → *lḥṣ* (press, # 4315); → *māṣôr* I (affliction, siege, # 5189); → *mrr* I (be bitter, distraught, afflict, # 5352); → *nega'* (plague, affliction, # 5596); → *ngś* (exact, # 5601); → *'nh* II (afflict, humble, afflict one's soul, fast, oppress, submit, # 6700); → *'wq* I (crush?, # 6421); → *'mr* II (deal tyrannically with, # 6683); → *'šq* I (wrong,

6943); → *ṣwq* I (constrain, press in/upon, harass, vex, # 7439); → *ṣwr* II (deal tyrannically with, # 7444); → *rhb* (assail, press, pester, alarm, confuse, # 8104); → *rṣṣ* (crush, # 8368); → *tôlāl* (oppressor, # 9354); → *tōk* (oppression, # 9412)
Enclosure: → *gnn* (enclose, protect, # 1713); → *ḥdr* I (surround, enclose, # 2539); → *sahar* (round enclosure, # 6044); → *ṣwr* I (besiege, enclose, # 7443); → *śwk* (hedge, shut in, # 8455)
Siege: → *m^{e}ḥî* (shock, blow, # 4693); → *ṣwr* I (besiege, enclose, # 7443); → *q^{e}bōl* (battering-ram, # 7692)

BIBLIOGRAPHY

TWAT 6:968-73; R. de Vaux, *AncIsr*, 1961, 236-38; C. Herzog and M. Gichon, *Battles of the Bible*, 1978; M. Noth, "Zur Anfertigung des 'Goldenes Kalbes,'" *VT* 9, 1959, 419-22; K. N. Schoville, "Siege," *ISBE* 4:503-5; Y. Yadin, *The Art of Warfare in Biblical Lands in the Light of Archaeological Study*, 1963.

P. P. Jenson

7444	צור

צור (*ṣwr* II), q. harass, cause distress, instigating someone into conflict or hostility (# 7444).

OT The object or victim of *ṣwr* is always a whole people, viz., the enemies of Israel (Exod 23:22-23), the Moabites (Deut 2:9), the Ammonites (Deut 2:19), the citizens of Shechem (Judg 9:31), and the Jewish population (Esth 8:11). Over against *ṣwr* I (→ # 7443) and *māṣôr,* which describe the actual oppressive siege of a whole population, *ṣwr* appears to express the psychological anguish of a people that is evoked by imminent war (Deut 2:9, 19; note the NIV's translation of *ṣwr* with "harass"). The appearance of *ṣrr* as object of *ṣwr* in Exod 23:22 suggests that *ṣwr* expresses the psychological side of affliction and oppression rather than the physical (→ *ṣrr* II, # 7675). In Judg 9:31 *ṣwr* expresses the act of instigating a city (viz., the citizens of Shechem) into hostility towards its dictator (Abimelech) whereby the latter's rule can be taken over by his opponents (Gaal and his brothers). In Esth 8:11 *ṣwr* describes the possible affliction and oppression of the Jewish population by armed forces within the Persian empire. Considering the proposed meaning of *ṣwr* in Exod 23:22 and Deut 2:9, 19, *ṣwr* in all probability not only expresses the physical hardship and slaughter of the Jews in Esth 8:11, but especially also psychological distress suffered by them. In Exod 23:22 *ṣwr* is furthermore used in the context of the covenant solidarity between Yahweh and Israel: if Israel is obedient to the will of Yahweh, he promises to cause distress (*ṣwr*) to those who cause distress (*ṣrr*) to his covenant people (cf. F. C. Fensham, *Exodus,* POT, 1970, 179).

Affliction, oppression: → *dḥq* (oppress, # 1895); → *ḥms* I (do violence, # 2803); → *ḥmṣ* II (oppress, # 2807); → *ynh* (oppress, # 3561); → *lḥṣ* (press, # 4315); → *māṣôr* I (affliction, siege, # 5189); → *mrr* I (be bitter, distraught, afflict, # 5352); → *nega'* (plague, affliction, # 5596); → *ngś* (exact, # 5601); → *'nh* II (afflict, humble, afflict one's soul, fast, oppress, submit, # 6700); → *'wq* I (crush?, # 6421); → *'mr* II (deal tyrannically with, # 6683); → *'šq* I (wrong, # 6943); → *ṣwq* I (constrain, press in/upon, harass, vex, # 7439); → *ṣwr* II (deal tyrannically with, # 7444); → *rhb* (assail, press, pester, alarm, confuse, # 8104); → *rṣṣ* (crush, # 8368); → *tôlāl* (oppressor, # 9354); → *tōk* (oppression, # 9412)

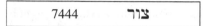

Bibliography

T. D. Hanks, *God So Loved the Third World: The Biblical Vocabulary of Oppression*, 1983, 3-39; Y. I. Kim, "The Vocabulary of Oppression in the Old Testament," Ph.D. diss. Drew University, 1981; C. F. Marriottini, "The Problem of Social Oppression in the Eighth Century Prophets," Ph.D. diss. Southern Baptist Theological Seminary, 1983; J. Miranda, *Communism in the Bible*, 1982, 37-39; J. Pons, *L'oppression dans l'Ancien Testament*, 1981; E. Tamez, *Bible of the Oppressed*, 1982, 1-30.

I. Swart

7445	צור

צור (*ṣwr* III), cast (metal) (# 7445).

ANE The vb. is known in Mish. Heb., various Aram. dialects, and Syr., meaning form, portray, or paint (*DISO*, 244). The nom. *ṣayyār*, Syr. *ṣayyārā'*, means painter. The Aram. *ṣwrh* means painting or picture.

OT The two pillars of Solomon's temple are cast (*wayyāṣar*) in bronze (1 Kgs 7:15). *BHS* suggests that this be emended to the more common *wayyiṣṣōq*, as might be suggested by the G (*echōneusen*); however, this vb. translates three other Heb. words of similar meaning, so this is hardly conclusive of a variant text. Montgomery proposes that *wayyāṣurû* in 2 Kgs 12:10[11] is the same vb. (*ṣwr*) and that the phrase is describing the minting and counting of the silver (429-30); this is based on an earlier suggestion of Torrey, that the *yōṣēr* of Zech 11:13 was a temple official who melted down contributions of precious metal for the temple (247-48). The two texts of Kgs together are strong evidence for a root *ṣwr* similar in form and meaning to *yṣr*, used to indicate the shaping of metals.

The phrase concerning the forming of the calf in Exod 32:4 is obscure; the vb. *wayyāṣar* can be read either as bind or form, and the instrument (*ḥereṭ*) can be an engraving tool (Isa 8:1) or a bag (cf. *ḥarîṭ*, 2 Kgs 5:23). Noth argued that the phrase referred to the silver that was bound in a bag as it was gathered (419-22), but this seems to distract from the focus on the calf. Another suggestion is that the silver was cast in a mold, but there is no evidence that *ḥereṭ* can carry this meaning. It seems best to take *ḥereṭ* as an engraving tool Aaron used to shape or form the gold in order to produce the image. This then would be an example of the root *ṣwr* with the meaning cast or form.

Holladay (20) suggests another possible occurrence of the word in what may be a double entendre at Jer 1:5. The Q reads *'eṣṣārkā* (*yṣr*), while the K reads *'aṣûrkā* (*ṣwr*); both mean, I formed you, but the latter may have a homonym meaning summon (cf. Ps 77:2[3], so Dahood, 225). If this is the case, the vb. *ṣwr* would be deliberate to add the sense of called in the womb to that of formed in the womb, a combination of ideas also found in Isa 49:1, 5. (For *ḥereṭ*, see Writing: Theology.)

P-B The Aram. vb. *ṣayyêr*, to form, shape, paint, or engrave, is common in the Tgs.

Metals: → *'ᵃnāk* (lead, # 643); → *bᵉdîl* (dross, # 974); → *barzel* (iron, # 1366); → *zāhāb* (gold, # 2298); → *ḥel'â* I (rust, # 2689); → *ḥašmal* (glow?, electrum, glowing metal, # 3133); → *kesep* (silver, money, # 4084); → *masgēr* II (metal worker, # 4994); → *ma'ᵃbeh* (foundry, # 5043); → *nᵉḥōšet* I (copper, bronze, # 5733); → *sîg* (lead oxide, # 6092); → *sēper* II (bronze, plate, # 6220); → *'ōperet* (lead, # 6769); → *paḥ* II (thin sheet, # 7063); → *pᵉlādōt* (steel?, # 7110);

→ *ṣwr* III (cast [metal], # 7445); → *ṣa'ᵃṣu'îm* (things formed by metal coating, # 7589); → *ṣph* II (arrange, overlay, plate, glaze, # 7596); → *ṣrp* (melt, smelt, refine, # 7671); → *qālāl* (polished metal, # 7838); → *šḥṭ* II (alloyed, # 8822)

BIBLIOGRAPHY
B. S. Childs, *The Book of Exodus*, OTL, 1974, 555-56; M. Dahood, *Psalms 51-100*, AB, 1968; W. L. Holladay, *Jeremiah 1*, 1986, 20; J. A. Montgomery, *The Books of Kings*, ICC, 1951, 429-30, 432; M. Noth, "Zur Anfertigung des "goldenen Kalbes," *VT* 9, 1959, 419-22; C. C. Torrey, "The Foundry of the Second Temple at Jerusalem," *JBL* 55, 1936, 247-48.

A. H. Konkel

7446	צור

צור (*ṣûr* I), boulder, large rock (# 7446).

ANE Among the several cognates, note the Aram. *ṭûr*, mountain (cf. Dan 2:35, 45).

OT 1. The word is found 74x in the OT and normally refers to boulders or large chunks of rock (e.g., 1 Sam 24:2[3]; Ps 78:15), but some contexts suggest smaller stones and rocks (e.g., Job 22:24; Jer 18:14). Large rocks and boulders were often used as hiding places or shelters (Exod 33:22; Job 24:8; Isa 2:10, 19, 21) and served other purposes, such as lookout points (Num 23:9), places of execution (Judg 7:25), and sacrifice (Judg 13:19).

2. Theologically, *ṣûr* is important in the OT for two reasons. First, Yahweh as the almighty Creator is able to make the rocks serve his redemptive purposes for Israel, especially during the desert sojourn after the Exodus when he produced water and oil for the Hebrews by splitting the rocks (Deut 8:15; 32:13; Ps 78:20; 105:41; 114:8). However, God's sovereign power in creation is even more graphically demonstrated in his judgment of the nations, when the very rocks are shattered in his presence (Nah 1:6). Second, and more important for the OT faithful, one of Yahweh's epithets is *Rock* (Deut 32:4; Ps 18:2[3]; etc.). Here Albright (*Yahweh and the Gods of Canaan*, 1968, 188-89) noted that *ṣûr* was a common appellative for deities in the OT world. He preferred to render the term "mountain" and argued that the Hebrews appropriated the epithet without borrowing the polytheistic baggage of their ancient counterparts. As Israel's "Rock," Yahweh was a unique God (1 Sam 2:2; Isa 44:8) and eternal God (Isa 26:4), their creator (Deut 32:18), their protection and salvation (Deut 32:15; Ps 62:6-7[7-8]; 94:22), their provider (Ps 81:16[17]; Isa 48:21), and a righteous judge (Hab 1:12; cf. D. N. Freedman's "Divine Names and Titles in Early Hebrew Poetry," in *Pottery, Poetry, and Prophecy*, 1980, 77-129, esp. 93, 114-15).

3. The prophet Isaiah calls Yahweh's Messiah "a rock that makes [people] fall" (Isa 8:14). The NT identifies this "stone of stumbling" as Jesus of Nazareth, who breaks and humbles some to repentance and crushes the rebellious in judgment (cf. Matt 21:42-44; Rom 9:32-33; 1 Peter 2:6-8). The apostle Paul understood that rock of provision during the Israelite desert trek to be that same "stone," preincarnate Jesus Christ (1 Cor 10:4).

Rock, stones: → *'eben* (stone, rock, # 74); → *gābîš* (rock-crystal, # 1486); → *ḥallāmîš* (flint, # 2734); → *ḥāṣāṣ* (gravel, # 2953); → *kēp* (rock, # 4091); → *sōḥeret* (mineral stone, # 6090); → *sela'* (rock, # 6152); → *sql* (throw stones, # 6232); → *ṣûr* I (rock, boulder, # 7446); → *ṣûr* II (pebble, flint, # 7447); → *ṣōr* I (flint knife, # 7644); → *rgm* (stone, # 8083); → *talpiyyôt* (courses of stones, # 9444)

God: → *'āb* (Father, # 3); → *'ābîr* (Mighty One, # 51); → *'ᵃdônāy* ([My] Lord, # 151); → *'ēl* V (God, # 446); → *'ᵉlōhîm* (God, # 466); → *ba'al* (Master, # 1251); → *gibbôr* (Divine Warrior, # 1475a); → *paḥad* I (Fear [of Isaac], # 7065); → *ṣûr* I (Rock, # 7446); → *qādôš* (Holy One, # 7705); → **Yahweh: Theology**

Bibliography

ISBE 3:205-6; 4:622-30; *NIDNTT* 2:731-34; 3:381-99; *THAT* 2:538-42; *TWOT* 2:762.

Andrew E. Hill

7447	צוּר

צוּר (*ṣûr* II), pebble, flint (# 7447).

ANE See Akk. *ṣurru* A, obsidian, flint (*CAD* 16:257-59).

OT The nom. occurs only in Job 22:24. Both Hartley's "stones of the wadi" (*Job*, NICOT, 1988, 333) and Pope's (*Job*, AB 15, 1973, 164) "pebbles of the brook" are superior to the NIV "rocks in the ravines," given the context.

Rock, stones: → *'eben* (stone, rock, # 74); → *gābîš* (rock-crystal, # 1486); → *ḥallāmîš* (flint, # 2734); → *ḥāṣāṣ* (gravel, # 2953); → *kēp* (rock, # 4091); → *sōḥeret* (mineral stone, # 6090); → *sela'* (rock, # 6152); → *sql* (throw stones, # 6232); → *ṣûr* I (rock, boulder, # 7446); → *ṣûr* II (pebble, flint, # 7447); → *ṣōr* I (flint knife, # 7644); → *rgm* (stone, # 8083); → *talpiyyôt* (courses of stones, # 9444)

Bibliography

ISBE 3:205-6; 4:622-30; *NIDNTT* 2:731-34; 3:381-99; *TWOT* 2:762.

Andrew E. Hill

7454	צַוָּרֹן

צַוָּרֹן (*ṣawwārōn*), = *ṣawwār* + dimin. end. *-ôn*; nom. necklace; only in pl. with suff. (# 7454); < צור (*ṣwr* I), q. tie up, bind; ni. part. enclosed (→ # 7443).

ANE Akk. *ṣawārum*, neck (cf. *AHw*, 1087a).

OT For occurrences, see S of Songs 4:9; Aram. *ṣawwa'r*, neck (Dan 5:7, 16, 29, # 10611).

For a discussion on jewelry, see *'dh* (put on ornaments, # 6335).

Malcolm J. A. Horsnell

7455	צות

צות (*ṣwt*), hi. light, kindle, ignite, set in flames (hapleg.; # 7455).

OT The hi. occurs once, in Isa 27:4, part of a passage (27:2-6) that seems to develop in reverse direction the motif of 5:1-7 (Whitehouse, 287-88; Skinner, 199; Gray, 453; Scott, 311; Bright, 508; Wright, 68; Herbert, 158; Watts, 349; Sheppard, 564; Seitz, 196-98; cf. Kaiser, 224, who, however, argues that the author of Isa 27:2-6 did not rest content with merely reversing the message of 5:1-7). Here, Yahweh, the assiduous keeper, protector and guardian of the vineyard (*kerem*; # 4142), first expresses the desire that the vine should be beset by thorns and briers so that he could do battle with them, and then gives the assurance that if these thorny intruders were to encroach on the vineyard, "I would set them all on fire (*ṣwt*)." The meaning of Isa 27:2-5 seems to be that Yahweh is longing to destroy the enemies (figuratively represented as thorns and briers; contrast 5:6, where briers and thorns are expressions of divine judgment on Judah) of Israel (his vineyard), but is prepared to spare them if they should cease from their hostility and turn to him (see, e.g., Whitehouse, 288; Skinner, 200; Thomson and Skinner, 99; Peake, 454; Kidner, 605; Oswalt, 495; Motyer, 222-23; Seitz, 198). As for Israel, she will flourish like a great vine and fill the whole world with fruit (v. 6).

However, not all commentators agree on the meaning of the individual references. For example, Watts (350) maintains that the briers and thorns are symbols of the void in the land left by Israel's evacuation, and some commentators think that it is Israel (see, e.g., Watts 350; Sheppard, 564) or an enemy group within the congregation of Israel (see, e.g., Kaiser, 225) that is twice urged in v. 5 to make peace with God. Again, although few would dispute that context can be of decisive importance in interpretation, there are conflicting opinions about the date of Isa 24-27.

Kindling: → *yṣt* (light, kindle, ignite, burn, scorch, # 3675); → *yqd* (burn, kindle, # 3678); → *nśq* (catch fire, be kindled, burn, # 5956); → *ṣwt* (light, kindle, ignite, set in flames, # 7455); → *qdḥ* (kindle, light, ignite, set ablaze, catch or take fire, # 7706)

BIBLIOGRAPHY

J. Bright, "Isaiah—I," in *Peake*, 1964, 489-515; G. B. Gray, *A Critical and Exegetical Commentary on the Book of Isaiah I-XXVII*, 1975; F. E. Greenspahn, *Hapax Legomena in Biblical Hebrew*, 1984; A. S. Herbert, *The Book of the Prophet Isaiah Chapters 1-39*, 1973; O. Kaiser, *Isaiah 13-39: A Commentary*, 1974; D. Kidner, "Isaiah," in *NBC*, 1972, 588-625; J. A. Motyer, *The Prophecy of Isaiah: An Introduction & Commentary*, 1993; J. N. Oswalt, *The Book of Isaiah Chapters 1-39*, 1986; A. S. Peake, "Isaiah I-XXXIX," in *Peake*, 1920, 436-59; R. B. Y. Scott, "The Book of Isaiah Chapters 1-39: Introduction and Exegesis," in R. B. Y. Scott and G. G. D. Kilpatrick, "The Book of Isaiah Chapters 1-39," in *IB*, 1956, 5:149-381; C. R. Seitz, *Isaiah 1-39*, 1993; G. T. Sheppard, "Isaiah 1-39," in *HBC*, 1988, 542-70; J. Skinner, *The Book of the Prophet Isaiah Chapters I-XXXIX*, 1909; C. H. Thomson and J. Skinner, *Isaiah I-XXXIX*, 1921; J. D. W. Watts, *Isaiah 1-33*, 1985; O. C. Whitehouse, *Isaiah I-XXXIX: Introduction Revised Version With Notes Index and Maps*, 1905; G. E. Wright, *Isaiah*, 1965.

Robin Wakely

7456 (*ṣaḥ*, scorching, radiant, clear), → # 7458

7458	צחח

צחח (*ṣḥḥ*), q. be dazzling (Lam 4:7; # 7458); צַח (*ṣaḥ*), adj. scorching, radiant, clear (Isa 18:4; 32:4; # 7456); צָחִיחַ (*ṣāḥîaḥ*), adj. shining, bare surface (Ezek 24:7, 8; # 7460); צְחִיחָה (*ṣ*ᵉ*ḥîḥâ*), nom. scorched land (Ps 68:7; # 7461); צַחְצָחָה (*ṣaḥṣāḥâ*), nom. scorched land (Isa 58:11; # 7463).

ANE Cognate with postbiblical Heb. *ṣihṣeah,* be smooth, polished, bright; Syr. *ṣaḥ,* be warm, glow; Arab. *ṣaḥṣaḥa,* glimmer, and *ṣaḥıḥ,* healthy; OSA *ṣḥḥ,* renew.

OT The vb. describes the brightness of healthy skin (Lam 4:7; cf. S of Songs 5:10) and may be used in Ps 73:7 of bright eyes (*yēṣaḥ* for *yāṣā'*, cf. Gunkel, *HALAT*). The adj. and noms. usually refer either to scorching heat (Isa 18:4; 58:11) or to places that have become barren through exposure to the sun (Neh 4:13[7]; Ezek 24:7, 8). The prophets use the imagery of a place that is sunscorched or bare to describe the effects of God's judgment (Isa 58:11; Ezek 26:4, 14; cf. Ps 68:6[7]).

Light, radiance, brightness: → *'wr* (be light, bright, shine, # 239); → *bāhîr* (bright, brilliant, # 986); → *zrḥ* I (rise [of sun], shine, # 2436); → *yp'* I (shine out, # 3649); → *ngh* (shine, cause to shine, # 5585); → *nhr* II (be radiant, # 5642); → *qrn* (send out rays, be radiant, # 7966)

Martin J. Selman

7460 (*ṣaḥîaḥ*, shining, bare surface), → # 7458

7461 (*ṣ^{e}ḥîḥâ*, scorched land), → # 7458

7462	צַחֲנָה

צַחֲנָה (*ṣaḥ^{a}nâ*), nom. stench (# 7462).

ANE Cognates in other Sem. languages suggest the meaning stinking for *ṣaḥ^{a}nâ* (*HALAT* 955).

OT The word is found only once in the HB, parallel to *b^{e}'ōš* (→ # 945) in Joel 2:20, where it describes the stench of the decomposing locusts driven into the sea, probably by a divinely ordained wind (cf. Exod 10:19). The repeated evocation of a terrible smell may emphasize the reality, horror, and finality of the divine judgment. These overtones remain if the verse is understood to apply not just to locusts (cf. Joel 1), but also to God's eschatological triumph over all his enemies.

P-B In Sir 11:12 God shakes the weak person free from the "stinking dust" (*'pr ṣḥnh*).

Smell, stench: → *b'š* (stink, become odious, # 944); → *zwr* III (stink, be offensive, # 2320); → *znḥ* II (become foul-smelling, # 2395); → *ḥnn* II (be stinking, loathsome, # 2859); → *srḥ* II (stink, spoil, # 6244); → *ṣaḥ^{a}nâ* (stench, # 7462); → *rwḥ* B (smell, # 8193); → **Smell: Theology**

P. Jenson

7463 (*ṣaḥṣāḥâ*, scorched land), → # 7458

7464	צחק

צחק (*ṣḥq*), q. laugh; pi. play, joke, insult, indulge in revelry (# 7464); nom. צְחֹק (*ṣ^{e}ḥōq*), laughter, derision (# 7465).

ANE There are cognates in Ugar. (*ṣḥq* and *ẓḥq*), Akk. (*ṣâḫu*), and Arab. (*ḍaḥika*), with the basic meaning laugh.

OT The term is used both positively and negatively.

1. Laughter can be associated with a positive change of fortune brought about by God for an individual. The aged Sarah reacted to the birth of Isaac by declaring "God has brought me laughter," a laughter of joy that others would share with her (Gen 21:6; for the interpretation of v. 6b see Westermann, 333-34). There is a play on the name "Isaac" (*yiṣḥāq*).

2. It is one of the ironies of the Samson narratives that his God-appointed work as judge to deliver Israel from the Philistine oppressors (Judg 13:5) was accomplished by the entertainment he was forced to provide, which led to their destruction (16:25).

3. In Exod 32:6 the vb. is used in connection with the worship of the golden calf (NIV indulge in revelry). This usage may correspond to that of *śḥq* (→ # 8471) for religious celebration (cf. Sasson, 152), but more likely it refers to a sexual orgy (Hvidberg, 148; Brenner, 47, 51; cf. Gen 26:8; 39:17).

4. There are instances of a negative connotation. In Gen 17:17 the vb. refers to Abraham's incredulous reaction to God's miraculous promise of a son, to which the name "Isaac" (17:19) would bear witness. In Gen 18:12, 13, 15 Sarah's laughter seems to reflect a more reprehensible measure of doubt and disbelief. (→ Abraham)

NT → *NIDNTT* 2:429-36.

Laughter, play, ridicule: → *l'g* (scorn, mock, # 4352); → *ṣḥq* (laugh, play, insult, # 7464); → *śḥq* (laugh, mock, rejoice, celebrate, dance, # 8471)

BIBLIOGRAPHY

TWAT 7:730-45; A. Brenner, "On the Semantic Field of Humour, Laughter and the Comic in the Old Testament," *On Humour and the Comic in the Hebrew Bible*, JSOTSup 92, 1990, 39-58; F. F. Hvidberg, *Weeping and Laughter in the Old Testament*, 1962; R. K. Johnston, *The Christian at Play*, 1983; G. von Rad, *Wisdom in Israel*, 1972; C. W. Reines, "Laughter in Biblical and Rabbinic Literature," *Judaism* 82, 1972, 176-83; J. M. Sasson, "The Worship of the Golden Calf," *Orient and Occident. Essays Presented to C. H. Gordon*, 1973, 151-59; G. Webster, *Laughter in the Bible*, 1960; C. Westermann, *Genesis 12-36*, 1985.

Leslie C. Allen

7465 (*ṣ^{e}ḥōq*, laughter, derision), → # 7464

7467	צָחֹר

צָחֹר (*ṣāḥōr*), adj. white (# 7467). Brenner defines *ṣāḥōr* as a secondary color (116-20) within the range of white: "light-colored" or "bright."

OT The adj. appears only in Deborah's Song (Judg 5:10) to describe the color of donkeys on which persons of the ruling class would ride (cf. 10:4; 12:14).

Colors—White: → *ḥwr* I (grow pale, # 2578); → *lbn* I (make white, # 4235); → *ṣāḥōr* (white, # 7467)

BIBLIOGRAPHY

A. Brenner, *Colour Terms in the Old Testament*, JSOT Sup, 1982; P. L. Garber, "Color," *ISBE* 1:729-32; R. Gradwohl, *Die Farben im Alten Testament*, BZAW 83, 1963.

Robert L. Alden

7469	צִי

צִי (*ṣî* I), warship (# 7469).

ANE Egyptian loanword *ḏ^{3}y*, river boat (cf. *HALAT* 956; and D. Jones, *A Glossary of Ancient Egyptian Nautical Titles and Terms*, 1988, 151). The term in Egyptian refers to a river boat, but in the OT a semantic shift took place and it is used for a warship.

According to Strömberg-Krantz, the original Egyp. river boat became part of the war flotilla (at a later stage—all OT references are from a later period) used to transport troops and goods, and for this reason it became a warship in Heb.

OT 1. The four occurrences appear primarily in prophecies of foreign attacks. In the oracles of Balaam the Kittim who come by ship subdue Asshur and Eber, but as with the other nations they are destroyed in the end, so that only Israel will prevail (Num 24:26[24]).

2. Isa 33:21 prophesies of the glory of Zion (→ Theology) when no *ṣî 'addîr* (NIV has "mighty ship") will come near.

3. In the oracle against Egypt, Ezekiel speaks of messengers on ships who will frighten the Kushites (Ezek 30:9).

4. Dan 11:30: Kittim ships oppose the king of the North. NIV identifies the king with Antiochus Epiphanes IV and the fleet with that of the Roman Popilius Laenas (note to Dan 11:30).

Ship, sailor: → *'^{o}nî/'^{o}niyyâ* (ship, # 639/41); → *ḥōbēl* (sailor, # 2480); → *mallāḥ* (mariner, sailor, # 4876); → *s^{e}pînâ* (ship, # 6208); → *ṣî* I (warship, # 7469)

Bibliography

TWAT 6:987; E. Strömberg-Krantz, *Des Schiffes Weg mitten im Meer. Beiträge zur Erforschung der nautischen Terminologie des Alten Testaments*, 1982, 66-69.

Izak Cornelius

7470	צִי

צִי (*ṣî* II), nom. desert dweller, crier, yelper, wild beast (# 7470).

OT This difficult nom. occurs only 5x (Ps 74:14; Isa 13:21; 23:13; 34:14; Jer 50:39; cf. possibly Ps 72:9). The identical, but unrelated, term *ṣî* I occurs 4x and is translated as ship (→ # 7469). It is difficult to determine the relationship between these two meanings. *ṣî* II is used to depict a specific animal, but of what kind it is unknown (BDB, 850). It is listed with other wild animals such as jackals, owls, and wild goats (Isa 13:21). This particular animal, being common enough, likely also represented some mystical or demonic force. Perhaps such an animal was thought to manifest certain animistic qualities (Isa 34:14).

Bibliography

J. Oswalt, *The Book of Isaiah, Chapters 1-39*, NICOT, 1986.

M. V. Van Pelt/W. C. Kaiser, Jr.

7472	צִיד

צִיד (*ṣyd*), hitp. provision o.s., outfit o.s. (for a journey) (hapleg. in Josh 9:12, 4[?]; # 7472; *HALAT* 956b); denom. < צַיִד (*ṣayid* II), masc. nom. (edible) provision(s), (food) supply (5x; # 7474; *HALAT* 957a); צֵידָה (*ṣêdâ*), nom. (edible) provision(s), (food) supply (10x; # 7476; *HALAT* 957a).

ANE There is reason for encountering difficulty when attempting to differentiate between Sem. roots *ġ/ṣ/zw/yd*, supply; make provision (for), and *ṣy/wd*, range, prowl, hunt; slaughter, owing probably to the reduction of Proto-Semitic /ṯ/ in the former root (written ǵ in Ugar.; Moscati, 28-29 [§8.16]) to /ṣ/ (as in Akk., Heb., Sam.) or, by dialectal diffusion, to /z/ (as in Aram. [e.g., Jewish Aram., Syr., Mand.] and Arab.) (cf. Moscati, 28 [§8.14]).

Akk. offers a vb. cognate in *ṣadû(m)*, take as provisions (*AHw* 3:1074a, attested only in Gtn and D. forms; cited as *ṣuddû*, to make provided [with food]; to provision, in *CAD, S*, 228b-29a). Other cognates of the vb. are attested in Sam. *zwd*, provide for, and Arab. *zwd* II, supply with journey provisions; provide for; equip, outfit (Wehr, 385b). Ben-Hayyim cites the equation of Sam. *zwdh*, make provision for (him), and Arab. (IV) *tzwyd*, you shall supply (him) with provisions, with the idiomatic Heb. hi. inf. const. + impf. *haʿ^{a}nêq taʿ^{a}nîq* (*lô*), you shall surely make a necklace (for him), a synecdoche meaning, you shall surely make provision (for him) (Deut 15:14; cf. BDB, 778b) (Ben-Hayyim, 2:555, no. 424).

For the nom. forms, cognates may be found in Akk. *ṣidītu(m)*, (journey) provisions (*CAD, Ṣ*, 172b-74a; *AHw* 3:1100a), and *ṣudû(m)* rations, (journey) provisions (*CAD, Ṣ*, 229b; *AHw* 3:1108b); and in Ugar. *mǵd* (/mṯd/) provisions; rations (in *UT*, Krt 84, 175 = *CTA* 14.ii.84, 175 = *KTU* 1.14.ii.31 and iv.12, each time ǁ *lḥm*, food; bread) (so de Moor, 195, 199; *CML*^{2} 84, 87, 151b; contra *UT*, # 1519, food, and Gray, 12, 38, food, which relate to the Arab. vb. *ġḏw*, nourish [*ǵdw* (sic) in Gray, 38], and nom. forms *maġḏā'* and *ġiḏā'*, nourishment, food [cf. Wehr, 667a]). Therefore, *pace* J. Aistleitner (*WUS*, ## 1626, 2134), the Ugar. nom. *mǵd* does not mean daybreak, as though related to a root **ġdw* (cf. Arab. *ġdw*, to go/come early in the morning [Weir, 666b]). Moreover, *pace HALAT* 957a and *RSP* 1, ii 473 (318), Ugar. *mṣd*, food/game (offering) (*WUS*, ## 1638, 2303; *CML*^{2}, 151b) is a cognate of Heb. *ṣwd*, hunt; slaughter, rather than of Heb. *ṣyd*, take provisions (indeed, *RSP*, 1, ii 473 [318] and 475 [319] wrongly translate *mṣd* as provisions [Krt 79] or feast [601:1b = *Ugaritica* 5, # 1:1b], as though synonymous with *'akl*, corn, grain [Krt 81], or *lḥm*, eat [601:2 = *Ugaritica* 5, # 1:2], respectively, whereas they rightly ǁ *dbḥ*, slaughter, sacrifice, in both instances [Krt 78; 601:1a = *Ugaritica* 5, # 1:1a]; cf. *RSP* 1, ii 474 [319]; S. E. Loewenstamm, *UF* 3, 1971, 357-59; Y. Avishur, *UF* 3, 1975, 44; and the use of nom. *ṣyd*, [animal] slaughtering, in the Punic construct *zbḥ ṣyd*, sacrifice of slaughtering [*KAI*, # 69, line 12]).

OT 1. The hitp. in Josh 9:12 offers the only undisputed attestation of the vb. in the MT: *zeh laḥmēnû ḥām hiṣṭayyadnû 'ōtô*, lit., "this bread of ours was warm when we provisioned ourselves with it," the Gibeonites thereby claiming to have outfitted themselves for a long journey. However, 9:4 in Codex Leningradensis (and its congeners) should probably be emended from *wayyiṣṭayyārû* (whether meaning [a] "they separated themselves/departed" [cf. OSA *ṣwr* III, separate oneself, leave; Arab. *ṣāra*, attain to, go], or [b] "they acted as a delegation" [NIV], "they disguised themselves" [NEB, REB] [cf. Heb. nom. *ṣyr*, messenger; Soggin, 108]; it should probably read *wayyiṣṭayyādû*, they provisioned themselves (so several Heb. MSS, LXX, Pesh., Vg.; BDB, 845a; *BHS*; RSV, JB, NAB, NRSV; Butler, 96-97).

2. The Heb. nom. forms *ṣayid* II and *ṣêdâ* are but masc. and fem. reflexes of the same lemma. In Heb. the masc. nom. *ṣayid* II, (edible) provisions, (food) supply, is a homograph of *ṣayid* I, hunting, game, but the two appear to derive from distinct lemmata and etymological streams (contra Butler, 97 n. 4. a). Heb. *ṣayid* II is used in Josh 9:5, 14 in reference to the Gibeonites' edible travel rations (which consisted of wine

and dry, moldy bread; cf. 9:4-5, 12-13). In Job 38:41, Yahweh queries rebukingly, "Who prepares for the raven its food supply (*ṣêdô*; ‖ nom. *'ōkel*)?" (author tr.). Similarly, Yahweh is portrayed as having promised always to bless Jerusalem with abundant "food supplies" (‖ nom. *lḥm*) for the sake of his covenant with David (Ps 132:15). Nehemiah forbids selling "food supplies," comprising a list of commodities such as grain, grapes, wine, and figs, in Jerusalem on the Sabbath (Neh 13:15).

3. The fem. nom. *ṣêdâ* is attested, with no significant difference in meaning, in Gen 27:3 (K, but read with the Q *ṣayid* I); 42:25; 45:21; Exod 12:39; Josh 1:11; 9:11; Judg 7:8; 20:10. In reference to manna, Ps 78:25 says that Yahweh allowed mortals to eat the bread (*lḥm*) of the mighty ones [i.e., angels] and to have sent them "(food) provisions" (‖ nom. *lḥm*) for their satiation. In its usage in 1 Sam 22:10, the "(edible) provisions" that Doeg reported that Ahimelech had given David included the consecrated bread from the tabernacle at Nob (cf. 1 Sam 21:4, 6[5, 7]).

P-B As to vb. cognates in the postbiblical period, Jewish Aram. *zwd* means in the pael (*zawwê/ēd*), make endowed/supplied; make provisioned/outfitted for, and in the itpaal (*'izdᵉwad*) (reflexively), supply/provision oneself (with), or to bundle (Jastrow, 1:384a); with similar sense, Syr. *zwd* occurs in the pael (*zawwed*) and etpaal (*'ezdawad*) (reflexively, sometimes figurative of receiving the viaticum when dying) (Payne Smith, 112a); so also Mand. *zud, zwd* (*MdD*, 164e).

Nom. cognates appear in postbiblical Heb. *ṣayid*, provision (Jastrow, 1274b), and *ṣêdâ*, provision; outfit (for traveling) (in 1QM 7:3 [cf. *KQT*, 187a]; Jastrow, 1274b, 2.); Jewish Aram. *zᵉwādā'*, support, provision; outfit, bag/bundle (Jastrow, 384a); Syr. *zᵉwādā'*, provision (for a journey), a viaticum; support (usually in the pl. *zᵉwādē'*; Payne Smith, 112a); and, with similar meaning, Mand. *zauada, zauda, zauadta* (*MdD* 157b).

Food: portion, provision: → *'kl* (eat, consume, devour, # 430); → *'ᵃruḥâ* (allowance, # 786); → *leḥem* (food, bread, # 4312); → *pat-bag* (food-quota, table-ration, # 7329); → *ṣyd* (provision oneself, outfit o.s, # 7472)

BIBLIOGRAPHY

Z. Ben-Hayyim, *The Literary and Oral Tradition of Hebrew and Aramaic Amongst the Samaritans,* 2 vols, Academy of the Hebrew Language 1-2, 1957, 2:555 [Hebrew]; T. C. Butler, *Joshua,* WBC 7, 1983, 96-97; J. C. de Moor, *An Anthology of Religious Texts from Ugarit,* Religious Texts Translation Series: Nisaba 16, 1987, 195; N. K. Gottwald, *Tribes of Yahweh,* 1979, 440, 455, 470 (on game); J. Gray, *The KRT Text in the Literature of Ras Shamra,* 2d ed., 1964, 12, 38 (re *mgd* in *UT*, Krt ii. 84); S. Moscati, ed., *An Introduction to the Comparative Grammar of the Semitic Languages,* 1969; J. Payne Smith, *A Compendious Syriac Dictionary,* 1903; J. F. Ross, "Food," *IDB* 2:(304b-8a) 305a; A. van Selms, "Food," *ISBE* 2:327a-331a; J. A. Soggin, *Joshua,* OTL, tr. R. A. Wilson, 1972, 108.

Robert H. O'Connell

7473 (*ṣayid* I, hunter, hunting), → # 7421

7474 (*ṣayid* II, provision, supply), → # 7472

7475 (*ṣayyād* I, hunter), → # 7421

7476 (*ṣêdâ*, provision), → # 7472

7480	צִיָּה

צִיָּה (*ṣiyyâ*), desert (16x) (# 7480).

OT This synonym of *midbār* and related terms is unclear in its precise semantic distinction. For etymology and cognates see *TWAT* 4:667; 6:991; *HALAT* 957; BDB, 851. For the theological significance, → Desert: Theology.

Desert, wilderness, wasteland: → *bōhû* (waste, # 983); → *bqq* I (lay waste, be agitated, # 1327); → *ḥorbâ* (ruin, waste, # 2999); → *y^e šîmôn* (wilderness, waste, # 3810); → *midbār* I (wilderness, # 4497); → *'^a rābâ* III (steppe, # 6858); → *ṣ^e ḥîḥâ* (scorched land, # 7461); → *ṣiyyâ* (desert, # 7480); → *š'h* I (lie waste, make s. th. into desolate, # 8615); → *šmm* (be desolate, deserted, lay waste, shudder, be horrified, # 9037); → **Desert: Theology**

A. R. Pete Diamond

7483	צִיּוּן

צִיּוּן (*ṣiyyûn*), nom. gravestone, road mark (# 7483).

OT The *ṣiyyûn* marks the spot of a grave (2 Kgs 23:17) or indicates the place where an unburied body lies (Ezek 39:15). In Jer 31:21 it signifies a road mark. This object could be set up (*nṣb*, Jer 31:21) or built (*bnh,* Ezek 39:15) and was probably a large stone or a heap of smaller ones. Jeremiah (31:21) encouraged the exiles to set up markers along the roads on their way to their destination so that at God's time they might speedily return to Zion. The similarity in sound of Zion (*ṣiyyôn* [→]) and *ṣiyyûn* should be noticed (Holladay, *Jeremiah*, 1989, 2:194).

P-B The word is used in Mish. Heb. of a whitewashed stone that indicates where there is a grave (*EncBib*, 2978). Compare also the Syr. *ṣ^e wāyā'*, heap of stones.

Mark: → *ṣiyyûn* (gravestone, roadmark, # 7483); → *t'h* (mark out, # 9292); → *twh* I (make a mark, # 9344); → *tamrûrîm* II (roadmarkers, signposts, # 9477)

Paul A. Kruger

7485 (*ṣînōq*, iron collar), → # 2414

7488 (*ṣîṣ* I, blossoms, flower), → # 7437

7491 (*ṣîṣâ*, blossoms, flower), → # 7437

7492	צִיצִת

צִיצִת (*ṣîṣit*), nom. hair, tassel (# 7492); < צִיץ (*ṣyṣ*), flower (→ 7488).

OT 1. In Num 15:38-39 this root refers to the tassels that were to be on the corners of the Israelites' garments. These tassels were visible reminders of Israel's special covenant status (v. 39).

2. In Ezek 8:3 the prophet felt himself picked up "by the hair" (*ṣîṣit*) of his head, while in a visionary trance.

Hair: → *zāqān* (beard, # 2417); → *maḥ^a lāpâ* (braid, # 4710); → *miqšeh* (well-dressed hair, # 5250); → *pr'* (untie hair, # 7277); → *ṣîṣit* (hair, tassel, # 7492); → *q^e wuṣṣôt* (hair, # 7767); → *ś'r* I (be appalled, # 8547); → *śāpām* (moustache, # 8559)

Bibliography
S. Bartman, "Tasseled Garments in the Ancient East Mediterranean," *BA* 24, 1961, 119-28; F. J. Stevens, "The Ancient Significance of Sisith," *JBL* 50, 1931, 59-71; G. A. te Stroete, "Ezekiel 24:15-27: The Meaning of a Symbolic Act," *Bijdr* 38, 1977, 163-65; H. Trav, N. Rubin, S. Vargon, "Symbolic Significance of Hair in the Biblical Narrative and the Law," *Koroth* 9, 1988, 173-79.

Robert Alden

7493 (*ṣyr*, send a delegation), → # 7495

7494	צִיר

צִיר (*ṣîr* I), door pivot (# 7494).

ANE Cognates include Akk. *ṣerru*, Jew. Aram. *ṣyr'*, Syr. *ṣyrt'*.

OT The cognates and context of this hapleg. in BH require the meaning, door pivot: "As a door turns on its hinges (pivot), so a sluggard turns on his bed" (Prov 26:14). A pivot is the shaft or hinge on which the door turns.

NT → *NIDNTT* 2:29-31.

Door, gate, threshold: → *'ayil* (doorpost, # 382); → *'ōmnâ* (pillar?, doorpost?, # 595); → *b^e^rîaḥ* (bar, # 1378); → *delet* (door, # 1946); → *lûl* (trapdoor, # 4294); → *m^e^zûzâ* (doorpost, # 4647); → *miptān* (threshold, # 5159); → *mašqôp* (lintel, # 5485); → *spp* (lie at threshold, # 6214); → *ṣîr* I (door pivot, # 7494); → *ša'ar* I (gate, # 9133)

Richard S. Hess

7495	צִיר

צִיר (*ṣîr* II), nom., envoy, messenger, ambassadors (# 7495); צִיר (*ṣyr*), q. send a delegation (# 7493).

ANE The proposed verbal root is *ṣyr*, become, go. Possibly related to Arab. *ṣāra*, went, came, became, or Egyp. *di-ir*, although some have suggested an association with Aram. *'iyr*, angel. Heb. *ṣîr* II is used 6x in the OT with the meaning delegation (Prov 13:17; 25:13; Jer 49:14; Isa 18:2; 57:9; Obad 1). The motif of messengers and their messages is a frequent one in the ANE and the OT (→ *bśr*, # 1413, and *b^e^śōrâ*, # 1415).

OT 1. The vb. *ṣyr* I, send a delegation (# 7493), refers once to a delegation that is a false front, or ruse, of the Gibeonites to Israel (a hitp. and hapleg., Josh 9:4). This example involves a textual question; considering that the verbal form is a hapleg., some mss. read the vb. as *ṣyd*, hunt or pack provisions (# 7472), and the LXX renders it with the vb. *sitizō*, prepare food (also NRSV). The essential meaning of preparation with deception is consistent with either reading.

2. The nom. is used to contrast a wicked envoy with a trustworthy envoy (Prov 13:17), as well as to describe a trustworthy messenger (25:13). In relation to this notion is the interesting use of *ṣîr* III (# 7494) in the graphic depiction of the sluggard who turns on his bed like a door on its hinges (26:14). This may carry some analogy to *ṣîr* I and II, in that the sluggard cannot move and would make an unreliable envoy.

Isa 18:2 describes messengers sent in papyrus boats by sea and on the Nile (ancient Cush). They represent the proud nations seeking help against Assyria (possibly envoys from Cush promising help); the message is a prophetic declaration that Assyria and all the nations standing against God's people will be delivered into the hand of the Lord. There is an ironic contrast between the envoys (*ṣîr* II), which represent the nations' collective strength, juxtaposed with the swift messengers (*mal'ākîm*), who will be sent to an unidentified, tall, and smooth-skinned people (18:2b). These latter messengers are subtly transformed from national envoys into a figure of the Lord's own prophetic condemnation of Israel's enemies (18:3).

A similarly negative portrayal of the proud machinations of ambassadors (*ṣîr* II) occurs in Isa 57:9, yet in this case it involves a condemnation of Israel's actions, regarding either their international delegations or idolatry (context allows for either derivation; possible a play on words). Their ambassadors of peace lead them into the grave itself (also 28:14-15). Prophetic messages of judgment are sent to Edom in Jer 49:14 and Obad 1-4. Once again the Lord condemns the futile efforts of the nations' envoys (particularly Edom) to incite trust in their own might.

3. The underlying nuance of *ṣîr* II in these examples generally suggests connotations of false versus truthful witnesses: i.e., those who represent the nations against the very word of the Lord himself.

P-B 1. As noted above, at Josh 9:4 the LXX renders the vb. *ṣyr* I with the vb. *sitizō*, prepare food, and numerous Heb. mss. attest to a possible haplography of *syd,* to hunt or pack provisions, with *ṣyr*. However, *sitizō* is placed in the context with *panougyrias*, duplicity, deceit (which the NT also uses in reference to Eve's deception, 2 Cor 11:3, and of the deceptive spies who tried to trap Jesus, Luke 20:19-23). The LXX understands that the preparations were done with trickery and deceit in mind, whether it was the sending of delegates or in the food preparation. The emphasis, however, is on the deception, not on the preparation itself.

2. The nom. in Prov 13:17; 25:13, a trustworthy envoy, the LXX translates *angelos* (cf. Jer 49:14[LXX 30:8]). Whereas Isa 18:2 reads "pledges and letters" (*homēra kai epistolas),* 57:9 is more straightforward with the translation *presbeis*, ambassadors. On the other hand, Obad 1 takes the same as *periochen*, a portion of a discourse. There is no apparent consistency or emphasis in the LXX renderings.

Message, messenger: → *bśr* (bring, proclaim [good, bad] news, # 1413); → *mal'āk* (angel, messenger, # 4855); → *ṣîr* II (messenger, # 7495); → *š^{e}mû'â* (news, report, message, # 9019)

Bibliography

HAW, 387; *NIDNTT* 1:126-28; *TWOT* 765; F. F. Bruce, "Travel and Communication in the Old Testament and New Testament World," AB 6:644-53; A. R. Hulst, *Old Testament Translation Problems*, 1960, 19; I. Mendelsohn, "Travel and Communication in the Old Testament," *IBD* 4:688-90; S. V. McCasland, "Travel and Communication in the NT," *IBD* 4:690-93; Zorrel, 691.

Stephen T. Hague

7496 (*ṣîr* III, birth pang), → # 2659

7498 (*ṣēl*, shade, shadow), → # 7511

7499 (*ṣlh*, roast), → Baking

7501 (*ṣ^{e}lûl*, circular cake), → Bread

7502/7503	צלח

צלח (*ṣlḥ*), q. be successful, be prosperous, be powerful (# 7502); hi. make successful, make prosperous (# 7503).

ANE The root *ṣlḥ* is attested in Phoen. and Pun. *ṣlḥ*, prosper, in Arab., *ṣalaḥa*, be in good condition, prosper, and in Aram., *ṣ^{e}laḥ*, be successful, make prosperous. Cf. Tigre *sälḥa*, succeed, prosper. See also its use in biblical Aram. (Ezra 5:8; 6:14; Dan 3:30; 6:29).

OT 1. In the OT, the Heb. term *ṣlḥ*, be successful or make successful, is used mainly as a vb. and occurs a total of 65x (25x in q. and 40x in hi.). It refers to successful activities in different areas of life, usually in the sense of accomplishing effectively what is intended. Besides describing a human or divine action, the vb. is also used with various subjects: a tree (thrives, Ps 1:3; Ezek 17:9), a weapon (prospers, Isa 54:17), a journey (succeeds, Judg 18:5), a waistcloth (is useful, Jer 13:7). Idiomatically, the vb. is used 7x in q. with *'al* or *'el* to describe God's Spirit "coming upon" his chosen one to empower the person for service, e.g., Samson (Judg 14:6), Saul (1 Sam 10:6), and David (16:13). The same expression is employed for "an evil spirit from God" (18:10). The hi. vb. is often followed by *derek*, way (8x), to describe making successful a journey or career.

2. Theologically, *ṣlḥ* emphasizes that God alone is the one who gives success, an emphasis well summarized in Nehemiah's words: "The God of heaven will give us success" (Neh 2:20). He gives success to those who obey his law (Josh 1:8; 1 Chron 22:13; Ps 1:3) and promises that his word will not return empty but what he desires will succeed (Isa 55:11). His will succeeds in the hand of the Suffering Servant (Isa 53:10). Though the wicked may also prosper (Ps 37:7; Jer 5:28; 12:1; Dan 11:27), their success is temporary and will be destroyed in time. It is important to note that success is often stated as merely God's grace, e.g., the reason for Joseph's success was simply stated as "the LORD was with Joseph" (Gen 39:2-3). God grants success to those who seek him diligently (2 Chron 26:5), to those who depend on his mercy and pray to him e.g., Abraham's servant (Gen 24:21, 40), Nehemiah (Neh 1:11), and the psalmist in Ps 118:25.

P-B Among the DSS, the term *ṣlḥ* is used in the epilogue of the Damascus Rule (13:21) to warn those who do not hold to the statutes set forth in the scroll that they will not "succeed" (or "thrive") in living in the land when the messianic age arrives. The LXX usually translates the vb. as *eudoō*. In Mish. Heb, the meaning "succeed/prosper" is still common to the root (see Jastrow 2:1283).

Success, skill: → *y'l* (profit, benefit, be useful, be helpful, # 3603); → *kšr* (succeed, prosper, be pleasing, # 4178); → *ṣlḥ* (be successful, be prosperous, be powerful, # 7502/03); → *śkl* I (have success, understand, make wise, act with insight, # 8505)

Bibliography

THAT 2:551-56; *TWOT* 2:766; E. Puech, "Sur la racine *ṣlḥ* en hébreu et en araméen," *Semitica* 21, 1971, 5-19; H. Tawil, "Hebrew צלחהצליח, Akkadian *ešeru/šūšuru*: A Lexicographical Note," *JBL* 95, 1976, 405-13.

Alex Luc

7504 (*ṣ^{e}lōḥît*, bow, jar, bottle, flask, jug), → # 3998

7505 (*ṣallaḥat*, bowl, pot, dish), → # 3998

7507 (*ṣālî*, roasted by fire), → Baking

7509	צלל

צלל (*ṣll* I), q. ring, quiver (4x; # 7509; *HALAT* 962b); nom. מְצִלָּה (*m^{e}ṣillâ*), bell, (bell-shaped) jingle (hapleg.; # 5197; *HALAT* 590a); מְצִלְתַּיִם (*m^{e}ṣiltayim*), paired (hand) cymbals (dual; 13x; # 5199; *HALAT* 590a); צְלָצַל (*ṣ^{e}lāṣal*), cricket (→ # 7526); whirring (< *ṣll* I or II?, Isa 18:1); צִלְצָל (*ṣilṣāl*), fishing gear (# 7528); צֶלְצְלִים (*ṣelṣelîm*), (finger/hand?) cymbals (3x; # 7529; *HALAT* 966a).

ANE The vb. occurs in Ugar. as a guild designation, *mṣlm*, cymbalists (*WUS* # 2318; *UT*, # 2164); Aram. *ṣ^{e}lal*, ring, clash; OSA *ṣalal* II, announce, herald (Müller, *ZAW* 75, 1963, 313); Arab. *ṣalla*, *ṣalṣala*, ring, clash. The nom. forms find cognates in Ugar. *mṣltm* (dual), paired cymbals (*WUS* # 2318; *UT* # 2164); Eth. *ṣanaṣlat* (pl. *ṣanāṣel[āt]*), cymbals (*LLA* 1293; *GVGSS* 1:247; Th. Nöldeke, *Neue Beiträge zur semitischen Sprachwissenschaft*, 1910, 42).

OT 1. The Heb. vb. *ṣll* I, meaning quiver, shake, is used only in Hab 3:16, "my lips quivered (‖ *rgz*, quiver, quake)," and in 1 Sam 3:11; 2 Kgs 21:12; Jer 19:3, about ears tingling, in all cases describing involuntary physiological responses to bad news (cf. D. R. Hillers, "A Convention in Hebrew Literature: The Reaction to Bad News," *ZAW* 77, 1965, 86-90).

2. The Heb. nom. *m^{e}ṣillâ* is used only in Zech 14:20, where it refers to a future day when horses' "bell-shaped jingles" would be inscribed with "HOLY TO THE LORD" (cf. the apotropaic use of *pa^{ʿa}mōnê zāhāb*, gold platelet-jingles, in Exod 28:33-35 [cf. 39:25-26] with the gold medallion inscribed, "HOLY TO THE LORD," in vv. 36-38). The dual nom. *m^{e}ṣiltayim* translates "paired (hand) cymbals." Both artifacts and the OT attest that such cymbals were generally made of bronze (1 Chron 15:19). The thirteen OT uses of *m^{e}ṣiltayim* appear only in the postexilic writings of Ezra, Nehemiah, and 1-2 Chronicles and always with other instruments used in connection with ritual worship (usually *n^{e}bālîm*, [large] lyres/harps, and *kinnōrôt*, [small] lyres, sometimes *tuppîm*, frame drums, *šôpār*, horn, and *ḥ^{a}ṣōṣ^{e}rôt,* trumpets), though it is uncertain whether all these instruments were thought to have been played simultaneously. Except for Neh 12:27 (which describes the dedication of the walls of Jerusalem), all uses of these passages describe Levitical worship at the temple in Jerusalem.

3. The three OT uses of *ṣelṣelîm* refer to (finger/hand?) cymbals used in cultic worship. In 2 Sam 6:5 (= 1 Chron 13:8), it is mentioned among instruments used in a cultic processional ensemble, including *kinnōrôt*, (small) lyres, *n^{e}bālîm*, (large) lyres, *tuppîm*, frame drums, *m^{e}naʿanʿîm*, sistra/(pottery) rattles (= 1 Chron 13:8, *m^{e}ṣiltayim*,

paired [hand] cymbals), and *ṣelṣelîm*, (finger/hand?) cymbals (= 1 Chron 13:8 *ḥᵃṣōṣᵉrôt*, trumpets). Its parallel uses in Ps 150:5, *ṣilṣᵉlê šāma'*, sounding (finger/hand?) cymbals, ‖ *ṣilṣᵉlê tᵉrû'â*, resonating (finger/hand?) cymbals, need not suggest that we have here different sizes of cymbals (*pace HALAT* 966a)—it is simply that the same instrument is described using poetic variation.

4. For the nom. *ṣᵉlāṣal*, cricket, see *'arbeh*, locust (→ # 746).

5. For the nom. *ṣilṣāl*, fishing gear, see *dyg*, fish (→ # 1899).

P-B Postbiblical Heb. attests nom. *mᵉṣillâ,* bells (Jastrow, 826a); Jewish Aram. has nom. *mᵉṣelṣᵉlîn,* cymbals (Jastrow, 2:826b; Tg. 1 Chron 15:28), and *ṣelṣāl* cymbal (Jastrow, 2:1286a; PTalm Sukkah V, 55b-c); Syr. attests the vb. *ṣal,* tingle (J. Payne Smith, *A Compendious Syriac Dictionary*, 1903, 478a), and nom. *ṣiṣlâ,* cymbals, castenets, 483b).

Musical instruments/terms: → *gittît* (musical instrument?, # 1787); → *hemyâ* (sound, din, # 2166); → *ḥll* (make the pipe played, # 2727); → *ḥṣṣr* (make the trumpet sound, # 2955); → *yôbēl* (ram, # 3413); → *kinnôr* (lyre, # 4036); → *mēn* (string, # 4944); → *mᵉna'an'îm* (rattle, # 4983); → *nēbel* II (unstringed instrument, # 5575); → *ngn* (play the lyre, # 5594); → *'ûgāb* (flute?, # 6385); → *prṭ* (improvise, # 7260); → *ṣll* I (ring, quiver, # 7509); → *šôpār* (ram's horn, # 8795); → *šālîš* II (musical instrument, # 8956); → *šema'* I (sound, # 9049); → *tpp* (drum, beat, # 9528); → *tq'* (drive, thrust, clap one's hands, blow trumpet, pledge, # 9546)

BIBLIOGRAPHY

B. Bayer, "The Finds That Could Not Be," *BARev* 8/1, 1982, 24, 32; idem, *The Material Relics of Music in Ancient Palestine and Its Environs: An Archaeological Inventory*, 1963, Figs. 14-15; idem, "Music: History: Biblical Period, Second Temple Period," *EJ* 12, cols. 564, Figs. 1a, 1b and 2a; S. B. Finesinger, "Musical Instruments in OT," *HUCA* 3, 1926, 66-68; D. A. Foxvog and A. D. Kilmer, "Muscic," *ISBE* 3:444, 445a; J. E. Hartley, *TWOT* 2:766b-77a; E. Gerson-Kiwi, "Musique (dans la Bible)," *DBSup* 5, 1957, cols. 1433-34; H. Gressmann, *Musik und Musikinstrumente im AT*, 1903, 32; O. Keel, *The Symbolism of the Biblical World*, tr. T. J. Hallett, 1985, s.v. "Music and Song," 340, Figs. 452 and 455; E. Kolari, *Musikinstrumente und ihre Verwendung im AT*, 1947, 21-26; J. D. Prince, "Music," *EncBib* 3, col. 3227; C. Sachs, *History of Musical Instrumgents*, 1940, 121-23; O. R. Sellers, "Musical Instruments of Israel," *BA* 4, 1941, 43-44, Fig. 7a, 11 and 12c; D. G. Stradling and K. A. Kitchen, "Music and Musical Instruments," *IBD* 2:1032-33, 1039-40; G. Wallis, "Musik, Musikinstrumente," *BHH* 3, col. 1258, Fig. 8; M. Wegner, *Die Musikinstrumente des alten Orients*, 1950, 38-39, 41; E. Werner, "Musical Instruments," *IDB* 3:470b-71a.

Robert H. O'Connell

7510 צלל

צלל (*ṣll* II), q. sink (hapleg. in Exod 15:10; # 7510).

ANE Akk. *ṣalālu*, lie down; Arab. *ḍalla*; Eth. *ṣälälä*, vanish.

OT The word occurs only in Moses' Song of the Sea, celebrating Yahweh's defeat of Pharaoh and his army at the Sea of Reeds (Exod 15:10). All the major EVV agree here, understanding that Pharaoh's chariots and officers "sank like lead" as the God of Israel demonstrated he was a warrior for his people (Exod 15:3). Here "lead" (*'ōperet*), a natural symbol for weight, is a simile for "stone" in v. 5. Cole (*Exodus*, TOTC, 1975, 124) prefers the translation "went gurgling down." This demonstration of Yahweh's absolute sovereignty and awesome power over the Egyptians quite naturally prompted the following question/declaration, "Who among the gods is like you, O LORD?" (v. 11).

Sinking, settling: → *ṭbʻ* (sink, # 3190); → *mkk* (sink, settle down, # 4812); → *ṣll* II (sink, # 7510); → *šwḥ* (sink, # 8755); → *šqʻ* (settle, # 9205)

Andrew E. Hill

7511	צלל

צלל (*ṣll* III), q. be, grow dark; hi. cast a shadow (# 7511); צֵל (*ṣēl*), nom. shade, shadow (# 7498); צַלְמָוֶת (*ṣalmāwet*), nom. darkness, shadow of death (# 7516).

ANE The vb. is attested in Arab. *ẓll*, overshadow; in Geez *ṣälälä*, give shade; and in Old Aram. *ṭll*, overshadow. The nom. *ṣēl* is attested in Arab. *ẓill*, Akk. *ṣillu*, Ugar. *ẓl*, shade, and Tigre *ṣ*^{e}*lāl*, Aram./Syr. *ṭellālāʼ*, shade, shadow. The derivation of the nom. *ṣalmāwet* is controversial, but by popular etymology it is regarded as a compound word made up of *ṣēl*, shadow, and *māwet*, death, and the EVV are almost unanimous in tr. it as "shadow of death," with reference to the netherworld, so Hades (Job 38:17, LXX). Thus, it is consistently "shadow of death" in the AV. This seems to be supported by the Massoretic vocalization.

However, many modern philologists suggest that the word is derived from the nom. *ṣelem* II, shade, shadow (→ # 7513), which, in turn, comes from the root vb. *ṣlm* II, grow dark, attested in Akk. *ṣalāmu,* become dark, black; adj. *ṣallāmu/ṣalmu,* black, dark. Cf. Arab. *ẓalima*, be shady; nom. *ẓulmat*, darkness; and Ugar. *ẓlm*, be dark (?), and *ẓlmt*, darkness (?). Ringgren noted that in Ugar. "the messenger of the gods, *Gpn-w'ugr*, is called ... *bn ẓlmt,*" which means "son of darkness" (*TDOT* 5:248). It is postulated that the original form of *ṣlm* was *ṣalmu*, which was supplemented with *ût* to form the superlative *ṣalmût*, deep darkness. In support of this view, the word occurs in parallel with other words for darkness, such as *ḥōšek* (→ # 3125), *'ōpel* (→ # 694), and *laylâ,* night (→ # 4326); and it appears in opposition to *'ôr,* light (→ # 240), and *bōqer,* morning (→ # 1332); and the Jewish exegete Rashi equated *ṣalmāwet* with *ḥōšek*, darkness (→ # 3125). This view seems to be the choice of the NIV in most instances.

On the other hand, W. L. Mitchell regards the Massoretic vocalization as correct and defends the tr. "shadow of death." He points out that in Ugar. *ẓl*, shade, and *mt*, dead, or "the god *Môt,*" are frequent, but *ẓlm* is controversial. D. W. Thomas agrees but regards *māwet* as the sign of the superlative, so also M. Dahood. In support of this view, other compound names occur with *māwet,* such as *ḥ*^{a}*ṣarmāwet*, lit., "the court or village of death" (Gen 10:26; 1 Chron 1:20); *ʻazmāwet* (lit., "the strength of death," 2 Sam 23:31); also, *ṣalmāwet* occurs in parallel with "the gates of death" (Job 38:17). Furthermore, in most languages, the metaphor "shadow of death" seems to express the strong emotional aspect of the sorrow, fear, or danger implied by the given contexts much better than does "deep darkness."

OT 1. The vb. is used only twice in the OT. It occurs once in the q. stem to refer to the onset of darkness before the Sabbath: "When evening shadows fell (*ṣll*) on the gates of Jerusalem before the Sabbath, I ordered the doors to be shut and not opened until the Sabbath was over" (Neh 13:19). It is used once in the hi. stem to refer to trees shading a forest with their branches: "Consider Assyria, once a cedar in Lebanon, with beautiful branches overshadowing (*ṣll*) the forest; it towered on high, its top above the thick foliage" (Ezek 31:3).

2. *ṣēl*, nom. shade, shadow. The nom. is used literally of the shadow or shade cast by an object irradiated by the sun. Thus, it refers to the shadow of a gnomon cast on the face of a sundial: When King Hezekiah was sick, Isaiah gave him a sign to assure him of recovery: "This is the LORD's sign to you that the LORD will do what he has promised: Shall the shadow go forward ten steps, or shall it go back ten steps?" (2 Kgs 20:9; see also vv. 10, 11; Isa 38:8). The word may also refer to the shadow or shade used for protection from the heat of sun: (a) as cast by trees or plants: in Jotham's allegory against Abimelech, he said, "The thornbush said to the trees, 'If you really want to anoint me king over you, come and take refuge in my shade (*ṣēl*), but if not, then let fire come out of the thornbush and consume the cedars of Lebanon!'" (Judg 9:15; see also Job 40:22; Ps 80:10[11]; S of Songs 2:3; Ezek 17:23; 31:6, 12, 17; Hos 4:13; 14:7[8]; Jon 4:5-6); (b) it may also refer to a shadow as cast by a large rock: "Each man will be like a shelter from the wind and a refuge from the storm, like streams of water in the desert and the shadow (*ṣēl*) of a great rock in a thirsty land" (Isa 32:2); (c) and so it may refer to shade in general: "Does not man have hard service on earth? Are not his days like those of a hired man? Like a slave longing for the evening shadows (*ṣēl*), or a hired man waiting eagerly for his wages" (Job 7:1-2).

The word is used figuratively of protection from harm. It may mean protection in general: Joshua and Caleb encouraged the people not to fear the Canaanites, but to conquer their land, "Only do not rebel against the LORD. And do not be afraid of the people of the land, because we will swallow them up. Their protection (*ṣēl*) is gone, but the LORD is with us. Do not be afraid of them" (Num 14:9). It may refer to the protection provided by a king: "The LORD's anointed, our very life breath, was caught in their traps. We thought that under his shadow (*ṣēl*) we would live among the nations" (Lam 4:20). It may refer to protection by a human ally: The Lord pronounced woe on the obstinate Israelites "who go down to Egypt without consulting me; who look for help to Pharaoh's protection, to Egypt's shade (*ṣēl*) for refuge. But Pharaoh's protection will be to your shame, Egypt's shade (*ṣēl*) will bring you disgrace" (Isa 30:2-3). It may refer to protection by wisdom or money: "Wisdom is a shelter (*ṣēl*) as money is a shelter (*ṣēl*)" (Eccl 7:12); and to protection by a city: "In the shadow (*ṣēl*) of Heshbon the fugitives stand helpless, for a fire has gone out from Heshbon, a blaze from the midst of Sihon; it burns the foreheads of Moab, the skulls of the noisy boasters" (Jer 48:45). It may refer to the protection provided when one enters a friend's or neighbor's home [lit., comes under the shadow of his roof]—thus, Lot sought to protect the angels who visited him (Gen 19:8).

Particularly, the word may refer to the protection provided by the LORD: "He who dwells in the shelter of the Most High will rest in the shadow (*ṣēl*) of the Almighty" (Ps 91:1; see also 121:5; Isa 16:3). His protection may be under the shadow of his wings: "Keep me as the apple of your eye; hide me in the shadow (*ṣēl*) of your wings" (Ps 17:8; see also 36:7[8]; 57:1[2]; 63:7[8]). In the eschatological kingdom, his protection will be the Shekinah glory: "Then the LORD will create over all of

Mount Zion and over those who assemble there a cloud of smoke by day and a glow of flaming fire by night; over all the glory will be a canopy. It will be a shelter and a shade (*ṣēl*) from the heat of the day, and a refuge and a hiding place from the storm and rain" (Isa 4:5-6; see also 25:4). The word is used figuratively of the transitoriness of life: "For we were born only yesterday and know nothing, and our days on earth are but a shadow (*ṣēl*)" (Job 8:9; see also 14:2; Ps 102:11[12]; 109:23; 144:4; Eccl 6:12; 8:13). The word is used figuratively of the members of the body emaciated by disease: "My eyes have grown dim with grief; my whole frame is but a shadow (*ṣēl*)" (Job 17:7).

3. The nom. *ṣalmāwet*, darkness, shadow of death, occurs 18x in the OT, always in poetry. It refers to literal darkness in opposition to light, usually with an implied sorrow or fear: Cursing the day of his birth, Job said of it, "That day—may it turn to darkness (*ḥōšek*); may God above not care about it; may no light shine upon it. May darkness (*ḥōšek*) and deep shadow (*ṣalmāwet*) claim it once more; may a cloud (*ʿanānâ*) settle over it; may blackness (*kamrîr*) overwhelm its light" (Job 3:4-5 [NIV]; see also 28:3; 34:22; Amos 5:8). It is often used figuratively. Thus, it can express deep sorrow: "My face is red with weeping, deep shadows (*ṣalmāwet*) ring my eyes" (Job 16:16 NIV). It is used figuratively of terror: "For all of them, deep darkness (*ṣalmāwet*) is their morning; they make friends with the terrors of darkness (*ṣalmāwet*)" (Job 24:17 [NIV]). It is used figuratively of deep gloom: "Some sat in darkness (*ḥōšek*) and the deepest gloom (*ṣalmāwet*), prisoners suffering in iron chains, . . . He brought them out of darkness (*ḥōšek*) and deepest gloom (*ṣalmāwet*) and broke away their chains" (Ps 107:10, 14 [NIV]). It is used of extreme danger: "Even though I walk through the valley of the shadow of death, I will fear no evil, for you are with me" (Ps 23:4; see also Jer 2:6). It is used of deep distress: "The people walking in darkness (*ḥōšek*) have seen a great light; on those living in the land of the shadow of death (*ṣalmāwet*) a light has dawned" (Isa 9:2[1]; see also Ps 44:19[20]).

It is also used figuratively of the deep mysteries of evil: "He reveals the deep things of darkness (*ḥōšek*) and brings deep shadows (*ṣalmāwet*) into the light" (Job 12:22 [NIV]). It is used of the deep darkness of the grave or the netherworld: In Job's complaint to God, he said, "Are not my few days almost over? Turn away from me so I can have a moment's joy before I go to the place of no return, to the land of gloom (*ḥōšek*) and deep shadow (*ṣalmāwet),* to the land of deepest (*'ōpel*) night (*'êpātâ*), of deep shadow (*ṣalmāwet*) and disorder, where even the light is like darkness (*'ōpel*)" (Job 10:20-22 [NIV]). "Have the gates of death been shown to you? Have you seen the gates of the shadow of death?" (Job 38:17 [NIV]). In most of these references, NIV has opted to view *ṣalmāwet* as darkness rather than the shadow of death. However, in each case the shadow of death adds the emotional aspect of fear, sorrow, or danger that fits the expectation of the context. Thus, the NKJV and NASV consistently translate the word as shadow of death along with the KJV.

P-B The vb. and the noms. *ṣēl* and *ṣalmawet* are found in the QL with much the same meaning as in the OT. In the RL *ṣēl* has essentially the same meaning, and *ṣalmāwet* is related to Gehenna and hell.

Darkness: → *'ōpel* (darkness, gloom, # 694); → *'ešûn* (approach of darkness, # 854); → *ḥšk* (be, grow dark, grow dim, darken, conceal, confuse, # 3124); → *ṭuḥôt* (darkness, obscurity, inward parts, # 3219); → *kamrîr* (blackness, deep gloom, # 4025); → *laylâ* (night, # 4326); → *nešep* (twilight, darkness, # 5974); → *'wp* II (be dark, # 6415); → *'alāṭâ* (darkness, dusk, # 6602);

→ ʿ*mm* II (darken, dim, # 6670); → ʿ*ᵃrāpel* (deep darkness, thick darkness, heavy cloud, # 6906); → *ṣll* III (be/grow dark, cast a shadow, # 7511); → *ṣalmāwet* (darkness, shadow of death, # 7516); → *qdr* (be dark, mourn, # 7722)

BIBLIOGRAPHY

TDOT 5:248; *TWOT* 2:767; W. L. Mitchell, "*ṣlmwt*, 'Deep Darkness' or 'Shadow of Death'?," *Biblical Research* 29, 1984, 5-20; D. W. Thomas, "*ṢLMWT* in the Old Testament," *JSS* 7, 1962, 191-200; R. F. Youngblood, "Qoheleth's 'Dark House' (Eccl 12:5)," *JETS* 29, 1986, 397-410; M. Dahood, *Psalms I*, AB, 147; W. McKane, *Jeremiah I*, ICC, 32, 52.

James D. Price

7512 (*ṣelem* I, statue, model, image), → Form

7513	צֶלֶם

צֶלֶם (*ṣelem* II), shade, shadow (# 7513).

ANE The nom. possibly comes from a vb. *ṣlm* II, to be shady, dark, not used in Heb., but attested in Akk. *ṣalāmu*, become dark, black, and Arab. *ẓalima*, be dark. The nom. is attested in Akk. *ṣallāmu/ṣalmu*, black, dark, late Aram. *ṣalmā'*, shadow, and possibly Ugar. *ẓlm*, become dark, *ẓlmt*, darkness. See the discussion of *ṣalmāwet*, darkness, shadow of death (# 7516) under *ṣll* (# 7511).

OT The word occurs only 2x in the OT and is thought to mean shade or shadow. It is translated in the NIV as "phantom" (Ps 39:6[7]) and "fantasies" (Ps 73:20), whereas others translate it as shadow, image, form. BDB relates this word to *ṣelem* I, image, likeness (→ # 7512), because a shadow is the image or likeness of the object casting it (so also *HALAT* 964).

P-B RL uses the word with essentially the same meaning. Jastrow 2:1284-85 includes "shadow" and "image" under the same root, in agreement with BDB.

Shade, shadow: → *skk* I (cover, guard, overshadow, protect, # 6114); → *ṣll* III (be/grow dark, cast a shadow, # 7511); → *ṣelem* II (shade, shadow, # 7513)

BIBLIOGRAPHY

THAT 2:558; M. Dahood, *Psalms II*, AB, 193-94.

James D. Price

7516 (*ṣalmāwet*, darkness, shadow of death), → # 7511

7519	צלע

צלע (*ṣl*ʿ I), q. limp, be lame (# 7519); צֶלַע (*ṣela*ʿ), nom. stumbling (# 7520).

OT 1. The vb. *ṣl*ʿ describes a limping condition, such as that of Jacob after he wrestled with the stranger (Gen 32:32), and the lame (figuratively speaking), who will become strong when the Lord delivers his people in the last days (Mic 4:6-7; Zeph 3:19).

2. The nom. *ṣela*ʿ is used to speak of the downfall of the wicked (Job 18:12) and of David's stumbling before his mocking enemies (Ps 35:15; cf. 38:17[18]). Jeremiah says that his enemies too are just waiting for him to slip (Jer 20:10).

3. The nom. *ṣela‘*, rib, side, most likely derives from the vb. *ṣl‘* II, be bent (*HALAT* 965; → # 7521).

Handicaps, disfigurement, blind, lame, stammer, speechless: → *’illēm* (speechlessness, # 522); → *gibbēn* (hunchbacked, # 1492); → *ḥārûṣ* IV (mutilation [animal], # 3024); → *ḥērēš* (speechless, # 3094); → *kšḥ* (be lame, crippled, # 4171); → *mûm* (blemish, # 4583); → *mišḥāt* (disfigured, # 5425); → *nākeh* (crippled, smitten, # 5783); → *‘wr* I (be blind, # 6422); → *‘illēg* (stammering, stuttering, # 6589); → *psḥ* (be lame, crippled, # 7174); → *ṣl‘* I (limping condition, # 7519); → *qlṭ* I (defective [animal], # 7832); → *śr‘* (deformed, mutilated, # 8594); → *t^eballul* (white spot in eye, # 9319)

R. K. Harrison/E. H. Merrill

7520 (*ṣela‘*, stumbling), → # 7519

7521	צֵלָע

צֵלָע (*ṣēlā‘* I), side, side chamber, rib (# 7521).

OT 1. The nom. occurs primarily in relation to architectural descriptions of the ark (Exod 25:12), tabernacle (26:20), altar (27:7), and side chambers of the temple (1 Kgs 6:5; Ezek 41:5).

2. The nom. occurs twice in Gen 2:21-22, where it denotes the part of the man's body used to form the woman. Only Hamilton (*The Book of Genesis: Chapters 1-17*, 178) retains the general translation "side" here. Most commentators, scholars, and translations take the word as a reference to the rib. According to Hamilton, this meaning of *ṣēlā‘*, with which he disagrees, is "traceable to an Arabic root meaning 'to curve, deviate'; hence, *ṣēlā‘* is a curved bone" (cf. G. R. Driver).

It has been argued that the suggestion for this picture of the woman arose from the close connection between the Sumerian word for "life" (*ti*[*l*]) and the word for "rib" (*ti*). Kramer (149) draws attention to the Sumerian Dilmun poem where the goddess created for healing Enki's rib is called Ninti(l), "the Lady of the rib" or "the Lady who makes live." So Eve, the mother of all human beings, was made from the man's rib.

No matter what the etymology, the biblical picture of Eve's creation shows the intimate and mutually dependent nature of the relationship between the sexes. She is truly bone of his bone and one flesh.

Bone: → *gerem* (bone, # 1752); → *‘eṣem* I (bone, skin, body, self, # 6795)

Bibliography

G. R. Driver, "Notes and Studies," *JTS* 47, 1946, 161-62; V. P. Hamilton, *The Book of Genesis: Chapters 1-17*, 1990; S. N. Kramer, *The Sumerians*, 1963; G. J. Wenham, *Genesis 1-15*, 1987; C. Westermann, *Genesis 1-11*, 1984.

Gordon H. Matties/Tremper Longman III

7526 (*ṣ^elāṣal*, cricket), → # 746

7528 (*ṣilṣāl*, fishing gear), → # 1899

7529 (*ṣelṣ^elîm*, cymbals), → # 7509

7532	צמא

צמא (*ṣm'*), q. be thirsty (# 7532); צָמָא (*ṣāmā'*), nom. thirst (# 7533); צָמֵא (*ṣāmē'*), adj. thirsty (# 7534); צִמְאָה (*ṣim'â*), nom. thirst (hapleg.; Jer 2:25) (# 7535); צִמָּאוֹן (*ṣimmā'ôn*), nom. waterless region (# 7536). In all its forms, the root occurs 41x (vb. 11x, nom. 17x, adj. 9x; *ṣimmā'ôn* 3x; hapleg. *ṣim'â*). The occurrences are fairly well distributed throughout the biblical corpus, with perhaps some prominence given to Ps and Isa

ANE The adj. is well attested in Akk. *ṣummû*, *ṣūmu[m]*, *ṣūmmu*, as is the vb. *ṣamû*. Likewise, Eth. attests both the adj. *ṣĕmū'* and the vb. *ṣam'a*, as does Arab. *ẓim'*, *ẓama'*, *ẓamā'*, *ẓāmi'a*. The Heb. *ṣimmā'ôn* also has an Akk. cognate, *ṣumāmîlētu(m)*, *ṣumāmu*.

OT The concept of thirst in the OT has both a literal and figurative dimension. These two dimensions are employed in describing both human thirst and dry land.

1. *Literal.* It should be no surprise that in the arid environs of the ANE the Bible should make more than occasional reference to the issue of thirst. In military contexts, Sisera (4:19), Samson (Judg 15:18), and David's men (2 Sam 17:29) thirst following their exploits. We also see the provision of water as an act of kindness (Ruth 2:9; Prov 25:21). Most prominent perhaps is the Israelites' thirst in the desert after their departure from Egypt (Exod 17:3; see also Neh 9:15, 20; perhaps Ps 107:5-9). The Israelites also experienced thirst during the desert trek that accompanied the departure from Babylon, which Isaiah portrays as a second exodus (Isa 48:21). Although both of these events concern themselves with physical thirst, it is not too difficult to see these events additionally as metaphors for the thirst of God's people that can be quenched only by the Lord's provision (see sec. 2 below). Furthermore, not only do people thirst, but the arid land itself is also referred to as thirsty (Deut 8:15; 29:18). Thirst is also seen as a form of God's punishment upon (a) his people (Deut 28:48) or the land itself (Ps 107:33-34) for covenant disobedience, and (b) Israel's enemies (Isa 65:13) or their land (Jer 48:18) for their opposition to God's people.

2. *Figurative.* Apart from the literal meaning, thirst also describes the intense yearning of the faithful for God, a metaphor laden with meaning in a region where the supply of water could never be taken for granted. The Psalms in particular describe the faithful as thirsting after God. In Ps 42:1-2[2-3], the psalmist's thirst for God is like a deer's panting (*'rg*, → # 6864) for streams of water (see also 119:131 [*š'p*, → # 8634]). In 63:1[2], David's earnest seeking (*šḥr*, → # 8838) after God is like one's thirst "in a dry and weary land where there is no water." A similar notion is seen in 143:6 (although the root *ṣm'* is not used): "my soul thirsts for you like a parched land." In Isa 55:1, the prophet extends an invitation to the exiles to enter into covenant with Yahweh: "Come, all you who are thirsty, come to the waters."

3. There are also several passages where thirst carries both literal and figurative meanings, a fact that serves to locate the theological import of the metaphor (figurative meaning) in everyday reality (literal meaning). Isa 44:3, for example, which speaks of the impending return from exile, promises water to be poured (*yṣq*, pour, → # 3668) on the "thirsty land, and streams on the dry ground." Although this seems to suggest simply the provision of water on their homeward journey, the verse follows by continuing the image, but juxtaposes an unambiguous figurative dimension: "I will pour out (*yṣq*) my Spirit on your offspring." A similar double meaning may also be seen in Isa 5:13; 41:17; 49:10.

Isaiah also links the provision of water for the returning exiles to the provision of water in the desert for the exodus generation (Isa 43:14-19; 48:20-21), thereby establishing a typological connection between the two events. The theological significance of this typology appears to be in the fact that the redemption of God's people at two of the more prominent junctures of redemptive-historical significance in the OT (exodus and exile) is closely tied to the "quenching of thirst," a theme that applies also to personal deliverance, as seen above.

We see then that in both literal and figurative terms God is the one who provides the most basic physical and spiritual needs of his people, although in punishment he may withhold that provision. Any punishment, however, is not merely an end in itself but a means of chastening to bring about repentance and the realization of one's complete dependence on God's goodness.

P-B This figurative meaning is also attested in DSS. 1QH 4:11 describes the "teachers of lies and seers of falsehood" as "withholding the drink of knowledge from the thirsty and quenching their thirst with vinegar (false teaching)" instead. 1QS 2:14 speaks of a "parched spirit" (cf. Deut 29:18). 1QpHab describes the wicked priest as deserving of God's cup of wrath for having quenched his thirst in shameful ways.

NT Although the literal sense is present in the NT (Matt 25:35, 37, 42, 44; Rom 12:20; 1 Cor 4:11), the figurative sense is prominent. The Lord's blessing on those who "hunger and thirst for righteousness" (Matt 5:6) fits nicely into the development of this theme seen above. Christ's offer of water in John 4:13-15; 6:35; 7:37 likewise presents the desire to know God in terms of quenching of thirst (see also Ps 36:9[10]; Jer 2:13; 17:13). Beyond the personal and immediate significance of these passages, they also carry decided eschatological overtones in that their thirst will be forever sated (John 4:14), and Jesus, in providing water to those who ask, implicitly claims to serve as the focal point of OT law (Lev 23:34) and prophecy (Isa 55:1). These eschatological overtones are more explicit in Rev 7:17; 21:6; 22:17, where the faithful in the world to come are promised living water (see also Isa 49:10; Ezek 47; Joel 3:18[4:18]; Zech 14:8). In both the OT and NT, the quenching of the thirst of the righteous is realized both in the present (e.g., Ps 63:1[2]; John 4:4, 13-15) and in the future state (Zech 14:8; Rev 21-22). This theme comes into sharp focus in the NT through the person and work of Christ, by whose invitation believers drink from the well of living water both now and for all eternity.

Drinking, drawing water, drenching: → *gm'* (swallow, drink, # 1686); → *gr'* II (draw up [drops of water], # 1758); → *dlh* I (draw water, # 1926); → *yrh* II (give to drink, # 3722); → *l'*' II (drink noisily, # 4363); → *lqq* (lick, lap, # 4379); → *mṣṣ* (drink, quaff, # 5209); → *rwh* (drink one's fill, drench, # 8115); → *š'b* (draw [water], # 8612); → *šqh* (drink, refreshment, # 9197); → *šth* II (drinking, # 9272)

BIBLIOGRAPHY

TWAT 6:1065-68; *TWOT* 2:768-69; D. C. Allison, Jr., "The Living Water (John 4:10-14; 6:35c; 7:37g-39)," *Saint Vladimir's Theological Quarterly* 30, 1986, 143-57; B. H. Grigsby, "'If Any Man Thirsts...': Observations on the Rabbinic Background of John 7:37-39," *Bib* 67, 1986, 101-8; L. Ruppert, "Dürsten nach Gott: Ein psalmistiches Motiv im religionsphänomenologischen Vergleich," *Die alttestamentlichen Botschaft als Wegweisung*, 1990, 237-51; A. Sicari,

"The Hunger and Thirst of Christ," *Communio: International Catholic Review* 18, 1991, 590-602.

Peter Enns

7533 (*ṣāmā'*, thirst), → # 7532

7534 (*ṣāmē'*, thirsty), → # 7532

7535 (*ṣim'â*, dry, thirst), → # 7532

7536 (*ṣimmā'ôn*, waterless region), → # 7532

7537	צמד

צמד (*ṣmd*), n. be attached, attach o.s.; pu. be bound; hi. attach (# 7537); צֶמֶד (*ṣemed*), nom. yoke, team, area of land, acre (# 7538).

ANE Akk. *ṣamādu*, bind, harness; Ugar. *ṣmdm*, harness, yoke; Aram.-Syr. *ṣemad*, bind up, bind together; Arab. *ḍamada*, to bind, dress a wound; Eth. *ḍamada*, harness; nom. Akk. *ṣimdu*, bandage, team (of draft animals), arrangement; Ugar. *ṣmd*, stick, club; Phoen. *ṣmd*, mace, club; Arab. *miḍmadat*, yoke.

OT 1. The nom. *ṣemed* is only used literally with reference to a pair of animals (Judg 19:10; 1 Sam 11:7; 1 Kgs 19:19, 21; 2 Kgs 5:17; 9:25; Job 1:3; 42:12; Isa 21:7, 9) or to a field, perhaps an area that could be plowed by a pair of oxen in one day (1 Sam 14:14; Isa 5:10).

2. Outside of 2 Sam 20:8, where the vb. *ṣmd* is used literally with reference to the way that Joab's sword was fastened to him, the term is used figuratively for Israel's attaching itself to the Baal of Peor (Num 25:3, 5; Ps 106:28); so also, God accuses the wicked of having a tongue that is bound to evil (Ps 50:19).

NT The nom. *zeugos*, pair, yoke, which is a translation of *ṣemed* in the LXX, refers to two doves (Luke 2:24) and to a pair of oxen (14:19). The vb. *heterozygeō*, to be unevenly yoked, mismated, occurs in Paul's exhortation to the Corinthians to refrain from being closely associated with unbelievers (2 Cor 6:14).

Yoke: → *môṭâ* (yoke, carrying pole, # 4574); → *'ōl* (yoke, # 6585); → *ṣmd* (be attached, attach oneself, # 7537)

Band, tie: → *'pd* (put on tightly, # 679); → *'ᵃpēr* (bandage, # 710); → *'eṣ'ādâ* (band, # 731); → *ḥbš* (tie up, saddle, imprison, bind, # 2502); → *ḥgr* (bind, gird, # 2520); → *ḥāšûq* (clasp ring, # 3122); → *ḥtl* (be swaddled, # 3156); → *keset* (band [for magic purposes], # 4086); → *migbā'â* (head-band, # 4457); → *'nd* (wind, tie s.t., # 6698); → *'qd* (tie up, # 6818); → *ṣrr* I (bind, tie up, # 7674); → *qšr* (ally together, conspire, bind, # 8003); → *rks* (bind, tie, # 8220); → *rtm* (tie up, # 8412)

BIBLIOGRAPHY

TDNT 2:43, 901; C. L. Tyer, "The Yoke in Ancient Near Eastern, Hebrew and New Testament Materials," Ph.D. Diss.: Vanderbilt, 1963.

John E. Harvey

7538 (*ṣemed*, yoke, team, area of land, acre), → # 7537

7539	צַמָּה

צַמָּה (*ṣammâ*), nom. veil (# 7539).

OT The nom. *ṣammâ* occurs 4x, 3x in S of Songs, where the lover praises the beloved for her eyes (4:1) and cheeks (4:3; 6:7) that lie behind the veil. Three kinds of veil have been suggested: (1) a diaphanous muslin gauze (M. Goulder, *The Song of Fourteen Songs,* JSOTSup 36, 1986, 33); (2) a veil concealing the lower part of the face and so dividing the cheeks into a darker lower half and a lighter upper half (the comparison with pomegranates [4:3; 6:7] would refer to the contrast between the dark red inner and bright red outer parts as portrayed on Egyptian paintings [M. Pope, *Song of Songs,* 1977, 457]); (3) an opaque veil with only eye holes (a *yashmak*). The lover's imagination or memory, rather than his sight, is at work (J. Snaith, *Song of Songs,* 1993, 61). A veil not only conceals, it can also function erotically to invite an imaginatively enhanced beauty.

The only other occurrence of the word is in a prophetic judgment on Babylon (Isa 47:2), where most translations understand a comparison with the enslavement of a refined virgin commanded to remove her veil (*gallî ṣammātēk*), symbolizing the loss of wealth, leisure, and honor. However, C. R. North (*The Second Isaiah*, 1964, 170) points out that *gll* means uncover rather than remove and argues that here and in S of Songs *ṣammâ* refers to the loosing of long hair (cf. NEB "uncover your tresses"; see 1 Cor 11:2-13) through the removal of the veil.

Veil: → *dōq* (veil, gauze, # 1988); → *ḥebyôn* (covering, # 2470); → *miṭpaḥat* (veil, cloak, # 4762); → *masweh* (veil, # 5003); → *massēkâ* II (veil, sheet, blanket, # 5012); → *mispāḥâ* (veil, # 5029); → *ṣammâ* (veil, # 7539); → *ṣā'îp* (veil, # 7581); → *rᵉdîd* (veil, # 8100); → *rᵉ'ālâ* (veil, # 8304)

Bibliography

R. de Vaux, "Sur le voile des femmes dans l'Orient ancien," *RB* 44, 1935, 397-412.

P. Jenson

7541	צמח

צמח (*ṣmḥ*), q. sprout, spring up, grow, prosper, make grow; pi.; hi (# 7541); צֶמַח (*ṣemaḥ*), nom. growth, shoot, bud (# 7542).

ANE Aram. with same meaning; Phoen. *ṣmḥ,* sprout, offshoot, posterity; Syr. *ṣᵉmaḥ,* shine forth; *ṣemḥā',* shining, sprout.

OT 1. Of the 33x the vb. *ṣmḥ* occurs, 14x denote the literal sprouting of a plant. The subject of the intransitive q. is that which sprouts: shrub of the field (Gen 2:5), heads of grain (41:6, 23), and trees (Exod 10:5; Eccl 2:6). The hi. has as its subject either God in contexts of blessing (Gen 2:9; Job 38:27; Ps 104:14; 147:8) or the earth in the context of curse (Gen 3:18; Deut 29:23[22]). Literal growth is used as a figure for the produce of God's word (Isa 55:10), righteousness and praise (61:11), and Israel (Ezek 17:6[9]).

(a) Sprouting also occurs in a metaphorical sense of the springing or bringing forth of salvation and desire (2 Sam 23:5), righteousness (Isa 45:8; 61:11), fulfillment of prophecy (42:9; 43:19), Israel's descendants (44:4), healing (58:8), truth (Ps 85:11[12]), trouble (Job 5:6), strength (Ezek 29:21), and men from the dust to take the place of the one who forgets God (Job 8:19). Instances of the hi. (2 Sam 23:5; Isa 45:8; 61:11) suggest that God is best understood as the ultimate author even in the q.

(b) An important use of the metaphorical sense occurs in connection with the Branch (*ṣemaḥ*) of David. This clearly messianic figure is made to sprout forth by the Lord (Jer 33:15) to execute justice and righteousness in the land, and as Zech 6:12 attests, sets out to build the temple of the Lord. It is possible that the reference of Ps 132:17 to the horn (*qeren*) of David, which the Lord causes to spring forth, is to be understood in a messianic sense, although, as with Ezek 29:21, it more likely denotes the great strength of the Davidic dynasty.

(c) Hair or beard growth is denoted in all four cases of the pi. (Judg 16:22; 2 Sam 10:5; 1 Chron 19:5; Ezek 16:7) and once by the q. (Lev 13:37).

2. Of the 12x the nom. *ṣemaḥ* occurs, 7x denote a shoot or growth in the literal sense. Of these, only Ps 65:10[11], in reference to God's care for the earth and its growth, is not employed as a figure. Isa 61:11 likens the sprouts brought forth by the earth to the righteousness and praise God causes to sprout before the nations. The remaining figures occur in poetic exhortations to obedience. Ezek 16:7 relates Israel's promising beginning to the numerous sprouts after sowing. In 17:9, 10, the vine that is Israel is in danger of having its new growth whither because the people have broken the covenant. Hos 8:7 likens the stalk with no head to Israel's rebellion: it will produce no fruit.

A distinctly different concept is introduced at Isa 4:2, "In that day the Branch of the LORD will be beautiful and glorious." Most modern commentators have determined that the verse refers only to the restoration of the land and suggest that the following parallel phrase, "and the fruit of the land will be the pride and glory of the survivors in Israel," substantiates this interpretation. Others have posited a messianic interpretation for the passage, a determination that finds early support in the Tg.: *mešîḥā' da*^{a}*dōnāy,* Messiah of the Lord. There can be little doubt that the nom. *ṣemaḥ* denotes the Messiah, the Branch of David, in Jer 23:5 and 33:15. Zech 3:8, "my servant, the Branch," and 6:12, "Here is the man whose name is Branch," further highlight the messianic import of the term. The LXX translates *ṣemaḥ* at Jer 23:5; Zech 3:8; 6:12 with *anatolē,* rising, sunrise, east. Although the LXX appears to have altered the image suggested by *ṣemaḥ,* W. Kaiser (*TWOT* 2:770) has suggested that Luke 1:78, "by which the rising sun (= branch?) will come to us from heaven," is to be linked conceptually to the Branch motif in the OT through *anatolē*. In this regard, it is of note that the Pesh. of Isa 4:2; Zech 3:8; 6:12; and Luke 1:78 use the word *denḥā'*, which also indicates the rising of the sun or stars. This word is also commonly used metaphorically to denote a theophany, a manifestation of God; or the epiphany, the manifestation of Christ in the flesh. A parallel to Jer 23:5 and 33:15 is found in a Phoenician inscription from Lapethos on Cyprus (*KAI* 43:11). This inscription, incised on a statue pedestal and dated to the third century BC, refers to Ptolemy II Philadelphus as *ṣemaḥ ṣedeq*, the righteous (legitimate?) shoot.

P-B The RL and Sir 14:18 continue the literal sense of sprouting plants, as do the Qumran texts (4Q423 2 3). In addition, copies of CDam found in Cave 4 at Qumran use *ṣmḥ* to denote an eruption of the skin (4Q269 8 2; 4Q272 1 i 6, 7; 4Q273 1 ii 4), whereas Lev 13, the biblical model, refers to the action of spreading (Lev 13:5, *pśh*). A report of the sect's history (CDam 1:7) refers to the Essene (Qumran) community as the "plant root" that "sprouted forth from Israel and Aaron." Although W. Kaiser's (*TWOT* 2:770) suggestion that Heb 7:14 should be translated "Our Lord sprang forth (or sprouted [*anatellō*]) from Judah," is intriguing, it would appear that neither the Qumran concept of community nor the OT messianic sense is present in the NT with relation to the vb. *ṣmḥ*.

Sir uses *ṣemaḥ* to denote the shoots of grain (Sir 40:22) or of new grass (43:21), as does 4Q418 107 5. 4Q252 (Pesher Genesis a) 1 v. 3-4, a commentary on Gen 49:10, interprets "until Shiloh (*šîlōh*; NIV he ... to whom it belongs) comes" as "until the Righteous Messiah comes, the Branch of David" (cf. 4Q174 1:11; 4Q285 5 3).

Growth, greatness, luxuriance, ripening, sprouting: → *bqq* II (grow luxuriantly, # 1328); → *gdl* I (grow up, become great, make great, boast, # 1540); → *nwb* (grow, prosper, flourish, # 5649); → *sāḥîš* (what grows on its own accord, # 6084); → *sāpîaḥ* I (what grows on its own accord, # 6206); → *ṣmḥ* (sprout, spring up, grow, prosper, make grow, # 7541); → *r'n* (be luxuriant, green, # 8315); → *śg'/śgh* (grow great, increase, exalt, # 8434/8436)

BIBLIOGRAPHY

TDNT 1:351-53; *THAT* 2:563-66; *TWAT* 6:1068-72; *TWOT* 2:769-70; J. G. Baldwin, "*ṣemah* as a Technical Term in the Prophets," *VT* 14, 1964, 93-97; J. Bright, *Jeremiah,* AB, 1965; J. H. Thompson, *The Book of Jeremiah*, NICOT, 1980; A. van den Branden, "Titoli tolemaic ['ŠāRā', *ṣmḥ ṣdq e* ἀνατολὴν δικίαν," *BibOr* 6, 1964, 60-72.

M. G. Abegg, Jr.

7542 (*ṣemaḥ*, growth, shoot, bud), → # 7541

7543	צָמִיד

צָמִיד (*ṣāmîd* I), nom. bracelet (of woman) (# 7543); < צמד (*ṣmd*), ni. commit/attach o.s.; pu. be fastened; hi. hitch up (an animal, used figuratively) (→ # 7537).

ANE Akk. *ṣamādu*, to tie, yoke, harness (*CAD* 16, 89; cf. *AHw*, 1080); Aram. *ṣ^emad*, bind; Ugar. *ṣmd*, harness (*UT*, 2169; *HALAT* 967).

OT For occurrences, see Gen 24:22, 30, 47 and Num 31:50. It is used as a metaphor in Ezekiel as God's gracious provision of the people of Judah: "I put bracelets on your arms" (Ezek 16:11), but also of the manner in which Samaria (Oholah) and Jerusalem (Oholibah) followed the nations who rewarded them with "bracelets" (23:42).

For a discussion on jewelry, see *'dh* (put on ornaments, # 6335).

Malcolm J. A. Horsnell

7544 (*ṣāmid* II, lid), → # 4059

7547	צֶמֶר

צֶמֶר (*ṣemer*), wool, woolen (# 7547).

ANE Eth. *ḍamr*, Aram. *'^amar*, Syr. *'amrā'*, Mand. *aqamra*.

OT 1. Wool comes from sheep, and sheep, along with goats, were the most abundant domestic animals. After the sheep were sheared, the wool was bleached, then tufted onto distaffs, and spun with spindles into thread. The shepherds' wives sometimes dyed the wool before or after it was made into thread, and then wove it on looms to produce a warm and heavy fabric. From that fabric the most basic garments were made. For fabric made from the hair of goats or camels (cf. Zech 13:4), see *kābîr* (hair of goats, # 3889); *śēʿār* (hair, # 8552).

2. Four of the 16x *ṣemer* occurs are in the regulations concerning fungus (Lev 13:47-48, 52, 59). Others are scattered through the Former Prophets, poetical books, and Latter Prophets. For example, Gideon put a wool fleece on a threshing floor for God to dampen as a sign of coming deliverance (Judg 6:37). King Mesha of Moab had to supply to Joram of Israel the wool of 100,000 rams as tribute (2 Kgs 3:4).

The word occurs several times in the Prophets. Hosea charged unfaithful Israel with accepting gifts, including wool as payment from her lovers (Hos 2:5[7]). In retaliation God promised to take back his wool and linen (2:9[11]). Isaiah likens forgiveness and cleansing to wool (Isa 1:18). But, the unrepentant are like wool in that "the worm will devour them like wool" (51:8).

Ezekiel also spoke of wool (3x). It was one of the goods Damascus traded with the Tyrians (Ezek 27:18). He charged the abusive shepherds of Israel with wrongfully using the wool of the sheep (34:3). And woolen garments are forbidden for priests who will serve in the eschatological temple (44:17), probably because this would make them sweat, and this, in turn, was probably a form of ceremonial uncleanness.

Four times wool is mentioned in poetic passages in Ps, Prov, and Isa. God "spreads the snow like wool" according to Ps 147:16. The wife of noble character diligently "selects wool and flax" (Prov 31:13).

Spinning, sewing, weaving, embroidering: → *ʾrg* (spin, weave, # 755); → *dallâ* I (hair, thrum, loom, # 1929); → *ḥōšēb* (weaver, # 3110); → *ṭwh* (spin, # 3211); → *kîšôr* (distaff, # 3969); → *mānôr* (rod, # 4962); → *skk* II (weave, intertwine, # 6115); → *ʿēreb* I (knitted material, # 6849); → *pelek* I (spindle-whorl, # 7134); → *rqm* (embroider, weave together, # 8387); → *śᵉrād* (woven, # 8573); → *šbṣ* I (weave, # 8687); → *šᵉtî* I (woven material, # 9274); → *tpr* (sew, # 9529)

Robert L. Alden

7550	צַמֶּרֶת

צַמֶּרֶת(*ṣammeret*), [tree-]top (# 7550).

ANE There are no cognates except possibly Arab.

OT The Heb. word is used 5x, only in Ezekiel: 17:3, 22; 31:3, 10, 14. The basic meaning of *ṣammeret* is top, highest branch and is translated similarly by all translations in all these passages. This is based mostly on usage in this context. The "top of a cedar" in Ezek 17:3 is generally accepted as a reference to Jehoiachin, and the "land of merchants" (v. 4) is applied to Babylonia.

Trees: → *ʾēlâ* I (mighty tree, # 461); → *ʾerez* (cedar, # 780); → *ʾōren* I (pine, # 815); → *ʾēšel* (tamarisk, # 869); → *bᵉrôš* (juniper, # 1360); → *lûz* I (almond-tree, # 4280); → *ʿēṣ* (trees, tree, wood, timber, sticks, # 6770); → *ʿarʿār* (juniper, # 6899); → *ṣammeret* (acacia, [tree-]top, # 7550); → *šāqēd* (almond, # 9196); → *šiqmâ* (sycamore-[fig-] tree, # 9204); → *tᵉʾaššûr* (cypress, # 9309); → *tāmār* I (date-palm, # 9469); → *tirzâ* (unknown tree, # 9560); (→ **Tree of Knowledge/Life: Theology**)

Larry L. Walker

7551	צמת

צמת (*ṣmt*), q., pilp. and hi. silence; ni. be silenced (# 7551); צְמִיתֻת (*ṣ^e^mîtut*), nom. forfeiture of the right of repurchase (# 7552).

ANE In Ugar. this root means destroy, and is paralleled with *mḫṣ*, strike. In Aram. it means press together, in Syr. to silence, and in Arab. be speechless.

OT 1. Like *dmh* II (→ # 1949), this root connotes silencing in a more or less permanent way. Thus, in the majority of its vb. occurrences NIV translates as destroy (cf. Ugar.). It is used especially frequently with regard to enemies who either seek to silence the speaker or are being themselves silenced (2 Sam 22:41; ‖ Ps 18:41; 54:5[7]; 69:4[5]; 73:27; 88:17; 94:23 [2x]; 101:5, 8; 143:12; Lam 3:53). The remaining refs. are to streams that grow silent in the dry season (a comparison to fickle human friends, Job 6:17), and to a zeal for God's word that is utterly exhausting as it seeks to get others to stop ignoring that word (Ps 119:139).

2. The nom. occurs only twice, both in Lev 25 (vv. 23, 30), where it is apparently a technical term for silence concerning repurchase of property. That is, if land in the countryside is sold, the family may always "speak up" to repurchase that land. On the other hand, if property in a walled city is sold, the heirs have no future claim and must be silent about such a claim in the future.

Rest, silence: → *dûmâ* I (silence, # 1872); → *dmh* II (come to an end, rest, be dumb, silent, # 1949); → *dmm* I (stand still, be motionless, silent, # 1957); → *ḥp'* (do s.t. secretly, # 2901); → *ḥšh* (keep silence, command to be silent, # 3120); → *ḥrš* II (be deaf, keep still, remain inactive, make silent, # 3087); → *ṣmṯ* (silence, # 7551)

John N. Oswalt

7552 (*ṣ^e^mîtut*, forfeiture of right of repurchase), → # 7551

7557	צִנָּה

צִנָּה (*ṣinnâ* I), coolness (hapleg.) (#7557).

OT A trustworthy messenger is compared to the "coolness" of snow at harvest time because he is refreshing (Prov 25:13). An apocryphal occurrence refers to the cold wind from the north (Sir 43:20).

Cold, cool: → *ṣinnâ* I (coolness, # 7557); → *qrr* II (be cold, # 7981)

Bill T. Arnold

7558	צִנָּה

צִנָּה (*ṣinnâ* II), long shield, body shield (# 7558).

ANE *HALAT* lists only a possible Akk. cognate *ṣinnatum*. However, *CAD* 16, 201 gives this word a different meaning.

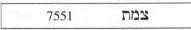

OT A *ṣinnâ* is a special kind of shield used to protect the entire body. The word likely refers to the shield used during the siege of cities, particularly when warriors are trying to undermine the walls. Often a shield bearer will have sole responsibility of moving the shield in order to protect himself and an archer who accompanies him. These shields often have a little overhang that protects the warrior from arrows shot from an elevation, like the top of a city wall. See illustrations in Yadin (406 far right, 418, 462).

In half of its occurrences *ṣinnâ* appears with *māgēn*, apparently referring to the normal or small shield as well as the large shield. This word pair functions as a merism covering all shields. These passages lack theological import (Ezek 23:24; 38:4). The same is true for a number of passages in which *ṣinnâ* stands alone (1 Kgs 10:16 [2x]; Ezek 26:8). However, there are a limited number of instances in which the word carries the same kind of theological import that *māgēn* I occasionally carries. Ps 91:4 is representative: "His (God's) faithfulness will be your shield and rampart."

Shield: → *māgēn* I (shield, protection, # 4482); → *ʿᵃgîlâ* (round shield, # 6317); → *ṣinnâ* II (long shield, # 7558); → *šeleṭ* (shield, # 8949)

BIBLIOGRAPHY

TWAT 4:646-59; O. Keel, *The Symbolism of the Biblical World*, 1978, 222-25; Y. Yadin, *The Art of Warfare in Biblical Lands*, 1963.

Tremper Longman

7560 (*ṣānûaʿ*, with modesty), → # 7570

7562 (*ṣinnôr*, water-spout? cataract? watershaft?), → # 5643

7563 (*ṣnḥ*, clap the hands, drive), → # 3338

7564	צְנִינִים

צְנִינִים (*ṣᵉnînîm*), thorns (# 7564).

OT It is possible that the *ṣᵉnînîm* should be identified with the bramble (*Rubus sanguineus*; Zohary, 157). The word occurs only in Num 33:55 and Josh 23:13, where it speaks of the judgment that God will bring on the Israelites if they do not drive out completely the Canaanites. The Canaanites that remain will be thorns in the eyes and backs (inverted between the two passages). The *ṣᵉnînîm* may be in view in Luke 6:44.

Thornbush, nettle, sting, thistle, thorn: → *'āṭād* (thornbush, # 353); → *barqōn* (thorn, brier, # 1402); → *deber* II (thorny sting, # 1823); → *dardar* (thistle, # 1998); → *ḥēdeq* (brier, # 2537); → *ḥôaḥ* I (thorn, # 2560); → *mᵉsûkâ* (thorn hedge, # 5004); → *naʿᵃṣûṣ* (thornbush, # 5848); → *sîrâ* (thorny bush, # 6106); → *sillôn* (thorn, # 6141); → *sᵉneh* (thorny shrub, # 6174); → *sirpād* (stinging nettle, # 6252); → *ṣe'ᵉlîm* (thorny lotus, # 7365); → *ṣᵉnînîm* (thorns, # 7564); → *qôṣ* I (thornbush, # 7764); → *qimmôś* (weeds, nettles, # 7853); → *śēk* (thorn, splinter, # 8493); → *šāmîr* I (Christ's thorn, # 9031)

BIBLIOGRAPHY

TWOT 2:771; I. and W. Jacob, "Flora," *ABD*, 1992, 2:815; M. Zohary, *Plants of the Bible*, 1982, 157.

K. Lawson Younger, Jr.

7565	צָנִיף

צָנִיף (*ṣānîp*), nom. turban (# 7565); מִצְנֶפֶת (*miṣnepet*), nom. that which is wound about; turban (NIV; # 5200); < צנף (*ṣnp*), wrap, put on (→ # 7571).

ANE A cognate in Arab., *ṣinf*, signifies hem or fringe; Syr. *maṣnaptā'*, turban.

OT 1. The vb. *ṣnp* occurs in finite form twice only and both times in q., with the sense to wind, wrap, or twist. It is used of the high priest (NIV) putting on (lit., winding on) the sacred turban (Lev 16:4). Shebna, in rebuke for his pride, is told that "(the Lord) *will roll you up tightly* like a ball and throw you into a large country" that is, "discard you as rubbish" (Isa 22:18). The phrase "will roll you up tightly" (NIV) consists of three words, an infinitive, a finite vb., and a nom. from the same root *ṣnp*.

2. The nom. *ṣānîp*, turban, occurs 4x in postexilic texts; except in Isa 3:23, the term is a parallel to *miṣnepet*. The *miṣnepet*, wrapping, formed by binding a strip of linen about the head in the fashion of a turban, was worn by the high priest and his sons as one of a number of sacred garments (Exod 28:4; 39:28; Lev 16:4). Made of linen, it bore a plate (→ *nēzer*, # 5694) inscribed "HOLY TO THE LORD" (Exod 28:36-38; 29:6; 39:30-31; Lev 16:4). Milgrom (511) notes that outside P, the OT uses *ṣānîp* for the high priest's headdress (Zech 3:5), for an article of luxurious fem. wear (Isa 3:23), for the royal headdress (Isa 62:3), and figuratively for justice (Job 29:14). He suggests that *miṣnepet* is a coinage by P to prevent confusion with any secular headwear. If this be so, the *miṣnepet* of Ezek 21:26[31] would be a badge of priestly office; the prophecy would entail the fall of both sacred and political power. The total reversal of Israelite life in the rest of v. 26 (cf. 1 Sam 2:4-10) suggests that the reference is to both the sacred and the secular.

3. Jerusalem is called a "royal diadem" (*ʿᵃṭārā*), which links the priestly symbol (*ṣānîp*) with the regal power (Isa 62:3; cf. Ezek 21:26; Zech 6:10-11). The extent of the postexilic high priest's power, its relation to the secular arm, and his use of former royal symbols are all debated. See further *AncIsr*, 398-401; Ackroyd, 195-97. For an outline of kingship ideas in OT times, cf. Eaton, "Kingship"; Cross, 219-65. Although throughout ANE kingship among gods and humans was symbolized by the wearing of a crown, nowhere in the Bible is God said to have worn one. The biblical writers in this way may have differentiated the kingship exercised by Yahweh from the political institution and its Canaanite origins.

P-B Mish. Yoma 7:5 says the turban was worn by all the priests but that only the high priest wore the *nēzer*.

Clothing—Turban: → *ṭᵉbûlîm* (turban, # 3178); → *miṣnepet* (turban, diadem, # 5200); → *nēzer* (diadem, # 5694); → *ṣānîp* (turban, diadem, # 7565)
Crown: → *ktr* III (wear as ornament, # 4194); → *ʿṭr* (surround, crown, # 6496/7)

BIBLIOGRAPHY

P. R. Ackroyd, *Exile and Restoration*, 1968, 195-97; F. M. Cross, *Canaanite Myth and Hebrew Epic*, 1973, 219-65; J. H. Eaton, "Kingship," *DBI*, 379-82; J. Milgrom, *Leviticus*, AB 3, 1991, 511; R. de Vaux, *AncIsr*, 1961, 398, 401-14.

Robert J. Way

7568 צָנֻם

צָנֻם (*ṣānum*), hard, barren (ears of grain) (# 7568).

OT This word is probably derived from the vb. *ṣnm*, meaning "dry up, harden," and is used only once in the OT, where it describes the withered ears of the seven years of famine in Pharaoh's dream (Gen 41:23). It is translated in the LXX with the G word *anemophthoroi,* meaning "dried up," and later Aram. and Syr. use the word *ṣûnāmā'* with the same meaning.

Grain, barley, millet, rice, etc.: → *'ābîb* (ears of grain, # 26); → *biṣqālôn* (fresh stalks [cj.], # 1303); → *bar* III (grain, corn, # 1339); → *gādîš* I (stack of grain, # 1538); → *gereś* (grits, # 1762); → *dāgān* (grain, # 1841); → *dōḥan* (sorghum, millet, # 1893); → *ḥiṭṭâ* (wheat, # 2636); → *kussemet* (emmer-wheat, # 4081); → *karmel* IV (grain, fresh, newly ripened grain, # 4152); → *m^e lîlâ* (grain, grains, # 4884); → *minnît* (rice, # 4976); → *mōṣ* (chaff, # 5161); → *sōlet* (wheat flour, # 6159); → *pannāg* (parched? grain, meal or flour, # 7154); → *ṣebet* (grain, bundle of grain, # 7395); → *ṣānum* (hard, barren [ears of grain], # 7568); → *qālî* (parched grain, # 7833); → *qāmâ* (crops, grain, standing grain, # 7850); → *śôrâ* (millet, # 8463); → *ś^e 'ōrâ* (barley, # 8555); → *šibbōlet* I (ear of grain, # 8672); → *šeber* II (grain, # 8692)

BIBLIOGRAPHY

F. E. Greenspahn, *Hapax Legomena in Biblical Hebrew*, 154.

Paul D. Wegner

7570	צנע

צנע (*ṣn'*), hi. be modest (# 7570); צָנוּעַ (*ṣānûa'*), with modesty (# 7560).

OT In the classic prophetic summary of the teaching of the eighth-century prophets that occurs at Mic 6:8, the phrase *haṣnēa' leket* occurs; this is normally translated "walk humbly" (RSV, NIV, NJPSV, TEV). The phrase is of somewhat uncertain meaning and has in recent commentaries been interpreted as "walk wisely," largely based on the Qumran Manual of Discipline rendering and the use of the root in Ecclesiasticus. But at the only other occurrence of the root in the OT (Prov 11:2), the nom. is used of the reticent wise (LXX *tapeinos*; Vg. *humilitas*). In modern Heb. the phrase is used of modest behavior, though this may be a biblical borrowing from Mic 6:8. The "humility" that Micah enjoins is linked with "acting justly" (*mišpāṭ*) and "loving faithfully" (*ḥesed*). If the traditional translation ("walk humbly") may stand, the phrase is the climax of the verse and is a most powerful assertion of the importance of humility.

Humble: → *kn'* (be subdued, be humbled, humble o.s., # 4044); → *'nh* II (afflict, humble, afflict one's soul, fast, oppress, submit, # 6700)

W. J. Dumbrell

7571	צנף

צנף (*ṣnp* I), q., wrap, turn (# 7571); nom. צָנִיף (*ṣānîp*), turban, diadem (→ # 7565); מִצְנֶפֶת (*miṣnepet*), turban, diadem (# 5200).

OT 1. The vb. occurs twice in Isa 22:18 in an inf. abs. construction with the meaning "roll up tightly" (NIV). Otherwise it appears only in Lev 16:4 in a cognate acc. construction with the nom. form *miṣnepet*, "turbaned with a turban."

2. The nom. *ṣānîp* occurs 5x: Job 29:14; Isa 3:23; 62:3; and twice in Zech 3:5. In Job it is parallel with *m^e 'îl*, robe. It is in the catalog of fem. finery with many of the items defying certain identification (Isa 3:18-23). In 62:3 it is parallel with *'^a ṭārâ*, crown. The Zech references are to the crown put on the head of Joshua, the high priest. The clean turban represents the reinstatement of a legitimate and ceremonially clean

high priest so that Israel once again has representation before God. A plate engraved with "HOLY TO THE LORD" is attached to the front of this turban (Exod 28:36; 39:30).

3. Eleven of the twelve occurrences of *miṣnepet* are in those sections of Exod and Lev describing the headgear of the high priest. Because *miṣnepet* is made of linen (e.g., Exod 39:28 or Lev 16:4), turban is the best translation. Exod 29:6 complicates the picture, however. "Put the turban (*miṣnepet*) on his head and attach the sacred diadem (*nezer*) to the turban (*miṣnepet*)." The *nēzer* must be what is elsewhere the *ṣîṣ*; the NIV renders both as "diadem." It is the item on which is engraved "HOLY TO THE LORD." Lev 8:9 presents a similar problem (cf. Exod 28:36-37). In Ezek 21:26[31] *miṣnepet* is parallel to *ʿᵃṭārâ*, crown (cf. Isa 62:3).

Clothing—Turban: → *ṭᵉbûlîm* (turban, # 3178); → *miṣnepet* (turban, diadem, # 5200); → *nēzer* (diadem, # 5694); → *ṣānîp* (turban, diadem, # 7565)
Clothing—Wear clothes: → *lbš* (put on, clothe, wear, # 4252); → *ʿṭh* I (cover, wrap, # 6486); → *ʿṭp* I (wrap, # 6493); → *ṣnp* I (wrap, turn, # 7571)
Priests and levites: → *ʾabnēṭ* (sash, esp. of priests, # 77); → *ʾēpôd* I (ephod, priestly garment, cult object, # 680); → *ḥōšen* (breast-piece of highpriest, # 3136); → *khn* (perform the duties of a priest, # 3912); → *kōmer* (pagan priest, # 4024); → *lēwî* (levite, # 4290); → *migbāʿâ* (head-band, # 4457); → *miknāsayim* (trousers, # 4829); → *paʿᵃmôn* (bell [on priest's robe], # 7194); → *tašbēṣ* (checkered work, # 9587); → **Aaron: Theology**; → **Priests and Levites: Theology**

BIBLIOGRAPHY
ABD 2:232-38; *ANEP*, figs. 1-66; *ISBE* 2:401-7; A. F. L. Beeston, "Hebrew *šibbolet* and *šobel* (Isa 47:2)," *JSS* 24, 1979, 175-77; M. Dahood, "To Pawn One's Cloak," *Bib* 42, 1961, 359-66; G. Dalman, *Arbeit und Sitte in Palästina*, 1987 (repr. 1937), 5:199-356; E. Dhorme, *L'emploi métaphorique des noms de parties du corps en hébreu et en akkadien,* 1963; M. Görg, "Zum sogenannten priesterlichen Obergewand," *BZ* 20, 1976, 242-46; H. W. Hönig, "Die Bekleidung des Hebräers: Eine biblisch-archäologische Untersuchung," diss. Zürich, 1957; M. G. Houston, *Ancient Egyptian and Persian Costume and Decoration*, 1954[2]; A. Jirku, "Zur magischen Bedeutung der Kleidung in Israel," *ZAW* 37, 1917/18, 109-25; H. F. Lutz, *Textiles and Customs Among the People of the Ancient Near East*, 1923; J. W. McKay, "My Glory—A Mantle of Praise," *SJT* 31, 1978, 167-72; W. Magass, "Texte und Textilien," *LB* 34, 1975, 23-36; J. Ruppert, *Le costume juif depuis les temps patriarchaux jusqu'à la dispersion (Le costume historique des peuples de l'antiquité)*, 1938.

Robert L. Alden

7573 (*ṣinṣenet*, jar, jug, basket), → # 3998

7575	צעד

צעד (*ṣʿd*), q. step, march; hi. make s.o. march (# 7575); **אֶצְעָדָה** (*ʾeṣʿādâ*), band (→ # 731); **מִצְעָד** (*miṣʿād*), step, train (# 5202); **צַעַד** (*ṣaʿad*), marching, pace, steps (# 7576); **צְעָדָה** (*ṣᵉʿādâ*), marching, step-chains (on the ankles) (# 7577).

ANE The vb. is cognate with Arab. *ṣaʿida*, climb out. It might also be cognate with Ugar. *ṣġd*. Thus, Gibson (124) translates line 30 of "Shahar and Shalim and the Gracious Gods," *[il yṣ]i gp ym wyṣġd gp thm*, "[El wen]t out to the shore of the sea, and *advanced* to the shore of the ocean."

OT 1. All instances of the vb. are in the q. except for the hi. in Job 18:14 (but with pass. sense): "he [viz., the wicked] is ... marched off to the king of terrors." Related to the vb. is the nom. "marching," found only in 2 Sam 5:24 (= 1 Chron 14:15), "As soon as you hear the sound of marching [of the Philistines]...."

2. A similarly written nom., *ṣ^{e}'ādâ*, ankle chain(s), anklets, appears in Isa 3:20 in a list of apparently expensive and ostentatious adornments that God is about to strip off the daughters of Jerusalem (→).

3. The nom. *miṣ'ād*, step, occurs in Ps 37:23 (God makes one's steps firm); Prov 20:24 (God directs a man's steps); and Dan 11:43 (NIV's "in submission" is strange; read something like "in his train").

4. The most frequent nom. built off the vb. is *ṣa'ad*, step, pace, stride. It may be used literally: 2 Sam 6:13 ("six steps"); 22:37 ("you broaden the path beneath me," ∥ Ps 18:36[37]); Prov 30:29 ("there are three things that are stately in their stride").

More frequent is the figurative use of *ṣa'ad*. The wise father says to his child about the way of wisdom, "when you walk, your steps will not be hampered" (Prov 4:12). Both in 16:9 and Jer 10:23 *ṣa'ad* is used with *derek*. Twice the same point is made, i.e., humankind is functioning at its best when we recognize that we are not in control of our own destiny, that we are not self-guides, and that such matters are best left to an infinitely wise God. See also Job, who believes that God both "counts" (14:16) and "sees" (31:4) his steps/ways. Elihu agrees (Job 34:21).

5. The vb. *ṣ'd* may have as its subject: Yahweh (Judg 5:4; Ps 68:7[8]; Isa 63:1; Hab 3:12); persons (2 Sam 6:13; Prov 7:8); a variety of animals (Prov 30:29-31); idols (Jer 10:5); branches/tendrils [?] (Gen 49:22, and see below).

(a) When Yahweh marches, he marches in indignation (Hab 3:12), to save his people (Isa 63:1) and to lead them through enemy territory toward the Land of Promise (Judg 5:4; Ps 68:7[8]). In the latter two references the language of one is similar to the other ("earth shook, the heavens poured, before God/Yahweh, the One of Sinai"), suggesting literary dependence of some kind. Furthermore, both Judg 5 and Ps 68 are identified as *šîr*, a song. God's marching is to be celebrated.

(b) While the warlike marching of deities is a common enough theme in ANE literature as in the OT, one must remember that "the enemies of the former are the mythological monsters of the private ocean, those of the latter are players on the stage of real history. Here [viz., Judg 5] and in Ps 68 the theophany is a triumphant procession to a real destination marked by triumphs which history records" (Blenkinsopp, 65).

(c) Prov 30:29-31 reminds that "there are three things that are stately in their stride, four that move with stately bearing: a lion ... a strutting rooster, a he-goat, and a king with his army around him." Here is a reflection on kingship rooted in the world of nature. In the human realm the king is supreme, and in public his stately stride at the head of his army befits his royalty. One can see how easy it was to transfer this idea from the regal marching of the head-of-state to the marching of the King of creation.

(d) Jacob's blessing over Joseph (Gen 49:22) begins: "Joseph is a fruitful vine, a fruitful vine near a spring, whose branches [*bānôt*, lit., "daughters"] climb (*ṣā'^{a}dâ*) over a wall" (NIV). Apart from the problems in the first two lines, one encounters no fewer than three problems in the third line: (1) How does one obtain "branches" from "daughters"? (2) how does one expand the meaning of *ṣā'ad* from "walk, step, march" to "climb over"? (for which see Zobel, 21 and 21 n.110, who connects the root with Ugar. *ṣġd* [IV AB III, 8] "climb, allow to climb"), and (3) why is a 3d fem. sing. vb. (*ṣā*[a]*dâ*) used with a fem. pl. subj. (*bānôt*), unless the vb. represents an old 3d pl. fem. ending? This also is the one place in Gen 49 where Jacob uses a plant metaphor rather than an animal metaphor when addressing his sons. In any case, Jacob's words to Joseph form a prayer and a blessing. Joseph and his own descendants have and are experiencing growth, so much so that his descendants are growing and climbing over walls that cannot contain the vines.

Marching, stepping: → *ḥšl* (unfit to march, straggle, shatter, # 3129); → *nḥt* (march down, descend, penetrate, settle, # 5737); → *s'n* (tramp along, tread, # 6008); → *pś'* I (step forth, march, # 7314); → *ṣ'd* (step, march, # 7575)

BIBLIOGRAPHY

J. Blenkinsopp, "Ballad Style and Psalm Style in the Song of Deborah: A Discussion," *Bib* 42, 1961, 61-76; S. Gevirtz, "Of Patriarchs and Puns: Joseph at the Fountain, Jacob at the Ford," *HUCA* 46, 1975, 35-49; L. Kopf, "Arabische Etymologien und Parallelen Zum Bibelworterbuch," *VT* 8, 1958, 161-215 (esp. 198); H.-J. Zobel, "Stammesspruch und Geschichte," *BZAW* 95, 1965.

Victor P. Hamilton

7576 (*ṣa'ad*, marching, pace, steps), → # 7575

7577	צְעָדָה

צְעָדָה (*ṣ*[e]*'ādâ*), nom. pl. anklets (# 7577); **אֶצְעָדָה** (*'eṣ'ādâ*), pace-chain, armlet (→ # 731); < **צעד** (*ṣ'd*), q. walk, step; hi. make s.o. walk (→ # 7575).

ANE Akk. *ṣâdu*, prowl, turn/roam about (*CAD* 16, 57).

OT For a representative use of the word group, see Isa 3:20; Num 31:50; and 2 Sam 1:10.

For a discussion on jewelry, see *'dh* (put on ornaments, # 6335).

Malcolm J. A. Horsnell

7579	צעה

צעה (*ṣ'h*), q. cower, rawl; tip (# 7579).

OT This vb. primarily represents a sprawling or stooped over position. It describes the knocking over of vessels (Jer 2:20) and the stooped or sprawling position of the subjugated (51:14), who hope for deliverance.

With its unique reference to the divine Warrior (→ Theology) in Isa 63:1, the vb. is usually emended to *ṣ'd*, walk (cf. NIV striding forward), but, according to J. D. W. Watts, this is unnecessary: "stooping under the weight of his armor" (*Isaiah 34-66*, WBC 25, 315-16).

Low, humble, flat, level: → *kr'* (crouch, squat, # 4156); → *'nh* II (humble, oppress, overpower, # 6700); → *šḥḥ* (stoop, crouch, humble, # 8820); → *špl* (be low, be levelled, humiliate, bring low, # 9164)

T. Desmond Alexander

7581	צָעִיף

צָעִיף (*ṣā'îp*), nom. veil (# 7581).

ANE Perhaps the term is related to an Arab. and Eth. root meaning, make double.

OT All three occurrences of *ṣā'îp* are in Genesis. Rebekah covered herself with a veil just before she met Isaac for the first time (Gen 24:65). Tamar, Judah's seductive daughter-in-law, posed as a prostitute, disguising herself with a veil (Gen 38:14, 19). Two things can be deduced about this veil. It sufficiently covered the wearer so that her identity was not obvious. It apparently was a symbol of an unmarried woman.

Veil: → *dōq* (veil, gauze, # 1988); → *ḥebyôn* (covering, # 2470); → *miṭpaḥat* (veil, cloak, # 4762); → *masweh* (veil, # 5003); → *massēkâ* II (veil, sheet, blanket, # 5012); → *mispāḥâ* (veil, # 5029); → *ṣammâ* (veil, # 7539); → *ṣā'îp* (veil, # 7581); → *r^edîd* (veil, # 8100); → *r^e'ālâ* (veil, # 8304)

Robert L. Alden

7582 (*ṣā'îr* I, little, small, young, trifling), → # 7592

7584 (*ṣ^e'îrâ*, youth), → # 7592

7585	צען

צען (*ṣ'n*), q. (have to) pack up; break down (hapleg.; # 7585).

ANE This root is a variant of *ṭ'n* II, which has cognates in Akk., Arab., OSA, Syr., and Eth. (*HALAT* 361, 975; cf. Delcor, 310-11; Greenspan, 154).

OT The term occurs in Isa 33:20 (in conjunction with *ns'* and *ntq*) to describe a tent that will not be moved or broken down. (See under *ns'* [→ # 5825]; for arguments not to emend *yiṣ'ān* in Isa 33:20, see H. Wildberger, *Jesaja*, BKAT X/3, 1310.)

Separation, breaking down, removal: → *'ṣl* (set apart, withdraw, shorten, # 724); → *bdl* (separate o.s., # 976); → *br'* I (create, separate, # 1343); → *hgh* II (separate, remove, # 2048); → *mwš* II (depart, remove, take away, # 4631); → *ns'* (tear out, march out, # 5825); → *ntq* (tear away, # 5998); → *prq* (pull away, # 7293); → *ṣ'n* (pack up, # 7585); → *rḥq* (be far away, remove, # 8178)

BIBLIOGRAPHY
M. Delcor, "Quelques cas de survivances du vocabulaire nomade en hébreu biblique," *VT* 25, 1975, 307-22, esp. 310-12; F. E. Greenspan, *Hapax Legomena in Biblical Hebrew*, SBLDS 74, 1984, passim, see index on 206.

Cornelis Van Dam

7589	צַעֲצֻעִים

צַעֲצֻעִים (*ṣa^aṣū'îm*), nom. things formed by metal coating (# 7589).

ANE The Arab. vb. *ṣāġa* (*ṣwġ*) has the meaning of form or shape.

OT The nom. is an hapleg. at 2 Chron 3:10, where the Chronicler substitutes this word for the wood of 1 Kgs 6:23 in the description of the cherubim. The G has retained the word "wood," but this is not indicative of a different text since the Vrs. are coping with a difficult word. The cherubim were carved from wood and overlaid with gold (1 Kgs 6:23, 28); the sense in 2 Chron 3:10 is that they were sculpted and fashioned with the overlay of gold.

P-B The Talm. appears to connect this to *ṣ'yr* or *z'yr,* meaning small, and describes the cherubs in the temple as having the form of babes (Jastrow, 2:1294).

Metals: → *'ᵃnāk* (lead, # 643); → *bᵉdîl* (dross, # 974); → *barzel* (iron, # 1366); → *zāhāb* (gold, # 2298); → *ḥel'â* I (rust, # 2689); → *ḥašmal* (glow?, electrum, glowing metal, # 3133); → *kesep* (silver, money, # 4084); → *masgēr* II (metal worker, # 4994); → *ma'ᵃbeh* (foundry, # 5043); → *nᵉḥōšet* I (copper, bronze, # 5733); → *sîg* (lead oxide, # 6092); → *sēper* II (bronze, plate, # 6220); → *'ōperet* (lead, # 6769); → *paḥ* II (thin sheet, # 7063); → *pᵉlādōt* (steel?, # 7110); → *ṣwr* III (cast [metal], # 7445); → *ṣa'ᵃṣu'îm* (things formed by metal coating, # 7589); → *ṣph* II (arrange, overlay, plate, glaze, # 7596); → *ṣrp* (melt, smelt, refine, # 7671); → *qālāl* (polished metal, # 7838); → *šḥṭ* II (alloyed, # 8822)

BIBLIOGRAPHY

R. B. Dillard, *2 Chronicles*, WBC, 1987; H. G. M. Williamson, *1 and 2 Chronicles*, NCBC, 1982.

A. H. Konkel

7590	צעק

צעק (*ṣ'q*), q. cry out, raise a cry of wailing, summon, call together; ni. be summoned, be called together; pi. to cry repeatedly; hi. summon, call together (# 7590); צְעָקָה (*ṣᵉ'āqâ*), nom. wailing, call for help (# 7591).

ANE The vb. *ṣ'q* is found in the Egyptian papyrus *APFC* 52, 6, which is a fragmented text consisting mostly of names and a few isolated vbs. (*DISO*, 246). It is also found in OSA meaning cry out, proclaim, or entreat; the Arab. *ṣa'aqa* means to strike with lightning, strike down, or daze. The Arab. *ṣa'iqa* can mean the loss of consciousness, and *ṣa'iq*, an outcry. The nom. *ṣᵉ'āqâ* may be restored in an eighth-century Sefire inscription (*KAI* 223 A 8), based on possible parallels to a related account (*KAI* 222 A 29), but the text is too broken to provide a secure context (cf. *DISO*, 246). It is likely that *ṣ'q* is a dialectical variation of *z'q* (*THAT* 2:568).

OT 1. The vb. *ṣ'q* is found 47x in the q. with the general sense of a cry for help or relief from injustice and suffering. It is used frequently for the call of Israel to be delivered from the Egyptians (Num 20:16; Deut 26:7; Neh 9:27; Isa 19:20) or other oppressors (Judg 10:12). It is also used frequently for a prayer of distress (Ps 34:17[18]; 77:1[2]; 88:1[2]) or a cry to God in a specific crisis (Exod 8:8; 14:15; 15:25; 17:4; Num 12:13; Josh 24:6; 2 Chron 13:14); such a cry is also made to idols (Isa 46:7). It can also be a cry for help (Gen 41:55; Num 11:2; Deut 22:27; 2 Kgs 4:1; 6:26), and even if it is a call for attention, it is because of apparent need (1 Kgs 20:39). The cry for help is often for justice (2 Kgs 8:3, 5); an incentive for such a cry is that God will hear the call of the oppressed (Exod 22:22, 26). God hears the blood of Abel, which cries out from the ground (Gen 4:10). Job finds no justice for his cry (Job 19:7), which Elihu explains is because of pride (35:12). The servant of God does not so cry, but rather brings justice to the earth (Isa 42:2).

2. The vb. is hardly a technical term for a cry for what is just and right (*THAT* 2:571-72). The cry of injustice is also one of lament (→) when the situation cannot be reversed, such as the cry of Esau when he realized he had lost his birthright (Gen 27:34). A cry of fear when a borrowed axhead is lost is also one of lament (2 Kgs 6:5); a similar cry is that of the prophets when they discover their food is poisonous (4:40). The outcry because judgment has come is at the same time a lament for the desolation of the land (Isa 33:7). Jeremiah describes the lament for the king buried like an animal (Jer 22:18-19) and the outcry for the destruction of the lands around (22:20). Rivers of tears flow day and night because of the destruction of Jerusalem (Lam 2:18). The unrighteous servants judged by the Lord will cry out in pain, especially as they see the blessings of the righteous (Isa 65:14). The vb. occurs once in the pi. to describe the repeated cries of Elisha at the translation of Elijah (2 Kgs 2:12). In the ni. the vb. is used to describe the gathering of an army for war (Judg 7:23, 24; 12:1; 1 Sam 13:4), and in the hi. for the gathering of an assembly (1 Sam 10:16).

3. The nom. occurs 21x, often as a description of the cry. In Gen 27:34 the lament of Esau is described as loud and bitter; in a similar manner the lament of the Egyptians for the loss of the firstborn is loud and widespread (Exod 11:6; 12:30). The laments of the nations because of their destruction is a loud cry; that of Moab reaches to Zoar (Jer 48:3-4; cf. LXX); the cry of the fall of Edom makes the earth shake and is heard to the Sea of Reeds (Jer 49:21). The cry of fallen Jerusalem will be heard throughout the doomed city (Zeph 1:10). The sound of the cry of the judged nations is that of wailing because their territory has been laid waste (Jer 25:36); the cry of Moab is also a weeping (48:5). The cry may be that of confusion and consternation, as heard by Eli when the ark was captured by the Philistines (1 Sam 4:14). The wickedness of Sodom is an outcry that God hears (Gen 18:21; 19:13), as is the injustice in the city of Jerusalem (Isa 5:7). The cry, of course, may be that of the oppressed, who expect help from God (Job 34:28; Ps 9:12[13]), though the wicked will not find it (Job 27:9). The cry of the Israelites in Egypt (Exod 3:7, 9) is one of pain and oppression, which incites the judgment of God against the Egyptians.

4. The lament cry is always loud and emotionally charged, a sound that may be compared to the shouting of a despot in contrast to the quiet cerebral words of wisdom (Eccl 9:17). The expression of anguish or alarm is characterized as being loud and bitter (Gen 27:34; Exod 11:6; 12:30; cf. *z'q* in 1 Sam 28:12; 2 Sam 19:4[5]; Neh 9:4; Ezek 11:13). Its force does not consist of needing to be heard at a distance, but is uttered in the extreme circumstance of need or trouble (*THAT* 2:569). It is, however, not simply the emotional cry of pain or grief, such as sigh (*'nh*), weep (*bkh*), or wail (*yll*), but is an appeal that has the potential to provide a change in the circumstance of distress. The appeal is directed either explicitly or implicitly to someone who can help (in two-thirds of the instances the object is indicated, usually by the preposition *'el*, but sometimes with l^e or the accusative). The root *ṣ'q* is both a cry of pain and a cry for assistance; *ṣ'q* is parallel with *šw'* pi. (to call for help) in Job 19:7; Lam 3:8; and Hab 1:2. Either aspect of a cry of pain or a cry for assistance may have predominance. The impetus of the lament cry is generated by the consciousness of a common human dependency, through which the cry of someone in need brings a sense of urgency to provide help.

The lament cry is directed to human intervention in a variety of circumstances. In time of famine the Egyptians cried out to Pharaoh for bread (Gen 41:55), and in the wilderness the people complained to Moses (Num 11:1-2). The woman who lost her husband cried out to Elisha when the creditors came to take her children (2 Kgs 4:1), and the prophets cried out to him when they discovered poisonous food (4:40) and when the borrowed axhead was lost (6:5). The cry of a woman sexually assaulted by a man serves as evidence that this was not a case of complicity (Deut 22:24, 27).

In almost half of the occurrences of *ṣ'q/z'q* the cry is explicitly or implicitly made to God. This is significant to the OT concept of prayer. The vb. is used in conjuction with various words for prayer to express deep emotions (*pll* hitp. in 2 Chron 32:20; *ḥnn* hitp. in Ps 142:1[2]; *šw'* pi. in Hab 1:2 and Lam 3:8; and *'tr* in Exod 8:8[4], 9[5], 12[8]). Its broad usage indicates that in prayer no essential difference was perceived between daily needs and the cry for justice or relief from oppression. This outcry in the OT was not primarily in the realm of liturgical laments, but was an expression of urgency in acute situations, such as that of the Israelites under Egyptian affliction (Exod 2:23; 3:7, 9). This sense of crying out was not lost even though the word did come to be used to express urgency in situations of liturgical communal lament (Joel 1:14) or penitence (Neh 9:4).

The cry to God in the OT is heard by God (Exod 3:7; Num 20:16; Ps 34:17[18]); God answers (1 Sam 7:9; Ps 77:1[2]; Isa 30:19), and God intervenes (Judg 10:12, 14; 1 Sam 7:8; 2 Chron 18:31; 20:9; Ps 22:5[6]; 34:17[18], 18[19]). The response of God was not in any sense capricious or simply obligation, but one of feeling for the distress of his people (*THAT* 2:574). The cry of lament in Egypt activated God as he saw their oppression (Num 20:16; Deut 26:7). This knowledge was the basis for the plea of the individual (Ps 9:12[13]; 22:5[6]; 34:17[18]) and the community (107:6, 13, 19, 28); it served as the foundation for the confession of trust and praise in psalms of lament. Obedience, of course, is a fundamental requisite for the response of God. God's failure to respond to the cry of the Israelites was the basis of the prophetic declaration of the disobedience of the people (1 Sam 8:18; Jer 11:11; Mic 3:4), who no longer cried to God from their heart (Hos 7:14; 8:2-3). The response of God was by no means limited to the Israelites; he would also hear the Egyptians when they cried (Isa 19:20). The story of the people of God is permeated with God's providing deliverance when they cry to him in their time of distress. (→ Lament: Theology)

P-B The vb. is found in the Tgs., and the nom. in the Talm. (Jastrow, 1294). The nom. is also found in a Qumran fragment (1Q Noah 1 1.4), which may be a copy of the lost Book of Noah related to the Book of Enoch. In all these instances it is a cry of complaint.

NT The LXX uses *boaō* and *krazō* to translate the root *ṣ'q*, in all the various forms of each. The nom. *boē* corresponds to the various nuances of *ṣ^{e}'āqâ*, such as alarm, complaint, and call for help. The cries (*boai*) of the oppressed laborers (James 5:4) express a call for justice, which the Lord of hosts will hear. Just as the complaint of the widow in the story of the unjust judge is heard (Luke 18:1-8), so God will hear the cries (*boōntōn*) of his elect. Jesus quotes Ps 22:1[2] when he cried out (*eboēsen*) from the cross, the supreme demonstration of God identifying fully with human suffering in order to provide ultimate deliverance from it. These NT examples show the same spontaneity and immediacy as the OT lament, with the same expectation of divine intervention and deliverance.

Calling, proclamation, summons: → *z'q* (call for help, call to arms, assemble, utter a plaintive cry, # 2410); → *ṣrḥ* (yell, call shrilly, raise the war-cry, # 7658); → *qr'* I (call, invoke, summon, proclaim, # 7924)
Cry: → *g'r* (roar, shout, bellow, cry out, rebuke, reprimand, # 1721); → *ṣrḥ* (yell, call shrilly, raise the war-cry, # 7658); → *qôl* (voice, sound, thunder, cry, # 7754); → *rw'* (shout, give war-cry, # 8131)
Lament, mourning: → *'bl* I (mourn, observe mourning rites, # 61); → *'nh* I (lament, # 627); → *bkh* (weep, bewail, # 1134); → *dm'* (shed tears, # 1963); → *z'q* (call for help, call to arms, assemble, utter a plaintive cry, # 2410); → *nhh* I (lament, # 5629); → *spd* (sound of lament, mourn, # 6199); → *qdr* (be dark, mourn, # 7722); → *qînâ* I (dirge, # 7806); → **Lament: Theology**

BIBLIOGRAPHY

THAT 2:568-75; H. Irsigler, "Äquivalenz in Poesie. Die kontextuellen Synonyme *ṣå'aqā-yålalā-šibr-gadu(w)l* in Zef. 1:10c,d,e," *BZ* 22, 1978, 221-35.

A. H. Konkel

7591 (*ṣ^{e}'āqâ*, wailing, call for help), → # 7590

7592	צער

צער (*ṣ'r*), q. be trifling, insignificant, become trifling (# 7592); מִצְעָר (*miṣ'ār* I), nom. small quantity, modest (# 5203); צָעִיר (*ṣā'îr* I), nom./adj. little, small, young, trifling (# 7582); צְעִירָה (*ṣ^{e}'îrâ*), nom. youth (# 7584).

ANE The root is common among Sem. languages. Akk. *ṣeḫēru/ṣaḫāru* means "to be, become small, young" (*AHw*, 1087-89). Ugar. *ṣġr* denotes "small, young." An interesting parallel to the biblical model of the younger supplanting the elder appears in the Epic of Krt, where the future youngest daughter of the hero is promised the blessing of the firstborn by the god Ilu (*KTU* 1.15, III, 16). Lowenstamm proposes, based on Ugar. evidence, that the two roots *sġr* (Ugar. shepherd) and *ṣġr* (the Proto-Sem. root of *ṣā'îr*) were later conflated in Heb. His suggestion to translate certain passages with "shepherd" has implications esp. for Zech 13:7 (see NEB; *BHS* note, NIV the little ones); Jer 14:3; 48:4 (for both, note K/Q, NIV).

OT 1. The vb. is found clearly only in Job 14:21 and Jer 30:19 and signifies "be, become insignificant." In the latter text the vb. is in parallel with *m'ṭ* (→ # 5070). Zech 13:7 is disputed (see Loewenstamm).

2. The notion of being small, which is expressed by the nom./adj. *ṣā'îr* (23x), often includes the sense of a lack of importance or prestige. This connotation is evident, e.g., in references to the least significant of the clans (1 Sam 9:21), tribes (Ps 68:27[28]), towns (Mic 5:2[1]), and horns (Dan 8:9). This reality is particularly emphasized where the term is paired with similar words, such as *dal* (→ # 1924; Judg 6:15), *qāṭān* (→ # 7783; 1 Sam 9:21), and *qāṭōn* (→ # 7785; Isa 60:22).

The young (-er, -est) are many times contrasted with older siblings (*b^{e}kōr, b^{e}kîrâ* [→ # 1142, # 1147]), where the import of order or social standing can come into play. Lot's younger daughter lies with him only after the elder daughter has

(Gen 19:31, 34-35); the morning after the ruse of the wedding night Laban reveals to Jacob the custom of marrying off the elder daughter before the younger (29:26); the brothers are seated according to age (much to their amazement!) at Joseph's table (43:33). The focus on the younger can also carry theological significance. The divine purpose can involve selecting the younger over the elder brother (Jacob/Esau, 25:23; Ephraim/Manasseh, 48:14), or those of obscure origin and background in place of the prominent (Gideon, Judg 6:15; Saul, 1 Sam 9:21; the tribe of Benjamin, Ps 68:27[28]; Bethlehem, Mic 5:2[1]) for a singular task or role within sacred history. This model of Yahweh's working is also reflected by the terms *qāṭān, qāṭōn* (→ # 7781).

3. The nom. *ṣᵉʿîrâ* is attested only in Gen 43:33 and appears with *ṣāʿîr*.

4. The nom. *miṣʾār* is found in four passages (*miṣʿār* in Ps 42:6[7] is probably a proper name). In keeping with the connotation of the other terms, the sense of inconsequence is understood as concomitant with the lack of size (Gen 19:20 [2x]; 2 Chron 24:24), a short time span (Isa 63:18), and a low social position (Job 8:7, NIV humble).

P-B A variety of words translate this word group in the LXX, the most important of which are *neōteros* (12x) and *mikros* (6x). For a discussion of these terms in the NT → *qṭn* (# 7781).

Little, trifle, insignificant: → *ʾēš* II (little, trifle, # 837); → *dll* I (be small, unimportant, # 1937); → *zᵉʿêr* (little, # 2402); → *ḥwr* II (become less, # 2579); → *ḥsr* (diminish, decrease, deprive, # 2893); → *ḥrh* II (disappear, be few in number, # 3014); → *mʿṭ* (be few, diminish, become small, few, # 5070); → *ṣʿr* (be trifling, insignificant, become trifling, # 7592); → *qṭn* (be small, trifling, make small, # 7781); → *škk* (go down, abate, allay from upon, # 8896); → *šēmeṣ* (little, # 9066)

BIBLIOGRAPHY

ISBE 3:97; *NIDNTT* 2:674-76; *TWAT* 6:1083-87; *TWOT* 2:773; S. E. Loewenstamm, "The Noun sᶜr (Kᵉtib) saᶜir (Qᵉre)," *Comparative Studies in Biblical and Ancient Oriental Literatures, AOAT* 204, 1980, 249-55.

M. Daniel Carroll R.

7595	צפה

צפה (*ṣph* I), q. keep guard, watch attentively; pi. watch, wait expectantly (# 7595); ; מִצְפֶּה (*miṣpeh* I), nom. watchtower, lookout point (# 5205); צְפִיָּה (*ṣippiyyâ*), nom. lookout post (# 7610).

ANE Akk. *ṣubbu*, look at; Pun. *ṣpʾ*, seer; Ugar. *ṣpy*, view.

OT Most of the 36x *ṣph* occurs are part. functioning nominally, signifying watchmen. Watchmen carried grave responsibilities. The root carries the implicit meaning of alert and active watching rather than simply gazing, for the safety of others depended on diligence, and the lackadaisical watchman would suffer the consequences (Ezek 33:2-6). The weight of Ezekiel's prophetic call was to be a watchman for his people (33:7). It is with this same intent gaze that the Lord watches the nations (Ps 66:7) and individuals, both good and evil (Prov 15:3).

The intensity implicit in *ṣph* is exhibited with the anxious Eli, who was looking intently down the road for the return of the ark (1 Sam 4:13). The empowered woman in Prov 31:27 intently and efficiently saw to the affairs of her household. This was also the appropriate word chosen by Laban when he departed from Jacob (Gen 31:49). Intense expectation is reflected by the psalmist as he daily ordered his prayers and watched for the Lord's response (Ps 5:3[4]). The same dependence on the Lord in the face of social corruption imbues the prophet's words (Mic 7:7).

P-B *ṣph* appears in DSS sectarian documents, 1QS 9,25; 1QH 12,21; as well as CD 1,18. In 1QS the Master must always be on watch for the judgment of God. The Cairo Damascus Rule notes that those who sought smooth things watched (*ṣph*) for breaks, alluding to Isa 30:13. The writer of the Thanksgiving Hymns notes that the children of God's grace "watch for thy goodness." The element of intensity permeates these pious expressions.

By Mishnaic times, *ṣph* is used increasingly for to foresee, have a vision; a related form, *ṣpy*, however, continued to connote look out, wait.

Guarding, watching: → *nṭr* (keep, # 5757); → *nṣr* I (watch, guard, keep, # 5915); → *ṣph* I (keep guard, watch attentively, post, # 7595); → *šmr* I (watch, guard, revere, # 9068); → *šqd* (watch, wake, # 9193)

BIBLIOGRAPHY

TWOT 2:773; A. E. Rüthy, "Wächter und Späher im AT: מְצַפֶּהצוֹפֶהשׁעֵרשׁוֹמֵר" *TZ* 21, 1965, 300-309.

Keith N. Schoville

7596	צפה

צפה (*ṣph* II), q. arrange, order; overlay, plate; glaze (# 7596); צִפּוּי (*ṣippûy*), nom. plating (# 7599); צֶפֶת (*ṣepet*), nom. capital (# 7633).

ANE The vb. *ṣph* occurs in a Ugar. text describing royal war chariots, some of which were gilded (*UT*, 475). In a late Punic inscription the fem. pl. nom. *ṣp't* is found with reference to a purple striped toga (*KAI*, 126.6). In OSA *ṣwf* describes fitted stones; in Eth. the vb. *ṣafṣafa* means plaster; the Arab. *ṣaffa* means to set up in a row or line.

OT The vb. is found 47x in the OT; it always has the meaning of overlaying or adorning, depending on the substances involved. It occurs most commonly in articles of the tabernacle or temple (e.g., gold, Exod 25:11, 24; 1 Kgs 6:22; precious stones, 2 Chron 3:6; wood, 1 Kgs 6:15). The text in 1 Kgs 6:20 is in question; it is possible that with the G the last phrase should say, "he also made an altar of cedar" (*BHS*). The vb. occurs in Prov 26:23, where the hot (fervent, or more likely smooth) lips of an evil heart are like a white glazed (cf. Ugar. *spsg*) clay pot. The meaning of Isa 21:5 is completely uncertain; it seems to indicate the spreading of a covering on a banquet table or perhaps arranging the cushions of the seating (Wildberger 2:765); the Vrs. are equally uncertain, but it is probably not to be related to *ṣph* I with the sense of setting a watch (contra Gesenius).

The nom. *ṣippûy* is found 5x in the OT; in Isa 30:22 it refers to silver-covered images, in Exod 38:17, 19 the tops of the pillars are covered with silver. The significance of Num 16:38-39[17:3-4] is unclear; the fire pans of the Korahites who sinned are hammered into bronze plates for the altar to serve as a warning. Since the altar was already plated (Exod 27:2; 38:2), this appears to be a contradiction, as indicated by the G, which provides a gloss of this verse in the Exodus account; however, the text may simply indicate that the altar was plated a second time to serve as a warning (Milgrom, 140).

The nom. *ṣepet* is found at 2 Chron 3:15 as metonymy for the capitals on the two great pillars at the entrance to the temple, which were ornately plated and decorated. The metal overlays associated with the temple were theologically significant. The temple as a whole represented the presence of God as experienced at the mountain. Majesty and holiness were central to the concept of the presence of God. In the temple this was signified by a gradation of precious metals; everything associated with the throne room itself was gold plated, while the surrounding court contained platings of silver and bronze on the various furnishings. This, accompanied by the sacrifices and the whole purification system, served as a theological statement expressing the incomparable holiness and power of the One who occupied the throne room and who could never be approached without mediation of priests and sacrifices.

P-B In the Talm. the nom. *ṣîpā'* is found for the fleshy covering of the date stones or for a reed mat used for sleeping or sitting. The nom. *ṣîppûy* is found for the covering of the mouth piece of a musical instrument or for the overlay of an altar. The vb. *ṣph* is found in the Temple Scroll at Qumran (e.g., 11QT 31.6 speaks of gold overlays to the upper chamber).

Metals: → *'ᵃnāk* (lead, # 643); → *bᵉdîl* (dross, # 974); → *barzel* (iron, # 1366); → *zāhāb* (gold, # 2298); → *ḥel'â* I (rust, # 2689); → *ḥašmal* (glow?, electrum, glowing metal, # 3133); → *kesep* (silver, money, # 4084); → *masgēr* II (metal worker, # 4994); → *ma'ᵃbeh* (foundry, # 5043); → *nᵉḥōšet* I (copper, bronze, # 5733); → *sîg* (lead oxide, # 6092); → *sēper* II (bronze, plate, # 6220); → *'ōperet* (lead, # 6769); → *paḥ* II (thin sheet, # 7063); → *pᵉlādōt* (steel?, # 7110); → *ṣwr* III (cast [metal], # 7445); → *ṣa'ᵃṣu'îm* (things formed by metal coating, # 7589); → *ṣph* II (arrange, overlay, plate, glaze, # 7596); → *ṣrp* (melt, smelt, refine, # 7671); → *qālāl* (polished metal, # 7838); → *šḥṭ* II (alloyed, # 8822)

BIBLIOGRAPHY
M. Haran, "The Priestly Image of the Tabernacle," *HUCA* 36, 1965, 191-226; J. Milgrom, *Numbers*, 1990, 140; J. N. Oswalt, *The Book of Isaiah: Chapters 1-34*, NICOT, 1986; H. Wildberger, *Jesaja*, BKAT X/2, 1978, 2:765.

A. H. Konkel

7597	צָפָה

צָפָה (*ṣāpâ*), discharge, pus (?) (# 7597).

OT A rare word occurring only in Ezek 32:6 and rendered "flowing blood" by NIV, NEB. The sense appears to point to some sort of discharge, but probably of a more purulent form than blood, as for example, ichorous pus, which contains fragments of sloughing tissue and often has a fetid odor.

Disease—blister, boil, skin disease, scar, wound: → *'ᵃba'bu'ōt* (blisters, # 81); → *bōhaq* (skin condition, # 993); → *baheret* (white patch on skin, # 994); → *gārāb* (festering eruption, # 1734); → *zrr* I (press out [wounds], # 2452); → *ḥeres* I (itch, # 3063); → *yabbelet* (wart?, # 3301); → *yallepet* (skin disease, # 3539); → *yᵉraqraq* (discoloration, # 3768); → *kᵉwiyya* (scar, # 3918); → *m'r* (be sore, # 4421); → *māzôr* I (boil, # 4649); → *makkâ* (blow, # 4804);

→ *mispaḥat* (skin eruption, # 5030); → *mrḥ* (rub, polish, # 5302); → *neteq* (scalp infection, # 5999); → *sappaḥat* (hair disease, # 6204); → *ʿōpel* I (abscesses, # 6754); → *ʿāš* II (pus, # 6932); → *ṣāpâ* (pus?, # 7597); → *ṣarebet* (scar, # 7648); → *ṣrʿ* (suffer from skin disease, # 7665); → *śeʾēt* II (swelling, # 8421); → *śtr* (break out [tumor], # 8609); → *šeḥîn* (boil, # 8825). For related entries → *ḥlh* I (become weak, tired, ill, # 2703)

Bibliography

ISBE 1:532, 953-60; 3:103-6.

R. K. Harrison

7599 (*ṣippûy*, plating), → # 7596

7600	צָפוֹן

צָפוֹן (*ṣāpôn* I), north (# 7600); צְפוֹנִי (*ṣepônî* I), northerner (# 7603).

ANE Regardless of the "root meaning" (Grave, 227-28), it is felt that the basic reference of the word was to the mountain, "Mount Saphon"; i.e., Mount Casius of the Greek world, Hazzi in Akkadian and Hittite treaties (Clifford, 58), or Jebel el' Aqraʿ, as is called in modern times. This 1770 meter mountain is in Syria and formed the natural northern boarder of Syria-Palestine (*TWAT* 6:1095; *TWOT* 2:774).

The most frequent use of the word occurs in Ugar., where it generally refers to Mount Saphon as the dwelling place of Baal (see Clifford, 58-97; *TWAT* 6:1096-98; WUS, 269 for references). It was on this mountain that the gods were to have gathered and held their sessions (*TWAT* 6:1096).

OT 1. The basic meaning of the word in the OT is "north" in the geographical sense, but it also can be used of geographical places named "Saphon." The other word for "north" is *śemôʾl* (literally "left" or "on the left side") but it only occurs in a few passages (Gen 14:15; Josh 19:27; Job 23:9; Ezek 16:46) (*HAHAT*, 787).

2. The geographical meaning is used in various contexts.

(a) The word "north" occurs in connection with the land that God promised to Abraham and his seed. In Gen 13:14 Abraham was told to look "to the *north* and south, east and west," and the land that he saw would be given to him and his seed forever (see 1QapGen 21:8-19; Gen 28:14; Deut 3:27). Although Israel was driven out of the land because of disobedience to the covenant and the "covenant curses" took effect (Deut 28:15-68), the Lord will gather the redeemed "from east and west, from *north* and south" (Ps 107:3; see also Isa 43:6).

(b) The word is used in connection with the instructions concerning the tabernacle, indicating the northern side or direction (e.g., Exod 26:20, 35; 27:11; 36:25; 38:11; 40:22; Lev 1:11). For a discussion of the exact location of the "north side" and which offerings were to be sacrificed there, see esp. R. Rendtorff, *Leviticus*, BKAT, 1985, 71-72; Mish. Zebahim 5:1-4; b. Zebahim 48a.b.

(c) The word is used to describe an enemy, which comes from the north. It is not necessary to see any "mythological" connections in such a usage (see Childs, 187-98), for the normal geographical conditions of Palestine made it natural that the enemies would march into the land from the north (Assyrians, Babylonians), or from the south (Egyptians) (see *TWAT* 6:1100-11). For this reason there is not just one specific "enemy from the north" (see *THAT* 2:579 for common characteristics of the "enemy from the north"). In Isa 14:31 the Assyrian army is coming from the north to destroy the coastal region of Palestine, whereas in Jer 1:13-15 the threatening enemy from the north is certainly Babylon (see also Ezek 26:7), even though other suggestions have been made (see W. McKane, *Jeremiah*, ICC, 1986, 1:18-21; S. Herrmann, *Jeremia*, BKAT, 1986, 1:76; D. R. Jones, *Jeremiah*, NCB, 1992, 74-76). The identification of the "disaster from the north" in Jer 4:6; 6:1, 22; 10:22; 13:20; 15:12; 46:20, 24 has been the subject of much controversy (see W. L. Holladay, *Jeremiah*, Hermeneia, 1986, 1:42-43; Harrison, *IOT*, 803-4; W. Thiel, 1989, 231-45). B. Duhm popularized Hermann Venema's view that the enemy from the north was the Scythians, who, according to his understanding of Herodotus (*Hist.* 1:103-6), invaded Palestine around 625 BC. Even though this view is still accepted by some, many have rejected the theory, explaining that the evidence from Herodotus was not properly understood (see R. P. Vaggione, 1973, 523-30). In addition, it seems that the evidence fits the Babylonians better (see C. L. Feinberg, "Jeremiah," *EBC*, 1986, 6:361-62; *HAIJ*, 382-83; A. R. Millard, "Scythians," *ISBE* 4:364-66). In Ezek 32:30 the "princes of the north" may refer to the Syrians along the northern coast of Phoenicia (J. B. Taylor, *Ezekiel*, TOTC, 1969, 212) or to the Babylonian satellite kings (see S. Fisch, *Ezekiel*, Soncino Books of the Bible, 1972, 220).

In Ezek 38:6, 15 and 39:2 the prophecy concerns nations that will march against Israel. Gomer and Beth Togarmah are to come from the north along with Gog, Persia, Cush, and Put to attack Israel (for a discussion of this passage, see W. Zimmerli, *Ezechiel*, BKAT, 1969, 2:921-75; Fisch, *Ezekiel*, 1972, 253). The identification of this "foe" is difficult, because the context has eschatological overtones. Some hold that these people will occupy the geographical areas in the "last days" (see C. H. Dyer, *The Bible Knowledge Commentary*, 1985, 1299-1300). Others see in the structural development of Ezek 36-39 God's assurance that regardless of the opposition, represented by the enemies from the north, God will restore his people, console them, and establish his kingdom (W. A. VanGemeren, *Interpreting the Prophetic Word*, 1990, 334-35).

Another "enemy" that should be included here is the one described by the word *ṣ^{e}pônî*, northerner, in Joel 2:20 (*HALAT* 980; *BL*, 501; *THAT* 2:581; *TWAT* 6:1102; Waltke, *IBHS*, 92). The term has the "gentilic ending," indicating that the one in view "belongs" to the north; that is, "a northerner." The identification of this group is not certain. Many view the term as a reference to the "locust" as described in Joel 1 (see Rev 9:1-21); others see the reference as a description of an actual army, either an unnamed foe, or the same enemy from the north as described by Jeremiah and Ezekiel (see H. W. Wolff, *Joel Amos*, BKAT, 1969, 2:73-74; W. Rudolph, *Joel-Amos-Obadja-Jona*, KAT, 1971, 2:64-5). Still others view this as a "mythical enemy," relating it to the "mythical" religion of the Canaanites (A. S. Kapelrud, *Joel Studies*: UUÅ, 1948, 106-8).

In Dan 11:6, 7, 8, 11, 13, 15, 40 the words "king of the North" are used to describe the Seleucid kings and their struggles with the Ptolemaic rulers, "the king of the South" (11:1-35). Some project that it also refers to the "king of the North," along with "the king of the South," who opposes the "Antichrist" in the "end time" (Dan 11:40) (see G. L. Archer, "Daniel," *EBC*, 1985, 7:129-49; *TWAT* 6:1101-2; T. Fischer, *Seleukiden und Makkabäer*, 1980; E. R. Bevan, *The House of Seleucus*, 1985; Bevan, *The House of Ptolemy*, 1985; L. Wood, A *Commentary on Daniel*, 1978, 283-314).

Others understand these oracles to apply to the whole history of opposition to God's kingdom, including Greece, the Seleucids, the Romans, etc. (VanGemeren, *Interpreting the Prophetic Word*, 1990, 346-7; E. J. Young, *The Prophecy of Daniel*, 1957, 234-53; for the relation of the Seleucid kings to "the mountain of Saphon" and the god Baal, see *TWAT* 6:1101).

(d) The word is used to describe the "north wind" (e.g., Prov 25:23; S of Songs 4:16). According to Sir 43:20, "the icy blast of the north wind" is caused by the Lord. The "whirlwind" or "electrical storm" (R. H. Alexander, *EBC* 1986, 6:757) that Ezekiel saw coming from the north need not be considered to be "mythological" trappings influenced by Canaanite religion (see *TWAT* 6:1099), but is a part of the vision that the prophet saw. In the ancient world it was felt that the north wind cleared the sky and brought good visibility; therefore, it "must have been a constant subject for prayers offered up by merchants and sea-captains in Ugarit, while they were waiting to set out with heavily loaded ships for the main trade targets in the South and Egypt" (C. Grave, *UF* 12, 1980, 227-28).

3. The word is also used as the name of geographical places called "Zaphon."

(a) In Exod 14:2, 9 and Num 33:7, a place called "Baal Zephon" is mentioned. This was the area where Israel camped as the armies of Pharaoh were approaching. The exact location is not certain, but it seems that it could be one of two places: Tell Defneh (ancient "Tahpanhes"; see Jer 2:16; 43:7-9; 44:1; 46:14; Ezek 30:18; *ANET*, 249-50; *TWAT* 6:1097-98; J. P. Hyatt, *Exodus*, NCBC, 1980, 151, 156-61), or Ras Kasrun (see also *HALAT* 138; Ges[18], 163; Y. Aharoni, 1962, 179; "Baal-Zephon," *ISBE* 1:381; U. Cassuto, A *Commentary on the Book of Exodus*, 1967, 159-60). Regardless of the exact identification, it seems clear that the Canaanite Baal Zaphon was worshiped also in Egypt (*TWAT* 6:1097-98; *ANET* 249-50).

(b) In Josh 13:27 and Judg 12:1 the word refers to a place called "Zaphon" that was near Succoth in the territory of Gad (see Z. Kallai, 1986, 262-71).

(c) The word is used in Ps 48:2[3], where Mount Zion is compared to the "heights of Zaphon." Many take this to be a reference to the mythological mountain in Ugarit and feel that "the psalmist affirms, in effect, that the aspirations of all peoples for a place on earth where God's presence could be experienced were fulfilled in Mount Zion, the true Zaphon" (P. C. Craigie, *Psalms 1-50*, WBC, 1983, 353; see also *TWAT* 6:1099; Clifford, 1972, 141-49; J. J. M. Roberts, "The Davidic Origin of the Zion Tradition," *JBL* 92, 1973, 334). The occurrence in Isa 14:13 ("utmost heights of the sacred mountain [lit., north])" may also be a reference to the mythological Mount Zaphon (see *TWAT* 6:1099).

Directions: → *dārôm* (south, # 1999); → *yām* (west, sea, # 3542); → *yāmîn* I (right, south, # 3545); → *mizrāḥ* (sunrise, east, # 4667); → *ma'ᵃrāb* II (west, # 5115); → *negeb* (south, Negev, # 5582); → *ṣāpôn* I (north, # 7600); → *qādîm* (east side, east wind, # 7708); → *śᵉmō'l* (left side, left hand, unlucky, northwards, # 8520); → *têmān* I (south, # 9402)

BIBLIOGRAPHY

ISBE 3:550-51; *THAT* 2:575-82; *TWAT* 6:1094-1102; B. S. Childs, "The Enemy from the North and the Chaos Tradition," *JBL* 78, 1959, 187-98; R. J. Clifford, *The Cosmic Mountain in Canaan and the Old Testament*, 1972; M. Dietrich & O. Loretz, "Ugaritisch *srrt spn, srry* hebräisch *yrkty spwn*," *UF* 22, 1990; O. Eissfeldt, *Baal Zaphon, Zeus Kasios, und der Durchzug der Israeliten durchs Meer*, 1932; C. Grave, "The Etymolgy of Northwest Semitic *ṣapānu*," *UF* 12, 1980,

227-28; W. L. Holladay, *Jeremiah*, 1:42-43; D. R. Jones, *Jeremiah NCBC*, 1992, 74-76; A. S. Kapelrud, *Joel Studies:* UUÅ, 1948, 93-108; W. Thiel, "'Vom Norden her wird das Unheil eröffnet'. Zu Jeremia 1,11-16," *FS Kaiser*, 1989, 231-45; R. P. Vaggione, "Over All Asia? The Extent of the Scythian Domination in Herodotus," *JBL* 92, 1973, 523-30.

Cleon L. Rogers, Jr.

7603 (*ṣ^epônî* I, northerner), → # 7600

7606	צִפּוֹר

צִפּוֹר (*ṣippôr* I), birds (# 7606).

ANE Sem. cognates: Ugar. *'ṣr*, Akk. *iṣṣūru*, *ṣibāru*, Aram. *ṣippar*, Syr. *ṣepp^erā'*, Arab. *'uṣfūr*.

OT In the OT this word appears 40x. Conceptually, *ṣippôr* is included in *'ôp* (→ # 6416). The occurrences of *ṣippôr* in the OT can be divided largely into two categories: cultic spheres and poetical metaphors.

1. *Cultic spheres.* In the cultic sphere the birds first appear in the covenant God made with Abraham (Gen 15:10). Here the birds, referring to the turtledove and the pigeon (→ *gôzāl*) in v. 9, are generally taken as representing Israel, as opposed to the "birds of prey" in v. 11, representing foreign nations. The *ṣippôr* was not severed into two like the animals that were offered with them. Exegetes have generally referred to the rite in Lev 1:17 and adopted the view that this was because of their small size.

In sacrificial rites of the priestly literature the turtledove (*tôr* II, # 9367, NIV dove) and the pigeon (*yônâ* I, → # 3433) are ordinary sacrificial birds. Lev 1:16 prescribes that the priest is to remove the entrails (*mur'â*, # 5263, NIV the crop) by its feathers (*nôṣâ* I, # 5901 NIV contents; cf. Milgrom, *Leviticus*, 169-71). Birds (*ṣippôr*) occur extensively in Lev 14 (13x), which prescribes the purification of the so-called leper (vv. 1-32) and the infected house (vv. 48-53) and play a significant part in the rituals. As J. Milgrom has commented, the choice of the term *ṣippôr* (and not turtledove or pigeon explicitly) appears deliberate; the prescription would mean wild (v. 4, NIV live) birds that carry the impurity of the leper to a distant place away from the human community without returning. The ritual assumes that the uncleanness the first slain bird bears is devolved upon the second one, a relationship resembling that of the two goats on the Day of Atonement ritual (Lev 16).

2. *Poetic metaphors.* Three kinds of poetical metaphors merit special attention. Birds fluttering without direction is the metaphor for an undeserved curse (Prov 26:2) or a man who strays from his home (27:8). Frequent mention of snares is also found in the sense of a bird being caught in a snare (7:23; Eccl 9:12; Amos 3:5) and escaping from a snare (Ps 124:7; Prov 6:5), both of which signify a sudden and unexpected turn of fate for life or death. The psalmist heightens his yearning toward the house of the Lord by being reminded of the intimacy or homeyness that the bird (*d^erôr* I, # 2000; NIV swallow) presumed to have toward its nest (Ps 84:3).

At the downfall of Gog in the last day (Ezek 39), birds of prey are summoned, along with beasts, to eat the flesh and drink the blood at the great sacrificial feast that God will provide for them (vv. 4, 17). Here "sacrifice" (v. 18) is mentioned in an unusual or ironic way (if not, it may have a *ḥērem* character [Hengstenberg]), since the sacrifices are the dead mighty men and princes, while the Lord's guests are presumably unclean animals and birds.

3. *Cleanness/uncleanness.* Unlike the case of the animals, no explicit criterion is given for unclean birds (Lev 11:13-19; Deut 14:12-18). However, the rationale behind the cleanness/uncleanness law regarding birds appears much more evident. The majority of birds listed cannot be identified with certainty:

'ayyâ, black kite (# 370); *'ᵃnāpâ*, heron (# 649); *dā'â*, red kite (# 1798); *dûkîpāt*, hoopoe (# 1871); *dayyâ*, falcon (# 1901); *yanšûp*, great owl (# 3568); *kôs* II, little owl (# 3927); *'ozniyyâ*, black vulture (# 6465); *peres*, vulture (# 7272); *qā'at*, desert owl (# 7684); *rā'â*, red kite (# 8012); *rāḥām/rāḥāmâ*, osprey (# 8164/8168); *šālāk*, cormorant (# 8960); *šaḥap*, gull (# 8830); *taḥmās*, screech owl (# 9379); *tinšemet* II, white owl (# 9492);

The following birds are birds of prey or eaters of carrion: eagles (*nešer,* # 5979), ravens (*'ōrēb,* # 6854), ostriches (*ya'ᵃnâ,* # 3612 [in the form of *bat ya'ᵃnâ*]), and falcons (*nēṣ* II, # 5891). Solely from this standpoint, bats (*'ᵃṭāllēp*, # 6491) may present a problem in that they are insectivores.

However, sundry explanations emanate (see Wenham, *Leviticus*, 174), reflecting the general attitude toward the concept of uncleanness (→ *ḥayyâ* # 2651). Some take birds of prey or eaters of carrion as meaning dangerous disease carriers, while others take the image of preying on other animals as polluting. From the structuralist's point of view, M. Douglas points out that in Israel animals are required to keep the covenant just as humankind in the Sabbath (Exod 20:10) and in the handling of the firstborn animals (22:29-30). Because these birds eat flesh with blood in it, they are declared unclean, just as people who do the same are declared unclean (Lev 17).

As in the case of animals, the rationale of uncleanness depends on how the concept "unclean" is viewed; it should not be viewed only in connection with birds but must be seen comprehensively, taking other cases of uncleanness into perspective. It is likely that the uncleanness represents varying degrees of the aura of death (Wenham, 1983). In this respect, those birds listed in Lev 11:13-19 as unclean are at least carnivorous, and in levitical worldview, related to death on that score.

It seems far simpler, therefore, to conclude that the birds of prey are unclean because, being eaters or carriers of carrion, they are associated with death.

P-B The nom. occurs in DSS (e.g., 11QT 65:2). In LXX *ṣippōr* is rendered mostly as *peteinon* (→ *'ōp,* # 6416). In RL the term *ṣippōr* appears extensively in cultic contexts (cf. BTalm Ḥullin 139 a,b; Bezah 8b; Berakot 56b). Conforming to the Creator (e.g., Isa 31:5), rabbis held that it is good to show mercy toward the birds (Mish. Berakot 5:3; Megilla 4:9).

Birds, flying creatures: → *'br* (fly, # 87); → *bêṣâ* (egg, # 1070); → *barbur* (species of fowl, # 1350); → *gôzāl* (young bird, # 1578); → *dgr* (hatch eggs, # 1842); → *ḥᵃsîdâ* (stork, # 2884); → *yônâ* I (dove, # 3433); → *ya'ᵃnâ* (ostrich, eagle-owl?, # 3613); → *kānāp* (wing, skirt, outermost edge, # 4053); → *nešer/nᵉšar* (vulture [eagle], # 5979); → *'ôp* (flying creatures, # 6416); → *'ayiṭ* (birds of prey [collective], # 6514); → *'ōrēb* I (raven, # 6854); → *ṣippôr* I (birds, # 7606); → *qōrē'* I (partridge, # 7926); → *śᵉlāw* (quails, # 8513)

Clean, pure: → *brr* I (purge out, sort, keep pure, sift, # 1405); → *zkh* (be pure, clean oneself, # 2342); → *ḥap* I (pure: clean, # 2899); → *ṭhr* (clean, cleanse, purify, # 3197)

Uncleanness, defilement, pollution: → *g'l* II (be defiled, desecrate, stain, # 1458); → *ḥnp* I (be godless, be defiled, # 2866); → *ṭm'* (be/come ceremonially unclean, defile o.s., desecrate, # 3237); → *piggûl* (unclean meat, # 7002)

BIBLIOGRAPHY

TWOT 2:775; *ABD* 6:1109-67; B. Landsberger, "The Fauna of Ancient Mesopotamia, Second Part," *MSL* 8, 1962; M. Douglas, *Purity in Danger*, 1966; J. Milgrom, *Leviticus 1-16*, 1991; G. J. Wenham, *Leviticus,* 1979; idem, "Why Does Sexual Intercourse Defile (Lev 15:18)?" *ZAW* 95, 1983, 432-34.

N. Kiuchi

7608 (*ṣappaḥat*, juglet, jar, flask), → # 3998

7610 (*ṣippiyyâ*, lookout post), → # 7595

7613 (*ṣappîḥit*, wafer), → Bread

7616	צָפִיעַ

צָפִיעַ (*ṣāpîa'*), nom. dung (of cattle) (# 7616).

OT The nom. *ṣāpîa'*, dung, is found only in Ezek 4:15. Ezekiel is allowed to substitute cow manure for the human excrement first commanded: "Bake your bread over cow manure."

Dung, excrement, refuse, urine: → *'ašpōt* (ash-heap, refuse-heap, dung-hill, # 883); → *gll* II (befoul, dirty o.s., # 1671); → *dōmen* (dung, manure, # 1961); → *ḥ^a^rā'îm* (dung, # 2989); → *yešaḥ* (filth, diarrhea, # 3803); → *madmēnâ* I (dung pit, # 4523); → *sûḥâ* (offal, # 6054); → *pereš* I (offal, contents of stomach, # 7302); → *ṣē'â* (filth, human excrement, # 7362); → *ṣāpîa'* (dung [of cattle], # 7616); → *śîg* (excrement, # 8485); → *šyn* (urinate, # 8874)

Roy E. Hayden

7618 (*ṣāpîr*, he-goat), → # 7366

7620	צָפִית

צָפִית (*ṣāpît*), nom. rug (# 7620); possibly < צפה (*ṣph* II, spread out, # 7596).

OT NIV "set the rugs" (Isa 21:5) refers to the carefree manner of the Babylonians banqueting (Oswalt, *Isaiah*, 393) at the table (→ *šulḥān*; # 7620).

Furniture: → *h^a^dōm* (footstool, # 2071); → *kebeš* (footstool, # 3900); → *kissē'* (chair, throne, # 4058); → *šulḥān* (table, # 8947)

I. Cornelius

7621	צפן

צפן (*ṣpn*), q. hide; ni. be hidden; hi. hide (# 7621); nom. מַצְפּוֹן (*maṣpôn*), hidden treasure (hapleg. in Obad 6; → # 5208). Of the 32x it appears in OT, 25x are poetic texts. See the variant form *śpn*, conceal (→ # 8561).

ANE Cognates include the Akk. *ṣapānu,* to hide (*CAD* 16:96); Arab. *ṣafana,* to hide.

OT 1. The root *ṣpn* primarily means to hide or conceal, either for purposes of protection and safety or for more sinister reasons like an ambush. For example, the baby Moses was concealed in a papyrus basket to spare him death according to Pharaoh's edict (Exod 2:3), Rahab hid the Hebrew spies in Jericho to prevent their discovery (Josh 2:4), and God hides the righteous in the shelter of his presence (Ps 31:20[21]). On the contrary, the wicked hide or lie in wait (NIV) for the righteous in order to destroy them (Ps 56:7; Prov 1:11, 18), but their deeds are not hidden from God (Jer 16:17).

2. *ṣpn* may also mean hide in the sense of treasure, store up, or reserve as in the judgment for sin that God stores up against the wicked (Job 15:20; 20:26; 21:19; Hos 13:12), the wisdom and knowledge God treasures for the upright (Prov 2:7; cf. 10:14), or even the fruits of love the maiden reserves for her beloved (S of Songs 7:13[14]).

3. In a theological sense, *ṣpn* may refer to the inscrutability of God (Job 10:13; 24:1) and the mystery of his ways in creation (17:4).

4. The vb. *ṣpn* takes on the technical meaning of memorizing the commandments of God (Job 23:12; Ps 119:11; Prov 2:1; 7:1).

5. Once the q. past part. (*ṣ^{e}pûnî*) is used to describe the treasured place or temple of Yahweh in Jerusalem (Ezek 7:22).

6. In Prov 27:16, *ṣpn* means hide in the sense of restraining the quarrelsome wife.

7. The myth of Edom's impregnable defenses will be shattered even as the nation is obliterated and her hidden treasures (*maṣpôn*) are ransacked in the day of Yahweh's judgment (Obad 6).

8. The MT *ûṣ^{e}pyyn^{e}kā* (Ps 17:14) is usually read *ṣ^{e}pûn^{e}kā* (q. past part., treasured ones; so NIV those cherished; cf. Dahood, *Psalms 1-50*, AB 16, 1965, 99, and Craigie, *Psalms 1-50*, WBC 19, 1983, 161). The entire verse evidences some corruption and disorder in the mss. Either the psalmist describes covenant blessings for the righteous or calls covenant curses and divine vengeance upon the wicked (so NRSV; cf. Anderson, *Psalms 1-71*, NCB, 1972, 151-52).

Hiding: → *ḥb'* (hide, conceal, # 2461); → *ḥbh* (hide, # 2464); → *ḥāgû* (refuge, cleft, # 2511); → *ḥpp* I (screen, shelter, # 2910); → *ṭmn* (hide, # 3243); → *kḥd* (be hidden, hide, # 3948); → *knp* (hide oneself, # 4052); → *sōk* (hiding-place, shelter, thicket, hut, # 6108); → *str* (hide, kept secret, # 6259); → *'lm* (hidden things, secrets, # 6623); → *ṣpn* (hide, # 7621); → *śpn* (conceal, # 8561)

BIBLIOGRAPHY

ISBE 2:705-7; *NIDNTT* 2:211-20; 3:553-56; *THAT* 2:174-82, 575-81; *TWAT* 4:165-71; 5:342-44; R. Gordis, "Studies in Hebrew Roots of Contrasted Meanings," *JQR* 27, 1936-37, 33-58; J. A. Thompson, "The Root *'-l-m* in Semitic Languages and Some Proposed New Translations in Ugaritic and Hebrew," in *A Tribute to Arthur Voobus: Studies in Early Christian Literature and Its Environment, Primarily in the Syrian East*, R. H. Fischer, ed., 1977; R. F. Youngblood, "Qoheleth's 'Dark House' (Eccl 12:5)," *JETS* 29, 1986, 397-410.

Andrew E. Hill

7625 (*ṣepa'*, viper), → # 5729

7626 (*ṣip'ōnî*, viper), → # 5729

7627	צפף

צפף (*ṣpp* I), pilp. whisper, chirp (as a sorcerer) (# 7627).

ANE Arab. *ṣafṣafa*, twitter, chirp.

OT The complete listing of the term's occurrence is Isa 8:19; 10:14; 29:4; 38:14. For a discussion on mantic practices, see *qsm*, practice divination (# 7876).

P-B Heb. *ṣipṣēp* II, scream, shriek, chirp (e.g., in prayer, of the dead who want to come up out of Gehenna) (Jastrow, 2:1298).

Malcolm J. A. Horsnell

7628 (*ṣapṣāpâ*, willow tree), → # 6770

7630	צְפַרְדֵּעַ

צְפַרְדֵּעַ(*ṣᵉpardēʿa*), frog (# 7630).

ANE This word is attested in various Sem. languages: Akk. *muṣaʾʾirānu*, Syr. *ʿurdᵉʿā*, Arab. *ḍifdiʿ*.

OT In the OT it appears 13x, and all exclusively in passages dealing with the Exodus (e.g., Exod 8:2[7:27]; Ps 78:45; 105:30). Some commentators (Cassuto) see in the plague of frogs by the Lord a defeat of the Egyptian god, *ḥeqt*, the frog-headed goddess. Furthermore, since the goddess was supposed to assist women at childbirth, Sarna comments that the plague is retribution for what the Egyptians did to the Hebrew midwives in trying to kill newborn babies. But against this approach Durham, while he thinks it is possible, comments that this should not be pressed, for this requires of the compiler of the text or the readership a rather sufficient knowledge of the Egyptian theology, whereas the defeat of the Egyptian deity cannot be ascertained from anywhere in the OT. Over against this is the witness of Exod 12:12, according to which the Exodus is God's victory over the Egyptian deities. (→ Plagues: Theology)

P-B LXX renders the word *batrachos* (cf. also Wisd 19:10). In the NT this G term occurs once in Rev 16:13, where frogs appear "as the form in which unclean spirits appeared" (*BAGD*, 137). In RL "frog" also appears in contexts discussing the Exodus. It is considered as an unclean amphibian (e.g., Mish. Toh 5:1,4).

Animals: → *bᵉhēmâ* (quadrupeds, # 989); → *zānāb* (tail, # 2387); → *ḥᵃzîr* (pig, # 2614); → *ḥayyâ* I (animal, # 2651); → *keleb* (dog, # 3978); → *ʿakbār* (mouse, # 6572); → *ṣᵉpardēaʿ* (frog, # 7630); → *qippod* (hedgehog/owl?, # 7887); → *rmś* (creep, swarm, # 8253); → *šrṣ* (swarm, teem, # 9237); → *tan* (jackal, # 9478); → **Reptiles: Theology**; see the Index for Birds; Camel; Deer; Donkey; Dove; Flock; Gazelle; Insects; Lion; Maggot; Snake, etc.

BIBLIOGRAPHY

EMiqr 6:762-63; U. Cassuto, *A Commentary on the Book of Exodus*, 1967; J. I. Durham, *Exodus*, 1987; N. Sarna, *Exodus*, 1991.

N. Kiuchi

7633 (*ṣepet*, capital), → # 7596

7639 (*ṣar* I, narrow, scarce, adversity, anguish), → # 7674

7640 (*ṣar* II, adversary), → # 7675

7644	צֹר

צֹר (*ṣōr* I), pebble, flint (# 7644); צְרוֹר (*ṣ^{e}rôr* II), pebble (# 7656).

ANE See the Akk. *ṣurru* A, flint, obsidian, flint blade (*CAD* 16:257-59).

OT 1. Israel's recalcitrance before Yahweh, divinely confirmed and intensified for purposes of judgment, is likened to a "forehead ... harder than flint" (Ezek 3:9). Isaiah mentions the flint-like hoofs of the Assyrian horses, a picture of the tireless and seemingly unbreakable Assyrian military machine (Isa 5:28).

2. Elsewhere, *ṣōr* is used of a flint knife for performing circumcision (Exod 4:25; Josh 5:2-3).

3. The nom. *ṣ^{e}rôr* is probably a variant of *ṣōr* and occurs only in 2 Sam 17:13; Amos 9:9. Both texts refer to utter destruction to the degree that not even pebbles will remain as indicators of habitation. In the one case, Hushai advised Absalom to amass an army to root out David (2 Sam 17:13); in the other, the prophet warns Israel of the thoroughness of divine judgment (Amos 9:9).

Rock, stones: → *'eben* (stone, rock, # 74); → *gābîš* (rock-crystal, # 1486); → *ḥallāmîš* (flint, # 2734); → *ḥāṣāṣ* (gravel, # 2953); → *kēp* (rock, # 4091); → *sōḥeret* (mineral stone, # 6090); → *sela'* (rock, # 6152); → *sql* (throw stones, # 6232); → *ṣûr* I (rock, boulder, # 7446); → *ṣûr* II (pebble, flint, # 7447); → *ṣōr* I (flint knife, # 7644); → *rgm* (stone, # 8083); → *talpiyyôt* (courses of stones, # 9444)

Bibliography
ISBE 3:205-6; 4:622-30; *NIDNTT* 2:731-34; 3:381-99.

Andrew E. Hill

7646	צרב

צרב (*ṣrb*), ni. be scorched (hapleg., # 7646); צָרָב (*ṣārāb*), adj. scorching (hapleg., # 7647).

ANE Akk. *ṣarāpu,* to burn; Phoen. (Lidz. 42); Aram. *ṣ^{e}rab.*

OT 1. The vb. appears only in Ezek 20:47[21:3]: "This is what the Sovereign Lord says: I am about to set fire to you . . . and every face (or, the whole surface) from south to north will be scorched by it." Fire is here a symbol of God's judgment against disobedient Judah. "Scorch" should not be regarded here as a mild form of a burn, but rather as the result of an especially severe and complete conflagration.

2. The adj. *ṣārāb*, scorching, is used in Prov 16:27 to describe the destructive fire that is found on the lips of the "scoundrel" (or "worthless one," Heb. *'îš b^{e}lîya'al*; → # 1175). Apparently the reference is to a gossip: such a person is picturesquely said to "dig up" or "plot" (*krh*; → # 4125) trouble.

Heat, scorching: → *ḥmm* (be warm, hot, keep warm, # 2801); → *ḥ^{a}rîšî* (scorching?, # 3046); → *ḥrr* I (be hot, scorched, burn, be hoarse, # 3081); → *yṣt* (light, kindle, ignite, burn, scorch, # 3675); → *ṣrb* (be scorched, # 7646); → *śrp* (burn, scorch, cauterize, # 8596); → *šdp* (scorch, # 8728); → *šārāb* (scorching heat, # 9220)

Bibliography
G. A. Cooke, *The Book of Ezekiel,* 1936; W. McKane, *Proverbs,* OTL, 1970; C. H. Toy, *Proverbs,* ICC, 1899, 331.

Anthony Tomasino

7647 (*ṣārāb*, scorching), → # 7646

7648	צָרֶבֶת

צָרֶבֶת (*ṣārebet*), scar (= scorching; # 7648); < צרב (*ṣrb*), scorch, (→ # 7646).

ANE Akk. *ṣarāpu*, burn.

OT The word is only used in Lev 13:23, 28 to denote a scar that has resulted from a burn.

Disease—blister, boil, skin disease, scar, wound: → *'ᵃbaʿbuʿōt* (blisters, # 81); → *bōhaq* (skin condition, # 993); → *baheret* (white patch on skin, # 994); → *gārāb* (festering eruption, # 1734); → *zrr* I (press out [wounds], # 2452); → *ḥeres* I (itch, # 3063); → *yabbelet* (wart?, # 3301); → *yallepet* (skin disease, # 3539); → *yᵉraqraq* (discoloration, # 3768); → *kᵉwiyya* (scar, # 3918); → *m'r* (be sore, # 4421); → *māzôr* I (boil, # 4649); → *makkâ* (blow, # 4804); → *mispaḥat* (skin eruption, # 5030); → *mrḥ* (rub, polish, # 5302); → *neteq* (scalp infection, # 5999); → *sappaḥat* (hair disease, # 6204); → *ʿōpel* I (abscesses, # 6754); → *ʿāš* II (pus, # 6932); → *ṣāpâ* (pus?, # 7597); → *ṣarebet* (scar, # 7648); → *ṣrʿ* (suffer from skin disease, # 7665); → *śᵉ'ēt* II (swelling, # 8421); → *śtr* (break out [tumor], # 8609); → *šᵉḥîn* (boil, # 8825). For related entries → *ḥlh* I (become weak, tired, ill, # 2703)

R. K. Harrison

7650 (*ṣārâ* I, misery, anguish, affliction, trouble), → # 7674

7651 (*ṣārâ* II, rival wife), → # 7675

7655	צְרוֹר

צְרוֹר (*ṣᵉrôr* I), nom. pouch; bag; purse; bundle; sachet (# 7655).

ANE Jew. Aram., Syr., *ṣᵉrārā'*; Arab. *ṣurrat, ṣirār*.

OT The word refers to a pouch/small bundle containing money (Gen 42:35), placed within a larger sack (*śaq*) (cf. Prov 7:20). It contained enough money for traveling. Because of her rebellion and sin Israel's money bags (*ṣᵉrôr*) had become tattered with holes (Hag 1:6). It is used metaphorically to describe a container for Job's offenses/sins (Job 14:17) and to depict those who are in God's care (1 Sam 25:29) and safekeeping. In S of Songs 1:13 the sachet (*ṣᵉrôr*) of myrrh represents the lover. This item was clearly of general and great personal value, much as a purse or wallet is today.

P-B The LXX translates using two different roots, (1) *(en)/(apo)/desmos* and (2) *ballantion*, each meaning bag, pouch, purse. The word is found in Sir 6:15 and in *KQT*, 188.

Bag, pouch: → *'argaz* (saddlebag, # 761); → *ḥārîṭ* (bag, # 3038); → *yalqûṭ* (shepherd's pouch, # 3541); → *kîs* (bag, # 3967); → *kar* III (saddle-bag, # 4121); → *mešek* I (pouch, bag, # 5433); → *mišpᵉtayim* (two saddle-bags, sheepfolds, # 5478); → *ṣᵉrôr* I (pouch, bag, # 7655)

Eugene Carpenter

7656 (*ṣᵉrôr* II, pebble), → # 7644

7658	צרח

צרח (*ṣrḥ*), q. yell, call shrilly; hi., raise the war cry (# 7658); צֶרַח (*ṣeraḥ*), nom., war cry, shriek (# 7659).

OT 1. Zeph 1:14 is the hapleg. of the vb. in the q. and signifies the shout of the warrior. It occurs in a description of the appearance of the Lord on the Day of the Lord.

The hi. appears once in Isa 42:13, in close conjunction with the vb. *rw'*. This passage too occurs in a context describing the appearance of the divine warrior (→), who gives a shout as he engages in battle with his enemies.

2. The nom. *ṣeraḥ* is conjectured to appear in Ezek 21:22[27]. The MT has *reṣaḥ* (# 8358), but the context and the Septuagint argue for a case of metathesis. The context again is one of warfare. Some (see *BHS* apparatus) also suggest an emendation in Jer 4:31 from *ṣrh* to *ṣrḥ*, but here the meaning distress is possible.

Shout, (war-)cry, yell: → *hêdād* (shout, # 2116); → *ṣwḥ* (shout, # 7423); → *ṣrḥ* (yell, call shrilly, raise the war-cry, # 7658); → *rw'* (shout, give war-cry, # 8131); → *rnn* (yell, shout [w. joy], moan, # 8264)

Tremper Longman III

7659 (*ṣeraḥ*, war cry), → # 7658

7661	צְרִי/צֳרִי

צְרִי/צֳרִי (*ṣºrî/ṣᵉrî*), nom. balm, resin (# 7661). The exact nature of this resin is uncertain; perhaps it is a resin-like gum of the mastic tree. Zohary proposes the storax tree.

OT 1. Geographically this resin is associated with the Gilead of the Transjordan (Gen 37:25; 43:11; Ezek 27:17), but no trees currently grow in that area that would produce the gum. They may have in ancient times.

The resin seems to have been widely associated with healing properties. Such resins would soothe the wound and provide a pleasant aroma to counteract the smell of the rotting flesh of the wound. Jeremiah announces that these properties are not enough to heal the wounds that will be left by God's judgment, whether it be Egypt (Jer 46:11), Babylon (51:8), or Judah herself (8:22). Jeremiah expected healing for Judah; after all, they were God's people. However, their wound—the fatal wound of idolatry—was too terrible. Idolatry was not just any sin, it was apostasy, a deliberate covenant-breaking act. Spiritual illness was not susceptible to physical amelioration, even by the best of medicaments.

2. Other related, rare words include: *lōt*, nom. myrrh or laudanum (# 4320); Gen 37:25; 43:11; *nᵉkō't*, nom. spices (# 5780); 37:25; 43:11. Both are some sort of aromatic gums. *bᵉdōlaḥ*, nom. gum resin, bdellium (# 978); Gen 2:12; Num 11:7.

Resin, balm, myrrh: → *mōr* (myrrh, # 5255); → *nāṭāp* (gum resin, # 5753); → *ṣ*ᵒ*rî*/*ṣ*ᵉ*rî* (balm, resin, # 7661); → *q*ᵉ*ṣîa'* (cassia, # 7904)
Incense: → *l*ᵉ*bōnâ* I (frankincense, white resin, # 4247); → *qṭr* (let go up in smoke, # 7787)

BIBLIOGRAPHY
I. and W. Jacob, "Flora," *ABD*, 2:803-17; M. Zohary, *Plants of the Bible*, 1982; United Bible Societies, *Fauna and Flora of the Bible*, 1972.

Gary H. Hall

7663	צְרִיחַ

צְרִיחַ (*ṣ*ᵉ*rîaḥ*), nom. cellar, vault; pits; stronghold (# 7663).

ANE Jew Aram. *ṣ*ᵉ*rîḥā'*, hall stronghold; Nab. *ṣryḥ*, hall, room; OSA *ṣrḥ*; Eth. *ṣerḥ*, upper room; Arab. *ṣarḥ*, high building, castle; *ḍaraḥa*, a hole dug for the dead; *ḍariḥ*, a hole, grave.

OT The word refers to the stronghold in the house of El-Berith in Shechem, where the wicked men of Shechem were burned by Abimelech and his men in fulfillment of Jotham's curse (Judg 9:46, 49, 50-57; cf. 9:20, 57). The men of Israel hid in pits (NIV; tombs, RSV) in fear of the Philistines (1 Sam 13:6). In both cases the *ṣ*ᵉ*rîaḥ* was a place where persons sought additional security for either defensive or offensive purposes.

Cellar: → *ḥānût* (vaulted cell, vault, dungeon, # 2844); → *niškâ* (storeroom(s), cell, room, # 5969); → *ṣ*ᵉ*rîaḥ* (cellar, vault, pit, stronghold, # 7663)
Stronghold: → *'armōn* (citadel, # 810); → *bîrâ* (citadel, acropolis, # 1072); → *bṣr* III (be inaccessible, # 1307); → *dāyēq* (siege-mound, # 1911); → *ḥêl* (rampart, # 2658); → *millô'* (terrace, # 4864); → *misgeret* (stronghold, dungeon, rim, table, # 4995); → *m*ᵉ*ṣād* (stronghold, # 5171); → *māṣôr* II (fortification, fortified city, # 5190); → *sōḥērâ* (rampart, # 6089); → *sōkēk* (mantelet, # 6116); → *ṣ*ᵉ*rîaḥ* (cellar, vault, pit, stronghold, # 7663); → *śgb* (be high, fortified, protect, # 8435); → **Fortification: Theology**

Eugene Carpenter/Michael A. Grisanti

7664	צֹרֶךְ

צֹרֶךְ (*ṣōrek*), nom. need (# 7664).

OT Although the root appears frequently in later Heb. (and is attested in Arab., Aram., and Ugar.), it is found only as a nom. in the OT in a single late passage (2 Chron 2:16[15]) that is part of a free retelling of 1 Kgs 5:1-12[15-26]. The earlier text, which stressed Solomon's "want" or "desire" (*ḥpṣ* [→ # 2911], 1 Kgs 5:8[22], 10[24]; cf. v. 9[23]), is rewritten in 2 Chron with a stress upon Solomon's "need." In contrast to *ḥsr*, lack, the most common Heb. root for this semantic field, *ṣrk* tends to focus on an available remedy to resolve the inadequacy (*ḥsr* focuses on the problem and not the solution), and to identify an object or quality without which an enterprise is impossible (*ḥsr* may allow for the enterprise to continue but at a substandard level).

Lack, need, want: → *ḥsr* (diminish, decrease, lack, deprive, # 2893); → *ḥpṣ* I (want, desire, wish, care, # 2911); → *'dr* III (be missing, lacking, # 6372); → *ṣōrek* (need, # 7664)

Sam Meier

7665	צרע

צרע (*ṣr'*), q. suffer from a skin disease; pu. struck with a skin disease (# 7665); צָרַעַת (*ṣāra'at*), nom. skin disease, leprosy (# 7669).

OT This word group forms a generic term for a variety of cutaneous diseases, most of which were benign, with one being malignant in character. The nom. is usually rendered "leprosy," which serves as a comprehensive designation for a wide variety of skin afflictions in the same general sense that "cancer" is employed to describe both sarcomas and carcinomas.

The hygienic regulations concerning leprosy in Lev 13-14 contain obscure terminology, making for difficulties in translation. *ṣāra'at* could affect both persons and material things such as houses (Lev 14:44) leather goods (14:55) and clothing (13:47, 59). The priest, acting as the community's medical officer of health, followed a carefully-defined diagnostic procedure in order to separate benign conditions such as acne, psoriasis, and vitiligo from the malignant form of *ṣāra'at* known to modern medicine as Hansen's disease (clinical leprosy). When a person's friends discovered in him indications of localized inflammation, an encrusted or a pinkish-red swollen area of skin, he was brought to the priest for diagnosis (13:9). A period of isolation enabled the priest to consider possible diagnostic alternatives, but in practice was only a formality, since clinical leprosy would already have been sufficiently advanced to make a ready diagnosis possible. Leprosy was indicated if the suspicious cutaneous spot penetrated the skin and the local hair had turned white.

When diagnosed the leper was declared ceremonially unclean and expelled from the community to preserve its holiness and to limit the spread of the disease. While most critical scholarship has denied the identification of malignant *ṣāra'at* with clinical leprosy, without, incidentally, suggesting a convincing alternative—a comparison of signs and symptoms in Leviticus with those of modern Hansen's disease dispels any reasonable doubt on the matter. The fact is that a minimum of any two symptoms is sufficient to establish the existence of leprosy, ancient or modern. While Bible expositors have often understood leprosy to be a type of human sin, the MT does not promote this interpretation speaking instead of sin in terms of hardness of heart, blindness, and obstinacy, not of being afflicted with *ṣāra'at*. Uzziah of Judah appears to have succumbed to Hansen's disease (2 Chron 26:21) as a punishment from God for usurping priestly functions.

Disease—blister, boil, skin disease, scar, wound: → *'ᵃba'bu'ōt* (blisters, # 81); → *bōhaq* (skin condition, # 993); → *baheret* (white patch on skin, # 994); → *gārāb* (festering eruption, # 1734); → *zrr* I (press out [wounds], # 2452); → *ḥeres* I (itch, # 3063); → *yabbelet* (wart?, # 3301); → *yallepet* (skin disease, # 3539); → *yᵉraqraq* (discoloration, # 3768); → *kᵉwiyya* (scar, # 3918); → *m'r* (be sore, # 4421); → *māzôr* I (boil, # 4649); → *makkâ* (blow, # 4804); → *mispaḥat* (skin eruption, # 5030); → *mrḥ* (rub, polish, # 5302); → *neteq* (scalp infection, # 5999); → *sappaḥat* (hair disease, # 6204); → *'ōpel* I (abscesses, # 6754); → *'āš* II (pus, # 6932); → *ṣāpâ* (pus?, # 7597); → *ṣarebet* (scar, # 7648); → *ṣr'* (suffer from skin disease, # 7665); → *śᵉ'ēt* II (swelling, # 8421); → *śtr* (break out [tumor], # 8609); → *šᵉḥîn* (boil, # 8825). For related entries → *ḥlh* I (become weak, tired, ill, # 2703)

Bibliography

ISBE 1:532, 953-60; 3:103-06; S. G. Browne, *Leprosy in the Bible*, 1970; E. V. Hulse, "The Nature of Biblical 'Leprosy' and the Use of Alternative Medical Terms in Modern Translations of the Bible," *PEQ* 107, 1975, 87-105; G. J. Wenham, *The Book of Leviticus*, NICOT, 1979, 189-214.

R. K. Harrison

7667	צִרְעָה

צִרְעָה (*ṣir'â*), nom. hornet; destruction; fear, terror; depression, discouragement; panic, terror (# 7667).

ANE Some have suggested a relationship with Arab. *ḍara'a*, dejected (see *HALAT* 989).

OT The word is found only 3x in the OT. All three vv. refer to God's driving out the peoples in Canaan before Israel. The reference may be taken literally, hornet's nest, wasp's nest; hornet, wasp (so LXX, *sphēkia*, wasp's nest; cf. *sphēks*, a wasp), or figuratively. Yahweh's sting may well have been the dread/fear of him upon the inhabitants when they heard of what he did to Egypt. The report psychologically incapacitated them much as a wasp's/hornet's sting does (Josh 2:10-11). Exodus 23:27 (*'êmâ*, terror) may support this view if considered to be parallel in thought with v. 28. But v. 28 could be a further (synthetic) development of v. 27, adding the means for the dread, terror. The hornet may be the messenger of the Lord, who leads Israel (Exod 23:20).

P-B The LXX translates *ṣir'â* each time with *sphēkia*. In LH the term is taken literally. There were supposedly two attacks/plagues of hornets, one in Moses' day, one in Joshua's day (*Sot.* 36[a]. Hornets were considered dangerous to life and could be killed on the Sabbath (cf. Jastrow 2:1303).

Insects: → *d^ebôrâ* I (bee, wasp, # 1805); → *kēn* V (mosquito, gnat, louse, # 4031); → *'ṭh* II (delouse, # 6487); → *'aqrāb* (scorpion, # 6832); → *'ārōb* (fly, swarm of flies, flying insects, # 6856); → *'āš* I (moth, # 6931); → *ṣir'â* (hornet, destruction, fear, terror, depression, discouragement, # 7667); → *qml* (wither, become moldy, musty, infected w. insects, # 7857)

Bibliography

IDB 2:246-56, 645; J. Sawyer, "Note on the Etymology of *ṢĀRA'AT*," *VT* 26, 1976, 241-45; *Fauna and Flora of the Bible*, 1980[2].

Eugene Carpenter/Michael A. Grisanti

7669 (*ṣāra'at*, skin disease), → # 7665

7671	צרף

צרף (*ṣrp*), q. melt, dissolve, liquefy, smelt, fuse, blend; cleanse, purify, purge, refine; sift, winnow, test, examine; ni. be melted, smelted; be purified, purged, refined; pi. part. purifier, refiner (# 7671); מַצְרֵף (*maṣrēp*), nom. crucible (→ # 5214); צֹרְפִי (*ṣōr^epî*), nom. collective goldsmiths (hapleg. # 7672); צָרְפַת (*ṣār^epat*), PN loc. Zarephath (# 7673).

ANE Both verbal and nom. forms are well attested, being found in Sam. (with the meaning try, test, examine, assay); Egyp. Aram., Phoen. (metal smelter); Ugar.

(silversmith; crucible; burn, cauterize; purify, refine); Akk. (*ṣarāpu*, fire-red colored; *ṣārip dušê*, leather dyer; pl. *ṣāripūtu*, metal smelters); Syr. (*ṣ^{e}rap*, purify, refine), Mandean (melt, smelt, purify, refine); and OSA (*ṣrp*, silver). The PN loc. *ḏa-ar-pá-ta* is found in Egyp., and the same place is referred to in Phoen. as *ṣarafand*. The nom. *mṣrp*, crucible, occurs in Ugar.

OT 1. The vb. *ṣrp* occurs with reference to metal smiths and their work. In only one text is the nom. *ṣōr^{e}pî*, goldsmiths, used (Neh 3:31, where the MT *ben-haṣṣōr^{e}pî* is usually emended to *ben-haṣṣōr^{e}pîm*, son of the goldsmiths, i.e., a member of the professional guild of goldsmiths; see, e.g., *BHS*; Williamson, 198; Blenkinsopp, 231). In all other passages, it is the q. act. part. that is used of goldsmiths and silversmiths (Judg 17:4; Neh 3:8, 32; Prov 25:4 [though here some follow LXX, which reads the ni. part., *niṣrāp*, purified, for MT *laṣṣōrēp*, to the smith; on this, see, e.g., McKane, 1970, 590-91]; Isa 40:19; 41:7; 46:6; Jer 10:9, 14; 51:17).

Significantly, all the latter passages, with the exception of the verses in Prov and Neh, refer to the manufacture of idols. The authors of Isa 40:18-31; 46:1-13; and Jer 10:1-16 expose the absurdity of comparing a man-made idol (even one overlaid with gold!) with Yahweh, the unique, the incomparable, the immeasurable, the incomprehensible, the inexhaustible God of creation (cf. e.g., Scullion, 24, 26). All idols, however expensively made and aesthetically pleasing they may be, are false, worthless, works of delusion (Jer 51:17-18). They are completely lifeless (10:14b; 51:17b), mute (10:5a), impotent (10:5), and motionless (Isa 46:7; Jer 10:5). They have to be carefully secured to prevent them from falling over (Isa 41:7; 46:7; Jer 10:4)! The maker of the universe is beyond representation (cf. Clifford, 574). An object symbolizing the heavenly being not only denies the transcendent nature of God (Clements, 68), but can also become the object worshiped (cf. Ackroyd, 354; Watts, 91-92). An image can delude people into believing that the deity is knowable through it alone (Sawyer, 103). Those whose focus is directed on idols tend to want to keep their deity captive and to manipulate the divine will in accordance with their own (cf. Watts, 167; Davidson, 1986, 94-95). On some forms of idolatry that persist in the modern world, see Davidson (1985, 159).

The sing. form of the q. act. part. occurs in Judg 17:4, which relates how the mother of a man named Micah expiated her son's theft of a substantial amount of her silver by donating part of the restored money to a silversmith to make a silver image (the text refers to a *pesel* and a *massēkâ*, but it is probable that only one object, possibly an image of Yahweh [O'Connor, 143], is meant). The comment in v. 6 may express the view of a later editor that the manufacture of an image and other cultic appurtenances and their installation in a private shrine were aberrations that were possible only because of the near anarchy of the times (cf. e.g., Moore, 369; May and Metzger, 317; Cundall, 185). However, the woman seems to have acted in good faith and in ignorance of the commandment prohibiting the use of graven and molten images in Exod 20:4, 23; 34:17; Deut 5:8 (cf. Deut 27:15). According to Judg 18:27-31, the silver image was later moved to the shrine at Dan, and some (cf. e.g., Hoppe, 191-93) think that the purpose of 17:1-6 was to discredit this sanctuary by stressing that its venerated image was made from stolen silver; that the greater part of the restored money, though dedicated to Yahweh, was fraudulently withheld; and that the idol itself was stolen by the Danites from its original owner. Others (e.g., Moore, 370) are sceptical of the claim that this was the author's prime motive.

2. *ṣrp* is used of refining metal by removing dross (Ps 12:6[7]; Prov 25:4). On the process of refining silver, see, e.g., Robinson. Ps 12:6[7] confidently asserts that, in fundamental contrast to the deceitful, betraying words of human falsehood (see esp. Weiser, 160; Stuhlmueller, 102-5), the promises of Yawheh are pure (i.e., true and dependable, containing no hidden dross or deceit; see, e.g., Rogerson and McKay, 1977a, 57) "like silver refined in a furnace of clay, purified seven times" (seven being a number of completeness and perfection). There was a time in antiquity when silver was considered to be more valuable than gold. However, some (e.g., NEB; REB; Craigie, 136) emend MT *lā'āreṣ* in Ps 12:6[7], "to the earth/land/ground" (NIV to clay), to *ḥārûṣ*, "gold," and translate "silver refined in a furnace, gold purified seven times." The assurance that the word of God proves true is also given in 2 Sam 22:31 (par. Ps 18:30[31]); Ps 119:140; and Prov 30:5, which all use the q. pass. part. *ṣ^{e}rûpâ* (without dross/unalloyed/well tested [JB]; flawless/thoroughly tested [NIV]; proves true/well tried [RSV; NRSV]; has stood the test/has been tested through and through [NEB; cf. REB]). Like gold or other precious metal that has been thoroughly tried by fire, Yahweh's word is of proved authenticity and precious (McKane, 1970, 648; cf. Baldwin, 1988, 289).

Most occurrences of the vb. (q.) are in passages that describe the process of testing or refining people. In Judg 7:4, Yahweh announces that in order to reduce the number of Gideon's warriors, thereby heightening the miraculous character of the deliverance to follow (May and Metzger, 302; Hoppe, 148), he is going to test the people, i.e., sort/thin them out, as a goldsmith assays pure metal (J. Gray, 1967, 304; Hoppe, 146). In Isa 1:25, Yahweh warns his people that in the furnace of his punitive and purifying judgment, he will smelt away their dross and remove all their alloy. Although unsupported by MSS or versions, many commentators emend MT *kabbōr*, as with lye, either to *bakkûr*, in the furnace, or to *kakkûr*, as in the furnace (e.g., G. B. Gray, 31, 35; Whitehouse, 1905, 96; Skinner, 11; Kissane, 16-17, 19). Good and bad alike will suffer in the severe punishment to be unleashed against them, but at the end of the refining process the impurities (i.e., the godless) will have been destroyed and the pure gold or silver (i.e., the faithful righteous) will have been preserved, redeemed, and restored (see, e.g., G. B. Gray, 35; Kaiser, 20-21). A similar picture of Judah being forced to endure the furnace of judgment in order to have its impurities removed is found in Ezek 22:17-22, although *ṣrp* is not used in this passage.

In Isa 48:10, Yahweh refers to the Exile as the furnace of affliction in which he has refined his people. The Exile was considered another Egypt, and the Egyptian bondage was likened to an iron furnace (Deut 4:20; 1 Kgs 8:51; Jer 11:4). Curiously, in Isa 48:10, MT reads "I have refined you but not with silver." Some (e.g., RSV; NRSV) emend the preposition *b^{e}* to *k^{e}* and read "[but not] like silver," meaning that the refining process was not as severe as with silver since that would have meant Israel's total destruction. Others (e.g., JB; McKenzie, 94; Westermann, 195; Ackroyd, 360) go further and omit the negative, reading "I have refined (Westermann has "refine") you (JB has "put you in the fire") like silver." North (178-79; cf. Scullion, 93) thinks that the preposition may be the *bêt* of price, in which case the meaning would be that Yahweh has assayed Israel, but not for any pleasure or profit (silver). More often, the preposition is taken as *bêth essentiae*, as silver; in this case the meaning is that the refining process of defeat and exile has produced not silver, but dross (Muilenburg, 557; D. R. Jones, 524; cf. RV; Whitehouse, 1908, 146; Dummelow, 444). Wardle (465) suggests that we read "I have tried thee in the furnace in vain." The text in Isa 48:10 can be understood to say that, despite the failure to smelt out any silver (i.e., any vestige of intrinsic goodness), God remains committed to using this people to accomplish his purpose (Knight, 1984, 118-19).

In Jer three figures are used to describe Yahweh's persistent efforts to locate one faithful Judahite who would justify sparing the nation from destruction. The prophet scours the streets of Jerusalem (Jer 5:1-9); he is a gleaner of grapes (6:9-12); and he is an assayer (6:27-30). According to 6:29, despite intense efforts to refine the metal, it remains so impregnated with impurities and dross as to be worthless. The process to try to separate the righteous in the community from the wicked has failed completely (McKane, 1986, 157). The wickedness of the people is so deeply ingrained that they are useless for God's purpose and must be rejected as his instruments (cf. e.g., Achtemeier, 39-40). In 9:7[6], however, Yahweh announces that he will refine his people. It may be that this passage is describing how, in both great weariness with their sin but also with great patience, Yahweh himself will undertake the arduous task of melting out the impurities (adultery, duplicity, dishonesty, mendacity, and cruelty are identified in vv. 2b-6[1b-5]; see Green, 69) of his people (cf. e.g., Achtemeier, 48-49). On the other hand, if the image is to be taken as a prediction, then this v. anticipates the burning of Israel's cities by an enemy striking from the north (Boadt, 80). Either way, the refining will be done in the crucible of suffering and humiliation (Davidson, 1986, 87).

According to Zech 13:9, in order to forge a new community, those (constituting a third of the people) who will survive the sword will be placed in the fire and refined. The purified remnant will worship Yahweh in sincerity, the covenant will be reconstituted, and true and undisturbed relations between God and his people will be restored. The vb. is used in parallelism with *bḥn*, try, prove, examine (→ # 1043), in Ps 17 and 26. In 17:3, the verbal forms *bāḥantā*, *pāqadtā*, and *ṣ*[e]*raptanî* may well be precative perfects equivalent to the preceding imperatives and jussives of MT (Dahood, 1966, 94; cf. Anderson, 148; *pace*, e.g., Oesterley, 158-59; NEB; REB; TEV; Rogerson and McKay, 1977a, 71; Craigie, 159). If this be correct, then both here and in 26:2, an individual petitioning for vindication against false accusers invites Yahweh to subject him to probing scrutiny so that his innocence may be proved (the metaphor of refining and testing is discussed by Keel, 183-86). Craigie (226-28) rightly stresses that while the author of Ps 26 affirms his integrity, he recognizes that more is required, and therefore he prays for purification (v. 11) so that he may proceed into the divine presence and participate in worship. The integrity that both psalmists claim to possess is not self-righteousness or legalism, but wholehearted devotion to Yahweh and unwavering trust in his steadfast love and faithfulness (Mays, 127-30; cf. Weiser, 180-81, 242-44; Rogerson and McKay, 1977a, 117-19; Knight, 1982, 128-30).

The combination of *ṣrp* and *bḥn* occurs again in Ps 66:10. Here Yahweh, who had tried his people as silver is tried (v. 10), is thanked by the members of the congregation for having sustained them during their corporate travail in the crucible of affliction when they were subjected to many dangers and ordeals. This text reminds us that the way to salvation and freedom is characterized by temptations, trials, oppression, suffering, humiliations, defeats, failure, and despair; furthermore, it is only by the grace of God that the faithful are sustained in their afflictions and delivered and purged from their sin (Weiser, 468-72).

The vb. is again found in Ps 105:19, part of a pericope (vv. 16-22) that describes how Joseph had to endure the severe testing imposed by God in order to become capable of fulfilling the task he had been appointed to carry out. The sufferings of Joseph were those of Israel in miniature; but just as this patriarch eventually won blessing, so too would the Israel of the psalmist's generation (cf. Rogerson and McKay, 1977b, 37; Allen, 43). Some exegetes (e.g., Kraus, 306-7) emend MT *ṣ^erāpāt^ehû*, it (i.e., the word of Yahweh) tested him, to *niṣrāpâ*, it (the word of Yahweh) was tested (i.e., proved true). Dahood (1970, 50, 58) suggests that the consonantal *ṣrpthw* be pointed as the q. pass. part. followed by the dative suffix of agency, yielding the sense, "Yahweh's promise was proved true by him." However, there are no convincing grounds for doubting MT. JB translates, "Yahweh's word proved him right"; TEV has "The word of the LORD proved him right"; and NIV reads "till the word of the LORD proved him true." Although "prove right/true" is, of course, a legitimate translation of the vb. (see, e.g., Bratcher and Reyburn, 896) and gives good parallelism here (Allen, 38), it does not seem as compelling as "test/try" (cf. Delitzsch, 145; Kirkpatrick, 619; Buttenwieser, 803).

The q. and the ni. are used in Dan 11:35 and 12:10, respectively, with the meaning refined. Dan 11:35 refers to the fate of martyrs (possibly the Maccabees, though this identification is not accepted by, e.g., Collins, 1984, 101; 1993, 386), whose death at the hands of the oppressor (almost certainly Antiochus IV Epiphanes) tested and developed the faith of the mass of the people (cf. e.g., Bevan, 195; Charles, 133; Driver, 190, 193; Dummelow, 543; Andrews, 532; Montgomery, 459; *pace* Collins, 1993, 386, 400, who argues that only the martyrs were purified). The slaughter of many pious leaders who proved their loyalty in the fires of persecution is part of the divine plan and is aimed at testing and purifying the community (Jeffery, 533-34), eliminating the faithless, and heartening the faithful (Montgomery, 459). By giving the assurance that their suffering is neither accidental nor meaningless but has the purpose of purifying, purging, and refining God's people, the concern of 12:10 seems to be to console persecuted Jews and to exhort those among them who may be tempted to yield in the face of seemingly overwhelming opposition to remain steadfast in their faithfulness (Baldwin, 1978, 208; cf. Goldingay, 319).

The pi. part. is used in Mal 3:2-3. As Smith (328), for one, points out, there is some confusion about the identity of the figure referred to in this passage: Is it God or one of his human or supernatural agents? It seems most probable that these vv. describe the action of Yahweh himself (see, e.g., Glazier-McDonald, 132, 142-43, *et passim*), who, coming in judgment, is likened first to a refiner's fire (v. 2) and then to a refiner and purifier of silver (v. 3). The process of purifying the people will begin with the thorough cleansing of the priests from their impurities in the crucible of suffering. God's judgment falls first on the priests because, by virtue of their position of high privilege and responsibility, they are the most guilty (Bennett, 388).

3. The nom. *maṣrēp*, crucible, occurs twice in Prov (17:3; 27:21) in the phrase "the crucible for silver and the furnace for gold." In 17:3, a comparison is drawn

between the process of refining precious metals and the way in which Yahweh tries human hearts to determine their true nature and motives (see, e.g., McKane, 1970, 511). In 27:21, the object of comparison is disputed. It may be the reputation (praise) that a person earns and that is considered an excellent index of character (see, e.g., McKane, 1970, 608-9). Other possibilities exist. Some (e.g., Scott, 162-63; cf. Walls, 568) think that the reference is to flattery and one's response to it rather than to reputation (one's reaction to praise is certainly a severe test of character, but see McKane, 1970, 608-9). Another possible meaning is that one's character is best revealed by the things one holds dear (Martin, 175; Walls, 568).

4. The name *ṣārᵉpat*, Zarephath, occurs in 1 Kgs 17:9-10 and Obad v. 20. Zarephath, modern *Ras ṣarafand*, was a town on the Phoenician coast about seven miles south of Sidon (see, e.g., J. Gray, 1970, 380; G. H. Jones, 305; de Vries, 217).

P-B The vb. occurs in both Heb. *ṣrp*, (smelt, melt, refine, purify, try; tighten, harden; change; pi. smelt; refine; tighten, harden; meld, weld, combine, join; ni. be smelted, tried; hitp. be joined, combined, counted in) and Aram. *ṣᵉrap*, *ṣᵉrêp* (smelt, refine, try; contract, sponge (cloth); pa. smelt, refine, torment; join, attach; mix earth with alum; ithpa. be joined; join). The following nom. forms occur: *ṣᵉrap*, junction (with adv. force, in immediate succession); *ṣārāpā'*, refining pot, crucible; *ṣārᵉpît*, the woman of Zarephath (another word, *ṣārᵉpît*, belonging to the goldsmith's shop, is also found); and *ṣārᵉpat*, Zarephath (Jastrow 2:1303-4).

Gold: → *'ôpîr* (gold of Ophir, # 234); → *beṣer* I (gold ore, # 1309); → *zāhāb* (gold, # 2298); → *ḥārûṣ* I (gold, # 3021); → *ketem* (gold, # 4188); → *sāgûr* (pure gold, # 6034); → *paz* (pure gold, # 7058; *pzz* I, set w. pure gold, # 7059); → *ṣrp* (melt, smelt, refine, # 7671)
Melting, dissolution: → *dônag* (wax [metaphor for melting], # 1880); → *mwg* (melt, reel, waver, lose courage, # 4570); → *mss* (lose courage, melt, become weak, # 5022); → *msh* (melt, drench, # 4998); → *šyḥ* (melt away, be in despair, # 8863)
Test, trial, discipline: → *bḥn* (test, # 1043); → *nsh* (test, train, exercise, # 5814); → *ṣrp* (smelt, refine, test, # 7671); → *twh* II (trouble, provoke, # 9345)

BIBLIOGRAPHY

TDOT 4:30-32; E. A. Achtemeier, *Jeremiah*, 1987; P. R. Ackroyd, "The Book of Isaiah," in *The Interpreter's One-Volume Commentary on the Bible*, 1971, 329-71; L. C. Allen, *Psalms 101-150*, WBC, 1983; A. A. Anderson, *The Book of Psalms. Volume I: Introduction and Psalms 1-72*, NCBC, 1972; H. T. Andrews, "Daniel," in *Peake*, 1920, 522-33; J. G. Baldwin, *Daniel: An Introduction and Commentary*, TOTC, 1978; idem, *1 and 2 Samuel: An Introduction and Commentary*, 1988; T. M. Bennett, "Malachi," in *BBC*, 1972, 7:366-94; A. A. Bevan, *A Short Commentary on the Book of Daniel*, 1892; J. Blenkinsopp, *Ezra-Nehemiah: A Commentary*, OTL, 1988; L. Boadt, *Jeremiah 1-25*, OTM, 1982; R. G. Bratcher and W. D. Reyburn, *A Translator's Handbook on the Book of Psalms*, 1991; M. Buttenwieser, *The Psalms Chronologically Treated With a New Translation*, 1969; R. H. Charles, *The Book of Daniel*, CB, 1913; R. E. Clements, *Jeremiah*, Interpretation, 1988; R. J. Clifford, "Isaiah 40-66," in *HBC*, 1988, 571-96; J. J. Collins, *Daniel With an Introduction to Apocalyptic Literature*, FOTL, 1984; idem, *A Commentary on the Book of Daniel*, Hermeneia, 1993; P. C. Craigie, *Psalms 1-50*, WBC, 1983; A. E. Cundall, "Judges: An Introduction and Commentary," in *Judges and Ruth*, TOTC, 1973; M. Dahood, *Psalms I: 1-50. Introduction, Translation, and Notes*, AB, 1966; idem, *Psalms III: 101-150*, AB, 1970; R. Davidson, *Jeremiah Volume 2 and Lamentations*, 1985; idem, *Jeremiah. Volume 1*, 1986; F. Delitzsch, *Biblical Commentary on the Psalms. Vol. III*, KD, 2d ed., 1885;

S. R. Driver, *The Book of Daniel With Introduction and Notes*, 1922; J. R. Dummelow, ed., *A Commentary on the Holy Bible*, 1909; B. Glazier-McDonald, *Malachi: The Divine Messenger*, 1987; J. E. Goldingay, *Daniel*, WBC, 1989; G. B. Gray, *A Critical and Exegetical Commentary on the Book of Isaiah I-XXVII*, ICC, 1975; J. Gray, *Joshua, Judges and Ruth*, NCBC, 1967; idem, *I & II Kings: A Commentary*, OTL, 2d, rev. ed., 1970; J. L. Green, "Jeremiah," in *BBC*, 1972, 6:1-202; L. Hoppe, *Joshua, Judges With an Excursus on Charismatic Leadership in Israel*, 1982; A. Jeffery, "The Book of Daniel: Introduction and Exegesis," *IB*, 1956, 6:339-549; D. R. Jones, "Isaiah—II and III," in *Peake*, 1964, 516-36; G. H. Jones, *1 and 2 Kings. Volume II: 1 Kings 17:1-2 Kings 25:30*, NCBC, 1984; O. Kaiser, *Isaiah 1-12: A Commentary*, OTL, 1977; O. Keel, *The Symbolism of the Biblical World: Ancient Near Eastern Iconography and the Book of Psalms*, 1978; A. F. Kirkpatrick, *The Book of Psalms*, CBSC, 1957; E. J. Kissane, *The Book of Isaiah Translated From a Critically Revised Hebrew Text With Commentary. Vol. 1 (I-XXXIX)*, 1960; G. A. F. Knight, *The Psalms. Volume 1*, DSB,1982; idem, *Servant Theology: A Commentary on the Book of Isaiah 40-55*, ITC, 1984; H.-J. Kraus, *Psalms 60-150: A Commentary*, 1989; W. McKane, *Proverbs: A New Approach*, OTL, 1970; idem, *A Critical and Exegetical Commentary on Jeremiah. Volume 1: An Introduction and Commentary on Jeremiah I-XXV*, ICC, 1986; J. L. McKenzie, *Second Isaiah: Introduction, Translation, and Notes*, AB, 1968; G. C. Martin, *Proverbs, Ecclesiastes and Song of Songs*, 1908; H. G. May and B. M. Metzger, eds., *The New Oxford Annotated Bible*, 1973; J. L. Mays, *Psalms*, Interpretation, 1994; J. A. Montgomery, *A Critical and Exegetical Commentary on the Book of Daniel*, ICC, 1964; G. F. Moore, *A Critical and Exegetical Commentary on Judges*, ICC, 2d ed., 1918; J. Muilenburg, "The Book of Isaiah Chapters 40-66: Introduction and Exegesis," in *IB*, 1956, 5:381-773; C. R. North, *The Second Isaiah: Introduction, Translation and Commentary to Chapters XL-LV*, 1967; M. O'Connor, "Judges," in *NJBC*, 1990, 132-44; W. O. E. Oesterley, *The Psalms Translated With Text-Critical and Exegetical Notes*, 1959; A. Robinson, "God the Refiner of Silver," *CBQ* 11, 1949, 188-90; J. W. Rogerson and J. W. McKay, *Psalms 1-50*, 1977 (1977a); idem, *Psalms 101-150*, 1977 (1977b); J. F. A. Sawyer, *Isaiah. Volume 2*, DSB, 1986; R. B. Y. Scott, *Proverbs, Ecclesiastes: Introduction, Translation, and Notes*, AB, 1965; J. Scullion, *Isaiah 40-66*, OTM, 1982; J. Skinner, *The Book of the Prophet Isaiah Chapters I-XXXIX*, WBSC, 1909; R. L. Smith, *Micah-Malachi*, WBC, 1984; C. Stuhlmueller, *Psalms 1 (Psalms 1-72)*, OTM, 1985; S. J. de Vries, *1 Kings*, WBC, 1985; A. F. Walls, "Proverbs," in *NBC*, 1972, 548-69; W. L. Wardle, "Isaiah XL-LXVI," in *Peake*, 1920, 460-73; J. D. W. Watts, *Isaiah 34-66*, WBC, 1987; A. Weiser, *The Psalms: A Commentary*, OTL, 1965; C. Westermann, *Isaiah 40-66: A Commentary*, OTL, 1969; O. C. Whitehouse, *Isaiah I-XXXIX*, CB, 1905; idem, *Isaiah XL-LXVI*, CB, 1908; H. G. M. Williamson, *Ezra, Nehemiah*, WBC, 1985.

Robin Wakely

7672 (*ṣōrpî*, goldsmith's guild), → # 7671

7674	צרר

צרר (*ṣrr* I), A trans.: q. bind, tie up, wrap, shut up; pu. be tied up. B intrans.: q. be narrow, scant, cramped, impeded, restricted, in straits, distress, tribulation; hi. make narrow, press hard, cause distress to, hamper, besiege (# 7674); מֵצַר (*mēṣar*), nom. straits, distress, affliction, oppression (# 5210); צַר (*ṣar* I), adj. narrow, tight, scarce; nom. narrowness, tight corner, adversity, anguish, fear, alarm, anxiety (# 7639); צָרָה (*ṣārâ* I), nom. misery, anguish, anxiety, distress, dismay, plight, affliction, calamity, hardship, trouble, oppression, fear, fright, terror (# 7650); צְרוֹר (*ṣ*[e]*rôr* I), bundle (→ # 7655).

ANE The vb. is found in Syr. *ṣar;* Arab. *ṣarra,* lace/cord up, bind, tie, chain, knot; Akk. *ṣarārum,* envelop, wrap; and OSA *ṣr,* close, press in/upon, vex, harass. The nom. occurs in Akk. *ṣerretu(m),* guide rope, leash, bridle; Ugar. *mṣrrt*, wrap; OSA *ṣr*; Tigre *ṣarra*, tie up (the udder of a camel).

OT 1. The verbal, nominal, and adjectival forms express the opposite idea from that conveyed by those words that denote spaciousness and that are applied either literally to physical dimensions or metaphorically to human experiences in contexts of physical danger, psychological anxiety, or spiritual distress (Sawyer). The forms derived from *ṣrr* are applied to any kind of restricting, claustrophobic experience. Thus, the q. is used of the distress caused by military defeat (e.g., Judg 2:15; 10:9) and near revolt (1 Sam 30:6); the frustration of an individual tortured by unsatisfied lust (2 Sam 13:2); the foreboding and uncertainty experienced in response to an approaching danger (Gen 32:7[8]); the anxiety suffered by the unscrupulous, avaricious person who undergoes a radical reversal of fortune at the very summit of success (Job 20:22); the fear, frustration, and cramped progress of one who rejects the unimpeded path of wisdom and righteousness in favor of folly and wickedness, which lead only to restriction, darkness, and death (Prov 4:12; cf. Job 18:7).

Especially in the Psalms the distress caused by personal foes is indicated. The distress of the psalmist often prompts a cry (→ *lḥṣ*; # 4315) to God for deliverance (Ps 18:6[7]; 34:17[18]; 102:1-2[2-3]; 106:44). Personal circumstances of individuals also cause distress, e.g., the death of a beloved friend (2 Sam 1:26), the suffering of the righteous and God's incomprehensible treatment of them (Job 7:11), obsessive passion (2 Sam 13:2), fear of death (Gen 42:21), etc. The distress expressed in these texts is commonly an indication of God's judgment of his unfaithful people (Judg 2:15; Isa 5:30; Jer 10:18; Hos 5:15). God, however, is also the one who delivers the anguished and distressed who do not renounce their faith in him (Gen 35:3; Ps 37:39; 50:15; Isa 25:4). Furthermore, in Prov 11:8; 12:13 it is stated that the righteous man, who follows the ways of wisdom, is safeguarded against distress (*ṣārâ*).

2. Affliction (which also includes a wide range of concepts such as hurt, injury, oppression, violence, wrong) in the OT is expressed by a significant number of Heb. words. It occurs broadly on two levels. First, there is affliction at an international level, viz., of a weaker nation by a powerful nation. This form of affliction contributes to the theme of OT salvation history when it is used by God to punish the unfaithfulness of Israel and make them an obedient people. Second, there is affliction within the community, viz., social injustice perpetrated by a certain group in society, but also including individual acts inflicted on one's fellow human being. The Heb. words for affliction describe both external (physical) and internal (psychological) forms of affliction. However, the OT does not primarily have in mind "spiritual affliction." The victims suffer exploitation, physical torture, and death. But these people may also be the objects of God's deliverance: the usage of the various Heb. words shows that the OT theology of affliction and oppression is in its innermost nature not humanistic or horizontal. Although the words for affliction also reflect the theological problem of a God who afflicts the suffering righteous one, he is more characteristically experienced as the personal, infinite God who hears the prayers and cries of the afflicted and delivers them out of their distress, or who undertakes to deliver them in the age to come.

3. The hi. is used of someone pressing another person hard, either by oppression or by siege (Deut. 28:52 [twice]; 1 Kgs 8:37; 2 Chron 28:20, 22 [cf. NEB and REB]; Jer 10:18). It is also applied to the acute distress induced by a troubled conscience (2 Chron 33:12) or by the disciplinary judgment of God (Neh 9:27; Zeph 1:17).

4. In several cases, the nom. *ṣar* is linked with other words that denote calamity of one kind or another (e.g., Job 38:23; Ps 107:6, 13, 19, 28; 119:143; Isa 5:30). The nom. suggests narrowness, constriction, physical and/or mental claustrophobia, being hemmed in by enemies or by circumstances, as opposed to "width" (from *rḥb*, be or grow wide/large [→ # 8143]), which conveys the idea of space, freedom of movement and thought, and well-being. In Ps 4:1[2], the psalmist says: "I was pressed hard, and thou didst set me at large" (NEB [cf. REB; RSV], taking *hirḥabtā* as an ordinary perfect rather than a precative or optative perfect [on which, see NIV; Dahood, 23; Anderson, 77; Craigie, 78]). The psalmist bases his confidence in Yahweh's ability and willingness to liberate him from oppression on his past experience of having been rescued from a tight corner. As C. A. and E. G. Briggs (30; cf. Davison, 56-57) comment: "Distress is here a being constrained into narrow limits; pressed from rightful freedom, and shut in on every side. The antith. is the removal of such restraint and pressure, giving room and freedom."

5. The nom. *ṣar* is also used of the distress inflicted by God in response to faithlessness, failure, disobedience, obduracy, and rebellion (Deut 4:30; 1 Sam 2:32; 2 Chron 15:4; Ps 106:44). Such conduct leads to the distress of divine abandonment (Hos 5:15) and divine judgment (Isa 5:30). Paradoxically, however, the conviction on the part of those caught in the crucible of affliction that God is the author of the distress being experienced invariably goes hand in hand with the deep-seated belief that only God's saving grace, enduring love, and continuing covenant loyalty—not the worthless help of humankind (Ps 60:11[13]); 108:12[13]—can effect deliverance and transform anxiety and doubt into peace and confidence (e.g., Deut 4:30-31; 2 Chron 15:3-4; Ps 106:40-46, esp. v. 44). The immutably merciful God is a fortress and refuge for the needy in times of distress (Ps 59:16[17]; Isa 25:4), a protective hiding place preserving them from trouble and encompassing them with deliverance (Ps 32:7). The afflicted beg to be rescued from their torment (e.g., Ps 18:6[7] ‖ 2 Sam 22:7; Ps 102:2[3]), and those who are delivered from life-threatening situations celebrate their divinely engineered escapes in liturgies of praise and thanksgiving (e.g., Ps 66:13-15, esp. v. 14; 107:6, 13, 19, 28). In the abyss of despair, mortal danger, and even death (when, humanly speaking, deliverance is impossible), God can raise the faithful up and disperse with his glorious light the gloom that continually threatens to reverse the work of creation (Isa 26:16-19).

6. Of even greater theological significance, perhaps, are those passages that seem to indicate that God himself suffers whenever his people are in the throes of affliction. In a problematic text, Isa 63:9, the words *b^e^kol-ṣārātām lô'* [*Q*] *ṣār* are translated by RSV (cf. NEB; JB; NIV) as "in all their affliction he was afflicted," suggesting that the sufferers were saved by God's loving presence and compassionate participation in his people's affliction (see Fretheim, 146).

7. Like the masc. nom., the fem. nom. *ṣārâ* is frequently linked with other words denoting adversity (e.g., 2 Kgs 19:3; Prov 1:27; Isa 8:22; 30:6; Jer 15:11; 49:24; Obad 12-14; Jon 2:2[3]; Zeph 1:15-16) The word describes the tribulation and

resulting enfeeblement from which it is fervently hoped and/or confidently expected that God will deliver (e.g., 1 Sam 26:24; Job 5:19; Ps 25:22; 120:1; Isa 33:2). The consequences of being in *ṣārâ* are well described in Prov 24:10, where the nom. *ṣārâ* and the adj. *ṣar*, small (lit., narrow, tight) are juxtaposed: the limitations of a person's resources of physical endurance, mental strength, and moral courage will be exposed when one is tightly hemmed in by a critical, harrowing crisis (McKane, 400). The inveterately wicked, who refuse to repent, are warned that God will not respond to their cry when trouble overtakes them (Job 27:8-9; Ps 50; Isa 65:13-16; Nah 1:7-10). The majority of the faithful, on the other hand, express supreme confidence in the ability of God, their "ever-present help in trouble" (Ps 46:1[2]; cf. Jer 16:19), to effect deliverance in the present as he has in the past (e.g., Neh 9:26-37; Ps 71; 81:7[8]). God responds even to the cry for deliverance out of distress uttered by one who has already descended into "the depths of the grave" (Jon 2:2[3]). And when God intervenes in a time of adversity, the person whose innermost being is in straits experiences a liberation. The paraphrase "Make wide the straits of my heart" (Kraus, 322) well captures the meaning of Ps 25:17, where the word *hirḥîbû* (NIV [they have] multiplied) should almost certainly be emended to *harḥêb*, relieve (see, e.g., *BHS*, 1107; RSV; NEB; REB; JB). As Luther, quoted by Kraus, says: "As affliction is the narrow place that oppresses us and makes us sad, so God's help is the wide open space that makes us free and joyful."

8. What causes *ṣārâ*? Sometimes it is the inevitable result of forsaking God and breaking the covenant (Deut 31:17, 21). Frequently it is considered a chastening test, a form of corrective discipline used by God for an unimpeachable purpose and accepted by the sufferer as an educative spiritual training exercise (e.g., Job 5:17-19). Occasionally, sufferers engage in remorseful self-recrimination and acknowledge that their present plight is the inexorable result of their own sin (e.g., Gen 42:21).

9. In some laments, however, confession of disobedience and guilt fades into the background as supplicants, verging on panic and blasphemy, complain about God's seeming indifference to their particular crisis or his apparent inability to effect deliverance (e.g., Jer 14:8). Often, suffering is experienced as profound God-forsakenness (e.g., Ps 22:11[12]). In most cases, however, faith triumphs over despair. In Ps 9 and 10 (which, printed as a single psalm in the LXX, constitute a complex composition in terms of structure, mood, and genre), a psalmist is perplexed by a perennial problem: How can faith and confidence in a loving, just, and holy God be sustained when actual experience seems to show that justice is dormant, that those who have jettisoned faith and morality are secure and prosperous, and that the innocent poor and needy are not only ruthlessly exploited and oppressed by the wicked, but also abandoned in the hour of their distress (Ps 10:1) by the very one who is traditionally praised for being "a refuge for the oppressed, a stronghold in times of trouble" (Ps 9:9[10])? Somehow this psalmist is enabled to accept that Yahweh does indeed respond to the desire of the afflicted, empowering and defending them (Ps 10:17-18).

There are many other laments (e.g., Ps 31 and 77) in which the *deus absconditus* becomes the *deus revelatus* (Weiser, 532-33) for those in "distress" (31:7[8]; 77:2[3]). Passages (e.g., 37:39) that assure those dispirited by the injustices of the world that Yahweh really is a refuge for the afflicted righteous are neither philosophical discourses nor reasoned doctrinal statements. Rather, each is a testimony, a pastoral counsel, an aid to faith that seeks to sustain the righteous by assuring them that peace and confidence can be acquired only by cultivating the presence of God, trusting in him (37:3, 5), and committing one's way to him (37:5) in expectant hope (37:7, 9, 34). The twofold assurance that God's protective presence is with the brokenhearted and crushed in spirit (34:17-18[18-19]; 86:7) and that he equips the faithful with the necessary resources to cope with adversity (Gen 35:3; Ps 91:2, 15), may not inspire a sense of gratitude among the prosperous, untroubled, and lackadaisical (e.g., 1 Sam 10:19), but it does instill fresh courage and hope in the victimized of every generation.

10. An interesting use of the nom. *ṣārâ* is in the phrase *[bᵉyôm] ṣārâ*, "[in the day of] distress." In Ps 20, it is recognized that, at such a time (v. 1[2]), deliverance is wholly dependent on God's presence and participation (v. 7[8]; cf. 44:1-8 [2-9]). The term *yôm ṣārâ* is used of the imminent calamity to be inflicted by the warrior God not only on an enemy invader (Hab 3:16), but also on Israel (Zeph 1:15). Elsewhere, though, the assurance is given that while Israelites will suffer panic and pain in that day, God will eventually deliver them (Jer 30:7). In Dan 12:1, the promise is made that, after the great tribulation, Michael, Israel's patron prince, who fights its legal and military battles, will deliver all those whose names are recorded in the register of the saints (cf. Exod 32:32; Ps 69:28[29]; Isa 4:3; Mal 3:16; Phil 4:3; Rev 3:5; 13:8; 17:8; 20:12, 15; 21:27; 1 En 47:3; 81:1-2; 103:2; 108:3). The words "a time of distress such as has not happened from the beginning" (Dan 12:1) became the classic description of the last times (1 Macc 9:27; Asm. M. 8:1; Matt 24:21; Mark 13:19; cf., Exod 9:18; Rev 16:18).

11. The nom. *mēṣar* occurs in Lam 1:3, where the phrase *bên hammᵉṣārîm*, "in the midst of her distress," describes how the exiles are like hunted animals pursued and cornered in a narrow space with no possibility of escape. In Ps 118:5, God is thanked for substituting an individual's chokingly restricted "anguish" with the broad, roomy place of freedom. Ps 116 relates how one entangled by the cords of death and ensnared in the *mᵉṣārê šᵉ'ôl* (v. 3), the constricting pangs or nooses of Sheol, while despairing of humankind (v. 11), clung steadfastly to his faith in the Lord (v. 10), who led him into the land of the living (v. 9) and loosed the chains that bound him (v. 16). See further # 5210.

P-B 1. This group of words is frequently used in QL to express the distress of the community. As in the OT these words also represent the psychological side of affliction, caused by individual (personal) foes (cf. the OT Psalms) (1QH 5:12; 9:28; 15:16), the Angel of Darkness (1QS 3:23), and military foes (1QM 10:7; 1QpHab 5:6). In other postbiblical Jewish texts, the verbal, nominative, and adjectival forms are all well attested: Heb. *ṣārar*, q. surround, wrap, tie up, be narrow, be distressed, worry; hi. be distressed, worry, feel sorry, distress, oppress, persecute, narrow, close; ho. become distressing, be painful; ni. be tied up, gathered; Aram. *ṣᵉrar*, tie up, enclose; *ṣar* and *ṣārâ*, adj. narrow, and nom. anguish, trouble, distress, persecution, oppressor, adversary; *ṣērûr*, nom. enmity; *ṣᵉrôr*, nom. knot, bundle, bag; *mēṣar*, *mêṣar*, nom. narrow pass, distress (Jastrow 2:828, 1299, 1300, 1305).

2. The many Heb. words in the semantic field of affliction in the OT are rendered in the LXX by a great number of G words (see E. Hatch and H. A. Redpath, *A Concordance to the Septuagint and the Other Greek Versions of the Old Testament,* 1897; Supplements by H. A. Redpath, 1900-1906). The words *thlibō* and *thlipsis,* especially, merit further comment since they are the common rendering for several Heb.

words for affliction, especially *ṣrr,* be distressed; *lḥṣ,* press; *ṣārâ,* anguish; *ṣar,* anguish; *laḥaṣ,* oppression, but also *ynh,* be violent; *ṣwq,* distress; *'šq,* wrong; *rṣṣ,* crush; *m^eṣûqâ,* stress; *māṣôq,* hardship; *'ōšeq,* extortion; *'āqâ,* misery. These Heb. words are thus in some sense formally unified in the LXX by their common rendering with *thlibō* and *thlipsis* (*TDNT* 3:140-43).

NT In the NT the tribulation (*thlipsis*) of Israel and of the individual righteous in the OT has become the tribulation of the church and of the apostles (1 Cor 4:9-13; 1 Thess 3:3-4) in the eschatological period. This tribulation is the suffering of Christ borne in solidarity with him (2 Cor 4:10-12; Col 1:24; 1 Peter 2:21) and is a necessary prelude to the kingdom (Acts 14:22). In God's plan of salvation it produces perseverance and hope (Rom 5:3-5). In the last judgment, *thlipsis* will be the destiny of the unrighteous (Rom 2:9) and of those who bring *thlipsis* upon the church (2 Thess 1:6; *NIDNTT* 2:808-9; *TDNT* 3:143-48).

NT → *NIDNTT* 2:805-9; 3:719-25.

Despair, discouragement, grief, trouble: → *'āgēm* (sad, grieved, distressed, # 108); → *y'š* (despair, be hopeless, # 3286); → *mwg* (melt, reel, waver, lose courage, # 4570); → *mss* (waste away, melt, dissolve, lose courage, # 5022); → *'gm* (be afflicted, distressed, grieved, # 6327); → *ṣwq* I (constrain, press in/upon, harass, vex, # 7439); → *ṣrr* I (bind, shut up, be narrow, in straits, distress, # 7674); → *mwg* (melt, reel, waver, lose courage, # 4570); → *qṣr* II (be short, be/become discouraged, worn out, # 7918); → *rph* (become slack, lose heart, discourage, # 8332); → *šyḥ* (melt away, be in despair, # 8863)

Affliction, oppression: → *dḥq* (oppress, # 1895); → *ḥms* I (do violence, # 2803); → *ḥmṣ* II (oppress, # 2807); → *ynh* (oppress, # 3561); → *lḥṣ* (press, # 4315); → *māṣôr* I (affliction, siege, # 5189); → *mrr* I (be bitter, distraught, afflict, # 5352); → *nega'* (plague, affliction, # 5596); → *ngś* (exact, # 5601); → *'nh* II (afflict, humble, afflict one's soul, fast, oppress, submit, # 6700); → *'wq* I (crush?, # 6421); → *'mr* II (deal tyrannically with, # 6683); → *'šq* I (wrong, # 6943); → *ṣwq* I (constrain, press in/upon, harass, vex, # 7439); → *ṣwr* II (deal tyrannically with, # 7444); → *rhb* (assail, press, pester, alarm, confuse, # 8104); → *rṣṣ* (crush, # 8368); → *tôlāl* (oppressor, # 9354); → *tōk* (oppression, # 9412)

BIBLIOGRAPHY

THAT 2:582-83; *TWOT* 2:778-79; W. F. Albright, "Palestinian Inscriptions," in *ANET*, 1969, 320-22; A. A. Anderson, *The Book of Psalms. Volume 1: Introduction and Psalms 1-72,* 1972; C. A. and E. G. Briggs, *A Critical and Exegetical Commentary on the Book of Psalms,* 1, 1960; B. S. Childs, *Exodus: A Commentary,* 1974; R. A. Cole, *Exodus: An Introduction and Commentary,* 1973; P. C. Craigie, *Psalms 1-50,* 1983; M. Dahood, *Psalms I: 1-50. Introduction, Translation, and Notes,* 1966; W. T. Davison, *The Psalms: I-LXXII,* n.d.; E. Dhorme, *A Commentary on the Book of Job,* 1967; T. E. Fretheim, *The Suffering of God: An Old Testament Perspective,* 1984; T. D. Hanks, *God So Loved the Third World: The Biblical Vocabulary of Oppression,* 1983, 3-39; Y. I. Kim, "The Vocabulary of Oppression in the Old Testament," Ph.D. diss. Drew University, 1981; A. F. Kirkpatrick, *The Book of Psalms,* 1957; H.-J. Kraus, *Psalms 1-59: A Commentary,* 1988; C. F. Marriottini, "The Problem of Social Oppression in the Eighth Century Prophets," Ph.D. diss. Southern Baptist Theological Seminary, 1983; W. McKane, *Proverbs: A New Approach,* 1970; J. Miranda, *Communism in the Bible*, 1982, 37-39; J. Pons, *L'oppression dans l'Ancien Testament,* 1981; J. F. A. Sawyer, "Spaciousness: An Important Feature of Language about Salvation in the Old Testament," *ASTI* 6, 1967-68, 20-34; E. Tamez, *Bible of the*

Oppressed, 1982, 1-30; A. Weiser, *The Psalms: A Commentary,* 1965; H. W. Wolff, *Anthropology of the Old Testament,* 1974.

I. Swart/Robin Wakely

7675	צרר

צרר (*ṣrr* II), q. be hostile (# 7675); nom. צָר (*ṣār* II), adversary (# 7640); צָרָה (*ṣārâ* IIA), rival wife (# 7651); צָרָה (*ṣārâ* IIB), enmity (# 7650).

ANE Cognates occur in Ugar. *ṣrr*, hurt; Akk. *ṣerru*, enemy; and Arab. *ḍarra*, inflict harm; cf. Geez *'aḍrärä*, show hostility; *'aḍḍrār*, enemy.

OT 1. The root appears in OT contexts in the standard fashion discussed under *'yb*, be an enemy (→ # 366). Many of the data given there are drawn from this root. Thus, whether nom. or vb., it is used of Israel's enemies (Num 10:9; 25:17-18; cf. Ps 129:1-2), from whom God gave deliverance (Ps 44:7[8]). Key to such deliverance was Israel's obedience and prayer to God (1 Kgs 8:37-40; 2 Chron 6:28-31; Neh 9:26-27). In addition, the root is employed of human enemies of the individual (2 Sam 24:13; Job 6:23), from whom God can be implored for deliverance (2 Chron 33:12; Ps 27:2, 12).

God is also said to have enemies (Deut 32:41-43) on whom he vents his righteous wrath (Nah 1:2). The enemies of an obedient Israel can be God's (Ps 78:42), but a disobedient Israel could find that God had become its enemy (Isa 1:24-26; Ezek 39:23). Ultimately, God will deal with all his enemies in that eschatological day when he restores the fortunes of his people (Isa 11:10-16; Zeph 1:14-18).

2. The part. form *ṣōrēr* is similarly used, whether of God's wicked (Ps 10:5) individual enemies (Ps 8:2 [3]) or those of his people (Exod 23:22; Ps 74:4, 22-23). It is often employed of the psalmist's enemies (e.g., Ps 31:11-13 [12-14]), who find occasion to demean God himself (42:10 [11]; 143:11-12). Nevertheless, the psalmist takes comfort in the God of all provision (23:5) and deliverance (6:7 [8]).

3. The nom. *ṣārâ* (cf. Syr. *'artā'*; Arab. *ḍarratun*) is used once of a rival wife (1 Sam 1:6; cf. Lev 18:18) and occurs 3x with the sense "adversary" (Ps 57:7 [9]; 138:7; 143:11-12). All three cases are conjectural, however, the meaning being assigned on the basis of a term for foe in the parallel member.

Animosity, enmity, hostility: → *'yb* (be an enemy, # 366); → *ṣrr* II (be hostile, # 7675); → *śṭm* (hate, # 8475); → *śāṭān* (accuser, satan, # 8477); → *śn'* (hate, one who is an enemy, # 8533); → *šôrēr* (adversary, # 8806); → **Animosity: Theology**

BIBLIOGRAPHY

THAT 2:582-83

Bruce Baloian

ק

7683 (*qēʼ*, vomit), → # 7794

7684 (*qāʼat*, desert owl), → # 7606

7685 (*qab*, kab), → # 406

7686	קבב

קבב (*qbb*), curse (# 7686); נקב (*nqḇ*), curse (→ # 5918).

OT The vbs. *qbb* and *nqb* are evidently byforms, with the only certain occurrences of the latter in Lev 24:16, in connection with blaspheming the name of God. Eight of the occurrences of *qbb* feature in Balaam's attempted cursing of Israel as described in Num 22-24.

NT → *NIDNTT* 1:413-18

Curse: → *ʼlh* I (swear, curse, put under oath, # 457); → *ʼrr* (curse, be cursed, # 826); → *brk* (bless [euph. for curse], # 1385a); → *gdp* (revile, blaspheme, # 1552); → *zʻm* (be angry, curse, # 2404); → *nqb* (pierce, bore, distinguish, curse, # 5918); → *qbb* (curse, # 7686); → *qll* (be slight, swift, appear trifling, treat with contempt, # 7837); → **Curse: Theology**

BIBLIOGRAPHY

S. H. Blank, "The Curse, Blasphemy, the Spell, and the Oath," *HUCA* 23/1, 1950-51, 73-95; H. C. Brichto, *The Problem of "Curse" in the Hebrew Bible*, 1963; T. G. Crawford, *Blessing and Curse in Syro-Palestinian Inscriptions of the Iron Age*, 1992.

Robert P. Gordon

7687	קֵבָה

קֵבָה (*qēbâ*), belly, maw (# 7687).

OT The basic meaning of the word is "cavity" or "hollow" (*WTM* 4:233), and it is used of the "rennet stomach" of ruminants (Deut 18:3), which was to be the share of the priest (see Mish. Ḥullin 10:1; BTalm Ḥullin 130a).

Abdomen, belly: → *ʼûl* (belly, body, # 214); → *beṭen* I (belly, # 1061); → *gāḥôn* (belly [of a reptile], # 1623); → *ḥōmeš* II (belly, # 2824); → *kārēś* (belly [of an animal], # 4160); → *mēʻeh* (body, bowels, # 5055); → *qēbâ* (belly, maw, # 7687); → *šōr* (navel, umbilical cord, # 9219)

Bibliography
A. Murtonen, *Hebrew in its West Semitic Setting*. Part One: A *Comparative Lexicon* Section Ba: *Root System: Hebrew Material*, 1988.

Cleon L. Rogers, Jr.

7688	קֻבָּה

קֻבָּה (*qubbâ*), nom. vaulted tent, women's quarters (# 7688).

ANE Cognates appear in several ANE languages. The Arab. *qubbâ* was a portable shrine, a much smaller version of the Israelite "Tent of Meeting." The Latin *cupola* (dim. of *cupa)* may also be etymologically related.

OT The nom. appears only in Num 25:8, where Phinehas follows an Israelite man who had taken a Midianite woman into the *qubbâ* and kills the two of them. The text seems to imply that it was a marital tent, a special dwelling set aside for newlyweds (Morgenstern, 260; Milgrom, 215). The dwelling may also have had some cultic significance, as with the Arab. *qubbâ*, so that the Israelite man's sin was not only intermarriage, but also apostasy (a state frequently associated with intermarriage; cf. Deut 7:3-4; 1 Kgs 11:1-4). A probable wordplay appears in the MT, linking the *qubbâ*, in which the couple enters, with the belly, *qēbâ*, through which the two are pierced; *BHS*, however, suggests a textual corruption here.

P-B The nom. is used in RL of a vaulted-roof tent, to which the heavens are compared in Ta'anit 8b. It designates an arch shape in Menaḥot 31b. It is also used, probably under the influence of Num 25:8, of a tent of prostitution (Abodah Zerah 17b).

Tent, curtain: → *'ōhel* (tent, tent-dweller, # 185); → *y^erî'â* (curtain, tent fabric, # 3749); → *yātēd* (peg, pin, nail, # 3845); → *qubbâ* (vaulted tent, women's quarters, # 7688); → *ś^emîkâ* (curtain, covering, # 8526); → *šaprîr* (state-tent?, # 9188)

Bibliography
IDB 2:4; R. K. Harrison, *Numbers*, 1990, 337-38; J. Milgrom, *Numbers,* 1990; J. Morgenstern, "The Ark, the Ephod, and the 'Tent of Meeting'," *HUCA* 17, 1942/3, 153-266, and 18, 1944, 1-45.

Anthony Tomasino

7689 (*qibbûṣ*, collection), → # 7695

7690 (*q^ebûrâ*, grave, burial), → # 7699

7691	קבל

קבל (*qbl*), pi. receive, take; hi. be opposite (# 7691).

ANE *qbl* is widespread in other Sem. languages but occurs much less in the HB (OT) than *lqḥ*. Akk.; Sabean: as a vb.: accept; Sabean: as a prep: in view of (cf. Corpus Inscript Semiticorum: IV, no. 79, 11.2.3.5.8); Arab.: *qabila*, be in front, opposite; *qabala*, accept, admit; Eth., esp. III. 2: go to meet, accept.

OT 1. The vb. occurs 14x, mostly in the pi., which have the following for objects: discipline, *mussār* (Prov 19:20); a gift (Esth 4:4); donation (8:30); blood (subj. priests)

(2 Chron 29:22); unclean things (29:16); newcomers (1 Chron 12:18[19]); good (*ṭôb*), trouble (*rāʿ*) as in Job 2:10, "Shall we accept good from God, and not trouble?" Theologically, Job's correction of his wife's advice is meaningful as a reminder that trust in the Lord must be total and submissive regardless of his circumstances. "The verb ... describes an active, positive participation in what God decrees, not mere passive reception" (Hartley, 84).

One may also accept or assume an obligation (Esth 9:23, 28 [+ *ʿal* reflex.]) or take in the sense of making a choice (1 Chron 21:11).

2. *qbl* occurs only twice in the hi. in the OT, in the form of a fem. part. with the meaning to be directly opposite, one to the other/to correspond to (Exod 26:5); curtain loops of the tabernacle (36:12).

P-B Heb.: accuse; Aram.: as preposition: *(l)q^ebîl* in front; Bib. Aram.: *l^eqābēl* before; Old Aram./Palmyrene *lqbl*, over against; Nab., over against; in view of (cf. Corpus Inscript. Semiticorum: IV, no 79, II.2.4.5.8.).

Receiving: → *ḥth* (take, fetch, # 3149); → *lqḥ* (take, grasp, be removed, # 4374); → *qbl* (receive, take, # 7691)

P. J. J. S. Els

7692	קְבֹל

קְבֹל (*q^ebōl*), nom. battering ram (# 7692).

OT This word occurs in Ezek 26:9 in the description of Nebuchadn(r)ezzar's siege of Tyre. The absolute form has been vocalized either as *q^ebōl* or *qōbel* (*HALAT* 993; BL, 582). Battering ram (cf. Vg. *arietes*; see also Y. Yadin, *The Art of Warfare in Biblical Lands in the Light of Archaeological Study,* 1963, 390-93) fits the context of a siege instrument that strikes against walls. LXX ("before you") may have read the Aram. *q^obēl* (in front of, before), and some LXX manuscripts have a similar translation in the only other occurrence, 2 Kgs 15:10 (cf. "before [the] people" AV; "in public" NRSV). However, an Aram. meaning is unlikely, and we would expect an article before *ʿām*, people. Other conspiracy accounts make us expect a note of the place of assassination, so most consider this a textual error for "at Ibleam" (cf. 2 Kgs 9:27), although T. R. Hobbs (*2 Kings,* 1985, 196) argues for an unknown Kabal-am.

Siege: → *m^eḥî* (shock, blow, # 4693); → *ṣwr* I (besiege, enclose, # 7443); → *q^ebōl* (battering-ram, # 7692)

P. Jenson

7694 (*qubbaʿat*, cup, bowl), → # 3998

7695	קבץ

קבץ (*qbṣ*), q. and pi. gather; ni. and pu., be gathered; hitp. gather together (# 7695); קִבּוּץ (*qibbûṣ*), collection (Isa 57:3; # 7689); קְבֻצָה (*q^ebuṣâ*), gathering (hapleg. in Ezek 22:20; # 7697).

ANE Ugar. *qbṣ* is used for an assembly (*KTU* 1.15:3:15). Cognates exist in Arab. *qabaḍa*, take, and Eth. *qabṣa*, draw together.

OT The word is used in the OT some 127x (perhaps 129x, cf. J. F. A. Sawyer, *THAT* 2:584), occurring in q., ni., pi., pu., and hitp. The vb. *qbṣ*, gather, has a wide range of usages (*THAT* 2:583-86). It is used for the collecting of the grain by Joseph for the coming lean years of famine (Gen 41:35, 48), the gathering of animals (Isa 34:15-16; Ezek 39:17), money for the repair of the temple (2 Chron 24:5), immoral grants (Mic 1:7), and the plunder obtained from cities worshiping idols (Deut 13:16[17]). People are gathered, referring to the sons of Jacob (Gen 49:2), Judah in distress (2 Chron 20:4), foreign nations, and Israel when the idols are rejected (Isa 45:20; 48:14).

1. Generally the subject of the vb. in q. is not God but human beings, which stands in contrast to the subject in pi. (Mommer, *TWAT* 6:1146).

(a) There are only 3x where the q. has God as the subject (Ezek 22:19, 20; Zeph 3:8). In Ezek 22:19-20 God says that because Israel has become dross and are like the copper, tin, iron, and lead gathered into a furnance, he will gather them into Jerusalem and in his anger and wrath melt them! Zeph 3:8 is another prophecy concerning God's judgment, but this time God says, "I have decided to assemble the nations, to gather the kingdoms and to pour out my fierce anger" (NIV). Here it is used parallel with *'sp*, which also means "to gather." In each passage the right of God to exercise judgment is stressed. He will judge his people, for they have rebelled and broken the stipulations of the Mosaic covenant. He will, however, gather the nations who oppose Jerusalem together for judgment.

(b) There are numerous usages of the word with a human being as the subject (see *HALAT* 994). (i) There is the gathering of things, such as the gathering of grain (Gen 41:35, 48), the gathering of spoils of an idolatrous town to destroy it (Deut 13:16[17]), the gathering of silver (money NIV) for the repair of the temple (2 Chron 24:5), and the gathering of possessions (Prov 13:11, money NIV; 28:8, wealth NIV). (ii) There is the gathering of people for various reasons. Generally, it is a group that has common qualifications or common interest (Mommer, *TWAT* 6:1146; see Jenni, 186). Men were gathered together for military reasons (Judg 12:4; 1 Sam 28:1, 4; 29:1; 2 Sam 2:30; 3:21; 1 Kgs 20:1; 2 Kgs 6:24; 2 Chron 25:5; 32:6). People were gathered for political reasons (1 Sam 8:4; 2 Sam 3:21; 1 Chron 11:1), for work on the walls (Neh 5:16), for social/political reasons (Esth 2:3), and for religious reasons (1 Kgs 18:19, 20; 2 Kgs 10:18; 2 Chron 15:9; 18:5; Joel 2:16).

2. The ni. usages are either reflexive (to assemble oneself) or passive (to be gathered) (see Siebesma, *The Function of the Niph'al in Biblical Hebrew*, 1991); the reflexive is predominant (Mommer, *TWAT* 6:1146; BDB, 867; but see *HALAT* 994-95).

3. Although there are some examples of the pi. with human beings as the subject (Isa 13:14; 22:9; 62:9; Nah 3:18; Hos 9:6; Mic 1:7), the majority of the passages have God as the subject and have to do with God's restoration of Israel to the Land of Promise (Jenni, *Pi'el*, 187-88). It is Deut 30:1-10 (compare 4:25-31) that forms the basis for the prophetic proclamation that God will scatter his people, but will again gather them into the land that he had given them (see Weinfeld, *Deuteronomy and the Deuteronomic School*, 346-61, 366-70; Sehmsdorf, "Studien zur Redaktionsgeschichte von Jesaia 56-66 (1)," 517-62, esp. 547-49). In connection with the covenant promises and the covenant curses, Moses speaks of the time when the curses of the Law will

come upon Israel because of disobedience (Deut 30:1-4). The curses of the Mosaic covenant will lead to the banishment of Israel from the land, but the covenant promises of the Abrahamic covenant will bring them back, and they will experience the blessings of the new covenant (Deut 30:6). The concepts connected with *qbṣ* in the pi., when used of God's gathering Israel, are "covenant (Mosaic)," "covenant curse," specifically, *ndḥ*, to scatter, to drive away (*HALAT* 636), *pwṣ*, to scatter (*HALAT* 868). Note also *'zb*, forsake (see Mommer 6:1148). Other words indicate the return, bringing back, or gathering of those expelled from the land; for example: *lqḥ min*, to take from; *'sp*, gather; *bw'*, bring back (hi.); *šwb*, return, cause to return, to bring back (hi.). Note also *nṣl*, rescue; *yṣ'*, lead out; *yš'*, save (see Mommer 6:1148). The place "from" which they are brought and the land "to" which they are gathered round out the accompanying ideas. Such words are used to describe the process of covenant punishment and restoration.

Isaiah uses the word a number of times in the pi. within the context of bringing Israel back into the land (Isa 43:5; 54:7; 56:8; Jer 31:8, 10; Mic 2:12; 4:6; cf. also Deut 30:3-4; Isa 49:18; 60:4). In Isa 11:12 Yahweh says he will reach out a second time and "will assemble the scattered people of Judah from the four quarters of the earth" (NIV). Although some have viewed this as referring to the return of the captives from Babylon, others have suggested that the passage refers to the final gathering of Israel by the Messiah.

The tender picture of a shepherd gathering the lambs in his arms and carrying them close to his heart is found in Isa 40:11 (see also Jer 31:10; Ezek 34:13; 37:21; Zeph 3:20; Mic 2:12), which could refer to the return from Babylon or to a future gathering (Mommer, *TWAT* 6:1148).

Isa 43:5 speaks of Yahweh's "gathering" his people from the around the world, from the east, west, north, and south. In 54:5-7 the prophet uses the picture of marriage. The Lord has put away Israel because of unfaithfulness, but this was not a permanent situation, for he will "gather her" back with great compassion (see 56:8). In Ezek 11:17 the prophet conveys the message of the Lord to his people just before he sees the "glory of the LORD" leave the city of Jerusalem (11:23). It is a prophecy that he will bring them back into the land, even though he has driven them out. Again, its fulfillment may have taken place in Israel's return from Babylon. Others see in the promise of the cleansing of the land from idols, and especially the terms relating to the "new covenant" (11:18-21; 36:24-28), a reference to an eschatological gathering of Israel (see also 20:41). Ezek 37:21 indicates that when God gathers his people, it will be the *whole* nation of Israel, joined together as a "stick of wood"; there will be one nation under one king, that is, King David, who will shepherd them (37:22, 24-28; see also Ps 106:47; 107:3).

There are also passages that speak of God's gathering the wicked together for judgment. In Ezek 16:37 God says that he is going to gather together Israel's lovers and expose her shame before them. Ezek 20:34 states that the Lord will gather the people from the nations and lead them into judgment; Hos 8:10 is similar in meaning, in that the context seems to point to God's gathering his people together for judgment. Andersen and Freedman point out that the word here is "ambivalent," but the "threat of judgment" is present (Andersen and Freedman, *Hosea*, AB, 1980, 506). Judgment is certainly the case in 9:6, where it is said that Egypt will "gather them" for burial. It might be that the word here is a euphemism for killing (Andersen & Freedman, *Hosea*, 530).

4. The pu. is used 1x (Ezek 38:8).

5. The hitp. is used 8x (Josh 9:2; Judg 9:47; 1 Sam 7:7; 8:4; 22:2; 2 Sam 2:25; Isa 44:11; Jer 49:14) and indicates that a group of people have come together for a common cause, or are called upon to get together for a common cause.

NT In the NT there is reference to the gathering of animals, things, and people; but it is also used in the sense of judgment between the wicked and the just (the goats will be separated from the sheep) (Matt 25:32, *synagō*; other references in *NIDNTT* 2:33).

Gathering: → *'sp* (gather, harvest, # 665); → *bṣr* (harvest grapes, # 1305); → *ḥṭb* (gather, cut, # 2634); → *kns* (gather, # 4043); → *lqṭ* (gather, # 4377); → *'ēdâ* I (community, gathering, band, # 6337); → *'mr* (gather grain, # 6682); → *qbṣ* (gather, # 7695); → *qᵉhillâ* (community, gathering, # 7737); → *qwh* II (gather, # 7748); → *qšš* (gather, collect, # 8006)
Harvest, gleaning: → *'sp* (gather, harvest, # 665); → *bṣr* (harvest grapes, # 1305); → *yᵉbûl* (produce, yield, # 3292); → *lqṭ* (reap, harvest, # 4377); → *'ll* I (glean, # 6618); → *'mr* (gather grain, # 6682); → *qbṣ* (gather, # 7695); → *qṣr* (harvest, # 7917); → *tᵉbû'â* (crop, yield, # 9311); → *tᵉnûbâ*, produce, # 9482)

BIBLIOGRAPHY

THAT 2:583-86; *TWAT* 6:1144-49; *TWOT* 2:783-84; E. Jenni, *Das hebräische Pi'el*, 1968, 188; H. Dietrich Preuss, *Theologie des Alten Testaments*, 1991, 1:137-39; M. Weinfeld, *Deuteronomy and the Deuteronomic School*, 1983, 346-61, 366-70; E. Sehmsdorf, "Studien zur Redaktionsgeschichte von Jesaia 56-66 (1)," *ZAW* 84, 1972, 517-62; esp. 547-49.

Cleon L. Rogers, Jr./I. Cornelius

7697 (*qᵉbuṣâ*, gathering), → # 7695

7699	קבר

קבר (*qbr*), q., pi. bury; ni., pu. be buried (# 7699); קְבוּרָה (*qᵉbûrâ*), nom. grave, burial (# 7690); קֶבֶר (*qeber*), nom. grave, tomb, burial ground (# 7700).

ANE The root *qbr* occurs in the main branches of the Sem. languages with the meaning bury (*HALAT* 995).

OT 1. The root *qbr* in the OT is always related to the burial of people, never animals or lifeless objects. Among the ancient Israelites it was customary to bury their dead in either a natural cave or a chamber hewn out of soft rock, with each family having their own burial tomb for the interment of deceased relatives.

2. Up to the monarchic period it was important for an individual to be buried in the tomb of his father (Gen 47:29-30; 49:29-31; Judg 8:32; 16:31; 2 Sam 2:32; 17:23; 21:14). Although this custom continued, some of the later kings of Judah constructed new tombs for themselves close to the tombs of their ancestors (2 Kgs 15:7 = 2 Chron 26:23; 2 Kgs 21:18 = 2 Chron 33:20; 2 Chron 28:27; 32:33). Notice the stereotyped phrase in Chronicles, "Then he rested with his fathers and was buried in the city of David his father" (2 Chron 9:31; cf. 21:20; 24:16, 25).

3. It is sometimes suggested that the existence of family tombs accounts for the idioms "to be gathered to one's people" (cf. Gen 35:29; 49:29) and "to rest with one's

fathers" (e.g., 47:30; 1 Kgs 2:10; 11:43). Yet, although these expressions occur in the context of death, they are not directly associated with burial. On the one hand, Jacob clearly implies that he will rest with his fathers long before he is buried beside them: "When I rest with my fathers, carry me out of Egypt and bury me where they are buried" (Gen 47:30). On the other hand, it is stated that Jehoram, Uzziah, Ahaz, and Manasseh rested with their fathers, although they were not buried in the same family tomb (2 Chron 21:20; cf. 2 Kgs 8:24; 26:23; 28:27; 33:20; cf. 21:18). Nowhere is burial in the family tomb a prerequisite for resting with or being gathered to one's fathers.

The existence of a family tomb appears to have indicated permanent ownership of the surrounding land. This explains the significance of the detailed account in Gen 23 of Abraham's purchase of the field of Machpelah as a burial site for his wife Sarah. By permitting Abraham to use the cave for the burial of Sarah, the inhabitants of Hebron granted him and his descendants permanent possession of the property. The desire of his descendants to be buried at Machpelah reveals the importance they attached to retaining their family's inheritance right to the land (49:29, 31; 50:13). Similarly, the locations of the burials of Jacob (49:29-32; 50:5-14; etc.), Joshua (Josh 24:30; Judg 2:9), and Joseph (Josh 24:32) are associated directly with the land that their descendants will inherit.

4. It was important for the dead to be buried because the exposure of human corpses desecrated the land (Deut 21:22, 23; cf. Josh 8:29; Ezek 39:11-16). Anyone touching a corpse became unclean for seven days (Num 19:11-16). Not to be properly buried was a sign of shame (2 Kgs 9:10, 34, 35; Jer 8:2; 14:16; 16:4, 6; 25:33; cf. 1 Kgs 14:13; Ps 79:3; Eccl 6:3; Isa 14:19-20); to bury someone was an act of kindness (2 Sam 2:4, 5).

5. The "burning" of the corpses of Saul and his sons by the people of Jabesh Gilead (1 Sam 31:12) may suggest cremation (for several explanations see Klein, *I Samuel*, 289-90). Gordon rejects the idea of cremation in favor of the funerary ritual of burning incense (*I & II Samuel*, 204-5). Similarly, the funeral fires mentioned in 2 Chron 16:14; 21:19; Jer 34:5 are not for cremation but possibly for the burning of incense and perfumes in honor of the deceased.

There is little evidence in the OT concerning the practice of cremation. It was restricted to severe offenders (Lev 20:14; 21:9; Isa 30:33). Rabbinic interpretation affirmed the necessity of burial from Deut 21:23, "Be sure to bury him that same day, because anyone who is hung on a tree is under God's curse. You must not desecrate the land the LORD your God is giving you as an inheritance." While other nations may have practiced cremation to a limited extent, it was viewed with some abhorrence (Amos 2:1). Wolff observes, "The mere fact that the remains of a human being were so desecrated, that a man had been treated as material, was of itself sufficient cause for Amos' indictment" (*Joel and Amos*, 163).

6. While most of the occurrences of *qbr* are in Genesis, Judg, 1 & 2 Sam, 1 & 2 Kgs, and 1 & 2 Chron, the prophets occasionally speak of burial as a divine punishment.

Jeremiah proclaims the impending judgment on Judah and her exile in a parabolic action at the potter's house. By it, the Lord declared, "I will smash this nation and this city just as this potter's jar is smashed and cannot be repaired. They will bury the dead in Topheth until there is no more room" (Jer 19:11). The fall of Jerusalem was a manifestation of the Day of the Lord (25:30-32), ending in a judgment on all the nations; "At that time those slain by the LORD will be everywhere—from one end of the earth to the other. They will not be mourned or gathered up or buried, but will be like refuse lying on the ground" (25:33; cf. 16:4).

Ezekiel prophesies the end of Gog in terms of a massive slaughter and burial, "On that day I will give Gog a burial place (*qeber*) in Israel, in the valley of those who travel east toward the Sea. ... Gog and all his hordes will be buried (*qbr*) there" (Ezek 39:11-12). So massive will be the slaughter that the prophet speaks of a seven months burial process and purification of the land (vv. 13-15).

7. The common Heb. term for grave or tomb (*qeber*) occurs 67x in the OT. It normally denotes an opening, natural or artificial, that is used for the burial of human corpses (e.g., Gen 23:9; Isa 22:16). Because of their association with death, graves are viewed as unclean (Isa 65:4). Even touching a grave defiled an individual so as to render him unclean for seven days (Num 19:18-19).

In several passages *qeber* is used metaphorically, always with negative overtones. The "throat" of the wicked is an "open grave" (Ps 5:9[10]). So are the Babylonians, whom the Lord is raising up against Judah, "Their quivers are like an open grave; all of them are mighty warriors" (Jer 5:16).

Jeremiah, in his confessions, questioning why he did not die while in the womb, compares the womb to a grave, "For he did not kill me in the womb, with my mother as my grave, her womb enlarged forever" (Jer 20:17). Because it parallels *šaḥat* (pit, grave, netherworld) in Ps 88:11[12], *qeber* may denote here the netherworld; however, it could equally well be taken to mean grave.

8. The nom. *qᵉbûrâ* occurs 14x in the OT. Apart from Jer 22:19, where it describes the grave of a donkey, *qᵉbûrâ* always denotes a human grave. The burial place (*qᵉbûrâ*) of Rachel (Gen 35:20) remained a marker for later generations (1 Sam 10:2). However, no such marker was left at Moses' burial ground, "to this day no one knows where his grave (*qᵉbûrâ*) is" (Deut 34:6).

Death: → *'bd* I (perish, # 6); → *'ᵃdāmâ* (ground, piece of land, soil, earth, realm of the dead, # 141); → *'āsôn* (mortal accident, # 656); → *gw'* (expire, die, # 1588); → *hrg* (kill, murder, # 2222); → *zrm* I (put an end to life, # 2441); → *ḥedel* (realm of the dead, # 2535); → *ḥnṭ* II (embalm, embalming, # 2846); → *mwt* (die, kill, execute, # 4637); → *qṭl* (murder, slay, # 7779); → *rᵉpā'îm* I (shades, departed spirits, # 8327); → *šᵉ'ôl* (sheol, netherworld, # 8619); → *šaḥat* (pit, grave, # 8846)
Corpse: → *gᵉwiyyâ* (body, corpse, # 1581); → *gûpâ* (corpse, # 1590); → *mappelet* (carcass, # 5147); → *nᵉbēlâ* (carcass, corpse, # 5577); → *peger* (carcass, corpse, # 7007)

BIBLIOGRAPHY

TWAT 6:1150-55; T. D. Alexander, "The Psalms and the Afterlife," *IBS*, 1987, 2-17; R. E. Cooley, "Gathered to His People: A Study of a Dothan Family Tomb," *FS Samuel J. Schultz*, 1983, 47-58; G. Garbini, "La Tomba di Rachele ed ebr. * *bērâ* 'ora doppia di cammino'," *BibOr*, 1977, 45-48; J. Illmann, *Old Testament Formulas About Death*, 1979, 37-48; K. M. Kenyon, *Digging Up Jericho*, 1957, 233-55; O. Loretz, "Vom kanaanäischen Totenkult zur jüdischen Patriarchen- und Elternehrung," JARG 3, 1978, 149-204; E. Meyers, "Tomb," *IDBSup*, 904-8; J. B. Payne, "Burial," *ISBE* 1:556-61; L. Y. Rahmani, "Ancient Jerusalem's Funerary Customs and Tombs," *BA* 45, 1982, 43-53; S. Talmon, "The Sectarian יחד—A Biblical noun," *VT* 3, 1953,

133-40; N. J. Tromp, *Primitive Conceptions of Death and the Nether World in the Old Testament*, *BibOr*, 1969; R. de Vaux, *AncIsr*, 56-61.

T. Desmond Alexander

7700 (*qeber*, grave, burial ground, burial), → # 7699

7702	קדד

קדד (*qdd*), q. bow down, kneel down (# 7702).

ANE The root with the same meaning is attested in Akk. (see *TWAT* 6:1157; *HALAT* 996).

OT The vb. *qdd* appears 15x, only in q. impf. and always preceding *ḥwh* (→ # 2556). The vb. more closely specifies the bodily act of prostration preparatory to the worship of God (9x, including the angel of the Lord by Balaam, Num 22:31), on the part of both individuals (4x) and Israel (in Exod 4:31; 12:27 and Chron-Neh, where it is a part of a fuller worship service, e.g., 2 Chron 29:30). Or, it precedes the act of obeisance before a royal or prophetic figure, on the part of a group (before Joseph, Gen 43:28) or an individual (before Saul, 1 Sam 24:9; Samuel, 1 Sam 28:14; and David, 1 Kgs 1:16, 31). In 1 Chron 29:20, Israel prostates itself before both Yahweh and the king.

Worship, bow down, serve: → *ghr* (down, bend over, # 1566); → *ḥwh* II (worship, bow, make obeisance, # 2556); → *kpp* (bow down, bow oneself down, # 4104); → *kr'* (bend, # 4156); → *sgd* (bow down, # 6032); → *'bd* (work, serve, worship, # 6268); → *qdd* (bow down, kneel down, # 7702); → *šrt* (wait on, be an attendant, serve, minister, # 9250)

Bibliography

TWAT 6:1157-59.

Terence E. Fretheim

7703 (*qiddâ*, cassia buds), → # 7255

7704 (*q^e dûmîm*, unexpl. hapleg.), → # 7709

7705 (*qādôš*/*qādōš*, be holy, separated, ordained), → # 7727

7706	קדח

קדח (*qdḥ*), kindle, light, ignite, set ablaze, catch or take fire (# 7706); קַדַּחַת (*qaddaḥat*), nom. kindling, ignition, inflammation, fever (→ # 7707).

ANE The vb. occurs in Punic *qdḥ* (pi. or jif.), light, kindle, ignite; Syr. *q^e daḥ*, light, kindle, ignite, catch or take fire, be ignited. The following verbal forms are also found: Arab. *qadaḥa* and Eth. *daqḥa*. Nom. forms occur in Ugar. *qdḥm*, lighter or tow, oakum; Sam. *qādēt*, kindling, ignition, inflammation; Syr. *q^e dāḥā*, flame, blaze, fire.

OT 1. Isa 63:15-64:12[63:15-64:11] has been described by Westermann (392) as "probably the most powerful psalm of communal lamentation in the Bible." The central part of this psalm (or sermon/prayer; see Watts, 329-37) is 64:1-4[63:19b-64:3], in which Yahweh is implored to impress Israel's adversaries by revealing himself in power in the same kind of spectacular theophany (→) as had characterized his activity in the past, rending the heavens and causing the mountains to shake (64:1[63:19b]), even as "fire sets twigs ablaze" (64:2[64:1], NIV).

2. The vb. is most often found in passages describing the divine wrath against Israel (Deut 32:22; Isa 50:11; Jer 15:14; 17:4). Deut 32:19-27 is part of the song of Moses (31:30-32:43). Ungrateful, rebellious, and forgetful Israel is here warned that Yahweh's righteous indignation has been provoked by his people's shameful idolatry. According to v. 22, a fire that has been kindled by the divine anger will consume the earth, burning to the depths of Sheol and setting ablaze the foundations of the mountains (popularly thought to be sunk in the subterranean ocean and to support the bowl of the firmament). Those who had rejected God's love must now suffer the scorching fire of his awesome wrath. However, the audience to whom this poem was addressed is not left without hope. The assurance is given of eventual vindication and restoration beyond judgment (see, esp., 32:36, 43). The thoroughly deserved punishment will run its course, but it will stop short of annihilation, and, afterwards, God will respond favorably to all who turn to him in loyalty and obedience (Nelson, 233). The desolation, destruction, and displacement suffered as the result of the people's infidelity would not mean the termination of their relationship with God. He would continue to offer them the choice between life, health, and blessing and curse, sickness, and death.

In Isa 50:11, which closely follows the third Servant Song (vv. 4-9), those who kindle a fire and provide themselves with flaming torches to illuminate their path are warned that they will be punished by God, who will make them lie down in torment. The identity of those to whom reference is made in this verse is obscure, but various suggestions have been made, including the following: the recalcitrant (North, 205-6) and wilfully disobedient (Sawyer, 132); those who are skeptical about the prophetic word and who sow discord among the community (McKenzie, 116-17); those who resist Yahweh and attack his prophets with weapons (e.g., Dummelow, 445; Westermann, 235); those who kindle the flames of persecution and strife and who will become the victims of their own fire (e.g., Wardle, 466); the apostate (Whitehouse, 174; Muilenburg, 588; Ackroyd, 361; Herbert, 97; Stuhlmueller, 340) or crypto-Israelites (Stuhlmueller, 340); the self-sufficient, who trust in their own strength (Ackroyd, 361; Kidner, 617); the heathen nations, who do not know that Yahweh is the true light and source of all fire (Knight, 147; however, see McKenzie, 117).

In Jer 15:14, part of Jeremiah's second personal lament (vv. 10-21), and 17:4, part of a passage (vv. 1-4) describing Judah's indelible sin (idolatrous practices), the people are warned that in Yahweh's anger an inextinguishable fire is kindled, as a result of which they will pay for their iniquity, losing their land (and all their wealth, 15:13; 17:3) and suffering deportation and enslavement. The two passages are almost identical. Because of the abrupt shift in the person addressed in Jer 15:13-14, many (e.g., Peake, 211; Robinson, 1920, 483; Hyatt, 941, 950; Paterson, 548; Bright, 109, 111, 119; Cunliffe-Jones, 124; Boadt, 131; Overholt, 622; Clements, 98; Couturier, 280; cf. Driver, 89-90) consider these verses to be misplaced, even irrelevant, in the context of ch. 15, but to fit correctly in their position in Jer 17 (see, however, Carroll, 328-29, who argues that the subtle differences which have been detected in the two sets of variants justify treating them separately).

3. The nom. occurs twice. In common with many ANE treaty texts and law codes, both the Holiness Code and the Deuteronomic Code conclude with divine

warnings and promises, with the penalties pronounced on disobedience greatly outnumbering the rewards for fidelity. The people are warned that disobedience and obstinacy will be met with God's hostile action: Yahweh will smite them with various afflictions, including fever (Lev 26:16 and Deut 28:22). It is true that, generally, people are more attentive to horror than to blessing and that fear is usually a more potent stimulant to the will than love (Davies, 269; Allis, 166; Thompson, 268; cf. Wenham, 330). However, while the aim of the crescendo of curses (Davies, 269; cf. Faley, 78) was certainly to motivate or enforce obedience, the preponderance of the penalties over the blessings also emphasizes the urgency of Israel's need to reform in the periods in which these texts were written (Nelson, 231; Faley, 78) and may well reflect the horrors of the Babylonian conquest (Robinson, 1907, 194; von Rad, 173; Noth, 120, 130-31; Phillips, 190; cf. Payne, 155-56; Miller, 189-90, 194). (For a different perspective on the dating of Deuteronomy, see McConville, 15-64.) Noth makes the interesting point that there is no place for the view that a reward may be earned by good, meritorious works. The blessing is not earned, but freely promised. However, by acting independently, there is only one possibility and that is transgression and defection, which are followed by curse and judgment.

P-B Verbal and nominative forms are well attested. The Aram. vb. *q^edaḥ* usually means bore, perforate [break through], grow forth, sprout (af. dig out, make a path for), but it also occurs with the meaning be inflamed. The following nouns are also found: *qedaḥ*, inflammation, blister; *qidḥā'*, *qîdḥā'*, inflammation; *qadḥûtā'*, *qaddaḥtā'*, fever, inflammation of the eye; and *q^edîḥûtā'*, burning, inflammation (Jastrow 2:1315).

Burning, blazing, glowing, scorching, singeing: → *b'r* I (burn, blaze up, be consumed, # 1277); → *gaḥelet* (burning charcoal, # 1625); → *dlq* (set on fire, burn, hotly pursue, # 1944); → *ḥmr* III (be in ferment, be heated, be red, glow, blaze, # 2813); → *ḥrr* I (glow, blaze, # 3081); → *yṣt* (light, kindle, ignite, burn, scorch, # 3675); → *yqd* (burn, kindle, # 3678); → *kwh* (burn, blaze, singe, # 3917); → *lhṭ* I (burn, glow, blaze, # 4265); → *nśq* (catch fire, be kindled, burn, # 5956); → *ṣwt* (light, kindle, ignite, set in flames, # 7455); → *qdḥ* (kindle, light, ignite, set ablaze, catch or take fire, # 7706); → *śrp* (burn, scorch, cauterize, # 8596)

BIBLIOGRAPHY

P. R. Ackroyd, "The Book of Isaiah," in *The Interpreter's One-Volume Commentary on the Bible*, 1971, 329-71; O. T. Allis, "Leviticus," in *NBC*, 1972, 140-67; L. Boadt, *Jeremiah 1-25*, 1982; J. Bright, *Jeremiah: Introduction, Translation, and Notes*, 1965; R. P. Carroll, *Jeremiah: A Commentary*, 1986; R. E. Clements, *Jeremiah*, 1988; G. P. Couturier, "Jeremiah," in *NJBC*, 1990, 265-97; H. Cunliffe-Jones, *Jeremiah: God in History*, 2d ed., 1972; G. H. Davies, "Deuteronomy," in *Peake*, 1964, 269-84; S. R. Driver, *The Book of the Prophet Jeremiah: A Revised Translation With Introductions and Short Explanations*, 1906; J. R. Dummelow (ed.), *A Commentary on the Holy Bible by Various Writers*, 1909; R. J. Faley, "Leviticus," in *NJBC*, 1990, 61-79; A. S. Herbert, *The Book of the Prophet Isaiah Chapters 40-66*, 1975; J. P. Hyatt, "The Book of Jeremiah: Introduction and Exegesis," in J. P. Hyatt and S. R. Hopper, "The Book of Jeremiah," in *IB*, 1956, 5:775-1142; D. Kidner, "Isaiah," in *NBC*, 1972, 588-625; G. A. F. Knight, *Servant Theology: A Commentary on the Book of Isaiah 40-55*, 1984; J. G. McConville, *Grace in the End: A Study in Deuteronomic Theology*, 1993; J. L. McKenzie, *Second Isaiah: Introduction, Translation, and Notes*, 1968; P. D. Miller, *Deuteronomy*, 1990; J. Muilenburg, "The Book of Isaiah Chapters 40-66: Introduction and Exegesis," in *HBC*, 1988, 209-34; R. D. Nelson, *First and Second Kings*, 1987; C. R. North, *The Second Isaiah: Introduction, Translation and Commentary to Chapters XL-LV*, 1967; M. Noth, "For All Who Rely on Works of the Law are Under a Curse," in his *The Laws in the Pentateuch and Other Studies*, 1967, 118-31; T. W. Overholt, "Jeremiah," in *HBC*, 1988, 597-645; J. Paterson, "Jeremiah," in *Peake*, 1964, 537-62; D. F. Payne, *Deuteronomy*, 1985; A. S. Peake, *Jeremiah. Vol. 1: Jeremiah I-XXIV. Introduction Revised Version With Notes, Map, and Index*, 1910; A. Phillips, *Deuteronomy*, 1973; G. von Rad, *Deuteronomy: A Commentary*, 1966; H. W. Robinson, *Deuteronomy and Joshua Introductions Revised Version With Notes, Map, and Index*, 1907; idem, "Jeremiah," in *Peake*, 1920, 474-95; J. F. A. Sawyer, *Isaiah. Volume 2*, 1986; C. Stuhlmueller, "Deutero-Isaiah and Trito-Isaiah," in *NJBC*, 1990, 329-48; J. A. Thompson, *Deuteronomy: An Introduction and Commentary*, 1974; W. L. Wardle, "Isaiah XL-LXVI," in *Peake*, 1920, 460-73; J. D. W. Watts, *Isaiah 34-66*, 1987; G. J. Wenham, *The Book of Leviticus*, 1979; C. Westermann, *Isaiah 40-66: A Commentary*, 1969; O. C. Whitehouse, *Isaiah XL-LXVI*, 2, 1908.

Robin Wakely

7707	קַדַּחַת

קַדַּחַת (*qaddaḥat*), inflammation, fever (# 7707); < קדח (*qdḥ*), be kindled (→ # 7706).

OT The term was used to describe a febrile condition (only in Lev 26:16; Deut 28:22), perhaps that of tertian or quartan malaria. But since the LXX of Lev 26:16 read *ikteros*, jaundice, it is possible that the disease was acute infectious hepatitis.

Disease—fever, illness, infirmity: → *'nš* I (be in poor health, # 653); → *dwb* (wear away, # 1853); → *dalleqet* (fever, # 1945); → *zôb* (discharge, # 2308); → *ḥl'* (fall ill, # 2688); → *ḥlh* I (become weak, tired, ill, # 2703); → *ḥarḥur* (heat of fever, # 3031); → *madeweh* II (disease, # 4504); → *pśh* (spread [of disease], # 7313); → *qaddaḥat* (fever, # 7707); → *šaḥepet* (illness, # 8831). For related entries → *ṣr'* (suffer from skin disease, # 7665)

Bibliography

ISBE 1:532, 953-60; 3:103-6; G. J. Wenham, *The Book of Leviticus*, NICOT, 1979, 189-214.

R. K. Harrison

7708	קָדִים

קָדִים (*qādîm*), east, east side, east wind; eastern (# 7708); קֶדֶם (*qedem*), before, east (# 7710); קַדְמֹנִי (*qadmōnî* I), eastern, former, former things (# 7719); < קדם (*qdm*, come before, meet; → 7709).

OT 1. *qādîm* has the meaning east, east side, and is used often in this sense in Ezek (some 52x) and especially in Ezek 40-48, where it appears in connection with the new temple and the new land (*TWAT* 6:1160). As Ezekiel is taken by the Spirit to the temple in Jerusalem, he is transported to the eastern gate on the eastern side of the temple (Ezek 11:1), and he sees how the glory of the Lord has left the temple and pauses on the mountain east of the temple, that is, the Mount of Olives (Ezek 11:23). It has been suggested that the glory of the Lord pauses here, either to give Israel a chance to repent (Fisch, *Ezekiel*, 1972, 62), or to go on to Babylon (Taylor, *Ezekiel*, 1969, 113). It is also through the eastern gate that the glory of the Lord will return (43:1-4), and the eastern gate is to be shut and remain closed, "because the LORD, the God of Israel, has entered through it" (44:1-2). It has been suggested that the reason the gate is to remain closed is because the glory of the Lord is never to leave the temple again (Fisch, 1972, 301-2), or because the eastern gate to the temples in Mesopotamia were kept closed and only used for the entrance of deities (*TWAT* 6:1161-62; for a discussion of both views, see Zimmerli, *Ezechiel* 2, BKAT, 1969, 2:1110-12). According to 44:3-4 the "prince" is the only one who may sit in the eastern gateway, but he is not to enter through the eastern gate. At the time of the second temple, the eastern gate is used only by the high priest and those helping him lead the "red heifer" to the Mount of Olives (Middoth 1.3). In 46:1 the eastern gate of the future temple is to remain closed except for the Sabbath and on the day of the new moon. (→ Ezekiel: Theology)

2. The word *qadîm* is also used of the "east wind." Since Yahweh is the one who controls nature, the east wind is under his control and can be used to accomplish his purposes (see *TWAT* 6:1162). The psalmist expresses this truth as he recounts the wonders of Yahweh for his people in the wilderness. He writes, "He let loose the *east* wind from heaven and led forth the south wind by his power" (Ps 78:26). In Exod 10:13 (cf. v. 18) God brings a plague of locusts to Egypt with an east wind. In 14:21 Yahweh uses a strong east wind to dry up the Red Sea so that Israel can cross over on dry land. The prophets predict that Yahweh will judge his people with a east wind (Ezek 17:10; 19:12; Hos 13:15). The devastating effect of the east wind is graphically described as withering a vine (Ezek 17:10; 19:12) or shattering ships (27:26; Ps 48:7[8]). The Lord sent a scorching east wind along with the blazing sun to the angry and disappointed prophet Jonah in order to teach the prophet a lesson (Jon 4:8). As God promises his people deliverance through the prophet Isaiah, he says that the punishment he gave them was not as severe as that which he did to their enemies (Isa 27:7), but it was a punishment like "on a day the east wind blows" (Isa 27:8). It was certainly as severe as the powerful east wind, but as the wind, it was only temporary and of a passing nature (E. J. Young, *Isaiah*, 2:245; see also H. Wildberger, *Jesaia*, BKAT, 1014-19). The unpleasant effect of the "sirocco" (east wind) is felt even today in Palestine (D. Baly, 67-70). The wind comes between April-June and Sept.-Oct. and lasts three or four days, followed by a sudden change of wind to the west and a rise in humidity.

3. The basic meaning of *qedem* is "in front of," and the developed meaning "east" arose from the idea of facing the rising sun or that which was in front (see *TWAT* 6:1165). The word is used in the OT as an adverb with the meaning "in front of," "before" (Ps 136:5), or in a temporal sense "of old" (74:2; 119:152). (See further # 7709)

(a) As a nom. *qedem* can have a temporal meaning, "ancient," "before time" (see Deut 33:27; Ps 143:5; Prov 8:22-23; Mic 5:2[1]; *THAT* 2:588; *TWAT* 6:1167-68; → *'ôlām*).

(b) *qedem* can refer to regions east of Palestine.

(i) It is used of the "Garden of Eden" (Gen 2:8), which is generally understood to be "somewhere in Mesopotamia or Arabia" (G. J. Wenham, *Genesis 1-15*, WBC, 1987, 61). The word also occurs in 3:24, where it is stated that God stationed cherubim "on the east of Eden," "to guard the way to the tree of life" (NIV). This seems to suggest that the entrance and exit to the garden was to be found on its eastern side (U. Cassuto, A *Commentary on the Book of Genesis*, 1961, 1:174).

(ii) In Gen 11:2 it is stated that the human race "journeyed *miqqedem*." This could mean "from east to west" ("east of Eden," cf. Gen 4:16; Rashi, *Pentateuch*, 1929, 1:44); "toward the east" (B. Jacob, *Genesis*, 1934, 297); "in the east" ("they wandered around in the east," Cassuto, 240). It was in the Plain of Shinar, located in the Mesopotamia region "east of the land of Israel," that men built the tower of Babel.

(iii) In Isa 2:6 the word seems to refer to the magic practices of the Mesopotamian area. The meaning could be "your land is full from the east," in the sense that the goods from the east have been brought in and filled the land (for this and the text problem, see G. B. Gray, *Isaiah I-XXVII*, ICC, 1912, 52-54, 58; H. Wildberger, *Jesaja*, BKAT, 1972, 93, 98-99). The parallelism, however, points more to the divination of the east that the people of Israel have adopted (see E. Reiner, "Fortune-Telling in Mesopotamia," *JNES* 19, 1960, 23-35; W. Farber, H. M. Kümmel, W. H. Ph. Römer, *Texte aus der Umwelt des Alten Testaments*, 1988, 2:163-281).

(c) The word *qedem* is used in the expression "sons of the east" (Gen 29:1; Judg 6:3, 33; 7:12; 8:10; 1 Kgs 4:30[5:10]; Job 1:3; Isa 11:14; Jer 49:28; Ezek 25:4, 10). The expression seems to refer to several different groups, depending on the context:

(i) The people of Mesopotamia. According to 1 Kgs 4:30[5:10] Solomon's wisdom was greater than that of the "sons of the east" and that of the Egyptians. Since the wisdom of Mesopotamia was world famous, but that of the desert was not, the reference seems to be to the people of Mesopotamia.

(ii) The nomadic tribes of the desert, which are associates with the peoples east of the Jordan River. In the book of Judges *qedem* refers to the people of the Transjordan region, i.e., the Syrian, or Arabian of the desert tribes (see *HALAT*, 1000; H. P. Müller, *ZDPV* 94, 1978, 61). As the riches of Job are described (sheep, camels, donkeys, etc.), it is said of him that he was the "greatest man among all the people of the East" (Job 1:3 NIV). This is the wealth of a nomad and evidently refers to the people of the desert (see E. Dhorme, *Job*, 1967, 3). The people of the desert are also referred to in Isa 11:14; Jer 49:28; Ezek 25:4, 10, and by the word *qadmōnî* in Job 18:20.

4. *qadmōnî* has the meaning "eastern" in describing the eastern sea (Dead Sea) and the eastern gate of the temple (Ezek 10:19; 11:1). Ezekiel, Joel, and Zechariah look at the Dead Sea as an eschatological symbol. On the one hand, Joel speaks of the drowning of the last enemy in the Dead Sea (Joel 2:20; H. W. Wolff, *Joel and Amos*, 1977, 62). On the other hand, Ezekiel and Zechariah express the hope for the transformation of creation in the imagery of the change of the Dead Sea to a sea full of living water (Ezek 47:18; Zech 14:8).

Directions: → *dārôm* (south, # 1999); → *yām* (west, sea, # 3542); → *yāmîn* I (right, south, # 3545); → *mizrāḥ* (sunrise, east, # 4667); → *maʿᵃrāb* II (west, # 5115); → *negeb* (south, Negev, # 5582); → *ṣāpôn* I (north, # 7600); → *qādîm* (east side, east wind, # 7708); → *śᵉmō'l* (left side, left hand, unlucky, northwards, # 8520); → *têmān* I (south, # 9402)

BIBLIOGRAPHY

THAT 2:575-82, 587-89; *TWAT* 6:1159-63, 1163-70; D. Baly, *The Geography of the Bible*, 1957, 67-70.

Cleon L. Rogers, Jr.

7709	קדם

קדם (*qdm*), pi. be before, meet, confront; hi. confront (# 7709); קְדוּמִים (*q^e dûmîm*), unexpl. hapleg. (Judg 5:21; # 7704); קָדִים (*qādîm*), east (→ # 7708); קֶדֶם (*qedem*), front, before, earlier, east (# 7710); קֵדֶם (*qēdem*), eastward (# 7711); קַדְמָה (*qadmâ*), origin, former condition (# 7712); קִדְמָה (*qidmâ*), in front of (# 7713); קַדְמוֹן (*qadmôn*), eastern (# 7716); קַדְמֹנִי (*qadmōnî* I), eastern, former (→ # 7719).

ANE In many Sem. languages cognates of *qdm* have a spatial (before, in front, east) and chronological (before, previous, former) reference (*HALAT* 999-1000). The prepositional use of the root (e.g., Akk. *qudmu,* Aram. *q^o dām*) is served in Heb. by *lipnê*, before.

OT 1. About half the occurrences of *qedem* have a chronological reference. "Before" or "in front" can refer to the relative or the absolute past (the primeval era). The "days of old" (*ye mê qedem*), refers to a particular era in the past whose duration and character depends on context. It could be the time of the patriarchs (Mic 7:20), the birth of the nation (Ps 74:2), the conquest of the land (Ps 44:1[2]), the days of David and Asaph (Neh 12:46; cf. Mic 5:2[1]), or the whole course of Israel's history (Ps 78:2). After the Exile, the restoration of the prosperity of former times was the object of prayer (Lam 1:7; 5:21) and was promised by the prophets (Jer 30:20; 46:26; cf. Ezek 16:55; 36:11). In expressions of complaint the sages recall the past when God had worked mightily (Ps 74:2; Job 29:2, "months of old"). Remembrance of them serves as an encouragement and a plea to God to restore the former times of prosperity. The fulfillment of former prophecies of the destruction of Babylon witness to the trustworthiness of God (Isa 45:21; 46:10).

2. Especially in poetry, *miqqedem*, from old (often ‖ *'ôlām* [→ # 6409]) evokes the primeval past, often with mythological overtones. The city of Tyre has ancient foundations (*qadmâ*, Isa 23:7). The praises of Israel affirm that God is king from of old (Ps 55:19[20]; cf. Deut 33:27), witnessed in his victory over the monsters in the primeval time of creation (Ps 74:12; Isa 51:9). In Prov 8:22-23 only wisdom is alongside God in the time before the world was created. *qedem* in the construct state describes the most ancient elements of creation (heavens, Ps 68:33[34]; mountains, Deut 33:15). (See further # 7708)

3. The denom. vb. occurs mostly in the pi. (hi. only Job 41:11[3]; Amos 9:10). The pi. (meet, come before) describes the action that results in the state of being in front or before, whether in time or in space. The psalmist comes before God in prayer at dawn (Ps 119:147). God is the only source of help when various dangers come before those who call upon him, such as death (18:5[6]), enemies (18[19]; 2 Kgs 19:32 = Isa 37:33), and pain (Job 30:27). God meets the psalmist to save (Ps 59:10[11]) and to grant blessing (21:3[4]). The preeminent occasion for coming before God is worship in the temple, to which all are summoned (Ps 95:2). There are moral and religious preconditions before the worshiper can come before God (Mic 6:6). In Ps 89:14[15] love and faithfulness, personified attributes of God, come before his presence.

P-B In 1QH 13:10-12 God is praised for establishing the world from eternity (*miqqedem 'ôlām*), but also for replacing the ancient things with new ones. Transgressors will not abide, since God has not chosen them from eternity (CD 2:7).

Early, former, front: → *qdm* (be before, meet, confront, # 7709); → *škm* (be early, rise early, be eager, # 8899)
Happening, meeting, attack: → *'nh* III (happen, # 628); → *hwh* II (become, # 2093); → *hyh* (be, become, happen, # 2118); → *y'd* (appoint, appear, come, meet, # 3585); → *ng'* (touch, hurt, # 5595); → *pg'* (encounter, attack, # 7003); → *pgš* (meet, # 7008); → *qdm* (be before, meet, confront, # 7709); → *qr'* II (happen, # 7925); → *qrh* I (happen, build, odain, direct, select, # 7936)

BIBLIOGRAPHY
THAT 2:587-89; *TWAT* 6:1163-74

P. P. Jenson

7710 (*qedem*, east, before), → # 7708, # 7709

7711 (*qēdem*, eastward), → # 7709

7712 (*qadmâ*, origin, former condition), → # 7709

7713 (*qidmâ*, in front of), → # 7709

7716 (*qadmôn*, eastern), → # 7709

7719 (*qadmônî*, eastern, former), → # 7708

7721	קָדְקֹד

קָדְקֹד (*qodqōd*), crown of head (# 7721).

ANE The nom. appears in Akk. (*qaqqadu*) and Ugar. (*qdqd*) with the meaning head or skull. The Akk. nom. can also refer to a sum of money (capital).

OT The nom. appears 11x in the OT, only in poetic contexts or idiomatic expressions, usually referring to the skull or crown of the head of a human being (cf. Deut 28:35; Jer 48:45). It is used, like *rō'š*, in the idiomatic expression "from the top of his head to the sole of his feet" (2 Sam 14:25; Job 2:7). In Ps 68:21[22] it refers to the skull as the base for hair (cf. also Jer 2:16). In Gen 49:26; Deut 33:16; Ps 7:16[17] is used par. to *rō'š* and probably refers to the head as a whole. In Deut 33:20 it is used metonymically for the head. In Isa 3:17 it is the place on which sores appear, referring not to the skull but to the top of the head. The shaving of the skull was a sign of humiliation.

Head: → *'ap* (face, anger, # 678); → *gulgōlet* (scull, # 1653); → *l^{e}ḥî* I (eye, nose, jawbone, chin, cheek, # 4305); → *mēṣaḥ* (forehead, # 5195); → *m^{e}tall^{e}'ôt* (jawbone, # 5506); → *pānîm* (face, visible, assault, # 7156); → *pōt* (front, forehead, # 7327); → *qodqōd* (crown of head, # 7721); → *rō'š* I (head, chief, beginning, # 8031); → *raqqâ* (temple [of head], # 8377)

BIBLIOGRAPHY
TWAT 6:1174-76.

Harry F. van Rooy

7722	קדר

קדר (*qdr*), q. be dark, mourn; hi. darken, cause to mourn; hitp. grow dark (# 7722); קַדְרוּת (*qadrût*), nom. darkness, blackness (# 7725); קְדֹרַנִּית (*q^{e}dōrannît*), nom. mourners (# 7726).

ANE The vb. is attested in Aram. q^e*dar*, be dark, and Arab. *qaḏira*, be dirty.

OT 1. In the q. the vb. is used 13x, only in poetry with the sense of "grow dark." Jeremiah pronounced the Lord's judgment in which "the earth will mourn and the heavens above grow dark" (Jer 4:28). Joel recorded a locust plague God sent on Israel in which "the sun and moon are darkened (*qdr*), and the stars no longer shine" (Joel 2:10; 4:15). Job likened his three unhelpful friends to a turbulent stream "darkened (*qdr*) by thawing ice and swollen with melting snow" (Job 6:16). Micah foretold a judgment in which Israel would experience a loss (darkening) of prophetic vision: "Therefore night will come over you, without visions, and darkness, without divination. The sun will set for the prophets, and the day will go dark (*qdr*) for them" (Mic 3:6). Speaking of persons, the q. stem means to mourn (Job 5:11; 30:28; Ps 35:14; 38:7[6]; 42:10[9]; 43:2; Jer 8:21; 14:2).

2. In the hi. the vb. is used 3x in the OT, only in Ezekiel. Speaking of things, the hi. means to darken the thing. In Ezekiel's lament over Pharaoh, he recorded the Lord's curse upon him: "When I snuff you out, I will cover the heavens and darken (*qdr*) their stars; I will cover the sun with a cloud, and the moon will not give its light. All the shining lights in the heavens I will darken (*qdr*) over you; I will bring darkness over your land" (Ezek 32:7-8). Speaking of persons or nations, it means to cause them to mourn: Describing the downfall of Lebanon, the LORD said, "On the day it was brought down to the grave I covered the deep springs with mourning for it; I held back its streams, and its abundant waters were restrained. Because of it I clothed Lebanon with gloom (*qdr*), and all the trees of the field withered away" (Ezek 31:15).

3. In the hitp. the vb. occurs only once on the OT, with the meaning grow dark. Elijah prayed for rain, so "the sky grew black (*qdr*) with clouds, the wind rose, a heavy rain came on and Ahab rode off to Jezreel" (1 Kgs 18:45).

4. The nom. *qadrût*, darkness, blackness, occurs only once in the OT (Isa 50:3) "I clothe the sky with darkness" [NIV] in ǁ (*šaq*) sackcloth.

5. The nom. q^e*dōrannît*, mourners, occurs only once in the OT. The impudent people had said in their hearts, "It is futile to serve God. What did we gain by carrying out his requirements and going about like mourners before the LORD Almighty?" (Mal 3:14). BDB identifies the word as an adverb, but its form is that of a nom. (GKC 85u), and here the nom. functions as an adverbial accusative.

P-B In Mish. Heb. *qadrût* was used to refer to an eclipse of the sun (*qadrût haššemeš*) and of the moon (*qadrût hayyārēaḥ*). In RL the vb. has essentially the same meaning.

Darkness: → *'ōpel* (darkness, gloom, # 694); → *'^{e}šûn* (approach of darkness, # 854); → *ḥšk* (be, grow dark, grow dim, darken, conceal, confuse, # 3124); → *ṭuḥôt* (darkness, obscurity, inward parts, # 3219); → *kamrîr* (blackness, deep gloom, # 4025); → *laylâ* (night, # 4326); → *nešep* (twilight, darkness, # 5974); → *'wp* II (be dark, # 6415); → *'^{a}lāṭâ* (darkness, dusk, # 6602); → *'mm* II (darken, dim, # 6670); → *'^{a}rāpel* (deep darkness, thick darkness, heavy cloud, # 6906); → *ṣll* III (be/grow dark, cast a shadow, # 7511); → *ṣalmāwet* (darkness, shadow of death, # 7516); → *qdr* (be dark, mourn, # 7722)

BIBLIOGRAPHY

TWOT 2:786; L. Delekat, "Zum hebräischen Wörterbuch," *VT* 14, 1964, 7-66.

James D. Price

7725 (*qadrût*, darkness, blackness), → # 7722

7726 (*q^{e}dōrannît*, mourners), → # 7722

7727	קדשׁ

קדשׁ (*qdš*), q. be holy, withheld from ordinary use, treated with special care, belonging to the sanctuary; ni. show, prove oneself holy, be treated as holy; pi. put something into a state of holiness, i.e., treat according to the procedures of worship, dedicate for use by God, pronounce something to be holy, put someone into a state of holiness, consecrate, establish, appoint a holy period of time, transfer or convey holiness, treat as holy; pu. be made holy; hi. designate as made holy, treat as made holy, God's declaration of s.o./s.t. to be holy to him, take God to be holy, give as votive offerings; hitp. behave as consecrated, prove o.s. to be holy, put o.s. into the state of dedication (# 7727); מִקְדָּשׁ (*miqdāš*), nom. sanctuary (→ # 5219); קָדֵשׁ (*qādēš* I), nom. sacred person, temple prostitute (# 7728); קֹדֶשׁ/קוֹדֶשׁ (*qôdeš/qōdeš*), nom. thing filled with holiness, therefore be treated carefully, consecrated gifts, offerings, God's holiness, something most holy (# 7731); קָדֹשׁ/קָדוֹשׁ (*qādōš/qādôš*), adj. holy, causing anxiety, separated, ordained for (# 7705).

ANE 1. The Sum. *ku₃*, holy, which does not function as a nom. but rather as an adj., qualifies affairs that pertain/belong to the realm of the divine. It also implies that a certain awesomeness is associated with objects, beings, or times so designated. The temple is referred to as being holy (Wilson, 5-24). In addition to the concept of sanctity applied to the temple in a general sense, however, it is possible to distinguish particular parts of the temple complex that are specified as being sacred (e.g., the adytum that is called the holy place (*ki-ku$_3$*), UE VI/I 103 1:33; the ABZU, which is called a holy sanctuary (*eš$_3$-ku$_3$*), UE VI/I 105 1:2; and the holy interior (*ša$_3$-ku$_3$*), UE VI/I 105 1:4, 16, while other parts do not appear to be so designated. Objects (e.g., plates, bowls, vessels, tables) typified as holy are similar in type to the temple utensils that are called *qōdeš* in the OT. That is to say, they all pertain to the temple in some way and almost all are used in rituals (Wilson, 24-30). Although one might expect the gods to be called holy, that does not occur often. That epithet is most commonly associated with the divinity Inanna. As goddess of fertility she is very important in the Mesopotamian pantheon.

The word *ku$_3$* is more commonly associated with divine body parts, e.g., Gudea Cyl B VI 25 mentions the holy hand (*šu-ku$_3$*) of Ningirsu. Similarly, Gudea is mentioned as having been chosen in the holy heart of the goddess Baba in statue E I 18-20. It would seem likely that the body parts of the gods are called holy in order to emphasize that these are not the body parts of mere mortals, and to thus maintain a certain distance and respect. Occasionally, if an animal is used as a symbol for a god, it is called holy, presumably to indicate that reference is made to some deity. In terms of holiness as a possible state for mortals, except for the priest, none of the temple personnel have the element of *ku$_3$* in their titles. By declaring that he himself is holy, the priest states his right to participate in the realm of the divine (Wilson, 30-32). The cultic festival is referred to as holy and thereby related to this realm of the divine, which in this case is represented by the temple, where the feast takes place. The songs of the priests are also called holy, because they are sung within the sacred precincts of the temple. Fire and water are used in the sanctification process. The sanctification of people, which enabled them to enter the presence of deity, was accomplished by means of the *šu-luḫ* ceremony, which marked the transition from the profane outer areas into the holy inner portions of the temple (Wilson, 32-40).

2. The Akk. vb. *qadāšu* and its derived adj. *qašdu(m)* indicate respectively a transition to and a state of purity, which implies freedom from pollutants (*CAD* 13:46-47). They are used in both a cultic and noncultic sense. In a noncultic sense they indicate freedom from dirt (in the case of clothes) or impurities not belonging to the same class as the object in question (e.g., impurities in metals), or freedom from legal claims. In a cultic sense, where the pollutant is specified, that pollutant is, in many cases, perhaps even always, evil spirits (Bettenzoli, 26-29). So *qadāšu* and *qašdu(m)* have a different linguistic range from Sum. ku_3. Whereas the latter basically designates a state of pertaining to the realm of the divine, the former indicates either freedom from physical pollutants or else freedom from unwanted supernatural influences. In other words, in Akk. there does not appear to be any word for holy in the sense of Sum. ku_3, or in the sense of Heb. *qōdeš* or *qādôš* (in either the concrete or abstract sense). That would explain why temple utensils are not called *qašdu* to the extent that they are called ku_3 in Sum. or *qōdeš* in Heb. Even when cedar is called *qašdu,* what is stressed is its purifying quality rather than any supernatural aspect.

3. In Ugar. *qdš*, holy, refers to the divine self in the case of El and Athirat, but not in the case of Baal (Pope, 43-44). In the phrase *bn qdš*, sons of holiness, *qdš* is used as an epithet of the god El (*THAT* 2:591). Thus, the phrase refers to the sons of El, namely, the gods (*KTU* 1.2 III:6). Athirat is sometimes referred to as the holy one (*KTU* 1.2 1.16 I:11, 22). In the case of Baal (and other gods) *qdš* is not used as a direct attribute, but qualified characteristics or possessions of Baal (Bettenzoli, 34). Body parts of gods, e.g., Baal's voice, are typified as holy (*KTU* 1.4 V:29). Places pertaining/belonging to the realm of the divine are typified as holy: "The rocks of Baal weep for you, father Zephon, the holy circuit (as place of pilgrimage and processions), the vast circuit is groaning (for you), the far-flung circuit" (*KTU* 1.16 I:7). The throne is typified as holy: "Come and I myself will search it out within my rock El Zephon, in (my) holy place, in the rock of my heritage, in (my) pleasant place, in the hill of my victory" (*KTU* 1.3 III:27). The nom. *qdš* also denotes a sanctuary: "They went a day and a second; afterwards with the sun on the third (day) he came to the sanctuary of Athirat of the two Tyres and to (the sanctuary of) Elat of the Sidonians" (*KTU* 1.14 IV:197).

OT By far the most extensive occurrences of the word group are to be found in the cultic and ritual texts which many scholars trace back only to the exilic and postexilic periods (Exod 25-Num 10; Ezek 40-48; and parts of 1 and 2 Chron). Jeremiah made very little use of the word group.

1. *The nom. qōdeš*. (a) At the lexical level the nom. is best typified in terms of its most important related but opposite terms as the many-faceted parallelism in Lev 10:10 suggests: "You must distinguish between the holy and the common (*ḥōl*; → # 2687), between the unclean (*ṭāmē'*; → # 3227) and the clean (*ṭāhôr*; → # 3196)." First, each leg of the parallelism contains an opposed pair, namely, holy and common/profane on the one side, and clean and unclean on the other side (cf. also 11:47; Ezek 22:26; 42:20; 44:23). Thus, common/profane is the nom.'s technical antonym.

Second, the legs of the parallelism are also opposed. Thus, while the nom. (and its opposite, common/profane) represents the divine relation (positively and negatively) to the ordered world, clean (with its opposite, unclean) embraces the normal state of human existence in the earthly realm (Jenson, 47). Third, the parallelism forms a chiastic structure, with the result that the nom. and clean can be aligned (Barr, 15). While it is true that common/profane is its technical antonym, the parallelism also shows that unclean is a state opposed and detrimental to the nom. These relationships suggest that the nom. and its opposites form a spectrum that refers to levels of holiness ranging from extreme sanctity to extreme uncleanness (very holy, holy, clean, unclean, very unclean). This spectrum is employed in spatial, personal, ritual, and temporal dimensions of the cult and reflects a graded conception of the world (Jensen, 56-88).

(b) The nom. in the genitive, instead of the adj., is used most frequently after another nom., but is rendered like an adj., holy (Isa 65:11, 25). It qualifies all those things that in any way pertain to God or his worship, e.g., holy day = Sabbath (Isa 58:13). Rarely only is it to be taken as an abstract nom. to be rendered as holiness (Ps 29:2; 89:35[36]). Concretely the nom. denotes a holy person, thing, place, or time, something sacred, consecrated to God.

(c) The major loci to which the nom. refers are as follows: God (Exod 15:11), his spirit (Isa 63:10), his name (Lev 20:3; 22:2, 32), his arm (Isa 52:10), his ways (Ps 77:13[14]); humans: priests (Lev 21:6), Levites (2 Chron 23:6); objects: offerings (Exod 29:33) and gifts (28:38), sanctuary furniture (1 Kgs 8:4), priestly clothing (Exod 29:29), sanctuary treasury (Lam 4:1; cf. Exod 30:13, 24), oil (Num 35:25), anointing oil (Exod 30:25), incense (30:35); places: sanctuaries (Lev 10:4, 17, 18), places of theophany (Exod 3:5; Josh 5:15), Zion (Isa 11:9), Jerusalem (48:2), Ezekiel's sacred district (Ezek 45:1), the divine habitation/heaven/throne (Deut 26:15; Ps 20:6[7]; Isa 63:15); and time: Sabbath (Exod 31:14, 15), Jubilee (Lev 25:12), and feasts (cf. also *ABD* 3:237-49).

(d) God is considered to be the source of holiness. The nom. connotes the essential nature that belongs to the sphere of God's being or activity and that is distinct from the common or profane. This might correspond to a claim of ownership, a statement of close association, or proximity to his cultic presence. It is first of all associated with the Lord (1 Chron 16:29; 2 Chron 20:21; Ps 96:9) and can be used almost as a synonym of deity. The nom., in the expression his holy name, can be put on a par with divine, his divine name, which in this context is nearly synonymous with his honor, reputation, and glory (Ezek 39:7; Amos 2:7). The Lord's holy name contrasts with everything creaturely. The nom. also typifies the Lord's Spirit (Ps 51:11[13]). In Isa 63:10-11 the Spirit referred to is the Spirit God sent among his people during the Exodus, but who was grieved by Israel through their rebellion. God's holiness thus becomes an expression for his perfection of being that transcends everything creaturely. Because God is holy by nature and separate from moral imperfection, he can be trusted to be faithful to his promises (Ps 105:42). Because of his holiness, God can accomplish the deliverance of his people (Exod 15:11).

(e) Holiness is not inherent in creation but comes by God's dictates. While the realm of the holy was conceptually distinct from the world with its imperfections, it could nevertheless operate within the world as long as its integrity was strictly maintained. An inviolable distinction between the spheres of the sacred and the common or profane had to be maintained (Ezek 39:7; 42:20). That which was inherently holy or designated so by divine decree or cultic rite was not to be treated as common. The maintenance of the integrity of holiness was a function of the Israelite cult. The regulations and prescriptions were designed to maintain the purity of holiness that characterized God's essential nature.

This principle was recognized even before the establishment of the levitical system (Exod 3:5). The Sabbath was holy, and the restrictions connected with that day served to maintain its distinctive nature and to guard against its being treated as common (16:23; Isa 58:13). Special restrictions were placed on the priests to guard against profanation of their holy status (Lev 21:6; 2 Chron 23:6). Only those who are holy will dwell on God's holy hill (Ps 15:1). Sexual intercourse was not considered immoral, but it did affect a state of levitical defilement, which prohibited contact with that which was holy (1 Sam 21:4[5]). The same principle applied to the fellowship offering (Lev 19:8), the holy oil (Exod 30:31-32) and holy incense (30:37). Holy objects, therefore, are those with no cultic pollution, which is symbolic of moral pollution. They are not merely dedicated, but dedicated to what is good and kept from what is evil. The ethical connotations of the nom. find their basis in the prescriptions against profaning that belong to the sphere of the sacred (Lev 22:32).

(f) That which was dedicated to God was regarded as entering the sphere of the divine. This included the various elements of levitical worship called holy things (Lev 5:15, 16), the produce of the land (19:24), real estate (27:14), personal property (27:28), and spoils obtained in military action (Josh 6:19). Doing so made them holy to the Lord, i.e., the property of the sanctuary and priests. The sacrifices that were to be eaten only by the priests are typified by the nom. by virtue of their absolute dedication to the sphere of the sacred (Lev 19:8).

(g) Everything that belonged to the realm of the cult was typified by the nom. Typical examples are the numerous holy occasions/sacred assemblies, e.g., the great feasts, New Moons, Sabbaths, Year of Jubilee (Lev 23:2, 3, 4, 7, 8, 21, 24, 27, 35, 36, 37); all the places and objects that serve the cult, e.g., temple (Isa 43:28), tabernacle (Exod 40:9), and ark (2 Chron 35:3), altars and their equipment (Exod 40:10) and offerings (Neh 10:33[34]).

Although all things referring to the cult are typified by the nom., they are not of equal status but show a gradation of holiness (cf. also Haran, 175-88). Aaron and his sons are designated as most holy (1 Chron 23:13) in apparent contrast to the Levites, who are referred to as holy (2 Chron 23:6). Offerings fall into two main groups, namely, most holy and less holy. Those called most holy are the grain offering (Lev 2:3, 10), the sin offering (Lev 6:25[18], 29[22]), and guilt offering (Lev 6:17[10]; 7:1, 6). A mark of most holy offerings is that only the priests may eat them and then only in the sanctuary court. In some passages less holy offerings are distinguished technically from most holy offerings by calling them simply holy offerings (Num 18:8, 9, 10, 19; Deut 12:26; 2 Chron 29:33; Ezek 36:38). The designation of spoils of war as most holy (Lev 27:28) is probably to emphasize their irredeemable nature. Sacrificial meat can be called holy flesh (Jer 11:15). Six pieces of cultic furniture are designated most holy: the ark, the incense altar, lampstand, bread table, the outer or burnt offering altar, and basin (Exod 29:37; 30:10, 26-29; 40:10; Num 4:4, 19). The other furniture may simply be labeled holy (Num 4:15).

Location, materials, lethality, and the cultic importance of the pieces suggest a gradation of holiness, with the ark being the highest, the outer altar and basin being the lowest. The high priest's clothing has an elevated degree of holiness. Only the high priest's clothing is called holy clothing (Exod 28:2, 4; 29:29; 31:10; 35:19, 21; 39:1, 41; 40:13). The golden plate is called holy (Exod 29:6; Lev 8:9). Aaron's sons' clothing is categorized thus only once (Exod 28:4), but the context shows that the high priest's clothing is meant. When performing the blood rites in the adytum, shrine, and court on the Day of Atonement, the high priest wears a plain linen tunic, breeches, waistband, and headdress called holy (Lev 16:4, 32). This may be utilitarian to prevent the soiling of regular priestly clothing, and at the same time befitting the holiness of the altar. Ezekiel's clothing for the priests is called holy (Ezek 42:14; cf. also 44:19) and had the power to render laypersons who touched it holy.

Terminology shows a gradation of different parts of the tabernacle. Technically speaking the adytum was called the Most Holy Place and the shrine simply the Holy Place (Exod 26:33, 34; 1 Chron 6:49[34]; Lev 16:33). But the entire tent structure could be called most holy, which indicates that its collective holiness is greater than the rest of the sanctuary area (Exod 30:29). Less technically speaking, both rooms were called the holy place (Exod 38:24, 27). The sanctuary area in general or the court was called the holy place (Exod 35:19; 36:1, 3, 4, 6; 39:1, 41; Lev 10:4, 18; Num 8:19; 28:7). The entire area of Solomon's temple, the second temple, and Ezekiel's visionary temple were also called holy places (Ps 74:3; 1 Chron 24:5; 2 Chron 29:5, 7).

(h) There is a crucial distinction between holy objects and holy persons. The holiness of objects is permanent, and they can never again enter the profane sphere. Thus, the bronze censers of the sons of Korah rendered holy by use (vb. *qdš*) became part of the permanent furniture of the cult (Num 16:37-40[17:2-5]). Priests, on the other hand, lived both in the profane and holy spheres, though at different times. In order to minister in the holy sanctuary, the priests had to be holy themselves, and to this end were consecrated at Mount Sinai (Lev 8-10). But in contrast to holy objects, their holiness was active only in the holy area, and there was no penalty if a priest became unclean outside the sanctuary. Yet priestly holiness was more than a mere potential, and it affected certain kinds of behavior outside the sanctuary.

2. *The adj. qādôš*. (a) The nom. and adj. are not used in the same contexts, i.e., the one is not just the adjectival form of the other, but they rather have linguistic ranges that do not overlap significantly (Wilson, 87-88). The adj. is used only in connection with the following: Divine beings (1 Sam 6:20; Isa 43:3; Hab 1:12), human beings (Deut 14:2; 26:19), the sacrificial court (Exod 29:31; Lev 6:16[9], 26[19]; 7:6; 10:13; 24:9; Ezek 42:13), the day on which Ezra read the law (Neh 8:9, 10, 11), and the water used to test the woman suspected of adultery (Num 5:17). Most of the things typified by the nom., such as the furnishings in the tabernacle, the sacrifices and garments, are never typified by the adj. Those things that are typified by the adj. are not normally typified by the nom., the exception being the court, which also is qualified by the nom. because it was part of the tabernacle complex.

There is a dynamism associated with those objects typified by the adj. that is missing in those typified by the nom. While the nom. simply denotes a state of belonging to the realm of the divine, those things that are typified by the adj. all possess the ability to move things or people into, or at least toward, the realm of the divine. God, as the source of holiness, is also the primary agent of sanctification, but human beings can participate in the rituals of sanctification (e.g., of Aaron and his sons) and therefore is qualified by the adj. The water in Num 5 is qualified by the adj. because it moves the suspected adulteress either into one sphere (i.e., that of impurity) or the other (i.e., that of the pure, and possibly even the sphere of the holy, at least to the extent that all Israel can be considered holy under ideal circumstances). In that sense the water is also dynamic. Finally, the day on which Ezra read the law could be qualified by the adj. because it was a day on which Israel was moved toward a state of holiness by heeding the law. Therefore, there was also a dynamism in that day. Thus, there is a conceptual difference between the nom. and adj., with the latter containing a dynamic quality, while the former merely denotes a state of belonging to the realm of the divine or, in a more concrete sense, to the temple/tabernacle complex.

(b) The title "Holy One of Israel" occurs only in Isaiah apart from a few dependent passages (2 Kgs 19:22; Jer 50:29; 51:5; Ezek 39:7). It reflects the Lord's supremacy over any competitors, his eternal being, as well as the fact that he is the sole object of Israel's devotion. It serves to place the sins of Isaiah's society in contrast to God's moral perfection (Isa 30:12) and expresses God's absolute separation from evil (17:7). The title functions in two contexts. First, instead of leaning on the Holy One of Israel, the people have relied on horses and chariots (31:1 versus 10:20; 30:15). But as the Holy One, the Lord himself intends to obtain justice in war for his people. Second, the sinful people, laden with guilt, have despised the Holy One of Israel (1:4; 30:12) and will therefore be smitten by him. The Holy One, the Creator of Israel (43:15; 45:11), who will redeem Israel out of slavery like a kinsman (43:14), is at the same time the Creator of the world and the Lord of the nations (40:25). As such he is sufficiently removed from his people to punish them without bias, but he is also sufficiently powerful to create something utterly new after the punishment. Therefore, nations will run to the Holy One of Israel because he will glorify Israel (55:5) (cf. also Anderson, 3-19).

(c) The adj. is also used in the title, Holy One (Hos 11:9; 11:12[12:1]; Hab 1:12). Hos 11:9 has perhaps a similar message as the Isa passages. The Lord, the Holy One in the midst of his people, is nonetheless not a destroyer or demon, even when the people have been guilty of great profanity, but intends purification through a devastating catastrophe. His purpose is not destruction, but a new future for Israel. Because God is holy, he is free from the moral imperfections and frailties common to humanity (Hos 11:9) and can be counted on to be faithful to his promises (Ps 22:3[4]). This aspect of God's character forms the basis of Habakkuk's hope that his people would not perish (Hab 1:12). This title does not occur frequently in the oldest sources. The Lord is once called "this holy God" by the Philistines because they were exposed to great disaster when they did not show proper respect for the ark of the covenant (1 Sam 6:19-20). The Lord is terrible and holy (Ps 99:3). None of the gods is holy as he is, for none casts down the exalted and raises the humble as he does (1 Sam 2:2).

(d) God is intrinsically holy and calls his people to be holy, providing for them the standard of obedience whereby that holiness may be maintained (Lev 19:2). According to R. Otto, the adj. points to five characteristics of the human experience of the divine: awe, majesty, vitality, otherness, and compelling fascination. Gammie (6-8) carries these ideas of Otto one step further, suggesting that the experience of holiness calls for the human response of purity and cleanness. Thus, the priestly tradition requires the cleanness of proper ritual and the maintenance of separation; the prophetic tradition demands the cleanness of social justice; the wisdom tradition stresses the cleanness of inner integrity and individual moral acts. The adj. typifies not only the mystery of God's power, but also his character as totally good and entirely without evil. The experience of God revealing himself as ethically holy calls for the human response to a holiness resembling his own (Lev 20:7).

But lay Israelites did not share the same holy status as priests. On special occasions, when Israel as a whole was involved, they attained the broader holiness that was not permanent and ceased as a natural consequence of time. Yet though they were denied priestly holiness attained through inaugural rites and genealogical right, they were charged to achieve another type of holiness: that which comes by obedience. Because God is holy, the Israelites could not serve him when they persisted in their idolatrous practices (Josh 24:19). They were to be separate from all that was unholy (Lev 11:44-45). Stipulations were imposed on them that they might not engage in practices common to other peoples (Num 15:40). Their call to holiness was based on the fact that they had become God's possession by virtue of his separating them from the nations (Lev 20:26). Thus, holiness should characterize Israel in its distinctiveness in relation to the nations with regard to purity laws (Lev 11:44-45) or moral behavior (Lev 19). The same aspect of holiness pertains to the deut. formula, the holy people. In so far as the people are holy to the Lord, their God (Deut 7:6; 14:2, 21; 26:19), the formula explains their separation from the practices and cult objects of foreign religions; not eating what dies of itself; destroying altars, Asherim, graven images, etc. Deut 26:19 declares that through keeping the whole law Israel will become a people holy to the Lord.

(e) God is not the only divine being typified by the adj. Subordinate divine beings are also qualified by the nom. (Job 5:1; 15:15; Ps 16:3; 89:5[6], 7[8]; Dan 8:13; Zech 14:5). The holy ones, saints, are heavenly companions of God. In Dan 7:18 (Aram.) they are those who stand by their God in the war between the Lord and the world powers, and who receive the kingdom.

(f) A ritual that relates the potential holiness of all Israelites to the specific cultic holiness of the priests is found in Num 6. The status of the Nazirite vow is typified by the adj. (Num 6:5, 8). The Nazirite vow was open to all Israelites, male or female, priest or lay. The holiness of the Nazirite was only temporary and noncommunicable and so not confined to the sanctuary or to the priesthood. Nevertheless, he or she was subject to restrictions during their vows, which put them on a par with a ministering high priest.

(g) The holiness of prophets is typified meagerly by the adj. Elisha is called a holy man of God (2 Kgs 4:9).

3. *The vb. qdš.* (a) The vb. refers to a state or the transition into/move towards a particular grade of holiness. The use of the vb. is more uniform in the context of its setting than the nom. and the adj.

(b) The q. connotes the state of that which belongs to the sphere of the sacred. Thus such a subject is in a state distinct from the common or profane. The pf. q. is used most frequently to describe the state of consecration effected by levitical ritual. In Exod 29:21 Aaron, his sons, and their garments were consecrated and were thus recognized as belonging to the realm of the sacred. The censers of the Korahites were regarded as holy because they had been devoted to the Lord (Num 16:37[17:2]). Accordingly, they were regarded as having entered the sphere of the sacred by virtue of cultic ritual and were accorded a special place in the sanctuary (Num 16:38[17:3]). The devotion of the censers seems to have created a condition of inviolable holiness that would not allow for their being treated in a common way. The impf. q. is used to depict the transmission of the state of holiness to whatever touched a person or object so consecrated (Exod 29:37; 30:29; Lev 6:18[11], 27[20]; cf. Hag 2:12). This process does not necessarily imply that a transferable divine energy exists in the idea of the vb. Rather, it seems that such a person or object entered the state of holiness in the sense of becoming subject to cultic restrictions, as were other holy persons or objects. Stipulations are in place to avoid defilement of the state of the sacred (Deut 22:9; 1 Sam 21:5[6]; Isa 65:5). It seems best to see the vb. in the q. as serving to delineate the sphere of the divine.

(c) The ni. of the vb., of which God is usually the subject, denotes the self-representation of his holiness in Israel in the face of the gentile world (Ezek 20:41; 28:25; 39:27). God demonstrates his holiness by judging sin (Lev 10:3; Num 20:13; Ezek 28:22) or by adhering to his promises (Isa 5:16; Ezek 38:16). The clearest example is Ezek 36:23. The Lord's holy name had been profaned through the scattering of the people, and the exiles had contributed to its further profanation. But when the Lord gathers his people from the four corners of the earth, he will manifest himself in them before all the nations as the Holy One, and the nations will acknowledge that he is the Lord. This means that they will recognize the Lord as God, even if he had not been. The acknowledgment of God as holy is also expressed by the ni. (Lev 22:32). The ni. can also connote the passive of the factitive, to be consecrated/to be brought into a state of holiness (Exod 29:43).

(d) But since the normal state of earthly things is common (*ḥōl*, → # 2687), it requires a special act to bring a thing or person into a state of holiness. The factitive of the vb., to set in a state of holiness, is denoted most frequently by the pi. The focus is on the result of the act of consecration. The subject of the vb. may be God or a person. God made Israel holy (Exod 31:13; Lev 20:8; 21:8; 22:32), restored the holiness of Israel (Ezek 20:12; 37:28), sanctified his name, which was defiled by Israel in the eyes of the nations (Ezek 36:23), and declared the Sabbath to be holy (Gen 2:3). Moses (Exod 19:10, 14), Joshua (Josh 7:13), Job (Job 1:5), and Samuel (1 Sam 16:5) sanctified either the nation or individuals. Solomon consecrated the middle part of the courtyard in front of the temple (1 Kgs 8:64; 2 Chron 7:7). In strict accord with the divine instruction Moses anointed both the sanctuary with its furnishings and the priests with the holy anointing oil (Exod 29:44; 40:9-11, 13; Lev 8:10; Num 7:1). The filling of the sanctuary by the glory of God at the consecration emphasized the limitation of the purely human construction.

A requisite for Aaron and his sons to serve as priests was the act of consecration, which inter alia entailed dressing in the sacred garments, anointing, ordaining, and eating of the ordination offerings (Exod 28:3, 41; 29:1, 33; 30:30). The priests had to take care not to consecrate the people by means of their garments (Ezek 44:19). Therefore, other garments were to be worn outside the sanctuary for ordinary life. For consecration the altar had to be brought into a state of purity. It was thus necessary to cleanse/purify the altar from the uncleanness of the Israelites. It was performed by the sprinkling of blood and resulted in the atonement of the altar (Exod 29:36; Lev 8:15; 16:19). After this act, the anointing by oil was necessary to bring the altar into a state of holiness. If this process was repeated, the altar became most holy (Exod 29:37; 40:10).

Other matters that were consecrated were the temple (by removing all defilement) (2 Chron 29:5, 17); the Jubilee Year (Lev 25:10); every firstborn male (Exod 13:2); the assembly (Joel 2:16); and parts of the ordination ram that belonged to Aaron and his sons, namely, the breast and the thigh (Exod 29:27), thereby placing them at God's disposal. In Exod 19:23 the consecration of Mount Sinai by establishing boundaries around it served to keep out all that might have profaned God's holy presence. The pi. is also used to denote the cultic preparations for going to war (Jer 6:4; 51:27, 28; Joel 3:9[4:9]; Mic 3:5), for calling an assembly (2 Kgs 10:20) or for appointing a holy period of time, e.g., a fast (Joel 1:14; 2:15).

(e) The consecration consists of a double movement, since the initiation of a new relationship with the divine realm entails a corresponding separation from the earthly sphere (Jenson, 48). Separateness is often thought to be the basic meaning of holiness, but it is more its necessary consequence. Consecration is a separation to God rather than a separation from the world. The theory that the original etymology was separation is now abandoned. The suggestion that the vb. is derived from an original biliteral *qd*, cut, is attractive but tenuous in view of the uncertainties surrounding the transmission of biliteral roots to the triliteral form. The meaning to separate is favored by many scholars, but the fact that the vb. rarely if ever occurs in a secular sense makes any positive conclusion in this regard difficult, because of the limited evidence on which to base philological comparison.

(f) The pi. is also used to depict the conservation of the holiness of God (Deut 32:51) or the result of the act of consecration. The Israelites are instructed to keep the Sabbath holy (Exod 20:8; Deut 5:12) by refraining from work or carrying loads on the Sabbath (Jer 17:22, 24, 27); it is a sign between them and God (Ezek 20:20; 36:23).

(g) The pu. part. is used like a nom. or adj. to depict or qualify subjects as being put into a state of holiness, e.g., angels (Isa 13:3), the priests (2 Chron 26:18; Ezek 48:11), feasts (Ezra 3:5), and contributions for worship (2 Chron 31:6).

(h) The hitp. denotes the entering of a state of holiness through one's own fault. In these cases nothing more than cultic qualification is implied. A person consecrated himself when he had been temporarily excluded from the life of the community by uncleanness, or when he came into contact with God. Bathsheba purified herself from her uncleanness after David slept with her (2 Sam 11:4). Priests and Levites had to consecrate themselves when they approached God or performed cultic duties (Exod 19:22; 1 Chron 15:12, 14; 2 Chron 5:11; 29:5, 34; 30:3, 15, 24). Jesse and his sons consecrated themselves for the family sacrifice (1 Sam 16:5). The people had to consecrate themselves to prepare for the deeds that the Lord would perform among them (Lev 11:44; 20:7; Num 11:18; Josh 3:5; 7:13). When God is the subject of the vb., the hitp. denotes God's self-display of his holiness (Ezek 38:23). The hitp. is also used to depict the celebration of a holy festival (Isa 30:29).

(i) The hi. has the sense of dedication, not with the implication of cultic qualification, but rather of transfer to the possession of God, to whom the person or thing dedicated now exclusively belongs. The hi. focuses on the process of dedication. The dedicated oblations that could not be offered in sacrifice consist of houses (Lev 27:14, 15) and fields (Lev 27:16, 17, 18, 19, 22). It is to be observed that in most cases no actual change of ownership takes place. If an owner dedicated his house and wished to redeem it, he had to pay an additional one-fifth of the estimated value of the property to be restored. The case of the field was much more complicated, since it involved the question of the Jubilee. But the owner could redeem it by adding one-fifth. Firstlings already belonged to the Lord, so they could not be dedicated (Lev 27:26; Num 3:13; 8:17; Deut 15:19). The sacred offerings that the Israelites dedicated to the Lord had to be treated according to the procedures of worship (Lev 22:2, 3). In Judg 17:3, when Micah acknowledged that he had taken the money and restored it to the purpose to which his mother had dedicated it, she neutralized the curse by invoking a blessing on him. Spoils of war (2 Sam 8:11; 1 Chron 18:11; 26:27) and the temple (2 Chron 2:4[3]) were dedicated to the Lord.

(j) Finally, the hi. is also used to denote the act by which God is honored as holy (Num 20:12; 27:14; Isa 8:13; 29:23) and the act of setting subjects apart for a certain divine purpose (Neh 12:47; Jer 12:3). According to the directions given in the law of Moses, six cities of refuge were set apart (hi.) for the asylum of those who had unintentionally committed homicide (Josh 20:7). Before conception, and between conception and birth, divine intimate awareness and divine separating action (hi.) led up to the moment of appointment of Jeremiah as prophet (Jer 1:5).

4. *The nom. qādēš.* The nom. has as reference the shrine/cultic/religious prostitute (Gen 38:21). The nom. appears in a passage that describes the building of high places, pillars, and Asherim (1 Kgs 14:24). However, Asa put the male shrine prostitutes out of the land (1 Kgs 15:12), and Jehoshaphat exterminated the rest of the male shrine prostitutes (1 Kgs 22:46[47]). A law in Deut prohibits the practice of cult prostitution by the daughters of Israel and likewise by the sons (Deut 23:17[18]). Apart from the bare allusion to these, always in connection with actual or implied condemnation, nothing is told about their function. This must be inferred from extrabiblical material. Many considered that the processes of nature were controlled by the relations between gods and goddesses. By engaging in sexual intercourse with devotees of the shrine they believed was that this would encourage the gods and goddesses to do likewise, with the result that a person's desire for increase in herds and fields, as well as in his own family, could be realized.

P-B 1. The Qumran community was an apocalyptic, priestly community in which the ordinances of purification that were originally obligatory only for the priests were made binding on all the members. The temple cult was replaced by special ways of obedience, such as washing, cultic meals, and especially observance of the calendar. The nom. and adj. were used for the self-designation of the community. The community described itself as the saints (1QM 6:6), God's holy people (1QM 14:12), men of holiness (1QS 8:17), and the council of holiness (1QS 8:21). It is the eschatological temple, a house of holiness for Israel, an assembly of supreme holiness for Aaron (1QS 8:5). Its members formed a unity with the heavenly community of angels, who were likewise called holy ones (1QS 11:8; 1QH 11:12) (*NIDNTT* 2:228; cf. also Naudé).

2. The context of the book of *Enoch* shows that suffering qualifies the righteous as holy (*Eth. En.* 48:7).

3. The term *saints* was also used for the members of the Jerusalem cultic community. Antiochus's men wanted to profane the sanctuary and the saints, i.e., those who were true to the law and had by their suffering demonstrated that they steadfastly belonged to the Lord (1 Macc 1:46).

4. Israel's writings were now also called holy (1 Macc 12:9). From now on the Scriptures were to form the new pivotal point for the system of holiness in Judaism, thereby replacing the cult. Hence, those who obeyed the Torah were in particular regarded as holy. Holiness focused more and more on daily life (*NIDNTT* 2:227).

5. In rabbinic Judaism the application of the word group is for the most part controlled by the OT. Occasionally new constructions were ventured, like the holiness of the hair to indicate that the Nazirites had to cut off their hair because it was dedicated to God. Because of the holiness of the name of God it was never pronounced. The holiness of the Torah is seen supremely in the fact that the reading of it stands at the heart of synagogue worship, encircled by a series of prayers referring to it. The particular expression for the holiness of the scrolls in RL is that they make the hands unclean (*Zabim* 5:12). A cultic washing of the hands was necessary after touching them—the hands having become holy through the holiness of Scripture and needing to be made unclean again after contact. The person who fulfills God's commandments and leads a pious life pleasing to God is often called holy (cf. also *TDNT* 1:97-100).

NT In the NT God is seldom described as holy (John 17:11; 1 Peter 1:15; Rev 4:8; 6:10). Christ is only once called holy in the same sense as God (Rev 3:7). The concept of holiness in the NT is determined rather by the Holy Spirit. Following from this, the proper sphere of the holy in the NT is not the cult but the prophetic. The sacred no longer belongs to things, places, or rites, but to the manifestations of life produced by the Spirit (Stronstad, 5-28).

Holy, ban, consecration: → *ḥrm* I (banish, devote to the ban, # 3049); → *nzr* (dedicate oneself to a deity, # 5692); → *qdš* (be holy, consecrate, # 7727)

BIBLIOGRAPHY

ABD 3:237-49; *CAD* 13:46-47; *NIDNTT* 2:223-32; *TDNT* 1:88-110; *THAT* 2:589-609; *TWOT* 2:786-89; B. W. Anderson, "The Holy One of Israel," *Justice and the Holy*, 1989, 3-19; J. Barr, "Semantics and Biblical Theology—A Contribution to the Discussion," *VTSup* 22, 1972, 11-19; G. Bettenzoli, *Geist der Heiligkeit. Traditionsgeschichtliche Untersuchung des QDŠ-Begriffes in Buch Ezekiel*, 1979; M. Eliade, *The Sacred and the Profane*, 1957; J. G. Gammie, *Holiness in Israel*, 1989; M. Haran, *Temples and Temple-Service in Ancient Israel*, 1985; P. P. Jenson, *Graded Holiness: A Key to the Priestly Conception of the World*, 1992; J. A. Naudé, *QDS in die Kumrangeskrifte*, 1985; M. H. Pope, *El in the Ugaritic Texts*, 1955; W. R. Smith, *Die Religion der Semite*, 1967; R. Stronstad, "Unity and Diversity: New Testament Perspectives on the Holy Spirit," *Paraclete* 23, 1989, 15-28; E. J. Wilson, *'Holiness' and 'Purity' in Mesopotamia*, 1994.

Jackie A. Naudé

7728 (*qādēš* I, sacred person, temple prostitute), → # 7727

7731 (*qōdeš/qôdeš*, thing filled with holiness, offerings), → # 7727

7733	קהה

קהה (*qhh*), q., pi. be blunt (# 7733); nom. קֵהָיוֹן (*qēhāyôn*), bluntness (# 7734).

OT 1. The vb. is used of teeth (Jer 31:29-30; Ezek 18:2) and (pi.) of iron (Eccl 10:10). The nom. is only found in Amos 4:6 as reconstructed by Lagarde, reading *qēhāyôn*, bluntness, for *niqqāyôn*, cleanness (of teeth). The phrase means famine (cf. NIV empty stomachs) and needs no emendation. This nom. is not found in *HALAT*. The root is present also in Aram. and Syr. (including the modern Kurdish dialect) with the same meaning.

2. EVV render the q. vb. (in Jer and Ezek) as "set on edge." The three verses each repeat a proverb: "The fathers have eaten sour grapes, and the children's teeth are set on edge." This is not the root meaning of the vb., but it may be required by the context. A theological point is being made, namely, that the people should no longer view God's judgements as a result of their ancestors' sins, but rather as earned by their own iniquities (cf. Deut 24:16). In such a context "bluntness" is less appropriate than a vb. indicating some form of personal distress. The translation "rasp" (cf. J. Bright, 276) represents this ambiguity well. The theological insight of the exilic age (also present in Gen 18:25) stands in marked contrast to the preexilic sense of corporate responsibility evidenced in Exod 20:5-6.

Sharp: → *brr* II (sharpen, # 1406); → *ḥdd* (be sharp, keen, # 2523); → *lṭš* (sharpen, # 4323); → *qillᵉšôn* (sharp object?, # 7849); → *šnn* I (sharpen, pierce, # 9111); **Blunt:** → *pᵉṣîrâ* (blunt?, # 7201); → *qhh* (be blunt, # 7733)

BIBLIOGRAPHY

J. Bright, *Jeremiah*, AB, 1965; J. A. Thompson, *The Book of Jeremiah*, NICOT, 578-79.

P. J. M. Southwell

7734 (*qēhāyôn*, bluntness), → # 7733

7735	קהל

קהל (*qhl*), ni. gather together, assemble; hi. call together, bring together, convoke (# 7735); nom. מַקְהֵל (*maqhēl*), gathering, assembly, throng, great assembly, congregation (# 5220); nom. קָהָל (*qāhāl*), assembly, community, horde, army, religious community, congregation, mob, crowd, alliance, people (# 7736); nom. קְהִלָּה (*qᵉhillâ*), gathering, community, assembly (# 7737); nom. קֹהֶלֶת (*qōhelet*), convener, leader of the congregation or community (# 7738).

ANE Sam. *qāl*; M. Heb., Jew. Aram. *qᵉhālā'*; OSA *qhl/qhlt*; vb. Syr. *qhl*; M. Heb. *qhl*. Within the Northwest Sem. languages the root was indigenous only in Heb. The uses found elsewhere all depend on Heb. Akk. used the root *paḫāru(m)* II, "gather together," lacking this Heb. root; nom. *puḫru(m)*; cf. Aram. *kᵉnîštā'*.

OT 1. The vb. *qhl,* a denominative, is found 39x. In the ni. it was largely reflexive. Moses gave a command to gather, and the congregation (*hā'edâ*) gathered itself (Lev 8:4). Solomon (1 Kgs 8:2) likewise summoned the people and they came together. The place or persons to which/at which the group or assembly is gathered is noted by the prepositions *'el, 'al, lᵉ*, or merely by an accusative (e.g., Shiloh, Josh 18:1) or by no case or preposition (i.e., absol.). It can designate profane as well as religious groups (2 Sam 20:14).

2. The nom. *qāhāl* occurs most often of this group (123x) and is used as a general word that is given definiteness by its larger context. The word itself is neither positive nor negative. The main areas of use are delineated below.

(a) It is often used to designate persons gathered for or because of a military issue. This group of assembled persons can be all Israelites (Gen 49:6; Judg 20:2; 21:5, 8; 2 Chron 28:14), Israelites/non-Israelites (1 Sam 17:47), or non-Israelites/enemies of Israel seeking her destruction (Ezek 38:4, hoard; Jer 50:9, alliance, gathering). Various expressions are used to designate these groups: the gathering/assembly of the people of God (*qᵉhal ʿam hāʾᵉlōhîm*); numerous gatherings/hoards (*qāhāl rāb*); great assembly (*qāhāl gādôl*); assembly of nations (*qᵉhal gôyîm*).

(b) Groups were assembled by the Lord for the purpose of carrying out justice against his people (Ezek 23:47, "the mob will stone them"; cf. 16:40).

(c) The word is employed in various expressions to designate Israel, the people, and the nation in various ways.

(i) Korah and representatives of Israel's leadership refer to the assembly or congregation of Yahweh (*qᵉhal yhwh* ‖ *ʿēdā*) as all the people, who are as holy as Moses (Num 16:3). The Lord's community opposed Moses and Aaron at Kadesh and refer to themselves as the *qᵉhal yhwh* (Num 20:4) that has been misled by Moses and Aaron. The Lord's assembly is reserved for some and membership is forbidden to others (emasculated, married improperly); the Amorite and Moabite may not enter, but Edomites and Egyptians may (see Deut 23:1-8[2-9]).

(ii) The term *qᵉhal yiśrāʾēl*, assembly or congregation of Israel, refers to the people in various situations: gathered before the tabernacle (Lev 16:17), before Moses to hear his song (Deut 31:30), and before Joshua with the people standing before Mount Ebal and Mount Gerizim (Josh 8:33-35). In Exod 12:6 *qᵉhal* is compounded with *ʿēdā* to designate the "gathered community of Israel" (*qᵉhal ʿᵃdat yiśrāʾēl*); cf. Num 14:5). Its use continued into postexilic times ("a large crowd of Israelites ... gathered" [Ezra 10:1]). The assembly of Yahweh stands for all Israel in 1 Chron 28:8.

(iii) The assembly of the people is often related to specific and various occasions: when the ark was brought to the temple of Solomon (1 Kgs 8:14), the whole assembly was blessed by Solomon (cf. Ezra 10:8; Neh 5:7). The whole exilic assembly built booths and lived in them to celebrate the Feast of Tabernacles (Neh 8:17; cf. 2 Chron 30:13-20). Job cries for help in the assembly (*baqqāhāl*; Job 30:28), possibly a town council (or religious assembly?). The assembly (*haqqāhāl*) Israel at Sinai (Deut 9:10) was a special group that received the Torah on a special day. In a similar vein the gathered Israelites in the desert were recognized (Exod 16:3; Lev 16:33; Num 14:5; 16:47[17:12]; 20:12) as a special group who saw Yahweh's wonders in the desert.

(iv) The community gathered for worship deserves special mention. The individual psalmist praises the name of Yahweh while in the midst of the congregation (Ps 22:22, 25[23, 26]; 35:18). The assembly of the people (*qᵉhal-ʿam*) is a more general term used (107:32). The *qᵉhal ḥᵃsîdîm*, the assembly of the pious, probably refers to the worshiping community of Israel (149:1). In contrast to this group is the assembly of the rebellious/evildoers (26:5). The whole congregation blessed the Lord God at times, bowed, and worshiped at the instruction of a leader (1 Chron 29:20). The assembly is called to proper consecration/holiness in Joel 2:16. In Numbers it is called together by trumpets (Num 10:7).

(d) Various miscellaneous groups of people are referred to by *qāhāl*. Isaac blesses Jacob and calls for a community/hoard of nations (*q^e hal gôyim*) to come from him (cf. Gen 35:11). Israel is referred to as a hoard/gathering/collection of people in the march toward Canaan (Num 22:4). An assembly of holy ones (*q^e dōšîm*) (Ps 89:5[6]) designates divine beings who praise God for his wonders. A group of rebellious men, a large group/assembly, is mentioned in Jer 44:15. In Prov 21:16 the company of the shades/dead (*r^e pā'îm*) is the final resting place for one who strays from the path of prudence.

(e) Several constructions occur describing the relationship of persons with the *qāhāl*, assembly. Korah, Dathan, and Abiram perish from the midst of the community (Num 16:33). A person could be "cut off" from the community (Num 19:20) or expelled (Ezra 10:8). Some were forbidden to come into the assembly of Israel (Deut 23:1, 3-8[2, 4-9]); Lam 1:10b; cf. Ezek 44:7, 9), some of whom were not allowed to do so by the Lord.

2. The nom. *q^e hillâ* is a synonym used twice. It designated the assembly of Jacob (*q^e hillat ya'^a qōb*) that had the unique possession of Yahweh's Torah, given to them by Moses (Deut 33:4), while in Neh 5:7 it describes an assembly called together to deal with the leading men of Israel, a large gathering (*q^e hillâ g^e dôlâ*). *maqhēl* is used of the assembly where the Lord/God will be praised (*brk*) (Ps 26:12; 68:26[27]).

3. The q. act. part., of *qhl*, *qōhelet* is found 7x and seems to mean the convener or leader of the congregation or community. All occurrences are in Eccl (1:1, 2, 12; 7:27; 12:8; 12:9, 10). In 12:8 only it occurs with the definite article. The speaker is a man, the son of David. He was king over Israel (1:12) and spoke words of wisdom (1:13) that he had searched out, (cf. 7:27, which has a fem. vb. form, but the reading is problematic; all other refs. have a masc. form of a vb./adj. defining the nom.). He sought to inculcate wisdom (12:9, *ḥkm*) in a palatable way (*ḥēpeṣ*, 12:10). He was one who called people to wisdom primarily, then one who evidently convened persons to hear his words.

4. In the hi. *qhl* indicates the directing or calling of an assembly, as when David summoned the Israelites to gather to get the ark (1 Chron 13:5). Various groups are thus summoned: all of Israel (1 Chron 15:3), the elders of Israel (1 Kgs 8:1), the princes/nobles of Israel (1 Chron 28:1), or the elders and the officers of Israel (Deut 31:28). Exod 35:1/Num 8:9 have as object the whole congregation (*'ēdâ*) of the sons of Israel.

P-B The LXX rendered the vb. *qhl* with *ekklēsiazō*, to hold assembly, sit in assembly, summon to assemble; *synagō*, to bring together, assemble; (*syn*) *athroizō*, to muster (together); *synistēmi*, to place or set together, to unite, combine; *episystrephō*, to run together. Some would argue that the various words used are the result of various translators, not original semantic choices made by the translator (*TWAT* 6:1221).

The words used to translate the nom. are various. The two used most often are *ekklēsia* (68x) and *synagōgē* (36x). Four other words are used at least once. While *'ēdâ*, congegation (→ # 6337), is translated 132x by *synagōgē*, it is never translated by *ekklēsia*. This may indicate that *qāhāl* is the proper forerunner of the NT *ekklēsia*. Fabry (*TWAT* 6:1222) would, however, challenge this. Much of this depends on dating the OT materials. See *'edâ*, which is usually considered the proper forerunner of the Jewish synagogue. Others find the proper background for these words in Hellenistic Jewish Christianity (Fabry, *TWAT* 6:1222).

In the DSS literature the root *qhl* is found about 50x, the vb. only 5x. The meaning of the root is rather broad. It refers to the entire community (4QMMT). The word is used in a more technical sense later, e.g., the hoard of Gog (1QM 11:16; Ezek 38:7), the nations, the evildoers (1QM 14:5; 15:10). The word itself is neutral in its meaning, but various *q^ehālîm*, as in the OT, are possible. In the CD and the TR the community (*qāhāl*) takes on a more specific aspect; e.g., it is the worshiping community (Temple Scroll 16:15-18; 18:7; 26:7-9).

In Mish. Heb. the root *qhl* in the rabbinic literature stood for the twelve tribes of Israel or for each tribe as a part of the total assembly. Adar 13 became the day of the assembly (*qhl*). The word stood for the ideal community. In later literature *qhl* stood for the synagogue assembly (*TWAT* 6:1221). The vb. continued to mean "to call." In addition to the ni. and hi. it was used in the hitp. (Gen R.s. 99). The nom. was used as noted above (JTalm Hor. 1:46a[Num 15:24]). Four communities (*qhl*) are to be designated by Deut 23:2-4, 9: priests, Levites, Israelites, proselytes (for ref. see Jastrow 2:1322-23). *qōhelet* was considered Solomon's surname since his words were presented in public to assemblies. The root is also used in Sir 44:15; 46:7 to refer to the assembly of Israel.

NT In the NT the community was most often designated as the *ekklēsia*. Many see *qāhāl* as the OT (LXX) background for this word (see comments to LXX above). *ekklēsia* may be rather a unique construction of the Hellenistic Christian community, though *'ēdâ* may be preferable (*THAT* 2:619).

Congregation, community, society: → *gēw* II (community, society, # 1569); → *yḥd* (join, # 3479); → *y'd* (determine, designate, appoint, assemble, # 3585); → *s^egullâ* (property, treasured possession, # 6035); → *'ēdâ* I (community, gathering, band, # 6337); → *qhl* (assemble, summon, # 7735)

BIBLIOGRAPHY

NIDNTT 1:270-73, 291-93, 295-304, 306; *THAT* 2:610-19; *TWAT* 6:1204-22; W. F. Albright, "The High Place in Ancient Palestine," *SVT* 4, 1957, 256; G. W. Anderson, "Israel: Amphictyony: 'AM; KAHAL; 'EDAH," P. Azzi, *"La Notion d'assemblée' dans l'AT*, Melta Récherches Orientales 1, 1995, 5-23; H. Bauer, "Die hebräischen Eigennamen als sprachliche Erhenntnisquelle," *ZAW* 48, 1930, 75; K. Berger, *Volksversammlung und Gemeinde Gottes. Zu den Anfängen der Christlichen Vervendung von Ekklesia*," *ZThK* 73, 1976, 167-207; J. Y. Campbell, "The Origin and Meaning of the Christian Use of the Word ἐκκλησία," *JThSt* 49, 1948, 130-42; also *FS H. G. May*, Nashville, 1970, 135-51; W. J. Dumbrell, "The Meaning and Use of Ekklesia in the New Testament with Special Reference to its Old Testament Background," Dissertation, London, 1956; H. J. Fabry, "Studien zur Ekklesiologie des AT und der Qumrangemeinde," Dissertation, Bonn, 1979, 200-12; Z. W. Falk, "Those Excluded from the Congregation," *BethM* 20, 1974/75, 342-51; 438; R. Köbert, "qhl (pal.—aram.) - λάος - ἐκκλησία," *Bib* 46, 1965, 464; L. Rost, *Die Vorstufen von Kirche und Synagoge in Alten Testament*, BWANT 76, 1938; T. Willi, "Kirche als Gottesvolk? Überlegungen zu einem Verstandnis von Kirche im Kontext alttestamentlich-Gottesreich," *TZ* 49, 1993, 289-310; H. W. Wolff, "Volksgemeidnde und Glaubensgemeinde im Alten Bund," *EvT* 9, 1949/50, 65-82; W. P. Wood, "The Congregation of Yahweh,"

Dissertation, Richmond, 1974; F. Zimmerman, "The Root *kahal* in Some Scriptural Passages," *JBL* 50, 1931, 311.

Eugene Carpenter

7736 (*qāhāl*, assembly, community, horde, army), → # 7735

7737 (*q*^{e}*hillâ*, community, gathering), → # 7735

7738 (*qōhelet*, convener), → # 7735

7740 (*q*^{e}*hat, q*^{o}*hat*, Kohath), → Kohath

7742	קַו

קַו (*qaw* I), measuring cord (# 7742), viewed either as a primary nom. (*HALAT* 1010) or nom. from קוה (*qwh* I, wait for; BDB, 857). Not to be confused with the disputed homonyms, קַו II (Isa 18:2, 7; NIV "aggressive [nation]") and קַו III (Isa 28:10, 13; NIV rule [in the phrase "rule on rule"; see further *HALAT* 1011).

OT For a discussion of etymological alternatives see *THAT* 2:619; *TWAT* 6:1223. Less frequent than *ḥebel* II (25x), it is a synonym of a more restricted semantic range: a "measuring cord or string." Theological interest relates to the rhetoric of judgment and restoration in prophetic oracles. As one measures or marks off a person's allotment/portion/lot (cf. 2 Sam 8:2), so God or his agent "stretched out a measuring line" (Lam 2:8) over Israel or some other nation (Isa 34:17) to ruin them (Isa 34:11; cf. Isa 28:17; 2 Kgs 21:13). Cf. Amos 7:17, "your land shall be shared out by a line (*ḥebel*)" (NRSV); and cf. Idrimi 95, *eblūm limdūdūššu,* "may they (the gods) measure his land with a line" (M. Tsevat, "Alalakhiana," *HUCA* 29, 1958, 124). Conversely, God promises to stretch a line in the future for Israel's/Jerusalem's restoration (Zech 1:16; cf. Jer 31:39; Ezek 40:3; Zech 2:1[5]). Related synonyms develop similar figures of judgment and restoration (Isa 3:24; 33:20; 54:2; Jer 10:20).

Cord, rope: → *gādil* (tassel, # 1544); → *ḥebel* II (cord, rope, land, region, # 2475); → *n*^{e}*'ōret* (tow, # 5861); → *niqpâ* (cord, rope, # 5940); → *'*^{a}*bōt* (twisted cord, # 6310); → *qaw* I (measuring cord, # 7742)
Measurement, standard, rule: → *zrh* II (measure, # 2431); → *mdd* (measure, measure off, # 4499); → *š'r* (calculate, # 9132); → *tkn* (regulate by weighing or measuring, # 9419). **For measurements of weight/volume:** → *'êpâ* (an ephah, # 406), **for measurements of length:** → *'ammâ* I (cubit, ell, forearm, # 564)

Bibliography

NIDNTT 3:591-92, 858; *TDNT* 2:43, 896-901; *TDOT* 4:172-79; *TWAT* 6:1223-25; R. J. Forbes, *Studies in Ancient Technology*, IV, 1956, 2-80.

A. R. Pete Diamond

7746 (*qôba'*, helmet), → # 5976

7747	קוה

קוה (*qwh* I), q. tarry, wait, hope; pi. hope (expectantly), await, wait for, expect (# 7747); מִקְוֶה (*miqweh*), hope (# 5223); תִּקְוָה (*tiqwâ*), hope, endurance, expectation (# 9536).

ANE Though possibly linked to, even derived from, the Heb. nom. *qāw*; see Akk. *qû*, rope, thread, string (*HALAT*, but see *THAT* 2:619), it is etymologically still uncertain whether a connection between *qwh* and *qāw* exists at all (*TWAT* 6:1226). If so, the basic meaning of *qwh* I would be, be tight, tense. Other possible cognates under discussion are: *qwh* II and Akk. *qu'û(m)*, expect, wait for, and Syr. *qawwî*, remain, expect (*TWAT* 6:1226).

OT 1. The root *qwh* I appears some 80x, most often in the intensive form (pi. 41x; 19x with *l*^{e}, 5x with *'el*, 16x with *'et*) and in the nom. form *tiqwâ* (32x). The rest of its occurences are: q. (all act. part.) 6x and the other nom. form, *miqweh* (5x).

2. Found only once in the Pentateuch (Gen 49:18) and never in the Former Prophets, the root is most commonly used in the Latter Prophets (29x) and in the Writings (47x). Thus, *qwh* figures among the more prominent roots in poetic expression.

3. Especially in the Psalms (some 20x; e.g., Ps 25:3; 69:7[6]; 130:5; cf. Prov 20:22; Lam 3:25), but also in various prophetic books (Isa 8:17; 25:9 [2x]; 26:8; 33:2; 40:31; 49:23; 51:5; 60:9; Jer 14:22; Hos 12:6[7]), God himself is the explicit object of the vb. hope (implicit: Ps 39:7[8]; cf. Isa 51:5). Twice *qwh* signifies one of his deeds (salvation, Gen 49:18; awesome things, Isa 64:3[2]), and once his name (Ps 52:9[11]). As to the nom., of the five occurrences of *miqweh*, three have God as their object: he is Israel's (Jer 14:8; 17:13) or their fathers' (50:7) hope, yet twice (1 Chron 29:15; Ezra 10:29) there is no object. Of the 32x *tiqwâ* occurs (see below), God is only once the explicit (Ps 71:5) and a few times the implicit object of hope (Job 5:16; 6:8; 11:18; Prov 23:18; Lam 3:29). Yet, all in all, no other person (or thing, for that matter) is as often the object of the root *qwh* as God himself.

4. In a few prophetic books (Jer 29:11; 31:17; Ezek 19:5; 37:11; Hos 2:15[17]; Zech 9:12) and especially in Job and Proverbs (Job 8:13; 17:15; 19:10; 27:8; Prov 11:7; 19:18; 24:14; 26:12; 29:20) hope seems to be an end in itself, i.e., no particular object is in view. Only when hope is linked (or used in parallel) to other words, noms. especially, is it possible to determine an object of hope (something good in the prophets; mostly not good in Job and Proverbs). Israel once believed that her expectation (*yḥl*, ni.) and hope were simply gone (Ezek 19:5; 37:11), but for those in Exile there was hope and a future (*'*^{a}*ḥarît*), viz., in their return (Jer 29:11; 31:17). The Valley of Achor (which means trouble and refers to the Exile) will be made into a door of hope (Hos 2:15[17]) for the exiles, who will later even become prisoners of hope, viz., at the appearing of their king (Zech 9:12). There is a future hope (*'aḥ*^{a}*rît*), a hope (*tiqwâ*) that will not be cut off (*krt*; → # 4162) for those who fear the Lord (Prov 23:18; 24:14). While the prospect (*tôḥelet*) of the righteous is joy, the hopes (*tiqwâ*) of the wicked come to nothing (*'bd*, 10:28; cf. 11:7). According to Eliphaz and Zophar, the hope (*tiqwâ*) and the confidence (*kislâ*, Job 4:6; *beṭaḥ*, 11:18; cf. Ps 71:5) of Job is obviously to get out of trouble, but for the godless, hope (with no parallel word) is bland and amounts to nothing (*'bd*, Job 8:13; 11:20; 27:8; Prov 10:28; cf. 11:7, 23), to mere survival for the poor (Job 5:16; Ps 9:19[18]), or to new life for a felled tree only, not for a dead man (Job 14:7), because, for mere mortals, hope ceases (*klh*; → # 3983) with life's end (7:6) or is destroyed (*'bd*; → # 6) altogether (14:19).

5. In a few instances, evenly distributed over the Latter Prophets and Writings, what amounts to abstractions make up the objects of hope, as in these examples: though Job hoped for (the) good, evil came (Job 30:26); though Yahweh looked for

(expected) justice, he saw (only) bloodshed (Isa 5:7); and when the repentant hoped for justice, there was none (59:11). Though Jeremiah hoped for peace, there was none, only terror (Jer 8:15; 14:19); though the psalmist looked for sympathy (*nwd*; → # 5653), there was none (Ps 69:20[21]).

6. As with *yḥl*, *qwh* may signify futile hope or pointless waiting, because either a point of no return has been reached (Isaiah and Jeremiah) or a situation has become desperate (Job). Thus, the vineyard grower who eagerly awaited a crop of good grapes hoped in vain, because the yield was worthless (Isa 5:2, 4). The repentant vainly hope that God will execute justice and rightousness for them (59:9); or the light the captives vainly hoped for will have been turned into thick darkness (Jer 13:16). Job wished that the morning stars of the day of his birth had waited in vain for daylight to come (Job 3:9)—such is his despondency about his very birth (3:1-26). Job complains that, unlike the hope a hired man can have to obtain his wages at the end of a long day's work, his own hope is that of unending misery only (7:2), or worse still, that of Sheol alone (17:13). Similarly, Naomi has no hope left to remarry and have sons again in view of her advanced age (Ruth 1:12).

7. Finally, there is eager, expectant waiting, though not necessarily for commendable things. The enemies of Jerusalem rejoice over its destruction, a day they have eagerly awaited (Lam 2:16), and so the psalmist's enemies eagerly wait to take his life (Ps 56:6[7]; 119:95). In a different way, dew from the Lord or showers on the grass do not wait expectantly for humankind, i.e., (probably) to be appreciated (Mic 5:7[6]).

8. Hope in the Old Testament.

(a) The study of hope or expectant waiting is not limited to a core semantic field (→ *ḥkh*, *yḥl*, *qwh*, and *śbr*). Hope is an attitude, a disposition, or a state of mind that is expressed in many different ways (see below).

(b) God himself is most often the ultimate source of hope. While there is such a thing as mere hope, hope as an abstraction, or futile hope (above all in Job), in the majority of cases there is an underlying belief in a continuity based on a strong belief in God and in his being active in history, even against all odds.

(c) Hope and expectant waiting on God are most often expressed when humans are particularly aware of their finiteness and God's infiniteness (Ps 39:4-7). This permeates so many texts that the distinction between sacred and profane hope is elusive.

(d) Hope and expectant waiting are linked to people's need to draw upon God's resources, especially when confronted with the question of goals in life.

(e) Hope owes much to God's numerous promises. Believers expect them to be unfailing. There are the covenant promises made by God to Noah, Abraham, Moses, and David, and the renewal of those covenant promises made to the prophets, especially to Jeremiah (Jer 31-33; thus, "God of hope," 14:8; 17:13). Even divided, Israel will one day be one again, under a single ruler (Ezek 37:15-23; cf. Isa 11:13). True enough, such promises give hope to a remnant only (e.g., Isa 7-8), but it is hope nevertheless. "Hope hopes in God, the God whose freedom we do not take away by hoping no matter how immovably certain they are of the promise of God to his own" (Zimmerli, 150).

(f) There are some notable contrasts. While the book of Job shows the most severe criticism of a hopeful existence, the book of Psalms is a collection of impressive sayings of hope. Even in psalms that show little hope (e.g., Ps 39), there hope is found in God (39:7). But all in all, the psalmists have an audacious certainty about them that seems to be substantiated by nothing but God (27:1). Even the book of Lamentations, perhaps the epitome of despair, sounds a profound note of hope (Lam 3:18-29). So does Qohelet, the apparent pagan and sarcastic, when he comments on hope (*biṭṭāḥôn*) (Eccl 9:4).

(g) Though hope might be deferred and/or not specified, there remains an expectancy (cf. Isa 8:17; Mic 7:7; Ps 42:5[6]). Even the eschatological/apocalyptic material with its imagery communicates, albeit imprecisely, continuity in history, and with that hope and expectancy (Isa 25:6-8). The imminent end, so characteristically expected, sounds a note of hope even amid current national trouble (Joel 3:15-16; Mal 4:5-6). "Faith in the sovereignty of the covenant God, obedience to the restored law of Moses, patience to wait for a vision postponed, confidence in the ultimate vindication of their purposes in history, and expectation of the expansion of God's kingdom despite all signs to the contrary—these were the responses of Israel's finest sons and daugters in circumstances that tried them almost to breaking-point" (Hubbard, 48).

P-B 1. In the LXX, while *qwh* I is most often (some 20x) translated with the vb. (*hypo-*)*menō* and only twice (Isa 25:9; 26:8) with *elpizō*, the nom. *tiqwâ* is translated some 20x with *elpis*, 4x with *hypomonē* (Job 14:19; Ps 9:19 Q; 62:5[6]; 71:4[5]) and twice with *hypostasis* (Ruth 1:12; Ezek 19:5); the other nom., *miqweh*, is always (4x) translated with *hypomonē* (once, in Jer 50:7 [LXX=27:7] it is not translated at all).

2. The QL confirms the prevalence of the roots *yḥl* and *qwh* when it comes to expressing hope and endurance. Equally rare as in BH are *ḥkh* and *śbr*. There is only one occurence of *ḥkh* so far, in 1QpHab 7.9, a quote of Hab 2:3, whereas *śbr* has yet to appear on a Qumran document.

Verbal forms of *yḥl* appear in 4Q 521 ("all of you who wait patiently in your hearts"), in 4Q 252pG^{a}, which is a quote of Gen 8:12, and in 4Q 266D^{a} (context uncertain). The nom. *tôḥelet* is found on 4Q 509 (actually the only legible word), in 11QPs 22.9 (noncanonical), and in 1QH 9.14, which has God as the addressee: "I know that there is hope thanks to your kindness and trust through the fulness of your strength."

As in BH, *qwh* the most frequently used root is in the QL. Verbal forms occur in 4Q 384papApocJerB (context uncertain), and in 4QHa, where "hope for knowledge" (through the study of the Scriptures) is expressed. The nom. *miqweh,* known from 1QH (3.20; 6.6; 9.14), appears on (tiny fragment) 4Q 382 (legible along with only one other word), whereas *tiqwâ,* also known from 1QH (3.27; 6.32; 9.12) and 1QM 11.9 (close to Hos 2:17) occurs in 4Q 221, a copy of *Jubilee,* in which "hope on earth" is expressed. Finally, without being able to determine any context, mostly because of the fragmentary nature of the document, yet the reading is ascertained, *tiqwah* is found in 4Q 365RP^{c}, in 4Q 378PsJ^{a}, in 4QHf 432, and in 4Q 434Barki Nafschi^{a}.

Though 1QH 3.2 and 6.32 state that hope can be lost through judgment, all in all, Qumran occurrences confirm the fact that hope is most often oriented towards God and/or something he is expected to do. When canonical texts containing a root expressing hope and endurance are cited, then it is most often in direct application to the Qumran community (e.g., 4QpPs37 2.4 & 4.10, citing Ps 37:9, 34).

NT For several NT writers the OT contained many promises that they believed were being fulfilled (cf. the *hina plērōthē* [= so that it might be fulfilled] formula, 10x and 4x respectively in Matt and John). Most of all, of course, they regarded the hope for a future Davidic king, the Messiah (→ *mšḥ*), fulfilled in Jesus. The messianic hope from the period of the classical prophets forward was one of the major hopes, if not the major hope of Israel (Luke 1:67-79; 2:25-38).

Hope, waiting: → *ḥkh* (wait, endure, expect, hope, # 2675); → *yḥl* (wait, hope, endure, long, # 3498); → *qwh* I (tarry, wait, hope, wait for, # 7747); → *śbr* (test, investigate, hope, wait, examine, # 8432)

BIBLIOGRAPHY

ISBE 2:80, 751-52; *NIDNNT* 2:238-41; *THAT* 2:619-29; *TWAT* 6:1225-34; *TWOT* 2:791; R. E. Clements, *Old Testament Theology: A Fresh Approach*, 1974, ch. 6; D. A. Hubbard, "Hope in the OT," *TynB*, 1983, 33-59; H.-W. Wolff, *Anthropologie des Alten Testaments*, 1973, 221-30 (Eng. *Anthropology of the OT*, 1974, 149-55); W. Zimmerli, *Man and his Hope in the OT*, SBT 20, 1971.

Daniel Schibler

7748	קוה

קוה (*qwh* II), ni. gather, be gathered (# 7748); מִקְוֶה (*miqweh* II), accumulation of water (→ # 5224); מִקְוָה (*miqwâ*), reservoir (# 5225).

OT The vb. occurs in the ni. 2x. In Gen 1:9 it is used of the gathering of the water under the sky, which is then called "sea." This shows that the Lord is the one who created the sea by the word of his mouth. In Jer 3:17 the word occurs in a prophecy concerning the time when the Lord will bring both Israel and Judah, who have been unfaithful, back into the land that he had given them. Perhaps the idea is that the nations will be brought together as the water was gathered together to form the sea (note Mic 4:1).

2. The nom. *miqweh* occurs in the OT 3x. In Gen 1:10 it is used of the waters that were gathered together. In Exod 7:19 it refers to the "pools" or "reservoirs of water" of the Egyptians that were turned to blood. This was evidently water collected or reserved for special purposes (J. I. Durham, *Exodus* WBC, 94). Although the reservoirs could be a reference to the "Crocodile" god, Sobek, who was worshiped in Egypt in the Middle Kingdom (see G. Posener, *Lexikon der Ägyptischen Kultur*, 1960, 136-37; A. Eggebrecht, *Das alte Ägyptien*, 1984, 271), it is more probable that *miqweh* refers to the irrigation system used by the Egyptians. There were not only the canals, but various dams with large and small reservoirs, which were opened and closed according to need when the Nile overflowed (see Eggebrecht, 388; and esp. A. Erman and H. Ranke, *Ägyptien und ägyptisches Leben im Altertum*, 1981). The plague struck at the very heart of the Egyptian agricultural life-line! In Lev 11:36 the context has to do with that which is clean, or unclean. If an unclean animal falls into a spring or a cistern for collecting water, it remains clean.

3. The word *miqwâ* is used once in the OT, Isa 22:11. This occurs in a prophecy against the city of Jerusalem. The leaders have sought to fortify the city against attack by building a reservoir. The prophet says, "You built a reservoir between the two walls

for the water of the Old Pool, but you did not look to the One who made it, or have regard for the One who planned it long ago" (NIV). Some feel that this "reservoir between the two walls" is the present-day "Pool of Siloam," which is at the end of Hezekiah's tunnel (see E. J. Young, *The Book of Isaiah*, NICOT, 2:98-99; J. N. Oswalt, *The Book of Isaiah Chapters 1-39*, NICOT, 413; see also H. Wildberger, *Jesaja*, BKAT, 1978, X, ii, 822-24). Regardless of the location, the point of the prophecy is that the city is depending on human efforts to save her, rather than relying on the Lord!

P-B In RL the word was used for the ritual bathing pool or reservoir ("immersion pools") as described in the Mishnah tractate Mikwaoth (see Danby, *Mishnah*, 732-45; *WTM* 3:218-19). For a description of the archaeological finds of such pools, see La Sor.

Gathering: → *'sp* (gather, harvest, # 665); → *bṣr* (harvest grapes, # 1305); → *ḥṭb* (gather, cut, # 2634); → *kns* (gather, # 4043); → *lqṭ* (gather, # 4377); → *'ēdâ* I (community, gathering, band, # 6337); → *'mr* (gather grain, # 6682); → *qbṣ* (gather, # 7695); → *qᵉhillâ* (community, gathering, # 7737); → *qwh* II (gather, # 7748); → *qšš* (gather, collect, # 8006)
Harvest, gleaning: → *'sp* (gather, harvest, # 665); → *bṣr* (harvest grapes, # 1305); → *yᵉbûl* (produce, yield, # 3292); → *lqṭ* (reap, harvest, # 4377); → *'ll* I (glean, # 6618); → *'mr* (gather grain, # 6682); → *qbṣ* (gather, # 7695); → *qṣr* (harvest, # 7917); → *tᵉbû'â* (crop, yield, # 9311); → *tᵉnûbâ*, produce, # 9482)

BIBLIOGRAPHY
W. S. LaSor, "Discovering What Jewish *Miqva'ot* Can Tell Us About Christian Baptism," *BARev* 13, 1987, 52-59.

Cleon L. Rogers, Jr.

7752	קוט

קוט (*qwṭ*), q. feel disgust; ni. feel disgust; hitpolal loathe (# 7752).

ANE Ugar. *qṭ* II/*qwṭ*, have an aversion for, loathe, *qṭṭ*, loathing, aversion; Mish. Heb. *qûṭ*, to feel an aversion for, be disgusted. BH *qwṭ* and *qwṣ* are etymological equivalents (due to the common Sem. *ṭ/ṣ* interchange—e.g., Heb. *ṣûr*, rock = Aram. *ṭûr*, rock).

OT The vb. *qwṭ* occurs 7x (Job 10:1; Ps 95:10; 119:158; 139:21; Ezek 6:9; 20:43; 36:31) and appears as a ni. 4x, hitpol. 2x, and q. only once. In every case a *bᵉ* preposition is prefixed to the object of loathing.

1. The byforms, *qwṭ* and *qwṣ* (→ # 7762), are nearly identical in semantic nuance. For example, Job (10:1, *qwṭ*, ni.) and Rebekah (Gen 27:46, *qwṣ*) were weary of certain aspects of life (Job's experience of suffering as an "innocent" man and Rebekah's frustration with Hittite women) to the point of disgust. During their wilderness wanderings, the Israelites became weary of their monotonous diet of manna, to the point of detesting it (Num 21:5, *qwṣ*).

2. Both roots (*qwṭ/qwṣ*) also describe Yahweh's loathing or hostile rejection of a people. Yahweh warned Israel against conforming to the abhorrent practices of the Canaanites. Those activities constituted the ground of his loathing of those pagans and resulted in his intention to drive them out of the land of promise (Lev 20:23, *qwṣ*). The Israelites themselves had experienced divine loathing in their wilderness wanderings, provoked by their inability to recognize and appreciate Yahweh's salvific activity on

their behalf (Ps 95:10, *qwṭ*, q.). Doubtless, Yahweh's loathing a people has severe punitive consequences.

3. The other occurrences of *qwṭ* connote human loathing in two realms that *qwṣ* does not signify. In his confession of loyalty to Yahweh, the psalmist affirms that he despises the faithless/treacherous because of their refusal to obey God (Ps 119:158). As an indication of covenant solidarity (cf. the treaty between Muršiliš II and Duppi-Teššub [Thompson, 16], "with my friend you shall be friend, and with my enemy you shall be enemy"), the psalmist declares that he loathes all those who rebel against Yahweh. Some scholars (e.g., *BHS*, Krause, 510-11) unnecessarily emend the MT *ûbitqôm^{e}mêkā*, those who rise up against you, to *ûb^{e}mitqôṭ^{a}ṭêkā*, those who despise you, in order to enhance the parellelism of this bicola.

4. The three occurrences of *qwṭ* (ni., followed by *bipp^{e}nê* denoting a reflexive nuance) in Ezek all describe Israel's self-loathing during their experience of exile (Ezek 6:9), after deliverance from exile (20:43), and in the eschaton (36:31). Ezekiel affirms to God's people that as they contemplate the *tô'ēbâ* (abomination, see # 9359) they committed, which occasioned their experience of Yahweh's wrath, they will loathe themselves for their reprehensible conduct.

Contempt, disdain, disgust, loathing: → *bwz* (show contempt for, # 996); → *bzh* (be contemptible, think lightly of, despise, # 1022); → *bḥl* (become tired of, disdain, # 1041); → *g'l* (abhor, be defiled, fail, # 1718); → *zhm* (make s.t. loathsome, # 2299); → *zwr* III (be offensive, # 2320); → *zll* I (be frivolous, be despised, # 2361); → *znh* II (feel a dislike for, # 2389); → *zārā'* (sickness, nausea, # 2426); → *ḥnn* II (be stinking, loathsome, # 2859); → *yq'* (turn aside, # 3697); → *nq'* (disengage, # 5936); → *qwṭ* (feel disgust, # 7752); → *qll* (be slight, swift, appear trifling, treat with contempt, # 7837); → *šwṭ* II (slight, despise, # 8764); → *šqṣ* (make o.s. detestable, # 9210); → *t'b* (be detestable, be loathed, loathe, abhor, # 9493)

Bibliography

TWAT 6:1234-37; *TWOT* 2:792; H.-J. Kraus, *Psalms 60-150*, 1989; J. Thompson, *The Ancient Near Eastern Treaties and the Old Testament*, 1964.

Michael A. Grisanti

7754	קוֹל

קוֹל (*qôl*), nom. voice, sound, obedience, thunder, noise, cry (# 7754).

ANE Several cognates occur, include Ugar. *ql*, voice, thunder, Akk. *qâlu*, speech, and Arab. *qawl*, word, saying.

OT 1. Three major roots make up the semantic domain of noise, viz., *qôl*, voice or noise (# 7754); *hmh*, make a noise (→ # 2159), and *hāmôn*, noise (# 2162), most often of natural rather than human noises; *š'h*, roar (# 8616), and *šā'ôn*, uproar (# 8623), implying most often the noise of a crowd (tumult). All three terms probably had onomatopoeic origins. See also *dbr*, speak, word (# 1819).

2. *qôl* is found only in the nom. form and occurs some 505x (so *HALAT*, but *NIVEC* 506x) in the OT, and is translated in the NIV by over 100 Eng. words and expressions, the bulk of which are only used once. In 23 cases, the word is left untranslated. On several occasions *qôl* is rendered by the NIV as an interjection, "Listen! (Gen 4:10 and Isa 52:8; cf. *TWAT* 6:1247). Common expressions include the following:

Obey (lit., hear . . . voice), with *šm'* hear (# 9048; e.g., Josh 24:24); cry for mercy with *taḥ^{a}nûn* (# 9384; e.g., Ps 28:2); cry aloud (lit., give [*ntn*, # 5989] voice; e.g., Prov 2:3); thunders (also with *ntn* [# 5989], give voice), (e.g., Jer 10:13); called out (lit., call with a loud voice) with *gādôl*, big (# 1524); and *qr'*, call (# 7924; e.g., 2 Chron 32:18). The most important theological contribution that *qôl* makes is in terms of the voice of God as a critical factor in the revelation of God, and the background that this supplies for both the rabbinic *bath-qôl* and the NT equivalent found in the gospels. The revelation of God, albeit accompanied by a vision, is essentially an oral experience!

3. *qôl* occurs over 100x in the Pent. The expression "lift up one's voice and weep" marks times of happiness (tears of joy), as in the first meeting between Jacob and Rebekah (Gen 29:11), as well as times of sadness (tears of sorrow), as when Esau discovers his brother's duplicity (27:38). The NIV rendering as "weep aloud" does not really do justice to a situation where "wept tears of joy" would be more appropriate. No words are indicated in these instances, so that one may understand that *qôl* is not restricted to the intelligible content of the voice. *qôl* may, in fact, mean an unintelligible noise, as in the incident of the golden calf. Moses and Joshua hear a *qôl*, which is neither the "sound (*qôl*) of victory ... [nor that] of defeat" (Exod 32:18). *qôl* may also imply simply the sound of someone moving. Thus, in the Garden of Eden, the man and the woman hear the sound (*qôl*) of the Lord in the garden, in the cool of the evening (lit., at the breeze of the day, Gen 3:8). That sound awakens Adam's guilt (v. 10). Following the murder of Abel, God searches out Cain and says, "Listen (*qôl*)!" His brother's blood is calling out, presumably for revenge (4:10). In the Exodus account of the plagues, *qôl* is used for thunder (Exod 9:23-34). In the account of the theophany at Sinai, *qôl* is used both for the thunder and the very loud voice (*qôl*) of the shofar (NIV a very loud trumpet blast, 19:16). Such auditory descriptions would, in time, become integral to accounts of the theophany of God.

4. In the most common expression, "to obey (lit., hear) the voice of the LORD," we may discern a sense of the authority and revelation of God. In the covenant formula as found in Deuteronomy, obedience to the voice of God is understood primarily as obedience to the covenant stipulations (Deut 27:26, cf. 28:15, where listening to God's voice is coupled with keeping his commandments and statutes; cf. Weinfeld, *TDOT* 2:266-78). In 27:10, prior to the listing of covenantal curses, and in 28:1 (obey fully, doubling of the vb. *šm'* [# 9048]), in preparation for the covenantal blessings, the people are exhorted to obey the voice of God. The conj. *b^{e}* (# 928) does service as the link between the action of listening (*šm'*) and the voice (*qôl*) of God, as with other vbs., implying paying close sensory attention (see BDB, 90). Obedience will result in blessings, such as fertility of family and of the fields (Deut 28:4), and in the responsibility of being designated God's holy people (v. 9). This combination of law, covenant, land, and obedience to the voice of God forms perhaps the most important of the themes in the history of the Deuteronomist and in other writings. So in Gen 26:5 the same linking of law (for which no less than four different Heb. terms are present in this verse) and obedience to God's voice is found, but with reference to Abraham, whose reward is the land (v. 3) and progeny (v. 4).

5. *qôl* in the historical collection of the Deuteronomist may be translated as voice, whether of God (Josh 5:6), of the people (Judg 2:4), or of an individual like David (1 Sam 26:17). The word is also used for the shout of triumph when the ark

entered the camp of the Israelites (1 Sam 4:6), for trumpets (Josh 6:5), for thunder (1 Sam 12:17, 18), and for the bleating of sheep and the lowing of cattle (1 Sam 15:14), while 2 Kings 7:6 speaks of the rumble of chariots by which God frightened away the besiegers of Samaria. Probably the most striking story is that of Elijah's refuge in a cave on Mount Horeb (1 Kgs 19:12), when God came to him as a gentle whisper (so NIV; lit., the sound [*qôl*] of silence [*d*ᵉ*māmâ*], # 1960). Standing in the cave mouth, Elijah received his instructions from a voice, subsequently identified as God speaking (1 Kings 19:13; cf. v. 15); the following chapters recount his obedience. Obedience to the voice of God (Josh 22:2; 24:24) or, more often, disobedience (Judg 2:2; 6:10; 1 Sam 15:19) represents one of the main themes of this collection of texts.

6. The Chronicler makes use of what appears to be a set phrase, rendered as "to issue or to send (lit., give, *ntn* (# 5989), a proclamation, *qôl*)." So in 2 Chron 24:9 a proclamation is made in Jerusalem regarding taxation, in 30:5 regarding the celebration of Passover, and in Neh 8:15, concerning Sukkoth. Ezra 1:1 speaks of the decree of Cyrus, which was made orally, but also taken down in writing (Ezra 1:1, cf. vv. 2-4).

7. *qôl* occurs over 200x in the prophets, mainly in Jeremiah, Ezekiel, and Isaiah. Isaiah uses *qôl* in both the personal and impersonal senses. In the vision of his call, the prophet Isaiah hears the voice of God asking, "Whom shall I send? And who will go for us?" (Isa 6:8). The idea of the divine council of God (cf. Jer 23:18-22) and the divine voice are important aspects of both the call narratives and of the later theophanies (cf. Habel, "The Form and Significance," 297-323, and Mullen, *The Assembly of the Gods*, 209-25). The voice of God is majestic and crushes Assyria (Isa 30:30-31). Such sounds of God's judgment form an important element that will recur in the apocalyptic literature. In describing the devastation of the earth, Isaiah uses the phrase "the voice of fear" (NIV sound of terror), which is made more frightening by its abstract and nonspecific quality (24:18). Similarly, in the woe to Ariel, the prophet warns that God will suddenly come with thunder (*ra'am*, → # 8308), earthquake, a great noise (*qôl*), windstorm, tempest, and flames of fire (29:6). Isaiah uses *qôl* of God's messenger (40:3) who prepares the way of God in the wilderness for the returning exiles. The imperative "cry" has sometimes been seen as the call of this anonymous prophet (v. 6). The servant of God will not cause his voice to be heard in the street (42:2, cf. does not open his mouth, 53:7). God commends those who obey the servant's voice (50:10). Other renderings of *qôl* include the sound of singing (48:20) and melody (51:3), and the sound of weeping will be heard no more in the messianic kingdom (65:19). The texture of the prophetic expressions of the coming reign of God included both sight and sound. In reference to God's vengeance, the prophet uses *qôl* 3x to describe the din (*qôl šā'ôn*, # 8263) that emanates from the temple, the sounds of God repaying his enemies for what they deserve (66:6).

8. The keys to Jeremiah's use of *qôl* are the twin ideas of obedience and disobedience. No less than 13x, the prophet declares that the people have not heeded the voice of God (e.g., Jer 3:13, 25), a commonplace expression deeply woven into the fabric of his prophecy. A key verse for Jeremiah's theology is found in 7:23, where God calls out, "Obey me (lit., voice), and I will be your God," an imperative repeated by the prophet (11:4, 7; 26:13; 38:20). The people are caught between the voice of God and the deceptive words of the popular religion, which combined elements of Yahwism and Baalism. As the spokesperson for the prophetic minority, Jeremiah calls

upon the people to worship God alone. Three times Jeremiah warns that God will bring an end to the sound (*qôl*) of joy and of gladness and to the voice (*qôl*) of the bride and bridegroom in the towns and streets of Judah (7:34; 16:9; 25:10). Instead, the people will hear the noises of war like the sound (*qôl*) of the trumpet (4:19, 21), the sound (*qôl*) of horsemen and archers, and the sound (*qôl*) of the neighing of stallions (8:16b).

9. In the theophanies of Ezekiel, one hears of the sound (*qôl*) of wings, like the roar (*qôl*) of rushing water, the voice (*qôl*) of the Almighty like the tumult (*qôl*) of an army (Ezek 1:24). To the ancient oriental mind the roar of the waves were reminders of the supernatural warriors of the forces of the deep (Zimmerli, *Ezekiel* I, 131). Sound also plays a significant role in other visionary experiences (cf. Ezek 3:12-13; 10:5; 43:2). In God's judgment on the idolatry within the temple, he warns ominously that even if the people shout (lit., cry in my ears with a great voice), he will not listen to them (8:18).

10. In the Writings, *qôl* is used mainly in the Psalms (over 50x) and Job (21x). In the majority of cases Job uses *qôl* literally of human voices, as in the expression "lift up (*nś'*, # 5951) their voices and weep" (Job 2:12), of animal noises (4:10), the flute (21:12), the thunderbolt (28:26), and the trumpet (39:24). Theologically significant is Elihu's dramatic description of God's voice, which roars (37:2), thunders, and resounds (v. 4), and thunders in marvelous ways (v. 5). Such parallels with the Baal texts are striking (see Pope, 240-46 and Day). However, the similarity ends there. The God of Elihu is not limited to being the personification of the natural phenomena, as Baal was, but is the creator of all things (37:18), as Job comes to see (38:4-11). In similar vein, Ps 29 speaks of the voice of the Lord thundering upon the waters (v. 3), powerful and majestic (v. 4), breaking the cedars of Lebanon (v. 5), striking with flashes of lightning (v. 7), shaking the desert of Kadesh (v. 8), and making the hinds give birth (better, twisting the oaks, v. 9). Dahood, *Psalms 1-50,* 174-80, details a significant series of parallels with the Ugaritic texts.

11. One of the theological lessons to be learnt from a study of *qôl* in the Psalms is that of answered prayer. Several times the psalmist cries out to God to hear his or her prayer (lit., voice e.g., Ps 27:7; 28:2), and correspondingly we have the cry of affirmation, that the Lord has heard his/her voice (e.g., Ps 6:8[9]; 18:6[7]; 28:6). With the wilderness experience as context, God calls out, "Today, if you hear his voice, do not harden your hearts." To do so would mean not entering into God's rest (95:7b-8a, 11). Proverbs use of *qôl* (7x) speaks most importantly of wisdom's voice (Prov 1:20), which calls to humankind to discover the wisdom of God (from her mouth comes knowledge and understanding [2:6]).

12. Throughout the OT, *qôl* is primarily associated with intelligible sounds, of which the revelation of God's voice takes precedence. God speaks, and it is the duty of humankind to obey. Such obedience is expressed most often in the sense of keeping of God's covenant. But *qôl* is also related to inarticulate noise, of which the sounds that accompany the theophany of God are the most striking.

P-B The LXX generally translates *qôl* with either the G nom. *phonē*, meaning sound, noise, or language, or the vb. *phoneō*, make a sound, call. The nom. was used in Classical G to represent the noise of living creatures, either human or animal, while the vb. could do service also for inanimate objects like musical instruments (see *TDNT* 2:954-55; 9:278-303). In RL *qôl* meant a voice, call, or sound (Ker 6a). The enjoyment of sound, sight, or smell does not come under the category of the misuse of sacred property (Pes 26a). In Ex R. 5 the expression *haqqôl* implies the voice of revelation. In the first century following, the rabbinic *bat-qôl* (daughter of voice) described the echo, audible on earth, of the divine voice, which served to bring divine pronouncements. *qôl* is also used regularly in QL (see *KKT*, 191-92) in ways reminiscent of the OT, such as the roaring of the enemy like the sound of many waters (1QH 2:16, 27), the clamor of the enemy (1QH 3:13), trumpets (1QM 8:5), or the exhortation to heed the voice of God (CD 3:7-8) and of the teacher of righteousness (CD 20:28-32).

NT The nom. *phōnē*, sound, and the vb. *phōneō*, produce a sound, occur regularly in the NT. The most significant element from the OT to surface in the NT is that of the voice of God (see *NIDNTT* 3:113-14), which is heard at important moments in Jesus' lifetime. Hearing the voice of Jesus is also important, especially in John's gospel (e.g., John 10:27). Finally *phōnē*, sound, supplies the oral texture for the book of Revelation, as consistent with BH's understanding of the voice from heaven.

Noise, roar, voice: → *g'r* (roar, shout, bellow, cry out, rebuke, reprimand, # 1721); → *hmh* (make a noise, uproar, sound, be restless, # 2159); → *hmm* (rumble, crush, # 2169); → *nhm* (growl, groan, # 5637); → *qôl* (voice, sound, thunder, cry, # 7754); → *rgš* (be restless, # 8093); → *š'g* (roar, # 8613); → *š'h* II (roar, # 8616)

BIBLIOGRAPHY

THAT 2:629-34; *TWAT* 6:1237-51; *TWOT* 2:792-93; F. M. Cross, "The Council of Yahweh in Second Isaiah," *JNES* 12, 1953, 274-77; J. Day, *God's Conflict with the Dragon and the Sea*, 1985; N. Habel, "The Form and Significance of the Call Narratives, *ZAW* 77, 1965, 297-323; J. Jeremias, *Theophanie*, 1965; E. C. Kingsbury, "The Prophets and the Council of Yahweh" *JBL* 83, 1964, 279-86; I. Konowitz, *The God Idea in Jewish Tradition*, 1989, 39-50; C. J. Labuschagne, *The Incomparability of Yahweh*, 1966; B. Lang, *Monotheism and the Prophetic Minority*, 1983; J. Lindblom, "Die Vorstellung vom Sprechen Jahwes zu den Menschen im AT," *ZAW* 75, 1963, 263-88; B. Long, "Prophet Call Traditions and Reports of Visions," *ZAW* 84, 1972, 494-500; E. T. Mullen, *The Assembly of the Gods*, 1980; M. Pope, *Job*, AB, 1965.

W. R. Domeris

7756	קוּם

קוּם (*qwm*), q. stand up, stand upright, stand (last, continue), arise, rise up, get up (in the morning), come about; pi. raise up, make (a word) come true, confirm, institute, direct; pil. raise up, present o.s.; hi. set up, erect, carry out, perform, make stand, establish, raise up, help up; polel raise up, ho. be erected, be carried out, be appointed; hitp. rise up, rebel (# 7756); יְקוּם (*yeqûm*), living thing (→ # 3685); מָקוֹם (*māqôm*), nom. place, location, space, region, area, town, site, dwelling place, holy place (# 5226); קוֹמָה (*qômâ*), nom. height (# 7757); קוֹמְמִיּוּת (*qômemiyyût*), erect (→ # 7758); קִים (*qîm*), adversary (hapleg. in Job 22:20; # 7799); קִימָה (*qîmâ*), nom. standing up (# 7800); קָמָה (*qāmâ*), nom., standing grain (→ # 7850); תְּקוּמָה (*teqûmâ*), nom. power to stand before enemies (# 9538).

ANE The vb. is well attested in Akk. *qamāmu*, raise oneself up; in Arab. *qāma*, and in Ugar. *qm*.

OT 1. With more than 600 occurrences, the vb., primarily in q. and hi. form, is found in most books and in many genres, especially in narrative, since *qwm* functions idiomatically as "begin to do something" (e.g. "rose up [stood] and worshiped," Exod 33:10; "got up to glean," Ruth 2:15). So the awkward combination in English of "rise, sit down" (lit.) is an idiom meaning, "Rise up, sit enthroned" (Isa 52:2; cf. B. A. Rebera, "'He Got Up'—Or Did He? [1 Samuel 20:25]," *BT* 40, 1989, 212-18). God gets judgment under way (lit. "rise [*qwm*] to judge") (Ps 76:9[10]; 82:8; Isa 2:19). The vb. signifies to set up (e.g. images, Judg 18:30; altars, 2 Kgs 21:3), but it has acquired several technical nuances.

2. God has knowledge of "when I sit and when I rise" (Ps 139:2; cf. Deut 6:7). One antithesis of "rise up" (*qwm*) from everyday usage, also transmuted to God, is sleep, lying down, or inactivity. God himself is pictured as one sleeping (Ps 44:23[24]), as inactive, as one who has not gone out with the armies (44:9[10]). Hence the call, "Rise up (*qumâ*) and help us" (44:26[27]; cf. 78:65). A. Weiser thinks that *qwm* is a technical term for a theophany and cites 3:7[8]; 7:6[7]; 9:19[20]; 46:10[11]; 76:9[10]). God's appearance at the annual covenant renewal ceremony guaranteed his blessing in the coming year (A. Weiser, *Hiob*, 150) (→ *b*ᵉ*rît*, covenant, # 1382).

3. When God arises, he seizes the initiative, often in settings of military encounters. Verbs associated with "rise up" have to do with enemies: terrify (Isa 2:19, 21), help (Ps 35:2; 44:26[27]), save (3:7[8]), and deliver (17:13). The expression "rise against" (*qwm 'al*) used with God as subject occurs three times (Isa 14:22; 31:2; Amos 7:9). Since in many passages *qwm* is followed by the idea of going into battle and/or fighting (e.g. Josh 8:3; 24:9; Judg 4:14; 5:12; 2 Sam 2:14) J. T. Willis concludes that "*qwm* is used frequently in military contexts describing both human and divine activity" and that *qwm* in these contexts especially means to "swing into action" (Willis, "Qumah YHWH," 213). When God "arises," the enemies are scattered (Num 10:35; cf. Ps 68:1[2]). (→ Divine Warrior)

4. The vb. *qwm* is also found, though less frequently, in legal-like texts. Where God is the subject, the vb. is followed by four vbs. that have legal overtones: judge (Ps 76:8-9[9-10]; 82:8), witness (Zeph 3:8), contest (Ps 74:22, and visit, examine (Job 31:14) (Willis, "Qumah YHWH," 208-9). "The counsel of the Lord stands (*qwm*)" (Prov 19:21, "prevails" NIV; cf. Isa 14:24). The ungodly shall "not stand" (*qwm*), i.e. survive in judgment (Ps 1:5), or "prevail in a lawsuit" (so S. M. Paul, "Unrecognized Biblical Legal Idioms in the Light of Comparative Akkadian Expressions," *RB* 86, 1979, 231-39). The vb. functions on a human plane in the sense of confirmation. Abraham's purchase of field and cave was "established," i.e. "made sure" (*qwm*; Gen 23:17). Vows taken by women were not necessarily "binding" (*qwm*) (Num 30:4[5], 9[10], 11[12]). The opposite of reliability would be for words to fall to the ground (1 Sam 3:19).

5. A more technical usage of *qwm* in the sense of "establishing" and "following through" is found in conjunction with oath (e.g. Jer 11:5) and especially in the hi. form, with covenant. To Noah God said, "I will establish (hi. *qwm*) my covenant with you" (Gen 6:18). Similar language using hi. *qwm* is found with the Abrahamic covenant (Gen 17:7, 19; Exod 6:4; cf. Lev 26:9) and with the future covenant (Ezek 16:62). In three different vb. forms *qwm* refers to God's word: q. (e.g. "The word of our God stands (*qwm*) forever," Isa 40:8), pi. (e.g. "I have taken an oath and confirmed (*qwm*)

it," Ps 119:106), and hi. (e.g. "I will . . . fulfill my gracious promise," lit. "raise up (*qwm*) my good word," Jer 29:10; cf. Num 23:19; 1 Kgs 8:20).

6. *qwm* can mean to endure, survive, or even oppose. The prophet asks, "Who can endure (*qwm*, parallel to *'md*, stand) his fierce anger?" (Nah 1:6a). "Stand" in Amos 7:2, 5 when referring to Jacob, is intended as "survive" (so NIV). To "rise up" is understood as "oppose," "revolt" (e.g. Judg 9:18). False witnesses oppose (Ps 27:12); the proud oppose (Ps 86:14). The q. part. "uprisers" becomes a term for the enemies of Israel (e.g Deut 28:7).

7. *qwm* also figures in eschatological texts as in the messianic prophecies in Balaam's oracle: "A scepter will rise (*qwm*) out of Israel" (Num 24:17). In a confession rather than a prophecy Job declares, "I know that my Redeemer lives, and that in the end he will stand upon (*qwm*) the earth" (Job 19:25). Associated with *ḥyh*, live (→ # 2649), the term *qwm* signifies a restoration (Hos 6:2, "restore us," hi. *qwm*), or resurrection (Isa 26:19; cf. J. F. A. Sawyer, "Hebrew Words for the Resurrection from the Dead," *VT* 23, 1973, 218-34). M. L. Barré argues against resurrection for Hosea 6 ("Balluta-rabi's Hymn to Gula and Hosea 6:1-2," *Or* 50, 1981, 241-45).

8. The pi. form has somewhat of a specialized meaning in the sense of ordain or appoint and is used several times in Esth but not theologically (e.g. Esth 9:27, 32).

9. The term *māqôm* occurs in numerous Northwest Semitic inscriptions (e.g. *DISO*, 165).

(a) Instructions about offerings in Lev and Num are laced with *māqôm*, place, (Lev 6:26[19]; 14:13). The land of Palestine as "this place" (Jer 7:3, 7) is closely tied with God's promises and with his punishments (Jer 19:3). Of all the OT books, the noun occurs most often in Jer.

(b) Theophanies (→) mark a "place" as unique; one's behavior must conform to divine instructions (Exod 3:5; Josh 5:15). Setting up markers memorializes the place (Gen 28:16).

(c) The tabernacle and the temple specified a most holy place, the room most remote from the entrance. With the ark as a footstool and the cherubim as guardians, this sacred room was the locus, most directly, of God's dwelling (Exod 25:22; 26:33-34; 1 Kgs 8:6-7). Devout Israelites prayed toward "this place" (1 Kgs 8:30).

(d) The term *māqôm*, place, has been crucial in a controversy about centralizing worship (Deut 12, *māqôm* 9x). Sacrifices are to be offered at a specified place where God's name has been put (Deut 12:5; cf. 14:23-25; 15:20; 16:2). Some (e.g. S. R. Driver, *Deuteronomy*, 1901, 140; M. Noth, *OTS* 8, 1950, 46) hold that this "place" in Deut 12:5 and elsewhere is Jerusalem. Another view is that the "place" where God causes his name to dwell need not be a single place but could be multiple places so that other worship centers were not precluded (J. Niehaus, "The Central Sanctuary: Where and When?" *TynBul* 43, 1992, 3-30). The debate hinges on "Name Theology" (→ *šēm*, name, # 9005) and authorship questions about Deut. (→ Deuteronomy: Theology)

Stand, station: → *yṣb* (stand, take stand, # 3656); → *kwn* (stand firm, stand fast, be durable, prepare, establish, # 3922); → *nṣb* I (stand, station oneself, stand firm, # 5893); → *'md* (stand, take one's stand, station, appoint, # 6641); → *qwm* (stand up, stand upright, arise, perform, # 7756)

Animosity, enmity, hostility: → *'yb* (be an enemy, # 366); → *ṣrr* II (be hostile, # 7675); → *śṭm* (hate, # 8475); → *śāṭān* (accuser, satan, # 8477); → *śn'* (hate, one who is an enemy, # 8533); → *šôrēr* (adversary, # 8806); → **Animosity: Theology**
Tabernacle, tent, temple: → *'ōhel* (tent, tent-dweller, # 185); → *d^e^bîr* I (Most Holy Place, # 1808); → *mô'ēd* (meeting-place, assembly, tent of meeting, # 4595b); → *miqdāš* (sanctuary, # 5219); → *miškān* (sanctuary, # 5438); → *pārōket* (curtain in front of Most Holy, # 7267); → *sukkâ* (tabernacle, tent, hut, shelter, # 6109); → **Aaron: Theology**; → **Priests and Levites: Theology**

BIBLIOGRAPHY
NIDNTT 3:224; *TDNT* 7:641-46; 8:193-202; *THAT* 2:635-41; *TWOT* 2:793-94; M. L. Barré, "A Note on Job 19,25," *VT* 29, 1979, 107-10; idem, "New Light on the Interpretation of Hos 6:2," *VT* 28, 1978, 129-41; F. Schnutenhaus, "Das Kommen und Erscheinen Gottes im Alten Testament," *ZAW* 76, 1964, 6-8; Roger W. Cowley, "Technical Terms in Biblical Hebrew," *TynBul* 37, 1986, 21-28, esp. 22, 26; J. T. Willis, "Qûmāh YHWH," *JNSL* 16, 1990, 207-21.

Elmer A. Martens

7757 (*qômâ*, height), → # 7756

7758	קוֹמְמִיּוּת

קוֹמְמִיּוּת (*qôm^e^miyyût*), adv., (walk) erect with head held high (hapleg.) (# 7758).

OT The word describes the state of freedom (as opposed to slavery) that the Israelites experienced subsequent to their redemption from Egyptian slavery. "I broke the bars of your yoke and enabled you to walk with heads held high" (Lev 26:13). Cf. the idiomatic expression *nś' rō'š* (2 Kgs 25:27), which also means "to release (from prison)."

Freedom, innocence, cleanness, liberation: → *d^e^rôr* III (release, freedom, # 2002); → *ḥpš* (freed, # 2926); → *ḥōr* I (free man, freeborn, # 2985); → *nqh* (be free, exempt from guilt, remain unpunished, # 5927); → *ntr* III (set free, # 6002); → *qôm^e^miyyût* (walk erect, # 7758); → *rwḥ* A (become wide or spacious, be spacious, # 8118)

J. P. J. Olivier

7761 (*qôp*, ape), → # 989

7762	קוץ

קוץ (*qwṣ* I), q. feel disgust; hi. to frighten, cause dread (# 7762).

ANE Mish. Heb., Jewish Aram., *qwṣ*, feel an aversion for, loathe, hate. Heb. *qwṭ* and *qwṣ* are etymological equivalents (due to the common Sem. *ṭ/ṣ* interchange—e.g., Heb. *ṣûr*, rock = Aram. *ṭûr*, rock).

OT The vb. *qwṣ* occurs 9x (Gen 27:46; Exod 1:12; Lev 20:23; Num 21:5; 22:3; 1 Kgs 11:25; Prov 3:11; Isa 7:6, 16) and appears in q. in all but one instance. The prefixed preposition *b^e^* or the collocation *mipp^e^nê* demarcates the loathed object (→ *qwṭ* [# 7752]) for a fuller overview of the similarities of these two byforms.

1. *qwṣ* shares with *qwṭ* the nuance of weariness with something that is so intense it occasions revulsion (Gen 27:46; Num 21:5; cf. Job 10:1, *qwṭ*) as well as the

loathing Yahweh manifests toward a rebellious people that occasions rejection (Lev 20:23; cf. Ps 95:10, *qwṭ*).

The writer of Proverbs reverses this latter aspect (loathing = rejection) with regard to one's reception of divine discipline. The father figure exhorts his son to not loathe divine instruction/correction (Prov 3:11). He wants his son to bear this instruction with patience rather than withdraw from it or reject it.

2. The three instances in which *mippᵉnê* follows *qwṣ* (Exod 1:12; Num 22:3; Isa 7:16) denote a people's fear of another people because of the potential outbreak of hostilities.

3. On two occasions *qwṣ* signifies a hostile or defiant attitude. As long as Rezin (Rezon) ruled over Samaria, he acted in defiance (loathing) toward Israel (1 Kgs 11:25). The only occurrence of a hi. form (Isa 7:6) delineates Pekah's and Rezin's intention to strike terror in Judah. Drawing on Orlinsky's work (65), Speier (xiv) contends that this occurrence of *qwṣ* is an example of *qwṣ* II, tear apart (cf. NIV). This suggestion faces two problems. Although a hi. form of *qwṣ* is not attested elsewhere in the OT, *qwṣ* II is not attested anywhere in BH. Beyond this, Pekah and Rezin intended to control Jerusalem, not destroy it (Wildberger, 284).

Contempt, disdain, disgust, loathing: → *bwz* (show contempt for, # 996); → *bzh* (be contemptible, think lightly of, despise, # 1022); → *bḥl* (become tired of, disdain, # 1041); → *g'l* (abhor, be defiled, fail, # 1718); → *zhm* (make s.t. loathsome, # 2299); → *zwr* III (be offensive, # 2320); → *zll* I (be frivolous, be despised, # 2361); → *znh* II (feel a dislike for, # 2389); → *zārā'* (sickness, nausea, # 2426); → *ḥnn* II (be stinking, loathsome, # 2859); → *yq'* (turn aside, # 3697); → *nq'* (disengage, # 5936); → *qwṭ* (feel disgust, # 7752); → *qll* (be slight, swift, appear trifling, treat with contempt, # 7837); → *šwṭ* II (slight, despise, # 8764); → *šqṣ* (make o.s. detestable, # 9210); → *t'b* (be detestable, be loathed, loathe, abhor, # 9493)

Bibliography

TWAT 6:1234-37; *TWOT* 2:794; H. Orlinsky, "The Hebrew and Greek Texts of Job 14.12," *JQR* 38, 1937/38, 57-68; S. Speier, "*Uneqiṣennah*, Isaiah 7:6a," *JBL* 72, 1953, xiv; H. Wildberger, *Isaiah 1-12*, 1991.

Michael A. Grisanti

7763	קוץ

קוץ (*qwṣ* II), hi. tear apart (intrans., of the heavens, Job 14:12 (# 7763); trans., of the walls, Isa 7:6); קוֹץ (*qôṣ*), nom. shreds of a wick (2 Sam 23:6; # 7765).

OT 1. The meaning of the terms remains problematic. The vb. *qwṣ* II has been justified on the basis of apparent cognates in Akk. *kâṣu* and Arab. *qāḍa* (*qwḍ*). However, in Job 14:12 reading the root *qyṣ* (hi.), awake (→ # 7810), suits the context (par. *'wr* [→ # 6424], ni. be aroused) and is supported by Aquila (E. Dhorme, *Job*, 1984, 200-201; but cf. G. R. Driver, "Problems in the Hebrew Text of Job," *VTSup*, 3, 1955, 77).

Isa 7:6 has the other usage of the vb.. Here the nations come against Judah, saying: "Let us tear it apart." However, *qwṣ* I, terrify (→ # 7762), also makes sense (RSV). Nevertheless, the use of *bq'* (hi.), take possession by storm, in the parallel expression (NIV divide it among ourselves) supports the rendering of *qwṣ* II.

Cf. J. J. M. Roberts, 194, n 1; J. D. W. Watts, *Isaiah 1-33*, 1985, 89, and H. Wildberger, *Isaiah 1-12*, 1991, 284.

2. *HALAT* proposes "shreds of a wick" (*qôṣ* II) in 2 Sam 23:6, instead of the more widely attested meaning "thorn" (→ # 7764; so also LXX). The traditional rendering continues to enjoy wide support (A. A. Anderson, *2 Samuel*, 1989, 267, NIV, and NRSV).

Tearing, prey: → *gzr* II (cut, slaughter, tear, prey, # 1616); → *ḥth* (take, fetch, # 3149); → *ṭrp* (tear in pieces, # 3271); → *mlḥ* I (be torn in pieces, dissipate, # 4872); → *nsḥ* (tear down, tear away, # 5815); → *ns'* (tear out, # 5825); → *ntṣ* (tear down, # 5997); → *ntq* (tear away, # 5998); → *pšḥ* (pluck, pull, leave fallow, # 7318); → *qwṣ* II (tear apart, # 7763); → *qr'* (tear up, # 7973); → *šs'* (tear, divide, # 9117)

Bibliography

J. J. M. Roberts, "Isaiah and His Children," in A. Kort and S. Morschauser, eds., *Biblical and Related Studies Presented to Samuel Iwry*, 1985, 193-203, esp. 194.

Cornelis Van Dam

7764	קוץ

קוץ (*qôṣ* I), thornbush (# 7764).

ANE Possible cognates occur in Akk. *giṣṣu* and Egyp. *qḏ* (*HALAT* 834).

OT 1. The word *qôṣ* occurs 12x in BH and indicates a "thornbush" (e.g., Exod 22:5; Ps 118:12; Isa 33:12; Jer 4:3; 12:13; Ezek 28:24). It is occasionally paired with *dardar* or *barqōn*: Gen 3:18; Judg 8:7, 16; Hos 10:8.

2. Hebrew plant names, in many instances, were originally specific. But with time and usage, they became often conceptual or collective (e.g., *'ēšel* for both "tamarisk" and "tree," *šûšan* for both "lily" and "flower"). In the case of thorns, there are more than seventy species of spiny plants in the flora of Israel. Those occurring in pairs are hendiadys and simply strengthen the concept of thorniness (e.g., *šāmîr wa-šayit*, or *qôṣ we-dardar*; see Zohary, 153). There is significant overlap, so that many names assigned in BH to thorns or thistles were synonyms, loose collectives, or vestiges of archaic phraseology.

P-B The term *qôṣ* is possibly found in the pi. verbal form *qwṣ*, meaning "to clear of thorns, weed" (see *Mo'ed Qaṭ.* 6a).

Thornbush, nettle, sting, thistle, thorn: → *'āṭād* (thornbush, # 353); → *barqōn* (thorn, brier, # 1402); → *deber* II (thorny sting, # 1823); → *dardar* (thistle, # 1998); → *ḥēdeq* (brier, # 2537); → *ḥôaḥ* I (thorn, # 2560); → *m^e^sûkâ* (thorn hedge, # 5004); → *na'^a^ṣûṣ* (thornbush, # 5848); → *sîrâ* (thorny bush, # 6106); → *sillôn* (thorn, # 6141); → *s^e^neh* (thorny shrub, # 6174); → *sirpād* (stinging nettle, # 6252); → *ṣe'^e^lîm* (thorny lotus, # 7365); → *ṣ^e^nînîm* (thorns, # 7564); → *qôṣ* I (thornbush, # 7764); → *qimmôś* (weeds, nettles, # 7853); → *śēk* (thorn, splinter, # 8493); → *šāmîr* I (Christ's thorn, # 9031)

Bibliography

TWOT 2:794; I. and W. Jacob, "Flora," *ABD*, 1992, 2:803-17; I. Löw, *Die Flora der Juden*, 1928; H. and A. Moldenke, *Plants of the Bible*, 1952, 165; M. Zohary, *Plants of the Bible*, 1982, 166.

K. Lawson Younger, Jr.

7765 (*qôṣ* II, shreds of a wick), → # 7763

7767	קְוֻצּוֹת

קְוֻצּוֹת (*qᵉwuṣṣôt*), hair (# 7767).

OT The meaning of *qᵉwuṣṣôt* as hair (only in S of Songs 5:2, 11) is "probable," according to R. O. Murphy (*Song of Songs*, Hermeneia, 1990, 165, n. 2). The beloved hears her lover say (in a dream), "My head is drenched with dew, my hair with the dampness of the night" (v. 2). The woman speaks of her lover in the most glorious manner, "His head is purest gold; his hair (*qᵉwuṣṣôt*) is wavy and black as a raven" (v. 11).

Hair: → *zāqān* (beard, # 2417); → *maḥᵃlāpâ* (braid, # 4710); → *miqšeh* (well-dressed hair, # 5250); → *pr'* (untie hair, # 7277); → *ṣîṣit* (hair, tassel, # 7492); → *qᵉwuṣṣôt* (hair, # 7767); → *ś'r* I (be appalled, # 8547); → *śāpām* (moustache, # 8559)

Robert L. Alden

7769	קור

קור (*qwr* I), q. dig (well); hi. bubble (# 7769); nom. מָקוֹר (*māqôr*), fountain, source of water (→ # 5227).

ANE Cognates to the vb. occur in Eth. *wäqärä*, dig, excavate; ESA *wqr*, inscribe, carve; and Arab. *qāra* II, make a round hole, hollow out, cut round. Ugar. attests the substantive *qr*. It appears in the Keret epic *KTU* 1.16.i27 in the construction *qr 'nk* as a description of weeping, perhaps "the well of your eyes" (*CML*, 95) or "the fountain of your eyes" (Caquot, Sznycer, and Herdner, 552; de Moor, 212).

OT 1. In two parallel passages Isaiah mocks Assyria's arrogant boast of digging wells and of drinking water from them in foreign lands (2 Kgs 19:23-24; Isa 37:24-25). 2 Kgs 19:24 describes the water as "strange water" (*mayim zārîm*) (cf. 1QIsaᵃ). The emphasis of the digging is less on the process and more on the goal attained, the waters. Thus, the translation "tap" is more accurate than dig. Tsevat (109) argues for a translation, be cooled off, from a different root, *qrr*. He bases this on a passage from the Sennacherib prism that expresses a parallel sentiment in which the king drinks cold *(ka-ṣu-te/ti)* water.

2. Disputed occurrences of *qwr* in the hi. appear in Jer 6:7, which describes Jerusalem in a simile. As a well (Q *bayir*; K *bwr* pit, cistern) bubbles water, Jerusalem "bubbles" evil (Rudolph, 42). Carroll, 192-93, Holladay, 204, and McKane, 142-43 argue for a root *qrr* II (→ # 7981) for the two hi. forms (*hqyr*, *hqrh*), with a translation such as "keeps cold," here understood to mean keeping water fresh. Holladay argues for this root because the context calls for a vb. appropriate to water, whereas the *qwr* root describes the process of digging. However, the Ugar. and Heb. occurrences of this vb. attest to its association with water. Thus a *qwr* root is best understood here, perhaps with a hi. force stressing the abundance of water produced (Hess).

Digging: → *ḥpr* I (dig, seek out, # 2916); → *ḥṣb* (quarry, hew out, dig, # 2933); → *ḥtr* (dig, break through, # 3168); → *krh* I (dig, be dug, # 4125); → *nqr* (pick out, hew out, dig out, # 5941); → *qwr* I (dig, bubble, # 7769)

BIBLIOGRAPHY
A. Caquot, M. Sznycer, and A. Herdner, *Textes ougaritiques. Tome I: Mythes et légendes*, 1974; R. P. Carroll, *Jeremiah. A Commentary*, OTL, 1986; J. C. de Moor, *An Anthology of Religious Texts from Ugarit*, 1987; R. S. Hess, "Hiphil forms of *qwr* in Jeremiah vi 7," *VT* 41, 1991, 347-50; W. L. Holladay, *Jeremiah 1*, Hermeneia, 1986; W. McKane, *Jeremiah*, ICC, 1986; W. Rudolph, *Jeremia*³, 1968; M. Tsevat, "Some Biblical Notes," *HUCA* 24, 1952-53, 107-14.

Richard S. Hess

7770 (*qûr*, spider-web), → # 6856

7771	קוֹרָה

קוֹרָה (*qôrâ*), nom. pole, beam; rafter; timber work; roof (# 7771).

ANE Syr. *qārîtā'*; Akk. *qarītu(m)*; Arab. *qarīyat.*

OT The word means roof in Gen 19:8 or possibly stands for house. The two messengers of the Lord had come into the shadow/shelter (*ṣēl*) of Lot's roof/house (*qôrâ*; cf. S of Song 1:17). Elsewhere it means beam, rafter, timber work, pole, log (2 Kgs 6:2, 5; 2 Chron 3:7). It is conjectured in 2 Kgs 6:15, but unnecessarily for *hā'îr*, the city (cf. v. 14).

P-B The LXX employs *dokos*, wooden beam, bar, shaft.

Beam, rafter, frame, board: → *kᵉrutôt* (beam, # 4164); → *mᵉqāreh* (timberwork, roof, # 5248); → *qrh* II (lay the beams, # 7936); → *qereš* (board, frame, # 7983); → *rāhîṭ* (beam, rafter, # 8112)

Eugene Carpenter

7774 (*qaḥ*, willow), → # 6770

7776	קֶטֶב

קֶטֶב (*qeṭeb*), destructive sting or plague (# 7776) (also var. spelling קֹטֶב).

ANE Cognates occur in Arab. and Eth. (*HALAT* 834).

OT The word denotes often a "destructive plague." This is clearest in Deut 32:34, where it is paired with *rešep*, pestilence (cf. Ps 91:6, where it is paired with *deber* II, sting). In Hos 13:14, it describes death's stinging plague (cf. 1 Cor 15:55). Finally, in Isa 28:2 it is employed as an adj.: *śa'ar qeṭeb*, a destructive storm.

P-B The term does not appear in P-B.

Disease—plague: → *deber* I (bubonic plague, # 1822); → *ṭᵉḥōrîm* (plague, # 3224); → *maggēpâ* (plague, # 4487); → *nega'* (plague, affliction, # 5596); → *rešep* I (pestilence, # 8404); → *ṣr'* (suffer from skin disease, # 7665). For related entries → *ḥlh* I (become weak, tired, ill, # 2703); → **Plagues: Theology**

BIBLIOGRAPHY
TWOT 2:795.

K. Lawson Younger, Jr.

7777 (q^e*ṭôrâ*, smoke [of burning sacrifice), → # 7787

7779	קטל

קטל (*qṭl*), q. murder, slay (# 7779); קֶטֶל (*qeṭel*), nom. murder (hapleg.; # 7780).

ANE In addition to the Aram. *qṭl* found in Daniel, there are Eth. and Arab. cognates.

OT The Heb. vb. occurs only 3x (Job 13:15; 24:14; Ps 139:19). In one of the great affirmations of the book, Job cries out in the face of his friends' blind orthodoxy and in defiance of his suffering, "Though he slay me, yet will I hope in him" (Job 13:15). The Aram. *qṭl* (14x in Daniel) has the sense of kill, be killed. Unlike *hrg*, which sometimes carries a metaphorical sense, *qṭl* (like *rṣḥ*) only renders the literal act of taking someone's life.

Kill, murder, massacre: → *hrg* (kill, murder, # 2222); → *qṭl* (murder, slay, # 7779); → *rṣḥ* (murder, kill, # 8357)

BIBLIOGRAPHY
G. von Rad, *Wisdom in Israel*, 1972.

W. R. Domeris

7780 (*qeṭel*, murder), → # 7779

7781	קטן

קטן (*qṭn*), q. be small, trifling; hi. make small (# 7781); קֹטֶן (*qōṭen*), nom. little finger (# 7782); קָטָן (*qāṭān* I), adj. little, small, young (# 7783); קָטֹן (*qāṭōn*) adj. small, trifling, young (# 7785).

ANE The root *qṭn* is attested in Akk. as *qatānu(m)*, be or become thin, weak. The adj. (thin, weak) is *qatnu(m)*.

OT 1. The vb. appears only 4x. In the three passages where the q. occurs, *qṭn* means "to be trifling, insignificant" and is used to confess a sense of unworthiness before the undeserved goodness of God (Gen 32:10[11]; 2 Sam 7:19 = 1 Chron 17:17). The hi. also is attested only in a quote, although in this case in the mouth of unscrupulous merchants who make the standard measure smaller (Amos 8:5).

2. The two adjs. *qāṭān* and *qāṭōn* are used a total of 101x. They can refer to the size of an object, such as the luminaries (Gen 1:16), a garment (1 Sam 2:19), an altar (1 Kgs 8:64), a cloud (1 Kgs 18:44), or a city (Eccl 9:14). In several cases where an animal is described, the small creature serves as a moral lesson either to foster a sense of outrage and then guilt (2 Sam 12:3), or as an example of wisdom (Prov 30:24). The "little foxes" of S of Songs 2:15 are apparently metaphorical. R. E. Murphy (*The Song of Songs*, Hermeneia, 1990, 141) speculates that it is a catchy folk-tune or a saucy retort by the girl that she is not totally inaccessible. Interpreters differ as to the meaning of the phrase (see M. H. Pope, *The Song of Songs,* AB 7C, 1977, 402-5; G. H. Jones, *Song of Songs,* NCB, 1993, 41).

Besides the notion of size, these terms can signify "insignificant" or "weak." Thus, a tribe (1 Sam 9:21), one's social standing or prominence (1 Sam 15:17; Isa

22:24), or the reconstruction efforts of the returning exiles (Zech 4:10) can be perceived as inferior or unworthy. In Amos 7:2, 5 the prophet declares that Jacob "is small." Some see here the recognition of Israel's dependence on Yahweh and an appeal to the covenant commitment of the deity (Brueggemann), though perhaps in the context of the book an allusion to the nation's economic precariousness (Paul) or a realistic appraisal of its military power (Carroll R.) is a more appropriate interpretation. In Jer 49:15 and Obad 2 the judgment of Yahweh is to make Edom small: this nation will be humiliated because of its arrogance and cruelty exhibited to the people of God.

qāṭān and *qāṭōn* often appear with *gādôl* in a wide variety of contexts as a merism, an idiom of inclusiveness, which points to everyone or everything under consideration (e.g., Gen 44:12; 1 Sam 5:9; 2 Kgs 23:2; 2 Chron 36:18; Jer 44:12). In Deut 1:17 this idiom is used by Moses to charge the judges appointed in the trek to Canaan to demonstrate equity in all of their deliberations, irrespective of race or prominence.

The concept of small or little can also point to age, i.e., to those "little" in years, the youth (e.g., 1 Sam 20:35; 1 Kgs 3:7; 2 Kgs 2:23; S of Songs 8:8). In a number of narratives, against all familial and cultural expectations, Yahweh sovereignly elects a younger son to fulfill a task for his people or to receive a special word of blessing (→ *ṣ'r*, # 7592). Jacob usurps the place of Esau (Gen 27:15, 42); Joseph is his father's favorite and is later replaced by Benjamin as Jacob's preferred son (42:13, 32; 44:20, 23, 26); the patriarch switches his hands to bless the younger Ephraim over the older Manasseh (48:19); David is chosen over his brothers as the future king of Israel (1 Sam 16:11), and, as the youngest, challenges Goliath, much to the chagrin of his siblings (17:14). This recurring pattern of selecting a younger son underscores that Yahweh will carry out his plans in unexpected ways through individuals of his own choosing. Not only demonstrations of his grace, these surprising choices emphasize that the successful unfolding of the historical process will depend ultimately on his power and thus redound to his glory alone.

3. The nom. *qōṭen* is used twice (1 Kgs 12:10 = 2 Chron 10:10). The words of Rehoboam's friends are difficult to interpret. Though the term usually has been taken to refer to the king's little finger, others, seeing a more vulgar challenge to the complaints of the northern tribes, take it as an allusion to his penis and thus a brash assertion of his strength and authority (e.g., G. H. Jones, *1 and 2 Kings,* NCB, 1984, 1:251-52; *HALAT* 1022).

P-B 1. The many issues dealt with in the OT are also alluded to in a broad spectrum of later literature, of which the following is a sample. The LXX utilizes primarily *mikros*, "small," and *oligos*, few, little, to translate the adjs. *qāṭān* and *qāṭōn,* as well as *m^e'aṭ* (→ # 5070). The comparative *neōteros*, "the younger," is used 36x to translate *qāṭān* and *qāṭōn*. The apocryphal literature echoes OT usage: e.g., smallness can relate to quantity (*oligos,* amount of guilt accrued to the Egyptians, Wisd 13:6; few possessions and the importance of moderation, Sir 19:1; 31:19) or to a brief time span, such as of human life (*oligos,* Wisd 2:1, 15:8; *mikros,* Sir 18:10) or of a period of testing (*oligos,* Wisd 3:5; 16:3, 6; *mikros,* Sir 6:19; 51:16, 27).

2. The terms of the Heb. word group are used by the rabbis in much the same way as in the OT (*TDNT* 6:649-50; note also the references in M. Jastrow, *A Dictionary of the Targumim, the Talmud Babli and Yerushalmi, and the Midrashic Literature,* 1950, 1350-51). The vb. in its several roots can refer, e.g., to being inferior or to

making something smaller, and *qāṭān* and *qāṭōn* can denote children. Interestingly, "little ones" is used for young, immature disciples of the rabbis. The importance of the proper order of inheritance within a family is underscored by the detailed prescriptions of the Mishnah (Mish. Baba Bathra 8-9, Order Nezikim).

NT In the NT *oligos* appears 40x and can mean a few in number (Matt 7:14; 9:37; 1 Peter 3:20), a small quantity (1 Tim 5:23), a little distance (Mark 1:19), or a short time (Rev 12:12). *mikros* is used to refer to the size of people and things (Matt 13:31-32 and par.; Luke 19:3), importance or worth (Matt 11:11; John 2:10), quantity (1 Cor 5:6; Gal 5:9), and age (Matt 18:6, 10, 14). The temporal nuance, which is found primarily in John (13:33; 14:19; 16:16-19; Heb 10:37), is also present, as is the combination of great and small to signify everyone of a group (Acts 8:10; 26:22; Rev 19:5, 18).

Children are a focus of Jesus' affection but also are a model of the humble and dependent character required of a disciple. Jesus utilizes these "little ones" in his teaching about what true greatness means in the kingdom: his followers are to serve others and to seek neither prestige nor positions (Matt 18:1-9 and par.; Luke 7:28). Service to the afflicted of the community of faith ("the little ones"/ "the least of these") will bring future reward (Matt 10:42; 25:40, 45). The mustard seed that grows into a large tree is another example of the small-great reversal of the sovereign workings of God (Matt 13:31-32 and par.).

In the NT *neōteros* refers to either younger men or women (e.g., 1 Tim 5:1-2).

Little, trifle, insignificant: → *'ēš* II (little, trifle, # 837); → *dll* I (be small, unimportant, # 1937); → *zᵉ'êr* (little, # 2402); → *ḥwr* II (become less, # 2579); → *ḥsr* (diminish, decrease, deprive, # 2893); → *ḥrh* II (disappear, be few in number, # 3014); → *m'ṭ* (be few, diminish, become small, few, # 5070); → *ṣ'r* (be trifling, insignificant, become trifling, # 7592); → *qṭn* (be small, trifling, make small, # 7781); → *škk* (go down, abate, allay from upon, # 8896); → *šēmeṣ* (little, # 9066)

Bibliography

ISBE 3:97; *NIDNTT* 2:427-29, 674-76; *TDNT* 4:648-59; 5:171-73; *TWAT* 7:3-10; *TWOT* 2:795; W. Brueggemann, "Amos' Intercessory Formula," *VT* 19, 1969, 385-99; H. W. Wolff, *Anthropology of the Old Testament,* (Eng) 1974, 119-27; M. Schwantes, "Jacob el pequeño. Visiones de Amos 7-9," *Revista de Interpretación Bíblica Latinoamericana* 1, 1988, 87-99; S. M. Paul, *Amos,* Hermeneia, 1991, 229-30; M. D. Carroll R., "The Prophetic Text and the Literature of Dissent in Latin America: Amos, García Márquez, and Cabrera Infante Dismantle Militarism," *Biblical Interpretation,* 4/1, 1996, 76-100.

M. Daniel Carroll R.

7782 (*qōṭen*, finger), → # 7781

7783 (*qāṭān* I, little, small, young), → # 7781

7785 (*qāṭōn*, small, trifling, young), → # 7781

7786	קטף

קטף (*qṭp*), q. pick, pluck, break off; ni. be picked (# 7786).

OT The actions of plucking ears of grain (Deut 23:25[26]), picking herbs (Job 30:4), cutting flowers (ni., Job 8:12), and breaking off twigs or shoots (Ezek 17:4, 22) are all conveyed with this vb. The first example in Ezek 17 is part of a parable and graphically portrays God's judgment. As an eagle plucks off the topmost shoot of a cedar and carries it away, so Nebuchadnezzar did to Jehoiachin, breaking him from the royal house of Israel and planting him humiliated in Babylon (vv. 4, 12). In v. 22 the same image is used in a comforting messianic prophecy. God will break off a tender sprig from the top of the cedar of the Davidic dynasty and make a new start by planting it on "a high and lofty mountain" (probably Mount Zion) so that it will become a splendid tree.

Breaking [off], pinching, plucking: → *'rh* II (pluck, # 768); → *mlq* (pinch, # 4916); → *qṭp* (pick, pluck, # 7786); → *qrṣ* (pinch, wink, # 7975)

BIBLIOGRAPHY

M. Dahood, "Hebrew-Ugaritic Lexicography IX," *Bib* 52, 1971, 346-47.

Cornelis Van Dam

7787	קטר

קטר (*qṭr*), pi. let go up in smoke; pu. perfumed, fumigated; hi. make go up in smoke; ho. be made to go up in smoke (# 7787); מִקְטָר (*miqṭār*), nom. burning, (# 5230); מִקְטֶרֶת (*miqṭeret*), nom. incense (# 5231); מֻקְטָר (*muqṭār*), nom. incense, (# 5233); קְטוֹרָה (*qᵉṭôrâ*), nom. burning incense (# 7777); קְטֹרֶת (*qᵉṭōret*), nom. smoke, incense (# 7792); קִיטוֹר (*qîṭôr*), smoke, cloud (# 7798).

ANE 1. Akk. has the vb. *qatāru*, rise, billow; (D-stem) cause something to smoke, make an incense offering; (Š-causative stem) cause to smoke, cause incense to billow (*CAD* Q, 166-68), plus a number of nom. derivatives (e.g., *qutru* A, smoke, fume, fog, *CAD* Q, 326-27; *qutrinnu*, censer, incense, *CAD* Q, 323-25; etc.). The same basic root with closely associated meanings is found in Arab., OSA, Eth., and Syr. (see *HALAT* 1022b; *TWAT* 7:11-12).

2. A nom. *qṭr* occurs 3x in Ugar. (possibly a couple more times if certain passages are properly restored; see Whitaker, 548). One expression refers to the freeing of a man's "spirit from the earth" after his death (*CML* 104, 17 i 28; possibly also p. 105 17 i 47). Another refers to "a vapor" that goes forth from one's nose when he dies (*CML* 112, 18 iv 26, 37). It is possible that these references refer to one's incense, which is related to one's breath or spirit (*CML* 104 n. 5; cf. *UT* 477; *WUS* 275). It is now well known that the use of incense in cultic worship (and probably also in secular life) went back to prehistoric times in Egypt and that it also had a long history of usage in Syro-Mesopotamia from Middle Babylonian times forward (Nielsen, 1986, 3-33).

OT 1. The most common general term for incense is *qᵉṭōret*, which occurs a total of 60x in the OT. Most of the time it refers to the special incense that was burned on the incense altar (see e.g., Exod 30:1-10, 27, 34-37; Lev 4:7; Num 4:16; 1 Chron 6:49[34]; 28:18; 2 Chron 13:11; 26:16, 19; contrast frankincense in particular, which was only one of the ingredients in this special incense, → *lᵉbōnâ* [# 4247]; cf. also *mizbēaḥ*, altar [# 4640], for a discussion of the incense altar in the OT). In Exod 30:34 the term spices, *sammîm*, occurs 2x surrounding "gum resin, onycha (*šiḥēlet*) and galbanum (*ḥelb^e^nâ*)." These three terms refer to the ingredients that probably made up one part of the holy incense and *l^e^bōnâ*, frankincense, the other part, with salt added for incendiary purposes (cf. Hurowitz).

2. The nom. *miqṭār*, burning, occurs only in Exod 30:1 in the phrase *miqṭar q^e^ṭōret*, burning of incense, as a term for the place of burning the incense (i.e., the incense altar; *HALOT* 627).

3. The nom. *muqṭār*, incense, occurs only in Mal 1:11: "In every place incense and pure offerings will be brought to my name." The form is a ho. part. of *qṭr*, meaning that which is made to smoke (Baldwin, 228-29). It may refer to the burning of offerings (esp. burnt offerings). The passage could be translated, "and in every place an oblation is offered to my name—a pure offering" (Smith, 308-9), or, more likely, "the smoke of burning incense" (Baldwin, 229).

4. The nom. *qîṭôr*, smoke, cloud, occurs 4x in the OT, referring to the smoke of the burning of Sodom and Gomorrah (Gen 19:28 [2x]), the hanging of a wineskin in the smoke (Ps 119:83; see Perowne, 2:358), and the smoke-like clouds or mist of a storm (Ps 148:8).

5. Ezek 8:10-11 uses *q^e^ṭōret* in a way that suggests the independent use of incense as an offering within the Israelite cultural milieu: "So I went in and looked, and I saw portrayed all over the walls all kinds of crawling things and detestable animals and all the idols of the house of Israel. In front of them stood seventy elders of the house of Israel, and Jaazaniah son of Shaphan was standing among them. Each had a censer (*miqṭeret*; occurs only here and 2 Chron 26:19), in his hand, and a fragrant cloud of incense (*q^e^ṭōret*) was rising." To be sure, this passage refers to idol worship, but it reflects what appears to have been a relatively common practice of offering incense as offerings in handheld censers not only in the ANE but also in Canaan and by the Israelites (see Haran, 231-41; Nielsen, 1986; see esp. the sketches of censers on pp. 4, 28, but also the archaeological data and textual issues discussed throughout the volume).

According to Lev 10:1; 16:12-13; Num 16:7, 17, such carrying of incense was well known as a practice in Israel. Haran has argued that we should distinguish between the special incense used on the incense altar in the Holy Place (Exod 30:34-38) and that which was sometimes carried in censers outside in the tabernacle courtyard or elsewhere (Haran, 231-45). Nielsen objects and argues instead that the same incense was used on censers in the tabernacle complex as was used in the Holy Place on the altar of incense (Nielsen, 1986, 69-70). The latter view seems more likely. The incense of Num 16 and Lev 10 and 16 is the same. In fact, it can be argued that Nadab and Abihu used this incense but took the fire on which it was burned from the wrong place (Lev 10:1, "Aaron's sons Nadab and Abihu took their censers ... offered unauthorized fire before the LORD"). They should have taken the fire from the burnt offering altar in the court of the tabernacle (cf. 16:12; the remarks in Milgrom, 1025; Nielsen, 1986, 78).

It is interesting to compare the incident in Num 16:41-50[17:6-15] with that in the Day of Atonement incense procedure in Lev 16:12-13. According to 16:13b, Aaron was to take the incense with him into the Most Holy Place "so that he will not die." It was a protective screen. The essentially protective nature of the incense appears also in Num 16:48[7:13], where Aaron "stood between the living and the dead, and the plague stopped." In both cases the same special incense was apparently used (cf. also

Num 16:1-35 just previously). In both cases the fire was taken from the altar of burnt offering (Lev 16:12; Num 16:46[7:11]). In both cases the purpose was protection. The point is that this special incense was created specifically to be used in the cult, never in the common Israelite home (Exod 30:37-38). It could be taken into the Most Holy Place to protect the high priest, but it could also be taken outside of the tabernacle complex to protect the people. The priests were holy and could therefore handle the holy incense but, at the same time, the entire nation was a "kingdom of priests and a holy nation" (Exod 19:6) and could therefore receive protection by the priestly ministration of incense, in the tabernacle and, on occasion, even in the community (Num 16:41-50[17:6-15]).

6. There are only a few instances where the nom. *qeṭōret* refers to the burning of sacrifices. For example, in Ps 66:15 the psalmist vows: "I will sacrifice fat animals to you and an offering (*qeṭōret*) of rams; I will offer bulls and goats" (cf. Isa 1:13). The vb. *qṭr*, however, esp. in the hi. stem, often refers to the burning of offerings, not incense, esp. in the priestly literature of the Pentateuch (see Lev 1:9, the burnt offering; 2:2, 9; 5:12, the grain offering; 3:5, the peace offering; 4:10, the sin offering; and 7:5, the guilt offering; but see offering incense in Num 16:40[17:5]). Some argue that this could be explained by the practice of putting incense also on the fire for animal offerings (Haran, 230), but this seems questionable. It is more likely that it was the offering as "an aroma pleasing to the LORD" (Lev 1:9 and many times) that explains this connection. In a few instances it is used for sacrificial or incense offerings to foreign gods (1 Kgs 11:8; Jer 48:35; Hos 2:15[13]; note 2 Chron 34:25; Q has pi., but K has hi.). There are only 2 ho. occurrences (Lev 6:15 and Mal 1:11; for the latter see sec. 3).

Normally the pi. vb. is used in the context of burning incense, but this is only outside the Pentateuch and almost exclusively in the context of illegitimate idol worship (see 1 Kgs 22:43; 2 Kgs 23:8; Jer 44:3, 5, 8, 15, 17-19, 21, 23, 25). There are only two exceptions. 1 Sam 2:16 uses the pi. for the burning of the sacrificial fat before distributing portions of meat to the priests. In Amos 4:5 the prophet sarcastically commands apostate Israel: "Burn (*qṭr* [pi.]) leavened bread as a thank offering." The pu. occurs only in S of Songs 3:16, where Solomon's carriage is described as "perfumed (*qṭr*) with myrrh and incense made from all the spices of the merchant."

These relatively consistent and distinctive patterns of the usage of the vb. led Wellhausen to argue that the offering of incense was a later development in Israel (see Wellhausen, 64-68; → *mizbēaḥ*, altar, # 4640). This view has now been thoroughly refuted from both archaeological and textual evidence (see Nielsen, 1986, 51, 87, 101-7). 1 Sam 2:28 (burn incense) and Deut 33:10 (the only usage of *qeṭōrâ*, burning incense) provide good evidence for the early use of incense in Israel.

7. There is one instance of *qeṭōret* being used figuratively: "May my prayer be set before you like incense; may the lifting up of my hands be like the evening sacrifice" (Ps 141:2). For extensions of this usage see P-B sec. 2 and NT.

8. In Exod 30:34-35 several other words for spices and perfumes occur together with *qeṭōret*: "Take fragrant spices (*sam*; # 6160)—gum resin (*nāṭāp*; # 5753), onycha (*šiḥēlet*) and galbanum (*ḥelbenâ*)—and pure frankincense (*lebōnâ*, # 4247), all in equal amounts, and make a fragrant blend of incense (*qeṭōret*), the work of a perfumer (*rqḥ*, # 8379). It is to be salted and pure and sacred."

(a) *ḥelb^{e}nâ*, galbanum, resin used in incense (# 2697), is the milky juice (the term is derived from Heb. *ḥālāb*, milk [# 2692], *HALOT* 316a) from which comes the "resin of various species of the Ferula" plant (Nielsen, 1992, 66). It is known also in Jewish Aram. (Jastrow, 464), Mand., Syr., Arab. (*HALOT* 316a) and is transliterated in the LXX as *chalbanē*.

(b) *šiḥēlet*, onycha, ingredient of incense (# 8829), is difficult to classify. Some have suggested that it is related to Aram. *taḥlē* (Jastrow, 1661) and Akk. *saḥlu* (*CAD* S1, 62-65; it had medical and ritual uses), which refer to the cress plant. It also occurs in reference to some vegetable in Ugar. *šḥlt* (*UT* 488). It is commonly rendered onycha. *šiḥēlet* occurs only in Exod 30:34, as does *ḥelb^{e}nâ*.

(c) For the words *l^{e}bōnâ* (# 4247); *nāṭāp* (# 5753), and *sam* (# 6160), see the relevant entries.

P-B 1. The root *qṭr* occurs 19x in the Qumran Temple Scroll, referring to the burning of the fat, meat, cereal, and even wine of offerings on the altar (e.g., 11QTS 16:6, 18; 34:13; Yadin 2:69, 72, 147). Curiously, the Temple Scroll uses this root to refer to neither incense nor the burning thereof.

2. The War Scroll uses *qṭr* only one time: "These are the men who shall attend at holocausts and sacrifices to prepare sweet-smelling incense for the good pleasure of God, to atone for all His congregation" (Vermes, 106).

NT The usual LXX rendering of Heb. *q^{e}ṭōret* is G *thymiama*, incense. It occurs in Luke 1:10-11 referring to the incense that Zachariah was offering on the incense altar when he received the revelation of the conception of his son, John the Baptist (see also *thymbioō*, burn incense, in Luke 1:9). Rev 18:13 refers to the incense trade, but Rev 5:8 and 8:3-4 identify the offering of incense with the "prayers of the saints." *Thymiatērion* occurs in Heb 9:4, referring to "the golden altar of incense."

Incense: → *l^{e}bōnâ* I (frankincense, white resin, # 4247); → *qṭr* (let go up in smoke, # 7787)

BIBLIOGRAPHY

TWAT 4:454-60; 7:10-18; J. G. Baldwin, *Haggai, Zechariah, Malachi*, TOTC, 1972; L. F. DeVries, "Cult Stands: A Bewildering Variety of Shapes and Sizes," *BARev* 13:4, 1987, 27-37; D. Edelman, "The Meaning of *qiṭṭēr*," *VT* 35, 1985, 395-404; M. D. Fowler, "Incense Altars," *ABD*, 1992, 3:409-10; K. Galling, "Incense Altar," *IDB*, 1962, 2:699-700; M. Haran, *Temples and Temple-Service in Ancient Israel*, 1978; V. Hurowitz, "Salted Incense—Exodus 30, 35; Maqlu VI 111-113; IX 118-120," *Bib* 68, 1987, 178-94; C. Meyers, "Censers," *ABD*, 1992, 1:882; idem, "Incense Dish," *ABD*, 1992, 3:410; J. Milgrom, *Leviticus 1-16*, AB, 1991; K. Nielsen, "Ancient Aromas Good and Bad," *BibRev* 7:3, 1991, 26-33; idem, "Incense," *ABD*, 1992, 3:404-9; idem, *Incense in Ancient Israel*, VTSup 38, 1986; J. S. S. Perowne, *The Book of Psalms*, 2 vols., 1878^4; R. L. Smith, *Micah-Malachi*, WBC, 1984; J. Wellhausen, *Prolegomena to the History of Ancient Israel*, ET, 1878; Y. Yadin (ed.), *The Temple Scroll*, 2 vols., 1983.

Richard E. Averbeck

7792 (*q^{e}ṭōret*, incense), → # 7787

7794	קיא

קיא (*qy'*), q. vomit, disgorge; hi. vomit something (# 7794); nom. קִיא (*qî'*), vomit (# 7795); קֵא (*qē'*), vomit (# 7683).

ANE Other Sem. languages have the same root, cf. Akk. *kâ'u*, spew, vomit; Arab. *qā'a*, vomit.

OT The word is used in both literal and metaphorical senses.

1. To eat greedily leads only to vomiting (Prov 23:8; 25:16; cf. Isa 19:14; 28:8 of the vomiting of drunkards). In Prov 26:11 there is the proverb about the dog returning to its own vomit, indicating "the unteachability of the fool" (OTL); it is quoted in the NT in 2 Peter 2:22 in relation to those who "have escaped the corruption of the world" but have become "again entangled in it and overcome" by it (v. 20).

2. In Jon 2:10[11] the great fish that the Lord had created vomited Jonah on the dry land.

3. Job 20:15 speaks of vomiting up riches, in the sense of God's forcibly showing the impermanence of earthly possessions and in particular of the wicked being forced to surrender possessions that they have acquired wrongfully.

4. Theologically the most significant use of the word is in relation to the way that the land of Canaan is said to have been defiled by its inhabitants and thus vomited them up so that they could live there no longer (Lev 18:25). Then the warning is given that it could do the same to Israel if they defiled the land by failing to live according to the ways of the Lord (18:28).

5. Jeremiah, like several other prophets, speaks of God's judgment in terms of the drinking of a "cup filled with the wine of (his) wrath" (Jer 25:15). It is in this sense that 48:26 speaks of Moab as "drunken," and thus the prophetic word is, "Let Moab wallow in her vomit, let her be an object of ridicule." There is some doubt, however, about the meaning of the vb. *spq* II, be in abundance (→ # 6216), translated by NIV and NRSV as "wallow." The normal meaning of the root is "slap" or "clap," and BDB takes it as meaning "splash into his vomit." AB, translating "vomit helplessly," understands it as a matter of clapping because of his vomit. The NEB translation "until he overflows with his vomit" is based on G. R. Driver's linking of the root with Aram. and especially Syr. *spq* with the sense of "vomit."

BIBLIOGRAPHY

TWAT 7:18-19.

Francis Foulkes

7795 (*qî'*, vomit), → # 7794

7798 (*qîṭôr*, smoke), → # 7787

7799 (*qîm*, adversary), → # 7756

7800 (*qîmâ*, standing up), → # 7756

7801 (*qyn*, sing a dirge), → Lament

7802 (*qayin* I, spearhead), → # 2851

7803 (*qayin* II, Cain), → Cain

7806 (*qînâ* I, dirge), → Lament

7810	קִיץ

קִיץ (*qyṣ* II), hi. awake; unlike *yqṣ*, which appears only in q., *qyṣ* appears only in hi. (# 7810). For the q. meaning of *qyṣ* I, spend the summer, see # 7811.

ANE There are no clear ANE cognates to this lexeme.

OT 1. There are several similar uses for *qyṣ* and *yqṣ*.

(a) Both vbs. may have people as subj. (*qyṣ*: 1 Sam 26:12; Ps 3:5[6]; *yqṣ*: Judg 16:14, 20). (b) Both vbs. may employ God as subj. (*qyṣ*: Ps 35:23; 44:23[24]; 59:5[6]; *yqṣ*: 78:65). (c) Both vbs. are used to refer to awaking from a dream (*qyṣ*: Ps 73:20; Isa 29:8; *yqṣ*: Gen 28:16; 41:4, 7, 21). (d) Both vbs. are used to refer to awaking from the stupor of drunkenness (*qyṣ*: Ps 78:65; Prov 23:35; Jon 1:5; *yqṣ*: Gen 9:24). (e) Both vbs. are used to refer to waking the sleeping idols or gods (*qyṣ*: Hab 2:19; *yqṣ*: 1 Kgs 18:27).

2. Only *qyṣ* occurs in prayers where the writer/prayer asks God to awake, rouse himself, bestir himself (Ps 35:23; 44:23[24]; 59:5[6]). Each of these requests comes in a psalm of lamentation in which the writer is being abused by another, and apparently God is doing nothing to stop the persecution. The writer desires God's manifestation and intervention on his behalf. These are, of course, vivid poetic passages, and attempts to see in such psalms (as argued by G. Widengren, *Myth, Ritual, and Kingship*, 191, and "Sakarales Königtum im Alten Testament," in *Franz Delitzsch-Vorlesungen*, 1955, 67) a concept of a dying/sleeping and rising of Yahweh confuse a formal parallel with a parallel in meaning.

3. A strange use of the vb. appears in Jer 31:26. After receiving some comforting words from Yahweh about the return of the exiles from Babylon and the restoration of Judah (31:16-25), Jeremiah says, "At this I awoke and looked around. My sleep had been pleasant to me." Now there is no reference to Jeremiah actually falling asleep and receiving this revelation in a dream or vision. The prophet's words must be "a dream-like scenario of healing reality, not yet in hand, but already assured by the power of God" (W. Brueggemann, *To Build, To Plant, Jeremiah 26-52*, ITC, 1991, 67).

4. There are a few instances in which *qyṣ* refers to awaking from the sleep of death, i.e., resuscitation (2 Kgs 4:31) or resurrection (Job 14:12; Jer 51:39, 57, all of which speak of sleeping forever and not awaking). On the other hand, verses like Ps 17:15 ("...when I awake, I will be satisfied with seeing your likeness") or 139:18 ("when I awake, I am still with you," rendered by Dahood, *Psalms*, AB, 3, 296 as "May I rise and my continuance be with you") may point to the gift of resurrection and eternal fellowship with God.

Although these verses lend themselves to other interpretations, *qyṣ* is clearly so used in Dan 12:2 ("Multitudes who sleep in the dust of the earth will awake: some to everlasting life, others to shame and everlasting contempt") and in Isa 26:19 ("But your dead will live; their bodies will rise. You who dwell in the dust, wake up and shout for joy"). One writer has stated, "Along with [Isa 25:8] it [26:19] represents the highest conception of resurrection in the Old Testament" (J. Oswalt, *Isaiah 1-39*, NICOT, 1986, 485).

NT Paul in Rom 8 makes an interesting use of one of these "Arouse yourself, O Lord" psalms. In Rom 8:36 he quotes Ps 44:22[23], "For your sake we face death all day long; we are considered as sheep to be slaughtered," to explain the persecution to which followers of Jesus will be subjected. What is of interest is that Paul in Rom 8 does *not* go on to quote the next v. of the psalm, "Awake, O Lord! Why do you sleep? Rouse yourself! Do not reject us forever" (v. 23[24]). For the OT writer the persecution of the godly, who are supposed to be blessed and prosperous and victorious, represents an enigma. For Paul, persecution is the lot for all who will live godly in Christ Jesus. Hence, there is no reason for the apostle to ask God to rouse himself from his tranquility and indifference.

Stirring, waking up: → *yqṣ* (awake, # 3699); → *'wr* II (stir oneself, # 6424); → *qyṣ* II (awake, # 7810)

BIBLIOGRAPHY

TWOT 2:798; J. Barr, *The Garden of Eden and the Hope of Immortality*, 1992; H. Birkeland, "The Belief in the Resurrection of the Dead in the Old Testament," *ST* 3, 1949, 60-78; W. Eichrodt, *TOT*, 1967, 2:496-529; J. F. A. Sawyer, "Hebrew Words for the Resurrection of the Dead," *VT* 23, 1973, 218-34.

Victor P. Hamilton

7811	קַיִץ

קַיִץ (*qayiṣ*), nom. summer, summer fruit (# 7811); קיץ (*qyṣ* I), q. spend the summer (# 7810); Aram. קַיִט (*qayiṭ*), nom. summer (# 10627).

ANE The vb. is attested in Arab. *qyẓ*, to be very hot. The nom. is widely attested with cognates for summer or summer fruit: Ugar. *qẓ*, Akk. *ebūru*, Can. *qēṣu*, OSA *qyẓ*, Arab. *qāẓa*, Syr. *qaiṭā'*, Old Aram. *kyṣ'*, Sam. Aram. *qeṣ*, Jud. Aram. *q(y)ṭ*.

OT 1. All 21 occurrences of the Heb. vb. and nom. relate to the summer as one of the two seasons of the year, the other season being winter (→ *ḥrp* I, # 3069).

2. The one occurrence of the denom. vb. refers to birds of prey surviving through the summer by feeding on the remains of a people (usually interpreted as the Assyrians) whom God judged (Isa 18:6).

3. The Heb. nom. is used with winter to refer to God's creation of the seasons (Ps 74:17) and to the constant fulfillment of divine promises through summer and winter, i.e., for all time (Gen 8:22; Zech 14:8).

4. The hot and dry climate of the summer provides metaphors in two passages. Prov 26:1 states that honor is as fitting to a fool as snow is to summer, and Ps 32:4 says that the displeasure of God is like the summer heat that saps one's strength (or dries the tongue). Because of the summer heat some wealthy Israelites evidently built separate residences for the summer, corresponding to winter houses for the cold months. Amos predicted that divine judgment would come on these houses because of their owners' sins (Amos 3:15).

5. God created summer as the season of harvest (*qayiṣ* and *qāṣîr* [harvest] are word pairs in Prov 6:8; 10:5; Jer 8:20). Consequently, a wise son gathers food in the summer (Prov 10:5), as docs the industrious ant (6:8; 30:25). While the harvest of summer is normally a symbol of hope, it is associated with divine judgment in two passages. In Isa 28:4 Samaria (or perhaps Gerazim) is depicted as an early fig (i.e., one that comes before the usual summer harvest) that is greedily eaten by her enemies.

Jer 8:20 contains a lament that while the summer harvest has come and gone, divine salvation has not appeared for unrepentant Judah.

6. The Heb. nom. sometimes refers to the fruit that is harvested in the summer. When David fled Jerusalem, Ziba provided summer fruit (*qayiṣ*) and other food for his entourage (2 Sam 16:1-2). The context suggests the fruit may have been figs. After the fall of Jerusalem the scattered Judeans, encouraged by Gedaliah, returned home to harvest the summer fruit (Jer 40:10, 12). This harvest was a sign of hope. In contrast the failure to harvest summer fruit is a sign of disaster. Micah compared his situation of being in a land devoid of godly people to being in an orchard where there is no summer fruit to harvest (Mic 7:1). Similarly, judgment on Moab is depicted in terms of the destruction of summer fruit before the harvest (Isa 16:9; Jer 48:32).

7. In his fourth vision Amos saw a basket of *qayiṣ*, which served as a sign that the *qēṣ* (usually translated "end" [→ # 7891]) had come for Israel (8:1-2). One interpretation of the vision is that Amos saw ripe fruit that symbolized that the time was ripe for the end, i.e., judgment. Another view suggests that *qayiṣ* and *qēṣ* are interchangeable words, both referring to harvest (rather than the latter meaning "end"). Thus, the basket of harvested grain (*qayiṣ*) is a sign of harvest (*qēṣ*) or judgment for the nation. A related approach also understands that *qayiṣ* means harvest, but it suggests that the basket Amos saw was an empty basket in the sense of a basket for harvesting—an indication that judgment was imminent. The best interpretation recognizes a paronomasia involving *qayiṣ* and *qēṣ*. Amos said he saw the summer fruit (*qayiṣ*); therefore God said the end (*qēṣ*) has come. The word play is intensified by the probability that *qayiṣ* was pronounced the same as *qēṣ* in the dialect of the northern kingdom. Accordingly, the normally hopeful symbol of harvested summer fruit was turned into a symbol of judgment.

8. The Aram. nom. *qayiṭ* appears in Dan 2:35, where the crushed statue in Nebuchadnezzar's dream becomes like chaff swept away by wind in the summer. Job 8:14 has the difficult hapleg *yāqôṭ*. Some also find *qayiṭ* here by emending the MT to read "summer thread" or "gossamer" (NEB, NRSV, KBL). It seems more likely that the hapleg comes from a conjectured root *qûṭ*, to be cut off (Tg., Pesh., KJV, RSV, BDB), or *qṭṭ*, to be short (BHS).

P-B The use of the Heb. nom. as the summer season or its harvest is echoed in Sir 50:8 and often in Qumran. The LXX renders the nom. with various terms relating to summer, its heat, or harvest.

Seasons: → *ḥrp* I (spend the winter, # 3069); → *qayiṣ* (summer, summer-fruit, # 7811); → *t*^{e}*qûpâ* (turning point, change of seasons, # 9543)

Harvest, gleaning: → *'sp* (gather, harvest, # 665); → *bṣr* (harvest grapes, # 1305); → *y*^{e}*bûl* (produce, yield, # 3292); → *lqṭ* (reap, harvest, # 4377); → *'ll* I (glean, # 6618); → *'mr* (gather grain, # 6682); → *qbṣ* (gather, # 7695); → *qṣr* (harvest, # 7917); → *t*^{e}*bû'â* (crop, yield, # 9311); → *t*^{e}*nûbâ*, produce, # 9482)

BIBLIOGRAPHY

TWAT 7:26-30; D. Clines, *Job 1-20,* WBC, 199-200; G. Dalman, *Arbeit und Sitte in Palästina*, 1, 34-50; S. M. Paul, *Amos*, Hermeneia, 253-54; B. Rahtjen, "A Critical Note on Amos 8:1-2," *JBL*

83, 1964, 416-17; K. Koch, *The Prophets*, 1:40; A. Wolters, "Wordplay and Dialect in Amos 8:1-2," *JETS* 31, 1988, 407-10.

Robert R. Ellis

7812 (*qîṣôn*, outermost), → # 7915

7813	קִיקָיוֹן

קִיקָיוֹן(*qîqāyôn*), nom. a plant of uncertain identity (# 7813).

ANE The word occurs in other Sem. languages. Akk. *kukkānītu* refers to a medicinal plant that may be the same as *qîqāyôn*. Aram. *qîqāyôn* and *qîqôs* (< G *kīkeōs*); Syr. *qîq'ôs* and *qîqî* (cf. G and Copt. *kīki*; Egyp. *k3k3,* bush).

OT *qîqāyôn* appears only 5x in the OT, all in Jon 4 (vv. 6*bis*, 7, 9, 10), where it is described as a plant capable of rapid growth and having leafy foliage adequate for providing Jonah with relief from the oppressive heat of the sun. The plant was also susceptible to rapid demise, ironically leaving the disobedient prophet with a greater sense of loss than he had experienced over the announced destruction of Nineveh's sizable human population. This plant is probably the *Ricinus communis*, or castor oil tree, which commonly reaches heights of 12-15 feet. According to M. de Waal it can attain a height of 40 feet (*Medicinal Herbs in the Bible*, 77). The plant is sometimes called Palma Christi, since its leaves have been likened to Christ's hands held forth to bless. Its oil was used as a fuel for lamps and as a lubricant for making soap. Its seeds are inedible and, in fact, poisonous.

A less likely, though ancient, suggestion regarding its identity is that the *qîqāyôn* is the *Cucurbita lagenaria*, or bottle gourd. This seems to be the way the word was understood in Jonah by LXX (G *kolokuntha*) and Pesh. (Syr. *šᵉrûrā' dᵉqar'ā'*). Both Symm. (G *kissos*) and Vg. (Lat. *hedera*) have "ivy" in Jonah (cf. Douay version). Jerome was strongly criticized for this translation and, in fact, he himself had misgivings about its suitability. The Old Latin has *cucurbita*. Aq. and Th. simply transliterated the term (*kikeōna*). Other suggested identifications, all problematic, include the gourd *cucurbita pepo*, the crookneck squash *cucurbita moschata*, the white-flowered gourd *lagenaria leucantha*, or the winter squash *cucurbita maxima*.

P-B The plant is referred to in the Talmud for its medicinal properties. Herodotus (2.94) and Pliny (*Natural History*, 15.7) describe a castor oil plant in Egypt called the *kīki*, which is probably a variety of this plant. According to Zohary, its modern uses include manufacture of plastics and aircraft lubricants (*Plants of the Bible*, 193). In modern pharmaceutical usage *oleum ricini* is a laxative. In modern Heb. *qîqāyôn* is the name of the castor oil plant, and *qîqāyônî* means ephemeral or short-lived.

Vegetation: → *'ēzôb* (hyssop, # 257); → *dš'* (become green, sprout, # 2012); → *zr'* (sow, scatter seed, form seed, # 2445); → *ḥāṣîr* I (grass, # 2945); → *ḥᵃšaš* (dry grass, # 3143); → *yereq* (green, greenness, # 3764); → *nṭ'* (plant, establish, drive, # 5749); → *'āleh* (leaf, leafage, # 6591); → *'ēśeb* (herb, herbage, weed, # 6912); → *qîqāyôn* (plant of uncertain identity, # 7813); → *rō'š* II (bitter and poisonous herb, # 8032); → *śîaḥ* I (bush, shrub, # 8489); → *šiṭṭâ* (acacia, # 8847)

Bibliography
ABD 2:803-17; *HDB* 2:250; *IDB* 2:298; *ISBE* 2:536; G. Dalman, *Arbeit und Sitte in Palästina*, 1928-1942, 2:269; *Fauna and Flora of the Bible*, 1972, 106-7; I. Löw, *Die Flora der Juden*, 1924, 1:208n, 219, 545, 608-11; B. P. Robinson, "Jonah's Qiqayon Plant," *ZAW* 97, 1985, 390-403; Y. Ṣmudi, "Jonah's Gourd," *BMik* 28, 1982-1983, 44-48 [Heb.]; M. Stol, "The Cucurbitacae in the Cuneiform Texts," *Bulletin on Sumerian Agriculture* 3, 1987, 81-92; M. de Waal, *Medicinal Herbs in the Bible*, 1980, 76-77; M. Zohary, *Flora Palaestina*, 1966-1986, 2:269; idem, *Plants of the Bible*, 1982, 193.

Richard A. Taylor

7814	קִיקָלוֹן

קִיקָלוֹן (*qîqālôn*), nom. disgrace (# 7814); < קלל (*qll*), q. be slight, swift; ni. appear trifling; pi. curse; pu. be cursed; hi. treat with contempt (→ # 7837).

ANE The vb. *qll* is attested in Aram. nom. *qᵉlālâ*, disgrace (cf. Beyer, 683). In Syr. the form *qeyqaltā'* also occurs. These occurrences lend support to the possibility that the Heb. *qîqālôn* can be seen as a derivative of the vb. *qll*.

OT The nom. *qîqalôn* occurs only in Hab 2:16. According to *HALAT* 1027 and 1032 the nom. can be considered as a reduplicated derivative of the vb. *qll*, treat with contempt or have a poor opinion of someone. From the context of the surrounding lexemes in Hab 2:16 it is justifiable to translate it as "disgrace" or "shame." This woe oracle is against he (Babylon? cf. Elliger, 47) who behaves morally indecent by inebriating his neighbors (v. 15) in order to profit from their condition. The Lord himself will transform that person's honor (*kābôd*) to disgrace. In a comparable instance (Ps 4:3) the nom. *kᵉlimmâ* is used to indicate the turning of *kābôd* to disgrace.

Shame, disgrace, humiliation, scorn: → *bwz* (show contempt for, # 996); → *bwš* I (be ashamed, put to shame, behave shamefully, # 1017); → *ḥsd* I (insult, reproach, # 2873); → *ḥpr* II (be dismayed, feel ashamed, # 2917); → *ḥrp* II (taunt, mock, insult, defy, # 3070); → *klm* (be shamed, humiliated, hurt, # 4007); → *l'g* (scorn, mock, # 4352); → *n'ṣ* (reject, disdain, treat disrespectfully, # 5540); → *qîqālôn* (disgrace, # 7814); → *qlh* II (be of low esteem, treat with contempt, dishonor, detest, # 7829)

Bibliography
BDB, 876; *HALAT*, 1024, 1026-27; K. Beyer, *Die aramäischen Texte vom Toten Meer*, 1984; K. Elliger, *Das Buch der zwölf Kleinen Propheten*, ATD 25, 1975; R. Patterson, *Nahum, Habakkuk, Zephaniah*, 1991, 203.

Philip J. Nel

7815	קִיר

קִיר (*qîr* I), wall (# 7815).

ANE Possibly related to Akk. *qīru*, Syr. *qīrā'*, and Arab. *qīr*, all associated with asphalt. The word also appears in Ugar. and other NW Sem. texts.

OT 1. In its 74 occurrences, *qîr* has a wider range of meaning than *ḥômâ* (# 2570). It often refers to the walls of a city (Num 35:4), but also of residential structures (2 Kgs 20:2) and of the temple (1 Kgs 6:5). In Ezek 41:22 the nom. signifies the sides of the altar. Jer 4:19 expresses the pain of the author over the impending doom of Judah. His distress is so great that it presses against the *qîrôt*, walls, of his heart, causing him great pain. In a psalm attributed to David, he compares his battering by opponents to those who assail a leaning wall (Ps 62:3[4]), a tottering fence (cf. *gādēr*, # 1555).

2. *qiryâ*, the synonym for *'îr*, (walled) city, is likely derived from *qîr*, wall, rather than from *qrh*, meet or happen. Thus, the main feature of a fortified center underlies the general name for such a site.

P-B The pl. nom. occurs twice in the DSS. In 1QH 3, 13 the poet foresees a messianic revenge on the conceivers of vanity, when the foundations of the wall will rock like a ship on the face of the waters. In a subsequent hymn (1QH 7, 9) he thanks the Lord for making him like a strong tower, a high wall ... and all his ramparts are a tried wall. The Lord has fortified him for his calling.

qîr continues to appear in postbiblical literature connoting a wall, recess, or chamber.

Wall, heap of stones: → *gdr* (erect a wall, # 1553); → *ḥômâ* (wall, # 2570); → *ḥayiṣ* (flimsy wall, # 2666); → *ṭîrâ* (row of stones, # 3227); → *kōtel* (wall, # 4185); → *nēd* (heap, wall, # 5603); → *qîr* (wall, # 7815); → *šûr* I (wall, # 8803)

Keith N. Schoville

7824	קַל

קַל (*qal*), nom. light, agile, quick, swift (# 7824); קֹל (*qōl*), lighthearted (hapleg., Jer 3:9, # 7825); < קלל (*qll*), be slight, swift, appear trifling, treat with contempt (→ # 7837).

ANE Mish. Heb. *ql*, light, lowly, poor, quick; Ugar. *ql*, runner (= messenger); Akk. *qallu(m)*, light, small; Jewish Aram. *qallîlā'*, light, quick; Egyp.-Aram. *qlyl*, swift, light; Syr. *qallīlā'*, light, swift, little; Mand. *qalil*, light, swift; OSA *qll*, little; Eth. *qalīl*, small, little; Arab. *qalīl*, little, small; Jewish Aram. *qullā'*, relief, frivolity, flippancy.

OT 1. Derived from *qll*, be slight, the adj. *qal* and *qōl* occur 13x and 1x respectively. The more common adj. (*qal*) serves as a substantive (5x) and an adverb (2x) in addition to its customary adj. function (6x). In each case, *qal* signifies the speed of the person, thing, or action it modifies, whether it be a runner seeking victory (2 Sam 2:18; Eccl 9:11), a messenger hastening to complete his task (Isa 18:2), soldiers fleeing for their lives (Jer 46:6; Amos 2:14-15), the flight of an animal (Isa 30:16; Jer 2:23), the arrival of attacking nations (Isa 5:26; Lam 4:19), or the passage of a cloud overhead (Isa 19:1).

In all but three instances, *qal* concerns some aspect of the experience of judgment. Destruction sent by Yahweh against a wayward people (whether Israel [Isa 5:26], Egypt [19:1], or Tyre, Sidon, and Philistia [Joel 3:4(4:4)]) occurs with devastating swiftness. From this kind of swift punishment there is no escape. The speed, strength, and weaponry of soldiers, all important to their success, will be of no avail (Isa 30:16; Jer 46:6; Amos 2:14-15).

In response to Judah's protestations of innocence, Yahweh (Jer 2:23) likens Judah to an unreliable female camel that dashes about swiftly (*qal*) in any direction at the slightest provocation (Bailey and Holladay, 258). After his friends accuse him of wickedness, Job seeks to delineate the characteristics of a truly wicked man. They are like a light object (*qal*), easily carried away by the strong current of a river (Job 24:18).

2. Although KB (839) derives *qōl* (hapleg.) in Jer 3:9 from *qôl* (voice—rumor; i.e., noise in a pejorative sense), all EVV favor a derivation from *qll*, be light, frivolous. The prophet Jeremiah declares that God's people thought harlotry was a trifling matter. Even though the Mosaic covenant demanded absolute allegiance of Israel to Yahweh, her apostasy had so diminished Israel's sensitivity to Yahweh's covenantal expectations that she regarded adultery as something insignificant (Thompson, 196).

Hurry, speed: → *'wṣ* (urge, # 237); → *dḥp* (hurrying, # 1894); → *ḥwš* (hurry, # 2590); → *ḥpz* (be in a hurry, # 2905); → *ṭwś* (rush, dart, # 3216); → *mhr* I (hurry, # 4554); → *qal* (light, agile, quick, swift, # 7824)

BIBLIOGRAPHY

TWOT 2:800-801; K. Bailey and W. Holladay, "The 'Young Camel' and 'Wild Ass' in Jer 2:23-25," *VT* 18, 1968, 256-60; E. Dhorme, *A Commentary on the Book of Job*, 1967; R. Gordis, *The Book of Job*, 1978; J. Hartley, *The Book of Job*, NICOT, 1988; W. McKane, *A Critical and Exegetical Commentary on Jeremiah*, 1986; S. Paul, *Amos*, 1991; J. Thompson, *The Book of Jeremiah*, NICOT, 1980.

Michael A. Grisanti

7825 (*qōl*, light-hearted), → # 7824

7828 (*qlh* I, parch, burn [w. fever]), → Baking

7829	קלה

קלה (*qlh* II), be of low esteem, treat with contempt, dishonor, detest (# 7829); קָלוֹן (*qālôn*), nom. shame, dishonor, contempt (# 7830).

ANE The vb. *qlh* II (Aram. *q^{e}la'* or *q^{e}ley*) with the meaning "to be disgraced" is attested only in RH, late Aram. and Syr., cf., e.g., Targ O. Deut 25:3 (Jastrow 2:1375). The nom. *qālôn* in RH may also refer to the disgrace of prostitution (Jastrow 2:1373).

OT 1. The vb. *qlh* II occurs 5x in the ni. formation and once in the hi. In Deut 27:16 the hi. part. of *qlh* occurs amongst the Levite curses on sacral offenses. Specifically it refers to a child who despises his parents, in other words, who violates their honor. The meaning of *qlh* is clear from Prov 12:9, where it is used in opposition to "be somebody," in other words, "be a nobody" (cf. also 1 Sam 18:23). Negatively, the ni. part. also refers to the loss of or degrading of honor and splendor of a person or a people (cf. Deut 25:3; Isa 3:5; 16:14). From Deut 25:1-3 it is clear that the inappropriate or excessive application of judicial punishment for crime might also lead to the shaming of a person. Warning is given against the excessive forms of shaming that violate the essential dignity of a person (cf. Bechtel, 62 and Daube, 41-47).

2. The nom. *qālôn* refers to the human condition opposite to pride and honor, i.e., dishonor and disgrace (Ps 83:16[17]; Prov 3:35; 13:18; Hos 4:7; Hab 2:16). In most of these instances it functions as an antonym of *kābôd* (honor). In Hab 2:16 and Hos 4:18 the disgrace results from the participation of people in activities that are morally shocking. Of these forms of conduct drinking and adultery are the foremost. In an absolute sense it refers to the removal of all pride and importance of a nation

(Isa 22:18; Jer 46:12). This ultimate dishonor is also expressed in the use of *qālôn* as a metaphor for the "nakedness" of a city (Jerusalem and Nineveh). The exposure of the nakedness is seen as an extreme form of dishonoring a person. The sexual connotation here is evident.

In Prov *qālôn* frequently occurs to denote the injury or loss of honor and respect of the wicked or fools (Prov 3:35; 11:2; 22:10). Scorn (*ḥerpâ*) often arises with the loss of honor (6:33; 18:3). The wise, on the other hand, are portrayed as those who can overlook an injury to their honor and do not react foolishly (12:16).

Shame, disgrace, humiliation, scorn: → *bwz* (show contempt for, # 996); → *bwš* I (be ashamed, put to shame, behave shamefully, # 1017); → *ḥsd* I (insult, reproach, # 2873); → *ḥpr* II (be dismayed, feel ashamed, # 2917); → *ḥrp* II (taunt, mock, insult, defy, # 3070); → *klm* (be shamed, humiliated, hurt, # 4007); → *l'g* (scorn, mock, # 4352); → *n'ṣ* (reject, disdain, treat disrespectfully, # 5540); → *qîqālôn* (disgrace, # 7814); → *qlh* II (be of low esteem, treat with contempt, dishonor, detest, # 7829)

BIBLIOGRAPHY

IDB 4:305-6; *TDNT* 1:189-91; *TDOT* 2:50-60; *THAT* 1:269-70; *TWOT* 1:222-23, 311-12, 442-43; 2:799; L. M. Bechtel, "Shame as a Sanction of Social Control in Biblical Israel: Judicial, Political, and Social Shaming," *JSOT* 49, 1991, 47-76; K. Beyer, *Die Aramäischen Texte vom Toten Meer*, 1984; D. Daube, "The Culture of Deuteronomy," *Orita* 3, 1969, 27-52; A. Lacque, "Sin and Guilt," *RE* 13:325-31; Th. C. Vriezen, "Sünde und Schuld im AT," *RGG* 6, 478-82.

Philip J. Nel

7830 (*qālôn*, shame, dishonor), → # 7829

7831	קַלַּחַת

קַלַּחַת (*qallaḥat*), nom. pot, caldron (# 7831).

ANE The term comes from Egypt and may possibly be related to Ugar. (*HALAT* 1030).

OT *qallaḥat* is found in a list describing the type of vessel that was used to cook meat outside the tabernacle in Shiloh (1 Sam 2:14; third in a list with *dûd*, *kiyyôr*, and *pārûr*). It also functions as part of a metaphor describing the evil conduct of the rulers of Israel who deny justice to God's people and so chop them up like meat for the pot (Mic 3:3; ‖ *sîr*, cooking pot, # 6105).

Pan, pot: → *'ᵃgarṭāl* (bowl, basin, # 113); → *dûd* (cooking pot, # 1857); → *maḥtâ* (censer, fire pan/tray, # 4746); → *marḥešet* (baking pan, # 5306); → *maśrēt* (baking pan, # 5389); → *sîr* (cooking pot, # 6105); → *pārûr* (cooking pot, # 7248); → *qallaḥat* (pot, # 7831)

BIBLIOGRAPHY

R. Amiran, *Ancient Pottery of the Holy Land*, 1970; A. M. Honeyman, "The Pottery Vessels of the Old Testament," *PEQ* 71, 1939, 90; J. L. Kelso, "The Ceramic Vocabulary of the Old Testament," *BASORSup*, nos. 5-6, 1948, esp. § 76; idem, "Pottery," *IDB* 3:846-53, esp. 850.

Cornelis Van Dam

7832	קלט

קלט (*qlṭ* I), (q. passv. ptc. or adj.) shortened tail? (# 7832).

OT The word occurs only in Lev 22:23 to describe a defective animal, perhaps one stunted in growth or having an unusually short tail, which would be especially noticeable in the case of fat-tailed sheep. Such deformity disqualified the animal from sacrifice inasmuch as it was disharmonious with the perfections of Yahweh.

Handicaps, disfigurement, blind, lame, stammer, speechless: → *'illēm* (speechlessness, # 522); → *gibbēn* (hunchbacked, # 1492); → *ḥārûṣ* IV (mutilation [animal], # 3024); → *ḥērēš* (speechless, # 3094); → *kšḥ* (be lame, crippled, # 4171); → *mûm* (blemish, # 4583); → *mišḥāt* (disfigured, # 5425); → *nākeh* (crippled, smitten, # 5783); → *'wr* I (be blind, # 6422); → *'illēg* (stammering, stuttering, # 6589); → *psḥ* (be lame, crippled, # 7174); → *ṣl'* I (limping condition, # 7519); → *qlṭ* I (defective [animal], # 7832); → *śr'* (deformed, mutilated, # 8594); → *t^eballul* (white spot in eye, # 9319)

BIBLIOGRAPHY
J. Hartley, *Leviticus,* WBC 4, 1992, 361.

R. K. Harrison/E. H. Merrill

7833	קָלִי

קָלִי (*qālî*), parched grain (# 7833).

OT This word may have derived from the vb. *qlh*, meaning "to roast or parch," and it has a cognate in Akk. *qalitu*, roasted grain. The LXX uses the phrase *pephrygmena chidra nea,* meaning new parched grain, for this word, and it continued to be used in later Heb. *qālî* and Aram. *qalyā'*, roasted ears (of grain). Each of its six occurrences in the OT suggests that roasted grain was a main dietary staple in Israel (Lev 23:14; Ruth 2:14; 1 Sam 17:17; 25:18; 2 Sam 17:28). It was the primary part of the offering (*minḥâ*) of the firstfruits (Lev 2:14) and, unless there is a mistake (see LXX), 2 Sam 17:28 uses this word twice in a list of provisions distinguishing the ways of preparing grain (i.e., wheat and barley can be roasted or ground into flour and beans can be dried or parched).

Grain, barley, millet, rice, etc.: → *'ābîb* (ears of grain, # 26); → *biṣqālôn* (fresh stalks [cj.], # 1303); → *bar* III (grain, corn, # 1339); → *gādîš* I (stack of grain, # 1538); → *gereś* (grits, # 1762); → *dāgān* (grain, # 1841); → *dōḥan* (sorghum, millet, # 1893); → *ḥiṭṭâ* (wheat, # 2636); → *kussemet* (emmer-wheat, # 4081); → *karmel* IV (grain, fresh, newly ripened grain, # 4152); → *m^elîlâ* (grain, grains, # 4884); → *minnît* (rice, # 4976); → *mōṣ* (chaff, # 5161); → *sōlet* (wheat flour, # 6159); → *pannāg* (parched? grain, meal or flour, # 7154); → *ṣebet* (grain, bundle of grain, # 7395); → *ṣānum* (hard, barren [ears of grain], # 7568); → *qālî* (parched grain, # 7833); → *qāmâ* (crops, grain, standing grain, # 7850); → *śôrâ* (millet, # 8463); → *$ś^e$'ōrâ* (barley, # 8555); → *šibbōlet* I (ear of grain, # 8672); → *šeber* II (grain, # 8692)

BIBLIOGRAPHY
R. L. Hubbard, *The Book of Ruth*, 1988, 174-75; J. Milgrom, *Leviticus 1-16*, AB, 1991, 194.

Paul D. Wegner

7837	קלל

קלל (*qll*), q. be slight, swift; ni. appear trifling; pi. curse; pu. be cursed; hi. treat with contempt (# 7837); nom. קִיקָלוֹן (*qîqālôn*), unusual nom. disgrace (→ # 7814); קְלָלָה (*q^elālâ*), curse (# 7839); קְלֹקֵל (*q^elōqēl*), worthless, contemptible? (→ # 7848).

ANE The Akk. *qalālu* means "discredit," which meaning is also within the semantic range of the cognates in Arab., Eth., and Syr. The Aram. *q^e lal* may, in addition, mean "curse."

OT 1. There are approx. 43 occurrences of *qll* (pi., pu.) with the meaning "curse." The cursing of authority figures, whether God, parents, or king, features frequently (Exod 21:17; 22:28[27]; Lev 20:9; 24:11, 15; 2 Sam 16:5-13, etc.). Scribal piety is probably responsible for the statement in 1 Sam 3:13 that Eli's sons were "blaspheming for themselves," MT *lāhem* having replaced an original *'^e lōhîm*, God (cf. C. McCarthy, *The Tiqqune Sopherim*, OBO 36, 1981, 77-79). The curse could have deadly effect (2 Kgs 2:24; cf. Prov 30:10), though one uttered without good cause is doomed to be ineffective (2 Sam 16:12; Prov 26:2). According to Isa 65:20 the person who, in the era of salvation, fails to reach a hundred years will be adjudged to have come under a curse. The idea of premature death as the result of a curse is paralleled in the following from a Babylonian text: *ina la ūmešu ar-rat niši ikaššadsu*, "the curse of the people will overtake him before his time" (cf. W. G. Lambert, *Babylonian Wisdom Literature*, 1960, 132:114).

2. As with the *'ālâ*, curse (→ # 460), there is a degree of flexibility attaching to the curse. When Jacob demurs at the thought of deceiving his father and possibly incurring a curse, Rebekah responds with, "My son, let the curse fall on me" (Gen 27:13).

3. There is a an instance of metonymy, by which the person cursed is called "a curse," with this root; so also *'ālâ* (# 460). A person exposed on a tree is described as "under God's curse (*qil^e lat '^e lohîm*)" (Deut 21:23), which designation underlies the statement in Gal 3:13 that "Christ redeemed us from the curse of the law by becoming a curse for us."

Curse: → *'lh* I (swear, curse, put under oath, # 457); → *'rr* (curse, be cursed, # 826); → *brk* (bless [euph. for curse], # 1385a); → *gdp* (revile, blaspheme, # 1552); → *z'm* (be angry, curse, # 2404); → *nqb* (pierce, bore, distinguish, curse, # 5918); → *qbb* (curse, # 7686); → *qll* (be slight, swift, appear trifling, treat with contempt, # 7837); → **Curse: Theology**

BIBLIOGRAPHY

S. H. Blank, "The Curse, Blasphemy, the Spell, and the Oath," *HUCA* 23/1, 1950-51, 73-95; H. C. Brichto, *The Problem of "Curse" in the Hebrew Bible*, 1963; T. G. Crawford, *Blessing and Curse in Syro-Palestinian Inscriptions of the Iron Age*, 1992; M. Noth, "For All Who Rely on Works of the Law Are Under a Curse," in *The Laws in the Pentateuch and Other Studies* (ET), 1966, 118-31; A. C. Thiselton, "The Supposed Power of Words in the Biblical Writings," *JTS* ns 25, 1974, 283-99.

Robert P. Gordon

7838	קָלָל

קָלָל (*qālāl*), polished metal (# 7838).

ANE The vb. *qll* is common in Can., Ugar., meaning to fall; the Akk. *qalālu* means to be light or to make light.

OT The adj. is found as a description of the living creatures that sparkle as the gleam of polished bronze (Ezek 1:7); it is not clear whether the description is of the legs (in which case the genders disagree) or of the whole entity under consideration. The meaning of the adj. can only be conjectured, but it is probably from a root meaning slight or swift and may have a technical sense when applied to metals, like the polished bronze in 1 Kgs 7:45. The G renders this *exastraptōn* (flashing; cf. Luke 9:29), but then adds a second translation as an attempt to give a more strictly etymological equivalent to say their wings were light, i.e., swift. The expression is taken over in Dan 10:6, where it applies to the arms and legs of the man in the vision.

P-B The vb. *qᵉlāl* with the meaning of being light or swift is common in Aram.

Metals: → *'ᵃnāk* (lead, # 643); → *bᵉdîl* (dross, # 974); → *barzel* (iron, # 1366); → *zāhāb* (gold, # 2298); → *ḥel'â* I (rust, # 2689); → *ḥašmal* (glow?, electrum, glowing metal, # 3133); → *kesep* (silver, money, # 4084); → *masgēr* II (metal worker, # 4994); → *maᶜᵃbeh* (foundry, # 5043); → *nᵉḥōšet* I (copper, bronze, # 5733); → *sîg* (lead oxide, # 6092); → *sēper* II (bronze, plate, # 6220); → *ʿōperet* (lead, # 6769); → *paḥ* II (thin sheet, # 7063); → *pᵉlādōt* (steel?, # 7110); → *ṣwr* III (cast [metal], # 7445); → *ṣaᶜᵃṣuʿîm* (things formed by metal coating, # 7589); → *ṣph* II (arrange, overlay, plate, glaze, # 7596); → *ṣrp* (melt, smelt, refine, # 7671); → *qālāl* (polished metal, # 7838); → *šḥṭ* II (alloyed, # 8822)

BIBLIOGRAPHY

L. Allen, *Ezekiel 1-19*, WBC, 1994; G. A. Cooke, *The Book of Ezekiel*, ICC, 1936.

A. H. Konkel

7839 (*qᵉlālâ*, curse), → # 7837

7840	קלס

קלס (*qls*), pi. disdain, scoff, jeer, make fun of; hitp. mock, deride (# 7840); קֶלֶס (*qeles*), nom. derision (# 7841); קַלָּסָה (*qallāsâ*), nom. derision (# 7842).

ANE The root is not widely attested beyond the eight OT occurrences. Ugar. provides a near cognate in *qlṣ*, which Gordon (*UT*, Glossary, # 2234) renders "restraint" and connects with Arab. *qalaṣa*, to contract, shrink (cf. Dahood, *Bib* 52, 1971, 348; *TWOT* 2:801).

OT 1. The vb. occurs 4x in the OT. The pi. in Ezek 16:31 emphasizes the despicable nature of Jerusalem's sin. Her faithlessness before Yahweh, in spite of his love and mercy, is worse than that of a whoring wife: "You were unlike a prostitute, because you *scorned* payment." So debased is Jerusalem's behavior that she is likened to a whorish wife, driven by a lust for illicit affection and fleeting acceptance, who gives away her entire dowry, demanding absolutely nothing but momentary pleasure in return (Eichrodt).

2. The hitp. form of the vb. occurs 3x. Each occurrence illustrates the usage of the hitp. as indicating an action "performed with regard to or for oneself, in one's own personal interest" (GKC, 150). The youths from Bethel who tease and taunt the prophet Elisha about his physical appearance (2 Kgs 2:23) gain a perverted satisfaction at another's expense. Their actions and attitudes demonstrate a disdain for authority, in this case disdain for Yahweh's prophet and, hence, for Yahweh himself. Their subsequent discipline (2:24) underscores the seriousness and the sinfulness of their actions.

In Hab 1:10, the vb. forms part of God's answer to the prophet's initial complaint of the violence, injustice, and anarchy that run roughshod across the land of Judah. God is raising up the Babylonians, a ruthless people who "*deride* kings and scoff at rulers." Contempt for all authority is a characteristic of the Babylonian forces. Their derision of kings and rulers reveals their contempt for all authority and their attitude of superiority over all peoples.

In Ezek 22:5, the guilt of Jerusalem results in a pronouncement of divine judgment. So complete will be Jerusalem's demise that "those who are near and those who are far away will *mock* you." The privileged position of which Jerusalem was so proud would be replaced by ruin, reproach, and mockery. Her willingness to make a mockery of the covenant she enjoyed with Yahweh (cf. 22:1-4) results in punishment that reduces her to an object of mockery among the nations.

3. The nom. *qallāsâ* occurs in the same context (Ezek 22:4). Combined with *ḥerpâ*, it describes Jerusalem's ruined reputation in the eyes of surrounding peoples: "I will make you an object of scorn to the nations and a *laughingstock* to all the countries." "When a righteous people follow the world's ways, as Judah had done, the world ends up laughing at her" (Alexander).

4. In Jer 20:8, the nom. *qeles* forms part of Jeremiah's complaint over the difficulty and the indignity of his calling. He continues to proclaim the message of the Lord faithfully, but the burden is exceedingly heavy: "The word of the LORD has brought me insult and *reproach* all day long." In Ps 44:13[14] and Ps 79:4, *qeles* is coupled with *ḥerpâ* and *la'ag* in the language of lament to describe the pitiful condition of a downtrodden, defeated people: "You [God] have made us a reproach to our neighbors, the scorn and *derision* of those around us" (Ps 44:13).

5. Each occurrence of this root describes actions that either contradict customary practices (e.g., Ezek 16:31) or flaunt acceptable standards (e.g., 2 Kgs 2:23; Jer 20:8; Hab 1:10). The attitude of disdain and its accompanying behavior are consistently directed toward authority figures, especially when individuals are the perpetrators (e.g., 2 Kgs 2:23; Jer 20:8). When nations engage in mockery, the object of their disdain is other nations. In the latter cases, Yahweh is involved in creating the occasion that leads to the mockery, invariably as an expression of his judgment for national sins (e.g., Ps 44:13[14]; 79:4; Ezek 16:31; 22:4; Hab 1:10).

P-B LXX uses various words meaning ridicule to translate the vb. *qls*: *katapaizō* (2 Kgs 2:23), *entryphaō* (Hab 1:10; cf. 2 Pet 2:13), *empaizō* (Ezek 22:5). The nom. derivatives are rendered by *chleuasmos* in Jer 20:8; Ps 43:12; 78:4 and by *empaigmos* at Ezek 22:4. In Sir 11:4, *qls* is translated by *epairomai*, indicating a slight shift in sense to boast; "the hubris motif replaces that of scorn" (*TDNT* 5:631). Forms of the vb. *empaizō* appear frequently in the NT, most often with reference to the mocking of Jesus (e.g., Matt 27:29, 31; Mark 10:34; 15:20).

Mocking, ridicule, scoffing, stammering: → *gdp* (revile, blaspheme, # 1552); → *htl* (deceive, mock, # 2252); → *ḥrp* II (taunt, mock, insult, defy, # 3070); → *lyṣ* (scorn, talk big, mock, ridicule, # 4329); → *l'b* (jest, play, # 4351); → *l'g* (stutter, mock, deride, # 4352); → *lṣṣ* (rebel, scoff, # 4372); → *mwq* (mock, scoff, deride, # 4610); → *qls* (disdain, scoff, jeer, # 7840); → *śḥq* (laugh, mock, rejoice, celebrate, dance, # 8471); → *tll* (deceive, mock, trifle, # 9438); → *t''* (mock, deceive, # 9506); → *ta'tu'îm* (errors, mockery, # 9511)

Taunt: → *ḥrp* II (taunt, mock, insult, defy, # 3070); → *mangînâ* (taunting song, # 4947); → *š^e nînâ*, taunt, # 9110)

BIBLIOGRAPHY

R. Alexander, "Ezekiel," *EBC*, 1986, 6:847; W. Eichrodt, *Ezekiel: A Commentary*, OTL, 1970, 208.

Tim Powell

7841 (*qeles*, derision), → # 7840

7842 (*qallāsâ*, derision), → # 7840

7843	קלע

קלע (*ql'* I), q. and p. to sling, hurl out, hurl away (# 7843); קֶלַע (*qela'*), nom. sling, slingstones (# 7845); קַלָּע (*qallā'*), nom. men armed with slings (hapleg.; # 7847).

ANE 1. *Philology*. Although occurrences of these terms are relatively rare in the OT, the root is nevertheless attested in Arab., Eth., Syr., and later Jewish Aram. with the same meaning as BH.

2. *History*. Although no examples of ancient slings have survived, we obtain a relatively clear picture of the history of the sling dating back to prehistoric times from wall paintings, reliefs, and statues. The sling has been used as a weapon since at least 8000 BC. Before its adaptation to the field of battle, it appeared first as the common weapon of herdsmen, where it was employed to protect animals from predators. This use is also attested in both the Bible and in Homer's *Iliad*. As early as the Middle Bronze Age, however, units of slingmen were regularly found among the light infantry in Egypt. This evidence coincides with the period of the patriarchs, which suggests that the sling was a military weapon in the ANE throughout the biblical period.

3. *Usage*. The sling and bow appear as the two main weapons developed for long-range firepower. The sling seems to have had longer range than the bow, sometimes reaching as far as 600 feet. The wall paintings of Beni-Hasan, for example, show the slingers behind the archers (Yadin 1:158-9; 2:297). Hobbs states that this positioning suggests the slingers were more accurate than the bowmen (127; cf. Judg 20:16). Thus, battles were normally commenced by the slingers, followed by the archers, then the wielders of medium- and short-range weapons. Thus, slingers can be seen to have had a decided tactical advantage when pitted against soldiers outfitted with short-range weapons (cf. 1 Sam 17:40-51). Although a major advantage of the sling was its adaptability to any terrain, slingers were especially effective in siege operations as slings possessed the capacity for rapid, high-angled fire. The sling was in use by most people groups in the ANE, with the possible exception of the Philistines (cf. OT section 1 below).

4. *Description*. The sling consisted of two thongs composed of rushes, animal sinews, leather, cloth, or even hair attached to either side of a wider pocket (*kaf-haqqāla'*, 1 Sam 25:29), which held the projectile. The projectile was placed in the pocket and swung above the head one to three times. When the desired centrifugal force had been generated one thong was released, thus discharging the missile. Unlike many other weapons of antiquity, the sling was inexpensively manufactured and required little technical know-how to produce or employ. Optimum accuracy,

however, was achieved only by years of dedicated practice. Ammunition generally consisted of stones, which were in plentiful supply. Clay and lead projectiles, however, have also been discovered in abundance. Slingstones (*'abnê qᵉlā'îm*, 2 Chron 26:14; cf. Job 41:20; Zech 9:15) were carried into battle in a bag (1 Sam 17:40) or during a siege were piled at the slinger's feet (Yadin 2:297, 430, 431, 436, 452). Projectiles were normally 6 centimeters in diameter (slightly smaller than a tennis ball) and weighed between 13 and 185 grams (Korfmann, 38).

5. *Effectiveness*. The intent of the slinger was to incapacitate the enemy so that the fatal blow could be delivered by the infantry. In his treatise *De Medicina*, the ancient writer Celsus included instructions for extracting lead and stone missiles from the bodies of wounded soldiers. There are numerous reports, however, of slingstones being the actual cause of death. Hobbs notes that the impact of the common slingstone had the capacity to smash bone and even kill (124-25). For example, the ancient author Vegetius noted that biconical missiles could pierce armor, and even if penetration did not result, the impact could cause fatal internal injury (Korfmann, 40).

OT 1. *Literal*. In the premonarchial period it is clear that the Israelites were technologically inferior to the Philistines and Canaanites. These enemies appear to have held a monopoly on metallurgy, and thus weaponry, over the more primitive Israelites. The Israelites were therefore forced to rely upon ruse, captured weapons, and unconventional weapons such as farm implements and slings (Judg 3:31; 4:21; 5:8; 5:26; 9:53; 14:6; 15:5, 15; 20:16; 1 Sam 13:19, 22; 21:8-9). In light of prohibitions such as in Deut 17:16; 20:1; Josh 11:6; Judg 7:2; Zech 4:6, it is possible that this situation existed as part of God's testing of his people to ensure that they would trust in him and not in their own might (cf. 1 Sam 17:45, 47; Ps 2; 20:7[8]; 33:16-17; 44:1-3[2-4], 5-7[6-8]; 60:12[14]; Isa 63:1-9; etc.). It was not until the time of David, who had probably learned Philistine tactics and technology during his time as a mercenary, that Israel actually adopted Iron Age weaponry on a massive scale (Matthews, 144-46). Prior to this the sling seems to have been the main conventional weapon (Moyer, 46).

From the time of the Judges, units of slingers as well as archers and heavy infantry were organized according to tribal identities (Judg 20:16; 1 Chron 8:40; 12:2, 8-15, 24, 33, 34, etc.). Korfmann provides evidence that this was common among ancient peoples, and particularly with respect to slingers (40). Special units of slingers continued to function in the monarchial period and beyond (Hobbs, 125; cf. 2 Kgs 3:25; 2 Chron 26:14). Many of these units became legendary, which testifies to the effectiveness of the sling when used in military operations (Judg 20:16; 2 Kgs 3:25; 1 Chron 12:2; cf. 2 below).

The most celebrated use of the sling in the Bible comes from the account of David and Goliath (1 Sam 17:40-51). Each detail conforms with what we know of the use of the sling during this period. Goliath appears as a heavily-armed hoplite in the traditional Aegean fashion. His weapons are those used in close, hand-to-hand combat. It appears that long-range weaponry was not in use among the Philistines (Gonen, 41; Yadin 2:250, 336-7; cf. Goliath's negative attitude toward David's armaments in v. 43 and the lack of biblical reference to Philistine use of the sling). The shepherd David, on the other hand, is pictured as a lightly-armed auxiliary, possessing only the tools of his trade, which included the sling. His choice of missiles was typical, yet deadly (cf. ANE, secs. 4 and 5). Possession of long-range weaponry negated the superior strength, equipment, and experience of Goliath; marksmanship honed by years of practice afforded David a fighting chance. Nevertheless, it was God in whom David trusted and who directed the first missile to its intended target. The missile penetrated, yet only stunned the giant. David had to strike the death blow with Goliath's own sword, a short-range weapon (Hobbs, 126). The intent of the biblical author, therefore, is not to extol David's prowess with the sling, but rather to present David as the paradigm of righteousness, who trusts in God rather than the superiority of arms to give the victory (vv. 45, 47).

2. *Metaphorical.* 1 Sam 25:29 and Jer 10:18 picture God as a slinger, slinging the rebellious from his presence. The first passage speaks of the removal of David's enemies; the second speaks of the imminent exile of Judah to Babylon.

In Job 41, the author describes the prowess of leviathan. In so doing, he portrays the ineffectiveness of the most powerful offensive weapons upon him. In this context the Scripture states, "Slingstones are like chaff to him" (v. 28[20]; n.b. 4 and 5 above).

Zech 9:15 speaks of the victory God will give to his people in terms of conquest by means of the sling ("They will destroy and overcome with slingstones") or in terms of the people of God overcoming the slingers ("They shall devour and tread down the slingers," RSV). The syntax of the Heb. presents a difficulty at this point, and for this reason many have suggested emending the text; thus, the difference in translation (Merrill, 261-62). If the RSV is correct, this passage would paint a vivid picture of complete victory, since the slingers were positioned at the rear of the attacking army and would be the last unit overrun in a counter-offensive (cf. ANE sec. 3).

3. Prov 26:8 compares giving honor to a fool to tying a stone in the pocket of a sling, *margēmâ* (# 5275). One action is as illogical as the other. The word *margēmâ* is not semantically connected to the terms listed above and indeed is somewhat problematic to translators as it occurs only once. Most translations, including the NIV, follow the LXX, rendering the term "sling."

P-B The literary and archeological records indicate continued use of the sling throughout the intertestamental and NT periods (cf. 1QM 8:1; Jdt 6:12; 9:7; 1 Macc 9:11). Sir 47:4 emphasizes the sling to the exclusion of all other weapons mentioned in the biblical account of David and Goliath (contra LXX Ps 151:7). Josephus records the use of the sling by both sides in the first Jewish revolt against Rome (*War* 2:423; 3:211; 4:14, etc.).

NT The NT makes no use of these terms or those used by the translators of the LXX. It is possible, however, that passages such as Matt 8:12; 22:13; 25:30; Rev 20:10, 14, 15 find conceptual parallels in texts such as 1 Sam 25:29 and Jer 10:18 (cf. OT sec. 2).

Hurling: → *ṭwl* (throw, # 3214); → *ql'* I (sling, hurl, # 7843); → *šlk* I (throw, hurl, # 8959)

Bibliography

R. Gonen, *Weapons of the Ancient World*, 1975; T. R. Hobbs, *A Time for War*, 1989; M. Korfmann, "The Sling as a Weapon," *Scientific American Resource Library; Readings in the Physical Sciences and Technology* 229, 1973, 34-42; V. Matthews, *Manners and Customs in the Bible*, 1988; E. Merrill, *Haggai, Zechariah, Malachi*, 1994; J. Moyer, "Weapons and Warfare in the

Book of Judges," *Discovering the Bible*, 1986; Y. Yadin, *The Art of Warfare in Biblical Lands*, 1963.

W. E. Nunnally

7844	קלע

קלע (*ql'* II), q. carve (# 7844); מִקְלַעַת (*miqla'at*), nom. carving (# 5237).

OT From earliest times people have decorated their surroundings and equipment with carvings or engravings. Where ancient texts describe these activities, it can be difficult to know exactly what is meant unless there are further details.

The cedar-paneled walls and wooden doors of Solomon's temple were decorated in the manner this vb. describes, with the derived nom. naming the result (1 Kgs 6:18, 29, 32, 35). The usual rendering "carve" is most likely, the additional qualification *pittûaḥ* in 6:29 perhaps indicating engraved enhancement of the cherubim displayed on the walls. The nom. *miqla'at* occurs in the same connection (1 Kgs 6:18, 29, 32; 7:31).

Carving, incision, inscription: → *ḥqh* (be incised, # 2977); → *ḥrt* (incise, # 3100); → *ptḥ* II (carve, # 7338); → *ql'* II (carve, # 7844)

Alan Millard

7845 (*qela'* I, sling, sling-stones), → # 7843

7846 (*qela'* II, curtain), → # 4595b

7847 (*qallā'*, man armed with sling), → # 7843

7848	קְלֹקֵל

קְלֹקֵל (q^e*lōqēl*), adj. of uncertain meaning: worthless(?), contemptible(?); nom. designating a plant/plant product(?) (hapleg.; # 7848; *HALAT* 1034a).

ANE Several possible etymological streams may be (or have been) suggested for the Heb. q^e*lōqēl*. They fall into two broad categories: those that regard q^e*lōqēl* as a quadraliteral nom. (requiring an emendation in the MT) and one that regards q^e*lōqēl* as a participial adj. (deriving from Heb. *qll*, be light, slight, contemptible).

First, we may consider those etymological streams that relate to nom. forms and that require an emendation of MT Num 21:5, *balleḥem haqq*^{e}*lōqēl*, to *b^e*leḥem haqq-l-q-l-* (cf. GKC § 128o and n. 3). The first nom. etymology relates to a supposed Akk. nom. **qalqaltu*, hunger; scant rations (cf. now *bubūtu(m)* I, hunger, *AHw* 1:135b [= *bubūtu* A, famine, hunger, sustenance, *CAD*, B, 301a-2b]; or *galgal(la)tu, kalkaltu*, hunger, *AHw* 1:274b [= *galgaltu* A, hunger, *CAD*, G, 14a-b]) (so Klein, 579a; cf. Gray, 277). Semantically, the sense required by the context and supplied by most versional translations is close enough to that of "bread of hunger, hunger rations," to allow such a derivation, but not so as to require it (see below). Formally, this etymology is less secure because the Heb. form preserved in the MT does not easily align with that of the Akk. nom. (properly *galgal(la)tu, kalkaltu* or *bubūtu*).

A second group of nom. etymologies relates to the identity of the plant substance from which the bread may have been derived. Several scholars have suggested a connection with Akk. *qulqulliānu/qulqullânu*, (a kind of) cassia (*Cassia tora,* Thompson?) (*AHw* 2:927a; *CAD,* Q, 301a-b [a plant]; cf. Holma, 81-83; KB 841b). A cognate may be found in Ugar. *qlql,* referring to an herb fed to horses (*WUS* # 2415; *UT* # 2235, on Text 55:8 = *CTA* # 160, 8), which A. Herdner compares to Arab. *qilqil*, cassia (*CTA* 246 n. 4; cf. Dietrich-Loretz-Sanmartín, 45; Huehnergard, 174). Syllabic Ugar. *qi-i-lu* (RS 20.123 + [*Ugaritica* V, 242-43] II:27') appears to refer to an herb from which a dye might be extruded (J. M. Sasson, "Flora, Fauna and Minerals," in *RSP*, 1, iii 108 [443]). Alternative etymological streams that relate to plant names or products may be (or have been) suggested. One relates to Akk. *qāqullu*, cardamom (*Elettaria cardamomum*) (*AHw*, 2:901b; *CAD,* Q, 124a-b 1. [a plant]; Contenau, 14, cress; Holma, 81-83); Arab. *qāqūlla*, cardamom (Wehr, 736a); and (postbiblical) Aram. *qāqûlā'*, cardamom (Jastrow, 1409b). Another relates to Arab. *qulqulān*, a leguminous plant (*Assahal hippocrepis bicontorta* [Philby, 1:311; KB 841b]). Another relates to Arab. *quliaqulān* (*Saviznya aegyptiaca*) (J. J. Hess, so KB 841b). Yet another relates to Akk. *qalqālu*, a kind of flour/meal (loanword from Sum.) (*AHw* 2:895a; *CAD*, Q, 67b [mng. uncert.]). Any of these nom. etymologies, while requiring emendation of MT Num 21:5, has the advantage of being formally close to the MT. Moreover, the nature of manna described elsewhere in the OT as resembling "coriander seed" (Exod 16:31; Num 11:7) makes plausible a metaphorical description of it here as "the bread of [a nom. designating a plant/plant product]."

All the foregoing nom. etymologies suffer for want of conformity to the syntax of MT Num 21:5, which requires that *qᵉlōqēl* be an adj. Thus, the second stream of etymology, the one that follows the MT, derives *qᵉlōqēl* as an adj. from the Heb. stative *qll*, be light, slight, contemptible (*HALAT* 1030b-32a; cf. Olshausen, §189f; Barth, 160; BDB 887a; so Gray, 277; L. J. Coppes, *TWOT* 2:800a-1a; Budd, 234). The Sam. Pent. attests *qålqål* (cf. Sam. *qlql,* which Ben-Hayyim logs as semantically equivalent to the Arab. adj. *saḫīf*, feeble, despicable [2:588, # 284]).

OT The only OT usage of this adj. occurs in the context of Num 21:5, the foremost instance of Israel's spurning of Yahweh's provision of manna. It is used in the expression *leḥem qᵉlōqēl*: "They spoke against God and against Moses, saying, '. . . There is neither food (*leḥem*)! nor water—and we detest this miserable/wretched bread (*balleḥem haqqᵉlōqēl*) [specifically, re manna]'" (author tr.) (so KD, 1:138; NIV, NRSV, REB). The LXX of Num. 21:5, which likewise interprets *qᵉlōqēl* as an adj. related to the vb. *qll*, be light, slight, contemptible, translates with the G adj. *diakenos*, empty, hollow: "our soul loathes this light bread."

P-B Cognates may also be found in postbiblical Heb. *qîlqûl* (< the pilpel *qilqel*, damage, ruin) and Jewish Aram. *qîlqûlā'* (< the palpel *qalqēl*, ruin), both nom. forms meaning deterioration, spoilage (Jastrow, 1361a).

Contempt, disdain, disgust, loathing: → *bwz* (show contempt for, # 996); → *bzh* (be contemptible, think lightly of, despise, # 1022); → *bḥl* (become tired of, disdain, # 1041); → *g'l* (abhor, be defiled, fail, # 1718); → *zhm* (make s.th. loathsome, # 2299); → *zwr* III (be offensive, # 2320); → *zll* I (be frivolous, be despised, # 2361); → *znh* II (feel a dislike for, # 2389); → *zārā'* (sickness, nausea, # 2426); → *ḥnn* II (be stinking, loathsome, # 2859); → *yq'* (turn aside, # 3697); → *nq'* (disengage, # 5936); → *qwṭ* (feel disgust, # 7752); → *qll* (be slight, swift, appear trifling, treat with contempt, # 7837); → *šwṭ* II (slight, despise, # 8764); → *šqṣ* (make o.s. detestable, # 9210); → *tʿb* (be detestable, be loathed, loathe, abhor, # 9493)

BIBLIOGRAPHY

TWOT 2:800a-801a; J. Barth, *Die Nominalbildung in den semitischen Sprachen,* 2d ed., 1894, 160; Z. Ben-Hayyim, *The Literary and Oral Tradition of Hebrew and Aramaic Amongst the Samaritans,* Academy of the Hebrew Language 1-2, 1957, 2:581, 588 [Hebrew]; P. J. Budd, *Numbers,* WBC 5, 1984, 234; G. Contenau, "Drogues de Canaan, d'Amurru et jardins botaniques," in *Mélanges Syriens offerts à monsieur René Dussaud,* 2 vols., FS R. Dussaud, Bibliothêque archéologique et historique 30, 1939, 1:(11-14) 14; M. Dietrich, O. Loretz, and J. Sanmartín, "Zur ugaritischen Lexicographie (XII)," *UF* 6, 1974, (39-45) 45, no. 26; G. B. Gray, *Numbers,* ICC, 1903, 277; H. Holma, *Kleine Beiträge zum assyrischen Lexikon,* Annales academiae scientiarum fennicae, ser. B, vol. 7, # 2, 1913, 81-83; J. Huehnergard, *Ugaritic Vocabulary in Syllabic Transcription,* HSS 32, 1987, 174; E. D. Klein, *A Comprehensive Etymological Dictionary of the Hebrew Language for Readers of English,* 1987, 579a; J. Olshausen, *Lehrbuch der hebräischen Sprache,* 1861, 2 vols., §189f; H. St. J. B. Philby, *The Heart of Arabia,* 2 vols., 1922, 1:311; J. F. Ross, "Food," *IDB* 2:304b-8a.

Robert H. O'Connell

7850	קָמָה

קָמָה (*qāmâ*), crops, grain, standing grain (# 7850); < קום (*qwm,* rise, → # 7756).

OT This word occurs 8x in the OT and appears to be derived from the vb. *qwm,* rise up, which has many cognates from other Sem. languages (e.g., Aram. *qwm;* Arab. *qāma;* Ugar. *qm;* etc.); however, apart from Aram. *qāmᵉtāʾ* there are no specific cognates that refer to "standing grain." The LXX uses several phrases to translate this word (*stachys orthos,* standing ears [Judg 15:5]; *amētos hestēkōs,* standing grain [Isa 17:5]). In Exod 22:5[6], a distinction is made between stacked grain and standing grain, and in Deut 16:9 the Feast of Tabernacles is determined from the time that the Israelites began to cut the standing grain. Other biblical passages make it clear that this is a general word referring to any kind of standing grain or a plant (Deut 23:25[26]; Judg 15:5; 2 Kgs 19:26; Isa 17:5; 37:27; Hos 8:7).

The word occurs 3x in oracles of judgment (Isa 17:5; 37:28; Hos 8:7), indicating that one clear sign of judgment is the removal of standing grain, and consequently the suffering of the people, "The stalk has no head; it will produce no flour. Were it to yield grain, foreigners would swallow it up" (Hos 8:7).

Grain, barley, millet, rice, etc.: → *ʾābîb* (ears of grain, # 26); → *biṣqālôn* (fresh stalks [cj.], # 1303); → *bar* III (grain, corn, # 1339); → *gādîš* I (stack of grain, # 1538); → *gereś* (grits, # 1762); → *dāgān* (grain, # 1841); → *dōḥan* (sorghum, millet, # 1893); → *ḥiṭṭâ* (wheat, # 2636); → *kussemet* (emmer-wheat, # 4081); → *karmel* IV (grain, fresh, newly ripened grain, # 4152); → *mᵉlîlâ* (grain, grains, # 4884); → *minnît* (rice, # 4976); → *mōṣ* (chaff, # 5161); → *sōlet* (wheat flour, # 6159); → *pannāg* (parched? grain, meal or flour, # 7154); → *ṣebet* (grain, bundle of grain, # 7395); → *ṣānum* (hard, barren [ears of grain], # 7568); → *qālî* (parched grain, # 7833); → *qāmâ* (crops, grain, standing grain, # 7850); → *śôrâ* (millet, # 8463); → *śᵉʿōrâ* (barley, # 8555); → *šibbōlet* I (ear of grain, # 8672); → *šeber* II (grain, # 8692)

Paul D. Wegner

7853	קִמּוֹשׂ

קִמּוֹשׂ (*qimmôś*), weeds (nettles) (# 7853).

ANE A cognate to *qimmôś* occurs in Arab. (*HALAT* 842).

OT *qimmôś* is used in two contexts in parallel to *ḥôaḥ*: Hos 9:6 in connection with the judgment of Memphis, and Isa 34:13 in connection with the judgment of Edom. In Prov 24:31 it is employed in the description of the field of the slothful—a field of all kind of weeds (contrasted to the righteous).

Thornbush, nettle, sting, thistle, thorn: → *'āṭād* (thornbush, # 353); → *barqōn* (thorn, brier, # 1402); → *deber* II (thorny sting, # 1823); → *dardar* (thistle, # 1998); → *ḥēdeq* (brier, # 2537); → *ḥôaḥ* I (thorn, # 2560); → *m^esûkâ* (thorn hedge, # 5004); → *na'^aṣûṣ* (thornbush, # 5848); → *sîrâ* (thorny bush, # 6106); → *sillôn* (thorn, # 6141); → *s^eneh* (thorny shrub, # 6174); → *sirpād* (stinging nettle, # 6252); → *ṣe'^elîm* (thorny lotus, # 7365); → *ṣ^enînîm* (thorns, # 7564); → *qôṣ* I (thornbush, # 7764); → *qimmôś* (weeds, nettles, # 7853); → *śēk* (thorn, splinter, # 8493); → *šāmîr* I (Christ's thorn, # 9031)

Bibliography

TWOT 2:802; H. and A. Moldenke, *Plants of the Bible*, 1952, 245.

K. Lawson Younger, Jr.

7854 (*qemaḥ*, flour), → Bread

7855	קמט

קמט (*qmṭ*), q. seize (# 7855).

ANE The Akk. vb. *qamādu*(m) is found in Old Babylonian and Old Assyrian with the sense of making full (e.g., days full of hardship); it is also found in the Amarna tablets to speak of packing weapons (*AHw*, 896). It is possible that the personal name *qmṭn* is found in Ugar.; the interpretation depends on the word division of a broken text (*UT*, 19.2238; cf. *KTU*, 4.44 xx). The Syr. *q^emaṭ* means to bind together, hold, or press; the Mand. *gmṭ* means to seize, hold fast, press; the Eth. *taqamaṭa* means to settle down; and the Arab. *qamaṭa* means to wrap up a diaper.

OT The vb. *qmṭ* occurs twice, both times in Job, and both variously interpreted. In Job 22:16 Eliphaz speaks of the evil ones who die before their time. Some commentators (e.g., Gordis) follow the meaning of Mish. Heb. and take the meaning to be cut off (247-48); he takes this to be a different root from 16:8. However it is logical, based on the Aram. and other cognates, to say the evil are seized or bound before their time, assuming the same vb. as 16:8 (Fohrer, 351). In the latter verse Job says that God has bound him or wrapped him up; Clines prefers wrinkled, based on a Syr. and Late Heb. meaning and synonymous with emaciated in the parallel line (370). The variation between second and third person (vv. 7-9) is "frequent and virtually normal" (Gordis, 175), so emendation is unwarranted.

P-B The vb. *qmṭ* occurs in later Aram. meaning press, but in the Talm. carries additional metaphorical meanings such as bound or constipated, or the sense of shrinking in feelings of aversion.

Seizing, grasping, taking hold of: → *'ḥz* I (seize, settled, # 296); → *ḥṭp* (seize and take away, # 2642); → *ḥth* (take, fetch, # 3149); → *kwl* (lay hold of, seize, contain, # 3920); → *lkd* (catch, capture, # 4334); → *lpt* (take hold of, grasp, clasp, turn around, # 4369); → *mšk* (seize, drag off, delay, # 5432); → *qmṭ* (seize, # 7855); → *tmk* (take hold of, grasp, # 9461); → *tpś* (capture, occupy, # 9530)

BIBLIOGRAPHY

D. J. A. Clines, *Job 1-20*, WBC 17, 1989, 370; G. Fohrer, *Das Buch Hiob*, KAT 16, 1963, 280, 351; R. Gordis, *The Book of Job*, 1978, 175-76, 247-48.

A. H. Konkel

7857	קמל

קמל (*qml*), q., wither(s), to become moldy, musty; infected with insects (?) (# 7857).

ANE Arab. *qamila*, become black speckled; OA, Arab. *qml*; Eth., *quĕmāl*; Tigre, *qamlat*, louse.

OT The word is used twice. In both cases (Isa 19:6; 33:9) the context suggests strongly that the word means to dry, wither away, become desiccated, dark, rather than infected with insects, although insects may be a partial cause of the effect. In both cases the effect is pictured as a part of Yahweh's judgment.

P-B The LXX does not translate *qml* in 19:6, evidently considering it to mean "to dry up" (*chēranthēsetai* = it will dry up in every marsh of reeds and rushes). Galilee and Carmel are reported as *phanera*, a nom. that means to become evident, open, bare (?) in the sense of, perhaps, "drying up" (33:9).

Dry, withering, parched: → *'bl* II (dry up, # 62); → *baṣṣārâ* (dearth, destitution, # 1314); → *zrb* (cease, dry up, # 2427); → *ḥrb* I (be dry or desolate, ruined, # 2990); → *ḥrr* II (be parched, # 3081a); → *ybš* (be dry, dried up, withered, dry up, # 3312); → *mll* I (wither, be dry, # 4908); → *nšt* (dry, parched, # 5980); → *qml* (wither, become moldy, musty, infected w. insects, # 7857)

Eugene Carpenter/Michael A. Grisanti

7858 (*qmṣ*, take a handful), → # 3338

7859 (*qōmeṣ*, handful), → # 3338

7860 (*qēn*, nest, nestlings), → # 7873

7861	קנא

קנא (*qn'*), pi. be jealous, envious, zealous, furious; hi. excite one's jealousy, anger (# 7861); adj. קַנָּא (*qannā'*), zealous, jealous (# 7862); nom. קִנְאָה (*qin'â*), jealousy, envy, zeal, ardor (# 7863); קַנּוֹא (*qannô'*), zealous, jealous (# 7868).

ANE Formerly, an etymological relationship between Heb. *qn'* and Akk. *uqnû*, lapis lazuli, or the Arab. *qana'a*, be red/black, was assumed (see J. Pedersen, *Israel: Its Life and Culture I-II*, 1926, 236). The existence of *qn'* in Ugar. is questionable (cf. *UT*, no. 2246; *KTU* 1.23.21). The meanings of cognates in other Sem. languages roughly correspond to the semantic range of the Heb. root.

OT 1. The root *qn'* appears 85x in the OT and has a wide range of meanings. The word can occur both in a positive sense (advocate zealously for the benefit of someone else) and in a negative sense (bear a grudge against, resent). The various usages share the notion of an intense, energetic state of mind, urging towards action. The cause of the *qn'* actions is the (possibly imagined) infringement of someone's rights or injury to the subject's honor. It is noteworthy that the human *qin'â* is discussed predominantly in the Wisdom literature, whereas the divine *qin'â* is an issue in the prophetic literature. The construction *qn'* + b^e (preposition), which has a negative connotation (be jealous), is never used in connection with the divine *qin'â*.

2. The human *qin'â* can appear in various guises, e.g., passion (S of Songs 8:6), anger (Prov 14:30, 27:4), jealousy (Gen 26:14; Ezek 31:9), competition (Eccl 4:4), devotion (Num 11:29). Several times *qin'â* is parallel to *ḥēmâ* and *'ēš*. In two places *qin'â* is used in connection with marriage and adultery: Prov 6:34 and Num 5 (the law on jealousy). In the Wisdom literature *qin'â* is often warned against as a destructive emotion (cf. Job 5:2).

3. Of more distinct theological interest are those places where the *qin'â* of the religious believers against the *r^ešā'îm* (the ungodly, wicked) is involved. The prosperity and pride of the ungodly can become a mystery, a temptation and cause jealousy for the miserable *ṣaddîq*. The *respice finem*, however, should prevent anger and jealousy (Ps 37:1; 73:3; Prov 3:31; 23:17; 24:1, 19). Also of importance are those passages in which *qin'â* is used to express religious fervor, impassionate devotion to God. Phinehas identified himself with God's cause by his strong-willed behavior against Zimri, to such an extent that he executed on his behalf God's *qin'â* (Num 25:11, 13; cf. 2 Cor 11:2). Elijah and Jehu also passionately stand up for the name and honor of their God (1 Kgs 19:10, 14; 2 Kgs 10:16 respectively; but cf. Hos 1:4). The fervor for God (God's home, God's law) completely occupies the faithful and "devours" him (Ps 69:10 [*'kl,* eat, # 430]; 119:139 [*ṣmt*, wear out, # 7551]).

4. The theologoumenon of the "zeal of the LORD" is one of the basic elements of the OT conception of God (W. Eichrodt, *Theologie des Alten Testaments*, 1, 1968[8], 133). God can be called simply "zealous" (Exod 34:14) or, by a very old formula (F. M. Cross, *TDOT* 1:257), "the zealous God" (7x, *'ēl qannā'/ qannô'*). From this it appears that the expression *qin'at yhwh* not merely expresses an affect, but an essential element in God (von Rad, *Theologie des Alten Testaments*, OTT, 1987[9], 1:220, calls the *qin'at yhwh* "the most personal revelation of God's being").

5. In a large number of texts the *qin'â* relates to Israel's idolatry (e.g., 1 Kgs 14:22; Ps 78:58; Ezek 8:3-4, etc.). God's *qin'â* is the fiery, angry reaction to the infringement of his rights *vis-à-vis* Israel and to the violation of the *b^erît* (cf. Isa 42:8; 48:10). Israel is God's people, and he is Israel's God. Anyone outside the circle of the covenant is "non-people" (*lō' 'ām*) and "no-god" (*lō' ēl*) (Deut 32:21). Inside the covenant circle God demands of his people a completely exclusive worship (cf. 6:4). His love for Israel totally excludes any other gods. The formula *'ēl qannā'/qannô'* is, therefore, used in the context of the covenant: Exod 34:14 (against the covenant with the Canaanites), 20:5/Deut 5:9 (the decalogue as covenant document), Deut 4:24; 6:15; Josh 24:19. In Exod 20:5/Deut 5:9, the clause *kî 'ēl qannā' hû'* functions as the basis of the first and second commandments; the *qin'â* of God is unfolded, showing its negative effect (*pōqēd 'āwôn*) and its positive effect (*'ōśeh ḥesed*). That the *qin'â* of God

usually implies the notion of "punishment" is made clear not only by the frequent parallelism with words such as *'ap/ḥēmâ, 'ēš* (Deut 4:24, God as *'ēl qannā'* and *'ēš 'ōkᵉlâ*), or *nāqām*, Isa 59:17; Nah 1:2), but also by its relation to the notion of the holiness of God in Josh 24:19. The *qin'â* of God is the self-preservation of the sovereign, unapproachable, holy God (cf. von Rad 1:217), who speaks of "zeal" and "holiness" as the reverse sides of one and the same property of God.

6. Any association with self-centered pettiness, fear of losing property, envy, or jealousy is absent in the context of the manifestation of the *qin'â* of God. The translation "jealous" is, therefore, inadequate (*pace* E. Reuter, *TWAT* 7:58; cf. B. E. Baloian, *The Aspect of Anger in the Old Testament*, 1988, 281). God's "jealousy" is not directed against the idols, but against the disloyal covenant partner. His *qin'â* is not like that of the deceived husband against his rival, but rather like that of the lord/sovereign who does not tolerate anyone else next to him in the covenant with his subjects, and in that way he claims and maintains the exclusive relationship with his people. Idolatry is preeminently a violation of covenant. Only in Ezek 16:38, 42 and 23:25 does the metaphor of marriage play a role, but here also the divine *qin'â* is not directed, as a "jealousy," against competitors. The *qin'â* of God, therefore, differs radically from the envy of gods known from the surrounding areas, which can be aimed at fellow gods or at worshipers. Whereas in the surrounding areas a fundamental religious tolerance prevailed (to such an extent that in one temple different gods could be worshiped), God's *qin'â* completely excludes other gods. The notion of the *qin'â* of God is, therefore, of importance in assessing the question whether, and if so to what extent, Israel's religion was monotheistic.

7. The divine *qin'â* can also be directed against the external threat to the covenant, and in that case it means a punishing fiery wrath against the enemy of Israel (especially in the exilic and postexilic prophets; e.g., Isa 42:13; Ezek 36:5-6; 38:19; Nah 1:2). In Zeph 1:18 and 3:8 the issue is the universal judgment. In prophecies of the saving acts of God, the *qin'â* of God has evident positive meaning: as a consequence of his compassion (Ezek 39:25) and pity (Joel 2:18) God devoted himself to his land and people (cf. Zech 1:14). This divine devotion is earnestly sought in Isa 63:15. The eschatological scope of these texts shows most clearly in Isa 9:6; 37:22; and 2 Kgs 19:31, where God's *qin'â* is the stimulating force behind the decisive turn in redemptive history: the "small remnant" and the coming of the Messiah are the result of God's burning love (= *qin'â*) for Israel.

P-B In the literature of Qumran and in Zealotry, the notion of *qin'â* as "devotion to God" has taken a particularly important position. The LXX has translated *qn'* rather consistently by the word *zēlos*.

NT → *NIDNTT* 3:1166-69.

Anger, rage, wrath: → *'np* (be angry, # 647); → *z'm* (curse, be angry, # 2406); → *z'p* I (rage, # 2406); → *ḥēmâ* (rage, # 2779); → *ḥrh* I (be hot, become angry, # 3013); → *k's* (be irritated, angry, # 4087); → *'br* II (show anger, # 6297); → *qṣp* I (become angry, # 7911); → *rgz* (shake, agitate, # 8074); → **Anger: Theology**

Desire, coveting, craving, delight, happiness, longing, pleasure: → *'ᵃrešet* (desire, request, # 830); → *ḥmd* (desire, crave, long for, covet, treasure, # 2773); → *ḥpṣ* I (want, desire, wish, care, # 2911); → *ḥšq* (desire, longing, lust, # 3137); → *y'b* (long for, yearn, desire, # 3277);

→ *kāleh* (longing, # 3985); → *kmh* (long after, lust for, # 4014); → *ksp* II (desire, long after, # 4083); → *môrāš* II (wish, desire, # 4626); → *'rg* (long after, pant after, # 6864); → *š'l* (ask, request, wish, # 8626); → *t'b* I (desire, long after, # 9289); → *t^eš̂ûqâ* (desire, longing, appetite, # 9592)

Bibliography

TDNT 2:879-90; *THAT* 2:647-50; *TWAT* 7:51-62; W. Berg, "Die Eifersucht Gottes - Ein problematischer Zug des alttestamentlichen Gottesbildes?" *BZ* 23, 1979, 197-211; H. A. Brongers, "Der Eifer des Herrn Zebaoth," *VT* 13, 1963, 269-84; C. Dohmen, "Eifersüchtig ist sein Name" (Exod 34:14): Ursprung und Beteutung der alttestamentlichen Rede von Gottes Eifersucht," *TZ* 46, 1990, 289-304; E. Haag (ed), *Gott, der einzige: Zur Entstehung des Monotheismus in Israel, QD* 104, 1985; J. Halbe, *Das Privilegrecht Jahwes Ex.34,10-26: Gestalt und Wesen, Herkunft und Wirken in vordeuteronomischer Zeit,* FRLANT, 114, 1975, 134-40; F. Küchler, "Der Gedanke des Eifers Jahwes im Alten Testament," *ZAW* 28, 1908, 42-52; J. C. de Moor, *The Rise of Yahwism: The Roots of Israelite Monotheism,* BETL 91, 1990, 227-29; G. von Rad, *OTT,* 216-25; B. Renaud, *Je suis un Dieu jaloux: Evolution sémantique et signification théologique de qin^e'ah,* 1963.

H. G. L. Peels

7862 (*qannā'*, zealous, jealous), → # 7861

7863 (*qin'â*, jealousy, envy, zeal, ardor), → # 7861

7864/7865	קנה

קנה (*qnh*), q. acquire, buy, create (cf. 3 below), produce, ni. be bought, hi. bought (# 7864/7865); קִנְיָן (*qinyān*), nom. something acquired; creatures (coll., hapleg. in this sense; Ps 104:24; # 7871). The prep. *min* indicates the seller and *l^e* the purchaser. *qnh* is the opposite of *mkr*, sell. Aram. קנה (*qnh*), buy (hapleg. in Ezra 7:17).

ANE Ugar. *qny*; Aram. *qnh* (*DISO*, 260 = *APFC*, no. 30:16); Akk. *qanû*, gain, acquire (*AHw*, 898b; *HAL*³, 1038).

OT 1. The word is used for the buying of land, such as the purchase of the burial place of Abraham (Gen 25:10; cf. 49:30; 50:13; Josh 24:32), Jacob bought land from the Shechemites (Gen 33:19) and Joseph as vizier of Egypt bought up all the land in Egypt in the time of famine (47:19-23), excluding temple land. David bought Araunah's field (2 Sam 24:21, 24 = 1 Chron 21:24), and Omri bought the hill of Samaria (1 Kgs 16:24). For the repairs to the temple, the reformers Joash and Josiah bought timber (2 Kgs 12:12[13]; 22:6 = 2 Chron 34:11). Nehemiah boasted that he and his officials did not buy any land (5:16), indicating that he performed his duties properly.

2. The vb. is used with reference to *people*. Joseph was bought as a slave by Potiphar (Gen 39:1). The teacher of Eccleciastes bought many slaves (2:7), which indicates his status. The pentateuchal laws deal with the purchasing of slaves. Priests may buy slaves (Lev 22:11), but a Hebrew slave that was bought is to be set free after seven years (Exod 21:2). The Jubilee laws in Lev 25 deal with the return of property and slaves (cf. R. de Vaux, *Ancient Israel,* 1960, 87-88). Boaz as kinsmen-redeemer acquired the field of Naomi (Ruth 4) in accordance with the laws of Lev 25:25-28.

Nehemiah blames the Jews for buying their brothers as slaves (Neh 5:8). Amos (8:6) preaches against those who buy the poor (cf. 2:6 with *mkr*), and in Zech 11:5 the Jews are sold by their leaders. In the day that is coming the false prophets will try to hide their identity by saying that they were bought as slaves when they were young (Zech 13:5).

3. Many texts deal with the *theological* idea that God bought (i.e., redeemed) Israel, e.g., Exod 15:16 and Ps 74:2: "Remember the people you purchased *(qnh)* of old, the tribe of your inheritance, whom you redeemed (*g'l*)" (also in Isa 11:11). The vb. can also be used of the land bought by God for Israel (Ps 78:54). In contrast to this stands the curse in Deut 28:68. The root *qnh* in the sense "create" is much disputed (Vawter; *THAT*, s.v.), but is to be maintained on grounds of the comparative linguistic and religious evidence (De Moor for Ugaritic; cf. *KAI* III 22a) and of its use and parallels in context (Gen 14:19, 22; Deut 32:6; Ps 139:13; Prov 8:22; cf. Westermann on Gen 4:1). Semantically, the range of *qnh* is similar to that of "get" and "beget" in Eng. (both mean acquire and procreate, see *OED* s.v.). The metaphoric imagery of procreation can be used to express the divine activity of creation (cf. De Moor). When used for divine creation in the OT, the procreative sense of *qnh* has generally become a dead metaphor. Yet in the crucial passage, Prov 8:22, where Yahweh's "creates" (*qnh*) Wisdom, the *metaphor* of procreation remains active through the use of *ḥyl* I (be in labor, tremble, → # 2655) in vv. 24-25 (cf. Deut 32:6, 18; Ps 90:2).

4. The prophets use the purchase imagery: Isaiah hereby expresses the obstinacy of God's people: "an ox knows his master (*qnh*; lit., "buyer")...my people do not understand" (Isa 1:3). In the coming judgment there will be no difference between buyer and seller (24:2); they will both suffer (cf. Ezek 7:12). The prophet Jeremiah bought things as a symbolic act (cf. G. Fohrer, *Die symbolischen Händlungen der Propheten*, 1953, 26-33), complementing his preaching: a belt (Jer 13:1-2, 4), which he buried to indicate that what bound God and his people will cease; a clay jar (19:1), which he broke to indicate the destruction of Judah; and the field from his uncle to indicate that the exiles will return (32:8-9).

5. The vb. is used in Proverbs to indicate the importance of obtaining wisdom, that is, in a noncommercial sense (Prov 1:5; 4:5, 7; 15:32; 17:16; 18:15; 19:8; 23:23), although 16:16 has: "How much better to get wisdom than gold." Buyer imagery is used in 20:14 for the buyer who bargains well by questioning the quality of the merchandise in order to get a better price (cf. W. McKane, *Proverbs*, 1970, 542).

6. Artaxerxes orders Ezra to buy sacrifices for God (Ezra 7:17 [Aram.]).

P-B One should not ask advice about selling (*mkr*) from a buyer (Sir 37:11).

Trade, merchandise, buying, selling: → *k^ena'an* (trader, # 4047); → *krh* (get by trade, # 4126); → *m^eḥîr* I (price, payment, # 4697); → *mkr* I (trade, sell, # 4835); → *sḥr* (travel, trade, # 6086); → *qnh* (acquire, buy, # 7864); → *rkl* (trade, # 8217); → *šbr* II (buy, # 8690)

Creation: → *br'* I (create, separate, # 1343); → *yṣr* (form, shape, create, # 3670) → *'śh* I (make, do, prepare, create, work, service, # 6913); → *p'l* (do, make, produce, practice, # 7188); → *qnh* (get, beget, create, # 7864)

BIBLIOGRAPHY

THAT 2:652-55 (3b and 4a); *TWAT* 7:63-65; J. C. De Moor, "El, the Creator," in *The Bible World: Essays in Honor of Cyrus H. Gordon*, eds., G. Rendsburg, R. Adler, M. Arfa,

N. H. Winter, 1980, 171-87; P. Humbert, "Qānā en Hébreu Biblique," in *Opuscules d'un hébraïsant*, 1958, 166-74; P. Katz, "The Meaning of the Root QNH," *JJS* 5, 1954, 126-31; B. Vawter, "Prov. 8:22: Wisdom and Creation," *JBL* 99, 1980, 205-16; C. Westermann, *Genesis 1-11: A Commentary*, translated by J. J. Scullion, 1984.

Izak Cornelius/Raymond C. Van Leeuwen

7865 (*qnh*, create), → # 7864

7866	קָנֶה

קָנֶה (*qāneh*), reed (# 7866).

ANE The cognate occurs in Akk. *qanû*, reed; Aram./Syr. *qanyā'*, reed; cf. Arab. *qanā'*, spear-shaft; Eth. *qanōt*, goad.

OT Reeds and rushes of various sorts grow in the Near East wherever there is a steady source of water. The biblical writers recognized this reality as evidenced by Bildad's rhetorical question, "Can papyrus (*gōme'*) grow tall where there is no marsh? Can reeds (*'āḥû*, # 286) thrive without water?" (Job 8:11; cf. Isa 19:5-6). While the papyrus plant, a type of reed, grows predominately in the Nile Valley, it did grow around ancient Lake Huleh in northern Canaan ("Flora," *ABD* 2:814), but probably was not used for paper. The people of Israel well knew that papyrus grew in marshy areas along the Nile (Isa 18:2).

The terms *qāneh* and *'agmôn* (# 109) appear to be generic terms for reeds (*Phragmites communis*). Reeds and rushes were widely used in the biblical world for making baskets (Exod 2:3) and when dried out, they could be used for kindling (Job 41:20). Surviving arrow shafts from ancient Egypt were made of reeds (W. McLeod, *Self Bows and Other Archery Tackle from the Tomb of Tut'ankhamun*, Tut'ankamun's Tomb Series IV, 1982, plate II), and thicker reeds could be used for staves (2 Kgs 18:21; Isa 36:6). The word *qāneh* is used as a measuring rod in Ezekiel (e.g., Ezek 40:3, 5, 6, 7), apparently another usage for the reed.

Metaphorically, reeds take on several meanings in the OT. Since taller reeds bend over under their own weight, Isa 58:5 likens such bending to one's being humble before the Lord as a gesture of repentance. The concept of humility is also found in 42:3: "A bruised reed he will not break." These words describe the Messiah showing his gentle and compassionate treatment of the weak and down trodden. The Lord Jesus quotes this passage, and the surrounding verse, as being fulfilled in him (Matt 12:15-21).

The flimsy condition of reeds is behind the picture in 1 Kgs 14:15, where the Lord's punishment on Israel would make the nation would be "like a reed swaying in the water." Similarly, just as a reed is easily cut, so God will cut off Israel (Isa 9:14[13]). While a thick, dried out reed might be used as a staff, it clearly could not sustain a significant weight. This idea is behind the Assyrian officer's mockery of Egypt's impotence when compared with the might of Assyria: "Look now, you (Judah) are depending on Egypt, that splintered reed of a staff, which pierces a man's hand and wounds him if he leans on it! Such is Pharaoh king of Egypt to all who depend on him" (36:6). Clearly, Egypt could not be depended upon for military support, just as a reed could not be counted on to support the weight of a man. Ezek 29:6 also uses this same motif to describe Israel's historical dependency on unreliable Egypt (see Egypt [# 5213] and Israel).

The Sea of Reeds (*yām sûp*, → # 6068) is the name of the body of water through which the Hebrews pass when leaving Egypt in the Exodus in the MT. This body of water was likely like one of the lakes that separated Egypt from Sinai (e.g. Timsah, el-Ballah, Bitter). *sûp* is cognate with the Egyptian word *ṯwfy,* papyrus (see Ward, "The Semitic Biconsonantal Root SP"). When God led Israel through the Sea of Reeds, their sojourn and suffering in Egypt ended. Conceivably, from this salvific event at *yam sûp*, the meaning of the vb. *swp*, come to an end (→ # 6066), had its origin (cf. Ps 73:19; Amos 3:15; Isa 66:17). At the end of the forty years of wandering in the wilderness, Moses and the Israelites camped at a site named *sûp* (Deut 1:1), suggesting that at this place, this period of Israelite history came to an end.

Vegetation: → *'ēzôb* (hyssop, # 257); → *dš'* (become green, sprout, # 2012); → *zr'* (sow, scatter seed, form seed, # 2445); → *ḥāṣîr* I (grass, # 2945); → *ḥ^{a}šaš* (dry grass, # 3143); → *yereq* (green, greenness, # 3764); → *nṭ'* (plant, establish, drive, # 5749); → *'āleh* (leaf, leafage, # 6591); → *'ēśeb* (herb, herbage, weed, # 6912); → *qîqāyôn* (plant of uncertain identity, # 7813); → *rō'š* II (bitter and poisonous herb, # 8032); → *śîaḥ* I (bush, shrub, # 8489); → *šiṭṭâ* (acacia, # 8847)

BIBLIOGRAPHY

TWOT 2:620, 2:804-5; W. Ward, "The Semitic Biconsonantal Root SP and the Common Origin of Egyptian *ČWF* and Hebrew *SÛP* 'Marsh (-plant),'" *VT* 24, 1974, 339-49.

James K. Hoffmeier

7868 (*qannô'*, zealous, jealous), → # 7861

7871 (*qinyān*, thing purchased or acquired, acquisition), → # 5238

7872	קִנָּמוֹן

קִנָּמוֹן (*qinnāmôn*), nom. cinnamon, *Cinnanomum zeylanicum* (# 7872).

ANE The word, most likely of Indian or Malayan origin, is not attested in ANE literature.

OT Cinnamon, obtained from the inner bark of small trees grown in Ceylon and India, was evidently prized in biblical times primarily for its fragrance. It is an ingredient in the oil of anointing (Exod 30:23); it perfumes the bed of the adulteress (Prov 7:17), and it is in a list of expensive perfumes (S of Songs 4:14).

P-B The LXX uses a G word of the same origin, *kinnamōmon.*

NT Rev 18:13 includes cinnamon in a list of merchandise of Babylon the Great.

Herbs, spices: → *'ôrâ* II (herb, mallow, # 246); → *gad* I (coriander, # 1512); → *kammōn* (cumin, # 4021); → *qinnāmôn* (cinnamon, # 7872); → *qeṣaḥ* (black cumin, # 7902); → *q^{e}ṣîa'* (cassia, # 7904); → *reqaḥ* (spice, # 8380)

BIBLIOGRAPHY

W. E. Shewell-Cooper, "Cinnamon," *ZPEB*, 1:866; M. Zohary, *Plants of the Bible,* 1982, 202.

M. G. Abegg, Jr.

7873	קנן

קנן (*qnn*), denom. pi. nest, make a nest; pu. nest (# 7873); קֵן (*qēn*), nom. nest, nestlings (# 7860).

ANE The Akk. *qinnu* has the literal meaning of nest, with a derived sense of family. The Akk. *qanānu* means to build (a nest). The Aram. *qinnā'* and Syr. *qennā'* mean nest.

OT 1. The forms *qēn* and *qnn* occur in their literal sense (e.g., birds nesting in the forests of Lebanon, Ps 104:17). In an attempt to preserve the balance of nature, Moses instructs the person who finds and empties a nest of its eggs or fledglings to leave unharmed the mother bird (Deut 22:6). More often, these terms are used in a figurative or metaphorical way, often pointing to the sense of safety basic to a nest, hence too, of the protective nature of God.

2. The blessing of Moses (Deut 32-33) describes God's finding Jacob (the people of Israel) in a desert land (32:10) and becoming their shield and protector. As the eagle stirs up its nest and catches its young in its talons (v. 11), so God carries his people through the desert—a powerful affirmation of God's loving care. By contrast, the Kenites who rest securely, or so they believe (like birds in nests upon a rock face), are warned that a dreadful fate awaits them (Num 24:21).

3. In the prophetic corpus, the comfort and security of a bird's nest is juxtaposed with the violence of God's judgment (e.g., Ezek 31:6). Some of the imagery is drawn from those birds found in the desert, like rock doves and swallows, who make their nests in rock overhangs and in the mouths of caves (Jer 48:28; cf. Cansdale, 170), or like eagles, high on the face of rocky cliffs (Jer 49:16 of Edom; Hab 2:9 of the wicked, who by unjust means sets their nest on high). The forest birds are also present. The rich kings who nest in Lebanon (i.e., Jerusalem; cf. 1 Kgs 7:2) will find judgment coming suddenly upon them (Jer 22:23-24). God will shatter such a false sense of security, bringing the wicked down, even if they nest among the stars (Obad 4). The security basic to a bird's nest serves as a foil for the inescapable judgment of God (like the comfortable women of Moab in Isa 16:2); the helplessness of the fledglings is highly illustrative (no one flaps or chirps, so helpless is Assyria at God's hand, Isa 10:14). Edom's cities will be ruins where owl and falcon nest (Isa 34:15).

4. The psalmist speaks of the sparrows and swallows, who love to build their nests near to human habitation, and who in this instance nest in the temple beside the altar (Ps 84:3[4]). The writer longs for the same sense of spiritual closeness to God. *qēn* in Job 29:18 should be read as house (so NIV) in the light of Gen 6:14 (rooms in Noah's ark, *qinnîm*).

P-B In RL *qēn* and *qnn* occur both with their literal sense (Ḥullin 12:1 and Ketubot 111b) and figuratively of Israel's finding a nest (home) for themselves (Exod R 20; cf. Ps 84:4). The Aram. form (*qn'*) may mean nest (Tg. Isa 10:14) or places close together (BTalm Baba Qamma 58b).

NT Jesus drew upon the idea of the protective nature of God when he compared himself to a mother hen gathering her chickens (Matt 23:37; cf. Deut 32:11). The nom. *kataskēnōsis* is found in Jesus' contrast between his fugitive lifestyle and the security of foxes' lairs and birds' nests (Matt 8:20; Luke 9:58); *kataskēnoō* is used for birds living in nests (Matt 13:32 and par.).

Birds, flying creatures: → *'br* (fly, # 87); → *bêṣâ* (egg, # 1070); → *barbur* (species of fowl, # 1350); → *gôzāl* (young bird, # 1578); → *dgr* (hatch eggs, # 1842); → *ḥ^{a}sîdâ* (stork, # 2884); → *yônâ* I (dove, # 3433); → *ya'^{a}nâ* (ostrich, eagle-owl?, # 3613); → *kānāp* (wing, skirt, outermost edge, # 4053); → *nešer/n^{e}šar* (vulture [eagle], # 5979); → *'ôp* (flying creatures, # 6416); → *'ayiṭ* (birds of prey [collective], # 6514); → *'ōrēb* I (raven, # 6854); → *ṣippôr* I (birds, # 7606); → *qōrē'* I (partridge, # 7926); → *ś^{e}lāw* (quails, # 8513)

BIBLIOGRAPHY
G. S. Cansdale, *Animals of Bible Lands,* 1970; A. Parmelee, *All the Birds of the Bible,* 1959.

W. R. Domeris

7876	קסם

קסם (*qsm*), q. practice divination in general without indication of means (sometimes through casting lots with arrows, consulting idols, and examining the liver [Ezek 21:21(26)], or through conjuring up the dead [1 Sam 28:8]) (# 7876); מִקְסָם(*miqsām*), occurs only in const. *miqsam*, bestowal of an oracle (# 5241); קֶסֶם (*qesem*), nom. divination, reconnaissance of the future, decision (through an oracle) (# 7877).

ANE Arab. *qasama*, divide, distribute, decide (by God or by fate); *qism*, part, share; *qismat*, division, part, share, lot, fate; Eth. *qäsämä*, practice divination, question through an oracle; *maqsĕm*, *maqsam*, divination by lot; Aram. *qismā'*, magic, sorcery; Syr. *qeṣmā'*, lot, fate, divination.

OT 1. Verbal and nominal forms of *qsm* occur in the following texts: Num 22:7; 23:23; Deut 18:10, 14; Josh 13:22; 1 Sam 6:2; 15:23; 28:8; 2 Kgs 17:17; Prov 16:10; Isa 2:6; 3:2; 44:25; Jer 14:14; 27:9; 29:8; Ezek 12:24; 13:6, 7, 9, 23; 21:21, 22, 23, 29[26, 27, 28, 34]; 22:28; Mic 3:6, 7, 11; Zech 10:2.

2. Mantic or divination was widespread in the ANE. Mantic/divination attempted to tell the future or bring to light hidden knowledge through various means, including the interpretation of signs or omens, communication with the dead, or the use of magical powers. The latter shows that divination was not completely distinct from magic; this is shown in the OT in passages where magic is spoken of along with mantic, indicating the interrelatedness of both practices (Exod 7:11; Lev 19:26; Deut 18:10-14; 2 Kgs 21:6 ‖ 2 Chron 33:6; Dan 2:2; Isa 2:6 [reading *miqsām* for *miqqedem*]; Isa 47:9, 12).

Mantic was a constant temptation to ancient Israel and Judah. That they succumbed to the influence of mantic so that it became widespread among them is shown by the strong legal, deuteronomistic, and prophetic prohibitions against its practice because it was seen as illegal, antisocial, and anti-Yahwistic. The intensity of these prohibitions is shown especially in those texts that denounce it along with other unacceptable practices (Lev 19:26-31; Deut 18:9-14; 2 Kgs 21:1-7 ‖ 2 Chron 33:1-7, etc.) The uniqueness of the Israelite faith in the context of the ANE is shown by these attempts to eradicate mantic from the practice of their religion. The Wisdom movement showed no special interest in mantic, apart from a reference to the snake "charmer" (Eccl 10:11; cf. Jer 8:17), in which the practice is neither condemned nor approved.

3. The OT reflects a number of ANE mantic practices that interpreted diverse types of phenomena as signs or omens (Isa 44:25, *'ōtôt*; 1 Kgs 20:33, *y^{e}naḥ^{a}šû*, "they

were looking for a sign/omen" [my trans.]): (a) astrology (study of heavenly bodies, Isa 47:13; Dan 2:2, 4); (b) hepatoscopy (inspection of liver of sacrificial animal, cf. Num 23:1-2, 14, where Balaam received no omens from the sacrificial animals, but a word of prophecy from the Lord instead; Ezek 21:21[26]); (c) natural phenomena; (d) birthing; (e) cup divination (cf. Joseph, who is said to have used a cup for divination, Gen 44:5); (f) casting lots (Prov 16:33; cf. the use of the sacred lots Urim and Thumim, Exod 28:30; Num 27:21; 1 Sam 23:9-12); (g) necromancy (communication with spirits of the dead; 1 Sam 28:7-19; Isa 8:19; cf. 1 Sam 15:23, "divination"; Isa 29:4); (h) observation of arrows shot (Ezek 21:21[26]; cf. 1 Sam 20:18-42; 2 Kgs 13:14-19); (i) observation of animals and birds; (j) interpretation of dreams (Gen 41:9-13; Dan 1:17; 2:24-28); (k) oracles from idols (Ezek 21:21[26]; Hos 4:12; Zech 10:2); (l) use of rods (Hos 4:12); (m) use of teraphim (cultic images; Ezek 21:21; Zech 10:2).

4. Some of these forms of omen divination appear to have been accepted in ancient Israel without condemnation (e.g., cups, lots, arrows, and dreams). Note, the personal name *hallôḥēš* occurs twice in Nehemiah (Neh 3:12; 10:24[25]) and is composed of the definite article plus q. act. part. of *lḥš*, "one who whispers/conjures" (my trans.). Laban "learned by divination" (*nḥš*) that God had blessed him because of Jacob's service with him (Gen 30:27). In spite of this apparent acceptance, the primary intended means of knowing the purposes of God was the divine word communicated through prophetic inspiration.

That some forms of omen divination (see also 8, below, in the cult) were accepted in Israel whereas magic was consistently condemned is difficult to explain, but it may in part be due to the difference in nature between magic and divination. Magic sought to manipulate the divine world to satisfy human needs; it was more human centered. In contrast, divination sought revelation from the divine world; it was more divinely centered. Ancient Israel's Yahwistic faith allowed for divine revelation but not for the manipulation of the divine world.

That some forms of divination were accepted in spite of the strong overall canonical (esp. legal, deuteronomistic, and prophetic) condemnation of divination is harder to explain. However, an explanation may lie in the fact that Israel inevitably absorbed practices and ideas from the cultural milieu of the ANE in which she lived; one may draw many religious, cultic, legal, sociological, and political parallels between the practices and ideas of Israel and those of the ANE. Of fundamental importance, however, are the ways in which true Yahwism (a) discriminated what was borrowed and (b) made those assimilated practices and ideas do service to Yahwism. With respect to those forms of divination accepted in Israel, it might be argued that the contexts in which this occurred supported true Yahwism or at least did not pervert it. When divination was perceived to be a direct threat to the purity of Yahwism and ceased to be a means of justifiable revelation, it was denounced as unacceptable; magic was always denounced because it was always a threat by its fundamentally manipulative nature.

5. Mantic is denounced by the Law of Moses. Leviticus forbids Israelites to "practice divination" (*tᵉnaḥᵃšû*) or "sorcery" (Lev 19:26) so that they may be holy (v. 1). Neither are they to "turn to mediums" (*'ōbōt*) or "seek out spiritists" (*yiddᵉ'ōnîm*) because they defile the people and the Lord is God of Israel, i.e., they are pagan practices (19:31).

A significant text in Deut forbids a variety of practices associated with divination and magic (Deut 18:9-13); it shows that inherent in the gift of the Promised Land was the temptation to engage in the practices of the prior nations in the land. Those practices are listed as the sacrificing of son or daughter in the fire, "practicing divination" (*qōsēm qᵉsāmîm*), "practicing sorcery" (*mᵉʿōnēn*), "interpreting omens" (*mᵉnaḥēš*), "engaging in witchcraft" (*mᵉkaššēp*), "casting spells" (*ḥōber ḥeber*), being a "medium" (*šōʾēl ʾôb*) or "spiritist"/soothsayer (*yiddᵉʿōnî*), or "consulting the dead" (*dōreš ʾel-hammētîm*). Such practices are "detestable," for which the Lord will "drive out those nations." An Israelite engaging in them is "detestable to the LORD." God's people are to be "blameless before the LORD [their] God" by rejecting such practices.

6. Mantic is denounced by the deuteronomistic historian. He condemns King Ahaz of Judah because "he did not do what was right in the eyes of the LORD his God" (1 Kgs 16:2) in that he appears to have engaged in pagan practice by using a bronze altar for inspection of a sacrifice (*bqr*, → # 1329) through omens, i.e., signs read from the entrails of sacrificial animals (2 Kgs 16:15). It might be argued that the contexts in which this occurred supported true Yahwism, i.e., that it was a form of divination accepted in Israel. Similarly, Manasseh "did much evil in the eyes of the LORD, provoking him to anger" because he practiced "divination" (*nḥš*, # 5727) and "consulted mediums" (*ʿśh ʾôb* [# 200]) and "spiritists" (*yiddᵉʿōnîm* [# 3362]; 2 Kgs 21:6 ‖ 2 Chron 33:6).

God judged Israel through Assyria because they "practiced divination" (*qsm qᵉsāmîm*) and "sorcery," sought or gave omens (*nḥš*, i.e., "seeking omens"), and thus "sold themselves to do evil in the eyes of the LORD, provoking him to anger" (2 Kgs 17:17). Samuel tells Saul that rebellion and the sin of "divination" (*qesem*) are akin (1 Sam 15:23). Saul's ultimate sin is his going to the medium at Endor to consult the dead spirit of Samuel (28:7-19).

7. Mantic is denounced by the prophets, who often associate divination with false prophecy.

(a) In Isa the Lord of creation speaks with hymnic phraseology of himself because he turns the "learning" of "false prophets"/oracle priests (*baddîm*) and "diviners" (*qōsᵉmîm*) into "nonsense" (Isa 44:24-25). The Babylonian "astrologers" (*hōbᵉrê šāmayim*; read *hōbᵉrē* according to the Qere; 1QIsa[a] has *hôbᵉrê*) and "stargazers" are ridiculed, with the implication that they are powerless to save the Babylonians from the coming judgment of God (47:13-15). God will judge Judah by taking away the clever "enchanter" (*laḥaš*), along with the "soothsayer" (*qōsēm*), "hero," "warrior," "judge," "prophet," "elder," "captain of fifty," "man of rank," "counselor," and "skilled craftsman" (3:1-3).

(b) Jeremiah denounces the Babylonians, whose "false prophets"/oracle priests (*baddîm*) will become "fools" (Jer 50:36). He equates false prophecy with "divination" (*qesem*), idolatry, and "delusions of their own minds" (14:14). False prophets, "diviners" (*qōsᵉmîm*), interpreters of dreams, mediums, and sorcerers all provide Judah with false hopes that they will "not serve the king of Babylon" (27:9). Prophets and "diviners" (*qōsᵉmîm*) deceive Judah; they prophesy lies and are not sent by the Lord (29:8).

(c) Ezekiel declares that Jerusalem's prophets see "false visions" and utter "lying divinations" (*qōsᵉmîm kāzāb*) (Ezek 22:28). He emphasizes the nearness of divine judgment by denouncing "false visions" and "flattering divinations" (*miqsam ḥălāq*) that seek to put off judgment (12:24). The false prophets' "visions" are "false" and their "divinations" (*qesem*) are a "lie"; they utter "lying divinations" (*miqsam kāzāb*) (Ezek 13:6, 7, 9, 23), but the Lord will save his people from their power in the eschaton; then they "will know that I am the LORD" (v. 23).

(d) Micah denounces false prophets, "seers," and "diviners" (*qōsᵉmîm*), who will not escape judgment, and prophets "who tell fortunes" (*yiqsōmû*) (Mic 3:7, 11). Zechariah declares that "diviners" (*qōsᵉmîm*) see "visions that lie" and tell "dreams that are false" (Zech 10:2).

8. The mantic is sometimes not far removed from the cult. Ps 27:4 is rendered: "to seek him in his temple" (the Heb. is more literally rendered according to RSV, "to inquire in his temple"). In Ps 5 there may be a play on words: "In the morning (*bōqer*), O LORD, you hear my voice" (3a[4a]) makes good sense, but v. 3b[4b] could read, "an omen sacrifice I prepare for you and watch/wait expectantly" (my trans.). The vb. *'rk*, prepare, does not in itself mean "I prepare a sacrifice" (RSV) or "I lay my requests" (NIV). The vb. is transitive, not intrans.; in the context it needs an object, and the only possibility is *bōqer*, but then it cannot mean "morning," but "sacrifice" (*bōqer* I). The NIV and RSV translations appear to circumvent the theological problem created. In another text, the psalmists enemies "whisper" (*yitlaḥᵃšû*) together against him (41:7[8]); this latter reference is akin to magic.

9. Necromancy (mediums, spiritists) is mentioned in the OT, but is not sanctioned.

(a) *'ôb* strictly means a "spirit of the dead" who communicates with humankind. But since in necromancy the spirit of the dead takes control of the body of, and speaks through, the medium, the distinction between the *'ôb* (→ # 200) and the medium may blur so that *'ôb* may refer to the medium; in a number of contexts the meaning is ambiguous and could refer to either the spirit of the dead or the medium. The same is true of *yiddᵉ'ōnî* (→ # 3362).

(b) According to the law, a "medium" (*'ôb*) or "spiritist" (*yiddᵉ'ōnî*) was to be put to death (Lev 20:27). To seek "mediums" (*'ōbōt*) or "spiritists" (*yiddᵉ'ōnîm*) was to be defiled by them, for "I am the LORD your God" (19:31). A person who seeks mediums or spiritists "prostitutes himself," and the Lord will "set [his] face against him" and "cut him off from his people" (20:6). Being a medium and consulting the dead are prohibited (Deut 18:9-13) because such practices are "detestable," and anyone who engages in them becomes "detestable to the LORD."

(c) The deuteronomistic history cites instances of necromancy. Saul, even after having removed "mediums" (*'ōbôt*) and "spiritists" (*yiddᵉ'ōnîm*) from the land, when threatened by the Philistines and having received no word from the Lord, capitulated to pagan practice and sought out "a woman who is a medium" (*baᵃlat-'ôb*) and told her to consult (*qsm*) the spirit of Samuel for him. But Samuel, instead of advising him concerning the Philistines, pronounced a word of divine judgment on Saul, confirming that the Lord was no longer with him (1 Sam 28:6-19).

David noticed his servants "whispering among themselves" (*mitlaḥᵃšîm*) at the death of his child (2 Sam 12:19). Manasseh "did much evil in the eyes of the LORD, provoking him to anger" because he "consulted mediums" (*'āśâ 'ôb*) and "spiritists" (*yiddᵉ'ōnîm*) (2 Kgs 21:6 ‖ 2 Chron 33:6), whereas Josiah is commended by the historian because he removed "mediums" (*'ōbôt*) and "spiritists" (*yiddᵉ'ōnîm*) and "all the other detestable things" in order "to fulfill the requirements of the law" (2 Kgs 23:24).

(d) Prophets address necromancy. Isaiah proclaims that there is no need for Judah to consult "mediums" (*'ōbôt*) and "spiritists" (*yidd^{e}'ōnîm*); God's people should consult the Lord (Isa 8:19). "Mediums" (*'ōbôt*) and "spiritists" (*yidd^{e}'ōnîm*) will not be able to prevent the Lord's judgment on Egypt (19:3). Isaiah pictures "mediums" and "spiritists" as people who "whisper" (*ṣpp*) (8:19). Judeans killed in the Babylonian destruction of Jerusalem will "whisper" (*ṣpp*) from the dust (29:4). This whispering appears to be a form of muttering speech comparable to the chirping of birds (cf. 10:14; 38:14).

10. The practice of divination in other nations impinged on Israel's life. Balak, king of Moab, sent messengers to Balaam to put a curse on Israel (Num 22-24). Balaam sought an answer from the Lord, who told him not to curse Israel for she was blessed. The messengers took with them a "fee for divination" (22:7, *q^{e}sāmîm* in this context appears to refer to the "fee"). Balaam's oracle announced that there was no pagan "sorcery"/magic curse, omen (*naḥaš*), or "divination" (*qesem*) that might be effective against Israel, for God was with her (23:23). When Balaam saw that God was blessing Israel, he ceased using "sorcery" (24:1, *neḥāšîm*), i.e., he realized it would be ineffectual.

Israel was forbidden to engage in "divination" (*qōsēm q^{e}sāmîm*; *qōs^{e}mîm*), practiced by other nations (Deut 18:10, 14). The strength of the prohibition against divination is suggested by the fact that Balaam, even though he had blessed Israel instead of cursing her, was ultimately put to death at the time of the Israelite conquest of Palestine because he "practiced divination" (*qōsēm*) (Josh 13:22).

The ark, captured by the Philistines, caused them so much trouble that they called for the priests and "diviners" (*qōs^{e}mîm*) to find out what to do (1 Sam 6:2). Isaiah was aware that the Philistines practiced "superstitions"/divinations (Isa 2:6, reading *miqsām* for *miqqedem*). When Ahab, king of Israel, had defeated Ben-Hadad in battle, Ben-Hadad sent a deputation to Ahab to seek mercy. The deputation looked for omens (*y^{e}naḥ^{a}šû*) arising from the conversation to indicate Ahab's attitude to their king (1 Kgs 20:33). The king of Babylon, God's means of judgment on Judah, will "seek an omen" (*liqsām-qāsem*), and this is associated with casting lots with arrows, consulting idols, and examining livers (Ezek 21:21[26]).

11. Diviners were part of the court of pagan kings. In the book of Daniel they function as a foil for Daniel, who is wise because the Spirit of God, who alone can give wisdom and enable people to interpret mysteries, is in him. All references to *'aššāp*, Aram. *'āšap*, *ḥarṭōm*, *kaśdîm*, Aram. *kaśdāyy'ē,* and Aram. *gāz^{e}rîn* are in Genesis, Exodus, and Daniel, i.e., in the context of Mesopotamian and Egyptian culture.

In Daniel "magicians" (*ḥarṭummîm*) and "enchanters" (*'aššāpîm*) functioned in the Babylonian court (Dan 1:20). These people, along with "astrologers" (*kaśdîm*; Aram. *kaśdā'ē*) and "sorcerers," are summoned to reveal Nebuchadnezzar's dream (Dan 2:2, 4[5, 10]).

It was "too difficult" for the Babylonian "magicians" (*ḥarṭōm*), "enchanters" (*'šp*), "astrologers" (*kaśdāy*), and "diviners" (Dan 2; 4) to reveal the interpretation of Nebuchadnezzar's dream. Only the "God in heaven," and those in whom is the Spirit of God, can reveal such mysteries (2:10, 27; 4:7, 9, 18[4, 6, 15]). In Dan 5 Belshazzar called for the "enchanters" (*'āš^e payyā'*), "astrologers" (*kaśdā'ē*), and "diviners" (*gāz^e rayyā'*) to interpret the writing on the wall but they could not (5:7, 15). Daniel is said by the king to be the "chief" (*rāb*) of the "magicians," "enchanters," "astrologers," and "diviners" (4:9[6]; cf. 5:11).

High officials in Egypt, including Joseph, used cups (in Joseph's case a silver cup) for divination (*nḥs*) (Gen 44:2a, 4b, 5). Joseph himself indicated that he engaged in such a practice (v. 15). When Pharaoh called the Egyptian "magicians" (*ḥarṭummîm*, i.e., soothsayer priests) to interpret his dream of seven full and seven lean cows and his dream of seven healthy and seven unhealthy heads of grain, they were unable to explain them (41:8, 24), but Joseph through the help of God was able (vv. 15-16).

"Magicians" (*ḥarṭummîm*) and "sorcerers," who were part of Pharaoh's court, used their "secret arts" to try to copy the miracles performed by Moses and Aaron (Exod 7:11, 22; 8:7, 18-19[3, 14-15]). Initially they were successful (snake becomes a staff, plagues of blood and of frogs), but they failed to duplicate the plague of gnats. As for the subsequent plagues (of flies, against livestock, of boils, of hail, of locusts, of darkness, against the firstborn), they did not even attempt to copy them nor were they able to prevent or reverse them; they were powerless. In these texts mantic is not explicitly condemned, but in Exodus and Daniel it is shown to be ineffectual against the power and wisdom of God.

12. Charms/amulets belong to mantic paraphernalia. "Charms" (*l^e ḥašîm*), one of the items of fine jewelry, used to protect against evil powers, will be taken away when God judges Judah (Isa 3:20).

NT Acts 16:16-19 is the one clear reference to divination in the NT. In this text a slave girl earns money for her keepers by telling (*manteuomai*) the future by means of a spirit that possessed her. Paul commanded the evil spirit to leave her, thus showing the superiority of the power of God through Paul.

In Acts 1:26 the casting of lots is used to determine who should succeed Judas as one of the twelve apostles (cf. the casting of lots in the OT [Prov 16:33] and the use of the sacred lots Urim and Thumim (Exod 28:30; Num 27:21; 1 Sam 23:9-12).

In Matt 2:1, 7, 16 the astrologers from the East (*magoi*, "magi" [NIV], "wise men" [RSV], who read omens from the stars, used without negative evaluation) are able to interpret the stars as to the time and place of the birth of Jesus.

In Gal 4:3 and Col 2:20 some believe that "the basic principles of the world" (NIV), "the elemental spirits of the universe" (RSV) (*ta stoicheia tou kosmou*), may be a reference to astrological determinations (cf. J. S. Wright, *ISBE* 1:343), to which Christians, through the freeing power of the gospel, no longer need to submit. Luke records as to how the practitioners of sorcery publicly burned scrolls on divination as evidence of how much impact the gospel made at Ephesus (Acts 19:20).

Mantic, divination: → *'aššāp* (conjurer, # 879); → *bad* V (diviner, # 967); → *ḥbr* (engage in astrology, # 2042); → *ḥarṭōm* (soothsayer priest, # 3033); → *yidd^e 'ōnî* (soothsayer, # 3362); → *kaśdîm* (Chaldeans, astrologers, # 4169); → *lḥš* (conjure, whisper, # 4317); → *nḥš* I (practice divination, # 5727); → *ṣpp* I (whisper, chirp, # 7627); → *qsm* (practice divination, # 7876)

Spirit, ghost, demon: → *'ôb* II (medium, spiritist, necromancer, ghost, # 200); → *'iṭṭîm* I (ghosts, ghosts of the dead, spirits, # 356); → *lîlît* (night monster, night creature, # 4327); → *'^a zā'zēl* (Azazel, demon, scapegoat, # 6439); → *ṣî* II (desert dweller, crier, yelper, wild beast, # 7470); → *rûaḥ* (wind, breath, transitoriness, volition, disposition, temper, spirit, Spirit,

8120); → *rᵉpāʾîm* I (shades, departed spirits, # 8327); → *śāʿîr* III (satyr, goat demon, goat idol, # 8539); → *šēd* (demon, # 8717)

BIBLIOGRAPHY

D. E. Aune, "Divination," *ISBE* 1:971-74; A. Caquot, *La divination*, 1968; G. Contenau, *La divination chez les Assyriens et les Babyloniens*, 1940; *Everyday Life in Babylon and Assyria*, 1966, 281-90; T. W. Davies, *Magic, Divination and Demonology Among the Hebrews and Their Neighbors*, 1898; M. Dietrich and O. Loretz, *Mantik in Ugariti Keilalphabetische Texte der Opferschau, Omensammbungen Nekromantie*, 1990; A. Guillaume, *Prophecy and Divination Among the Hebrews and Other Semites*, 1938; Joanne K. Kuemmerlin-McLean, "Magic, Old Testament," *ABD* 4, 468-71; E. Lipinski, "Urim and Tummim," *VT* 20, 1970, 495-96; B. O. Long, "Astrology," *IDBSup*, 76-78; idem, "Divination," *IDBSup*, 214-43; idem, "The Effect of Divination Upon Israelite Literature," *JBL*, 1973, 489-97; L. MacNeice, *Astrology*, 1964; I. Mendelsohn, "Divination," *IDB* 1, 856-58; J. Nougayrol (ed.), *La Divination en Mésopotamie et dans les régions voisines*, 1966; A. L. Oppenheim, *The Interpretation of Dreams in the Ancient Near East*, 1956; idem, *Ancient Mesopotamia*, 1964/1977, 206-27; H. W. F. Saggs, *The Greatness That Was Babylon*, 1962, 320-28; J. S. Wright, "Astrology," *ISBE* 1:341-44.

Malcolm J. A. Horsnell

7877 (*qesem*, divination), → # 7876

7878	קסס

קסס (*qss*), po. strip away; pick (# 7878).

OT This vb. is used effectively to describe the plundering and carrying away of Judah by Babylon in a powerful parable of destruction (Ezek 17:9). Judah, a tender but protected vine (cf. Isa 5:1-6), flourished as long as it remained loyal to Nebuchadnezzar. But its turning to Egypt (v. 7) would result in its being uprooted and "transplanted" in Babylon.

P-B Found in Tg., *yqtp*, "he will pluck." The word continued to be used into Mish. Heb. in the po. to mean "to cut" (JTalm Berakot VI, 10b); "to taste sharp, cut" (JTalm Pesaḥhim II); "wine" (part.); and even "to turn sour." It was used in the hi. and pi. as well. For refs. see Jastrow 2:1397.

Plunder, spoil, robbing, stealing: → *bzz* (plunder, spoil, # 1024); → *gzl* (steal, rob, # 1608); → *gnb* (steal, rob, # 1704); → *pārîṣ* II (burglar, robber, # 7265); → *pereq* (crossroad?, plunder, # 7294); → *šll* II (take plunder, seize, # 8964); → *šsh* (plunder, loot, # 9115)

BIBLIOGRAPHY

ISBE 4:1068-72; L. Cooper, *Ezekiel*, NAC, 1994, 181-82; F. Greenspahn, *Hapax Legomena in Biblical Hebrew*, 1984.

Eugene Carpenter

7879 (*qeset*, scribe's palette), → Writing

7882	קַעֲקַע

קַעֲקַע (*qaʿᵃqaʿ*), nom. tattoo, incision (hapleg.; # 7882).

OT 1. The nom. may be derived from **qʿʿ* or **qwʿ*. The etymological derivation, by reduplication, of *qaʿᵃqa* from *qʿʿ* or *qwʿ* is uncertain (*HALAT* 1042-43).

2. The nom. occurs only in Lev 19:28, "Do not . . . put tattoo marks [k^e*tōbet qa*^{ʿa}*qa*ʿ] on yourselves." It is a prohibition against following the pagan practice by cutting oneself in mourning for the dead. Wenham comments, "Man is not to disfigure the divine likeness implanted in him by scarring his body" (*Leviticus*, 272). The phrase (k^e*tōbet qa*^{ʿa}*qa*ʿ, lit., a cutting of *qa*^{ʿa}*qa*ʿ) appears to be synonymous with *śereṭ* . . . *bib*^{e}*śarkem* (lit., "an incision/cutting (*śrṭ*, → # 8581) in your flesh/body/skin" (v. 28a).

The Israelites were forbidden to engage in this practice because it was a pagan religious ritual. The Israelites, as God's chosen, covenant people, were to be holy, separated unto the Lord, to whom alone they owed worship. For priests to engage in this rite meant profanation of the name of God. The prohibition was based on the Hebrew understanding of the sacredness of life and the human body.

Incision, cut, tattoo: → *gdd* I (inflict cuts, make incisions, # 1517); → *ḥārûṣ* IV (mutilation, # 3024); → *qa*^{ʿa}*qa*ʿ (tattoo, incision, # 7882); → *śrṭ* (cut, make incisions, be cut up, # 8581)

Malcolm J. A. Horsnell

7883 (q^e*ʿārâ*, dish, bowl, platter), → # 3998

7884	קפא

קפא (*qp'*) q. thicken, congeal; hi. cause to congeal, curdle (# 7884); קִפָּאוֹן (*qippā'ôn*) frost, as congealing of water (# 7885).

ANE Syr. and Aram. have the same root with similar meaning.

OT 1. Exod 15:8, in describing Israel's crossing of the Red Sea, speaks of the waters piling up, and, parallel to "the surging waters stood firm like a wall," it is said that "the deep waters congealed in the heart of the sea." Whatever the physical means, storm or earthquake, the people crossed over the sea to safety by Yahweh's enabling.

2. Job speaks (in Job 10:10-11) of the wonder of his own creation in the words, "Did you not pour me out like milk and curdle (*qp'*) me like cheese, clothe me with skin and flesh and knit me together with bones and sinews?"

3. In Zeph 1:12 judgment is pronounced on those in Jerusalem who are "complacent ... who think, 'The LORD will do nothing, either good or bad,'" who are "like wine left on its dregs (lit., thickened on their lees)" (cf. the use of *ʿbh* in Deut 32:15).

4. The nom. is used only in the Q of Zech 14:6 for "frost" (and LXX and other versions and most modern translations follow this). The K has a part of the vb. *qp'* following the fem. pl. of the adj. *yqr*, which would have to be translated in some such way as "the splendid ones will congeal," taken by Baldwin (*TOTC*) with reference to the stars losing their brightness; NASB has "the luminaries will dwindle." Read according to the Q, the passage says that in the day of the Lord there will be "no cold or frost," and the next verse goes on to describe that day as like no other day: "It will be a unique day, without daytime or nighttime—a day known to the LORD. When evening comes, there will be light."

Thick: → *ʿbh* (be thick, # 6286); → *qp'* (thicken, congeal, # 7884)
Snow, frost, ice: → *'elgābîš* (hail or ice crystals, # 453); → k^e*pôr* II (frost, hoar-frost, # 4095); → *qippā'ôn* (frost, # 7885); → *qeraḥ* (ice, # 7943); → *šeleg* I (snow, # 8920)

Bibliography

D. Baly, *The Geography of the Bible*, 50-52.

Francis Foulkes

7885 (*qippāʼôn*, frost), → # 7884

7886	קפד

קפד (*qpd*), pi. roll up (# 7886); קְפָדָה (*q^e^pādâ*), anguish (# 7888).

ANE The Syr. reflexive means to be wrinkled or shrivelled; the Arab. *qafada* means to bind tightly.

OT This vb. is a hapleg. in Isa 38:12, in the psalm of Hezekiah that speaks of life being rolled up. The text is difficult; "Like a weaver I have rolled up my life" is hardly a transparent metaphor. It is often suggested the vb. should be second person, with reference to Yahweh (so *BHS*), the corruption to first person possibly having taken place when the *yod* from the abbreviated tetragrammaton was joined to the vb. Following the lead of the Syr. and Tgs., Begrich thinks that the vb. refers to the fabric that was folded or rolled during the weaving and cut off when it was finished (28-32); this corresponds better with the second line, which speaks of being cut off from the thrum of the loom. It is also possible that the first bicola of v. 12 should be emended to say, "My dwelling is plucked up and rolled up like the tent of a shepherd," reading the ni. of *gll* (Begrich, 27-28; cf. Isa 34:4 for the form); this provides much more consistent imagery, comparing life to the nomadic herdsmen (cf. Job 4:21). The two bicola then become powerful complementing images of the end of life as the rolling up of a shepherd's tent or a weaver's cloth. Given the difficult state of the text and the evidence of the Syr. and Tgs., it is probable that this is how the metaphors should be understood, an apt description of the experience of human life in relation to the eternal God.

2. The nom. *q^e^pādâ*, anguish, is a hapleg. and refers to anguish associated with divine judgment (Ezek 7:25). Various cognate possibilities are noted in *HALAT* 1043.

P-B In Mish. Heb. *qpd* means to draw together or contract; in Sir 4:31 it refers to the closing of the hand. In the hi. of Mish. Heb. the sense of compressing is a metaphor for becoming angry or insulting, or to be strict and particular (Jastrow, 1398); the Aram. vb. also means to be angry or particular, and in the reflexive it can mean to be contracted or shortened.

Rolling: → *gll* I (roll, roll away, flow down, drag, wallow, # 1670); → *glm* (roll up [mantle], # 1676); → *plš* (roll, # 7147); → *qpd* (roll up, # 7886)

Pain, pangs: → *ḥbl* IV (be pregnant, travail, # 2473); → *ḥyl* I (be in labor, tremble, # 2655); → *kʼb* (be in pain, cause pain, ruin, # 3872); → *mrṣ* (be hurtful, painful, irritate, # 5344); → *ʻṣb* II (hurt, grieve, offend, # 6772)

Bibliography

J. Begrich, *Der Psalm des Hiskia*, FRLANT 42, 1926; J. N. Oswalt, *The Book of Isaiah, Chapter 1-39*, NICOT, 1986; J. A. Motyer, *The Prophecy of Isaiah*, 1993.

A. H. Konkel/Terence E. Fretheim

7887	קִפֹּד

קִפֹּד (*qippōd*), hedgehog/owl? (# 7887).

ANE The following cognates are known: Syr. *quppᵉdā'*, Arab. *qunfuḏ*.

OT The nom. occurs 3x in the OT. It is not certain if this is an animal or a short-eared owl (*HALAT* 1585). The meaning hedgehog can be traced to the LXX (*echinos*), whereas the medieval commentator Rashi understood the term in Isa 34:11 and Zeph 2:14 (NIV the screech owl in both places) as a kind of bird. *HALAT* favors the meaning hedgehog in Isa 14:23 and 34:11, and short-eared owl in Zeph 2:14 and possibly Isa 34:11.

In all three passages the nom. symbolizes desolation. In the Isa passages it is associated with the root *yrš*, inherit (→ # 3769). In 14:23 God says concerning Babylon, "I will turn her into a place of owls and into swampland" (NIV) as over against the possibility of the wicked "inheriting" the land (v. 21b).

Animals: → *bᵉhēmâ* (quadrupeds, # 989); → *zānāb* (tail, # 2387); → *ḥᵃzîr* (pig, # 2614); → *ḥayyâ* I (animal, # 2651); → *keleb* (dog, # 3978); → *'akbār* (mouse, # 6572); → *ṣᵉpardēa'* (frog, # 7630); → *qippod* (hedgehog/owl?, # 7887); → *rmś* (creep, swarm, # 8253); → *šrṣ* (swarm, teem, # 9237); → *tan* (jackal, # 9478); → **Reptiles: Theology**; see the Index for Birds; Camel; Deer; Donkey; Dove; Flock; Gazelle; Insects; Lion; Maggot; Snake, etc.

Bibliography

EMiqr 7:210-11.

N. Kiuchi

7888 (*qᵉpādâ*, anguish), → # 7886

7889 (*qippôz*, snake?), → # 5729

7890	קפץ

קפץ (*qpṣ* I), q. draw together, shut (# 7890). The hapleg. קפץ (*qpṣ* II), pi. leap, bound (# 7890) occurs only in S of Songs 2:8 and is discussed under *ḥwl*, whirl about (→ # 2565).

ANE Akk. attests *kapāṣu*; Ugar. *qbṣ*; Arab. *qafaṣa*.

OT 1. The Heb. is used to refer to the closing of one's mouth or hand, much as the Akk. *kap/bāṣ/su* may be used of closing other parts of one's body: eyes, ears, navel, etc. (*AHw*, 443). While the upright rejoice in the enumerated blessings of Yahweh, the wicked shut their mouths in silence (Job 5:16; Ps 107:42). Kings will shut their mouths in speechless astonishment at the sudden exaltation of the suffering servant, risen so high, so quickly (Isa 52:15).

2. This vb. may also designate closing off or withholding. Thus, God does not withhold his tender mercies (Ps 77:10), and the righteous Israelite is commanded not to withhold his hand (sustenance) from a needy brother, which is tantamount to hardening one's heart (Deut 15:7-8). Job uses the only OT example of the ni. to describe the wicked, who are exalted temporarily but are eventually "gathered up" like everyone else (Job 24:24, but the text is difficult and may not have originally contained this root).

Closing, shutting: → *'ṭm* (stopped up, # 357); → *'ṭr* (close [mouth], # 358); → *gwp* I (shut, close, # 1589); → *ṭḥḥ* (besmeared, stuck, shut, # 3220); → *ṭmh* (stopped up, # 3241); → *n'l* I (tie, lock, # 5835); → *sgr* I (shut, close, deliver up, # 6037); → *stm* (stop up, # 6258); → *'ṣh* I (shut, # 6781); → *'ṣm* III (shut one's eyes, # 6794); → *ṣrr* I (bind, shut up, be narrow, in straits, distress, # 7674); → *qpṣ* I (draw together, shut, # 7890); → *š''* I (smear, smooth, shut, # 9129)

Bill T. Arnold

7891	קֵץ

קֵץ (*qes*), nom. end, limit, boundary (# 7891); < קָצַץ (*qss* I), q., pi. cut off; pu. maim (→ # 7915).

ANE The Heb. word *qēṣ* is related to Ugar. *qṣ*, end; and Akk. *qaṣāṣu*, cut off, cut down, trim (see the discussion under *gaṣāṣu*, *CAD* 5:53).

OT 1. Unlike *qāṣeh*, end (→ # 7894), the word *qēṣ* is rarely used of spatial boundaries (cf. Jer 50:26). This nom. may refer to the "end" of life (Gen 6:13), "after" in a temporal sense (8:6; Esth 2:12), "limit" (to perfection, Ps 119:96, or human endurance, Job 6:11), or even "remotest" (boundary, 2 Kgs 19:23).

2. Theologically, the word often appears in the context of divine judgment (e.g., the Flood in Gen 6:13; as part of a wordplay in Amos 8:2 announcing the end of Israel and of Judah (cf. Ezek 7:3). Elsewhere, Daniel uses *qēṣ* to signify the eschaton, the end time, of human history (Dan 8:17, 19; 11:40; 12:4, 6). An end of wrongdoing is also envisioned by the prophets (Ezek 21:25, 29[30, 34]), just as a time of peace without end is expected (Isa 9:7[6]).

Border, boundary, corner, edge, rim: → *gbl* I (bound, border, # 1487); → *zāwît* (corner, # 2312); → *kānāp* (wing, skirt, outermost edge, # 4053); → *karkōb* (rim, edge, # 4136); → *mḥh* II (border on, # 4682); → *swg* II (border by, # 6048); → *pē'â* I (corner, # 6991); → *pinnâ* (corner, # 7157); → *ṣad* (side, # 7396); → *ṣēlā'* I (side, rib, side-chamber, # 7521); → *qēṣ* (limit, boundary, # 7891); → *qāṣeh* (end, border, # 7895); → *qṣ'* II (made with corners, # 7910)
End, cessation, outcome: → *'aḥ^{a}rît* (end, outcome, # 344); → *'ps* (cease, come to an end, # 699); → *bṭl* (cease working, # 1060); → *gmr* (be at an end, cease, fail, # 1698); → *ḥdl* I (end, stop, # 2532); → *swp* (come to an end, # 6066); → *sārâ* I (stopping, # 6239); → *qēṣ* (end, limit, boundary, # 7891); → *qṣh* I (bring about the end, shorten, # 7894)

BIBLIOGRAPHY
THAT 2:654-63; A. Wolters, "Wordplay and Dialect in Amos 8:2," *JETS* 31, 1988, 407-10.

Andrew E. Hill/Gordon H. Matties

7892	קצב

קצב (*qṣb*), q. cut off, shear; chop (# 7892); קֶצֶב (*qeṣeb*), nom. form, shape, mold; roots/bottom (# 7893).

ANE Syr. *qaṣṣābā'*; Palm. *qṣb'*; Akk. *kaṣābu*; Arab. *qaṣaba*.

OT 1. The vb. occurs 2x, the nom. 3x in the OT. The vb. refers to the simple act of cutting (2 Kgs 6:6, Elisha cutting a stick/piece of wood) and to the shearing of sheep (S of Songs 4:2).

2. The nom. means one size or one shape (1 Kgs 7:37), standing with *mûṣāq*, casting (→ # 4607), and *middâ*, measure (→ # 4500), all limited by the numerical adjective one. It is also used to indicate the size/shape of the cherubs (→ # 4131; 1 Kgs 6:25, used with *middā* again). It bears a different meaning in Jon 2:6[7], but its exact meaning is in doubt. Jonah descended to the lowest parts of the sea as far as the *qiṣ*^e^*bê* of the mountains. It could mean the extremities, lowest forms of the mountains under water (cf. NIV, roots; RSV, roots) or the base of the mountains (L. Allen, *The Books of Joel, Obadiah, Jonah and Micah*, 1976, 214, n. 3).

P-B The LXX renders it *eis schismas oreōn*, into the clefts of the mountains. The same word occurs in Sir 16:19, paralleling "foundations of the world." *BHS*'s suggested emendation to "ends of" (*qaṣ*^e^*wê*) is unwarranted.

Cutting, destruction, extermination, shearing, trimming: → *bṣ'* (cut away, get gain, cut off, break up, # 1298); → *br'* III (clear out trees, cut, destroy, # 1345); → *btr* (cut into pieces, # 1439); → *gd'* (cut short, # 1548); → *gzh* (bring forth, # 1602); → *gzz* (cut, shear, # 1605); → *gzr* I (cut, take away, # 1615); → *grz* (be cut off, # 1746); → *gr'* I (cut out, reduce, # 1757); → *ḥlp* II (cut through, pierce, # 2737); → *ksḥ* (cut, cut down, # 4065); → *krsm* (make cropped, trimmed off, # 4155); → *krt* (cut, cut off, exterminate, cut a covenant, circumcise, # 4162); → *melqāḥāyim* (snuffers for trimming/cleaning of lights/lamps, # 4920); → *nqp* I (cut/chop down, destroy, # 5937); → *ntḥ* (cut in pieces, # 5983); → *qṣb* (cut off, shear, # 7892); → *šsp* (hew into pieces, # 9119); → *tzz* (cut away, # 9372)

Eugene Carpenter

7893 (*qeṣeb*, form, shape), → # 7892

7894	קצה

קצה (*qṣh* I), q., pi., trim off, maim, shorten; hi. scrape (?) (# 7894); קָצֶה (*qāṣeh*), nom. end, edge, border, extremity (→ # 7895); קָצָה (*qāṣâ*, pl. *q*^e^*ṣôt*), nom. end, tip (→ # 7896); קֵצֶה (*qēṣeh*), without end (# 7897); קָצוּ (*qāṣû*), ends (of the earth) (# 7898); קְצָת (*q*^e^*ṣât*), nom. end, extremity (# 7921).

ANE The vb. has cognates in Phoen. *qṣh*, cut off, exterminate; Aram. *qṣ'*; Syr. *q*^e^*ṣā'*, break (bread); Arab. *qaṣā*, to be distant, bob the point from an animal's ear; cf. Tigrinya *qäčäyä*, cut off (ears of corn).

OT 1. Unlike the vb. *qṣr* (# 7918), which can mean shortening of spatial or temporal limits, *qṣh* is not used of time. It is used of reducing quantities in Hab 2:10, where the Chaldeans are accused of cutting off (*qṣh* q.) many peoples, i.e., reducing their numbers. In 2 Kgs 10:32, the Lord began to cut off parts of Israel's territory as a penalty for the sins of her kings (*qṣh* pi. + b, used here with partitive force; see Gray, 563). Prov 26:6 warns that sending a message by a fool is like cutting off one's feet: rather than gaining a pair of feet to add to one's own, the effect is precisely the opposite, tantamount to rendering one lame (Scott, 159).

2. The vb. is used in the hi. stem in Lev 14:41, 43 for scraping mildew from the walls of a house. The procedure would involve cutting away the plaster from the inside of the walls. *BHS* and BDB suggest reading here instead *hqṣy'* (hi. of *qṣ'*, scrape off; → # 7909), which has some manuscript support and is so used in postbiblical Heb.

3. The nom. *qāṣeh,* always used in the sing., often means the end or tip of a physical object. In Exod 26:5 (= 36:12), it refers to the end of a curtain in the tabernacle. In Judg 6:21, *qāṣeh* denotes the end of a staff, while in 2 Sam 14:27, 43, it designates the end of a rod. In Isa 7:3, the Lord tells Isaiah to meet King Ahaz at the end of a water conduit. More frequently, *qāṣeh* means a perimeter or border, such as the perimeter of a camp (Num 11:1; Judg 7:17) or a city (Josh 4:19). It often means the border of some geographical region, such as the border of the land of Canaan (Exod 16:33; Num 20:16), Edom (Num 33:37), Egypt (Gen 47:21), or the wilderness (Exod 13:20; Num 33:6). Jeremiah states that the sword of the Lord devours the land "from one end to the other," describing the total destruction that God's judgment would bring upon the land of Judah (Jer 12:12). The nom. is also used to designate borders of geographical formations, such as mountains (Exod 19:12; Josh 1:16) or valleys (Josh 15:18), and often designates the banks of bodies of water, such as the Salt Sea (Num 34:3) or Sea of Kinnereth (Josh 13:27). In Josh 3:8, 15, the Jordan River parted as the feet of the priests touched its edge. This miracle marked a major turning point in the history of Israel, from their time of hopelessness to the beginning of life in the land of Canaan.

4. A common use of the nom. is in the phrase "end of the earth." Usually the phrase means the most distant part of the world (cf. Ps 61:2[3]). Sometimes, it means the horizon, the most distant visible land, from which the Hebrews believed the clouds arose (Ps 135:7; Jer 10:13). Most often, however, the end of the earth is the realm of foreign peoples. The Israelites are cautioned against worshiping the gods of peoples "from one end of the land to the other" (Deut 13:7[8]), or else they will be scattered among them (28:64). If Israel does fall into apostasy, the Lord will bring armies from the end of the earth to chastise them (28:49; Isa 5:26). Those who have been carried away into exile will be brought back from the end of the earth (Isa 43:6), on account of God's special love for his people. Frequently, BH affirms that the praise and knowledge of the Lord is not to be confined to Israel, but to reach the end of the earth (Ps 19:4; Isa 42:10; 62:11). It is an insufficient task for the Servant of the Lord to proclaim deliverance to Israel alone; he is also to take God's salvation to the Gentiles at the end of the earth (49:6). (Paul took this verse as the basis for his mission to the Gentiles; Acts 13:47.) This universalistic hope is also found in Ps 46:9[10], that the Lord causes wars to end at the end of the earth, among the distant Gentile nations.

5. Similar, but even more distant, is "the end of the heavens," where the sun rises (Ps 19:6[7]). This construction is a rare hyperbolic alternative to "end of the earth": it is from here that the armies come that devastate the land (i.e., the Babylonians; Isa 13:5). Even if Israel is exiled to the end of the heavens, the Lord will bring them back to their land, if they repent (Deut 30:4; Neh 1:9).

6. The nom. can also mean a part or division, especially of a group of people. Thus, in Num 22:41 and 23:13, Balaam sees some of (NIV part of) the people of Israel. In Ezek 33:2, the meaning is apparently similar, but the nom. is usually untranslated.

7. With the preposition *min* + a period of time, the phrase means "after so much time had passed," as in Gen 8:3: "At the end of (*miqṣēh*) the hundred and fifty days the water had gone down." It is used with a variety of time periods, including days (Josh 3:2; Ezek 3:16), months (2 Sam 24:8; Ezek 39:14), and years (Deut 14:28; 2 Kgs 8:3).

8. The nom. *qāṣâ,* end, tip, appears in the sg. form only in Exod 25:19 = 37:8 (2x each v.), where it designates either end of the cover of the ark of the covenant, and 26:4 = 36:11, where it designates either end of the curtain. Elsewhere, it is used only in the pl. const. form *qᵉṣôt.* It designates the ends of various tabernacle fixtures and priestly paraphernalia in the book of Exodus: the ends of the ark cover (25:18 = 37:7); the ephod (28:7 = 39:4); the breastplate (28:23, 24, 26 = 39:16, 17, 19); the chains (28:25 = 39:18); and the grating (27:4). The nom. also designates the tips of the cherubim's wings (on the cover of the ark) in 1 Kgs 6:24 (2x).

Elsewhere, the term is used with cosmological significance. In Jer 49:36, the four ends of the heavens are the sources of the winds that God will bring as a judgment on Elam. The nom. is also used in the expression "the ends of the earth," i.e., the remotest parts of the diaspora, from whence God calls Israel, his servant, in Isa 41:9 (see also v. 5). In Job 28:24 the expression "the ends of the earth" means not its extremities but its entirety, since the expression stands in parallelism with "everything that is under heaven." Probably this usage is an example of metonymy, the ends signifying the whole. The same meaning is likely found in Isa 40:28, where the Lord is called "the Creator of the ends of the earth," i.e., the whole world. The passage links God's role as Creator of all to his ability to deliver those who trust him (40:29-31). A similar example of metonymy is found in 1 Kgs 12:31 and 13:33, which state that Jeroboam anointed priests "from all sorts of people, even though they were not Levites" (cf. also "They also appointed all sorts of their own people to officiate for them as priests in the shrines at the high places" (2 Kgs 17:32), and "They selected five men from the ends of the people" (lit., Judg 18:2). The expression here probably means the people as a whole. A more metaphorical use of the nom. appears in Job 26:14. Here, after describing some of the mighty works of God, Job claims that "these are (but) the ends of his ways," apparently meaning the basest of his deeds. In contrast to these, Job remarks, his greatest works are totally incomprehensible to humanity.

9. Used with the partitive preposition *min* (i.e., *miqṣāt*), the construction can mean some of, as in Neh 7:70[69] ("some of the heads of the fathers") and Dan 1:2 ("some of the articles from the temple of God"). The same expression, however, is used to mean "at the end of" a period of time, as in Dan 1:15 ("at the end of the three days"). The nom. is used with a compound preposition in 1:18, the phrase *miqṣāt* preceded by the preposition *lᵉ*, but its meaning appears to be the same as in 1:15 ("at the end of the time set by the king"). (→ # 7895)

10. The nom. *qēṣeh* appears only in the phrase *'ên qēṣeh,* "without end." Isa 2:7 says that there is no end to the riches of Israel, while Nah 2:9[10] says there is no end to the store of Nineveh. Nahum predicts the destruction of Nineveh, with no end to the corpses (3:3). In 3:9, the city of Cush is described as receiving endless strength from Egypt, and yet it went into exile; the example serves as a sign to Nineveh of its impending doom.

11. The nom. *qāṣû*, end, is used only in the phrase *qāṣwê 'ereṣ*. In Ps 48:10[11], the praise of God is said to extend to the ends of the earth, expressing the belief that the worship of God in the temple held significance for the entire world, and not for Israel alone. The Lord is the hope of the ends of the earth, because it is he who maintains the order of nature (Ps 65:5[6]). In Isa 26:15, *'ereṣ* is parallel with "nation," in a description of the eschatological blessing to be poured out on Israel. Here, the phrase

qaṣwê 'ereṣ evidently means the borders of the land of Judah, which the Lord enlarges as a sign of his renewed favor.

P-B In RL the vb. means to harvest, to carry off, or to reduce in the q. stem; in the ho., it means to be cut off or separated. The pl. const. nom. *qaṣwôt* appears in 1QM 1.8, "to the ends of the world," meaning its farthest reaches.

Short: → *qṣh* I (trim off, maim, shorten, scrape, # 7894); → *qṣṣ* (cut off, trim, cut off, cut to pieces, # 7915); → *qṣr* II (be short, shorten, # 7918)
Scraping: → *grd* (scrape oneself, # 1740); → *mll* IV (scrape, # 4911); → *sḥh* (scrape away, # 6081); → *qṣh* I (trim off, maim, shorten, scrape off, # 7894); → *qṣ'* I (scrape off, # 7909); → *rdh* II (scrape out, # 8098)

Bibliography
TWOT 2:807; M. Cassuto, *Commentary on the Book of the Exodus*, 1967; B. S. Childs, *The Book of Exodus*, OTL, 1974; G. A. Cooke, *The Book of Ezekiel*, 1936; J. Gray, *1 and 2 Kings*, OTL, 1976; idem, *Joshua, Judges, Ruth*, NCBC, 1986; R. B. Y. Scott, *Proverbs-Ecclesiastes*, AB, 1985; W. Zimmerli, *Ezekiel 2: A Commmentary on the Book of the Prophet Ezekiel, Chapters 25-48,* Hermeneia, 1983.

Anthony Tomasino

7895	קָצֶה

קָצֶה (*qāṣeh*), nom. end, border, extremity, shore (# 7895); קָצָה (*qāṣâ*), nom. end, border, edge, extremity (# 7896); < קצה (*qṣh* I), bring to an end (→ # 7894).

OT 1. The word *qāṣeh* is used of the end or extremity of objects, including the earth (Deut 28:49; Ps 46:9[10]; Isa 5:26) and heaven (universe?) (Deut 4:32), as well as the border regions of cities and camps (Num 11:1; 1 Sam 9:27). The texts cited that speak of "the ends of the earth" or "the end of the heavens" evoke an awareness that the entire cosmos is Yahweh's domain and emphasize his sovereignty in the world of the nations. His cosmic sovereignty includes the expectation that he will bring all warfare to an end (Ps 46:9[10]). The word also has a temporal use, "at the end" of a period of time (Gen 8:3; Deut 14:28).

The prophet Isaiah uses the word in the context of his oracles of salvation. It fits in with his emphasis on the universal rule of Yahweh. God's good news of salvation reaches the "ends of the earth" (*miqṣēh hā'āreṣ*, Isa 48:20). Not only the news, but the salvation itself extends to the uttermost parts of the earth (49:6). Because of this, Isaiah calls on the "ends of the earth" to worship the Lord (42:10).

2. The word *qāṣâ* refers to the end or edge of a variety of objects, occurring predominantly in descriptions of cultic objects in the book of Exodus (e.g., Exod 25:18). Referring to people, the idiom *q*^{e}*ṣôt hā'ām*, the masses (1 Kgs 12:31; 13:33), implies a criticism of Jeroboam's appointing priests from outside the designated class of Levites. The word is also used in expressions referring to the "*ends* of the earth" (Isa 41:5) and "the four *quarters* of the heavens" (Jer 49:36). In their respective contexts, those texts utilize cosmological imagery to depict Yahweh's sovereign activity with or against imperial powers. Yahweh is both creator of the ends of the earth (Isa 40:28; cf. Job 28:24) and the one who has brought Israel from the ends of the earth (Isa 41:9). The

singularly provocative outburst by Job declares that God's creative ability reveals only "the outer *fringes* of his works" (Job 26:14).

Border, boundary, corner, edge, rim: → *gbl* I (bound, border, # 1487); → *zāwît* (corner, # 2312); → *kānāp* (wing, skirt, outermost edge, # 4053); → *karkōb* (rim, edge, # 4136); → *mḥh* II (border on, # 4682); → *swg* II (border by, # 6048); → *pē'â* I (corner, # 6991); → *pinnâ* (corner, # 7157); → *ṣad* (side, # 7396); → *ṣēlā'* I (side, rib, side-chamber, # 7521); → *qēṣ* (limit, boundary, # 7891); → *qāṣeh* (end, border, # 7895); → *qṣ'* II (made with corners, # 7910)

Bibliography
S. L. Stassen, "'Die Ende van die Aarde' in Jes 40:28[a], 41:5[a], 41:4[a]," *JSS* 2, 1990, 191-202.

Gordon H. Matties/Tremper Longman III

7896 (*qāṣâ*, end, border), → # 7895

7897 (*qēṣeh*, without end), → # 7894

7898 (*qāṣû*, ends), → # 7894

7900 (*qāṣûr*, shortened), → # 7918

7902	קֶצַח

קֶצַח (*qeṣaḥ*), nom. black cummin, *Nigella sativa* (# 7902).

ANE Not attested in ANE.

OT The word occurs 3x in the book of Isaiah as a seed that one sows rather than scatters and beats out of its pod with a rod rather than threshes (Isa 28:25, 27[2x]). This is a reference to black cummin (Arab. *kazḥa*) rather than "dill" (RSV, NASB), "fitch" (KJV), or "caraway" (NIV). The seeds were sprinkled on breads and cakes for added flavor.

P-B The LXX translates *qeṣaḥ* with *melanthion*, black cummin (*Nigella sativa*).

Herbs, spices: → *'ôrâ* II (herb, mallow, # 246); → *gad* I (coriander, # 1512); → *kammōn* (cumin, # 4021); → *qinnāmôn* (cinnamon, # 7872); → *qeṣaḥ* (black cumin, # 7902); → *qᵉṣîa'* (cassia, # 7904); → *reqaḥ* (spice, # 8380)

Bibliography
M. Zohary, *Plants of the Bible,* 1982, 91; W. E. Shewell-Cooper, "Fitch, Fitches," *ZPEB* 2:544.

M. G. Abegg, Jr.

7903	קָצִין

קָצִין (*qāṣîn*), commander, leader (# 7903).

ANE The word is cognate with Arab. *qāḍn*, judge (lit., decider).

OT The term, appearing 12x, may denote military commanders (Josh 10:24; Judg 11:6) or leaders in general (cf. Prov 6:7; 25:15).

1. The word (‖ *rā'šîm*, heads) designates the civil and juridical leaders of Jerusalem (Mic 3:1, 9). They are condemned for failing to uphold justice at the courts they preside over: they "despise justice and distort all that is right" (v. 9). Their conduct

towards the people is graphically portrayed as an act of cannibalism (vv. 2-3). The expression "who build Zion with bloodshed" (v. 10) suggests that Naboth's fate was not exceptional (1 Kgs 21; → *zāqēn*, # 2418). The description of their position as "leaders of the house of Israel" (Mic 3:9) serves to remind them their victims are God's people and to place their conduct in the light of God's covenant demands for the administration of justice (cf. Exod 23:6-8; Deut 16:18-20). Probably the same leaders are also the subject of Isaiah's appeal to the "rulers of Sodom" to pay heed to God's teaching (*tôrâ*, Isa 1:10) and to mend their ways (vv. 16-17). "Of Sodom" evokes both their wickedness (cf. 3:9) and the threat of total destruction that looms over a city under sentence of God's judgment (cf. 1:9; Mic 3:12).

2. The word recurs in the prospect of judgment in Isa 3:6-7. These verses depict the state of chaos and confusion in Jerusalem after its leadership has been swept away in divine judgment (vv. 1-3). So great will be the extent of Jerusalem's ruin that none can be persuaded to become "leader," but will protest "I have no remedy" (lit., "not a binder [of wounds]," *ḥōbēš*). This expression looks back to 1:6 (*ḥubbašû*, NIV bandaged) and forward to 30:26, when God himself "binds up the bruises of his people and heals the wounds he inflicted."

P-B The LXX mostly trans. *qāṣîn* by *archēgos* (Isa 3:6) or *archōn* (1:10). In Prov 25:15 it is rendered *basileus*, king.

Leaders: → *'ādôn* (lord, master, # 123); → *'allûp* II (tribal chief, # 477); → *'āṣîl* II (eminent, noble, # 722); → *zāqēn* (elder, # 2418); → *ḥōr* I, free man, freeborn, # 2985); → *maptēaḥ* (badge of office, # 5158); → *nāgîd* (prince, ruler, leader, # 5592); → *nāśî'* I (chief, king, # 5954); → *sārîs* (eunuch, court official, # 6247); → *seren* II (Philistine prince, # 6249); → *'attûd* (he-goat, leader, # 6966); → *peḥâ* (governor, # 7068); → *pāqîd* (officer, # 7224); → *qāṣîn* (commander, leader, # 7903); → *rab* II (captain, chief, # 8042); → *rzn* (rule, # 8142); → *šôa'* I (noble, # 8777)

BIBLIOGRAPHY
TWAT 7:93-95.

Kenneth T. Aitken

7904	קְצִיעָה

קְצִיעָה (*qᵉṣî'â*), cassia (# 7904).

OT The nom. *qᵉṣî'â*, cassia, cinnamon flowers (for incense) refers to some kind of cinnamon and may derive from the flowers and fruits of the *Cinnamomum zeylanicum* variety known as cassia. Some have suggested that the term itself has a Chinese origin, but others argue that it is more likely to be related to the Heb. vb. *qṣ'*, scrape off, referring to the scraping of the bark of the cassia tree (Nielsen, 1992, 65). The nom. is a hapleg., which occurs in Ps 45:8[9], referring to the scenting of the king's robes for the marriage ceremony, "All your robes are fragrant with myrrh and aloes and cassia; from palaces adorned with ivory the music of the strings makes you glad."

Resin, balm, myrrh: → *mōr* (myrrh, # 5255); → *nāṭāp* (gum resin, # 5753); → *ṣᵒrî/ṣᵉrî* (balm, resin, # 7661); → *qᵉṣîa'* (cassia, # 7904)
Spices, herbs: → *'ôrâ* II (herb, mallow, # 246); → *gad* I (coriander, # 1512); → *kammōn* (cumin, # 4021); → *qinnāmôn* (cinnamon, # 7872); → *qeṣaḥ* (black cumin, # 7902); → *qᵉṣîa'* (cassia, # 7904); → *reqaḥ* (spice, # 8380)

Bibliography

K. Nielsen, *Incense in Ancient Israel*, SVT 38, 1986.

Richard E. Averbeck

7907 (*qāṣîr* I, harvest), → # 7917

7908 (*qāṣîr* II), bough), → # 580

7909	קצע

קצע (*qṣʿ* I), hi. scrape (hapleg.; # 7909); מַקְצֻעָה (*maqṣuʿâ*), nom. scraping tool, plane, chisel (hapleg.; → # 5244).

OT As part of the process of cleansing a building from mildew, the priest "must have all the inside walls ... scraped (*yaqṣiaʿ*) and the material that is scraped off (*hiqṣû*) dumped into an unclean place outside the town" (Lev 14:41). He must tear the house down if the mildew "reappears ... after the stones have been torn out and the house scraped (*hiqṣôt*) and plastered" (v. 43). Note that the root *qṣh* I (hi. scrape [off], # 7894) is used only in Lev 14:41b, 43 in assonance with *qṣʿ* I.

Perhaps the tools employed in the scraping process were similar or identical to the chisels (*maqṣuʿâ*, → # 5244) used by carpenters in roughing out the detestable idols they often made (Isa 44:13).

Scraping: → *grd* (scrape oneself, # 1740); → *mll* IV (scrape, # 4911); → *sḥh* (scrape away, # 6081); → *qṣh* I (trim off, maim, shorten, scrape off, # 7894); → *qṣʿ* I (scrape off, # 7909); → *rdh* II (scrape out, # 8098)

Ronald Youngblood

7910	קצע

קצע (*qṣʿ* II), pu., ho. made with corners (# 7910); nom. מִקְצוֹעַ (*miqṣôaʿ*), corner (# 5243).

OT Verbal forms refer to tabernacle and temple construction (Exod 26:23; 36:28; Ezek 46:22). The nom. refers to corners of the altar (Exod 26:24) and court (Ezek 46:21), and an area in Jerusalem (2 Chron 26:9; Neh 3:19-20).

Border, boundary, corner, edge, rim: → *gbl* I (bound, border, # 1487); → *zāwît* (corner, # 2312); → *kānāp* (wing, skirt, outermost edge, # 4053); → *karkōb* (rim, edge, # 4136); → *mḥh* II (border on, # 4682); → *swg* II (border by, # 6048); → *pēʾâ* I (corner, # 6991); → *pinnâ* (corner, # 7157); → *ṣad* (side, # 7396); → *ṣēlāʿ* I (side, rib, side-chamber, # 7521); → *qēṣ* (limit, boundary, # 7891); → *qāṣeh* (end, border, # 7895); → *qṣʿ* II (made with corners, # 7910)

Gordon H. Matties

7911	קצף

קצף (*qṣp*), q. wrathful; hi. provoke to wrath (# 7911); קֶצֶף (*qeṣep* I), nom. annoyance, irritation, displeasure; anger (# 7912).

ANE The vb. in Akk. is *kaṣāpu/keṣēpu*, become worried (*HALAT* 1049b, *THAT* 2:663); cf. Syr. *qᵉṣap*, be irritated, anxious, worried.

OT 1. The nom. *qeṣep* occurs 28x, almost exclusively with reference to the Lord. The nom. occurs 4x in the Pent., 11x in the historical books, 3x in the poetical books, and 10x in the prophetic books. The vb. *qṣp*, be angry, occurs 34x. It occurs in the q. 28x, with the Lord as subject 17x. It is found 6x in the hi. stem with 1 occurrence of the Lord as the subject. The vb. is found 12x in the Pent., 6x in the historical books, 2x in the poetical books, and 14x in the prophetic books.

2. The phrase *qeṣep gādôl* occurs 6x (Deut 29:28[27]; 2 Kgs 3:27; Jer 21:5; 32:37; Zech 1:15; 7:12). The nom. *qeṣep* occurs 17x with the preposition *ʿal*, on, on account of. The nuances of this word are close to *ḥēmâ*, wrath. In three instances the nom. *ʾap*, *ḥēmâ*, and *qeṣep* are combined forming a phrase that builds in intensity. This phrase ends not simply with *qeṣep*, but *qeṣep gādôl*, great wrath (Deut 29:28[27]; Jer 21:5, 32:37). Deut 29:18-28[17-27] warns the people of the consequences of apostasy. Because the people will abandon the Lord's covenant and worship other gods, the Lord will uproot them from the land in anger and in wrath and in great wrath, *bᵉʾap ûbᵉḥēmâ ûbᵉqeṣep gādôl* (Deut 29:28[27]).

The second occurrence of this phrase is found in Jer 21:5, where the Lord himself will fight against Zedekiah and the inhabitants of the city. The Lord will fight in anger and wrath and great wrath (cf. Deut 29:28[27]). The final occurrence of this phrase is in the context of the Lord's promising restoration to the people. He has banished the people in his anger, wrath, and great wrath, yet he will "bring them back to this place and let them live in safety" (Jer 32:37).

Thus the three phrases are connected. The curse of Deut finds fulfillment in Jer. The words used for anger build in intensity until the final phrase, *qeṣep gādôl*, great wrath.

3. When free standing, *qeṣep* carries much the same force as *ḥēmâ*. *qeṣep* without any modifiers appears in a context in which the people had abandoned the temple of the Lord and were worshiping Asherah poles and idols (2 Chron 24:18). For this reason wrath was on Judah and Jerusalem. Another instance of *qeṣep* without modifiers is found in 32:24-26, which tells of Hezekiah's healing. Yet, his heart was proud, and he did not "respond to the kindness shown him." On account of this, wrath was on Hezekiah, Judah, and Jerusalem. By his repentance he averted the Lord's wrath (*qeṣep*, v. 26). These examples illustrate the similarity in meaning between *qeṣep* and *ḥēmâ*.

P-B The Aram. vb. *qṣp* signifies be angry, arouse to anger, excite, incite (Jastrow, 2:1406b). The nom. in Aram., *qeṣep*, denotes anger, destruction, harm (Jastrow, 2:1406b). The LXX translates *qṣp* with a variety of words, including *orgizomai*, *lupeō*, or *thymoō*. *qeṣep* is usually translated by either *thymos* or *orgē*.

Anger, rage, wrath: → *ʾnp* (be angry, # 647); → *zʿm* (curse, be angry, # 2406); → *zʿp* I (rage, # 2406); → *ḥēmâ* (rage, # 2779); → *ḥrh* I (be hot, become angry, # 3013); → *kʿs* (be irritated, angry, # 4087); → *ʿbr* II (show anger, # 6297); → *qṣp* I (become angry, # 7911); → *rgz* (shake, agitate, # 8074); → **Anger: Theology**

BIBLIOGRAPHY

THAT 2:663-66; *TWOT* 2:808-9; B. E. Baloian, *Anger in the Old Testament*, 1992; S. Erlandsson, "The Wrath of YHWH," *TynBul* 23, 1973, 111-16; A. J. Heschel, *The Prophets*, v 2, 1962; L. Morris, "The Wrath of God," *ExpTim* 63, 1952, 142-45.

Gale B. Struthers

7912 (*qeṣep* I, anger), → # 7911

7915	קצץ

קצץ (*qṣṣ* I), vb. q. cut off, trim; pi. cut off, cut to pieces (# 7915); קֵץ (*qēṣ*), nom. end (→ # 7891); קִיצוֹן (*qîṣôn*), adj. outermost (# 7812).

ANE The root is widely attested in the ANE: Akk. *gaṣāṣu,* to cut off; Ugar. *qṣ,* end of a garment; ends of the earth; slice of meat (KTU 1.16, 1.3, 1.4); Aram., Syr., Arab. *qṣṣ,* cut off; Eth. *qäṣqäṣä,* be cut, broken.

OT 1. The vb. is frequently used in the pi. stem meaning to cut something into pieces. The golden vessels of the temple were cut to pieces by King Ahaz (2 Chron 28:24) and later by King Nebuchadnezzar (2 Kgs 24:13). Gold leaf was cut into thin threads for use in the high priest's vestments (Exod 39:3). In Ps 46:9[10] the Lord is said to cut to pieces the spear, symbolic of the peace that he brings to the entire earth. The Lord cuts to pieces the cords of the wicked, probably referring to the ropes by which a yoke is held (Ps 129:4). This image is therefore related to the frequent metaphor of breaking the yoke, symbolic of Israel's national liberation (cf. Isa 9:3; Jer 28:1-4; Ezek 34:27; Kraus, 462).

2. The vb. can also mean to cut off, in both the q. and pi. stems. King Ahaz cut off (pi.) the enclosure (or rim) of the "Sea" that was in the temple, apparently to give it as tribute to the king of Assyria (2 Kgs 16:17). Hezekiah cut (pi.) the gold plate off the temple doors for tribute to Assyria (18:16). The vb. can also mean to cut parts from the body. Jer 9:26[25]; 25:23; and 49:32 condemn a circumcised people of the desert who "clip the hair of their foreheads" (q. pass. part. cf. NIV marg. note), i.e., who shave their hair at the temples (a practice forbidden to the Israelites, Lev 19:27). The vb. is also used of cutting off the bodily extremities, a common ANE practice. The Judahites cut off (pi.) the thumbs and big toes of Adonibezek, king of the Canaanites and Perizzites, who himself had cut off the thumbs and big toes of seventy kings (Judg 1:6-7). The incident is thus presented as a case of poetic justice. David ordered that the men who had killed Ishbaal, the son of Saul, should themselves be executed. The hands and feet of their corpses were cut off (pi.), and their bodies hung in public display at Hebron. Such a display was surely designed to demonstrate David's outrage at the murder of Saul's son and to remove any suspicions that he was behind the act (2 Sam 4:12). In Deut 25:11-12 a unique example of casuistic law is found: if two men are struggling, and the wife of one of them seeks to rescue her husband by seizing the genitals of the other man, her hand is to be cut off (vb. in q. stem). While the penalty of maiming or disfigurement was common in ANE law codes (see Driver, 343-67), this is the only case in biblical law (apart from the *lex talionis,* Deut 19:21) prescribing such a penalty. Craigie (315-16) sees here a specific application of the *lex talionis* (Deut 19:21): since the woman has no external genitalia, the cutting off of the hand was regarded as equal compensation for the injury to the man's genitalia. It should also be noted that this severe penalty was not inspired primarily by excessive Israelite modesty; in a society where offspring were valued as highly as they were in ancient Israel, damaging a man's reproductive potential was one of the most heinous crimes imaginable.

3. The nom. *qēṣ* is used in a variety of BH constructions. It sometimes designates a border or boundary, as in Jer 50:26, where it refers to the borders of Chaldaea (cf. borders of Lebanon [Isa 37:24]). A more metaphorical use of the nom. with this sense appears in Job 28:3: "Man puts an end to the darkness; he searches the farthest recesses for one in the blackest darkness." This passage speaks of miners, who place a limit on the darkness by means of lamps. Ps 119:96 notes that on every (human) perfection there is a boundary (*qēṣ*), but the commandment of God by contrast is broad (i.e., unbounded).

4. Usually, however, the nom. refers to the end of a period of time. A common expression (occurring 22x) is *miqqēṣ x,* the preposition *min* (or sometimes *l*ᵉ) + X period of time. The phrase means "At the end of X time . . .", or, "After X time had passed . . ." It can be used of a period of days, as in Gen 8:6 ("after forty days"); of months, as in Judg 11:39 ("after the two months"); or of years, as in Exod 12:41 ("at the end of the 430 years"). The phrase *miqqēṣ yammîm,* "at the end of days" (e.g., Gen 4:3; 1 Kgs 17:7) or *l*ᵉ*qēṣ šānîm,* "at the end of years" (Neh 13:6; 2 Chron 18:2; Dan 11:6, 13) both mean after some time passes (had passed).

5. The nom. also designates the end of events or activities of limited duration. In some instances the end is welcome. Job 18:2 asks, "When will you end these speeches?" while Qohelet laments that there is no end to the writing of many books (Eccl 12:12). The nom. is also used of the end of the human life span (Job 6:11; Ps 39:4[5]; Dan 9:26; 11:45), or even the end of the existence of all flesh (Gen 6:13; but note Wallenstein, 212-13, who suggests translating *qēṣ* here "season"). The end of Babylon's existence is predicted in Jer 51:13; while Israel's end is foretold in Amos 8:2 (with a word play on *qayiṣ*, summer fruit, cf. Lam 4:18; Ezek 7:2-3, 6). Ezek 21:25[30]; 21:29[34]; 35:5 say that the day had come for Israel's "punishment of the end," i.e., the punishment that would bring the end of her national existence (cf. Zimmerli, 203-4, who considers *qēṣ* an important catchword in Ezekiel). This end, however, is only of the then-existing, sinful nation, for these prophets also predict the restoration of the Davidic throne and kingdom (e.g., Ezek 34:23-31; Amos 9:11-15). Of the peace of this kingdom, says Isaiah, there will be no end (Isa 9:7[6]).

6. In the book of Daniel, and perhaps also in Hab 2:3, the nom. *qēṣ* is used as a technical term for the eschaton. It does not refer to the end point of the world, but rather a period of time of some length that culminates in the consummation of human history (Collins, 93). In Dan 8-12, the term *qēṣ* occurs 14x, although it is used as a technical term only 10x. Twice (9:26 and 12:13) it is used alone. In 8:19 and 11:27, 35, it is used with the nom. *mô'ēd*, appointed time, thus "the appointed time of the end" (a possible allusion to Hab 2:3, where *qēṣ* is also used with *mô'ēd*). The similar phrase *'ēt qēṣ,* time of the end, appears in Dan 8:17; 11:35, 40; 12:4, 9. In Daniel, therefore, the end time commences at a predetermined point in history, which can be discerned by the insightful (see esp. 9:24-27). It involves a series of events, including spreading wars (9:26, but especially the campaigns of the "king of the North"; 11:40), a time of distress for the people of God (12:1), the destruction of the earthly powers (9:27; 11:45), and the resurrection of the dead (12:13).

7. The adj. *qîṣōn,* outermost, derived from the nom. *qēṣ*, is found only in Exod 26:4, 10, and the parallel passages in 36:11, 17. It describes the ends of the goat-hair curtains that comprised the walls of the Tent of Meeting, in which loops were to be set.

P-B The nom. *qēṣ* is an important technical term in many of the DSS, sometimes meaning "season, time period" (cf. its meaning in some rabbinic texts, "predetermined time" [Jastrow]), but also meaning "the end time," as in Daniel. The Community Rule tells how the spirits of light and darkness struggle with one another "until the final end" (1QS 4.16), "for God has established a time for the end of falsehood" (4.18). The Habakkuk Commentary states that God revealed all the mysteries of the prophets to the Teacher of Righteousness, but "the closing of the end he did not make known to him" (i.e., the exact time of the eschaton; 1QpHab 7.2). The statement, "The final end will be extended" (7.7), indicates that the end was viewed as a period, as in Daniel, instead of a point in time.

NT The NT also reflects Daniel's understanding of the end. In Matt 24, when Jesus is asked what will be the signs of "the end of the age" (Matt 24:3), the only prophet quoted by name is Daniel (v. 15, quoting Dan 9:27). Like Daniel, the NT also views the "end of the age" as a period of time, beginning with the coming of Jesus (Heb 9:26; 1 Peter 1:20). Paul, like Daniel, associates the end with the resurrection of the dead (1 Cor 15:20-24).

Border, boundary, corner, edge, rim: → *gbl* I (bound, border, # 1487); → *zāwît* (corner, # 2312); → *kānāp* (wing, skirt, outermost edge, # 4053); → *karkōb* (rim, edge, # 4136); → *mḥh* II (border on, # 4682); → *swg* II (border by, # 6048); → *pē'â* I (corner, # 6991); → *pinnâ* (corner, # 7157); → *ṣad* (side, # 7396); → *ṣēlā'* I (side, rib, side-chamber, # 7521); → *qēṣ* (limit, boundary, # 7891); → *qāṣeh* (end, border, # 7895); → *qṣ'* II (made with corners, # 7910)
Cutting, destruction, extermination, shearing, trimming: → *bṣ'* (cut away, get gain, cut off, break up, # 1298); → *br'* III (clear out trees, cut, destroy, # 1345); → *btr* (cut into pieces, # 1439); → *gd'* (cut short, # 1548); → *gzh* (bring forth, # 1602); → *gzz* (cut, shear, # 1605); → *gzr* I (cut, take away, # 1615); → *grz* (be cut off, # 1746); → *gr'* I (cut out, reduce, # 1757); → *ḥlp* II (cut through, pierce, # 2737); → *ksḥ* (cut, cut down, # 4065); → *krsm* (make cropped, trimmed off, # 4155); → *krt* (cut, cut off, exterminate, cut a covenant, circumcise, # 4162); → *melqāḥāyim* (snuffers for trimming/cleaning of lights/lamps, # 4920); → *nqp* I (cut/chop down, destroy, # 5937); → *ntḥ* (cut in pieces, # 5983); → *qṣb* (cut off, shear, # 7892); → *šsp* (hew into pieces, # 9119); → *tzz* (cut away, # 9372)
End, cessation, outcome: → *'aḥ^{a}rît* (end, outcome, # 344); → *'ps* (cease, come to an end, # 699); → *bṭl* (cease working, # 1060); → *gmr* (be at an end, cease, fail, # 1698); → *ḥdl* I (end, stop, # 2532); → *swp* (come to an end, # 6066); → *sārâ* I (stopping, # 6239); → *qēṣ* (end, limit, boundary, # 7891); → *qṣh* I (bring about the end, shorten, # 7894)
Short: → *qṣh* I (trim off, maim, shorten, scrape, # 7894); → *qṣṣ* (cut off, trim, cut off, cut to pieces, # 7915); → *qṣr* II (be short, shorten, # 7918)

BIBLIOGRAPHY

THAT 2:659-63; *TWAT* 7:84-92; J. Collins, "The Meaning of 'the End' in the Book of Daniel," in *Of Scribes and Scrolls,* ed. Harold Attridge, John Collins, and Thomas Tobin, 1990, 91-98; G. A. Cooke, *The Book of Ezekiel,* 1936; P. Craigie, *The Book of Deuteronomy,* NICOT, 1976; G. R. Driver, *The Assyrian Laws,* 1935; J. E. Goldingay, *Daniel,* WBC, 1989; H.-J. Kraus, *Psalms 60-150: A Commentary,* 1989; M. Wallenstein, "Some Lexical Material in the Judaean Scrolls," *VT* 4, 1954, 211-14; N. Wieder, "The Term קץ in the Dead Sea Scrolls and in Hebrew Liturgical Poetry," *JJS* 5, 1954, 22-31; W. Zimmerli, *Ezekiel 2: A Commmentary on the Book of the Prophet Ezekiel, Chapters 25-48,* Hermeneia, 1983.

Anthony Tomasino

7917	קצר

קצר (*qṣr* I), q. harvest, gather, assemble; part. harvester (# 7917); קָצִיר (*qāṣîr* I), nom. harvest (# 7907).

ANE In the Gezer calendar *qṣr* refers to the harvesting of grain (*KAI* 182 I 4-5). Akk. *kaṣāru*, tie, gather, is likely a cognate (*HALAT* 1051).

OT 1. Harvesting refers to the gathering of the produce: i.e., cereals (grain) or fruit (grapes and figs); the harvesting of the crop (Gen 45:6; Exod 34:21; Ruth 2:21, 23; 1 Sam 8:12). The harvest time was one of the signs of cosmic order (Gen 8:22). Some texts use the time of harvesting to indicate a time period (Josh 3:15; Judg 15:1; Ruth 1:22, etc.). Legislation provided for gleanings in the interest of the poor (Lev 19:9-10; Deut 24:19). Jer 8:20 refers to the end of the harvest (*qāyiṣ*, → # 7811; i.e., in August-September; cf. Gezer calendar *KAI* 182 I 7), but the absence of deliverance.

2. The theological meaning of harvest lies in part in the fact that harvest was regarded as a blessing from God and a joyous occasion. The cultic meaning of harvest revolved around the Feast of the Harvest, also known as the Feast of Weeks (Exod 34:22-24; Num 28:26). Its name in G, Pentecost, derived from the count of fifty days from the first Sabbath of Passover (Lev 23:16). At the harvest a sheaf of the first grain was to be brought to the priest, who dedicated it to the Lord (23:10-11). Harvesting ceased on the Sabbath (Exod 34:21). There was no harvesting in the Sabbath Year and the Jubilee (Lev 25:5, 11). The cultic rituals underlined the role of Yahweh in the fertility that resulted in harvest. That role is indicated by the use of the phrase "I am the LORD your God" (Lev 23:22, cf. v. 43). Only after God as the Provider was honored through the sheaf dedication (vv. 10-11) could the worshiper enjoy of the produce himself.

3. Metaphorically the figure of harvest is employed in morality. The sowing of righteousness will result in a harvest of loving-kindness (*ḥesed*, → # 2876; Hos 10:12; cf. Ps 126:5). The opposite will be true if one sows unrighteously (Job 4:8; Hos 10:13; 8:7).

4. God's judgment is described in terms of cutting down, as in a harvest. The judgment of the nations in general is described as a sickle swung for the ripe harvest (Joel 4:13[3:13]; cf. Matt. 3:12). Despair will replace the joy over harvest (Isa 16:9; 17:11), especially on the Day of the Lord (Joel 1:11). Other judgments with the figure of harvest are: Judah (Hos 6:11), Israel (Isa 17:5), Ethiopians (Isa 18:4-5), and Babylon (Jer 51:33).

5. Salvation for restored Israel is depicted in harvest terms with a cornucopia of plenty (Isa 62:9). In agriculture there will be overproduction (Amos 9:13: Cornelius, *JNSL* 14, 1988, 49; *TWOT* 2:809 is incorrect in connecting this v. with judgment).

6. In sum, the theological meaning of the harvest/harvesting operates in three spheres: (a) a blessing from God in which the poor and landless partake; (b) a metaphor for the judgment of God when God harvests Israel or the nations, or when he punishes the Israelites in the form of a meager harvest, and (c) a symbol of hope, when Israel gathered from the Exile will enjoy rich yields in the age to come.

P-B LXX translates the Heb. with *therismos* (vb. with *therizō*). Jewish apocalyptic literature also developed the theme of the harvest as divine judgment—in the apocalyptic end of the world there will be a harvest of good and evil (2 Bar 70:2). Philo developed the moral-ethical meaning of the harvest (→ *NIDNTT* 3:526). In the NT (→ *NIDNTT* 3:526-27; *TDNT* 3:132-33) the harvest (*therismos*) is used literally, but also in an extended meaning for the fruit of the Christian mission (Matt 9:37-38) and divine judgment (Matt 3:12; Rev 14:15-20; cf. Joel 4:13[3:13]).

Harvest, gleaning: → *'sp* (gather, harvest, # 665); → *bṣr* (harvest grapes, # 1305); → *y^e^bûl* (produce, yield, # 3292); → *lqṭ* (reap, harvest, # 4377); → *'ll* I (glean, # 6618); → *'mr* (gather grain, # 6682); → *qbṣ* (gather, # 7695); → *qṣr* (harvest, # 7917); → *t^e^bû'â* (crop, yield, # 9311); → *t^e^nûbâ*, produce, # 9482)

Bibliography
ABD 3:63-64; *ISBE* 2:619; *NIDNTT* 3:525-27; *TDNT* 3:132-33; *TWOT* 2:783-84, 809-10.

I. Cornelius

7918	קצר

קצר (*qṣr* II), q. be short; pi., hi. to shorten (# 7918); קָצוּר (*qāṣûr*), adj. shortened (# 7900); קֹצֶר (*qōṣer*), nom. shortness; with "spirit," impatience, dejectedness, pusillanimity (# 7919); קָצֵר (*qāṣēr*), adj. short (# 7920).

ANE The root is attested in Aram. *qṣr*, be short; Arab. *qaṣura,* short, shorten; and in Mand. *QṣR,* be short. The vb. appears in the Ugar. phrases, "My days will be short" (*KTU* 1.103), and *qṣr npš,* be impatient (*KTU* 1.40), a clear parallel to the BH usage of the phrase noted below (cf. van Selms, 240). Leslau (48) suggests a comparison with Eth. *ḫṣr,* be short.

OT 1. In the q. stem, the vb. can mean to be short in length or duration. Jerusalem is warned against trusting in her "covenant with death" (i.e., alliance with Egypt; Isa 28:15), because "the bed is too short to stretch out in" (28:20). Apparently this proverbial saying is a metaphor for the insufficient security that Egypt will provide when the Lord goes forth in judgment. Anticipating their premature destruction by the hand of the Lord, a sage warns that "the years of the wicked are cut short" (Prov 10:27). Because of his wrath, apparently arising because of some unnamed sin, the Lord cut short the youth of the Davidic prince (Ps 89:45[46], where the hi. is used; cf. Ps 102:23[24], which expresses much the same idea using the vb. in the pi. stem [see below, section 4]).

2. More frequently, the vb. is used in the idiomatic expression, his soul (*nepeš*) or his spirit (*rûaḥ*) was short. The phrase is generally translated "be impatient." Num 21:4 states that the "soul of the people was shortened" (NIV the people became impatient) as they had to pass the long way around Edom, and they grumbled against God and Moses. Samson's "soul was shortened" because of the constant pestering of Delilah (Judg 16:16). God's spirit, too, can become short. When Israel repented and put away their foreign gods, God became impatient because of their suffering and delivered them from their oppressors (Judg 10:16). Mic 2:7 asks rhetorically, "Is the Spirit of the LORD angry (lit., shortened)?" The question demands the answer "no"; God will still bless those who are upright (Mic 2:7b). Wolff believes there to be a phenomenological basis behind this figure of speech: one who is impatient becomes short of breath in his or her excitement (Wolff, 37). Haak seeks to distinguish between this meaning of

qṣr nepeš and one based on the Ugar., to be weak. He believes that the Ugar. nuance can be discerned in Job 21:4, which is usually rendered "Is my complaint directed to man? Why should I not be impatient?" Haak (164) holds that Job was lamenting his weakness. It is equally likely, however, that Job was expressing his vexation over what he perceived to be injustice in God's dealing with humanity.

3. Another figure of speech involving this vb. is "short of hand," meaning to be weak. This expression is used with the adj. in 2 Kgs 19:26 to describe the inhabitants of cities besieged by Sennacherib. With the vb., however, the phrase is only used of God, and only in rhetorical questions or negative statements. Thus, in Num 11:23, when Moses questions how God can feed all the people of Israel, God asks, "Is the LORD's arm too short?" The Isaianic corpus also asks, "Was my arm too short to ransom you?" (Isa 50:2), and later answers, "Surely the arm of the LORD is not so short to save" (59:1). This expression probably derives from the equation of the hand with power or authority (Wolff, 67-68), and the shortening of the hand with the curtailing of power. It could also stand in contrast to "stretching forth the hand," a frequent expression for the exercise of power.

4. The pi. is used in Ps 102:23[24], part of the prayer of an afflicted, demoralized, ostracized, and persecuted individual (*contra* those commentators, e.g., Eaton, 244, who argue that the entire psalm is a prayer offered by a representative spokesperson on behalf of the Jerusalem community). The psalmist, who is desolate, solitary, and beset by intense pain and enmity, pours out his complaint to, and against, God, whom he considers the real cause of his sorrow. In v. 23[24], God, the one who possesses endless years (v. 24[25]), is accused of having drained the psalmist's vitality and of having "cut short" his days (the suggestion made by Kraus, 282-83, that the 3d person common pl. pu. pf. be read is not compelling; on the LXX text, which retains the Heb. consonants but changes the vowels and verse-division of vv. 23-24[24-25], see, e.g., Kidner, 362-63). Although Ps 102 is classified in church liturgy as the fifth of the seven so-called "penitential psalms," the psalmist makes no confession of sin or explicit expression of penitence. He complains that God, in great wrath, cruelly picked him up and flung him aside (v. 10[11]) and is now hiding his face, refusing to listen to the psalmist's cry for help (vv. 1-2[2-3]. Some commentators (e.g., Buttenwieser, 382-92) argue that the text of this psalm has suffered dislocation in the course of transmission, but others (e.g., Anderson, 704; Durham, 376; Kraus, 284) defend the unity of the composition. In its present form, the protest in v. 23[24] is preceded by a recitation that looks forward to the time in the future when Yahweh will again be moved to compassion for the people of Israel, responding to the prayer of the destitute and releasing the prisoners and those condemned to death (vv. 12-22[13-23]). This suggests that the psalmist's need for healing did not fade into the background as he contemplated the future restoration of afflicted Israel. Rather, the psalmist seems to hope that God will apply these corporate promises to his particular plight: just as God will restore the nation from its affliction, so too the psalmist will experience divine deliverance from his distress (cf. Rogerson and McKay, 18, 22; Anderson, 704; Broyles, 211). Verse 23[24] is followed by a petition (v. 24a[25a]), in which the psalmist beseeches God to spare him from a premature death. The psalm concludes with a majestic hymn of praise (vv. 24b-28[25b-29]), which celebrates the fact that, despite the transience of the natural world, God's enduring presence offers finite humanity the possibility of being

established (v. 28[29]; cf. Westermann, 116; Rogerson and McKay, 22). As White (155) comments: "The lives of the godly do not pass into oblivion, but through their children and successors shall endure and be established, through future years, before the unchanging God."

5. The adj. *qāṣûr,* describing the upper chambers of Ezekiel's visionary temple, appears only in Ezek 42:5. The NIV translates the adj. "narrower," but Zimmerli translates the term more literally as "foreshortened" (Zimmerli, 393). The adj. clearly means that the size of these chambers was reduced by the building's galleries.

6. The adj. *qāṣēr* is used in some of the same constructions as the vb. The use of the adj. in the phrase "short of hand" in 2 Kgs 19:26 has been noted above. In Job 14:1, mortals are described as "short of days," i.e., short-lived. In Prov 14:29, he who is short of spirit (*qᵉṣar-rûaḥ*, i.e., an impatient hothead) is contrasted with one who is slow to anger (*'erek 'appayîm*).

7. In Exod 6:9, the nom. occurs in the phrase *miqqōṣer rûaḥ* (lit.: "out of shortness of spirit/breath"), which is variously translated, faintheartedness (LXX); discouragement (NIV); anguish of spirit (AV); broken spirit (RSV and NRSV); depths of despair (REB); crushed ... spirit (JB). While some prefer "impatience" (e.g., NEB; Cole, 86; Childs, 110) or even "anger" (Cole, 86), the context suggests that the people are disheartened and demoralized by the cruel hardships of slavery.

P-B Heb. and Aram. verbal, nominative, and adjectival forms are well attested: *qṣr*, q. cut, reap, be short, be impatient, be vexed, be sick of; pi. shorten, be brief in doing; hitp. and nitp. be shortened, be impatient, sick; *qᵉṣar*, q. be short, shorten; pi. shorten; itp. be shortened, reduced; *qāṣēr*, adj. short; *qaṣṣār*, *qaṣrā'*, nom. [one who causes shrinking], fuller, washer; *qôṣer*, nom. shortness (Jastrow 2:1408, 1340).

Sir 30:24 warns that jealousy and anger "shorten days," (cf. Ps 89:45[46]; 102:23[24], where it is the Lord who cuts short the days of those who sin). In Sir 7:10 (Manuscript A), the sage enjoins his readers not to be short (*ttqṣr*) in their prayers. (This hitp. form of the vb., although not found in BH, is attested in rabbinic texts.) The Community Rule of the Dead Sea Scrolls condemns shortness of temper (*qᵉṣûr 'appayîm*) as one of the "works of darkness," the sins engendered by the spirit of falsehood (1QS 4.10; cf. Gal 5:19-21; James 1:19-20).

Short: → *qṣh* I (trim off, maim, shorten, scrape, # 7894); → *qṣṣ* (cut off, trim, cut off, cut to pieces, # 7915); → *qṣr* II (be short, shorten, # 7918)
Extinguishing: → *d'k* (snuff out, extinguish, vanish, # 1980); → *z'k* (be extinguished, # 2403); → *kbh* (be extinguished, put out, # 3882)

BIBLIOGRAPHY

A. A. Anderson, *The Book of Psalms: Volume 2 Psalms, 73-150*, 1972; C. C. Broyles, *The Conflict of Faith and Experience in the Psalms: A Form-Critical and Theological Study*, 1989; M. Buttenwieser, *The Psalms Chronologically Treated with a New Translation*, 1969; B. S. Childs, *Exodus: A Commentary*, 1974; R. A. Cole, *Exodus: An Introduction and Commentary*, 1973; G. A. Cooke, *Critical and Exegetical Commentary on the Book of Ezekiel*, ICC, 1936; J. I. Durham, "Psalms," in *Esther-Psalms*, 1972, 4:153-464; J. H. Eaton, *Psalms: Introduction and Commentary*, 1972; R. Haak, "A Study and New Interpretation of *QSR NPS*," *JBL* 101, 1982, 161-67; D. Kidner, *Psalms 73-150: A Commentary on Books III-V of the Psalms*, 1977; H.-J. Kraus, *Psalms 60-150: A Commentary*, 1989; J. L. McKenzie, *Second Isaiah: Introduction,*

Translation, and Notes, 1968; C. R. North, *The Second Isaiah: Introduction, Translation and Commentary to Chapters XL-LV*, 1967; J. W. Rogerson and J. W. McKay, *Psalms 101-150*, 1977; A. van Selms, "CTA 32: A Prophetic Liturgy," *UF* 3, 1971, 235-48; C. Westermann, *Isaiah 40-66: A Commentary*, 1969; idem, *The Living Psalms*, 1989; R. E. O. White, *A Christian Handbook to the Psalms*, 1984; H. W. Wolff, *Anthropology of the Old Testament*, 1973; W. Zimmerli, *Ezekiel 2: A Commmentary on the Book of the Prophet Ezekiel, Chapters 25-48*, Hermeneia, 1983.

Anthony Tomasino/Robin Wakely

7919 (*qōṣer*, shortness; impatience, dejectedness), → # 7918

7920 (*qāṣēr*, short, feeble, impatient, irascible), → # 7918

7921 (*q^eṣāt*, end, far away), → # 7915

7922 (*qar*, cool), → # 7981

7923 (*qōr*, cold), → # 7981

7924	קרא

קרא (*qr'* I), q. call, invoke, summon, proclaim, appeal to; ni. be called, be proclaimed; pu. be called, be proclaimed (# 7924); מִקְרָא (*miqrā'*), nom. calling, assembly, reading of Scripture (# 5246); קָרִיא (*qārî'*), nom. a called/summoned person, delegate (# 7951); קְרִיאָה(*q^erî'â*), nom. proclamation (hapleg.; # 7952).

ANE With the exception of Eth. the vb. is well attested in all Sem. languages: Ugar. *qr'*, call, invite; Old Aram. *qr'*, call; Phoen. *qr'*, call; Akk. *qerû,* call, invite; Tigre *qar'a*, read (prayers), recite; Arab. *qara'a,* recite, read, announce, proclaim. The BH expression in Deut 20:10 *qr' l^ešālom 'el X* is a formula of vindication that is par. to the Akk. (*ana bīt X šasūm*) and Hitt. (*parnaššea šuwaizzi*) expressions (cf. Otto, 94-96).

OT 1. The basic meaning of *qr'* is to draw attention to oneself by the audible use of one's voice in order to establish contact with someone else. The reaction of the called person is normally expressed by the vbs. *'nh*, answer (→ # 6699), and *šm'*, hear (→ # 9048). The vb. *qr'* occurs in only a few cases with an animal as subj. (e.g., Ps 147:9 "[He feeds] the young ravens when they call"). With the exception of 1x in Ps (42:7[8]) and 6x in Prov (1:21, 24; 8:1, 4; 9:3, 15), *qr'* is never used in a figurative or metaphorical sense.

2. Certain special uses of the vb. *qr'* deserve mentioning. In several cases the use of the vb. should be understood as an announcement or proclamation: "Aaron ... announced [*qr' l^e*]: 'Tomorrow there will be a festival to honor the LORD'" (e.g., Exod 32:5; see *THAT* 2:669; Miller, 611-12, for a discussion of the usage of *qr' d^erôr* in Jer 34:8-22 [→ # 2002]; this expression serves as an example of a declared correspondence between sin/crime and judgment/punishment in prophetic literature). Another common use of the vb. is with the meaning to invite. In this case the vb. *šlḥ*, send (→ # 8938), often precedes *qr'*, and the invited person(s) is usually indicated with the acc. or by prepositional constructions with *'el* and *l^e*. *qr'* is also used with the judicial meaning "to summon before a court" (e.g., 1 Sam 22:11; Isa 59:4), or in a military sense, "to call up for military service" (e.g., Judg 8:1; Jer 4:5). In numerous contexts

the vb. *qr'* means read, often, to read audibly/in public. In later Heb. usage the vb. came to be used for reading from Scripture, with the nom. *miqrā'* ("Holy Scriptures") developing from this usage (see section 10 below).

3. One of the theologically important uses of the vb. *qr'* in the OT is with Yahweh as subj. The meaning then is "to call someone to be in service of Yahweh." Numerous examples occur in the prophetic literature. Note the similarity in use between *dbr* and *qr'*. Zimmerli (109-10) describes the usage of *qr'* with Yahweh as subj. in Isa. Numerous obj. occur: the stars (Isa 40:26), human generations (41:4), Abraham (51:2), Israel (41:9; 42:1), Cyrus (45:3), etc. When Yahweh calls persons/objects, he proclaims his sovereignty over them, he takes possession of them in order to use them for special service, and he remains the "primary author" behind their actions. This expression indicates a close relationship between Yahweh and the called person (cf. *THAT* 2:670).

4. The vb. *qr'* is also used to designate "to call unto Yahweh"; 47 of the 89x are found in Psalms. This use, which does not always occur in a cultic context, renders numerous modes of communication with Yahweh, e.g., thanksgiving, praise, lament, to call for help (cf. also *THAT* 2:951-52). With this meaning the vb. is normally used either in a prepositional construction with *lᵉ* or *'el,* or in combination with *šēm* (acc.) or *bᵉšēm yhwh* (see 6b).

5. In the prophetic literature the vb. *qr'* is a technical term for the proclamation of Yahweh's will (e.g., 1 Kgs 13:32; 2 Kgs 23:16, 17; Isa 40:2, 6; 58:1; Jer 2:2; 3:12; 7:2; 11:6; 19:2; 20:8; 49:29; Jon 1:2; 3:2, 4; Zech 1:4, 14, 17). In some cases the vb. used with this meaning also occurs in combination with *šēm yhwh* (to be distinguished from the uses in 6).

6. *qr'* in combination with "on the name of Yahweh" (*bᵉšēm yhwh*).

(a) This combination is often a technical expression of worship of Yahweh (e.g., Gen 4:26; 12:8; 13:4; 21:33; 26:25), but also generally (and not strictly in cultic contexts), an indication of Yahweh worship (e.g., Ps 79:6; Jer 10:25).

(b) When a reply is expected from Yahweh, this expression means "to ask Yahweh's help" (e.g., 1 Kgs 18:24; Zech 13:9) or "to intercede with Yahweh" (e.g., 2 Kgs 5:11; Ps 99:6).

(c) In doxological contexts this expression means "to glorify Yahweh's name" (e.g., Ps 116:17; Isa 12:4).

(d) In isolated cases the expression *qr' bᵉšēm yhwh* is used as a legitimizing formula. Cf. par. expressions with the vbs. *brk*, bless (→ # 1385; e.g., Deut 10:8; 21:5), *qll*, curse (→ # 7837; e.g., 2 Kgs 2:24), and *šb'*, swear (→ # 8678; e.g., Lev 19:12; Deut 6:13; 10:20).

7. *qr'* in combination with *šēm*, name (→ # 9005).

(a) The act of name-giving is usually depicted by one of the following constructions: *qr' šēm* + acc. of the name (e.g., Gen 3:20; 4:25, 26; 5:2, 3, 29, etc.); *qr' šēm lᵉ / 'el* (Gen 2:20; 26:18; Ruth 4:17; Ps 147:4; Isa 65:15); or just *qr' lᵉ / 'el* (Gen 1:5, 8, 10; 2:19; 33:20, etc.). It is commonly observed that the act of bestowing a name on a person or a place is a demonstration of authority over that person or place (cf. von Rad, *Genesis,* 1972, 83). In reaction to Trible's argument that the naming of the woman in Gen 2:23 is not, in fact, an example of naming and that the v. may not, therefore, be used to support a view of male supremacy, Ramsey (24-35) studied the name-giving constructions with *qr'*. His conclusion is: "Taken all together, the evidence indicates that, instead of thinking of name-giving as a *determiner* of an entity's essence, the Hebrews regarded naming as commonly *determined by* circumstances. The naming *results from* events which have occurred. This is a generalization which is based on the actual naming passages of the OT. The OT narratives report that circumstances frequently influence the way people name individuals and places, but it is very difficult to identify a passage where the narrator suggests that the name given is intended to shape the character of the recipient" (34). He, therefore, asserts that Gen 2:23 is, in fact, an act of name-giving, but here it is an act of discernment, rather than an act of domination.

(b) The technical construction *qr'* (ni.) *šēm 'al* is used to indicate the judicial right of possession; e.g., when property is transferred from one party to another, the name of the new owner is called over the property (cf. 2 Sam 12:28; Isa 4:1). In cases where the name of Yahweh is called out over Israel, the temple, etc. (e.g., Deut 28:10; 2 Sam 6:2; Jer 15:16; 32:34; Dan 9:18, 19; Amos 9:12), it is suggested that Yahweh has authority over these people/objects.

(c) To mention a person's name after his/her death (e.g., Gen 48:16; Ruth 4:14) means that this particular person lives on (with the occasional nuance of "being famous"). When someone's name is not mentioned after his/her death (e.g., Isa 14:20), that person's identity fades into oblivion.

8. *miqrā'* is normally understood as "the assembly of Israelite people" (e.g., Exod 12:16; Lev 23:2, 4, 7, 27, 35). However, both Kutsch (247-53) and Katz (253-55) argue that *miqrā'* should not be understood as a festive gathering, but rather as holiday or festal season. The development of the semantic value of the nom. more or less took place as follows: (a) originally *miqrā'* denoted the call (nom.); (b) from the meaning of *qr'*, to call together, to assemble, developed the nuance of *miqrā'* as assembly/calling together of people; (c) from the meaning of *qr'*, proclaim, developed the nuance of *miqrā'* as proclamation (of a day of festivity), or even, feast; (d) from the meaning of *qr'*, read, developed the nuance of *miqrā'* as "reading." In later BH and postbiblical Heb. *miqrā'* came to be understood as "Scripture reading," or even "Scripture" itself (Neh 8:8).

9. *qārî'*, which occurs only in Num, always designates a person acting as delegate of the Israelite community (cf. Num 1:16; 16:2; 26:9).

10. *q^{e}rî'â*, a hapleg. (Jon 3:2) means "message/proclamation of Yahweh." The LXX translates it with *kērygma*.

P-B In the Qumran texts the vb. *qr'* (20x) is used similarly to the OT usage. In several instances the Tgs. translate the OT idiom *qr' 'el* as *šly qdm* ("pray before"). Cf., for example, Deut 4:7 and Tg. Jon. Judg 1:28; 15:18; 1 Sam 12:17; 1 Kgs 8:52; 2 Kgs 20:11; Jer 11:14. The OT vb. *qr'*, used with the name of God, without an intervening particle, indicates prayer and is translated in the Tgs. as *šly qdm* (cf., for example, 2 Sam 22:4, 7; Ps 18:3, 6[4, 7]). The vb. on its own, and without explicit mention of the name of God, can also refer to prayer. In such cases it can be rendered in the Tgs. by *šly qdm* (cf. for example, Ps 34:6[7]; Isa 58:9; 65:24; Zech 7:13) (cf. Maher, 239-42). In the LXX the vb. *qr'* is mostly translated with *kaleō*, but occasionally also with *boaō*, *kērussō*, and *anaginōskō*. See also the NT usage of *kaleô* as an act of name-giving (cf. Louw and Nida, 33.131).

Calling, proclamation, summons: → *z'q* (call for help, call to arms, assemble, utter a plaintive cry, # 2410); → *ṣrḥ* (yell, call shrilly, raise the war-cry, # 7658); → *qr'* I (call, invoke, summon, proclaim, # 7924)

Bibliography

THAT 2:666-74, 951-53; C. Cohen, "The Idiom *qr' bšm* in Second Isaiah," *JANESCU*, 1968, 32-34; P. Katz, "'Mikra' in der griechischen und lateinischen Bibel," *ZAW* 65, 1953, 253-55; E. Kutsch, "Mikra," *ZAW* 65, 1953, 247-53; C. J. Labuschagne, "Pentateuchal Patterns: A Reply to P. R. Davies and D. M. Gunn," *VT* 34/4, 1984, 407-13; J. P. Louw and E. A. Nida, *Greek-English Lexicon of the New Testament based on Semantic Domains,* 1988, 33.129, 33.131, 33.307, 33.312, 33.315; M. Maher, "The Meturgemanim and Prayer," *JJS* 41, 1990, 226-46; P. D. Miller, "Sin and Judgment in Jeremiah 34:17-19," *JBL* 103, 1984, 611-23; E. Otto, "Die keilschriftlichen Parallelen der Vindikationsformel in Dtn 20,10," *ZAW* 102, 1990, 94-96; G. W. Ramsey, "Is Name-Giving an Act of Domination in Genesis 2:23 and Elsewhere?" *CBQ* 50, 1988, 24-35; W. Zimmerli, "Jahwes Wort bei Deuterojesaja," *VT* 32, 1982, 104-24.

Louis Jonker

7925	קרא

קרא (*qr'* II), q. happen, come to s.o. (# 7925).

ANE This root is not widely attested: Jewish-Aram. *qr'*, happen, do accidentally; Syr. *q^erā'* II, meet, encounter; Mand. *qra* II, meet, encounter; Arab. *qara'a*, gather, bring together. The infinitival form occurs in the Siloam inscription, "crew pressing toward (*lqr't*) crew" (4th line; cf. Sasson, 111).

OT The verbal roots *qr'* II and *qrh* (→ # 7936) constitute close synonyms (a close relationship between final *he* and final *aleph* root occurs with several other verbal pairs [GKC, 216-17, §5rr]). Although several theological wordbooks treat them under one heading (e.g., *THAT*, *TWAT*, and *TWOT*), they receive separate consideration here. As with *qrh*, *qr'* II can signify accidental or intentional happenings in everyday life or in the context of covenantal relationship.

1. *Description of the general happenings of life.* Ten of the sixteen occurrences of the finite vb. connote events experienced by people, sometimes coincidental (from a human perspective) and others intentional. Jacob worried that harm might happen to Benjamin during an anticipated trip to Egypt (Gen 42:4, 38; cf. *qrh* in 44:29). *qr'* II also signifies chance encounters (Deut 22:6; 2 Sam 1:6; 18:9; 20:1) or describes the potential of war happening (Exod 1:10), the experience of personal tragedy (divine judgment, Lev 10:19), or emotions occasioned by an ominous dream (Job 4:14).

2. *Divine-human encounter.* As part of his request that Pharaoh release the Israelite men for a brief trip to worship Yahweh, Moses mentions that Yahweh "met" with them (cf. treatment of Exod 3:18 under # 7936, where Yahweh instructs Moses to say this, but with *qrh*).

3. *Manifestations of divine sovereignty.* Before his death, Jacob provides for his sons a glimpse of God's future dealings with them (Gen 49:1). Moses anticipates (Deut 31:29) and the prophets seek to direct Israel's attention toward their experience of divine judgment (Isa 51:19; Jer 13:22; 44:23). Jer 32:23, the only hi. occurrence of *qr'* II, places emphasis on divine causation.

4. *A "frozen" inf. form.* The construction *liqra't* occurs 121x, most often with various vbs. of motion (see *HALAT* 1056), but also in nom. clauses. It can mean to

meet on friendly terms (Gen 18:2; Judg 4:18), for political benefit (Josh 9:11; 2 Sam 19:15[16]; 2 Kgs 10:15; 16:10), to assist (Ps 59:4[5]) or, most often, to engage the enemy in warfare (Num 21:23; Josh 8:14; 11:20; Judg 7:24; 20:31; 1 Sam 4:1-2; et al.). It can also function as the preposition "against" (Gen 15:10; Exod 14:27; Judg 14:5; 1 Sam 17:21; 2 Sam 10:9; Ps 35:3) or "toward" (1 Sam 9:14; 25:20). One of its most debated instances is in the expression, "Prepare to meet your God" (Amos 4:12). Drawing on imagery from Exod 19:11-17, Amos announces to Israel that they will have a face to face confrontation with Yahweh (see Smith, 133-36, 146-67, for a helpful overview of views with regard to this phrase).

Happening, meeting, attack: → *'nh* III (happen, # 628); → *hwh* II (become, # 2093); → *hyh* (be, become, happen, # 2118); → *y'd* (appoint, appear, come, meet, # 3585); → *ng'* (touch, hurt, # 5595); → *pg'* (encounter, attack, # 7003); → *pgš* (meet, # 7008); → *qdm* (be before, meet, confront, # 7709); → *qr'* II (happen, # 7925); → *qrh* I (happen, build, odain, direct, select, # 7936)

BIBLIOGRAPHY

THAT 2:681-84; *TWAT* 7:172-75; *TWOT* 2:811; V. Sasson, "The Siloam Tunnel Inscription," *PEQ* 114, 1982, 111-17; G. Smith, *Amos*, 1989.

Michael A. Grisanti

7926	קֹרֵא

קֹרֵא (*qōrē'* I), partridge (# 7926).

ANE No clear cognate is found in other Sem. languages.

OT In the OT this word appears in 1 Sam 26:20 and Jer 17:11. For Jer 17:11a, two divergent views have been advanced. The problem revolves around the meaning of *dgr* (→ # 1842) and *yld*, give birth (→ # 3528), but partly about the habit of the partridge. The majority view (W. McKane) is reflected in the translation, "Like a partridge hatching what she did not lay" (JPSV). A minority view (recently Sawyer) is to translate something like, "The partridge broods on its eggs, but hatches none." The former describes the treacherous nature of the partridge, whereas the latter describes its vulnerability. Though some arguments are advanced against the former view, the parallelistic balance with the second half seems to require that *w^e lō' yālad* should be circumstantial to the preceding. Thus, the verse could be translated: "The partridge hatches an egg, while she does not lay them."

P-B LXX renders *qōre'* in Jer 17:11 as *perdix* but the same term in 1 Sam 26:20 by *nyktikorax*. The former G term *perdix* occurs in Sir 11:30 as a bird having an evil intention. As Mish. Heb. it is also attested in Mish. Ḥullin 12:2, where it is presumed that the partridge hatches an egg which she has not laid.

Birds, flying creatures: → *'br* (fly, # 87); → *bêṣâ* (egg, # 1070); → *barbur* (species of fowl, # 1350); → *gôzāl* (young bird, # 1578); → *dgr* (hatch eggs, # 1842); → *ḥ^a sîdâ* (stork, # 2884); → *yônâ* I (dove, # 3433); → *ya^a nâ* (ostrich, eagle-owl?, # 3613); → *kānāp* (wing, skirt, outermost edge, # 4053); → *nešer/n^e šar* (vulture [eagle], # 5979); → *'ôp* (flying creatures, # 6416); → *'ayiṭ* (birds of prey [collective], # 6514); → *'ōrēb* I (raven, # 6854); → *ṣippôr* I (birds, # 7606); → *qōrē'* I (partridge, # 7926); → *ś^e lāw* (quails, # 8513)

Bibliography
EMiqr 7:215-16; W. McKane, *Jeremiah,* 1986; J. A. Thompson, *The Book of Jeremiah,* NICOT, 1980.

N. Kiuchi

7928	קרב

קרב (*qrb*), q. come near, approach, draw near; ni. be brought near; pi. cause to approach, bring near; hi. bring near, present, offer (# 7928); קָרֵב (*qārēb*), adj. approaching (# 7929); קִרְבָה (*qir^e bâ*), approaching (# 7932); קָרְבָּן (*qorbān*), nom. offering (→ # 7933); קֻרְבָּן (*qurbān*), offering (# 7934); קָרוֹב (*qārôb* I), near, imminent (# 7940); קָרוֹב (*qārôb* II), warlike, warrior (only in Ezek 23:5, 12; # 7940).

ANE This root is attested throughout the range of Sem. languages and is used commonly in northwest Sem. (*DISO*, 264-65) and Akk. (*AHw*, 915-17) with meanings similar to Heb.

OT 1. The motion inherent in this root involves being near or in close proximity to an object and is a bit more restricted than the broader *bw'*. The numerous q. occurrences entail physical movement, as when Moses drew near the camp (NIV's approached, Exod 32:19). Moving into close proximity may be a prelude for a second action, so that one draws near in preparation for hearing (*šm'*, Deut 5:27; Isa 34:1). Often that which approaches is a unit of time ("days," "years," or "times"), and in this sense *qrb* emphasizes the imminence of some important event (1 Kgs 2:1; Ezek 12:23). The q. may refer to sexual relations (Lev 18:14).

As with *bw',* the hi. of *qrb* is a so-called "two-place Hiphil," meaning it has both a subject and an object (see *bw'*, # 995). Typically, the subject is simply causing the object to draw near, so that the hi.'s meanings are closely related to the q. Occasionally, *qrb* may also be a "one-place Hiphil," in which the subject and object are the same, so that the double-status subject causes itself to be near: "As Pharaoh approached, the Israelites looked up" (Exod 14:10, and see Waltke-O'Connor, *IBHS* 439-41). The ni. occurs twice as the simple pass. of the q., and the pi. occurs 7x, usually with a causal-factitive meaning (Isa 46:13).

2. As with *bw', qrb* has special theological significance when God draws near to humans. The psalmist longs for Yahweh to "come near and rescue" him (Ps 69:18[19]). God's approaching can be for judgment (Mal 3:5) or for comfort (Lam 3:57), depending on the circumstances at his arrival.

3. As with *bw',* humans may approach (*qrb*) God. Drawing near to God is the privilege of the priests who serve him (Lev 9:7), and the hi. is common in Leviticus for bringing offerings to the tabernacle. At Korah's rebellion, Moses wondered why Korah would abuse his Levitical privilege, since God had brought him near himself "to do the work at the LORD's tabernacle" (Num 16:9-10).

Beyond the cultic contexts, approaching God can have metaphorical implications. The poetic parallelism of Zeph 3:2 makes it clear that drawing near to God is synonymous with trusting him.

4. The adj. *qārôb* is a common designation for close, spatial proximity. Houses may be near each other (Exod 12:4), as may cities, such as Sodom and Zoar

(Gen 19:20). In some cases, the nearness may actually be physical contact with the object. Naboth's vineyard was contiguous to Ahab's summer palace (1 Kgs 21:2).

This adj. is also used to designate nearness of relationship (Lev 21:3; Ruth 2:20). Thus it is possible for Israel to be called a people close to God (Ps 148:14). Yahweh is the God who is near whenever his people call to him (Deut 4:7; Ps 34:18[19]; 145:18). Isaiah used this as motivation for seeking God, implying that he would not always be near those who refuse to call on him: "Seek the LORD while he may be found, call on him while he is near" (Isa 55:6). Likewise, Yahweh's word is near his people, in their mouths and in their hearts (Deut 30:14).

The adj. is frequently coupled with its semantic antonym *rāḥôq* (distant, far) in typical Sem. merism, "near and far," to indicate inclusion of all the items of a series (Jer 25:26). Ezekiel includes all Israel in his prophecy that pestilence will strike those far away and the sword those nearby, "and he that survives...will die of famine" (Ezek 6:12, and see Daniel's confession of Israel's national guilt, Dan 9:7). Isaiah uses this antonymic pair in issuing his broad summons: "You who are far away, hear what I have done; you who are near, acknowledge my power!" (Isa 33:13).

As the adjective by itself is a useful metaphor for intimate relationship, so this antonymic word pair is full of theological import. The psalmist asks God not to be far from him, because trouble is near (Ps 22:11[12]). Jeremiah complained that Yahweh was always near to the lips of the wicked (on their lips, NIV), but far from their hearts (Jer 12:2, and see the parallel in Isa 29:13, where the synonym *ngš* is used). Jeremiah also used this word pair in emphasizing the transcendence of Yahweh in order to impress his hearers with God's omnipresence and omniscience: "'Am I only a God nearby,' declares the LORD, 'and not a God far away?'" (Jer 23:23) .

The part. *qārēb* may also be used as an adj. and is used several times in cultic contexts. Priests and Levites are given the special responsibility of approaching the tabernacle or temple (Ezek 40:46; 45:4), but no one else was permitted to draw near (Num 1:51).

5. The nom. *qorbān* occurs 79x, all in the cultic settings of Leviticus, Numbers, and Ezekiel. It designates that which is brought to the Lord for dedication, either as a sacrifice (Lev 1:3) or for service in the temple (Num 31:50). This nom. illustrates the principle of sacrificing the best or most desirable to Yahweh. If the *qorbān* is an animal, it must be without blemish (Lev 1:3). If vegetable, it must be of the finest variety (2:1). Furthermore, in order for the offering to be acceptable to Yahweh, it must also be offered in the right manner, both in ritual and attitude (1:9, and the entire unit Lev 1-7). Nehemiah appears to have had his own pronunciation of this nom., which occurs twice as *qurbān* (Neh 10:34[35]; 13:31). See further # 7933.

NT In the NT, the term *qorbān* came to mean anything verbally dedicated to God, but not actually given. Jesus condemned the selfish practice of pronouncing "Corban" (or "dedicated to God") over resources needed by one's parents in order to retain them for personal use (Matt 15:5; Mark 7:11).

Coming, approaching, entering: → *'th* (come, bring, # 910); → *bw'* (go, come, arrive, enter, # 995); → *zrq* II (creep in, # 2451); → *ngš* (draw near, approach, offer, # 5602); → *qrb* (draw near, approach, offer, # 7928)

Sacrifice, Offering: → *'azkārâ* (sign-offering, # 260); → *'iššeh* (offering by fire, # 852); → *'āšām* (guilt offering, # 871); → *zbḥ* (slaughter, sacrifice, # 2284); → *ḥaṭṭā'at* (sin offering,

2633); → *ṭbḥ* (slaughter, # 3180); → *minḥâ* (gift, present, offering, sacrifice, # 4966); → *ma*^{a}*śēr* (tithe, # 5130); → *ndr* (make a vow, # 5623); → *nwp* I (move back and forth, wave, # 5677); → *nsk* I (pour out, be consecrated, libation, # 5818); → *'ōlâ* I (burntoffering, # 6592); → *'*^{a}*rîsâ* (meal/dough offering, # 6881); → *qorbān* (offering, gift, # 7933); → *šḥṭ* I (slaughter, # 8821); → *šelem* (settlement sacrifice, # 8968); → *tāmîd* (regular offering, # 9458); → *t*^{e}*rûmâ* (tribute, contribution, # 9556); → **Aaron: Theology**; → **Offering: Theology**; → **Priests and Levites: Theology**

BIBLIOGRAPHY

TDNT 3:860-66; *THAT* 1:264-69, 674-81; *TWOT* 2:811-13; J. A. Fitzmyer, "More About Elijah Coming First," *JBL* 104, 1985, 295-96; H. Fleddermann, "John and the Coming One (Matt 3:11-12—Luke 3:16-17)," *Society of Biblical Literature: Seminar Papers,* 1984, 377-84; E. Jenni, "'Kommen' im theologischen Sprachgebrauch des AT," *Wort-Gebot-Glaube. W. Eichrodt zum 80.Geburtstag. ATANT* 59, 1970, 251-61; F. Schnutenhaus, "Das Kommen und Erscheinen Gottes im AT," *ZAW* 76, 1964, 1-21; E. A. Speiser, "'Coming' and 'Going' at the City Gate," *BASOR* 144, 1956, 20-23; G. von Rad, "The Origin of the Day of the Yahweh," *JSS* 4, 1959, 97-108.

Bill T. Arnold

7929 (*qārēb*, approaching), → # 7928

7930	קְרָב

קְרָב (*q*^{e}*rāb*), nom. battle (# 7930); < קרב (*qrb*), draw near, approach, offer (→ # 7928).

ANE Akk. attests a word nom. formed from the same verbal root as the Heb. cognate, *taqrubtu*, which means war.

OT 1. The nom. is formed from the verbal root *qrb,* which means to approach. In a military context this approach can be hostile and can result in battle. Its appearance as a near synonymn of *milḥāmâ* confirms the meaning (Job 38:23).

2. The nom. refers to past battles in Ps 78:9, which recounts Ephraim's reluctance to enter the battle, and 55:18[19], which celebrates God's deliverance from battle. In 144:1 the psalmist rejoices in the fact that God gives him skill in battle.

3. The word is used in an eschatological context in Zech 14:3. The prophet sees a future day where God will do battle against the forces of evil that range against God's people.

War, army, battle, fight: → *gdd* II (band together, # 1518); → *ḥmš* (organized for war, # 2821); → *lḥm* I (do battle, fight, # 4309); → *maḥ*^{a}*neh* (camp, encampment, war, # 4722); → *ma*^{a}*rākâ* (battle-line, # 5120); → *ṣb'* (go to war, serve, muster, conscript, # 7371); → *ṣî* (warship, # 7469); → *ṣrḥ* (yell, call shrilly, raise the war-cry, # 7658); → *q*^{e}*rāb* (battle, # 7930); → *rkb* (ride/mount, # 8206); → *rw'* (shout, give war-cry, # 8131); → *šālîš* III (third man in war-chariot, adjutant, # 8957)

Tremper Longman III

7931	קֶרֶב

קֶרֶב (*qereb*), inner organs, body, inner being, mind (# 7931).

ANE Aram., Moab., Ugar. *qrb*, Akk. *qerbu(m)*, Arab. *qur(u)b*. As in Heb., Akk *qerbu(m)* is sometimes used as the heart/mind. See *CAD* 13:227.

OT 1. This word often refers to the inner organs of the human body, including the heart (1 Sam 25:37; Jer 23:9) and stomach (Job 20:14), and to the human psychic center (1 Kgs 3:28; Ps 94:19; Jer 4:14). As the location of the heart (*lēb*), one's inner being is viewed as the seat of the emotions (Ps 39:3[4]; 55:4[5]; 109:22; Isa 16:11; Lam 1:20), thoughts (Ps 36:1[2]; 64:6[7]), and will (Jer 31:33). Though the heart/inner being can contain God-given wisdom (1 Kgs 3:28; Prov 14:33), it is also the source of evil, deceitful, and hostile thoughts (Ps 5:9[10]; 62:4[5]; Prov 26:24; Jer 4:14; 9:8[7]).

2. The inner being (*qereb*) also contains the divinely created breath of physical life (*rûaḥ*) (Zech 12:1). As the location of the human *rûaḥ*, one's inner being is also viewed as the seat of volition and moral character (Isa 19:3; 26:9). For this reason the author of Ps 51, overwhelmed by his sinfulness, begs the Lord to transform his inner being by giving him "a steadfast spirit" (v. 10[12]).

3. In conjunction with the eschatological new covenant, the Lord will write his law on the "minds" (*qereb*) and hearts of his people (i.e., he will transform their moral character) so that they might willingly obey him (Jer 31:33; cf. also Ezek 11:19; 36:26-27).

Body: → *bāśār* (meat, food, flesh, # 1414); → *g^{e}wiyyâ* (body, corpse, # 1581); → *gîd* (sinew, tendon, # 1630); → *gap* II (body, # 1727); → *ḥōb* (bosom, # 2460); → *ḥêq* (lap, chest, # 2668); → *kābēd* II (liver, # 3879); → *kilyâ* (kidney, # 4000); → *l^{e}ḥûm* (entrails?, # 4302); → *mē'eh* (body, bowels, # 5055); → *mipśā'â* (buttocks, # 5156); → *'eṣem* I (bone, skin, body, self, # 6795); → *qereb* (inner organs, # 7931)

BIBLIOGRAPHY

THAT 2:674-81; *TWAT* 7:161-65; W. Eichrodt, *TOT*, 145-46; A. Johnson, *The Vitality of the Individual in the Thought of Ancient Israel*, 1964, 73, n.6; H. W. Wolff, *Anthropology of the Old Testament*, 1981, 63-64.

Robert B. Chisholm

7932 (*qirbâ*, approaching), → # 7928

7933	קָרְבָּן

קָרְבָּן (*qorbān*), nom. offering, gift (# 7933); < קרב (*qrb*), approach, offer (→ # 7928).

ANE The root of this nom. is the common Sem. *qrb*. The vb. *qrb* (# 7928), esp. in the hi. stem, commonly takes *qorbān* as its cognate acc. object. For a full discussion of the vb. as it relates to the presentation of offerings see Bravman, 465-77, who points out that the q. vb. means to be or draw near and the hi. to bring near, present as an offering. According to him a "linguistic taboo" underlies the use of this vb. in the sense that reverence is expressed by the notion that the offering draws near, the person who brings it near being placed in the background.

OT 1. This nom. is used 80x in the OT: 40x in Leviticus, 38x in Numbers, and 2x in Ezekiel. For the latter, see Ezek 20:28 referring to the idolatrous "offerings that provoked me (the Lord) to anger" on the high places, and 40:43 in reference to "the tables (in Ezekiel's future temple that) were for the flesh of the (burnt) offerings." Clearly, the distribution of the term shows its direct and exclusive connection to the sacrificial cult. Elsewhere *minḥâ* (→ # 4966) was the common term for a gift, present, or offering to the Lord (e.g., Gen 4:4-5) and to others (see Gen 32:13[14]), but within the priestly literature *minḥâ* was used almost exclusively for the grain offering (see e.g., Lev 2 and the discussion in Anderson, 27-34, esp. 32).

2. The use of this nom. with its corresponding cognate vb. (see ANE above for the vb.) at the beginning and end of the main offerings section in Lev 1-7 is indicative of its broad application to all the categories of offerings included within the priestly system. Thus, according to 1:2b-3, "When any of you brings (*yaqrîb*) an offering (*qorbān*) to the LORD, bring (*taqrîbû*) as your offering (*qorbān*) an animal from either the herd or the flock. If the offering (*qorbān*) is a burnt offering (*'ōlâ*, # 6592) from the herd, he is to offer (*yaqrîbennû*) a male without defect. He must present (*yaqrîb*) it at the entrance to the Tent of Meeting so that it will be acceptable to the LORD." Similarly, 7:38 seals off this section of the book of Lev as follows: "(These are all the regulations) which the LORD gave Moses on Mount Sinai on the day he commanded the Israelites to bring (*lᵉhaqrîb*) their offerings (*qorbᵉnêhem*) to the LORD, in the Desert of Sinai." The people could bring (the vb.) all sorts of offerings, all of which are referred to in general by the nom. *qorbān* (1:2b), but for any of the various kinds of offerings there were specific regulations.

3. In Lev 2:1a we can see how this term relates to the term that is used elsewhere for gift, present, or offering (i.e., *minḥâ* outside of the priestly materials of the OT): "When someone brings a grain offering (*taqrîb qorban minḥâ*, lit., brings an offering of a grain offering; note that *qorban* has a short *a* and is, therefore, const. to *minḥâ*) to the LORD, his offering (*qorbān*) is to be of fine flour. . . ." The genitive relationship here treats *qorbān* as the larger category that is further defined by the term *minḥâ*.

Thus, *qorbān* is used many times as the general category that includes burnt offerings, grain offerings, peace (fellowship) offerings (Lev 3:1), sin offerings (4:23), and guilt offerings (Num 18:9). The offering(s) of the "sheaf of the first grain you harvest" (Lev 23:10) is also included (v. 14) as well as the "grain offering for jealousy" (Num 5:15), the Passover offering (9:7, 13), the combination of offerings for the successful completion of a Nazirite vow (6:21) and the supplying of the tabernacle (7:3, 10), and the articles of gold contributed as a means of atonement for taking a census (31:50).

4. Any particular animal that fell into the category of clean animals and had been vowed to the Lord was permanently holy—it could not be redeemed (Lev 27:9; contrast v. 11 for unclean animals, cf. Hartley, 481-82 for explanation). Some of them were even most holy, that is, they could only be consumed by the priests themselves in the tabernacle (Num 18:9-10; cf. Lev 10:12-13), not their families with them (for the latter see Lev 10:14-15; Num 18:11; these were only holy [cf. Lev 27:9], not most holy). Still others were "the food for my (i.e., the Lord's) offerings (*qorbān*) made by fire, as an aroma pleasing to me" (Num 28:2b). Such offerings were consumed on the altar itself as the Lord's food (see the remarks on this issue of the food of God in Offerings and Sacrifices: Theology).

Overall, *qorbān* is one of the most important terms for understanding the gift aspect of the nature of offerings and sacrifices in the OT.

P-B 1. The nom. *qorbān* appears nowhere in the Qumran literature, although the hi. vb. is commonly used for the presentation of offerings to the Lord in the Temple Scroll (e.g., "And they shall offer [*qrb*] any cereal offering that is offered with a drink offering"; Yadin 2:88).

2. The LXX virtually always uses G *dōron*, gift, to render Heb. *qorbān*, but either *prospherō*, offer, present, or *prosagō*, bring near, for the rendering of the hi. vb. of the same Heb. root in combination with the nom. With regard to the vb., *prosagō* occurs often in the LXX with *dōron* but infrequently in the NT. *Prospherō*, however, is common in the context of presenting offerings both in the LXX and in the NT, and the corresponding nom. is *prosphora*, offering, sacrifice, gift; act of offering; grain offering (Sir 14:11; 9x in the NT).

In the Apocrypha we find several instances of the latter nom. and vb. combination in suitable usage for our concerns here. For example, in the book of Sirach: (a) Sir 14:11: "My son, treat yourself well, according to your means, and present worthy offerings (*prosphora*) to the Lord" (RSV, Metzger, 146); (b) 34:18: "If one sacrifices (*thysiaṣō*) from what has been wrongfully obtained, the offering (*prosphora*) is blemished; the gifts of the lawless are not acceptable" (RSV, Metzger, 173); (c) 34:19: "The Most High is not pleased with the offerings (*prosphora*) of the ungodly; and he is not propitiated for sins by a multitude of sacrifices (*thysia*)" (RSV, Metzger, 173); (d) 35:1-2: "He who keeps the law makes many offerings (*prosphora*); he who heeds the commandments sacrifices (*thysiazō*) a peace offering. He who returns a kindness offers (*prospherō*) fine flour, and he who gives alms sacrifices (*thysiazō*) a thank offering" (RSV, Metzger, 173); (e) 35:6: "The offering (*prosphora*) of a righteous man anoints the altar, and its pleasing odor rises before the Most High" (RSV, Metzger, 173); and (f) 50:13-14: "all the sons of Aaron in their splendor with the Lord's offering (*prosphora*) in their hands, before the whole congregation of Israel. Finishing the service at the altars, and arranging the offering (*prosphora*) to the Most High, the Almighty" (RSV, Metzger, 195).

3. The usage of the Heb. vb. in the Mish. and Talm. is treated by Bravman (465-77). The nom. is, of course, used multitudes of times. One of the most important concentrations of the term is in tractate *Nedarim* (vows; see NT sec. 2).

NT 1. G *dōron*, gift, the nom. that normally renders Heb. *qorbān* in the LXX, occurs 19x in the NT and sixteen of which refer to sacrificial gifts or offerings to God in terms of: (a) offerings at the Jerusalem temple burnt offering altar (Matt 5:23-24; 8:4; 15:5; 23:18; cf. "gifts and sacrifices" in Heb 5:1; 8:3-4; 9:9), (b) gifts to the temple treasury (Luke 21:1, 4), or (c) gifts offered to God in the OT (Heb 11:4; cf. Gen 4:3-5, Cain and Abel).

2. One of the most important instances of *dōron* is in Mark 7:11-12, where we also find *qorbān* in G transliteration: "... you say that if a man says to his father or mother: 'Whatever help you might otherwise have received from me is Corban' (that is, a gift [*dōron*] devoted to God), then you no longer let him do anything for his father or mother." In the context Jesus rebukes the Pharisees saying: "You have let go of the commands of God and are holding on to the traditions of men.... You have a fine way of setting aside the commands of God in order to observe your own traditions!"

The general background for this is the matter of vowing things to the Lord that, therefore, become holy to the Lord and cannot be consumed by people (see OT sec. 4;

see also esp. Mishnah Nedarim 1-3, Danby, 264-68). The particular tradition in Mark 7:11 does not seem to appear in the Mishnah, but one can see the general pattern in the following: "If a man saw others eating [his] figs and said, 'May they be *Korban* to you!' and they were found to be his father and brothers and others with them, the School of Shammai say: ..." (Nedarim 3:2, Danby, 266).

Offering, sacrifice: → *'azkārâ* (sign-offering, # 260); → *'iššeh* (offering by fire, # 852); → *'āšām* (guilt offering, # 871); → *zbḥ* (slaughter, sacrifice, # 2284); → *ḥaṭṭā'at* (sin offering, # 2633); → *ṭbḥ* (slaughter, # 3180); → *minḥâ* (gift, present, offering, sacrifice, # 4966); → *ma'ᵃśēr* (tithe, # 5130); → *ndr* (make a vow, # 5623); → *nwp* I (move back and forth, wave, # 5677); → *nsk* I (pour out, be consecrated, libation, # 5818); → *'ōlâ* I (burnt offering, # 6592); → *'ᵃrîsâ* (meal/dough offering, # 6881); → *qorbān* (offering, gift, # 7933); → *šḥṭ* I (slaughter, # 8821); → *šelem* (settlement sacrifice, # 8968); → *tāmîd* (regular offering, # 9458); → *tᵉrûmâ* (tribute, contribution, # 9556); → **Aaron: Theology**; → **Offering: Theology**; → **Priests and Levites: Theology**

BIBLIOGRAPHY

G. A. Anderson, *Sacrifices and Offerings in Ancient Israel*, HSM, 41, 1987; M. M. Bravman, *Studies in Semitic Philology*, 1977; H. Danby, *The Mishnah*, 1933; J. E. Hartley, *Leviticus*, WBC, 1992; B. A. Levine, *Leviticus*, The JPS Torah Commentary, 1989; B. M. Metzger (ed.), *The Apocrypha*, 1977; J. Milgrom, *Leviticus 1-16*, AB, 1991; J.-M. de Tarragon, *Le culte à Ugarit*, 1980; Y. Yadin, *The Temple Scroll*, vols. 1-2, 1983.

Richard E. Averbeck

7934 (*qurbān*, offering), → # 7928

7935 קַרְדֹּם	קַרְדֹּם (*qardōm*), nom. axe, adze (# 7935).

ANE In the Baal Cycle the *qardōm* is a weapon in Baal's left hand; the word also appears in his epithet *aliy qrdm,* but perhaps there it means "mighty hero" (Akk. *qarrādu,* Wyatt).

OT 1. *Vocabulary for axe, chisel, and saw.* (a) In biblical literature the *qardōm* as a tool was used on trees (Judg 9:48; 1 Sam 13:20-21; Ps 74:5; Jer 46:22). For a time the Philistines held a monopoly on sharpening this and other agricultural tools.

(b) Other words for "axe" are: גַּרְזֶן (*garzen*), nom. axe, chisel (# 1749); כֵּילַף (*kêlāp*), hatchet (hapleg.; # 3965); כַּשִּׁיל (*kaššîl*), nom. axe, hand axe (hapleg.; # 4172); מַגְזֵרָה (*magzērâ*), nom. axe (hapleg.; # 4477); סְגָר/סָגָר (*sᵉgōr/sāgār*), nom. double axe or javelin (hapleg.; # 6038). Two words for "saw" used in conjunction with "axe" are: מְגֵרָה (*mᵉgērâ*), a stone saw (# 4490), and מַשּׂוֹר (*maśśôr*), nom. saw (hapleg.; # 5373). The tools *garzen, qardōm, kaššîl,* and *maśśôr* are widely attested in Sem. languages.

The *garzen* was used for chopping wood or stone (Deut 19:5; 20:19; 1 Kgs 6:7; Isa 10:15). According to the inscription, it was used by Hezekiah's men to hew out the Siloam Tunnel in the late eighth century BC (cf. 2 Kgs 20:20; 2 Chron 32:30).

The *magzērâ* (2 Sam 12:31 ‖ 1 Chron 20:3 as emended) was a type of axe and used together with the *mᵉgērâ* (2 Sam 12:31 ‖ 1 Chron 20:3; 1 Kgs 7:9), a saw for cutting blocks of limestone, which is relatively soft when first quarried. David put

Ammonites to this kind of labor (2 Sam 12:31), but Solomon conscripted native Israelites (1 Kgs 5:13-18[27-32]). The vb. suggests cutting by saws.

The *kaššîl* may have been a smaller axe; it appears together with the *kêlāp*, hatchet (hapleg.; Ps 74:6; # 3965) as a tool for destroying the temple's interior paneling.

Many conjecture the *s*^{e}*gōr* (Isa 35:3) to be *sāgār* (Akk. *šikru*) and, thus, related to the Scythian double-axe, the *sagaris,* although in 1QM 5:7, 9 it seems to be the metal clasp or socket that joins the blade of a spear to its staff (Yadin, 137-38). This hapleg. appears parallel to the *ḥ*^{a}*nît,* spear, and may be a javelin (NIV). The word could also be construed as a vb. (q. impv. of *sgr,* shut), yielding the translation, "Brandish spear and block the way" (NIV; Ps 35:3, note).

The *maśśôr* is a wood saw (Isa 10:15).

2. *Discussion.* (a) These implements can function as weapons and appear in prophetic oracles of punishment. Although Egypt had known great power, Jeremiah prophesied its flight before Nebuchadnezzar and his Babylonian forces, acting like lumberjacks who would go to work not on trees, but on the soldiers of Pharaoh Neco's army (Jer 46:22). Isaiah condemned the king of Assyria for failing to recognize that he was only a tool in the hand of Yahweh and had no right to attribute his stunning victories boastfully to his own strength and wisdom (Isa 10:15). As judgment, Yahweh would reduce the number of the "trees of his forest" by personally cutting down his "lofty trees" and "forest thickets" (10:18-19, 33-34). While actual tools of destruction were used to chop up the paneling of the temple (Ps 74:5-6), the Assyrian campaign against Judah effectively chopped down the Davidic family tree, the royal dynasty. In contrast to the immense power of Assyria now marked for felling, a "shoot" would sprout from the lone "stump of Jesse," becoming a fruitful "Branch" (Isa 11:1), who would be eminently endowed with the Spirit of Yahweh and equipped to rule the world with righteousness (cf. 4:2; 53:2; Jer 33:15-16; Ezek 17:22; John 1:32-34).

(b) A miracle story about Elisha features a floating axe-head (*habbarzel*, the iron, 2 Kgs 6:5-7), and a dull axe illustrates the need for more strength when skill is lacking (Eccl 10:10).

NT Heb 11:37 mentions being sawed in two as only one of the many ends met by ancient heroes of faith. John the Baptist and Jesus continued the prophetic tradition of using the axe as a metaphor of divine judgment (Matt 3:10 ‖ Luke 3:9; Matt 7:19; Luke 13:6-9).

P-B The nom. *m*^{e}*gērâ* and *massār* occur with the meaning wood saw.

Axe, chisel: → *'ēt* III (plowshare?, axe, # 908); → *garzen* (axe, chisel, # 1749); → *kaššîl* (axe, hand axe, # 4172); → *magzērâ* (axe, # 4477); → *m*^{e}*gērâ* (stone saw, # 4490); → *maśśôr* (saw, # 5373); → *ndḥ* II (wield [with an axe], # 5616); → *s*^{e}*gōr/sāgār* (double axe or javelin, # 6038); → *qardōm* (axe, adze, # 7935)

Bibliography

ISBE 1:373-74; 4:347-48; *TDOT* 2:459-61; *TWAT* 5:253-60; J. H. Charlesworth, ed., *The Old Testament Pseudepigrapha,* 1985, 2:143-76; G. R. Driver, "Hebrew Roots and Words," *WO* 1,

1947/1952, 406-15; N. Wyatt, "A Further Weapon for Baal," *UF* 22, 1990, 459-65; Y. Yadin, *The Scroll of the War of the Sons of Light Against The Sons of Darkness,* 1962, 137-38.

Robert C. Stallman

7936	קרה

קרה (*qrh* I), q. happen; ni. make o.s. available, ordain, happen to be; pi. build w. beams (*qrh* II ? see below); hi. ordain, direct, select (# 7936); מִקְרֶה (*miqreh*), nom. happening, occurrence, fate, fortune (# 5247); קָרֶה (*qāreh*), nom. nocturnal emission (# 7937); קְרִי (*q*ᵉ*rî*), nom. encounter (# 7950).

ANE The vb. is well attested: Ugar. *qry*, meet, present; Arab. *qarā*, receive a person as a guest; Eth. *'aqāraya*, bring, carry; Egypt.-Aram. *qrh*, happen; OSA *qrw*, strive for; Egypt. *qri*, come near. The cognate noms. *qerî* (Mish. Heb. and Jewish Aram. *qaryā'*, Syr. and Arab. *qry*, encounter) and *qāreh* (Syr. *qeryā'*, accident; Arab. *qar'/qur'*, menstruation) are also attested.

OT 1. *Description of the general happenings of life*. Among the 27x *qrh* occurs, several passages describe miscellaneous happenings of life without an explicit indication of causation (see *hyh*, # 2118, for other instances of "happen, come to pass"). This use of *qrh* depicts the events it describes as accidental, i.e., unplanned. Upon the return from a trying time in Egypt, Jacob's twelve sons told him "all that had happened to them" (Gen 42:29). Mordecai (Esth 4:7) and Haman (Esth 6:13) also provide a summary of unexpected events they had encountered.

Jacob expresses concern that his son Benjamin might encounter harm on an upcoming trip to Egypt (Gen 44:29; cf. *qr'* II in 42:4, 38), and Saul assured the witch of Endor that no harm would happen to her (1 Sam 28:10). The Israelites experienced a surprise attack by the Amalekites during the wilderness wanderings (Deut 25:18). After Saul's death an Amalekite claimed that he "just happened" to be on Mount Gilboa when he discovered King Saul (2 Sam 1:6; notice the unique combination of *qr'* II and *qrh* in an inf. abs. + finite vb. construction).

As Ruth sought for a field in which to glean, "she found herself" working in a field belonging to Boaz (Ruth 2:3). Only here and one other passage (Eccl 2:14-15, where the vb. and nom. occur twice) do the vb. *qrh* and its cognate nom. (*miqreh*) occur together to underscore the unexpected or unplanned nature of Ruth's choice (see below for further discussion of *miqreh*). Rather than emphasizing the accidental nature of this event, the expression highlights the lack of human intent. This event happened *to* Ruth, not *because of* her (Hubbard, 141; cf. Hals, 11-12; contra Sasson, 45). In fact, the expression constitutes hyperbolic understatement to stress divine, rather than human, involvement.

The cognate nom. *miqreh* generally means "something that happens," i.e., an event unplanned and unexpected, but not something random. Outside of Ruth 2:3, this nom. occurs twice in 1 Sam and 7x in Eccl (2:14, 15; 3:19[3x]; 9:2, 3). The author of Eccl utilizes all seven instances of *miqreh* to denote the destiny faced by all of humanity (*miqreh 'eḥād*, 2:14; 3:19; 9:2, 3), regardless of their wisdom or morality—death. Once again, however, *miqreh* does not connote that which is purely accidental or a fate that is mysterious. This event, beyond the control of those who experience it, remains part of God's intentions.

According to a Philistine, the route taken by the cart carrying the ark of the covenant would indicate whether their recent experience of affliction was by Yahweh's hand or simply by chance (1 Sam 6:9). Even though this Philistine wondered about the intentional or coincidental nature of their suffering, the surrounding narrative clearly demonstrates Yahweh's superintendence in all these events. Finally, Saul explained David's absence from a ritual meal with the expression, "something must have happened" to David (lit., "it is a happening"; 1 Sam 20:26). Saul appears to allude to a possible act of defilement that prevented David from attending. Another nom. derived from *qrh*, *qāreh*, signifies a nocturnal emission in Deut 23:10[11] (lit., "an event/happening of the night"). A par. passage (Lev 15:16) demonstrates that *qāreh* probably refers euphemistically to a seminal discharge.

2. *Expectation of divine involvement.* Yahweh answers Moses' expression of skepticism in light of the daunting task of providing food for all Israel with the statement, "You will now see whether or not what I say will come true (*qrh*) for you" (Num 11:23). The proof of a true God is whether he can make his affirmations a reality. Isaiah challenges the pagan gods' claim to divinity by means of this very argument. The prophet demonstrates Yahweh's incomparability by emphasizing the fact that Yahweh alone predicts and brings to pass future events (cf. Dan 10:14). To help set apart Yahweh from the various other gods, Isaiah challenges them to predict the future, i.e., to tell what will happen (*qrh*) in the future (Isa 41:22).

3. *Explicit statement of divine intervention in human affairs.* The 3 occurrences of the hi. emphasize causation, whether human or divine. Both Eliezer, in his search for a wife for Abraham (Gen 24:12), and Jacob, in his supposed quest for meat for his father Isaac (Gen 27:20), recognize that God makes it happen or grants success. Yahweh exhorts Moses to make happen or bring into being (*qrh*) the cities of refuge (Num 35:11), emphasizing human causation.

4. *Divine-human encounters.* As grounds for his request that Pharaoh release the men of Israel for a brief trip to worship Yahweh in the wilderness region (Houtman, 376), Moses points out that Yahweh had "met" with them (Exod 3:18, all Israel by means of corporate solidarity with Moses). Moses apparently uses *qrh* rather than the customary *r'h* (→ # 8011) in order to conform with Gentile thinking (in ANE religious practice an encounter with a god was not an assured thing; and cf. Ugar., where *qry* signifies a theophany in *KTU* 1.17.VI:43-44 [*CML*, 110]). When describing Yahweh's appearance to Israelites in the preceding context, Moses uses a ni. form of *r'h*. He seems to use *qrh* to emphasize the sudden and unexpected nature of this divine encounter, explaining to the Pharaoh why no such request had been made earlier (Sarna, 18).

In Numbers 23 *qrh* occurs in an account describing a theophany before a non-Israelite, Balaam (Num 23:3-4, 15-16). The presence of *qrh* in these two pairs of desire-fulfillment statements ("Perhaps the LORD will come to meet with me ... God met with him ... Stay here while I meet with him ... The LORD met with Balaam....") stresses the element of chance. Balaam was unable to coerce Yahweh's appearance; rather, Yahweh allowed himself to be encountered (Milgrom, 198).

5. *An expression of covenant rebellion.* Another cognate nom., $q^e r\hat{i}$, occurs 7x in the idiomatic expression "be/remain hostile toward..." (*hlk 'im [*b^e*]* $q^e r\hat{i}$, lit., "walk with/away from me in hostility," Lev 26:21, 23, 24, 27, 28, 40, 41). As with Deut 28,

Moses presents Israel with a choice: blessing for covenant fidelity or cursing for covenant rebellion. The phrase "if you follow (*hlk*) my decrees" introduces the blessing for obedience section (Lev 26:3-13). As part of the covenant blessing, Yahweh promises that he will walk (*hlk*) among them and be their God (v. 12). Four of the seven instances of *q*^{e}*rî* (26:21, 23, 27, 40) depict the arrogance of Israel's covenant treachery: "if you defy me"/"if you walk obstinately"/"if you remain hostile" (Levine [186] derives *q*^{e}*rî* from the Heb. root *qrr* II, "be cold," consequently, "walk with coldness"). The three remaining occurrences (26:24, 28, 41) describe Yahweh's appropriate reaction, i.e., he will oppose them. Just as the promise of his presence constitutes the epitome of covenant blessing, his withdrawl from their midst and his intention to severely judge them denotes the climax of covenant cursing.

6. *A demonstrative verb*. Derived from the nom. *qôrâ*, beams, the vb. *qrh* (II) appears 5x (*HALAT* lists this vb. as *qrh* II, while KB and several theological wordbooks [*THAT*, *TWAT*, and *TWOT*] discuss it under *qrh* I). This root means "to build with beams" and occurs with reference to the refurbishing of the temple in the time of King Josiah (2 Chron 34:11), the rebuilding of Jerusalem's walls under Nehemiah (Neh 2:8; 3:3, 6), and Yahweh's erection of his heavenly palace (Ps 104:3).

Happening, meeting, attack: → *'nh* III (happen, # 628); → *hwh* II (become, # 2093); → *hyh* (be, become, happen, # 2118); → *y'd* (appoint, appear, come, meet, # 3585); → *ng'* (touch, hurt, # 5595); → *pg'* (encounter, attack, # 7003); → *pgš* (meet, # 7008); → *qdm* (be before, meet, confront, # 7709); → *qr'* II (happen, # 7925); → *qrh* I (happen, build, odain, direct, select, # 7936)

Bibliography

THAT 2:681-84; *TWAT* 7:172-75; *TWOT* 1:813-15; R. Hals, *The Theology of the Book of Ruth*, 1969; C. Houtman, *Exodus*, 1993; R. Hubbard, *The Book of Ruth*, 1988; B. Levine, *Leviticus*, 1989; J. Milgrom, *Numbers*, 1990; N. Sarna, *Exodus*, 1991; J. Sasson, *Ruth*, 1989.

Michael A. Grisanti

7937 (*qāreh*, nocturnal emission), → # 7936

7938 (*qārâ*, cold), → # 7981

7940 (*qārôb* I, near, imminent; *qārôb* II, warlike, warrior), → # 7928

7941 (*qārût*, cold), → # 7981

7942 קרח

קרח (*qrḥ*) q. shave bald; ni., hi. shave o.s. bald; ho. shaved bald (# 7942); nom. קֵרֵחַ (*qērēaḥ*), bald head (# 7944); nom. קָרְחָה (*qorḥâ*), baldness (# 7947); nom. קָרַחַת (*qāraḥat*), bald head (# 7949).

ANE The root has cognates in Aram., Arab., and Eth., where the meaning is essentially the same.

OT 1. As a vb., *qrḥ* appears only 5x (Mic 1:16 in the q. impv., Lev 21:5 in the q. impf., Jer 16:6 in the ni. impf., Ezek 27:31 in the hi. perf., and 29:18 in the ho. part.). In Micah, Jeremiah, and the first of the Ezekiel passages, making oneself bald is in a context of mourning. The Leviticus passage forbids priests to shave their heads, perhaps as a symbol of mourning, though this is not made explicit. Ezek 29:18 seems to be describing baldness caused by the constant wearing of war helmets. The parallel is "every shoulder made raw" (→ *mrṭ*).

2. The fem. nom. *qorḥâ*, baldness, occurs 11x, mostly in the prophets. In Lev 21:5 it is a cognate accusative of the vb. *qrḥ* (see # 1 above): lit., "They (the priests) must not make bald any baldness on their heads . . ." Despite the prohibition in Deut 14:1 about shaving the head in mourning, God in Isa 22:12 called Jerusalem to mourning by baldness and the wearing of sackcloth. Jeremiah's two uses of this nom. are in his oracles against Philistia and Moab respectively (Jer 47:5; 48:37). Ezekiel used the language of baldness in his lament over Tyre (Ezek 27:31) as well as in his apocalyptic description of doomed Jerusalem (7:18). Amos' oracle against the northern kingdom of Israel is similar with its references to head shaving, sackcloth wearing, weeping, and mourning (Amos 8:10).

3. The second form of the fem. nom., *qāraḥat*, appears exclusively in Lev 13:42 (2x), 43, and 55. Lev 13:40-44 deals with infectious skin diseases that break out on bald heads (*qāraḥat*) or foreheads (*gabbaḥat*, → # 1478). Persons so afflicted were to cry out, "Unclean! Unclean!" Verse 55 is in a pericope dealing with mildew in garments. Again both synonyms appear, but translations vary widely in their efforts to render this awkward expression. KJV has "bare within or without." RSV has "on the back or on the front." NIV has "one side or the other." JB has "through and through." NEB has "the right side or the wrong." NASB remained with the "bald head-bald forehead" idea of the other passages: "bareness on the top or on the front of it."

4. *qērēaḥ* occurs twice in the OT, once in Lev 13:40 (see preceding paragraph) and once in the well-known 2 Kings 2:23. There forty-two youths taunted Elisha the prophet, who had just seen Elijah carried off in a chariot of fire, with the words twice repeated, "Go on up, baldhead!" Some say that Elisha's retaliation (two bears attacked the boys) was due to the phrase, "go on up," rather than the "baldhead" taunt. The youths were either urging him to leave their city of Bethel to go to Samaria, or they were wishing he would disappear as Elijah had just done so spectacularly.

Baldness, shaving: → *gibbēaḥ* (bald in forehead, # 1477); → *mlṭ* II (be bald, # 4881); → *mrṭ* (pull out hair, hairless, # 5307); → *qrḥ* (shave bald, # 7942)

BIBLIOGRAPHY

TWOT 2:815.

Robert L. Alden

7943	קֶרַח

קֶרַח (*qeraḥ*), frost, ice, crystal (# 7943).

ANE Akk. attests *qarḫu*, ice (*CAD* 13:131); cf. Aram. *qarḥā'*, ice.

OT This word is used in passages in which exposure to temperature extremes is in view (e.g., frost, *qeraḥ*, and heat, *ḥōreb*). In Gen 31:40 Jacob describes the conditions under which he had labored in caring for Laban's flocks. In Jer 36:30 Jeremiah indicates how, after Jehoiakim's unlamented death, his unburied body will be left exposed to the elements.

2. *qeraḥ* is also used with the signification "ice" in Job 6:16; 37:10; 38:29; Ps 147:17 (in this last passage NIV translates "hail").

3. *qeraḥ* (understood by some to mean "crystal," in this case) is used as an object of comparison in describing the appearance of the platform of the throne of God, which is over the cherubim in Ezek 1:22. It is a means of representing the fact that Ezekiel sees the glory of God from a human perspective on earth. God reigns in heaven, while working through the cherubim to do his will on earth. Note here Exod 24:10, in which God is described as having under his feet "something like a pavement made of sapphire, clear as the sky itself.

NT In Rev 4:6 the throne of God has before it "what looked like a sea of glass, clear as crystal" (NIV). Here John has been transported to heaven itself and sees the throne of God, not through the platform that separates it from earth, but above it, as represented by the sea of glass.

Snow, frost, ice: → *'elgābîš* (hail or ice crystals, # 453); → *k^{e}pôr* II (frost, hoar-frost, # 4095); → *qippā'ôn* (frost, # 7885); → *qeraḥ* (ice, # 7943); → *šeleg* I (snow, # 8920)

BIBLIOGRAPHY

D. Baly, *The Geography of the Bible*, 50-52.

Hermann J. Austel

7944 (*qērēaḥ*, bald head), → # 7942

7946 (*qōraḥ*, Korah), → Korah

7947 (*qorḥâ*, baldness), → # 7942

7949 (*qāraḥat*, bald head), → # 7942

7950 (*q^{e}rî*, encounter), → # 7936

7951 (*qārî'*, called, summoned person, delegate), → # 7924

7952 (*q^{e}rî'â*, proclamation), → # 7924

7953	קִרְיָה

קִרְיָה (*qiryâ*), nom. town, city (# 7953); קֶרֶת (*qeret*), nom. town, city (# 7984).

ANE The nom. *qiryâ* may be derived from *qrh* I, meet (→ # 7936), or from *qîr* I, wall (→ # 7851). The etymology remains problematic (*HALAT* 1065). The nom. is attested in Phoen. *qrt*, town; Aram. *qiryā'*, village; Ugar. *qry*, *qryt*, and *qrt* (a variant of *qryt*), city; and in Arab. *qaryat*, city. Dahood noted that "in Canaanite mythology, Death's subterranean domain is called *qrt*, 'city' (*UT* 51:8:11)."

OT 1. The nom. *qiryâ*, town, city, a synonym of *'îr*, occurs 29x in the OT and is used mainly in poetry and passages in higher literary style. It may refer to towns or cities in general: "Not one town (*qiryâ*) was too strong for us. The LORD our God gave us all of them" (Deut 2:36). "At that time we took all his cities (*'îr*). There was not one of the sixty cities (*qiryâ*) that we did not take from them—the whole region of Argob, Og's kingdom in Bashan" (3:4). It may refer to specific towns, such as (a) Gilead: "Gilead is a city of wicked men (*qiryat pō'alê 'āwen*) [lit., a town of doers of wickedness], stained with footprints of blood" (Hos 6:8); (b) Heshbon: "Fire went out from

Heshbon, a blaze from the city (*qiryâ*) of Sihon" (Num 21:28); (c) Damascus: "Why has the city of renown (*'îr t^ehillâ*) not been abandoned, the town (*qiryâ*) in which I delight?" (Jer 49:25); (d) Jerusalem: "the city (*qiryâ*) of the Great King" (Ps 48:2[3]); "Afterward you will be called the City of Righteousness (*'îr haṣṣedeq*), the Faithful City (*qiryâ ne'^emānâ*)" (Isa 1:26); "Woe to you, Ariel, Ariel, the city (*qiryâ*) where David settled!" (Isa 29:1); a city of tumult and revelry (Isa 22:2; 32:13); "Look upon Zion, the city (*qiryâ*) of our festivals; your eyes will see Jerusalem, a peaceful abode, a tent that will not be moved" (Isa 33:20; see also Lam 2:11; Mic 4:10). In Isa 24-26, the word is used collectively referring to various representative cities, such as a ruined city (lit., city of confusion) (24:10); a fortified town (25:2; cf. Prov 10:15; 18:11, 19); cities of ruthless nations (25:3); and a lofty city (26:5); see also Hab 2:8^b=17^b.

Sometimes the word refers to an indefinite city (Job 39:7; Prov 29:8; Hab 2:12), and at times it refers figuratively to the inhabitants of a city (1 Kgs 1:41, 45; Prov 11:10; Isa 1:21).

2. The word *qeret*, town, city, occurs 5x and is found only in poetry in the OT. It may be a contraction of *qiryâ*, with the same meaning. It is used in reference to Job's city (Job 29:7), of an indefinite city (Prov 8:3; 9:3, 14), and figuratively of the inhabitants of an indefinite city (11:11).

P-B In RL the nom. *qôrâ* is confirmed with the additional meaning "the trunk of a tree." The nom. *qiryâ* occurs in the QL with reference to Jerusalem (1QpHab 12:7).

NT The village Kerioth (*q^eriyyôt*; # 7954) is traditionally associated with Judas Iscariot (*'îš qeriyyôt*, lit., "a man of Kerioth"). Kerioth is a village in the territory of Judah (Josh 15:25); NIV combines Kerioth with the name that follows, Hezron, to form a compound name, Kerioth Hezron, as do NASB and RSV; but the two Heb. words are divided by the disjunctive accent *zaqeph,* which marks the words as separate names, much like an English comma between them would do (cf. AV and NKJV).

City, village, country: → *ḥûṣ* (outside, street, # 2575); → *ḥāṣēr* (enclosure, court, settlement, village, # 2958); → *kāpār* (village, # 4107); → *māqôm* (place, town, site, dwelling place, holy place, # 5226); → *miqlāṭ* (city of refuge, asylum, # 5236); → *'îr* I (city, town, # 6551); → *p^erāzôn* (fertile field, # 7251); → *qiryâ* (town, city, # 7953); → *r^eḥōb* I (broad open place, plaza, # 8148); → *šûq* (street [in a town], # 8798)

Bibliography

TWOT 2:814-15; M. Dahood, *Psalms II*, AB, 194.

James D. Price

7965 (*qrm*, cover), → # 4059

7966 קרן

קרן (*qrn*), q. send out rays, be radiant; hi. have horns (Ps 69:31[32]) (# 7966); קֶרֶן (*qeren*), nom. horn (→ # 7967).

ANE The nom. is well known throughout ANE as Akk. *qarnu*, Aram., Syr. *qarnā'*, Arab., Eth., Phoen., *qrn*, all meaning horn. The vb. remains unparalleled.

OT *qrn* describes the condition of Moses' face after meeting with God (Exod 34:29, 30, 35). The nom. *qeren,* horn, is also applied to God's hand (Hab 3:4). Though medieval and modern interpreters have taken this as a reference to actual horns (cf. Michaelangelo's portrayal of Moses), it probably describes an impression of rays of light caused by God's reflected glory.

Light, radiance, brightness: → *'wr* (be light, bright, shine, # 239); → *bāhîr* (bright, brilliant, # 986); → *zrḥ* I (rise [of sun], shine, # 2436); → *yp'* I (shine out, # 3649); → *ngh* (shine, cause to shine, # 5585); → *nhr* II (be radiant, # 5642); → *qrn* (send out rays, be radiant, # 7966)

BIBLIOGRAPHY

TWOT 2:815-16; R. W. L. Moberly, *At the Mountain of God*, JSOTSup 22, 1983, 108-9; J. M. Sasson, "Bovine Symbolism in the Exodus Narrative," *VT* 18, 1968, 385-87.

Martin J. Selman

7967 קֶרֶן

קֶרֶן (*qeren*), nom. horn (of animal; altar); hill? (Isa 5:1); often used fig., esp. in Psalms, as a symbol of strength (# 7967; Bib. Aram. # 10641); > קרן (*qrn*), q. send out rays, shine (Exod 34:29, 30, 35); hi. have horns (Ps 69:31[32]) (# 7966).

ANE The nom. *qeren*, horn, has cognates in Akk., Ugar., Phoen., Aram., Syr., Arab., and Eth. For discussion of Ugar. *b'l qrnm wḏnb*, cf. *UF* 7, 1975, 109-10, 113; cf. further G *keras*; Lat. *cornu*, apparent Indo-Germanic cognates. There are no known cognates to the denominative vb. *qrn*.

OT 1. The nom. *qeren* occurs 90x in the OT (including 14x in Bib. Aram.), with all usage ultimately flowing from the basic meaning of horn (i.e., of an animal); cf. Gen 22:13; Deut 33:17. Such horns could be used as musical instruments (Josh 6:5; cf. Dan 3:5, 7, 10, 15) or flasks (1 Sam 16:13; 1 Kgs 1:39), while the forceful image of an animal goring with its horns was adapted prophetically (cf. 1 Kgs 22:11 ‖ 2 Chron 18:10; cf. Mic 4:13; Ezek 34:21 [with ref. to the faithless shepherds]). Although certain animal horns were widely believed to have special magical and medicinal powers (cf. *TWAT* 7:182-83, and note to this day the Asian market for rhino horns), there is no hint of this in the OT usage.

(a) The nom. *qeren* occurs most frequently in the context of the horn-like protrusions of the altar (see Exod 27:2; 38:2; Ps 118:27), a self-evident meaning now confirmed by archaeology (cf. *BA* 37, 1974, 2-6); cf. also the biting sarcasm of Jer 17:1, with reference to the horns of the illicit altars. In cultic ritual, the blood was often applied to the horns of the altar (e.g., Lev 4:7), and it was to these altar horns that Adonijah and Joab clung, having incurred the wrath of David and Solomon (1 Kgs 1:50-51; 2:28). However, while clinging to the altar itself was, in a sense, the ultimate public appeal for mercy, it is not clear that any theological significance should be attached to the fact that these men specifically held on to the *horns* of the altar (cf., however, Keil KD on 1 Kgs 1:50; and note Montgomery and Gehman, 80, who state that the "horns were the most sacred part of the altar"). Rather, they may have clung to the altar's horns simply because they were easily grasped.

(b) There are several important metaphorical images related to *qeren*, associated in particular with the vbs. *rwm*, lift up, exalt, and *gd'*, cut off, cut down, and based on the picture of an animal (esp. the *r^e'ēm*, wild ox; cf. Deut 33:17; Ps 22:21[22]), either with head and horns held high, a symbol of triumph, or with horns cut off, an image of humiliation and defeat. Thus Hannah rejoices, saying, "in the LORD my horn is lifted high" (1 Sam 2:1; *rāmâ qarnî*); indeed, the Lord will "exalt the horn of his anointed" (2:10; *w^e yārēm qeren m^e šîḥô*); cf. similarly Ps 89:17[18], 24[25]; 92:10[11] (*kir'êm*); 112:9. According to P. K. McCarter, 72, "the expression 'exalt the horn' implies a significant elevation in condition involving some kind of visible distinction; in certain instances it refers specifically to the establishment of the lasting distinction of posterity" (note also M. H. Tate on Ps 75:5, 256, and cf. *'aṣmîaḥ qeren* in Ps 132:17; Ezek 29:21; cf. also Ps 148:14; Luke 1:69). The proud, however, are self-exaltant, and the Lord will bring them down. Thus Ps 75:5 warns, "Do not lift your horns against heaven" (*'al-tārîmû qāren*), and 75:10[11] declares, "I will cut off [*'^a gaddēa'*] the horns of all the wicked [cf. Jer 48:25, with ref. to Moab; note also Amos 3:14, with ref. to the horns of the altar], but the horns of the righteous will be lifted up [*t^e rômamnâ*]." Thus the picture presented in Lam 2:3, 17 is colored with bitter irony: In his fierce anger, the Lord "has cut off every horn of Israel" (v. 3), while "he has let the enemy gloat over you, he has exalted the horn of your foes" (v. 17). Cf. also the picture of utter abasement in Job 16:15, where the NIV's "I ... buried my brow in the dust" renders *'ōlaltî be'āpār qarnî.*

(c) In Isa 5:1, *qeren* seems to mean hill or mountain spur (apparently, land that protrudes and is prominent; cf. the LXX's *keras*, and note LSJ), and this may provide the clue to 2 Sam 22:3 ‖ Ps 18:2[3], where the psalmist describes the Lord as *qeren yišî*. While this construct phrase is normally rendered "the horn of my salvation," *qeren* here may mean "mountain" or the like (cf. McCarter's "peak of safety," 452), akin to descriptions of God as *ṣûr*, rock, etc. (note also the overall imagery of the verse, and cf. *ṣûr yiš'î*, 2 Sam 22:47; Ps 95:1; cf. also Tg.'s *ṭûr rām* for *qeren* in Isa 5:1). In any case, a rendering such as the NJPSV 's "my mighty champion," in spite of its imprecision, is to be preferred to the almost universal—but too literal—"horn of my salvation," which fails to translate the meaning of the metaphor (contrast also the NIV and the NJPSV in 1 Sam 2:1); cf. further *TWAT* 7:184, for noteworthy renderings of *qeren* in the LXX and Tg., and see Olofsson.

(d) In prophetic vision, where various animals symbolize different nations, the horns, accordingly, refer to leaders; cf. Dan 7:7-8:21; note also Zech 2:1-4. (Note, however, that such imagery may suggest itself even outside of such symbolic contexts; hence the future Davidic king can be characterized as *qeren*; cf. Ps 132:17, although *qeren* there may simply mean posterity.)

2. Verbal usage of *qrn* is denom., and if, in fact, it does mean shine; be radiant in the much discussed account in Exod 34:29, 30, 35 (the skin of Moses' face shone when he came down from Mount Sinai), then the sense would apparently be to send out rays (cf. # 7966, *qrn*, and see Hab 3:4, "His splendor was like the sunrise; rays [*qarnayim*] flashed from his hand, where his power was hidden"). There was a striking, luminous protrusion from Moses' face (cf. the common rabbinic explanation that refers to *qarnê hahôd*, lit., horns of splendor; see, e.g., Exod. Rab. 47:6). Thus J. I. Durham tentatively suggests that *qrn* was used rather than *hē'îr* "because the narrator intended to suggest a light or a shining that was separate from Moses' own person, an appendage-light, an exterior light, a light that was a gift to Moses from Yahweh, a sign precisely of an authority that was his by virtue of his special fellowship with Yahweh" (467; see ibid., 464, for lit.). Less likely is the suggestion of Propp, that Moses' skin

actually protruded and became disfigured, although his discussion underscores the difficulties involved in determining with precision the significance of the verbal usage. Ps 69:31[32], with the hi., is straightforward, meaning having horns (par. with *maprîs*, having hooves).

P-B The usage of *qeren* in the DSS is consonant with the range of meanings found in the OT; cf. 1 QH 7:22-24; 1 QM 1:4; 5:14. RL expands on some of the OT's important metaphorical and theological imagery of *qeren* (cf., e.g., Gen. Rab. 99:2), also expanding the semantic range to refer to other kinds of projections (e.g., the handle of a staff) or corners; note also the meanings of principal, fullness, and essence in both the Heb. and Aram.

Horn: → *qeren* (horn, # 7967); → *šôpār* (ram's horn, # 8795)

BIBLIOGRAPHY

TWAT 7:181-89 (with lit.); *HALAT* 3:1067-69; 5:1771; J. I. Durham, *Exodus*, WBC, 1987; J. A. Montgomery and H. S. Gehman, *The Books of Kings*, ICC, 1951; P. K. McCarter, Jr., *I Samuel*, AB, 1980; J. Morgenstern, "Moses With the Shining Face," *HUCA* 2, 1925, 1-27; S. Olofsson, *God Is My Rock: A Study of Translation Technique and Theological Exegesis in the Septuagint*, ConBOT 31, 1990; P. A. Porter, *Metaphors and Monsters: A Literary-Critical Study of Daniel 7 and 8*, ConBOT 20, 1982, 64-69; W. H. Prossp, "The Skin of Moses' Face—Transfigured or Disfigured?" *CBQ* 49, 1987, 375-86; M. L. Süring, *Horn-Motif in the Hebrew Bible and Related Ancient Literature and Iconography*, 1982; M. Tate, *Psalms 51-100*, WBC, 1990; M. Tsevat, "*Qāran 'Ôr Pānāyw*," ErIsr 16, 1982, 163-67 (Heb.).

Michael L. Brown

7970	קרס

קרס (*qrs*), q. bend over, cringe (# 7970); קֶרֶס (*qeres*), hook (# 7971).

OT From the word *qeres* used in Exod 26:6, 11, 33; 35:11; 36:13, 18; 39:33 to denote a hook comes the denominative vb. (*qrs*) found in Isa 46:1-2, where it appears in company with *kr'*, apparently meaning to "bend over."

Kneel, bend: → *brk* I (kneel, # 1384); → *kr'* (crouch, squat, # 4156); → *qrs* (bend over, # 7970)

William C. Williams

7971 (*qeres*, hook), → # 4595b, # 7970

7972	קַרְסֹל

קַרְסֹל (*qarsōl*), ankle (# 7972).

ANE Cognates are Syr. *qurṣ^{e}lā* and Akk. *kursinnu* (*CAD* 8:566-67), both of which mean "anklebone."

OT The word appears only in 2 Sam 22:37 (= Ps 18:36[37]), "you broaden the path beneath me, so that my ankles do not turn."

Leg, loins, foot, thigh: → *b^{e}hôn* (thumb, big toe, # 984); → *ḥ^{a}lāṣayim* (loins, # 2743); → *yārēk* (thigh, leg, # 3751); → *kesel* I (loins, flank/side, # 4072); → *midrāk* (foot-print, # 4534); → *marg^{e}lôt* (place of feet, # 5274); → *motnayim* (loins, hips, # 5516); → *na'al* (sandal, # 5837);

→ *paḥad* II (thigh, # 7066); → *pa'am* (foot, step, time, # 7193); → *qarsōl* (ankle, # 7972); → *regel* (foot, # 8079); → *šôq* (thigh, leg, # 8797)

Victor P. Hamilton

7973	קרע

קרע (*qr'*), q. tear up; tear away; enlarge; ni. be torn up (# 7973); קְרָעִים (*qᵉrā'îm*), nom. rags (# 7974).

ANE Cognates exist in Mand. and Arab. (*HALAT* 1069b).

OT 1. Most often (39x) this vb. is used to describe the tearing of garments. This rending of clothes (no particular piece appears to have preference) indicates intense grief and is often an immediate reaction to a disaster. Jacob so responds to news of Joseph's apparent death (q., Gen 37:34; cf. v. 29). In a similar fashion, for example, Joshua responds to defeat in battle (q., Josh 7:6), Job to the death and calamities that befell his house (q., Job 1:20), his friends to Job's miserable condition (q., 2:12), David to news of Saul's death (q., 2 Sam 1:11, cf. v. 2), and Ezra shocked by the mixed marriages (q., Ezra 9:3). Such an action could be accompanied by donning sackcloth (Gen 37:34), putting dust on the head (Josh 7:6; Job 2:12), and fasting (2 Sam 1:12). See De Ward (8-10) on tearing clothes and mourning.

With respect to grief for sin, God is not satisfied with a mere outward sign of sorrow like torn clothes. "Rend [*qr'*] your heart and not your garments" (Joel 2:13). In judgment God will tear open the enclosure of the heart of his people (q., Hos 13:8).

2. The tearing of clothes also occurs in other contexts. The part of a garment that had been contaminated by mildew is to be torn out (q., Lev 13:56) and the uncleanness removed. The prophet Ahijah tore (*qr'*) his new garment into twelve pieces (*qᵉrā'îm*) and so symbolically divided up the kingdom into two parts, because Yahweh was about to tear (*qr'*) the kingdom from Solomon (1 Kgs 11:30-31; cf. vv. 12-13; 1 Sam 15:28; 28:17; 1 Kgs 14:8; 2 Kgs 17:21).

3. Other uses include the graphic prayer for Yahweh's descent from heaven. "Oh that you would rend [*qr'*] the heavens and come down" (Isa 64:1[63:19]).

When something is torn, it separates and so enlarges. Thus *qr'* can mean "to enlarge." Paint and makeup around the eyes is said to enlarge them. "Why shade (enlarge, *qr'*) your eyes with paint?" (Jer 4:30; cf. 22:14; see Holladay, *Jeremiah*, 170, 595).

Tearing, prey: → *gzr* II (cut, slaughter, tear, prey, # 1616); → *ḥth* (take, fetch, # 3149); → *ṭrp* (tear in pieces, # 3271); → *mlḥ* I (be torn in pieces, dissipate, # 4872); → *nsḥ* (tear down, tear away, # 5815); → *ns'* (tear out, # 5825); → *ntṣ* (tear down, # 5997); → *ntq* (tear away, # 5998); → *pšḥ* (pluck, pull, leave fallow, # 7318); → *qwṣ* II (tear apart, # 7763); → *qr'* (tear up, # 7973); → *šs'* (tear, divide, # 9117)

BIBLIOGRAPHY

E. F. De Ward, "Mourning Customs in 1, 2 Samuel," *JJS* 23, 1972, 1-27, 145-66, esp. 8-10.

Cornelis Van Dam

7974 (*qᵉrā'îm*, rags), → # 7973

7975	קרץ

קרץ (*qrṣ*), q. wink; pu. be pinched off (# 7975).

OT The root *qrṣ* occurs in Ps 35:19; Prov 6:13; 10:10, and has the basic meaning "pinch." The contexts support a rendering such as "wink maliciously" (NIV), because it is the wicked or the fool who does this.

Eye, wink: → *'îšôn* (pupil of eye, # 413); → *bābâ* (pupil of eye, # 949); → *'yn* (view with suspicion, # 6523); → *'ap'appayim* (flashing of eye, # 6757); → *qrṣ* (wink, pinch, # 7975); → *rzm* (flash, # 8141); → *t^eballul* (spot in eye, # 9319)

Allan M. Harman

7976 (*qereṣ*, gadfly), → # 6856

7977	קַרְקַע

קַרְקַע (*qarqa'* I), nom. floor, bottom (# 7977).

ANE Akk. *qaqqaru(m)* denotes earth; cf. Arab. *qarqar/qariq*, level ground.

OT 1. The word occurs 6x (*HALAT* 1071) to designate, e.g., the floor/pavement of the tabernacle (Num 5:17) or the floor of Solomon's palace (1 Kgs 7:7). The dust off the floor, mixed with holy water, was used in the ritual of trying a suspected adulteress (NIV; overlaid RSV). The inner/outer rooms of Solomon's temple had floors covered with gold, the favorite metal of the gods in the ANE (1 Kgs 6:15, 16, 30). The under floors of the temple were cedar/pine, suggesting that gold was an overlay. In Amos the term describes the bottom of the sea as a useless place for God's guilty people to hide, for he will find and judge them even there (Amos 9:3). Finally, the nom. is used in Josh 15:3 as a city name (*qarqa'* II).

2. Two other words meaning floor/flooring, clay/mortar occur one time each. The hapleg. nom. *dar* (# 1993) is found only in Esth 1:6, where it probably means mother-of-pearl or costly flooring, further describing *riṣpâ*, the more general term used earlier in the same verse. The hapleg. nom. *meleṭ* (# 4879) means clay/clay flooring or mortar (NJPS) in Jer 43:9, where Jeremiah commands the people in Tahpanhes to imbed large stones in the mortar/clay of the floor/brick structure (*malbēn*) before Pharaoh's palace. Nebuchadnezzar was to be made ruler over these very stones in Egypt at Yahweh's bidding (43:8-11).

Floor, pavement: → *qarqa'* I (inlaid floor, floor(s), bottom, # 7977); → *riṣpâ* (pavement, stone pavement, mosaic pavement, # 8367)

Eugene Carpenter/Michael A. Grisanti

7981	קרר

קרר (*qrr* II), hi. be cold (# 7981); מְקֵרָה (*m^eqērâ*), coolness (# 5249); קֹר (*qōr*), cold (# 7923); קָרָה (*qārâ*), cold (# 7938); adj. קַר (*qar*), cool (# 7922); nom. קָרוּת (*qārût*), cold (conj., Zech 14:6; # 7941).

ANE This root has cognates in the more distantly related languages (Arab., Eth., and Syr.).

OT 1. Noms. from this root designate a low temperature on earth (Gen 8:22, where *ḥōm*, heat, is its antonym). The continuity of the alternating seasons of cool and hot temperatures is a sign of God's faithfulness to keep his promises. Although the text of Jer 18:14 is in question, the adj. appears to modify water. It symbolizes the dependability of God's grace and benevolence to the land of Israel. In contrast to God's action is Israel's unfaithfulness to him. The adj. is used in Prov 25:25 in a simile comparing good news from a distant land to "cold water" for a weary soul.

2. The expression "cool of spirit" (*rûaḥ*, Prov 17:27) appears to indicate an even-tempered, self-composed individual who can control his speech (but Q has a slightly different nuance, "composed spirit"). But, no human can stand before Yahweh's *qārâ* ("icy blast," Ps 147:17, NIV), though they can praise him for his sovereign control of nature in the cold as well as the warm seasons of the year. This nom. may be used in construct state to modify "day" (Prov 25:20) or independently for the abstract "the cold" (Job 24:7). On the strength of ancient versions (LXX, Pesh., Symm., Tg., Vg.), *qārût*, "cold," is restored in the difficult text of Zech 14:6b, where cosmic changes on the Day of the Lord are described when all the temperature extremes will cease (cf. JB, NEB, NIV, and RSV).

3. The verbal root may occur in Jer 6:7, referring to fresh cool water (Holladay, *Jeremiah,* 1:204), but some treat it as a form of *qwr,* to dig (a well), thus the gushing forth of water from a spring is like the gushing forth of wickedness from Jerusalem (*KD* 8:137-38).

4. The "cool chamber" (*m^eqērâ*) of a house is "the inner room" (Judg 3:24).

Cold, cool: → *ṣinnâ* I (coolness, # 7557); → *qrr* II (be cold, # 7981)

Bibliography

R. P. Gordon, "Targumic *'dy* (Zechariah 14:6) and the Not So Common 'Cold,'" *VT* 39, 1989, 77-81.

Bill T. Arnold

7983	קֶרֶשׁ

קֶרֶשׁ (*qereš*), nom. board(s); frame(s); deck (# 7983).

ANE Ugar. *qrš* (the meaning is doubtful; *UT*, # 2283); Akk. *qarāšu qeršu(m)*; Arab. *qarisa* II.

OT This word describes the material used for the supporting framework of the tabernacle. It is used most often to refer to the *qereš/qerāšîm* used to construct the tabernacle in Exod 26:15-19; 35:11; 36:20-34; 40:18; Num 3:36; 4:31. The translation boards is uncertain, but useful. Other suggestions have been: planks, panels, (upright) frames, supports. These boards/frames/supports were overlaid (*ṣph*) with gold (Exod 26:29; 36:34). In the construction of the tabernacle these frames were made (*'śh*), brought to their proper locations (*bw'*), and put in place (*śym*) (Exod 26:15; 39:33; 40:18). It is best translated as deck in Ezek 27:6, which has ivory worked in.

P-B The LXX usually translates using *stylos*, pillar; post; beam; mast (of ship).

Beam, rafter, frame, board: → *k*^e^*rutôt* (beam, # 4164); → *m*^e^*qāreh* (timberwork, roof, # 5248); → *qrh* II (lay the beams, # 7936); → *qereš* (board, frame, # 7983); → *rāhîṭ* (beam, rafter, # 8112)

BIBLIOGRAPHY
B. Childs, *Exodus*, 525; J. Durham, *Exodus*, WBC, 366-67; W. Zimmerli, *Ezekiel*, 627.

Eugene Carpenter

7984 (*qeret*, town, city), → # 7953

7987 (*qaśwâ*, jug, jar, pitcher), → # 3998

7988 קְשִׂיטָה	קְשִׂיטָה(*q*^e^*śîṭâ*), nom. unknown weight (# 7988).

OT The word occurs only in Gen 33:19; Josh 24:32; Job 42:11. For a discussion on weights → *šql,* weigh, weigh out, pay, # 9202.

Jerry E. Shepherd

7990 קַשׁ	קַשׁ (*qaš*), nom. chaff, stubble (# 7990); < קשׁשׁ (*qšš*), po. gather (→ # 8006).

ANE *qaš* is related to Arab. *qaṯṯa*, pull out; Ugar. *qṯṯ*, tear out; and Syr. *qeššᵉtā'*, straw (*HALAT* 1073, 1077).

OT *qaš* refers to chaff as opposed to straw (Exod 5:12; see Dalman, 1:137; Durham, 62) and can be used, therefore, as a metaphor for that which is worthless (Isa 33:11). *qaš* is predominantly used in metaphors pertaining to divine judgment. In some texts the metaphor is chaff driven away by the wind of divine judgment (e.g., Isa 40:24); the wind (*rûaḥ*, → # 8120) driving the chaff is the east wind (Jer 13:24; see Fitzgerald, 248-50), which is itself a frequent image of divine judgment. In other texts the metaphor is chaff consumed by the fire of divine judgment (e.g., Isa 5:24). Chaff driven by the wind and consumed by fire are related metaphors in that the driving east wind is often presented as hyperbolically hot enough to set things ablaze (e.g., Amos 1:14; see Fitzgerald, 253-54). This interface between the metaphors explains a text like Ps 83:13-15, where the psalmist prays for God's enemies to be made like *qaš* driven before the wind (v. 13) and to be consumed by fire (v. 14) set by the east wind (v. 15; see Fitzgerald, 190-93).

Grass, plants: → *dš'* (become green, sprout, # 2012); → *ḥāṣîr* I (grass, # 2945); → *ḥ*^a^*šaš* (dry grass, # 3143); → *yrq* II (be green, # 3762b); → *leqeš* (late grass, # 4381); → *'ēśeb* (green plants, # 6912)
Winnow: → *zrh* I (scatter, winnow, # 2430); → *nāpâ* I (sieve, # 5864); → *raḥat* (winnowing shovel, # 8181)

BIBLIOGRAPHY
G. Dalman, *Arbeit und Sitte*, 1928-42; J. Durham, *Exodus*, WBC, 1987; A. Fitzgerald, "Lord of the East Wind," diss. Pontifical Biblical Institute, 1983.

Mark D. Futato

7992	קשׁב

קשׁב (*qšb*), q. (hapleg.), hi. be attentive, pay attention, listen (# 7992); nom. קֶשֶׁב (*qešeb*), attentiveness (# 7993); adj. קַשָּׁב (*qaššāb*), attentive (# 7994); קַשֻּׁב (*qaššub*), attentive (# 7995).

OT 1. The vb. is found only in Heb. It is primarily used in the impv. as a poetic synonym of *šm'* or *'zn* (hi.), in the sense of listen attentively (see *'zn*; # 263). However, whereas these vbs. invariably denote paying attention to what is heard, the root *qšb* can also denote paying attention to what is seen. In Isa 21:7 the hi. with *qešeb* as nom. obj. is used of the close attention the watchman must give when he sees something ("when he sees chariots... let him be alert, fully alert"). More generally, the phrase *'ēn qešeb* denotes the lack of "response" not only of a lifeless Baal to the shouts of his prophets (1 Kgs 18:29), but also of the lifeless boy to the prodding of Elisha's staff (2 Kgs 4:31). In late passages, the expression "let your ear be attentive" (*qaššāb*, Neh 1:6, 11; *qaššub*, 2 Chron 6:40; Ps 130:2) replaces the impv. in appeals to God to answer prayer (see *šm'*, section 7 [c]).

2. As a synonym of *sm'*, the vb. can also denote giving heed, being obedient (1 Sam 15:22), esp. to God's words (2 Chron 33:10; Jer 6:19) and his commandments (Neh 9:34; Isa 48:18; see *šm'*, section 6). In Jer 6:10 the prophet reflects on Israel's failure to respond to his preaching. Israel is unable to pay heed because their "ears are uncircumcised" (NIV marg.) and God's words are offensive to them (cf. Zech 7:11). God had appointed watchmen to sound a warning, but Israel would not heed the warning (Jer 6:17; see *šm'*, section 6 [b]). In 8:6 God listens attentively but in vain for words of repentance from Israel. By contrast, in Mal 3:16 he listens to the conversation of those who fear him and approves.

P-B At Qumran, the vb. occurs in 6QD 8:41-42 and 4QDibHam 5:21 with reference to Mal 3:16 and Isa 48:18, respectively. In the LXX it is usually trans. *prosechō,* "pay attention."

Hearing, listening, obedience, rumor: → *'zn* I (listen, # 263); → *qšb* (be attentive, # 7992); → *šm'* (hear, listen, understand, heed, obey, # 9048)

BIBLIOGRAPHY
NIDNTT 3:172-80; *THAT* 2:684-89; *TWAT* 7:197-205.

K. T. Aitken

7993 (*qešeb*, attentiveness), → # 7992

7994 (*qaššāb*, attentive), → # 7992

7995 (*qaššub*, attentive), → # 7992

7996	קשׁה

קשׁה (*qšh* I), q. be hard, severe; ni. be hard pressed; pi. have severe labor; hi. make hard, heavy (# 7996); קָשֶׁה (*qāšeh*), adj. hard, cruel, severe, fierce (# 7997); קְשִׁי (*q^e šî*), nom. stubbornness (hapleg.; # 8001).

ANE Syr. *q^e šā'*, be hard; Arab. *qasā,* be hard, cruel.

OT 1. The vb. appears 29x and expresses the basic meaning of to be hard. It occurs in q. (5x), ni (1x), pi. (1x), hi. (21x; with the obj. *'ôrep*, neck, 11x; with the obj. *lēb[āb]*, heart, 3x). The adj. occurs 36x (7x in connection with *'ôrep*, neck; 5x with *'ᵃbōdâ*, work, service, and 6x as a substantival fem. adj., two of which are in pl.).

(a) The vb. is used of Rachel when she had hard labor (Gen 35:16). It is also used of a hard case to judge (Deut 1:17). In 15:18 it is used in the sense of difficulty or hardship: "Do not consider it a hardship to set your servant free." In Isa 8:21 *qšh* is used along with the word *rā'ēb,* hungry, starving (→ # 8279), to describe the severe suffering that Israel would experience under the Assyrian yoke. In Job 30:25 *qāšeh* describes the harsh suffering of the poor.

(b) In a number of passages vb. and adj. describe the harsh and tyrannic oppression of a whole people by a tyrannic oppressor. In this meaning they are frequently used with the words *'ᵃbōdâ*, labor or servitude (→ # 6275), and *'ōl,* yoke (→ # 7537). In Egypt (Exod 1:14; 6:9; Deut 26:6) and under Babylonian tyranny (Isa 14:3) the people of Israel were forced into cruel and oppressive servitude. In the reign of Solomon the native population of Israel had to bear a heavy yoke and do harsh labor on account of Solomon's heavy taxation and conscription to work on royal projects (1 Kgs 12:4; 2 Chron 10:4).

(c) The word *qšh* is used in the sense of stiff-necked (Deut 10:16; 2 Kgs 17:14; 2 Chron 30:8; 36:13; Neh 9:16, 17, 29; Jer 7:26; 17:23; 19:15; Prov 28:14; 29:1). Its use in connection with Pharaoh's heart has been especially noted; e.g., Exod 7:3, "I will harden Pharaoh's heart"; 13:15, "When Pharaoh stubbornly refused to let us go." Scripture says both that God hardened Pharaoh's heart (*qšh*, 7:3; *ḥzq*, 14:4; *kbd*, 10:1) and that Pharaoh hardened his own heart (9:34, 35; 13:15). The word *'mṣ*, be strong (→ # 599), occurs together with *qšh* to express the obstinacy of one's heart (Deut 2:30; 2 Chron 36:13). The Lord described his people to Moses as stiff-necked (Exod 32:9; cf. 33:3, 5; 34:9; Deut 9:6, 13). In Deut 31:27 the Lord says of his people, "I know how rebellious and stiff-necked (*qšh*, # 7997) you are."

2. The adj. *qāšeh* is found 36x. (a) It is used of heavy-handed treatment and heavy work in 1 Kgs 12:4: "Your father put a heavy (*qāšeh*) yoke on us, but now lighten the harsh (*qāšeh*) labor and the heavy yoke he put us us."

(b) It is used of a hard person in 1 Sam 25:3, where Nabal is described as "surly (*qāšeh*) and mean in his dealings."

(c) The term is sometimes used to describe harsh speaking. In Gen 42:7 Joseph spoke harshly to his brothers, and when they reported it to their father (v. 30), they used the same word to describe the manner in which Joseph had spoken to them. In 1 Sam 20:10 David asks Jonathan, "Who will tell me if your father answers you harshly?" It is used of the harsh answer given by King Rehoboam: "The king answered the people harshly (*qāšeh*)" (1 Kgs 12:13).

3. In 1 Sam 1:15 Hannah described herself as "a woman who is deeply troubled (*qšh*)." The unusual use here may refer to her harsh emotional state, her cruel experience. The new translations vary: "deeply troubled" (NRSV), "heart-broken" (REB), "unhappy" (NAB), and "in great trouble" (NJPSV).

4. It can be used of a fierce battle. In a battle between the houses of David and Saul the battle is described as "fierce, and Abner and the men of Israel were defeated by David's men" (2 Sam 2:17).

5. The word can also be used in the sense of bad news, as in 1 Kgs 14:6, when Ahijah tells the wife of Jeroboam that he has bad news for her. The versions render this a variety of ways: "heavy tidings" (NRSV), "heavy news" (REB), and "bitter news" (NAB).

6. It is used in the sense of hard times, when the psalmist says to the Lord, "You have shown your people desperate times" (Ps 60:3), or, as the NAB puts it, "made your people go through hardship."

7. The word is used to describe jealous love in S of Songs 8:6, "love is as strong as death, its jealousy unyielding (*qāšeh*) as the grave." Other versions render: "[its] passion fierce as the grave" (NRSV), "[its] passion cruel as the grave" (REB). The unusual use of the term in this context is complicated by the question of another word, jealousy (*qin'āh*; # 7863). This term can refer to that which is jealous or zealous, to jealousy or zeal (cf. # 7863).

8. In a few instances the adj. describes the fierceness of God's judgment: Yahweh will hand Egypt over to a tyrannic master (*'ªdōnîm qāšeh*) (Isa 19:4); 27:1 states that God will slay the sea monster Leviathan with his fierce sword, *ḥarbô haqqāšâ* (see further 27:8). In this context the meaning of harsh, cruel, fierce is preferred to "hard" sword, which would give a different idea.

9. The word *qᵉšî* is used only in Deut 9:27, where Moses entreats the Lord to "overlook the stubbornness (*qᵉšî*) of this people."

Hard, harsh, difficult, severe: → *'akzār* (cruel, # 425); → *ḥzq* (be strong, seize, # 2616); → *ḥms* I (do violence, # 2803); → *kbd* (be heavy, unresponsive, honored, # 3877); → *perek* (brutal, ruthless, # 7266); → *qšh* I (be hard, severe, be stiff-necked, # 7996); → *qšḥ* (treat harshly, harden, # 7998)

Rebellion, conspiracy, stubbornness, obstinacy: → *ysd* II (conspire together, # 3570); → *kśh* (become stubborn, headstrong, # 4170); → *lāṣôn* (bragging, foolish talk, # 4371); → *lṣṣ* (rebel, scoff, # 4372); → *mrd* (revolt, rebel, # 5277); → *mrh* (be refractory, obstinate, # 5286); → *srr* I (be stubborn, rebellious, # 6253); → *'bt* (conspire together, # 6309); → *'ēṣâ* II (disobedience?, revolt?, # 6784); → *'ātāq* (old, hard, stubborn, arrogant, # 6981); → *pš'* (revolt, rebel, # 7321); → *qᵉšî* (stubbornness, # 8001); → *qšr* (ally together, conspire, bind, # 8003); → *šᵉrîrût* (stubbornness, # 9244)

BIBLIOGRAPHY

T. D. Hanks, *God So Loved the Third World: The Biblical Vocabulary of Oppression*, 1983, 3-39; Y. I. Kim, "The Vocabulary of Oppression in the Old Testament," Ph.D. diss. Drew University, 1981; C. F. Marriottini, "The Problem of Social Oppression in the Eighth Century Prophets," Ph.D. diss. Southern Baptist Theological Seminary, 1983; J. Miranda, *Communism in the Bible*, 1982, 37-39; J. Pons, *L'oppression dans l'Ancien Testament*, 1981; E. Tamez, *Bible of the Oppressed*, 1982, 1-30.

Larry Walker/I. Swart

7997 (*qāšeh*, hard, heavy, difficult, stiff-necked), → # 7996

7998	קשׁח

קשׁח (*qšḥ*), hi. treat harshly, harden (# 7998).

OT Used only twice with the same basic meaning as the similar root *qšh*. Job 39:16 tells us that the ostrich "treats her young harshly (*qšḥ*), as if they were not hers." The prophet Isaiah interceded, "Why, O LORD, do you make us wander from your ways and harden (*qšḥ*) our hearts so we do not revere you?" (Isa 63:17).

Hard, harsh, difficult, severe: → *'akzār* (cruel, # 425); → *ḥzq* (be strong, seize, # 2616); → *ḥms* I (do violence, # 2803); → *kbd* (be heavy, unresponsive, honored, # 3877); → *perek* (brutal, ruthless, # 7266); → *qšh* I (be hard, severe, be stiff-necked, # 7996); → *qšḥ* (treat harshly, harden, # 7998)

Larry Walker

8000 (*qōšeṭ*, bow), → # 8008

8001 (*qᵉšî*, stubbornness), → # 7996

8003	קשר

קשר (*qšr*), q. bind together; ally together, conspire; to bind; ni. to be bound together, to be fitted together, fastened; pi. to bind, fasten together; to gird up, to tie up with; pu. healthy, robust; hitp. to take allegiance to each other/against (# 8003); קֶשֶׁר (*qešer*), nom. conspiracy, coming together (# 8004); קִשֻּׁרִים (*qiššurîm*), sashes, gossamer (→ # 8005).

ANE Akk. *kašāru(m), kešēru*, restore, reestablish.

OT The vb. occurs 44x in the OT. Drawing on the physical act of binding/tying, several instances of the vb. and its cognates signify figurative binding as well as binding in human relationships (positive and negative connotations).

1. *Literal binding*. The foundational meaning for *qšr* is a lit. binding or tying something to something else. This vb. signifies the tying of a string around an infant's wrist by a midwife, Rahab's securing a scarlet cord to hang from her window (Josh 2:18, 21), and the instructions received by Jeremiah to tie a stone to the scroll before tossing it into the Euphrates River (Jer 51:63).

2. *Figurative binding*. In several passages the act of binding is juxtaposed with a body part (Deut 6:8; 11:18, hand; Prov 3:3, neck; 6:21; 22:15, heart; 7:3, fingers) and seems to signify the internalization of something. The father figure in Prov encourages his son to bind steadfast love and faithfulness around his neck and to write them on his heart (3:3), i.e., to make them part of his character just as they are part of God's nature. He also demands that they internalize parental commands (6:21) as well as divine mandates (7:3). According to the wise sage, discipline is a tool to break the cords that bind foolishness to a child's heart (22:15). The prophet Isaiah (Isa 49:18) assures despondent Zion, bereft of her children, that Yahweh will regather her children around her. She will revel in their presence in pride, like a bride who proudly puts on a special piece of her bridal attire.

Although some scholars argue that Deut 6:8 and 11:18 refer to a literal phenomenon (Weinfeld, 342-43) or are undecided whether the binding is literal or figurative (Christensen, 144; Craigie, 171), the figurative interpretation appears to be most accurate. Since "these commandments" in 6:6 refer not only to 6:6-9 but to the Mosaic stipulations in general, a literal application appears to be impossible. Consequently, the binding of "these commandments" represents "another figurative way of expressing the centrality of the covenant to everyday life" (Merrill, 167).

In his rebuke of Job, Yahweh queries Job as to whether he is able to control the course of heavenly constellations (Job 38:31), guide a wild ox in plowing a straight furrow (39:10), or domesticate the powerful Leviathan (41:5[40:29]). The obvious answer to all these questions is a resounding "no."

3. "*Stronger.*" In two instances (Gen 30:41-42) the vb. root appears as a part. (adjectival; v. 41, pu. part.; v. 42, q. pass. part.) with the meaning stronger. They occur in a passage that describes Jacob's strategy for crossbreeding the animals in his flock. It appears that the literal idea, those who are bound together/knit together, refers to those animals that are firm and compact (KD 1:294) or well-knit, i.e., vigorous or stronger (Hamilton, 281, n. 24).

4. *Binding in human relationships*. In the context of human relationships, *qšr* can signify either a relationship between two people that is characterized by devotion or the binding together of individuals for the sake of rebellion.

(a) A relationship characterized by devotion. Drawing on the covenantal/political nuance signified by *'hb* in ANE treaties (Moran, 78-79; Thompson, 334-38), Ackroyd (213-14) suggests that *qšr* carries a double entendre of personal devotion as well as political alliance in 1 Sam 18:1. This conclusion also draws on Saul's estimation of David's and Jonathan's relationship as a conspiracy (22:8, 13). Although David's friendship with Jonathan heightened Saul's fear of David as a threat to his throne (and consequently part of a plot against him), the use of *qšr* in 18:1 most likely refers to the devoted affection that existed between Jonathan and David. Jonathan's relationship with David never approximated that of a king and subject. A better backdrop for this description is the par. expression in Gen 44:30, where Judah pleads that Benjamin's life be spared (because the stolen cup was discovered in Benjamin's sack). As part of his entreaty, Judah declares that the loss of Benjamin would precipitate his father Jacob's death since his father's life is closely bound up with the life of Benjamin (*nepeš ... qšr ... nepeš*). The binding together of *nepeš* signifies a bond of affection, i.e., devotion in affection and loyalty (McCarter, 305).

(b) Plotting together for the sake of rebellion. *qšr* occurs 25x to connote some kind of rebellious conniving, i.e., it refers to people planning together an attempt to overthrow a ruling figure. The nom. *qešer* occurs 16x and refers to a conspiracy/rebellion of some sort in each instance. On six occasions it is juxtaposed with the vb. as a cognate accusative (1 Kgs 16:20; 2 Kgs 12:20[21]; 14:19; 15:15, 30; 2 Chron 25:27). The vb. (and its cognate nom.) refers to threats against the ruling king in the united monarchy (Saul vs. David, 1 Sam 22:8, 13; David vs. Absalom, 2 Sam 15:12, 31) as well as various attempts to revolt against the king during the divided monarchy: within the northern kingdom (1 Kgs 15:27; 16:9, 16, 20; 2 Kgs 10:9; 15:10, 15, 25, 30), within the southern kingdom (2 Kgs 11:14; 12:20[21]; 14:19; 21:23-24 [= 2 Chron 33:24-25]; 2 Chron 23:13; 24:25-26; 25:27), and between the northern and southern kingdoms (2 Kgs 9:14). It also describes Israel's unsuccessful attempt, during the reign of Hoshea, to throw off the yoke of Assyrian domination (17:4) and the disconcerting threat by the Samaritan rabble to interfere with the rebuilding of Jerusalem's walls under Nehemiah (Neh 4:8[2]).

(c) In addition to these conspiracies for political rebellion, *qšr* also signifies conspiracies directed explicitly against Yahweh. The Chronicler calls the plans to slay a true prophet (because his rebuke angered the disobedient king) a conspiracy

(2 Chron 24:21). One of the northern kingdom's counterfeit priests described the prophet Amos's ministry as a reprehensible conspiracy against Israel (Amos 7:10). Yahweh describes Israel's conduct toward him (abandoning him and worshiping other gods) a conspiracy as well (Jer 11:19; cf. Ezek 22:25). In the face of the threat from external powers, Yahweh exhorts the prophet Isaiah in Isa 8:12 against joining the popular clamor for "the supposed safety of political alliance and worldly armed strength" (Motyer, 95). Instead, he was to rely on God's orchestration of world affairs. Driver's suggestion (82-84) of "difficulty" does not do justice to the normal or contextual meaning of *qešer*. The emendation of the MT's *taqdîšû* (sanctify, regard as holy) to *taqrîšû* (hi. impf., you shall identify as conspiracy) (cf. Driver, 83-84; Wildberger, 355, 357-58) is unnecessary. The transition from referring to a conspiracy to drawing attention to Yahweh's holiness is appropriate since forming a covenant pagan nation constitutes a failure to sanctify Yahweh (Evans, 113). Isaiah probably utilized the similarity in sound (*qrš/qdš*) for rhetorical effect (Clements, 99).

5. Another cognate nom., *qiššurîm*, occurs twice and signifies something worn by a woman (Isa 3:20; Jer 2:32). A survey of commentaries and translations demonstrates the divergence of opinion on this term's meaning. It clearly refers to something bound/tied on the woman, although its precise nature is difficult to ascertain.

6. *Stubborn* (*qᵉšî*). A cognate nom. from the vb. *qšh* (see # 8001), *qᵉšî* (hapleg., Deut 9:27), occurs in Moses' prayer that Yahweh will not destroy his covenant nation in spite of their stubbornness (*qᵉšî*), wickedness (*reša'*), and sin (*ḥaṭṭā't*).

P-B The meaning of the words in Sir 7:8; 11:31; 13:12 as given by R. Smend (*TWAT* 7:1:297) as evil/to commit evil is suspect. Sir 7:8 understands a sin committed twice to become one's own, bound to them. Conspiracy is perhaps a good translation of Sir 11:31 (*qešer*).

The verbal root is found in the DSS, but only in the ni. bound (KQT 196: CD 13:19, ni. part.). For the nom. see CD 13:10. The word refers to the binding together of the members of the Qumran community, but the text is unclear about what the binding involves. The nom. is used figuratively for social pressures/compulsions.

In LH the use of the nom. is found meaning union, conspiracy (*Sanh* 26a, ref. to Isa 8:12; see further Jastrow 2:1432-33).

Rebellion, conspiracy, stubbornness, obstinacy: → *ysd* II (conspire together, # 3570); → *kśh* (become stubborn, headstrong, # 4170); → *lāṣôn* (bragging, foolish talk, # 4371); → *lṣṣ* (rebel, scoff, # 4372); → *mrd* (revolt, rebel, # 5277); → *mrh* (be refractory, obstinate, # 5286); → *srr* I (be stubborn, rebellious, # 6253); → *'bt* (conspire together, # 6309); → *'ēṣâ* II (disobedience?, revolt?, # 6784); → *'ātāq* (old, hard, stubborn, arrogant, # 6981); → *pš'* (revolt, rebel, # 7321); → *qᵉšî* (stubbornness, # 8001); → *qšr* (ally together, conspire, bind, # 8003); → *šᵉrîrût* (stubbornness, # 9244)

Band, tie: → *'pd* (put on tightly, # 679); → *'ᵃpēr* (bandage, # 710); → *'eṣ'ādâ* (band, # 731); → *ḥbš* (tie up, saddle, imprison, bind, # 2502); → *ḥgr* (bind, gird, # 2520); → *ḥāšûq* (clasp ring, # 3122); → *ḥtl* (be swaddled, # 3156); → *keset* (band [for magic purposes], # 4086); → *migbā'â* (head-band, # 4457); → *'nd* (wind, tie s.t., # 6698); → *'qd* (tie up, # 6818); → *ṣrr* I (bind, tie up, # 7674); → *qšr* (ally together, conspire, bind, # 8003); → *rks* (bind, tie, # 8220); → *rtm* (tie up, # 8412)

BIBLIOGRAPHY
TWAT 7:211-17; *TWOT* 2:818-19; P. R. Ackroyd, "The Verb Love—*'āhēb* in the David-Jonathan-Narratives," *VT* 25, 1975, 213-14; D. Christensen, *Deuteronomy 1-11*, 1991; R. Clements, *Isaiah 1-39*, 1980; P. Craigie, *Deuteronomy*, 1976; G. Driver, "Two Misunderstood Passages of the Old Testament," *JTS* 6, 1955, 82-87; C. Evans, "An Interpretation of Isa 8,11-15 Unamended," *ZAW* 97, 1985, 112-13; V. Hamilton, *The Book of Genesis, Chapters 18-50*, 1995; P. McCarter, *1 Samuel*, 1980; E. Merrill, *Deuteronomy*, 1994; W. Moran, "The Ancient Near Eastern Background of the Love of God in Deuteronomy," *CBQ* 25, 1963, 77-87; J. Motyer, *The Prophecy of Isaiah*, 1993; J. Thompson, "The Significance of the Verb *Love* in the David-Jonathan Narratives in 1 Samuel," *VT* 24, 1974, 334-38; H. Wildberger, *Isaiah 1-12*, 1991.

Eugene Carpenter/Michael A. Grisanti

8004 (*qešer*, conspiracy), → # 8003

8005	קִשֻּׁרִים

קִשֻּׁרִים (*qiššurîm*), nom. breast-bands (# 8005); < קשׁר (*qšr*), q. tie up, bind, conspire; ni. be bound; pi. bind; pu. sturdy (→ # 8003).

ANE Cognates to Heb. *qšr* exist in Syr. and Eth.

OT *qiššurîm* refers to part of a woman's dress, possibly sashes (Isa 3:20; Jer 2:32).

Band, tie: → *'pd* (put on tightly, # 679); → *'ᵃpēr* (bandage, # 710); → *'eṣ'ādâ* (band, # 731); → *ḥbš* (tie up, saddle, imprison, bind, # 2502); → *ḥgr* (bind, gird, # 2520); → *ḥāšûq* (clasp ring, # 3122); → *ḥtl* (be swaddled, # 3156); → *keset* (band [for magic purposes], # 4086); → *migbā'â* (head-band, # 4457); → *'nd* (wind, tie s.t., # 6698); → *'qd* (tie up, # 6818); → *ṣrr* I (bind, tie up, # 7674); → *qšr* (ally together, conspire, bind, # 8003); → *rks* (bind, tie, # 8220); → *rtm* (tie up, # 8412)

T. Desmond Alexander

8006	קשׁשׁ

קשׁשׁ (*qšš*), q. assemble?; polel collect; hitpolel gather together? (# 8006); קַשׁ (*qaš*), chaff (→ # 7990).

OT The word is used in q. (Zeph 2:1); 6x in polel (Exod 5:7, 12; Num 15:32, 33; 1 Kgs 17:10, 12), and 1x hitpol. (Zeph 2:1). The term is evidently a diminutive from *qaš*, straw or chaff. It occurs in the polel as causative with the meaning gather, perhaps with the overtones of gathering that which is small and insignificant. The polel is used in Exod 5:7, where Pharaoh orders the overseers not to give the people any more straw for the making of bricks. The Egyptians used mud and sand from the Nile, mixed with chopped straw, to make the bricks (Cassuto, *Exodus*, 68; *ANEP*, 35, # 115), but now the people are to go and "gather their own straw." Num 15:32-33 has to do with a man who was found "gathering wood on the Sabbath day." In the hithpolel in the phrase "gather together, O shameful nation" signifies a public expression of contrition (Zeph 2:1). The idea seems to be "gather yourselves together as straw, recognizing your poor condition, for the burning wrath of God is coming and will consume you as fire does chaff."

P-B In RL the word occurs in connection with Num 15:32, the man "gathering sticks" on the Sabbath (*WTM*, 4:400; see b Sabb. 96b; p Sanh V, 22d).

Gathering: → *'sp* (gather, harvest, # 665); → *bṣr* (harvest grapes, # 1305); → *ḥṭb* (gather, cut, # 2634); → *kns* (gather, # 4043); → *lqṭ* (gather, # 4377); → *'ēdâ* I (community, gathering, band, # 6337); → *'mr* (gather grain, # 6682); → *qbṣ* (gather, # 7695); → *q^ehillâ* (community, gathering, # 7737); → *qwh* II (gather, # 7748); → *qšš* (gather, collect, # 8006)
Harvest, gleaning: → *'sp* (gather, harvest, # 665); → *bṣr* (harvest grapes, # 1305); → *y^ebûl* (produce, yield, # 3292); → *lqṭ* (reap, harvest, # 4377); → *'ll* I (glean, # 6618); → *'mr* (gather grain, # 6682); → *qbṣ* (gather, # 7695); → *qṣr* (harvest, # 7917); → *t^ebû'â* (crop, yield, # 9311); → *t^enûbâ*, produce, # 9482)

BIBLIOGRAPHY

R. D. Patterson, *Nahum, Habakkuk, Zephaniah*, 1991, 328-33; J. J. M. Roberts, *Nahum, Habakkuk, and Zephaniah*, 1991, 186-90.

Cleon L. Rogers, Jr.

8008	קֶשֶׁת

קֶשֶׁת (*qešet*), bow (# 8008); קֹשֶׁט (*qôšeṭ*), bow, a variant spelling of *qešet*, occurs only in Ps 60:4[6] with the meaning "bow" (# 8000); קַשָּׁת (*qaššāt*), archer (# 8009).

ANE This term is found extensively in various Sem. languages of the ANE. Cf. Ugar. *qšt*; Akk. *qaštu*; Old Aram. *qaštā'*; Arab. *qaus*; Eth. *qast* (*HALAT* 1077).

OT 1. In the ANE, technologically advanced bows were composite (cf. McEwen, Miller and Bergman, 78-79; Haas, 27-41). In its classic form the composite bow consisted of a thin wooden core with sinew glued to the back and a horn, usually of a bull, glued to the belly (McEwen, 76-82). In an Ugar. mythical text, Aqhat made a composite bow. He used sinews from wild oxen, tendons from the hocks of a bull, horns from mountain goats, and some wood from Lebanon (cf. *KTU* 1.17:21-23). In a few instances bows were made of other materials (perhaps for ceremonial reasons?). For example, "a bow of bronze" is mentioned in 2 Sam 22:35 (= Ps 18:34[35]), which David claims to be able to bend.

2. As a literal bow (weapon), *qešet* is used to describe the bow of the hunter (Gen 27:3; Isa 7:24) and frequently the bow of the warrior (e.g., Gen 21:20; 48:22; Josh 24:12; 1 Sam 18:4; 2 Sam 1:22; 1 Kgs 22:34; 2 Kgs 6:22; 9:24; 13:15; 1 Chron 12:2; 2 Chron 17:17; 18:33; 26:14; Job 29:20; Ps 7:12[13]; 11:2[3]; 44:6[7]; 78:9; Isa 5:28; 7:24; 13:18; 22:3; 41:2; Jer 4:29; 6:23; 49:35; 50:42; Ezek 39:3, 9; Hos 1:7; 2:18[20]; Amos 2:15; Hab 3:9; Zech 9:10; 10:4).

3. *qešet* is used metaphorically to describe the rainbow. After the Flood, God states: "I have set my bow (*qešet*) in the cloud" (Gen 9:13-16). The only other time that *qešet* is used in BH for the rainbow is in Ezek 1:28, where the vision of glory of Yahweh is compared to a meteorological phenomenon, "like the appearance of a rainbow in the clouds on a rainy day." An example of a postbiblical Heb. usage can be found in Sir 50:7, where Simon the high priest is compared with the rainbow and many other things that elsewhere are applied to God (cf. also Sir 43:11). Later, in the book of Revelation, John uses Ezekiel's rainbow metaphor to describe both God (Rev 4:3) and an angel (Rev 10:1).

4. In a few instances, *qešet* is used as a metonymy. For example, in Job 20:24, it is put in the place for "a bronze-tipped arrow" (lit. "bow of bronze") that pierces Job (cf. Job 41:28: *ben qešet*; see also Ps 76:3[4]: *rišpê qešet,* "flashing arrows," and *ḥēṣ,* "arrowhead"). *qešet* is sometimes used as a metonymy for "archer" (Isa 21:17; 66:19). The term is used in the phrase *ṭāḥâ qešet* to describe a "measure of distance," i.e., "the distance of a bowshot" (Gen 21:16).

5. Lamenting Saul's and Jonathan's death, David composed the dirge titled, according to the vocalization of the MT, *qāšet,* "Bow" (2 Sam 1:18). Recently, Fokkelman has argued that the consonants should be vocalized *qāšōt*, hard things, or better "painful realities" (650-51). The dirge was preserved in the Book of Yashar.

6. As the most fragile piece of military equipment, the bow can be retired by being faulty, by being broken, or by being hung up. Instances of "faulty bows" can be seen in Ps 78:57 and Hos 7:16. In the case of the breaking of bows, if it is one's own bow, this is a disastrous curse; if it is the enemy's bow, a blessing indeed. In the OT, Yahweh breaks both. Yahweh promises to punish Israel by breaking the bow (Hos 1:5); and he promises to punish the wicked (Ps 37:15; 46:9[10]) and specific enemy nations by breaking their bows (e.g., Babylon: Jer 51:56; Elam: 49:35).

7. In the ANE, the breaking of the bow was often connected to a treaty (Waldman, 82-88). For example, in the Aram. treaty of Sefîre the parties agree that "Just as [this] bow and these arrows are broken, so may In[ur]ta and Hadad break [the bow of Mati-ilu] and the bow of his nobles" (*KAI* 222 A.38-39).

8. When in the OT the breaking of the bow occurs as bringing promised blessing in a covenant or treaty context, two themes can be discerned. Since the bow is primarily that of the enemy, who is likely to be a vassal on whom such a one as Esarhaddon imposed a vassal treaty, its breaking to the benefit of Israel can be interpreted as a punishment for the ruler's having infringed the justice of Yahweh and his own oath. But since Yahweh punishes his own people through the hands of their enemies, the bow can also be interpreted as that of Yahweh, which after Israel's repentance is now being hung up, as after the Flood in the covenant with Noah (Hos 2:18; Zech 9:10).

9. By extension, the phrase "breaking of the bow" comes to represent vigor generally (e.g., 1 Sam 2:4; this passage also contains clear treaty terminology). A further extension is encountered in Job 29:20, where it stands for sexual vigor. While *qešet* is feminine, as a symbol it works often as masculine, since the arrow is "the son of the bow" (Job 41:20).

10. *qaššāt* is used once in the OT with the meaning "archer" (Gen 21:20).

Bow, arrow, archery: → *'ašpâ* (quiver, # 880); → *zîqôt* (flaming arrow, # 2338); → *ḥēṣ* (arrow, # 2932); → *ṭḥh* (distance of bowshot, # 3217); → *yôreh* I (archer, # 3452); → *yeter* II (bowstring, # 3857); → *qešet* (bow, # 8008); → *rbb* II (shoot, # 8046); → *rbh* II (archer, # 8050); → *t^elî* (quiver, # 9437); → **Warfare: Theology**

Bibliography

TWOT 2:819; J. P. Brown, "Archery in the Ancient World: 'Its Name Is Life, Its Work Is Death'," *BZ* 37, 1993, 26-42; J. P. Fokkelman, *Narrative Art and Poetry in the Books of Samuel,* Studia Semitica Neerlandica, 2, 1986; V. Haas, "Kompositibogen und Bogenschieṣen als Weltkampf im Alten Orient," *Kikephoros* 2, 1989, 27-41; W. W. Hallo, "More on Bows," in *Yigael Yadin Volume*, ed. A. Malamet, *ErIsr* 20, 1989, 68-71; J. K. Hoffmeier, "Some Egyptian Motifs

Related to Enemies and Warfare and Their Old Testament Counterparts," in *Egyptological Miscellanies: A Tribute to Professor Ronald J. Williams*, Ancient World 6, 1983, 53-70; O. Keel, "Der Bogen als Herrschaftsymbol," *ZDPV* 93, 1977, 141-77; E. McEwen, R. L. Miller, and C. A. Bergman, "Early Bow Design and Construction," *Scientific American* 264, 1991, 76-82; Udo Rüterswörden, "Der Bogen in Genesis 9: Militär-historische und traditionsgeschichtliche Erwagungen zu einem biblischen Symbol," *UF* 20, 1988, 247-63; E. Salonen, "Bogen," *StudOr* 33, 1966, 40-42; N. M. Waldman, "The Breaking of the Bow," *JQR* 69, 1978-1979, 82-88.

K. Lawson Younger, Jr.

8009 (*qaššāt*, archer), → # 8008

ר

8011	ראה

ראה (*r'h*), q. see, have visions, see!, look at, see = go to, choose, select, perceive; ni. be seen, appear, make oneself visible; pu. to be seen; hi. cause to see, cause to know, to experience; ho. to be caused to see; hitp. look at each other, measure one's strength against another (# 8011); מַרְאֶה (*mar'eh*), nom. sight, appearance, supernatural vision, flare (# 5260); מַרְאָה (*mar'â*), appearance, vision, mirror (# 5261); רֹאֶה (*rō'eh* I), seer (# 8014); רֹאֶה (*rō'eh* II), nom. vision (# 8015); רַאֲוָה (*ra'^{a}wâ*), nom. seeing (# 8019); רְאוּת (*r^{e}'ût*, txt. problem), nom. look, sight (# 8021); רְאִי (*r^{e}'î*), nom. mirror (# 8023); רֳאִי (*r^{o}'î*), nom. appearance, spectacle (# 8024).

ANE While the root occurs throughout Sem. the meaning to see occurs only in Akk., Ugar., and Ge'ez.

OT 1. *The meanings of the vb. r'h.* (a) Generally the vb. denotes the physical sense perception with the eyes. The q. denotes the act of seeing/perceiving/watching/looking with one's own eyes. Eve perceived that the fruit of the tree was good (Gen 3:6). In 6:2 the sons of God saw that the daughters of men were beautiful. Isaac called for Esau when Isaac's eyes were so weak that he could no longer see (27:1). The hitp. denotes the reflexive, to look at each other. Because Jacob's sons just looked at one another in such a helpless and undecided manner during the famine, Jacob exhorted them to fetch corn from Egypt to preserve his family from starvation (42:1). The act of letting see, show, display, is expressed by the hi. Abram was to leave all and to follow the Lord into the land he would show him (Gen 12:1). The ni. denotes the reflexive of the causative, to present oneself (= let oneself see). In the case of a skin disease, one was to present oneself to the priest for examination (Lev 13:19). The ho. denotes the passive of the causative, to be shown. Moses had to make the lampstand according to the pattern shown to him on the mountain (Exod 25:40). Thus, the literal sense of the vb. calls for no special comment, for it is the common word for seeing with the eyes. But the vb. has extended and metaphorical meanings (cf. also Riekert, 128-38).

(b) The vb. is also used in the sense of becoming psychologically visionary conscious, seeing in a vision, receiving a revelation. This sense is expressed by the q. Balaam declared that he had received a vision from the Almighty in which he saw Israel in the future when the star of Jacob would arise and the tribes of Israel would crush Moab

(Num 24:17). To express the reflexive of this meaning, the ni. is used, appear in a vision, to reveal oneself. The assurance of the possession of the land of Canaan for Abram's descendants was made by means of an appearance of the Lord as a sign that this land was henceforth to be the scene of the manifestation of the Lord (Gen 12:7). The causative, to show in a vision, reveal, is expressed by the hi. The Lord showed the prophet a vision of the means by which the promises of a glorious future for the city and people of God were to be achieved (Zech 3:1).

(c) The vb. in the q. can also mean to become mentally aware of, realize, take note of. In these cases the vb. refers to perception by means of other senses, e.g., understanding or hearing. When Hagar became aware of her pregnancy by Abram, she despised her mistress Sarai (Gen 16:4-5). In Samuel's final address to Israel a miraculous sign of thunder and rain, virtually unknown in Palestine at this time of the year, ratified the renewal of the covenant. By experiencing this sign Israel would see/realize what an evil thing they had done in the eyes of the Lord when they asked for a king (1 Sam 12:17). The Lord saw/took note of the distress of Israel (Ps 106:44). In his promise to restore the people, the Lord asked Jeremiah whether he had not noticed the people's sayings on the rejection of the kingdoms/families. These sayings could only be heard (Jer 33:24).

(d) The vb. in the q. has the sense of experiencing or an activity or state. The Lord would not let the faithful one see/experience Sheol, which signified that dreaded death under divine wrath and rejection, i.e., decay (Ps 16:10; cf. also 89:48[49]). In 34:8[9] the psalmist is exhorted to taste and see that the Lord is good. In a graphic description of God's protecting care, it is said that the offspring of Israel did not experience the discipline of the Lord like their parents (Deut 11:2). The causative, cause to experience, is expressed by the hi. The prophet Habakkuk was troubled because God had made him experience the presence of injustice among Israel (Hab 1:3).

(e) The q. also denotes the act of inquiring into, investigating into, inspecting. Joseph was sent to Shechem by Jacob to inquire after the welfare of his brothers and their flocks (Gen 37:14).

(f) The q. is used to express the act of taking care of, looking after. The Lord was with Joseph, with the result that the warden entrusted all the prisoners to the care of Joseph and did not trouble himself about/took care of anything that fell under his control (Gen 39:23).

(g) As marker the impv. of the q. is used to draw attention to a situation that a speaker regards as existing or that he assumes his audience may regard as existing. In Gen 27:27 the marker was used by Isaac to draw attention to the fact that he was an old man when he sent for Esau.

(h) The q. denotes the act of visiting. David's absence at Saul's sacrificial meal was due to the permission Jonathan gave him to go and see/visit his brothers (1 Sam 20:29).

(i) The q. can also mean to select. God admonished the Israelites to beware of offering sacrifices in every place that they might see/choose (Deut 12:13). Moses said about the tribe Gad that it chose the best land for itself (33:21). The Lord sent Samuel to Jesse of Bethlehem to choose one of his sons to be king (1 Sam 16:1). Saul ordered his attendants to choose someone who could play a harp (16:17).

(j) To provide is another meaning of the vb. When Abraham was tested, the q. was used to assure Isaac that God himself would provide the lamb for the burnt offering (Gen 22:8, 14). The passive, to be provided, is expressed by the ni. The place of testing was called, "On the mountain of the Lord it will be provided" (Gen 22:14).

(k) Two other meanings in the q. are attested each 1x. The first is to distinguish. The restoration of the moral order is typified as distinguishing between the righteous and the wicked (Mal 3:18). The second is to despise. The newcomer to a harem was subject to the contemptuous looks of the other women (S of Songs 1:6). She apologized for her tanned appearance by stating that her brothers had sent her day after day to work under the relentless sun in the family vineyards. All this led to the neglect of the vineyard of her own complexion.

(l) The vb. is also used in idioms. To see someone's face (*pānîm*; → # 7156) can be interpreted to meet someone, as in 2 Sam 3:13, where David demanded that Abner return Michal when he came to see his face; or to be allowed in the presence of someone, as in Gen 43:3, 5 where Joseph solemnly warned that his brothers would not see his face unless accompanied by their youngest brother. To see the sun in Eccl 7:11 means to be alive. Wisdom benefits those who see the sun, i.e., those who are alive. To appear before the face of God (Exod 23:15, 17) means to serve God in his sanctuary. To meet someone face to face means either to fight against each other or to consult with each other in a meeting (2 Kgs 14:8; 2 Chron 25:17). Thus, it is important to note that the vb. embraces a whole series of meanings which have little to do with seeing.

2. *The theological significance of the vb.* (a) On the one hand, God sees and watches people. In the instances in which God is said to see, the vb. must be interpreted anthropomorphically. In Gen 6:12 God saw how corrupt the earth had become. God would look at the rainbow which is a divine guarantee to human beings and a reminder to God of his commitments as Protector of the world (9:16). God descended to see the pinnacle at Babel (11:5). The Lord saw that Moses had gone over to look at the burning bush (Exod 3:4). When the Lord saw the blood on the top and at the sides of the doorframes at the time of the ending of the bondage in Egypt, he passed over that doorway (12:13, 23). The Lord's tender mercy, which is keenly awaited, is expressed as his looking down from heaven (Lam 3:50). In Jer 23:24 the omniscience of the Lord is expressed by the question: "Can anyone hide in secret places so that I cannot see him?" God sees into a person's innermost being (1 Sam 16:7). He also sees the death of his prophet (2 Chron 24:22). The statements that the Lord had heard the prayer of Hezekiah and seen his tears (Isa 38:5) or is on high but looks upon the lowly (Ps 138:6) refer to God acting in mercy.

(b) On the other hand, God lets himself be seen, disclosed, or revealed in theophanies (cf. Tournay). In Exod 6:3 it is stated that God appeared to Abraham, Isaac, and Jacob (although there are no accounts of theophanies to Isaac). In 3:2 the angel of the Lord appeared to Moses. From 3:4 on reference is made to the Lord himself rather than to the angel. In particular, the description of these manifestations extends the bodily imagery on God—e.g., Isa 6:1, in which it is stated that Isaiah saw the Lord seated on a throne. The parts of God's form that are mentioned (the eye, ear, and hand) illustrate his faithfulness and care (Exod 33:23). Through these actions the one who sees, as well as the hearer, is encouraged or commissioned. Even though the OT speaks of God's becoming visible in theophanies, these are never indicative of inquisitive speculation into God's form. Rather, the OT seeks to disclose God's nature but not to provide any concrete visual images of him. As a matter of fact, the Lord was always thought of as having a human form like that of a man (von Rad, 145, 219). These anthropomorphic modes of speech show how people used to recognize and understand God's nature and how they conceived of it. It is significant that qualities such as those attributed to the Greek gods (like sexuality) are not ascribed to God in the OT.

(c) The face of God denotes the very person of God, not just that side of him that is turned towards us (cf. Smith, 171-83). In Ps 42:2[3] the expression "to see the face of God" is used to express the yearning for communion with God himself. Jacob called the place where he had wrestled with God Peniel, because he had seen God face to face (Gen 32:30[31]). Here it expressed familiarity beyond previous visions or divine appearances. However, God's holiness and majesty prevent a person from seeing his face because it referred to knowledge of God that exceeds the abilities and hopes of humankind. At the burning bush Moses veiled his face because he was afraid to look at God (Exod 3:6). It may appear that God could have been seen but that Moses did not avail himself of the opportunity. Though Moses did not see God, it is said that God appeared to him (3:16). Thus God met Moses and talked to him in some glorious representation that fell short of a full unveiling of his face.

God's face could slay a person. But in Exod 33:18 Moses asked to see the very face of the Lord to obtain full assurance of the Lord's renewed grace to him and to the Israelites. The Lord warned that at such a vision Moses would instantly die (33:20). Yet, as a special confirmation of his personal favor and presence, the Lord promised that he would reveal his back to Moses, without showing his face. Therefore the Lord would cover him with his hand until he had passed by. When he removed his hand, Moses would see his back, but his face might not be seen (33:23). Moses was to see the afterglow of the theophany, which was a reliable indication of what his full splendor is like (Kaiser, 84). When Gideon lamented that he had seen the angel of the Lord face to face, he was assured that he was not going to die (Judg 6:22). In some theophanies God's glory was revealed and seen by human beings (Exod 33:18; Num 14:22). Heaven opened, the transcendent broke through and was visible (Ezek 1:1). Supernatural brightness (Ps 18:12[13]; 50:2; Hab 3:4) and the likeness of sunrise (Hos 6:3), storm, and tempest (Job 38:1; Nah 1:3) are mentioned as phenomena that accompany God's presence. A person's consciousness of guilt leads to a consciousness of distance (Isa 6:5).

(d) The vb. is connected with revelations during sleep. In Jacob's appeal to his wives to leave Laban he stated that he had seen in a dream that the male goats that were mating with the flock were streaked, speckled, or spotted (Gen 31:10-12). The angel of God explained this event to him as a sign to go back to his native land. In his dreams Pharaoh saw seven heads of corn, full and good, growing on a single stalk (Gen 41:22). These dreams were purely visual, with the result that the pictures and images had to be interpreted by individuals. Such dreams were normally regarded as revelations, as impartations of the divine will and knowledge.

(e) The vb. is one of the characteristic words used for visionary-ecstatic prophetic seeing, including hallucinatory or inner perceptions that could occur either by day or by night, e.g., the so-called night visions of Zech (Zech 1:8; cf. also Isa 6:1;

Jer 1:11, 12, 13; Ezek 1:1, 4, 15, 27, 28; 2:9; 8:2, 6, 7, 10, 15; 10:1, 9; 11:1; cf. also Reiterer, 156-75). Three main types occur. (i) Oracle vision, where the visionary image is simple and provides occasion for typical prophetic oracles (e.g., Amos 8:1, 2). (ii) Dramatic word vision, depicting a heavenly scene taken as a portent of the future (e.g., 1 Kgs 22:17). (iii) Revelatory mystery vision, which conveys esoteric messages about divine activity and the future (e.g., Zech 2:1[5]). The reports of visions were connected with prophetic divination (Long, 353-65).

The authenticity of visions is the same as that of the prophetic messages of revelation in general. In particular, the principle holds good that humanity is always the recipient and never the author of revelation. There is no human process, whether prayer, sacrifice, or a specific technique, whereby a person can bring about a theophany. God himself showed the prophets visions; e.g., the Lord showed Amos a locust plague of such intensity that national survival would be out of the question; a devouring fire that would eat up even the very land itself; and a wall that had been built with a plumb line, and the testing of it was not by some other standard, but by the same standard that the builders were supposed to use (Amos 7:1, 4, 7). Every vision is introduced by the statement that this was what the Lord showed him.

(f) The vb. refers to the bare act of intellectual perception of the message of the prophet (Isa 52:10, 15). In 6:9-10 the impv. with the inf. abs. of the vb. is used in the utterance, "Be ever seeing, but never perceiving." The instruction to Isaiah to close their eyes is also added. This utterance sums up not the content of Isaiah's public preaching, but its effect as intended by God. The commission to blind does not mean that the truth is merely withheld from the sinful people. It is proclaimed through the prophet, but only in order to speed the coming judgment. Every word of the prophet would make them more determined not to abandon their own thoughts. However, they had come to the point where one more rejection of the truth would finally condemn them to inevitable judgment. The dilemma of the prophet was that there was no way of saving sinners but by the very truth, the rejection of which would condemn them utterly.

(g) In the utterance of the Lord to Noah, that he had found him righteous in this generation, the vb. refers to the act of acceptance, especially on the part of God (Gen 7:1). Another example is Num 23:21, where the Lord had not looked on the wrongs found in Israel. By this statement Balaam declared that he could discern no misfortune for God's people since the Lord was with them.

3. *The nom. mar'eh.* (a) Being derived directly from the vb. by addition of a nom.-making prefix, this nom. bears much of the variety of significance of the vb. It normally refers to the outward appearance/looks of a person (Gen 39:6), object (Ezek 1:13), or event (Num 9:16). In 1 Sam 16:7 the nom. denotes appearance in the sense of how someone appears to be on the outside as opposed to inner reality. The external appearance of skin disease (Lev 13:3, 4, 12, 20, 25, 30, 31, 32, 34, 43), phenomena such as the burning bush (Exod 3:3), the cloud above the tabernacle (Num 9:15), sights (Deut 28:34, 67), flashes of lightning (Ezek 1:14), and the glory of the Lord (Exod 24:17) are denoted by the nom.

(b) The nom. refers to the act of looking (Isa 11:3; Josh 22:10) and the faculty or function of seeing (Eccl 6:9; 11:9). The nom is used to denote transparency. In Num 12:8 the Lord states that he spoke with Moses face to face clearly and not in riddles.

(c) The nom. also refers to the pattern the Lord had shown Moses, according to which the lampstand was made (Num 8:4). In 2 Sam 23:21 the nom. denotes a huge man and in Job 4:16 an image. The nom. expresses the common notion of face or countenance, the part of a person visible to the eye (1 Sam 16:7; S of Songs 2:14; 5:15).

(d) Qualifications for fair and desirable as well as ugly and undesirable are commonly used with the nom. All the trees in the garden that the Lord grew out of the ground are qualified as pleasant to the sight (Gen 2:9). The looks of Sarai were described by Abram as beautiful (12:11). The same pertains to the complexion of Rebekah, fair to look upon (24:16; 26:7), and Rachel, beautiful to look upon (29:17). The shape of the gaunt oxen in Pharaoh's dream is described as ugly (41:3, 4, 21).

(e) The nom. is used to typify the nature of the solitary figure in Isaiah's fourth Servant Song (Isa 52:12-53:12; → *'ebed*, servant; # 6269). His appearance is so disfigured beyond that of any person (Isa 52:14). There is nothing in his appearance that a person should desire him (Isa 53:2). The servant's perfection, dignity, and privilege are most thoroughly degraded, not by smashing him physically, but by destroying all evidence of the perfection, dignity, and privilege that a person has by convicting him as a criminal, torturing him as a thief, abusing him as being of no status whatsoever, and ignoring him while executioners amused themselves with his attire. The suffering of the servant is symbolic of the suffering of Israel, who had to suffer to create a new future for the new generation.

This servant passage was understood by NT writers as prophesying Christ because it portrays those qualities which accorded with messiahship as they understood it: Christ not only encountered and accepted suffering in the course of his work; in the final phase suffering became the means whereby he accomplished his work, and it was effective in the salvation of others by making himself an offering of sin like the servant. Since the Jews found difficulty in conceiving of a suffering Messiah, they adopted the collective theory, that the servant was Israel. Later historical individual theories (which have no wide following today) were put forward. Among kings, Hezekiah, Uzziah, Jehoiachim, Zerubbabel, and Cyrus have been suggested; among prophets, Isaiah, Jeremiah, Moses as ruler, or an unknown contemporary of Deutero-Isaiah. (Cf. also Motyer, 422-44; VanGemeren, 280 and *EBC* 6:17-20, 298-307.)

(f) With reference to prophecy, the nom. also denotes visions (Ezek 8:4; 11:24; Dan 8:16, 26, 27; 9:23; 10:1). In the visions the auditive aspect is predominant over the visual element. It is revelation by word instead of picture. What is to be heard is God himself, who gives his word to the prophet in the vision. Of Ezekiel's many visions, only three are termed *mar'ôt 'ᵉlōhîm,* visions of God: The vocation of the prophet (Ezek 1:1-3:15), the judgment on Jerusalem (8:1-11:25), and the program for a restored Israel (40:1-48:35) (cf. Van Dyke Parunak, 61-74).

4. *The nom. mar'â.* (a) This nom. is distinguished from the nom. *mar'eh* only by the second vowel. It is used almost exclusively for vision(s) as a vehicle of divine revelation to prophets (Ezek 1:1; 8:3; 40:2; Dan 10:7, 8, 16). The words alternate in this sense in Ezekiel and Daniel. The call of Samuel was depicted as a vision (1 Sam 3:15). This experience can be classified as an auditory message dream (Gnuse, 379-90).

(b) In Num 12:6 it is said that the Lord would make himself known to a prophet in visions. The theme and content of the visual side of prophetic visions is not God himself. What is to be heard is God himself, who speaks to the prophet in the vision. What is to be seen are persons, animals, objects, processes such as occur in nature and life, sometimes with mythological or heavenly features, but never God himself.

(c) God spoke to Jacob in a vision by dispelling any lingering uncertainty concerning his duty; in Egypt itself the promises would begin to be fulfilled (Gen 46:2).

(d) In Exod 38:8 the nom. refers to the mirrors of the women out of which the bronze basin and its bronze stand were made.

5. *The nom. rō'eh II.* (a) This nom. is properly a q. part. of the vb., seeing or one who sees. As a part. it is used in this general sense. As a nom., it is used 12x and refers to the spokesperson who experienced the act of seeing God's message (by dreams or visions), i.e., a seer (1 Sam 9:9, 11, 18, 19), whose name is also given: Samuel, Zadok, Hanani. It is always used with the article except in 2 Sam 15:27. It can have the full or defective form.

(b) The nom. alternates with the nom. *ḥōzeh*, used 16x, a word with almost the same meaning. Apparently *rō'eh* is the earliest. In 1 Sam 9:9 it is stated that the contemporary prophet (*nābî'*) used to be called by the nom. *rō'eh.* Gad was called both *nābî'* and *ḥōzeh* (2 Sam 24:11). These three terms are used together in 1 Chron 29:29, where it is stated that the acts of King David are written in the history of Samuel the seer (*rō'eh*), and in the history of Nathan the prophet (*nābî'*), and in the history of Gad the seer (*ḥōzeh*). The nom. *nābî'* stresses the objective or active work of the messenger of the Lord in speaking forth God's message. The terms *rō'eh* and *ḥōzeh* emphasize the subjective element, namely, the receiving of divine revelation by seeing.

(c) In Isa 28:7 the nom. refers to the act of seeing, a prophetic vision.

6. *Other derivatives.* (a) The nom. *ra'^{a}wâ* refers to a spectacle. In Ezek 28:17 the casting out of the king of Tyre from the heights of heaven—i.e., the reducing of the king who enjoyed such high regard to a miserable helpless creature—is typified by the nom. The deceitfulness of riches is the actual reason leading to contempt for the will of God, and that again turns beauty and wisdom into a snare. The profaner of the mountain of God is spoiled of his dignity by God himself and expelled from the heavenly sphere (Eichrodt, 394-95).

(b) The nom. *r^{e}'î* refers to a mirror. Job is challenged to spread out the clouds solid as a mirror of cast metal (Job 37:18). The context makes it clear that the reference is not to a primordial act of creating the firmament that holds back the celestial waters, but to control of the weather and of the clouds in particular (Habel, 501).

(c) The nom. *r^{o}'î* refers to perception, appearance, and spectacle. It is utilized in Hagar's name for the Lord, "God who sees me" (Gen 16:13). In Hagar's explanation of the name it is probably correct to center the idea not on God's seeing her, but her seeing God, and that without fatal consequence. Suffering may deprive a person of one's appetite and one's firm, healthy flesh so that he or she cannot be perceived any longer (Job 33:21). In 1 Sam 16:12 the nom. refers to the appearance of David, which is qualified as fine. The nom. depicts the spectacle whereby Nineveh, who endeavored to build herself up as a center of world commerce, would be destroyed (Nah 3:6).

(d) The nom. *r^{e}'ût* refers to look/sight. It is used in the context to show the vanity of riches and human destiny; the benefit to the owner of the increase in goods is only for his sight (Eccl 5:11[10]).

P-B 1. In late Judaism seeing gave way to hearing. The vb. is used in the sense of meeting with/coming to: he who sees (comes to) a place (Mish. Berakot 9:1); considering/reflecting/reasoning: the central vine trees were considered as if not existing (Baba Batra 83a); seeing the reason of: I see the opinion of Admon (Ketubot 13:3). The hi. of the vb. is used in the sense of becoming fit for use, appearing reasonable/convincing by clear argument or visiting.

2. In Philo this group of words took on a spiritualized meaning (cf. *TDNT* 5:334-38). Seeing is frequently separated from the grasping of sense-perceptions (Leg. All. 3:100-103). Besides the general meaning of to know, seeing and its derivatives can mean to obtain knowledge and also, occasionally, to see God.

3. The main equivalents for the vb. in the LXX are *horaō*, *hoptanō*, *theaomai*, *theōreō*, and *blepō*, see, perceive. With regard to the distinction between sensual and spiritual seeing, the compass of the vbs. of seeing is much the same in Heb. and G. Thus, the LXX translators were not confronted by any serious difficulties. Exceptions are Gen 39:23; 41:33; Isa 5:12. Many compounds of vbs. for seeing used in the LXX often correspond to Heb. words that have nothing whatsoever to do with seeing, e.g., *anablepō* (*TDNT* 5:324-28). *Horaō* and *eidon* are the characteristic words used for visionary or ecstatic prophetic seeing.

4. If anyone in Scripture is described as seeing God, he must have seen the image of God, and probably that image took the form of a man. Paul, in his midrash on Exod 34 in 2 Cor 3:7-18, understood Moses to have seen the preexistent Christ in the tabernacle, and probably Paul believed that Christ appeared in the form of man (cf. Phil 2:7-8). This will mean that, according to Paul, Moses veiled his face in order that the Israelites should not recognize the glory of the preexistent Christ (Hanson, 2-28).

5. Theophanies are not found in the NT. Appearances of angels are mentioned in connection with Jesus' coming (Luke 2:13), the temptation (Matt 4:11), the passion (Luke 22:43), and the resurrection (Matt 28:2, 5). Revelatory dreams are mentioned only in the prefaces (Matt 1:20; 2:13, 19). The NT knows nothing about any experiences of the risen Christ in dreams, but there are repeated accounts of visions. These are given by God, who causes them to be seen (Acts 9:10, 12; 10:3; 2 Cor 12:1) (*NIDNTT* 3:517).

6. In the Qumran texts the vb. mainly denotes the physical sense perception with the eyes. Certain stipulations must be followed if a person sins against the law, and his fellow person sees/detects him when he is alone (CD 9:17). In 1QH 7:2 the complaint is that the eyes are blind from having seen evil. No immodest nakedness may be seen during meetings or in the surroundings of the camp (1QS 7:14; 1QM 7:7). The vb. is also used in the sense of experiencing an activity or state. The community members are commanded to open their eyes so that they can see and understand the deeds of God (CD 2:14). Because they had taken refuge in his holy name, God would atone for the community members so that they could see his salvation (CD 20:34). The Israelites are accused of not keeping apart in accordance with the law, but instead lying with a woman who sees the blood of her menstrual flow (CD 5:7).

Look, observation, perception, sight, vision, watch: → *ḥdh* II (gaze on, appear, # 2526); → *ḥzh* (see, perceive, behold, # 2600); → *ḥmh* I (see, watch out for, become visible, # 2778); → *nbṭ* (look around, accept as an act of grace, # 5564); → *pls* II (observe, # 7143); → *ṣwṣ* II (look at, # 7438); → *r'h* (see, have visions, choose, perceive, # 8011); → *rṣd* (keep one's eye on,

8353); → *śqd* (take note of, # 8567); → *š'h* III (stand gazing, # 8617); → *šgḥ* (gaze, stare, # 8708); → *šwr* I (gaze on, regard, see, # 8800); → *šzp* (catch sight of, tan, scorch, # 8812); → *š'h* (look, care about, gaze about, # 9120); → *šqp* (look down, # 9207); → *št'* (gaze, look, regard, look anxiously about, # 9283)

Bibliography

EBC 6:17-20, 298-307; *IDBSup*, 896-98; *NIDNTT* 3:511-21; *TDNT* 5:324-40; *THAT* 2:692-701; G. L. Archer, *Encyclopedia of Bible Difficulties*, 1982; W. Eichrodt, *Ezekiel: A Commentary*, 1970; R. Gnuse, "A Reconsideration of the Form-Critical Structure in 1 Samuel 3: An Ancient Near Eastern Dream Theophany," *ZAW* 92, 379-90, 1970; N. C. Habel, *The Book of Job. A Commentary*, 1985; A. T. Hanson, "The Midrash in 2 Corinthians 3: A Reconsideration," *JSNT* 19, 2-28; W. C. Kaiser, *Hard Sayings of the Old Testament*, 1991; B. O. Long, "Reports of Visions Among the Prophets," *JBL* 95, 1976, 353-65; J. Motyer, *The Prophecy of Isaiah*, 1993; F. V. Reiterer, "Ekstase-Besessenheit-Vision: Anmerkungen aus der Sicht des Alten Testaments," *Kairos* 25, 1983, 156-75; S. J. Riekert, "Probleme en herbesinning in die soektog na 'n bevredigende leksikografiese paradigma van die betekenisse van *ra'ah*," *Acta Academica* 22, 1987, 128-38; M. S. Smith, "'Seeing God' in the Psalms: The Background to the Beatific Vision in the Hebrew Bible," *CBQ* 50, 1988, 171-83; R. J. Tournay, *Seeing and Hearing God with the Psalms: The Prophetic Liturgy of the Second Temple in Jerusalem*, 1991; H. van Dyke Parunak, "The Literary Architecture of Ezekiel's *mar'ôt 'elōhîm*," *JBL*, 1980, 61-74; W. VanGemeren, *Interpreting the Prophetic Word*, 1990.

Jackie A. Naudé

8012 (*rā'â*, red kite), → # 7606

8014 (*rō'eh* I, seer), → # 8011; Prophecy

8015 (*rō'eh* II, vision), → # 8014, Prophecy

8015 (*rō'eh* II, vision), → # 8011; Prophecy

8019 (*ra'ᵃwâ*, seeing), → # 8011

8021 (*rᵉ'ût*, look, sight), → # 8011

8023 (*rᵉ'î*, mirror), → # 8011

8024 (*rᵒ'î*, appearance, spectacle), → # 8011

8031	ראשׁ

ראשׁ (*rō'š*), head, hair of head, top, beginning, chief, leader, total amount, branch (# 8031); מְרַאֲשׁוֹת (*mᵉra'ᵃšôt*), headrest (→ # 5265); רִאשָׁה (*ri'šâ*), former situation (hapleg. in Ezek 36:11; → # 8035); רֹאשָׁה (*rō'šâ*), top (hapleg. in Zech 4:7; → # 8036); adj. רִאשׁוֹן (*ri'šôn*), first, former situation, preceding, former (→ # 8037); רִאשֹׁנִי (*ri'šōnî*), first (hapleg., Jer 25:1; → # 8038); רֵאשִׁית (*rē'šît*), nom. beginning, starting point, first, best, firstfruits (→ # 8040).

ANE The nom. *rō'š* appears in most of the Sem. languages, and the meaning in the different languages is fairly consistent. In biblical Aram. *rē'š* is used for the head of a human (Dan 2:28), the head of a statue (2:32), metaphorically for leaders (Ezra 5:10), and for the beginning or the substance of a dream (Dan 7:6). The word also appears in Phoenician and Punic, in Moabite (Mesha 20 for a division of an army), and in Ugar. (for head, the summit of a mountain, and with the same use as in Ezra 5:10). The same meaning appears also in Arab. (*ra's*), Syr. (*ryš*), and Akk. (*rāšum* and *rēšum*).

OT 1. *Head of a human.* The nom. is often used with this meaning in the OT. The expression from head to foot is used to denote a human's whole body (cf. Lev 13:12; Isa 1:6). Things can be carried on the head (Gen 40:16-17). Special provision was made for sores on the head as part of the provisions for ceremonial cleansing (cf. Lev 13:29-30, 44). In the case of the ceremonial cleansing of infectious skin diseases, the head had to be shaven and oil poured on the head of the person who is cleansed (Lev 14:9, 18, 29). In certain rituals the head also had an important role. When somebody blessed somebody else, his hands were laid on the head of the other person (Gen 48:14-18). The laying of hands on somebody's head could, however, also have a totally different significance. In Lev 24:10-23 the stoning of a blasphemer is related. All those who heard his blasphemy had to lay their hands on his head to confirm their testimony (24:14).

In Lev 19 a number of laws dealing with holiness are found. They include a stipulation that the hair on the side of the head may not be shaven (19:27). Priests were forbidden to shave their hair (21:5), and so also Nazirites (Num 6:5; Judg 13:5). The unshaven head served as a symbol of the Nazirite's consecration to the Lord (Num 6:7). When the period of separation has passed, the hair had to be shaven and placed in the fire under the sacrifice of the fellowship offering (6:18-19). In the same way the head of a captured woman also had to be shaven (Deut 21:12).

People in certain offices had their heads decorated. In Ezek 13:18 judgment is pronounced on the women who adorned their heads with veils in order to ensnare people. Figuratively, wisdom is described as an adornment for somebody's head (Prov 1:9). The priest received a turban on his head (Exod 29:6). Oil was poured on the priest's head as sign of his consecration (29:7; Lev 21:10). In the same way a king was also anointed (cf. 1 Sam 10:1; 2 Kgs 9:3, 6; Ps 23:5). A crown on the head of a king or queen indicated their royal dignity (1 Chron 20:2; Esth 2:17). When the crown of the high priest was taken away from him (Zech 6:11), it signified the removal of his honor. In Deut 28:23 "over your head" refers spatially to that which is above one (the sky in this case). In 33:16 reference is made to blessings that will come on somebody's head, i.e., that will become his. On the other hand, a storm that will come on one's head is a sign of judgment (Jer 23:19). In battle the head was regarded as an easy target. For this reason it was often protected with a helmet (1 Sam 17:5). The head of a slain enemy was regarded as a war trophy (17:57; 29:4). In Ezek 29:18 a head rubbed bare was regarded as a sign of heavy service in the army.

2. *The head of an animal.* The word is also used for the heads of animals. This is often the case with animals used in sacrifices. The Passover lamb had to be roasted in its entirety, including the head, legs, and inner parts (Exod 12:9). During the consecration of priests a young bull and two lambs were to be sacrificed. Before slaughtering the bull, Aaron and his sons had to lay their hands on the bull's head (29:10). The same had to be done with both the lambs (vv. 15, 19). This laying of the hands before a sacrifice appears frequently in Lev. In Lev 1:4 the sacrificer is commanded to lay his hand on the head of the burnt offering. Different explanations have been offered, such as

transference of the sins to the animal, declaration of the purpose of the sacrifice or of innocence, or ownership. In the case of Lev 1:4 only one hand was used, while two were used in the case of the scapegoat in 16:21. In the latter text, transference is probably the right explanation. In 1:4 and related instances the action probably refers to the ownership of the offering by the sacrificer. This action is omitted when the sacrificer could carry the offering. In the case of the scapegoat, the guilt of Israel was transferred to the scapegoat and then he was driven into the desert to carry the guilt of Israel away. When a dove was sacrificed, the priest had to wring his head from his body, sometimes completely (1:15) and sometimes partially (5:8).

In 2 Sam 3:8 the head of a dog is used in a derogatory reference to a person. In 2 Kgs 6:25 the value attached to a donkey's head denoted the severity of a famine.

3. *Head of statue or idol.* In 1 Sam 5:4 the word refers to the head of the statue of Dagon that was broken off before the ark of the Covenant.

4. *Head of other things.* Cherubim also had heads (Ezek 10:1, 11). Also the sea monsters and the Leviathan had heads (Job 41:7[40:31]; Ps 74:13, 14). In Ps 24:7, 9 gates are personified in the reference that they must lift their heads.

5. *Metonymically for hair, individual, or person.* The expression "to shave someone's head," meaning to shave his hair, appears frequently (cf. 2 Sam 14:26; Ezek 44:20). In Ps 140:7[8] it is said that the Lord will protect the head of the poet, head referring metonymically to his life. Also in 1 Chron 12:20 the word denotes life in the expression, "It will cost us our heads." In 2 Sam 2:16 reference is made to youths who grabbed each other's head (= hair) in battle. In 1 Sam 28:2 a bodyguard is called (lit.) "the keeper of my head."

6. *The nom. in conjunction with vbs. denoting gestures.* In particular, the shaking of the head is important. In Jer 18:16 the shaking of the head is a sign of amazement. In Ps 44:14[15] it is a sign of scorn and derision. In Job 16:4 it expresses mocking (cf. also 2 Kgs 19:21).

7. *Leader.* For a full discussion of the use of the word in this meaning, cf. Bartlett (1969). This nom. is frequently used to denote different kinds of leaders. It can denote leaders in general (cf. Num 25:4; Deut 29:10[9]; 33:5; Josh 23:2; 24:1; Job 29:25), important people in society (Isa 9:14, 15[13, 14]), or leaders of specific groups. It is used frequently for heads of families (Exod 6:14, 25; Num 7:2) and the heads of the tribes of Israel (Num 1:16; 32:28; Deut 1:15; 1 Kgs 8:1; 2 Chron 5:2). There are also references to the leaders of Jacob (Mic 3:1), the leaders of the house of Judah (3:9), the leaders of the people (Neh 10:14[15]), and provincial leaders (11:3).

Jephthah is called a head in Judg 11:4-11. It must denote more than just a military leader in this instance, perhaps something like a governor. Saul is also called the leader of the tribes of Israel (1 Sam 15:17). The word is also used for leaders of non-Israelite tribes (Num 25:15) or of the world in general (Job 12:24). Moses elected leaders, on the recommendation of Jethro, to assist him in judging cases (Exod 18:25, 26). The king of Israel is denoted by this word as the one who is a leader amongst the nations (2 Sam 22:44; Ps 18:43[44]; Jer 31:7). The word is often used in military contexts, e.g., for the head of the army (1 Chron 11:6) the leader of the Three (2 Sam 23:8, 18), and the thirty leaders of David's army (2 Sam 23:13). It is used for the high priest (2 Kgs 25:18; Jer 52:54) as well as for other important leading priests (Neh 12:7), and also for leaders of the Levites (Neh 12:24). In the cult a leader in thanksgiving and prayer is mentioned (Neh 11:17), and also leaders (directors) for the singers (Neh 12:46).

Even a city can be called the leading city in an area or among a group of cities (Josh 11:10; Isa 7:8, 9), and so also the mountain of the Lord's temple as chief among the mountains (Isa 2:2).

In connection with this use, the expression "to put at a group's head" denotes the appointment of somebody as leader (Deut 1:13, 15; 20:9). It is also used for a first-born son (1 Chron 23:8, 11, 16) or a son who received the privileges of a firstborn (26:10).

8. *Temporally: beginning.* The nom. can also be used temporally, to denote the beginning of time (Prov 8:23), the first month of the year (Exod 12:12), the first day of a month (Num 28:11), and the beginning of a year (Ezek 40:1). It is also used for the beginning of a watch (Judg 7:19; Lam 2:19). It can also be used in an abs. sense, for the beginning (Isa 40:21; 41:4, 26), also in opposition to the end of something (Eccl 3:11).

9. *Spatially: summit of a mountain, topside.* The nom. is used for the upper end of an object. It is often used for the summit of mountains or hills (Gen 8:5; Num 14:40; Isa 42:11). In Exod 34:2 God met Moses on the summit of a mountain. The summit of the temple mountain was regarded as holy (Ezek 43:12). This is probably related to the fact that the summit of a mountain was often used for sacrifices (Hos 4:13).

The word is also used for the top of a rock (Gen 28:18), the top of the stand in the temple (1 Kgs 7:35-36), of the pillars in the temple (2 Chron 3:15, 16), of a throne (1 Kgs 10:19), of a lampstand (Zech 4:2), of a tower (Gen 11:4), of a ladder (28:12), of the posts in the tabernacle (Exod 36:38), and of a tree (Ezek 17:4) or other plants (2 Sam 5:24). In Job 24:24 "the heads of grain" refers to the ears of crops. In Job 22:12 the word is used to denote the highest stars. The head of a table was regarded as a position of honor (1 Sam 9:22).

10. *Best or highest example of something.* Finest spices are often denoted by use of *b*^{e}*śāmîm rō'š* (cf. Exod 30:23; Ezek 27:22). It is also used absolutely for the best things (Deut 33:15). In Ps 137:6 it is used for the highest joy.

11. *The head of God or of the Lord.* The nom. is used infrequently with respect to God. In the vision of the Ancient of Days in Dan 7:9 God is represented as an old man whose hair is gray, as a sign of wisdom and knowledge. In the imagery in Isa 59:17 God's head is also mentioned, but evidently as part of an extended metaphor where God is pictured as an armored soldier, ready for vengeance. In 1 Chron 29:11 God is called the head of all, expressing his dominion. This is related to the use of the nom. to denote leaders. In 2 Chron 13:12 the Lord is called the leader of the people.

12. *Mourning rites.* The head played an important role in the mourning rites of Israel. The first rite was usually to throw dust, soil, or ashes on the head (Josh 7:6; 1 Sam 4:12; 2 Sam 1:2; 15:32; Job 2:12; Lam 2:10; Ezek 27:30). To put the hand on the head was regarded as a sign of sorrow (2 Sam 13:19, with a reference to Tamar's actions after being raped by Amnon; cf. also Jer 2:37). Ben-Hadad and his men tied ropes around their heads in addition to wearing sackcloth for their surrender to Israel (1 Kgs 20:31-32). It was also customary to shave the hair of the head as sign of mourning (Isa 15:2; Jer 48:37; Ezek 7:18). The head was also covered (2 Sam 15:30; Esth 6:12; Jer 14:3-4). When the hair was not shaved, it could be left to hang loose

(Lev 10:6) or left unkempt (2 Sam 15:30). To pull the hair from the head is also mentioned in this regard (Ezra 9:3).

13. *Head, total amount, sum.* In Num 5:7 the nom. refers to the sum of money to be paid as restitution, i.e., the capital amount on which interest must be reckoned. In Ps 119:160 and 139:17 the word refers to the sum or total of the Lord's words.

14. *Head, division, partition.* In Gen 2:10 the nom. is used to denote the four headwaters of the river running from Eden. The nom. is commonly used as a military term for different military formations or units (cf. Judg 7:16, 20; 9:34, 37, 43-44; 1 Sam 11:11; 13:17-18; Job 1:17).

15. The nom. refers to a main cornerstone in Ps 118:22, in the expression *rō'š pinnâ.*

16. *Idiomatic expressions.* The head of a person is also used in different idiomatic expressions, sometimes with a positive and sometimes with a negative sense. In Eccl 2:14 the wise person is typified as the one who has his eyes in his head, while the fool walks in darkness. This image is related to the opposition between light and darkness that appears frequently in the Wisdom literature to describe the two groups (wise people and fools). To heap burning coals on someone's head is an idiomatic expression taken over by many languages (Prov 25:22). This is a controversial idiom. The image used refers to severe pain. The pain could be the pain of contrition or sorrow caused by the good deed as payment for a bad deed. Some commentators refer to an Egyptian ritual in which live coals on the head of a penitent person was a mark of contrition. Others refer to an Old-Assyr. law with a similar punishment for a whore. A good deed can cause an evildoer to repent. The expression, "not a hair of his head will fall to the ground," meaning that a person will come to no harm (1 Sam 14:45), also became idiomatic in many languages. The expression "more than the hair of my head" is used to express a large number (Ps 40:12[13]).

The expression, "your blood be on your own head," is used to denote that something is somebody's own fault (2 Sam 1:16; cf. Ezek 33:4). If somebody is, however, responsible for something that happened to somebody else, esp. if it caused the other's death, the expression is used to denote the guilt of that party ("his blood will be on his own head," Josh 2:19; "may his blood fall upon ...," 2 Sam 3:29; "The LORD will repay him for the blood he shed...," 1 Kgs 2:32-33). In the last instance it is stated that the guilt will rest on "the head of Joab and his descendants forever." To let something return on someone's head (NIV to make someone pay for something, Judg 9:57) means to repay someone for what he did. It is mostly used with a negative sense, such as to repay someone for the evil he did (9:57; 1 Sam 25:39), for his insults (Neh 4:4[3:36]), for his way (1 Kgs 8:32), or for what he did (Joel 3:4, 7[4:4, 7]). To humiliate someone is expressed by the expression "to trample on the heads of ..." (Amos 2:7).

The expression "my head will be exalted" denotes a position of honor and the certainty of victory (Ps 27:6). Related to this is the expression "to lift up someone's head." It denotes the appointment to a position of honor (cf. Gen 40:13), although it can also be used ironically to denote that someone was hanged (40:19-20). In the last case the addition of the prepositional phrase *m'lyk* makes it clear that the expression has an ironic meaning (cf. Marcus, 1989, for a discussion of this usage of the nom.). The same expression is also used for the taking of a census (Exod 30:12; Num 1:2, 49; 4:2, 22). A nation that was humiliated and subjected is unable to raise its head

(Judg 8:28; cf. also Job 10:15; Ps 3:3[4]; 83:2[3]; Zech 1:21[2:4]). Jehoiachin's release from prison is denoted by the same expression (2 Kgs 25:27). Marcus (1990, 21) distinguishes four meanings for this expression: (a) to take off someone's head, to carry it off (1 Chron 10:9); (b) to take a census; (c) to be happy or to assert oneself; and (d) as in the case of Jehoiachin, it perhaps has the meaning to review a case. The expression that someone's head touches the clouds denotes human pride (Job 20:6).

The head of a street denotes one end of a street (Isa 51:20; Ezek 16:25). Cf. also the head of a valley (Isa 28:1) and the head of a passage (Prov 1:21; Ezek 42:12). The word is also used for the tip of a scepter (Esth 5:2) or of poles (1 Kgs 8:8).

17. The nom. *m^{e}ra'^{a}šôt*, headrest, refers to a rock used by Jacob as a pillow (Gen 28:11, 18), to the head end of a bed (1 Sam 19:13), and to the place at Saul's head on the ground, where he planted his spear for the night and where his water jug stood (1 Sam 26:7, 11-12, 16; cf. 1 Kgs 19:6).

P-B In Mish. Heb. the word is used in the same way as in the OT. In the LXX it is usually translated with *kephalē*. Other translations are also possible, reflecting the use of the nom. in the Heb., e.g., *archē* in Ps 137[136]:6 and *prōtotokos* in 1 Chron 5:12.

NT In the NT *kephalē* is used mainly for the head of a human, but also for animals and demons. It is also used in connection with fasting and penitence (Matt 6:17; Acts 18:18; Rev 18:19). Eph 4 is esp. important, where Christ is described as the head and the church as the body. This emphasizes the authority of Christ.

Head: → *'ap* (face, anger, # 678); → *gulgōlet* (scull, # 1653); → *l^{e}ḥî* I (eye, nose, jawbone, chin, cheek, # 4305); → *mēṣaḥ* (forehead, # 5195); → *m^{e}tall^e'ôt* (jawbone, # 5506); → *pānîm* (face, visible, assault, # 7156); → *pōt* (front, forehead, # 7327); → *qodqōd* (crown of head, # 7721); → *rō'š* I (head, chief, beginning, # 8031); → *raqqâ* (temple [of head], # 8377)
Beginning: → *ḥnk* (train, inaugurate, # 2852); → *rō'š* I (head, chief, beginning, # 8031); → *t^{e}ḥillâ* (beginning, # 9378)

Bibliography

NIDNTT 2:156-63; *TDNT* 3:673-82; *THAT* 2:701-15; *TWAT* 7:271-84; J. R. Bartlett, "The Use of the Word ראש as a Title in the Old Testament," *VT* 19, 1969, 1-10; D. Marcus, "The Bargaining Between Jephtah and the Elders (Judges 11:4-11)," *JANESCU* 19, 1989, 95-100; idem, "'Lifting Up the Head': On the Trail of a Word Play in Genesis 40," *Prooftexts* 10, 1990, 17-27; J. Milgrom, *Leviticus 1-16*, AB, 1991, 150-53, 1041-43.

Harry F. van Rooy

8031a	ראש חֹדֶשׁ

ראש חֹדֶשׁ (*rō'š ḥōdeš*), Festival of the New Moon (# 8031a); for the nom. see *ḥōdeš* (month, new moon; → # 2544) and *rō'š* I (head, chief, beginning; → # 8031).

OT 1. *Usage*. References to the new moon occur 22x in the Bible and is usually linked with other days of veneration. In four-name lists it is named in conjunction with Sabbaths (Num 28:11-15; Ezek 45:17; Hos 2:11[13]; 1 Macc 10:34; *Jub*. 1:14), Feasts of Passover and Weeks (Num 28:16-31), and generic references to feasts and appointed feasts (Ezek 45:17; Hos 2:11[3]; 1 Macc 10:34). New Moon(s) occur 8x in three-name sequences, usually preceded by Sabbath and followed by a reference to unspecified feasts (McKay, 17). Although the New Moon celebration is only described in one narrative as an important cultic event (1 Sam 20:5-34), rituals such as trumpet blowing and sacrifice are specified in detail in numerous contexts (Lev 23:24; Num 10:10; 28:11-15; 29:1-6; Ps 81:3[4]; Ezek 46:6).

2. *Theological interpretation.* Kraus (79-80) considered the New Moon to be a monthly festival that was established early in Israel's family life. It was a monthly day of cultic celebration in preexilic Israel, during which sacrifices were brought to the temple or sanctuary (Hasel, 38-39). Frequent references in 1 and 2 Chron create the impression that New Moon festivals gained popularity after the exile (1 Chron 23:31; 2 Chron 2:4[3]; 8:13; Ezra 3:5 and Neh 10:33[34]). This impression is further enhanced by the New Moon's importance in Lev 23:24-25, but caution must be exercised to accept a New Moon festival as the forerunner of the New Year festival (*TREg* 11:103).

The possibility that some form of moon worship caused the New Moon day to be celebrated merits exploration. Numerous seals have been found in Palestine that depict signs and symbols associated with a moon cult, parallel to artifacts connected with the moon god Sin excavated in Harran (Northern Syria). Albertz (190) is convinced that the moon cult was the result of strong Aramaean religious influences flooding into Judah after the Assyrian occupation.

It seems as if the aspect of renewal might have played an important role in the commemoration of the festival of the New Moon and that it was later linked to the eschatological renewal of the covenant by God (*TDOT* 4:244).

P-B The Mishnah (Megilla 4:2) indicates that at the start of each month special services were held in the synagogue (Thornton, 97). Josephus (*Ant*) as well as Judith (8:6) and 1 Macc (10:34) incorporated New Moon festivals in their lists of Jewish feasts. There is a legend that explains the *Rosh Hodesh* as a holiday for Jewish women as a reward for their refusal to take part in the making of the golden calf (Adelman, 155).

NT The fact that the beginning of the New Moon celebrations was determined by the empirical sighting of the moon may be alluded to in Gal 4:10, where the observation of days and months is mentioned (Thornton, 99).

Feasts & festivals: → *bikkûrîm* (early or firstfruits, # 1137); → *ḥag* (procession, round dance, festival, feast, # 2504); → *ḥanukkâ* (dedication, Feast of Dedication, # 2853); → *mô'ēd* (appointed time, # 4595); → *maṣṣôt* (Feast of the Unleavened Bread, # 5174a); → *marzēaḥ* (cultic feast, funeral meal, # 5301); → *sukkôt* (Feast of Tabernacles, # 6109a); → *'aṣārâ* (festive assembly, # 6809); → *pûrîm* (festival of Purim, # 7052a); → *pesaḥ* (Feast or sacrifice of Passover, # 7175 [→ **Passover: Theology**]); → *rō'š ḥōdeš* (festival of the new Moon, # 8031a); → *rō'š haššānâ* (beginning of the year, # 8031b); → *šābu'ôt* (feast of Weeks, # 8651a); → *šabbāt* (sabbath, # 8701 [→ **Sabbath: Theology**])

BIBLIOGRAPHY

TDOT 4:225-44; *TREg* 11:103; P. V. Adelman, "A Drink from Miriam's Cup. Invention of Tradition Among Jewish Women, " *Journal of Feminist Studies in Religion*, 10, 1994, 151-66; R. Albertz, *A History of Israelite Religion in the Old Testament Period I*, 1994; G. F. Hasel, "'New Moon and Sabbath' in Eighth Century Israelite Prophetic Writings (Isa 1:13; Hos 2:13; Amos 8:5)," in *Wünschet Jerusalem Frieden*, eds, M. Augustin & K. D. Schunck, 1988, 37-64; H.-J. Kraus, *Worship in Israel*, 1966; H. A. McKay, "New Moon or Sabbath?" in *The Sabbath in*

Jewish and Christian Traditions, ed., T. Eskenazi, 1991, 12-27; T. C. G. Thornton, "Jewish New Moon Festivals, Galatians 4:3-11 and Colossians 2:16," *JTS* 40, 1989, 97-100.

Hendrik L. Bosman

8031b	ראשׁ הַשָּׁנָה

ראשׁ הַשָּׁנָה (*rō'š haššānâ*), beginning of the year; lit. head of the year (# 8031b); for the nom. see *rō'š* I (head, hair of head, chief, leader; → # 8031) and *šānâ* (year; → # 9102).

ANE Various ANE cultures observed some form of New Year celebration, and according to several scholars, significant examples of these type of festivities can be found in Mesopotamia and Canaan. The *akītu* festival in Babylon has been most frequently referred to as a possible analogy for an Israelite New Year festival. Van der Toorn (332-39) has pointed out that there were two *akītu* a year and that it functioned as the divine ratification or confirmation of the royal mandate, not as the reenactment of a supposed creation combat.

OT 1. *Usage*. The term *rō'š haššānâ* occurs only 1x in the OT (Ezek 40:1). Ezekiel dates his vision of the future temple on the 10th day of the beginning of the year, a day that coincides with the Day of Atonement (Lev 25:9). It is possible that we here find an older date for the New Year with an Israelite year beginning in the autumn, but it is still obscure why the beginning of the year was on the 10th and not on the 1st of the month (Zimmerli, 1983, 346). The reference to "the beginning of the year" in Ezek 40:1 is ambiguous, but there might be a symbolic reference to the Jubilee Year (celebrated every fifty years), with the additional chronological indication that the vision took place twenty-five years after the deportation of Jehoiachin in 597 (Fuhs, 226; Allen, 229).

2. *A New Year feast in the OT?* Mowinckel developed a theory that Israel began its new year in autumn with the seventh month (Tishri), which coincided with the wine harvest. This New Year feast was celebrated as a symbolic reenthronement of God through the king as his earthly representative. He found evidence for this celebration in the royal psalms and those psalms where the enthronement of Yahweh is mentioned. A comparative study of Canaanite and Israelite sources on New Year festivals led de Moor (28-29) to the conclusion that Israel took over this festival from the Canaanites in a critical way by making it acceptable to Yahwism.

(a) No New Year festival is described in the OT, and no explicit reference can be found in any of the cultic calendars or the narratives. Festivals like the Day of Trumpets, Day of Atonement, and the Feast of Succoth took place during the seventh month, but no one of them can be associated beyond any doubt with an autumn New Year feast (Grabbe, 98-99). There are certain similarities between the Feast of Succoth, seen as an autumn festival, and the Babylonian *akītu* (van der Toorn, 340-43). Despite their common agrarian origins, solemn procession, and legitimation of kingship, there is still no proof that this autumn festival was *the* New Year festival in Israel. There might have been an observance of a New Year festival at the royal court in Jerusalem, but it never became theologically significant enough to be mentioned in the cultic calendars of Israel (Zimmerli, 1984, 129).

(b) Clines (22-40) has argued for a new year starting in spring during preexilic times. Although different calendars were in use, the most consistent time for the beginning of the new year in the OT seems to be in the spring, not in autumn.

P-B 1. *LXX. rō'š haššānâ* is translated *en tō prōtō mēni;* this indicates that the LXX interpreted it to be merely an approximate indication of the date so that no information about the month is given (Zimmerli, 1983, 330, 345).

2. *Rabbinical literature.* Although Josephus and Philo never mention a New Year feast, the New Year feast was so important to the early Jews that the Mishnah devotes a whole tractate (Roš Haššana) to it. They kept the feast on the first of Tishri, when a shofar was sounded and songs of praise were sung (de Vaux, 502). It was seen as a day of judgment or penitence (*Yom ha-Din*), when each person had to give an account of his or her actions during the past year, and as a day of remembrance (*Yom ha-Zikkaron*) when the deeds (successes and failures) of previous generations were commemorated (Gaster, 107-34).

NT Despite the Roman calendar being the official one, events were frequently referred to with reference to the Jewish religious year; it is remarkable that no mention is made of any form of New Year celebration in the NT (*ISBE* 3:532).

Feasts & festivals: → *bikkûrîm* (early or firstfruits, # 1137); → *ḥag* (procession, round dance, festival, feast, # 2504); → *ḥ^{a}nukkâ* (dedication, Feast of Dedication, # 2853); → *mô'ēd* (appointed time, # 4595); → *maṣṣôt* (Feast of the Unleavened Bread, # 5174a); → *marzēaḥ* (cultic feast, funeral meal, # 5301); → *sukkôt* (Feast of Tabernacles, # 6109a); → *'^{a}ṣārâ* (festive assembly, # 6809); → *pûrîm* (festival of Purim, # 7052a); → *pesaḥ* (Feast or sacrifice of Passover, # 7175 [→ **Passover: Theology**]); → *rō'š ḥōdeš* (festival of the new Moon, # 8031a); → *rō'š haššānâ* (beginning of the year, # 8031b); → *šābu'ôt* (feast of Weeks, # 8651a); → *šabbāt* (sabbath, # 8701 [→ **Sabbath: Theology**])

BIBLIOGRAPHY

ABD 1:138-40; *IDB* 544-46; *ISBE* 3:529-32; *THAT* 2:711-14; *TWAT* 7:271-82; L. C. Allen, *Ezekiel 20-48*, WBC, 1990; D. J. A. Clines, "The Evidence for an Autumnal New Year in Pre-Exilic Israel Reconsidered," *JBL* 93, 1974, 22-40; J. C. de Moor, *New Year with Canaanites and Israelites*, 1972; R. de Vaux, *AncIsr*, 1961, 502-6; H. F. Fuhs, *Ezechiel* II, 1988; T. H. Gaster, *Festivals of the Jewish Year*, 1978; L. L. Grabbe, *Leviticus*, 1993; S. Mowinckel, *Psalmenstudien II. Das Thronbesteigungsfest Jahwäs und der Ursprung der Eschatologie*, 1922; K. van der Toorn, "The Babylonian New Year Festival: New Insights from the Cuneiform Texts and Their Bearing on Old Testament Study," *Congress Volume Leuven*, 1989, ed. J. A. Emerton, 1991, 331-44; W. Zimmerli, *Ezekiel*, Hermeneia, 1983; idem, *OTTO*, 1984.

Hendrik L. Bosman

8032	ראשׁ

ראשׁ (*rō'š* II), or רושׁ (*rôš*), nom. a bitter and poisonous herb (# 8032).

ANE Cf. Aram. *rêšā'*, poison.

OT The word occurs 12x in the OT. Usually it has in view a bitter and poisonous plant, but twice it refers to the venom of snakes (Deut 32:33; Job 20:16). The exact identity of this plant is not certain; at times the word seems to have assumed a sense of poison in general. In every OT instance the word is used figuratively. Jeremiah likens God's wrath to poisonous water that the people were made to drink (Jer 8:14; 9:15[14]; 23:15; cf. Lam 3:5, 19). Idolatry is a root that sprouts poisonous and bitter growth (Deut 29:18[17]). Justice or litigation can be turned into poison, as it were (Hos 10:4; Amos 6:12), and the treatment received from enemies can be tantamount to poison (Deut 32:32; Ps 69:21[22]). In the last reference "gall in my food" is parallel to "vinegar for my thirst." The verse takes on Christological significance in connection with a detail of Jesus' crucifixion recorded by all four Gospels (Matt 27:34, 48; Mark 15:36; Luke 23:36; John 19:29).

Some scholars think that the biblical *rō'š* is the perennial or biennial *Conium maculatum*, which has medicinal use as a sedative and as a preventative for spasms. According to many this plant may also be the source of the poison hemlock administered, among others, to Socrates.

P-B Heb. *rôš* and Aram. *rêš* occur in RL and in the Targumim; e.g., the word occurs in *Esth. Rab.* 1:1 in reference to a poisonous drink. In the LXX *rō'š* is rendered 6x by *cholē*, gall (Deut 29:17; 32:32; Jer 8:14; 9:14; Ps 69[68]:22; Lam 3:19). Other renderings are *thymos*, anger (Deut 32:33; Job 20:16; Amos 6:12); *agrōstis*, dog's-tooth grass (Hos 10:4); *pikros*, pungent (Jer 23:15). In one instance the Greek translator understood *rō'š* to be the homonym meaning head, which he translated by *kephalē* (Lam 3:5). The word also occurs in the DSS (e.g., CD 8:9-10; 19:22, citing Deut 32:33; 1QH 4:14).

Vegetation: → *'ēzôb* (hyssop, # 257); → *dš'* (become green, sprout, # 2012); → *zr'* (sow, scatter seed, form seed, # 2445); → *ḥāṣîr* I (grass, # 2945); → *ḥ^ašaš* (dry grass, # 3143); → *yereq* (green, greenness, # 3764); → *nṭ'* (plant, establish, drive, # 5749); → *'āleh* (leaf, leafage, # 6591); → *'ēśeb* (herb, herbage, weed, # 6912); → *qîqāyôn* (plant of uncertain identity, # 7813); → *rō'š* II (bitter and poisonous herb, # 8032); → *śîaḥ* I (bush, shrub, # 8489); → *šiṭṭâ* (acacia, # 8847)

BIBLIOGRAPHY

ABD 2:817; *IDB* 2:297; *ISBE* 3:899-900; *TWAT* 7:284-87; *TWOT* 2:826; *Fauna and Flora of the Bible*, 1972, 167-68; N. Feinbrun-Dothan, *Flora Palaestina*, 1966-86, 3:405-6; R. K. Harrison, *Healing Herbs of the Bible*, 1966, 35; I. Löw, *Die Flora der Juden*, 1924, 1:725; 2:364; 3:48; 4:155; W. McKane, "Poison, Trial by Ordeal and the Cup of Wrath," *VT* 30, 1980, 474-92, esp. 478-87; H. N. and A. L. Moldenke, *Plants of the Bible*, 1952, 48-50, 78-80, 279; M. de Waal, *Medicinal Herbs of the Bible*, 1980, 46-47; W. Walker, *All the Plants of the Bible*, 1957, 98-99; M. Zohary, *Plants of the Bible*, 1982, 186.

Richard A. Taylor

8035 (*ri'šâ*, former situation), → # 8031

8036 (*rō'šâ*, top), → # 8040

8037 (*ri'šôn*, first, preceding, former), → # 8040

8038 (*ri'šōnî*, first), → # 8040

8040	רֵאשִׁית

רֵאשִׁית (*rē'šît*), nom. beginning, starting point, first, best, firstfruits (# 8040); רֹאשׁ (*rō'š* I), nom. head, chief, beginning (# 8031); מְרַאֲשׁוֹת ($m^e ra'^a$*šôt*), headrest (# 5265); רִאשָׁה (*ri'šâ*), former situation (hapleg. in Ezek 36:11; # 8035); רֹאשָׁה (*rō'šâ*), top (hapleg. in Zech 4:7; # 8036); adj. רִאשׁוֹן (*ri'šôn*), first, former situation, preceding, former (# 8037); רִאשֹׁנִי (*ri'šōnî*), first (hapleg., Jer 25:1; # 8038).

ANE A common Sem. root (see *HALAT* 1086). All but one of the fourteen occurrences of *rē'š* in bibl. Aram. (Dan 7:1 being the exception) denote the bodily "head" (as in the last line of the Siloam Inscription, *ANET*[3], 321) In an eighth century BC Phoenician inscription from Cyprus, *rē'šît* means either the first yield of copper from a new mine or the choicest copper (cf. Gibson, *TSSI* 3:66-68). Akk. speakers also used noms. from this root for firstborn, beginning, or objects of high quality (*AHw* 972-73).

OT 1. The Bible's first word, *rē'šît*, beginning, presents a complicated and unique problem. The nom. *rē'šît* occurs 51x, 19x indicating something's beginning (wisdom, strife, sin, etc.). In 78 percent of its total occurrences (40x), it appears as the first of two noms. bound in a construct state indicating the genitive relationship. In another 5x, it is made definite by the use of a pronominal suffix. It is used in an absolute, independent construction 5x, only one of which carries the meaning "beginning" (Isa 46:10).

2. The exact form in Gen 1:1 (prepositional phrase b^e*rē'šît*) occurs elsewhere only in Jeremiah, where it is always in bound construction with the same nom. (or cognates of the nom. "kingdom," Jer 26:1; 27:1; 28:1; 49:34). In Gen 1:1, however, *rē'šît* is doubly peculiar since it is followed by the vb. "created" and is indefinite. Its traditional interpretation as an independent clause (see KJV) is a peculiar grammatical phenomenon in bibl. Heb. Some, therefore, reject the traditional interpretation supported by all ancient versions (LXX, Vg., Aq., Th., Symm., Tg. Onk.), and translate it as a dependent clause on the basis of parallels with the Babylonian creation account: "When God set about to create..." (Speiser, *Genesis* AB, 1964, 1, 3 with arguments on 12-13; see also JPSV and NEB). Such an interpretation suggests that God began his creation with primordial matter, instead of creating *ex nihilo*. (→ *br'* I, create, # 1343)

Though the dependent interpretation is possible lexically and grammatically, it is not necessary since time designations in adverbial expressions do not require the definite article (Heidel, *The Babylonian Genesis: The Story of Creation*, 2d ed., 1963, 92). Furthermore, the laconic style of Gen 1 is not likely to have begun with the convoluted syntax of a lengthy, dependent clause related to v. 2 or v. 3 (Hamilton, *The Book of Genesis*, NICOT, 1990, 107-8). More to the point, von Rad has aptly observed "syntactically perhaps both translations are possible, but not theologically" (*Genesis*, OTL, 1972, 48). The biblical witness is univocal in its support of *creatio ex nihilo*, the ancient doctrine that God created the universe from nothing by his great power (see for example Ps 33:6, 9; Heb 11:3). In this light, it is significant that the only other independent occurrence of *rē'šît* (i.e., absolute, and not in construct with another nom.) meaning "beginning" is in Isa 46:9-10: "I am God, and there is none like me. I make known the end from *the beginning*, from ancient times, what is still to come." Thus the reason the first word in Gen 1:1 is grammatically peculiar and syntactically unique may be because the author (like Isaiah) is describing a unique event. Unlike the beginning of a king's reign or the beginning of wisdom, strength, or sin, describing the beginning of

God's creative activity required atypical language. So the form and use of *rē'šît* in Gen 1:1 and Isa 46:10 are unique, but they should not be surprising. (→ Genesis: Theology)

Later in Israel's history the nom. *rē'šît* began to be used in eschatological contexts. It was used with its antonym *'aḥarît* to mark the temporal parameters of something, as in Deut 11:12: "...from the beginning of the year to its end" (so see Job 8:7; 42:12; Eccl 7:8; Isa 46:10). There were other words available for the first in a series of items (see *teḥillâ*), but only *rē'šît* holds the "end" in view from the "beginning" (for more detail see Sailhamer, "Genesis," *EBC*, 1990, 2:20-23). In contradistinction to Israel's neighbors, the first verse in the Bible focuses on a timeline for history that has definite parameters and becomes an instrument of divine revelation. Yahweh is the God of that history.

3. The nom. *rō'š* occurs 596x, 230 of which designate the physical head, whether of man or beast (for book-by-book statistical analysis, see *THAT* 2:703). David cut off Goliath's head with the Philistine's own sword (1 Sam 17:51, 54; see also 2 Sam 4:8; 20:22). Isaiah used a bodily metaphor in describing Israel as diseased from the sole of the foot to the head (Isa 1:6). Hands were laid on the head of sacrificial animals, symbolizing the transference of guilt (Exod 29:10; Lev 1:4). This literal sense lends itself naturally to designate the top of a hill, mountain, rock, or pillar as its "head" or "top" (Exod 19:20 and 87 more times). See further # 8031.

Spices and oil may be modified as *rō'š,* meaning "best" or of "high quality" (Ps 141:5; Jer 22:6). The exilic believer prefers Jerusalem above his choicest joy (Ps 137:6). "Head" can mean first in sequence (Exod 12:2) and therefore "beginning" when used in time or space designations (Judg 7:19; Ezek 16:25, respectively). Humankind cannot fathom what God has done "from beginning to end" (Eccl 3:11). "From the beginning" is especially noticeable in Isaiah (40:21, 41:4, 26; 48:16).

B. S. Childs (*IOTS*, 1979, 311-38) believes the "former things" refer to the prophecies in Isaiah 1-39, but the "first/former" in 48:16 seems to refer to earlier prophecies about Cyrus, or in 40:21 and 41:3 to the creation of the world. The Exodus event seems to be the "former things" in 43:18, but the common aspect in all these passages is God's ability to act and reveal his will in the future as well as the past. That ability brings comfort, for he is sovereign over history and time, planning and executing his powerful will to bring all people to himself. This nom. is frequently used to specify the chief or leader of a tribe, city, or nation, especially in the expression "head of the house of (his) fathers" (Num 1:4; Hos 1:11[2:2]). This is the common identification for the head or "chief priest" (1 Chron 27:5). The stone that was at one time rejected has become the "head of the corner" (Ps 118:22), a statement Jesus applied to himself (Luke 20:17).

When combined with the vb. *nś'*, *rō'š* forms an idiom ("lift up the head") with a multitude of meanings: enumerate, honor, or act haughtily. This idiom lends itself to wordplay (Gen 40:13, 19-20). Wagging one's head was a sign of derision and scorn (2 Kgs 19:21; Ps 22:7[8]), and baldness on every head was a sign of universal calamity (Jer 48:37; Amos 8:10).

4. The adj. *ri'šôn* occurs 182x modifying the first of two or more items ranging from brothers (Gen 25:25) to the stone tablets of the Decalogue (Exod 34:1). This adj. is especially common with words of time (such as "month," Gen 8:13, and "day," Exod 12:15). The ages of antiquity begin with the "former days" when God created

humankind on the earth (Deut 4:32; notice the "later days" of v. 30, which are in Israel's future). Occasionally used with its antonym ("last" [*'aḥ^{a}rôn*]), this adj. forms a merism typical in Sem. languages, in which polar extremes describe totality. In Isaiah's expression of monotheism, Yahweh is both "the first" and "the last," meaning the only (probably an enumeration in which he is the only number, Isa 44:6, and see also 41:4; Neh 8:18; Rev 1:8).

5. The nom. *rē'šît* occurs frequently as the "firstfruits" of produce (Lev 2:12, see *bkr*, → # 1144). Israel was thus wholly the Lord's, the firstfruits of his harvest (Jer 3:2). It can also be descriptive of the highest quality, as in "wisdom is supreme" (Prov 4:7, similarly to *rō'š*).

6. In Wisdom texts the fear of the Lord is said to be the "beginning, first principle" of wisdom (Ps 111:10; Prov 1:7; 9:10). This is more than the motto of wisdom; it is the essential or chief part (Bronger, 167), the sum or firstfruits of wisdom, or the first and controlling principle of wisdom (Kidner, *Proverbs*, TOTC, 1964, 59). Fearing God is where wisdom begins (Ps 111:10, *teḥillâ*), but it is not left behind by the wise person, for it continues to guide and offer control and first principles for all of life's decisions.

7. Two other nom. derivatives designate "former" or "first." God promises the barren and destitute mountains of Israel they will once again be cultivated and populated with Israelites as in the past (*ri'šâ*, their former situation, used in parallel with *qadmâ*, Ezek 36:11). The "top" or "headstone" of Zech 4:7 (*hā'eben hārō'šâ*) was probably a "former stone" preserved from Solomon's temple and used by Zerubbabel as a building deposit in the second temple. Such a stone served to underscore sacred continuity with the previous temple, just as the *libittu maḫrītu*, "the first (or former) brick," was used in Mesopotamian building practices (see Ellis, *Foundation Deposits in Ancient Mesopotamia*, 1968, 13, 26-29).

8. The nom. *m^{e}ra'^{a}šôt* occurs 9x for "headrest." Most references are to make-shift sleeping arrangements for nights spent out-of-doors. Elijah fled from Jezebel and hoped to die in a remote desert of Judah, but slept instead. When he awoke, an angel provided bread and water for him at his headrest (1 Kgs 19:6). Jacob used a stone at Bethel for his headrest while he slept and dreamed of Yahweh's ladder. The next morning he set up the headrest as a sacred monument (*maṣṣēbâ*) commemorating the event (Gen 28:11, 18). See also # 5265.

David's wife Michal used goat's hair at the head of his bed in her ruse to deceive Saul's men (1 Sam 19:13, 16). The occurrence of this nom. in Jer 13:18 is due to a misinterpretation of the Masoretic scribes, as the evidence in all the ancient versions testifies (W. L. Holladay, *Jeremiah* 1, Hermeneia, 1986, 408).

NT → *NIDNTT* 1:164-69.

Beginning: → *ḥnk* (train, inaugurate, # 2852); → *rō'š* I (head, chief, beginning, # 8031); → *t^{e}ḥillâ* (beginning, # 9378)

BIBLIOGRAPHY

THAT 2:701-15; *AncIsr* 380-81, 404, 441-46, 490-93; J. R. Bartlett, "The Use of the Word *rō'š* as a Title in the Old Testament," *VT* 19, 1969, 1-10; J. Becker, *Gottesfurcht im Alten Testament,* AnBib, 1965; H. Blocher, "The Fear of the Lord as the Principle of Wisdom," *TynBul* 28, 1977, 3-28; A. Brongers, "La Crainte du Seigneur (Jir'at Jhwh, Jir'at 'Elohim)," *OTS* V, 1948, 158-63;

G. F. Hasel, "Recent Translations of Gen 1:1: A Critical Look," *BT* 22, 1971, 154-67; C. R. North, "The 'Former Thing' and the 'New Things' in Isaiah 40-48," in *Studies in OT Prophecy: FS for T. H. Robinson*, ed. H. H. Rowley, 1950, 111-26; D. H. Odendaal, "The 'Former' and 'Latter Things' in the Prophecies of Deutero-Isaiah," *Tarbiz* 14, 1942, 19-25; N. H. Ridderbos, "Gen 1:1 and 2," *OTS* 12, 1958, 214-60; A. Schoors, "Les choses antérieures et les choses nouvelles dans les oracles Deutéro-Isaïens," *Ephemerides Theologicae Lovanīenses* 40, 1964, 19-47; B. K. Waltke, "The Creation Account in Genesis 1:1-3: Part III: The Initial Chaos Theory and the Precreation Chaos Theory," *BSac* 132, 1975, 216-28.

Bill T. Arnold

8041 (*rab* I, numerous, plentiful, abounding), → # 8045

8042	רַב

רַב (*rab* II), nom. captain, chief, commander, ruler (# 8042); רַב (*rab* I), adj. great, important (→ # 8041); רֹב (*rōb*), nom. greatness, multitude (# 8044); < רבה (*rbh* I), multiply, be great (→ # 8049).

ANE 1. The nom. *rab* is common Sem., originally East Sem. and adopted in West-Sem.: Akk. *rabū,* great one, chief, captain, commander, official; PS *rb,* chief, foreman; OSA *rb,* master, lord; Ugar. *rabu,* chief, captain, leader, commander; Phoen. *rab,* chief, commander, officer; Pun. *rab,* chief, commander; Neo-Pun. *rab,* commanding officer, chief, head; Moab. (pl.) *rbn,* captain, commander; Old Aram. *rab,* chief, captain; Aram. *rab,* chief, commander, officer; Emp. Aram. *rab,* chief, captain; *rbh,* officer; JAram. *rbh,* chief, captain, master, employer, teacher, instructor; JPAram. *rab,* chief, master, teacher; Egyp. Aram. *rab,* official, director, chief, head, headmaster, commanding officer; Syr. *rab,* chief, master; Palm. *rab,* chief, captain, commanding officer; Hatra *rb,* chief; Nab. *rb,* chief, captain; Arab. *rabba,* master, lord, ruler, governer, official, commander.

2. *rab* often appears in construct with a following genitive, forming a title designating authority in five areas: (a) vocational: supervisor, foreman, chief; (b) cultic: chief priest; (c) judicial: chief magistrate; (d) military: officer, captain, commander; and (e) governmental: royal official, ruler (*AHw*, 933-38; *DISO*, 270-72).

3. *Political/administrative titles.* Akk. *rab mugi,* chief prince; *rab ša rēši šarri* (lit., chief who is at the head of a king), chief official; *rab šaqû,* chief cupbearer; *rab āli,* mayor of city; *rab ālāni,* ruler of sub-district; *rabi ekalle,* palace inspector; *rabi urtānē,* master of treasury; *rabi alaḫḫini,* chief tax collector; *rabi abulli,* gate official (*AHw*, 933-38); Ugar. *rb qrt,* chief of town (mayor) (*UT*, 2297; *WUS*, 2482); Phoen. *rb 'rṣ,* ruler of land/district; *rb srsrm,* chief courtier (*GPL*, 145-46); Emp. Aram. *rb srs,* chief official (eunuch?) (*DISO*, 270-72).

4. *Military titles.* Akk. *rab kiṣri,* commander of army; *rab ḫanše,* captain of fifty; *rab šaqû,* commandant, commander of march (*AHw*, 933-38; Saggs, 260); Ugar. *rb 'šrt,* chief of ten (corporal); *rb m't,* chief of 100 (captain) (*UT*, 2297; *WGU*, 2482); Moab. (pl.) *rbn,* captain, commander (Meṣa 5); Emp. Aram. *rb šwq,* inspector of the march (*DISO*, 272); Phoen. *rb m't,* chief of 100 (centurion); *rb smy,'* holder of the banner; Pun. *rb mšryt',* captain of the camp; *rb mšṭrt,* chief quartermaster; *rb smy',* holder of the banner; Neo-Pun. *rb ḥyl',* commander of garrison; *rb m't,* centurion, commander

of 100; *rb mḥnt,* consul, captain of army; *rb t'ḥt,* proconsul, captain of guards (*DISO,* 270-72; *GPL,* 145-46).

5. *Vocational titles.* Akk. *rab aškapē,* inspector of leatherworkers; *rabi puḫri,* chief judge; *rab zammārē,* director of musicians (*AHw,* 933-38); PS *rb nqbnm,* chief miner, foreman (Albright 1:43); Ugar. *rb nqdm,* chief of herdsmen (overshepherd); *rb ḥršm,* chief of craftsmen (foreman); *rb kzym,* chief of grooms (*UT,* 2297; *WGU,* 2482); Emp. Aram. *rb šyrt',* captain of caravan; Phoen. *rb hsprm,* chief of the scribes; *rb ḥyš,* foreman, chief architect; *rb ḥrš,* chief of construction (foreman) (*GPL,* 145-46); Pun. *rb hsprm,* chief of the scribes; *rb š'rm,* chief porter; Neo-Pun. *rb byt',* household manager, chief butler; Syr. *rab baytā* household manager, chief butler (*DISO,* 270-72).

6. *Cultic titles.* Ugar. *rb khnm,* chief of priests; Phoen. *rb khnm,* chief of priests; *rb ḥz'nm,* chief of omen-sacrifices (*AHw,* 933-38; *DISO,* 270-72; *UT,* 2297; *WGU,* 2482).

7. *Polite address.* In Northwest Sem., the first sing. suffixed form *rby* is often used as a polite title of address: "Sir" (*DISO,* 270-71). This is reflected in OT, postbiblical Heb., and NT (see below).

OT 1. As in the Sem. world, *rab* designates royal officials, military commanders, and professional supervisors. *rab* is a synonym for *śar* (# 8569), who was the upper-level official in the monarchial administration (Rüterswörden, 4-19, 92-95). Interestingly, *rab* only refers to non-Israelite foreign leaders (esp. Assyrian, Babylonian, and Persian); it never designates their Israelite counterparts, which are usually introduced by *gādôl* (great) instead. Thus, *rab* is a foreign loanword in BH, offering a unique reflection of technical titles used in surrounding Semitic cultures.

2. The referents of *rab* essentially parallel those attested in the Sem. languages: (a) royal officials and administrative rulers (Jer 39:3, 13; 41:1; Dan 1:3; 2:48; 5:1); (b) household managers or palace stewards (Esth 1:8); (c) military commanders or captains (2 Kgs 18:17, 19, 26-28, 37; 19:4, 8; 25:8, 10-12, 15, 18, 20; Isa 36:2, 4, 11-13, 22; 37:4, 8; Jer 39:9-11, 13; 40:1, 2, 5; 41:10; 43:6; 52:12, 14-16, 19, 24, 26, 30; Dan 2:14); (d) high ranking professionals (Dan 4:6[9]; 5:11); and (e) foremen of workers (Jon 1:6).

3. *Phoenician vocational title.* Jon 1:6 *rab haḥōbēl,* captain of the sailors (*HALAT* 1:287), is a loanword from Phoen. *rb hḥbl,* captain of the sailors (*DISO,* 81; *GPL,* 89; Wolff, 89). Jonah did not set sail on a Hebrew ship but a Phoenician merchant vessel. This title parallels other ANE titles for vocational foremen/captains, e.g., PS *rb nqbnm,* foreman of miners; Ugar. *rb nqdm,* chief of herdsmen; Egyp. Aram *rb šyrt',* captain of caravan (see ANE sec. 5).

4. *Assyrian military titles.* 2 Kgs 18:17 lists three Neo-Assyrian military officials who played a role in Sennacherib's siege of Jerusalem in 701: *tartān,* supreme commander, *rab sārîs,* chief officer, and *rab šāqēh,* field commander (NIV). These are not personal names (as KJV), but are loanwords from Neo-Assyrian titles for high-ranking military officials, similar to *rab kiṣri,* commander of the army, and *rab ḫanše,* captain of fifty (Grayson, 605; Tadmor, 279-85; Patterson-Austel, 259; Saggs, 260). The title *tartān,* supreme field commander (# 9580), is a loanword from Akk. *turtannu/tartanu,* who was a high military and administrative official, second in rank only to the king (*KAJI,* 245:17; Unger, 204-10). The title *rab sārîs* is from Akk. *rabû ša rēši* (*šarri*) (lit. chief who is at the head of the king), military commander or chief

eunuch (*AHw*, 974; *GAG* §46d; *MSL* 8:1:74; Zimmern, 116; → # 6247). Both nuances were used in Neo-Assyr., but the other titles in 2 Kgs 18:17 suggest a military connotation. However, eunuchs did play important roles in the Neo-Assyr. bureaucracy, and perhaps this military commander was a eunuch (Grayson, 605). The titles are reflected in Ugar. *ša rēšu šarri,* he who is at the head of the king (*PRU*, 4:237, 22; 203, 13); Nuzi *ša rēši,* he who is the head (*HSS*, 14, 99, 17); Phoen. *rb srsrm,* chief of eunuchs (*RES*, 1206. 1-3); and Emp. Aram. *rb srs,* chief eunuch (*CIS* 2:38. 6; *AHw*, 974; *DISO*, 271). The title *rab šāqēh,* field commander, is from Akk. *rab šaqû,* chief officer, commandant, chief cupbearer, commander of the march (*AHw*, 933-38, 1182; Saggs, 260; Klauber, 73-75; Ellenbogen, 152). This is reflected in Emp. Aram. *rb šwq,* chief of the march (*CIS* 2:3932. 5; *DISO*, 271). Assyrian records indicate that the *rab šaqû* (cupbearer of the king) occupied an important position in the economy of royal affairs (Grayson, 605; Weidner, 264-65). Jewish tradition records that Esarhaddon made his cupbearer (Ahikar) second to himself in the administration of his kingdom (Tobit 1:22), and the well-known Greek historian says that the office of cupbearer was honored among the Persians (Herodotus 3:34).

5. *Babylonian political/administrative titles.* Jer 39:3, 13 lists three Babylonian officials who established control of Jerusalem after it fell to Nebuchadnezzar in 586: *nērgal śar-'eṣer samgar-n^ebû,* Neriglissar, a district ruler; *n^ebûšaz-bān rab-sārîm,* Nebu-Sheziban, a chief officer; and *nērgal śar-'eṣer rab-māg*, Neriglissar, a chief prince. They are explicitly identified as Babylonian political/royal officials: *śārê melek-bābel,* officials of the king of Babylon (39:3); and *rabbê hāmmelek bābel,* high officials of the king of Babylon (Jer 39:3, 13).

While accurately preserving the consonants, MT accentuation and vocalization obscured the three sets of long-forgotten names and titles, suggesting six personal names (so LXX, Josephus, KJV). However, *BHS* editors and others redivide and revocalize to restore three sets of well-known Babylonian names and titles (Grayson, 605; Tadmor, 279-85; *HALAT* 2:759; *TWOT* 2:827): (a) *nērgal śar-'eṣer samgar,* Neriglissar, a high district ruler, or Nergal-Sharezer of Samgar: *nērgal śar-'eṣer* reflects the personal name *Nergal-šar-uṣur* (= Neriglissar), "Nergal, protect the king!" (Schalit, 90; Tallqvist, 219-20; *HALAT* 2:723, 759), and *samgar* reflects the title *simmagir* (*AHw*, 1045), referring either to the district of Sin-magir (*TWOT* 2:827) or the highest ranking official of a district (*AHw*, 85-86; *HALAT* 2:759); (b) *n^ebûšaz-bān rab-sārîm* Nebu-Sheziban, a chief officer: *n^ebû-šazbān* (conj., cf. Jer 39:13) reflects the personal name *Nabū-šēzibanni,* "Nabu, save me!" (Tallqvist, 160; Stamm, 170; Zimmern, 399-401), and *rab-sārîm* reflects the title *rab ša rēši* (lit., chief who is at the head), a political official who became provincial governor of newly conquered provinces (*AHw*, 974; *GAG*, 46d; *MLS* 8/1:74; *HALAT* 2:769-70; Zimmern, 116; Selmsdorf, 557) (see # 6247); (c) *nērgal śar-'eṣer rab-māg*, Neriglissar, chief prince: *nērgal śar-'eṣer* is the personal name Neriglissar (see above), and *rab-māg* reflects the royal title *rab-mugu,* chief prince (*AHw*, 667; *RLA* 1:463), which designated the officer of highest rank beneath the king (Saggs, 260; Grayson, 605; Tadmor, 279-85; Klauber 2:73-75; Zimmern, 36; idem., *ZDMG*, 116-18; Ellenbogen, 151-52). It is possible that this was the Neriglissar who eventually succeeded Nebuchadnezzar in 560-556 BC (Schnabel, 273-74; Schalit, 90; Unger, 282-84; *ANET*, 308; *AHw*, 85-86; Reicke, 1302; *HALAT* 2:723).

6. *Babylonian military title.* After Nebuchadnezzar conquered Jerusalem, control of the city was turned over to Nebuzaradan: *rab ṭabbāḥîm*, the captain of the imperial guard (2 Kgs 25:8, 10-12, 15, 18, 20; Jer 39:9, 10, 11, 13; 40:1-2, 5-6; 41:10; 43:6; 52:12, 14-16, 19, 24, 26, 30). This is a Babylonian loanword that designates the executive officer in charge of a military detachment (Klauber, 2:73-75; Zimmern, 6; *ZDMG*, 116-18; Ellenbogen, 151-52).

7. *Babylonian political title.* The title *rab signîn,* ruler of prefects (NIV: Dan 2:48) is derived from Akk. *rab šaknu,* which designates a Babylonian official who governed a vassal state that had submitted to Babylonian suzerainty (*AHw*, 1141; Zimmern, 16; Saggs, 254-60), in contrast to a provincial governor (*bēl pīḫâti*), who ruled directly over a once recalcitrant area that was now annexed as a Babylonian territory (*AHw*, 862; Saggs, 241-47; Grayson, 750).

8. *Babylonian palace/administrative title.* Ashpenaz, the Babylonian official assigned to care for the exiled Judean royality, is called *rab sārîsîm* chief of the court officials (Dan 1:3), and elsewhere *śār hassārîsîm,* captain of the court officials (1:7-11). This title is a loan from Akk. *rab ša rēši,* lit., chief who is the head (*GAG*, §46d; *MSL*, 8/1:74; Jensen, 91-93; Zimmern, 116), which designates a palace steward, household manager, superintendent and later eunuch (*AHw*, 974a). This title is also attested in Emp. Aram. *rb srs,* chief eunuch (*CIS* 2:38. 6; *DISO*, 271) and Phoen. *rb srsrm,* chief of the courtiers (*RES*, 1206. 1-3; *DISO*, 271). Ashpenaz was either the chief overseer of the palace officials or the head eunuch, who was the personal attendant of the royal family and nobles.

9. *Persian administrative title.* Esth 1:8 *rab bêtô* (lit., chief of his house) designates the household manager or palace steward (*THAT* 2:721; Gerleman, 61). This title is identical to Neo-Pun. *rb byt',* and Syr. *rab baytā,* household manager (*DISO*, 270-72).

P-B 1. *rb* II (chief) appears in several ancient Heb. inscriptions (Frey, 900. 2; 994b. 2; 1218). In DSS *rb* II (master, lord; teacher, instructor) occurs in several Jewish Aramaic texts from Qumran (11QtgJob 19:3[Job 29:4]; 25:1[Job 34:24]) (KQT 198-99).

2. Rabbinic literature: *rab,* adj. great, described someone who occupied a high and respected position (Levy 4:409). *rab* nom. had a threefold range of meanings: (a) chief, head, e.g., head of the Jews (*Sanhedrin* 20d. 13), chief of the spirits (*Sheqalim* 49b. 2); (b) master, often with antonym *'ebed* slave (*Aboth* 1:3; *Giṭṭin* 22a,43b,46a); (c) teacher (*B'rakhoth* 63b; *Aboth* 1:16); "Rab" as title of the Babylonian Amoraim (*P'saḥim* 52b) and surname of Abba Arekha, founder of the academy of Sura in Babylonia (*Hullin* 95b; *Abodah Zarah* 10b; *Peah* 6:19c; *Erubin* 50b; *Niddah* 24b). The pl. was used always with first pl. suffix: *rabbôtênû,* our teachers (*Ta'anith* 7a; *Sh'buoth* 47a; *Giṭṭin* 7:48d; *Sabbath* 5:7c; *Betsah* 2:61c; *Megillah* 1:70d) (Dalman, 395; Jastrow, 1438; Levy, 409-10; Sokoloff, 512).

3. In JAram, JPAram, and postbiblical Heb., *rab* developed a specialized nuance (master = teacher) when used as absolute without a following genitive. This is the semantic background of the NT and RL use of *rab,* master = teacher. Derived from *rab,* teacher: first sing. suffixed form as title *rabbî,* Rabbi (= my teacher, my master), title of scholars, especially of the Tannaim and Palestinian Amoraim (*Baba M'tsi'a* 84a, 85a; *Abodah Zarah* 17b), and the title of Rabbi Judah han-Naṣi (*Giṭṭin* 59a; *B'rakhoth* 13a; *Soṭah* 32b; *Baba M'tsi'a* 85a) (Dalman, 395; Jastrow, 1442; Levy, 410;

Sokoloff, 513). In origin a title of authority, Heb. *rabbî* became a title as well as a mode of polite address by the first century (Doeve, 1541-42; *TDNT* 6:962-66). In RL the term *rab* was used to designate the master of a slave (e.g., *Pesaḥ* 8. 1-2; *Giṭṭin* 4. 4) and to designate a teacher, even before AD 70 (e.g., *Pesaḥ* 4. 13-14) and before AD 135 (e.g., *Yad.* 4. 3; *'Ed.* 8. 7). The terms *rabbî* and *rabbān* are also used in the mode of address; nearly all occurrences are about figures associated with the period before AD 135.

4. As early as ca. 110 BC, *rab* was used to denote teacher in the saying handed down by Jehoshua ben Perachiah: "Get a teacher (*rab*) and find a fellow-student" (*Aboth* 1:6). The pupil followed his teacher with obedience and respect and expressed this by addressing him as *rabbî,* my master and my teacher (RH 2. 9; *Ned.* 9:5; BQ 8. 6). From the middle of the first century AD the suffix increasingly lost its pronominal significance, and examples of *rabbî* as a general title begin to appear. For example, the earliest evidence for *rabbî* as a title attached to a proper name (e.g., Rab Hana) occurs on Jerusalem ossuaries that apparently date from before AD 100 (*CII* 2:249, 275-79). The oldest example that can be dated with certainty is a Jerusalem ossuary from before 70 AD that has *didaskalos* and the name of the deceased.

5. The inscriptions that date from AD 100-400 indicate that men entitled *rabbî* were probably wealthy. Generally, the inscriptions indicate that this title should be thought of as an honorific title, roughly equivalent to "sir," with no explicit connection to either teaching or adjudication. In RL personages associated with the period before AD 70 are not referred to with a title (e.g., Hillel, Shammai), while those associated with the later periods are titled (e.g., Rabbi Aqiba, etc.).

NT 1. The term *rabbî* is transliterated 17x as *rhabbi* and 2x as *rhabbouni/rhabboni.* It is used 3x as the honorific title Rabbi as in RL: Teacher, Master (Matt 23:7-8). It is used 16x as a polite address in the vocative (Matt 26:25, 49; Mark 9:5; 10:51; 11:21; 14:45; John 1:38[39], 49[50]; 3:2, 26; 4:31; 6:25; 9:2; 11:8; 20:16). While some are merely equivalent to "Sir," many connote the authority of Jesus as Lord and Teacher. For example, when the two disciples address Jesus as *rhabbi,* this is glossed as *didaskalos,* teacher (John 1:36-38). Nathaniel addresses Jesus as Rabbi and Son of God and king of Israel (John 1:49). Nicodemus addresses Jesus as Rabbi, a teacher from God (John 3:2). When Mary Magdalene mistook Jesus as a gardener, she called him *kyrios,* "Sir" (John 20:15); but when she recognized him, she called him "Rabboni," which is glossed as *didaskalos* "Teacher." These suggest that when Jesus was called Rabbi elsewhere by the people and his disciples, the more authoritative title Master, Lord is connoted (John 3:26; 4:31; 6:25; 9:2; 11:8).

2. The use of Rabbi in Matt 23:7-8 reveals a startling contrast between the teaching ministry of Jesus and the rabbinic teachers. In Judaism, when a pupil joined himself to a teacher, he was bound to him for the rest of his life (*TDNT* 6:962). When after several years of association with his master he had become familiar with the oral tradition, he could be addressed as Rabbi. Since the scribes and theologians were generally called Rabbi, it gradually became the exclusive term for those who had completed their studies and had been ordained as teachers of the Law (*TDNT* 6:963). Jesus alludes to this and censures the desire of the scribes to be greeted with respect and addressed as Rabbi (Matt 23:7-8). When Jesus is called Rabbi by his disciples and others, this shows that, like the Jewish scribes, he taught Scripture to the people. His

disciples stood to him in the relation of students to their master and showed him the respect due by calling him Rabbi. However, there was a basic difference between the relation of Jesus to his disciples and that of scribes to their pupils, for Jesus had called them to discipleship and was their Lord. They were expressly forbidden to call themselves Rabbi (23:8). Rather than simply being their Rabbi in the Jewish sense, he was also their Lord and King (*TDNT* 6:965).

Leaders: → *'ādôn* (lord, master, # 123); → *'allûp* II (tribal chief, # 477); → *'āṣîl* II (eminent, noble, # 722); → *zāqēn* (elder, # 2418); → *ḥōr* I, free man, freeborn, # 2985); → *maptēaḥ* (badge of office, # 5158); → *nāgîd* (prince, ruler, leader, # 5592); → *nāśî'* I (chief, king, # 5954); → *sārîs* (eunuch, court official, # 6247); → *seren* II (Philistine prince, # 6249); → *'attûd* (he-goat, leader, # 6966); → *peḥâ* (governor, # 7068); → *pāqîd* (officer, # 7224); → *qāṣîn* (commander, leader, # 7903); → *rab* II (captain, chief, # 8042); → *rzn* (rule, # 8142); → *šôa'* I (noble, # 8777)

BIBLIOGRAPHY

AHw, 933; *DISO*, 270-71; *GPL*, 145; *HALAT* 4:1094; *KAI*, 3:22-23; *TDNT* 6:692-96; *THAT* 2:715-26; *TWOT* 2:827; *UT*, §2297; *WGU*, §2482; W. F. Albright, *The Proto-Sinaitic Inscriptions and Their Decipherments*, 1966, 1:43; J. C. Biella, *Dictionary of Old South Arabic*, 1982, 216; C. Cohen, "Neo-Assyrian Elements in the First Speech of the Biblical Rab-šāqê," *IOS* 9, 1979, 32-48; S. J. D. Cohen, "Epigraphical Rabbis," *JQR* 72, 1981, 1-17; R. Conti, *Chrestomathia Arabica Meridionalis Epigraphica*, 1931, 235; G. A. Cooke, *A Textbook of Northwest Inscriptions*, 1923, 29; G. H. Dalman, *Aramäisch-neuhebräisches Handwörterbuch zu Targum, Talmud und Midrash*, 1967, 395; E. Ebeling, "Keilschrifttexte aus Assur juristischen Inhalts," *WVDOG* 1, 1927, 245:17; M. Ellenbogen, *Foreign Words in the Old Testament: Their Origin and Etymology*, 1962, 151-52; E. Forrer, *Die Provinzeinteilung des assyrischen Reiches*, 1920, 60-63; J. B. Frey, *Inscripionum Iudaicarum*, 900. 2; 994b. 2; A. Kirk Grayson, "Mesopotamia, History of: Administration," *ABD*, 1992, 4:732-77; idem, "The Walters Art Gallery Sennacherib Inscription," *AfO* 20, 1963, 96, 120; idem, "History and Culture of Assyria," *ABD*, 1992, 4:732-55; idem, "Rabshakeh," *ABD*, 5:605; idem, "Rabsaris," *ABD*, 1992, 5:605; idem, "Rabmag," *ABD*, 1992, 5:605; M. Jastrow, *Dictionary of the Targumim, Talmud Babli, Yerushalmi and Midrashic Literature*, 1982. 1438; M. Heltzel, *The Internal Organization of the Kingdom of Ugarit*, 1982, 99-100; C. F. Jean-J. Hoftijzer, *Dictionnaire des inscriptions sémitiques de l'ouest*, 1965, 197; E. G. Klauber, *Assyrischen Beamtentum nach Briefen aus der Sargonidenzeit*, 1910, 73-76; K. G. Kuhn, *Konkordanz zur des Qumrantexten*, 1960,198-99; H. Lapin, "Rabbi," *ABD*, 1992, 5:600-602; P. Leander, *Laut- und Formenlehre des Agyptisch-Aramäischen*, 1928, 43; J. Levy, *Wörterbuch über die Talmudim und Midraschim*, 1924, 409-10; P. Machinist, "Palestine, Administration of (Assyro-Babylonian)," *ABD*, 1992, 5:69-81; S. E. McEvenue, "The Political Structure in Judah from Cyrus to Nehemiah," *CBQ* 43, 1981, 5-64; R. North, "Palestine, Administration of (Judean Officials)," *ABD*, 1992, 5:86-90; R. D. Patterson and H. J. Austel, "1 and 2 Kings," *EBC*, 1988, 4:259; J. Pecirkova, "The Administrative Organization of the Neo-Assyrian Empire," *ArOr* 45, 1977, 211-28; idem, "The Administrative Methods of Assyrian Imperialism," *ArOr* 55, 1987, 162-75; J. van der Ploeg, "Les chefs du peuple d'Israel et leurs noms," *RB* 57, 1950, 40-61; J. N. Postgate, "Assyrian Deeds and Documents," *Iraq* 32, 1970, 148; idem, "The Place of the *šaknu* in Assyrian Government," *AnSt* 30, 1980, 67-76; B. Reicke and L. Rost, *Biblisch-historisches Handwörterbuch*, 1962-66, 1302; K. C. Rossini, *Chrestomathia Arabica Meridionalis Epigraphica*, 1931, 235; U. Rüterswörden, *Die Beamten der israelitischen Konigszeit*, 1985, 4-19, 92-95; H. W. F. Saggs, *The Greatness That*

Was Babylon, 1969, 233-68; A. Schalit, *Namenwörterbuch zu Flavius Josephus*, 1968, 90; P. Schnabel, *Berossos und die babylonisch-hellenistische Literatur*, 1923, 273-74; H. Shanks, "Is the Title 'Rabbi' Anachronistic in the Bible?" *JQR* 5, 1963, 37-45; idem, "On the Origin of the Title 'Rabbi'," *JQR* 59, 1968, 152-57; M. Sokoloff, *A Dictionary of Jewish Palestinian Aramaic of the Byzantine Period*, 1990, 512; J. J. Stamm, *Die akkadische Namengebung*, 1939, 170; H. Tadmor, "Rab-Saris and Rab-Shekah in 2 Kings 18," in *The Word of the Lord Shall Go Forth*, 1983, 279-85; K. L. Tallqvist, *Assyrian Personal Names*, 1914, 219-20; J. Teixidor, "Les fonctions de *rab* et de suffixe en Phöenicie," *Sem* 29, 1979, 9-17; E. Unger, *Babylon*, 1958, 282-84; R. de Vaux, "Titres et fonctionnaires égyptiens à la cour de David et de Salomon," *RB* 48, 1939, 394-405; B. T. Viviano, "Rabbouni and Mark 9:5," *RB* 97, 1990, 207-18; E. Weidner, "Hof- und Harems-Erlasse assyricher Könige," *AfO* 17, 1956, 264-65; H. Wildberger, "Die rede des Rabsake vor Jerusalem," *TZ* 5, 1979, 5-47; S. Zeitlin, "A Reply [to Shanks]," *JQR* 53, 1963, 345-49; idem, "The Title Rabbi in the Gospels Is Anachronistic," *JQR* 59, 1968, 158-60; H. Zimmern, *Akkadische Fremdwörter als Beweise für babylonische Kultureinfluss*, 1917, 116.

Gordon H. Johnston

8043 (*rab* III, archer), → # 8046

8044 (*rōb*, great number, abundance), → # 8045

8045	רבב

רבב (*rbb* I), q. become numerous, much, great; pu. increased ten-thousand fold (# 8045); רַב (*rab*, I), adj. numerous, much, plentiful, abounding (# 8041); רֹב (*rōb*), nom. great number, abundance (# 8044); רְבָבָה (r^e*bābâ*), nom. great multitude, legion, ten thousand (# 8047); רִבּוֹ(א) (*ribbô/ribbô'*), ten thousand (# 8052).

ANE The root *rbb* is common in both East (Akk. *rabû/rabbu*—be great, grow/great, many) and West Sem. languages (Ug. *rbb*, II/*rbt*, myriad, ten thousand; *rbb*, III/*rb*, to be great/great, many).

OT 1. The verbal root occurs some 24x in the OT, with all but five found in poetic style texts (Gen 6:1; 18:20; Exod 23:29; Deut 7:7; 1 Sam 25:10). The word denotes the rapid growth of human (Gen 6:1) or animal populations (Exod 23:29), and the increase of crops (Ps 4:7[8]) and material goods (Eccl 5:11[10]). More frequently, the prophets use it to describe the multitude of Israel's transgressions before God (Isa 59:12; Jer 5:6; 14:7), or the psalmist laments continually increasing number of enemies arrayed against the righteous (Ps 3:1[2]; 25:19; 38:19[20]).

Two texts deserve special mention. The first concerns the psalmist's declaration in praise of the "many" works of God (Ps 104:24). Here *rbb* may be correctly rendered "manifold," as the works of God are both numerous and variegated. The second involves the vb. in the pu. in 144:13, where the understanding "ten thousand" or "myriads" is appropriate, given the context of poetic parallelism with *m.l'*, be full (→ # 4848).

2. The adj. *rab* occurs over 400x in the OT and predominantly means "much, many" (e.g., Deut 15:6; Josh 11:4) or "great" (1 Sam 26:13; 2 Chron 21:3). The word describes the extent of the wickedness of humanity prompting the Flood (Gen 6:5), as well as the depths of the subterranean waters that overflowed the earth as God brought

divine judgment on human sin (7:11). In the Psalms, the term depicts the magnitude of God's mercy, truth, goodness, and power (Ps 31:19[20]; 86:15; 103:8; 145:7; 147:5). The prophets employ this particle to describe both the extent of evil that occasions Yahweh's judgment (Joel 3:13[4:13]) and the pervasiveness of the peace and righteousness when the Lord restores the fortunes of Israel (Isa 54:13; 63:7).

Elsewhere, special usages of the word *rab* include the meaning "enough" (Gen 33:9), "abundant" (Exod 34:6; Num 20:11), "too much" (as in 1 Kgs 12:28), and even "abound" (Prov 28:20; 29:22).

3. The nom. *rōb*, a derivative of *rbb,* is normally translated by "abundance (e.g., 2 Chron 32:5, 29) or "multitude" (Isa 1:11; 47:9). Of the nearly 150 occurrences of the word in the OT, only a few call for a special understanding. For example, "greatness of your majesty" in Exod 15:7, "long" as in journey (Josh 9:13) or time (2 Chron 30:5), "immense" or "huge" army in 2 Chron 16:8, and "excellent" or "surpassing greatness" in Ps 150:2. Of supreme importance theologically is the emphasis on Yahweh's omnipotence in accomplishing Israel's deliverance at the Sea (Exod 15:6-8). According to D. N. Freedman, Yahweh's unrivaled might is showcased in this cosmic conflict symbolically by two key themes of Canaanite myth: the divine messengers who perform the will of the sovereign deity (*rōb gā'ôn*) and the personified weapons of the deity (*rōb ḥārôn*). Thus, the poet affirms the unique majesty and singular prerogatives of this King of the gods (Freedman, 205).

4. The nom. *rᵉbābâ* ("multitude") occurs 16x in the OT. It signifies an enormous number of descendants (Gen 24:60), troops (Deut 32:30), or angels (33:2). This word is in poetic parallelism with "thousand" (*'elep*) in David's victory song touting his military prowess (1 Sam 18:7, 21:11[12]; 29:5; Ps 91:7). Theologically the term both suggests Yahweh's blessing for the abounding growth of the Israelite population (Gen 24:60; Ezek 16:7; cf. Gen 12:1-3) and affirms his ability to deliver the righteous in the face of overwhelming odds (Ps 3:6[7]; 91:7). See further # 8047.

5. The nom. *ribbô/ribbô'* is a later Aramaizing synonym of *rᵉbābâ* and is generally found in numbering materials and peoples. Great is the Lord's compassion on the thousands of children in Nineveh (Jon 4:11).

Abundance, multiplication, sufficiency: → *dgh* (multiply, # 1835); → *day* (sufficiency, overflowing supply, # 1896); → *ysp* (add, continue, increase, # 3578); → *kbr* I (make many, be in abundant supply, # 3892); → *mᵉgammâ* (totality, abundance, # 4480); → *rbb* I (become numerous, much, great, # 8045); → *rbh* I (become numerous, multiply, increase, # 8049); → *r'š* II, be abundant, # 8322); → *śg'/śgh* (grow great, increase, exalt, # 8434/8436); → *śpq* II (suffice, be enough, # 8563); → *šwq* I (overflow, bestow abundantly, # 8796); → *šepa'* (super-abundance, # 9179)

Andrew E. Hill

8046	רבב

רבב (*rbb* II), shoot (hapleg., # 8046); רַב (*rab* III), archer (# 8043).

OT 1. Three times *rab* is used in the OT with the nuance of "one who shoots." In Jer 50:29, it is parallel to the phrase "those who draw the bow"; hence, the translation "archer" in this context as in Gen 49:23 and Job 16:13 (*HALAT* 868-69).

2. In Ps 18:14[15], the vb. (q.) has the meaning "shoot (arrows)" (for this context, see *ḥēṣ*).

Bow, arrow, archery: → *'ašpâ* (quiver, # 880); → *zîqôt* (flaming arrow, # 2338); → *ḥēṣ* (arrow, # 2932); → *ṭḥh* (distance of bowshot, # 3217); → *yôreh* I (archer, # 3452); → *yeter* II (bowstring, # 3857); → *qešet* (bow, # 8008); → *rbb* II (shoot, # 8046); → *rbh* II (archer, # 8050); → *t^elî* (quiver, # 9437); → **Warfare: Theology**
Shooting, throwing: → *dḥh* (push, overthrow, be cast down, # 1890); → *ṭwl* (throw, # 3214); → *ydh* I (shoot, # 3343); → *yrh* I (shoot, throw, # 3721); → *mgr* (throw, # 4489); → *rbb* II (shoot, # 8046); → *rmh* I (throw, shoot, # 8227); → *šlk* I (throw, hurl, # 8959); → *šmṭ* (release, remit, drop, throw down, # 9023)

BIBLIOGRAPHY
TWOT 2:827.

K. Lawson Younger, Jr.

8047	רְבָבָה

רְבָבָה (*r^ebābâ*), nom. ten thousand, myriad (# 8047); < רבב (*rbb*), be many, abound (→ # 8045); רִבּוֹ, רִבּוֹא (*ribbô', ribbô*) (→ # 8052).

OT 1. The forms *ribbô* and *ribbō'* are found primarily in late texts and were used in combination with other numbers to indicate large numbers (Ezra 2:64; Neh 7:66). Earlier texts use *'elep* for more precise counts (Judg 1:4; Ezek 48:10), leaving *r^ebābâ* to indicate quality rather than quantity. N. Gottwald (*The Tribes of Yahweh,* 1979, 278-82) has suggested that in early poetic texts, *r^ebābâ,* like *'elep*, is not a number but rather means a multitude (Gen 24:60; Num 10:36; Deut 33:2, 17).

2. The three cognates generally tend to signify an extremely large and undetermined number. Arithmetical precision is not of great significance in traditional cultures except in specialized genres, such as censuses and military reports. Such large numbers were particularly suited for use in the hyperbolic language of court speech (2 Sam 18:3), love poetry (S of Songs 5:10), and expressions of trust in God when threatened by a myriad of enemies (Ps 3:6[7]; 91:7). God's power, dignity, and status make it fitting that he be accompanied by myriads of chariots (68:17[18]) and holy ones (Deut 33:2). The blessing on Rebekah (Gen 24:60) is for thousands of ten thousands of progeny, numerous children being the source of power and status in many cultures.

3. Where the first part of a poetic line has "thousands," the second part often includes a heightened and intensified "ten thousand." Saul was understandably sensitive to the political as well as military implications of being in this way subordinated to David (1 Sam 18:7-8). Such high numbers appropriately accompanied the praise and presence of divinity. A double multiplication and heightening (thousands of thousands to ten thousands of ten thousands) tends towards infinity in the portrayal of the number of God's servants in the heavenly throneroom (Dan 7:10; 1 En. 1:9; 14:22). In Ugaritic mythology Baal's palace extends over a "thousand tracts/ten thousand spaces" (*'alp/rbt*; *CTA* 4 v 118-19; *CML*², 62).

P-B In 1QM 3:16; 4:16 the ten thousand (*rbw'*) is a military grouping between the thousand and the tribe.

NT The largest number (*myrios*) is used in hyperbolical stories (Matt 18:24) and rhetorical contrasts (1 Cor 15; cf. 14:19) or intensifications (Rev 5:11). It is found in apocalyptic texts describing the numbers of angels in the divine throne room (1 En. 14:22; Rev 5:11) and the military forces of the last battle (Jude 14; Rev 9:16).

Numbers: → *'eḥād* (one, # 285); → *'elep* II (thousand, military contingent, # 547); → *'arba'* (four, # 752); → *ḥāmēš* (five, # 2822); → *mē'â* I (hundred, # 4395); → *'eśer* (ten, # 6924); → *r^ebābâ* (ten thousand, myriad, # 8047/8052); → *šeba'* I (seven, # 8679); → *šālōš, š^elōšâ* (three, a three, # 8993); → *š^emōneh* (eight, # 9046); → *š^enayim* (two, # 9109); → *šēš* I (six, # 9252); → *tēša'* (nine, # 9596)
Numbering, counting: → *kss* (reckon, apportion, # 4082); → *mnh* (count, # 4948); → *spr* I (count, number, reckon, rehearse, # 6218); → *pqd* (number, appoint, # 7212)

BIBLIOGRAPHY
THAT 2:715-26; *TWAT* 7:294-320; Jastrow 2:1439, 1440; M. S. Smith, "Divine Form and Size in Ugaritic and Pre-exilic Israelite Religion," *ZAW* 100, 1988, 424-27.

P. P. Jenson

8048	רבד

רבד (*rbd*), q. prepare a bed (# 8048); nom. מַרְבַד (*marbad*), covering (# 5267).

ANE The vb. *rbd* appears in Ugar. with an unclear meaning (*UT*, 482), though a cognate word occurs in Arab. with the meaning to bind, fold in layers (BDB, 914). It is tempting to compare it with *rpd* (with a *b/p* interchange), which is better attested (BDB, 951) and is illustrated by the vb. (pi.) used in Job 17:13, where Job spreads out his bed in darkness (→ *yāṣûa'*; cf. Pope 325-26, 380-81).

OT *rbd* appears in Scripture only in Prov 7:16, where the promiscuous woman has bedecked (*rbd*) her bed (*'ereś*) with coverings or a canopy (*marbaddîm*; cf. Ugar. *mrbdt*), ironically something the virtuous woman is said to make (Prov 31:22). Judging from the related nom. *rābîd*, necklace, a meaning nuanced toward "ornament, decorate" may be appropriate.

Bed: → *yṣ'* (spread out a bed, # 3667); → *miṭṭâ* (bed, # 4753); → *miškāb* (bed, # 5435); → *'ereś* (bedstead, # 6911); → *pē'â* II (luxury [of a couch], # 6991); → *rbd* (prepare a bed, # 8048)

BIBLIOGRAPHY
M. H. Pope, *Song of Songs*, AB, 1977, 325-27, 380-81.

William C. Williams

8049	רבה

רבה (*rbh*, I), q. become numerous, increase, multiply; pi., hi. increase (# 8049); אַרְבֶּה (*'arbeh*), nom. locust (→ # 746); הַרְבֵּה (*harbēh*), hi. inf. abs. great number, many, much (# 2221); מַרְבֶּה (*marbeh*), nom. abundance, increase (only Isa 9:7[6]; 33:23) (# 5269); מַרְבִּית (*marbît*), nom. multitude, majority (# 5270); תַּרְבּוּת (*tarbût*), nom. breed (→ # 9551); תַּרְבִּית (*tarbît*), nom. interest, increase (# 9552).

OT 1. Several different Heb. words convey the idea of multiplication in the OT. Predominant are *ysp* and *rbh*. There is some overlap here with roots like *rbb* I and *r'š* II, meaning abundance. The wide variance of meanings in Eng. for the Heb. roots demonstrate both the latitude of meaning associated with the original Heb. roots and the inconsistency of the NIV in translating the same root word. The root *rbh* occurs over 200x in the OT, 60x in the q. and 160x in the hi. The NIV translates *rbh* with more than eighty separate Eng. words or phrases, the most prominent being increase (54x), many (17x), numerous (14x), and multiply (12x).

2. The root *rbh* in the q. frequently has a quantitative sense, as in the creation account when God commands the living creatures to fruitful (*p^e rû*) and become numerous or multiply (*r^e bû*; NIV increase in number, Gen 1:22, 28). The same word describes the increasing volume of water in the great Flood (7:17-18). Likewise, the divine imperative to replenish the earth after the Flood repeats the original creation mandate, using *rbh* (8:17; 9:7).

Elsewhere, the quantitative *rbh* is applied to the process of time (Gen 38:12; NIV after a long time), the divine wonders multiplied against Egypt (Exod 11:9), the extension of human life (Deut 11:21), the increase of material possessions (8:13), the length of a journey (19:6; NIV the distance is too great), the magnitude of slaughter in battle (1 Sam 14:30), the greatness of Solomon's wisdom (1 Kgs 4:30[5:10]), and the increase of human posterity (whether an individual [Job 27:14] or the nation of Israel [Exod 1:7]).

Theologically, Elihu employs *rbh* to describe the transcendence of God in rebuking Job (Job 33:12). The psalmist observed that "sorrows increase" for those who chase after false gods (Ps 16:4), and those who have increased in wealth and splendor take nothing with them when they die (49:16-17). Finally, the sage acknowledged the righteous "thrive" when the wicked perish (Prov 28:28), but when the wicked thrive, so does sin (29:16).

3. The root *rbh* appears 4x in the pi., referring to the increase of an army (Judg 9:29; NIV whole army), the rearing of young (Lam 2:22; Ezek 19:2), and turning a profit on a sale (Ps 44:12[13]; NIV gained). In contrast to the q., the pi. of *rbh* refers to the process of increasing rather than the result or product of "becoming many."

4. The hi. *rbh* most often means make numerous or multiply. These forms especially portray the abundance of God's giving and the fullness of his mercy: in the promise to multiply the patriarchs into a great nation (Gen 17:2, 20; 22:17; 26:4; 48:4; Exod 32:13; Lev 26:9; Deut 1:10; 7:13), in the multiplication of signs and wonders to his glory and the destruction of Egypt (Exod 7:3), and in his gracious redemption (Ps 78:38; Isa 55:7). Conversely, Israel and all humanity stand before God continually multiplying sin, wickedness, and rebellion (Gen 3:16; Ezra 10:13; Ezek 16:25, 26, 29). The remedy for the human malady is not found in multiplying possessions (as the Hebrew kings attempted, cf. Deut 17:16-17). Rather, God must wash and cleanse the sinner thoroughly (*rbh*, NIV wash away all; Ps 51:2[4]). Then the sinner may understand, along with the poet David, how God stoops down to make the righteous great (*rbh*, 2 Sam 22:36 ‖ Ps 18:35[36]).

The hi. *rbh* can also mean many or increase, like the many gardens of Israel divinely destroyed by blight and mildew (Amos 4:9; NIV reads the proposed emendation *heḥ^e rabtî*, "many times I struck"), or the increase that comes from saving money little by little (Prov 13:11). Here *rbh* is to be understood as a gradual or steady increase, or larger sums compared to multitudes. See further *harbēh*.

The hi. *rbh* + l^e + inf can mean do something frequently, copiously, continually. For example, Hannah prayed continually to the Lord for a son (1 Sam 1:12; NIV kept on), the woman of Tekoa begged David to prevent continued killing of her family (2 Sam 14:11; NIV adding to the destruction), King Manasseh provoked God's wrath with the continual practice of evil (2 Kgs 21:6 ‖ 2 Chron 33:6), as did Amon his son (2 Chron 33:23) and all the people of Judah (36:14).

Even as the Leviathan (→ # 4293) does not "keep begging" for mercy (Job 41:3[40:27]), so the Lord has stopped listening to the continual prayers of his people (Isa 1:15). Yet if the wicked repent, stop doing wrong, and learn to do right, God will copiously pardon (Isa 55:7; NIV freely pardon)—just as he has done continually throughout Israelite history (Ps 78:38; NIV time after time he restrained his anger).

5. *HALAT* lists the hi. inf. abs. *harbēh* as an independent entry. The form occurs 49x in the MT, fifteen in Eccl alone. This form is coupled with *m*^{e}*'ōd*, very, some 18x, and with the exception of Eccl the term is found in predominantly prose narrative texts.

harbēh is used as a subject ("many...fell and died," 2 Sam 1:4), an object ("you planted much," Hag 1:6), in apposition ("very great insight," 1 Kgs 4:29[5:9]), and adverbially ("very much afraid," Neh 2:2; "greatly incensed," 4:1[3:33]). In two instances *harbēh* conveys the comparative sense of "more than" (2 Chron 25:9; Jon 4:11). *harbēh* also functions hyperbolically, as in Jehu's ruse to "serve Baal much" (2 Kgs 10:18), or Qoheleth's exaggeration of his wisdom and wealth (Eccl 1:16; 2:7) and the emptiness of life (5:16; 11:8), or even King Manasseh's wickedness (2 Kgs 21:16).

Theologically, three texts deserve mention. In Gen 15:1 the predicate construction *ś*^{e}*kārkā harbēh me'ōd* reveals God as "your very great reward" to Abram. Given the context (Abram's victory over the kings of the plain, Gen 14), Wenham connects the phrase with the military metaphor (shield) in the couplet and understands reward (*śākār*) as mercenary's pay or soldier's booty (*Genesis* 1-15, WBC 1, 327). In contrast, Hamilton emends *māgēn*, shield, to *māgān*, benefactor (→ # 4481), and while not denying the material nature of Abram's reward, rightly connects *śākār* to the reward of posterity (*Genesis 1-17*, NICOT, 419). (→ *śkr*, reward, # 8509).

In the second text, Isaiah satirically announced "Assyria's funeral pyre. . . has stood ready from ancient days" (Oswalt, *Isaiah 1-39*, NICOT, 569)—an "abundance" (*harbēh*) of wood and fire has been prepared (Isa 30:33)! Here the prophet assured the Hebrews that God's sovereignty extended into Mesopotamia as well.

Lastly, the psalmist used *harbēh* to describe the extent or abundance of Yahweh's love and redemption for Israel (NIV full redemption, Ps 130:7). Despite his great sin, the poet knows there is forgiveness and plenteous redemption (RSV) with God; "and though he has again and again to pass through nights of anguish caused by sin, his life guided by God's hand is nevertheless a way from redemption to redemption" (Weiser, *Psalms*, OTL, 775). Weiser also recognized the important connection between the individual (vv. 1-6) and the community (Israel, vv. 7-8) for both the knowledge and assurance of Yahweh's plenteous redemption.

6. According to Isaiah, the Ideal King (an eschatological figure) will possess and rule an ever increasing dominion—in contrast to the decreasing domain of Israel and Judah, given Assyrian aggression during the 8th cent. BC (Isa 9:7[6]). The word *marbeh* in the MT is written with a final *mem*, prompting the emendation *rabbâ*

(reading *lm* as dittography with *šālôm*, peace, of v. 6[5]); see further Watts, *Isaiah 1-33*, WBC 24, 131-132, n. 6a.).

Elsewhere, *marbēh* occurs only in Isa 33:23, where Jerusalem is portrayed as a ship yet unseaworthy and thus dependent upon Yahweh for deliverance (v. 22, so NIV). Others interpret the ship in disarray as Assyria about to be plundered by Judah (cf. Oswalt, *Isaiah 1-39*, NICOT, 604-5). In either case, there is spoil aplenty for God's people, to the point that even the lame will carry off their share. Hayes and Irvine are probably correct here in understanding the events of Isa 33 as the aftermath of a failed coup in Samaria against Assyria in 726-725 BC (*Isaiah*, 360-70). In a festival liturgy the prophet welcomes the Israelite refugees from the northern kingdom with his prophetic description of the reversal of Israelite (and Judean?) fortunes (33:17-20), to which the refugees responded with an oath of allegiance (33:21-24). Some identify the destruction of the Assyrian army in 701 BC as the event permitting Jerusalem to cart off great spoil, thus fulfilling Isaiah's prophecy (e.g., Wolf, *Interpreting Isaiah*, 164; cf. 2 Kgs 19:20-37).

7. The hi. part. *marbît* occurs 5x in the MT with three different technical meanings. The term signifies the majority (most, NIV) of Benjaminites loyal to Saul (1 Chron 12:29[30]), and the northern tribesmen who participated in Hezekiah's Passover ceremonially unclean (2 Chron 30:18).

The expected meaning increase, abundance is found in the Queen of Sheba's recital of Solomon's "greatness of wisdom" (2 Chron 9:6), and in the man of God's curse against the "increase" of Eli's household (i.e., the next generation, 1 Sam 2:33).

In the priestly legislation against usury, *marbît* is coupled with *nešek* (interest, usury) and is usually rendered interest (so NIV) or profit (so NRSV). Israel was unique in the ancient world in totally prohibiting interest payments on loans of money and food to the poor (cf. Wenham, *Leviticus*, NICOT, 322, n. 17).

8. The fem. nom. *tarbît* occurs 6x in the OT, always paired with *nešek* (usury, interest). Twice the prophet Ezekiel includes the taking of *tarbît* among the sins of Jerusalem (Ezek 18:13; 22:12). Conversely, the refusal to take *tarbît* is cited among the virtures of the righteous (18:8, 17).

The sage also denounces the collecting of exorbitant interest, noting it is amassed only for another who in kindness will give it to the poor (Prov 28:8). The injunction against taking *tarbît* is found in Lev 25:36. Following Speiser, *nešek* represents "first" interest, while *tarbît* is "added" or penalty interest (*Oriental and Biblical Studies*, 1967, 131-41)—hence the NIV translation "excessive interest." No interest was to be charged to the poor for loans of money or food, and no excessive interest was to be added to legitimate loans (cf. Exod 22:25-27; Deut 24:10-13). These economic principles were rooted in the gracious character of Yahweh, who redeemed Israel from servitude (and indebtedness) in Egypt (e.g., Lev 25:38, 55).

Abundance, multiplication, sufficiency: → *dgh* (multiply, # 1835); → *day* (sufficiency, overflowing supply, # 1896); → *ysp* (add, continue, increase, # 3578); → *kbr* I (make many, be in abundant supply, # 3892); → *m^{e}gammâ* (totality, abundance, # 4480); → *rbb* I (become numerous, much, great, # 8045); → *rbh* I (become numerous, multiply, increase, # 8049); → *r'š* II, be abundant, # 8322); → *śg'/śgh* (grow great, increase, exalt, # 8434/8436); → *śpq* II (suffice, be enough, # 8563); → *šwq* I (overflow, bestow abundantly, # 8796); → *šepa'* (super-abundance, # 9179)

BIBLIOGRAPHY

NIDNTT 1:728-44; 2:128-31; 3:136-38; *THAT* 2:715-26; *TWOT* 2:828-29; M. Gilbert, "Soyes feconds et multipliez (Gen 1:28)," *NRT* 96, 1974, 729-42; I. Nowell, "The Narrative Context of Blessing in the Old Testament," in *Blessing and Power*, 1988, 3-12.

Andrew E. Hill

8050	רבה

רבה (*rbh* II), archer (# 8050).

OT *rbh* occurs as a q. part. in Gen 21:20, with the meaning of one who shoots (i.e., an "archer"; see *HALAT* 870).

Bow, arrow, archery: → *'ašpâ* (quiver, # 880); → *zîqôt* (flaming arrow, # 2338); → *ḥēṣ* (arrow, # 2932); → *ṭḥh* (distance of bowshot, # 3217); → *yôreh* I (archer, # 3452); → *yeter* II (bowstring, # 3857); → *qešet* (bow, # 8008); → *rbb* II (shoot, # 8046); → *rbh* II (archer, # 8050); → *t^elî* (quiver, # 9437); → **Warfare: Theology**

BIBLIOGRAPHY

TWOT 2:829.

K. Lawson Younger, Jr.

8052 (*ribbô/ribbô'*), ten thousand), → # 8045, # 8047

8053	רְבִיבִים

רְבִיבִים (*r^ebîbîm*), showers (# 8053).

ANE *r^ebîbîm* is related to Ugar. *rbb* and *rb*, drizzle, (*HALAT* 1099).

OT 1. *r^ebîbîm* refers to light showers or drizzle (Reymond, 22; *THAT* 2:722), more typical of the early and late rains than of the heavier rains of Dec. through Feb. *r^ebîbîm* is used for the first rains of fall that soften the soil for plowing and planting (Ps 65:11; see Futato, 176, and Dalman, 1:164), and is also parallel to *malqôš* (late rains) in Jer 3:3.

2. The king is like *r^ebîbîm* watering the earth and resulting in prosperity (Ps 72:6). The remnant of Judah spread throughout the nations is like life-giving *r^ebîbîm* on grass (Mic 5:6[7]). Neither the idols of the nations nor impersonal laws of nature send down *r^ebîbîm*, but the Lord God of Israel brings rain, so Israel must hope in him (Jer 14:22).

Rain, dew, drizzle, hail, showers: → *'ēgel* (drop [of dew], # 103); → *brd* I (hail, # 1351); → *gšm* (make rain, # 1772); → *zrm* II ([clouds] pour out [water], # 2442); → *ḥ^anāmal* (sleet, hail?, # 2857); → *ṭal* (dew, light rain, drizzle, # 3228); → *yrh* II (give drink, cause rain, # 3722); → *mṭr* (make rain, # 4763); → *malqôš* (late rain, # 4919); → *sagrîr* (downpour, # 6039); → *sāpîaḥ* II (violent storm, # 6207); → *r^ebîbîm* (showers, # 8053); → *rāsîs* (dew drop, # 8268); → *r'p* (drip, flow, rain, # 8319); → *śā'îr* IV (heavy rain, # 8540); → *šikbâ* (layer of dew, emission/ discharge of seed, # 8887)

BIBLIOGRAPHY

G. Dalman, *Arbeit und Sitte*, 1928-42; M. Futato, "A Meteorological Analysis of Psalms 104, 65, and 29," diss. The Catholic University of America, Washington, D.C., 1984; P. Reymond, *L'eau, sa vie, et sa signification dans l'AT*, 1958; R. Scott, "Meteorological Phenomena and Terminology of the OT," *ZAW* 64, 1952, 11-25.

Mark D. Futato

8054	רָבִיד

רָבִיד (*rābîd*), nom. necklace (# 8054); < רבד (*rbd*), q. prepare (a couch) (→ # 8048).

ANE Ugar. *rbd*, furnish (a bed) with covers (*UT*, 2300; *KAI* 124), *mrbd(t)* (cf. *HALAT* 1097).

OT For examples, see Gen 41:42; Ezek 16:11; 2 Chron 3:16(?). For a discussion on jewelry, see *'dh*, put on ornaments (# 6335).

P-B Tg. *rôbēdā'*, pavement (cf. BDB, 914); Mish. Heb. *rôbed*, pavement, paved terrace (BDB, 914).

Malcolm J. A. Horsnell

8055 (r^e*bî'î,* fourth), → # 752

8057	רבך

רבך (*rbk*), mix, mingle, stir (only ho. participle; # 8057).

ANE Arab. *rabaka*, mix, mingle, Akk. *rabāku*, make a concoction; Egypt. *rbk*, Sam Pent. *amrubbēkat.*

OT The fem. part. *murbeket* (ho. from *rbk*) occurs 3x in BH: Lev 6:21[14]; 7:12; 1 Chron 23:29, always in the context of ritual offerings. In Lev 6:21 the instruction to prepare flour and oil for an offering as a part of the ordination ritual for Aaron and his progeny is followed by a command that the mixture be burned completely as a "soothing odor for Yahweh." Milgrom (*Leviticus*, AB, 400) suggests (on the basis of the Akk. cognate) a process whereby a product emerges from the boiling down of its ingredients. He argues for the same meaning in Lev 7:12 and 1 Chron 23:29. In Lev 7:12 the context is the peace offering ritual, which requires that the mixed cake of flour and oil be given to the priest. The reference in Chronicles lists responsibilities of the Levites, which are said to include "the mixture" or "the mixing" (NIV). In the first two references the mixing is to take place so that flour can be made into the more presentable form of a cake or bread.

Mixing, mingling, mixture: → *bll* (confuse, mix, # 1176); → *kil'ayim* (two kinds, # 3977); → *msk* (mix, # 5007); → *'rb* II (associate with, mingle with, be intermixed with, # 6843); → *rbk* (stirred, mixed, # 8057); → *rqḥ* (blend, mix, # 8379)

Wilma A. Bailey

8061	רבע

רבע (*rb'* I), q. lie down, lie with, copulate, mate; hi. cause to lie down (# 8061).

ANE At one time *rb'* I was thought to be an Aram. form of *rbṣ* (so BDB, 918). The evidence from Ugar. now appears to distinguish between *rbṣ*, lie down, and *rb'*, mate, with a *rb'* III, indicating "go" or "way" (Ps 139:3).

OT 1. In Lev 18:23 and 20:16, the vb. is used of copulation, particularly of a woman with an animal. Perhaps Margalit (391) overstates the case in concluding that *rbṣ*, lie down, and *rb'*, mate, have nothing in common, for the two ideas may be connected, both in Heb. and in Eng. But he is certainly correct in seeing that relationship as one that has, by the time of BH, faded into the background.

2. Dahood argues convincingly that *'orḥî* and *wᵉrib'î* in Ps 139:3 to be rendered "my departure" and "my arrival" and not, as conventionally, "my going and my lying down" (as NIV). If this is correct (the parallelism in the verse would appear to support it), there must be a *rb'* III in Heb. that, like its Ugar. cognate, means to come, arrive (Dahood, 286-87), or perhaps, "my going" and "my return."

Lying down, copulation, rape: → *rb'* I (lie down, copulate, # 8061); → *rbṣ* (lie down, # 8069); → *šgl* (sleep, be ravished, # 8711); → *škb* (lie down, be ravished, be bedded down, # 8886)

Bed: → *yṣ'* (spread out a bed, # 3667); → *miṭṭâ* (bed, # 4753); → *miškāb* (bed, # 5435); → *'ereś* (bedstead, # 6911); → *pē'â* II (luxury [of a couch], # 6991); → *rbd* (prepare a bed, # 8048)

BIBLIOGRAPHY

M. Dahood, *Psalms III: 101-150*, AB, 1970; B. Margalit, "Ugaritic Contributions to Hebrew Lexicography (*with special reference to the poem of Aqht*)," *ZAW* 99, 1987, 391-404.

William C. Williams

8062 (*rb'* II, square), → # 752

8063 (*reba'* I, fourth part, four sides), → # 752

8065 (*rōba'* I, fourth part), → # 752

8066	רֹבַע

רֹבַע (*rōba'* II), nom., dust, rubbish (# 8066).

OT *HALAT* lists an Akk. cognate, *turbu/ttu*, dust, cloud. BDB lists the meaning fourth part (978). If we follow KBL, the oracle of Balaam has parallel lines: "Who can count the dust of Jacob or number the rubble (*rōba'*, dust, cloud) of Israel?" (Num 23:10). Most translations interpret the word to mean "fourth part" (cf. 2 Kgs 6:25).

Dust, clay, dirt, loose soil: → *'ābāq* (dust, # 85); → *'ēper* (ashes, loose soil, # 709); → *ḥōmer* II (mud, clay, mortar, # 2817); → *ṭîṭ* (mud, mire, clay, # 3226); → *ṭnp* (dirty, # 3245); → *'pr* (dust, # 6759); → *rōba'* II (dust, rubbish, # 8066); → *regeb* (clods of earth, # 8073); → *šᵉḥôr* (soot, blackness, # 8818); → *šaḥaq* (dust, clouds of dust, # 8836)

Roy E. Hayden

8067	רִבֵּעַ

רִבֵּעַ (*ribbēa'*), member of the fourth generation (4x, always pl.; # 8067; *HALAT* 1102a).

ANE In the Aram. inscriptions, the pleonasm *bny rb'* means "members of the fourth generation" (*KAI* # 226; cf. *DISO* 273).

OT BH *ribbē'îm* always follows *šillēšîm*, "members of the third generation" (Exod 20:5 [= Deut 5:9]; 34:7; Num 14:18). See *šillēš* (→ # 9000).

Family, relative, citizen: → *'āb* (father, # 3); → *'aḥ* II (brother, kinsman, relative, countryman, # 278); → *'ēm* (mother, # 562); → *bēn* I (son, grandson, member of a group, # 1201); → *bat* I (daughter, granddaughter, # 1426); → *dôd* (uncle, # 1856); → *ḥām* I (father-in-law, # 2767); → *ḥtn* (become intermarried, become a son-in-law, # 3161); → *mōdā'* (kinsman, relative, # 4530); → *mišpāḥâ* (clan, kind, # 5476); → *'am* I (citizen, kinsman, relative, # 6638); → *ribbēa'* (member of fourth generation, # 8067); → *šillēš* (member of sixth generation, # 9000)

Robert H. O'Connell

8069	רבץ

רבץ (*rbṣ*), q. lie down, couch, hi. make to lie down (# 8069); מַרְבֵּץ (*marbēṣ*), fold, lair (→ # 5271); רֵבֶץ (*rēbeṣ*), resting place [for animals] (# 8070).

ANE The root *rbṣ* is well attested in nearly every Sem. language (e.g., Akk. *rabāṣu*, to settle down; see BDB, 918), including Ugar., where it appears in the causative *š*-form in the sense of "cause to mate" (Margalit, 391).

OT 1. When Jacob arrives in the land of the Easterners, he finds three flocks of sheep bedded down (*rbṣ*) beside a well (Gen 29:2). Judah sits on his haunches (*rbṣ*) like a lion before lying down with his chest to the ground (Gen 49:9), but in the nearly identical language about Balaam in Num 24:9, the vb. *škb* is used in place of *rbṣ*.

2. Sin couches (*rbṣ*) like a lion at Cain's door (Gen 4:7, although some take *rbṣ* as the name of a demon, cf. Akk. *rābiṣu*). The vb. can also speak of an animal collapsed beneath a burden too heavy for it (Exod 23:5; cf. Gen 49:14) or a mother bird brooding over eggs or chicks (Deut 29:19). *rbṣ* can describe inanimate objects such as *t*ᵉ*hôm*, stretched out beneath the sky (and perhaps the land, Gen 49:25). A curse can settle (*rbṣ*) on a person who disobeys Yahweh (Deut 29:19[20]). In the hi., *rbṣ* can describe a shepherd bedding down his flock (Ps 23:2) or an architect building a city (Isa 54:11, parallel to *ysd*, found [→ # 3569]).

Lying down, copulation, rape: → *rb'* I (lie down, copulate, # 8061); → *rbṣ* (lie down, # 8069); → *šgl* (sleep, be ravished, # 8711); → *škb* (lie down, be ravished, be bedded down, # 8886)

BIBLIOGRAPHY

R. Davidson, *Genesis 1-11*, 1973; J. D. Heck, "Issachar: Slave or Freeman? (Gen 49:14-15)," *JETS* 29, 1986, 385-96; J. S. Kselman, "A Note on Jer 49,20 and Ze 2,6-7," *CBQ* 32, 1970, 579-81; Baruch Margalit, "Ugaritic Contributions to Hebrew Lexicography (*with special reference to the poem of Aqht*)," *ZAW* 99, 1987, 391-404; H. G. M. Williamson, "A Reconsideration of עזב in Biblical Hebrew," *ZAW* 97, 1985, 74-85.

William C. Williams

8070 (*rēbeṣ*, resting place), → # 8069

8071 (*ribqâ*, Rebekah), → Isaac

8073	רֶגֶב

רֶגֶב (*regeb*), nom., clods of earth, soil (# 8073).

OT Job, commenting on his observation of the wicked, says that "the soil (*regeb*) in the valley is sweet to him" (21:33). Elsewhere God replies to Job by asking who it is that can bring rain when "the clods of earth stick together" (38:38).

Dust, clay, dirt, loose soil: → *'ābāq* (dust, # 85); → *'ēper* (ashes, loose soil, # 709); → *ḥōmer* II (mud, clay, mortar, # 2817); → *ṭîṭ* (mud, mire, clay, # 3226); → *ṭnp* (dirty, # 3245); → *'pr* (dust, # 6759); → *rōba'* II (dust, rubbish, # 8066); → *regeb* (clods of earth, # 8073); → *šᵉḥôr* (soot, blackness, # 8818); → *šaḥaq* (dust, clouds of dust, # 8836)

Roy E. Hayden

8074	רגז

רגז (*rgz*), q. agitate, quiver, shake, excite; hi. make shake, rouse up, agitate; hitp. excite oneself (# 8074); רֹגֶז (*rōgez*), nom. agitation, excitement, turmoil (# 8075); רַגָּז (*raggāz*), adj. agitated, shaking (# 8076); רָגְזָה (*rogzâ*), nom. agitation (# 8077).

ANE Aram. *rᵉgaz*, tremble, rage; Arab. *rağaza*, thunder, roar (sea).

OT The vb. *rgz* occurs 41x throughout the OT, most frequently in Isa, 11x. Fundamentally this word expresses the idea of physical shaking. The development of this root, however, has extended beyond its original boundary and is able to express the ideas of rebellion, fear, trouble, rage, and excitement.

1. The shaking of the earth, both *'ereṣ* (→ # 824) and *tēbēl* (→ # 9315), is a common theme. The wrath or anger of Yahweh is typically described as the reason for such shaking (1 Sam 14:15; 2 Sam 22:8; Ps 18:7[8]; Amos 8:8). Along with the earth, the mountains, heavens, nations, kingdoms, and their inhabitants also shake or tremble at the wrath of Yahweh (1 Sam 13:13; Isa 5:25; 23:11; 64:2). This same idea is also connected with the theophanic presence of Yahweh (Jer 33:9) and the great and terrible Day of the Lord (Joel 2:1, 10). Some of the synonyms appearing in this context are *ḥrd* and *r'š*.

2. The physical trembling of the body is often associated with extreme fear or anxiety: "I heard and my heart pounded, my lips *quivered* at the sound; decay crept into my bones, and my legs *trembled*" (Hab 3:16). The context is one of theophany (→). The Israelites evoked such a response in others as they began to conquer the land of Canaan (Exod 15:14; Deut 2:25). A conquered army surrenders in tremendous fear (Mic 7:17). The devastating affects of drought and famine are said to cause such fear (Isa 32:10), as is the luminous, royal presence of Yahweh (Ps 77:16, 18[17, 19]; 99:1). Some of the synonyms appearing in this context are *pḥd* and *ḥwl*.

3. In a few instances this vb. can mean to disturb, agitate, or excite. Samuel asks the question of Saul: "Why have you *disturbed* me by bringing me up?" in the unusual story of Saul's illicit consultation of a medium or witch (1 Sam 28:15). That the Israelites would not be disturbed or shaken from their land was one of Yahweh's promises (2 Sam 7:10; 1 Chron 17:9). This term is also applied to King David as he wept or was disturbed over the loss of his son (2 Sam 18:33[19:1]). It is used of Yahweh as he rouses or excites himself to battle (Isa 28:21).

4. To shake against someone or something is to rebel or rage against that person or thing. This is how a foolish person responds to a controversy with a wise person (Prov 29:9), or how a nation rebels against God (2 Kgs 19:27, 28; Isa 37:28, 29). Israel by her sinfulness stirred Yahweh to such wrath: "But because our fathers *angered* the God of heaven, he handed them over to Nebuchadnezzar the Chaldean, king of Babylon" (Ezra 5:12). In an unusual instance, Joseph uses this term when ordering his

brothers not to argue or quarrel while traveling home. In such instances it seems that *rgz* has come to function as a term denoting personal animosity between two parties.

5. Eight times the masc. nom. form, *rōgez,* of this root appears, which can express the type of fierce anger that is often accompanied by shaking (Hab 3:2; Dan 3:13). It can also represent tremendous anguish and suffering. The antonyms *nwḥ* (→ # 5663), to rest, and *šqṭ* (→ # 9200), to be quiet, express the exact opposite idea communicated by *rgz* (Job 3:17, 26; 14:1; Isa 14:3). The nom. form of *rgz* can simply represent a very loud noise (Job 37:2). The one occurrence of the fem. nom. form is used in the sense of fear and anxiety (Ezek 12:18). In a related sense, the root appears once as a adjective (*raggāz*), modifying heart to express profound anxiety (Deut 28:65).

Shaking, terror, trembling: → *g'š* (rise and fall noisily, swell, surge, # 1723); → *zw'* (tremble, quake, be afraid, # 2316); → *zll* II (shake, quake, tremble, # 2362); → *ḥalḥālâ* (shaking, trembling, anguish, # 2714); → *ḥrg* (come out trembling, # 3004); → *ḥrd* (tremble, shudder, startle, # 3006); → *yr'* (tremble, be fainthearted, # 3760); → *mwṭ* (waver, reel, stagger, shake, reel, # 4572); → *m'd* (slip, slide, shake, totter, # 5048); → *nwd* (shake, totter, waiver, wander, mourn, flee, # 5653); → *nwṭ* (shake, quake, # 5667); → *nw'* (shake, tremble, stagger, totter, wave, # 5675); → *n'r* II (shake, shake off, # 5850); → *smr* (shudder, have goose-bumps, bristle, # 6169); → *'iw'îm* (distortion, stagger, dizzy, # 6413); → *pwq* I (stagger, wobble, reel, totter, # 7048); → *pḥd* I (tremble, be in dread, # 7064); → *plṣ* (shudder, shake, tremble, # 7145); → *qwṣ* I (feel disgust, frighten, cause dread, # 7762); → *rgz* (agitate, quiver, shake, excite, rouse up, agitate, # 8074); → *rnh* I (rattle, # 8261); → *r'd* (tremble, shake, tremble, # 8283); → *r'l* I (brandish, make to quiver, # 8302); → *r'š* I (quake, shake, leap, # 8321); → *rpp* (shake, quake, rock, # 8344); → *rᵉtēt* (terror, panic, trembling, # 8417); → *ś'r* I (be afraid, terrified, bristle with horror, # 8547)

Anger, rage, wrath: → *'np* (be angry, # 647); → *z'm* (curse, be angry, # 2406); → *z'p* I (rage, # 2406); → *ḥēmâ* (rage, # 2779); → *ḥrh* I (be hot, become angry, # 3013); → *k's* (be irritated, angry, # 4087); → *'br* II (show anger, # 6297); → *qṣp* I (become angry, # 7911); → *rgz* (shake, agitate, # 8074); → **Anger: Theology**

BIBLIOGRAPHY

TWOT 2:830.

M. V. Van Pelt/W. C. Kaiser, Jr.

8075 (*rōgez*, agitation, excitement, turmoil), → # 8074

8076 (*raggāz*, agitated, shaking), → # 8074

8077 (*rogzâ*, agitation), → # 8074

8078	רגל

רגל (*rgl*), q. slander; pi. spy, slander; tiph. teach to walk, guide (# 8078).

ANE The vb. is a denom. of *regel,* foot, a nom. with cognates in Eth., Arab.

OT The vb. *rgl* occurs most frequently with mundane uses, that is, to speak of spies or spying. Of twenty-six attestations (q. 1x, pi. 24x, tiph. 1x), twelve are part. serving either as noms., spies, or verbals, spying. On two occasions (2 Sam 19:27[28] pi.; Ps 15:3 q.) the meaning is slander or the like, perhaps alluding to the stealthy or secretive nature of such talk. Once (Hos 11:3) the connotation is that of instruction or guidance in walking.

1. *The vb. with the meaning spy.* The earliest occurrence of vb. *rgl* in this sense is in Gen 42, where Joseph accuses his brothers of being spies (part. *m^{e}ragg^{e}lîm)* in Egypt (vv. 9, 11, 14, 31, 34, all pi. part.). The furtiveness of their activity (and hence the meaning spies) is clear from Joseph's allegation that they have come to exploit Egypt's weaknesses. The part. appears also in 42:30 as a verbal (spying on the land). The pi. part. is used in the same way to describe the infiltrators whom Joshua sent into Canaan (Josh 2:1, spies) and their activity (6:22-23, spying). Elsewhere *rgl* part. describes David's spies in the Negev (1 Sam 26:4) and Absalom's secret messengers (2 Sam 15:10).

Apart from the part. the vb. is attested also in inf. const. to describe the sending out of persons for the purpose of espionage. Moses sent out spies to Jazer (Num 21:32), Joshua dispatched some to Jericho (Josh 6:25), Caleb testified that he had been sent out to explore Canaan before the conquest (14:7), the Danites sent out scouts to Laish (Judg 18:2, 14, 17), and David was accused by the Ammonites of having sent out spies rather than ambassadors to celebrate the accession of their new king (2 Sam 10:3 = 1 Chron 19:3). The preterite occurs twice (Deut 1:24; Josh 7:2) to recount that spies were sent forth. The use in Josh 7:2 is the response to the impv. in the same verse: "Go up and spy out the region" (NIV). Though Yahweh never appears as the subject of the vb. or even as directly initiating the action, it is clear that spying, as surreptitious as it must, of necessity, be, is an appropriate action when carried out at the command of God's agents such as Moses and Joshua. Nevertheless, in other circumstances spying inevitably is viewed pejoratively.

2. *The vb. with the meaning slander.* The psalmist (Ps 15:3) says that the one qualified to live in God's sanctuary "has no slander on his tongue" (NIV; lit., does not slander [q.] by means of [*'al*] his tongue). The par. in v. 2c ("speaks the truth from his heart") solidifies the meaning slander in v. 3. In 2 Sam 19:27[28] Mephibosheth complains to David that Ziba has slandered him—that is, he has lied about him behind his back. The form here is the pi. + prep. *b^e* + *'abd^{e}kâ*, "he has slandered with reference to your servant." The connection to *rgl*, spy, is obvious: slander, like spying, is stealthy and hidden.

3. *The vb. with the meaning teach to walk.* The vb. *rgl* occurs in Hos 11:3 in the *tiph'el* stem (*GKC* 55h), perhaps factitive meaning, put the feet in the right position, that is, lead or teach to walk. Andersen and Freedman suggest, however, that since Ephraim here is a *na'ar,* a youth, "teach to walk" is inappropriate. Rather, the idea is "I [Yahweh] was a guide for Israel" (579).

P-B LXX renders *rgl* by either (vb.) *kataskopeō* or (nom.) *kataskopos.*

Bibliography

TWAT 7:330-46; F. I. Andersen and D. N. Freedman, *Hosea,* AB, 1980; H. Englander, "Rashi's Grammatical Comments," *HUCA* 17, 1942-43; S. Wagner, "Die Kundschaftergeschichten im Alten Testament," *ZAW* 76, 1964, 255-69; H. W. Wolf, *Hosea,* Hermeneia, 1974.

E. H. Merrill

8079	רֶגֶל

רֶגֶל (*regel*), foot (# 8079); מַרְגְּלוֹת (*marg*e*lôt*), place of feet (# 5274); רגל (*rgl*), denom. vb. slander, spy (→ # 8078); רַגְלִי (*raglî*), on foot, soldier (# 8081).

ANE The nom. appears in Aram. *riglā'*; OSA *rgl*; Eth. *'ĕgr*; and Arab. (*riğl*). See section 2.

OT 1. While used most frequently to refer to human feet, *regel* also is used for the feet of birds (Gen 8:9), quadrupeds (Lev 11:21, 23, 42), seraphs (Isa 6:2), cherubs (Ezek 1:7), physical objects (Exod 25:26; 37:13), and even God's feet (Exod 24:10; 2 Sam 22:10/Ps 18:9[10]; 99:5; 132:7; Isa 60:13; 66:1; Nah 1:3; Hab 3:5; Zech 14:4).

2. The nom. *regel* is used with "head" to indicate the extremes of the body, and as a literary merism meaning "all over one's body." *regel* may be the first listed body part, as in "from the soles of your feet to the top of your head" (Deut 28:35; Job 2:7; Isa 1:6), or it may be the second listed body part, as in "from head to foot" (Lev 13:12; 2 Sam 14:25). The equivalent in Akk. for the first is *ištu ṣuprim adi šārtim ša qaqqadim* (*AHw*, 1113a), and for the second *ultu qaqqadišu adi kibis šēpēšu*, an expression that occurs in Akk. medical texts (*CAD*, s.v. *qaqqadu* 1:10).

3. Feet are the means of locomotion. Without good feet one is rendered almost immobile (2 Sam 4:4; 9:3, 13). So Mephibosheth is the opposite of the fleet-footed mentioned in 2 Sam 2:18 and Amos 2:15.

4. Lev 21:16-24 lists the various bodily defects that disqualify a priest from officiating in the sacrificial cult. One of these is lameness or a broken leg/foot (*šeber regel*, v. 19). Leviticus insists on physical soundness both for the sacrificial victim and the officiating clergy. Neither a blemished animal nor an imperfect person is to enter his immediate presence.

5. Similarly, the priest is to wash his feet and hands before entering the tent or presiding before the altar (Exod 30:19, 21; 40:31). To fail to do so is to invite death. By Second Temple times this responsibility was encumbent on the priest after he finished offering the sacrifice as well (Jub 21:16). Only on the Day of Atonement was the high priest required to bathe his entire body, at the beginning of his ministration (Lev 16:4) and after its completion (16:26), for entering into the Most Holy place demands a more thoroughgoing purification.

6. On occasion in the OT "feet" may be a euphemism for the genitalia, male (Exod 4:25; Judg 3:24; 1 Sam 24:3[4]; posssibly Ruth 3:4, 7), female (Deut 28:57; Ezek 16:25), or heavenly creatures (Isa 6:2). In 2 Kgs 18:27/‖ Isa 36:12 urine is called "water of feet." The clearest reference to this anatomically euphemistic use of *regel* is Isa 7:20. The king of Assyria, as God's hired razor to judge his people, will come and "shave your head and the hair of your legs (*śa'ar hāraglāyim*, NIV)." The objects of shaving could also be translated "shave the head and the genital hair" (Wildberger, *Isaiah 1-12*, 319), i.e., public and private hair.

7. The nom. *marg*e*lôt* occurs 5x in the OT, four of which are in Ruth (3:4, 7, 8, 14), and the fifth in Daniel (10:6). The translation "legs" seems preferable in Dan 10:6, where it is used in conjunction with "arms" to describe the body parts of the man Daniel saw in his vision. In Ruth, however, the translation "place of feet" is preferable to NIV's "feet" (GKC, par.124ab identifies the *-ôt* ending as "a plural of local

extension" and compares this word with *m^era'^ašôt*, place of head). Apart from the choice in Ruth of the word *marg^elôt*, derived from *regel*, foot (which is at times a euphemism for the pudenda), the use of other nearby words like "uncover" and "lie down" heighten the sexual overtones of this first encounter between Ruth and Boaz (Hubbard, 203, n30; Sasson, 69-71; DeWaard and Nida, 50, 94-95).

8. The word *raglî*, on foot, soldier, is almost always used with large numbers. In ascending size the numbers are 10,000 (2 Kgs 13:7); 20,000 (2 Sam 8:4; 10:6; 1 Chron 18:4); 30,000 (1 Sam 4:10); 40,000 (1 Chron 19:18); 100,000 (1 Kgs 20:29); 200,000 (1 Sam 15:4); 400,000 (Judg 20:2); 600,000 (Exod 12:37; Num 11:21).

The word is used by God in his blunt response to Jeremiah's complaint about abuse and the prosperous wicked (Jer 12:1-4). The first part of God's rejoinder (12:5a) is, "If you have raced with men on foot and they have worn you out, how can you compete with horses?" The worse is yet to come. The real battles are still in the future.

While earlier texts (Exod 12:37; Num 11:21) may refer simply to the number of adult males "on the march," and not necessarily to infantry in a technical sense, other references, such as 1 Kgs 20:29, appear to have infantry in mind. The infantry was divided into four groups: archers (1 Chron 12:2; Jer 50:14); slingers (2 Kgs 3:25; 1 Chron 12:2); spearmen (1 Chron 12:8[9]; and auxiliaries. The spearmen, the assault troops of the infantry, defended themselves with shields, unlike the archers or slingers. Unlike the cavalry, which took part only in open field engagements, the infantry participated in assaults against fortified cities as well.

Leg, loins, foot, thigh: → *b^ehôn* (thumb, big toe, # 984); → *ḥ^alāṣayim* (loins, # 2743); → *yārēk* (thigh, leg, # 3751); → *kesel* I (loins, flank/side, # 4072); → *midrāk* (foot-print, # 4534); → *marg^elôt* (place of feet, # 5274); → *motnayim* (loins, hips, # 5516); → *na'al* (sandal, # 5837); → *paḥad* II (thigh, # 7066); → *pa'am* (foot, step, time, # 7193); → *qarsōl* (ankle, # 7972); → *regel* (foot, # 8079); → *šôq* (thigh, leg, # 8797)

BIBLIOGRAPHY

R. deVaux, *AncIsr*, 1965, 1:213-28; J. DeWaard and E. A. Nida, *A Translator's Handbook on the Book of Ruth*, 1973; R. Hubbard, *The Book of Ruth*, NICOT, 1988; J. Sasson, *Ruth: A New Translation with a Philological Commentary and a Formalist-Folklorist Interpretation*, 1979; Y. Yadin, *The Art of Warfare in Biblical Lands*, 1963.

Victor P. Hamilton

8081	רַגְלִי

רַגְלִי (*raglî*), on foot, soldier (# 8081); < רֶגֶל (*regel*), foot (→ # 8079).

ANE The nom. appears in Aram. (*riglā'*), OSA (*rgl*), Eth. (*'egr*), and Arab. (*riǧl*).

OT 1. Almost always this word is used with large numbers. In ascending size the numbers are 10,000 (2 Kgs 13:7); 20,000 (2 Sam 8:4; 10:6); 30,000 (1 Sam 4:10); 100,000 (1 Kgs 20:29); 200,000 (1 Sam 15:4); 400,000 (Judg 20:8); 600,000 (Exod 12:37; Num 11:21).

2. The word is used by God in his blunt response to Jeremiah's complaint about abuse and the prosperous wicked (Jer 12:1-4). The first part of God's rejoinder (12:5a) is, "If you have raced with men on foot and they have worn you out, how can you compete with horses?" The worst is yet to come. The real battles are still in the future.

War, army, battle, fight: → *gdd* II (band together, # 1518); → *ḥmš* (organized for war, # 2821); → *lḥm* I (do battle, fight, # 4309); → *maḥ*^{a}*neh* (camp, encampment, war, # 4722); → *ma*$^{'a}$*rākâ* (battle-line, # 5120); → *ṣb'* (go to war, serve, muster, conscript, # 7371); → *ṣî* (warship, # 7469); → *ṣrḥ* (yell, call shrilly, raise the war-cry, # 7658); → *q*^{e}*rāb* (battle, # 7930); → *rkb* (ride/mount, # 8206); → *rw'* (shout, give war-cry, # 8131); → *šālîš* III (third man in war-chariot, adjutant, # 8957)

Victor P. Hamilton

8083	רגם

רגם (*rgm*), q. (only) stone, throw stones (# 8083); מַרְגֵּמָה (*margēmâ*), meaning uncertain (# 5275), only Prov 26:8; רִגְמָה (*rigmâ*), throng (→ # 8086).

ANE Aram. *rgm*, stone, shoot, throw.

OT 1. The root *rgm* occurs 16x in the OT, and like *sql* (→ # 6232) the word is used primarily in legal texts for execution by stoning. For instance, Mosaic law decrees death by stoning (*rgm*) for blasphemy (Lev 24:14, 16, 23), Sabbath violation (Num 15:35-36), the practice of spiritism (Lev 20:27), child sacrifice to Molech (Lev 20:2), persistent disobedience to parents (Deut 21:21), and violation of the holy war ban on booty (Josh 7:25). The legal act of stoning as a form of capital punishment was a corporate responsibility (cf. Num 15:35; Deut 21:21), demonstrating the solidarity of the covenant community in its response to sin.

2. On two occasions stoning was an act of rebellion against authority—against that of King Rehoboam in the stoning of his official Adoniram (1 Kgs 12:18 = 2 Chron 10:18), and against that of Yahweh in the stoning of the priest Zechariah (2 Chron 24:21).

3. The prophet Ezekiel includes death by stoning in his catalog of atrocities committed by the Babylonians against those living in Jerusalem (Ezek 16:40; 23:47).

4. The nom. *margēmâ* in Prov 26:8 is obscure. The NIV follows the LXX and translates "sling," but *HALAT* suggests "heap of stones." McKane (*Proverbs*, 1970, 598) insists that *margēmâ* must be translated "sling" or "cairn."

Rock, stones: → *'eben* (stone, rock, # 74); → *gābîš* (rock-crystal, # 1486); → *ḥallāmîš* (flint, # 2734); → *ḥāṣāṣ* (gravel, # 2953); → *kēp* (rock, # 4091); → *sōḥeret* (mineral stone, # 6090); → *sela'* (rock, # 6152); → *sql* (throw stones, # 6232); → *ṣûr* I (rock, boulder, # 7446); → *ṣûr* II (pebble, flint, # 7447); → *ṣōr* I (flint knife, # 7644); → *rgm* (stone, # 8083); → *talpiyyôt* (courses of stones, # 9444)
Shooting, throwing: → *dḥh* (push, overthrow, be cast down, # 1890); → *ṭwl* (throw, # 3214); → *ydh* I (shoot, # 3343); → *yrh* I (shoot, throw, # 3721); → *mgr* (throw, # 4489); → *rbb* II (shoot, # 8046); → *rmh* I (throw, shoot, # 8227); → *šlk* I (throw, hurl, # 8959); → *šmṭ* (release, remit, drop, throw down, # 9023)

BIBLIOGRAPHY
ISBE 3:205-6; 4:622-30; *NIDNTT* 2:731-34; 3:381-99; *TWOT* 2:832.

Andrew E. Hill

8086	רִגְמָה

רִגְמָה (*rigmâ*), nom. noise, shout; noisy crowd, shouting crowd (hapleg., # 8086).

ANE 1. Scholars have proposed several possible etymologies: *rgm* I, stone (# 8083); *rgm* II, shout, noise; *r'm* roar, thunder (# 8306); *rgš*, be in commotion (# 8093) (see ANE # 2-5 and OT # 2-3).

2. The root *rgm* I is limited to WestSem.: Arab. *rāgama*, throw stones, heap up stones; Eth. *ragama*, throw stones; Aram. *r^{e}gam*, stone, throw; Syr. *r^{e}gam*, stone, throw stones, heap up stones. (See OT # 2.)

3. The root *rgm* II is widespread and well attested: Ugar. *rgm*, speak, talk; report, inform, tell; *rgm*, word, speech, utterance; news, message, report, account; Arab. *rāgāmu*, noisy crowd; Bab. *rigmu*, shout, scream; clanking of weapons, noise of army; Akk. *ragāmu*, call, summon, cry out, shout; *rugummû*, complaint, lament; *rigmu*, voice, shout, noise. Note: The Akk. nom. *rigim* is used in reference to the noise of populuous humanity in the Atraḫasis Epic: "the noise (*rigim*) made by man (*ameluti*) has become too great for me" (*CTA* 15 49 iii 6). (See OT # 3.)

4. The root *r'm* is limited to WestSem.: Aram. *r^e'ēm*, thunder (of words), roar, rage; Syr. *r^e'ēm*, thunder forth sound (of words), resound; clamor; be enraged, angry, indignant; Arab. *raġima*, vex, dislike; Eth. *ra'ama*, thunder (of words). (See OT # 2.)

5. The root *rgš* is well attested and widespread: Akk. *ragāšum*, get worked out into excitement; fly into a rage; Aram. *r^{e}gaš*, be excited, turbulent; Emp. Aram. *rgš*, be excited; ecstatic (*DISO*, 275); Syr. *r^{e}gaš*, be in an uproar; *regōš*, uproar; *r^{e}gešōt*, rustling noise; movement; Arab. *ragasu*, vehement noise (of an animal: camel, elephant); Arab. *rāǧasa*, make a vehement noise. (See OT # 2.)

OT 1. Psalm 68 is a processional liturgy celebrating God's triumph over his enemies and his kingship over Israel and the nations. Verses 1-18 describe his triumphal and historical march from Mount Sinai (in the days of Moses) to Mount Zion (in the days of David). Verses 19-35 describes the entrance of the procession into the sanctuary and the enthronement of God in the sanctuary at the time of the dedication of the temple. In verses 24-27[25-28] the procession has come into view of the worshipers and is about to enter the sanctuary. All Israel is represented at this celebration, including delegates from the small tribe of Benjamin to the powerful tribe of Judah, from the most northern tribes (Zebulun and Naphtali) to the most southern tribes (Benjamin and Judah).

The enigmatic nom. *rigmātām* > *rigmâ* in Ps 68:27[28] is a hapleg. The stanza of vv. 24-27[25-28] pictures a liturgical procession approaching the temple, singing and playing musical instruments. A plethora of participants is detailed: procession (*h^{a}lîkôteykā*), singers (*šārîm*), musicians (*nōg^{e}nîm*), maidens (*'^{a}lāmôt*), congregation (*maqhēlôt*), and assembly (*mimm^{e}qôr*). Thus, *rigmâ* is often understood as referring to a noisy crowd or throng (see LePeau, 192-97). NIV renders vv. 24-27[25-28] thus:

Your procession has come into view, O God,
the procession of my God and King into the sanctuary.
In front are the singers, after them the musicians;
with them are the maidens playing tambourines.
Praise God in the great congregation,
praise the LORD in the assembly of Israel.
There is the little tribe of Benjamin, leading them,
there the great throng of Judah's princes (*rigmātām*),
and there the princes of Zebulun and of Naphtali.

2. Early lexicographers suggested that *rigmâ* is derived from the common Heb. root *rgm* I (stone) and that it denotes heap of stones (lit.), hence, crowd of people (fig.) (BDB, 920; König, *HAW* 9, 432; Briggs, 111). (See ANE 2.) More recent lexicographers and scholars relate *rigmâ* to Ugar. *rgm* and Akk. *ragămu*, to shout (see ANE 2) and suggest "shouting crowd" (*HALAT*, 873; König, 432; Gesenius, 745; Kraus, 45-47). (See ANE # 3.) Others suggest that it is a variable spelling of the Heb. nom. *r'm*, noise, thunder, and posit the metonymy, noisy crowd (e.g., Cheyne, 156). (See ANE # 4.) Still others posit that *rigmâ* is a textual corruption of *rigšâ*, noise; throng, tumultuous throng (BDB, 920-21; Zorell, 757). Orthographic confusion between *m* and *š* is possible because they were similar in the paleo-Heb. script. The nom. *rigšâ* refers to a "throng" of worshipers walking in procession to the temple (Ps 55:15). The vb. *rgš* denotes to be in tumult, commotion; to throng tumultuously (Ps 2:1), and *r^egaš* denotes to assemble, throng together tumultously (Dan 6:6[7], 11[12], 15[16]). (See ANE # 5.)

If, however, the nom. is derived from Ugar. and Akk. *rgm*, shout (see ANE # 3), MT *rigmātām* might simply denote "their shout." This would refer to the cultic praise mentioned in v. 26[27] or singing in v. 25[26]. The line could be rendered, "The little tribe of Benjamin is leading them, the princes of Judah in their shout."

3. Several Heb. MSS read *b^eriqmātām* (in their variegated clothes) from *riqmâ*, variegated, embroidered material (BDB, 955; *HALAT* 909-10). LXX reads *a'tån*, their leaders, which reflects *rōz^enêhem* (so *BHS*), which may only represent a desperate attempt to interpret *rigmātām* as a reference to the tribal leaders of Judah in v. 27[28].

P-B Although the root *rgm* I (stone) is common in P-B, the homonymic root *rgm* II (shout, noisy crowd) does not appear in P-B in either the DSS or RL. Rabbinic exegesis mistakenly treated *rigmātām* as the vb. *rgm*, stone: "The princes of Judah stoned them [the tribe of Benjamin]" (Braude 2:547).

NT The NT term *ochlos*, crowd, parallels Heb. *rigmâ*, shouting crowd, when it describes a festive throng playing musical instruments or shouting out in worship (Matt 9:23; 21:8, 46; Mark 3:7; Acts 2:6).

Crowd of people, congregation, rabble: → *'^asapsup* (rabble, # 671); → *hāmôn* (noise, crowd, agitation, bustle, turmoil, # 2162); → *h^amullâ* (noise, noisy crowd, crowd, # 2167); → *sāk* (number, multitude, throng, # 6107); → *'^aṣārâ* (festive assembly, # 6809); → *qhl* (assemble, summon, # 7735); → *rigmâ* (noise, noisy crowd, # 8086)

Bibliography

J. Aistleitner, "Zu Ps. 68," *BZ* 19, 1931, 29-41; W. G. Braude, *Midrash on the Psalms*, 1959, 2:547; C. A. Briggs, *The Book of Psalms*, 1917, 2:111; A. Caquot, "Le Psaume LXVIII," *RHR* 177, 1970, 147-82; T. K. Cheyne, "On Ps 68,28. 31," *ZAW* 19, 1899, 156-57; G. R. Driver, "Studies in the Vocabulary of the OT IV," *JTS* 33, 1931-32, 38-47; idem, "Zeitschriftenschau," *ZAW* 50, 1932, 176-77; J. Gray, "A Cantata of the Autumn Festival: Psalm LXVIII," *JSS* 22, 1977, 2-26; A. R. Johnson, *Sacral Kingship in Ancient Israel*, 1955, 68-77; E. Klein, *A Comprehensive Etymological Dictionary of the Hebrew Language*, 1987, 606; H.-J. Kraus, *Psalms 60-150: A Commentary*, 1989, 45-47; J. P. LePeau, "Psalm 68: An Exegetical and Theological Study," Ph. D. Diss. University of Iowa, 1981, 192-97; M. E. Tate, *Psalms 51-100*, 1992, 168; A. Weiser, *The Psalms*, 1962, 479.

Gordon H. Johnston

8087	רגן

רגן (*rgn*), q., ni., murmur, complain (# 8087).

OT 1. Deut 1:27 and Ps 106:25 use this root when they refer back to the tradition of the Israelites grumbling because of the spies' report at Kadesh Barnea (Num 13-14). This kind of murmuring is more clandestine and behind the scene (they murmured in their tents) whereas *lwn* is complaining in an open confrontation (Coats, *Rebellion in the Wilderness*, 192-93). This murmuring was related to the peoples' unbelief, their unwillingness to listen to the word of the Lord, and their assumption that the Lord hated them.

2. The ni. part., used substantively, is used 4x in Proverbs describing the evil speech of the foolish person. It refers to murmuring about another person behind their back rather than openly complaining about their behavior. This kind of gossip could cause a deep separation between friends (Prov 16:28; 18:8; 26:20, 22).

P-B The LXX frequently translates *rgn* as *gongyzō* or one of its derivatives. The term refers to an attitude of dissatisfaction when a group of people believe that God did not deal with them fairly or justly (*TDNT* 1:730). When Philo and Josephus discuss the rebellion of the Israelites in the wilderness, they employ this word to refer to the murmuring of the people.

NT The NT uses *gongyzō* when it makes a direct reference to the grumbling of the Israelites (1 Cor 10:10). It describes the complaining of workers who thought that they were not paid enough for their work (Matt 20:11) and the rebellious attitude of the Jews who disliked what Jesus said and did (John 6:41, 43; 7:12). Believers are warned against grumbling (Phil 2:14). Jude 15-16 defines grumbling as harsh things that the ungodly speak or illegitimate faultfinding.

Complaint, grumbling: → *'nn* (complain, # 645); → *lwn* I (howl, grumble, # 4296); → *rgn* (murmur, complain, # 8087)

BIBLIOGRAPHY

TDNT 1:728-37; G. W. Coats, *Rebellion in the Wilderness*, 1968; S. J. DeVries, "The Origin of the Murmuring Tradition," *JBL* 87, 1968, 51-58.

Gary V. Smith

8088/8089	רגע

רגע (*rg'*), q. crust over, stir up, come to rest; ni. be quiet; hi. cause a person to rest, act in a moment (# 8088, # 8089); מַרְגּוֹעַ (*margôa'*), nom. resting place (# 5273); מַרְגֵּעָה (*margē'â*), nom. resting place (# 5276); רָגֵעַ (*rāgēa'*), nom. quiet, resting (# 8091); רֶגַע (*rega'*), nom. period, instant, suddenly, every moment (# 8092).

ANE No cognates are known.

OT 1. While KBL recognizes only one root having these consonants, BDB and the *NIV Exhaustive Concordance* recognize two, and this seems more probable. The first meaning (# 8089) is to act hastily, in a moment (Prov 12:19; Jer 49:19; 50:44), or to stir up the sea (Job 26:12; Isa 51:15; Jer 31:35). The second meaning (# 8088) has to do with being at rest or in repose (Deut 28:65; Job 7:5; Isa 34:14; 51:4; Jer 31:2; 47:6;

50:34). Job 7:5 may offer the basic idea or it may be anomolous. NIV (with KJV) translates "my skin is *broken* and festering." If this is the correct rendering, it is difficult to see what this has to do with repose—or with hasty action, for that matter. KBL, however, suggests that the idea is "to crust over," and NRSV and NASB, which both have "my skin *hardens*," reflect that understanding. If that rendering is correct, then it is possible that the basic idea of *rg'* (II) is to cease activity. This is certainly seen in Jer 47:6, where the sword is called to return to its scabbard and "*cease* and be still (*dmh*)." However, the overall range of connotations for this second meaning is similar to that of *nwḥ*. So it means to find repose in Deut 28:65 and Isa 34:14, where it is paralleled with *mānôaḥ*, place of rest. The Lord "places" his justice as a light to the peoples (Isa 51:4). God promises to "give rest," that is, procure relief for his people and their land after the horrors of the Exile (Jer 31:2; 50:34).

2. The nom. *rāgēa'*, *margôa'*, and *margē'â* each occur once (Ps 35:20; Isa 28:12; Jer 6:16; resp.), and all have to do with being in repose, with experiencing the tranquility that results from having ceased one's own efforts and from having found security through trust in God. On the other hand, all the occurrences (22x) of *rega'* (nom.) partake of the other meaning of the root: to act suddenly. This word regularly connotes a moment of time. In a few instances it is used adverbially and is translated "suddenly" (e.g., Ps 73:19) or even, "continually" (lit., to moments, Isa 27:3), but all of these relate to sudden, momentary action and have no connotation pertaining to rest or silence.

Rest, quiet, repose: → *dmh* II (come to an end, rest, be dumb, silent, # 1949); → *nwh* I (rest, # 5657); → *nwḥ* I (settle, take a rest, wait, station, deposit, # 5663); → *rg'* (crust over, come to rest, be quiet, # 8088/89); → *š'n* (be at ease, untroubled, # 8631); → *šbḥ* II (hush, soothe, quiet, # 8656); → *šebet* (sitting quietly, rest, # 8699, 8700); → *štq* (become calm, # 9284)

BIBLIOGRAPHY
TWOT 2:832-33.

John N. Oswalt

8091 (*rāgēa'*, quiet, resting), → # 8088

8092 (*rega'*, period, instant, suddenly, every moment), → # 8088

8093	רגשׁ

רגשׁ (*rgš*), q. be restless (# 8093); רֶגֶשׁ (*regeš*), nom. unrest (# 8094); רִגְשָׁה (*rigšâ*), nom. commotion (# 8095).

OT This word occurs 3x, once in each of the forms noted above. The vb. describes the restless nations that "conspire" against the Lord and his Messiah (Ps 2:1). The two nom. forms refer to noisy crowds, whether of worshipers in Jerusalem (Ps 55:14[15]), or of evildoers seeking to do harm to the psalmist (Ps 64:2[3]).

Noise, roar, voice: → *g'r* (roar, shout, bellow, cry out, rebuke, reprimand, # 1721); → *hmh* (make a noise, uproar, sound, be restless, # 2159); → *hmm* (rumble, crush, # 2169); → *nhm* (growl, groan, # 5637); → *qôl* (voice, sound, thunder, cry, # 7754); → *rgš* (be restless, # 8093); → *š'g* (roar, # 8613); → *š'h* II (roar, # 8616)

John N. Oswalt

8094 (*regeš*, unrest), → # 8093

8095 (*rigšâ*, commotion), → # 8093

8096	רדד

רדד (*rdd*), q. repel, subdue, obtain control; hi. hammer out (gold); ho. be troubled (# 8096). This vb. is a root variant of רדה (*rdh* I), rule, govern (→ # 8097).

ANE In Akk. the vb. *radādu* means pursue or chase (*AHw*, 940), and in Arab. *radda*, send, force back. In RL the vb. is maintained with meanings that correlate with OT usage (cf. Jastrow 2:1451).

OT In two instances (i.e., 1 Kgs 6:32 and Ps 55:2[3]) the vb. *rdd* has meanings quite different from its regular meaning as indicated above. The former occurrence refers to the flattening of gold and the latter to a state of mind, being worried or troubled. For the rest the vb. has a meaning similar to *rdh* I, subdue, but occurs mainly with Yahweh as the subject. It is he who subdues the nations, and does so on behalf of a particular king (Isa 45:1; 41:2; Ps 144:2).

Kingship, rule, supervision, dominion: → *b'l* I (marry, rule over, own, # 1249); → *g^ebîrâ/g^eberet* (lady, queen, mistress, # 1485/1509); → *ykḥ* (dispute, reason together, prove, judge, rule, reprove, # 3519); → *kbš* (make subservient, subdue, # 3899); → *mlk* I (rule, # 4887); → *mšl* II (rule, govern, # 5440); → *nṣḥ* (supervise, # 5904); → *rdd* (repel, subdue, # 8096); → *rdh* I (rule, govern, # 8097); → *r'h* I (feed, graze, shepherd, rule, # 8286); → *śrr* I (rule, direct, superintend, # 8606); → *šlṭ* (gain power, # 8948); → *špṭ* (get justice, act as a judge, rule, # 9149)

Philip J. Nel

8097	רדה

רדה (*rdh* I), q. rule, govern, tread, have dominion (# 8097).

ANE The vb. *redû* in Akk. means to walk, to drive (animals), or to guide. The nom. *redûm* may refer to an attendant, to an army, or to a troop of police (*AHw*, 966-68).

OT The vb. *rdh* stresses the act of dominance by force and overlaps accordingly with the comparable nuance of meaning of *mšl*. In 1 Kgs 4:24[5:4] it occurs with *mšl* and emphasizes the Israelite king's dominance over other kingdoms and enemies of the state (cf. Ps 72:8; 110:2). The negative connotation of the vb. is evident from those instances where the Israelite community is warned against the subduing of countrymen (Lev 25:43, 46, 53; Ezek 34:4). Its negative meaning also correlates with that of *slṭ* (→ # 8949).

In Gen 1:26, 28 the vb. occurs with a positive meaning when it is stated that humanity, created in God's own image, should subdue (*kbš*, → # 3890) the earth and rule over (*rdh*) all animals. Humankind is given the responsibility for God's creation, as is evident from the fact that his command to them is part of his blessing (1:28).

P-B In Rabb. Heb. and the Targumim *rdh* (Aram. *rd'* or *rdy*) is commonly associated with the meanings to stamp, tread, chastise, or rule (e.g., Tg. Lev 26:17). In the Qumran texts it maintains the meaning to rule or govern (1QS 9:23).

Kingship, rule, supervision, dominion: → *b'l* I (marry, rule over, own, # 1249); → *g*^e^*bîrâ/g*^e^*beret* (lady, queen, mistress, # 1485/1509); → *ykḥ* (dispute, reason together, prove, judge, rule, reprove, # 3519); → *kbš* (make subservient, subdue, # 3899); → *mlk* I (rule, # 4887); → *mšl* II (rule, govern, # 5440); → *nṣḥ* (supervise, # 5904); → *rdd* (repel, subdue, # 8096); → *rdh* I (rule, govern, # 8097); → *r'h* I (feed, graze, shepherd, rule, # 8286); → *śrr* I (rule, direct, superintend, # 8606); → *šlṭ* (gain power, # 8948); → *špṭ* (get justice, act as a judge, rule, # 9149)

Philip J. Nel

8098	רדה

רדה (*rdh* II), q. scrape out, scoop out (# 8098).

OT In a lion's carcass Samson found some honey, "which he scooped out (*wayyirdēhû*) with his hands and ate as he went along.... But he did not tell (his parents) that he had taken (*rādâ*) the honey from the lion's carcass" (Judg 14:9). Samson should not have eaten anything ceremonially unclean (Lev 2:11) or that had been contaminated by contact with a carcass (11:39-40)—especially since he had been a Nazirite from birth (Judg 13:4-5, 7). This fact lends credence to Holladay's suggestion that Jer 5:31 ("The prophets prophesy lies, the priests rule [*yirdû*] by their own authority ['*al-y*^e^*dêhem*]") should be translated: "The prophets prophesy lies, the priests deconsecrate themselves." Noting that the enigmatic expression "fill the hands of" is used 17x in OT for the installation or consecration of a priest, Holladay proposes that just as the prophets in Jer 5:31 are doing the opposite of what they are supposed to do, so also the priests are doing the opposite of "filling their hands": "(they) are scraping out whatever it is with which their hands have been filled at the time of their consecration."

Scraping: → *grd* (scrape oneself, # 1740); → *mll* IV (scrape, # 4911); → *sḥh* (scrape away, # 6081); → *qṣh* I (trim off, maim, shorten, scrape off, # 7894); → *qṣ'* I (scrape off, # 7909); → *rdh* II (scrape out, # 8098)

BIBLIOGRAPHY

W. L. Holladay, "'The Priests Scrape Out on Their Hands,' Jeremiah v 31," *VT* 15, 1965, 111-13.

Ronald Youngblood

8100	רְדִיד

רְדִיד (*r*^e^*dîd*), nom. veil, cloak (# 8100); רדד (*rdd*), beat (→ # 8096).

ANE This word has cognates in Arab. and Syr., with similar meaning.

OT The vb. *rdd* means to beat out, so perhaps this veil is a large one that covers more than the face, hence "cloak" in some modern translations. The two places where it occurs are Isa 3:23, the prophet's list of women's clothing, and in S of Songs 5:7, the article of clothing that the guards so rudely took from the searching maiden.

Veil: → *dōq* (veil, gauze, # 1988); → *ḥebyôn* (covering, # 2470); → *miṭpaḥat* (veil, cloak, # 4762); → *masweh* (veil, # 5003); → *massēkâ* II (veil, sheet, blanket, # 5012); → *mispāḥâ* (veil, # 5029); → *ṣammâ* (veil, # 7539); → *ṣā'îp* (veil, # 7581); → *r*^e^*dîd* (veil, # 8100); → *r*^e^*'ālâ* (veil, # 8304)

Robert L. Alden

8101	רדם

רדם (*rdm*), ni. go to sleep (# 8101); תַּרְדֵּמָה (*tardēmâ*), deep sleep (# 9554).

ANE The etymology of the root *rdm* is uncertain, but appears to be connected to a more primitive biradical root (*d/ṭ/tam*), meaning "stop up, close" (cf. Arab. *radama*, "stop up"), and thus indicates a heavy sleep in which one is shut off from the outer world (Thomson, 423), making one open to revelation from God (Gordis, 48-49). *HALAT* gives the definition "stunned" for Psalm 76:6[7]; Dan 8:18; 10:9. Moreover, Bos suggests that the difficult *w^ehû'-nirdām wayyā'ap wayyamōt* in Judges 4:21 be translated to show Sisera first stunned, then collapsing, then dying (50-52). In Psalm 76:6 (Heb 7) the vb. bespeaks death: *nirdām w^erekeb wāsûs*; NIV—both horse and chariot lie still.

OT God sends both *tardēmâ* (Gen 2:21) and *šēnâ* (1 Sam 26:12), in which may come dreams (e.g., Eliphaz, Job 4:13) or prophetic messages (Isa 29:10) from the Lord. Note, for example, Job 33:15: *baḥ^alôm ḥezyôn laylâ, bin^epōl tardēmâ 'al-'^anāšîm* (NIV In a dream, in a vision of the night, when deep sleep falls on men [as they slumber in their beds]). Gordis suggests that the use of *tardēmâ* in Jonah 1:5-6 may be ironic, pointing to a prophet who fell asleep, "not in order to establish contact with God, but to escape it" (48-49). Yahweh causes a deep sleep to fall on people to allow him to do his work without interference (Gen 2:21; 1 Sam 26:12; Isa 29:10) or reveal himself in a special way (Gen 15:12; Job 4:13; 33:15; Dan 8:18; 10:9). The best-known instances of revelation through sleep happen to Abraham (*tardēmâ*, Gen 15:12-21), Jacob (28:10-22), Solomon at Gibeon (1 Kgs 3:4-15), and Balaam (Num 22:8-13).

Sleep: → *dlp* II (be sleepless, # 1941); → *yšn* I (sleep, # 3822); → *nwm* (sleep, # 5670); → *rdm* I (go to sleep, # 8101)

Bibliography

TWOT 2:833-34; R. Gordis, *The Book of Job*, 1978; T. H. McAlpine, *Sleep, Divine and Human, in the Old Testament*, JSOTSup 38, 1987; J. G. S. S. Thomson, "Sleep: An Aspect of Jewish Anthropology," *VTS*, 1955, 421-33.

William C. Williams

8103	רדף

רדף (*rdp*), q. be behind, be after, pursue, persecute; ni. be pursued; pi. pursue hotly; pu. be driven out (# 8103); מֻרְדָּף (*murdāp*), nom. persecution (# 5284).

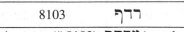

OT 1. The Christian church was not the first institution to experience attack. Judaism, the matrix in which Christianity was born, had her full share of sufferings. Ps 129:1-2 tells the story of Jewish suffering. Israel's history was one long tale of oppression and suppression and violence both from within and without. But persecution within Israel/Judah for religious reasons of those who refused the then royal policy of Baal/Yahweh syncretism and official toleration of injustice and pagan immoralities only became frequent from Elijah's period on. It is noteworthy that although 1 Kgs 18:4 suggests that it was Jezebel who cut off the prophets of Yahweh, Elijah's complaint in 1 Kgs 19:10, 14 is that the people of Israel had slain the prophets. Here we see

the beginnings of the belief that Israel as a whole is responsible for the death of her prophets and must bear the guilt corporately. This is the meaning of the indictment of Jer 2:30, "Your sword has devoured your prophets." With this we may compare the generalization found in 2 Chron 36:15-16, where the reference is not to violence but to ridicule. This generalization is easily understood as an explanation of the destruction of the nation by the Babylonians in the sixth century. Whatever the origin of the martyr traditions associated with the various prophets, these traditions were apparently widely accepted in the first century AD.

2. Prophets arose in times of national crises, whether that took the form of national apostasy or the form of imminent war. In such crises anyone who did not reflect the current and predominant outlook was considered a saboteur and consequently came under affliction and hardship. It should therefore occasion no surprise that many a prophet met with bitter opposition and personal violence, some even meeting death. Historically speaking several prophets suffered maltreatment or, to use later terminology, were "confessors": Elijah, Micaiah (1 Kgs 22:13-28), Amos, and Jeremiah (cf. Neh 9:26, 30, 32; Lam 2:20). Few prophets were actually put to death for their faith, as were Zechariah (2 Chron 24:20-21; cf. Josephus, *Ant* 9.168-71) and Uriah (Jer 26:20-23). Many are unknown by name (1 Kings 19:10; cf. Josephus, *Ant* 8.330, 334; 2 Kgs 21:16; cf. Josephus, *Ant* 20.38). In later Jewish tradition this motif underwent a development, and martyrdom became indispensable for the prophetic vocation. Therefore every prophet was regarded as having undergone a martyr's death. Therefore, Micaiah not only suffers but dies a martyr (*Asc. Isa.* 2:16). Jeremiah dies by stoning in Egypt (Tertullian, *Scorpiace*, 1:8; *Acts of Phil.*, 83). Similarly, Isaiah was sawn asunder by Manasseh (*Martyrdom of Isaiah*). Even Abel, who was killed by his brother Cain, came to be referred to as a martyr prophet (4 Macc. 18:14). In Mandaen sources and Kabbalistic circles Abel is referred to as a prophet (J. S. Pobee, 124, n. 40); so was Jonah, according to a tradition dating from AD 350 (Strack-Billerbeck 1:643). Amos and Ezekiel were allegedly executed (*Vitae Prophetarum*, 38, 52). Indeed according to a midrash in the name of R. Jose b. Nehonai the following were the persecuted prophets: Abel, Noah, Abraham, Isaac, Jacob, Joseph, Moses, Saul, David, and Israel (Pobee, 28, 124 n. 43).

3. Later prophets as spokesmen of uncompromising truth and the claims of divine law suffered severely at the hands of the ruling classes, so that persecution became in Jewish eyes the hallmark of the true prophet (2 Chron 36:16; Matt 5:12; 23:29-37; Acts 7:52; Heb 11:32-38). Christians had inherited the view from Judaism that Israel had persistently persecuted her own prophets. In the *Vitae Prophetarum* (AD) six prophets are associated with unnatural death (Amos, Micah, Isaiah, Jeremiah, Ezekiel, and Zechariah ben Johoiada). This theme persisted in rabbinic circles. Josephus gives evidence of the view that suffering was the prophet's lot. In *Ant* 9.13 (264-67) Josephus, reproducing the story of the sending of messengers to the northern kingdom by Hezekiah (2 Chron 30:1), adds to the biblical narrative the following: "And when their prophets exhorted them in like manner, and foretold that they would suffer if they did not alter their course to one of piety towards God, they poured scorn (lit., spat) upon them and finally seized them and killed them." In *Ant* 10.3 (Pobee, 38) he speaks of Manasseh's daily slaughter of the prophets; although it is the king and not the people who are here responsible, the exaggeration nevertheless indicates the role

played by the theme in the popular mind. The popularity of the tradition further indicates that in the time of Jesus, shrines were erected on the supposed sites of prophetic martyrdoms. But historical research has indicated that the number of prophetic martyrdoms was greatly exaggerated in popular tradition. The ill-treatment of Israel in Egypt, like her later oppression by the Philistines, Midianites, and others, had economic and political grounds.

4. The period of the great empires (Persian, Grecian, Roman) provides the classic examples of persecution. The age of Judaism that emerged from the Babylonian captivity as a church-state had a traumatic experience of persecutions to a degree unparalleled in its history. Scholars have long pointed out the connection between persecutions and the literary genre of apocalyptic emerging definitively during that period. The problem of the period was not the existence of God; rather it was the question of what God, who was almighty, sovereign, good, and just, was doing when his chosen race, and more those who were zealous for him and his laws, were trampled over or indeed put to death by the heathen. Had the God of Israel relinquished his control over history? What made the persecutions even more difficult to understand was that the imperial persecutors, who were apparently the victor by the standards of the world, were unbelievers and heathen.

5. The Psalms especially present religious persecution as an offense of the persecutors (see Ps 7:1, 5; 31:15; 35:3; 71:11; 109:16; 119:84, 86; cf. Jer 15:15; 20:11). But the primary source for exilic persecutions is the book of Daniel. There are numerous references to Daniel as the prototype and ideal martyr (1 Macc 2:60; 4 Macc. 13:9; 16:3, 21; 18:13; Heb 11:34; Jos., *Ant* 10:260-63; Gen Rabbah 34). Daniel's stories illustrate the incidence of persecution at that time. There are also numerous Talmudic and midrashic references to the three companions of Daniel: Hananiah, Mishael, and Azariah. More striking are the amplifications of the text that heighten the martyrological aspect. Thus in the LXX is added at the end of Daniel, Bel and the Dragon, which probably goes back to an Aramaic or Hebrew original. The G versions, followed by the Latin, Syriac, and Arabic versions, places the Song of the Three Children after Dan 3:23 (Pobee, 14). All this attests a lively interest in martyrdom in the later period.

6. Shadrach, Meshach, and Abednego, before being thrown into the fiery furnace for refusing to worship the golden image set up in the plains of Dura, gave a short speech affirming their devotion to God, his power, and his ability to deliver them from the hands of the persecutors. By the martyr's witness through suffering he seeks to witness to God and to convert others to his God. Consequently, we learn through the documents of the conversion of the persecutor as a result of the suffering. Thus, according to Daniel 3:26-29, Nebuchadnezzar, as a result of the deliverance of the three men from the fiery furnace, came to acknowledge them as "servants of the Most High God"; he also blessed the God of Shadrach, Meshach, and Abednego and passed a decree to destroy all who spoke evil of that God. Similarly King Darius came to recognize the God of Daniel 6:25-27 (cf. Bel and the Dragon, 41).

7. The suffering of devotees of God at the hands of the Gentiles raises problems for faith. Often the sufferings undergone were considered chastisements for the sins of the nation. So in Dan 9, in the midst of Daniel's prayer in connection with the mystery of seventy years, the following confession is made: "O LORD, we and our kings, our princes and our fathers are covered with shame because we have sinned against you"

(Dan 9:8). In other words, the untold suffering of Daniel and his companions was God's punishment of the sins of the people of God, high and low alike. The sentiment is again expressed at Dan 9:16, "O Lord, in keeping with all your righteous acts, turn away your anger and your wrath from Jerusalem, your city, your holy hill. Our sins and the iniquities of our father have made Jerusalem and your people an object of scorn to all those around." Israel's afflictions were considered God's just punishment for her sins (Isa 40:2), yet the sufferings were considered as evidence of the love of God. Unlike the nations for whom wrath is stored up, Israel's punishments come in the here and now. They are evidence of God's goodness in the sense that God does not tolerate evil or sin. Israel's calamities are not vindictive punishment but corrective in intent, for the chastening of the nations. To that extent they are evidences of God's love. And such early punishment is a mark of God's blessing, God's special favor to Israel. Instead of letting Israel continue in her wickedness like all the other nations, who will realize only at the last day that they are doomed for destruction, God has made a timely intervention to arrest Israel's progression to final destruction and to put her on the right path to fellowship with himself. Thus Israel's calamities are chastisements of love. Those whom God loves, he punishes early.

On the return under foreign rule strict Jews (saints, holy ones, the righteous poor) sought to preserve the nations' identity and religion amid alien pressures and compromises of lax Jews anxious for accommodations and prosperity. The result was social oppression and harassment, which is echoed in the repeated pleas for vindication and divine intervention in the Psalms. The persecutions reached a horrifying climax of cruelty during the Maccabaean age, provoking armed resistance in response (2 Macc 6:7). Thus, despite her confidence in God's sovereignty and protection, Israel learned that right does not always prosper in God's world, that faithfulness to truth did not ensure immunity from suffering, sacrifice, or martyrdom.

As God's people reflected on persecution, the sacrificial motive became a further martyr motivation. One metaphor for suffering was refining (cf. Prov 17:3; 27:21; Isa 48:10; Zech 13:9; Mal 3:3). Another application was that of cleansing (Pobee, 37; cf. Dan 11:35, "some of the wise will stumble [i.e., be martyrs] so that they may be refined, purified, and made spotless"). Thus their martyrdom is a cleansing (cf. Dan 12:10), and important for later theology is the recognition that *katharizō* is sometimes used (Exod 29:37 LXX) as a translation of *kpr* (→ # 4105), the word so often used for atonement. Expressing the sacrificial idea and that of martyrdom in Isa 53:5 is the verb *'šm* (→ # 870), to provide a guilt offering, i.e., a sacrifice that atones for sin. The suffering of the zealous nation later acquires atoning efficacy (Pobee, 37).

8. The problem raised by the death of the faithful persecuted with no apparent vindication was resolved by eschatology. Martyrs possessed zeal for Yahweh and suffered death in consequence of that zeal for the Lord. They thus looked beyond the present and earthly human circumstances to the kingdom of God. Zeal for the Lord that refused to count the cost was rooted in a deep conviction about the sovereign omnipotence of God. The confessor looked to the future for the vindication of God, who controlled all history, if such vindication was absent from the present. The book of Daniel makes sweeps into history in order to establish that the God of the martyrs was the sovereign Lord of history. The faithful were conscious of history moving lineally towards a great denouement, the Day of the Lord. God would intervene and on that Day sum up

human history, and the judgment that gave expression to the accountability of all humanity would then take place. Thereby rewards would accrue to the believers but punishment to the wicked. Pobee (38) has pointed out the diverse forms and different ideas which the eschatological vindication of God's purposes would take. One approach, especially in apocalyptic Judaism, took the general line that the sufferings of the present time were expressions of the tribulations that must precede the great Day; these were part of the so-called messianic woes out of the birth pangs of which the messianic age would be born (Isa 26:17; 66:7; Jer 22:23; Hos 13:13; Mic 4:9-10). These sufferings would take the principal form of persecution and apostasy (Dan 8:23-26; 9:24; 11:33; 12:1). The period just preceding the end would show a tremendous resurgence of evil since the full tale of the messianic sufferings must be reflected in the historical period and finished before the end (Dan 8:23). Wickedness had to reach its zenith. Then God would break into history and introduce the kingdom of God, which would replace such incarnations of the end time as the empires under which the people of Israel lived after the Exile. Similarly in Dan 9:24 the eschaton can only come when the full measure of sins was filled up, a process that was taking place in the persecutions principally in Daniel's day.

9. The book of Daniel clearly enunciated the doctrine of the afterlife but did so in a context of oppression and tribulation directed at the faithful. The doctrine of the afterlife is broached in Dan 12 as a concept that would vindicate the stance of the confessors before heathen political power as well also as the faith of Israel itself. Since the persecution of believers was a matter of continued difficulty for the postexilic Jewish community, the doctrine of an afterlife gave the mark of assent to the fidelity of God to his covenant with Abraham and Israel. The persecutors and their abettors and those who had compromised the faith would be exposed to dire punishment. Their plight in Dan 12:2 takes the form of shame (*ḥ^{a}rāpôt*) and everlasting contempt (*dir'ôn*). The contempt involved the repugnance of exposed and decomposing bodies (Isa 66:24 [*dir'ôn*]). To be denied such burial precluded the possibility of fellowship with God after the grave, the hope of every pious Jew (cf. Dan 12:1-4). It is also thus appropriate that one quarter of Sheol was reserved for persecutors (1 En. 91:11, 19; 94:1, 6, 7; 95:6; 96:1, 6, 8; Pobee, 40). The fate of the persecutors also bore a direct connection with their treatment of Israel/Israelites (cf. 2 Chron 24:22; see also Josephus, *Ant* 11.171, where the murder of Joash is punishment for his murder of Zechariah [cf. Esth 7:10; Jos. *Ant* 11:267-68]).

God in his sovereign concern for believers would not permit persecutions to be unrequited. Evil could not ultimately be left unpunished. The punishment of persecutors would make the ultimate control of all history as under the shaping hand of God clear. Since the primary reason for persecution was the faith the confessors bore, persecution was an attack on the honor of God himself. Here the much celebrated blood of Abel, who was considered in late Judaism as the first martyr, cried out to heaven for vengeance so plaintively that the earth refused his blood (Gen R. 22.22; Sibyl Or iii.311; Pobee 41).

10. The eschatological fate of the martyrs presents a very diverse array of ideas. They are to be rewarded. But the nature of the reward is one of variety. They may be exalted to share in the messianic age, appearing as assessors at the judgment. An example of this theology is Dan 7:22(21, LXX), where judgment was given to the saints;

i.e., they became judges (cf. 12:3, where the righteous perhaps act as assessors at the last judgment).

Another idea in the expectation of rewards is the suggestion of immortality (Dan 12:1-3). By his steadfast conduct in the face of dire adversity the confessor became an example to his contemporaries and to posterity. The martyrs were immortalized through feasts as well. Here the feasts of Hanukkah and Purim come immediately to mind. The feast of Hanukkah, celebrating the occasion of the rededication of the temple (165 BC), came to celebrate the valor of the martyrs shown during that period. Similarly, the feast of Purim celebrated the triumph of faith over the might of the Persian Empire when Ahasuerus (Xerxes) afflicted the Jews (ca. 483 BC) (Esth 3:12-15).

But the book of Daniel does not commit itself to the concept of a general resurrection (Dan 12:1-3). Only *many* of the dead (*rabbîm miyy*^{e}*šēnê 'admat-'āpār yāqîṣû*) are to be raised. Not all mortals who died will be raised to everlasting life but only those community members denominated, who are described as *maskilîm* (12:3, 10; 1:4). These may be the wise leaders of the community. Thus one group to be raised are those whose fidelity to their faith and extraordinary goodness in times of persecution is attested by their martyrdom. Those whose extraordinary wickedness is attested by their persecution of the true religion are not raised but their bodies lie exposed and unburied (Dan 12:2; cf. Isa 66:24). Resurrection is thus a sign of the in-breaking of the kingdom of Yahweh into this age of evil.

Also in the book of Daniel persecution and martyrdoms occur within the context of earthly battles that are themselves manifestations of cosmic war. Thus the plight of the saints was explained as an earthly manifestation of the involvement in conflict of the angel of Persia (Dan 10:13) and the angel of Greece (10:20), on the one hand, and the angel of the Jews on the other. When the little horn "grew ... it reached the host of the heavens, and it threw some of the starry host down to the earth and trampled on them" (Dan 8:10). The host of heaven seems to mean here the stars (cf. Deut 4:19; Jer 33:22). But in this context there is a close relationship with the martyrs, who form part of God's army against the pagan threat and heavenly resources. There may indeed, as has been suggested, be an assimilation between the stars and the men on earth. Since the reality behind the conflict involves war between God and Satan, heavenly protectors may be sent to offer aid to the persecuted. Thus the angel of God intervened to protect Shadrach, Meshach, and Abednego from the fiery furnace (Dan 3:28), and the angel of the Lord intervened to rescue Daniel from the jaws of the lion (6:22). But by the end of the biblical period a body of ideas was beginning to develop that would grow in the Maccabaean period into a martyr theology. This would contribute towards the Christian understanding of the implications of the gospel message.

Persecution, pursuit: → *brḥ* II (drive away, injure, # 1369); → *dbr* I (turn/drive away, # 1818); → *rdp* (be behind, pursue, persecute, # 8103)

BIBLIOGRAPHY

D. R. A. Hare, *The Theme of Jewish Persecution of Christian in the Gospel According to St. Matthew*, 1967; J. S. Pobee, *Persecution and Martyrdom in the Theology of Paul*, 1985; H. L. Strack and P. Billerbeck, *Kommentar zum Neuen Testament aus Talmud und Midrasch*, 1922.

W. J. Dumbrell

8104	רהב

רהב (*rhb*), q. press, assail; hi. excite (# 8104); רֹ֫הַב (*rōhab*), nom. pride (?). (# 8106); רַהַב (*rahab*), nom. Rahab (# 8105; → Rahab: Theology); arrogant (# 8107).

ANE A cognate vb. is attested in Akk. *ra'ābu*. It means either shake or be angry, fume. Its semantic range is fixed from Old Babylonian through New Babylonian. An Aram. cognate appears in Targumic texts, meaning to submit to (pe.); to do homage to (ha.). An Arab. vb. occurs, meaning fear.

OT 1. The vb. *rhb* occurs 4x in the HB. The translation of the vb. is dictated by context, according to the nuances appearing above. These occurrences are roughly coterminous. It is impossible to offer a single lexeme to translate this vb.

(a) In Isaiah 3:5, the vb. has the nuance be arrogant (cf. Mish. verbal usages and the Targumic usage below). Yahweh declares the coming political and societal chaos accompanying the military collapse of Judah as judgment: "And I will make boys their officials; mere children will govern them.... The young will rise up against (be arrogant toward) the old, the base against the honorable" (3:4-5). The lawlessness of the oppression of others is underscored by the employment of this nom., as insolence replaces societal order. The Mishnah proclaims that of the eighteen punishments inflicted upon Judah by Yahweh in Isaiah, this is the pinnacle (*Ḥagiga* 84).

(b) The vb. occurs twice in Wisdom literature. In S of Songs 6:5 the male betrothed exclaims, "Turn your eyes from me, they overwhelm me" (NIV). The speaker is overcome by the eyes of his beloved. This may well be related to the Akk. nuance meaning, tremble.

(c) In Prov 6:3 the nom. appears as an expansion of the preceding line. Unfortunately, neither line is easily understood. The MT *lēk hitrappēs ûr^{e}hab rē'eykā* is translated "Go and humble (lit. "repeatedly muddy") yourself and submit to your neighbor" (lit.). An emendation has been offered, *l^{e}kâ ṭārēp (w^e)sarhēb* (see Sam. and Targumic noms. below) *rē'eykā*, translated "Go seize and press yourself upon your neighbor." The vb. *ṭrp*, seize, is a legal term for seizing property. However, there is no precedent for confusing the *ṭet* with a *taw*. The NIV employs the latter half of the emendation, rendering the couplet as "Go and humble yourself; press your plea with your neighbor." This may be the best way to capture the context of the passage. This circumstance is followed by the analogy with the ant, underscoring the need to be active. However, the nuance may well be that of submission to the rash pledge (as above) and working oneself out of especially adverse circumstances. Either suggestion makes sense. However, the latter suggestion leaves the MT as is, while the former still has the MT *waw* between the *samek* and the *hē* to explain.

(d) Finally, the vb. appears in Ps 138:3: (lit.) "On the day that I called, you answered me; you *rhb* my soul (in/by/with) strength." The verse is problematic. Most translators soften the vb. *rhb* to "encourage" (JPS) or "embolden" (NIV), etc., as a parallel process to becoming arrogant, something akin to gaining (a comparatively moderate amount of) self-confidence. Others favor emending the text. For example, Kraus wishes to change the text from *trhbny* to *trbh* (following the LXX *poluōrēseis*, "you will pay attention to," and Tg.) in interpreting the vb. as metathesized in the MT. The resulting vb. from *rbh* (# 8049) would render this verse, "you increased my soul."

2. The hapleg. *rōhab* is problematic: "The length of our days is seventy years—or eighty, if we have the strength; yet their span (*rōhab*; NIV mg. note "yet the best of them") is but trouble and sorrow, for they quickly pass, and we fly away" (Ps 90:10). Most commentators emend this word to *w^e rubbām*, "and the bulk of them," see NIV. This is a contextually wonderful suggestion. However, there are no obvious text critical mechanisms to explain this insertion by the MT.

Others (e.g., Kraus) hold that the nom. is a derivative of *rhb* (# 8104). This derivative would mean something like "(point of) pride" or "glory." The implication is that the span is not long, not pleasant, and is the antithesis of a point of pride. Dahood revocalizes the nom. *r^e hābîm*, arrogance. In this context the implication is that humans do not have time to engage in arrogance. Either works contextually in the course of a passage, which underscores the timelessness of Yahweh and the fleeting nature of human life. None of the options are preferable.

3. The nom. *rahab* is used both in the wider sense of "pride" and as an appellative epithet for the mythological chaos monster. By extension, the latter meaning is also used to denote Egypt. (→ Rahab [monster]: Theology)

(a) Psalm 40:4[5] is the lone example of the former meaning of the nom.: "Blessed is the man who makes the LORD his trust, who does not look to the proud, to those who turn aside to false gods."

(b) Job 26:12-13 makes reference to the battle scene in which Yahweh is seen as the victor over chaos. "By his power he churned up the sea; by his wisdom he cut Rahab in pieces. By his breath the skies became fair; his hand pierced the gliding serpent." This verse appears in a grand cosmological declaration of Yahweh's complete control over and access to all of the universe (vv. 5-14). Psalm 89:9-10[10-11] echoes this deed in the context of Yahweh's power over the universe (vv. 5-14), "You rule over the surging sea. . . you crushed Rahab like one of the slain; with your strong arm you scattered your enemies." In a declaration of the power of Yahweh over his creation, Job acknowledges that "God does not restrain his anger; even the cohorts of Rahab cowered at his feet" (Job 9:13)—a reference to the helpers of the chaos monster (cf. Tiamat's helpers in the Enuma Elish 4:107; Yam also had helpers, *KTU* 1.3.III.37ff.). This verse occurs in the context of Job's legal case against Yahweh, in that he is just as powerless before Yahweh as were the helpers of Rahab.

The extension of this concept to the nation of Egypt is demonstrated in Isa 51:9-10:

Awake, awake! Clothe yourself with strength,
  O arm of the LORD;
awake, as in days gone by,
  as in generations of old.
Was it not you who cut Rahab to pieces,
  who pierced that monster through?
Was it not you who dried up the sea,
  the waters of the great deep,
who made a road in the depths of the sea
  so that the redeemed might cross over?

The theological significance of juxtaposing these concepts is rich. The creation of the earth is implied in the conquest of the chaos monster. It is this same symbolic process that gives birth to the nation of Israel, for the depths are forced to acquiesce to Yahweh's creative desires as the earth emerges from the waters. The gods of Egypt, including the pharaoh, are powerless before his power of creation. The waters are stilled to allow Israelite passage and then become chaotic at the command of Yahweh, who controls all natural phenomena. Egypt, as Rahab, is powerless before Yahweh. The appellative Rahab better suits the actions of Pharaoh in the Exodus narrative sequence than other names used for the chaos monster (*tannîn*, # 9490; Leviathan, # 4293). Given the hardening of Pharaoh's heart, in the sense of arrogance, the nominal nuance of pride resounds in the employment of this label. This mythopoeic language occurs in the larger context of the promise of eventual return from exile in Babylon, another re-creation of the nation. The miracle involved in political restoration would be on the level of recreating human order, thus the appeal to divine intervention expressed in mythopoeic language.

Egypt (→) is called Rahab in two passages. Psalm 87:4, in the context of declaring the day when all nations will acknowledge the glory of Zion, lists Egypt among the nations, "I will record Rahab and Babylon among those who acknowledge me—Philistia too, and Tyre, along with Cush." Isaiah 30:7 occurs in the course of the Assyrian crisis, as Yahweh lambastes his people for trusting in Egypt, rather than Yahweh, for protection, "Egypt, whose help is utterly useless. Therefore I call her Rahab the Do-nothing" (reading *hammōšbāt* for the semantically empty MT *hēm šābet*). The implication of the epithet is that Rahab, the monster of chaos, has been stilled in her defeat by Yahweh (a definitional impossibility, as chaos must be moving); Rahab is dead. Trust in Rahab is thus misplaced, since only Yahweh, the defeater and stiller of this monster, can provide aid.

How the imagery fits into Israelite religion is a matter of debate. The stilling of the chaos monster myth is attested in Mesopotamian, Egyp., and Ugar. religious texts. These texts were familiar (at the very least) to the literate inhabitants of Israel (e.g., a copy of the Enuma Elish was found at Taanach). This has led a number of scholars to posit that the Israelites had incorporated this myth into their religion, with Yahweh becoming the champion of the gods through this combat and creation possible after the establishment of order. Other scholars hold that the myth was a primary Sem. myth, possessed by all in the region. Other scholars posit that the references are figurative, that Yahweh was inserted into the role of champion in what was understood by the audience to be a foreign myth with readily understood metaphorical vivancy. Some see in the reference to Egypt a historicizing of an original myth so as to demonstrate Yahweh's control of events in the mundane time/space continuum. In any scenario, what is clear is that Yahweh stills the monster with little effort. It is not a struggle, but simply an expression of will as he defeats the monster with his understanding (*t*^{e}*bûnâ*, Job 26:12). Yahweh not only is the most potent force in the universe, but he has no rival.

P-B 1. The vb. is well attested in postbiblical works. It appears in Mish. and Targum as be arrogant; a second Targumic nuance is strain, be overbearing; and the Syr. cognate has the meanings of run, tremble. In Sam., Mish., and Targum the related vb. *sarhēb* appears, meaning press, intrude (Mish.); hurry (Targum).

2. The LXX translates this nom. with *kētos* in Job (Aq. also does so in Isa 51:9; Th. also does in 27:1). The G nom. generically means big fish. By this era it is often used for whale. It is used to translate the normal Heb. noms. for fish, *dāg* (# 1834) and *dāgâ* (# 1836), as well as the other appellatives for the chaos monster, *liwyātān* and *tannîn*. The Heb. nom. is rendered *hyperēphanos,* arrogant one, in Ps 89:10, a translation based on a literal rendering of the verbal root. Ps 87:4 is simply a transliterated GN, *Raab.*

Though Rahab does not appear by name in later literature, the concept of creation and re-creation expressed through the myth of conflict with the dragon continues. Daniel's apocalyptic vision of the beast and the varied cosmological imagery of Revelation are examples (nondragon examples include *1 En.*, *4 Ezra*, *2* and *3 Bar*., and the Qumran War Scroll). The same type of disenchantment with political and societal institutions translates into similar mythological representations of Yahweh's power and his ability to right the chaos brought on by humanity for the sake of his oppressed people. This cosmic power is to be manifested on the historical plane to enable his own to exist once again.

Affliction, oppression: → *dḥq* (oppress, # 1895); → *ḥms* I (do violence, # 2803); → *ḥmṣ* II (oppress, # 2807); → *ynh* (oppress, # 3561); → *lḥṣ* (press, # 4315); → *māṣôr* I (affliction, siege, # 5189); → *mrr* I (be bitter, distraught, afflict, # 5352); → *nega'* (plague, affliction, # 5596); → *ngś* (exact, # 5601); → *'nh* II (afflict, humble, afflict one's soul, fast, oppress, submit, # 6700); → *'wq* I (crush?, # 6421); → *'mr* II (deal tyrannically with, # 6683); → *'šq* I (wrong, # 6943); → *ṣwq* I (constrain, press in/upon, harass, vex, # 7439); → *ṣwr* II (deal tyrannically with, # 7444); → *rhb* (assail, press, pester, alarm, confuse, # 8104); → *rṣṣ* (crush, # 8368); → *tôlāl* (oppressor, # 9354); → *tōk* (oppression, # 9412)

Arrogance, pride, presumption: → *g'h* (rise up, be exalted, # 1448); → *zyd* (act presumptuously, prepare food, # 2326); → *yāhîr* (haughty, # 3400); → *sll* (lift up, exalt, # 6148); → *'pl* (swell, lift up, # 6752); → *'ātāq* (old, arrogant, # 6981); → *pḥz* (be reckless, arrogant, # 7069); → *rwm* (be high, exalted, proud, # 8123); → *šaḥaṣ* (pride, # 8832)

BIBLIOGRAPHY

ABD 1:279-88, 5:610-11; *IDB* 1:725-32; 4:6; *TDNT* 8:525-29; *TWOT* 2:840-41; B. Batto, *Slaying the Dragon*, 1992; B. Childs, *Myth and Reality in the Old Testament*, 1962; F. Cross, *Canaanite Myth and Hebrew Epic*, 1973, esp. 135-44; M. Dahood, *Psalms*, AB, 1968, 1:243-46; 2:298-300, 308-20, 321-27; 3:275-82; J. Day, *God's Conflict with the Sea*, 1985; N. Habel, *Job*, OTL, 1985, 190-92, 372-75; W. Kaiser, *Isaiah 1-12*, OTL, 1981, tr. 1983, 71; H.-J. Kraus, *Psalms*, 1978, tr. 1989, 2:184-89, 197-218, 505-8; W. McKane, *Proverbs*, OTL, 1970, 1977, 320-23; R. Murphy, *Song of Songs*, Hermeneia, 1990, 174-77; J. Oswalt, *Isaiah 1-39*, NICOT, 1986, 133; M. Pope *Job*, AB, 1964, 70-71, 180-86; idem, *Song of Songs*, AB, 1964, 564-67; C. Westermann, *Isaiah 40-66*, OTL, 1969, 1977, 238-42.

Mark Anthony Phelps

8105 (*rāhāb*, Rahab), → Rahab [monster]

8106 (*rōhab*, pride?), → # 8104

8107 (*rahab*, arrogant), → # 8104

8110	רַהַט

רַהַט (*rahaṭ* I), nom. trough (for watering cattle) (# 8110).

ANE A vb. *rhṭ* is not known in biblical Hebrew, but cognate languages have verbs with the meaning "collect," gather," and Syr. has a nom *rā/ḥaṭâ*, conduit; Akk. *rāṭu*, channel.

OT There is no theological significance in this word's use in Gen 30:38, 41 and Exod 2:16 of Jacob and Moses feeding flocks.

Trough: → *'ēbûs* (feeding trough, # 17); → *yeqeb* (wine vat/trough, winepress, # 3676); → *miš'eret* (kneading trough, # 5400); → *pûrâ* (trough [winepress], # 7053); → *rahaṭ* (watering trough, # 8110); → *šōqet* (watering trough, # 9216)

Francis Foulkes

8112	רָהִיט

רָהִיט (*rāhîṭ*), nom. beam, rafter(s) (# 8112).

ANE Cf. Syr. *rā/ahṭā'*, board.

OT The word is found only in S of Songs 1:17 in parallel with *qôrôt*, beam(s), rafters. The sophistication and luxury of the lovers' house lies in its beauty and quality, with rafters (*rhṭ*) of fir/cypress and beams (*qôrôt*) of cedar. The K is *rḥyṭ*, the Q *rhyṭ* in *BHS*.

P-B The Tg. reads *rhyṭ*. The LXX renders it with *phatnōma*, vaulted ceilings; Vg., *laquearia*, paneled ceiling.

Beam, rafter, frame, board: → *k^{e}rutôt* (beam, # 4164); → *m^{e}qāreh* (timberwork, roof, # 5248); → *qrh* II (lay the beams, # 7936); → *qereš* (board, frame, # 7983); → *rāhîṭ* (beam, rafter, # 8112)

Eugene Carpenter

8113	רוד

רוד (*rwd*), q. freely move around, roam; hi. free oneself (# 8113); מָרוּד (*mārûd*), homelessness (# 5291).

ANE Arab. *rāda* (*rwd*), go here and there; Akk. *râdu(m)*, quake.

OT 1. Several of the limited occurrences of the vb. (less than six) are under dispute, either as to textual reading or as to the root derivative (e.g., *yrd*, *rdd*, *rdh*). So, for example, Hos 11:12[12:1] is rendered variously as "Judah is unruly (*rād*)" (NIV), or "Judah still walks (*rād*) with God" (NKJV; cf. H. W. Wolff, *Hosea*, 205, 210, "goes with God"; G. I. Emmerson, *Hosea*, 114-15). In Jeremiah Judah is reported as flaunting God by saying, "We are free to roam" (Jer 2:31). An uncertain reading is found in Ps 55:2[3]: "My thoughts trouble me."

2. The nom. *mārûd*, wandering, occurs 3x. Jerusalem remembers her wandering (*mārûd*), where the nom. is coordinate with *'^{o}nî*, affliction (→ # 6700; Lam 1:7; 3:19).

A list of ethical behavior, descriptive of true fasting, includes providing "the poor wanderer (*mārûd*, though *BHS* lists alternatives) with shelter" (Isa 58:7).

Roaming, wandering, homeless: → *hl'* (stray, be removed far off, # 2133); → *ṭ'h* (roam around, lead astray, # 3246); → *ndd* I (flee, stray, wander, # 5610); → *nwd* (sway, be homeless, # 5653); → *nwṣ* (flee, # 5680); → *rwd* (roam, # 8113); → *šgh* (stray, err, go/do wrong, mislead, # 8706); → *šwṭ* I (roam, # 8763); → *t'h* (wander off, # 9494)

Elmer A. Martens

8115	רוה

רוה (*rwh*), q. be saturated/drenched (of things); be sated (of beings; always of beverages); pi. make saturated, sated; hi., cause to be saturated, sated; ho., be made saturated, sated; be drunk (14x + 2x [*yrh* II]; # 8115; *HALAT* 1114b-15b); adj. רָוֶה (*rāweh*), saturated/drenched; watered/irrigated(?); sated (3x + Job 10:15[?]; # 8116; *HALAT* 1115b, cf. 416b); nom. רִי (*rî*), moisture/wetness (hapleg., Job 37:11; → # 8188; *HALAT* 1141b) and רְוָיָה (*r^e^wāyâ*), overflow (Ps 23:5 [hapleg.?] + MT Ps 66:12 [so NIV, REB; but LXX, Pesh., Tg., *BHS,* NAB, NRSV read/restore **r^e^wāḥâ*, spacious place]; → # 8122; *HALAT* 1121b).

ANE The proto-Semitic root *rwy* finds reflexes throughout North- and Southwest Sem. languages in both intransitive and transitive senses. Ugar. has the vb. *rwy*, saturate, sate (*KTU,* 1.16 II 15-16, III 2; J. C. de Moor, "The Speech of Mot in *KTU*, 1.5 I," *UF* 11, 1979, [640-53] 645-46, though his translation, "refresh," may reflect a metonymical, rather than lexical, sense) and nom. *(bn) rwy,* irrigator(?) (*PTU*, 312, 409a; unless a proper nom., cf. *WUS* # 2493; *UT* # 2310). Aram. texts from Deir 'Alla (*ATDA*, 221, 223, 307b) attest the vb. forms (*'lmh*) *rwy* (*ddn*), (maiden) ... sated (with affection) (II 4; ‖ *'kl*, eat, II 3; cf. *nirweh dōdîm* in Prov 7:18), and pael *yrwy*, will/may make (himself) sated (II 6; cf. H.-P. Müller, "Die aramäische Inschrift von Deir 'Allā und die älteren Bileamsprüche," *ZAW* 94, 1982, (214-44) 217, 232). Achaemenid Aram. may attest, in Aḥīqar 189, an itpael impf. *ttrwh* < *rwy*, be saturated/sated (with wine[?]—context damaged; *DISO* 275).

In OSA the vb. *rwy* I, h-stem provide with irrigation, and nom. forms *rwym,* well, watering place, *mrw/mryt*(?), sweet well are attested (Biella, 482-83). Arab. preserves the vb. forms *rawīya,* drink one's fill/have one's thirst quenched, be irrigated; *rawāy,* give (water) to drink, saturate; II/IV make (thirst) quenched, make irrigated, make saturated (Wehr, 369b); and nom. forms *riyy,* quenching, watering, wetting; *rawî,* thirst-quenching; *rayyān,* sated (with drink), well-watered/irrigated; *'irwa'ī,* irrigational, irrigated (Wehr, 369b-70a). Vb. forms appear also in Eth. *rawaya, rawya,* drink fully; irrigate; *arwaya* II,1, make drunk (*LLA* 306-7); Tigriña (so Müller, 217); and Tigre *rawā,* drink one's fill (TigrWb, 159a). The adj. finds cognates in Eth. *rĕwūy,* sated (with drink) (*LLA* 307); and Tigre *rāwī,* sated (TigrWb 159a).

OT 1. The vb. appears only in OT poetic or prophetic books, even when the text is disputed. Not surprisingly, therefore, its uses often carry a metonymical significance, be satisfied, or, refresh oneself, though its lexical sense seems limited to the meanings be saturated (of things); sated (of beings) (cf. contexts where *rwh* parallels *śb'*, eat fully, be satiated (usually of solid foods) [Jer 31:14; 46:10; Lam 3:15 (hi.); Job 10:15(?)] or *ml'* [pi.], make full/filled [Jer 31:25]).

2. The lexical sense "be saturated (of things)" seems clear in Isa 55:10-11, where the hi. is used to describe a condition of the earth that results from precipitation: *kî 'im-hrwh 't h'rṣ,* "(for just as) the rain and the snow descend from the heavens, and do not return (there) until they have caused the earth to be satiated (... so my word that goes forth from my mouth)" (author tr.). Correspondingly, the lexical sense "be sated (of beings)" occurs in Ps 36:8[9], in a context where Yahweh's salvation is figuratively compared to his providence of seasonal rains: "They [humans] are sated (*yirw^{e}yun*) with the oil [a hypocatastasis for water, as a luxurious fluid] [that flows] from your house; you let them drink (*tašqēm*) at the channel [that flows] [with] your delights/[at] your appointed seasons (*'^{a}dāneykâ;* cf. Akk. *adannu*, time at the end of a specified period, period...of predetermined length [*CAD*, A/1, 976]; Ugar. *'dn*, season {*UT* # 1823])" (author tr.) (cf. Jer 31:14). Parallelism with a reflexive/reciprocal hitp., in Prov 7:18, suggests that the coh. of *rwh* may carry a reflexive force: "Come, let us sate ourselves (*nirweh*) with affection until morning, let us enjoy ourselves/each other in love-making" (lit. tr.).

In Jer 46:10, the sword of Yahweh's retribution (against Egypt) is personified as eating (flesh) and drinking (blood) to the full: "the sword will devour till it is satiated (*w^{e}śāb[^{e}]'â*), till it has quenched its thirst (q. *w^{e}rāw[^{e}]tâ*) with blood" (cf. Isa 34:7, against Edom, whose land [personified] was to be sated with blood). In Lam 3:15, Jerusalem personified laments: "(Yahweh) has filled me (*hiśbî'anî*) with bitter herbs and sated me (hi. *hirwanî*) with gall (i.e., something undrinkable)."

It is doubtful whether **r^e'ô/*rā'ô*, being/to be sated/drunk (inf. const./abs. < *r'w/rww*), should be restored from *'ô* in MT Prov 31:4 (so Thomas; Gray, 284); if repointed as **'āw,* to desire (pi. inf. const., apocopated < **'awwēh;* cf. GKC §75*k, bb),* we have: "The drinking of wine is not for kings, nor is the desiring of brew for rulers." However, in several places, vb. or nom. forms of *rwh* may be restored *mutatis mutandis* from *r'h* (e.g., Job 10:15; Prov 23:31; cf. G. R. Driver, "L'interprétation du texte masorétique à la lumière de la lexicographie hébraïque," *ETL* 26, 1950, (337-53) 351; *HALAT* 1081b-82a, q. §16). On a conjectured hi. impf. **yarweh* in Hos 6:3, and on *yôre'* as an Aramaicized byform of ho. impf. *yôreh* in Prov 11:25, see *yrh* II (→ # 3722).

3. The adj. *rāweh* is used in both Isa 58:11 and Jer 31:12 in similes that compare restored Israel to an irrigated garden. The adj. in Deut 29:19[18] is used substantively of irrigated (hence, metonymically, fertile) land/ground: "he will bring disaster on the watered [land] as well as the dry"—a hypocatastasis for obedient and disobedient people (cf. LXX). If *r^e'ēh* in Job 10:15 were restored to **r^{e}wēh,* then we would have the parallelism: "[I am] satiated/filled (*ś^{e}ba'*) with shame and sated/soaked (*ûr^{e}wēh*) with/in my affliction" (author tr.).

P-B Taking into consideration the caveat that definitions such as "satisfy" or "refresh" by postbiblical times may still reflect metonymical, rather than lexical, meanings, verbal cognates occur in postbiblical Heb. *rwh,* be saturated/moist; pi., make saturated, make refreshed[?]; nitpael, be saturated, be refreshed(?) (Jastrow, 2:1459a); and Jewish Aram. *rwy/rw'/rwh*, be saturated, be drunken (Jastrow, 2:1459a). Nom. cognates are attested in postbiblical Heb. *r^{e}wîyâ,* saturation, satisfaction(?); *r^{e}wāyâ,* overflow (Jastrow, 2:1459b); and Jewish Aram. *rawwê/rawyā',* drunken one, drunkard; *rawyû,* drunkenness; *rawyā(y)tā',* intoxicating (drink/state); *r^{e}witā'* overflowing

(Jastrow, 2:1459b). The vb. appears in Syr. r^{e}*wā'*/r^{e}*wî,* be drunk/intoxicated; aphel give to drink, irrigate, make drunk (*LexSyr*, 719-20); and Mand. *rwa* I, drink one's fill, be drunk/refreshed(?); refresh oneself(?) (*MdD*, 427b). The adj. finds a cognate in Syr. *rawwāyā',* drunk.

Drinking, drawing water, drenching: → *gm'* (swallow, drink, # 1686); → *gr'* II (draw up [drops of water], # 1758); → *dlh* I (draw water, # 1926); → *yrh* II (give to drink, # 3722); → *l"* II (drink noisily, # 4363); → *lqq* (lick, lap, # 4379); → *mṣṣ* (drink, quaff, # 5209); → *rwh* (drink one's fill, drench, # 8115); → *š'b* (draw [water], # 8612); → *šqh* (drink, refreshment, # 9197); → *šth* II (drinking, # 9272)

BIBLIOGRAPHY

M. Dahood, "Hebrew-Ugaritic Lexicography X," *Bib* 53, 1972, [386-403] 389; D. M. Edwards, "Drunkenness," *ISBE*, 1915, 2:880b-81b; J. Gray, *Legacy of Canaan,* 2nd ed., 1965; P. Mailberger, *TWAT* 7:378-81; D. E. Smith, "Drink," *ISBE*, 1979, 1:992b-93a; D. W. Thomas, "אֵו in Proverbs xxxi 4," *VT* 12, 1962, 499-500; W. White, *TWOT* 2:835b-36a. Cf. S. Wagner, *TWAT* 3:916-20; ET: *TDOT* 6:336-39.

Robert H. O'Connell

8116 (*rāweh*, saturated, drenched), → # 8115

8118 רוח

רוח (*rwḥ*), *rwḥ* A, q. become wide or spacious; pu. be spacious (*HALAT* 1116; # 8118); der. nom. רֶוַח (*rewaḥ*), space, liberation (only in Gen 32:16[17]; Esth 4:14; # 8119); רוּחַ (*rûaḥ*), air, breath, temper, spirit, Spirit (→ # 8120); רְוָחָה (r^{e}*wāḥâ*), respite, relief (only in Exod 8:15[11]; Lam 3:56; # 8121); *rwḥ* B, hi. smell (# 8193); der. nom. רֵיחַ (*rêaḥ*), smell, odor, scent (# 8194; see *HALAT* 1115-16).

ANE The relation of *rêaḥ* to *rûaḥ* is uncertain, both in Heb. and in other Sem. languages (*TWAT* 7:382). For example, in Ugar. *rḥ* can mean scent (*KTU* 1.3, II.2) as well as wind.

OT 1. The vb. *rwḥ* A, like the cognate Aram. and Arab., conveys the notion to be wide, spacious (cf. Jer 22:14 [pu. part.]). In Heb. it also means to feel relieved (1 Sam 16:23; Job 32:20).

The denom. vb. *rwḥ* B is found 11x, all in the hi. Some distinguish this from the occurrences of the vb. in the q. (1 Sam 16:23; Job 32:20) and pu. (Jer 22:14), where the vb. means to be wide or to be relieved. Those who argue for one root point out that other Sem. roots have a similar semantic range (e.g., Akk. *napāšu*; see *HALAT* 1115-16; *TWAT* 7:383). De Boer (1968, 1972) has challenged the traditional translations by arguing that the nom. refers to a smell given out, while the vb. can express the giving out of a smell as well as its reception. Thus, in Job 39:25 the war horse does not smell war from afar, but gives out the scent of war even from afar. People may be tempted to make the holy incense in Exod 30:38 not to smell of it (l^{e}*hārîaḥ bāh*), but to give forth scent with it. However, de Boer's theories are less satisfactory for the cultic use of *rêaḥ nîḥōaḥ,* and he has failed to persuade the majority of commentators.

2. The nom. *rewaḥ* denotes spaciousness and relief: "keep some space between the herds" (Gen 32:16[17]). In Esth 4:14 it is used in conjunction with *haṣṣālâ* (< *nṣl* [→ # 5928]): "relief and deliverance."

3. The nom. *r*^{e}*wāḥâ* occurs in Exod 8:15[11] indicating the relief from the plague of frogs and, consequently, the respite from God's impending judgment. Its usage in Lam 3:56 is not quite clear (*THAT* 2:727) but may at best be interpreted as an outcry for relief from the realm of the netherworld (Kraus, *Klagelieder*, 67). In Ps 66:12, the word *r*^{e}*wāyâ*, saturation (cf. Ps 23:5), may be read as *r*^{e}*wāḥâ*. Accordingly it has been proposed to interpret the phrase *yṣ' lār*^{e}*wāḥâ* (cf. Vrs.), to lead to a place of relief; freedom (Kraus, *Psalmen*, 1:456). The term *rwḥ* (and its derivatives) is, however, not a common word for freedom or liberty.

4. *rêaḥ* is a primary nom., found 58x, but of these, 43x occur in the cultic technical term *rêaḥ nîḥōaḥ*. This phrase is often interchangeable with *'iššeh*, and R. Rendtorff (*Leviticus 1-3,* 1985, 68) suggests that there is a complementary relation, *'iššeh* highlighting the human role in giving the sacrifice and *rêaḥ nîḥōaḥ* the divine response in accepting it. In Gen 8:21 God smells the *rêaḥ nîḥōaḥ*, which suggests that it refers to the "pleasing aroma" of a sacrifice that is offered to Yahweh for him to smell. Those embarrassed at such anthropomorphism suggest that it is a traditional phrase that has lost its literal meaning, or that it is a remnant of an early, primitive view of God. However, the senses of smell and taste need be no more anthropomorphic than the senses of sight, hearing, and touch. Ezekiel refers to "fragrant incense" only in the context of idolatry (Ezek 6:13; 16:19; 20:28), but this is more likely to be an echo of the curse of Lev 26:30-31 than a concern to spiritualize the concept. God is said metaphorically to accept the aroma of those gathered from exile (Ezek 20:41).

A more positive approach is to relate "smell worship" (Durham) to the way in which Israel's worship employs all the senses in constructing a rich, multimedia experience of God. The overall theological framework provides the interpretative limits for these and similar material symbols and expressions (e.g., Num 28:2). Indeed, the invisible yet potent nature of smell makes it an appropriate mediating expression of God's presence at the sacrifice (cf. Josephus, *Ant* 8:101-2). The divine presence is the reason why the smell of sacrifice may be associated with blessing and life, not any independent or magical quality in the smell.

(a) The meaning of *rêaḥ nîḥōaḥ* is disputed, possibly because a smell may signify different things according to context. Some argue for a propitiatory meaning ("soothing odor," REB), so that the smoke calms or removes God's anger (cf. 1 Sam 26:19) and so gives rest (the hi. of *nwḥ* is used in Ezek 5:13). When God smells Noah's sacrifices after the Flood (Gen 8:21), it soothes his wrath. However, the texts are not conclusive, and others have argued that the sacrifice was a thanksgiving for salvation, with God's response being correspondingly positive (cf. translations such as "pleasing aroma," NIV). G. J. Wenham (*Genesis 1-15,* 1987, 189) argues that both propitiation and thanksgiving can be associated with the burnt offering and the *rêaḥ nîḥōaḥ*. However, in the priestly texts *rêaḥ nîḥōaḥ* almost always describes the effect of burnt offerings (Lev 1:9), grain offerings (2:2), peace offerings (3:5), and libations (Num 15:7) rather than the reparation or purification offerings (Lev 4:31 is an exception). It may be argued that these particular sacrifices strengthen the relation between God and the offerer, with a range of associations including thanksgiving, celebration, dedication, or honor (see also Sir 35:8). The use of a technical sacrificial term in Gen 8:21 may be a redactional indication that the sacrifice was legitimate, or even that it was a prototype of the later sacrificial system (Wenham, 190).

(b) Smell is one of the essential human senses and thus characteristic of the living God of Israel (Gen 8:21), but not of idols (Deut 4:28; Ps 115:6). Being the least material sense, it is an appropriate medium for God's regular interaction with the cult; for God to smell the sacrifice is equivalent to accepting the offering (1 Sam 26:19). In Amos 5:21 God refuses to smell (NRSV, "takes no delight in") the solemn assemblies of the Israelites, indicating that injustice nullifies the provisions of Israel's sacrificial system (cf. Lev 26:31). The ability of the God of the Israelites to prevent even the smell of fire attaching to the bodies of the three Hebrews is the climactic recognition of his power in Dan 3:27.

(c) The nom. comes 7x in the sensual celebrations of the S of Songs, describing the oils and perfumes of the woman (S of Songs 4:10). Similes comparing her garments to the scent of Lebanon (4:11) suggest strength and majesty, and the association with spring fruits (2:13; 7:8[9], 13[14]) fertility and beauty. The smell of a person can reflect, *pars pro toto,* their character and relationship, so that the lover yearns for the scent of the woman's breath (7:8[9]).

However, in Exod 5:21 Moses and Aaron's demands have made the Israelites' smell before Pharaoh offensive (hi. of *b'š*). There is a subtle play on the relative reliabilities of the senses of sight, touch, and smell in Gen 27, when Jacob borrows the smell of the field (v. 27) to trick Isaac. Isa 11:3 (lit., "his smelling is in the fear of *yhwh*") is difficult and does not fit the context well, so it is often considered a corrupt repetition of v. 2b. The sense of smell does complement references to the senses of sight and hearing in v. 3b in the received text, and could be understood to refer to a satisfied and persistent experience of God (hence "his delight" in translations).

P-B *rêaḥ nîḥōaḥ* occurs frequently in the Temple Scroll in accounts of sacrifices at festivals and is associated with the offerings on the altar in 11QT 34:14. In 1QS 8:9 the community is the holy dwelling in which Aaron may offer the pleasing aroma.

NT In the NT Paul uses the LXX translation of *rêaḥ nîḥōaḥ, osmē euōdias,* to describe the sacrifice of Christ (Eph 5:2) and also the gifts of the Philippian congregation to Paul (Phil 4:18).

→ *NIDNTT* 2:719-23.

Freedom, innocence, cleanness, liberation: → *d^e^rôr* III (release, freedom, # 2002); → *ḥpš* (freed, # 2926); → *ḥōr* I (free man, freeborn, # 2985); → *nqh* (be free, exempt from guilt, remain unpunished, # 5927); → *ntr* III (set free, # 6002); → *qôm^e^miyyût* (walk erect, # 7758); → *rwḥ* A (become wide or spacious, be spacious, # 8118)
Broad, open, spacious, wide, extensive: → *p'r* (open wide, # 7196); → *ptḥ* I (open, conquer, surrender, set free, loosen, break up, # 7337); → *rwḥ* A (become wide or spacious, be spacious, # 8118); → *rḥb* (open wide, broaden, # 8143)
Smell, stench: → *b'š* (stink, become odious, # 944); → *zwr* III (stink, be offensive, # 2320); → *znḥ* I (become foul-smelling, # 2395); → *ḥnn* II (be stinking, loathsome, # 2859); → *srḥ* II (stink, spoil, # 6244); → *ṣaḥ^a^nâ* (stench, # 7462); → *rwḥ* B (smell, # 8193); → **Smell: Theology**

Bibliography

TDNT 2:808-10; *TWAT* 7:382-85; G. A. Anderson, *Sacrifices and Offerings in Ancient Israel: Studies in Their Social and Political Importance*, 1987; P. A. H. de Boer, "ומרחוק יריח מלחמה—Job 39:25," in *Words and Meanings: Essays Presented to David Winton Thomas*, 1968, 29-38; idem, "An Aspect of Sacrifice," VTSup 23, 1972, 27-47; J. I. Durham, *The Senses Touch, Taste, and Smell in Old Testament Religion,* 1963; G. B. Gray, *Sacrifice in the Old Testament: Its Theory and Practice,* 1925; J. Hoftijzer, "Das sogenannte Feueropfer," VTSup 16, 1967, 114-34; M. Haran, "The Uses of Incense in the Ancient Israelite Ritual," *VT* 10, 1960, 113-29; H.-J. Kraus, *Klagelieder <Threni>*, BKAT, 1968; idem, *Psalmen 1-59,* BKAT, 1978; idem, *Psalmen 60-150,* BKAT, 1978; R. Rendtorff, *Studien zur Geschichte des Opfers im alten Israel,* WMANT 24, 1967; G. L. Young, "The Smelling of the Sweet Savor of Noah's Sacrifice," *BibS* NS 3, 1905, 64-67.

Philip Jenson/J. P. J. Olivier

8119 (*rewaḥ*, space, liberation), → # 8118

8120	רוּחַ

רוּחַ (*rûaḥ*), nom. wind, breath, transitoriness, volition, disposition, temper, spirit, Spirit (# 8120).

ANE The Heb. nom. *rûaḥ* occurs 387x in the OT. "It is best considered a primitive nom., related to an *ayin*-vowel root *ruḥ* 'to breathe'" (Payne, *TDOT* 2:836; cf. BDB, 924). Aram. *rûaḥ,* Syr. *rāḥ*. Similar roots are accounted for in the Ugar. *rḥ,* Phoen. *rḥ,* and the Arab. *rîḥ*, wind, and *rûḥ*, spirit, which are both derived from *rāḥa*, to blow; cf. Eth. *roḥa*, make a slight wind. The LXX renders this word as *pneuma*, wind, spirit, 264x and as *anemos*, wind, 49x.

OT The most basic meaning of *rûaḥ* is variously defined as "blowing" (Kamlah, *NIDNTT,* 690), "air in motion" (*TDOT* 2:836; Reiling, *DDD*, 792), and "wind" (Koch, 872). The first two definitions attempt to express the actual phenomenological properties manifested by *rûaḥ*; i.e., the verbal properties of the nom. The third definition, however, simply names the phenomenon without any reference to its essence. The establishment of both a fundamental and then a universally acceptable definition is extremely difficult for two reasons. First, since *rûaḥ* has such a broad range of meanings, it is difficult to capture its semantic breadth with a single term or phrase. Second, what is invisible or unseen is difficult to define. As Kamlah observes, "The idea behind *rûaḥ* is the extraordinary fact that something as intangible as air should move; at the same time it is not the movement *per se* which excites attention, but rather the energy manifested by such movement" (*NIDNTT* 3:690). In other words, the invisible essence of *ruaḥ* is known primarily by its effect on the visible world, by which we can then attempt to perceive its essence. Thus, *rûaḥ* is a term representing something unseen in order that the visible effect of this invisible force might be adequately apprehended. The following discussion of *rûaḥ* is divided into 6, sometimes related, categories: (1) wind, (2) compass point, (3) breath, (4) disposition, (5) seat of cognition and volition, and (6) spirit.

1. When *rûaḥ* refers to the wind, we read of the trees shaking (Isa 7:2), the chaff being driven from the wheat (41:16), and the rain or clouds associated with a storm (1 Kgs 18:45; 2 Kgs 3:17). In this context *rûaḥ* simply refers to the force of nature commonly known as wind. The OT affirms, however, that this invisible, unpredictable force of nature is under the divine and sovereign control of Yahweh (Num 11:31). On numerous occasions reference is made to what is called the "east wind" (Exod 10:13). This is the hot, scorching wind of the desert. This east wind is typically associated with

the judgment, punishment, or wrath of Yahweh (Ps 48:7[8]; Jer 18:17; Ezek 17:10; Hos 13:15; Jon 4:8). In contrast, the west wind brings relief and deliverance (Exod 10:19). *rûaḥ* as wind can also be used to depict powerlessness, worthlessness, or vanity. The author of Ecclesiastes makes the repeated assertion on ten different occasions that the pursuit of fleeting pleasures is vanity, "a chasing after the wind" (1:6, 14, 17; 2:11, 17, 26; 4:4, 6, 16; 6:9). Similarly, those who chase after the wind are called fools (Mic 2:11). The prophets use this term to mock the forged images of idols, referring to their impotence as "wind and confusion" (Isa 41:29). Like idols, false prophets are also said to be "like wind," or of no real substance. Our modern expression "full of hot air" is a rough equivalent to these prophetic taunts.

2. In a derived sense *rûaḥ* is also used of the four compass points. This usage is implied in phrases like (lit.) "to every wind," viz., in every direction (Ezek 5:10-12; 12:14; 17:21), but is explicitly expressed in the idiom "the four winds" (Jer 49:36; Ezek 37:9; Zech 2:6[10]; Dan 7:2). Like the semantic cognate in Akk., *šari erbetti*, and the native idiom, "four corners of the earth," the expression reflects the hypothetical division of the earth into four quadrants. Accordingly, to be "scattered to the winds" means to be dispersed in all the earth, the most severe exile imaginable (Jer 49:32; Ezek 12:14; 17:21). This tendency for *rûaḥ* to mean compass point culminates in the application of the term to "side," as in the four sides of the sanctuary (Ezek 42:16-20; cf. 1 Chron 9:24).

3. The rendering of *rûaḥ* as breath is similar to wind in that breath also connotes the movement of air. Occurring 10x in connection with *n*ᵉ*šāmâ*, breath (→ # 5972), *rûaḥ* can be used to refer to the life-sustaining function called breathing or breath. This breath is the essence of life (Gen 6:17; Job 12:10; Isa 38:16; 42:5; Ezek 37:5-14; Mal 2:15-16). As such the OT is clear in its teaching that such breath is a direct result of the divine, creative power of Yahweh graciously bestowed upon his creation (Job 27:3; 33:4; Ps 104:29, 30; Zech 12:1). Thus, to possess this breath is life, but the departure of this breath is death (Ps 146:4; Eccl 12:7). Symbolically, the expression "the *breath* of Yahweh's nostrils" (probably referring to the wind) is used to describe the ominous force of Yahweh's power, typically employed in judgment, "At the *breath of God* they are destroyed; at the *blast of his anger* [nose] they perish" (Job 4:9; cf. Exod 15:8; 2 Sam 22:16; Ps 18:15[16]; Isa 30:28; 33:11; 40:7; also "breath of his lips" in Isa 11:4).

4. An extension of this use of the nom. perceives the *rûaḥ* as a person's or group's disposition, attitude, mood, inclination, as an approximate synonym of *nepeš*, appetite, disposition, person (cf. Deut 6:4). Accordingly, to speak of one's *rûaḥ* is to discuss his/her character, nature, or condition. This principle is effectively illustrated in Isa 19:3, "Then the *spirit of the Egyptians* will be demoralized within them; and I will confound their strategy, so that they will resort to idols and ghosts of the dead, and to mediums and spiritists" (NASB). Yahweh is literally going to empty or demoralize the Egyptian *rûaḥ*. As a result, the Egyptians will lose heart and will try to encourage themselves by resorting to spiritism in all its aspects. In this way the Egyptians are subsequently characterized as those who possess a "spirit of idolatry," that is, a *rûaḥ* inclined by nature towards such.

Such designations in Heb. are typically constructed by associating the appropriate adj. with the nom. *rûaḥ*. According to this pattern a bitter spirit depicts grief

(Gen 26:35) or anger (Ezek 3:14), a sinking spirit depression (1 Kgs 21:5), or a short spirit discouragement (Exod 6:9). A short spirit can also express a lack of patience or a quick temper (Job 21:4; Prov 14:29). A person who has a high spirit exhibits pride, but a person of low spirit is said to be humble (Prov 16:18-19; Isa 66:2). Unfaithfulness is characterized as a spirit of harlotry or adultery (Hos 4:12; 5:4). Further examples include an oppressed spirit (1 Sam 1:15), staggering spirit (Isa 19:14), grieving spirit (Isa 54:6), and a trustworthy spirit (Prov 11:13).

5. Frequently *rûaḥ* denotes the seat of cognition and volition, those activities involved in thinking, aptitude, and decision-making. The knowledge and ability to perform a particular task is one clear example of this use of *rûaḥ*. In this way the construction of the tabernacle was carried out by those who possessed the spirit of wisdom, that is, the ability suited to such a task (Exod 28:3). Furthermore, the endowment of the "Spirit of God" associated with such ability is described as consisting of wisdom, knowledge, understanding, and workmanship—all of which are associated with cognitive faculties (Exod 31:3; 35:31; cf. Isa 11:2). Often *rûaḥ* actually means mind, as in Isa 29:24, where the nom. *rûaḥ* appears in connection with the two vbs. *yd'*, to know and *lmd*, to learn: "And those who err in *mind* will *know* the truth, and those who criticize will accept *instruction*" (NASB; cf. 1 Chron 28:12; Ezek 11:5-6; 20:32; 38:10). In 21 instances, *rûaḥ* and the nom. *lbb*, heart, occur together as synonyms of one another. In Heb. the heart depicts not only the seat of emotions, but also of intellectual thinking, skills moderns normally associate with the mind. (The more emotional concept of heart and the subconscious is expressed in Heb. by kidney, liver, bowels.) Ps 77:6[7] notes that we meditate with our heart and ponder with our *rûaḥ*. In a more profound sense, Ezekiel predicts that Yahweh will give his people a "new heart" and a "new spirit," that they might obey his law (Ezek 11:19, 20; 18:31; 36:26-27). When *rûaḥ* and heart are used together, the subsequent discussion typically consists of deliberate actions, not emotional descriptions (Exod 28:3; Ps 51:10[12]; Isa 65:14; Dan 5:20).

6. Theologically, in the OT the most significant usage of *rûaḥ* involves its representation of the metaphysical or numinous, specifically the "Spirit of God/the LORD." The expression "Spirit of God" actually appears only 11x, "Spirit of the LORD" 25x, and "Holy Spirit" 3x (Ps 51:11[13]; Isa 63:10, 11). However, the operation of the Spirit of the Lord is both pervasive and diverse.

The Spirit of God is the agent of creation (Ps 104:29; Job 33:4). His Spirit was active not only at the original creation (Gen 1:2) and at the re-creation after the Flood (8:1), but also at the creation of the people of Israel (in the form of wind, Exod 14:19-20; 15:10) and at the creation of the church (Acts 2:1-4). While the precise role of the Spirit in these events is not equally clear, biblical authors speak of the Spirit as both omnipresent (Ps 139:7) and omniscient (Isa 40:13). Often the divine *rûaḥ* functions as the alter ego of Yahweh, dwelling in the midst of Israel like the divine Glory (Hag 2:5).

Frequently the Spirit of God represents the agent/agency by which God exercises his sovereign control over individuals. Occasionally the effects are calamitous, as in those instances where the LORD's Spirit is described as destructive or disruptive (not evil in a moral sense; Judg 9:23; 1 Sam 16:14-16, 23; 18:10; 19:9). But usually God's Spirit operates on behalf of his people by energizing them (Ezek 2:2), transporting them (1 Kgs 18:12; 2 Kgs 2:16; Ezek 3:12, 14; 8:3; 11:24; 37:1, though sometimes in visionary form), endowing ("filling") them with his Spirit, and giving them special gifts and power for sacred service (Exod 35:31; Mic 3:8). Often the Spirit of God comes/falls on those divinely chosen and commissioned for the work of God. This was particularly true of those who prophesied under the inspiration of the Lord (the seventy elders, Num 11:17, 25; Saul, 1 Sam 10:6, 10), as opposed to false prophets, who were inspired from within (Ezek 13:3), though occasionally the Scriptures speak of the Lord deceitfully inspiring false prophets (1 Kgs 22:21-23; cf. Ezek 14:9).

In Hos 9:7 the prophet is aptly called (lit.) a "man of the spirit," i.e., "an inspired man." Through the Spirit prophets speak on behalf of Yahweh, execute his lawsuits, judge, and deliver the people of God (Num 24:2; 2 Sam 23:2; Neh 9:20, 30; Ezek 11:5; Zech 7:12). Of special interest is the divine empowerment of military leaders by his Spirit coming/falling on them or clothing them, so that people who are neither spiritually nor physically equipped for divine military service are able to win great victories over the enemies of God (Judg 6:34; 13:25; 14:6, 19; 15:14; 1 Sam 11:6; 1 Chron 12:18). In other instances the presence of the Spirit of the Lord not only empowers, but also authorizes a person for leadership of God's people in a more general sense (Joshua, Deut 34:9; the "saviors" of Israel, Judg 3:10; 11:29, etc.).

David's special experience of the Spirit of God seems to have been linked with his position as the divinely chosen king of Israel (the "man after God's own heart," viz., of God's own choosing, 1 Sam 13:14). To be sure, Saul was both anointed (*mšḥ*, 10:1) and empowered by the Spirit so that he could prophesy (10:6-10) and lead Israel in battle (11:6). However, not only were his anointing and spiritual endowment chronologically separate; the Lord expressly withdrew the Spirit of kingship from him and replaced it with "an evil spirit" (16:14). In David's case the anointing with oil and the spiritual anointing occurred simultaneously (16:13), and the effects of both were permanent. Not only does the liquid anointing symbolize the divine spiritual anointing. This divine anointing provides the basis for David's adoption as God's son (Ps 2), hence the bearer of all subsequent messianic hopes (cf. Isa 11:2; 42:1; 61:1). Accordingly, the descent of the Spirit of God as a dove on Jesus at his baptism and the heavenly voice's declaration that the person baptized was "my Son, whom I love" represent the divine affirmation of Jesus as the Christ, the Messiah, the Anointed One par excellence (Matt 3:16-17; Mark 1:10-11; Luke 3:22).

To be distinguished from the empowering presence of the Spirit upon an individual for the performance of a specific task or the exercise of an office is the indwelling transforming presence of the Spirit. While many argue that the latter is a distinctly NT phenomenon, this conclusion is open to question. From Jesus' conversation with Nicodemus (John 3) it is evident that this learned Jew should have known that entrance into the kingdom of God has always been through the transforming power of the Spirit of God. Specific evidence for this doctrine may be found in David's association of a steadfast spirit with a clean heart and his fear of rejection by the Lord, that is, the removal of the Holy Spirit (Ps 51:10-11[12-13]). Even more telling is Ezekiel's vision of a day when the Lord will perform a heart transplant on his people as a whole and will infuse them with his own Spirit, transforming them into the living, obedience community of faith. The essence of what he envisions is not new. Since all life depends on the animating power of the spirit (cf. Gen 2:7), this is certainly true of the spiritual community. What is new about his vision is that finally the physical boundaries of the nation of Israel will be coterminous with its spiritual boundaries. No longer will the regenerated people consist of the isolated few like himself, but Israel as a nation will be revived by God's Spirit (Block, 37-41).

Finally, in the prophets' eschatological visions they foresee a time when God will pour out his Holy Spirit on his people in unprecedented fashion. This liquid imagery occurs four times, always in the context of Israel's restoration and covenant renewal (Isa 32:15; 44:3-4; Ezek 39:29; Joel 2:28[31]). While the effects of this event are compared to a desert becoming a fertile field (Isa 32:15, Karmel, # 4149) and the dry ground a flourishing stream (44:3-4), in each case the pouring out of God's Spirit represents the definitive act whereby the Lord claims and seals the restored Israel as his own covenant people. The Spirit of the Lord poured out on them serves as a permanent witness of the "covenant of peace" and the "covenant of eternity" (Block, 46-48).

NT As one moves from the operation of the *rûaḥ* in the OT to the *pneuma* in the NT, one is struck more by the continuity of the work of the Spirit of God than its discontinuity. Although the focus tends to shift to the incarnate Son of God, especially in creation, most of the previously noted dimensions of the Spirit's work are still in evidence. Through the Spirit individuals are transformed and enter the kingdom of God (John 3), are sealed as the people of God (Eph 1:13), are authorized for divine service (John 20:22-23), are inspired to prophesy (Acts 4:8), and are empowered to fight the enemies of God (Eph 6:17). Through the Spirit Jesus is authenticated as the Messiah of God, and through this same Spirit he authorizes and commissions his disciples (John 14:26; 15:26-27; 16:7-15; 20:22-23).

Of special interest is the manner in which the OT prophecies of the outpouring of the Holy Spirit are seen to be fulfilled in the book of Acts. It is hardly accidental that the commencement of each new stage in the advancement of the gospel and the incorporation into the community of faith of new groups of people are signaled by the special manifestation of the Spirit. Thus the Spirit is explicitly described as being poured out upon the Jews gathered in Jerusalem (Acts 2:4, 33, 38), but the evidences are repeated when the gospel reaches the Samaritans (8:14-17), the Gentile proselytes in the land of Judaea (10:44-48; cf. 11:16), and the Gentiles of Asia Minor (19:6). Each of these events marks the expansion of the boundaries of the people of God—Jews first, then Samaritans, God-fearers in the land of Israel, and converted pagans on foreign soil. The seal of the Spirit confirms that the ethnic borders of Israel as the people of God have been sprung, as God's transforming power is felt all over the world.

Breath, life: → *hebel* I (breath, # 2039); → *nepeš* (breath, life, desire, # 5883); → *n^{e}šāmâ* (breath, # 5972); → *š'p* I (pant, gasp, # 8634)
Spirit, ghost, demon: → *'ôb* II (medium, spiritist, necromancer, ghost, # 200); → *'iṭṭîm* I (ghosts, ghosts of the dead, spirits, # 356); → *lîlît* (night monster, night creature, # 4327); → *'^{a}zā'zēl* (Azazel, demon, scapegoat, # 6439); → *ṣî* II (desert dweller, crier, yelper, wild beast, # 7470); → *rûaḥ* (wind, breath, transitoriness, volition, disposition, temper, spirit, Spirit, # 8120); → *r^{e}pā'îm* I (shades, departed spirits, # 8327); → *śā'îr* III (satyr, goat demon, goat idol, # 8539); → *šēd* (demon, # 8717)

BIBLIOGRAPHY

DDD, 791-804; *NIDNTT* 3:689-709; *TDNT* 6:359-68; *THAT* 2:726-54; *TWOT* 2:836-37; C. Armerding, "The Holy Spirit in the Old Testament," *BSac* 92, 1935, 277-91, 433-41; D. I. Block,

"The Prophet of the Spirit: The Use of *RWH* in the Book of Ezekiel," *JETS* 32, 1989, 27-49; idem, "Empowered by the Spirit: The Holy Spirit in the Historical Writings of the Old Testament, *Southern Baptist Theological Journal* 1, 1997; I. Blythin, "A Note on Genesis 1:2," *VT* 12, 1962, 120-21; E. D. Burton, *Spirit, Soul, and Flesh*, 1918; P. S. Cripps, "The Holy Spirit in the Old Testament," *Theology* 24, 1932, 272-80; M. Dreytza, *Der Theologische Gebrauch von RUAH im Altem Testament*, 1992; R. Dussaud, "La nephesh et la rouah dans le 'Livre de Job,'" *Revue de l'Histoire des Religions* 129, 1945, 17-30; J. Hehn, "Zum Problem des Geistes im alten Orient und im A.T.," *ZAW* 43, 1925, 218-25; W. Hildebrandt, *An Old Testament Theology of the Spirit of God*, 1995; M. G. Kline, *Images of the Spirit*, 1986; R. Koch, "Spirit," *Sacramentum Verbi: An Encyclopedia of Biblical Theology*, ed. J. B. Bauer, 1970; W. McClellan, "The Meaning of *ruach 'elohim* in Gen 1:2," *Bib* 15, 1934, 517-27; S. Moscati, "The Wind in Biblical and Phoenician Cosmology," *JBL* 56, 1947, 305-10; S. Mowinckel, "The 'Spirit' and the 'Word' in the Pre-exilic Reforming Prophets," *JBL* 53, 1934, 199-227; 56, 1937, 261-65; L. Neve, *The Spirit of God in the Old Testament*, 1972; H. Orlinsky, "The Plain Meaning of Ruach in Gen 1:2," *JQR* 48, 1957-58, 157/8, 174-82; J. P. Peters, "The Wind of God," *JBL* 30, 1911, 44-54; 33, 1914, 81-86; H. Schlüngel-Straumann, *Ruah bewegt die Welt*, 1992; W. R. Shoemaker, "The Use of רוח in the Old Testament and πνευμα in the New Testament," *JBL* 23, 1904, 13-67; W. A. VanGemeren, "The Spirit of Restoration," *WTJ* 50, 1988, 81-102; L. Waterman, "Cosmogonic Affinities in Genesis 1:2," *AJSL* 43, 1927, 175-84; H. W. Wolff, *Anthropology of the Old Testament*, 1974; L. Wood, *The Holy Spirit in the Old Testament*, 1976; I. F. Wood, *The Spirit of God in Biblical Literature*, 1904; E. J. Young, "The Interpretation of Gen 1:2," *WTJ* 23, 1960/61, 151-78.

M. V. Van Pelt/W. C. Kaiser, Jr./D. I. Block

8121 (r^e*wāḥâ*, respite, relief), → # 8118

8122	רְוָיָה

רְוָיָה (r^e*wāyâ*), overflow (Ps 23:5 [hapleg.?] + MT Ps 66:12 [so NIV, REB; but LXX, Pesh., Tg., *BHS,* NAB, NRSV read/restore *r^e*wāḥâ,* spacious place]; # 8122; *HALAT* 1121b); < רוה (*rwh*) (→ # 8115).

OT The nom. r^e*wāyâ*, overflow, superabundance (hapleg.), occurs only in Ps 23:5, where the "overflowing cup" of the banquet prepared by God symbolically celebrates the bounty and blessing of Yahweh's covenant love experienced by the psalmist during his life (see P. C. Craigie, *Psalms 1-50*, WBC, 1983, 208).

Abundance, multiplication, sufficiency: → *dgh* (multiply, # 1835); → *day* (sufficiency, overflowing supply, # 1896); → *ysp* (add, continue, increase, # 3578); → *kbr* I (make many, be in abundant supply, # 3892); → m^e*gammâ* (totality, abundance, # 4480); → *rbb* I (become numerous, much, great, # 8045); → *rbh* I (become numerous, multiply, increase, # 8049); → *r'š* II, be abundant, # 8322); → *śg'/śgh* (grow great, increase, exalt, # 8434/8436); → *śpq* II (suffice, be enough, # 8563); → *šwq* I (overflow, bestow abundantly, # 8796); → *šepa'* (super-abundance, # 9179)

Andrew E. Hill/Robert H. O'Connell

8123	רום

רום (*rwm*), q. to be high, exalted, proud; polel/polal to raise up; exalt; hi. lift up, exalt; ho.

be exalted, be removed; hitpol. to exalt oneself (hapleg. in Dan 11:36) (# 8123); רוֹמֵם (*rômēm*), pol. exalt; polal be exalted (→ # 8123a); מָרוֹם (*mārôm*), nom. height, high status, pride (# 5294); רוֹמָם (*rômām*), nom. praise (→ # 8123b); רוּם (*rûm*), nom. height, haughtiness (# 8124); רוֹם (*rôm*), adj. high (# 8125); רוֹמָה (*rômâ*), adv. haughtily, proudly (hapleg. in Mic 2:3; # 8127); רוֹמֵמֻת (*rômēmut*), lifting up (Isa 33:3; # 8129); רָמָה (*rāmâ* I), nom. height, high place (# 8229); תְּרוּמָה (*t^erûmâ*), contribution (→ # 9556) רָמוּת (*rāmût*), rubbish, heap? (text. problem; Ezek 32:5); Aram. רום (*rwm*), vb. to lift up, exalt, be arrogant (# 10659); רוּם (*rûm*), nom. height (# 10660).

ANE This is a common root found in many of the ANE languages, including proper names in Eblaite meaning "my god is exalted" (*HALAT*). In Ugar. *rw/ym* is found in reference to erecting or making high a building (*UT*, 2311). In Arab. and Aram. the root also means to be high (*DISO*, 275-76, 280).

OT 1. The vb. can communicate the process of lifting or moving things higher, or it may have the stative sense when describing things that are high or exalted. Highways were lifted up to make a smooth road (Isa 49:11), voices were lifted up with a loud sound (Gen 39:15, 18; Deut 27:14; Isa 40:9), the ark of Noah was lifted up by the water (Gen 7:17), stones were lifted up from the Jordan to make a memorial (Josh 4:5), and sacrifices were lifted up or presented to God (Num 15:20; Ezek 45:13).

The stative usage describes things that are already high or lifted up. God is a rock who is higher than humankind (Ps 61:2[3]); his throne is high and lifted up (Isa 6:1); and the stars are high in the heavens (Job 22:12). The nom. *mārôm* has the literal meaning of the high places in connection with the field (Judg 5:18) or with a mountain (2 Kgs 19:23). It refers to heaven where God dwells (Job 16:19; 31:2; Isa 33:5), the place from which God's Spirit comes (Isa 32:15).

2. The literal lifting up of a person's hand was a symbolic gesture of power and pride (Deut 32:27; Mic 5:8). God has a strong high hand to accomplish his purposes (Ps 89:13[14]). In Exod 14:8 (and cf. Num 33:3) the Israelites marched out of Egypt "boldly, defiantly," (lit. "with a high hand," *b^eyād rāmâ*). When a person defiantly chooses to do something (with a high hand) contrary to God's command, that person is defying God and must be judged more severely than the person who does something in ignorance (Num 15:29-31). More than likely this metaphorical expression is to be understood in light of depictions of ANE deities, sculptured with an uplifted hand, menacingly brandishing some kind of weapon (*ANEP*, # 466, 480-84, 490-97). Thus, the expression may be used of a threatening gesture of the deity against his enemies or for the sinner who commits his act in brazen defiance of God (Num 15:30).

As with other roots meaning "to be high," *rwm* is frequently used with parts of the body in order to describe an attitude: the heart (Deut 8:14; 17:20; [NIV consider himself better than]; Jer 48:29 [‖ *g'h*; *gbh*]; Ezek 31:10; Dan 5:20; 11:12; Hos 13:6); the eyes (2 Kings 19:22 [= Isa 37:23]; Ps 18:27[28]; 131:1; Prov 6:17; 21:4; 30:13; Isa 10:12); the head (Ps 110:7). It is presumptuous and arrogant to lift up one's heart and become arrogant when one is rich, since everything that one has is God's gracious provision (Deut 8:13-15; Hos 13:6). God hates people who lift up their eyes in pride (Ps 131:1; Prov 6:17), and he will judge the haughty (Ps 18:27[28]). The wicked exalt themselves and speak against God (Dan 11:36).

A frequent object of *rwm* is *qeren*, horn (→ # 7967), which is a metaphor for strength and pride both in the OT and in ANE literature (Dhorme). Sometimes *rwm qeren* is used negatively (Ps 75:4, 5[5, 6]; Lam 2:17 [God "has cut off every horn (or strength) of Israel," and "he has exalted the horn (or strength) of your foes"]). More frequently it carries a positive nuance, i.e., God gives strength to those who have no strength in themselves (1 Sam 2:1, 10; Ps 75:10[11]; 89:17[18], 24[25]; 92:10[11]; 112:9).

3. People are to exalt (lift up) the name of God for all his wondrous deeds and worship him as king (Exod 15:2; 99:5, 9; Isa 25:1; he will exalt them with blessing (Ps 37:34) and deliver them from their enemies (Ps 30:1[2]).

4. The nom. *rûm* has the meaning of height when referring to the heavens (Prov 25:3), but it has the figurative sense of haughtiness or arrogance when describing the heart of those who boast (the Moabites in Jer 48:29 ‖ *g'h*; *gbh*) or the exaggerated claims of the proud (e.g., the Assyrians in Isa 10:12) who think that they can destroy with their own power. The adv. *rômâ* is used in Mic 2:3 to describe the powerful people who arrogantly seize the houses of the poor. On the Day of the Lord all who lift themselves up in pride and haughtiness will be removed, all people will be humbled, and God alone will be exalted (Isa 2:11, 17).

5. Other derivatives of the vb. include *rāmâ* I, height, high, high ground (7x: 1 Sam 19:22, 23; 20:1; 22:6; Ezek 16:25, 31, 39); *mārôm*, place on high, height (54x [Isa 16x; Ps 13x]).

P-B The literal usages of this root (high hill) are frequently rendered in the LXX with *hypsoō,* raise up, exalt; *hypsos,* height, high; *hypsēlos,* high, proud; or a derivative. Judg 5:18 translates *mārôm*, the heights of the field, with *hypsos*, the heights. These roots can refer to heaven, where God dwells, or to the arrogance of humankind (Isa 2:11, 17).

NT In the NT *hypsos* can refer to heaven or the heavenly city (Luke 1:78; 24:49; Rev 21:16) while *hypsēlos* refers to those who are haughty and arrogant (Rom 12:16).

Arrogance, pride, presumption: → *g'h* (rise up, be exalted, # 1448); → *zyd* (act presumptuously, prepare food, # 2326); → *yāhîr* (haughty, # 3400); → *sll* (lift up, exalt, # 6148); → *'pl* (swell, lift up, # 6752); → *'ātāq* (old, arrogant, # 6981); → *pḥz* (be reckless, arrogant, # 7069); → *rwm* (be high, exalted, proud, # 8123); → *šaḥaṣ* (pride, # 8832)

Height: → *g'h* (rise up, be exalted, # 1448); → *gbh* (be high, exalt, be haughty, # 1467); → *gēwâ* I (pride, # 1575); → *nś'* (lift, raise high, pardon, bear, exalt o.s., # 5951); → *sll* (lift up, exalt, # 6148); → *rwm* (be high, exalted, proud, # 8123)

BIBLIOGRAPHY

THAT 2:753-761; *TWAT* 8:600-619; *TWOT* 2:837-39; G. Bertram, "'Hochmut' und verwandte Begriffe im griechischen und hebräischen Alten Testament," *WO* 3, 1964, 32-43; E. P. Dhorme, "L'emploi métaphorique des noms de parties du corps en hébreu et en akkkadien," *RB* 29, 1920, 465-506; 30, 1921, 347-99, 517-40; 31, 1922, 215-33, 489-547; 32, 1923, 185-212; D. E. Gowan, *When Man Becomes God: Humanism and Hybris in the Old Testament,* 1975; P. Humbert, "Demesure et chute dans l'Ancien Testament," *Hommage á Wilhelm Vischer*, 1960, 63-82.

Gary V. Smith/Victor Hamilton

8123a	רוֹמֵם

רוֹמֵם (*rômēm*), pol. exalt; polal be exalted (# 8123a); Aram. pol. exalt (# 10659); רוֹמָם (*rômām*), nom. praise (# 8123b); < רום (*rwm*), q. to be high, exalted, proud; polel/polal to raise up; exalt; hi. lift up, exalt; ho. be exalted, be removed; hitpolel to exalt oneself (hapleg. in Dan 11:36) (→ # 8123).

OT 1. This vb. belongs to the general vocabulary of praise; it appears predominantly in the Psalms. It is used to introduce sections of a communal hymn at Ps 99:5, 9, a solo hymn at 145:1, and an eschatological hymn at Isa 25:1. In Neh 9:5 it features in hymnic praise at the beginning of a prayer of confession.

2. It introduces a thanksgiving song in Ps 30:1[2] and concludes another in 118:28 (cf. 107:32), while in Dan 4:34[37] it concludes a prayer of thanksgiving. In Ps 34:3[4] the congregation is encouraged to exalt God's name for his deliverance of the individual singer. In 66:17, on the other hand, the nom. refers back to a readiness to praise God in the context of a lament, so certain was the psalmist that he would be delivered.

3. In Ps 149:6 the nom. appears in an eschatological hymn, with reference to praise during battle against the nations.

P-B In 1QM 4:8 one of the banners carried by the victorious army was to be inscribed *rwmm 'l,* "praise of God," an echo of Ps 149:6. The victors were to sing a hymn of praise, in which the vb. occurs twice, in praise of God's name (1QM 14:4), as in Ps 34:3[4], and of his mighty acts (1QM 14:13). In 1QH 11:15 "I will exalt you, my Rock" recalls expressions in other psalms.

Praising, singing, thanksgiving: → *hll* II (praise, be praiseworthy, boast, exult, # 2146); → *zmr* I (make music, sing praise, # 2376); → *ydh* II (acknowledge, give thanks, praise, # 3344); → *nwh* II (praise, # 5658); → *'nh* IV (sing, # 6702); → *psḥ* I (break forth with or break into singing, # 7200); → *rômēm* (exalt, # 8123a); → *šbḥ* I (commend, praise, honor, # 8655); → *šyr* (sing, # 8876); → *tnh* (recite, commemorate, # 9480)

Bibliography

THAT 2:760-61.

Leslie C. Allen

8124 (*rûm*, height, haughtiness), → # 8123

8125 (*rôm*, high), → # 8123

8127 (*rômâ*, haughtily, proudly), → # 8123

8129 (*rômēmut*, lifting up), → # 8123

8131	רוע

רוע (*rw'*), q. to shout (in victory); to shout (in the anguish of defeat); to shout loudly; to give a war cry (# 8131); רֵעַ (*rēa'* I), nom., shouting (# 8275); תְּרוּעָה (*tᵉrû'â*), nom., a signal; a shout (in the anguish of defeat); a shout (in victory; # 9558).

ANE The root does not occur in any other ancient Sem. languages, though it does possibly occur in postbiblical Arab. (*raǵa*).

OT 1. (a) The vb. *rwʿ* is close to the meaning of *rnn,* with which the vb. often appears in parallel (Job 38:7; Ps 81:1[2]; Isa 16:10; 44:23); indeed, they are so close it is difficult to provide a meaningfully nuanced translation. They both indicate a loud sound by the human voice, or perhaps by a trumpet or musical horn, that often has the function of a signal. They both are connected, especially in the latter sense, with the battlefield. Further, they both indicate responses to victory and to defeat on the battlefield. Thus, the basic meaning of *rwʿ*, like *rnn*, seems to be to shout or to make a loud noise. When the two vbs. appear in parallel (as in the above verses), *rnn* occurs first, perhaps indicating that *rwʿ* is less used than *rnn* (a fact bolstered by its 33x, compared to *rnn*'s 53x).

(b) It is true, however, that a much higher percentage of this vb.'s use is associated with warfare. Many of the vb.'s occurrences are found in the narratives of battles. The vb. plays an important role in the description of the battle of Jericho. The shout not only signals the commencement of battle but also causes the walls to fall (Josh 6:10 [3x], 16, 20 [2x]). At the time the tribes of Israel fought against the Philistines under the leadership of Hophni and Phinehas, the Israelites shouted loudly when the ark came into the camp (1 Sam 4:5), but to no avail, since they apparently treated it as a mechanical talisman rather than as a symbol of the presence of the divine warrior (→). The vb. also has a part in the narrative of David's fight with Goliath. As the young man approaches the battlefield, he hears the shouts of battle (1 Sam 17:20), and then after he defeats Goliath, the Israelites followed up on his victory by rushing the Philistine army, shouting as they approached.

One final example will suffice. In the Chronicler's account of Abijah's struggle against Jeroboam, the Judaean king is pictured as a faithful follower of Yahweh. At the beginning of his victorious battle against the Israelite king, the vb. describes the signal given by the priests to initiate the battle. In this case it is interesting to note that the sound is emitted not by the human voice, but by trumpets (*ḥ*^{a}*ṣōṣ*^{e}*rôt*; cf. 2 Chron 13:12, 15). This leads us back to the Pentateuch, where in Num 10:9 we read that Aaron and his sons are charged with the use of the trumpet to signal the beginning of warfare.

(c) The prophets pick up the language of warfare in their description of God, who fights on behalf of his people when they are obedient to him, but who fights against them when they reject him as their God. Isaiah (42:13) pictures God marching out "like a warrior" against his enemies. As he goes out, he gives a "shout" that signals the beginning of the battle.

(d) It is interesting, in addition, to note the connection between the vb. and descriptions of the Day of the Lord in two prophetic passages. The Day of the Lord is a day of battle, so it is appropriate that Joel 2:1 sees it signaled by the sounding of the alarm (*hārîʿû*). In Zeph 1:16 the "battle cry" (the nom. *t*^{e}*rûʿâ*) is also associated with the battle on the Day of the Lord.

(e) The vb. is also used 11x in the Psalms. While occasionally it is used to indicate the shout before or after a battle (Ps 60:8[10]; 108:9[10]), it is sometimes used more generally to simply indicate a joyful exclamation in response to God. In this sense, it is found in the call to worship at the beginning of hymns (47:1[2]; 95:1, 2; 100:1).

(f) Lastly, the vb. is used, rarely, to indicate not a joyful noise but a mournful or alarmed noise. In battle contexts, the vb. describes the response to defeat, not to victory. Illustrative is Judg 7:21, where the Midianites shout as they retreat at the ruse of Gideon (see also Job 30:5; Mic 4:9).

2. (a) The nom. *t^e^rû'â* has a similar semantic range to the vb. *rw'*. Indeed, the nom. is frequently used in the same clause (often as cognate accusative) with the vb. (cf. Josh 6:5, 20; 1 Sam 4:5; in all three cases the nom. is modified by "great" [*g^e^dôlâ*]). It indicates a shout, occasionally a trumpet blast, that is often associated with warfare. We will see, however, a more frequent association with the formal worship of Israel. As with the vb., the nom. has positive as well as negative connotations.

(b) Perhaps the most frequent use of the nom. is in connection with the formal worship of Israel. In particular, it is associated with the Feast of Trumpets (Lev 23:24; Num 29:1). Indeed, our nom. is the word used to indicate that the feast began with a trumpet blast. In the Year of Jubilee, on the Day of Atonement, the trumpet blast reverberates throughout the land (Lev 25:9).

But the word is not just associated with specific feasts. As God blesses the psalmist and rescues him from his enemies, he will respond by offering sacrifices and with shouts of joy (Ps 27:6). Indeed, more precisely, the grammatical construction is construct (*zibḥê t^e^rû'â*), lit., "sacrifices of shouts of joy." In 150:5 *t^e^rû'â* is in construct with "cymbals," qualifying that instrument as loud and joyous (resounding cymbals NIV).

The nom. is also associated with a specific, one-time cultic occasion, the moving of the ark from the house of Obed-Edom to Jerusalem (2 Sam 6:15; 1 Chron 15:28).

(c) The nom., like the vb., is often associated with warfare. It can refer to a signal (vocal or instrumental) that initiates battle (Num 31:6; Josh 6:5, 20) or simply the sound of screaming and yelling as soldiers clash (1 Sam 4:5, 6; Ezek 21:22[27]; Amos 1:14; 2:2). Even here we may speak of a cultic function of the battle cry at least in certain instances. After all, it was often the priests who gave the shout or sounded the trumpet to initiate battle (2 Chron 13:12). Battle was a form of worship in the OT.

(d) The book of Job offers examples of a nonmilitary shout of joy. In Job 8:21 Bildad offers Job the hope that God will once again fill his mouth with "shouts of joy." In Job 33:26 Elihu describes the person who turns to God again and is restored. He sees God's face and "shouts for joy."

(e) The nom. *t^e^rû'â* takes on a negative cast in Jer 20:16. Jeremiah, in his bitter depression, castigates the person who brought the news of his birth. He wishes him ill by saying, "May he hear wailing in the morning, a battle cry (*t^e^rû'â*) at noon." The nom. has clearly negative connotations since the battle cry is directed at the person. He is the recipient of violence.

3. *rēa'* I is a second nom. formed from the verbal root *rw'*, which occurs 3x in the HB (Exod 32:17; Job 36:33; Mic 4:9). In Exod 32:17 Joshua descends from Mount Sinai with Moses after receiving the Ten Commandments. As they descend, they hear the people as they celebrate in the worship of a false god, the golden calf. Joshua hears

the shouting (*rēa'*) and mistakes it for the sound of war (*qôl milḥāmâ*), thus showing again the connection between the root *rw'* and warfare.

P-B In the Qumran materials the vb. in the hi. and the nom. *t^erû'â* occur exclusively in war contexts (1 WM 1,11). In the Septuagint the vb. is translated by a wide variety of G vbs. including *alalatzō, samainō, boaō, kpazō* and *salpizō*. The nom. is most frequently translated with *alalagmos* and *kraugē*.

Shout, (war-)cry, yell: → *hêdād* (shout, # 2116); → *ṣwḥ* (shout, # 7423); → *ṣrḥ* (yell, call shrilly, raise the war-cry, # 7658); → *rw'* (shout, give war-cry, # 8131); → *rnn* (yell, shout [w. joy], moan, # 8264)

BIBLIOGRAPHY

TWAT 7:434-38; P. Humbert, *La 'terou'a.' Analyse d'un rite biblique*, 1946; Ihroni, "Die Haufung der Verben des Jubelns Zephanja III 14f., 16-18," *VT* 33, 1983, 106-10; R. Schmid, "Opfer mit Jubel. Die *zibḥe t^erû'â* von Ps. 27,6," *TZ* 35, 1979, 48-54.

Tremper Longman III

8132	רוץ

רוץ (*rwṣ*), q. run, be busy; pol. to dash to and fro; hi. cause to run, to fetch quickly, to chase someone quickly off (# 8132); מֵרוֹץ (*mērôṣ*), מְרוּצָה (*m^erûṣâ* I), nom. running, manner of running, course (# 5296/5297).

ANE Par. forms of the vb. *rwṣ* are well attested in other Sem. languages. There are two Ugar. vbs. that are normally mentioned as cognates to the Heb. vb. *rwṣ*. The first one, *rẓ*, means run. The following quotation from *KTU* 1.6 I 50 serves as example: *dq 'anm lyrẓ 'm b'l* (literally: he who is powerless cannot run like Baal). The second vb. is *rẓẓ*, hasten. Cf. *KTU* 1.16 I 49 [w] *yqrb trzzh* (he approached quickly). Other cognates are: Akk. *râṣu(m)*; Syr. *r^ehēṭ*; Mand. *RHṬ*; Eth. *rōṣa*; and Amh. *rōṭa*. All these forms have the meaning "run." The Arab. form *rāḍa*, however, means to train (an animal); to exercise. The consonantal changes of the Aram. form *rhṭ* are noteworthy.

OT 1. The vb. *rwṣ* is used only once in the OT with animals as subj. In Amos 6:12 *sûsîm*, horses, function as subj. of the vb. A variety of scholarly discussions have been devoted to this verse. The rendering of the second phrase, in particular, is problematic, as Loretz (1989, 240-41) has pointed out. Michaelis emended the MT's second phrase: *'m yhrwš bbqrym* to read *'m yhrwṣ bbqr ym* and translated as follows: "or does one plough with the cattle of the sea?" Dahood emended the phrase according to the Ugar. usage of the prep. *b* (from, without) to read *'m yhrwṣ bbqrym*: "or can one plough with oxen?" Loretz takes the parallelism and symmetry between the first and second phrases of the verse into account. He provides a text critical explanation for his reading of the second phrase *'m yhrwṣ bym bqr*; "or do the oxen plough in the sea?" A triple parallelism thus exists between the two halves of the verse: *yrwṣwn* ‖ *yhrwṣ*; *bsl'* ‖ *bym*; *swsym* ‖ *bqr*. The argumentation of this verse can be summarized as follows: just as senseless as it would be for horses to gallop on rocks or for oxen to plough the sea, so foolish it is for Israel to turn justice into poison and bitterness.

2. The vb. *rwṣ* most often occurs with people as subj. The vb. occurs on its own (e.g., 1 Sam 20:36; 2 Sam 18:21, 22, 23, 26), in conjunction with another vb. (but

without *w*) (e.g., *rwṣ mṣ'* [1 Sam 20:36]; *rwṣ dbr* [Zech 2:8]), in conjunction with a following impf. cons. (e.g., Gen 24:28; 29:12; Num 11:27), in conjunction with impf. + *w* (e.g., 2 Sam 18:19; Ps 59:4[5]), in conjunction with an acc. of place (e.g., 1 Sam 17:22; 2 Sam 18:23), and in conjunction with various prep. (e.g., *'el* [Gen 18:7]; *'ad* [2 Kgs 4:22]; *l^e* [Prov 1:16]; *b^e* [Amos 6:12]; *min* [1 Sam 4:12]; *liqrā't* [Gen 18:2]; *lipnê* [1 Sam 8:11]). The vb. also occurs together with the nom. *derek* (→ # 2006; cf. Ps 119:32) to designate doing the will of Yahweh. This combination thus expresses theologically the mode of life desired by God, the life *coram Deo*.

3. The part. of the vb. *rāṣ* (sing.) and *rāṣîm* (pl.) are used as nom. (runner, messenger), e.g., in 1 Sam 22:17 (in Israel or Judah) and in Esth 3:13, 15 (in the Persian kingdom).

4. The hi. form of the vb. *rwṣ* has the nuance of a swift action, e.g., Jer 49:19 (chase away quickly), Gen 41:14 (fetch quickly), and 1 Sam 17:17 (bring quickly).

5. The nom. *mērôṣ* and *m^erûṣâ* I occur in only a few verses in the OT. The form *mērôṣ* appears only in Eccl 9:11, where it functions as subj. of the sentence and means the running, the race.

Three verses contain the nom. *m^erûṣâ*, namely, 2 Sam 18:27 (2x), Jer 8:6 (Q), and 23:10. The two occurrences in 2 Sam 18:27 both refer to the physical style of people's running. In Jer, however, the nom. is used figuratively. The context of Jer 8:6 is Yahweh's accusing his people by the mouth of his prophet of turning away from him. Their course away from him is then compared to a horse storming away from a battle. The nom. thus refers to their evil lifestyle and their lack of commitment to Yahweh. The occurrence in Jer 23:10 has much the same nuance. Here the prophets are accused of an evil course of life. Therefore, Yahweh pronounces his wrath on them.

Hurry, speed: → *'wṣ* (urge, # 237); → *dḥp* (hurrying, # 1894); → *ḥwš* (hurry, # 2590); → *ḥpz* (be in a hurry, # 2905); → *ṭwś* (rush, dart, # 3216); → *mhr* I (hurry, # 4554); → *qal* (light, agile, quick, swift, # 7824)

BIBLIOGRAPHY

TDNT 8:226-35; O. Loretz, "Amos VI 12," *VT* 39/2, 1989, 240-41.

Louis Jonker

8133	רושׁ

רושׁ (*rwš*), q. become poor, oppressed, weak; hitpol. make oneself poor (# 8133); רֵישׁ (*rêš*), poverty (# 8203).

ANE No cognates of any significance have been adduced.

OT 1. The God of the Bible is a God with a passionate concern for those whom society has dehumanized or whose lack of power and status has made them especially vulnerable to exploitation—widows, orphans, and the poor (and since the two groups were often linked, e.g., Isa 58:6-7, also the oppressed). In the absence of an earthly kinsman-redeemer, God stands as their protector and guardian (see D. Daube, *Studies in Biblical Law*, 46).

2. The root *rwš* and its derivatives (which occur some 31x) are found mainly in the Wisdom material and denote destitution. In the Prophets the term is used literally in Nathan's famous parable against David (2 Sam 12:1, 3, 4) and figuratively in David's

love song to Michal indicating his unworthiness but willingness to marry her (1 Sam 18:23).

3. Eccl contains a vivid picture of poverty and oppression. "If you see the poor oppressed in a district, and justice and rights denied, do not be surprised," says Eccl 5:8[7]. Such is the nature of an oppressive society. Oppressor and oppressed are both victims (Eccl 4:1). Proverbs illustrates something of the ambiguity that surrounds wealth and poverty. On the one hand, we read that people may become needy through laziness (Prov 10:4); on the other, that the poor are the victims of oppression. When their fields produce crops, injustice sweeps it away (13:23). They are often unsupported by family, friends, and neighbors (14:20; 19:7). They receive little mercy from the rich (18:23), who rule over them and make them servants of their creditors (22:7). No room exists here for a vow of poverty. Here is only hunger, thirst, and the unending cycle of working to eat and eating to work, in a world that seems blind to those, like the poor, who have no honor or status.

4. God, however, is neither blind nor deaf (Isa 59:1). The one who mocks the poor mocks God himself, and those who gloat over another's disaster will be punished (Prov 17:5). In God's eyes the upright poor have more honor than the rich fool, who is perverse (19:1; 28:6) or a liar (19:22). All people are equal in the eyes of God, for he made them all (22:2). So there is an obligation on those who have to give to the poor (28:27).

P-B 1. Sirach reflects the same ambiguity in the understanding of poverty as does Proverbs. In Sir 13:1-14:2 he details the relationship between rich and poor. They have different attitudes towards doing wrong (13:3—one boasts and the other seeks forgiveness). The rich abuse those who have less status (vv. 4-7). Enmity exists between rich and poor like that between a hyena and a dog (v. 18). The poor (*dallîm*) are feeding grounds for the rich, and in times of trouble they are without friends (v. 21). The wise poor are taken much less seriously than the rich fool (vv. 22-23).

2. *rwš* is one of the terms used by the writer of the Hymn Scroll from Qumran as a self-description, in line with the sect's use of poverty as a spiritual category to depict their dependence on God (1QH 5:14).

In Num R 10, which refers to Prov 31:7, *riš* is used of a person who is due to be executed and so supersedes purely physical loss, to include a sense of misery and lack of hope. One is reminded here of the similar lack of hope that attends people who suffer from abject poverty.

Poor, crushed, needy: → *'ebyôn* (poor, needy, # 36); → *dk'* (crush, be crushed, # 1917); → *dal* II (scanty, helpless, powerless, insignificant, dejected, # 1924); → *dqq* (crush, # 1990); → *mwk* (depressed, grow poor, # 4575); → *miskēn* (poor man, # 5014); → *'ānāw* (poor, humble, # 6705); → *'ānî* (humble, # 6714); → *ṣn'* (be modest, humble, # 7570); → *rwš* (become poor, oppressed, # 8133)

Bibliography

TWAT 7:445-49; F. C. Fensham, "Widow, Orphan and the Poor in Ancient Near Eastern Legal and Wisdom Literature" *JNES* 21, 1962, 129-39; W. McKane, *Proverbs*, OTL, 1970; J. D. Pleins, "Poverty in the Social World of the Wise" *JSOT* 37, 1987, 61-78; P. W. Skehan and A. A. di Lella, *The Wisdom of Ben Sira*, AB, 1987; R. N. Whybray, "Poverty, Wealth and Point of View in Proverbs," *ExpTim* 100, 1988/89; G. H. Wittenberg, "The Lexical Content of the Terminology for 'Poor' in the Book of Proverbs," *Scriptura* 2, 1986, 40-85.

W. R. Domeris

8135	רזה

רזה (*rzh*), q. destroy, waste away; ni. shrink away; pi. let shrink away (→ # 8135); רָזֶה (*rāzeh*), adj. lean, poor (# 8136); רָזוֹן (*rāzôn* I), nom. emaciation, leanness, wasting (# 8137).

ANE The vb. is connected with the Jewish Aram. *rz'*, making it unpleasant; Syr. *rz'*, grow lean; Arab. *raza'a/razi'a*, to take, to diminish; *radija*, weak, powerless. The adj. can be linked to the Sam. *rāza*, lean.

OT The vb. is only found twice in prophetic literature (Isa 17:4; Zeph 2:11); the adj. is used in Num 13:20 and Ezek 34:20 and the nom. in Ps 106:15; Isa 10:16; and Mic 6:10.

In Num 13:20 Moses instructs the spies to compile a thorough report on Canaan. Some of the crucial questions were: How is the soil? Is it fertile (lit., fat) or poor (lit., lean)? (Milgrom, 102). The adj. is used here as a metaphoric reference to poor or infertile soil.

Isa 10:16 forms part of a prophecy on the coming destruction of the Assyrians (vv. 16-19); the nom. *rāzôn* refers to a threat about a wasting disease drawn from 17:4 (Clements, 113-14). This reference can be seen in close connection with the sick man who "wastes away" in 10:18 and is related to the punishment of the Assyrian forces in 701 outside Jerusalem (Seitz, 94). Isa 17:4 is the first of three oracles concerning Jacob/Israel, all starting with "in that day" (17:4, 7, 9). The use of *rzh* portrays the grim results of judgment inflicted upon Israel—most probably anticipating the Assyrian destruction of the northern kingdom (Clements, 158-59). Ezek 34:20 contains a judgment that distinguishes between fat and lean animals/sheep in close connection with a depiction of the intimidation of weak sheep in v. 21 (Zimmerli, 209, 217). While the whole of ch. 34 is united by the theme of shepherding, vv. 17-24 introduce the concept of justice as an essential element of leadership. God will see to it that justice is done between those with power and the powerless in the anticipated reunited Israel after the Exile (Blenkinsopp, 159).

Micah's oracle contains a curse on a city where the rich cheated the poor (Mic 6:9-16; Hillers, 80-81). Part of this dishonest behavior involved the use of the short/scant/emaciated *rāzôn*, ephah (v. 10), an unlawful reduction of the ephah, and so the deception of the buyer who would get less than was agreed upon (Wolff, 192-93). Zephaniah's judgments on Moab and Ammon in Zeph 2:8-11 uses *rzh* to describe how God destroys/shrivels all the foreign gods by constricting the land over which they have dominion. Such action is a demonstration of the Lord's superiority (v. 11; Patterson, 344, 348; Berlin, 110). When Ammon and Moab are devastated, they will produce no food and their gods will become thin and starve (Roberts, 201-2).

Israel's ingratitude during the time of their wandering in the wilderness is the subject in Ps 106. The use of *rzh* refers to Israel receiving a wasting disease (v. 15; Anderson, 741; Gray, 133). It is possible that the events refered to in Num 11:33 are suggested by Ps 106 and that the "wasting disease" forms part of Israel's punishment as a result of their failure to trust the Lord (Booij, 252-53; Mays, 340-43).

P-B 1. *LXX*. The vb. is tr. in Isa 17:4 with *seiō*, shake, tremble and in Zeph 2:11 with *exolethreuō*, destroy completely. The adj. is tr. in Num 13:20 with *ponēra*, bad or worthless. In Ezek 34:20 the contrast between fat and lean is absent in the G. The nom. is tr. in Isa 10:16 with *atimia*, dishonor; in Mic 6:10 the reference to the short ephah is tr. with a reference to the pride of unrighteousness, and in Ps 106:15 the wasting disease is not reflected in the tr. "and sent fullness into their souls."

2. *Rabbinical literature*. In the Midr. *Tanhduma Sh'lah* 6 *rzh* is used in the phrase: "If the ground is clayish, the fruit are lean."

NT *seiō*, shake, cause to quake is used as part of the earthquake motif in Matt and as a topos in stories of miraculous deliverance in Acts 16:26 (*EDNT* 3:236-37). *exolethreuō*, root out, is used in Acts 3:23 to indicate the rooting out of those who do not listen to prophets (*TDNT* 5:171). *ponēros*, in troubled condition, bad, worthless, evil, malicious, wicked, is used 78x, 26x in Matt and 21x in Luke-Acts (*THAT* 2:794-803). *atimia*, dishonor or shame, occurs almost exclusively in Paul; a good example can be found in Rom 1:21-27 (*EDNT* 1:177).

Feeble, despair, faint, frail, tender: → *'ml* I (be weak, be feeble, languish, # 581); → *ḥlh* I (become weak, tired, ill, # 2703); → *ylh* (languish, # 3532); → *k'h* (be disheartened, frightened, # 3874); → *nbl* I (wither, fade, languish, dishonor, # 5570); → *'ṭp* II (grow weak, faint, be feeble, # 6494); → *'lp* (cover, faint, # 6634); → *'šš* (become weak, # 6949); → *pwg* (be feeble, numb, be prostrated, # 7028); → *rzh* (destroy, waste away, # 8135); → *rkk* (be tender, timid, gentle, # 8216); → *rph* (become slack, lose heart, discourage, # 8332)
Thin: → *daq* (thin, # 1987); → *rzh* (destroy, waste away, # 8135); → *raq* I (thin, # 8369)

Bibliography

EDNT 1:177; 3:236-37; A. A. Anderson, *The Book of Psalms II*, 1992; A. Berlin, *Zephaniah*, 1994; J. Blenkinsopp, *Ezekiel*, 1990; T. Booij, *Psalmen III*, 1994; R. E Clements, *Isaiah 1-39*, NCBC, 1987; M. D. Gray, "Ps 106, 15b: Did the Children of Israel Get What They Asked for?" *SJOT* 7, 1993, 125-33; D. R. Hillers, *Micah*, Hermeneia, 1984; J. L. Mays, *Psalms*, 1994; J. Milgrom, *Numbers*, AB, 1990; R. D. Patterson, *Nahum, Habakkuk, Zephaniah*, 1991; J. J. M. Roberts, *Nahum, Habakkuk and Zephaniah*, OTL, 1991; C. R. Seitz, *Isaiah 1-39*, 1993; H. W. Wolff, *Micah*, 1990; W. Zimmerli, *Ezekiel 2*, Hermenia, 1983.

Hendrik L. Bosman

8136 (*rāzeh*, lean, poor), → # 8135

8137 (*rāzôn* I, emaciation), → # 8135

8138 (*rāzôn* II, dignitary), → # 8142

8141	רזם

רזם (*rzm*), q. flash (# 8141).

OT In Job 15:12 *rzm* occurs in connection with anger, and a translation more like "flash" is preferable to "wink." Only rarely in the OT are the eyes mentioned in connection with either sleeping or waking.

Eye, wink: → *'îšôn* (pupil of eye, # 413); → *bābâ* (pupil of eye, # 949); → *'yn* (view with suspicion, # 6523); → *'ap'appayim* (flashing of eye, # 6757); → *qrṣ* (wink, pinch, # 7975); → *rzm* (flash, # 8141); → *t^eballul* (spot in eye, # 9319)

Allan M. Harman

8142	רזן

רזן (*rzn*), q. act. part. rule (# 8142); רָזוֹן (*rāzôn* II), dignitary, ruler (hapleg. in Prov 14:28; # 8138).

ANE In form, *rôzēn* is the act. part. of a vb. otherwise unattested in Heb., but perhaps cognate with Arab. *razuna*, be weighty. Phoen. *rzn* has the same meaning as Heb. *rôzēn.*

OT The lexeme is found only in poetry and the pl. as a parallel to kings or to judges (*šôp^eṭîm*) in the sense of rulers (Isa 40:23). The vb. occurs 6x and *rāzôn* once (Prov 14:28).

1. In Prov, the term is used in the context of royal wisdom (Prov 14:28). Through divinely given wisdom kings reign and "rulers" decree what is just (8:15). Since the exercise of justice and the defense of the oppressed requires a clear mind, the wise ruler must not be given to strong drink (31:4). The point of the saying is evidently that the true glory of a ruler lies in the well-being of his subjects.

2. In several passages, the term designates "rulers" hostile or potentially hostile to God. In Judg 5 kings and "rulers" are summoned as interested parties to listen to Deborah's song (v. 3), celebrating God's march from Sinai as divine warrior, and Deborah's victory over "the kings of Canaan" (v. 19). Warning is given that all of God's enemies will likewise perish (v. 31). More explicitly, Ps 2 affirms God's sovereign rule over kings and "rulers" of the earth who plot against God and the Davidic king (v. 2). The wisdom of kings and rulers (*šôp^eṭîm*) is to serve God with reverence and to submit to the authority of his anointed king in Zion (vv. 10-12). The theme is expressed succinctly in Isa 40:23: "he brings princes to naught." Ps 2:2 is quoted in Acts 4:26 and applied to the conspiracy of Herod and Pilate against Jesus, and of the chief priests and elders against the apostles. Here, as in Isa 40, faith in God's sovereign rule over human potentates is reinforced by recalling God's work of creation.

P-B The LXX variously trans. this word by *archōn* (Ps 2:2), *dynastēs* (Prov 8:15), *satrapēs* (Judg 5:3), and *tyrannos* (Hab 1:10).

Leaders: → *'ādôn* (lord, master, # 123); → *'allûp* II (tribal chief, # 477); → *'āṣîl* II (eminent, noble, # 722); → *zāqēn* (elder, # 2418); → *ḥōr* I, free man, freeborn, # 2985); → *mapteaḥ* (badge of office, # 5158); → *nāgîd* (prince, ruler, leader, # 5592); → *nāśî'* I (chief, king, # 5954); → *sārîs* (eunuch, court official, # 6247); → *seren* II (Philistine prince, # 6249); → *'attûd* (he-goat, leader, # 6966); → *peḥâ* (governor, # 7068); → *pāqîd* (officer, # 7224); → *qāṣîn* (commander, leader, # 7903); → *rab* II (captain, chief, # 8042); → *rzn* (rule, # 8142); → *šôa'* I (noble, # 8777)

Kenneth T. Aitken

8143	רחב

רחב (*rḥb*), q. open wide; ni. part. broad, wide; hi. make wide, broaden, extend, provide wide room for (# 8143); מֶרְחָב (*merḥāb*), nom. wideness, open space (# 5303); רַחַב (*raḥab*), nom. wide space, width (# 8144); רֹחַב (*rōḥāb*), nom. width (of a land), breadth (# 8145); רָחָב (*rāḥāb*), adj. wide, broad, extended, open, extensive (# 8146); רְחֹב (*r^eḥōb*), broad place (→ # 8148).

ANE The vb. *rḥb* is well attested in the languages of the ANE. The vb. occurs in the yifil form in Phoen. with the meaning make wider. In Ugar. it occurs as adj. (*rḥb*, wide) and as nom. (*rḥbt*, barrel). In Ebla the verbal root is used to form a personal name. The Mand. cognate is *RḤB* II (to be wide/broad). In ESA it occurs both as vb. (*rḥb*, to be wide/broad) and as nom. (width). This is also the case in Eth. (vb., *rĕḥĕba*, be wide/broad; adj., *reḥib*, wide; nom., *reḥeb*, *raḥeb*, *reḥbat*, *marḥeb*), in Tigre (vb., *raḥaba*; adj., *rĕḥīb*; nom., *mĕrḥāb*), and in Arab. (vb., *raḥiba*, *raḥuba*, be wide/broad; adj., *raḥb*, *raḥīb*, *ruḥab*, wide; nom., *ruḥb*, *raḥab*, width; nom., *raḥbat*, *raḥabat*, open space; nom., *raḥābat*, width). From these ANE cognates it is clear that the vb., as well as its derivatives, almost always fall within the semantic field of "openness, wideness." Note also the numerous par. to the Heb. derivatives *rōḥab*, *rāḥāb*, and *merḥāb*.

OT 1. According to Lisowsky's *Concordance of the Hebrew OT* (1981^2) the vb. *rḥb* appears 3x in the q. (1 Sam 2:1; Isa 60:5; Ezek 41:7), once in the ni. (part. in Isa 30:23), and 21x in the hi. (once each in Gen, Exod, 2 Sam, Prov, Amos, Mic, Hab; 3x in Deut; 5x in Isa; 6x in Ps). Significant is that nine of the occurrences in the hi. have Yahweh as subj. Gen 26:22 appears in the context of Isaac reestablishing himself in the area where his father Abraham once had dominion. He dug two wells, but the Philistines quarreled over them. When Isaac dug a third well in another area, nobody quarreled there over it, and he called the well "open space." The motivation behind the name is then furnished by Isaac: "Now the LORD has given us room and we will flourish in the land." The gift of the land is thus interpreted as Yahweh providing the space and means to live. Exod 34:24 also has the promise of the land as context. Yahweh promises that he will extend (*rḥb*) the boundaries to secure their territory. The same expression appears in Deut 12:20 and 19:8.

The following five occurrences all appear in poetic texts. In Deut 33:20 Moses (in the Song of Moses before his death) pronounces blessings on the one who provided space for the tribe Gad (*marḥîb gad*), implying Yahweh. The context is thus again Yahweh's promise of the land. In 2 Sam 22:37 and Ps 18:37 (where the same phrase appears) Yahweh's action is interpreted personally. Literally this phrase can be translated by "you have broadened my steps underneath me." This refers to the existential experience of protection by the Lord. Ps 4:2 also has the experience of the individual believer in the context of lament, as the psalmist cries out, "Give me relief" (NKJV "you have relieved me"). This could be interpreted as God saving the individual or providing freedom. In Ps 119:32 the poet states that he wants to live according to Yahweh's commandments, because he has broadened his heart (lit.). This means that Yahweh has provided insight and understanding.

From these examples it seems that the vb. *rḥb* with Yahweh as subj. normally functions in one of two contexts: (1) the context of the Lord's promise of the land, and

(2) the experience of the individual believer that the Lord is actively involved in his/her life.

2. The nom. *rōḥāb* normally functions as a technical term to indicate dimension. There are mainly three contexts in the OT where this technical term appears: (a) The context of the institution of the first semipermanent Israelite sanctuary, namely, the tabernacle and all the sacred utensils associated therewith. Numerous references in Exod 25-39 use *rōḥāb* to state the dimensions of these constructions. (b) In the prescriptions for the building of Solomon's temple (1 Kgs 6-7) this technical term appears several times. (c) The passage where *rōḥāb* is most frequently used is Ezek 40-48. These chapters contain Ezekiel's vision of the temple. (→ Ezekiel: Theology)

3. *merḥāb* appears 6x in the OT, always in a poetic context. All these cases are related to Yahweh's actions. The references in 2 Sam 22:20 and Ps 18:20; 31:9; 118:5 especially emphasize God's protection and sustenance. He is the One who provides open space (metaphorically spoken, "freedom") in distress. Cf. the second context mentioned above in section 1.

4. The adj. *rāḥāb* is often used in connection with the spacious land that Israel received as gift from Yahweh (cf. Exod 3:8; Neh 9:35). As the geographical proportions of this land was not really spacious, this term should rather be understood metaphorically. The land in which Yahweh provided freedom and sustenance, and which their children will inherit, was experienced as wide, open, and spacious. The adj. used in this sense therefore often appears in conjunction with *yādayim* (lit. hands), on both sides. This phrase emphasizes the sense of freedom the land left with the Israelites.

The adj. *rāḥāb* is also used to describe physical phenomena. The walls of Jerusalem (Neh 3:8; 12:38) and of Babel (Jer 51:58), *inter alia*, are described as *rāḥāb* (broad). However, abstract phenomena are also characterized by *rāḥāb*: e.g., *miṣwôtᵉkā*, your commandments (Ps 119:96) are comprehensive; *hammᵉlā'kâ*, the task (Neh 4:19[13]) is spread out over a distance; *lēb/lebab*, heart (Ps 101:5; Prov 21:4)—meaning proud/arrogant; *nepeš*, soul (Prov 28:25)—meaning selfish.

5. *rāḥāb* is also used as personal name in the OT. In Josh 2:1, 3; 6:17, 23, 25 this name is used to refer to Rahab, the woman of Jericho who saved the Israelite spies' lives and was, therefore, pardoned during the destruction of the city. Josh 2:1 describes this woman as *'iššâ zônâ*, a prostitute. Interestingly enough Matt 1:5 also refers to this woman as one of the ancestors of Jesus, the Messiah. Barstad in an interesting article (*SEÅ* 54, 1989, 43-49) investigates the origin of this name. After providing several arguments (following J. A. Montgomery), *inter alia* from Ugar. par., he states that the term *rāḥāb* has something to do with the feminine genitalia. Cf. the par. term *zkrwn* (male genitalia). He thus comes to the conclusion that *rāḥāb*, as it appears as personal name in the book of Josh, is not a real personal name, but a nickname, which is a harsh indication of the woman's profession. (→ Rahab)

6. The nom. *raḥab* occurs only in Job. In 36:16 *raḥab* is qualified with the phrase *lo'-mûṣāq taḥteyhā* ("a spacious place free from restriction"). In 38:18 it is used in a construct form together with *'ereṣ* ("the vast expanses of the earth").

P-B In numerous cases the LXX translates the Heb. vb. *rḥb* with *platynō*, widen/broaden.

NT This G vb., as well as its derivatives (nom. *platos*, adj. *platys*), also occurs in the NT (e.g., Matt 7:13; 23:5; Rev 21:16).

Broad, open, spacious, wide, extensive: → *p'r* (open wide, # 7196); → *ptḥ* I (open, conquer, surrender, set free, loosen, break up, # 7337); → *rwḥ* A (become wide or spacious, be spacious, # 8118); → *rḥb* (open wide, broaden, # 8143)

Bibliography

ABD 1:408-19; 3:308-18; H. M. Barstad, "The Old Testament Feminine Personal Name *rahab*: An Onomastic Note," *SEÅ* 54, 1989, 43-49.

Louis Jonker

8144 (*raḥab*, spacious), → # 8143

8145 (*rōḥab*, width), → # 8143

8146 (*rāḥāb* I, wide, broad, open, extensive), → # 8143

8147 (*rāḥāb*, Rahab), → Rahab [harlot]

8148	רְחֹב

רְחֹב (*r^eḥōb* I), nom. a broad open place, plaza, public square (# 8148); < רחב (*rḥb*), open wide (→ # 8143).

ANE The nom. is derived from the root vb. *rḥb* I, be, grow wide, large (→ # 8143), which is attested in Arab. *raḥiba/raḥuba*, Eth. *rĕḥĕba,* and Aram./Syr. *r^eḥab*., OSA *rḥb*. The nom. is attested in Akk. *rebītu*, Aram. *r^eḥôb*, and Arab. *raḥ(a)bat*. Although *rḥb* occurs in Ugar. it does not seem to be related to this word (*UT*, # 2317).

OT The word refers to a broad open place in a city or village. It was an essential part of a city (Deut 13:16[17]; Dan 9:25), usually near a city gate (2 Chron 32:6; Neh 8:1, 3, 16; Job 29:7) and interconnected with its streets (S of Songs 3:2 ‖ *šûq*; Jer 5:1; 9:21[20]). It was used for various public and private purposes such as: (a) public assemblies (2 Chron 29:4; 32:6; Ezra 10:9; Neh 8:1, 3); (b) public proclamations (Esth 6:9, 11); (c) public speeches (Prov 1:20); (d) public lamentations (Esth 4:6, cf. vv. 1-3; Ps 144:14; Isa 15:3; Jer 48:38; Amos 5:16); (e) social life (Prov 5:16; 7:12; Zech 8:4, 5); (f) a public encampment where travelers could lodge (Gen 19:2; Judg 19:15, 17, 20); (g) public hanging of enemies and criminals (2 Sam 21:12); (h) public inquiry (Jer 5:1); (i) a location for pagan shrines and high places (Ezek 16:24, 31); (j) public celebration of the Feast of Tabernacles (Neh 8:16); (k) public service by important individuals (Job 29:7); (l) and figuratively of a place representative of public opinion (Ps 55:11[12]; Isa 59:14). BDB suggests that Nah 2:4[5] uses *r^eḥōb* of an open place *outside* the city, but the context does not support this, as the versions indicate.

At times the word seems to refer simply to city streets (Prov 22:13; 26:13; Jer 49:26; 50:30; Lam 2:11-12; 4:18).

P-B The nom. is used in the QL and postbiblical Heb. with essentially the same meaning.

City, village, country: → *ḥûṣ* (outside, street, # 2575); → *ḥāṣēr* (enclosure, court, settlement, village, # 2958); → *kāpār* (village, # 4107); → *māqôm* (place, town, site, dwelling place, holy place, # 5226); → *miqlāṭ* (city of refuge, asylum, # 5236); → *'îr* I (city, town, # 6551); → *p^e rāzôn* (fertile field, # 7251); → *qiryâ* (town, city, # 7953); → *r^e ḥōb* I (broad open place, plaza, # 8148); → *šûq* (street [in a town], # 8798)

BIBLIOGRAPHY
TWOT 2:841; M. Dahood, *Psalms II*, AB, 33.

James D. Price

8154 (*r^e ḥab'ām*, Rehoboam), → Rehoboam

8157 (*raḥûm*, compassionate), → # 8163

8158 (*rāḥôq*, distant, remote, far off, long ago), → # 8178

8161 (*raḥēl* I, ewe lamb), → # 7366

8163	רחם

רחם (*rḥm*), denom; q. love (dubious hapleg.); pi. have compassion; pu. be shown compassion (# 8163); רַחוּם (*raḥûm*), adj. compassionate (# 8157); רֶחֶם (*reḥem*), nom. womb (# 8167); רַחֲמִים (*raḥ^a mîm*), compassion (intensive pl.) (# 8171); and רַחֲמָנִי (*raḥ^a mānî*), adj. compassionate (hapleg., # 8172).

ANE The words in this group are all derived from the nom. *reḥem*, womb (→ # 8167). Words found in cognate languages show a connection between "womb" and "compassion." See BDB, 933, *HALAT* 1134-35.

OT 1. In the OT *reḥem/raḥam* is often used in parallel with *beṭen* (belly, body, womb; → *beṭen*; # 1061). Both words are used metaphorically, but the range of meanings is different. The root *rḥm* and its derivatives belong to the realm of grace and hope, expressing someone's willingness to show favor.

(a) The singular *reḥem/raḥam* may always be translated womb, even though it often has a further significance. For example, the phrase "open the womb" is used to describe Leah's and Rachel's giving birth after a period of distress (Gen 29:31; 30:22), and in an expression denoting the firstborn (Exod 13:2, 12, 15; 34:19). "From the womb" indicates the very beginning of a person's existence (Job 3:11; Ps 22:9[11]; 58:3[4]; Jer 1:5; 20:17-18). A closed womb is a serious judgment or misfortune and a miscarrying womb may be a curse (Gen 20:18; 1 Sam 1:5-6; Hos 9:14). (Male infertility is not much discussed in the OT.)

(b) The "womb" carries with it a picture of the tender care bestowed on an infant when it is most vulnerable. Possibly the significance of Job 24:20, "the womb forgets them" (an assertion of the three friends, which Job rejects), is that the wicked are in such a bad state that even their own mothers, who have the most involved concern for them, forget them. See further # 8167.

2. In any case it is easy to see the transition from the literal "womb" to the meaning of the pl. nom. *raḥ^a mîm*, compassion.

(a) In 1 Kgs 3:26 a prostitute, who was the real mother, showed her love for the child at risk, i.e., "her compassion grew warm (*kmr*) over her son" (cf. NIV, was filled with compassion for her son, and NRSV, her heart yearned for her son). This nom. and vb. (*kmr*) combination also occurs in Gen 43:30, where we are told that Joseph's compassion grew warm toward his brother Benjamin, so that, to avoid being overcome by emotion in the presence of his brothers, he rushed out to his own chamber to weep. Hosea gives an anthropomorphic picture of God's love in similar terms: "How can I give you up, O Ephraim ... My heart is changed within me, all my compassion (*niḥûmāy*) is aroused (*kmr,* lit. grows warm)" (Hos 11:8). Though *rḥm* does not occur here, the roots *rḥm* and *nḥm* are semantically parallel. The nom. *niḥûm* occurs in two other places, also in the pl., with the meaning "comfort" (Isa 57:18; Zech 1:13).

(b) Clearly *raḥ*^{a}*mîm* signifies emotion. It frequently occurs with other synonyms. In Isa 63:15 it is parallel to *h*^{a}*môn mē'eykā* (lit. "murmur of your inward parts"). The prophet complains that God's zeal and other signs of his emotional involvement with his people are withheld. In Jer 16:5 Jeremiah is commanded not to enter the house of mourning to identify with and to comfort the mourner because Yahweh has taken away his "blessing ... love and ... pity."

(c) Often *raḥ*^{a}*mîm* is contrasted with anger, for example, in the reference to Edom "stifling all compassion, because his anger raged continually and his fury flamed unchecked" (Amos 1:11). Zech 1:2 puts great stress on the anger of God with the fathers: the root *qṣp* occurs as the first and last words of this brief verse. The climax of the chapter is reached in vv. 12-17. How long is there to be anger and no mercy? The Lord's anger is now turned upon the nations, and he has returned to Jerusalem with compassion. Compare also Ps 77:9[10]; 79:8.

(d) *raḥ*^{a}*mîm* is used to signify something that goes beyond what ought to be given (→ *ḥws*, # 2571). So Jacob sends his sons back to Joseph with Benjamin, praying without assurance that God may "grant (them) mercy before the man" (Gen 43:14). In 2 Sam 24:14 David chooses to put himself in God's hands and hope for the best, because "his mercy is great." The same situation occurs when Israel has fallen into sin and turns to Yahweh in repentance (1 Kgs 8:50). In Ps 51:1[3] the ground of the prayer for forgiveness is "your great compassion" (*rōb raḥ*^{a}*meykā*, in parallel to "your unfailing love," *ḥasdekā*).

(e) It is noteworthy that God often gives a person *raḥ*^{a}*mîm* in the sight of another (more powerful) person (Neh 1:11; Ps 106:46; Dan 1:9). As with the vb. *ḥnn*, God is said to "give compassion" (Gen 43:14; Jer 42:12). In Ps 106:46 Yahweh gives *raḥ*^{a}*mîm* to Israel before their captors, and in Dan 1:9, to Daniel in the sight of the chief eunuch.

(f) The basic meaning of the root is made clear by these examples. It signifies a warm compassion, a compassion which goes the second mile, which is ready to forgive sin, to replace judgment with grace. It is found with words from other significant roots (*ḥsd*, be faithful [→ # 2874]; *ḥnn*, be gracious to [→ # 2858]; *nḥm*, comfort [→ # 5714]).

3. The adj. *raḥûm* carries the same nuances. In eleven of its thirteen occurrences it is linked with *ḥannûn*, gracious, often as part of a long liturgical formula that spells out the divine attributes: "the compassionate (*raḥûm*) and gracious (*ḥannûn*) God, slow to anger, abounding in love and faithfulness" (Exod 34:6; Ps 86:15; 103:8; and with the first two adjectives reversed: Neh 9:17; Ps 145:8; Joel 2:13; Jon 4:2; cf. the shorter formulas in Neh 9:31; 2 Chron 30:9; Ps 111:4; 112:4). Deut 4:30-31 envisages repentance in exile and concludes, "You will return to the LORD your God and obey him. For the LORD your God is a merciful (*raḥûm*) God."

These are mostly liturgical formulas, yet they retain their force. The piling up of words expressing related ideas gives emphasis to the picture of Israel's God who forgives and saves, who hangs on to his people even when they have consistently rebelled against him and have broken the covenant he had graciously made with them.

4. *raḥ^{a}mānî* occurs only in Lam 4:10: "With their own hands compassionate women have cooked their own children" (cf. *raḥ^{a}mîm*, 1 Kgs 3:26 above).

5. The vb. *rḥm* is usually found in pi. (39x) and pu. (4x). There is one doubtful occurrence of the q. in Ps 18:1[2], "I love you, O LORD"; the verse does not appear in the parallel in 2 Sam 22. The vb. could easily be emended to pi., but it would be without parallel for a person to say this to God.

(a) The most common use for this vb. is of God as either having compassion (Exod 34:19; Deut 13:17; 30:3; 2 Kgs 13:23; Isa 14:1) or not having compassion (Isa 27:11) on his people. In the latter case its use shows the seriousness of Israel's plight in that "their Maker has no compassion (*rḥm*) on them, and their Creator shows them no favor (*ḥnn*)." Yet the compassionate God cannot leave his people in a state of alienation. This is the message of hope given by the prophets. For example, Jeremiah proclaimed, "Is not Ephraim my dear son, the child in whom I delight? Though I often speak against him, I still remember him. Therefore my heart yearns for him; I have great compassion (*rḥm*) for him" (Jer 31:20). The book of Zechariah encourages the postexilic community to keep their hope fixed on Yahweh: "I will strengthen the house of Judah and save the house of Joseph. I will restore them because I have compassion (*rḥm*) on them. They will be as though I had not rejected them, for I am the LORD their God and I will answer them" (Zech 10:6). W. L. Holladay refers to a group of passages in which "return" (*šwb*, → # 8740) is associated with a vb. denoting "covenantal sustaining" (*The Root ŠÛBH in the Old Testament*, 1958, 69). The occasional association of "return"/"restore" with the phrase "in compassion," in both biblical and extrabiblical texts, is noted by R. P. Gordon in K. J. Cathcart, R. P. Gordon, *The Targum of the Minor Prophets Aramaic Bible* 14, 1989, 172.

(b) The vb. *rḥm* is also used of human beings, usually as regards their behavior as conquerors (BDB, 933). Isa 13:18 refers to the Medes who will "have no mercy on infants nor will they look with compassion on children" (cf. Jer 6:23; 21:7; 50:42).

This root and its derivatives goes beyond the realm of legal right into the realm of grace and hope, and dependence on the willingness of another party to show favor.

NT → *NIDNTT* 1:327-29, 567-73; 2:593-601.

Compassion, comfort, consolation: → *ḥws* (pity, look upon with compassion or regret, # 2571); → *ḥml* (spare, have compassion, # 2798); → *ma'^{a}dannîm* (dainties, comfort, delight, # 5052); → *nḥm* (be sorry, comfort, have compassion, repent, # 5714); → *'gm* (have pity, # 6327); → *rḥm* (love, have compassion, # 8163); → *ta'^{a}nûg* (comfort, delight, enjoyment, # 9503)

BIBLIOGRAPHY

THAT 2:762-67; A. H. Friedlander, "Judaism and the Concept of Forgiving," *Christian Jewish Relations* 19, 1986, 6-13.

Mike Butterworth

8164 (*rāḥām*, osprey), → # 7606

8167	רֶחֶם

רֶחֶם (*reḥem*), womb, a physical organ unique to the female (# 8167) and from which in the Heb. language developed the vb. *rḥm*, have compassion, the nom. *rāḥămîm*, compassion, mercies, and the adj. *raḥûm*, compassionate, merciful; → *rḥm* (# 8163).

ANE Although Akk. distinguishes between two vbs. *ra'āmu*, love (from *r'm*), and *rêmu*, have compassion (from *rḥm)*, in both Heb. and Aram. these two vbs. coalesce as *rḥm*, love, have compassion (Muffs, 132-35, but for a contrary view, cf. Sperling, 149-59). The Ugar. texts (49: II: 27) provide one instance of *rḥm* as girl, maiden, a meaning for Heb. *reḥem* found only in Judg 5:30. Cf. also Arab. *raḥuma*, to be tender, Aram. *raḥmā'*, mother love. In the Aram. inscription from Deir 'Allā (II:13), approximately 750-650 BC, the phrase *'al rḥm* is used as to refer to the fetus enclosed in the mother's body (Müller, 217, 236). Also, both Syr. *raḥmā'* and Arab. *raḥim, riḥm* carry the meaning mother love and compassion.

OT 1. *reḥem* is to be distinguished from *beṭen* (→ # 1061), with which it is often in parallelism (Job 3:11; 10:18, 19; Ps 22:10[11]; 58:3[4]; Isa 46:3; Jer 1:5). The latter refers not specifically to the womb but to the larger abdominal area of the body.

2. *reḥem* is to be distinguished from *mē'îm* (→ # 5055), which does translate as "womb" in Gen 25:23; Ruth 1:11; Ps 71:6; Isa 49:1. The latter also refers not exclusively to the womb but to the stomach, belly (2 Sam 20:10), and frequently to the male reproductive organs (Gen 15:4; 2 Sam 7:12; 16:11).

3. In several instances God sets apart his chosen vessel even while that vessel is still in the mother's womb. This is true of the call of Jeremiah (Jer 1:5) and the chosen servant of the Lord (Isa 49:5). These two calls are the prototype for St. Paul's statement of his own prenatal call to apostolic ministry (Gal 1:15).

4. ANE literature provides similar instances of a divine call from the womb, but restricts such legitimizations to kings. Thus, Shulgi of the Third Dynasty of Ur (ca. 2050 BC) states in a royal hymn, "A king am I; from the womb I have become a hero" (Kramer, 14 n.1). Similarly, Assurbanipal (668-627 BC) claims, "I am Assurbanipal ... whom they (viz., the gods Assur and Sin) formed in his mother's womb for the rulership of Assyria" (Luckenbill 2:291, sec. 765). And from Egypt, the god Amun says to Pianchi, pharaoh of the 25th dynasty (ca. 751-730 BC), "It was in the belly/womb of your mother that I said to you that you were to be ruler of Egypt, it was as seed and while you were in the egg that I knew you, that you were to be Lord" (Gilula, 114).

5. God is both womb closer (Gen 20:18; 1 Sam 1:5, 6) and womb opener (29:31; 30:22). The former action may have a moral explanation (20:18) or simply be a mystery (1 Sam 1:5-6).

6. The frequent phrase "the first offspring of every womb among the Israelites belongs to me," or a variant (Exod 13:2, 12, 15; 34:19; Num 3:12; 8:16; 18:15), demonstrates that it was the firstborn of the mother, provided that it was male, who held sacred status, although inheritance rights were claimed by the firstborn of the father (Deut 21:15-17). Thus, Num 18:15 intentionally used the vb. "offer" (*qrb*) rather than some vb. like "give" (*ntn*) when speaking of bringing the first issue of the womb to Yahweh, for the firstborn of the mother are Yahweh's innate property. The OT appears to say that the firstborn son owes his position to the fact that he was his *father's* first issue, i.e., the first of *the father's* procreative power (Gen 49:3; Deut 21:17; cf.

Ps 78:51; 105:36). Because a husband could have more than one wife, it was *his* first issue that counted rather than the firstborn of any wife. Ultimately, of course, the firstborn was God's, because he was the firstfruits of the marriage.

7. The connection noted above between "womb" and "have compassion," a vb. for which often God is the subject, suggests the possibility of a maternal metaphor for God. That is, as a place of care and protection, the womb is a metaphor of divine compassion. Thus, one scholar renders God's words in Jer 31:20, "I have great compassion [*rḥm*] for him, declares the LORD" [NIV]) as, "I will surely have motherly compassion on him, says the LORD" (Trible 368-69; cf. Andersen 473; Carroll, *Jeremiah*, OTL, 1986, 597). This assumes that Jeremiah was aware of the etymological relationship between *rḥm*, have compassion, and *reḥem*, womb, a fact possibly to which nonnative speakers of a language would be more sensitive than would native speakers (Gruber, 5 & n.6). Also, we may note that if indeed the prophet is saying that Yahweh will exercise motherly compassion, he is not thereby insinuating that he believes Yahweh to be mother. In fact, there is no text anywhere in the OT that uses the metaphor "Mother" for God as it does "Father." When female imagery is used for God, it takes the form of simile (which compares one characteristic of something to another [God's compassion and a mother's compassion are like each other]), rather than metaphor (which compares the totality of one thing to the totality of another thing; see Achtemeier, 19). (→ *rḥm* [love, have compassion, # 8163; *raḥûm*, compassionate, # 8157; *reḥem*, womb, # 8167; *raḥ^{a}mîm*, compassion, # 8171; *raḥ^{a}mānî*, compassionate, # 8172].)

P-B Charlesworth's concordance lists abundant examples of *rḥm* in the DSS. Jastrow 2:1467 notes some interesting occurrences in Jewish literature. See also *NIDNTT* 1:169, 667-69.

Womb: → *reḥem* (mouth of the womb, # 8167); → *mašbēr* (breach, # 5402)
Birth, conception, pregnancy: → *hrh* (be pregnant, conceive, # 2225); → *ḥyl* I (be in labor, tremble, # 2655); → *yld* (bear, bring forth, be borne, # 3528)

BIBLIOGRAPHY

THAT 2:762, 765-66; *TWOT* 2:841-43; E. Achtemeier, "Why God Is Not Mother," *CT*, Aug 16, 1993, 17-23; B. Anderson, "'The Lord Has Created Something New': A Stylistic Study of Jer 31:15-22," *CBQ* 40, 1978, 463-78; M. Dahood, "Denominative *riḥḥam*, 'To Conceive, Enwomb,'" *Bib* 44, 1963, 204-5; M. Gilula, "An Egyptian Parallel to Jeremiah 1:4-5," *VT* 17, 1967, 114; R. Gordis, "More on *mrḥm bn bṭnh* (Isa 49:15)," *Tarbiz* 53, 1983-84, 137-38; M. I. Gruber, "Can a Woman Forget Her Sucking Child?," *Tarbiz* 51, 1981-82, 491-92; idem, *The Motherhood of God and Other Studies*, 1992; J. Kegler, "Beobachtungen zur Körpererfahrung in der hebräischen Bibel," in *Was ist der Mensch...? Beitrage zur Anthropologie des Alten Testaments. Hans Walter Wolff zum 80. Geburtstag*, 1992, 28-41; S. N. Kramer, "The Oldest Literary Catalogue," *BASOR* 88, 1942, 10-19; D. Luckenbill, *Ancient Records of Assyria and Babylon*, 1927, rep. 1967; H.-P. Müller, "Die aramäische Inschrift von Deir 'Alla und die älteren Bileamsprüche," *ZAW* 94, 1982, 214-44; Y. Muffs, *Studies in the Aramaic Legal Papyri from Elephantine*, 1969; S. D. Sperling, "Biblical *rḥm* I and *rḥm* II," *JANESCU* 19, 1989, 149-59; P. Trible, "God, Nature of, in the OT," *IDBSup* 368-69.

Victor Hamilton

8168 (*rāḥāmâ*, osprey), → # 7606

8171 (*raḥ^{a}mîm*, compassion), → # 8163

8172 (*raḥ^{a}mānî*, compassionate), → # 8163

8173	רחף

רחף (*rḥp*), q. shake, tremble; pi. hover (# 8173).

ANE The etymology is debated. An Egyptian original for the expression in Gen 1:2 has been proposed. In Ugar. *rḥp*, applied to a winged goddess, means to honor. The Syr. *r^{e}ḥep* means to brood, protect.

OT *rḥp* appears only 3x in the OT (pi., Gen 1:2; Deut 32:11; q., Jer 23:9) In Gen 1:2 it describes the activity/location of the Spirit of God in relationship to the primeval waters at the outset of the creative ordering of this world. The Song of Moses in Deut 32:11 employs this same vb. to depict the *hovering* movement of an eagle. This eagle metaphor describes the theophanic presence of Yahweh, the pillar of cloud by day and fire by night, as he led Israel through the barren wilderness. In both instances *rḥp* characterizes the activity of the Spirit of God, the first with regard to the creation of the cosmos and the second with regard to the creation of a people. In Jeremiah *rḥp* is used to describe the trembling of a drunken man (Jer 23:9). This metaphor is applied to the prophet himself as one who has experienced the judicial presence of the Lord, received his holy word, and subsequently trembles as a human participant in this wholly divine phenomenon.

M. V. Van Pelt/W. C. Kaiser, Jr.

8175	רחץ

רחץ (*rḥṣ*), q. wash with water, wash off, bathe; pu. be washed; hitp. wash oneself (# 8175); רַחַץ (*raḥaṣ*), nom. wash basin (# 8176); רַחְצָה (*raḥṣâ*), nom. washing (# 8177).

ANE Egyp. *rḫt* and Ugar. *rḥṣ*, wash. Akk. *raḫaṣu*, overflow, is philologically but not semantically cognate.

OT 1. As a routine word for cleansing the body or its parts—hands (Job 9:30), face (Gen 43:31), feet (19:2)—the vb. is found in several narratives. The courtesy of washing the guest's feet belonged to hospitality (Gen 18:4; 24:32; 43:24; Judg 19:21). Hospitality was an expression of faithfulness to God (Isa 58:7), and failure to extend it amounted to wrongdoing, for which God brought punishment (Deut 23:3-4).

2. Washing or bathing are critical for the plots of several OT narratives. Pharaoh's daughter, while bathing, found Moses, Israel's future deliverer (Exod 2:5). David saw Bathsheba bathing (*rḥṣ*) (2 Sam 11:2); adultery and murder eventually followed. Another story, salvific in nature, is of Naaman, the Syrian captain, whose skin disease (*ṣr'*, suffer from a skin disease; → # 7665) disappeared when he followed the prophet Elisha's instruction to bathe in the Jordan (2 Kgs 5:10).

3. The vb. is frequent in priestly legislation with instructions for the ceremonial washing of priests, and sometimes the washing of parts of the sacrifice (Num 19:7, 8; Lev 1:9, 13; 9:14). At their investiture and also on the Day of Atonement priests were to wash their bodies (Exod 29:4; Lev 8:6; 16:4, 24, 26). Before stepping to the altar or into the tent of meeting, priests were to wash hands and feet on penalty of death

(Exod 30:19-21). Lavers for the tabernacle (30:18) and a brass "Sea" in Solomon's temple (2 Chron 4:6) facilitated the ritual. Such washing rituals were not only obedient responses to God (Exod 40:32), but reinforced the requirement for cleanness of those ministering in worship.

4. Ceremonial washings readmitted "unclean" persons into the community. Skin disorders represented departures from the normal. Holiness was "symbolized by wholeness" (G. Wenham, *Leviticus*, 203, 212). The return to the community of quarantined persons required priestly inspection, sacrifice, and body bathing (one-fifth of the 70 occurrences of the vb. cluster in Lev 14-15). Men and women with discharges (sexually related or otherwise) or who had cohabited were regarded as unclean, and though not removed from the community, were required to wash and to wait for specified periods before participating in divine worship at the tabernacle (e.g., 15:27, 31).

5. In poetry especially the ceremonial washings became metaphors for cleansing from sin. The washing of one's hands was a declaration of innocence (Ps 26:6; 73:13; cf. Deut 21:6). Isaiah protested his uncleanness by urging, "Wash and make yourselves clean" (Isa 1:16). By this he meant, "Eradicate evil and wrongdoing." The sage Agur wrote of people who think of themselves as pure but who "are not cleansed (*rḥṣ*) of their filth" (Prov 30:12; cf. Job 9:30; Acts 22:16).

6. Washings were sometimes of a cosmetic nature (S of Songs 5:12) and were preparatory to love-making (S of Songs 4:2; 5:3; cf. Ruth 3:3).

P-B In the Qumran community, full members engaged in a daily rite of washing in one of the larger cisterns, in order to cleanse the body by water and the heart by the Holy Spirit (1QS 3:2-9). Baths were also taken before the common meal.

Wash, washing: → *bōr* II (potash, # 1342); → *dwḥ* (rinse, # 1866); → *ṭbl* I (immerse, # 3188); → *kbs* (wash, pound, # 3891); → *neter* (nitre, # 6003); → *rḥṣ* (wash, # 8175); → *šeleg* II (soapwort, # 8921)

BIBLIOGRAPHY

NIDNTT 1:144, 151, 225; *TDNT* 4:300-302; *TWOT* 2:843; G. Wenham, *The Book of Leviticus*, 1979.

Elmer A. Martens

8176 (*raḥaṣ*, wash basin), → # 8175

8177 (*raḥṣâ*, washing), → # 8175

8178	רחק

רחק (*rḥq*), q. be distant, remote (29x); ni. be removed (hapleg., Eccl 12:6 [K: *yirḥaq*; Q: *yērāḥēq*]; + Mic 7:11?); pi. make distant, removed (4x); hi. put away, remove (24x) (58x for vb.; # 8178; *HALAT* 1139a-40a); מֶרְחָק (*merḥāq*), nom. distant place, distance (18x; # 5305; *HALAT* 599b-600a); רָחוֹק (*rāḥôq*), adj. distant, remote, far off, long ago (85x; # 8158; *HALAT* 1133a-34b); רָחֵק (*rāḥēq*), stative adj. being/keeping distant, far (hapleg., Ps 73:27; # 8179; *HALAT* 1140a).

ANE Semitic cognates of the vb. include Akk. *rêqu(m)*, be far, become distant, remove oneself (*AHw* 2:971a-72a); Ugar. *rḥq*, be distant, withdraw (*WUS* # 2505; *UT* # 2324; *CML*[2] 157b); Ancient Aram. *rḥq*, be distant (*DISO*, 278-79); OSA (Sab.) *rḥq*, be distant, removed (*CIS*, 4, # 95, # 98; Conti Rossini, 240); Eth. *reḥeqa*, be distant, remote (*LLA* 271-72); and Tigre *raḥaqa*, become distant, remove oneself. In Arab., the vb. and its derivatives have been displaced almost entirely by the root *bʿd*, be distant, far off; II, remove, banish (Wehr, 65b-66b).

Nom. cognates may be found in the Ugar. nom. *mrḥq/mrḥqt,* distance (with enclitic *m*, *mrḥqm/mrḥqtm*, from afar [so *WUS* # 2505; *UT* # 2324; Aartun, *UF* 14, 1982, 3]; in future [so Dietrich-Loretz, 172, line 31]); the Egyp. Aram. nom. *mrḥq*, renunciation (*DISO*, 168); the Aram. nom. *rḥq*, separation (attested at Deir ʿAlla; *ATDA* 218, 307); the Arab. nom. *raḥīqun*, exotic/imported wine, nectar (Fraenkel, 158; Wehr, 331a); the Eth. nom. *reḥeq/reḥqat*, distance, interval (*LLA* 271); and the Tigre nom. forms *reḥeq* and *merḥāq*, separation (*TigrWb* 146-47).

Cognates related to the adj. appear in the Akk. adj. forms *rēqu(m)* and *rūqu(m)*, far (*AHw* 2:971a, 995); *rēqēnum*, from afar; and the locative/adv. forms *rēqiš*, far away, and *rūqiš*, from afar (*AHw* 2:971a, 995a); the Ugar. adj. *rḥq*, far, distant (*WUS* # 2505; *CML*^{2} 157b); the Ammonite adj. *rḥq*, long, in the expression *šnt rḥqt*, long year (inscription from Tell Siran, line 8; cf. Loretz, *UF* 9, 1977, 169-71); the Phoen. adj. *rḥq*, distant, in the expression *drkm rḥqm*, distant roads (inscription from Byblos; cf. Röllig in Degen-Müller-Röllig, 2, line 3); the Ancient Aram. adj. *rḥyq*, distant, alienated (*DISO*, 279); the OSA (Sab.) adj. *rḥq*, far (Biella, 486); the Eth. adj. *reḥūq*, remote, distant (*LLA*, 272); and the Tigre adj. *reḥūq*, far.

OT 1. As in Akk. and Ugar., the Heb. root *rḥq*, be distant, remote, may be used with either spatial or temporal significance, though the Heb. vb. itself tends to be used mainly in the spatial sense. Obvious spatial usages of the vb. include those that refer to distances to/from places, whether they be specified locations (Exod 33:7; Josh 3:16; Ezek 8:6; 11:15 [where *yhwh* stands metonymically for the land of his habitation]) or unspecified locations (Deut 12:21; 14:24, referring to some place [*māqôm*] too distant). The spatial sense applies even to persons, as when "all a poor man's relatives hate him, so surely his friends keep distant (*rāḥ*^{a}*qû*) from him" (Prov 19:7a, author's tr.), and sometimes the vb. may be used to indicate someone's complete absence: "Far from me is (*rāḥaq mimmennî*) any comforter, any restorer of my soul" (Lam 1:16a, author's tr.). In the sense of abstaining from something, the vb. appears in Exod 23:7a: "You shall keep away from the false charge" (author's tr.; cf. also Eccl 3:5). In an example of the vb. being used of cultic separation, Ezekiel denounces the Levites who went far (*rāḥ*^{a}*qû*) from Yahweh through their idolatry (Ezek 44:10; cf. Jer 2:5).

2. The nom. form *merḥāq*, distant place, distance, occurs often together with the nom. *'ereṣ*. For example, as part of a threat against the nations that attack God's people (Isa 8:9-10), Isa 8:9 speaks of distant lands (*merḥaqqê-'āreṣ*, lit., distances of land) being shattered militarily. The nom. is used in a (non)salvific sense in Ps 138:6: "Though Yahweh is on high, he attends to the lowly; but the haughty he knows only from a distance (*mimmerḥāq*)" (author's tr.).

3. The adj. *rāḥôq*, distant, remote, far off, may signify a relationship of distance that is either spatial or temporal.

(a) Used spatially, the adj. appears in Gen 22:4, where Abraham sees from afar (*mērāḥôq*) the place where Isaac should be offered up. Similarly, in Josh 9:6, the Gibeonites speak of their homeland as a distant country (*'ereṣ r*^{e}*ḥôqâ*).

(b) Temporal uses of the adj. may indicate either the distant past (*mērāḥôq*, [from] long ago, in Isa 22:11b; 25:1) or the distant future. Referring to the distant past, Yahweh declares: "Have you not heard? Long ago (*lᵉmērāḥôq*) I ordained it. In days of old I planned it" (Isa 37:26 [= 2 Kgs 19:25]). Correspondingly, an example of the adj. referring to the future may be found in David's response to the words of Yahweh's covenant with him: "You have spoken about the [distant] future (*lᵉmērāḥôq*, lit., from afar) of the house of your servant" (2 Sam 7:19 [= 1 Chron 17:17]).

(c) In other contexts the adj. may form part of a portrayal of God or his affairs as being in or emanating from the distance. In such theological contexts one frequently finds *rāḥôq*, distant (sometimes contrasted with *qārôb*, near), referring alternatively to Yahweh's revelation, transcendence, salvation, or proximity as mediated by the cult (cf. Lemke). Referring to Yahweh's revelation, the negated adj. appears in Deut 30:11-14 in parallelism with the adj. *qārôb*, near: "For this commandment that I am giving you today is neither too difficult nor too remote (*rᵉḥōqâ*) for you. It is neither in heaven ... nor is it beyond the sea.... Rather, the word is very near (*qārôb*) you, in your mouth and in your heart, so that you may perform it" (author's tr.). The context speaks of the accessibility of God's covenant stipulations.

In regard to the transcendence of Yahweh's abode, the psalmist declares: "You know when I sit and when I rise; you perceive my thoughts from afar (*mērāḥôq*)" (Ps 139:2; cf. Job 36:3). The MT of Jer 23:23-24 conforms to this notion of Yahweh's transcendence (and hence, omniscience): "'Am I a god nearby (*miqqārōb*)?' declares Yahweh, 'and not a god far off (*mērāḥōq*)? Can anyone hide in hidden places and I not find him?' declares Yahweh. 'Do I not fill both heaven and earth?' declares Yahweh" (author's tr.). In context, this passage affirms Yahweh's transcendent knowledge of Judah's sinfulness, a sinfulness ignored by Jeremiah's rivals, who also claim access to Yahweh's council (vv. 16-22; cf. Lemke, 553-55). Remarkably, by ignoring the interrogative, the LXX of Jer 23:23 reverses Yahweh's claim: "I am a god nearby, says the Lord, and not a god far off," so as to make the theological point—one that conforms to the deuteronomic notion of the proximity of Yahweh's revelation—that Yahweh is indeed at hand in the form of his word to the prophet Jeremiah (cf. Lemke, 551-53, 555).

In Ps 22:1[2], the psalmist uses the adj. in a (non)salvific sense, complaining: "My God, my God! Why have you forsaken me? Far (*rāḥôq*) from my salvation are the words of my groaning!" (author's tr.), which suggests that the psalmist senses alienation either from deliverance or, as seems more likely, from his deliverer (by metonymy of effect for cause) (cf. v. 2[3]: "O my God, I cry out by day, but you do not answer, by night, and am not silent"; v. 11[12], "Do not be far [*'al-tirḥaq*] from me, for trouble is near and there is no one to help"; v. 19a[20a], "But you, O LORD, be not far off [*'al-tirḥāq*]"). Although the B-colon of v. 1[2] is usually read as continuing the erotesis: "[Why are you so] far from saving me, [so far from] the words of my groaning?" (cf. NAB, NIV, NRSV, REB), the tradition of supplying this stepwise ellipsis in translation is not required to make sense of the Heb. colon.

(d) Often in the OT the adj. is used in contexts where the notion of distance is cultic in nature. An example that compares the spatial use of the adj. with a cultic use of the hi., meaning remove, appears in Ps 103:12a: "as far (*kirḥōq*) as the east is from the west, [so far] has he removed (*hirḥîq*) our trangressions from us."

(e) An example of the adverbial use of *rāḥôq* occurs in Prov 31:10: "A noble wife who can find? Yea, far (*rāḥōq*) above jewels is her value" (author's tr.).

4. The stative adj. *rāḥēq*, being/keeping distant, is attested only in Ps 73:27-28a, where its usage clearly relates to cultic conformity (‖ *kōl-zôneh*, anyone whoring/apostatizing): "Those who remain far from you (*rᵉḥēqeykā*) will perish; you destroy anyone who goes awhoring from you (*kōl-zôneh mimmekkā*). But for me, the nearness (*qirᵃbat*) of God is to my benefit" (author's tr.).

P-B Postbiblical Heb. witnesses the vb. *rḥq*, be distant, removed (Jastrow, 1469a-b). The DSS also attest usage of the vb. (*KQT* 204). Other postbiblical cognates of the vb. include Jewish Aram. *rᵉḥēq*, be distant, removed (Jastrow, 1469b); and Syr. *rᵉhaq*, become distant (*LexSyr* 725; J. Payne Smith, *A Compendious Syriac Dictionary*, 1903, 538a-b).

Postbiblical Heb. retains the nom. *merḥāq*, distance (Jastrow, 841b). Other cognates of the nom. include the Jewish Aram. nom. *mᵉraḥᵃqā'*, abomination (Jastrow, 841b), and nom. *rᵉḥûqâ*, alienation (Jastrow, 1465b); and the Syr. nom. forms *rūḥqā'*, distance, antiquity; *rᵉḥūqyā'*, renunciation; and *raḥīqūtā'*, remoteness, separation, immunity (Payne Smith, 534a, 537a).

The postbiblical Heb. adj. *rāḥôq* sustains the sense of distant, removed (Jastrow, 1465b). Other cognates of the adj. include the Jewish Aram. adj. *mᵉrāḥaq*, abominable, unclean (Jastrow, 841b); and the Syr. adj. *raḥīq*, far off, remote (Payne Smith, 537a).

Removal, banishment, scattering, expulsion: → *brḥ* II (drive away, injure, # 1369); → *grš* I (banish, drive out, divorce, # 1763); → *dbr* I (turn/drive away, # 1818); → *hgh* II (separate, remove, # 2048); → *ḥlṣ* (remove, make strong, # 2741); → *ḥrm* I (banish, devote to the ban, # 3049); → *ygh* II (carry off, # 3325); → *yrš* I (take possession of, be dispossessed, drive out, destroy, # 3769); → *ndh* (exclude, # 5612); → *ndḥ* I (banish, be scattered, be cast out, seduce, # 5615); → *nšl* (slip off, drop, clear away, # 5970); → *rḥq* (be distant, remote, # 8178)

BIBLIOGRAPHY

THAT 2:768-71; *TWAT* 7:490b-96b; *TWOT* 2:843b-44b; K. Aartun, "Präpositionale Ausdrücke im Ugaritischen als Ersatz für semitisch *min*: Eine kontrastive und sprachgeschichtliche Analyse," *UF* 14, 1982, (1-14) 3; idem, *Die Partikeln des Ugaritischen I*, AOAT 21/1, 1974, 12 (on the Ugar. subst.); K. Conti Rossini, *Chrestomathia arabica meridionalis epigraphica*, 1931, 240; M. Dahood, "Hebrew-Ugaritic Lexicography X," *Bib* 53, 1972, (386-403) 387-88; R. Degen, W. W. Müller, and W. Röllig, *Neue Ephemeris für semitische Epigraphik*, 2, 1974; M. Dietrich and O. Loretz, "Beschriftete Lungen- und Liebermodelle aus Ugarit," *Ugaritica* 6, 1969, (165-79) 172, line 31; S. Fraenkel, *Die aramäischen Fremdwörter im Arabischen*, 1886, 158; P. Fronzaroli, "[Review of] *Ugaritica VI* ... Paris 1969," *JSS* 16, 1971, (214-21) 216 (Italian); A. L. Kristensen, "Ugaritic Epistolary Formulas: A Comparative Study of the Ugaritic Epistolary Formulas in the Context of the Contemporary Akkadian Formulas in the Letters from Ugarit and Amarna," *UF* 9, 1977, (143-58) 148 (on the Ugar. subst.); W. E. Lemke, "The Near and the Distant God: A Study of Jer 23:23-24 in Its Biblical Theological Context," *JBL* 100, 1981, 541-55; O. Loretz, "Die ammonitische Inschrift von Tell Siran," *UF* 9, 1977, 169-71; S. E. Loewenstamm, *Comparative Studies in Biblical and Ancient Oriental Literatures*, AOAT 204, 1980, 246-48 (on the Ugar. subst.); H. Preisker, μακράν, μακρόθεν," in *Theologisches Wörterbuch zum Neuen Testament*, ed. G. Kittel and G. Friedrich, 10 vols., 1932-1979, 4:372-74; ET: *TDNT* 4:372-74.

Robert H. O'Connell

8179 (*rāḥēq*, far), → # 8178

8180	רחשׁ

רחשׁ (*rḥš*), be stirred up [hapleg.] (# 8180); מַרְחֶשֶׁת (*marḥešet*), pan (→ # 5306).

ANE Aram. *rḥš* means to move, stir oneself, as does Syr. and Sam. *r^eḥeš*. Cf. also Arab. *raḥaša*, be aroused.

OT Ps 45:1[2], a psalm written in praise of a king on his wedding day relates, "My heart is stirred (*rḥš*) by a noble theme as I recite my verses for the king...." Cf. the translation of H.-J. Kraus (*Psalms 1-59*, 1988, 450), "My heart overflows about good news...." M. J. Dahood (*Psalms*, AB, 1966, 1:270) understands *rḥš* as a metathetic form of *ḥrš* II (engrave, work metal), but here, compose, improvise. Dahood renders the Heb., "My heart has composed a sweet melody."

Stirring, tossing: → *grš* II (toss up, # 1764); → *ḥmr* II (foam, surge, # 2812); → *swk* I (stir up, # 6056); → *'wr* II (stir oneself, # 6424); → *rḥš* (be stirred up, # 8180)

Victor P. Hamilton

8181	רַחַת

רַחַת (*raḥat*), winnowing shovel (# 8181).

ANE *raḥat* is related to Ugar. *rḥtm*, handmills, and Arab. *rāḥat*, winnowing shovel, see *HALAT* 1140.

OT *raḥat* occurs only in Isa 30:24, where it is paired with *mizreh*. *raḥat* refers to the winnowing shovel used in the second stage of winnowing, as opposed to *mizreh*, a winnowing fork used in the first stage.

Winnow: → *zrh* I (scatter, winnow, # 2430); → *nāpâ* I (sieve, # 5864); → *raḥat* (winnowing shovel, # 8181)

Bibliography

ABD 1:95-98; J. Feliks, "Agricultural Implements in Ancient Ereṣ Israel," *EJ*, 1971; S. Paul and W. Dever, *Biblical Archaeology: Library of Jewish Knowledge*, 1974.

Mark D. Futato

8182	רטב

רטב (*rṭb*), q. be moist (# 8182); רָטֹב (*rāṭōb*), adj. wet (# 8183).

ANE The root *rṭb* is widely attested. Akk. *raṭābu*, be/become moist, fresh; Aram., Arab., Eth., be moist. In Akk., the adj. *raṭbu*, moist, fresh, also occurs.

OT 1. The vb. occurs only in Job 24:8 (q. impf.), in which the poor are said to wander about naked like wild donkeys (cf. 24:5), drenched by mountain rains. The passage refers to the plight of the impoverished, who are reduced to an animal-like state by their unjust oppressors.

2. The adj. *rāṭôb* occurs only in Job 8:16, where a man who forgets God is compared to a "well-watered plant in the sunshine," but withers away when uprooted (8:19). Moisture here symbolizes prosperity in favorable times, like the freshness of a plant in good weather. In biblical use, *rāṭôb* is a veritable synonym for *laḥ* (# 4300), but postbiblical Heb. uses *rāṭôb* almost exclusively in describing plant life, while *laḥ* is used for both plants and liquids.

Wet, moist: → *laḥ* (moist, # 4300); → *rwh* (drink one's fill, drench, # 8115); → *rṭb* (be moist, # 8182); → *rss* I (moisten, # 8272)

Bibliography
M. Pope, *Job*, 1974.

Anthony Tomasino

8183 (*rāṭōb*, wet), → # 8182

8187	רטשׁ

רטשׁ (*rṭš*), 6x, vb. pi. smash/dash to pieces, strike down; pu. be dashed/smashed to pieces (# 8187).

ANE Tg. Aram. *r^{e}ṭaš/r^{e}ṭêš*, abandon, drive out, pa. abandon, scatter, dash to pieces.

OT Without exception the root in BH refers to atrocity committed against people as part of warfare. The details of the atrocity are not clear, but in one text, Isa 13:18, bows accomplish the action. Elsewhere (e.g., 2 Kgs 8:12; Isa 13:16; Hos 13:16[14:1]) the root seems to refer to dashing infants to the ground, an atrocity common in ancient warfare.

P-B *rāṭûš* is attested in Tosefta and Talm., referring to an emigrant or fugitive whose estate is abandoned.

Shattering, breaking, destroying: → *mḥq* (strike, # 4735); → *npṣ* I (break, smash, # 5879); → *pṣṣ* (pulverize, crush, # 7207); → *rṭš* (smash, strike down, # 8187); → *r'ṣ* (shatter, # 8320); → *ršš* (destroy, crushed, # 8406); → *šbr* I (break, shatter, # 8689)

Bibliography
TWOT 2:844.

Gary Alan Long

8188	רִי

רִי (*rî*), nom. moisture (# 8188); < רוה (*rwh*), be saturated, drink one's fill (→ # 8115).

ANE The root is attested in Aram., Arab., and Eth., but the nom. is not attested.

OT The nom. appears only in Job 37:11: "He loads the clouds with moisture (*b^{e}rî*)." The text, however, is possibly defective, since this reading is not supported by the versions. Suggested emendations include *bārād*, hail (→ # 1352), and *bārāq*, lightning (→ # 1389) (see Pope, 282).

Wet, moist: → *laḥ* (moist, # 4300); → *rwh* (drink one's fill, drench, # 8115); → *rṭb* (be moist, # 8182); → *rss* I (moisten, # 8272)

Bibliography
M. Pope, *Job*, 1974.

Anthony Tomasino

8189	ריב

ריב (*ryb*), q. strive, quarrel, conduct a legal suit; hi. contend against (# 8189); nom. יָרִיב (*yārîb* I), adversary (# 3742); מְרִיבָה (*m^e rîbâ* I), strife (# 5312); רִיב (*rîb*), strife, dispute, controversy (case at law) (# 8190); nom. רִיבָה (*rîbâ*), contest, case (# 8191).

ANE The Heb. *ryb* has etymological connections with the Akk. *râbu*, replace, reimburse, but also with the Arab. *rāba*, disturb, upset, disrupt, and Syr. *rāb*, cry, yell.

OT 1. The root *ryb* in both verbal and nominal forms is used to describe a quarrel or strife among humans, though the conflict that is narrated often has theological significance. E.g., in Gen 13:7-8, the nom. forms *rîb* and *m^e rîbâ* are used to describe the conflict between the herdsman of Abraham and Lot. Theologically, this quarrel represents human conflict in the midst of which Yahweh grants his blessing to Abraham (see Coats; cf. Gen 26:20-32).

2. In Prov, the nom. forms *rîb* and *m^e rîbâ* refer to human conflict and the problems it creates. Repeatedly, the admonition of the proverbs is to avoid "strife" (e.g., Prov 17:1, 14; 18:6, 17; 26:17, 21; 30:33; on the theological significance of human conflict in Prov, see von Rad, 74-96, 190-206).

3. In laments of the prophets Jeremiah and Habakkuk, the combination *rîb* and *mādôn* (→ # 4506) describes the prophets' conflicted situation. In the case of Habakkuk, the prophet laments because the Lord does not respond though "there is strife, and conflict abounds" (Hab 1:3). Jeremiah complains that the word of the Lord has made him "a man with whom the whole land strives and contends" (Jer 15:10).

4. In a number of OT texts, particularly within legal codes, *rîb* refers to a dispute to be adjudicated by judges and/or priests (e.g., Exod 23:2, where both NIV and NRSV translate *rîb* as lawsuit; Deut 19:17; 21:5; 25:1, where NIV and NRSV translate *rîb* as dispute). Similarly, in 2 Sam 15:1-6, Absalom adjudicates "complaints" (*rîb*) that people bring to him. Since the form-critical work of Gunkel, it has often been held that such occurrences of *rîb* referred technically to a lawsuit. However, this claim is now disputed (see M. DeRoche and literature cited there; cf. *TWAT* 6:496-501).

5. Particularly in prophetic literature a *rîb* is between Israel and Yahweh. Among the prominent examples are Jer 2:5-9; Hos 2:4-25; 4:1-3; Mic 6:1-8. In each case, the *rîb* of Yahweh leads to a pronouncement of judgment. It has been argued that the use of *rîb* in prophetic texts such as those cited here indicates a technical "prophetic lawsuit" form. However, this is now widely disputed (see DeRoche).

6. Related to Yahweh's *rîb* against Israel are two texts, Ps 103:9 and Isa 57:16, in which Yahweh declares, "I will not accuse (*'ārîb*) forever/always ..." and which develop in context themes of Yahweh's forgiveness, healing, and compassion.

7. In the OT Yahweh is the one who defends the cause (*rîb*, NIV) of God's people and saves them. In these cases, *rîb* implies conflict and imperilment. This use of *rîb* is evident particularly in exilic literature (e.g., Isa 49:25; Mic 7:9) as an expression of hope, and in lament psalms as a petition for God to save (e.g., Ps 35:1; 43:1; 119:154;

cf. Lam 3:58). Ps 74:22 is interesting as a plea to Yahweh to defend his own cause from those who mock him.

8. Even as the OT affirms Yahweh as the defender of Israel's cause, the OT affirms that Israel has an ethical obligation to defend the cause (*rîb*) of persons who are vulnerable. Such affirmations are found in legal traditions (e.g., Exod 23:6), in prophetic literature (e.g., Isa 1:17, 23) and in Wisdom traditions (e.g., Prov 23:11).

9. In Job both nominal and verbal forms of *ryb* are used frequently. In several instances, Job demands to know God's case against him (Job 10:2; 13:8); in other instances there is acknowledgment of the futility of contending with God (9:3; 33:13). In 40:2 God demands an answer from Job, "who contends with the Almighty" to convict him, an answer Job cannot give (see von Rad, 206-26).

Contention, strife, struggle: → *gl'* (break out in a dispute, # 1679); → *grh* (stir up strife, # 1741); → *nṣh* I (struggle, # 5897); → *ptl* (twist, be wily, shrewd, # 7349); → *ryb* (strive, # 8189); → *r^e'ût* II (longing, striving, # 8296); → *śrh* I (contend, struggle, # 8575)

BIBLIOGRAPHY
TWAT 6:496-501; G. Coats, "Lot: A Foil in the Abraham Saga," in *Understanding the Word*, 1985, 113-32; M. De Roche, "Yahweh's *rîb* Against Israel: A Re-assessment of the So-Called 'Prophetic Lawsuit' in Pre-exilic Prophets," *JBL* 102, 1983, 563-74; G. von Rad, *Wisdom in Israel*, 1972.

John M. Bracke

8190 (*rîb*, strife), → # 8189

8191 (*rîbâ*, contest), → # 8189

8193 (*rwḥ* B, smell), → # 8118

8194 (*rêaḥ*, scent), → # 8118

8197	ריק

ריק (*ryq*), hi. empty out, pour out, draw; ho. be poured out (# 8197); רִיק (*rîq*), nom./adj. emptiness, worthlessness, empty, worthless (# 8198); רֵק/רֵיק (*rêq*; *rēq*), nom./adj. empty, unsatisfied, unprincipled, vain (# 8199); רֵיקָם (*rêqām*), adv. empty-handed, without success, without property, without cause (# 8200).

ANE The root *ryq* and its derivatives are well attested in other Sem. languages: Akk. *riāqû*/*râqû*, be empty, *riqû*, empty, idle, *riqussû*, empty-handed; Arab. *rjq*, empty, *rāqa*, pour out; Aram. *rêqā'*/*rêqān*, empty out.

OT 1. The vb., which occurs only in the causative stems (hi. 17x, ho. 2x), basically relates to the idea of emptying. The acc. of the vb. can be either the container that is being emptied (e.g., sacks in Gen 42:35), or the contents of the container (e.g., oil in Zech 4:12; cf. S of Songs 1:3). Clouds pour out rain on the earth (Eccl 11:3). In Isa 32:6, the wicked fool leaves the hungry empty (lit., he empties the soul [*nepeš*] of the hungry).

2. The vb. is used to refer to the literal drawing of swords, i.e., emptying the sword out of the scabbard, in Exod 15:9; Ezek 5:2, 12; 28:7; 30:11 (cf. Ps 35:3). In

Ezek 30:11 there is an interesting wordplay in that Nebuchadnezzar's armies will empty (*ryq*) their swords against Egypt, and then use them to "fill (*ml'*) the land with the slain."

3. More remote from the idea of emptying is the use of the vb. in Gen 14:14 in reference to Abram's calling out of his 318 trained men to pursue his relatives' captors.

4. Metaphorically the vb. is used in Mal 3:10 to refer to how the Lord will pour out a blessing on his repentant people.

5. The dominant note, however, in the figurative usage of the vb. is that of judgment. The psalmist declares that the Lord defeated his enemies by pouring them out "like mud in the streets" (Ps 18:42[43]). In Jer 48:11-12 Moab, a nation that "has been at rest from youth," is referred to as "not poured from one jar to another," i.e., "she has not gone into exile." But the Lord promises to send men against her who will "pour (her) out" (*ṣ'h*) and "empty (*ryq*) her jars," i.e., send her into exile. In Lev 26:33 the Lord promises to "draw out (his) sword" against his own people if they refuse to obey him (cf. Ezek 5:12; 12:14).

6. Of the twelve occurrences of the nom./adj. *rîq*, only once does it refer to a literally physically empty object (Jer 51:34), and even then it serves a metaphorical purpose: "Nebuchadnezzar ... has made us an empty jar." Otherwise it always signifies that which is useless, to no purpose, in vain. In Isa 30:7 the term, in hendiadys with *hebel* (as recognized by the NIV's rendering "utterly useless"), describes the worthlessness of any assistance that Egypt might offer Judah against Babylon. When the Lord sends calamity against Babylon, its people will "exhaust themselves for nothing (*rîq*)" in trying to resist (Jer 51:58; cf. Hab 2:13). Those who plot against the Lord and his Anointed One do so only "in vain" (Ps 2:1; but note Dahood's suggestion that the word here means "troops"). The psalmist complains that he has kept himself pure "in vain" (73:13). The word is used to describe labor that is spent in vain in Lev 26:16, 20; Job 39:16. In Isa 49:4 the servant of the Lord complains that he has labored to "no purpose" (*rîq*); the term occurs here in parallel with *hebel*, vanity (# 2039), and *tôhû*, waste (# 9332). In 65:23 the inhabitants of the new Jerusalem will no longer "toil in vain" (*rîq*). A possible moral connotation attaches to the term in Ps 4:2[3], when the psalmist complains that his enemies love delusions (*rîq*) and seek falsehood (*kāzāb* [# 3942]; NIV's "false gods" is probably reading too much into the text).

7. The nom./adj. *rêq* occurs 14x in the OT, in several instances having approximately the same sense as *rîq*. It is used to describe either the emptiness of physical objects (Gen 37:24; Ezek 24:11; 2 Kgs 4:3) or their worthlessness (Gen 41:27). It refers to physical hunger in Isa 29:8. Moses presses on the Israelites that his words of instruction (*dibrê hattôrâ*) from the Lord are not just empty or idle (*rēq*) words (Deut 32:47). Prov 12:11 and 28:19 warn against those who show lack of judgment in pursuing *rêqîm* (fantasies or delusions).

But in addition to these usages it is also employed to refer to empty persons. In Judg 9:4 Abimelech hires empty and undisciplined men (*'^{a}nāšîm rêqîm ûpōḥ^{a}zîm*, NIV: reckless adventurers) to help him in his attempt to become king. In Judg 11:3 *'^{a}nāšîm rêqîm* (NIV: adventurers) join themselves to Jephthah after he flees from his brothers (in both these cases Dahood argues that *rêqîm* is a term for troops, but he has not been generally followed). In 2 Chron 13:7 *'^{a}nāšîm rêqîm* occurs in apposition to *b^{e}nê b^{e}liyya'al*, sons of Belial, to describe the "worthless scoundrels" (NIV) who gathered around Jeroboam (the text is ambiguous as to whether it was Jeroboam or actually Rehoboam; see R. B. Dillard, 107-8). Michal rebukes David for dancing and exposing himself like "any vulgar fellow" (*'aḥad hārēqîm*, 2 Sam 6:20).

8. The adv. *rêqām* is used 16x in a variety of contexts. Several times it is best translated as empty-handed; the Lord declares that no one is to appear before him *rêqām*, i.e., without an offering (Exod 23:15; 34:20; Deut 16:16). Some understanding of this probably lies behind the Philistines' concern that the ark should not be returned to the Israelites empty (1 Sam 6:3).

(a) When a slave is released in the seventh year, he is not to be sent away *rêqām*, i.e., without provision (Deut 15:13). In Job 22:9 Eliphaz accuses Job of having sent widows away *rêqām*, empty-handed. For similar uses cf. Gen 31:42; Exod 3:21; Ruth 1:21; 3:17; Jer 14:3.

(b) In military contexts it is said of swords, arrows, and skilled warriors that they did not return *rêqām* (2 Sam 1:22; Jer 50:9). Similarly, the Lord declares that his words will not return to him empty, but will achieve the purposes he intended for them (Isa 55:11).

(c) Two ambiguous and possibly distinct uses of the term occur in Psalms. In Ps 7:4[5], the psalmist asserts that he is not guilty of having robbed his foe "without cause" (*rêqām*). Similarly, 25:3 says that those who are "treacherous without excuse (*rêqām*)" will be put to shame. Though most translations and commentaries agree on this rendering, others argue that since (i) *ḥinnām* would have more clearly conveyed the idea of "without cause," and (ii) *rêqām* nowhere else carries this meaning, an understanding of the word's meaning more compatible with its other usages should be sought. For 7:4[5] BDB suggests "those who were my adversaries in vain." Craigie and Tigay retranslate 7:4[5] so that it reads, "if I have repaid my ally with treachery, and rescued his adversary empty-handed"; Dahood renders both passages with the phrase "idle talk."

P-B The root and its derivatives are amply attested in the postbiblical literature and in DSS with basically the same meanings as in the OT. 1QpHab 10:8 in its commentary on Hab 2:12-13 notes how the nations strive in vain (*ryq*). 1QpHab 6:8 uses the vb. to refer to the Kittim who draw (*ryq*) their swords to massacre innocent and helpless peoples.

The LXX uses various words to render the terms. The vb. is most frequently translated by *ekkenoō*. The derivative forms are most frequently rendered by *kenos*.

NT It is possible that the hapleg. *rhaka* (NIV "Raca") in Matt 5:22 is related to the Aram. *rêqā'*, fool, idiot, blockhead, and that both are related to *rêq* (for discussion see *NIDNTT* 1:417-18; *TDNT* 6:973-76).

Worthless, vain: → *hbl* (be worthless, # 2038); → *slh* I (treat as worthless, # 6136); → *ryq* (empty out, pour out, draw, # 8188); → *šw'* (treat badly, # 8735)

Bibliography

NIDNTT 1:417-18, 546-53; 3:659-62; *TDNT* 3:659-62; 6:973-76; *TWOT* 2:846; P. C. Craigie, *Psalms 1-50*, WBC 19, 1983, 96-98, 100; M. J. Dahood, *Psalms 1-50*, AB 16, 1965, 7-8, 40, 42,

154, 156; R. B. Dillard, *2 Chronicles*, WBC 15, 1987, 107-8; J. Tigay, "Psalm 7:5 and Ancient Near Eastern Treaties," *JBL* 89, 1970, 179-80.

Jerry Shepherd

8198 (*rîq*, emptiness, worthlessness, empty, worthless), → # 8197

8199 (*rêq*, empty, unsatisfied, unprincipled, vain), → # 8197

8200 (*rêqām*, empty-handed, without success, without property, without cause), → # 8197

8201	ריר

ריר (*ryr*), q. flow (# 8201); רִיר (*rîr*), nom. saliva, slime (# 8202).

ANE Cf. Syr. *rîrā'*, saliva, mucus; Mish. Heb. and Aram. (*ryr/rîr*), run flow; spittle.

OT 1. The q. verbal form, *rār,* occurs in Lev 15:3. It describes a human disease in which a discharge flows from the body.

2. In 1 Sam 21:13[14] the nom. form occurs. There David acts insane, "letting saliva run down his beard." The nom. also occurs in Job 6:6, a text describing the lack of taste "in the juice of mallows" (Clines, 155, 158). Apparently referring to an unidentified plant (Millard), the "juice" or "slime" from this plant is an organic substance. This fact, as well as the colorless nature of the material, seems to be shared by all three instances of the root.

Dripping, flowing, trickling: → *'ēgel* (drop, # 103); → *dlp* I (drip, # 1940); → *zwb* (flow, # 2307); → *ṭrd* (continuous dripping, # 3265); → *mar* II (drop, # 5254); → *ngr* (flow, gush forth, pour out, # 5599); → *nzl* (flow, trickle, # 5688); → *nṭp* (drip, pour, # 5752); → *'rp* I (drip, # 6903); → *pkh* (trickle, # 7096); → *r^ewāyâ* (overflow, # 8122); → *ryr* (flow, # 8201); → *rss* I (moisten, # 8272); → *r'p* (drip, flow, rain, # 8319)
Spittle, saliva: → *yrq* I (spit, spew, # 3762a); → *rîr* (spittle, juice, slime, # 8202); → *rqq* (spit at, spit, # 8394); → *tōpet* I (spit, # 9531)

BIBLIOGRAPHY
D. J. A. Clines, *Job 1-20*, WBC 17, 1989; A. R. Millard, "What Has No Taste? (Job 6:6)," *UF*, 1969, 1:210.

Richard S. Hess

8202 (*rîr*, saliva, slime), → # 8201

8203 (*rêš*, poverty), → # 8133

8204 (*rōk*, being soft, weak, tender), → # 8216

8205 (*rak*, tender, frail, weak, pampered, tender), → # 8216

8206	רכב

רכב (*rkb*), q. ride/mount (a horse/donkey) (# 8206); מֶרְכָּב (*merkāb*), nom. war chariot park, saddle-seat (# 5323); מֶרְכָּבָה (*merkābâ*), nom. war chariot, chariot (# 5324); רֶכֶב (*rekeb*), nom. chariotry (used collectively for chariots, as well as for charioteers), upper millstone (# 8207); רַכָּב (*rakkāb*), nom. charioteer (driver), horseman (# 8208); רִכְבָּה (*rikbâ*), nom. riding (# 8210); רְכוּב (r^e*kûb*), nom. vehicle, chariot (# 8213).

ANE 1. The vb. *rkb* is well attested in the languages of the ANE. The Ugar. par. is used with the meaning mount or ride. The vb. often occurs in the word combination *rkb ʿrpt* (riding on the clouds), which normally qualifies Baʿal. (Cf. *HALAT* 1147-48 for a discussion of the various possibilities to translate this Ugar. expression; cf. also Ps 68:5, where this expression occurs in Heb. as a qualification of Yahweh.) Cognate forms of the vb. also occur in Akk. *rakābu(m)*, mount a cart/ship, drive a cart, to ride a donkey/horse; in Syr. r^e*keb*, drive, mount; in Palm. *mrkb*, mount, ride a horse; in Mand. *rkb*, mount, ride; in Eth. *räkäbä*, manage something; and in Aram. *rakiba*, ride, mount, drive. The vb. occurs in several languages as part of a personal name, e.g., in Ugar. *rakub-baʿl, ilimarakub*; and in Amor. *Yarkab-*^{d}*/M(Addu)*. In OSA the vb. *rkb* occurs as part of a place name (*rkbn*) and as part of an ethnic name (*rkbyn*).

2. The nom. *merkābâ* has cognates in Ugar. *mrkbt*, Akk. *narkabtu*, in Egyp. *mrkbt* (a further development from the Akk. form), and in Aram./Syr. *markabtâ*. Cognate forms are also attested in the ANE languages for the Heb. nom. *rekeb, rakkāb, rikbâ,* and r^e*kûb*.

OT 1. *General.* James (109) advocates a thorough assessment of the influence the chariot had on the people of the various countries to which it diffused over and above its obvious military uses. He states that it is insufficient to describe the chariot only in terms of the political circumstances, the time and the place in which it developed. A study of the chariot should rather take into account that “the advent of this first of the world’s really very complex mechanisms with the speed and power and magnification of certain human qualities which it brought, (changed) the course of human life and behavior forever more.”

2. *Purpose.* Throughout the ANE chariots/carts were used for different purposes. Although it seems that they were mainly used for military purposes, various texts, reliefs, and archaeological finds bear witness that they also served for hunting (cf. Egyptian depictions in particular), for transportation of people (cf. Gen 46:5—Jacob and his family traveled to Egypt on *ʿ*^{a}*gālôt*, carts [# 6322]; 2 Kgs 5:21—Naaman traveled on a *merkābâ*), on ceremonial occasions (cf. Gen 41:43—Joseph traveled in the Pharaoh’s *merkābâ* to receive honor), or for cultic purposes (cf. 1 Chron 28:18—a *merkābâ* was included among the temple utensils).

However, the main purpose of chariots/carts was to provide mobility in military battle (cf. Yadin, 1963). It served as a mobile firing platform within the battlefield, from which relatively limited firepower could be rushed to and brought to bear on decisive spots in the midst of the fighting. Due to its design, it did not primarily serve as a means of transport from a distant base to the battlefield. Not to be underestimated is its psychological value in battle. Chariots charging into the enemy ranks were employed for their shock value. To fulfil its major function of providing a mobile firing platform in battle, the chariot had to offer speed and maneuverability, as well as stability for the firing of weapons. These prerequisites had to be taken into account in the design (cf. following paragraph). Due to their design chariots could not operate optimally in irregular terrain. They were obviously more efficient in campaigns on flat country and in open plains.

3. *Design and constituting parts.* The needs of maneuverability and stability are contradictory. The first need is best provided by a small and light chariot, while a stable firing platform demands a heavier and more spacious vehicle. Throughout the historical development of the chariot these two rival claims dominated the minds of military designers. Material used for the manufacturing of chariots was mainly wood (special kinds for each part), strips of leather, and various metals. Because of the high technological and manufacturing skills, as well as costly materials, chariots were expensive vehicles (cf. Hauer, 63-73). Therefore Yadin (5) states: "It was not an instrument common to the equipment of all armies. It could be fashioned only by nations commanding rich resources and advanced techniques."

A long history of the technological development of chariots can be traced (for extensive discussions, cf. Yadin, and, in particular, Littauer and Crouwel). The first evidence of wheeled vehicles comes from the site of Uruk in southern Mesopotamia (dating back to the late fourth millennium BC). They were more like sledges with either two rollers or four disk wheels. There is no firm evidence of two-wheelers at this period. However, evidence for both four- and two-wheelers becomes plentiful during the early part of the third millennium BC in Mesopotamia. During this period two types of two-wheelers, each carrying a single person, appear. It was only during the early part of the second millennium BC that a light, two-wheeled, horse-drawn vehicle with spoked wheels, the chariot, evolved and was generally adopted in the Near East. Modifications were performed to earlier two-wheeled versions to provide increased stability and eventually to allow a crew of two to stand abreast. The later second millennium BC provides ample evidence for the widespread use of fast, horse-drawn chariots. Evidence (depiction of the Battle of Kadesh) shows that the Hittites and their Asiatic allies had chariots big enough to permit a third man to stand behind the others. It seems that there was a trend early in the first millennium BC towards a bigger, heavier, and higher-sided chariot. This development probably reflects a modification in the vehicle's military role. More horses (often a team of four, all under yoke) were used to draw a chariot. Some reliefs of this period show that the contemporary chariot design often provided for a crew of four. Illustrations of wagons and carts from the late first millennium BC are rare. During this period chariots are shown in strictly Western Asiatic, chiefly Achaemenid, figured documents and also in Graeco-Persian ones. Evidence of this period shows that the chariot almost completely ceased to function as mobile firing platform during battle. Mounted troops were by now taking over the traditional role of the light, fast chariotry.

Chariots normally carried bow cases and arrows for the archer(s). Javelins or short, light spears could also be used as distance weapons and could serve for thrusting if the chariot was brought to a standstill.

Several parts are associated with carts or chariots (cf. James for an extensive description of chariot fittings from Late Bronze Age Beth Shan). The wheel (*gilgāl* I [# 1651], *'ôpan* [# 236]) also had a long history of development. Initially tree logs were used as rollers underneath sledges. Gradually, however, disc wheels evolved, and eventually spoked wheels (*ḥiššuq* [# 3140]) of various shapes. The design and position of the axle (*seren* I [# 6248]) varied. Initially the wheels were attached to a revolving axle, but later a fixed axle with differentially turning wheels evolved. The position of the axle on a two-wheeled vehicle had an effect on the maneuverability thereof.

4. *Crew.* Initially chariots were designed to carry only a single soldier. However, later designs provided for crews of two (a driver and an archer), three (a driver, an archer and a shield bearer) or even four (with an extra shield bearer). The third soldier in the three-man team was called, in Assyrian, *šalšu rakbu* or *tašlīšu.* Heb. references to *šālîš* (# 8957; e.g., 1 Kgs 9:22 and 2 Kgs 10:25) are then normally taken as the military term for the third man in an Israelite chariot. (Mastin disagrees with this identification. He conjectures that *šālîš* refers to the king's adjutant, who was given this designation because he was "of the third rank.") The driver of a chariot was called *rakkāb* (cf. 1 Kgs 22:34).

5. *Israel.* Although the OT contains numerous references to chariots, there are not even fragmentary remains from Palestine. The only representation of a Palestinian chariot is on an Assyrian relief of the conquest of Lachish by Sennacherib. Textual evidence shows that Israel did not have chariots before the reign of David, albeit a small chariot force. The situation was quite different under Solomon (cf. Hauer), whose army had an extensive chariot arm.

Although different numbers are provided in the OT, it can be assumed that Solomon's total chariot strength was 1400 (cf. 1 Kgs 10:26). Various chariot cities were designed so that horses could be kept. (The stables at Megiddo were once ascribed to Solomon's building efforts, but later archaeological evidence showed that these constructions rather belonged to the time of King Ahab.) The chariotry continued to play a significant military role in the divided kingdom. However, the large chariot forces of the kings of Judah and of Israel in the ninth century became progressively smaller and poorer until, by the end of the century, in the reign of Jehoahaz, son of Jehu, the army numbered only "fifty horsemen, and ten chariots, and ten thousand footmen" (2 Kgs 13:7).

6. *Biblical references.* The most common Heb. word for chariot, used over 100x in the OT, is *rekeb. merkābâ* occurs 44x, *rikbâ* (Ezek 27:20), and *r^ekûb* (Ps 104:3) once each. *merkāb* refers to "chariot" in 1 Kgs 4:26[5:6], but should be understood as "saddle-seat" in Lev 15:9 and S of Songs 3:10. It seems that *ᵃgālâ* rather refers to "wagon/cart" (e.g., Gen 45:19; 1 Sam 6:7; Isa 5:18; Amos 2:13).

There is an interesting biblical reference to chariot wheels in Exod 14:25. Stek investigates the question as to what happened to the wheels of the Egyptian chariots while they were chasing the Israelites through the Reed Sea. He proposes that the spoked wheels of these chariots got jammed in the tall, wet seaweed or reeds, causing them to drag.

Another significant biblical reference is the mentioning of iron chariots in Judg 4:13-16. Littauer and Crowel (*ABD* 1:890) discuss the development of chariotry in the ANE. During the tribal period the Israelites had neither use for nor the means of producing and maintaining chariotry. They also did not have iron at the time. Iron was only introduced to them by the Sea People, who arrived in this part of the world approximately 1100 BC. However, Judg 4:13-16 make clear that the Canaanites already had iron chariots during the tribal period. Because the Israelites had no iron themselves at the time (cf. *CAH* 2/2:516), it may have seemed remarkable to them that Sisera's chariots had some iron components, no matter how small. Even a small amount of iron might have been sufficient for them to categorize the whole vehicle as such.

2 Kgs 2:11-12 describes Elijah's ascension in a fire chariot and horses. H. A. Brongers (*II Koningen, POT*, 1982, 23) is of the opinion that this should be understood as a theophany. In v. 12 the epithet *rekeb yiśrā'ēl ûpārāšayw* is used for Elijah. This is strange, because Elijah was, as far as we know, never involved in military activity. Joash and Elisha also received this epithet. Galling (129-48) advanced the opinion that Elisha was actually called as such, and that Elijah only received it secondarily.

7. *merkābâ mysticism.* The term *merkābâ* is often used as a description of the divine throne-chariot mentioned in Ezekiel's (Ezek 1 and 10) and Isaiah's (Isa 6) visions. From this usage the so-called *merkābâ* mysticism developed. Ezekiel in his visions allowed the development of a mystical theosophy. This developed into *merkābâ* mysticism, which consisted of the practice of an ecstatic ascent to heaven to gaze upon the enthroned Deity. Rowland (in *DBI*, 441) describes it as the rabbinic continuation of apocalyptic, because *merkābâ* mysticism relates closely to the apocalyptic tradition of Second Temple Judaism. Although there is uncertainty about how early this ecstatic practice began, there seems to be indications that "already in the period of the Second Temple (i.e., before AD 70), there were a number of teachers practicing such heavenly ascents, and this practice was then continued by the first rabbis..." (Rowland, 441).

8. *The vb. rkb. HALAT* and Ficker (*THAT* 2:780) mention that the OT Heb. vb. *rkb* does not primarily mean mount (the more prominent meaning in other Sem. languages, e.g., Akk. and Ugar.), but rather ride. Only in a few cases where *rkb* occurs together with *hlk* can the meaning mount be considered (cf. Gen 24:61; 1 Sam 25:42; 2 Sam 19:27; 1 Kgs 13:13; 18:45; 2 Kgs 9:16).

Ficker (*THAT* 2:780) makes an interesting observation that riding was not a common practice for everyone. He refers to certain OT passages to argue that riding was normally practiced by privileged and distinguished people, e.g., a king (cf. 1 Kgs 18:45; Zech 9:9), princes (cf. 2 Sam 13:29; 18:9; 19:27; 1 Kgs 1:33, 38, 44), wealthy women (cf. 1 Sam 25:20, 42), and distinguished gentlemen (cf. Gen 41:43; Esth 6:9, 11).

The vb. *rkb* often appears in the OT with *yhwh* or *'elohîm* as subj. These passages normally describe the appearance of God to help his people or to fend off his enemies. Yahweh is often described as riding on clouds (cf. Ps 68:5) or riding into heaven (cf. Deut 33:26). This portrayal of God is closely associated with the portrayal of Baal in certain Ugar. texts (see ANE above).

P-B The vb. *rkb* occurs in QL (1QM). Jastrow (2:844) mentions a few occurrences of the nom. *merkābâ* in postbiblical Heb. literature. Interestingly enough, the majority of these cases are used in connection with *merkābâ* mysticism (see above). The vb. *rkb*, according to Jastrow (2:1478-79), normally means to ride, but in a few cases also to combine, join, or even to inoculate (a tree). The nom. *rekeb* accordingly can either mean wagon or chariot or a branch for inoculation. The LXX translates more than half of the occurrences of the q. vb. *rkb* with *epibainō*. The nom. *merkābâ* and *rekeb* are almost always translated in the LXX with *harma*. This word also occurs in the NT (e.g., in Acts 8:28, 38; Rev 9:9).

Chariot, cart, wagon, riding: → *rkb* (ride/mount, # 8206); → *šālîš* III (third man in war-chariot, adjutant, # 8957); → **Warfare: Theology**

Horse: → *dhr* (gallop, # 1851); → *sûs* I (horse, # 6061); → *pārāš* (horseman, rider, horse, # 7304); → *rekeš* (team of horses, # 8224); → *ra'mâ* II (mane, # 8310); → *š^{e}'ātâ* (stamping [of hoofs], # 9121)

BIBLIOGRAPHY

ABD 1:888-92; 6:893-95; *BHH* 3:2127-30; CAH 2/2:516; *DBI* 440-41; *NBD* 204-6; *TDOT* 3:20-23; *THAT* 2:777-81; M. A. Beek, "The Chariots and the Horsemen of Israel (II Kings 2, 12)," *OTS* 17, 1972, 1-10; R. de Vaux, *AncIsr*, 1961, 222-25; K. Galling, "Der Ehrenname Elisas und die Entrückung Elias," *ZThK* 53, 1956, 129-48; C. Hauer, Jr., "The Economics of National Security in Solomonic Israel," *JSOT* 18, 1980, 63-73; F. James, "Chariot Fittings from Late Bronze Age Beth Shan," in R. Moorey and P. Parr (eds.), *Archaeology in the Levant. Essays for Kathleen Kenyon,* 1978, 102-15; M. A. Littauer and J. H. Crouwel, *Wheeled Vehicles and Ridden Animals in the Ancient Near East,* 1979; B. A. Mastin, "Was the *ŠALÎŠ* the Third Man in the Chariot?" in J. A. Emerton (ed.), "Studies in the Historical Books of the Old Testament," SVT 30, 1979, 125-54; J. H. Stek, "What Happened to the Chariot Wheels in Exod 14:25?" *JBL* 105, 1986, 293-302; Y. Yadin, *The Art of Warfare in Biblical Lands in the Light of Archaeological Discovery,* 1963.

Louis Jonker

8207 (*rekeb*, chariotry, upper millstone), → # 8206

8208 (*rakkāb*, charioteer), → # 8206

8210 (*rikbâ*, riding), → # 8206

8211 (*rēkābî*, Rechabite), → Rechabite

8213 (*r^{e}kûb*, vehicle, chariot), → # 8206

8215	רָכִיל

רָכִיל (*rākîl*), peddler, huckster, hawker; deceiver; slanderer, defamer(?) (6x + Ps 31:21[?]; # 8215; *HALAT* 1153a-b).

ANE The Heb. nom. *rākîl* finds a nom. cognate only in Sam. *rēkel* (Sam. Pent. Lev 19:16), which may be only a calque on the biblical word (cf. MT Lev 19:16).

OT 1. The etymology of the nom. within Heb. is ambiguous. Some authorities suggest a derivation from the vb. *rkl* I, travel about; conduct trade (cf. *HALAT* 1153b-54a), a vb. probably related to the denom. vb. *rgl*, q. go about (e.g., Ps 15:3, "who does not go about with his tongue" [author tr.]) or pi. make traveled, explored, spied out, exposed, defamed (e.g., 2 Sam 19:27[28], "He has slandered [*way(^{e})raggēl b-*] your servant to my lord the king") (cf. BDB, 920a, 940a; *HALAT* 1104a-5a, though elsewhere *HALAT* relates *rākîl* to a hypothetical root *rkl* II [1154a]). Bühlmann has suggested that, in the preexilic period, Heb. *rākîl* had the meaning gossip (Prov 11:13; 20:19; Jer 6:28; 9:4[3]) and only later took on the sense slander, defamation (Lev 19:16; Ezek 22:9). Others have argued that designations such as "gossip" seem too light for these OT contexts (W. White, *TWOT* 2:848b).

2. Five of the six examples use some form of the idiomatic syntagm *hlk rākîl*, go about as a huckster/deceiver/defamer (so Lev 19:16; Prov 11:13; 20:19; Jer 6:28; 9:3), which may allude to the reputation of the *rākîl* as a deceptive door-to-door

peddler/hawker (so Lipiński, 522). Accordingly, Lev 19:16 presents an apodictic prohibition, *lō'-tēlēk rākîl be'ammêkā*, "You shall not go about as a huckster/deceiver/defamer among/against your people" (author tr). Given the possibility of bloodshed described in the context and the syntagm of *rgl* + *b-* (cf. 2 Sam 19:27[28]), the preposition *b-* here may be adversative (against), not just locative (among) (so Maier, 307). On Prov 11:13 and 21:19, cf. Bühlmann, 238-44.

Ezek 22:9 offers the only OT usage of *rākîl* that is unaccompanied by *hlk*, go, which shows how in later Heb. this *nomen agentis* had come to be identified with its pejorative connotation. Addressing the bloody city of Jerusalem, the prophet cries: *'an(e)šē rākîl hayû bāk*, "Men of deceit/slander are in you [to shed blood]" (author tr.). This inner Heb. semantic development parallels that whereby Arab. *makîr*, trader, came to mean deceiver (Lipiński, 522).

P-B Postbiblical cognates of the nom. appear in traditions that are dependent on BH. See postbiblical Heb. *rekîlût*, going about, exploring, exposing, slandering (Jastrow, 1479b) and attestations in the DSS (cf. K. G. Kuhn, *Konkordanz zu den Qumrantexten*, 1960, 205). The Qumran Temple scroll holds a Heb. use of *rākîl* in the expression *'yš rkyl*, man of deceit (cf. 11Q19 64.6-13). *rkyl* appears also in the Aram. Genesis Apocryphon (1QapGen 2.9).

Deception, falsehood, fraud, guile, iniquity, lie: → *'āwen* (mischief, iniquity, deception, # 224); → *bd'* (invent, devise, lie, # 968); → *kzb* I (lie, be a liar, deceive, # 3941); → *kḥš* (fail, deceive, grow lean, # 3950); → *nkl* (knave, deceiver, cheat, # 5792); → *nš'* II (be deceived, deceive, cause a deception, # 5958); → *sārâ* II (rebellion, crime, revolt, falsehood, # 6240); → *'qb* I (seize the heel, overreach, deceive, # 6810); → *rmh* II (betray, deal treacherously with, # 8228); → *śwṭ* (turn away to falsehood, entangled in lies, # 8454); → *šqr* (deal/act falsely, betray, # 9213); → *tll* (deceive, mock, trifle, # 9438)
Slander: → *bl'* II (make conveyed, reported, # 1181); → *dopî* (blemish, stain, fault, slander, # 1984); → *lāšôn* (tongue, language, # 4383) → *rgl* (slander, spy, # 8078); → *rākîl* (peddler, huckster, deceiver, slanderer, # 8215)

Bibliography

TWAT 7:521-23; *TWOT* 2:848a-b; W. Bühlmann, *Vom rechten Reden und Schweigen: Studien zu Proverbien 10-31*, OBO 12, 1976, 238-44; E. Lipiński, "Products and Brokers of Tyre According to Ezekiel 27," *Phoenicia and Its Neighbours*, Studia Phoenicia 3, 1985, 213-20; J. Maier, "Verleumder oder Verräter: Zur jüdischen Auslegungsgeschichte von Lev 19,16," in *Altes Testament—Forschung und Wirkung*, FS H. G. Reventlow, 1994, 307-11.

Robert H. O'Connell

8216	רכך

רכך (*rkk*), q. be tender, timid, gentle; pu. be softened; hi. make timid (# 8216); מֹרֶךְ (*mōrek*), despondency (# 5322); רֹךְ (*rōk*), being soft, weak, tender (# 8204); רַךְ (*rak*), nom./adj. tender, frail, weak, sensitive, pampered, timid (# 8205).

ANE The vb. is widely attested: Ugar. *rk*, being soft, gentle (*WUS*, 2510), but that the impf. *yrk* is used in *KTU* 1.10 III 27 is contested (*TWAT* 7:519); Phoen. *ṣdyrk*, (the god) *ṣd* is gentle (*PNPHPI*, 177); Syr. *rak*, being soft; Mand. adj. *rakīk*, tender; Arab. *rakka*, weak, thin. The adj. *rak* is also found in: Sam. *råk*, soft, thin; Aram. *rkyk* (*DISO*,

280); Syr. *rakkīkā'*, Mand. *rakīk*, soft and gentle; Arab. *rakīk*, powerless, thin (*Wehr*, 322a). *rōk* is a hapleg. in OT and attested in Syr. and Sam. (*HALAT* 1147).

OT 1. *Distribution*. The vb. *rkk* is found in seven books of the OT: 3x in narrative texts (Deut 20:3; 2 Kgs 22:19; 2 Chron 34:27), 3x in prophetic literature (Isa 1:6; 7:4; Jer 51:46), and one each in Wisdom and lyrical literature (Job 23:16; Ps 55:21[22]). The nom./adj. *rak* occurs 16x in the OT and is used in nine books, with the highest concentration being in the narrative and Wisdom literature: 10x in narrative texts (Gen 18:7; 29:17; 33:13; Deut 20:8; 28:54, 56; 2 Sam 3:39; 1 Chron 22:5; 29:1; 2 Chron 13:7), 2x in prophetic literature (Isa 47:1; Ezek 17:22), and 4x in Wisdom literature (Job 41:3[40:27]; Prov 4:3; 15:1; 25:15). *rok* is used once (Deut 28:56) and *mōrek* is found only in Lev 26:36.

2. *Narrative literature*. Gen 18:7 uses *rak* to refer to a tender calf that Abraham selects as the main dish for the three visiting strangers. The tender calf was "a rare delicacy and a sign of princely hospitality among pastoralists" (Sarna, 129). Similar entertainment is mentioned with regards to the divine messenger in the Ugar. Dan'el epic (Westermann, 279). The fem. pl. *rakkôt* describes the weak, gentle eyes of Leah in Gen 29:17. In this context where Leah is contrasted with the beautiful Rachel, the meaning dull, lusterless might fit better (*GKC* 145n; Wenham, 233). Lustrous eyes were a sign of beauty in the ANE (1 Sam 16:12; S of Songs 4:1, 9). The cautious Jacob disengages himself from Esau by pointing out that the children are tender/frail/weak (Gen 33:13; Sarna, 230). This observation is juxtaposed with Esau's group of 400 men mentioned in 33:1 (Westermann, 526).

mōrek is only used in Lev 26:36, where it describes the heart's faintness/fear/despondency that God will cause Israel to experience in the land of their enemies. The cowardly are also called fainthearted (Deut 20:8) and are considered unfit for military service (Levine, 190). This curse is the opposite of Deut 20:2-4, where Israel is exhorted not to be timid, while in Lev 26:36 they will flee at the sound of a windblown leaf (Hartley, 468).

In the laws concerning war, the divine presence causes Israel not to be fainthearted or afraid because the conflict is identified as the Lord's (Deut 20:1-20; Merrill, 281-83). The section on the exemption from military service (20:5-9) contains a case where the interest of the army is put first. Any fainthearted soldiers must go home before they undermine the morale of their fellow soldiers (v. 8; cf. Gideon's army in Judg 7:3; Labuschagne, 163). Deut 28:15-68 contains different curses for disobedience to God's commands, including the curse of military siege (vv. 47-57; Merrill, 364-68) and acts of cannibalism during siege (vv. 53-57); *rak* (and *rōk*, fem.) is mentioned 2x for the most gentle and sensitive man (v. 54) and woman (v. 56) who do not even refrain from these unspeakable deeds; the woman is so gentle that she would not touch the ground with bare feet. Much of the material here is reflected in ANE curse formulations attached to treaties and dramatically represents the dire consequences of covenantal disobedience (Miller, 196-98; Mayes, 351).

A narrative about David and Abner is found in 2 Sam 3, in which the last section (vv. 28-39) indicates that David did not have anything to do with the murder of Abner by Joab (Anderson, 1989, 55). In v. 39 there is a certain balance between "And today . . . I am weak" (*rak*) and "these sons of Zeruiah are too strong for me." This balance favors the MT despite the reading of the LXX: "and that he (Abner) was today a kinsman," because the LXX presupposes a confusion between *rk* and *rd,* which was possible in the scripts of many periods but does not warrant the emendation of the MT (McCarter, 111-12).

The temple repairs and the discovery of the Book of the Law during the reign of Josiah is reported in 2 Kgs 22:1-23:1 (Jones, 607). In 2 Kgs 22:19 and 2 Chron 34:27 Huldah refers to the delay in judgment because of the repentance of Josiah, which echoes God's response to Hezekiah (Priest, 366-68; Hobbs, 327). *rak l^{e}bāb^{e}kā*, lit., your heart was soft, is an idiom used in parallel to vbs. of timidity and fear. Here it describes how the penitent Josiah was responsive to the warnings in the rediscovered book (Cogan & Tadmor, 284). He is set as an example, and the reward promised as a result of his obedient penitence is held out as further encouragement to follow suit (Williamson, 402). 2 Chron 34:27 omits some of the hard words concerning the curse in 2 Kgs 22:19 and adds a second reference to the king's humility. This indicates what theological importance the author attached to humility as an element of Josiah's example (Japhet, 1035).

1 Chron 22:5 explains why David made such lavish material provision for the building of the temple in Jerusalem: it was because Solomon was "young and inexperienced/weak" (Williamson, 153). *na'ar wārāk*, young and inexperienced, is repeated not only in 29:1, but also in 2 Chron 13:7, where it reflects an excuse for Rehoboam for his part in the schism of the unified kingdom of Israel—although according to 12:13 the "young" Rehoboam was 41 years old when he became king (Braun, 220; Japhet, 395). The expression "young and inexperienced" is a metaphor for a morally immature personality, not a reflection of age (Japhet, 692).

3. *Prophetic literature*. In Isa 1:6 the pu. pf. *rukk^{e}kâ* is used in the description of sickness as metaphor for the sin of Judah and Jerusalem as "wounds and welts and open sores" that are not "bandaged or softened/soothed with oil" (Sweeney, 105). Another metaphor is used in 7:4 to equate the kings of Israel and Syria that plotted to invade Judah with two smoldering stubs of firewood (Oswalt, 200; Werlitz, 143-48). There is, therefore, no need for Ahaz to have a weak/timid heart, because God assures him that the invasion will not take place (v. 7; Seitz, 76-77). Babylon is addressed in the style of the oracles against nations as a virgin daughter that will no longer be called tender or delicate (47:1; McKenzie, 91; Van Oorschot, 152-56). The portrayal of the fall of Babylon with the metaphor of the delicate daughter that will have to do hard labor and who will no longer be called tender/delicate follows the familiar biblical motif of reversal (Hanson, 117-18).

Jer 51:46 is the only independent clause in Jer introduced with *pen,* and its tone of reassurance, "do not" or "be sure not to," suggests a context of continual bad news (Holladay, 399, 430). Despite rumors the exiles are encouraged not to lose heart or let the heart faint, because (v. 49) the time will come that Babylon must fall (Carroll, 850-51).

A forecast of the renovation of the kingdom of Judah is attached by Ezekiel to the preceding prediction of God's punishment (Ezek 17:22-24; cf. 19:21; Greenberg, 319). The tender sprig in v. 22 refers to the highest and newest growth of the cedar and acts as a lofty counter to the action of the eagle in vv. 3-4 (Zimmerli, 367).

4. *Wisdom literature*. Prov 4:1-9 emphasizes the importance of traditional wisdom in which the voice of experience (vv. 1-5), and in this case the father's

reminiscence of his own education (vv. 3-5), receives special attention (Whybray, 74-75). The reference to tender in v. 3 probably refers to inexperience and youth. McKane (303) considers the plain meaning of v. 3 to be that parents (the mother is also mentioned) transmit to their children the learning or teaching that they received from their parents—even at an early or tender age (1 Chron 22:5; 29:1). Prov 15:1 is one of the many antithetic sentences in ch. 15 that deal with the use and abuse of speech. The power of the spoken word can promote harmony or cause disruption (Whybray, 225). The soft/gentle word/answer implies a conciliatory attitude and not appeasement at any cost (McKane, 476-77). A similar statement about the power of speech is found in 25:15b, where the impact of a "soft/gentle tongue" finds hyperbolic expression in "can break a bone" (Whybray, 365). The same principle is found in v. 15a, which reflects the view that a ruler can also be persuaded.

Job ends his speech in Job 23 poised between the poles of compulsion and fear (Habel, 351). The phrase "made my heart faint" in v. 16a refers to the fear that God causes in Job and that is expressed more strongly in the parallel v. 16b (compare the same intensification between God and Almighty—Alden, 244). Job 41:3[40:27] contains ironic questions about the mighty leviathan (crocodile or chaos dragon?) begging for mercy (v. 3a) and speaking soft/gentle words (v. 3b; Alden, 401). This forms part of a group of rhetorical questions in 40:24-41:7[40:24-31], reminding Job that God is the master of the mighty leviathan.

5. *Lyrical literature*. Ps 55 provides a description of the unfaithful friend in vv. 20-21[21-22] who breaks his covenant/oath (Tate, 58). According to v. 21[22], this unfaithful friend has speech smoother than butter and words more gentle/soothing than oil. Both expressions describe flattering and hypocritical words (Anderson, 1992, 419).

P-B 1. *Qumran*. 1 QM X 3 uses *rkk* with "heart" (*yrk lbbkmh*) to indicate a softening of attitude. 1QM VI 12 uses *rky ph* to refer to the "soft mouths" of horses.

2. *Rabbinical literature*. The Talmud (*Keth*. 46a) comments on Lev 19:16 that the court should not be soft/lenient (*rak*) to one and hard to another. The *Exodus Rabba* uses soft speech in a play on words to indicate persuasive speech (Jastrow 2:1478). In the Palestinian Talmud (*Sabb*. VIII. 11b) *rakkîkayyâ* is used for soft skins and *rakkîkattā'* for soft bristles (Jastrow 2:1479).

NT *apalos* is used for the new twigs and leaves sprouting in summer in Matt 24:31 and Mark 13:28 (*EDNT* 1:114). *epieikēs* refers to the demand of slaves in 1 Pet 2:18 to be gentle (*EDNT* 2:26). *malakos* describes how people of high standing are dressed in soft clothing (Matt 11:8; Luke 7:25) and in the vice catalog of 1 Cor 6:9 it refers to soft people/weaklings (*EDNT* 2:381). *oligopsychos* is used in 1 Thess 5:14 for the timid who need comforting (*EDNT* 2:507).

Feeble, despair, faint, frail, tender: → *'ml* I (be weak, be feeble, languish, # 581); → *ḥlh* I (become weak, tired, ill, # 2703); → *ylh* (languish, # 3532); → *k'h* (be disheartened, frightened, # 3874); → *nbl* I (wither, fade, languish, dishonor, # 5570); → *'tp* II (grow weak, faint, be feeble, # 6494); → *'lp* (cover, faint, # 6634); → *'šš* (become weak, # 6949); → *pwg* (be feeble, numb, be prostrated, # 7028); → *rzh* (destroy, waste away, # 8135); → *rkk* (be tender, timid, gentle, # 8216); → *rph* (become slack, lose heart, discourage, # 8332)

Tired, exhausted, feeble, weak, weary: → *'ml* I (be weak, be feeble, languish, # 581); → *ḥlh* I (become weak, tired, ill, # 2703); → *ḥlš* I (be enfeebled, be weakened, # 2764);

→ *ḥallāš*, weakling, # 2766); → *yg'* (be tired, # 3333); → *mss* (lose courage, melt, become weak, # 5022); → *nṣb* II (wretched, exhausted [animal], # 5894); → *pgr* (be too feeble, tired, # 7006); → *'yp* (be weary, # 6545); → *rph* (become slack, lose heart, discourage, # 8332)

Bibliography

EDNT 1:114; 2:26, 381, 507; *TWAT* 7:519-21; *TWOT* 2:848; R. L. Alden, *Job*, NAC, 1993; A. A. Anderson, *2 Samuel*, 1989; idem, *The Book of Psalms I*, 1992; R. Braun, *1 Chronicles*, 1986; R. P. Carroll, *Jeremiah*, OTL, 1986; M. Cogan & H. Tadmor, *1 Kings*, 1988; M. Greenberg, *Ezechiel 1-20*, 1983; N. C. Habel, *The Book of Job*, OTL, 1985; P. D. Hanson, *Isaiah 40-66*, 1995; J. E. Hartley, *Leviticus*, 1992; T. R. Hobbs, *2 Kings*, AB, 1985; S. Japhet, *I & II Chronicles*, 1993; G. H. Jones, *1 and 2 Kings II*, NCBC, 1984; C. J. Labuschagne, *Deuteronomy II*, 1990; B. A. Levine, *Leviticus*, AB, 1989; A. D. H. Mayes, *Deuteronomy*, NCBC, 1991; P. K. McCarter, *II Samuel*, AB, 1984; W. McKane, *Proverbs*, OTL, 1970; J. L. McKenzie, *Second Isaiah*, AB, 1968; P. D. Miller, *Deuteronomy*, 1990; J. N. Oswalt, *The Book of Isaiah 1-39*, NICOT, 1986; J. Priest, "Huldah's Oracle," *VT* 30, 1980, 366-68; N. M. Sarna, *Genesis*, 1989; C. R. Seitz, *Isaiah 1-39*, 1993; M. A. Sweeney, *Isaiah 1-4 and the Post-Exilic Understanding of the Isaianic Tradition*, 1988; M. E. Tate, *Psalms 51-100*, WBC, 1990; J. Van Oorschot, *Von Babel zum: Zion*, 1993; G. J. Wenham, *Genesis 16-50*, WBC, 1994; J. Werlitz, *Studien zur literarkritischen Methode. Gericht und Heil in Jesaja 7, 1-17 und 29, 1-8*, 1992; C. Westermann, *Genesis 12-36*, 1985; R. N. Whybray, *Proverbs*, NCBC, 1994; H. G. M. Williamson, *1 and 2 Chronicles*, NCBC, 1987; W. Zimmerli, *Ezechiel 1*, Hermeneia, 1979.

Hendrik L. Bosman

8217	רכל

רכל (*rkl* I), vb. go about, trade (# 8217), part. רֹכֵל (*rōkēl*), trader; מַרְכֹּלֶת (*markōlet*), trading (# 5326); רְכֻלָּה (*r^{e}kullâ*), trade, merchandise (# 8219).

OT 1. The goods and the group appear in the description of the great trading center Tyre (Ezek 27-28, cf. 27:3ab: *rōkelet hā'ammîm 'el-'iyyîm rabbîm*, merchant of peoples on many coasts), skillful, with widespread interests including various commodities, but violent and dishonest in trade. Babylon is also described as a trader in Ezek 17:4 and Nineveh has more traders than the stars, but this will not help in the coming calamity (Nah 3:16). Other foreign traders are also indicated by *rōkēl* in Ezek 27: Judah, Israel, Assyria, Sheba, etc. The term is used to describe a market (Ezek 27:24) (markets are also indicated by the term *ḥûṣôt*, streets [→ # 2575], in 1 Kgs 20:34, where Ben-Hadad agrees to let Ahab set up "market areas" [NIV] in Damascus as his father did in Samaria [Elat, 543-44]; cf. on the whole matter M. Silver, *Economic Structures of the Ancient Near East*, 1985). Tyre is cursed, and the enemy will steal their goods (Ezek 26:12). The traders brought in Solomon's revenue (1 Kgs 10:15) and had a quarter in Jerusalem, and later some waited outside to do business on the Sabbath (Neh 3:31-32; 13:20). Landsberger made them small traders, but this is rejected (Elat).

2. The carriage of Solomon is perfumed with the scent-dust (scent-powder in *HALAT* 8a; NIV spices) of the trader (S of Songs 3:6; NIV note: imported); presumably from markets in Sheba/Saba (Ezek 27:22; cf. O. Keel, *Das Hohelied*, 1992, 120).

3. Other terms: *ma^{a}rāb* and *'izbônîm* (Akk. *uzub(b)u*) are also used for various types of merchandise in Ezek 27 to describe its wealth, but this will come to nought when these sink into the sea and are shattered by the waves (vv. 27, 34). There will be

no trading in goods (*maqqāḥôt*) on the Sabbath according to the agreement in Neh 10:31[32].

Trade, merchandise, buying, selling: → *k^{e}na'an* (trader, # 4047); → *krh* (get by trade, # 4126); → *m^{e}ḥîr* I (price, payment, # 4697); → *mkr* I (trade, sell, # 4835); → *sḥr* (travel, trade, # 6086); → *qnh* (acquire, buy, # 7864); → *rkl* (trade, # 8217); → *šbr* II (buy, # 8690)

BIBLIOGRAPHY

TWAT 7:521-23; M. Elat, "The Monarchy and the Development of Trade in Ancient Israel," *State and Temple Economy in the Ancient Near East,* 2, 1979, 531 note 17; B. Landsberger, in *Hebräische Wortforschung*, 1967, 187.

Izak Cornelius

8219 (*r^{e}kûllâ*, trade, merchandise), → # 8217

8220	רכס

רכס (*rks),* q. bind, tie (# 8220); רֶכֶס (*rekes),* nom. rugged ground (hapleg.; → # 8221); רֹכֶס (*rōkes),* band, league (hapleg. in Ps 31:20[21], NIV intrigues; # 8222).

OT The vb. is used twice in Exodus in the description of the priestly garments: "The rings ... are to be tied ..." (Exod 28:28; cf. 39:21).

Band, tie: → *'pd* (put on tightly, # 679); → *'^{a}pēr* (bandage, # 710); → *'eṣ'ādâ* (band, # 731); → *ḥbš* (tie up, saddle, imprison, bind, # 2502); → *ḥgr* (bind, gird, # 2520); → *ḥāšûq* (clasp ring, # 3122); → *ḥtl* (be swaddled, # 3156); → *keset* (band [for magic purposes], # 4086); → *migbā'â* (head-band, # 4457); → *'nd* (wind, tie s.t., # 6698); → *'qd* (tie up, # 6818); → *ṣrr* I (bind, tie up, # 7674); → *qšr* (ally together, conspire, bind, # 8003); → *rks* (bind, tie, # 8220); → *rtm* (tie up, # 8412)

T. Desmond Alexander

8221	רֶכֶס

רֶכֶס (*rekes*), nom. rugged ground (hapleg., Isa 40:4, # 8221).

OT This hapleg. apparently derives from the vb. *rks*, to bind (Exod 28:28; 39:21, binding the priest's breastplate to his ephod). 1QIsa^a slightly changed the vocalization of the word, inserting the vowel *w* between the *resh* and *kaph* (*hrwksym*). Ravenna (69; cf. Elliger, 2, 19) contends that in light of 1QIsa^a, the nom. *rks* in Isa 40:4 must be related to another hapleg. found in Ps 31:20[21] (translated in various ways: KJV, pride; NASB, conspiracies; NIV, intrigues; NRSV, plots). Ravenna (69) offers "hindrances" as a translation of *rekes* in Isa 40:4. However, keep in mind the contrast repeated throughout the verse: "Every valley shall be raised up, every mountain and hill made low, the rough ground shall become level, the *rekes* (shall become) a plain." The antonymic counterpart of *rekes*, *biq'â* (valley, plain; → # 1326) suggests another topographical term that is opposite in meaning (e.g., KJV, rough places; NASB, rugged terrain; NIV, rugged places). As with *'āqōb* (→ # 6815), *rekes* represents a topographical obstacle (whether real or metaphorical) that will be removed in preparation for the Lord's coming.

P-B Mish. Heb. *rekes*, walls of beaten earth, mounds, embankments; Jewish Aram. *rîksâ*, stone fortifications.

Field, ground, rural area: → *'ādām* IV (ground, # 135); → *bar* IV (wild, open country, # 1340); → *gāzēr* (infertile land, # 1620); → *ḥûṣôt* (open fields, # 2575a); → *yāgēb* (field, # 3321); → *m^e lēḥâ* (barren land, salt-plain, # 4877); → *mimšāq* (ground overrun with weeds, # 4940); → *m^e 'ārâ* II (bare field, # 5118); → *nîr* II (ground newly broken & cleared, # 5776); → *'āqob* (ground [uneven and bumpy], crafty heart, # 6815); → *p^e rāzôn* (fertile field, # 7251); → *rekes* (rugged ground, # 8221); → *śādeh* (open country, open field, fields, domain, # 8441); → *š^e dēmâ* (terrace, # 8727); → *šāmān* (fertile field, # 9044)

Bibliography

K. Elliger, *Deuterojesaja*, 1978; A. Ravenna, "Is 40,4 e Ps 31,21," *Rivista Biblica Italiana* 1, 1953, 69-70.

Michael A. Grisanti

8222 (*rōkes*, band, league), → # 8220

8223	רכשׁ

רכשׁ (*rkš*), q. acquire property (# 8223); רְכוּשׁ (*r^e kûš*), property, goods, outfit, equipment, domain (# 8214).

ANE An original connection between the Sem. roots *rkb* and *rkš* is probable (cf. Akk. *rukūbu* and *rukūšu*). It may be assumed that the nom. *r^e kûš* is related to the vb. *rkš*, collect, gather property.

OT 1. The vb. occurs 5x in the OT, each time in q. (Gen 12:5; 31:18 (2x); 36:6; 46:6). The word indicates the acquiring of possessions that are movable, as in Gen 12:5, which records the obedience of Abram to God's command for him to leave his father's house. "He took his wife Sarai, his nephew Lot, all of the possessions they had accumulated and the people they had acquired in Haran, and they set out for the land of Canaan." This does not say how the possessions were acquired, nor what they were; it is, however, obvious that the possessions were "movable." Instead, it points to the place and land where the possessions were acquired and to where they were taken (B. Jacob, *Das erste Buch der Torah: Genesis*, 340).

2. At times the word *r^e kûš* is used specifically to indicate domesticated animals—the flocks and herds that formed the backbone of the people's agricultural existence throughout the various periods of Israelite history (cf. Gen 13:6; 31:18; 36:7; Num 35:3; 2 Chron 31:3; 35:7; cf. also 1 Chron 27:31; 28:1). The term, within its given context, is often indicative of wealth and affluence.

3. In some texts the term *r^e kûš* refers more widely to various forms of movable property, often including but not limited to cattle and livestock. Also included in such references could be articles of household furnishings, utensils, tools, and implements (cf. Gen 12:5; 13:6; 14:11, 12, 16, 21; 15:14; 31:18; 46:6; Num 16:32; 35:3; 2 Chron 21:14, 17; 32:29; Ezra 1:4, 6; 8:21; 10:8).

4. Booty and spoils of war are referred to by this term in 2 Chron 20:25; Dan 11:24, 28. Here, too, there is a connotation of vast riches, in this case the magnitude of the plunder.

Property, possession: → *'ᵃḥuzzâ* (property, # 299); → *b'l* I (marry, rule over, own, # 1249); → *miqneh* (livestock, property, # 5238); → *rkš* (acquire property, # 8223)

Cleon L. Rogers, Jr./William T. Koopmans

8224	רֶכֶשׁ

רֶכֶשׁ (*rekeš*), team of horses (# 8224).

ANE Jewish Aram. *rikša'*, Syr. *rakšā'*, Man. *rakša.*

OT The term is used of Solomon's war horses (1 Kgs 4:28[5:8]), the Assyrian war horses harnessed to chariots (Mic 1:13), and the swift horses used by the Persian couriers (Esth 8:10, 14). The term does not contribute in any significant way to the theological message of these passages.

Horse: → *dhr* (gallop, # 1851); → *sûs* I (horse, # 6061); → *pārāš* (horseman, rider, horse, # 7304); → *rekeš* (team of horses, # 8224); → *ra'mâ* II (mane, # 8310); → *šᵉ'ātâ* (stamping [of hoofs], # 9121)

Robert B. Chisholm

8227	רמה

רמה (*rmh* I), q. throw, shoot (arrow) (# 8227); Aram. רמא (*rm'*), pe. throw, impose; pe'il be thrown, set in place (of thrones); hitp. be thrown (# 10667).

ANE Aram. *rm'*, Ugar. *rmy* (?), Akk. *ramû(m)*, Eth. *rämäyä*, strike, Arab. *ramā(y)*.

OT Both Moses and Miriam used this vb. to describe how the Lord destroyed Pharaoh's armies in the sea (Exod 15:1, 21). Ten of the twelve occurrences of the biblical Aram. cognate are in the stories of the fiery furnace (Dan 3) and the lions' den (Dan 6).

Shooting, throwing: → *dḥh* (push, overthrow, be cast down, # 1890); → *ṭwl* (throw, # 3214); → *ydh* I (shoot, # 3343); → *yrh* I (shoot, throw, # 3721); → *mgr* (throw, # 4489); → *rbb* II (shoot, # 8046); → *rmh* I (throw, shoot, # 8227); → *šlk* I (throw, hurl, # 8959); → *šmṭ* (release, remit, drop, throw down, # 9023)

Robert B. Chisholm

8228	רמה

רמה (*rmh* II), pi. betray, deal treacherously with (# 8228); מִרְמָה (*mirmâ* I), betrayal, fraud, deceit (# 5327); רְמִיָּה (*rᵉmiyyâ*), nom. deceit, treachery (# 8245); תָּרְמָה (*tormâ*), under cover, treacherously (?) (# 9564); תַּרְמִית (*tarmît*), deceitfulness, deceit (# 9567).

ANE Akk. *ramû(m)* III, relax, become slack, become exhausted; Arab. *ramj* VI, lazy, be slow; Aram. *rᵉmā'*, throw; Syr. *rᵉmā'*, throw. Several different roots may be involved.

OT 1. In the OT the vb. *rmh* II is found 8x and regularly means some kind of betrayal, deceit, or treachery carried out by various parties against another party: Laban's deception of Jacob over Rachel (Gen 29:25), the Gibeonites' deception of Israel in making a covenant with them (Josh 9:22, which still stood nevertheless), and Saul's supposed betrayal of the witch of Endor (1 Sam 28:12; cf. 2 Sam 19:26[27];

Prov 26:19). In each situation an attempt is made to give a false representation, making something to appear to be what it is not.

2. The nom. *mirmâ* is found 40x and describes false scales (Prov 11:1; Amos 8:5), which God abhors (Mic 6:11), and treacherous and crafty dealings with others (Gen 34:13; 2 Kgs 9:23). Treacherous lips are especially depicted by the word (Ps 17:1; 52:4[6]), including swearing falsely (24:4). Fools, false witness, and deceit are inseparably linked (Prov 12:17; 14:8). Israel as a people had become like bird cages full of deceit (Jer 5:27). The womb of the evil produces deceit (Job 15:35); producing peace is the opposite of producing evil (*ra'*; → # 8273). Joy (*śimḥâ*; → # 8525) is the result of the former, deceit (*mirmâ*) the result of the latter (Prov 12:20). The destroyer of God's people is a master of deceit/treachery (cf. Gen 3:13; Dan 8:25). The servant of Yahweh is notable, for no deceit was found in his mouth (Isa 53:9). Anyone who desires a successful life must refrain from speaking lies (Job 31:5-6; Ps 17:1; 34:13[14]).

3. The other three words are used in the same semantic range and describe the moral, ethical, spiritual, and religious corruption of God's people.

(a) The nom. *r^{e}miyyâ* occurs 15x with the basic meaning of deceit/treachery. Micah (Mic 6:12) describes the rich of Israel with par. terms, meaning the violent, liars, and persons whose tongues speak deceit (cf. Job 13:7; 27:4; Ps 52:2[4]; 101:7; 120:2, 3). This nom. can also signify the untrustworthy nature of a lazy person (Prov 10:4; 12:24, 27; 19:15; Jer 48:10) or a faulty bow (Ps 78:57; Hos 7:16).

(b) A less common nom., *tarmît* (5x), highlights Israel's penchant to cling to delusions rather than Yahweh's messengers (Ps 119:18; Jer 8:5; 14:14; 23:26; Zeph 3:13). Jeremiah (Jer 8:5) depicts the people of Jerusalem as persons who cling to deceit, i.e., not knowing/following the demands/requirements of the Lord (v. 7). *r^{e}miyyâ* and *tarmît* are synonymous terms, although the first describes the presentation of deceit while the second depicts the deceit as an accomplished fact.

(c) The occurrence of *b^{e}tormâ* in Judg 9:31 has occasioned several interpretive suggestions. Gevirtz (59-60) contends that *tormâ* is a hapleg. derived from *trm,* to remove, set apart. Consequently, the nom. could mean separation, deviation, secret, which would be translated "in secret." It could also be a nom. derived from *rmh,* with the translation "by a ruse" (REB, Boling, 178; Cundall, 132). Boling (178; cf. Driver, 15) argues that if this nom. is derived from *rmh* (to deceive), the translation "secretly" (NKJV) or "under cover" (NIV) is unlikely. Several scholars either regard the word as a corruption (Moore, 259) or emend it to read the place name Arumah (cf. Judg 9:41; Gray, 323; Burney, 281). The translation "by a ruse" clearly manifests the attempt to cloak one's intentions and would allow for the translation "under cover."

DSS The vb. is found in 1QS 7:6 in the hitp. 6x, meaning to act carelessly, and in 1QH 17:7. The noms. are found 23x referring to: the godless, orders of the community, men in general, and with respect to the truthfulness of God (cf. Kartveit, *TWAT* 7:527, for references).

P-B Late Heb. continued the pi. usage of the word meaning to be cunning; to impose upon (for refs. see Jastrow 2:1482).

Deception, falsehood, fraud, guile, iniquity, lie: → *'āwen* (mischief, iniquity, deception, # 224); → *bd'* (invent, devise, lie, # 968); → *kzb* I (lie, be a liar, deceive, # 3941); → *kḥš* (fail, deceive, grow lean, # 3950); → *nkl* (knave, deceiver, cheat, # 5792); → *nš'* II (be deceived, deceive, cause a deception, # 5958); → *sārâ* II (rebellion, crime, revolt, falsehood, # 6240); → *'qb* I (seize the heel, overreach, deceive, # 6810); → *rmh* II (betray, deal treacherously with, # 8228); → *śwṭ* (turn away to falsehood, entangled in lies, # 8454); → *šqr* (deal/act falsely, betray, # 9213); → *tll* (deceive, mock, trifle, # 9438)

Bibliography
NIDNTT 2:457-63, 470-74; *TWAT* 7:523-27; *TWOT* 2:849; R. Boling, *Judges*, AB, 1975; C. Burney, *The Book of Judges*, 1920; A. Cundall, *Judges: An Introduction and Commentary*, TOTC, 1968; G. Driver, "Problems in Judges Newly Discussed," *ALUOS* 4, 1962-1963, 6-25; S. Gevirtz, "The *Hapax Legomenon* תרמה (Judg. 9:31)," *JNES* 17, 1958, 59-60; J. Gray, *Joshua, Judges and Ruth*, NCBC, 1967; M. Klopfenstein, *Die Lüge nach dem Alten Testament*, 1964; G. Moore, *Judges*, ICC, 1895.

Eugene Carpenter/Michael A. Grisanti

8229 (*rāmâ* I, height, high place), → # 8123

8231 (*rimmâ*, worm, maggot), → # 8249, 9357

8232 (*rimmôn* I, pomegranate tree), → # 6770

8242 (*rōmaḥ*, spear), → # 2851

8244	רְמִיָּה

רְמִיָּה (*r^e^miyyâ*), nom. slackness, looseness (# 8244).

ANE *HALAT* regards *remiyyâ* as having a meaning both of laxness, looseness, and deceit. BDB separates these concepts by positing *remiyyâ* I (deceit) and II (slackness). The Akk. *rimūtu,* referring to an art of dissembling, is suggested as cognate (*HALAT* 4:1159).

OT 1. The lazy (*remiyyâ*) do not roast their game (i.e., they failed to hunt), but the diligent man prizes his possession (Prov 12:27). A further contrast between lazy hands and diligent hands is made in 10:4. Laziness brings poverty, diligence makes rich. The contrast is likely drawn by observing human behavior, quite apart from a divine revelation. Two references to a slack or loose bow (*remiyyâ*) provide an apt metaphor for a moral condition of laxity (Ps 78:57; Hos 7:16).

An adverbial use of the word appears in the phrase to act neglectfully (lax, or deceitfully [?]) in reference to carelessness (deception [?]) in doing the Lord's work (Jer 48:10).

2. For a nuance of the word with the meaning of deceit, see Job 13:7 (cf. 27:4; Ps 32:2; 52:2[4]; 101:7; 120:2, 3; Mic 6:12).

Lazy, slow, slack: → *'rk* I (become long, # 799); → *'ṣl* (be sluggish, # 6788); → *r^e^miyyâ* (slackness, # 8244); → *rph* (become slack, lose heart, discourage, # 8332)

Bibliography
TWOT 2:849; W. McKane, *Proverbs*, OTL, 1978.

J. A. Thompson/Elmer A. Martens

8245 (*r^e^miyyâ*, deceit, treachery), → # 8228; # 8244

8247 (*rammākâ*, swift mare), → # 6061

8249	רמם

רמם (*rmm* I), rot, be full of worms (# 8249); רִמָּה (*rimmâ*), nom. maggot (# 8231).

ANE According to de Moor the reflexive of *rmm* is found in Ugar. in *KTU* 1.12 iv 3 with the sense of being full of maggots (126, 133). He argues that the god Yammu is suffering from vermin found in his own body, as found for instance in Gilgamesh. This sense is also followed by Fisher (*RSP* 1:340, # 521; cf. *yrm*, Exod 16:20). However, the Ugar. form *'rt* commonly means breast (*UT*, 365, # 326), the meaning followed by Gibson (142; cf. Akk. *irtu*), who translates "lungs of death" (43). Gibson finds the nom. *rmmh* at *KTU* 1.12 i 11 in the Ugar. *mrm* (152), but this is highly conjectural; de Moor translates this as "bitter pain" (129). The word *rmh* in the text of Deir 'Alla II 8 may be vermin (Hoftijzer and van der Kooij, 226-27, 307). The nom. maggot may be found in the Akk. *rimmatum* (*AHw*, 986).

OT 1. The vb. *rmm* is found only at Exod 16:20, where the bread left until morning rots with worms. The nom. *rimmâ* is found 7x in the MT. Exod 16:24 is parallel to the use of the vb. in reference to the Sabbath food, which had no worms. The nom. is found 5x in Job. In 7:5 Job describes his body as covered with worms; in 17:14 and 21:26 being consumed by maggots is parallel with decaying in the grave. In 25:6 Bildad describes humankind as a maggot; the word *rimmâ* is parallel with worm (*tôlē'a*, # 9357). The text of 24:20 is difficult, but emendations as those proposed by Fohrer, to say the sinner's name will not be remembered (368-69), are not an improvement; the MT appears to say that the worm will find the sinner sweet (Gordis, 270), again a reference to the grave.

In Isa 14:11 the king of Babylon is brought down to Sheol, to a bed of maggots (*rimmâ*) and a covering of worms (*tôlē'a*). Based on this parallel and the versions, *rimmâ* has also been proposed for Isa 41:14 as a description of Israel, reading *rmt* for *mt* in the second line. There also seems to be a textual problem at Ezek 32:5, which according to Syr. and Vg. should speak of filling the valley with corpses, possibly reading *rimmâ* as a metonym for decaying bodies rather than *rāmût* (height); however, the derivation of the word is uncertain.

2. Apart from the Exod references, the biblical use of maggot is metaphorical for death and the grave, or for the pitiful state of human existence (Job 25:6). It is a graphic image for the judgment of death.

P-B The vb. *rmm* is known in Arab. (*ramma*, to become rotten). The nom. *rimmâ* is found in Late Heb. and Aram. It is found in the DSS in the Rule of the Community (1QS 11:21) to speak of the grave as the destiny of humans. The nom. is also found in Syr., Mand., and Arab.

Rotting, decay: → *mqq* (putrefy, rot, dwindle away, # 5245); → *māśôś* II (something rotten, # 5376); → *rmm* I (rot, be full of worms, # 8249); → *rqb* (rot, become worm eaten, # 8372)

Bibliography

G. Fohrer, *Das Buch Hiob*, 1989, 368-69; J. C. L. Gibson, *CML*[2], 43, 142, 152; R. Gordis, *The Book of Job*, 1978, 270; J. Hoftijzer and G. van der Kooij, *Aramaic Texts from Deir Alla*, 1976,

226-27, 307; J. C. de Moor, *The Seasonal Pattern in the Ugaritic Myth of Ba'lu*, AOAT 16, 1971, 126, 133; idem, *An Anthology of Religious Texts from Ugarit*, 1987, 38, 129.

A. H. Konkel

8250	רמם

רמם (*rmm* II), q. rise up; ni. rise up; be exalted; go away from (# 8250).

OT *rmm*, to rise upward (e.g., cherubim, Ezek 10:15), is applied theologically in one instance to God's right hand (ni. be exalted, Ps 118:16).

Exaltation, height: → *zbl* (exalt, honor, # 2290); → *sll* (lift up, exalt, # 6148); → *rwm* (be high, exalted, proud, # 8123); → *rmm* II (rise up, be exalted, # 8250); → *śg'/śgh* (grow great, increase, exalt, # 8434/8436)

Elmer A. Martens

8252	רמס

רמס (*rms*), q. trample; ni. be trampled (# 8252); מִרְמָס (*mirmās*), ground trampled down, trampling (# 5330).

ANE The root is known in other Sem. languages.

OT Both vb. and nom. are used to speak of human aggression, the trampling of enemies, but also of the powerful action of God in judgment.

1. The words are used of those who were aggressors against Israel or other nations, such as the "goat" and its "horn" in Dan 8:7, 10; this particular aggression involved the trampling underfoot of the sanctuary (Dan 8:13). Ezek 34:18-19 speaks of aggressors within God's people, using the picture of those of the flock who trampled the pasture and muddied the drinking water for others.

2. The prophets stress that God will surely punish those who are proud and aggressive towards others, whether within Israel or among the nations who oppress them. "The pride of Ephraim's drunkards, will be trampled underfoot" (Isa 28:3). Isa 63:3-4 speaks in terms of God's trampling out the vintage. He had to tread that winepress alone, but he could say, "I trampled them in my anger and trod them down in my wrath.... For the day of vengeance was in my heart, and the year of my redemption has come."

3. God used heathen nations in the trampling down of his vineyard (Isa 5:5). Feet trample down the proud city (26:6). In 10:6 the Assyrians in particular are used to trample others down "like mud in the streets," but it is made clear that they themselves must, in turn, be vanquished. In 41:25 it is the one stirred up from the north who will "tread on rulers as if they were mortar," so that the Lord's people might be set free. In 2 Kgs 7:17, 20 we read of the unbelieving officer who was trampled underfoot during a stampede when it was realized that the Syrians had left their camp. 2 Kgs 9:33 speaks of Queen Jezebel trodden under foot when Jehu finally compassed her death. In the oath of innocence in Psalm 7:4-5[5-6] the psalmist invites such a judgment on himself, "If I have done evil to him who is at peace with me ... then let my enemy pursue and overtake me; let him trample my life to the ground...."

4. There are then the promises that those who trust in the Lord will be enabled to trample on their enemies, even "like a lion among the beasts of the forest" (Mic 5:8[7]). In Ps 91:13 it is put, "you will tread upon the lion and the cobra, you will trample the great lion and the serpent."

5. Finally, there is quite a different use of the vb. in Isaiah 1:12, where it is said that those who come to offer sacrifices in the temple, but are living lives contrary to the will of God, are merely trampling the courts of the temple.

Trampling, treading, subjugation: → *bws* (tread down, # 1008); → *dbr* I (turn/drive away, # 1818); → *dwš* (trample, thresh, # 1889); → *hdk* (tread down, # 2070); → *kbš* (make subservient, subdue, # 3899); → *kpš* (make cower, # 4115); → *lkd* (catch, capture, # 4334); → *'ss* (tread down, # 6748); → *rms* (trample, # 8252); → *rpś* (trample, # 8346)

BIBLIOGRAPHY

TWAT 7:532-34

Francis Foulkes

8253	רמשׂ

רמשׂ (*rmś*), q. move, creep, swarm, teem (# 8253); nom. רֶמֶשׂ (*remeś*), small animals, reptiles (coll.) (# 8254).

ANE According to *HALAT*, the Heb. root *rmś* may be related to the Arab. *ramaša* (touch gently?) and the Akk. *namāšû*, break open; *nammaštu*, creeping things.

OT 1. The root *rmś* occurs 17x in the OT, 10x in Gen alone. The term is a Heb. classifier of animal life. The vb. essentially depicts the locomotion of small ground animals, since *rmś* is frequently joined with *'al-hā'āreṣ* (Gen 1:26, 28, 30; 7:14, 21; 8:17, 19) or *'ᵃdāmâ* (Gen 9:2; Lev 20:25). Yet, *rmś* is used to describe the prowling beasts of the forest (Ps 104:20, NIV) and the movement of water creatures (Gen 1:21; Ps 69:34[35]). J. Milgrom summarizes, "The verb *rāmaś* can mean 'move, stir' and, hence, apply to all animals and not just to creepers" (*Leviticus 1-16*, AB 3, 687).

The animal category *rmś* or "moving things" (NIV) was a part of God's good creation (Gen 1:21). They were originally plant eaters (1:30) and were among those animal groups over which humanity was to exercise dominion (1:26, 28). Those in the *rmś* animal category were among the creatures preserved on the ark and later released to replenish the earth after the Flood waters receded (7:8, 14; 8:17, 19).

After the great Flood, the *rmś* animal group became a divinely ordained part of the food chain for human beings (Gen 9:2). Subsequent Levitical law prohibited the eating of *rmś* animals (Lev 20:25). In fact, the *rmś* category represents all the unclean foods that compromise personal holiness and ritually defile people (Lev 11:44, 46). Deuteronomic law forbids idols cast in the image of *rmś* animals (Deut 4:18).

2. The nom. *remeś* occurs 17x in the OT, with ten of those citations in Gen. Like the vb., it functions as a Heb. classifier for living creatures, but restricts the category to small creeping animals. The word overlaps with the Heb. *šereṣ* in that both *remeś* and *šereṣ* are creatures that multiply quickly and in great numbers. However, *remeś* as a classification of animal life identifies primarily small creeping rodents and reptiles (creatures that move on the ground, NIV; Gen 1:24-26). By contrast, *šereṣ* identifies primarily swarming aquatic creatures and insects (see *šrṣ*, # 9237). In two

exceptional cases *remeś* refers to sea creatures (Ps 104:25; Hab 1:14). The report of King Solomon's scientific discourses also includes his investigation of the *remeś*, usually rendered reptiles (so NIV, NRSV; 1 Kgs 4:33[5:13]). Wenham summarizes that *remeś* or "creeping things refers to mice, reptiles, insects, and any other little creatures that keep close to the ground" (*Genesis 1-15*, WBC 1, 25).

Heb. law outlawed certain creatures in the category of *remeś* as ritually unclean for hygienic and cultic reasons (Lev 11:44, 46). Ezekiel's vision of unclean *remeś* in the murals profaning the walls of the temple suggests their association with pagan idol worship (Ezek 8:10). Finally, as part of God's good creation the psalmist calls upon the *remeś* to praise the Lord (Ps 148:10), and the day of the Lord will see a covenant between God's people and the (crop-destroying) *remeś* (i.e., nature and humanity will be at peace, Hos 2:18[20]).

Abundance, multiplication, sufficiency: → *dgh* (multiply, # 1835); → *day* (sufficiency, overflowing supply, # 1896); → *ysp* (add, continue, increase, # 3578); → *kbr* I (make many, be in abundant supply, # 3892); → *m^{e}gammâ* (totality, abundance, # 4480); → *rbb* I (become numerous, much, great, # 8045); → *rbh* I (become numerous, multiply, increase, # 8049); → *r'š* II, be abundant, # 8322); → *śg'/śgh* (grow great, increase, exalt, # 8434/8436); → *śpq* II (suffice, be enough, # 8563); → *šwq* I (overflow, bestow abundantly, # 8796); → *šepa'* (super-abundance, # 9179)

BIBLIOGRAPHY

NIDNTT 1:728-44; 2:128-31; 3:136-38; *TWOT* 2:850; M. Gilbert, "Soyes feconds et multipliez (Gen 1:28)," *NRT* 96, 1974, 729-42; I. Nowell, "The Narrative Context of Blessing in the Old Testament" in *Blessing and Power*, 1988, 3-12.

Andrew E. Hill

8254 (*remeś*, small animals, reptiles), → # 8253

8260 (*rōn*, shouts), → # 8264

8261	רנה

רנה (*rnh* I), q. rattle (# 8261).

OT *rnh* occurs only once (q. impf.) and describes the rattling of battle equipment arrayed upon a charging horse prepared for battle. It is possibly onomatopoeic (Job 39:23).

BIBLIOGRAPHY

RSP 3:153; J. E. Hartley, *The Book of Job*, NICOT, 1988.

M. V. Van Pelt/W. C. Kaiser, Jr.

8262 (*rinnâ* I, shout of joy, moan), → # 8264

8264	רנן

רנן (*rnn*), q. to yell, to shout with joy, to moan; pi. to shout with joy, to proclaim with shouts of joy; pu. to shout for joy (only Isa 16:10); hi. to make someone shout with joy (# 8264); רוֹן (*rôn*), shouts (Ps 32:7; # 8260); רִנָּה (*rinnâ*), nom. shout of joy, moan (# 8262); רְנָנָה (*r^{e}nānâ*), shout of joy (Job 3:7; 20:5; Ps 63:5[6]; 100:2; # 8265).

ANE The root occurs with essentially the same meaning in Ugar. (M. J. Dahood, 13-36 and M. Astour, 13-36), Aram., Arab., and postbiblical Heb. Von Soden (*AHw*, 242-43) identifies a similar Akk. word (*ernettu(m)*), but its existence is doubtful and not recognized by the *CAD*.

OT 1. (a) The vb. *rnn* often indicates a loud, enthusiastic, and joyful shout. However, in at least two cases, it clearly lacks joy, but is either a moan of despair (Lam 2:19) or an expression of yearning for God's presence (Ps 84:2[3]). For this reason we may speculate that the root's basic meaning is yell (see Prov 1:20 and 8:3 for this basic meaning), the tone determined by the context. However, in over fifty other occurrences, in q., pi., pu., and hi., it expresses happiness, joy, or relief, occurring in association with other vbs. that express a similar joyful emotion (i.e., *śmḥ* [Ps 5:11(12); 92:4(5), *rwʿ* [Ps 95:1], *ʿlz* [Ps 96:12; 149:5], *zmr* [Ps 71:23], *šyr* [Ps 59:16(17)] among others).

(b) Most of the 53x the vb. occurs are found in Ps (26x) and Isa (14x). The former is not surprising since it is a book that includes many songs of praise. In the Psalms we find only one use of the q. (Ps 35:27) and three of the hi. (32:11; 65:8[9]; 81:1[2]); the rest of the time the vb. is in the pi. With the exception of 65:8[9], which presents a clearly causative meaning of the root, no real difference can be discovered between these different stems. Wagner (436) suggests that the use in the Psalms indicates "some cultic shout which was offered at the appropriate place in the worship."

(c) By far the predominant object of the shout of joy in all its OT occurrences is Yahweh (for those few exceptions see 1[g]). The reasons that evoke this response are numerous.

(i) God's creation of the universe elicits a shout of joy. In Job 38:7 the morning stars respond to God's laying the foundation of the earth with a shout of joy (see Dahood, 391). In Ps 65:8[9] the one who "formed the mountains" (v. 6) is the recipient of shouts of joy. Other passages that call for a shout of joy also describe God as Creator (Ps 95:1).

(ii) More frequently God evokes shouts of joy in response to his acts of redemption. God will rescue his people from their dispersion among the nations, and they will respond with shouts of joy especially as they see the tremendous bounty of grain, wine, and oil that God will provide for them. On a more personal level, in Ps 51:14[16] the psalmist calls on God to save him from his "bloodguilt," promising to respond with shouts of joy. The very heavens and earth are called upon to shout and sing with joy because God redeemed Israel by sweeping away their sins (Isa 44:23; 49:13).

(iii) In a number of cases where the vb. *rnn* occurs God's salvation is linked with his appearance as a divine warrior (→). So much so, it is tempting to think that in certain contexts the vb. has the narrower meaning of to give a victory shout. Zeph 3:14 calls on Israel to give a shout since God has beaten off their enemy. Zech 2:10[14] invites Zion to "shout and be glad" since God will avenge Israel against those who plundered them. He will save them from their oppression and live among them. Ps 20:5[6] clearly illustrates how the joyful shouting is a response to the successful waging of warfare, "We will shout for joy when you are victorious...."

In the light of the connection between the shout for joy and warfare, it is interesting to note that the vb. occurs in most of the OT contexts where the phrase "new song" occurs. Elsewhere (Longman and Reid, 45, 191) it has been suggested that "new song" refers to a song sung in the light of a victory in warfare. Through warfare God has created new situations to the advantage of his people as he frees them from oppression. The vb. *rnn* is found in the context of "new song" in Ps 33:1; 96:12; 98:4, 8; 149:15. This association heightens the connection between warfare and the shout.

(iv) The vb. signifies the proper response of the people to the appearance of God's glory, even in nonmilitary settings. After the ordination of Aaron and his sons as priests in Israel, as they begin their sacrificial ministry, God appeared in his glory and the people "shouted for joy" (Lev 9:24). In Isa 35:2 the wilderness will burst into bloom at the appearance of God's glory and will "shout for joy" (see also Ps 63:7[8]).

(v) Not only do people shout for joy because God is Creator, Savior, victor, but also because he is the provider of material bounty. According to Jer 31:12, those on the heights of Zion will rejoice because God gives them grain, new wine, herds, and oil.

(vi) Ps 89:12[13] combines a number of these themes. Tabor and Hermon sing for joy at God's name in a context that celebrates God as Creator (v. 11[12]) and Savior, specifically as the divine warrior (vv. 9-10[10-11], 13[14]).

(d) A multitude of voices shout for joy to God in the Bible. Most often the ones who shout are God's people. Indeed, according to Prov 29:6 it is only the righteous who can shout for joy; the wicked are unable because of their sin. In one unusual but theologically provocative passage, the dead rise out of their dusty graves to "shout for joy" before the Lord (Isa 26:19). Job 38:7 describes the angels as shouting for joy at the sight of God creating the world. Different parts of God's inanimate creation also take part in the symphony of praise (the desert [Isa 35:2]; the heavens [44:23; 49:13]; the mountains [Ps 98:8]; the trees [96:12]; Tabor and Hermon [89:12(13)]; and Lady Wisdom [Prov 1:20; 8:3]).

(e) Certain contexts make it clear that the shout of joy takes place within a formal cultic setting (Lev 9:24; Ps 63:7[8]; 132:9), but the vast majority of cases have no clear connection to the formal worship apparatus of Israel. One may praise God both formally and informally.

(f) The vb. occurs in one strange context that deserves special mention. Ps 78 provides a theologically charged history of Israel from the time of the wilderness wanderings to the eve of the Davidic dynasty. In vv. 56-64 it describes God's anger against the tribe of Ephraim, with disastrous consequences for Israel. Verse 65 recounts the reversal. God comes to save his people from his enemies. The change from the absence to the presence of God is described as God's waking from sleep. The second line intensifies the thought of the first. Not only was God asleep; he was in a wine-induced deep sleep. The vb. used to describe God's action in the second colon is from *rnn*. The NIV obscures this by translating the vb. "wakes," which has no justification. Rather, God wakes up, "like a man shouting from wine." It is hard to tell from the context, but this image may be referring to God's slow arousal and the vb. may refer to the loud moan of a person who wakes up with a hangover. If so, then this use of *rnn* is similar to those described in 1(h).

(g) On most occasions the vb. describes an emotional and physical response to the presence and provision of God. In two instances, however, other factors motivate the shout. In the first place, as Job describes his life before his affliction, he enumerates the ways in which his life helped other people. In Job 29:13 he says that his actions caused the heart of the widow to sing for joy. In Isa 16:10 Moab's desolation results in the absence of shouts of joy in its orchards and vineyards. Apparently, then, when they were thriving and blossoming, it was the fertility of the land that evoked such a response.

(h) As anticipated above, in two instances the shout is not one of joy, but one of sadness. In Ps 84:2[3] the psalmist, apparently separated from the temple where God's presence is felt, moans for that experience once again. In Lam 2:19 the author moans because of the devastation and lack in Jerusalem since God abandoned them and then attacked them.

2. (a) The nom. *rinnâ* shows the same semantic disparity as the vb. That is, in a majority of cases it means a shout of joy, even a victory shout (see 2[b-f]) but in a number of cases, proportionally more than the vb., it means moan (see 2[g]). The nom. occurs 33x, and, like the vb., predominantly in Psalms (15x) and Isaiah (9x). The nom. often occurs in the same context, even the same line, as the vb. (Isa 44:23; 54:1).

(b) As with the vb., God is the object of the shout. He is the one who receives the shout of praise (2[f]) as well as the plea for help (2[g]). There is one striking exception to this in Zeph 3:17. Here Jerusalem is told that, in response to his rescuing of the city, God "will rejoice over you with singing" (*b^{e}rinnâ*). God is the one who shouts for joy.

(c) The people sing shouts of joy in response to God's saving action in their life (Ps 105:43; Isa 49:13). In two notable places in the Psalms God's action causes the transformation of weeping into the rejoicing shouts of the saved (Ps 30:5[6]; 126:5, 6).

(d) Many of the contexts in which Israel responds to God's saving action with a shout of joy specifically describe God as the divine warrior (Ps 118:15; Isa 14:7; 48:20; 51:11). Prov 11:10 associates the shout of joy as the right response when evil people are destroyed. Most of these are responses to winning a battle with God's aid. Thus, the shout of joy is a kind of victory shout. However, in 2 Chron 20:22 Jehoshaphat's army sings these songs as they march into battle, perhaps anticipating victory, since they know that God is fighting on their side.

(e) Also like the vb., the nom. is occasionally found in clearly cultic contexts. In Ps 42:4[5] the psalmist thinks back to the good times in the past when he was able to participate in the formal worship of Israel. He thinks of the processions at the temple when he sang songs of joy with the community of worshipers before the Lord. The songs of joy are associated with the thank offerings in 107:22.

(f) Many different people, creatures, and even inanimate objects offer a shout for joy before God. Not only people (Isa 48:20) but also the mountains (49:13) as well as the nations (Ps 47:1[2]) shout joyfully in his presence. Mention has already been made (see 2[b]) of God's singing in Zeph 3:17.

(g) On the opposite side of the emotional spectrum, *rinnâ* can mean, not shouts of joy or happiness, but sadness or desire or yearning. Solomon calls on God to pay attention to his cry for help as he directs it toward his presence in the temple (1 Kgs 8:28), many psalms use the term in the context of an appeal to God for help or in need (Ps 17:1; 61:1[2]; 88:2[3]; 106:44; 119:169; 142:6[7]), and Jeremiah also uses the word in this way (Jer 7:16; 11:14; 14:12). There is also one clear military context in which the word refers to the shouting or singing after the battle, but since it is a defeat and not a victory, the word is rightly understood as a cry (1 Kgs 22:36).

3. The nom. r^e*nānâ* occurs in four texts (Job 3:7; 20:5; Ps 6:6[5]; 100:2). In all four cases the word means joyful song or joyful shout.

4. In Ps 32:7 we have the only occurrence of a nom. *rôn* with the same meaning as the noms. *rinnâ* and r^e*nānâ*. The psalmist praises God for surrounding him with songs of deliverance. See Craigie, *Psalms 1-50*, WBC, 1983, 265, for a critical discussion of attempted emendations of this word.

P-B According to Jastrow (1484) the root has the same two meanings (praise or complaint) in Mishnaic Heb. (occurrences are in the pi.). The root is also fairly frequent at Qumran in praise contexts (1QM 4, 4; 14, 2.6; 19, 7; 1QH 3, 23; 11, 5.14.26; 1QS 10, 14.17; 1QSb 2, 25 [see *TWAT* 7:545]). The Septuagint translates the root *rnn* in a variety of ways, but in the Psalms most frequently with *agalliaomai* and in Isaiah with *euphrainō*.

Shout, (war-)cry, yell: → *hêdād* (shout, # 2116); → *ṣwḥ* (shout, # 7423); → *ṣrḥ* (yell, call shrilly, raise the war-cry, # 7658); → *rw'* (shout, give war-cry, # 8131); → *rnn* (yell, shout [w. joy], moan, # 8264)

Bibliography

THAT 2:781-86; *TWAT* 7:538-45; M. Astour, "Two Ugaritic Serpent Charms," *JNES* 27, 1968, 13-36; F. Crüsemann, *Studien zur Formgeschichte von Hymnus und Danklied in Israel*, WMANT 32, 1969, 38-82; M. J. Dahood, "Hebrew-Ugaritic Lexicography X," *Bib* 53, 1972, 386-403; T. Longman and D. G. Reid, *God Is a Warrior*, 1995; N. E. Wagner, "*rinnâ* in the Psalter," *VT* 10, 1960, 435-41.

Tremper Longman III

8265 (r^e*nānâ*, shout of joy), → # 8264

8266 (r^e*nānîm*, ostrich), → # 6416

8268 (*rāsîs* I, dew drops), → # 8272

8270	רֶסֶן

רֶסֶן (*resen* I), nom. a mouthpiece, a harness perhaps of rope for use with animals, restraint (# 8270).

ANE Aram. *risnā'*, bridle; Arab. *rasan*, halter.

OT As a harness by which an animal was controlled, the term *resen* came to stand for restraint (e.g Job 30:11 NIV; cf. "leash," Job 41:13[5]). God will place his harness or bridle on the mouth of nations which, like horses not yet "broken" or domesticated, will by a jerk be tossed to their destruction (Isa 30:28; see J. Oswalt, *Isaiah 1-39*, 566-67). *resen* and *meteg*, bridle (→ # 5496), each occur 4x; they occur together in Ps 32:9.

Restraint, muzzle, bridle, mouth piece: → *blm* (restrain, # 1178); → *ḥsm* (muzzle, # 2888); → *meteg* (bridle, # 5496); → *resen* I (mouth piece, # 8270)

Elmer A. Martens

8272	רסס

רסס (*rss* I), q. moisten (# 8272); רָסִיס (*rāsîs*), nom. dew drops (# 8268).

ANE Sem. attestations may reflect two homonymic roots: one with a basic meaning of crushing (Old Akk., Mish. Heb., and Aram.) and the other involving the sprinkling of a liquid (Arab. and Syr.). Although interpreted in other ways, in the Ugar. myth of Baal and Mot (*KTU* 1.5), line 4 contains the expression *krs*. This has been understood as the preposition *k* (as, like, in), followed by *rs*, cognate to *r*[e]*sîsîm* (perspiration, Caquot and Sznycer [240]), describing the heavens as inflamed and dripping like the perspiration from your garment or breaking, crushing (Gibson, 68, describing how Mot will crush Baal).

OT The q. vb. appears as an inf. in a description of a temple offering in Ezek 46:14: "a third of a hin of oil to moisten (*rss*) the flour." The nom. form with the similar meaning of dampness is found in S of Songs 5:2: "My head is drenched with dew, my hair with the dampness of the night." While in the above two examples the context requires a meaning of wetness, the remaining example, Amos 6:11, allows for no such meaning: "He will smite the great house into pieces (*r*[e]*sîsîm*), and the small house into bits (*r*[e]*sîsîm*)." This distinction in usage has led to speculation of a homonymous root (Andersen and Freedman, 576; BDB, 944).

Dripping, flowing, trickling: → *'ēgel* (drop, # 103); → *dlp* I (drip, # 1940); → *zwb* (flow, # 2307); → *ṭrd* (continuous dripping, # 3265); → *mar* II (drop, # 5254); → *ngr* (flow, gush forth, pour out, # 5599); → *nzl* (flow, trickle, # 5688); → *nṭp* (drip, pour, # 5752); → *'rp* I (drip, # 6903); → *pkh* (trickle, # 7096); → *r*[e]*wāyâ* (overflow, # 8122); → *ryr* (flow, # 8201); → *rss* I (moisten, # 8272); → *r'p* (drip, flow, rain, # 8319)

BIBLIOGRAPHY

F. I. Andersen and D. N. Freedman, *Amos: A New Translation with Introduction and Commentary*, AB, 1989; A. Caquot and M. Sznycer, *Textes Ougaritiques, Tome I: Mythes et légendes*, Litteratures anciennes du proche-orient 7, 1974; J. C. L. Gibson, *Canaanite Myths and Legends*, 1978.

Richard S. Hess

8273 (*ra'*, bad, evil), → # 8317

8275 (*rēa'* I, shouting), → # 8131

8276 (*rêa'* II, neighbor, friend), → # 8287

8278 (*rōa'*, ugliness), → # 8317

8279	רעב

רעב (*r'b*), q. to be hungry, famished, starving; to hunger, go hungry; hi. (twice only) to cause to hunger, to let go hungry (# 8279); רָעָב (*rā'āb*), nom. famine, hunger, starvation (# 8280); רָעֵב (*rā'ēb*), adj. hungry (# 8281); רְעָבוֹן (*r*[e]*'ābôn*), starving (# 8282).

ANE Cognates are found in Ugar. *rġb*, be hungry; Eth. (*rĕḫbä*), be hungry; and Arab. (*raġuba*), be voracious.

OT 1. *r'b* denotes lack of food or of water (Amos 8:11; 1 Kgs 18:1, 2); it is paired with thirst (*ṣm'*; → # 7532) only in Deut 28:48; Neh 9:15; 2 Chron 32:11; Isa 5:13; Amos 8:11. In biblical times the majority of Israelites eked out a marginal existence from the fields. As in all marginal societies food production lay at the heart of the economy, and any upset in climatic or political continuity could plunge the country into famine. The descent into Egypt by the patriarchs (Gen 37-50) reflects the way in which Canaan, a land directly dependent on local precipitation, could suffer famine while Egypt, which gathered precipitation from a large area via the Nile, could still produce crops. The Amarna letters reflect a period of warfare and its associated shortages (Moran). The failure of early or late rain (Deut 11:14), as well as unseasonal or immoderate precipitation (Exod 9:25), parasitic plague (Exod 10:14; Amos 4:9), and scorched earth policies in war (2 Kgs 3:19; cf. Deut 20:19, 20) were recognized as causes of famine (1 Kgs 8:37). Hunger is only one of many evils that may afflict humankind, and it is linked in the OT with thirst and shame (Isa 65:13); loss of moral restraint (Isa 8:21); plague and war (Jer 42:14-17); nakedness and want (Deut 28:48); pestilence (Deut 32:24); death, sword, captivity (Jer 15:2); and wild beasts (Job 5:20, 22; Ezek 5:17). Ezekiel's quartet of disasters—sword, famine, wild beasts, and plague (Ezek 14:21)—echo the interrelated nature of such events in contemporary experience. This passage undergirds John's vision of the apocalyptic horsemen (Rev 6:1-8).

Palestine is crossed by the border between the desert and the sea. Small variations in precipitation result in large shifts in its locus. The early Iron Age appears to have been a dry period in the Near East (Shea). The incursion of the Midianites (Judg 6:2-6, 11) and the migration of Ruth may reflect population movements triggered by famine, though this must remain speculative. David's three-year famine falls within this period (2 Sam 21:1). Famines are attested in Mesopotamia in these centuries (Neumann and Parpola). Extrabiblical attestation for such conditions in the time of Elijah and Elisha, however, is lacking (1 Kgs 17:1; 2 Kgs 8:1-3). The drought mentioned in the Persian period by Haggai (Hag 1:10, 11) was local so far as is known, but the lack of supplies (Hag 1:6; 2:16) was probably partly due to social misorganization (Hag 1:1-5). In postbiblical literature, partly supported by Josephus (*Ant* 12:378), it is noted that keeping the sabbatical law for the land may lead to a shortage of food and hence to political danger (1 Macc 6:48-54; cf. Lev 25:1-7; Exod 23:10, 11). The Mishnah ('Abot 5:8) asserts that failure to keep the law of a Sabbath for the land brings pestilence. Josephus records Herod the Great's purchase of corn from Egypt at his own expense for common consumption during the drought of 25-24 BCE (*Ant* 15:299-316). Josephus tells also of Queen Helena of Adiabene making corn available in the period 44-48 AD (*Ant* 20:49-52, 101; cf. Acts 11:27-30).

2. Israel developed its understanding of God's relation to the fertilizing forces of nature alongside other nations, who credited these forces to various different gods. It is inevitable that both similarities and differences should be seen between the separate traditions (Cross, 147-69; Miller, 1987, 59-60; Greenfield; 67-70; Millard and Bordreuil, 1982). Israel's belief that God directly controlled natural forces made rainfall and the soil's fertility a matter of central religious concern. It was Israel's conviction that God gave the land fertility out of his love (Deut 7:12-13) and out of concern for his honor (Ezek 36:22-30; Weinfeld, 316-19).

Genesis (1:1-2:4; 8:22) presents the normative Israelite belief, viz., a picture of the natural world whose various members and forces, regarded as having divine status by the neighboring nations, were secularized but still under the control of God. The biblical understanding is that God could give rain and the soil's fertility as a blessing or withhold them as a sanction (Deut 28). The contest on Carmel between Elijah and the priests of Baal is evidence that the orthodox view was not always held by all Israelites (1 Kgs 18:1-36).

God's concern for the moral welfare of his people is at one with his purpose for their material well-being, hence the OT teaching that godly obedience leads to material plenty (Lev 26:3-12) and moral disobedience leads to material lack (Lev 26:14-20). These sanctions formed part of God's covenant with his people. The righteous understood such actions as a testimony to the love of God and as a rebuke to the ungodly (Ps 107:33-42). This assumption made it natural for the prophets to move from a statement of fact about failed crops to a prayer of confession of sin (Jer 14:1-10). The existence of such God-given sanctions invited repentance (Amos 4:6-11); the prophets' task was to issue the summons.

Those who prefer the empty visions of diviners to the testimony given by God are given empty stomachs and are emptied of hope (Isa 8:19-22). The experience of the Exile and of the Return failed to convince Israel of this truth, and the warning had to be repeated (Isa 65:11-15). Deuteronomy includes hunger among the curses awaiting those who disobey God's Law (Deut 28:48); and the Song of Moses, which in its present form appears to reflect the experience of the Exile, reinforces this message (32:19-27). Jeremiah even regards refusal to submit to the invading Babylonians as a resistance to God, which will invoke the same penalty (Jer 42:13-17). The drought in Elijah's time was also sent by God (1 Kgs 17:1) and announced by the prophet. Its purpose was not only to summon individuals to righteousness, but to effect a change in the established religious and political pattern (1 Kgs 18:39-40; 19:15-18).

The confident connection of want with ungodliness does not go unchallenged in the OT. The book of Job and such passages as Ps 73 and Eccl 5:8-12[7-11] reflect an awareness that human experience does not always follow neat formulae. Our Lord's words in Luke 13:1-5 and John 9:1-3 show how persistent such rigid expectations can be, and he endorses the openness to experience expressed by such writers. Paul takes the same view, asserting that hunger does not separate believers from God (Rom 8:35-33).

3. Amos uses *rā'āb* as a metaphor for the desperation of those who perversely seek the knowledge of God in places where he is not to be found (Amos 8:11-14; cf. Deut 30:11-14; Jer 2:13). H. W. Wolff (330) observes that the phrase "I will send" (hi. *šlḥ*) is always used in the OT of God's sending a disaster, in this case, the denial of his word to those who refuse to hear it (cf. Ezek 33:30-33; 2 Cor 3:12-18). Andersen and Freedman (*Amos*, ad.loc) note that the punishment is to be unable to hear the word of God. This they take to mean the withholding of prophets who will make Mosaic teaching plain.

Deut 8:3 draws on a similar connection between God's word and humanity's well-being when adducing a contemporary relevance to the story of the manna in the desert. However, here it may allude not merely to the speech of God in the Law or by the prophets, but to the whole creative initiative of God (H. Brunner, *VT* 8, 428-29;

cf. von Rad, 18-19, footnote). Jesus' use of Deut 8:3 is conditioned by his circumstance and the function of the temptation in his determination of the priorities for his ministry (Matt 4:4; Luke 4:4).

4. The nom. *r*[e]*'ābôn* (GKC 85u; Moscati, 12:21.) occurs only in Gen 42:19, 33 and Ps 37:19. In Gen it is used of the supplies that Jacob's sons took back to Canaan from Egypt, i.e., "grain/food ... for your starving households." Ps 37:19 says, "In days of famine (*r*[e]*'ābôn*; i.e., in days when famine relief is needed) they (the blameless) will enjoy plenty."

5. Theological reflections on hunger.

(a) The effect of hunger on those who suffer it varies. The godly have their trust confirmed by their experience; the ungodly are confirmed in their wayward disposition (Ps 107:42; Isa 8:21). The hunger of an enemy creates a chance for the godly man to create a new state of affairs (Prov 25:21; cf. Isa 58:10; Rom 12:20). To relieve hunger was a godly duty (Ezek 18:7, 16), while to hide from fulfilling it, especially behind a cloak of piety (Isa 58:5, 7), was to reject God (cf. Job 22:4-11). That reminders were needed reveals that the duty was often neglected.

In all periods of history prolonged hunger has distorted normal human reactions (Isa 29:8) and brought about the collapse of normal moral restraint (Isa 29:8; 2 Kgs 6:25-29; cf. Josephus, *Wars* 5:424-38, 571; 6:1-3, 193-213; Weinfeld, 126-29). Hunger has also been a major universal spur to migration (cf. Gen 42:1-5; Ruth 1:1; Carpenter, 59-66).

(b) Freedom from hunger and thirst was a mark of the promised golden age of restoration (Isa 4:2; 25:6-8; Hos 2:21-22[23, 24]; Amos 9:13) and of the restoration after the Exile (Ezek 34:29; 36:29, 30). The experience of the returned exiles, however, did not match up to these hopes (Hag 1:6, 9-11; Neh 5:1-3).

Freedom from hunger, historically, brought its own danger of complacency (Deut 6:10-12). The provision of plenty is a gift bestowed by God out of his own gracious initiative (Ps 107:4-9, 35-42) and is the particular privilege of those who hope in God (37:18-19; 146:5, 7), even though they be of non-Israelite stock (146:9). The initiative of God must be held in tension with human responsiveness as the ground for deliverance from hunger (33:12-19). This makes both fatalism and self-rescue entirely by one's own efforts equally inadequate responses in times of need.

(c) God is one and has made humankind in his own image. From this it follows that human life is linked at all levels; the moral character of people and their physical experience are connected. True or false action in one sphere of life can be expected to lead to prosperity or degradation in another. God is one and those made in his image cannot erect effective partitions either within themselves or between themselves and others. This necessary interaction holds on the basic level of an individual's inner experience, on the broader level of interpersonal action, and on the sum of both, which makes up the nation's life and character. However, the time lag between action and consequence, and the possible incidence of the consequence upon those who have no fault, give rise to the universal human complaint that God has forgotten justice. The biblical writers themselves voice this.

There is, however, another reaction on their part, and this is to assert those moral connections within life that the doubters question. This is what Ezekiel does by connecting moral renewal with fruitful crops and the removal of political shame

(Ezek 36:24-31) at a time when the nation's hopes seemed to have been denied. Jeremiah, interestingly, gives the mirror image of this by connecting refusal to obey, attempted avoidance of the consequences of disobedience, and the ultimate suffering of war, famine, and plague (Jer 42:13-17). The assertion of the moral connection is a part of the biblical understanding of the place of hunger and other evils in human experience. The pattern of cause and effect is usually held to act in the direction from moral mischoice to experiential consequence. It can also operate in the opposite direction, to a pattern of moral existence extending to all people and across the time limits of single human lives.

From this it follows that all people, not only God's people, are involved in it; and that people often experience the consequences of actions that were not their own. This is reflected in 2 Sam 21:1-9. The situation is presented by the author as a wholly impersonal complex of events. Suffering is being borne by those who have committed no crime themselves, and the operative fault—the slaughter by Saul—is atoned for by those who carry no blame. This passage raises theological perplexities that may be eased by considering the origin of the acts recorded. It is possible that the victims' deaths were connected with a non-Israelite fertility sacrifice (v. 9; cf. 1 Kgs 16:29-34; 2 Kgs 3:21-27). Such a worldview has been abolished by OT faith itself (cf. Hertzberg, 384-85).

Hunger: → *kāpān* (poverty of diet, # 4103); → *māzeh* (wasting, # 4642); → *r'b* (hungry, famished, # 8279; *rā'āb*, famine, # 8280; *r^e'abôn*, starving, # 8282)

BIBLIOGRAPHY

F. I. Andersen and D. N. Freedman, *Amos*, AB 24a, 1989; H. Brunner, "Was aus dem Munde Gottes geht," *VT* 8, 1958; E. Carpenter, *Discontinuity in Greek Civilisation*, 1966; F. M. Cross, *Canaanite Myth and Hebrew Epic*, 1973; A. D. Crown, "Towards a Reconstruction of the Climate of Palestine 8000BC—O BC," *JNES* 31, 1972, 312-30; J. C. Greenfield, "Aspects of Aramean Religion," *Ancient Israelite Religion*, FS F. M. Cross, 1987; H. W. Hertzberg, *I and II Samuel*, OTL, 1964; Josephus, *Antiquities*, 1943; idem, *Wars*, 1927; A. R. Millard and P. Bordreuil, "A Statue with Assyrian and Aramaic Inscriptions," *BA* 45, 1982, 135-41; P. D. Miller, Jr., "Aspects of the Religion of Ugarit," *Ancient Israelite Religion*, Festschrift F. M. Cross, 1987; W. L. Moran, *Les Lettres d'El Amarna*, 1987; S. Moscati (ed.), *An Introduction to the Comparative Grammar of the Semitic Languageis*, 1964; J. Neumann and S. Parpola, "Climate Change and the Eleventh Century Eclipse of Assyria and Babylonia," *JNES* 46, 1987, 161-82; M. H. Pope, *Job*, AB 15, 1974; G. von Rad, *Genesis*, OTL, 1961; W. H. Shea, "Famine," *ABD* 2, 1992, 769-73; M. Weinfeld, *Deuteronomy and the Deuteronomic School*, 1972; C. Westermann, *Genesis 37-50*, SPCK, 1987; H. W. Wolff, *Joel and Amos*, Hermeneia, 1977.

Robert J. Way

8280 (*rā'āb*, famine), → # 8279

8281 (*rā'ēb*, hungry), → # 8279

8282 (*r^e'ābôn*, starving), → # 8279

8283	רעד

רעד (*r'd*), q. tremble; hi. shake, tremble (# 8283); רַעַד (*ra'ad*), nom. trembling, shaking (# 8284); רְעָדָה (*r^e'ādâ*), nom. trembling, shaking (# 8285).

OT 1. The Heb. root *r'd* appears 9x: 3x as a vb. (Ezra 10:9; Ps 104:32; Dan 10:11), 2x as a masculine nom. (Exod 15:15; Ps 55:5[6]), and 4x as a fem. nom. (Job 4:14; Ps 2:11; 48:6[7]; Isa 33:14). This Heb. root represents a condition of such immense terror as to produce physical trembling in both human beings and nature.

Characteristic of many of the words in this semantic field, the verbal form of *r'd* depicts the trembling of the earth at the theophanic presence of Yahweh, "he [Yahweh] who looks at the earth, and it *trembles*, who touches the mountains, and they smoke" (Ps 104:32). Similarly, Daniel's response to the word of the numinous being was that of trembling (*mār'îd*, hi. part.) (Dan 10:11). The term *r'd* is used to describe the lamenting condition of a penitent people (*mār'îdîm*, hi. ptc.) (Ezra 10:9).

2. As a nom., the trembling of *r'd* is characteristically depicted as something that seizes (*'ḥz* [→ # 296], Exod 15:15; Ps 48:6[7]; Isa 33:14) or comes upon (*bw'* [→ # 995] in Ps 55:5[55:6 MT] and *qr'*, call [NIV seized; → # 7925] in Job 4:14) a person. This type of terror is attributed to those overwhelmed by an enemy, sinners before God, and one in the midst of tremendous suffering.

Shaking, terror, trembling: → *g'š* (rise and fall noisily, swell, surge, # 1723); → *zw'* (tremble, quake, be afraid, # 2316); → *zll* II (shake, quake, tremble, # 2362); → *ḥalḥālâ* (shaking, trembling, anguish, # 2714); → *ḥrg* (come out trembling, # 3004); → *ḥrd* (tremble, shudder, startle, # 3006); → *yr'* (tremble, be fainthearted, # 3760); → *mwṭ* (waver, reel, stagger, shake, reel, # 4572); → *m'd* (slip, slide, shake, totter, # 5048); → *nwd* (shake, totter, waiver, wander, mourn, flee, # 5653); → *nwṭ* (shake, quake, # 5667); → *nw'* (shake, tremble, stagger, totter, wave, # 5675); → *n'r* II (shake, shake off, # 5850); → *smr* (shudder, have goose-bumps, bristle, # 6169); → *'iw'îm* (distortion, stagger, dizzy, # 6413); → *pwq* I (stagger, wobble, reel, totter, # 7048); → *pḥd* I (tremble, be in dread, # 7064); → *plṣ* (shudder, shake, tremble, # 7145); → *qwṣ* I (feel disgust, frighten, cause dread, # 7762); → *rgz* (agitate, quiver, shake, excite, rouse up, agitate, # 8074); → *rnh* I (rattle, # 8261); → *r'd* (tremble, shake, tremble, # 8283); → *r'l* I (brandish, make to quiver, # 8302); → *r'š* I (quake, shake, leap, # 8321); → *rpp* (shake, quake, rock, # 8344); → *r^etēt* (terror, panic, trembling, # 8417); → *ś'r* I (be afraid, terrified, bristle with horror, # 8547)

Bibliography

TWOT 2:852.

M. V. Van Pelt/W. C. Kaiser, Jr.

8284 (*ra'ad*, trembling, shaking), → # 8283

8285 (*r^e'adâ*, trembling, shaking), → # 8283

8286	רעה

רעה (*r'h* I), q. to feed, graze, pasture, tend, shepherd; also metaphorically: to lead a people, to rule (# 8286); מִרְעֶה (*mir'eh*), nom. pasture, pasturage (# 5337); מַרְעִית (*mar'ît*), nom. pasturage (# 5338); רְעִי (*r^e'î*), nom. pasture (# 8297). Related words are: אהל (*'hl* I), q. to obtain pasturing rights (# 182); בער (*b'r* II), pi. graze (a field), ruin, sweep away;

hi. be grazed (# 1278); דֹּבֶר (*dōber*), nom. remote place, pasture (# 1824); כַּר (*kar* II), nom. pasture (# 4120); מִגְרָשׁ (*migrāš*), nom. open space around city or sanctuary, pastureland (# 4494); מִשְׁלָח (*mišlāḥ*), nom. pastureland (→ # 5448); נָוֶה (*naweh*), nom. pastureland, abode, residence (→ # 5661); נָוָה (*nawā*), nom. pastureland, abode, residence (→ # 5659); נֹקֵד (*nōqēd*), nom. shepherd (→ # 5924).

ANE 1. *r'h and derivatives.* Equivalent forms of the vb. *r'h* occur in numerous ANE languages; e.g., in Akk. *re'u(m)*, Syr. *rᵉ'ā'*, Mand. *RAA* I, *r'ia*, ESA *r'y*, Eth. *rĕ'ĕya, rĕaya,* and Arab. *ra'ā* from *r'y*. The nom. *ro'eh*, shepherd (q. part.), also has numerous cognates: in Phoen. *r'm* (pl.), Egyp. Aram. *r'y'*, Ugar. *r'y* sing., Akk. *re'û(m)* (masc.), *rē'ītu(m)* (fem.), Syr. *rā'yā'* (masc.), *rā'ītā'* (fem.), Copt. *r'y'*, Mand. *r'ia/r'iia*, ESA *r'y*, and Arab. *rā'in*. Variations of the vb. and nom. further occur in personal names. The equivalent of the nom. *mir'eh* occurs in a MS of the Samar. Pent. *mērī*. The nom. *mar'ît* has cognates in Eth. *mar'ēt* and Tigre *mar'īt*.

2. *Nom. meaning pasturage, pastureland, abode, residence.* Various forms of the nom. *naweh* and *nawâ* occur in cognate languages, e.g., in Sam. *nābe*, Arab. *nawan, niyyat*, Akk. *naw/mûm*, and Syr. *nāwītā'*. Cf. Malamat (168-72) and Ringgren (*TWAT* 5:293) on the use of *naweh* and its par. form in the Mari documents, *nawûm*.

3. *Nom. meaning shepherd.* Equivalents of *nōqēd* occur in Ugar. (*nqd* is also used as a title for an eminent official), Akk. (*nāqidu*, originally used for shepherd in distinction of *re'u*, keeper of cattle), and Arab. (*naqqād*).

4. *Vb. meaning to obtain pasturing rights.* The Arab. vb. *'ahila* has the same meaning as the Heb. form.

OT 1. *Literal usage.* (a) *r'h* and derivatives. The q. form of *r'h* occurs 168x in the OT. Nearly half of these occurrences (83x) appear in the masc. subst. part. form (*rō'eh*). The fem. part. *rō'â* (female shepherd) occurs once (Gen 29:9). Significant chapters seem to be: Ezek 34, where the vb. occurs 31x, and Zech 11, where it occurs 10x. The derivatives of *r'h* occur less commonly: *mir'eh* (13x), *mar'ît* (10x), and *rᵉ'î* (1x).

The vb. *r'h* normally occurs with two types of subj.: (i) People as subj.: *r'h* can then be translated to feed, to tend, to shepherd. The subst. part. *rō'eh* and *rō'â* fall in this category. In the nomadic society of the patriarchal period the shepherd's task was preferably fulfilled by members of the family (by the daughters only in the immediate vicinity of the dwelling) (*NIDNTT* 3:564). Another word (*nōqēd*) is used twice in the OT (2 Kgs 3:4 and Amos 1:1) as a designation for an animal-keeper. (ii) Animals as subj.: In this case *r'h* can be translated to graze (intransitive). Another vb., *b'r*, also falls in this category but is used transitively (to graze a field, to destroy).

The animals most often associated with the vb. *r'h* (274x in the OT) are *ṣō'n* (collective term for sheep and goat; → # 7366). In a number of cases (183x in the OT) *bāqār*, cattle, (→ # 1330), occurs with the vb., sometimes also in conjunction with *ṣō'n*. The term most often used for a shepherd's herd/flock is *'ēder* (39x in the OT [→ # 6373]).

(b) Places of pasturage. A number of Heb. words are used to designate the place where animals graze and where shepherds tend their flock. A few of them have already been mentioned as derivatives of the vb. *r'h*: *mir'eh* (13x in the OT), *mar'ît* (10x), and *rᵉ'î* (1x).

With the exception of 2 Sam 7:8, *nāweh* always occurs in poetic texts (*TWAT* 5:293). This nom. has an unusual pl., *nā'ôt,* which occurs only as st. constr. From the contexts where this nom. is used, as well as from its combinations with other nom., it is clear that the nom. most frequently designates a place of pasturage for animals. In a few cases (e.g., Isa 27:10 and Ezek 25:5) *nāweh* (among other words) is used threateningly to warn that Yahweh will destroy the settled areas of his enemies so that these areas will become places of pasturage for animals. In some texts *nāweh* stands par. to *bayit,* house, and *'ōhel,* tent. In these cases the nom. might have the meaning of "place of settlement." (This also applies to the use of *nāwâ* and *nāwôt* in the OT. These nom. refer both to places of pasturage and places of settlement.) In a few instances this nom. seems to refer to Yahweh's home on Mount Zion (e.g., 2 Sam 15:25). In Isa 33:20 *nāweh* is used with the adj. *ša'ᵃnān* to denote the steadfastness of the future Jerusalem.

migrāš, traditionally rendered pasture, pastureland, is particularly common in the lists of the Levitical cities (Josh 21; 1 Chron 6). Barr (21-25) cites several objections to the common supposition that the meaning of *migrāš* is pastureland. He mentions four arguments: (i) *migrāš* never occurs in texts about shepherds and flocks. The word then obviously does not belong to this semantic field. (ii) The ancient versions (the LXX in particular) never translate *migrāš* with the equivalent for "pasture," but rather render this word with the equivalents for "open lands, suburban areas, neighboring areas." (iii) There is no indication that Ezekiel's usage of *migrāš* in his description of the future temple and city involves pasturing of flocks. It seems more likely that a separating or protecting zone around the city is meant here. (iv) *migrāš* does not derive from the root *grš* (to drive out cattle). This erroneous derivation stimulated and supported the premise that pastureland was the actual meaning of *migrāš*. From these arguments Barr then concludes: "The one thing we know clearly about it is that it is a demarcated area outside the wall of cities" (Barr, 25). Barr then continues to describe the important historical implications of this rendering of the nom. He traces the historical development of land usage around an inhabited city. The role of the Levites in this development, in particular, is taken into consideration. This argumentation probably motivated the translation of KJV, which consistently renders it "suburbs."

(c) Pasturing rights. Traditionally the vb. *'hl* is translated with to pitch a tent (cf. the associated nom. *'ōhel*). Riggans (230-38) provides an interesting perspective on the usage of the phrase "to your tents, Israel" in Exod 32 and 1 Kgs 12. He argues that the phrase *lᵉ'ōhāleyka yiśrā'ēl* in 1 Kgs 12:16 (which constitutes a play of words with the passage in 1 Kgs 12:28, *hinnēh 'ᵉlōheykā yiśrā'ēl*) should be understood as a challenge of the authority of God's leaders (cf. also *TDOT* 1:118-30). In two cases, however, the vb. is translated better with "to obtain pasturing rights" (Gen 13:12, 18). Gen 13 discusses the negotiations between Abram and Lot on the issue of land rights. Lot chose the fertile Jordan Valley. According to v. 12 Lot and his people occupied territory up to Sodom. Abram, on the other hand, extended his territory up to Hebron (v. 18). This narrative clearly suggests a judicial context. Westermann classifies this narrative as "Streiterzählung," which should be understood against the background of patriarchal family life (202; see de Vaux's discussion of the Israelite family, *AncIsr*, 1961, 1:19-23). Wolf (*IDB* 3:558) mentions that pasturing territory was defined and remained the property of specific families. The seminomadic existence of the patriarchs should be understood against this background. To break up one's tents and to pitch them in another location was not a haphazard process of traveling from one place to another, but happened according to the contemporary pasturing customs and rights (cf. also *ABD* 1:634-38; *BHH* 1:209-10; 2:1319; 3:2108-9).

2. *Metaphorical usage.* (a) Human leaders as shepherds. In a pastoral community it is obvious that shepherd would also have a metaphorical usage. Although God was always regarded as Israel's principal shepherd (cf. next paragraph), its leaders were often regarded as shepherds. They had to tend to their flock, God's people. This metaphorical usage of *rō'eh* is understandable since shepherds were expected to show caution, patient care, and honesty towards their flock. These values, albeit on another level, also had to distinguish Israelite leaders. Although no Israelite king is ever explicitly called "shepherd," this metaphor is implied by several contexts. According to 2 Sam 5:2, e.g., David feeds or shepherds Israel. It is clear, however, that, unlike the usage in other ANE contexts, the title *shepherd* is never used in the OT to denote a deified king or human leader.

In the book of Jeremiah the image includes both political and religious leaders of varying rank and authority. It shows that by this time it was a well-established and regular designation for the ruling nobility. It was not only Israelite leaders who were referred to by this title. The most vivid example is the Persian king Cyrus, who is anointed as God's servant and chosen as his shepherd to rebuild Jerusalem and the temple (Isa 44:28).

A significant OT passage in this regard is Ezek 34 (cf. among others, Nielsen, 130). In this chapter the prophet is told to prophesy against the unjust leaders of Israel. These leaders are called the shepherds who do not tend to their flock but feed themselves instead. They are compared to evil shepherds, who slaughter the fattest animals to eat their fat and clothe themselves with their wool. They do not strengthen the weak, they do not heal the sick, they do not bring back the strayed, they do not seek the lost, and they have ruled them with force and harshness. Yahweh therefore directs his wrath against the evil shepherds. He promises to rescue his sheep from their mouths. He undertakes to make an end to the rule of the evil shepherds, the leaders of Israel.

(b) God as Shepherd. The depiction of Yahweh as Shepherd of his flock, Israel, is also not surprising in the OT context. The tradition of God as Israel's Shepherd originated in Israel's life in the desert. Although he is seldom explicitly called Shepherd, it is clear from several contexts that he should be understood as such. God is often portrayed with animals in his bosom that cannot keep up; he is mindful of the sheep that have young lambs and takes care not to overdrive them (cf. Gen 33:13; Isa 40:11; Ps 28:9). "The acknowledgment that Yahweh was the shepherd of Israel grew out of the living religious experience of the people and is thus to be distinguished from the cold courtly style of the ancient East. In invocation, in praise, in prayer for forgiveness, but also in temptation and despair, the worshippers know that they are still safe in the care of God the faithful shepherd.... At the same time the thought of God's unlimited sovereignty over his flock is not absent. In these contexts it co-exists in creative tension with the overwhelming consciousness of God's spontaneous love" (*NIDNTT* 3:565).

The symbol of God as Shepherd was common for depicting the Exodus. In several contexts (e.g., Exod 15:13, 17) this saving act of Yahweh portrays a shepherd who leads his flock to safe pastures. He is also described as a powerful leader who drives out other nations and makes room for his own flock (cf. Ps 78:52-55, 70-72). In some contexts (cf. Isa 40:11; 49:9-13; Jer 23:1-8; 31:8-14) the return from the Babylonian exile is described in similar metaphorical terms.

One of the classical OT passages depicting Yahweh as Shepherd is Ps 23. "Through the ages and every day anew, Psalm xxiii pre-eminently has afforded consolation and support to the believer. The words and imagery of this short and rich text will certainly accompany the faithful reader 'all the days of (his) life'" (Van Uchelen, 156). In this psalm we encounter an individual who confesses trust in the good Shepherd who will provide in all circumstances.

The shepherd motif underwent an interesting development in the exilic and postexilic era. A Shepherd, who is identified with David, is promised. He will be a leader and servant of God, who will reestablish the new Israel (cf. Ezek 34:23-24; 37:24-25). Bauer (*Enc. of Bibl. Theol.* 3:845) interprets these statements messianically: "The Messiah who is to come from the house of David is the first to whom (the term *shepherd*) is applied. He will exercise the function of a shepherd, and he alone as the only shepherd will pasture his people...." Zimmerli (849) states that Ezekiel does not elaborate on the relationship between the old covenant and the promised new covenant. He only designates the coming ruler as Shepherd—a good shepherd who will not continue the injustices of the preexilic shepherd-kings, who did not tend to the needs of their flock. The promised Shepherd will not, like his earthly predecessors, exploit the lives of his sheep, but will offer his life for them. The shepherding of the promised Shepherd "would this time be compatible with Yahweh's covenant relationship with his people" (Allen, 163). The aim of the shepherd motif's usage in the context of the new covenant thus accentuates the ethical and social role of the promised leader. "In this way the more ethical and social aspect of the task of the messianic ruler who is to come is set in contrast to a purely political understanding of the Messiah ..." (Bauer, *Enc. of Bibl. Theol.* 3:845).

It should be clear from this discussion why the messianic interpretation of the shepherd motif in some OT passages provided the seedbed for the flowering of Jesus' teachings on the shepherd. Cf. the discussion under NT.

3. *Summary.* From the above discussion it is clear that there are several Heb. nom. that could be translated by "pasture." These terms are *mir'eh*, *mar'ît*, *r^e'î*, *kar* II, *mišlāḥ*, *dōber*, *migrāš*, *nāweh*, and *nāwâ*. Although these terms could be used more or less synonymously, some of them have a special connotation. *dōber* also refers to "a remote place." *nāweh* and *nāwâ* could also be translated with "abode/residence." *migrāš* (as was shown above) refers to "open space around a city or a sanctuary," or even "suburb."

The vb. *r'h* I and *b'r* II both refer to the grazing of livestock. Used transitively, *r'h* refers to the feeding of sheep, while *b'r* refers to the grazing of a field. *b'r* (in the pi.) has a destructive connotation (to ruin, sweep away). *r'h* also differs from *b'r* in the sense that *r'h* could also be used metaphorically (to lead people).

P-B The G vbs. most often used in the LXX to translate the meanings to pasture/to shepherd are *nemō* and *poimainō*, with the associated nom. for pasture and shepherd, *nomē* and *poimēn*. Significantly, the LXX renders the occurrence of *migrāš* in Ezek with *diastema*. Barr (23), with reference to Zimmerli's remark on this translation, comments: "But this means that the LXX with its *diastema* was not here employing a *Verlegenheitswort*: this was not a rough expedient because the translator was unsure of the meaning, but was a correct rendition of the essential sense, 'a separation, an interval.'" Cf. the discussion of *migrāš* above.

In the Apocalypse of Hermas (from approximately the middle of the second century AD) an angel in the image of a shepherd functions as mediator of the revelation. As a result, this apocalypse came to be known as Pastor Hermae. A shepherd who functions as mediator is unknown to NT literature.

NT The shepherd metaphor also plays a significant role in the NT (cf. Nielsen). The shepherds in Jesus' birth narrative are well known. However, the metaphorical use of the shepherd as designation of God (cf. Luke 15:4-7, par. Matt 18:12-14) who seeks his lost sheep until he finds it is of equal importance. In John 10 this metaphor indicates that Jesus Christ is the Good Shepherd. Nielsen (131), who regards John 10 as a reinterpretation of Ezek 34 (cf. also *TWNT* 6:406), points out that the metaphor of the Good Shepherd has been adapted on one important point. Where Ezek 34 states that the shepherd only defends his flock against wild beasts, John 10 portrays Jesus Christ as the Good Shepherd who gives his life for the sheep. The Good Shepherd is both shepherd and sacrificial lamb. The proclamation of Christ as the Good Shepherd became a living experience for the NT church and acquired pastoral significance. Cf. Beyreuther's description of *poimēn* (*NIDNTT* 3:564-69).

Shepherd: → *nwh* I (rest, # 5657); → *ṣō'n* (flock, small cattle, # 7366); → *r'h* I (feed, graze, shepherd, rule, # 8286)

Bibliography

ABD 1:634-38; 5:1187-90; *BHH* 1:209-10; 2:1319; 3:2108-9; *Encyclopedia of Biblical Theology*, 3:844-46; *IDB* 3:558; *NBD* 1175-76; *NIDNTT* 3:564-69; *TDOT* 1:118-30; *THAT* 2:791-94; *TWAT* 5:293-97; *TWNT* 6:484-501; L. C. Allen, *Ezekiel 20-48*, WBC, 1990, 29; J. Barr, "*MIGRAŠ* in the Old Testament," *JSS* 29/1, 1984, 15-31; A. Malamat, "Pre-Monarchical Social Institutions in Israel in the Light of Mari," SVT 40, 1988, 165-76; K. Nielsen, "Shepherd, Lamb, and Blood," *ST* 46, 1992, 121-32; W. Riggans, "Gods, Tents, and Authority: A Study of Exodus 32 and I Kings 12," *JBQ* 19, 1990/1, 230-38; N. A. van Uchelen, "Psalm xxiii. Some Regulative Linguistic Evidence," *OTS* 25, 1989, 156-62; C. Westermann, *Genesis 12-36*, BK I/2, 1981; W. Zimmerli, *Ezechiel 25-48*, BK 13/2.

Louis Jonker

8286a	רֹעֶה/רֹעָה

רֹעֶה/רֹעָה (*rō'eh, rō'â*), shepherd(ess) (# 8286a); < רעה (*r'h* I), graze, pasture, shepherd (→ # 8286).

ANE Akk. *rē'û* (*AHw*, 977-78), common royal and divine epithet (*RLA* 4:424); Ugar. *r'y* as epithet of Baal (*KTU* 1.21:II:6; cf. J. C. de Moor, *An Anthology of Religious Texts from Ugarit*, 1987, 266, n. 269) and used in Egypt for kings and deities (Grapow, 156-57).

OT 1. Abel was a shepherd (Gen 4:2), as were the patriarchs of Israel (13:7-8; 26:20; 46:32, 34; 47:3), and David before he became king (1 Sam 17:34, 40; cf. Exod 2:17, 19; 1 Sam 21:7[8]; 25:7).

2. The image is used figuratively in prophecies of doom: Isa 13:20; 38:12; Jer 6:3; 12:10; 33:12; 51:23; Amos 1:2; Zeph 2:6; cf. in addition Eccl 12:11; Isa 31:4; Jer 49:19; 50:44; Amos 3:12; Zech 11.

3. The common ANE royal title is used for foreign rulers such as the leaders of Assyria (Nah 3:18) in a threatening way (cf. Nebuchadnezzar, Jer 43:12), and positively of Cyrus of Persia (Isa 44:28), who is called by Yahweh "my shepherd" because he permitted the return of Israel to the Holy Land. No known monarch of the kingdoms of Israel and Judah (but cf. Joshua, Num 27:17) has the title "shepherd." The reason may be because they are criticized for not acting as true shepherds (leaders) (1 Kgs 22:17 = 2 Chron 18:16; Isa 56:11; Jer 10:21; 23:1-2; 50:6; esp. Ezek 34; Zech 10:2-3).

4. As a common ANE divine epithet, it is scarcely used of Yahweh by Jacob (Gen 48:15; 49:24); for Israel in the future (Ps 80:1[2]; Jer 31:10); and individually (Ps 23:1). The main theological point is the caring of the shepherd for his flock and the trust it places in him.

5. Because the leaders of Israel failed as shepherds, Yahweh will give them trustworthy shepherds (i.e. leaders: Jer 3:15; 23:4) after his heart. He himself will look after them as shepherd and appoint one (Ezek 34:23): *'eḥād*) messianic shepherd, his future servant David (Ezek 34:12, 23, who becomes in the postexilic period the suffering servant (Zech 13:7; cf. 12:10; Mic 5:5[4]).

P-B The idea of God as a shepherd bringing back his flock is found in Sir 18:13. In QL the *m^e^baqqēr* is a shepherd (CD 13:9), and later Judaism transferred the metaphor to the Messiah (Pss. Sol. 17:45). RL is negative about shepherds, although the term is used for Moses and David as true shepherds (*TDNT* 6:488-89). Philo uses it typologically, and a more positive use of the term is found in the NT → *NIDNTT* 3:566-68; *TDNT* 6:485-502.

Arts, crafts, professions: → *'ommān* (craftsman, # 588); → *'ōpeh* (baker, # 685); → *gōdēr* (mason, # 1553); → *gallāb* (barber, # 1647); → *dayyāg* (fisherman, # 1900); → *ḥōṣēb* (stonecutter, # 2935); → *ḥārāš* (craftsman, # 3093); → *ḥōšēb* (weaver, # 3110); → *ṭabbāḥ* (butcher, # 3184); → *yôṣēr* (potter, # 3450); → *yāqûš* (fowler, # 3687); → *kbs* (wash, # 3891); → *kōrēm* (vinedresser, # 4144); → *mašqeh* (butler, # 5482); → *nōqēd* (shepherd?, # 5924); → *ṣayyād* I (hunter, # 7475); → *ṣōrēp* (goldsmith, # 7671); → *rō'eh* (shepherd, # 8286a); → *rōqēaḥ* (ointment-mixer, # 8382)
Pasture: → *nwh* I (rest, # 5657); → *r'h* I (feed, graze, shepherd, rule, # 8286)

Bibliography
THAT 2:791-94; G. Dalman, *Arbeit und Sitte in Palästina*, I-VII, 1928-42, repr. 1964; R. de Vaux, *Ancient Israel*, 1974, 76-78; H. Grapow, *Die Bildlichen Ausdrücke des Ägyptischen*, 1983; H. Hodges, *Technology in the Ancient World*, 1970; O. Keel, *The Symbolism of the Biblical World*, 1978.

I. Cornelius

8287	רעה

רעה (*r'h* II), q. associate with (BDB, 945); pi. be best man (only in Judg 14:20); hitp. make friends with (# 8287); מֵרֵעַ (*mērēa'* I), nom. official member of court or loyal companion (# 5335); רֵעַ (*rēa'* II), nom. other person, neighbor, friend (# 8276); רֵעֶה (*rē'eh* I), nom. official friend (# 8291); רֵעָה (*rē'â*), nom. female friend (# 8292); רְעוּת (*r^e^'ût* I), nom. female companion, friend (# 8295); רַעְיָה (*ra'yâ*), nom. female friend (# 8299).

ANE Akk. *rū'u* I, companion; Ugar. *r'*, friend, assistant. The OT usage of "other person" (see below) occurs in the eighth-century BC Siloam Tunnel inscription with the sense of "the other"—*'l r'w* (to the other, 2x in ll. 2, 3)—and *'š lqr' 'l r'w*, one towards another (l. 4). The contexts are those of the two groups of laborers approaching one another in completing the digging of the tunnel. The work groups approach one another, they call to one another, and finally their picks meet.

R. de Vaux identified *rē'eh* followed by the king's name or *hammelek*, the king, as derived from the Egyptian honorific *rḫ nsw*, friend of the king (de Vaux, 403-5; McCarter, 372). The Egyptian term also occurs in the Amarna correspondence from Jerusalem, in EA 288.11, *ru-ḫi šarri*, friend of the king.

OT 1. *General.* The terms used to describe the concept of friendship are numerous. The basic root for this concept is *r'h* II, associate with. The most frequent nom. *rēa'*, other person, neighbor, friend, is also the widest in terms of application. It represents the entire range of usages found in other terms. On the side of friendship as a distant or official association are *mērēa'*, official member of court or [dis]loyal companion, and *rē'eh*, official friend, both used as titles for official positions. The same is true of the Aram. loanword *keₙāt*, colleague. Cf. also *'āmît*, citizen, community member. This term describes a closer association of identification by tribe or other ethnic affiliation. Still closer in terms of friendship are the noms. *re'ût,* female companion, friend, and *ra'yâ*, female lover. Though referring to personal friends, *re'ût* is also used as other person. It corresponds to the range of the masc. nom. *rēa'*. Other synonymous expressions are: *'ōhēb*, friend (→ # 170); *'āḥ*, brother (→ # 278); *'allûp*, familiar, confidant (→ # 476); *ḥeber* I, company; *dôd*, lover (# 1856); *yd'*, know (→ # 3359); *nkr*, be acquainted (→ # 5795); and *qārôb*, one who is near (→ # 7940).

2. *The vb. r'h.* (a) There is dispute concerning the appearance of the q. of *r'h* II in Ps 37:3, in the phrase "cherish faithfulness" (*re'ēh 'emûnâ*). The LXX, NIV, and others (Craigie, 294) read here the *r'h* I, pasture root. Elsewhere in the q. the part. is used, but always with reference to undesirable associations, whether fools (Prov 13:20), gluttons (28:7), or prostitutes (29:3).

(b) The pi. is used only in Judg 14:20 with reference to Samson's friend who had served as the best man at the wedding (NIV who had attended him at his wedding). Boling renders the phrase "whom he had befriended" (229).

(c) Hitp. Prov 22:24 warns, "Do not make friends with a hot-tempered man." This also describes a negative association (cf. above on q.).

3. *The nom.* rēa' *often denotes other human beings.*

(a) Other person. (i) Of the many usages of *rēa'*, the most frequent is its appearance together with "person" (*'îš*) to describe mutuality or reciprocity in idiomatic expressions, such as *'îš 'el rē'ēhû*, each other (Gen 11:3); *'îš berē'ēhû*, each against the other (Judg 7:22); *'îš lerē'ēhû*, each other (Exod 18:7), etc. The usage of *rēa'* in Prov 18:17 also seems to carry the idea of another or a second, who follows the first to present his case. A related expression is that of *'ēšet*, wife of, or *nešê*, wives of (Jer 29:23), in construct with *rēa'*. The reference is one of prohibition of adultery (in the law, e.g., Exod 20:17) or the condemnation of the practice (in the Prophets, e.g., Ezek 18:6, it is especially common in Ezekiel). A similar idea is found in Jer 3:1, where *rēa'* describes the lovers with whom Israel has lived as a prostitute. In the context of Hos 3:1 Hosea is commanded to love "the woman loved by another." The other is the lover whom Gomer has lusted after and with whom she has committed adultery (Wolf, 60). Job (31:9) claims innocence of the offense of adultery and of lying at the door of his *rēaʿ*: "If my heart has been enticed by a woman, or if I have lurked at my neighbor's door...."

(ii) A usage such as Exod 18:16, which describes adversaries who are brought before a judge, suggests that this category need not refer to a friend or imply any special relationship. When *rēaʿ* appears a second time in the context of such an idiom, it can again refer to another person, without any specification of a special relationship. This is true in Judg 7:14, following the idiom in v. 13. Two people in the enemy camp are speaking but the narrative is unconcerned with who they are or what their relationship to one another is.

(iii) Another usage occurs in Hab 2:15, where, in the midst of a series of woes against Babylon, the nation is described as one that makes drunk its *rēaʿ*, friend, in order to see the friend's nakedness. This refers to the nation(s) conquered by Babylon.

(b) Association by location. The two groups of warriors at the pool of Gibeon who kill one another are so described (2 Sam 2:16). *rēaʿ* appears in parallel with *šākēn*, neighbor (→ # 8907), in Jer 6:21.

(c) Association by ethnic/tribal identity. The two Hebrews Moses comes upon in Egypt are ethnically associated (Exod 2:13). More often this category includes the appearance of *rēaʿ* in legal material in the Pent. and elsewhere. Consideration of one's neighbor includes the prohibitions against false testimony or slander against one's neighbor (Exod 20:16; Deut 5:20; Ps 101:5; Job 17:5; Prov 3:28; 11:9, 12; 24:28; 26:19; Jer 9:8[7]), coveting a neighbor's property (Exod 20:17; Deut 5:21), theft (Exod 22:7, 8, 10, 26[6, 7, 9, 25]; Lev 19:13; Deut 19:14; 23:24-25[25-26]; 27:17), extortion (Deut 15:2; 24:10; Jer 22:13), and death (Exod 32:27; Lev 19:16; Deut 4:42; 19:4, 5; 27:24; Josh 20:5). Positively, one is expected to love one's neighbor (Lev 19:18; on the meaning of *rēaʿ*, see Mathys), "but love your neighbor as yourself" (cf. Matt 22:39-40; Rom 13:9). Wenham comments, "*Love* and *neighbor* are as wide-ranging in their scope and meaning in Hebrew as the corresponding English terms" (269).

In the Psalms and Wisdom literature there are also occurrences of *rēaʿ* in ethical contexts referring to proper and improper treatment of one's fellow (Job 6:27; Ps 28:3; Prov 3:29; 14:20, 21; 16:29; 21:10; 22:11). For example, "What you have seen with your eyes do not bring hastily to court, for what will you do in the end if your neighbor puts you to shame? If you argue your case with a neighbor, do not betray another man's confidence" (Prov 25:7b-9).

Samuel's prophecy against Saul, that God has taken away his kingdom and given it to his *rēaʿ*, fits this category (1 Sam 15:28; 28:17). The same sense is applied to God's judgment of David in 2 Sam 12:11, a *rēaʿ* will lie with David's wives. It seems that the use of *rēaʿ* to describe the elders of Judah to whom David sends tribute is intended to contrast with "the LORD's enemies," the Amalekites, from whom the plunder was taken (1 Sam 30:26). *rēaʿ* can refer to one who traps someone in debt (Prov 6:1-3, where it appears in parallel with *zār*, stranger, cf. 17:18).

(d) Companion on a journey or task. Hirah accompanies Judah (Gen 38:12, 20). One of the sons of the prophets asks his friend to hit him (1 Kgs 20:35). The associates of the high priest Joshua sit before him (Zech 3:8). Job's three "friends" are companions in his "journey" of suffering (Job 2:11; 12:4; 19:21; 32:3; 35:4; 42:7, 10).

(e) Close friend. This usage is specified in the prohibition against apostasy, which could include, along with one's own family, *rē'ᵃkā 'ᵃšer kᵉnapšᵉkā* (your friend who is like yourself, Deut 13:6[7]). Amnon's friend in whom he confides is Jonadab (2 Sam 13:3). Elah's destruction of Baasha's family includes his friends (1 Kgs 16:11). The term is used in parallel with *'allûp* III, friend, confidant, in Mic 7:5.

The word *rēa'* appears in the Psalms and Wisdom literature in parallel with *'ōhēb*, loved one (Ps 38:11[12]; 88:18[19]; cf. Lam 1:2 in reference to Jerusalem); with *'āḥ*, brother (Job 30:29; Ps 35:14; 122:8; Prov 17:17), and with *qārôb*, one who is near (Ps 15:3). In Prov 27 a friend's counsel is praised (v. 6), and a friend is regarded as better than a *'āḥ*, brother, in times of distress (v. 10). Parallelism occurs in S of Songs with *dôdîm*, lovers (5:1), and with *dôdî*, my love (5:16).

(f) Fairweather friend. Of special interest is Prov 18:24, where *rēa'* appears in the expression "a man of many companions may come to ruin." This is followed by a contrastive usage of *'ōhēb*, friend, in "but there is a friend who sticks closer than a brother." The emphasis of the two clauses contrasts the broader circle of "acquaintances" with a special "friend." The "friends" of the wealthy and of the gift giver in Prov 19:4 and 6 also fit here.

(g) Other. A sarcastic usage appears twice in 2 Sam 16:17. There Absalom addresses Hushai and refers to his *rēa'*, David. He asks why Hushai did not go with his friend in retreat from Jerusalem. In the passage (v. 16), Hushai is designated by the title *rē'eh dāwid* (friend of David). See *rē'eh.*

4. *The nom. mērēa', official member of court or loyal companion.* (a) Official position. Ahuzzath is a *mērēa'*, usually understood as an adviser, who accompanies Abimelech (Gen 26:26; cf. Sarna, 187). This position may be similar to the thirty companions (*mērēa'*) given to Samson in Judg 14:11. They appear to be functionaries of some sort, possibly related to other such groups of thirty (2 Sam 23:13; see Talmon, 33, n21; Boling, 231). The word describes officials of Saul's court as well, as used by Abner in 2 Sam 3:8.

(b) Boling (232) describes the *mērēa'* of Samson to whom his wife is given as "best man" (Judg 14:20; 15:2, 6). Clearly this figure is distinct from the thirty of 14:11.

(c) Close to Samson's "best man" is the usage of *mērēa'* in the Wisdom literature. It also appears in contexts concerned with loyalty. A poor man's *mērēa'* deserts him (Prov 19:4, 7). Job's friends lack loyalty (*ḥesed*; Clines, 178).

5. *The nom. rē'eh refers to an official friend.* Thus, the usage of *rē'eh* in describing Hushai (in relation to David) is one in which Hushai is a recognized official in the court of David (2 Sam 15:37; 16:16). The same is true of Zabud son of Nathan, in the court of Solomon (1 Kgs 4:5). If the K is followed in Prov 27:10, its appearance there may be as a poetic synonym to *rēa'*, neighbor, friend (→ # 8276), which also occurs.

6. The expression *rᵉ'ût*, female companion, friend, is the specifically female equivalent of *rēa'*, companion. Thus, it has similar usages as are found under that expression. (a) Other person. The word is found with the sense of reciprocity (see *rēa'*). It is used of falcons (Isa 34:15-16), of flesh of sheep (Zech 11:9), and of neighbors (Exod 11:2). In the judgment against Vashti, her position is to be given to someone else, lit. her associate (Esth 1:19).

(b) Close friend. This includes the usage of *rēʿâ* in Judg 11:37-38, where the daughter of Jephthah roams the hills and mourns with her "friends." It also may occur in Ps 45:14[15] to describe the companions who accompany the bride of the king. However, as with references to official positions of friend of the king, here there may be a royal class of friends of the queen.

7. The appearances of *raʿyâ* are confined to the S of Songs. They are used to address the lover (5:2), most often in contexts praising her beauty (1:9, 15; 2:2, 10, 13; 4:1, 7; 6:4).

P-B 1. *Other person.* Similar idioms exist as in BH: *'yš mlpny r'yhw*, one before the other (1QpHab 4.12); *'yš lr'hw*, toward each other (1QS 2.25; 5.21, 23; 6.7; 1QSb 4.24); *'yš lpny r'hw*, one after the other (1QS 5.23); *'yš 't r'hw*, each other (1QS 5.25; 6.2; 8.20; 9.19; CD 8.6); *'yš 'l r'hw*, one against another (1QS 6.1; 11QT LXVI 7); *'yš btwk dbry r'hw*, each in his turn (1QS 6.10); *'yš 'm r'hw*, with one another (1QS 8.2); *'yš mr'hw*, one more than another (1QH 10.28; 1QSa 1.18). There is a similar example without the initial *'îš*: *'šr yšwb 't r'hw* (who answers his neighbor) (1QS 6.26). As in the Bible, *rēaʿ* can refer to something other than persons; e.g., nations (1Q27 1.1.11). It is also used in the construction *'ēšet*, wife of (11QT LXVI 3) with reference to adultery.

2. *Association by ethnic/tribal identity.* At Qumran the correspondent is a member of the community. Thus, the references from 1QS under the first category could be included here. In addition, the prohibitions against slander, deception, lack of concern, hatred, interruption, and nakedness (1QS 7.4-17) with reference toward a *rēaʿ* fit here. The *rēaʿ* is to report any sin that his friend commits (CD 9.17). However, this is not trustworthy if the *rēaʿ* has sinned (CD 10.2). The *rēaʿ* is forbidden to discuss or perform any transactions involving money or labor on the Sabbath (CD 10.18).

3. *Close friend.* In the context of *'whb 'mwnh*, faithful friendship, Sir 6:17 *ky kmwhw kn r'hw* (that like himself so is his friend) is an expression similar to Lev 19:18. The friends and *mwd'y*, my acquaintances, of 1QH 4.9 are those from whom the psalmist is banished. The friends of the psalmist in 1QH 5.23 have become those who oppose him.

4. *Other.* CD 16.15 quotes Mic 7:2, replacing *'aḥîw*, his brother, with, his friend.

NT → *NIDNTT* 1:254-60 (Brother); 2:547-50 (Love: friend).

Friend, companion, colleague, community member: → *'allûp* I (familiar, friend, # 476); → *ḥbr* II (unite, be joined, charm, make an alliance with, # 2489); → *k^{e}nāt* (collaegue, # 4056); → *ʿāmît* (citizen, community member, # 6660); → *r'h* II (associate with, be best man, make friends with, # 8287)

Brother, sister: → *'āḥ* II (brother, kinsman, relative, countryman, # 278); → *'aḥ^{a}wâ* I (brotherhood, # 288); → *'āḥôt* (sister, beloved, # 295); → *yābām* (brother-in-law, # 3303)

Bibliography

R. Boling, *Judges*, AB, 1975; D. J. A. Clines, *Job 1-20*, WBC, 1989; P. C. Craigie, *Psalms 1-50*, WBC, 1983; J. Fichtner, "Der Begriff des 'Nächsten' im AT," *WD* 4, 1955, 25-52; P. K. McCarter, Jr., *II Samuel*, AB, 1984; H.-P. Mathys, *Liebe deinen Nächsten wie dich selbst: Untersuchungen zum alttestamentlichen Gebot der Gottesliebe (Lev 19,18)*, OBO, 1986; N. Sarna, *Genesis: The Traditional Hebrew Text with the New JPS Translation*, 1989; A. van Selms, "The Origin of the Title 'The King's Friend' (1 Kgs 4:2-6)," *JNES* 16, 1957, 118-23; S. Talmon, "The

New Hebrew Letter from the Seventh Century B.C. in Historical Perspective," *BASOR* 76, 1964, 29-38; R. de Vaux, "Titres et fonctionnaires égyptiens à la cour de David et de Salomon," *RB* 48, 1939, 394-405; G. J. Wenham, *The Book of Leviticus*, NICOT, 1979; H. W. Wolf, *Hosea*, Hermeneia, 1974.

Richard S. Hess

8288 (*rā'â* I, evil), → # 8317

8291 (*rē'eh*, official friend), → # 8287

8292 (*rē'â*, female friend), → # 8287

8295 (*rᵉ'ût* I, female friend), → # 8287

8296	רְעוּת

רְעוּת(*rᵉ'ût* II), longing, striving (# 8296); רַעְיוֹן (*ra'yôn*), longing, striving (# 8301).

ANE There is uncertainty about the derivation for the words here considered and about their meaning. While some hold the derivation to be from the root *r'h,* tend, graze cattle, others relate these to the common Aram. vb. *rᵉ'ā'*, desire (see G. Barton, 85-86; R. N. Whybray, 49-50); *HALAT* derives these forms from *r'h* III (1177, 1180).

OT The two words discussed here are seemingly used interchangeably in Eccl, where they occur exclusively. With only one exception (Eccl 2:22), the words are used in conjunction with *rûaḥ,* and so mean either to tend the wind or to strive after the wind. Fortunately, either rendering of the phrase results in a similar sense of the text: an impossible, futile task is indicated. Such is the judgment of the Teacher about human wisdom and accomplishment: they are futile and meaningless (see von Rad, 226-39). (→ Ecclesiastes: Theology)

Contention, strife, struggle: → *gl'* (break out in a dispute, # 1679); → *grh* (stir up strife, # 1741); → *nṣh* I (struggle, # 5897); → *ptl* (twist, be wily, shrewd, # 7349); → *ryb* (strive, # 8189); → *rᵉ'ût* II (longing, striving, # 8296); → *śrh* I (contend, struggle, # 8575)

BIBLIOGRAPHY

G. Barton, *Ecclesiastes,* ICC 17, 1909; G. von Rad, *Wisdom in Israel*, 1972; R. N. Whybray, *Ecclesiastes,* NCBC, 1989.

John M. Bracke

8297 (*rᵉ'î*, pasture), → # 8286

8299 (*ra'yâ*, female friend), → # 8287

8301 (*ra'yôn*, longing, striving), → # 8296

8302	רעל

רעל (*r'l* I), ho. brandish, make to quiver (# 8302); רַעַל (*ra'al*), nom. staggering, reeling, (# 8303); תַּרְעֵלָה(*tar'ēlâ*), nom. reeling, staggering (# 9570).

OT The Heb. root *r'l* occurs only once as a vb., in the ho. form, to describe the appearance of a warrior's spear (Nah 2:3[4]). In Zech 12:2 it is used as a masculine nom., in the phrase "cup of reeling" (*sap ra'al*). The fem. nom. form, *tar'ēlâ*, occurs 3x (Ps 60:3[5]; Isa 51:17; 51:22): twice in construct with, *kôs* cup, and once with *yāyin*, wine. In every instance this root is used in the theological context of judgment.

BIBLIOGRAPHY
TWOT 2:853; J. J. M. Roberts, *Nahum, Habakkuk, Zephaniah*, OTL, 1991.

M. V. Van Pelt & W. C. Kaiser, Jr.

8303 (*ra'al*, staggering, reeling, veil), → # 8302

8304	רְעָלָה

רְעָלָה(*rᵉ'ālâ*), nom. veil (# 8304).

OT The meaning of *rᵉ'ālâ* is uncertain, since it comes only in the list of ornaments in Isa 3:19 (NIV the earrings and bracelets and *veils*, the headdresses ...). Other translations have scarfs (NRSV), coronets (REB), trinkets (NJPSV). The word may be derived from *r'l* I, shake, swing (→ # 8302; describing the movement of a veil, although it might also suggest small bells), or *r'l* II, cover (the veil as covering the face; or might it be some other part of the body?). Platt (198) argues from the context that it should describe a neck ornament, such as droplet beads.

Veil: → *dōq* (veil, gauze, # 1988); → *ḥebyôn* (covering, # 2470); → *miṭpaḥat* (veil, cloak, # 4762); → *masweh* (veil, # 5003); → *massēkâ* II (veil, sheet, blanket, # 5012); → *mispāḥâ* (veil, # 5029); → *ṣammâ* (veil, # 7539); → *ṣā'îp* (veil, # 7581); → *rᵉdîd* (veil, # 8100); → *rᵉ'ālâ* (veil, # 8304)

BIBLIOGRAPHY
E. E. Platt, "Jewelry of Biblical Times and the Catalog of Isa 3:18-23," *AUSS* 17, 1979, 71-84, 189-201.

Philip Jenson

8306	רעם

רעם (*r'm* I), q. storm, thunder; hi. cause it to storm, thunder (# 8306); nom. רַעַם (*ra'am*), thunder (# 8308).

ANE *r'm* is related to Ugar. *rġm*, thunder, and Eth. *ra'äma*, thunder, see *HALAT* 1181.

OT 1. Thunderstorms brew over the Mediterranean (Ps 29:3), cross the hill country (29:5-7), and dissipate over the eastern desert (29:8; see Futato, 211-18, and Loretz, 87-92). Ps 29:3-9 testifies to the power of thunder (see Dalman, 1:215): thunder breaks cedars (v. 5), makes mountains tremble (v. 6), and shakes the desert (v. 8). While features of a genuine thunderstorm are evident in the storm described in Ps 29, hyperbole is also at work, as this storm is a theophany of Yahweh (see Cross, *Canaanite Myth*, 151-56, and Loretz, 135-45), a theophany that implicitly contrasts the power and glory of Yahweh with "the weakness of the inimical Baal" (Craigie, 246). The apologetic power of Ps 29 is intensified if the psalm was originally a hymn to Baal (for surveys of the evidence see Craigie, 243-45, and Loretz, 12-22). While certainty is not possible, some evidence does point to a Canaanite original. The geographical setting of the psalm (Lebanon [v. 5], Sirion/Hermon [v. 6], Kadesh [v. 8]) is north of the area effectively occupied by Israel (see Futato, 215-18). If *yhwh* is replaced with *b'l*, striking alliterative patterns emerge (see Fitzgerald, 61-63). (→ Baal)

2. The phrase "Let the sea roar/thunder" (*yir'am hayyām*) in Ps 96:11 and 98:7 also refers to a thunderstorm. The sea does not actually thunder, but the association of thunder and the sea (see Ps 29) is sufficient to explain this metonymy. The fields are jubilant and the trees are singing for joy (96:12-13) as a result of the rains brought by the thunderstorm. So too the rushing rivers recently filled from the thunderstorm sound like a grand audience clapping hands, and the rain-drenched mountains sing for joy (98:8). As in Ps 29, this storm is a theophany of the Lord, who comes to judge the earth (96:13; 98:9).

3. Since thunder is powerful (see Ps 29), it serves as a weapon wielded by the Lord against his enemies. In Hannah's song, when the Lord comes to judge the earth, he thunders (*yar'ēm*) against those who oppose him (1 Sam 2:10). This general statement finds specificity in 7:10, where the Lord thundered (*wayyar'ēm*) against the Philistines and thereby routed them. David's deliverance from Saul is also described in terms of a thunderstorm theophany in 2 Sam 22:10-20 ॥ Ps 18:10-20. The Lord thundered (*yar'ēm*, v. 14) from heaven and routed the enemy (v. 15). The bottom of the sea was then exposed (v. 16), and the Lord drew David out of the deep waters (v. 17) and brought him into a spacious place (v. 20). These last three actions are reminiscent of the Exodus, when the Lord made a path through the sea and brought Israel through the sea and into the Promised Land. The language of deliverance through a thunderstorm (1 Sam 2:10; 2 Sam 22:10-20 ॥ Ps 18:10-20) is rooted in the prior thundering of God against the Egyptians at the Red Sea. Ps 77:16-19 describes the theophanic presence of God that delivered his people (see v. 15) at the sea (v. 19) in terms of a thunderstorm. The clouds resounded with thunder (*qôl nāṭᵉnû šᵉḥāqîm*, v. 18) and the sound of God's thunder was heard in the whirlwind (*qôl ra'amᵉkā baggalgal*, v. 19). So too, when God says in 81:8a that he rescued Israel from distress by answering out of a thunder cloud (*bᵉsēter ra'am*), the reference is to the deliverance at the sea (see the reference to the wilderness in v. 8b).

As the deliverance of Hannah, of the Israelites from the Philistines, and of David from Saul is rooted in the prior deliverance of Israel from the Egyptians at the sea, the deliverance at the sea is itself rooted in God's prior vanquishing of the deep at the time of creation (→ *br'* I, create, separate, # 1343). In describing God's creation of the world, Ps 104:6 says the waters (*mayim*) of the deep (*tᵉhôm*) covered the earth as a garment, but then at God's rebuke (*gaᵃrātᵉkā*, v. 7a), at the sound of his thunder (*qôl ra'amᵉkā*, v. 7b; see 77:19), the waters were put to flight and were contained in the designated place (vv. 8-9; see Futato, 19-30). The God who created the dry land by thundering against the waters at the time of creation is the God who redeemed his people by thundering against all who opposed him. (For *qôl*, the most frequent Heb. term for thunder, → # 7754.)

4. Job understood thunder to be God's voice: "He thunders with his majestic voice.... God's voice thunders in marvelous ways; he does great things beyond our understanding" (Job 37:4-5). Moderns understand more about the nature of thunder than Job did. Thunder is the sound waves produced by air rapidly expanding as a result of being superheated by the release of tremendous electrical charges (lightning); thunderstorms are produced by the rapid uplifting of moist air. But moderns understand less

about the nature of thunder than Job did, if his perspective is lost: "At this my heart pounds and leaps from its place. Listen! Listen to the roar of his voice, to the rumbling that comes from his mouth" (Job 37:1-2). (→ Job: Theology)

5. Because of the association of thunder and storms that brought life-giving rain (→ *gešem*, # 1772) to the Promised Land, thunder was theologically significant in the world of the OT. For example, Baal, the most prominent god of the Canaanites, the perennial rival to the Lord God of Israel, and the storm god on whose rain the land supposedly depended, was also known as Hadad (Thunderer). In one myth Baal used two clubs symbolizing thunder and lightning to defeat Yam/Sea (Day, 545). The language of such mythology is used in the OT to demonstrate that Yahweh, not Baal, is the Lord of creation. For example, thunder and lightning are a pair of weapons used jointly in both Ps 77:18 and 18:13-15. The language of Baal's defeat of Yam with two clubs symbolizing thunder and lightning is used to assert the supremacy of Yahweh.

Thunder: → *hēd* (thunderclap?, # 2059); → *ḥāzîz* (cloud, strong wind, thunderclap, # 2613); → *qôl* (voice, sound, thunder, cry, # 7754); → *r'm* I (storm, thunder, # 8306)
Cloud: → *ḥāzîz* (cloud, strong wind, thunderclap, # 2613); → *miplāś* (spreading [of a cloud], # 5146); → *'wb* (cover w. cloud, # 6380); → *'ānān* (clouds, # 6727); → *'ᵃrāpel* (deep darkness, thick darkness, heavy cloud, # 6906); → *šaḥaq* (dust, clouds of dust, # 8836)

BIBLIOGRAPHY

P. Craigie, *Psalms*, 1983; F. Cross, *Canaanite Myth and Hebrew Epic*, 1973; G. Dalman, *Arbeit und Sitte*, 1928-42; J. Day, "Baal," *ABD*, 1992; A. Fitzgerald, "A Note on Psalm 29," *BASOR*, 1974, 61-63; M. Futato, "A Meteorological Analysis of Psalms 104, 65, and 29," diss. The Catholic University of America, Washington, D.C., 1984; O. Loretz, *Psalm 29*, 1984.

Mark D. Futato

8307	רעם

רעם (*r'm* II), q. be agitated, be confused; hi. upset (# 8307).

OT The vb. *r'm* II appears 2x in the OT, 1x in the q. and 1x in the hi. In the q. it appears in Ezek 27:35, together with "face." It points to the expression on the faces of people whose faces are distorted because of what they see. They are appalled and shudder with horror while their faces are distorted. In the hi. the vb. refers to the irritation Peninnah caused for Hannah when she kept on provoking her (1 Sam 1:6).

Confusion, agitation: → *bwk* (be agitated, wander in agitation, # 1003); → *bll* (confuse, mix, # 1176); → *bl'* III (be confused, confused, # 1182); → *hwm* (throw into confusion, be in uproar, # 2101); → *kmr* (agitated, # 4023); → *'wh* (disturb, distress, agitate, pervert, do wrong, # 6390); → *p'm* (be disturbed, feel disturbed, # 7192); → *rhb* (assail, press, pester, alarm, confuse, # 8104); → *r'm* II (be agitated, be confused, # 8307); → *tmh* (be benumbed, be stunned, shocked, gaze, # 9449)

Harry F. van Rooy

8308 (*ra'am*, thunder), → # 8306

8310	רַעְמָה

רַעְמָה (*ra'mâ* II), mane (hapleg. in Job 39:19; # 8310).

ANE Arab. *ri'm.*

OT The term appears only in Job 39:19, where God points to the horse and its mane as another of the many examples of his creative power and design.

Horse: → *dhr* (gallop, # 1851); → *sûs* I (horse, # 6061); → *pārāš* (horseman, rider, horse, # 7304); → *rekeš* (team of horses, # 8224); → *ra'mâ* II (mane, # 8310); → *š^e'āṭâ* (stamping [of hoofs], # 9121)

Robert B. Chisholm

8315	רען

רען (*r'n*), pa'lal be luxuriant, green (hapleg.; # 8315); רַעֲנָן (*ra'^{a}nān*), adj. luxuriant, full of leaves (# 8316).

ANE In addition to Aram. *ra'^{a}nan*, flourishing (Dan 4:4[1]), the root is attested in Syr. *rô'^{a}nā'*, a wild herb.

OT 1. The vb. occurs once in the pa'lal (GKC §55d), meaning be luxuriant, green (Job 15:32).

2. The adj. *ra'^{a}nān* means luxuriant, green and is almost exclusively used to describe trees. The dominant theme is that of the spreading or green tree that was considered sacred in Canaanite religion. Jeremiah 2:20b, "and under every spreading tree you lay down as a prostitute," is not metaphorical but an evidence that the practice associated with these sites was basically sexual. The sexual activity of the worshipers was believed to influence the fertility of the gods, which in turn increased the fertility of the land. Israel was warned against becoming involved in this abhorrent practice and was commanded to destroy these cult locations (Deut 12:2). 1 Kgs 14:23 testifies that Israel established their own cultic sites beneath "every spreading tree" (2 Kgs 16:4; 17:10; 2 Chron 28:4) and were condemned by the prophets because of it (Isa 57:5; Jer 2:20; 3:6, 13; 17:2; Ezek 6:13). With a touch of irony, God likens himself to a spreading cypress, who provides fruit for his people (Hos 14:8[9]).

The picture of a luxuriant, spreading tree is also used to describe the prosperity of Judah, the righteous person (Ps 52:8[10]; 92:14[15]; Jer 17:8), and even the outwardly prosperous wicked (Ps 37:35; cf. Dan 4:4[1]).

Finally, the adj. is used in a more general sense of fresh in describing oil (Ps 92:10 [11]) and of luxurious in describing the bed of lovers (S of Songs 1:16).

P-B The metaphorical use of the adj. continues in the RL and in DSS, 1QH 10:25, the only occurrence of *ra'^{a}nān* in the Qumran scrolls, where the righteous are likened to the spreading tree (Ps 1:3; Jer 17:8).

Growth, greatness, luxuriance, ripening, sprouting: → *bqq* II (grow luxuriantly, # 1328); → *gdl* I (grow up, become great, make great, boast, # 1540); → *nwb* (grow, prosper, flourish, # 5649); → *sāḥîš* (what grows on its own accord, # 6084); → *sāpîaḥ* I (what grows on its own accord, # 6206); → *ṣmḥ* (sprout, spring up, grow, prosper, make grow, # 7541); → *r'n* (be luxuriant, green, # 8315); → *śg'/śgh* (grow great, increase, exalt, # 8434/8436)

M. G. Abegg, Jr.

8316 (*ra'^{a}nān*, luxuriant, full of leaves), → # 8315

8317	רעע

רעע (*r*“ I), q. be bad, be displeasing, look coldly on (see *HALAT* 1184); ni. suffer; hi. do evil, hurt, injure, harm, bring calamity, commit an evil deed (# 8317); מֵרַע (*mēra*‘), evil, atrocity (# 5334); רַע (*ra*‘), adj. of bad quality, inferior, disagreeable, displeasing, vicious, harmful, bad, evil (# 8273a); רַע (*ra*‘), subst. evil (# 8273b); רֹעַ (*rō‘a*), nom. bad quality, ugliness, bad humor, perverseness, malice (# 8278); רָעָה (*rā‘â* I), evil, harm, wickedness, perverseness, misery, trouble, disaster (# 8288). The substantives *ra‘/rā‘ā* are gender doublets with no difference in meaning (*IBHS* 6.4.3).

The foundational meaning of the root concerns an action or state that is detrimental to life or its fullness. It and its antonym *ṭôb*, good, are associated with “death” and “life” respectively (Deut 30:15). The detriment can be physical, literal death or abnormality of the body, or moral injury to the spirit or to a relationship. Both aspects concern a departure from that which is ideal and desired for fulness and enjoyment of life.

ANE Akk., not having an exact phonetic equivalent to the guttural /‘/, has the cognate root *rgg*. The oldest attested form of the root is the adj. *raggu,* bad, evil. This occurs in the Old Assyr. and Old Babylonian and is clear through the latest periods of the language (*AHw*, 942). That the verbal form *ragāgu* only occurs rarely, and that in late texts (*AHw,* 941-42), suggests that it is probably a denominative vb.

The nom./adj. form occurs in Phoen. (*DISO*, 281), and possibly in Imperial Aram., though the latter is uncertain (*DISO*, 168 sub *mēra*‘). The root occurs in a much later Arab. form (rabble, riffraff; Wehr, 1966, 345), but this could well be borrowed from another Sem. language, possibly even Heb., since it is so rare that it does not appear to be native Arab.

OT 1. The preponderance of nominal and adjectival forms of the root in the OT suggests a denominative origin of the vb. here also (BDB, 949; *IBHS*, 24.4).

The adj. *ra*‘ occurs several times in the immediate context of *ṭôb,* good, indicating opposite poles of a spectrum (Lev 27:10, 12, 14; Num 13:19; Isa 5:20; see *THAT* 795), or a merism, in which the two extremes indicate a totality (Gen 2:9, 17). This usage is clear in Prov 15:3, where God watches everyone, “the wicked and the good.”

In some cases there is no moral censure involved in the adj. Animals are “wild” (Ezek 5:17; 14:15, 21), with their ferocity part of their untamed nature, not something that is condemnable (Gen 37:20, 33: Lev 26:6), so the translation “vicious” of the NIV comes across too harshly. Things of low quality and limited use are described as poor (figs—Jer 24:2, 8), ugly (cows—Gen 41:3, 19), or bad (water—2 Kgs 2:19; land—Num 13:19; cf. 20:5). This departure from the norm for the fullness of life is also evident when the face is described as “sad” (Gen 40:7; Neh 2:2).

At times the adj. is used to accentuate the grievousness of something that is intrinsically harmful to one’s physical well-being, even though no moral judgment is being made by the use of the adj. itself. For example, a flaw is serious (Deut 15:21), an event is disastrous (1 Kgs 5:4[18]), boils and other maladies are painful or severe (Deut 28:35, 59; Job 2:7; cf. Deut 7:15; 2 Chron 21:19), and the arrows of famine are deadly (Ezek 5:16). Even something that is ultimately beneficial can appear to its recipient to be bad or stern, such as Yahweh’s discipline that befalls a sinner (Prov 15:10).

Most commonly, the adj. is applied to people and their activities in contexts that indicate moral turpitude. This is a uniting into one word of what in English is expressed by two words, physical (bad) and moral (evil). Both abrogate in some way the fullness of life. An individual such as Haman is vile (*ra'*) because of his despicable plot to harm others (Esth 7:6; 9:25; cf. 1 Sam 30:22). The very heart of humankind is now evil (Jer 3:17; 7:24), as are their inclinations (*yēṣer*; Gen 8:21). Humanity's way of life is evil (Ps 119:101; Prov 4:14), as are his methods, deeds, and practices (1 Kgs 13:33; Neh 9:35; Prov 8:13; Eccl 4:3; Isa 32:7; Jer 18:11; Zech 1:4). Humankind in groups is also evil, whether as a community (Num 14:27), a nation (Jer 8:3; 13:10; Ezek 7:24), or a generation (Deut 1:35). As a result of humanity's wickedness and wicked nature, the good but holy and righteous God will send judgment, which, from the perspective of the one who is its object, is dreadful (*ra'*) (Ezek 14:21; cf. Exod 33:4; Deut 6:22).

A useful picture of the nature of "evil" as designated by the adj. is painted by looking at words that are used synonymously with it, as well as those with which it is in contrast. Evil is associated closely with guilt (Ezra 9:13), sin (Gen 13:13; Jer 36:3), and perversity (Prov 2:12; 8:13). It can involve arrogant pride (Prov 8:13), slander (Deut 22:14, 19), and betrayal (Judg 9:23) of the covenant relationship with God by turning to other gods (Jer 13:10; 25:6-7; 35:15) and foreign cultic practices (2 Kgs 17:11). Unlike God himself, who is morally pure, evil involves uncleanness (Deut 23:9-10[10-11]). Attitudes associated with evil include anger (Ps 78:49), wickedness (141:4; Prov 4:14), stubbornness (Jer 3:17), and indignation (Ps 78:49). It makes one an enemy of both God (Neh 13:17; Ps 78:49) and other people (Esth 7:6).

In contrast, rather than following our evil nature, we should fear the Lord (Prov 8:13), keeping his commands (2 Kgs 17:13; Eccl 8:5; cf. Ps 119:101) and obeying him in everything (Jer 16:12). In this way one does well, living a life of good (Josh 23:15) in righteousness (Prov 12:12; 29:6), upright blamelessness (28:10), and safety (Ezek 34:25), guided by God's Spirit (1 Sam 16:14-16). Rather than looking to oneself for guidance, one should look to God in humble prayer (2 Chron 7:14). All of these provide a marked contrast to a life of evil.

At times the evaluation expressed by the word is relative, as, for example, when something is "bad in the eyes (opinion) of someone" (Gen 28:8; Exod 21:8; Num 22:34; Josh 24:15; Jer 40:4). The force of the construction is in relation to a person's view rather than to some external, objective standard. The latter, however, is in evidence when the opposite construction is used, as when Israel did "what was right in their own eyes" (lit. trans. of Judg 17:6; 21:25; cf. Deut 12:8), in implicit contrast to the only truly absolute standard, the good in the eyes of God (cf. Deut 6:18; 12:25).

A type of relativity or "just desserts" may have been seen in a double entendre in Prov 1:16, where the wicked rush in to do evil and harm to others, to their own physical hurt. In doing this, they are in fact bringing this injury down upon themselves.

2. The nom. *rā'â*, an abstract nom. (*IBHS*, 6.4.2b) marked for the fem. grammatical gender, occurs 319x in the OT. It finds its field of use in relation to humans who are involved in actions or states of being that are not acceptable. It describes not only their deeds, but also the results of them when they receive punishment and disaster (*rā'â*) falls.

As could be expected, wicked people do wickedness or evil (Job 20:12; Prov 26:26). Often the nom. is applied to Israel's enemies who mistreated her, acting either as individuals (Haman—Esth 8:3) or as national bodies (Assyria—Nah 3:19, and its capital Nineveh—Jon 1:2; Syria and her king—1 Kgs 20:7). Israel itself is not without blame, however, since she committed evil deeds (Isa 3:9; Jer 6:7; 11:17; Ezek 16:57; Hos 7:2). Individuals or groups within the nation also do wrong (Joseph's brothers, Gen 50:15, 17; Saul, 1 Sam 20:7, 9, 13; David, 2 Sam 12:11; Benjamin, Judg 20:3, 12).

As a result of evil actions, evil results will fall upon the perpetrators. These are understood as calamity, disaster, or harm. In prophetic passages this falls on Israel's enemies (Isa 47:11; Jer 2:3; 48:2, 16; 49:37), as well as Israel itself or members of it in other texts (Deut 31:29; Judg 20:34, 41; 2 Sam 17:14; 1 Kgs 22:23). It is in this context that one reads Isa 45:7. God is the creator of all things, light and well-being on the one hand, and darkness and woe or disaster on the other. This is exemplified by God's use in this passage of his anointed servant, the pagan Cyrus, to bless some nations and punish others by bringing God's disaster on them.

Due to its rich use of parallelism, Heb. poetry provides many synonymous terms in elucidating the poet's understanding of the nature of evil. It is sinful (Gen 39:9; Judg 11:27; 1 Sam 12:19; 24:11[12]) and perverse (Prov 16:30). Its results are the violence and destruction of war (2 Kgs 8:12; Ps 140:2[3]; Jer 5:12; 6:7). It leads to feeling God's fierce anger (Jer 49:37) like that of a storm (25:32), ending in calamity (Isa 47:11), disaster (Ps 91:10), and ultimately death (1 Kgs 1:52).

Evil is contrasted to the presence of Yahweh (Mic 3:11), in whom is no evil at all. It is antithetical to everything that is good (Gen 50:20; 1 Sam 24:17[18]; Prov 11:27; Jer 18:20) and upright (1 Sam 29:6). Evil is incompatible with righteousness, purity, and truth (Ps 15:2-3). In its presence and practice one can find no peace (Jer 23:17), ease (Prov 1:33) nor pleasure (Eccl 12:1).

Two proverbs clearly show the danger of evil's pursuit. If one should seek to pursue it, death will result (Prov 11:19), but as fallen people, it pursues us, resulting in misfortune unless we forsake our own evil and seek righteousness (13:21).

3. The nom. *mēra'* occurs only once in the OT, in a discussion of two opposing kings (Dan 11:27). They not only lie to each other, but their very "hearts [are] bent on evil." The specific nature of the wrong is not spelled out, but both are violently opposed to God and his people, as the context shows (Dan 11).

4. The nom. *rōa'* has similar uses to that of *rā'â*. It describes bad fruit (Jer 24:2, 3) and ugly cows (Gen 41:19), as well as a sad heart (Neh 2:2; cf. Eccl 7:3). Most often it describes the ugly, evil or wicked deeds of human beings. David's heart is wicked (1 Sam 17:28) according to his brothers, when he came to visit them in the battle. More frequently, Israel's outright sin and wicked actions are called evil (Isa 1:16; Jer 4:4; 25:5; cf. Deut 28:20).

5. The vb. *r''* occurs only in the q. (25x) and hi. (68x) stems in the OT. In the former, the vb. is stative, describing a characteristic or quality of the verb's subject as being evil (*IBHS*, 22.2.2), while the latter designates causing to be evil (*IBHS*, 27.4a).

In the q., the subject's mental state is described as troubled, downhearted, or distressed (Gen 21:11, 12; Num 11:10). An example is Hannah's disconsolation at being barren (1 Sam 1:8), where the situation does not render her morally culpable, but does detract from the state of well-being that should be expected within a family, especially one dedicated to the service of God.

At other times the feeling of anger or active displeasure comes out, a matter of increased emotion compared to the last use (Gen 48:17; 1 Sam 8:6; 18:8; Neh 2:10; 13:8; Isa 59:15; Jon 4:1). Finally, at the more malevolent end of the spectrum, a person's actions or state of mind are actively evil or wicked, such as Onan's *coitus interruptus* (Gen 38:10), or a person of means withholding aid from those who are not able to provide for themselves (Deut 15:9, 10; 28:54, 56; cf. 1 Chron 21:7).

In the hi., the vb. is often used in contrast to do good (*yṭb*) in a merism describing any kind of action "whether good or evil" (Lev 5:4, regarding any oaths; Isa 41:23, regarding the inability of idols to act; cf. Jer 10:5; Zeph 1:12, where God is wrongly described as doing nothing). The contrast and mutual incompatibility of the two concepts is clear in Jer 13:23, where one who is accustomed to evildoing is not capable of good deeds. The habit, if not the nature, of humankind is to choose the ill rather than the good (Eichrodt, *TOT*, 2:389; W. L. Holladay, *Jeremiah 1*, 1986, 415).

This contrast to good is spelled out in other terms used in the context. Evil and keeping the commandments of God are in opposition (Ps 119:115), as are evil and God's holy, messianic kingdom (Isa 11:9; 65:25). The evildoer is also contrasted to the blameless (Job 8:20) and to those who hope in Yahweh (Ps 37:9).

The vb., when accompanied by the preposition "to" (Heb. *l^e*), can indicate an emotion or action coming from outside the subject (*IBHS*, 376-7, n. 43). For example, God brings trouble or deals harshly with people (Exod 5:22, 23; Num 11:11; Ruth 1:21), as do other people at times (Gen 43:6). Actual mistreatment can be meant, such as that desired by the Sodomites (Gen 19:9; cf. the Egyptians' treatment of Israel—Num 20:15). Foreign kings are also warned against harming or even laying a finger on the prophets, who were God's representatives (Ps 105:15; cf. 1 Chron 16:22, with the preposition "against" [Heb. *b^e*]). God can ultimately step in and punish those who oppose him. This appears as evil, or at least disaster, to those who are being punished (Josh 24:20; Zech 8:14).

There are times where the vb. seems to indicate physical distress, where, for example "those whom I [Yahweh] have brought to grief" are explained as the "exiles" and the "lame" (Mic 4:6; a possible *waw explicativum*; Baker, 1980, 129-36). There also is a clear contrast in Gen 31:7 between fiscal maltreatment by Jacob at the hands of Laban, which Jacob acknowledges, and "harm" (*l^ehāra'*). The latter seems to be saying that, although he was defrauded, he was not assaulted.

The vb. is used in parallel with other vbs. designating various levels of wrongdoing that cannot be attributed to external factors. Moses denies any wrong on his side against the Israelites, even to the misappropriation of a donkey (Num 16:15), while the Israelites under Egypt were faced with more severe treatment, including suffering and hard labor (Deut 26:6). The mistreatment even goes as far as taking life (1 Kgs 17:20). Specific sins are described as evil, such as theft (Gen 44:5), idolatry (1 Kgs 14:9; 2 Kgs 21:11), David's sin of taking a census (1 Chron 21:17), and homosexuality (Gen 19:7; Judg 19:23). This last perversity as practiced at Sodom appears to have become a paradigm of evil, against which later deeds were judged (Jer 23:14).

Those who habitually practice evil, most commonly, though not exclusively, designated through the use of the part. (*IBHS*, 37.1e), are called dogs (Ps 22:16[17]), wicked (26:5), enemies and foes (27:2; cf. 92:11[12]), evildoers (Ps 64:2[3]; 94:16; Isa 31:2), senseless fools (Jer 4:22), and destructive killers (Isa 14:20). They do not listen to God (Jer 7:26), but mistreat his messengers (38:9). But God is faithful in that he rescues the poor from the power of the wicked (Jer 20:13) and brings down disaster on those who oppose him. This can include war (Jer 25:29), but in the most detailed description of the punishment of God, the Lord describes the disaster as uprooting, tearing down, overthrowing, and destroying (Jer 31:28). In contrast, when his people had finally turned back to him, he restored them, building and planting (31:28), since it is not his final will that his people Israel, or any nation, be utterly destroyed; "words of judgment are replaced by words of restoration" (W. L. Holladay, *Jeremiah 2*, 1989, 197).

P-B The rabbis did not add significantly to the wide range of usage of the nom. forms of this root already evident in the OT; in fact, they seemed to use it in all of its riches. Instead of the heart being grudging (Deut 15:10), a later idiom spoke of the illiberal eye (Mish. 'Abot 2:11; 5:13). There also developed the idea of the evil eye, defined as bewitchment (Jastrow 2:1071).

The vb. in Mish. Heb. takes on a different nuance in addition to that mentioned already. Here it denotes breaking, cracking, or shattering something (ibid., 2:1488), a use not apparent in the OT.

Bad, vicious, wicked: → *zmm* (plan, purpose, plan evil, # 2372); → *kîlay* (scoundrel, # 3964); → *'wl* I (act wrongly, # 6401); → *ṣdh* I (act intentionally, # 7399); → *r''* I (be bad, injure, # 8317); → *rš'* (act wickedly, unrighteously, be guilty, pronounce guilty, # 8399)

BIBLIOGRAPHY

NIDNTT 1:561-68; *TDOT* 3:464-87; 6:546-66; *THAT* 2:794-803; *TWOT* 2:854-56; D. W. Baker, "Further Examples of the Waw Explicativum," *VT* 30, 1980, 129-36; W. L. Holladay, *Jeremiah 1*, Hermeneia, 1986; idem, *Jeremiah 2*, Hermeneia, 1989.

David W. Baker

8318	רעע

רעע (*r''* II), q. break in pieces; hitpo. be broken up; be broken in pieces (# 8318). A loanword from Aram. (= Heb. *rṣṣ*; → *rṣṣ* [crush, mash, break, # 8368; *m^e rûṣâ*, oppression, # 5298]). See also רעץ (*r'ṣ*), dash to pieces, shatter (→ # 8320).

OT 1. This vb. depicts the judgment of Yahweh's king in shattering in pieces the nations as when pottery is smashed (q., Ps 2:9, par. *npṣ*, smash), and God's breaking mighty men in Job 34:24 (q.) and the earth in Isa 24:19 (q., hitpo.). "Iron from the north," the foe, is difficult to smash (q., Jer 15:12), but a kingdom as strong as iron can break in pieces (Dan 2:40 [Aram.]; peal, pael).

2. In Mic 5:6[5] *w^e rā'û* (NIV they will rule; mg. note, crush) is best understood from *r'h*, shepherd, rule (→ # 8286), rather than *r''*, in light of *rō'îm*, shepherds, in v. 5[4] (K. J. Cathcart, *Bib* 59, 1978, 43).

3. In Prov 18:24a *hitrō'ēa'* has been derived from *r''* II (e.g., *HALAT* 1185) and translated "(A man of many companions) may come to ruin" (NIV). The derivation, however, remains disputed. G. R. Driver has suggested the root *rw'*, to shout, used in the weakened sense as found in Syr. and meaning chatter (Driver, 183-84). Another

suggestion is to read *hitrā'ôt* (from *r'h*, have dealings with someone) and to render it seek society (*BHS*). See the discussion in Whybray, 274, McKane, 518-19, and Hulst, 125.

In Prov 25:19, *rō'â* has been understood as a contracted part. form from *r''* II (GKC, 67s) and rendered broken (tooth), or it has been repointed as *rā'â* and translated bad (tooth) (*BHS*).

Split, breach, slice: → *bq'* (split, break open, # 1324); → *ḥrm* II (split, # 3050); → *ḥtr* (break through, # 3168); → *miśpāḥ* (breach of law, # 5384); → *plḥ* (cut into slices, split open, # 7114); → *pṣm* (split open, # 7204); → *prṣ* I (break through, burst out, be broken down, # 7287); → *r''* II (break in pieces, # 8318); → *rṣṣ* (crush, mash, break, # 8368); → *šbr* I (break, break down, smash, shatter, # 8689)

BIBLIOGRAPHY

TWOT 2:856-57; G. R. Driver, "Problems in the Hebrew Text of Proverbs," *Bib* 32, 1951, 173-97; M. Dahood, "Hebrew-Ugaritic Lexicography X," *Bib* 53, 1972, 394; A. R. Hulst, *Old Testament Translation Problems*, 1960, 175; W. McKane, *Proverbs*, 1970; R. N. Whybray, *Proverbs*, NCB, 1994.

Cornelis Van Dam

8319	רעף

רעף (*r'p*), q., hi. drip, flow (# 8319).

OT This vb. occurs in poetry, 4x in the q. and once in the hi. (Isa 45:8). Subjects include your carts (Ps 65:11[12]), grasslands (65:12[13]), *š^{e}ḥāqîm*, clouds (Prov 3:20; cf. Job 36:28, where the subject *rāb* [abundance] refers to the clouds of the first half of the v.), and heavens (Isa 45:8). The objects include righteousness (Isa) and dew (Prov). *nzl* appears twice in synonymous parallelism (Isa and Job). The vb. always describes the blessings of abundance and fruitfulness provided by God and nature.

Dripping, flowing, trickling: → *'ēgel* (drop, # 103); → *dlp* I (drip, # 1940); → *zwb* (flow, # 2307); → *ṭrd* (continuous dripping, # 3265); → *mar* II (drop, # 5254); → *ngr* (flow, gush forth, pour out, # 5599); → *nzl* (flow, trickle, # 5688); → *nṭp* (drip, pour, # 5752); → *'rp* I (drip, # 6903); → *pkh* (trickle, # 7096); → *r^{e}wāyâ* (overflow, # 8122); → *ryr* (flow, # 8201); → *rss* I (moisten, # 8272); → *r'p* (drip, flow, rain, # 8319)

Richard S. Hess

8320	רעץ

רעץ (*r'ṣ*), q. shatter (bisleg., # 8320).

ANE Tg. Aram. *r^{e}'aṣ/r^{e}'ēṣ*, break, shatter.

OT In the Song of Moses Yahweh's right hand carries out the action of this vb. against the enemy (Exod 15:6). The judge Jephthah responds to the Philistine and Ammonite persecution after they "shattered (*r'ṣ*) and crushed (*rṣṣ*)" the Israelites (Judg 10:8).

P-B The vb. occurs in the q. in Yalqut Exodus 24,6 with the same sense as in BH.

רעשׁ (# 8321)

Shattering, breaking, destroying: → *mḥq* (strike, # 4735); → *npṣ* I (break, smash, # 5879); → *pṣṣ* (pulverize, crush, # 7207); → *rṭš* (smash, strike down, # 8187); → *r'ṣ* (shatter, # 8320); → *ršš* (destroy, crushed, # 8406); → *šbr* I (break, shatter, # 8689)

Gary Alan Long

8321	רעשׁ

רעשׁ (*r'š* I), q. quake, shake; hi. cause to shake, quake, leap (# 8321); רַעַשׁ (*ra'aš*), nom. quaking, clatter, commotion (# 8323).

ANE Aram. *r^e'aš*, toss, rage; Arab. tremble, quiver, quake; Akk. *rêšu*, exult.

OT The Heb. vb. *r'š* occurs 30x in the OT. This root appears exclusively in the Prophets and Writings. The things that shake are: foreign nations, the earth, heavens, and various weapons of war. Such shaking occurs primarily for two reasons: (1) as a description of battle or destruction, and (2) as a description of nature's cosmic response to Yahweh's theophanic presence. On one occasion this vb. has a milder nuance. In Ps 72:16 *r'š* is used to describe the swaying heads of wheat blown about by the wind. Some (cf. M. Dahood, *Psalms 51-100*, AB, 183-84) have suggested an alternative root, but such speculation as yet is not convincing (cf. *HALAT* 4:1186; *TWOT* 2:857).

1. When depicting the mass destruction of battle, *r'š* is used figuratively to describe this type of devastation: "The snorting of the enemy's horses is heard from Dan; at the neighing of their stallions the whole land *trembles*. They have come to devour the land and everything in it, the city and all who live there" (Jer 8:16). At times Yahweh is the author of such destruction for the sake of judgment: "But the LORD is the true God; he is the living God, the eternal King. When he is angry, the earth *trembles*; the nations cannot endure his wrath" (10:10). Cavalry, chariots, and wagons in stampeding fashion also cause the earth to quake (Ps 77:18[19]; Ezek 26:10).

2. In many instances the quaking and shaking (*r'š*) is associated with the theophanic presence of Yahweh: "The fish of the sea, the birds of the air, the beasts of the field, every creature that moves along the ground, and all the people on the face of the earth will *tremble* at my presence" (Ezek 38:20; cf. Judg 5:4; 2 Sam 22:8; [bis] Ps 68:8[9]; Isa 13:13; Hag 2:6). This theophanic presence brings both doom upon Yahweh's enemies (Jer 51:29) and comfort to his chosen people (Joel 3:16[4:16]).

The cosmic shaking associated with God's theophanic presence (→ Theophany) occurs in the context of the eschatological Day of the Lord. Drawing upon the language of past theophanic descriptions (cf. Exod 19:18; Judg 5:4-5; Ps 68:6; Hab 3:6), the prophet Haggai describes a future day of shaking that will bring all things perishable to a ghastly end: "In a little while I will *once more shake* the heavens and the earth, the sea and the dry land. I will *shake* all nations" (Hag 2:6-7). The author of the book of Hebrews explains that "the words 'once more' indicate the removing of what can be shaken—that is, created things—so that what cannot be shaken may remain" (Heb 12:26-27). In this way, the people of God look forward to a secure inheritance, to life in a "kingdom that cannot be shaken" (12:28). In part, this last day has begun (Matt 27:51-54). We do, however, continue to look for the sure consummation of this day (Rev 21:1-5).

3. The masc. nom. form of this vb., *ra'aš*, occurs 17x. In Ezek 12:18 this nom. describes the physical shaking caused by extreme fear or anxiety. It is used again by Ezekiel to describe the rattling of the dry bones as they once again form whole bodies (37:7). The term can also be used both generally to describe the sound of battle (Isa 9:5; Jer 10:22) or more specifically of the particular weapons used in battle: the warrior's boot (Isa 9:5[4]), the chariot (Jer 47:3; Nah 3:2), and the javelin (Job 41:29[21]). This nom. is used 7x as the term for an earthquake (1 Kgs 19:11 [bis], 12; Isa 29:6; Ezek 38:19; Amos 1:1; Zech 14:5). These earthquakes are variously depicted as a simple natural catastrophe, a means of divine judgment, and as a cosmic witness to Yahweh's theophanic presence (cf. Ezek 3:12).

Shaking, terror, trembling: → *g'š* (rise and fall noisily, swell, surge, # 1723); → *zw'* (tremble, quake, be afraid, # 2316); → *zll* II (shake, quake, tremble, # 2362); → *ḥalḥālâ* (shaking, trembling, anguish, # 2714); → *ḥrg* (come out trembling, # 3004); → *ḥrd* (tremble, shudder, startle, # 3006); → *yr'* (tremble, be fainthearted, # 3760); → *mwṭ* (waver, reel, stagger, shake, reel, # 4572); → *m'd* (slip, slide, shake, totter, # 5048); → *nwd* (shake, totter, waiver, wander, mourn, flee, # 5653); → *nwṭ* (shake, quake, # 5667); → *nw'* (shake, tremble, stagger, totter, wave, # 5675); → *n'r* II (shake, shake off, # 5850); → *smr* (shudder, have goose-bumps, bristle, # 6169); → *'iw'îm* (distortion, stagger, dizzy, # 6413); → *pwq* I (stagger, wobble, reel, totter, # 7048); → *pḥd* I (tremble, be in dread, # 7064); → *plṣ* (shudder, shake, tremble, # 7145); → *qwṣ* I (feel disgust, frighten, cause dread, # 7762); → *rgz* (agitate, quiver, shake, excite, rouse up, agitate, # 8074); → *rnh* I (rattle, # 8261); → *r'd* (tremble, shake, tremble, # 8283); → *r'l* I (brandish, make to quiver, # 8302); → *r'š* I (quake, shake, leap, # 8321); → *rpp* (shake, quake, rock, # 8344); → *r^eṭēt* (terror, panic, trembling, # 8417); → *ś'r* I (be afraid, terrified, bristle with horror, # 8547)

M. V. Van Pelt/W. C. Kaiser, Jr.

8322	רעשׁ

רעשׁ (*r'š* II), q. be abundant (hapleg.) (# 8322).

ANE The vb. *r'š* II has no ANE cognates. According to G. R. Driver, the term is not to be associated with the common Heb. vb. *r'š* I, shake, quake, but with the Arab. *raǵasa*, give abundantly (*JTS* 33, 1932, 43). Dahood (*Psalms 51-100*, 183) related this word to Ugar. *ġt* and Arab. *raġaṭa*, suck, meaning that the grass crops on the mountain tops were so abundant that the flocks might pasture there and suckle their young.

OT The vb. occurs only in Ps 72:16, where the prayers of the people for divine blessing upon the king of Israel include the petition for an abundance of grain in the land. The passage echoes the psalmist's praise for the rich blessings upon Davidic kingship, which no doubt originated in the blessings (and curses) attached to the stipulations of Yahweh's covenant law (Lev 26:1-26; Deut 28:1-46).

Abundance, multiplication, sufficiency: → *dgh* (multiply, # 1835); → *day* (sufficiency, overflowing supply, # 1896); → *ysp* (add, continue, increase, # 3578); → *kbr* I (make many, be in abundant supply, # 3892); → *m^egammâ* (totality, abundance, # 4480); → *rbb* I (become numerous, much, great, # 8045); → *rbh* I (become numerous, multiply, increase, # 8049); → *r'š* II, be abundant, # 8322); → *śg'/śgh* (grow great, increase, exalt, # 8434/8436); → *śpq* II (suffice, be enough, # 8563); → *šwq* I (overflow, bestow abundantly, # 8796); → *šepa'* (super-abundance, # 9179)

Andrew E. Hill

8323 (*ra'aš*, quaking, clatter), → # 8321

8324	רפא

רפא (*rp'*), q. heal; restore; mend (the earth's fissures); part. healer; physician; ni. be healed; be cured/remitted (with *nega' ṣārā'at* in person or house); be repaired, fixed (of a piece of shattered pottery); be made wholesome (of undrinkable, salt water); pi. heal; treat (medically); repair (a broken-down altar); make wholesome (of undrinkable, salt water); hitp. recover (of wounds), be healed (# 8324); מַרְפֵּא (*marpē'* I; sometimes written as *marpēh*), remedy, cure, healing (# 5340); רִפְאוּת (*rip'ût*), healing; medicine (# 8326); רְפוּאָה (*r^epû'â*; always pl., *r^epu'ôt*), medicine; remedy (# 8337); תְּרוּפָה (*t^erûpâ*), healing, medicine (# 9559). The root is also found in several personal names: *rāpû'*, healed; *r^epā'ēl*, God healed; *r^epāyâ*, Yah healed. It is also attested in the place-name *yirp^e'ēl* (Josh 18:27).

ANE *rp'* is attested among the main Sem. language groups, although it is properly classified as WestSem. (*THAT* 2:803; *TWAT* 7:617-20), since it is not found in Akk. with the exception of one WestSem. loanword (*ripûtu* [healing or medicine] in EA 269:17), and personal names in peripheral Akk. sources (Ugar., Mari, Taanak, etc.). It is also common in Amor. personal names (most notably Hammurapi), as well as in personal names in Ugar., Phoen.-Pun., Aram., and Arab. In Ugar., verbal *rp'*, to heal, is attested with certainty only once (*KTU* 1:114.28).

Although the *rpum* are often designated by scholars as healers and the deity *rpu* as healer (cf. esp. de Moor), this derivation is far from certain; see further *r^epā'îm* I, # 8327 and cf. Brown, "Asklepios." Both verbal and participial forms of *rp'* are found in Phoen. and Pun. (to heal; physician). In Aram., it appears that *rp'* was used in the older phases of the language until being displaced by the Akk. loanword *asû* (physician) > Aram. *'sy'*, physician; *'sy*, heal. The root is found once or twice in Ahiqar (lines 100, 154); once in the DSS (4QEnastr^c 1,II,2); and once as a clearly learned (or, nonce) word in the writings of Ephraem the Syrian, in which *rp'* serves in a wordplay with *rpy* (to loose, be slack). It is therefore somewhat misleading to speak of Aram. *rp'* (since it is entirely absent from the rabbinic writings and all other later phases and dialects of Aram.), while it is actually incorrect to refer to Syr. *rp'*, heal (based, as it were, on only one preserved occurrence in the entire history of Syr. literature), although this error is perpetuated in the major lexicons (e.g., BDB; *HALAT*; see *TWAT* 7:618 for further details). In OSA, *rf'* is attested twice verbally, meaning heal (contra Biella, who posits favor); elsewhere in South Sem., the root is primarily attested in the semantic complex of repairing, mending; cf. Arab. *rf'*, to mend, darn, repair. Also attested in Arab. are: to pull a ship to shore; to appease, affect a reconciliation; although these may possibly be related to different or homonymous roots. Eth. (Ge'ez) attests meanings related to sewing; but cf. the noun *rafa'i*, helper, protector, or, possibly, healer.

Those scholars who derive all South Sem. occurrences of *rf'* from *rf'* I (= *rp'* I) generally posit a Proto-Sem. meaning of bring together, put together for the root. While this linguistic development may be plausible, it has led to the unsupported, yet widely held belief that a *rôpē'* (physician) was so-called because he patched up or stitched up his patient (cf. *ISBE* 2:645; cf. also the unlikely, albeit common, theory that the shades [*r^epā'îm*] were so-called because they were "gathered together" in death; cf. *r^epā'îm* I, # 8327). A more likely view is that Proto-Sem. *rp'* meant to put [anything] back together > to restore. This semantic base readily explains the various meanings for *rp'* attested with certainty in the different branches of Sem.

OT 1. *Distribution.* The vb. *rp'* occurs 67x in the OT: q. 38x; ni. 17x; pi. 9x; hitp. 3x. The total occurrences by individual books are as follows: 13x in Jer; 7x each in Ps and Isa; 6x in 2 Kgs; 5x in Hos; 4x each in 2 Chron, Lev, Ezek; 3x each in Exod, Gen, Deut; 2x in Job; once each in Eccl, Lam, 1 Sam, Zech, 1 Kgs. In nom. forms, *marpē'* (or, sometimes *marpēh*) occurs 16x: 8x in Prov; 4x in Jer; 2x in 2 Chron; once each in Eccl and Mal. *r*^{e}*pû'â* (always pl.—*r*^{e}*pu'ôt*) occurs 3x: 2x in Jer; once in Ezek; *t*^{e}*rûpâ* occurs once (Ezek 47:12; and cf. Ben Sira 38:4); *rip'ût* occurs once (Prov 3:8).

2. *Semantic range.* The fundamental meaning of Heb. *rp'* is restore, make whole (Brown, *Healer*, 25-31). Specific nuances include: (a) repair or fix; cf. Jer 19:11, "This is what the LORD Almighty says: I will smash this nation and this city just as this potter's jar is smashed and cannot be repaired" (cf. also 1 Kgs 18:30); (b) make fresh, wholesome, pertaining to deadly salt water (2 Kgs 2:21-22; Ezek 47:8-9; note also *t*^{e}*rûpâ* in 47:12); (c) mend (but never sew, stitch!): "You have shaken the land and torn it open; mend its fractures, for it is quaking," Ps 60:2[4]; (d) most commonly, heal, in terms of physical disease or wounds, e.g., Miriam's *ṣārāʿat*, Num 12:10; the Philistines' tumors (*ʿ*^{o}*pālîm*, 1 Sam 5:6; the exact meaning of this term is disputed; see also *ṭ*^{e}*ḥōrîm*, 1 Sam 6:11-17); Hezekiah's boil (*š*^{e}*ḥîn*), 2 Kgs 20:8; Jehoram's wounds, 2 Kgs 8:29 [‖ 2 Chron 22:6]; and diseases (*taḥ*^{a}*lumîm*), Ps 103:3. In Lev 13-14, the ni. of *rp'* (*w*^{e}*nirpā'*) is used 4x with *negaʿ-haṣṣārāʿat* as the subject, 3x with reference to humans (13:18, 37; 14:3) and once with reference to houses (14:48), suggesting that remit may serve as a more appropriate and uniform rendering here than heal, cure.

God heals Abimelech and his household, all of whom had been smitten with infertility (Gen 20:17; cf. also 12:17). This usage, however, does not indicate that *rp'* includes the nuance of "refertilizing," as some scholars have argued (e.g., Pope; see also the bibliography to *r*^{e}*pā'îm* I, # 8327); rather, barrenness, impotency, and infertility were perceived as maladies that needed to be healed (or as defective conditions that needed to be made whole). This is in keeping with the covenantal understanding that equated health and fertility with divine blessing (Exod 15:26; 23:25-26; Deut 7:12-15) and sickness and infertility with divine curses (see especially Deut 28:27, 35, which threaten *incurable* diseases as a consequence of covenantal breach, since God, Israel's Healer, was rejected, a theme common in the ANE; cf. also *'ên marpē'//l*^{e}*'ên marpē'*, without remedy, with reference to the nation [2 Chron 36:16] or individuals [e.g., Prov 29:1] whose recalcitrance has resulted in a condition of judgment that is beyond cure).

While it is possible that 2 Chron 7:14 pictures the drought-stricken and locust-ravaged land as sickly (cf. Deut 29:22) and hence in need of healing, it is hardly proper in Eng. to speak of healing *land*; thus the broader meaning of restore is correct here (accordingly render: "then will I hear from heaven and forgive their sin and restore their land"). As to the specific nature of the healing granted by God in answer to Hezekiah's prayer (2 Chron 30:20), the context is ambiguous and the commentaries divided: Does the text presuppose that God had already smitten the people because of their ritual impurity, or does *rp'* here simply indicate that God did *not* smite the people (cf. also Exod 15:26, interpreted in similar fashion by some; e.g., A. B. Ehrlich, *Randglossen*, 1:323, 192; 7:377; cf. also his *Mikra' Ki-Pheshuto*, 1:104; S. Japheth,

I & II Chronicles, OTL)—equating healing with withholding punishment? Or does *rp'* mean heal in the sense of restore from impurity (a usage elsewhere unattested)?

The q. of *rp'* (*rōpē'*) is used for human physicians (e.g., 2 Chron 16:12; in Gen 50:2 [*bis*] it is used for the Egyptian physicians who embalmed Jacob; cf. Spiegelberg) as well as for the Lord as Israel's Healer (Exod 15:26; Ps 103:3; 147:3); see below, 5.

3. *Synonyms and antonyms.* In Hos 5:13, *rp'* is used synonymously with *ghh*, be free from sickness (cf. the Syr.), cure (→ # 1564), but it is impossible to determine with precision the difference between the two words in actual usage. *rp'* occurs 5x with *ḥbš*, to bind up; see Ezek 30:21 ("I have broken the arm of Pharaoh [which] has not been bound up [*ḥbš*] for healing [*r^epû'â*])"; see also Hos 6:1 ("Come, let us return to the LORD. He has torn us to pieces but he will heal [*rp'*] us; he has injured us but he will bind up [*ḥbš*] our wounds"); Ps 147:3 (God "heals [*rp'*] the brokenhearted and binds up [*ḥbš*] their wounds"); Isa 30:26; Ezek 34:4 (cf. also Zech 11:16). Other lexemes that relate to the semantic complex of healing include: *ḥyh*, to live, be alive; recover; make alive, quicken (pi.; cf. with Akk. *bulluṭu* and see *TWAT* 7:617-18); for usage with *rp'*, see Deut 32:39; also Gen 20:7 with 20:17 (to live means to be healed and not die; e.g., Num 21:8–9; see further *ḥyh*, # 2649); for *rp'* with *ḥayyîm*, cf. below, 4(d); *'^arûkâ,* lit., new skin; healing; restoration (# 776; always with *'lh*, to arise; see Jer 8:22; 30:17; 33:6, all with *rp'*); cf. also Isa 58:8 (with *śmḥ*); see also Neh 4:1; 2 Chron 24:13, in nonhealing contexts; cf. also *t^e'ālâ* (from *'lh*, also meaning new skin on a wound > healing; Jer 30:13; 46:11, both times with *t^e'ālâ 'ên lāk*, immediately following *r^epu'ôt*); *ḥlm* I, to be(come) healthy, strong, only at Isa 38:16; *rp'* is sometimes found in proximity to or parallel with *šālôm* (Isa 57:18-19; cf. also Jer 6:14 ‖ 8:11; 14:19; 33:6).

The most frequent antonym of *rp'* is *šbr* I, break, smash, fracture (→ # 8689), a root that occurs prominently in Jeremiah (over one-third of all OT occurrences). A comparison of the similar (antithetical) semantic ranges of the roots *šbr* and *rp'* in Jeremiah is illuminating: with reference to a clay jar, "smashed-repaired" (Jer 19:11); with reference to a bone, "fractured-treated" (Jer 6:14; 8:11); with reference to a body, "injured-healed" (Jer 30:12-13). Of course, the significance of the images is metaphorical: The potter's jar that is smashed beyond repair and the sickly, wounded body symbolize the condition of the city of Jerusalem under judgment; and the false prophets were guilty of superficially treating the people's fracture (*šeber*) by prophesying that all was well when nothing, in fact, was well (*šālôm šālôm w^e'ên šālôm*; Jer 6:14; 8:11; it is possible, of course, to translate this in a more overtly political fashion: "'Peace! Peace!' When there is no peace"). Thus Judah's national injuries were incurable until corporate repentance—the source of healing and restoration—would spring forth (Jer 30:12-13; 33:6-9; cf. again Deut 28:27, 35; 2 Chron 36:16, and see further below, 6). Thus, by extension, the city-wide or national dimensions reflected in Jeremiah's usage of *šbr/rp'* work out to mean "collapsed-restored." Closely related to this is Lam 2:13 ("What can I say for you? With what can I compare you, O Daughter of Jerusalem? To what can I liken you, that I may comfort you, O Virgin Daughter of Zion? Your wound [or, breech; *šeber*], is as deep as the sea [*mišbar*; lit., breaker]. Who can heal you?"), a condition that the author of Lamentations blames on the sin of the false prophets whose misleading and worthless visions failed to "expose your sin to ward off your captivity"

(Lam 2:14). For further examples of *rp'/šbr* see Ps 147:3; Isa 30:26; Jer 51:8; Zech 11:16.

Other antonyms include: *mḥṣ*, wound, strike (→ # 4730); cf. Deut 32:39: "I have wounded (*mḥṣ*) but I myself will heal" (*wa'ᵃnî 'erpā'*); see also Job 5:18; Isa 30:26; *nkh*, strike, smite (→ # 5782); see 2 Kgs 8:29 (∥ 2 Chron 22:6); 9:15; Jer 14:19; again Isa 30:26; *ḥlh*, be sick, infirm (→ # 2703); see 2 Kgs 20:8; Ps 103:3; Ezek 34:4; *ṭrp*, tear (→ # 3271); see Hos 6:1 (referring back to the divine tearing of 5:13-14); *ngp*, smite, strike (→ # 5597); see Isa 19:22, the prophetic text promising future restoration to Egypt: "The LORD will strike Egypt with a plague; he will strike them and heal them. They will turn to the LORD, and he will respond to their pleas and heal them" (contrast Ezek 30:21, also with Egypt; Jer 51:8-9, with Babylon; and see below, 4[b]); *hrg* kill (→ # 2222), opposite *rp'* only in Eccl 3:3, "a time to kill, a time to heal," where the reference is apparently to those wounded in battle (the only appropriate time to kill?—see Targ.); otherwise, one would not expect to find *rp'* with *hrg*, since those who are killed are not candidates for healing.

4. *The question of "figurative" or "spiritual" healing.* It is common to classify the usage of *rp'* in contexts that do not specifically deal with bodily ailments as "figurative," but this needs to be qualified and, at times, corrected. This is due to the fact that, in the OT, the usage of *rp'* is decidedly holistic (cf. the similar usage of *sōzō* in the NT, where the range of meanings includes deliverance from sickness, demons, death, and sin, sometimes within two chapters of the same book; cf. Luke 7:50; 8:36, 48, 50). In the OT, there was a wide range of conditions that were candidates for healing, and one must ask if, to the biblical mind, the restoration of an individual's health would be seen as literal while the restoration of a nation's health would be understood to be figurative. Would a semantic distinction even be perceived?

At times, the problem is one of reading biblical concepts in terms of our compartmentalized canons of thinking as opposed to adjusting our thinking to the Bible's more holistic outlook. Moreover, it is inappropriate to presuppose that every occurrence of *rp'* in the OT proceeded from a fundamental meaning of to heal physical disease, as if, when Elijah *repaired* the Lord's broken-down altar (1 Kgs 18:30, with *rp'* in the pi.), the root was used because repairing an altar was analogous to healing a body. (Note that it is rendered with *bᵉnā'*, built, in the Targ., but with *iasato* [!], healed, in the LXX; cf. the similar, but incorrect listing in *HALAT* 903, and, even more strikingly, in W. L. Holladay's Eng. abridgement, 344.) Rather, 1 Kgs 18:30 reflects the earlier (and broader) semantic range of the root, reflected especially in South Sem. usage, before it became associated almost exclusively with the semantic domain of healing in the late biblical and postbiblical Heb. language (see below, P-B); cf. also the Tg. (note also the Pesh.) to Isa 6:10, and see Mark 4:12.

(a) In certain prophetic contexts, *rp'* is used for the healing of sin and apostasy, presupposing the figure of sin as a serious illness (Jer 3:22; Hos 14:3). Thus, Israel's *mᵉšûbâ* (unfaithfulness, waywardness, backsliding) is a dangerous condition that only God can cure. In this case, the translation of heal should be retained (as opposed to forgive, as per some translators and commentators), although it is acceptable to speak of figurative usage here, since the specific object of *rp'* is abstract (viz., the people's sinful condition pictured as an illness rather than the people and nation pictured as ill, for which see immediately below, 4[b]).

(b) Frequently, the prophets used *rp'* in terms of divine restoration for the nation after a time of judgment and chastisement (e.g., Isa 6:10; Jer 30:17; Hos 5:13; 6:1), thereby expanding on the imagery discussed immediately above. However, to speak of this usage as figurative or spiritual can be misleading, since the reality of the promised restoration had to be just as real as that of the devastating judgments inflicted. That is to say, the literality of the healing had to correspond to the literality of the smiting. While it is true that the prophets could describe Israel as a sin-sick people needing healing (cf. Isa 1:4-7), and while their emphasis was certainly on repentance and reconciliation, they knew that there were serious consequences to sin, including social upheaval, military defeat, economic collapse, famine, plague, the destruction of the temple, war, and even exile and captivity (cf. also below, sec. 6). For the prophets, the promised healing would have to be equally comprehensive and, in this sense, hardly figurative.

Verses such as Isa 30:26 ("The moon will shine like the sun, and the sunlight will be seven times brighter, like the light of seven full days, when the LORD binds up the bruises of his people and heals the wounds he inflicted") were not just read as beautiful poetry. They offered concrete promises for a people whose condition at times appeared terminal. The metaphorical imagery, powerfully expressed through vivid figures such as Israel's "new skin" arising (e.g., Jer 30:17; 33:6, not rendered expressively in the NIV), or a physician applying healing balm (8:22; 46:11; 51:8; cf. also Isa 1:6), must therefore be seen as inclusive and not as exclusive (in other words, healing of physical diseases was certainly not excluded from the wider metaphor of national healing and restoration). Thus, to say here that the prophetic usage of *rp'* was metaphorical is not to say that it was merely figurative or spiritual in nature (in contrast with 4[a]). The hope of the prophets was nothing less than the whole man wholly healed, classically expressed in Isa 53:4-5, "Surely he took up our infirmities and carried our sorrows, yet we considered him stricken by God, smitten by him, and afflicted. But he was pierced for our transgressions, he was crushed for our iniquities; the punishment that brought us peace was upon him, and by his wounds we are healed." The depth of meaning in these verses can be seen by comparing the spiritualizing rendering of 53:4a in the LXX ("This man bore our sins and was pained because of them") and Targ. Jon. ("Then for our sins he will pray and our iniquities will be forgiven because of him") with Matthew's literal rendering in Matt 8:17b ("He took up our infirmities and carried our diseases") in the context of healing the sick (8:16-17a). Both concepts are present in the Heb. text, as J. A. Motyer noted with ref. to Isa 53:5: "Isaiah uses 'healing' in a total sense: the healing of the person, restoring fullness and completeness, a mark of the Messianic day (19:22; 30:26)" (*The Prophecy of Isaiah*, 1993, 436).

(c) In the Psalms, *rp'* is virtually always used with reference to literal, physical healing (cf. Ps 6:3; 30:3; 41:4[5]; 103:3; 107:20, and note especially H.-J. Kraus, BKAT, to Ps 6; 30; 41; see further Brown, *Healer*, 119-44; Ps 147:3 refers to the healing of the brokenhearted). However, because of the close connection in these psalms between sin and sickness, on the one hand, and forgiveness and healing on the other hand, these texts have often been understood as if healed simply meant forgiven. Rather, to cite one clear example, the cry of the psalmist in 41:4(5), "Heal me, for I have sinned against you," cannot be reduced to a prayer for forgiveness alone. The context, which begins with an indisputably literal promise of health and restoration

(vv. 1-3[2-4]), makes it clear that the psalmist was bedridden, stricken with what looked to be a terminal illness, interpreted to be the apparent result of personal sin (cf. John 5:14; James 5:14-15; see also Matt 9:2), to the derision and delight of his detractors. Forgiveness of sin and healing of disease would thus go hand in hand, sickness being perceived as the fruit of disobedience and healing as the fruit of repentance. Accordingly, the promise of future glory for Zion in Isa 33:15-24, ends with: "No one living in Zion will say, 'I am ill'; and the sins of those who dwell there will be forgiven." It should also be noted that the overly wooden renderings of, e.g., the AV, NKJV, and NASB, all of which translate with "Heal my soul," have contributed to the common misunderstanding of the usage of *rp'* in the Psalms (see also *nepeš*); similar to this is the medieval Jewish exegesis of the passage, which understood healing of the soul to be equivalent to repentance (see, e.g., David Kimchi, and note BTalm Megilla 17b, where it is stated that the petition for healing is placed in the Shemoneh Esreh [i.e., Eighteen Benedictions] because it is not a prayer for [physical] healing of sickness, but rather for [spiritual] healing through forgiveness).

(d) An obvious principle that can be deduced from the examples cited immediately above is that the literality of the usage of *rp'* is directly related to the literality of the immediate context. This is brought into focus in Proverbs, where *rp'* brings healing to a wide variety of conditions. In at least two prominent cases, there is no reason to deny that the healing promised as a result of godly living is bodily: "Do not be wise in your own eyes; fear the LORD and shun evil. This will bring health [*rip'ût*, better rendered healing, or, according to some, medicine, based on the parallelism with *šiqqûy*—nourishment or tonic?] to your body and nourishment to your bones" (Prov 3:7-8); "My son, pay attention to what I say; listen closely to my words. Do not let them out of your sight, keep them within your heart; for they are life to those who find them and health (*marpē'*, better rendered healing) to a man's whole body" (4:20-22).

The book of Proverbs, in keeping with Wisdom literature in general—not to mention the OT as a whole—sees godliness as the very real path to life and well-being while godlessness is the sure road to death and destruction. In this light, and with physical referents such as flesh (*š^e'ēr*; the precise meaning of the Heb. is uncertain) and bones (*'^{a}ṣāmôt*) in 3:8 and body (*bāśār*, flesh) in 4:22, the force of the verses is clear: Godly living is a key to healing and health. Elsewhere in Prov, in keeping with the general imagery of the OT, *'ên marpē'* speaks of the disastrous state of those whose defiant sinfulness takes them beyond the brink of possible recovery: They "will suddenly be destroyed—without remedy" (*peta' yiššābēr w^e'ên marpē'* in both 6:15 and 29:1). In positive contexts, Prov 12:18 states that "the tongue of the wise brings healing" to the sword-like wounds inflicted by a chatterbox; according to 13:17, in contrast to the wicked messenger who always falls into trouble, "a trustworthy envoy brings healing" (*ṣîr '^{e}mûnîm marpē'*—i.e., by faithfully delivering his message), while 16:24 notes that "pleasant words are a honeycomb, sweet to the soul [*nepeš*, better rendered here palate] and healing to the bones." Cf. also 15:4a, "The tongue that brings healing is a tree of life," underscoring the healing power of the words of the wise, first seen in 4:20-22, where *marpē'* occurred in close proximity to *ḥayyîm*. (Note that it is best to understand *marpē'* in 14:30 as *marpēh*, hence, "The heart at rest is the life of the body," in spite of the presence again of *ḥayyîm*; → *rph*, # 8332; note, however, that the

LXX relates *marpē'* here to *rp'*.) Thus, in Prov, *marpē'* (or, *rip'ût*) is the concrete remedy for physical or emotional wounding and collapse.

5. *Human physicians* (*rōpᵉ'îm*) *and the divine healer* (*rôpē'*). In distinct contrast to their Mesopotamian and Egyp. neighbors, the people of Israel preserved almost no ancient medical literature of any kind (cf. the lone reference to [*lṭbšlm*] *bn zkr hrp'*, "to PN son of Zkr, the physician," in a later seventh/early sixth-century bulla from the City of David; see *IEJ* 36, 1986, 28-29, no. 4). This may be due in part to the fact that ANE medical literature was rarely, if ever, purely "scientific" (cf., however, Civil, for the two extant Sumerian medical texts); rather, it demonstrated a complete intertwining of magic, medicine, and religion (cf. esp. Ritter, as well as general bibl. related to ANE medicine, below). Thus, involvement with physicians often meant involvement with pagan deities and foreign practices proscribed by the Torah. In fact, Exod 15:26, the *locus classicus* in which God reveals himself to be Israel's Healer, must be seen as directed more against rival healing deities than against earthly physicians. Nonetheless, for basic outward medical care, such as setting of fractures and treating of wounds, it seems that physicians were accepted as religiously neutral. The more mysterious inner workings of disease and recovery were apparently understood in spiritual terms, and in the case of *ṣārā'at* (serious skin disease), the priests functioned only as observers and hygienists.

(a) Human physicians (*rōpᵉ'îm*). There is legislation in Exod 21:18-19 (cf. the parallel in the Code of Hammurabi, 206) dealing with the case of injuries caused by a fight: If the injured man does not die, then the one who struck him "must pay the injured man for the loss of his time and see that he is completely healed" (21:19b; *rappō' yᵉrappē'*). The final clause is interpreted in the LXX and Targums to mean, pay the physician's fee; cf. also BTalm Baba Qamma 85a. Thus, "professional" medical care is mandated in case law in the Book of the Covenant. There are several references to treating wounds and broken bones in the prophetic books (Jer 6:14; 8:11; 46:11; 51:8; Ezek 30:21; and with ref. to sheep, Ezek 34:4; Zech 11:16), all with metaphorical application, but all presupposing the prevalent nature of such practices, either by physicians (or, in the specific case of the flocks, by shepherds) or as common folk practices. Jer 8:22, again in a metaphorical context, asks if there is no balm in Gilead or no physician there, suggesting that the presence of a physician was routinely expected, at least in Gilead, famous for its healing balm (*ṣᵒrî*); cf. also the sarcastic reference to "worthless physicians" in Job 13:4.

Of special interest is 2 Chron 16:12, the classic text quoted in popular religious circles to support the position that it is a sin for true believers to go to doctors instead of simply trusting the Lord. As rendered in the NIV, and reflecting the common understanding of the passage, the verse states: "In the thirty-ninth year of his reign Asa was afflicted with a disease in his feet. Though his disease was severe, even in his illness he did not seek help from the LORD, but only from the physicians." However, the greater context needs to be observed, as well as the specific idiom of v. 12. That is to say, 2 Chron 16:12 is the climax of chs. 14-16, which describe Asa's reign, marked by the fervent way in which he commanded the people to seek the Lord (*lidrôš 'et-yhwh*; see esp. 14:4-7), especially in the midst of a great military crisis. Asa put his trust in the Lord rather than in earthly help, and the Lord delivered him (14:8-15), resulting in a national decree that whoever would not seek the Lord would be put to death (15:1-15).

Sometime later, in a new military crisis, rather than seek the Lord's help, Asa hired a foreign army to fight for him, paying them with the temple treasuries and resulting in a sharp prophetic rebuke, which Asa brutally rejected (16:1-9). It was only at this point that he was smitten with a severe foot disease (gout? see DeVries and Weinberger), in the midst of which he still refused to seek the Lord but rather *consulted* (i.e., in an oracular sense) the physicians, meaning idolatrous or magical practitioners, expressed with biting conciseness in the words *lō' dāraš 'et-yhwh kî bārōp^{e}'îm* (*dāraš 'ēt* is simply to seek, whereas *dāraš b-* is to consult; cf. 2 Chron 10:10). Thus, 16:12 does not proscribe medical help in general, but rather deals with the issue of trusting in the help of God instead of leaning on sinful, human support; cf. Hasel, and see W. Rudolph, *Chronikbücher*, HAT, 249. Interestingly, however, verbal *rp'* never occurs in the OT with both a human subject and object (excluding metaphorical contexts such as Jer 6:14; Hos 5:13-14); the Lord is virtually always the subject of *rp'* (cf. e.g., Gen 20:17; Deut 32:39; and *passim*).

(b) The divine Physician. Virtually all ancient deities were believed to have healing powers (cf. Jayne; von Baudissin; Sigerist, 134), since spiritual, material, and physical well-being were equally attributed to the deity's blessing, while spiritual, material, and physical breakdowns were attributed to the deity's wrath or to demonic powers. A god who was not thought to have healing powers would hardly be worthy of divine stature, any more than a god who could not forgive sins or send rain would be considered worthy of adoration. In this light, it is interesting to note that both Jesus and Asklepios, the preeminent Greco-Roman healing deity, were hailed by their followers as both *sōtēr* (savior) and *iatros* (physician), while in ancient Babylon, Marduk could be hailed as *asû* and *ašipu* (physician and exorcist/magical expert; cf. also *bēl ašiputi*—chief exorcist/magical expert) and Gula, the preeminent female healing deity, as *azugallatu* (the great [lady] physician; cf. Lambert). Some would also argue that the Ugar. deity *rpu* (equated by de Moor with Baal, but by most scholars with either El, another known Ugar. deity, or simply a deity named Rapi'u or Rapa'u; see also *r^{e}pā'îm* I, # 8327), was so designated because he was known as the paramount healer of the pantheon. This much is sure: For the people of Israel, there was to be one main source for healing, deliverance, and salvation, viz., the Lord. As healer (a rendering that points to a wider range of activity than does "physician") he promised to remove sickness from their midst, bless their food and drink, grant them fertile wombs and productive lands, and give them a full life span—if they would only heed his voice (the foundational Torah texts are Exod 15:26; 23:25-26; Deut 7:12-15).

The OT records several instances of (apparently) miraculous physical healings (or, resurrections) in answer to prayer (or through following specific prophetic direction), generally without any medical intervention (cf. Gen 20:17-18; Num 12:9-15; 21:6-9; 1 Kgs 17:17-24; 2 Kgs 4:8-36; 5:1-14; cf. also 6:18-20), although, according to 2 Kgs 20:1-11 ‖ Isa 38:1-8, the Lord told Isaiah to apply a lump of figs (commonly used for medicinal purposes in the ANE) to Hezekiah's boil, after which he recovered (cf. also 1 Tim 5:23, where wine is recommended for Timothy's stomach ailments, albeit without any hint of divine healing in the context). Cf. further 2 Kgs 2:19-22, where undrinkable, salt water is made wholesome (*rp'* in pi. and ni.) through Elisha's divinely inspired words and actions (using salt as a medium; cf. also Ezek 47:1-12, with *rp'* in ni.; and note Exod 15:22-25, the immediate context of 15:26). Thus the psalmist praised him who forgave all sin, healed all disease, and delivered from death (Ps 103:1-5), clearly interrelated concepts in the biblical mentality, and no doubt reflecting general Israelite piety. And it was to the Lord, Israel's divine Healer, that the prophets looked for the ultimate restoration of their divinely afflicted nation (cf. above, 4[b]).

The fact that Yahweh is pictured more as a smiter than a healer in the OT is due to the historically sinful character of the people, not to any lack of beneficence in the character of the Lord. In this light, Deut 32:39 states, "See now that I myself am He! There is no god besides me. I put to death and I bring to life [speaking in general terms of God's sovereign power], I have wounded [a prophetic-perfect statement, looking back on God's future smiting of his disobedient people] and I will heal [upon repentance], and no one can deliver out of my hand" (cf. Brown, *Healer*, 87-93, 99-112). Thus, the messianic promises burst with the hope of a profusion of miracles of renewal and restoration (cf. Isa 35:1-5), a hope that begins to see its fulfillment in the coming of Jesus the Messiah into the world (note especially Luke 7:17-22). As expressed by Malachi, "But for you who revere my name, the sun of righteousness will rise with healing [*marpē'*] in its wings. And you will go out and leap like calves released from the stall" (Mal 4:2[3:20]).

6. *Theological reflections.* The issue of physical healing in the Bible transcends earthly, medical concerns, touching on various aspects of Israelite piety and belief. Related concepts include: the mental, emotional, social, and spiritual state of the seriously ill (e.g., tormented within and without, one foot in the grave, cut off from the land of the living, in the grip of Sheol, a laughingstock to his enemies, separated from the sanctuary and corporate worship, and, frequently, conscious of guilt and sin); sickness as a manifestation of guilt (where personal sin was clearly known) and healing as a manifestation of grace (signaling that all was well, bringing personal vindication in the presence of one's enemies [e.g., Ps 41:10-11(11-12)], and restoring to intimacy and divine favor [e.g., Ps 41:12(13)]); healing as deliverance from death and the grave [e.g., 30:1-3(2-4)]; sickness as chastisement (serious sickness, viewed as incipient death, served as the perfect wake-up call to the sinning servant of the Lord, indicating clearly that something was wrong, that he had strayed from the path of life; cf. Job 5:17-18; 33:14-30); and healing as a manifestation of the power and nature of the *living* God (it is the living who praise him!—cf. Isa 38:16-19).

Such subjects, which relate in particular to individual sickness and healing, can only be touched on in the briefest of terms. They do, however, provide the conceptual background to the larger prophetic picture of divine healing and restoration, which takes in national, covenantal issues and focuses for the most part on corporate restoration, often in the context of corporate repentance (for *rp'* and *šwb* used in close conjunction, cf. Isa 6:10; Jer 3:22; Hos 6:1; 6:11b-7:1a). At times, however, there seemed to be no hope of healing (cf. Jer 14:19); the smiting was too severe and the sinful condition of the patient irremediable: "This is what the LORD has said: 'Your fracture is grievous, your wound is incurable [again *šeber* and *makkâ*: *'ānûš lᵉšibrēk naḥlâ makkātēk*; cf. also Mic 1:9]. No one pleads your cause; there is no healing for your sore, no fresh skin for you [*'ên-dān dînēk lᵉmāzôr rᵉpu'ôt-tᵉ 'ālâ 'ên lāk*].'. . . Why do you cry out over your wound? Your pain is incurable. Because of the greatness of your guilt and your sins which were so many I have done these things to you’" (Jer 30:12-13, 15, my translation).

Yet even in the midst of this hopeless prognosis light was about to dawn. Israel’s divine Healer promised to act: "Surely I will bring you restoration, and will heal you of your wounds" (*kî ’a^{a}leh ’^{a}rukâ lāk ûmimmakkôtayik ’erpā’ēk*, again, my translation, 30:17). And to the city of Jerusalem, "‘I will bring health and healing to it; I will heal my people and will let them enjoy abundant peace and security. I will bring Judah and Israel back from captivity and will rebuild them as they were before. I will cleanse them from all the sin they have committed against me and will forgive all their sins of rebellion against me. Then this city will bring me renown, joy, praise and honor before all nations on earth that hear of all the good things I do for it; and they will be in awe and will tremble at the abundant prosperity and peace I provide for it’" (Jer 33:6-9). In the end, mercy would triumph over judgment and healing over smiting.

P-B The most important single postbiblical healing text is Ecclus 38, reflecting a Hellenized outlook on medicine and doctors, in which the doctor is God’s agent for healing, using the (herbal) medicines that the Lord has put in the earth (38:4 with *t^{e}rûpôt* in the Heb. original, clearly harking back to Ezek 47:12; cf. also Rev 22:2). The patient should "pray to the Lord" (38:9), "leave off from sin" (38:10), and "then give place to the physician" (38:12), who will also pray to the Lord for success (38:14). For the healing of Tobit’s eyes by the hand of the angel Raphael, cf. Tob 2:10; 3:17; 7:7; 11:7-16 (see 6:6-8); 12:1-15; 14:2; note also that his affliction and subsequent healing serves as a tacit portrait of Israel’s present distress and future restoration (against the backdrop of the Assyrian exile).

In the DSS, the root *rp’* is attested to date 3x verbally and 5x nominally (cf. 1QH 9, 25; 1QS 4, 6; CD 8, 4; and cf. Deut 28:28 with 4Q DibHam^{a} 1-2,II, 14; for *l’yn mrp’*, cf. 1QH 2, 26; and note *w’yn rwp’* in 4Q 509, 12-13, 4). In rabbinic Heb., *rôpē’* is the standard word for physician (generally thought of in positive terms [cf. e.g., BTalm Berakot 60a, where God, however, is still the "reliable Physician"]; but see also Mish. Qiddušin 4:14), although the q. of *rp’* is no longer used for heal, giving way to the pi., while the ni. has been displaced by the hitp. and nit. conjugations. Key healing vocables in the NT include: *iaomai* and its nominal forms (almost always the LXX equivalents to *rp’*); *therapeuō*; *sōzō* (cf. also *diasozō*); *hygiainō* (and related forms).

Healing, health, healthful: → *ghh* (heal, # 1564); → *rp’* (heal, make healthy, drinkable, # 8324); → *šālôm* (peace, friendship, happiness, prosperity, health, salvation, # 8934)
Sickness: → *ḥl’* (fall ill, # 2688); → *ḥlh* I (become weak, tired, ill, # 2703)

BIBLIOGRAPHY

ABD 4:659-64; *DBSup* 5:957-68; *EMiqr* 7:407-25; *ERE* 4:723-31, 755-57; 6:540-56; *IDB* 2:541-48; *ISBE* 2:640-48; *NIDNTT* 2:163-72; *TDNT* 3:128-32, 194-215; *THAT* 2:803-9; *TWAT* 7:618-25; *TWOT* 2:857; *ZPEB* 3:54-58; D. W. Amundsen and G. B. Ferngren, "Medicine and Religion: Pre-Christian Antiquity," in *Health/Medicine and the Faith Traditions: An Inquiry Into Religion and Medicine*, 1982, 53-92; M. Asaf, ed. *HaRefu’a BaMekorot*, 1982; H. Avalos, *Illness and Health Care in the Ancient Near East: The Role of the Temple in Greece, Mesopotamia, and Israel*, 1995; M. L. Barré, "Bulluṭsa-rābi’s Hymn to Gula and Hosea 6:1-2," *Or* 50, 1981, 241-45; C. Barth, *Die Erretung vom Tode in den individuellen Klage- und Dankliedern des Altes Testament*, 1947; J. Z. Baruch, "The Relation Between Sin and Disease in the Old Testament,"

Hanas: Revue Internationale de l'historie des sciences 5, 1964, 295-302; R. D. Biggs, "Babylonien," in *Krankheit, Heilkunst, Heilung*, 91-114; idem, "Medicine in Ancient Mesopotamia," in *History of Science*, 1969, 8:94-105; idem, "Medizin. A. In Mesopotamien," *RLA* 7:623-29; J. D. Bleich, "The Obligation to Heal in the Judaic Tradition: A Comparative Analysis," repr. in F. Rosner and J. D. Bleich, eds., *Jewish Bioethics*, 1979, 1-44; W. K. Bokovay, "The Relationship of Physical Healing to the Atonement," *Didaskalia* 3, 1991, 24-39; M. L. Brown, *Israel's Divine Healer*, SOTBT 1995; idem, "Was There a West Semitic Asklepios?" *UF* forthcoming; J. B. Burns, "The Chastening of the Just in Job 5:17-23: Four Strikes of Erra," *Proceedings, Eastern Great Lakes and Midwest Bible Societies* 10, 1990, 18-30; M. Civil, "Une nouvelle prescription médicale sumérienne," *RA* 55, 1961, 91-94; idem, "Prescriptions médicales sumeriénnes," *RA* 54, 1960, 57-72; W. R. Dawson, "The Egyptian Medical Papyri," repr. in *Diseases in Antiquity*, 1967; H. de Meulenaere, "Arzt," *LÄ* 1:455-59; idem, "Arzteschule," in *LÄ* 1:79-80; J. C. de Moor, "Rāpi'ūma—Rephaim," *ZAW* 88, 1976, 323-45; A. DeVries, and A. Weinberger, "King Asa's Presumed Gout: Twentieth Century A.D. Discussion of Ninth Century B.C. Biblical Patient," *NY State Medical Journal* 75, 1975, 452-55; W. Ebstein, *Die Medizin im Alten Testament*, 1965; E. Edel, *Ägyptische Arzte und ägyptische Medizin am hethitischen Königshof: Neue Funde von Keilschriftbriefen Ramses' II aus Bogazkoy*, 1976; E. J. Edelstein, and L. Edelstein, eds., *Asclepios: Testimonies*, 1945; J. W. Estes, *The Medical Skills of Ancient Egypt*, 1989; D. M. Feldman, *Health and Medicine in the Jewish Tradition*, 1986; D. Flusser, "The Role of the Doctor According to Ben-Sira," (Heb.), *Mahanayim* 122, 1970, 48-55; H. Friedenwald, *The Jews and Medicine*, 3 vols, 1967; P. Ghalioungui, *The Physicians of Ancient Egypt*, 1983; idem, *The House of Life—Per Hankh: Magic and Medical Science in Ancient Egypt*, 1973; H. Grapow, *Untersuchungen über die altägyptischen medizinischen Papyri*, 1935-36; idem, and H. von Deines, W. Westendorf, *Grundriss der Medizin der alten Ägypter*, 9 Vols., 1954-73; M. Hamilton, *Incubation, or the Cure of Disease in Pagan Temples and Christian Churches*, 1906; R. K. Harrison, *The Healing Herbs of the Bible*, 1966; G. F. Hasel, "Health and Healing in the Old Testament," *AUSS* 21, 1983, 191-202; J. Hempel, *Heilung als Symbol und Wirklichkeit im biblischen Schriftum*, 1958; idem, "Ich bin der Herr dein Arzt," *TLZ* 82, 1957, 809-26; L. Hogan, "A Note on Healing and Ignorance in the Bible," *Koroth* 9/1-2, 1985, 107-12; P. Humbert, "Maladie et médecine dans l'Ancien Testament," *RHPhR* 44, 1964, 1-29; W. T. Im der Smitten, "Patient und Arzt. Die Welt des Kranken im Alten Testament," *Janus* 61, 1974, 103-29; I. Jacob, and W. Jacob. *The Healing Past: Pharmaceuticals in the Biblical and Rabbinic World*, 1993; W. A. Jayne, *Healing Gods of Ancient Civilizations*, 1979 (repr.); M. T. Kelsey, *Healing and Christianity*, 1973; C. Kerenyi, *Asklepios: Archetypal Image of the Physician's Existence*, 1959; S. Kim, "The Concepts of Health, Disease and Healing: Theological Perspective," in *The Proceedings of the Consultation on the Study Program of the Healing Ministry*, 27-35; J. V. Kinnier-Wilson, "Medicine in the Land and Times of the Old Testament," in *Studies in the Period of David and Solomon*, 1982, 337-65; F. Kocher, *Die babylonische-assyrische Medizin in Texten und Untersuchungen*, 1963-; S. S. Kottek, *Medicine and Hygiene in the Works of Flavius Josephus*, 1994; R. Labat, *Traité akkadien de diagnostics et prognostics médicaux*, Vol. 1, *Transcription et Traduction*, Vol. 2, *Planches*, 1951; W. G. Lambert, "The Gula Hymn of Bulluṭsa-rābi," *Or*, n.s. 36, 1967, 105-32; S. Levin, "Hezekiah's Boil," *Judaism* 42, 1993, 214-17; B. A. Levine, and J.-M. de Tarragon, O.P. "'Shapshu Cries Out in Heaven': Dealing with Snake-Bites at Ugarit," *RB* 95, 1988, 481-518; F. Lindström, *Suffering and Sin: Interpretations of Illness in the Individual Complaint Psalms*, ConBOT, OTS 37, 1994; E. Lipiński, "Eshmun, 'Healer'," *Annali dell'Istituto orientale di Napoli* 23, 1973, 161-83; A. Lods, "Les idées des Israélites sur la maladie, ses causes et ses remèdes," in *Vom Alten Testament*, 181-93 (= K. Marti Festscrhift, *BZAW* 41, 1925); N. Lohfink, "'Ich bin Jahwe, dein Arzt' (Ex 15,26). Gott, Gesselschaft und menschliche Gesundheit in einer nachexilischen Pentateuchbearbeitung (Ex 15, 25b.26)," in *Ich Will euer Gott werden: Beispiele biblischen Redens von Gott*, SBS 100, 1981, 11-73; O. Loretz, "Tod und Leben nach altorientalischer und kanaanaäisch-biblischer Anschauung in Hos 6, 1-3," *BN* 17, 1982, 37-42; D. S. Margulis, *Lashon u-refuah ba-Tanakh*, 1949; R. Martin-Achard, "La prière des malades dans le psautier d'Israēl," *Lumière et Vie* 86, 1968, 25-43; F. Michaeli, "Les malades et le temple dans l'Ancien Testament," *Église et Théologie* 21, 1958, 3-12; E. Neufeld, "Hygiene Conditions in Ancient Israel (Iron Age)," *BA* 34, 1971, 42-66; H. Niehr, "JHWH als Arzt. Herkunft und Geschichte einer alttestamentlichen Gottesprädikation," *BZ* 35, 1991, 3-17; D. Noy, "The Talmudic-Midrashic Healing Stories as a Narrative Genre," *Koroth* 9, Special Issue, 1988, 124-46; B. Palmer, ed., *Medicine and the Bible*, 1986; M. H. Pope, "Notes on the Ugaritic Rephaim Texts," in *Essays on the Ancient Near East in Memory of Jacob Joel Finkelstein*, 1977, 163-82; J. Preuss, *Biblical and Talmudic Medicine*, 1978, 18-31; P. Prioreschi, *A History of Medicine: Volume 1, Primitive and Ancient Medicine*, 1991; E. K. Ritter, "Magical-expert (= *ašipu*) and Physician (= *asû*). Notes on Two Complementary Professions in Babylonian Medicine," in *Studies in Honor of Benno Landsberger on His 75 Birthday*, Assyriological Studies 16, 1965; F. Rosner, "The Illness of King Hezekiah and 'The Book of Remedies' Which He Hid," *Koroth* 9/1-2, 1985, 191-93; idem, *Medicine in the Bible and Talmud*, 1977; R. Rouillard, "*El rofé* en *Nombres* 12,13," *Sem* 37, 1987, 17-46; H. Schipperges, and E. Seidler, P. U. Unschuld, eds., *Krankheit, Heilkunst, Heilung*, 1978; K. Seybold, *Das Gebet des Kranken in Alten Testament: Untersuchungen zur Bestimmung und Zuordnung der Krankheits- und Heilungspsalmen*, BWANT 99, 1973; idem, "Krankheit und Heilung. Soziale Aspekte in dem Psalmen," *BK* 20, 1971, 107-11; idem, and U. B. Mueller, *Sickness and Healing*, 1981; H. E. Sigerist, *Civilization and Disease*, 1943; D. J. Simundson, "Mental Health in the Bible," *Word & World* 9, 1989, 140-46; idem, "Health and Healing in the Bible," *Word & World* 2, 1982, 330-39; W. Speigelberg, "Die Beisetzung des Patriarchen Jacob (Gen 50, 2ff.) in Licht der agypt. Quellen," *OLZ* 26, 1923, 421-24; D. Sperber, "Weak Waters," *ZAW* 82, 1970, 114-16; J. J. Stamm, "Erlosen und Vergeben im Alten Testament," diss. Basel, 1940; K. Stendahl, "Gamla Testaments föreställningar om helandet. Rafa'-utsagorna i kontext och ideologi," *Svensk Exegetisk Årsbok* 15, 1950, 5-33; T. Struys, *Ziekte en Genezing in het Oude Testament*, 1968; A. M. Sweet, "A Theology of Healing," *TBT* 20, 1982, 145-49; F. Vattioni, "Mal. 3,20 e un mese del calendario fenicio," *Bib* 40, 1959, 1012-15; W. W. G. von Baudissin, *Adonis und Esmun: Eine Untersuchung zur Geschichte des Glaubens an Auferstehungsgötter und an Heilgötter*, 1911; C. Westermann, "Heilung und Heil in der Gemeinde aus der Sicht des Alten Testaments," *Wege zum Menschen* 27, 1975, 12-25; D. J. Wiseman, "Medicine in the Old Testament," in *Medicine and the Bible*, 1986, 13-42; A. S. Yahuda, "Medical and Anatomical Terms in the Pentateuch in the Light of Egyptian Medical Papyri," *Journal of the History of Medicine* 2, 1947, 549-74; H. J. Zimmels, *Magicians, Theologians, and Doctors: Studies in Folk-Medicine and Folklore As Reflected in the Rabbinic Responsa*, 1952.

Alan Kam-Yau Chan and Thomas B. Song/Michael L. Brown

8326 (*rip'ût*, recovery, remedy), → # 8324

8327	רְפָאִים

רְפָאִים (*r^e pā'îm* I), nom., always pl., shades, departed spirits, inhabitants of the netherworld

(*Totengeister*; # 8327); see also r^e*pā'îm* II, the ethnic Rephaim (# 8328); for the possible relationship between the two, see sec. 3 below.

ANE Cognates to Heb. r^e*pā'îm*, shades, departed spirits, are attested only in Phoen.-Pun. and Ugar., but the texts are relevant to the OT. In the fifth-century Phoen. royal sarcophagus inscriptions of Tabnit and Eshmunazzar (*KAI* 13:7-8 and 14:7-8), the identical imprecation occurs, viz., that anyone who would disturb the king's coffin (note the usage of *škb-mškb* in this context in both inscriptions) would have no resting place among the shades (*'l ykn lk/lm mškb 't rp'm*; both curses contain the "neither roots nor fruits" formula, i.e., no seed [or son] among the living and no resting place [or burial] among the dead). The other attestation (*KAI* 117), a bilingual text from El Amruni dating from the first century AD, translates Pun. *l'l[nm] 'r'p'm* (the divine shades/*rephaim*) with Lat. *D(is) M(anibus) SAC(rum)*, "sacred shades" (see *TWAT* 7:627; the reading of *l'l[n]' r'p'm*, the gods of the shades/*rephaim*, is less likely). This apparently points to some kind of deified status of the dead; see further sec. 3 below.

The Ugar. texts are more ambiguous (cf. in particular *KTU* 1.120-22), since, for the most part, neither the identity nor function of the *rpum* are clearly spelled out and the texts remain somewhat obscure, in spite of the fact that they have received a great amount of attention (for overviews, cf. Dietrich, Loretz, Sanmartín; *RSP* 3; *DBSup*; *TWAT*; for a new edition of the primary texts, cf. Pitard, 1992). Scholars are therefore divided in their views, and the *rpum* have been variously categorized as dead kings and heroes, divinized ancestors, healers, savior shades, a guild of (deceased?) warriors, and devotees of the god *rpu*. M. H. Tate (*Psalms 51-100*, WBC, 397-98, n. 11.b., with reference to Spronk), states what may be called the conglomerate—and at times, tenuous—scholarly assessment: the *rpum* are "the privileged dead, royal ancestors, who live as the dead, but sometimes in the roles of warriors and healers, who have superior power; functioning like lower deities in the underworld. The *rp'um* may come up from the netherworld on occasion, as in a new year festival, and the living ruler may be counted among the *rp'um*." However, the evidence for the Ugar. *rpum* as healers is meager (see *KTU* 1.161; cf. de Moor; Spronk; otherwise, Brown). The god *rpu* (El? Baal? Maliku? or simply Rapi'u?) is not featured in the Ugar. literature as a healer, *KTU* 1.108 notwithstanding. Thus, the observation of S. E. Loewenstamm (*EMiqr* 7:406 [Heb.]) with regard to the ANE and OT *rp'ym*, viz., that "there is not in any text a clear reference to an act of healing [r^e*pû'â*], be it healing the sick, reviving the dead, or restoring fertility to man or earth" must still be taken seriously.

OT 1. *Etymology.* Prior to the discovery of the cognate material, it was generally thought that Heb. r^e*pā'îm* was to be derived from *rph* (→ # 8332), to be/become weak, feeble, slack. Hence, the r^e*pā'îm* were either those who had sunken down in death (cf. Prov 2:18 with reference to those who go down to death, *šāḥâ 'el māwet*, par. with r^e*pā'îm*; see further M. Held, *JANESCU* 5, 1973, 178-81) or those who as shades now languished in the netherworld (cf. the common German rendering "die Schwachen," and note also that Eng. "shades" speaks of the shadowy existence of these disembodied spirits). The final *aleph* in *rp'ym* was therefore regarded simply as an orthographic development in BH, not impossible with final weak verbs. However, the discovery of the ANE material, all of which attests final *aleph*, makes the derivation from *rph* far less likely (cf. however, *TWOT*; note the comment of J. N. Oswalt, *Isaiah 1-39*,

NICOT, 318, n. 15, which is still representative of many scholars: "The dead are called *r^e^pā'îm*, 'the slack ones'"; see further *HALAT* 4:1191, sub *rph* II, with reference to 2 Sam 21:20, 22; 1 Chron 20:6, 8).

It is true that F. Delitzsch (*Proverbs*, KD 5/1:261-62, to Prov 12:18) and R. Gordis (*JQR* 27, 1936, 55-56) posited a direct relationship between *rph* and *rp'*, deriving both from a biliteral **rp* and arguing for a polar development of the two roots (*rph*—to become weak; *rp'*—to make strong). However, the roots *rph* and *rp'* do not, in fact, evidence a clear, polar semantic development, since *rp'* fundamentally means put back together, restore, heal (as opposed to make strong), while *rph* is not primarily related to being sick, broken, or torn (→ further *rp'*, # 8324); moreover, even if the two roots did issue from a common biliteral source, this would not alter the fact that *rp'ym* is most probably to be derived from a root with final *aleph* as opposed to final *hēh* or *yōd*. More recent discussion has therefore centered in on the relationship between the *rp'ym* and the root *rp'*, with theories including: the *rp'ym* are so-called because they are gathered together in death (cf. the biblical idiom, "to be gathered to one's fathers"), based on alleged S. Sem. usage of *rp'*; through death they have taken on special powers, preeminently healing (or, fertilizing); they are "healed" through death; they are devotees of the god *rpu*.

None of these theories, however, is compelling, and each theory presents certain difficulties: (a) Although the Bible attests such idioms as *q^e^hal r^e^pā'îm*, the assembly of shades, Prov 21:16 (cf. also the parallelism in Ugar. texts between *rpi arṣ*, the shades of the netherworld, and *qbṣ dtn*, the clan of Dtn), the root *rp'* (S. Sem. *rf'*) never simply means gather, gather together (see *rp'*, # 8324; the closest S. Sem. usage is put [something] back together, such as by darning or mending; cf. also to pull a ship to shore, although some Arab. lexicographers trace this meaning to a different root). Note also that there is no known Sem. idiom that uses the root *rp'* with regard to being gathered to one's people in death. (b) As noted above, neither the OT nor ANE material specially portrays the *rp'ym* as healers, although in different cultures, some special powers are attributed to the dead (see sec. 3; generally speaking, it is claimed that there is "an organic association between the notions of the Nether World—the chthonic cycle—and of healing, i.e., granting health, strength, fertility, and fecundity" [M. C. Astour, cited in *RSP* 3:464], but such an assertion, which may be widely supported by the religious texts and oral traditions of other cultures, is hardly supported by the extant *rp'ym* material from the OT and ANE). (c) In no Sem. language does *rp'* ever mean fertilize, make fertile (contra Pope; Gray; similarly, Lipiński; cf. Brown for details). (d) Death itself (or, more accurately, the state of being dead) is hardly viewed as a healing in the ANE or OT, especially if the dead are thought to carry on a shadowy existence in the netherworld. The more plausible theory that the shades were designated as healed ones in a euphemistic sense presupposes a passive vocalization, but the (admittedly late) Pun. epigraphic evidence (*r'p'm*) seems to favor an active vocalization (i.e., *rōp^e^'îm*, *rāpi'ūma*, as opposed to MT's *r^e^pā'îm*, which would then be seen as a polemical revocalization, although it is fruitless to speculate as to which nominal pattern was being followed—suggestions including *r^e^šā'îm*, wicked, and *ṭ^e^lā'îm*, lambs—seeing that the form is the common segholate m. pl.). Also, if the association with *rp'* was merely euphemistic, then it would tell us absolutely nothing about the alleged activities or powers of the *rp'ym*. (e) Although the OT makes reference to the *y^e^lîdê hārāpâ/ā'*

(2 Sam 21:16, 18; cf. also 1 Chron 20:4), it is highly unlikely that BH *hārāpâlā'* (cf. Ugar. *rpu*) speaks of a deity (contrast L'Hereux, 1976), neither is it clear from the Ugar. texts that the *rpum* were specially related to the deity *rpu*.

Of course, there may in fact be an original etymological connection between *rp'*, put back together, restore, heal, and *rp'ym*, shades, but at this point nothing certain can be said. It should also be noted that the older readings of Keret 1.7 with *rpat*, taken to mean became shades, died out (thus pointing to a *rp'* II; cf., e.g., *ANET*; *TO*; *CML*[1] and *CML*[2]), have generally been abandoned, and *KTU* 1.14.7 reads instead *'*(?)rwt*, apparently to be rendered stripped naked (cf. J. C. de Moor, *An Anthology of Religious Texts From Ugarit*, 1987, 192, n. 4). The etymological suggestion of G. Mendenhall, positing "an archaic north Syrian root *rp'* meaning 'lord'" (*The Tenth Generation*, 1973, 160, n. 47) is interesting, as it would correlate the ANE and OT *rp'ym* with a *rp'* II, unrelated to the semantic domain of healing and restoration; however, no solid evidence for such a root has been forthcoming (cf., however, the relevant study of Heltzer).

2. *Usage and meaning.* While the etymology of *r^epā'îm* is unclear and the historical and/or ideological connection between the shades, ethnic Rephaim, and Ugar. *rpum* (if there was, in fact, such a connection) remains difficult to reconstruct (see sec. 3), the eight OT occurrences of *rᵉpā'îm* as shades are fairly straightforward, as indicated by the context. In Isa 26:14; 26:19; Ps 88:10[11] the *rᵉpā'îm* occur in parallelism or close association with *mētîm*, the dead, while in Prov 2:18 they are in parallelism with *māwet*, death (→ # 4926). In Isa 14:9 and Prov 9:18 the *rᵉpā'îm* are associated with *šᵉ'ôl*, the grave/netherworld (→ # 8619), while the immediate context of Job 26:5 (viz., 26:6) relates the *rᵉpā'îm* to *šᵉ'ôl* and *'ᵃbaddôn* (→ # 11). Interestingly, all these examples occur in poetic contexts, while references to the ethnic Rephaim are found exclusively in historical narrative passages.

Moreover, the usage of *rᵉpā'îm* is in keeping with the representative themes of each book. In Prov, it is the house of the seductive woman that "leads down to death, and her paths to the shades" (2:18, NRSV; cf. NIV's spirits of the dead); and when the foolish woman gives her appealing call, the undiscerning man does not know that the shades (NIV, the dead) are there and that her guests "are in the depths of Sheol" (9:18, NRSV; cf. 1 Tim 5:6). Thus, "A man who strays from the path of understanding comes to rest in the company of the dead" (21:16; better, shades), meaning that he will soon find himself among the deceased, with no comfort intended in the concept of coming to rest. (Contrast with this the Phoen. sarcophagi texts cited above, wishing the offender no resting place [*mškb*] with the shades, assuming some kind of continued existence for the dead, but calling for a harried, tormented afterlife for the miscreant.)

The only usage of *rᵉpā'îm* in Psalms occurs in the midst of an important and recurring theme: Can the dead praise Yahweh? And can he continue to demonstrate his salvific deeds for those in the netherworld? Thus the psalmist asks: "Do you show your wonders to the dead? Do those who are dead [*rᵉpā'îm*; again, render, the shades] rise up and praise you?" (Ps 88:10[11]). Cf. further vv. 11-12[12-13]: "Is your love declared in the grave, your faithfulness in Destruction? Are your wonders known in the place of darkness, or your righteous deeds in the land of oblivion?" All this undergirds the psalmist's urgent plea that the Lord act on his behalf *now*. If he dies (was he suffering from a life-threatening illness?), he can no longer offer public praise (cf. Isa 38:19);

once he is gone from this world, Yahweh can no longer intervene on his behalf; see sec. 4 for the LXX's rendering here.

Job 26:5, which is somewhat obscure (but not as obscure as the AV's "Dead *things* are formed from under the waters, and the inhabitants thereof"), locates the *r^e^pā'îm* spatially along with the inhabitants under the waters. Whether they tremble or are in deep anguish (NIV, rendering *y^e^ḥôlālû*) is not critical. Rather, dwelling beneath the subterranean waters (cf. 2 Sam 22:5; Ps 88:6-7[7-8] for the imagery, and note N. C. Habel, *Job*, OTL, 370: "The pit of the underworld was located deep in the watery abyss"), the shades are among those who are not hidden from the Lord. Yes, "Death is naked before God; Destruction lies uncovered" (Job 26:6). He is the one who created the earth and skies, subduing all hostile powers. Indeed, "these are but the outer fringe of his works; how faint the whisper we hear of him! Who then can understand the thunder of his power?" (26:14).

Isa 14:9, once again a fairly straightforward text, has received special attention because it is the only OT passage that might preserve the memory of the shades as deceased kings or leaders (cf. Levine and de Tarragon; *ABD*). In vivid poetic language, the prophet describes the descent of the once mighty king of Babylon (meaning Assyria?) into Sheol: "The grave below is all astir to meet you at your coming; it rouses the spirits of the departed [*r^e^pā'îm*] to greet you—all those who were leaders in the world; it makes them rise from their thrones—all those who were kings over the nations. They will all respond, they will say to you, 'You also have become weak [*ḥulêtā*], as we are; you have become like us'" (14:9-10). The question is, does the text simply move from the general to the specific, i.e., from the spirits of the departed to a specific group among them (viz., the leaders and kings), or does the reference to leaders and kings follow naturally from the meaning of *r^e^pā'îm* as dead kings and heroes? If the latter is correct, then this text would suggest that there was, in fact, a connection between the ethnic Rephaim, remembered as giants, and the shades; for an apposite, pre-Ugaritic observation, cf. Driver and Gray, *Job*, ICC, 1:219.

The remaining Isaianic *r^e^pā'îm* passages are of greater theological significance, occurring as they do in one of the most important resurrection passages in the OT (cf. also Dan 12:1-2). As for those who oppressed the people of God in the past, the verdict is gloomy: "They are now dead [*mētîm*], they live no more; those departed spirits [*r^e^pā'îm*] do not rise. You punished them and brought them to ruin; you wiped out all memory of them" (Isa 26:14). But for the people of the Lord, the picture is glorious. It is true that there had been protracted and futile labor: "We were with child, we writhed—it is as though we had given birth to wind. We have won no victory on earth [or, we have not brought salvation to the earth]; the inhabitants of the world have not come to life [*bal-yiplû*]" (26:18, NJPSV). Here is both a recognition of Israel's eschatological calling—to bring about final salvation and even resurrection—and a confession of her failure to succeed in that mission. Yet through God's intervention, the promise is sure: "Your dead will live! [Your] corpses will rise! [Read *n^e^bēlōt y^e^qûmûn*, taking the *yōdh* of *n^e^bēlātî* as arising through dittography with the following *y^e^qûmûn*.] Wake up and shout for joy, you who dwell in the dust, for your dew is like the fresh morning dew [*ṭal 'ôrōt,* lit., the dew of lights]; and the earth [or, underworld; see *'ereṣ*, # 824 and cf. Ugar. *rpi arṣ*] will give birth [*tappîl*] to the shades [*r^e^pā'îm*]" (26:19, my tr.; for *tappîl*, lit., cast forth, in the sense of bring to birth, cause to come alive, cf. v. 14, and see the commentaries). In contrast with Isa 26:14, where the ungodly dead would not (or, simply, do not) live, here the dead will live. In 26:14, it is the *r^e pā'îm* who would not (or do not) rise; here it is the corpses that will rise, and the term *r^e pā'îm* is thus saved for the final clause: "the earth/netherworld will give birth to the shades." G. B. Gray (*Isaiah 1-27*, ICC, 446) is therefore correct in calling this a "remarkable expression of what must have been already a well-defined and clear belief in a bodily resurrection of Jews who had died before the New Age began (cp. Dn 12[1])," although his view that it promises only the Jews a future resurrection—in distinction from "the common lot of man (v.[14])"—is overstated. The *r^e pā'îm*, no longer disembodied spirits dwelling in the shadowy realms beneath the earth, mere "diminished selfhoods which survive death" (Tate, ibid., 397), but fully clothed and renewed, would rise with shouts of joy. Indeed, they are *commanded* to do so; see below, P-B.

3. *Shades and Rephaim.* The OT makes no direct connection between the shades and the ethnic Rephaim, and, despite a profusion of scholarship on the Ugar. *rpum* and their relationship to the OT *r^e pā'îm*, we have advanced little beyond the definitions provided by BDB, 952: "1) shades, ghosts, name of dead in Sheol; 2) old race of giants; ancient inhab. of Canaan (W. of Jordan?)." As noted immediately above, some scholars have pointed to Isa 14:9 for the conceptual link between the shades and the ancient giants. Thus, it would seem that the fame of a race (or guild or line) of kings/warriors/heroes continued after their death. They then took on deified status in some circles, eventually becoming synonymous with the dead in general.

However, as emphasized above, there is no OT evidence that the *r^e pā'îm* had special powers, although the prohibitions against necromancy, along with passages such as 1 Sam 28:13 with *'^e lōhîm* (cf. Hutter; Loretz), and, as interpreted by some, Isa 8:19 (so, e.g., H. Wildberger, BKAT; NJPSV ; contrast NIV; Oswalt, NICOT; note also *KAI* 117, treated above, and cf. 1QIs[a] to Isa 8:19), do point to various beliefs about the oracular powers of the deceased (for recent studies, cf. Lewis; Spronk; Bloch-Smith; Schmidt; Johnston; there is no valid reason, however, to emend *rōp^e'îm* at 2 Chron 16:12 to *r^e pā'îm*, as per M. Jastrow, *JBL* 28, 1909, 42-56; *ABD* 5:675; see *rp'*, # 8324). Unfortunately, scholars have often interpreted the fairly straightforward OT material in light of the much more difficult Ugar. data, thus reading extraneous ideas into the biblical text. Cf., e.g., M. H. Tate, *Psalms 51-100*, WBC, 397-98, n. 11.b., who takes "the sense in Ps 88:11 to retain an element of the old idea of the *rephaim* as the elite, the heroic ones, among the dead, which the strong *-'m* construction tends to support: 'Do *even* the Rephaim rise (and) praise you?' Perhaps the strong 'healers' among the dead should be able to do what the ordinary dead cannot, but they are as weak as all the dead." As stated above, however, it is uncertain that the Ugar. *rpum* were healers, while it is completely unsupported that the OT *r^e pā'îm*, shades, were viewed as such (cf. also A. van Selms, cited in *RSP* 3:465; note further that the grammar of Ps 88:10[11], with interrogative *h^a*—followed by *'im*—is normal for a double rhetorical question; cf. M. Held, "Rhetorical Questions in Ugaritic and Biblical Hebrew," ErIsr 9, 1969, 71-79).

In any case, the ideological relationship between the Rephaim of hoary antiquity and the shades remains unclear (cf. the agnostic position of H. Wildberger, *Jesaja 13-27,* BK, 549, as cited by J. W. W. Watts, *Isaiah 1-33*, WBC, 209), although in terms of simple exegesis, the OT shades passages are fairly lucid.

4. *r^{e}pā'îm in the ancient versions.* The LXX three times renders *r^{e}pā'îm*, shades, with *gigantēs* (Job 26:5; Prov 21:16; Isa 14:9; cf. also the Vg. to these verses with *gigantēs* [note Prov 9:18 as well] and the Targ. to Job 26:5; Prov 2:18; Isa 14:9; 26:14 with *gibārāyā'*), apparently influenced by the biblical record describing the ethnic Rephaim as giants (→ Giants: Theology; cf., e.g., the LXX to Josh 12:4; 13:12; 1 Chron 11:15; 14:9; 20:4; the Vg. to Deut 2:20; and the Tg. to Gen 15:20), but in terms of a translation for "shades," very much inappropriate. Interestingly, at Ps 88:10[11; LXX 87:11] and Isa 26:14, the LXX (cf. also the Old Lat. to Ps 87:11) renders MT *r^{e}pā'îm* with *iatroi*, as if reading *rōp^e'îm*; cf. further the Sam. Targ. to Deut 2:20; 3:13, rendering MT's *'ereṣ r^{e}pā'îm* with *'r' 'shym* (land of the physicians); note Pirke d'R. Eliezer, 34, which equates *r^{e}pā'îm* in Isa 26:19 with healing (*'ereṣ r^{e}pā'îm tappîl* is interpreted to mean *nôtēn r^{e}pû'ôt lā'āreṣ*, brings healing to the earth).

Relying primarily on the LXX renderings or based on comparative religious phenomenology, scholars as early as M. Lagrange in 1905 (cf. *TWAT* 7:628-29) sought to portray the *r^{e}pā'îm* as the equivalent of the G *heros iatros* (cf. M. Weinfeld, *Deuteronomy 1-11*, AB, 162: "*Heros* is the name of a legendary hero as well as the spirit of the dead for whom memorial rites were performed"). There are, however, problems with this theory (cf. Brown; for the most full presentation of the evidence, see de Moor), while the data from the versions is either inconsistent (cf., e.g., the LXX's *asebon*, impious, for *r^{e}pā'îm* at Isa 26:19 [see also Tg. Jon.], and note Aquila's transliteration of *raphain* at Isa 26:14, which argues against the *rōp^e'îm* vocalization), subject to a different interpretation (e.g., the LXX renderings of Isa 26:14 and Ps 88:10[11] have been read as a polemic against physicians, seeing that both contexts state that they will *not* rise; cf. also Abot d'Rab. Nat. 36:5, m. Qid. 4:14), or simply an example of a free midrashic interpretation (so Pirke d'R. Eliezer). In sum, given the ambiguous relationship between the shades and the Rephaim, and in light of the consonantal similarity between *r^{e}pā'îm* and *rōp^e'îm*, some confusion in the rendering of the ancient versions is not surprising and too much should not be read into the data.

P-B While the *r^{e}pā'îm* do not have a significant afterlife in postbiblical literature, the concept of *calling forth* the dead from their graves (cf. Isa 26:19)—with no specific reference to shades—is taken up in the NT. Interestingly, in each resurrection account in the Gospels and Acts, the dead are addressed directly and commanded to rise (cf. Mark 5:41-42, Jairus' daughter; Luke 7:14-15, the widow's son; John 11:43-44, Lazarus; Acts 9:40, Tabitha). In this age, those who are spiritually dead and "hear the voice of the Son of God . . . will live" (John 5:25); in the eschaton, "all who are in their graves will hear his voice and come out—those who have done good will rise to live, and those who have done evil will rise to be condemned" (5:28-29; cf. also 1 Thess 4:16). Thus, the resurrection call will be for all; for some it will be life, for others condemnation. The so-called intermediate state for believers (i.e., after death but before resurrection) also receives greater clarity in the NT (cf. 2 Tim 1:10), and those who are in Christ are certain that to depart from this body is to be with him (Phil 1:20-24), although they still eagerly await the final resurrection (cf. 2 Cor 5:4, "We do not wish to be unclothed but to be clothed with our heavenly dwelling, so that what is mortal may be swallowed up by life"). Thus death has already lost its sting (1 Cor 15:51-57; cf. John 5:24).

Spirit, ghost, demon: → *'ôb* II (medium, spiritist, necromancer, ghost, # 200); → *'iṭṭîm* I (ghosts, ghosts of the dead, spirits, # 356); → *lîlît* (night monster, night creature, # 4327); → *ʿazā'zēl* (Azazel, demon, scapegoat, # 6439); → *ṣî* II (desert dweller, crier, yelper, wild beast, # 7470); → *rûaḥ* (wind, breath, transitoriness, volition, disposition, temper, spirit, Spirit, # 8120); → *repā'îm* I (shades, departed spirits, # 8327); → *śā'ir* III (satyr, goat demon, goat idol, # 8539); → *šēd* (demon, # 8717)

Bibliography

ABD 5:674-76; *DBSup* 10:344-57; *EJ* 14:79; *EMiqr* 7:404-7; *IDB* 4:35; *IDBSup*, 739-40; *ISBE* 4:440; *RSP* 3:460-67; *THAT* 2:803-9; *TWAT* 7:626-36; *TWOT* 2:858; E. Bloch-Smith, *Judahite Burial Practices and Beliefs About the Dead*, JSOTSup 123, 1992; M. Brown, "Was There a West Semitic Asklepios?" forthcoming, *UF*; A. Caquot, "Les Rephaim Ougaritiques," *Syria* 37, 1960, 75-93; M. Dietrich and O. Loretz, "Baal *RPU* in KTU 1.108; 1.113 und nach 1.17 VI 25-33," *UF* 12, 1980, 170-82; idem, and J. Sanmartín, "Die ugaritischen Totengeister *Rpu(m)* und die biblischen Rephaim," *UF* 8, 1976, 45-52; J. Gray, "The Rephaim," *PEQ* 84, 1949, 127-39; idem, "*DTN* and *RPUM* in Ancient Ugarit," *PEQ* 84, 1952, 39-41; J. F. Healey, "Ritual Text KTU 1.161—Translation and Notes," *UF* 10, 1978, 83-88; idem, "*MLKM/RP'UM* and the *KISPUM*," *UF* 10, 1978, 89-91; idem, "The Last of the Rephaim," in idem and K. J. Cathcart, eds., *Back to the Sources: Biblical and Near Eastern Studies*, 1989, 33-34; M. Heltzer, "The *RABBA'UM* in Mari and the *RPI(M)* in Ugarit," OLP 9, 1978, 5-20; W. J. Horwitz, "The Significance of the Rephaim," *JNSL* 7, 1979, 37-43; M. Hutter, "Religionsgeschichtliche Erwagungen zu אלהים in 1Sam 28,13," *BN* 21, 1983, 32-36; P. Johnston, "The Underworld and the Dead in the Old Testament," *TynBul* 45, 1994, 415-19 (summarizing his 1993 Cambridge dissertation); P. Karge, *Rephaim: Die vorgeschichtliche Kultur Palästinas und Phöniziens*, 2d ed., 1925; B. A. Levine and J.-M. de Tarragon, "Dead Kings and Rephaim: The Patrons of the Ugaritic Dynasty," *JAOS* 104, 1984, 649-59; T. J. Lewis, *Cults of the Dead in Ancient Israel and Ugarit*, HSM 39, 1989; C. E. L'Heureux, "The Ugaritic and Biblical Rephaim," *HTR* 67, 1974, 265-74; idem, "The *yelîdê hārāpā'*—A Cultic Association of Warriors," *BASOR* 221, 1976, 83-85; idem, *Rank Among the Canaanite Gods: El, Ba'al, and the Repha'im*, HSM 21, 1979; E. Lipiński, "Ditanu," in Y. Avishur and J. Blau, eds., *Studies in Bible and the Ancient Near East*, 1978, 91-110; O. Loretz, "Die Teraphim als 'Ahnen-Götter-Figur(in)en' im Lichte der Texte aus Emar, Nuzi, und Ugarit. Anmerkungen zu *ilānu/ilh, ilhm/'lhym*, und DINGER.ERÍN.MEŠ/*inš ilm*," *UF* 24, 1992, 133-78; J. C. de Moor, "Rāpi'ūma-Rephaim," *ZAW* 88, 1976, 323-45; S. B. Parker, "The Ugaritic Deity Rāpi'u," *UF* 4, 1972, 97-104; W. T. Pitard, "The Ugaritic Funerary Text RS 34.126," *BASOR* 232, 1978, 65-75; idem, "A New Edition of the 'Rāpi'ūma' Texts: KTU 1.20-22," *BASOR* 285, 1992, 33-77; M. H. Pope, "Notes on the Rephaim Texts from Ugarit," in M. de Jong Ellis, ed., *Essays on the Ancient Near East in Memory of Jacob Joel Finkelstein*, 1977, 163-82; idem, "The Cult of the Dead at Ugarit," in G. D. Young, ed., *Ugarit in Retrospect: Fifty Years of Ugarit and Ugaritic*, 1981, 159-79; D. J. Ryan, "Rpum and Rephaim: A Study in the Relationship Between the *rpum* of Ugarit and the Rephaim of the Old Testament," diss. Ireland, 1954; B. B. Schmidt, *Israel's Beneficent Dead: Ancestor Cult and Necromancy in Ancient Israelite Religion and Tradition*, FAT 11, 1994; K. Spronk, *Beatific Afterlife in Ancient Israel and in the Ancient Near East*, AOAT 219; 1986; S. Talmon, "Biblical *repā'îm* and Ugaritic *rpu/i*(m)," *HAR* 7, 1983, 235-49.

Michael L. Brown

8328 (*repā'îm* II, Rephaites), → Giants

8331	רפד

רפד (*rpd*), spread out, support, refresh (# 8331); רְפִידָה (r^e*pîdâ*), support (of litter) or covering (# 8339).

ANE The vb. is cognate with Akk. *rapādu*, roam about. In Lachish letter IV:5 the phrase *byt hrpd* is to be rendered the bedding house or sleeping house.

OT 1. The basic meaning of the vb. is spread, underlay and hence, support. The vb. occurs once in the q. (Job 41:30[22], Leviathan "leaves a trail in the mud like a threshing sledge," a reference to the creature's scales spreading the mud). It occurs twice in the pi.: Job 17:13 ("if I spread out my bed in darkness"); and S of Songs 2:5 ("Refresh/support me with apples").

2. The nom. r^e*pîdâ*, support (of litter) or covering (# 8339), is in S of Songs 3:10, "Its posts he made of silver, its base of gold." Heb. r^e*pîdâ* may be compared with Arab. *rifadah*, "saddle-blanket," i.e., something spread out and over.

Spreading, extending, stretching: → *hdh* (stretch out the hands, # 2063); → *zrh* I (scatter, sprinkle, spread, # 2430); → *ṭph* I (spread out, # 3253); → *yšṭ* (hold out, extend, # 3804); → *mtḥ* (spread out, # 5501); → *nṭh* (extend, # 5742); → *npṣ* II (spread out, scatter, be dispersed, # 5880); → *pwṣ* (scatter, disperse, be spread, dispersed, # 7046); → *pzr* (scatter, scatter, spread, be scattered, # 7061); → *prś* (spread out, spread, # 7298); → *pśh* (spread [of disease], # 7313); → *rpd* (spread out, support, refresh, # 8331); → *šṭḥ* (spread out, pour out, # 8848)

BIBLIOGRAPHY

M. Pope, *Song of Songs*, AB, 1977, 380.

Victor P. Hamilton

8332	רפה

רפה (*rph*), q. sink, slacken, relax, decline, drop, be drooping; with hands, lose heart/courage/energy; ni. (part.) idle, indolent; pi. let drop, make slack, limp/drooping, loosen, weaken, enfeeble, discourage, dishearten, unnerve, deject, depress; hi. let drop, let go, relax, refrain, cease, abandon, forsake, desert, leave in the lurch; hitp. show oneself slack, lazy/indolent/idle/disheartened (# 8332); רָפֶה (*rāpeh*), adj. slack, feeble, faint, languid, disheartened (# 8333); רִפָּיוֹן (*rippāyôn*), nom. relaxation, slackness (hapleg. # 8342).

ANE The vb. is well attested: e.g., Ugar. *rpy, trp;* Akk. *ramû(m)*; Assyr. *ramā'u(m),* relax; Syr. r^e*pā',* be slack, loose; Eth. *'a'räfä,* rest, repose; Arab. *rafā(w),* appease, mollify, pacify. The adj. occurs in Sam. *arfi;* Akk. *ramû(m),* prostrate; Syr. *rapyā',* slack, lazy, indolent, slothful; Eth. *'erūf,* quiescent; Arab. *rafāhat,* at ease, lazy. The nom. is found in Syr. *rapyūtā',* softness, weakness, indolence, and *ruppāyā',* softening.

OT 1. The q. is used in Jer 49:24 to describe how Damascus, as a result of divine judgment, becomes enfeebled by panic, anguish, and pain. The q. is commonly used with hands as the subject. Whereas raising the hand can signal a revolutionary uprising (e.g., 1 Kgs 11:26-27), the dropping of the hands can signify fear, or despair, or both (cf. the similar expressions that occur in Sir 2:12 [REB] and Heb 12:12 [RSV]). The verbal picture of hands hanging limply is used to convey the enervation that can be caused by the dissemination of false allegations (Neh 6:9); the demoralization created by disturbing news (2 Sam 4:1); the nervous collapse and physical paralysis induced by the proximity of an enemy (Jer 6:24; 50:43) or by the approaching day of Yahweh (Isa 13:7; Ezek 7:17; 21:7[12]); and the failure of nerve that can result from the absence of encouragement (cf. 2 Chron 15:7; Zeph 3:16).

2. The pi. is used in Jer 38:4, where state officials accuse Jeremiah of subverting the war effort by unnerving (lit. weakening the hands of) both troops and civilians. Ironically, in Lachish Ostracon Vl, a similar phrase is used by an anonymous patriotic official who charges some Jerusalem nobles of seditiously undermining morale (Albright, 322). The expression occurs again in Ezra 4:4 to describe how those rebuffed by Zerubbabel, Jeshua, and the rest of the leaders of Israel attempted to discourage the people of Judah (Patterson, 378, 382-83).

3. The hi. is used in a variety of contexts. In Ps 46:10a[11a], the impv. *harpû,* "Be still" (NIV; RSV), is probably a word of comfort to the faithful who are advised to relax, confident in the knowledge that their great protector destroys the instruments of war (v. 9[10]) and establishes peace and security throughout the world *(contra* those [e.g., Kirkpatrick, 258] who take it as a rebuke to wild and unruly peoples). The hi., sometimes in conjunction with hands (to let one's hands fall), also means to abandon (Deut 4:31; Josh 10:6; Ps 138:8). The assurance of Yahweh's unfailing protective presence (*lōʾ yarp^{e}kā*, "he will not fail you," RSV; NRSV; JB; TEV) constitutes the basis for an appeal to both the nation (Deut 31:6) and individuals (Joshua, Deut 31:8 [cf. Josh 1:5; Heb 13:5]; Solomon, 1 Chron 28:20) to be strong and courageous.

4. The hitp. is used in Prov 24:10, which seems to say that the true test of strength is whether or not a person falters in times of adversity (*hitrappîtā b^{e}yôm ṣārâ ṣar kōḥekâ*, If you faint in the day of adversity, your strength is small).

5. The adj. *rāpeh* is also used in combination with hands. Those who are slack of hands are demoralized (2 Sam 17:2, RSV) or, possibly, exhausted (NIV). To strengthen feeble hands is to steady the dispirited, who, under the onslaught of adversity, are collapsing into a state of helpless despondency (Job 4:3; Isa 35:3).

6. The phrase *mēripyôn yādāyim* (lit. from slackness of hands) occurs in Jer 47:3, where vivid staccato language reproduces the frightening roar of pounding hooves and rumbling chariot wheels, which will create such panic among the Philistines that unnerved fathers will either abandon their children in a futile effort to escape or will be rendered incapable of assisting their offspring because of their terror-induced feebleness.

P-B The hi. with the nom. hands occurs in 1QpHab VII 11, and the pi. with hands, weaken/slacken the hands = discourage, dishearten, unnerve, is found in the Lachish Ostraca (6, 6).

Feeble, despair, faint, frail, tender: → *ʾml* I (be weak, be feeble, languish, # 581); → *ḥlh* I (become weak, tired, ill, # 2703); → *ylh* (languish, # 3532); → *kʾh* (be disheartened, frightened, # 3874); → *nbl* I (wither, fade, languish, dishonor, # 5570); → *ʿṭp* II (grow weak, faint, be feeble, # 6494); → *ʿlp* (cover, faint, # 6634); → *ʿšš* (become weak, # 6949); → *pwg* (be feeble, numb, be prostrated, # 7028); → *rzh* (destroy, waste away, # 8135); → *rkk* (be tender, timid, gentle, # 8216); → *rph* (become slack, lose heart, discourage, # 8332)

Despair, discouragement, grief, trouble: → *ʾāgēm* (sad, grieved, distressed, # 108); → *yʾš* (despair, be hopeless, # 3286); → *mwg* (melt, reel, waver, lose courage, # 4570); → *mss* (waste away, melt, dissolve, lose courage, # 5022); → *'gm* (be afflicted, distressed, grieved, # 6327); → *ṣwq* I (constrain, press in/upon, harass, vex, # 7439); → *ṣrr* I (bind, shut up, be narrow, in straits, distress, # 7674); → *mwg* (melt, reel, waver, lose courage, # 4570); → *qṣr* II (be short, be/become discouraged, worn out, # 7918); → *rph* (become slack, lose heart, discourage, # 8332); → *šyḥ* (melt away, be in despair, # 8863)

BIBLIOGRAPHY

W. F. Albright, "Palestinian Inscriptions," *ANET*, 1969, 320-22; A. F. Kirkpatrick, *The Book of Psalms*, 1957; R. D. Patterson, *Nahum, Habakkuk, Zephaniah*, 1991.

Robin Wakely

8333 (*rāpeh*, slack, faint, languid, disheartened), → # 8332

8337 (*r^epû'â*, healing, remedy), → # 8324

8339 (*r^epîdâ*, support (of litter) or covering), → # 8331

8342 (*rippāyôn*, relaxation, slackness), → # 8332

8344	רפף

רפף (*rpp*), po. shake, quake, rock (# 8344).

OT *rpp* occurs only once in Job 26:11: "The pillars of the heavens *quake*, aghast at his rebuke." The response to the sovereign power or awesome presence of Yahweh is typically described in terms of physical quaking and shaking. Even more astonishing, however, are the words of Job subsequent to the above description found in v. 14: "And these are but the outer fringe of his works; how faint the whisper we hear of him! Who then can understand the thunder of his power?"

Shaking, terror, trembling: → *g'š* (rise and fall noisily, swell, surge, # 1723); → *zw'* (tremble, quake, be afraid, # 2316); → *zll* II (shake, quake, tremble, # 2362); → *ḥalḥālâ* (shaking, trembling, anguish, # 2714); → *ḥrg* (come out trembling, # 3004); → *ḥrd* (tremble, shudder, startle, # 3006); → *yr'* (tremble, be fainthearted, # 3760); → *mwṭ* (waver, reel, stagger, shake, reel, # 4572); → *m'd* (slip, slide, shake, totter, # 5048); → *nwd* (shake, totter, waiver, wander, mourn, flee, # 5653); → *nwṭ* (shake, quake, # 5667); → *nw'* (shake, tremble, stagger, totter, wave, # 5675); → *n'r* II (shake, shake off, # 5850); → *smr* (shudder, have goose-bumps, bristle, # 6169); → *'iw'îm* (distortion, stagger, dizzy, # 6413); → *pwq* I (stagger, wobble, reel, totter, # 7048); → *pḥd* I (tremble, be in dread, # 7064); → *plṣ* (shudder, shake, tremble, # 7145); → *qwṣ* I (feel disgust, frighten, cause dread, # 7762); → *rgz* (agitate, quiver, shake, excite, rouse up, agitate, # 8074); → *rnh* I (rattle, # 8261); → *r'd* (tremble, shake, tremble, # 8283); → *r'l* I (brandish, make to quiver, # 8302); → *r'š* I (quake, shake, leap, # 8321); → *rpp* (shake, quake, rock, # 8344); → *r^etēt* (terror, panic, trembling, # 8417); → *ś'r* I (be afraid, terrified, bristle with horror, # 8547)

BIBLIOGRAPHY

TWOT 2:859; J. Jeremias, *Theophanie*, WMANT 10, 1965, 67-68; F. E. Greenspahn, *Hapax Legomena in Biblical Hebrew*, 1984.

M. V. Van Pelt/W. C. Kaiser, Jr.

8345	רפק

רפק (*rpq*), hitp. lean (# 8345).

OT This root is only used in S of Songs 8:5, where the beloved is described as coming up from the desert leaning on her lover.

Help, support, sustenance: → *zqp* (rise, lift up, # 2422); → *smk* (support, lean, refresh, # 6164); → *s'd* (sustain, support, # 6184); → *'zr* (help, support, find help, # 6468); → *rpq* (lean, # 8345); → *š'n* (lean, depend on, # 9128)

Bibliography

F. E. Greenspahn, *Hapax Legomena in Biblical Hebrew*, 1984, 157.

Allan M. Harman

8346	רפשׂ

רפשׂ (*rpś*), or רפס (*rps*), trample, with the sense of befouling or troubling the object and usually with the object as some form of water (# 8346), occurs 5x; מִרְפָּשׂ (*mirpāś*), nom. pool muddied by trampling (# 5343).

ANE The vb. is represented in Akk. *rapāsu*, beat, and is well attested in Syr. where it means to trample or beat the ground (often in dancing), though Syr. here more accurately is cognate to the sense of BH *rms*, trample (not used of water). The vb. occurs in Ugar. in a fragment of a line in which land (*ḥwt*) is the object (*šumma izbu* omen series, line 50 of text *UF* 7, 1975).

OT Ezek 34:18 provides perhaps the best context, since in this v. the action is undertaken by the feet and the expression *rpś brgl* is parallel to *rms brgl*, the difference being that *rms* is used with the trampling of pastures and *rpś* with the fouling of waters (the nom. *mirpāś* occurs in the next v.). Prov 25:26 also has the object as water as well as a parallel with *šḥt*, ruined, and Ezek 32:2 has the object as water (see # 1931 for its parallel *dlḥ*). The hitp. of *rps* in Prov 6:3 does not mean trample yourself or let yourself be trampled (= humble yourself), but rather should find its meaning in q., trample with the sense of troubling, because of its parallel *rhb*, to storm against (R. Giese, "Strength Through Wisdom and the Bee in LXX-Prov 6,8[a-c]," *Bib* 73, 1992, 406). The vb. in Ps 68:30[31] should also be taken with the q. sense of trample. The nom. *repeš*, mire, in Isa 57:20, though taken into modern Heb. pointed the same, should be taken as the nom. *repeś* related to the root above.

P-B The same nom. occurs in 1QH 2:12; 3:32; and 8:15 (the first is based on Isa 57:20).

Mud, mire, swamp: → *bōṣ/biṣṣâ* (swamp, # 1288/1289); → *dlḥ* (trouble [water], # 1931); → *ṭîṭ* (mud, mire, clay, # 3226); → *yāwēn* (mud, # 3431); → *rpś* (trample, # 8346)

Ronald L. Giese, Jr.

8348	רֶפֶת

רֶפֶת (*repet*), enclosure for cattle, is a hapleg. (# 8348) in Hab 3:17, "... though there are no sheep in the pen and no cattle in the *stalls*."

OT Though a hapleg., it may be related to postbiblical *repet*, cattle shed, stall. The word occurs near the end of Habakkuk, the last three verses of which are a moving affirmation of triumphant trust in Yahweh, even when life looks grim, disconsoling, and unpromising. It is about doxology rising above circumstances.

The word stable (→ *'urwâ,* # 774) may be a sign of God's blessing on those who are righteousness. But the absence of stables (*repet*) is not a sign of the absence of God's favor. In fact, stables (*marbēṣ*) may point to God's judgment on unrighteousness. A stable, after all, may be occupied by work and draught animals (*'urwâ*, *repet*) or by ravenous animals (*marbēṣ*).

Stable, lair, pen, stall: → *'urwâ* (stable, # 774); → *miklā'/miklâ* (pen, # 4813); → *marbēṣ* (fold, lair, # 5271); → *repet* (enclosure of cattle, # 8348)

Victor P. Hamilton

8353	רצד

רצד (*rṣd*), pi. keep one's eye on (# 8353).

ANE Akk. *raṣādu(m)*, watch, peep at; Arab. *raṣada*, look after.

OT The vb. denotes the act of gazing in envy or hostility. In Ps 68:16[17] the mountains of Bashan, probably the towering, snow-capped Mount Hermon, gaze in envy at Mount Zion. The reason for this envy is that the claims of the rival sanctuary in the north had been disposed of forcibly in favor of those of Mount Zion and its temple, which God himself has chosen as his eternal dwelling-place (Weiser, 489). Honor, however, lies not in physical majesty but in spiritual dignity, and this the Lord has conferred on Mount Zion alone.

P-B In the RL the vb. denotes the act of lying in wait or watching.

Look, observation, perception, sight, vision, watch: → *ḥdh* II (gaze on, appear, # 2526); → *ḥzh* (see, perceive, behold, # 2600); → *ḥmh* I (see, watch out for, become visible, # 2778); → *nbṭ* (look around, accept as an act of grace, # 5564); → *pls* II (observe, # 7143); → *ṣwṣ* II (look at, # 7438); → *r'h* (see, have visions, choose, perceive, # 8011); → *rṣd* (keep one's eye on, # 8353); → *śqd* (take note of, # 8567); → *š'h* III (stand gazing, # 8617); → *šgḥ* (gaze, stare, # 8708); → *šwr* I (gaze on, regard, see, # 8800); → *šzp* (catch sight of, tan, scorch, # 8812); → *š'h* (look, care about, gaze about, # 9120); → *šqp* (look down, # 9207); → *št'* (gaze, look, regard, look anxiously about, # 9283)

BIBLIOGRAPHY

U. Cassuto, "Psalm lxviii," *Biblical and Oriental Studies*, 1973, 1:263-65; F. E. Greenspahn, *Hapax Legomena in Biblical Hebrew*, 1984; A. Weiser, *The Psalms: A Commentary*, 1962.

Jackie A. Naudé

8354	רצה

רצה (*rṣh* I), q. to be pleased with, to treat favorably; ni. be accepted; pi. beg; hitp. make oneself pleasing (# 8354); nom. רָצוֹן (*rāṣôn*), favor, what is acceptable (# 8356).

ANE The root occurs in other WestSem. languages. A probable etymological connection is with Aram. *r'h* (cf. *r^e'û*, will; Ezra 5:17; 7:18). In the Qumran texts *rāṣôn* is used for the divine will (e.g., 1QS 5,1).

OT 1. The vb. *rṣh* occurs primarily in the q. (42x; 13x in Psalms), also in the ni. (6x; all in Lev.), and once each in pi. and hitp. It is used both of God and human beings. The nom. *rāṣôn* appears 56x (14x in Prov; 13x in Ps). It is used both for divine (39x) and human dispositions or attitudes.

2. *For human beings. rāṣôn* may be either negative (Gen 49:6; Dan 11:3) or positive, as favor (Prov 16:13, 15) or a desire to seek God (2 Chron 15:15) or God's blessings (Ps 145:16). The vb. is also used for human favor or receptivity (Gen 33:10; Deut 33:24) or a delighting in good (God's ways, Prov 23:26; the temple, 1 Chron 29:3; cf. Ps 102:14[15]) or evil (falsehood, 62:4[5]).

3. *For God. rāṣôn* is divine acceptance and favor (Deut 33:11, 16), which can be open to questioning (Ps 77:7[8]; cf. Job 34:9). In its most basic sense, *rāṣôn* is the divine goodwill that reaches out to others in mercy and compassion (Isa 60:10). Such favor may assume concrete form, such as a wife (Prov 18:22), saving help (Ps 106:4), or general benefits (Deut 33:23). It is used in anticipation of a time of God's gracious activity: time of favor (Ps 69:13[14]; Isa 49:8) or year of favor (Isa 61:2). It also refers to the will of God as that which is taught (Ps 143:10) and done (40:8[9]; 103:21). God is pleased with those who do his will and visits them with favor and peace (Prov 12:2; 16:7).

4. Both vb. and nom. are used some 30x in contexts of worship regarding that which is (or is not) pleasing to God, especially sacrifices (nom.: Lev 1:3; 19:5; 22:19-21; Ps 51:16[18]; Isa 56:7; 58:5; Jer 6:20; vb.: Lev 1:4; 7:18; Isa 60:7; Jer 14:12; Hos 8:13; Amos 5:22; Mic 6:7). More generally, certain persons are a delight to God (king, 1 Chron 28:4; servant, Isa 42:1; those who fear him, Ps 147:11) as are certain behaviors: uprightness (1 Chron 29:17; Prov 11:20), seeking good (Prov 11:27), praying (15:8; cf. Job 33:26), building the temple (Hag 1:8). God has no pleasure in sinners (Jer 14:10), those who do not worship well (Mal 1:10-13), or those who rely on nondivine strength (Ps 147:10). In the new creation, God will accept his people (Ezek 20:40-41; 43:27). The striking language of God's delighting—the subjective side of the divine will—demonstrates that feelings are not foreign to his experience of the world.

Pleasing: → *ṭwb* (please, be in favor, be joyous, be valuable, # 3201); → *rṣh* I (be pleased with, to treat favorably, # 8354)

Bibliography

TDOT 4:22-36; *TWOT* 2:860; D. R. Ap-Thomas, "Some Aspects of the Root HNN in the Old Testament," *JSS* 2, 1957, 128-48; R. M. Hals, *Grace and Faith in the Old Testament*; W. F. Lofthouse, "*ḥen* and *ḥesed* in the Old Testament," *ZAW* 51, 1933, 29-35; W. L. Reed, "Some Implications of HEN for Old Testament Religion," *JBL* 73, 1954, 36-41.

Terence E. Fretheim

8355	רצה

רצה (*rṣh* II), q. pay for, make good; ni. be paid for, made good; pi. make amends (# 8355).

ANE 1. Those who argue for separating the occurrences of *rṣh* into two roots rely partially on the ANE cognates for support (see e.g., *HALAT* 1195b). According to *AHw* (960a) an Old Babylonian vb. *raṣûm* (only 1x cited) is related to a Canaanite root *rāṣā* II and means perhaps to give (a house) in payment. Contrast the Old Babylonian nom. *tarṣiātum,* meaning perhaps enjoyment, which is also known from only a single occurrence and is thought to be related to WestSem. *rd/ṣî,* have enjoyment (*AHw,* 1331b).

2. OSA also seems to support a *rṣh* II from a word *rdym.* It has been argued from this cognate that the original Sem. root for Heb. *rṣh* II might have been *rdh* as opposed to the original root *rṣh* for Heb. *rṣh* I (Müller, 315). Compare also Jewish Aram. *r*'', pay, according to Müller (followed in *HALAT* 1195b).

3. In that connection, according to the standard lexicons, in late Jewish Aram. *r*'' means delight in, favor, be acceptable (see e.g., Jastrow, 2:1486) as opposed to *rṣ'*, to appease (Jastrow, 2:1494). Furthermore, as in the HB, the semantic range of Late Heb. *rṣh* seems to reflect a combination of the two Jewish Aram. roots cited above (Jastrow, 2:1493-94): q. to favor, pardon, please; pi. to appease, procure pardon; ni. to be acceptable, accepted, appeased; hi. to satisfy a debt; etc. For Qumran and more on Late Jewish Aram. and Heb. see P-B below.

OT 1. Whether or not *rṣh* II exists as a separate root distinct from *rṣh* I (to accept; be accepted, acceptable; be pleased with, enjoy, # 8354) is still debated by lexicographers. The brief review of some of the most important ANE materials above (including postbiblical Heb. and Aram.) suggests that there may be some reason to believe that two original words are represented in HB *rṣh* (see e.g., *HALAT* 1195b). According to *HALAT* there are eight occurrences of *rṣh* II, five of them in Lev 26:34 (2x), 41, and 43 (2x; note that in *HALAT* under hi., 26:34a should read 26:34b): 4 or 5x in q. (26:41b and 43b, to pay for; 26:34a; 2 Chron 36:21; and according to the MT also Lev 26:43a, to make up for; cf. hi. below), 1x ni. (Isa 40:2, to be paid for), 1x pi. (Job 20:10, to restore, make good), and 1 or 2x in hi. (Lev 26:34b, to make up for; and possibly also 26:43a is hi. rather than q. according to the Sam. Pent.; cf. *BHS* v. 43 n. a and *HALAT*).

The NIV handles only four of these occurrences as if they were from a *rṣh* II: Lev 26:41b and 43b q. "(when) they (the rebellious Israelites) pay for their sin(s)"; Job 20:10, "His (i.e., the wicked man's) children must make amends to the poor;" and Isa 40:2, "her (i.e., Jerusalem's) sin has been paid for." It treats the other three occurrences differently (i.e., according to *rṣh* I): Lev 26:34a, 43a; and 2 Chron 36:21 refer to the land enjoying its Sabbaths, not making good (or making up for) its Sabbaths.

2. It should be observed, however, that this distinction between two *rṣh* roots is by no means accepted by all modern lexicographers. Some argue that the HB usage and the LXX translations of *rṣh* betray a rather broad semantic range for a single root (see e.g., *TWAT* 7:646-47; *THAT* 2:810-11; and Even-Shoshan, 1090; cf. BDB, 953). According to this view, one should take the supposed instances of *rṣh* II as falling within the extended semantic range of *rṣh* I, to accept.

Those who take this approach often argue that there is a play on words in Lev 26:34, 41, and 43 (see e.g., *TWAT* 7:646-47 and esp. *THAT* 2:811). The Israelites must "*accept* (the punishment for) their iniquity" that will come in the form of their exile from the land (vv. 41b and 43b; cf. BDB, 730, for *'āwōn* as iniquity or punishment for iniquity; see also the explanation of Isa 40:2 below), and the land must *accept* those years of exile as the Sabbaths (i.e., the sabbatical years) that are due to it (vv. 34 and 43a; cf. 2 Chron 36:21). *HALAT* (1195) treats the pi. of *rṣh* in Job 20:10 under both *rṣh* I, to make (oneself) acceptable (to), seek the favor of, the poor (acceptable, *TWAT* and

THAT) versus *rṣh* II, to restore, make amends to, the poor (not acceptable, *TWAT* and *THAT*). The ni. form of this vb. in Isa 40:2 would mean not that Jerusalem's iniquity "has been paid for" (NIV, see OT sec. 1), but instead, that Jerusalem's iniquity "has been accepted" in the sense that the punishment for their iniquity that they had already received has been accepted as adequate (*TWAT* 7:646 and *THAT* 2:811).

P-B At Qumran there are two occurrences of the vb. *rṣh* with *'āwōn* as its direct object (cf. OT sec. 2, esp. Lev 26:41b, 43b; Isa 40:2). Once again *HALAT* (1195b) takes them as evidence for a *rṣh* II, pay for, but others take the expression to mean that those involved have had their punishment for iniquity accepted (see OT sec. 2, esp. *TWAT* 7:651a). The two occurrences are in the *Manual of Discipline* (1QS 8:3), where the Council of the Community "shall atone for sin (*wlrṣt 'wwn*) by the practice of justice and by suffering the sorrows of affliction" (Vermes, 72), and in *The Words of the Heavenly Lights* (4Q504 or 4QDibHam[a] VI 4-6; DJD VII, 148), "Now, on the day when our heart is humbled, we expiate our iniquity (*rṣynw 't 'wwnnw*) and the iniquity of our fathers, together with our unfaithfulness and rebellion" (Vermes, 219).

It appears that in Late Heb. and Aram. this usage of *rṣh,* meaning pay for, satisfy, make up for, continues to occur in the Midr., Mish., and Talm. literature (see ANE sec. 3). For example, see the reference to Lev 26:34 (Heb. hi., Jastrow, 2:1493b), "the land shall rest ... until it shall have made up (*'d štarṣeh*) before me for all the Sabbatical years which it owes me," and (Aram. Ithpe., Jastrow, 2:1494a), "peradventure the Lord will be appeased and send rain."

Atonement: → *kpr* I (cover, paint, smear, atone, appease, # 4105); → *rṣh* II (pay for, make good, make amends, # 8355)
Payment, rent, reward, wages: → *'ᵃgôrâ* (payment, # 102); → *'eškār* (tribute, payment, # 868); → *mᵉḥîr* I (price, payment, # 4697); → *sl'* (be paid, # 6131); → *slh* II (be paid, # 6137); → *pᵉ'ullâ* (wages, punishment, reward, payment, # 7190); → *rṣh* II (pay for, make good, make amends, # 8355); → *śkr* (hire, # 8509); → *šlm* (repay, reward, retribute, make peace, # 8966); → **Retribution: Theology**

BIBLIOGRAPHY

THAT 2:810-11; *TWAT* 7:646-47; W. W. Müller, "Altsüdarabische Beiträge zum Hebräischen Lexicon," *ZAW* 75, 1963, 304-16; G. Vermes, *The Dead Sea Scrolls in English*, 3d ed., 1987.

Richard E. Averbeck

8356 (*rāṣôn*, favor, what is acceptable), → # 8354

8357	רצח

רצח (*rṣḥ*), q. murder, kill; ni. be murdered, killed; pi. murder, murderer; pu. be killed (# 8357); רֶצַח (*reṣaḥ*), nom. slaughter (# 8358).

ANE The Heb. root has no obvious cognates in the languages of the ANE.

OT 1. The root *rṣḥ* (38x) carries the sense of killing or murdering. B. S. Childs (*Exodus,* 1974, 419-21) finds the origins of this term in the practice of blood vengeance. In the Decalogue, *rṣḥ* is used in the sixth commandment (Exod 20:13; Deut 5:17), where it is rendered by the NIV as "You shall not murder." As it stands, it is a blanket prohibition against the taking of a person's life by an individual or by a mob, who target an individual, with all the attendant savagery. In the wider context of the OT, the prohibition may be defined more narrowly as the taking of a life outside of the parameters (as in the case of war or capital punishment), laid down by God (cf. W. Zimmerli, *Old Testament Theology in Outline*, 1978, 135).

Human life, even more than other forms of life, has a unique value in the sight of God. To take a life, outside of the perimeters set by God, therefore, requires some form of restitution. At times in the OT such a taking of a life was punished by the courts, at other times by the tribal practice of blood vengeance. Thus was Israel required to order her society in obedience to God's justice. Most importantly she was to take steps to curtail the ever-present danger of the cycle of violence, which still today threatens to destroy our fragile societies (→ *hrg*, # 2222).

2. The priestly record in Num 35 (where *rṣḥ* occurs 20x) deals with the cities of refuge set up perhaps in the early period of the monarchy (cf. R. de Vaux, *AncIsr*, 1961, 158-63) and addressed (again) during the time of the deuteronomic reform (cf. Deut 19:1-13 and Josh 20). The intention was to provide safety for perpetrators of accidental manslaughter (Num 35:11, 22, 23) and more importantly to stem the tide the revenge killing (cf. Exod 21:13 and L. Schweinhorst-Schönberger, 384-86). In tribal societies today, it still happens that a single incident, like the rape of a woman, can precipitate a cycle of violence leaving thirty or forty people dead and many others injured. Num 35 ends on a dramatic note: "Bloodshed pollutes the land, and atonement cannot be made for the land on which blood has been shed, except by the blood of the one who shed it" (v. 33). Bloodguilt might attach itself to a person/family (1 Kgs 2:28-34) or to a place (Deut 19:10). In the case of an accidental murder, the person involved was not free to leave his/her refuge until the death of a high priest (Num 35:32), while in the event of an unsolved murder, the community was purged from guilt by the slaughter of a heifer (Deut 21:1-9).

3. In the prophetic corpus *rṣḥ* (like *hrg*) renders the idea of literal killing, whether accidental (Josh 20:3-6) or intentional (Jer 7:9). Often a sense of the judgment of God is present. For example, in the story of Naboth's vineyard, Elijah confronts Ahab with the words, "Have you not murdered a man and seized his property?" (1 Kgs 21:19). *rṣḥ* expresses the full horror and violence of the murder as well as the bloodguilt that now comes to rest on Ahab and Jezebel.

4. In the Wisdom corpus, the killing of the weak by the powerful is vividly depicted in Job 24:14: "When daylight is gone, the murderer rises up and kills the poor and needy; in the night he steals forth like a thief." On a different note, Prov speaks of the person who is afraid to venture from his/her home in search of honest labor with the excuse that there may be a lion in the street or someone waiting to kill him or her (Prov 22:13).

P-B The LXX makes use of the vb. *phoeneuō* and its nom. *phoneutēs*, murderer, in its rendering of *rṣḥ*. In the NT citations of the Ten Commandments (e.g., Rom 13:9; James 2:11) *phoneuō* is again used.

NT Significantly, Jesus ranks humiliation, degradation, and dehumanization along with murder (Matt 5:22).

Kill, murder, massacre: → *hrg* (kill, murder, # 2222); → *qṭl* (murder, slay, # 7779); → *rṣḥ* (murder, kill, # 8357)

Bibliography

B. S. Childs, *Exodus,* 1974; A. Philips, *Ancient Israel's Criminal Code*, 1970; L. Schweinhorst-Schönberger, *Das Bundesbuch*, BZAW, 1989; R. de Vaux, *AncIsr*, 1964; W. Zimmerli, *Old Testament Theology in Outline*, 1978.

W. R. Domeris

8358 (*reṣaḥ*, slaughter), → # 8357

8361	רצע

רצע (*rṣ'*), q. bore, pierce (# 8361); מַרְצֵעַ (*marṣēa'*), nom. awl, piercing tool (# 5345).

ANE Perhaps Akk. (neo-Babyl.) subst. *marṣā'u* awl(?), from the root *raṣā'u* (*AHw*, 613), the Sumerian equivalent signifies a tool to loosen and tighten (*CAD M*/1, 290); the same Akk. subst. was thought to occur in EA 120:21 in a cotext of goods and tools, where *ma-a[r]-[ṣ]a-ú* was read (*CAD M*/1, 617), but this lexical item is now read *ma-ar-⌈ba⌉-d[u]*, blanket (Moran, 199, citing Rainey and Bonkamp); (Pal.) Arab. *raṣa'a,* to press, perforate, *'arṣa'a* (IV-stem), to wound (with a spear); Tg. Aram. *'arṣa'*, aphel pierce (used to translate Exod 21:6).

OT 1. The vb. occurs only in Exod 21:6. The textual environment cites ordinances about slavery. If a slave desired to work for his master for the rest of his life, the master was to bring the slave before God, then to a door or doorpost and "pierce" (*rṣ'*) his ear "with an awl" (*marṣēa'*).

2. The subst. *marṣēa'*, awl, piercing tool, occurs in Exod 21:6 and Deut 15:17. Both texts speak to the issue of a slave who desired to work permanently for a master (see 1).

The ceremony of ear-piercing recorded in Exod 21:6 and Deut 15:17 is similar, though if one follows the MT in Exod 21:6, the ceremony prescribed there appears more religious in that the MT reads that the slave was to be brought *to God,* perhaps referring to a ceremony in the sanctuary. The same religious procedure might be implicit in the Deuteronomy account, though nothing is said there about being brought to God. Perhaps the deut. account envisions a simple symbolic rite among the family circle (Thompson, 191). The ancient translations of Exod 21:6, however, seem to envision a more civil ceremony since in them the slave was to be brought before "judges" (LXX, Pesh., and Targ.).

P-B The root is attested in the q., ni., and pi. stems with senses of press, flatten, perforate, and lash. As a nom. the root is attested in *raṣ'ān*, leather-worker, shoemaker (Jastrow, 2:1494b).

Penetration: → *nḥt* (march down, descend, penetrate, settle, # 5737)

Bibliography

W. L. Moran, ed. and trans., *The Amarna Letters*, 1992; A. F. Rainey, *AOAT*^{2}, 81; J. A. Thompson, *Deuteronomy*, TOTC, 1974.

Gary Alan Long

8363	רֶצֶף

רֶצֶף (*reṣep* I), nom. live coal (# 8363).

OT 1. The nom. refers to hot live coals (1 Kgs 19:6).

2. The coal in Isa 6:6 symbolizes the altar from which it came, and inferentially that the penalty of sin was paid by a substitute offered in the sinner's place. The symbol, applied to Isaiah's lips, the point at which his need was most pressing, assures him of personal forgiveness.

Fire, flame: → *'ûd* (log, burning stick, # 202); → *'ēš* I (fire, # 836); → *b'r* I (burn, blaze up, be consumed, # 1277); → *gaḥelet* (burning charcoal, # 1625); → *goprît* (sulphur, # 1730); → *yṣt* (kindle, burn, set on fire, # 3675); → *yqd* (burn, be burning, kindled, # 3678); → *kîdôd* (spark, # 3958); → *lbb* II (bake cakes, # 4221); → *lahab* (flame, blade, # 4258); → *lhṭ* I (glow, burn, # 4265); → *lappîd* (torch, lightning, # 4365); → *nîṣôṣ* (spark, # 5773); → *peḥām* (charcoal, # 7073); → *reṣep* I (live coal, # 8363); → *rešep* I (flame, glow, arrow, plague, # 8404); → *śrp* (burn, be burnt, # 8596); → *šābîb* (flame, # 8663)

Jackie A. Naudé

8367	רִצְפָּה

רִצְפָּה (*riṣpâ*), nom. pavement, stone pavement, mosaic pavement (# 8367); nom. מַרְצֶפֶת (*marṣepet*), stone pavement, base (# 5346).

ANE Akk. *riṣpu, riṣiptu; raṣāpu,* fit stones together; cf. Aram. *riṣp^{e}tā'*, pavement; *r^{e}ṣap*, arrange in a line.

OT 1. The nom. *riṣpâ* occurs 6x in the OT. Its major use is to describe: the floor in Xerxes' palace in Susa, which was a mosaic of various stones (marble, mother-of-pearl, and other stones; Esth 1:6); the pavement of Solomon's temple (2 Chron 7:3); and the floor/pavement around the outer court of Ezekiel's visionary temple (Ezek 40:17, 18; 42:3). The splendor and beauty of the palaces are stressed each time.

2. The nom. *marṣepet* indicates the base, most likely a stone pavement (cf. NIV, base; cf. NJPS), on which Ahaz set the brass Sea after he removed it from the bronze bulls on which it had been resting (2 Kgs 16:17). All of this was done under pressure from the Assyrian king, Tiglath-Pileser (16:18).

NT A pavement of stone is mentioned in connection with Jesus' trial (John 19:13); a stone pavement is also a feature of the New Jerusalem (Rev 21:9-21).

Floor, pavement: → *qarqa'* I (inlaid floor, floor(s), bottom, # 7977); → *riṣpâ* (pavement, stone pavement, mosaic pavement, # 8367)

Eugene Carpenter/Michael A. Grisanti

8368	רצץ

רצץ (*rṣṣ*), q. crush, smash up; ill-treat, abuse; ni. crack, break; hi. and pi. crush in pieces; po. oppress; hitpo. crush each other (# 8368); nom. מְרוּצָה (*m^{e}rûṣâ* II), oppression (Jer 22:17; # 5298).

ANE The meaning of the Akk. *raṣāṣu* is unclear (*AHw*, 960a), but the Arab. cognate, *raḍḍa*, means pulverize.

OT 1. In its most basic and literal sense, *rṣṣ* can describe the breaking of a bowl, a wheel (q. and ni., both in Eccl 12:6, where they are part of graphic imagery describing death), the broken reed (q., 2 Kgs 18:21; Isa 36:6; cf. ni., Ezek 29:7), and the crushing of the skull of Abimelech by a millstone (hi., Judg 9:53).

2. *rṣṣ* and its derivative are also used to describe the oppression of the socially weak in Israelite society (q., 1 Sam 12:3, 4; pi. Job 20:19; q., Amos 4:1 [par. *'šq*]; cf. Jer 22:17 [*m*ᵉ*rûṣâ*; par. *'ōšeq*]) as well as God's just judgment over his people (q., Deut 28:33 [par. *'šq*]; po. Judg 10:8 [par. *r'ṣ*]; q., Hos 5:11 [par. *'šq*]; cf. pi. 2 Chron 16:10). It becomes clear from the various contexts of social oppression that *rṣṣ*, like *'šq*, reflects the exploitation and despoliation of the poor (1 Sam 12:3-4; Job 20:19; Amos 4:1). In Isa 58:6-7 the relieving of oppression is set forth as the prerequisite for divine blessing (recorded in vv. 8-12): "To loose the chains of injustice and untie the cords of the yoke, to set the oppressed (*r*ᵉ*ṣûṣîm*) free and break every yoke ... to share your food with the hungry and to provide the poor wanderer with shelter—when you see the naked, to clothe him." This passage refers to the Year of Jubilee and the Sabbath Year (cf. 61:1-2), when those who fell into slavery were to be freed, all properties were to be returned to their original owners, poverty was to be expelled from society, and the social order was to be restored (Lev 25). God, too, would set the oppressed free (*r*ᵉ*ṣûṣîm*) and break every yoke (cf. 58:6).

3. In a few instances *rṣṣ* describes oppression of Israel by other nations, which was at the same time the means whereby God executed his judgment on his unfaithful people (Deut 28:33; Judg 10:8; Hos 5:11 [cf. v. 14]). In Deut 28:33 *rṣṣ* reflects the idea of the physical privation that Israel would suffer as result of a foreign nation eating the fruit of the ground and the produce of Israel's labor (cf. Deut 28:8, 11).

4. With respect to the Servant of Yahweh, *rṣṣ* is used effectively to bring out his greatness: "A bruised (*rṣṣ*) reed he will not break, and a smoldering wick he will not snuff out. In faithfulness he will bring forth justice; he will not falter (*khh*) or be discouraged (i.e., crushed; *rṣṣ*) till he establishes justice on earth" (Isa 42:3-4). (On *yārûṣ* as q. impf. of *rṣṣ* see *GKC* § 67q. It is thus not necessary to read *yērôṣ*; cf. *BHS*.)

5. It was noteworthy that Esau and Jacob "jostled each other" (*rṣṣ*) in the womb before their birth (Gen 25:22). Alarmed, Rebekah inquired of Yahweh for an explanation. He said: "Two nations are in your womb, and two peoples within you will be separated; one people will be stronger than the other, and the older will serve the younger" (v. 23). Thus, the prebirth friction would carry over into later conflict. The LXX renders *rṣṣ* (v. 22) by *skirtaō*. This vb. also occurs in Luke 1:41, 44, where it is used of the baby (John the Baptist) in Elizabeth's womb. Here the action carries a positive message.

6. In Ps 74, God's greatness as king victorious over Egypt is poetically recounted in the words: "You broke (*šbr*) the heads of the monster in the waters. It was you who crushed (*rṣṣ*) the heads of Leviathan" (vv. 13-14). Egypt is described as a sea monster elsewhere too (Ezek 29:3; 32:2). (For the argument that one should read creation language in these verses, see e.g., M. E. Tate, *Psalms 51-100*, 1990, 251-52.)

P-B In CD 8:10 the rule for the Guardian of the Congregation is given: "He shall loosen all the fetters which bind them that in his Congregation there may be none that are oppressed (*'āšûq*) or broken (*rāṣûṣ*)" (Vermes, 115; → *'šq*). This task of the Guardian calls to mind the duty of the king in Israel and in the ANE to protect the inhabitants of their land, especially the socially weak, from oppression.

Split, breach, slice: → *bq'* (split, break open, # 1324); → *ḥrm* II (split, # 3050); → *ḥtr* (break through, # 3168); → *miśpāḥ* (breach of law, # 5384); → *plḥ* (cut into slices, split open, # 7114); → *pṣm* (split open, # 7204); → *prṣ* I (break through, burst out, be broken down, # 7287); → *r''* II (break in pieces, # 8318); → *rṣṣ* (crush, mash, break, # 8368); → *šbr* I (break, break down, smash, shatter, # 8689)
Affliction, oppression: → *dḥq* (oppress, # 1895); → *ḥms* I (do violence, # 2803); → *ḥmṣ* II (oppress, # 2807); → *ynh* (oppress, # 3561); → *lḥṣ* (press, # 4315); → *māṣôr* I (affliction, siege, # 5189); → *mrr* I (be bitter, distraught, afflict, # 5352); → *nega'* (plague, affliction, # 5596); → *ngś* (exact, # 5601); → *'nh* II (afflict, humble, afflict one's soul, fast, oppress, submit, # 6700); → *'wq* I (crush?, # 6421); → *'mr* II (deal tyrannically with, # 6683); → *'šq* I (wrong, # 6943); → *ṣwq* I (constrain, press in/upon, harass, vex, # 7439); → *ṣwr* II (deal tyrannically with, # 7444); → *rhb* (assail, press, pester, alarm, confuse, # 8104); → *rṣṣ* (crush, # 8368); → *tôlāl* (oppressor, # 9354); → *tōk* (oppression, # 9412)

BIBLIOGRAPHY

T. D. Hanks, *God So Loved the Third World: The Biblical Vocabulary of Oppression*, 1983, 3-39; Y. I. Kim, "The Vocabulary of Oppression in the Old Testament," Ph.D. diss. Drew University, 1981; M. A. Knibb, *The Qumran Community*, 1987; C. F. Marriottini, "The Problem of Social Oppression in the Eighth Century Prophets," Ph.D. diss. Southern Baptist Theological Seminary, 1983; J. Miranda, *Communism in the Bible*, 1982, 37-39; J. Pons, *L'oppression dans l'Ancien Testament*, 1981; E. Tamez, *Bible of the Oppressed*, 1982, 1-30.

Cornelis Van Dam/I. Swart

8369	רַק

רַק (*raq* I), thin (# 8369).

OT The word is used in the OT only in Gen 41:19, 20, 27 of the thin cows in Pharoah's dream. The word *daq*, thin, is also used of the lean cows and the thin ears of corn, and in the verses mentioned *daqqôt* is a variant reading for *raqqôt*.

Thin: → *daq* (thin, # 1987); → *rzh* (destroy, waste away, # 8135); → *raq* I (thin, # 8369)

Francis Foulkes

8370 (*raq* II, only), → Particles

8371 (*rōq*, spittle or saliva), → # 8394

8372	רקב

רקב (*rqb*), q. rot, become worm eaten (# 8372); רָקָב (*rāqāb*), nom. rottenness (# 8373); רִקָּבוֹן (*riqqābôn*), nom. rottenness (# 8375).

ANE The vb. *rqb* occurs in Akk. as a causative (*raqābu*; *AHw*, 957), as well as the Akk. nom. *ruqb/pu*, *ruqbūtu* (*AHw*, 994).

OT 1. The vb. *rqb* is found 2x in the MT; in Isa 40:20 it describes solid wood (not rotten) chosen for the base of an idol. It is used metaphorically in Prov 10:7 to describe the reputation of the wicked. It has also been proposed for Ps 49:14[15], where the MT reads "the upright will rule over them in the morning (*bqr*)"; by simple metathesis to *rqb*, a redivision of the letters and revocalization of the words, the line would say "they will justly go down to rot." However, there are other problems, and Kraus asserts that "a logically based reconstruction of the second part of v. 14 is impossible" (480). The vb. has also been proposed for Job 5:3, emending *w'qqwb* (I declared accursed) to *wrqb* or *wyyrqb,* to say of the wicked, "His abode rotted suddenly" (Fohrer, 128, 132); however, Gordis argues that the MT is a better parallel with the first line (52).

2. The nom. *rāqāb* is found 5x in the MT. It appears to serve as a metaphor to describe the emotional effects of distress as a "rottenness in the bones" (Prov 12:4; 14:30; Hab 3:16); Hos 5:12 describes the judgment of God as rottenness. The occurrence of *rqb* at Job 13:28, describing the failure of human flesh, should be translated "wineskin" as in G, cf. Aram. *r(w)qb'* and Sir 43:20; "rottenness" does not suit the vb., which would make the line read something to the effect that "he will waste away like rottenness" (Fohrer, 239). The nom. *riqqābôn* is found only at Job 41:19, where bronze is to Leviathan as rotten wood. Rottenness is a weakening that indicates a loss of life. It renders material useless and is an apt metaphor for the sins and ailments that destroy human life.

P-B The inf. *rqb* is found at Sir 14:19; the Midr. and Talm. have the nom. *rāqēb* and the vb. *r^{e}qēb*. The nom. *riqbā'*, which also includes the sense of rust, is found in the Tgs. and Talm.

Rotting, decay: → *mqq* (putrefy, rot, dwindle away, # 5245); → *māśôś* II (something rotten, # 5376); → *rmm* I (rot, be full of worms, # 8249); → *rqb* (rot, become worm eaten, # 8372)

BIBLIOGRAPHY

P. Casetti, "Gibt es ein Leben vor dem Tod? Eine Auslegung von Psalm 49," *OBO* 44, 1982, 138-40; G. Fohrer, *Das Buch Hiob*, 1989, 128, 132, 239; R. Gordis, *The Book of Job*, 52; H.-J. Kraus, *Psalms 1-59*, 1988, 480.

A. H. Konkel

8373 (*rāqāb*, rottenness), → # 8372

8374	רֹקֶב

רֹקֶב (*rōqeb*), nom. leather (hapleg.; # 8374). This is a conjectured revocalization of the MT in Job 13:28, which has *rāqāb*, rottenness (→ # 8373).

ANE Arab. *qirbat*, waterskin; Tg. Aram. *rûqbā'*, goatskin made into a bag or bottle; Syr. *raqbā'*, leather skin for carrying liquid.

OT If the revocalization of the MT is accepted, a seemingly closer semantic parallel is created: *rōqeb*, leather item ‖ *beged*, garment (Job 13:28). NIV, however, follows the MT, which has *rāqāb*, rottenness, and translates, "So man wastes away like something rotten, like a garment eaten by moths."

Skin, leather: → *'ādām* II (leather, # 133); → *'ah^a^bâ* II (leather, # 174); → *'ôb* I (wine-skin, # 199); → *gēled* (skin, # 1654); → *ḥēmet* (waterskin, # 2827); → *nō'd* (bottle, scroll, # 5532); → *'ôr* (skin, hide, # 6425); → *ṣhl* II (shine [of healthy skin], # 7413); → *taḥrā'* (leather collar?, # 9389); → *taḥaš* I (leather?, # 9391)

Gary Alan Long

8375 (*riqqābôn*, rottenness), → # 8372

8376	רקד

רקד (*rqd*), q, pi., hi. skip about, to leap (# 8376).

ANE The Akk. cognate *raqādu* pictures military troops gathering like a flock of sheep. The Syr. equivalent root term, *rqd*, meant either dance or mourn.

OT The idea of skipping is denoted in the Heb. vb. *rqd*. It can refer to the activity of animals: rams (Ps 114:4, 6), calves (29:6), and he-goats (Isa 13:21). This vb. is used in 1 Chron 15:29 to describe David's dancing before the LORD. "There is a time to dance (*rqd*)" in Eccl 3:4 and the children of the wicked are described as dancing about in Job 21:11. It also describes children's merriment (Job 21:11) and is the opposite of mourning (Eccl 3:4).

Dance, whirl: → *ḥwl* I (whirl around, dance, # 2565); → *krr* II (whirl, # 4159); → *rqd* (skip, leap, # 8376)

David S. Dockery

8377	רַקָּה

רַקָּה (*raqqâ*), temple (of head) (# 8377).

ANE The nom. appears also in Jewish Aram. and Ugar., with the same meaning as in Heb. Also the Akk. nom. *raqqatum* has the same meaning.

OT The nom. appears only 5x in the OT. Three of the cases (Judg 4:21, 22; 5:26) refers to Jael, who hammered a tent peg through Sisera's temple. She chose that spot because it is a soft spot in the skull, facilitating the driving of a peg through the skull. The other two instances are in S of Songs (4:3; 6:7). In both cases the same words are used to compare the bride's temple behind her veil with a pomegranate.

Head: → *'ap* (face, anger, # 678); → *gulgōlet* (scull, # 1653); → *l^e^ḥî* I (eye, nose, jawbone, chin, cheek, # 4305); → *mēṣaḥ* (forehead, # 5195); → *m^e^tall^e^'ôt* (jawbone, # 5506); → *pānîm* (face, visible, assault, # 7156); → *pōt* (front, forehead, # 7327); → *qodqōd* (crown of head, # 7721); → *rō'š* I (head, chief, beginning, # 8031); → *raqqâ* (temple [of head], # 8377)

BIBLIOGRAPHY

R. Boling, *Judges*, AB, 1975, 99; E. W. Nicholson, "The Problem of צנח," *ZAW* 89, 1977, 257-66; M. Pope, *Song of Songs*, AB, 1977, 464; R. D. Patterson, "The Song of Deborah," in *Tradition and Testament: Essays in Honor of Charles Lee Feinberg*, 1981, 140-41.

Harry F. van Rooy

8379	רקח

רקח (*rqḥ*), q. blend, mix ointments; pu. blended, mixed ointments; hi. mix in (# 8379); מִרְקַחַת

(*mirqaḥat*), nom. mixture of ointments (# 5351); רַקָּח (*raqqaḥ*), nom. ointment mixer (# 8382); רִקֻּחַ (*riqquaḥ*), nom. ointment, perfume (# 8383). Terms related to the field of perfumery: אֲבָקָה (*'ᵃbāqâ*), nom. aromatic powders (# 86); בֹּשֶׂם (*bōśem*), nom. balsam (shrub), balsam (oil), perfume (→ # 1411); כחל (*kḥl*), vb. paint (eyes) (# 3949); מְרוּקִים (*mᵉrûqîm*), nom. cosmetic treatment (# 5299); נֵרְדְּ (*nērd*), nom. aromatic ointment (# 5948); נֶשֶׁק (*nešeq* II), nom. fragrant substance (# 5978); סַם (*sam*), nom. fragrant perfumes (# 6160); עָתָר (*'ātār*), nom. fragrance (# 6986); פּוּךְ (*pûk*), nom. black eye-paint, hard cement (# 7037); תַּמְרוּק (*tamrûq*), nom. massage and ointment (# 9475).

ANE 1. The numerous terms from the root *rqḥ* derive from a root vb. meaning pound, mix spices or perfumes (*DNWSI*, 1083). It has background in Akk. *riqqu*, perfume, fragrant wood (*AHw*, 988; cf. also *ruqqu*, fine oil, pressed oil, *AHw*, 995, and other derivatives given there). The root occurs in Ugar., Phoen., Punic, and Deir 'Alla Aram. for the occupation of a perfumer (*UT* 486; Tomback, 306-7; *DNWSI*, 1083). It also occurs in Ugar. as a substantive ointment, perfume, and in other forms and usages (see *HALAT* 1202 and the extensive literature cited there).

2. Heb. *sam*, fragrant perfumes, has background in Akk. *šammu*, plant, grass, herb, medicinal plant (*CAD* Š/1, 315-21). The term occurs also in Jewish Aram. (Jastrow, 998), Syr., Mand., and Arab. (*HALOT* 759; Nielsen, 1986, 67).

OT 1. (a) The vb. *rqḥ* occurs only 8x, but it has sundry nom. derivatives (see the list above). It refers to mixing spices in making anointing oil (Exod 30:33), esp. the perfumer who mixed the holy anointing oil and incense for the tabernacle (Exod 30:25, 35; 37:29; cf. 1 Chron 9:30; also *mirqaḥat* in Exod 30:25; 1 Chron 9:30 referring to mixture of ointments used in making anointing oil and burial spices; and *raqqāḥ*, ointment mixer, in Neh 3:8), and for the tomb of Asa (2 Chron 16:14; note also *mirqaḥat* again here). Eccl 10:1 refers to perfuming in a proverbial statement: "As dead flies give perfume a bad smell, so a little folly outweighs wisdom and honor."

(b) The Lord's wrath against Israel is the occasion for a note that reflects the practice of perfuming or spicing meat (Ezek 24:10, "So heap on the wood and kindle the fire. Cook the meat well, mixing in [hi. of *rqḥ*] the spices; and let the bones be charred"; cf. *riqquaḥ* in Isa 57:9a, "You went to Molech with olive oil and increased your perfumes"). Ezek 8:11 uses *'ātār*, fragrance, to refer to illegitimate incense offerings to idols, "Each had a censer in his hand, and a fragrant cloud of incense was rising" (see v. 12 for the reference to the idols; cf. *HALOT* 906, for the Arab., OSA, Eth., and Syr. cognates to this term).

2. Related terms.

(a) Heb. *'ᵃbāqâ* (1x), referring to the traveling vehicle of Solomon as being "perfumed with myrrh and incense made from all the *spices* of the merchant" (S of Songs 3:6), shows that this is not limited to women.

(b) The vb. *kḥl* is used of faithless Israel in the figure of women who "sent messengers for men who came from far away, and when they arrived you bathed yourself for them, *painted your eyes* and put on your jewelry" (Ezek 23:40).

(c) *mᵉrûqîm* and the cognate *tamrûqîm* occur in Esth 2:12, together with other terms for cosmetics: "Before a girl's turn came to go in to King Xerxes, she had to complete twelve months of beauty treatments (*mᵉrûqîm* [# 5299]) prescribed for the

women, six months with oil of myrrh (*mōr*, # 5255) and six with perfumes (*bōśem*, # 1411) and cosmetics (*tamrûqîm* [# 9475])" (cf. S of Songs 4:10, 14, 16; 8:14; on the latter verse see Pope, 699). *tamrûq* in Esth 2:3, 9, 12 refers to women's "beauty treatments" (NIV) by massaging of ointments (cf. the root *mrq*, polish, rub; Prov 20:30 is textually difficult).

(d) The nom. *nērd*, aromatic ointment, was also important in this regard (S of Songs 1:12; 4:13-14; cf. *HALOT* 723-24 for its Sanskrit etymology and its source in the Himalayas).

(e) The nom. *sam*, fragrant perfumes, occurs together with *q*ᵉ*tōret*, incense (→ # 7792), in the phrase *q*ᵉ*tōret hassammîm* (Exod 25:6; 31:11; Lev 4:7; Num 4:16, etc.).

(f) The nom. *pûk*, black eye-paint, hard cement, refers to both the painting of women's eyes (both instances negative: 2 Kgs 9:30 of Jezebel, and the context in Jer 4:30) and of some sort of colored stones (1 Chron 29:2; Isa 54:11; the meaning is still unclear according to *HALAT* 868).

P-B Sir 24:15 refers to wisdom figuratively as the perfume of life: "Like cassia and camel's thorn I gave forth perfume, and like choice myrrh I spread my fragrance, like galbanum, onycha, and stacte, and like the odor of incense in the tent."

NT In 2 Cor 2:14 Paul thanks the Lord that "through us spreads everywhere the fragrance (*osmē*) of the knowledge of him" (cf. vv. 15-16; John 12:3). The same kind of figurative use of this term is found in references to the fragrant aroma of Christ's sacrifice on our behalf (Eph 5:2) and to the sacrificial commitment that the Philippians showed Paul (Phil 4:18).

Perfume, ointment: → *bōśem* (balsam [shrub], balsam [oil], perfume, # 1411); → *rqḥ* (blend, mix ointment, mixed, # 8379)

BIBLIOGRAPHY

ABD 5:226-28; *IDB* 3:730-32, 593-95; G. Dalman, *Arbeit und Sitte in Palästina*, I-VII, 1928-42, repr. 1964; R. de Vaux, *Ancient Israel*, 1974, 76-78; R. J. Forbes "Professions and Crafts in Ancient Egypt," *Archives internationales d'histoire des sciences* 12, 1950, 599-618; idem, *Studies in Ancient Technology*, III-VI; VIII-IX, 1955-1958; 1964; H. Grapow, *Die Bildlichen Ausdrücke des Ägyptischen*, 1983; H. Hodges, *Technology in the Ancient World*, 1970; O. Keel, *The Symbolism of the Biblical World*, 1978; H. N. Moldenke and A. L. Moldenke, *Plants of the Bible*, 1952; K. Nielsen, "Ancient Aromas Good and Bad," *BibRev* 7, 1991, 26-33; idem, "Incense," *ABD*, 1992, 3:404-9; idem, *Incense in Ancient Israel*, VTSup 38, 1986; M. Pope, *Song of Songs*, AB, 1977; R. S. Tomback, *A Comparative Lexicon of the Phoenician and Punic Languages*, SBLDS 32, 1978; M. Zohary, *Plants of the Bible*, 1982, 56-57.

Richard E. Averbeck

8380	רֶקַח

רֶקַח (*reqaḥ*), nom. spice (added to wine) (hapleg.; # 8380); מֶרְקָח (*merqāḥ*), nom. aromatic herbs (hapleg.; # 5349); רֹקַח (*rōqaḥ*), nom. spice, perfume (# 8381); < רקח (*rqḥ*), blend, mix ointment (→ # 8379).

ANE The root *rqḥ* is attested in Ugar., meaning "perfumer."

OT 1. *rōqaḥ*, spice, is used to indicate the compound formed by blending various spices. Mixed with olive oil, it was used to anoint the Tent of Meeting and the ark of the Testimony; as a powder it was placed before the Testimony in the Tent of Meeting (Exod 30:25, 35).

2. The hapleg. *merqaḥ*, aromatic herbs, is likely a general term for aromatic herbs or spices (S of Songs 5:13).

3. *reqaḥ*, spice, which refers to a mixture of various spices, appears only in construct with wine at S of Songs 8:2. Spiced or mingled wines were of numerous varieties in the ANE.

P-B The LXX uses *myron*, ointment, for *rōqaḥ* at Exod 30:25, a term used 13x in the NT (cf. Mark 14:5). The LXX translates *merqaḥ* as *myrepsikos,* a word with a similar general reference to aromatic elements.

Herbs, spices: → *'ôrâ* II (herb, mallow, # 246); → *gad* I (coriander, # 1512); → *kammōn* (cumin, # 4021); → *qinnāmôn* (cinnamon, # 7872); → *qeṣaḥ* (black cumin, # 7902); → *q^eṣîa'* (cassia, # 7904); → *reqaḥ* (spice, # 8380)

BIBLIOGRAPHY

J. P. Brown, "The Mediterranean Vocabulary of the Vine," *VT* 19, 1969, 146-70; I. Low, *Die Flora der Juden*, 1924-34, 3441-47; L. L. Walker, "Perfume," *ZPEB* 4:698-99; G. W. Van Beek, "Frankincense and Myrrh in Ancient South Arabia," *JAOS*, 1958, 141-52.

M. G. Abegg Jr.

8381 (*rōqaḥ*, spice, perfume), → # 8380

8382 (*raqqāḥ*, ointment mixer), → # 8379

8383 (*riqquaḥ*, ointment, perfume), → # 8379

8385	רָקִיעַ

רָקִיעַ (*rāqîa'*), firmament, plate (# 8385).

OT This term, often rendered as firmament, is translated as expanse (Gen 1:6; Ezek 1:22; 10:1, etc.), skies (Ps 19:1[2] *šāmayim*, heavens), or heavens (Ps 150:1; Dan 12:3) in NIV. In Gen 1:8, God called the expanse, *šāmayim*. The term is hyponymous to *šāmayim*; i.e., what *rāqîa'* refers to is included in what *šāmayim* refers to, as in the expanse of the sky (Gen 1:14, 15, 17, 20). Cf. Akk. *burūmû*, firmament (of the heavens) (*CAD* B:344-45).

The verbal root of *rāqîa'* is *rq'*, hammer out (pi.); its nom. form means the hammered-out plate (*HALAT* 1203; P. Collini, *SEL* 4, 1987, 19; also M. C. A. Korpel, *UF* 23, 1991, 220). The vb. describes God's creative actions of spreading out the earth (Ps 136:6; Isa 42:5; 44:24) or the skies (*š^eḥāqîm*, Job 37:18). The last passage mentions the skies as "hard as a mirror of cast bronze." The sky and the ground turn like iron ‖ bronze as God's punishment (Lev 26:19b; Deut 28:23). In Ezek 1:22 the living creatures are under and God is far above the expanse.

A synonym for *rāqîa'* is *'^aguddâ*, firmament (→ # 99). The term in this sense appears only in Amos 9:6. Its meaning is uncertain (NIV foundation). Cf. vault (RSV); (Himmels-) Gewölbe (*HALAT* 10).

David Toshio Tsumura

8386 (*rāqîq*, wafer), → Bread

8387	רקם

רקם (*rqm*), q. do the work of an embroiderer, pu. woven together (# 8387); רִקְמָה (*riqmâ*), nom. embroidered (garment, dress, work) (# 8391).

ANE Arab., Eth, and Syr. all have cognates with the same meaning as in Heb.

OT 1. The q. part. occurs 8x in Exodus describing the tabernacle curtains (26:36; 27:16; 36:37; 38:18), the high priest's sash (28:39; 39:29), and the skills of Bezalel and Oholiab (35:35; 38:23).

2. The sole occurrence of the pu. vb. shows God's special care for the psalmist, "I was woven together in the depths of the earth" (Ps 139:15).

3. The nom. *riqmâ* occurs 12x. It specifically refers to embroidered fabric (Judg 5:30; Ps 45:14[15]); Ezek 16:10, 13, 18; 26:16; 27:7, 16, 24). In two places it has to do with different colored semiprecious stones (1 Chron 29:2) and with variegated feathers (Ezek 17:3).

Spinning, sewing, weaving, embroidering: → *'rg* (spin, weave, # 755); → *dallâ* I (hair, thrum, loom, # 1929); → *ḥōšēb* (weaver, # 3110); → *ṭwh* (spin, # 3211); → *kîšôr* (distaff, # 3969); → *mānôr* (rod, # 4962); → *skk* II (weave, intertwine, # 6115); → *'ēreb* I (knitted material, # 6849); → *pelek* I (spindle-whorl, # 7134); → *rqm* (embroider, weave together, # 8387); → *š^{e}rād* (woven, # 8573); → *šbṣ* I (weave, # 8687); → *š^{e}tî* I (woven material, # 9274); → *tpr* (sew, # 9529)

BIBLIOGRAPHY

ANEP, figs. 1-66; *ISBE* 2:401-7; H. F. Lutz, *Textiles and Customs Among the People of the Ancient Near East*, 1923; W. Magass, "Texte und Textilien," *LB* 34, 1975, 23-36; J. Ruppert, *Le costume juif depuis les temps patriarchaux jusqu'à la dispersion (Le costume historique des peuples de l'antiquité)*, 1938.

Robert E. Alden

8391 (*riqmâ*, embroidered garment), → # 8387

8392	רקע

רקע (*rq'*), stamp, hammer out, spread out, beat into plates (# 8392); רָקִיעַ (*rāqîa'*), expanse (→ # 8385); רִקֻּעַ (*riqqua'*), expanse, hammered surface (# 8393).

OT 1. The vb. *rq'* has three distinctive usages in BH. (a) In the q. stem, *rq'* is used by Ezekiel when he stamps his feet as a gesture of God's anger (Ezek 6:11; 25:6; Zimmerli, *Ezekiel 1*, 184). In 2 Sam 22:43 David describes how he smashes (*rq'*) his enemies "like mud in the streets" (the parallel vb., *dqq*, crush, does not appear in 4QSam^{a}; cf. McCarter, *II Samuel*, 461).

(b) In the pi. stem, *rq'* is used of hammering out metals into sheets (Exod 39:3; Num 16:39[17:4]) for purposes of plating objects (Isa 40:19; pu. Jer 10:9). Altars (Num 16:39[17:4]) or idols (Isa 40:19; Fitzgerald, "Isaiah 40:19-20 + 41:6-7," 438) may be plated with bronze or gold.

(c) In both q. and hi. stems, *rqʻ* describes the spreading out of the expanse of the earth (Ps 136:6; Isa 42:5; 44:24) and of the skies (hi. Job 37:18). In these examples, *rqʻ* resembles its nominal form, *rāqîaʻ*, firmament, familiar from Gen 1, where it divides the waters.

2. The term *riqquaʻ*, hammered surface, appears only in Num 16:38[17:3]. It describes the form into which censers are to be made: "Hammer the censers into sheets to overlay the altar." *paḥ* is also associated with the vb. (pi. stem) *rqʻ* in Exod 39:3.

P-B *rqʻ* appears in the Thanksgiving Hymns (1QH) from Qumran. It is probably most closely related to *riqquaʻ* among the forms of *rqʻ* found in the Bible. In col. 3, line 31, it describes the expanse of the *yabbāšâ*, dry land.

Hammer, hammered work: → *halmût* (hammer, # 2153); → *maqqebet* (hollow, hammer, # 5216/17); → *miqšâ* I (hammered work, # 5251); → *paṭṭîš* (hammer, # 7079); → *rqʻ* (hammer out, # 8392)

Bibliography

A. Fitzgerald, "The Technology of Isaiah 40:19-20 + 41:6-7," *CBQ* 51, 1989, 426-46; P. K. McCarter, Jr., *II Samuel: A New Translation with Introduction and Commentary*, AB 9, 1984; W. Zimmerli, *Ezekiel 1: A Commentary on the Book of the Prophet Ezekiel, Chapters 1-24*, Hermeneia, 1979.

Richard S. Hess

8393 (*riqquaʻ*, expanse), → # 8392

8394	רקק

רקק (*rqq*), q. spit at, spit (# 8394); רֹק (*rōq*), nom. masc. spittle or saliva (# 8371).

ANE Sam. Pent. *yrq(q)*, spit; Syr. *raq*, spit.

OT 1. The vb. is found solely in Lev 15:8. When a person who is unclean spits on one who is clean, the heretofore clean person is rendered unclean. Levine understands this verse to be both a matter of health and holiness. He writes, "Spittle was considered to carry infection and disease" (Levine, *Leviticus*, 94). Elsewhere, he notes, "Any prevailing impurity within the Israelite community, threatened ... the purity of the sanctuary" (93). Unclean individuals were always prohibited access to the sanctuary regardless of the type of impurity involved.

2. The nom. *rōq* is found twice in Job 30:10 and once in Job 7:19 and Isa 50:6. The coupling of *k^e^limmôt* (insults) with *rōq* in Isa may be understood as a hendiadys, meaning all kind of insults, both verbal and acted out. In Isa and Job, God is the ultimate cause of the mistreatment of the prophet and Job by others. In Job 7:19, spittle is used in a phrase indicating a brief period of time: "Will you never ... let me alone even for an instant?"

Spittle, saliva: → *yrq* I (spit, spew, # 3762a); → *rîr* (spittle, juice, slime, # 8202); → *rqq* (spit at, spit, # 8394); → *tōpet* I (spit, # 9531)

Bibliography

B. A. Levine, *The JPS Torah Commentary Leviticus*, 1989.

Wilma Ann Bailey

8398 (*ršm*, written), → Writing

8399	רשׁע

רשׁע (*rš‘*), q. act wickedly, unrighteously, to be guilty, wicked; hi. pronounce guilty, in the wrong (# 8399); מִרְשַׁעַת (*mirša‘at*), nom. wicked, wicked woman (hapleg., 2 Chron 24:7, # 5360); רֶשַׁע (*reša‘*), nom. wickedness, evil, unrighteousness (# 8400); רָשָׁע (*rāšā‘*), adj. evil person, wicked, evil, unjust, wrong (# 8401); רִשְׁעָה (*riš‘â*), nom. guilt, wickedness, evil (# 8402).

ANE Cognates have been suggested in Ugar. *rš‘*, transgress; Aram. *r*^{e}*ša‘*, be wicked; Syr. *r*^{e}*ša‘*, act wickedly; *rašî‘*, wicked.

OT The use of *rš‘* always includes the idea of wickedness, evil intent, and injustice against God or persons. The vb. and its cognates occur 343x in the OT, most frequently in Job (40x), Ps (92x), Prov (87x), and Ezek (37x). Its most appropriate antonym is *ṣdq* (# 7405), to act, do righteously. In contrast to *ṣdq*, *rāšā‘* signifies negative behavior of evil thoughts, words, and deeds that are not only contrary to God's character, but are also hostile to the surrounding community. At times *rāšā‘* manifests the inner disharmony and unrest of a man (Isa 48:22; 57:20) (*THAT* 2:814). The vb. *rš‘* can delineate ruptures in social (Deut 25:1; Ps 94:21) or international relationships (1 Sam 14:47) or serve as a reference to conduct contrary to God's laws (1 Kgs 8:32; Prov 17:15; Dan 12:10).

1. *Judicial pronouncement of guilt/wickedness.* The vb. occurs 34x (q.-9x, hi.-25x; various lexical sources identify *l*^{e}*riš‘â* in Ezek 5:6 as an inf. const. rather than an instance of the noun *riš‘â* and consequently find 35 examples of the vb.) and appears to be a denom. vb. derived from the nom. *rešā‘*. In the q. it refers to wicked conduct, while in the hi. it can connote either wicked conduct or the pronouncement of guilt.

Several instances of the hi. denote the pronouncement of guilt against a judicial background. A forensic nuance is esp. prominent in Deut 25:1, where a tribal court adjudicates an interpersonal dispute, acquitting the innocent (*ṣdq ... ṣaddîq*) and condemning the guilty (*rš‘... rāšā‘*), and in Exod 22:9[8], where judges pronounce guilt in cases of misappropriated property (cf. 1 Kgs 8:32). Any reversal of true justice, i.e., acquitting the guilty and condemning the innocent (Prov 17:15, the above pattern is perverted, *ṣdq ... rāšā‘ ... rš‘... ṣaddîq*) constitutes an abomination before Yahweh (cf. Isa 50:9). Job describes his experience of affliction in courtroom terms when he refers to his suffering as a divine guilty verdict (Job 9:29; 10:2).

2. *Acting wickedly/wickedness.* Most of the q. and some of the hi. forms of *rš‘* signify conduct that is wicked. Several Heb. kings during the divided monarchy period were renowned for their wicked lifestyle (2 Chron 20:35; 22:3). In his song of praise, David does not claim to be sinless but affirms that he never departed from Yahweh by acting wickedly (2 Sam 22:22). The sincere confession of wicked conduct is an integral part of covenant renewal (1 Kgs 8:47 = 2 Chron 6:37; Neh 9:33; Dan 9:5).

The nom. forms *reša‘* (30x) and *riš‘â* (15x) denote an abstract sense of wickedness or an act of wickedness. Like the adj. *rāšā‘* (see below), the nom. *reša‘* occurs most frequently in Wisdom literature (17x) and Ezek (4x) and represents the precise opposite of righteousness (*ṣedeq/ṣ*^{e}*dāqâ*, → # 7406/7407). It also refers to treasures gained through wickedness (Mic 6:10) and false scales (scales of wickedness, Mic 6:11). The less common nom. *riš'â* refers to the wickedness of Canaanite peoples (Deut 9:4-5) and the wicked conduct of God's people that occasioned their exile from Jerusalem (Ezek 5:6; 18:20, 27; 33:12, 19). In two passages it serves as the par. antonym for *ṣ^{e}dāqâ* (Prov 11:5; 13:6). Malachi (1:4) applies the title "Wicked Land," lit., territory of wickedness (*g^{e}bûl riš'â*), to Edom because they will continually face Yahweh's wrath and judgment.

3. *The wicked person.* The adj. *rāšā'* is the most frequently occurring cognate, occurring 263x. Out of the nineteen OT books in which it appears, the vast majority of instances (214x) occur in Wisdom literature (Job-26x, Ps-82x, Prov-78x) and Ezek (28x). Although the adj. can mean guilty, criminal, or godless, most often it serves as a reference to those who are characterized by wickedness.

The wicked person is equated or compared by means of par. to workers of iniquity (*pō'^{a}lê 'āwen*, Ps 28:3; 92:7[8]; 101:8; 141:9-10), evildoers (*m^{e}rē'îm*, 26:5; 37:9-10; Prov 24:19), evil men (*rā'*, Ps 10:15; Prov 4:14; 14:19; 24:20), the ruthless (*'ārîṣ*, Job 15:20; 27:13; Isa 13:11), sinners (*ḥaṭā'ṭ*, Ps 1:1, 5; 104:35), scorners (*lēṣ*, Ps 1:1; Prov 9:7), liars (*mirmâ*, Ps 58:3[4]; 109:2), transgressors (*bōgēd*, Prov 2:22; 21:18; Jer 12:1; Hab 1:13), and the enemy (*'ōyēb*, Job 27:7; Ps 3:7[8]; 17:9; 55:3[4]).

(a) *Psalms.* In the Psalter *rāšā'* designates the wicked person who stands diametrically opposed to the *ṣaddîq* (→ # 7404), i.e., God's saints (37:28), those who love God (145:20), and those who wait on the Lord (32:10). In a word, he is the archenemy of the godly individual (68:2[3]). In fact, he hates the righteous (34:21[22]).

This wicked person lives as a practical atheist. There is no room in his thoughts for God (Ps 10:4), nor is there any fear of God in his eyes (36:1[2]). As the enemy of Yahweh (37:20), he hates God (68:1-2[2-3]). His mouth is full of curses and threats (10:7). In arrogance, he reviles God (10:3). He has no worries that God might intervene with his perversion (10:13). Since God has forgotten and does not see the wicked man's conduct (10:11), his innocent victims are without defense.

In addition to being the enemy of God's people, he is the oppressor of the poor (Ps 10:2; 37:14), needy (37:14; 82:4), widows, orphans, and strangers (a triad that occurs twice, in 94:3-6, as the object of the wicked person's hatred). The day will come when his own children will become fatherless and his wife a widow (109:9, 12). While Yahweh will watch over the widows, orphans, and strangers, he will frustrate the ways of the wicked (the other occurrence of this triad, 146:9).

Kraus (130-31) points out three metaphors in Ps that illustrate the uncanny and gruesome attacks of the wicked (and other enemies of God's people) upon the righteous. (i) The *rāšā'* are likened to a hostile army that attacks the helpless and surrounds them with overwhelming forces (Ps 3:7[8]; cf. 27:3; 55:18[19]; 56:1[2]; 59:1-3[2-4]). (ii) The enemies of godly individuals are compared with hunters or fishermen who seek their prey (9:15-16[16-17]; 10:8-10; 140:4-5[5-6]). (iii) The wicked are depicted as wild, ravenous animals (like a lion, 17:12), having sharp teeth for tearing the flesh of their victims (3:7[8]).

(b) *Proverbs.* As with Ps, *ṣaddîq* and *rāšā'* serve as bipolar terms throughout Prov (45x). While, on the one hand, *ṣaddîq* delineates loyal, reliable conduct based on a commitment to God and his covenant (Hubbard, 143), *rāšā'* represents the opposite of *ṣaddîq*. It connotes disloyalty to Yahweh, rebellion against the covenant standards, and total disregard for the welfare of fellow citizens (Hubbard, 143). Like wisdom and folly, righteousness and wickedness do not refer to specific acts performed in a moment of decision. Rather, they signify chosen patterns of life and ingrained attitudes/dispositions. The wicked person's rejection of any divine expectations and hostility toward fellow members of the covenant community parallels that of Ps (see above).

Proverbs provides several insights into the fate of the wicked. Their reputation will be like rotten wood (Prov 10:7). God will reject all their desires (10:3), and all their hopes will come to nothing (10:28; 11:8, 10). Their worst fears will be realized (10:24). The wicked person will know nothing but calamity (12:21, depicted as a relentless hunter in 11:19), as well as contempt and reproach (18:3). He will flee even when there are no pursuers (28:1) and eventually will be driven off to death (14:32). Without a future dwelling place awaiting him (10:30), he is overthrown by God (21:12) and is swept away like chaff (10:25).

(c) *Job*. The adj. *rāšā'* appears 26x, most often in one of Job's speeches (13x). In his dialogue or disputation with his three friends (Job 3-27), Bildad (8:22; 18:5), Zophar (11:20; 20:5, 29), and Eliphaz (15:20) refer to the wicked as an illustration to help Job understand their belief that his wickedness has occasioned his present suffering. According to them, the wicked experience nothing but torment (15:20) and only short bursts of joy (20:5). Their hope is like a dying gasp (11:20) because God will snuff out their lives (18:5; cf. 8:22; 20:29).

Job knew about the customary fate of the wicked (Job 3:17; 27:13), but found his own experience of suffering and accusations of wickedness unsettling. He realized that his friends' statements about the destiny of the wicked did not always come to pass (21:7, 17). He complained that God oppressed him while giving the wicked freedom to carry out their vile schemes (10:3). Job came to the conclusion that God brought destruction upon the blameless and wicked alike (9:22). Elihu sought to guide Job toward a proper understanding of God's dealings with humankind. God knows who the wicked are (34:18), punishing them accordingly (34:26; 36:6), and he delivers the afflicted from their suffering (36:6). Elihu exhorted Job to respond to his suffering (painfully similar to that promised to the wicked) properly (36:17).

Yahweh has the final word about the wicked. He does not violate his character by overlooking the sin of the wicked person, but judges them severely (Job 38:13, 15; 40:12).

4. *The nom. miršaʿat*. This hapleg. serves as a descriptive term for Queen Athaliah, who was the embodiment of wickedness.

5. *rš' and other Heb. words for sin* (see *ABD*, 6:31-32; Eichrodt, 2:380-81; Oehler, 160). The most common Heb. roots for sin are *ḥaṭṭa't* (# 2633), *'āwōn* (# 6411), and *peša'* (# 7322). Building on the basic meaning to miss the mark, *ḥaṭṭa't* refers to a failure with regard to a norm, i.e., falling short of a standard. It signifies both intentional and unintentional sins. The nom. *'āwōn* primarily designates the character of an action rather than act itself. It highlights a deviation or twisting of a standard (with full knowledge of its significance). *peša'* draws on the language of politics for its fundamental meaning. It represents some kind of rebellion or revolt against God's laws or, more specifically, the covenant. Consequently, it connotes more than a legal offense but signifies covenant treachery. Like *ṣaddîq*, *rš'* draws on juristic concepts

where the person is vindicated by the court or pronounced guilty. However, it is more than a legal term. It connotes the inner nature of the guilty person when evil has become a habitual feature of one's disposition and actions. Finally, *'šm* (# 870) emphasizes the idea of culpability, primarily in the context of Israelite regulations concerning sacrifices. The terms *'āwōn* and *'šm* can encompass the sin itself or the resultant guilt, as well as its punishment. Both *ḥaṭṭa't* and *'šm* can encompass both intentional and unintentional sin.

P-B *rš'* and its cognates occur widely in LH and are attested about 180x in the DSS (*rš'*-30x, *rāšā'*-over 60x, *rešā'/riš'â*-90x). In QL this word family does not serve primarily as an antonym for righteousness. Rather, these terms focus on the Qumranic dualism between the Teacher of Righteousness and the wicked priest (*hakkōhēn hārāšā'*), who stands out among all the opponents of the Qumran community. The wicked priest apparently served as the leader of a group that broke away from the Teacher of Righteousness and eventually caused several to defect. A number of passages attribute various sins to this wicked priest, including abusive treatment of the Teacher of Righteousness (1QPHab 5:9; 8:8; 9:1, 9, 11; 10:5; 11:4; 12:2, 8; 4QPIsa^c 30:3; 4QpPs 37:4, 8). The Thanksgiving Hymns describe various experiences of a religious teacher (probably the Teacher of Righteousness). Because he lived in the midst of wickedness (1QH 2:8; 3:24), the community of sinners stormed against him (1QH 2:12), casting affliction (1QH 5:17), fright (1QH 2:36), and slander (1QH 2:10) his way. In spite of this intense opposition, he enjoyed God's strength (1QH 7:7) and rested in the knowledge that God had condemned the wicked (1QH 2:24).

Guilt, evil, unrighteousness: → *'šm* (become guilty, incur guilt, bear guilt, pronounce guilty, # 870); → *dām* (blood, bloodshed, blood-guilt, murder, # 1947); → *wāzār* (unjust, laden with guilt, # 2261); → *ḥwb* (be the cause of guilt, # 2549); → *ḥēṭ'* (sin, guilt, punishment of sin, # 2628); → *nqh* (be free, exempt from guilt, remain unpunished, # 5927); → *rš'* (act wickedly, unrighteously, be guilty, pronounce guilty, # 8399)
Sin, guilt, rebellion, transgression, wrong: → *'āwen* (mischief, iniquity, deception, # 224); → *ḥṭ'* (sin, commit a sin, purify, # 2627); → *'wh* (do wrong, pervert, # 6390); → *'wl* I (act wrongly, # 6401); → *pš'* (rebel, violate, transgress, # 7321); → **Fall: Theology**

BIBLIOGRAPHY

ABD 6:31-40; *IDB* 4:361-76; *THAT* 2:813-18; *TWAT* 7:675-84; *TWOT* 2:863-64; W. Eichrodt, *Theology of the Old Testament*, 1967; D. Hubbard, *Proverbs*, 1989; H.-J. Kraus, *Theology of the Psalms*, 1986; G. Oehler, *TOT*, 1883.

Eugene Carpenter/Michael A. Grisanti

8400 (*reša'*, wickedness, evil, unrighteousness), → # 8399

8401 (*rāšā'*, evil person, wicked, unjust, wrong), → # 8399

8402 (*riš'â*, guilt, wickedness, evil), → # 8399

8404	רֶשֶׁף

רֶשֶׁף (*rešep* I), nom. flame, glow, arrow, plague (# 8404).

OT 1. The nom. has as referents bolts of lightning (Ps 78:48), sparks of a fire (Job 5:7), flames or glow of a fire (S of Songs 8:6), or arrows (= flashes of a bow) (Ps 76:3[4]).

2. This name for a Ugaritic deity carried in Israel the meaning of "flame" (*KAI* # 15; *KTU* 1, 91, 11; M. de Tarragon, *Le culte à Ugarit,* 1980, 108). It was also used metaphorically for a devastating disease, identified with pestilence or plague as a punishment for apostasy (Deut 32:24; Hab 3:5). See Craigie, *The Book of Deuteronomy*, 384-85.

Fire, flame: → *'ûd* (log, burning stick, # 202); → *'ēš* I (fire, # 836); → *b'r* I (burn, blaze up, be consumed, # 1277); → *gaḥelet* (burning charcoal, # 1625); → *goprît* (sulphur, # 1730); → *yṣt* (kindle, burn, set on fire, # 3675); → *yqd* (burn, be burning, kindled, # 3678); → *kîdôd* (spark, # 3958); → *lbb* II (bake cakes, # 4221); → *lahab* (flame, blade, # 4258); → *lhṭ* I (glow, burn, # 4265); → *lappîd* (torch, lightning, # 4365); → *nîṣôṣ* (spark, # 5773); → *peḥām* (charcoal, # 7073); → *reṣep* I (live coal, # 8363); → *rešep* I (flame, glow, arrow, plague, # 8404); → *śrp* (burn, be burnt, # 8596); → *šābîb* (flame, # 8663)
Disease—plague: → *deber* I (bubonic plague, # 1822); → *ṭᵉḥōrîm* (plague, # 3224); → *maggēpâ* (plague, # 4487); → *nega'* (plague, affliction, # 5596); → *rešep* I (pestilence, # 8404); → *ṣr'* (suffer from skin disease, # 7665). For related entries → *ḥlh* I (become weak, tired, ill, # 2703); → **Plagues: Theology**

BIBLIOGRAPHY
ISBE 1:532, 953-60; 3:103-6.

Jackie A. Naudé/R. K. Harrison

8406	רשׁשׁ

רשׁשׁ (*ršš*), po. cut/break apart = destroy; pu. be broken apart = crushed (# 8406).

ANE Syr. *raš*, ethpe. be pounded, beaten, hammered; pa. crush, chew; ethp. be husked; ettap. be broken small; Ugar. *rš*, crushed (*KTU* 1.14 i 10; either G or Gp).

OT The vb. occurs in Jer 5:17 in the poel stem, where it takes a direct object. Here, in a prophecy of disaster, Yahweh claims that a distant nation will come against Judah creating havoc and destruction; indeed, it will come with a sword that will cut/break apart, i.e., "destroy the fortified cities" (NIV). In the very next verse, however, Yahweh promises that Judah will not be destroyed completely. In Mal 1:4 Edom claims that though they have been crushed, i.e., broken apart, they will rebuild the ruins, a claim immediately countered by Yahweh.

P-B The root occurs in the hitpol. stem with the sense of being stamped upon or crushed. A substantive *rᵉšāšîn* refers to clods of broken earth in need of crushing (Niddah 8).

Shattering, breaking, destroying: → *mḥq* (strike, # 4735); → *npṣ* I (break, smash, # 5879); → *pṣṣ* (pulverize, crush, # 7207); → *rṭš* (smash, strike down, # 8187); → *r'ṣ* (shatter, # 8320); → *ršš* (destroy, crushed, # 8406); → *šbr* I (break, shatter, # 8689)

Gary Alan Long

8407	רֶשֶׁת

רֶשֶׁת (*rešet*), nom. net, network (# 8407); possibly deriving from the root ירשׁ (*yrš*), take possession of (→ # 3769).

OT 1. The most common word for a net, including fishing nets, is the nom. *rešet*, which is found 22x in the OT. Theologically the term is most often used in the context of the plots of the wicked to catch the righteous (e.g., Ps 10:9; Prov 29:5; Hos 5:1). The righteous, however, put their trust in God for deliverance and at times for revenge, that the wicked may be caught in their own traps (Ps 9:15[16]; cf. 35:7-8, where the action of setting nets and digging pits form a poetic balance).

2. *rešet* is used of God's punishment particularly upon his people Israel (e.g., Lam 1:13). Ezek 12:13 speaks of God's catching the prince of Israel in his net (see also 17:20); in similar vein 32:3 describes God's netting Pharaoh (see *ANEP*, 288, with a Mesop. king catching prisoners in a net). So *rešet* is related strongly to the idea of the judgment of God.

P-B The NT uses three different words for net: *sagēnē*, with the sense of a dragnet (Matt 13:47-50); *amphiblēstron*, which is used for a casting net in Matt 4:18, along with the more common term for fishing nets, *diktuon* (John 21:6). The nets used today on Galilee are throw-nets weighted at the edges, and these may well be the same as those of NT times. In the parable of the net (Matt 13:47-50), which Jesus uses to describe the coming reign of God, a strong sense of judgment is again present.

Hunting: → *yqš* (lay a trip wire, set a trap, # 3704); → *paḥ* I (trap, snare, # 7062); → *ṣwd* (hunt, # 7421); → *rešet* (net, # 8407); → *šûḥâ* I (pit, # 8757)

BIBLIOGRAPHY
A. Negev, ed., *Archaeological Encyclopaedia of the Holy Land*, 1972, 149-50.

W. R. Domeris

8408 (*rattôq*, chain), → # 8415

8409 (*rtḥ*, bring to a boil), → Baking

8410 (*retaḥ*, boiling), → Baking

8412	רתם

רתם (*rtm*), q. tie up (hapleg.; # 8412).

OT Micah calls on the people of Lachish to prepare for war by hitching (*rtm*) horses to chariots (Mic 1:13).

Band, tie: → *'pd* (put on tightly, # 679); → *'ᵃpēr* (bandage, # 710); → *'eṣ'ādâ* (band, # 731); → *ḥbš* (tie up, saddle, imprison, bind, # 2502); → *ḥgr* (bind, gird, # 2520); → *ḥāšûq* (clasp ring, # 3122); → *ḥtl* (be swaddled, # 3156); → *keset* (band [for magic purposes], # 4086); → *migbā'â* (head-band, # 4457); → *'nd* (wind, tie s.t., # 6698); → *'qd* (tie up, # 6818); → *ṣrr* I (bind, tie up, # 7674); → *qšr* (ally together, conspire, bind, # 8003); → *rks* (bind, tie, # 8220); → *rtm* (tie up, # 8412)

T. Desmond Alexander

8415	רתק

רתק (*rtq*), pu. be bound (# 8415); רַתּוֹק (*rattôq*), nom. chain (txt. problem?; # 8408); רַתּוּקָה (*rattûqâ*), nom. chain (hapleg. in 1 Kgs 6:21; # 8408); רְתֻקָה (r^e*tuqâ*), nom. chain (# 8416).

OT 1. The vb. *rtq* expresses the fate of exiles, "Yet she (Thebes) was taken captive and went into exile. Her infants were dashed to pieces at the head of every street. Lots were cast for her nobles, and all her great men were put in chains" (Nah 3:10). The Q. in Eccl 12:6 has a privative ni. form (Gordis, 347), with the meaning sever: "Remember him—before the silver cord is severed."

2. For a discussion of the problem of *rattôq* in Ezekiel 7:23, according to which the Judeans will go and be bound in chains into exile because of their sinfulness, see Brownlee, *Ezekiel 1-19*, 113.

3. Decorative gold chains (*rattûqâ*) extended across "the front of the inner sanctuary" of the Solomonic temple (1 Kgs 6:21).

4. The word r^e*tuqâ* occurs only in Isa 40:19 in the polemic against idolatry, "As for an idol, a craftsman casts it, and a goldsmith overlays it with gold and fashions silver chains for it."

Chain, fetter: → *'sr* (bind, imprison, fetter, hitch, # 673); → *zēq* I (chain, fetter, # 2414); → *ḥarṣōb* (chain, fetter, # 3078); → *kebel* (shackle, # 3890); → *migbālôt* (chains, # 4456); → *mahpeket* (stocks, # 4551); → *mōsēr* (fetters, chains, # 4591); → *sad* (stocks, shackles, # 6040); → *pḥḥ* (be captured, chained, # 7072); → *rtq* (be bound, # 8415); → *šarš*^{e}*râ* (chain, # 9249)
Idolatry: → *'*^{e}*lîl* (Nothing, # 496); → *'*^{a}*šērâ* (wooden cult-object, pole, goddess, # 895); → *gillûlîm* (images, idols, # 1658); → *dāgôn* (Dagon, # 1837); → *k*^{e}*môš* (Chemosh [god of the Moabites], # 4019); → *mōlek* (Molech, # 4891); → *massēkâ* I (cast statuette, # 5011); → *mipleṣet* (terrible thing, dreadful object, # 5145); → *semel* (image, # 6166); → *'āṣāb* (god-image, # 6773); → *'aštōret* (Astarte, # 6956); → *pesel* (cultic image, statue of a god, # 7181); → *tōmer* II (scarecrow, # 9473); → *t*^{e}*rāpîm* (figurines, mask, # 9572); → **Idolatry: Theology**
Prison, restraint, closure: → *'*^{a}*sēpâ* (imprisonment, # 669); → *'sr* (bind, imprison, fetter, hitch, # 673); → *kl'* I (detain, imprison, close, shut up, # 3973); → *misgeret* (stronghold, dungeon, rim, table, # 4995); → *sgr* (close, # 6037); → *sōhar* (prison, # 6045); → *'ṣr* (restrain, imprison, stop, close, # 6806)

T. Desmond Alexander

8416 (r^e*tuqâ*, chain), → # 8415

8417	רְתֵת

רְתֵת (r^e*tēt*), nom. terror, panic, trembling (# 8417).

OT r^e*tēt* occurs only in Hos 13:1. The LXX, however, records *dikaiōmata*, ordinances, reading (by transposition of the first two root letters) the more frequently occurring *tôrôt*, laws (→ *tôrâ*, # 9368). Wolff, supporting the MT, explains that "this word is now attested in 1QH 4, 33, with the meaning horror, as also found in ancient Greek versions" (Wolff, 219). Thus the integrity of the MT is also supported.

Shaking, terror, trembling: → *g'š* (rise and fall noisily, swell, surge, # 1723); → *zw'* (tremble, quake, be afraid, # 2316); → *zll* II (shake, quake, tremble, # 2362); → *ḥalḥālâ* (shaking, trembling, anguish, # 2714); → *ḥrg* (come out trembling, # 3004); → *ḥrd* (tremble, shudder, startle, # 3006); → *yr'* (tremble, be fainthearted, # 3760); → *mwṭ* (waver, reel, stagger, shake, reel, # 4572); → *m'd* (slip, slide, shake, totter, # 5048); → *nwd* (shake, totter, waiver, wander, mourn, flee, # 5653); → *nwṭ* (shake, quake, # 5667); → *nw'* (shake, tremble, stagger, totter, wave, # 5675); → *n'r* II (shake, shake off, # 5850); → *smr* (shudder, have goose-bumps, bristle, # 6169); → *'iw'îm* (distortion, stagger, dizzy, # 6413); → *pwq* I (stagger, wobble, reel, totter, # 7048); → *pḥd* I (tremble, be in dread, # 7064); → *plṣ* (shudder, shake, tremble, # 7145); → *qwṣ* I (feel disgust, frighten, cause dread, # 7762); → *rgz* (agitate, quiver, shake, excite, rouse up, agitate, # 8074); → *rnh* I (rattle, # 8261); → *r'd* (tremble, shake, tremble, # 8283); → *r'l* I (brandish, make to quiver, # 8302); → *r'š* I (quake, shake, leap, # 8321); → *rpp* (shake, quake, rock, # 8344); → *r^{e}tēt* (terror, panic, trembling, # 8417); → *ś'r* I (be afraid, terrified, bristle with horror, # 8547)

BIBLIOGRAPHY

F. I. Anderson and D. N. Freedman, *Hosea*, AB, 1980; H. W. Wolff, *Hosea*, Hermeneia, 1974.

M. V. Van Pelt/W. C. Kaiser, Jr.

שׂ

8419 (ś^e'ōr, leaven), → Bread

8421 שְׂאֵת

שְׂאֵת (ś^e'ēt II), swelling, blotch (# 8421).

OT This condition, mentioned in Lev 13:2-43; 14:56, would be regarded by the priest on examination as potentially malignant. It appears to have been some form of blotch, i.e., a pimple (papule) or a small pustule that had potential for growth. But so little is known about the term that it could have been applied equally well to any minor cutaneous lesion. Because of the potential for infection, anyone exhibiting this swelling was required to submit to priestly examination so that the ceremonial purity of the people would not be threatened. Milgrom prefers "discoloration," observing that it cannot refer to swelling since it is lower than the surrounding skin (*Leviticus 1-16*, AB, 773).

Disease—blister, boil, skin disease, scar, wound: → *'^{a}ba'bu'ōt* (blisters, # 81); → *bōhaq* (skin condition, # 993); → *baheret* (white patch on skin, # 994); → *gārāb* (festering eruption, # 1734); → *zrr* I (press out [wounds], # 2452); → *ḥeres* I (itch, # 3063); → *yabbelet* (wart?, # 3301); → *yallepet* (skin disease, # 3539); → *y^{e}raqraq* (discoloration, # 3768); → *k^{e}wiyya* (scar, # 3918); → *m'r* (be sore, # 4421); → *māzôr* I (boil, # 4649); → *makkâ* (blow, # 4804); → *mispaḥat* (skin eruption, # 5030); → *mrḥ* (rub, polish, # 5302); → *neteq* (scalp infection, # 5999); → *sappaḥat* (hair disease, # 6204); → *'ōpel* I (abscesses, # 6754); → *'āš* II (pus, # 6932); → *ṣāpâ* (pus?, # 7597); → *ṣarebet* (scar, # 7648); → *ṣr'* (suffer from skin disease, # 7665); → *ś^e'ēt* II (swelling, # 8421); → *śtr* (break out [tumor], # 8609); → *š^{e}ḥîn* (boil, # 8825). For related entries → *ḥlh* I (become weak, tired, ill, # 2703)

BIBLIOGRAPHY

ISBE 1:532, 953-60; 3:103-6; G. J. Wenham, *The Book of Leviticus*, NICOT, 1979, 189-214.

R. K. Harrison

8422 (ś^{e}bākâ, lattice, net), → # 580; 2707; 8449

8425 שׂבע

שׂבע (śb'), q. be satiated; be satisfied (with solid foods or potable liquids) (78x); ni. be satisfied (hapleg.); pi. make satiated/satisfied (2x), hi. let/make . . . be satiated/satisfied (16x) (vb. 97x; # 8425; *HALAT* 1214b-15b); adj. שָׂבֵעַ(*śābēa'*), satiated; satisfied (10x; # 8428; *HALAT* 1215b-16a); nom. שָׂבָע (*śābā'*), satiety; plenty; produce/grain(?) (8x; # 8426; *HALAT* 1216a); שֹׂבַע (*śōba'*), satiety, plenty (8x; # 8427; *HALAT* 1216a); שָׂבְעָה(*śob'â*), satiety, plenty (6x; # 8429; *HALAT* 1216a-b); שִׂבְעָה(*śib'â*), byform of *śob'â*; satiety (hapleg.; # 8430; *HALAT* 1216b).

ANE Cognates of the Heb. vb. *śb'* are widely attested among the Sem. languages, though reflexes of the sibilant vary (cf. Voigt, 111). Vb. cognates may be found in Akk. *šebû(m),* satiate oneself, be satiated (*AHw* 3:1207a-b; *CAD*, *Š*/2, 251b-55b); an Eblaite personal nom. *áš-ba-il*, "I was satisfied, O El" (Pettinato, 187; Müller, 226); Ugar. *šb'*, be satiated; satisfied (*WUS* # 2579; *UT* # 2380; *CML*[2], 158a); Ancient Aram. *šb'*, be satiated; satisfied (*KAI* 3:42b; *DISO* 289; on *š* for *ś*, see Degen, § 57 [68]; cf. *śb'* in Rosenthal, *Aramaic Handbook*, I/2, 6b); Egyp. Aram. *šb'*, be satiated; satisfied (*DISO* 289; on *š* for *ś*, see Leander, 10p); Palmyrene *šb'*, be satiated; satisfied (*DISO* 289; cf. Cantineau, 42; Rosenthal, *Sprache*, 38f.); Sam. *s/śb'*, be satisfied; Ma'lūla *śb'* (Bergstrasser, 69); OSA *šb'*, sate (with water for irrigation); satisfy (Conti-Rossini, 247; Biella, 510-11; Beeston et al., *Sabaic*, 131); Arab. *šabi'a,* be satiated, full; satisfied (Wehr, 452a); Eth. *ṣagba* (*LLA*, col. 1315f; *GVGSS*, 1:169dβ, 239 §88a; cf. Ge'ez *šabḥa,* be/grow fat [*LLA*, col. 248; Tomback, 311]). The Ugar. vb. *šb'*, be satiated, forms a word pair with the vb. *šty*, drink (*RSP*, 3, i 296a-c, g [154-55]; cf. *mlk* reign ‖ *šb'*, satisfy, in *RSP*, 1, ii 364a-d [267]; *mr'u*, be fat ‖ *šb'*, satisfy, in *RSP*, 2, i 39a-d, f [22-23]).

Cognates of the adj. appear in Akk. *šē/ebû(m),* filling, satisfying (*AHw* 3:1207b; *CAD*, *Š*/2, 251b), and Old Babylonian (Mari) *šabī'u(m)*, satiated (one); satisfied (one) (*AHw* 3:1120a; *CAD*, *Š*/1, 11b); Sam. *s/śbîa',* satisfied, full (cf. Sam. Pent. *šēbi*); OSA *šb'*, sufficient, copious, abundant, overflowing (Beeston, "Correspondence," 56); and in Arab. *šab'ān,* satiated, sated; rich, and (part.) *mušabba',* satiated, saturated (with); replete, filled (with) (Wehr, 452b).

A nom. cognate seems attested in Akk. *šib'um*, *šību* (II), satiety, satisfaction (*AHw* 3:1229b; *CAD*, *Š*/2, 389b). Ugar. may have a nom. *šb'*, satiety (in RS 24. 258, Obv. 3, 16 [= *KTU* 1. 114 3, 16]; so Segert, 201b; de Moor, 135, 136), though some sources cite these attestations as verbal (so *RSP*, 3, i 296d-f [155]). Although Ugar. *šb't*, in *KTU* 1. 3 II 19, was regarded as a nom. by C. H. Gordon (*UT*, # 2380, re *'nt* II, 19), most now understand it to be a fem. vb., as also the same form in *KTU* 1. 17 II 6, 20 (see *CML*[2] 104; de Moor, 230, 231; contra *HALAT* 1216b). The use of a nom. *šb'* in *KTU* 1. 17 I 31 is also disputed (*pace HALAT* 1216a; see *CML*[2] 104; de Moor, 228). Phoen. has a nom. *šb'*, satiety, produce/grain, which may be related to the Heb. nom. *śābā'*, satiety, plenty, produce/grain(?) (Prov 3:10?) (*DISO* 289; Tomback, 311; on *š* for *ś*, see Harris, 21; Friedrich, §44). Punic has a nom. *šb't*, abundance, plenty (*DISO* 289). Sam. has nom. *s/śb'*, satiety; fertility (cf. Sam. Pent. *šāba*). OSA has nom. *šb'(m),* satiety; satisfaction (Conti-Rossini, 247; Biella, 511; cf. Beeston, "Correspondence," 56); Arab. has nom. forms *šab',* satiety, fullness, plenty; *šib',* something that fills, satisfies; *šub'a(t),* a filling, sufficient amount; and *'išbā',* satiation, filling, satisfaction (cf. Wehr, 452b).

OT 1. A state of satiation is the result of having eaten or drunk to the point of fullness (cf. contexts where *śb'* follows/parallels *'kl*, eat: e.g., Exod 16:8; Deut 8:10;

Isa 44:16; or *šth*, drink [Hab 2:16]; or *škr*, be drunk [Hag 1:6]). In contexts where *rwh*, be saturated, sated (→ # 8115), refers to the effect of drinking potable liquids, its parallel, *śb'*, be satiated, refers to the state resulting from eating solid foods (Job 10:15[?]; Jer 31:14; 46:10; Lam 3:15 [hi.]). Similarly, the Heb. vb. *śb'*, be satiated (→ # 8425), may refer to the effect of drinking liquids, when forming a word pair with the vb. *šth*, drink (→ # 9272; Hab 2:16 [of drink]; Amos 4:8 [of water]) (*RSP*, 3, i 296h, j, l [155]; though, contra 3, i 296i, *śb'* in Hag 1:6 forms a word pair with *škr*, be drunk (→ # 8910), not with *šth*).

In the OT Yahweh/God is portrayed as the Creator-Provider, who satiates/satisfies the earth with rain (Ps 104:13), trees with water (104:16), animals with "what is good" (*ṭôb*, 104:28 ‖ *'oklām*, their food, v. 27b), and his people with food (Exod 16:8; Jer 50:19 [as sheep that graze]; cf. Ps 37:19; *ṭûbî*, my goods/produce [‖ *dešen*, fatness], Jer 31:14)—and he requires acknowledgment for such (Deut 6:11b-12; 8:10, 12[-17]; cf. 31:20; Hos 13:6 [2x]).

However, satiation is not always a desirable state—especially when it involves self-indulgence. Because satiety was charactistically the domain of kings, OT royal proverbs warn against knavish kings who indulge undeservedly this privilege of rank. To that end, the Heb. vb. *mlk*, reign ‖ *śb'*, be satiated, in a numerical proverb that includes, among the four things under which a land collapses, "a servant when he reigns, and a fool when he is satisfied with food" (author tr.) (Prov 30:22) (*RSP*, 1, ii 364e [267]). One may compare the synonymous adj./nom. *šetî*, satiety/drunkenness, which appears in an analogous royal saying, commending a land whose king and princes "eat at a proper time—for strength and not for drunkenness (*šᵉtî*)" (Eccl 10:17).

Sometimes *śb'* connotes having to endure something to the brink of what is tolerable. In a disputational rejection of ritual compensation, Yahweh protests: "I Amos satiated (*śāba'tî*; i.e., fed up) with offerings of rams and the fat of fatlings" (author tr.) (Isa 1:11; though, contra M. Dahood [*RSP*, 2, i 39e-f (22-23)], the Heb. nom. *mᵉrî'*, fatling, does not here form a word pair with the vb. *śb'*, be sated).

2. The vb. is used in various contexts where Yahweh/God acts as an adversarial judge. Ironically, he satiates personified Jerusalem with the bitter herbs of his wrath (Lam 3:15); or carrion-eating birds and beasts with the carcasses of Gog's horses, charioteers, and soldiers (Ezek 39:20); or by his wisdom surfeits the fool with his own devices (Prov 1:31). To those who would make their neighbor drink wine only to take advantage of him when drunk, Yahweh counters, "You will be filled (*śāba'tā*) with shame, instead of glory ... drink (*šᵉtēh*) and stagger (*wᵉhērā'ēl*, with DSS, LXX, Aq., Tg., Pesh., Vg; as NAB, NRSV, REB)/be exposed (MT: *wᵉhē'ārēl*, as NIV) (Hab 2:15-16).

Many OT passages that negate the vb. depict people in want of something desirable, often when under Yahweh's judgment. As the result of a drought brought upon Israel by Yahweh, two or three towns might wander to one town to drink water, but not be satiated (Amos 4:8). To the people of Judah who lived in paneled houses, while Yahweh's house lay in ruins, Haggai said, "[There is] eating, but not so as to be satiated (*wᵉ'ên-lᵉśāb'â*); [there is] drinking, but not so as to become drunk (*wᵉ'ên-lᵉšākrâ*)" (author tr.) (Hag 1:6; cf. Ps 59:15[16]; Isa 9:20[19]; Hos 4:10). In one numerical proverb, the sages taught: "Three things are never satiated (*lō' tiśba'nâ*); four never say, 'Enough! (*hôn*)': the grave, the barren womb, the earth never satiated (*lō' śāb<^{e}>'â*) with water, and fire, which never says, 'Enough! (*hôn*)'" (author tr.) (Prov 30:15-16).

In idiomatic (metonymical) usage, the vb. may take on the sense "satisfy." The psalmist says that what satisfies him is Yahweh (Ps 17:15; 63:5[6]). Isaiah anticipates that all who nurse at the breast of the purified Jerusalem will be satiated/satisfied (Isa 66:11). The ni. hapleg. appears in the context of Job's righteous disavowal of vengeance-taking and should therefore probably be rendered: "(I [Job] have not let my jaw [synecdoche of part for the whole, self] sin by requesting his [my adversary's] life with a curse); the members of my tent have never said, 'Though one should give/pay [even] of/with his flesh, he [Job] would not be satisfied (*niśbā'*)!'" (author tr.) (Job 31:[30-]31; contra NIV, NRSV, REB).

In Isa 53:11, after the suffering of the servant of Yahweh, he is prophesied to "see light" and "be satisfied." The former is an idiom meaning "to live/revive" (cf. Job 3:16b; 33:28; Ps 36:9[10];Ps 49:19[20]); the latter may be related either to the idiom "be satisfied with days" (*śāba' yāmîm*, 1 Chron 23:1; 2 Chron 24:15), meaning here "live long" (note the parallelism with v. 10) or, less probably, to the idea of being satisfied with the result when one is vindicated or rewarded.

3. The adj. *śābēa'*, satiated, satisfied, may denote the state resulting from eating to fullness: "Those who were full (*ś^{e}bē'îm*) hire themselves out for food (*balleḥem*), but those who were hungry hunger no more (**ḥād<^{e}>lû '<ô>d*; so NIV)/have ceased to toil(?) (**ḥād<^{e}>lû ^{a}bōd*; cf. Driver, 25)/have become fat with food(!) (**ḥād<^{e}>lû 'ad*; cf. Arab. *ḫadu/ila* be fat, Old Babylonian adj. *ḫuddulu* fat; Ugar. *lḥm* bread/food ‖ *mġd* food; so Thomas; Calderone; McCarter, 72; NAB, NRSV; cf. REB)" (1 Sam 2:5; cf. Judg 5:7; Job 14:6). Metonymically, it may denote the satisfaction that results from fearing Yahweh (Prov 19:23) or receiving his favor: "Naphtali is satiated/satisfied with favor (*ś^{e}ba' rāṣôn*); and filled (*ûmālē'*) with Yahweh's blessing" (author tr.) (Deut 33:23). The adj. *śābēa'* is used as part of an idiom (metonymy), *ś^{e}ba' yāmîm,* satiated/satisfied with days (i.e., full of years), typical of death-notice formulae: "Then Abraham breathed his last and died at a good age, an old man and full of days (*ûś^{e}ba' yāmîm*; so some Heb. MSS, Sam. Pent., LXX, Pesh., a Tg. MS)" (Gen 25:8; cf. 35:29; Job 42:17; 1 Chron 29:28).

4. OT attestations of the nom. *śābā',* satiety; plenty, produce/grain(?), include one usage that seems to pun on the amphibology of *śābā'*: "Sleep is sweet for the laborer, whether he eats little or much; but the satiety/abundance of the rich man allows him no freedom to sleep" (author tr.) (Eccl 5:12[11]). A further six uses—all pertaining to the seven years of abundant produce/grain (Gen 41:29, 30, 31, 34, 47, 53)—could be translated in either sense, plenty/bounty, or, produce/grain (cf. the Phoen. cognate [Dunand, 32; Tomback, 311; Dahood, "Hebrew-Ugaritic," 397-98]; and antonym *rā'āb*, famine, in vv. 30, 34). Again, in the context of Prov 3:(9-)10, *śābā'* may denote either "plenty" (so NIV, NRSV) or "grain" (so LXX *sitoulō,* "of/with grain," NAB, NEB, REB): "Honor the LORD with your wealth, with the first-fruits of all your crops; then your barns will be filled with plenty/grain, and your vats will brim over with wine."

5. The (segholate) masc. nom. *śōba'* and fem. nom. *śob'â* are but masc. and fem. reflexes of the same lexeme, meaning satiety; plenty (cf. GKC §§ 93 and 94, Paradigm I of both). The basic sense is attested in Ezek 39:19, where *śob'â* ‖ nom.

šikkārôn, drunkenness (*pace RSP*, 3, i 296k [155], which says nom. *śob'â* ‖ the vb. *šth*, drink): "You [carrion eating birds and beasts] will eat fat to [the point of] satiety, and drink blood to [the point of] drunkenness" (cf., similarly, *śob'â* in Isa 23:18; 55:1-2 [hypocatastasis]; 56:11; and *śōba'* in Exod 16:3; Lev 25:19; Deut 23:24[25]; Ruth 2:18; Ps 78:25; Prov 13:25). The derived sense, plenty, fullness, is attested in Ezek 16:49, which criticizes Jerusalem's sister Sodom for having had *śib'at-leḥem,* abundance of food (const. < **śib'â*, a byform of *śob'â*), yet not having aided the poor and needy (cf., similarly, *śob'â* in Ezek 16:28; *śōba'* in Ps 16:11).

P-B The DSS attest the postbiblical Heb. vb. *śb'*, and nom. *śb'h* (*KQT*, 211). Mish. Heb. has the stative vb. and adj. form *śābēa'* (Jastrow, 2:1516a), and the nom. forms *śebî'â* (Jastrow, 2:1514b), and *śôba'*, satiation, plenty (Jastrow, 2:1529a). Jewish Aram. has a vb. *s/ś^{e}ba'* (Jastrow, 2:951a, 2:1516a-b), (part.) adj. *s/śbîa'*, satisfied (Jastrow, 2:949b, 2:1516a-b), and nom. forms *sib'ā'*, plenty (Jastrow, 2:951b), *s/śub'ā'*, satiation, plenty (Jastrow, 2:1529a), and *śôb'ā'*, satiation, plenty (Jastrow, 2:1529a). Syr. has the vb. *s^{e}ba'*, be satiated, filled, satisfied (Payne Smith, 358b-59a), adj. *sab'ā'*, full, satisfied (Payne Smith, 359a), and nom. forms *sab'ā'*, satiety, fulness; plenty; overflow (of water), and *sab'ūtā'*, plenty, abundance (Payne Smith, 359a). Mand. has the vb. *sba* (*MdD* 316a), adj. *saba*, full; satisfying, satisfactory (*MdD* 308a), and nom. *siba*, satiety; overflow (*MdD* 324a).

Satisfaction, abundance, plenty: → *śb'* (be satiated, # 8425); → *šlm* (have satisfaction, repay, reward, retribute, make peace, # 8966)

BIBLIOGRAPHY

THAT 2:819-21; 7:693-704; *TWAT* 7:693-704; *TWOT* 2:869a-70a; A. F. L. Beeston, "The Correspondence of Hebrew *s* to ESA *s*²" *JSS* 22, 1977, 50-57; idem, et al., *Sabaic Dictionary-Dictionnaire Sabéen*, 1982; G. Bergstrasser, *Glossar des neuaramäischen Dialekts von Ma'lūla*, 1921; P. J. Calderone, "*ḤDL*-II in Poetic Texts," *CBQ* 23, 1961, 451-60; J. Cantineau, *Grammaire du Palmyrénien épigraphique*, 1935; C. Conti-Rossini, *Chrestomathia arabica meridionalis epigraphica*, 1931; M. Dahood, "Hebrew-Ugaritic Lexicography X," *Bib* 53, 1972, 386-403; idem, "Qoheleth and Northwest Semitic Philology," *Bib* 43, 1962, (349-65) 349-50; R. Degen, *Altaramäische Grammatik der Inschriften des 10.-8. Jh.s v. Chr.*, Heidelberger Studien zum AT, 1969; J. C. de Moor, *An Anthology of Religious Texts from Ugarit*, Religious Texts Translation Series: Nisaba 16, 1987; S. R. Driver, *Notes on the Hebrew Text of Samuel*, 2nd ed., 1913, 25; M. Dunand, *Bulletin du Musée de Beyrouth* 8, 1946-48, 32; J. Friedrich, *Phönizische-Punische Grammatik*, AnOr 32, 1951; Z. S. Harris, *A Grammar of the Phoenician Language*, AOS 8, 1936; I. Kottsieper, "Zur Etymologie von hebräischer *śb'* I," *UF* 22, 1990, 149-68; P. Leander, *Laut- und Formenlehre des Ägyptisch-Aramäischen*, 1928; P. K. McCarter, *I Samuel*, AB 8, 1980, 72; H. P. Müller, "Das eblaitische Verbalsystem nach den bisher veröffentlichten Personennamen," in L. Cagni (ed.), *La lingua di Ebla*, 1981, 211-33; J. Payne Smith, *A Compendious Syriac Dictionary*, 1903; G. Pettinato, *The Archives of Ebla*, 1981; M. H. Pope, "A Divine Banquet at Ugarit," in J. M. Efird, (ed.), *The Use of the OT in the New and Other Essays*, FS W. S. Stinespring, 1972, 170-203 (on RS 24. 258); F. Rosenthal, *An Aramaic Handbook*, Porta Linguarum Orientalium NS 10, 1967; idem, *Sprache der palmyrenischen Inschriften*, 1936; D. W. Thomas, "Some Observations on the Root *ḥdl*," *SVT* 4, 1957, 8-16; R. S. Tomback, *A*

Comparative Semitic Lexicon of the Phoenician and Punic Languages, SBLDS 32, 1978; R. M. Voigt, "Die Laterale im Semitischen," *WO* 10, 1979, 93-114.

Robert H. O'Connell

8426 (*śābāʿ*, satiety; plenty; produce, grain), → # 8425

8427 (*śōbaʿ*, satiety; plenty), → # 8425

8428 (*śābēaʿ*, satiated; satisfied), → # 8425

8429 (*śobʿâ*, satiety; plenty), → # 8425

8430 (*śibʿâ*, satiety), → # 8425

8432	שׂבר

שׂבר (*śbr*), q. test, investigate; pi. hope, wait; examine, wait, expect, hope (# 8432); שֵׂבֶר (*śēber*), hope (# 8433).

ANE No known similar root outside Heb. and Aram. (cf. *śbr*: Dan 7:25) exists; one derivative is *śēber* (nom.).

OT 1. Of all the verbal roots denoting hope or expectation (→ *ḥkh*, # 2675; → *yḥl*, # 3498; → *qwh* # 7747), *śbr* is the least frequent (9x): q. (with prep. b^e Neh 2:13, 15), pi. (with prep. *'el*, Ps 104:27; 145:15; Isa 38:18; with l^e Ruth 1:13; Esth 9:1; Ps 119:166) and the nom. in Ps 119:116 and 146:5.

2. The primary idea of the root is that of examining, digging out, and exploring (*HALAT*). Nehemiah nightly examined (*śbr*) the walls of Jerusalem that had been broken down (Neh 2:13, 15), probably to get an idea of their condition.

3. It is the more pervasive intensive form (pi) that conveys the added notion of hope and expectancy. As with this family of vbs. (*ḥkh* ; *yḥl*; *qwh*), the person concerned is looking mostly to God to provide what is hoped for. Thus, the psalmist says people and animals alike look to God to provide food (Ps 104:27; 145:15; nothing divergent about that usage here, *contra THAT* 1:627); indeed, happy are those whose hope (*śēber*) is the Lord (Ps 146:5); they hope for his salvation (y^e*šûʿâ*, Ps 119:166).

4. But in prose, the intensive form of *śbr* denotes futile hope or vain waiting (→ *yḥl*; *qwh*). Thus, Naomi is sure that her daughters-in-law, widows like her, would not want to wait unduly for new husbands (Ruth 1:13), whereas in Esther's time, such was God's providence that the enemies of the Jews had been vainly waiting, albeit expectantly (hoping), to overpower them (Esth 9:1).

Hope, waiting: → *ḥkh* (wait, endure, expect, hope, # 2675); → *yḥl* (wait, hope, endure, long, # 3498); → *qwh* I (tarry, wait, hope, wait for, # 7747); → *śbr* (test, investigate, hope, wait, examine, # 8432)

BIBLIOGRAPHY

THAT 2:620, 627; *TWAT* 6:1228.

Daniel Schibler

8433 (*śēber*, hope), → # 8432

8434	שׂגא

שׂגא, שׂגה (*śg'/ śgh*), q. grow great, increase; hi. make great, exalt (# 8434, 8436); שַׂגִּיא (*śaggî'*), adj. exalted, great (# 8438); Aram. שְׂגָא (*$ś^e$gā'*), pe'al grow great, increase (# 10677); שַׂגִּיא (*śaggî'*), adj. great, many; adv. very, exceedingly (# 10678).

ANE The adj. of this root, meaning much, many, is used in Aram., Syr., and Phoen. (R. Tomback, *A Comparative Semitic Lexicon of the Phoenician and Punic Languages*, 1988, 314).

OT 1. The Heb. vbs. *śg'/śgh* appear to be orthographic variations of the same root. These vb. forms are found 6x in Job and Psalms. The idea is the opposite of becoming insignificant (Job 8:7). The root describes the literal growth of a plant (8:11), an increase in a person's wealth (Ps 73:12), or the expansion of a nation into a world power (Job 12:23). The Aram. adj. refers to the multiplicity or increased number of years, gifts, fruit, flesh, the great honor of a person, or the great height of an object (Dan 2:6, 48; 4:10, 12, 21[7, 9, 18]; 7:5). Sometimes God is recognized as the sovereign power that causes this great growth, but at other times this issue is ignored.

2. Although God does not increase in greatness, his reputation grows greater when people proclaim the greatness of his deeds or his power (Job 36:24).

The nom./adj. forms are used twice in Job (36:26; 37:23) to remind Job that the God whom he wishes to question is an exalted, all-powerful, just, totally other being who is beyond human comprehension. Although God is partially unknowable, Elihu concludes that his exalted nature provides Job with a solid basis for trusting God rather than questioning his justice.

3. The Aram. sections of Ezra and Daniel use *$ś^e$gā'* to express a strong positive or negative desire for another person. It is found in the positive context of the traditional greeting to the king, "May you prosper greatly" (Dan 4:1[3:31]; 6:25[26]), as well as the negative context of fearing increased damage to the king's reputation and financial position (Ezra 4:22). The adverb serves to heighten the degree of anger or pleasure of a person to an exalted level (Dan 5:9; 6:14, 23[15, 24]; 7:28). The king was very, exceedingly, or increasingly angry with the wise men of Babylon because they could not tell or interpret his dream. Therefore he ordered that they be killed (Dan 2:12).

Exaltation, height: → *zbl* (exalt, honor, # 2290); → *sll* (lift up, exalt, # 6148); → *rwm* (be high, exalted, proud, # 8123); → *rmm* II (rise up, be exalted, # 8250); → *śg'/śgh* (grow great, increase, exalt, # 8434/8436)

Abundance, multiplication, sufficiency: → *dgh* (multiply, # 1835); → *day* (sufficiency, overflowing supply, # 1896); → *ysp* (add, continue, increase, # 3578); → *kbr* I (make many, be in abundant supply, # 3892); → *m^egammâ* (totality, abundance, # 4480); → *rbb* I (become numerous, much, great, # 8045); → *rbh* I (become numerous, multiply, increase, # 8049); → *r'š* II, be abundant, # 8322); → *śg'/śgh* (grow great, increase, exalt, # 8434/8436); → *śpq* II (suffice, be enough, # 8563); → *šwq* I (overflow, bestow abundantly, # 8796); → *šepa'* (super-abundance, # 9179)

Gary V. Smith

8435	שׂגב

שׂגב (*śgb*), q. be (inaccessibly) high, fortified; ni. be high, be exalted; pi. make high, protect; pu. be protected; hi. be too great (# 8435); מִשְׂגָּב (*miśgāb*), high spot, refuge (# 5369).

ANE In Old Aram. *śgbwh*, pl. suff. form refers to magnates, "the high and mighty."

OT 1. Verbal forms of *śgb* occur 20x, mainly connoting being "high, exalted, lofty," and with related meanings: kept safe, protected, strong, safe, and once, unscalable. Apart from two occurrences in Job, two in Prov, and one in Deut, the remainder are used in Isa and Ps.

2. Forms of the nom. *miśgāb* are employed 17x. Except for an occurrence in 2 Sam and another in Jer, the remainder are found in Isa and Ps. Clearly the inspired poets envisioned God as the ultimate security. The nom. *miśgabbî*, my fortress, expressed the need of the troubled psalmist for a refuge in oppressive circumstances (e.g., Ps 9:9[10]; 59:9, 16-17[10, 17-18]; 62:2[3], 6[7]).

P-B For Mish. Heb. see Jastrow 2:1520-21; for DSS see 1QH 6,25.

Fortification, citadel, siege-mound, stronghold: → *'armōn* (citadel, # 810); → *bîrâ* (citadel, acropolis, # 1072); → *bṣr* III (be inaccessible, # 1307); → *dāyēq* (siege-mound, # 1911); → *ḥêl* (rampart, # 2658); → *millô'* (terrace, # 4864); → *misgeret* (stronghold, dungeon, rim, table, # 4995); → *m^eṣād* (stronghold, # 5171); → *māṣôr* II (fortification, fortified city, # 5190); → *sōḥērâ* (rampart, # 6089); → *sōkēk* (mantelet, # 6116); → *ṣ^erîaḥ* (cellar, vault, pit, stronghold, # 7663); → *śgb* (be high, fortified, protect, # 8435); → **Fortification: Theology**

BIBLIOGRAPHY

TWOT 2:871; E. Klein, *A Comprehensive Etymological Dictionary of the Hebrew Language for Readers of English*, 1987, 639; K. N. Schoville, "Fortification," *ISBE* 2:346-54; Y. Yadin, *The Art of Warfare in Biblical Lands*, 1963.

Keith N. Schoville

8436 (*śgh*, grow great, increase; exalt), → # 8434

8438 (*śaggî'*, exalted, great), → # 8434

8440	שׂדד

שׂדד (*śdd*), pi. harrow. # 8440.

OT The vb. *śdd* is used with "plowing" and "breaking up soil" (Isa 28:24); the action referred to, which follows plowing (→ *ḥrš*, # 3086) and precedes planting (Hos 10:11), is the harrowing of newly plowed fields. The farmer used the harrow to beat the clods and to level the ground in preparation for planting or sowing (H. W. Wolff, *Hosea*, Hermeneia, 1974, 185).

Agriculture—farming: → *'ikkār* (farmer, # 438); → *ygb* (be a farmer, # 3320); → *'dr* I (be weeded, # 6371); → *'zq* (break up, loosen, # 6466); → *śdd* (harrow, # 8440)
Plowing: → *'ēt* III (plowshare?, axe, # 908); → *g^edûd* I (ridge, # 1521); → *ḥrš* I (plow, engrave, prepare, plan, # 3086); → *ma'^anâ* (furrow-length, # 5103); → *nyr* II (break up [unplowed ground], # 5774); → *telem* (furrow, # 9439)

Mark D. Futato

8441/8442	שָׂדֶה/שָׂדַי

שָׂדֶה/שָׂדַי (*śādeh/śāday*), open country, open fields, fields, domain (# 8441/8442).

ANE The nom. *śādeh* as well as its poetic form, *śāday*, derives from the same etymon as Akk. *šadû(m)*, "mountain, open country." *šd* occurs in Old Can., Can., Phoen., and Pun. with the meaning "field, plain" while *s²dw* is found in OSA for "hill, terraced land," and Ugar. attests *šd* for "field, individual field, mountain."

In spite of the wide diffusion of cognate forms throughout Sem. languages, the etymology remains somewhat unclear. As stated above, most scholars derive *śādeh/śāday* from Akk. *šadû(m)*, mountain, open plain. Dhorme (229-31) and Albright (183-84) suggested that *śādeh/śāday* derive from the Proto-Sem. root **ṯdw*, breast, through the Akk. *šadû(m)*. Propp (232) provides five reasons why the Akk. *šadû(m)* does not derive from **ṯdw*, confirming the likelihood of a *śādeh/śāday* and *šadû(m)* connection with the meaning, open field, hill, or highland. The Northwest Sem. evidence points to an original biradical form that expanded to the present nom. by adding a *yodh* or *he*.

OT The nom. *śādeh* occurs 320x while its poetic counterpart, *śāday*, is found only 13x (Deut 32:13; Ps 8:7[8]; 50:11; 80:13[14]; 96:12; 104:11; Isa 56:9; Jer 4:17; 18:14; Lam 4:9; Hos 10:4; 12:12; Joel 2:22). The more common term *śādeh* appears most frequently in Gen (48x), Exod (22x), Lev (25x), 1 and 2 Sam (35x), Jer (25x), and Ezek (26x), and is esp. concentrated in the short book of Ruth (16x). Both forms are absent from Ezra, Esth, Dan, Amos, Jon, Nah, Hab, Zeph, and Hag.

1. *Open, wide land.* In contrast to the inhabited ground of a village or city, *śādeh* serves as a general term for open fields located outside cities and villages. At times it describes land immediately around a city (*śᵉdēh hā'îr*, Gen 41:48; Lev 25:34; Josh 21:12; 1 Chron 6:56[41]; Neh 11:30; 12:29, 44). Herbs (Gen 2:5; 3:18; Exod 9:22, 25; 10:15), trees (Exod 9:25; Deut 20:19; Isa 55:12; Jer 7:20; Ezek 17:24; 31:4, 5, 15; 34:27; Joel 1:12, 19), flowers (Ps 103:15; Isa 40:6), and various other plant life grow in these open spaces. The *śādeh* can serve as shelter and refuge (1 Sam 20:5, 24), find use as a burial ground (Gen 23:11, 17, 19; 49:29-30; 50:13), or be a place for battle (Judg 9:32, 43; 2 Sam 11:23; 18:6; Jer 6:25).

The phrase wild animals (*ḥayyat haśśādeh*, lit., animals of the field) refers to undomesticated animals in general (Gen 2:19, 20; 3:1) and destructive carnivores in certain instances (Lev 26:22; 2 Sam 21:10; Jer 12:9; Ezek 34:5, 8; Hos 13:8; cf. *bahᵃmôt śādeh/śādāy*, Ps 8:7[8]; Joel 1:20; 2:22).

2. *Cultivable fields.* Since not all *śādeh* will produce useful agricultural products, *śādeh* can also more specifically denote cultivable land (in contrast to *midbār*). It signifies land for raising crops (Exod 23:16; Lev 19:19; 25:3-4; Ps 107:37) and grazing cattle (Gen 34:5, 28; Exod 9:19) and sheep (Gen 29:2; 31:4; Exod 9:3). Several biblical writers juxtapose fields (*śādeh*) and vineyards (*kerem*) as general reference to agricultural resources (Exod 22:5[4]; Lev 25:3-4; Num 16:14; 20:17; 21:22; Judg 9:27; 1 Sam 8:14; 22:7; Neh 5:3-5; 5:11; Job 24:6; Ps 107:37; Prov 24:30; 31:16; Jer 32:15; 35:9; Mic 1:6).

3. *The region of a people, tribe, or family.* The expression the fields of, followed by a national (land of Israel, Judg 20:6; land of Moab, Gen 36:35; Num 21:20; Ruth 1:1, 2, 6; 2:6; 4:3; 1 Chron 1:46; 8:8; land of Syria, Hos 12:12[13]; land of

Philistines, 1 Sam 6:1; 27:7, 11; and field of Zoan, Ps 78:43) or tribal name (land of Ephraim, Obad 19), carries with it territorial connotations (region/domain).

This connection of *śādeh* with territorial names carries over to the idea of personal property owned by an individual or a family (e.g., Joshua, 1 Sam 6:14; Caleb, Josh 21:12). The expression a parcel of ground (*ḥelqat haśśādeh*, Gen 33:19; Ruth 2:3; 4:3; 2 Sam 23:11; 1 Chron 11:13) normally highlights ownership. The concentration of *śādeh* in Ruth arises from that book's focus on harvesting in the fields and Boaz's attempt to redeem Naomi's *śādeh* (Ruth 4:3, 5). Fields were commonly bought (*qnh*, Gen 25:10; 33:19; 49:30; 50:13; Josh 24:32) and sold (*mkr*, Gen 47:20) (see below for covenantal stipulations governing these activities).

4. *Mainland*. The city of Tyre, located on the Mediterranean Sea one hundred miles north of Jerusalem, consisted of three elements. A short distance offshore from the main part of the city were two island harbors. In light of this layout, Ezekiel's prophecy that an invading army would slay the daughters of Tyre in the *śādeh* (Ezek 26:6, 8) clearly refers to the mainland region in contrast to the islands (Schwarzenbach, 85).

5. *Highland*. Propp (230-36) has suggested that lexicographers add the meaning highland to the semantic range of *śādeh/śāday* in a number of passages (Num 23:14; Judg 5:18; 2 Sam 1:21; Job 40:20; Ps 50:11; Jer 13:27; 17:3; 18:14), primarily on contextual grounds (cf. Heidel, 233-35). Of the examples offered by Propp, Job 40:20 is the least likely example of this nuance.

6. *Covenantal stipulations*. A number of passages delineate the manner in which the Israelites were to care for their *śādeh*. Even in this legislation about fields, certain important truths concerning God's expectations of his covenant nation stand prominent. The Israelites needed to understand that their *śādeh* was received by divine grant and was essential to the continued existence of each tribe (and family). Consequently, each Israelite was to provide for his family from proper use of the land, provide assistance for fellow Israelites who were poor and needy, fatherless, or widowed, and beyond that, was to manifest gratitude to Yahweh by giving a tithe of produce and by bringing offerings to the central sanctuary. The divine allotment of land left no room for coveting or stealing land from a fellow Israelite.

Moses' specific instructions about the treatment of a neighbor's land (Exod 22:5-6[4-5]) indicate the compassion that was to characterize landowners in Israel. Every sabbatical and Jubilee year the land was to remain unplanted (Lev 25:3-4; 25:12). Any fields sold outside the family would automatically return to the original owner at the Year of Jubilee (25:31). Since land around the cities and villages was essential to providing sustenance for urban dwellers, that land could not be sold (25:34). Even land dedicated to holy service (use by priesthood) would normally return to the original owner at the Jubilee year (27:16-28). In gratitude for God's abundant provision (of the land itself as well as each harvest), the Israelites were to be satisfied with their land allotment (not coveting the land of others, Deut 5:21[18]), leave gleanings for the less fortunate (Lev 19:9; 23:22; Deut 24:19), and present a tithe (Deut 14:22), an offering of firstfruits (Exod 23:16), and other non-blood offerings from each harvest.

In order to maintain the land's purity (consecrated status), the priests conducted a special purification ceremony when a corpse was discovered in the *śādeh* and the precise cause of death was unknown (Lev 14:7, 53; Num 19:16; Deut 21:1-9).

Finally, as with *'ᵃdāmâ* (# 141), the productivity or barrenness of Israel's *śādeh* was connected to Israel's covenant obedience or treachery. Yahweh is the one ultimately responsible for the abundant productivity of *śādeh* (Lev 26:4; Ezek 17:24; 34:27). Micah (2:2) refers to Israel's penchant for coveting their neighbor's fields as an example of their covenant rebellion. As part of covenant curse, Yahweh promised to make Israel's fields barren (Deut 28:38) and a place for violent death before an invading army (Ezek 7:15; 33:27; 34:5, 8) or in the jaws of a wild beast (*ḥayyat haśśādeh*, Lev 26:22; Jer 12:9; Ezek 34:5, 8). In their description of the judgment coming against Israel, certain prophets depict Zion as plowed like a field (Jer 26:18; Mic 3:12).

In the context of covenant blessings and curses, the city (*'îr*) and country (*śādeh*) contrast serves as a merism to delineate the entire nation of Israel (Deut 28:3, 16; Ezek 7:15; cf. Gen 34:28).

7. *Comparison of śādeh with 'ereṣ (→ # 824) and 'ᵃdāmâ* (→ # 141). When *'ereṣ* signifies the land of Israel, *śādeh* serves as a subset of *'ereṣ* (seen in the juxtaposition of *śādeh* and *bā'āreṣ*, Gen 2:5; Exod 9:22; Jer 32:43). When they connote a parcel of land, *'ᵃdāmâ*, *'ereṣ*, and *śādeh* can be synonyms (Ezek 32:4; 38:20; Hos 2:18[20]; Joel 1:10; Mal 3:11).

Unlike *'ᵃdāmâ*, *śādeh* can denote barren and uncultivable land (Josh 8:24; Ezek 29:5; Joel 1:19). Although almost identical in form, the phrase *'al penê haśśādeh* (→ # 141) never has universal significance. It simply serves as an ambiguous reference to the open fields (11x, Lev 14:7; 17:5; Num 19:16; et al.; cf. similar phrase, *'el pᵉnê haśśādeh*, Lev 14:53; Ezek 16:5).

8. *Conclusion*. For an Israelite, *śādeh* serves as a realm in which all aspects of life take place. Its fertile soil provides sustenance for human existence and refuge from danger and holds a significant place in the life of any Israelites as part of their inheritance. The fields also serve as gory battlefields and scenes of horrendous atrocities. Many of God's activities on behalf of, through, and against his elect nation play out against the background of *śādeh*.

Field, ground, rural area: → *'ādām* IV (ground, # 135); → *bar* IV (wild, open country, # 1340); → *gāzēr* (infertile land, # 1620); → *ḥûṣôt* (open fields, # 2575a); → *yāgēb* (field, # 3321); → *mᵉlēḥâ* (barren land, salt-plain, # 4877); → *mimšāq* (ground overrun with weeds, # 4940); → *mᵉ'ārâ* II (bare field, # 5118); → *nîr* II (ground newly broken & cleared, # 5776); → *'āqob* (ground [uneven and bumpy], crafty heart, # 6815); → *pᵉrāzôn* (fertile field, # 7251); → *rekes* (rugged ground, # 8221); → *śādeh* (open country, open field, fields, domain, # 8441); → *šᵉdēmâ* (terrace, # 8727); → *šāmān* (fertile field, # 9044)

BIBLIOGRAPHY

TWAT 6:709-18; *TWOT* 2:871; W. Albright, "The Names *Shaddai* and *Abram*," *JBL* 54, 1935, 173-204; P. Dhorme, "L'emploi métaphorique des noms de parties du corps en hébreu et en akkadien (suite)," *RB* 31, 1922, 215-33; A. Heidel, "A Special Usage of the Akkadian Term *Šadû*," *JNES* 8, 1949, 233-35; W. Propp, "On Hebrew *Śāde(h)*, 'Highland,'" *VT* 37, 1987, 230-36; A. Schwarzenbach, *Die Geographische Terminologie im Hebräischen des Alten Testaments*, 1954.

Michael A. Grisanti

8442 (*śāday*, open country, open field, fields, domain), → # 8441

8444 (*śᵉdērâ*, unexplained [NIV beams, ranks]), → # 1215

8446	שָׂהֵד

שָׂהֵד (*śāhēd*), witness (# 8446).

ANE Old Aram. *śhd,* Jewish Aram. *śᵉhad/sᵉhad*; Syr. *shd*, Arab. *šahida*. In an Old Aram. inscription from Sefire (see I A 12) the word refers to the divine witnesses to the treaty between Bir-Gayah and Matiel. (See *KAI* 222A:11-12; *ANET*, 659, and J. Fitzmyer, *The Aramaic Inscriptions of Sefire,* 12-13, 39.)

OT 1. The Aram. cognate occurs in Gen 31:47, where it refers to the heap of stones set up by Jacob and Laban as a reminder of their covenant. Jacob called the stone heap Galeed (*Gal'ēd*), witness heap or the heap is a witness, while Laban gave it the equivalent Aram. name, Jegar Sahaduta (*yᵉgar śāhᵃdûtā'*).

2. The term also appears parallel to *'ēd*, witness (# 6332), in Job's confident affirmation that he has a witness/advocate in heaven who will plead his case before God (Job 16:19). Some identify Job's advocate as God himself (see Hartley, *Job,* 264, and Veijola, *JBL* 107, 1988, 417), but, as Pope points out, "the heavenly witness, guarantor, friend can scarcely be God who is already Accuser, Judge, and Executioner" (125). It is true, as Clines observes, that God proves to be Job's witness in the end, but it is unlikely that Job anticipates such an ironic development at this point in his experience (389). Clines sees the witness as Job's "protestation of innocence" that "has been placed on record in the heavenly court" and demands a response (390; cf. Beaucamp, 309-10). Curtis proposes that Job's mediator is his own personal deity who will oppose Yahweh (549-62), while Habel suggests that the advocate is one of the angels of the heavenly council who is the counterpart to the accuser/Satan (275). Elihu's statement about the possibility of an angelic mediator (Job 33:23), as well as the book's other references and allusions to the heavenly assembly (1:6; 2:1; 5:1; 15:15; 38:7), make Habel's proposal the most attractive interpretive option.

Witness: → *yāpēaḥ* (witness?, # 3641); → *'wd* (surround, encircle, admonish, call to witness, # 6386); → *śāhēd* (witness, # 8446)

BIBLIOGRAPHY

E. Beaucamp, "Le *goēl* de Jb 19, 25," *LTP* 33, 1977, 309-10; D. J. Clines, *Job*, 1989, 1:389-90; J. B. Curtis, "On Job's Witness in Heaven," *JBL* 102, 1983, 549-62; N. Habel, *Job*, 1985, 274-76; J. Hartley, *Job*, NICOT, 1988, 264; W. Irwin, "Job's Redeemer," *JBL* 81, 1962, 217-24; S. Mowinckel, "Hiobs *go'el* und Zeuge im Himmel," in *Vom Alten Testament: Festschrift fur Karl Marti,* 1925, 207-12; E. T. Mullen, Jr., "The Divine Witness and the Davidic Royal Grant: Ps 89:37-38," *JBL* 102, 1983, 217-18; M. Pope, *Job*, AB, 1965, 125; T. Veijola, "The Witness in the Clouds: Ps 89:38," *JBL* 107, 1988, 417.

Robert B. Chisholm

8448	שַׂהֲרֹנִים

שַׂהֲרוֹנִים (*śahᵃrônîm*) = *sahar* + dimin. end. *-ôn*, pl. crescents, small moon-shaped ornaments (# 8448).

ANE Akk. *sa'uru*, a type of jewelry? (*CAD* 15, 202); Aram. *sêh^arā'*, *sah^arā'* moon; Old Aram. *šhr*, moon-god; cf. Arab., Eth., Syr. cognates meaning moon/new moon/moon-god (BDB 962; *HALAT* 1222).

OT The terms occur in Judg 8:21, 26; and 3:18.
For a discussion on jewelry, see *'dh* (put on ornaments, # 6335).

Malcolm J. A. Horsnell

8449	שׂוֹבֶךְ

שׂוֹבֶךְ (*śôbek*), tangle of branches (8449); שְׂבָכָה (*ś^ebākâ*), lattice, net (# 8422).

ANE Attested by Akk. *šabikû*, headgear (*CAD*, 17:11); Arab. *šabaka*, entangle. The vb. *śbk* is not found in BH, but from its derivatives and from the cognate languages it can be understood to have had the meaning, interweave.

OT 1. *śôbek* is used for the network of branches in which Absalom was caught and met his death (2 Sam 18:9).

2. *ś^ebākâ* is used in Job 18:8 for an animal trap, probably a network of branches spread over a pit, and in 2 Kgs 1:2 for the latticework through which King Ahaziah fell and was mortally injured. Especially significant is its use for the beautiful "network of interwoven chains" or interwoven pomegranate branches on the pillars of Solomon's temple (1 Kgs 7:17-18, 41-42; 2 Kgs 25:17; 2 Chron 4:12-13; Jer 52:22-23).

Intertwining, twisting: → *gablut* (interwoven, twisted work, # 1491); → *śôbek* (tangle of branches, # 8449); → *śrg* (intertwine, # 8571); → *śrk* (twist, # 8592)

Francis Foulkes

8454	שׂוט

שׂוט (*śwṭ*), q. to turn away to falsehood, to become entangled in lies, falsehood (hapleg., Ps 40:4[5]; # 8454; cf. # 8474).

ANE Arab. *šāṭa*, to run after falsehood; Akk. *šâṭu*, rebel; Eth. *šōṭa*, restore.

OT This word is used only 1x in the OT in a q. part. in Ps 40:4[5]. It is, of course, difficult to know what it means. It may be related to *śṭh* (→ # 8474), turn aside (cf. also *swt*; → # 6077). The usual translation of the passage is "those who turn aside to falsehood." The NIV has "those who turn aside to false gods," while the NJPSV renders the line "who turns not to the arrogant or to followers of falsehood (*w^eśāṭê kāzāb*)." Since *kzb* (# 3942) is used to stand for lie/idol, both renderings are possible (cf. Amos 2:4). The context indicates persons who are somehow given to falsehood/idols/false gods. Craigie suggests "and has not turned to the *defiant*, the *fabricators* of *falsehood*," but observes that the expression is of uncertain meaning (312-13; emphasis mine). These individuals will not be blessed (v. 4a[5a]) in the same manner as will those who put their trust in Yahweh.

P-B Late *sṭy* = biblical Heb. and *śṭy* mean to deviate, to turn to/from (Koh R 1:16, *hlb sōṭeh*, "The heart turns to evil (deviates)." For refs. see Jastrow 2:972-73. This development supports the trans. suggested above.

Deception, falsehood, fraud, guile, iniquity, lie: → *'āwen* (mischief, iniquity, deception, # 224); → *bd'* (invent, devise, lie, # 968); → *kzb* I (lie, be a liar, deceive, # 3941); → *kḥš* (fail, deceive, grow lean, # 3950); → *nkl* (knave, deceiver, cheat, # 5792); → *nš'* II (be deceived, deceive, cause a deception, # 5958); → *sārâ* II (rebellion, crime, revolt, falsehood, # 6240); → *'qb* I (seize the heel, overreach, deceive, # 6810); → *rmh* II (betray, deal treacherously with, # 8228); → *śwṭ* (turn away to falsehood, entangled in lies, # 8454); → *šqr* (deal/act falsely, betray, # 9213); → *tll* (deceive, mock, trifle, # 9438)

Bibliography
P. Craigie, *Psalms 1-50*, WBC, 1983.

Eugene Carpenter/Michael A. Grisanti

8455	שׂוּךְ

שׂוּךְ (*śwk*), q. hedge, shut in (# 8455); מְסוּכָה (*m^e sûkâ*), nom. thorn hedge (hapleg. Mic 7:4; → # 5004), < *swk* I or *skk/śkk* (*HALAT* 572); מְשׂוּכָּה (*m^e śûkkâ,* only Isa 5:5; → # 5372), nom. hedge; < *śwk* II/*swk* (*HALAT* 605); מְשֻׂכָה (*m^e śûkâ,* only in Prov 15:19; → # 5379), nom. thorn hedge (NIV blocked), alternate form of מְשׂוּכָּה (*m^e śûkkâ, HALAT* 605).

OT 1. *swk* I and *śwk* are normally regarded as byforms (*HALAT* 1223), although *HALAT* 712 treats Job 3:23; 38:8 under *skk* I, screen, and J. Hartley (*Job*, 1989, 493) derives the vb. in Job 38:8 from *skk* II, weave (cf. Ps 139:13b). In Ezek 28:13 H. J. van Dijk (*Ezekiel's Prophecy on Tyre*, 1968) relates the nom. *m^e sukāteka* to *swk* (your defense), rather than *skk* I (your covering). The precious stones are then the protective wall of the garden. However, he has not been followed by commentators and translators.

2. A hedge is useful for someone dwelling in a hostile environment, but it becomes an obstacle if there is a way to be traveled (D. J. A. Clines, *Job 1-20*, 101). Satan complains that God's hedging Job from trouble has made piety too easy for him (Job 1:10). Ironically, in 3:23 Job complains at the one hedge that remains, his life. Job yearns for the way to the grave, but God has blocked the path to it (cf. 19:8). However, in 38:8 God asks Job who has hedged in the sea with doors. The vital cosmic barriers that restrain the sea/chaos monster (→ *tannîm* [sea creatures, # 9490]) suggest that Job is to regard God's hedges as an expression of his sovereign wisdom.

3. The people are the hedge (*m^e sûkâ*) in Mic 7:4, so corrupt that even the best are a thorny obstacle to the attainment of God's purposes. In Hos 2:6[8], the hedge is God's punishment, barring Israel's way to her lovers. The lazy find their way blocked by a thorn hedge, or perhaps behave as if it was (Prov 15:19).

Enclosure: → *gnn* (enclose, protect, # 1713); → *ḥdr* I (surround, enclose, # 2539); → *sahar* (round enclosure, # 6044); → *ṣwr* I (besiege, enclose, # 7443); → *śwk* (hedge, shut in, # 8455)

P. P. Jenson

8463	שׂוֹרָה

שׂוֹרָה (*śôrâ*), millet (# 8463).

OT This word occurs only in Isa 28:25 but has several ANE cognates (Arab. *ḏurrat*, millet; and Early Aram., where the word [*swrh*] occurs in the inscriptions of Zinjirli

[N. Syria] in a list of cereal grains). The LXX translates it as *kenchros*, millet, and Isa 28:25 indicates that it is either a type of grain (millet: O. Kaiser, *Isaiah 13-39*, 1974, 257) or planted "in rows" (R. E. Clements, *Isaiah 1-39*, 1980, 234). The latter option is most likely, given the structure of the passage. If another grain were intended, normally the *wāw* would connect *śôrâ* with the preceding *ḥiṭṭâ*, wheat (→ # 2636).

Grain, barley, millet, rice, etc.: → *'ābîb* (ears of grain, # 26); → *biṣqālôn* (fresh stalks [cj.], # 1303); → *bar* III (grain, corn, # 1339); → *gādîš* I (stack of grain, # 1538); → *gereś* (grits, # 1762); → *dāgān* (grain, # 1841); → *dōḥan* (sorghum, millet, # 1893); → *ḥiṭṭâ* (wheat, # 2636); → *kussemet* (emmer-wheat, # 4081); → *karmel* IV (grain, fresh, newly ripened grain, # 4152); → *m^elîlâ* (grain, grains, # 4884); → *minnît* (rice, # 4976); → *mōṣ* (chaff, # 5161); → *sōlet* (wheat flour, # 6159); → *pannāg* (parched? grain, meal or flour, # 7154); → *ṣebet* (grain, bundle of grain, # 7395); → *ṣānum* (hard, barren [ears of grain], # 7568); → *qālî* (parched grain, # 7833); → *qāmâ* (crops, grain, standing grain, # 7850); → *śôrâ* (millet, # 8463); → *ś^e'ōrâ* (barley, # 8555); → *šibbōlet* I (ear of grain, # 8672); → *šeber* II (grain, # 8692)

Bibliography
J. Oswalt, *The Book of Isaiah: Chapters 1-39*, NICOT, 1986, 521, 523.

Paul D. Wegner

8464	שׂושׂ

שׂושׂ (*śwś*), q. rejoice (# 8464); מָשׂוֹשׂ (*māśôś* I), nom. joy (# 5375); שָׂשׂוֹן (*śāśôn*), nom. exultation (# 8607).

ANE There is no apparent Sem. eytmology for *śwś*.

OT The vb. *śwś* occurs 27x, most often in Isa (9x, 8x in Isa 61-66), Ps (7x), and Deut (4x). A preposition (*b^e*—8x, *'al*—8x, *k^e*—3x, *'et*—1x) frequently marks the object of rejoicing.

1. *Indicator of the status of Israel's covenant relationship.* The four instances of *śwś* in Deut delineate two potential divine responses to Israel's conduct, i.e., blessing and cursing. In the midst of a litany of covenant curses, Moses affirms that Yahweh can take delight in prospering or devastating his vassal nation, depending on their response to the covenant stipulations (Deut 28:63). Deut 30:9 envisions the day when Yahweh will regather his scattered people and restore their fortunes, delighting in them just as he had delighted in the patriarchs.

The prophets look forward to a day when Yahweh will once again rejoice over Israel (Isa 62:5; 65:19; Jer 32:41; Zeph 3:17 [cf. *gyl*, # 1635]), and this will cause his restored people to rejoice concerning his deeds on their behalf (Isa 65:18; 66:10, 14; cf. Zeph 3:14—*śmḥ* [# 8523] and *'lz*, [# 6600]). Isa 62:5 compares this divine rejoicing to a bridegroom's jubilation over his bride (a common comparison in judgment statements, cf. *śmḥ* [# 8523] and *gyl* [# 1635]). Yahweh's rejoicing over his covenant nation will replace the sounds of weeping (Isa 65:19). Isaiah describes the future transformation of the world by personifying nature: "the desert and the parched land will be glad" (35:1).

2. *A characteristic of an obedient spirit.* The psalmist confesses to and pleads for rejoicing in Yahweh (Ps 40:16[17]; 70:4[5]), divine salvation (35:9), and jubilation itself (68:3[4]). The psalmist declares that he delights in divine statutes as a person would rejoice about great wealth (119:14) or abundant booty (119:162).

3. *Malicious joy*. As with other vbs. of rejoicing (cf. *śmḥ* [# 8523] and *gyl* [# 1635]), *śwś* can connote the gloating of an enemy over the misfortune of an adversary (Lam 1:21). Edom, who rejoiced over Judah's devastation (Obad 12 [*śmḥ*, # 8523]; Lam 4:21), will also drink from the cup of devastation.

4. *Other uses*. The writer of Job and the psalmist refer to rejoicing in strength to describe the power of a war horse (Job 39:21) or the intensity and swiftness of the sun (Ps 19:5[6]). Some who feel overwhelmed by adversity rejoice at the prospect of release from physical existence (Job 3:22; see *śmḥ* [# 8523] for a fuller treatment).

5. *The nom. māśôś*. This nom. occurs 17x, 10x in Isa, twice in Lam, and once in Job, Ps, Jer, Ezek, and Hos. Positively, *māśôś* connotes the joyfulness that accompanies music (Isa 24:8). Biblical writers describe Zion as the joy of the whole earth (Ps 48:2[3]; Lam 2:15), the rejoicing of all generations (Isa 60:15), and the joy of the Babylonian exiles (Ezek 24:25) (Zion functions metonymically as the object that causes joy). Yahweh affirms that he will cause his chosen people to become a delight (Isa 65:18) and will rejoice over his people as a groom rejoices over his bride (62:5). Negatively, the absence of rejoicing serves as a stark indication of divine judgment (Isa 24:11; Jer 49:25). Yahweh promises to bring an end to Israel's celebrations (religious festivals, Hos 2:11[13]), while the survivors of Jerusalem's destruction bemoan the departure of joy from their hearts (Lam 5:15). The prophet Isaiah provides a wordplay in his repetition of *māśôś* in Isa 32:13-14. While the surviving remnant will mourn the loss of their houses of *māśôś*, the structures of Jerusalem will serve as the *māśôś* of donkeys.

6. *The conjectured existence of māśôś* II. Certain lexical works (e.g., *TWAT* 7:722; *HALAT*, 605) posit the existence of *māśôś* II, derived from *mss*, to dissolve, melt (→ # 5022). In the first of these instances, Isa 8:6, the unique form of *māśôś* (*m^eśôś*, a const. form followed by a prep. [*'et*] rather than an abs. element) and its problematic relationship to the immediate context has occasioned significant discussion. Most scholars interpret the larger pericope (8:5-8) against the background of the impending invasion by the Syro-Ephraimite coalition. In light of this, rejoicing over Rezin (king of Syria) does not appear to be an appropriate response from Judah, Rezin's adversary. Only four of the various suggestions that have been offered receive brief mention below (see Sweeney, 43-45; Irvine, 185-87, for a helpful overview of the interpretive options).

Hayes and Irvine (146-49) and Watts (116-17) revocalize *m^eśôś* to *māśôś*, an abs. form ("a joy to Rezin and Remaliah's son"). Watts contends that "this people" (Isa 8:6) refers primarily to the northern kingdom (Israel) and suggests that *m^eśôś* articulates Rezin's joy over Israel's willingness to participate in the uprising against Assyria. Hayes and Irvine argue that a significant part of the Judean population ("this people," 8:6; or the Judean political elite, Gitay, 220) vehemently opposed Ahaz's refusal to join the coalition against Assyria. Consequently, they rejoiced at the impending invasion by Rezin and the potential removal of Ahaz from kingship.

Several writers replace the MT *m^eśôś*, rejoice, with a homophone *māsôs*, melt (with fear, Clements, 96; Kaiser, 112; Wildberger, 1991, 341) to describe Judah's dismay over the approaching invasion by the Syro-Ephraimite coalition.

Sweeney (48-52) retains the MT form and affirms that *m^eśôś* expresses Judah's willingness to submit to the forces of Samaria and Syria. Auret (113-14; cf. Young,

1:305; Grogan, 67; Oswalt, 225-26), who also retains the MT form, suggests that Tiglath-Pileser's invasion of Syria and Israel, rather than the threatening Syro-Ephraimite coalition, provides the backdrop for 8:6. Consequently, Isaiah's audience ("this people" = Judah; cf. Sweeney, 51, n. 1) rejoices over the fruit of their secret alliance with Assyria, i.e., with regard to the demise of Rezin and Pekah. However, Ahaz and his fellow Judeans are totally unprepared for the trauma they will soon experience at the hands of the same Assyrian ruler (8:7-8).

Another potential example of *māśôś* II occurs in Job 8:19, a passage that has stymied many scholars. This passage belongs to Bildad's delineation of the ultimate fate of the wicked. If *māśôś* II occurs here (or the homophone *māsôs* should be read), Bildad refers to the easily forgotten demise of the wicked. Clines (198, 200) translates the first bicolon, "That is the dissolution (*m*ᵉ*śôś*, from *mss*) of its life" (cf. Smick, 907-8; Fohrer, 189; Horst, 134). Although others have proposed various additional emendations (cf. Michel, 196-97, n. 120, for a brief overview of these suggestions), it appears best to retain the MT as the more difficult reading. The phrase, the joy of his way, either serves as an ironic description of the short-lived nature of the wicked person's joy (Driver and Gray, 82; Habel, 169, 178; Rowley, 74; Pope, 65), or it functions as part of an illustration of triumph over hardship that Bildad offers to bolster Job's spirits (Hartley, 160, n. 7, 162-63).

7. *The nom. śāśôn.* Eighteen of *śāśôn*'s 22x appear in the Ps (5x), Isa (6x), and Jer (7x) (cf. Esth, 2x; Joel, 1x; Zech, 1x). The cognate nom. *śimḥâ* is juxtaposed with *śāśôn* 13x, with *śāśôn* occurring first in all but two instances (Esth 8:16-17) while *rinnâ* serves as a par. term only once (Ps 105:43).

When *śāśôn* stands alone (without a par. cognate), it signifies rejoicing that accompanies the experience of the benefits of salvation (Ps 51:12[14]; Isa 12:3), an attitude toward divine statutes (Ps 119:11; cf. Jer 15:16), as well as future joy instead of sorrow that Yahweh will provide for his beloved people (Jer 31:13; 33:9). The expression "oil of joy" figuratively depicts Yahweh's bestowal of abundant joy on a Davidic ruler (Ps 45:7[8]) and on his covenant people (Isa 61:3). Drawing on contextual descriptions of withered (and fruitless) vines and trees, Joel depicts the devastation of the coming judgment by affirming that joy (*śāśôn*) from humankind will wither away.

The juxtaposition of *śāśôn* with a par. cognate term connotes enthusiastic celebration. The Jews joyfully celebrated their deliverance from Egypt (Ps 105:43, *śāśôn* ... *rinnâ*) and from certain massacre by the Persians (Esth 8:16-17, *śimḥâ* ... *śāśôn*).

In addition to the psalmist's desire to hear (know) once again joy and gladness (Ps 51:8[10]), and the prophet's affirmation of joyful reliance on Yahweh's revelation (Jer 15:16), the par. of *śāśôn* and *śimḥâ* delineates aspects of Israel's covenantal relationship with Yahweh. Of the 4x this pair occurs in Isa, three instances describe the festive celebration that will accompany Yahweh's glorious restoration of his people (Isa 35:10; 51:3, 11; cf. Zech 8:19). Isa 22:13 depicts the arrogant celebration of God's people who, in the face of an impending invasion, refused to turn to Yahweh in faith, but rather satisfy their physical desires in the last moments available to them. The expression "the sounds of joy and gladness" (*qôl śāśôn w*ᵉ*qôl śimḥâ*) occurs 4x in Jer (7:34; 16:9; 25:10; 33:11). A tangible example of festive celebration accompanies each of these cognate pairs ("the voices of bride and bridegroom"). In order to demonstrate the sobering impact of the coming covenantal judgment, Yahweh promises to bring to an end (*šbt*) and banish (*'bd*) all such rejoicing (7:34; 16:9; 25:10). In his description of his future restoration of Israel Yahweh promises that these sounds of jubilation will be heard once more (33:11).

Happiness, joy, rejoicing: → *'šr* II (be fortunate, # 887); → *blg* (be cheerful, happy, # 1158); → *gad* II (luck, fortune, # 1513); → *gyl* (exult, # 1635); → *ḥdh* (gladden, rejoice, make happy, # 2525); → *'lz* (exult, # 6600); → *'ls* (enjoy, appear glad, # 6632); → *'lṣ* (rejoice, # 6636); → *śwś* (rejoice, # 8464); → *śmḥ* (rejoice, make glad, # 8523)

BIBLIOGRAPHY

TWAT 7:721-29; *TWOT* 2:873; A. Auret, "Another Look at ומשושin Isaiah 8:6," *Old Testament Essays* 3, 1990, 107-14; R. Clements, *Isaiah 1-39*, NCBC, 1980; D. Clines, *Job 1-20*, 1989; S. Driver and G. Gray, *A Critical and Exegetical Commentary on the Book of Job*, ICC, 1921; G. Fohrer, *Das Buch Hiob*, 1963; Y. Gitay, "Isaiah and the Syro-Ephraimite Crisis," *The Book of Isaiah*, 1989, 217-30; G. Grogan, "Isaiah," *EBC*, 1986, 6:1-354; N. Habel, *The Book of Job*, OTL, 1985; J. Hartley, *The Book of Job*, NICOT, 1988; J. Hayes and S. Irvine, *Isaiah the Eighth-Century Prophet: His Times and His Preaching*, 1987; F. Horst, *Hiob*, 1968; S. Irvine, *Isaiah, Ahaz, and the Syro-Ephraimite Crisis*, 1990; O. Kaiser, *Isaiah 1-12*, OTL, 1979; W. Michel, *Job in the Light of Northwest Semitic*, 1987; J. Oswalt, *The Book of Isaiah, Chapters 1-39*, NICOT, 1986; M. Pope, *Job*, AB, 1973; H. Rowley, *Job*, NCBC, 1976; E. Smick, "Job," *EBC*, 1988, 4:843-1060; M. Sweeney, "On *ûm^{e}śôś* in Isaiah 8:6," *Among the Prophets: Language, Image and Structure in the Prophetic Writings*, 1993, 42-54; J. Watts, *Isaiah 1-33*, WBC, 1985; H. Wildberger, *Isaiah 1-12*, 1991; idem, *Jesaja*, 1982; E. Young, *The Book of Isaiah*, 1970.

Michael A. Grisanti

8465	שֵׂחַ

שֵׂחַ (*śēaḥ*), nom. thought, plan (hapleg.; # 8465); < שִׂיחַ (*śyḥ* II, complain, → # 8490).

OT Amos uses this nom. for Yahweh's plan or purpose that he declares to humans (Amos 4:13). "Plan" in this text surely includes his law as well as his will made known through the prophets (cf. 3:7). The great God clearly communicates with humans.

Plan, thought, meditation, scheming: → *'zn* II (weigh, consider carefully, # 264); → *bd'* (devise, imagine, # 968); → *higgāyôn* (melody, thought, # 2053); → *zmm* (plan, purpose, plan evil, # 2372); → *ḥms* II (think, invent, # 2804); → *ḥšb* (count, compute, calculate, think, plan, # 3108); → *yēṣer* I (frame of mind, disposition, # 3671); → *'št* I (think, consider, # 6951); → *śîḥâ* (meditation, study, # 8491); → *ś^{e}'ippîm* (disquieting thoughts, worries, # 8546); → *tar'ît* (thought, # 9569)

John E. Hartley

8466	שׂחה

שׂחה (*śḥh*), q. swim; hi. make swim, overflow (# 8466); der. שָׂחוּ (*śāḥû*), swimming (# 8467).

OT 1. The radical *śḥh* occurs twice as a vb. and once as a substantive in the OT. As a vb. it appears in the q. (Isa 25:11) and hi. (Ps 6:7) formation.

2. This word can be used in a literal sense where it refers to physical swimming. In the Isaiah passage it functions in a context of divine judgment on the land of Moab in contrast to God's salvation, which is extended to Israel (cf. Isa 25:9-10). Moab as an enemy will be trampled down under Yahweh as straw is trampled down in manure water. In their attempt to escape they will instinctively spread out their hands as swimmers. Yet all their efforts will be of no avail because God will bring them down, despite the cleverness of their hands. Here we have a metaphorical expression of Moab's attempt to escape their fate (i.e., to escape from the manure pile into which Yahweh has pushed them), but their response to the impending danger is described in a physical sense. Hence, the vb. *śḥh* has the literal meaning of swimming. It describes Moab's feeble attempt to survive a death-threatening situation.

3. It can also be used in a metaphorical or figurative sense. This is especially the case in Ps 6:6[7]. Here we have a hyperbolic description of great sadness that the psalmist is currently experiencing. A synonymous parallelism is employed to relate something of the intensity of this pain and suffering: "Every night I make my bed swim, I drench my couch with tears" (lit. tr.). Once again the vb. conveys the meaning (to cause to) swim. Unlike the first occurrence, *śḥh* does not describe swimming as a physical act (cf. Isa 25:11), but conveys an exaggerated account of a negative experience, called a hyperbole. In this way, the audience is enabled to share in the mental anguish of the suppliant. Here the vb. *śḥh* should rather be interpreted as (to cause to) "float," instead of "swim." This brings out the intended meaning and is more true to the context in which it appears.

4. The nom. *śāhû* is used in a literal sense (Ezek 47:5), i.e., "rising waters for swimming." The prophet gives a description of an amount of water that is deep enough to allow someone to swim in it. Perhaps the prophet had in mind a contrast between this and the Kidron Valley, which was usually a dry wash. This dry riverbed is now compared with a new stream of water that is constantly increasing. This life-giving effect of the new waters becomes more graphic as the waters freshen and the fish return to it (cf. Ezek 47:1-7).

Overflow: → *day* (sufficiency, overflowing supply, # 1896); → *r^e^wāyâ* (overflow, # 8122); → *śḥh* (swim, make swim, overflow, # 8466); → *šwq* I (overflow, bestow abundantly, # 8796); → *šṭp* (wash away, flood, overflow, # 8851)

BIBLIOGRAPHY

F. I. Anderson & A. D. Forbes, *The Vocabulary of the Old Testament*, 1992, 235.

P. J. J. S. Els

8467 (*śāḥû*, swimming), → # 8466

8468 (*ś^e^ḥôq*, laughter, playing, pleasure), → # 8471

8469	שׂחט

שׂחט (*śḥṭ*), q. squeeze, press out (grapes) (# 8469).

ANE Mish. Heb. *sḥṭ*; Jew. Aram. *s^e^ḥaṭ*; Akk. *ṣaḫātu(m)*.

OT This hapleg. occurs in the q. in Gen 40:11 to describe what the chief cupbearer for Pharaoh did. He took the grapes (*ʿēnāb*) and, he said, "I squeezed (*śḥṭ*) them into Pharaoh's cup." Then he served the cup to Pharaoh.

NT The LXX renders it to mean that the cupbearer took a "bunch of grapes" (*staphylē*) and pressed/crushed (*ekthlibō*) them. It is certain that the position required a person whom the Pharaoh could trust with his life.

Grapes—juice, wine: → *gat* I (wine press, # 1780); → *demaʿ* (juice from wine vat, # 1964); → *ḥōmeṣ* (vinegar, wine, beer, # 2810); → *ḥemer* (wine, foaming wine, # 2815); → *yayin* (wine, # 3516); → *yeqeb* (wine vat/trough, winepress, # 3676); → *yrš* II (tread the wine press/grapes, # 3770); → *mhl* (adulterated wine, # 4543); → *mezeg* (spiced/blended/mixed wine, # 4641); → *mišrâ* (juice, # 5489); → *ʿāsîs* (grape juice, # 6747); → *śḥṭ* (squeeze, to press out grapes, # 8469); → *šemer* I (dregs, aged wine, # 9069); → *tîrôš* (fresh wine, # 9408)

BIBLIOGRAPHY

KB 4:1226; D. Marcus, "'Lifting Up the Head': On the Trait of a Word Play in Gen 40," *Prooftexts* 10, 1990, 17-27.

Eugene Carpenter

8471	שׂחק

שׂחק (*śḥq*), q. laugh, mock; pi. play, rejoice, revel, celebrate, dance, engage in a military contest; hi. scorn (# 8471); nom. מִשְׂחָק (*miśḥāq*), object of ridicule (# 5377); שְׂחוֹק (*ś^eḥôq*), שְׂחֹק (*s^eḥōq*), laughter, laughingstock, playing, pleasure (# 8468).

ANE A cognate form is found only in Eth. (*šäḥaqä*, laugh), unless Akk. *šeḫēqu*, sneeze, is related.

OT This byform mainly replaces *ṣḥq* (→ # 7464) in exilic and postexilic Heb. and in Mish. Heb. (Brenner, 47-48). This term, too, has positive and negative usages.

1. It conveys the notion of ordinary human happiness. Life is inexorably divided by God into a series of changing scenes, which are described in Eccl 3:4 as "a time to weep and a time to laugh." Jeremiah complained to God that his grim vocation as prophet of divine judgment cut him off from those who indulged in normal social pleasures (revelers, Jer 15:17). The restored Jerusalem was again to echo with the sound of "rejoicing" (Jer 30:19; cf. 31:4[3]), and its streets would be filled with children playing (Zech 8:5).

2. As with *ṣḥq*, the term can be used to refer to positive changes in fortune brought about by God for an individual or the community. Bildad assured Job that God would turn the tide of his suffering and fill his mouth with laughter (Job 8:21). Likewise, a divine change of national fortunes caused the Judeans' mouths to be filled with laughter (Ps 126:2).

3. In Prov 8:30-31, in a description of wisdom's role in creation that enhances its importance as the object of human pursuit, personified wisdom is portrayed as actively present with God in his work of creation, "rejoicing" in the world he made (cf. von Rad, 151-55; Keel, 25-30).

4. For the usage concerning Samson's entertainment of the Philistines in Judg 16:27 see *ṣḥq* (laugh, mock, # 7464).

5. In Ps 104:26 the "leviathan" or large sea creature, which might otherwise be the object of fear (cf. Isa 27:1), is transformed in the psalmist's God-oriented view of the world into a playful, dolphin-like creature.

6. In Israelite worship "celebrating," as NIV renders, seems to have been a term for dancing (Gruber, 354). Thus, David's determination to "celebrate before the LORD" the movement of the ark to Jerusalem in 2 Sam 6:21 refers to his "leaping and dancing before the LORD" in v. 16, while in 1 Chron 15:29 the "dancing" of 2 Sam 6:16 is paraphrased as "celebrating" (cf. 2 Sam 6:5; 1 Chron 13:8).

7. In the wisdom teaching of Prov and Eccl, laughter and pleasure have limitations. Laughter and sorrow are not far away from each other (Prov 14:13). A warning is sounded against a light attitude to life (Eccl 2:2), while sorrow is commended for the lessons it can teach (7:3). The empty laughter of fools is deprecated (7:6), and so is their pleasure in evil conduct (Prov 10:23).

8. Laughter may have a negative, hostile connotation of derision and ridicule, as the frequent parallelism with *l'g*, mock, shows (e.g., 2 Chron 30:10; Ps 2:4; 59:8[9]; Prov 1:26; Jer 20:7). Thus it is used in lament contexts, in pitiful descriptions of the attitude of personal or national enemies to sufferers (Job 12:4; 30:1; Jer 20:7; Lam 1:7; 3:14).

9. In Hab 1:10 it is used of the wicked power of the Babylonians over smaller nations, in the course of Habakkuk's protest that God should use such a means to accomplish his purposes.

10. In 2 Chron 30:10 those among the northern tribes who repudiated Hezekiah's invitation to worship at the temple in Jerusalem are described as laughing his couriers to scorn.

11. However, the godly may rightly indulge in negative laughter, as an oblique expression of divine blessing. It is possible to laugh at, and so disregard, untoward prospects or circumstances that would otherwise fill one with alarm. Thus, the wise woman is so prepared that the future poses no problem for her household (Prov 31:25; cf. Job 39:18, 22; 41:29[21]).

12. Faith in God's eventual purposes may be so expressed. In Ps 52:6[8] evildoers are cut down to size with the observation that the righteous will live to laugh at their destruction through God's hands. In Prov 1:26 personified wisdom threatens to laugh at the disastrous end of those who ignore her teaching.

13. Similarly, several psalms bring the assurance that God will have the last laugh. "Yahweh laughs as an expression of his complete and sovereign superiority to his opponents and those who will not bow to him" (Hvidberg, 154). Thus, the heavenly king laughs at ultimately futile attempts to conspire against the Davidic king (Ps 2:4). In a wisdom poem the doom of the wicked is celebrated in terms of God's laughter (Ps 37:13). An affirmation of faith Ps 59:8[9] envisions in similar terms the future downfall of persecutors.

Laughter, play, ridicule: → *l'g* (scorn, mock, # 4352); → *ṣhq* (laugh, play, insult, # 7464); → *śḥq* (laugh, mock, rejoice, celebrate, dance, # 8471)

Dance, whirl: → *ḥwl* I (whirl around, dance, # 2565); → *krr* II (whirl, # 4159); → *rqd* (skip, leap, # 8376)

Happiness, joy, rejoicing: → *'šr* II (be fortunate, # 887); → *blg* (be cheerful, happy, # 1158); → *gad* II (luck, fortune, # 1513); → *gyl* (exult, # 1635); → *ḥdh* (gladden, rejoice, make happy,

2525); → *'lz* (exult, # 6600); → *'ls* (enjoy, appear glad, # 6632); → *'lṣ* (rejoice, # 6636); → *śwś* (rejoice, # 8464); → *śmḥ* (rejoice, make glad, # 8523)
Mocking, ridicule, scoffing, stammering: → *gdp* (revile, blaspheme, # 1552); → *htl* (deceive, mock, # 2252); → *ḥrp* II (taunt, mock, insult, defy, # 3070); → *lyṣ* (scorn, talk big, mock, ridicule, # 4329); → *l'b* (jest, play, # 4351); → *l'g* (stutter, mock, deride, # 4352); → *lṣṣ* (rebel, scoff, # 4372); → *mwq* (mock, scoff, deride, # 4610); → *qls* (disdain, scoff, jeer, # 7840); → *śḥq* (laugh, mock, rejoice, celebrate, dance, # 8471); → *tll* (deceive, mock, trifle, # 9438); → *t''* (mock, deceive, # 9506); → *ta'tu'îm* (errors, mockery, # 9511)
Sorrow, affliction, grief: → *d'b* (sorrow, # 1790); → *ygh* I (sorrow, grief, # 3324); → *mûṣāq* (distress, affliction, grief, trial, # 4608); → *ṣrr* I (bind, shut up, be narrow, in straits, distress, # 7674)

Bibliography

TWAT 7:730-45; A. Brenner, "On the Semantic Field of Humour, Laughter and the Comic in the Old Testament," *On Humour and the Comic in the Hebrew Bible*, JSOTSup 92, 1990, 39-58; M. I. Gruber, "Ten Dance-Derived Expressions in the Hebrew Bible," *Bib* 62, 1981, 328-46; F. F. Hvidberg, *Weeping and Laughter in the Old Testament*, 1962; R. K. Johnston, *The Christian at Play*, 1983; O. Keel, *Die Weisheit "spielt" vor Gott*, 1974; G. von Rad, *Wisdom in Israel*, 1972; C. W. Reines, "Laughter in Biblical and Rabbinic Literature," *Judaism* 82, 1972, 176-83; G. Webster, *Laughter in the Bible*, 1960; C. Westermann, *Genesis 12-36*, 1985.

Leslie C. Allen

8474	שׂטה

שׂטה (*śṭh*), q. turn aside, turn aside from, go astray (# 8474).

ANE Cognates are attested in Aram. *ś^{e}tā'*, Aram./Syr. *s^{e}tā'*, err, and in Eth. *šāṭäyä*, be led away from the right path, and Arab., *šaṭṭa*, to overstep limits.

OT The vb. appears primarily in the Torah legislation about a wayward wife, whose waywardness consists in adulterous relationships (Num 5:12, 19, 20, 29). In Wisdom literature the meaning is more general: warnings to abstain from wicked ways (Prov 4:15), esp. the temptations to adultery (7:25).

Turning, apostasy, returning, faithlessness, repentance: → *zwr* II (turn away, # 2319); → *ḥmq* (turn aside, # 2811); → *yq'* (turn aside, # 3697); → *nq'* (disengage, # 5936); → *sbb* (turn, go round, surround, # 6015); → *swr* (turn aside, # 6073); → *pnh* (turn to the side, # 7155); → *śṭh* (turn aside, # 8474); → *šwb* I (repent, turn, return, revert, withdraw, # 8740); → *t^{e}qûpâ* (turning point, # 9543)

Bibliography

TWOT 2:874; H. C. Brichto, "The Case of the Sota and a Reconsidertion of Biblical Law," *HUCA* 46, 1975, 55-70; M. Fishbane, "Accusations of Adultery: A Study of Law and Scribal Practice in Num 5:11-31," *HUCA* 45, 1974, 25-45.

J. A. Thompson

8475	שׂטם

שׂטם (*śṭm*), q. hate, show enmity, persecute (# 8475); מַשְׂטֵמָה (*maśṭēmâ*), nom. the result of enmity or animosity (# 5378). A related form is *śāṭān* (→ # 8477).

OT 1. The vb. appears 6x and has the sense of strong hostility (Ps 55:3[4], bear a grudge (BDB, 966). It is thus particularly suitable for Esau's strong feelings against Jacob and the concern of Joseph's brothers that he would similarly view them for their selling him into slavery (Gen 49:23; 50:15). It is also used of Job's thoughts as to how God regarded him (Job 16:9; 30:21).

2. Hosea employs the nom. twice of sinful Israel's settled hostility against God and his prophets (Hos 9:7-8). (→ Anomisity: Theology)

Animosity, enmity, hostility: → *'yb* (be an enemy, # 366); → *ṣrr* II (be hostile, # 7675); → *śṭm* (hate, # 8475); → *śāṭān* (accuser, satan, # 8477); → *śn'* (hate, one who is an enemy, # 8533); → *šôrēr* (adversary, # 8806); → **Animosity: Theology**

Bruce Baloian

8476 (*śṭn*, be hostile, accuse), → # 8477

8477	שָׂטָן

שָׂטָן (*śāṭān*), nom. accuser, Satan (# 8477); שׂטן (*śṭn*), denom. vb. q. be hostile, accuse (# 8476); שִׂטְנָה (*šiṭnâ* I), accusation (hapleg. in Ezra 4:6; # 8478).

ANE Cognates occur in Arab. *šaiṭān*, and Eth. *s/šaiṭan*; Tigr. *šēṭān*.

OT 1. The vb. form is found only 6x. It has a distinctive usage that does not allow it to be translated merely as enemy, but often has the distinct nuance of one who verbally accuses (Ps 38:20[21]; 71:13; 109:4, 20, 29; Zech 3:1).

2. Special note needs to be taken of the term *śāṭān*, which has had extensive development theologically in the NT. Though the term basically means adversary, or in a legal sense, accuser, it functions in the Psalms as enemies or adversaries with the added nuance of verbal accusation (Ps 38:20[21]; 71:13; 109:4, 6, 20, 29). In the narrative portions, as in the Psalms, *śāṭān* seems to function with the meaning: one who is in opposition (Num 22:22, 32; 1 Sam 29:4; 2 Sam 19:23; 1 Kgs 5:18; 11:14, 23, 25). However, in Job 1 and 2 and perhaps in Zech 3:1-2 *śāṭān* has clearly the meaning of a heavenly accuser, but it is improbable that a specific demonic being is referred to (a possible exception may be 1 Chron 21:1). In Job, for instance, *śāṭān* is merely a member of the heavenly court with a role similar to a district attorney.

The development of the idea of an express leader of the forces of evil is not found within the OT itself but took place in the Apocrypha and Pseudepigrapha. However, there is a hint of demonic character in Gen 3, 6:1-4; Isa 14:12; Hos 4:12; 5:4; and Zech 13:2. Eichrodt (207-8) speculates that the original pagan ideas of an antagonistic supernatural personal being in the above texts are borrowed from pagan mythology. Such ideas are suppressed under monotheism, as is much else that is borrowed from pagan mythology, and sublimated to Yahweh's sovereignty and rule over all aspects of reality. Note the claim, "I am the LORD, and there is no other; apart from me there is no God.... I form the light and create darkness, I bring prosperity and create disaster; I, the LORD, do all these things" (Isa 45:5a, 7). The OT does not see the satanic aspect as forming part of its theodicy. A "satan" is not portrayed as the origin or cause of evil.

P-B The subsequent development in later Judaism (cf. 1 En. 15-16) has often been attributed to Persian influences coming out of Zoroastrianism. Here one has a personalized demonic being. For example, in Wisd 2:4 the serpent in the garden is identified with Satan, and this interpretation is followed up in the NT (Rev 12:1; 20:2). This development is not found within the OT, but neither is it in opposition to the OT and its view of the need of humans to choose between good and evil. The development of a head devil and his cohorts existing in the spiritual world does contrast sharply with God and gives a metaphysical grounding to the polarities of human choices. However, such ontological contrasts increase human responsibility, not lighten or eliminate it. Humans are responsible to choose with which spiritual power they will side. The exclusive monotheistic demands found within the OT are carried over into the NT.

Animosity, enmity, hostility: → *'yb* (be an enemy, # 366); → *ṣrr* II (be hostile, # 7675); → *śṭm* (hate, # 8475); → *śāṭān* (accuser, satan, # 8477); → *śn'* (hate, one who is an enemy, # 8533); → *šōrēr* (adversary, # 8806); → **Animosity: Theology**

BIBLIOGRAPHY
NIDNTT 3:468-69; *TDNT* 2:73-75; *THAT* 2:822-23; W. Eichrodt, *TOT*, 2:205-9; T. H. Gaster, "Satan," *IDB*, 4:224-28; E. Langton, *Essentials of Demonology*, 1949; E. Pagels, "The Social History of Satan, the Intimate 'Enemy': A Preliminary Sketch," *HTR* 84, 1991, 105-28; R. R. Scharf, "Die Gestalt des Satans im AT," diss. Zurich, 1948; W. Vosloog, "Die Ou-Testament oor Demone en die Satan," *In die Skriflig*, 26, 1992, 387-96.

Bruce Baloian

8478 (*śiṭnâ*, accusation), → # 8477

8482	שׂיב

שׂיב (*śyb*), q. be gray, be old (# 8482); שֵׂיב (*śêb*), nom. old age (# 8483); שֵׂיבָה (*śêbâ*), gray-headedness, gray-headed person (# 8484).

ANE The root has several cognates in ANE languages: Ugar. *šb*, pl. *šbm*, old; Akk. *šību(m)*, gray hair, old; Aram. *sîbā'*, old; *sêbā'*, old age; Geez *šebä*, grow gray, old. *sêbâ* has cognates in many ANE languages: Ugar. *šbt*, gray hair; Akk. *šībtu[m]*, gray hair, old woman; pl. *šibâtum;* Mand. *sibuta;* Pal. *sybw*, old; Eth. *šībat;* Tigr. *šīb, šībat*, gray hair.

OT 1. The word *śêbâ* occurs 20x in the OT and generally emphasizes that a person's hair has grayed (cf. Job 41:32[24]) and that, in deference to the person's wisdom, honor and respect should be shown (Lev 19:32; Prov 16:31; 20:29). Sometimes the adj. *ṭôb*, good, is added to *śêbâ* to describe a long, pleasant life blessed by God (Gen 15:15; 25:8; Judg 8:32; 1 Chron 29:28), but unwise choices or other circumstances could cause this time to be one of great sadness and sorrow (Gen 42:38; 44:29, 31; 1 Kgs 2:6, 9). Several times *zāqēn*, old, is used as a synonym for *śêbâ* (Lev 19:32; Isa 46:4); *yônēq*, suckling, nursling, is its antonym (Deut 32:25). This word generally refers to "old age," and the context may emphasize a positive sense of the honor and respect due to an older person (Gen 15:15; 25:8; Lev 19:32; etc.) or a negative sense of a person's weak or senile condition (Hos 7:9). The contexts in which this word is used indicate that God is the one who blesses a person with a long life (Gen 15:15; 25:8) and that even when the body fails, God will not forsake the elderly (Ps 71:18; 92:14[15]; Isa 46:4).

2. J. G. Harris states, "Languages throughout the ANE use 'white hair' (wool) to refer to one of optimum age and wisdom" (*ABD* 5:10). Ahijah is described as old, *śêb*; because of his advanced age, his eyesight was failing (1 Kgs 14:4).

P-B 1. The author of the LXX translates *śêb* by *presbyteros*, elder, older, advanced in years.

2. *sêbâ* had continued use with a similar meaning in the DSS (K. G. Kuhn, *Konkordanz zum der Qumrantexten,* 1960, p. 211); 1QH 4, 30, "old age or grey hair"; Sam. *šiba* [Gen 42:38]) and in Aram. The LXX translates this word either as *gēras*, old age (Gen 15:15; 25:8; 42:38; 44:29; etc.), *presbyteros*, old man (Deut 32:25; 2 Sam 19:34, etc.), or *polios*, gray-headed (Lev 19:32; Ruth 4:15, etc.).

Old, aged: → *zqn* (be old, grow old, # 2416); → *yašîš* (elderly, very aged, # 3813); → *yšn* II (become old, # 3823); → *'tq* (move, become old, to move, # 6980); → *śyb* (be gray, old, # 8482)

Bibliography
ABD 5:10; J. G. Harris, *Biblical Perspectives on Aging: God and the Elderly,* 1987; M. Sokoloff, "'*Amar Neqe'*, Lamb's Wool (Dan 7:9)," *JBL* 95, 1976, 277-79.

Paul D. Wegner

8483 (*śêb*, old age), → # 8482

8484 (*śêbâ*, gray-headedness), → # 8482

8485	שִׂיג

שִׂיג (*śîg*), nom. excrement, or possibly, departure (# 8485).

OT The nom. *śîg*, excrement, is found only in 1 Kgs 18:27. Elijah chides the prophets of Baal and makes several suggestions, one of which is that Baal may be relieving himself (*śîg*) (NIV busy).

Dung, excrement, refuse, urine: → *'ašpōt* (ash-heap, refuse-heap, dung-hill, # 883); → *gll* II (befoul, dirty o.s., # 1671); → *dōmen* (dung, manure, # 1961); → *ḥ^{a}rā'îm* (dung, # 2989); → *yešaḥ* (filth, diarrhea, # 3803); → *madmēnâ* I (dung pit, # 4523); → *sûḥâ* (offal, # 6054); → *pereš* I (offal, contents of stomach, # 7302); → *ṣē'â* (filth, human excrement, # 7362); → *ṣāpîa'* (dung [of cattle], # 7616); → *śîg* (excrement, # 8485); → *šyn* (urinate, # 8874)

Bibliography
H. D. Preuss, *Die Verspottung fremder religionen im Alten Testament,* BWANT 92, 1971, 86.

Roy E. Hayden

8486	שׂיד

שׂיד (*śyd*), q. plaster, whitewash (# 8486), denom. vb.; nom. שִׂיד (*śîd*), plaster (# 8487).

OT 1. The vb. occurs only in Deut 27:2, 4, where Israel, having crossed the Jordan, is to erect a pile of stones and plaster them with plaster (*śîd*), on which could be written the words of the Law of Moses (27:3, 8). Since early plaster was made of lime, lime and plaster are often differentiated only by usage, with plaster being used to protect the mud walls of houses from the elements.

2. Both Isaiah and Amos speak of people whose bones are burned into lime (*śîd*; Isa 33:12; Amos 2:1). In Isaiah the figure alludes to the practice of burning limestone to produce lime and thus bespeaks the fierceness of God's judgment on the nations round about Judah (Oswalt, 598). Amos refers to burning the bones of the king of Edom as an unspeakable atrocity, with the words "to lime" (*laśśîd*) stressing the totality of the destruction. Wolff suggests that the Targum is probably correct in interpreting the expression to mean that the Moabites had made whitewash from the ashes of the king's bones and used it to cover their houses (162-63). See BDB, 966, for etymologies.

Lime, chalk, plaster: → *gir* (chalk, # 1732); → *ṭwḥ* (plaster, coat, overlay, paint, # 3212); → *ṭpl* (smear, plaster, # 3260); → *śyd* (plaster, whitewash, # 8486); → *śered* (chalk, # 8574); → *šayiš* (alabaster, # 8880); → *tāpēl* II (mud-plaster, whitewash, # 9521)

Bibliography
J. N. Oswalt, *The Book of Isaiah: Chapters 1-39*, NICOT, 1986; H. W. Wolff, *Joel and Amos*, 1977; W. Zimmerli, *Ezekiel 1*, 1979.

William C. Williams

8487 (*śîd*, plaster), → # 8486

8488	שׂיח

שׂיח (*śyḥ* II), denom. vb., q. complain, muse, study, talk; pilp. meditate, consider (# 8488); nom. שֵׂחַ (*śēaḥ*), thought (hapleg.; → # 8465); nom. שִׂיחַ (*śîaḥ* II), complaint, musing (# 8490); nom. שִׂיחָה (*śîḥâ*), complaint, musing (# 8491).

OT 1. Fluctuating between the act of speaking and thinking, *śyḥ* takes on more specific connotations in contextual usage (cf. Judg 5:10; Job 12:8; Ps 55:17[18]; 69:12[13]; 119:15, 23, 27; Isa 53:8). Attested cognates exhibit the same semantic interplay (BDB, 966; *HALAT* 4:1230-31; on 1 Kgs 18:27 see Gary A. Rendsburg, "The Mock of Baal in 1 Kgs 18:27," *CBQ* 50, 1988, 414-17). For synonyms see *THAT* 1:510, 839; 2:81, 900. It is its use in the vocabulary of worship that generates theological interest.

2. In the Psalms, the vb. is used by the psalmist primarily in a transitive sense (11x), for reflection on the saving deeds of Yahweh on behalf of Israel, and secondarily in an intransitive sense (2x), to speak of the psalmist's act of complaint or lamentation (55:17[18]; 77:3[4]; cf. Job 7:11; see below on the nom.). Specific context determines whether the focus is on thought (77:6[7]) or speech (105:2). In either case, the action in view ranges from dramatic action depicted within the psalm to the psalm itself and its recitation in cultic worship. This mental/verbal reflection on Yahweh's saving deeds identifies the psalmist as a deserving suppliant for divine aid (143:5), provides the basis for comfort and encouragement in context of suffering (77:12[13]), and gives the motive for and substance of communal praise of Israel's God (105:2; 145:5). Within the context of Israel's ritual psalmody, *śyḥ* constitutes one of the vbs. of worship. Its principal object, Yahweh's deeds (77:12[13] *ʿᵃlîlôt*, works; 105:2 *niplāʾôt*, wonders; 143:5 *maʿᵃśê yādeykā*, works of your hands; 145:5 *dibrê niplᵉʾôteykā*, reports of your wonders, but cf. *BHS*), anchors Israel's worship in the reverent recollection and personal reappropriation of her story of national origin as a history of divine love and

deliverance within the election-promise-exodus-divine guidance-conquest/inheritance framework. (→ Psalms: Theology)

The late Psalm 119 extends the concept of reflection on Yahweh's saving deeds to take in study of the Torah—more specifically, v. 15 *piqqudeykā*, your precepts, v. 23 *ḥuqqeykā*, your statutes, v. 148 *'imrōteykā*, your words. Significantly, "your wonders," *nipl^e'ôteykā,* is paralleled to "your precepts," *piqqûdeykā* (v. 27). Covenantal law has become a constituent of Yahweh's saving acts, or perhaps better, his saving miracles. Torah study has become a cultic act of worship and the practical demonstration of righteousness in the framework of a Torah-centered piety. (→ Law of God: Theology)

3. The nominal formations, *śîaḥ* and *śîḥâ*, mirror the vb. (→ # 8491). They refer, on the one hand, to the psalmist's meditation—i.e., his hymn of praise in celebration of Yahweh as Creator (Ps 104:34), or his loving study of the Torah (119:97, 99). Thus as an act of worship, *śîḥâ* functions as a related term to the appropriate religious posture of reverential fear (Job 15:4, ‖ *yir'â,* fear; on the fear of God, see further, *THAT* 1:765-78). On the other hand, the two words refer to the psalmist's complaint (cf. the intransitive use of the vb. above), modulating between the verbal act or the cause for it, and his suffering/troubles (4x: Ps 55:2[3]; 64:1[2]; 102:title[1]; 142:2[3]; cf. 5x: Job 7:13; 9:27; 10:1; 21:4; 23:2). As a term for the psalm of complaint (cf. the title on 102:1), or as a label for the dramatic description of trouble and consequent petition for deliverance, complaint also constitutes part of Israel's ritual prayer in the cult. Thus, rather than an act opposed to worship, complaint is one of the appropriate poles within Israel's idiom of worship. It, too, ironically, is a way of honoring and praising Yahweh (see further, C. Westermann, *Praise and Lament in the Psalms,* 1981, 52-81; H.-J. Kraus, *Theology of the Psalms,* 1986, 84-100, 137-43).

Concern, business, occupation, trouble: → *d'g* (be anxious, concerned, fear, dread, # 1793); → *'nh* III (be troubled, busy with, # 6701); → *ṣrr* I (bind, shut up, be narrow, in straits, distress, # 7674); → *śyḥ*, complain, muse, study, talk, meditate, # 8488)

Fear, dread, terror: → *'āyōm* (terrible, awesome, majestic, # 398); → *'êmâ* (terror, dread, # 399); → *bhl* (be dismayed, terrified, dismay, terrify, hasten, hurry, # 987); → *b't* (overtaken by sudden terror, stupefied, be terrified, assail, # 1286); → *gwr* III (be afraid of, dread, stand in awe, # 1593); → *d'g* (be anxious, concerned, fear, dread, # 1793); → *zḥl* II (fear, be afraid, # 2324); → *ḥrd* (tremble, shudder, startle, # 3006); → *ḥtt* (be shattered, dismayed, terrified, scare, terrify, # 3169); → *ygr* (fear, dread, terror, # 3336); → *yr'* I (fear, be afraid, held in honor, # 3707); → *yrh* (be afraid, terrified, paralyzed with fright, # 3724); → *'rṣ* (be alarmed, terrified, dreadful, dreadful, be in terror, # 6907); → *pḥd* I (tremble, be in dread, # 7064); → *qwṣ* I (feel disgust, frighten, cause dread, # 7762)

Praising, singing, thanksgiving: → *hll* II (praise, be praiseworthy, boast, exult, # 2146); → *zmr* I (make music, sing praise, # 2376); → *ydh* II (acknowledge, give thanks, praise, # 3344); → *nwh* II (praise, # 5658); → *'nh* IV (sing, # 6702); → *pṣḥ* I (break forth with or break into singing, # 7200); → *rômēm* (exalt, # 8123a); → *šbḥ* I (commend, praise, honor, # 8655); → *šyr* (sing, # 8876); → *tnh* (recite, commemorate, # 9480)

Bibliography

W. Brueggemann, *Israel's Praise: Doxology, Idolatry and Ideology,* 1988; idem, *Abiding Astonishment: Psalms, Modernity, and the Making of History,* 1991.

A. R. Pete Diamond

8489	שִׂיחַ

שִׂיחַ (*śîaḥ* II, *HALAT śîaḥ* I), nom. bush, shrub, plant (# 8489).

ANE Aram., *šîḥ,* plant or tree; Syr., *sîḥā'*, shrub; Punic, *śḥ*.

OT The word occurs 4x in the OT. Gen 2:5 speaks of a time at the beginning of the Lord's creative work when no plant of the field (*śîaḥ haśśādeh*) had yet appeared. In 21:15 Hagar leaves her child to die under one of the bushes. In Job 30:4 the outcasts of society have only such things as the leaves of bushes (*'alê-śîaḥ*) to eat. Such people were forced to live among the bushes, according to 30:7.

P-B The word appears in RL as a general word for plant or tree, and in Syr. literature in reference to a shrub. The LXX is inconsistent in the way it renders the word.

Vegetation: → *'ēzôb* (hyssop, # 257); → *dš'* (become green, sprout, # 2012); → *zr'* (sow, scatter seed, form seed, # 2445); → *ḥāṣîr* I (grass, # 2945); → *ḥašaš* (dry grass, # 3143); → *yereq* (green, greenness, # 3764); → *nṭ'* (plant, establish, drive, # 5749); → *'āleh* (leaf, leafage, # 6591); → *'ēśeb* (herb, herbage, weed, # 6912); → *qîqāyôn* (plant of uncertain identity, # 7813); → *rō'š* II (bitter and poisonous herb, # 8032); → *śîaḥ* I (bush, shrub, # 8489); → *šiṭṭâ* (acacia, # 8847)

Bibliography

ISBE 1:561; I. Löw, *Die Flora der Juden*, 1924, 1:382-83, 387; 2:470; 3:39; 4:32-34, 36, 62, 76, 155.

Richard A. Taylor

8490 (*śîaḥ* II, complaint, musing), → # 8488

8491	שִׂיחָה

שִׂיחָה (*śîḥâ*), nom. meditation, study, speech, discourse (# 8491); שֵׂחַ (*śēaḥ*), nom. thought, plan (hapleg.; # 8465); < שׂיח (*śyḥ* II), muse, study (→ # 8488).

OT 1. The root *śyḥ* is distinctly used in Ps 119; twice this nom. occurs with the sense, meditation, study (vv 97, 99); the law (*tôrâ*) and the testimonies (*'ēdôt*) are the content of the psalmist's study, which makes him wiser than all his teachers. The other OT occurrence of this nom. comes in Eliphaz's scathing attack against Job for diminishing or esteeming lightly meditation on or wise discourse about God; *śîḥâ* stands parallel to *yir'â*, fear [of Yahweh] (Job 15:4). Here the nom. may mean either meditation (Mowinckel, 6) or wise discourse (Müller, 368). The latter fits the context of the dialogue best; the meaning, then, is that Job is undermining the wise discourse of his comforters with his challenge of their interpretation of the doctrine of retribution, and thus he is abandoning faith. In Ben Sira this nom. means learned discourse, being parallel to *ḥîdôt*, riddles (8:8) and *mešal bînâ*, a proverb of discernment (6:34[35]). An important path to wisdom is listening with delight to the discourse of the wise (Sir 6:34-35; 8:8). Good etiquette, furthermore, holds that discourse of the wise may not be interrupted (11:8).

2. Amos uses *śēaḥ* for Yahweh's plan or purpose, which he declares to humans (Amos 4:13). "Thoughts" or "plans" in this text surely includes his law as well as his

will made known through the prophets (cf. 3:7). The great God clearly communicates with humans.

Plan, thought, meditation, scheming: → *'zn* II (weigh, consider carefully, # 264); → *bd'* (devise, imagine, # 968); → *higgāyôn* (melody, thought, # 2053); → *zmm* (plan, purpose, plan evil, # 2372); → *ḥms* II (think, invent, # 2804); → *ḥšb* (count, compute, calculate, think, plan, # 3108); → *yēṣer* I (frame of mind, disposition, # 3671); → *'št* I (think, consider, # 6951); → *śîḥâ* (meditation, study, # 8491); → *śᵉ'ippîm* (disquieting thoughts, worries, # 8546); → *tar'ît* (thought, # 9569)

BIBLIOGRAPHY

S. Mowinckel, "The verb *śiᵃḥ* and the Nouns *śiᵃḥ, śiḥā*," *ST* 15, 1961, 1-10; H.-P. Müller, "Die hebräische Wurzel שׂיח," *VT* 19, 1969, 361-71.

John E. Hartley

8492	שׂים

שׂים (*śym* I), q. put, set, place; set up; impose; appoint; lay, put; pick up; deposit; inflict; fix; hi. put, place; ho. be set, placed (# 8492); תְּשׂוּמֶת (*tᵉśûmâ*), joint property (hapleg. in Lev 5:21; → # 9582).

ANE Among the vbs. that mean set, place, in Heb., only *śym* I (the most common root in Heb.) is broadly attested in the Sem. languages (Phoen., Eth., Ugar., Akk., Aram., ESA). *šyt* is attested as a vb. elsewhere only in Phoen., Ugar., and Akk., and *šwh* only in Aram.; *yṣg* appears nowhere else.

OT 1. As a vb. describing spatial displacement, it is characteristically associated with prepositions that specify the kind of location. When one positions objects or persons, their new location is specified with respect to other objects: one places objects in (*šyt*, Ruth 4:16; *śym*, Gen 31:34), beside (*yṣg*, 1 Sam 5:2), in front of (see 4(c), below), upon (Gen 9:23; 22:6; Judg 9:48; 16:3; 2 Kgs 4:29, 31), under (*šyt*, Ps 8:6[7]; *śym*, 2 Kgs 9:13), or between (*šyt*, Gen 3:15; *śym*, 30:36; 32:16[17]; Exod 8:19; Deut 14:1; Josh 24:7) other objects.

2. The role of this vb. in positioning an object in space or time accounts for its extensive use in forming similes and metaphors: when a writer juxtaposes different semantic fields, this is literally the "placing" of one concept in the domain of another (Jenni, 139-40). Thus, one treats families like flocks (Ps 107:41), a ruler like a signet ring (Hag 2:23), a beloved like a seal (S of Songs 8:6), a pulverized enemy like dust (2 Kgs 13:7), the sea like a jar with its contents (Job 41:31[23]), one person's life like another's (1 Kgs 19:2), or walls like rubies (Isa 54:12). Vivid blessings and curses capitalize on this juxtaposition in seeking to motivate or warn people so that they become like heroes or villains of the past (*śym*, like Manasseh and Ephraim in Gen 48:20; like Zedekiah in Jer 29:22; *šyt*, like Oreb and Zeeb in Ps 83:11[12]).

3. The vb. figures prominently in describing the spatial requisites of the cult. One sets up idols (Deut 27:15; Judg 18:31; 1 Kgs 12:29; 2 Kgs 21:7 ‖ 2 Chron 33:7; Ezek 14:4, 7) in the same way that one puts into place legitimate cultic monuments (Gen 28:18, 22; 1 Sam 7:12). A similar usage appears—and is peculiarly appropriate—with the root *yṣg* (Judg 8:27; 2 Sam 6:17 ‖ 1 Chron 16:1). Because the tabernacle precincts enclose sacred space, everything must be carefully situated in its appropriate

place: blood (Exod 24:6), sacred stones (28:12; 39:7), gold rings (28:26, 37; 39:19), priestly garments (Lev 8:8-9), and all of the objects that facilitate the cult (Exod 26:35; 40:3, 5, 8, 18, 19 *et passim*; Num 4:6, 8, 11, 14; Deut 10:2, 5; 31:26).

4. (a) In placing parts of one's body in particular poses or places, one can communicate nonverbal messages: a hand on one's own head signifies mourning (2 Sam 13:19), a right hand on another's head indicates blessing (*šyt*, Gen 48:14, 17; *śym*, 48:18), a hand under another's thigh signifies an oath (24:2, 9; 47:29), a hand on one's own mouth connotes silence, acquiescence, shame, or astonishment (Judg 18:19; Job 21:5; 29:9; 40:4; Mic 7:16). Because the hand is a symbol of strength, the metaphorical placing of the hand upon nations signifies the dominion and sovereignty of God and his king (Ps 89:25[26]; Ezek 39:21).

(b) When one sets one's face in a particular direction, it can signal the intent to undertake a journey in that direction (Gen 31:21; 2 Kgs 12:17[18]; Jer 42:15, 17; 44:12; Dan 11:17, 18). Ezekiel aligns his face toward persons or nations about whom he is preparing to deliver an oracle of doom (Ezek 6:2; 13:17; 20:46[21:2]; 21:2[7]; 25:2; 28:21; 29:2; 35:2; 38:2), echoing the posture of God, who sets his face against persons or groups who are hostile to him (*śym b-*, Lev 20:5; Jer 21:10; Ezek 15:7). Balaam, on the other hand, aligns his face toward those whom he intends to bless (*šyt*, Num 24:1).

(c) Setting one's eyes upon something can mean anything from simply neutral observation (Gen 44:21) to looking favorably (Jer 24:6; 39:12; 40:4) or with hostility (*śym*, Amos 9:4; *šyt*, Ps 17:11). A reciprocal action that accomplishes the same end is to set something before one's eyes or face for observation or careful scrutiny (*yṣg*, Gen 43:9; 47:2; *šyt*, Ps 101:3; *śym*, Exod 19:7; 21:1; Deut 4:44).

(d) An individual can metaphorically place one's heart toward or upon (or place upon one's heart: Isa 42:25; 47:7; 57:1, 11; Jer 12:11; Dan 1:8; Mal 2:2) an infinite variety of objects or abstractions. In so doing, one is mentally focusing on the object or issue in question, paying careful attention to it or considering its importance (*śym*, Exod 9:21; Deut 32:46; Job 1:8; *šyt*, Exod 7:23; Job 7:17).

(e) A graphic image of a daring initiative that exposes an individual's life to mortal danger is to place one's throat ("life") in one's hand (Judg 12:3; 1 Sam 19:5; 28:21; Job 13:14).

5. One is exercising power and authority over whatever one relocates to another position. The object or person placed in a new position need not be moved easily, or even willingly, but the fact that it is accomplished implies that the one who effects the movement has either the requisite authority or the competence to achieve the task. This dimension of authority attributed to the subject of the vb. is easily observed on those occasions where one individual places another in a position of power and status. One can predict that in most cases, the one who appoints is socially superior to both the position and the individual appointed: queens (Esth 8:2) and kings appoint lesser officials (1 Sam 8:12; 18:5, 13; 28:2; 2 Sam 17:25; 18:1; 23:23 = 1 Chron 11:25; 2 Chron 33:14), officials position commoners (Gen 47:6), fathers position sons (Gen 27:37), brothers position sisters (S of Songs 1:6), and God positions humans (*šyt*, 1 Kgs 11:34; *śym*, Gen 45:8-9; 1 Kgs 10:9). In this light it is important to note the superior status of the prophet as one who appoints the king to his position (1 Sam 8:5; 10:19). However, it is peculiar to find in the context of the thoroughly monarchic ANE that the people

can be depicted as appointing their own leaders (Deut 17:14-15; Judg 11:11; Hos 1:11[2:2]).

6. The object of the vb. in these cases reflects the transforming dimension of the concept, for the person appointed enters into a new sphere of influence and power (one is often appointed over or above (*'l*) other individuals (*śym*, Exod 1:11; *šyt*, Gen 41:33). This transformation cannot occur until a legitimate or sufficiently powerful external authority transfers the individual's identity into a new sphere. Without this external authority, if one wishes to remain within accepted cultural bounds, one can only wait and hope for eventual investiture (2 Sam 15:4) or be prepared for opposition if one acts without fully sanctioned authority (Exod 2:14). The person so transformed may resist the appointment (Isa 3:7).

7. To put or place an already existing object or person implies that the person or object is removed from one sphere of reality in order to be transported to another (cf. the juxtaposition of *lqḥ* and *śym* in 2 Kgs 9:13; Ezek 19:5). These vbs. identify a transformation particularly when the sentence structure is of the form "transform (lit. place) X into (l^e)/like (k^e) Y." These transformations can take place on a number of levels.

(a) The transformations can be complete such that the new reality negates the former: there is nothing in the new that corresponds to the old. This happens when God turns darkness into light (*śym*, Isa 42:16 [cf. Job 17:12]; *šyt*, Jer 13:16).

(b) The transformation may be one of function. In these instances, little or nothing in the transformed object changes, for it is only the object's role or task that is modified: God places the sand as a boundary for the sea (Jer 5:22); God is said to set a human up for target practice (Job 7:20). A building that once served as a temple for Baal is turned into a latrine (2 Kgs 10:27). Humans have a choice in making God their refuge and source of strength (*śym*, Ps 40:4[5]; 52:7[9]; 91:9; *šyt*, Ps 73:28; cf. *šwh*, Ps 16:8). This last case suggests that when a social inferior is the subject of the vb. and a social superior is the object, the vb. describes the activation of an already existing reality: nothing about God changes when a person turns to God for help, for he has always been available for assistance. It is only his role that is new with respect to the person in question. On the other hand, when the subject of the vb. is a social superior and the object is a social inferior (as discussed above), the vb. describes the bringing into being of the new reality.

(c) The vbs. sometimes focus on a transformation of quality. The object retains its essential identity but either becomes debased or enhanced in value or ability: God can turn Israel into something repulsive (*śym*, Ps 44:13, 14[14,15]; 80:6[7]; cf. *šyt*, Ps 88:8[9]) or something praiseworthy (Isa 60:15; 62:7). Israel turned God's inheritance into an abomination (Jer 2:7). God makes human feet as dexterous as the deer (Hab 3:19). Each of these objects remains the same in essence, modified only in quality. One must be cautious with such transformations, since many apparent essential transformations are merely qualitative: the metamorphosis of human hearts into stone is a metaphor for a change of quality (i.e., what is pliable becomes unyielding) and not a change of essence (Zech 7:12). Similarly, God's transformation of Israel's horns and hoofs into iron and bronze identifies enhanced durability (Mic 4:13, 13).

(d) One of the most frequent qualitative modifications is associated with either inhabited or uninhabited land. Although God can take inhabited, fruitful, and well-watered land and place it in the category of desolation (*šyt*, Isa 5:6; Jer 22:6;

Hos 2:3[5]; *śym*, Ps 107:33; Isa 42:15; 50:2; Hos 2:3[5]), he can also do the opposite, taking the wilderness and putting it into the category of well-watered land (Ps 107:35; Isa 41:18; 51:3). Humans are described as doing only the former (*śym*, Josh 8:28; Ps 79:1; Isa 23:13; Jer 4:7; 10:22; 12:11; *šyt*, Jer 2:15; 50:3).

(e) Another transformation may reflect a natural development or growth that is encouraged and nurtured by another. One can speak of turning a lion cub into a mature lion (Ezek 19:5), transforming cultivated land into a forest (Hos 2:12[14]), or multiplying individuals into a nation (Gen 21:13, 18; 46:3).

(f) A final transformation entails the fashioning of a raw material into a product, as when one turns timber into rafts (1 Kgs 5:9[23]). In this category belong those occasions where God transforms humans into a variety of objects that function as tools for God to use. God transforms humans (or human features) into offensive weapons that he employs against his foes: threshing sledges (Isa 41:15), swords (Isa 49:2; Zech 9:13), arrows (Isa 49:2), or war horses (Zech 10:3).

(g) One cannot deduce from the vb. itself the degree of stability of the transformation or the new placement that is described: there is no reason why the new reality cannot readily be undone. Nevertheless, in a number of contexts where God is the subject of the vb., a nuance of permanence or longevity is deducible from the type of transformation described or the specific use of words that affirm inertia. When God sets global (*šyt*, Exod 23:31) and cosmic boundaries (*śym*, Job 38:5; Ps 104:9; Jer 33:25), or when one describes the transformations associated with the ruling house of David (*šyt*, Ps 21:6[7]; *śym*, 2 Sam 23:5; Ps 89:29[30]), the objects of these divine transformations transcend the vicissitudes of time and become markers of divine faithfulness and stability.

8. *śym* and *šyt* are synonyms that can be interchangeable (Gen 48:14, 17, 18; cf. alternations in above discussion) and appear in poetic parallelism (Jer 13:16; Hos 2:3[5]). *śym* can also substitute for *ntn*, give (Gen 41:33, 41; Deut 7:15; 1 Kgs 12:29; 18:23; 2 Kgs 18:14; Hos 11:8), particularly when one speaks of ascribing glory to God (*śym*, Josh 7:19; Ps 66:2; Isa 42:12; cf. 1 Sam 6:5; Ps 115:1; Jer 13:16; Mal 2:2). Nevertheless, some general distinctions may be occasionally defensible in a comparison of these three vbs. when each is complemented by the same direct object: *šyt*, the most infrequent, appears primarily in poetry, and *ntn* (→ # 5989) is more likely than *śym* to appear in prose, Ezek, Late BH, Deut, and deut. related literature (cf. Job 1:22 with 24:12, Hag 2:9 with Num 6:26, 2 Chron 18:22 with Isa 63:11, Deut 6:22 with Ps 78:43). Diachronic and synchronic (dialect) variation may account for these distinctions where *śym* appears less colloquial than *ntn*, and *šyt* seems the most exotic of the three (cf. Eng., "place," less colloquial and more formal than its synonym "put," though both are interchangeable).

Placement, appointment, stand, station: → *yṣg* (set, bring s.o. forward, # 3657); → *kwn* (stand firm, prepare, establish, # 3922); → *nṣb* I (stand, station oneself, stand firm, # 5893); → *ntn* (give, present, offer, # 5989); → *'md* (stand, take one's stand, station, appoint, # 6641); → *'rk* (set, put in rows, enter into battle, # 6885); → *qwm* (stand up, stand upright, arise, perform, # 7756); → *śym* I (put, set, place, set up, impose, # 8492); → *šwh* II (place, put, # 8751); → *šyt* (put, set, lay, appoint, # 8883)

BIBLIOGRAPHY
TWAT 5:696-97; 7:761-81, 1296-1306; P. W. Coxon, "The Distribution of Synonyms in Biblical Aramaic in the Light of Official Aramaic and the Aramaic of Qumran," *RevQ* 9, 1977-78, 497-512; H. J. Van Dijk, "A Neglected Connotation of Three Hebrew Verbs," *VT* 18, 1968, 16-30; E. Jenni, "Zur Semantik der hebräischen Personen-, Tier- und Dingvergleiche," *ZAH* 3, 1990, 133-66; S. Layton, "Biblical Hebrew 'To Set the Face', in Light of Akkadian and Ugaritic," *UF* 17, 1987, 169-81.

Sam Meier

8493	שֵׂךְ

שֵׂךְ (*śēk*), thorn, splinter (# 8493).

ANE Two Akk. cognates can be cited: *šakāku*, to harrow, thread (*CAD*, 17:113-16), and *sikkatu*, nail point. There is also an Arab. cognate (*HALAT* 1236).

OT This term occurs only in Num 33:55, where the Israelites are warned that if they do not drive out the inhabitants of the land, those inhabitants that remain "will become thorns (*śēk*; NIV barbs) in your eyes." In Josh 23:13, *ṣ^eninîm*, thorns, is used in the place of *śēk*. Num 33:55 is alluded to in Judg 2:3, but *śēk* is either an ellipsis or has fallen out of the text through a copyist's error.

P-B Cognates *śak*, thicket or wild growth (thorns) (often referring to overgrowth); and *śôk*, bough, thornbush, occur numerous times in the postbiblical period (e.g., *midr. Lam.* 1.17; *y. Keth.* 2.27).

Thornbush, nettle, sting, thistle, thorn: → *'āṭād* (thornbush, # 353); → *barqōn* (thorn, brier, # 1402); → *deber* II (thorny sting, # 1823); → *dardar* (thistle, # 1998); → *ḥēdeq* (brier, # 2537); → *ḥôaḥ* I (thorn, # 2560); → *m^esûkâ* (thorn hedge, # 5004); → *na'^aṣûṣ* (thornbush, # 5848); → *sîrâ* (thorny bush, # 6106); → *sillôn* (thorn, # 6141); → *s^eneh* (thorny shrub, # 6174); → *sirpād* (stinging nettle, # 6252); → *ṣe'^elîm* (thorny lotus, # 7365); → *ṣ^enînîm* (thorns, # 7564); → *qôṣ* I (thornbush, # 7764); → *qimmôś* (weeds, nettles, # 7853); → *śēk* (thorn, splinter, # 8493); → *šāmîr* I (Christ's thorn, # 9031)

BIBLIOGRAPHY
TWOT 2:877.

K. Lawson Younger, Jr.

8495	שׂכה

שׂכה (*śkh*), q. lie in wait for (# 8495).

ANE The root is proposed for Ps 35:12 on the basis of common later Heb. and Aram. usage. It is unattested in ancient Sem.

OT The text of Ps 35:12 presents a considerable difficulty. In this complaint against threatening enemies the first half of the verse is clear: they repay me evil for good. The MT text of the second half of the verse is literally "childlessness (*š^ekôl*) for my soul." Dahood proposed a shaphel form of *klh* (spent, destroyed), based on the Ugar. *škllt*, which he took to be a certain class of person who makes disease pass away (213). However, his reference (*KTU* 1.16 ii 29) is uncertain. Gibson proposes "enclosure" in reference to a grave (*CML*^{2}, 97, 158), based on the Akk. *šuklultu*, but de Moor translates "like women in labour" (215) in relation to lamentation. Soggin suggested an archaic causative of *kll,* translating "my very essence is destroyed" (67-68). However, the search for a shaphel form may be misguided; it seems best with Kraus (391) to treat the lamed of *škwl* as dittography, and to read *śkw*, based on the root *śkh*, meaning, "they look out for (my life)"; this may be translated "they lie in wait for my life" (Craigie, 283). Being on the lookout for the life of the psalmist in the sense of trying to trap him is a sensible sequel to the evil witnesses of v. 11. Though watching for one's life should be positive, in the case of the evil witnesses it is a malicious intent. This seems to be the best approach to the text, which then describes a watching of one's life for the negative purpose of ambush.

P-B The vb. *śkh* (*sky*, *skh*), meaning to look, see, or forsee, is common in later Heb. and Aram.; the Aram. and Syr. of the vb. *sky/sk'* extends the meaning to look for or hope. The nom. *sakwā'āh* means watchman or prophet.

Ambush: → *'rb* (lie in ambush, lay an ambush, # 741); → *ṣ^{e}diyyâ* (ambush, malice, # 7402); → *śkh* (lie in wait, # 8495)

Bibliography

M. Dahood, *Psalms I; 1-50*, 1966, 213; P. C. Craigie, *Psalms 1-50*, 1983, 283, 285; J. C. de Moor, *An Anthology of Religious Texts from Ugarit*, 1987, 217; J. C. L. Gibson, *CML²*, 97, 158; H.-J. Kraus, *Psalms 1-59*, 1988, 391; J. A. Soggin, "Skwl nel Salmo 35,12," *BibOr* 9, 1967, 67-68.

A. H. Konkel

8496	שְׂכָּה

שְׂכָּה (*śukkâ*), harpoon (# 8496).

ANE No cognates are found (*HALAT* 921).

OT The word is used only in Job 40:31 in speaking of putting a "harpoon" in leviathan.

P-B The term does not occur in P-B.

Bibliography

TWOT 2:877.

K. Lawson Younger, Jr.

8498 (*śekwî,* cock?), → # 6416

8501	שַׂכִּין

שַׂכִּין (*śakkîn*), knife (# 8501).

ANE Probable Aram. loanword; root dubious. Aram. *sakkîn* generally refers to a knife used for slaughtering animals.

OT The nom. appears only in Prov 23:2, where the glutton is admonished to hold a *śakkîn* to his throat when dining at a king's table. The apparent intent is that the threat to life will keep the appetite in check, so to avoid giving offense to the king.

Knife, razor, chisel: → *garzen* (axe, chisel, # 1749); → *ma'^{a}kelet* (butcher-knife, # 4408); → *ma'^{a}ṣād* (bill-hook, chisel, # 5108); → *maqṣu'â* (carving knife, # 5244); → *śakkîn* (knife, # 8501); → *ta'ar* (razor, pen-knife, # 9509)

BIBLIOGRAPHY
IDB 3:42, 711; *NIDBA* 281; C. Corswant, *A Dictionary of Life in Bible Times*, 1956, 164.

Anthony Tomasino

8502 (*śākîr*, rented, day-laborer), → # 8509

8505	שׂכל

שׂכל (*śkl* I), q. have success; hi. understand, see, make wise, have success, act with insight or devotion (# 8505); שֶׂכֶל/שֵׂכֶל (*śekel/śēkel*), nom. insight, understanding (# 8507).

ANE The root occurs elsewhere in Aram. (see Dan 5:11-12, 14; 7:8) and Syr., in Sir 21x, and in the QL.

OT 1. Except for q. in 1 Sam 18:30, the vb. occurs only in hi. (59x, plus 14x as *maśkîl*, hi. ptc. form used in psalm superscriptions and 47:7[8]), 16x in Job-Proverbs, 11x in Psalms, 9x in Daniel. The nom. occurs 16x (7x in Job-Proverbs; 6x in the Chronicler). The word is commonly used in literature associated with wisdom. The vb. belongs to the same semantic field as those below and is sometimes parallel to *byn* (Deut 32:29), *yd'* (Isa 41:20), and *de'â* (Jer 3:15); the nom. is parallel to *bînâ* (1 Chron 22:12) and *ḥokmâ* (Ps 111:10).

2. The general usage of the vb. has various senses, especially: to understand (Isa 44:18), to have insight (Jer 9:23), and to be wise (Prov 15:24). It can often focus on the results of having insight, e.g., wise dealing (1:3), instruction (21:11), good skill (2 Chron 30:22), judicious speech (Prov 16:23), prudent action (10:5, 19), success (1 Sam 18:5), and prosperity (Prov 17:8). The nom. form has the sense of being wise (1 Sam 25:3), having good sense (Prov 19:11) and insight (12:8), with favorable effects (3:4). It can also have a negative sense (cunning, Dan 8:25).

3. The theological use includes the giving of insight by God (1 Chron 22:12; 28:19; Dan 1:17; 9:22; cf. Prov 19:14), whose good Spirit instructs the people (Neh 9:20); so the faithful are to do, given their experience of God's grace (Ps 32:8). In Gen 3:6, the way humans acquire wisdom becomes the issue, not acknowledging the one who gives wisdom. The people of God are to consider carefully God's deeds (Ps 64:9[10]; 106:7; Isa 41:20) and God's ways (Neh 8:13; Ps 101:2; 119:99), wherein their lives can prosper (1 Kgs 2:3). God's presence and action in the lives of the obedient can issue in good success (Josh 1:7-8; 1 Sam 18:14, 30), but a lack of success can befall those who do not attend to the Lord (Jer 10:21), who observes the house of the wicked (Prov 21:12). The move to action can be seen in the careful consideration of the poor (Ps 41:1[2]). Insight is characteristic of the coming Messiah (Jer 23:5; cf. Jer 3:15); God will make the way of the suffering servant prosper (Isa 52:13). The wise will participate in the resurrection (Dan 12:3).

Knowledge, discernment, shrewd, wisdom: → *byn* (understand, discern, # 1067); → *ḥkm* (become wise, act wisely, # 2681); → *ṭ'm* (taste, test, sense, discern, # 3247); → *yd'* I (observe, care about, # 3359); → *nkr* (pretend, be recognized, # 5795); → *'rm* II (be cunning, be crafty, make crafty, # 6891); → *śkl* I (have success, understand, make wise, act with insight, # 8505)

BIBLIOGRAPHY
THAT 2:824-28; *TWAT* 7:781-95.

Terence E. Fretheim

8506 (*śkl* II, cross), → # 3338

8507 (*śekel*, insight, understanding), → # 8505

8508 (*śiklût*, foolishness), → # 6118

8509	שׂכר

שׂכר (*śkr*), q. hire (s.o. for wages); ni. (have to) hire o.s. out; hitp. hire o.s. out (# 8509); מַשְׂכֹּרֶת (*maśkōret*), nom. wages (# 5382); שָׂכִיר (*śākîr*), adj. rented, hired; nom. day laborer, hired laborer, wage-earner (# 8502); שָׂכָר (*śākār* I), nom. wages; reward; fare; expenses; maintenance (# 8510); שֶׂכֶר (*śeker*), nom. wages (# 8512).

ANE This root is widely attested. According to *HALAT* 1239-40, cognates have been identified in Ugar., Arab., OSA, and Eth. (Geez). *TWAT* (7:795-97) also includes Akk., Amorite, Aram., and Phoen., but questions Ugar.

OT 1. The basic meaning of the vb. (q.) is the granting of payment for labor, services, or almost any type of benefit received from someone. Thus, in the vb.'s first occurrence, Leah hired Jacob for the price of mandrakes given to Rachel in order to sleep with him (Gen 30:16). When she conceived and bore a son, she said (lit.): "God has given me my wages (*śkr*)," and she called him Issachar (apparently related to *'îš śākār*; 30:18). The vb. is also used for hiring skilled workers (2 Chron 24:12; Isa 46:6). In the tumultuous days of the judges, upstart Abimelech hired worthless fellows in an attempt to realize his political ambitions (Judg 9:4), and in a different age, the Ammonites hired outside help against David (2 Sam 10:6; 1 Chron 19:6-7). King Amaziah was chastised by God for hiring mercenaries from outside Judah rather than trusting in God (2 Chron 25:6-8).

Prov 26:10 is difficult textually. NIV follows a widely accepted interpretation: "Like the archer who wounds at random is he who hires a fool or any passer-by." For a detailed discussion and another proposal, see Snell, 350-56.

2. Israel's enemies could hire a diviner or prophet to curse or harm God's people. The Mesopotamian diviner Balaam (→) was hired (*śkr*) by Balak, king of Moab, to curse Israel before that nation entered the promised land (Deut 23:5; Neh 13:2), but God, who is sovereign and watches over his people, made him bless his nation instead (Num 22:12; 23-24). Balaam became a symbol of a false spokesman of God who "loved the wages of wickedness" (2 Peter 2:15; cf. Jude 11). Tobiah and Sanballat, the foes of Nehemiah, hired (*śkr*) Shemaiah to prophesy against Nehemiah (Neh 6:12-13). Nehemiah realized he was a false prophet, for he suggested Nehemiah go where the law forbade him to go in the temple, to save his life (Neh 6:10-13; cf. Deut 18:20).

The hiring of religious personnel was also found within Israel. In the period of decadence preceding the monarchy, a Levite was hired (*śkr*) and installed to be a private priest for a family (Judg 18:4; cf. 17:10-12). When better opportunities came, he gladly went to serve an entire tribe (18:20). Such open hiring of Levites for a private or tribal sanctuary which Yahweh had not chosen was illicit (cf. Deut 12:1-14; Judg 17:6; 18:1), but it also seemed to bear testimony to the fact that the nation was neglecting to provide for the Levitical tribe as demanded by the law (Num 18:24; Deut 12:19; cf. also how the Levite was looking for a place to stay, presumably where he would be provided for, Judg 17:8; cf. Mic 3:11).

3. To work for wages (*śkr*, hitp.) without putting God first is like putting the earnings (*śkr*, hitp.) into a purse with holes (Hag 1:6). In the futility of work, God's covenant curse is experienced (cf. Deut 28:38-39; Hag 1:6).

4. The wages one receives can be indicated by nom. *śeker* (of laborers, Isa 19:10), *śākār* (of shepherd, Gen 30:28-33; of servants, Deut 24:15; of wet nurse, Exod 2:9; of an animal, Zech 8:10), and *maśkōret* (of a shepherd, Gen 31:7, 41). *sākîr*, adj. and used as subst., indicates the one hired, be it as a laborer (Deut 24:14), mercenary soldier (Jer 46:21), or an animal (Exod 22:15[14]). God will use the king of Assyria as a hired (*śᵉkîrâ*) razor to shave Judah completely (Isa 7:20) (E. J. Young, *Isaiah*, 1, 1965, 297-98; cf. Lipiński, 799-800).

Wages could be paid in kind (e.g., sheep and daughters!, Gen 30:28-34; cf. 29:15-19; war spoil for the army, Ezek 29:18) or with money (e.g., thirty pieces of silver, Zech 11:12).

The meaning of Exod 22:15[14] concerning what happens when a hired animal is injured or dies is well rendered in NIV: "If the animal was hired (*śākîr*), the money paid for the hire (*śākār*) covers the loss." This does not absolve the one hiring the animal of all responsibility. "Only the obligation to make good injuries and death caused during the use of the hired animal was excluded" (Falk, 108-9; cf. Lipiński, 799).

5. The hired worker (*śākîr*) may be a poor foreigner (Exod 12:45; see Houtman, 191) or an Israelite who had lost his possessions, including his land (Deut 24:14; also cf. Horst, 114), and his anxious lot was not a joyous one (cf. Job 7:1-2). This very poor and vulnerable part of society was protected by God's law. The hired man had to be paid the same day (Lev 19:13; Deut 24:15; cf. Mal 3:5). The OT gives no indication of what the wages were. Unlike the slave, the hired worker retains his own identity. Thus, if he lives with the priest, he is not to eat of the sacred offering, but a slave who belongs to the priest is considered part of the priestly household and he may eat of it (Lev 22:10).

6. When God gives *śākār* to his people, the term is usually trans. "reward" or the like. God does not hire and, thus, does not pay his people wages, for they are like a son and bride to him (Exod 4:22-23; Ezek 16). What he as sovereign God and Redeemer gives is a free gift. It is noteworthy that after Abram refused to receive riches from the king of Sodom and so implied that only the Lord could make him prosper (Gen 14:21-24), God assured Abram that his reward would be very great (15:1; cf. O. Kaiser, *ZAW*, 70, 1958, 115). Significantly, children too are a reward (*śākār*) from God (Ps 127:3; par. *naḥᵃlat yhwh*, "the heritage of Yahweh"). God rewards obedience to him (2 Chron 15:7). "The wicked man earns deceptive wages, but he who sows righteousness reaps a sure reward (*śeker*)" (Prov 11:18, NIV).

7. In Zech 11:12, Zechariah asks for his wages (*śākār*) after shepherding God's wayward people faithfully. The nation that detested him paid him the price of a slave, thirty shekels (Exod 21:32), thus insulting the Lord whom he represented. This was the same amount Judas later received to betray Jesus (Matt 26:15), and so Zech 11:12-13 was fulfilled in the rejection of the Messiah (Matt 27:3-10).

P-B 1. The rare usage of *śkr* follows OT patterns. In CD 12:11, *śwrkw*, his tenant (usually corrected to *śkyrw*, his hired hand), is included with the slave and maidservant as those who cannot be urged to work on the Sabbath. In CD 14:12, *śkr* refers to wages of two days per month given to support orphans and other needy. See C. Rabin, *The*

Zadokite Documents, 1958, 56-57, 70-71. In 11QPs[a] 22:1 (corresponding to Sir 51:30), *śkr* denotes reward.

2. The usage of the terms *śākîr* and *śākār* in RL mirrors the OT usage, with the exception that with the vb. *śkr* the additional theme of hi. (to lease, to let; to cause to profit, to benefit) is found, and the other themes have slightly different meanings (ni. to be rewarded, to have the advantage; hitp. to profit, to deal in) (Jastrow, 2:1576).

Payment, rent, reward, wages: → *'ᵃgôrâ* (payment, # 102); → *'eškār* (tribute, payment, # 868); → *mᵉḥîr* I (price, payment, # 4697); → *sl'* (be paid, # 6131); → *slh* II (be paid, # 6137); → *pᵉ'ullâ* (wages, punishment, reward, payment, # 7190); → *rṣh* II (pay for, make good, make amends, # 8355); → *śkr* (hire, # 8509); → *šlm* (repay, reward, retribute, make peace, # 8966); → **Retribution: Theology**

BIBLIOGRAPHY

NIDNTT 3:138-41; R. de Vaux, *AncIsr*, 1, 1961, 76; Z. W. Falk, *Hebrew Law in Biblical Times*, 1964, 107-10; C. Houtman, *Exodus*, 2, COT, 1989; F. Horst, *Hiob*, BKAT, 1968, 113-14; E. Lipiński in *TWAT* 7:795-801; H. Preisker and E. Würthwein in *TDNT* 4:695-728; D. C. Snell, "The Most Obscure Verse in Proverbs: Proverbs xxvi 10," *VT* 41, 1991, 350-56.

Cornelis Van Dam

8510 (*śākār* I, wages, expenses), → # 8509

8512 (*śeker*, wages, hired laborers), → # 8509

8513	שְׂלָו

שְׂלָו (*śᵉlāw*), quail (# 8513).

ANE Sem. cognates: Aram. Tg. (*sᵉlāyw*), Syr. (*salway*), and Arab. (*salwā*).

OT In the OT this word appears only in the specific context that deals with God's provision in the wilderness in response to the people's request (Exod 16:13; Num 11:31, 32; Ps 105:40). While the quail in Exod 16 was, in addition to manna, God's gracious gift for the Israelites, the provision of the quail in Num 11 is expressive of the wrath of God against the grumbling people, desirous of returning to Egypt (cf. Ps 78:26-31).

Birds, flying creatures: → *'br* (fly, # 87); → *bêṣâ* (egg, # 1070); → *barbur* (species of fowl, # 1350); → *gôzāl* (young bird, # 1578); → *dgr* (hatch eggs, # 1842); → *ḥᵃsîdâ* (stork, # 2884); → *yônâ* I (dove, # 3433); → *ya'ᵃnâ* (ostrich, eagle-owl?, # 3613); → *kānāp* (wing, skirt, outermost edge, # 4053); → *nešer/nᵉšar* (vulture [eagle], # 5979); → *'ôp* (flying creatures, # 6416); → *'ayiṭ* (birds of prey [collective], # 6514); → *'ōrēb* I (raven, # 6854); → *ṣippôr* I (birds, # 7606); → *qōrē'* I (partridge, # 7926); → *śᵉlāw* (quails, # 8513)

BIBLIOGRAPHY

J. Milgrom, *Numbers*, 1990.

N. Kiuchi

8515 (*śalmâ*, garment, cloth), → # 8529

8520 (*śᵉmō'l*, left side, left hand, northwards), → # 8521

8521	שׂמאל

שׂמאל (*śm'l*), hi. go to the left, use the left hand (# 8521); שְׂמֹאל (*ś^{e}mō'l*), nom./adj. left side, left hand, unlucky, northwards (# 8520); שְׂמָאלִי (*ś^{e}mā'lî*), adj. (on the) left, north (# 8522).

ANE The root *śm'l* is well attested in ANE literature. In Akk. *šumēlu* conveys the meaning left side, left hand, left wing of an army, or neighbor to the left (*AHw*, 1271; *CAD* 17/3: 267-72). The Ugar. *šm'al*, the Aram. *s^{e}mā'lā'*, and the Syr. *semmālā'* convey the same meaning as the Heb. *śm'l* (*HALAT* 1242; *LexSyr*, 481; *WUS*, 307). The OSA *hš'ml* (IV Form) can be linked to the Heb. *śm'l*, the Arab. *šimāl* can be translated with north, northwards or left side and *šamāl* with northerly wind (*TWAT* 7:804; Müller, 315; Beeston, 56). The Arab. *šimāl* conveys both the meaning left hand and the negative connotation bad omen (*EncJud* 14:179).

The words left and right are often used together in ANE literature (cf. CAD 17/3: 268).

OT 1. *Statistics.* The hi. form of the root *śm'l* occurs only 5x in the OT (Gen 13:9; 2 Sam 14:19; 1 Chron 12:2; Isa 30:21; Ezek 21:21), the nom./adj. *ś^{e}mō'l* 54x (27x written with *waw ś^{e}mō'wl*), and the adj. *ś^{e}mā'lî* 9x (Even-Shoshan, 1166-67). *śm'l* must be understood in relation to the terms *yāmîn* (right) and *yād* (hand). The expression *yāmîn-ûś^{e}mō'l*, right and left, are used 37x in the OT, and *yad ś^{e}mō'l*, left hand, only in Judg 3:21; 7:20; Ezek 39:3 (*TWAT* 7:805).

2. *Left as opposed to right.* Left refers to that which is in the left direction as opposed to the right: "and on his left (*ûmiśś^{e}mō'l*) were Pedaiah ..." (Neh 8:4). Left and right play an important role in Jacob's final blessing of his grandsons, Ephraim and Manasseh (Gen 48:12-20). Joseph placed Ephraim on Jacob's left hand and Manasseh on Jacob's right hand, expecting his father to place his right hand on Manasseh, the eldest (v. 13). Joseph's careful preparations were changed by Jacob as he crossed his hands, laying his right on Ephraim's head (v. 14). The blind Isaac was tricked into blessing his younger son Jacob (Gen 27), but this time the blind Jacob deliberately chose to bless the younger Ephraim (48:18-19) (Westermann, 188; Wenham, 464-65).

Left refers to the left side of someone's body. The OT mentions the peculiarity that the Benjaminites were frequently left-handed (Judg 3:15; 20:16; 1 Chron 12:2). Judg 20:16 says that there were 700 among the warriors of Benjamin (Braun, 165). Halpern (41) believes that these warriors of Benjamin were not only left-handed, but ambidextrous. It is ironic that the Benjaminites used their left hand as well as their right hand because the name Benjamin literally means "son of the right hand." There are three different hypotheses concerning the meaning of the name Benjamin: (a) It may be linked to Judg 3:15 and 20:16, where the expression "impeded in his right hand" conveys the meaning left-handedness (*TWAT* 7:806). (b) The right hand refers to the southerly direction, because Benjamin was the southernmost tribe of the house of Joseph (2 Sam 19:17-21) (*EncJud* 14:178; Schunk, 671). (c) It may indicate something like "specially favored" or "lucky" (*IBD* 1:185; Drinkard, 723). Although the last two hypotheses are probably the most correct, the matter is still unresolved.

3. *Left as metaphor for weakness.* God's right hand is often spoken of symbolically, especially in Psalms. It is, therefore, significant that the term *śm'l* does not appear in Psalms at all. The right hand provides support (Ps 18:35[36]; 98:1) and

victory (Exod 15:6, 12; Ps 17:7; 44:4; 118:15; Isa 62:8). It is the right hand that God grasps as a symbol of election (Ps 73:23; Isa 41:13) and expresses the omnipresence of God (Ps 139:10). In contrast with this *śm'l* is never used in connection with God.

The place at a man's right hand is important as a place of honor (1 Kgs 2:19; Ps 45:9[10]; Zech 3:1), and the right hand was the hand of special blessing (Gen 48:13-20). The right side of a man is the side on which God marches when assisting him in battle (Ps 109:31; 110:1, 5; Isa 63:12) (*EncJud* 14:178; *NIDNTT* 2:146; Drinkard, 724).

In Eccl 10:2 the right is portrayed as the good side and the left side as the evil one: "The heart of the wise inclines to the right, but the heart of the fool to the left (*liś^e mō'lô*)." The right and left hands have been seen as lucky and unlucky, good and bad. There were also blessings of the right and of the left, differing in degree (cf. Gen 48:13-14) (Kidner, 88-89). Likewise the NT suggests a negative connotation to the left in the separation of the sheep from the goats (Matt 25:33, 41): the goats who will be condemned are placed on the left, while the sheep who will be blessed are placed on the right (*NIDNTT* 2:148; Drinkard, 274). This negative connotation is further conveyed by the Latin word "sinister" (left-handed) (Kidner, 89).

4. *Left as indication of a northerly direction.* The Hebrews oriented themselves according to the place where the sun rises. Therefore in many OT passages *śm'l* refers to the north, the direction to one's left when one faces east. In this sense "right hand" means south, "before" east, and "behind" west (*EncJud* 14:177; *TWOT* 2:879).

The NIV translates *ś^e mō'l* 8x and the adj. *ś^e mā'lî* 4x with the word "north." Job 23:9 says the following: "When he is at work in the north (*ś^e mō'l*), I do not see him; when he turns to the south, I catch no glimpse of him" (cf. Gen 13:14; 14:15; Josh 19:27; 1 Kgs 7:21; 2 Chron 3:17; etc.).

Some passages translated as "left" may indicate the northerly direction. In Gen 13:9 Abraham says to Lot: "If you go to the left (*haśś^e mō'l*), I'll go to the right; if you go to the right, I'll go to the left" (*EncJud* 14:177).

5. *Left as suggestion of completeness (both/and).* Most often in the OT neither right nor left is given a special connotation. In many cases, the path is a straight one from which one is not to depart, either to the right or to the left. Deut 5:32 says: "So be careful to do what the LORD your God has commanded you; do not turn aside to the right or to the left (*ś^e mō'l*)" (cf. also Num 20:17; 22:26; Deut 2:27; 17:11, 20; 28:14; Josh 1:7; 23:6; Isa 30:21) (Drinkard, 274). In contrast to this 2 Sam 14:19 refers to the will of the earthly king, not the will of Yahweh.

The above *śm'l* passages refer to the straight path in a figurative sense, that is, to do the will of Yahweh and obey his commandments. In other instances *śm'l* is used literally: "Then the cows went straight up toward Beth Shemesh, keeping on the road and lowing all the way; they did not turn to the right or to the left (*ś^e mō'l*)" (1 Sam 6:12).

A few *śm'l* passages convey the meaning "everywhere": 1 Kgs 22:19; Isa 9:20[19]; Zech 12:6; etc. (*EncJud* 14:179). Isa 9:20[19] says that right and left are equally evil: "On the right they will devour, but still be hungry; on the left (*ś^e mō'wl*) they will eat, but not be satisfied. Each will feed on the flesh of his own offspring" (*TWOT* 2:878).

6. *Left and left-handedness in a positive sense.* (a) In OT times the right hand held the major weapon (e.g., the sword), while the left hand held the defensive weapon (e.g., the shield). Some specially skilled warriors were trained to use their left hand. 1 Chron 12:2 says the following: "they were armed with bows and were able to shoot arrows or to sling stones right-handed or left-handed (*maśmi'lîm*); they were kinsmen of Saul from the tribe of Benjamin."

Ehud the Benjaminite was probably such a left-handed or perhaps ambidextrous warrior (Drinkard, 274). The fact that he used his left hand allowed him to assassinate Eglon, king of Moab. The guards would have noticed that he had no sword on his left thigh, the usual side. He concealed it at his right side. Finally Ehud struck Eglon from the unexpected side: "Ehud reached with his left hand (*'et-yad śᵉmō'lô*), drew the sword from his right thigh and plunged it into the king's belly" (Judg 3:21) (Gray, 250).

In a similar way Joab killed Amasa, the commander of Absalom's rebel army (cf. 2 Sam 9-10). Joab took Amasa by the beard with his right hand and stabbed him unexpectedly with the dagger in his left hand (*TWAT* 7:806).

(b) The names and meaning of the two pillars mentioned in 1 Kgs 7:21 (= 2 Chron 3:17) may indicate a more positive connotation to the left (north) than to the right (south): "He erected the pillars at the portico of the temple. The pillar to the south he named Jakin and the one to the north (*haśśᵉmā'lî*) Boaz." Scholars have a wide variety of opinions concerning the names of the two pillars. Jakin may convey the meaning "he establishes, he shall uphold" and the name Boaz "in him is strength" or "may strength be in him" (Dillard, 30). If this hypothesis is correct, it indicates that the pillar on the left side (Boaz) is not seen as weaker or less important.

(c) Prov 3:16 says: "Long life is in her right hand; in her left hand (*biśmō'wlâ*) are riches and honor." Court (225) assumes a more negative connotation to the left than to the right: "but for those who go to the left hand thereof there is riches and honor, but not length of days." This negative connotation to the left hand is probably incorrect. Riches and honor are not set against a long life, but are equally good (*TWOT* 2:879; Snijders, 39). Prov 3:16 may refer to the Egyp. goddess Maat, who holds a symbol of life in her one hand and a scepter symbolizing wealth and dignity in the other (McKane, 295).

(d) Ezek 1:10 mentions the "four faces" of the living creatures Ezekiel saw in his vision. On the right side were the face of a lion and on the left the face of an ox. The ox is seen as a symbol of strength, not weakness (cf. Deut 33:17) (Brownlee, 11).

(e) Whereas it was usual to lift one's hand in taking an oath (Gen 14:22; Exod 6:8; Ezek 20:5), Dan 12:7 says the following: "The man clothed in linen, who was above the waters of the river, lifted his right hand and his left hand (*śᵉmō'l*) toward heaven, and I heard him swear by him who lives for ever ..." (Baldwin, 207).

7. Louw and Nida (98) states the following on the use of the expression left hand: "The left hand is designated in a number of languages by an idiomatic phrase which normally contrasts with expressions for the right hand. For example, one may often speak of the left hand as the 'bad hand' or the 'weak hand,' and in some instances as the 'anus hand,' since this is the hand used in cleansing the body after defecation." (cf. also Hertz, 3-31 in his study of the preeminence of the right hand in different religions).

Most of the OT *śm'l* passages (except Eccl 10:2) do not reflect the same negative connotations as in many other languages, cultures, or religions (*TWAT* 7:807). The left hand is not seen as unholy, because the priests were allowed to use their left hands in the holy offerings (Lev 14:15-16, 26-27). Both hands are spread to the Lord in prayer (1 Kgs 8:22) and in the blessing (Num 9:22). Lev 16:21 describes how Aaron is laying both hands on the head of the live goat and confesses over it all the sins of the Israelites (Wright, 48).

P-B In the Tgs., Talm., and Midr. literature *śm'l* conveys the same meaning as in the OT, i.e., left side, left hand, to go to the left, to be on the left side and go wrong (Jastrow, 2:1591). Although *śm'l* can be translated with "go wrong," Rabinowitz (*EncJud* 14:179) believes that there is no evidence in the Talm. literature that the left was regarded as sinister. The general opinion in both the *halakhah* and *aggadah* is merely that the right is more important and significant than the left.

According to Kellermann (*TWAT* 7:807) the root *śm'l* occurs at least 15x in the Heb. texts (1QS 1.15; 3.10; 7:15; 1QM 6.8; etc.) and 7x in the Aram. texts of Qumran (1 QapGen 21.8; 22.10; etc.). The QL echoes the OT usage of *śm'l*, e.g. in 1QapGen 21.8 and 22.10 *śm'l* conveys the meaning "north" and in 5QJN 1.12 and 2.2 the meaning "left side" (Charlesworth, 504; Martīnez, 132, 234-36).

The Heb. *śᵉmō'l* is normally translated by the G term *aristeros* (51x in LXX), but *euōnumos* (16x in LXX) is also used.

According to the Slavonic *Book of Enoch* the angel Gabriel is situated on God's left hand (*Sl. Enoch* 24:1) while the NT says that Jesus Christ is seated on God's right hand (Eph 1:20; Col 3:1) (*NIDNTT* 1:103).

Hand, arm, finger: → *'eṣba'* (finger, # 720); → *hdh* (stretch out the hands, # 2063); → *zᵉrôa'* (arm, forearm, # 2432); → *yād* (hand, power, side, # 3338); → *kap* (hand, hollow hand, # 4090); → *tq'* (drive, thrust, clap one's hands, blow trumpet, pledge, # 9546)
Right: → *yāmîn* I (right, south, # 3545)

BIBLIOGRAPHY

AHw, 1271; *CAD* 17/3: 267-72; *EncJud* 14:177-80; *IBD* 1:185-86; Jastrow, 1591; *HALAT* 1242-43; *LexSyr*, 481; *NIDNTT* 2:148; *TWAT* 7:804-8; *TWOT* 2:878-79; *WUS*, 307; J. G. Baldwin, *Daniel*, 1978; A. F. L. Beeston, "On the Correspondence of Hebrew *s* to ESA s^2," *JSS* 22, 1977, 50-57; R. Braun, *1 Chronicles*, 1986; W. H. Brownlee, *Ezekiel 1-19*, 1986; J. H. Charlesworth (ed.), *Graphic Concordance to the Dead Sea Scrolls*, 1991; J. M. Court, "Right and Left: The Implications for Matthew 25.31-46," *NTS* 31, 1985, 223-33; R. B. Dillard, *2 Chronicles*, 1987; J. F. Drinkard, "Left, Left Hand," *ABD* 4, 1992, 273-74; idem, "Right, Right Hand," *ABD* 5, 1992, 724; A. Even-Shoshan (ed.), *A New Concordance of the Bible*, 1990; J. Gray, *Joshua, Judges, Ruth*, 1986; B. Halpern, *The First Historians*, 1988; R. Hertz, "The Pre-eminence of the Right Hand: A Study in Religious Polarity," *Right and Left: Essays on Dual Symbolic Classification*, 1973, 3-31; D. Kidner, *The Message of Ecclesiastes*, 1976; J. P. Louw & E. A. Nida, *Greek-English Lexicon of the New Testament*, 1988; F. G. Martīnez, *The Dead Sea Scrolls Translated* (ET), 1994; W. McKane, *Proverbs*, 1985; V. W. Müller, "Altsüdarabische Beiträge zum hebräischen Lexicon," *ZAW* 75, 1963, 304-17; K. D. Schunck, "Benjamin," *ABD* 1, 1992, 671-73; L. A. Snijders, *Spreuken*, 1984; G. Wenham, *Genesis 16-50*, 1994; C. Westermann, *Genesis 37-50* (ET), 1986; D. P. Wright, "Hands, Laying on of," *ABD* 3, 1992, 47-48.

D. F. O'Kennedy

8522 (*ś^{e}mā'lî*, on the left, north), → # 8521

8523	שׂמח

שׂמח (*śmḥ*), q. rejoice, be joyful; pi. make s.o. glad, allow s.o. to rejoice; hi. make s.o. to rejoice (# 8523); שָׂמֵחַ (*śāmēaḥ*), vb. adj. filled with joy, glad (# 8524); שִׂמְחָה (*śimḥâ*), nom./adj. joy (# 8525).

ANE Mish. Heb. *smḥ*, gladden; Ammonite *smḥ*, be happy; Ugar. *šmḫ*; *iš-mu-ḫu* (# 109, l. 50), succeed (Mercer, 1:369), be arrogant (Moran, 183); Punic *isthymihi*, be happy; Ugar. *šmḫt*, joy; Amor. *simḫ* (in theophoric personal name, *simḫi*—^{d}Dagan [rejoicing of Dagan]; cf. Huffmon, 250).

Several scholars suggest that the meaning of *śmḥ* cannot be restricted to be happy, rejoice. According to them, the diverse meanings in Ugar., be happy (most common) and shine (1.17:II:8-9—"On Dan'el's head the brow did brighten [*tšmḫ*]. Above, his countenance did shine" [Margalit, 146])—appear to carry over into a few instances of Heb. *śmḥ* (e.g., Ps 104:15; Prov 13:9; Isa 60:5; cf. Greenfield, 147-48; Ginsberg, 72-73).

Scholars (e.g., Greenfield, 141-51; Kopf, 249, 276; Clines, 10-11; Grossberg, 550-52) also debate whether Heb. *śmḥ* should be derived from Akk. *šamāḫu(m)*, to grow high, flourish, and Arab. *šamaḫa*, to be high, proud. Greenfield (148-49) cites several occurrences of *śmḥ* (pi. and hi.) that signify to be high, to elevate (e.g., 2 Chron 20:27; Ps 89:42[43]; Lam 2:17). He contends that both *śmḥ* and *ṣmḥ* derive from the Akk. and Arab. cognates, and that the former connotes to be high, to glow, to rejoice, and the latter primarily means to grow.

While it is granted that one's understanding of certain passages benefits from the recognition of a wider semantic range for *śmḥ*, many of the passages cited as illustrations easily signify the nuance, to rejoice.

OT The vb. *śmḥ* and its derivatives occur in every OT book except Josh, Ruth, Dan, Hag, and Mal. The vb. form occurs 158x (q. 129x, pi. 28x, hi. 1x), while the nom. *śimḥâ* and the vb. adj. *śāmēaḥ* occur 97x and 20x respectively. The Psalter contains one quarter of the instances of *śmḥ* and its derivatives.

1. *Nontheological uses*. *śmḥ* and its derivatives signify a spontaneous and vocal expression of joy rather than a restrained frame of mind. The juxtaposition of *śmḥ* with the following vbs. suggests the expressive nature of the vb.: to lift up one's voice (*l^{e}hārîm b^{e}qôl*—1 Chron 15:16; Ezra 3:12), singing (*šîr*—Gen 31:27; 2 Chron 23:18; Ps 137:3), and singing praise (*zmr*—Ps 9:2[3]; 68:3-4[4-5]). It often serves as part of a festive celebration that entails eating and drinking (Deut 12:18; 14:26; 16:14; 27:7; 1 Chron 29:22; Neh 8:12; Esth 8:17; 9:18-19, 22; Ps 104:15; Eccl 8:15; 9:7; Isa 22:13; 65:13) and the playing of various instruments (Gen 31:27; Num 10:10; 1 Kgs 1:40; 1 Chron 15:16; 2 Chron 30:21; Neh 12:17; Job 21:12; Isa 30:29). Other expressive activities that occur along with *śmḥ* are dancing (2 Sam 6:14-16), clapping the hands (Isa 55:12; Ezek 25:6), frolicking (Jer 50:11) and stamping the feet (Ezek 25:6). The root serves as the polar opposite for mourning (Ps 30:11[12]) and gloom (Isa 24:11).

A number of events, things, and activities constitute the occasion for expressing *śmḥ*. Meeting a loved one (Exod 4:14; Judg 9:13), receiving good news (1 Sam 11:9; 19:5; 2 Sam 1:20; 1 Kgs 5:7[21]; 1 Chron 29:9; Jer 20:15), protection from the elements (Jon 4:6), release from imprisonment (Jer 41:13), victory over an enemy (1 Sam 19:5; 2 Sam 1:20; Amos 6:13), great wealth (Job 31:25), the ruin/misfortune of an enemy (22:19; 31:29), fulfillment of a significant task (Neh 12:43), and a generous-hearted attitude in giving cause *śmḥ*. Commodities like perfume (Prov 27:9), music (Job 21:12; Ps 45:8[9]), and wine (Judg 9:13; Ps 104:15; Eccl 10:19; Zech 10:7) and events like the ingathering of the harvest (Ps 4:7[8]; Isa 16:10), a wedding (S of Songs 3:11; Jer 7:34; 16:9; 25:10; 33:11), farewell festivities (Gen 31:27), and the erection and dedication of the temple in Jerusalem (Ezra 3:12-13; Neh 12:27, 43-44) evoke joy. The absence of joy like that normally expressed at a wedding (Jer 7:34; 16:9; 25:10) or harvest (Isa 16:10) serves as a prophetic description of a coming devastation. Simple yet important things like a kind word (Prov 12:25), a cheerful look (15:30), and an apt reply (15:23) can bring joy to a person. God and his activities on behalf of Israel serves as the foundational occasion for the expression of joy (see below).

Some of the various subjects that experience this joy (*śmḥ*) are the Lord (Ps 104:31), king (45:8[9]; 63:11[12]), poor (69:32[33]), humble (Ps 34:2[3]), wicked (35:15, 19, 24), pilgrims (122:1), Mount Zion (48:11[12]), Jacob and Israel (53:6[7]), nations (67:4[5]), heavens (1 Chron 16:31; Ps 96:11), earth (Ps 97:1), fir trees (Isa 14:8), and Egypt (Ps 105:38). The juxtaposition of heart (Exod 4:14; 1 Chron 16:10; Ps 16:9; 19:8[9]; 33:21; 105:3; Prov 12:25; 15:30; 23:15; 27:9, 11; Zech 10:7) and soul (Ps 86:4; Ezek 25:6) with *śmḥ* connotes the comprehensive extent of this disposition, pervading the whole person.

Joy should also be prominent in family relationships. Moses exhorts the new husband to devote himself to making his wife happy (Deut 24:5), and the sage counsels the husband to rejoice in the wife of his youth (Prov 5:18). Although the father of a fool cannot rejoice (Prov 17:21), a wise son brings great joy and delight to his father (10:1; 15:20; 23:24-25; 27:11; 29:3).

2. *Theological uses*. The vb. and its derivatives fall into four primary categories of theological usage: joyfulness in relation to Israel's worship calendar, rejoicing grounded in the character and activity of God, the gloating/joyfulness of the wicked over the affliction of the righteous, and the joyful anticipation of future salvation.

(a) Rejoicing at festivals. Moses mandates tangible expressions of joy as part of the Israelites' celebration of feast days, offering sacrifices and tithes, or other national gatherings. The expression "before Yahweh" (*lipnê yhwh*) at the very least connotes Yahweh's presence at these celebrations and may signify his participation as a covenant partner with Israel (D. Sheriffs, 61-65). This expression occurs 7x in connection with the celebration of the Feast of Tabernacles (Lev 23:40), Feast of Weeks (Deut 16:11), fellowship offerings (27:7), tithing (14:26), and national convocations (for covenant reaffirmation and renewal, see 12:7, 12, 18). This idea is implied in other exhortations to/demonstrations of joyfulness in the celebration of religious feasts (Feast of Tabernacles—Deut 16:14; Neh 8:17; Passover and Feast of Unleavened Bread —2 Chron 30:21, 23, 25-26; Ezra 6:22; Firstfruits—Deut 26:11; Feast of Purim—Esth 8:16-17; 9:17-19, 22), fasting (Zech 8:19), all worship activities (Num 10:10), and coronation ceremonies (1 Sam 11:15). In a few contexts, the feast day is called a day of rejoicing (*yôm śimḥâ*—Num 10:10; Esth 9:17-18; cf. 9:19, 22).

gyl (→ # 1635) and *śmḥ* form a standard fixed pair of terms denoting the fall harvest festival revelries of dancing, singing, shouting, etc., both for the benefit and enjoyment of the people and as an act of devotion to Yahweh (Exod 23:16; Lev 23:33-43; Deut 16:13-17) (Stuart, 142).

(b) Rejoicing in Psalms. The Psalter is replete with exhortations to rejoice in Yahweh/God (Ps 9:2[3]; 32:11; 33:21; 34:2[3]; 40:16[17]; 43:4; 63:11[12]; 64:10[11]; 70:4[5]; 97:12; 104:34; 105:3; 149:2). The grounds for this joyfulness are God's presence (16:9, 11; 21:6[7]; 69:32[33]), divine refuge (5:11[12]; 107:30), his provision of abundant blessings for his chosen people (14:7; 46:4[5]; 53:6[7]; 85:6[7]; cf. Isa 9:3[2]; 65:13), his strength (Ps 21:1[2]), his precepts (19:8[9]), his love (31:7[8]; 90:14-15), his rule (67:4[5]; 96:11; 97:1), and his vindication of his people by intervening on their behalf (2 Kgs 11:20 = 2 Chron 23:21; 2 Chron 20:27; 29:36; Ps 35:27; 48:11[12]; 58:10[11]; 66:6; 92:4[5]; 97:8; 107:42; 118:24). God himself rejoices over his works (creation, 104:31) and over his chosen nation (Zeph 3:17); he will give foreigners joy (Isa 56:7), but takes no pleasure in the wicked (Isa 9:17[16]).

(c) Misguided rejoicing. *śmḥ* signifies gloating in several contexts where an adversary delights in the affliction of another (individual or people), whether it be Babylon (Isa 14:8), the nation of Israel (Ezek 25:6; 35:14; 36:5; Obad 12; Hab 1:15), or an individual Israelite (Ps 35:15). The gloating of Ammon (Ezek 25:6) and Edom (35:14; 36:5; Obad 12) constituted the grounds for God's judgment of them. The psalmist prays that God will prevent the wicked from gloating over his distress (Ps 35:19, 24; 38:16[17]; Mic 7:8) and praises God for preventing this abuse in a certain situation (Ps 30:1[2]), while the sage warns against gloating over the demise of one's enemy (Prov 24:17). Because of Israel's covenant treachery, God caused Israel's enemies to gloat over his covenant people (Ps 89:42[43]; Lam 2:17).

(d) Future rejoicing. The prophet Jeremiah (Jer 33:11) affirms that the day when Yahweh restores Israel to her land inheritance will be a day of joy (*śāśôn*, → # 8607) and gladness (*śimḥâ*). Zech 8:19 draws attention to the abundant blessings awaiting Israel by making a contrast between the present days of fasting and future feast days. The Lord will transform the fasts that commemorate dark days in Israel's history into joyful days of feasting. Instead of mourning, joyfulness and festive celebration will characterize these days because of the redemption Yahweh will accomplish on Israel's behalf (Ps 14:7; 126:3; Isa 25:9; 29:19; 30:29; 51:3, 11; 55:12; 61:7; 65:13; 66:10; Zeph 3:14; Zech 10:7). God himself will rejoice over his covenant people (Zeph 3:17).

3. *śmḥ in Eccl.* The use of *śmḥ* in Eccl (esp. 3:12, 22; 5:19[18]; 8:15; cf. *śimḥâ*, 2:26; 5:20[19]; 8:15; 9:7) provides a significant complement to the emphasis on vanity (*hebel*, # 2039) in that section of Wisdom literature. On the one hand, the Teacher (Qohelet) depicts human inability to master one's own destiny (a vanity verdict; Hubbard, 22-23). He seeks to convince humankind that God has arranged all things according to his own purposes. On the other hand, in addition to accepting God's wisdom and sovereignty and his own limitations, a person should enjoy (*śmḥ*) life as God gives it (an alternative conclusion; Hubbard, 22, 92-97). Enjoying (*śmḥ*) what God provides and allows is integral to a life that is not dominated by *hebel*, vanity. While vanity demarcates the limits of human ability to understand and change the way life works,

joy (*śmḥ*) offers relief in the midst of life's frustrations (Hubbard, 22; cf. Whybray, 87-98).

4. *Do not rejoice! (Hos 9:1).* In sharp contrast to the repeated exhortations to joyful celebration in the OT, the prophet Hosea (Hos 9:1) commands Israel to refrain from rejoicing like other nations. From the following context, Hosea apparently referred to the celebrations that customarily follow an abundant harvest (9:2-3). Although this was common among all agriculturally oriented nations, such joyful expressions had special significance for Israel. Moses had affirmed that Israel's agricultural prosperity directly depended on her covenant loyalty to Yahweh (Deut 28:1-14), and he warned that idolatry would occasion drought and exile (28:15-19, 22-24, 36-42, 64-67). In their abhorrent mixture of Yahweh worship and Baal worship, Israel probably participated in some Canaanite fertility practices and treated Yahweh like Baal, a god motivated to bless them because of their conduct. Because of Israel's spiritual fornication (cf. Stuart, 142), God's chosen people would not be able to celebrate over the abundant harvest or remain in the land. Rather, they would eat unclean food in the land of their oppressor (Assyria).

P-B *śmḥ* and its derivatives occur over 90x in DSS (60x in the fragments from cave 4). It is most common in hymnic material (e.g., 4Q508, 20:2; 1QM 12:13; 19:5; 4Q492, 1, 5). The Qumran community is exhorted to exult God's name in a joyful chorus (1QM 14:4; 4Q502, 4, 3) and personified Justice rejoices (1QM 17:8) (cf. *TWAT* 7:822). 11 QPs^{a} (21:12b = Sir 51:15) refers to grapes that "gladden the heart" (Sanders, 80-81).

Happiness, joy, rejoicing: → *'šr* II (be fortunate, # 887); → *blg* (be cheerful, happy, # 1158); → *gad* II (luck, fortune, # 1513); → *gyl* (exult, # 1635); → *ḥdh* (gladden, rejoice, make happy, # 2525); → *'lz* (exult, # 6600); → *'ls* (enjoy, appear glad, # 6632); → *'lṣ* (rejoice, # 6636); → *śwś* (rejoice, # 8464); → *śmḥ* (rejoice, make glad, # 8523)

BIBLIOGRAPHY

THAT 2:828-35; *TWAT* 7:808-22; *TWOT* 2:879; G. Ahlström, "The Tell Sīrān Bottle Inscription," *PEQ* 116, 1984, 12-15; F. Andersen and D. Freedman, *Hosea*, AB, 1980; D. Clines, "The Tree of Knowledge and the Law of Yahweh (Psalm 19)," *VT* 24, 1974, 8-14; A. Gianto, "The Theme of Enjoyment in Qohelet," *Bib* 73, 1992, 528-32; H. Ginsberg, "Lexicographical Notes," in *Hebräische Wortforschung*, FS W. Baumgartner, SVT 16, 1967, 71-82; J. Greenfield, "Lexicographical Notes II," *HUCA* 30, 1959, 141-51; D. Grossberg, "The Dual Glow/Grow Motif," *Bib* 67, 1986, 547-54; D. Harvey, "'Rejoice Not, O Israel,'" in *Israel's Prophetic Heritage*, FS J. Muilenburg, eds. B. Anderson, and W. Harrelson, 1962, 116-27; D. Hubbard, *Ecclesiastes, Song of Solomon*, WBC, 1991; H. Huffmon, *Amorite Personal Names in the Mari Texts*, 1965; L. Kopf, "Arabische Etymologien und Parallelen zum Bibel Wörterbuch," *VT* 9, 1959, 247-87; H. Lenowitz, "The Mock-*śimḥâ* of Psalm 137," in *Directions in Biblical Hebrew Poetry*, 1987, 149-59; B. Margalit, *The Ugaritic Poem of AQHT*, 1989; S. Mercer, ed., *The Tell El Amarna Tablets*, 1939; W. Moran, ed. and trans., *The Amarna Letters*, 1992; J. Sanders, *The Psalm Scroll of Qumrân Cave 11 (11QPs^{a})*, DJD # 4, 1965; D. Sheriffs, "The Phrases *ina IGI DN* and *lip^{e}nēy yhwh* in Treaty and Covenant Contexts," *JNSL* 7, 1979, 61-65; D. Stuart, *Hosea-Jonah*, WBC, 1987; R. Whybray, "Qoheleth, Preacher of Joy," *JSOT* 23, 1982, 87-98; H. Wolff, *Hosea*, Hermeneia, 1974.

Michael A. Grisanti

8524 (*śāmēaḥ*, filled with joy, glad), → # 8523

8525 (*śimḥâ*, joy), → # 8523

8526	שְׂמִיכָה

שְׂמִיכָה(*śᵉmîkâ*), nom. curtain, covering (?; hapleg., # 8526); < perhaps סמך (*smk*), q. lean upon, rest on (→ # 6164).

ANE The nom. is not attested, although the possible root *smk* is found widely, with similar meaning to the Heb.

OT The nom. occurs only in Judg 4:18, where Jael covers Sisera with a *śᵉmîkâ* before killing him in her tent. The meaning of the term is uncertain. The ancient versions vary widely (e.g., layer [LXX], cover [Vg.], leather covering [OG]), apparently guessing at the meaning from the context. Moore suggests rug (123), but Burney rightly notes that if it were Jael's intention to make Sisera comfortable, she would hardly cover him with a rug after his long hot flight. He suggests instead flynet (92). Boling argues that a flynet would do little to conceal Sisera and concludes that the word remains unclear (97). But it should also be noted that it is not certain whether Jael intended to conceal Sisera with the *śᵉmîkâ* or merely to make him comfortable, so that he would be off guard when she killed him. Gray (260) suggests a screened quarter for women.

P-B The nom. is unattested in QL. For its use in RL, which is obscure, see Jastrow 2:1595.

Tent, curtain: → *'ōhel* (tent, tent-dweller, # 185); → *'āzēn* (equipment, # 266); → *yᵉrî'â* (curtain, tent fabric, # 3749); → *yātēd* (peg, pin, nail, # 3845); → *qubbâ* (vaulted tent, women's quarters, # 7688); → *śᵉmîkâ* (curtain, covering, # 8526); → *šaprîr* (state-tent?, # 9188)

BIBLIOGRAPHY

R. Boling, *Judges*, AB, 1975; C. F. Burney, *The Book of Judges,* 1918; J. Gray, *Joshua, Judges, Ruth*, NCBC, 1986; G. F. Moore, *Judges,* ICC, 1895.

Anthony Tomasino

8529	שִׂמְלָה

שַׂלְמָה, שִׂמְלָה (*śimlâ*, *śalmâ*), nom. garment, cloth, clothes, clothing, apparel (# 8529). The second word (# 8515) is a metathesized form of the first (# 8529). There is no cognate vb. in Heb.

OT 1. *śimlâ* occurs 29x, mainly in the historical books. It is a general word and seems not to be limited to any particular article of clothing. It is what Shem and Japheth covered themselves with to avoid embarrassing their father, Noah (Gen 9:23). The term occurs 5x in the Joseph narratives (37:34; 41:14; 44:13; 45:22 [2x]).

Exod 3:22 and 12:35 suggest that such garments were of value, being listed in conjunction with Egyptian jewelry in those two places. Exod 22:27[26] uses the word to describe the outer coat that must not be denied a debtor, no matter how extreme his poverty. A *śimlâ* is what Joshua tore in response to Achan's sin (Josh 7:6) and what Naomi urged Ruth to wear for her nocturnal encounter with Boaz (Ruth 3:3).

2. The only figurative use of *śimlâ* is in Prov 30:4, where Agur asks rhetorically, "Who has wrapped up the waters in his cloak?"

3. *śalmâ* occurs 16x with a distribution similar to that of *śimlâ*. Apparently the two words were interchangeable throughout the biblical period. Exod 22:27[26] and Deut 24:13 both address the poor debtor, yet use different spellings of this word. Deut 8:4; 29:5[4]; Neh 9:21 exhibit the same curiosity. *śalmâ* describes the old clothes the Gibeonites wore to deceive Joshua (Josh 9:5, 13), and the new cloak that Ahijah the prophet wore and then tore into twelve pieces in front of Jeroboam to illustrate the division of the tribes (1 Kgs 11:29-30). It is the word for the pleasant-smelling clothing of the Shulammite (S of Songs 4:11). Ps 104:2 is the only figurative use of *śalmâ*; there God is described as wrapping himself in light as with a garment.

Clothing, garment: → *beged* II (clothes, garment, # 955); → *g^elôm* (garment, # 1659); → *ḥob* (fold of garment, # 2460); → *ḥōṣen* (fold of garment, # 2950); → *k^etonet* (garment, # 4189); → *lbš* (put on, clothe, wear, # 4252); → *mad* (garment, clothes, # 4496); → *madeweh* I (garment, # 4504); → *maḥ^alaṣot* (festive garments, # 4711); → *meltāḥâ* (wardrobe, # 4921); → *meši* (costly garments, # 5429); → *sādîn* (costly garments, # 6041); → *sut* (garment, # 6078); → *p^etîgîl* (fine clothing, # 7345); → *ṣeba'* (colorful garments, # 7389); → *śimlâ* (garment, cloth, # 8529); → *šōbel* (flowing skirt, # 8670); → *šît* (garment, attire, # 8884)

BIBLIOGRAPHY

ABD 2:232-38; *ANEP*, figs. 1-66; *ISBE* 2:401-7; A. F. L. Beeston, "Hebrew *šibbolet* and *šobel* (Isa 47:2)," *JSS* 24, 1979, 175-77; M. Dahood, "To Pawn One's Cloak," *Bib* 42, 1961, 359-66; G. Dalman, *Arbeit und Sitte in Palästina*, 1987 (repr. 1937), 5:199-356; E. Dhorme, *L'emploi métaphorique des noms de parties du corps en hébreu et en akkadien,* 1963; M. Görg, "Zum sogenannten priesterlichen Obergewand," *BZ* 20, 1976, 242-46; H. W. Hönig, "Die Bekleidung des Hebräers: Eine biblisch-archäologische Untersuchung," diss. Zürich, 1957; M. G. Houston, *Ancient Egyptian and Persian Costume and Decoration*, 1954^2; A. Jirku, "Zur magischen Bedeutung der Kleidung in Israel," *ZAW* 37, 1917/18, 109-25; H. F. Lutz, *Textiles and Customs among the People of the Ancient Near East*, 1923; J. W. McKay, "My Glory—A Mantle of Praise," *SJT* 31, 1978, 167-72; W. Magass, "Texte und Textilien," *LB* 34, 1975, 23-36; J. Ruppert, *Le costume juif depuis les temps patriarchaux jusqu'à la dispersion (Le costume historique des peuples de l'antiquité)*, 1938.

Robert L. Alden

8532 (*ś^emāmît*, lizard), → Reptiles

8533	שׂנא

שׂנא (*śn'*), q. hate, one who is an enemy; ni. be hated; pi. be an enemy (# 8533); שִׂנְאָה (*śin'â*), hatred (# 8534); שָׂנִיא (*śānî'*), disdained, slighted (# 8535).

ANE The root *śn'* is not found in Akk., in which *zêru(m)* (dislike, refuse, hate) has corresponding meanings (*AHw*, 1522). The word *šūnû* III is found as a Can. loanword in a cuneiform inscription from Boghazkoi with the sense of hateful one (*AHw*, 1590). The Ugar. vb. *šn'* describes the sacrifices Baal hates (*KTU* 1.4 iii 17) and as a part. describes the enemies of Baal (*KTU* 1.4 vii 36). Both the text and meaning of the Ugar. *(š)n'itk* (*KTU* 2.72 36) is uncertain; it might refer to enemies (Pardee 4, 20) or to divorce (Brooke 70, 80). The vb. occurs as a part. in the Moabite inscription (*KAI*

181.4) as Mesha claims to look in triumph over his enemies (cf. Ps 118:7); the same part. form is found 5x in the Sefire inscriptions in reference to enemies (*KAI* 222 B 26; 223 B 14; 224.10, 11, 12). In Aram. this form is conjectured for Ahiqar line 176, though it is disputed (*AP* 246); in line 132 the words of a liar are described as "his hatefulness" (*šn'th*). The Aram. papyri further uses the vb. as a metonymy for divorce (e.g., APFC 9.8; 15.23, 27; cf. Deut 24:3); the nom. *šn'h* is used for the deed of the divorce (*AP* 18.1). The root is found throughout the northwest Sem. languages in all periods (*DISO*, 311; *THAT* 2:835; *HALAT* 1247).

OT 1. The gamut of feelings of dislike are included in the scope of *śn'*; it may express the most intense hatred of the enemies of God (Ps 139:21-22), or that of a violent enemy (25:19), but it may simply express that which is to be avoided, such as serving as a guarantor for a debt (Prov 11:15), the feelings of aversion for a poor man (19:7), or the aggravation of a neighbor who visits too often (25:17). At times the vb. carries the ingressive sense of begin to hate, as God's hatred of Ephraim at Gilgal (Hos 9:15) or his making Jerusalem, his beloved, an object of prey (Jer 12:8). Love (Heb. *'hb*, → # 217) is the opposite of hate; often the two words are found in contrast. Ammon hated Tamar, after raping her, with an intensity that was as great as his passion had been for her (2 Sam 13:15); but on a less intense scale, hate may simply express the feelings of affection for one wife in contrast to the aversion for another (Deut 21:15, 17).

The two words form a poetic word pair frequently found in antithesis: There is a time to love and a time to hate (Eccl 3:8); the Lord hates those who love violence (Ps 11:5); the psalmist hates the company of evildoers, but loves the house of the Lord (26:5, 8); the Lord loves righteousness but hates iniquity (45:7[8]); those who love discipline love knowledge, and those who hate reproof are stupid (Prov 12:1), etc. The hate of *śn'* is synonymous with detest or abhor (Heb. *t'b*, → # 9493); so the psalmist says "I hate and abhor falsehood, but I love your law" (Ps 119:163). The greedy hate the one who seeks justice in the gate and abhor the one who speaks with integrity (Amos 5:10); the Lord loathes the pride of Jacob, he hates their fortifications (6:8, cf. *BHS*). There are six things the Lord hates, seven that are abominable (nom. *tw'bh*, # 9359) to him (Prov 6:16). In the q. the vb. has the general sense of hate; usually the object is enemies, but the vb. may take an object, such as the desire for profit (Exod 18:21; cf. Prov 28:16), or may even be used absolutely as "a time to hate" (Eccl 3:8).

The use of loved and hated to describe the attitude toward a preferred wife as opposed to the one who was tolerated or even rejected (Gen 29:31, 33) lends to hate the sense of being unloved or not chosen, or even abandoned and rejected. The unloved (*śᵉnû'â*) woman who marries shakes the very foundations of order (Prov 30:23). In the metaphorical extension of the conjugal relationship Jerusalem is described as an abandoned bride (Isa 54:6), as a city abandoned and rejected (*śᵉnû'â*; Isa 60:15); Ezekiel describes Jerusalem as the prostitute whose lover (Assyria) now hates her, leaving her stripped and naked (Ezek 23:28-29). When the prophet Malachi says "I have loved Jacob, but Esau I have hated" (Mal 1:2-3), he is emphasizing the sovereign choice of God (*THAT* 2:836); nevertheless, the rejection of Esau leads further to their judgment.

The anthropological language of hate is extended to God in a number of ways. God hates the abominable heathen practices (Deut 12:31; 16:22) as well as the ritualistic festivals observed amidst injustice (Isa 1:14; Amos 5:21); the Lord loves justice but hates robbery with a burnt offering (Isa 61:8 MT). God hates pride, arrogance, the way of evil, and perverted speech (Prov 8:13).

God is obliquely made the object of hatred in reference to his enemies, that is, those who hate him (Exod 20:5 = Deut 5:9; Num 10:35; cf. Deut 7:10 2x; 2 Chron 19:2; Ps 68:1[2]; 81:15[16]; 83:2[3]; 139:21). The part. of *śn'* is also used in the application of justice before God. A person who "hates his neighbor" describes the motive by which willful murder is judged (Deut 19:11); on the other hand, the absence of such malice and a scheme to kill indicates that this is not willful murder (4:42; 19:4, 6; Josh 20:5). In solemn affirmation God forbids anyone to have an attitude of hatred towards a brother (Lev 19:17), but requires the love one has for himself (19:18). So Prov 25:21 teaches that if the one who hates you is hungry, you are to give him food.

The use of hate in Mal 2:16 is a crux; the text, syntax, and general meaning are all in question. A summary of the exegetical questions and the major approaches adopted is provided by Hugenberger (51-76). Though there are those who have taken a completely agnostic approach, and others who think the offense is an idolatrous ritual or the maltreatment of a second wife, it seems tolerably clear based on the comparison of terminology with Babylonian law, Aram. papyri, and other OT passages that this is a reference to divorce. A further question is the subject of the vb. *śn'*; the vb. occurs as a third person in the direct discourse of Yahweh. It seems best to take the subject of *śn'* as the one divorcing his wife, in an asyndetic relationship with the vb. for divorce (*šlḥ,* # 8938). Westbrook has shown that the use of the term hate for divorce in the Aram. papyri is an abbreviation of a longer formula (1986, 400-402). In the full formula, as found in Mal 2:16, hate provides a motive for the divorce, i.e., the cause is not misconduct. Hugenberger concludes that the text of Mal 2:16 should not be emended; the subject of *śn'* is indefinite and is modified by the pi. inf. abs. of *šlḥ* to speak of one who divorces his wife out of hatred (70-76). The vb. *śn'* provides the reason why the divorce under consideration is an unacceptable violence.

2. The Heb. vb. *śn'* is found in the q. 129x; this includes 34x as an active part. to mean an enemy, and 9x as a passive part. meaning unloved or abandoned. Two occurrences are textually questionable. The text of Ezek 35:6 should read "you have become guilty (Heb. *'šm,* # 870) in blood," following the G (cf. *BHS*), rather than "you hate blood." Several Greek codices also lack the phrase "I will prepare you for blood and blood will pursue you."

It is probable that Ps 9:13a[14a] should read the vocative to say, "Look at my suffering, the one who lifts me up" (*BHS*) rather than "from those who hate me" (MT); the change involves the simple metathesis of two letters (*mnś'y* rather than *mśn'y*), which then provides a parallel to v. 13b[14b], (lit.) "the one who raises me from the gates of death." A similar metathesis at Prov 26:28 (*BHS*) to alter "A lying tongue hates those it hurts" to "rouses noise" (cf. Ps 93:3) is much less likely.

The ni. of *śn'* is found in Prov 14:20: "The poor are shunned even by their friends." It is also found at 14:17 in the MT, which says, "One with discretion is hated," but the sense is questionable. The line would seem to form a contrast with the preceding, "A quick-tempered man does foolish things," and the Vrs. suggest a sense of being patient or at peace. The ni. is distinct from the q. pass. in that the latter is always with reference to the spurned wife (cf. Gen 29:31, 33; Deut 21:15-17). The Q of

2 Sam 5:8 is read as a q. pass., but it is likely to be read with Qumran texts as a q. pf. fem.

The vb. occurs in the pi. 15x; it is always found as a part., meaning an enemy. The enemy may be personal (Job 31:29), even an individual thought to be a friend (Ps 55:12[13]); most often the enemy is a political adversary (Ps 18:40[41] = 2 Sam 22:41; cf. Deut 33:11; Ps 44:7[8], 10[11]; 89:23[24]). Such enemies are the object of God's judgment (Deut 32:41; Ps 68:1[2]; 83:2[3]). In Prov 8:36 the enemy of wisdom is one who loves death.

3. The nom. *śin'â* occurs 17x. In Ps 139:22 and 2 Sam 13:15 it serves adverbially as the object of *śn'* to indicate the intensity of hatred. The nom. is also used to describe the motivation for murder (Num 35:20) or the hatred that leads one nation to destroy another (Ezek 25:11). The Israelites might perceive themselves as objects of God's hatred (Deut 1:27; 9:28) when they faced his judgment in the wilderness.

In contrast to love, *śin'â* describes animosity between individuals (Ps 109:5; cf. v. 3), or, as the opposite of love, it stirs up strife (Prov 10:12, cf. v. 18); it is better to have a simple meal with love than a fatted ox with hatred (15:17). The Teacher observes that love and hate are part of the human experience (Eccl 9:1, 6), with no observable discrimination in how it affects the good and the bad.

The nom. *śānî'* is found in Deut 21:15 to refer to the spurned wife. It is synonymous with the pass. q. fem. part., which is the reading of the Sam. text.

P-B 1. The root *śn'* is found in all phases of later Heb. and Aram. In a Palmyrene inscription *rwh' śnyn* refers to a hateful spirit, but the context is damaged and the form is uncertain (*DISO*, 311). The vb. *s^{e}nê* (*s^{e}nā'*) is common in later Aram., often describing an attitude toward others; in one text it has the particular sense of ugly (Jastrow, 1007). The nom. *śan'ûtā'* designates an object of hatred, enemies (Jastrow, 1604).

2. In the Qumran texts the meaning is mostly within the range of the opposition between good and evil. In the Damascus document those outside the covenant whom God hates he allows to go astray (CD 2.13, 15). In the Hymns the psalmist prays that he may walk in what God loves and loathe what he hates (1QH 17.24 = Martinez 4.24). In the Mysteries the people are said to loathe (*śn'w*) sin (1 1.9), yet they all walk about under its influence. In the Temple Scroll *śn'* is used of a husband rejecting his wife, accusing her of not being a virgin after he has rejected her (11Q 65.11).

3. In the LXX *śn'* is rendered almost exclusively with *miseō*. In Luke 14:26 (cf. Matt 10:37) the requirement of Jesus that one hate the members of one's own household in order to be a disciple must be understood as a Semitic expression emphasizing the comparatively greater commitment required for the kingdom (Jeremias, 1:215). In Rom 9:13 Paul quotes Mal 1:2-3, "Jacob I loved, but Esau I hated," in order to express the elective purposes of God in the fulfillment of his promises; the apostle simply applies the expression of Malachi to his contemporary situation.

Animosity, enmity, hostility: → *'yb* (be an enemy, # 366); → *ṣrr* II (be hostile, # 7675); → *śṭm* (hate, # 8475); → *śāṭān* (accuser, satan, # 8477); → *śn'* (hate, one who is an enemy, # 8533); → *šôrēr* (adversary, # 8806); → **Animosity: Theology**

BIBLIOGRAPHY

TDNT 4:683-94; *THAT* 2:835-37; G. Brooke, *UF* 11, 1979, 70, 80; G. P. Hugenberger, *Marriage As a Covenant: A Study of Biblical Law & Ethics Governing Marriage, Developed from the*

Perspective of Malachi, SVT 52, 1994, 51-73; J. Jeremias, *Neutestamentliche Theologie*, 1971, 1:215; F. G. Martinez, *The Dead Sea Scrolls Translated*, 1994, 34, 178, 318, 399; D. Pardee, *BO* 34, 1977, 4, 20; R. Westbrook, "The Prohibition on Restoration of Marriage in Deuteronomy 24:1-4," ScrHier 31, 1968, 399-403.

A. H. Konkel

8534 (*śin'â*, hatred), → # 8533

8535 (*śānî'*, disdained, slighted), → # 8533

8537 (*śā'îr* I, hairy), → # 8547

8538 (*śā'îr* II, hairy goat), → # 7366

8539	שָׂעִיר

שָׂעִיר (*śā'îr* III), nom. satyr, goat demon, goat idol (# 8539).

OT *sā'îr* III occurs only 4x (Lev 17:7; 2 Chron 11:15; Isa 13:21; 34:14; cf. also possibly 2 Kgs 23:8) in the OT. Scholars suggest that this nom. depicts some type of demon that exhibited the likeness of a goat and was closely associated with idolatry and the high places. The first appearance occurs in Lev 17:7, which states that sacrifices for the "goat idols" (NIV) or "goat demons" (NASB) are strictly forbidden: "They must no longer offer any of their sacrifices to the *goat idols* to whom they prostitute themselves. This is to be a lasting ordinance for them and for the generations to come." The context suggests that such a prohibition pertains primarily to the appropriate method for sacrifice, so as to avoid both the appearance and practice of inappropriate cultic behavior. The remaining occurrences of this word simply expand on and apply this initial prohibition. 2 Chron 11:15 (cf. 2 Kgs 23:8, cj.) records the violation of this prohibition. The occurrences in Isaiah are somewhat ironic descriptions of judgment. In both instances Isaiah taunts his audience by stating that the very demons and ghosts to which they sacrifice will eventually remain as the only inhabitants of the land they now occupy.

Spirit, ghost, demon: → *'ôb* II (medium, spiritist, necromancer, ghost, # 200); → *'iṭṭîm* I (ghosts, ghosts of the dead, spirits, # 356); → *lîlît* (night monster, night creature, # 4327); → *'^{a}zā'zēl* (Azazel, demon, scapegoat, # 6439); → *ṣî* II (desert dweller, crier, yelper, wild beast, # 7470); → *rûaḥ* (wind, breath, transitoriness, volition, disposition, temper, spirit, Spirit, # 8120); → *r^{e}pā'îm* I (shades, departed spirits, # 8327); → *śā'îr* III (satyr, goat demon, goat idol, # 8539); → *šēd* (demon, # 8717)

BIBLIOGRAPHY

M. A. M. Juárez, "El diablo y los demonios. Le fe del antiguo Israel," *Biblia y Fe* 56, 1993, 36-54; J. H. Motyer, *The Prophecy of Isaiah*, 1993; J. Oswalt, *The Book of Isaiah, Chapters 1-39*, NICOT, 1986.

M. V. Van Pelt / W. C. Kaiser, Jr.

8540	שָׂעִיר

שָׂעִיר (*śā'îr* IV), heavy rain (# 8540); < שׂער (*ś'r* II), storm (→ # 8548).

OT *śā'îr* is related to *s^e'ārâ* (heavy wind storm) and occurs only in Deut 32:2 as one of four terms for rain used in a simile for Moses' word: "Let my teaching fall like rain (*māṭār*) and my words descend like dew (*ṭal*), like showers (*śā'îr*) on new grass, like abundant rain (*r^ebîbîm*) on tender plants" (see P. C. Craigie, *Deuteronomy*, 1976).

Rain, dew, drizzle, hail, showers: → *'ēgel* (drop [of dew], # 103); → *brd* I (hail, # 1351); → *gšm* (make rain, # 1772); → *zrm* II ([clouds] pour out [water], # 2442); → *ḥ^anāmal* (sleet, hail?, # 2857); → *ṭal* (dew, light rain, drizzle, # 3228); → *yrh* II (give drink, cause rain, # 3722); → *mṭr* (make rain, # 4763); → *malqôš* (late rain, # 4919); → *sagrîr* (downpour, # 6039); → *sāpîaḥ* II (violent storm, # 6207); → *r^ebîbîm* (showers, # 8053); → *rāsîs* (dew drop, # 8268); → *r'p* (drip, flow, rain, # 8319); → *śā'îr* IV (heavy rain, # 8540); → *šikbâ* (layer of dew, emission/ discharge of seed, # 8887)

Mark D. Futato

8541 (*śē'îr* I, Seir), → Edom

8542 (*śē'îr* II, Mt. Seir), → Edom

8544 (*ś^e'îrâ* I, hairy goat), → # 7366

8546	שְׂעִפִּים

שְׂעִפִּים (*ś^e'ippîm*; nom. disquieting or excited thoughts, worries, anxiety (# 8546); also spelled with an epenthetic *reš*, שַׂרְעַפִּים[*śar'appîm* (# 8595)], and it is the same word as *sā'îp* = *sar'appâ* [branch]).

ANE Syr. *sar'epītā*, branches, fork; Arab. *šaġafa*, be disquieted.

OT The nom. stands for troubled, anxious thoughts that are produced in many ways, including night visions (Job 4:13), hearing rhetoric that defames one (20:2), and fear of falling as a result of mistreatment by others (Ps 94:19). These thoughts, which inflict harsh pain (*ḥwš* II; Job 20:2; → # 2591), are deep inside a person (Ps 94:19); thus this nom. stands parallel to *rûaḥ mibbînātî* ("impulse from my understanding" tr. D. Clines, *Job 1-20*, 1989, 471; 20:2a ‖ 20:3b). The comforts or consolations (*tanḥûmîm*; → # 9488) provided by God enable a person to overcome the anxiety of such thoughts (94:19). In this light the psalmist prays that God may search him and know his troubled thoughts in order to remove any harmful way within him so that he might traverse the everlasting way (139:23-24).

Plan, thought, meditation, scheming: → *'zn* II (weigh, consider carefully, # 264); → *bd'* (devise, imagine, # 968); → *higgāyôn* (melody, thought, # 2053); → *zmm* (plan, purpose, plan evil, # 2372); → *ḥms* II (think, invent, # 2804); → *ḥšb* (count, compute, calculate, think, plan, # 3108); → *yēṣer* I (frame of mind, disposition, # 3671); → *'št* I (think, consider, # 6951); → *śîḥâ* (meditation, study, # 8491); → *ś^e'ippîm* (disquieting thoughts, worries, # 8546); → *tar'ît* (thought, # 9569)

John E. Hartley

8547	שׂער

שׂער (*ś'r* I), q. have one's hair stand upright; be appalled (# 8547); שָׂעִיר (*śā'îr* I), nom. hairy (# 8537); שַׂעַר (*śa'ar* I), nom. bristling, shudder (→ # 8550); שֵׂעָר (*śē'ār*), nom. hair (# 8552); שַׂעֲרָה(*śa^{'a}râ*), nom. hair (# 8553); שְׂעַר (*ś^e'ar*), Aram. nom. hair (# 10687).

ANE The derivation of the root is uncertain. For several suggestions, see *HALAT* 1252.

OT 1. The vb. occurs only 3x to denote an appalled or horrified reaction to Judah's shocking apostasy from the Lord (Jer 2:12), the unbelievable fall of the wealthy and powerful city of Tyre (Ezek 27:35), and God's astonishing destruction of Egypt (32:10).

2. The nom. *śēʿār* is the most common word for hair (28x). Some people were known for their long hair: the Nazirites (Num 6:5, 18), Samson (Judg 16:22), and Absalom (2 Sam 14:26). Elijah was called a hairy man (2 Kgs 1:8), but some have associated this with his hairy mantle. (Zech 13:4 associates the hairy mantle with other prophets; see 2 Kgs 1:8: "He was a man with a garment of hair," cf. Hobbs, *2 Kings*, 10.)

(a) Fifteen times *śēʿār* occurs in the priestly regulations detailing infectious skin diseases (Lev 13-14). According to 13:20, the priest, after examining a person whose skin is affected and whose hair "has turned white," must declare him unclean and ineligible to come into the temple/tabernacle to worship in the presence of God. These regulations detail the color of the hair, whether it be white (13:3-4, 10, 21, 25, 26), yellow (13:30, 32, 36), or black (13:31, 37).

(b) The cases of the Nazirites (→ # 5687) and Samson, a Nazirite from birth, is of theological significance (→ Samson: Theology). The regulations pertaining to the Nazirite vow are given in Num 6:1-21. Three stipulations applied to their hair. (i) He could not shave his hair during the period of his consecration, to demonstrate that he is holy and separated to God during this time (v. 5). (ii) If he was defiled, he must shave off his hair, undergo a period of ritual purification, make an offering, and let the hair grow again. The period of consecration began anew upon his completion of these requirements (vv. 9-12). (iii) At the fulfillment of his vow, he must shave off his hair and undergo a ritual celebrating the completion of his vow (v. 19).

(c) The "hairy crowns" are parallel with "heads" in Ps 68:21[22], in which the psalmist affirms his faith in God's justice, "Surely God will crush the heads of his enemies, the hairy crowns of those who go on in their sins." For the exegetical problems, see Anderson, *Psalms*, 1:493.

(d) Ezra pulled out his hair as a gesture of disgust to show how horrified he was because of the intermarriage between the people of Israel and their pagan neighbors (Ezra 9:3). Twice the lover of S of Songs describes the hair of the Shulammite as a flock of goats (S of Songs 4:1; 6:5). R. O. Murphy suggests that this analogy may be based on "the color and the undulating flow of the hair from head to shoulders" (*Song of Songs*, Hermeneia, 1990, 159). The root refers to pubic hair in Ezek 16:7 (a sign of maturity) and possibly in Isa 7:20 (a sign of judgment, see below).

3. The fem. form, *śaʿᵃrâ*, points to single hairs. The expression "not one hair will fall" appears in 1 Sam 14:45; 2 Sam 14:11; 1 Kgs 1:52, in oaths that promise God's absolute protection—even to one hair of the head. Ps 40:12[13] and 69:4[5] both have the expression "more than the hairs of my head" in reference to the multitude of trouble or enemies. The seven hundred left-handed Benjamites, famous for their accuracy, "could sling a stone at a hair and not miss" (Judg 20:16).

The rendering of Job 4:15 in the NIV, "A spirit glided past my face, and the hair on my body stood on end," leads one to imagine that Eliphaz, one of Job's counselors, was so shaken that his hair stood on end. Many commentators render the form *śaʿarat* as "whirlwind" to keep the parallelism with "wind" (*rûaḥ*, NIV "spirit"). For suggestions, see D. J. A. Clines, *Job 1-20*, WBC, 1989, 111, n. 15.c.

4. The word *śāʿir* describes Esau, in contrast to his smooth-skinned brother Jacob, as a hairy man (Gen 27:11, 23). The hairy quality of his skin required Jacob to deceive his blind father Isaac in order to steal the blessing from Esau.

5. The Aram. word *śeʿar* occurs in Dan 3:27 (the unsinged hair of Daniel's three friends, who trusted God for deliverance and protection from the fire), 4:33[30] (the long hair of the temporarily insane Nebuchadnezzar, who refused to recognize that God was the ruler over all humanity), and 7:9 (the white, like wool, hair of the Ancient of Days, who will destroy the forces that persecute the saints of God). The description of 7:9 is a most interesting description of God as the Ancient of Days, seated on a throne: "His clothing was as white as snow; the hair of his head was white like wool. His throne was flaming with fire, and its wheels were all ablaze" (cf. Rev 1:14).

Hair: → *zāqān* (beard, # 2417); → *maḥalāpâ* (braid, # 4710); → *miqšeh* (well-dressed hair, # 5250); → *prʿ* (untie hair, # 7277); → *ṣîṣit* (hair, tassel, # 7492); → *qewuṣṣôt* (hair, # 7767); → *śʿr* I (be appalled, # 8547); → *śāpām* (moustache, # 8559)
Shaving, trimming: → *glḥ* (shave, # 1662); → *ksm* (trim hair, # 4080)

BIBLIOGRAPHY
ISBE 2:596-99; *TDOT* 3:5-20; *THAT* 2:50-53; M. Dahood, "*ŚʿRT* 'Storm' in Job 4:15," *Bib* 48, 1967, 544-45; F. C. Fensham, "The Shaving of Samson: A Note on Judges 16:19," *EvQ* 31, 1959, 97ff.; J. Lust, "A Stormy Vision: Some Remarks on Job 4, 12-16," *Bijdr* 36, 1975, 308-11; O. Margalith, "Samson's Riddle and Samson's Magic Locks," *VT* 36, 1986, 225-34; S. M. Paul, "Job 4:15—A Hair Raising Encounter," *ZAW* 95, 1983, 119-21; C. Sherlock, "Ezekiel's Dumbness," *ExpTim* 94, 1982/83, 296-98; H. Trav, N. Rubin, S. Vargon, "Symbolic Significance of Hair in the Biblical Narrative and the Law," *Koroth* 9, 1988, 173-79; Z. Weisman, "The Biblical Nazirite, Its Types and Roots," *Tarbiz* 36, 1967, 207-20.

Robert L. Alden

8548	שׂער

שׂער (*śʿr* II), q. carry off in a windstorm; ni. it is stormy; pi. sweep away in a gale; hitp. storm against (# 8548); שַׂעַר (*śaʿar* II), nom. gale, storm (# 8551); שְׂעָרָה (*śeʿārâ*), nom. fem. gale, storm (# 8554). Also סער (*sʿr* I), q. be stormy; ni. be raged (be stirred up); pi. blow off in a storm (# 6192); סַעַר (*saʿar*), nom. gale, tempest (# 6193); סְעָרָה (*seʿārâ*), nom. fem. gale, tempest (# 6194).

ANE There seems to have been a nom. Sem. root *ś/sʿr*. Akk. *šāru*, wind, storm, breath (*AHw* 3:1192-93). The connection Akk. *šāru*—Heb. *saʿar* may be doubtful (Fabry, 893). The root occurs in the Egyp. PN *yasʿar-kuna* of the Execration Texts and the Heb. PN (*sʿryhw*) of the Arad-Ostraca 31,4 (7 Cent. BC): "Yahweh has caused a storm."

OT 1. The noms. *śaʿar* (only Isa 28:2), *saʿar* (8x), *śeʿārā* (only Job 9:17; Nah 1, 3), *seʿārā* (16x) belong to the meteorological sphere. They are used in connection with other words for weather phenomena: *bārād*, hail (→ # 135, Ezek 13:11); *gešem*, rain, downpour (→ # 1773); *sûpâ,* windstorm (→ # 6070, Isa 29:6; Amos 1:14); *qîṭôr*, smoke, mist (→ # 7798, Ps 148:8); *ra'ad*, thunder, roar (→ # 8284; Isa 29:6); *ra'am* (→ # 8308); *šeleg*, snow (→ # 8920). Its synonym is *rûaḥ*, wind, breath, spirit (→ # 8120). The fem. *s^e'ārâ* seems to be a *nomen unitatis*. The fem. form may be combined in a construct state with *rûaḥ*. The construct *rūaḥ s^e'arā*, windstorm, which does not occur in the opposite order, shows that *sa'ar/s^e'arā*, like *anemos* in G, is the older (?) or at least more precise designation of the wind, while *rūaḥ* as a process-nom. ("the blowing") needs a specification. The antonym to *sa'ar* is *d^emāmâ*, silence, whisper (# 1960, Ps 107:29).

Palestine belongs to the Mediterranean climate zone with mostly subtropic climate. The year is divided into two seasons: a rainy winter and a rainless summer (just as in southern Spain, Shanghai, or Georgia, USA). The winds mainly come from the west (Mediterranean Sea), bringing rain and coolness. During the winter north winds can bring cold. During the change of seasons hot eastern winds (khamsin, scirocco) from the Syro-Arabian Desert bring oppressive heat and stifling air. These phenomena determine the metaphoric color of the semantic field. The words for wind mostly have a destructive connotation.

2. Like *sûpâ* (→ # 6070) the lexeme is found in three kinds of OT texts.

(a) The storm may be an agent accompanying God's theophany: Job 38:1; 40:6; Ezek 1:4. This feature is missing from Sinai theophany (only earthquake, lightning, thunder, fire, and smoke; cf. Exod 19:16-18). Elijah went up (*'lh*, → # 6590) to heaven in a whirlwind (2 Kgs 2:1, 11). In NT apocalyptic texts the windstorm is not a specifically mentioned sign of God's coming, whereas lightning, thunder, earthquake still are: Rev 4:5; 8:5; 11:19; 16:17-21. Mark 4:35-41 shows Jesus acting in the authority of the Creator, calming the storm.

(b) The few occurrences where the lexeme denotes a storm do not lack a theological implication. The Heb. description of nature as creation included God's sovereignty over all phenomena. Even in describing the force of a storm at sea, the writer of Ps 107 knows about God's power to rouse and calm a storm (vv. 25, 29). Even windstorms must do "his bidding" (148:8; cf. Jon 1:4, 12). In Jonah 1:4 *sa'ar gādôl* cannot mean "high waves" (contra Fabry, 896), at best it could denote the raging of the sea, according to the basic meaning of the vb. *s'r*, rage.

(c) Because of the destructive nature of a storm, the Heb. words are combined with a negative connotation. Thus the storm becomes an agent for God's wrath. He will come to scatter and destroy his and Israel's enemies (Ps 83:15[16]; Isa 29:6; 40:24; 41:16; Jer 23:19 = 30:23; Zech 9:14). He will also come for judgment against false prophets and his deceived people (Ezek 13:11, 13). The speaker of Ps 55:8[9] desires to find shelter before "the tempest and storm" (*mērūaḥ sō'â missā'ar*).

P-B The LXX translates *sa'ar* with many different words, thus trying to interpret precisely the individual weather phenomena.

Wind, storm: → *zal'āpâ* (scorching [wind], # 2363); → *ḥāzîz* (cloud, strong wind, thunderclap, # 2613); → *yôm* II (wind, storm, breath, # 3428); → *m^ezārîm* (north-winds, # 4668); → *sûpâ* I (destructive wind-storm, whirlwind, # 6070); → *s'h* (calumniate, rush [storm], # 6185); → *rûaḥ* (wind, Spirit, # 8120); → *r'm* I (storm, thunder, # 8306); → *ś'r* II (carry off in a storm-wind, # 8548)

Bibliography

TWAT 5:893-98; H. Lugt, "Wirbelstürme im Alten Testament," *BZ* 19, 1975, 195-204; R. B. Y. Scott, "Meteorological Phenomena and Terminology in the Old Testament," *ZAW* 64, 1952, 11-25.

Manfred Dreytza

8550	שַׂעַר

שַׂעַר (*śa'ar* I), nom. bristling, shudder (# 8550); שׂער (*ś'r* I), q. be afraid, terrified, appalled, bristle with horror (→ # 8547).

OT 1. The verbal root *ś'r* I appears only 4x, all in q. (Deut 32:17; Jer 2:12; Ezek 27:35; 32:10). A frequently appearing synonym of this form (except Deut 32:17) is *šmm,* meaning to be desolate or appalled (see also Job 18:20). The source of such horror or disgust is willful sin (Jer 2:12), more specifically idolatry (Deut 32:17), and the fate of Yahweh's enemies (Ezek 27:35; 32:10).

2. The nom. derivative *śa'ar* appears only 3x. On two occasions it functions as an adverbial accusative (shudder with horror) when employed with its verbal parent (Ezek 27:35; 32:10). Thus *śā'ᵃrû śa'ar* in Ezek 27:35 is aptly rendered "are horribly afraid" (NASB) or "shudder with horror" (NIV). In Job 18:20 it is once again used in connection with *šmm* and is characterized as something that unexpectedly seizes (*'ḥz,* → # 296) a person when observing the fate of the wicked.

Trembling, shaking: → *g'š* (rise and fall noisily, swell, surge, # 1723); → *zw'* (tremble, quake, be afraid, # 2316); → *zll* II (shake, quake, tremble, # 2362); → *ḥalḥālâ* (shaking, trembling, anguish, # 2714); → *ḥrg* (come out trembling, # 3004); → *ḥrd* (tremble, shudder, startle, # 3006); → *yr'* (tremble, be fainthearted, # 3760); → *mwṭ* (waver, reel, stagger, shake, reel, # 4572); → *m'd* (slip, slide, shake, totter, # 5048); → *nwd* (shake, totter, waiver, wander, mourn, flee, # 5653); → *nwṭ* (shake, quake, # 5667); → *nw'* (shake, tremble, stagger, totter, wave, # 5675); → *n'r* II (shake, shake off, # 5850); → *smr* (shudder, have goose-bumps, bristle, # 6169); → *'iw'îm* (distortion, stagger, dizzy, # 6413); → *pwq* I (stagger, wobble, reel, totter, # 7048); → *pḥd* I (tremble, be in dread, # 7064); → *plṣ* (shudder, shake, tremble, # 7145); → *rgz* (agitate, quiver, shake, excite, rouse up, agitate, # 8074); → *rnh* I (rattle, # 8261); → *r'd* (tremble, shake, tremble, # 8283); → *r'l* I (brandish, make to quiver, # 8302); → *r'š* I (quake, shake, leap, # 8321); → *rpp* (shake, quake, rock, # 8344); → *rᵉṭēt* (terror, panic, trembling, # 8417); → *ś'r* I (be afraid, terrified, bristle with horror, # 8547)

Bibliography

TWOT 2:946; J. E. Hartley, *The Book of Job*, NICOT, 1988.

M. V. Van Pelt/W. C. Kaiser, Jr.

8551 (*śa'ar* II, gale, storm), → # 8548

8552 (*śē'ār*, hair), → # 8547

8553 (*śa'ᵃrâ*, hair), → # 8547

8554 (*śᵉ'ārâ*, gale, storm), → # 8548

8555	שְׂעֹרָה

שְׂעֹרָה (*śᵉ'ōrâ*), barley (# 8555).

OT This word occurs 34x and has cognates in many ANE languages (Ugar. *š'r*; pl. *š'rm*; Old Aram. *ś'rh*; *ś'rîm/n*; *s'ry'*; Arab. *ša'īr*; OSA *š'r* II; Tigre *ša'ar*, each meaning barley). It is also found in the early Heb. of the Gezer Calender (line 4), indicating when barley was to be harvested (March-April). The LXX translates this word as *krithē* or *krithinos,* both meaning barley, and the Aram. Targ. (*s^e'ār^etā'*) and later Heb. (*ś^e'ôrâ*) employ words related to *ś^e'ōrâ* for barley. This word may have derived from the word "hairy" because of the long awns that project from the seeds (J. C. Trever, 1:355; *HALAT* 4:1254). Barley and wheat appear to have been the two major grain crops in Israel (Deut 8:8; Job 31:40; Jer 41:8; Joel 1:11), though barley ripened about four weeks earlier than wheat (Exod 9:31; Ruth 2:23). Barley was rarely required for cereal offerings (Num 5:15; Ezek 45:13) and was possibly less expensive than wheat (2 Kgs 7:1, 16, 18), which would explain why it was used to feed to animals (1 Kgs 4:28[5:8]). Similarly, the barley loaf in the dream of Judg 7:13 may have confirmed to the Midianite that it was a reference to Gideon, because barley was the staple crop of Israel's poor farmer (A. E. Cundall, *Judges and Ruth,* 1968, 111-12; J. Gray, *Joshua, Judges, Ruth,* 1986, 292).

Grain, barley, millet, rice, etc.: → *'ābîb* (ears of grain, # 26); → *bisqālôn* (fresh stalks [cj.], # 1303); → *bar* III (grain, corn, # 1339); → *gādîš* I (stack of grain, # 1538); → *gereś* (grits, # 1762); → *dāgān* (grain, # 1841); → *dōḥan* (sorghum, millet, # 1893); → *ḥiṭṭâ* (wheat, # 2636); → *kussemet* (emmer-wheat, # 4081); → *karmel* IV (grain, fresh, newly ripened grain, # 4152); → *m^elîlâ* (grain, grains, # 4884); → *minnît* (rice, # 4976); → *mōṣ* (chaff, # 5161); → *sōlet* (wheat flour, # 6159); → *pannāg* (parched? grain, meal or flour, # 7154); → *ṣebet* (grain, bundle of grain, # 7395); → *ṣānum* (hard, barren [ears of grain], # 7568); → *qālî* (parched grain, # 7833); → *qāmâ* (crops, grain, standing grain, # 7850); → *śôrâ* (millet, # 8463); → *ś^e'ōrâ* (barley, # 8555); → *šibbōlet* I (ear of grain, # 8672); → *šeber* II (grain, # 8692)

BIBLIOGRAPHY
IDB 1:355; M. Zohary, *Plants of the Bible,* 1982.

Paul D. Wegner

8557	שָׂפָה

שָׂפָה (*śāpâ*), nom. lip, language, shore, bank (# 8557).

ANE With both literal and figurative meaning, *śāpâ* is common Sem. It is widely attested in Akk. *šaptu* (*CAD*, 17:483-87) with the meanings lip, utterance, speech, edge, rim; in Ugar. *špt* (*WUS* # 2663) as lip (*CTA* 23, 61-62; 24, 46; 22, B 4; 2, iv 6), always referring to the human face; and in Aram *śph* (*KAI* 224, 14-15, 16 = *Sfîre* III, 15-16), again the bodily organ. Cf. Tigrin *šänfäf*, lip; also Arab. *šafat*, Egyp. *śpt*.

OT 1. The nom. *śāpâ* occurs ca. 175x in the OT, overwhelmingly with reference to the human lip or lips as synonymous with mouth or as the organ of speech (*HALAT* 1255-56). Little theological value attaches to most of these occurrences; in some cases, however, especially when used figuratively of speech itself, usually idiomatically, its use affords interesting exegetical insight. In a strictly metaphorical sense *śāpâ* describes the shore of a sea (Gen 22:17; Exod 14:30; Judg 7:12; 1 Kgs 4:29[5:9]; 9:26) or the bank of a river (Gen 41:3; Exod 2:3; 7:15; 2 Kgs 2:13; Dan 12:5). It also refers to the edge of something, such as a curtain (Exod 26:4, 10), a garment (28:26, 32), or a territory (Judg 7:22). Finally, it speaks of the brim of the Sea by the temple (1 Kgs 7:23, 26) and the outer edge of the great altar in Ezekiel's temple (Ezek 43:13).

2. The word *śāpâ* as a synonym for *peh*, mouth (→ # 7033), is clearly seen in Ps 51:15[17] and 66:14, where the two are parallel or in synonymous juxtaposition.

3. The most instructive examples of *śāpâ* meaning "language" or "speech" are in the Babel narrative of Gen 11. In v. 1, *śāpâ* is synonymous with *d^ebārîm*, words, and in v. 6 Yahweh says that all humanity has "one lip," i.e., is speaking one language. To redress the problem of failure to disperse, Yahweh says he will confuse their "lip" so that no one will be able any longer to understand the "lip" of his neighbor (v. 7). The language of Egypt is also described as an "unknown lip" (Ps 81:5[6]), but, ironically, the day will come when Egyptians will speak the "lip of Canaan" (i.e., Hebrew, Isa 19:18). The Akk. language of Assyria is described as *'imqê śāpâ*, unintelligible of lip (Isa 33:19; cf. Ezek 3:5, 6). Finally, Isaiah tells of a day when God will speak to Israel with *la'^agê śāpâ ûb^elāšôn 'aḥeret,* foreign lips and strange tongues (Isa 28:11).

4. As speech or speaking *śāpâ*, like *lāšôn*, tongue (→ # 4383), appears predominantly in Wisdom and poetic literature. Thus, of 176 occurrences with variations of meaning, twelve are in Job, twenty-eight in Psalms, and forty-five in Proverbs; in the great majority the reference is to lips as metonymy for verbal communication. For the most part, *śāpâ* is associated with negative or harmful speech. There are lying (*šeqer* → # 9214) lips (Ps 31:18[19]; 120:2; Prov 10:18; 12:22), and those that are deceitful (*mirmâ*, Ps 17:1), flattering (*ḥ^alaqôt*, 12:2[3]), and perverse (*'iqqēš*, Prov 19:1). Isaiah, viewing God in his holiness, saw himself as a man with "unclean lips" (*'îš ṭ^emē' ś^epātayim*), i.e., as one cultically impure and unable to speak for Yahweh (Isa 6:5). Moses described himself as one with "uncircumcised lips" (*'^aral ś^epātayim*), also suggesting impurity and disqualification for service to a holy God (Exod 6:12, 30). One who speaks without thinking is called a "man of lips" (Job 11:2), and his talk is scornfully described as "word of lips" (2 Kgs 18:20; Prov 14:23; Isa 36:5), i.e., speech without forethought. Such people are fools (*'^ewîl ś^epātayim*, foolish of lips, Prov 10:8, 10; cf. 18:6). The lips can, of course, be used in positive forms of speech. They can tell truth (Prov 12:19, ‖ lying tongue), utter gracious words (22:11), and sing the praises of Yahweh (Ps 63:5[6]). The reason for praise in this last verse is the love of God (i.e., his covenant favor) for David, as pointed out in v. 3[4].

P-B Mish. Heb. *śāpâ*, lip, speech, edge; Aram. *spt'*, lip, edge; LXX *cheilos*, lip, shore, bank.

Language, tongue, speech: → *l'z* (speak unintelligibly, # 4357); → *lāšôn* (tongue, language, # 4383); → *lšn* (slander, # 4387); → *śāpâ* (language, lip, shore, # 8557)

BIBLIOGRAPHY

TWAT 7:840-49; *TWOT* 2:882; K. Albrecht, "Das Geschlecht der hebräischen Hauptwörter," *ZAW* 16, 1896, 41-121; A. Beeston, "The Hebrew verb *špt*," *VT* 8, 1958, 216-17; D. Block, "The Role of Language in Ancient Israelite Perceptions of National Identity," *JBL* 103, 1984, 321-40; M. Dahood, "Deuteronomy 35, 19 and UT, 52:61-63," *Or* 47, 1978, 263-64; N. Graetz, "Miriam: Guilty or Not Guilty," *Judaism* 40, 1991, 184-92; M. Gruber, *Aspects of Nonverbal Communication in the Ancient Near East*, 1980, 1:328-29; M. Jastrow 2:1613-14; H. W. Wolff, *Anthropology of the Old Testament*, 1974, 77.

Eugene H. Merrill

8559	שָׂפָם

שָׂפָם (*śāpām*), nom. mustache, lower part of the face (# 8559).

OT 1. *śāpām* denotes the lower part of the face and sometimes the moustache specifically. In Lev 13:45 persons with certain infectious skin diseases were to wear torn clothes, let their hair be unkempt, cover the lower part of their faces, and cry out "Unclean! Unclean!" According to Micah, false prophets will have to cover their faces because of the disgrace of not receiving a word from God (Mic 3:7; cf. Zech 13:4).

2. Trimming the mustache was a customary form of good grooming. The absence was remarkable and pointed to a deep distress, as was the case of Mephibosheth, Saul's grandson, during David's temporary exile from Jerusalem: "(he) also went down to meet the king. He had not taken care of his feet or trimmed his mustache or washed his clothes from the day the king left until the day he returned safely" (2 Sam 19:24[25]). Only here does *śāpām* require the rendering mustache.

3. The word is used in the context of mourning in Ezek 24:17, 22. The Lord instructed his servant that he could not give himself to public mourning over the loss of his wife (v. 17; cf. v. 22). Ezekiel's mission as a public watchman over Israel kept him from engaging in the public mourning rituals. (→ Ezekiel: Theology)

Hair: → *zāqān* (beard, # 2417); → *maḥ^{a}lāpâ* (braid, # 4710); → *miqšeh* (well-dressed hair, # 5250); → *pr'* (untie hair, # 7277); → *ṣîṣit* (hair, tassel, # 7492); → *q^{e}wuṣṣôt* (hair, # 7767); → *ś'r* I (be appalled, # 8547); → *śāpām* (moustache, # 8559)
Shaving, trimming: → *glḥ* (shave, # 1662); → *ksm* (trim hair, # 4080)

Bibliography

ISBE 2:596-99; *TDOT* 3:5-20; C. Sherlock, "Ezekiel's Dumbness," *ExpTim* 94, 1982/83, 296-98; G. A. te Stroete, "Ezekiel 24:15-27: The Meaning of a Symbolic Act," *Bijdr* 38, 1977, 163-65; H. Trav, N. Rubin, S. Vargon, "Symbolic Significance of Hair in the Biblical Narrative and the Law," *Koroth* 9, 1988, 173-79; R. R. Wilson, "An Interpretation of Ezekiel's Dumbness," *VT* 22, 1972, 91-104.

Robert L. Alden

8561	שׂפן

שׂפן (*śpn*), q. conceal, hide (hapleg. in Deut 33:19; an orthographic variation of the Heb. *ṣpn*, cover or roof; → # 7621) (# 8561).

ANE The Heb. root *śpn* is cognate with the Akk. *ṣapānu* (to hide, EA 147:10; see *CAD* 16:96); cf. Phoen. *mspnt* (roof; *KAI* 10, 6).

OT The word occurs as part of Moses' farewell blessing of the tribes of Issachar and Zebulun. They "will feast on the abundance of the seas, on the treasures hidden in the sand" (Deut 33:19). S. R. Driver *(Deuteronomy*, ICC, 1901, 410) and P. C. Craigie (*Deuteronomy*, NICOT, 1976, 399) associate the "treasure hidden in the sand" with the seacoast industries of shellfish dye and glass making. A. D. H. Mayes (*Deuteronomy*, NCBC, 1979, 407) emends the first of the two passive participles in combination and reads, "and they draw out the treasures of the sand" (see NEB). He connects the reference to caravan trade as a source of wealth for the tribes. In any case, the abundance of God's creation will make Issachar and Zebulun prosperous.

Hiding: → *ḥb'* (hide, conceal, # 2461); → *ḥbh* (hide, # 2464); → *ḥāgû* (refuge, cleft, # 2511); → *ḥpp* I (screen, shelter, # 2910); → *ṭmn* (hide, # 3243); → *kḥd* (be hidden, hide, # 3948); → *knp* (hide oneself, # 4052); → *sōk* (hiding-place, shelter, thicket, hut, # 6108); → *str* (hide, kept secret, # 6259); → *'lm* (hidden things, secrets, # 6623); → *ṣpn* (hide, # 7621); → *śpn* (conceal, # 8561)

BIBLIOGRAPHY

NIDNTT 2:211-20; 3:553-56; S. E. Balentine, "A Description of the Semantic Field of Hebrew Words for Hide," *VT* 30, 1980, 137-53; R. Gordis, "Studies in Hebrew Roots of Contrasted Meanings," *JQR* 27, 1936-37, 33-58.

Andrew E. Hill

8562 (*śpq* I, clap one's hand), → # 3338

8563	שׂפק

שׂפק (*śpq*, II), q. suffice, be enough (only in 1 Kgs 20:10); hi. abound (?) (only in Isa 2:6) (# 8563); שֶׂפֶק (*śepeq*), nom. abundance (only in Job 20:22; # 8564); שֵׂפֶק (*śēpeq*), nom. overflow (# 8565). Related forms: ספק (*spq II*), be in abundance (only in Jer 48:26; # 6216); סֶפֶק (*sepeq*), nom. abundance (or hand-clapping in mockery; only in Job 36:18; # 6217).

ANE See the Akk. cognate *sapāqu,* be enough, sufficient (*CAD* 15:161, and Arab.).

OT 1. Ben-Hadad boasted his superior manpower would reduce Samaria to dust, with even this residue of rubble so insignificant the huge Aramean army might carry it off by the handful (1 Kgs 20:10). Of course Ben-Hadad's bravado was premature since the king and his troops fled from King Ahab and the Israelites in the face of battle.

2. The array of translations in the versions for Isa 2:6 emphasizes the difficulty of the text. Compare, "many foreign children were born to them" (LXX), "with the children of foreigners everywhere" (NEB), and "clasp hands with pagans" (NIV). At issue is the underlying root, whether it be from *śpq* II, abound, or *śpq* I, clap hands (→ # 8562). Oswalt (*Isaiah 1-39*, 122) notes that while the meaning "clap hands" (*śpq* I) in the sense of making alliances with other nations is not attested elsewhere, the MT should not be emended (cf. *TWAT* 5:910).

3. The noms. (*śēpeq, śepeq*) occur only in Job 20:22 and 36:18. The meaning in 20:22 is unambiguous, "In the midst of his plenty, distress will overtake him." But the meaning in 36:18 is doubtful. Pope (*Job*, AB, 271) connects the word to the root meaning suffice, abound (*śpq* II), rather than clap the hands (*śpq* I, so NIV). In both instances a warning against greed provides the context for the usage of the expression.

Abundance, multiplication, sufficiency: → *dgh* (multiply, # 1835); → *day* (sufficiency, overflowing supply, # 1896); → *ysp* (add, continue, increase, # 3578); → *kbr* I (make many, be in abundant supply, # 3892); → *m^{e}gammâ* (totality, abundance, # 4480); → *rbb* I (become numerous, much, great, # 8045); → *rbh* I (become numerous, multiply, increase, # 8049); → *r'š* II, be abundant, # 8322); → *śg'/śgh* (grow great, increase, exalt, # 8434/8436); → *śpq* II (suffice, be enough, # 8563); → *šwq* I (overflow, bestow abundantly, # 8796); → *šepa'* (super-abundance, # 9179)

Andrew E. Hill

8564 (*śepeq*, abundance), → # 8563

8565 (*śēpeq*, abundance), → # 8563

8566	שַׂק

שַׂק (*śaq*), nom. sack, sackcloth (# 8566).

ANE Jew. Aram. *saqqā'*; Egyp. Aram. *śq*; Akk. *s/šaqqu(m)*, sack; Eth. *šaq*; Egyp. *śg*, woolen blanket; Copt. *sok*, sack.

OT 1. Sack/sackcloth was worn when persons mourned for various reasons. In the time of national calamity sackcloth could be worn (2 Kgs 6:30-32; cf. 1 Kgs 21:27; Lam 2:10). It also was a sign of grief and mourning in the time of personal tragedy (Gen 37:34; Job 16:15; Joel 1:8), as when David mourned for Abner (2 Sam 3:31; cf. 12:20). The practice of wearing sackcloth and ashes together with fasting constituted the ritual process of mourning and seeking mercy from the Lord (Dan 9:3). The wearing of sackcloth is coupled with humility in the Psalms (Ps 35:13; cf. 1 Kgs 21:27). The Lord can remove one's sackcloth (grief) and replace it with gladness (Ps 30:11[12]). Kings, elders, priests, common people—all classes and even animals could be clothed in sackcloth (2 Chron 21:16; Jon 3:5). Its shape was possibly similar to a bean bag or a loincloth. The cloth was likely dark in color (cf. Isa 50:3; Rev 6:12) and made of goat hair. It was used figuratively by Isaiah to describe the darkening of the sky, "sackcloth its covering" (Isa 50:3). (→ Lament: Theology)

2. The sack or sackcloth along with the mournful demeanor and gestures of the wearer represented the pain, grief, sorrow, or lack of or loss of hope, or the coming of tragedy. Sackcloth was the opposite of festal garments that were worn in times of joy and celebration. The dark color of sackcloth represented the absence of color; color signified glory, honor, and jubilation. Wearing sackcloth could represent the tragedy of an external event or the throes of an internal condition of the heart and soul.

NT The NT continues this same usage (Matt 11:21; Luke 10:13; Rev 6:12; 11:3).

Sack: → *'amtaḥat* (sack, bag, burden, pack, # 623); → *śaq* (sack, sack-cloth, # 8566)

BIBLIOGRAPHY

TWAT 7:849-55.

Eugene Carpenter/Michael A. Grisanti

8567	שׂקד

שׂקד (*śqd*), ni. take note of (# 8567).

OT The vb. is attested 1x. The meaning is uncertain. According to the context of Lam 1:14 it is normally interpreted as meaning bound. Another suggestion is that it means to take note of/watch. According to this suggestion, the vb. in Lam 1:14 can be interpreted that the Lord took note of/set himself as a watch over the transgressions of Jerusalem and tied them all together. *HALAT* suggested (together with various manuscripts and the LXX) that *śqd* must be amended to *šqd*, which is the normal word for watching. The last two suggestions also imply that the vocalization of the following word *'ōl*, yoke, must change to *'al*, on/over (cf. Renkema, 116).

Look, observation, perception, sight, vision, watch: → *ḥdh* II (gaze on, appear, # 2526); → *ḥzh* (see, perceive, behold, # 2600); → *ḥmh* I (see, watch out for, become visible, # 2778); → *nbṭ* (look around, accept as an act of grace, # 5564); → *pls* II (observe, # 7143); → *ṣwṣ* II (look at, # 7438); → *r'h* (see, have visions, choose, perceive, # 8011); → *rṣd* (keep one's eye on, # 8353); → *śqd* (take note of, # 8567); → *š'h* III (stand gazing, # 8617); → *šgḥ* (gaze, stare, # 8708); → *šwr* I (gaze on, regard, see, # 8800); → *šzp* (catch sight of, tan, scorch, # 8812); → *š'h* (look, care about, gaze about, # 9120); → *šqp* (look down, # 9207); → *št'* (gaze, look, regard, look anxiously about, # 9283)

Bibliography
F. E. Greenspahn, *Hapax Legomena in Biblical Hebrew*, 1984; J. Renkema, *Klaagliederen*, 1993.

Jackie A. Naudé

8569 (*śar*, official, chieftain, leader, prince), → # 8606

8571	שׂרג

שׂרג (*śrg*), pu. be intertwined; hitp. intertwine o.s. (# 8571).

ANE The cognate *s^erag* in Syr. has the meaning of a path entangled with stumbling blocks.

OT This root is used of the "close-knit" sinews (Job 40:17) of behemoth (40:15-19) to demonstrate the power and mystery of God's great creature, which is far beyond human control or rule. In Lam 1:14 Israel's sins are "woven together" as a net holding them fast; they are an inescapable yoke, which brings destruction.

Intertwining, twisting: → *gablut* (interwoven, twisted work, # 1491); → *śôbek* (tangle of branches, # 8449); → *śrg* (intertwine, # 8571); → *śrk* (twist, # 8592)

Bibliography
J. G. Gammie, "Behemoth and Leviathan: On the Didactic and Theological Significance of Job 40:15-41:26," in *Israelite Wisdom*, ed. J. G. Gammie, et al., 1978, 217-31.

Francis Foulkes

8572	שׂרד

שׂרד (*śrd*), q. run away, escape (# 8572); שָׂרִיד (*śārîd* I), nom. escapee, survivor of battle (# 8586).

ANE Cognate forms of the vb. *śrd* occur in Syr. *s^erad* and Mand. *SNDR*. In both these languages the vb. has the meaning to be scared. The Arab. form *šarada*, in contrast, has the same meaning as the Heb. vb., run away, flee. The Syr. nom. *s^erîdā'*, survivor, escapee corresponds to the Heb. nom. *śārîd*.

OT The vb. *śrd* occurs only once in the OT (Josh 10:20, escape). The nom. that is derived from this vb. (*śārîd*) occurs, however, 28x, but it is often difficult to tell whether the nom. refers to escapees or to a place-name. One such *crux interpretum* occurs in Judg 5:13 (*'az y^erad śārîd l^e'addîrîm 'am yhwh y^erad-lî baggibbôrîm*). The meaning of *śārîd* and its relation to *'addîr* (# 129) is not clear. Na'aman (423-26) discusses the various attempts to translate or emend the verse. He argues that the particle *'az* is used in vv. 8, 11, 13, 19, and 22 of Judg 5 every time that a new stage of the battle is introduced. From this he concludes that *śārîd* refers to a place-name. Sarid is a well-known Israelite town on the southern border of Zebulun (cf. Josh 19:10, 12). Greenberg (*ABD* 5:985) mentions that the town has been identified with Tel Shadud in the northern Jezreel Valley. The town of Sarid was used as an assembly point for the Israelite army, from where attacks were launched on the Canaanite forces who assembled nearby (about 10 km away) at Taanach, by the waters of Megiddo.

According to Ruprecht (*THAT* 2:424) the nom. *śārîd* often occurs in conjunction with or par. to the nom. *pālîṭ* (Josh 8:22; Jer 42:17; 44:14; Lam 2:22; Obad 1:14). They are normally synonymous, both having the meaning of "someone who was able to escape a sword-death on a battle-field." In a few cases (Gen 14:13; Ezek 24:26; 33:21), however, *pālîṭ* designates "an escapee who brings the message of defeat in battle."

Wildberger (*THAT* 2:846) contends that these nom. could also be related to the noms. *šᵉ'ār* and *šᵉ'ērît*, remnant (→ # 8637, # 8642). The latter words acquired a theological nuance in the postexilic Israelite community to designate Yahweh's people who were saved from extinction by his grace. It is doubtful whether *śārîd* underwent the same theological shift in meaning. However, some prophetic references (cf. in particular, Isa 1:9 and Jer 31:2) suggest such a shift.

P-B In numerous cases the LXX uses variants of the vb. (*dia-*, *ana-*)*sōzō* to translate the vb. *śrd* and the nom. *śārîd*. Often the conjunction *śārîd ûpālîṭ* is translated by the LXX with only one word (normally a part. form of *sōzō*). Cf. Fohrer's discussion (*TWNT* 7:970-81) of equivalents of *sōzō* and *sōtēria* in the OT. In his discussion of the LXX's translation of these words he does not account for the fact that *sōzō* is sometimes used to translate the combination of *sarîd ûpālîṭ*, and not only of the vb. *pl*.

Refuge, escape: → *ḥsh* (seek refuge, # 2879); → *mālôn* (lodging place, # 4869); → *mānôs* (place of escape, # 4960); → *miqlāṭ* (refuge, asylum, # 5236); → *'wz* (take refuge, # 6395); → *plṭ* (save, bring to safety, # 7117); → *śrd* (run away, escape, # 8572)

BIBLIOGRAPHY

ABD 5:985; *THAT* 2:419-27, 843-55; *TWNT* 7:966-1024; N. Na'aman, "Literary and Topographical Notes on the Battle of Kishon (Judges IV-V)," *VT* 40/4, 1990, 423-36.

Louis Jonker

8573	שְׂרָד

שְׂרָד (*śᵉrād*), nom. woven (# 8573).

ANE Aram. *srd'*, plaiting, is a cognate.

OT All four occurrences of this nom. refer to the priestly garments in Exod and are always compounded with *beged* II, garment (Exod 31:10; 35:19; 39:1, 41; → # 955). KJV rendered it "cloths of *service*," but NIV, following the LXX, renders the phrase: "*woven* garments." Childs reads "stitched vestments."

Spinning, sewing, weaving, embroidering: → *'rg* (spin, weave, # 755); → *dallâ* I (hair, thrum, loom, # 1929); → *ḥōšēb* (weaver, # 3110); → *ṭwh* (spin, # 3211); → *kîšôr* (distaff, # 3969); → *mānôr* (rod, # 4962); → *skk* II (weave, intertwine, # 6115); → *'ēreb* I (knitted material,

6849); → *pelek* I (spindle-whorl, # 7134); → *rqm* (embroider, weave together, # 8387); → *śᵉrād* (woven, # 8573); → *šbṣ* I (weave, # 8687); → *šᵉtî* I (woven material, # 9274); → *tpr* (sew, # 9529)

Bibliography

M. Haran, "The Priestly Image of the Tabernacle," *HUCA* 36, 1965, 213-15; B. Childs, *Exodus*, OTL, 1974, 522, 529.

Robert L. Alden

8574	שֶׂרֶד

שֶׂרֶד (*śered*), traditionally "reddle" (red chalk) (# 8574).

OT Of uncertain derivation and used only in Isa 44:13, this word possibly denotes the marker used by a craftsman in laying out a piece of wood about to become an idol. The precise kind of marker is disputed (cf. *HALAT* 1262). A likely Arab. cognate *sirād* points to the meaning awl.

William C. Williams

8575	שׂרה

שׂרה (*śrh* I), q. contend, struggle (# 8575).

OT *śrh* occurs only 3x in the OT, all in reference to Jacob's wrestling with the divine being in Gen 32 (Hos 12:4-5 refers to this tradition, using *śrh* twice). The primary occurrence is in Gen 32:29: "Your name will no longer be Jacob, but Israel, because you struggled (*śārîtā*) with God and with men and have overcome" (NIV). *śrh* is used here as an etymology for Israel. The purpose of the text is to make a theological claim about God's transformation of Jacob (→), the former trickster (see E. Speiser, 255; cf. G. Vermes, 12-13).

Contention, strife, struggle: → *gl'* (break out in a dispute, # 1679); → *grh* (stir up strife, # 1741); → *nṣh* I (struggle, # 5897); → *ptl* (twist, be wily, shrewd, # 7349); → *ryb* (strive, # 8189); → *rᵉ'ût* II (longing, striving, # 8296); → *śrh* I (contend, struggle, # 8575)

Bibliography

E. Speiser, *Genesis*, AB 1, 1964; G. Vermes, "The Impact of the Dead Sea Scrolls on Jewish Studies During the Last Twenty-Five Years," *JJS* 26, 1-14.

John M. Bracke

8576 (*sarâ* I, princess; noble, lady), → # 8606

8577 (*śārâ*, Sarah), → Sarah

8579 (*śᵉrôk*, sandal-strap), → # 8592

8581	שׂרט

שׂרט (*śrṭ*), q. cut, make incisions (tattoo); ni. be cut up, get cut up (# 8581); nom. שֶׂרֶט (*śereṭ*), incision, cutting (in one's body/flesh; # 8582); שָׂרֶטֶת (*śāreṭeṭ*), incision, cutting (in one's body; # 8583).

OT 1. Priests were prohibited from cutting their bodies, along with shaving their heads and trimming their beards (Lev 21:5), because they were holy to their God and would, by such activity, profane the name of God.

2. The people of Israel were prohibited from cutting their bodies in mourning for the dead (Lev 19:28) because "I am the LORD," i.e., the Israelites owed exclusive allegiance and worship to Yahweh, and to mourn for the dead in this way was to engage in a pagan religious practice.

3. Eschatologically, the passive or reflexive ni. form of the vb., together with the emphatic q. inf. abs., is used to describe the judgment (i.e., grievously cut up) that the nations will bring upon themselves when they gather together to overthrow Jerusalem (Zech 12:3). The use of the vb. *śrṭ* in this eschatological context may be the prophet's effective way of turning the nations' own pagan practices back on their own heads; their pagan practices will, in an intensified way, be the means of their punishment in the eschaton.

NT Paul refers to Jewish legalists as "mutilators of the flesh" (Phil 3:2) and says "those agitators ... I wish they would ... emasculate (mutilate/*apokopsountai*) themselves" (Gal 5:12) (see W. L. Reed in *IDB*, K-Q, 477). *apokoptō*, being a derivative of *koptō*, strike, beat the breast in mourning, may have a ritual mourning significance (see *NIDNTT* 2:417-19). For Paul, the gospel has freed the believer from ritual and legalistic observances as signs of one's covenant relationship with God.

Incision, cut, tattoo: → *gdd* I (inflict cuts, make incisions, # 1517); → *ḥārûṣ* IV (mutilation, # 3024); → *qaʿᵃqaʿ* (tattoo, incision, # 7882); → *śrṭ* (cut, make incisions, be cut up, # 8581)
Shaving, trimming: → *glḥ* (shave, # 1662); → *ksm* (trim hair, # 4080)

Malcolm J. A. Horsnell

8582 (*śereṭ*, incision, cutting), → # 8581

8583 (*śāreṭeṭ*, incision, cutting), → # 8581

8584 (*śāray*, Sarai), → Abraham

8585	שָׂרִיג

שָׂרִיג (*śārîg*), nom. branch, tendril, climber (# 8585).

ANE Arab. *sarǧ*; Mid. Heb, *śārîg*; Jew. Aram. *sᵉrîgā'*.

OT The word is used 3x in the OT. In Gen 40:10, 12 it is used figuratively in the chief cupbearer's dream to signify three days, since three tendrils/branches (*śārîgîm*) appeared on the vine (*gepen*). After three days the chief cupbearer was restored to his place before Pharaoh. In Joel 1:7d the word is again used to describe the effect of a locust plague upon the vines (*gepen*) and the vine branches (*śārîgeyhā*) of the Lord's land. These branches are "white" from the devastation, i.e., dried up and dying.

P-B The LXX uses *klēma*, shoot, vine twig (Joel 1:7), and *pythmēn*, root, stem (Gen 40:10, 12).

Grapes—viticulture: → *bṣr* I (gather grapes, tread down, vine-dresser, # 1305); → *gepen* (vine, grapevine, # 1728); → *kerem* I (vineyard, # 4142); → *qss* (strip away, pick, # 7878); → *śārîg* (branch, tendril, climber, # 8585); → *śōrēq* II (choice vine, # 8603); → *śᵉrēqā* (vine with the best grapes, # 8605)

Eugene Carpenter

8586 (*śārîd* I, escapee, survivor of battle), → # 8572

8592	שׂרך

שׂרך (*śrk*), pi. twist (# 8592); nom. שְׂרוֹךְ (*śᵉrôk*), sandal-strap (twisted over the foot) (# 8579).

OT The vb. is used in Jer 2:23 of a "restive young camel interlacing her tracks" (NRSV), picturing Israel's restless running after the Baals. When Israel sinfully pursues its own will, aimless and purposeless behavior results.

Intertwining, twisting: → *gablut* (interwoven, twisted work, # 1491); → *śôbek* (tangle of branches, # 8449); → *śrg* (intertwine, # 8571); → *śrk* (twist, # 8592)

Bibliography

K. E. Bailey and W. L. Holladay, "The 'Young Camel' and 'Wild Ass' in Jeremiah ii, 23-25," *VT* 18, 1968, 256-60.

Francis Foulkes

8594	שׂרע

שׂרע (*śr'*), q. deformed, mutilated; hitp. stretch o.s. (Isa 28:20) (# 8594).

OT 1. This term occurs exclusively in Leviticus to describe some physical deformity that disqualified a man from being admitted to the priesthood (Lev 21:18), since otherwise the ceremonial purity of the Lord's ministers would be compromised. Deformed or mutilated animals were not permitted as burnt offerings to the Lord (Lev 22:22), since only the highest quality animal could serve adequately in this capacity. At the same time, a deformed sheep or cow could serve acceptably as a freewill offering (Lev 22:23). Hartley (350) suggests that the deformity consists of "having a member of the body malformed, too short or too long, or possibly having something extra like an extra finger or possibly having slit ears."

2. The hitp. inf., stretch o.s. (Isa 28:20), has no reference to a natural deformity.

Handicaps, disfigurement, blind, lame, stammer, speechless: → *'illēm* (speechlessness, # 522); → *gibbēn* (hunchbacked, # 1492); → *ḥārûṣ* IV (mutilation [animal], # 3024); → *ḥērēš* (speechless, # 3094); → *kšḥ* (be lame, crippled, # 4171); → *mûm* (blemish, # 4583); → *mišḥāt* (disfigured, # 5425); → *nākeh* (crippled, smitten, # 5783); → *'wr* I (be blind, # 6422); → *'illēg* (stammering, stuttering, # 6589); → *psḥ* (be lame, crippled, # 7174); → *ṣl'* I (limping condition, # 7519); → *qlṭ* I (defective [animal], # 7832); → *śr'* (deformed, mutilated, # 8594); → *tᵉballul* (white spot in eye, # 9319)

Bibliography

J. Hartley, *Leviticus,* WBC 4, 1992, 350.

R. K. Harrison/E. H. Merrill

8595 (*śᵉr'appîm*, disquieting thoughts, worries), → # 8546

8596	שׂרף

שׂרף (*śrp*), q. burn, scorch, cauterize; ni. be, become burnt; pu. be, become burnt (# 8596); מִשְׂרָפוֹת (*miśrāpôt*), nom. burning, combustion (→ # 5386); שָׂרָף (*śārāp*), nom. seraph, snake, serpent (→ # 8597); שְׂרֵפָה (*śᵉrēpâ*), nom. fire, conflagration, burning, combustion, burned-out place (→ # 8599); סרף (*srp*), pi. burn (hapleg.; # 6251).

ANE The vb. is found in Ugar. *šrp*; Akk. *šarāpu(m)*, burn, scorch; Egyp. Aram. *śrf*, be warm, hot. The nom. occurs in Eblaite *sà-ra-pá-tum*, Ugar. *šrp*, Akk. *šurpu(m)* and *šuruptu(m)*, and Sam., *šērīfa*, burning, combustion, firewood. The Eblaite *sà-ra-pá-tum* may also mean burnt offering.

OT 1. The vb. is used of straightforward acts of burning, as, for example, in Isa 44:16, 19, part of a brilliant, caustic, satire on idolatry (44:9-20), which exposes the absurd inconsistency of using as fuel for warmth, baking, and cooking the same perishable tree from which a "god" to be worshiped has been assiduously carved (cf. Wisd 13:11-13; Horace's *Satires*, I, viii, 1-3).

The q. occurs with the nom. in the paronomastic phrase *wᵉniśrᵉpâ liśᵉrēpâ*, and [let us] bake them [bricks] hard (NEB; REB; TEV), in Gen 11:3, part of the tower of Babel (→) story, which relates the dissolution, as a consequence of human hubris and rebellion, of the harmony and unity created by God. Bricks were normally sun-dried in Palestine, but the firing process used often in Babylonia ensured greater strength and durability (Hertz, 39; Westermann, 546; Wenham, 1987, 239; Gowan, 117).

According to the problematic text of Neh 4:2[3:34], Sanballat asked his associates and/or allies if the "feeble Jews" were going to use the burned stones out of the rubble heaps as building materials. When subjected to fire, slabs of stone may become weakened and cracked. Limestone in particular has a tendency to crumble when subjected to moderately intense heat (Williamson, 216). The mention of the burned rubble has been taken to refer to the increased difficulty of acquiring sufficient building material for the task of restoration from the mass of fire-damaged debris (Batten, 226). However, the implication of Neh 4:2-3[3:34-35] seems to be that the reconstructed wall will be a jerry-built structure that will collapse under the slightest strain (Cundall, 406). It has been suggested that Sanballat would have considered the stones blackened by fire to have been cursed, which in turn would have precluded their use in the restoration project (Fensham, 1983, 180-81), but this seems unlikely.

The vb. *śrp* occurs in Jer 36:25, 27, 28, 29, 32, part of a dramatic narrative describing how, each time Jehudi read three or four columns of the scroll dictated to Baruch by Jeremiah, Jehoiakim cut them off with a penknife and threw them into the fire of a brazier (2 Kgs 22:3-23:24; on this, see, e.g., Carroll, 1986, 663-64). If, however, Jehoiakim thought that by destroying them in an apotropaic act of execration (Couturier, 292; cf. Carroll, 1981, 152-53; 1986, 663) he could neutralize the power of these prophetic words to effect their own fulfillment, he was mistaken; instead of destroying the threats and curses in the scroll, his action released them (Carroll, 1986, 663, 667-68). Neither royal power nor consuming flame is effective in preventing the operation of the prophetic word.

The vb. is also used of the funerary rite of burning spices in Jer 34:5, where the prophet assures Zedekiah of a peaceful death and customary ceremonial funeral rites, and in 2 Chron 16:14, which describes how spices were burned for Asa. It was considered a great dishonor for a person to be denied proper burial rites (cf. 1 Kgs 13:22; Jer 22:19; 2 Chron 21:19).

2. According to the biblical narrative, Israel's recidivist tendencies toward idolatry can be traced back to the foot of Sinai, where the people entered into covenant with God. Exod 32:20 and Deut 9:21 relate how, on his return to the camp after his long vigil on the summit of Sinai, Moses took the golden calf before which the people had been dancing, burned it, and then ground it to powder. In the Exodus account, he then scattered the fine dust of the pulverized metal upon the water and made the people drink it. This could have been a form of retribution (Dummelow, 82), making the people ingest their own sin (Clifford, 59), or the subjection of the Israelites to a trial by ordeal in order to discriminate between the innocent and the guilty (see, e.g., Num 5:16-28; Rylaarsdam, 1068; G. H. Davies, 1967, 233; Gray, 1971, 64; Clements, 1972, 208; May and Metzger, 110; cf. McCarter, 154), or a kind of sin offering (Gray, 1971, 64).

3. The vb. appears frequently in cultic contexts. In Exod 12:10, the Israelites are commanded to burn, before morning, whatever remains from the feast of the sacrificed Passover lamb. As regards the background and motive of the instruction to dispose of the food left over, several suggestions have been made. Some (e.g., Clements, 1972, 72) consider this to be a strong indication that, in its original form, the Passover was a nocturnal festival in which the moon figured prominently, possibly as the symbol of the divine presence. Several commentators think that the motive for the command may have been to avoid profanation of sacred flesh by persons in an unsanctified state or at an unsanctified time (Dummelow, 58; S. R. Driver, 1953, 91-92; Stalker, 219; Noth, 96; G. H. Davies, 1967, 112; Gray, 1971, 45; Hyatt, 1971, 133; cf. Hertz, 255). Another suggestion is that it was aimed at discouraging magical practices (Cole, 107). H. R. Jones (127) maintains that the total consumption by eating and burning signified the complete consecration of the paschal sacrifice to a holy purpose. At any rate, burning was the standard procedure for disposal of the remains of a sacrificial animal (see Exod 29:34; Lev 7:17; 19:6 [what remains of the flesh of a votive offering, a freewill offering, or a sacrifice of fellowship offerings on the third day must be burned]; 8:32 [the burning of the remainder of the flesh and bread used at the ordination of Aaron and his sons]; see also 4:12, 21; 8:17; 9:8-11; 16:27-28; Ezek 43:21 [only the sacred, vital parts of the bull, calf, or goat of the sin offering are to be sacrificed and the remainder, contaminated by contact with the sinner's hands, must be burned outside the camp or sacred area of the temple]). Burning was also prescribed in the case of flesh that had been contaminated by any unclean thing (Lev 7:19).

According to Lev 6:23, every cereal offering of a priest had to be burned. The flesh of the sin offering in respect of a ruler or ordinary person was eaten by the priests (6:6), but those who were ordained to the priesthood were forbidden from eating their own sin offering (4:1-12) or that of the whole community (4:13-21); instead, these offerings had to be burned completely (cf. 6:30[23]). Milgrom (1976) has argued that both the eaten and the burnt sin offerings had a purificatory purpose: The eaten sin offering (*ḥaṭṭā't*) purged the outer altar of the malignant impurity caused by inadvertent sins of the individual; the burnt sin offering (*ḥaṭṭā't*) purged the dangerously contagious impurity created by unintentional or presumptuous sins committed by the high priest and/or the community. If not neutralized, this impurity would have been sufficiently powerful to penetrate into the shrine and adytum. Zohar (1988) disagrees with Milgrom that only the sanctuary was purified by the sin offering sacrifices. He contends that the sinner's personal purification was also effected by the sin offering (*ḥaṭṭā't*) ritual: both atonement and the purification of the sanctuary were achieved as a result of God's forgiving response to the disowned impurity that had been brought before him.

The vb. *śrp* is also used in Num 19:5, 8, part of a section (19:1-22) dealing with rites for purifying a person defiled by contact with, or proximity to, a corpse. The people were instructed to bring an unblemished red heifer that had never been used for ploughing or pulling a cart (v. 2) to the priest, Eleazar, before whom the animal was to be slaughtered outside the camp (v. 3) to produce ash with purificatory properties, which would then be fortified by adding other potent cleansing agents. Two facts seem to denote a nonsacrificial burning here: The incineration of the heifer takes place outside the camp, and the vb. used is *śrp* instead of *qṭr* (# 7782), turn into incense, which is used of burning on the altar (Wenham, 1981, 146; cf. Milgrom, 1981, 63). Thc incineration of the dead heifer's skin, flesh, blood, and dung was to take place in the sight of Eleazar (v. 5), after he had sprinkled some of the animal's blood seven times in the direction of the front of the Tent of Meeting (v. 4). The person who had been entrusted with the task of burning the carcass was to wash his clothes and bathe himself, but would remain unclean until evening (v. 8). The ashes of the heifer were then to be deposited outside the camp in a clean place and preserved as a kind of instant sin offering (Milgrom, 1981; Wenham, 1981, 147) for the congregation for use in the water of cleansing, a physical agent that effected purification from sin (v. 9; on the origin, purpose, and significance of this rite, see, especially, Kennedy, 1906). The paradox of that which cleanses the defiled defiling the clean has long been recognized (see, e.g., Snaith, 1964, 263; Milgrom, 1981). Milgrom (1981, 64-65, 67) argues that, by absorbing the maleficent impurity of the object that it has purged, the burnt *ḥaṭṭā't* transmitted impurity from the purified to the purifier: The ashes defiled their handlers and purified their recipients.

śrp is used in the context of cultic reforms that involve the burning of foreign images and/or cult vessels, which are irreconcilable with faith in Yahweh. In Deut 7:5, 25; 12:3, Israelites are instructed to exterminate the native peoples of Canaan, to demolish their cultic apparatus, and to burn the images of their gods (7:5, 25) and their Asherim (12:3; probably wooden emblems of the Canaanite goddess Asherah [T. W. Davies, 235; G. H. Davies, 1964, 274, 276; Manley and Harrison, 216; Mayes, 184]; possibly stylized representations of the female figure [Blenkinsopp, 1990b, 99]).

According to 2 Kgs 10:26, after the treacherous slaughter of the devotees of Baal, who had been enticed by guile and subterfuge into the temple of Baal in Samaria, Jehu's officers removed the pillar (emending the pl. of MT to the singular form in agreement with the suffix appended to the vb. *śrp*) from the temple of Baal in Samaria and burned it (cf. 2 Kgs 3:2, which describes how this object had previously been removed by Jehoram). Some (e.g., Stade, 278; Skinner, 334; cf. *BHS*) argue that since a stone pillar cannot be burned, the object must have been an *'ᵃšērâ* rather than a *maṣṣēbâ*. However, others (e.g., Gray, 1970, 558; cf. G. H. Jones, 1984b, 471) favor the retention of "the pillar" for two reasons: (a) the etymology of *maṣṣēbâ* signifies any standing object, which may include a wooden image; and (b) an effective way to shatter a standing stone is by heating it and then rapidly reducing its temperature by pouring cold water over it.

In 1 Kgs 15:13 (‖ 2 Chron 15:16), Asa, the first in a series of four repentant, cult-reforming kings, is commended for having cut down and burned (in the Kidron valley, where later reforming kings of Judah also destroyed idolatrous cult objects) the "abominable image" that had been made for Asherah, the mother goddess of the Canaanite fertility cult and consort of Baal, by Maacah, the queen mother. The vb. is also used in 2 Kgs 23:4, 6, 11, 15, part of the description of the reforms implemented by the last and most celebrated of the cult reformers, Josiah, the exemplar of genuine faith, fidelity, and trust. Josiah ordered the removal (from the Jerusalem temple) and burning of "all the articles made for Baal and Asherah and all the starry hosts" (2 Kgs 23:4, NEB), burned the Asherah, which had been in the temple (v. 6), burned "the chariots of the sun" (part of the paraphernalia used in the solar cult), which had also been located at the temple (v. 11), and burned the Asherah at Bethel (v. 15). Burning was the usual method of disposing of the appurtenances of apostasy, but it may be that this action was as much symbolic as physical, at least in the case of those objects that, constructed from stone or metal, would have been difficult to burn (Hobbs, 333, 336).

4. *śrp* is often used in the context of war and conflict. References to the burning (*śrp*) of cities include the following: the burning of Ziklag by marauding Amalekites (1 Sam 30:1, 3, 14); Pharaoh's burning of Gezer (1 Kgs 9:16); the burning of Judah's fortified cities by the invading Assyrians, perhaps during the campaign of Sennacherib in 701 BC (Isa 1:7); the threat that the Babylonians would burn Jerusalem if Zedekiah did not surrender (Jer 38:17, 18, 23); and the actual burning of the temple, the palace, and all the houses of Jerusalem by Nebuzaradan, captain of King Nebuchadrezzar's bodyguard (2 Kgs 25:9 ‖ Jer 52:13; cf. 2 Chron 36:19; Jer 39:8). In Jer 43:12-13, the prophet in Tahpanhes, an Egyptian border fortress, is reported as having issued a warning that Nebuchadrezzar would destroy by fire the temples of the Egyptian gods. 1 Chron 14:12 relates how, after his defeat of the Philistines at Baal Perazim, David ordered the enemy's gods to be burned (cf. Deut 7:5, 25; 12:3, which stipulate that the cultic equipment and accessories of those peoples defeated in battle must be destroyed). In 2 Sam 5:21, however, David and his men are said to have carried the Philistine gods away, presumably as booty (Coggins, 82; Braun, 179).

The vb. *śrp* occurs several times in Judges. Immediately prior to being mortally wounded by an anonymous, female, would-be assassin who crushed his skull with a well-aimed millstone, Abimelech drew near to the door of the besieged tower in the city of Thebez, where the city's inhabitants had taken refuge, with the intention of burning it (Judg 9:52), a tactic he had successfully employed earlier against the tower of Shechem (vv. 48-49). In 12:1, the querulous Ephraimites, enraged that Jephthah had won a great military victory without their assistance, threatened to burn Jephthah's house over him. Judg 14:15 relates how Samson's wife was threatened by the wedding guests that if she failed to discover and disclose the key to her husband's riddle, she and her father's house would be burned. When the Philistines discovered Samson's revenge for being denied his wife, they burned the woman and her father (15:6; or, her father's house, i.e., family, following some Heb., G, and Syr. MSS).

The vb. is used in Ps 74:8 is an impassioned prayer for deliverance from an enemy who has devastated and burned the temple (vv. 4-7) and "burned every place where God was worshiped in the land" (v. 8; there is no need to emend the MT, *śārᵉpû*, they burned, to *našbîtâ*, let us put an end to, as Oesterley, 347 [cf. C. A. and E. G. Briggs, 150, 154, 159; Kissane, 331-34] has suggested). Surveying the scene of devastation, the author bombards the creator God (vv. 12-17), who now seems strangely indifferent, inactive, even absent, with accusatory questions and complaints (Tate, 253). He boldly orders God to remember and have regard for the Mosaic covenant and the promises made in respect of Jerusalem (vv. 2, 20); to walk through the ruins and acquaint himself with the extent of the destruction wreaked by the arrogant, blaspheming invaders, who have trespassed and defiled the holy dwelling place (v. 3); to remember the enemy's scoffing (vv. 18, 22b) and clamor (v. 23); to arise and defend the divine cause (v. 22a); and to protect the lives of his afflicted people (v. 19).

In Ps 80, another prayer for deliverance from national enemies God is urgently entreated to restore the vine (his people) that he had carefully transplanted from Egypt and assiduously cultivated (vv. 8-13[9-14]), but which the enemy has cut down and burned (v. 16[17]), reading either the MT *śᵉrupâ*, it is burned, or the emendation *śᵉrāpuhā*, they burned it (see, e.g., *BHS*; Kraus, 139). Kissane (1964, 369, 371) emends to *śōrᵉpeyhā*, those who burned it, but this is not compelling.

The vb. is also used in the context of holy war, when an enemy was placed under the sacrificial ban (on which, see, e.g., Exod 17:8-16, especially v. 14), annihilated in the name of religion (Deut 20:1-20, particularly vv. 16-18), and offered as a sacrifice to Yahweh (see, e.g., 1 Sam 15). Deuteronomy's demand for total destruction was part of a utopian ideology that stands in complete contradiction to the picture given by the accounts in Judg 1 and the parallels in Joshua, which describe how Canaanite inhabitants continued to occupy coastal cities and substantial sections of the lowlands. In other narratives the following cities are said to have been devoted to destruction as a holocaust to Yahweh: Jericho (Josh 6:24), Ai (8:28), and Hazor (11:6, 9, 11, 13). In Judg 18:27, part of a narrative recording how, owing to pressure from the Philistines, the tribe of Dan was forced to migrate from the southwest (Josh 19:40-46; Judg 1:34; 13:2), to the far north of the land, the Danites killed the inhabitants of Laish and then burned their city. According to Deut 13:16[17], after the inhabitants of a city who have been seduced into idolatry have been exterminated, together with their cattle (v. 15[16]), the city itself along with all its spoil is to be burned "as a whole burnt offering to the LORD your God," and the site must not be reoccupied since even the ground has become contaminated by the city's pollution (Phillips, 96).

5. *śrp* is frequently used to describe God's burning fire of judgment. 2 Sam 23:7 contains a warning that the fate of the godless is to be consumed with fire as worthless thorns. Lev 10:1-20 recounts how two of Aaron's sons, Nadab and Abihu, made an unauthorized offering of fire to Yahweh (possibly in defiance of God's instructions regulating the preparation and use of incense such as those given in Exod 30:1-10, 34-38, though see Chapman and Streane, 54). It is impossible to determine the precise nature of the trespass they committed, but, because they infringed God's law by offering unholy (RSV, NRSV; cf. TEV) or unlawful (JB) or illicit (NEB; REB) or unauthorized (NIV) fire (v. 1), they were immediately consumed by a conflagration that came forth from the presence of Yahweh (vv. 1-2).

In Num 16, which describes two mutinies against Yahweh's appointed leaders, God's fire of judgment consumed the rebellious Korah and his 250 followers immediately after they had taken their censers, lit them, and laid incense in them.

Mic 1:6-7 announces that, because of her corruption, Samaria will be destroyed (v. 6), her images will be broken to pieces, her idols laid waste, and her hires (RSV) or earnings (JB)—that is, the wages of the sacred prostitutes (so, JB; Thomas, 631), or the produce of the land that was regarded as the gift of the Baalim (so, Robinson, 560), or the offerings at the idol shrines (so, Dummelow, 580)—will be committed to the fire (v. 7).

śrp is used in Ezek 5:4, part of a difficult (see, e.g., Brownlee, 1986, 80-86) passage describing how, at God's command, the prophet was to shave his head and face and use the shorn hair to portray, as an efficacious representation and actualization of what God wills to be (Eichrodt, 81-82; Cody, 35), the unrelenting severity and total degradation of the divinely willed disaster created by the coming siege of Jerusalem (5:1-17). The hair, normally a sign of strength and dignity (Judg 16-17; 2 Sam 10:4-5; see, e.g., Boadt, 312) but here, being shorn, an emblem of shame and devastation (cf. Isa 7:20; 2 Sam 10:4-5; Isa 15:2; Jer 41:5; 48:37) was to be meticulously divided into three portions. To symbolize the various fates to be suffered by the inhabitants of the city and the inexorable ruthlessness of the punishment to be inflicted by Yahweh for the cardinal sins of disobedience, rebellion, and defilement of the sanctuary (Muilenburg, 573), one portion of the hair was destined to be burned in the fire (v. 2 [root *b'r*]), signifying, as in v. 12, death by pestilence and famine); the second part was to be cut up with the sword (v. 2, denoting, as v. 12 indicates, the doom of the city's defenders); and the third piece was to be scattered in the wind (v. 2, representing dispersement and exile [cf. v. 12]). The few hairs that were to be retrieved from those scattered to the wind and sewn into or onto the hem or fold(s) of the prophet's robe (5:3) probably symbolize a handful of survivors (Brownlee, 1986, 83, thinks the swatch of hair represents those who remember to do the will of God), but even some of these are later to die violently, for the prophet is commanded to take some of the surviving hairs and "throw them into the fire and burn them up (*śrp*)" (5:4, NIV; NRSV). The words "[a] fire will spread from there to the whole house of Israel" (v. 4b) are problematic. Some commentators think that v. 4 may contain a slight hint that the destructive divine fire that burns the remnant in exile is redemptive for the rest of Israel (see, e.g., Wilson, 666). However, others (e.g., A. B. Davidson, 37) argue that, as in Ezek 19:14, the fire that goes out from the remnant is not purifying, but destructive for the entire house of Israel. As Taylor (85-86) comments, the view that the fire was for the purpose of purification and not judgment is plausible if the phrase is interpreted as a late gloss, but it would not naturally fit the context for the word fire to have two such different meanings. Elsewhere in Ezekiel, Jerusalem is condemned for her degenerate conduct and infidelity and threatened with destruction by fire (Ezek 16:41; 23:47).

In the oracle against Zedekiah and Jerusalem (Jer 21:1-10), the inhabitants of the besieged city are warned that, in accordance with the will of Yahweh, Jerusalem will be captured by the king of Babylon, God's servant (cf. 27:6; 43:10), who will destroy it with fire (v. 10; cf. 11:16; 32:29; 34:2, 22; 37:8, 10; 38:18, 23). Since it is Yahweh himself who fights against them (v. 5), the city's inhabitants are urged to cease their resistance and to surrender peacefully to God's agents of judgment

(vv. 8-9). Moderns, who confuse patriotism with loyalty to God, are uneasy about the stand taken here by Jeremiah. However, the prophet was not pro-Babylonian, but pro-Yahweh (R. Davidson, 11-12). Far from being a traitor, he stated openly and unequivocally his conviction that Israel merited divine punishment. Since surrender to Babylon was nothing less than acceptance of God's will, Jeremiah was not prepared to give a reassuring oracle or to forecast a miraculous deliverance of Jerusalem (McKane, 1986, 496).

śrp is also found in Jer 51:32, where insolent Babylon, the "destroying mountain" (51:25), is threatened with destruction by God's fire. As a result of its own evildoing, the former instrument of God's punishment is now to become the object of the divine vengeance (Dummelow, 481). The vb. is also used in Isa 47:14, a superb taunt song in which Babylon, accused of having overstepped its divine mandate to chastise Israel (v. 6), is stripped by God of her royalty and forced into the menial service of a slave girl (vv. 1-4), censured for her pretentious pride and ambition (vv. 5-7), condemned for her arrogant presumption of divinity (vv. 8b, 10b) and claim to ultimate power, and likened unto stubble, which will be consumed by the irresistible devouring conflagration from the power of whose flame no one can be delivered (v. 14). Other prophetic references to the destruction of cities by God's fire of judgment include Amos 1:4 (Damascus), 1:7 (Gaza), 1:10 (Tyre), 1:12 (Teman and Bozrah), 1:14 (Rabbah), 2:2 (Kerioth), and 2:5 (Jerusalem).

śrp is also used of God's destruction of the weapons of war. Ps 46:9[10] indicates that Yahweh is not only the one who fights against evil as a mighty warrior, but also the one who establishes peace, making wars to cease, breaking the bow, shattering the spear, and burning chariots (RSV) or wagons (Davison, 242; Addis, 380; Craigie, 1983b, 342), or shields (*BHS*; NIV; NEB; JB; NRSV; REB; TEV; Buttenwieser, 513, 517; Oesterley, 256; NEB [sing.]), reading *ʿagilot* or *ʿagîlôt* [→ # 6317], following LXX, Tg. and Vg., for MT *ʿagālôt*). Ps 46 is powerful testimony to the OT faith in the power of God to afford the faithful refuge and protection, even during cataclysmic cosmic tumults and turbulent political upheavals. God destroys the weapons of war, silences the strident sounds of conflict (cf. Stuhlmueller, 455), and establishes universal peace.

6. The vb. *śrp* is used often with reference to the burning of human beings. Sometimes burning is the punishment prescribed for certain sexual offenses. In ancient Israel the usual punishment for harlotry was stoning (cf. Deut 22:23-24). Death by burning was normally the penalty reserved for the daughter of a priest who was found guilty of prostitution (cf. Lev 21:9). However, in Gen 38:24, Judah, on being informed that his daughter-in-law, Tamar, had played the harlot, ordered her to be brought out and burned. However, just before the sentence of death was enforced, Tamar revealed to Judah the elaborate ruse she had engineered to ensure that her father-in-law would fulfil his legal obligation to her by performing the levirate duty, whereupon Judah acknowledged that she was in the right and he was in the wrong. The vb. is also used in Lev 20:14, according to which a man found guilty of having sexual relations with a woman and the woman's mother incurred the penalty of death by burning for both himself and the two women concerned.

The vb. is found again in Josh 7, a passage that not only illustrates "the penalty of solidarity" (Dummelow, 145), but also highlights for moderns the continuing importance of corporate responsibility (Rast, 239). The first five verses relate how Israel lost the battle for Ai because of Achan's violation of the oath of destruction at Jericho. Verses 10-26 describe how Joshua implemented Yahweh's instructions that resulted in the discovery and punishment of the culprit. The command is given in v. 15 that the individual who transgressed the covenant had to be burned together with all that he had. To expiate the sin and to purge Israel of the contaminating guilt, thereby appeasing the divine wrath, Achan and all the human and animal members of his family group were stoned and burned (v. 25). Bright (1953, 590) thinks the victims were burned to death and then covered with a cairn of stones, whereas Gray (1986, 84-92) maintains that the reference to stoning was incorporated in response to the need to explain the cairn associated with Achan in the plain of Achor.

śrp occurs in several passages (Deut 12:31; 2 Kgs 17:31; Jer 7:31; 19:5), which describe the cultic burning of sons and daughters. Deut 12:29-31 contains a stern warning to the Israelites to take great care not to become ensnared into adopting the abominable cultic practices of the indigenous peoples of Canaan, which even included the detestable rite of burning offspring in the fire as sacrifices to their gods. The people of Phoenicia and Carthage are known to have dedicated children to a god by burning (de Vaux, 445-46; Day, 86-91; Blenkinsopp, 1990b, 101; see further Heider [93-222], who furnishes a much more comprehensive review of the literary and epigraphic evidence from the surrounding ANE civilizations). This gruesome aberration was apparently introduced late in the history of Israel and was resorted to from time to time during the monarchic period (see, e.g., 2 Kgs 16:3; 17:17, 31; 21:6).

The deity mentioned in this context is called Molech. This name seems to be the word *melek*, king, pointed with the vowels of the word *bōšet*, shame (see, e.g., W. R. Smith, 372, n. 1; S. R. Driver, 1965, 223; Phillips, 92; Blenkinsopp, 1990b, 101). However, Heider (223-28) disagrees, arguing (226-27) that *mōlek* could be the original vocalization, possibly a "frozen" participial form with the stress on the penultimate syllable. De Vaux (444-46) thinks the sacrifices concerned were either offered to a god called Moloch or were offered as *molk*, which was the name by which such a sacrifice was known in both Phoenicia and Carthage. Eissfeldt seems to have been the first to have argued that the Heb. *mōlek* was a sacrificial term cognate with Punic *molk*. However, two more recent studies by Heider and Day, respectively have argued that an underworld deity Molech was worshiped and that his cultus included the immolation of children.

Lev 18:21 strictly forbids the sacrifice of children by fire to Molech, and 20:2-3 demands the death penalty for any man found guilty of making such a sacrifice. Deut 18:10 prohibits the practice of passing a child through the fire, which is probably a reference to some kind of practice associated with the cult of Molech. It has been claimed that the phrase "makes ... pass through the fire" (lit.) here and elsewhere (cf., e.g., Lev 18:21; 2 Kgs 17:17; 21:6; Jer 32:35; Ezek 20:26) referred to an ordeal by fire that occasionally failed (see, e.g., S. R. Driver, 1965, 222; Wright, 447-48; Gottwald, 112), but others think it more probable that the reference is to child sacrifice (see, e.g., G. A. Smith, 174; Cunliffe-Jones, 111; Blair, 57; Phillips, 125; Day, 20; Miller, 151), possibly for the purpose of discerning or determining the future (Craigie, 1983a, 260). Heider (256, 266) suggests that the vb., the hi. of *'br*, had a legal/cultic technical meaning, designating the transfer of ownership or control.

At any rate, 2 Kgs 23:10 records that one of the reforms implemented by Josiah was the defilement of Topheth (a burning platform translated "roaster" by de Vaux, 444), located in the Valley of Ben Hinnom near Jerusalem, in an effort to prevent any further child sacrifices to Molech. In Jer 7:16-8:3, the sacrifice of children by fire is one of Judah's abuses in worship that is severely censured (7:31). In 19:5, the people of Judah are condemned for offering their children as burnt offerings to Baal. In 32:26-44 the prophet is told of Yahweh's decision to deliver Jerusalem into the hands of the Babylonians because of all the ways in which his people have provoked him to anger, including offering up their children to Molech (32:35). In Ezek 16:15-22, Jerusalem, Yahweh's unfaithful wife, is condemned for her unfaithfulness and degenerate practices, including the slaughter of children as burnt offerings to other gods.

śrp is used once in the context of suicide. 1 Kgs 16:8-20 describes how an army officer called Zimri, who commanded half the chariotry, led an insurrection, murdered Elah king of Israel, seized the throne, and then eliminated all the members of his predecessor's family, the house of Baasha. However, after Zimri had reigned a mere week in Tirzah, the newly elected king of Israel, Omri, led an army that besieged the city. When he saw that Tirzah had been taken, Zimri entered the citadel of the royal palace "and burned the king's house over him with fire, and died" (1 Kgs 16:18, RSV).

In several texts the vb. is used of the burning of the dead (1 Sam 31:12; 1 Kgs 13:2; 2 Kgs 23:16, 20; Amos 2:1; 6:10). In most cases, the reference is to an act of desecration. 1 Kgs 13—a "much misinterpreted narrative" (de Vries, 1978, 60); "a puzzle to exegetes as well as to theologians" (de Vries, 1985, 168); "a complex and intriguing story" (Nelson, 83; see Crenshaw, 39-49, for an insightful exposition of this chapter)—begins by recounting how an anonymous prophet denounced the altar at Bethel, beside which Jeroboam was standing to burn incense. The prophet warned that a future king, Josiah by name, would desecrate the altar by burning human bones upon it (v. 2). 2 Kgs 23:16, 20 and 2 Chron 34:5 describe the fulfillment of this prophecy. In Amos 2:1-3, an oracle of judgment against Moab, the Moabites are condemned for having "burned to lime (ashes) the bones of the king of Edom" (v. 1; see RSV; NRSV). There is debate about whether this refers to the burning alive of the Edomite king or to the burning of the victim after he had been killed or buried (Harper, 40).

There is also uncertainty (see, especially, Harper, 40) about whether the words usually translated "to lime" (cf. Isa 33:12) refer to the manner of burning (as lime is burned), to the result of the intensity of the heat (reduction of the bones to fine white powdered dust, as Vg.; Oswalt, 598), or to the purpose (to produce an ingredient for either plaster, as Tg., or whitewash, as Wolff, 162-63; Hubbard, 137). What is perfectly clear, however, is that the Moabites were guilty of a monstrous act of desecration, which earned the indictment of Yahweh, the God of all nations, who punishes all such atrocious crimes against humanity. This gross, sacrilegious indignity, clearly a mark of unrelenting hate and vindictiveness (S. R. Driver, 1901, 143), may have been designed, actually or symbolically, to prevent the Edomite king from being "gathered to his fathers" (Harper, 41; Dummelow, 564; Gwynn, 7-8; Stuart, 314-15). The abuse of the corpse may have been a deliberate attempt to make a final end of the person (Snaith, 1960, 17), or (as suggested by Dummelow, 565) to cause suffering for the spirit of the victim (cf. Isa 66:24), or perhaps to be "a sort of impotent grasping at eternal vengeance" (Pusey, 170). Significantly, Yahweh's punishment of this crime and of the transgressions of Israel's other neighbors, including Judah, is described in terms of the divine fire that, once released, consumes strongholds, causing their inhabitants to suffer either exile or death. (In Amos 2:13-16, the punishment inflicted on Israel itself is described in terms of crushing military defeat.)

1 Sam 31:11-13 records the act of fidelity performed by the valiant men of Jabesh Gilead, after hearing that the Philistines had removed the corpses of Saul and his three sons from Mount Gilboa, decapitated (postmortem) the Israelite king and then affixed his body and the bodies of his three sons to the wall of Beth Shan. Because of their abiding loyalty and gratitude to Saul, who had delivered their town from the Ammonites in the first battle of his career (1 Sam 11:1-11), these men from across the Jordan traveled through the night to transfer the remains of Saul and his sons to Jabesh, where they burned them (v. 12; the reference to cremation is omitted by the Chronicler, 1 Chron 10:12) and then buried the bones in Jabesh. Because the customary Hebrew practice was to bury rather than burn corpses, some commentators, preferring to assume another meaning for the vb. *śrp*, have translated the last phrase of v. 12 as "they anointed them with spices" (see, e.g., G. R. Driver; NEB; Mauchline, 1971, 193; Hertzberg, 233; Brockington, 330; Ackroyd, 1971, 229; Wevers, 1971, 169). The vb. *spd* means mourn, wail, lament, and Kennedy (1905, 190), following Klostermann, Budde and others, emends the text of v. 12 to read "and made lamentation for them there," instead of "and burnt them there." However, neither of these readings is convincing.

If it be accepted that there are no good grounds for departing from MT (H. P. Smith, 253-54), then how is one to explain this act of cremation? It is impossible to be certain, but various suggestions have been made. The bodies may have been burned because they were in an advanced state of decomposition (Goldman, 185 and Hertzberg, 231, 233, following Kimchi). Pusey (207; see further, Kirkpatrick, 233; Myers, 176) argues that burning was chosen out of fear that the Philistines would disinter the bodies to inflict further defilement on them. However, W. R. Smith (372, n. 3; cf. Dummelow, 195), while conceding that the cremation may have been to prevent the bodies from being exhumed and further desecrated by the Philistines, deems it more likely that it had a religious intention, almost as an act of worship, given that the bones were interred under the sacred tamarisk at Jabesh (v. 13). Another interpretation has been advanced by McKane (1963, 174), who suggests that the cremation may have been motivated by the need to destroy the defilement that Saul's body, at least, had suffered at the hands of the Philistines. Budde (cited by Klein, 290) argues that the reference to burning was added by a scribe to denigrate the memory of Saul. Rainey (cited by Klein, 290) has suggested that the burial rites described here are the same as those carried out in honor of Greek heroes.

An interesting use of the pi. part. of *srp* occurs in Amos 6:10, which, with v. 9, seems to describe the horrors of a plague during or immediately after a siege (see, however, Hubbard, 196, who argues that there is no explicit reference to pestilence or plague). One of the relatives of the deceased, who has the task of removing the corpses from the building where death has occurred, is described as *m*^{e}*sār*^{e}*pô*. The root *srp* occurs only here and the text of v. 10 presents difficulties. Understandably, therefore, this word has been translated in different ways. TEV (cf. Duhm, 72; Snaith, 1958, 115; 1960, 41) has "the one in charge of the funeral," which is much too vague. RSV,

NRSV, and NIV take the word to signify the person responsible for cremating the corpses (although NRSV has, as an alternative reading, "who makes a burning for him"). Following G. R. Driver and T. H. Robinson, Mays (1976, 118-19; cf. Mauchline, 1971, 193; Stuart, 361-62; Hubbard, 197) thinks that *m^e^sār^e^pô* is a synonym of *dôdô* and refers to a kinsman on the mother's side. G. R. Driver (cf. Mauchline, 1971, 193) has argued for the existence of a common Semitic root *srp* with the meaning anoint, embalm, and NEB, REB, and Paul (213, 215-16) translate the word as embalmer. In support of this translation, Paul (215-16) points out the existence in rabbinic Heb. of the nom. *ś^e^rāp* (sometimes *s^e^rāp*), meaning resin, from which a denominative vb. is derived meaning "smear with resin." Moreover, in Sam. Aram. the vb. *srp* is a *vario lectio* for Heb. *swk*, anoint (→ # 6057), in Deut 28:40. Paul concludes that the *m^e^sārēp* would have been one whose profession was to anoint the dead with *s^e^rāp* (probably aromatic spices).

JB considers the Heb. of Amos 6:10 unintelligible, and commentators who agree have suggested a variety of emendations, the least radical of which are Ehrlich's proposal (cited by Canney, 552) to change MT *ûm^e^sār^e^pô* to *ûm^e^sapp^e^rô*, and the one who removes him (*spr* = Arab. *safara*, sweep [a house]), and the reading *um^e^sapp^e^dô/ûmaspîdô*, and his mourner, recommended by Nowack and Tur-Sinai (both cited by Paul, 215). Others have proposed emending the first three words of the verse (see, e.g., *BHS*; cf. Harper, 152, who lists various attempts that have been made to reconstruct the text). However, if MT be correct and if the translation rendered by RSV, NRSV, and NIV be accepted, then why are the corpses disposed of by cremation rather than by interment? S. R. Driver (1901, 197) and Harper (154; cf. Canney, 552; Hyatt, 1964, 623; Vawter, 63; Finley, 271-72) maintain that the reference is to the burning of spices, as in 2 Chron 16:14; 21:19; Jer 34:5. However, Hayes (1988b, 189-90; cf. McKenzie, 108; Kitchen, 171) disagrees, arguing that Amos 6:10 is to be interpreted on the analogy of 1 Sam 31:8-13. Whereas 2 Chron 16:14; 21:19; Jer 34:5 refer to the burning of spices in honor of deceased monarchs, 1 Sam 31:8-13 describes a means of stifling the stench of rotting flesh and rendering human remains into a form that could be handled. Several other commentators (e.g., Pusey, 207; Dummelow, 569; Hyatt, 1964, 623; Kraft, 474; McKeating, 51; G. V. Smith, 208) believe that the special circumstances demanded burning: It would have been necessary to take steps to prevent contagion from the plague-ravaged corpses.

7. In Lev 13:52, 55, 57, *śrp* is used in connection with the instructions issued for dealing with what is described as a leprous disease in woolen, linen, or skin garments, a reference, presumably, to fungus or mildew that causes discoloration and corrosion, effects superficially similar to those created by leprosy (Dummelow, 93). Any garment showing signs of the leprous disease had to be examined by the priest who, if necessary, would place it in quarantine for a period of seven days. If, after the week-long confinement, the disease had spread, it had to be burned (vv. 47-52). If the disease had not spread, the garment was to be washed and then isolated for a further period of seven days, after which it was reexamined. Should the affected area not have changed color, the garment had to be burned (vv. 53-55). However, should the color of the relevant spot have dulled, then that spot would be torn out of the garment. If, after the spot had been removed, discoloration were to appear elsewhere on the material, the garment

had to be burned. On the other hand, if the disease did not reappear, then the garment had to be washed a second time, after which it was deemed to be clean (vv. 56-58).

P-B Both verbal and nominal forms are well attested. The vb. occurs in both Heb. *śārap*, sip, absorb; consume, burn; ni. be burnt; and Aram. *śᵉrap*, consume, burn; ithpa., be burned. The following nom. forms are also found: *śārāp*, burning, venomous serpent; *śᵉrāp*, acrid substance, esp. vegetable sap made thick by inspissation; resin, gum (secreted by the heat of the sun); *śᵉrēpâ*, *śᵉrêpâ*, burning, fire (Jastrow 2:1632-33).

BIBLIOGRAPHY

NIDNTT 1:509-10; *TDNT* 5:566-82; *TWOT* 2:884; P. R. Ackroyd, *The First Book of Samuel*, 1971; W. E. Addis, "The Psalms," in *Peake*, 1920, 366-96; L. W. Batten, *A Critical and Exegetical Commentary on the Books of Ezra and Nehemiah*, 1961; E. P. Blair, *Deuteronomy, Joshua*, 1964; J. Blenkinsopp, *Ezekiel*, 1990a; idem, "Deuteronomy," in *NJBC*, 1990b, 94-109; L. Boadt, "Ezekiel," in *NJBC*, 1990, 305-28; R. L. Braun, *1 Chronicles*, 1986; C. A. Briggs and E. G. Briggs, *A Critical and Exegetical Commentary on the Book of Psalms*, 2, 1960; J. Bright, "The Book of Joshua: Introduction and Exegesis," in *IB*, 1953, 2:539-673; idem, "Isaiah-I," in *Peake*, 1964, 489-515; idem, *Covenant and Promise*, 1977; L. H. Brockington, "I and II Samuel," in *Peake*, 1964, 318-37; W. H. Brownlee, "The Book of Ezekiel," in *The Interpreter's One-Volume Commentary on the Bible*, 1971, 411-35; idem, *Ezekiel 1-19*, 1986; M. Buttenwieser, *The Psalms Chronologically Treated with a New Translation*, 1969; M. A. Canney, "Amos," in *Peake*, 1920, 547-54; R. P. Carroll, *From Chaos to Covenant: Uses of Prophecy in the Book of Jeremiah*, 1981; idem, *Jeremiah: A Commentary*, 1986; idem, *Jeremiah*, 1989; A. T. Chapman and A. W. Streane, *The Book of Leviticus*, 1914; R. E. Clements, *God's Chosen People: A Theological Interpretation of the Book of Deuteronomy*, 1968; idem, *Exodus*, 1972; idem, *Jeremiah*, 1988; idem, *Deuteronomy*, 1989; R. J. Clifford, "Exodus," in *NJBC*, 1990, 44-60; A. Cody, *Ezekiel, With an Excursus on Old Testament Priesthood*, 1984; R. J. Coggins, *The First and Second Books of the Chronicles*, 1976; R. A. Cole, *Exodus: An Introduction and Commentary*, 1973; G. P. Couturier, "Jeremiah," in *NJBC*, 1990, 265-97; P. C. Craigie, *The Book of Deuteronomy*, 1983 (1983a); idem, *Psalms 1-50*, 1983 (1983b); J. L. Crenshaw, *Prophetic Conflict: Its Effect upon Israelite Religion*, 1971; A. E. Cundall, "Ezra and Nehemiah," in *NBC*, 1972, 395-411; H. Cunliffe-Jones, *Deuteronomy: Introduction and Commentary*, 1964; A. B. Davidson, *The Book of the Prophet Ezekiel, with Notes and Introduction*, 1892; R. Davidson, *Jeremiah Volume 2 and Lamentations*, 1985; G. H. Davies, "Deuteronomy," in *Peake*, 1964, 269-84; idem, *Exodus: Introduction and Commentary*, 1967; T. W. Davies, "Deuteronomy," in *Peake*, 1920, 231-43; W. T. Davison, *The Psalms I-LXXII*, 1904; J. Day, *Molech: A God of Human Sacrifice in the Old Testament*, 1989; G. R. Driver, "A Hebrew Burial Custom," *ZAW* 66, 1954, 314-15; S. R. Driver, *The Books of Joel and Amos With Introduction and Notes*, 1901; idem, *A Critical and Exegetical Commentary on Deuteronomy*, 3rd ed., 1965; idem, *The Book of Exodus in the Revised Version With Introduction and Notes*, 1953; B. Duhm, *The Twelve Prophets: A Version in the Various Poetical Measures of the Original Writings*, 1912; J. R. Dummelow (ed.), *A Commentary on the Holy Bible*, 1909; W. Eichrodt, *Ezekiel: A Commentary*, 1979; O. Eissfeldt, *Molk als Opferbegriff im Punischen und Hebräischen und das Ende des Gottes Moloch*, 1935; F. C. Fensham, "The Burning of the Golden Calf and Ugarit," *IEJ* 16, 1966, 191-93; idem, *The Books of Ezra and Nehemiah*, 1983; T. J. Finley, *Joel, Amos, Obadiah*, 1990; S. Goldman, *Samuel: Hebrew Text and English Translation With an Introduction and Commentary*, 1962; N. K. Gottwald,

"The Book of Deuteronomy," in *The Interpreter's One-Volume Commentary on the Bible*, 1971, 100-121; D. E. Gowan, *From Eden to Babel: A Commentary on the Book of Genesis 1-11*, 1988; J. Gray, *I & II Kings: A Commentary*, rev., ed., 1970; idem, "The Book of Exodus," in C. M. Laymon (ed.), *The Interpreter's One-Volume Commentary on the Bible*, 1971, 33-67; idem, *Joshua, Judges, Ruth*, NCBC, 1986; R. M. Gwynn, *The Book of Amos*, 1958; W. R. Harper, *A Critical and Exegetical Commentary on Amos and Hosea*, 1966; J. H. Hayes, "Leviticus," in *HBC*, 1988, 157-81 (1988a); idem, *Amos The Eighth Century Prophet: His Times and His Preaching*, 1988 (1988b); G. C. Heider, *The Cult of Molek: A Reassessment*, 1985; J. H. Hertz (ed.), *The Pentateuch and Haftorahs: Hebrew Text, English Translation and Commentary*, 2d ed., 1969; H. W. Hertzberg, *I & II Samuel: A Commentary*, 1974; T. R. Hobbs, *2 Kings*, 1985; D. A. Hubbard, *Joel and Amos: An Introduction and Commentary*, 1989; J. P. Hyatt, "Amos," in *Peake*, 1964, 617-25; idem, *Exodus*, 1971; G. H. Jones, *1 and 2 Kings. Volume 1: 1 Kings 1-16:34*, 1984 [1984a]; idem, *1 and 2 Kings. Volume II: 1 Kings 17:1-2 Kings 25:30*, 1984 [1984b]; H. R. Jones, "Exodus," in *NBC*, 1972, 115-39; A. R. S. Kennedy, *Samuel*, 1905; idem, "Red Heifer," in *HDB*, 1906, 4:207-10; A. F. Kirkpatrick, *The First Book of Samuel, With Map, Notes and Introduction*, 1899; E. J. Kissane, *The Book of Psalms Translated from a Critically Revised Hebrew Text with a Commentary*, 1964; K. A. Kitchen, "Burial and Mourning 1: In the Old Testament," in *NBD*, 1975, 170-72; R. W. Klein, *1 Samuel*, 1983; C. F. Kraft, "The Book of Amos," in *The Interpreter's One-Volume Commentary on the Bible*, 1971, 465-76; H.-J. Kraus, *Psalms 60-150: A Commentary*, 1989; P. K. McCarter, "Exodus," in *HBC*, 1988, 129-56; W. McKane, *I & II Samuel: Introduction and Commentary*, 1963; idem, *A Critical and Exegetical Commentary on Jeremiah. Volume 1: Introduction and Commentary on Jeremiah I-XXV*, ICC, 1986; H. McKeating, *The Books of Amos, Hosea and Micah*, 1971; J. L. McKenzie, *Dictionary of the Bible*, 1968; G. T. Manley and R. K. Harrison, "Deuteronomy," in *NBC*, 1972, 201-29; J. Mauchline, *1 and 2 Samuel*, 1971; H. G. May and B. M. Metzger (eds.), *The New Oxford Annotated Bible*, 1973; A. D. H. Mayes, *Deuteronomy*, 1979; J. L. Mays, *Amos: A Commentary*, 1976; J. Milgrom, "Two Kinds of *HATTA'T*," *VT* 26, 1976, 333-37; idem, "The Paradox of the Red Cow (Num. XIX)," *VT* 31, 1981, 62-72; P. D. Miller, *Deuteronomy*, 1990; J. Muilenburg, "Ezekiel," in *Peake*, 1964, 568-90; A. C. Myers (ed.), *The Eerdmans Bible Dictionary*, 1993; R. D. Nelson, *First and Second Kings*, 1987; M. Noth, *Exodus: A Commentary*, 1966; W. O. E. Oesterley, *The Psalms Translated With Text-Critical and Exegetical Notes*, 1959; J. N. Oswalt, *The Book of Isaiah Chapters 1-39*, 1986; S. M. Paul, *Amos*, 1991; A. Phillips, *Deuteronomy*, 1973; E. B. Pusey, *The Minor Prophets With a Commentary Explanatory and Practical and Introductions to the Several Books*, 1891; W. E. Rast, "Joshua," in *HBC*, 1988, 235-44; H. W. Robinson, "Micah," in *Peake*, 1920, 559-63; J. C. Rylaarsdam, "The Book of Exodus: Introduction and Exegesis," in *IB*, 1952, 1:831-1099; J. Skinner, *Kings*, 1893; G. A. Smith, *The Book of Deuteronomy*, 1918; G. V. Smith, *Amos, a Commentary*, 1989; H. P. Smith, *A Critical and Exegetical Commentary on the Books of Samuel*, 1961; W. R. Smith, *Lectures on the Religion of the Semites. First Series: The Fundamental Institutions*, rev. ed., 1914; N. H. Snaith, *The Book of Amos. Part Two: Translation and Notes*, 1958; idem, *Amos, Hosea and Micah*, 1960; idem, "Numbers," in *Peake*, 1964, 254-68; B. Stade, "Anmerkungen zu 2 Kö. 10-14," *ZAW* 5, 1885, 275-97; D. M. G. Stalker, "Exodus," in *Peake*, 1964, 208-40; D. Stuart, *Hosea-Jonah*, 1987; C. Stuhlmueller, "Psalms," in *HBC*, 1988, 433-94; M. E. Tate, *Psalms 51-100*, 1990; J. B. Taylor, *Ezekiel: An Introduction and Commentary*, 1971; D. W. Thomas, "Micah," in *Peake*, 1964, 630-36; R. de Vaux, *AncIsr*, 1968; B. Vawter, *Amos, Hosea, Micah, With an Introduction to Classical Prophecy*, 1981; S. J. de Vries, *Prophet Against Prophet: The Role of the Micaiah*

Narrative (1 Kings 22) in the Development of Early Prophetic Tradition, 1978; idem, *1 Kings*, 1985; G. J. Wenham, *Numbers: An Introduction and Commentary*, TOTC, 1981; idem, *Genesis 1-15*, 1987; C. Westermann, *Genesis 1-11: A Commentary*, 1987; J. W. Wevers, *Ezekiel*, 1969; idem, "The First Book of Samuel," in *The Interpreter's One-Volume Commentary on the Bible*, 1971, 155-69; H. G. M. Williamson, *Ezra, Nehemiah*, WBC, 1985; R. R. Wilson, "Ezekiel," in *HBC*, 1988, 652-94; H. W. Wolff, *Joel and Amos: A Commentary on the Books of the Prophets Joel and Amos*, 1977; G. E. Wright, "The Book of Deuteronomy: Introduction and Exegesis," in *IB*, 1953, 2:309-537; N. Zohar, "Repentance and Purification: The Significance and Semantics of חטאת in the Pentateuch," *JBL* 107, 1988, 609-18.

Robin Wakely

8597	שָׂרָף

שָׂרָף (*śārāp*), nom. seraph, snake, serpent (# 8597); < שׂרף (*śrp* I), q. burn, scorch, cauterize; ni. be, become burnt; pu. be, become burnt (→ # 8596).

ANE See *śrp* (→ # 8596).

OT The nom. is used in apposition with the word *nāḥāš* in Num 21:6 and Deut 8:15 with the meaning fiery serpent(s). The term seems to be applied either to the nature of the venom of the snakes or to the burning inflammation resulting from a snakebite (see, e.g., Craigie, 1983, 188, n. 8 and the literature cited there). However, Coats (117, n. 51), followed by Budd (234), has argued that it is possible that the word *śārāp* (pl. *ś^{e}rāpîm*) has no connection with either snakebite or the painful result of such a bite, but is, rather, the name of mythological creatures that were thought to have a burning appearance. Coats' own preference, though, is to take the word as a term borrowed by the Israelites that has nothing to do with the Heb. root *śrp*. This suggestion, however, seems unlikely. In his comment on the occurrence of the word in Deut 8:15, G. A. Smith (122) does not exclude the possibility that *śārāp* may be a foreign word meaning "dragon" or the like (see, too, JB, below, on Isa 14:29 and 30:6).

In Num 21:8, where, however, the reference is to an inanimate object, the nom. occurs on its own with the meaning, fiery serpent ("serpent" has to be understood here; cf Sam, G. See, however, NEB which, under the influence of v. 9, translates "a serpent of bronze"; TEV has "a metal snake"). Num 21:8-9, which reflects the principle of inversion (see, e.g., Wade, 223; Wenham, 158), may echo the notion of sympathetic magic. Those bitten by snakes are to be saved from death merely by gazing at the bronze serpent affixed to the top of a pole. Wenham (157-58) has advanced the intriguing view that (bronze/)copper may have been used in the manufacture of the snake in v. 9 because the red hue of this metal not only matched the color of the inflammation caused by snakebite, but also symbolized atonement and purification (cf. the narrative of the red heifer in 19:1-10).

A plausible explanation of the text is offered by those (e.g., Rowley, 132; cf., Joines, 1968; Burns, 266-67; Budd, 233-35) who argue that Num 21:4-9 is mainly an aetiology designed to explain why, as 2 Kgs 18:4 indicates, the bronze serpent, Nehushtan (which name is explained through connection with *n^{e}ḥōšet*, bronze), was venerated in temple worship during the monarchic period. According to Rowley (132-41), the bronze serpent destroyed by Hezekiah during his reformation (2 Kgs 18:4) originally represented a Canaanite deity. Nehushtan, he maintains, was a Jebusite sacred symbol, probably the symbol of the shrine guarded by the priest Zadok prior to David's capture of Jerusalem, which was then adopted by the Israelites and transferred to the temple. At any rate, this story in Num 21:4-9 is allegorized in Wisd 16:7, where any hint of magical piety is corrected by the assertion that the bronze serpent had no power of itself: whosoever turned toward the "symbol of deliverance" (v. 6, NRSV) "was saved, not by what he looked at but by you, the saviour of all" (REB). In John 3:14, the lifting up of the serpent by Moses is used to symbolize Christ's crucifixion (see, e.g., Wade, 223).

Twice in Isaiah (Isa 14:29; 30:6), the nom. occurs followed by the pi. part. *m*^{e}*'ôpēp*, with the meaning "a flying fiery serpent" (NRSV translation of Isa 14:29) or "a flying serpent" (RSV translation of both occurrences [cf., NEB; REB] and NRSV translation of the words in Isa 30:6; NIV translates "darting, venomous serpent" in 14:29 and "darting snakes" in 30:6). According to Skinner (44), the reference to a flying serpent is an allusion to a widely diffused mythological notion. JB translates the words in 14:29 as "a flying dragon" and has a footnote (in connection with Num 21:6) suggesting that the reference in Isa 30:6 may also be to a dragon. In both 14:29 and 30:6, Whitehouse (122) and Kaiser (49, 54, 290) take *śārāp* to mean "fiery dragon." In 14:29, the reference is to an(other), even more formidable, oppressor who will arise to destroy Philistia, root and remnant (v. 30). In 30:6, the flying serpent is one of the dangers encountered by those traversing the Negev.

In Isa 6:2, 6, the pl. is used of supernatural creatures associated with the glory of Yahweh (or holiness, so Oswalt, 178-79). Motyer (76) thinks these heavenly beings were named seraphs because the prophet experienced their burning ministry. Lacheman thinks that what Isaiah saw was the cherubim glinting in the sunlight. Gray (105) and Herbert (58) have ventured that the bronze serpent in the temple may have been the stimulation for the entire visionary experience. Some (see, e.g., Whitehouse, 122-23; Thomson and Skinner, 21; Gray, 105; May and Metzger, 830) suggest that the word translated "seraphim" or "seraphs" may have been applied to griffin-like creatures. Peake (441; see, Thomson and Skinner, 21; Snaith, 1964, 264; 1967, 280; Kaiser, 76, especially n. c) has argued that if the cherubim represented thunder clouds, then the seraphim were personifications of the forked serpent-like lightning, although in Isa 6 they have lost their serpent form, having faces, voices, hands, and sexual organs (but see Motyer [76] who, purely on the ground that it would be inappropriate to attribute sexuality to heavenly beings, objects that the word "feet" in v. 2 is not, as in many other contexts, a euphemism for genitalia). Joines (1967) thinks that the seraphim were like the protective uraeus-deities of Egypt. As regards their function, the duty of the seraphim was not only to sing God's praise, but also to guard the entrance to his presence (see, e.g., Whitehouse, 123; Peake, 441; Bright, 495).

Burning, blazing, glowing, scorching, singeing: → *b'r* I (burn, blaze up, be consumed, # 1277); → *gaḥelet* (burning charcoal, # 1625); → *dlq* (set on fire, burn, hotly pursue, # 1944); → *ḥmr* III (be in ferment, be heated, be red, glow, blaze, # 2813); → *ḥrr* I (glow, blaze, # 3081); → *yṣt* (light, kindle, ignite, burn, scorch, # 3675); → *yqd* (burn, kindle, # 3678); → *kwh* (burn, blaze, singe, # 3917); → *lhṭ* I (burn, glow, blaze, # 4265); → *nśq* (catch fire, be kindled, burn, # 5956); → *ṣwt* (light, kindle, ignite, set in flames, # 7455); → *qdḥ* (kindle, light, ignite, set ablaze, catch or take fire, # 7706); → *śrp* (burn, scorch, cauterize, # 8596)

BIBLIOGRAPHY

J. Bright, "Isaiah—I," in *Peake*, 1964, 489-515; P. J. Budd, *Numbers*, 1984; R. J. Burns, *Exodus, Leviticus, Numbers, with Excurses on Feasts/Ritual and Typology*, 1983; G. W. Coats, *Rebellion in the Wilderness*, 1968; P. C. Craigie, *The Book of Deuteronomy*, 1983; G. B. Gray, *A Critical and Exegetical Commentary on the Book of Isaiah I-XXVII*, 1975; A. S. Herbert, *The Book of the Prophet Isaiah Chapters 1-39*, 1973; K. R. Joines, "Winged Serpents in Isaiah's Inaugural Vision," *JBL*, 86, 1967, 410-15; idem, "The Bronze Serpent in the Israelite Cult," *JBL*, 87, 1968, 245-56; O. Kaiser, *Isaiah 1-12: A Commentary*, 1977; E. R. Lacheman, "The Seraphim of Isaiah 6," *JQR* 59, 1968, 7-8; H. G. May and B. M. Metzger eds., *The New Oxford Annotated Bible*, 1973; J. A. Motyer, *The Prophecy of Isaiah: An Introduction & Commentary*, 1993; J. N. Oswalt, *The Book of Isaiah Chapters 1-39*, 1986; A. S. Peake, "Isaiah I-XXXIX," in *Peake*, 1920, 436-59; H. H. Rowley, "Zadok and Nehushtan," *JBL* 58, 1939, 113-41; J. Skinner, *The Book of the Prophet Isaiah Chapters I-XXXIX*, 1909; G. A. Smith, *The Book of Deuteronomy*, 1918; G. V. Smith, *Amos, A Commentary*, 1989; N. H. Snaith, "Numbers," in *Peake*, 1964, 254-68; idem, *Leviticus and Numbers*, 1967; C. H. Thomson and J. Skinner, *Isaiah I-XXXIX*, 1921; G. W. Wade, "Numbers," in *Peake*, 1920, 213-30; G. J. Wenham, *Numbers: An Introduction and Commentary*, TOTC, 1981; O. C. Whitehouse, *Isaiah I-XXXIX*, 1905.

Robin Wakely

8599	שְׂרֵפָה

שְׂרֵפָה (*śerēpâ*), nom. fire, conflagration, burning, combustion, burned-out place (# 8599); < שׂרף (*śrp* I), q. burn, scorch, cauterize; ni. be, become burnt; pu. be, become burnt (→ # 8596).

ANE See *śrp* (→ # 8596).

OT 1. The nom. *śᵉrēpâ* is used in Numbers of a blaze (Num 16:37[17:2]), of the burning of a heifer as part of a rite to purify a person defiled by a corpse (19:6), and of a burnt (sin) offering (19:17). The word is found once in Deut, where the people are warned that violation of Yahweh's covenant will be met with judgment, which, like a scorching fire, will transform their land into a burnt-out waste ("blasted landscape," Nelson, 232), like that of Sodom and Gomorrah, where nothing can grow (Deut 29:23[22]). According to Weinfeld (110), the conventional punishment in the ANE for breach of treaty was the destruction by fire of the offenders' city, which was then sown with salt and brimstone.

The word occurs twice in Isaiah (Isa 9:5[4]; 64:11[10]). In 9:5[4] it refers to the burning of the former oppressor's military equipment, which is the prelude to the inauguration of an era of idyllic justice, righteousness, peace, and prosperity. Isa 64:8-12[7-11] is a petition in which, in penitence and faith, Yahweh is earnestly entreated to have compassion on desolate Jerusalem and its once beautiful temple, which has now been burned to the ground (v. 11[10]) as a result of the divine anger, which was roused by the people's sin. The word is also used in Amos 4:11. Amos 4:6-12, a "litany of unrepentance" (Barré, 213) or "litany of judgment" (Hubbard, 160), describes a series of divinely inflicted, but unheeded, judgments aimed at chastising the people for their stubborn infidelity and inducing them to return to God. Amos 4:11 refers to one of these catastrophes, from which severely damaged Israel emerged like a charred piece of wood "plucked out of the burning" (RSV). As a result of her obdurate refusal to respond to the divine warnings, Israel is heading for a direct encounter with Yahweh (4:12), which will have even more drastic consequences.

2. In 2 Chron 16:14, a verse not found in the account in Kings, the nom. is used of the magnificent funeral pyre made in honor of Asa, the former king of Judah. The word occurs again in 21:19, which records disdainfully that the unpopular Jehoram was not thought to merit such a fire in his honor when he died because this king had incurred the wrath of Yahweh. The overwhelming majority of commentators (e.g., Elmslie, 235; Curtis and Madsen, 390, 418; Fritsch, 216; Ellison, 388; Dillard, 127, 169) maintain that what is referred to in 16:14 and 21:19 is not cremation, but the burning of spices (cf. Jer 34:5). However, as Coggins (207) rightly points out, little is known of burial practice in ancient Israel.

2 Chron 16:14 is the more intriguing of the two passages. Myers (92) translates *wayyaškîbuhû bammiškāb* as "they laid him in the crypt," which, if accepted, would preclude the possibility of cremation. Bloch-Smith (786-87) follows a similar tack, translating *bammiškāb* as "in the resting place" and then treating the fire referred to in the last part of the verse as being separate from the actual burial. RSV and NRSV, too, by inserting a semicolon instead of a comma, separate the reference to the very great fire from the previous part of v. 14. NEB and REB go even further by linking the reference to Asa's being laid on a bier directly to his burial in the tomb. On the other hand, the translations of 16:14 which are given by NIV ("they laid him on a bier") and by JB ("they laid him on a couch") seem to leave open the possibility that the Chronicler was speaking about cremation. Sensibly, JB points out in a footnote that while the reference is probably to the burning of spices, the possibility that cremation is meant cannot be ruled out.

Burning, blazing, glowing, scorching, singeing: → *bʿr* I (burn, blaze up, be consumed, # 1277); → *gaḥelet* (burning charcoal, # 1625); → *dlq* (set on fire, burn, hotly pursue, # 1944); → *ḥmr* III (be in ferment, be heated, be red, glow, blaze, # 2813); → *ḥrr* I (glow, blaze, # 3081); → *yṣt* (light, kindle, ignite, burn, scorch, # 3675); → *yqd* (burn, kindle, # 3678); → *kwh* (burn, blaze, singe, # 3917); → *lhṭ* I (burn, glow, blaze, # 4265); → *nśq* (catch fire, be kindled, burn, # 5956); → *ṣwt* (light, kindle, ignite, set in flames, # 7455); → *qdḥ* (kindle, light, ignite, set ablaze, catch or take fire, # 7706); → *śrp* (burn, scorch, cauterize, # 8596)

BIBLIOGRAPHY

M. L. Barré, "Amos," in *NJBC*, 1990, 209-16; E. Bloch-Smith, "Burials: Israelite," in *ABD*, 1992, 1:785-89; R. J. Coggins, *The First and Second Books of the Chronicles*, CBC, 1976; E. L. Curtis and A. A. Madsen, *A Critical and Exegetical Commentary on the Books of Chronicles*, 1965; R. B. Dillard, *2 Chronicles*, 1987; H. L. Ellison, "1 and 2 Chronicles," in *NBC*, 1972, 369-94; W. A. L. Elmslie, *The Books of Chronicles With Maps, Notes and Introduction*, 1916; C. T. Fritsch, "The Second Book of the Chronicles," in *The Interpreter's One-Volume Commentary on the Bible*, 1971, 214-19; D. A. Hubbard, *Joel and Amos: An Introduction and Commentary*, 1989; J. M. Myers, *II Chronicles: Introduction, Translation, and Notes*, 1973; R. D. Nelson, "Deuteronomy," in *HBC*, 1988, 209-34; M. Weinfeld, *Deuteronomy and the Deuteronomic School*, 1972.

Robin Wakely

8601	שָׂרֹק

שָׂרֹק (*śārōq*), adj. brownish red (# 8601); Brenner defines *śārōq* as a secondary color (114-15) within the range of red: reddish brown or sorrel.

ANE Akk. *šarku*, red, blood; Arab. and Sabean connect it with the red of the sunrise.

OT This adj. occurs but once, and that to describe one of the horses in Zechariah's vision (Zech 1:8). The words for the colors of the horses in Zechariah's first and eighth vision differ from each other. Compare, "and there before me was a man riding a red (*'ādōm*) horse! ... Behind him were red (*'ādōm*), brown (*śārōq*) and white (*lābān*) horses" (1:8), and "The first chariot had red (*'ādōm*) horses, the second black (*šāḥōr*), the third white (*lābān*), and the fourth dappled (*bārōd*)—all of them powerful (*'āmōṣ*, or pie-bald)" (6:2-3; cf. vv. 6-7).

J. Baldwin explains the difference between the colors in 1:8 and 6:2-3, 6-7 by the changed perception of things during the sunset (1:8) and dawn (6:2-3, 6-7). As the colors of the morning are more vivid, she argues, "a new era is dawning for Judah and the world, for God's purposes as set out in the visions are about to be fulfilled" (*Haggai, Zechariah, Malachi*, 130, see also 138-40). D. L. Petersen rightly challenges this view by asking how we may know whether dappled is the color of the dawn or sunset (*Haggai and Zechariah 1-8*, 141-43, 269). In both visions in Zechariah, the colors of the horses are not interpreted or given any theological significance. (→ Zechariah: Theology)

Smith tends to agree with McHardy that the visions have reference to four primary colors—red, sorrel (greenish yellow, gray), white, black (*Micah-Malachi*, 214). Further, he relates these to the horses in Rev 6:2-8—the horsemen ride out on white, red, black, and pale horses—and to the significance of the colors: white for victory, red for war, black for famine, and pale for death.

Colors—Red: → *'dm* (be red, # 131); → *'argāmān* (purple, # 763); → *karmîl* (crimson, # 4147); → *šārōq* (brownish red, # 8601); → *šānî* I (scarlet, # 9106); → *šāšar* (vermillion/red, # 9266); → *tl'* II (clad in scarlet material, # 9433)

BIBLIOGRAPHY

A. Brenner, *Colour Terms in the Old Testament*, JSOT, 1982; R. Gradwohl, *Die Farben im Alten Testament*, BZAW 83, 1963; W. D. McHardy, "The Horses in Zechariah," *BZAW* 103, 1968, 174-79.

Robert L. Alden

8603	שׂוֹרֵק

שׂוֹרֵק (*śôrēq* II), nom. choice vine (# 8603).

OT The word is used 3x in the OT, twice in a metaphorical sense. In Isa 5:2 it refers to the choice vine the Lord planted in the most fertile place possible (v. 1) in his newly prepared vineyard. The vine, however, brought forth wild or unworthy grapes/fruit, an unexpected result because of the excellent quality of the vine he had planted (v. 2), as clearly indicated from the context (vv. 1-3). Jer 2:21 extends the discussion, indicating that Israel was a *śrq*, but changed with respect to the Lord, turning to become an alien/corrupt vine (*gepen nokriyyā*) that could not change her nature (v. 22). The third use is in the name given to the valley where Delilah lived, the Valley of Sorek

(Judg 16:4), a clear indication of irony in the story, for Samson, a Nazirite, would be overcome in the Valley of the Choice Vine.

P-B The LXX transliterates the word 2x (Isa/Judg), but translates with *ampelos*, vine, vineyard, in Jer.

Grapes—viticulture: → *bṣr* I (gather grapes, tread down, vine-dresser, # 1305); → *gepen* (vine, grapevine, # 1728); → *kerem* I (vineyard, # 4142); → *qss* (strip away, pick, # 7878); → *śārîg* (branch, tendril, climber, # 8585); → *śōrēq* II (choice vine, # 8603); → *śᵉrēqā* (vine with the best grapes, # 8605)

Eugene Carpenter

8605	שְׂרֵקָה

שְׂרֵקָה (*śᵉrēqâ*), nom. choice(est) vine; vine with the best grapes (# 8605).

OT This nom., a hapleg., is found in Gen 49:11, where it is parallel to *gepen* (→ # 1728). If this is synthetic parallelism, then it is reasonable to assume that the advance is: vine → (choice) vine, rather than the branch of the vine. Both noms. are preceded by *lᵉ* and the definite article. However, the LXX uses *ampelos*, vine (*gepen*), parallel *heliks*, tendril (*śᵉrēqâ*) (cf. NIV). The Vg. follows a similar pattern (*vinea* parallel *vitis*).

Grapes—viticulture: → *bṣr* I (gather grapes, tread down, vine-dresser, # 1305); → *gepen* (vine, grapevine, # 1728); → *kerem* I (vineyard, # 4142); → *qss* (strip away, pick, # 7878); → *śārîg* (branch, tendril, climber, # 8585); → *śōrēq* II (choice vine, # 8603); → *śᵉrēqā* (vine with the best grapes, # 8605)

Eugene Carpenter

8606	שׂרר

שׂרר (*śrr* I), q. rule, direct, superintend; hi. cause to rule; hitp. lord it over (# 8606); מִשְׂרָה (*miśrâ*), dominion (disleg. Isa 5:6, 7[5, 6]; # 5385); שַׂר (*śar*), nom. official, chieftain, leader, prince (# 8569); שָׂרָה (*śārâ* I), princess; noble lady (# 8576).

ANE In Palm., the vb. deals with deciding, resolving in an official context (*DISO*, 320-21). The noms. *šarrum* (king, noble man, ruler) and *šarratum* (queen, noble lady) are frequently employed in Akk. when referring to the royal family, to rulers in general, and for attributions of various gods (*AHw*, 1188-1190). The nom. vb. *šarāru* is, however, absent. C. H. Gordon (*UT*, 494) assumes the presence of the nom. *šr* in Ugaritic. It also occurs in other Northwest Sem. languages, e.g., *KAI* Nr 196:4; 200:1, 12. The use of the masc. and fem. form of the nom. *śar* continue in Mid. Hebr. and Aram. The vb. occurs seldom.

OT 1. The vb. *śrr* I is a denominative from *śar* and has a low frequency (6x). It designates the act of ruling or governing by a king or an official (Prov 8:16). In Isa 32:1 the reign (*mlk*) of the king is clearly distinguished from the rule (*śrr*) of the rulers (*śārîm*).

The vb.'s basic concern is with exercising rule and authority like a king or prince. Abimelech did this for three years over the city-state of Shechem before he was overthrown (Judg 9:22). This exercise of direction and authority is to be done with justice and righteousness (Isa 32:1) and by the wisdom of God (Prov 8:16). This royal activity is extended by analogy to describe the authority that Persian men were expected to demonstrate within their own homes (Esth 1:22), an authority flaunted by Vashti. It was feared that her unacceptable insubordination might spread throughout the Persian empire, so she was banished (1:10-22).

In one instance, the vb. is used in the hitp. form, a form that has a reflexive sense in which one does an action on one's own behalf, or else esteems oneself to be in a certain state (Waltke, *IHBS*, 1990, 430). In Num 16:13, Dathan and Abiram deny Moses any true authority, claiming that he is "lording it over" them. In this case, the form is used with an understanding that Moses on his own was making a claim to authority that he did not actually hold. God showed the truth of Moses' claims, however, by stepping in and annihilating his accusers and their families (16:23-25).

The unique hif. occurrence of the vb., showing the causative function of this form (*IHBS*, 433-46), is also used in a context where the action is wrongfully done. The Israelites are accused by God of wrongfully enthroning and delegating authority to people not chosen for this honor by God (Hos 8:4). Israel was forgetting that God is their ultimate King as well as their authoritative king-maker.

2. The WestSem. word *śar*, frequently in the pl. *śārîm* and *śārôt* (fem.), has a broad semantic range of reference. In general it does not refer to the Israelite king himself, but to the advisers of the king, namely, city officials, military officials, and royal officials and functionaries in general (e.g., Gen 12:15; 1 Chron 22:17; Esth 1:18; Jer 24:1). In Isa 10:8 the Assyrian leaders (*śārîm*) were identified as kings (*m^elākîm*). Originally *śar* could have been a reference to a clan leader or military leader (Gen 21:22; Judg 4:7; 7:25; 8:3; 1 Sam 18:30; 1 Kgs 15:20). In Isa 9:5 the word has a peculiar usage when the future Davidic leader is called *śar šālôm*, prince of peace.

Kingship, rule, supervision, dominion: → *b'l* I (marry, rule over, own, # 1249); → *g^ebîrâ/g^eberet* (lady, queen, mistress, # 1485/1509); → *ykḥ* (dispute, reason together, prove, judge, rule, reprove, # 3519); → *kbš* (make subservient, subdue, # 3899); → *mlk* I (rule, # 4887); → *mšl* II (rule, govern, # 5440); → *nṣḥ* (supervise, # 5904); → *rdd* (repel, subdue, # 8096); → *rdh* I (rule, govern, # 8097); → *r'h* I (feed, graze, shepherd, rule, # 8286); → *śrr* I (rule, direct, superintend, # 8606); → *šlṭ* (gain power, # 8948); → *špṭ* (get justice, act as a judge, rule, # 9149)

BIBLIOGRAPHY

TWOT 2:284-85.

David W. Baker/Philip J. Nel

8607 (*śāśôn*, exultation), → # 8464

8609	שׂתר

שׂתר (*śtr*), break out (tumor; # 8609).

ANE Akk. *šutturu*, break down, break out.

OT This rare word was employed solely to describe the outbreak of tumors in 1 Sam 5:9, consequent upon the Philistine's capture of the ark of the covenant and its transfer to Gath.

Disease—blister, boil, skin disease, scar, wound: → *'^aba'bu'ōt* (blisters, # 81); → *bōhaq* (skin condition, # 993); → *baheret* (white patch on skin, # 994); → *gārāb* (festering eruption, # 1734);

→ *zrr* I (press out [wounds], # 2452); → *ḥeres* I (itch, # 3063); → *yabbelet* (wart?, # 3301); → *yallepet* (skin disease, # 3539); → *y*^{e}*raqraq* (discoloration, # 3768); → *k*^{e}*wiyya* (scar, # 3918); → *m'r* (be sore, # 4421); → *māzôr* I (boil, # 4649); → *makkâ* (blow, # 4804); → *mispaḥat* (skin eruption, # 5030); → *mrḥ* (rub, polish, # 5302); → *neteq* (scalp infection, # 5999); → *sappaḥat* (hair disease, # 6204); → *'ōpel* I (abscesses, # 6754); → *'āš* II (pus, # 6932); → *ṣāpâ* (pus?, # 7597); → *ṣarebet* (scar, # 7648); → *ṣr'* (suffer from skin disease, # 7665); → *ś*^{e}*'ēt* II (swelling, # 8421); → *śtr* (break out [tumor], # 8609); → *š*^{e}*ḥîn* (boil, # 8825). For related entries → *ḥlh* I (become weak, tired, ill, # 2703)

Bibliography

ISBE 1:532, 953-60; 3:103-6.

R. K. Harrison

New International
Dictionary of New Testament Theology

4 Volume Set

"Has proved its worth."
—*F. F. Bruce*

"Indispensable for advanced theological students and scholars as well as ordinary Bible students."
—*Christianity Today*

The *New International Dictionary of New Testament Theology* is, first, a basic translation, and then an extensive revision and considerable enlargement of the German *Theologisches Begriffslexikon zum Neuen Testament.* On its first publication in German it was recognized as a major reference work and has since become more and more widely acclaimed as an important tool for understanding the theology and message of the Bible. Its translation and publication in English, together with the extensive revisions and additions, provide a unique source of information, invaluable to ministers, teachers, and anyone interested in the study as well as the teaching of the Bible.

Some of its main features are:

- Concise discussions of the major theological terms of the Bible
- Arranged in English alphabetical order
- Does not require knowledge of Greek and Hebrew
- Discusses the use of each key term in classical Greek, the Old Testament, the rabbinic writings, and the New Testament
- Glossary of technical terms
- Full bibliographies
- Complete indexes that make the wealth of information in these volumes readily accessible.